# THE NEW INTERPRETER'S® BIBLE

## IN TWELVE VOLUMES

# Volume Ten

THE ACTS OF THE APOSTLES

INTRODUCTION TO EPISTOLARY
LITERATURE

THE LETTER TO THE ROMANS

THE FIRST LETTER TO THE
CORINTHIANS

# EDITORIAL BOARD

# THE NEW INTERPRETER'S® BIBLE

GENERAL ARTICLES
&
INTRODUCTION, COMMENTARY, & REFLECTIONS
FOR EACH BOOK OF THE BIBLE
INCLUDING
THE APOCRYPHAL/DEUTEROCANONICAL BOOKS
IN
TWELVE VOLUMES

VOLUME
X

ABINGDON PRESS
Nashville

THE NEW INTERPRETER'S BIBLE
VOLUME X

Library of Congress Cataloging-in-Publication Data
    The New Interpreter's Bible: general articles & introduction,
    commentary, & reflections for each book of the Bible, including the
    Apocryphal/Deuterocanonical books.
        p.  cm.
    Full texts and critical notes of the New International Version and
the New Revised Standard Version of the Bible in parallel columns.
    Includes bibliographical references.
        ISBN 0-687-27823-6 (v. 10: alk. paper)
        1. Bible—Commentaries.  2. Abingdon Press.  I. Bible.  English.
New International.  1994.  II. Bible.  English.  New Revised
Standard.  1994.
BS491.2.N484 1994
220.7'7—dc20      94-21092
        CIP

The HebraicaII® and GraecaII® fonts used to print this work are available from Linguist's Software, Inc., PO Box 580, Edmonds, WA 98020-0580. Tel (425) 775-1130. Web www.linguistsoftware.com

PUBLICATION STAFF
President and Publisher: Neil M. Alexander
Editorial Director: Harriett Jane Olson
Senior Editor of Reference Resources: Michael R. Russell
Production Editor: Linda S. Allen
Hebrew and Greek Editor/Assistant Editor: Lynn Allan Kauppi
Production and Design Manager: Walter E. Wynne
Designer: J. S. Laughbaum
Copy Processing Manager: Sylvia S. Street
Composition Specialist: Kathy M. Harding
Prepress Manager: Glenn R. Hinton
Prepress Systems Technicians: J. Calvin Buckner
                            Phillip D. Elliott
Director of Production Processes: James E. Leath
                            Billy W. Murphy
Scheduling: Laurene M. Martin
            Tracey D. Craddock
Print Procurement Coordinator: Martha K. Taylor

02 03 04 05 06 07 08 09 10 11 — 10 9 8 7 6 5 4 3 2 1

MANUFACTURED IN THE UNITED STATES OF AMERICA

# CONSULTANTS

NEIL M. ALEXANDER
President and Publisher
The United Methodist Publishing House
Nashville, Tennessee

OWEN F. CAMPION
Associate Publisher
*Our Sunday Visitor*
Huntington, Indiana

MINERVA G. CARCAÑO
Director
Mexican American Program
Perkins School of Theology
Southern Methodist University
Dallas, Texas

V. L. DAUGHTERY, JR.
Retired Pastor
South Georgia Conference
The United Methodist Church

SHARON NEUFER EMSWILER
Pastor
First United Methodist Church
Rock Island, Illinois

JUAN G. FELICIANO VALERA
Director
Development Office
Evangelical Seminary of Puerto Rico
San Juan, Puerto Rico

CELIA BREWER MARSHALL
Lecturer
University of North Carolina at Charlotte
Charlotte, North Carolina

NANCY C. MILLER-HERRON
Attorney and clergy member of
the Tennessee Conference
The United Methodist Church
Dresden, Tennessee

ROBERT C. SCHNASE
Pastor
First United Methodist Church
McAllen, Texas

BILL SHERMAN
Pastor Emeritus
Woodmont Baptist Church
Nashville, Tennessee

RODNEY T. SMOTHERS
Pastor
Ousley United Methodist Church
Lithonia, Georgia

WILLIAM D. WATLEY
Pastor
St. James African Methodist Episcopal Church
Newark, New Jersey

TALLULAH FISHER WILLIAMS[†]
Superintendent
Chicago Northwestern District
The United Methodist Church
Chicago, Illinois

SUK-CHONG YU
Superintendent
Nevada-Sierra District
The United Methodist Church
Reno, Nevada

[†] *deceased*

vii

# CONTRIBUTORS

ELIZABETH ACHTEMEIER
Adjunct Professor of Bible and Homiletics
Union Theological Seminary in Virginia
Richmond, Virginia
(Presbyterian Church [U.S.A.])
*Joel*

LESLIE C. ALLEN
Professor of Old Testament
Fuller Theological Seminary
Pasadena, California
(Baptist)
*1 & 2 Chronicles*

GARY A. ANDERSON
Associate Professor of Religious Studies
University of Virginia
Charlottesville, Virginia
(The Roman Catholic Church)
*Introduction to Israelite Religion*

DAVID L. BARTLETT
Lantz Professor of Preaching and
Communication
The Divinity School
Yale University
New Haven, Connecticut
(American Baptist Churches in the U.S.A.)
*1 Peter*

ROBERT A. BENNETT, PH.D.
Cambridge, Massachusetts
(The Episcopal Church)
*Zephaniah*

ADELE BERLIN
Robert H. Smith Professor of Hebrew Bible
Associate Provost for Faculty Affairs
University of Maryland
College Park, Maryland
*Introduction to Hebrew Poetry*

BRUCE C. BIRCH
Dean and Woodrow W. and Mildred B. Miller
Professor of Biblical Theology
Wesley Theological Seminary
Washington, DC
(The United Methodist Church)
*1 & 2 Samuel*

PHYLLIS A. BIRD
Associate Professor of Old Testament
Interpretation
Garrett-Evangelical Theological Seminary
Evanston, Illinois
(The United Methodist Church)
*The Authority of the Bible*

C. CLIFTON BLACK
Professor of New Testament
Perkins School of Theology
Southern Methodist University
Dallas, Texas
(The United Methodist Church)
*1, 2, & 3 John*

JOSEPH BLENKINSOPP
John A. O'Brien Professor of Biblical Studies
Department of Theology
University of Notre Dame
Notre Dame, Indiana
(The Roman Catholic Church)
*Introduction to the Pentateuch*

M. EUGENE BORING
I. Wylie and Elizabeth M. Briscoe Professor of
New Testament
Brite Divinity School
Texas Christian University
Fort Worth, Texas
(Christian Church [Disciples of Christ])
*Matthew*

ix

WALTER BRUEGGEMANN
William Marcellus McPheeters Professor of
Old Testament
Columbia Theological Seminary
Decatur, Georgia
(United Church of Christ)
*Exodus*

DAVID G. BUTTRICK
Professor of Homiletics and Liturgics
The Divinity School
Vanderbilt University
Nashville, Tennessee
(United Church of Christ)
*The Use of the Bible in Preaching*

RONALD E. CLEMENTS
Samuel Davidson Professor of Old Testament
King's College
University of London
London, England
(Baptist Union of Great Britain and Ireland)
*Deuteronomy*

RICHARD J. CLIFFORD, S.J.
Professor of Old Testament
Weston Jesuit School of Theology
Cambridge, Massachusetts
(The Roman Catholic Church)
*Introduction to Wisdom Literature*

JOHN J. COLLINS
Holmes Professor of Old Testament
Criticism and Interpretation
Yale University Divinity School
New Haven, Connecticut
(The Roman Catholic Church)
*Introduction to Early Jewish Religion*

ROBERT B. COOTE
Professor of Old Testament
San Francisco Theological Seminary
San Anselmo, California
(Presbyterian Church [U.S.A.])
*Joshua*

FRED B. CRADDOCK
Bandy Distinguished Professor of Preaching
and New Testament, Emeritus
Candler School of Theology
Emory University
Atlanta, Georgia
(Christian Church [Disciples of Christ])
*Hebrews*

† *deceased*

SIDNIE WHITE CRAWFORD
Associate Professor of Hebrew Bible
and Chair of the Department of Classics
University of Nebraska—Lincoln
Lincoln, Nebraska
(The Episcopal Church)
*Esther; Additions to Esther*

JAMES L. CRENSHAW
Robert L. Flowers Professor of
Old Testament
The Divinity School
Duke University
Durham, North Carolina
(Baptist)
*Sirach*

KEITH R. CRIM†
Pastor
New Concord Presbyterian Church
Concord, Virginia
(Presbyterian Church [U.S.A.])
*Modern English Versions of the Bible*

R. ALAN CULPEPPER
Dean
The School of Theology
Mercer University
Atlanta, Georgia
(Southern Baptist Convention)
*Luke*

KATHERYN PFISTERER DARR
Associate Professor of Hebrew Bible
The School of Theology
Boston University
Boston, Massachusetts
(The United Methodist Church)
*Ezekiel*

ROBERT DORAN
Professor of Religion
Amherst College
Amherst, Massachusetts
*1 & 2 Maccabees*

THOMAS B. DOZEMAN
Professor of Old Testament
United Theological Seminary
Dayton, Ohio
(Presbyterian Church [U.S.A.])
*Numbers*

JAMES D. G. DUNN
Lightfoot Professor of Divinity
Department of Theology
University of Durham
Durham, England
(The Methodist Church [Great Britain])
*1 & 2 Timothy; Titus*

ELDON JAY EPP
Harkness Professor of Biblical Literature and
Chairman of the Department of Religion
Case Western Reserve University
Cleveland, Ohio
(The Episcopal Church)
*Ancient Texts and Versions of the New
Testament*

KATHLEEN A. ROBERTSON FARMER
Professor of Old Testament
United Theological Seminary
Dayton, Ohio
(The United Methodist Church)
*Ruth*

CAIN HOPE FELDER
Professor of New Testament Language
and Literature
The School of Divinity
Howard University
Washington, DC
(The United Methodist Church)
*Philemon*

TERENCE E. FRETHEIM
Professor of Old Testament
Luther Seminary
Saint Paul, Minnesota
(Evangelical Lutheran Church in America)
*Genesis*

FRANCISCO O. GARCÍA-TRETO
Professor of Religion and Chair of the
Department of Religion
Trinity University
San Antonio, Texas
(Presbyterian Church [U.S.A.])
*Nahum*

CATHERINE GUNSALUS GONZÁLEZ
Professor of Church History
Columbia Theological Seminary
Decatur, Georgia
(Presbyterian Church [U.S.A.])
*The Use of the Bible in Hymns, Liturgy,
and Education*

JUSTO L. GONZÁLEZ
Adjunct Professor of Church History
Columbia Theological Seminary
Decatur, Georgia
(The United Methodist Church)
*How the Bible Has Been Interpreted in
Christian Tradition*

DONALD E. GOWAN
Robert Cleveland Holland Professor of Old
Testament
Pittsburgh Theological Seminary
Pittsburgh, Pennsylvania
(Presbyterian Church [U.S.A.])
*Amos*

DANIEL J. HARRINGTON, S.J.
Professor of New Testament
Weston School of Theology
Cambridge, Massachusetts
(The Roman Catholic Church)
*Introduction to the Canon*

RICHARD B. HAYS
Professor of New Testament
The Divinity School
Duke University
Durham, North Carolina
(The United Methodist Church)
*Galatians*

THEODORE HIEBERT
Professor of Old Testament
McCormick Theological Seminary
Chicago, Illinois
(Mennonite Church)
*Habakkuk*

CARL R. HOLLADAY
Professor of New Testament
Candler School of Theology
Emory University
Atlanta, Georgia
*Contemporary Methods of Reading the
Bible*

MORNA D. HOOKER
Lady Margaret's Professor of Divinity, Emeritus
The Divinity School
University of Cambridge
Cambridge, England
(The Methodist Church [Great Britain])
*Philippians*

DAVID C. HOPKINS
Professor of Old Testament
Wesley Theological Seminary
Washington, DC
(United Church of Christ)
*Life in Ancient Palestine*

LUKE T. JOHNSON
Robert W. Woodruff Professor of New
Testament and Christian Origins
Candler School of Theology
Emory University
Atlanta, Georgia
(The Roman Catholic Church)
*James*

WALTER C. KAISER, JR.
President and Colman M. Mockler
Distinguished Professor of Old Testament
Gordon-Conwell Theological Seminary
South Hamilton, Massachusetts
(The Evangelical Free Church of America)
*Leviticus*

LEANDER E. KECK
Winkley Professor of Biblical Theology,
Emeritus
Yale University Divinity School
New Haven, Connecticut
(Christian Church [Disciples of Christ])
*Introduction to The New Interpreter's Bible*

CHAN-HIE KIM
Professor of New Testament and Director of
Korean Studies
The School of Theology at Claremont
Claremont, California
(The United Methodist Church)
*Reading the Bible as Asian Americans*

RALPH W. KLEIN
Christ Seminary-Seminex Professor of Old
Testament
Lutheran School of Theology at Chicago
Chicago, Illinois
(Evangelical Lutheran Church in America)
*Ezra; Nehemiah*

MICHAEL KOLARCIK, S.J.
Associate Professor of Old Testament
Regis College
Toronto, Ontario
Canada
(The Roman Catholic Church)
*Book of Wisdom*

ANDREW T. LINCOLN
Professor of New Testament
Wycliffe College
University of Toronto
Toronto, Ontario
Canada
(The Church of England)
*Colossians*

J. CLINTON MCCANN, JR.
Evangelical Professor of Biblical Interpretation
Eden Theological Seminary
St. Louis, Missouri
(Presbyterian Church [U.S.A.])
*Psalms*

ABRAHAM J. MALHERBE
Buckingham Professor of New Testament
Criticism and Interpretation, Emeritus
The Divinity School
Yale University
New Haven, Connecticut
(Church of Christ)
*The Cultural Context of the New
Testament: The Greco-Roman World*

W. EUGENE MARCH
Dean and Arnold Black Rhodes Professor of
Old Testament
Louisville Presbyterian Theological Seminary
Louisville, Kentucky
(Presbyterian Church [U.S.A.])
*Haggai*

JAMES EARL MASSEY
Dean Emeritus and
Distinguished Professor-at-Large
The School of Theology
Anderson University
(Church of God [Anderson, Ind.])
*Reading the Bible from Particular Social
Locations: An Introduction; Reading the
Bible as African Americans*

J. MAXWELL MILLER
Professor of Old Testament, Emeritus
Candler School of Theology
Emory University
Atlanta, Georgia
(The United Methodist Church)
*Introduction to the History of Ancient
Israel*

PATRICK D. MILLER
Charles T. Haley Professor of Old Testament
Theology
Princeton Theological Seminary
Princeton, New Jersey
(Presbyterian Church [U.S.A.])
*Jeremiah*

PETER D. MISCALL
Adjunct Faculty
The Iliff School of Theology
Denver, Colorado
(The Episcopal Church)
*Introduction to Narrative Literature*

FREDERICK J. MURPHY
Professor
Department of Religious Studies
College of the Holy Cross
Worcester, Massachusetts
(The Roman Catholic Church)
*Introduction to Apocalyptic Literature*

CAROL A. NEWSOM
Professor of Old Testament
Candler School of Theology
Emory University
Atlanta, Georgia
(The Episcopal Church)
*Job*

GEORGE W. E. NICKELSBURG
Professor of Christian Origins and
Early Judaism
School of Religion
University of Iowa
Iowa City, Iowa
(Evangelical Lutheran Church in America)
*The Jewish Context of the New
Testament*

IRENE NOWELL, O.S.B.
Community Formation Director
Mount St. Scholasticas
Atchison, Kansas
(The Roman Catholic Church)
*Tobit*

KATHLEEN M. O'CONNOR
Professor of Old Testament Language,
Literature, and Exegesis
Columbia Theological Seminary
Decatur, Georgia
(The Roman Catholic Church)
*Lamentations*

GAIL R. O'DAY
Almar H. Shatford Professor of Preaching
and New Testament
Candler School of Theology
Emory University
Atlanta, Georgia
(United Church of Christ)
*John*

BEN C. OLLENBURGER
Professor of Biblical Theology
Associated Mennonite Biblical Seminary
Elkhart, Indiana
(Mennonite Church)
*Zechariah*

DENNIS T. OLSON
Associate Professor of Old Testament
Princeton Theological Seminary
Princeton, New Jersey
(Evangelical Lutheran Church in America)
*Judges*

CAROLYN OSIEK
Professor of New Testament
Department of Biblical Languages and
Literature
Catholic Theological Union
Chicago, Illinois
(The Roman Catholic Church)
*Reading the Bible as Women*

SAMUEL PAGAN
President
Evangelical Seminary of Puerto Rico
San Juan, Puerto Rico
(Christian Church [Disciples of Christ])
*Obadiah*

SIMON B. PARKER
Professor of Hebrew Bible and Harrell F. Beck
Scholar in Hebrew Scripture
The School of Theology
Boston University
Boston, Massachusetts
(The United Methodist Church)
*The Ancient Near Eastern Literary
Background of the Old Testament*

PHEME PERKINS
Professor of New Testament
Boston College
Chestnut Hill, Massachusetts
(The Roman Catholic Church)
*Mark; Ephesians*

DAVID L. PETERSEN
Clifford E. Baldridge Professor of Biblical
Studies
The Iliff School of Theology
Denver, Colorado
(Presbyterian Church [U.S.A.])
*Introduction to Prophetic Literature*

CHRISTOPHER C. ROWLAND
Dean Ireland's Professor of the Exegesis of
Holy Scripture
The Queen's College
Oxford, England
(The Church of England)
*Revelation*

ANTHONY J. SALDARINI
Professor of Biblical Studies
Boston College
Chestnut Hill, Massachusetts
(The Roman Catholic Church)
*Baruch; Letter of Jeremiah*

J. PAUL SAMPLEY
Professor of New Testament and
Christian Origins
The School of Theology and The Graduate
Division
Boston University
Boston, Massachusetts
(The United Methodist Church)
*1 Corinthians; 2 Corinthians*

JUDITH E. SANDERSON
Assistant Professor of Hebrew Bible
Department of Theology and Religious Studies
Seattle University
Seattle, Washington
*Ancient Texts and Versions of the Old
Testament*

EILEEN M. SCHULLER, O.S.U.
Professor
Department of Religious Studies
McMaster University
Hamilton, Ontario
Canada
(The Roman Catholic Church)
*Malachi*

FERNANDO F. SEGOVIA
Professor of New Testament and Early
Christianity
The Divinity School
Vanderbilt University
Nashville, Tennessee
(The Roman Catholic Church)
*Reading the Bible as Hispanic Americans*

CHRISTOPHER R. SEITZ
Professor of Old Testament and Theological
Studies
St Mary's College
University of St. Andrews
Fife, Scotland
(The Episcopal Church)
*Isaiah 40–66*

CHOON-LEONG SEOW
Henry Snyder Gehman Professor of Old
Testament Language and Literature
Princeton Theological Seminary
Princeton, New Jersey
(Presbyterian Church [U.S.A.])
*1 & 2 Kings*

MICHAEL A. SIGNER
Abrams Professor of Jewish Thought
and Culture
Department of Theology
University of Notre Dame
Notre Dame, Indiana
*How the Bible Has Been Interpreted in
Jewish Tradition*

MOISÉS SILVA
Professor of New Testament
Westminster Theological Seminary
Philadelphia, Pennsylvania
(The Orthodox Presbyterian Church)
*Contemporary Theories of Biblical
Interpretation*

DANIEL J. SIMUNDSON
Professor of Old Testament
Luther Seminary
Saint Paul, Minnesota
(Evangelical Lutheran Church in America)
*Micah*

ABRAHAM SMITH
Associate Professor of New Testament
Andover Newton Theological School
Newton Centre, Massachusetts
(The National Baptist Convention, USA, Inc.)
*1 & 2 Thessalonians*

DANIEL L. SMITH-CHRISTOPHER
Associate Professor of Theological Studies
Department of Theology
Loyola Marymount University
Los Angeles, California
(The Society of Friends [Quaker])
*Daniel; Bel and the Dragon; Prayer of Azariah; Susannah*

ROBERT C. TANNEHILL
Academic Dean and Harold B. Williams
Professor of Biblical Studies
Methodist Theological School in Ohio
Delaware, Ohio
(The United Methodist Church)
*The Gospels and Narrative Literature*

GEORGE E. TINKER
Professor of American Indian Cultures
and Religious Traditions
The Iliff School of Theology
Denver, Colorado
(Evangelical Lutheran Church in America)
*Reading the Bible as Native Americans*

W. SIBLEY TOWNER
The Reverend Archibald McFadyen Professor
of Biblical Interpretation
Union Theological Seminary in Virginia
Richmond, Virginia
(Presbyterian Church [U.S.A.])
*Ecclesiastes*

PHYLLIS TRIBLE
Professor of Biblical Studies
The Divinity School
Wake Forest University
Winston-Salem, North Carolina
*Jonah*

GENE M. TUCKER
Professor of Old Testament, Emeritus
Candler School of Theology
Emory University
Atlanta, Georgia
(The United Methodist Church)
*Isaiah 1–39*

CHRISTOPHER M. TUCKETT
Rylands Professor of Biblical Criticism and
Exegesis
Faculty of Theology
University of Manchester
Manchester, England
(The Church of England)
*Jesus and the Gospels*

RAYMOND C. VAN LEEUWEN
Professor of Religion and Theology
Eastern College
Saint Davids, Pennsylvania
(Christian Reformed Church in North America)
*Proverbs*

ROBERT W. WALL
Professor of Biblical Studies
Department of Religion
Seattle Pacific University
Seattle, Washington
(Free Methodist Church of North America)
*Acts; Introduction to Epistolary Literature*

DUANE F. WATSON
Associate Professor of New Testament Studies
Department of Religion and Philosophy
Malone College
Canton, Ohio
(The United Methodist Church)
*2 Peter; Jude*

RENITA J. WEEMS
Associate Professor of Hebrew Bible
The Divinity School
Vanderbilt University
Nashville, Tennessee
(African Methodist Episcopal Church)
*Song of Songs*

LAWRENCE M. WILLS
Associate Professor of Biblical Studies
The Episcopal Divinity School
Cambridge, Massachusetts
(The Episcopal Church)
*Judith*

VINCENT L. WIMBUSH
Professor of New Testament and
Christian Origins
Union Theological Seminary
New York, New York
(Progressive National Baptist Convention, Inc.)
*The Ecclesiastical Context of the New Testament*

N. Thomas Wright
Canon Theologian
Westminster Abbey
London, England
(The Church of England)
*Romans*

Gale A. Yee
Professor of Hebrew Bible and
Director of Feminist Liberation Theologies
Episcopal Divinity School
Cambridge, Massachusetts
(The Roman Catholic Church)
*Hosea*

# FEATURES OF
# THE NEW INTERPRETER'S® BIBLE

The general aim of *The New Interpreter's Bible* is to bring the best in contemporary biblical scholarship into the service of the church to enhance preaching, teaching, and study of the Scriptures. To accomplish that general aim, the design of *The New Interpreter's Bible* has been shaped by two controlling principles: (1) form serves function, and (2) maximize ease of use.

General articles provide the reader with concise, up-to-date, balanced introductions and assessments of selected topics. In most cases, a brief bibliography points the way to further exploration of a topic. Many of the general articles are placed in volumes 1 and 8, at the beginning of the coverage of the Old and New Testaments, respectively. Others have been inserted in those volumes where the reader will encounter the corresponding type of literature (e.g., "Introduction to Prophetic Literature" appears in Volume 6 alongside several of the prophetic books).

Coverage of each biblical book begins with an "Introduction" that acquaints the reader with the essential historical, sociocultural, literary, and theological issues necessary to understand the biblical book. A short bibliography and an outline of the biblical book are found at the end of each Introduction. The introductory sections are the only material in *The New Interpreter's Bible* printed in a single wide-column format.

The biblical text is divided into coherent and manageable primary units, which are located within larger sections of Scripture. At the opening discussion of any large section of Scripture, readers will often find material identified as "Overview," which includes remarks applicable to the large section of text. The primary unit of text may be as short as a few verses or as long as a chapter or more. This is the point at which the biblical text itself is reprinted in *The New Interpreter's Bible*. Dealing with Scripture in terms of these primary units allows discussion of important issues that are overlooked in a verse-by-verse treatment. Each scriptural unit is identified by text citation and a short title.

The full texts and critical notes of the New International Version and the New Revised Standard Version of the Bible are presented in parallel columns for quick reference. (For the Apocryphal/Deuterocanonical works, the NIV is replaced by The New American Bible.) Since every translation is to some extent an interpretation as well, the inclusion of these widely known and influential modern translations provides an easy comparison that in many cases will lead to a better understanding of a passage. Biblical passages are set in a two-column format and placed in green tint-blocks to make it easy to recognize them at a glance. The NAB, NIV, and NRSV material is clearly identified on each page on which the text appears.

Immediately following each biblical text is a section marked "Commentary," which provides an exegetical analysis informed by linguistic, text-critical, historical-critical, literary, social-scientific, and theological methods. The Commentary serves as a reliable, judicious guide through the text, pointing out the critical problems as well as key interpretive issues.

The exegetical approach is "text-centered." That is, the commentators focus primarily on the text in its final form rather than on (a) a meticulous rehearsal of problems of scholarship associated with a text, (b) a thorough reconstruction of the pre-history of the text, or (c) an exhaustive rehearsal of the text's interpretive history. Of course, some attention to scholarly problems, to the pre-history of a text, and to historic interpretations that have shaped streams of tradition is important in particular cases precisely in order to illumine the several levels of meaning in the final form of the text. But the *primary* focus is on the canonical text itself. Moreover, the Commentary not only describes pertinent aspects of the text, but also teaches the reader what to look for in the text so as to develop the reader's own capacity to analyze and interpret the text.

Commentary material runs serially for a few paragraphs or a few pages, depending on what is required by the biblical passage under discussion.

Commentary material is set in a two-column format. Occasional subheads appear in a bold green font. The next level of subdivisions appears as bold black fonts and a third level as black italic fonts. Footnotes are placed at the bottom of the column in which the superscripts appear.

Key words in Hebrew, Aramaic, or Greek are printed in the original-language font, accompanied by a transliteration and a translation or explanation.

Immediately following the Commentary, in most cases, is the section called "Reflections." A detailed exposition growing directly out of the discussion and issues dealt with in the Commentary, the Reflections are geared specifically toward helping those who interpret Scripture in the life of the church by providing "handles" for grasping the significance of Scripture for faith and life today. Recognizing that the text has the capacity to shape the life of the Christian community, this section presents multiple possibilities for preaching and teaching in light of each biblical text. That is, instead of providing the preacher or teacher full illustrations, poems, outlines, and the like, the Reflections offer *several* trajectories of possible interpretation that connect with the situation of the contemporary listeners. Recognizing the power of Scripture to speak anew to diverse situations, not all of the suggested trajectories could be appropriated on any one occasion. Preachers and teachers want some specificity about the implications of the text, but not so much specificity that the work is done for them. The ideas in the Reflections are meant to stimulate the thought of preachers and teachers, not to replace it.

Three-quarter width columns distinguish Reflections materials from biblical text and Commentary.

Occasional excursuses have been inserted in some volumes to address topics of special importance that are best treated apart from the flow of Commentary and Reflections on specific passages. Set in three-quarter width columns, excursuses are identified graphically by a green color bar that runs down the outside margin of the page.

Occasional maps, charts, and illustrations appear throughout the volumes at points where they are most likely to be immediately useful to the reader.

# CONTENTS

## VOLUME X

# THE ACTS OF THE APOSTLES

INTRODUCTION, COMMENTARY, AND REFLECTIONS

BY

ROBERT W. WALL

# THE ACTS OF THE
# APOSTLES

## INTRODUCTION

The Acts of the Apostles is one of the most exciting and challenging books in the Christian Bible. Here we find a highly evocative story of the church's beginnings that traces its dramatic growth from sacred Jerusalem to imperial Rome. Because of its continuing importance in shaping the identity of today's church, Acts demands our most careful reading and thoughtful interpretation.

The importance of Acts for Christian formation is belied, however, by its sparse use in the church's lectionary, which assigns but a few of its most colorful episodes from the early chapters for use during the seven weeks leading from Easter to Pentecost. While liturgical practice reflects the book's keen stress on the Lord's resurrection and God's Spirit, I will argue for a much thicker portfolio of lessons, drawn from the entire narrative and included throughout the year, to enhance the teaching ministry of the church.

In order to draw fully upon the resources brought forward from the book of Acts, especially in this postmodern era of Bible study when methodological imperialism has been replaced by methodological pluralism, the student of Scripture should examine every biblical text in the light of different interpretive interests and cultural sensibilities. What follows seeks to introduce readers to this methodological pluralism by considering various topics from the book's origins to its inclusion within the NT canon. Layers of the text's full meaning are found at each of four different locations where interpreters pause for instruction in guiding the church's reflection upon God's Word for today. The critical admission of a text's multivalency, or variety of meaning, need not imply that the

The Eastern Early Roman Empire

meaning is relative to an individual interpreter. What must finally regulate a faithful reading of Acts at every location—whether "behind the text" or "in the text" or "in front of the text"—are those core convictions of Christian confession and those distinctive practices that mark out Christian κοινωνία (*koinonia*, "community"). When every element of Scripture study aims at theological understanding, the community of interpreters moves toward obedience to the divine will.

## ACTS AS CONVERSATION: READING ACTS AS HISTORY

The Acts of the Apostles began its life as the written conversation between a storyteller (Luke) and his story's first reader (Theophilus). Modern commentaries on Acts are generally interested in reconstructing the circumstances of this correspondence as the most direct angle of vision to the text's intended meaning. To learn about the personal identities of the narrator and the first readers, their location, the circumstances that occasioned the writing of the book, and its date and communicative intention is not the disinterested pursuit of historians. Attending to such queries can make today's interpreters more aware of the book's continuing relevance and religious authority. To be sure, the historian's interest in the narrative of Acts does not necessarily supply us with accurate historical information about the origins of Christianity or of the narrator's purpose in telling his story. Such a presumption would be anachronistic, for Luke's task is to interpret and grant theological significance to past events rather than to describe them objectively or with factual precision suitable for his modern readers.[1]

Acts is an anonymous book. Even though the traditions of the ancient church assert that the evangelist Luke wrote both the Third Gospel and Acts—and there is no hard evidence to deny his authorship—knowing his identity or even that he was a sometimes traveling companion of Paul adds hardly anything to our understanding of his narrative. We can, perhaps, sketch the basic features of the nameless author of this narrative: He was an educated and well-traveled Greek who may well have converted to Judaism years before he became a Christian missionary; perhaps he was even an associate of Paul.[2] As a matter of literary fact, however, this narrator does not insinuate himself into his story, nor does he even bother to identify himself when joining Paul's company during the apostle's European mission (16:10-17; 20:5-16; 21:1-18; 27:1–28:16). Some modern scholars have come to base their historical judgment of Luke's authorship and the reliability of his story about Paul on these so-called we passages and the perceived intimacy they reflect between the narrator and the apostle.[3] The ambivalence of current opinion over both the reliability of Luke's sources and his authorship of Acts reflects the

1. See J. Green, "Internal Repetition in Luke-Acts," in *History, Literature and Society in the Book of Acts,* ed. B. Witherington (Cambridge: Cambridge University Press, 1996) 283-99.

2. For this line of evidence, see A. Culpepper, "The Gospel of Luke," in *The New Interpreter's Bible,* 12 vols. (Nashville: Abingdon, 1994–2002) 9:4-10.

3. For a positive assessment of the relationship between the Paul of Acts and the historical Paul, see M. Hengel and A. Schwemer, *Paul Between Damascus and Antioch* (Louisville: Westminster John Knox, 1997) 1-23.

Jerusalem at the Time of Paul

CP = Court of Priests
CW = Court of Women
CI = Court of Israel
G = Gate

N

**Jerusalem at the
Time of Paul**

Approximate lines of City Walls:

under Herod the Great
added by Agrippa I

0   100   200   300
Meters

0   100   200   300
Yards

G

FORTRESS
ANTONIA

TEMPLE

CI

Soloman's
Portico

G

CP

Beautiful
Gate?

G

CW
Court
of
Gentiles

Bridge

Portico

G

Royal Portico

G

ROYAL
PALACE
PRAETORIUM

G   G   G

G

Herodian Street

G

G

Hinnom

Valley

Tyropoeon   Valley

Kidron   Valley

Mount of Olives
(Mt. Olivet)

indeterminacy of these matters. In any case, the anonymity of Acts indicates that the narrator's focus is on the story rather than on his own identity.

The date and provenance of Acts, while important for determining its original social location, also cannot be determined with precision. Even if a date for Luke's Gospel from the mid-80s is likely and the narrative unity of Luke and Acts is presumed, this critical conclusion does not guarantee that Acts came from the same time and place as the Gospel. The argument that the same narrator must have written Acts with his Gospel depends largely on the claims that both the Gospel of Luke and Acts share (1) common language, (2) consistent theology, and (3) an ignorance of a second-century corpus of Pauline letters. Each of these claims, however, has been challenged; each is at day's end indeterminate.[4]

Once again the reader's sense of the time and place of Acts must arise from a close reading of the narrative. Luke probably wrote at a time when stressing the church's Jewish roots was necessary for both theological and political reasons. On the one hand, Rome should allow the church the same political freedoms it allowed Judaism; on the other hand, believers should retain their Jewish Scriptures and practices in order to be fully Christian. This later emphasis would have been especially pertinent if the theological tendency of Luke's church was toward supersessionism or some other theological expression that reflected the general failure of the church's mission to the Jews of the diaspora.[5] This would explain Luke's principal concern regarding the health of the church's Jewish legacy.

Perhaps we can discern more about the world behind Acts by considering the first reader, Theophilus (see 1:1; Luke 1:3), who is otherwise unknown to us. Evidently Theophilus is a new, although socially prominent, believer. Some have speculated that his name, which in Greek means "dear to God," is Luke's clever metaphor for every new Christian seeking theological instruction. However, it is more likely that Theophilus is a wealthy patron who has provided funds to enable Luke to write a detailed narrative of the church's beginnings for public consumption. Both his Greek name and his apparent spiritual immaturity (see Luke 1:4), especially when considered with the writer's honorific appellation "most excellent Theophilus" (Luke 1:3), suggest that Luke's first

4. See R. Maddox, *The Purpose of Luke-Acts* (Edinburgh: T. & T. Clark, 1982) 6-9. D. Trobisch, *Paul's Letter Collection* (Minneapolis: Fortress, 1994), has argued that Paul (or a close associate) placed a collection of his letters into circulation at Ephesus, perhaps as early as the mid-60s. Whether Luke knew of a collection of Paul's letters in any case cannot be so easily dismissed if allusions to (rather than citations of) them are credible evidence. The Commentary will argue at several points on the second half of Acts that Luke may well be alluding to one or more Pauline letters (e.g., Romans; 1–2 Corinthians) and not simply to common Pauline traditions used in both Acts and certain (esp. later/deutero-) Pauline correspondence (e.g., Ephesians; 1–2 Timothy). See also W. Walker, "Acts and the Pauline Corpus Reconsidered," *JSNT* 24 (1985) 3-23, who argues that Luke surely knew a collection of Paul's letters, was influenced by them, but had none open before him when writing Acts. This later conclusion is now revised in W. Walker, "Acts and the Pauline Corpus Revisited," in *Essays in Honor of Joseph B. Tyson,* ed. R. Thompson and T. Phillips (Macon: Mercer University Press, 1998) 77-86.

5. Any attempt to "update" religious conviction in the light of present contingencies is a kind of supersessionism— e.g., Judaism's efforts in rereading its Scriptures to take into account the destruction of the Temple/priesthood and its result in moving early Judaism toward its rabbinical expression is a kind of supersessionism. For this reason, R. Gordon, *Hebrews* (Sheffield: Sheffield Academic, 2000) 27-28, compares favorably the supersessionism evident in the Letter to the Hebrews with respect to the Scriptures with that taking place in contemporary Judaism.

reader was an affluent Greek, perhaps a God-fearer before converting to Jesus,[6] who desires a useful story to confirm his faith in the face of mounting confusions and challenges. It is reasonable for us to imagine that he found the transition from one symbolic world to another profoundly difficult.

While the narrative unity between the Gospel and Acts links Luke's story of Jesus to the events that follow his departure, the commentary will treat Acts as an independent biblical writing with its own literary, theological, and canonical integrity. While not disconnected from the purpose of his Gospel, Luke's reasons for writing a second book may be inferred from the distinctive theological emphases in Acts. Powell usefully summarizes these emphases in six categories: irenic, polemical, apologetic, evangelistic, pastoral, and theological.[7] His index catalogs those historical contingencies at the end of the first century that occasioned and helped shape this narrative as edifying communication from Luke for Theophilus.

(1) Acts was written to consolidate disparate faith communions. Luke's *irenic* spirit is no doubt an idealized feature of his theological vision. At the same time, his ecumenicity is never divorced from the hard pragmatics of the first church's mission in the world (see 6:1-7; 11:1-18; 14:27–15:29). A religious movement that lacks solidarity within its diverse membership will be ineffective in advancing its claims. Moreover, in the wider Roman culture, riddled with conflict and controversy of all kinds, a community of shared goods (material and spiritual) would embody evidence for the transforming power of God's saving grace. Surely the historical referent of this narrative theme is intended to compel Theophilus to locate himself within a community that practices reconciliation as the way of God.

(2) Acts was written as a *polemic* against idolatry. Scholars have long argued that Luke wrote Acts to challenge certain heretical forms of Christianity or even formative Judaism. That is doubtful. Rather, Luke responds positively to the concerns voiced by James at the Jerusalem Council over the "gentilizing" of the church (see 15:20-21, 28-29; see also the Commentary on 15:13–28:28). Agreeing with Paul's epistolary advice to the Corinthians (see 1 Corinthians 8–10), Luke's narrative sounds a cautionary note. Adding uncircumcised, uncatechized Gentiles to the church's rolls while the church's mission carries the Word of God farther and farther from the holy city may very well incline a pragmatic leadership (perhaps including Theophilus) to accommodate pagan religious practices and secular values that will corrupt its Jewish heritage.

(3) Acts was written as an *apologia* for Christianity. Read as a narrative about people, Luke's portrayal of Christian leaders underscores the authority and importance of their traditions for the future of the church. This is especially true of Paul, whose standing within the ancient church was contested into the second century. Luke does not locate Paul's religious authority in his apostolicity (see 1:21-22), as he does in his letters (e.g.,

6. Cf. J. Nolland, *Luke 1–9*, WBC (Dallas: Word, 1989) xxxii-xxxiii.
7. M. Powell, *What Are They Saying About Acts?* (New York: Paulist, 1991) 13-19.

Galatians 1–2). Rather, Paul's importance for the church is guaranteed by his prophetic vocation and performance (see 20:17-35).

Read as a political narrative, Luke's ambivalent depiction of Rome (and of Paul's Roman citizenship) in Acts may intend to define citizen Theophilus's relations with a non-Christian Roman world. While it is possible for a strong believer to be a good citizen (e.g., Paul), loyalty to the gospel or the church's missionary vocation must never be compromised by the obligations of citizenship.[8] Paul's defense speeches (see Acts 22–26; 28) are not concerned with his relationship to Rome; his *apologia* in Acts is funded by a rehearsal of his Jewish background and practices, along with a description of his prophetic vocation as a teacher of Israel. For this reason, neither repentant nor unrepentant Israel should have a problem with him or with the Christian congregations he has founded. Such a defense would be especially crucial if Theophilus belongs, as seems likely, to a congregation founded by Paul's mission. The Paul of Acts embraces his Roman and Tarsain citizenship without apology, and so should Theophilus when appropriate; the more important commitment, however, is to the church's Jewish roots. The Pauline legacy shapes a future that is closer to Israel than to Rome.

(4) Acts was written as a tool of the church's evangelistic *mission.* Clearly the literary theme that follows the triumph of the Word of God from Jerusalem to Rome testifies to the power and necessity of the proclaimed gospel. The prophetic boldness and effectiveness of the church's mission, superintended by God's Spirit, expresses this same theme. If the missionary episodes are read as indicating normative patterns of outreach for subsequent generations of Christians, then Acts may have been written for Theophilus to invigorate his congregation's missionary vocation or to teach him how to convert others in continuity with the missionaries of the earliest church.

The natural shift of the church's geographical epicenter from Jerusalem to Rome following the fall of Jerusalem would have instigated different concerns from those earlier between the Gentile mission and the Jewish church (see 11:1-18; 15:13-29; 21:17-26). The pressures on Luke's first readers would have been most keenly felt from the pervasive paganism of Roman cities. His response to this new missionary situation, however, is reactionary rather than progressive. When Paul finally arrives in Rome, he does not carry God's Word to its pagan population but first establishes his Jewish credentials (see 28:17-22) in order to convert religious Jews to Jesus (28:23-25). Luke does not perceive paganism as the church's principal threat; rather, the church's outreach is substantially weakened by the loss of its connection with the core beliefs and practices of repentant Israel.

(5) Acts was written to deepen the fragile faith of new believers such as Theophilus. Luke's *pastoral* intent for writing this narrative may have been to characterize Christian

8. This ambivalence is reflected in competing assessments of the church's relationship with Rome in Acts. P. Walaskay, *"And So We Came to Rome": The Political Perspective of Acts,* SNTSMS 49 (Cambridge: Cambridge University Press, 1983), argues that Acts defends Rome to the church, while R. Cassidy, *Society and Politics in the Acts of the Apostles* (Maryknoll, N.Y.: Orbis, 1987), argues that the church is a counterculture that brooks no political allegiance with Rome.

discipleship in response to his patron's particular struggles, with implications for all who share Theophilus's social status within the church. This motive underlies several narrative themes. For example, Acts provides a basic chronology of the religious roots of Christianity that may have enabled Theophilus and other new believers to locate themselves within space and time as participants of a real historical movement.[9] More important, Acts' distinct emphasis on the community of goods and description of well-known role models, such as Barnabas, may well have commended to affluent believers like Theophilus the sharing of their wealth with the community's poor as a Christian practice (see 2:42-47; 4:32-37; 11:27-30). This and other distinctive resurrection practices envisage a counterculture that may have proved a difficult life-style for the empire's rich and famous. That is, Acts was written to encourage members of urban congregations, such as Theophilus, to spearhead the redistribution of wealth as the guiding principle of the church's welfare program (cf. 1 Timothy 5–6). Further, the content and narrative significance of the speeches in Acts may have reassured the well-educated Theophilus that the gospel has intellectual integrity (see 17:22-31).

(6) Acts was written in response to a *theological* crisis. It is only a slight exaggeration to say that every NT book is occasioned by a theological crisis—a confusion over or misappropriation of some core conviction of God's Word that threatens to subvert the audience's Christian formation and witness. Several important interpreters of Acts have considered the occasion of Luke's narrative from this angle of vision. For example, H. Conzelmann famously opined that Acts was written to correct the apocalyptic eschatology of a church troubled by an internal conflict over end-time fanaticism and doubt. For this reason, Luke edited out most eschatological speculation from his sources and creatively shaped a narrative that emphasizes mission and church growth in a "real" world.[10]

The theological crisis that occasioned the writing of Acts, however, is similar to that of Paul's Letter to the Romans; it concerns whether "there is any unrighteousness on God's part" (Rom 9:14) with respect to unbelieving Israel (Romans 9–11).[11] The rousing success of Paul's urban mission in the diaspora among God-fearing Gentiles, coupled with his relative lack of success among Jews who remained divided in their response to the risen Jesus (see 28:16-28), may have prompted some Jewish believers to wonder whether the church's mission actually subverted God's promise to restore historic Israel: "Has Israel stumbled so as to fall?" (Rom 11:11). The church's missionary reports, combined with the destruction of the Jerusalem Temple, the placing of Palestine to direct Roman rule by Roman governors, and the virtual cessation of the Jerusalem church by end of the first century, provided the necessary warrants for some believers in Luke's

9. See B. Witherington, *The Acts of the Apostles: A Socio-Rhetorical Commentary* (Grand Rapids: Eerdmans, 1998) 77-97, for a full discussion of Acts' chronology.

10. H. Conzelmann, *The Acts of the Apostles,* trans. J. Limburg et al., ed. E. J. Epp and C. R. Matthews, Hermeneia (Philadelphia: Fortress, 1987) xlv-xlvii.

11. See R. Wall, "Israel and the Gentile Mission According to Acts and Paul: A Canonical Approach," in *Witness to the Gospel: The Theology of the Book of Acts,* ed. I. Howard Marshall and D. Peterson (Grand Rapids: Eerdmans, 1998) 437-58.

church to argue that the relevant symbols of covenant renewal between God and a "true" Israel no longer should include the traditional expressions of Jewish identity and holiness. These believers may have even appealed to Jesus' prediction of Jerusalem's destruction by Rome as the just deserts of Israel's rejection of him as Messiah (see 6:14; cf. Matt 24:1-2; Luke 19:41-48). The worrisome consequence was the attenuation of the church's Jewish legacy, without which the church could not be the church.

We should note that Luke's response in Acts is different from Paul's in Romans; Paul wrote a generation earlier when this internal threat was not so keenly felt. While both contend that only a remnant within Israel ever repented of sin and turned to God in faith (Rom 9:6-29), Paul is clearly dissatisfied with a divided Israel as a permanent solution. He, therefore, posits the full restoration of historic Israel at the return of Jesus following the Gentile mission (see Rom 11:25-36).[12] Acts does not register so sharp a dichotomy between the Jewish rejection of the gospel and the Gentiles embrace of it as found in Romans (see Rom 11:11-24). Rather, Luke is resigned to a divided Israel as a permanent feature of God's plan of salvation (see 3:19-23). The promise of a faithful God to restore Israel has *already* been realized in the church's mission to the entire household of Israel (Acts 2–8). For Luke, unlike for Paul, the return of Christ inaugurates a season of "universal restoration" (3:21); and for him, unlike for Paul, the promise of Israel's "refreshment" has already been fulfilled among repentant Jews (see 3:19-20). In the meantime, the pattern of God's faithfulness to Israel agrees with (rather than reverses) biblical prophecy: Israel is restored first and only when repentant Gentiles are "grafted in their place to share the rich root of the olive tree" (Rom 11:17).

This same difference is also reflected by the principal opponents of Paul's Gentile mission within the church. In the Pauline letters, Paul is opposed by "Judaizers"—Jewish Christians who stipulated that all Gentile converts must also be catechized and circumcised according to the traditions of the Judaizers' ancestral religion. As a working symbol of his opposition to this "Judaizing" movement within the church, he refused to circumcise Titus, a Greek convert (see Acts 15:1-2; cf. Gal 2:1-10). When Luke wrote Acts, however, the principal internal threat to the church's faith were "Gentilizers" who threatened to erase anything Jewish from the church's core identity. To mark this different context, Luke tells the story of Paul's circumcision of Timothy, who symbolizes the mission's resistance to the gentilizing of the church's Jewish legacy (see 16:1-5; cf. 15:19-21, 28-29; 21:25). Surely Luke was right to worry; the attenuation of the church's Jewish legacy led to Marcionism in the next generation and has cultivated the anti-Semitism that continues to debilitate our own.

## ACTS AS COMPOSITION: READING ACTS AS LITERATURE

The principal interest of those interpreters who approach Acts as a composition is to construct the literary world within the text rather than to reconstruct the ancient world

12. See C. Hill, "Romans," *Oxford Bible Commentary* (Oxford: Oxford University Press, 2001).

behind it. Some "in-the-text" readings of Acts are vitally interested with historical questions too—with those first-century exigencies and communicative intentions that contributed to the narrator's choice of literary genre and narrative aim. Other literary explorations into Acts detach the literary text from these historical moorings in order to consider its intertextuality, linguistics, or creative storytelling in ways that treat Acts' historical context as largely irrelevant to the theological points it scores.

For the majority of interpreters of Acts, the most important literary query concerns its *genre:* Is Acts a history, a biography, a novel, an apologia, or a variety of literature without ancient parallel?[13] The stakes in answering this question are large, since what one concludes about a book's genre influences what one concludes about its overarching purpose—that is, function follows literary form. The literary critic typically begins with the recognition that Acts is the second of two volumes whose interpretation requires a prior decision about its narrative unity with Luke's Gospel. Until recently most commentators have simply affirmed the unity of Luke and Acts and extended this unity to a common genre. In this case, the genre of "Luke-Acts" is introduced by the preface to Luke's Gospel (1:1-4), which is then alluded to in the preface to Acts (1:1-2). That is, Acts is the second volume of a continuous *diēgēsis*—a historical narrative of some sort—about "the things fulfilled among us" (Luke 1:1).

At the very least, however, this consensus must now be qualified in several ways. Simply put, Acts is not a gospel. Luke's Gospel is more like ancient biographical literature that tells the story of a person's life and career. This biography is "gospel" because it tells the life story of the Savior from conception to ascension. Acts, on the other hand, sketches the origins of a religious movement, itself full of miracles and magic but without telling the story of only one heroic character. Moreover, the narrative of this second volume is deliberately set within a chronological and geographical framework similar to historical monographs produced in antiquity (see 1:8). Acts is hardly "secular" history, since its narrator structures the progress of this movement as a commentary on biblical prophecy. Read from this literary perspective, the story of the successive missions of various prophets-like-Jesus who carry the Word of God from Jerusalem to Rome and from Jew to Gentile has been scripted by God according to Israel's Scriptures (see 2:14-21; 15:13-21; 28:25-28).

A number of studies have demonstrated that Acts is best read as a genre of ancient *historiography,* itself quite fluid in form and function. Luke's narrative is a selective account of what happened—a "history" shaped and signified according to his personal theological beliefs and pastoral purposes (see above, "Acts as Conversation"). History, whether ancient or modern, is almost always written with a language and within a framework that reflects the historian's discrete perspective on the meaning of events. In the case of Acts, then, Luke selects and arranges a series of events that he narrates for

13. Cf. M. Parsons and R. Pervo, *Rethinking the Unity of Luke and Acts* (Minneapolis: Fortress, 1993). See also Witherington, *The Acts of the Apostles,* 2-39, for a careful review of Parsons and Pervo's work. The editorial tendency of many modern commentary series to assign both Luke and Acts to the same scholar reifies the assumption that common authorship presumes a common theological conception.

his reader(s) in order to give meaning to the church's mission and message as a history that accords with God's redemptive plans for Israel and the nations.

Since Luke was not himself an eyewitness to much of what he recounts and interprets, he depended upon sources for his relevant information.[14] The content and nature of these sources, whether oral or written; their identity; and Luke's reception and handling of them are all matters of considered and continuing speculation. Dibelius's verdict that Acts is largely the creative work of its author, whose access to reliable material was limited at best, has keenly influenced the modern discussion.[15] On this view, for example, the speeches of Acts are not based on notes taken by auditors but are Luke's literary creations. Even the "we" passages of Acts are not the accounts of an eyewitness but reflect the rhetorical artistry of a narrator who inserts himself into the narrative world in order to influence the reader's impressions of what is read (see 16:10-16). This older view has been substantially revised by new appreciation for the artistry of ancient historiographers, whose representations of a real event cohere not only with other literary elements of their composition but also with available information about that event as recalled by reliable (and often firsthand) witnesses. Many scholars, therefore, are inclined to accept Luke as one of Paul's team whose memory (or personal diaries) is the principal (but not the only) source he draws upon when shaping his story of Paul's mission and trials. While it remains another matter to assess the historical credibility of what is written in the first person or the nature of Luke's personal relationship with Paul, the narrator's presence as "credible witness" to events narrated in several passages has a measured rhetorical effect on the reader. Luke must have realized this, or else he would have surely erased every trace of himself from Acts. Instead, he chooses to address certain reservations about Paul or the results of his mission by placing himself unobtrusively in the story to help relieve the suspicions about a controversial Paul.[16]

In this light, another important interest of literary criticism is to determine how the various elements of Luke's story form a coherent plotline: How does Acts work as a narrative?[17] Simply stated, the plot of Acts unfolds in support of Luke's theological aim. On the one hand, he designs his story according to a specific geographical and chronological framework. The action begins in Jerusalem before moving beyond the holy city into the neighboring provinces of Samaria and Judea before moving into the nations and peoples beyond Palestine (see the Overview to Acts 9–28). Many have found this geographical outline indexed by Jesus' programmatic prophecy in Acts 1:8. In addition, Acts traces the key events with brief glimpses of the most important leaders of earliest

14. For a competent review of Luke's use of various sources when writing Acts, see J. A. Fitzmyer, *The Acts of the Apostles,* AB 31 (Garden City, N.Y.: Doubleday, 1998) 80-90. I will take up more specific problems with Luke's sources when apropos to the discussion of specific texts.

15. M. Dibelius, *Studies in the Acts of the Apostles,* ed. H. Greek (New York: Scribner's, 1956).

16. Cf. S. Porter, *The Paul of Acts,* WUNT 115 (Tübingen: Mohr Siebeck, 1999) 10-66, who argues that the use of "we" in Acts cues the reader to an independent and continuous Pauline source (which may be, but probably is not, Luke) whose favorable view of Paul was of special usefulness in advancing the narrator's apologetic interests.

17. For good examples of reading Acts as narrative, see R. Tannehill, *The Narrative Unity of Luke-Acts,* vol. 2 (Minneapolis: Fortress, 1990); F. S. Spencer, *Acts,* Readings: A New Biblical Commentary (Sheffield: Sheffield Academic, 1997).

Christianity to establish a general chronology of the church's origins. On the other hand, this historical conception provides the framework for two grand thematic movements ("conversion" and "consecration"), each scripted by extended citations of Scripture (see 2:17-21; 15:16-18) that narrate how the redemptive purposes of God are realized through the church's mission (see "Acts as Theology," below).

Among the many narrative elements that make up the plot of Acts, the speeches are especially important.[18] They make up roughly one-third of the composition and often signal programmatic movements in the plot while providing summaries of the narrator's core theological commitments. The speeches of Acts typically provoke further responses to the gospel that move the story's action from setting to setting in a "logical" manner. As such they supply an interpretive matrix by which the narrative's aim is made clearer. The most important and often debated of these speeches serve missionary ends. Peter's Pentecost sermon (see 2:14-41), the inaugural sermon of Paul's mission to the nations at Pisidian Antioch (see 13:16-41), and Paul's sharply stated Socratic retort at the Athenian Aeropagus (see 17:22-31) are good examples of missionary discourse that serve the narrator's programmatic concerns. Other speeches shaped according to the conventions of different rhetorical genre are important to the plotline of Acts. For example, Stephen's apologia as a prophet-like-Jesus stipulates the nature of the prophetic vocation that details the conflict between Christian preaching and Jewish tradition (see 7:1-53). Paul's so-called farewell speech defines the sort of person who best serves an orderly succession of future leaders in the fledgling church his mission has founded (see 20:18-35). Finally, the various defense speeches of the Paul of Acts at the book's end (see 22:1-21; 24:10-21; 26:2-23; 28:17-20) serve to defend his spiritual authority within emergent Christianity and within the Christian biblical canon of the Pauline letters that follow.

Even though reflecting different rhetorical conventions to serve different narrative settings, the speeches of Acts draw from a common pool of images and ideas.[19] The result is a profound sense of continuity both in the *content* of Christian proclamation from the risen Jesus (see 1:3) to the imprisoned Paul (see 28:30-31) and in the *vocation* of Christian preachers inspired by the Holy Spirit to perform competently, faithfully, and boldly all the tasks of the prophet-like-Jesus. Thus every speech in Acts—whether missionary, apologetic, or edifying—is centered by the non-negotiable content of God's saving word. Jesus performs signs and wonders as God's Messiah; he then suffers and is crucified; and finally he is resurrected and exalted by God to confirm that "there is no other name under heaven by which we must be saved" (4:12). To show that this messianic "event" conforms to the script of God's salvation, proofs from prophecy are

18. See M. Soards, *The Speeches in Acts: Their Content, Context, and Concerns* (Louisville: Westminster/John Knox, 1994).

19. I will consider the implications of the rhetorical shaping of the speeches of Acts in some detail when commenting upon specific passages. For a useful introduction to this literary element, especially as it relates to ancient models of public speaking, see the relevant essays gathered together in *The Book of Acts in Its First Century Setting*, vol. 1, ed. B. Winter and A. Clarke (Grand Rapids: Eerdmans, 1993).

layered into the speeches. Eyewitness testimony, whether of the risen Jesus (e.g., 2:32; 26:8, 15-16, 26), of personal experience of God's presence (e.g., 15:7-11, 12), or of an exemplary life (e.g., 20:18-21), complements Scripture's witness. Religious experience is glossed by Scripture's interpretation to prove the trustworthiness of the Gospel's claims about the Lord's messiahship and the faithfulness of God to promises of redemption. Other narrative elements, such as Luke's summaries (see 2:42-47; 4:32-35) and interludes (see 6:1-7), perform roles within Acts similar to the speeches. These elements underwrite the most important literary themes and provide a retrospective on previous events in preparation for the future.

Luke's use of repetition is another important literary convention of his narrative. For instance, the triadic telling of important episodes underscores their value in the narrative world (e.g., Paul's call, 9:9-19; Cornelius's conversion, 10:1-44). In addition, the repeated uses of prophetic catchwords (e.g., παρρησία parrēsia, "boldness") and phrases (e.g., σημεῖα καὶ τέρατα sēmeia kai terata, "signs and wonders" or ἔσχατος τῆς γῆς eschatos tēs gēs, "end of the earth"), of kerygmatic motifs (e.g., ἄφεσις aphesis, "forgiveness" or βασιλεία τοῦ θεοῦ basileia tou theou, "kingdom of God"), of literary themes (e.g., ἄπαντα κοινά hapanta koina, community of goods) and narrative actions (e.g., mixed response to the gospel or mass conversions) are important for several reasons. The entire range of meaning unfolds by each repetition of a word or literary theme in new compositional settings. More important, the *intratextuality* within Acts invites a more reflexive or unified reading of the story. Through repeated words or images the reader is reminded of earlier episodes or texts that are then recalled and brought into a mutually informing dialogue with the current text or episode. For example, in the testimony that God did "signs and wonders" among the Gentiles (15:12), the reader recognizes that the use of "signs and wonders" recalls Joel's prediction concerning the last days (Joel 2:19). In this way, the reader recovers the theological subtext of Paul's (and Peter's) testimony: God's promise of salvation is extended to include everyone, Jew and now Gentile, who repents and turns to the Lord Jesus in faith. Luke's use of repetition forges a literary coherence that aims disparate pieces of the narrative toward a common theological purpose.

Similar to the phenomenon of intratextuality within Acts, the *intertextuality* between Acts and antecedent sacred tradition supports and adds an inherent depth of understanding to Luke's narrative aim.[20] Even a cursory reading of Acts reflects Luke's routine use of sacred tradition, both biblical (LXX) and kerygmatic. He needs only to mention a familiar biblical phrase or employ a familiar prophetic typology (e.g., God's judgment of unrepentant Israel) to evoke other biblical texts and stories where that phrase is used or follows a typological pattern. Sometimes these texts are actually cited (e.g., 2:17-21), but more often Scripture is echoed by reference to common words or narrative elements

---

20. See R. Wall, "Intertextuality, Biblical," in *Dictionary of New Testament Background,* ed. C. Evans and S. Porter (Downers Grove: InterVarsity, 2000) 541-51.

(e.g., people, places, events). The "diverse components of the biblical anthology share a common worldview, [where] innumerable strands link together the constitutive units [to form] a literary and ideological entity."[21] The anticipated result of finding these citations or hearing those echoes of an earlier text when reading another is to link these two texts together as partners in a reflexive, mutually informing conversation—hence, the label "intertextuality." Significantly, the cited or echoed text recalls not only a particular story or idea but also a history of reception (both within and external to Scripture) that adds still additional layers of information to the interpretive matrix. The result is that the reader is able to discern a fuller, richer meaning.[22]

While Luke's rereading of his sacred tradition is also shaped by the currents of his Greco-Roman world, his use of Scripture in Acts is essentially Jewish. Thus he employs tradition in a way consonant with the church's Jewish heritage. The idea of Scripture that lies behind its appropriation in Acts is that the cited or echoed text is produced by the Spirit of God. This same Spirit leads interpreters to render Scripture's divinely intended meaning in public proclamation (17:3). In this way, Scripture (or Jesus tradition) is rightly used to supply evidence that "these things that have happened among us" follow God's prophesied plan for Israel's promised restoration. That is, Luke does not use Scripture in defense of the faith ("proof from prophecy") but as integral to his story's theological meaning. This particular quality of Lukan composition is similar to Jewish midrashic literature.[23] Modern interpreters, alert to the principles of Jewish exegesis, will recognize, for example, that Luke's composition of Peter's Pentecost sermon is midrash-like: the citation of a relevant biblical text (Joel's prophecy, Joel 2:28:32 [LXX 3:1-5]) is followed by commentary on its contemporary meaning (see Joel 2:14-21, 22-41) and the inclusion of biblical commentaries (*midrashim*) on Pss 16:8-11 and 110:1. Luke's use of catchwords and phrases from biblical texts throughout his narrative suggests a sustained and reflexive dialogue with Israel's Scriptures—that is, between his text and the biblical text—that is characteristic of midrashic literature. The intent is to lead us into a fuller and more contemporary understanding of God's Word.[24]

No introduction to the literary fabric of Acts is complete without mentioning the artistry of Luke's storytelling. His effective use of romance[25] and dramatic episodes involving divine speech and action,[26] his use of local color to add realism to the most

21. S. Talmon, "Emendation of Biblical Texts on the Basis of Ugaritic Parallels," in *Studies in the Bible,* ed. S. Japhet (Jerusalem: Magnes, 1986) 279.

22. According to R. Hays, *Echoes of Scripture in the Letters of Paul* (New Haven: Yale University Press, 1989) 18-19, the critical task of finding echoing predecessors prevents a version of intertextuality that is purely literary and of the present moment.

23. For Luke's narrative style as midrash-like, see Evans and Sanders, *Luke and Scripture,* 1-13.

24. Cf. D. Boyarin, *Intertextuality and the Reading of Midrash* (Bloomington: Indiana University Press, 1990) 1-21; M. Fishbane, *The Garments of Torah* (Bloomington: Indiana University Press, 1989) 16-18.

25. See R. Pervo, *Profit with Delight* (Philadelphia: Fortress, 1987); D. Edwards, *Religion and Power* (New York: Oxford, 1996).

26. See J. Thomas, *The Devil, Disease and Deliverance,* JPTSS 5 (Sheffield: Sheffield Academic, 1998); H. Kee, *Medicine, Miracle and Magic in the NT Times,* SNTSMS 55 (Cambridge: Cambridge University Press, 1986).

crucial episodes of Paul's mission (27:1–28:10), and the lively wit he brings to his storytelling (20:7-12), sometimes to mock the early church's competition (see 19:28-34), all contribute to a well-told story that entertains as well as edifies.

Finally, this commentary will often call attention to the complex textual history of Acts.[27] R. Brown comments that "Acts has a textual problem more acute than that of any other NT book."[28] In addition to the standard set of textual variants, the ancient Greek manuscripts of Acts include a distinctive group best exemplified by the bilingual (Latin and Greek) Codex Bezae (D), known as "the Western text of Acts."[29] One must decide whether this Western text or another prominent family of manuscripts, the so-called Alexandrian text of Acts, most nearly represents the Acts written by Luke and thus the narrative used for this study. The majority of textual scholars believe that the most distinctive features of the Western text are scribal interpolations added long after Luke's death; for this reason such scholars prefer to use the Alexandrian text as the basis of modern translations (including both the NIV and the NRSV).

Some scholars, however, have proposed that both texts of Acts were put into circulation roughly at the beginning of the canonical process toward the end of the second century, when Luke's reasons for writing Acts were replaced or qualified by still other concerns of the emerging church catholic. Significantly, the Western text of Acts, which expands Luke's narrative (more than the speeches) to reflect the theological tendencies of this church, betrays its concern to distinguish Christianity from Judaism as two discrete religious and theological options. In doing so, this popular version of Acts became an "anti-Judaic" narrative. The hostility of unrepentant Jews and their leaders is intensified in the text, while the institutions and traditions of Judaism are diminished in importance. A large number of "Western" variants contribute to this negative impression; thus, in Epp's words, "the Jews come out rather poorly in the D-text."[30] Further, Western scribes added narrative materials to enhance Paul's already powerful profile. Not only are his deeds made even more spectacular and his character more virtuous, but also he is routinely protected by the Holy Spirit against the evil machinations of his Jewish opponents, who are powerless against him in any case. While these later interpolations may well reflect an early scribal commentary on Luke's Acts in the service of the canonical process,[31] they helped to foster a supersessionist theology and anti-Semitic

27. See C. K. Barrett, *A Critical and Exegetical Commentary on the Acts of the Apostles,* 2 vols., ICC (Edinburgh: T. & T. Clark, 1994, 1998) 1:2-29. The most important textual problems will be considered in the footnotes to this commentary.

28. R. Brown, *An Introduction to the New Testament* (New York: Doubleday, 1997) 327. For a full account of the history of this textual problem, see W. Strange, *The Problem of the Text of Acts,* SNTSMS 71 (Cambridge: Cambridge University Press, 1992).

29. See E. Epp, *The Theological Tendency of Codex Bezae Cantabrigiensis in Acts,* SNTSMS 3 (Cambridge: Cambridge University Press, 1966). The most balanced discussion of how this version of Acts compares with the other principal Greek text of Acts, the so-called Alexandrian text, is P. Head, "Acts and the Problem of Its Texts," in Winter and Clarke, *The Book of Acts in Its First Century Setting,* 1:415-44.

30. Cf. Epp, *The Theological Tendency of Codex Bezae Cantabrigiensis in Acts,* 166.

31. Cf. B. Childs, *Introduction to the Old Testament as Scripture* (Philadelphia: Fortress, 1979) 84-106.

prejudice within the church that remains to this day. For the contemporary church, reading the story of Paul in Acts in the light of Luke's original theological agenda may provide a necessary corrective to this dark side of the canonical project.

## ACTS AS CONFESSION: READING ACTS AS THEOLOGY

The decisions one makes about reading Acts as literature influences one's reading of Acts as a theological narrative.[32] Biblical narrative envisages the narrator's confession of faith—his core Christian beliefs—in narrative form. B. Gaventa's salient point is worth keeping in mind: "Luke's theology is intricately and irreversibly bound up with the story he tells and cannot be separated from it. An attempt to do justice to the theology of Acts must struggle to reclaim the character of Acts as a narrative."[33] At the same time, the theology of Acts contributes to a fuller biblical theology that monitors and molds the church's confession of faith according to its rule of faith.[34] For this reason, reading Acts as theology is an important project for any interpreter whose faith seeks theological understanding.

The theological substructure of Luke's narrative world is an antecedent "master" story about what God has done to bring salvation to the world according to the Scriptures. The inner logic of this foundational narrative and the substance of its core themes are introduced into Acts by the story of the first Pentecostal outpouring of the Holy Spirit (2:1-47) and are then developed within the rest of Acts by subsequent stories of the church's mission and speeches of a succession of prophets-like-Jesus. That is, the theological coherence of Acts is not found in a system of propositions about God or the way of God's salvation, but in the integral elements of a Christian story about how God's redemptive promises, prophesied by Scripture, are fulfilled. The following outline of this master story is intended only to orient the reader to the principal elements of a more theological reading of Acts.

(1) *God, the only God, has a plan of salvation disclosed in Israel's Scriptures.* God's sovereign presence and God's saving activities, according to Acts, are inextricably linked to God's redemptive plan (see 2:23; 13:36; 20:27). While God is not a character in the narrative, the narrated events occur as a "divine necessity" ($\delta\epsilon\hat{\iota}$ *dei;* see 1:16; 3:18; 5:38; 13:27; 27:24), whether they result in great successes or puzzling tragedies. The narrative world of Acts is underwritten by a faithful God who works through an

---

32. In organizing the theological conception of Luke's Gospel, Culpepper, *Luke,* 13-30, considers a range of "christological emphases" before treating a "compendium" of the gospel's most important theological themes. I would advise readers to peruse Culpepper's considered discussion of the theology of Luke's Gospel in conjunction with my outline of the theology of Luke's book Acts. The reader should keep in mind, however, that while various themes of Luke's Gospel do recur in Acts, the theological unity between them is much more dynamic. Luke's "confession of faith" in Acts adapts itself to a different historical setting and genre of literature; but his faith, reflected in the story he narrates, has also developed in consideration of new theological concerns facing his church. The theology of Acts is not redundant and makes its own distinctive contribution to a NT theology.

33. B. R. Gaventa, "Toward a Theology of Acts: Reading and Rereading," *Int.* 42 (1988) 150.

34. See R. Wall, "The 'Rule of Faith' in Theological Hermeneutics," in *Between Two Horizons,* ed. J. Green and M. Turner (Grand Rapids: Eerdmans, 2000) 88-107.

---

empowered church to fulfill promises made both to Israel and to all "the families of the earth" (3:25).

God promises to restore repentant Israel first of all (1:6). For this reason the church's mission begins in the holy city among devout Jews from "every nation under heaven" (see 2:5-11) and religious status (2:10b; 6:1-7; 8:4-25, 26-40). God is Israel's God, and God's salvation is promised to the "people" (λαός *laos*) of Israel and is first experienced by repentant Jews before moving out to include believers from every nation (chaps. 1–8; see esp. 3:17-26).[35] When the Word of God is finally carried beyond Palestine to the nations, the foundation of every new congregation is the church's Jewish legacy (15:19-21, 28-29; see also chaps. 16–28). Indeed, Israel's God is the sovereign Creator of all things (see 4:24) who alone determines the destiny of every nation (see 14:15-17; 17:22-31). It is this God who promised Abraham that all the nations would be blessed (see 3:25-26; cf. 7:5). For this reason the terms and aim of God's Word are never circumscribed by nationalistic or ethnocentric commitments, nor can any one sacred place domesticate a transcendent God or a people's covenant with such a God (see 7:44-50). The universal scope of God's salvation is predicated on the success of the church's mission among repentant Jews whose vocation is as "light to the nations to the end of the earth" (see 13:44-47). Repentant Gentiles who are added to the church membership rolls share in blessings promised to Israel, not because unrepentant Israel rejected the gospel but because a remnant of repentant Jews within Israel accepted its assertion that the resurrected Jesus is the Messiah of God.

The God of Acts orchestrates Christian history. The surety of God's redemptive purpose is central to the theology of Acts. Good planning not only envisions the prospect of what a people might become but it also implements and actively brings its purpose to realization in people's lives. Thus the God who makes promises also keeps them by carefully choreographing the events that accomplish redemption in the history of the repentant community. God's Spirit is poured out on this community as a gift of salvation, and, just as critically in Acts, the Spirit enables and directs members of the community in missionary activity according to God's plan.

This divine plan is revealed by the Scriptures of Israel, especially its prophetic texts and typologies. Jervell has famously asserted that "Luke is the fundamentalist within the New Testament,"[36] because Luke believes that Scripture vocalizes the intentions of God and predicts the history of God's salvation. God's Spirit and Israel's Scriptures are two

---

35. This summary follows the lead of J. Jervell, whose "theology of Acts" is found in several of his publications, especially *The Theology of the Acts of the Apostles* (Cambridge: Cambridge University Press, 1996). I disagree, however, with his description that repentant Gentiles *in every case* are found in the synagogue where their Jewish sensibilities have been cultivated prior to hearing the Christian gospel proclaimed. However, there are instances of pagans responding to the gospel in Acts (e.g., 14:8-9). Moreover, the point of Paul's proclamation to the pagans of Lystra (14:15-17) and Athens (16:22-33) is that God, the only God, is the God of every nation who desires to forgive everyone who calls upon the Lord for salvation.

36. Ibid., 61. Jervell contends that this "fundamentalism" extends from Luke's idea of Scripture's absolute authority and the validity of its teaching to his pervasive use of Scripture in support of his narrative's plotline.

parts of an integral whole in Acts. The Spirit can guide the church's mission and make its message effective only when witness is grounded in the wisdom of Scripture as rightly interpreted by Spirit-inspired prophets-like-Jesus (see 2:4; also, e.g., Peter, 4:8; Stephen, 6:3, 10; Philip, 8:4-6, 11-13; Paul, 13:4-12; James, 15:28). The conflict within Israel is essentially over which community is custodian of the christological interpretation of Scripture (see 17:2-3). In this sense, Scripture not only is interpreted by the Spirit-filled community in the light of the risen Jesus but also interprets and authorizes the community's mission in the Spirit's power and message about the Lord's resurrection.

(2) *According to prophecy's script, Jesus of Nazareth is God's Messiah, the only Savior, who realizes God's redemptive purpose as attested by his prophetic ministry and resurrection.*[37] The redemptive partnership between God, who takes complete responsibility for creation's promised restoration, and Jesus, who ushers its fulfillment into history, is at the epicenter of the theological conception of Acts. Jesus is God's Messiah, whose divine appointment as the world's Savior is at God's direction and according to God's plan as disclosed in Scripture (see 2:22-23, 36; 10:34-43). God alone can attest to Jesus' redemptive role and does so by the powerful deeds and persuasive word that God effects through him (see 2:22; 10:38). God's ultimate confirmation of Jesus' messiahship is disclosed in God's resurrection of him (see 2:36). God has made Jesus reigning Lord (2:36; cf. 1:9-11; 5:30-31); all must call upon his name for their salvation (see 2:21; 4:12).

God's faithful response to Jesus is reciprocal of Jesus' costly faithfulness to God, indicated by his suffering. The narrative of Jesus enshrined in the missionary speeches of Acts echoes both Jesus tradition and Scripture to render the Lord's suffering and death as faithful to God's redemptive purpose (see 5:30; 10:39). In this sense, God's resurrection of Jesus is more than a vindication of his messiahship; it is also symbolic of Christian mission and discipleship that demands bold obedience to God's divine purpose in order to participate in its forward movement to the end of earth and time (see 14:22).

The kerymatic Jesus of Acts reflects a fairly robust christology. While the terms of the church's proclamation emphasize his suffering and resurrection, details of Jesus' entire messianic career are included (1:22; 10:37-38), as is his parousia, when he will come to restore (3:19-21) and judge (17:30-31) all humanity (10:42). Luke's profile is consistent with the Gospel's story about Jesus and clearly assumes his readers' familiarity with it (1:1). Luke's theology of the cross is more prophetic than salvific. That is, rather than emphasizing Jesus' death as a sacrifice for sin (= Pauline), Acts interprets the crucifixion as symbolic of unrepentant Israel's obduracy about Jesus' mission (3:22; cf. 7:37).

37. See C. F. D. Moule, "The Christology of Acts," in *Studies in Luke-Acts,* ed. L. Keck and L. Martyn (Philadelphia: Fortress, 1980) 159-85, who argues that the developing christology the careful reader notes when moving from Luke's Gospel to Acts is integral to a realistic narrative that reflects changes in the church's confession of Christ in a post-Easter setting. Thus, e.g., the frequency of "Lordship" language in Acts (see 2:36) and the description of Jesus as the heavenly recipient of the church's petitions (see 7:59-60) is possible only *after* the events of the Gospel narrative are in "the past of Jesus."

The question may well be asked, then, In what sense is the Jesus of Acts the Savior of the world? The profile given above suggests various activities at different stages of his messianic career: in his past as the prophetic carrier of God's saving word (see 3:22; 7:37); during his present as exalted Lord with divine authority to save all who call upon him (see 2:21; cf. 7:56, 60); and in his future as returning agent of God's final restoration and judgment of all people (see 3:20-21; 17:31). The departure of the living Jesus at the beginning of Acts is a condition for a mission that continues what he has begun to do and say (see 1:1-2, 9-11). His bodily absence, however, does not mean that his redemptive influence is effectively in the past or that he is experienced as exalted Savior only in the words of the proclaimed gospel. The emphasis on the Lord's resurrection in Acts underwrites his living presence and active participation in the church's mission.[38] Thus, while Jesus does not dwell within the believer or the community "in him" (as in Pauline thought), he does exist beyond the church's kerygma. For instance, he reappears in visionary guise at strategic moments in the church's mission to disclose God's purpose for particular people (especially Paul) and places (see 7:55; 9:3-6, 10-16; 23:11), and the mere mention of his name revitalizes those who come into its power (see 4:8-12). It is incorrect, therefore, to speak of Jesus as a passive figure during the church's present mission. While God's Spirit has replaced God's Messiah as the principal agent of salvation during "these last days" (see 2:17-19), the exalted Lord continues as a sometimes participant in the church's mission.

(3) *All who earnestly repent and call upon the living Jesus will be saved, the Jew first and also the Gentile.* All who hear the gospel, whether Jewish or Gentile, are divided into two groups: the repentant and the unrepentant (see "Acts as Conversation," above). Indeed, the common identifying mark of all who belong to Jesus is their positive response to the saving call of God issued in the proclamation of the gospel and their reception of the Holy Spirit (see 15:7-11). Likewise, the spiritual crisis facing Israel (most especially) and the nations is their ignorance of the gospel: People cannot convert to the light if they continue to live in darkness. The prophet's imperative is grounded in this practical reality (see 3:17; 13:27; 17:30).

Converting to Jesus means calling him "Lord" (see 2:21) and confessing that he is the promised Savior God has sent forth into the world to rescue us from our enemies and— especially—to forgive our sins (see 2:38; 3:19; 5:31; 13:38-39; 15:9) and so to liberate us from eternal death (see 13:46). But salvation also involves healing the sick (see 3:7-8; 4:8-12; 28:7-9), illuminating the ignorant (see 3:17; 13:27; 17:30), rescuing the vulnerable from political threat (see 12:4-11; 16:30-31) and material poverty/hunger (see 4:33-34), guarding against demonic powers (see 5:16; 16:16-18; 19:11-20; 26:17-18), and protecting from natural catastrophe (see 27:21-26, 31-44). Each expression of saving grace heralds God's commitment to keep the biblical promise of a "universal restoration" (see 3:21).

38. Cf. R. O'Toole, *The Unity of Luke's Theology,* GNS 9 (Wilmington, Del.: Glazier, 1984) 38-61.

At the same time, each act of divine benefaction responds to a deliberate act of faith commensurate with need. Repentance is an intellectual reorientation—a change of one's mind—away from any ordering of one's life that opposes the reign of God and toward the truth claims of God's Word. The repentant Jews who asked Peter following Pentecost, "What shall we do?" vocalize the decisive question that is implied throughout Acts in different narrative settings: How shall a needy people respond to the gospel's invitation to enter into a new life with God? The answer comes in a series of imperatives: listen (2:22; 7:2; 8:6; 13:7, 16; 15:13; 19:10; 28:28); believe (3:16; 8:12-13, 37; 11:17, 21; 13:12; 14:23; 15:11; 18:8); be baptized (2:41; 8:38; 9:18; 16:15, 33; 19:1-5); turn to God (3:19; 9:35; 11:21; 20:21; 26:20); request instruction (8:31; 9:5; 10:30-33; 24:24; 26:17-18); show hospitality to strangers (16:15, 33-34; 28:7-10). Indeed, there are some who will respond more eagerly to the Word of God because of conscientious study (17:11) or faithfulness to Jewish training (15:21), both of which indicate readiness to receive God's truth.

The clear impression left by this glossary of salvation is its all-encompassing holistic nature. God's grace saves people from disease, disaster, demons, death, and destitution; and it also forgives people of sin. This penetration of divine grace into human life symbolizes the biblical conception of salvation—one that reroutes a broken and battered creation back toward the original intentions of its Creator, beginning with Israel's restoration (3:19-21).

(4) *Those who repent and belong to the Lord Jesus Christ receive the Holy Spirit and are initiated into a community of goods.* The third person of the Holy Trinity is disclosed at Pentecost as the Spirit of prophecy who empowers persons to bear a persuasive and insightful witness to the risen Jesus (see 2:4). As the reader of Acts should expect, this is not very different from the idea of God's Spirit in Israel's Scriptures.[39] However, the powerful influence of the Holy Spirit in Acts extends to all believers and reflects the characteristics of a personal deity. The Spirit speaks (8:29; 10:19; 13:2) and guides (13:4; 15:28; 16:6-7), and people can lie to (5:3), test (5:9), and resist (7:51) God's Spirit. The Spirit is not external to those it influences (cf. 11:15) but is "poured out" to "fill up" (2:4; 4:8, 31; 6:3, 5; 7:55; 9:17; 11:24; 13:9) those it empowers for ministry.

The Holy Spirit enables the Lord's successors to continue to do and say what he began during his messianic career (1:1-8). That is, the Spirit's presence within the community of believers provides the essential resource for obeying its missionary vocation (1:8; 2:1-4, 17-21). As Jervell notes, "the church does not lead and guide itself: God does through the Spirit."[40] In particular, the Spirit funds the religious authority of a succession of prophetic leaders (8:14-19) who interpret the prophecies of Scripture (2:4), speak the

39. See R. Stronstad, *The Charismatic Theology of St. Luke* (Peabody, Mass.: Hendrickson, 1984), and *The Prophethood of All Believers,* JPTSS 16 (Sheffield: Sheffield Academic, 1999); cf. Jervell, *The Theology of the Acts of the Apostles,* 43-54.

40. Jervell, *The Theology of the Acts of the Apostles,* 51.

Word of God persuasively (4:8) and boldly (4:29-31; 9:27, 29; 19:8; 28:31; cf. 18:26), and perform mighty signs and wonders (5:12-16; 8:13; 14:3). All of these activities are in continuity with Jesus and the OT prophets before him.

Peter's programmatic reference to the "gift of the Holy Spirit" at Pentecost (2:38) is important in two ways for filling out Luke's idea of the Spirit. First, the Spirit of prophecy is also the transforming Spirit of God, whose work is especially realized in the resurrection practices of the repentant community.[41] Second, salvation is marked out within history by a concrete experience of the Spirit's reception (see 8:14-17, 39-40; 9:17; 10:43-44; 19:5-6). Neither the protocol nor the experience of being filled with the Spirit follows a common pattern, and the narrator stresses different literary themes in each episode. Nevertheless, it is clear from Acts that God's salvation and the reception of God's Spirit are integral elements of any real experience of God's benefaction, to which the community bears witness in the manner of its life together (see 2:47).

The church of Acts is a community of goods. Its united witness to the Messiah's resurrection is not only proclaimed but is also embodied in its common life under the aegis of the Holy Spirit. The community's "resurrection practice" includes four discrete elements: economic, spiritual, religious, and social. As economic κοινωνία (*koinōnia*), the community reorders its possessions according to the principle of Jubilee (see Luke 4:16-18) so that its generosity toward the needy reciprocates God's generosity in the gift of salvation (see 2:44-45; 4:32–5:11; 6:1-6; 11:27-30). Likewise, the gift of God's salvation is embodied as the gift of God's Spirit. As with material possessions, the Holy Spirit is the common property of an inclusive community, so that its Pentecostal coming upon repentant Jews is repeated on repentant Samaritans (see 8:14-16) and Gentiles (see 10:44; cf. 11:17; 15:9). Living boldly under its powerful influence is a second resurrection practice of those who follow Jesus. The religious dimension of the community's solidarity is expressed most profoundly by a prohibition: Abstain from things polluted by idols (15:20; see also 15:29; 21:25). The concern of Acts is not so much the inward, spiritual purification of individual believers but the political purity of a community's identity. The sin of idolatry undermines Scripture's legacy as that which gives shape to a people's worship of and allegiance to God (see 7:38-44). Those who practice idolatry—who substitute alternative deities for worship of Israel's God, the only God—demonstrate their ignorance of God's redemptive purpose (14:14-18; 17:22, 24-29; 19:26). A prophetic community is a counterculture to the surrounding order. A sociology of external conflict requires all the more a sociology of internal unity. This is possible to maintain only by a carefully managed protocol of conciliation that forges unity between its disparate groups (see 6:1-6; 14:27–15:29). The solidarity of believers is emphatic within Acts: Believers are "together" when at worship and in mission.

41. See M. Turner, *Power from on High: The Spirit in Israel's Restoration and Witness in Luke-Acts,* JPTSS 9 (Sheffield: Sheffield Academic, 1996).

The religious authority of the community's leadership team receives particular stress in Acts even as it does in the so-called Pastoral Letters of the Pauline corpus (1–2 Timothy and Titus). The emphasis is not on ecclesiastical orders so that a succession of male leaders is placed at the top of an institutional hierarchy/patriarchy. Rather, the religious authority of the Lord's successors is practical, prophetic, and personal. Further, it is ever adaptable to the changing landscape of the church's mission, for no one model of leadership is found in Acts. Yet Peter (4:32–5:16), Priscilla (18:1-28), and Paul (20:18-35) are surely the principal prophetic exemplars of Acts.[42] In particular, the similarities between Luke's portraits of the apostle Peter in the first half of Acts and the missionary Paul in the second half suggest that God grants spiritual authority predicated by a common prophetic vocation that is commissioned by and in continuity with the risen Lord. Moreover, the confirmation of this authority is by persuasive word and powerful deeds that are enabled by the Holy Spirit rather than by individual talent or education (see 4:13). Both Peter and Paul stand out as individuals. The moral value of their personal portraits in Acts should not be underestimated. Each embodies characteristics that are critical to the future leaders of the church: Their courageous and costly obedience to their calling, stewardship of possessions, theological perspicuity, religious observance, and personal piety are marks of the faithful disciple (see 20:18-35).

There are also real differences between the Twelve, represented by Peter, and their successors, represented by Stephen, Philip, James, and Paul. Although the matter remains contested among scholars of Acts, I want to emphasize the special significance of the Twelve—and Peter in particular—within the economy of God's salvation. They are close friends of the historical and resurrected Jesus and thus warrant being considered his apostolic successors (see 1:3-11, 21-22); and their commission to prophetic ministry and spiritual authority are glossed by Jesus' earlier prophecy that they would act as regents and judges of Israel (see chaps. 3–5; cf. Luke 22:29-30). Their inspired ministry is the medium through which the kingdom is restored to repentant Israel. Further, every decisive movement in the church's mission to the end of the earth is initiated or confirmed by apostolic authorization. While the Paul of Acts embodies most fully the vocation of repentant Israel as light to the nations, it is the Peter of Acts who both inaugurates (10:1–11:18) and confirms it (15:6-11). The continuity between Peter and Paul can function as an important element of Luke's apologia for Paul precisely because of Peter's key role in God's plan of salvation.

(5) *The community's resurrection hope during the last days is for the return of Jesus and the promised season of universal restoration he will fulfill.* Acts is a narrative about "the last days" (see 2:17; 3:19-26); in fact, every element of this "master story" is ultimately understood against an eschatological horizon. This theological conception may come as a surprise to those who note that while Acts opens in a resounding eschatological key (see 1:6-8, 10-11), the remaining narrative rarely sounds another futuristic

42. Cf. L. T. Johnson, *The Acts of the Apostles,* SP 5 (Collegeville, Minn.: Liturgical, 1992) 12-14.

note (see 3:19-21; cf. 7:31; 10:42; 17:30-31). Nowhere is there a discourse on the future as found everywhere else in the NT. Of course, Luke presumes a prior reading of his Gospel and knowledge of its prediction of the Lord's return, confirmed at Jesus' ascension. Further, Peter's reference to a future "time of universal restoration" (3:21) and Paul's prophecy of endtime judgment (see 17:31) point to God's cosmic triumph at the Lord's return to earth. Although scholars continue to debate the meaning of these texts, the narrator's theology is not shaped by a concern to correct some mistaken escha- tology—for example, a perceived delay in Christ's return or an apocalyptic faction within his church. The focus of Luke's eschatology in both his Gospel and Acts is God's commitment to promises made according to Scripture. Therefore, the primary theologi- cal problem addressed by the book is *theodicy,* the vindication of God's justice.

Acts envisages both the Lord's return (1:10-11) and the outpouring of the Holy Spirit (2:17) as eschatological events. The central theme in Luke's reckoning of this eschato- logical moment, however, is neither a detailed chronology nor the apocalyptic cast of the future (see 1:7); rather, his emphasis shifts to the historical means by which God's peo- ple will make their way under the aegis of the Spirit from Pentecost to parousia. The nar- rative framework of the church's movement toward God's ordained future consists of two integral motifs: the church's Spirit-led mission from Jerusalem to Rome, the princi- pal cities of two symbolic worlds that represent all people for all time, and an interpre- tive strategy that warrants each episode of this mission as fulfilling the promises of Israel's Scripture. The historic reality that confirms God's faithfulness is that a portion of Israel is restored (see 2:40; 3:19-23; cf. Rom 9:1-29). Despite the recurrent hostility of unrepentant Jews and Gentiles, this restored Israel, led first by the apostles and ulti- mately personified by the Paul of Acts, becomes "a light to the nations" from Jerusalem to Rome (see 3:25-26; 13:47; cf. 1:6-8).

The mode by which the Lord bids the covenant community to journey from Pentecost to parousia is to bear powerful witness to his resurrection (see 1:8). Scripture's promise of a restored Israel is not realized within "national" Israel—as many Jews antic- ipated—but within a remnant of repentant Jews (see 3:23) whom God calls out of Israel through the church's mission (see 2:37-41). Indeed, the church's mission to the whole household of Israel has already carried the Word of God to every group within the household of Israel (see 2:5-11): Hebrews and Hellenists (Acts 2–7), Samaritans and proselytes (Acts 8), those inside and those outside of the holy land. The conflict and mixed results that this mission has provoked fulfill Scripture's prophecies (see 28:25-27), and Paul personifies the prophesied vocation of repentant Israel in his mission as "light to the nations" (see 13:47; see also chaps. 9–28).

The church's hope in God's coming triumph is expressed through daily proclamation of God's faithfulness, in continuity with the risen Messiah and the prophetic community that succeeded him in this ministry of the Word. The ending of Acts (28:30-31), which summarizes Paul's mission in Rome, serves to facilitate the transition from the book's narrative world to the readers' real worlds. The book bids its audience to move ever forward to God's coming triumph by engaging in Spirit-enabled witness in the world.

## ACTS AS CANON

Approaching Acts in search of the Word of God requires more than a rigorous analysis of the book's social world, literary artistry, and theological conception. For the most part, modern interpreters concentrate on reconstructing the book's point of origin, whether in historical, literary, or theological categories. From their perspective, Acts is typically read as the second volume of Luke's continuous narrative. This narrative is shaped by his pastoral intentions, composed with ancient literary, rhetorical, and historiographical conventions and informed by his theological convictions to serve in the Christian formation of his first readers and the church. This critical construction, however, is often based on scholarly conjecture and runs the risk of freezing *the* meaning of Acts in an ancient world far removed from that of its current readers.

Even on historical grounds, Acts followed a separate and more difficult course into the biblical canon from the one taken by the Third Gospel. Those who formed the church's Scriptures for future generations of believers evidently did not think it necessary or even profitable to read Luke and Acts together. More likely, the pre-canonical Acts circulated with different collections of letters, both catholic and Pauline. For this reason, by the time the canonical process had concluded a few centuries later, the canonical Acts had its own peculiar function within the biblical canon, different from that of the Third Gospel. The importance of its role *as Scripture* thereby underwrites a particular approach to the study of Acts and its distinctive deposit to the biblical witness.

**Reading the Book of Acts as Scripture.** In the Commentary to follow, the central critical question raised is, *What do Luke's reasons for writing Acts have to do with the church's reasons for reading Acts as Scripture?* Any interpreter must try to bridge these two hermeneutical horizons. However, they are in constant flux due both to new insights about Luke's world and his writing and to changes in the time and location of his various interpreters. In particular, this text's movement from personal "conversation" to the church's "canon" sharply resets the interpreter's angle of vision toward Acts.[43] Several implications of this shift should be briefly noted:

(1) Reading Acts as Scripture recognizes the importance of different literary relationships within the New Testament. The intracanonical relationships between Acts and the four Gospels and between Acts and the two collections of letters (especially Pauline) that follow it are elevated in importance within canonical context. The "canon logic" envisaged

43. See R. Wall, "Canonical Context and Canonical Conversations," in *Between Two Horizons,* ed. J. Green and M. Turner (Grand Rapids: Eerdmans, 2000) 165-82.

by the arrangement of the different parts within the NT whole, and sometimes even of individual writings within these canonical parts, stipulates important markers in guiding the reader's approach to the NT. According to this arrangement, then, the fourfold gospel (not just Luke's Gospel) is perceived as prerequisite reading for the study of Acts, and the study of Acts under the gospel's light is prerequisite reading for the study of the letters that follow. The implications of this "canon logic" will be teased out in the Commentary.

(2) These new intracanonical relationships forged by the canonical process are also valuable when assessing the distinctive importance of the theology of Acts within the NT. No longer does the biblical theologian consider the thematic interests of Acts only in terms of their congruence with those found in Luke's Gospel. Rather, the theological contribution Acts makes to *biblical* theology is now measured as an indispensable part of an integral whole. Put in different words, upon consideration of the various theologies that make up the NT's entire theological conception, the interpreter is now pressed to imagine what a biblical witness to God might lack if it did not include Acts. What distorted idea of the church's faith, its religious or social identity, or of its vocation in the world might result from a conversation with a body of sacred writings that did not include this book? What thin reading of the Pauline letters would result if the interpreter failed to prepare by first reading the story of the canonical Paul of Acts? Simply put, reading Acts within its biblical setting reminds us that any theological understanding lacking the witness of Acts will distort Christian faith and life.

(3) The Paul of Acts is valued more keenly from this canonical perspective than when his role is reduced to a cameo appearance in the modern quest of the historical Paul. At stake in following the story of the Paul of Acts is not so much the historical accuracy of Luke's portrait—even though this is currently being reconsidered—or even the important questions about his credibility within earliest Christianity. The most important issues from a canonical angle of vision are theological ones: What does the Paul of Acts have to say about the future of the church? How does Paul's story in Acts orient its readers to the implied author of the Pauline letters that follow and the Pauline witness they enshrine (see the Overview to 15:13–28:28)?

(4) The church's conflict with the synagogue at the end of the canonical process was no doubt different from Luke's assessment when he wrote Acts (see "Acts as Conversation," above). What began as an intramural "Jewish problem" had become a "Judaism problem" by the end of the second century. Keen competition had developed between two "world religions," a problem made all the more prickly by their common history and theological conception. The scribal emendations to the Western version of Acts, with a more negative characterization of unrepentant Israel, may well reflect the canonizing community's heightened sensitivity to its relationship with Judaism and its sense of the canon's function to clearly delineate the church's identity (see "Acts as Composition," above). In a different sense, the portrait of Israel found in Acts clarifies

the difference between Christianity and Judaism in christological rather than nationalistic or ethnocentric terms. Thus Acts subverts any "Christian" prejudice against Jews on ethnic grounds (= anti-Semitism) or on the mistaken presumption that God has either reneged on promises made to historic Israel according to the Scriptures or has replaced Jews with Christians in the economy of salvation (= supersessionism). God's faithfulness to Israel remains inviolate; therefore, today's church must become more—not less—Jewish in order to be fully Christian in its worship and witness.

(5) The "primitivism" of Acts simply reflects the ecclesial experience of the earliest church, which fashioned itself after the diaspora synagogues and other voluntary organizations of the Roman world. Worship consisted of prayer meetings and teaching, with Christian fellowship centered in the homes of believers. The sociology of the church dramatically changed during the canonical process; these loosely confederated house congregations became in time participants of an emerging church catholic. For this reason, the ongoing interest in the images and ideas of "church" in Acts should focus on emulating its missionary vocation and prophetic message, its resurrection practices, and the nature of its spiritual leadership—important claims on any congregation in every age—rather than on replicating outward forms of governance and worship or other time-conditioned practices.

(6) In this regard, reading Acts as Scripture seeks to insinuate its narrative world into the changing "real" worlds of current readers. New layers of meaning hitherto hidden are discovered whenever sacred texts are allowed to penetrate and interpret the world of their interpreters. For example, contemporary readers will more easily discern the relevance of the Ethiopian eunuch's story (8:26-40) for reflecting upon the relationship between the church and its homosexual membership or more readily recognize the example of Priscilla in chap. 18 (as well as other women in Acts) as a role model for prophetic ministry in congregations that once were reluctant to encourage women in ministry. The vivid snapshots of the community of goods or repeated episodes that depict Paul's relations with Rome may challenge today's congregations to a more prophetic understanding of church as counterculture. Read as Scripture, Acts provides an important element of a wider "canonical context" in which the faithful community gathers to reflect on those issues that either undermine or underscore God's presence in today's world.

(7) Finally, reading Acts as Scripture cultivates a fresh sense of sacred time and space. The church continues to live in "the last days," betwixt Pentecost and parousia, when the Spirit of God empowers Christ's disciples to bear witness to the resurrection throughout the world in anticipation of God's coming triumph and creation's final restoration (see 3:20-21). The book of Acts has continuing authority to form a church that proclaims God's word and embodies a witness to its truth, heralding that coming day.

**Reading the Book of Acts Within Scripture.** If Acts is approached as a narrative written for and relevant to only its first readers, then the book's current readers will find little of value for their own Christian formation. Perhaps it was precisely a concern for subsequent readers of sacred texts that guided the canonical process that produced the NT in its present form. For example, in its canonical setting the book of Acts is detached from Luke's Gospel, which is now read as one of a set of four. If Acts is read in its current canonical placement rather than as the second volume of Luke-Acts, then the reader will naturally reflect upon its narrative as continuing the story of Jesus presented by the four Gospels. The reader's understanding of "all that Jesus began to do and teach" will be greatly expanded and enriched by a fourfold presentation.

The book of Acts acquired two properties during the process of canonical development that continue to help readers envisage its distinctive role within the NT: (1) its title, "The Acts of the Apostles," and (2) its placement as a bridge between the Gospels, on one side, and the two collections of letters, Pauline and catholic, on the other. Most people begin reading a book by considering its title, for a book's subject matter is typically indicated by its title and/or its subtitle. Consider the curious title of this book, "The Acts of the Apostles." Commentators routinely adjure that Luke's story is inappropriately titled. The book is about the activity of the Holy Spirit, they claim, rather than that of the apostles. Or, if read as Luke-Acts, the "mighty acts" of Acts are best understood as the continuation of Luke's historical narrative about Jesus. Against this conjecture, the effect of recognizing the superscription of Acts as a canonical property is to call attention to a new set of orienting concerns for readers of Acts as Scripture.[44]

Canonically, the two halves of the title each function to signal a key concept about the role of the apostles in Acts. First, the literary genre of πράξεις (*praxeis,* "acts")[45] tells stories of people, real or imagined, who are divinely favored to act in powerful ways on behalf of their community or nation. Such an aretology, or "folk" story, also functions as social commentary, since supernatural powers are given to heroes as evidence of their special status (and by extension, the special status of those communities or nations they helped to found). Their mighty deeds are not of their own making but testify to divine favor, and anyone who links his or her destiny to these heroic characters is assured of divine favor.

In the case of the book of Acts, the canonical process recognized the importance of Jesus' successors, whose persuasive words and powerful deeds founded the church and formed its rule of faith. The second half of the title—"of the apostles"—identifies those heroes of the faith whose special status and divinely ordained destiny ensures the salvation of all who submit to their spiritual authority (chaps. 4–5; 20:18-35). While it may seem theologically prudent to think of these characters as merely the means of the Holy

44. See R. Wall, "The Acts of the Apostles in the Context of the New Testament Canon," *BTB* 18 (1988) 15-23.
45. See J. A. Fitzmyer, *The Acts of the Apostles,* AB 31 (Garden City, N.Y.: Doubleday, 1998) 47-49.

Spirit's work, the effect of the canonical title is to shift the reader's interest from the Spirit's baptism to those prophetic successors of the Lord whom the Spirit fills for ministry. This concern to attach the church to its apostolic forebears reflects the sociology of the emergent "one holy catholic and apostolic church." This church's claims of special status in the economy of God's order were contested by rivals both within the church (Gnosticism, Montanism) and outside it (formative Judaism).[46] The book of Acts reminds its confessing readers that the church's sacred memories of the Lord's apostolic successors (including Paul) exemplify a vocation, character, message, and faith that all Christians must imitate in demonstrating their obedience to God.

The strategic placement of Acts between the Gospels and the letters suggests the transitional role it performs within the NT. The narrative of Acts continues and concludes the authorized biography of Jesus while introducing the Bible's readers to the apostolic writings that follow. Acts functions as a bridge connecting Gospels and letters in a logical relationship that mirrors the ultimate aim of the NT: to nurture Christian discipleship after the pattern of Jesus.

Acts can first of all be read as "commentary" on Jesus' story narrated in the four Gospels. Not only does the story Acts tells offer substantial proof of Jesus' resurrection as Lord and Messiah (cf. Acts 2:36), but it also issues Scripture's response to the theological crisis occasioned by his bodily absence from the Christian community (see John 13:31–14:31). Those disciples who follow after the exalted Lord are to continue in the power of the Holy Spirit to do and to say what Jesus began (see Acts 1:1-2). In this regard, the importance of retaining the final shape of the NT rather than combining Luke and Acts as a single narrative is indicated by the significant roles performed by Peter and the Holy Spirit in Acts where Jesus is absent—roles for which Luke's Gospel does not adequately prepare the reader of Acts. Peter's rehabilitation at the end of John (John 21:15-17) as well as the teaching about the Spirit's post-Easter role by John's Jesus (John 14–16) signify the important role that John's Gospel performs in preparing the reader for the story of Acts. Moreover, what it means to be a "witness" of the risen Jesus (Acts 1:8) is more fully understood by the biblical reader in the context of John's Gospel (John 15:26-27; cf. Luke 24:48).

The relationship between Acts and the following two collections of letters is more difficult for the interpreter to order. The conventions of epistolary literature are different from those of narrative literature and thus the differences between Acts and the letters are readily discernible. For example, Luke's portrait of Paul is sometimes at odds with Paul's self-understanding or missionary itinerary as given in his letters. Further, Luke

---

46. Some scholars use the expression "early catholicism" when referring to an emergent Christianity whose principal concern was to delineate the theological boundaries of the faith—by means of a "rule of faith"—to regulate Christian preaching and preserve the core beliefs of the apostolic traditions from their internal and external religious rivals. See E. Käsemann, "Paul and Early Catholicism," in *New Testament Questions of Today* (Philadelphia: Fortress, 1969) 236-51.

does not quote any of Paul's letters. Reading Acts as Scripture, however, compels a dialogue between the Paul of Acts and the Pauline letters of the NT.[47] The potential gains of this perspective may be illustrated when considering the canonical "seam" that connets the final passage in Acts, which portrays a missionary Paul in Rome (see 28:17-31), to the opening text of the first Pauline letter, that to the Romans, which introduces biblical readers to a missionary-minded apostle who is eager "to proclaim the gospel to you also who are in Rome" (Rom 1:15).[48] The interplay between the ending of Acts and the beginning of Romans underscores the primary concern of Luke's Paul, who is not found in a secluded study writing dense Christian theology but on city streets or in living rooms of rented apartments relating the Christian gospel to life in practical and persuasive ways.

Perhaps the most important role Acts performs within the NT is to proffer biographical introductions to the implied authors of the letters that follow. In canonical context, such biographies serve a theological purpose by orienting readers to the religious and moral authority of apostolic authors as trustworthy carriers of the word of God. While the historical accuracy of Luke's narrative of Paul and other leaders of earliest Christianity may be challenged, the rhetorical and ethical power of these figures confirms and commends the importance of their letters. The salient issue is not whether Acts fails as a historical record but that it succeeds as a theological resource, contributing to the church's understanding of its vocation and identity in the world.

In this regard, Acts provides an angle of vision into the Pauline and catholic epistolary collections that follow.[49] For instance, the relations among Peter, John, James, and Paul and their respective missions, as depicted in Acts, suggest how the interpreter arranges the intracanonical dialogue between those NT writings attached to each leader. Similarities and dissimilarities in emphasis and theological conception found when comparing the catholic and Pauline letters may actually correspond to the manner by which Acts narrates the negotiations on theological convictions and social conventions between different missions (e.g., Acts 2:42-47; 9:15-16; 11:1-18; 12:17; 15:12-29; 21:17-26). The modern discussion has emphasized how a narrator committed to the practical requirements of an "early catholic" church softens the disagreements between the leaders of earliest Christianity. But what is often overlooked is that the church collected and eventually canonized a Pauline corpus whose principal letters are often polemical and potentially divisive. The question is never raised as to why these Pauline letters were included in the canon of an "early catholic" church if the aim was to shape theological uniformity. Might it not be the case that the church recognized the importance of Acts in introducing the apostolic writings not so much to smooth their disagreeable edges as to interpret them?

---

47. For a comprehensive listing and analysis of the intertextual echoes of Pauline letters in Acts, see D. Wenham, "Acts and the Pauline Corpus," in *The Book of Acts in Its First Century Setting: Ancient Literary Setting,* ed. B. Winter and A. Clarke (Grand Rapids: Eerdmans, 1993) 215-58.

48. See R. Wall, "Romans 1:1-15: An Introduction to the Pauline Corpus of the New Testament," in *The New Testament as Canon,* ed. R. Wall and E. Lemcio, JSNTSup 76 (Sheffield: JSOT, 1992) 142-60.

49. See R. Wall, "Introduction to Epistolary Literature," in *The New Interpreter's Bible,* 12 vols. (Nashville: Abingdon, 1994–2002) 10:XXX.

Indeed, perhaps the canonical role Acts best performs is to explain rather than to temper the diversity found in the two collections of biblical letters. According to Acts, the church that claims its continuity with the first apostles tolerates a rich pluralism even as the apostles did, not without controversy and confusion. What was achieved at the Jerusalem Council is a kind of theological understanding rather than a theological consensus. The divine revelation given to the apostles, according to Acts, forms a pluralizing monotheism that in turn informs two distinct missions and appropriate proclamations, Jewish and Gentile (see Gal 2:7-10). Thus, sharply put, Acts interprets the two collections of letters in a more sectarian fashion: The Pauline corpus reflects the gospel of a Gentile mission, while the catholic collection reflects the gospel(s) of a Jewish mission. However, rather than causing division within the church, such a theological diversity is now perceived as normative and necessary for the work of the One who calls both Jews and Gentiles to be the people of God. As a context for theological reflection, Acts forces us to interpret the letters in the light of two guiding principles. First, we should expect to find kerygmatic diversity as we move from the Pauline to the catholic letters. Second, we should expect such a diversity to be useful in forming a single people of God. Against a critical hermeneutics that tends to select a "canon within the canon" from among the various possibilities, the Bible's own recommendation is for an interpretive strategy characterized by a mutually illuminating and self-correcting conversation among biblical theologies.

Finally, the dominant theological commitments of Acts guide theological reflection upon the letters. The point is not that a theology of Acts determines or even anticipates the various theologies found in the letters. Rather, Acts shapes a particular perspective, a practical concern, an abiding interest that influences the interpretation of the letters. For example, if according to Acts the church's vocation is to continue what Jesus began to do and to say, then a subsequent reading of the letters should bring to sharper focus the identity and praxis of a missionary people who respond to the Lord's demand to be his witness to the ends of the earth. This same perspective holds true of the catholic epistles, where believers constitute a community of "resident aliens" whose vocation is a costly faithfulness to God rather than that of the missionary witness to a needy world found in the Pauline letters. How does the catholicity of Acts deepen our understanding of God's people as a community of "resident aliens"? The canonical approach presumes that the connection is complementary rather than adversarial. In this case, the Pauline church, which may be inclined to accommodate itself to the mainstream of the world in order to more effectively spread the gospel (see 1 Cor 9:12b-23), is reminded by the catholic witness that it must take care not to be corrupted by the values and behaviors of that world (see Jas 1:27). That is, the synergism effected by the dominant theological commitments of Acts suggests that the diverse theologies ingredient in the biblical canon compose a dynamic, self-correcting system, preventing theological distortion.[50]

50. For a defense of this interpretive strategy and illustrations of its usefulness for reading across the NT canon, see R. Wall and E. Lemcio, *The New Testament as Canon,* JSNTSup 69 (Sheffield: JSOT, 1992).

## BIBLIOGRAPHY

Commentaries:

Barrett, C. K. *A Critical and Exegetical Commentary on the Acts of the Apostles.* 2 vols. ICC. Edinburgh: T. & T. Clark, 1994–98. The standard technical commentary on the Greek text in the English language. Offers valuable insight on the philology, grammar, transmission and translation, and history of interpreting Acts. Both volumes include comprehensive introductions with bibliographies covering every aspect of Acts criticism.

Bruce, F. F. *The Acts of the Apostles.* Rev. ed. NICNT. Grand Rapids: Eerdmans, 1988. An informed and helpful exposition of Acts that defends the historical accuracy of Luke's narrative.

Dunn, J. D. G. *The Acts of the Apostles.* Valley Forge, Pa.: Trinity, 1996. A highly readable commentary on the narrative plotline of Acts; written for preachers and teachers.

Fitzmyer, J. A. *The Acts of the Apostles.* AB 31. Garden City, N.Y.: Doubleday, 1998. This sparse commentary on Acts, which presumes information found in Fitzmyer's commentary on Luke's Gospel in the same series, contains informed summaries of introductory matters and current bibliographies of value to students. Fitzmyer's translation of Acts is highly recommended.

Haenchen, E. *The Acts of the Apostles.* Philadelphia: Westminster, 1971. Haenchen's masterful commentary reflects the interests and traditions of modern German scholarship. Alhough he is skeptical of the historical value of Acts, his commentary is rich with insight; and most recent interpreters use it as the starting point for their own studies.

Jervell, J. *Die Apostelgeschichte.* KEK 3. Göttingen: Vandenhoeck & Ruprecht, 1998. Innovative and controversial, Jervell's commentary (which replaces Haenchen's in the KEK series) defends the Jewish character of Acts against the critical consensus that Luke's story reflects a Gentile (and largely anti-Jewish) perspective.

Johnson, L. T. *The Acts of the Apostles.* SP 5. Collegeville, Minn.: Liturgical, 1992. Theologically profound and written in lively prose; integrates technical fluency with practical insight. Johnson's understanding of how Luke's prophetic theology informs the telling of his story is highly recommended for both preacher and scholar.

Kee, H. C. *To Every Nation Under Heaven: The Acts of the Apostles.* NTC. Valley Forge, Pa.: Trinity, 1997. A nontechnical commentary that seeks to understand Acts in the context of Luke's social and political world; several illuminating excurses on various topics are included throughout, and Kee concludes with a topical bibliography of recent research.

Spencer, F. S. *Acts.* Readings: A New Biblical Commentary. Sheffield: Sheffield Academic, 1997. An excellent nontechnical commentary that highlights Luke's evocative narrative style. Especially useful for those interested in reading Acts as literature.

Tannehill, R. C. *The Acts of the Apostles.* Vol. 2 of *The Narrative Unity of Luke-Acts: A Literary Interpretation.* Minneapolis: Fortress, 1990. The second volume of Tannehill's influential study of Luke's narrative argues that Acts continues the plotline of the Gospel to underwrite Luke's distinctive account of God's redemptive plan.

Witherington, B. *The Acts of the Apostles: A Socio-Rhetorical Commentary.* Grand Rapids: Eerdmans, 1998. Considers a massive amount of secondary literature in order to comment on a wide range of pertinent issues, often summarizing his research in judicious excurses and nontechnical appendixes that are well worth consulting.

Specialized Studies:

Cassidy, R. J. *Society and Politics in the Acts of the Apostles.* Maryknoll, N.Y.: Orbis, 1987. This provocative collection of short studies analyzes various social and political controversies provoked by the community's ministry within and beyond Palestine. Contends that Luke's characterization of the church as opposed to the political and social world of the day continues from and is warranted by the prophetic Jesus of his Gospel.

Evans, C. A., and J. A. Sanders. *Luke and Scripture: The Function of Sacred Tradition in Luke-Acts.* Minneapolis: Fortress, 1993. Contends that Luke-Acts is a narrative commentary on select portions of Israel's Scriptures that are either cited or alluded to in order to underwrite the claim that Jesus is the Christ of God according to biblical promise.

Hill, C. C. *Hellenists and Hebrews: Reappraising Division within the Earliest Church.* Minneapolis: Fortress, 1992. Responding to the modern consensus that the earliest church was deeply divided by competing theological commitments concerning Temple and Torah purity, Hill argues that first-century Judaism and Christianity were much too variegated and fluid to allow for simple cataloging of traditions.

Jervell, J. *The Theology of the Acts of the Apostles.* NTT. Cambridge: Cambridge University Press, 1996. This more accessible companion volume to Jervell's commentary (see above) summarizes the themes of a theology of Acts.

Marshall, I. H., and D. Peterson, eds. *Witness to the Gospel: The Theology of Acts.* Grand Rapids: Eerdmans, 1998. Treats the main theological themes of Acts from a variety of methodological perspectives and in an expository style that intends to clarify the meaning of the *text* of Acts.

Martin, C. J. "The Acts of the Apostles." In *Searching the Scriptures: A Feminist Commentary.* Vol. 2. Edited by E. Schüssler Fiorenza. London: SCM, 1995. Martin's illuminating "womanist" readings of select passages in Acts are combined with an introduction that surveys Luke's characterization of women.

Parsons, M., and R. Pervo. *Rethinking the Unity of Luke and Acts.* Minneapolis: Fortress, 1990. A fresh introduction to a vexing issue of Lukan scholarship.

Porter, S. E. *The Paul of Acts.* WUNT 115. Tübingen: Mohr Sebeck, 1999. First sifts through and evaluates recent scholarship on the role Paul performs in Acts and his relationship to Luke and the Holy Spirit then seeks to interpret the relationship between Luke's Paul and the portrait of Paul found in his letters.

Powell, M. A. *What Are They Saying About Acts?* New York: Paulist, 1991. Reviews and synthesizes scholarly opinion concerning the unity of Luke-Acts, the distinctive literary makeup and core theological themes of Acts, and the history of its interpretation in both the church and the scholarly guild.

Soards, M. L. *The Speeches in Acts: Their Content, Context, and Concerns.* Louisville: Westminster/John Knox, 1994. Written in response to M. Dibelius's programmatic form-critical analysis of Acts; examines the literary structure and narrative role of every speech in Acts in the light of an oral culture shaped by Greco-Roman rhetorical conventions.

Winter, B. W., and A. Clarke, eds. *The Book of Acts in Its First Century Setting.* 6 vols. Grand Rapids: Eerdmans, 1993–. This series seeks to reconstruct the cultural and historical context of Acts. An indispensable resource for any student who seeks to interpret Acts guided by knowledge of the ancient world behind the text.

# OUTLINE OF ACTS

I. Acts 1:1-2, The Prologue

II. Acts 1:3–2:13, Preparing to Continue the Ministry of Jesus

   A. 1:3-14, The Apostolic Succession

   B. 1:15-26, And Then There Were Twelve

   C. 2:1-13, Pentecost: The Spirit of Prophecy Falls upon the Community

III. Acts 2:14–15:12, Part One: A Narrative of Conversion

   A. 2:14-41, Peter's Pentecost Proclamation

   B. 2:42-47, The Community of the Uncommon Life

   C. 3:1–8:3, "You Shall Be My Witnesses in Jerusalem": The Jerusalem Mission

      3:1–4:4, Story One: The Apostles Heal the Lame of Israel
      4:5-31, Story Two: The Apostles vs. the Sanhedrin, Round One
      4:32–5:16, Interlude: "One Holy and Apostolic Church"
      5:17-42, Story Three: The Apostles vs. the Sanhedrin, Round Two
      6:1-7, Interlude: Resolving Conflict Within the Community of Goods
      6:8–8:3, Story Four: Stephen, a Prophet Mighty in Word and Deed

   D. 8:4-40, "And in All Judea and Samaria": Philip's Mission to Outcasts Beyond Jerusalem

      8:4-25, Philip's Mission to the "Outcasts of Israel": The Samaritans
      8:26-40, Philip's Mission to the "Outcasts of Israel": The Eunuch from Ethiopia

   E. 9:1–15:12, "And to the End of the Earth": Paul's Mission as "Light for the Nations"

      9:1-31, The Conversion and Commissioning of Saul
      9:32–11:18, Back to the Future: Peter's Prophetic Ministry Beyond Jerusalem
      11:19–12:25, The Succession of the Twelve
      13:1–14:26, Paul's Mission to the Nations
      14:27–15:5, The Jerusalem Council: Report and Reaction to Paul's Mission
      15:6-12, The Jerusalem Council: Evidence That Demands a Verdict

## THE PROLOGUE

NIV

1 In my former book, Theophilus, I wrote about all that Jesus began to do and to teach ²until the day he was taken up to heaven, after giving instructions through the Holy Spirit to the apostles he had chosen.

NRSV

1 In the first book, Theophilus, I wrote about all that Jesus did and taught from the beginning ²until the day when he was taken up to heaven, after giving instructions through the Holy Spirit to the apostles whom he had chosen.

## COMMENTARY

In antiquity prefatory sentences aroused interest and put readers on notice what to expect in the story that follows; the first sentence of Acts is such a sentence.[51] The narrator begins in the conventional way of second volumes: Luke addresses his reader, Theophilus, in the first person by sharply summarizing the content of his first volume.[52] Theophilus's identity and role in the production of Acts remain indeterminate, although likely the name refers to an actual person rather than to a symbolic audience (see Introduction, "Acts as Conversation," 5-11).

Acts lacks, however, the narrator's conventional summary of the second volume. Luke is content to review what he has already written and Theophilus has read: the gospel story of what "Jesus began to do and to teach." In doing so, he introduces Acts within a wider narrative that infers a working "intertext" between Luke's Gospel and Acts, the first influencing and expanding the meaning of the second. The introduction includes a caveat: The reader who attempts to follow the plotline of Acts without benefit of "the first book" will have missed much that is utterly essential for reading the second volume. The story of Jesus' messianic career is the narrative subtext of Acts; the stories must be read together as a whole greater than the sum of its two integral parts (see Introduction, "Acts as Canon," 26-32).

Verse 2 emits three signals that alert the reader to the importance of the events that will soon follow. First, the awkward reference to the Lord's ascension, which at first seems unnecessary here, actually helps to introduce the succession of the apostles to Jesus' ministry (see also 1:3-14). As the concluding event of his earthly ministry, the ascension of the risen Jesus inaugurates the ministry of his apostles, who will continue to do and teach what he has begun (see 1:9-11). But this passing reference to the Lord's departure also frames the religious crisis it occasions: Will the new age of God's promised salvation, which dawned with the Messiah, continue to unfold in his absence?

Second, although his Gospel lacks detail in this regard, Luke understands that all Jesus did as God's Messiah is "through the Holy Spirit." The Holy Spirit is "the Spirit of prophecy" who calls forth, empowers, and authorizes the Messiah's prophetic ministry and will ensure continuity in his absence. The Lord's instructions to his apostles are given "through the Holy Spirit," since only by the Spirit's power and direction will they fulfill their vocation as prophets-like-Jesus (see 1:8; cf. Luke 24:46-49).

Third, Luke finally mentions "the apostles whom Jesus had chosen" who will continue to do and to speak what the Lord has begun.[53] The title

51. There is no end to the various ways commentators divide the preface to Acts from its main story. I separate 1:1-2 from the rest of Acts for special consideration as Luke's *literary* introduction to his second book, which he then begins with the story of apostolic succession in 1:3-14.

52. See L. C. A. Alexander, *The Preface to Luke's Gospel: Literary Convention and Social Context in Luke 1.1-4 and Acts 1.1*, SNTSMS 78 (Cambridge: Cambridge University Press, 1993).

53. The phrase "whom [Jesus] had chosen" presumes the reader knows something of Luke's earlier narrative of the selection process by which Jesus "elected" the Twelve (Luke 6:12-16). Critical in the Gospel account is that Jesus first prayed to God—on the mountain and all night—to learn precisely God's will in this matter. Prayer is an important narrative thematic in Luke's Gospel and Acts and functions as a theological metaphor for God's sovereign control over those events that fulfill God's promised salvation.

ἀπόστολος (*apostolos,* "apostle") derives from the verb ἀποστέλλω (*apostellō,* "to send"), denoting someone who is "sent out" with something important to give another—in this case, with a word of salvation to proclaim and mighty works to perform in Jesus' name. The images conjured up by this concept are similar to those associated with OT stories of the commissioning of God's prophets. Indeed, apostles bear a striking family resemblance to OT prophets in both their vocation and their suffering.[54] The reference to their selection by Jesus recalls that he chose them with God's provident help (see Luke 6:13) and gave them special responsibilities and a privileged status within a restored Israel (see Luke 22:30), detailed now in this second book.

54. Agnew's review of discussion of the concept of apostleship commends an understanding based on an OT description of the prophetic vocation. See F. H. Agnew, "The Origin of the NT Apostle-Concept," *JBL* 105 (1986) 75-96.

# REFLECTIONS

**1.** "I wrote about all that Jesus began to do and to teach" (1:1 NIV). The clear signal emitted by that declaration is that what Jesus began, his successors will continue, not in dutiful practice but in sincere devotion to the sublime truth disclosed in that messianic life. The purpose of Acts is to tell a story that bids its living readers to continue what Christ began in their own time and hence to the end of history. The apostles continued the Messiah's mission without repeating its unique importance in the economy of God's salvation. However, the pattern of his life and work shapes the direction of theirs as prophets-like-Jesus. This core conviction of Luke's is made evident in the literary shaping of Acts.

**2.** "Giving instructions through the Holy Spirit to the apostles whom he had chosen" (1:2 NRSV). The catchphrases "through the Holy Spirit" and "the apostles whom Jesus had chosen" introduce the key elements of this continuity. The Spirit and the apostles are both the appointed successors of God's Messiah, and through their sacred partnership, divine and human, the promised salvation of God continues to be fulfilled in history. This is the first mention of the Spirit's agency in Acts and cues the reader both to Jesus' imminent departure and the coming of the Spirit at Pentecost, when both the need for continuity and its means will be disclosed. It is important to note that the Spirit is introduced in connection with the Lord's instruction. This is the "Spirit of prophecy" whose prominent role in the OT is maintained in Acts—the instrument by whom prophets are raised up, commissioned, instructed, and inspired to carry God's word to God's people. In Acts, the Lord's apostolic successors, and their successors in turn, are God's Spirit-filled prophets, the principal interpreters of Scripture and of the course of salvation's history scripted by biblical prophecy.

What are the marks of Spirit-filled prophets today? Surely those, whether well known or anonymous, who help the community experience God's love, know God's Word, and discern God's will are the successors of the earliest believers. At times their activities may be grand events; more often, leadership is exercised in the everyday faith and practice of the community.

# PREPARING TO CONTINUE THE MINISTRY OF JESUS

## ACTS 1:3-14, THE APOSTOLIC SUCCESSION

**NIV**

[3]After his suffering, he showed himself to these men and gave many convincing proofs that he was alive. He appeared to them over a period of forty days and spoke about the kingdom of God. [4]On one occasion, while he was eating with them, he gave them this command: "Do not leave Jerusalem, but wait for the gift my Father promised, which you have heard me speak about. [5]For John baptized with[a] water, but in a few days you will be baptized with the Holy Spirit."

[6]So when they met together, they asked him, "Lord, are you at this time going to restore the kingdom to Israel?"

[7]He said to them: "It is not for you to know the times or dates the Father has set by his own authority. [8]But you will receive power when the Holy Spirit comes on you; and you will be my witnesses in Jerusalem, and in all Judea and Samaria, and to the ends of the earth."

[9]After he said this, he was taken up before their very eyes, and a cloud hid him from their sight.

[10]They were looking intently up into the sky as he was going, when suddenly two men dressed in white stood beside them. [11]"Men of Galilee," they said, "why do you stand here looking into the sky? This same Jesus, who has been taken from you into heaven, will come back in the same way you have seen him go into heaven."

[12]Then they returned to Jerusalem from the hill called the Mount of Olives, a Sabbath day's walk[b] from the city. [13]When they arrived, they went upstairs to the room where they were staying. Those present were Peter, John, James and Andrew; Philip and Thomas, Bartholomew and Matthew; James son of Alphaeus and Simon the

[a] 5 Or in   [b] 12 That is, about 3/4 mile (about 1,100 meters)

**NRSV**

[3]After his suffering he presented himself alive to them by many convincing proofs, appearing to them during forty days and speaking about the kingdom of God. [4]While staying[a] with them, he ordered them not to leave Jerusalem, but to wait there for the promise of the Father. "This," he said, "is what you have heard from me; [5]for John baptized with water, but you will be baptized with[b] the Holy Spirit not many days from now."

[6]So when they had come together, they asked him, "Lord, is this the time when you will restore the kingdom to Israel?" [7]He replied, "It is not for you to know the times or periods that the Father has set by his own authority. [8]But you will receive power when the Holy Spirit has come upon you; and you will be my witnesses in Jerusalem, in all Judea and Samaria, and to the ends of the earth." [9]When he had said this, as they were watching, he was lifted up, and a cloud took him out of their sight. [10]While he was going and they were gazing up toward heaven, suddenly two men in white robes stood by them. [11]They said, "Men of Galilee, why do you stand looking up toward heaven? This Jesus, who has been taken up from you into heaven, will come in the same way as you saw him go into heaven."

[12]Then they returned to Jerusalem from the mount called Olivet, which is near Jerusalem, a sabbath day's journey away. [13]When they had entered the city, they went to the room upstairs where they were staying, Peter, and John, and James, and Andrew, Philip and Thomas, Bartholomew and Matthew, James son of Alphaeus, and Simon the Zealot, and Judas son of[c] James. [14]All these were constantly devoting them-

[a] Or eating   [b] Or by   [c] Or the brother of

NIV

Zealot, and Judas son of James. [14]They all joined together constantly in prayer, along with the women and Mary the mother of Jesus, and with his brothers.

NRSV

selves to prayer, together with certain women, including Mary the mother of Jesus, as well as his brothers.

# COMMENTARY

The prefatory sentence of Acts is followed by a brief summary of what Jesus does and says over the forty days between his resurrection and ascension (1:3). Luke recapitulates the conclusion to Jesus' messianic mission according to Luke's Gospel (cf. Luke 24:36-53), recalling in particular those memories that will be elaborated in this second book. Here are the Lord's final instructions to his apostles that function as his "last will and testament" and lend authority to the future work of his chosen successors.[55]

The central moment of the narrative is the prophecy of the coming of God's Spirit (1:4-5), whose arrival in the holy city portends the restoration of Israel (1:6) and empowers the mission of the church (1:7-8). According to Acts, the hope of Israel's restoration and the mission of the church are integral features of "the last days" of salvation's history soon to be inaugurated by God during Pentecost (see 2:1-4). The departure of the glorified Jesus into the heavens (1:9-11) concludes the first stage of his messianic mission and creates the circumstance that requires an apostolic succession. But the succession from Messiah to his apostles is not without problems. The messianic community left behind gathers for prayer (1:14) to wait for God to act on the Lord's promise of the Spirit. Yet we note that it includes only *eleven* apostles (1:13). How will God's salvation go forward without the requisite twelve "to sit on thrones judging the twelve tribes of Israel" (Luke 22:30)?

**1:3-8.** The brevity of v. 3 presumes that the reader of Acts will be familiar with the Gospel account of Jesus' resurrection and his teaching about the reign of God. The idiom of Luke's summary, however, is provocative. The term he uses

for the living Lord's "many convincing proofs" (τεκμήριον *tekmērion*) is found only here in the NT. In ancient rhetoric this same word is used of the hard evidence that convinces the skeptic or confirms the authority of the apologist. Used here in Acts, the Lord's "proofs" confirm his resurrection, perhaps for those disciples who still doubt it (cf. Matt 28:17), and underwrite the propriety of his instructions (1:2) that prepare his followers for their mission soon to be at hand.

The resurrection of Jesus is a theme of enormous importance for Acts. It testifies to Jesus' faithfulness to God and confirms him as Lord and Christ (see 2:36). The authority of Jesus is deeply rooted in his faithfulness to God as God's servant and his relationship with God as God's Son. Jesus not only understands God's redemptive plans but interprets Scripture's disclosure of those plans faithfully. His "suffering" is the signature of the Lord's costly obedience, which is requisite of Messiah's faithful service to God, as the resurrected Jesus himself points out (Luke 24:26).

Unlike the Gospel narrative, in which the details of Jesus' Easter appearances are recounted in the course of a very long and exciting day, Acts simply says that Jesus "appeared" to his disciples over an extended period of "forty days" (1:3). Some interpreters think Luke's reference to forty days is his rhetorical marker that extends the compressed last day of the Gospel's Jesus to a more leisurely forty days in Acts. Others think Luke adds "forty days" to fill out the chronology from Easter to Ascension, and then finally on to Pentecost some ten days later. Various OT writings, which Luke knew, refer to forty days/years as a period of preparation during which God fully instructs people for their future work (e.g., Exod 24:12-18; 34:28; 1 Kgs 19:8). In Luke's Gospel the Spirit leads Jesus into the wilderness for forty days of testing (Luke 4:1-13). The reference to "forty

55. J. A. Fitzmyer, *The Acts of the Apostles,* AB 31 (Garden City, N.Y.: Doubleday, 1998) 199.

days," then, probably symbolizes an extended period of preparation and examination for the difficult work ahead.[56]

The Lord first instructs his apostolic successors about the "kingdom of God," which is the central idiom of Jesus' preaching ministry, according to Luke's Gospel. While not as prominent in the speeches of Acts, it is used here and at the book's end as a literary inclusio (see 28:31). The reader is put on notice that the triumph of God's reign is the subtext of the narrative sandwiched between. However, nowhere does Acts supply a normative definition of God's "kingdom." Elements of a definition are perhaps best inferred from its uses in the fourfold gospel and from the images and ideas of Luke's theological perspective in Acts. For example, Luke's narrative is centered upon God, who alone reigns and who, as the divine choreographer of history, is not detached from this history but is powerfully present to heal and restore those who trust God. In this context God promises to bless all nations through the mission of a restored Israel (see 1:8).

Jesus' second instruction is "not to leave Jerusalem" (1:4*a*). According to Luke's narrative map, all roads leading into God's salvation are to or from Jerusalem. It is a city built with the bricks of prophecy, and the fate of all creation depends on what happens there. This has already proved true for the Messiah, for whom Jerusalem was the city of his destiny and now is the site of his imminent departure (cf. Luke 9:51). So, too, will it be for his successors, since Jerusalem is the point of their departure into the world, carrying the word of the Lord forth to the "ends of the earth" (1:8; cf. Luke 24:47).

The third and climactic instruction is to "wait for the promise of the Father" (1:4*b*), which is "you will be baptized with the Holy Spirit" (1:5). The John the Baptist's prophecy of the Messiah's Spirit-filling, unfulfilled in the Gospel, is now recalled and prophesied again by Jesus. The Lord calls the Spirit "the promise of the Father" because the Spirit is God's Spirit, who continues to mediate God's word before, through, and after Christ (2:33). There is continuity between the prophetic ministry of Jesus and his apostolic successors because each is baptized into the realm of this same Spirit of prophecy who empowers an effective ministry of word and living witness.[57] Jesus' response to the provocative question posed by his apostles (1:6) indicates that the role of the Holy Spirit in Acts is more functional than soteriological: Initiation into the realm of the Spirit enables the believers to bring an effective witness of the risen Jesus to the world (1:7-8). Unlike the Pauline emphasis on the Spirit's mediation of God's salvation-creating grace, then, the images and ideas of the Spirit's role are almost always tied to the apostles' mission or to the authority of their leadership. The kind of interpretive myopia that privileges the Pauline idea to the exclusion of Acts, or the reverse, is corrected within canonical context where these different emphases are brought into a mutually enriching relationship. The Pauline conception of the "spiritual life," which emphasizes the Spirit's role in enabling believers to live in new ways, is complemented by Acts' conception of the Spirit as the invigorating source of the community's witness in the world.

Luke follows Jesus' instruction with the apostles' question: "Lord, is this the time when you will restore the kingdom [of God] to Israel?" (1:6). All that has happened since the Lord's passion has convinced them of God's triumph. However, Jesus had not yet engaged in those messianic actions that would redeem Israel (cf. Luke 24:21). Was the arrival of the promised Spirit Israel's redemptive moment? Recalling that their minds had been opened by the resurrected Lord to understand the meaning of Scripture (cf. Luke 24:44-45) and that they have just spent the past forty days learning about the kingdom of God from him (see 1:3), we should presume that the apostles are correct in drawing the implication they do from Jesus' prophecy of the Spirit's outpouring: The Spirit signals the fulfillment of Scripture's prophecy of Israel's restoration (cf. Isa 32:14-20).[58] Jesus' vague response to their query is nothing like "an indirect denial that it is Israel to whom the Kingdom will be given."[59] Nor does it point to

56. C. H. Talbert, *Reading Acts* (New York: Crossroad, 1997) 23-24.

57. See Roger Stronstad, *The Prophethood of All Believers,* Journal of Pentecostal Theology Supplemental Series 16 (Sheffield: Sheffield Academic, 1999).

58. For the importance of the Spirit of prophecy in Israel's restoration theology, see M. Turner, *Power from on High,* JPTSS 9 (Sheffield: Sheffield Academic, 1996).

59. R. Maddox, *The Purpose of Luke-Acts* (Edinburgh: T. & T. Clark, 1982) 106.

"the rule of God over human hearts,"[60] since Acts steadfastly refuses to substitute a distinctively Christian or spiritualized meaning for the more traditional Jewish hope of Israel's restoration.[61] The apparent intention of Jesus' answer is not to set aside the implicit connection between Pentecost and the promise of Israel's restoration but rather to clarify the terms of its fulfillment at Pentecost.

Jesus' final instruction is prefaced by the claim that God's plan to restore Israel does not become the special knowledge of insiders: "It is not for you to know" (1:7). Many scholars suppose that this stern word responds to the painful disappointments experienced within the ancient church over unrealized predictions of Christ's return. Some speculate that Luke has in mind Christian prophets who claimed personal insight into the "times and periods" of endtime events and had gathered a cult-like and divisive congregation around themselves. I doubt this. Jesus does not respond to speculation surrounding what is "not yet" but insists that his disciples engage in a mission "right now." He points out that the disciples are not waiting for the Spirit within some apocalyptic time zone, where saving events come from heaven and erupt into human history in the "twinkling of an eye." The apostles are to wait for a different redemptive reality. Jesus defines in a paradigmatic way the relationship between the Spirit's outpouring and Israel's restoration. He prophesies that "you will receive power when the Holy Spirit has come upon you" (1:8)—a prediction that echoes Isaiah's prophecy of the pouring out of the Spirit to renew Israel's eternal covenant with God (so Isa 32:15). While Jesus thereby agrees with the theological subtext of the apostles' query—the Spirit's outpouring does indeed signal the season of Israel's restoration—he applies it to their vocation: God's reign will be reestablished among God's people not by some apocalypse from heaven but by a mission on earth.

The word Luke uses for "power" is δύναμις (*dynamis*), which denotes a robust force at work in demonstrative ways for all to see and feel. Such a "power" comes with the Spirit of prophecy. The Spirit does not confer a political authority upon the apostles but rather new competencies that enable them to perform the tasks given them, whether through their inspired words, their miraculous works, or their leadership within the community's common life (see 2:42-47; 4:32-35). For this reason, the Lord stipulates emphatically that this power will reside upon "you" (= apostles) to enable the apostles to "be my witnesses." They are to continue "all that Jesus began to do and teach" (1:1).

When Jesus turns the expectation of Israel's restoration from an indeterminate chronology to the means of its realization within the church's missionary history, the theological subtext of Acts is established. He then provides a geographical index to underwrite this history's eventual progress. The plotline of Acts follows this same index, beginning "in Jerusalem [Acts 2–7], in all Judea and Samaria [Acts 8], and to the end of the earth [Acts 9–28]."[62] The Spirit's outpouring empowers a global mission as the divinely intended means by which God's covenant with a repentant Israel is renewed and Israel is called as "a light to the nations" so that repentant Gentiles also can share in the blessings of Israel's salvation (see 3:19-26; 13:44-47; cf. Luke 2:32).

**1:9-11.** The two accounts of Jesus' ascension here and in Luke 24:51 are unique in the NT. Jesus' ascension further validates his resurrection (see 1:3) and vindicates the claim that he is God's Messiah (see 2:21, 36). Unlike others who are resuscitated to life (e.g., Lazarus), Jesus is brought back to life never again to die. The Gospels report only the discovery of an empty tomb followed by

---

60. L. T. Johnson, *The Acts of the Apostles,* SP 5 (Collegeville, Minn.: Liturgical, 1992) 29.

61. J. Jervell, *The Theology of the Acts of the Apostles,* NTT (Cambridge: Cambridge University Press, 1996) 18-43.

62. Significantly, the final phrase (ἕως ἐσχάτου τῆς γῆς *heōs eschatou tēs gēs*) is singular, "the *end* of the earth," and probably echoes Isa 49:6 and its prophecy of Israel's identity as a "light to the nations" (see Acts 13:47). See J. Dupont, *The Salvation of the Gentiles* (New York: Paulist, 1979) 17-19. Others, such as H. Conzelmann, *The Acts of the Apostles,* trans. J. Limburg et al., ed. E. J. Epp and C. R. Matthews, Hermeneia (Philadelphia: Fortress, 1987) 7, find the phrase's referent, quite possibly Rome, in the narrative itself and, therefore, view the phrase as another element of the story's inclusio: Even as Jesus teaches the "kingdom of God" to his apostles at Acts' beginning (1:3) for their mission to the "end of the earth," so also Paul continues his teaching of the "kingdom of God" at the "end of the earth" (Rome) at its conclusion (28:31). In this sense, Jesus' commission is ultimately carried out (and on) by Paul; indeed, the commission is an essential feature of the story's Pauline apologia. R. C. Tannehill, *The Acts of the Apostles,* vol. 2 of *The Narrative Unity of Luke-Acts: A Literary Interpretation* (Minneapolis: Fortress, 1990) 2:102-112, argues, however, that the Ethiopian eunuch (8:26-39) represents those at the "end of the earth," formally bringing to conclusion the narrative of the Lord's apostolic successors indexed by Acts 1:8 and preparing the reader for the story of Paul beginning in Acts 9.

various post-resurrection epiphanies of the risen Jesus; but there are no witnesses to the resurrection itself. Perhaps for this reason, the verbs Luke employs in Acts stress the availability of the ascension to eyewitnesses: they "were watching" until he was "out of their sight" (1:9), continuing to "gaze" (1:10) while two men asked them why they were "looking."

In Jewish literature the biblical story of Elijah's dramatic departure in a fiery chariot (2 Kgs 2:11) is followed by the apocalyptic retelling of Enoch's ascension in whirlwinds to the very "end of the heavens" (*1 Enoch* 39:3-4) and also by Philo's description of Moses' ascension to God while still proclaiming God's word.[63] Luke's story of the ascension glosses this important Jewish tradition of exalting God's prophets: Jesus is the prophet-like-Moses Messiah (cf. Deut 18:15-22), powerful in word and work (cf. Luke 24:19; Acts 7:22), whom God sent to announce the arrival of God's salvation and to broker it on behalf of the world.[64]

The ascension also provides the implied religious motive for the apostles' testimony to Jesus (1:8). While they are not eyewitnesses to his resurrection, the apostles are eyewitnesses to his ascension, lending credibility to their proclamation that he is alive. Significantly, the "cloud" ($\nu\epsilon\phi\acute{\epsilon}\lambda\eta$ *nephelē*) that carries Jesus heavenward (1:9) recalls the use of a "cloud" to symbolize God's faithful presence among the liberated people in the OT story of Israel's exodus (see Exod 16:10; 19:9; 24:15-18).[65] If Luke adds *nephelē* to make this allusion, he also implies that the apostolic proclamation about the living Jesus further confirms God's commitment to fulfill promises made to Israel (see 1:6-8).

The "two men in white robes" redirect our line of vision from the past of Jesus to his future with the words "this Jesus . . . will come in the same way" (1:11). Their eschatological commentary on Jesus' ascension makes two different, although complementary, points. Their words cultivate the haunting awareness of Jesus' bodily absence from his disciples. In its canonical setting, the theological

crisis occasioned by the Lord's departure is addressed in a farewell speech of John's Jesus (John 14–16), when he tells his followers that his departure results in the "coming of the Counselor to you" (John 16:7) to "bear witness to me" (John 15:26) and to "teach you all things and bring to remembrance what I have said to you" (John 14:26). By this exhortation, Jesus encourages the disciples to find their way in the world without him and to shoulder the tasks of the messianic movement he had begun. Jesus' departure is the formal condition of their succession, even as it is the material condition of the Spirit's empowerment. In fact, the Lord's instructions given over the past forty days (Acts 1:3) become sheer nonsense without his bodily departure.

Yet, the eschatological horizon of the church's mission is the Lord's return from heaven to complete his messianic vocation (see John 14:3). The church's mission, which continues the past of Jesus, is motivated by the hope of his future (see 3:19-21; 10:42). Much has been made of the lack of clear references to Christ's return in the speeches of Acts. Certainly this lack is all the more remarkable when these speeches are compared to the frequency of references to the second coming found in the letters and gospel traditions. While Luke diminishes the "not yet" of Jesus in favor of the "right now" of the church's mission, this narrative opening that asserts "this Jesus . . . will come" frames the entire story with future expectation (see Introduction, "Acts as Confession," 18-26).

Most interpreters claim that the two "men" symbolize the Torah's requirement that two witnesses must confirm the veracity of an alleged event (see Deut 19:15). Given the integral connection of ascension and resurrection, the reader should assume that these "men" are the same two who also appeared to the women in the empty tomb to confirm his prediction of execution and resurrection (Luke 24:4-7). Perhaps we should also take them as angelic witnesses to heaven's confirmation of the living Jesus, as Cleopas did (Luke 24:23). Earlier in the Gospel, however, Elijah and Moses—both of whom ascended into heaven, according to well-known Jewish legends—appear at the Son's transfiguration and speak of his "departure" from Jerusalem (see Luke 9:30-31). The echoes of familiar traditions about

---

63. Philo *Life of Moses* 2:291.

64. For this see M. Parsons, *The Departure of Jesus in Luke-Acts*, JSNTSup 21 (Sheffield: JSOT, 1987), who views the ascension as a literary device that helps the reader from Gospel into Acts, its sequel. The function of this hinge-narrative is to form impressions of the triumph of the risen Jesus, which is the christological subtext for reading Acts.

65. Fitzmyer, *The Acts of the Apostles*, 209-10.

Elijah and Moses that reverberate throughout Acts provide good reason to think that the identity of the "two men" is not angelic but "Jesus'" prophetic predecessors who ascended, Moses and Elijah.[66] In either case, they provide "official" testimony to the Lord's importance that will fund the apostles' proclamation about him.

**1:12-14.** With the departure of the Messiah and his "official" succession to them now complete, the apostles are left to wait for the promised Spirit to empower their mission. Whether they are able to continue what their Lord began depends on their faithfulness to God. Luke is careful to depict them as observant Jews who journey only "a sabbath's day" from Jerusalem (cf. Exod 16:27-30).[67] They are also faithful to Jesus who instructed them to wait in Jerusalem for the Spirit's outpouring (1:4), and they "constantly devoted themselves to prayer" (1:14). Typically in Luke's narrative world, true believers gather together for prayer to wait upon God to act at critical moments of their history (cf. 1:24-25; 4:24-30; 6:6; 8:15; 9:11; 12:12; 13:3; 14:23; 16:25; 20:36; 28:8). This prayerful waiting upon the Lord

not only characterizes the church of Acts; it also underscores the implicit importance of Pentecost when God will deliver them the Holy Spirit as promised.

The community's constituency is noteworthy. The listing of apostles (1:13) is a literary convention of succession narratives and is expected here: These are the names of those who form the community's leadership and will provide the messianic community's leadership in the Messiah's absence. Only eleven apostles are named, members of an incomplete apostolic circle. This narrative detail explains the purpose of the subsequent account of Judas's demise (see 1:15-20*a*) and his replacement's selection (1:20*b*-26). The inclusion of "certain women, including Mary the mother of Jesus" recalls the importance of various women in Jesus' ministry (cf. Luke 8:1-3; 24:1-11; John 4; 11) and makes clear that women will continue to play a significant role in the church's mission to the end of the earth (see Acts 18). Finally, Luke's curious reference to Jesus' "brothers" has led some commentators to find here a metaphor for all other disciples that make up the messianic community at Pentecost. It is more likely, given the central importance of the resurrection in the opening of Acts, that this final phrase alludes to the Lord's Easter day appearances to members of his own family (James, Jude) according to tradition (cf. 1 Cor 15:7).

---

66. Johnson, *The Acts of the Apostles,* 31.
67. Luke locates Mt. Olivet in Bethany (Luke 19:29), a suburb of Jerusalem that John's Gospel reports is two miles from the city center (John 11:18), well beyond the limit prescribed for a sabbath's walk. If we use the same map as Josephus, we find Mt. Olivet in the Kidron ravine on the city's southeastern edge and well within the distance allowed for the "Sabbath day's journey" stipulated in Acts.

# REFLECTIONS

**1.** "They were looking intently up into the sky as he was going" (1:10 NIV). Jesus gathers his followers after Easter to prepare them for their future without him. The initial spiritual crisis concerns their discipleship and whether they can follow after Jesus without seeing or hearing him, drawing strength from his physical presence among them. The same remains true today: How can we live as earnest disciples of a now-departed Lord? Jesus prepared his followers to continue in the pattern of ministry that he had begun. According to Acts, discipleship is defined in terms of an active witness to the risen Jesus rather than a deeply affecting relationship with him. While any biblical definition of discipleship must include those prophetic tasks in continuity with what Jesus did and said, Acts' overemphasis in the life of the church can replace the centrality of an abiding relationship with the living Jesus that ultimately saps the spiritual energy believers draw from him. We live in an activist's age in which participation in good deeds is keenly encouraged, even demanded of the "committed person." For this reason the biblical interpreter must take care to bring together the "task discipleship" of Acts with teaching of a more contemplative pattern of discipleship from, for example, John's Gospel (John 14–17), where God's Spirit is given to cultivate an intimate relationship with the living Jesus.

---

**2.** "After his suffering . . . he appeared to them during forty days" (1:3 NRSV). Jesus' curriculum in preparing his followers to continue his mission concerns "the many proofs" of his resurrection and instruction about "the kingdom of God" (1:3). What must be noted first is that the Lord consecrates a period of time to prepare his followers *fully* for their future ministry, symbolized by the number "forty." Their witness will be guided and empowered by the Spirit (1:8), but they are thoroughly briefed by Jesus to understand *accurately* what they have seen and its theological significance. The Holy Spirit does not work in an intellectual vacuum; nor is Christian witness effective if it merely testifies to the experience of God's salvation without being able to interpret meaning for all of life. Impoverishment of theological understanding in the church diminishes the community's influence on its surrounding culture.

**3.** "He presented himself alive to them by many convincing proofs" (1:3 NRSV). The gospel that is preached and embodied in life is not funded by fictions or theological abstractions but is predicated on various proofs—the hard evidence—that Jesus appears to real people as really alive. From the fourfold gospel tradition, the interpreter can list what these proofs are: He "appeared" to them over several days to share table fellowship with them and show them his wounded hands and feet; he interpreted Scripture for them and commissioned them for ministry; and he made promises to them that were realized in their transformed lives. The horizon of Christian life and practice is fashioned by the credibility of Jesus' resurrection and by the continuing experience of the living Jesus. The Gospel stories of Easter tell us of the apostles' initial confusion and incredulity at the report of the Lord's resurrection. This period of preparation therefore engenders their confidence that what they will announce to others is true; and also confirms their spiritual authority to do so. And at its very essence, this time of preparation presumes that those who know that Jesus lives will want to tell others the good news.

**4.** He "spoke [to them] about the kingdom of God" (1:3 NIV). Any reflection on the Lord's goodness to his disciples must include this season of preparation, making clear to them what to expect and how to best use their time without him. He does not leave them to discover these practical truths on their own. Therefore, in addition to this robust portfolio of experiences with the living Jesus, he schools them to teach the kingdom of God, now informed by his passion and resurrection, and to recognize or discern its disclosure during the course of their mission. The kingdom of God is ordered by God's benevolent presence and redemptive purposes. Although God rarely appears as a character in Acts, God's plan for human history controls the plotline of the story.

**5.** "Wait in Jerusalem for the promise of the Father" (see 1:4). After instructing the apostles, Jesus directs them to wait for the Father to send them the promised Spirit. Waiting for this dynamic future to unfold involves a measure of uncertainty and urgency. What makes it possible for them to hope for tomorrow's best is God's past faithfulness to Jesus. His resurrection and ascension are reflections of God faithfulness both to him and to promises made to Israel because of him. Our capacity to wait expectantly for God to act according to "the promise" is cultivated by memory of the record of God's faithfulness in the history of others.

**6.** Waiting for God to act is also a community's project. Waiting with others is an act of solidarity with friends. The apostles do not scatter and go their separate ways to await a private Spirit-filling or a personal experience of divine faithfulness. They "were joined together" in a specific place to await God's action on them all.

**7.** "They all joined together constantly in prayer" (1:14 NIV). Waiting on the Lord to act is not a passive inactivity: They waited by praying (1:14) and studying Scripture together (1:15-22). Prayers are not offered to solicit God's benefaction, which they have already experienced, nor to ensure that God would fulfill what is promised them. Praying together publicly demonstrates the importance of their spiritual unity and resolve in accomplishing their missionary vocation as Jesus prophesied it and as God will continue to clarify it to them. As is often the case in Acts, however, prayer precedes doing the tasks given by the Spirit's power. Experiencing the living Jesus and knowing thoroughly the content of the Gospel is not sufficient for effective ministry. The community will have nothing to say that matters without God's full participation in all that they do. The substance of what we proclaim and live as good news must first of all be grounded in a community that is given over to constant prayer and worship.

**8.** "But you will receive power when the Holy Spirit has come upon you" (1:8 NRSV). This passage introduces the Holy Spirit as the "Father's promise" and the receptacle of "power" that enables the progress of the gospel to go forward from sacred Jerusalem to profane Rome. The Spirit's role within the faith community is central to Acts, but it is carefully circumscribed. This Spirit is the "Spirit of prophecy," poured out upon God's people, according to Scripture's promise, in order to enable them to perform the various tasks of mission. The church routinely neglects teaching believers that they live in the realm and under the influence of a more mission-minded Spirit whose presence empowers an effective, responsible witness for Jesus in the world. The Christianity shaped by Acts is neither quiet or passive but aggressive, assertive, challenging, and countercultural in calling upon everyone everywhere to repent and turn to Jesus in faith. However, the interpreter must aim at a balanced theology of the Spirit that includes Paul's teaching of its transforming spiritual and moral effect in the individual believer's life.

**9.** " 'Lord, is this the time when you will restore the kingdom to Israel?' " (1:6 NRSV). With minds opened by Jesus to understand the witness of Scripture to the salvation of Israel, the disciples ask Jesus whether God's promise of the Spirit is coordinate with God's promise to restore the kingdom to Israel (1:6). Jesus is instructive both in what he says and in what he does not say in response (1:7-8). He does not reprove the apostles for they are right in making this connection: Pentecost has *everything* to do with God's fidelity to the biblical promises made to the Jews. Nowhere does Jesus suggest that God's promise to restore "real" Israel has been reclaimed and given to the church as a spiritual or "true" Israel. Christianity has not superseded Israel in the plan of God's salvation so that God's future now belongs to the church. Jesus rather indicates to his apostles that the fulfillment of God's promise to revitalize Israel is not a matter of "when" (1:7) but "how" (1:8): God's concern for what happens at the "end of the earth" or at its very center in Jerusalem is evinced by the church's *mission.* The Gentile mission is *not* the result of Jewish rejection. It is God's idea from the very beginning according to biblical prophecy, and it is made possible only because of God's prior saving work among repentant Jews mediated by the church's *Jewish* mission.

**10.** So much of this passage involves believers' "coming together" in order to learn, to wait upon God, to pray in preparation to witness in Jesus' name by the Spirit's power. This fairly extensive collocation of images and ideas formulates a particular understanding of the church's identity and vocation: The church of Acts is a missionary community called together by God's Messiah and sent out into the world by the power of God's Spirit to interpret the importance of Jesus' resurrection for all people everywhere. Of course, the various resources of our canonical heritage teach us that to be the church we should seek a complement of witnesses. Thus the witness of the Confessing Church in Nazi Germany and that of Martin Luther King, Jr., in a racially divided United States speak to the importance and power of Jesus' resurrection in modern life. The distinctive contribution Acts makes to our understanding of mission is that the risen Lord bids and fills us with the Spirit to witness to him publicly and boldly in all that we do and say.

**11.** "This same Jesus . . . will come back in the same way you have seen him go into heaven" (1:11 NIV). The seventh and final Sunday of Easter is Ascension Sunday, and this passage is its principal lection. What do we really believe when we confess together the good news that Jesus "ascended into heaven"? Simply put, it is our affirmation that Jesus is *still* alive and *presently* metes out the Spirit's power for ministry (2:33) and God's grace for forgiveness (5:31) until he returns for "the restoration of all things" (3:21). In addition the ascension story in Acts (unlike Luke's Gospel) is directly tied to the forty days required by Jesus to prepare his apostles for their succession to his ministry. They are now "on the clock"—a formidable challenge, but one realistically envisaged by the promised Spirit.

**12.** Just as Acts is preeminently a theological book, so also the first images of God presented in the book are particularly important. No matter how vague or incomplete they are, these initial impressions of God in the opening paragraphs of Acts shape how its readers interpret God's subsequent appearances in its narrative world. God is faithful to Jesus (1:3, 9-11). God makes promises to Israel and plans to keep them (1:4-6). God's people gather to worship and pray to God, confident that God will act as promised (1:12-14). Perhaps keener than any other image, however, is that the God of Acts has a redemptive purpose to accomplish and a plan already worked out according to the promises of Scripture. The missionary vocation of the apostles, and by implication of the community they lead, is a task-centered one: The community will be enabled by God's Spirit to witness to God's Messiah—to preach persuasively and teach boldly, to interpret Scripture after the mind of God, and to perform miracles to awaken people to the benevolence of God's rule (1:8).

# ACTS 1:15-26, AND THEN THERE WERE TWELVE

NIV

[15]In those days Peter stood up among the believers[a] (a group numbering about a hundred and twenty) [16]and said, "Brothers, the Scripture had to be fulfilled which the Holy Spirit spoke long ago through the mouth of David concerning Judas, who served as guide for those who arrested Jesus— [17]he was one of our number and shared in this ministry."

[18](With the reward he got for his wickedness, Judas bought a field; there he fell headlong, his body burst open and all his intestines spilled out. [19]Everyone in Jerusalem heard about this, so they called that field in their language Akeldama, that is, Field of Blood.)

[20]"For," said Peter, "it is written in the book of Psalms,

" 'May his place be deserted;
    let there be no one to dwell in it,'[b] and,

" 'May another take his place of leadership.'[c]

[21]Therefore it is necessary to choose one of the men who have been with us the whole time the Lord Jesus went in and out among us, [22]beginning from John's baptism to the time when Jesus was

NRSV

15In those days Peter stood up among the believers[a] (together the crowd numbered about one hundred twenty persons) and said, [16]"Friends,[b] the scripture had to be fulfilled, which the Holy Spirit through David foretold concerning Judas, who became a guide for those who arrested Jesus— [17]for he was numbered among us and was allotted his share in this ministry." [18](Now this man acquired a field with the reward of his wickedness; and falling headlong,[c] he burst open in the middle and all his bowels gushed out. [19]This became known to all the residents of Jerusalem, so that the field was called in their language Hakeldama, that is, Field of Blood.) [20]"For it is written in the book of Psalms,

'Let his homestead become desolate,
    and let there be no one to live in it';
and

'Let another take his position of overseer.'

[21]So one of the men who have accompanied us during all the time that the Lord Jesus went in and out among us, [22]beginning from the baptism of John until the day when he was taken up from

[a] 15 Greek *brothers*    [b] 20 Psalm 69:25    [c] 20 Psalm 109:8

[a] Gk *brothers*    [b] Gk *Men, brothers*    [c] Or *swelling up*

NIV

taken up from us. For one of these must become a witness with us of his resurrection."

²³So they proposed two men: Joseph called Barsabbas (also known as Justus) and Matthias. ²⁴Then they prayed, "Lord, you know everyone's heart. Show us which of these two you have chosen ²⁵to take over this apostolic ministry, which Judas left to go where he belongs." ²⁶Then they cast lots, and the lot fell to Matthias; so he was added to the eleven apostles.

NRSV

us—one of these must become a witness with us to his resurrection." ²³So they proposed two, Joseph called Barsabbas, who was also known as Justus, and Matthias. ²⁴Then they prayed and said, "Lord, you know everyone's heart. Show us which one of these two you have chosen ²⁵to take the place*a* in this ministry and apostleship from which Judas turned aside to go to his own place." ²⁶And they cast lots for them, and the lot fell on Matthias; and he was added to the eleven apostles.

*a* Other ancient authorities read *the share*

# COMMENTARY

Symbols are important to biblical stories because they provide theological markers for their readers. There is hardly a more important numerical symbol in Scripture than twelve. Simply put, the number twelve stands for Israel as God's people. The significance of twelve apostles is elevated in Acts because Luke's Jesus had placed the prospect of Israel's restoration in the hands of his apostolic successors (see Luke 22:28-30; see also Acts 1:6-8). In this sense the restoration of the Apostolate to Twelve symbolizes (and is a necessary condition of) Israel's restoration. The stories of Judas's demise (1:15-20*a*) and Matthias's selection to replace him (1:20*b*-26), so laden with theological import and interpretive problems, are related here to explain how God acts to restore the Twelve. The group's return to its full complement heralds the apostles' inspired roles as agents of God's plan to restore the "twelve tribes of Israel." Moreover, the stories symbolize a divided Israel (see Luke 2:34-35) and therefore also the pattern of Israel's restoration. Even as Judas represents unrepentant Israel who rejects Messiah and is therefore rejected by God (see 13:44-47), Matthias, who unlike Judas is a "witness with us to his resurrection" (1:22*b*), represents a repentant Israel in whose life God's reign is present through the gift of the Spirit.

**1:15-20a.** The problem facing the interpreter of Judas's demise according to Acts has been framed and freighted in two ways. The NT reader approaches it with Matthew's version already in

mind (see Matt 27:3-10). Matthew's Judas is paradigmatic of the unrepentant disciple and contrasted to Peter who is rehabilitated because of his earnest repentance (see Matt 26:57-75; John 21:15-17). Upon closer reading, however, many discrepancies are noted between the Matthean and Acts' versions, not only in detail but in theological motivation as well.[68] Imaginative harmonies of Judas's death have been created in response to these discrepancies and then put forward as "authorized"—ironically, to preserve the authority of the very Scripture they displace! At the very least, the interpreter should take care to understand each account of Judas's death within its particular context. The different meanings should then be cobbled together as integral parts of a fuller, more textured understanding of Judas's death (see below).

Those who have read both Matthew's amd Luke's Gospels before Acts may be puzzled as to why Luke delays telling this story rather than including it in his Gospel. However, Luke's placement of the story in the introductory material of Acts envisages its strategic role. Luke understands that Judas's betrayal has greater theological significance than the spiritual failure of a particular

68. Read in terms of Matthew's theological conception, the contrasting responses of remorseful Peter and an equally remorseful Judas to their betrayal of Jesus illustrates the nature of spiritual conflict: Peter is penitent because he failed Jesus (26:75), whereas Judas's remorse is evoked by a private sense of guilt (27:4) that turns him inward rather than back to Jesus and the community for forgiveness (see Matt 18:20-22).

disciple; indeed, Judas's failure and demise appear to pose a real threat to the destiny of the messianic community itself. This seems especially true if Luke composes Acts to address a question concerning God's faithfulness in keeping promises made to Israel, for God's fidelity will be embodied in the apostles' future career as the Lord's successors (see 1:3-8). Jesus himself prophesied that the Twelve would rule over the "twelve tribes of Israel" in his absence (Luke 22:28-30). In this light, then, the reader of Acts realizes that Judas's demise fractures the Twelve and thereby undermines God's future plans: They are currently only the "eleven" and the divine plans cannot go forward (see 1:13).[69] If God's plans have gone awry because of Judas's defection—an apostle that God had chosen (see 1:2)—we may be inclined to ask further about God's faithfulness or to question whether God really has sovereign control over salvation's history. By this story, Luke rescues God from embarrassment!

Quite apart from any symbolic significance that the reference to "one hundred and twenty persons" (= a multiple of twelve) may suggest (1:15), Peter may have convened these believers as an official body to hear relevant testimony leading to an important decision or action. Peter's first speech in Acts provides testimony in two parts (1:16-20a and 1:20b-22) necessary to render a verdict in favor of God. He prefaces his remarks with two claims of Scripture's authority as the context in which such deliberation takes place. Peter begins his speech by asserting that "the scripture had [δεῖ *dei*] to be fulfilled." Luke characteristically uses the "*dei* of divine necessity" to mark out certain events as ordained by God (see Luke 22:37; 24:26, 44; Acts 3:21; 17:3); and Scripture is cited or alluded to as an independent testimony that these events are, indeed, written into the divine script by biblical prophecy as elements of God's plan of salvation. Computed by this redemptive calculus, then, Peter will logically contend that both Judas's death and the selection of Matthias are prophesied by Scripture (see 1:20) and must be viewed by the community as "necessary" for the realization of God's purposes and

even included in the script of God's salvation—even though by public perception these events have an awkward feel and accidental look.

Indeed, Peter claims "the Holy Spirit spoke long ago through David concerning Judas." That is, the Spirit's production of biblical prophecy through inspired prophets such as David[70] and the recovery of its contemporary meaning by inspired interpreters such as Peter ensure that the divinely intended meaning of Scripture is transmitted to the faith community. This careful staging of Peter's comments about Judas's death and the importance of selecting a replacement, justified by his reading of Scripture, presume that the production and interpretation of Scripture are by the same Spirit of God and therefore espouse a single truth: Judas's accidental death and Matthias's selection by chance are executed according to divine purpose.

Peter explains that Judas "was numbered among us and was allotted a share in this ministry" (1:17). The verbs used place Judas under the provident care of a sovereign God, note the happy beginning of a tragic story, and make clearer that his defection from "this ministry" is by his choice and not God's. The parenthetical description of Judas's death in vv. 18-19[71] examines his spiritual failure and casts blame on him, thereby justifying God's rejection of Judas as the one who betrayed the Messiah and reneged on his portion of the apostolic ministry—all for the "reward of his wickedness" (1:18). In sharp contrast to Matthew, Peter does not claim a remorseful Judas returned the money; here Judas chooses instead to purchase "a field" (= a "small farm"), perhaps to buy his way into a higher social class. Judas's choice of money over Messiah is paradigmatic of spiritual failure in Acts. In contrast to the exercise of spiritual authority and maturity within the community of goods, exemplified by the glad sharing of material wealth with others (see 2:42-47; 4:32-35), Judas's rejection of Jesus and defection from his apostolic duties is embodied in his use of ill-begotten money for a personal end. This act supplies ample proof of his alienation from

---

69. See J. Jervell, *Luke and the People of God* (Minneapolis: Augsburg, 1972) 75-112, esp. 88-96.

70. In Acts, David is "the prophet par excellence, the central figure in Scripture" according to J. Jervell, *The Unknown Paul* (Minneapolis: Augsburg, 1984) 126.

71. Since punctuation marks are not used in the Greek text, the writer must revert to syntactical markers to introduce a narrative parenthesis. Luke uses the transitional phrase οὗτος μὲν οὖν (*houtos men oun,* "Now this man") in 1:18 to signal this to the reader.

God.[72] Noteworthy is Peter's use of Ps 69:25 (Ps 68:26 LXX), which is prophetic of Judas's *land* and not his death: "Let his homestead become desolate, and let there be no one to live in it" (1:20*a*).[73] Luke employs the symbolism of property to underscore that the money paid Judas ultimately bought land used to bury the dead rather than land used to house the living. Likewise, the person who chooses money over Messiah actually makes a choice for death rather than for life.

The vivid description of Judas's death is also shaped for its theological effect: "he burst open in the middle and all his bowels gushed out" (1:18). Luke shapes his story after familiar Jewish (and secular) death stories of the wicked in which the more wicked the deed the more graphic and inopportune the death (see Acts 12:20-23; see also Josh 7; 2 Sam 20:4-13; 2 Macc 9:5-6).[74] Moreover, the burst "bowels" (σπλάγχνον *splanchnon*) of Judas may allude to famous exemplars of his opposites in Luke's Gospel: the "good Samaritan" who is "moved by pity" (σπλαγχνίζοναι *splanchnizomai,* Luke 10:33) to care for the wounded stranger and the caring father who is "filled with compassion" (*splanchnizomai,* Luke 15:20) when welcoming his prodigal son home. This Lukan intertext cultivates the reader's impression of Judas as a tragic symbol of religious disaffection whose self-absorption wins out over mercy.

Finally, the discrepant versions of Judas's fate found in Matt 27:3-10 and Acts 1:18-20 are actually complementary within a canonical whole.

Rather than viewing them as contradictory and in need of some kind of exegetical arbitration, the interpreter should think of them as the discrete yet collateral interpretations of Judas's death that the church has included within its Scriptures to be read together and reflexively. In this way the very differences found in one text frame a fresh angle of vision into the other text, allowing the interpreter to detect hitherto hidden layers of meaning. For example, commentators on Acts routinely fail to find an implicit contrast between Peter and Judas (as noted above). With Matthew's sharpened contrast in mind, the reader approaches Peter's speech about Judas's demise quite differently: The living Jesus has fullest effect in a restored Peter who has now succeeded him as Israel's primary interpreter of Scripture.[75] Given Matthew's description of the contrasting responses of Peter and Judas to their betrayal of the Lord, Peter's speech may also fulfill Jesus' prediction that Peter's betrayal would yield a greater faith, one that would enable him to lead the messianic community (see Luke 22:31-34). In this way, the contrasting destinies of Judas and Peter that Matthew introduces at the moment of their common failure are lifted up in the opening of Acts to underscore the continuity of all that Jesus had begun.

**1:20b-26.** Part two of Peter's speech (1:20*b*-22) outlines the requirements of the qualified replacement for Judas with an aim of restoring the apostolic circle according to God's prophesied plan.[76] The "*dei* of divine necessity" (1:21) stipulates two credentials: The successful candidate will (1) "have accompanied us all the time that the Lord Jesus went in and out among us, beginning from the baptism of John until the day when he was taken up from us;" and will (2) "become a witness with us to his resurrection." Peter's job description contrasts with the prior failure of Judas: The successful candidate must be a "witness with us," unlike Judas, who was an apostate from the apostolic circle; and this candidate must have "accompanied us all the time—until the day he was taken from us," unlike Judas, whose death occurred prior to the Lord's passion and ascension.

---

72. According to L. Johnson's literary analysis, *The Literary Function of Possessions in Luke-Acts,* SBLDS 39 (Missoula, Mont.: Scholars Press, 1977) esp. 173-222, Luke's view of the use and misuse of possessions constitutes an important theological symbol in the narrative world of Acts. The pattern of divine judgment and future blessing is routinely linked to money. Possessions symbolize the condition of a person's relations with God and neighbor. The roots of such a motif are deeply set in the prophetic tradition of Israel's Scriptures and in contemporary Greek philosophy (Stoic, Cynic) that valued the sharing of possessions as a public expression of friendship.

73. H. C. Kee, *To Every Nation Under Heaven: The Acts of the Apostles,* NTC (Valley Forge, Pa.: Trinity, 1997) 40, suggests that blood spilled on land renders it impure and off limits to the observant Jew, analogous to the woman whose loss of blood at childbirth requires that she go through a period of purification in order to be restored to the community (see Leviticus 12).

74. The Acts account may echo the well-known legend of Antiochus's fatal illness (2 Macc 9:1-12; 1 Macc 6:1-16). In 2 Maccabees, a theological lesson is drawn from the manner of a person's death, whether the death of a righteous martyr or of a wicked foe. In the case of wicked Antiochus, his "bowels" (σπλάγχνον *splanchnon*) become painfully infected—"justly so" because he had tortured the "bowels" of observant Jews who refused to compromise their community's devotion to God (2 Macc 6:9). The connection to Judas's death is clear enough; the reader now is able to see a similar lesson in the Acts narrative of Judas's death.

75. Tannehill, *The Acts of the Apostles,* 20.

76. Johnson, *The Acts of the Apostles,* 36, notes that Luke's use of Ps 109:8, "Let another take his position as overseer," works well here only because the LXX renders the Hebrew word פקדה (*pĕqûdâ*) by the Greek ἐπισκοπή (*episkopē*), a word that designates an office of ecclesial leadership as in Acts 20:28 (cf. 1 Tim 3:11).

Neither of the two candidates, Justus and Matthias, is ever again mentioned in the NT. The importance of this story has nothing to do with the two people involved; it illustrates the theological principle that the God who "knows everyone's heart" (1:24) controls the course of salvation's history. Equally important is the conviction that God collaborates with others in the progress of salvation toward its ordained end. Thus the community is a full partner in the decision-making process: First they petition God to make the tough decision (1:24-25) and then they cast lots as the means by which God's decision is made known (1:26). As with Judas's demise, which those outside the community would surely classify as an accidental death or bad luck, outsiders would think the casting of lots brings Matthias good fortune. The faith community knows differently, since lot casting was a traditional and widespread practice for disclosing God's will (see Josh 19:1-40; Jonah 1:7-8). Moreover, God's will is discerned by a community whose decision process values Scripture (1:20), a close relationship with Jesus (1:21-22), and prayerful petition (1:24-25). The concluding phrase that Matthias "was added to the eleven apostles" suggests that a vote was taken to ratify God's evident choice.

# REFLECTIONS

**1.** "So one of the men who have accompanied us during all the time that the Lord Jesus went in and out among us" (1:21 NRSV). The twelve apostolic successors to Jesus are colleagues of Jesus and witnesses of what he did and said from beginning to end (1:21-22). This close and comprehensive knowledge of Jesus ensures the reliability of what is said about him to others in his absence. From the ancient church forward the comprehensiveness, consistency, and integrity of the Rule of Faith (*regula fidei*), which measures every claim that is called "Christian," is predicated on its source: We have received our confession from the apostles who were taught it by Jesus. Thus, for Irenaeus, the church's rule of faith predates Scripture (and every other canonical text) and is funded by the precious memories of Jesus that were received from his apostles,[77] and then preserved and passed on to the "one holy, catholic and *apostolic* church" through a succession of its canonical episcopate.[78] The authority of Scripture's teaching or the theological perspicuity of its interpretation is warranted by analogy to this Rule of Faith, which has its origins in leaders who knew Jesus personally and intimately.

**2.** "The Scripture had to be fulfilled" (1:16 NIV). This "δεῖ [*dei*] of divine necessity" is a literary theme of importance in Acts. Luke employs it to make certain readers understand that this or that event is a necessary bit or piece of God's plan of salvation according to Scripture. Judas's demise and Matthias's selection to replace him in the circle of the Twelve are the first instances of this use of *dei* in Acts (1:16, 21); both accord with God's plans and redemptive purposes. But how is this so? Judas was "chosen" by Jesus (1:2) in consultation with a sovereign God (cf. Luke 6:13). How is it possible that someone handpicked to lead the people of God as a member of the apostolic circle then dies in accordance with God's scripted plans? God's selection is never coercive but collaborative. Tasks are given with the requisite resources to accomplish them. The emphasis on character in Acts, however, leads the reader to presume that God's instructions are provisional and must be obeyed to be implemented. God's sovereignty is never at the expense of human freedom. Thus, even though Judas's "accidental" death and Matthias's "lucky" selection are in some sense God's actions and accord with biblical prophecy, God can act only because of freely made human choices.

**3.** "The lot fell on Matthias; and he was added to the eleven apostles" (1:26 NRSV). Various models for selecting leaders are found in Scripture. In this case, Matthias's selection follows a

---

77. Irenaeus *Against Heresies* 1.10.1.
78. Ibid., 3.3.3.

protocol of discernment by which a game of chance is used to complement corporate prayer in discerning God's will. In his letters, Paul claims to hold the gift of apostleship (Rom 1:5) by virtue of his Damascus road calling (Gal 1:11-17; see also Acts 9:10-19) and witness of the living Jesus (1 Cor 15:7-8; see also Acts 9:3-9). Paul's résumé is similar to that of the Old Testament prophets, who were also called by God through visionary episodes. This is still different from the protocol used for selecting the seven (see 6:1-7) or for "appointing" congregational elders (see 14:23). According to Pauline instruction, found in 1 Timothy 3 and Titus 1, the "overseer/elder" is identified by scrutinizing the sort of person he is rather than according to his acquaintance with the historical (= Matthias) or resurrected (= Paul) Jesus. It should be noted that the requirements for apostleship given in Acts 1:21-22 would disqualify even the Paul of Acts who did not accompany the Twelve "during all the time that the Lord Jesus went in and out among us" (1:21). Different situations require different processes for selecting a congregation's leaders. In every case, however, some institutional means for discerning God's will is established to ensure that those selected are of God's choosing rather than of our own.

# ACTS 2:1-13, PENTECOST: THE SPIRIT OF PROPHECY FALLS UPON THE COMMUNITY

## NIV

2 When the day of Pentecost came, they were all together in one place. [2]Suddenly a sound like the blowing of a violent wind came from heaven and filled the whole house where they were sitting. [3]They saw what seemed to be tongues of fire that separated and came to rest on each of them. [4]All of them were filled with the Holy Spirit and began to speak in other tongues[a] as the Spirit enabled them.

[5]Now there were staying in Jerusalem God-fearing Jews from every nation under heaven. [6]When they heard this sound, a crowd came together in bewilderment, because each one heard them speaking in his own language. [7]Utterly amazed, they asked: "Are not all these men who are speaking Galileans? [8]Then how is it that each of us hears them in his own native language? [9]Parthians, Medes and Elamites; residents of Mesopotamia, Judea and Cappadocia, Pontus and Asia, [10]Phrygia and Pamphylia, Egypt and the parts of Libya near Cyrene; visitors from Rome [11](both Jews and converts to Judaism); Cretans and Arabs—we hear them declaring the wonders of God in our own tongues!" [12]Amazed and perplexed, they asked one another, "What does this mean?"

[13]Some, however, made fun of them and said, "They have had too much wine.[b]"

## NRSV

2 When the day of Pentecost had come, they were all together in one place. [2]And suddenly from heaven there came a sound like the rush of a violent wind, and it filled the entire house where they were sitting. [3]Divided tongues, as of fire, appeared among them, and a tongue rested on each of them. [4]All of them were filled with the Holy Spirit and began to speak in other languages, as the Spirit gave them ability.

[5]Now there were devout Jews from every nation under heaven living in Jerusalem. [6]And at this sound the crowd gathered and was bewildered, because each one heard them speaking in the native language of each. [7]Amazed and astonished, they asked, "Are not all these who are speaking Galileans? [8]And how is it that we hear, each of us, in our own native language? [9]Parthians, Medes, Elamites, and residents of Mesopotamia, Judea and Cappadocia, Pontus and Asia, [10]Phrygia and Pamphylia, Egypt and the parts of Libya belonging to Cyrene, and visitors from Rome, both Jews and proselytes, [11]Cretans and Arabs—in our own languages we hear them speaking about God's deeds of power." [12]All were amazed and perplexed, saying to one another, "What does this mean?" [13]But others sneered and said, "They are filled with new wine."

[a] 4 Or languages; also in verse 11    [b] 13 Or sweet wine

# COMMENTARY

The succession from the now-departed Messiah to the Twelve is made complete with the arrival of God's promised Spirit. First John the Baptist (in Luke 3:16) and then the risen Jesus (in Acts 1:4-5) predicted this high moment in the church's history (see 1:6-8). Not surprisingly, then, this passage is structured to reflect Jesus' earlier prophecy: The reception of God's Spirit (2:1-4) enables the community to carry an inspired word about God's risen Messiah to the entire household of Israel (2:5-13).[79]

**2:1-4.** No episode narrated in Acts has received more attention than this one. Such scrutiny is deserved for several reasons: the importance Jesus gives the Spirit's role in his final instructions to the apostles (see 1:4-8), the passage's highly evocative description,[80] the way certain faith traditions and religious movements have drawn on this passage to warrant their religious experience and theological contribution, and the fact that this text frames and informs the church's observance of its Pentecost season when believers gather together in heightened expectation of being renewed and reborn by the power of God's Spirit. Yet, the attraction to Pentecost is also surprising. Luke alone among biblical writers has the Spirit's arrival as his "great theme," without which "there would be no story to tell."[81] To be sure, John's Gospel makes passing reference to the risen Jesus bestowing the Holy Spirit upon his disciples (20:22) and Paul draws upon a tradition about the Lord's appearance to five hundred at one time (1 Cor 15:6), perhaps in the form of his "life-giving Spirit" (1 Cor 15:45). But neither witness seems to know the particular tradition Luke uses in composing his story of the coming of

God's Spirit.[82] The reader is doubly surprised, then, to find the account of so important an event so "slender and spare."[83] Perhaps its telescoping to a scant four verses intends to move the reader more quickly to the story of the Spirit's powerful effect in the community's mission to Israel (see 2:5-13), which is more central to Luke's theological program.

According to the opening phrase of this passage, the entire community is baptized into the realm of the Spirit "when the day of Pentecost had come."[84] This is evidently the particular day for which the community had been instructed to "wait" (see 1:4). The word for "Pentecost" (lit., "fiftieth day") was used by Diaspora Jews for a day-long harvest festival more commonly known as the "Feast of Weeks" (*Shavuot*) and scheduled fifty days following Passover (Exod 23:16; 34:22; Lev 23:15-21; Num 28:26; Deut 16:9-12). Luke's staging of the Spirit's outpouring and miracle of tongues may be explained in part by the subsequent "list of nations" (2:9-10), since Pentecost was one of three pilgrimage feasts when the entire household of Israel gathered in Jerusalem to celebrate the goodness of God toward the nation (cf. 2:11).

Some interpreters of this passage have heard echoes of Scripture's narrative of the Sinai theophany

---

79. C. K. Barrett, *A Critical and Exegetical Commentary on the Acts of the Apostles,* 2 vols, ICC (Edinburgh: T. & T. Clark, 1994, 1998) 108, suggests that Luke's purpose in this narrative is concentrated on the universalism of Jesus' commission. Even though occurring in Jerusalem and observed only by Jews, the coming of the Spirit effectively transforms the community into a "universal society in which a universal communication is possible."

80. According to H. Conzelmann, *The Acts of the Apostles,* trans. J. Limburg et al., ed. E. J. Epp and C. R. Matthews, Hermeneia (Philadelphia: Fortress, 1987) 15, "Luke has fashioned [the Pentecost narrative] into its present form as an episode with a burlesque impact."

81. J. D. G. Dunn, *The Acts of the Apostles* (Valley Forge, Pa.: Trinity, 1996) 22.

82. Barrett, *Acts,* 108, notes that this is especially problematic when considering Paul, for whom the Spirit's role in the community's life is of special significance. However, G. Lüdemann, *Early Christianity According to the Traditions in Acts* (Minneapolis: Fortress, 1989) 42-43, contends that these three NT accounts may well reflect elements of a common tradition that link christophany with the giving of the Spirit. Two other factors suggest an even fuller memory reflected by the "Pentecost" stories of John and Acts (and perhaps even known to Paul). The timing of the promised Spirit in both narratives falls after and points to the exaltation of Jesus—in John immediately following his resurrection and in Acts soon after his ascension. Further, in both cases the gift of the Spirit climaxes succession narratives, when the Spirit empowers the community to continue the Lord's work—in John to forgive sin (John 20:23; cf. 16:8-9) and in Acts to do and teach what Jesus began (Acts 1:1).

83. So L. T. Johnson, *The Acts of the Apostles,* SP 5 (Collegeville, Minn.: Liturgical, 1992) 45.

84. Luke leaves unattended the evident tension between the apostolic provenance of the Lord's (and his Father's!) original promise of the Spirit according to 1:4-5 and the corporate realization of this promise according to 2:1-4. Clearly more than the Twelve are gathered together, and all are given the ability by the Spirit to proclaim the good news of God's deeds of power in different languages. This same tension is unresolved in Acts criticism. Some scholars, such as Fitzmyer, speak only of the apostles as baptized with the Spirit; others, such as R. Stronstad, *The Prophethood of All Believers,* JPTSS 16 (Sheffield: Sheffield Academic, 1999), press for a more communitarian baptism.

and the giving of Torah (Exod 19:16-19; Deut 5:4-5); on this basis they claim its typological significance for Luke's theology of the Holy Spirit. The Sinai typology contains two key elements: the giving of the Torah occurred roughly fifty days after Passover (so Exod 19:1) as an act of covenant renewal, and the Torah-based covenant renewal of Israel was mediated through Moses. Whereas Jewish interpreters vest Pentecost with the importance of the Torah of Moses for Israel's future with God, Christian interpreters posit that a new dispensation has dawned when the Holy Spirit through the Messiah mediates a new covenant with repentant Israel (see Jer 31:31-34; Rom 8:2). Both interpretations of Pentecost, however, are now contested. The specific question is whether the symbolism that links Pentecost and Sinai was available to Luke when he wrote Acts. Most scholars have concluded that Israel's commemoration of the gift of Torah during Pentecost reflects a later rabbinical practice, appearing in Jewish writings only after Luke wrote Acts.[85] Still, both *Jubilees* and Philo imply this connection between Pentecost and Sinai, if only vaguely so. Further, Luke uses familiar OT symbols of theophany, similar to Moses' experience on Sinai (e.g., fire, sound, speech), to describe the Spirit's outpouring at Pentecost; and elsewhere in Acts he makes reference to Moses and the Exodus when defending the importance of Jesus' messiahship for the renewal of Israel's covenant with God (see 3:19-24; 7:35-38). So Luke's careful staging of this event on a particular day may reflect his own theological innovation.[86]

In any case, the inbreaking of heaven into human affairs is a salient feature of Luke's narrative world. The reader of Acts is hardly surprised, then, that the promised Spirit arrives from heaven with special effects, sounding like a "violent wind" and appearing like "tongues of fire." Significantly, the community's reception of God's Spirit is perceptible; and the Lord's prophecy is fulfilled beyond doubt. The church's mission can and must

begin. This passage does not claim the Holy Spirit *is* a "wind" or *is* a "fire"; rather, the Spirit is compared to the sound wind makes (cf. Gen 1:2)[87] and to the flames fire produces (cf. Exod 3:2; Ps 104:4). The narrator's intent is to create a vivid impression of the Spirit's presence among the community of the Lord's disciples as its distinguishing mark.[88]

The image of "tongues of fire" (γλῶσσαι ὡσεὶ πυρός *glōssai hōsei pyros*) heralds the gift of speaking in foreign languages (2:4) as the Spirit enables the community, especially the apostles, to testify publicly to Israel. This connection of Spirit and proclamation does not yet concern the content of the message but rather the powerful and persuasive manner by which the gospel is boldly preached (see 2:29; 4:13; 9:27-8; 14:3). J. Levison has argued, however, that "fire" (πῦρ *pyr*) was frequently used in contemporary Jewish (e.g., Philo, Pseudo-Philo) and Greco-Roman popular writings (e.g., Quintillian, Plutarch) as a metaphor for the physiological experiences of prophetic inspiration (i.e., inflammation and agitation in combination) that occurred when the spirit of prophecy awakened and elevated the prophet's ability to think, reason, and speak.[89] That is, Luke's symbolism of the Spirit's fiery presence not only signifies the power to speak the word of God effectively but also to think about God in fresh and "inspired" ways.

In this regard, Levison's study also illumines how we should take the prophetic idiom "filled with the Holy Spirit" (2:4). While certainly reflecting Luke's insistence that God guides the witnessing community through the Holy Spirit, we can no longer limit the meaning of Spirit baptism to prophetic demeanor—to the boldness or even the persuasive rhetoric of the community's (and especially their

---

85. The best summary of the evidence for this position is provided by Barrett, *Acts,* 111-12. Yet even his review omits important countervailing evidence. For example, while he is correct in setting aside the reference to the "Feast of Weeks" in *Jub.* 6:17-21 as referring to the Noahic rather than the Mosaic covenant, *Jub.* 1:1 nevertheless suggests that God's covenant with Noah is glossed by God's covenant with Moses at Sinai. See C. H. Talbert, *Reading Acts* (New York: Crossroad, 1997) 40.

86. Johnson, *The Acts of the Apostles,* 46.

87. The depiction of the Spirit as "wind" may well recall the creation story to posit yet another typological rendering of the baptism with the Spirit—namely, that the creative power of the Spirit results in the birth of a new creation or even new life. This subtext could very well be intended by John 20:22, referring to Jesus' "breathing" upon the disciples (so alluding to the creation of human life in Gen 2:7), especially given the theological importance of the "new creation" motif in John's Gospel. In this case, the "fire" symbolism in Acts 2:3 could infer the cleansing purification of the old, fallen order brought by the Spirit at Pentecost. Nonetheless, I doubt this meaning is present in Acts, where the coming of the Spirit is so keenly linked to the community's vocation as witness to Jesus.

88. J. Jervell, *The Theology of the Acts of the Apostles,* NTT (Cambridge: Cambridge University Press, 1996) 45.

89. J. R. Levison, *The Spirit in First Century Judaism,* AGAJU 29 (Leiden: Brill, 1997) 114-21, 245-46.

apostles') missionary proclamation. The Spirit also gives extraordinary insight to those it fills. The prophet who is filled with the Spirit of prophecy is able to set aside the processes of human intellect, such as conjecture and guesswork, and replace them with "true" knowledge of a divinely inspired intellect.[90] The practical result, according to Philo, is that the Spirit-filled prophet is given an enriched capacity to exegete Scripture—to interpret the biblical word after the mind of God.[91] Surely Luke understands the baptism or "filling" by the Spirit in this way. Thus, the Spirit is the power by which the Scriptures are written through the inspired prophets of old (1:16; 4:25; 28:25); and these same biblical words inspired by the Spirit are rendered accurately and with keen insight into the human (and especially Israel's) condition by the power of this same Spirit. Acts does not depict the Spirit's filling, then, in a manner that is disconnected from Scripture.[92] Charismatic (i.e., inspired) utterance is deeply rooted in charismatic exegesis.

Although concentrated in the apostles (following OT teaching), this Spirit of prophecy is neither the private property of an enlightened few nor a transitory presence. This Spirit belongs to a people of God as their shared, permanent property. Luke makes this point clearer by repetition: "they were all together" in a "whole house where all were sitting," when the Spirit came to rest on "each of them" so that "all of them were filled."[93] The power of the Spirit in this case evinces an extraor-

dinary ability for them to "speak in other languages"—that is, in foreign languages unknown to them.[94] This "gift of tongues" should not be confused with the spiritual gift of *glossolalia* that concerns Paul in 1 Corinthians 12–14. The relevant issue at stake is not the source or the linguistic structure of this gift, whether "of men or of angels" (1 Cor 13:1); nor does Luke's use of "other" (ἑτέρα *hetera*) distinguish this from subsequent episodes of extraordinary speeches in Acts (e.g., 10:45-46; 19:6).[95] The key difference is between competing purposes. According to Pauline teaching, the gifts of the Spirit are used to empower Christian ministry to other believers for the purpose of Christian formation. Thus the Pauline meaning of *glossolalia* denotes a special language given to a few believers by the Spirit (so 1 Cor 12:14-30) to edify the entire congregation (so 1 Cor 14:5)—a purpose quite different from that of Luke.

**2:5-13.** The crowd of "devout Jews" (2:5) hears "this sound" (2:6), whose source is "Galileans" (2:7)—notorious for their lack of linguistic talent—"speaking in the native language of each" (2:6, 8, 11) about "God's deeds of power" (2:11).[96] This is the first of over fifty references to the "Jews" in Acts and has paradigmatic value for the reader.[97] Jews occupy the center stage of

90. Ibid., 168-89.

91. Ibid., 190-211.

92. The actual phrase "baptism with the Spirit" is nowhere used in Scripture. Luke uses the verb "baptize" (βαπτίζω *baptizō*) with "Spirit" (πνεῦμα *pneuma*) in only Acts 1:5; 11:16; and probably in 9:18; and interchangeably with "fill" (πίμπλημι *pimplēmi*) in Acts 2:4; 4:8, 31; 9:17; 13:9) as the idiom of the Spirit's enabling those chosen by God to do the tasks of the prophet-like-Jesus. My use of "baptism with the Spirit" is a nontechnical reference to the prophecy of Jesus (1:8) that his witnesses will receive (i.e., be "baptized into" or "filled" with) the Spirit, which will enable them to do the tasks given them by God: persuasive preaching to nonbelievers, edifying teaching of believers, inspired interpretation of Scripture, miraculous "signs and wonders," and the like. Throughout this commentary, I understand the gift of the Spirit primarily (although not exclusively) in functional or missional terms.

93. The implicit contrast in Acts between the evident importance of particular Spirit-filled apostles, who are inspired to preach, interpret Scripture, perform miracles and lead the church, and rank-and-file believers who are also Spirit-filled but not central to the church's mission has led Turner to distinguish between the transforming power of the Spirit, which is experienced by all believers, and the more functional empowerment of the Spirit, which is experienced only by the prophets-like-Jesus (e.g., Peter, Stephen, Paul). See M. Turner, *Power from on High: The Spirit in Israel's Restoration and Witness in Luke-Acts,* JPTSS 9 (Sheffield: Sheffield Academic, 1996) 314-427.

94. Many interpreters, ancient and modern, find in this miracle of *glossolalia* an allusion to the OT story of Babel in Gen 11:1-9, where the division of speech is the hallmark of human creation's rebellion against the Creator. Here the use of multiple languages by a cohesive community to present a coherent message is the hallmark of the Creator's initiative to reverse Babel's curse. The emphasis of 2:5-13, however, is upon the *hearing* of (see 2:6, 8, 11) rather than the *speaking* of different languages (see 2:4). In fact, the Babel typology might be more effectively understood if the real miracle envisaged by this story is rather one of hearing a *single* language of the Spirit but in multiple declensions. Nevertheless, the Commentary on 2:5-13 unfolds from my analysis of 2:4, which stipulates that the miracle of Pentecost is the enabling of these Spirit-filled Galileans to speak in multiple languages.

95. So J. A. Fitzmyer, *The Acts of the Apostles,* AB 31 (Garden City, N.Y.: Doubleday, 1998) 239.

96. The language of "power" may refer specifically to Pentecost and the power of the Spirit that now transforms the community, or more generally to the "power" that enables the community to proclaim a word about the redemptive acts of God in Jesus. I take it that this latter meaning as intended here: the power of the Pentecostal Spirit enables proclamation.

97. See the helpful excursus on " 'The Jews' in Acts" in H. C. Kee, *To Every Nation Under Heaven: The Acts of the Apostles,* NTC (Valley Forge, Pa.: Trinity, 1997) 45-47. See also J. Jervell, *The Theology of the Acts of the Apostles,* NTT (Cambridge: Cambridge University Press, 1996) 18-54; J. Jervell, *Die Apostelgeschichte,* KEK 3 (Göttingen: Vandenhoeck & Ruprecht, 1998) 92-93, where Jervell asserts that in Acts God's people and God's promises for them always refer to the entire household of Israel. In this sense, the church of Acts *is* Israel. Unlike Jervell, Kee (with most other interpreters) divides references to Jews into two semantic fields, roughly according to the two parts of Acts. In (*cont.*)

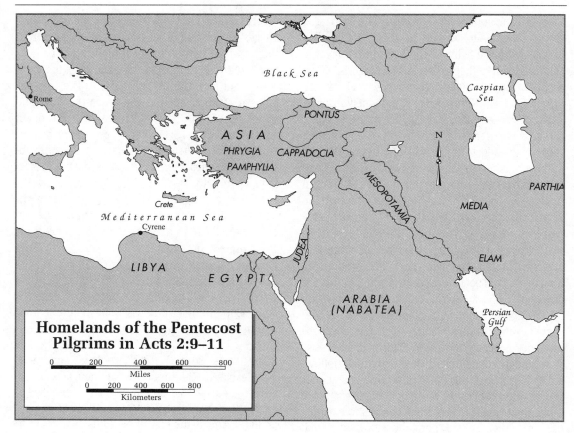

**Homelands of the Pentecost Pilgrims in Acts 2:9–11**

Luke's narrative world; for this reason, we must be alert to the nuances of his usage here. In particular, they are "devout" Jews. The church's proclamation of the mighty acts of God begins with faithful Jews. Significantly, the catalogue of nations (2:9-11)[98] indicates that these Jews constitute an international assembly. Luke's hyperbole captures this nicely: "every nation under heaven" (2:5). In effect, the entire household of Israel, including "both Jews and proselytes"[99] (2:10), is present to hear this inspired witness to God's faithfulness to Israel.[100]

---

(*continued from previous page*)

the book's first half (chaps. 1–15), concluding with the Jerusalem Council, "the Jews" refer to those committed to Israel's Torah and Jewish religious traditions as the very foundation for maintaining good relations with God as well as working relations with the wider society. In the book's second half (chaps. 16–28), which follows missionary Paul to the "end of the earth" (Rome), "the Jews" are more narrowly circumscribed as the ruling elite of "official" Israel and are generally hostile to "the sect of the Nazarenes" (24:5). Jervell, *The Theology of the Acts of the Apostles,* 34-43, rightly deduces that both groups are players, for good and ill, in resolving (or not) the central crisis facing the Jewish people, which is the division *within* Israel between messianic and non-messianic Jews. In this sense, then, Israel has not rejected the gospel that the Messiah has come as the risen Jesus of Nazareth; rather, Jews are divided over the issue and this theological conflict plots the action of Acts.

98. The so-called list of nations is routinely identified as a critical problem by modern interpreters. See, e.g., E. Haenchen, E. *The Acts of the Apostles* (Philadelphia: Westminster, 1971) 172-75; H. Conzelmann, *The Acts of the Apostles,* trans. J. Limburg et al., ed. E. J. Epp and C. R. Matthews, Hermeneia (Philadelphia: Fortress, 1987) 14-15. For example, the inclusion of "Judea" (2:9) seems strange since

they would speak (roughly) the same language as the Galileans. Further, the list includes various "ancient" nations no longer in existence when Luke wrote Acts (e.g., Parthians, Elamites), and the Cretans or Arabians are better understood as groups rather than nations. But Luke knew all of this! The narrative function of the list is theological, defining the inclusive boundaries of the household of Israel for whom the promise of restoration is now going forth from the community of the Spirit.

99. The word for "proselyte" (προσήλυτος *prosēlytos*) refers to "one who has come over," or the Gentile who has converted to Judaism. Scot McKnight, *A Light Among the Gentiles: Jewish Missionary Activity in the Second Temple Period* (Minneapolis: Fortress, 1991), has demonstrated that while Gentiles converted to Judaism during the Second Temple period, there was no organized Jewish mission to the Gentiles. Contra Fitzmyer, *The Acts of the Apostles,* 243. Since there was no Jewish mission to the Gentiles, these converts were first "God seekers" who were attracted to Jewish faith because of its teachings and way of life. This is an important group of Jews in Acts, perhaps because Luke was a proselyte before becoming a believer. In any case, the concerns raised about Paul's Gentile mission, which is the first organized Jewish mission to the Gentiles, according to Acts, are concerns about *how* (and not *that*) Gentiles convert. These are concerns settled at the Jerusalem Council (Acts 15:13-21). Perhaps the reference to "proselytes" in 2:10 hints at Paul's mission to the outsiders and the Gentile constituency of a restored Israel. See also R. Zehnle, *Peter's Pentecost Discourse Tradition and Lukan Reinterpretation in Peter's Speeches of Acts 2 and 3,* SBLMS 15 (Nashville: Abingdon, 1971).

100. Those who comment that this catalog of nations implies a universal mission, which ultimately will conclude in Rome (Acts 28; see also 2:10), are doubtless correct. Jesus' commission (1:8) has already provided the reader with such a geographical index and its implication for the church's missionary endeavor. However, it is more critical that the catalog of nations depicts the extent of a restored Israel, which will consist of Jews and proselytes from every nation.

Moreover, these Jews are "bewildered" (2:6), "amazed and astonished" (2:7), and "perplexed" (2:12) by what they hear. The present crisis facing Israel is their divided house: Some have the promised Spirit but others do not and therefore remain ignorant of Scripture's confirmation that Jesus is God's Messiah (see 2:14-36; 3:17-24). Their amazement also reflects their spiritual predicament: Who will show them the way? The short-term consequence of their ignorance is to write off the importance of what they have heard as a case of inebriation: "They are filled with new wine" (2:13). Their confusion leads Peter to interpret the divine audition they have witnessed while dispelling their ignorance about the Messiah, for it is the task of the prophet-like-Jesus to show Israel the way of the Lord.

# REFLECTIONS

**1.** "When the day of Pentecost had come" (2:1 NRSV). The Spirit arrives in Jerusalem on the day of Pentecost as the fulfillment of prophecy and as the answer to the community's expectant prayers; it is a clear sign of God's faithfulness. Earlier Jesus told his apostles that God has "marked" the crucial dates of salvation's history (see 1:7). The entire household of Israel had gathered in the holy city on Pentecost to celebrate God's provident care. The gift of the Holy Spirit is another concrete example of God's goodness to Israel, and it models God's faithfulness in keeping divine promises.

**2.** The Pentecost experience of God's Spirit is repeated in Acts; its images are routinely recalled to interpret subsequent outpourings of God's Spirit as the constant testimony to God's continuing faithfulness (8:17; 10:44–11:18; 19:1-6). While a special moment in salvation's history, this Pentecostal outpouring of the purifying, empowering Spirit upon God's people is not a unique event from a time long ago. Luke's narrative of this wondrous action symbolizes the powerful and effective nature of God's ongoing presence among those who follow after God's Messiah.

**3.** "They were all together in one place" (2:1 NIV and NRSV). God's Spirit is poured out upon a community of believers. The Holy Spirit is not a "personal" gift from God that each believer privatizes—"you can have your Spirit if I can have mine." This same Spirit of one God "appeared among them—on each of them" as the distinguishing mark of a *people* belonging to God. The restoration of Israel is the work of this Spirit sent by God as promised (see 1:6), which is why the first auditors of the miracle of tongues were "devout Jews from every nation" (2:5).

**4.** "And at this sound the crowd gathered" (2:6 NRSV). The church has always tended toward *bitarianism,* worshiping the Father and the Son while regarding the Spirit as a marginal member of the Holy Trinity. The Holy Spirit is kept to the interior region of individual devotion and only under special circumstances makes a public appearance in the form of odd religious experiences that frighten away the uninitiated. However, it is clear from this story that the arrival of the Holy Spirit is anything but private and hidden from view, nor does it prompt folks to run from its illuminating power. The Spirit's arrival is a noisy affair with special effects that draws an interested public "from every nation" to the community in amazement.

**5.** "All of them were filled with the Holy Spirit and began to speak in other languages" (2:4 NRSV). The presence of the Holy Spirit in the community's life is indicated first of all by the miracle of speaking in unknown foreign languages. In explaining why this is so, the interpreter should begin with the obvious: The miracle occasions proclamation, which is central to the community's vocation as a witness to the risen Messiah (1:8). The dramatic speech is neither ecstatic nor unintelligible; it is language that communicates to others "the wonders of God" (2:11). Moreover, this miracle of speech is not just good rhetoric but the result of the Spirit's "filling" that issues in elevated insight. The community is filled with the Spirit to express the wonders of God in intelligible and intelligent tongues.

**6.** "Are not all these who are speaking Galileans?" (2:7 NRSV). The Jewish auditors, amazed and perplexed, recognize the community's familiar Galilean dialect. The language of the Spirit is not communicated with perfect or heavenly diction, free from the marks of human identity; it is the language of particular human groups, spoken in their idiom. God works in collaboration with real people—people who are filled with the Spirit to work on God's behalf in their own world.

**7.** Preaching during the season of Pentecost should take its principal cues from Luke's story of the first Pentecost. Yet John's narrative of the Spirit's arrival provides another angle of vision into the meaning of Pentecost (see John 20:19-23). While the plotline of the church's liturgical life follows Luke's theological instincts and separates Easter from Pentecost, John's Gospel combines them. It is still Easter and John's Jesus has not yet departed "for his Father's house" when he presents himself to the community of his disciples. They receive from their Lord his benediction of peace and the gift of the Holy Spirit. There is theological value in John's perspective because it resists any attempt to detach the resurrection of Jesus from the mission of his disciples whose motive derives from Easter. For this reason John's story of the Spirit's arrival is read and preached during both Easter and Pentecost seasons. At the same time John leaves vague what the Spirit's role is in the mission of the church. Acts sharpens the reader's understanding by clearly connecting the outpouring of the Spirit with the dynamic power that enables the church to give effective witness to the living Jesus.

**8.** The story of the Spirit's arrival in John's Gospel recalls Jesus' farewell discourse (John 14–17), where the Holy Spirit is introduced as teacher and comforter of the disciples in the Lord's absence. While these ideas are introduced in terms of cultivating an "abiding" relationship between disciples and Lord (rather than empowerment for world mission), the reader of Acts is better prepared to understand the ultimate importance of the Spirit's arrival at Pentecost having first read John's Gospel.

# ACTS 2:14–15:12

## PART ONE: A NARRATIVE OF CONVERSION

### OVERVIEW

Peter's initial response to his mocking audience is to quote a prophecy from Joel 2:28-32 (3:1-5 LXX; Acts 2:17-21) to prove that the outpouring of the Spirit is the inaugural event of Israel's "last days" during which "everyone who calls upon the name of the Lord will be saved." This theological insight also frames what comes next in the narrative.[101] Parallel with Acts' geographical structure (1:8), Luke leads his readers to the Jerusalem Council by telling stories of different people in ever-changing geographical settings who all call upon the Lord's name and are saved.[102] These converts form a variegated community that witnesses to God's faithfulness in keeping promises made. When read reflexively with Joel's prophecy, Acts' constant repetition of the prophecy's catchphrases (e.g., "signs and wonders") and concepts (e.g., Spirit baptism/filling, inspired prophets, conversion) expands the full significance of the Spirit's outpouring at Pentecost.

Luke's narrative commentary on Joel's prophecy is, then, a narrative of conversion, marked out and enclosed by two parallel verses, Acts 2:22 and 15:12. According to 2:22, Peter addresses the Jews in Jerusalem about "Jesus of Nazareth, a man attested to you by God with [1] deeds of power, wonders, and signs [2] that God did [3] through him [4] among you [Israel]." By the time the narrator informs readers in 15:12 that another assembly of devout Jews gathered once again in Jerusalem and "listened to Barnabas and Paul as they told of all the [1] signs and wonders [2] that God had done [3] through them [4] among the Gentiles," the shift from Peter to Paul and from Jews to Gentiles corresponds to a fuller understanding of Joel's prophecy provided by the intervening chapters. Beginning in Jerusalem (Acts 2–7), then beyond the holy city into the surrounding provinces of Samaria and Judea (Acts 8) before leaving Palestine for "the ends of the earth" (Acts 13–14), Spirit-filled prophets-like-Jesus proclaim the word of God to Jews first and then to Gentiles. In each geographical region of the gospel's progress, hidden contours of the prophecy's messianic meaning are exposed to endorse Luke's belief that the promised blessings of God (= forgiveness, eternal life, gift of the Spirit) extend to everyone who does truly repent and believe the gospel about the living Jesus.

The church's intramural conflict that surfaces in Antioch (15:1-2) and Jerusalem (15:4-5; cf. 11:1-18) reflects the contested nature of God's universal salvation within the household of Israel. The pivotal testimonies presented before the assembly of elders in Jerusalem (15:6-11, 12) consolidates the normative meaning of salvation. When opponents to Paul's mission in Antioch insist that uncircumcised Gentiles "cannot be saved" (15:1), no new argument comes forth to refute their claim: the whole narrative supplies implicit evidence that requires no additional comment. Peter summarizes the past and concludes that "we believe that

101. See S. Walton, "Where Does the Beginning of Acts End?" in *The Unity of Luke-Acts,* ed. J. Verheyden, BETL 142 (Leuven: Leuven University Press, 1999) 447-67. After reviewing six different proposals for delimiting the preface to Acts from Acts "proper," Walton uses a complex linguistic analysis of Lukan vocabulary to argue that Acts 1–2 marks the beginning of Acts, primarily due to the perceived role these two chapters perform within Luke-Acts (as "bridge" between Luke's stories of Jesus and church) and within Acts (as "overture," where the principal themes of Acts are introduced). He admits, however, that the boundary between the beginning of Acts and the rest of the book is kept "fuzzy" by Luke as an implicit exhortation for his readers to keep the whole narrative pointing ever forward to the "end of the earth."

102. In Barrett's words, "there can be little doubt—that it was Luke's intention in these opening chapters (Acts 1–14) to describe a decisive step by which the faith of a group of Jews, and the Gospel that had been committed to them, were communicated to men who were of a different religious and racial background." See C. K. Barrett, *A Critical and Exegetical Commentary on the Acts of the Apostles,* 2 vols, ICC (Edinburgh: T. & T. Clark, 1994, 1998) 1:49.

we shall be saved through the grace of the Lord Jesus, just as [Gentiles] will" (15:11). The adumbrations of Peter's clear statement of divine grace have already appeared throughout the intervening narrative.

If Acts is written to defend the faithfulness of God toward historic Israel, the first half of the narrative offers Luke's preliminary response. The movement of the gospel from Jerusalem to the nations is scripted by Scripture's prophecy and therefore accords with God's purposes. Prophecy's fulfillment symbolizes divine faithfulness. Moreover, repentant Israel's mission to the nations,

inaugurated by Peter and spearheaded by Paul, does not require the "Judaizing" of uncircumcised Gentile converts. Whatever protests had been voiced in this regard, whether in Antioch or in Jerusalem, have now been silenced. The problem that remains is whether the church will become so thoroughly "Gentilized" that the church's Jewish legacy will be truncated or abandoned, which would be a tacit denial of God's faithfulness to historic Israel. This version of the problem of theodicy shapes the plotline of the second half of Acts (see 15:13-29).

# ACTS 2:14-41, PETER'S PENTECOST PROCLAMATION

## NIV

[14]Then Peter stood up with the Eleven, raised his voice and addressed the crowd: "Fellow Jews and all of you who live in Jerusalem, let me explain this to you; listen carefully to what I say. [15]These men are not drunk, as you suppose. It's only nine in the morning! [16]No, this is what was spoken by the prophet Joel:

[17] " 'In the last days, God says,
  I will pour out my Spirit on all people.
Your sons and daughters will prophesy,
  your young men will see visions,
  your old men will dream dreams.
[18] Even on my servants, both men and women,
  I will pour out my Spirit in those days,
  and they will prophesy.
[19] I will show wonders in the heaven above
  and signs on the earth below,
  blood and fire and billows of smoke.
[20] The sun will be turned to darkness
  and the moon to blood
  before the coming of the great and glorious
    day of the Lord.
[21] And everyone who calls
  on the name of the Lord will be saved.' [a]

[22]"Men of Israel, listen to this: Jesus of Nazareth was a man accredited by God to you by miracles, wonders and signs, which God did

[a] 21 Joel 2:28-32

## NRSV

14But Peter, standing with the eleven, raised his voice and addressed them, "Men of Judea and all who live in Jerusalem, let this be known to you, and listen to what I say. [15]Indeed, these are not drunk, as you suppose, for it is only nine o'clock in the morning. [16]No, this is what was spoken through the prophet Joel:

[17] 'In the last days it will be, God declares,
  that I will pour out my Spirit upon all flesh,
    and your sons and your daughters shall
      prophesy,
  and your young men shall see visions,
    and your old men shall dream dreams.
[18] Even upon my slaves, both men and women,
    in those days I will pour out my Spirit;
      and they shall prophesy.
[19] And I will show portents in the heaven above
    and signs on the earth below,
      blood, and fire, and smoky mist.
[20] The sun shall be turned to darkness
    and the moon to blood,
      before the coming of the Lord's great
        and glorious day.
[21] Then everyone who calls on the name of the
    Lord shall be saved.'

22"You that are Israelites, [a] listen to what I have to say: Jesus of Nazareth, [b] a man attested to you

[a] Gk Men, Israelites    [b] Gk the Nazorean

NIV

among you through him, as you yourselves know. [23]This man was handed over to you by God's set purpose and foreknowledge; and you, with the help of wicked men,[a] put him to death by nailing him to the cross. [24]But God raised him from the dead, freeing him from the agony of death, because it was impossible for death to keep its hold on him. [25]David said about him:

" 'I saw the Lord always before me.
   Because he is at my right hand,
   I will not be shaken.
[26] Therefore my heart is glad and my tongue
       rejoices;
   my body also will live in hope,
[27] because you will not abandon me to the
       grave,
   nor will you let your Holy One see decay.
[28] You have made known to me the paths of life;
   you will fill me with joy in your presence.'[b]

[29]"Brothers, I can tell you confidently that the patriarch David died and was buried, and his tomb is here to this day. [30]But he was a prophet and knew that God had promised him on oath that he would place one of his descendants on his throne. [31]Seeing what was ahead, he spoke of the resurrection of the Christ,[c] that he was not abandoned to the grave, nor did his body see decay. [32]God has raised this Jesus to life, and we are all witnesses of the fact. [33]Exalted to the right hand of God, he has received from the Father the promised Holy Spirit and has poured out what you now see and hear. [34]For David did not ascend to heaven, and yet he said,

" 'The Lord said to my Lord:
   "Sit at my right hand
[35] until I make your enemies
   a footstool for your feet." '[d]

[36]"Therefore let all Israel be assured of this: God has made this Jesus, whom you crucified, both Lord and Christ."

[37]When the people heard this, they were cut to the heart and said to Peter and the other apostles, "Brothers, what shall we do?"

[a] 23 Or of those not having the law (that is, Gentiles)  [b] 28 Psalm 16:8-11   [c] 31 Or Messiah. "The Christ" (Greek) and "the Messiah" (Hebrew) both mean "the Anointed One"; also in verse 36. [d] 35 Psalm 110:1

NRSV

by God with deeds of power, wonders, and signs that God did through him among you, as you yourselves know— [23]this man, handed over to you according to the definite plan and foreknowledge of God, you crucified and killed by the hands of those outside the law. [24]But God raised him up, having freed him from death,[a] because it was impossible for him to be held in its power. [25]For David says concerning him,

'I saw the Lord always before me,
   for he is at my right hand so that I will not
       be shaken;
[26] therefore my heart was glad, and my tongue
       rejoiced;
   moreover my flesh will live in hope.
[27] For you will not abandon my soul to Hades,
   or let your Holy One experience
       corruption.
[28] You have made known to me the ways of life;
   you will make me full of gladness with
       your presence.'

[29]"Fellow Israelites,[b] I may say to you confidently of our ancestor David that he both died and was buried, and his tomb is with us to this day. [30]Since he was a prophet, he knew that God had sworn with an oath to him that he would put one of his descendants on his throne. [31]Foreseeing this, David[c] spoke of the resurrection of the Messiah,[d] saying,

'He was not abandoned to Hades,
   nor did his flesh experience corruption.'
[32]This Jesus God raised up, and of that all of us are witnesses. [33]Being therefore exalted at[e] the right hand of God, and having received from the Father the promise of the Holy Spirit, he has poured out this that you both see and hear. [34]For David did not ascend into the heavens, but he himself says,

'The Lord said to my Lord,
   "Sit at my right hand,
[35]    until I make your enemies your footstool." '
[36]Therefore let the entire house of Israel know with certainty that God has made him both Lord and Messiah,[f] this Jesus whom you crucified."

[37]Now when they heard this, they were cut to the heart and said to Peter and to the other apostles,

[a] Gk the pains of death    [b] Gk Men, brothers    [c] Gk he
[d] Or the Christ    [e] Or by    [f] Or Christ

NIV

³⁸Peter replied, "Repent and be baptized, every one of you, in the name of Jesus Christ for the forgiveness of your sins. And you will receive the gift of the Holy Spirit. ³⁹The promise is for you and your children and for all who are far off—for all whom the Lord our God will call."

⁴⁰With many other words he warned them; and he pleaded with them, "Save yourselves from this corrupt generation." ⁴¹Those who accepted his message were baptized, and about three thousand were added to their number that day.

NRSV

"Brothers,ᵃ what should we do?" ³⁸Peter said to them, "Repent, and be baptized every one of you in the name of Jesus Christ so that your sins may be forgiven; and you will receive the gift of the Holy Spirit. ³⁹For the promise is for you, for your children, and for all who are far away, everyone whom the Lord our God calls to him." ⁴⁰And he testified with many other arguments and exhorted them, saying, "Save yourselves from this corrupt generation." ⁴¹So those who welcomed his message were baptized, and that day about three thousand persons were added.

ᵃ Gk *Men, brothers*

# COMMENTARY

Almost a third of the book of Acts consists of speeches. Although different in many ways, most of these speeches seek to convince their auditors of the gospel's central claims: God's resurrection of Jesus confirms him as Messiah and through him God has acted faithfully to the biblical promise to save the world from sin and death. The speeches are "missionary speeches," the principal expression of the church's obedience to Jesus' commission (1:8); and they are Luke's compositions, although most reflect his use of reliable sources. When reading a speech from Peter or Paul, then, the reader should not infer that the narrator has transcribed it verbatim. Rather, every speech functions as a element of Luke's narrative world and serves to make sense of his narrative aim.[103]

103. The extent to which these speeches are the product of Luke's creative imagination remains contested. In this case, the historical problem is whether Luke's composition of Peter's sermon is in line with what the real Peter actually taught. Dibelius considers the speeches of Acts as Lukan literary creations, there only to advance Luke's theological agenda without any interest in an historical referent. See M. Dibelius, "The Speeches in Acts and Ancient Historiography," in *Studies in the Acts of the Apostles* (London: SCM, 1956) 138-85. While there are no historical conventions to follow when composing stories of real people or events that include speeches, Witherington notes that if Luke is accepted as a "careful historian in the mold of Thucydides and Polybius," then we may expect his speeches to be accurate summaries of the major points that were spoken. See B. Witherington, *The Acts of the Apostles: A Socio-Rhetorical Commentary* (Grand Rapids: Eerdmans, 1998) 117. On balance, the speeches of Acts report substantial historical information, gleaned from reliable sources, that are then reshaped and positioned into Acts to serve Luke's rhetorical and theological purposes. See L. T. Johnson, *The Acts of the Apostles,* SP 5 (Collegeville, Minn.: Liturgical, 1992) 5-9.

Peter's sermon plays a paradigmatic role within Acts. From the opening of the book, the reader is made alert to the narrative's redemptive calculus: A Spirit-empowered witness to the risen Jesus is the means by which God's purposes are realized. The departure of Jesus has made witness to him necessary, while the Pentecostal baptism with the Spirit has made it possible. In this setting the attentive reader recognizes that Peter's speech is exemplary of the community's witness and is made possible by the filling of the Spirit. Only the inspired prophet can recover the plan of God's salvation from Scripture, according to which Jesus dies (2:22, 25-28) and is raised again (2:23, 34-35) to confirm him as Messiah and Lord (2:36). He is the "Lord" on whose name everyone must call in order to be saved (2:21). The Spirit of God empowers persuasive speeches for specific audiences and not ecstatic events that convince no one in particular. Persuasive preaching is not a matter of being "filled [μεστόω *mestoō*] with new wine" (2:13) but being "filled [πίμπλημι *pimplēmi*] with the Holy Spirit" (2:4).

Like other speeches in Acts that address a Jewish audience, Peter's Pentecost sermon is Jewish midrash (or commentary) on Scripture. He begins by echoing the preceding prophecy and then goes on to provide a persuasive commentary on its messianic meaning (2:22-40) in order to address the present crisis—namely, ignorance of the importance of the present moment in salvation's history (i.e., Messiah has come and gone; God's Spirit has come to replace him).[104] The miracle of *xenolalia* (speaking foreign languages; see 2:12) has confused these devout Jews, producing a mocking retort (2:13-15) rather than a faithful response (cf. 2:41).

The speeches of Acts are also composed with attention to well-regarded Greco-Roman rules of persuasive speaking, rules that regulate what is said in terms of the particular audience addressed, the specific crisis that occasions the speech, and the subject matter.[105] Accordingly, Peter's speech reaches its climax in 2:36 in a stylized manner that seems logical, even necessary because of the evidence he marshals: scriptural testimony from David plus the testimony of eyewitnesses to the Lord's signs and wonders (2:22), his resurrection (2:31-32), and his exhaltation (2:36).[106] Peter is not careless with evidence but carefully crafts it into a persuasive speech that deals with the immediate crisis of Israel's skepticism. For this reason, he is able to lead some into faith. One implication of the rhetorical shaping of this speech is that faith (2:41) is the *logical* response to Peter's persuasive speech. John Wesley called gospel preaching an "awakening experience." Good preaching compels people to deeper reflection and courageous action, and under the aegis of the Spirit can even transform scoffers into believers.

We should also note the importance of this narrative within the New Testament. O. Cullmann argues that the portrait of Peter in Acts introduces the NT reader to his spiritual authority and that his speeches introduce his theological conception.[107] For all the critical attention that concentrates on the relationship between the Paul of Acts and the Pauline letters, Cullmann's study reminds the interpreter that the rehabilitated Peter of Acts provides the NT's introduction to the implied "voice" of the Petrine letters as well. While Peter's authorship of the Petrine letters is disputed, these images of his spiritual authority in Acts cultivate a keen impression of the canonical authority of their implied author. As an introduction to a distinctively Petrine theological conception within the NT, Peter's identification of Jesus as Isaiah's suffering Servant (3:13, 26; 4:27, 30) introduces the reader to the most important christological vocabulary of 1 Peter (1 Pet 2:21-25). A reflexive reading may also bring together the apocalyptic eschatology of 2 Peter 3 with Peter's programmatic teaching about the future of God's salvation in Acts 3:21-26, the one expanding the central ideas of the other (see the Commentary on 3:1–4:4).[108]

**2:14-15.** Peter heads the apostolic Twelve and so continues the Messiah's magisterial office (see 1:15-20).[109] His address boldly circumscribes his audience: "Fellow Jews (or Judeans) and all those living in Jerusalem; let this be known to you (who) listen to what I say." Israel's ignorance about their Messiah, which has provoked derision rather than confession, will be reversed only if they listen well to the prophet's message. Careful "listening" is an important literary theme in Acts and sometimes functions as a narrative marker, preparing the reader for an important moment in the story's plotline (see 15:13; 28:28). In this case, Luke employs an unusual Septuagintal term for "listen" (ἐνωτίζομαι *enōtizomai*) that literally means "let me place it [= the word of God] into your ears" (cf. Exod 15:26). In his Gospel, Luke uses a similar expression at a critical point when Jesus tells his audience in Nazareth that "today" the prophet's promise of good news for the poor would be fulfilled among those "with ears" (ἐν ὠσίν *en ōsin*, 4:21).

---

104. See Dodd's, which now must be put forward only in a highly qualified manner, is that Peter's sermon not only reflects the theological commitments of the Jerusalem mission at its very beginning but is quintessentially Christian, providing a broad outline for NT theology and Christian proclamation (or *kerygma*). See C. H. Dodd, *The Apostolic Preaching and Its Developments* (New York: Harper and Bros., 1937) 21.

105. B. Mack's comment about the inadequacy of this sermon's evidence to convince anyone but the faithful readers of Acts (and by implication *not* the sophisticated nonbeliever) points out, if unwittingly, the rhetorical importance of audience. See B. Mack, *Rhetoric and the New Testament,* GBS (Minneapolis: Fortress, 1990) 91-92. That is, a good speech "works" because it addresses particular auditors at a particular moment in time about a relevant issue at hand; and it can do so because of appeals to accepted authority. Peter's sermon thus would not convince Mack's implied audience of secular intellectuals—who are not, in fact, the audience for this speech.

106. Witherington's rhetorical analysis of Acts is helpful at this point. He regards the main speech (2:14-36) as a kind of "forensic rhetoric" by which Peter refutes the charge that the apostles are drunks. A second speech of "deliberative rhetoric" follows (2:37-40), by which Peter responds to his audience's remorse (2:37) by encouraging them to take a particular course of action leading to their salvation (2:38-40). See Witherington, *The Acts of the Apostles,* 138.

107. O. Cullmann, *Peter: Disciple-Apostles-Martyr* (London: SCM, 1953) 33-69.

108. See R. W. Wall, "The Canonical Function of 2 Peter," *BibInt* 9 (2001) 64-81.

109. G. Lüdemann, *Early Christianity According to the Traditions in Acts* (Minneapolis: Fortress, 1989) 49, admits that Peter played a leading role from the beginning and would have probably been the one to give such a speech.

The immediate point Peter must make defends the community's Pentecostal experience against the charge that it must result from a round of drunken debauchery. Evidently in popular culture "nine o'clock in the morning" was an hour inhabited only by those who intend no good.[110] Using a retort (2:15) dripping with comic irony, Peter corrects their misunderstanding before moving on to address his audience as their teacher by interpreting the Scriptures in order to interpret the Pentecostal experience.

**2:16-21.** Peter explains that what the household of Israel has experienced has been prophesied by Joel as the "outpouring of the Spirit" that inaugurates "the last days" of salvation's history when "everyone who calls upon the name of the Lord will be saved." Peter quotes from the Greek version (LXX) of Joel 3:1-5. The Greek rendering allows Luke's Peter to use this text in support of his kerygmatic claim that Jesus is "Lord." When the prophet claims that "everyone who calls upon the name of the Lord [κύριος *kyrios*] shall be saved" (2:21), *kyrios* translates here the Hebrew word for God[111] and therefore allows Peter to argue that this "Lord" is the risen Jesus (so 2:36). Israel must call upon Jesus for the salvation they anticipate will come with God's messianic ruler.[112]

**2:16-17a.** Peter "rewrites" Joel's prophecy in still other ways to adapt it more precisely to this Pentecostal setting. Two important changes are made in the opening line: He substitutes "in the last days" (ἐν ταῖς ἐσχάταις ἡμέραις *en tais eschatais hēmepais*) for "after these things" (μετὰ ταῦτα *meta tauta*),[113] and he then adds the phrase "God declares" (λέγει ὁ θεός *legei ho theos*) to clarify the earlier prophetic formula (2:16). Especially

when read within its wider NT context, the catch-phrase "in the last days" (cf. 1 Tim 3:1; Heb 1:2; Jas 5:3; 2 Pet 3:3) locates the outpouring of the Spirit against a new eschatological horizon. Simply put, Pentecost initiates Israel into a new epoch—"the last days"—of God's salvation history, when things said and done by Jesus' successors take on added urgency, not of an imminent apocalypse in the case of Acts but rather of a mission to restore God's kingdom to Israel (see 1:6-8).

The addition of "God declares" to the biblical citation underscores the premise of all prophetic texts in Acts: Events that fulfill biblical prophecy are in God's script of salvation.[114] The intensification of this very emphasis stands behind Luke's addition of the phrase "and they shall prophesy" (προφητεύσουσι *prophēteusousi*) to 2:18. The community's forward movement toward God's eschatological horizon of a restored Israel is fundamentally a *prophetic* movement, a movement of empowered and illumined proclamation (2:18); and Pentecost is fundamentally the pouring out of the Spirit of prophecy as the distinguishing mark of that movement.

**2:17b-18.** Much has been made in recent years of the inclusiveness of this prophetic community and rightly so: "I will pour out my Spirit on *all* flesh" (2:17). The entire membership receives God's Spirit and will speak like prophets (2:18). Peter adds "my" (μου *mou*) here to the LXX, which is especially suggestive of the grand reversal wrought at Pentecost, when even household slaves are transformed into "my servants" (δοῦλος μου *doulos mou*) and given important prophetic tasks to perform. This revolutionary feature of the eschatological community Joel depicts anticipates subsequent episodes in Acts that will draw out its fuller meaning.

**2:19-20.** The special effects that accompany the outpouring of Spirit are also noteworthy. In their original prophetic setting, these dramatic occurrences signal the imminent arrival of the "Day of the Lord" in judgment of the nations that treated Israel shamefully. Not so in Acts. In this new setting, the "signs and wonders" (σημεῖα καὶ τέρατα *sēmeia kai terata*) mark the presence and progress of the Spirit who prepares the way for

---

110. See Conzelmann, *Acts,* 19, followed by many others. However, the point may be simply that to be drunk at such an early hour is a sign of shiftless debauchery.

111. *Kyrios* is the referent used most frequently in Acts for Jesus; it is also the only title used for both Jesus and God. I suspect this indicates that Luke regarded Jesus and God as co-collaborators in the salvation of reconstituted Israel. In that the Spirit is the "Father's promise" and is sent forth according to God's timing (1:4-7), Jesus' messianic mission, now followed by the community of his successors, is redemptive work that is subordinate to God's provident care for Israel.

112. E. Haenchen, *The Acts of the Apostles* (Philadelphia: Westminster, 1971) 179n. 5.

113. The transmission of the text of Acts is corrupted at this point. *B* (Vaticanus), one of the earliest witnesses to Acts, reads μετα ταυτα (*meta tauta,* "after this") and so returns the text back to the sense of its LXX original. Most critics, especially those who conclude that Peter's Pentecost speech is largely Luke's composition, prefer the majority reading "in the last days," since its eschatological horizon better frames Luke's theological agenda in Acts.

114. For this interpretation see Johnson, *The Acts of the Apostles,* 49, 54.

the church's missionary work (see 2:43; 4:16, 22, 30; 5:12; 6:8; 8:6, 13; 14:3; 15:12).[115] In this context, then, "the coming of the Lord's great and glorious day" no longer conjures up images of God's imminent retribution but instead that of Pentecost, with its promise of empowered witness and God's salvation.[116]

**2:21.** Typically, the most important phrase of a quoted text is the last one read, which lingers in the auditor's ear; "everyone who calls upon the name of the Lord shall be saved" (2:21) is such a phrase. Its full meaning is the interpretive project of the first half of Acts (see the Overview above). By the time the reader arrives at the depiction of the Jerusalem Council in Acts 15 the meaning of Joel's prophecy of Israel's salvation will be understood differently than it had been by the prophecy's original Judean audience or even those Jewish pilgrims who heard Peter's recitation on Pentecost. Then, on the other side of Paul's mission to the Gentiles, the meaning of Joel's "everyone" will have been embellished to include every repentant Jew and Gentile (see the Overview above). The adumbration of "salvation" through the first half of Acts will clearly indicate that at the epicenter of Luke's theological conception of Israel's restoration is a God who forgives every person who names Jesus as their Lord and confesses him as God's Messiah (see 2:38; cf. 4:12; 7:25; 13:23, 26, 47; 15:11).[117]

Frankly, Acts is much clearer in addressing the questions, "What must one do to get saved?" and "Who does the saving?" than the corollary "What happens when one gets saved?" The near context of the prophecy emphasizes forgiveness from sins for those who repent and believe, complemented by the repentant believer's initiation into life with God's Spirit (see 2:38-39). Insofar as the community of goods exhibits a distinctive social life, we are also led to believe that salvation results in a new way of living one with another (see 2:42-47). As we will find in the story that follows, however, divine forgiveness and human healing form an integral whole in Acts: to be saved from sins means to be healed from sickness (see 3:1-8; 4:9-12; 14:8-10). While this connection can be and has been pressed in dangerous directions, the theological note sounded by the various healing and prison-escape episodes in Acts makes clear the close relationship in Luke's mind between the Lord's spiritual and physical rescue from internal and external threat. Even as his conception of God's salvation is international in scope it is also holistic in consequence.

**2:22-36.** Peter's commentary on the quoted Scripture (midrash) is in two parts, linked together by his stunned audience's pertinent question, "What should we do?" (2:37). The first part (2:22-36) appeals to his Jewish auditors (2:22*a*) to listen and consider his witness to "Jesus of Nazareth" (2:23-24)[118] in the light of the substantial evidence put forward from his eyewitness reflection (2:22*b*) and from Scripture (2:25-35) in support of the gospel's claim that "God has made this Jesus whom you crucified both Lord and Messiah" (2:36).[119] It is imperative that we follow Peter's speech to its christological climax as a midrash on Joel's prophecy that seeks to clarify the relevance of the Spirit's outpouring at Pentecost for this Jewish audience.

115. Johnson, ibid., 50, notes that "signs and wonders" is associated with the prophetic role that Moses performed during the exodus. Since Luke routinely portrays Jesus as the "prophet-like-Moses" in both his Gospel and in Acts (3:22; 7:36-37), Johnson is inclined to find the purpose of this catchphrase in the Pentecost speech rather than in its association with the "signs and wonders" Jesus performs according to 2:22. I take it that the succession theme of Acts, and the role Pentecost plays in its development, would allow the reader to make the interpretive move from the "signs and wonders" of prophetic Jesus to his Spirit-filled successors.

116. Notably, Luke edits out Joel's prophecy of God's judgment of the nations in order to underscore Pentecost as a redemptive event. At the same time, Luke's Peter turns his Jewish audience back to Joel's judgment theme in concluding his speech in 2:40: "Save yourselves from this corrupt generation." Clearly, the reference to "save yourselves" picks up Joel's salvation idiom and renders it more closely to his original meaning, which was an exhortation for faithful Israel to turn to God during a season of international calamity when God would destroy the nations, including unfaithful Israel—"the crooked generation" in Peter's words (cf. Deut 32:5)—while protecting and restoring the fortunes of the faithful nation.

117. Although he undervalues the prophetic aspect of the community's mission, Marshall is especially clear on this point: The witness of the prophetic community to the Messiah is for the world's salvation. See I. H. Marshall, *The Acts of the Apostles*, NTG (Sheffield: JSOT, 1992) 47-63. See also Witherington's apt summary of this narrative theme, *The Acts of the Apostles*, 143-44.

118. According to Conzelmann, the community's preaching (*kerygma*) or formal confessions about Jesus include his name, his pre-crucifixion works, his death, and his resurrection, all of which are elements present in this speech. See H. Conzelmann, *The Acts of the Apostles,* trans. J. Limburg et al., ed. E. J. Epp and C. R. Matthews, Hermeneia (Philadelphia: Fortress, 1987) 20. Behind this speech, then, the careful reader already discovers the later (Pauline?) notion of saving faith, which is to accept the beliefs of Christian proclamation as true.

119. The well-known charge of anti-Semitism posited against 2:36—that Jews killed Jesus—is substantially qualified in near context by 2:23, "you crucified—by the hands of those outside the law." This earlier detail recalls and glosses the gospel story of Jesus' crucifixion, itself a Roman and not Jewish form of political execution. The Jewish decision to execute Jesus was possible only through the agency of pagan Roman authority.

**2:22-24.** This observation seems evident from the opening line, where testimony to the "signs and wonders" of Jesus picks up Luke's rewriting of Joel's prophecy about the "signs and wonders" of the Spirit (2:19). If the interpreter considers this intertext rhetorically, Peter is simply asking his auditors to remember and apply what some in his audience first heard and saw performed by Jesus the Nazarene—what "you know" to be his divine authorization (2:22*b*)—to this most recent episode of Pentecostal "signs and wonders," which must be assumed as divinely accredited as well. But the implied theological claim is much more telling than its rhetorical intent: what Jesus began did not end with his crucifixion but continues in his absence under the aegis of God's Spirit in the life and mission of this community. This implied claim is what is good news! Joel's prophecy of Pentecost is really a prophecy about a season of salvation that has already begun with Messiah (see 1:1) and continues on as the prospect of this community's transformed life (see 2:42-47) and empowered mission (see 1:8).

The appeal to God's "definite plan and foreknowledge" (2:23) does not envisage a predestinarian notion of divine providence but Luke's logical deduction from his idea of Scripture. That is, if the Jesus event and the Spirit's outpouring both follow the biblical script of God's salvation, then God must have known about both in advance of their occurrence. In this regard, then, the biblical texts from the LXX psalter that Peter quotes (Pss 18:4-6 [17:4-6 LXX] = 2:24; 16:8-11 [15:8-11 LXX] = 2:25-28; 132:11 [132:11 LXX] = 2:30; 110:1 [109:1 LXX] = 2:34-35) supplies additional biblical testimony in support of the community's claim that the Jesus event in all its tragic and glorious aspects is intended by God as messianic.

**2:25-33.** Peter's clever rereading of these psalms assumes first that King David is a type of the coming Messiah and, therefore, a principal participant in Israel's future plans (2:25*a*).[120] Peter also claims that David is God's prophet (2:30; cf. 1:16, 20) with keen insight into the future of Israel

and the identity of the Messiah (cf. Acts 4:25; 13:33-36). He finally claims that David is Israel's "patriarch" (2:29 NIV), obligating the household of Israel to give proper respect to David's voice.[121] This last point is made with considerable irony, since every ancestor or patriarch, although important to Israel's history, remained dead, as their famous tombs memorialized.[122] The Messiah, on the other hand, gets resurrected and stays alive (2:31-33)!

**2:34-36.** The readers of Acts will recognize the powerful logic of Peter's point that while Israel's great king-prophet-patriarch David "did not ascend into the heavens" (2:34), Jesus did (see 1:10-11). As midrash, however, Peter's chain of citations from the biblical psalter funds his christological commentary on God's intended meaning of Joel's prophecy that salvation comes to those who call on the "Lord" (see 2:21). For this reason his appeal to the "my Lord" of Ps 110:1 (109:1 LXX), well used elsewhere in the NT to support christological claims (cf., Mark 12:36; 14:62; 16:19; Luke 20:42; Rom 8:34; 1 Cor 15:25; Eph 1:20; Col 3:1; Heb 1:3, 13; 8:1; 10:12),[123] supports his climactic point that God has made the risen Jesus to rule over Israel as its "Lord" (2:36). David's "Lord" is this risen Lord Jesus of Joel's prophecy on whose name everyone must call for their salvation from sin and death (see 2:21).

**2:37-40.** The crowd understands the implications of Peter's dramatic claim that the crucified Jesus of Nazareth is, in fact, the risen Christ of God. Luke tells us "they were cut to the heart." Perhaps the crowd's emotional response is simply recognition of their own guilt in the matter of Jesus' death.[124] In any case, Peter concludes his sermon by calling these enlightened auditors to conversion.

**2:37.** The crowd's question, "What shall we do?" is more than rhetorical; it makes a sincere request for instruction that will lead to forgiveness

---

120. See J. Jervell, *Die Apostelgeschichte,* KEK 3 (Göttingen: Vandenhoeck & Ruprecht, 1998) 147-48. We know by an earlier text (see 1:16, 20) that what David says is actually the voice of the Holy Spirit and that what is spoken by the Holy Spirit must be fulfilled. This feature of Peter's speech is deeply rooted in Luke's conception of Scripture and the prophetic role to recover God's intended or eschatological meaning from the biblical text.

121. Peter bestows on David the title of patriarch to ensure his audience's respect for David's prophecy of Jesus. See Haenchen, *The Acts of the Apostles,* 182; Jervell, *Die Apostelgeschichte,* 147.

122. For David's tomb, see Josephus *The Jewish War* 1:61. See also J. A. Fitzmyer, *The Acts of the Apostles,* AB 31 (Garden City, N.Y.: Doubleday, 1998) 257.

123. For the NT use of Ps 110:1 LXX as Christian apoligia, see M. Black, "The Christological Use of the Old Testament in the New Testament," *NTS* 18 (1971-72) 6-11. See also C. K. Barrett, *A Critical and Exegetical Commentary on the Acts of the Apostles,* 2 vols, ICC (Edinburgh: T. & T. Clark, 1994, 1998) 150-51.

124. So Haenchen, *The Acts of the Apostles,* 183.

and restoration. As such, the theological subtext of their question of Peter is this: Will God forgive and restore them even if they do repent of their participation in Messiah's death? The reader rightly raises this question in light of Judas's demise since God apparently refused him a second chance (see 1:16-20; cf. 5:1-10). Why did Peter continue beyond v. 36 and its implicit indictment of Israel's guilt in rejecting the Messiah? In canonical context, the reader imagines that this rehabilitated Peter knows from personal experience that God gives betrayers second chances (see 1:15-20; cf. John 21:15-17). The outpouring of God's Spirit at Pentecost is God's second chance to Israel. If the Jesus and Spirit events are scripted by God as the climactic pieces of the plan to restore Israel, Peter cannot now turn his back on these Jews who want to know what to do in response.

**2:38a.** Peter stipulates the basis by which his audience may be saved (2:38*a*) and anticipates the results of their salvation (2:38*b*-40). In doing so he demands nothing different from what John the Baptist did prior to Easter and Pentecost (cf. Luke 3:10 with Acts 2:37). Of course, the subtext of Peter's response is that Easter and Pentecost have since occurred; they provide spiritual resources for Israel's conversion that were not present to John the Baptist. While Peter's speech at this point echoes John's redemptive protocol—"repent and be baptized"—the theological implications of Peter's invitation are substantially different.

In shaping Peter's evangelical appeal, Luke emphasizes a repentant response to the gospel message (cf. "repent" [μετανοέω *metanoeō*] in Luke 10:13; 11:32; 13:3, 5; 15:7, 10; 16:30; 17:3, 4; Acts 3:19; 8:22; 17:30; 26:20; and "repentance" [μετάνοια *metanoia*] in Luke 3:3, 8; 5:32; 15:7; 24:47; Acts 5:31; 11:18; 13:24; 19:4; 20:21; 26:20). Jesus earlier predicted that his successors would preach "repentance in his name" (cf. Luke 24:47). Literally, "to repent" denotes a radical change of mind. Spiritual reform is possible only with an intellectual reorientation—how one thinks and what angle of vision one takes when looking at the "real world." After all, the wrong-headed response of Israel to Jesus can only be explained by their ignorance of him—ignorance now dispelled by Peter's sermon and Israel's witness to the outpouring of God's Spirit. Significantly, "repent" is plural in form, which indicates that Peter's demand

is addressed to the entire household of Israel; the second demand, "be baptized," is stipulated only of those individual Jews who convert. The baptism of converts makes personal what should be true of all Israel. The interpreter should observe the tension in Acts between national and individual repentance. The promise of Israel's restoration obtains only to those baptized *individuals* within Israel who repent and turn to Christ in faith. These converts are those who constitute a repentant (= restored) Israel in whose history the promised blessings of God will be realized.

The significance of a rite of baptism probably stems from John the Baptist's mission, and its symbolism is brought forward with new and greater meaning by command of Jesus (cf. Matt 28:19; Mark 16:16). Christian baptism remains a rite of initiation into a new life under a different Lord with membership in a community of common faith in him and a new future with God. As the central symbol of this new orientation, the convert is baptized "in the name of Jesus Christ" (see 2:21). No believer goes unbaptized in Acts simply because no believer exists outside of the Messiah's community into which every new believer is initiated. Yet, in this narrative setting Peter issues his demand for baptism *because* of Pentecost and the community's experience of the baptism with the Spirit. Baptism, then, is initiation into a community that lives within the powerful realm of God's Spirit. Sharply put, Christian baptism assumes Spirit baptism in Acts and the readiness of the converted for the work of witness.[125]

**2:38b-40.** Repentance and Christian baptism result in the "forgiveness of your sins" (ἄφεσις τῶν ἁμαρτιῶν ὑμῶν *aphesis tōn hamartiōn hymōn*) and "the gift of the Holy Spirit" (ἡ δωρεά τοῦ ἁγίου πνεύματος *hē dōrea tou hagiou pneumatos* 2:38*b*). The word for "forgiveness" (*aphesis*) means "pardon," and in Acts it typically is combined with "sins." Forgiveness of financial debts is one connotation of this phrase and perhaps reflects the sociology of salvation, so that believers are members of a community of goods where those pardoned of sin pardon the debts of others (see 2:42-47; cf. Luke 11:1-13).[126] The

125. J. D. G. Dunn, *The Acts of the Apostles* (Valley Forge, Pa.: Trinity, 1996) 32-33.

126. See S. Ringe, *Jesus, Liberation, and the Biblical Jubilee: Images for Ethics and Christology,* OBT 19 (Philadelphia: Fortress, 1985).

second phrase, "gift of the Holy Spirit," is exceptional. Peter does not have in mind the role the Spirit performs in a charismatic congregation (1 Corinthians 12–14), where according to Paul the Spirit supplies different spiritual gifts that enable each believer to edify the faith of the others. The Spirit of Acts is not an intrinsic member of the community as "Lord" (*kyrios;* cf. 2 Cor 3:17), nor often the agent of the community's transformed existence as God's new creation (cf. Gal 5:16-26). Again, the Spirit of Acts is more like the Spirit of OT prophecy who fills believers with an explosive power that enables them to perform the church's missionary vocation.

The principal difficulty in the history of the interpretation of this text is whether Christian baptism is a condition for or a consequence of the "forgiveness of your sins" and thus the reception of the "gift of the Holy Spirit." The problem turns on the causal use of the preposition εἰς (*eis*): "for [*eis*] the forgiveness of your sins." However, Barrett reminds us that Luke does not use this preposition consistently, nor does he place much value on it in any case.[127] Moreover, Acts evinces a variety of grammatical formulas when speaking of God's forgiveness and baptism together (see 8:16; 10:44; 19:5; cf. 8:38-39; 18:26). Peter's formulation of these different demands therefore is not technical and in no way establishes a theological norm.

More important, baptism "in the name of Jesus Christ" (ἐπὶ τῷ ὀνόματι Ἰησοῦ Χριστοῦ *epi tō onomati Iēsou Christou*) and "forgiveness of sins" are joined by Peter to embellish the meaning of Joel's prophecy, which concludes by linking "the name of Jesus Christ" with salvation.[128] The saving power of the "name" is hardly magical but is rather a metaphor for Joel's announcement of salvation, which has arrived from God in the form of forgiveness because of Jesus. For this reason, Christian baptism after Pentecost initiates the repentant believers into a new spiritual reality that John the Baptist could only predict (so Luke 3:16) but in which neither he nor his baptized followers could participate, even though their sins were forgiven (cf. Luke 3:3). In addition, the Baptist's exhortation to do "works in keeping with repentance" is glossed in this new setting as those missionary tasks that pertain to the community's vocation.

127. Barrett, *Acts,* 1:154.
128. See J. Roloff, *Die Apostelgeschichte* (Göttingen: Vandenhoeck & Ruprecht, 1981) 61.

The referent of Israel's "promise" (ἡ ἐπαγγελία *hē epangelia,* 2:39) is Israel's restoration (see 1:6). The phrase "for all who are far away" (πᾶς ὁ εἰς μακράν *pas ho eis makran*) in this setting is a faint echo of Isaiah's promise that "the wind [Spirit?] of the Lord" (57:19) will bring exiled Jews back to Israel to become members of the restored community. If intentional, the intertextual echo intensifies Peter's address to those of his audience from the diaspora, perhaps anticipating Paul's mission to the diaspora.[129] The interplay between Joel's promise of salvation to "everyone who calls upon the name of the Lord" and Peter's exhortation that God's promise belongs to "everyone whom the Lord our God calls to him" (ὅσους ἂν προσκαλέσηται κύριος ὁ Θεὸς ἡμῶν *hosous an proskalesētai kyrios ho theos hēmōn*) reminds the reader of the reciprocal nature of salvation: God calls everyone into the blessings of salvation (forgiveness, Spirit), which then are experienced by everyone who calls upon the Lord.

Peter's haunting words to "save yourselves from this crooked generation" (2:40) round off his midrash on Joel's prophecy. The repentant Jews who save themselves realize Joel's promise that those who call upon the Lord will be saved. The effect of its iteration is to sound a warning to all those Jews who refuse to repent: They will not participate in the blessings of a restored Israel. Rather, they belong to "this crooked generation" (ἡ γενεὰ τῆς σκολιᾶς ταύτης *hē genea tēs skolias tautēs*), a phrase that echoes a memorable lyric from Moses' farewell song (Deut 32:5), in which God's faithfulness to Israel is contrasted with the faithlessness of "this crooked generation" of unrepentant Jews (see Acts 7:35-43).

**2:41.** The purpose of Luke's numerical summary of Peter's first evangelistic preaching is to make a good impression on the reader rather than to provide readers with an accurate count of new converts.[130] Prior to Pentecost, the community's

129. It is highly unlikely that this phrase hints at the future Gentile mission. Luke's narrative theme is to give all of Israel a second chance to be restored to God. See R. Denova, *The Things Accomplished Among Us,* JSNTSup 141 (Sheffield: Sheffield Academic, 1997) 155-77.
130. Haenchen, *Acts,* 188-89, and others following him have called attention to the practical and political problems that a mass conversion would have created for this fledgling movement. Witherington, *The Acts of the Apostles,* 156, rightly cautions against dismissing Luke's poll as unlikely, when evidence exists that makes it possible. The question remains as to what is the function of Luke's summaries, such as this one, within Acts. See Witherington's discussion, *Acts,* 157-59.

membership stood at one hundred and twenty (1:15); and now it stands at over three thousand— a vigorous growth spurt that commends the gospel's truth. Peter's persuasive powers, granted him by the Spirit of prophecy, are significant, which commends his spiritual authority as the community's leader and anticipates his coming

conflict with those in authority over "official" Israel. Finally, the growth of the community implies that it will enjoy a strong public presence in Jerusalem and will be noticed by outsiders (2:47).[131]

131. G. Schneider, *Die Apostelgeschichte*, 2 vols., HTK (Freiburg am Breisgau: Herder, 1981–82) 1:279.

# REFLECTIONS

**1.** "This is what was spoken through the prophet Joel" (2:16 NRSV). Jacob Jervell calls Luke the "Fundamentalist within the New Testament."[132] That is, Luke believes that all Scripture is divinely given and therefore binding upon human life and religious faith. At the center of Israel's Scriptures are the prophecies of God's salvation that "script" Luke's narrative of Israel's restoration and its mission to the nations. Given this perspective, it is appropriate that Peter should appeal to Joel's prophecy to explain the outpouring of God's Spirit. Scripture and Spirit are the indispensable instruments by which the way of salvation is marked out for the church to trod. The Spirit not only inspires Scripture but also inspires its proper interpretation. This interpretation of Scripture, mediated by the successors to Jesus, is inviting and invigorating of salvation. Scripture functions as canonical context within which we comprehend the grand truth that "God has made Jesus Lord and Christ." However, only the repentant are ushered into understanding by the Spirit.

**2.** Joel's prophecy shapes the church's mission in Acts. God's Spirit, the Spirit of prophecy, has been poured out to inaugurate "the last days" of salvation's history—those days that are urgent harbinger of "the Lord's great and glorious [= terrifying] day" (2:20), a future day of "universal restoration" (3:21). These are no longer days of waiting but days set apart for mission. God's Spirit is poured out upon the community's entire membership in order to prophesy, see visions, and dream dreams (2:17-18). As the meaning of Joel's prophecy unfolds in the narrative world of Acts, these prophetic activities (or others like them) clarify and direct the church's overarching vocation of giving witness to the risen Jesus. Following the passage from Joel, the shape of this witness includes two primary tasks: the mediation of God's "wonders" or "portents" and "signs" (2:19) and the proclamation of God's word that issues an invitation to "everyone who calls on the name of the Lord shall be saved" (2:21 NRSV). Without this prophetic awareness, the ministry of the church is corrupted by self-interest and its presence in the world ceases to matter.

**3.** The speeches in Acts are not abstract, homiletically crafted sermons featuring an attention-grabbing introduction and a tear-jerking conclusion. They are typically responses to theological challenges, sometimes made by those who mock, as here, and sometimes made by those ignorant of truth but earnest to find it. Not surprisingly, then, the speeches of Acts center upon God. The rhetor's logic is truly *theo*logical. Evidence is claimed from religious experience and sacred texts; however, the essential points always concern God's eternal plans and purposes and are rooted in a firm conviction about God's faithful benevolence to all.

**4.** "They were cut to the heart and asked, 'What must we do?'" (see 2:37). What should we make of this account of the crowd's response to Peter's speech? Every dissonant voice is removed; initial scorn is quickly turned to vital interest. Peter never stumbles, his voice never breaks; the crowd never raises objections to his interpretation of Scripture or his witness to the risen Jesus. Their question of Peter "what should we do?" does not seem peculiar or out of place.

132. J. Jervell, *The Theology of the Acts of the Apostles*, NTT (Cambridge: Cambridge University Press, 1996) 61.

It aptly frames a universal and timeless search for relevant answers to the ultimate questions of life, and Peter's message to these devout Jews speaks to their questions—that is, to their life with God. The question, "What should we do?" continues to express concern for "the relevant" or "the real" in life. The church's response should not be to offer the gospel with apology but to do so with the confidence that we are presenting the words of eternal life.

**5.** "Repent, and be baptized, every one of you, in the name of Jesus" (2:38 NRSV). Peter is asked by his audience to relate the practical relevance of the gospel proclamation just given. He offers no helpful hints on living a more fulfilling life, no useful projects to work on, no feel-good platitudes; rather, he calls people to conversion. Further, he does not require a particular mode of baptism according to an exact liturgical formulation. What is important is his demand that they turn from competing beliefs and values toward Jesus in faith that God has made him Lord and Savior—in short, that they repent.

**6.** Repentance is the internal and intellectual act of exchanging old beliefs for new ones. In Acts the Evangelist's call to conversion comes only after careful attention is paid to evidence. For example, in Luke's narrative of Paul's mission expressions for serious study of Scripture strengthen the perception that turning to God in faith is not an irrational act (e.g., 17:2-3). Bringing the non-believer into the faith often requires critical investigation of texts and careful study of the Christian religion. Moreover, this turning to God unfolds over time. Peter's call to conversion is placed alongside a passage that summarizes the religious practices of the community of converts. These activities, such as study and worship, nurture faith and facilitate the catechesis of the newly repentant. Those congregations that are active in the work of evangelism must also develop an infrastructure that fully initiates the baptized believer into the faith tradition. Many converts are lost to the faith for the lack of attention to a *process* of repentance that includes participation in committed fellowship with other believers who attend to "the apostles' teaching" and to daily prayers (see 2:42-47).

# ACTS 2:42-47, THE COMMUNITY OF THE UNCOMMON LIFE

## NIV

[42]They devoted themselves to the apostles' teaching and to the fellowship, to the breaking of bread and to prayer. [43]Everyone was filled with awe, and many wonders and miraculous signs were done by the apostles. [44]All the believers were together and had everything in common. [45]Selling their possessions and goods, they gave to anyone as he had need. [46]Every day they continued to meet together in the temple courts. They broke bread in their homes and ate together with glad and sincere hearts, [47]praising God and enjoying the favor of all the people. And the Lord added to their number daily those who were being saved.

## NRSV

[42]They devoted themselves to the apostles' teaching and fellowship, to the breaking of bread and the prayers.

43Awe came upon everyone, because many wonders and signs were being done by the apostles. [44]All who believed were together and had all things in common; [45]they would sell their possessions and goods and distribute the proceeds[a] to all, as any had need. [46]Day by day, as they spent much time together in the temple, they broke bread at home[b] and ate their food with glad and generous[c] hearts, [47]praising God and having the goodwill of all the people. And day by day the Lord added to their number those who were being saved.

[a] Gk *them*   [b] Or *from house to house*   [c] Or *sincere*

# COMMENTARY

The early chapters of Acts include several important summaries of the community's life and mission in Jerusalem (see 4:32–5:16; 6:1-7). These "snapshots" are touched up and colorized by Luke—some say considerably so[133]—to form a portfolio of biblical images paradigmatic of the church's corporate witness. While evangelism is certainly one effect of their life together (see 2:47), the primary purpose of their common life is to nurture Christian community.[134]

**2:42.** Luke writes stories to instruct his readers about normative matters of the faith rather than merely to set the historical record straight.[135] The Christian norm reflected in this text, and others like it in Acts, is that believers who share a common geographical address are also to share a common religious life. The chief characteristics of this common life are listed in v. 42 and elaborated in the following verses: "apostles" teaching (v. 43, ἡ διδαχὴ τῶν ἀποστόλων *hē didachē tōn apostolōn*), fellowship (v. 44, κοινωνία *koinōnia*), the breaking of bread (vv. 45-46, ἡ κλάσις τοῦ ἄρτου *hē klasis tou artou*), and prayer (v. 47*a*, προσευχή *proseuchē*).[136] These same characteristics are

repeated throughout Acts as the hallmarks of an ever-expanding people of God (2:47*b*).[137]

**2:43.** That the believers in Jerusalem should "devote themselves to the apostles' teaching" in not surprising, for the apostles are not only the principal successors to Jesus but also the principal depositories of the Spirit's power. The "many wonders and signs" (πολλά τέρατα καὶ σημεῖα *polla terata kai sēmeia*) they perform bear witness to their spiritual authority. This phrase recalls Joel's prophecy (2:19) of the outpouring of the Spirit to mark them out as important participants in a new epoch of salvation's history. In fact, they are the heirs of Jesus' authority, which he earlier demonstrated by the "wonders and signs that God did through him among you" (2:22; cf. Luke 9:1-2; 24:19). The effect of their authority within the community is confirmed both by adherence to their instruction but also by the "awe (that) came upon everyone." "Awe" translates φόβος (*phobos;* lit., "fear"), which Luke routinely uses to summarize even the outsider's response to God's activity (cf. Luke 2:9; 8:37; Acts 19:17). The performance of these same "signs and wonders" of Jesus is the evident result of their baptism with God's Spirit that enables them to do and teach in continuity with their Lord (cf. 1:1-2). In fact, 2:43 glosses 2:19 as well, indicating the "signs and wonders" of the Spirit will continue in the community's life through the presence of the apostles.

**2:44.** "Fellowship" (*koinōnia*) is used only here in Acts, but for Paul it is an important idiom of the community that is initiated into newness of life in partnership with the Spirit (cf. 2 Cor 13:13; Phil 2:1). In this case, however, God's gift of the Spirit to the community suggests a transforming presence that unites the different believers into a common *koinōnia*.[138] In elaboration, Luke uses a well-known phrase from Greek philosophy indicating friendship: "all things in common." A fellowship of believers shares more than common beliefs and core values; they display a profound

---

133. The critical problem with this text (and with all of Luke's so-called narrative summaries) is whether it is Luke's utopian fiction (see E. Haenchen, E. *The Acts of the Apostles* [Philadelphia: Westminster, 1971] 193-96) or reports based upon reliable traditions (see B. Capper, "The Palestinian Cultural Context of Earliest Christian Community of Goods," in *The Book of Acts in Its Palestinian Setting,* ed. R. Bauckham [Grand Rapids: Eerdmans, 1995] 323-56). Most scholars (including Capper) agree that Luke's portrait of this first Christian congregation is "obviously idealized" (L. T. Johnson, *The Acts of the Apostles,* SP 5 [Collegeville, Minn.: Liturgical, 1992] 61) but that Luke also intends to leave impressions of the community's common life. In sum, there is no good reason to think Luke's narrative summaries are figments of his creative imagination, written only for his readers' religious edification or moral instruction.

134. This community of goods is characteristic of great religious renewals when spiritual enthusiasm generates a robust common life and communal practices, of both an ordinary (e.g., eating together) and a religious (e.g., worshiping together) kind. See J. D. G. Dunn, *The Acts of the Apostles* (Valley Forge, Pa.: Trinity, 1996) 34-35.

135. F. Horn argues that this summary and the one found in 4:32-37 serve Luke's paraenetic and pragmatic interests for maintaining a distinctive form of Christian fellowship (*koinōnia*). What the reader finds in these summaries, then, are the most important topics of catechesis not only for the first converts but for all other converts as well. See F. Horn, *Glaube und Handeln in der Theologie des Lukas,* GTA 26 (Göttingen: Vandenhoeck & Ruprecht, 1983) 36-49.

136. Jeremias argues that the four are given in a liturgical sequence proper to the order of Christian worship in the ancient church and represent the earliest tradition Luke draws upon for his summary. See J. Jeremias, *The Eucharistic Words of Jesus* (Philadelphia: Fortress, 1977) 118-21.

137. The opening phrase of 2:42, "they devoted themselves" (ἦσαν προσκαρτεροῦντες *ēsan proskarterountes*), literally means that they "held fast to" or "persevered in" these disciplines enumerated. The sense is of enduring practices.

138. See R. Wall, "Community (NT)" in *The Anchor Bible Dictionary,* 6 vols. (Garden City, N.Y.: Doubleday, 1992) 1:1103-1110.

---

regard for one another's spiritual and physical well-being as a community of friends. The Jewish community at Qumran, for example, tied its rituals of purification to this same ideal of friendship[139] in a manner recalling 1 Peter's exhortation that the "purification of souls" issuing from Jesus' passion should form a community of friends (cf. 1 Pet 1:19-22).

**2:45-46.** The formation of believers into a community of goods is an important theme in Acts. Popular sentiment may well have led Luke to emphasize more traditional elements of public piety—the contented soul of Stoic thought or the civility of Platonic theory. While no doubt Luke knew these popular Greco-Roman notions of true friendship,[140] his ideals are more deeply rooted in the prophetic typology of Jubilee (cf. Lev 25:10)—Isaiah's "favorable year of the LORD" (Isa 61:2a; cf. Luke 4:19)—that had previously shaped his Gospel narratives of Jesus' ministry among the poor (see, e.g., Luke 4:16-21; 6:20-36; 12:22-34; 15:1–16:31; 17:20–18:4; 19:1-10). According to this biblical pattern, the redistribution of proceeds from sold property reflects the social character of God's kingdom, where all share equally in the good gifts of God.[141] The community of goods of Acts is indicative of those economic practices of the restored Israel of God.

Luke's reference to temple observance is not a bid to take it over for Christian worship or to advance the church's claim that it is the "true Israel."[142] Rather, his point is that worship is a resurrection practice of repentant Israel. The reference to the joyful practice of "breaking bread at home" (κλῶντές . . . κατ᾽ οἶκον ἄρτον *klōntes . . . kat' oikon arton*), the perfect evidence of life in the Spirit, should not be interpreted as a Christian sacrament (i.e., the Lord's supper)[143] or some other distinctly Christian discipline.[144] Rather Luke recalls the practice of devout Jewish families who following temple worship would share meals together as symbolic of their social and spiritual solidarity.[145] The decisions the community makes about "bread"—how to sell it, distribute it to those with needs, and share it without rank or rankle—manifests the effect of the Spirit in its common life.

**2:47.** The community's worship is characterized by the people's praise of God (2:47a; see also 3:8). The community has no material needs, no intramural conflicts, no broken hearts for which to petition God for tender mercy. This will come soon enough. At the beginning of its mission there are only success stories and a community of friends filled with gladness. The reader's lingering impression of the daily rhythm of this community of the uncommon life is that it is both growing "day by day" and worshiping in the Temple "day by day." Indeed, the formation and practices of this community of goods testify to God's commitment to Israel's restoration.

---

139. Johnson, *The Acts of the Apostles*, 58-59.

140. R. C. Tannehill, *The Acts of the Apostles*, vol. 2 of *The Narrative Unity of Luke-Acts: A Literary Interpretation* (Minneapolis: Fortress, 1990) 2:45; Johnson, *The Acts of the Apostles*, 62.

141. See R. North, *Sociology of the Biblical Jubilee*, AnBib 4 (Rome: Pontifical Biblical Institute, 1954) 225-31, who argues that Luke's appropriation of the Jubilee typology found in Isaiah's prophecy is messianic and "improves" upon the OT ideal by mapping the kind of life, individual and corporate, that has arrived because of Jesus.

142. So H. Conzelmann, *The Acts of the Apostles*, trans. J. Limburg et al., ed. E. J. Epp and C. R. Matthews, Hermeneia (Philadelphia: Fortress, 1987) 24.

143. J. A. Fitzmyer, *The Acts of the Apostles*, AB 31 (Garden City, N.Y.: Doubleday, 1998) 271, with others.

144. Johnson, *The Acts of the Apostles*, 59; Roloff, *Die Apostelgeschichte*, 67.

145. J. Jervell, *Die Apostelgeschichte*, KEK 3 (Göttingen: Vandenhoeck & Ruprecht, 1998) 157.

# REFLECTIONS

**1.** "All who believed were together and had all things in common" (2:44 NRSV). At the beginning of his Gospel, Luke uses an Isaianic prophecy about "the favorable year of the Lord" to introduce the principal themes of Jesus' anointed ministry (Luke 4:16-18). In particular, Jesus' actions among the poor and powerless in identifying with their marginal status within Israel and announcing their deliverance are taken as the fulfillment this prophecy of the Lord's Jubilee (Luke 4:21). Jesus' teaching about sharing possessions envisages the social character of God's kingdom where the conditions of the least, lame, lost, and last are transformed. God's grace does not privilege the rich and famous; God's liberating love extends to everyone who calls on the name of the Lord for salvation. However, this Jubilee is possible only *because* of the empty tomb and only *after* Pentecost. The community of converts formed on the Day of Pentecost is a repentant Israel to whom the kingdom of God has been restored. God's kingdom reflects solidarity and mutuality rather than a class system; therefore, believers live together and have "all things in common."

**2.** Teaching, fellowship, sharing goods, and prayers are the religious practices of repentant Israel. Each is a concrete expression of forgiveness of sins and the reception of the Spirit; each is made possible only because of conversion, and together they make possible the convert's continued formation toward maturity. This is so because these practices are much too demanding to implement without the habits of a repentant mind and purified heart. They are also too demanding for the individual believer; therefore, the initial images of conversion in Acts are those of a community and of shared practices and goods.

**3.** These are religious practices that envisage a steady and lasting obedience. The popular conception of a Pentecostal outpouring of the Holy Spirit or of a great revival featuring many conversion experiences is of religious phenomena characterized by fleeting spiritual intensity. The religious practices of the converted in Acts suggest a different enthusiasm, one that is more disciplined and holistic. The spiritual authority of the Twelve, exercised by their teaching and miracle working, is coupled with corporate worship and prayer. The traditional Jewish routines of temple observance are paired with meetings in believers' homes. The Acts' model of Christian community is one of common worship, common practice, common good, and common witness.

**4.** "They would sell their possessions and goods and distribute the proceeds to all" (2:45 NRSV). The most distinctive practice of the community's common life is the sharing of goods. It should be noted that Luke is not interested in the production of goods but rather that these goods already possessed are now shared with other believers. In an economic culture shaped by individual acquisitiveness, this resurrection practice seems idealistic and even scandalous. All the institutions and mythologies of the present order teach us to value *private* property as the principal motive of hard work, invention, and national wealth. Yet, for Luke the kingdom of God *is* the real world; there can be no economic policy more prudent, therefore, than one that cultivates a community of goods in which class divisions are dismantled under the aegis of the Holy Spirit. Why should this be so? Social inequity of any sort fosters no good thing. It is impossible (and finally impractical) to achieve a lasting unity, no matter how important the cause, if inequality persists. This is precisely why Luke is so keen to press the inclusiveness of God's salvation.

# ACTS 3:1–8:3, "YOU SHALL BE MY WITNESSES IN JERUSALEM": THE JERUSALEM MISSION

## OVERVIEW

This narrative unit reflects the increasing demands placed on the apostles and their fierce rivalry with the priesthood of "official" Judaism for the affections of "the people" (4:5-22; 5:17-39; 6:8–8:3). But there is also intramural conflict within the faith community over the distribution of goods (4:32–5:16; 6:1-2). With each new conflict, external or internal, the apostles are forced to discern afresh the ways of Israel's God and to call the emerging church back to worship and to reliance on the spiritual resources God has made available to them (4:23-31; 5:40-42; 6:3-7). God's faithfulness to Israel and the spiritual authority of these prophets-like-Jesus who rule over a restored Israel are the predominant themes of Luke's narrative of the Jerusalem mission. Both are easily detected in the cycle of the stories told. Each episode consists of four elements, closely following the plotline of the paradigmatic events of the earlier Pentecost drama:

(1) God initiates mission by acting in powerful and public ways (3:1-8; 4:5-12; 5:17-23; 6:8-10; cf. 2:1-11) to compel those living in Jerusalem to deal with the nature of God's rule and the meaning of God's promise to restore that rule in Israel (see 1:6).

(2) The crowds who witness these mighty acts of God are ignorant of their significance for Israel (3:17); thus, the people are puzzled—even scornful—and typically mistaken in their perceptions. Their bewilderment about the miracles they witness and the opposition of their own religious leaders toward the Jesus movement prompts more information (3:9-11; 4:13-18; 5:24-28; 6:11–7:1; cf. 2:12-13).

(3) Beginning with and framed by Peter's programmatic sermon on Pentecost, the apostolic proclamation of the gospel is the centerpiece of the church's mission. The authority of the Spirit-filled apostles is demonstrated by their keen ability to respond to questions the crowd raises, questions displaying the crowd's misunderstanding of God's salvation and the character of God's reign in Israel (3:12-26; 4:19-20; 5:29-32; 7:2-53; cf. 2:14-40). Each sermon appeals to Scripture and religious experience to contribute yet another element to the church's *kerygma,* or gospel. Some of the speeches of Acts are spare (see 4:19-20) and presume the reader's recollection of earlier sermons, while others such as Stephen's masterpiece are more full-bodied and self-standing (see 7:2-53).

(4) The final element of this literary pattern of mission turns the story back to the crowd and describes a variety of responses provoked by the proclamation of the gospel (4:1-4, 21-31; 5:33-42; 7:54–8:3; cf. 2:41). The results are mixed. The community's prophetic leaders are arrested and thrown into prison; Stephen is executed; the rank-and-file are persecuted. The word of God is disagreeable to some, especially those priests in charge of "official Judaism," who are annoyed by the movement's popular appeal and alarmed by what it asserts (4:1-2). At the same time, thousands believe (including some priests; 6:7) and the movement continues to grow and gain in influence among the people of God. Conflict is the theme of this narrative.

Two fascinating interludes (4:32–5:16; 6:1-7; cf. 2:42-47), or "summaries," are strategically placed within this narrative to add depth to Luke's profile of the Jerusalem community. Their principal role is to remind the reader that repentant Jews are beneficiaries of God's promise to bless a restored Israel; it is here and only here that the gift of the Spirit is experienced "day by day." But these blessings come at a price: There are intramural conflicts that challenge the very practices that organize the community's common life (2:42) and, therefore, its public witness (2:47). Central to its common life is the resurrection practice of sharing goods (4:32-35; cf. 2:45-46), which is first threatened by the deception of Ananias and Sapphira (5:1-11) and then by an unequal redistribution of food among the growing community's most marginal membership (6:1). This threat precipitated two others: a breakdown in Christian fellowship ("the Hellenists complained against the Hebrews," 6:1; cf. 2:44) and the frustration of the apostles' prophetic vocation ("it is not right that we should neglect the word of God to wait on tables," 6:2; cf. 2:43). Significantly, regular worship is the one resurrection practice that the worshiping community does *not* neglect.

# Acts 3:1–4:4, Story One: The Apostles Heal the Lame of Israel

**NIV**

3 One day Peter and John were going up to the temple at the time of prayer—at three in the afternoon. [2]Now a man crippled from birth was being carried to the temple gate called Beautiful, where he was put every day to beg from those going into the temple courts. [3]When he saw Peter and John about to enter, he asked them for money. [4]Peter looked straight at him, as did John. Then Peter said, "Look at us!" [5]So the man gave them his attention, expecting to get something from them.

[6]Then Peter said, "Silver or gold I do not have, but what I have I give you. In the name of Jesus Christ of Nazareth, walk." [7]Taking him by the right hand, he helped him up, and instantly the man's feet and ankles became strong. [8]He jumped to his feet and began to walk. Then he went with them into the temple courts, walking and jumping, and praising God. [9]When all the people saw him walking and praising God, [10]they recognized him as the same man who used to sit begging at the temple gate called Beautiful, and they were filled with wonder and amazement at what had happened to him.

[11]While the beggar held on to Peter and John, all the people were astonished and came running to them in the place called Solomon's Colonnade. [12]When Peter saw this, he said to them: "Men of Israel, why does this surprise you? Why do you stare at us as if by our own power or godliness we had made this man walk? [13]The God of Abraham, Isaac and Jacob, the God of our fathers, has glorified his servant Jesus. You handed him over to be killed, and you disowned him before Pilate, though he had decided to let him go. [14]You disowned the Holy and Righteous One and asked that a murderer be released to you. [15]You killed the author of life, but God raised him from the dead. We are witnesses of this. [16]By faith in the name of Jesus, this man whom you see and know was made strong. It is Jesus' name and the faith that comes through him that has given this complete healing to him, as you can all see.

[17]"Now, brothers, I know that you acted in ignorance, as did your leaders. [18]But this is how

**NRSV**

3 One day Peter and John were going up to the temple at the hour of prayer, at three o'clock in the afternoon. [2]And a man lame from birth was being carried in. People would lay him daily at the gate of the temple called the Beautiful Gate so that he could ask for alms from those entering the temple. [3]When he saw Peter and John about to go into the temple, he asked them for alms. [4]Peter looked intently at him, as did John, and said, "Look at us." [5]And he fixed his attention on them, expecting to receive something from them. [6]But Peter said, "I have no silver or gold, but what I have I give you; in the name of Jesus Christ of Nazareth,[a] stand up and walk." [7]And he took him by the right hand and raised him up; and immediately his feet and ankles were made strong. [8]Jumping up, he stood and began to walk, and he entered the temple with them, walking and leaping and praising God. [9]All the people saw him walking and praising God, [10]and they recognized him as the one who used to sit and ask for alms at the Beautiful Gate of the temple; and they were filled with wonder and amazement at what had happened to him.

[11]While he clung to Peter and John, all the people ran together to them in the portico called Solomon's Portico, utterly astonished. [12]When Peter saw it, he addressed the people, "You Israelites,[b] why do you wonder at this, or why do you stare at us, as though by our own power or piety we had made him walk? [13]The God of Abraham, the God of Isaac, and the God of Jacob, the God of our ancestors has glorified his servant[c] Jesus, whom you handed over and rejected in the presence of Pilate, though he had decided to release him. [14]But you rejected the Holy and Righteous One and asked to have a murderer given to you, [15]and you killed the Author of life, whom God raised from the dead. To this we are witnesses. [16]And by faith in his name, his name itself has made this man strong, whom you see and know; and the faith that is through Jesus[d] has given him this perfect health in the presence of all of you.

[a] Gk the Nazorean   [b] Gk Men, Israelites   [c] Or child   [d] Gk him

## NIV

God fulfilled what he had foretold through all the prophets, saying that his Christ[a] would suffer. [19]Repent, then, and turn to God, so that your sins may be wiped out, that times of refreshing may come from the Lord, [20]and that he may send the Christ, who has been appointed for you—even Jesus. [21]He must remain in heaven until the time comes for God to restore everything, as he promised long ago through his holy prophets. [22]For Moses said, 'The Lord your God will raise up for you a prophet like me from among your own people; you must listen to everything he tells you. [23]Anyone who does not listen to him will be completely cut off from among his people.'[b]

[24]"Indeed, all the prophets from Samuel on, as many as have spoken, have foretold these days. [25]And you are heirs of the prophets and of the covenant God made with your fathers. He said to Abraham, 'Through your offspring all peoples on earth will be blessed.'[c] [26]When God raised up his servant, he sent him first to you to bless you by turning each of you from your wicked ways."

4 The priests and the captain of the temple guard and the Sadducees came up to Peter and John while they were speaking to the people. [2]They were greatly disturbed because the apostles were teaching the people and proclaiming in Jesus the resurrection of the dead. [3]They seized Peter and John, and because it was evening, they put them in jail until the next day. [4]But many who heard the message believed, and the number of men grew to about five thousand.

[a] 18 Or Messiah; also in verse 20   [b] 23 Deut. 18:15,18,19
[c] 25 Gen. 22:18; 26:4

## NRSV

17"And now, friends,[a] I know that you acted in ignorance, as did also your rulers. [18]In this way God fulfilled what he had foretold through all the prophets, that his Messiah[b] would suffer. [19]Repent therefore, and turn to God so that your sins may be wiped out, [20]so that times of refreshing may come from the presence of the Lord, and that he may send the Messiah[c] appointed for you, that is, Jesus, [21]who must remain in heaven until the time of universal restoration that God announced long ago through his holy prophets. [22]Moses said, 'The Lord your God will raise up for you from your own people[a] a prophet like me. You must listen to whatever he tells you. [23]And it will be that everyone who does not listen to that prophet will be utterly rooted out of the people.' [24]And all the prophets, as many as have spoken, from Samuel and those after him, also predicted these days. [25]You are the descendants of the prophets and of the covenant that God gave to your ancestors, saying to Abraham, 'And in your descendants all the families of the earth shall be blessed.' [26]When God raised up his servant,[d] he sent him first to you, to bless you by turning each of you from your wicked ways."

4 While Peter and John[e] were speaking to the people, the priests, the captain of the temple, and the Sadducees came to them, [2]much annoyed because they were teaching the people and proclaiming that in Jesus there is the resurrection of the dead. [3]So they arrested them and put them in custody until the next day, for it was already evening. [4]But many of those who heard the word believed; and they numbered about five thousand.

[a] Gk brothers   [b] Or his Christ   [c] Or the Christ   [d] Or child
[e] Gk While they

# COMMENTARY

The first story of the Jerusalem mission begins abruptly. The literary pattern and images recall the earlier story of Pentecost, suggesting that the two should be read together reflexively, the one expanding the meaning of the other. The first panel (3:1-8) portrays the devout Peter and John on their way to the Temple for evening prayers (see 2:46-47). A beggar asks them for money but they have none to give since their possessions are now the shared property of the community (see 2:45). But as practitioners of "signs and wonders" (see 2:43), they respond to the beggar's request for money by healing him "in the name of Jesus Christ of Nazareth." The lame man—now healed—leaps up and walks into the Temple in praise of God (see 2:47a) to pray with the apostles. His healing provokes puzzlement among those who see him walking (3:9-11). Instead of mocking the apostles as before (see 2:12-13), the crowd rushes to Peter and John for their commentary on this mighty act of God. Peter's explanatory speech in response reveals the depth of their ignorance about God's redemptive plans for Israel (3:12-17). This healing in Jesus' name is evidence that Scripture's prophecy of God's refreshing forgiveness is fulfilled (3:18-20; cf. 2:38) and is a harbinger of the Messiah's return for a season of universal restoration, fulfilled first in Israel through him (3:21-26). The final panel concludes this missionary drama with images of a divided Israel (4:1-4). On the one hand, unrepentant Sadducees arrest Peter and John; on the other hand, Luke's last word is that "many of those who heard the word believed" (4:4; cf. 2:41). This happy report is what the reader carries into the next story of Acts.

**3:1-8.** While John now accompanies Peter to the Temple for "evening" prayers (actually in mid-afternoon) and daily sacrifice,[146] he is given a limited speaking role in Acts (see 4:19-20). Luke includes him to make a theological rather than historical point: The two most important apostles are depicted here as colleagues and pious Jews, unimpeachable witnesses to the miracle about to occur.[147] The object of the miracle is a beggar they encounter on the incline leading up to the Temple. His résumé is carefully drafted by Luke to depict someone in need of a savior: He is "a man" who has been "lame from birth" and was "daily carried by people" and placed "at the temple gate called 'the Beautiful Gate,' where he asked for alms from those entering the temple" (3:2). Since the combination of temple prayers and alms-giving

characterizes Jewish piety, beggars are found outside the Temple at three o'clock in the afternoon, for those headed for evening prayers are the most likely to give alms to the poor.

L. T. Johnson reminds us that the narrated details of the beggar's existence are hardly arbitrary for another reason: They recall similar accounts both of Jesus before them (e.g., Luke 5:17-26) and of the biblical prophets before Jesus (e.g., 1 Kgs 17:17-24; 2 Kgs 4:32-37).[148] In this case, the healing of a lame beggar in public view of other devout Jews is surely controversial. According to current Jewish practice his physical condition marks him as an "outsider" to the temple community (cf. Lev 21:17-20; *mSabb.* 6:8). By contrast, his healing and entrance into the Temple for prayer symbolize the dawning of a messianic epoch when the conditions of "the poor, the maimed, the lame, the blind" are reversed so that they too can participate in the blessings of God's kingdom (cf. Luke 7:22). Scripture's special concern for the last and least of Israel (see Lev 25; Deut 24:10-22; Isa 58:6-7; 61:1-2), then, is a piece of God's bold promise that the boundaries of Israel will one day be redrawn to include repentant beggars and the restored lame as constituents of the covenant community.

The precise location of the Beautiful Gate in the Temple's courtyard remains debated among scholars.[149] Luke's chief concern, in any case, is to describe the daily routine by which the lame beggar is placed *outside* this temple gate and thus to contrast it with that of those Jews entering the Temple for prayer and with the man's eventual entrance following his healing. This crucial narrative detail suggests that the lame man was excluded from the Temple and all it symbolized in Israel under the current temple leadership. Conflict with Jewish authority is inevitable, and it explains the movement of the plotline toward

---

146. The sacrifice is called "Tamid" and is a continual offering of supplicants made in demonstration of their devotion to God (cf. Exod 29:38-42; Ezek 46:13-15). The Ezekiel reference is especially revealing, since Tamid is featured as part of the sacrificial practice of the eschatological Temple. Perhaps the time of daily prayers is added by Luke to evoke another symbol of "the last days" that Pentecost has inaugurated.

147. Many scholars think that Luke adds John here and elsewhere in Acts (4:13, 19; 8:14; cf. Luke 22:8) to make clear the plurality of the apostolate (so 2:42) and to supply the story with a necessary second witness to confirm what is said and done in witness to the name of Jesus. See O. Bauernfeind, *Die Apostelgeschichte*, THKTT 5 (Leipzig: Deichert, 1939) 60. Bruce considers them as leaders of the apostolate by their "special association with the Lord," which would give this story added weight with a Christian readership. See F. F. Bruce, *The Acts of the Apostles*, rev. ed., NICNT (Grand Rapids: Eerdmans, 1988) 135.

148. L. T. Johnson, *The Acts of the Apostles*, SP 5 (Collegeville, Minn.: Liturgical, 1992) 71-72. The striking parallels between this story and the later story of Paul's healing miracle in Lystra (14:8-18) draws a similar conclusion: Paul continues the prophetic ministry of Peter and John before him. A feature of Luke's telling of miracle stories that is important for his theological program is the contribution others make to those who receive God's mercy. Similar to the friends who dropped the paralytic man through the roof for Jesus to heal (Luke 5:18-19 and par.), the lame beggar "was being carried" by others and placed by them in a setting where he would be healed (Acts 3:2).

149. See J. A. Fitzmyer, *The Acts of the Apostles*, AB 31 (Garden City, N.Y.: Doubleday, 1998) 277 for the alternatives. See also E. Haenchen, *The Acts of the Apostles* (Philadelphia: Westminster, 1971) 198n. 12.

the second story of this narrative cycle (see 4:5-31).

Luke makes much in this story of Peter's eye contact (cf. 3:4-5). Why does Peter "look intently" at the lame man (3:4) and command him to "look at us," which naturally compels the mans to "fix his attention" on the apostles? The demonstration of divine mercy is always a personal concern: Peter's line of sight is set squarely upon a particular individual whose brokenness is in need of repair (cf. Luke 10:32-34). The beggar's obedience to Peter's demand is prompted by his business savvy (3:5b): He wants money from them. His ignorance of their spiritual authority characterizes all who first hear the gospel, whether they are devout Jews or destitute beggars. Given Luke's interest in the outcast, perhaps it is not surprising that an outsider helps mark out the path that leads into God's salvation. The man adheres to the apostles' demand and once healed joins them in the Temple to praise God (3:8; cf. 3:11).

Luke's description of the man's healing symbolizes one who finds salvation. First is Luke's vivid narration: "he stood and began to walk . . . walking, leaping" (3:8). The reality that healing happened is confirmed. Luke is also careful to establish the theological implications of healing: "he . . . entered the temple with them . . . and praised God" (3:8). The restored man is now a member of a restored Israel whose new identity is "with them" (σὺν αὐτοῖς *syn autois*, "the apostles"; see 2:42-43) and whose worship of God is characterized by prayers of praise and Temple fellowship (see 2:46-47). This story also demonstrates Luke's use of possessions to contrast what the apostles do not have (money) and the miracle-working power they do have: The power to heal the sick in "the name of Jesus Christ of Nazareth."[150] It will be this power that is put on trial in the next story of this Jerusalem cycle (see 4:5-31).

**3:9-11.** The man who is restored both to health and to Israel "clings" (κρατέω *krateō*) to Peter and John (3:11), thereby intimately identifying with them as his healers and with the move-

ment they are authorized by God to lead.[151] They have become the center of all the people's attention—and for good reason. Luke is careful to provide the reader with a "police report" of precisely what the crowd witnessed, which confirms the details of the prior account (3:9-10a). It is noteworthy that Luke twice refers to this crowd of witnesses as "all the people" (3:9, 11). Rather than a story-teller's hyperbole, Luke's repetition of this phrase indicates its theological purchase. Luke's uses "people" (λαός *laos*) to recall OT references to Israel as a people belonging to God. As with "all" who witnessed the "signs and wonders" of Pentecost (cf. 2:12), this second congregation of devout Jews represent the whole house of Israel for whom God has promised renewal and restoration (see below).[152]

The intention of Luke's elaborate description of the crowd's response to the healing miracle is almost certainly indicated by the ironical phrase, "filled with wonder and amazement [ἐπλήσθησαν θάμβους καὶ ἐκστάσεως *eplēsthēsan thambous kai ekstaseōs*]" (3:10b). The verb, a favorite of Luke's, recalls his earlier story of Pentecost when Peter and John and the other believers were "filled [*eplēsthēsan*] with the Holy Spirit" (2:4). Israel's persistent unbelief is indicated by the implicit contrast between the Pentecost experience and their "filling": They are "filled with wonder" rather than with the Holy Spirit.

Luke's striking choice of ἔκστασις (*ekstasis*) for "amazement," which figures into subsequent stories of those confused by the implications of the Spirit's "signs and wonders" (cf. 8:9, 11, 13; 10:45), nicely captures the crowd's spiritual ambivalence. They have had a powerful, ecstatic experience that has transported them from the

---

150. Johnson puts it this way: "possessions are being used simply as a negative foil, to point out the enormity of what the Apostles did possess, the power to heal in the Name of Jesus." See L. Johnson, *The Literary Function of Possessions in Luke-Acts,* SBLDS 39 (Missoula, Mont.: Scholars Press, 1977) 190-91.

151. The addition of "Solomon's Portico" (3:11) to the scene's description is problematical. According to Josephus (*Antiquities of the Jews* 15.396-401; *The Jewish War* 5:184-85), the portico was a shelter primarily for Greek visitors to the holy city and, therefore, was built outside the Temple, although its precise location remains uncertain. Yet Luke's narrative places Peter and John, along with the healed man, inside the Temple for prayers (3:8). To resolve this disagreement, the Western text (D) provides a different topology, placing the portico outside the Beautiful Gate, where the apostles and the man had since retreated—which Bruce, *The Acts of the Apostles,* 138, considers historically correct. Whether or not Luke's knowledge of the Temple is suspect, as some think, the purpose of his reference may be to recall an important site of Christian witness, as is clear from 5:12. What is important to his narrative world is that Solomon's Portico is a Christian "shrine" remembered for apostolic "signs and wonders" and witnessing and for the conversions that resulted.

152. J. Jervell, *Die Apostelgeschichte,* KEK 3 (Göttingen: Vandenhoeck & Ruprecht, 1998) 163.

ordinary into an encounter with God. Such experiences typically provoke theological reflection that requires a change of mind. As before, the reader is led to ask: How will this Israel respond to its encounter with God?

**3:12-26.** Actually the stakes may have reached a critical stage for these Jews. In Luke's narrative world, God anoints and then sends prophet Peter to "all the people" to give them a second chance to repent and turn to God in faith. If they rebuff the prophet's word a second time, God will send them into exile and delay the fulfillment of their restoration.[153] If this story is read as structurally and thematically parallel to his Pentecost narrative and if Luke's emphasis on "all the people" relates this crowd to the Israelites Peter addressed on the day of Pentecost, then the implication is that these are those Jews who refused his earlier invitation of salvation and this speech may well be their second chance to respond favorably. Clearly Peter's second speech to them, which provides the additional testimony of the healed man, is more sharply worded and the call to conversion is more urgently proffered. The question asked earlier of the stunned crowd at Pentecost (see 2:37) is even more pressing now: How will this Israel respond to Peter's second sermon, based on its second hearing of the gospel message?

The circumstances of Peter's second sermon to Israel are similar to those of his first (see 2:14-40): The whole household of Israel—"all the people"—has witnessed God's mighty work and has congregated around Peter for his commentary on their experience.[154] This sermon, too, is a missionary speech in two parts about the importance of the resurrection of Jesus (3:12-16) that intends to convert its auditors to him as their Lord and God's Christ (3:17-26).[155]

**3:12.** The purposeful interplay between these first two missionary speeches in Acts is indicated by the repetition of Peter's opening address, "Men of Israel" (cf. 2:22). The reader of this speech knows to have the Pentecost speech in mind when reflecting on what is now proclaimed. Yet, the differences between the addresses make for a fuller understanding of the gospel. For example, Peter's judgments of Israel's guilt in Jesus' execution are much more harshly drawn than before (3:13-15; cf. 2:23). He also makes explicit the charge of Israel's ignorance (3:17), which has led to their wickedness (3:26) and away from God's purposes as articulated in the promise to Abraham (3:25). This sharp condemnation compels keener attention to Peter's interpretation of Scripture (midrash) and makes more urgent its reception. If the whole Pentecost narrative is more idealistic and pastoral in tone, this speech is more polemical and prophetic. This is Israel's second chance; the urgency of Peter's appeal underscores their theological crisis.

Peter's sermon is prompted again by misunderstanding, although certainly more good-hearted than before. His audience does not mock what they have just witnessed (cf. 2:13-15) and their honest mistake concerns the nature of Peter's spiritual authority in effecting the man's cure (3:12b). Peter and John *do* exercise enormous power as God's chosen prophets and their piety is well documented by the preceding narrative. Peter is concerned that the crowd understand that these are not attributes apostles themselves have cultivated over time, qualities that can manipulate a sovereign

153. L. T. Johnson, *The Acts of the Apostles*, SP 5 (Collegeville, Minn.: Liturgical, 1992) 13, contends that such second visits are an important narrative theme of Acts and supply one element of its "prophetic structure." According to Johnson, the account of Moses (Acts 7:22-50) in Stephen's speech is patterned after Luke's story of Jesus and provides an exposition of the theme that the prophet is sent to save Israel, but out of ignorance the people reject him. The prophet returns to offer salvation to the same people a second time. If the people reject the prophet again, they will be sent into exile. While my reading of Peter's second sermon follows Johnson's lead in general, several differences should be noted. Peter's Jewish audience is the entire household of Israel, including Jews of the diaspora. Further, the decision of Jews in a synagogue of a particular city (e.g., Jerusalem, Pisidian Antioch) does not determine the fate of all Israel, but only that of those particular Jews who hear the prophetic word and refuse to obey its demands. Finally, this "second visitation" theme is joined by another—namely, the "divided house of Israel." The restoration of repentant Israel unfolds over time in response to the prophetic word in various locations, sometimes proclaimed in two visits (see 13:44), even as does the harsh exclusion of unrepentant Israel (3:23; cf. 13:45-47).

154. Luke's shaping of the traditions of this second sermon, as with the first, reflect his own linguistic choices and theological intentions. Again, the interpreter should read this text as the recounting of an event, the memories of which have been preserved and transmitted to Luke but whose significance is his to tell.

155. These two parts are rhetorically similar to Peter's Pentecost speech, combining "judicial" (or "explanation," 3:12-16) with "deliberative" (or "appeal," 3:17-26) conventions. See M. L. Soards, *The Speeches in Acts: Their Content, Context, and Concerns* (Louisville: Westminster/John Knox, 1994) 40-44, for analysis and alternate outlines. In this second speech, however, Peter combines traditions differently than he did on Pentecost; he uses *kerygma* rather than proof from prophecy to address the problem of Israel's rejection of the Messiah (cf. 2:22-36), while his missionary appeal is to Israel's Scripture rather than to the Christian *kerygma* (cf. 2:38-40).

God's prerogative. Peter's cautionary note reminds the reader that healing is "in the name of Jesus Christ of Nazareth" (3:6 b) and is mediated by the saving power vested in and released by that name according to Scripture (cf. 2:21; 4:7-12). This theme persists into the next story, where Peter's audience consists of Israel's rulers, who are also guilty of "ignorance" (3:17) but whose response is more cynical and political than that of rank-and-file Jews.

**3:13-16.** Peter's correction concerning the protocol of the prophet's exercise of power leads naturally and immediately to Christian *kerygma*:[156] To understand the meaning of the miracle (3:16) is to come to grips with who Jesus is (3:13-15). The entire sermon is framed by Abraham's promise of universal salvation (3:13, 25) and, therefore, by Israel's role toward that redemptive end. The traditional appeal to "the God of our ancestors" expresses Peter's confidence in God's faithfulness to aid Israel in fulfilling that role.[157] Indeed, God has acted faithfully toward Israel in Jesus, God's glorified "servant" (δοῦλος [*doulos*]; 3:13, 26).[158] While the precise meaning of Jesus' identification as God's servant is unclear (see below), the reference to Jesus no doubt reminds the audience that the healing miracle was done in his name. That Jesus is "glorified" (δοξάζω *doxazo*) probably

alludes to his resurrection and ascension[159] and envisages his vindication as God's faithful "servant."[160]

Peter quickly moves to clarify Israel's guilt for rejecting Jesus, which is more sharply and elaborately stated here than in his first sermon. Notice five new details Peter adds to his legal brief against Israel (see 3:13c-15b; cf. 2:23): Even though Jesus is (1) "the Holy and Righteous One," (2) they handed him over to Pilate (3) when Pilate wanted him released; (4) they exchanged him for a murderer, (5) which occasioned the execution of "the Author of life." The reference to Pilate's role in Jesus' trial and death is generally consistent with its synoptic narration (see Luke 23:1-25 and par.; cf. Acts 4:27; 13:28). With a prior reading of the gospel narrative in mind, however, the reader knows that pagan Pilate had little interest in intramural Jewish conflict and therefore in the final disposition of Jesus. He cedes Jesus to his Jewish opponents for political reasons. In any case, Peter's point is less to depict Rome's passive stance toward Jesus and more to depict unrepentant Israel's active participation in bringing about his execution.

Twice Peter mentions that Israel "rejected" Jesus (3:13-14), using the verb ἀρνέομαι (*arneomai*), which means "to deny" or "to disown" someone. Peter presumes that Jesus belongs to Israel in some special way and that Israel betrayed that relationship by participating in his execution. The two titles of Jesus used here in rapid succession—"the Holy and Righteous One [ὁ ἅγιος καὶ ὁ δίκαιος *ho hagios kai ho dikaios*]" (3:14) and "the Author of life [ὁ ἀρχηγὸς τῆς ζωῆς *ho archēgos tēs zōēs*]" (3:15)—draw upon important OT/Gospel terms to define the nature of that relationship and therefore also the enormity of Israel's treason. The first title follows from Peter's reference to Jesus as God's glorified servant by recalling the Roman centurion's ironic commentary on the death of Jesus, whom he asserts is "innocent" (or "righteous," *ho dikaios*, Luke 23:47). In the Gospel setting, as here, *ho dikaios* alludes to Isaiah's depiction of the suffering servant as *ho dikaios* (Isa 53:11 LXX) and so as having

---

156. Fitzmyer, *The Acts of the Apostles*, 282, lists the kerygmatic elements of this speech as follows: (1) miracle is the work of Israel's faithful God (3:13ab), not powerful and pious prophets (3:12b); (2) miracle witnesses to Jesus and thus to the ignorance of Israel about him (3:13c-19); (3) Israel's restoration is predicated on Jesus' resurrection (3:20-21), which is (4) proved by biblical prophecy (3:22-26).

157. D. Bock, *Proclamation*, 187-88. Bock argues that the precise formula of Peter's appeal in 3:13a intentionally recalls the same confession used in Exod 3:6, 15 in the famous exchange between God and Moses. There God commends Israel's confidence in the exodus event due to God's prior faithfulness to their ancestors. A similar justification project is in view here, where Peter's use of the traditional formula of Israel's confidence is posited for the resurrection where God has acted faithfully in Christ to restore Israel.

158. There is an intriguing connection between Peter's use of God's "servant" (παῖς *pais*) in this sermon (3:13, 26) and the important and clear allusions to Isaiah's "suffering servant" in 1 Peter 2 (in this case with reference to household). See O. Cullmann, "Jesus serviteur de Dieu," *Dieu vivant: perspectives religieuses et philosophiques* 16 (1950) 17-34. Both texts allude to Isaiah's prophecy of God's servant (Isa 52:13), who suffers as Israel or on Israel's behalf. Bruce, *The Acts of the Apostles*, 139-40, suggests that this connection between Peter's speech and 1 Peter's use of servant indicates the historical accuracy of Luke's narrative, while others, such as J. Jeremias, *TDNT*, 5:677-717, are more reserved and allow that both Acts 3 and 1 Peter 2 reflect a very early christology stemming from Peter himself, although in the case of Acts without the redemptive value it has in 1 Peter. In my view, the combination of "servant" and "the Holy and Righteous One" in this speech almost certainly alludes to Isaiah 53's Suffering Servant, perhaps not to forward a theology of the cross but to relate servant Jesus and Israel together in a redemptive way.

159. So Haenchen, *The Acts of the Apostles*, 205.

160. Most scholars still think that "servant" is not used as a messianic title in the NT. See M. D. Hooker, *Jesus and the Servant* (London: SPCK, 1959). Even if this view is right, that the Messiah is exalted by God and worshiped by the church as Lord because of his faithful service to God seems clear enough from the NT (e.g., Phil 2:5-11; Revelation 5).

divine authority to bear Israel's sins. In this sense, Peter interprets Jesus' passion as the expression of his faithful service for Israel, which Israel then rejected—and so too the salvation that attends it.

The latter title is repeated in Acts 5:31 for the glorified Jesus.[161] This speech contrasts Israel's action of taking life with Jesus' action of authoring life, and perhaps also with God's bringing Jesus back to life (3:15). Thereby Israel demonstrates its robust ignorance of God's purposes by removing the very source of its promised life! On Pentecost, Peter marshals proofs from biblical prophecy to commend his eyewitness of the risen Jesus. He makes the same claim as before that "we are witnesses" (3:16; see also 2:32), but here Peter speaks of Israel's rejection of Jesus rather than of the resurrection.

Peter's response to the misunderstanding of his prophetic powers (3:16; cf. 3:12a) uses the crucial phrase "by faith in his name" (ἐπὶ τῇ πίστει τοῦ ὀνόματος αὐτοῦ epi tē pistei tou onomatos autou), which brings together the objective reality of the man's "perfect health" with the subjective faith "that is through Jesus."[162] The reference to "the name" that "made the man strong" recalls the circumstances of the healing miracles (see 3:6) and the promise of Joel's prophecy that those who call upon the *name* of the Lord will be saved (= healed). In this larger sense, healing heralds the fulfillment of prophecy and provides additional evidence of God's faithfulness.

**3:17.** By pointing to the Lord's authority, Peter has set the stage for his appeal to his auditors to repent and believe in order to become members of a "healed" Israel. He begins graciously by excusing their treachery: "I know that you acted in ignorance as did also your rulers" (3:17). With these words Luke succinctly sets forth the theological crisis facing a devout but divided household: They

are "ignorant" (ἄγνοια *agnoia,* 7:25; 13:37; 17:30; cf. Luke 19:44; 23:34; Acts 7:60). In particular, Israel is divided over Jesus because of its ignorance of Scripture that would indicate his messianic identity and mission. Peter adds "as did also your rulers" (3:17b) as a prophet's emphasis, since the ignorance of leaders transfers to the people they lead. The leaders' obduracy will become increasingly clear as the narrative of the community's Jerusalem mission depicts the conflict between the apostolic leaders of restored Israel and the priestly leaders of "official" Israel. Of course, the reader of Acts is well aware that the Spirit has filled the apostles and has thereby elevated their intellectual abilities to discern Scripture's meaning. They alone are enabled to know God's intended meaning in Scripture and to make clear God's redemptive purposes for Israel. In a word, they are Israel's rightful spiritual leaders during these last days of salvation's progress to its consummation.

**3:18-21.** Peter now reissues his call to conversion: "repent therefore and turn to God"[163] (3:19a; see 2:38). Repentance embraces a different interpretation of Scripture—the one that Peter has just provided his auditors.[164] The primary purpose of repentance is "so that your sins are wiped out" (cf. Isa 43:25), which will then usher repentant Israel into "times of refreshing" and trigger the return of Messiah (3:20) from heaven (cf. 1:11) to inaugurate "the time of universal restoration" (3:21).[165] Peter's argument stakes out the

---

161. The meaning of *archēgos* is unclear. Most accept the translation "author" and yet question how this translation fits easily with Luke's strong views of God's sovereign and provident control of salvation's history, expressed in the opening of Peter's Pentecost sermon. For this reason, Bauernfeind, *Die Apostelgeschichte,* 63-64, understands by the expression that Jesus is *Lebensführer,* "leader into life," to make the evident contrast between life and death more vivid.

162. It remains unclear whether the lame man's faith was required and, therefore, preceded his healing or whether the apostles' faith "in the name of Jesus Christ of Nazareth" resulted in the man's healing and then his faith. The logic of the earlier healing story suggests the latter: It is *the apostles'* faith in his name" that "has made this man strong—and has given him perfect health." While the power to heal resides in Jesus, Peter claims that the requisite faith in Jesus that heals resides in the apostles (see 3:12a).

163. J. D. G. Dunn, *The Acts of the Apostles* (Valley Forge, Pa.: Trinity, 1996) 46, contends with others that Luke combines the imperatives μετανοήσατε *metanoēsate* ("repent") with ἐπιστρέψατε *epistrepsate* ("to turn") to clarify the experience of conversion called for by the gospel. On the one hand, the gospel requires a "change of mind" (in what one believes about God); but on the other hand, it also requires a radical change of direction (in how one lives for God). The logic of conversion, which moves from changing what one thinks or believes about God to changing the way one lives with others, is already implied by the Pentecost narrative. There the 3,000 who converted (2:41) formed a community whose common life enjoyed favor with all (2:42-47).

164. According to Jervell the theme of Israel's repentance in Acts can only be understood in continuity with Luke's Gospel, where Jesus' mission was to begin a process of healing a divided Israel. See esp. J. Jervell, "The Divided People of God," in *Luke and the People of God* (Minneapolis: Augsburg, 1972) 41-74.

165. Although the two phrases Luke uses in 3:20-21 of eschatological "seasons"—"the times of refreshing" and "the time of universal restoration"—are clearly related, they do not refer to the same saving season but to a *sequence* of saving seasons. J. A. Fitzmyer, *The Acts of the Apostles,* AB 31 (Garden City, N.Y.: Doubleday, 1998) 288, contends, correctly, that the temporal word καιροί (*kairoi*) that Luke uses in "the times of refreshing" denotes the *beginning* of a season, whereas his use of χρόνος (*chronos*) in the second phrase denotes "the duration of it." Luke is commenting on conversion as the initiation into the first of "the last days" of salvation's history which will conclude at the parousia in the cosmic triumph of God's reign.

enormous purchase of Israel's repentance, since the restoration of Israel is the pre-condition that leads to God's universal blessing.

The eschatology of Luke is predicated on God's faithfulness to the promises "announced long ago through his holy prophets" to Israel (3:21).[166] He does not have in mind a detailed timetable of specific dates when this or that event will happen (cf. 1:7). The reader knows only that "the last days" of salvation's history have been inaugurated by the suffering of God's Messiah (3:18) and the Spirit's arrival at Pentecost (see 2:17-21), and that Jesus will return at the consummation of history (see 1:11). Between these two eschatological markers unfolds the Spirit-enabled mission of the Lord's successors as his witness to Israel and the nations to the end of the earth and history.

The present text sharpens the Messiah's future horizon and its importance as the religious motive of the church's mission in Jerusalem and beyond. The Lord's return to earth to complete his messianic mission is heralded by "times of refreshing that come from the presence of the Lord" (3:20). This first reference to a season of redemption refers to the present blessings of repentant Jews, which are both spiritual (see 2:38) and material (see 2:42-47). This, too, is the immediate objective of the church's vocation: to reestablish God's presence—"the kingdom" (see 1:6)—within the community of a restored Israel during the "last days" of salvation's history (see 2:17).

According to Peter, these days of mission culminate in God's dispatch of the glorified Messiah, Jesus, "who must remain in heaven until the time of universal restoration." The phrase "time of universal restoration" (NRSV) translates χρόνων ἀποκαταστάσεως πάντων (chronōn apokatastaseōs pantōn) to recall and gloss the apostles' decisive question that begins Acts: "Lord, is this the time [chronos] when you will restore [ἀποκαθιστάνεις apokathistaneis] the kingdom to Israel?" (see 1:6). Peter now extends the scope of God's plan for restoring Israel to include

creation and in doing so underscores the universal importance of Israel's repentance.

Luke emphasizes that God's promise of "refreshing times" for a repentant Israel has already been fulfilled and is the necessary precondition for the Lord's coming triumph and creation's restoration. In fact, the church's mission to the "families of the earth" as agent of God's faithfulness to Abraham's promise (3:25) is also preconditioned on Israel's repentance (3:26).[167]

Peter's earlier reference to the man's "perfect health" (3:16) is expanded in its significance as the eschatological metaphor of creation's perfection in the coming age. That is, the healed man is the herald of a broken and battered creation's being made whole again. While Peter's kerygmatic announcement of Messiah's return and creation's restoration is the last we hear of it in Luke's narrative, he provides the three broad movements of God's future plans: (1) These "last days" consist of a mission to heal Israel, which will result in a divided household; (2) God's promise of "refreshing times" will nevertheless be fulfilled among repentant Jews who will carry the gospel to the Gentiles so they too can share in Israel's blessings; and (3) then the Day of the Lord will come, which will inaugurate "the time of universal restoration."

**3:22-23.** Peter's eschatological program for repentant Israel is sharpened by combining the promise of "a prophet-like-Moses" (3:22-23a; cf. Deut 18:15-19 LXX) with a levitical warning of excommunication for those who are unprepared for the Day of Atonement (3:23b; Lev 23:29). Although not widely attested during the Second Temple period, the deuteronomic expectation of a prophet to succeed Moses does find currency in an important Qumran text.[168] Peter follows this same interpretive line by claiming that God has "raised up" Jesus (3:26; cf. 2:36) as indication that a Moses prophet has been "raised up for you." The significance of Peter's identification of Messiah

---

166. The "must" in the phrase "[Jesus] *must* remain in heaven" translates the Greek particle δεῖ (*dei*), which functions in Acts as a catchword of prophetic fulfillment. Luke has already used it in the Gospel's prediction of Jesus' passion (Luke 9:22; 17:25) and in the report of its fulfillment (Luke 22:27; 24:7, 44). As the critical eschatological elements of this same divine purpose, Jesus "must" remain in heaven and "must" return to earth to inaugurate God's restoration of all creation, because this is what "all the biblical prophets" predict according to apostolic (i.e., Spirit inspired) interpretation.

167. According to Paul, the completion of the Gentile mission is the necessary precondition for the Lord's return, at which time "all Israel will be saved" (cf. Rom 11:25-27) and creation repaired (cf. 8:18-25). Of course, the Evangelist knows what the apostle did not know when writing Romans: Paul would not complete his mission to the nations and would not live to see Jesus return.

168. *4QTestim* 7/4Q175.5-8. It should be pointed out that unlike traditional Judaism this "prophet-like-Moses" figured prominently in Samaritan religion, which some suggest is Luke's source for what becomes the foundation of his Moses christology. See C. C. Hill, *Hellenists and Hebrews: Reappraising Division Within the Earliest Church* (Minneapolis: Fortress, 1992) 87.

with the prophetic ministry of Moses is that each discloses God's word for Israel. Whether or not one "listens to that prophet"[169] determines one's membership in the covenant community where the refreshing presence of God may be experienced. Put negatively, those who refuse to listen to God's prophetic word are "utterly rooted out of the people [λαός *laos*]" (3:23) and excluded from the experience of God's refreshing grace. During these "last days" of salvation's history, Israel remains divided over this apostolic word about Jesus; however, God's redemptive purpose moves inexorably toward the coming age by the witness of repentant Jews.

**3:24-26.** The division within Israel between those who heed (or not) the prophet's call to conversion implies an essential internal characteristic of Israel prior to the Messiah's return. The reader of Acts should anticipate still other expressions of a divided house and should not be distracted by them. Clearly God's present blessing of faithful Jews—this "time of refreshing" (3:20)—is sufficient evidence that God has faithfully kept the promise to restore Israel, and on this basis the gospel's advance to "all the families of the earth" is also anticipated but awaits Paul's mission to bring "light to the nations" for its fuller narration. At this early moment in the church's mission, however, Peter can only iterate the premise of God's redemptive plan (3:24) that the things that are happening (e.g., the healing of the lame outsider) herald the realization of what God has foretold through "all the prophets" (cf. 3:18).

Samuel, who is the first prophet following Moses by Peter's counting, and all "those (biblical prophets) after him predicted these days"—that is, "the last days" beginning at Pentecost (cf. 2:17). This leads to an expansion of previous themes in reverse order. The future prospect of "universal restoration" (3:21) is now interpreted in the terms of God's promise to Abraham (3:25) that "in your descendants [lit., "seed" = Jews] all the families [= Gentiles] of the earth shall be blessed" (cf. Gen 22:18)—a promise whose fulfillment requires, then, the conversion of these very Jews since they are "the descendants of the prophets" (3:25). Perhaps for this reason Peter's final note repeats

the present prospect of Israel's "refreshing" (3:20) for which Messiah was sent "first to you, to bless you by turning each of you from your wicked ways" (3:26; see 3:19).

Throughout this passage, Luke carefully and creatively adapts his language to order and commend his view of salvation history. He shifts the terminology in 3:20-21 from "times/time" (καιροί/χρόνος *kairoi/chronos*) to "these days" (αὗται ἡμέραι *hautai hēmerai*), thus recalling the earlier reference to Joel's prophecy of the "last days" (2:17). This shift returns the auditors and readers from future speculation to the present moment in order to address their situation in light of Scripture: What is the meaning of this man's healing? How can one enjoy God's promised blessing? What or who is the ground of repentance? Moreover, Luke changes the contextual sense of ἐνευλογηθήσονται (*eneulogēthēsontai*, "will bless themselves") in Gen 22:18 (LXX) from a middle to a passive voice—"will be blessed"—to underscore God's future act of blessing the "nations." Finally, he substitutes "families" (πατριαί *patriai*) for "nations" (ἔθνη *ethnē*) without changing the universal sense of the promised salvation that will come in some unknown future. In Luke's presentation, than, Peter's appeal has mostly to do with his hearers' participation in current blessing, beginning with their sins being "wiped out" (3:19) and "turning from your wicked ways" (3:26), as the focal moment in the larger plan.

**4:1-4.** Luke frequently tells stories of interrupted speeches or actions (e.g., 2:37; 7:54; 8:39-40; 10:44; 17:32; 22:22; 26:24). This literary device often introduces important elements into the story—a leading question, a principal player, a theological problem.[170] The interrupted speech also serves to connect consecutive episodes as logically related. Thus when the Sadducees (4:1-3), who will become the movement's most hostile opponents, interrupt Peter's speech, the stage is set for Peter's defense of the gospel before a hostile tribunal consisting largely of Sadducees (4:5-31).

Three groups are mentioned as approaching John and Peter while Peter concludes his speech (3:12-26): "the priests, the captain of the temple,

---

169. Johnson, *The Acts of the Apostles*, 70, notes that Luke's rewriting of the LXX text suggests that the verb "listens" (ἀκούω *akouō*) connotes obedience and is better translated "obeys."

170. See H. Conzelmann, *The Acts of the Apostles*, trans. J. Limburg et al., ed. E. J. Epp and C. R. Matthews, Hermeneia (Philadelphia: Fortress, 1987) 22.

and the Sadducees."[171] The first two represent the Temple, the central symbol of "official" Israel; it is in their responsibility to protect the Temple's interests, especially matters of ritual purity. This is the first reference to Sadducees in Acts; while demonized in the Gospels and here, not much is actually known about them or the nature of their authority in Jerusalem.[172] In the ancient world behind Luke's story, the Sadducees were probably devout laity from wealthy (mainly priestly) Jerusalem families who were close to the political and financial institutions of Judean culture but who were without any direct power over temple protocol.[173] Within Luke's narrative world of Acts, however, Sadducees are portrayed as "flat characters" with flawed personae and incorrect theology. In fact, they represent the Jewish group most responsible for a divided Israel—in particular, for unrepentant Israel's resistance to the church's testimony to the word in Jerusalem. In effect, the negative depictions of the church's opposition are neatly summarized in verses 2-3: The opponents are "annoyed" (διαπονέομαι *diaponeomai*) because of the people's welcome response to the

apostles' proclamation "that in Jesus there is the resurrection of the dead,"[174] and for this reason "they arrested [the apostles]." Putting prophets into prison is commonplace in Acts; this is the first of several conflicts that result in arrest and incarceration.

In contrast to the response of the temple establishment, five thousand who heard the word believed (4:4; see 2:41). Luke frequently uses "the word" (ὁ λόγος *ho logos*) in Acts for the Christian *kerygma,* or gospel. The movement of the word through Acts is sometimes surprising (see 8:4) and always expansive, whether from Jew to Gentile or from Jerusalem to the "end of the earth." To "believe" (πιστεύω *pisteuō*) in this word is Luke's shorthand for obeying the gospel imperatives to "repent and turn to God" by believing in what the apostles proclaim about the risen Jesus and in how they support their christological claims by Scripture (see 3:19; cf. Matt 4:17 and par.).

171. Some early MSS (B, C) read instead "chief-priests" (ἀρχιερεῖς *archiepeis*), which would be consistent with Luke's identification of both Jesus' hostile opponents in the Gospel and the apostles' opponents in the next story in Acts (see 4:23). "Priests" (ἱερεῖς *hiereis*) is the preferred term here because it is the more difficult to explain and thus presumed to be earlier.

172. Fitzmyer, *The Acts of the Apostles,* 297-98. The name "Sadducees" is related to the Hebrew word for "righteous" and the OT "Zadok," the name of an Aaronid priest (2 Sam 2:17; Ezek 40:46). Sadducees are thought to be contemporary descendants of Zadok and the Zadokite priesthood, keenly influenced by Hellenistic culture and philosophy and quite sophisticated—perhaps the reason why they were so impressed by the speech of "uneducated and ordinary men" (4:13).

173. See Roloff, *Die Apostelgeschichte,* 80-81.

174. This is Luke's succinct, but difficult, summary of the gospel. The point and problem of Luke's phrase is that the apostles nowhere claim that "in [or by] Jesus" the dead are raised but rather than he is raised from the dead. See C. K. Barrett, *A Critical and Exegetical Commentary on the Acts of the Apostles,* 2 vols, ICC (Edinburgh: T. & T. Clark, 1994, 1998) 219-20. The Sadducees did not possess a robust notion of a restored Israel or believe in the "resurrection from the dead" (see 23:8). Their Bible contained only the Torah, and not the prophecies (such as Isaiah) that script God's plan of salvation, according to Luke. They expressed their hope for Israel's salvation in terms of temple observance by which Israel's covenant purity with God is faithfully maintained. Luke's phrase reflects, rather, the core belief of the Pharisees, who understood Israel's hope in terms of the endtime resurrection of the dead; and it envisages the intramural conflict within religious Israel between these two groups (see 23:6-10). The eventual triumph and spread of the Pharisees' influence and the concurrent demise of the Sadducees in post-70 CE Judaism, certainly known to Luke when he wrote Acts, lend tacit support that the church's proclamation of the risen Jesus is the hope of Israel.

# REFLECTIONS

**1.** "In the name of Jesus Christ of Nazareth, walk" (3:6 NIV). Peter's command is not the incantation of a magician, as though healing powers were released by the mere mention of a sacred "name," but a believer's confession of the continuing authority of the living Jesus. In the Gospels, Jesus admonished his followers for having "little faith" (cf. Matt 6:30; 8:26) since the proper exercise of trusting God is a powerful force, strong enough to "move mountains" (cf. Matt 17:20; 1 Cor 13:2). Peter's words to the crippled beggar are words that issue in new life precisely because they are words of profound confidence in the present authority of Jesus to heal the lame and save the lost.

**2.** "He stood and began to walk, and he entered the temple with them" (3:8 NRSV). In his farewell speech, Jesus commissions his apostles to a Spirit empowered witness (1:8); the implied result of their witness is the restoration of God's reign to repentant Israel (1:6). The Lord's interplay between vocation and restoration provides the reader with the interpretive key for understanding why Luke features healing miracles in Acts and narrates them with a similar resonance (5:14-16; 9:32-34; 36-41; 14:8-10; 16:16-18; 19:11-12; 20:7-13; 28:7-9). The healing of crippled beggars "in the name of Jesus Christ of Nazareth" in order to restore them physically also restores them to membership within the restored Israel of God. The beggar's entrance into the Temple to the shouts of holy praise symbolizes a *religious* restoration, since he is now restored to a community of faith and able to worship God with them.

**3.** "And they recognized him as the one who used to sit and ask for alms . . . and they were filled with wonder and amazement at what had happened to him" (3:10 NRSV). Healing is the principal "sign and wonder" performed by God's Spirit through the prophets-like-Jesus of Acts. Healing miracles are "enacted parables" of the manner or experience of God's saving grace. For this reason, Luke sometimes uses the verb "to save" for "to heal" (see Luke 7:50; 8:36, 48, 50; Acts 4:9; 14:9). This is not because sin precipitates in bodily infirmity under the curse of God. God's redemptive intention is to liberate people from whatever debilitates them and prevents them from enjoying the good things created for them. The interpreter of Acts sometimes makes the distinction between spiritual sickness (= sin), from which one is healed by the salve of divine forgiveness, and physical sickness (= lameness), from which one is healed by God's miracle-working power. The one is more public and spectacular but no more exceptional than the other. They are two sides of a common coin, minted by grace and received in faith.

**4.** God "glorified his servant Jesus, whom you handed over and rejected in the presence of Pilate" (3:13 NRSV). Luke makes the execution of Jesus the primary symbol of unrepentant Israel, even as believing that Jesus is God's Messiah is the primary mark of repentant Israel. Peter's presentation of the gospel highlights the ultimate importance of choosing for Jesus, since to reject him is to reject all the blessings of grace that God metes out to us because of him. When unrepentant Israel turns to Pilate—a disinterested, cynical ruler who represents a pagan power—from an interested God, they freely choose death rather than life. Their bad choice represents every bad choice people make when rejecting the words of eternal life in favor of competitors that are disinterested in our future with God.

**5.** "I know that you acted in ignorance, as did your leaders" (3:17 NIV). In the first century of the new millennium, most religious people are theologically and biblically illiterate. They believe in God, but they are not clear as to why they believe. At the same time, because of secular culture's pervasive awareness of and profound interest in God, the popular media routinely feature stories on religious beliefs, miracles and angels, and the universal importance of Jesus. How can the church contribute to the wider discussion—that is, how can the church respond to awareness and interest in things spiritual—if believers are ignorant of their own faith?

**6.** Jesus "must remain in heaven until the time of universal restoration" (3:21 NRSV). Modern interpreters of Acts often point out that the book's emphasis on the church's present mission has the effect of diminishing the sense of eschatological intensity. Salvation is today and only the expectation of God's universal judgment is delayed to the end of history (see 10:42; 17:31). The future is "fixed" in God's mind and therefore removed as a principal concern of ours. While the surface level of the narrative does stess the church's present mission, the future of God's salvation provides a theme of enormous importance for the theological "superstructure" of Luke's story. Indeed, salvation history provides the "authorial motive" that explains the direction the story takes from beginning to end. Peter's speech in particular suggests that the church's mission is coordinated with salvation's future. Thus the mission is first to Jews (3:17-19, 26) whose repentance are so "your sins may be wiped out" (3:19 NRSV) and "times of refreshing may come" (3:20 NRSV). The restoration of repentant Israel in these last days (3:24) is the condition for a Gentile mission (3:25), the completion of which will trigger the return of the glorified Jesus at the end of history (cf. 1:11) for "the time of universal restoration" (3:21; cf. Rom 11:25-26). Genuine mission activity is always part of the larger and longer plan of God's salvation.

**7.** "So they arrested them and put them in custody until the next day" (4:3 NRSV). Institutional authority is always concerned with deviant voices and movements. Those in elected or established positions of power act in self-interest to protect the interests of those they represent. However, we should guard against the facile collapse of private and public morality. Good people are sometimes caught doing bad things—things that are against their own moral code—for the good of those that employ or elect them.[175] The Sadducees are the antagonists of Luke's narrative world whose exercise of authoritarian (and some might even say "responsible") leadership is repressive and sometimes even murderous. These horrific public actions should not lead us to make negative judgments about the Judaism they represent. To do so is a source of the anti-Semitism that has shaped the destructive relations between Jews and Christians for two millennia.

175. See R. Niebuhr, *Moral Man and Immoral Society* (New York: Macmillan, 1983).

# Acts 4:5-31, Story Two: The Apostles vs. the Sanhedrin, Round One

## NIV

[5]The next day the rulers, elders and teachers of the law met in Jerusalem. [6]Annas the high priest was there, and so were Caiaphas, John, Alexander and the other men of the high priest's family. [7]They had Peter and John brought before them and began to question them: "By what power or what name did you do this?"

[8]Then Peter, filled with the Holy Spirit, said to them: "Rulers and elders of the people! [9]If we are being called to account today for an act of kindness shown to a cripple and are asked how he was healed, [10]then know this, you and all the people of Israel: It is by the name of Jesus Christ of Nazareth, whom you crucified but whom God raised from the dead, that this man stands before you healed. [11]He is

" 'the stone you builders rejected,
which has become the capstone.'[a][b]

[12]Salvation is found in no one else, for there is no other name under heaven given to men by which we must be saved."

[13]When they saw the courage of Peter and John and realized that they were unschooled, ordinary men, they were astonished and they took note that these men had been with Jesus. [14]But since they could see the man who had been healed

[a] 11 Or *cornerstone*    [b] 11 Psalm 118:22

## NRSV

[5]The next day their rulers, elders, and scribes assembled in Jerusalem, [6]with Annas the high priest, Caiaphas, John,[a] and Alexander, and all who were of the high-priestly family. [7]When they had made the prisoners[b] stand in their midst, they inquired, "By what power or by what name did you do this?" [8]Then Peter, filled with the Holy Spirit, said to them, "Rulers of the people and elders, [9]if we are questioned today because of a good deed done to someone who was sick and are asked how this man has been healed, [10]let it be known to all of you, and to all the people of Israel, that this man is standing before you in good health by the name of Jesus Christ of Nazareth,[c] whom you crucified, whom God raised from the dead. [11]This Jesus[d] is

'the stone that was rejected by you, the
builders;
it has become the cornerstone.'[e]

[12]There is salvation in no one else, for there is no other name under heaven given among mortals by which we must be saved."

[13]Now when they saw the boldness of Peter and John and realized that they were uneducated and ordinary men, they were amazed and recog-

[a] Other ancient authorities read *Jonathan*    [b] Gk *them*    [c] Gk *the Nazorean*    [d] Gk *This*    [e] Or *keystone*

## NIV

standing there with them, there was nothing they could say. [15]So they ordered them to withdraw from the Sanhedrin and then conferred together. [16]"What are we going to do with these men?" they asked. "Everybody living in Jerusalem knows they have done an outstanding miracle, and we cannot deny it. [17]But to stop this thing from spreading any further among the people, we must warn these men to speak no longer to anyone in this name."

[18]Then they called them in again and commanded them not to speak or teach at all in the name of Jesus. [19]But Peter and John replied, "Judge for yourselves whether it is right in God's sight to obey you rather than God. [20]For we cannot help speaking about what we have seen and heard."

[21]After further threats they let them go. They could not decide how to punish them, because all the people were praising God for what had happened. [22]For the man who was miraculously healed was over forty years old.

[23]On their release, Peter and John went back to their own people and reported all that the chief priests and elders had said to them. [24]When they heard this, they raised their voices together in prayer to God. "Sovereign Lord," they said, "you made the heaven and the earth and the sea, and everything in them. [25]You spoke by the Holy Spirit through the mouth of your servant, our father David:

" 'Why do the nations rage
 and the peoples plot in vain?
[26] The kings of the earth take their stand
 and the rulers gather together
against the Lord
 and against his Anointed One.[a], [b]

[27]Indeed Herod and Pontius Pilate met together with the Gentiles and the people[c] of Israel in this city to conspire against your holy servant Jesus, whom you anointed. [28]They did what your power and will had decided beforehand should happen. [29]Now, Lord, consider their threats and enable your servants to speak your word with great boldness. [30]Stretch out your hand to heal and perform

[a] 26 That is, Christ or Messiah    [b] 26 Psalm 2:1,2    [c] 27 The Greek is plural.

## NRSV

nized them as companions of Jesus. [14]When they saw the man who had been cured standing beside them, they had nothing to say in opposition. [15]So they ordered them to leave the council while they discussed the matter with one another. [16]They said, "What will we do with them? For it is obvious to all who live in Jerusalem that a notable sign has been done through them; we cannot deny it. [17]But to keep it from spreading further among the people, let us warn them to speak no more to anyone in this name." [18]So they called them and ordered them not to speak or teach at all in the name of Jesus. [19]But Peter and John answered them, "Whether it is right in God's sight to listen to you rather than to God, you must judge; [20]for we cannot keep from speaking about what we have seen and heard." [21]After threatening them again, they let them go, finding no way to punish them because of the people, for all of them praised God for what had happened. [22]For the man on whom this sign of healing had been performed was more than forty years old.

[23]After they were released, they went to their friends[a] and reported what the chief priests and the elders had said to them. [24]When they heard it, they raised their voices together to God and said, "Sovereign Lord, who made the heaven and the earth, the sea, and everything in them, [25]it is you who said by the Holy Spirit through our ancestor David, your servant:[b]

'Why did the Gentiles rage,
 and the peoples imagine vain things?
[26] The kings of the earth took their stand,
 and the rulers have gathered together
 against the Lord and against his
 Messiah.'[c]

[27]For in this city, in fact, both Herod and Pontius Pilate, with the Gentiles and the peoples of Israel, gathered together against your holy servant[b] Jesus, whom you anointed, [28]to do whatever your hand and your plan had predestined to take place. [29]And now, Lord, look at their threats, and grant to your servants[d] to speak your word with all boldness, [30]while you stretch out your hand to heal, and signs and wonders are performed

[a] Gk their own    [b] Or child    [c] Or his Christ    [d] Gk slaves

NIV

miraculous signs and wonders through the name of your holy servant Jesus."

[31]After they prayed, the place where they were meeting was shaken. And they were all filled with the Holy Spirit and spoke the word of God boldly.

NRSV

through the name of your holy servant[a] Jesus." [31]When they had prayed, the place in which they were gathered together was shaken; and they were all filled with the Holy Spirit and spoke the word of God with boldness.

[a] Or *child*

# COMMENTARY

Peter and John are arrested because they testify to Jesus, by whom, they claim, there is "the resurrection of the dead" (4:1-3). They are detained overnight, perhaps to give the authorities opportunity to build their case against the apostles, since so many devout Jews in Jerusalem have come to believe "the word" they proclaim (4:4). But the new political reality is this: The apostles are under arrest (4:3) and the movement they lead is under attack by hostile forces with the political power and financial resources to threaten the Jerusalem mission. Thus Luke shapes this narrative of the apostles' defense against the charges leveled against them to underscore those divine actions that safeguard the mission and are responsible for its continuing success.

By following the literary pattern of Luke's Jerusalem story cycle, the reader is aided in understanding his theological purpose. Once again Luke's narrative is severely gapped and its full meaning depends upon a prior reading of all that has preceded it (see the Overview for 2:14–15:12). With this in mind, then, the first panel (4:5-12) recounts how Peter and John are asked by a council of Jerusalem's "rulers" (4:5; cf. 3:17) to explain the "the power of the name" that has apparently healed the crippled beggar (see 3:1-8). Peter does so in the power of the Holy Spirit (4:8; cf. 2:4; 1:8). The narrative's second panel (4:13-20) briefly tells of the outsiders' reaction; as with Peter's other audiences, "they are amazed" (4:13; cf. 2:12; 3:9-11). Their puzzlement at Peter's rhetorical ability is only deepened by the presence of the healed man standing before them, whom they admit is "a notable sign [= evidence] . . . we cannot deny" (4:16; see also 3:1-8). But their amazement shows their profound ignorance (cf. 3:17) of what they observe but fail to compre-

hend. In turn, they suppose they can squelch the "power of the name" and silence the apostles' witness to it. In response, then, John and Peter add a firm judicial statement (4:19-20) as epilogue to their earlier speech (cf. 4:9-12). The summary of their speech clarifies both the imperative and the motive of their witness to Jesus and makes clear why silencing or subverting the word is impossibile. The final panel of this story (4:21-31) testifies again to a divided Israel. The leaders of unrepentant Israel threaten the apostles (4:21*a*) but will not punish them because of their popular support (4:21*b*-22). The apostles' spiritual authority is aptly envisaged in their benediction that seeks God's "bold" grace to lead all the peoples of Israel (4:24-30). By these responses Luke clarifies the challenges and choices that are occasioned by the apostles' ministry of the word (4:31).

**4:5-12.** Not much is known about the legality of the case that is brought against Peter and John or of the tribunal that hears it. As with many trials depicted in Acts, this one has the informality of a pre-trial hearing when judges and lawyers gather to determine whether there is sufficient evidence to prosecute. This assembly of different "rulers, elders, and scribes" (4:5) makes up the Jerusalem law-court that Luke later identifies by its technical name, "the Sanhedrin" (4:15; cf. 5:21, 27, 34, 41; 6:12, 15; 22:30; 23:1-28; 24:20). Their collective authority in Jerusalem is made cohesive by the high priest, whom Luke identifies as "Annas" (4:6),[176] and its membership is based on their family pedigree (priests), social prominence (elders), and education (scribes). Court opinions were

---

176. Annas was actually high priest emeritus, since he held the office only until 15 CE; he was succeeded eventually (in 17 CE) by his son-in-law Caiaphas, whom Luke also mentions. Caiaphas was probably the high priest when this event took place.

rendered by those most interested and knowledgeable in the issues being debated. For example, legal matters relating to ethical issues (*halakhah*) were routinely deferred to the Pharisees in attendance, even though Sadducees maintained control over most other matters (as well as over the majority of the Sanhedrin's seventy-one members).[177] In every case, however, a vital relationship to the Temple and its politics was central to membership and participation. Thus, the arresting group (4:1) exercised influence upon the Sanhedrin and their concerns eventuated this pre-trial hearing.[178]

The council poses the relevant question: "By what power or by what name did you do this?" (4:7). But the antecedent of "this" (τοῦτο *touto*) is intentionally unclear and may indicate a trick question. On the one hand, "this" could refer to Peter's healing of the man (3:1-8); on the other hand, "this" could refer to Peter's "teaching the people" in and around the Temple (3:12-26) that had resulted in much controversy and many converts (4:1-4). In the narrative context, the question regarding "this" refers to a name rather than to a magical power—to "the name of Jesus Christ" by whom the man is healed in fulfillment of Joel's prophecy (see 3:6; cf. 2:21).

Peter is "filled with the Holy Spirit" (4:8*a;* see 2:4)[179] to give a persuasive and powerful response to whatever accusation is implied by the council's question. In fact, the following speech (4:9-12) is actually a compressed rehearsal of what has already been proclaimed by Peter both on Pentecost (2:22-40) and at Solomon's Portico (3:12-26): the Spirit inspires Peter to define the "this" of the council's leading question in kerygmatic

terms. Before he presents his christological evidence, however, he interprets what occurred as a "good deed" (εὐεργεσία *euergesia*) done to a sick man who is now healed, realizing correctly that the primary purpose of this hearing is to examine the hard evidence of a purported healing (4:9).[180] The healed man himself has already been placed on exhibit (see 4:14) and the purity of Peter's motive is irreproachable—healing is "a good deed done to someone" (4:9), the sort performed by any law-abiding, civil-minded Jew.[181] The true focus of Peter's opening statement is indicated by his word for "healed": σώζω (*sōzō*), which means "saved." Throughout Acts this verb has the double sense of "to heal" and "to save." It echoes the salvation theme of Joel's prophecy (see 2:21), which theme has already been glossed by its previous soundings (see 2:40, 47). The subtext of Peter's explanation, then, is theological rather than legal, and his primary evidence is biblical, not "scientific."

Peter's speech is addressed to the very "rulers" he earlier accused of acting in ignorance regarding Scripture's prophecies about Jesus (see 3:17-18). While he does not actually demand their repentance in this case (cf. 3:19), the sharpened contrast between "Jesus . . . whom you crucified" and "Jesus . . . whom God raised from the dead" (4:10) makes clear that these rulers are not aligned with God's purposes. The unstated implication is that they must "repent and turn to God so that their sins may be wiped out" (3:19).[182] Peter appeals to Ps 118:22 (Ps 117:22 LXX) for proof that their conflict has a divine purpose (see 4:11). Luke cites this same text in his Gospel's parable of the vineyard (Luke 20:17; cf. 1 Pet 2:4, 7) in a collocation of texts gathered around the catchword "stone" (ὁ λίθος *ho lithos*) to warn these same leaders that to reject Jesus is to reject the "cornerstone" of Israel's promised salvation. The intertext forged with Acts implies this same warning. However, in this post-resurrection setting where "the stone" is clearly a messianic metaphor of

---

177. This may explain why the Pharisee Gamaliel, even though a member of the minority party, is asked to give the "majority opinion" in the Sanhedrin's closing argument against the apostles (Acts 5:33-42).

178. The NRSV translation of the ambiguous Greek αὐτοὺς (*autous;* lit., "them") as "prisoners" (4:7; the NIV translates it "Peter and John") seems to stretch the textual and historical evidence. With the semi-circular courtroom in mind, the KJV translation gets it right: "And when they had set them in the midst. . . ."

179. Does this second reference in Acts to the Spirit's filling suggest that the power of Spirit baptism that came with Pentecost is temporary? Jervell is no doubt right when saying that "the speech is understood here to result from the Spirit's miracle-working power." See J. Jervell, *Die Apostelgeschichte,* KEK 3 (Göttingen: Vandenhoeck & Ruprecht, 1998) 178. At moments such as this one in Israel's history, the Spirit of God has enabled the prophets of God to speak with power and insight in order to set Israel on the way of righteousness. The Spirit does not withdraw from the apostles after this speech is finished; that is clear by the "signs and wonders" they continue to perform (5:12). Dunn suggests that this phrase envisages "an occasional 'topping up' of a Spirit once bestowed at Pentecost." See J. D. G. Dunn, *The Acts of the Apostles* (Valley Forge, Pa.: Trinity, 1996) 52-53.

180. Both translations obscure the juridical aspect of this pre-trial hearing by translating ἀνακρίνω (*anakrinō,* "called to account," NIV; "questioned," NRSV) instead of its more literal sense, "critically examined."

181. The term *euergesia* denotes benefaction, which agrees with Luke's general understanding of saving grace. The use of the Greek word for "save" (*sōzō*) for "healing" already commends a more theological accounting of the miracle event.

182. G. Krodel, *Acts,* ACNT (Minneapolis: Augsburg, 1986) 110.

Jesus, the rulers of "official" Israel can no longer be excused for their ignorance (see 3:17). This is their second chance, and to reject the apostolic word is to forfeit their participation in Israel's promised blessings (see 3:12-26; 7:35-42).

The final line of Peter's speech, awkwardly but emphatically stated, offers another synthesis of Luke's theology of salvation with echoes of Joel's prophecy: "There is salvation in no one else, for no other *name* under heaven is given by which *we must be saved* [= healed]" (4:12, italics added). Peter deflects attention from apostolic authority or the miracle to the christological meaning of this redemptive moment. The statement's subtext is easily discerned by the repetition of catchwords from Joel's prophecy ("name," ὄνομα *onoma;* "save," *sōzō;* "heaven," οὐρανός *ouranos*), which is here combined with Luke's δεῖ (*dei,* "must") of divine necessity to confirm that Israel's Scripture testifies to the universal importance of Peter's kerygmatic claims (see 1:16). In this sense, the redemptive significance of the healed man is once again extended beyond the rulers of Jerusalem and "all the people" of Israel to include humankind (see 3:25).

**4:13-18.** What will be the rulers' response to the gospel? Will they repent and turn to God for forgiveness of their sins or remain unrepentant and therefore excluded from the "season of refreshing" that has come with Pentecost (see 3:19-21)? The reader should not be surprised that their initial reaction to Peter's "bold" proclamation is "amazement" (4:13).[183] Nor should we be surprised that their amazement is rooted in mistaken identity (cf. 2:13-15; 3:9-12): They are impressed with the rhetorical ability of "uneducated and ordinary men,"[184] which we know "is due to the

work of the Spirit." The rulers fail to recognize that Peter is an inspired prophet-like-Jesus and that the "filling with the Holy Spirit" (4:8) had elevated his intellectual and rhetorical abilities without benefit of theological training or academic schooling (see 2:4).

Therefore, the council debates the wrong things even though asking the right questions. They have heard and seen the evidence but can offer no countervailing opinion (4:14): "a notable sign has been done through them; we cannot deny it" (4:16b).[185] Rather than repent in faith, they retire into "executive session" where they "discussed the matter with one another" (4:15)! Their discussion finally turns on a political solution, ironically stipulated by Luke's prophetic idiom: "let us warn them to speak no more *in this name* [ἐπί τῷ ὀνόματι τούτῳ *epi tō onomati touto*]" (4:17, italics added). The council's strict ban, motivated by the perceived interests of the city, actually restates and legitimizes Joel's "in the name" formula (2:21): The apostles have won the argument! By failing to recognize them as prophets who carry an inspired word from God to proclaim to Jerusalem, the council seeks to separate the merit of the "good deed" performed "in this name" from its kerygmatic commentary (4:18).[186] In doing so, the rulers seek to keep Israel ignorant of the very means by which "all the people" (see 3:9-11) and "also your rulers" (see 3:17) are guided into a season of refreshment (see 3:19).

**4:19-20.** The apostles famously defy the council's verdict rather than their prophetic commission.[187] Soards calls their response an "epilogue" to Peter's previous speech, continuing its final,

---

183. The glossary of terms Luke uses to describe Peter's speech and the rulers' reaction in 4:13 almost always is used to narrate this sort of encounter between the proclaimed word of God and its Jewish auditors. For example, Luke employs the term παρρησία (*parrēsia,* "boldness") in its various forms to describe the manner of prophetic or inspired proclamation (2:29; 4:29, 31; 9:27-28; 13:46; 18:26; 19:28; 26:26; 28:31), which is possible because of Spirit baptism. Likewise, we anticipate the initial reaction of devout but unbelieving Jews to such bold preaching will be θαυμάζω (*thaumazō,* "amazement"; 2:7; 3:12; 7:31; 13:41). That is, they recognize the numinous because of their loyalty to Israel's God and Scriptures, but they fail to "get it" and so are amazed instead of repentant. These qualities reflect Greco-Roman notions of powerful and persuasive public speaking.

184. These terms are probably not to be taken literally as though Peter were unschooled and could not write or read. They simply recognize the profound difference in social class between those sitting in judgment and the apostles.

185. The helplessness of the Sanhedrin's situation is made more apparent by Luke's use of σημεῖον (*sēmeion* sign) as the idiom for "proof from (Joel's) prophecy" (2:19; cf. Acts 2:22, 43; 4:22, 30; 5:12; 15:12). The profound conflict to which these rulers of "official" Israel are party is between spiritual and political realities, between what God reveals and the city's "mean streets" require of them.

186. Witherington notes that nothing is said in 4:17-18 about preventing the apostles from performing healing miracles, which the council assumes they have power to do. See B. Witherington, *The Acts of the Apostles: A Socio-Rhetorical Commentary* (Grand Rapids: Eerdmans, 1998) 196. This implicit separation of healing miracle from gospel proclamation not only clarifies the antecedent of the ambiguous "this" in the council's opening question (4:7)—the real issue at stake *is* kerygmatic—but the nature of their theological "ignorance" as well.

187. Luke's educated first readers would have known Plato's famous account of Socrates' trial and his courageous (and civil) response to his Athenian jury: "I will obey the god rather than you—and never cease from the practice and teaching of philosophy." Plato *Apology* 29d. Examples of such courage in similar settings are easily found in Jewish writings as well (e.g., Dan 3:16-18; 2 Macc 7:2; Josephus *Antiquities of the Jews* 17.158-59).

firm statement (4:12), and therefore judicial and kerygmatic in substance.[188] "To listen" translates the Greek ἀκούω (akouō), which also connotes obedience in Acts. That is, John and Peter's decision is to obey God's command rather than the council's. In narrative context this command must surely refer to their prophetic vocation, issued by the risen Jesus (see 1:8), which is "to speak about what we have seen and heard" (4:20).[189] From the beginning, the community's mission has been to bear witness to Jesus' resurrection and its redemptive significance for Israel. The "signs and wonders" that outsiders have also witnessed simply supply the platform for their inspired proclamation of the gospel. The subtext of this epilogue, however, includes a political criticism of the council's ability to lead Israel: Its members are unable to speak for God because they are unable to understand (akouō, "listen") the proclamation of God's word or the meaning of the healed man. There is considerable irony, then, in Peter's exhortation to these judges that they "must judge" (κρίνω krinō) for themselves, since to do so would lead to self-condemnation.[190]

**4:21-31.** The concluding panel of this episode is shaped by Luke's assessment of the council's paltry reaction to Peter's bold comment (4:21-22), which contrasts sharply with the apostles' prayerful response (4:23-31). In fact, Luke's shaping of their prayer of thanksgiving (4:24c-30) functions as an important theological commentary that deepens the reader's understanding of Peter's speech before the council, especially its dramatic epilogue.

**4:21-23.** Luke provides the motive of the council's timid decision: They responded "because of the people" (διὰ τὸν λαόν dia ton laon; 4:21; cf. Luke 20:19; Matt 21:26). The reason why the apostles go unpunished, then, is not due to the council's devotion to the law, which might have

constrained them;[191] their repeated threats and their evident desire to teach them a lesson they would not soon forget are frustrated "because of the people," all of whom are praising God. The reader is now in a position to return to 3:17 for a more wakeful reading of Luke's phrasing "I know that [all] you [people] acted in ignorance, *as did your rulers*" (italics added). The contrasting responses drawn here between the Jerusalem's rulers and the "people" of whom they are fearful (cf. 4:25, 27) makes clear that the rulers remain ignorant and therefore fail to "repent and turn to God" (3:19). Not only is there a deep division between the people and their religious rulers, which will make it politically difficult for them to lead, there is also a deep theological division between the rulers and God, which will make it impossible for them to guide Israel through the latter days into the promised season of refreshment. That is, the members of the Sanhedrin, no matter how dedicated they are to Torah and Temple, are unable to bridge the division between repentant and unrepentant Israel; and it is due time for the Twelve to mount Israel's thrones to shepherd all the people of Israel (cf. Luke 22:30).[192] For this reason, Johnson contends—rightly, in my view—that the destination of the apostles' return "to their friends"[193] to report the council's verdict is the apostolate rather than the entire community. These are matters that concern the identity of Israel's leaders and therefore the apostolic circle.[194]

**4:24-30.** Luke's reshaping of his biblical traditions and of this apostolic memory nicely captures the mood and circumstances of the moment (cf. 2:42, 46-47a).[195] The apostles' benedictory recognizes the importance of their spiritual authority and prophetic vocation (see 4:29). As with other speeches in Jewish settings, this one too is a collection of biblical interpretations (midrashim) on alluded and cited biblical texts that interpret the

---

188. M. L. Soards, *The Speeches in Acts: Their Content, Context, and Concerns* (Louisville: Westminster/John Knox, 1994) 47.

189. See P. Anderson, *The Christology of the Fourth Gospel* (Valley Forge, Pa.: Trinity, 1996) 274-77, who persuasively argues that 4:20 reflects the "seeing and hearing" idiom of John's Jesus and preserves the central motifs of the Johannine "witness motif" (cf. John 3:32; 1 John 1:1-3). More interesting to the readers of Acts is Anderson's conclusion that Luke has preserved a memory of Peter's retort (in 4:19) and then also of John's (in 4:20).

190. J. Jervell, *Die Apostelgeschichte,* KEK 3 (Göttingen: Vandenhoeck & Ruprecht, 1998) 181. See also Schneider, *Die Apostelgeschichte,* 1:351-52.

191. So Dunn, *The Acts of the Apostles,* 55.

192. See J. Jervell, *Luke and the People of God* (Minneapolis: Augsburg, 1972) 75-112.

193. This phrase translates πρὸς τοὺς ἰδίους (*pros tous idious,* "to their own") and is unclear. Does "friends" refer to all members of the community or to apostolic colleagues? The NIV's "to their own people" is clearer but mistaken in meaning.

194. L. T. Johnson, *The Acts of the Apostles,* SP 5 (Collegeville, Minn.: Liturgical, 1992) 90.

195. I. H. Marshall, *The Acts of the Apostles,* NTG (Sheffield: JSOT, 1992) 103-4.

---

apostles' conflict with the rulers of "official" Israel and make clear God's intended meaning for all of Israel. The principal text that supplies the canonical context for the apostles' prayer is Ps 2:1-2, cited verbatim in vv. 25b-26. In its biblical setting, Psalm 2 celebrates the enthronement of Israel's king (= David) as God's son, yet the competition is already at work to plot his overthrow—a setting roughly analogous to the one facing the apostles.[196] It is introduced in Acts by an address to and ascription of God as "Sovereign Lord" (Δέσποτα Despota), the Creator of all things (4:24b; cf. 14:15; 17:24), and indicates that the prayer is deeply rooted in a belief in God's provident care over creation and God's plan to restore it (see 3:21; cf. 4:30). David is again introduced as a prophet of God whose words cited from the psalm are words of the Holy Spirit that carry divine authority (4:25a; see 1:16; cf. 2:25-27, 30-31).[197]

The following prayer offers an inspired interpretation of their apostolic/prophetic vocation in terms of the earlier conflict between Jerusalem's leaders, apostolic and priestly. The relevant meaning of their midrash-prayer is in its petition (4:29-30) that is introduced by a new salutation, "And now, Lord" (4:29a). Their petition is for a continuation of the Spirit's power "to speak your word with all boldness"—the very attribute recognized by the Sanhedrin (cf. 4:13)—and for a continuation of the Spirit's "signs and wonders" (4:30) according to Joel's prophecy (cf. 2:19; see 2:22). In simple terms, Luke's shaping of the apostles' petition enshrines the principal theme of his narrative: Apostolic successors live boldly within their vocation where the resources of the Holy Spirit will empower them to continue to do and to teach what the Lord Jesus had begun (1:1).

**4:31.** The Lord God's response to the apostles' petition for power is immediate, dramatic, and confirming: "they were filled with the Holy Spirit and spoke the word of God with boldness" (4:31; see 2:1-4).[198]

---

196. Although there is no evidence of a messianic reading of this psalm prior to Jesus, a christological midrash of this point would surely find here a prophecy of Israel's rejection of Jesus—a principal topic of Peter's speeches to this point in Acts.

197. The word order of this formula has been corrupted, making it difficult to understand. See C. K. Barrett, *A Critical and Exegetical Commentary on the Acts of the Apostles*, 2 vols, ICC (Edinburgh: T. & T. Clark, 1994, 1998) 244-45; J. A. Fitzmyer, *The Acts of the Apostles*, AB 31 (Garden City, N.Y.: Doubleday, 1998) 308-9. The meaning of παῖς (*pais*), translated "servant" and applied here to David, was earlier applied to Jesus (3:13, 26) and could mean "child/son" in reference to his royal status as Israel's king and ancestor to Messiah, God's "child/Son." This latter meaning makes sense in the light of the intended function of Psalm 2 to install the king of Israel as God's son and ruler in God's place over God's people. The continuity between David and Jesus, both God's servant-son, underscores the implied meaning of this difficult phrase: The Holy Spirit inspired David to write this psalm and now inspires the apostles of Jesus to render it.

198. Commentators debate the composition of the recipients of the Holy Spirit in this text. E.g., R. Stronstad, *The Prophethood of All Believers*, JPTSS 16 (Sheffield: Sheffield Academic, 1999) 55-59, 73-75, argues that it must include every believer (now numbering in the thousands) and locates "the place where they were gathered" as the Temple. However, if the petition is made by the apostles to embolden their prophetic ministry, then the theophany that responds to their prayer is restricted to them.

# REFLECTIONS

**1.** "Then filled with the Holy Spirit, Peter said to them . . . and when they realized he was an uneducated and ordinary man, they were amazed" (see 4:8, 13). Jesus warned his disciples to expect the very crisis that Peter and John here encounter: "When they bring you before the synagogues, the rulers, and the authorities, do not worry about how you are to defend yourselves or what you are to say; for the Holy Spirit will teach you at that very hour what you ought to say" (Luke 12:11-12). One of the cultural affectations that has always influenced the religious politics of the church is the value placed upon the educated person and informed opinion. Typically those who aspire to positions of spiritual authority in the life of the church must spend years being properly trained. No one should deny the importance of education in the production of a thoughtful, competent Christian leadership. Yet this story in Acts reminds us that spiritual authority is primarily the result of the Spirit's work in human life and is therefore subject to spiritual disciplines that make us more available to the Spirit's filling. Peter was an ordinary man who did extraordinary things to influence thousands of people because he was "filled with the Holy Spirit." While talent and a fine education are worthy attributes of a Christian leader, there is simply no substitute for the spiritually mature believer whose leadership reflects the rule of the Spirit in her life.

**2.** "There is salvation in no one else" (4:12 NRSV). While the hallmark of the theological conception of Acts is its universalism, whereby the blessings of God's salvation are extended to all people, there is but a single route that leads into life with God. This is sometimes taken as an offense in a day of cultural pluralism that commends diversity and variety. The monotheism of biblical religion is only elevated and intensified by the theocentrism of Acts: God, the only God, has a single plan according to which no one except Jesus can mediate salvation to all people. Today's challenge is to interpret the exclusivity of this way to divine blessing in an idiom that is relevant to all people, no matter what else might characterize them as individuals.

**3.** They "commanded them not to speak or teach at all in the name of Jesus" (4:18 NIV). All of us know from hard experience the foolishness of the children's saying that "sticks and stones may break my bones but words never harm me." Words carry enormous power to do good and evil. They hold sway over us, and all appreciate the political wisdom that whoever controls the "words" influences what goes on in the townsquare and marketplace. The struggle for people/power in Jerusalem between the apostles and the Sanhedrin is over the right to speak and the content of what is said. The most precious civil right of a liberal democracy is the right to free speech, which allows the prophet to afflict the comfortable without fear of reprisal and give equal right to the priest to comfort the afflicted without fear of ridicule. Tragically, this is often not the case within the church. A pundit once remarked that the church is the only army that kills its wounded. The community of believers transformed by God's grace should exemplify the kind of tolerance that will allow thoughtful opinion to be voiced, if only then to be challenged by the prophets among us.

**4.** "When they had prayed, the place in which they were gathered together was shaken" (4:31 NRSV). In response to the official efforts to repress their preaching ministry, the apostles prayed together for ability "to speak your word with great boldness" (4:28). Their prayer (4:24-30) is exemplary of how to petition God when under pressure to silence the gospel. The interpreter should take note first of the effective interplay between worship and witness. The two form an integral whole in Acts and mark out together the community's identity and vocation: Vital witness is not possible without fervent worship. In their prayer the apostles first invoke God's presence (4:24-28). In this confession of who God is and what God has done a particular idea of God emerges that is appropriate for the difficult situation they find themselves in. God is the Creator who is sovereign over and in control of all things. While this does not prevent the "nations to rage" or frustrate the conspiracy against the Messiah, it does mean that God's redemptive plan will finally succeed. Further, this confident trust in God's ultimate triumph issues in a petition for a bold and aggressive witness even in the presence of threats (4:29-30). If the church is too timid of what others may think and does not ask God for enough "boldness" for ministry, it must have timid convictions about who God is, what God has done, and what God will do.

# Acts 4:32–5:16, Interlude: "One Holy and Apostolic Church"

NIV

³²All the believers were one in heart and mind. No one claimed that any of his possessions was his own, but they shared everything they had. ³³With great power the apostles continued to testify to the resurrection of the Lord Jesus, and much grace was upon them all. ³⁴There were no needy persons among them. For from time to time those who owned lands or houses sold them, brought the money from the sales ³⁵and put it at the apostles' feet, and it was distributed to anyone as he had need.

³⁶Joseph, a Levite from Cyprus, whom the apostles called Barnabas (which means Son of Encouragement), ³⁷sold a field he owned and brought the money and put it at the apostles' feet.

5 Now a man named Ananias, together with his wife Sapphira, also sold a piece of property. ²With his wife's full knowledge he kept back part of the money for himself, but brought the rest and put it at the apostles' feet.

³Then Peter said, "Ananias, how is it that Satan has so filled your heart that you have lied to the Holy Spirit and have kept for yourself some of the money you received for the land? ⁴Didn't it belong to you before it was sold? And after it was sold, wasn't the money at your disposal? What made you think of doing such a thing? You have not lied to men but to God."

⁵When Ananias heard this, he fell down and died. And great fear seized all who heard what had happened. ⁶Then the young men came forward, wrapped up his body, and carried him out and buried him.

⁷About three hours later his wife came in, not knowing what had happened. ⁸Peter asked her, "Tell me, is this the price you and Ananias got for the land?"

"Yes," she said, "that is the price."

⁹Peter said to her, "How could you agree to test the Spirit of the Lord? Look! The feet of the men who buried your husband are at the door, and they will carry you out also."

¹⁰At that moment she fell down at his feet and died. Then the young men came in and, finding her dead, carried her out and buried her beside

NRSV

32Now the whole group of those who believed were of one heart and soul, and no one claimed private ownership of any possessions, but everything they owned was held in common. ³³With great power the apostles gave their testimony to the resurrection of the Lord Jesus, and great grace was upon them all. ³⁴There was not a needy person among them, for as many as owned lands or houses sold them and brought the proceeds of what was sold. ³⁵They laid it at the apostles' feet, and it was distributed to each as any had need. ³⁶There was a Levite, a native of Cyprus, Joseph, to whom the apostles gave the name Barnabas (which means "son of encouragement"). ³⁷He sold a field that belonged to him, then brought the money, and laid it at the apostles' feet.

5 But a man named Ananias, with the consent of his wife Sapphira, sold a piece of property; ²with his wife's knowledge, he kept back some of the proceeds, and brought only a part and laid it at the apostles' feet. ³"Ananias," Peter asked, "why has Satan filled your heart to lie to the Holy Spirit and to keep back part of the proceeds of the land? ⁴While it remained unsold, did it not remain your own? And after it was sold, were not the proceeds at your disposal? How is it that you have contrived this deed in your heart? You did not lie to us*ᵃ* but to God!" ⁵Now when Ananias heard these words, he fell down and died. And great fear seized all who heard of it. ⁶The young men came and wrapped up his body,*ᵇ* then carried him out and buried him.

7After an interval of about three hours his wife came in, not knowing what had happened. ⁸Peter said to her, "Tell me whether you and your husband sold the land for such and such a price." And she said, "Yes, that was the price." ⁹Then Peter said to her, "How is it that you have agreed together to put the Spirit of the Lord to the test? Look, the feet of those who have buried your husband are at the door, and they will carry you out." ¹⁰Immediately she fell down at his feet and died. When the young men came in they found her dead, so they carried her out and buried her

*ᵃ* Gk *to men*     *ᵇ* Meaning of Gk uncertain

## NIV

her husband. [11]Great fear seized the whole church and all who heard about these events.

[12]The apostles performed many miraculous signs and wonders among the people. And all the believers used to meet together in Solomon's Colonnade. [13]No one else dared join them, even though they were highly regarded by the people. [14]Nevertheless, more and more men and women believed in the Lord and were added to their number. [15]As a result, people brought the sick into the streets and laid them on beds and mats so that at least Peter's shadow might fall on some of them as he passed by. [16]Crowds gathered also from the towns around Jerusalem, bringing their sick and those tormented by evil[a] spirits, and all of them were healed.

[a] 16 Greek unclean

## NRSV

beside her husband. [11]And great fear seized the whole church and all who heard of these things.

12Now many signs and wonders were done among the people through the apostles. And they were all together in Solomon's Portico. [13]None of the rest dared to join them, but the people held them in high esteem. [14]Yet more than ever believers were added to the Lord, great numbers of both men and women, [15]so that they even carried out the sick into the streets, and laid them on cots and mats, in order that Peter's shadow might fall on some of them as he came by. [16]A great number of people would also gather from the towns around Jerusalem, bringing the sick and those tormented by unclean spirits, and they were all cured.

# COMMENTARY

The apostolic leaders have now been singled out by the religious authorities of Jerusalem for special attention. Their spiritual authority and prophetic practices have disturbed and challenged those with power in the holy city (4:1-2), resulting in the arrest of Peter and John (4:3) and a hearing before the Sanhedrin court (4:5-20). The controversies and conflict provoked by the church's Jerusalem mission will only increase as the narrative unfolds, even though the reader knows that God favors, and God's Spirit empowers, the apostolic leadership team. Although the battle lines are just now drawn, we already know the eventual outcome (see 4:31). Luke's takes pause in his story to continue his keen interest in the Jerusalem community's inner life and especially its communal practice of sharing its possessions with one another. Similar to his first narrative summary (see 2:42-47),[199] this interlude looks back to retrieve

important images of what the church should look like in every age. The reader of Acts is reminded that the church's internal witness is centered by the sharing of goods, even as its external witness is centered by the proclamation of the gospel. Both activities attract favorable attention from "the people," for they publicly demonstrate the church's common life and shared purpose under the aegis of the Holy Spirit.

Luke's second description of the Jerusalem church's common life (4:32-35) is rounded off by contrasting examples of the community's most distinctive internal practice (4:36–5:11): the redistribution of proceeds from the sale of possessions. These proceeds are "laid at the apostles' feet" (4:35, 37; 5:2) in acknowledgment of their spiritual authority and then redistributed to other members according to their financial situation so that "there was not a needy person among them" (4:34a). Barnabas is an exemplar of this practice (4:36-37), while Ananias and Sapphira are negative examples whose tragic deaths underscore the vital importance of this practice as social marker and spiritual barometer for this community (5:1-11).

This interlude concludes by shifting attention

199. See the Commentary on 2:42-47. The ongoing critical problem is whether these summaries are Luke's creations, and essentially "edifying fictions," or idealized, theologized portraits of what actually occurred in earliest Christianity. In the particular example of Barnabas (4:36-37), who became an important figure in earliest Christianity, Luke's narrative almost certainly reworks a personal tradition that is historically accurate and relevant. The subsequent, contrasting case of Ananias and Sapphira (5:1-10) is more difficult to assess. See Conzelmann, *Acts,* 37. However, the authority of Peter and the importance of the rule of common goods form an historical nucleus.

once again from the post-resurrection practices of the faith community to its apostles, whose performance of "signs and wonders" (see 2:19) not only reconfirms God's favorable response to their petition for power (see 4:29-30) but also reconfirms, despite recent internal setbacks and increasing external tension, that the mission they lead continues forward under the direction and power of the Holy Spirit.

**4:32-35.** Luke uses a well-known rhetorical device called chiasmus[200] to summarize the Jerusalem community's internal life in a way that locates the center of its theological gravity. The apostles' magisterial office leads Luke's first summary (see 2:42-43). He begins this second summary by paying special attention to the church's distinctive practice of sharing goods (see 2:44-45) and so brackets the entire unit with the assertion that this community of believers is "of one heart and soul" (καρδία καὶ ψυχὴ μία *kardia kai psychē mia*)—they live together as loving neighbors[201]—as indicated by repudiation of private ownership and by sharing of goods (A = 4:32), redistributing them according to financial need (A´= 4:35 *b*).

In this narrative setting, where the question of who should lead Israel has been placed squarely before the reader, Luke logically continues to point us to the spiritual authority of the Twelve. Renewed in the Spirit's power (see 4:29-31), the apostles witness "to the resurrection of the Lord Jesus" (see 1:8; cf. 4:2) "with great power [δύναμις *dynamis*]" (B = 4:33 *a*). Indeed, now

even the radical economic practices of the community are subject to the apostles' authority: "they laid [the proceeds of what was sold] at the apostles' feet"[202] (B´ = 4:34 *b*-35 *a*).

The resurrection practice of holding everything in common, which enjoys favorable public reputation (see 2:47), is now used as evidence of the apostles' increasing grip on the inner life and destiny of all believers. The repetition of "power" in Acts signals their competency to be prophets-like-Jesus, the medium of God's word in the world. Their power does not derive from their education or social status; it is mediated only "in the name of Jesus" (so 4:7). The function of their "great power" is to bear witness to the risen Jesus (so 1:8) and, therefore, serves only the redemptive purposes of God in continuity with Jesus (so 2:22) according to the Scriptures (cf. 2:19). Given the meaning of "power" supplied by this narrative setting, the reader resists the temptation to think of the apostles as deities and the gifts placed at their feet the equivalent of votive offerings deposited at the feet of religious shrines by pagan worshipers. They are prophets baptized with the Holy Spirit to bear powerful and effective witness of the Sovereign Creator (cf. 4:24), first to the whole house of Israel.

Luke's theological commentary on the community's internal practices is inserted at the center of this vignette to give it principal importance (4:33 *b*-34 *a*). At this point in Acts Luke significantly turns his earlier reference that the community enjoyed the "favor [χάρις *charis*] with all the people" (see 2:47 *a*) toward God's favor: "and [God's] great grace [*charis*] was upon them all" (4:33 *b*; cf. Exod 3:21; 33:12-13).[203] The interplay between these two texts fills out Luke's theology of grace: The effective power of God's grace "upon" the assembly

---

200. The term "chiasmus" derives from the Greek letter χ, which looks like an "X" and indicates that the focus of a reader's attention should be placed at that point where "X marks the spot." As a rhetorical device, then, a chiasmus orders the details of a particular narrative unit into an inverted parallelism (ABB´A´), but then places a distinctive element of the story at its center (or "vertex")—that is, its focal point. Typically, the elements the narrator locates at the beginning and end of the unit (A//A´) "bracket" its overall importance and establish a meaningful interplay with the detail the reader finds at the unit's vertex (C). In this case, the community's social solidarity, indicated by its sharing of goods (4:32//4:35 *b*) is the result of appropriating God's grace and results in the abolition of the poverty that offends God (4:33 *b*-44). (Letters in parentheses refer to elements in this passage's chiastic pattern.)

201. Luke is drawing on popular Greek literature for these images, in which the intimacy of close friendship was often characterized as sharing "one heart and soul" and also personal possessions. The combination of "heart and soul" also finds currency in the OT, notably in the *Shema* (Deut 6:5), to characterize Israel's love for God, which Jesus then applies to neighborly love (Luke 10:27)—even extending to strangers and enemies (Luke 10:29-37). While the Greek ideal included the practical necessity of reciprocity, Luke's description in continuity with the Lord's instruction indicates that there is no thought of payback: Sharing is a spiritual convention that is obligated out of love for God.

202. The practice of placing goods at the apostles' feet, no doubt an element of early Christian liturgy, is a nonverbal way of demonstrating submission to another of higher authority.

203. Luke's expression "grace *upon* [ἐπί *epi*] them all" (4:33 *b*, italics added) is similar to Paul's conception of divine grace in that it denotes "the active favour of God" (Barrett, *Acts,* 254) and is the by-product of the Holy Spirit's work within the community. There is an important difference between Luke and Paul as well. Luke's idea of divine grace probably does not refer to the personal transformation of believers "in Christ" as in Pauline thought. Note that Luke's phrase is not "grace *in* them all" but rather "grace *upon* them all." This phrase suggests that grace functions more like an "impulse" or influence that God has "upon" the entire community to move believers in God's direction. This idea is much closer to the OT idea of God's Spirit or even the more contemporary Jewish idea of a "יצר [*yēṣir,* "impulse"] of righteousness."

of believers enables it to produce those public behaviors that cultivate good will and interest (i.e., civic "favor") among outsiders. Jerusalem's rulers, otherwise upset with the apostles' teaching, did not resent the "good deed" of healing the lame man (see 4:9, 16-17).

More critically, Luke insinuates God's grace upon the community's social life so that "there was not a needy person among them." The practice of landowners selling their property and giving the proceeds over to the apostles for redistribution embodies a sociology of divine grace (4:34b). This summary recalls an element of what Jesus began to teach at Nazareth (cf. Luke 4:16-30). Different words for "favor" are repeated in that narrative to draw attention to Isaiah's promise of eschatological blessing to the poor: The promise of the Lord's "favorable year" for the poor (cf. 4:18-19; Isa 61:1-2a) is already underway among those who "hear" (or believe) the Messiah's prophetic announcement of its arrival (cf. 4:21). Before the Nazarenes turn against Jesus, they confirm the truth of his prophetic commentary as words about God's grace (4:22). The people's ironical response to the Lord's announcement is now recalled by the reader of Acts: The gift of the Holy Spirit given at Pentecost effectively mediates God's "great grace upon them all" that reforms and reshapes them into a community of goods.

**4:36-37.** An early exemplar of this practice is Barnabas. He is evidently influenced by God's "great grace" to sell a field and give the proceeds over to the apostles' for redistribution (4:37). But first Luke provides three salient features of Barnabas's résumé to aid a fuller understanding his action. How so? Barnabas is a Levite. Members of the Levitical household were to be dedicated to the Lord and Israel's spiritual well-being rather than to the stewardship or cultivation of the promised land (Deut 12:12; Josh 14:3-4; cf. Josh 21). Even though the historical record tells us this stipulation was rarely practiced in Jewish history,[204] the inclusion of this detail in the story to illustrate the benefaction of landowners is ironical and may well deepen Luke's sense that an economic reversal has begun with Jesus and Pentecost.

Barnabas is "a native of Cyprus." That is, he is a diaspora Jew, who has become a member of the Jerusalem community. The point certainly continues from Pentecost, when many converts were from the diaspora. However, this feature of his résumé will become more important in Acts when Barnabas defends and then teams with Paul in their mission to the diaspora. Barnabas's submission to the Twelve (4:37) is harbinger of his important role as mediator between Paul and the apostles of the Jerusalem church. If Paul is something of a "loose cannon" and always suspect, Barnabas is not and adds credibility to Paul's witness in Jerusalem.

Barnabas is called Joseph, "to whom the apostles gave the name Barnabas (which means 'son of encouragement')."[205] This action echoes biblical stories of name changes, including Peter's own from "Barjona" (cf. Matt 16:17-19). Typically names change with vocational changes and indicate God's favor, as does Barnabas's obedience to the rule of this community of goods (see 4:33b-34). That the apostles changed Joseph's name underscores once again their religious authority; and thereby, Luke shows that these are social conventions of the apostolic church.

**5:1-11.** The story of Ananias and Sapphira survives in ignominy.[206] Luke finds it useful as a negative example of community life: If Barnabas's actions embody God's favor, then Ananias and Sapphira's actions embody God's disfavor. But does Barnabas's good example imply that the redistribution of goods is voluntary or obligatory? Can God's efficacious grace be resisted and if so what are the consequences? Finally, what is the relationship between God's grace and the community's practice? The answers to these important questions are forthcoming in this story.

204. See Josephus *Life* 68-83.

205. Luke's parenthetical comment is problematic, since the meaning of the second part of his Aramaic name, *nabas,* does not mean "consolation"; the name literally means "Son (*Bar-*) of Nebo (*nabas*)" (see Isa 46:1). I take it that Luke knew as much and that the purpose of his parenthetical comment is to stipulate the *motive* of the name change (i.e., its connotative meaning) rather than its literal meaning.

206. Fitzmyer, *The Acts of the Apostles,* 317, says that this story is "the main incident in Acts that raises questions about the historical value of the Lucan narrative as a whole." Because it relates to the community's practice of redistributing goods, the story's essential plotline seems likely; although composed as an "edifying tale," it nevertheless tells of a known couple and something that happened to them. Without question, Luke reworks the story delivered him by his Jerusalem sources, whatever its form and substance, to fit well into his narrative and illustrate his theological conception.

**5:1-2.** Ananias and Barnabas belong to the same social class: They are landowners and believers who sell their property according to the community's practice of common goods and bring the proceeds to the apostles for redistribution (5:1-2). Unlike Barnabas (cf. 4:37) and subversive of the community's common practice (see 4:34*b*), Ananias "kept back some of the proceeds" (5:2) with his wife's consent (5:1) and knowledge (5:2). Aware that a sin has been committed, the reader may want to know whether there exists in this community a protocol for restoring a sinful believer to fellowship (cf. Matt 18:15-17). Luke's narrative returns only "blanks": we are told nothing of what transpired between verses 2 and 3, how Peter came to know what was in Ananias's "heart" (5:3; cf. 4:32) or whether Ananias was given a chance to repent and be restored (as was Simon the Samaritan, for instance; cf. 8:18-24). Luke's interests are focused on the nature of Ananias's deception and his tragic end—and on what this may teach us about the working of divine grace within the faith community.

**5:3-6.** Peter's rebuke of Ananias carries the weight of a death sentence (cf. 5:5), and it introduces two new elements into the story. Assuming his prophetic perspicuity, the rebuke first of all expresses God's assessment of Ananias's action:[207] His sin is prompted by Satan's filling of "his heart"[208] (5:3) rather than by the Spirit's "filling" (see 2:4), exemplified by Barnabas's generosity. The cosmic struggle between Satan and Spirit has its historical precipitate in Ananias's decision to depart from the community's practice, to remove himself out from "under" God's "great grace" (χάρις μεγάλη *charis megalē* 4:33*b*), and to deceive the apostles and therefore the Spirit.[209]

Moreover, Ananias is deceived because he remains ignorant of the participatory nature of God's "great grace." Peter tells him that the believer retains ownership of property and the personal freedom to do with it what he wants. Thus, if surrendered to the apostles, it is by voluntary action and the result of a individual choice rather than by apostolic coercion (5:4).[210] Ananias is not charged with failure to sell his property or to place the proceeds at the apostles' feet (cf. 5:1-2) but with deception. His act undermines the accord of the community of goods and the authority of the apostles.[211]

A further question from Peter reveals that Ananias is also engaged in a theological deception: "How is it that you have contrived this deed in your heart?" (5:4). His deception of the community (and its Spirit) is finally not Satan's handiwork but the result of a decision that Ananias himself makes by resisting the influence of God's "great grace" (4:33*b*), without which such promises are impossible to keep.[212] The practices of the common life cannot be obeyed out of a sense of duty or as a requirement of saving grace; compliance results as the believer freely responds to the prompting of God's grace.

In hearing Peter's verdict, Ananias dropped dead and was buried, and "great fear seized all who heard of it" (5:5; see 2:43). The reader must presume his is not an accidental or coincidental death. Rather, Peter's words are a death sentence, and Ananias is removed from the community of goods.[213]

**5:7-11.** The second new element follows the first: Three hours after Ananias's death, his unwitting wife, Sapphira, comes before the apostle (5:7).

---

207. This is not to say that Peter is a "divine man" who can read hearts; the narrative does not indicate how he came to know Ananias's motives and is not important to the story. Peter is an inspired prophet whose analysis is "of God." See ibid., 322-23.

208. The "heart" symbolizes one's internal decision-making apparatus. When "Satan," who personifies evil in Luke's narrative world (Luke 10:18; 11:18; 13:16; 22:3, 31; Acts 26:18), enters the believer's heart the result will be to turn that person toward apostasy and treachery. This reference to "heart" probably cues the earlier reference to the community's "one heart" (4:32): Ananias's action was not in solidarity with other believers; however, the presumption of this story is that he is a full member of the faith community.

209. The parallelism between Luke's stories of Ananias and Judas (see 1:16-20) is often noted by commentators: Both are insiders who are cursed by God because of actions taken against the community for love of money—in Judas's case, to betray God's Messiah, and in Ananias's case to lie to God's Spirit. Of course, the shift of referent to the Spirit in Luke's narrative of Ananias's deception makes sense only after Pentecost.

210. The community of goods is often compared to the Essene community at Qumran. Luke's narrative, however, makes clear an important difference between the two: The Essenes required the surrender of all property upon admission to membership as an element of their vow to deny the world; the Jerusalem community did not require compliance to the rule of common goods for membership. Evidently, this was a choice that each made in counsel with the Holy Spirit.

211. L. T. Johnson, *The Acts of the Apostles,* SP 5 (Collegeville, Minn.: Liturgical, 1992) 88.

212. Why Ananias resists God's grace is not stated. Luke's use of possessions as a narrative theme suggests that he is deeply concerned to spell out the spiritual pitfalls of trying to juggle the secular socioeconomic values with a vital piety. Therefore, the interpreter may reasonably assume that Ananias falls victim to theological deception and resists the influence of God's grace because of his undue acquisitiveness.

213. B. Witherington, *The Acts of the Apostles: A Socio-Rhetorical Commentary* (Grand Rapids: Eerdmans, 1998) 216, constructs a plausible historical explanation: Ananias suffers a fatal heart attack resulting from being publicly unmasked and shamed by Peter's words.

She, too, receives his rebuke (5:9; cf. 5:3-4), and she also dies upon hearing it and is buried "beside her husband" (5:10; cf. 5:6). The second act concludes on the same note: "Great fear seized the whole church and all who heard about these events" (5:11; cf. 5:5). Critically, the flow of this parallelism is interrupted, however, by Peter's initial query of her: "Tell me, is this the price you and Ananias got for the land?" (5:8). The reader knows that even though Sapphira entered "not knowing" what had happened to her husband (5:7), she did know his deception fully (cf. 5:2). That is, Peter exposes her as Ananias's accomplice. Yet, at another level, Peter's question invites Sapphira's repentance and restoration. Had she not lied in response, Peter's judgment would not have been rendered. Again, his questioning of Sapphria underscores the importance of the believer's choices in determining the outcome of God's provident care of God's people.

**5:12-16.** The final pericope of Luke's interlude concentrates the reader's attention even more keenly on the Twelve, their prophetic powers, and their growing influence among "the people" of God that now stretches beyond the city limits of Jerusalem (5:16). Luke is preparing the reader for the next story of the church's Jerusalem mission when the apostles' authority comes under attack again.

Much of this summary is familiar to the reader of Acts: The theological implication of the phrase "signs and wonders" (5:12) is deduced by its earlier uses (see 2:22, 43; 4:16, 22, 30) as the continuing realization of Joel's prophecy about the Spirit's outpouring in "the last days" of Israel's history (see 2:19). The apostles, through whom the Spirit's "signs and wonders" are performed in Jerusalem, are God's endtime prophets who are called and empowered to gather Israel together for the day of their salvation. While their prophetic ministry to this point in Acts has focused on their inspired interpretation of Scripture and powerful proclamation of the word, here Luke adds a more detailed summary of their healing ministry that brings them more completely into continuity with the Lord Jesus, who similarly healed and cast out the demons of those who came to him from surrounding towns (5:15-16; cf. Luke 4:40-41 and par.). Despite the disapproval of the rulers of "official" Israel (see 4:5-31), their prophetic ministry evidently continues with increasing success "among the people" (5:12; cf. 4:17). Indeed, Luke tells us that "more and more believed in the Lord" (5:14; cf. 2:41; 4:4). These numinous images are used to persuade us of the Twelve's enormous and compelling powers. Indeed, they are so astounding—even extending to Peter's shadow (5:15)![214]—and intimidating that "the rest" of the people are too afraid to believe and "dared not join" (5:13) the congregation gathered at the Temple's Solomon's Portico for worship (see 3:11). Why does Luke add this puzzling reference to "the rest" (τὰ λοιπά *ta loipa*) who "dared not join" (οὐδεὶς ἐτόλμα κολλᾶσθαι *oudeis etolma kollasthai*) the remnant community for worship (5:13a)?[215] Unlike the hostile rulers of Jerusalem these nonbelieving Jews "held the apostles in high regard" (5:13b). Despite the apostles' great success and growing public acclaim, "the rest" of Israel did not join the faithful remnant at Solomon's Portico because they had not yet called upon the name of the Lord and were not yet saved.

214. The referent behind "Peter's shadow" is uncertain and is perhaps closest to the gospel's story of the woman touching Jesus' garment as he walked by (Luke 8:43 and par.) or Greek myths of "divine men." While no doubt hyperbolic, the reader cannot miss Luke's point: Peter radiates the power of God for the purpose of witness and (now) leadership.

215. E. Haenchen, *The Acts of the Apostles* (Philadelphia: Westminster, 1971) 242, admits that the exegete is "helpless" in determining the meaning of Luke's phrase "the rest who dared not join." H. Conzelmann, *The Acts of the Apostles,* trans. J. Limburg et al., ed. E. J. Epp and C. R. Matthews, Hermeneia (Philadelphia: Fortress, 1987) 39, blames Luke for a "clumsy" narrative. In any case, it is doubtful that "the rest" refers to those believers who are not apostles. So R. Pesch, *Die Apostelgeschichte,* 2 vols., EKKNT 5 (Zurich: Benziger, 1986) 1:206; Johnson, *The Acts of the Apostles,* 95), since they are contrasted with "all" the believers of 5:12. With Barrett and others, then, it seems best to understand "the rest" as nonbelievers. See C. K. Barrett, *A Critical and Exegetical Commentary on the Acts of the Apostles,* 2 vols, ICC (Edinburgh: T. & T. Clark, 1994, 1998) 274. Perhaps Luke has in mind the implied distinction in the OT prophetic writings between a faithful remnant within Israel and "the rest" (or unfaithful) Israel (e.g., Isa 11:11; 37:31-32; Jer 6:9; 44:7, 12-13, 28).

# REFLECTIONS

**1.** "With great power the apostles gave their testimony to the resurrection of the Lord Jesus" (4:33*a* NRSV). Acts 4:32-35 is read on the Second Sunday of Easter with John's account of the Spirit's arrival—the so-called Johannine Pentecost (cf. John 20:19-31). This Gospel lesson includes the poignant and important exchange between Jesus and Thomas, who demands and is given the hard evidence of the Lord's resurrection. Their conversation together on the evening of the first Easter concludes with Jesus' pronouncement of blessing on those who believe without seeing him in the flesh. The earlier arrival of the Spirit helps the interpreter understand what Jesus implies: The Spirit's life within the community of disciples in the Lord's absence will help shape and fortify relationships between them that will cultivate faith and bring others to faith. A vital and vigorous faith in the living Jesus can only be formed within a community of the Spirit. This lesson from the Gospel is the pretext for this lesson from Acts. The powerful images collected together in this passage—among the most radical in Scripture related to our possessions—are interpreted under the light of Easter and Pentecost. Indeed, the formation of a community of goods is a *realistic* prospect only because God's transforming benevolence symbolized by the resurrection is now realized wherever the Holy Spirit resides.

**2.** "There was not a needy person among them" (4:34 NRSV). Possessions are an important symbol of power. How possessions are used provide important social markers about the nature of human relations within particular groups, whether families or churches. The value we place on private ownership, not only on what we purchase but the motives for acquiring particular brands or models, is an expression of our inmost and utmost loyalties. Few biblical books are as important as Acts in providing the church with teaching and exemplars about the proper use of our wealth. Other books, such as James, are important in helping their faithful readers form proper attitudes and responses while struggling with the poverty and powerlessness of a socially marginal existence. This is not the case with Acts, whose implied audience has wealth to share with others and whose poverty is more spiritual than social. Both the positive (Barnabas) and negative (Ananias and Sapphira) examples have wealth; moreover, their stories pay little attention to the effects of their generosity or greed upon the community's poor. The importance of this passage and others like it in Acts (see the Reflections at 2:42-47), then, is to provide its readers with principles and illustrations that encourage the formation of a community of goods that exemplifies friendship and spiritual maturity by the manner it handles its wealth.

**3.** "Those who believed were of one heart and soul" (4:32 NRSV). The first principle the community of goods follows is one of perspective. A way of thinking is decisive to a way of doing. This is especially true of human relationships, which his why in Matthew's Sermon on the Mount Jesus ratchets up the manner of a "righteous" life by giving equal moral weight to the way the disciple thinks of another (see Matt 5:21-48). Luke begins his summary of the community's life together with this familiar description of friendship among Greek moral philosophers. "All is shared between friends," Aristotle taught. Congregational solidarity evinces more than shared beliefs; to share "one heart and soul" implies a level of intimacy with and commitment to others that blurs the boundaries of personal rights or private property. A community of goods is a community full of friends. It is important, therefore, to cultivate a way of thinking about other believers as precious friends, as "soulmates." To the extent we come to value others and what they need more than we do our possessions and what we want, we will come to think of what we own as "common property."

**4.** "As many as owned lands or houses sold them and brought the proceeds of what was sold. They laid it at the apostles' feet, and it was distributed to each as any had need" (4:34*b*-35 NRSV). The proper exercise of spiritual authority is crucial in the formation of a community of friends. It is difficult to mobilize a people to "practice resurrection" in their common life without having competent leaders who instruct and exemplify the principles that warrant such a practice. The apostles lead by example in a manner that inspires trust and reverence and prompts the believers to submit to them for the good of the whole. They are also the distribution center of the community's life; they are in a position to know all who have need and they have the maturity to discern what an equitable distribution of goods entails. What would it mean in our own time for Christian leaders to invigorate and inspire the church by their teaching and example to act against the grain of an acquisitive and materialistic culture?

**5.** "And great grace was upon them all" (4:33b NRSV). The act of laying proceeds at the apostles' feet not only symbolizes submission to their religious authority over the community's life, it also symbolizes a self-emptying spirituality that follows the pattern of Jesus' suffering for the salvation of others. One does not just do generosity; new habits of mind and spirit must be developed before new religious practices occur. The problem with the Greek pattern of friendship according to which all things were shared between kindred spirits is that human will left to itself rarely accommodates such an ideal. The experience of God's transforming grace—God's "great grace"—enables believers to work in partnership with God through dispossession of their self-interest.

**6.** "Tell me whether you and your husband sold the land for such and such a price" (5:8 NRSV). J. Polhill remarks that the teacher of this hard passage "must not pass (it) off—as an adjunct to Luke's ideal portrait of the church. If the incident makes us feel uncomfortable, it should. It deals with money—and the pitfalls of wealth."[216] Peter's question to Sapphira cuts to the heart of the lessons learned in this story. The community of goods must first of all be a community of friends. The religious practice of generosity envisages new and elevated way of seeing other believers that is possible only by reliance upon the grace of God. Peter gives Sapphira the chance to retreat from her earlier conspiracy with her husband to choose greed over grace. Her marital relationship with Ananias is the most intimate friendship possible between human beings; the interpreter must imagine how difficult it is to choose against one's spouse. Yet her apostasy is precisely that she chose in favor of him rather than God, breaking the circle of friendship that joined their community in "one heart and soul."

**7.** "But the people held them in high esteem" (5:13 NRSV). What is it that nonbelievers— "the people"—recognized about the apostles? Clearly they offered a charismatic leadership in a different key from that sounded by other leaders in Jerusalem. But new patterns of leadership, as with most fads, wear quickly. Luke's profile of the apostles in this passage concentrates on two enduring attributes that galvanize a public's attention. First, they were power brokers: Acts displaying God's resurrection power were "done among the people through the apostles" (5:12a) and "they were all cured" (5:16b). The exercise of these "signs and wonders" is not for self-promotion, which was evidently of little concern to the apostles. They mediated God's power to make *others* whole. Second, they were found in Solomon's Portico at the Temple (5:12b; see 3:11) doing what was forbidden by those in charge of public propriety. Later Peter will tell the Sanhedrin simply and modestly that "we must obey God rather than human authority" (see 5:29). The courage of one's core convictions is the substance of which heroes are made. This was certainly true in Luke's world; it is true is our own day as well. Thus, while the people largely ignore the council's authority (cf. 5:41-42), Peter's presence evokes the fear of God (5:11).

216. J. P. Polhill, *The Acts of the Apostles* (Nashville: Broadman, 1992) 162.

# Acts 5:17-42, Story Three: The Apostles vs. the Sanhedrin, Round Two

## NIV

[17]Then the high priest and all his associates, who were members of the party of the Sadducees, were filled with jealousy. [18]They arrested the apostles and put them in the public jail. [19]But during the night an angel of the Lord opened the doors of the jail and brought them out. [20]"Go, stand in the temple courts," he said, "and tell the people the full message of this new life."

[21]At daybreak they entered the temple courts, as they had been told, and began to teach the people.

When the high priest and his associates arrived, they called together the Sanhedrin—the full assembly of the elders of Israel—and sent to the jail for the apostles. [22]But on arriving at the jail, the officers did not find them there. So they went back and reported, [23]"We found the jail securely locked, with the guards standing at the doors; but when we opened them, we found no one inside." [24]On hearing this report, the captain of the temple guard and the chief priests were puzzled, wondering what would come of this.

[25]Then someone came and said, "Look! The men you put in jail are standing in the temple courts teaching the people." [26]At that, the captain went with his officers and brought the apostles. They did not use force, because they feared that the people would stone them.

[27]Having brought the apostles, they made them appear before the Sanhedrin to be questioned by the high priest. [28]"We gave you strict orders not to teach in this name," he said. "Yet you have filled Jerusalem with your teaching and are determined to make us guilty of this man's blood."

[29]Peter and the other apostles replied: "We must obey God rather than men! [30]The God of our fathers raised Jesus from the dead—whom you had killed by hanging him on a tree. [31]God exalted him to his own right hand as Prince and Savior that he might give repentance and forgiveness of sins to Israel. [32]We are witnesses of these things, and so is the Holy Spirit, whom God has given to those who obey him."

## NRSV

17Then the high priest took action; he and all who were with him (that is, the sect of the Sadducees), being filled with jealousy, [18]arrested the apostles and put them in the public prison. [19]But during the night an angel of the Lord opened the prison doors, brought them out, and said, [20]"Go, stand in the temple and tell the people the whole message about this life." [21]When they heard this, they entered the temple at daybreak and went on with their teaching.

When the high priest and those with him arrived, they called together the council and the whole body of the elders of Israel, and sent to the prison to have them brought. [22]But when the temple police went there, they did not find them in the prison; so they returned and reported, [23]"We found the prison securely locked and the guards standing at the doors, but when we opened them, we found no one inside." [24]Now when the captain of the temple and the chief priests heard these words, they were perplexed about them, wondering what might be going on. [25]Then someone arrived and announced, "Look, the men whom you put in prison are standing in the temple and teaching the people!" [26]Then the captain went with the temple police and brought them, but without violence, for they were afraid of being stoned by the people.

27When they had brought them, they had them stand before the council. The high priest questioned them, [28]saying, "We gave you strict orders not to teach in this name,[a] yet here you have filled Jerusalem with your teaching and you are determined to bring this man's blood on us." [29]But Peter and the apostles answered, "We must obey God rather than any human authority.[b] [30]The God of our ancestors raised up Jesus, whom you had killed by hanging him on a tree. [31]God exalted him at his right hand as Leader and Savior that he might give repentance to Israel and forgiveness of sins. [32]And we are witnesses to these things, and so is the Holy Spirit whom God has given to those who obey him."

[a] Other ancient authorities read *Did we not give you strict orders not to teach in this name?* [b] Gk *than men*

## NIV

33When they heard this, they were furious and wanted to put them to death. 34But a Pharisee named Gamaliel, a teacher of the law, who was honored by all the people, stood up in the Sanhedrin and ordered that the men be put outside for a little while. 35Then he addressed them: "Men of Israel, consider carefully what you intend to do to these men. 36Some time ago Theudas appeared, claiming to be somebody, and about four hundred men rallied to him. He was killed, all his followers were dispersed, and it all came to nothing. 37After him, Judas the Galilean appeared in the days of the census and led a band of people in revolt. He too was killed, and all his followers were scattered. 38Therefore, in the present case I advise you: Leave these men alone! Let them go! For if their purpose or activity is of human origin, it will fail. 39But if it is from God, you will not be able to stop these men; you will only find yourselves fighting against God."

40His speech persuaded them. They called the apostles in and had them flogged. Then they ordered them not to speak in the name of Jesus, and let them go.

41The apostles left the Sanhedrin, rejoicing because they had been counted worthy of suffering disgrace for the Name. 42Day after day, in the temple courts and from house to house, they never stopped teaching and proclaiming the good news that Jesus is the Christ.[a]

[a] 42 Or Messiah

## NRSV

33When they heard this, they were enraged and wanted to kill them. 34But a Pharisee in the council named Gamaliel, a teacher of the law, respected by all the people, stood up and ordered the men to be put outside for a short time. 35Then he said to them, "Fellow Israelites,[a] consider carefully what you propose to do to these men. 36For some time ago Theudas rose up, claiming to be somebody, and a number of men, about four hundred, joined him; but he was killed, and all who followed him were dispersed and disappeared. 37After him Judas the Galilean rose up at the time of the census and got people to follow him; he also perished, and all who followed him were scattered. 38So in the present case, I tell you, keep away from these men and let them alone; because if this plan or this undertaking is of human origin, it will fail; 39but if it is of God, you will not be able to overthrow them—in that case you may even be found fighting against God!"

They were convinced by him, 40and when they had called in the apostles, they had them flogged. Then they ordered them not to speak in the name of Jesus, and let them go. 41As they left the council, they rejoiced that they were considered worthy to suffer dishonor for the sake of the name. 42And every day in the temple and at home[b] they did not cease to teach and proclaim Jesus as the Messiah.[c]

[a] Gk Men, Israelites    [b] Or from house to house    [c] Or the Christ

# COMMENTARY

The plotline and logic of the third story of Luke's Jerusalem cycle unfolds according to its missionary pattern: (1) The opening episode (5:17-23) tells of God's wondrous intervention on behalf of the imprisoned apostles, (2) whose unexplained escape "perplexes" their hostile captors (5:24-28). (3) The result is to mistake the motive and content of the apostles' teaching ministry in Jerusalem, which leads to Peter's kerygmatic clarification (5:29-32). (4) Peter's gospel proclamation occasions both increased conflict between the opposing leaders of a divided Israel (5:33-40) and the joyful obedience of the apostles (5:41-42).

The elements of this narrative unit are broadly reminiscent of Luke's second story (see 4:5-31), which suggests that they were written to be read together as mutually interpreting narratives of apostolic vocation and authority.[217] Yet Luke

217. Such literary doublets are characteristic of Luke's narrative art—e.g., the broad parallelism between the story of Pentecost in Acts and the subsequent story of Peter and John's healing of the lame man. The modern discussion of Lukan doublets puzzle over whether there is a single historical referent behind them or whether there are sufficient differences in detail and sources to warrant the conclusion that these stories are of two different events. See Fitzmyer, *Acts*, 332. Whatever one's conclusion is on this point, it seems evident that Luke's intention is for his readers to read similar stories reflexively, the details of the one filling in the narrative gaps and thickening the meaning of the other.

introduces new themes into this account, two of which are noteworthy in expanding our understanding of the apostles' prophetic vocation and spiritual authority. The "angel of the Lord" (ἄγγελος κυρίου *angelos kyriou*) makes its first appearance in Acts (5:19; cf. 7:30, 35, 38; 8:26; 10:3; 12:7-11, 23; 27:23). Although a few commentators suggest that a Hellenistic motif supplies a working model for the angel's role in Acts,[218] angelic intervention is also a common literary theme of biblical narrative. Angels are not merely agents of divine power who are able to reorder historical circumstances according to God's plans; they also deliver messages that disclose the theological particulars of God's word. These narrated angelic activities insinuate God's provident control into events that seem out of control or to be threatening God's redemptive plans.

The other new feature of this story is Gamaliel's speech (5:34-40). The protocol that allows for his speech and reaction to it provides an important perspective on the Sanhedrin. But Gamaliel speaks as a Pharisee. Depending on whether the reader perceives the motive of his speech to be ironic or supportive of the apostles' mission, Luke's subtext may intend to set the political programs and intentions of the Sadducean and Pharisaic parties at odds for future reference (see 22:30–23:10). The reader could suppose at the outset of this story that the Pharisees, whose core beliefs (Messiah, resurrection, restored Israel, a coming new order, spirit world) are similar to those already proclaimed by Peter and later by Paul, would naturally be more supportive of the apostles' teaching ministry than the Sadducees; this story may confirm such a suspicion.[219] In any case, the profile of the Pharisees in Acts, where some become believers (15:5) and Paul professes loyalty to his Pharisaic roots (23:6-9; 26:5), is in sharp contrast to that of the Gospels, where Pharisees unite with other religious and political groups in opposition to Jesus (see Matt 22:23–23:39; cf. Luke 13:31).[220]

**5:17-23.** There is good reason for the high priest, the chief justice of the Sanhedrin and leader of "the sect of the Sadducees"[221] (5:17), to be upset with the apostles. Earlier this same council had demanded their silence (cf. 4:21), perhaps even implying their acquiescence to the Sadducees' political authority in Jerusalem. Their demand went unheeded. In fact, the incorrigible apostles petitioned God for even greater prophetic boldness (cf. 4:24-30), with dramatic results evident in both internal (4:31–5:11) and external (5:12-16) venues. Sharply put, the people feared the apostles and were attracted to their message in increasing numbers, while the Sadducees were "filled with jealousy"[222] (5:17). The result is as we might anticipate: they arrest the apostles, not only Peter and John as before, and lock them all up in "the public prison" (τήρησις δημοσία *tēresis dēmosia* 5:18).[223]

Luke's clipped narrative of the angel's jailhouse intervention includes the two essential components of divine assistance: the liberating act and the commanding word (cf. Gen 16:7-11; 22:10-18; 31:11-13; Exod 3:2-6).[224] Under the cover of night, an angel is dispatched by Jesus to free his apostles from jail.[225] The "prison escape" is a literary

---

218. E.g., Johnson, *The Acts of the Apostles*, 97, mentions Euripides' tale of Bacchus liberating a group of his persecuted followers from prison. See also Euripides *Bacchae* 346-640.

219. H. C. Kee, *To Every Nation Under Heaven: The Acts of the Apostles*, NTC (Valley Forge, Pa.: Trinity, 1997) 83-84, reminds us that the Pharisees were hardly the "pious nitpickers" or rigid legalists of popular distain, but were rather devout believers who sought to live life in conformity with the Law of Moses as Scripture taught it ("written law") and as they interpreted it ("oral law"). They often met in informal groups for Bible study and prayer, and demanded rigorous attention to religious and moral purity in obedience to God.

220. See R. C. Tannehill, *The Acts of the Apostles*, vol. 2 of *The Narrative Unity of Luke-Acts: A Literary Interpretation* (Minneapolis: Fortress, 1990) 2:67.

221. Even though the word "sect" (αἵρεσις *hairesis*) is the root of "heresy," and may denote this in Paul's judicial although ironical use in 24:14 (cf. 24:5), its meaning here is political and refers to a party (so also 15:5). See Conzelmann, *Acts*, 41.

222. "Jealousy" translates ζῆλος (*zēlos*), a term that typically appears in contemporary catalogues of moral vices. While some interpreters want to give it a religious meaning—a zeal for the truth (see Barrett, *Acts*, 283)—Luke's use of it in Acts is clearly a negative judgment on the moral character of those to whom it is assigned (cf. 13:45). This observation is made more important by Luke's connection of character with one's ability to discern truth. Johnson, *The Acts of the Apostles*, 98, notes that "envy" is often the chief motive for murder in Hellenistic moral philosophy, which may explain the Sanhedrin's murderous reaction to Peter's speech in 5:33.

223. The phrase "the public prison" has two plausible meanings, and scholars are divided as to which is best here. Both the NIV and the NRSV take *dēmosia* as an adjective, "public," modifying "prison"; but others take *dēmosia* as an adverb to emphasize the more public or demonstrative nature of the arrest. See Haenchen, *The Acts of the Apostles*, 249.

224. Dunn is puzzled by Luke's matter-of-fact and abbreviated narrative of this episode, when compared to the later and more fulsome parallel story of Peter's prison escape (12:6-11; cf. 16:23-24). He suggests that the jailbreak of 5:17-18 was the bold work of a sympathizer on the prison staff, whose role in the church's retelling of the story was likened to the "angel of the Lord." See J. D. G. Dunn, *The Acts of the Apostles* (Valley Forge, Pa.: Trinity, 1996) 67-68.

225. The phrase "of the Lord" translates the genitive noun *kyriou* (Jesus; 2:36) and denotes here the source from which the "angel" (*angelos*) derives rather than the angelic appearance of the exalted Lord Jesus.

theme that symbolizes the futile attempt to subvert the redemptive purposes of God by silencing God's prophetic word. In this setting, where those attached to the Temple are responsible for their arrest, the apostles are instructed to continue their ministry "in the temple." They and not the Sanhedrin elders are the legitimate leaders of Israel; they are the ones who are called and empowered by God to teach the people. The liberation of the apostles to preach the gospel "in the temple" makes clear the triumph of "the whole message about this life" they proclaim over all other alternatives.[226] Obedient to the angel's (= the Lord's) instruction, the apostles return to the Temple "at daybreak and went on with their teaching"[227] (5:21a).

The following panel paints a somewhat sarcastic portrait of the high priest and his Sadducean entourage (cf. 5:17). They arrive prepared to indict their prisoners (5:21b), only to find them missing (5:22) without reasonable explanation (5:23; the literary intent is the rough equivalent of "rubbing it in"). The Sadducees, who convened this assembly to demonstrate their confidence and authority, are shamed before their judicial and cultural peers.[228] Indeed, at the very moment of their humiliation, the apostles are teaching the people of Jerusalem in the Temple—the one place the Sadducees presumed to have control!

**5:24-28.** The central character of this brief episode is "the captain of the temple" (5:24, 26). He is responsible for the safeguard of the prisoners and is especially affected by the apostles' disappearance. He is "perplexed," no doubt because he worries what will become of his career and the future of those he serves and who serve him. The reader of Acts, however, is familiar with this response to the activity of God. In fact, the very word that translates "perplexed" (διαπορέω

diaporeō) is used earlier by Luke to describe the response of pious Jews to the miraculous speech at Pentecost (see 2:12). There as here, perplexity is the response of an eyewitness who lacks understanding to interpret the theological significance of a miracle for the future of Israel.

When the captain and his assistants receive the report that the prisoners "are standing in the temple and teaching the people" according to the angel's instruction, their initial response is as it should be: Police are duty-bound to retrieve their prisoners and bring them to "stand before the council." But Luke's description suggests anything but the ordinary! What seems strange, even comical, is that the captain takes extraordinary precaution "because they were afraid of being stoned by the people" (5:26). Surely their fear is another indication of the apostles' popular support in Jerusalem. However, the precise nature of their fear—"of being stoned" by pious Jews—indicates that the support for the apostles is *religious* in nature. Execution by stoning, while illegal in Roman provinces, might be carried out on the sly by devout Jews on any other Jew suspected of blasphemy. This emotional response of the temple police to the apostles is further evidence that at the popular level religious authority in Jerusalem has shifted to the apostles; the Sanhedrin has every reason to be concerned.

This new political reality is the subtext of the high priest's scolding of the apostles: "We ordered you to stop teaching in this name" (5:28). They have disobeyed the Council's ban (see 4:18) in obedience to God's command with the result of increased power and widespread popularity—such that even now the opponents fear for their lives! The high priest's accusation reflects his theological obduracy as well and underscores the real reason for the shift of religious power in Jerusalem. His comment that the apostles "are determined to bring this man's blood *upon us*"[229] (5:28, italics added) not only reflects the arrogance of his institutional authority but also the mistaken presumption that the actions of the apostles are politically motivated. However, the apostles teach because it

---

226. "This life" probably recalls Peter's earlier title for Jesus, "Author of life" (ἀρχηγὸς τῆς ζωῆς archēgos tēs zōēs; see 3:15) and indicates "the new life offered by Jesus," which is similar in meaning to Paul's subsequent phrase "message of this salvation" in 13:26. The angel's reference to "people" (ὁ λαός ho laos) refers to the "people of Israel," who are the first recipients of this good news (see 3:17). See Barrett, *Acts*, 284.

227. Josephus *Antiquities of the Jews* 18.29 tells us that while the gates to the Temple remained open through the night, faithful Jews began their day of worship "at daybreak." Luke no doubt adds this small detail to his narrative to emphasize the piety of the apostles and their spiritual authority to lead faithful Israel.

228. See E. Haenchen, *The Acts of the Apostles* (Philadelphia: Westminster, 1971) 250-51.

229. The antecedent of "upon us" (ἐφ' ἡμᾶς eph' hēmas) is unclear, since in earlier teaching Peter blamed the Jewish people generally (see 2:23; 3:13) but notably their rulers as well (3:17). Almost certainly in this comment, however, the high priest has only the Sanhedrin in mind. See Barrett, *Acts*, 288.

is their prophetic vocation to do so; and they teach in the temple's courtyard because they are instructed to do so by the "angel of the Lord."

**5:29-32.** As in the prior stories of Acts, Peter is prompted to speak out to correct mistakes made by perplexed nonbelievers (see 2:13; 3:11; 4:13-17). Luke adds "and the apostles" to Peter's answer, not because all of them spoke in unison but because they stood united in agreement with what Peter said, acknowledging his apostolic authority for saying it. In this setting, the mistake made by the high priest is to assume that he is the political target of an opposition party led by these apostles: They were teaching in the Temple to provoke a popular uprising against Sanhedrin (or Saduccean) authority in order to replace the council with the Apostolate as the center of religious (and political) authority in Jerusalem.[230] Peter's famous and provocative reply attempts to make clear the true motive: "We must obey God rather than men [i.e., the men—no women!—seated on the Sanhedrin]!" (5:29; see 4:19-20; cf. Num 22:38). Even though it is a more sharply stated version of what was said before to the Council, Peter's reply is puzzling because it does not directly respond to the high priest's accusation, as one might expect of a judicial retort. It is more puzzling because on face value Peter's statement is tautological in a Jewish setting: The high priest, a dedicated monotheist, would surely not disagree with Peter's claim, nor with Peter's assumption that it is biblically based. Peter's opening comment reminds the council that the principal concern of religious leadership is theological, not political or institutional or personal.[231] Indeed, Gamaliel's exhortation that follows (see 5:33-39) provides additional commentary on Peter's assertion and essentially agrees with it.

What follows in Peter's speech, however, commends a missionary motive: In a wonderfully concise way, Peter preaches the gospel to the council![232] By repeating "God," Luke shapes this speech to provide a normative definition of obedience "to God rather than men." Simply put, to obey God means to confirm as true the claims of the Christian gospel. This seems so because "the God of our ancestors raised up Jesus" (5:30) and "exalted him . . . that he might give repentance to Israel" (5:31) and give the Holy Spirit "to those who obey [God]" (5:32). From beginning to end, the claims of the apostles about Israel's restoration are framed by God's decisive and determinative action. The claims are in continuity with Israel's traditions and interests—the God who restores Israel through Jesus is the same "God of our ancestors." To "obey God" rather than human authority is to obey the demands of this gospel to repent and be baptized (see 2:38).

These claims are stated here in outline much like a confession of faith, since Peter has already addressed each point in earlier speeches (see 2:22-40; 3:12-26; 4:8-12, 19-20). Yet, this speech is more prophetic and provocative than those that have come before. Peter's reference to Jesus' death—"whom you had killed by hanging him on a tree"—is graphic in a way the earlier speeches were not. The verb translated as "you had killed" (διεχειρίσασθε *diecheirisasthe;* cf. 26:21) is a judicial charge of premeditated murder made in a courtroom, a charge made only slightly less severe by reversing the order of Jesus' death and resurrection. That is, the Sanhedrin's decision about Jesus was not God's and therefore—fortunately for them—not final or permanent. Peter also calls Jesus' crucifixion a lynching—"you had [him] killed by hanging him on a tree" (5:30). The phrase clearly alludes to the prescription found in Deut 21:22-23 about the burial of Israel's worst criminals who are cursed by God.[233] Used in this speech before a council that had condemned Jesus to death, the intertextual echo deepens the enor-

---

230. Haenchen, *The Acts of the Apostles,* 251, thinks the high priest may also be worried that the apostles are calling upon God to punish the Sanhedrin for their role in the execution of Jesus, which would certainly be in keeping with their role as Israel's judges (cf. Luke 22:30) and consistent with the narrator's explanation of Judas's demise (see 1:16-19).

231. Haenchen, ibid., rightly adds that Peter's response "stands as an example to all readers of how the Apostles bear witness before the authorities, whose guilt in the death of Jesus they fearlessly expose."

232. Peter's speech serves as Luke's summary of Peter's prior kerygmatic speeches to his Jewish audiences. He emphasizes here as before the Jewish rejection of Jesus, and his resulting death, resurrection, and ascension as the enactment of God's plan for restoring Israel. Luke uses these speeches to ameliorate the ignorance of the Jewish people and their rulers (3:17), which will lead to their repentance and conversion (3:19) and finally to their prophesied role as healing agent in God's repair of all creation (3:20).

233. J. A. Fitzmyer, *The Acts of the Apostles,* AB 31 (Garden City, N.Y.: Doubleday, 1998) 337, refers to a citation of the Deuteronomy text in the Temple Scroll of Qumran (11QT 64:7-12) that reserves death by "hanging on a tree" for those found guilty of treason against the people of Israel. If Luke is aware of this use of Deut 21:23, the irony of Peter's statement is deepened significantly, especially if the council has in mind to charge the apostles with treason. In fact, it is the council that has acted against God's best interests for the people of Israel.

mity of their previous error: Rather than Israel's traitor cursed by God, Jesus is Israel's "Leader and Savior" (ἀρχηγός καὶ σωτήρ *archēgos kai sōtēr*) exalted by God (5:31; cf. 2:36).

This is the first time the title "Savior" (*sōtēr*) is used for Jesus in Acts (cf. Luke 2:11; Acts 13:23). Its importance for Luke is indicated not only by the appended "that he might give repentance to Israel and forgiveness of sins" (5:31; see 2:38) but also by recalling Joel's prophecy that salvation comes to those who "call upon the name of the Lord" (see 2:21; cf. 2:38).[234] We are reminded again that God must be obeyed because the kerygmatic claims that map Israel's repentance accord with the prophecies of Israel's Scripture.

Peter's speech concludes by claiming, "we are witnesses to these things," which connects his summary of the gospel with the apostolic vocation as commissioned by this same Jesus (see 1:8) and with various speeches since (see 2:32; 3:15; 4:33). The familiar connection of apostolic testimony with the Holy Spirit glosses Peter's opening statement that the apostles obey God rather than Sanhedrin, not only because their testimony is also centered on God's redemptive activity but also because it is inspired by God's Spirit. Peter's appeal to the Spirit as given by God "to those who obey God" (5:32) authorizes both what the apostles teach and the results of their teaching, since the verb "has given" (ἔδωκεν *edōken*) recalls the giving of the Spirit at Pentecost (see 2:38). More provocatively, however, Peter may well be suggesting that without the gift of the Holy Spirit, the Sanhedrin lacks the spiritual resources to understand the claims he has just made.

**5:33-42.** The final panel of this story describes the Council's reaction to Peter's speech. At first its membership is "enraged and wanted to kill [the apostles]" (5:33; see 5:17). Not only were the apostles insubordinate by refusing to obey the Sanhedrin's ban against their public teaching, but Peter's speech effectively exposed the illegitimacy of their claim to lead God's people. The Temple and all that it symbolizes—including the religious authority of the Sadducees—has been given over to the apostles for their teaching ministry (see 5:20). This excludes the Council not only from

political power but also from participation in the restored Israel and its blessings!

It is left to Rabban Gamaliel to bring peace. Not much is known about this Gamaliel, the purported teacher of Paul (so Acts 22:3), other than what Luke gives us in 5:34: He was "a Pharisee in the council—a teacher of the law and respected by all the people."[235] More critically, the motive of his speech remains unclear. Its plain intent appears to be conciliatory and supportive of Luke's theological emphasis on God's sovereignty, expressed aptly by Peter's earlier retort "we must obey God rather than men"—and this is how most scholars take it.[236] If we are to assume from 5:33 that the threat to kill the apostles is real, even though unlikely given their popularity, then Gamaliel's persuasive speech may well have had a conciliatory intention.

L. T. Johnson, however, has challenged this consensus in a penetrating analysis of Gamaliel's "little speech."[237] According to Johnson, the first readers of Luke-Acts recall that a malevolent Gamaliel had previously participated in various damning decisions resulting in Jesus' death, to which Peter has just referred, and the flogging of his apostles. Peter excuses no one sitting on the Sanhedrin from these previous crimes (5:30-31); and, Johnson contends, neither should the reader. Further, the historical examples of Theudas (5:36) and Judas (5:37) that Gamaliel uses to argue his case have the rhetorical effect of "reducing Jesus to the status of those 'would-be' prophets and kings."[238] Johnson finds Gamaliel's advice, there-

---

234. Jesus' dying and rising gives Israel "the opportunity" for repentance; God does not restore Israel independent of its repentance. See H. Conzelmann, *The Acts of the Apostles*, trans. J. Limburg et al., ed. E. J. Epp and C. R. Matthews, Hermeneia (Philadelphia: Fortress, 1987) 42. Further, Luke assumes the necessity of Peter's kerygmatic proclamation; the opportunity to convert to Jesus does not present itself outside of the apostolic mission.

235. It was said of Gamaliel upon his death that "when Rabban Gamaliel the Elder died, the glory of the law ceased, and purity and abstinence died" (*m.Sotah* 9:15); see also Fitzmyer, *The Acts of the Apostles,* 339.

236. See B. Witherington, *The Acts of the Apostles: A Socio-Rhetorical Commentary* (Grand Rapids: Eerdmans, 1998) 233-35 for a summary of this consensus.

237. L. T. Johnson, *The Acts of the Apostles,* SP 5 (Collegeville, Minn.: Liturgical, 1992) 99-103.

238. Ibid., 103. Johnson notes that the verbal ideas Luke uses echo both the prophetic ministry and resurrection of Jesus in a way that discredits him. Thus, Theudas "rose up—but was killed"; and then Judas "rose up—and also perished." I would add that the order in both Luke's references to these insurrectionists is first to their "rising up" and then to their death, which follows the order of Peter's speech (see 5:30-31) as if to mock his kerygmatic claims for Jesus. The notorious critical problem raised about Luke's misdating of Theudas's popular uprising—it actually took place in the mid-40s according to Josephus, about ten years after Gamaliel's speech!—and reversing its order with the earlier one led by Judas falls within the literary conventions of ancient historiography and does not finally subvert the point he has Gamaliel make in this speech. See J. D. G. Dunn, *The Acts of the Apostles* (Valley Forge, Pa.: Trinity, 1996) 73. Bruce's solution that Gamaliel may be referring to a different Theudas seems like special pleading. See F. F. Bruce, *The Acts of the Apostles,* rev. ed., NICNT (Grand Rapids: Eerdmans, 1988) 176.

fore, disingenuous. He is a leading example of the hypocrisy of the Pharisees who aspire to prudence but who then refuse to obey the word of God (Matt 23:13-29; Luke 11:44).[239] The reader also may wonder why the high priest, a Sadducee, would allow Gamaliel, a Pharisee, to address the Council on a non-halakic case unless he anticipated his support. If Johnson's interpretation is accepted, the necessary conclusion is that unrepentant Gamaliel expects the apostles to fail and his verdict is a cynical one: "if it is of God, you will not be able to overthrow them—in that case you may even be found fighting against God" (5:39a). That the council is "convinced" by a disingenuous Gamaliel only indicates the depth of their obduracy (5:39b)![240]

And so the apostles are released—but not before they are "flogged—and ordered not to speak in the name of Jesus" (5:40; cf. 4:18). Their joyful response to suffering is in stark contrast to the Council's response to them and expands their profile as prophets of God and leaders of restored Israel, who are "worthy to suffer dishonor for the sake of the name" (5:41).[241] Whether in the Temple or in the households (see 2:46) the apostles continue to live within their prophetic vocation "to teach and proclaim Jesus as the Messiah" (5:42). These concluding words have a "rounding off effect" on the reader.[242] Not only has Luke supplied a succinct summary of Peter's missionary speeches in Acts (5:29-32), here he describes the practical results of obeying God rather than humans. The community's priestly opposition, while continuing to wield judicial authority, can do nothing to deter the apostles from continuing to proclaim "the name of Jesus." At the end of this day, the conflict between these two groups of leaders dissolves in favor of the apostles.

---

239. Luke's use of "plan" (ἡ βουλή hē boulē) in 5:38 ironically echoes its earlier uses in 2:23 and 4:28 of God's plan disclosed in the death and resurrection of Jesus (cf. Luke 7:29). That is, Gamaliel speaks of the apostolic mission as "this plan," which the faithful reader understands as God's plan but which Gamaliel thinks is of human derivation.

240. Luke's use of a language of "power" to conclude Gamaliel's speech ("you will not be able to overthrow [δύναμαι dynamai, lit., "to have power"] them") reflects God's ultimate control over human affairs but also echoes the apostles' appropriation of the Spirit's "power" (δύναμις dynamis) in service of God (see 1:8). While Gamaliel believes in God's sovereign power, he is evidently unconvinced that God's power and authority—God's dynamis—are vested in either Jesus or his apostles.

241. The pattern of suffering as a result of proclaiming the word of the Lord is distinctively Lukan. It will be a decisive motive in shaping the plotline of his story of Paul's mission (see 9:15-16) and generally reflects Luke's understanding of prophetic ministry according to his Scriptures (cf. Luke 11:45-52).

242. Dunn, *The Acts of the Apostles,* 73-74; cf. J. Jervell, *Die Apostelgeschichte,* KEK 3 (Göttingen: Vandenhoeck & Ruprecht, 1998) 212-13.

# REFLECTIONS

**1.** "During the night an angel of the Lord opened the prison doors [and] brought them out" (5:19 NRSV). There are three jailbreak stories in Acts (cf. 12:6-11; 16:25-34). Every narrative "triad" in Acts sends a signal to the reader of its theological importance. The primary meaning of the apostles' heavenly deliverance from prison is clear: In spite of public appearances to the contrary, God remains in firm control over the particulars of the church's mission and intends to safeguard the apostles against all foes. No one or no thing can intrude upon the forward movement of the gospel according to God's plan of salvation. Three other details of this brief episode nuance this theological principle. The prison symbolizes hostility against God's redemptive plan; it is the location of spiritual warfare between good and evil. The angel's command to "Go and stand in the temple and tell the people the words of life" is a call to a provocative boldness, which takes center stage in the very place of the apostles' opponents, the priestly establishment. There is no break to a safehouse but to battle. The second detail is the befuddlement of the captors whose confusion is testimony both to God's liberating presence and to their ignorance of God's presence. These are the "Keystone Kops" of Acts; their role is to exemplify the incompetence of God's opposition. Finally, the apostles willingly make themselves available for re-arrest. This has nothing to do with their respect—or lack thereof—for civil authority and everything to do with their sublime confidence in God's provident care.

**2.** "We must obey God rather than any human authority" (5:29 NRSV). Peter's heroic retort to the high priest is Scripture's leading justification for civil disobedience. The interpreter must take care, however, to use it in full awareness of its near and wider canonical context. In Acts, Peter's response is toward a particular kind of political authority, carefully drawn by the narrator. Hostile, unrepentant, tyrannical, envious, clearly unfit to lead the people, who seem to recognize what the narrator does! In our worlds, political authority is rarely so sharply drawn, and a response like Peter's is rarely so glibly made. Such defiance is possible only with several qualifications. In Acts, Peter's comment introduces kerygma, gospel. That is, his expression of civil disobedience does not serve political but rather missionary ends. He does not define himself or his religious authority in terms of protest but as a witness to God's salvation of Israel. He is not the leader of a movement of protest but a movement of God.

In wider canonical context, the interpreter should note the variety of ways in which Scripture defines the relationship between church and state. For example, Paul in Romans speaks with respect (and possibility with irony?) of how civil (= Roman) authority is divinely sanctioned to serve the good purposes of God in the world. Peace is maintained; troublemakers are locked up; good neighbors are rewarded. In a word, the church supports civil authority to make it possible for the church to be the church (cf. Rom 13:1-10). Yet, the book of Revelation speaks with apocalyptic cynicism of a political "Babylon" that is ruled by an unholy trinity, where the people of God are persecuted and even martyred because of their courageous opposition. In this biblical context, the church stands opposed to a civil authority whose self-interest is contrary to the purposes of God (cf. Revelation 13; 17–18). Within the New Testament, Acts takes a stand between these two extremes to help maintain their self-correcting interplay. Scripture seems to suggest that the uneasy relationship between the church as counterculture and the state as custodian of cultural order will remain uneasy.

**3.** "If it is from God, you will not be able to stop these men" (5:39 NIV). Gamaliel's cautionary note, however motivated, sounds a practical perspective for judging religious claims. The truth of God embodied in the church's witness in the world should look, act, and sound peculiar to the outsider. There is nothing stranger than the God of Scripture! This may be especially the case of truth that demands one's repentance. The thoughtful person will take longer to test the gospel's claims, for the risks and costs of trusting them are much greater. At the same time, it seems that the apostles recognize the problem with Gamaliel's "wait and see" argument. His pragmatic test could lead to the kind of inactive determinism that waits for God to triumph at the end of the day. There are challenges the church must face squarely. To wait and see is to allow evil its momentary victory in this person's or that group's life. Wait in confidence of God's coming triumph, yes—but "wait and *act*," as did the apostles who left their court appearance to continue their prophetic vocation (5:42).

**4.** "They rejoiced that they were considered worthy to suffer dishonor for the sake of the name" (5:41 NRSV). The prophetic vocation is a call to share in the suffering of Jesus. The Lord predicted that his disciples would suffer and pronounced God's blessing to those persecuted because of him (cf. Luke 6:22-23). Suffering is the "downward" way of discipleship and is a hard concept to embrace (let alone embody) for those in the "upward" middle class, who enjoy a relatively secure and comfortable life-style. Stories like this one have produced an extraordinary amount of guilt in believers who do not suffer at the hands of oppressive foes—perhaps even a sanctified masochism that substitutes self-inflicted suffering for the suffering envisaged here. In adapting this text to the contemporary church, the interpreter should note that suffering is the result of ministry not masochism. Peter does seek to suffer; he seeks to obey God and to execute the tasks God has given him with grace and courage. His joy is not in his suffering but in his service. The costs of Peter's discipleship are peculiar to his prophetic tasks, spiritual authority, and special role as the Lord's apostolic successor in salvation's history. However, what he models for all believers in every situation is the nonnegotiable importance of serving the interests of God whatever the cost, wherever the occasion.

# Acts 6:1-7, Interlude: Resolving Conflict Within the Community of Goods

## NIV

6 In those days when the number of disciples was increasing, the Grecian Jews among them complained against the Hebraic Jews because their widows were being overlooked in the daily distribution of food. [2]So the Twelve gathered all the disciples together and said, "It would not be right for us to neglect the ministry of the word of God in order to wait on tables. [3]Brothers, choose seven men from among you who are known to be full of the Spirit and wisdom. We will turn this responsibility over to them [4]and will give our attention to prayer and the ministry of the word."

[5]This proposal pleased the whole group. They chose Stephen, a man full of faith and of the Holy Spirit; also Philip, Procorus, Nicanor, Timon, Parmenas, and Nicolas from Antioch, a convert to Judaism. [6]They presented these men to the apostles, who prayed and laid their hands on them.

[7]So the word of God spread. The number of disciples in Jerusalem increased rapidly, and a large number of priests became obedient to the faith.

## NRSV

6 Now during those days, when the disciples were increasing in number, the Hellenists complained against the Hebrews because their widows were being neglected in the daily distribution of food. [2]And the twelve called together the whole community of the disciples and said, "It is not right that we should neglect the word of God in order to wait on tables.[a] [3]Therefore, friends,[b] select from among yourselves seven men of good standing, full of the Spirit and of wisdom, whom we may appoint to this task, [4]while we, for our part, will devote ourselves to prayer and to serving the word." [5]What they said pleased the whole community, and they chose Stephen, a man full of faith and the Holy Spirit, together with Philip, Prochorus, Nicanor, Timon, Parmenas, and Nicolaus, a proselyte of Antioch. [6]They had these men stand before the apostles, who prayed and laid their hands on them.

[7]The word of God continued to spread; the number of the disciples increased greatly in Jerusalem, and a great many of the priests became obedient to the faith.

[a] Or keep accounts    [b] Gk brothers

# COMMENTARY

Interludes generally help make transitions from one story to the next. Accordingly, Luke uses this episode to introduce elements that trigger a sequence of events bringing the Jerusalem mission to conclusion and so beginning the next stage of the church's mission, beyond the holy city (see 8:4-40; cf. 1:8).[243] Interludes also underwrite previous points. For example, this passage concerns the distinctive practice of sharing goods so that "there was not a needy person among them" (4:34a), indicating to all the presence of God's "great grace upon" the community (4:33b; cf. 2:47). New procedures are introduced into the

community due to its vigorous growth and the problem of supply and demand that growth has created. One group in particular—the widows from among "the Hellenists" (οἱ Ἑλληνισταί hoi Hellēnistai)—is adversely affected, and their neglect is blamed on "the Hebrews" (οἱ Ἑβραῖοι hoi Hebraioi). The circumstances that have given rise to this accusation are unstated, and Luke's interest seems more practical than political—that is, he is concerned with the ineffective infrastructure that has resulted in unmet needs within the community of goods.

The apostles understand the nature of the problem and have a strategy for its effective resolution. However, they curiously use this intramural con-

243. See E. Richard, *Acts 6:1–8:4: The Author's Method of Composition*, SBLDS 41 (Missoula, Mont.: Scholars Press, 1978).

flict to remind the community that their vocation is to be prophets-like-Jesus rather than waiters on tables[244] (6:2). The present threat to the widows' welfare, therefore, is defined in two ways: On the one hand, the most needy members of the community are being neglected; on the other hand, the apostles find themselves spending more time in administrative matters than in the ministry of the word to which they are called (6:4; see 1:8). To resolve this vocational conflict the apostles gather "the whole community of disciples" to recommend "seven from among yourselves" who will assume responsibility for food distribution (6:3). These seven are commissioned by the Twelve (6:6), and so "the word of God continued to spread" and new converts were added to the church (6:7).[245]

**6:1-2.** While Luke has emphasized the resurrection practice of sharing goods with the needy, the personal tragedies of Judas (see 1:6-20) and then Ananias and Sapphira (see 5:1-11) have prepared the reader to recognize that the community's witness is threatened by the problems that believers have with their possessions. Heretofore, when problems arise the offending parties are simply "excommunicated" (see 5:1-11) without indicating how these problems could be resolved more constructively. The importance of this episode in Acts, then, is to introduce a pattern for resolving congregational conflict, which is then repeated as a strategic element of the church's mission (see 11:1-18; 14:27–15:29; 21:17-26).

At its root this conflict envisages the economic disparity between members that threatens any rapidly growing community no matter how cohesive they are in mind and practice: "the disciples were increasing in number" and so their "widows were being neglected in the daily distribution" (6:1). Rapid growth imperils the performance of the biblical injunction to take special care to meet the material requirements of the community's most vulnerable members—widows, orphans, resident aliens, the destitute, and the powerless (cf. Lev 19; 25; Deut 16:11; Mal 3:5; 1 Tim 5:3-16; Jas 1:22–2:17).[246] The prophets make clear that the treatment of its poor and powerless effectively gauges Israel's relationship with God (Mal 3:5; Zech 7:10) and heralds repentant Israel's renewed covenant with God (Isa 47:8). For this reason, the Hellenists were right to lodge their complaint.

Despite the story's importance within the narrative, the reader may still puzzle over several of its details. The first is to identify "the Hellenists" and the source of their grievance with "the Hebrews." The interpreter must avoid the kind of pigeonholing that places each group into a rigidly defined social class or ideological camp; there is little basis in the text, or behind it, for doing so.[247] The reader should presume that the Hellenists and Hebrews "were of one heart and soul" (see 4:32) and *in principle* shared equally in the blessings of a restored Israel. The present complaint stems from the realization that one group *in practice* has not yet fully participated in the community of goods according to its rule of faith (see 4:32-35).

The terms "the Hellenists" and "the Hebrews" are used together only in this passage, and their wider currency in contemporary Jewish literature is of little help in understanding their use in Acts. Luke's use of the adjective form of "Hebrew" ( Ἐβραῖος *Hebraios*) suggests that these terms refer to a spoken language. Paul, for example, some-

---

244. The interpreter should note that Luke's use of διακονέω/διακονία (*diakoneō/diakonia*, "to wait (on tables)/distribution") in this passage follows its plotline. The failure is stated as a breakdown in the daily *diakonia* ("distribution") of food (6:1). Luke's subsequent use of the verbal form *diakoneō* (6:2) assesses this conflict: food is not being "distributed" to the needy. Finally, the repetition of *diakonia* in 6:4 introduces the resolution of this conflict: the apostles are no longer diverted by administrative tasks and are now fully engaged in their *diakonia* ("ministry") of the word. Significantly, both food "distribution" and the "ministry" of the word are a *diakonia*.

245. C. K. Barrett, *A Critical and Exegetical Commentary on the Acts of the Apostles,* 2 vols, ICC (Edinburgh: T. & T. Clark, 1994, 1998) 1:305.

246. Johnson, *The Acts of the Apostles,* 105-6. The Hellenist "widows" of Acts combine two welfare classes: they are widows and resident aliens, without family or national support. If by "Hellenist" Luke means those who speak mostly Greek in a Semitic culture, their inability to speak the native language would push these widows to Jerusalem's social and economic fringe. Because of the conflict between the temple elites and the Twelve, the welfare system operated by the Temple might also have been placed outside the grasp of these poorest of the poor. See E. Haenchen, *The Acts of the Apostles* (Philadelphia: Westminster, 1971) 260-61.

247. The most important study of this issue is by C. Hill, *Hellenists and Hebrews* (Minneapolis: Fortress, 1992). Hill's thesis is that the old consensus that divided these groups by competing theological commitments concerning Temple and especially Torah purity is mistaken. First-century Judaism is simply too complex and fluid a religious phenomenon for an easy cataloging of its various subgroups; and Jewish Christianity reflects the pluriform Judaism that mothered it. There is no evidence from the NT that Luke's depiction of intramural strife in Acts is deeply rooted in age-old prejudices against "the Hellenists" who were therefore singled out for mistreatment in Jerusalem. Contra Dunn, *The Acts of the Apostles,* 82. At least according to Acts, "official" Judaism's persecution of the community's leaders is not selective: the Twelve, who were from among "the Hebrews," are opposed (4:5) by the same antagonists who later oppose Stephen, who came from among "the Hellenists" (6:12; 7:1).

times speaks in "Hebrew" to his Palestinian audiences (Acts 21:40; 22:2; 26:14). The division inferred here, then, is between language groups rather than theological outlooks: "The Hellenists" speak mostly Greek, "the Hebrews" speak mostly Aramaic, and the language barrier between them may explain in part why the practice of food distribution was impeded.

But different languages often involve other, more subtle differences. Just as diaspora Jews have been an important constituency of Israel in Acts since Pentecost (see 2:5-11), so also Luke's "Hellenists" may be Jews who have come to Jerusalem from the diaspora and have settled in ethnic enclaves throughout Jerusalem, where they maintain their own cultural conventions. Many became believers (see 2:41) and perhaps since Pentecost had even established Greek-speaking congregations in their neighborhoods while recognizing the religious authority of the Twelve.[248] If this construction of the story behind the story is accurate, their "complaint"[249] against the Hebrews may well reflect other, more cultural barriers that now divide different congregations within the Jerusalem church.

Another important and somewhat puzzling feature of this passage is its turn toward a second team of seven leaders, two of whom (Stephen, Philip) are given prophetic tasks to perform similar to those of the powerful Twelve. The previous narrative has settled the public debate over Israel's leadership in favor of the apostles (see 5:40-42) whose authority within the faith community is unrivaled (see 4:32–5:16). Their prominence is predicated on two important roles effectively performed. The first is their prophetic ministry of the word and mediation of the Spirit's "signs and wonders." Their second role, however, is to redistribute goods to the community's needy. They now rank their prophetic tasks ahead of their administrative role[250] and are even willing to share their spiritual authority—which the redistribution of goods symbolizes (see 4:32–5:16)—with other members of the wider community. Before this crisis the Twelve acted only in collaboration with the Holy Spirit; now, the community's growth and ethnic diversity prompts the realization that their performance standards have not been met. Their mature recognition signals the redistribution of their authority to others within the community. Ironically, then, the selection of the seven will substantially qualify the reader's understanding the Twelve: Although they continue to do and teach what Jesus began, their authority to do so now extends to different leaders of the next generation and from a different constituency of believers.

A final interpretive puzzle is the identity and purpose of those who belong to "the whole community of disciples" (6:2, 5).[251] This text is the first to mention "disciples" in Acts.[252] In the Gospels, of course, a "disciple" is a follower or student of Jesus, and the same is true here. Luke introduces this term into Acts, however, in connection with the Hellenists' complaint, and for this reason "disciples" probably refers to the Greek-speaking believers in Jerusalem, many of whom are new to the faith (6:1). The impression made by the translations of this text is that the Twelve "called together/gathered" the "whole/all" the "disciples"—now well into the thousands—for a discussion of the problem. More likely, this "community of disciples" refers to a much smaller representative "group" of Hellenists who are more mature in the faith and have been given responsibility for the care of their constituents.

**6:3-6.** The charge given to this advisory group is to "select from among yourselves seven men"

---

248. H. Conzelmann, *The Acts of the Apostles,* trans. J. Limburg et al., ed. E. J. Epp and C. R. Matthews, Hermeneia (Philadelphia: Fortress, 1987) 45, suspects that preferences in everyday language extended to worship and Scripture; so that "the Hellenists" read the Septuagint (rather than the Hebrew Scriptures) and prayed publicly in Greek. His point seems right; and since everyday language is decisive in shaping a general cultural orientation, differences of other kinds may well be implied by Luke's term. See H. C. Kee, *To Every Nation Under Heaven: The Acts of the Apostles,* NTC (Valley Forge, Pa.: Trinity, 1997) 88; Dunn, *The Acts of the Apostles,* 81-82.

249. Johnson, *The Acts of the Apostles,* 105, contends that "slighted" better translates παραθεωρέω (*paratheoreō*) in this passage because it better judges the nature of discrimination in this case than the more pejorative "complained."

250. Luke uses the phrase "preaching the word of God" in 6:2 of the apostles' principal activity, which certainly is consistent with his portrait of them to this point in Acts. In 6:4, however, he adds prayer to "the ministry of the word," perhaps recalling their effective petition in 4:24-30 and its connection with "bold" preaching. In Luke's mind, these two prophetic actions of praying and preaching are inseparably linked.

251. "Community" translates πλῆθος (*plēthos*), which denotes a particular subgroup within the community—one that is assembled for deliberation and decision making. Some commentators contend that the reference to "disciples" (μαθητής *mathētēs*) belongs to Luke's primary source and that he simply retains this reference without added meaning or import. This, however, is unlikely given Luke's intentional shaping of his traditions to tell his story and forward his theological vision, and given the repeated use of "disciples" from this point on in Acts.

252. The Western text of Acts, followed by the KJV, substitutes "disciples" for "believers" in 1:15.

(6:3). The number seven is not arbitrary but reflects the Jewish practice of choosing seven members to provide oversight to local congregations (cf. Exod 18:21; Num 27:18-19 LXX). Nor is the process of selecting leadership an arbitrary one. The verb ἐπισκέπτομαι (*episkeptomai*, "select") is from a word family used of critical and prudent judgments; this decision is made only after careful deliberation by mature believers.

The community is asked to investigate potential leaders on the basis of three personal attributes, which differ from those used for selecting the Twelve (see 1:21-22) but are deemed most important in meeting the urgent demands of this appointment: "good standing, full of the Spirit and of wisdom" (6:3). Each attribute is important for "waiting on tables" and also foreshadows the seven's talent in providing competent oversight within the church. The participle translated "good standing" (μαρτυρουμένος *martyroumenos*) suggests a good reputation that is based upon the favorable "testimony" of others; it is a crucial feature of leading others (cf. Acts 15:14, 36). The combination of "full" (πλήρης *plērēs*) with "Spirit" (πνεῦμα *pneuma*) denotes evidence of a candidate's mature faith (so 2:38) and implies the capacity for prophetic ministry (so 2:4; cf. 6:5; cf. Num 11:16-17). The final characteristic, "wisdom," may refer to organizational talent; but in combination with the Holy Spirit it suggests spiritual authority. Seven from among the Hellenists meet these criteria and are selected. Luke provides the reader with a list of their Greek names, highlighting for future reference the appointments of Stephen ("a man full of faith and the Holy Spirit"; 6:5)[253] and Philip (see Acts 8). The presence of "Nicolaus, a proselyte of Antioch" among the seven indicates a diversity that extends across the entire household of Israel (see 2:11); it also is a harbinger of the church's Antiochene mission to that city's large population of Hellenists (see 11:20).

The apostolic vocation is here defined as devotion "to prayer and to serving the word" (6:4). Luke uses "word" (λόγος *logos*) as a catchword for the full range of the prophet's tasks—the keen interpretation of Scripture, the persuasive proclamation of the gospel, and the performance of the Spirit's "signs and wonders" that provide the eschatological setting for biblical interpretation and evangelistic preaching according to Acts (see 4:31; 6:7; cf. 8:4, 14; 11:1; 12:24; 13:48; 19:20). The petition of apostolic prayers seeks greater power from God to make certain these various prophetic tasks will be boldly and effectively executed (see 4:23-30).

Commentators have made much of the Twelve's gesture of "laying their hands on" the seven Hellenists who "stand before" them (6:6).[254] This service of installation indicates their religious authority to govern the community's internal life and sanction its decisions. The reader of biblical texts also recognizes that this gesture often signals a succession of authority from one leader to the next (cf. Num 27:18, 23; Deut 34:9). Ironically, only the apostles have the authority to transfer their power to others, and here they do so to preserve the most distinctive practice of the community of goods and in order to safeguard their prophetic vocation.

**6:7.** Luke encloses this interlude with an optimistic note: "The number of disciples increased greatly in Jerusalem" (see 6:1). The reader is thereby assured that the present problem has been effectively handled so that the Jerusalem mission moves ever forward (see 2:41, 47; 4:4; 5:14).

This latest notice of the community's success is especially noteworthy for two curious phrases. First, "the word of God continued to spread" personifies the apostles' proclamation of the gospel, shifting the reader's focus from the power and authority of those who preach it (the apostles) to the power and authority of what is preached (the word of God). By leaving open the identity of the prophetic carrier of the word the reader is made

---

253. Luke's introduction of Stephen into the narrative uses the same verb ("they chose [ἐκλέγομαι *eklegomai*] Stephen") used earlier in Acts of the apostles (see 1:2). The implied meaning of this phrase is that his principal vocation is *not* to wait on tables but to join the line of prophets in continuity with Jesus and his apostolic successors to preach the gospel (6:10) and do "signs and wonders" (6:8) in witness to God's reign. Luke also adds "full of faith" (πλήρης πίστεως *plērēs pisteōs*) to Stephen's attributes for ministry, a characteristic phrase that denotes faithfulness to God.

254. Some take the antecedent of v. 6 to be the advisory committee mentioned in v. 5, which may lead the reader to suppose that this committee joined the Twelve to lay hands on and consecrate the seven for their sacred task (cf. Num 8:10). See Barrett, *Acts*, 315-16. My sense of the wider context leads me to understand that it was the Twelve who laid their hands on the seven as a function of their apostolic authority—although not without first "pleasing" the advisory group from the Hellenists (see 6:5).

even more alert to the diminishing attention Acts will pay to the story of the Twelve and to the progress of the word of God to the end of earth—no matter who proclaims it.

Second, the verse claims that "a great many of the priests became obedient to the faith."[255] Given the apostles' past grievances with the priestly establishment of Jerusalem, this phrase initially strikes the reader as confirming once for all the reversal of religious leadership within Israel (see

255. Some commentators find Paul's influence in Luke's phrase "obedient to the faith" (ὑπήκουον τῇ πίστει hypēkouon tē pistei). Paul's parallel phrase is "for an obedience of faith" (εἰς ὑπακοὴν πίστεως eis hypakoēn pisteōs; Rom 1:5; 16:26) and reflects the central claim of his Gentile mission: The sinner's profession of trust that "Jesus is Lord" saves (10:9). In the context of Acts, Luke's phrase "obedient to the faith" envisages a response to "the word of God" that requires the new convert to "repent" and be "baptized" into the community of goods.

5:17-42). Closer attention to the historical referent, however, suggests otherwise. Haenchen estimates that upwards of 18,000 priests were living in Jerusalem at the time, most with minimal responsibilities in their service of the Temple and, held in low public esteem, with little or no income.[256] Their attraction to the Jesus movement indicates that the ministry of the apostles proffers nothing that is offensive to traditional Jewish sensibilities; however, they may have been drawn to the community by the availability of food. This too implies the favorable result of the community's welfare program that is now administered by the seven.

256. Haenchen, *The Acts of the Apostles,* 264. Josephus claims that some priests without means even starved to death during famine. See also Josephus *Antiquities of the Jews* 20.181.

# REFLECTIONS

**1.** "The Hellenists complained . . . because their widows were being neglected in the daily distribution of food" (6:1 NRSV). Disputes within the fellowship of believers are especially painful, because close friends often find themselves on different sides of an issue and upset with each other for that reason. Nevertheless complaints must be voiced with civility to initiate the community's practice of reconciliation. The most important internal conflicts to settle are those that go to the heart of a community's identity; these are the most passionately contested because more is at stake. In this passage, the practice of distributing food among the Jerusalem community's most needy and vulnerable members—its displaced widows—has apparently broken down. Besides the prior concern for the welfare of its membership, the congregation's public identity for sharing goods according to need is being challenged. The vocation of the church is to extend that witness to the entire household of Israel (see 2:1-13). The scope of God's promise to restore all of Israel is threatened by this apparent division along ethnic and language lines. The church's witness to the holy city is subverted as a result of this internal crisis. The protocol followed, which both addresses the problem and preserves the prophetic vocation, is a biblical model to guide conflict resolution in today's church, in particular conflict issuing from ethnic, class, or gender divisions.

**2.** "And the twelve called together the whole community of the disciples" (6:2a NRSV). The first step in resolving this internal conflict is to bring together all those involved and include them as parties to a remedy. The implied subtext of this account in Acts is that all are members of a cohesive congregation whose regular experience is serving God together with "one heart and soul" (see 4:32). There is the presumption of solidarity—of shared faith and abiding friendship—that provides the groundwork for this meeting. The "community of disciples" convened are the most mature representatives of the parties involved. This is not a "town hall" meeting that gives voice to any and every grievance. Instead, the Twelve solicit a representative assembly of members who have registered the crisis and have their collective finger on the pulse of the problem at issue.

**3.** "It is not right that we should neglect the word of God in order to wait on tables" (6:2b NRSV). As is often the case, at the nub of the conflict is a failure of leadership. Almost certainly there is more to the complaint of the Hellenists than that the increasing demands of a growing community have outpaced the ability of the apostles to exercise their spiritual authority in the distribution of goods. Growth requires change, and change comes slowly to any culture, but especially to a religious movement that is indebted to past memories and ancestral traditions, preserved and transmitted to others. To change with the times is a function of an agile leadership team. The practical failure of apostolic leadership to administrate effectively the community's food bank occasions the next triumph of their leadership: They received a report from the leaders and recognized their inability to preach and do all the bookkeeping at the same time. It is time to redefine the job description of an apostle. Others outside of the circle of the Twelve need to share in their religious authority for the good of their common life and witness. The Twelve clearly recognize the importance of a congregation's infrastructure for maintaining its spiritual and physical health as a community of goods. A staff of competent people is selected to wait on tables so that the welfare of the most needy believers is attended. Once settled, the outreach ministry of the church continues to flourish (see 6:7).

One should also note that the Twelve recognize that the "real" problem of their leadership is that they are unable to live within their vocation because of their increasing administrative duties (see also 6:4). The pastor and the congregation should ever be alert to those crises occasioned when the administrative demands of running a church eat into the time one must devote in preparing for those tasks to which the pastor is called—most especially the ministry of the word.

**4.** "Select from among yourselves seven men" (6:3 NRSV). When an organization such as a church or university opens a search to find strong candidates to fill a vacancy, a list of qualifications and special talents is drawn up that envisions the job to be done. If a congregation requires a strong preacher, the search committee catalogs the attributes of good preaching to guide them in finding and evaluating possible candidates. Today's orientation toward work emphasizes the required tasks or expected activities of the vacated post. This is as it must be in the current job market. However, in Acts the emphasis is on *character* not task, whether a person is of "good standing, full of the Spirit and of wisdom." Luke's bias reflects his Greek intellectual culture, which championed the notion that habitual virtue—the sort of person one is—is the most important credential when considering people for leadership positions. This emphasis is found in the so-called "Pastoral Letters" of the New Testament (1–2 Timothy, Titus), where instructions for appointing congregational leaders concern exclusively whether one is known as a person of moral character and mature faith.

**5.** "The word of God continued to spread; the number of the disciples increased greatly" (6:7 NRSV). Within the fourfold Gospel tradition, a similar interplay between the community's outreach and "in-reach" is found. For example, the Synoptic Gospels define the love commandment in terms of caring for the "enemy" (cf. Matt 5:43-48 and par.) and the Lord's parting commission instructs his disciples to go out into the nations with the gospel in witness to nonbelievers (cf. Matt 28:18-20 and par.). The Fourth Gospel defines the love command in terms of caring for other disciples (cf. John 13:34) and the Lord's parting admonition to Peter is for him to take care of other believers (cf. John 21:15-17). How does the interpreter engage these different emphases as parts of a coherent, constructive whole? Luke's summary of the results of resolving the intramural squabble between the Hellenists and Hebrews of the Jerusalem community may give us a clue. With unity restored through careful attention to the welfare of all believers first of all (John's concern), the community's outreach ministry flourishes and its membership rolls increase, especially among those who earlier had felt marginalized (synoptic concern)! Congregational leaders would do well to build and fund an infrastructure that maintains the spiritual and material care of the entire congregation as the foundation and condition for an effective outreach program.

# Acts 6:8–8:3, Story Four: Stephen, a Prophet Mighty in Word and Deed

## NIV

[8] Now Stephen, a man full of God's grace and power, did great wonders and miraculous signs among the people. [9] Opposition arose, however, from members of the Synagogue of the Freedmen (as it was called)—Jews of Cyrene and Alexandria as well as the provinces of Cilicia and Asia. These men began to argue with Stephen, [10] but they could not stand up against his wisdom or the Spirit by whom he spoke.

[11] Then they secretly persuaded some men to say, "We have heard Stephen speak words of blasphemy against Moses and against God."

[12] So they stirred up the people and the elders and the teachers of the law. They seized Stephen and brought him before the Sanhedrin. [13] They produced false witnesses, who testified, "This fellow never stops speaking against this holy place and against the law. [14] For we have heard him say that this Jesus of Nazareth will destroy this place and change the customs Moses handed down to us."

[15] All who were sitting in the Sanhedrin looked intently at Stephen, and they saw that his face was like the face of an angel.

Then the high priest asked him, "Are these charges true?"

[7] [2] To this he replied: "Brothers and fathers, listen to me! The God of glory appeared to our father Abraham while he was still in Mesopotamia, before he lived in Haran. [3] 'Leave your country and your people,' God said, 'and go to the land I will show you.'[a]

[4] "So he left the land of the Chaldeans and settled in Haran. After the death of his father, God sent him to this land where you are now living. [5] He gave him no inheritance here, not even a foot of ground. But God promised him that he and his descendants after him would possess the land, even though at that time Abraham had no child. [6] God spoke to him in this way: 'Your descendants will be strangers in a country not their own, and they will be enslaved and mistreated four hundred years. [7] But I will punish the nation they

a 3 Gen. 12:1

## NRSV

[8] Stephen, full of grace and power, did great wonders and signs among the people. [9] Then some of those who belonged to the synagogue of the Freedmen (as it was called), Cyrenians, Alexandrians, and others of those from Cilicia and Asia, stood up and argued with Stephen. [10] But they could not withstand the wisdom and the Spirit[a] with which he spoke. [11] Then they secretly instigated some men to say, "We have heard him speak blasphemous words against Moses and God." [12] They stirred up the people as well as the elders and the scribes; then they suddenly confronted him, seized him, and brought him before the council. [13] They set up false witnesses who said, "This man never stops saying things against this holy place and the law; [14] for we have heard him say that this Jesus of Nazareth[b] will destroy this place and will change the customs that Moses handed on to us." [15] And all who sat in the council looked intently at him, and they saw that his face was like the face of an angel.

[7] Then the high priest asked him, "Are these things so?" [2] And Stephen replied:

"Brothers[c] and fathers, listen to me. The God of glory appeared to our ancestor Abraham when he was in Mesopotamia, before he lived in Haran, [3] and said to him, 'Leave your country and your relatives and go to the land that I will show you.' [4] Then he left the country of the Chaldeans and settled in Haran. After his father died, God had him move from there to this country in which you are now living. [5] He did not give him any of it as a heritage, not even a foot's length, but promised to give it to him as his possession and to his descendants after him, even though he had no child. [6] And God spoke in these terms, that his descendants would be resident aliens in a country belonging to others, who would enslave them and mistreat them during four hundred years. [7] 'But I will judge the nation that they serve,' said God, 'and after that they shall come out and worship me in this place.' [8] Then he gave him the covenant

a Or spirit    b Gk the Nazorean    c Gk Men, brothers

## NIV

serve as slaves,' God said, 'and afterward they will come out of that country and worship me in this place.'[a] [8]Then he gave Abraham the covenant of circumcision. And Abraham became the father of Isaac and circumcised him eight days after his birth. Later Isaac became the father of Jacob, and Jacob became the father of the twelve patriarchs.

[9]"Because the patriarchs were jealous of Joseph, they sold him as a slave into Egypt. But God was with him [10]and rescued him from all his troubles. He gave Joseph wisdom and enabled him to gain the goodwill of Pharaoh king of Egypt; so he made him ruler over Egypt and all his palace.

[11]"Then a famine struck all Egypt and Canaan, bringing great suffering, and our fathers could not find food. [12]When Jacob heard that there was grain in Egypt, he sent our fathers on their first visit. [13]On their second visit, Joseph told his brothers who he was, and Pharaoh learned about Joseph's family. [14]After this, Joseph sent for his father Jacob and his whole family, seventy-five in all. [15]Then Jacob went down to Egypt, where he and our fathers died. [16]Their bodies were brought back to Shechem and placed in the tomb that Abraham had bought from the sons of Hamor at Shechem for a certain sum of money.

[17]"As the time drew near for God to fulfill his promise to Abraham, the number of our people in Egypt greatly increased. [18]Then another king, who knew nothing about Joseph, became ruler of Egypt. [19]He dealt treacherously with our people and oppressed our forefathers by forcing them to throw out their newborn babies so that they would die.

[20]"At that time Moses was born, and he was no ordinary child.[b] For three months he was cared for in his father's house. [21]When he was placed outside, Pharaoh's daughter took him and brought him up as her own son. [22]Moses was educated in all the wisdom of the Egyptians and was powerful in speech and action.

[23]"When Moses was forty years old, he decided to visit his fellow Israelites. [24]He saw one of them being mistreated by an Egyptian, so he went to his defense and avenged him by killing the Egyptian.

[a] 7 Gen. 15:13,14    [b] 20 Or was fair in the sight of God

## NRSV

of circumcision. And so Abraham[a] became the father of Isaac and circumcised him on the eighth day; and Isaac became the father of Jacob, and Jacob of the twelve patriarchs.

[9]"The patriarchs, jealous of Joseph, sold him into Egypt; but God was with him, [10]and rescued him from all his afflictions, and enabled him to win favor and to show wisdom when he stood before Pharaoh, king of Egypt, who appointed him ruler over Egypt and over all his household. [11]Now there came a famine throughout Egypt and Canaan, and great suffering, and our ancestors could find no food. [12]But when Jacob heard that there was grain in Egypt, he sent our ancestors there on their first visit. [13]On the second visit Joseph made himself known to his brothers, and Joseph's family became known to Pharaoh. [14]Then Joseph sent and invited his father Jacob and all his relatives to come to him, seventy-five in all; [15]so Jacob went down to Egypt. He himself died there as well as our ancestors, [16]and their bodies[b] were brought back to Shechem and laid in the tomb that Abraham had bought for a sum of silver from the sons of Hamor in Shechem.

[17]"But as the time drew near for the fulfillment of the promise that God had made to Abraham, our people in Egypt increased and multiplied [18]until another king who had not known Joseph ruled over Egypt. [19]He dealt craftily with our race and forced our ancestors to abandon their infants so that they would die. [20]At this time Moses was born, and he was beautiful before God. For three months he was brought up in his father's house; [21]and when he was abandoned, Pharaoh's daughter adopted him and brought him up as her own son. [22]So Moses was instructed in all the wisdom of the Egyptians and was powerful in his words and deeds.

[23]"When he was forty years old, it came into his heart to visit his relatives, the Israelites.[c] [24]When he saw one of them being wronged, he defended the oppressed man and avenged him by striking down the Egyptian. [25]He supposed that his kinsfolk would understand that God through him was rescuing them, but they did not understand. [26]The next day he came to some of them as

[a] Gk he    [b] Gk they    [c] Gk his brothers, the sons of Israel

## NIV

<sup>25</sup>Moses thought that his own people would realize that God was using him to rescue them, but they did not. <sup>26</sup>The next day Moses came upon two Israelites who were fighting. He tried to reconcile them by saying, 'Men, you are brothers; why do you want to hurt each other?'

<sup>27</sup>"But the man who was mistreating the other pushed Moses aside and said, 'Who made you ruler and judge over us? <sup>28</sup>Do you want to kill me as you killed the Egyptian yesterday?'<sup>a</sup> <sup>29</sup>When Moses heard this, he fled to Midian, where he settled as a foreigner and had two sons.

<sup>30</sup>"After forty years had passed, an angel appeared to Moses in the flames of a burning bush in the desert near Mount Sinai. <sup>31</sup>When he saw this, he was amazed at the sight. As he went over to look more closely, he heard the Lord's voice: <sup>32</sup>'I am the God of your fathers, the God of Abraham, Isaac and Jacob.'<sup>b</sup> Moses trembled with fear and did not dare to look.

<sup>33</sup>"Then the Lord said to him, 'Take off your sandals; the place where you are standing is holy ground. <sup>34</sup>I have indeed seen the oppression of my people in Egypt. I have heard their groaning and have come down to set them free. Now come, I will send you back to Egypt.'<sup>c</sup>

<sup>35</sup>"This is the same Moses whom they had rejected with the words, 'Who made you ruler and judge?' He was sent to be their ruler and deliverer by God himself, through the angel who appeared to him in the bush. <sup>36</sup>He led them out of Egypt and did wonders and miraculous signs in Egypt, at the Red Sea<sup>d</sup> and for forty years in the desert.

<sup>37</sup>"This is that Moses who told the Israelites, 'God will send you a prophet like me from your own people.'<sup>e</sup> <sup>38</sup>He was in the assembly in the desert, with the angel who spoke to him on Mount Sinai, and with our fathers; and he received living words to pass on to us.

<sup>39</sup>"But our fathers refused to obey him. Instead, they rejected him and in their hearts turned back to Egypt. <sup>40</sup>They told Aaron, 'Make us gods who will go before us. As for this fellow Moses who led us out of Egypt—we don't know what has

<sup>a</sup> 28 Exodus 2:14    <sup>b</sup> 32 Exodus 3:6    <sup>c</sup> 34 Exodus 3:5,7,8,10
<sup>d</sup> 36 That is, Sea of Reeds    <sup>e</sup> 37 Deut. 18:15

## NRSV

they were quarreling and tried to reconcile them, saying, 'Men, you are brothers; why do you wrong each other?' <sup>27</sup>But the man who was wronging his neighbor pushed Moses<sup>a</sup> aside, saying, 'Who made you a ruler and a judge over us? <sup>28</sup>Do you want to kill me as you killed the Egyptian yesterday?' <sup>29</sup>When he heard this, Moses fled and became a resident alien in the land of Midian. There he became the father of two sons.

<sup>30</sup>"Now when forty years had passed, an angel appeared to him in the wilderness of Mount Sinai, in the flame of a burning bush. <sup>31</sup>When Moses saw it, he was amazed at the sight; and as he approached to look, there came the voice of the Lord: <sup>32</sup>'I am the God of your ancestors, the God of Abraham, Isaac, and Jacob.' Moses began to tremble and did not dare to look. <sup>33</sup>Then the Lord said to him, 'Take off the sandals from your feet, for the place where you are standing is holy ground. <sup>34</sup>I have surely seen the mistreatment of my people who are in Egypt and have heard their groaning, and I have come down to rescue them. Come now, I will send you to Egypt.'

<sup>35</sup>"It was this Moses whom they rejected when they said, 'Who made you a ruler and a judge?' and whom God now sent as both ruler and liberator through the angel who appeared to him in the bush. <sup>36</sup>He led them out, having performed wonders and signs in Egypt, at the Red Sea, and in the wilderness for forty years. <sup>37</sup>This is the Moses who said to the Israelites, 'God will raise up a prophet for you from your own people<sup>b</sup> as he raised me up.' <sup>38</sup>He is the one who was in the congregation in the wilderness with the angel who spoke to him at Mount Sinai, and with our ancestors; and he received living oracles to give to us. <sup>39</sup>Our ancestors were unwilling to obey him; instead, they pushed him aside, and in their hearts they turned back to Egypt, <sup>40</sup>saying to Aaron, 'Make gods for us who will lead the way for us; as for this Moses who led us out from the land of Egypt, we do not know what has happened to him.' <sup>41</sup>At that time they made a calf, offered a sacrifice to the idol, and reveled in the works of their hands. <sup>42</sup>But God turned away from them and handed them over to worship the host of

<sup>a</sup> Gk him    <sup>b</sup> Gk your brothers

## NIV

happened to him!'[a] [41]That was the time they made an idol in the form of a calf. They brought sacrifices to it and held a celebration in honor of what their hands had made. [42]But God turned away and gave them over to the worship of the heavenly bodies. This agrees with what is written in the book of the prophets:

" 'Did you bring me sacrifices and offerings
    forty years in the desert, O house of Israel?
[43] You have lifted up the shrine of Molech
    and the star of your god Rephan,
    the idols you made to worship.
Therefore I will send you into exile'[b] beyond
    Babylon.

[44]"Our forefathers had the tabernacle of the Testimony with them in the desert. It had been made as God directed Moses, according to the pattern he had seen. [45]Having received the tabernacle, our fathers under Joshua brought it with them when they took the land from the nations God drove out before them. It remained in the land until the time of David, [46]who enjoyed God's favor and asked that he might provide a dwelling place for the God of Jacob.[c] [47]But it was Solomon who built the house for him.

[48]"However, the Most High does not live in houses made by men. As the prophet says:

[49] " 'Heaven is my throne,
    and the earth is my footstool.
What kind of house will you build for me?
                                    says the Lord.
    Or where will my resting place be?
[50] Has not my hand made all these things?'[d]

[51]"You stiff-necked people, with uncircumcised hearts and ears! You are just like your fathers: You always resist the Holy Spirit! [52]Was there ever a prophet your fathers did not persecute? They even killed those who predicted the coming of the Righteous One. And now you have betrayed and murdered him— [53]you who have received the law that was put into effect through angels but have not obeyed it."

[54]When they heard this, they were furious and gnashed their teeth at him. [55]But Stephen, full of the Holy Spirit, looked up to heaven and saw the

## NRSV

heaven, as it is written in the book of the prophets:

'Did you offer to me slain victims and sacri-
    fices
    forty years in the wilderness, O house of
    Israel?
[43] No; you took along the tent of Moloch,
    and the star of your god Rephan,
    the images that you made to worship;
so I will remove you beyond Babylon.'

[44]"Our ancestors had the tent of testimony in the wilderness, as God[a] directed when he spoke to Moses, ordering him to make it according to the pattern he had seen. [45]Our ancestors in turn brought it in with Joshua when they dispossessed the nations that God drove out before our ancestors. And it was there until the time of David, [46]who found favor with God and asked that he might find a dwelling place for the house of Jacob.[b] [47]But it was Solomon who built a house for him. [48]Yet the Most High does not dwell in houses made with human hands;[c] as the prophet says,

[49] 'Heaven is my throne,
    and the earth is my footstool.
What kind of house will you build for me,
    says the Lord,
    or what is the place of my rest?
[50] Did not my hand make all these things?'

[51]"You stiff-necked people, uncircumcised in heart and ears, you are forever opposing the Holy Spirit, just as your ancestors used to do. [52]Which of the prophets did your ancestors not persecute? They killed those who foretold the coming of the Righteous One, and now you have become his betrayers and murderers. [53]You are the ones that received the law as ordained by angels, and yet you have not kept it."

[54]When they heard these things, they became enraged and ground their teeth at Stephen.[d] [55]But filled with the Holy Spirit, he gazed into heaven and saw the glory of God and Jesus standing at the right hand of God. [56]"Look," he said, "I see the heavens opened and the Son of Man standing at the right hand of God!" [57]But they covered their ears, and with a loud shout all rushed together

[a] 40 Exodus 32:1    [b] 43 Amos 5:25-27    [c] 46 Some early manuscripts the house of Jacob    [d] 50 Isaiah 66:1,2

[a] Gk he    [b] Other ancient authorities read for the God of Jacob    [c] Gk with hands    [d] Gk him

## NIV

glory of God, and Jesus standing at the right hand of God. [56]"Look," he said, "I see heaven open and the Son of Man standing at the right hand of God."

[57]At this they covered their ears and, yelling at the top of their voices, they all rushed at him, [58]dragged him out of the city and began to stone him. Meanwhile, the witnesses laid their clothes at the feet of a young man named Saul.

[59]While they were stoning him, Stephen prayed, "Lord Jesus, receive my spirit." [60]Then he fell on his knees and cried out, "Lord, do not hold this sin against them." When he had said this, he fell asleep.

8 And Saul was there, giving approval to his death.

On that day a great persecution broke out against the church at Jerusalem, and all except the apostles were scattered throughout Judea and Samaria. [2]Godly men buried Stephen and mourned deeply for him. [3]But Saul began to destroy the church. Going from house to house, he dragged off men and women and put them in prison.

## NRSV

against him. [58]Then they dragged him out of the city and began to stone him; and the witnesses laid their coats at the feet of a young man named Saul. [59]While they were stoning Stephen, he prayed, "Lord Jesus, receive my spirit." [60]Then he knelt down and cried out in a loud voice, "Lord, do not hold this sin against them." When he had said this, he died.[a] 8 [1]And Saul approved of their killing him.

That day a severe persecution began against the church in Jerusalem, and all except the apostles were scattered throughout the countryside of Judea and Samaria. [2]Devout men buried Stephen and made loud lamentation over him. [3]But Saul was ravaging the church by entering house after house; dragging off both men and women, he committed them to prison.

[a] Gk *fell asleep*

# COMMENTARY

The final episode of Luke's Jerusalem cycle features Stephen of the seven rather than Peter of the Twelve. The earlier interlude signals this narrative shift to the charismatic Stephen, who succeeds Peter to lead another constituency of disciples and continue what the Messiah "began to do and teach" among them (1:1).

Luke shapes his story of Stephen according to the literary pattern of this cycle of missionary stories (see the Overview to 3:1–8:3).[257] (1) The first narrative panel profiles a powerful Stephen, whose résumé indicates that he is a prophet-like-Jesus

who provokes public scrutiny (6:8-10). (2) The official response to his ministry, however, is ever more hostile (6:11-15). Added to the coalition of Jewish opponents to Jesus and his apostolic successors—the elders, scribes, and Sanhedrin—is a more aggressive and malevolent contingent from the diaspora's "synagogue of Freedmen." This group of Hellenists agitates unrest and sets up "false witnesses" against Stephen, one of their own. (3) Like Peter, Stephen responds to this mistake in a speech. His speech (7:1-53) is the longest in Acts and counts among the most significant for

257. The debate over the reliability of Luke's sources and the extent to which he edits them continues unabated. The literary parallelism between the events leading up to Stephen's speech (6:8–7:1) with those that follow it (7:54–8:3) lead some to conclude that Luke received his information about Stephen from a single source but then thoroughly reshaped it for his own theological purposes (Dibelius, Haenchen, Conzelmann, Lüdemann). Others emphasize the reliability of this single

source and conclude that Luke does not modify it much in interest of historical accuracy that reflects the importance of Stephen's martyrdom for earliest Christianity (Bruce, Marshall, Witherington). The truth is probably found somewhere between. While allowing that Luke exercised considerable freedom in shaping his story to suit his narrative aim, it seems likely that the memory of Stephen's martyrdom is precisely the sort that would have been preserved and transmitted, not only for its moral value but also because it witnesses to a decisive turning point in the relations between Christianity and Judaism (Fitzmyer, Johnson, Jervell, Barrett, Kee, Soards).

understanding the theological contribution the book makes to Christian faith. It is a stunning retort to his opponents, who falsely claim that he opposes "Moses and God" (6:11), the two central characters of his biblical retelling of Israel's history. (4) The story's final panel depicts a variety of responses to Stephen's speech (7:54–8:3). His martyrdom envisages the prophet's exemplary response to the truth of God's Word even as his executioners' hostile response to that Word confirms the accuracy of Stephen's characterization of unrepentant Israel.

**6:8-10.** Luke alerts his readers to Stephen's spiritual authority: "Stephen [is] a man full of faith and the Holy Spirit" (6:5)—he is a prophet-like-Jesus among his peers. Stephen's persona is filled out by the present text, which adds that he is "full of grace and power" (v. 8) with competence to defend the word of God "with wisdom and the Spirit" (v. 10) and to perform "great wonders and signs among the people" (v. 8).[258] This profile is surprising given Stephen's recent selection to assume the administrative duties of the Twelve (see 6:4). Clearly the Spirit has now marked him out also for a ministry of the word that will continue what Jesus (see Luke 2:40, 52) and his apostolic successors (see Acts 5:12) had begun in Jerusalem.[259] Toward this end, Luke's repetition of the catchphrase "signs and wonders" recalls Joel's prophecy of the last days (see 2:17-21; cf. 2:22, 43; 4:16, 30; 5:12) and enables the reader to discern Stephen's true vocation. Both his wonders and his inspired words are prophetic instruments used in service of an effective witness to the resurrected Lord. Such an inspired ministry specializes in the spoken word; it is finally what the prophet says to the people that provokes a protest from unrepentant Jews. They "argued with Stephen" (6:9) but could not withstand the combination of wisdom and Spirit "with which he spoke" (6:10).[260]

Stephen's opponents "belonged to the so-called synagogue of the Freedmen" (v. 9).[261] The reference to "synagogue" is neither to a particular building nor a local institution but to a religious movement within diaspora Judaism, which included vast regions of the Roman Empire, including Asia and Africa.[262] The word that is translated "Freedmen" is Λιβερτῖνος (Libertinos), a transliteration of the Latin word for "former slaves" (libertinus). A few of these "freedmen" became Roman citizens with influence in the political arena related to Judaism. Apparently a substantial number had settled in Jerusalem out of a sense of religious devotion and had founded a local chapter, or "synagogue," of this religious movement.[263]

This is Luke's first reference to the movement, and its appearance here implies its connection with "the disciples" from among "the Hellenists" (6:1), who now are led by Stephen and are enjoying great success in the Greek-speaking neighborhoods of Jerusalem (6:7). This latest round of conflict suggests that there are rival factions among "the Hellenists" that parallel the standing rivalry among "the Hebrews" between the Sanhedrin and the Twelve.[264]

**6:11-15.** Since fair debate fails Stephen's opponents, they resort to dirty tricks to subvert his influence. They do so by underhanded rabble-rousing, which pegs them as unfit representatives of diaspora Jews. The accusations they level against Stephen are three: (1) He speaks "blasphemous words against Moses and God" (6:11); (2) he

---

258. Luke's phrase "among the people [λαός *laos*]" (6:8; see also 2:12; 3:9-12; 5:12) places Stephen's ministry among and for Israel as the "people of God." See J. Jervell, *Die Apostelgeschichte*, KEK 3 (Göttingen: Vandenhoeck & Ruprecht, 1998) 224-25. I would sharpen the focus of this biblical idiom within this passage so that the "people" are from "among the Hellenists" (see 6:1) who have not yet become Christian "disciples" (see 6:1, 7).

259. The Western text of Acts amends v. 8 by adding "in the name of Jesus Christ" and v. 10 by adding "with all boldness [παρρησία *parrēsia*] so that they were refuted by him, unable to deal with the truth ἀλήθεια *alētheia*]." Both emendations forge greater agreement between Luke's portrait of Stephen's ministry and the prophetic "boldness" of the apostles' ministry.

260. Jesus predicted that his witnesses would be characterized by "words and wisdom that none of your opponents will be able to withstand" (Luke 21:15). This prophecy is here fulfilled by Stephen. The point is that it no longer matters whether Stephen's ministry is authorized by the apostles by the laying on of hands; it is sanctioned by prophecy of the Lord.

261. Barrett calls attention to the repetition of the article (τήν . . . τήν *tēn* . . . *tēn*) in 6:9 and suggests that two different groups of diaspora Jews are in view; the first are members of a "synagogue of Freedmen" as distinguished from a second who are unattached to this particular assembly but join them against Stephen. See C. K. Barrett, *A Critical and Exegetical Commentary on the Acts of the Apostles*, 2 vols., ICC (Edinburgh: T. & T. Clark, 1994, 1998) 323.

262. H. C. Kee, *To Every Nation Under Heaven: The Acts of the Apostles*, NTC (Valley Forge, Pa.: Trinity Press International, 1997) 317n. 3.

263. See J. A. Fitzmyer, *The Acts of the Apostles*, AB 31 (Garden City, N.Y.: Doubleday, 1998) 356-58.

264. So R. Pesch, *Die Apostelgeschichte*, EKKNT 5, 2 vols. (Zurich: Benziger, 1986) 237, who says that "jealousy" remains the primary motive of the Jewish opposition to the church.

"never stops saying things against this holy place and the law" (6:13); and (3) he claims that "Jesus of Nazareth will destroy this place and change the customs of Moses" (6:14).

**6:11-12.** The initial charge is both surprising and revealing. It is surprising because "blasphemy against Moses" is not illegal, and yet the opponents mention it before charging him with blaspheming God, which is illegal. Luke's phrasing of this twofold accusation may intend to put the reader on notice that the substance of the legal case against Stephen is bogus.

By posting a previous concern for what Stephen teaches about Moses, his opponents prepare the reader for two "legitimate" allegations that they place before the council for judicial deliberation, which concern "the customs that Moses handed on to us" (6:14). The real issue at stake, then, is over Mosaic prescriptions concerning the sanctity of the Temple rather than the orthodoxy of Stephen's theology. In any case, Stephen will defend his loyalty to both "Moses and God" as the two principal characters in his provocative recital of Israel's history that follows (see 7:2-53).

Luke shapes his story of Stephen's trial to parallel the story of Jesus' trial. Thus the freedmen's charge of blasphemy alludes to a similar accusation leveled against Jesus (see Matt 26:65; Mark 14:57-8).[265] The deceit of Jesus' accusers is similar to that of Stephen's as well: While "falsely" accusing Stephen of breaking the law that prohibits blasphemy against God (Lev 24:11-26), they break the law that forbids bringing false witness against another (Exod 20:16).[266] Luke's literary interplay implies that Stephen is a prophet-like-Jesus whose vocation is to bring the Word of God to Israel but whose destiny is rejection and death (see Luke 45–52).

**6:13.** His accusers bring Stephen before a tribunal, which had already threatened and flogged the apostles without just cause, in order to hear the claims of "false" witnesses. The chances of Stephen's receiving a fair hearing are nil to none! Both accusations heard by the Sanhedrin delimit the earlier charge that Stephen blasphemes against Israel's Mosaic traditions. In the first offense, his accusers claim that Stephen teaches against "this holy place and the law" (6:13). Since the Temple and the Torah form an integral pair of Mosaic traditions, what is actually alleged is that Stephen's teaching about the role of the Temple in God's salvation cuts against the grain of traditional Jewish practice as legislated by scribal "oral torah" (traditional *halakhah*).[267]

**6:14.** But the real climax of the court case against Stephen is scored by the second "false" accusation: "we heard him say that this Jesus of Nazareth will destroy this place." Significantly, this is the first negative appraisal of Jesus' suffering found in Acts and is proffered by these opponents of the church's mission. To this point we have heard only from Peter, who accuses unrepentant Israel of participating with Rome in the Messiah's death. The charge against Stephen not only implies a rejection of the church's gospel but also represents a considered political opinion that both the Jewish charge against Jesus for blasphemy and his subsequent Roman execution are legitimate consequences of his teaching against the Temple and Torah. In this regard, N. T. Wright has argued that Jesus' actions in the Temple were motivated by the conviction that his messianic role and authority for Israel had replaced both Temple and Torah as the central symbols of a Jewish way of life and faith. According to Stephen's Jesus, then, God's promise to purify and then restore an eschatological Israel does not include the Temple at all

---

265. Luke's version of Jesus' trial does not include the testimony of false witnesses. Dunn explains this omission as characteristic of Luke's narrative strategy, which delays certain gospel stories to Acts, where they perform a more important role than in the gospel tradition. This explanation presumes without hard evidence that Luke knew he would write Acts when composing his Gospel. If that is the case, this element of Jesus' trial may have been delayed to the present episode in order to underscore the history of an unrepentant Israel, who persists in rejecting God's offer of salvation at every stage of its history. See J. D. G. Dunn, *The Acts of the Apostles* (Valley Forge, Pa.: Trinity Press International, 1996) 88. See also L. T. Johnson, *The Acts of the Apostles*, SP 5 (Collegeville, Minn.: Liturgical, 1992) *Acts*, 112.

266. This characterization of witnesses as "false" is a narrative device, since the council could not have known this at the time (see below).

267. Fitzmyer, *The Acts of the Apostles*, 359. Among Pharisees a distinction was made between written Torah and oral Torah—what Josephus called "ancestral rules" (*The Jewish War* 7.10.2), the Mishnah labels "sayings of the fathers," or what Luke referred to as "the customs that Moses handed down" (6:14). This "oral torah" is based on case study and reflects the pious attempts of Pharisaic scholars to adapt written Torah to their congregational setting. Of course, there was no unanimity within Pharisaic Judaism over these matters. Other devout diaspora Jews were living in Jerusalem at the time of Stephen who were not believers and yet probably would have sided with him against the temple hierarchy in order to elevate practical "piety" over temple protocol (see 8:2).

but is, rather, fulfilled through Jesus' messianic activity alone.[268]

Perhaps Luke's emphasis on the Temple as the principal location of apostolic proclamation and subversive authority in Jerusalem continues this element of the Lord's apologia (see 3:11; 5:12, 20-21). Those who oppose the church's witness, such as these freedmen, seek to maintain the centrality of the Temple to Israel's national identity and destiny. While their actions certainly intend to counteract Stephen's growing influence among their compatriots in the holy city, the various allusions to the story of Jesus suggest that their hostility toward Stephen is rooted in a historical memory of Jesus' troubling actions in the Temple (see John 2:13-22 and par.) and his prediction of its destruction (see Luke 21:20-24 and par.).[269]

If Stephen's proclamation of Jesus included, if only implicitly, a denial of the Temple's centrality in Israel's future relations with God, in what sense is this second accusation against Stephen false? Are these witnesses "false" because they never really heard him say what they allege? Is the substance of their accusations "false" because Stephen never said or practiced what they allege? Or are they "false" witnesses from the narrator's perspective because they claim that Stephen is blasphemous when he is not? This latter option seems best. Stephen's subsequent speech does not criticize either the Temple or Torah but an unrepentant Israel whose zeal for the Temple prevents

them from believing that Jesus is the Messiah.[270] In continuity with the teaching and actions of Jesus, then, Stephen denies the Temple its pivotal role in "the last days" of salvation's history, when Israel's purification and restoration will result from turning to God's Messiah rather than by observing the practices of temple purity (see 3:17-23; cf. 7:44-50). While these allegations against Stephen may have misstated what he actually said about Jesus' troubled relations with the temple leadership and are in this limited sense "false," they accurately summarize the essence of Stephen's position, which the unrepentant Sanhedrin and freedmen would deem "false."

**6:15.** Stephen's transfiguration before his accusers, who "saw that his face was like the face of an angel," echoes the OT story of Moses' descent from Mt. Sinai, tablets in hand, when "his face shone because he had been talking with God" (Exod 34:29 LXX; cf. Matt 17:2; 2 Cor 3:10). This intertextual echo glosses Stephen's trial with the irony that it is Stephen, accused of blasphemy against Moses, and not the Sanhedrin, who is Israel's authorized interpreter of Moses. Stephen's speech that follows should be read not as a defense but as this prophet's inspired midrash on the biblical traditions of Moses for "the last days." Stephen, then, is hardly critical of Torah; he is, rather, an interpreter of these same "living oracles" (7:38), which can lead those who listen to the Messiah.[271]

**7:1-53.** Barrett claims that Stephen's is "the most important speech in Acts";[272] and many agree with this verdict. Johnson, for example, claims that "it provides the reader with the key to understanding everything that had happened in [Luke's] story of Jesus and the apostles up to this point."[273] But it is also the most perplexing and

---

268. N. T. Wright, *Jesus and the Victory of God* (Minneapolis: Augsburg Fortress, 1996) 405-27. The inference drawn from Jesus' *actions* within the Temple about what his *teaching* against the Temple might include is difficult to ascertain. Luke's Jesus predicts the Temple's destruction (Luke 21:6) but at the hands of pagans (21:24); and John's Jesus cryptically replies to the request for a sign: "Destroy this temple and in three days I will raise it up" (2:19). Jesus does not say "*I* will destroy this temple and *I* will rebuild it in three days." Perhaps in the ears of priestly loyalists to temple purity and scribes equally loyal to torah purity, Jesus' words were misconstrued—especially since he routinely pronounced the forgiveness of the unforgivable. Likewise, nowhere does Jesus teach against the law; indeed, he demands that his disciples obey all of it. However, his interpretation and practice of the law challenge and even change its current status within Israel—a point that was offensive to his scribal conversation partners.

269. The Temple had been destroyed by the Romans well before Luke wrote Acts, and the public debate about building its replacement as an eschatological sign was a lively one within diaspora Judaism. The historical subtext of the present passage sounds an unwritten note of Stephen's vindication. It may explain why Luke uses the future tense in stating the charge that Jesus "will destroy this place" (6:14) when, in fact, Jesus' prediction has already come true. But it also presumes a specifically Christian (or messianic) opinion about the building of a "third" Temple and an explanation about why Israel had been defeated by a pagan power and its Temple destroyed. See C. Giblin, *The Destruction of Jerusalem According to Luke's Gospel,* AnBib 107 (Rome: Pontifical Biblical Institute, 1985).

270. As Hill points out, Stephen does not actually criticize the "institution of the temple" but rather Jewish unbelief that resulted in the Temple's destruction. See C. C. Hill, *Hellenists and Hebrews: Reappraising Division Within the Earliest Church* (Minneapolis: Fortress, 1992) 69. If Acts 6:1–8:3 is dated *after* the Temple's destruction, Luke's probable intent is to draw an analogy between Israel's rejection of Moses and its dire consequences (see 7:35-50; cf. 3:22-23) and Israel's rejection of Jesus and its implied tragic consequence, the destruction of the Temple. See C. C. Hill, "Acts 6:1–8:4: Division or Diversity," in *History, Literature, and Society in the Book of Acts,* ed. B. Witherington (Cambridge: Cambridge University Press, 1996) 129-53.

271. R. C. Tannehill, *The Acts of the Apostles,* vol. 2 of *The Narrative Unity of Luke-Acts: A Literary Interpretation* (Minneapolis: Fortress, 1990) 2:85-87, notes how Stephen constructs his history of unrepentant Israel by quoting Moses ten times.

272. Barrett, *Acts,* 334.

273. Johnson, *The Acts of the Apostles,* 137.

difficult speech of Acts to analyze, as the history of its interpretation surely attests.[274]

Speeches in Acts typically respond to a theological mistake. Stephen's is no exception: The question, "Are these things so?" is asked by a hostile court in consideration of "false" testimony (see above). On the face of it, however, Stephen's speech is hardly an apologia in either form or motive; nowhere does he *directly* respond to the charges brought against him. Nor is his speech kerygmatic, since nowhere does he draw together biblical passages in support of the church's proclamation that the risen Jesus is God's promised Messiah. Rather, he tells a story of unrepentant Israel. Johnson reminds us that similar prophetic recitals of Israel's history were commonplace within biblical and contemporary Jewish literature. The manner of the storyteller's retelling of that sacred history—what is included or omitted and in what sequence—presents a particular line of vision into Israel's faith and destiny.[275] Apart from its brevity, the principal literary convention that distinguishes this historiography from secular counterparts (e.g., Herodotus, Thucydides, Josephus) is its biblical diction and citation: Stephen's speech is midrashic—that is, he retells Israel's history by recalling a selection of biblical stories that carry his theological freight—a prophet's exposure of Israel's need for repentance and restoration.[276] He only indirectly responds to the charges leveled against him as an element of this theological perspective, and the central themes of his speech are those of a pious Jew who would never blaspheme God or Moses (see 6:11).[277] The following summary should help to orient readers to Stephen's story.

(1) *God is the principal subject of Israel's story, and God's provident care throughout Israel's history is its main predicate.*[278] God has persistently acted in the history of "our ancestors" to reverse evil with good, to make and keep promises, and to see (7:34), hear (7:34), appear (7:2), speak, (7:3, 6, 33) and come down (7:34) to rescue (7:10, 34) Israel from despair and death. This is the God who judges those who oppress Israel (7:7) and who turns from an unfaithful Israel in sorrow (7:42). No fair-minded assembly of Jewish jurists could seriously entertain the freedmen's original accusation that Stephen blasphemed against God.[279]

(2) *God grants wisdom, special insight, and "signs and wonders" to those chosen and called by God to lead the repentant Israel (7:10, 22, 36).* The liberators of Israel are prophets of God. Even before Israel was Israel, God raised up prophets, such as Joseph, who suffered at the hands of hostile authorities; and when Israel became Israel, God chose and empowered prophets-like-Moses (and Jesus) to deliver God's word to an Israel that routinely misunderstood and denounced them. In fact, while "the pharaohs" recognized their prophetic gifts (7:11, 22), these servants of God were rejected within Israel. Stephen's ministry and martyrdom are exemplary of these prophetic leaders of God's people.

(3) *Unrepentant Israel is a "stiff-necked people" (7:51).* As a pattern expressive of God's persistent concern for Israel and its persistent disregard for God's saving word, God sends the prophetic carrier of God's saving word twice to Israel (7:12-13, 35-36). An ignorant Israel fails to obey the first time and will listen to him only upon

---

274. The secondary literature on Stephen's speech is vast, reflecting the variety of critical issues at stake. See Fitzmyer, *The Acts of the Apostles,* 386-88, for a working bibliography. Haenchen admits that "experts have cudgeled their brains" in trying to sort these issues out. See E. Haenchen, *The Acts of the Apostles* (Philadelphia: Westminster, 1971) 286. For a summary of these scholarly debates, see M. L. Soards, *The Speeches in Acts: Their Content, Context, and Concerns* (Louisville: Westminster/John Knox, 1994) 58-70; Witherington, *The Acts of the Apostles,* 259-64.

275. Johnson, *The Acts of the Apostles,* 120.

276. Luke's quotation or allusions of Scripture are in line with his use of Scripture elsewhere in Acts. He does not distort the theological intent of the cited/echoed biblical (LXX) text but interprets its current meaning to fit into his narrative. The impression that lingers after this speech is that Stephen's verdict of those who accuse him is also God's verdict as scripted and sanctioned by the Scriptures.

277. Soards, *The Speeches in Acts,* 58, notes that the speech, although incomplete, is a kind of judicial rhetoric called "counteraccusation." The defendant does not offer countervailing evidence to overturn an indictment or even seek acquittal on some other grounds. Rather, the defendant takes the offensive to indict his accusers as the guilty party. Naturally, since the accusers generally hold judicial power and the indicted defendant has none, the audience should not expect the defendant to be acquitted, and Stephen isn't.

278. Krodel claims that the opening phrase of Stephen's speech, which invokes God as "God of glory," introduces divine transcendence as the organizing theme of the speech, which for this reason is enclosed by Stephen's final vision of "the glory of God" (7:55). See G. Krodel, *Acts,* ACNT (Minneapolis: Augsburg, 1986) 140.

279. See J. D. G. Dunn, *The Acts of the Apostles* (Valley Forge, Pa.: Trinity Press International, 1996) 92.

his return—but only with short-term results.[280] Whereas the community that shares goods lives together (most of the time) with "one heart and soul," disobedient Israel is a divided people; this makes it impossible to hear the word of God (7:9, 26, 39-41). The execution of Stephen is this Israel's second rejection of God's prophet, and so the word will depart Jerusalem for another place.[281]

(4) *The Lord God's activity on behalf of Israel is not bounded by a particular place of worship or time of salvation.* Clearly the distinction between "true" and "false" worship is an important theme of Stephen's speech; "true" worship of a transcendent God can never be domesticated into cultic prescription, to handmade artifacts, or to an institutionalized protocol.[282] The vital texture of his speech is provided by the perpetual motion that marks Israel's relations with God: It moves constantly from place to place, from land to land, while God's promise given to Abraham, reissued by the prophets to this constantly changing environment, remains the fixed constant. Against those who accuse him, then, Stephen's concluding point about the tent *cum* Temple is not to criticize the Temple as a sacred site for worshiping God but only the Sanhedrin's temple politics, which divide the house of Israel and blind the people of God to the truth about Jesus.

In his concluding words, Stephen clearly understands that there is a christological component to temple politics. The resurrection of Jesus has confirmed him as God's Messiah and the central symbol of Jewish faith and life—not the Temple, not the Torah, not any institution of Jewish national life or religious cult. But temple politics are a politics of power. The subtext of Stephen's accusation of official Israel's "stiff-necked" leadership is to

challenge their presumption that a transcendent God, the only God, can be contained within a sacred place or particular parcel of land and regulated by a powerful group of self-appointed people. The God of Stephen's speech is constantly on the move from heaven to earth, and upon earth from place to place, making surprising choices at every turn in fulfilling the promise of salvation.

**7:1-16. The "Patriarchal" Epoch of God's Promise.** Stephen begins his story of Israel's history with God's promise to Abraham (vv. 2-8). Peter's earlier speech provides initial commentary on Abraham's promise both to lay claim on God's ultimate intent to bless "all the families of the earth" and to condition this universal salvation upon Israel's repentance (see 3:19-26). Stephen's rehearsal of God's promise to Abraham reflects a similar theme in that the promise is not realized during the patriarch's lifetime but points to its future fulfillment for "his descendants after him" (vv. 6-7). He depicts a wandering Abraham as following God's directions from place to place (vv. 3-4; cf. Gen 11:31–12:5), even being removed from the promised land, of which "God did not give him any of it . . . not even a foot's length" (v. 5; cf. Gen 15:7; 22:17; Deut 2:5).[283] Stephen also depicts this future posterity of promise as "resident aliens in a country not their own, and they will be enslaved and mistreated for four hundred years" (v. 6; cf. Gen 15:13; see 3:25). But he does not indicate that their eventual experience of divine blessing reverses these social misfortunes; rather, the essential characteristic of blessing is that "they will worship me in this place" (v. 7; cf. Gen 15:14; Exod 3:12 LXX).[284] Stephen's reference to Abraham as "our ancestor" (7:2; cf. 7:11-12, 19, 38, 44-45), coupled with his striking phrase "covenant of circumcision" (7:8; cf. Genesis 17), reflects his position on the point currently debated

280. According to Johnson's "two visitation" hypothesis, the Gospel story of Luke's Jesus tells of God's messianic prophet sent forth a first time to save Israel. Because of their ignorance, Israel rejects him and he is forced into exile (i.e., his ascension). Acts narrates the "second visitation" and second offering of God's salvation to Israel. In Acts, however, Jesus' role is resumed by his Spirit-filled successors—substitutes for the glorified Jesus and armed with his Spirit's "signs and wonders" and inspired word. In hearing the word of God proclaimed a second time, Israel can no longer plead ignorance. Israel will no longer be excused as Peter accused them earlier in Acts (3:17). The stakes are elevated for Israel: If they reject the prophet's second offer of salvation, they and not he will be sent into exile. See L. T. Johnson, *The Acts of the Apostles*, SP 5 (Collegeville, Minn.: Liturgical, 1992) 13.

281. Ibid., 136.

282. B. Witherington, *The Acts of the Apostles: A Socio-Rhetorical Commentary* (Grand Rapids: Eerdmans, 1998) 271.

283. The Genesis narrative indicates that God promises Abraham "this land as your inheritance" (Gen 15:7). Luke presumes that God's promise was not realized by Abraham (Deut 2:5) and believes that it has only recently been realized for Abraham's progeny since the resurrection of Jesus (so Acts 3:25-26; cf. Romans 9–11; Gal 3:15-20).

284. Luke rewrites Gen 15:13-14 LXX by editing out its final phrase "with vast possessions" and substituting a modified phrase from Exod 3:12 that substitutes τόπος οὗτος (*topos houtos,* "this place [= Canaan]") for τόπος ὄρος (*topos oros,* "this mountain [= Sinai]"). The effect is to hear that God's purpose for Israel (and for all creation) is to "worship me in this place." While "this place" might anticipate Jerusalem's Temple, Luke is well aware that this Temple has long since been destroyed according to the Lord's prediction. The center of sacred worship has now shifted from a particular place to a particular person.

"within family": Israel's principal identifying mark is neither its fertile land nor its sacred sites but its covenant relationship with God.[285]

Consistent with his interpretive key, Stephen's account of Joseph portrays him as a type of prophet (vv. 9-16) whose story typifies all prophets, including Jesus and now Stephen. The "patriarchs" are "jealous" (ζηλόω zēloō) of Joseph and sell him into slavery (v. 9; cf. Genesis 37). But God rescues him and enables him to "win favor and to show wisdom" with the pagan pharaoh (v. 10; cf. Genesis 41). This same prophetic pattern of reversal was introduced earlier in Acts when the Sadducees were "filled with jealousy" (ζῆλος zēlos) because of the popularity of the apostles (5:17), provoking their arrest and their miraculous rescue (5:18-19). Moreover, that a pagan ruler discerns Joseph's prophetic gifts when Israel's patriarchs do not is another kind of reversal that will be prominent in Luke's story of Paul, when Rome safeguards him from malevolent Jewish opposition (see 18:12-17).

Stephen's attribution of Joseph's "wisdom" and his success at winning the pharaoh's "favor" recalls Luke's description of him as "full of grace" (6:8) and "wisdom" (6:10). Joseph is a biblical exemplar whom Stephen follows. As with Joseph, Stephen's destiny is in the hands of God. Joseph is enabled by God's Spirit to deliver his brothers from death (cf. Gen 41:38-39); likewise, Stephen's mission is to deliver "his brothers and fathers" (v. 2) from death. Yet, unlike Joseph's brothers, who finally respond to him on their second visit to Egypt (v. 13), God's saving grace is not mediated through this prophet-like-Jesus because Stephen's brothers refuse to heed his word. In the context of God's promise to Abraham, these seemingly unrelated experiences of Joseph and his brothers prepare Israel "for the fulfillment of the promise that God had made to Abraham" (v. 17).

Stephen's inclusion of a burial story (vv. 15-16) is puzzling, especially since its details disagree with Scripture.[286] Apparently Luke has taken bits

and pieces from different biblical texts to feature Samaritan Shechem, a region scorned by Stephen's orthodox Jewish audience because Shechem is associated with Mt. Gerizim, the most sacred site of Samaritan religion and the chief competitor to the temple site in Jerusalem (v. 16; cf. Gen 33:18-20). Its reference here functions as another piece of his larger contention that true worship of God is not relegated to a single place, which is a form of idolatry. Characteristic of his narrative style, Luke may also mention Samaria to prepare his readers for the following account of Philip's highly provocative Samaritan mission as the legitimate concern of Israel's God (see 8:4-25).[287]

**7:17-43. The "Mosaic" Epoch of God's Prophet.** The second, longest, and most important section of Stephen's speech focuses on Moses as another exemplary prophet of God. Indeed, Moses is the prototype of the anticipated Messiah whom God will raise up to deliver God's people from death to lead them into newness of life (v. 37). This messianic prophet-like-Moses is, of course, Jesus (see 3:22-23).[288] Thus Stephen's account of Moses authorizes his gospel proclamation that Jesus is God's Messiah and at the same time provides his defense against the charge that he speaks "blasphemous words against Moses" (see 6:11).

**7:17-22.** Stephen's opening assertion places this episode of Israel's history within the broader movement of God's plan to save Abraham's international progeny: Moses was born at a time "for the fulfillment of the promise God had made to Abraham" (v. 17; see also v. 5). Moses was born at a time of political crisis as well, when God's prediction of Israel's oppression (v. 6) was being realized under the rule of "another king who had not known Joseph" (vv. 18-19; cf. Exod 1:8). God's recognition of Moses' "beauty"[289] (v. 20a; cf. Exod

285. Note at the same time that Stephen adds "in which *you* are now living" (7:4) to the biblical allusion to Judea/Jerusalem. While he locates himself among God's people, Stephen at the same time distances himself from the "land" and "place" of God's promise in keeping with the central theme of his speech.

286. Krodel, *Acts*, 143-44. However, the Genesis accounts of patriarchal burials are confusing and have led to different speculations about locations of burial sites. See C. K. Barrett, *A Critical and Exegetical Commentary on the Acts of the Apostles*, 2 vols., ICC (Edinburgh: T. & T. Clark, 1994, 1998) 350-51.

287. I. H. Marshall, *The Acts of the Apostles*, NTG (Sheffield: JSOT, 1992) 139. His solution seems more likely if Luke views Samaritans as "the lost tribes" of Israel.

288. For development of the "prophet-like-Moses" theme in Luke-Acts, see the various studies by D. Moessner, especially his programmatic essay, "The Christ Must Suffer," *NovT* 28 (1986) 220-56. Moessner cautions the interpreter that Luke's typological use of Moses neither elevates Moses to messianic level nor diminishes Jesus' role in Israel as analogous to Moses. Jesus' fulfillment as the prophet-like-Moses is unique and final; there can be for Luke no messianic predecessor or successor.

289. Although Kee, *To Every Nation Under Heaven*, 319, translates ἀστεῖος (*asteios*) as "well-pleasing" and proleptic of Moses' obedience to God, the tradition of Moses' physical attractiveness is widespread in Jewish literature (see Heb 11:23),

2:2 LXX) and Egypt's appraisal of his "wisdom" and "powerful words and deeds" (vv. 20b-22; see also 6:8, 10) confirm him as to the prophet's manner born.[290]

**7:23-29.** Stephen's résumé of the second forty years of Moses' life follows this same prophetic typos and is coincidental of Luke's important two-visitation motif (see 3:17-23).[291] Stephen recounts the intent of Moses' first visit to the Israelites (v. 23) as a failed attempt to fulfill God's promise. Even though Moses was the one through whom God would "rescue" Israel (v. 25a), "they did not understand" (v. 25b; see also v. 12; 3:17).[292] The Israelite who ironically accused Moses of being "a ruler and a judge over us" (v. 27) got it right, but then "pushed him aside" and thus frustrated God's initiative to reconcile a divided Israel (v. 26; cf. Exod 2:14).[293] Because of Israel's obduracy, Moses was sent into exile in the land of Midiam (vv. 28-29).

**7:30-34.** The recounting of the final forty years of Moses' life includes a second visitation and its tragic aftermath and is more critical to the overall aim of Stephen's speech (vv. 30-43). Exiled Moses is called back to Israel by divine revelation to rescue an afflicted people (v. 34; cf. Exod 3:7-10).[294] Luke's telling of Moses' theophany at the burning bush concentrates on the Lord's statement that "the place where you are standing is holy ground" (v. 33; cf. Exod 3:5-6). Johnson comments that

once again Stephen's speech relativizes the importance of a particular "holy place" (= temple site in Jerusalem; see also 6:13), since any place where God presides among God's people through the Holy Spirit is holy.[295]

**7:35-40.** God dispatches Moses on his second visit to Israel. Stephen frames his retelling of this visit by mentioning the poor results of the first visit: "It was this Moses whom they rejected—whom God now sends as both ruler and liberator" (v. 35).[296] This depiction of Moses, reminiscent of Peter's earlier proclamation of the gospel about Jesus (3:13-15; cf. 3:22), is combined with the familiar catchphrase "wonders and signs" (see 2:19, 22, 43; 4:30; 5:12; 6:8) to draw a close family resemblance among Moses, Jesus, and his prophetic successors. Prophets are all called by God and are imbued by the power of the Holy Spirit to proclaim God's word and perform mighty deeds that make clear God's intention to fulfill the promise to Sarah and Abraham.

The comparison between Moses and Jesus in the literature of the ancient church emphasizes how much Jesus outdistances Moses (cf. Heb 3:1-6).[297] Here, however, and in Peter's earlier speech (see 3:22), Moses is considered the prophet par excellence because he predicted the one who would fulfill Abraham's promise to be a messianic "prophet-like-me" (v. 37).[298] Notably, Stephen employs the Moses typology without including his role as a lawgiver, since Moses "received living oracles to give to us" that evidently remain in effect (v. 38). The importance attached to the OT story of Moses is vocational: The Messiah will be "like *me*" in ministry and result. Thus the pattern of Israel's response to Moses' prophetic ministry is insinuated into Messiah's career: "Our ancestors were unwilling to obey Moses" (v. 39a; cf. Exod 16:3) and "in their hearts turned back to Egypt" in spiritual disaffection (v. 39b; cf. Num 14:2-3 LXX; Ezek 20:8), claiming ignorance (to Aaron) that

290. Stephen's phrase "powerful in words and deeds" is the same one used of Jesus by his disciples in Luke 24:19 (cf. Acts 2:22) and is similar to Luke's description of Stephen in Acts 6:8. There is no support for this description of Moses either in the exodus narrative, which makes the opposite point (Exod 4:10), or in Jewish tradition. The phrase is Luke's, and its motive is typological: Moses is the proto-prophet-like-Jesus after whom Peter and now Stephen are modeled.

291. See Johnson, *The Acts of the Apostles,* 13, although the two visits of the prophet determine the destiny only of those repentant or unrepentant Jews in that particular location.

292. Stephen's comment that Moses first failed due to Israel's ignorance (7:25) is not in either the biblical narrative or any extant Jewish commentary on Exodus. His midrash reflects Luke's hand in adapting the biblical story to his "two visitation" typology, according to which the people of Israel are given another chance to repent and turn to God for salvation because of their leaders' ignorance (see 3:17; 7:12).

293. Stephen's assessment that Moses' act is motivated by reconciliation reflects Luke's assessment that the principal theological crisis facing Israel is its divided house (Luke 2:34). As with Moses' failed effort to reconcile divided Israelites, the Messiah's attempt to bring peace to Israel was also rebuffed, because "they did not understand" (see 3:17).

294. Stephen cites and alludes to several fragments from Exod 3:7-10, combining them in a more succinct version to emphasize God's sovereign initiative in calling Moses to rescue Israel. The repetition of "this Moses/one" in the following verses recalls "Come now, I will send you to Egypt" (7:34b) and underscores his mission according to divine necessity. The implication is that this is true of the Messiah's mission as well, since he is the prophet-like-Moses.

295. Johnson, *The Acts of the Apostles,* 128.

296. The vocabulary used of Moses' two visitations recycles the kerygmatic language used in 3:13-15. In doing so Luke draws an implicit parallel between Moses and Jesus, thereby aiming the reader ahead to the prophecy about the "prophet-like-Moses" fulfilled by Jesus. In Peter's speech this same proof from prophecy is used (3:22) as to indicate the fulfillment of Abraham's promise (3:25).

297. See M. Simon, *St. Stephen and the Hellenists* (London: Longmans, Green, 1958) 60-62.

298. J. Jervell, *Die Apostelgeschichte,* KEK 3 (Göttingen: Vandenhoeck & Ruprecht, 1998) 240.

"we do not know what happened to him" (v. 40). Roughly the same response characterizes a subsequent generation's response to God's Messiah, Jesus.

**7:41-43.** Stephen next describes the spiritual treachery that resulted because Israel rejected Moses' mission: "They made a calf, offered a sacrifice to the idol, and reveled in the works of their hands" (v. 41; cf. Exod 32:4-6).[299] Even though his second visitation had produced a saving result (v. 36), Israel's disaffection with God soon after and their desire to return to Egypt and offer sacrifice to idols committed them to a slavery of a different sort: "God turned away from them and handed them over to worship the host of heaven" (v. 42*a;* cf. Rom 1:24, 26, 28), captive to the consequences of their choice to live without God's grace and power.[300]

Stephen's quotation from the prophecy of Amos (Amos 5:25-27 LXX) to conclude his telling of the Moses story makes "the most astonishing jump in the speech."[301] Luke inserts the phrase "to worship" (προσκυνεῖν *proskynein* v. 43*c*) into the prophecy and changes Damascus to "Babylon" (v. 43*d*) to correct its history and make clear Scripture's lesson: If Israel rejects the prophet's second offering of God's salvation, it is the people and not the prophet of whom God says, "Therefore I will send you into exile" (v. 43*d*).[302]

**7:44-50. The "Temple" Epoch of God's Presence.** At last Stephen considers the Temple directly, moving with great rapidity from the "tent of testimony in the wilderness" (v. 44; cf. Exod 27:21) to Solomon, "who built a house [temple] for God" (v. 47; cf. 1 Kgs 5:1–7:51). He uses the regular Septuagint term for the tabernacle (ἡ σκηνή *hē skēnē*), which indicates its role within Israel is as a "testimony" (μαρτύριον *martyrion*) or witness to the "God of glory"—the same

prophetic role the apostles, and now Stephen, have assumed within Israel (see 1:8, 22; 2:32; 3:15; 5:32; 10:39, 41). Stephen's choice of "tent" instead of "Temple" envisages God's direct control over its construction and its easy movement in the wilderness journey from place to sacred place so that one particular site is unimportant. By contrast, Solomon's (and certainly Herod's) Temple was not built according to God's pattern and instruction and could not be easily moved in any case! The glossary of worship terminology Stephen employs—"land," "tent," "worship," "God," "our ancestors"—shifts the definition of worship from the routines of a permanent structure to the dynamic presence of a transcendent God. Stephen's ironic wordplay concludes that any definition of Israel's worship that fails to emphasize worshiping God (= "the tent of testimony") runs the risk of substituting a "*tent* for Moloch" for the "dwelling place for the *house* of Jacob" (v. 46, italics added; cf. Ps 131:5 LXX).[303]

Stephen's contrast between Solomon, who builds a "house for God" (v. 47), and a God who "does not dwell in houses made with human hands" (7:48) is the very nub of the prophet's criticism of his accusers (see 17:24-25).[304] Read in the context of Acts, his intent is *not* to criticize the Temple per se, since it continues to function as a worship center for the faith community (see 2:46; 3:8; 5:12).[305] Nor does Stephen demonize Solomon (or even Herod) for building a Temple to worship God; in fact, Solomon merely realizes his pious father's heartfelt petition when building the Temple (v. 47; cf. 2 Sam 7:2-7). Stephen's implied criticism is rather of any theological claim that domesticates God's transcendence, whether this obtains to the legalisms of observing an oral Torah or following a priestly protocol for purification. That is, God does not inhabit "houses" bound by space and time, since "the prophet says 'Heaven is

---

299. The sin of the golden calf is viewed within Judaism as Israel's archetypal sin—a kind of "original sin."

300. The phrase "host of heaven" (ἡ στρατιὰ τοῦ οὐρανοῦ *hē stratia tou ouranou*) derives from 1 Kgs 22:19//Jer 7:18 and probably denotes astral powers. Luke shapes his account of Israel's spiritual failure in the wilderness by describing a religion composed of handmade idols and human calculations, neither of which leads a people into communion with God.

301. Dunn, *The Acts of the Apostles,* 96.

302. Moloch and Rephan (7:43*a*) are deities to whom the Israelites offered sacrifices in the wilderness. Moloch is a Babylonian deity; Stephen's reference to "tent of Moloch" stipulates that Israel's Babylonian exile resulted from idolatry. See Johnson, *The Acts of the Apostles,* 132. The threat posed by idolatry will become an important motif in the narrative of Paul's mission and the formation of Christian congregations in pagan environs (see 15:20-21).

303. There is a significant textual problem with the NRSV's "the tent of Jacob," as indicated by the different translation found in the NIV, "the God of Jacob." For arguments in support of the NRSV reading, see B. Metzger, *A Textual Commentary on the Greek New Testament,* (Stuttgart: Deutsche Bibelgesellschaft, 1994) 351-53; for arguments in support of the NIV reading, see Johnson, *The Acts of the Apostles,* 132-33.

304. 7:48 begins with ἀλλά (*alla*) to signal such a contrast between 7:47 (Solomon's Temple) and 7:48-50, which claims that God dwells in heaven.

305. Contra Dunn, *The Acts of the Apostles,* 97, along with others.

---

my throne, and the earth is my footstool' " (7:49).[306]

Stephen's use of Isa 66:1 LXX to conclude his retelling of the Temple's history repeats earlier references to Israel's idolatry in the wilderness, when "our ancestors" built an idol sacrifice by "the works of their hands" (v. 41; cf. "made with human hands," v. 48) and turned from God "to worship the host of heaven" (v. 42; cf. "heaven is my throne," v. 49). This intertext clarifies the primary subtext of Stephen's speech, which does not polemicize against religious institutions (Temple, Torah) but against an unrepentant people who persist in refusing to believe the word of God's prophets (see v. 39)—Moses, Messiah, his apostolic successors, and now Stephen.[307]

**7:51-53. The Prophet-Like-Jesus Indicts Unrepentant Israel.** The charges against Stephen are without merit: He blasphemes neither Moses nor God. His charge against his accusers, however, is more serious and has merit. They are in danger of repeating Israel's wilderness sin and are thereby perilously close to being sent into spiritual exile. Stephen accuses them of four evils: (1) They are "stiff-necked" (σκληροτράχηλος *sklērotrachēlos*; this term repeats an angry Lord's condemnation of disobedient Israel in Exod 33:3, 5), (2) "uncircumcised of heart and ears,"[308] (3) "forever opposing the Holy Spirit" (echoing Isa 63:10, which remembers Israel's rebellion in the wilderness) and so (4) behave "just as *your* ancestors used to do"[309] (v. 51, italics added). These accusations pro-

vide court evidence for his stinging indictment: "You are the ones that received the law as ordained by angels and yet you have not kept it" (v. 53).[310]

The real issue at stake in marking out a people belonging to God is neither temple nor torah purity but obedience to God's command. In this regard, Stephen's shocking condemnation of his accusers as "betrayers and murderers" of "the Righteous One" (v. 52) brands them as law breakers and unable to live up to their own standard of covenant loyalty. His use of ὁ δίκαιος (*ho dikaios*, "the Righteous One") recalls the story of Jesus' death, when the centurion confessed Jesus as *dikaios* ("an innocent man," Luke 23:47). The reader of Acts knows to fill in the gaps of Stephen's accusation with details of Luke's story of Jesus' execution as an innocent man; the gospel tradition provides the evidence in support of Stephen's judgment that those who put him to death were "murderers" and therefore law breakers. But its use here is articular—*the* Righteous One—and so recalls Peter's title for Jesus (an allusion to Isaiah's suffering servant), "the Righteous One" (see 3:14; cf. Isa 53:11).[311] Of course, the word of God's prophet that unrepentant Israel rejects concerns the salvation brokered by Jesus. The harsh implication is that the priestly establishment has forged temple practices and manipulated torah observance into a kind of idolatry that keeps Israel in a spiritual wilderness without Jesus, the true medium of sacred worship.

**7:54–8:3.** The contrasting responses to Stephen's speech are anticipated: The prophet's criticism of opponents inevitably provokes rage and death. Stephen's martyrdom confirms what Acts has only hinted at in the earlier suffering of

306. Mark 14:58 also substitutes "house" for "temple." The use of the plural "houses" reflects Christian tradition and, as used here, perhaps refers to all temples, pagan and Jewish. See C. A. Evans and J. A. Sanders, *Luke and Scripture: The Function of Sacred Tradition in Luke-Acts* (Minneapolis: Fortress, 1993) 197n. 102.

307. Evans, ibid., 197-99, rightly adds that the "people" Stephen attacked were the temple hierarchy, who sought to place God in the Temple and then define the terms of Israel's worship of God. This subverts the sovereignty of God and constitutes idolatry.

308. The charge of being "uncircumcised in heart" reverses the deuteronomic definition of covenant renewal when "God will circumcise your heart" (Deut 30:6; cf. Rom 2:29). The phrase recalls Jeremiah's judgment of unfaithful Israel as having "ears that are uncircumcised/they cannot listen [= obey]" (Jer 6:10). Surely his accusation recalls Stephen's earlier retelling of God's promise to Abraham, when "the covenant of circumcision" (7:8) indicated God's commitment to fulfill the promise within the history of the covenant/circumcised people (7:17). In effect, then, the refusal to believe Jesus imperils one's membership in the covenant community.

309. To signal the rhetorical shift from defense to accusation, Stephen turns from a recital of traditions received from "*our* ancestor(s)" (ὁ πατήρ ἡμῶν *ho patēr hēmon*; 7:2, 11, 15, 17, 19, 38-39, 44-45) to an accusation that his auditors belong to a history of spiritual failure written and handed down by "*your* ancestors" (οἱ πατέρες ἡμῶν *hoi pateres hēmōn*), a Jewish tradition to which Stephen/Jesus does not belong.

310. The reference to "angels" continues an interesting *leitmotif* of Stephen's speech introduced in his retelling of Moses' story. In two different places—at his calling (7:30, 35) and at his giving of the Torah (7:38)—angels communicate the word of the Lord to Moses. While Luke may well be continuing here the practice of the Septuagint to substitute "angel" as a euphemism for God's personal name, the usage probably carries theological freight within Luke's narrative world, in which angels typically mediate between heaven and earth as brokers of divine transcendence. This symbolic value is elevated in Stephen's contrast between God's heavenly habitation (7:49) and God's alleged habitation in the Jerusalem Temple.

311. The reference to Jesus as "Righteous One" recalls the cluster of titles for Jesus in Peter's second missionary speech (see 3:13-16) on the basis of which Peter demands Israel's repentance. While Stephen's appeal to Jesus lacks kerygmatic details, in the context of Acts Peter's earlier speech forms the intertext with 7:52 and fills in these missing details.

the apostles: Prophets-like-Jesus will share in the passion of the suffering servant. The evident importance Luke attaches to Stephen's death may also reflect a common secular sensibility that self-sacrifice legitimates the truth of one's witness. Thus in his death Stephen exemplifies Christian discipleship. He is killed because of the shocking things he says about God's relations with an unrepentant Israel.

Stephen's death also marks a radical turning point in the Acts narrative of the church's mission. Clearly things are different now: "That day a severe persecution began" (8:1b). The church's mission is largely finished in the holy city because of Stephen's death. Never again will Acts narrate an evangelistic effort in Jerusalem, and the holy city will now become home to all kinds of forces that are opposed to God's plan of salvation. To be sure the Twelve (and presumably disciples from "the Hebrews") still live there (8:1b). But soon their ranks will dwindle through martyrdom and its threat (cf. Acts 12). And James will later report to Paul that mass conversions among the Jews still take place in Palestine (see 21:20). But the narrative's movement of mission from Stephen's martyrdom forward will push away from Jerusalem and toward Rome. Something has happened in God's relations with Jerusalem's Jews as a result of Stephen's death. Perhaps his speech represents the prophet's second visitation; perhaps his rejection and execution have sent these unrepentant Jews into spiritual exile and they now must await the return of the Messiah for their own return. Yet there is also the prospect of rebirth and renewal in death. And so it is that Stephen's death serves to spread the gospel to other regions where the experience of the Spirit's signs and wonders and the hearing of the gospel will add others to the restored Israel of God.

The narrative of Stephen's martyrdom also introduces us to Saul, who will become in time the featured character of Acts and his mission its central topic. Luke introduces Saul to the reader at a theologically significant point: immediately before Stephen's death and his extraordinary petition for the Lord's forgiveness of those complicit in his murder. The deep logic of Saul's commission as a witness to the risen Jesus is not his background in diaspora Judaism, his membership in its Pharisaic party, his rabbinical education, or his Roman citizenship—all of which are important details of his biographical sketch in Acts and his vocation as a teacher of Israel. His conversion to Jesus and calling as a prophet-like-Jesus are explained by Luke in gospel terms: Saul is a forgiven man. By his own testimony, Stephen's martyrdom was a significant feature of Saul's conversion (cf. 22:20), not only as a benchmark of his own theological reversal but also as the foreshadowing of divine forgiveness and his restoration to faithful Israel.

**7:54.** The reader must eavesdrop on several conversations that fashion this story. The loudest is between Stephen and the mob that will kill him. Nowhere in Acts is the contrast between those who disobey and those who obey God's will more sharply drawn. The effect on the reader is to experience more concretely Stephen's biblical retelling of Israel's story as a history of disobedience. This somber effect is intensified by constant echoes of both OT and gospel traditions, reminding us that the harsh response to Stephen's prophetic ministry is characteristic of God's people.

The "these things" heard by Stephen's accusers are words critical of disobedient people and not of Temple or Torah. Their initial response is as expected: "They became enraged [lit., "their hearts were ripped open"] and ground their teeth at Stephen." The rage of a judicial body was first experienced by Peter in 5:33 in response to a kerygmatic summary of the gospel (see 5:29-32). The angry reaction against Stephen is like Peter's before him: Disobedience to God is measured by a people's response to the gospel and not by maintaining temple or torah purity. The phrase "ground their teeth" (ἔβρυχον τοὺς ὀδόντας *ebrychon tous odontas*) is used in the psalter of the angry response of the wicked against God's servant (Pss 35:16; 37:12; 112:10; cf. Job 16:9) and in Matthew's Gospel of those excluded from the kingdom of heaven (Matt 8:12; 13:42, 50; 22:13; 24:51; 25:30). The testimony of the biblical witness glosses this expression of righteous indignation as evidence of the accusers' guilt and their status as outsiders of God's kingdom.

**7:55-56.** Stephen's response is Spirit-filled and exemplary: He accepts his fate as the prophets of God had before him (cf. 2 Chr 24:21). The phrase "filled with the Holy Spirit" (v. 55) designates him as one who is enabled by the Spirit to give bold and powerful witness to the risen Messiah (see

2:4; 4:8, 31; 6:5, 8). In this case, the Spirit elevates Stephen's prophetic consciousness to envision "the glory of God" (v. 55) and "the Son of Man standing at the right hand of God" (v. 56). His vision confirms his faithful testimony and prepares him for a martyr's death. Thus in seeing "the glory of God" Stephen is linked with Abraham, to whom "the God of glory" also appeared with promise of divine blessing (see 7:2). He is further associated with the death and rising of Jesus, whom Peter claimed was "glorified" by the God of this same Abraham (see 3:13), and also with his return "in a cloud with great glory" (Luke 21:27; cf. Acts 1:11). Good company, indeed!

Stephen is enabled by the Spirit of prophecy to envision "the Son of Man *standing*" (ἵστημι *histēmi;* v. 56, italics added).[312] While several interpretations seek to explain the posture of the exalted Son of Man,[313] the juridical cast of this setting suggests that Jesus now stands before heaven's jury to give convincing testimony in support of his servant Stephen.[314]

**7:57-58.** The council does not have a compelling capital case against Stephen, for he has not blasphemed Moses or God. But now they think their case has been made by Stephen's "blasphemous" claim that the Spirit had led him through heaven's portal and to the very throneroom of God.[315] In blind passion the mob "with a loud shout all rushed together against him" (v. 57). Luke combines the vivid expression "they covered their ears" with "uncircumcised in ears" (7:51) to form a vivid couplet expressive of the accusers' obdurate solidarity in opposition to God's word.[316] No formal verdict is rendered; their murderous response is an act of rage—in effect, a lynching.

There is a profound depth of irony in Luke's formulation of Stephen's execution: They "dragged

him out of the city and began to stone him" (v. 58*a*). In their fit of rage, the mob maintains their pious decorum and takes him "out of the city," according to Torah's proscription (cf. Lev 24:11-13; Num 15:35) against murdering an innocent person, laying their coats at the feet of Saul (7:58*b*) in accordance with rabbinical *halakhah*.[317]

**7:59-60.** And so Stephen dies in imitation of Jesus: He prays, "Receive my spirit"[318] (cf. Luke 23:46), and cries out, "Do not hold this sin against them"[319] (cf. Luke 23:34), and died (cf. Luke 23:46). Unlike Jesus, however, the object of Stephen's petitions is the glorified "Lord Jesus" himself, the one whom the martyr worships.

**8:1-3.** Luke's transitional narrative features Saul. Luke upgrades Saul's passive witness to Stephen's execution to the status of one who "approves of their killing him" (v. 1). Saul also assumes a more aggressive role in "ravaging the church by entering house after house; dragging off men and women and putting them in prison" (v. 3).[320] The apostles, along with other Hebrews, are momentarily exempt from this localized persecution because Saul's persecution follows the lead of Stephen's execution and probably concerns only disciples among the Hellenists.[321]

312. In both Acts and the Gospels, this "Son of Man" refers to Jesus. Contra E. Haenchen, *The Acts of the Apostles* (Philadelphia: Westminster, 1971) 295. As a title for Jesus, this is the only example of its use outside of the Gospels and Revelation (1:13; 14:14).

313. C. K. Barrett, *A Critical and Exegetical Commentary on the Acts of the Apostles,* 2 vols, ICC (Edinburgh: T. & T. Clark, 1994, 1998) 384-85, helpfully catalogs the various interpretations of "standing." He thinks it is an idiom of Christ's parousia: Jesus stands in preparation to come for Stephen in the same manner that he will come for all believers at the end of time. If so, "standing" envisages the Lord's readiness to return to complete his messianic task (see 1:11; 3:20).

314. B. Witherington, *The Acts of the Apostles: A Socio-Rhetorical Commentary* (Grand Rapids: Eerdmans, 1998) 275.

315. Barrett, *Acts,* 383.

316. L. T. Johnson, *The Acts of the Apostles,* SP 5 (Collegeville, Minn.: Liturgical, 1992) 140.

317. See *m.Sanh.* 6:1–7:10. Mishnaic rules governing such things as the execution of a blasphemer come from a later period; it may well be anachronistic to read them into Luke's narrative. On the other hand, many of these regulations recall case studies extended back to the Second Temple period, perhaps including the protocol followed here in Luke's narrative of Stephen's death.

318. Haenchen, *The Acts of the Apostles,* 296, says that Luke fashions these words after a short Jewish evening prayer based upon Ps 31:5 to commend pious Stephen's "spirit" to the Lord.

319. Stephen's petition that God forgive *him* reverses what we would usually expect from a condemned man. His petition for forgiveness of the sins of others reflects his personal righteousness in two ways: by the implication that he has no sins to forgive and by the depth of his mercy in forgiving those who falsely and illegally execute him.

320. The purpose and nature of Saul's persecution remain contested. What is on firm historical ground is that such a persecution took place and that it was precipitated by Stephen's death. What is also clear from contemporary Jewish literature from the Maccabean period is that a zeal for torah purity could lead to harsh demonstrations against those perceived as violating God's covenant with Israel. In this historical light, the reader of Acts is better able to understand that Saul's persecution of other diaspora Jews in Jerusalem is prompted by his own zeal for torah purity (see Phil 3:6) and by the perception that this messianic movement led by Stephen had transgressed the bounds of faithful Israel as measured by torah regulation of temple practices and prerogatives.

321. See Hill, *Hellenists and Hebrews,* 32-40, who thinks it unrealistic to suppose that business returned to normal following Stephen's death. Passions among the Hellenists within the church would have been every bit as fierce as those that precipitated their leader's execution—especially if their numbers were as large as 6:1, 7 suggests. Paul's severe persecution may well have been a court-sanctioned strategy to maintain peace in the Greek-speaking enclaves of Jerusalem (see Acts 22:4-5). See also Witherington, *The Acts of the Apostles,* 278.

These initial snapshots of Saul in Acts provide a critical background for reading Luke's story of his conversion and calling in Acts 9 and then of his subsequent career as a Christian missionary. Saul's earnest opposition to the church is of a kind with those who executed Stephen, and his malevolent evolution from passive bystander (7:58) to leading enemy of the church (8:3) will be stopped by his breathtaking transformation into a leader of the church's mission.

Sandwiched between narrative summaries of Saul's dreadful persecution of Hellenist Jewish believers (8:1 *b,* 3) are two comments that move the reader forward in Acts. First, the church is "scattered throughout the countryside of Judea and Samaria" (8:1 *b*). Will they advance the gospel beyond Jerusalem, as prophesied by the Lord (see Acts 1:8)? Second, "devout men buried Stephen and made loud lamentation over him" (8:2). Luke's vague description of "devout men" has led some to think that they are not believers but are either pious Jews interested in maintaining torah purity[322] or Jewish sympathizers who shared Stephen's opposition to the temple hierarchy. Johnson is probably correct that this comment echoes the Gospels' tradition about Joseph of Arimathea (see Luke 23:50; John 19:38-42); he also suggests that "a good and righteous" remnant still remains outside repentant Israel.[323]

322. See G. Schneider, *Die Apostelgeschichte,* 2 vols., HTK (Freiburg am Breisgau: Herder, 1981–82) 479. J. Jervell, *Die Apostelgeschichte,* KEK 3 (Göttingen: Vandenhoeck & Ruprecht, 1998) 255, thinks this is the first reference to "God-fearers" and foreshadows the conversion of Cornelius (similar to Pesch and Roloff).
323. See Johnson, *The Acts of the Apostles,* 141.

# REFLECTIONS

**1.** "For we have heard him say that this Jesus of Nazareth . . ." (6:14 NIV). The growing hostility provoked by Stephen's ministry is due to his likeness to Jesus. Similar to Luke's description of Jesus, Stephen is portrayed as a prophet full of "wisdom and Spirit," capable of performing "great wonders and signs." He continues what Jesus had begun to say and to do (see 1:1). The accusations brought against him are also similar in kind and are made by common opponents. Both Jesus and Stephen died as martyrs, ever obedient to God, whose chief concern in the end was the forgiveness of those responsible for their deaths. Stephen is like Jesus in character and conduct, and he is lionized by the church as exemplary of a Christlike obedience to the redemptive purposes of God. But Stephen is not the Messiah. The church's confession of Jesus as Savior and Lord underlines his unique role and status in the economy of God's salvation. To imitate the risen Jesus is not to assume for oneself his messianic calling or his heavenly status: "Salvation is found in no one else, for there is no other name under heaven given to men by which we must be saved" (4:12 NIV).

**2.** "The time drew near for the fulfillment of the promise that God had made to Abraham" (7:17 NRSV). Great sermons often mark turning points in the book of Acts as they do in the life of congregations. In Acts they are precipitous of either transformed lives or hostile actions because of the ideas they introduce about the nature and manner of God's salvation. This speech by Stephen marks such a moment, largely because of the two important ideas he presses for. The first is that the history of God's salvation, marked out by a recital of Old Testament events, pivots on the promise of God to Abraham. The surety of Israel's future is predicated on divine promise, not on political negotiation. The second is that God's salvation is brokered by prophets-like-Moses, who are marked out within Israel by their liberating works and living words. The good future promised is determined by Israel's response to the provocative ministry of God's inspired prophets. As the history of God's salvation continues into our day, this prophetic calculus for realizing the promises of God in the church's life remains the same. Who are the prophets-like-Jesus among us? And what is our response to their provocative words and powerful deeds?

**3.** "Make gods for us who will lead the way for us" (7:40*a* NRSV). When any congregation of a faithful God refuses to listen to honest warnings of their spiritual laxity, they inevitably turn away from the one true God to idols they have fabricated to validate their selfish values. In response to his accusers, who claim that he challenges the religious "customs" of Moses, Stephen considers the prophetic vocation of Moses as exemplary of faithful Israel. The Word of God not only offers people God's forgiveness and healing, but it also engages them in self-criticism. While the primary task of the prophet-like-Moses is to mediate God's gracious rescue of people from death (in its various forms), the prophet also is called to mediate God's indictment of a people's obduracy and ungratefulness. Israel's rejection of Moses and then Stephen illustrate how difficult it is for God's people to hear harsh and honest words that call us to repentance.

**4.** "The Most High does not dwell in houses made with human hands" (7:48 NRSV). One of the most provocative themes of Stephen's biting criticism of official Israel's religious practices is the exhaltation of a particular sacred place (i.e., the Temple in Jerusalem), a particular priesthood, and a particular protocol of purity as the medium of God's active presence among God's people. This theme continues for the rest of Acts. When James expresses anxiety about the relations between repentant Gentiles and Jews in the diaspora (see 15:20-21, 29), he reflects a similar sentiment to the one challenged by Stephen: Can spiritual formation take place outside those practices and institutions the church (or Judaism) has established for this purpose? Jesus' criticism of the Temple as the central symbol of Jewish faith, followed now by Stephen, is deeply rooted in Christianity's core conviction that we are a people gathered together and marked out by our faith in a person. Jesus Christ sanctifies the place—any place—where the congregation gathers for worship and instruction.

**5.** "While they were stoning him, Stephen prayed" (7:59 NIV). The manner of Stephen's death is exemplary of his costly obedience. His inspired vision of the exalted Lord, glossed by his faithful confession and earnest prayers at the very moment of his martyrdom, expresses a genuine piety. Yet the most compelling evidence of the depth of Stephen's spiritual life is the content of his prayers. Similar to Jesus' dying words, Stephen prays for the forgiveness of his enemies at the very moment of their apparent triumph over him and his witness. He does not ridicule his executioners, nor does he express regret for his untimely death. He prays for their salvation: It is what and for whom he prays, and not that he prays, that gives his death its most profound meaning.

Included among Stephen's enemies is Saul. Prayers that petition God for the forgiveness of another are important for Luke: They make second chances for spiritual renewal possible (cf. 1 John 5:14-16). Paul's later, seemingly passing reference to Stephen in his apologia (22:20) is laden with this realization: The earnest prayer of Saul's religious opponent supplies the context for his own calling to be, as Stephen was, a prophet-like-Jesus. For whom does the church pray today? And what is the concern of our intercession?

# ACTS 8:4-40, "AND IN ALL JUDEA AND SAMARIA": PHILIP'S MISSION TO OUTCASTS BEYOND JERUSALEM

## OVERVIEW

This passage narrates the beginnings of the church's mission beyond Jerusalem, thereby fulfilling Jesus' prophecy of Acts 1:8.[324] The holy city remains in the reader's rear view mirror—always in sight but now left behind: "all except the apostles were scattered throughout the countryside of Judea and Samaria" (8:1*b*). This passage also tells the story of Philip, another charismatic prophet-like-Jesus and one of the seven (see 6:5) who has evidently succeeded Stephen as leader of the persecuted Hellenists.[325] It is principally through his prophetic ministry that the word of God goes forward into these new territories and continues to flourish there (see 21:7-14).[326]

Despite the strategic importance of Philip's mission, Acts relates only two episodes. Their combined role within Acts is much debated, although it seems more like a transition or interlude that moves the reader from one significant moment (Stephen) to the next (Paul) by nuance rather than by bold and substantive contribution. In fact, the literary shaping of Luke's account of the Samaritan mission (8:4-25) recalls the pattern of the first interlude of Acts (see 4:32–5:16): (1) The passage begins with a summary of Philip's mission to underscore its continuity with the Jerusalem apostolate (cf. 8:4-8//4:32-35). (2) This summary is followed by the story of that curious figure, Simon the Great, whose contrasting responses to the powerful word of God illustrate the theme of its continuity beyond Jerusalem (see 8:9-19//4:36–5:11). (3) The interlude concludes with another vividly rendered portrait of apostolic authority (cf. 8:20-25//5:12-16). In this sense, then, the story of Philip's Samaritan mission gathers together in a compressed way the most important literary themes of Acts thus far, moving them beyond Jerusalem into a new territory in preparation for the dramatic stories of Saul's commission to carry the word beyond Israel (see 9:15) and Peter's conversion of an uncircumcised Gentile (see 10:1–11:18).[327]

The role of the second story (8:26-40), Philip's conversion of an Ethiopian eunuch, is more difficult to assess. Once again, the reader finds a critical clue in its literary pattern, which Luke shapes as a chiasmus to bring to clearer focus the eunuch's pertinent question, "About whom, may I ask you, does the prophet say this?" (8:34), and thereby also his idea of Scripture (see 1:16). The eunuch's question reflects what he presumes about the Isaianic prophecy he ruminates upon—that is, Scripture is prophetic of God's plan of salvation: "About whom, may I ask you, *does the prophet say this*?" He also believes that biblical prophecy can make sense of people, places, events, and protocols that are the variegated bits and

---

324. J. D. G. Dunn, *The Acts of the Apostles* (Valley Forge, Pa.: Trinity Press International, 1996) 102, claims that the initial expansion into Judea began in 5:16, but clearly "the towns around Jerusalem" refers to the suburbs of Jerusalem and are still within its city limits. On the other hand, R. C. Tannehill, *The Acts of the Apostles,* vol. 2 of *The Narrative Unity of Luke-Acts: A Literary Interpretation* (Minneapolis: Fortress, 1990) 2:108-9, sees the conversion of the eunuch (8:26-39), who comes to Jerusalem from Ethiopia (mythology's "end of the earth") as the fulfillment of Jesus' prophecy that the gospel would spread to the "end of the earth." In this sense, then, the conversion of the eunuch sounds a transitional note in the church's international mission and prepares the reader for the activities of Paul the evangelist. However, this, too, is an unlikely reading, since Jesus' prophecy in Acts 1:8 concerns the *geography* (not the biography) of mission—i.e., Philip's conversion of the eunuch is the first such episode *on Judean soil.*

325. The secondary literature on Philip is slender. See F. S. Spencer, *The Portrait of Philip in Acts,* JSNTSS 67 (Sheffield: JSOT, 1992); F. S. Spencer, *Acts,* Readings: A New Biblical Commentary (Sheffield: Sheffield Academic, 1997) 84-94. R. Pesch, *Die Apostelgeschichte,* EKKNT 5, 2 vols. (Zurich: Benziger, 1986) 288, suggests that this is not the Hellenist Philip of the seven but the Hebrew Philip of the Twelve (see 1:13). Indeed, as J. A. Fitzmyer, *The Acts of the Apostles,* AB 31 (Garden City, N.Y.: Doubleday, 1998) 410, argues, Luke considers it a "divine necessity" for each discrete stage of the church's mission to be initiated by one of the Lord's apostolic successors. But the textual evidence strongly argues that this is deacon Philip.

326. If Luke was Paul's traveling companion and visited Philip in Caesarea with him, it could be that he first heard these stories directly from Philip (21:8-10). If Luke did not know Paul or travel with him, then this narrative is more likely composed freestyle to advance his theological interests. As with most speculations about Luke's sources, the truth is probably somewhere between: Luke had and used reliable sources but shaped his story to advance his own theological perspective.

327. For the connection between Philip and the later portrait of Peter in Acts, see Spencer, *The Portrait of Philip in Acts,* 103-22.

pieces of this redemptive plan: "*About whom,* may I ask you, does the prophet say this?" But he finally recognizes that biblical prophecies require prophetic interpreters to recover their meaning: "About whom, *may I ask you,* does the prophet say this?" The Ethiopian has already admitted his dependence upon "someone [who] guides me" (8:31*a*). The eunuch's question of Philip is appropriate, and this second story of Philip's mission rounds off his prophetic résumé. In addition to the gospel that he proclaims and the signs and wonders that he performs, Philip is enabled by the Spirit to read sacred texts after the mind of God (see 2:4; 8:35).

Of equal importance are the surprising converts that are added to the church's rolls. Samaritans and Ethiopian eunuchs are marginal Jews, more removed from Israel's promised blessings than their geographical separation from Jerusalem suggests. While Samaritans are not proto-Gentiles,[328] they are "the lost sheep of Israel"[329] and religious renegades as well as racially "impure" according to more traditional Jews. While the second convert is a pious pilgrim, his geographical origin and sexual condition disclose a religious status that is far removed from the epicenter of Jewish life and faith.[330] In fact, the subtitle of this section—"the

outcasts of Israel"—comes from Isa 56:8, a prophecy echoed in Luke's story of the Ethiopian eunuch (see 8:27). According to this prophecy, God will gather the entire household of Israel, including both "foreigners" and "eunuchs," for worship in celebration of God's faithfulness to God's people. Philip's mission in Samaria and his conversion of the eunuch do *not* initiate the church's mission beyond Israel; they are, rather, the climactic episodes in Luke's narrative of Israel's restoration that began with Jesus' messianic mission to Israel.

Finally, this narrative of mission is shaped by a biblical conception of salvation's progress, which begins within Israel as a divine necessity before moving out to the nations (cf. Isa 2:3). By the time we reach Luke's concluding summary of Philip's mission (see 8:40), Acts will have recounted conversions from the various groups that constitute the *whole* household of Israel—resident Jews from Jerusalem to pilgrims from the most distant regions of the diaspora, pious Jews most devoted to their religious heritage to those most detached from it. Why? To prepare the reader for the Lord's shocking commission of another Jewish convert who will carry the word of God beyond Israel as "a light to the nations" (see 9:15).

328. Luke seems to locate Samaritans and this Ethiopian eunuch within historic Israel in 11:19 when he summarizes Philip's mission: "They spoke the word to no one except Jews."

329. See J. Jervell, "The Lost Sheep of the House of Israel," in *Luke and the People of God* (Minneapolis: Augsburg, 1972) 113-32.

330. The precise religious identity of the eunuch is a critical problem of long standing, since it determines his role within the story. Is he a Gentile, a God-fearer, a Jewish proselyte, a diaspora Jew, or a representative of all God "seekers"? C. K. Barrett, *A Critical and Exegetical Commentary on the Acts of the Apostles,* 2 vols, ICC (Edinburgh: T. & T. Clark, 1994, 1998) 425-26, summarizes the various options and con-

tends (with others) that the eunuch is the first Gentile convert. However, his portrait in Acts is certainly not that of a pagan Gentile, since he is linked to the Temple and to Scripture. Nor is he (at least in Luke's mind) a God-fearing Gentile like Cornelius, since Peter later claims him to be the first Gentile convert (Acts 15:7). J. A. Fitzmyer, *The Acts of the Apostles,* AB 31 (Garden City, N.Y.: Doubleday, 1998) 410, concludes that the eunuch is a Jewish proselyte—a Gentile who has converted to Judaism; but this is not his distinguishing mark within Acts, since other proselytes had come to the faith (see 2:10; 6:5). He represents the most marginal groups within the household of Israel, since he is a sexually castrated Jew, considered impure and, therefore, forbidden from participating in Jewish fellowship.

# Acts 8:4-25, Philip's Mission to the "Outcasts of Israel": The Samaritans

| NIV | NRSV |
|---|---|
| [4]Those who had been scattered preached the word wherever they went. [5]Philip went down to a city in Samaria and proclaimed the Christ[a] there. [6]When the crowds heard Philip and saw the miraculous signs he did, they all paid close attention to what he said. [7]With shrieks, evil[b] spirits | 4Now those who were scattered went from place to place, proclaiming the word. [5]Philip went down to the city[a] of Samaria and proclaimed the Messiah[b] to them. [6]The crowds with one accord listened eagerly to what was said by Philip, hearing and seeing the signs that he did, [7]for unclean |
| [a] 5 Or *Messiah*   [b] 7 Greek *unclean* | [a] Other ancient authorities read *a city*   [b] Or *the Christ* |

NIV

came out of many, and many paralytics and cripples were healed. [8]So there was great joy in that city.

[9]Now for some time a man named Simon had practiced sorcery in the city and amazed all the people of Samaria. He boasted that he was someone great, [10]and all the people, both high and low, gave him their attention and exclaimed, "This man is the divine power known as the Great Power." [11]They followed him because he had amazed them for a long time with his magic. [12]But when they believed Philip as he preached the good news of the kingdom of God and the name of Jesus Christ, they were baptized, both men and women. [13]Simon himself believed and was baptized. And he followed Philip everywhere, astonished by the great signs and miracles he saw.

[14]When the apostles in Jerusalem heard that Samaria had accepted the word of God, they sent Peter and John to them. [15]When they arrived, they prayed for them that they might receive the Holy Spirit, [16]because the Holy Spirit had not yet come upon any of them; they had simply been baptized into[a] the name of the Lord Jesus. [17]Then Peter and John placed their hands on them, and they received the Holy Spirit.

[18]When Simon saw that the Spirit was given at the laying on of the apostles' hands, he offered them money [19]and said, "Give me also this ability so that everyone on whom I lay my hands may receive the Holy Spirit."

[20]Peter answered: "May your money perish with you, because you thought you could buy the gift of God with money! [21]You have no part or share in this ministry, because your heart is not right before God. [22]Repent of this wickedness and pray to the Lord. Perhaps he will forgive you for having such a thought in your heart. [23]For I see that you are full of bitterness and captive to sin."

[24]Then Simon answered, "Pray to the Lord for me so that nothing you have said may happen to me."

[25]When they had testified and proclaimed the word of the Lord, Peter and John returned to Jerusalem, preaching the gospel in many Samaritan villages.

[a] 16 Or in

NRSV

spirits, crying with loud shrieks, came out of many who were possessed; and many others who were paralyzed or lame were cured. [8]So there was great joy in that city.

[9]Now a certain man named Simon had previously practiced magic in the city and amazed the people of Samaria, saying that he was someone great. [10]All of them, from the least to the greatest, listened to him eagerly, saying, "This man is the power of God that is called Great." [11]And they listened eagerly to him because for a long time he had amazed them with his magic. [12]But when they believed Philip, who was proclaiming the good news about the kingdom of God and the name of Jesus Christ, they were baptized, both men and women. [13]Even Simon himself believed. After being baptized, he stayed constantly with Philip and was amazed when he saw the signs and great miracles that took place.

[14]Now when the apostles at Jerusalem heard that Samaria had accepted the word of God, they sent Peter and John to them. [15]The two went down and prayed for them that they might receive the Holy Spirit [16](for as yet the Spirit had not come[a] upon any of them; they had only been baptized in the name of the Lord Jesus). [17]Then Peter and John[b] laid their hands on them, and they received the Holy Spirit. [18]Now when Simon saw that the Spirit was given through the laying on of the apostles' hands, he offered them money, [19]saying, "Give me also this power so that anyone on whom I lay my hands may receive the Holy Spirit." [20]But Peter said to him, "May your silver perish with you, because you thought you could obtain God's gift with money! [21]You have no part or share in this, for your heart is not right before God. [22]Repent therefore of this wickedness of yours, and pray to the Lord that, if possible, the intent of your heart may be forgiven you. [23]For I see that you are in the gall of bitterness and the chains of wickedness." [24]Simon answered, "Pray for me to the Lord, that nothing of what you[c] have said may happen to me."

[25]Now after Peter and John[d] had testified and spoken the word of the Lord, they returned to Jerusalem, proclaiming the good news to many villages of the Samaritans.

[a] Gk fallen    [b] Gk they    [c] The Greek word for you and the verb pray are plural    [d] Gk after they

# COMMENTARY

There was considerable antipathy between Samaritans and Judean Jews in the first century.[331] Samaritans were widely viewed by traditional Jews as racially "impure," religiously "heterodox," and politically treacherous—the gatekeepers of the Roman occupation in Palestine headquartered in Samarian Caesarea. Even though they worshiped the same God and followed a version of the same torah, Samaritans were outcasts within the household of Israel because the location of their temple was on a different mountain and in a different holy place. Most religious Samaritans were dedicated messianists, who hoped for the coming of the *Taheb,* the restorer of Samaritan fortunes, according to Deut 18:15. The Jesus of the Synoptic Gospels avoids traveling in Samaria altogether, although Luke's Jesus does rebuke his disciples for asking him to be like Elijah and call down heaven's fire to purge a rogue Samaria (cf. Luke 9:51-56). However, the story of Jesus' Samaritan mission found in John 4:1-42 prepares readers for Philip's Samaritan mission in the following ways:[332]

(1) John's story of Jesus' sojourn in Samaria is introduced by, "Jesus had to [ἔδει *edei*] go through Samaria" (John 4:4). The geographical necessity of Jesus' detour envisages its theological necessity: Jesus went through Samaria as part of God's redemptive plan.[333] In continuity with John's Jesus, then, this account of Philip's Samaritan mission is governed by divine purpose (see 1:8).

(2) Jesus' encounter with the Samaritan woman underscores its "shock value." The woman is surprised that Jesus would speak to her (John 4:9), not only because it violates long-standing social conventions that arrange male/female relations by a particular etiquette but also because it offends traditional religious beliefs that have long divided observant Jews from Samaritans. The Gospel's subtext, which is now worked out more fully in this story of Philip's mission, is that God's "living water" is for the Samaritans too (John 4:10, 13-14).

(3) Jesus' response to the woman's remark concerning the popular currents that locate the center of worship in different parts of Palestine (John 4:20-24) illumines the literary relationship that places this passage following the story of Stephen's dispute with the temple hierarchy over the right "place" of sacred worship. Both Stephen and John's Jesus direct our attention to a God who is worshiped in "spirit and truth" rather than upon a particular mountain and at a certain site.[334]

(4) At the same time Jesus reminds the Samaritan that God's salvation comes from "the Jews" (John 4:22*b*); the redemptive protocol insists that a Samaritan mission follow a Jerusalem mission. The woman's climactic confession that "I know the Messiah is coming" (John 4:25) recognizes that his saving word is prophetic (cf. John 4:19) of her own hope in a coming Messiah (John 4:25).

(5) The Lord's extraordinary confession that "I Am" the Messiah (John 4:26) discloses his true identity as "the Savior of the world" (John 4:42) to this outcast and provides the christological subtext of Philip's distinctive proclamation of "the Messiah" to the Samaritans (Acts 8:5). Even as the experience of God's salvation that comes in the name of this "Savior of the world" dissolves the social and economic barriers in the community of goods, so now in the Samaritan and Judean

---

331. Literature on this issue is divided. On the one hand, Samaritans are considered a Jewish problem, and as such their origins, history, beliefs, social status, and religious practices are all evaluated within the context of Jewish history. See A. Crown, ed., *The Samaritans* (Tübingen: J. C. B. Mohr [Paul Siebeck], 1989). On the other hand, Samaritans are considered a Christian problem, and their role in Acts is considered from the angle of Samaritan Christianity, whose influence on Luke is seen through his emphasis on themes linked to Samaritan beliefs—e.g., the messianic prophet-like-Moses, God's preferential option for the social outcast. See Hill, *Hellenists and Hebrews,* 95-99.

332. The following is an example of a "canonical conversation" that takes place *between* biblical texts rather than in the actual ancient world *behind* the text. Whether the historical Jesus ever conducted a Samaritan mission is not the principal interest of this conversation. If the reader follows a sequential (i.e., ideal) reading of Scripture, he or she would have already considered Jesus' provocative use of the "good Samaritans" in Luke 10:29-37 and 17:11-19 and then Jesus' Samaritan mission in John 4 before taking up Acts 8. The "canonical" task is to discern whether this prior reading of the Gospels informs and gives direction to the interpretation of Acts 8.

333. See G. R. O'Day, "John, Introduction, Commentary, and Reflections," in *NIB,* 9:565.

334. This Lukan collocation of two episodes from Philip's mission concerns groups viewed as marginal in relation to the Jerusalem Temple. Not only are Samaritans considered religious rogues because of the location of their "temple," but also the eunuch is prohibited by Torah from entering the Temple (see Deut 23). The Temple subtext plotted by Luke's narrative of the Jerusalem mission is brought forward—although more implicitly—into this next stage of mission.

missions of Philip long-standing religious barriers begin to crumble as well.

(6) More extraordinary still is that the Samaritan woman, now a convert, becomes a witness to Jesus (John 4:39-42). She is Philip's predecessor in Samaria, and her personal testimony of Jesus leads others into a shared experience with him. Yet this new faith is rooted in a personal encounter with Jesus (John 4:40-41) rather than public testimony about him (John 4:42). The confidence that these new Samaritan believers share the same experience of Jesus with those that come before is supported in Acts by the literary theme of succession: Philip is a prophet-like-Jesus vested with power by the Spirit to continue what Jesus began to say and do as Savior of the world.

**8:4-8.** The various panels of this episode are enclosed by Luke's characteristic use of the Greek phrase οἱ μὲν οὖν (*hoi men oun,* "Now those," v. 4; "Now after," v. 25), which indicates that his plotline has turned in a new direction.[335] This catchphrase begins the story by introducing a doublet that summarizes the church's Samaritan mission: "Those scattered [in Samaria; v. 1 b] preached [εὐαγγελίζω *euangelizō*] the word" (v. 4), and "Philip went to the city of Samaria and proclaimed [κηρύσσω *kēryssō*] the Messiah" (v. 5). The people of the city listen carefully ("with one accord") to what Philip says and watch closely what he does. Earlier missionary speeches fill in the gaps of what Philip proclaims and provide meaning of the "signs" he performs (v. 6; see also 2:19). The impression is clear: Philip is a prophet-like-Jesus who has come to Samaria to announce the arrival of God's salvation.

Yet, Philip proclaims a word in a different idiom for the citizens of a different city. A new stage of Christian mission is symbolized by a new sign: the exorcism of unclean spirits (v. 7), which recalls Jesus' ministry of exorcism as an expression of God's triumphant kingdom (cf. Luke 11:14-26). The Samaritans' "joyful" experience of God's salvation (v. 8) is also noted for the first time in Acts and is another symbol of the gospel's arrival in a

new territory.[336] Philip's success topples the wall of enmity between Samaritans and Jews, and Stephen's puzzling reference to the tombs of Samarian "shechem" (see 7:16) finally makes sense: The patriarchs buried here found an Israel that includes "the lost tribes of Israel" (= Samaritans).

**8:9-13.** To illustrate this new day, Luke recruits one of the most interesting characters of Acts, Simon the Great.[337] Carefully selected elements from his legendary biography are recalled by Luke in a brief narrative flashback: Previously Simon had "practiced magic" and "amazed Samaritans" of every kind, who "listened eagerly to him" and called him "Power of God" (δύναμις τοῦ θεοῦ *dynamis tou theou*) or simply "Great" (μέγας *megas* v. 9).[338] This résumé echoes Luke's portrait of the crowd who responds to Philip by "listening eagerly" (vv. 6, 11) to the gospel he proclaims. In this way, Luke links Simon and Philip as two brokers of a power that attracts people to them. Unlike Simon's case, however, the source of Philip's prophetic power is the Holy Spirit and its motive is redemptive rather than political. This contrast is implicit in Luke's use of the adversative δέ (*de,* "But," v. 12). The Samaritans "believed Philip"[339] and were "baptized" (v. 12; see 1:3; 2:38; 3:6-11; cf. 20:25; 28:31). Whatever rivalry existed between Simon

---

335. See G. Krodel, *Acts,* ACNT (Minneapolis: Augsburg, 1986) 160-61; Barrett, *Acts,* 400.

336. Luke introduces "proclaimed the Messiah" (ἐκήρυσσεν τὸν Χριστόν *ekēryssen ton Christon*), an important verb for gospel preaching, in this narrative summary and will repeat it in describing Saul's first and final preaching ministries in Acts (9:20; 28:31) and in Peter's mission to Cornelius to define the essential task of the Gentile mission (10:37, 42). The experience of "joy" (χαρά *chara*) is introduced into Acts here as well and is subsequently used in 13:52 and 15:3 (cf. 20:24) to summarize the experience of Paul's Gentile converts.

337. His alias, Simon the Magician (Simon Magus), is never used by Luke and is the creation of later church theologians who demonized Simon and attached his name to all kinds of heresies and subversive activities—a reputation that Simon the Great has been unable to shake. Compared to his apocryphal profile, Luke's Simon is a rather benign fellow whose character functions to illustrate the transforming power of God's saving grace as well as the dangers of immature faith.

338. Although their precise meaning remains debated, the names Luke gives to Simon suggest his deification. Luke follows Scripture and consigns "magic" to the demonic realm (e.g., Acts 13:10; 19:13-20). Magicians exercise real power and have real influence over people, but magic's form and result are spiritually oppressive and physically debilitating. Hence, exorcism demonstrates God's reign precisely because of its liberating effect in the demoniac who is freed from oppressive or physical ailment (see Luke 11:14-26). See R. W. Wall, "The 'Finger of God': Deuteronomy 9:10 and Luke 11:20," *NTS* 33 (1987) 144-50.

339. While the phrase "believed Philip" is exceptional, since Luke typically has either God or Jesus as the object of the convert's trust (see 5:14; 9:42; 10:43//11:17; 16:31-34), it undoubtedly is elliptical and means something similar to his earlier phrase, where converts "accepted Peter's message and were baptized" (see 2:41).

and Philip is now over: "Even Simon himself believed and was baptized" (v. 13*a*). This Simon whom the Samaritans "followed" everywhere (v. 11) now "follows Philip everywhere" (v. 13*a*)!

But Luke alerts the reader to a spiritual problem on the near horizon: "Simon was amazed at the signs and great miracles that took place" (v. 13*b*). This expression is characteristic in Acts of the *unbeliever's* response to their experience of God's mighty deeds through the Holy Spirit and typically comes *prior to* repentance. In his case the redemptive protocol is reversed: His amazement at the Spirit's "signs" comes after his conversion and not as a precondition of it. He seems more impressed by the spectacular than by the spiritual. This response to the Spirit's "signs and wonders" reflects Simon's theological mistake.

**8:14-17.** The plot thickens when Philip's role is assumed by the Jerusalem apostles, Peter and John. Their house call on this newly formed Samaritan congregation is an exercise of their spiritual authority and should take no one by surprise. To read a sinister motive into their Samaritan mission is simply unwarranted; they are clearly putting their apostolic powers to use in solidarity with Philip's mission.

The expression of their apostolic leadership within the church is a different expression of a familiar practice: Peter and John redistribute the Holy Spirit among believers in need of its spiritual powers, analogous to their redistribution of goods to the community's needy (see 4:32-35; cf. 2:44-45). The Samaritan believers had not yet been baptized with the Holy Spirit, even though they already have been "baptized in the name of the Lord Jesus" (8:16). Luke does not explain the delay between these two baptisms, and their relationship remains quite fluid in Acts in any case (see 2:38-41; 10:44-48; 19:1-6). We can only infer from Jesus' promise of Spirit baptism that believers are unable to participate fully in the community's missionary vocation without receiving the gift of the Holy Spirit (see 1:4-8). The aim of the apostles' mission in Samaria, then, is precisely as before: to form a religious community that shares all things in equal measure including their missionary vocation. Even their liturgical acts of "prayer" (v. 15; see also 6:4) and "laying their hands on them" (v. 17; see also 6:6) recall the role they performed when commissioning the seven to heal the grow-

ing rift between the "Hellenists" and "Hebrews" within the community of goods.

**8:18-19.** Nevertheless, the narrative's spotlight remains on Simon. "Now when Simon saw" (v. 18) shifts the story's action quickly back to him for his reaction to the apostles' actions. Nothing in the text indicates that Simon has been excluded from the Spirit's empowerment, but his political ambition solicits a different species of "power" that would qualify him to lead the community— an authority to rule that Jesus had given only to his apostolic successors (see 1:2). The word translated "power" (ἐξουσία *exousia,* v. 19) denotes the legal authority of decision making.[340] Simon offers money to purchase for himself a share of the apostles' *exousia,* with all the rights and privileges that obtain to their appointment as rulers over the restored Israel of God. His theological miscalculation is again symbolized by his offering of money in exchange for something he could possess and manipulate for himself in complete disregard for the community of goods (see 5:1-10).[341]

**8:20-24.** Simon's spiritual failure is sharply pointed out by Peter who exclaims, "May your money perish with you!" (v. 20).[342] The direction and purpose of God's Spirit (v. 20; see also 2:38) are divine prerogatives (see 1:2).[343] Spencer contends the implied subject of Peter's severe rebuke is not Simon's salvation but Peter's honor.[344] That is, Peter regards Simon's spiritual insolence as degrading of his apostolic rule—the mistaken

340. See W. Foerster, "ἐξουσία" *TDNT* 2:566-74.
341. L. Johnson, *The Literary Function of Possessions in Luke-Acts,* SBLDS 39 (Missoula, Mont.: Scholars Press, 1977) 216. For the parallelism in narrative details and theological significance between this story and Luke's earlier story of Ananias and Sapphira (see 5:1-11), see Johnson's fuller discussion in ibid., 213-17.
342. So E. Haenchen, *The Acts of the Apostles* (Philadelphia: Westminster, 1971) 304, who nicely captures the threat Simon's lust for power poses to his eternal salvation.
343. Several allusions clarify Peter's intention in rebuking Simon. His assertion that Simon has "no part [μερίς *meris*] or share [κλῆρος *klēros*] in this [gift]" (8:21*a*) recalls the story of Judas, who forsakes his "part" (*klēros*) of apostolic ministry by failing Jesus for money (1:17)—the same "part" that Matthias then plays in replacing him (1:25). Ironically, Simon offers money to gain the apostolic "part" of the mission that Judas lost because of money. The next phrase, "your heart is not right before God," echoes Ps 78:37 and its teaching that one who repents will be restored to God. The OT intertexts of "gall of bitterness" (see Deut 29:18; Heb 12:15-17) and "chains of wickedness" (see Isa 58:6) harshly condemn the practice of idolatry, and here one might infer that Peter's holds little hope for Simon's restoration. See C. K. Barrett, *A Critical and Exegetical Commentary on the Acts of the Apostles,* 2 vols, ICC (Edinburgh: T. & T. Clark, 1994, 1998) *Acts,* 417. These biblical intertexts supply Peter's rebuke with a kind of prophetic undercurrent that makes his appeal to Simon to repent more urgent.
344. F. S. Spencer, *Acts,* Readings: A New Biblical Commentary (Sheffield: Sheffield Academic, 1997) 88-89.

presumption that membership in the Apostolate can be purchased by someone who is so obviously unqualified (see 1:21-22). The subtext of Peter's retort and Simon's prompt acquiescence is recognition of the apostle's ultimate authority on earth to determine the terms of any believer's participation in God's salvation (cf. Matt 16:19). Thus again the practical objective of Peter's exercise of apostolic authority is to save people from the consequences of their sins, as in his earlier speech that associates Israel's ignorance (see 3:17) with its wickedness (see 3:26) and prompts his exhortation to "repent and turn to God so that your sins may be wiped out" (see 3:19). Read in this light, Peter's rebuke of Simon is considerably less severe than his earlier condemnation of Ananias, and the prognosis of Simon's restoration is more favorable. The apostle tacitly excuses Simon for being ignorant (or theologically immature), and the reader more clearly understands the motive of his exhortation that Simon "pray to the Lord" (v. 22). Peter evidently holds out hope for God's forgiveness and Simon's restoration (cf. v. 23).

**8:25.** The story that begins with Philip preaching the gospel as he departs Jerusalem with other persecuted believers (see 8:4) here concludes with the apostles retracing his evangelistic mission by preaching their way back to Jerusalem. The inclusio that frames this episode by a common phrase (οἱ μὲν οὖν *hoi men oun*) indicates the continuity between the church's missions in and beyond Jerusalem and relates the differences between them.[345] The different tasks performed in Samaria (e.g., the exorcism of demons), the proclamation of the gospel in a new idiom (e.g., preaching the Messiah or the kingdom of God), and even the time lapse between water and Spirit baptisms all aim at the same redemptive reality: the restoration of the whole house of Israel (see the Overview above).

345. F. S. Spencer, "The Ethiopian Eunuch and his Bible," *BTB* 22 (1992) 155-65, argues that 8:25 better forms an inclusio with 8:40, framing the story of his evangelistic tour of Judea and conversion of the eunuch as a nice complement to the story of his Samaritan mission, which is circumscribed by political bounds and social conventions of a particular Samaritan city.

# REFLECTIONS

**1.** "Those who were scattered went from place to place, proclaiming the word" (8:4 NRSV). Persecution does not stop proclamation. In fact, Luke's story of Philip employs many images of traveling and references to geography to create a vivid impression that the word of God is on the move beyond Jerusalem in productive ways. This passage also indicates and illustrates the three "big ideas" of Christian proclamation: Philip preached the good news about (1) *the kingdom of God* (8:12), (2) *the resurrection of Jesus Christ* (8:4-5, 12), and (3) *the gift of the Holy Spirit* (8:15-17). The complement of gospel preaching and miraculous "signs" has a galvanizing effect on those who "listened eagerly" to Philip (8:6). The fact that a program of religious repression fails to stop the word from spreading says something about both the character of those faithful witnesses who are scattered and the intention of a faithful God whose commitment to humanity's salvation cannot be subverted.

**2.** "Simon . . . followed Philip everywhere, astonished by the great signs and miracles he saw" (8:13 NIV). The Samaritan Simon of Acts is a compelling figure. Later theologians who wrongly identify him as the prototype of every Christian heretic rightly recognize that at the root of Simon's spiritual failure is a temptation every new believer must resist. From his conversion, he is attracted to the spectacular. He covets the religious authority that would allow him to broker the power of the Spirit. He knows from personal experience that the one with hold on the reins of the spectacular can control the entire community (see 8:9-10). Thus Simon does not follow Philip for instruction in the faith, as the Ethiopian eunuch later would (below); rather, he is attracted to Philip and then to Peter because of the miracles they perform by the power of the Spirit. While miracles are a frequent phenomenon in Luke's story world, the spectacular is always a means to draw people to hear the word of God.

# Acts 8:26-40, Philip's Mission to the "Outcasts of Israel": The Eunuch from Ethiopia

NIV

26Now an angel of the Lord said to Philip, "Go south to the road—the desert road—that goes down from Jerusalem to Gaza." 27So he started out, and on his way he met an Ethiopian[a] eunuch, an important official in charge of all the treasury of Candace, queen of the Ethiopians. This man had gone to Jerusalem to worship, 28and on his way home was sitting in his chariot reading the book of Isaiah the prophet. 29The Spirit told Philip, "Go to that chariot and stay near it."

30Then Philip ran up to the chariot and heard the man reading Isaiah the prophet. "Do you understand what you are reading?" Philip asked.

31"How can I," he said, "unless someone explains it to me?" So he invited Philip to come up and sit with him.

32The eunuch was reading this passage of Scripture:

"He was led like a sheep to the slaughter,
    and as a lamb before the shearer is silent,
    so he did not open his mouth.
33 In his humiliation he was deprived of justice.
    Who can speak of his descendants?
    For his life was taken from the earth."[b]

34The eunuch asked Philip, "Tell me, please, who is the prophet talking about, himself or someone else?" 35Then Philip began with that very passage of Scripture and told him the good news about Jesus.

36As they traveled along the road, they came to some water and the eunuch said, "Look, here is water. Why shouldn't I be baptized?"[c] 38And he gave orders to stop the chariot. Then both Philip and the eunuch went down into the water and Philip baptized him. 39When they came up out of the water, the Spirit of the Lord suddenly took Philip away, and the eunuch did not see him again, but went on his way rejoicing. 40Philip, however, appeared at Azotus and traveled about, preaching the gospel in all the towns until he reached Caesarea.

[a] 27 That is, from the upper Nile region   [b] 33 Isaiah 53:7,8
[c] 36 Some late manuscripts baptized?" 37Philip said, "If you believe with all your heart, you may." The eunuch answered, "I believe that Jesus Christ is the Son of God."

NRSV

26Then an angel of the Lord said to Philip, "Get up and go toward the south[a] to the road that goes down from Jerusalem to Gaza." (This is a wilderness road.) 27So he got up and went. Now there was an Ethiopian eunuch, a court official of the Candace, queen of the Ethiopians, in charge of her entire treasury. He had come to Jerusalem to worship 28and was returning home; seated in his chariot, he was reading the prophet Isaiah. 29Then the Spirit said to Philip, "Go over to this chariot and join it." 30So Philip ran up to it and heard him reading the prophet Isaiah. He asked, "Do you understand what you are reading?" 31He replied, "How can I, unless someone guides me?" And he invited Philip to get in and sit beside him. 32Now the passage of the scripture that he was reading was this:

"Like a sheep he was led to the slaughter,
    and like a lamb silent before its shearer,
        so he does not open his mouth.
33 In his humiliation justice was denied him.
    Who can describe his generation?
        For his life is taken away from the earth."

34The eunuch asked Philip, "About whom, may I ask you, does the prophet say this, about himself or about someone else?" 35Then Philip began to speak, and starting with this scripture, he proclaimed to him the good news about Jesus. 36As they were going along the road, they came to some water; and the eunuch said, "Look, here is water! What is to prevent me from being baptized?"[b] 38He commanded the chariot to stop, and both of them, Philip and the eunuch, went down into the water, and Philip[c] baptized him. 39When they came up out of the water, the Spirit of the Lord snatched Philip away; the eunuch saw him no more, and went on his way rejoicing. 40But Philip found himself at Azotus, and as he was passing through the region, he proclaimed the good news to all the towns until he came to Caesarea.

[a] Or go at noon   [b] Other ancient authorities add all or most of verse 37, And Philip said, "If you believe with all your heart, you may." And he replied, "I believe that Jesus Christ is the Son of God."
[c] Gk he

# COMMENTARY

Acts combines the narrative of Philip's urban mission in Samaria with the memorable story of his encounter with an Ethiopian eunuch. As a religious person the Ethiopian symbolizes what the Samaritan Simon is not: He is spiritual pilgrim from a distant land who is earnestly seeking to understand Scripture's prophecies of God's salvation. This eunuch shares the same status as the Samaritan, however, for he too is on the margins of mainstream Israel, excluded by law from full participation in the covenant community (see Deut 23:2 LXX; Lev 21:17-21). The unwritten conflict plotted by this story, then, is that this pious proselyte, who seeks to know the God's purposes more fully, has been excluded from the very religious community whose resources would illumine his quest (see the Overview to 8:4-40).

The resolution of this conflict puts Luke's well-known concern for God's preferential option of the poor and powerless in sharper focus. The crisis facing the eunuch is not so much his social standing—he is after all an "official" with solid political connections—as his spiritual standing with God. Nor is his spiritual poverty the consequence of his own lack of earnest dedication to find God—as is true of Simon. Rather it is his forbidden castration and perhaps his nationality, not his piety or his practices, which have compromised his religious standing. The essential task of the prophet, then, is to clarify membership requirements of those belonging to God, sometimes in ways that redraw Israel's boundaries to include the excluded ones. The Ethiopian eunuch symbolizes the eschatological horizon of the Israel in the last days that is now taking form because of Jesus under the aegis of the Holy Spirit.

The key in recovering this point from the present passage is its chiastic literary pattern. The reader finds it stated in the form of "the right question" at the intersection of and framed by an inverted parallelism. The commentary on this passage will try to pay attention to the clues provided by this pattern:[346]

A (vv. 26-27*a*): Philip "got up and went" from Samaria south to Gaza
   B (vv. 27*b*-28): the Ethiopian eunuch worships and reads Scripture (Isaiah 56)
      C (vv. 29-30*a*): Philip "runs" according to the Spirit's command
         D (vv. 30*b*-31): the eunuch queries prophet Philip
            E (vv. 32-33): Scripture (Isa 53:7-8) quoted
               F (v. 34): "About whom is the prophet talking?"
            E′ (v. 35): Scripture is interpreted by Philip
         D′ (vv. 36-38) the eunuch queries prophet Philip
      C′ (v. 39*a*): Philip snatched away by the Spirit
   B′ (v. 39*b*): the eunuch rejoices
A′ (v. 40): Philip passes through "all the towns" from Gaza north to Samaria

**8:26-33.** The elements of the first line of the chiasmus (A-E) introduce the principal players of this conversion drama—the Ethiopian eunuch and Philip. The encounter between the God-seeker and the prophet, complete with angelic visitations and chariot riding, are familiar to the OT reader of Elijah's story cycle (see 1 Kings 17–2 Kings 3). Luke's Jesus alludes to just such an encounter during his inaugural mission in Nazareth (see Luke 4:26-27). In addition, many commentators have noted the parallels between this story and Luke's story of Jesus' exchange with his two disciples on the Road to Emmaus (Luke 24).[347] These stories from the Gospels provide additional texture to this story of the eunuch's conversion, where Philip is a prophet-like-Jesus whose words and deeds continue to lead the church's mission "from place to place" (8:4) beyond Jerusalem.

Instead of preaching in a particular "city of Samaria," Philip is on the road; he is up north and needs to take a southbound route to Gaza—"the road that goes down from Jerusalem to Gaza." The narrator's aside that this is "a wilderness road"

---

346. See Krodel, *Acts,* 167. C. H. Talbert, *Reading Acts* (New York: Crossroad, 1997) 90-93, uses a similar strategy to reach a similar conclusion but through a different rhetorical design 90-93.

347. For a summary, see B. Witherington, *The Acts of the Apostles: A Socio-Rhetorical Commentary* (Grand Rapids: Eerdmans, 1998) 292.

(8:26) is puzzling because the road is not a desert route. The reader is left to wonder what this detail contributes to the story. Spencer suggests that it relocates the prophet and the eunuch in a "liminal zone off the beaten path of regular traffic," where serious theological reflection and personal transformation are more likely.[348] Perhaps. In any case, the presence of both "the angel of the Lord" (8:26; see 5:19) and "the Spirit" (8:29), who give Philip directions,[349] make clear the divine necessity of his encounter with the Ethiopian. The images of heaven's intervention in earth's work could hardly be clearer.

The eunuch's religious résumé is even more interesting and detailed. As with Philip, the narrator carefully locates him on Judea's map: "he had come to Jerusalem to worship" (v. 27 b) and "was returning home" (v. 28 a). He was evidently a proselyte from the diaspora who had recently made a hard pilgrimage as a mark of his profound religious devotion, since the farther one journeys the more devotion one exhibits. The reference to "worship" in Jerusalem is provocative since eunuchs were forbidden to enter the Temple for worship (see 3:8). By juxtaposing "eunuch" and "worship" the narrator perhaps imagines that the Ethiopian's recent "worship experience" has triggered a theological crisis over his future in the household of Israel. His social class—"a court official of Queen Candace in charge of her treasury" (v. 27 a)—only intensifies the impression that he is spiritually hungry and not materially impoverished.

The final feature of the eunuch's profile is that "he was reading the prophet Isaiah" (v. 28 b). Perhaps he dwells on Isaiah because of its hopeful references about Ethiopia's participation in the blessings of God (Isa 18:1; 45:15). The quoted prophecy from Isa 53:7-8 (see Acts 8:32-33) provides the prophetic intertext necessary for interpreting the *second* half of this story (see 8:35-40). However, the Ethiopian man's personal biography echoes a second Isaianic prophecy (Isa 56:3-8; cf. Ps 67:32), one that provides an important subtext that illumines the initial encounter between

prophet and convert (i.e., 8:26-33). According to this echoed prophecy, God promises to "gather the outcasts of Israel" (Isa 56:8), including those "eunuchs and foreigners" (Isa 56:3-4; cf. 39:7) who "keep the Sabbath and do not profane it" (Isa 56:6) and come to "my holy mountain//my house of prayer" (Isa 56:7), and to grant them a future with God. This Ethiopian eunuch who "has come to Jerusalem to worship" (v. 27) represents both these disenfranchised, disinherited groups of an exiled Israel as the choice recipient of God's promise.

Philip joins the Ethiopian eunuch by instruction of the Spirit of prophecy (vv. 29-30 a), and Philip's abrupt question is appropriate to his prophetic vocation: "Do you understand what you are reading?" (v. 30 b). At one level, such a question asked by a stranger of a literate man seems condescending and offensive. Philip's question, however, presumes that Scripture is more than a literary text, for this man is "reading the prophet Isaiah," who conveys information about God's plan of salvation. Moreover, the man's earnest piety suggests a likely interest in the text's theological meaning; thus, his retort is also apropos: "How can I unless someone guides me?" (v. 31).[350] His subsequent invitation that Philip "sit beside him" implies spiritual discernment that recognizes this stranger as his theological mentor who is authorized by God to comment on this biblical prophecy.

The cited prophecy is from Isaiah 53, whose history within Christianity commends its profound influence in shaping our core convictions about Jesus' death.[351] Its function in Acts, however, is to define more clearly why an Ethiopian eunuch should be interested in the Christian gospel. Luke quotes the prophecy verbatim from the

---

348. Spencer, *Acts,* 90-91. While, perhaps, another indication that Luke's geographical knowledge of Palestine is poor, this could be yet another example of Luke's use of geography to cue a theological interest in his story.

349. On the interchangeability of "Spirit" and "angel" in contemporary Jewish literature, see J. Levison, "The Prophetic Spirit as an Angel According to Philo," *HTR* 88 (1995) 189-207.

350. The eunuch's question is awkwardly stated and "corrected" by later scribes. Luke's intent is hardly to express the eunuch's slow wit, but his self-awareness that his prospects for understanding this Scripture are conditioned on the aid of a talented/inspired interpreter. See Haenchen, *The Acts of the Apostles,* 312. Barrett, *Acts,* 428, however, claims that the eunuch's Greek reflects his rhetorical elegance and literacy.

351. Isaiah 53 is rarely cited but often echoed in NT passages of Jesus' suffering (Matt 8:17; Luke 22:37; John 12:38; Rom 10:16; 1 Pet 2:21-25; Rev 14:5). Whether these intertextual echoes support later Christian use of Isaiah 53 as a prophecy of Jesus' atonement remains contested. See M. Hooker, *Jesus and the Servant* (London: SPCK, 1959) 113-14, who claims that Luke cites only Isa 53:7-8 in Acts 8 and, therefore, avoids any soteriological implication. See also M. Parsons, "Isaiah 53 and Acts 8," in *Jesus and the Suffering Servant: Isaiah 53 and Christian Origins,* ed. W. Bellinger and W. Farmer (Harrisburg, Pa.: Trinity, 1998) 104-24, who argues for a soteriological meaning in Luke's use in Acts 8.

Septuagint. At first glance, we note that only that portion of the prophecy that speaks of the servant's "humiliation" (ταπείνωσις *tapeinōsis,* v. 33) is mentioned. If the Servant's humiliation denotes social ostracism, the eunuch's situation is interpreted by Isaiah's suffering Servant because he too is a social outcast. Further, Johnson notes that this quotation departs from its Hebrew source in several important ways. The most dramatic and important deviation is found in the final phrase "for his life is taken from the earth" (8:33; the NIV translation, which renders the tense of the clause ὅτι [*hoti*] in the past ["for his life *was taken* (ὅτι αἴρεται *hoti airetai*) from earth"], is unwarranted).[352] While the Hebrew text claims that the servant is "cut off [גזר *gzr*] from the earth" (i.e., he dies), the Septuagint translation oddly renders *gzr* as "lifted up" (αἴρω *airō*) from the earth." This verbal shift allows Luke to interpret the Servant's humiliation as the means to his exaltation—he is "lifted up from earth" into heaven (see 1:9-11). If Luke takes this phrase to refer to the vindication (or "lifting up") of the humiliated Servant, then perhaps the reader should suppose that the eunuch's identification with the humiliated Servant might lead him to hope for a different future than the one consigned him by official Israel.

**8:34.** Found at the center of the chiasmus (see the Overview to 8:4-40) is the eunuch's question, which keys a redemptive encounter: "About whom, may I ask, does the prophet say this, about himself or about someone else?" Of three possible interpretations, he omits the nationalistic one most common in his day: faithful Israel. But naturally an outcast and foreigner is unlikely to include an interpretation, no matter how popular, that excludes him. Some contemporary sectarian movements within Judaism were interpreting this prophecy as pointing to God's eschatological prophet whom Isaiah "himself" represents. Given the response to Stephen's accusation that Israel persecutes and murders its prophets (see 7:52), including the "Righteous One" (see 7:53; cf. Isa 53:11), this second reading is entirely plausible.[353] But apparently the eunuch holds out for a "some-

one else" with whom the outcasts and aliens of Israel might more closely identify and then join in God's coming triumph.

**8:35-40.** The eunuch's conversion, recounted by the second line of this chiasmus (E[prime]-A[prime]), issues from the prophet's inspired response to his climactic question. "Then Philip began to speak" (v. 35*a*) translates a biblical expression for divinely inspired speech (ἀνοίξας . . . τὸ στόμα αὐτοῦ *anoixas . . . to stoma autou;* lit., "opening his mouth"; see 10:34; Exod 4:12; Ezek 3:27). In an encounter that is so evidently superintended by the Spirit, we are not surprised that Philip's answer is not his to give but God's. Luke's characteristic summary of Philip's response—"the good news about Jesus" (v. 35*b*)—is filled out by details from the other missionary speeches of Acts.

The conversion of the eunuch is recounted elliptically by his request to be baptized (v. 37), which presumes his public confession of faith "in the name of the Lord Jesus" (v. 16; see also 2:21, 38-41).[354] In the prior story of the Samaritan mission, water and Spirit baptism are discrete but integral media of divine grace (see 8:12-13, 16-17). Perhaps to preserve this pattern of Philip's mission a few scribes rewrote v. 39 this way: "When they came up out of the water, the Spirit fell upon the eunuch, but an angel carried Philip away." In any case, water baptism initiates new believers into the realm of the Spirit of prophecy whose filling empowers them for Christian ministry; conversion makes one dependent upon God's Spirit to perform the tasks of God's work. The evident and direct participation of the Spirit in this final panel of the story lends support to the importance of this theme in Acts. The reader is left to presume, then, that when Philip and the eunuch go their separate ways they both engage in Christian mission.

The text tells us nothing of what becomes of the Ethiopian.[355] However, we are told that the Spirit deposits Philip in Azotus, where he resumes his

---

352. L. T. Johnson, *The Acts of the Apostles,* SP 5 (Collegeville, Minn.: Liturgical, 1992) 156.

353. See J. Jeremias, παῖς θεοῦ *TDNT,* 5:684-89. But note Barrett's important criticisms, *Acts,* 1:430-31.

354. A few late MSS, agreeing with patristic commentary, add a v. 37 to make clear the protocol of Christian conversion, which requires a profession of faith as the condition of baptism. Both the NIV and the NRSV omit this verse for text-critical reasons, since the vast majority of MSS do not include it. In any case, this inference of faith is made without scribal assistance on the basis of Acts 2:38-41; 8:12-13.

355. There is no evidence of a first-century Ethiopian church, although Irenaeus claims—no doubt on the basis of a much earlier tradition—that the eunuch was responsible for the evangelization of Ethiopia. See Irenaeus *Against Heresies* 3.12.8-10.

mission by going from place to place (see 8:4), to the north up the coastline to Caesarea (8:40), where he establishes a family ministry of lasting importance (see 21:8-10).[356] The Spirit's action is reminiscent of the prophets Elijah (1 Kgs 18:12; 2 Kgs 2:16) and Ezekiel (Ezek 11:24), whose experiences with this same Spirit of prophecy effected compliance to God's plans. It is likewise here in Acts: Philip is "snatched up" and relocated to a place where God wanted him to resume his evangelical mission according to the Lord's commission (see 1:8).

356. Luke's narrative is consistent with his Scripture: The Spirit sometimes "snatches up" and moves prophets from place to place to facilitate the plans of God (see 2 Kgs 2:16; Ezek 11:24).

# REFLECTIONS

"How can I understand Scripture unless someone guides me?" (see 8:31). The Ethiopian eunuch is a double outcast within Israel, twice rejected by those in control of religious sentiment because of where he lives and because he has been castrated: his sexuality has excluded him from the assembly of God and his distance from the holy city makes for a difficult pilgrimage. Similar concerns continue to be impediments today for those from society's margins who seek after God. The way of the eunuch's salvation establishes a pattern of catechesis for the convert who must travel some distance to secure God's salvation. If the emphasis of Luke's story of Samaritan conversion is placed on reception of the Spirit, then the emphasis of his story of the eunuch's conversion is placed on reception of the Scripture. The two are decisively and strategically intertwined in Acts as the principal media of God's word and thus of the believer's theological formation. Certainly the images of the Spirit's detailed guidance of Philip in this narrative—giving him direction, inspiring his interpretation, transporting him from place to place—symbolize God's active presence in enabling the church's mission in the world, especially among those whom our religious traditions marginalize.

In each case those placed outside the borders of official religion turn to the prophet-like-Jesus to access to these powerful resources of Spirit and Scripture. The Spirit is distributed through the apostles to the Samaritan believers, and then the Scriptures are interpreted by the evangelist for the Ethiopian proselyte. For all the current debate about the authority of Scripture in the contemporary church, of equal importance in Luke's story world is the authority of Scripture's interpreter. The eunuch, who evidently understood the importance of Scripture in his search for God, recognized as well the importance of one who could interpret its meaning for him. Philip's authority to do so has already been evinced by his continuing obedience to God's calling.

Scriptures point us to God. The climax of Luke's story of the eunuch's conversion is Philip's response to his critical question of Scripture's referent: "About whom . . . does the prophet say this?" (8:34 NRSV). Philip then "proclaimed to him the good news about Jesus." When the Christian teacher is invited to mentor someone seeking to find God, she should do so by interpreting Scripture in theological terms.

# ACTS 9:1–15:12, "TO THE END OF THE EARTH": PAUL'S MISSION AS "LIGHT FOR THE NATIONS"

## OVERVIEW

No conversion to Jesus is more renowned than Saul's (alias Paul). Luke's account in Acts follows a carefully constructed sequence of events according to which Saul is introduced as a minor player at Stephen's execution (see 7:58). Although Luke relativizes Saul's participation in this treachery through Stephen's petition for divine forgiveness (see 7:59-60), Saul's solidarity with the church's opponents in Jerusalem is immediately evident by his persecution of the very community that Stephen once led (see 8:1-3). Therefore, when his story resumes in Acts, the reader is left to puzzle over how the Lord will cash Stephen's promissory note. Meanwhile, much has happened beyond Jerusalem since Stephen's martyrdom and Saul's purge of the holy city. In fact, Philip's successful mission has extended the gospel's influence north toward Syria (see 8:26-27*a*, 40), which explains why there are disciples in Syrian Damascus with a zealous Saul still in pursuit of them (see 9:1-2).

Philip's mission completed the evangelization of those marginal groups that constitute the whole household of a restored Israel (see 8:4-25, 26-40). Under the impress of Scripture's prophecy that salvation will spread from "the Jew first and then to the Greek [or non-Jew]" (cf. Rom 1:16; see Acts 3:25-26), now this narrative turns toward non-Jews. In the peculiar economy of God's salvation, the Lord responds to Stephen's petition for Saul's forgiveness by commissioning him as carrier of God's word "to the Jew first and then to the [Gentile]." Given the strategic role that Saul plays in Acts, Luke pays considerable attention to his conversion and commission. As with other pivotal moments in the church's mission, Luke narrates this dramatic episode three times (cf. 9:1-31; 22:3-16; 26:4-23), as he does the subsequent conversion story of the Roman centurion Cornelius (cf. 9:32–11:18; 15:6-11). The literary combination of these two conversion stories of a Jewish missionary and a Gentile convert provide a critical subtext for the remainder of Acts. Saul is called and empowered to carry the word of God to the Jew first and especially to "God-fearing" Gentiles, like Cornelius.

Even though Paul will spearhead the last stage of the church's mission, it begins with Peter (see Acts 9:32–10:48). The plotline of Acts unfolds according to a succession of prophetic leaders. Their continuity in ever-changing situations ensures the solidarity of the community's life and the integrity of its witness across space and time. The word Saul will proclaim about the resurrected Jesus is the very word Peter, Stephen, and Philip have proclaimed before him in an unbroken line of testimony to the faithfulness of God. In this light the stories of Peter's involvement in the conversion of Cornelius and of his escape from prison (see Acts 12:1-21) are elements of a "succession narrative" that authorizes Saul to continue the sacred role performed by the Twelve and the seven before him for another generation and in another place.

Luke orchestrates his composition of Saul's mission in several movements. He preaches God's gospel boldly and persuasively, interprets Israel's Scriptures properly and cogently, does miraculous "signs and wonders," wins arguments, and gets into conflict with unrepentant Jews and suffers because of it (see 9:16). Saul is now Paul (see Acts 13:9); his urban mission is centered in the city's synagogue where he encounters other devout Jews from the diaspora and more receptive God-fearing Gentiles (Acts 13:13–14:28). Paul's programmatic success among non-Jews extends even to pagans (Acts 14:8-10); however, he will find most of his Gentile converts in the diaspora synagogues where "Moses is read every sabbath" (15:21). His founding of this mission church provokes conflict among traditional Jews, even those within the church (see 14:27–15:5; cf. 11:1-2). In prayerful consideration of personal testimony and biblical prophecy, however, the elders of the Jewish church resolve to support Paul's mission to the nations while expecting him to maintain his commitment to the church's Jewish legacy (see Acts 15:6-29; cf. 11:3-18).

Following this Jerusalem Council, Paul never deviates from his prophetic vocation or from the pattern of mission established during his first evangelistic effort in Asia. He continues to extend the influence of the Word of God to the most important provinces and urban centers of the Roman Empire. His secular work as a "tentmaker" in Corinth would come to symbolize his sacred work that Amos prophesied: to repair and rebuild "the tent of David" (cf. Acts 15:16-18). His second mission westward to Macedonia (cf. Acts 15:30–17:15) and then southward to Greece (17:16–18:17) includes Athens, the intellectual center of Paul's world (see Acts 17:16-34), and Corinth, among its wealthiest (see Acts 18:1-17). Luke's narrative of his third mission (see Acts 18:18–21:16) considers Paul's evangelistic work in a single city, Ephesus, which would become a pivotal center in the succession of Paul's mission to the diaspora (see Acts 20:17-38).

When Paul finally returns to the holy city as a religious pilgrim (Acts 20:16), he faces increasing hostilities both within the church (see Acts 21:16-26) and within Judaism (see Acts 21:27-31; cf. 20:22-23; 21:11-14). Yet Rome, not Jerusalem, is the city of Paul's destiny; it is there at the mythic "end of the earth" that Paul fulfills Jesus' prophecy-commission (see 1:8) and God's ultimate plan for his life (see 19:21; 23:11; 27:24). His mission to Rome, however, is delayed (and ironically triggered) by his arrest in Jerusalem (see Acts 21:32-36) and the protracted legal case brought against him by the leadership of unrepentant Israel (see Acts 21:37–26:32). Even though Paul, a Roman citizen, ends formal litigation against him by appealing to the Caesar (cf. Acts 25:6-12), he arrives in Rome only after surviving the perils of a stormy sea (Acts 27) and a poisonous snake (Acts 28:1-10). Finally in Rome and still under house arrest, Paul resumes his missionary work in defense of his prophetic vocation and according to the biblical script of God's salvation (Acts 28:11-31).

Acts was placed before the Pauline letters during the canonical process to provide the church catholic with Scripture's own introduction to the Pauline letters. From this point forward, Acts forges impressions of Paul's vocation and authority, his prophetic persona, and his missionary purpose that provide a line of sight into the biblical letters that follow. By encountering the Paul of Acts as a central character in Luke's narrative, readers acquire a different although complementary perspective of the canonical Paul, one that is productive of a more faithful reading of his letters as Scripture (see Introduction, "Acts as Canon," 26-32).

# Acts 9:1-31, The Conversion and Commissioning of Saul

## NIV

9 Meanwhile, Saul was still breathing out murderous threats against the Lord's disciples. He went to the high priest [2]and asked him for letters to the synagogues in Damascus, so that if he found any there who belonged to the Way, whether men or women, he might take them as prisoners to Jerusalem. [3]As he neared Damascus on his journey, suddenly a light from heaven flashed around him. [4]He fell to the ground and heard a voice say to him, "Saul, Saul, why do you persecute me?"

[5]"Who are you, Lord?" Saul asked.

"I am Jesus, whom you are persecuting," he replied. [6]"Now get up and go into the city, and you will be told what you must do."

## NRSV

9 Meanwhile Saul, still breathing threats and murder against the disciples of the Lord, went to the high priest [2]and asked him for letters to the synagogues at Damascus, so that if he found any who belonged to the Way, men or women, he might bring them bound to Jerusalem. [3]Now as he was going along and approaching Damascus, suddenly a light from heaven flashed around him. [4]He fell to the ground and heard a voice saying to him, "Saul, Saul, why do you persecute me?" [5]He asked, "Who are you, Lord?" The reply came, "I am Jesus, whom you are persecuting. [6]But get up and enter the city, and you will be told what you are to do." [7]The men who

[7]The men traveling with Saul stood there speechless; they heard the sound but did not see anyone. [8]Saul got up from the ground, but when he opened his eyes he could see nothing. So they led him by the hand into Damascus. [9]For three days he was blind, and did not eat or drink anything.

[10]In Damascus there was a disciple named Ananias. The Lord called to him in a vision, "Ananias!"

"Yes, Lord," he answered.

[11]The Lord told him, "Go to the house of Judas on Straight Street and ask for a man from Tarsus named Saul, for he is praying. [12]In a vision he has seen a man named Ananias come and place his hands on him to restore his sight."

[13]"Lord," Ananias answered, "I have heard many reports about this man and all the harm he has done to your saints in Jerusalem. [14]And he has come here with authority from the chief priests to arrest all who call on your name."

[15]But the Lord said to Ananias, "Go! This man is my chosen instrument to carry my name before the Gentiles and their kings and before the people of Israel. [16]I will show him how much he must suffer for my name."

[17]Then Ananias went to the house and entered it. Placing his hands on Saul, he said, "Brother Saul, the Lord—Jesus, who appeared to you on the road as you were coming here—has sent me so that you may see again and be filled with the Holy Spirit." [18]Immediately, something like scales fell from Saul's eyes, and he could see again. He got up and was baptized, [19]and after taking some food, he regained his strength.

Saul spent several days with the disciples in Damascus. [20]At once he began to preach in the synagogues that Jesus is the Son of God. [21]All those who heard him were astonished and asked, "Isn't he the man who raised havoc in Jerusalem among those who call on this name? And hasn't he come here to take them as prisoners to the chief priests?" [22]Yet Saul grew more and more powerful and baffled the Jews living in Damascus by proving that Jesus is the Christ.[a]

[a] 22 Or Messiah

were traveling with him stood speechless because they heard the voice but saw no one. [8]Saul got up from the ground, and though his eyes were open, he could see nothing; so they led him by the hand and brought him into Damascus. [9]For three days he was without sight, and neither ate nor drank.

10Now there was a disciple in Damascus named Ananias. The Lord said to him in a vision, "Ananias." He answered, "Here I am, Lord." [11]The Lord said to him, "Get up and go to the street called Straight, and at the house of Judas look for a man of Tarsus named Saul. At this moment he is praying, [12]and he has seen in a vision[a] a man named Ananias come in and lay his hands on him so that he might regain his sight." [13]But Ananias answered, "Lord, I have heard from many about this man, how much evil he has done to your saints in Jerusalem; [14]and here he has authority from the chief priests to bind all who invoke your name." [15]But the Lord said to him, "Go, for he is an instrument whom I have chosen to bring my name before Gentiles and kings and before the people of Israel; [16]I myself will show him how much he must suffer for the sake of my name." [17]So Ananias went and entered the house. He laid his hands on Saul[b] and said, "Brother Saul, the Lord Jesus, who appeared to you on your way here, has sent me so that you may regain your sight and be filled with the Holy Spirit." [18]And immediately something like scales fell from his eyes, and his sight was restored. Then he got up and was baptized, [19]and after taking some food, he regained his strength.

For several days he was with the disciples in Damascus, [20]and immediately he began to proclaim Jesus in the synagogues, saying, "He is the Son of God." [21]All who heard him were amazed and said, "Is not this the man who made havoc in Jerusalem among those who invoked this name? And has he not come here for the purpose of bringing them bound before the chief priests?" [22]Saul became increasingly more powerful and confounded the Jews who lived in Damascus by proving that Jesus[c] was the Messiah.[d]

[a] Other ancient authorities lack *in a vision*    [b] Gk *him*    [c] Gk *that this*    [d] Or *the Christ*

NIV

²³After many days had gone by, the Jews conspired to kill him, ²⁴but Saul learned of their plan. Day and night they kept close watch on the city gates in order to kill him. ²⁵But his followers took him by night and lowered him in a basket through an opening in the wall.

²⁶When he came to Jerusalem, he tried to join the disciples, but they were all afraid of him, not believing that he really was a disciple. ²⁷But Barnabas took him and brought him to the apostles. He told them how Saul on his journey had seen the Lord and that the Lord had spoken to him, and how in Damascus he had preached fearlessly in the name of Jesus. ²⁸So Saul stayed with them and moved about freely in Jerusalem, speaking boldly in the name of the Lord. ²⁹He talked and debated with the Grecian Jews, but they tried to kill him. ³⁰When the brothers learned of this, they took him down to Caesarea and sent him off to Tarsus.

³¹Then the church throughout Judea, Galilee and Samaria enjoyed a time of peace. It was strengthened; and encouraged by the Holy Spirit, it grew in numbers, living in the fear of the Lord.

NRSV

23After some time had passed, the Jews plotted to kill him, 24but their plot became known to Saul. They were watching the gates day and night so that they might kill him; 25but his disciples took him by night and let him down through an opening in the wall,ᵃ lowering him in a basket.

26When he had come to Jerusalem, he attempted to join the disciples; and they were all afraid of him, for they did not believe that he was a disciple. 27But Barnabas took him, brought him to the apostles, and described for them how on the road he had seen the Lord, who had spoken to him, and how in Damascus he had spoken boldly in the name of Jesus. 28So he went in and out among them in Jerusalem, speaking boldly in the name of the Lord. 29He spoke and argued with the Hellenists; but they were attempting to kill him. 30When the believersᵇ learned of it, they brought him down to Caesarea and sent him off to Tarsus.

31Meanwhile the church throughout Judea, Galilee, and Samaria had peace and was built up. Living in the fear of the Lord and in the comfort of the Holy Spirit, it increased in numbers.

ᵃ Gk through the wall    ᵇ Gk brothers

# COMMENTARY

The literary importance and theological complexity of Saul's (= Paul's) Damascus road encounter with the risen Jesus is indicated by the fact that it is recounted three times, here in the narrator's voice and twice again in Paul's voice (see 22:3-16; 26:4-23). The primary problem facing the interpreter of Luke's narrative triad is not how best to harmonize or explain its discrepant details, but how its repetition more fully defines the prophetic vocation of the Paul of Acts.[357] It is impossible either to deny or to overestimate the transforming effect Jesus' visitation had on him and on his understanding of God's relations with

faithful Israel.[358] Yet, Saul's repentance and radical turn toward Jesus is only one element of a literary pattern that climaxes with his prophetic calling and baptism with the Spirit. Acts is more interested in Saul's calling than in his conversion, since it provides the impetus of his mission and the foundation of his future authority in the church.[359]

357. See B. Witherington, *The Acts of the Apostles: A Socio-Rhetorical Commentary* (Grand Rapids: Eerdmans, 1998) 305-15, for a detailed analysis of these discrepancies and possible explanations for them. See also J. Jervell, *Die Apostelgeschichte,* KEK 3 (Göttingen: Vandenhoeck & Ruprecht, 1998) 288-93, who pays close attention to the sources behind Luke's triadic narrative of Paul's mission statement.

358. The idea of Paul's "conversion" is important to reconsider in the light of K. Stendahl, "The Apostle Paul and the Introspective Conscience of the West," *HTR* 56 (1963) 199-215. While there was a radical and fundamental change in Paul's zeal (he stops persecuting the church and starts preaching about Jesus), it is not a conversion from Judaism to Christianity. The Paul of Acts remains an observant Jew and continues to live within his vocation as a teacher of Israel. See Jervell, *The Unknown Paul: Essays on Luke-Acts and Early Christian History* (Minneapolis: Augsburg, 1984) 71-72; A. Segal, *Paul the Convert* (New Haven: Yale University Press, 1990).

359. Paul himself regards this appearance of the risen Jesus as confirmation of his apostolic authority within the church—and he is the "last" to be so confirmed (1 Cor 15:8; cf. Gal 1:11-16). While the Saul of Acts does not qualify for membership in the apostolate (see 1:21-22) and is nowhere called an apostle (cf. 13:1-3), his prophetic vocation assigns an equal measure of authority to him, since all prophets-like-Jesus are granted similar tasks, powers, and responsibilities.

This passage is framed by an inclusio of characteristic irony: Even as Saul's persecution of the church (see 8:1-3) occasions Philip's mission beyond Jerusalem (see 8:4-40), so his conversion and departure brings a fresh season of shalom among believers living in the region (9:31; cf. 8:40). Enclosed between is the riveting drama of Saul's own "great reversal." On his way to persecute the Syrian church (9:1-2), he encounters the living Jesus who converts him (9:3-9) and prophesies his prophetic ministry (9:10-18). An obedient Saul takes two painful steps toward his destiny, the first in Damascus (9:19-25) and the second in Jerusalem (9:26-30), where he preaches the gospel and suffers in fulfillment of Jesus' prophecy (9:15-16).[360]

**9:1-2.** Saul's zealous persecution of the church has taken him from Jerusalem to Damascus, where he desires to continue and extend his hostilities among "any who belonged to the Way (9:2).[361] Evidently his efforts in this regard continue to be supported by those same religious elites who opposed and executed Stephen. The historical circumstances for his solicitation of letters of support from the high priest (probably Caiaphas) remain uncertain; however, their "legitimate" interest in Saul's mission in the synagogues of Damascus suggests that the membership of "the way" consists of devout Jewish believers, probably Hellenists, who have attached themselves to congregations of other diaspora Jews in that city.[362] Saul's mission is to "bind" believers and return them to Jerusalem for a religious inquisition, perhaps one patterned after Stephen's (see 6:11-14).

**9:3-9.** This passage recounts Saul's conversion to Jesus.[363] The day begins with Saul "approaching Damascus" (9:3) as a take-charge zealot who is "breathing threats and murder against the disciples of the Lord" (9:1).[364] By day's end, however, he is "led by hand into Damascus" (9:8), blind and utterly dependent upon others for food and drink (9:9). What occurs in the meantime is the stuff of legend: Saul the persecutor becomes Paul the prophet-like-Jesus. Here and in the other stories of his conversion in Acts, his personal encounter with the living Jesus is emphasized (see 1 Cor 9:1; 15:8).

The sudden appearance of "a light from heaven" (φῶς ἐκ τοῦ οὐρανοῦ *phōs ek tou ouranou* 9:3; cf. 22:6, 9) that is "brighter than the noon-day sun" (26:13; cf. 2 Cor 4:4-6) and that "flashed around him" (cf. 22:6; 26:13) are the special effects of a theophany when God meets a prophet (cf. Exod 19:16; Ezek 1:4, 7, 13, 28; Dan 10:6).[365] Similar to the prophet Ezekiel's response to his vision of God's glory (Ezek 1:28), Saul "fell to the ground" (9:4) in anticipation of hearing God speak to him. In this case, the "light" (φῶς *phōs* he sees is of the exalted Jesus, shrouded in the glory of God (cf. 7:55).

This epiphany is a divine audition (cf. Exod 3:4-10; Gen 31:11-13; see 2:5-13): Saul "heard a voice" (9:4*b*), and what he hears converts him to Jesus. The Lord's intent is evidently not to frighten him into obedience but to reveal a plan of action. The primary purpose of visionary episodes in Acts is not to convert non-believers—gospel preaching performs this role—but to commission prophets to missionary tasks (see 10:9-16; 16:6-10). Saul does not recognize the "voice" (φωνή *phōne*) he hears, and asks "Who are you, Lord?" (9:5*a*). His ironical use of "Lord" (κύριος *kyrios*) is not yet a confession of faith in Jesus but the honest query of a devout Jew who understands the significance of

360. Luke's narrative of Paul's conversion agrees with Paul's letters at every main point: the location, the visionary event, the effects, and the overarching importance of his calling. While the terms for Paul's mission are given to Ananias rather than to Paul (Acts 9:15), his Spirit-filling confirms that divine authority has been given him to enable this mission.

361. Luke's use of "the way" (ὁ ὁδός *ho hodos*) in Acts (19:9, 23; 22:4; 24:22) as a title for the church is distinctive within the NT. There is little doubt of its currency in earliest Christianity, especially among its Jewish opponents. Luke may use it here ironically, however, because of its theological resonance. According to the OT, "way" is a catchword for living in conformity with Moses (Exod 18:20; 32:8; Deut 26:17; Pss 1:1, 6 LXX; 118:1, 29) or to God (Isa 40:3). The term usually implies that such obedience is freely chosen (esp. the proverbial use of "way"; Prov 3:17; 10:17) and that the consequences of such are a choice justly dispensed. In Acts, the articular "way" circumscribes the church as a messianic sect within Judaism (so 24:14) that is marked out by a distinctive way believers live together and by its beliefs about Jesus. See J. A. Fitzmyer, *The Acts of the Apostles,* AB 31 (Garden City, N.Y.: Doubleday, 1998) 423-24.

362. Damascus was an important Syrian city about 135 miles to the north of Jerusalem. It was known for its former glory and for its role as strategic commercial center for the Roman Empire. Several important trade routes passed through Damascus, including the "Great North Road" on which Saul was traveling. Josephus reports in *The Jewish War* 2.20.2 that Damascus was home to a large population of Jews.

363. F. S. Spencer, *Acts,* Readings: A New Biblical Commentary (Sheffield: Sheffield Academic, 1997) 95-96, notes that Luke's repeated use of "bind" (δέω *deō*) in 9:2, 14, 21 to describe Saul's intended plan nicely captures the irony of his situation: He intends to "bind" believers, but it is he who is incapacitated and led by other believers to safety and service.

364. For historical background on Luke's strategic use of "disciples," see H. C. Kee, *To Every Nation Under Heaven: The Acts of the Apostles,* NTC (Valley Forge, Pa.: Trinity, 1997) 118-20.

365. B. Gaventa strategically links the "light" that blinds Paul with his subsequent mission as a "light to the nations" (εἰς φῶς ἐθνῶν *eis phōs ethnōn*) as the organizing image of Luke's story; *From Darkness to Light: Aspects of Conversion in the New Testament,* OBT (Philadelphia: Fortress, 1986) 52-95.

his experience from reading Scripture.[366] For this reason, Saul is absolutely attentive to what is said next: "I am Jesus, whom you are persecuting" (9:5*b*).

Saul's brief exchange with Jesus validates what will become the central claim of his gospel: God made the crucified Jesus alive as Messiah and Lord (see 26:8; cf. 2:36). Jesus could keep his retort brief because his very appearance exposes the ignorance that prompts Saul's mission to Damascus. Jesus is not another dead pretender to the messianic throne but is alive and is Christ indeed. What real choice does Saul have other than to embrace his future? The Lord's use of personal names and his direct appeal to Saul underscores the "personal character of the early Christian belief in the resurrection."[367] The living Jesus recruits him personally into the faith and then commissions him for ministry.[368]

The imperative of their encounter is introduced by the intensive "But" (ἀλλά *alla*, 9:6), which usually links contrasting statements. In this case, it makes more emphatic the purpose of this christophany: to send Paul on a mission. "Get up and enter the city and you will be told what you are to do" (9:6; cf. 22:10; 26:14). "He who a moment ago was so powerful has now become utterly powerless. But it is not the weakness of Saul so much as the power of Christ that Luke is concerned to show."[369]

Witnesses of this drama are in shock because they hear the living Jesus without seeing him (cf. 9:7; 22:9; 26:13; Deut 4:12; Dan 10:7).[370] Aware that something has happened to the posse's leader, they can only lead him into town. Saul's "blind obedience" to Jesus' imperative is indicated by a fast—"for three days . . . he neither ate nor drank" (9:9). On the one hand, Saul's condition is physical confirmation that a vision occurred, shocked him into blindness, and took away his appetite for food. On the other hand, "three days" of abstinence nicely symbolizes Saul's conversion to the *resurrected* Jesus. When he begins to eat again (see 9:19) and receives his sight (see 9:18), he will have been given time to begin an intense spiritual journey that will fortify him for the work ahead—though he once was blind, now he sees (cf. John 9:25).[371]

**9:10-19a.** The next narrative panel concerns what Saul is to do; it is for this reason that Jesus bids him go into Damascus (see 9:6). Coincidental to Saul's vision of his healing (v. 12), the Lord appears to Ananias[372] in a second vision (vv. 10-16).[373] Like Saul, he is a devout Jew (cf. 22:12); however, he is numbered among the believers Saul seeks to harm. Ironically, it is now Ananias who seeks out Saul to heal him and deliver the initial instructions of a new life (vv. 17-18).

Ananias's initial response to the Lord's bidding is the prompt reply, "Here I am Lord" (v. 10)—reminiscent of Samuel's (1 Sam 3:4, 10) and Abraham's (Gen 22:1-2) obedience to God's call. The Lord reveals Saul's name to Ananias and provides him with a specific address where he might be found.[374] Luke also provides an important biographical detail: Saul is "a man from Tarsus" (9:11)—a Jew of the diaspora.

Ananias's caveat in vv. 13-14 does not indicate spiritual failure or a concern for personal well-being. Rather, Luke adds it to prompt readers to

---

366. I am convinced that Luke shapes this narrative in the light of the Exodus story of Moses' commissioning. Jesus' address, "Saul, Saul," echoes the angel's address, "Moses, Moses" (Exod 3:4); and Jesus' response to Saul's query, "I am Jesus [ἐγὼ εἰμι Ἰησοῦς *egō eimi Iēsous*]," echoes God's response to Moses' similar question, "I am I AM [*egō eimi*]" (Exod 3:13-14). The logic of Luke's intertext reflects the importance of Moses in Acts as prototypical prophet-like-Jesus (see Acts 7:23-43).

367. Johnson, *The Acts of the Apostles*, 163.

368. S. Kim, *The Origin of Paul's Gospel*, WUNT 2/4 (Tübingen: J. C. B Mohr, 1984) 51-66, contends that Paul receives the essential terms of his gospel in this brief exchange and the following commissioning statement. Contra H. Conzelmann, *The Acts of the Apostles*, trans. J. Limburg et al., ed. E. J. Epp and C. R. Matthews, Hermeneia (Philadelphia: Fortress, 1987) 71.

369. E. Haenchen, *The Acts of the Apostles* (Philadelphia: Westminster, 1971) 322.

370. The three accounts of Paul's conversion disagree on this detail but agree in meaning "to reserve the appearance (of Jesus) to Paul alone." See ibid., 71.

371. Fitzmyer, *The Acts of the Apostles*, 426, allows that the meaning is primarily spiritual so that this is a fast in preparation for Christian baptism. However, see Johnson, *The Acts of the Apostles*, 164.

372. The repetition of the name "Ananias" in Acts may indicate that the reader should take these "Christian" stories together as mutually glossing commentaries on the meaning of the name, "God is merciful." The first Ananias is a disciple who does not obey God's word and is shamed, whereas the second Ananias is a disciple who obeys the Lord's word and is honored (22:12). The purpose of the interplay is to remind the reader that God's merciful response is conditioned upon the disciple's obedient response to God's word.

373. The literary convention of a "double vision" is a familiar feature of ancient stories. Luke uses visions in Acts to clarify God's call and a "double vision" to underscore God's control over the various details of the call—in this case, Saul's call. See C. Hedrick, "Paul's Conversion/Call," *JBL* 100 (1981) 415-32.

374. Luke's careful attention to detail in describing Ananias's vision reflects his use of a source carefully maintained and transmitted, in part because of the names and places it contains. Judas and Ananias are probably known to the first readers and Judas's home on Straight Street may well have housed an important synagogue of Jewish believers.

take special note of the radical turn of events that has just occurred with Saul's conversion (see 10:14-15). Since healing symbolizes salvation in Acts (see 3:1-8), his dismay evinces the "hard rationalist's" case against the fact of Saul's conversion and by implication therefore confirms its legitimacy.[375]

The climax of this narrative is the Lord's prophecy of Saul's forthcoming mission, which indexes the plotline of his mission in Acts and provides a glossary of its key terms that are repeated in his later speeches (13:46-47; 20:18-35; 22:14-15; 26:16-18).[376] Moreover, the Lord's reference to Saul as one "chosen" (ἐκλογή eklogē) for a task repeats the terms used for the work of the Twelve (see 1:2) and the seven (see 6:5) as instruments of salvation. This repetition emphasizes that the tasks the Lord gives to Saul "to bring my name before Gentiles and kings and before the people of Israel" (9:15) continue the church's witness to God's salvation.

Significantly, for the first time in Acts the international scope of the church's witness is clarified in terms of Saul's future mission. The order of "Gentiles and kings"[377] before "people of Israel" reverses the typical pattern of his urban mission, which usually begins in the synagogue and often on the Sabbath. In any case, Acts never depicts Paul aiming the gospel only at Gentiles or Jews; his mission is international in scope because God has promised to bless "all the families of the earth" (see 2:21; 3:25). The order here is probably for rhetorical effect to cue the narrative's turn toward a mission that will include non-Jews.

The second part of the Lord's programmatic prophecy of Saul's mission connects his witness to personal suffering, continuing this important literary theme. Saul's suffering is stipulated here as a divine necessity: "I will show him how much he must [δεῖ dei] suffer" (v. 16; see 1:16, 22; 3:21; 4:12). This suffering places Saul in continuity with the Messiah and his apostolic successors, and it shapes the way Acts tells his story. The dei—the "must" of divine necessity of Saul's suffering—reminds us that suffering is not incidental to salvation but in the prophet's case is instrumental in realizing God's promises according to the Scriptures (cf. 1 Pet 1:10-12). The repetition of "my name" (ὄνομά μου onoma mou) in both parts of this commissioning prophecy recalls Joel's prophecy that in the last days "everyone who calls upon the name of the Lord will be saved" (italics added; see 2:21).

The report of Ananias's mission rounds off this initial account of Saul's calling as a prophet-like-Jesus. His initial gesture of "laying his hands on Saul" (v. 17b) obeys the Lord's instruction (v. 12). Yet when read in context of Acts (see 6:6) in combination with his "Christian" greeting, "Brother Saul" (see 1:15) and the extraordinary exhortation for Saul "to be filled with the Holy Spirit" (v. 17c), Ananias's gesture connotes the community's confirmation of his salvation and vocation. Luke's idiom is pregnant with implicit information about Saul's destiny: The immediate restoration of Saul's sight (v. 18)[378] and his filling/baptism with the Holy Spirit symbolize God's confirmation of his salvation (cf. 2:21) and prophetic vocation (cf. 1:8).[379] His turn to action is indicated by ending his fast (9:19a).

**9:19b-25.** With his return to normalcy, Saul "began to proclaim Jesus in the synagogues" (v. 20). Luke's repeated use of "immediately" (εὐθέως eutheōs, vv. 18, 20) leaves the impres-

---

375. O. Bauernfeind, *Die Apostelgeschichte,* THKTT 5 (Leipzig: Deichert, 1939) 134, points out that Ananias's reluctance rightly reflects the ambiguity of Saul's situation—that Saul exists in a kind of "no man's land" between his conversion on the one hand and his triumphant mission on the other. Ananias's response to the Lord is noteworthy because it introduces "saints" (ἅγιοι *hagioi*) into Acts (cf. 9:32, 41; 26:10). It is used of Jerusalem's believers in Acts and has a similar referent in the Pauline letters (Rom 15:26; 1 Cor 16:1; 2 Cor 8:4; cf. Eph 2:19), which may indicate a semitechnical use in the Pauline mission. See C. K. Barrett, *A Critical and Exegetical Commentary on the Acts of the Apostles,* 2 vols, ICC (Edinburgh: T. & T. Clark, 1994, 1998) 1:455.

376. See R. C. Tannehill, *The Acts of the Apostles,* vol. 2 of *The Narrative Unity of Luke-Acts: A Literary Interpretation* (Minneapolis: Fortress, 1990) 2:118-20.

377. The prophecy that Paul would carry Christ's name to a plurality of "kings" is fulfilled in his speech to King Agrippa (cf. 25:23–26:29) and in anticipation of his audience with the Roman Caesar (cf. 27:24). Fitzmyer's argument, *The Acts of the Apostles,* 429, for combining "Gentiles and kings" as a discrete audience different from Paul's second audience, "the people of Israel," seems correct. The punctuation of this phrase is better rendered "before Gentiles and kings, and before the people of Israel."

378. The phrase "something like scales fell from his eyes" is probably contemporary medical parlance for the natural process of healing momentary blindness caused by a "bright light." See Haenchen, *The Acts of the Apostles,* 325.

379. Paul never mentions his baptism in his letters. The reference here is likely to his baptism with the Spirit (cf. 1 Cor 12:13). Luke's literary intention is to form a promise-fulfillment parallelism between Ananias's words (i.e., promise, 9:17) and the report (i.e., fulfillment, 9:18). The further implication of this literary conclusion is a theological claim: Paul's baptism is a baptism with the Spirit rather than a rite of initiation into the Damascus community. The point of this story is Paul's calling to prophetic ministry, which the filling/baptism with the Spirit enables and confirms.

sion of urgency.[380] We are not told, however, by whom or by what curriculum Saul is catechized to preach Jesus, which leaves the impression that this initial and urgent mission is prompted by his recent experience of the living Jesus (cf. Gal 1:11-17).[381] Although more details are provided later in Acts, Luke uses the narrative gaps effectively to underscore the importance of Saul's conversion.

Further, the location of his Damascus mission—"in the synagogues"—and the substance of what he says there—"Jesus is the Son of God" (v. 20; cf. Gal 1:16)—are compressed details of a pattern of ministry that will be expanded in considerable detail later in Acts. Moreover, his gospel proclamation is typically accompanied by a rigorous exegesis of Scripture that "amazes" (ἐξίστημι *existēmi*) and "confounds" (συγχέω *syncheō*) his opponents (so vv. 21-22), and the results are often hostile. Saul will proclaim that Jesus is God's Messiah, and unrepentant Israel will protest it. While his opposition often plots to get rid of him (cf. 14:19-20; 23:12-15), he inevitably escapes with the aid of others (sometimes heavenly) in order to continue the work for which he is called (so vv. 23-25).

The content of what Saul proclaims—that "Jesus is the Son of God"—is more difficult to explain. The interpreter should expect that these first words from a newly converted Saul are programmatic of any future missionary speech where the implications of this messianic title are developed in detail. Yet what is found instead is silence: this is the title's only kerygmatic use in Acts, even though it is routinely used both in the Gospels and in the Pauline letters (cf. Luke 1:32-35; 22:67-71; Rom 1:3; Gal 1:16; 2:20).[382] Because Paul's only other use of it in Acts is as part of a biblical citation (see 13:33; cf. Ps 2:7) to warrant his claim that Jesus is the Davidic Messiah (see 13:22-23), its use

here should be viewed as synonymous with the epithet of v. 22 that "Jesus was the Messiah."[383]

Neither the fact that gospel preaching provokes a divided Israel beyond Jerusalem—the Jews of Damascus "plotted to kill Saul" (v. 23)—or that Saul escapes them to preach another day is surprising.[384] Johnson points out that even the incredulity of Saul's auditors is expressed in words that Paul himself uses to explain his preconversion mission (cf. Gal 1:13, 23).[385] Yet the irony of this incident is envisaged by the reversal of his status within Israel. This episode began with him on the road to Damascus "breathing threats and murder against the disciples" on behalf of official Israel (v. 1) and now concludes with his former religious cohort seeking his death.[386] The persecutor has become the persecuted, fulfilling the Lord's prophecy that Saul would suffer for his name (see v. 16).

**9:26-30.** The persecuted Saul now heads south from Damascus to Jerusalem. The conflict experienced in the public square of Damascus now moves indoors where the church hesitates to embrace their new brother: "Saul attempted to join the disciples—they were afraid and did not believe that he was a disciple" (v. 26). Their suspicion is reasonable: Enemies do not become fast friends overnight! More important for Acts, the conflict is a harbinger of the profound difficulty the Jerusalem church will have with Paul's mission, whether to the Gentiles (so 15:4-5) or to the Jews (so 21:17-21). Intramural conflict over the nature of God's salvation, especially over acceptance of its revolutionary shape, is an important theme in Acts.

Barnabas, known to the readers of Acts for his generous spirit (see 4:36-37), intervenes and rehearses the evidence of Saul's conversion and

---

380. Paul writes that he came back to Damascus only after spending an indeterminate length of time in Arabia (cf. Gal 1:17). There have been various proposals to explain (or not) this chronological discrepancy. From a literary perspective, one can imagine that Luke had access to a fuller Pauline chronology from his source but telescopes his account to enhance the impression of the urgency of Paul's mission.

381. M. Hengel, *Paul Between Damascus and Antioch* (London: SCM Press, 1997) 43-47, finds agreement between Luke's telling of this episode and Paul's autobiography of his post-conversion experiences in Galatians 1, especially in maintaining Paul's independence from apostolic authorization to preach the gospel.

382. J. D. G. Dunn, *The Acts of the Apostles* (Valley Forge, Pa.: Trinity, 1996) 124-25, reviews the various historical constructions of the meaning of "Son of God" in earliest Christianity and its propriety for this particular setting in Acts.

383. See E. Haenchen, *The Acts of the Apostles* (Philadelphia: Westminster, 1971) 331.

384. The reference to "his disciples" (9:25) denotes something akin to "his colleagues."

385. L. T. Johnson, *The Acts of the Apostles,* SP 5 (Collegeville, Minn.: Liturgical, 1992) 171.

386. There may very well have been a coalition of religious and political factions that ganged up on Paul in Damascus. See V. Furnish, *II Corinthians,* AB (Garden City, N.Y.: Doubleday, 1984) 521-23, 540-42. Paul mentions only the Nabatean faction (2 Cor 11:32-33) and Luke only the Jewish faction to serve their respective rhetorical and theological interests. In Acts, Luke makes "the Jews" Saul's foes because he is keen to demonstrate that the conflict is theological and internal to Judaism. He features it at the beginning of Paul's ministry as programmatic of the species of suffering that he will experience during his career as a prophet-like-Jesus.

prophetic calling (v. 27). The consecutive καί (*kai*, "So," v. 28) suggests that Barnabas's intercession is effective and the Twelve confirm Saul's conversion and calling. Their official confirmation allows Saul to take a second missionary step in Jerusalem,[387] which results in a showdown with nonbelieving "Hellenists" (v. 29; see 6:1, 9-14) who attempt to kill him as they earlier had Stephen. We are left to imagine that their conflict with Saul is for similar reasons: His "bold speaking in the name of the Lord"[388] asserts the redemptive purchase of Jesus against a manner of purity that derives from temple routines or Torah observance. Of course, Saul was once a zealot among them and now has reversed his position. Such great reversals are certain to be noticed by friends and foes alike for their public appeal. Unlike Stephen, Saul escapes the Hellenists with a little help from his friends (9:30).[389]

**9:31.** This verse is another narrative summary and eases the transition to the "next stage" of the church's mission. Here we learn that the church founded by Philip's mission (see Acts 8) has entered into a period of "peace and build up"[390]— perhaps now because Saul is "off to Tarsus" (9:30)!

The reference to Galilee (the only time in Acts) is striking because it contrasts so sharply with the Gospel's geography of Jesus' Galilean mission. Perhaps Luke adds this detail to remind his readers that the church's mission is moving *from* Galilee and beyond the perimeter of the Lord's messianic mission toward still other territories. The phrase "comfort of the Holy Spirit" in connection with the "peace" and "fear" of the Palestinian church recalls the discourse on the Spirit by John's Jesus, who prophesied the coming of God's Παράκλητος (*Parakletos*), the Holy Spirit, to comfort the disciples in his absence (John 14:26). The comforting Spirit is the medium of God's peace, so there is no cause for fear of others (John 14:27). According to the Johannine text, the disciples' fear that threatens their relationship with the Lord is precipitated by those "who will put you out of the synagogues" (John 16:1-2). Readers of Acts who are familiar with John's Gospel add a layer of meaning to this narrative summary: The church experiences peace and stability by "fearing the Lord" rather than the synagogue's opposition and by "the comfort of the Holy Spirit" that the Lord has given them.

387. The apparent contradiction with Paul's own contention that he was unknown to the Judean church (Gal 1:22) is resolved by Luke's careful placement of Paul within the city limits of Jerusalem without any reference to a wider ministry. See Haenchen, *The Acts of the Apostles,* 332.

388. Luke's use of "bold" (παρρησιάζομαι *parrēsiazomai*), speaking of Paul, is strategic in Acts because it links the power of his public speaking with the apostle's earlier petition for "boldness" (παρρησία *parrēsia*) in 4:29 and the Spirit's subsequent filling to effect an ever bolder preaching (4:31). The reader presumes that Paul's Spirit-filling (9:17-18) has a similar result—a presumption borne out by Luke's repetitive use of *parrēsiazomai* in Acts with reference to Paul's rhetorical effectiveness (13:46; 14:3; 18:26; 19:8; 26:26; 28:31).

389. For the meaning of the articular "the believers" (οἱ ἀδελφοί *hoi adelphoi*) in Acts, see H. C. Kee, *To Every Nation Under Heaven: The Acts of the Apostles,* NTC (Valley Forge, Pa.: Trinity, 1997) 123.

390. "Peace" (εἰρήνη *eirēnē*) is an important result of God's salvation and marks the people belonging to God, according to Luke (cf. Luke 1:79; 2:14; 10:5-6; 12:51; 19:38, 42; Acts 10:36; 24:2). Likewise, the word for "build up" (οἰκοδομέω *oikodomeō*) will be featured in the second half of Acts with reference to Amos's prophecy of the rebuilding of the house of Israel (see 15:16-18). Its use here probably refers to Christian nurture, as in the Pauline letters.

# REFLECTIONS

**1.** "The reply came, 'I am Jesus, whom you are persecuting. But get up and enter the city, and you will be told what you are to do.' " (9:5*b*-6 NRSV). The story of Saul's/Paul's conversion and calling forms an important subtext of Acts. For generations readers have formed their impressions of conversion on the basis of this story or have read their own experiences of conversion into this text. Scholars continue to debate whether interpreters should universalize the relevance and manner of Paul's conversion experience; almost certainly Luke recognized the distinctive importance of what happened to Paul on his way to Damascus and even in his story is careful to restrict those who saw the same "light" or heard the "voice" as Paul. Perhaps the highly personal cast of their exchange and of Paul's experience indicates that the pattern of Christian conversion is neither preformed or universal: God finds people in a variety of ways.

Three elements of Paul's experience form the core of the story's different versions in Acts. First, Paul is converted to Jesus and not from one religion to another. There is no repudiation of his Jewish heritage when he turns to the Lord: Paul remains a pious Jew and a teacher of Israel. Nor is Paul led toward Jesus by the persuasive sermon of a talented preacher or the Christian nurture of loving parents. His change of mind is about Jesus and the realization that he is alive, not dead. The idea and experience of conversion in Acts concerns a coming to the Messiah in the confidence that God sent him into the world to rescue everyone from all that kills. That he is living confirms that he is God's promised salvation (see Luke 2:29-32). Second, Paul is changed—not immediately but over time—because of his encounter with the living Jesus. The "before-and-after" graphic is striking: Paul heads for Damascus with authority and purpose, but he is led by hand into the city helpless and blind. This one-time enemy of the church becomes its great champion. This persecutor of Jesus is then persecuted for proclaiming him. Personal transformation is the mark of genuine conversion; in some, like Paul, the changes are more dramatic and public. Finally, conversion is the means to a missionary end. Paul is converted for a calling. This pattern of Paul's salvation is typical of Acts: Personal transformation never collapses into sanctified self-absorption. Rather, conversion prepares the believer for performance of concrete tasks in the service of God.

**2.** "I will show him how much he must suffer for my name" (9:16 NIV); "Saul talked and debated with the Hellenists, but they tried to kill him" (see 9:29). Paul is called to preach the gospel to all people because God desires the salvation of all people. Yet as good as this theological sentiment feels, there are some who are determined to define God's salvation on more limited terms and to fight those who disagree with them. The Lord's prediction that Paul would suffer for proclaiming his name is not a condition of his calling but a consequence of his faithful exercise of it. Paul's fiercest opponents do not deny the integrity of his faith nor do they campaign in earnest against his personhood. Rather, they object to what he says about Jesus.

**3.** "All who heard [Saul] were amazed and said, 'Is not this the man who made havoc in Jerusalem among those who invoked this name?' " (9:21 NRSV). There are two dangers the church must guard against when regarding Christian conversion. On the one hand, believers should not presume that authentic Christianity is always characterized by conversion experiences resulting in radical personal transformation. Strong evangelism programs coupled with revivalist preaching often display this orientation toward dramatic transformation. However, many traditions teach that the child of faith gradually grows into Christian maturity, not through the giant leaps of conversion experiences but through the small steps fostered by a nurturing congregation. Many Christians cannot remember a time when they were not believers. On the other hand, believers should not diminish or ignore the resources God has given the church to transform people. Acts reminds its readers time and again that "we ignore the phenomenon of conversion at the peril of losing the church."[391] I am a Methodist with deep roots in the revivalist heritage of Wesleyan Holiness Christianity; while growing up I was "born again" and "purified" many times! The marvel of Luke's narrative is that both orientations are held together as integral elements of a mutually informing whole. Clearly Paul is converted to Jesus and his personal life is transformed as a result. This much is confirmed by his letters (see 1 Cor 15:3-11; Gal 1:11-19). Luke, however, is careful to place him within a faith community that confirms his salvation and safeguards his prophetic vocation.

Acts complements Paul's rehearsal of his conversion by reminding us that Christian discipleship is far too demanding for the individual. Only within a caring community will the believer find those resources and relationships that forge an enduring faith.

391. W. Willimon, *Acts* (Atlanta: John Knox, 1988) 104.

# Acts 9:32–11:18, Back to the Future: Peter's Prophetic Ministry Beyond Jerusalem

## NIV

[32]As Peter traveled about the country, he went to visit the saints in Lydda. [33]There he found a man named Aeneas, a paralytic who had been bedridden for eight years. [34]"Aeneas," Peter said to him, "Jesus Christ heals you. Get up and take care of your mat." Immediately Aeneas got up. [35]All those who lived in Lydda and Sharon saw him and turned to the Lord.

[36]In Joppa there was a disciple named Tabitha (which, when translated, is Dorcas[a]), who was always doing good and helping the poor. [37]About that time she became sick and died, and her body was washed and placed in an upstairs room. [38]Lydda was near Joppa; so when the disciples heard that Peter was in Lydda, they sent two men to him and urged him, "Please come at once!"

[39]Peter went with them, and when he arrived he was taken upstairs to the room. All the widows stood around him, crying and showing him the robes and other clothing that Dorcas had made while she was still with them.

[40]Peter sent them all out of the room; then he got down on his knees and prayed. Turning toward the dead woman, he said, "Tabitha, get up." She opened her eyes, and seeing Peter she sat up. [41]He took her by the hand and helped her to her feet. Then he called the believers and the widows and presented her to them alive. [42]This became known all over Joppa, and many people believed in the Lord. [43]Peter stayed in Joppa for some time with a tanner named Simon.

**10** At Caesarea there was a man named Cornelius, a centurion in what was known as the Italian Regiment. [2]He and all his family were devout and God-fearing; he gave generously to those in need and prayed to God regularly. [3]One day at about three in the afternoon he had a vision. He distinctly saw an angel of God, who came to him and said, "Cornelius!"

[4]Cornelius stared at him in fear. "What is it, Lord?" he asked.

The angel answered, "Your prayers and gifts to the poor have come up as a memorial offering

[a] 36 Both *Tabitha* (Aramaic) and *Dorcas* (Greek) mean *gazelle.*

## NRSV

[32]Now as Peter went here and there among all the believers,[a] he came down also to the saints living in Lydda. [33]There he found a man named Aeneas, who had been bedridden for eight years, for he was paralyzed. [34]Peter said to him, "Aeneas, Jesus Christ heals you; get up and make your bed!" And immediately he got up. [35]And all the residents of Lydda and Sharon saw him and turned to the Lord.

[36]Now in Joppa there was a disciple whose name was Tabitha, which in Greek is Dorcas.[b] She was devoted to good works and acts of charity. [37]At that time she became ill and died. When they had washed her, they laid her in a room upstairs. [38]Since Lydda was near Joppa, the disciples, who heard that Peter was there, sent two men to him with the request, "Please come to us without delay." [39]So Peter got up and went with them; and when he arrived, they took him to the room upstairs. All the widows stood beside him, weeping and showing tunics and other clothing that Dorcas had made while she was with them. [40]Peter put all of them outside, and then he knelt down and prayed. He turned to the body and said, "Tabitha, get up." Then she opened her eyes, and seeing Peter, she sat up. [41]He gave her his hand and helped her up. Then calling the saints and widows, he showed her to be alive. [42]This became known throughout Joppa, and many believed in the Lord. [43]Meanwhile he stayed in Joppa for some time with a certain Simon, a tanner.

**10** In Caesarea there was a man named Cornelius, a centurion of the Italian Cohort, as it was called. [2]He was a devout man who feared God with all his household; he gave alms generously to the people and prayed constantly to God. [3]One afternoon at about three o'clock he had a vision in which he clearly saw an angel of God coming in and saying to him, "Cornelius." [4]He stared at him in terror and said, "What is it, Lord?" He answered, "Your prayers and your alms have ascended as a memorial

[a] Gk *all of them*   [b] The name Tabitha in Aramaic and the name Dorcas in Greek mean *a gazelle*

## NIV

before God. ⁵Now send men to Joppa to bring back a man named Simon who is called Peter. ⁶He is staying with Simon the tanner, whose house is by the sea."

⁷When the angel who spoke to him had gone, Cornelius called two of his servants and a devout soldier who was one of his attendants. ⁸He told them everything that had happened and sent them to Joppa.

⁹About noon the following day as they were on their journey and approaching the city, Peter went up on the roof to pray. ¹⁰He became hungry and wanted something to eat, and while the meal was being prepared, he fell into a trance. ¹¹He saw heaven opened and something like a large sheet being let down to earth by its four corners. ¹²It contained all kinds of four-footed animals, as well as reptiles of the earth and birds of the air. ¹³Then a voice told him, "Get up, Peter. Kill and eat."

¹⁴"Surely not, Lord!" Peter replied. "I have never eaten anything impure or unclean."

¹⁵The voice spoke to him a second time, "Do not call anything impure that God has made clean."

¹⁶This happened three times, and immediately the sheet was taken back to heaven.

¹⁷While Peter was wondering about the meaning of the vision, the men sent by Cornelius found out where Simon's house was and stopped at the gate. ¹⁸They called out, asking if Simon who was known as Peter was staying there.

¹⁹While Peter was still thinking about the vision, the Spirit said to him, "Simon, three*ᵃ* men are looking for you. ²⁰So get up and go downstairs. Do not hesitate to go with them, for I have sent them."

²¹Peter went down and said to the men, "I'm the one you're looking for. Why have you come?"

²²The men replied, "We have come from Cornelius the centurion. He is a righteous and God-fearing man, who is respected by all the Jewish people. A holy angel told him to have you come to his house so that he could hear what you have to say." ²³Then Peter invited the men into the house to be his guests.

*ᵃ 19* One early manuscript *two;* other manuscripts do not have the number.

## NRSV

before God. ⁵Now send men to Joppa for a certain Simon who is called Peter; ⁶he is lodging with Simon, a tanner, whose house is by the seaside." ⁷When the angel who spoke to him had left, he called two of his slaves and a devout soldier from the ranks of those who served him, ⁸and after telling them everything, he sent them to Joppa.

9About noon the next day, as they were on their journey and approaching the city, Peter went up on the roof to pray. ¹⁰He became hungry and wanted something to eat; and while it was being prepared, he fell into a trance. ¹¹He saw the heaven opened and something like a large sheet coming down, being lowered to the ground by its four corners. ¹²In it were all kinds of four-footed creatures and reptiles and birds of the air. ¹³Then he heard a voice saying, "Get up, Peter; kill and eat." ¹⁴But Peter said, "By no means, Lord; for I have never eaten anything that is profane or unclean." ¹⁵The voice said to him again, a second time, "What God has made clean, you must not call profane." ¹⁶This happened three times, and the thing was suddenly taken up to heaven.

17Now while Peter was greatly puzzled about what to make of the vision that he had seen, suddenly the men sent by Cornelius appeared. They were asking for Simon's house and were standing by the gate. ¹⁸They called out to ask whether Simon, who was called Peter, was staying there. ¹⁹While Peter was still thinking about the vision, the Spirit said to him, "Look, three*ᵃ* men are searching for you. ²⁰Now get up, go down, and go with them without hesitation; for I have sent them." ²¹So Peter went down to the men and said, "I am the one you are looking for; what is the reason for your coming?" ²²They answered, "Cornelius, a centurion, an upright and God-fearing man, who is well spoken of by the whole Jewish nation, was directed by a holy angel to send for you to come to his house and to hear what you have to say." ²³So Peter*ᵇ* invited them in and gave them lodging.

The next day he got up and went with them, and some of the believers*ᶜ* from Joppa accompanied him. ²⁴The following day they came to Caesarea. Cornelius was expecting them and had

*ᵃ* One ancient authority reads *two;* others lack the word      *ᵇ* Gk *he*
*ᶜ* Gk *brothers*

The next day Peter started out with them, and some of the brothers from Joppa went along. [24]The following day he arrived in Caesarea. Cornelius was expecting them and had called together his relatives and close friends. [25]As Peter entered the house, Cornelius met him and fell at his feet in reverence. [26]But Peter made him get up. "Stand up," he said, "I am only a man myself."

[27]Talking with him, Peter went inside and found a large gathering of people. [28]He said to them: "You are well aware that it is against our law for a Jew to associate with a Gentile or visit him. But God has shown me that I should not call any man impure or unclean. [29]So when I was sent for, I came without raising any objection. May I ask why you sent for me?"

[30]Cornelius answered: "Four days ago I was in my house praying at this hour, at three in the afternoon. Suddenly a man in shining clothes stood before me [31]and said, 'Cornelius, God has heard your prayer and remembered your gifts to the poor. [32]Send to Joppa for Simon who is called Peter. He is a guest in the home of Simon the tanner, who lives by the sea.' [33]So I sent for you immediately, and it was good of you to come. Now we are all here in the presence of God to listen to everything the Lord has commanded you to tell us."

[34]Then Peter began to speak: "I now realize how true it is that God does not show favoritism [35]but accepts men from every nation who fear him and do what is right. [36]You know the message God sent to the people of Israel, telling the good news of peace through Jesus Christ, who is Lord of all. [37]You know what has happened throughout Judea, beginning in Galilee after the baptism that John preached— [38]how God anointed Jesus of Nazareth with the Holy Spirit and power, and how he went around doing good and healing all who were under the power of the devil, because God was with him.

[39]"We are witnesses of everything he did in the country of the Jews and in Jerusalem. They killed him by hanging him on a tree, [40]but God raised him from the dead on the third day and caused him to be seen. [41]He was not seen by all the peo-

called together his relatives and close friends. [25]On Peter's arrival Cornelius met him, and falling at his feet, worshiped him. [26]But Peter made him get up, saying, "Stand up; I am only a mortal." [27]And as he talked with him, he went in and found that many had assembled; [28]and he said to them, "You yourselves know that it is unlawful for a Jew to associate with or to visit a Gentile; but God has shown me that I should not call anyone profane or unclean. [29]So when I was sent for, I came without objection. Now may I ask why you sent for me?"

[30]Cornelius replied, "Four days ago at this very hour, at three o'clock, I was praying in my house when suddenly a man in dazzling clothes stood before me. [31]He said, 'Cornelius, your prayer has been heard and your alms have been remembered before God. [32]Send therefore to Joppa and ask for Simon, who is called Peter; he is staying in the home of Simon, a tanner, by the sea.' [33]Therefore I sent for you immediately, and you have been kind enough to come. So now all of us are here in the presence of God to listen to all that the Lord has commanded you to say."

[34]Then Peter began to speak to them: "I truly understand that God shows no partiality, [35]but in every nation anyone who fears him and does what is right is acceptable to him. [36]You know the message he sent to the people of Israel, preaching peace by Jesus Christ—he is Lord of all. [37]That message spread throughout Judea, beginning in Galilee after the baptism that John announced: [38]how God anointed Jesus of Nazareth with the Holy Spirit and with power; how he went about doing good and healing all who were oppressed by the devil, for God was with him. [39]We are witnesses to all that he did both in Judea and in Jerusalem. They put him to death by hanging him on a tree; [40]but God raised him on the third day and allowed him to appear, [41]not to all the people but to us who were chosen by God as witnesses, and who ate and drank with him after he rose from the dead. [42]He commanded us to preach to the people and to testify that he is the one ordained by God as judge of the living and the dead. [43]All the prophets testify about him that everyone who believes in him receives forgiveness of sins through his name."

## NIV

ple, but by witnesses whom God had already chosen—by us who ate and drank with him after he rose from the dead. ⁴²He commanded us to preach to the people and to testify that he is the one whom God appointed as judge of the living and the dead. ⁴³All the prophets testify about him that everyone who believes in him receives forgiveness of sins through his name."

⁴⁴While Peter was still speaking these words, the Holy Spirit came on all who heard the message. ⁴⁵The circumcised believers who had come with Peter were astonished that the gift of the Holy Spirit had been poured out even on the Gentiles. ⁴⁶For they heard them speaking in tongues*a* and praising God.

Then Peter said, ⁴⁷"Can anyone keep these people from being baptized with water? They have received the Holy Spirit just as we have." ⁴⁸So he ordered that they be baptized in the name of Jesus Christ. Then they asked Peter to stay with them for a few days.

**11** The apostles and the brothers throughout Judea heard that the Gentiles also had received the word of God. ²So when Peter went up to Jerusalem, the circumcised believers criticized him ³and said, "You went into the house of uncircumcised men and ate with them."

⁴Peter began and explained everything to them precisely as it had happened: ⁵"I was in the city of Joppa praying, and in a trance I saw a vision. I saw something like a large sheet being let down from heaven by its four corners, and it came down to where I was. ⁶I looked into it and saw four-footed animals of the earth, wild beasts, reptiles, and birds of the air. ⁷Then I heard a voice telling me, 'Get up, Peter. Kill and eat.'

⁸"I replied, 'Surely not, Lord! Nothing impure or unclean has ever entered my mouth.'

⁹"The voice spoke from heaven a second time, 'Do not call anything impure that God has made clean.' ¹⁰This happened three times, and then it was all pulled up to heaven again.

¹¹"Right then three men who had been sent to me from Caesarea stopped at the house where I was staying. ¹²The Spirit told me to have no hesitation about going with them. These six brothers

*a 46 Or other languages*

## NRSV

⁴⁴While Peter was still speaking, the Holy Spirit fell upon all who heard the word. ⁴⁵The circumcised believers who had come with Peter were astounded that the gift of the Holy Spirit had been poured out even on the Gentiles, ⁴⁶for they heard them speaking in tongues and extolling God. Then Peter said, ⁴⁷"Can anyone withhold the water for baptizing these people who have received the Holy Spirit just as we have?" ⁴⁸So he ordered them to be baptized in the name of Jesus Christ. Then they invited him to stay for several days.

**11** Now the apostles and the believers*a* who were in Judea heard that the Gentiles had also accepted the word of God. ²So when Peter went up to Jerusalem, the circumcised believers*b* criticized him, ³saying, "Why did you go to uncircumcised men and eat with them?" ⁴Then Peter began to explain it to them, step by step, saying, ⁵"I was in the city of Joppa praying, and in a trance I saw a vision. There was something like a large sheet coming down from heaven, being lowered by its four corners; and it came close to me. ⁶As I looked at it closely I saw four-footed animals, beasts of prey, reptiles, and birds of the air. ⁷I also heard a voice saying to me, 'Get up, Peter; kill and eat.' ⁸But I replied, 'By no means, Lord; for nothing profane or unclean has ever entered my mouth.' ⁹But a second time the voice answered from heaven, 'What God has made clean, you must not call profane.' ¹⁰This happened three times; then everything was pulled up again to heaven. ¹¹At that very moment three men, sent to me from Caesarea, arrived at the house where we were. ¹²The Spirit told me to go with them and not to make a distinction between them and us.*c* These six brothers also accompanied me, and we entered the man's house. ¹³He told us how he had seen the angel standing in his house and saying, 'Send to Joppa and bring Simon, who is called Peter; ¹⁴he will give you a message by which you and your entire household will be saved.' ¹⁵And as I began to speak, the Holy Spirit fell upon them just as it had upon us at the beginning. ¹⁶And I remembered the word of the Lord, how he had said, 'John baptized with water, but you will be

*a Gk brothers    b Gk lacks believers    c Or not to hesitate*

NIV

also went with me, and we entered the man's house. [13]He told us how he had seen an angel appear in his house and say, 'Send to Joppa for Simon who is called Peter. [14]He will bring you a message through which you and all your household will be saved.'

[15]"As I began to speak, the Holy Spirit came on them as he had come on us at the beginning. [16]Then I remembered what the Lord had said: 'John baptized with[a] water, but you will be baptized with the Holy Spirit.' [17]So if God gave them the same gift as he gave us, who believed in the Lord Jesus Christ, who was I to think that I could oppose God?"

[18]When they heard this, they had no further objections and praised God, saying, "So then, God has granted even the Gentiles repentance unto life."

[a] 16 Or in

NRSV

baptized with the Holy Spirit.' [17]If then God gave them the same gift that he gave us when we believed in the Lord Jesus Christ, who was I that I could hinder God?" [18]When they heard this, they were silenced. And they praised God, saying, "Then God has given even to the Gentiles the repentance that leads to life."

# COMMENTARY

Acts weaves together different narrative strands of the church's mission to the end of the earth. If Peter's story is the warp of Acts, then Paul's is its weft. Both men are prophets-like-Jesus who execute their commissioned tasks in different places with similar authority and effectiveness. As Saul departs to prepare for his future mission (see 9:30-31), the narrative resumes Peter's story, describing his mission beyond Jerusalem that also prepares for Saul's future endeavors.

Although a case can be made that Philip is forerunner to this stage of Peter's ministry,[392] the religious authority of the apostolic Twelve continues as an important theme in Acts. Peter and not Philip is the principal link between the risen Jesus and the messianic movement beyond Jerusalem that bears his name,[393] and the conversion of Cornelius, the first uncircumcised Gentile admitted into the faith, is considered his prerogative.

This claim leads to two brief observations. First, new snapshots of Peter are added to his portraiture to commend his personal charisma, which is actually *increasing* and in no way has been attenuated by Saul's arrival on the scene. Peter restores the paralytic Aeneas in Lydda (9:33-35; see 3:1-8) and the deceased Tabitha/Dorcas in Joppa (9:36-42) in a manner reminiscent of Jesus (cf. Luke 5:17-26) and the prophets before him (cf. 1 Kgs 17:17-24; 2 Kgs 4:19-27). These healings reestablish and even enhance Peter's spiritual authority, underwriting his mission to convert Cornelius's household and then to bear witness to the Spirit's "Gentile Pentecost" (cf. 10:44). The latter event confirms God's plan to allow uncircumcised but repentant Gentiles to experience the blessings of Israel's salvation (see 10:44; 11:15-18; 15:8-11) and defines the terms of Paul's future mission to the Gentiles.

Second, the theological subtext of Peter's mission to Cornelius is framed by Luke's allusion to the story of Jonah.[394] As with the OT prophet who

392. So F. S. Spencer, *The Portrait of Philip in Acts,* JSNTSS 67 (Sheffield: JSOT, 1992).

393. J. D. G. Dunn, *The Acts of the Apostles* (Valley Forge, Pa.: Trinity, 1996) 133, notes that Luke's Gospel avoids using Jesus tradition that considers clean and unclean foods and people (Gentiles), delaying it to Luke's narrative of the Gentile mission in Acts where these social boundaries are more properly considered.

394. See R. W. Wall, "Peter, 'Son of Jonah': The Conversion of Cornelius in the Context of Canon," *JSNT* 29 (1987) 79-90.

reluctantly received a call to take the word of God from Joppa to Gentile Nineveh (cf. Jonah 1:3), Peter is commissioned by the same God to carry the gospel from this same Joppa (see Acts 10:23; cf. 9:36, 43) to the home of Gentile Cornelius. Perhaps recollection of Peter's Aramaic name, Simon bar Jonah (Matt 16:17), led Luke to see Jonah's story repeated in Peter's. In any case, both prophets withdraw initial protests to their commissions only after God reveals more clearly the divine intention of their missions— after Jonah spends three days and nights in the belly of the great fish (Jonah 2:1) and after Peter hears a divine audition three times (Acts 10:15-16). Jonah's mission results in the repentance of Gentile Ninevites unto life (Jonah 3:1-10), to which the repentance and baptism of Cornelius's household corresponds (Acts 10:43, 47-48). The salvation of repentant Gentiles provokes a hostile response from "traditional" Israel (Jonah 4:1; see als Acts 11:1-2; cf. Acts 10:14), which then God refutes (Jonah 4:2-11; Acts 11:17-18; cf. Acts 15:13-21). Jonah's God is Peter's God; "the Gentile mission is from the beginning seen not as the work of men, even if they are Apostles, but of God (11:18)."[395]

**9:32-35.** The Plain of Sharon runs along the Mediterranean coastline from the twin cities, Lydda and Joppa, northward to Samarian Caesarea.[396] Peter is there, following in Philip's footprints (see 8:40), moving "here and there among all the believers" (v. 32; see 8:4). In Lydda, he finds himself in a situation similar to the early days of his Jerusalem mission when he healed the beggar (see 3:1-8): "Aeneas who had been bedridden for eight years, for he had been paralyzed" (v. 33). As before, Peter heals faithful Aeneas by invoking the name of Jesus: "Jesus Christ heals you" (v. 34; cf. 3:6; also, 10:38; 28:8).[397] In this instance, Peter removes himself as a broker of the Lord's healing grace and asserts that the Lord heals Aeneas.

The use of Aeneas's personal name—a Greek name for a diaspora Jew—roots the story in historical memory and reflects the expectation that God's salvation is experienced individually. The motive of the curious instruction to "get up and make your bed" is not the same as that of the frustrated parent of a lazy child; rather, Peter's instruction seeks confirmation by some responsible action that a healing has taken place. The effect of God's healing grace is both immediate and public, with the result that "all the residents . . . turned to the Lord" (v. 35).[398] As earlier with Jesus, Peter connects the truth of the gospel with the healing of a paralytic; but unlike Jesus, Peter's ministry is among the "saints" where healing does not incite controversy (see Luke 5:17-26).

**9:36-42.** This second healing story takes place in Joppa (modern Jaffa) and is linked to Peter's first healing by the geographical proximity of these twin cities (v. 38*a*). The situation in Joppa, however, is considerably more urgent: Another believer, Tabitha (= Dorcas),[399] "became ill and died" (v. 37*a*). For this reason, her congregation sends two witnesses of her demise to Peter with the extraordinary appeal to "come to us without delay" (v. 38*b*). Peter's widespread reputation as a healer, coupled with biblical accounts of dramatic healings that Luke's narrative echoes (cf. 1 Kgs 17:17-24; 2 Kgs 4:32-37), have cultivated an optimism of grace that believes even a dead woman already prepared for burial—"they had washed her and laid her out"[400]—can be resuscitated by the apostle.

There is even more at stake in Tabitha's restoration than in Aeneas's case, as the details of her public profile make clear. She is renowned for "good works and charity." The widows of her congregation cry out to Peter, showing him the

---

395. S. Wilson, *The Gentile and the Gentile Mission in Luke-Acts,* SNTMS 23 (Cambridge: Cambridge University Press, 1973) 177.

396. This region, known for its lush grazing areas (Isa 65:10), was an important commercial and political site during the Roman governance of Palestine; it would have been a natural area for Philip and then Peter to evangelize. Luke's repeated reference of "all the saints" (9:32) and "all the residents" (9:35), which encloses this first healing story, suggests that Peter's ministry takes place in a well-populated area.

397. The tense of the verbal idea of "Jesus Christ heals [ἰᾶται *iatai*] you" is debated, whether it is an aoristic present or perfect (ἴαται *iatai*) and whether in the indicative or subjunctive mood. C. K. Barrett, *A Critical and Exegetical Commentary on the Acts of the Apostles,* 2 vols, ICC (Edinburgh: T. & T. Clark, 1994, 1998) 481, weighs the various options and decides in favor of an aoristic present indicative, which intensifies the reality of a particular moment in time: Jesus Christ heals you *right now.*

398. With characteristic hyperbole Luke reminds the reader of the evangelical purpose of this current demonstration of Peter's apostolic powers. The residents of the Sharon valley are Jews since they "turned to the Lord [Jesus]" rather than to God. See Haenchen, *The Acts of the Apostles,* 338.

399. Luke uses the feminine form for "disciple" (μαθήτρια *mathētria*)— the only time it is used in the NT. The double naming of Tabitha, her Aramaic name, and the summary of her personal profile "she was devoted to good works and acts of charity" (9:36*b*) indicate her substantial reputation in the church. We learn nothing, however, about her marital or social status from this narrative.

400. The fact that Luke does *not* mention that her body was "anointed" with burial salts as expected may well indicate the community's confidence in her imminent resuscitation.

clothes she had made for them (v. 39b).[401] Her loss is keenly felt because of the community's responsibility for the welfare of its needy widows (see 6:1-2). Her healing bears additional witness to the importance of the community of goods. Yet the spotlight remains on Peter who "sends them all out of the room" (v. 40). Perhaps the reader has reason to wonder how he will respond to the weeping widows, given the earlier failure of the Twelve to respond adequately to the welfare of Hellenist widows. In his ministry beyond Jerusalem, Peter's response is more direct and empathetic: He hears the widows' lamentation, he prays, and then he resuscitates Tabitha (vv. 40-41).

Peter's command, "Tabitha, get up" (ἀνάστηθι anastēthi), and the narrator's refrain, "he presented her to them alive," recall the resurrection of Jesus (see 1:3). This refrain also glosses Peter's similar command of Aeneas (see v. 34b) and thus we now suppose that his earlier claim that "Jesus Christ heals you" (see v. 34a) is implied here as well. That is, Peter's prophetic role is to announce the availability of the Lord's healing power among those who believe (cf. Luke 8:49-56). Peter's power to heal is not an exercise of magic but a function of his close communion with the Lord of glory. Once again, the action of "helping her up" (v. 41) and returning her to the "saints and widows" confirms the resuscitation. And again as a result of this healing, "many people believed the Lord" (v. 42b; see also v. 35). Although the catalytic character of "signs and wonders" is characteristic of Acts, Luke's summaries of conversions are characteristically gapped and should be filled out with additional details culled from similar missionary episodes. In this way, the reader knows that the inference of every conversion is that people "turn to the Lord" (v. 35) and "believe in the Lord" (v. 42) in response to the proclamation of the gospel.

**9:43.** The impression left by this verse is one of a pause in preparation for the next episode. Two details are important in this regard. First, Peter "stayed in Joppa." The repetition of the city in the following story of Cornelius's conversion (10:6,

17, 32) commends the importance of "Joppa" to the story's meaning: Peter's location connects his prophetic mission and Jonah's, who also departed from Joppa on his fateful mission to Nineveh (see above). Second, Peter stays "with a certain Simon, a tanner." The symbolic importance of kosher purity in Luke's Cornelius story (see 10:14) is introduced here by reference to Simon's trade, since a tanner carries the odors and blood of animals that would make him "unclean."[402]

**10:1-8.** The taxonomy of God's universal salvation reaches a watershed moment with the introduction of God-fearing Roman Cornelius. The brief sketch of his résumé, completed by subsequent reports of close associates (see 10:22) and then by Cornelius himself (see 10:31), places him in Caesarea and identifies him as a ranking "centurion" attached to the "Italian Cohort" (v. 1).[403] Cornelius is the first person with Roman authority named in Acts. Religiously, he is "a devout man, who feared God—gave alms generously—and prayed constantly to God" (v. 2; cf. 10:22, 31). Although Luke attaches considerable importance to God-fearing Gentiles in Acts, we have no standard definition or precise classification of "God-fearing" from the ancient world.[404] Allowing for a technical difference between the non-Jewish believer who has completed the prescribed rite of initiation into Judaism ("proselyte"; cf. 6:5) and the non-Jewish seeker who is simply interested in the beliefs and practices of Judaism ("God-fearer"; see v. 2), references to the actual practices of Gentile proselytes (cf. 13:43) are roughly the same as of God-fearers in Acts. In any case, Luke's emphasis is on Cornelius's character rather than on his political or religious status—and implicitly on the causal relationship between his character

---

401. The middle voice of the participle "showed" (ἐπιδεικνύμεναι epideiknymenai) indicates that the widows are actually wearing clothes made for them by Dorcas, who distributes them among the most needy of the community in keeping with the principle of the community of goods (see 4:32-35).

402. Some scholars think this connection is too clever for Luke's readers if not for Luke. Others suggest that this negative reaction to a tanner's work stems from the casuistry of later rabbis and is probably not yet in Luke's social world. See J. McConnachie, "Simon a Tanner" (Acts ix.43; x.6, 32), *ExpT* 36 (1924-25) 90.

403. A centurion was a noncommissioned officer wo commanded one hundred soldiers; he was probably a Roman citizen. A "cohort" of soldiers typically numbers six hundred (one-tenth of a legion)—although this is contested by historians of the Roman army, as is the location, date, and precise role of the "Italian Cohort." See J. A. Fitzmyer, *The Acts of the Apostles*, AB 31 (Garden City, N.Y.: Doubleday, 1998) 449.

404. The scholarly literature on the status of Gentile God-fearers is extensive. For good summaries of the social and religious worlds of God-fearers see B. Witherington, *The Acts of the Apostles: A Socio-Rhetorical Commentary* (Grand Rapids: Eerdmans, 1998) 341-44; H. C. Kee, *To Every Nation Under Heaven: The Acts of the Apostles*, NTC (Valley Forge, Pa.: Trinity, 1997) 133-36.

and conversion. Thereby his piety is a "memorial before God"[405] (v. 4; cf. 10:31) and showing him to be the sort of pious Gentile that has favor with God.

God responds to Cornelius's prayers with a vision. The missionary function of visions in Acts is to locate a person in the right place at the right time in order to receive God's benefaction. In this light, the soldier is given marching orders to follow into salvation: "send men to Joppa" for a certain man who is staying in a particular house (vv. 5-6). Obedience to God's bidding is the hallmark of readiness to receive God's grace. Cornelius obeys God according to his own military conventions: He "called . . . a devout soldier from the ranks" whose experience is most like Cornelius's (see v. 2) and would therefore be best able to represent his interests to Peter, which he evidently does (v. 8).

References to the time of day are always theologically laden in this book: The pious Cornelius had a vision "one afternoon at about three o'clock" (v. 3; see also 3:1). This was a time of day set aside for religious observance among the faithful of Israel—in the middle of the afternoon for all to see. Once again a "double vision" is employed in Acts to get two people on God's page. Before both Saul and Ananias had separate visions about the same future (see 9:11-12); and here again Cornelius and "a certain Simon who is called Peter" will also have visionary experiences of the same future—God's future. Cornelius's response to the angel is the same as Saul's to Jesus—"What is it, Lord?" (v. 4; see also 9:5)—and for the same reason: He lacks understanding, which the vision then supplies.

**10:9-16.** "About noon the next day," as the caravan travels to Joppa, Peter has gone to a rooftop in Joppa to pray.[406] Luke adds that the apostle prays while hungry, an appropriate context for a vision about food. Peter's hunger is a function of his piety, since prayer likely is joined with a fast to underwrite his devotion to God. Peter's piety in turn might then explain both his "trance" (ἔκστασις *ekstasis*), which occasions prophetic ecstasy, and his subsequent hesitancy to kill and eat unclean foods.

The general role of visions in Acts is to clarify God's redemptive plan with regard to specific places and people. "This is the moment when new religions or sects are born—when what has hitherto been taken for granted as a fundamental and defining principle is called into question, and the question is heard as the voice of God."[407] In Peter's case a picnic blanket is envisaged, spread with various species of animals (vv. 11-12) without distinguishing clean from unclean.[408] Characteristically, what he sees is accompanied by what he hears: the Lord's instruction for him to "get up, kill and eat" (v. 13) the animals without proper attention to their kosher preparation (cf. Leviticus 11). Peter's negative response—"By no means, Lord"—should be anticipated by his Jewish piety (v. 14).[409] The subsequent repetition of this divine audition makes Peter's proper response clear: What was formerly "profane and unclean" is now clean and no longer profane. The second repetition of the divine audition (v. 15) explains the first and provides the essential message of the vision. Peter does not require the third audition, which serves a symbolic rather than an epistemic role.

The exchange between God and Peter only indirectly concerns traditions regarding clean and unclean foods, even though this is surely what prompts him to "puzzle greatly" and ponder the meaning of his vision (vv. 17, 19a).[410] Comprehension unfolds only with additional

---

405. This striking phrase alludes to OT offerings made to God whose fragrance ascends to God's "nostrils"—an anthropomorphism of divine pleasure (cf. Lev 2:2, 9, 16; 5:12; 6:15). While the content of Cornelius's prayers is unknown, it is reasonable to infer that the angelic vision is a response to prayer.

406. While not a fixed time of daily prayer for the pious Jew, Peter's noontime prayer may very well be part of a fast since it is associated with his hunger. Some later mss. read "three o'clock" instead of "noon" but this is clearly a scribal accommodation to the earlier reference to Cornelius's prayer and is in any case a better known time for demonstrations of Jewish piety (see 3:1).

407. J. D. G. Dunn, *The Acts of the Apostles* (Valley Forge, Pa.: Trinity, 1996) 138.

408. Reptiles (cf. Lev 11:29-38) and birds (cf. Lev 11:13-19) are especially unclean for a pious Jew.

409. The phrase "by no means" translates the adverb μηδαμῶς *medamos* and is found only here (and in Peter's retelling of this incident in 11:8) in the NT. The intensity of Peter's response is expressed by the addition of "never" (οὐδέποτε *oudepote*; lit., "at no time") and the pairing of "profane or unclean" (κοινὸν καὶ ἀκάθαρτον *koinon kai akatharton*)—synonyms for the unlawful taken from both Jewish ("unclean") and Greek ("profane") religious vocabularies.

410. The word for "puzzle" (διαπορέω *diaporeo*) is used only by Luke in the NT and typically of an inward response to divine revelation, whether in reference to nonbelievers (see Acts 2:12; 5:24; cf. Luke 9:7) or believers (cf. Luke 24:4). All have the inherent ability to perceive the importance of what they see or hear, even though without understanding.

information:[411] Peter's vision concerns his mission to fulfill God's purpose that unclean (= uncircumcised) Gentiles will also share Israel's blessings (see vv. 42-43).

**10:17-23a.** Several coincidental incidents occur that gradually illumine Peter's understanding of his vision. Cornelius's emissaries arrive from Caesarea and ask to see Peter (vv. 17-18). The clever literary interplay between two "Simons"— Simon the tanner (v. 17) at whose house "Simon who was called Peter" (v. 18) is staying—may intend to create the impression of confusion (related to Peter's understanding of the vision) that is then resolved by the Spirit's intervention (v. 19).

The Spirit's word to Peter serves both theological and practical ends: "Look, three men are searching for you" (10:19*b*). Peter is evidently lost in his meditation on the meaning of his vision and does not hear the three men knocking and calling for him from the gate. The Spirit's intervention to facilitate their meeting makes us expect that those who stand at the door knocking will somehow aid Peter in deciphering his vision. Further, its instruction for Peter to "go with them—for I have sent them" (v. 20) indicates that the message these men bring him accords with divine purpose.

Peter's question, "Why have you come?" (v. 21), seems to challenge the Spirit's earlier instruction, "Go with them without hesitation" (v. 20). The phrase translated "without hesitation" (μηδὲν διακρινόμενος *mēden diakrinomenos*) means to act without pausing to doubt its merit.[412] Peter's question, perhaps, functions as a literary prompt that occasions yet another sounding of God's reasons for saving Cornelius. The three messengers assert that "he is a righteous and God-fearing man, who is respected by all the Jewish people" and that he was "directed by a holy angel" to listen to what Peter says (v. 22). These details comprise both a confirmation and an expansion of Luke's earlier résumé (see vv. 1-4) and reflect an independent appraisal of Cornelius's fitness to receive God's salvation. Cornelius is described for Jewish Peter's benefit as a "righteous man" (replacing the earlier "devout man"), as though he lived his life according to Torah's precept.[413]

Significantly, Peter learns that they were "directed" by a "holy angel" with the tacit promise that Peter would go to Cornelius's home where a Gentile would listen to what the prophet would say to him. The verb χρηματίζω (*chrēmatizō*), translated "directed" (NRSV) or even more timidly as "told" (NIV), is a much stronger term that denotes a revelatory word from God (see Matt 2:12, 22; Luke 2:26; Heb 8:5; 11:7). For this reason, Peter is responsive to what his visitors tell him; indeed, the demonstration of his hospitality toward them—he "invited them in and gave them lodging" (v. 23)—is characteristic of one who is responsive to God's Word.[414] The reader must presume that Peter now understands the intent of his vision and has accepted the prospect of a Gentile mission as a feature of God's plan of salvation (see 10:28-29).

**10:23b-33.** This panel of Luke's story takes place "the next day," when Peter departs for Caesarea. He is joined by "some of the [Jewish] believers from Joppa" (v. 23*b*) who will later attest to Cornelius's conversion (see v. 45; 11:12). Cornelius has already been prepared for Peter's visit and "had called together his relatives and close friends" (v. 24) of his extended household.[415]

For all his religious devotion Cornelius is not yet a believer and still makes theological mistakes: "Cornelius, falling at Peter's feet, worshiped him" (10:25).[416] Given the importance the angel has attached to Peter, Cornelius's response seems reasonable since it proffers homage to someone

---

411. Peter's failure to "get" his vision is not the result of hardened resistance or spiritual obduracy (as perhaps is true with Jonah) but reflects the sheer difficulty of deciphering the symbols of God's message. Contra Dunn, *The Acts of the Apostles,* 138. Peter needs more information; and when he receives it, he understands.

412. Barrett, *Acts,* 511. It is noteworthy that Luke uses this same verb in Peter's review of this incident before the Jerusalem Council (15:9). In this later use, however, it is used of God who "makes no distinction" (οὐθὲν διέκρινεν *outhen diekrinen*) between Jews and Gentiles. The later glosses the earlier use so that the reader understands that the Spirit tells Peter to go "without hesitation" to a Gentile because God "makes no distinction" between Jew and non-Jew.

413. Fitzmyer, *The Acts of the Apostles,* 457.

414. L. T. Johnson, *The Acts of the Apostles,* SP 5 (Collegeville, Minn.: Liturgical, 1992) 185.

415. In Acts the "household" is an important location for the experience of God's saving power, as the use of οἶκος/οἰκία (*oikos/oikia,* "house") shows (see 2:2, 46; 5:42; 9:17; 10:22; 11:12-14; 16:31-32; 18:7-8; 20:20). A range of important literary themes in Acts are centered in the house, such as goods, hospitality, friendship, and worship. The reader should be alert, then, to the social fabric of salvation that is indicated by repeated references to the household, as here in the story of Cornelius's conversion where members of his extended household— including clients and friends—are not only witnesses to his salvation but participants in it.

416. The word "worship" (προσκυνέω *proskyneō*) denotes either homage given a deity or the profound respect one demonstrates toward an emissary sent by God. Peter's response suggests that Cornelius presumes that Peter is worthy of worship that is due God alone.

heaven has authorized to mediate the blessings of eternal life. Peter, however, has consistently refused to exercise his religious authority in a self-centered manner and always has subordinated it to the will and purposes of God (see 3:12; 9:40). Cornelius's honest mistake, then, is in supposing that Peter is in some sense directly responsible for his salvation; Peter's role, however, is to proclaim salvation, not to dispense it. His response testifies to this subordinate role in Cornelius's salvation: "Stand up; I am only a mortal" (10:26; cf. 14:14-15).

In all modesty, then, Peter's opening missionary address testifies to his own recent "conversion" (see 10:22-23a): "God has shown me that I should not call anyone profane or unclean" (10:28b; see 10:14-15). In fact, the process of divine disclosure began with Peter's missionary efforts beyond Jerusalem among marginal Jews (see 8:25; 9:32-42, 43). These missionary efforts beyond Jerusalem are now directed to those beyond Israel.[417] The temporal framework supplied by the narrative itself indicates that Peter's understanding of his Gentile mission unfolds over several days of visions (see 10:30), internal reflection (see 10:17, 19), and the reports of others (see 10:22). What God finally "shows" him is the subtext of this unusual house call, since an observant Jew deems it "unlawful to visit a Gentile" (10:28a)[418] and especially "without objection" (10:29a).

Peter's question, "May I ask why you sent for me?" (10:29b), and Cornelius's response (10:30-33) appear redundant (see 10:4-6, 22) and an unnecessary preface to the proclamation of the gospel. Such restatements are characteristic of Luke's narrative style, however, and are employed to elucidate and clarify important literary themes. For example, Cornelius's commentary on this

occasion emphasizes God's faithfulness more than his own religious résumé: "God has heard—and remembered"[419] (10:31; cf. 10:4b). Cornelius's goodwill (and earlier homage) toward Peter and submission to his spiritual authority are now explained by his desire to "listen to all that the Lord has commanded you to say" (10:33).

**10:34-43.** Peter and Cornelius share a premonition that a religious revolution is about to commence in Israel. For this reason, Peter's gospel presentation is not defensive but *epideictic* (= edifying) in tone and christological in substance.[420] Its chiastic shape (ABCB´A´) funnels its auditors to the speech's core kerygmatic elements (see 10:38-42a) to underline the continuity between his proclamation to Jew and now to Gentile.[421]

**10:34-35 (A).** Luke's opening formula, "Then Peter began to speak" (lit., "Peter then opened his mouth"; see 8:35) is a literary convention indicating that the speech is inspired prophecy. The full implication of his mission has now been made clear to him: "I now realize how true it is that God shows no partiality" between Jew and Gentile (v. 34b; see also vv. 28-29). Peter's lesson is about God and not the scope of his mission. Surely he knows from Israel's Scriptures that God is not a respecter of persons (cf. Deut 10:17; cf. Ps 81:2 LXX; Lev 19:15; 2 Chr 19:7); however, this conviction has acquired new dimensions of meaning in the light of recent events. Moreover, the biblical principle of divine impartiality comes with a critical aspect: Although God does not discriminate by ethnic group or nationality, God does indeed single out those "in every nation . . . who fear him and

---

417. The word translated "Gentile" in 10:28 is ἀλλόφυλος (*allophylos*); it is used only here in the NT but often as a pejorative in the LXX. The term denotes people of different or mixed ethnic grounds other than Jewish; its sense is not religious but racial.

418. Some scholars pose considerable problems with Peter's initial address to his Gentile audience since they claim his visitation of Gentiles is not unprecedented. Observant Jews did cultivate friendships and have social relations with non-Jews, especially in the diaspora. See E. Haenchen, *The Acts of the Apostles* (Philadelphia: Westminster, 1971) 350; Josephus *The Jewish War* 2.463. However, Peter's idiom is not relational but cultic. He merely restates the teaching of rabbis that it is ritually unclean for a "clean" (i.e., observant) Jew to enter the home of an "unclean" (i.e., non-observant) Gentile. See J. A. Fitzmyer, *The Acts of the Apostles*, AB 31 (Garden City, N.Y.: Doubleday, 1998) 457, 461. Cornelius is not a proselyte Jew or yet a believer. He is, therefore, "unclean" from Peter's perspective as an observant Jew.

419. Johnson, *The Acts of the Apostles*, 190-91, argues that the choice of "remember" intentionally recalls the OT idiom of God's covenant faithfulness, when God "remembers" Israel and blesses them. In this setting, then, God's act of remembering Cornelius is a response of God's faithfulness to the promise made to Abraham that Gentiles would share in Israel's blessings—rather than a per se response to Cornelius because of deeds he had done.

420. Peter's speeches in Acts follow a common literary pattern consisting of an opening address that connects with the audience (vv. 34-35), christological kerygma (vv. 36-41), scriptural proofs (v. 43), and a summons to repent (v. 42).

421. The chiastic pattern is as follows: A = 10:34-5 (God is not partial); A´ = 10:43b (God forgives all who believe); B = 10:36a (God sent the gospel to Israel first); B´ = 10:43a (God sends the gospel to Gentiles); C = 10:36b-37 (Jesus is Lord of all); C´] = 10:10:42b (Jesus is judge of all); and D = 10:38-42a (the gospel message: Jesus sent forth as Messiah).

do what is right" (v. 35).[422] Cornelius is a Roman exemplar of this theological principle (see 10:4-6, 31).[423]

**10:36-37 (B).** Peter's brief geographic review of the Messiah's career also argues for the fairness of God, although not without considerable irony.[424] Perhaps this element of Peter's speech responds to an unstated problem concerning the perceived partiality of Jesus' mission, which was only to Jews. His response is to claim that the biblical promise of peace is made first to Israel; therefore, the Messiah is sent first to Israel (v. 36) with a "message [ῥῆμα *rhēma,* "event"][425] spread throughout Judea, beginning with Galilee" (v. 37). Nevertheless, the implicit universal importance of Jesus' mission to Israel is ironically captured by Peter's parenthetical confession that "[Jesus Christ] is Lord of all" (v. 36).

**10:38-42a (C).** Peter brings his gospel to climax with a summary of "the message [ὁ λόγος *ho logos*] God sent to the people [lit., "children"] of Israel," of which "we are witnesses" (v. 39). Its familiar content in this rhetorical setting is yet another way to articulate the biblical principle of divine impartiality. Peter emphasizes not only the basis of Jesus' prophetic ministry ("with the Holy Spirit and with power")[426] but also its public venue and the dramatic manner by which "he went about doing good and healing all who were oppressed by the devil, for God was with him"

(v. 38). For this reason, his reputation for good works is already known by this Gentile audience (see "you know the message," v. 36). Moreover, Jesus has reliable "witnesses [μάρτυρες *martyres*] to all that he did both in Judea and Jerusalem" (v. 39; see also 1:21-22; 2:22-24; 3:13-15; 4:40; 5:30) and following his resurrection (vv. 40-41; see also 2:32). That is, the details of the Messiah's career—how and what he did—were not hidden from public view and now allow for the impartial dissemination of God's message to non-Jews.

Because these apostolic witnesses "were chosen by God" (v. 41; see 1:2) as the special audience to whom the risen Jesus appeared and with whom he "ate and drank" (see Luke 24:30-31, 41-43; John 21:12-13), the sense is that God operates from a predetermined plan with the relationship between the Messiah and his apostles at its center.[427] The implied point again is to underline the inherent authority of the apostles as witnesses and colleagues of the risen Jesus, and that through their ministry God's plan of salvation goes forward.

**10:42b-43a (B').** Peter's witness to the resurrected Jesus presumes a special relationship with him and a privileged knowledge of him, which obligates him "to testify" (διαμαρτύρασθαι *diamartyrasthai;* see 2:40; 8:25) to the Jewish "people" (see 2:47; 3:23; 10:2) after the pattern established by the Messiah's mission and biblical prophecy. It is noteworthy that Peter introduces Jesus' future role as Israel's "judge of the living and the dead" to a Gentile audience (cf. 17:29-31), which is, perhaps, another symbol of the principle of divine impartiality.

**10:43b (A').** Scripture's witness is added to Peter's testimony to complete his presentation of the gospel. Peter's appeal to Scripture makes sense only because Cornelius is God-fearing and would recognize the authority of Israel's Scriptures. There is no specific citation given; Peter's appeal to "all the prophets" is to the whole tenor of Scripture (cf. 3:18, 24; 7:42; 26:22; 28:23). All Scripture testifies to God's promise of salvation, which has been fulfilled in the Christ event, so

---

422. The phrase "what is right [δικαιοσύνη *dikaiosynē* ]" refers to practices that conform to God's law; Barrett, *Acts,* 1:520-21. Peter thereby allows that an uncircumcised Gentile like Cornelius can become a member of the covenant community, even though not a proselyte, because his life is characteristic of the faithful Jew.

423. The meaning of the predicate "God accepts" (NIV; NRSV, "is acceptable to God") is unclear. Has God already "accepted" Cornelius because of his acts of piety as a God-fearer (so NIV)? Or has his righteousness more simply made him "acceptable" to be saved (so NRSV)? The latter translation seems best here since salvation in Acts is impossible apart from a hearing of the gospel and a believing response to its kerygmatic claims (see 2:38).

424. For the difficult text critical, grammatical, and interpretative issues regarding 10:36-38, see Barrett, *Acts,* 521-25; G. Schneider, *Die Apostelgeschichte,* 2 vols., HTK (Freiburg am Breisgau: Herder, 1981–82) 2:76-77.

425. In this case *rhēma* is probably better rendered as "event" (i.e., the Christ event) as in Luke 2:15. See Haenchen, *The Acts of the Apostles,* 352.

426. Dunn, *The Acts of the Apostles,* 142-43, notes three OT allusions that together provide a prophetic co-text to clarify Luke's intended meaning for 10:36-38: Ps 107:20 ("he sent out his word and healed [the people of Israel]"); Isa 52:7 ("those who preach peace [to the people of Israel]"); and Isa 61:1 ("The Spirit of the Lord is upon [Jesus of Nazareth] because he has anointed [him] to preach good news [to the people of Israel]"; cf. Luke 4:18). Thus Peter's rehearsal of Jesus' messianic mission (the "Christ event") is understood as the concrete fulfillment of God's *biblical* promise to Israel.

427. The word translated "chosen" (προχειροτονέω *procheirotoneō*) is used only here in the NT, although it is similar to the word used in 3:20 for God's "choosing" of Jesus as Messiah (προχειρίζομαι *procheirizomai*). This vocabulary not only confirms that Peter's (= the Twelve's) ministry is a sign of God's provident care of the Jewish people, but that it also follows a carefully prearranged (*pro-*) script that inspires the audience's confidence in its completion.

that "*everyone* who believes in him receives forgiveness of sins through his *name*" (italics added). This final refrain echoes Joel's prophecy (see 2:21), which joins Jonah's prophecy as the implied biblical witnesses to the theological truth of Peter's proclamation to Cornelius. The Pauline phrase "believes in him" is found only here in Acts (cf. 13:39), which may cue the narrative's turn toward Paul's mission to the nations but here is still more clearly bound to the familiar themes of Peter's earlier preaching—"forgiveness of sins" (see 2:38; 3:18-19) and "through his name" (e.g., 2:38; 3:6; 4:10).

**10:44-48.** Although Acts mentions twice that Peter's speech is interrupted (v. 44*a;* see also 11:15), nothing important is left out and it stands as a complete presentation of the gospel. It is probably best to understand this "interrupted speech," then, as a literary convention employed earlier (cf. 2:37) and later (cf. 17:32; 22:22; 23:7; 26:24) for rhetorical effect—in this instance to showcase two important theological convictions. First, the Holy Spirit insinuates itself into Peter's preaching as a demonstration that God takes the lead in fulfilling the prophesied plan of salvation; in effect, God's Spirit intrudes upon Peter's ministry to illustrate a point he has just made about the testimony of prophets (see v. 43)!

More critical, however, is a second core conviction: God's Spirit interrupts Peter to empower *his* witness to the history of God's salvation, another theme of this speech (see v. 39). Peter's subsequent witness to this "Gentile Pentecost" will both complete the task God has given him and revolutionize how he thinks of Gentile admission into the covenant community. Indeed, from this moment forward whenever Peter is asked to interpret the status of uncircumcised Gentiles within the church or in relationship to Jews/Jerusalem, his final appeal will not be to his vision but to Cornelius's reception of the gift of the Holy Spirit. Peter is a witness not only to the historical Jesus (and so his apostle) but also to the initial outpouring of the Holy Spirit at Pentecost and its subsequent outpourings in Samaria and now upon the household of Cornelius, an uncircumcised Roman Gentile. Only Peter is in a position to recognize the strong family resemblance between them and to draw its soteriological significance from what he has observed (see 11:15). Perhaps for this reason

Luke shapes his account of the Gentile Pentecost after the sequence of events of Israel's Pentecost narrated in Acts 2: (1) "The Holy Spirit fell upon all who heard the word" (v. 44//2:4); (2) "the circumcised believers . . . were astounded . . . for they heard them speaking in tongues and extolling God" (vv. 45-46//2:11-12); (3) "Then Peter said, 'Can anyone withhold the water for baptizing these people who have received the Holy Spirit just as we have?' " (v. 47//2:38); and (4) they were "baptized in the name of Jesus Christ" (v. 48*a*//2:41).

This literary interplay within Acts between the Jerusalem and the Gentile "Pentecosts" guarantees an appropriate response to Peter's rhetorical question, "Can anyone withhold the water for baptizing these people?" (v. 47). The logical response must be a resounding no. There is nothing that should exclude these repentant Gentiles from their initiation into the faith community. The reader of Acts recalls, however, that the Spirit's outpouring had earlier "amazed" Jewish pilgrims in the holy city who out of ignorance mistook "God's deeds of power" for human folly (see 2:11-12). In a similar way, the "astonishment" of those "circumcised believers" who witnessed "that the gift of the Holy Spirit had been poured out even on the Gentiles" (v. 45) alerts the reader that other repentant Jews may not be prepared to readily embrace the revolution that Peter's mission to Cornelius has begun. Thus, even though the apostle "ordered them to be baptized" (v. 48*a*), there is hint of trouble brewing back home in the Jerusalem church (see 11:2). The question remains why the Spirit's baptism of Cornelius should have amazed Peter's Jewish cohort. Because of the church's prior experience with the Spirit's outpouring in both Jerusalem and Samaria, it is doubtful that their astonishment obtains to the phenomena of "speaking in tongues and extolling God" (v. 46). Moreover, they would have heard reports from both Peter and Cornelius of their coincidental "double vision" as testimony that God intends to include "unclean" Gentiles in the church. The surprising element of this incident of Spirit baptism must be that repentant Gentiles share the same gift of the Holy Spirit equally with repentant Jews—in Peter's words "these people who have received the Holy Spirit *just as we have*" (v. 47, italics added). The conclusion the

Peter of Acts draws from their common religious experience is that uncircumcised believers belong as fully to the messianic community as do these stunned "circumcised believers."

**11:1-17.** With every case of repetition, especially when it is of whole episodes as here, we must be on the lookout for changes in setting, in details, or in literary design that uncover the full importance that episode carries within the whole narrative. In this second telling of Cornelius's conversion, Peter is compelled to provide testimony to a council of church leaders in Jerusalem (vv. 1-3). Evidently, some believers are upset by reports that "Gentiles had also accepted the word of God" (v. 1; cf. 8:14). Peter's careful rehearsal of Cornelius's conversion (vv. 4-14) does not seek to defend his own actions but the actions of God who has saved an "unclean" Roman Gentile (vv. 15-18; see also 15:6-11).

**11:1-3.** The report of the favorable reception of the word by Gentiles was well received by Peter's apostolic colleagues who "praised God" (v. 18). Luke implies a division exists in the Judean church between "the apostles and the believers" and "the circumcised believers" (cf. 10:45) who "criticized" (διακρινόμενος *diakrinomenos*) Peter's actions in converting Cornelius (11:2; see 10:20). Ironically, their criticism of Peter echoes his own hesitancy to obey the directive of his divine audition to eat non-kosher foods (see 10:13-16) and then his anxiety over the "legality" of visiting a non-kosher household (see 10:28). Peter's earlier anxiety is now reflected by leading members of the Jewish church who worry that table fellowship with unclean Gentiles will defile them as well. Only time will tell whether their anxiety over the intermingling of clean and unclean people will also dissolve upon consideration of their common gift of the Holy Spirit.

The first Jerusalem assembly to consider controversies provoked by the Gentile mission is now convened, and will continue at a second Jerusalem assembly (15:4-5) that concludes the first part of Acts (see the Overview to 2:14–15:12). The irony of the present story is nicely captured by Luke's clever repetition of *diakrinō,* first of the Spirit's injunction for Peter to hear out Cornelius's emissaries and accompany them "without hestitation" (*diakrinō,* 10:20) and now here of Peter's opponents in Jerusalem who "criticize" (*diakrinō,* 11:2) him for doing so. If the anxiety of conservative

Jews is that they will become as Gentiles by sharing table fellowship with them, then their salve for this anxiety is that the Gentile convert must become as a Jew by following their purity laws. The real danger is to trivialize their anxiety and criticize these Jewish believers as "legalists" or worse. Their concern for purity is in reality a concern for the community's solidarity. This is after all a community of friends that has distinguished itself in Jerusalem's public life by living together with "one heart and soul" (see 4:32). Now, however, the currency of the community's solidarity is no longer merely sharing goods; the community's new currency minted by the Gentile Pentecost is the sharing of the same spiritual food, "the gift of the Holy Spirit," which purifies *everyone* who calls upon the risen "Lord of all." That is, while the stated anxiety is table fellowship, the implied and real anxiety is over sharing the Holy Spirit with unholy Gentiles. The tendency to embody the pattern of God's salvation, which privileges Jews (see 10:37-39), in the social practices of the faith community as symbolized by table fellowship is subverted by the shared experience of the Holy Spirit.

**11:4-14.** Peter's response to their question about his alleged table fellowship with Gentiles is characterized as an "explanation" (ἐκτίθημαι *ektithēmai,* v. 4). His primary motive is to set forth the chronological order of events in a straightforward fashion, and he does so in the first person as the principal witness to these events.

The summary of the double vision follows closely its initial narration in 10:9-33; there are, however, two substantial additions that gloss the earlier story. The first is Peter's reference to "these six brothers also accompanied me, and we entered the man's house" (v. 12). Even though it remains unclear from the earlier account whether these "circumcised believers" agreed with Peter's actions (see 10:45-48), he has now made them witnesses to confirm Peter's report as trustworthy. Clever politics indeed! The second and far more important change comes with Peter's retelling of Cornelius's report concerning what the angel had told him (see 10:31-32) in the light of what ultimately transpired. Cornelius mentioned nothing of an angelic promise that Peter's message would be the means "by which you and your entire household will be saved" (v. 14).

The angel's emphasis on *salvation* adds three new elements to the Cornelius tradition. (1) The prior concern that Gentiles follow Israel's purity code is redefined to invite reflection on God's "code" by which Gentiles participate in the blessings of Israel's salvation. (2) Peter's shift to the soteriological implications of Cornelius's conversion prepares us for a second Jerusalem council when Peter will refer to Cornelius's conversion and Spirit baptism (see 15:6-11) as paradigmatic of the conversion of uncircumcised Gentiles and their solidarity with Jewish believers (cf. 15:4-5). Peter concludes with the Paul-like assertion that "we believe that we [Jews] will be saved through the grace of the Lord Jesus, just as they [Gentiles] will" (15:11; cf. Eph 2:8-9). (3) The phrasing of Peter's "you will be saved" (σωθήση *sōthēsē*) recalls the final phrase of Joel's paradigmatic prophecy that everyone—now including God-fearing uncircumcised Gentiles—who believes in the Lord Jesus "will be saved" (σωθήσεται *sōthēsetai,* 2:21). This intertext glosses Peter's previous climactic claim that "all the prophets [Jonah and now Joel] testify about him that everyone who believes in him receives forgiveness of sins through his name" (10:43).

**11:15-17.** Peter's explanation emphasizes Cornelius's experience of Spirit baptism (see 10:44-48). Clearly this has become for him the hermeneutic key to understanding God's plan to save "unclean" Gentiles like Cornelius. He does not mention his speech; Peter's witness is not to a kerygma but to a religious experience. His use of a traditional saying, "John baptized with water, but you will be baptized with the Holy Spirit" (v. 16; cf. Luke 3:16), recalls the Lord's instruction of his apostolic successors at the beginning of Acts (see 1:5). However, neither Cornelius nor any member of his household engage in ministry following their Spirit baptism (cf. 1:8). The Gentile Pentecost presumes a different religious motive and effect that is redemptive and not vocational. In this regard, Peter asserts that "God gave them the same *gift* that he gave us when we believed in the Lord Jesus Christ" (v. 17, italics added; cf. 11:15*b*), which echoes his conviction that repentance occasions receiving the "*gift* of the Holy Spirit" (2:38, italics added) and initiation into the community of goods (see 2:42-47). The implied point is that repentant Gentiles are initiated into a community of goods that shares God's gift of the Holy Spirit with repentant Jews.

**11:18.** The Jewish believers' response to Peter's report and stunning conclusion is silence (v. 18*a*): Their initial objection (see 11:3) is considered an irrelevancy by their Apostle, who has skillfully turned the occasion into a theological platform to sound a programmatic note about Israel's mission to the Gentiles. The importance of the council's judgment that "God has granted even the Gentiles the repentance unto life" (v. 18*b*), which otherwise sounds redundant, is gleaned from two "repentance" texts found earlier in Acts and echoed here to "thicken" the importance of repentant Gentiles. In concluding his speech to Cornelius, Peter appeals to "all the prophets" for proof that "forgiveness of sins" is granted to "everyone who believes in Jesus" (10:43). In the light of the pairing of "repentance" with the reception of both "forgiveness of sins" and "the gift of the Spirit" in 2:38, the council's verdict is that the requirements and results of Gentile and Jewish repentance are the same. The full implication of their conclusion will be cashed out when this same council reconvenes to consider whether the repentant Gentiles of Paul's congregations in the diaspora should practice circumcision (see 14:27–15:29).

The second text alluded to is 5:30-32, where Peter famously addresses the Sanhedrin with the affirmation that "we must obey God rather than men" (5:29). Peter goes on to explain that his obedience to God is predicated on "the *God* of our ancestors [who] raised Jesus" (5:30, italics added] in order to "grant *repentance* to Israel and the forgiveness of sins" (5:31, italics added) and to give the Holy Spirit "to those who obey God" (5:32). That is, according to Peter, God's plan to bless a repentant Israel is signaled by the reception of the Holy Spirit. In concluding this first Jerusalem Council, then, those elders assembled agree that this fresh outpouring of the Spirit must mean that God has "*granted* even the Gentiles the *repentance* unto life" (italics added). Behind this verdict lies the critical recognition that Cornelius's repentance and Spirit baptism are not at odds with Jewish tradition but actually *agree* with it. In fact, the success of Peter's earlier mission to repentant Israel is the prior condition of his current success with repentant Cornelius. This raw belief stands now only in theory; its practical outworking will bring to surface other concerns that Paul, not Peter, will consider and respond to.

# REFLECTIONS

**1.** "Peter knelt down and prayed—Tabitha opened her eyes, and seeing Peter, she sat up" (see 9:40). In a single year I lost two dear colleagues to terminal illness. Both had requested prayers for healing, and earnestly, repeatedly we gathered together as believers and friends to petition God on their behalf. The practice of our prayers reflected a type of Christian realism that recognizes and depends upon God's transcendent love as our final hope. But our friends died anyway. Some of us were tempted to shrug it off, supposing our prayers did not work once again. Luke's account of Peter's healing ministry, repeated in Acts for emphasis, provides a biblical setting that helps us reflect upon "unanswered prayers." How is this true when Peter's prayers were answered? But this is the essential truth of our faith: God does heal the sick whether by medicine or miracle. More remarkably a gracious God intervenes to heal the least and last among us—widows such as Tabitha. There is something arresting about these stories of healings in Acts and the parallels found in the Gospels and the prophets. Peter says only "rise up." Nothing more is necessary but his simple claim on God's resurrection power. What confidence—but then Peter had seen the crucified Jesus alive!

What is sometimes missed in reading these healing stories, however, are the wider, more public consequences of being sick and of being healed. For example, Tabitha's sickness provided the occasion for renewing Peter's relations with the widows of the community, who themselves gathered for mutual consolation and to display the handiwork of their sick sister. There is more at stake in sickness than the miraculous cure of the one. It affords a grieving community the chance to express gratitude for someone else, to worship and weep together, to find a measure of God's comforting presence among them. In this case God does heal Tabitha. But once again Luke's story does not end with her but with others: "This became known throughout Joppa, and many believed in the Lord" (9:42 NRSV).

When I reflect upon the death of my friends, I cannot help feeling their haunting absence. Yet, I continue to seek God's help to look through a wider angle of vision that allows me to see other consequences of their sickness and death, consequences reflecting the evidence of God's active mercy. And I have, praise be to God.

**2.** "Cornelius, your prayers and alms have ascended as a memorial before God" (see 10:4). Luke's telling and retelling of Cornelius's conversion and the inauguration of the church's mission to the Gentiles (= nations) is shaped by an ancient conflict between the synagogue and church. Today's reader is alerted to importance of that tension by a world profoundly influenced by the tragedy of the Jewish Holocaust. While there are vast differences between the two, both are born by an intolerance conceived in ignorance and cultivated by nationalistic zeal. The conflict between the two as portrayed in Acts has its origins in God's "surprising" salvation of uncircumcised Gentiles who are granted the same religious status and Spirit given to repentant Jews. Luke's explanation of God's gracious decision is multifaceted and seeks to dispel the impression that the conversion of repentant Gentiles is a surprise. To do so, he characteristically appeals to the non-negotiable evidence supplied by Scripture (e.g., Jonah) and religious experience (e.g., visions, the Gentile Pentecost) according to the sound interpretation of the inspired prophet (= Peter). In this case, Jewish ignorance (and so intolerance) of repentant Gentiles who are saved because of God's benefaction is dispelled by relevant prophecy properly interpreted (see 10:43).

In the case of Cornelius, however, repeated references to his pious character suggest another reason (see 10:2, 4, 22, 30): He is saved because of the sort of person he is. An uncircumcised Gentile? Yes. A military commander of the despised Roman army? Yes again. Yet, God finds him anyway because he first made himself known to God by his prayers and gifts to the poor. The point is not that God saves Gentiles such as Cornelius because he is a pious person; rather, it is his pious acts that prove his spiritual competence to repent. Perhaps his attachment to Israel, if only as a God-fearer, has helped form him into such a person who is responsive to God's word. In any case, Luke's insistence throughout Acts on the importance of an outsider's good character is instructive for today's church. Although some unbelievers are simply unable to repent by their fundamental lack of spiritual goods, there are many others who come under the influence of the church's public witness even though they are not members of any congregation. This *indirect* witness to the culture at large by caring deeds and prophetic word may help form the sorts of persons who, like Cornelius, are responsive to the gospel's invitation to turn to God in faith.

**3.** "God has shown me that I should not call anyone profane or unclean" (10:28 NRSV). God's pastoral project is to bring us into an understanding of God's will so that we may better collaborate with God in the work of salvation. The conversion of Cornelius takes Peter by surprise but not because God decides at the last moment to save an uncircumcised Gentile. In fact, the universal embrace of divine love was promised to Abraham and prophesied by Scripture long before Cornelius was saved. Yet, for all his spiritual authority, Peter still did not "get it"; his religious parochialism prompted him to divide people into "clean" (repentant Jews) and "unclean" (uncircumcised Gentiles). God's redemptive purpose for Gentiles could not be realized unless the apostle changed his mind.

The theological crisis envisaged by this story, then, is the issue of by what manner an earnest believer like Peter learns God's will in order to obey it and serve God's redemptive interests. Even though Peter's case is exceptional, it also exemplifies two important elements in finding God's will for our lives. First, we learn of God's will from God rather than from our own resources: "God has shown me." The Lord is not a passive bystander or a disinterested partner but is committed to a process of disclosure by which God's will is made known to us. In fact, the urgency of this matter is indicated by the repetition of Peter's vision, which discloses something new to him about God's redemptive will that he otherwise could not have known on his own. Second, we typically learn God's will over time through a series of "aha" experiences. Peter's vision initially left him baffled. Peter's understanding of his Gentile mission unfolds as a result of "double visions" (see 10:30), internal reflection (see 10:17, 19), through the reports of others (see 10:22), and by Cornelius's hospitable reception of him and his word. Peter turned to Scripture for confirmation and clarification only after he learned by these multiple experiences over several days that God's forgiveness is offered to all people without partiality.

We live in a society that promises instant reward for self-sufficient people who know with certainty the way forward. These cultural values collide with the practical aim of Christian faith to know and act upon God's will. The process of getting on the same page with God is frequently confusing, profoundly dependent upon others and often takes a considerable time. But God will tell us the page number!

**4.** "I truly understand that God shows no partiality" (10:34 NRSV). The biblical idea that God has chosen a particular people as object of special regard cultivates the dangerous suspicion that God did not therefore choose others. Those believers who think themselves among God's "elect" are often inclined on this theological basis to think that God has not chosen anyone else who disagrees with their beliefs or customs. We pin labels on our disagreeable opponents to disenfranchise them: they are "liberal" or "conservative" or "homosexual" or "Jewish" or "Lutheran" or "female" or "laity" or "black" or "divorced." Yet, what has become crystal clear to Peter is that to do so is not the prerogative of pious Israel or anyone else: It is God alone who judges the living and the dead (10:42). One of the most surprising features of Acts is the diversity of people God calls to be included among God's people—all of whom are symbolized by uncircumcised Cornelius.

**5.** "If then God gave them the same gift that he gave us . . . who was I that I could hinder God?" (11:17 NRSV). There is little room for the importance of religious experience in the

Christian congregation that views Scripture as the only source of divine revelation. In fact, some faith traditions dismiss human experience of God's truth as inherently flawed by human depravity. Such a theological perspective is at odds with Acts, where God's word often takes the form of a surprising phenomenon rather than a biblical text. In fact, when testimony of God's new direction is asked for in Acts, the prophet-like-Jesus typically cites a saving event before a sacred text. Scripture is reread by experience. For all our proper attention to careful Bible study, God's prodding is sometimes felt within us or first observed in the bustle of life around us. Often our opinion is reversed for the Lord's sake by our existential encounters with the Holy Spirit in the mess and muck of ordinary living.

## Acts 11:19–12:25, The Succession of the Twelve

### NIV

[19]Now those who had been scattered by the persecution in connection with Stephen traveled as far as Phoenicia, Cyprus and Antioch, telling the message only to Jews. [20]Some of them, however, men from Cyprus and Cyrene, went to Antioch and began to speak to Greeks also, telling them the good news about the Lord Jesus. [21]The Lord's hand was with them, and a great number of people believed and turned to the Lord.

[22]News of this reached the ears of the church at Jerusalem, and they sent Barnabas to Antioch. [23]When he arrived and saw the evidence of the grace of God, he was glad and encouraged them all to remain true to the Lord with all their hearts. [24]He was a good man, full of the Holy Spirit and faith, and a great number of people were brought to the Lord.

[25]Then Barnabas went to Tarsus to look for Saul, [26]and when he found him, he brought him to Antioch. So for a whole year Barnabas and Saul met with the church and taught great numbers of people. The disciples were called Christians first at Antioch.

[27]During this time some prophets came down from Jerusalem to Antioch. [28]One of them, named Agabus, stood up and through the Spirit predicted that a severe famine would spread over the entire Roman world. (This happened during the reign of Claudius.) [29]The disciples, each according to his ability, decided to provide help for the brothers living in Judea. [30]This they did, sending their gift to the elders by Barnabas and Saul.

12 It was about this time that King Herod arrested some who belonged to the church, intending to persecute them. [2]He had

### NRSV

19Now those who were scattered because of the persecution that took place over Stephen traveled as far as Phoenicia, Cyprus, and Antioch, and they spoke the word to no one except Jews. [20]But among them were some men of Cyprus and Cyrene who, on coming to Antioch, spoke to the Hellenists[a] also, proclaiming the Lord Jesus. [21]The hand of the Lord was with them, and a great number became believers and turned to the Lord. [22]News of this came to the ears of the church in Jerusalem, and they sent Barnabas to Antioch. [23]When he came and saw the grace of God, he rejoiced, and he exhorted them all to remain faithful to the Lord with steadfast devotion; [24]for he was a good man, full of the Holy Spirit and of faith. And a great many people were brought to the Lord. [25]Then Barnabas went to Tarsus to look for Saul, [26]and when he had found him, he brought him to Antioch. So it was that for an entire year they met with[b] the church and taught a great many people, and it was in Antioch that the disciples were first called "Christians."

27At that time prophets came down from Jerusalem to Antioch. [28]One of them named Agabus stood up and predicted by the Spirit that there would be a severe famine over all the world; and this took place during the reign of Claudius. [29]The disciples determined that according to their ability, each would send relief to the believers[c] living in Judea; [30]this they did, sending it to the elders by Barnabas and Saul.

12 About that time King Herod laid violent hands upon some who belonged to the

[a] Other ancient authorities read *Greeks*     [b] Or *were guests of*
[c] Gk *brothers*

## NIV

James, the brother of John, put to death with the sword. ³When he saw that this pleased the Jews, he proceeded to seize Peter also. This happened during the Feast of Unleavened Bread. ⁴After arresting him, he put him in prison, handing him over to be guarded by four squads of four soldiers each. Herod intended to bring him out for public trial after the Passover.

⁵So Peter was kept in prison, but the church was earnestly praying to God for him.

⁶The night before Herod was to bring him to trial, Peter was sleeping between two soldiers, bound with two chains, and sentries stood guard at the entrance. ⁷Suddenly an angel of the Lord appeared and a light shone in the cell. He struck Peter on the side and woke him up. "Quick, get up!" he said, and the chains fell off Peter's wrists.

⁸Then the angel said to him, "Put on your clothes and sandals." And Peter did so. "Wrap your cloak around you and follow me," the angel told him. ⁹Peter followed him out of the prison, but he had no idea that what the angel was doing was really happening; he thought he was seeing a vision. ¹⁰They passed the first and second guards and came to the iron gate leading to the city. It opened for them by itself, and they went through it. When they had walked the length of one street, suddenly the angel left him.

¹¹Then Peter came to himself and said, "Now I know without a doubt that the Lord sent his angel and rescued me from Herod's clutches and from everything the Jewish people were anticipating."

¹²When this had dawned on him, he went to the house of Mary the mother of John, also called Mark, where many people had gathered and were praying. ¹³Peter knocked at the outer entrance, and a servant girl named Rhoda came to answer the door. ¹⁴When she recognized Peter's voice, she was so overjoyed she ran back without opening it and exclaimed, "Peter is at the door!"

¹⁵"You're out of your mind," they told her. When she kept insisting that it was so, they said, "It must be his angel."

¹⁶But Peter kept on knocking, and when they opened the door and saw him, they were astonished. ¹⁷Peter motioned with his hand for them to be quiet and described how the Lord had brought

## NRSV

church. ²He had James, the brother of John, killed with the sword. ³After he saw that it pleased the Jews, he proceeded to arrest Peter also. (This was during the festival of Unleavened Bread.) ⁴When he had seized him, he put him in prison and handed him over to four squads of soldiers to guard him, intending to bring him out to the people after the Passover. ⁵While Peter was kept in prison, the church prayed fervently to God for him.

6The very night before Herod was going to bring him out, Peter, bound with two chains, was sleeping between two soldiers, while guards in front of the door were keeping watch over the prison. ⁷Suddenly an angel of the Lord appeared and a light shone in the cell. He tapped Peter on the side and woke him, saying, "Get up quickly." And the chains fell off his wrists. ⁸The angel said to him, "Fasten your belt and put on your sandals." He did so. Then he said to him, "Wrap your cloak around you and follow me." ⁹Peter*ᵃ* went out and followed him; he did not realize that what was happening with the angel's help was real; he thought he was seeing a vision. ¹⁰After they had passed the first and the second guard, they came before the iron gate leading into the city. It opened for them of its own accord, and they went outside and walked along a lane, when suddenly the angel left him. ¹¹Then Peter came to himself and said, "Now I am sure that the Lord has sent his angel and rescued me from the hands of Herod and from all that the Jewish people were expecting."

12As soon as he realized this, he went to the house of Mary, the mother of John whose other name was Mark, where many had gathered and were praying. ¹³When he knocked at the outer gate, a maid named Rhoda came to answer. ¹⁴On recognizing Peter's voice, she was so overjoyed that, instead of opening the gate, she ran in and announced that Peter was standing at the gate. ¹⁵They said to her, "You are out of your mind!" But she insisted that it was so. They said, "It is his angel." ¹⁶Meanwhile Peter continued knocking; and when they opened the gate, they saw him and were amazed. ¹⁷He motioned to them with

ᵃ Gk *He*

NIV

him out of prison. "Tell James and the brothers about this," he said, and then he left for another place.

[18]In the morning, there was no small commotion among the soldiers as to what had become of Peter. [19]After Herod had a thorough search made for him and did not find him, he cross-examined the guards and ordered that they be executed.

Then Herod went from Judea to Caesarea and stayed there a while. [20]He had been quarreling with the people of Tyre and Sidon; they now joined together and sought an audience with him. Having secured the support of Blastus, a trusted personal servant of the king, they asked for peace, because they depended on the king's country for their food supply.

[21]On the appointed day Herod, wearing his royal robes, sat on his throne and delivered a public address to the people. [22]They shouted, "This is the voice of a god, not of a man." [23]Immediately, because Herod did not give praise to God, an angel of the Lord struck him down, and he was eaten by worms and died.

[24]But the word of God continued to increase and spread.

[25]When Barnabas and Saul had finished their mission, they returned from[a] Jerusalem, taking with them John, also called Mark.

[a] 25 Some manuscripts to

NRSV

his hand to be silent, and described for them how the Lord had brought him out of the prison. And he added, "Tell this to James and to the believers."[a] Then he left and went to another place.

[18]When morning came, there was no small commotion among the soldiers over what had become of Peter. [19]When Herod had searched for him and could not find him, he examined the guards and ordered them to be put to death. Then Peter[b] went down from Judea to Caesarea and stayed there.

[20]Now Herod was angry with the people of Tyre and Sidon. So they came to him in a body; and after winning over Blastus, the king's chamberlain, they asked for a reconciliation, because their country depended on the king's country for food. [21]On an appointed day Herod put on his royal robes, took his seat on the platform, and delivered a public address to them. [22]The people kept shouting, "The voice of a god, and not of a mortal!" [23]And immediately, because he had not given the glory to God, an angel of the Lord struck him down, and he was eaten by worms and died.

[24]But the word of God continued to advance and gain adherents. [25]Then after completing their mission Barnabas and Saul returned to[c] Jerusalem and brought with them John, whose other name was Mark.

[a] Gk brothers    [b] Gk he    [c] Other ancient authorities read from

# COMMENTARY

To this point in Acts, "the gospel road has been paved to the Gentiles, but the traffic remains sparse."[428] Coincidental to Jerusalem's confirmation of Peter's Gentile mission in Caesarea, however, a new mission among Gentiles has also begun in Syrian Antioch.[429] Not many details of its

origins are provided;[430] evidently it is the unexpected result of the scattering of believers that fol-

deities as well. Its strategic importance in Acts, however, is due to its pivotal role in the Jewish diaspora. Proselyte Jews were abundant in the city (so Josephus *The Jewish War* 7.45), which also enjoyed favorable relations with the Herodian family and so with Israel. All these historical details provide the raw material for an illuminating backdrop against which the outline of its cityscape in Acts is made more apparent.

430. The question of Luke's sources for "the Antioch Chronicles," as B. Witherington, *The Acts of the Apostles: A Socio-Rhetorical Commentary* (Grand Rapids: Eerdmans, 1998) 366-72, titles his discussion of Acts 11:19–15:35, remains indeterminate and problematic. Most are willing to admit that Luke depended upon some "Antiochene source" that had preserved the essential details of its founding and of Paul's involvement in its mission to the Diaspora. That is, this story is not a fiction. Few remain as convinced as Witherington, however, that Luke's "Antiochene source" is none other than Paul and thus reliably transmitted to Luke.

428. F. S. Spencer, *Acts*, Readings: A New Biblical Commentary (Sheffield: Sheffield Academic, 1997) 119.

429. The church in Antioch is second in importance within Luke's narrative world, surpassed only by the "mother church" in Jerusalem. For this reason, the reader of Acts should have in mind relevant information about this city. Founded in the third century BCE by Seleucus I as the capital city of his Assyrian Empire, Antioch was a large cosmopolitan city of great importance to the Roman Empire—the third largest in population and prosperity after Rome and Alexandria. In Luke's day, it was designated the capital city of Roman Syria and home to many political and commercial interests. Nearby were shrines to various pagan

lowed Stephen's death (11:19; see 8:4). In addition to the missions led by Philip and Peter, nameless others from Cyprus and Cyrene have continued the gospel's northward progress to Syrian Antioch, where they had successfully evangelized Gentiles, "proclaiming the Lord Jesus" to them as well as to Jews (11:20-21). Following the protocol established in response to Philip's Samaritan mission, the Jerusalem church dispatches Barnabas to bear witness to God's work in Antioch and to aid in the pastoral work there (11:22-23; cf. 8:14-25). The remarkable growth of this congregation soon required additional support staff, and so he departs for Tarsus to find Saul and bring him to Antioch—and back into his future (11:25-26a). Their team ministry lasted a year, at the end of which the Antiochene believers were "for the first time called 'Christians' " (11:26b).

The passage that follows looks at first to be a collocation of three seemingly unrelated episodes. The first recounts the prophet Agabus's prediction of a Judean famine and the Antiochene congregation's hospitable response to the church there (11:27-30). The final episode contrasts the community's feeding program with that of King Herod (12:20-24). These contrasting responses to material need enclose the second episode, the angel's dramatic rescue of Peter from Herod's prison (12:1-17). Luke shapes this story with constant allusions to the concluding story of the exalted Jesus in the Gospels in order to confirm Peter's religious authority a final time and prepare the way for his succession to both James (12:17) and Paul (12:25).[431]

**11:19-26.** The expression "now those who were scattered because of the persecution" picks up the unwoven threads of 8:4 to weave an account of the missionary activities of unnamed fugitives from the Jerusalem church. They have extended Philip's Samaritan and Peter's Caesarian missions into Syrian Antioch. The double reference to Cyprus (11:19-20) and then to the Cypriot Barnabas (see 4:36; 11:22) foreshadows the importance of Cyprus in Paul's first mission (cf. 13:4) and subsequently his split with Barnabas, who returns to Cyprus following the Jerusalem Council to some unwritten future (cf. 15:39).

Presumably the importance of Cyprus in Acts, which had been Barnabas's address before his conversion to Christ and participation in the Jerusalem community, is due to its large colony of diaspora Jews. This fact may also explain why missionaries from Cyprus and Cyrene "spoke the word to no one except Jews" (11:19).[432] In any case, the prophetic stipulation to move the word of God from "the Jew first and then to the Greek" is maintained in Antioch, since after bringing the gospel to the Jews they "began to speak to Greeks also" (11:20).[433]

The expression "the hand of the Lord" (11:21) recalls the petition of the apostles for God to "stretch out your hand" to perform mighty signs and wonders in fulfillment of Joel's prophecy (see Acts 2:19) and confirmation of their prophetic authority in Jerusalem (see 4:30-31). That earlier prayer continues to be answered by God in fresh ways and in new places. In this setting, the "Lord" (κύριος kyrios) refers to the exalted Jesus as the medium of divine power and mercy, who not only is the object of Christian proclamation (11:20) but also assists the mission in Antioch so that "a great number became believers and turned to the Lord" (11:21; see 2:41; 4:4; 6:7). The Lord Jesus' powerful presence and active participation confirms the legitimacy of this work and the importance of its future.

When Jerusalem hears of the founding of this new mission, they dispatch one of their own—Barnabas—not to assess or confirm what had taken place but to collaborate with the missionaries already at work (see 8:14-25). The decision to send Barnabas to Antioch as Jerusalem's emissary makes sense for two reasons: (1) He is from the same Cypriot community that produced the founders and unnamed leaders of this Antiochene congregation (so 4:36; 11:21), and (2) his spiritual authority is practically demonstrated by his earnest submission to the community's apostolic leader-

---

431. See R. W. Wall, "Successors to 'the Twelve' According to Acts 12:1-17," *CBQ* 53 (1991) 628-43.

432. Hill contends that they preached the gospel only to Jews because the church's Gentile mission had not yet "officially" begun. Further, the first Gentile converts in Antioch were doubtless similar to God-fearing Cornelius and were connected to the synagogues there. See C. C. Hill, *Hellenists and Hebrews: Reappraising Division Within the Earliest Church* (Minneapolis: Fortress, 1992) 137-38.

433. The text-critical problem of whether to read "Greeks" ("Ελληνας *Hellēnas*) or "Hellenists" (Ελληνιστάς *Hellēnistas*) is similar to 6:1, where "Hellenists" is preferred. In this case, "Greeks" is preferred due to context. J. A. Fitzmyer, *The Acts of the Apostles,* AB 31 (Garden City, N.Y.: Doubleday, 1998) 476, speaks for many scholars in saying "in this situation the reading 'Hellenists' makes little sense."

ship when sharing his possessions with the needy of the community of goods (see 4:36-37). He also ably defended Saul's conversion and calling before its leadership council (see 9:27). In the present text, Barnabas's positive profile is expanded by his characterization as "a good man, full of the Holy Spirit and faith" (11:24; see 6:5, 8; 7:55; cf. Luke 23:50), all familiar features of the prophet-like-Jesus, whose authority is concentrated on the task of testifying to the risen Jesus as Messiah.

Barnabas is a prophet-like-Jesus, cut from the same cloth as Stephen (11:24a; see 6:5). Thus the Spirit enables him to "see the grace of God" resting upon these new believers and to "exhort them all to remain faithful to the Lord with steadfast devotion" (11:23).[434] The important phrase "grace of God" (χάρις τοῦ θεου *charis tou theou*) denotes God's public and demonstrative benefaction on an entire community of believers (see 2:47; 4:33; cf. 14:26). In context of Acts, "grace" (*charis*) refers to a divine blessing promised Israel that arrives with the Messiah and is now poured out through the Holy Spirit. This benefaction is first visited on a restored Israel (2:47; 4:33) and then on believing Gentiles (so 10:44-46; cf. 15:8-11) as here in Antioch (cf. 14:3, 26). The responsibility of prophet Barnabas's presence in Antioch is to bear Israel's second witness that the saving grace of God now extends to Gentiles, who also experience the salvation God promised first to Israel. Further, Barnabas is restored as Israel's herald that its ordained role in these last days of salvation's history as "light to the nations" has begun.

While previous clues in Acts have shaped the reader's anticipation of Barnabas's successful ministry in Antioch, where "a great many people were brought to the Lord" (11:24b) under his ministry, what happens next is full of irony: "Barnabas went to Tarsus to look for Saul, and . . . brought him to Antioch" (11:25-26a). His patronage does not take us by complete surprise, however, since earlier Barnabas had "brought Saul to the apostles" (so 9:27) and probably was among those who encouraged him to return to Tarsus for further preparation (cf. 9:30). Here it appears that he acts on his

own without the approval of either Antioch or Jerusalem. But from the imagined perspective of the Antiochene parishioners, who knew nothing of what transpired on the Damascus road, their pastor's bold initiative must have seemed shocking: This Saul was the primary reason why they had "scattered because of the persecution." Their implied forgiveness and later their generosity to the endangered Judean church disclose character fashioned by the "grace of God."

In any case, the result is stated in pregnant terms: "and in Antioch the disciples were first called 'Christians' " (11:26c).[435] Why does Luke add this aside to an otherwise sparse account of the formation of this important congregation? While the origins of the designation "Christian" may well be the outsider's pejorative for the disciple of Christ, its connotation in this narrative setting is more neutral: It simply recognizes the *differences* between the Antioch and Jerusalem congregations. Surely there is a sociological difference between the Antiochene congregation, constituted by a mixture of Jewish and non-Jewish believers from various places, and the Jerusalem congregation, which continues to symbolize the restoration of the whole household of historic Israel and is constituted by Jews only (see 21:17-26). Perhaps more important, a theological difference is also implied, since the formation of this congregation is the result of instruction: "for an entire year [i.e., for a long time] they met with the church and taught a great many people" (11:26b). Could Luke's use of "Christians" as the name of a new congregation of believers signal future battles within the church over the *ordo salutis* ("order of salvation") that the Jerusalem Council is convened to resolve? I think so.

---

434. Luke employs wordplay to show that Barnabas's persona is ideally suited for the Antiochene setting, since his name means "son of encouragement" (παράκλησις *paraklēsis*; see 4:36) and here he "exhorted [παρεκάλει *parekalei*] them to be faithful to the Lord" (11:23).

435. See Fitzmyer, *The Acts of the Apostles*, 477. The Western text of Acts expands 11:25 by adding "[Barnabas] found [Saul] and exhorted him to come with him to Antioch," thereby stressing not only the independence of Barnabas's decision to recruit Saul as his co-workerr but also Saul's decision to share in his Antiochene ministry. Johnson suggests that this independence stands behind the concluding note that these Antiochene "disciples were for the first time called 'Christians,' " which indicates agitation rather than solidarity within the church. See L. T. Johnson, *The Acts of the Apostles*, SP 5 (Collegeville, Minn.: Liturgical, 1992) 204. Conzelmann is typical of those who suppose the historical referent behind the word "Christians" in 11:26 is a political (and hostile) reality: Rome had come to recognize that believers constituted a religious organization and as such were accountable to Roman law and prosecution. See H. Conzelmann, *The Acts of the Apostles*, trans. J. Limburg et al., ed. E. J. Epp and C. R. Matthews, Hermeneia (Philadelphia: Fortress, 1987) 88-89. However, the literary shaping of this account seems rather to underscore Antiochene Christianity's independence from Jerusalem, a result of Pauline teaching.

---

**11:27-30.** The story of the Antiochene relief effort to Judea introduces two classes of officers within the church: the Christian prophet, represented by Agabus, whom we will meet again in Acts 21,[436] and the elders of the Judean church, who apparently have replaced the seven with the administrative duty of food distribution within the community of goods (v. 30). Important features of their leadership are symbolized by Agabus, whom although apparently attached to a local congregation, is an itinerant charismatic enabled by the Holy Spirit to predict the future. The purpose of his ministry is similar to other prophetic figures who populate Luke's narrative world, such as Barnabas and Saul, whose prophetic tasks include the encouragement and instruction of believers. The special talents of Christian prophets are always tied to missionary tasks in Acts and are used as part and parcel of the church's vocation to bear witness to the risen Messiah. For this reason, Agabus's inspired ability to see into the future is not tied to self-promotion but serves the well-being of the community of goods.

Agabus came with other prophets "from Jerusalem to Antioch" (v. 27). Their mission helps to define the relationship between repentant Jews (= Jerusalem) and Gentiles (= Antioch), who share the messianic blessings equally. Appropriately, images of shared goods symbolize their partnership. The peril of being without food in a social world where a hand-to-mouth existence is the norm underscores the practical importance of sharing goods;[437] and no doubt this resurrection practice continues within a community pastored by Barnabas, who himself is an exemplar of sharing goods with the community's needy (see 4:36-37).[438]

Within the wider narrative setting of Acts, then, the prediction of Agabus sounds a fuller note: The future he predicts occasions a spiritual test for this new congregation of believers in Antioch. Will they be participants in a community of goods, whose solidarity with God and each other is exemplified by sharing their food with needy believers? The short answer is a resounding yes. In doing so, these Antiochene disciples follow the pattern of other collections mentioned in Pauline letters (see Rom 15:25-31; 1 Cor 16:1-4; 2 Corinthians 8–9; Gal 2:10) as well as in Acts (see 24:17).[439] Once a need within the community of goods is made known—in this case by a prophet's prediction of famine—a collection is gathered "according to their ability" (v. 29; cf. 4:35)[440] and is sent to the needy—in this case "to the believers living in Judea"—by congregational representatives—in this case "to the elders by Barnabas and Saul" (v. 30),[441] who will return to Antioch when their mission is complete (12:25). Thus the Antiochene congregation supplies additional testimony that the Lord's "great grace was upon them all" (see 4:33) and that they could be counted among those believers who "were of one heart and soul" (see 4:32).

In shaping this story Luke is careful to locate the fulfillment of Agabus's prophecy within secular history: "A severe famine over all the world . . . took place during the reign of Claudius" (v. 28). Such concrete reporting is a literary convention of the historian; and the measure of his report, whether ancient or modern, is whether he gets it right. The reliability of Luke's history has been

436. For a discussion of Christian prophets and prophecy, see R. Stronstad, *The Prophethood of All Believers*, JPTSS 16 (Sheffield: Sheffield Academic, 1999); D. Hill, *New Testament Prophecy* (London: Marshall, Morgan & Scott, 1979) esp. 94-109. See also the collection edited by J. Panagopoulos, *Prophethic Vocation in the New Testament and Today*, NovTestSup 45 (Leiden: Brill, 1977).

437. See B. Winter, "Acts and Food Shortages," in *The Book of Acts in Its First Century Setting*, ed. B. W. Winter and A. Clarke, 6 vols. (Grand Rapids: Eerdmans, 1993–98) 2:59-78.

438. Johnson commends the importance of this distribution of goods as carried out by Barnabas in the company of Saul, who has had no previous experience with such a practice. Indeed, even as the succession of spiritual authority from the Twelve to the seven is indicated by food distribution ("wait on tables," διακονέω *diakoneō*, 6:2) among needy widows (see 6:1-7), so again here the succession of spiritual authority to Saul/Paul is symbolized by food distribution ("relief," διακονία *diakonia,* 11:29). See L. Johnson, *The Literary Function of Possessions in Luke-Acts*, SBLDS 39 (Missoula, Mont.: Scholars Press, 1977) 217-20.

439. The interpreter should recognize the critical problem of reconciling Luke's report of a Gentile collection for the Jewish church and Paul's own report of a similar collection. It is unlikely that Acts 11:27-30 should be read by the light of Gal 2:10 (contra Witherington, *The Acts of the Apostles*, 375-76), since Paul's Jerusalem visit, mentioned in Gal 2:1, "is undoubtedly the same as the visit for the 'Council' in Acts 15:4." Fitzmyer, *The Acts of the Apostles*, 480.

440. This phrase translates καθὼς εὐπορεῖτό τις (*kathōs euporeito tis;* lit., "just as each is able") and recalls the phrase from 4:35 that distribution of goods was made "to each according to their need" (καθότι ἄν τις χρείαν εἶχεν *kathoti an tis chreian eichen*). The interplay between these two texts completes the calculus of giving, so that the offering of "each according to their ability" (11:29) is redistributed to "each as they have need" (4:35).

441. This is the first instance in Acts of "elders" (πρεσβύτεροι *presbyteroi*) used for the leadership team of Christian (although Jewish) congregations (cf. 14:23; 15:2, 4, 6, 22-23; 16:4; 20:17; 21:18). The role of the Judean elders is probably similar to the "elders" of Jewish synagogues; however, in this instance the elders have taken on the role of food distribution—a responsibility of the seven before their scattering from Judea with other Hellenists at the time of the "great persecution" (see 8:1-3). See R. A. Campbell, *The Elders* (Edinburgh: T. & T. Clark, 1994).

repeatedly challenged by modern Acts criticism, and this episode is another case in point.[442] Here the stakes are a bit higher for a *theological* reason, since the famine in question is predicted by an inspired prophet. The nub of the historical problem is not whether a famine occurred during the reign of Caesar Claudius, which is supported by reliable secular historians;[443] rather, it is the scope of the famine, whether it was "over all the world." If taken as objective reporting, Luke is surely mistaken, since famines are regional in scope. Johnson contends, however, that the word οἰκουμένη (*oikoumenē,* "world") better connotes "empire," and so this phrase could be rendered, "over all the empire."[444] If that is the case, the reader is still left to wonder why this famine had bypassed Antioch. Other scholars simply suggest the phrase is a metaphor for a "widespread" famine and thus a reliable report.

**12:1-17.** Once again the community's apostolic leadership is threatened in Jerusalem by the violent repression of political rivals—in this case King Herod, who had executed the apostle James and now arrested Peter (vv. 1-5a). The "hand of the Lord" is felt not only in a season of blessing and renewal (cf. 11:21) but also in this season of suffering and political reprisal, for Peter is rescued by the "angel of the Lord" (vv. 5b-11) in response to the community's earnest prayer. Peter's "great escape" is fitting conclusion to his prophetic ministry in Acts, and when he departs on the sly for another place (v. 17b)—to the great frustration of Herod (vv. 18-19)—his leadership in Jerusalem is transferred and continued by James the brother of Jesus (vv. 12-17a) and Saul (v. 25).

Stories of God's rescue operations are familiar to the reader of Acts.[445] In every case the forces of evil are pitted against the forces of good, with good prevailing by divine intervention. Luke's interest in such stories is to make clear the religious authority of the one rescued, which is not only indicated by God's intervention on his behalf or by the redemptive consequences of his miraculous escape but also by the literary shaping of the story itself. Characteristic of Luke's typological handling of the traditions of heroic individuals, Peter's escape takes on even greater significance by consistent and clear allusions to the story of Jesus' death and exaltation. Surely this episode supplies final proof that he is a prophet-like-Jesus par excellence whose memory continues to shape the faith and mission of the messianic community he helped to found.

**12:1-4.** To this point in Acts, the apostles of Jerusalem are keenly favored by the "people" of Israel and resisted only by the council—the "official" religious authority in the holy city. The reputation of the apostolate throughout Palestine has most recently attracted the malicious attention of Herod Agrippa I, client of Caesar Gaius and the principal political authority of the region. He is the third in a succession of kings named Herod to "[lay] violent hands upon some who belonged to the church" (v. 1): Herod the Great (see Luke 1:5) was followed by Herod Antipas (see Luke 23:7-15; Acts 4:27), whose exile in 39 CE led to King Herod Agrippa I's expanded domain over most of Palestine.[446] According to Josephus, his reign was characterized by violence and caprice,[447] which is vividly captured by the account of his death in Acts (see vv. 20-22). Perhaps this is sufficient evidence to fill in the historical gap left by the narrative, which tells the reader nothing of Herod's motive for this most recent attack upon the Judean church. Nor does Luke make clear why the apostle James is beheaded and the apostle Peter spared; presumably the church prayed for the release of both. The brief mention of James' martyrdom indicates the depth of difficulty Peter finds himself when Herod "proceeded to arrest Peter also" (v. 3). More important, however, James is not replaced as Judas was before him (see 1:15-26), and so the circle of the Twelve seems broken beyond repair with their rule at an end in

442. See S. Joubert, *Paul as Benefactor,* WUNT 124 (Tübingen: Mohr Siebeck, 2000) 91-93, who argues that a collection gathered and delivered by Paul prior to the Jerusalem Council (Acts 15; Galatians 2) would surely have been factored into its proceedings. The lack of clear reference to a collection by either Luke or Paul (but see Gal 2:10), however, is strong evidence against this conclusion.

443. See Fitzmyer, *The Acts of the Apostles,* 481-82; R. Riesner, *Paul's Early Period: Chronology, Mission Strategy, Theology,* trans. Doug Scott (Grand Rapids: Eerdmans, 1998) 128-30, who catalogs several regional famines throughout the empire based on these sources.

444. Johnson, *The Acts of the Apostles,* 205-6, 208.

445. Johnson, *The Acts of the Apostles,* 217, points out that similar stories are found in Hellenistic fiction as well, where they are used to illustrate virtuous character and divine favor.

446. Following the lead of J. Darr, Spencer contends that Luke-Acts forms a "composite Herodian profile" to cast the quintessential "villain" of the story, whose violent demise (see 12:20-22) is the just recompense of a fair-minded God. See F. S. Spencer, *Acts,* Readings: A New Biblical Commentary (Sheffield: Sheffield Academic, 1997) 123-25, 128-29.

447. Josephus *Antiquities of the Jews* 18.250-56; 19.6.1-4, 292-316.

Jerusalem. The succession of their spiritual authority appears necessary, since the Jerusalem mission must continue on under new leadership (= James the brother of Jesus) as Acts makes clear (see 15:4-29; 21:17-26).

Herod "had seized [Peter] . . . put him in prison and handed him over to four squads of soldiers to guard him" (v. 4) because "it pleased the Jews" that James was beheaded. Decapitation is the most severe form of execution and usually reserved for "murderers and a city's apostates,"[448] which James was not. We presume that his execution was warranted for illegitimate reasons similar to Stephen, and that the city's secular authority (= Herod) has now come to agree with its religious authority (= Sanhedrin) that the Jesus movement is detrimental to Israel.[449]

The circumstances of Peter's arrest and apparent fate, therefore, are similar to those that faced Jesus, especially given Herod's political motive for arresting Peter (cf. Luke 23:10-12). This parallelism extends to the timing of Peter's arrest "during the festival of Unleavened Bread" (v. 3; cf. Luke 22:1) and the ironic concern of his "pious" enemies to maintain the purity of Passover out of concern for what the "people" might think (cf. 12:4; Luke 23:1-5, 17).[450]

**12:5-11.** The transitional phrase μὲν οὖν (*men oun;* lit., "So therefore") marks the beginning of the climactic scene of this drama. In stark contrast to the hostile action of a powerful tyrant against its apostolic leadership, the "church prayed fervently to God for [Peter]" (v. 5; see also 1:14, 24; 2:42; 4:24-30). The narrator makes certain that the reader understands the extent of the evidence against Peter's possible escape: He is bound with two chains and sleeps between two soldiers, with additional guards stationed at every exit to prevent escape the "very night" before he is scheduled to suffer a fate similar to that of James (v. 6). That is, his situation is hopeless; there remains only heaven's help. On cue "an angel of the Lord appeared—in the cell" (v. 7a). In elabo-

rate detail, equal to that describing the jailhouse security system, the narrative rehearses the angel's rescue operation: first comes the "tap" on Peter's side to awaken him (v. 7b), followed by a series of commands—get up, get dressed, get going (vv. 7c-8).

The angel must still negotiate the prison's hallways, and do so with Peter still in his post-epiphany daze. They first pass the guards and then go through the prison's "iron gate" (πύλη *pulē*), which was miraculously open to them, and into the city and to freedom (v. 10). The reference to the iron gate is especially important to the story, not only because it symbolizes Herod's misbegotten initiative to subvert God's purposes and the community's prayers but also because it forms a wordplay with the "outer gate" (πυλών *pulōn*) that leads into the home where the community had gathered to pray for Peter's release (vv. 13-14). Going in through one gate and then out another marks out not only Peter's escape route but also the triumph of God over the community's enemies. Still, Peter "did not realize that what has happening with the angel's help was real; he thought he was seeing a vision" (v. 9). This dreamlike state during his escape explains why he "came to himself"; finally realizing that the "light shone in [his] cell" (v. 7a) meant that "the Lord has . . . rescued me" (v. 11a; see also 9:3).[451]

Acts offers no explanation of what exactly "the Jewish people" (ὁ λαός ὁ Ἰουδαῖος *ho laos ho Ioudaios*) had expected in Peter's case, although his execution is surely implied. There is no evidence in the text to assign malicious motive to the Jewish people or to suppose that they are "unrepentant" Jews who are Peter's religious adversaries. It is possible to read the phrase as quite benign and in terms of v. 4, where the "people" (*laos*) expect Herod to "bring Peter out" to them after Passover. If malicious motive is intended, then Peter's once vigorous public popularity in Jerusalem has fallen on hard times indeed (see vv. 18-19).

**12:12-17a.** After Peter recovers his sense and

---

448. *mSanh.* 9.1.

449. See F. F. Bruce, *The Acts of the Apostles*, rev. ed., NICNT (Grand Rapids: Eerdmans, 1988) 281-83.

450. See J. A. Fitzmyer, *The Acts of the Apostles*, AB 31 (Garden City, N.Y.: Doubleday, 1998) 487. Luke's reference to "the people" probably continues his thematic interest in the reactions of rank-and-file Jews to the community's apostolic leadership. Cf. L. T. Johnson, *The Acts of the Apostles*, SP 5 (Collegeville, Minn.: Liturgical, 1992) 216-17; C. Hill, "Acts 6:1–8:4," in *History, Literature, and Society in the Book of Acts*, ed. B. Witherington (Cambridge: Cambridge University Press, 1996) 135-36.

451. Given the Passover setting of this story, Luke's use of the verb "rescue" (ἐξαιρέω *exaireō*) is intentional and ironical, recalling God's rescue of Israel from Egyptian bondage (Exod 18:10), which was also led by the angel of the Lord (so Exod 14:19; Num 20:16; cf. Dan 3:28). See R. W. Wall, "Successors to 'the Twelve' According to Acts 12:1-17," 637; S. Garrett, "Exodus from Bondage: Luke 9:31 and Acts 12:1-24," *CBQ* 52 (1990) 656-80.

sensibility, he "went to the house of Mary . . . where many had gathered and were praying" (v. 12). These are characteristic features of the faith community in Acts: Believers have gathered in the home of another believer for prayer (see 1:14; 2:45-46; 5:42). The reader supposes that the subject of their petition is Peter's safety (see v. 4), even though they are as yet unaware that their prayers have been answered.

For the first time, the meetinghouse is specified by its owner—Mary, the mother of John Mark, who will have an important if ambiguous role in Acts (13:5, 13; 15:37-39). She is apparently an independent woman and is sufficiently wealthy to employ a maidservant. Luke's interest in "leading women" is well known, and this episode is another case in point. What is of greater interest to Luke, however, is the role performed by her servant Rhoda, whose voice is the first heard from a Christian woman in Acts. In attending to her household chores, she discovers Peter alive and well. In a manner reminiscent of risen Jesus' encounter with his unwitting disciples, Peter's verbal encounter with Rhoda produces her "recognition" (cf. Luke 24:31) and joyful report that he is alive (cf. Matt 28:8). But her good news of Peter's safety evokes a response of incredulity in other believers (cf. Luke 24:10-11, 41). Meanwhile Peter is left standing at the door, while his friends imagine that the voice Rhoda has heard actually belongs to his guardian angel (12:15)![452] To their mutual credit Peter persists in his knocking and Rhoda to her story, until at long last "they opened the gate, saw him and were amazed [ἐξίστημι existēmi]" (v. 16). Amazement is typically the result of a mistake (see 3:10)—in this case, of mistaking Peter for his guardian angel, which Peter corrects by rehearsing "how the Lord had brought him out of the prison" (v. 17a). His testimony alludes to the Lord's appearance before stunned disciples with persuasive proofs of his resurrection (cf. Luke 24:28-43; see also Acts 1:3).

**12:17b.** The story of the living Peter's exodus from certain death had not yet been told to "James and the brothers." The abrupt introduction of James into the narrative, typical of Luke's storytelling strategy, both presumes that the reader knows him to be "James the brother of the Lord" and leader of the Jewish church and hints at the importance of his future role in Acts.[453] The introduction of James into the narrative world of Acts is the complement of Peter's departure from it. Although Peter will make an important cameo appearance during the proceedings of the Jerusalem Synod (cf. 15:6-11), his role in the history of God's salvation has already been served when "he left and went [ἐπορεύθη eporeuthē] to another place."[454] This echoing of Jesus' "going [πορευομένου poreuomenou] . . . toward heaven" (see 1:10) at his ascension, which necessitates his apostolic succession, adds a layer of meaning to the concluding moment of Peter's mission in Jerusalem. The implied meaning is that the reins of spiritual authority have been transferred from Peter to James.

**12:18-19.** A new day dawns, and the prized prisoner is nowhere to be found: The soldiers attached to Herod "searched for Peter and could not find him"—naturally, since they were looking for him in the wrong city! The bewilderment of the prison guards echoes their response to an earlier escape in 5:22-26 and fills in the gaps of this story. Indeed, the captain of the guard had wondered in the aftermath of that earlier escape "what would come of this escape" (see 5:24); and the apostles did not hide nor did they resist re-arrest since they knew "the people" of Israel were on their side and feared they might turn violent against the temple guard (see 5:26). On this occasion, as the story turns back to King Herod, the reader realizes that the atmosphere in Jerusalem has changed dramatically since Acts 5. The circle of the Twelve, broken by Herod, has not been restored and those left evidently do not enjoy the

---

452. H. Conzelmann, *The Acts of the Apostles,* trans. J. Limburg et al., ed. E. J. Epp and C. R. Matthews, Hermeneia (Philadelphia: Fortress, 1987) 95, notes that Judaism regarded the guardian angel as a "celestial double" who could imitate a person's appearance and voice—in this case, the voice of Peter. The entire scene is rich comedy and only adds to the theological claim that stands behind the story: A sovereign God acts powerfully to reverse misfortune, even to the joyful surprise of God's people.

453. R. Bauckham, "James and the Jerusalem Church," in *The Book of Acts in Its First Century Setting,* 6 vols., ed. B. Winter and A. Clarke (Grand Rapids: Eerdmans, 1993–98) 4:427-50, argues that 12:17 is glossed by 11:30: Even as Peter's spiritual authority is transferred to James at this moment, so also this accords with a change already underway in the governance of the church from apostolic to elder rule.

454. The precise location of the "another place" where Peter ended is unknown, as is the role he assumed there. Ancient tradition tells us that Peter went to Rome and established a faith community there prior to Paul's arrival.

same level of public respect from "the people" as before (see vv. 4, 11). Further, the apostles' more benign religious opposition in Jerusalem has now been replaced by the graceless political tyranny of Herod, who "examined the guards and ordered them to be put to death."[455] Moreover, Herod's departure from Jerusalem for Caesarea immediately after Passover "to stay" at the capital of the Roman occupation of Palestine is indicative of his true loyalties.

**12:20-22.** While Herod's tyranny has already made him God's foe and destined him for harsh judgment, the final evidence is his response to a community's request for food. Nowhere is the reader made aware of the reason why "Herod was angry with the people of Tyre and Sidon" (v. 20a). The motive of Herod's anger is unimportant to the telling of this story; rather, the issue is his vile personality and inhospitable response to the desperate delegation from neighboring Syrian cities, which heap evidence upon evidence of his opposition to God's purposes in the world and supports the justice soon meted out to him. On the one hand, the more obvious act of Agrippa's rebellion against God's reign is his crude spectacle of self-aggrandizement that coerced the pitiable Phoenician delegation to worship and listen to him "on an appointed day."[456] On the other hand, a more subtle contrast is made that anticipates Herod's demise. Those emissaries that came to Herod through his chamberlain, Blastus, to negotiate a peace settlement were from Tyre and Sidon, free cities located on the Phoenician coastline. The ultimate purpose of this entreaty is for food distribution, since "their country depended upon the king's country for food" (v. 20b).

The reader should note that the Phoenician delegation came to Herod from the same region visited by the missionaries mentioned in 11:19 who later founded the congregation in Antioch (see 11:19-26). In effect, they are an unwitting witness to the vast differences between the secular and sacred as evinced by contrasting practices of food distribution. Unlike arrogant Herod's petulant response to the Phoenicians, the elders of the Antiochene church hospitably received the prophetic delegation from Jerusalem and responded immediately to Agabus's prophecy of a famine with an offering of food (see 11:27-30; cf. 12:25). The intent of this narrative interplay is not to engage in culture criticism—to portray the pretentious Herod as representative of society's rich and famous who typically exploit the weak and powerless and force them to submit to self-deification. The issue at stake is a theological one, consistent with all of Acts, that God posits spiritual authority in the community that gives all glory to God alone (see 3:12-13; 4:24; 10:25-26) and that is enabled to respond to its own needy with graceful benefaction (see 2:42-47; 4:32-35).

**12:23-25.** Two integral events summarize the fallout from Peter's escape "to another place." The death of a vile antagonist is commonplace in the happy endings of world literature—the more horrible the villain's death the more satisfying the story's ending. It is not surprising to the reader of Acts that Herod is "struck down" in horrific fashion. Luke's account is enhanced by his reference to an angel of death that carries out God's death sentence against Herod and by the "worms" that eat his flesh, which both allude to biblical stories of holy terror. In the first case, the angel of the Lord who earlier had tapped Peter to rescue him from Herod's death sentence now executes God's judgment by tapping Herod for death. The angel's activities throughout the chapter recall the first Passover when the heavenly "destroyer" delivered a deathblow against another king-like-Herod (cf. Exod 12:12, 23, 29) that occasioned Israel's exodus from the Pharaoh's death sentence. Likewise, Peter departs on his exodus from Jerusalem to another city (see 12:11; cf. Exod 14:19). Finally, the mode of Herod's demise—his flesh "was eaten by worms"[457]—reminds one of the Maccabean description of the gruesome death of Antiochus IV Epiphanes (2 Macc 9:9); it also recalls Isaiah's exhortation that in the light of the permanence of

---

455. The Greek is more ambiguous than either the NIV or the NRSV allows. The verb translated "execute/put to death" is ἀπάγω (apagō), a legal term that usually denotes "to make an arrest." The Western text substitutes the verb ἀποκτείνω (apokteinō, "to execute"). Given Luke's literary intent to cast Herod in a bad light, when added to his reputedly violent persona and the intolerance in the Roman world of a soldier's dereliction of duty, the present translation of the passage is certainly plausible.

456. Despite chronological differences, Josephus's account of the early death of Herod Agrippa I, in *Antiquities of the Jews* 19.343-53, is similar to Luke's. See also C. K. Barrett, *A Critical and Exegetical Commentary on the Acts of the Apostles,* 2 vols, ICC (Edinburgh: T. & T. Clark, 1994, 1998) 589-92.

457. The Western text of Acts embellishes the story of Herod's death by recasting it as a torture scene, so that the worms attack his body while he is still alive.

God's faithfulness God's people should not fear the attacks of their foes since "the worm will eat them like wool" (Isa 51:8). Such is the fate of God's foes.

In contrast to Herod's death, "the word of God continued to advance and gain adherents" (v. 24; see also 6:7). This summary underscores the plotline of Acts: the word of God flourishes in the face of hostile opposition in its unalterable advance to the end of the earth. Moreover, in contrast to the failure of Herod's approach to food distribution, "Barnabas and Saul returned from Jerusalem"[458] having completed their relief mission in service of the Judean church and according to the sacred practice of the community of goods (v. 25; see also 11:27-30). The successful completion of their mission complements the advance of the gospel in the region and serves on this basis to validate Paul's mission that is soon to commence.

458. The difference in translation of the prepositional phrase "from [ἐξ *ex* or ἀπό *apo*] Jerusalem" or "to [εἰς *eis*] Jerusalem" reflects its corrupted status in the Greek MSS of Acts. The NIV, which accepts *ex* on contextual rather than textual grounds, is preferred in this case; while *eis* is the best attested rendering, it does not make sense of the plotline.

# REFLECTIONS

**1.** "News of this came to the ears of the church in Jerusalem, and they sent Barnabas to Antioch" (11:22 NRSV). I belong to a church that has long valued ecclesiastical "connectionalism." While this means different things to different congregations, at its core is an abiding commitment of each congregation toward the well-being of others. When the church's mission moved beyond Jerusalem into new neighborhoods where marginal Jews and uncircumcised Gentiles were evangelized, its leaders realized that certain safeguards were needed to protect the gospel's sacred deposit from contamination. For this reason Peter and John are earlier sent to Samaria and Barnabas to Antioch. Certain theological norms, religious experiences and ecclesial practices—church "tradition"—are maintained to ensure solidarity of Christian fellowship and witness even between diverse congregations founded in different geographical locations. Even though Jerusalem retains a certain level of authority over Antioch, because it is still home to the Lord's apostolic successors, the generosity of the Antiochene congregation toward the Jerusalem church in its time of need reflects the dynamic and caring mutuality between congregations connected to each other by a common faith and witness. Simply because one fellowship is larger and richer or is perceived to have more mature communicants than another does not imply that it will dictate the terms of the other's life. Connectionalism is not coercive; it is caring toward the end of forming a faith founded on the gospel.

**2.** "About that time King Herod laid violent hands upon some who belonged to the church" (12:1 NRSV). The theme of the church's repression is important in Acts. The contemporary reader is tempted to read these stories of Herod's rampage in a detached way, especially if we live in a liberal democracy that values religious freedom. Yet even in North America religious sentiment is openly ridiculed at times, and modest public expressions of a thoughtful Christian faith are often arrogantly dismissed. What should be the church's response to such a culture?

Luke's story of Peter's "great escape" is full of symbols of transcendence: the rescuing angel, the community's earnest prayers, the Jewish celebration of Passover, even the gruesome details of Herod's demise. The church's response to any attempt to repress its public witness ought not be vengeful or prickly, nor ought it to be passive. There is nothing passive about praying for deliverance from our enemies and for their salvation. Prayer is a defiant act because it recognizes that the purpose of a sovereign God will win out in the end: "thy kingdom come, thy will be done on earth as it is in heaven." Prayer presumes a position of confident trust, believing that the God of the exodus has the power to release the captive and to reverse bad news to good. For all the silly arrogance of a malevolent Herod who seeks to stamp the church's leaders underfoot and bring glory to himself, Peter escapes while Herod dies. When it seems God's plan has been overtaken by enemies and/or events, we pray in faith for God's deliverance anyway. This story assures its readers that God hears our prayers and renders the final verdict: "the word of God continued to advance and gain adherents" (12:24).

## Acts 13:1–14:26, Paul's Mission to the Nations

### NIV

**13** In the church at Antioch there were prophets and teachers: Barnabas, Simeon called Niger, Lucius of Cyrene, Manaen (who had been brought up with Herod the tetrarch) and Saul. [2]While they were worshiping the Lord and fasting, the Holy Spirit said, "Set apart for me Barnabas and Saul for the work to which I have called them." [3]So after they had fasted and prayed, they placed their hands on them and sent them off.

[4]The two of them, sent on their way by the Holy Spirit, went down to Seleucia and sailed from there to Cyprus. [5]When they arrived at Salamis, they proclaimed the word of God in the Jewish synagogues. John was with them as their helper.

[6]They traveled through the whole island until they came to Paphos. There they met a Jewish sorcerer and false prophet named Bar-Jesus, [7]who was an attendant of the proconsul, Sergius Paulus. The proconsul, an intelligent man, sent for Barnabas and Saul because he wanted to hear the word of God. [8]But Elymas the sorcerer (for that is what his name means) opposed them and tried to turn the proconsul from the faith. [9]Then Saul, who was also called Paul, filled with the Holy Spirit, looked straight at Elymas and said, [10]"You are a child of the devil and an enemy of everything that is right! You are full of all kinds of deceit and trickery. Will you never stop perverting the right ways of the Lord? [11]Now the hand of the Lord is against you. You are going to be blind, and for a time you will be unable to see the light of the sun."

Immediately mist and darkness came over him, and he groped about, seeking someone to lead him by the hand. [12]When the proconsul saw what had happened, he believed, for he was amazed at the teaching about the Lord.

### NRSV

**13** Now in the church at Antioch there were prophets and teachers: Barnabas, Simeon who was called Niger, Lucius of Cyrene, Manaen a member of the court of Herod the ruler,[a] and Saul. [2]While they were worshiping the Lord and fasting, the Holy Spirit said, "Set apart for me Barnabas and Saul for the work to which I have called them." [3]Then after fasting and praying they laid their hands on them and sent them off.

4So, being sent out by the Holy Spirit, they went down to Seleucia; and from there they sailed to Cyprus. [5]When they arrived at Salamis, they proclaimed the word of God in the synagogues of the Jews. And they had John also to assist them. [6]When they had gone through the whole island as far as Paphos, they met a certain magician, a Jewish false prophet, named Bar-Jesus. [7]He was with the proconsul, Sergius Paulus, an intelligent man, who summoned Barnabas and Saul and wanted to hear the word of God. [8]But the magician Elymas (for that is the translation of his name) opposed them and tried to turn the proconsul away from the faith. [9]But Saul, also known as Paul, filled with the Holy Spirit, looked intently at him [10]and said, "You son of the devil, you enemy of all righteousness, full of all deceit and villainy, will you not stop making crooked the straight paths of the Lord? [11]And now listen—the hand of the Lord is against you, and you will be blind for a while, unable to see the sun." Immediately mist and darkness came over him, and he went about groping for someone to lead him by the hand. [12]When the proconsul saw what had happened, he believed, for he was astonished at the teaching about the Lord.

13Then Paul and his companions set sail from Paphos and came to Perga in Pamphylia. John, however, left them and returned to Jerusalem; [14]but they went on from Perga and came to

a Gk tetrarch

## NIV

[13]From Paphos, Paul and his companions sailed to Perga in Pamphylia, where John left them to return to Jerusalem. [14]From Perga they went on to Pisidian Antioch. On the Sabbath they entered the synagogue and sat down. [15]After the reading from the Law and the Prophets, the synagogue rulers sent word to them, saying, "Brothers, if you have a message of encouragement for the people, please speak."

[16]Standing up, Paul motioned with his hand and said: "Men of Israel and you Gentiles who worship God, listen to me! [17]The God of the people of Israel chose our fathers; he made the people prosper during their stay in Egypt, with mighty power he led them out of that country, [18]he endured their conduct[a] for about forty years in the desert, [19]he overthrew seven nations in Canaan and gave their land to his people as their inheritance. [20]All this took about 450 years.

"After this, God gave them judges until the time of Samuel the prophet. [21]Then the people asked for a king, and he gave them Saul son of Kish, of the tribe of Benjamin, who ruled forty years. [22]After removing Saul, he made David their king. He testified concerning him: 'I have found David son of Jesse a man after my own heart; he will do everything I want him to do.'

[23]"From this man's descendants God has brought to Israel the Savior Jesus, as he promised. [24]Before the coming of Jesus, John preached repentance and baptism to all the people of Israel. [25]As John was completing his work, he said: 'Who do you think I am? I am not that one. No, but he is coming after me, whose sandals I am not worthy to untie.'

[26]"Brothers, children of Abraham, and you God-fearing Gentiles, it is to us that this message of salvation has been sent. [27]The people of Jerusalem and their rulers did not recognize Jesus, yet in condemning him they fulfilled the words of the prophets that are read every Sabbath. [28]Though they found no proper ground for a death sentence, they asked Pilate to have him executed. [29]When they had carried out all that was written about him, they took him down from the tree and laid him in a tomb. [30]But God raised him from the

---

a [18] Some manuscripts *and cared for them*

## NRSV

Antioch in Pisidia. And on the sabbath day they went into the synagogue and sat down. [15]After the reading of the law and the prophets, the officials of the synagogue sent them a message, saying, "Brothers, if you have any word of exhortation for the people, give it." [16]So Paul stood up and with a gesture began to speak:

"You Israelites,[a] and others who fear God, listen. [17]The God of this people Israel chose our ancestors and made the people great during their stay in the land of Egypt, and with uplifted arm he led them out of it. [18]For about forty years he put up with[b] them in the wilderness. [19]After he had destroyed seven nations in the land of Canaan, he gave them their land as an inheritance [20]for about four hundred fifty years. After that he gave them judges until the time of the prophet Samuel. [21]Then they asked for a king; and God gave them Saul son of Kish, a man of the tribe of Benjamin, who reigned for forty years. [22]When he had removed him, he made David their king. In his testimony about him he said, 'I have found David, son of Jesse, to be a man after my heart, who will carry out all my wishes.' [23]Of this man's posterity God has brought to Israel a Savior, Jesus, as he promised; [24]before his coming John had already proclaimed a baptism of repentance to all the people of Israel. [25]And as John was finishing his work, he said, 'What do you suppose that I am? I am not he. No, but one is coming after me; I am not worthy to untie the thong of the sandals[c] on his feet.'

[26]"My brothers, you descendants of Abraham's family, and others who fear God, to us[d] the message of this salvation has been sent. [27]Because the residents of Jerusalem and their leaders did not recognize him or understand the words of the prophets that are read every sabbath, they fulfilled those words by condemning him. [28]Even though they found no cause for a sentence of death, they asked Pilate to have him killed. [29]When they had carried out everything that was written about him, they took him down from the tree and laid him in a tomb. [30]But God raised him from the dead; [31]and for many days he appeared to those who came up with him from Galilee to Jerusalem, and they are now his witnesses to the

---

a Gk *Men, Israelites*   b Other ancient authorities read *cared for*
c Gk *untie the sandals*   d Other ancient authorities read *you*

## NIV

dead, [31]and for many days he was seen by those who had traveled with him from Galilee to Jerusalem. They are now his witnesses to our people.

[32]"We tell you the good news: What God promised our fathers [33]he has fulfilled for us, their children, by raising up Jesus. As it is written in the second Psalm:

" 'You are my Son;
today I have become your Father.'[a][b]

[34]The fact that God raised him from the dead, never to decay, is stated in these words:

" 'I will give you the holy and sure blessings promised to David.'[c]

[35]So it is stated elsewhere:

" 'You will not let your Holy One see decay.'[d]

[36]"For when David had served God's purpose in his own generation, he fell asleep; he was buried with his fathers and his body decayed. [37]But the one whom God raised from the dead did not see decay.

[38]"Therefore, my brothers, I want you to know that through Jesus the forgiveness of sins is proclaimed to you. [39]Through him everyone who believes is justified from everything you could not be justified from by the law of Moses. [40]Take care that what the prophets have said does not happen to you:

[41] " 'Look, you scoffers,
wonder and perish,
for I am going to do something in your days
that you would never believe,
even if someone told you.'[e] "

[42]As Paul and Barnabas were leaving the synagogue, the people invited them to speak further about these things on the next Sabbath. [43]When the congregation was dismissed, many of the Jews and devout converts to Judaism followed Paul and Barnabas, who talked with them and urged them to continue in the grace of God.

[44]On the next Sabbath almost the whole city gathered to hear the word of the Lord. [45]When the Jews saw the crowds, they were filled with jealousy and talked abusively against what Paul was saying.

[a] 33 Or have begotten you    [b] 33 Psalm 2:7    [c] 34 Isaiah 55:3
[d] 35 Psalm 16:10    [e] 41 Hab. 1:5

## NRSV

people. [32]And we bring you the good news that what God promised to our ancestors [33]he has fulfilled for us, their children, by raising Jesus; as also it is written in the second psalm,

'You are my Son;
today I have begotten you.'

[34]As to his raising him from the dead, no more to return to corruption, he has spoken in this way,

'I will give you the holy promises made to David.'

[35]Therefore he has also said in another psalm,

'You will not let your Holy One experience corruption.'

[36]For David, after he had served the purpose of God in his own generation, died,[a] was laid beside his ancestors, and experienced corruption; [37]but he whom God raised up experienced no corruption. [38]Let it be known to you therefore, my brothers, that through this man forgiveness of sins is proclaimed to you; [39]by this Jesus[b] everyone who believes is set free from all those sins[c] from which you could not be freed by the law of Moses. [40]Beware, therefore, that what the prophets said does not happen to you:

[41] 'Look, you scoffers!
Be amazed and perish,
for in your days I am doing a work,
a work that you will never believe, even if someone tells you.' "

[42]As Paul and Barnabas[d] were going out, the people urged them to speak about these things again the next sabbath. [43]When the meeting of the synagogue broke up, many Jews and devout converts to Judaism followed Paul and Barnabas, who spoke to them and urged them to continue in the grace of God.

[44]The next sabbath almost the whole city gathered to hear the word of the Lord.[e] [45]But when the Jews saw the crowds, they were filled with jealousy; and blaspheming, they contradicted what was spoken by Paul. [46]Then both Paul and Barnabas spoke out boldly, saying, "It was necessary that the word of God should be spoken first to you. Since you reject it and judge yourselves to be unworthy of eternal life, we are now turning to

[a] Gk fell asleep    [b] Gk this    [c] Gk all    [d] Gk they    [e] Other ancient authorities read God

## NIV

⁴⁶Then Paul and Barnabas answered them boldly: "We had to speak the word of God to you first. Since you reject it and do not consider yourselves worthy of eternal life, we now turn to the Gentiles. ⁴⁷For this is what the Lord has commanded us:

" 'I have made you*ᵃ* a light for the Gentiles,
that you*ᵃ* may bring salvation to the ends of
the earth.'*ᵇ* "

⁴⁸When the Gentiles heard this, they were glad and honored the word of the Lord; and all who were appointed for eternal life believed.

⁴⁹The word of the Lord spread through the whole region. ⁵⁰But the Jews incited the God-fearing women of high standing and the leading men of the city. They stirred up persecution against Paul and Barnabas, and expelled them from their region. ⁵¹So they shook the dust from their feet in protest against them and went to Iconium. ⁵²And the disciples were filled with joy and with the Holy Spirit.

**14** At Iconium Paul and Barnabas went as usual into the Jewish synagogue. There they spoke so effectively that a great number of Jews and Gentiles believed. ²But the Jews who refused to believe stirred up the Gentiles and poisoned their minds against the brothers. ³So Paul and Barnabas spent considerable time there, speaking boldly for the Lord, who confirmed the message of his grace by enabling them to do miraculous signs and wonders. ⁴The people of the city were divided; some sided with the Jews, others with the apostles. ⁵There was a plot afoot among the Gentiles and Jews, together with their leaders, to mistreat them and stone them. ⁶But they found out about it and fled to the Lycaonian cities of Lystra and Derbe and to the surrounding country, ⁷where they continued to preach the good news.

⁸In Lystra there sat a man crippled in his feet, who was lame from birth and had never walked. ⁹He listened to Paul as he was speaking. Paul looked directly at him, saw that he had faith to be healed ¹⁰and called out, "Stand up on your feet!" At that, the man jumped up and began to walk.

¹¹When the crowd saw what Paul had done, they shouted in the Lycaonian language, "The

*ᵃ 47* The Greek is singular.    *ᵇ 47* Isaiah 49:6

## NRSV

the Gentiles. ⁴⁷For so the Lord has commanded us, saying,

'I have set you to be a light for the Gentiles,
so that you may bring salvation to the ends
of the earth.' "

⁴⁸When the Gentiles heard this, they were glad and praised the word of the Lord; and as many as had been destined for eternal life became believers. ⁴⁹Thus the word of the Lord spread throughout the region. ⁵⁰But the Jews incited the devout women of high standing and the leading men of the city, and stirred up persecution against Paul and Barnabas, and drove them out of their region. ⁵¹So they shook the dust off their feet in protest against them, and went to Iconium. ⁵²And the disciples were filled with joy and with the Holy Spirit.

**14** The same thing occurred in Iconium, where Paul and Barnabas*ᵃ* went into the Jewish synagogue and spoke in such a way that a great number of both Jews and Greeks became believers. ²But the unbelieving Jews stirred up the Gentiles and poisoned their minds against the brothers. ³So they remained for a long time, speaking boldly for the Lord, who testified to the word of his grace by granting signs and wonders to be done through them. ⁴But the residents of the city were divided; some sided with the Jews, and some with the apostles. ⁵And when an attempt was made by both Gentiles and Jews, with their rulers, to mistreat them and to stone them, ⁶the apostles*ᵃ* learned of it and fled to Lystra and Derbe, cities of Lycaonia, and to the surrounding country; ⁷and there they continued proclaiming the good news.

⁸In Lystra there was a man sitting who could not use his feet and had never walked, for he had been crippled from birth. ⁹He listened to Paul as he was speaking. And Paul, looking at him intently and seeing that he had faith to be healed, ¹⁰said in a loud voice, "Stand upright on your feet." And the man*ᵇ* sprang up and began to walk. ¹¹When the crowds saw what Paul had done, they shouted in the Lycaonian language, "The gods have come down to us in human form!" ¹²Barnabas they called Zeus, and Paul they called

*ᵃ* Gk *they*    *ᵇ* Gk *he*

NIV

gods have come down to us in human form!" [12]Barnabas they called Zeus, and Paul they called Hermes because he was the chief speaker. [13]The priest of Zeus, whose temple was just outside the city, brought bulls and wreaths to the city gates because he and the crowd wanted to offer sacrifices to them.

[14]But when the apostles Barnabas and Paul heard of this, they tore their clothes and rushed out into the crowd, shouting: [15]"Men, why are you doing this? We too are only men, human like you. We are bringing you good news, telling you to turn from these worthless things to the living God, who made heaven and earth and sea and everything in them. [16]In the past, he let all nations go their own way. [17]Yet he has not left himself without testimony: He has shown kindness by giving you rain from heaven and crops in their seasons; he provides you with plenty of food and fills your hearts with joy." [18]Even with these words, they had difficulty keeping the crowd from sacrificing to them.

[19]Then some Jews came from Antioch and Iconium and won the crowd over. They stoned Paul and dragged him outside the city, thinking he was dead. [20]But after the disciples had gathered around him, he got up and went back into the city. The next day he and Barnabas left for Derbe.

[21]They preached the good news in that city and won a large number of disciples. Then they returned to Lystra, Iconium and Antioch, [22]strengthening the disciples and encouraging them to remain true to the faith. "We must go through many hardships to enter the kingdom of God," they said. [23]Paul and Barnabas appointed elders[a] for them in each church and, with prayer and fasting, committed them to the Lord, in whom they had put their trust. [24]After going through Pisidia, they came into Pamphylia, [25]and when they had preached the word in Perga, they went down to Attalia.

[26]From Attalia they sailed back to Antioch, where they had been committed to the grace of God for the work they had now completed.

[a] 23 Or Barnabas ordained elders; or Barnabas had elders elected

NRSV

Hermes, because he was the chief speaker. [13]The priest of Zeus, whose temple was just outside the city,[a] brought oxen and garlands to the gates; he and the crowds wanted to offer sacrifice. [14]When the apostles Barnabas and Paul heard of it, they tore their clothes and rushed out into the crowd, shouting, [15]"Friends,[b] why are you doing this? We are mortals just like you, and we bring you good news, that you should turn from these worthless things to the living God, who made the heaven and the earth and the sea and all that is in them. [16]In past generations he allowed all the nations to follow their own ways; [17]yet he has not left himself without a witness in doing good—giving you rains from heaven and fruitful seasons, and filling you with food and your hearts with joy." [18]Even with these words, they scarcely restrained the crowds from offering sacrifice to them.

[19]But Jews came there from Antioch and Iconium and won over the crowds. Then they stoned Paul and dragged him out of the city, supposing that he was dead. [20]But when the disciples surrounded him, he got up and went into the city. The next day he went on with Barnabas to Derbe.

[21]After they had proclaimed the good news to that city and had made many disciples, they returned to Lystra, then on to Iconium and Antioch. [22]There they strengthened the souls of the disciples and encouraged them to continue in the faith, saying, "It is through many persecutions that we must enter the kingdom of God." [23]And after they had appointed elders for them in each church, with prayer and fasting they entrusted them to the Lord in whom they had come to believe.

[24]Then they passed through Pisidia and came to Pamphylia. [25]When they had spoken the word in Perga, they went down to Attalia. [26]From there they sailed back to Antioch, where they had been commended to the grace of God for the work[c] that they had completed.

[a] Or The priest of Zeus-Outside-the-City    [b] Gk Men    [c] Or committed in the grace of God to the work

# COMMENTARY

Luke's story of Paul's first mission is bracketed by Antioch, where he and Barnabas are commissioned for missionary service (13:1-4*a;* see 9:15-21) and where they then report "all that God had done through them" (14:21-26). Antioch has replaced Jerusalem as the center of the church's mission, and Paul (see 13:9) and Barnabas have replaced Peter and John[459] as the principal pair of prophetic witnesses to Jesus.

Between their departure from and return to Antioch, Paul and Barnabas are sent out under the aegis and at the behest of the Holy Spirit (13:2, 4*a*) to do "the work to which [God has] called them" (see 13:2; 14:26). They travel together to several important cities of Roman Asia (modern-day Turkey), including Cyprian Paphos (13:4-12), Pisidian Antioch (13:13-52), Lycaonian Iconium (14:1-7), and Lystra (14:8-20). This new missionary endeavor is marked by old practices and priorities: Paul proclaims the word of God (see 13:5, 7, 16-41, 44; 14:3, 7, 25) and performs prophetic "signs and wonders" (14:3; see 2:17-21; cf. 13:11; 14:8-10; 15:12) in the synagogues of urban centers (13:5, 14; 14:1) to mixed audiences (13:6-7, 42-48; 14:1-5, 27) and suffers because of it (cf. 13:50; 14:5, 19). While Paul shares in the suffering of Jesus (see 9:16), he also shares in the successes of the church's earlier missions. His evangelistic efforts in Asia typically result in many conversions among both Jews and Gentiles and in the founding of congregations similar to his sponsoring church in Syrian Antioch. On the way, he preaches the gospel, rebukes another practitioner of magic (Elymas; cf. Simon in Acts 8), converts a sympathetic Roman official (Sergius Paulus; cf. Cornelius in Acts 10), and commands the crippled to walk (cf. the lame man of Acts 3:1-8; 9:32-35). In each case, Paul replicates the actions of his prophetic predecessors. And like Peter (see 8:25), at the end of their mission Paul and Barnabas retrace their footsteps to encourage

new converts and to testify to the grace of God at work in the believers (cf. 14:21-26).

At the same time, a more radical dimension in both scope and effect characterizes Paul's missionary work. For example, Paul's religious authority is mistaken by pagans as divine in the shadow of their temple to Zeus (cf. 14:8-13) for doing precisely what Peter had done before him in the shadow of the Jerusalem Temple (see 3:1-8). Israel's mission as "light to the nations" is being realized through his mission, and different cultural symbols are being overturned as a result. Paul's climactic call to conversion in the synagogue at Pisidian Antioch (13:38-41), then, introduces a distinctive element to the gospel about Jesus: Forgiveness from sin comes through belief in Messiah Jesus rather than through Mosaic law (cf. 15:11). This idea so unsettles some devout Jews that they provoke Paul to clarify repentant Israel's prophesied mission as "light to the nations" (see 13:44-48)—a mission that he himself personifies in Acts.

The narrative of Paul's first mission has a "primacy effect" on its reader.[460] The impression that lingers on for the rest of Acts is that Paul is a central figure in God's plan of salvation, whose personal authority is envisaged by his résumé as a devout teacher of Israel, a virtuous man, a persuasive orator, and a person with recognized religious and social standing. This portraiture is different from that found in his letters, where his disinclination to speak of his apostolic charism reflects differences of literary genre and purpose. Also missing from Acts are accounts of Paul's controversies with other church leaders, although the narrator sometimes presumes these controversies as the narrative subtext that Acts itself seeks to answer.[461] The

---

459. Although Barnabas is a more robust character than John in Acts, his pairing with Paul serves a similar rhetorical role: Barnabas is to Paul as John is to Peter—his "silent partner" in their missionary outreach. Some have speculated that their religious authority is indexed by the order of their names, with Barnabas placed first as the leader of their mission. As such, e.g., it is speculated that he speaks for both when they appear before the church (e.g., in 15:12). The text is silent on this issue, however; in any case, Luke's story is now Paul's story, as earlier it was Peter's story.

460. So Tannehill, who understands 13:1-12 as a commissioning story that establishes the future concerns of God—the reader's orienting concerns—from the outset of Paul's mission. Further, commissions define the terms of mission and have a "primacy effect" upon the one sent out. Following the lead of B. Hubbard, Tannehill identifies seven elements in biblical narratives of commission: (1) introduction, (2) confrontation, (3) reaction, (4) commission, (5) protest, (6) reassurance, and (7) conclusion. See R. C. Tannehill, "Gospels and Narrative Literature," in *NIB*, 8:64-65. If the reader recalls the story of Saul's conversion from Acts 9:1-21 as co-text with this one, then Luke presents the reader with a full sense of what lies ahead for Paul in Acts.

461. The omission of any direct reference to Paul's letter writing in Acts is much less a problem than it once was in Acts criticism, for two reasons: (1) There are clear allusions to Pauline letters in Acts, and (2) it now seems possible that a collection of Paul's letters was placed in circulation—perhaps even by Paul himself—before the turn of the first century. It is simply inconceivable that Luke would not have known and read these letters, and therefore used them as a secondary source when writing Acts.

function of Paul's portrait in Acts within the NT, however, is to form a powerful impression of Paul's inspired persona that insinuates itself into his NT letters, resulting in a more attentive, trusting hearing of the word of God that is mediated there (see Introduction, "Acts as Canon," 26-32; see also the Overview to 15:13–28:28).

**13:1-4a.** Chapter 13 begins with a catalog of the leaders and their offices "in the church at Antioch," which signals a turning point in the narrative to the mission God has given this congregation. I doubt that this reference to Antioch's "prophets and teachers" indicates a departure from the organization of the Jewish church,[462] since the Twelve and Seven also engaged in teaching and prophetic ministry. If anything, it establishes the identity of those within the congregation who act as conduits for the Holy Spirit to make clear God's will for the congregation. More interesting is the cultural and social range of the leadership as evinced by the roll of names (see 11:19-20): "A Levite from Cyprus, a black man, a North African from Cyrene, a boyhood friend of Herod Antipas and a Pharisee educated under Gamaliel were acknowledged to be spiritual dynamos."[463]

In addition to sharing goods with the Jerusalem community (see 11:27-30), the resurrection practices of the Antiochene community also include "fasting and praying" (v. 3; see also 1:24; 6:6; 8:15; 12:12), which indicate their disciplined devotion to the Lord and capacity to discern his will (cf. 10:30; 14:23; Matt 6:5, 16; Luke 2:37). It is not surprising, then, that God's will is disclosed to them through the Holy Spirit: "Set apart for me Barnabas and Saul for the work to which I have called them" (v. 2). The verb ἀφορίζω (aphorizō, "set apart") denotes the separation of clean from unclean, typically for service or sacrifice to God (see Exod 13:12; 19:12, 23; Lev 13:4-5; Ezek 45:1-4). Luke's use of it in the commissioning of Barnabas and Saul sounds an important intertextual echo of two Pauline texts that describe the apostle's calling: Rom 1:1 and Gal 1:15. Paul's use of this verb in these texts recalls the biblical prophets whose commissioning is similar to his own (cf. Isa 49:1; Jer 1:5; As. Mos. 1:14; 1 Tim

1:12-16). Naturally, he also associates his missionary tasks with the prophet's vocation (cf. Rom 1:1-5; Gal 1:15-16). In the LXX this same verb is used for Israel's being "called" out of unclean nations to make a consecrated witness to God's salvation, even to the "ends of the earth" (Isa 52:10-11; cf. Lev 20:26). Both of these biblical connotations are combined in the present text where the Spirit of God calls Paul to a work among "unclean" nations (cf. Gal 1:15).[464]

The liturgy of commissioning, when church leaders "laid their hands on" Saul and Barnabas (v. 3), is used earlier in Acts 6:6 to symbolize apostolic authority. In this setting the Christian prophets and teachers of Antioch transmit the authority and benefaction of the Spirit to Barnabas and Saul in "sending them off." The reader should note that Paul's apostolic status in Acts (see 14:4, 14) is carefully qualified in deference to and distinction from the Twelve. While the Paul of Acts cannot claim apostolic status, since that is predicated on a personal relationship with the historical Jesus (see 1:21-22), he is "sent out by the Holy Spirit" (v. 4a)[465] and according to the prophecy of the resurrected Lord (see 9:15-16). Moreover, his religious authority is well established by the conclusion of his mission through the execution of those same tasks that other Spirit-filled prophets-like-Jesus have performed before him: inspired interpretation, persuasive preaching, and the performance of "signs and wonders" that result in mass conversions.

**13:4b-12.** One must have a map at hand when reading Acts, since geography serves Luke's theological purpose (see 1:8; see the map "The Early Eastern Roman Empire," 4). In this instance, the expedition party leaves Antioch and stops first on the island of Cyprus, where they arrive at Salamis, the principal port city on Cyprus's east coast and a logical place to begin their island campaign. They then cross the island to Paphos, the principal port on the west coast and the provincial capital, which is the logical place to

---

462. So J. D. G. Dunn, *The Acts of the Apostles* (Valley Forge, Pa.: Trinity, 1996) 172-73.

463. G. Krodel, *Acts,* ACNT (Minneapolis: Augsburg, 1986) 226.

464. See R. Wall, "Power and Purity in the Acts of the Apostles," *WTJ* 34 (1999) 64-82.

465. Luke does not use the more familiar "sending" verb ἀποστέλλω (apostellō), which would have called attention to the noun "apostle," but the rather unusual verb ἐκπέμπω (ekpempō, "send out"; cf. 17:10) to emphasize that this new mission was undertaken by *direct* instruction of the Spirit (rather than by the leadership of a local church). See Barrett, *Acts,* 1:610.

conclude and climax their campaign. Barnabas and Saul proclaim "the word of God in the Jewish synagogues" (v. 5; see 6:9),[466] and they are joined by John Mark as their "helper" (see 12:12, 25). He soon returns to Jerusalem (v. 13), however and becomes party in the later split between Barnabas and Paul (see 15:37-39).

Their mission to Paphos leads Saul and Barnabas to meet with the Roman proconsul stationed there, Sergius Paulus (46–48 CE), whom Luke describes as "an intelligent man."[467] Human virtue and receptivity of the divine word are often paired in Acts (see 17:11), even as are malicious character and spiritual failure. For example, the missionaries also encounter a "magician and Jewish false prophet, named Bar-Jesus" (v. 6),[468] who is likely an adviser to the proconsul. If Sergius is a type of Gentile convert, then Bar-Jesus is a type of Jewish opponent. Contrary to Sergius' intelligence, this false prophet is an "enemy of all righteousness [δικαιοσύνη *dikaiosynē;* cf. Luke 1:75; Matt 5:20] full of all deceit [δόλος *dolos;* cf. Deut 27:24 LXX; Rom 1:29; 1 Thess 2:3] and villainy [ῥαδιουργία *rhadiourgia;* cf. Acts 18:14]"—a catalog of vices suggesting that the principal motive of Jewish opposition is moral rather than theological. Sharply put, Bar-Jesus fears that Paul might intrude on his political relationship with Sergius Paulus and subvert his political influence.

His motive is not unlike that of Simon the Great, who offered to purchase the "political" authority of Peter and John when he encountered them during Philip's Samaritan crusade (see 8:19). In both episodes, the presence of missionaries is considered an invasion of the magician's territory, where he enjoys power and status.[469] As before, the magician's opposition occasions a sure demonstration of religious authority.[470] In this case, when the opposition is less benign, Saul "discerns the spirits," demonizes Bar-Jesus, and then as the authorized medium of "the hand of the Lord" (v. 11; see 11:21) blinds him. Saul's rhetorical question "will you not stop making crooked the straight paths of the Lord?" (v. 10*b*) combines phrases from different prophecies (Prov 10:9; Isa 40:3-4; 59:8; Hos 14:9; cf. Luke 3:4-5; see also Acts 8:21) to supply the biblical subtext of his curse: The false prophet seeks to make crooked what the true prophet of God makes straight.[471] Perhaps the magician's temporary blindness is a metaphor of the failure he and others like him have in blinding people to the course of God's salvation.

Significantly, at this moment of spiritual warfare, when Saul is "filled with the Holy Spirit" (v. 9; see also 4:8), Luke changes Saul's name to Paul and, for rhetorical effect, Bar-Jesus' name to Elymas. In both cases, Jewish names (Saul/Bar-Jesus) are exchanged for Gentile names (Paul/Elymas) to underscore the conversion of the Roman man Sergius Paulus. In this sense, name changes cue both the Gentile mission and the nature of the Jewish opposition to it. That is, Elymas (= unrepentant Jews) tries "to turn [Sergius Paulus] away from the faith" (v. 8) and so exposes himself as an "enemy of all righteousness, full of all deceit and villainy" (v. 10*a*). His blindness (v. 11*b*), the result of Paul's punitive word (vv. 10-11*a*), combined with Sergius Paulus's conversion, in response to Paul's prophetic word (v. 12), clearly indicates Paul's authority and predicts his mission's ultimate success.[472]

---

466. While "Jewish synagogues" may seem like a redundancy, the Greek word for "synagogue" (συναγωγή *synagōgē*) denotes a place for assembly and was used for other voluntary organizations in the Roman world. Luke's linguistic precision at this point reflects his theological precision: Paul's identity and mission are centered by the symbols of his Jewish world.

467. Luke uses the proper Greek title for a "proconsul" (ἀνθύπατος *anthypatos;* cf. 18:12) for the Roman official in charge of the island's governing senate, located in Paphos.

468. The combination of "magician" with "Jewish false prophet" may well envisage Luke's attempt to dissociate Christianity from a popular criticism of Judaism (and therefore Christianity) as a nonrational superstition.

469. Spencer's treatment of this story illumines the importance of its social cues, which extend from Roman/visible to cosmic/invisible worlds. See F. S. Spencer, *Acts,* Readings: A New Biblical Commentary (Sheffield: Sheffield Academic, 1997) 138-43.

470. L. T. Johnson, *The Acts of the Apostles,* SP 5 (Collegeville, Minn.: Liturgical, 1992) 226, sees the parallelism between this story and the story of Jesus' temptation following the outpouring of the Spirit on him at his baptism/commission. If Jesus' temptation proves that he has the mettle to be Messiah, Paul's quick defeat of Elymas, who evidently is the devil's agent (see 13:10), makes a similar point: Paul has the mettle to be a prophet-like-Jesus with the religious authority to carry the word of God to the end of the earth.

471. Tannehill argues that the intertextual echo is of John the Baptist's statement in Luke 3:4-5, which launches a "renewal movement based upon repentance and release of sins." This movement now continues with Paul's mission under the aegis of the glorified Messiah. See R. C. Tannehill, *The Acts of the Apostles,* vol. 2 of *The Narrative Unity of Luke-Acts: A Literary Interpretation* (Minneapolis: Fortress, 1990) 2:163.

472. I doubt that the conversion of Sergius Paulus begins Luke's apologia for a variety of "early catholic" Christianity that accommodates Roman rule, as is suggested by E. Haenchen, *The Acts of the Apostles* (Philadelphia: Westminster, 1971) 403-4, following others. Luke's portrait of Rome's relationship to Paul's mission is ambiguous at best, typically presenting it as utterly secular and self-interested.

**13:13-15.** From Cyprus, "Paul and his companions," which now include John Mark, set sail to the Asian coast of provincial Pamphylia, where they travel inland about eight miles to Perga (v. 13*a*). No journal is kept of their campaign there; the reader is expected to fill in this entry with details inferred from earlier mission stories. What is most noteworthy about this stop, however, is that John "left them and returned to Jerusalem" (v. 13*b;* see also v. 6) and his mother's house (see 12:12). No reason for his departure is given. Perhaps the first readers of Acts knew the reason and Luke was being polite in not mentioning it. Bruce speculates that Paul had displaced his cousin Barnabas as the mission's chief leader and Luke cues this change by mentioning Mark's departure.[473]

Following the pattern of Jesus before him (cf. Luke 4:1-30), Paul and Barnabas "went into the synagogue" (at Pisidian Antioch)[474] to worship God (v. 14) following the defeat of the evil one. The reference to the "reading of the law and the prophets" refers to the most essential moment during Jewish worship when lessons from the Torah (reading from the law of Moses) and the *Haftorah* (a related reading from the biblical prophecies) are recited, typically followed by a teacher's midrash—an interpretation of the recited Scriptures that seeks to explain both its contemporary relevance (*dĕrash*) and plain meaning (*pĕshat*) for the congregation. What is extraordinary about this scene is not that Paul worshiped with other pious Jews on sabbath, for this is his religious habit. Rather, it is that "the synagogue rulers" invited him to offer the morning's midrash or homily on the biblical lessons (13:15). Actually, "word of exhortation" (λόγος τῆς παρακλήσεως *logos tēs paraklēseōs*) is a technical term in Jewish homiletics for an edifying homily

concerning God's saving acts in the history of Israel.[475]

**13:16-41.** Paul will provide them a "word of exhortation" in vv. 17-25, perhaps even alluding to the morning's lessons—which Luke does not actually cite[476]—before expanding his exhortation to include Christian proclamation (vv. 26-37), an invitation to repent (vv. 38-39), and a warning of why his audience must do so (vv. 40-41). Commentators favorably compare the importance and rhetorical brilliance of Paul's speech with Peter's Pentecost address (see 2:22-40) and Stephen's speech (see 7:1-53). Besides numerous parallels in rhetorical design, literary detail, and theological substance, the paradigmatic role of each within Acts is similar. As Paul stands to speak and makes the rhetor's gesture for the congregation to quiet down (v. 16*a*) and "listen" (v. 16*b*), the reader of Acts also comes to the alert, knowing that his first speech is paradigmatic of every other speech Paul will give in Acts.

**13:16.** The congregation of the diaspora synagogue is different from those addressed during the church's Palestinian mission. Paul addresses not only "Israelites" (῎Ανδρες ᾿Ισραηλῖται *Andres Israēlitai;* lit., "men," "brothers," 2:22; 7:2; cf. 13:16*b*) but now also "others who fear God" (οἱ φοβούμενοι τὸν θεόν *hoi phoboumenoi ton theon* also in v. 26)—pious Gentiles such as Cornelius.[477]

**13:17-25.** The first section of Paul's speech retells Scripture's narrative of salvation's history in a manner similar to Stephen's speech (see 7:1-53). Paul, however, draws out Jesus' connection to the Davidic dynasty as royal Messiah rather than Stephen's primary emphasis on Jesus as the messianic prophet-like-Moses. Because Stephen has already said what must be said to the reader about Moses and the exodus, the Paul of Acts says few

---

473. F. F. Bruce, *The Acts of the Apostles*, rev. ed., NICNT (Grand Rapids: Eerdmans, 1988) 300. Johnson, *The Acts of the Apostles*, 229, finds a layer of possible meaning in the use of the verb ἀποχορέω (*apochōreō*, "to leave") in Jer 46:5 LXX, where it implies a cowardly retreat, or in 3 Macc 2:33, where it connotes apostasy. Paul evidently finds John Mark inadequate for the missionary task, whatever the reason (Acts 15:38-39).

474. Pisidian Antioch in Paul's day was a flourishing Roman colony located in central provincial Asia (modern Turkey). It was well known as home to powerful relatives of Caesar Tiberias and Herod, as well as to members of the Antiochene dynasty that had founded the city centuries earlier. For this reason, perhaps, Antioch had become a leading center of the imperial cult in Roman Asia. See S. Mitchell and M. Waelkens, *Pisidian Antioch* (London: Duckworth, 1998).

475. The "word of exhortation" might be what the Mishnah later calls a "priestly blessing," which follows the biblical recitations and concludes the worship service. See Fitzmyer, *The Acts of the Apostles*, 510; Barrett, *Acts,* 1:628-29; J. Bowker, "Speeches in Acts," *NTS* (1967-68) 96-111. What is more puzzling is why Paul is invited to encourage a congregation that he does not know. Luke's literary aim, however, is to show Paul engaging in his primary missionary activity—synagogue preaching—and to set forth in this inaugural speech an account of God's salvation that coheres with the theological aims of his narrative.

476. From his careful analysis of allusions in the speech with attention to contemporary Jewish hermeneutics, Bowker, "Speeches in Acts," 101-10, speculates that the Torah reading includes Deut 4:25-46 with 2 Sam 7:6-16 as the *Haftorah* reading.

477. Barrett, *Acts,* 630-31, takes "others who fear God" as referring to Gentile proselytes rather than mere Jewish sympathizers.

words in moving "this people Israel" from their divine election (v. 17a; see also 7:2-16) and exodus from Egypt (v. 17b; see also 7:17-34) through the wilderness (v. 18; see also 7:35-44) and into "their land as an inheritance for about four hundred fifty years" (vv. 19-20a; see also 7:45-50).

Although Paul pays careful attention to the various time periods of God's provident care of Israel's destiny, as did Stephen, he slows his pace at the mention of "the prophet Samuel" and the people's request made to him for a national king (vv. 20b-21a; cf. 1 Sam 8:5-9, 19-22). The climax of Paul's rehearsal of salvation's history is the founding of Israel's monarchy, for it is from Israel's kingly lineage that the Messiah will come: This prophet-like-Moses of Stephen's speech is also the messianic king-like-David. Paul's claim is rooted in the most traditional expression of Israel's expectation of a national savior, which Paul now asserts is realized in Jesus according to Scripture's testimony (v. 23). That is, the biblical story of David's ascendancy to Israel's throne (cf. 1 Samuel 10–16), when Saul is "removed" as Israel's unfaithful king and David is "made [ἐγείρω egeirō; lit., "raised up"] their king" (v. 22a; see also v. 30), is the biblical *typos* of God's "raising up" Jesus as Israel's messianic ruler (see 2:25-36). He is this prophesied Savior from David's royal household.

Because Scripture provides "testimony" (εἶπεν μαρτυρήσας eipen martyrēsas; see 10:43) of David's triumph, since God "found David" (cf. Ps 88:21) to be "a man after my heart, who will carry out all my wishes" (cf. 1 Sam 13:14; Isa 44:28), this typology supports Jesus' triumph as Israel's Messiah.[478] For this reason, Paul's segue to his proclamation about Jesus alludes to Scripture's promise of a Davidic heir to rule an eternal kingdom (v. 23; cf. 2 Sam 7:12-14). Jesus is this "posterity" (lit., "seed," see 2:30) who is destined to be Israel's "Savior" (see 5:31; cf. Luke 2:11) according to what God "promised" David (see 2:29-32; 3:21-25; 7:46-47)—that is, an eternal kingdom (cf. 2 Sam 22:51). According to Acts, however, this promised kingdom has already been realized within a repentant Israel (see 1:6) and is marked out by the presence of God's Spirit, who is also the

"Father's promise" (see 1:4). The flashback to John the Baptist is apropos of Paul's reference of divine promise because John the Baptist had predicted the promised Spirit's arrival with the Messiah (see 1:5). Paul's mention of his message when heard with these various intertextual echoes underscores the immediate relevance of the "repentance to all the people of Israel," including these members of this diaspora synagogue (cf. Luke 3:17, 23; John 1:20-21). John the Baptist also joins King David as a more contemporary prophetic witness to Paul's gospel about Jesus (cf. Luke 16:16).

**13:26-37.** The second section of Paul's speech reiterates his opening address to the devout Jews and God-fearers in attendance (see v. 16b), but now as recipients of "the message of this salvation" (v. 26). If his message concerns Jesus, who is "Savior" (so v. 23), then what is said about him pertains to God's salvation, which Joel's prophecy links with calling upon the name of that Savior (see 2:21). When Paul repeats the church's proclamation about Jesus' death and resurrection (vv. 27-30; see 2:22-24; 3:13-17), he adapts his message to a sabbath setting in a Jewish synagogue of the diaspora, where Israel's Scriptures are read and interpreted. So Paul clarifies that the Savior's rejection was by "the residents of Jerusalem and their leaders" (v. 27a), who were ignorant of "the words of the prophets that are read every sabbath" (v. 27b; see also v. 15; 3:17; 4:8, 26; cf. 15:21).

Paul stresses Jesus' innocence (v. 28), pointing out that "the words of the prophets" stipulate that "[Pilate, the Jerusalemites, and their leaders] had carried out everything that was written about him" (v. 29a; see 4:25-28). The gospel subtext expands the redemptive irony of the Christ-event: The malevolent killing of an innocent person triggers God's benevolent plan in raising Jesus from the dead, thereby reversing such evil for good. The elaboration of Jerusalem's guilt is new in Acts and no doubt intends to recall the earlier story of the Jerusalem church and the obduracy of the city's religious leaders in rejecting the proclamation of the Lord's apostolic successors. The narrative logic of this emphasis is "to open the way to a 'second chance' for these dwellers in the Diaspora."[479]

Paul marshals support for his gospel both from Israel's Scriptures and from those eyewitnesses

478. Johnson, *The Acts of the Apostles*, 232-38, argues that in shaping this speech Luke uses a rabbinical exegetical technique called *gezerah shewa* by which different biblical texts are combined by common words or figures, such as David.

479. Ibid., 238.

who encounter the living Jesus and are "witnesses to the people [λάος *laos*]" (v. 31; see also 1:8, 21-22; 10:41), proving "that what God promised to our ancestors he has fulfilled for us" (vv. 32*b*-33*a;* see also vv. 27, 29; cf. 2:25-36). The subtext of Paul's message is ironical because he was an agent of the very Jerusalem leadership he now condemns for rejecting the gospel's witness to the risen Jesus. His complicated midrash of Scripture brings into conversation three texts about David—two from the psalter (Pss 2:7; 16:10 [15:10 LXX] and another from Isaiah's prophecy (Isa 55:3). Together they supply the principal warrant for his proclamation that Jesus' resurrection is proof that he is the prophesied Davidic Messiah. The first prophecy, "written in the second psalm" (v. 33; cf. Ps 2:7), reiterates the promise made to "our ancestors" that is now fulfilled "for us, their children" (vv. 32-33; cf. Rom 1:4; Heb 1:5): Jesus' resurrection discloses that he is the Messiah (cf. 2:36). Paul offers no further reflection on the meaning of the cited psalm but assumes that this text would not make sense of a dead Jesus but only of one who "no more [returns to] corruption" (v. 34*a*). Isaiah's promise that God "will give [δώσεις *dōseis*] you the holy [ὅσιος *hosios*] promises made to David" (v. 34; cf. Isa 55:3) is then interpreted by a second Davidic psalm, which draws the inference about the living Jesus who does not "return to corruption" and must be the referent of David's promise that God did "not let *dōseis* your Holy One [ὁ ὅσιος *ho hosios*] experience corruption" (v. 35; cf. Ps 15:10 LXX). Surely David could not be its referent, since he "died, was laid beside his ancestors, and experienced corruption" (cf. 1 Kgs 2:10 LXX; see also Acts 2:27-31).

**13:38-41.** Paul begins the final section of his speech with his third appeal for "my brothers" to listen to his message (see vv. 16*b*, 26). This is his "altar call" (the *peroratio*)—a missionary's appeal for his or her auditors to convert to Jesus as Savior in order to be initiated into a new life with God. Haenchen contends that the critical phrase "through him everyone who believes is justified" is Luke's attempt to reproduce Pauline theology—or at least that portion of Pauline theology still accepted by Luke and his church.[480] However, this

definition of God's salvation is more typical of Paul's speeches in Acts than of his NT letters. In particular, the proclamation of "forgiveness of sins" (v. 38) is an implicit call to repent and turn to the risen Jesus as Savior, which is a distinctive theological emphasis of Luke-Acts (see 2:38; 10:43; cf. Luke 24:47). The vague reference to "the law of Moses" (13:39) strikes a note more loudly sounded in the earlier Stephen story (see 6:11, 14; 7:20, 53) and subsequent Jerusalem Council than in Pauline thought;[481] and, most important, the reference to "everyone who believes" (v. 39) cues Joel's prophecy as its theological referent in Acts (see 2:21; 10:43; however, see Rom 10:11-13). The point is that Luke shapes the *peroratio* of Paul's programmatic speech to confirm the theological sensibilities of *his* Paul, in continuity with *his* Jesus and the apostolic successors. In doing so Luke confirms Paul's religious authority and the trustworthiness of his message.

The caveat that concludes Paul's inaugural speech agrees broadly with the language and spirit of the prophecy in LXX Habakkuk.[482] The prophecy warns Judah to "believe" rather than "scoff" when the prophet "tells you" (ἐκδιηγέομαι *ekdiēgeomai,* "to report"; see 15:3) of God's "work." Paul uses the prophecy here to warn Jews in the Diaspora to believe his "report" of God's work (= gospel) or forfeit the promised blessing of eternal life (see vv. 44-46). By "reporting" the details of God's "work" through Messiah Jesus, Paul continues Habakkuk's prophetic ministry of announcing God's work to Israel. In this essential way, then, Luke's Paul uses Habakkuk to underscore the urgency of his "report" about God's work (= gospel) among them.

---

480. E. Haenchen, *The Acts of the Apostles* (Philadelphia: Westminster, 1971) 412.

481. The Protestant interpreter should not be too quick to contrast the two statements about "believes is justified" (NIV; NRSV, "believes is set free") and "law of Moses" in terms of Paul's distinctive contrast between the faith of/in Jesus and works of law, especially found in Romans (3:21-26; 9:28–10:13) and Galatians (2:11-16; 3:21-24; cf. Titus 3:4-7). See H. Conzelmann, *The Acts of the Apostles,* trans. J. Limburg et al., ed. E. J. Epp and C. R. Matthews, Hermeneia (Philadelphia: Fortress, 1987) 106. The meaning of Luke's reference to "the law of Moses" is unclear. He almost certainly is not suggesting that Torah observance subverts God's plan of salvation, nor is he introducing a "theology of the law"; rather, the "law of Moses" is mentioned in passing as performing a different role in the economy of God's salvation than that of the Savior; the law is Israel's "sign" that they are God's people. See J. Jervell, "The Law in Luke-Acts," in *Luke and the People of God* (Minneapolis: Augsburg, 1972) 133-51; and *Die Apostelgeschichte,* KEK 3 (Göttingen: Vandenhoeck & Ruprecht, 1998) 360-61.

482. See R. W. Wall, "The Function of LXX Habakkuk 1:5 in the Book of Acts," *BBR* 10 (2000) 247-58.

Although on balance the original meaning of the prophecy is not distorted, a close reading evinces slight modifications to update its meaning for Acts. Luke's most important addition is of a second ἔργον (ergon, "work"). This repetition emphasizes the importance of Paul's missionary "work" entrusted to him by the Holy Spirit (see v. 2), which is confirmed by the mission's success (see 14:26). The entire narrative of this inaugural mission is thereby enclosed by repeated reference to Barnabas and Paul's missionary "work" (13:2–14:26), which is to proclaim and mediate God's "work" of grace (14:26). The Habakkuk prophecy stands at the center of this inclusio to remind the reader of the peril of "scoffing" and "never believing" the prophet's warning; indeed, unrepentant Jews will refuse the prophet's message (v. 45), proving them "unworthy of eternal life" (v. 46).

**13:42-43.** The congregation's initial response is cautiously positive: Barnabas and Paul are invited to preach again in the synagogue the following sabbath (v. 42), while many "Jews and devout converts to Judaism" who heard him "followed Paul and Barnabas" and encouraged them "to continue in the grace of God" (v. 43). Luke does not provide precise definitions of each group within the synagogue. For example, even though the combination of "devout" (σεβόμενος sebomenos) with "convert" (προσήλυτος prosēlytos) is unique within Acts, it is not clear whether these Jewish proselytes are different from those "who fear God" mentioned earlier (vv. 16b, 26). In this context, however, they are likely viewed as recent converts to Christ who have now come to "follow" the truth of Paul's message—a situation perhaps similar to Luke's own experience.[483] If this is not the case their exhortation for Paul and Barnabas "to continue in the grace of God" makes

little sense, since in Acts the "grace of God" always refers to the concrete experience of divine faithfulness among those who repent (see 2:47; 4:33).

**13:44-47.** The next week, Paul and Barnabas return to the synagogue. Word of Paul's earlier sermon has filtered out into the Jewish community and so "almost the whole city gathered to hear the word of the Lord" (v. 44). The purpose of Luke's characteristic hyperbole is to create an impression of Paul's rhetorical powers in keeping with his religious authority; he also wants to explain why Paul's Jewish opponents "were filled with jealousy" (v. 45). They sense that Paul is their principal rival as teacher of the Jewish community of their city.

Their reaction recalls Elymas's earlier response to Paul, which is paradigmatic of all Jewish opposition during Paul's mission (see vv. 8-10). His "deceit and villainy" when seeking to subvert Paul's influence in Paphos resulted in blindness—a metaphor of his spiritual blindness. The real offense felt by local Jewish opponents to Paul's message, whether in the court of Sergius Paulus or in the synagogue of Pisidian Antioch, is not in what is said but in the influence exerted upon those "many Jews and devout converts" (v. 43) who had responded favorably to the word and now "followed Paul and Barnabas." Change is never easy, and any substantial change in what a community believes or values has wide-ranging social repercussions that are felt by the elites of the "old order."[484]

Yet the reaction of Paul's Jewish opposition in Pisidian Antioch also reflects their spiritual obduracy and anticipates the indictment that Paul and Barnabas issue them: "since you reject [ἀπωθέομαι apōtheomai] it [the word of God] and judge [κρίνω krinō] yourselves to be unworthy of eternal life" (v. 46). That they condemn their opponents "boldly" (παρρησιάζομαι parrēsiazomai) suggests that they do so in the power of God's Spirit (see 4:29). Paul's denunciation echoes his earlier use of krinō in describing Jerusalem's ignorant rejection of Jesus ("condemning him," v. 27) by which God's redemptive purposes are realized. The same irony stands behind the Jewish

---

483. Contra B. Witherington, *The Acts of the Apostles: A Socio-Rhetorical Commentary* (Grand Rapids: Eerdmans, 1998) 414, who, along with other commentators, assumes that no one in Paul's audience has yet been converted. But see I. Levinskaya, *The Book of Acts in Its Diaspora Setting*, in *The Book of Acts in First Century Setting*, ed. B. W. Winter and A. Clarke, 6 vols. (Grand Rapids: Eerdmans, 1993–98) 5:19-49. Her essential argument is that the combination of *prosēlytos,* ("convert") with *sebomenos* ("devout"; lit., "worshiping"), found only in 13:43, refers to a special group of God-fearing Gentiles who have become "Jewish" in outlook and religious observance. Moreover, she thinks that in combination "Jews and devout proselytes" form a discrete group within the synagogue that has *already* converted to Christianity and for this reason are now "followers" of Paul.

484. J. D. G. Dunn, *The Acts of the Apostles* (Valley Forge, Pa.: Trinity, 1996) 183-84.

rejection of Paul's synagogical preaching, since it leads to his Gentile mission. Further, Stephen had said that the word of God brought to the people by Moses was twice "pushed aside" (apōtheomai) by unrepentant Israel (see 7:27, 39), resulting in their idolatry and exile. Not only does their rejection of Paul's message a second time accomplish God's redemptive purposes among the Gentiles, it also marks Paul's Jewish opponents out as an unrepentant Israel who are "exiled" from the prospect of "eternal life."[485] These who "pushed aside" the "word of the Lord" proclaimed by this prophet-like-Jesus are themselves "pushed aside" from the coming age. A harsh verdict indeed!

This passage has performed an important, if sometimes notorious, role in the history of Acts criticism. On its basis, many have argued that Paul's Gentile mission is both occasioned and justified by Jewish rejection of his gospel, or that Paul's words express "a divorce between the gospel and Judaism."[486] Such general statements, however, typically fail to note that "many Jews" and proselytes are converted to Jesus (v. 43) and that Paul does not cease his mission to the synagogue in any case (see 14:1). The scope of his denunciation is local and pertains only to those Jews of Pisidian Antioch who have twice rejected the gospel (cf. 18:3; 28:28). According to Scripture's prophesied pattern Paul carries the Word of God to the Jews first, and then a second time if necessary; those who are still unrepentant are justly condemned by God (see 3:17-26; 10:34-43).[487] Moreover, Paul's "turning to the Gentiles" in Pisidian Antioch personifies the missionary vocation of repentant Israel. His statement, a defining moment in Acts, is ironical of divine sovereignty, since an episode of conflict both clarifies and accomplishes God's redemptive purposes rather than subvert them (see 13:27-30). Paul's turn toward the city's Gentiles, no doubt a practical move given the Jewish opposition there, satisfies Scripture's command that faithful Israel "be a light for the Gentiles, so that you may bring salva-

tion to the ends of the earth" (13:47; see 1:8; 9:15-16; 26:23; cf. Isa. 49:6; Luke 2:32).

In this light, note should be taken of the formula that introduces Isaiah's prophecy, "I have set you [ἐντέλλομαι entellomai] to be a light [φῶς phōs] for the Gentiles [= nations]." The word entellomai is a term of vocation (see 1:2), and Isaiah's original sense of it, carried over to Acts, is of faithful Israel's purpose in the world. While Paul appeals to Isaiah to justify his mission to the Gentiles, he does so ironically since he personifies the missionary identity of repentant Israel. The biblical metaphor of "light" refers to the theological illumination occasioned by the hearing of "the word of the Lord" (see 26:23; 13:44, 48-49). In Acts this proclaimed word is informed by memories of the risen Jesus and the prophet's inspired interpretation of Scripture. The matrix of important terms supplied by Isaiah's prophecy not only delineates the biblical justification of Paul's mission to the Gentiles but also will provide the subtext of his defense before Israel (see 22:21): He personifies the vocation of repentant Israel according to Scripture. This citation also picks up Simeon's prophecy of Jesus' messianic mission (cf. Luke 2:32), and the phrase "ends of the earth" recalls Jesus' commission that his apostles be his witnesses "to the end of the earth" (1:8). In fact, it will be Paul who will bear primary responsibility of bearing Jesus' witness to the "end of the earth" (= Rome; see 28:16-31). In this sense, Paul's urban mission continues the witness of Messiah and his apostolic successors to God's salvation. While God's salvation is a theme of his earlier sermon (see 13:26), its use here in a missionary text surely recalls Joel's prophecy that the blessings of salvation are extended to "everyone who calls upon the name of the Lord" (see 2:21).

**13:48-49.** Upon hearing Paul's response to his Jewish opposition, the Gentiles "were glad and praised the word of the Lord." The reader rightly assumes that these Gentiles are from Antioch and attached to its synagogue as either God fearers (vv. 16, 26) or devout proselytes (v. 43). Further, Luke's division of people is not primarily along ethnic lines; thus here it might seem to indicate that the Gentiles' happy response is inherently antisemitic. No more did all "the Gentiles" believe than did all "the Jews" reject the gospel. Luke typically divides audiences along religious lines according

---

485. The phrase "eternal life" (ἡ αἰωνία ζωή hē aiōnia zōē) is a synonym of "salvation" (σωτηρία sōtēria; see 13:38-39) and occurs only here in Acts (cf. Luke 10:25; 18:18, 30). It is, however, well used in first-century Judaism of life with God in the coming new creation. See 4Q181 1.4-6.

486. Haenchen, The Acts of the Apostles, 417; cf. Conzelmann, The Acts of the Apostles, 145.

487. Johnson, The Acts of the Apostles, 13.

to their different responses to God's promises. In this sense, then, the Gentiles of Antioch rejoice simply and rightly because Paul has come to them carrying the word of the Lord in fulfillment of Scripture's prophecy that eschatological Israel would invite the nations to share in the blessings of its salvation.[488]

The repetition of the phrase "word of the Lord/God" (ὁ λόγος τοῦ κυρίου/θεοῦ *ho logos tou kyriou/theou* vv. 44, 46, 48-49; see also vv. 5, 7; 4:31; 6:7; 8:25; 11:1; 12:24), culminating in a summary of its triumph "through the region" (v. 49), concentrates the reader's focus upon the message of salvation rather than on its prophetic messenger or on the ethnicity of his auditors; the message is the locus of God's visitation among the Gentiles and the legitimate cause of their joy. It is this saving word that calls *everyone* to repentance and trust, and not the ethnicity of the community's constituency (see 13:46); and so "as many as had been destined [passive, ἦσαν τεταγμένοι *ēsan tetagmenoi*] for eternal life became believers [ἐπίστευσαν *episteusan*]."

Barrett says about this hard text that it stands "as unqualified a statement of absolute predestination as is found anywhere in the NT."[489] Two characteristics of salvation, consistently and constantly employed by Luke, qualify every definition of salvation found in Acts: The plan and history of God's salvation are mapped by the prophecies of Scripture; and everyone who experiences salvation's blessings does so because he or she has turned to God in faith (see Introduction, "Acts as Confession," 18-26). The joy of the Antiochene Gentiles springs from Paul's inspired interpretation of Scripture that locates them in God's plan of salvation.[490] Their faithful response to the word of the Lord results in eternal life (rather than in condemnation or in nothing at all). Moreover, this inclusive salvation is the exclusive experience of all those who believe—whether Jew or Greek. The joy of these particular Gentiles, then, pre-

sumes they have believed the truth of the word of the Lord that Paul has delivered to them; and in accordance with the divine purpose they are made worthy of eternal life.[491]

**13:50-52.** The negative reaction toward Paul and Barnabas from a coalition of leading Jews and "devout women of high standing and the leading men of the city" is not surprising. The adjective σεβομέναι (*sebomenai*, "devout"), suggesting that the women were Jewish proselytes (see v. 43), combined with "the Jews" who instigated the protest, indicates that hostilities toward the Christian missionaries originated from within the synagogue and were motivated because of the leaders' "jealousy" (see v. 45).

Reference to the "persecution [διωγμός *diōgmos*] against Paul and Barnabas," however, reminds us of the theological context of Acts.[492] Jesus' prophecy of Paul's mission, which insinuates itself into the narrative pattern in Acts, defines both its universal scope (9:15) and Paul's suffering (9:16). Both Luke's social world and his theological conception shape a narrative, then, that elevates suffering as the consequence of mission—the collision of obedient proclamation and unrepentant hearts—but also as the mark of a new horizon. They "shook the dust off their feet in protest against them" and traveled down the road to Iconium. Theirs is not a fearful flight without fight, but one of prophetic protest and severance from a contaminated place (cf. Luke 9:4; 10:11).

The happy prospect of new converts now stands before Paul and Barnabas in Iconium, even though the haunting tragedy of a rejected salvation lay behind them in Antioch. It is not because of their departure that "the disciples were filled with joy and with the Holy Spirit"; rather, these are the marks of salvation and the founding of a new community of "disciples" (see 2:38; 4:31; 8:38; 10:44-46).[493] Thus, even though the missionaries

488. Whether diaspora Judaism was a missionary religion or whether Paul was the first Jew to launch an active mission to the Gentiles as Acts suggests remains a lively debate. E.g., Scot McKnight, *A Light Among the Gentiles: Jewish Missionary Activity in the Second Temple Period* (Minneapolis: Fortress, 1991), argues that diaspora Judaism was not a missionary religion and that the Acts portrait of Paul's controversial diaspora mission to the Gentiles is historically likely.

489. Barrett, *Acts*, 1:658. The NIV preserves the absolute sense of Luke's statement.

490. Marshall, *The Acts of the Apostles*, 231.

491. Cf. Haenchen, *The Acts of the Apostles*, 414, who argues that the word ὅσοι (*hosoi*, "as many as") indicates that not all Gentiles believed, which makes sense of the later conflict among other Gentile women and men (see 13:50). The "predestination" of Gentiles for salvation is thereby qualified by the faith of individuals freely given.

492. The Western text of Acts adds "a great tribulation and" before "persecution" to intensify the conflict and to recall the earlier use of "tribulation" (θλῖψις *thlipsis*) in 11:19, where the Antioch mission was first established as a consequence of the founding members' "tribulation."

493. Dunn, *The Acts of the Apostles*, 185, draws the unwarranted inference from the Lukan summary in 13:52 that the joyful experience of Spirit filling is exclusively felt among Gentiles (see 13:43) and is now possible because of the departure of Paul and Barnabas from Antioch.

have departed for another city, in their absence the Holy Spirit remains behind in Antioch to enable the disciples to advance the word of the Lord there (see 2:4) and to cultivate joy in their community.

**14:1-7.** Iconium, Lystra, and Derbe are neighboring cities in the Roman province of Galatia, roughly ninety miles southeast from Antioch on the Via Sebaste, the main roadway connecting the most important Roman cities of the area (see the map "The Early Eastern Roman Empire," 4). Paul's missionary pattern repeats itself in this Lycaonian district; the narrative of this mission has severe gaps and requires the reader to recall details from earlier stories. As before Paul and Barnabas "went into the Jewish synagogue and spoke" (v. 1*a*; see also 13:5, 14). Luke writes that they spoke "in such a way" (οὕτως *houtōs*) to cue readers to fill in the narrative at this point with details ascribed to Paul's ministry at Pisidian Antioch (see 13:16-47).[494] The immediate result is the same as well: "A great number of Jews and Greeks became believers" (v. 1*b*; see 13:43), again testifying to the universal cast of Paul's mission and message.

As before, "unbelieving Jews stirred up the Gentiles and poisoned their minds" (v. 2; see also 13:10, 44-45, 50). Characteristically in Acts, the household of Israel is divided by the proclamation of the gospel (v. 4; see also 4:1-4; cf. Luke 2:34) between those who repent and believe (14:1) and those who do not (v. 2). In this case, the counter-attack is fueled by some unspecified anti-Christian propaganda that "poisoned [κακόω *kakoō*; lit., "made evil"] their minds," a phrase that recalls Stephen's use of Exod 2:22 to characterize Egypt's reign of terror over Israel (see 7:6, 19)—in the present case, however, in reference to an intellectual rather than physical repression. Indeed, according to Acts the battle waged for the gospel is often for the mind, whether to overcome the ignorance that keeps people's minds numb to the truth (see 3:17) or to correct wrongheaded interpretations of the prophet's wisdom (see 6:8-10). The reader again should presume that the unstated motive of their "villainy" (see 13:10) is "jealousy" (see 13:45) over the growing influence

of Paul and Barnabas, including the duo's interpretation of Israel's Scriptures.[495]

Perhaps because of the threat this opposition posed for the new converts, "they remained [in Iconium] for a long time" (v. 3*a*)—narrative logic made clear by the use of the conjunction μὲν οὖν (*men oun;* lit., "so therefore") to link vv. 2-3. "Bold" (= inspired; see 4:29-31) proclamation of the "word of grace" and performance of "signs and wonders," all the tried and trusted tools, catalog their prophetic activity (see 2:19, 22, 43; 4:13, 16, 29-30; 5:12; 6:8; 9:27-28). This fresh outpouring of God's Spirit on pagan turf provides evidence that the prospect of salvation has arrived in another region, for the prophecy of Joel is fulfilled here too (see 2:17-21). In this particular Lukan formulation, however, the exalted Lord confirms their religious authority, as God had confirmed his (see 2:22) and the mission of the Twelve (see 2:43). Luke's subsequent use of "apostles," when dividing the assembly into rival factions (14:4), does not suggest Paul's/Barnabas's authority is due to the apostolic office but rather that it is evinced in the performance of their prophetic tasks.[496]

The escalation of tensions in Iconium that required Paul and Barnabas to make a mad dash for Lystra, Derbe, and "the surrounding country" (14:6) sounds a familiar note in Acts (see 13:50-51). As before in Antioch, the opposition party has united Jews and Gentiles against their mission (cf. Luke 23:6-12). In this case, however, the intent is not mere expulsion motivated by a sense of civic duty; the opponents seek "to mistreat them and to stone them" (14:5; see 14:19). The combination of infinitives makes certain we do not mistake their vile behavior as the result of Jewish legal procedure, where stoning is meted out to

---

494. Barrett, *Acts,* 1:668.

495. The Western text of Acts fills in the narrative gap to sharpen the conflict between Jewish leaders and Christian missionaries by substituting "the rulers of the Jewish synagogue and the leaders of the synagogues began persecuting the righteous" for the opening more ambiguous phrase, "The unbelieving Jews."

496. The curious reference to Paul and Barnabas as "apostles" is certainly non-titular, since neither meets the qualifications for membership in the apostolate established by 1:21-22. I doubt that Luke uses an Antiochene source here in which the term "the apostles" refers to commissioning by a local (= Antiochene) congregation, which "sent out" (apostles) Paul and Barnabas as missionaries. Indeed, Acts makes clear that Paul and Barnabas were sent out by the Holy Spirit and not by a local church (see 13:1-3). The best alternative is that "the apostles" is a term of continuity, which reminds the readers that the mission and message of Paul and Barnabas are grounded in the same religious authority and practices as were those of their prophetic (= apostolic) predecessors. See Barrett, *Acts,* 1:671-72; F. S. Spencer, *Acts,* Readings: A New Biblical Commentary (Sheffield: Sheffield Academic, 1997) 149.

blasphemers. The conflict over Paul is political, having to do with the exercise of power, and not theological, having to do with spiritual formation (see 13:44-45). In any case, the "good news" is irrepressible, and persecution only occasions its proclamation is still another urban venue (14:7).[497]

**14:8-20a.** The preceding paragraph had the feel of a missionary report, providing a general, mostly positive summary of Paul's mission in the Lycaonian district. The present passage complements this summary by narrating a specific incident in Lystra. The obvious literary parallelism between this healing story and Peter's healing of the lame man in Jerusalem (see 3:1-8) suggests a similar narrative role, which is to underscore that Paul's religious authority in the Diaspora is commensurate to Peter's authority in Palestine.[498] Moreover, the repetition of "apostles" at the climax of this story (v. 14; see also v. 4) may well point to this narrative intention. The persistence of Paul's concern for his legitimate apostolic authority, reflected by his letters (e.g., 2 Corinthians 11–12; Galatians 1–2), discloses the contested status of his authority during his lifetime. The issue at stake does not appear to be a fractious rivalry with Peter; rather, what matters is whether Paul possesses an authoritative (and independent) witness to Jesus and whether such a witness requires a personal relationship with him (see 1:21-22; cf. 22:15; 26:16). In the case of the Twelve, their physical proximity to the historical Jesus is supplemented by his prophecy of their reign over a restored Israel (cf. Luke 22:29-30)—a gospel tradition that Acts elevates in importance (see 1:1-14). If Paul's religious authority—and his persona, his teaching, and the pattern and results of his urban mission—is second-guessed for the future of Luke's church, then the Evangelist is rightly interested in clarifying and confirming it. If something

like this problem occasioned the writing of Acts (see Introduction, "Acts as Conversation," 5-11), then the purpose of this story is to account for Paul's authority on grounds other than "apostleship" that nonetheless legitimize his continuing importance for the church.

The literary template Luke earlier followed in narrating Peter's healing of the lame man in Jerusalem is employed here as well. By comparing the two stories in common sequence, the reader more easily detects both similarities and also the real differences in Paul's exercise of his religious authority. Accordingly, the church's mission proceeds from a public demonstration of God's benevolent rule: God's healing power is mediated first through Peter and here through Paul (see 3:1-8). Thus, "looking intently and seeing that [the lame man] had faith to be healed [σωθῆναι *sōthēnai*]" (v. 9*b;* see 3:4), Paul heals the man. Unlike the lame man Peter healed, however, this man's faith *precedes* his healing. This important difference makes clear the healed man had first "listened to Paul as he was speaking" (v. 9*a*), and thereby his faith is awakened by what Paul says—that is, by the gospel he proclaims. What is finally awakened in the man's heart results in his salvation symbolized by his healing (see 13:23; cf. 3:16): "And the man sprang up and began to walk" (v. 10; see also 3:8*a*), but not to enter into the nearby temple to worship God as before (see 3:8*b*) since the temple of Lystra belongs to Zeus. The demonstration of Paul's authority, then, is related to his prophetic vocation of preaching the Word of God.

The reader anticipates that those who witness this healing miracle will react in amazement (see v. 11; see also 3:9-10) and that their amazement exposes a theological mistake that the prophet-like-Jesus must correct (see 3:11). In this pagan setting, the crowd mistakes Paul and the silent Barnabas for deities: "Barnabas they called Zeus, and Paul they called Hermes, because he was the chief speaker" (v. 12). So powerful is this misguided impression of Paul that the priest of Zeus "brought oxen and garlands to the gates," ready to offer an appropriate sacrifice to them on behalf of the people (see v. 13). This comedy stands in stark contrast to the hostility of temple priests in Jerusalem toward Peter and reflects a vastly different theological sensibility from that of the observant Jew, who would never think to idolize a

497. Once again the Western text of Acts makes more explicit the popular success of their mission by adding to 14:7 "Every person in the entire crowd was astounded by their teaching."

498. The precise linguistic connections between these two Lukan stories suggest their intentional pairing within Acts: The recipients of God's healing grace are both "crippled from birth" (3:2//14:8); the agents of healing "look intently" at the lame men immediately before healing them (3:5//14:9); both healed men provide the same public evidence of the miracle—"leaping up and walking" (3:8//14:10); both healing miracles take place in the shadow of temple gates (3:2//14:13); both healing miracles illustrate saving faith (3:16//14:9)—in the first case of the apostles and in this case of the lame man; and both are subsequently interpreted in succinct missionary speeches that make clear the connection of faith and the healing/saving power/grace of God (4:8-12//14:15-17).

human being.[499] Ironically, only in this pagan setting at Lystra is it possible to reach "a highpoint in the demonstration of apostolic [sic] powers"[500]—or at least in the public's "appreciation" of them.

The public deification of Paul in the shadow of the temple of Zeus at Lystra sets the stage for a prophet's gesture and speech that clarify the nature of his religious authority. First, Paul and Barnabas "tore their clothes and rushed out into the crowd" (v. 14). This gesture typically reflects inward grief (cf. Gen 37:29-34) and is used in the Gospels to signal a perceived "blasphemy" (cf. Matt 26:65//Mark 14:63; see also Acts 22:23). Here it carries these same connotations as a public protest against pagan enthusiasm that is considered blasphemous by faithful Jews, who are represented here by Paul and Barnabas. The attribution of Barnabas and Paul's authority as "apostles" (v. 14), already expressed by their prophetic actions, is theocentric rather than egocentric or institutional.

Paul's speech underscores this point. He asserts three traditional Jewish beliefs (see 17:22-31): (1) He and Barnabas "are mortals [ὁμοιοπαθής homoiopathēs] just like you,"[501] and so as mortals they "bring you good news" (v. 15a; see also 10:26). (2) The subject of the good news is "the living God, who made the heaven and the earth and sea and all that is in them" (v. 15c; cf. 17:24-25; Exod 20:11), and its predicate is "that you should turn from these worthless things to the living God" (v. 15b). Although framed in a different idiom, presumably apropos to this pagan audience, the deep logic of Paul's message is the same as all other missionary speeches in Acts: Repent of your ignorance and turn to God (see 3:17-19a; 17:30-31). (3) This "living God" has graciously maintained a "witness" to the nations, even though they have routinely rejected God in ignorance "to

follow their own ways" (vv. 16-17a; cf. 2:28; 3:17; 13:27; 17:26-31; Psalm 1 LXX; see esp. Rom 1:18-31). God's good deeds are adumbrated as the "rains" that produce fruitful harvests of "food" that reproduce heart-felt "joy" (v. 17b). Paul's striking contention that these activities do not leave the nations "without a witness [μαρτύρος martyros]" to God's ordinary goodness recall the earlier uses in Acts of witnesses to God's good news (see 1:8; 2:43; 3:15; 5:32; 10:39-41; 13:31; cf. 7:44). If this brief speech offers a correction to the theological mistake made by ignorant pagans, its implied force is this: God's prior witness to the nations consists of nature's good works; but the Creator's divine goodness is now climaxed in a mission that brings the good news of salvation (= healing) to them. The aim of their witness is not hearts gladdened by a full stomach occasioned by a bountiful harvest but hearts gladdened by the Holy Spirit occasioned by forgiveness (see 13:52).

The crowd's responses to Paul all along have been curious. It is as though only the healed man listened to anything he said and is saved as the result. The act of deifying Paul and Barnabas surely cut against the grain of everything Paul had said initially; and now his clarifying speech has concluded and the pagans are still "scarcely restrained . . . from offering sacrifice to them" (v. 18; see also v. 13)—obviously they are still ignorant! Where are Paul's powers of persuasion when he really needs them? For all the local color that enriches this story, there is this note of realism: Not every Gentile audience is won over by Paul's rhetorical brilliance. Those in Lystra are not, perhaps due to the sheer depth of their theological ignorance.

The Jewish problem with Paul is not so benign. Their resistance to his witness in the diaspora has escalated to the point of violence. Evidently their new strategy is to follow Paul wherever he goes—in this case to pagan Lystra from Jewish Antioch (see 13:50) and Iconium (see 14:5)—and attempt to "[win] over the crowds" (14:19a). No reason is given why the once exuberant crowds at Lystra were so quickly turned against Paul: Was it something said but unrecorded? Or did he finally convince them he was a mere mortal after all? In any case, his Jewish opposition evidently succeeds: The crowds "stoned Paul and dragged him out of the city, supposing he was dead" (14:19b; see also

499. Commentators have made much of the literary allusions to Ovid's well-known myth told in *Metamorphoses* 8.617-725 of the elderly couple who wined and dined Zeus and Hermes—who were disguised as humans—without knowing their true identities and were rewarded for their hospitality with appointments as priests of the Phrygian temple of Zeus. See Haenchen, *The Acts of the Apostles*, 432-34. While the myth doubtless contributed to the final shape of Luke's story, his aim is less to explain the crowd's response and more to clarify Paul's religious authority.

500. Ibid., 433.

501. *Homoiopatheis* denotes "with the same [*homoi-*] nature *pathos*" and extends to emotional and psychological characteristics shared by all humans. "Fully human" may be another way of translating this word—"we are fully human just like you."

14:5). But they were wrong about Paul again; he is alive and so "got up and went into the city," from where he left with Barnabus for Derbe (14:20).

Luke's poignant imagery makes a subtle point concerning Paul's religious authority, a point revealed in the narrative gaps. Paul but *not* Barnabas is persecuted and then surrounded by the disciples. Luke has eyes for Paul only. Johnson rightly says Luke's portrayal of Paul's recovery from attack is not about his "irresistible power so much as his indefatigable faith and loyalty. Paul does not return to the city in triumph to best his opponents in a contest of wonders." He returns in the company of friends who have turned to Jesus because of his ministry.[502] This scene nicely captures another dimension of Paul's religious authority: He is able to build a network of supporters whose aid makes it possible to sustain his mission (cf. 14:22, 27-28).

**14:20b-23.** The importance of the final two paragraphs of the narrative of Paul's first mission has less to do with Paul himself and more to do with the protocol he followed in establishing Christian congregations in the diaspora—a social location that connotes separation and struggle. The plotline of this passage is the retracing of previous steps back to Antioch (vv. 20b-21) to strengthen and encourage new converts along the way (v. 22; see also 11:23; 13:43), while entrusting their spiritual leaders to the Lord through acts of prayer and fasting (v. 23). The aim of Paul's pastoral visit is to keep Christians "Christian" in an environment hostile to the faith—a hostility that Paul himself has recently experienced firsthand, in accordance with Jesus' prophecy (see 9:16).

For this reason Paul's message to them interprets their shared struggle: "We must [δεῖ *dei*] go through [διά *dia*] many hardships [θλῖψις *thlipsis*] to enter the kingdom of God" (v. 22; cf. Luke 18:24-25). The word *thlipsis* ("hardships," "persecutions") is used earlier in Acts to recall the circumstances that led to the founding of the Antiochene parish (see 11:19; cf. 8:1-3), the mother church of Paul's mission. Its use here implies that these new converts belong to a community whose roots and reputation are of faithful suffering. More critically, this use of *dei* reminds

502. Johnson, *The Acts of the Apostles,* 256.

one of Paul's synagogue preaching of the Lord's messianic affliction (see 13:27-30; cf. Luke 24:46) and the prophecy of his own mission (see 9:16). In context, then, the suffering of faithful believers is an element of God's plan of salvation and even the gateway (*dia*) through which salvation is entered (cf. 1 Pet 1:10-12). Although this idea of the divine necessity (*dei*) of entering God's kingdom "through many persecutions" helped to shape the cult of martyrs during the century following Luke, it is not so in Acts: God's kingdom has arrived with Christ and the kingdom has already been restored to a repentant Israel. Paul's mission as light to the nations bids Gentiles to share in Israel's blessings—right now, right here.

The appointment of elders (πρεσβύτεροι *presbyteroi*) "in each church" was attended to by prayer and fasting. Paul and Barnabas had also been sent out by the prayer and fasting of a congregation's leaders (see 13:1, 3); now they take responsibility for the selection of leaders for the congregations their mission had founded (cf. 20:17; 2 Cor 8:19; Titus 1:5). The interpreter makes a mistake to think this practice reflects a situation later than Paul—that Luke takes for granted the polity of his day, reflected, for example, in the Pauline Pastorals.[503] In fact, Luke's earlier reference to the "elders" of the Judean congregations (see 11:30) does not suggest novelty but compatibility and continuity between the Gentile and Jewish churches.

**14:24-26.** Barnabas and Paul return to Syrian Antioch (v. 26a), "preaching the word" along the way (v. 25), to conclude their mission where it had originated and where their congregational support lay (see 13:1, 3). With this passage Luke encloses his account of Paul's inaugural mission, using two important phrases—touch points for his entire account, by which we can review the "work" that Paul and Barnabas have been authorized to perform (see 13:2).

The first phrase is that "they had been com-

503. The standard treatment of this notion that the rule of elders over local congregations reflects the polity of the post-Pauline church is H. von Campenhausen, *Ecclesiastical Authority and Spiritual Power in the Church of the First Three Centuries,* trans. J. A. Baker (Stanford: Stanford University Press, 1969). This thesis is simply assumed by most modern commentators; however, the structure for governing the local congregation found in 14:23 (cf. 20:17) and in the Pauline use of "elders/bishops" (1 Timothy 3; 5; and Titus 1) is quite simple and draws its model from the governing structures of the diaspora synagogue (see 11:30) or other voluntary organizations of the Roman world.

mended [= "committed," NIV; παραδίδωμι *para-didōmi*] to the grace of God" (14:26*b*). Luke's choice of verbs is revealing, since in his Bible (the Septuagint) *paradidōmi* carries the negative connotation of being delivered to one's enemies with nasty results (cf. 27:1). He may intend to remind his readers of Paul's suffering provoked by his "work." At the same time, the surety of God's providence is given expression here, since Paul is routinely delivered from his enemies by "the grace of God" (cf. 15:40). At the outset of the story he and Barnabas were sent on their way "by the Holy Spirit" (13:2, 4), which is now replaced by a confessional idiom, "the grace of God." The pairing of God's Spirit and grace in this inclusio makes theological sense in Acts, where "the grace of God" often denotes the "graces" of prophetic ministry (preaching, performance of miraculous signs) that are executed by the inspiration of the Spirit, including in this narrative (see 13:43; 14:3). The second phrase, "for the work that they had completed," repeats "work" (see 13:2; cf. 13:41) as the primary catchword of Luke's inclusio. We are reminded that the work done is divinely authorized and enjoys the favor of God. That it has been "completed" validates God's choice (see 12:25).

## REFLECTIONS

**1.** "Then after fasting and praying they laid their hands on them and sent them off" (13:3 NRSV). The readers of Acts have an advantage over Paul: By eavesdropping on the Lord's prophecy to Ananias, they know something of Paul's future missionary task (see 9:15-16). The practical problem this text addresses is the manner by which Paul himself comes to discern his prophetic calling. Today's church would do well to follow a similar protocol of discernment when commissioning its workers for Christian ministry. What is clear from this text is that spiritual discernment is not a private matter. Paul and Barnabas are "sent off" by the "hands"—a personal touch—of the particular congregation that knows and cares for them. The disclosure that they are given missionary tasks to perform comes to this congregation's leadership from the Holy Spirit. For this reason, a positive discernment of God's clear direction is possible only when the congregation is actively engaged in spiritual practices—worship, fasting, prayer. The Spirit does not communicate with God's people by religious osmosis.

Luke's placement of Paul's encounter with the con artist Elymas (= Bar-Jesus) is strategic in this regard, for in context it confirms the congregation's discernment of Paul's calling. Elymas claims the capacity to divine truth by the power of his spirit; on this basis he seeks to influence the Roman Sergius Paulus. When competing claims of truth are placed on the table, how does one "test the spirits" to discriminate between the true and false prophet? We should follow the lead of an "intelligent" outsider, Sergius, who first gave thoughtful hearing to the "word of God" and then observed the results of the contest between the two prophets, which the Spirit-filled Paul clearly won. The coherence of the message complemented by the powerful consequences of the messenger's work confirmed Paul's calling as a true prophet.

**2.** "They were filled with jealousy and talked abusively against what Paul was saying" (13:45 NIV). How should the church respond to those who make it their public business to reject the gospel? Paul's message is powerfully preached but typically enjoys mixed results. While many who hear Paul's gospel respond by turning to God in faith, many others do not. Ancient narratives are full of action, but they rarely provide reasons for the actions that are taken. In this passage, however, Luke tells us that certain Jews in Pisidian Antioch viewed Paul as their rival and contended against his gospel to retain their political status within the synagogue—a status they share with powerful Gentiles who are attached to the synagogue (13:50). Still other Gentile auditors of Paul's preaching who are attached to the Zeus temple rather than the synagogue also reject the Word of God, but more out of ignorance than rivalry. In each case Paul challenges those who reject his mission by interpreting the eternal consequences for doing so (13:44-47) or by correcting the underlying reasons for his opponents' wrong-headed response (14:15-17).

More important, however, Paul is irrepressible; he boldly continues to do what he is called to do in spite of his public rejection, moving from location to location while seeking out those more responsive to the gospel for special attention (13:47; 14:21-26). While the church should expect opposition to the gospel, whether for political reasons or out of blind ignorance, its response is to be ever agile, willing and able to move to new places in order to minister to different groups who are responsive to its witness to God's good news.

**3.** "After they preached the good news to that city and had made many disciples, they returned to Lystra, then on to Iconium and Antioch" (see 14:21). Paul is an urban missionary. According to Acts, the church's mission is primarily concentrated in important cities, first in Palestine and then beginning with Paul, across the Roman Empire. Why? In part the reasons are sociological and practical: A wide range of people from different cultures and with diverse backgrounds congregated in cities because of their religious, financial, and political resources. Simply put, Paul evangelized cities because that is where concentrations of people were found. However, urban ministry also expresses the purpose of God to save all people. The city in Acts is a religious symbol of God's universal salvation. Nothing can be farther from Luke's theological point than for a congregation to gather in isolation from its surroundings without any interest in reaching out to diverse populations or institutions. The vocation of the urban congregation as exemplified by Paul is to bear witness to the risen Jesus to everyone from the least and last to the rich and famous. God wants us all to hear and receive the good news of salvation.

# Acts 14:27–15:5, The Jerusalem Council: Report and Reaction to Paul's Mission

NIV

27On arriving there, they gathered the church together and reported all that God had done through them and how he had opened the door of faith to the Gentiles. 28And they stayed there a long time with the disciples.

15 Some men came down from Judea to Antioch and were teaching the brothers: "Unless you are circumcised, according to the custom taught by Moses, you cannot be saved." 2This brought Paul and Barnabas into sharp dispute and debate with them. So Paul and Barnabas were appointed, along with some other believers, to go up to Jerusalem to see the apostles and elders about this question. 3The church sent them on their way, and as they traveled through Phoenicia and Samaria, they told how the Gentiles had been converted. This news made all the brothers very glad. 4When they came to Jerusalem, they were welcomed by the church and the apostles and elders, to whom they reported everything God had done through them.

5Then some of the believers who belonged to the party of the Pharisees stood up and said, "The

NRSV

27When they arrived, they called the church together and related all that God had done with them, and how he had opened a door of faith for the Gentiles. 28And they stayed there with the disciples for some time.

15 Then certain individuals came down from Judea and were teaching the brothers, "Unless you are circumcised according to the custom of Moses, you cannot be saved." 2And after Paul and Barnabas had no small dissension and debate with them, Paul and Barnabas and some of the others were appointed to go up to Jerusalem to discuss this question with the apostles and the elders. 3So they were sent on their way by the church, and as they passed through both Phoenicia and Samaria, they reported the conversion of the Gentiles, and brought great joy to all the believers.[a] 4When they came to Jerusalem, they were welcomed by the church and the apostles and the elders, and they reported all that God had done with them. 5But some believers who belonged to the sect of the Pharisees stood up and

a Gk brothers

| N IV | NRSV |
|------|------|
| Gentiles must be circumcised and required to obey the law of Moses." | said, "It is necessary for them to be circumcised and ordered to keep the law of Moses." |

# COMMENTARY

Even if Luke's account of the Jerusalem Council is not the watershed event of his book as many hold, it undoubtedly remains a storm center of modern Acts criticism.[504] Surely Haenchen is still right when commenting shortly after the Second World War that "nearly every scholar has hacked his own way through the jungle of problems, and often it was done in a thoroughly violent fashion."[505] Many simply point to the story's placement in the middle of Luke's narrative as symbolic of its centrality to his theological conception.[506] After all, they claim, here the Paul of Acts shucks off all associations with the Jerusalem church and points the gospel toward Rome as the new epicenter of God's symbolic universe.[507]

I am not convinced. The role this story performs in Acts is not paradigmatic; instead, it is similar to that of a narrative summary that reviews the past rather than introducing something new. That is, this passage provides a literary moratorium in the middle of the story where the reader can take pause to reflect upon the importance of earlier decisions made or actions taken in preparation for what lies ahead. For this purpose, then, the narrator of Acts convenes his central characters a final time to render "official" decisions that confirm the direction and character of God's salvation ever since Pentecost.

Two intramural conflicts over different, but related, matters—one in Antioch (14:27–15:2) and then another in Jerusalem (15:4-5)—occasion the second gathering of an assembly of church eld-

ers (see 11:1-18) to assess God's redemptive plans in light of mission reports (15:6-12) and biblical teaching (15:13-21). The result is a pastoral letter sent from Jerusalem to Antioch that lists general agreements made for the sake of Christian unity (15:22-29). But does their deliberation change the direction of the church's mission or its theological basis? Does James introduce a new pattern of salvation by which faith rather than Torah observance saves? No. The Judean protest in Antioch for a different pattern of salvation is glossed by Peter's citation of Joel's prophecy at Pentecost. This rehearsal stipulates a redemptive pattern from the beginning of these "last days" that emphasizes calling upon Jesus as Lord in order to save non-believers from sin and initiate them into a community of goods ruled over by the Spirit of God (see 2:17-21, 38). Although Luke does not tell us why the "question" carried by the Antiochene delegation to Jerusalem for deliberation (15:2) is set aside in Jerusalem (15:4-5), the reader presumes that such a question is finally considered irrelevant, given the course of salvation to this point in Acts and the unauthorized nature of the protest movement in Antioch (see 15:24).

The conflict in Jerusalem provoked by Pharisaic believers, while more constructive, is *halakhic* in nature, having to do with ethical norms for daily life (see the Commentary on 15:4-5). The objection to Paul's Gentile mission frames a "case study" regarding the appropriate practices of Gentile converts within the church. The issue here is not whether Israel's salvation should be shared with uncircumcised Gentile converts—a decision already affirmed at the first Jerusalem meeting following the conversion of Cornelius (see 11:1-18).[508] Even though Paul and Barnabas

---

504. See B. Witherington, *The Acts of the Apostles: A Socio-Rhetorical Commentary* (Grand Rapids: Eerdmans, 1998) 439-50, for a judicious introduction to the modern history of this scholarly debate. Also noteworthy is Haenchen's discussion of whether to identify this Jerusalem Council with the one mentioned by Paul in Galatians 2. See E. Haenchen, *The Acts of the Apostles* (Philadelphia: Westminster, 1971) 461-72.

505. Haenchen, *The Acts of the Apostles*, 455.

506. See I. H. Marshall, *The Acts of the Apostles*, NTG (Sheffield: JSOT, 1992) 242.

507. See H. Conzelmann, *The Acts of the Apostles*, trans. J. Limburg et al., ed. E. J. Epp and C. R. Matthews, Hermeneia (Philadelphia: Fortress, 1987) 121-22.

508. P. J. Achtemeier, *The Quest for Unity in the New Testament Church: A Study in Paul and Acts* (Philadelphia: Fortress, 1987) 49-55, suggests that Paul's version of the Jerusalem Council in Galatians 2 is actually closer to Acts 11:1-18 than to Acts 15:1-29. Not only are Paul's stated concerns closer to the issues provoked by Cornelius's conversion, but also the leadership of the Jerusalem church is still apostolic and has not yet been succeeded by James, which is clearly the case in Acts 15.

were not in attendance at that first meeting, the repercussions of the earlier decision are evident in their inaugural mission, when God-fearers and pagans alike came to faith in Christ (see 13:42-52; 14:8-10).

And what about Jerusalem, the location of this assembly? Is Haenchen correct that "up to Chapter 15 all roads lead to Jerusalem" and afterward to Rome? Do the council proceedings mark a geographical if not an ecclesiastical turning point?[509] No again. In fact, God's salvation has traveled on roads leading out of Jerusalem since Acts 8. Moreover, the association of the Jerusalem Twelve with various missions beyond the holy city is collaborative; there is no sense that missions led by other prophets-like-Jesus must be subordinate to Jerusalem's prerogatives for legitimacy (see 8:4-40). This is certainly true of the Antiochene mission, whose independence from Jerusalem is symbolized both by the effect of Paul's teaching at Antioch, which distinguishes believers there as "Christians" for the first time (see 11:25-26), and by the congregation's food offering for the Judean church (see 11:27-30). Moreover, the circle of the Jerusalem Apostolate has already been broken and was never repaired, leading to a succession of authority to other leaders (see 12:1-19; cf. 6:1-7). While it is true that Peter and Barnabas appear no more in Acts, the church continues its mission to the Jews in Palestine (see Acts 21:20-21).

The practical purpose of this and other meetings in Jerusalem, then, is an exercise not of religious authority but of corporate solidarity in fulfilling the church's vocation in the world. Paul makes no paradigmatic speech or symbolic gesture in this story, even though Peter makes a cameo appearance (see 15:6-11). He even continues to share the stage with Barnabas, who otherwise has been his silent partner (15:4, 12). The verdict James renders provides Scripture's validation to what God has already authorized and Paul has already realized (see 15:13-21); James offers nothing really new to the reader of Acts, even though he shifts the gravity of the debate from the practice of circumcision to the purity concerns of table fellowship (see 15:19-21). His rhetorical role is to clarify and confirm what the reader already knows, and his decision or the subsequent "decree" does not change

Paul's message or the pattern of his mission. The Paul of Acts is more polite than the Paul of Galatians, but he is just as resolved in his prophetic identity and missionary vocation. Thus, the reader of Acts is no more or no less confident of Paul's authority after Acts 15 than before, where the value of Paul's prophetic agency in the history of God's salvation is already made evident by the Lord's prophecy (see 9:15-16) and its fulfillment during Paul's first mission. All that is left to tell in Acts is the story of *how* Paul gets to "the end of the earth"; whether he will do so is never in doubt, before or after Jerusalem. Acts 15 is more a rest stop than a gateway toward that end.

Passing reference was made earlier to the troublesome relationship between Acts 15 and Galatians 2. Without minimizing the complexity or importance of the issues at stake, I suspect that most disagreements are in details that are responsibly explained as the literary reflection of Luke and Paul's different pastoral interests, historical perspectives, and theological commitments. These inform compositions of different genres written for different audiences. Fair-minded scholars acknowledge real disagreements between Acts and any Pauline letter, but to privilege either text is theologically and historically tendentious. In fact, when proper consideration is given the conciliatory bent of Luke and the polemics of Paul, the substance and ethos of their reports of a Jerusalem meeting are quite complementary. Both reports underscore the independence and authority of Paul's mission, and both agree that its results accord with God's redemptive purposes.

Among several insoluble disagreements between the two, the most serious is whether an "apostolic decree" (see 15:22-29) was ever issued. Paul never mentions an "official" decree in Galatians, and he claims that the Jerusalem accord promptly dissolves during the infamous "incident at Antioch" (Gal 2:11-14). Besides attempting to resolve various chronological issues, the interpreter should resist using the phrase "apostolic decree" to characterize the results of this meeting. Luke's account does not indicate that the accord reached in Jerusalem is then mandated upon rank-and-file believers in Antioch. The impression cultivated—especially with the invocation of the Spirit's partnership (see 15:28)—is that the publication of the council's agreements function like a

509. Haenchen, *The Acts of the Apostles,* 461.

pastoral exhortation and that they are joyfully embraced by other believers as such (see 15:31). How does this square with the more polemical tone and substance of Gal 2:11-14? Surely Paul would not have easily embraced the specific terms of the pastoral exhortation as stipulated in Acts 15:20-21, 29. Holmberg is probably right when suggesting that Luke conflates two different episodes—the council and the writing of the pastoral exhortation—as an integral whole, when in fact the Antioch incident that Paul speaks of in Gal 2:11-14 probably happened sometime between the two.[510]

**14:27-28.** This passage describes the initial report Paul and Barnabas make of their missionary adventure in the diaspora; they do so in Antioch, their home congregation. In solidarity with them, "they called the church together" to hear their mission report of "all that God had done with them," the theological substance of which is that "God had opened a door of faith to the Gentiles." Salvation is God's activity; and God's Spirit enables a working partnership with prophets-like-Jesus such as Paul and Barnabas, "with whom" God works in the world as witnesses to God's Messiah.

The use of the metaphor "door of faith" (θύρα πίστεως *thyra pisteōs*) nicely captures the thematic interest in faith—faith in the truth proclaimed as the word of the Lord is requisite for sharing in the messianic blessings promised by God (see 13:39, 48; 14:22, 23). "Door" suggests a divine openness to or opportunity given Gentiles to participate in the blessings God had promised Jews (cf. 1 Cor 16:9; 2 Cor 2:12; Col 4:3). The door is opened to repentant Gentiles not because of unrepentant Israel but because of a repentant, restored Israel, which is now able to lay hold of its prophesied vocation, embodied in Paul and Barnabas, to be "a light for the Gentiles" (13:47). This is an upbeat report, with mention made of the conflict that followed Paul from town to town. The reader's mind is concentrated upon what God has done in partnership with these prophets-like-Jesus to save repentant Gentiles.

**15:1-2.** The Jerusalem Council concerns conflict resolution—a more difficult project because there are actually two conflicts within two differ-

ent congregations that need resolution. The first intramural conflict takes place in Syrian Antioch, where Paul's mission report has apparently provoked protest from "certain individuals came down from Judea" (v. 1*a*). Their protest concerns the conversion of uncircumcised Gentiles, whether circumcision is necessary for their salvation: "Unless you are circumcised according to the custom of Moses, you cannot be saved" (v. 1*b*).

Among a range of possible responses to Pauline preaching within the Jewish church, theirs is a more conservative expression.[511] The subtext of their protest is a long-standing Jewish tradition that the rite of circumcision is central to the public identity of a covenant people (see Genesis 17). Thus, for example, when the Syrians attempted to suppress the practice of circumcision two centuries before, presumably for political reasons, Israel revolted under its Maccabean leadership (1 Macc 1:60-61) to assert circumcision as a national priority (1 Macc 2:46). To define one's Jewish identity on some other terms is tantamount to apostasy and grounds for exclusion from the covenant community (1 Macc 1:11-15). Naturally, then, circumcision was expected of every proselyte who expected to share in Israel's blessings according to the promise God made Abraham (see 3:25-26). Beyond Palestine in the diaspora, however, the literal observance of this initiatory rite was not always practiced. Paul's appeal— written a few decades before Acts—to the deuteronomic injunction of a spiritualized circumcision in Rom 2:29 (see also Deut 10:16; Jer 4:4; 9:25 LXX) may reflect the prevailing teaching of more liberal diaspora communities that did not require their proselytes to undergo the physically painful rite of circumcision. The rite of initiation was reduced to a symbolic exercise, more a matter of the heart than of the flesh.

This spiritualizing of the rite of circumcision may well have upset the more traditional Jews from Judea who believed that the apostasy of Maccabean Syria is revisiting Paul's mission and the believers in Syrian Antioch. The first Jerusalem Council, however, had already given tacit approval

---

510. B. Holmberg, *Paul and Power,* ConBNTS 11 (Lund: CWK Gleerup, 1978) 11-34, provides the best discussion of the critical problems.

511. These opponents of Paul, frequently noted in his letters (e.g., Rom 16:17-20; Gal 2:11-14; Phil 3:2, 18-19), are sometimes called "Judaizers." Luke portrays them as an extreme and unauthorized (see Acts 15:24) expression of the Jewish church's opposition to Paul's mission.

of the conversion of uncircumcised Cornelius (see 11:18). For this reason the protest movement in Antioch is made up of renegade rigorists who act "without portfolio" from their religious leaders in Jerusalem (see 15:24). Nonetheless, they have insinuated themselves into the mixed congregation in Antioch as custodians of Jewish tradition. The readers of Acts know they are wrong on the issue, since at Pentecost Peter cites the prophet Joel to establish that God's pattern of salvation includes everyone who "calls upon the name of the Lord" in faith—the very theological point developed from that moment forward in the narrative.

The result of their presence in Antioch is "no small dissension and debate." The congregation's constructive response is the formation of a delegation "to discuss this question with the apostles and elders" of Jerusalem (v. 2). Since these "certain individuals" from Judea are members of the Jerusalem church and are under the spiritual authority of its leaders, the decision is left for those leaders to make—not as an exercise in ecclesiastical authority but as an act of corporate solidarity.

**15:3.** The repeated pattern of a mission report (14:27-28//15:4) followed by contentious reaction (15:1-2//15:5) encloses and therefore highlights this oft-neglected travelogue sandwiched between. The careful design of Luke's account of the intramural dissension that occasioned this second Jerusalem assembly would seem to indicate the pivotal role of this verse.[512]

The reader is simply told that on the way from Antioch to Jerusalem the appointed delegation "reported [ἐκδιηγέομαι *ekdiēgeomai*] the conversion of the Gentiles." The implication is that their primary concern is not the dust-up back home—perhaps even that they dismiss the "question" about circumcision raised in Antioch by the Judean believers. Upon closer reading, however, the reader's attention is drawn not to the implied subject matter of the report, which we already know (see 14:27-28), but to the act of "reporting" it. Luke's use of an exceptional verb for "reporting" (*ekdiēgeomai*) is striking. It is used only here and in Acts 13:41 within the NT. This fact suggests that Luke echoes Acts 13:41 in order to

recall Paul's prophetic warning and the resulting dissension among *unrepentant* Jews (see 13:44-47) his ministry in Pisidian Antioch occasioned as as a context for reading the present story of dissension among *repentant* Jews. His earlier warning is recalled as the subtext of the subsequent gathering of the Jerusalem Council: To scoff at Paul's mission report runs the risk of divine judgment. The sense of urgency that pervades this meeting, then, is not whether traditional Jews embrace Paul's mission to the nations, nor even whether the purity and practices of uncircumcised Gentile believers will subvert the church's social solidarity or its Jewish legacy. The implied threat lies not with Paul's mission but with the obduracy of certain Jewish believers whose protests of Paul's mission threaten *their* membership within the restored Israel of God.

**15:4-5.** The pattern of mission report/reaction repeats itself in Jerusalem, although in softened tones. Paul and Barnabas are welcomed by the whole "church," which hears their mission report of "all that God had done with them" (v. 4//14:27-28). What is surprising here is that the floor is then given to Pharisees, who are evidently members of the Jewish church that has already welcomed Paul and Barnabas. Moreover, their opinion is not dismissed by the church leadership as marginal but is taken seriously, in marked contrast to the earlier protest in Antioch that apparently had been dismissed as unwarranted.

The Pharisees are concerned that believers live within carefully prescribed social and theological boundaries (= *halakhah*), especially when sharing table fellowship with impure sinners. Their earnest commitment in relating biblical teaching to the practices of true religion reflects a larger commitment to the community's purity before a Holy God and within a profane world (cf. Jas 1:27). Their angle of vision toward Gentile circumcision is slanted differently than Paul's opponents in Syrian Antioch, where the issue at stake obtains to the salvation of uncircumcised Gentiles. The Pharisees in the Jerusalem church are not troublemakers; they rightly press for an "official" interpretation regarding the religious *practices* of repentant Gentiles according to Israel's Scriptures, whether they should include the rite of circumcision. The question raised about uncircumcised but repentant Gentiles is not about their forgiveness;

---

512. See R. W. Wall, "The Function of LXX Habakkuk 1:5 in the Book of Acts," *BBR* 10/2 (2000) 247-58.

the text implies the Pharisees were part of the congregation's hospitable response to the Antioch delegation's arrival in Jerusalem (v. 4; cf. v. 24). The issue at stake has shifted, then, from soteriology to sociology—that is, to seeking clarification whether the practice of circumcision should remain the leading symbol of the proselyte's fellowship with repentant Jews within the whole church. The

Pharisees' assertion that "it is necessary [δεῖ *dei*] for them to be circumcised" is introduced by the familiar Lukan idiom of "divine necessity," which in turn frames the "case study" the council now convenes to consider: *Does the practice of circumcising repentant Gentiles in "the last days" of salvation's history accord with God's will?* (See Reflections at 15:6-12.)

## Acts 15:6-12, The Jerusalem Council: Evidence That Demands a Verdict

### NIV

⁶The apostles and elders met to consider this question. ⁷After much discussion, Peter got up and addressed them: "Brothers, you know that some time ago God made a choice among you that the Gentiles might hear from my lips the message of the gospel and believe. ⁸God, who knows the heart, showed that he accepted them by giving the Holy Spirit to them, just as he did to us. ⁹He made no distinction between us and them, for he purified their hearts by faith. ¹⁰Now then, why do you try to test God by putting on the necks of the disciples a yoke that neither we nor our fathers have been able to bear? ¹¹No! We believe it is through the grace of our Lord Jesus that we are saved, just as they are."

¹²The whole assembly became silent as they listened to Barnabas and Paul telling about the miraculous signs and wonders God had done among the Gentiles through them.

### NRSV

6The apostles and the elders met together to consider this matter. 7After there had been much debate, Peter stood up and said to them, "My brothers,[a] you know that in the early days God made a choice among you, that I should be the one through whom the Gentiles would hear the message of the good news and become believers. 8And God, who knows the human heart, testified to them by giving them the Holy Spirit, just as he did to us; 9and in cleansing their hearts by faith he has made no distinction between them and us. 10Now therefore why are you putting God to the test by placing on the neck of the disciples a yoke that neither our ancestors nor we have been able to bear? 11On the contrary, we believe that we will be saved through the grace of the Lord Jesus, just as they will."

12The whole assembly kept silence, and listened to Barnabas and Paul as they told of all the signs and wonders that God had done through them among the Gentiles.

[a] Gk *Men, brothers*

## COMMENTARY

Part one of Acts—a "narrative of conversion"—concludes in a setting vaguely reminiscent of a courtroom drama in which a jury of peers, consisting of "apostles and elders," gathers "to consider this matter [λόγος *logos*]" (v. 6). The case brought by certain Pharisaic members of the Jerusalem church is whether circumcision is a "divine necessity" for Gentile converts (see vv. 4-5). The evidence considered includes relevant tes-

timony from Peter, who rehearses the story of Cornelius's conversion (see vv. 7-11), and then from Barnabas and Paul, who summarize for a third time what "God had done through them among the Gentiles" (v. 12; see also v. 4; 14:27; cf. 2:22). Their combined witness to the nature of Gentile conversion will provide the raw material for James's commentary on a prophecy from Amos (see vv. 13-21).

**15:6.** Those who brought the case to public hearing are now excused for an "executive session" of the church's "apostles and elders" (cf. 6:1-2; 11:1-2). Too much has been made of the politics of this assembly, whether Luke's passing reference to "apostles and elders" says anything about a succession of leadership within the Jerusalem community from the apostles to its elders. In fact, the succession to new leadership within Jerusalem has already taken place (see 11:27–12:25). The apostle Peter, who no longer resides in Jerusalem (see 12:17), is present to provide testimony; it is elder James who interprets the evidence in settling the case before the council. Their activity is "to consider" (ἰδεῖν περί *idein peri;* lit., "to look into") this matter, which suggests that they have convened as a rabbinic lawcourt to deliberate over an issue of *halakhah.*[513]

**15:7-11.** Peter's portrait in Acts stands behind his testimony. Here is the friend of Jesus, his principal apostolic successor, whose powerful prophetic ministry had congregated a restored Israel in fulfillment of biblical prophecy. Here is the Peter whose miraculous escape from prison merely adds the climactic entry to the *vita* of his life's work. Here is the legendary prophet-like-Jesus par excellence whose witness is unimpeachable. He alone—not James or Paul—has the authority to supply the terms of Israel's future identity.

It is now commonplace to say that Luke's shaping of Peter's testimony is "Luke being Pauline."[514] Luke's unfolding portrait of Peter in Acts, however, should reflect the latter's theological development, especially in light of his own diverse missionary experiences and the growing influence of Paul upon the future of the church. To think that Luke composed Peter's testimony to impersonate Paul, presuming that the historical Peter remained unaffected by what was happening around him, is a highly dubious conjecture. Even so, the deep logic of Peter's speech and the idiom of his testimony are Pauline, and in fact they follow closely the argument found in Paul's Letter to the Romans. The careful reader will note, for instance, the following similarities: (1) Peter's claim that God

chose him to carry "the message of the good news" to the Gentiles, along with the pairing of their hearing and believing, loudly echoes Paul's own description of his apostolic vocation (v. 7*b;* cf. Rom 1:5); (2) his reference to God's investigation of the human heart (v. 8; cf. Rom 8:27), (3) without partiality (v. 9*b;* cf. Rom 2:11; 3:22) (4) according to a person's faith (v. 9*a;* cf. Rom 10:8-10); and (5) his contrast between the impossibility of carrying out all the law's demands (v. 10; cf. Rom 2:25-27) and the universal need for God's grace (v. 11), which nicely formulates a familiar Pauline teaching (13:38-39; cf. Rom 3:21-26; also Eph 2:5-8).

**15:7-9.** Peter reprises his decisive testimony at the first Jerusalem Council (see 11:4-17) by concentrating on God's prerogatives: "God made a choice [ἐκλέγομαι *eklegomai*] among you" (v. 7; cf. 11:5-14), "[God] testified to them by giving them the Holy Spirit" (v. 8; cf. 11:15), "[God] made no distinction between them [= Gentiles] and us [= Jews]" (v. 9; cf. 11:12, 17). God's will is publicly disclosed in the conversion of Cornelius, the circumstances of which have already been ratified by an earlier council in praise of God that "God has given even to the Gentiles the repentance that leads to life" (11:18). End of debate.

Peter's assertion that the church's mission to uncircumcised Gentiles is God's "choice" recalls other uses of *eklegomai* in Acts for initiatives that fulfill God's redemptive purposes (see 1:2, 24-25; 6:5; 13:17). In combination with the phrase "the message [*logos*] of the good news," which occurs only here in the NT (cf. 20:24), Peter underscores that the hearing and believing of the preached gospel are the principal means by which the divine purpose is achieved.[515]

Peter's mention of the reception of the Holy Spirit as divine confirmation (v. 8) perhaps alludes to the curious timing of the Gentile Pentecost, when the Spirit fell upon Cornelius before Peter had chance to finish his gospel presentation (see 10:44). No outward gesture of belief or conversion experience is noted by the narrative; God, "who knows the human heart . . . [gave] them the Holy Spirit" as testimony to what God found there. That this gift of salvation is predicated on inward trust

513. Barrett, *Acts,* 2:713.
514. G. Lüdemann, *Early Christianity According to the Traditions in Acts* (Minneapolis: Fortress, 1989) 167.

515. See L. T. Johnson, *The Acts of the Apostles,* SP 5 (Collegeville, Minn.: Liturgical, 1992) 262-63.

and not on some public confession or rite may very well insinuate a standard of "divine necessity" into this hearing that meets the Pharisees' implied requirement (see v. 5)—not that of circumcision, a public rite of initiation, but rather a heartfelt response to the gospel that only God need detect.

The final and most important element of Peter's theological reflection repeats in sharper fashion his earlier claim that "God has made no distinction [οὐθὲν διέκρινεν *outhen diekrinen*] between them [= Gentiles] and us [= Jews]" (see 10:34; 11:17; cf. Rom 2:11; 3:22; 10:12; Gal 2:6; Col 3:25//Eph 6:9). Significantly, his repetition of διακρίνω (*diakrinō*) recalls the ambivalence of Peter's initial struggle to understand his calling to uncircumcised Cornelius, when the Spirit instructed him to do so "without hesitation" (μηδὲν διακρινόμενος *mēden diakrinomenos,* 10:20) and then also "by circumcised believers" in Jerusalem who reacted to the report that Peter enjoyed table fellowship with Cornelius with criticism (διεκρίνοντο *diekrinonto,* 11:2). This string of textual connections rehearses the difficult history of the present debate but also reminds the reader of God's "judgment" that repentant Gentiles, even though uncircumcised, will share in the blessings of Israel's salvation.

This leads Peter to conclude climactically that God has cleansed the hearts of Gentiles by faith rather than by ritual purification, whether symbolized by circumcision or table fellowship (so 15:9). This emphasis again responds to the Pharisees who are rightly concerned with the purity (and perhaps parity) of uncircumcised Gentiles within the faith community but who want to define the issues at stake in traditional terms.

**15:10-11.** Peter's rhetorical question, "Why are you putting God to the test?" (v. 10), calls the council back to the relevant issue at stake: whether the circumcision of Gentiles is a necessary practice of Christian community. Peter's rhetoric should not be taken as polemical; this is a juridical hearing among colleagues who have to this point not even hinted at leaning one way or another. In context, then, the idea of testing God refers to the Apostle's just rendered theological judgments as establishing a norm for discerning God's will. To set aside his witness to God's activity is to subvert God's redemptive purpose since Pentecost.

Peter now prods the council in a manner that echoes Paul's definition of "the true Jew" in Romans (see Rom 2:25-29). Recalling Paul's argument helps to clarify the Lukan Peter's argument for the reader. Paul stipulates as a general principle the meaninglessness of circumcision as an initiation ritual if the observant Jew cannot then meet the legal obligations of the covenant community into which he is initiated: Such a Jew in effect becomes "uncircumcised" (see Rom 2:25) and is no better in God's view than the uncircumcised Gentile whose moral accomplishment is roughly the same (see Rom 2:26-27). The disciple's identity, whether Jew or Greek, must be predicated on grounds other than Torah purity; it must be evinced by a new life in the Spirit who circumcises the believer's heart and enables her to live in a transformed manner (see Rom 2:28-29). Paul's argument is neither novel nor revolutionary. He draws upon the Torah's own argument to warrant his claims: True circumcision is a matter of the heart (see Lev 26:41; Deut 10:16; 30:6; Jer 4:4; 9:26; Ezek 44:7-9). No doubt the eschatological horizon of this teaching is Jeremiah's prophecy of a "new covenant," when the restored Israel would live in covenant with God through a transformed (and therefore obedient) heart (so Jer 31:33). This eschatological horizon has been brought into view for everyone who repents because of Jesus. God's promise to Israel, then, is not revoked, and Israel's truest identity can now be realized because of the Messiah (see Romans 9–11).

Peter's conclusion addresses the purity of a Jewish social identity within an inclusive faith community. If Torah purity demands utter blamelessness and this state is impossible to attain, then the Pharisees' concern is misplaced even if sincere. More to his (and Paul's) point is that such a perspective actually subverts a Jewish identity marked by trusting a faithful God to "save [us] through the grace of the Lord Jesus" (v. 11).

**15:12.** Often overlooked in Luke's narrative of the Jerusalem Council, this verse functions strategically with Acts 2:22 to enclose Luke's narrative commentary of Joel's prophecy of the "last days" cited by Peter at Pentecost (see the Overview to 2:14–15:12). The assembly's "silence" is not due so much to their unspoken agreement with Peter's words but rather is a rhetorical device to direct the reader's attention to what is said next and to listen more carefully "to Barnabas and Paul as they told of all the signs and wonders that God had done through them among the Gentiles." Their final mission report of what "God had done" highlights the theme of Peter's speech that God's election of Peter to carry the gospel to the Gentiles and God's testimony to their salvation in the "Gentile Pentecost" is now consummated by the prophetic work done through Paul and Barnabas among the Gentiles (Acts 13–14).

With testimonies from Peter (vv. 6-11; cf. 11:1-18) and from Barnabas and Paul (v. 12; cf. 14:27-28; 15:3-4), Luke's "narrative of conversion" concludes and the full meaning of Joel's prophecy is clarified: God has poured out the Holy Spirit upon witnesses to carry God's word into the whole world, to the Jew first and then to the Gentile. All who repent and call upon the Lord Jesus in faith are saved from their sins and receive the gift of the Spirit in equal measure. The primary theological subtext of this first half of Acts is whether God is faithful to the biblical promise of a restored Israel (1:6; 3:19-20). The short answer is yes. According to Acts 2:22–15:12, the Spirit's repeated outpouring testifies to God's continuing faithfulness to Israel, not so much by its transforming presence as by its empowering agency that enables a people's compelling witness to the risen Messiah. The church's Spirit-filled mission goes first to the entire house of Israel to call out a community of repentant Jews for a "season of refreshment" (Acts 2–9). This same Spirit then empowers this community to fulfill God's call as "a light to the nations," beginning with Peter (Acts 10–12) and more fully personified in Paul (Acts 13–14). God's salvation of the Jew first and then the Gentile through common prophetic witness with shared blessings envisages the stunning impartiality of God's faithfulness (10:34-48).

# REFLECTIONS

"Paul and Barnabas and some of the others were appointed to go up to Jerusalem to discuss this question with the apostles and the elders" (15:2 NRSV). L. Johnson characterizes the Jerusalem Council as a "theological process" because the decisions made there determine how the church understands itself as a people belonging to God.[516] It is a long and reflective process characterized by sharp and sometimes heated conflict within the church. The importance of theological controversy for initiating a process of discernment is a literary theme of importance in Acts; yet, it sounds a dissonant note for most readers, who have been encouraged to agree with their leaders and conform to their religious traditions. In such situations, appeals are typically made to biblical texts that extol the importance of Christian unity to support uniformity. If agreement is not possible, the disgruntled are advised either to remain silent or to leave the congregation to find or form another. Especially within the Protestant church, church shopping and schisms are responses of first resort when theological debates are not resolved amicably. Tragically, some leave never again to return to a community of faith.

While sharp disagreement between believers is always hard and must be confronted and resolved in every case, the passionate exchange of different opinions is a crucial element of any process by which a faithful people seek to understand the will of God. Reform and renewal are sometimes the Spirit-led results of open protest and debate between earnest believers of the same congregation. Indeed, Acts considers this prospect with considerable optimism! The practical problem, however, is that the leaders of most congregations lack expertise or effective models to guide a congregation through intramural conflict toward a constructive end. Moreover, those on different sides of an issue often lack the kind of civility that resists demanding too much change at once. In my experience, this is especially true of the "liberal" who demands that the "conservative" change quickly and more completely than is practically possible.

If a more civil debate is welcomed, the relevant question is, What are the "rules of engage-

516. L. Johnson, *Decision Making in the Church* (Philadelphia: Fortress, 1983) 86-87.

ment" to guide participants toward a formative end? The following observations may be helpful in this regard.[517]

(1) The congregation should acknowledge that open disagreement between earnest believers is formative of Christian theological understanding. Constructive disagreements are finally *not* between believers over issues of power and personality but about God over issues of theological formation. Sometimes the most important pastoral task is to help members of the congregation distinguish between the *motives* that prompt their disagreement. Purposeful debate of the sort that should be encouraged is aimed at settling issues about who God is and how God acts in our midst. Disagreeable believers who debate issues out of pride, peevishness, or personal ambition allow their disagreements to destroy congregations and make reconciliation, which is God's work, impossible.

(2) Present disagreements between believers typically have a long prehistory. For instance, the strife in Antioch that prompted the convening of the Jerusalem Council began much earlier with the conversion and Spirit baptism of the uncircumcised Gentile, Cornelius. Then Paul's mission beyond Palestine and the congregations he founded there press the theological boundaries of the accord subsequently reached between Peter and the elders of the Jewish church. Reading the story of the Jerusalem Council in its narrative context reminds the reader that conflict resolution should include the "long view" of a particular issue, where its entire prehistory informs its present debate. To do so relativizes and contextualizes our disagreements by bringing other voices from different venues to the same table; the result often diminishes their animosity.

(3) The primary evidence offered is personal testimony, and personal testimony is largely shaped by one's experiences of God. First Peter (15:7-11) and then Barnabas and Paul (15:12) testify to the entire assembly what God has done through them; their audience keeps silent and listens carefully to their stories (15:12-13). Open and formative debate between earnest believers within a congregational setting is largely narrative in shape, existential in substance, and practical in aim. Public testimony is never a monologue intended to draw attention to the speaker. Rather, personal testimony is illustrative of a community's witness and serves to shape its identity and future direction.

(4) The primary authorization offered is scriptural. While public testimony of personal experience is decisive, it cannot settle debates between believers. God's will is made known finally by God's word. According to Acts, the teacher's faithful interpretation of Scripture and the leading of the Holy Spirit are intertwined. When James writes down his exhortation for the believers of Antioch and asserts that it agrees with what "seemed good to the Holy Spirit" (15:28), he recalls his reading of Scripture as the authoritative commentary on the personal testimony just heard. The congregation discerns the Spirit's direction when its teachers use Scripture to both warrant and explain their experience of God.

(5) James's interpretation of Scripture envisages something of a compromise solution that accepts the personal testimony of the missionaries to the Gentiles on the one hand and seeks to maintain the church's Jewish heritage on the other. It is often necessary for decision makers to forge careful compromises between two competing positions to preserve Christian unity, whenever each person or party makes a valuable contribution. It must be said that James does not bring both sides of the issue together as a political accommodation in which both sides make grudging concessions and wind up equally unhappy; he offers a theological affirmation of each as a critical part of a more robust whole. This result is characteristic of *good* theology: to propose constructive solutions that enable the church to go forward.

(6) The verdict that James renders is not only a compromise but it is also a corrective. That is, James not only recognizes that God has acted through both Peter and Paul to call Gentiles

---

517. My profound thanks are due Professor Richard B. Steele for his incisive (and private) comments on an earlier draft of this reflection.

into the covenant community but he also realizes the dangers of allowing uncircumcised Gentiles into a community whose heritage is Jewish. Good theology facilitates new ways of thinking about God when new situations require it; however, good theology is ever alert to the danger of discarding the non-negotiable "old" for the "new." While James says "no" to the Pharisaic believers, he also sounds the cautionary note to the missionaries to guard against facile cultural compromise that renders "Moses" irrelevant. Yes, Paul should continue to evangelize uncircumcised Gentiles, but he should search them out in places where Jewish traditions have helped to shape their religious sensibilities.

(7) While the community's leaders are convened as the "official" council to receive "this question" (15:2) or hear that protest (15:5) between believers, they communicate their decisions and offer appropriate exhortations and other resources to the entire church (15:22-29). Even disagreements between two individuals may spread to the entire congregation; therefore, their settlements should be communicated in all civility to everyone affected to guide future decisions.

(8) Present disagreements between believers typically have a long posthistory. Paul's bumpy relations with the Jewish church are not settled by the Jerusalem Council. Controversies continue to swirl around his mission as he extends the reach of the word of God in new settings. An ongoing review of James's decisive exhortation is required in order to update God's will for the present community of believers (see 21:25). Perhaps this is the final exam whether or not the community has properly discerned God's will: Does the settlement of a momentary disagreement between believers result in an understanding of God that influences the future of the entire congregation in positive ways?

# ACTS 15:13–28:28

# PART TWO: A NARRATIVE OF CONSECRATION

## OVERVIEW

The literary structure of Part Two of Acts is similar to that of Part One: James, Peter's successor, cites (15:16-18; cf. 2:17-21) and then interprets (15:19-21; cf. 2:22-36) Scripture's prophecy (specifically, Amos) of restored Israel, which supplies the theological substructure for the second half of Luke's narrative. The brackets of this narrative unit are again indicated by repetition of a catchword—in this case, "listen." Just as James bids his audience to "listen to me" (15:13), so also Paul concludes his haunting indictment of unrepentant Israel by predicting that God will include repentant Gentiles to share in Israel's salvation because "they will listen" to God's Word (28:28). The narrative within this inclusio recovers an expanded understanding of Amos's prophecy that in turn makes the reader ever more alert to what is at stake in "listening" to God's Word. Further, the Amos prophecy continues the narrative theme introduced by Joel and developed to this point in Acts: God's rebuilding of Israel will find a place for "all the Gentiles who are *called* by my *name*" (15:17, author's trans.; cf. 2:21; 3:19-26). In particular the repetition of the "call" upon the Savior's "name" confirms God's promise to bless "all the families of earth" is now being fulfilled through the church's mission.

James use of a different name for Peter signals a shift of thematic emphasis in Acts, much as the change from Saul to Paul had earlier cued a turn in plotline toward Rome (see 13:9): "*Simeon* has related how God first looked favorably on the Gentiles" (15:14).[518] In fact, James's commentary on biblical prophecy introduces new words and themes by which the reader can better track God's salvation to "the end of the earth." In particular, "rebuild" (ἀνοικοδομέω *anoikodomeō*, lit., "housing") is a restoration metaphor recalled again and again in the stories of various "households" (οἰκία *oikia*) and "houses" (οἶκος *oikos*) that provide a strategic locus of Paul's urban mission. Even the reference to a Davidic "tent" (σκηνή *skēnē*; NRSV, "dwelling") resonates with Paul the "tent-maker" (σκηνοποιός *skēnopoios*, 18:3) who is Israel's brightest "light" in God's new housing project.

More significant, James no longer appears interested in the original question of whether converted Gentiles should be circumcised according to Mosaic teaching. The matter of *halakhah* (teaching on legal matters) he now introduces concerns the purity of diaspora Christian congregations where uncircumcised Gentiles and repentant Jews worship together, with a potentially deleterious effect upon the authority of the Jewish legacy they share (15:19-21, 29; cf. 21:25). The vital issue of Gentile purity for James is not the same as for Peter, who claims that uncircumcised Gentiles were purified of heart by their faith in Christ (see 15:9). The relevant issue for James is ecclesiological—and more sociological than spiritual (see the Commentary on 15:19-21).[519] If the implied

Simeon's prophecy on the basis of the evidence just heard from Simon Peter. See R. Riesner, "James's Speech (Acts 15:13-21), Simeon's Hymn (Luke 2:29-32), and Luke's Sources," in *Jesus of Nazareth: Lord and Christ*, ed. J. Green and M. Turner (Grand Rapids: Eerdmans, 1994) 263-78. The case for viewing the *Nunc Dimittis* as the intertextual allusion of James's "Simeon" would be strengthened by extending the text to include Simeon's prophecy of a divided Israel in Luke 2:34-35, which is evidently fulfilled because of the Gentile mission as well.

519. The particular *halakhic* matter James has in mind when commenting upon the Amos prophecy is the levitical concern for the effect of "the practices of the nations" upon Jewish purity or when "resident aliens" mingle with faithful Jews (Leviticus 17–18). See R. Bauckham, "James and the Gentiles (Acts 15:13-21)," in *History, Literature, and Society in the Book of Acts*, ed. B. Witherington (Cambridge: Cambridge University Press, 1996).

518. There is no textual evidence to support the NIV's "Simon"; this translation simply recognizes the logic that James is apparently responding to Peter (and therefore to "Simon") and not to someone else named "Simeon." R. Riesner has rehabilitated an ancient interpretation (Chrysostom's) that James is not referring to Simon Peter but to the Simeon of Luke's Gospel, whose *Nunc Dimittis* prophecy (Luke 2:29-32) predicts that the salvation that comes with Jesus will extend "as a light to the nations." James is simply announcing here the fulfillment of

question raised by Jewish believers about the salvation (15:1) and solidarity (15:5) of uncircumcised Gentiles is whether repentant Gentiles should "become like Jews," then the thematic shift signaled by James's use of the Semitic form of Peter's name addresses the same question in reverse, whether repentant Jews (= "Simeon") should "become like Gentiles."

That this is an interpretive key for the second half of Acts is made clear when Paul returns to Jerusalem following his farewell tour through Roman Asia (Acts 21:17-26). While James is no longer concerned with the religious practices of uncircumcised Gentile converts, he is distressed over reports that Paul's urban mission has subverted important religious traditions among Jewish converts who live in a pervasively pagan culture: "You tell them not to circumcise their children or observe the [Mosaic] customs" (21:21). The relevant issue, then, turns on whether Paul's mission "gentilizes" repentant Jews. In response, Paul defends his mission in the manner of an observant Jew: He purifies himself for temple worship (see 21:24-26) and then appeals to his purity (24:18) to claim that his Jewish opponents have found no "impurity" (ἀδίκημα adikēma) in him (24:20; cf. 18:14). One subtext of his defense, then, is that his mission among "impure" Gentiles in no way imperils the "purity" of repentant Jews.

Luke is probably responding to the attenuation of the Jewish foundations of Christianity within his own church (see Introduction, "Acts as Conversation," 5-11). His conciliatory response to this rather thorny theological crisis cannot disguise the tension within the early church, or the anxiety felt by Jewish believers at the sudden influx of Gentiles into their fellowship or at the movement of the gospel farther and farther away from the holy city. In fact, Luke's interest in protecting the Jewish heritage of Christian faith is not wholly expected and must be viewed as somewhat radical given the evidence. Even as God does not require uncircumcised Gentile converts to follow conventional Jewish practices (i.e., circumcision) for Christian fellowship with Jewish believers, neither does God require repentant Jews to forsake their ancestral traditions out of loyalty to the Messiah. *The spiritual crisis as Luke sees it is the possible loss of a distinctively Jewish memory without which the church cannot be the church.*

In shaping the second half of his story as a response to this theological challenge, Luke composes accounts of three additional Pauline missions. It is here in Acts that he occasionally places himself within the narrative world—as eyewitness and reporter on Paul's newsbeat. The literary net effect of the "we" passages is to make his account more direct and reliable (see Introduction, "Acts as Composition," 11-18).[520] The first mission follows the aftermath of the Jerusalem Council (15:22-35) and extends the scope of Paul's urban mission beyond Roman Asia into Macedonia and Greece (15:36–18:17). The second narrative block is centered on Paul's Ephesian mission and includes panels of his "farewell tour" that ends in Jerusalem, once again before an assembly of church elders led by James (18:18–21:26). Significantly, this narrative is enclosed by acts of ritual purification that characterize Paul as an exemplar of holiness within traditional Judaism (18:18-21; 21:26). Paul's final mission is to Rome, the city of his destiny. His route there is circuitous and strategic: He is arrested in Jerusalem and put on "trial" (21:27–26:32), but he appeals to the Caesar to hear his case and journeys to Rome by ship with much intrigue but without a verdict yet rendered (27:1–28:16). His great adventure concludes in Rome, where he awaits his court appearance by engaging in prophetic ministry that, as we might anticipate, divides the house of Israel according to Scripture (28:17-28). Luke's second book then concludes with a curious summary, noting only that Paul's mission continues on but without any indication of what the Emperor decides (28:30-31). Perhaps this is only the beginning of the story![521]

---

520. The debate continues whether the narrator's use of "we" is purely literary and used to create an impression upon the reader or is drawn from the personal memory (perhaps even written in a diary) of an eyewitness. An aspect of the critical problem is the lack of precise "we" parallels in contemporary literature or historiography that could be used for comparison with Luke's Acts. Most commentators fall somewhere between, supposing that Luke actually was a participant in the "we" passages of Acts but that he places himself in the narrative for rhetorical or literary (rather than purely historical) ends. See B. Witherington, *The Acts of the Apostles: A Socio-Rhetorical Commentary* (Grand Rapids: Eerdmans, 1998) 480-86; C. K. Barrett, *A Critical and Exegetical Commentary on the Acts of the Apostles,* 2 vols, ICC (Edinburgh: T. & T. Clark, 1994, 1998) 2:xxv-xxx. Johnson adjures that "the presence of these first-person passages seems to have little impact on the development or meaning of the story." See L. T. Johnson, *The Acts of the Apostles,* SP 5 (Collegeville, Minn.: Liturgical, 1992) 297.

521. For this possibility, see L. Alexander, "Reading Luke-Acts from Back to Front," in *The Unity of Luke-Acts,* ed. J. Verheyden, BETA 152 (Leuven: Leuven University Press, 1999) 420-46.

The second half of Acts is a story of *consecration,* a word that derives from the Latin root for "sacred." Consecration denotes the act of separating someone or something for a sacred purpose. While Paul exemplifies consecrated service to God, the very idea of consecration evokes a constellation of images, ideas, and claims about purity staked out by James's commentary on Amos. Israel's "consecration" among the nations is publicly expressed by practicing those purity laws and national traditions that cultivate a distinctively Jewish ethos. Does Paul's mission to the nations contaminate this ethos? The Jewishness of Paul's profile in the second half of Acts, both in his religious practices and his missionary protocol, indicates that his witness to the risen Messiah does not displace his ancestral heritage but reshapes it in new and sometimes unconventional ways. Luke makes clear that neither Paul nor his mission sponsors the attenuation or contamination of Israel's social identity. In fact, there is reason to think that his mission to the nations worked hard to safeguard the church's Jewish legacy in those cultural settings where its future was anything but certain (see 16:11-40).

From a canonical perspective, the second half of Acts points the Bible's readers forward to the Pauline letters. The stories of Paul's urban missions in the great Roman cities of his day—Philippi, Thessalonica, Corinth, Ephesus, Rome—prepare readers for the related Pauline letters that follow in the NT. Although the intra-canonical relationship between Acts and the Pauline letters is laden with important historical questions, this commentary will continue to ask what these stories of Paul's mission in Acts contribute to our reading of Paul's letters *today,* as his legacy passes to his *living* readers (see Introduction, "Acts as Canon," 26-32).

My interpretive interest in this relationship between Acts and the NT letters is both rhetorical and theological. At a rhetorical level, great narratives such as Acts have the capacity to evoke powerful impressions that influence how we approach related, more discursive literature such as Pauline letters. Acts tells us something of the canonical Paul's persona, his circumstances, his vocation, and his religious motives, that enables the interpreter of his letters to fill in gaps imaginatively and in agreement with Pauline tradition. Acts is also a theological narrative that offers its own witness to God's gospel. While the contrast between the Jewish cast of Luke's Paul and the essentially Gentile cast of Paul's letters has long been recognized as a critical problem; in combination the two writings envisage the prophetic protocol that Acts sponsors. In particular, the founding of different congregations according to Acts is at its roots a Jewish enterprise: It begins in the synagogue with Jewish and Gentile converts who are attached to the synagogue. Even when Paul is forced to leave the confines of the synagogue to maintain the Christian character of his urban mission, he does not leave behind the congregation's Jewish practices or constituency (e.g., see 18:5-8). Even though the recipients of Paul's letters (e.g., 1–2 Corinthians) are primarily Gentile, their future with God is predicated on their congregation's Jewish roots—the very point that Acts illumines by its narrative emphasis. The connection between Acts and the Pauline letters suggests, then, that "to the Jew first, then the Greek" is an ecclesial calculus every bit as much as it is a prophetic protocol.

# ACTS 15:13-35, THE JERUSALEM COUNCIL: THE VERDICT OF JAMES

## NIV

13When they finished, James spoke up: "Brothers, listen to me. 14Simon[a] has described to us how God at first showed his concern by taking from the Gentiles a people for himself. 15The words of the prophets are in agreement with this, as it is written:

16 " 'After this I will return
and rebuild David's fallen tent.
Its ruins I will rebuild,
and I will restore it,
17 that the remnant of men may seek the Lord,
and all the Gentiles who bear my name,
says the Lord, who does these things'[b]
18     that have been known for ages.[c]

19"It is my judgment, therefore, that we should not make it difficult for the Gentiles who are turning to God. 20Instead we should write to them, telling them to abstain from food polluted by idols, from sexual immorality, from the meat of strangled animals and from blood. 21For Moses has been preached in every city from the earliest times and is read in the synagogues on every Sabbath."

22Then the apostles and elders, with the whole church, decided to choose some of their own men and send them to Antioch with Paul and Barnabas. They chose Judas (called Barsabbas) and Silas, two men who were leaders among the brothers. 23With them they sent the following letter:

The apostles and elders, your brothers,

To the Gentile believers in Antioch, Syria and Cilicia:

Greetings.

24We have heard that some went out from us without our authorization and disturbed you, troubling your minds by what they said. 25So we all agreed to choose some

a 14 Greek Simeon, a variant of Simon; that is, Peter    b 17 Amos 9:11,12    c 17,18 Some manuscripts things'— / 18known to the Lord for ages is his work

## NRSV

13After they finished speaking, James replied, "My brothers,[a] listen to me. 14Simeon has related how God first looked favorably on the Gentiles, to take from among them a people for his name. 15This agrees with the words of the prophets, as it is written,

16 'After this I will return,
and I will rebuild the dwelling of David,
which has fallen;
from its ruins I will rebuild it,
and I will set it up,
17 so that all other peoples may seek the Lord—
even all the Gentiles over whom my name
has been called.
Thus says the Lord, who has been
making these things 18known from
long ago.'[b]

19Therefore I have reached the decision that we should not trouble those Gentiles who are turning to God, 20but we should write to them to abstain only from things polluted by idols and from fornication and from whatever has been strangled[c] and from blood. 21For in every city, for generations past, Moses has had those who proclaim him, for he has been read aloud every sabbath in the synagogues."

22Then the apostles and the elders, with the consent of the whole church, decided to choose men from among their members[d] and to send them to Antioch with Paul and Barnabas. They sent Judas called Barsabbas, and Silas, leaders among the brothers, 23with the following letter: "The brothers, both the apostles and the elders, to the believers[e] of Gentile origin in Antioch and Syria and Cilicia, greetings. 24Since we have heard that certain persons who have gone out from us, though with no instructions from us, have said things to disturb you and have unsettled your minds,[f] 25we have decided unanimously to choose

a Gk Men, brothers    b Other ancient authorities read things. 18Known to God from of old are all his works.'    c Other ancient authorities lack and from whatever has been strangled    d Gk from among them    e Gk brothers    f Other ancient authorities add saying, 'You must be circumcised and keep the law,'

## NIV

men and send them to you with our dear friends Barnabas and Paul— [26]men who have risked their lives for the name of our Lord Jesus Christ. [27]Therefore we are sending Judas and Silas to confirm by word of mouth what we are writing. [28]It seemed good to the Holy Spirit and to us not to burden you with anything beyond the following requirements: [29]You are to abstain from food sacrificed to idols, from blood, from the meat of strangled animals and from sexual immorality. You will do well to avoid these things.

Farewell.

[30]The men were sent off and went down to Antioch, where they gathered the church together and delivered the letter. [31]The people read it and were glad for its encouraging message. [32]Judas and Silas, who themselves were prophets, said much to encourage and strengthen the brothers. [33]After spending some time there, they were sent off by the brothers with the blessing of peace to return to those who had sent them.[a] [35]But Paul and Barnabas remained in Antioch, where they and many others taught and preached the word of the Lord.

[a] 33 Some manuscripts them, [34]but Silas decided to remain there

## NRSV

representatives[a] and send them to you, along with our beloved Barnabas and Paul, [26]who have risked their lives for the sake of our Lord Jesus Christ. [27]We have therefore sent Judas and Silas, who themselves will tell you the same things by word of mouth. [28]For it has seemed good to the Holy Spirit and to us to impose on you no further burden than these essentials: [29]that you abstain from what has been sacrificed to idols and from blood and from what is strangled[b] and from fornication. If you keep yourselves from these, you will do well. Farewell."

[30]So they were sent off and went down to Antioch. When they gathered the congregation together, they delivered the letter. [31]When its members[c] read it, they rejoiced at the exhortation. [32]Judas and Silas, who were themselves prophets, said much to encourage and strengthen the believers.[d] [33]After they had been there for some time, they were sent off in peace by the believers[d] to those who had sent them.[e] [35]But Paul and Barnabas remained in Antioch, and there, with many others, they taught and proclaimed the word of the Lord.

[a] Gk men   [b] Other ancient authorities lack and from what is strangled   [c] Gk When they   [d] Gk brothers   [e] Other ancient authorities add verse 34, But it seemed good to Silas to remain there

## COMMENTARY

The inaugural event of the second half of Acts is actually the concluding event of the Jerusalem Council: the speech of James. Having heard all the relevant evidence from the mission field, the new leader of the Jerusalem church is prepared to render a verdict. The specific issue before the council is whether Gentile converts should be circumcised as a religious practice required by Torah (see 15:5). The theological method used by James considers first the religious experience testified to by Peter (see 15:6-11) as well as by Barnabas and Paul (see 15:12). Their combined missionary experiences appear to confirm God's intention to call out of all nations "a people for his name" (15:13-15). Such experiences of conversion, how-

ever, must finally be "read" by Scripture. Thus James turns from religious experience to Israel's Scripture, citing a prophecy from Amos that provides a context in which the testimony presented to the council might be considered a theological norm (15:16-18).

Earlier James referred to Peter by his Aramaic name, "Simeon" (15:14), to signal a change of direction (see the Overview). Neither his rehearsal of the available evidence nor his appeal to biblical prophecy give the reader any indication of what that new direction might be. His commentary on Amos, however, does (15:19-21). The question that had occasioned the council's deliberation is no longer of interest to James or anyone else since it seems clear that uncircumcised Gentiles (such as Cornelius) share equally in the blessings of Israel's salvation. The matter of *halakhah* that concerns James is instead the potentially deleterious effects that Gentile converts may have on repentant Jews with whom they share congregational life, and whether a "gentilizing" of the mission in the diaspora may even lead to the attenuation of the church's Jewish legacy. James's commentary on Amos is inscribed as a pastoral "exhortation" and sent to the Antiochene congregation (15:22-29). Their joyful response (15:30-31) cues the continuation of Paul and Barnabas's mission in Syrian Antioch (15:32-35).

**15:13-14.** Only the passing reference to James, when Peter departs Jerusalem following his miraculous escape from prison (see 12:17), provides the reader with any hint of the important role James will play in the second half of Acts. Here and later in Acts 21, he stands as the teaching authority of the Jewish church. His discernment of God's will proves decisive in settling the present conflict and for anticipating the potential problem of mixing uncircumcised and circumcised believers in the Christian congregations of the diaspora.

James addresses the council only "after they finished speaking"—that is, following the testimonies of Peter (see 5:6-11) and of Barnabas and Paul (v. 12), and in due consideration of them. Following his appeal for a reasoned "listening," James summarizes the previous testimony: "Simeon has related how God looked favorably on the Gentiles" (v. 14; see the Overview). His understanding of the evidence includes: (1) "God first," which echoes Peter's earlier temporal location "in the early days" (v. 14; see also v. 7) to place God's redemptive action within space and time, where God's will is more easy to detect. (2) That God "looked favorably on" (ἐπισκέπτομαι *episkeptomai*) repeats a verb used in Stephen's speech of God's visitation through Moses to deliver the Israelites from Egyptian oppression (see 7:23; cf. 6:3). The James of Acts admits, then, that Peter is a prophet-like-Moses through whom God's grace has delivered an uncircumcised Gentile from death to eternal life. (3) James's concluding expression, "a people [λαός *laos*] for his name" (15:14), recalls important literary themes in Acts. The term for "people" is an OT idiom for Israel

that Luke typically uses in Acts of Jews. Here the term is used for Gentiles, not because they are included into a spiritual or "true" Israel but because they share in equal measure the blessings of Israel's salvation from a God who is impartial (see 10:34-43).[522]

**15:15-18.** While the church's religious experience establishes a theological precedent, it must agree with and be explained by "the words of the prophets" (v. 15). This introductory formula of a prophetic citation reflects Luke's idea of Scripture: Prophecy scripts salvation and necessarily lends its support for and clarification of its progress (see Introduction, "Acts as Confession," 18-26). The use of plural "prophets" is perplexing since only Amos is mentioned. Upon closer reading, however, we find a pastiche of fragments mostly from Amos 9:11-12 LXX, but also including a bit from Jeremiah and another piece from Isaiah. More likely this is a consensual prophecy in which the testimony of "all the prophets" is implied even though a single prophetic witness is mentioned (see 3:24; 10:43).

The prophecy quoted and James's interpretation of it mark a storm center of Acts criticism. There are two related problems with which the interpreter must contend. The first problem concerns the significant differences between the Greek (LXX) translation of this Amos prophecy and its Hebrew (MT) version, which differences allow James to adapt Scripture to comment on the potential "gentilizing" of repentant Jews in the diaspora (see vv. 19-21). Additional changes are made to the LXX citation, two of which are important to mention.

(1) Luke substitutes "after this" (μετὰ ταῦτα *meta tauta*) for "on that day" (ἐν τῇ ἡμέρα *en tē hēmera*) to begin the citation (v. 16; cf. Amos 9:11). The editorial effect is that this prophecy responds to the timing of the earlier prophecy from Joel about "these last days" (see 2:17), insinuating that Israel's restoration, predicted by Joel, has now been fulfilled "after this"—that is, after the church's mission to Jews (Acts 2–8) and Gentiles (Acts 9–14).

522. J. Jervell, *Die Apostelgeschichte,* KEK 3 (Göttingen: Vandenhoeck & Ruprecht, 1998) 394; however, see Johnson, *The Acts of the Apostles,* 264. Bauckham, "James and the Gentiles," 169, contends that it is likely that this phrase alludes to Zech 2:11: "many nations shall join themselves to the Lord on that day, and shall be my people."

(2) According to Amos 9:12 MT, the promise of Israel's restoration is coupled with the promise that Israel would reclaim the lands of Edom and all the other nations as well. According to Amos 9:12 LXX, to which the James of Acts appeals, the promise of Israel's restoration makes it possible that "all other peoples may seek the Lord" (v. 17).[523] James is thereby able to confirm that the testimonies of Peter, Barnabas, and Paul agree with the prophesied plan of God: Following Israel's restoration, now realized, God will allow "all other peoples" (i.e., uncircumcised Gentiles) to share in Israel's blessings (i.e., forgiveness of sins, gift of the Spirit, eternal life) without first becoming proselytes.

The second problem concerns what role this prophecy performs within Acts. R. Bauckham has observed that the cited text is similar to other prophecies (Isa 45:21; Jer 12:16; Zech 2:11-15) that predict the rebuilding of an eschatological temple—the rebuilt "tent of David" (15:16)—that would signal and be a gathering point for the conversion of the nations. The story of Stephen has already reminded us that the Lord's symbolic actions within the Jerusalem Temple and prediction of its destruction transvaluate the role the Jerusalem Temple will play in Israel's future purification (see 6:13-14). The Messiah is the sole agent of Israel's rebuilding project. Amos's promise of a rebuilt "tent of David" is fulfilled by this Davidic Messiah; and the prospect of Israel's eschatological purification and the conversion of "all other peoples" have been transferred to him (see 3:19-20).[524]

The real worry of the Jewish church over Paul's mission to the nations, however, concerns those religious practices from which James exhorts repentant Gentiles to abstain (vv. 20, 29)—practices that are linked to pagan temples. If God's grace has been extended to "all other peoples," even those with a background in pagan religion who have not been properly catechized by Jewish teachers, they are obliged to embrace the "rules of polite company" set out in Leviticus 17–18, which delineates the respectful conduct of "resident aliens" living among the holy "house of Israel" (see below). The thematic interplay between this prophecy from Amos concerning the salvation of the nations and the Levitical injunctions against their "abominations" among Jews (cf. Lev 18:24-30) provides the biblical context for Luke's subsequent narrative of Paul's mission. Indeed, his mission among the pagans carries the considerable risk that repentant Gentiles, set free from the requirements of Jewish proselytism, will retain their former religious practices—idols, sexual immorality, food regulations—that will defile believing Jews who are members of their congregations (see below).[525]

**15:19-21.** James begins his commentary on the Amos prophecy with, "I have reached the decision." This is not a personal opinion but a reasoned judgment from someone with authority to render a verdict on behalf of the council. The "therefore" (διό *dio*) presumes his judgment that "we should not trouble those Gentiles who are turning to God" (v. 19) is based upon the preceding evidence of personal testimony (vv. 13-14; cf. vv. 6-12) and Scripture (vv. 15-18). The force of the word translated "trouble" (παρενοχλέω *parenochleō*) denotes pestering someone against the person's will. Read in light of Peter's earlier admonition that requiring circumcision of converted Gentiles puts God "to the test" (see v. 10), James may assume that to do so unduly "pesters" God against God's will. His *halakhah* is as straightforward as the evidence allows: God's intention is to purify the hearts of non-proselyte Gentiles.

But there is a proviso: James is unwilling to grant them *carte blanche*. The intent of his comment that "we should write to them" (v. 20) is debated by scholars, whether what is written serves as a pastoral "exhortation" to guide behavior or as an administrative "decree" to regulate behavior. If the reader takes this as Antioch's happy response, then he or she should perceive James's judgment as hortatory and pastoral (see v. 31).[526] Further, it is doubtful that the Jerusalem

523. The differences in translation are easily explained by the similar sounding words: "Edom" (אֱדוֹם *'ĕdôm*) is mistaken for "peoples/men" (אָדָם *'ādām*) and the Hebrew word for "possess" (יָרַשׁ *yāraś*) is mistaken for "seek" (דָּרַשׁ *dāraś*).

524. Cf. J. Dupont, "Je rebâtirai la cabane de David qui est tombée [Ac 15,16 = Am 9,11]," in *Glaube und Eschatologie,* E. Grässer and O. Merk (Tübingen: Mohr, 1985) 19-32. R. Bauckham, "James and the Gentiles (Acts 15:13-21)," in Witherington, ed., *History, Literature, and Society in the Book of Acts,* 164-66.

525. R. Bauckham, "James and the Gentiles (Acts 15:13-21)," in *History,* 154-84.

526. It is likely that this pastoral letter is Luke's primary source for his narrative of James's speech. If so, then his impressions of its purpose and effect given in 15:31 are instructive for how we understand the motive of Luke's James in rendering his oral judgment. See ibid., 178-84.

church is any longer in a position to demand Antioch's compliance to a "decree" (see 11:19-30).

The strong adversative conjunction ἀλλά (*alla,* "But") cues the shift in the gravity of James's concern from "Judaizing" repentant Gentiles to "gentilizing" repentant Jews. The importance of v. 20 within Acts should not be underestimated and requires the interpreter's most careful attention. As with some other significant matters in Acts, there are three versions of James's proviso that differ slightly in nuance (see also v. 29; 21:25). In this first instance, James encourages repentant Gentiles to abstain from four impurities observant Jews associated with the pagan world: (1) idolatry, (2) sexual immorality, and (3) eating either food with blood or (4) strangled food[527]—religious practices that are all associated with temple feasts.[528] In this regard, then, to abstain from "things polluted by idols" refers to the food offered in pagan temples, which is contaminated by contact with idol worship (cf. Mal 1:7). The second behavior, "fornication" (πορνεία *porneia*), has broad moral currency in Greco-Roman moral thought but probably refers to temple prostitution in this setting and may well anticipate issues at stake in Paul's later missions in both Corinth and Ephesus, which were well-known centers of this pagan religious practice. The final two impurities from which to abstain concern food laws: Do not eat food with "blood"[529] or "strangled food." The levitical injunctions regarding table fellowship extend not only to certain kinds of foods but also to food preparation, both of which were routinely broken during pagan feast days.

The biblical context for understanding the importance of these injunctions against pagan religious practices is Leviticus 17–18, a text from Moses that is "read aloud every sabbath in the synagogues" (Acts 15:21).[530] This text legislates the behaviors of "resident aliens" living in the holy land among Jews and sounds a cautionary note about possible effects of "aliens who sojourn in your midst" whose practices may defile and subvert the people's covenant relationship with God. The exhortation to avoid "the practices of the nations" is deeply rooted in the prophet's keen awareness that Israel's single-minded loyalty to God (and so its future) can be imperiled by the manner of a people's worship or fellowship in a heterogeneous culture.[531] This same concern is here adapted by James to guide the behaviors of converted Gentiles who share Christian fellowship with repentant Jews in the urban synagogues of the diaspora (cf. 15:21). In effect, James implies that Jews should treat uncircumcised Gentiles who otherwise share the same sacred space as "resident aliens." James offers guidelines to ensure that Christian fellowship in the mixed congregations of Paul's urban mission will nurture faith rather than contaminate it.[532] The lack of sensitivity to the church's Jewish legacy would surely have an adverse effect on a congregation's Jewish membership (cf. Romans 14; 1 Corinthians 8–10).

It may also be true that in Acts the only good Gentile is a "God-fearing" one—one who is attached to the synagogue. It is noteworthy that most Gentile converts are those whom Paul finds in the synagogue; moreover, the only reported failure from his first mission is at Lystra among the Zeus worshipers there (see 14:8-18). Even within the narrative world of Acts clear religious distinctions are made between Gentiles that indicate a preference for God-fearers as more ready to embrace the gospel and to live in appropriate ways with their Jewish sisters and brothers. Perhaps the missionary subtext of James's *halakhah* is that uncircumcised Gentiles attached to synagogues where Moses is preached every sabbath are to be privileged. If so, then certainly the Paul of Acts seems to agree, since he finds most of his Gentile converts in the urban synagogues of the Disapora.

Upon an initial reading, the interpreter may wonder how James's interest in table fellowship within the Christian synagogues of the diaspora relates to the biblical prophecy just cited. Is it part of his midrash on this Scripture or a pastoral exhortation detached from Scripture? If the Gentile believers in the church are the Gentiles of

---

527. In all 3 versions of this list, the Western version of Acts omits "strangled food" and adds the Golden Rule, perhaps to contemporize the list for a later time.

528. Witherington, *The Acts of the Apostles,* 462.

529. Although Barrett, *Acts,* 2:733, thinks "blood" refers to murder and is a prohibition against bloodshed rather than to animal blood left on eaten meat.

530. So R. Bauckham, "James and the Gentiles"; cf. Barrett, *Acts,* 2:734-35; Johnson, *The Acts of the Apostles,* 273.

531. See G. Wenham, *Leviticus,* NICOT (Grand Rapids: Eerdmans, 1979) 240-61.

532. S. G. Wilson, *Luke and the Law,* SNTSMS 50 (Cambridge: Cambridge University Press, 1983) 68-102.

the prophecy, whose salvation is then confirmed by prophecy (Amos), then his exhortation for them to remain pure according to Moses (Leviticus 17–18) should not be viewed as odd. The same Scripture that claims them for God also obligates their civility.[533]

**15:22-23a.** The foregoing commentary on biblical prophecy is offered by James alone, even though it expresses a wider concern within the Jewish church. The consensus reached by "the apostles and the elders, with the consent of the whole church" has to do with the dissemination of the council's verdict. They "choose" and "send" a delegation of men to the Antiochene church "with the following letter," presumably to publish for believers there. This delegation of witnesses includes another fascinating list of names, which serves to bring all of Acts around the contents of this letter. "Judas called Barsabbas," who shares the same name as a candidate for Judas's replacement (see 1:23), serves as a rhetorical link to the mission to the Jews narrated in the early chapters of Acts; mention of "Paul and Barnabas" and their initial mission to the nations brings "the narrative of conversion" to this midpoint; and "Silas" will play an important role as Paul's colleague during his forthcoming Macedonian mission (cf. 18:5). Silas and Judas are called "prophets" (15:32), apparently because the Spirit empowers them to engage in the prophetic tasks by which believers are "strengthened."[534]

**15:23b-29.** The literary convention of communicating an earlier decision by letter is similar to the "double vision" (see 9:10-18; 10:1-16) in that the letter reads back into the previous narrative and fills in gaps with added detail. The result in Acts is a more fully nuanced account of important moments that clarify God's purposes and the motives of those with whom God participates in the church's prophetic mission.

The members of the delegation are introduced and given credentials apropos to an important task: They are of one mind (v. 25a), beloved (v. 25b), "who have risked their lives" for the Lord's sake (v. 26), with the personal integrity to confirm orally the validity of what is written (v. 27). More important, however, what is written and carried to Antioch "has seemed good to the Holy Spirit" (v. 28). The content of James's reading of Scripture agrees with the intentions of its author, the Holy Spirit (see 1:16). Any interpretation of Scripture that is on target must enjoy a consensus that includes God's Spirit. The implied response to such an interpretation is obedience.

All this leads to the second iteration of the material in v. 20. The only differences in this statement of the "essentials" of ecclesial (= synagogal) solidarity are minor: The order of terms here places "fornication" last, and εἰδωλόθυτων (eidōlothytōn, "sacrificed to idols") replaces the phrase τῶν ἀλισγημάτων τῶν εἰδώλων (tōn alisgēmatōn tōn eidōlōn, "polluted by idols"), making more explicit the specific religious practice that would be considered a social pollutant if carried into a Christian synagogue.

The exhortation "if you keep yourselves from these, you will do well" (v. 29b) underscores the importance of reciprocity in any covenant relationship. Its conditionality commends the importance of human accountability to God's purposes, discerned by James from Scripture. This is not a pointless formality—a polite way of saying goodbye to friends. There will be other disputes within emergent Christianity that will require turning back to James's reading of Amos for support and clarity in moving the word of God forward. In opening "a door of faith for the Gentiles" (14:27), a set of other concerns has also been let in that will require constant cooperation between the faith community and the Holy Spirit.

**15:30-35.** Reading the letter occasioned rejoicing at the exhortation (15:31) among the community's membership. The word "strengthen" (ἐπιστηρίζω epistērizō) denotes fortifying believers to resist threats to their faith, usually through instruction and comfort (Luke 22:32; Rom 1:11; 1 Thess 3:2, 13; 1 Pet 5:10). This text is paradigmatic of follow-up ministry, where mature leadership stands alongside rank-and-file believers in working through the implications of new teaching. Luke's note of "peace" at the return of Silas and Judas to the elders and apostles of the Jerusalem church is his familiar idealism that always serves a larger theological purpose: The intention of James's speech is Christian solidarity for the sake of the

---

533. Cf. Bauckham, "James and the Gentiles (Acts 15:13-21)," 177-78.

534. The Western version of Acts adds "filled by the Holy Spirit" to 15:32 to make this Lukan point more clearly.

gospel.[535] This optimistic panel concludes with Paul and Barnabas together in ministry where it all began for them—"in Antioch . . . they taught and proclaimed the word of the Lord" (v. 35; see 11:25-26; cf. 4:31; 6:7)—and nicely rounds off this important narrative.

535. Some MSS add "Silas decided to stay there" and edit Silas out of v. 33 to keep him in Antioch with Paul until their departure in 15:40.

# REFLECTIONS

**1.** "After they finished speaking, James replied, 'My brothers, listen to me' " (15:13 NRSV). One of the most important roles that Acts performs within the New Testament is to provide its readers with "authorized" introductions of important people linked to the letters that follow (and to the interpretive traditions they envisage). Among these people is James. Details regarding the James of Acts provide an angle of vision toward the Letter of James and its implied author. When making sense of what Luke's James says at the Jerusalem Council, the interpreter should have the Letter of James open for reflexive reading. Thus, for example, the continuing importance James posits on the Moses tradition for repentant Jews (see 21:20-21) as well as for repentant Gentiles (15:21) prepares the reader for the texts and subtexts of the epistolary James where high value is posited on Torah purity as a distinctive mark of the faith community (see Jas 1:22–2:13). Moreover, his concern for the "gentilizing" (Paulinzing?) of the Jewish heritage in the diaspora church (15:20, 29) may shape an important perspective on the letter's teaching about "faith and works" (2:14-26). For every Pauline claim that our faith in the faithfulness of Jesus saves us for eternal life, there must be a complementary Jamesian claim that our faithfulness to Jesus maintains our membership in the covenant community.[536]

**2.** "Abstain . . . from things polluted by idols" (15:20 NRSV; cf. 15:29). L. T. Johnson notes that with the exhortation of James, "Luke has given fundamental and programmatic expression to the nature of Christianity as a people of faith."[537] At the very least, James recognizes that a convert to the faith must give up various practices. While the community welcomes all who truly repent—as God welcomes them—there are limits to what the community marks out as "Christian." The subtext of James's exhortation is the fear that as the church's mission carries the gospel farther and farther from the Holy Land, the social world in which the church must bear witness and worship will become increasingly pluralistic and secular. The reader of Acts will recognize this concern for the contaminating effect of idolatry registered by Paul also (1 Cor 10:14), in a passage that delineates an acceptable accommodation of a pluralizing and pagan culture without a correspondent compromising of the gospel's core beliefs and values (cf. 1 Cor 10:1-22). Paul alerts his readers to two present and integral dangers in a cultural setting "polluted by idols." Whether the believer is aware of it or not, the symbols (if no longer the practices) of "idol worship" have a profound effect in shaping one's loyalties and how one engages the culture for Christ's sake. Paul further contends that a jealous God will judge those whose witness is polluted by their worship of idols.

In today's culture believers no longer contend for Christ in a world dominated by pagan shrines or temples. Nonetheless, the polluting effect of idolatry continues, as witnessed in the unprincipled acquisition of wealth or in triumphal nationalism—and "temples" to these idols are found in our city's marketplaces and town squares. Whatever holds primary value in place of God is an idol, and related institutions function as its temples. Along with this understanding, the interpreter may translate James's remarks on purity, sexual and ritual, as symbolic of a discipleship that is ever alert to those competing interests that sully our daily walk with the Lord and our neighbors.

536. For these arguments and their practical implications, see R. Wall, *The Community of the Wise: The Letter of James,* New Testament in Context (Valley Forge: Trinity, 1997).
537. L. T. Johnson, *The Acts of the Apostles,* SP 5 (Collegeville, Minn.: Liturgical, 1992) 280.

**3.** "[Moses] has been read aloud every sabbath in the synagogues" (15:21 NRSV). If the "essence" of Christianity is insufficiently Jewish, one's interpretation and application of Scripture for daily living will tend to marginalize those ideas and ideals that are Jewish in character. The practical result of listening to Moses according to James is that people will be prepared for a right hearing of the gospel. In other words, those who are most likely to respond to the gospel and grow in God's grace are those attached to a congregation where the truth of Torah is embraced in faith and its core values embodied in human relations. The casual dismissal of this essential Jewish concern for fear that it somehow shapes a legalistic approach to the faith subverts the church's identity and its mission in the world. Time and again I have heard non-Christians tell me that they have decided against the faith because of the hypocrisy they see in the Christians they know. At the same time, believers tell me that they have decided in favor of Jesus while living or working or even worshiping alongside Christians, due to the coherence of their gospel witness with the integrity of their lives.

# ACTS 15:36–16:10, INTERLUDE: PAUL BEYOND ROMAN ASIA

## NIV

[36]Some time later Paul said to Barnabas, "Let us go back and visit the brothers in all the towns where we preached the word of the Lord and see how they are doing." [37]Barnabas wanted to take John, also called Mark, with them, [38]but Paul did not think it wise to take him, because he had deserted them in Pamphylia and had not continued with them in the work. [39]They had such a sharp disagreement that they parted company. Barnabas took Mark and sailed for Cyprus, [40]but Paul chose Silas and left, commended by the brothers to the grace of the Lord. [41]He went through Syria and Cilicia, strengthening the churches.

16 He came to Derbe and then to Lystra, where a disciple named Timothy lived, whose mother was a Jewess and a believer, but whose father was a Greek. [2]The brothers at Lystra and Iconium spoke well of him. [3]Paul wanted to take him along on the journey, so he circumcised him because of the Jews who lived in that area, for they all knew that his father was a Greek. [4]As they traveled from town to town, they delivered the decisions reached by the apostles and elders in Jerusalem for the people to obey. [5]So the churches were strengthened in the faith and grew daily in numbers.

## NRSV

36After some days Paul said to Barnabas, "Come, let us return and visit the believers[a] in every city where we proclaimed the word of the Lord and see how they are doing." [37]Barnabas wanted to take with them John called Mark. [38]But Paul decided not to take with them one who had deserted them in Pamphylia and had not accompanied them in the work. [39]The disagreement became so sharp that they parted company; Barnabas took Mark with him and sailed away to Cyprus. [40]But Paul chose Silas and set out, the believers[a] commending him to the grace of the Lord. [41]He went through Syria and Cilicia, strengthening the churches.

16 Paul[b] went on also to Derbe and to Lystra, where there was a disciple named Timothy, the son of a Jewish woman who was a believer; but his father was a Greek. [2]He was well spoken of by the believers[a] in Lystra and Iconium. [3]Paul wanted Timothy to accompany him; and he took him and had him circumcised because of the Jews who were in those places, for they all knew that his father was a Greek. [4]As they went from town to town, they delivered to them for observance the decisions that had been reached by the apostles and elders who were in Jerusalem. [5]So

[a] Gk brothers    [b] Gk He

NIV

⁶Paul and his companions traveled throughout the region of Phrygia and Galatia, having been kept by the Holy Spirit from preaching the word in the province of Asia. ⁷When they came to the border of Mysia, they tried to enter Bithynia, but the Spirit of Jesus would not allow them to. ⁸So they passed by Mysia and went down to Troas. ⁹During the night Paul had a vision of a man of Macedonia standing and begging him, "Come over to Macedonia and help us." ¹⁰After Paul had seen the vision, we got ready at once to leave for Macedonia, concluding that God had called us to preach the gospel to them.

NRSV

the churches were strengthened in the faith and increased in numbers daily.

6They went through the region of Phrygia and Galatia, having been forbidden by the Holy Spirit to speak the word in Asia. ⁷When they had come opposite Mysia, they attempted to go into Bithynia, but the Spirit of Jesus did not allow them; ⁸so, passing by Mysia, they went down to Troas. ⁹During the night Paul had a vision: there stood a man of Macedonia pleading with him and saying, "Come over to Macedonia and help us." ¹⁰When he had seen the vision, we immediately tried to cross over to Macedonia, being convinced that God had called us to proclaim the good news to them.

# COMMENTARY

With the conclusion of the Jerusalem Council, the narrator is now prepared to focus exclusively on Paul and his mission to bring "light to the nations." The present passage moves the reader quickly through several important events, which prepares the way for Paul to join different colleagues on a new mission field along the other shoreline of the Aegean Sea. The "interlude" has a twofold function in Acts. An interlude moves the reader from episode to episode in a "logical" manner, accounting for transitions in places and personnel.[538] In this instance, Silas replaces Barnabas as Paul's missionary colleague, and together they return to former venues, "strengthening the churches" (see 15:36-41; cf. 14:21-26). While traveling in the region of Lystra and Iconium (see Acts 14:7, 21-22), Paul adds Timothy to his team (see 16:1-5). Timothy personifies the issues just addressed in Jerusalem, at least as James finally understands it (see 15:20-21); therefore, he becomes a test case of its resolution: Paul circumcises him "because of the Jews" (cf. Gal 2:3). Significantly, there is also a transition in places. Although his mission in Roman Asia enjoys considerable success (see 16:5), Paul is called to

Macedonia (16:6-10), where he breaks new ground for the Word of the Lord.

Interludes also summarize common theological themes that link different narrative units as the bits and pieces of a narrative whole. What is true in Jerusalem at Pentecost continues in the synagogues of Macedonia, where prophetic ministry results in converts added to the membership rolls of local congregations (see 16:5; see also 2:41; 4:4; 5:14; 6:7; 14:21-23). Especially important is the intervention of the Holy Spirit (see 16:6-8) and an auditory vision to make clear the plans of God for Paul (see 16:9). The role of visions is not to convert the non-believer but to commission prophets-like-Jesus; likewise, the Spirit in Acts is the divine agent not so much of personal transformation but of prophetic power. The first instance of the narrator's use of first person plural occurs in this passage (see 16:10). Although inconsistently used and occurring only in the second half of Acts, such language allows the narrator to participate in some of the events he narrates; along with Silas and Timothy, he is another of Paul's traveling companions (see Introduction, "Acts as Composition," 11-18).

**15:36-41.** The close working relationship between Paul and Barnabas is an important theme in Acts to this point. It was Barnabas who supported the newly converted Saul when others did

538. J. A. Fitzmyer, *The Acts of the Apostles,* AB 31 (Garden City, N.Y.: Doubleday, 1998) 570, for instance, says that Luke begins the second half of Acts with this passage.

not trust him (see 9:27) and who later went to Tarsus and sought out Saul to help him with his fledging church at Antioch (see 11:25-26). Barnabas was Paul's colleague in the first mission to the nations (see chaps. 13–14) and stood with him when giving testimony to the Jerusalem Council of its success (see 15:12). Therefore, it comes as a stunning surprise when the successful team is split apart.

The historical referent behind the story in Acts remains indeterminate. Paul mentions Barnabas's failure of nerve in his reference to the infamous Antioch spat with Peter (cf. Gal 2:11-14) but in a way that contends for his religious independence and theological perspicuity more than his alienation from others. Luke mentions none of this. In Acts, the estrangement between these two colleagues concerns the failure of nerve of someone else, John Mark.

This episode begins with good resolve: " 'Let us return and visit the believers in every city where we proclaimed the word of the Lord and see how they are doing' " (v. 36; cf. 14:21-23). The impression is that Barnabas and Paul intend to continue their mission now that the council has settled the controversies that the mission provoked. It is Paul's initiative to do so and his suggestion to Barnabas neatly summarizes their earlier mission together: an urban mission in which the "word" was proclaimed by prophets-like-Jesus with conversions the result.

Barnabas wants to take John Mark along (v. 37). His motive is unknown and left to the reader's imagination. Perhaps it is for family reasons, since John Mark is Barnabas's cousin (cf. Col 4:10) or because John Mark's mother is the apostle Peter's patron (see Acts 12:12) or because Barnabas, who is generous of heart (see 4:36-37), is himself a patron of second chances. We simply do not know. What Luke does tell us, however, is that Paul will have none of it and his reasons are sound: John Mark "had deserted them in Pamphylia and had not accompanied them in the work" (v. 38; cf. 13:13). Paul's reasons are both theological and practical. The defection from community life and vocation carries the connotation of apostasy. For someone to quit on a mission field previously delineated by the Spirit's instruction (13:1-4a), and without good excuse, is tantamount to spiritual defection. Paul disqualifies John Mark for two rea-

sons: He lacks field experience—he is not a witness to "all the signs and wonders that God had done through them among the Gentiles" (v. 12)—and he is a defector, an apostate from a mission the Spirit had sanctioned.[539] Barnabas's "sharp disagreement" with Paul and his subsequent decision to take John Mark on an independent (and unsanctioned) mission to Cyprus (15:39) must finally be viewed as casting an unfavorable light upon Barnabas's otherwise idealized profile in Acts. Luke is too polite to say anything more; however, the word he selects for "sharp disagreement" (παροξυσμός paroxysmos) denotes a passionate, even bitter, exchange. Words were said that made this partnership impossible to continue. The reader should note that Luke takes Paul's side (for reasons mentioned above) and drops both Barnabas and John Mark from the narrative.

In Luke's narrative world, mission is usually in pairs (cf. Luke 10:1). For this reason Paul replaces Barnabas with Silas, who is commended by the believers "to the grace of the Lord" (15:40; cf. 14:26). Luke has already introduced Silas, who is called a "prophet" (15:32) and, therefore, qualifies for missionary work. Significantly, with this change of partners comes a change of plans. Rather than return to the cities of his first mission, Paul joins Silas in Syria and Cilicia, where Silas is already at work to "strengthening the churches" (see vv. 22-23). Nothing more is added to this summary. However, the implied motive for Paul's actions is that he wants to strengthen his relationship with Silas for the work ahead and does so on the latter's turf—in his comfort zone—before continuing on to Derbe and Lystra as originally planned.

**16:1-5.** The second part of this narrative interlude throws a spotlight on Timothy, whom Paul wanted to accompany him. Timothy proves to be a good find and in due course becomes one of the most important leaders of the Pauline church. He is mentioned with affection in several Pauline letters; and he is, of course, the implied recipient of 1–2 Timothy—two of the so-called Pastoral letters and among the most important resources in Scripture for organizing and nurturing a congregation of believers. For this reason, his mention in Acts takes on added importance.

---

539. Cf. Johnson, *The Acts of the Apostles,* 288.

Timothy is the personification of the diversity found in the Christian synagogues of the diaspora and embodies Paul's solution to the theological crisis James addresses at the Jerusalem Council (see 15:19-21, 28-29). He is an uncircumcised believer, the "son of a Jewish woman, who was a believer" and a Greek father (v. 1). This profile is confirmed in 2 Timothy, which reports that he learned "the sacred writings" (i.e., the Septuagint) during his childhood (so 3:15), presumably from his faithful mother (Lois) and grandmother (Eunice; see 1:5). Moses was preached to him from his "earliest times" every sabbath (see 15:21).

Even though his Jewish identity is guaranteed through his mother, Timothy is the product of a mixed marriage and his birthright is imperiled for this reason; indeed, he has Jewish ancestry but is not yet circumcised! The ambivalence among repentant Jews of the diaspora, symbolized by Timothy, is precisely the subtext of James's earlier verdict rendered at the Jerusalem Council (see 15:19-21). What makes this case pertinent is that Timothy's Jewish identity has not been cultivated at home "for they all knew that his father was a Greek" (v. 3). The sense of this phrase is that Timothy's Gentile father had prevented his circumcision;[540] his religious identity had been "gentilized" in a mixed home and neighborhood.

Paul's circumcision of Timothy "because of the Jews who were in those places" (v. 3) must be understood, then, as an accommodation to James.[541] This seems especially important given Luke's reference to Paul delivering "the decisions that had been reached by the apostles and elders who were in Jerusalem" from town to town (v. 4). His motive is not to make Timothy into an honest Jew, nor is he responding to Timothy's lack of circumcision from his Pharisaic background as a peril

to his salvation as a Jew.[542] An exemplary Paul circumcises Timothy to restore his Jewish identity in order to maintain good working relations between faithful Jews and Gentiles in the churches he founded. This religious motive agrees with James and will serve us again when he accuses Paul of preventing the circumcision of Jewish children (see 21:21). From Luke's perspective, Paul is as committed as James is to keeping the Jewish heritage of Christian faith alive and well. To confirm this fact, he notes that "the churches were strengthened in the faith and increased in numbers daily" (v. 5; see also 2:41; 6:7).

**16:6-10.** The story of Paul's turn toward Europe begins with a summary of his travels. The Holy Spirit is responsible for the plotline of church's mission, leading sometimes by divine speech and at other times by heavenly vision. In this case, the Spirit directs Paul by blocking doors in Asia rather than by opening them. Luke's earlier use of the verb κωλύω (kōlyō, "forbidden/kept from") in Acts (8:36; 10:47; 11:17) makes the positive point that God's redemptive plans, worked out in the church's mission, cannot be frustrated (see 11:17)—Gamaliel's ironic point made in different words (see 5:38-39). Yet here God frustrates Paul's plans, which he had announced to Barnabas (15:36) and begun to accomplish with Silas and Timothy's help. Perhaps there is in this text a faint echo of the circumstances of Peter's mission to Cornelius, which also began with resistance to God's plans for the Gentiles and were also challenged and overturned by visionary revelation.

The repetition of "Spirit" (πνεῦμα pneuma) is striking and reconfirms a theological conviction central to Acts: The Spirit guides as well as empowers the church's witness. This is the only occurrence of the expression "Spirit of Jesus" in Acts and probably cues the reader's recollection of Jesus' active role in Paul's conversion and commission (see Acts 9:1-20). There, Ananias received a vision of the Lord's prophecy of Paul's future mission and suffering (see 9:15-16). That earlier visionary appearance of Jesus supplies a subtext to this reference to

540. Ibid., 284, 289.

541. Whether the historical Paul would have circumcised Timothy remains contested. The relevant issue is not whether Paul *could* have circumcised Timothy, since circumcision could be performed by any Jew. See H. Conzelmann, *The Acts of the Apostles,* trans. J. Limburg et al., ed. E. J. Epp and C. R. Matthews, Hermeneia (Philadelphia: Fortress, 1987) 125. The difficulty is in understanding Paul's religious motive for doing so. G. Lüdemann, *Early Christianity According to the Traditions in Acts* (Minneapolis: Fortress, 1989) 176, appeals to Paul's missionary principle of accommodation in becoming a "Jew in order to win Jews" (1 Cor 9:19). That is, circumcision may have been necessary if Timothy was to accompany Paul in a mission that went first to the synagogue to preach the gospel.

542. M. Hengel, *Earliest Christianity* (London: SCM, 1986) 64, thinks it likely that Timothy would have been viewed as a Jewish apostate by other Jews rather than merely as an outsider like his father. In this sense, Paul's action rehabilitated Timothy's favorable status within Jewish society.

"the Spirit of Jesus" and prepares the reader for the following account of Paul's night vision of a certain Macedonian man.

Visions call prophets to mission. In Paul s vision, "there stood a man of Macedonia pleading with him and saying, 'Come over to Macedonia and help us' " (v. 9). Paul's epiphany is of a human and not a heavenly figure. His actions of standing and begging stress the human urgency of the situation, thereby qualifying the prior emphasis on the Spirit's control of Paul's mission by showing the importance of people's receptivity to the gospel. God does not produce faith in people as though the church is an "imperial juggernaut streaming its way to the ends of the earth."[543] Luke's use of βοηθέω (boētheō, "help") is almost prayer-like and recalls the invocative language of petitions for help in the psalter (e.g., Pss 5:2; 9:35; 12:1; 17:2; 18:6; 36:40; see also Acts 21:28; Heb 2:18; 4:16). The

543. F. S. Spencer, *Acts*, Readings: A New Biblical Commentary (Sheffield: Sheffield Academic, 1997) 162.

proclamation of the good news is in response to the urgent plea for help.

Paul's response is immediate: "We *immediately* tried to cross over to Macedonia, being *convinced* that God had called us to *proclaim* the good news to them" (v. 10, italics added). The rest of Acts hinges on this text. Luke joins Paul's mission to underscore its dramatic importance. Significantly, "vocation" words used here recall a similar matrix of vocation words used following Paul's Damascus road epiphany (see 9:18-22) and again at his Antiochene recommissioning (see 13:1-4*a*): Paul "immediately" responds to his calling by proclaiming the gospel and seeking to "convince" his auditors that Jesus is the Messiah. In both of these earlier texts, Paul's mission is superintended by the Holy Spirit. A reflexive reading of these three commissioning stories alerts the reader of this passage to the implied subtext—namely, that the "Spirit of Jesus," who had earlier closed the door to Asia, had now opened another for Paul to go to the people of Macedonia.

# REFLECTIONS

**1.** "Paul wanted Timothy to accompany him; and he took him and had him circumcised because of the Jews" (16:3 NRSV). If Barnabas is no longer a suitable colleague for Paul, then Timothy is. Clearly he meets the job description's minimum requirements: He is a "disciple" (16:1) who is "well spoken of by the believers" (16:2). But the details of Luke's description of Timothy would suggest that Paul is more interested that he is the progeny of a "mixed" marriage than in his religious credentials. Timothy is the right person for the work ahead because his ethnic mix envisages the very mixture of Paul's mission. As the church extends into new territories, new missionaries are added to the team to meet the new challenges that will be encountered. Although Acts underlines the importance of certain personal characteristics for those given tasks to perform in service of God's plan of salvation, there remains this pragmatic feature of the effective leader. Paul wanted Timothy as a traveling companion not because of his professional résumé but because he personifies and presumably has a grasp of the tensions between "being Greek" and "being Jewish" that will characterize the Pauline church. When choosing the right people to staff our ministries, congregations must consider issues of character and skill. However, the congregation should also search outside the "professional boxes" of religious culture to find those gifted leaders with instincts and personal histories that seem well suited for the tasks at hand.

**2.** "Come over to Macedonia and help us" (16:9 NRSV). Luke reports that the Spirit of Jesus both prevented Paul from going in one direction and allowed him to advance in another. Routinely in Acts the Spirit intervenes—we are not always told how—to guide, assist, and inspire the prophets-like-Jesus. In one sense these are images of divine sovereignty—the active presence of a faithful God to ensure that the plan of salvation is realized. In another sense, these are images of divine concern—the active presence of a caring God to move these prophetic agents of salvation to the places where grace is most needed. Paul's commitment to safeguard the faith of new congregations is a complement of this understanding of God's caring presence among us, helping us enter into and enjoy a strong relationship with God.

# ACTS 16:11-40, PAUL'S MISSION TO THE PHILIPPIANS

## NIV

[11]From Troas we put out to sea and sailed straight for Samothrace, and the next day on to Neapolis. [12]From there we traveled to Philippi, a Roman colony and the leading city of that district of Macedonia. And we stayed there several days.

[13]On the Sabbath we went outside the city gate to the river, where we expected to find a place of prayer. We sat down and began to speak to the women who had gathered there. [14]One of those listening was a woman named Lydia, a dealer in purple cloth from the city of Thyatira, who was a worshiper of God. The Lord opened her heart to respond to Paul's message. [15]When she and the members of her household were baptized, she invited us to her home. "If you consider me a believer in the Lord," she said, "come and stay at my house." And she persuaded us.

[16]Once when we were going to the place of prayer, we were met by a slave girl who had a spirit by which she predicted the future. She earned a great deal of money for her owners by fortune-telling. [17]This girl followed Paul and the rest of us, shouting, "These men are servants of the Most High God, who are telling you the way to be saved." [18]She kept this up for many days. Finally Paul became so troubled that he turned around and said to the spirit, "In the name of Jesus Christ I command you to come out of her!" At that moment the spirit left her.

[19]When the owners of the slave girl realized that their hope of making money was gone, they seized Paul and Silas and dragged them into the marketplace to face the authorities. [20]They brought them before the magistrates and said, "These men are Jews, and are throwing our city into an uproar [21]by advocating customs unlawful for us Romans to accept or practice."

[22]The crowd joined in the attack against Paul and Silas, and the magistrates ordered them to be stripped and beaten. [23]After they had been severely flogged, they were thrown into prison, and the jailer was commanded to guard them carefully. [24]Upon receiving such orders, he put

## NRSV

11We set sail from Troas and took a straight course to Samothrace, the following day to Neapolis, [12]and from there to Philippi, which is a leading city of the district[a] of Macedonia and a Roman colony. We remained in this city for some days. [13]On the sabbath day we went outside the gate by the river, where we supposed there was a place of prayer; and we sat down and spoke to the women who had gathered there. [14]A certain woman named Lydia, a worshiper of God, was listening to us; she was from the city of Thyatira and a dealer in purple cloth. The Lord opened her heart to listen eagerly to what was said by Paul. [15]When she and her household were baptized, she urged us, saying, "If you have judged me to be faithful to the Lord, come and stay at my home." And she prevailed upon us.

16One day, as we were going to the place of prayer, we met a slave-girl who had a spirit of divination and brought her owners a great deal of money by fortune-telling. [17]While she followed Paul and us, she would cry out, "These men are slaves of the Most High God, who proclaim to you[b] a way of salvation." [18]She kept doing this for many days. But Paul, very much annoyed, turned and said to the spirit, "I order you in the name of Jesus Christ to come out of her." And it came out that very hour.

19But when her owners saw that their hope of making money was gone, they seized Paul and Silas and dragged them into the marketplace before the authorities. [20]When they had brought them before the magistrates, they said, "These men are disturbing our city; they are Jews [21]and are advocating customs that are not lawful for us as Romans to adopt or observe." [22]The crowd joined in attacking them, and the magistrates had them stripped of their clothing and ordered them to be beaten with rods. [23]After they had given them a severe flogging, they threw them into prison and ordered the jailer to keep them

[a] Other authorities read *a city of the first district*     [b] Other ancient authorities read *to us*

## NIV

them in the inner cell and fastened their feet in the stocks.

25About midnight Paul and Silas were praying and singing hymns to God, and the other prisoners were listening to them. 26Suddenly there was such a violent earthquake that the foundations of the prison were shaken. At once all the prison doors flew open, and everybody's chains came loose. 27The jailer woke up, and when he saw the prison doors open, he drew his sword and was about to kill himself because he thought the prisoners had escaped. 28But Paul shouted, "Don't harm yourself! We are all here!"

29The jailer called for lights, rushed in and fell trembling before Paul and Silas. 30He then brought them out and asked, "Sirs, what must I do to be saved?"

31They replied, "Believe in the Lord Jesus, and you will be saved—you and your household." 32Then they spoke the word of the Lord to him and to all the others in his house. 33At that hour of the night the jailer took them and washed their wounds; then immediately he and all his family were baptized. 34The jailer brought them into his house and set a meal before them; he was filled with joy because he had come to believe in God—he and his whole family.

35When it was daylight, the magistrates sent their officers to the jailer with the order: "Release those men." 36The jailer told Paul, "The magistrates have ordered that you and Silas be released. Now you can leave. Go in peace."

37But Paul said to the officers: "They beat us publicly without a trial, even though we are Roman citizens, and threw us into prison. And now do they want to get rid of us quietly? No! Let them come themselves and escort us out."

38The officers reported this to the magistrates, and when they heard that Paul and Silas were Roman citizens, they were alarmed. 39They came to appease them and escorted them from the prison, requesting them to leave the city. 40After Paul and Silas came out of the prison, they went to Lydia's house, where they met with the brothers and encouraged them. Then they left.

## NRSV

securely. 24Following these instructions, he put them in the innermost cell and fastened their feet in the stocks.

25About midnight Paul and Silas were praying and singing hymns to God, and the prisoners were listening to them. 26Suddenly there was an earthquake, so violent that the foundations of the prison were shaken; and immediately all the doors were opened and everyone's chains were unfastened. 27When the jailer woke up and saw the prison doors wide open, he drew his sword and was about to kill himself, since he supposed that the prisoners had escaped. 28But Paul shouted in a loud voice, "Do not harm yourself, for we are all here." 29The jailer[a] called for lights, and rushing in, he fell down trembling before Paul and Silas. 30Then he brought them outside and said, "Sirs, what must I do to be saved?" 31They answered, "Believe on the Lord Jesus, and you will be saved, you and your household." 32They spoke the word of the Lord[b] to him and to all who were in his house. 33At the same hour of the night he took them and washed their wounds; then he and his entire family were baptized without delay. 34He brought them up into the house and set food before them; and he and his entire household rejoiced that he had become a believer in God.

35When morning came, the magistrates sent the police, saying, "Let those men go." 36And the jailer reported the message to Paul, saying, "The magistrates sent word to let you go; therefore come out now and go in peace." 37But Paul replied, "They have beaten us in public, uncondemned, men who are Roman citizens, and have thrown us into prison; and now are they going to discharge us in secret? Certainly not! Let them come and take us out themselves." 38The police reported these words to the magistrates, and they were afraid when they heard that they were Roman citizens; 39so they came and apologized to them. And they took them out and asked them to leave the city. 40After leaving the prison they went to Lydia's home; and when they had seen and encouraged the brothers and sisters[c] there, they departed.

[a] Gk He      [b] Other ancient authorities read word of God      [c] Gk brothers

# COMMENTARY

Even though Paul's urban mission remains centered in the synagogues of the diaspora, his turn toward the great cities of Europe reflects changes of cultural scenery and of missionary strategy. Compared to his mission in Roman Asia (see Acts 13–14), for example, Macedonia has a much smaller Jewish population and therefore a more pronounced pagan ethos. Paul's encounter with a clairvoyant slave girl in Philippi, whose unscrupulous handlers have influence over the city's rulers, is an evocative symbol of this region's spiritual state. Moreover, Paul had to leave the city to worship Israel's God, and he found that this same girl was the only "witness" within the city limits to the "Most High God"—empowered by "a spirit of divination" rather than by the Holy Spirit![544] At the end of his mission, the only "houses" that God rebuilt in Philippi are those belonging to Christian converts—first Lydia's and then the jailer's; in fact, Luke's story is enclosed by references to Lydia's "household" congregation (16:15, 40) and centered by the conversion of the jailer's "household" (16:30-34). The reader is reminded, not without considerable irony, of Amos's prophecy of God's housing project among the nations (see 15:16-18): The absence of a Jewish testimony to the "Most High God" in pagan Philippi is finally supplied by repentant Gentiles.

The plotline of this passage begins where most of Paul's efforts do: on a sabbath in a place of prayer with attentive God-fearing Gentiles in attendance (16:11-15). But this place is not an urban synagogue but an informal setting at a riverside outside the city limits, where the most responsive in a group of religious women is a Gentile merchant, Lydia. Paul's mission receives harsher treatment within the city limits, where he encounters the possessed slave girl (16:16-18; cf. 13:6-12) whose healing provokes a sharp legal challenge (16:19-24). As with the apostles before them (see 5:17-18; cf. 12:4-11), Paul and Silas are miraculously liberated from their shackles—in this case, by a timely earthquake rather than by

heaven's angel (16:25-26; see 5:19; cf. 4:31).[545] Unlike the Twelve, however, Silas and Paul remain in prison much to the surprise of the jailer who awakened to opened prison gates and the expectation of a nighttime jailbreak (16:27; see 5:20-26). This occasions the famous missionary exchange between the terrified jailer, who asks his ambiguous question, "What must I do to be saved?" Paul's retort, "Believe on the Lord Jesus, and you will be saved," results in the conversion of a second household of Gentiles (16:28-34). Paul and Silas are released from prison the next day (16:35-36), but rather than depart with grateful acquiescence, citizen Paul excoriates the city's magistrates for their abuse of Roman justice (16:37-38) before making a pastoral house call on Lydia's congregation and then leaving for another city (16:39-40).

The cache of common themes between this story and Paul's Letter to the Philippians commends its role within the NT as the letter's "canonical context." Paul's poignant reflection on his imprisonment and suffering in Philippians (Phil 1:12-14), especially in light of the Lord's humility (Phil 2:6-8), is provided a narrative context by the Acts account, even though it was not written at Philippi. In this regard, the detailed description of the legal apparatus leading to Paul's imprisonment may provide a set of images that enable a more powerful reading of Philippians 1. Paul's preaching of the gospel during his imprisonment is vividly portrayed in Acts, where he sings praises and witnesses to the other prisoners and the jailer. The opposition of pagan religion to Paul's teaching, perhaps even of the Roman imperial cult (Phil 2:9-11), that Paul indicates in his letter (Phil 2:15) is made more clear by Luke's unflattering portrait of Philippi. The significant christological teaching found in this letter (e.g., Phil 2:5-11) is framed by Paul's exhortation to "believe in the Lord Jesus and you will be saved" (Acts 16:31). In particular, this kerygmatic summary from the Paul of Acts captures nicely the central point Paul makes in Philippians against the potential threat of "the dogs" (Phil 3:2-4a) who boast of their nationality

---

544. There is no archival or archaeological evidence of a Jewish congregation in Philippi in Paul's day. See P. Pilhofer, *Philippi*, WUNT 87 (Tübingen: Mohr [Siebeck], 1995). M. Bockmuehl, *Philippians*, BNTC (London: Black, 1997) 6-8, argues that the religious threat Paul envisages in his letter is from pagan "folk" or indigenous religions.

545. For comparison of prison stories in Acts, see ibid., 167-69.

and ritual purity as the true marks of covenant renewal (Phil 3:4*b*-6) rather than of their faith in Christ (Phil 3:7-11). Finally, the poignant images of hospitality, which frame and center this story, may well help the interpreter of Philippians recover the important epistolary theme of the congregation's financial support of and partnership (κοινωνία *koinōnia*) with him in the ministry of the gospel (Phil 4:14-17; cf. 2 Cor 11:9). An element of that congregational partnership is the full participation of men and women in Paul's mission there (Phil 4:2-3), which may explain Luke's shaping of this story about the conversion of a woman and a man and their respective households.

**16:11-15.** A traveling itinerary (vv. 11-12) assures the reader that Paul arrives in Macedonia in response to his vision of the Macedonian man (vv. 8-10). Whatever reluctance Paul may have felt in leaving Roman Asia for Macedonia prior to his vision (see vv. 6-7) was probably not due to a difference in cultures or languages, since people on both sides of the Aegean Sea were thoroughly influenced by Greek culture and literature. The team's base of operations is Philippi, "a leading city of the district of Macedonia and a Roman colony."[546]

The plotline of the activities that follow is initially shaped by two encounters with two very different working women. The first is "a certain woman named Lydia" (v. 14). According to literary pattern, Paul meets Lydia on a sabbath in a makeshift synagogue—in this case located outside of town (v. 13) as a "place of prayer"—that he frequented while staying in Philippi (v. 16). Evidently there is no synagogue in the city. The term "place of prayer" (προσευχή *proseuchē*) is synonymous with "synagogue," even though in this case the term designates a marginal location *outside* the city gates and *beside* a small river on the southern edge of town. The more informal setting allows rabbi Paul to sit with Gentile women gathered

there, which may indicate the city lacks a quorum of ten Jewish males to congregate an assembly of Jews for worship.[547] That Paul only supposed this was a place of prayer may well symbolize the insignificance of a Jewish presence within the city, more than a lack of familiarity with the cityscape—since he had arrived days earlier. All these narrative details contextualize the anti-Semitic slur of the slave girl's owners (16:20).

Paul's posture toward these religious women may indicate the beginning of a worship service, with Paul acting as guest liturgist and rabbi. Lydia is among the women before whom he sits and speaks; her profile is sufficient to indicate the importance of her conversion for the wider Philippiain mission (see v. 40). One of the implied conclusions of James's paradigmatic commentary on Amos is that God-fearing Gentiles attached to synagogues are preferred converts (see 15:20-21). The details of her spiritual biography are therefore similar to God-fearing Cornelius:[548] she is a "worshiper of God, [who] was listening to us" (v. 14; cf. 10:1-8). Although Luke is ambiguous about her religious identity, it is more likely that she is a Gentile attracted to the synagogue than that she is a Jew, since his earlier use of similar wording in Acts 13:43 describes Gentile seekers who are attached to the local synagogue. Also, her personal name, "Lydia," is Greek rather than Jewish; she is named after an ancient city well known for the fabrics she sells. Her attention to Paul's message because "the Lord opened her heart" may well be the result of her good character, reflected in her hospitable reception of Paul (v. 15). The connection between hospitality—sharing goods with others—and responsiveness to the word of God is an important literary theme in both Luke and Acts (cf. Luke 24:29-31).[549] This is another indication of her spiritual authority as first convert and leader of the church in Philippi.

Several details of Lydia's professional résumé indicate her success: She owns her own business and her own home.[550] She is a "dealer in purple cloth" from Thyatira, a city well known for its

---

546. Luke's introduction of Philippi is awkward and its transmission corrupted. The two most likely readings are provided by the NIV, which has Philippi as "the leading city of that district of Macedonia," and the NRSV, which more ambiguously notes that Philippi is "a leading city." While Philippi was an important Roman colony with the privileged status of *ius italicum* (a Roman legal status exempting the colony from various taxes) it was *not* the leading city of its district; Amphipolis was. The NRSV follows the critical text more precisely, and its rendering (and implied meaning) is preferred: Philippi is one of four "leading" cities that made up Roman Macedonia. Luke emphasizes its importance in order to underscore its programmatic importance for Paul's European mission.

547. F. F. Bruce, *The Acts of the Apostles,* rev. ed., NICNT (Grand Rapids: Eerdmans, 1988) 358-59.

548. See Spencer, *Acts,* 164-65, for details of their comparison.

549. See Johnson, *The Acts of the Apostles,* 297.

550. No husband is mentioned, which may indicate that she is a single (divorced, widowed) woman or, if married, that her husband is not a believer.

textile industry (v. 14; cf. Rev 2:18-29). Purple clothing was destined for the rich and royal in the Roman world, where it symbolized power and influence. A merchant in purple cloth, then, is someone who rubbed shoulders daily with society's rich and famous. Luke's use of Lydia's personal name in his story may well indicate her social prominence.[551] In his narrative world, however, even the socially prominent are spiritually impoverished without Jesus; Lydia's eager response to the gospel is another illustration of this reality.

**16:16-18.** Paul's exorcism of the divining slave girl recalls a similar encounter found in Mark's Gospel (Mark 1:21-26; cf. Luke 4:41). At the beginning of his messianic mission, Jesus enters the synagogue at Capernaum to worship God. Among those in attendance is a demoniac who alone among the worshipers knows Jesus' messianic identity. Jesus' authority and, ironically, the truth of the gospel he proclaims are aptly demonstrated when he expels the demon from the worshiping community. Similar points are made by this episode in Acts. There is also the sense that the slave girl unwittingly has thrown down a gauntlet of sorts to Paul. His spiritual authority as a prophet-like-Jesus is thereby confirmed by this exorcism: Paul's Holy Spirit is greater than the unholy spirit who speaks through the girl. Moreover, her public divination that Paul and Silas are "slaves of the Most High God, who proclaim to you a way of salvation" (v. 17), which goes on "for several days," ironically introduces the kerygmatic theme that Paul's conversion of the Philippian jailer will later illustrate (see vv. 30-31). The term "Most High God" is also used in worship of Zeus, to whom her own handlers may be attached and she their "slave" as well. Paul, of course, is "slave" to the Most High God of Israel (see 7:48), and his exorcism of the girl's spirit is a demonstration of God's authority over Zeus and all other pagan gods of the Philippian pantheon. This demonstration clears the way for a fuller expression of Paul's prophetic authority and gospel when he leads the

jailer's household into the "way of salvation" (see 4:12; also 2:28; 9:2).

The species of the girl's unholy spirit is literally "a pythian spirit" and recalls the Greek Πυθῶν (Pythōn) myth of the dragon that guarded the Delphi oracle at Mt. Parnassus and was killed by Apollo. In Luke's day, its name and legend were attached to someone with clairvoyant powers or, perhaps, to the trickery of a ventriloquist.[552] The powers or trickery of this slave girl are apparently extraordinary or the Philippian public extremely gullible, since she "brought her owners a great deal of money by fortune-telling" (v. 16).

The formula Paul uses to expel the spirit from the slave girl recalls Peter's command for healing "in the name of Jesus Christ" (see 3:6, 16; 4:10). Then as here the prophet's use of "the name" to heal and make people whole again is not magical but confessional: Paul's rebuke of the spirit expresses his surety of God's triumph over evil. While an exercise of his spiritual authority, it is also symbolic of his kerygmatic claim that the risen Jesus is Messiah and Lord. This exorcism itself, then, aptly illustrates what Paul will later proclaim to the jailer, fulfilling the slave girl's own prophecy: The Most High God saves the lost.

**16:19-23.** The dispossession of "property" is an important literary theme in Acts, typically serving as a barometer of relations with God. Evident exploitation of another for profit is especially condemning, not only of the girl's owners but of the religious climate of Philippi that would support their religious profit-taking. The animus toward religious charlatans, especially those who exploited human "property" to satisfy their greed, is often expressed in Greco-Roman literature as well. The greedy owners' immediate response to the healing of their slave girl, then, is hardly happy: "They seized Paul and Silas and dragged them into the marketplace before the authorities" (16:19). Their motive for doing so is clearly financial; they saw that their profits "went out with the demon"![553]

551. B. Witherington, *The Acts of the Apostles: A Socio-Rhetorical Commentary* (Grand Rapids: Eerdmans, 1998) 491-92; however, see Spencer, *Acts*, 165, who follows Reimer's argument that Lydia's location within Philippian society is more marginal than most scholars assume. See I. Reimer's, *Women in the Acts of the Apostles: A Feminist Liberation Perspective* (Minneapolis: Fortress, 1995) 102-9.

552. C. K. Barrett, *A Critical and Exegetical Commentary on the Acts of the Apostles,* 2 vols, ICC (Edinburgh: T. & T. Clark, 1994, 1998) 2:785; however, see H. Conzelmann, *The Acts of the Apostles,* trans. J. Limburg et al., ed. E. J. Epp and C. R. Matthews, Hermeneia (Philadelphia: Fortress, 1987) 131.

553. L. T. Johnson, *The Acts of the Apostles,* SP 5 (Collegeville, Minn.: Liturgical, 1992) 295.

The juridical terms used by Luke in this passage indicate that a lawsuit is brought against Paul for this loss of income. The "marketplace" (ἀγορά agora) is the city's secular synagogue where people assemble to conduct various transactions, including legal ones. The greedy owners follow a precise protocol in bringing their claims to the court: They go first to the "authorities," who are responsible for public order, and turn Paul and Silas over to the local "magistrates," who are responsible for settling civil claims. Perhaps realizing that loss of income due to the loss of a pythian spirit would not work well in a public court, the clever owners bring a more mean-spirited yet appealing accusation before the magistrates in two parts: "They are Jews and are advocating customs that are not lawful for us" (16:20-21). The initial charge appeals to Roman anti-Semitism and is propagandistic without legal merit. The clear intent is to incite prejudice against Jews in a pagan marketplace, and it is this appeal that sparks the crowd's hostilities against Paul.

Their second charge appeals to the legal "principle of incompatibility" according to which it is considered unlawful within the premises of a Roman colony to proselytize converts to a non-Roman cult.[554] This charge is also without merit since by Paul's day the principle was no longer followed in legal practice. Further, there is every indication that Paul recruited converts *outside* the city limits at the place of prayer and therefore was not in violation of this law in any case—unless the slave girl's exorcism in Jesus' name is considered an act of proselytizing her.

It is significant that Paul's religious practices, which Luke carefully links to the place of prayer, are recognized as "Jewish" and in sharp contrast with the Roman customs of Philippi (v. 21). In fact, the mob reaction against Paul, obviously incited by their anti-Semitic sentiments, makes this point all the more clear. Once again Luke portrays Paul as an exemplar of James's primary concern for Jewish purity on pagan turf; Paul has not contaminated himself by accommodating to Gentile forms of religious observance. Paul is no "gentilized" Jew (see 15:20-21).

There is no indication of a court verdict, unless the violent crowd is considered a jury of sorts and

their attack on Paul and Silas constitutes an indictment of guilt. Without being granted any opportunity to defend their actions,[555] Paul and Silas are stripped and beaten with rods by the order of the court, the standard Roman legal procedure (v. 22). They are then thrown into prison and are securely guarded (v. 23). These injudicious actions, however, will come back to haunt the magistrates by story's end (see vv. 35-40).

**16:24-34.** The next scene introduces the city's jailer, who will play a complementary role to Lydia's in this drama. As its plotline unfolds he will personify the power of God's grace that Paul proclaims. He appears as a functionary of civil authority who "following these instructions" puts Paul and Silas in solitary confinement, their feet fastened "in the stocks" (v. 24). These images of harsh treatment and loneliness serve two purposes. They recall the Lord's prophecy that Paul would "suffer for the sake of my name" (9:16). Paul is imprisoned because he exorcized the girl's divining spirit "in the name of Jesus Christ" (see v. 18).

The jailer's actions also stage the miracle that follows: Surely there is no escape at "midnight" from "the innermost cell" when one's feet are "in the stocks."[556] The prison itself symbolizes a place where the cosmic and invisible battle between God and evil (or Zeus) is being waged. Paul and Silas are doing what exemplary believers must do when waiting for God to act: They are "praying and singing hymns to God" (v. 25; cf. 1:14). While observing their witness, the attention of their co-prisoners is directed to the source of liberating power; indeed, "that the other prisoners heard them proves—that the earthquake is God's answer."[557]

The earthquake strikes suddenly and opens the prison doors and unfastens the prisoners' chains (v. 26), but no one leaves. Luke does not give the reason for this unexpected response to God's intervention; however, had Paul and Silas left no one would have prevented the jailer from taking his life. The earthquake has also awakened him, but why he should consider taking his life prior to a

554. Barrett, *Acts*, 2:790.

555. This is no doubt the case because to this point Paul and Silas are unwelcome and Jewish "foreigners" without local rights. See Witherington, *The Acts of the Apostles*, 497.

556. Conzelmann, *Acts*, 132.

557. E. Haenchen, *The Acts of the Apostles* (Philadelphia: Westminster, 1971) 497.

check of the innermost cell is the stuff of legend! Nor is it clear in any case why he should resort to such a dramatic solution to his problem, unless living is a fate worse than death (see 12:17).

More likely, the jailer's decision to take his own life is due to his religious conviction. Especially since earthquakes were thought to be acts of divine intervention, he may have thought it was an act of judgment from which his salvation is unlikely. The jailer's response to Paul's saving call makes perfect sense against this backdrop. Initially, he "fell down trembling [ἔντρομος entromos] before Paul and Silas" (v. 29; see also 10:25). This jailer is scared because he has "seen" his fate and it is not good. The question he poses of his prisoners, whom he now recognizes as agents of divine power, is utterly pragmatic: "Sirs, what must I do to be saved?" (v. 30). That is, he wants to know whether or not his life can be spared by Paul's God.

The jailer's story parallels Paul's own story, which is the subtext of the gospel he now presents: "Believe on the Lord Jesus, and you will be saved, you and your household" (v. 31; cf. 1 Tim 1:12-14). This firm connection of belief and salvation is central to Luke's account of Paul's gospel (see 14:9; 15:11; cf. Rom 10:9), and it provides a succinct formulation of the "way of salvation" called for by the slave girl's oracle (see 16:17). The repetition of "household" (οἶκος oikos) both in Paul's gospel presentation and then again in Luke's following summary (16:32) recalls the images of "re-housed" Israel from Amos's prophecy to remind the reader that God has granted Gentiles a share of Israel's blessings (see 15:13-19). What is different about this second conversion story in Philippi, and yet complementary to Lydia's, is that the jailer is not a God-fearer attached to a local synagogue; he is a pagan attached to the city prison, a symbol of opposition to the church's mission. The referent of Amos's prophecy concerning "all the Gentiles over whom my name has been called" (15:17) is thereby expanded to include even those pagan converts God calls out of spiritually desolate places that are full of evil spirits, moral rogues, and anti-Semitic sentiments.

First a woman, now a man, and the households of both evince the universal scope of God's saving work. As before in Lydia's case (see v. 15), confirmation of the jailer's salvation is demonstrated by

his hospitality toward Paul and Silas. In this case, "he took them and washed their wounds . . . and brought them up into the house and set food before them" (vv. 33-34). With the festive meal, Luke adds that the "entire household rejoiced that he had become a believer in God." The combination of meal and joy strongly implies their celebration gathered around holy Eucharist, when Jesus' suffering is remembered as an act of redemption. The faithful reader likewise sees in Paul's suffering for the sake of Jesus' name a means of grace that brings the jailer and his family into the way of salvation.

**16:35-40.** The account of the jailer's salvation is sandwiched between episodes that tell of Paul and Silas's legal problems. The present passage continues from 16:23, describing events the morning after the great earthquake. Paul and Silas are back in jail. "The police" (οἱ ῥαβδοῦχοι hoi rhabdouchoi) are now involved as delegates of the court who carry messages from the magistrates to the jailer on prison-related matters. Their message in this case is highly compressed, since Luke is not interested in what prompts their decision to "let those men go" (v. 35)—even though we can imagine why.[558] Paul's response, however, reflects the honor/shame culture of his world. He does not want the magistrates to brush the crumbs of their shameful behavior under the carpet of public scrutiny, and so he lists the grievances that resulted in his humiliation: public flogging, condemnation, and incarceration of innocent Roman citizens, without benefit of trial or defense attorneys (16:37). Imprisoning and flogging a Roman citizen without benefit of a trial is illegal; to do so publicly is a criminal act worthy of execution. No wonder the magistrates "were afraid when they heard that they were Roman citizens" (v. 38).

The stunning new piece of information that Paul and Silas are both Roman citizens requires a rereading of Acts in two important ways. If Paul's suffering is not due to political questions about his Roman citizenship, then it must be due to his religious identity. In this sense, the anti-Semitism of the slaveowners, motivated by greed, is true to public form. Beyond Palestine and the Jewish

---

558. The Western version of Acts explains how the magistrates reconvened in the *agora* to reflect upon the previous evening's earthquake, determined it had something to do with Paul and Silas, and decided to release them to appease the gods.

synagogues of Roman cities, Paul suffers for being Jewish. Moreover, Acts tells us what the Letters do not: Paul is a Roman citizen, with all the rights and privileges due him. Even though the interpreter may set aside the historicity of Luke's claim,[559] Paul's citizenship is an important, although typically ironic, feature of his apologia in Acts. In this regard, Paul's acceptance of Philippi's official apology (see v. 39) symbolizes his general attitude toward Rome in Acts. His point is that Rome is unable to subvert the work of God's sal-

559. For an evaluation of Paul's claim of Roman citizenship, see A. Sherwin-White, *The Roman Citizenship*, 2nd ed. (Oxford: Clarendon, 1973). See also J. A. Fitzmyer, *The Acts of the Apostles*, AB 31 (Garden City, N.Y.: Doubleday, 1998) 144-45; G. Lüdemann, *Early Christianity According to the Traditions in Acts* (Minneapolis: Fortress, 1989) 240-41.

vation in the world; and even this great empire must come hat in hand to the prophets of the Most High God.

Paul and Silas depart the city only after having gone to Lydia's home to encourage "the brothers and sisters there" (v. 40). Luke's nice literary touch effectively encloses the narrative of the Philippian mission by mentioning hospitable Lydia's faithfulness to the Lord (see v. 15). The sequence of their departure from the city following their visit to the Christian congregation gathered in Lydia's home is deliberate and important—that is, her home lies *within* city limits. In absence of a quorum of male Jews to establish a urban synagogue (see vv. 13-14), believers now gather in the home of a God-fearing Gentile woman in witness to the gospel.

# REFLECTIONS

**1.** "A certain woman named Lydia, a worshiper of God, was listening to us" (16:14*a*). Much has been written about Luke's view of women. Although largely oriented toward males (e.g., the prophets-like-Jesus of Acts are all males, with the possible exception of Priscilla and the daughters of Philip), Luke's narrative world is still a location where females are given greater prominence and independence in comparison to his social world. Lydia is a literary example of a theological conviction: God's saving grace dismantles various social barriers that cultivate strife between people. Mutuality is the watchword of a community of goods! Upon closer reflection, the case of Lydia is especially invigorating as an example of the church's counterculture. She makes her entrance into Acts as a religious person without permission of or reference to her husband. The first place mentioned is not her home but a "place of prayer," and when she does mention her home it is by self-reference: It is "my" home. The impression is given that she is self-sufficient, a successful businesswoman with a decent income whose hospitality demonstrates her fine character. In all these ways, Luke has Lydia play the role of an ideal convert. His depiction of the easy relations between a male religious leader and a female outsider symbolizes a counterculture that remains impressive even for our modern liberal democracies. Indeed, it is her home that becomes the spiritual center for the entire city, and the story's presumption is that she becomes its spiritual leader. Yet Luke's principal point is not sociological but theological: Lydia is saved because "the Lord opened her heart to listen eagerly" (16:14*b*). For all her evident social accomplishment, she had a spiritual need satisfied by hearing God's word.

**2.** "What must I do to be saved?" (16:30 NIV and NRSV). Luke's marvelous telling of the Philippian jailer's improbable conversion is useful for reflection on the nature of Christian conversion. Paul and Silas's worshipful response to their jailhouse suffering and their refusal to escape strikes most readers as odd if not humorous. These missionaries are incorrigible! But is not this Luke's point? Typically, conversions are the by-product of the trenchant faithfulness of others, when believers are ever alert to the need and prospect of salvation. The polyvalence of the jailer's cry for help is also instructive. Luke resists the divorce between bodily and religious species of salvation: The God who saves the jailer from the executioner's sword is the same God who forgives him and his household of their sins. In fact, conversion often occurs at the intersection of the two wants, when the need for healing or physical rescue occasions the need to hear the gospel appeal, "Believe on the Lord Jesus, and you will be saved" (16:31 NRSV). Note also that an extended protocol of conversion suggests a way of salvation beyond gospel preaching that includes Christian instruction (16:32), baptism (16:33), and caring fellowship (16:34). These are all sacraments of grace that initiate new believers more fully into their life with God.

**3.** "They were afraid when they heard that they were Roman citizens" (16:38 NRSV). For the first time Paul appeals to his Romans citizenship, and he does so strategically. In many ways the Paul of Acts personifies the church's sometimes messy but potentially useful relations with the secular state, and this story narrates a case in point. The reader should first ask why Paul delayed insisting on his rights as a Roman citizenship until *after* his experiences of police brutality and illegal incarceration? Paul's strategic acceptance of their apology (16:39) suggests a reversal of power that has become an important political matter only *after* the households of faith have been established in Philippi. The proper role of civil authority is not to dictate terms so that the church becomes yet another institution of its power. Rather civil authority is now obliged to safeguard the deposit of faith in their city as an institution of divine power (cf. Rom 13:1-7). Luke's portrait of Rome in Acts is of the *inability* of secular authority to subvert the work of God's salvation in the world.

# ACTS 17:1-15, CONFLICT AND CONVERSION AMONG DIASPORA JEWS

NIV

**17** When they had passed through Amphipolis and Apollonia, they came to Thessalonica, where there was a Jewish synagogue. [2]As his custom was, Paul went into the synagogue, and on three Sabbath days he reasoned with them from the Scriptures, [3]explaining and proving that the Christ[a] had to suffer and rise from the dead. "This Jesus I am proclaiming to you is the Christ,[a]" he said. [4]Some of the Jews were persuaded and joined Paul and Silas, as did a large number of God-fearing Greeks and not a few prominent women.

[5]But the Jews were jealous; so they rounded up some bad characters from the marketplace, formed a mob and started a riot in the city. They rushed to Jason's house in search of Paul and Silas in order to bring them out to the crowd.[b] [6]But when they did not find them, they dragged Jason and some other brothers before the city officials, shouting: "These men who have caused trouble all over the world have now come here, [7]and Jason has welcomed them into his house. They are all defying Caesar's decrees, saying that there

[a] *3 Or* Messiah    [b] *5 Or the assembly of the people*

NRSV

**17** After Paul and Silas[a] had passed through Amphipolis and Apollonia, they came to Thessalonica, where there was a synagogue of the Jews. [2]And Paul went in, as was his custom, and on three sabbath days argued with them from the scriptures, [3]explaining and proving that it was necessary for the Messiah[b] to suffer and to rise from the dead, and saying, "This is the Messiah,[b] Jesus whom I am proclaiming to you." [4]Some of them were persuaded and joined Paul and Silas, as did a great many of the devout Greeks and not a few of the leading women. [5]But the Jews became jealous, and with the help of some ruffians in the marketplaces they formed a mob and set the city in an uproar. While they were searching for Paul and Silas to bring them out to the assembly, they attacked Jason's house. [6]When they could not find them, they dragged Jason and some believers[c] before the city authorities,[d] shouting, "These people who have been turning the world upside down have come here also, [7]and Jason has entertained them as guests. They are all acting contrary to the decrees of the emperor, say-

[a] *Gk they*    [b] *Or the Christ*    [c] *Gk brothers*    [d] *Gk politarchs*

NIV

is another king, one called Jesus." [8]When they heard this, the crowd and the city officials were thrown into turmoil. [9]Then they made Jason and the others post bond and let them go.

[10]As soon as it was night, the brothers sent Paul and Silas away to Berea. On arriving there, they went to the Jewish synagogue. [11]Now the Bereans were of more noble character than the Thessalonians, for they received the message with great eagerness and examined the Scriptures every day to see if what Paul said was true. [12]Many of the Jews believed, as did also a number of prominent Greek women and many Greek men.

[13]When the Jews in Thessalonica learned that Paul was preaching the word of God at Berea, they went there too, agitating the crowds and stirring them up. [14]The brothers immediately sent Paul to the coast, but Silas and Timothy stayed at Berea. [15]The men who escorted Paul brought him to Athens and then left with instructions for Silas and Timothy to join him as soon as possible.

NRSV

ing that there is another king named Jesus." [8]The people and the city officials were disturbed when they heard this, [9]and after they had taken bail from Jason and the others, they let them go.

[10]That very night the believers[a] sent Paul and Silas off to Beroea; and when they arrived, they went to the Jewish synagogue. [11]These Jews were more receptive than those in Thessalonica, for they welcomed the message very eagerly and examined the scriptures every day to see whether these things were so. [12]Many of them therefore believed, including not a few Greek women and men of high standing. [13]But when the Jews of Thessalonica learned that the word of God had been proclaimed by Paul in Beroea as well, they came there too, to stir up and incite the crowds. [14]Then the believers[a] immediately sent Paul away to the coast, but Silas and Timothy remained behind. [15]Those who conducted Paul brought him as far as Athens; and after receiving instructions to have Silas and Timothy join him as soon as possible, they left him.

[a] Gk brothers

# COMMENTARY

Acts next follows Paul's travel itinerary along the Via Egnatia from Philippi to Thessalonica (see the map, "The Early Eastern Roman Empire," 4), the most important city of Macedonia. The related narratives of his mission there (17:1-9) and then down the road in Beroea (17:10-15) are shaped by a familiar pattern: Paul begins his crusade in the city's synagogue (17:1, 10b) where he worships according to Jewish "custom" on successive sabbaths (17:2) and expounds the Scriptures to those in attendance (17:2-3, 11). Even though some Jews are convinced by Paul's teaching and are converted (17:4, 12), his argument from Scripture that Jesus is the Messiah divides the house of Israel. Other Jews do not repent and turn against Paul and his converts (17:5-6a, 13), bringing legal action against them (17:6b-9). Although he enjoys success among devout Gentiles attached to the local synagogue (17:4), this hostile response forces Paul and Silas to leave town "immediately" for the next venue of ministry (17:10a, 14-15).

The specific charges leveled against Paul repeat in different circumstances what earlier had taken place in Philippi (see 16:19-23). The involvement of the Roman legal system in his destiny will be a featured narrative element during the second half of Acts. The accusations brought to the city officials of Thessalonica by Paul's Jewish opponents are similar to those brought earlier to Philippi's rulers and magistrates by his pagan opponents. In both cases, Paul is accused of disturbing the peace in a way that goes against Roman political conventions. It should not surprise us that Paul's Philippian opponents would appeal to Rome in a jingoistic idiom and with materialistic intent—they are pagans. That Paul's *Jewish* opponents would bring similar charges to civil authority, however, is surprising. Perhaps Luke considers this an instance of James's anxiety about the "gentilizing" of repentant Jews—but with irony, since his worries are realized in *unrepentant* Jews whose legal maneuver evinces a thoroughly secular approach.

This story prepares the NT reader for the Thessalonian correspondence of the Pauline corpus that follows. On the one hand, "we find the highest degree of correspondence between Luke's narrative and the information given by Paul's letters."[560] Paul's sketch of his suffering and opposition in Thessalonica (1 Thess 2:1–3:2) follows the plotline of Luke's story. On the other hand, Luke's shaping of his story supports his own theological interests, which include not only the Jewish element of Paul's religious practices, his spiritual authority, and his mission, but also the character of the "devout Gentiles" attracted to Paul's preaching—in this case, prominent women. These are not unrelated to the themes of Paul's Thessalonians letters, especially their common concern that Paul's religious authority is deeply rooted in his heroic suffering. Further, the thematic connection between character and receptivity to the gospel, nicely illustrated in the story of Paul's Beroean mission (see 17:11), is envisaged in 1 Thessalonians, where Pauline paraenesis functions to describe a manner of life that both pleases God (cf. 1 Thess 4) and establishes a congregation firmly in the faith (cf. 1 Thess 3).

**17:1-4.** Amphipolis and Apollonia are cities along the main Roman road through the region, the Via Egnatia (see the map "The Early Eastern Roman Empire," 4). Nothing more is said of them in Acts, which has led some scholars to speculate that Paul made no missionary effort in these cities, perhaps because they had no synagogue.[561] In any case, Paul no doubt had included Thessalonica in his itinerary because of its importance to the region, and he found "a synagogue of the Jews" there (17:1).

An exemplar of repentant Israel, Paul "went in [the synagogue] on three sabbath days" (v. 2). His growing reputation among the Jewish communities in the diaspora is due to his authoritative Bible teaching. This feature of Paul's mission is nicely captured by this text, where he is said to perform a sequence of tasks apropos of a trained exegete of Scripture: "from the scriptures" (γραφαί *graphai;* see 1:16), he "argued" (διαλέγομαι *dialegomai*), "explained" (διανοίγω *dianoigō*), and "proved" (παρατίθημι *paratithēmi*). The first task should

not be viewed as argumentative but as that of the scholar who carefully sifts textual evidence is mounting a persuasive case. The second task refers to the interpretive act of recovering Scripture's contemporary meaning for its present readers. In the gospel this same word is used of the Lord's instruction following his resurrection, when he "opened" their minds to the messianic meaning of Scripture (cf. Luke 24:32, 45). The final task envisages the interpreter as a host who sets the table in preparation for a common meal. Here, then, Paul gathers together the fruit of his study and research, together with appropriate illustrations, to feed his congregation the gospel truth that "it was necessary [δεῖ *dei*] for the Messiah to suffer and to rise from the dead" (v. 3). We can fill in the kerygmatic gaps from earlier speeches in Acts; and we know the theological import of *dei,* which claims that the gospel agrees with Scripture's script of God's salvation (see 1:16; 3:18; cf. 2:22-23). Even so, Fitzmyer's observation bears repeating: These notions of a suffering and resurrected Messiah (rather than Israel) are foreign to the "plain" teaching of the OT, and it is this radical cast of Paul s argument from Scripture that explains the conflict and controversy he provokes among Thessalonica's Jews.[562]

In any case, Paul's proclamation that the Jesus who suffered is the living Messiah "persuaded" (πείθω *peithō;* see 5:36-37; 13:43) a few Jews into the faith, and they "joined" (προσκληράομαι *prosklēraomai;* lit., "cast their lot with") the Christian mission in their city. Presumably these Jewish converts include Jason and those meeting in his house (see 17:6). In addition to these repentant Jews, characteristically mentioned first by Luke, are "a great many of the devout Greeks and not a few of the leading women" (17:4). Probably nothing is indicated by Luke's separation of "devout" Gentiles from the important women who also converted; they are all attached to the synagogue. The impression of Jewish influence in high places of Thessalonian culture now extends to Paul's mission (see 13:50).[563]

**17:5-9.** "The Jews" (see 12:3; 13:45; 14:2)

---

560. Johnson, *The Acts of the Apostles,* 308.
561. Cf. Barrett, *Acts,* 2:809.

562. Fitzmyer, *The Acts of the Apostles,* 594.
563. In noting the contrasting responses between the "leading women" at Pisidian Antioch and here, Tannehill observes that Luke's literary tendency is to use common patterns in varying ways to give some sense of the varied results of Paul's mission. See R. C. Tannehill, *The Acts of the Apostles,* vol. 2 of *The Narrative Unity of Luke-Acts: A Literary Interpretation* (Minneapolis: Fortress, 1990) 2:208.

who reacted against Paul's teaching ministry did so in disagreement with his messianic reading of Scripture (see above), not because of Paul's growing influence in the city's synagogue (v. 5*a*; see also 5:17; 13:45; cf. 7:9). They hired some "ruffians" to form a mob in the agora that would "set the city in an uproar" (v. 5*b*), which thereby allows them to falsely accuse Paul and Silas of "turning the world upside down" (v. 6). Paul's opponents routinely use this tactic, using the riot they instigate as evidence against the church's mission. In this case, Paul's opponents wanted to bring him and Silas before the δῆμος (*dēmos,* "citizens' assembly") but could not locate them; and so they took their mischief to "Jason's house" (v. 5*c*) and "dragged Jason and some believers" before the city authorities to accuse Jason of having "entertained them as guests" (v. 7*a*), thereby bringing the virtue of hospitality to trial.

The "city authorities" (πολιτάρχαι *politarchai*) are local magistrates who formed the city's administrative council and whose tasks are similar to those of the Philippian "magistrates" (see 16:20). One of their principal duties is to make certain that proper respect and due loyalty are given to Caesar. For this reason the only politically relevant accusation leveled against Paul and Silas is the third, which claims that they say that there is "another king named Jesus" (v. 7*b*)—high treason against the empire and disrespect toward Caesar. Such a charge foreshadows Paul's Roman trial, when he will be accused of sedition by reason of preaching the gospel that Jesus is the Messiah (see 24:5). The legal challenge before this court is not whether Paul preaches that Jesus is the Davidic Messiah who rules as Lord over an invisible, cosmic kingdom; clearly he does (see 13:21-23; cf. Luke 1:33; 23:2-3). The relevant issue is whether Christian missionaries are free to do so in a secular empire where the only legitimate ruler is Caesar—a religious vigilance maintained under threat of social unrest (v. 5*a*).

Paul's Jewish opponents are disingenuous since their criticism of him is motivated by theological disagreement rather than political loyalty. For this reason, Rome does not take their court appearances and legal accusations seriously. More often than not, civic authority rightly recognizes this is a religious conflict and properly locates it within

Jewish community. While the court is "thrown into turmoil" (v. 8),[564] it nevertheless releases Jason and the other believers in receipt of bail money (v. 9) and refuses to give in to the will of the mob.

**17:10-12.** Realizing the imminent danger to Paul and Silas in Thessalonica, the believers send them by night to Beroea, a major city about fifty miles southwest of Thessalonica in the foothills of the Olympian mountains and the regional center of the imperial religion (v. 10*a*). The narrative is compressed, and so nothing more is known of Paul's activities upon arrival; the plotline moves him quickly into the synagogue (v. 10*b*), where Paul finds Jews "of more noble character [εὐγενέστεροι *eugenesteroi*] than the Thessalonians" (v. 11). Luke's comparative judgment of character, perhaps grounded in local knowledge,[565] explains the Beroean's responsiveness to the gospel: They took to Paul's teaching "eagerly" and studied with him every day.

Paul's Bible study in Beroea is a function of his prophetic vocation and is realized in synagogue study that follows the same sequence of interpretive tasks as in Thessalonica with the same christological aim: to call Jews to repent and turn to Jesus as God's Messiah (see 17:2-3). The new word introduced here, ἀνακρίνω (*anakrinō,* "examine"), is a legal term used nowhere else in the NT for the study of Scripture. Luke uses it here for Paul's appeal to Israel's Scriptures as a legal "witness" to warrant his gospel's claims about Jesus. That is, his claims about Jesus are not the by-product of an imaginative reading of Scripture. Rather, they are judicious and give competent testimony by which a fair verdict may be rendered by his auditors; indeed, "many of them therefore believed" (v. 12).[566]

**17:13-15.** Perhaps for this reason, when "the Jews of Thessalonica" hear of Paul's success in

564. The NRSV's translation of ταράσσω (*tarassō,* "disturbed") fails to pick up its primary connotation of being confused by different reports, which is better captured by the NIV. See Fitzmyer, *The Acts of the Apostles,* 597.

565. So Witherington, *The Acts of the Apostles,* 509.

566. The Western text significantly modifies Luke's expansive description of both Jewish and women conversions: Some Jews "believed while others did not; and from the Greeks and people of high standing, many men and women became believers."

Beroea, they arrive "to stir up and incite the crowds" (v. 13; see also vv. 5-9). Because the Thessalonian *politarchai* (or city authorities; see 17:6, 8) have no civic jurisdiction in Beroea, the Thessalonians cannot bring their legal brief with them; their mischief is localized and ad hoc. In fact, Luke mentions that Silas and Timothy remain in Beroea, perhaps because they are free to do so and the pastoral need there is great (v. 14).[567]

Once again, however, Paul is scurried away in haste toward the coast for his safety (17:14) before being brought overland to Athens (17:15)—a journey of over two hundred miles from Beroea.

567. Lüdemann, *Early Christianity According to the Traditions in Acts*, 188, argues that Paul's reference to Timothy in 1 Thess 3:2 assumes that he becomes Paul's colleague during his Athenian mission and was only then sent back to Thessalonica before finally joining him in Corinth. Acts seems to place Timothy in Beroea/Thessalonica prior to Athens. For this reason, Lüdemann claims that Luke's informa-tion is inaccurate. More likely, as Barrett, *Acts*, 2:820, points out, Timothy has been a "silent partner" since Lystra (see 16:1-3) and only now is entrusted with an important task. For this reason, Johnson, *The Acts of the Apostles*, 308, concludes that "the narrative corresponds exceptionally well with the information contained in 1 Thess 3:1-2."

# REFLECTIONS

**1.** Paul "argued with them from the scriptures, explaining and proving that it was necessary for the Messiah to suffer" (17:2-3*a* NRSV). Few passages in Acts so clearly express the impor-tance of Scripture in Christian preaching. In Thessalonica on successive sabbaths Paul argued and explained and proved the core claims of his gospel from the Scriptures, while the Jews of Beroea "examined the scriptures every day" with him (17:11). This pattern of proof from prophecy, which assumes that belief in Scripture's Messiah will lead the reasonable person to choose for Jesus, is a distinctive feature of Luke's apologia. Elsewhere in the New Testament, Scripture is merely cited as fulfilled by Jesus. According to Acts, however, Scripture supplies the working "script" that sets out the terms of God's salvation, which its inspired interpreters then relate logically both to Jesus and to their missionary experiences that are made necessary by divine ordination. In Luke's sense, biblical prophecy provides an authoritative context within which a messianic community gathers together to reflect on the redemptive importance of Jesus' death and resurrection. For the Jewish Paul of Acts, the Hebrew Bible is not some sacred text that can be bent at will but Israel's special witness to God's plan of salvation. That plan reaches its climax in the suffering and resurrection of Jesus (= the gospel) and continues to be disclosed in the church's mission (= Acts).

This story provides, however, two important qualifications to what has become for some believers the typical pattern of Christian apologetics—that is, the defense and/or proof of Christian belief. First, Paul's audiences in Thessalonica and Beroea consist of Bible-believing Jews. There are no pagans at his Bible studies. In this sense, then, his proof from prophecy argu-ments and the *theo*logic he presumes make sense only for those who agree that Scripture is the inspired medium of God's Word. For those who deny the authority of Scripture, Paul's argument that prophecy provides reason to believe that Jesus is the Messiah is without rational basis. Second, the response to Paul's apologia among Bible-believing Jews is mixed. That is, the con-troversy within the synagogue turned on competing conceptions of the "gospel" to which Scripture aims its interpreters. Not every religious person who accepts the authority of Scripture will interpret its theological meaning and practical relevance in the same way. The conflict between Paul and his opponents is not over his view or use of Scripture, which is thoroughly Jewish; rather, the unrepentant Jews who challenge Paul do so because they reject his belief that the risen Jesus is God's Messiah by whom God's biblical promises are approached and interpreted.

Believers are simply mistaken when they think that the contest for souls is settled by the battle for the Bible. Winning agreement over the precise terms of Scripture's authority is no guarantee for a right understanding of or a faithful response to gospel truth. While proof-from-prophecy provides an additional reason to consider the gospel message more carefully, it is finally the proclamation of the gospel and its embodiment in the community's life together that draw all people toward Christ in faith.

**2.** "The Bereans were of more noble character than the Thessalonians, for they received the message with great eagerness" (17:11 NIV). Is everyone who hears the gospel on equal footing to respond to its truth in faith? Evidently Luke would answer no. The inherent inequality between people, however, is not a matter of divine predestination according to which some are elect for salvation while others are not. Rather some are better able to receive the message of salvation with greater eagerness because of their more "noble character." This "nobility" is not a genetic disposition or an "accident of birth." But surely there are certain environments of family life, relationships, and even culture, as well as various personal habits of mind and heart, that nurture and shape the sort of person who is interested in the things of God. While salvation is surely the work of a faithful God in combination with an obedient church, every choice for Jesus is freely made by those who are moved to respond to the gospel. Luke's additional factor in this redemptive calculus is that some people are more responsive simply because of who they are.

# ACTS 17:16-34, PAUL'S ATHENIAN MISSION

## NIV

16While Paul was waiting for them in Athens, he was greatly distressed to see that the city was full of idols. 17So he reasoned in the synagogue with the Jews and the God-fearing Greeks, as well as in the marketplace day by day with those who happened to be there. 18A group of Epicurean and Stoic philosophers began to dispute with him. Some of them asked, "What is this babbler trying to say?" Others remarked, "He seems to be advocating foreign gods." They said this because Paul was preaching the good news about Jesus and the resurrection. 19Then they took him and brought him to a meeting of the Areopagus, where they said to him, "May we know what this new teaching is that you are presenting? 20You are bringing some strange ideas to our ears, and we want to know what they mean." 21(All the Athenians and the foreigners who lived there spent their time doing nothing but talking about and listening to the latest ideas.)

22Paul then stood up in the meeting of the Areopagus and said: "Men of Athens! I see that in every way you are very religious. 23For as I walked around and looked carefully at your objects of worship, I even found an altar with this inscription:

## NRSV

16While Paul was waiting for them in Athens, he was deeply distressed to see that the city was full of idols. 17So he argued in the synagogue with the Jews and the devout persons, and also in the marketplace[a] every day with those who happened to be there. 18Also some Epicurean and Stoic philosophers debated with him. Some said, "What does this babbler want to say?" Others said, "He seems to be a proclaimer of foreign divinities." (This was because he was telling the good news about Jesus and the resurrection.) 19So they took him and brought him to the Areopagus and asked him, "May we know what this new teaching is that you are presenting? 20It sounds rather strange to us, so we would like to know what it means." 21Now all the Athenians and the foreigners living there would spend their time in nothing but telling or hearing something new.

22Then Paul stood in front of the Areopagus and said, "Athenians, I see how extremely religious you are in every way. 23For as I went through the city and looked carefully at the objects of your worship, I found among them an altar with the inscription, 'To an unknown god.'

[a] Or *civic center*, Gk *agora*

## NIV

TO AN UNKNOWN GOD. Now what you worship as something unknown I am going to proclaim to you.

24"The God who made the world and everything in it is the Lord of heaven and earth and does not live in temples built by hands. 25And he is not served by human hands, as if he needed anything, because he himself gives all men life and breath and everything else. 26From one man he made every nation of men, that they should inhabit the whole earth; and he determined the times set for them and the exact places where they should live. 27God did this so that men would seek him and perhaps reach out for him and find him, though he is not far from each one of us. 28'For in him we live and move and have our being.' As some of your own poets have said, 'We are his offspring.'

29"Therefore since we are God's offspring, we should not think that the divine being is like gold or silver or stone—an image made by man's design and skill. 30In the past God overlooked such ignorance, but now he commands all people everywhere to repent. 31For he has set a day when he will judge the world with justice by the man he has appointed. He has given proof of this to all men by raising him from the dead."

32When they heard about the resurrection of the dead, some of them sneered, but others said, "We want to hear you again on this subject." 33At that, Paul left the Council. 34A few men became followers of Paul and believed. Among them was Dionysius, a member of the Areopagus, also a woman named Damaris, and a number of others.

## NRSV

What therefore you worship as unknown, this I proclaim to you. 24The God who made the world and everything in it, he who is Lord of heaven and earth, does not live in shrines made by human hands, 25nor is he served by human hands, as though he needed anything, since he himself gives to all mortals life and breath and all things. 26From one ancestor[a] he made all nations to inhabit the whole earth, and he allotted the times of their existence and the boundaries of the places where they would live, 27so that they would search for God[b] and perhaps grope for him and find him—though indeed he is not far from each one of us. 28For 'In him we live and move and have our being'; as even some of your own poets have said,

'For we too are his offspring.'

29Since we are God's offspring, we ought not to think that the deity is like gold, or silver, or stone, an image formed by the art and imagination of mortals. 30While God has overlooked the times of human ignorance, now he commands all people everywhere to repent, 31because he has fixed a day on which he will have the world judged in righteousness by a man whom he has appointed, and of this he has given assurance to all by raising him from the dead."

32When they heard of the resurrection of the dead, some scoffed; but others said, "We will hear you again about this." 33At that point Paul left them. 34But some of them joined him and became believers, including Dionysius the Areopagite and a woman named Damaris, and others with them.

[a] Gk From one; other ancient authorities read From one blood
[b] Other ancient authorities read the Lord

# COMMENTARY

The conflict plotted by this story is immediately introduced upon Paul's arrival in Athens: He sees idols everywhere and is distressed (17:16). The plot thickens when Paul characteristically visits the city's synagogue and then also the *agora,* arguing with those he finds in both places (17:17). The philosophers among Paul's auditors in the *agora* fail to fully grasp what he proclaims to them and so they make two errors of judgment: They ques-

tion his spiritual authority, calling him a "babbler," and they confuse the content of what he proclaims about Jesus and his resurrection (17:18). Their misunderstanding leads them to bring Paul to the Areopagus where he is asked by the city's intellectuals to explain his "new teaching" (17:19-21). Paul does so in a speech of uncommon power that both legitimizes his spiritual authority (17:22-23) and examines the claim that he teaches "foreign deities" (ξενία δαιμόνια *xenia daimonia*, 17:24-29), then he turns to his "new teaching" about Jesus and the resurrection (17:30-31). Characteristically, his call to conversion results in a divided house (17:32-34).

Fitzmyer and others claim that this is "the most important episode" of Luke's narrative of Paul's second mission.[568] The episode is important not because it evinces some missionary innovation or exposes a new angle of vision into Paul's message. In fact, Luke has already supplied a précis of Paul's important speech earlier at Lystra (see 14:15-17) and the pattern of Paul's missionary activity in Athens rings familiar.[569] The importance of this episode in Acts is rather due almost entirely to the *city* Athens.[570] Although a bit tattered by comparison to the golden age of Pericles and Socrates, Athens was still a great university town and symbolized the "high culture" where important ideas have value and are carefully considered by the intellectually curious. It is here that the Paul of Acts delivers one of his three major missionary speeches and the only one to non-believers.

The theological subtext of Paul's "Mars Hill" apologia is his distress over the city's pervasive idolatry (cf. 17:16). Great learning has not eliminated false religion from Athens, but neither has the city's synagogue, which apparently exerts little influence on the beliefs of its citizens (cf. 17:17). In wider context, Paul's distress over idolatry recalls James's earlier admonition concerning Gentile converts "polluted by idols" as a potential source of confusion for repentant Jews in the diaspora (see 15:20). James was worried that the Pauline mission might accommodate the religious practices of pagan temples; the present passage expands this concern to include the thought and practice of an entire city, for Paul finds "the *city* was full of idols" (17:16, italics added). The emotional response to what he sees and the terms of his subsequent speech indicate agreement with James's exhortation, though on a grander scale.

The principal critical problem facing the interpreter is whether the portrayal of Paul portrait and especially his speech as a philosopher-like-Socrates is Luke's invention, or whether Luke reliably preserves Paul's visit and speech in Athens. Those who argue that Luke has rendered an "authentic" Paul refer to 1 Thessalonians 3:1, where he mentions an Athenian visit. They then add that Paul does or says nothing in Athens that disagrees with anything he writes in his NT letters. In fact, the substance of his speech, if not its idiom, is confirmed in general terms by Romans 1:18-32 (cf. 1 Thess 1:9-10).[571] Further, his actions and speech seem to reflect a well practiced Jewish response to contemporary secular philosophy in the Diaspora.[572] If not an eyewitness to Paul's mission, Luke certainly draws upon reliable Pauline sources when shaping this story.[573]

While Paul's objection to idolatry and the theological conception of his speech in Athens are consistent with Pauline tradition found in the letters, the critic must still respond to the question whether the historical Paul would be drawn into an intellectual sparring match with Athenian philosophers. Most scholars say probably not. Paul seemed to have little use for such discussions, nor were "such negative themes the basis and prime content of his message."[574] Moreover, the apocalyptic cast of his missionary message in the letters

568. J. A. Fitzmyer, *The Acts of the Apostles*, AB 31 (Garden City, N.Y.: Doubleday, 1998) 600, 613-17. The scholarly literature on this passage is voluminous and comes from biblical scholars and theologians, ancient and modern—probably more than on any other passage in Acts.

569. R. C. Tannehill, *The Acts of the Apostles*, vol. 2 of *The Narrative Unity of Luke-Acts: A Literary Interpretation* (Minneapolis: Fortress, 1990) 2:211-12, carefully relates the various bits and pieces of this story with other stories in Acts, showing they are all of a single textured cloth. In this light, Schubert claims that when considered along with all other missionary speeches in Acts, Paul's Areopagus speech is the final and climactic element in Luke's exposition of God's plan to save all humanity. "The Place of the Areopagus Speech in the Composition of Acts," in *Transitions in Biblical Scholarship*, ed. J. Rylaarsdam (Chicago: University of Chicago Press, 1968) 260-61. Similarly, Tannehill, *The Acts of the Apostles*, 2:215, considers the speech paradigmatic of the gospel's encounter with secular culture.

570. Athens was a "free city" located in Roman Achaia. Most of the great public buildings from its days as capital city of Grecian Attica were destroyed during the Persian wars (480s BCE), and its population had dwindled to between 5,000 and 10,000 when Paul visited. Although Haenchen says that Athens "lived on its great past," Cicero and other intellectuals of the day spoke well of Athens as a place of great learning, and this tradition seems to have been its essential cultural identity when Luke wrote Acts. See E. Haenchen, *The Acts of the Apostles* (Philadelphia: Westminster, 1971) 517.

571. Cf. J. D. G. Dunn, *The Acts of the Apostles* (Valley Forge, Pa.: Trinity, 1996) 231-32; B. Witherington, *The Acts of the Apostles: A Socio-Rhetorical Commentary* (Grand Rapids: Eerdmans, 1998) 425-26; S. Porter, *The Paul of Acts*, WUNT 115 (Tübingen: Mohr Siebeck, 1999) 141-49. Cf. R. Maddox, *The Purpose of Luke-Acts* (Edinburgh: T. & T. Clark, 1982) 83-84, who rightly cautions against a facile analysis of Rom 1:18-32 and Paul's Areopagus speech.

572. Haenchen, *The Acts of the Apostles*, 522-23.

573. Dibelius's famous verdict that this speech "is absolutely foreign to Paul's theology" has been overturned by recent scholarship, but it still influences current discussion of Luke's Pauline sources. See M. Dibelius, "The Speeches in Acts and Ancient Historiography," in *Studies in the Acts of the Apostles* (London: SCM, 1956) 71-72.

574. C. K. Barrett, *A Critical and Exegetical Commentary on the Acts of the Apostles*, 2 vols, ICC (Edinburgh: T. & T. Clark, 1994, 1998) 2:826.

shapes an ecclesiology that did not compel him to spend his time in becoming "relevant" to the surrounding culture. This passage is rather an expression of Luke's authorial intentions; it reflects the narrator's "idealized version of what ought to have happened, so marvelously wrought that for its readers it provides the emblem of what possibly could happen."[575]

**17:16-17.** Upon arriving in Athens, Paul is "deeply distressed to see that the city was full of idols." Although these "idols" were often valued as great works of art, Paul's response to them is one of Jewish outrage. "Deeply" translates the phrase τὸ πνεῦμα αὐτοῦ ἐν αὐτῷ (*to pneuma autou en autō* lit., "his spirit within him") and refers to his inner life—his mind and soul. Evidently what is shocking to Paul is the sheer number of idols he finds in Athens. The word translated "full of idols" (κατείδωλος *kateidōlos*) is found only here in the NT and conjures up the image of a forest of idols. Although Athens has a Jewish synagogue, we infer that the misunderstanding of Paul's proclamation of Jesus in the *agora* (see 17:18) is due to an ignorance of Jewish history and religion, which have proved unimpressive to the citizens.

Following his missionary pattern, Paul "argues [διαλέγομαι *dialegomai*] in the synagogue with the Jews and the devout persons" (17:17; see 17:2, 10). In this cultural setting, Luke's word-choice "to argue" is strategic, recalling the memory of Socrates who often engaged ordinary citizens in the marketplace (*agora*) in philosophical debate. Earlier accounts of Paul's synagogal arguments allow the reader to fill in the gaps of this text; the assumption is that his arguments with Jews in the synagogue now spill over into the marketplace. Paul thereby performs the role of Socrates in this story, even though public debate with "those who happened by" has been a feature of his European mission since Philippi (see 16:19).

**17:18.** Among those in the *agora* are "Epicurean and Stoic philosophers" who debated [συμβάλλω *symballō*] with him. The style of discourse is indicated by Luke's choice of *symballō,* a favorite term of his, which denotes a collegial exchange toward a constructive end (see 4:15;

18:27; 20:14; cf. Luke 2:19; 14:31). The impression made, then, is that Paul is engaged in an honest, not hostile exchange with his "scholarly peers." They include members of divergent schools of thought, although both were interested in practical rather than theoretical discourse—the rhetorical bent of Luke's missionary Paul as well. In any case, their practical orientation toward intellectual discourse would certainly have included religion and in ways reflected in Paul's later speech to them. For example, Epicureans were materialists and believed that human life exists by natural chance. Avoidance of pain and suffering is the true aim of this life and not religious devotion, since a personal, provident god—a god who could make a practical difference in the outcome of a happy life—simply does not exist. Significantly, Epicureans were harsh critics of idolatry as well; their primary criticism of Athenian folk religion was that offering sacrifice to gods who are neither personal nor provident may be "religious" but it is also non-rational: Impersonal deities cannot produce personal happiness. Stoics, on the other hand, were hard rationalists, guided by their analytical observations and careful reasoning. They sought to live in harmony with the cosmos. Stoics believed in the solidarity of the human race and in a deity in whom "we live and move and have our being" (17:28), because, conversely, the deity is in all things, not transcendent, as is the Most High God.

The initial impression made on the audience overhearing their debate on "practical reason" is that Paul's proclamation of the risen Jesus is ill-conceived and intellectually impoverished—he is a "babbler" (σπερμόλογος *spermologos;* lit., "seed picker") of old ideas that are no longer relevant or important. This mocking term challenges Paul's spiritual authority to contend for a superior account of practical divinity.

The second and quite different challenge is that Paul lobbies for "foreign deities" (*xenia daimonia;* see 16:21).[576] The earlier allusion to Socrates as a

---

575. Cf. L. T. Johnson, *The Acts of the Apostles,* SP 5 (Collegeville, Minn.: Liturgical, 1992) 318-19.

576. R. Bultmann argued that upon first hearing Paul's proclamation, the Athenians mistook his claim of "resurrection" as a female fertility goddess (the Greek word for resurrection is the feminine noun, *anastasis*) paired with his male god, "Jesus"—hence the plural, "foreign deities," refers to "Jesus and Anastasis." See R. Bultmann, *Theology of the New Testament,* trans. K. Grobel (London: SCM 1952) 1:77. See also Tannehill, *The Acts of the Apostles,* 2:214. Paul's speech, then, is occasioned by a theological mistake.

public philosopher is now made clear by Luke: Like Socrates, Paul is charged with propagating strange gods in Athens. Johnson argues that the allusion to Socrates is especially strategic since his response to his accusers was widely recognized by contemporary philosophers as "the model for philosophical integrity."[577] In any case, Paul is a philosopher-like-Socrates who contends that Jesus is Messiah.

**17:19-21.** Paul's place in the marketplace of ideas has been challenged in the two ways most damning of the ancient philosopher: he is an incompetent "seed-picker" who traffics in strange religion. The best place to respond to such an accusation is the Areopagus of Athens, and that is where Paul is taken. The meaning of ἐπιλαμβάνομαι *epilambanomai* ("took"), however, is ambiguous: It can mean either "to arrest" (to take into police custody) or "to accompany" (to take along with) to the "Areopagus" (lit., "Mars" Hill).[578] Whether his speech there should read as a legal defense, a scholarly discussion, or something of both largely depends on how one understands "the Aeropagus" (17:22).

The "Areopagus" (ὁ Ἄρειος Πάγος *ho areios pagos*) is the name given to an elevated, open-air site just to the west of the acropolis in Athens. The Areopagus also denotes the equivalent of a city assembly or council that would hear public debates and render verdicts. In this sense the Areopagus enjoys a role and authority similar to all the other councils of Acts. In this light, then, Paul may well have been taken into custody to determine whether he has sufficient "intellectual" authority to bring his "strange teaching" into Athens.

His prosecutors and judges in this case are more intellectually curious than hostile.[579] The charges against Paul are restated with more civility than before and appear to reflect keen interest in learning something new from Paul: "May we know what this new teaching is that you are presenting?" (17:19). The potentially dangerous charge of teaching "foreign deities" has been dropped and replaced by the famous Athenian curiosity in the latest fad (τι καινότερον *ti kainoteron;* lit.,

"something new," 17:21). While their interest in Paul's message is promising, the council's disappointing response to his speech (see 17:32-34) reflects the narrator's irony. Luke's parenthetical comment about Athenian curiosity suggests that it both occasions Paul's speech and explains why his call to conversion is then rejected: The curious might find a definitive claim for ultimate truth unsettling.

**17:22-31.** The broad structure and content of Paul's Areopagus speech are similar to what is heard earlier at Lystra, where he championed "the living God who made the heaven, the earth and sea and all that is in them" and asserted its predicate "that you should turn from these worthless things to the living God" (14:15). But we are in Athens, not Lystra; and here before the Areopagus, Paul is asked to defend this new religion he is proclaiming throughout the city.

R. Garland recently has demonstrated that three claims were necessary to establish a new religion in Athens: (1) the sponsor must claim to represent a deity; (2) he must provide evidence that this deity is eager to reside in Athens; and (3) the deity's residence in Athens must benefit Athenians as a mark of its goodwill.[580] In this light, Paul's Areopagus speech may be read as an *apologia* (however subversive!) in response to these three criteria.[581] Accordingly, Paul introduces himself as an authorized herald (22-23) of a living deity whose transcendent residence above the earth requires no Athenian residence, priesthood or religious practices (24-29). Paul's deity does not therefore seek formal induction into the Athenian Pantheon—of this the Areogapus need not worry; rather, his God seeks to judge and save all repentant Athenians as disclosed in the Lord's resurrection—and of this they need worry (30-31)!

**17:22-23.** Characteristically Luke cues the speech by dramatic gesture: "Paul stood in front of the Areopagus" and addressed his auditors directly by name, "Athenians." Paul clarifies his motive by responding to the earlier charge that he is a "seed picker" (*spermologos*)—a babbler of secondhand ideas and therefore without scholarly credentials in the scholar's *agora* where Socrates once taught. The

577. Johnson, *The Acts of the Apostles*, 313.
578. Ares is the Greek god of war usually referred to by his Latinized name, Mars.
579. This explains in part why Soards refers to the rhetorical situation of Paul's speech as "judicial" while Paul's rhetorical motive is "deliberative." See M. L. Soards, *The Speeches in Acts: Their Content, Context, and Concerns* (Louisville: Westminster/John Knox, 1994) 96.

580. R. Garland, *Introducing New Gods: The Politics of Athenian Religion* (London: Duckworth, 1992) 18-19.
581. Cf. B. Winter, "On Introducing Gods to Athens: An Alternative Reading of Acts 17:18-20," *TynBull* 47.1 (1996) 71-90, esp. 84-87.

scholar's most important talent is the capacity to make careful observations. Paul's first words intend to cultivate the impression that he is a skilled practitioner of the scholar's trade who "went through the city" and "looked carefully at objects of your worship," concluding that the Athenians are "extremely religious [δεισιδαιμονέστερος deisidaimonesteros] in every way." The superlative deisidaimonesteros could mean that they are very superstitious or, more likely, that they are keenly pious—a characteristic of the educated person in the ancient world. Paul's opening words thereby intend to elicit a positive impression (rhetoricians regarded such an opening of a discourse as the captitio benevolentiae). They also help to cue his religious motive: He intends to address them as a religious audience in a religious idiom about religious matters in anticipation of a religious response (i.e., conversion). While doing so he challenges the perception that he lacks the scholar's talent, which would disqualify him from the marketplace of important ideas.

Paul is also accused of being "a proclaimer [καταγγελεύς katangeleus] of foreign divinities" (17:18)—or as the council more politely rephrases it, for presenting a "new teaching" that "sounds strange to us" (17:19-20). In reporting his most important observation from his tour of Athens, Paul notes an altar's inscription "To an unknown God" (Ἄγνωστος Θεός Agnōstos Theos). Paul is being ironical by providing evidence of his audience's superlative piety: You are so religious that you even worship gods you do not know! Paul's implied point is made clear by his subsequent claim that they live during "times of human ignorance" (see 17:30) when what is unknown about god is the hallmark of the intellectual's religious devotion. With this stunning observation of the non-rational cast of Athenian religion, Paul has positioned himself to declare boldly the purpose of his speech (and mission) before the Areopagus: This God whom you worship in ignorance, "I proclaim [katangellō] to you."

While his Athenian auditors could not have known the powerful resonance of Paul's assertion, readers of Acts will detect in his use of katangellō a richly textured meaning. This verb is repeatedly used for the church's prophetic witness, when the good news is proclaimed for conversion (see 3:24; 4:2; 13:5, 38; 15:36; 16:17; 17:3). In the guise of

a philosopher-like-Socrates, Paul discloses his true vocation as a prophet-like-Jesus;[582] and as such a prophet he defends his spiritual authority as the inspired medium of God's word, which exposes the ignorance of these learned people and bids them to repent and turn to the one true God for salvation.

**17:24-25.** Paul begins the main body of his speech with a series of theologically dense statements. Most scholars detect a prophet's theologic in his sequence, not unlike a Jewish confession of faith in the idiom of Greek philosophy. Axiomatic and essential to this logic is that God is one God: Paul's God is "the God" (ὁ θεός ho theos, 17:24), the definitive divinity, and is neither dependent upon another nor is divided by another. God does not depend upon Paul's claim that God has a "right" to exist in Athens. God is God and transcends such requirements.

It follows that God "made the world [κόσμος kosmos] and everything in it" (17:24a; see 4:24; 14:15; cf. Isa 42:5; Gen 1:1-23; Exod 20:11) without aid of another and is therefore "Lord of heaven and earth" (17:24b; cf. Luke 10:21). These first two assertions are logically related since the Creator God justifiably takes responsibility for what is created—a conclusion that appeals to the Stoics, whose belief in humanity's solidarity is predicated on a God who is the source for all of life (see 17:18). The deduction that Paul draws from this formulation of divine sovereignty is that no creature of the natural kosmos is capable of domesticating the Creator. This is, after all, a God who "does not live in shrines made by human hands" (17:24c)—the very point Stephen made about the Jerusalem Temple (see 7:48; cf. Isa 57:15-16). What is true for the Jews of Jerusalem is true for the intellectuals of Athens! Nor does God require the worshiper's religious gifts "as though [God] needed anything" (17:25a; cf. Amos 5:12-23)—a conclusion that appeals to the Epicureans, whose functional atheism is predicated on a belief that such a God would need nothing from anyone (see 17:18). God is rather a gracious Benefactor who "gives to all mortals life

---

582. Haenchen, *The Acts of the Apostles*, 521, notes that Paul's declaration of his intention shows that he introduces no new god but rather discloses one already known as "unknown," thereby distinguishing himself from Socrates who was accused of introducing brand new gods into Athens' religious culture.

and breath and all things" (17:25b; cf. Isa 42:5; Gen 2:7). This same assessment of God's goodness is envisaged in Peter's earlier theological assertion that Israel's God, the only God, freely dispenses the gifts of salvation to all who repent and believe without prejudice (see 10:34).

**17:26-28a.** On the foundation of these more general claims of God's benevolent lordship over all things, Paul narrows his focus to God's relations with human creation to make his most dramatic theological assertions. Even as Paul contends that from one God everything derives, so now he argues that from one human stock (i.e., Eve/Adam) many races/nations descend "to inhabit the whole earth" (17:26; cf. Gen 1:24-25; Rom 5:12-14). This pairing of one God with one species implies that the "many" who physically descend from common parents (some manuscripts read "from one blood") share an inherent religious sensibility, whether this God is recognized or not.[583] The initial implication Paul draws from his argument is that God allots "the times . . . and the boundaries" that circumscribe human existence (17:26). While Paul's comment is laden with contemporary philosophical and theological speculation, the point he makes is practical and straightforward: God who makes human life has a plan for it. He would be accused of muddled thinking to contend that a provident Lord who takes great care in making and sustaining human creation, then would abandon us to find our own way in a *kosmos* without coherent pattern or purpose (see 14:16-17).[584]

In this regard, the second implication Paul draws is axiomatic of biblical faith: God's intent for ordering human life with purpose and precision is "so that humans would search for God and perhaps grope for him and find him" (17:27a). God creates an environment that allows close participation with humanity in their history so that God "is not far from each one of us" (17:27b; cf. Rom 10:8; Ps 145:18). In setting forth this theological claim, Paul prepares the audience for his ultimate

move to Christian proclamation., where he will proclaim that the Creator God makes just such a world to deliver them all from divine judgment.

Paul's appeal to appropriate evidence is central to all speeches in Acts. For this audience of learned non-believers, Paul draws upon Greek poetry to confirm his theological point: "In him [ἐν αὐτῷ *en autō*] we live and move and have our being" (17:28a; cf. Titus 1:12).[585] Although the Stoics in his audience may well have taken this poetic source as confirmation of their pantheism that God is near us because we are in him, the Paul of Acts almost certainly would have understood *en autō* as instrumental: Human existence depends upon God, "*by whom* we live and move and have our being."[586]

**17:28b-29.** Paul's second citation from a philosopher-poet uses "offspring," a term whose meaning he exploits: "Since we are God's *offspring*, we ought not to think that the deity is . . . an image formed by the art and imagination of mortals" (17:29). In its wider narrative setting, Paul's commentary on Athenian idolatry adds a layer of meaning to James's earlier condemnation of the "pollutions of idols" as an expression of his principal concern to preserve the church's Jewish identity (see 15:20). At the same time, it prepares the reader for Luke's forthcoming account of Demetrius's polemic against Paul during his Ephesian campaign (cf. 19:23-27). Paul's contribution to both episodes is to expose the faulty logic of religious devotion whose chief symbols—shrines, idols, foods offered to gods, pagan rituals—are inconsistent to the inherent character of God's relations with humankind. God must be worshiped in accordance with who God is; and religious practices must reflect humanity's kinship with God. The substitution of inanimate materials for a God who is transcendent and animate makes no sense.

---

583. Cf. Fitzmyer, *The Acts of the Apostles,* 609 for a discussion of the difficult syntax and various translations of the awkward phrase that "From one [ancestor] God made all nations to inhabit the whole earth." He translates the phrase, "From one [stock] God made the whole human race inhabit the whole earth."

584. H. Conzelmann, *The Acts of the Apostles,* trans. J. Limburg et al., ed. E. J. Epp and C. R. Matthews, Hermeneia (Philadelphia: Fortress, 1987) 142-44.

585. The anonymous citation of sources is a convention of ancient rhetoric, whether of secular poets or biblical prophets. The audience would almost certainly know their identity and recognize the authority of their words. Although a growing number of scholars think that Luke composed the first poetic citation, most scholars believe that it comes from a Stoic philosopher. There is a consensus from Clement forward that the second citation is from the Stoic philosopher Aratus, c. 310 BCE, *Phenomena* 5.

586. So Johnson, *The Acts of the Apostles,* 316; Witherington, *The Acts of the Apostles,* 529; cf. K. Lake and H. J. Cadbury, *The Acts of the Apostles,* vol. 4 of The Beginnings of Christianity, ed. F. J. Foakes Jackson and K. Lake (Grand Rapids: Baker, 1979).

**17:30-31.** In a sharply stated conclusion Paul wonderfully captures the essence of the biblical conception of a God who is at once transcendent yet personal, sovereign and fully engaged in human life. He thereby exposes the logical flaw of Athenian religion, suggesting that the inward distress he experienced when observing the pervasiveness of Athenian idolatry was both spiritual and intellectual in origin. Idolatry evinces "times of human ignorance [ἄγνοια *agnoia*]," recalling Peter's criticism of pious Jews whose continued "ignorance" (*agnoia;* see 3:17) about Jesus subverted the prospect of their repentance for the forgiveness of sins and participation in Israel's "times of refreshing" (3:19). Paul tells his audience, much like Peter before him, that a benevolent God "overlooks" ignorance and has brought a prophet to them with the word of God (17:30; see 3:17). The theological subtext of Peter's earlier warning, however, is God's faithfulness to the promise of Israel's restoration, whereas the subtext of Paul's speech is the universality of God's salvation. The terms used in his missionary appeal—"times of ignorance," "repent," "day of judgment"—are glossed by this universality to include those of the Athenian Areopagus. When the similar appeals of Peter and Paul are combined, one arrives at a theological conception not unlike Paul's argument in Romans 1:18–3:26 for the universal need of salvation and a Savior. To this the Paul of Acts may well add that the ultimate reason any person—whether religious Jew or secular intellectual—fails to repent and turn to God in faith is attachment to cultural idols and an ignorance of God's gospel.

The warrant for turning to God and away from idolatry is that God "will have the world [οἰκουμένη *oikoumenē*) judged in righteousness" (17:31; cf. Amos 5:18; Pss 9:8; 67:4; 96:13; 99:9). Paul's turn to the future is yet another feature of his gospel appeal that follows the deep logic of Peter's second missionary speech (see 3:17-26). Paul's emphasis, however, is on universal judgment rather than "the time of universal restoration" (see 3:21). Envisaged by both prophetic speeches is universality concentrated on the Lord's return both to judge (= purify) and to restore the *oikoumenē*—the inhabited world (see 11:28; 17:6; cf. Luke 21:26). The righteousness of this judgment implies that the criterion used will be fairly employed and there will be no need for an Areopagus to intervene on the final "day of judgment" to render a verdict about the fairness, legitimacy, or authority of God's judgment about people.

What is left unstated is the content of that eschatological criterion by which a "righteous" or evenhanded verdict will be rendered. The reader of Acts will draw the unstated implication from the exhortation to repent that the criterion is whether people repent of the "pollutions of idols" and turn to the living God in faith. Paul is more interested to press for the urgency of the matter. This day of universal judgment (and restoration, 3:21) is assured by the resurrection of "a man whom God has appointed" (i.e., Messiah; see 2:22-24, 36).

**17:32-34.** The response to Paul's exhortation to repent on the basis of the resurrection is mixed, as the reader of Acts would expect. Clearly the resurrection remains a "strange teaching" to the Athenian scoffers (17:32*a*), even though now wrapped up in a robust common ground of theological and philosophical ideas. That these ideas are generally accepted and found stimulating may well be indicated by the response of others who say, " 'We will hear you again about this' " (17:32*b*). Significantly, Paul is not mocked nor disabused of his authority to argue his case; even though the response is not great, he "left them" a free man (17:33). Luke notes two converts: Dionysius, a member of the Areopagus, and Damaris. Although this mission report shows only modest gains, Luke wants to assure the reader that the foundations for an Athenian parish are of highest quality.[587]

---

587. The Western version of Acts adds that Damaris is a "respected" woman, which implies her social prominence.

# REFLECTIONS

**1.** "What does this babbler want to say?" (17:18 NRSV). Luke's story re-imagines Paul for a "post-Pauline" venue, where his letters are read in response to a similar "culture war" in which the gospel is challenged by cities "full of idols" and where the church is asked to respond to the important questions of secular intellectuals. In this regard, we should take care to consider the continuing relevance of the initial objections to Paul's proclamation of Jesus and the resurrection. The first objection questions his spiritual authority in the Athenian marketplace: he is only a "babbler" of secondhand religious propaganda. Paul's response lays claim to the prophet's inspired powers to "see" and to "proclaim" God's truth (see 17:22b-23). It is on this basis that the church reads his letters with confidence that their teaching carries sufficient intellectual insight to engage the thinking public.

The skeptics also question whether he teaches "foreign deities," which contain irrelevant or incomprehensible subject matter. His speech makes clear that belief in his God is reasonable and practical, while exposing the fraud of a society's idols. Confident that Paul's judgment extends to his letters, their reader approaches these writings as sacred witness to a God who is neither "foreign" to outsiders nor tolerant of their various idolatries. Simply put, Paul's Mars Hill speech in Acts reminds students of his NT letters that the church intends their teaching to have universal appeal. Luke does not "invent" this encounter between Paul and the secular intellectuals of his day; he composes a story that is faithful to both Athenian secular culture and to Pauline tradition. For this reason his story has paradigmatic value for the church's continuing teaching of the Pauline letters.

**2.** "So that they would search for God and perhaps grope for him and find him" (17:27 NRSV). Does Paul's speech to the Athenians offer contemporary readers a model for engaging the secular intellectuals of our day? Many think so. While different language and ideas are required to contemporize Paul's message, his core ideas about religious culture and God remain relevant and important. This prospect challenges two assumptions still prevalent about the gospel. On the one hand, by playing the role of Socrates in a university town Paul challenges the anti-intellectualism among believers today who are deeply suspicious of secular "learning." On the other hand, believers should not be intimidated by those pundits who characterize the Christian gospel as unintelligible superstition or as an equal among many religious options. Especially in our day when ideologies once considered on the margins for lack of evidence and common sense have become mainstream, the gospel thoughtfully presented has never sounded more attractive to those earnestly searching for ultimate answers.

The rhetorical design of Paul's speech is noteworthy because of its comprehensiveness and internal coherence. Each statement by turns calls his auditors for a conversion of sorts; and every "small" conversion leads them step-by-step toward the risen Christ. Paul's opening observations about idolatry call for an admission that even pagans seek spiritual satisfaction, although "groping" in ignorance. While we should admit that some skeptics reject out of hand the very idea of a spiritual reality, most do give expression to their spiritual yearning by their adherence to the values and core convictions of one or another "ism"—scientism, materialism, individualism, nationalism, naturalism, humanism, and so on. A commitment to any of these worldviews shapes loyalties and informs decisions. Following Paul's pattern, then, the initial moment in conversion is a people's recognition that they order their lives according to some ultimate loyalty, staking their futures on something or someone in which they believe. In this sense, all people are religious. Such an agreement about religious pluralism marks the beginning point of a conversation that narrows the choices to Christ.

Admission of God's knowability comes next, followed by a robust summary of what then can be known about God: God is Creator, Sustainer, Sovereign, Benefactor, Judge. We should also take note that while Paul does not cite Scripture and uses language suitable for this academic setting and secular audience, the content of his theological summary is thoroughly biblical. True to the core biblical idea, then, God is transcendent yet personal, vastly superior to some detached deity that consigns humankind to the vicissitudes of fortune. God is not some provincial deity, the God of a few; nor is God unmoved and unconcerned about the struggles of real people in particular places. God is truly worthy of worship.

Yet Paul regards philosophical speculation as the means to a missionary end. Although the church cannot preach the risen Jesus without a comprehensive profile of the biblical God persuasively presented, neither can the church be content to construct new and more relevant models of God for popular consumption without also calling for repentance and faith in Christ. Thus, Paul's speech concludes with a call to repentance that is predicated on the meaning of Christ's resurrection, God's ultimate judgment of sin and death.

To agree with this concluding claim is not a matter of theological proofs but of personal faith. Even those who may have agreed with everything Paul has said to this point about God will find a final decision in favor of his gospel profoundly difficult to make. Those Athenians who scornfully interrupt Paul at the very moment he turns his speech toward the resurrection of Jesus and God's coming triumph are indicative of the scandal of faith (cf. 1 Cor 1:18-25). I doubt that the real difficulty with the gospel is finally one of knowledge: there is no lack of evidence or intellectual integrity in Paul's presentation. The problem provoked by Paul's appeal to the resurrection is a more practical one, since it calls for a complete reordering of what one thinks and how one lives. The confession that the living Jesus is the only Messiah and the one Lord (see 2:36) means that all other competing loyalties and practices must be set aside in order to begin a new life with him. Most in Athens are unable to do this, and secular intellectuals today face a similar challenge when they encounter the gospel.

# ACTS 18:1-17, PAUL'S CORINTHIAN MISSION

## NIV

**18** After this, Paul left Athens and went to Corinth. ²There he met a Jew named Aquila, a native of Pontus, who had recently come from Italy with his wife Priscilla, because Claudius had ordered all the Jews to leave Rome. Paul went to see them, ³and because he was a tentmaker as they were, he stayed and worked with them. ⁴Every Sabbath he reasoned in the synagogue, trying to persuade Jews and Greeks.

⁵When Silas and Timothy came from Macedonia, Paul devoted himself exclusively to preaching, testifying to the Jews that Jesus was the Christ.[a] ⁶But when the Jews opposed Paul and became abusive, he shook out his clothes in protest and said to them, "Your blood be on your own heads! I am clear of my responsibility. From now on I will go to the Gentiles."

[a] 5 Or Messiah; also in verse 28

## NRSV

**18** After this Paul[a] left Athens and went to Corinth. ²There he found a Jew named Aquila, a native of Pontus, who had recently come from Italy with his wife Priscilla, because Claudius had ordered all Jews to leave Rome. Paul[b] went to see them, ³and, because he was of the same trade, he stayed with them, and they worked together—by trade they were tentmakers. ⁴Every sabbath he would argue in the synagogue and would try to convince Jews and Greeks.

5When Silas and Timothy arrived from Macedonia, Paul was occupied with proclaiming the word,[c] testifying to the Jews that the Messiah[d] was Jesus. ⁶When they opposed and reviled him, in protest he shook the dust from his clothes[e] and

[a] Gk he   [b] Gk He   [c] Gk with the word   [d] Or the Christ
[e] Gk reviled him, he shook out his clothes

## NIV

[7]Then Paul left the synagogue and went next door to the house of Titius Justus, a worshiper of God. [8]Crispus, the synagogue ruler, and his entire household believed in the Lord; and many of the Corinthians who heard him believed and were baptized.

[9]One night the Lord spoke to Paul in a vision: "Do not be afraid; keep on speaking, do not be silent. [10]For I am with you, and no one is going to attack and harm you, because I have many people in this city." [11]So Paul stayed for a year and a half, teaching them the word of God.

[12]While Gallio was proconsul of Achaia, the Jews made a united attack on Paul and brought him into court. [13]"This man," they charged, "is persuading the people to worship God in ways contrary to the law."

[14]Just as Paul was about to speak, Gallio said to the Jews, "If you Jews were making a complaint about some misdemeanor or serious crime, it would be reasonable for me to listen to you. [15]But since it involves questions about words and names and your own law—settle the matter yourselves. I will not be a judge of such things." [16]So he had them ejected from the court. [17]Then they all turned on Sosthenes the synagogue ruler and beat him in front of the court. But Gallio showed no concern whatever.

## NRSV

said to them, "Your blood be on your own heads! I am innocent. From now on I will go to the Gentiles." [7]Then he left the synagogue[a] and went to the house of a man named Titius[b] Justus, a worshiper of God; his house was next door to the synagogue. [8]Crispus, the official of the synagogue, became a believer in the Lord, together with all his household; and many of the Corinthians who heard Paul became believers and were baptized. [9]One night the Lord said to Paul in a vision, "Do not be afraid, but speak and do not be silent; [10]for I am with you, and no one will lay a hand on you to harm you, for there are many in this city who are my people." [11]He stayed there a year and six months, teaching the word of God among them.

[12]But when Gallio was proconsul of Achaia, the Jews made a united attack on Paul and brought him before the tribunal. [13]They said, "This man is persuading people to worship God in ways that are contrary to the law." [14]Just as Paul was about to speak, Gallio said to the Jews, "If it were a matter of crime or serious villainy, I would be justified in accepting the complaint of you Jews; [15]but since it is a matter of questions about words and names and your own law, see to it yourselves; I do not wish to be a judge of these matters." [16]And he dismissed them from the tribunal. [17]Then all of them[c] seized Sosthenes, the official of the synagogue, and beat him in front of the tribunal. But Gallio paid no attention to any of these things.

[a] Gk *left there*    [b] Other ancient authorities read *Titus*    [c] Other ancient authorities read *all the Greeks*

# COMMENTARY

In shaping his account of Paul's mission to Corinth,[588] Luke provides several new details of

588. The city of Corinth is fifty miles west of Athens and is its rival in reputation. While not Athen's equal as a cultural center, ancient Corinth was the capital city of Roman Achaia and a leading commercial center overlooking two ports, which allowed for easy access to the Aegean and Ionian seas and beyond. The many important civic and religious buildings surrounding the city's *agora* were known throughout the world, as was the city's reputation for sexual perversion. Ancient Corinth (or Roman "Neocorinth") is an important archaeological site today. The literature that describes various archaeological expeditions is extensive; for bibliography and abstract of these findings, see Fitzmyer, *The Acts of the Apostles*, 623-24, 631-32.

the everyday conditions of the missionary's life. For example, we find out that Paul works by day in the leather shop of Priscilla and Aquila to sustain himself financially (18:2-3). While Paul's mission is still centered in the city's Jewish synagogue where he teaches, there is indication of a transition to another venue—namely, a "household" of Gentiles attached to the synagogue (18:4-8). Paul's previous visits to important European cities were short term, due either to political pressure or lack of success. He spends a longer period of time in

Corinth to establish a congregation of believers there (18:11). Earlier hints of Rome's benign attitude toward Paul's mission are realized in Corinth as Achaia's proconsul Gallio intervenes to rule that Paul's message and church planting activity falls within Judaism's protected boundaries. Thus, the conflict between him and unrepentant Jews is a Jewish and not a Roman affair (18:12-17).

Paul's Corinthian mission, however, is carefully circumscribed by familiar patterns found elsewhere in Acts. He continues his sabbath routine of worshiping in the city synagogue where he argues that Jesus is Messiah (18:4). He faces Jewish resistance to his message there (18:5-6a) but still enjoys modest success among other Jews (18:8) as well as with God-fearing Gentiles attached to the synagogue (18:6b-7). There is no mission in Acts without suffering (18:9), nor one that is not superintended by a provident Sovereign (18:10).

The disassociation of Paul's mission from the Jewish synagogue and its new association with "the house [οἰκία oikia] of a man named Titius Justus, a worshiper of God" (18:7) once again echoes the Amos prophecy of a "re-housed" Israel and its interpretation by James (see 15:16-21). The passing reference to Paul's trade as a "tentmaker" (σκηνοποιός skēnopoios; 18:3) may well echo Amos' critical catchphrase of Israel's restoration, "the tent (skēnē) of David" (see 15:16), since it is Paul the tentmaker who best personifies the restored Israel's vocation as a "light to the nations." In particular, however, these intratextual echoes recall James's understanding of the real theological crisis provoked by Paul's mission, which is not the Judaizing of repentant Gentiles but the "gentilizing" of repentant Jews in the Diaspora synagogues (see 15:19-21, 28-29).

In this regard, the present story alerts the reader to the deepening rift between Paul and his Jewish opponents who sharply disagree with his *Christian* proclamation that Jesus is Messiah. Gallio's benign neutrality makes him the perfect referee of this conflict, for it is really an intramural debate between religious Jews over a messianic interpretation of Israel's Scriptures. Paul's departure from the synagogue for Titius's house may well indicate something of a solution in maintaining the fragile accommodation of his Christian beliefs with his Jewish practices, which is the hallmark of his mission in Acts (cf. 1 Cor 9:16-23). Indeed, the par-

ticipants in this new house congregation—Paul, Silas, Timothy, Priscilla and Aquila (cf. 1 Cor 16:19), Titius, Crispus (cf. 1 Cor 1:14), Sosthenes (cf. 1 Cor 1:1)—are all former members of the Corinthian synagogue who follow Paul's example and would presumably want to preserve Jewish traditions in this new setting. Reading the text by the light of the Jerusalem Council adds an additional layer of meaning to this movement: Leaving the synagogue may afford the best chance of preserving what is Jewish for the future church.

Finally, this story provides a canonical context for studying Paul's Corinthian letters. On the face of it, it lacks mention of several important themes found in the letters; this is perhaps due to the generic differences between Luke's narrative and Pauline letters that are written as rejoinders to the practical problems of a divided church more pagan than Jewish in religious background. A number of these problems result from the socioeconomic diversity within an urban church that made creating Christian solidarity in witness and fellowship difficult. Moreover, Paul's defense of his religious authority weaves together his apostolic office, charismatic power, and exemplary persona into a seamless whole, whereas the authority of the Paul of Acts derives from his prophetic vocation. Nevertheless, this account of his founding of the Corinthian church in Acts prepares the reader of 1–2 Corinthians by providing the following important impressions of his work there.[589]

(1) The present passage narrates the origins of Corinthian Christianity and adds details to Paul's own more allusive account in 1 Corinthians 3–4. In this regard, Paul's enigmatic references to his colleague Apollos in 1 Corinthians (1:12; 3:5-9; 4:6-13) may be illumined against the background of his story in Acts (see 18:24-28). Even though some modern interpreters of 1 Corinthians suppose a bitter rivalry existed between them (cf. 1 Cor 1:12), there is no evidence of such rivalry and Paul seems to make the contrary point: Where we expect to find a power struggle between two gifted men, we discover a commitment to each other

---

589. Johnson, *The Acts of the Apostles,* 324, contends that the agreements between Acts and the Corinthian correspondence confirm the reliability of the Acts account while the disagreements between them suggest that Luke did not use the letters as sources when writing his narrative.

and to the missionary tasks each is given.[590] Paul's point in 1 Corinthians is confirmed by Acts; however, Luke contrasts Paul's spiritual authority to the individual talent of Apollos, whose powerful gifts are not due to his Spirit baptism but to his Alexandrian education (cf. 1 Cor 4:13).

(2) The impression that Paul's mission took place in a milieu of conflict (18:6-7, 9-10) is also evident in the Corinthian letters (cf. 1 Cor 1:10-17). Two kinds of conflict are envisaged. The first is more implicit and obtains to Paul's troubled relationship with the congregation. If at the heart of Paul's troubles in Corinth is the rejection of his religious authority (cf. 1 Cor 4:1-21; 9:1-27; 2 Cor 10-13), then the story of the church's founding in Acts may function as an apologia to underscore his foundational importance for the church's future.

(3) The second conflict concerns various problems that Paul responds to especially in 1 Corinthians, including sexual practices (chaps. 5–7) and foods sacrificed to idols (chaps. 8–10). The reader may well wonder how a congregation founded by Jews (= Acts) had evolved some four or five years later (= 1–2 Corinthians) into a congregation that is largely pagan in background and without keen awareness of the gospel's debt to the church's Jewish heritage. Paul's declaration that "from now on I will go to the Gentiles" (18:6) may help explain this sociological phenomenon. More important, however, the lack of a Jewish touchstone opens the church's witness to contamination from the very practices that were of concern to James and his Jewish church: eating food "polluted by idols" and sexual immorality (15:20, 29; 21:25). The purpose of the canonical conversation between Acts and 1 Corinthians is simply to remind the reader of the vital importance to resist the "gentilizing" of the church's Jewish legacy in order to be the church.

(4) Among the topics of contention within the Corinthian community, central is the conviction of Christ's lordship over any other lordship, political or religious. Cultural predilections and social norms have been voided by the Lord's death and resurrection and replaced by the community's relationship with him in a way that regulates every dimension of human existence (1 Cor 7:22-24;

8:5-6; 12:2-3). Is not this the subtext of the charges against Paul heard by Gallio? The litigious Jews ironically are guilty of a religious lawlessness (see 18:12-17) according to which they reject the word of God (see 18:11).

**18:1-3.** Luke's reference to Caesar Claudius's edict for "all Jews to leave Rome" (18:2) is an important chronological marker in Acts. Most place the date at 49 CE, following the Roman historian Suetonius, who chronicled Claudius's career and wrote that his expulsion of Jews from Rome was "because of their constant disturbances at the instigation of *Chrestus* (= Christ)."[591] While it is unlikely that he would expel Rome's entire Jewish community, then numbering about 40,000 people, it is likely that those sent packing would include the most active participants in these "disturbances," and some of those were probably believers.[592] Aquila and Priscilla were evidently among them, arriving in Corinth around 50 CE, probably as mature believers, suggesting the presence of a Christian community in both Corinth and Rome before Paul's arrival in each city.

Paul's reasons for searching out Aquila and Priscilla were twofold: They shared both the same faith and the same trade: "by trade they were tentmakers" (18:3). The social setting of Acts layers this phrase with important nuances. Paul was a member of a trade guild, which provided a context of financial support and friendship. R. Hock has argued that Paul's trade would have occupied him through most of the day. At least in those cities where he remained a considerable amount of time, such as Corinth, he no doubt spent more hours in his workshop than in the city's *agora* preaching the gospel.[593] The lack of social esteem given to the city's working class would have been sharply qualified by Paul's own Jewish sensibilities, since working creatively with one's hands to pay the bills is an important value of the teacher of Israel (cf. 1 Cor 4:12; 1 Thess 2:9; 2 Thess 3:6-8).

590. Cf. R. Hays, *First Corinthians,* IBC (Louisville: John Knox, 1997) 67-73.

591. Suetonius *Claudius* 25.4. This edict was rescinded upon the accession of the next emperor, Nero, in 54 CE, which dates Paul's Corinthian mission sometime in the early 50s CE.

592. Cf. R. Brändle and E. Stegemann, "The Formation of the First 'Christian Congregations' in Rome," in *Judaism and Christianity in First Century Rome,* ed. K. Donfried and P. Richardson (Grand Rapids: Eerdmans, 2000) 125-26. For a helpful discussion of Rome's attitude toward the Jews, see Witherington, *Acts,* 539-44.

593. R. Hock, *The Social Context of Paul's Ministry: Teaching and Apostleship* (Philadelphia: Fortress, 1980).

**18:4-5.** If Paul's weekly schedule included a long day working alongside Priscilla and Aquila in their tentmaking shop, then they worshiped alongside each other every sabbath when Paul "would argue in the synagogue and would try to convince Jews and Greeks" (18:4).[594] The reader can recover relevant details of Paul's sabbath ministry from earlier episodes to fill in the gaps of this summary (see 13:14-47; 17:2-3, 10-11, 17).

With the arrival of Silas and Timothy from Macedonia (see 17:15; cf. 1 Cor 16:10-11; 2 Cor 1:19), Paul "was occupied with proclaiming of the word . . . that the Messiah was Jesus" (18:5). Paul's experiment with bivocationalism has apparently ended; his occupation has shifted from tentmaking to evangelism, perhaps facilitated by funds brought by Silas and Timothy from the Macedonian congregations (cf. Phil 4:15; 2 Cor 11:9).[595] This text repeats the core content of his synagogue discussions to the Jews and God-fearing Greeks every sabbath, which has become the central feature of his daily teaching in the city.

**18:6-8.** For a second time Paul's frustration with unrepentant Jews who "opposed and reviled him" is recounted (18:6*a*). Paul's prophetic gesture—"he shook the dust from his clothes" (see 13:51; cf. Neh 5:13)—signals their apostasy in rejecting the word of God.[596] If Paul's transition to full-time ministry is a variation of Luke's "second visitation" prophetic motif (see 7:35),[597] Paul's gesture and declaration of intention that follows render God's verdict on the spiritual failure of Corinthian Jews. They have been given every opportunity to hear Paul's message in full and in repetition, and their continuing opposition to him confirms their unwillingness to repent, disqualifying them from participating in the blessings of Israel's restoration (see 13:44-47).

His fierce rebuke that "Your blood be on your own heads" is an intertextual echo of Ezek 33:4, where Jewish "blood" flows because they do not heed God's warning proclaimed through the prophet. Paul's earlier denunciation of unrepentant Jews at Pisidian Antioch used a similar prophecy from Habakkuk to warn hostile Jews that to deny his teaching that Jesus is God's Messiah would result in the loss of eternal life (see 13:46). The message of that earlier incident is implied in this one.

Paul's declaration that "from now on I will go to the Gentiles" should be understood in context. On the one hand, Paul is turning from those Jews who continue to reject his message and revile him to those who are more responsive. The declaration is a statement of fact rather than of resolve; indeed, God-fearing Gentiles in Corinth have been more responsive to the gospel. Luke's Acts is interested in stipulating *that* it is so not *why* it is so. On the other hand, Paul does not turn from Corinthian Jews in general since he enjoys some stunning successes, including two "officials of the synagogue," Crispus (18:8) and Sosthenes (18:17).

The failure of Paul's mission to the Jews of the Corinthian synagogue precipitates moving the location of his teaching ministry to a different house, one in the shadow of the synagogue (see 6:9).[598] This fledging congregation met in the home of Titius Justus, whose home is the second noted in Acts (Lydia's in the first) where believers meet for worship. However, the congregants of Titius's house church are not only Gentiles formerly attached to the synagogue; the Jewish leader Crispus "became a believer in the Lord together with all his household [οἶκος *oikos*]," along with many other Corinthians (18:8). Although the text does not identify these Corinthians, they are probably attached to the synagogue and join Crispus upon hearing of his conversion.

This transition from synagogue to house must also be understood in terms of the concerns raised by James at the Jerusalem Council. Whatever confidence James has that a diaspora congregation of

---

594. The Western version depicts a subversive Paul who "inserted" the name of the Lord Jesus into the Scripture lessons, probably as substitute for "Lord," when reading and teaching them. The variant also implies that Greeks in attendance were Paul's principal audience, again reflecting its anti-Semitic bias.

595. Conzelmann, *The Acts of the Apostles,* 152; Dunn, *The Acts of the Apostles,* 242.

596. Cf. Haenchen, *The Acts of the Apostles,* 535.

597. Johnson, *The Acts of the Apostles,* 13.

598. Luke's proximity of Titius's house "next door to the synagogue" (18:8) symbolizes the congregation's continuity with the religious practices of the synagogue—more likely since the distance of houses to meeting places allowed members of the synagogue to observe sabbath *halakhah* (see 1:12).

mixed constituency will retain its Jewish heritage is predicated on a mission that is synagogue-based, since there Moses will be preached every Sabbath (see 15:21). God-fearing Gentiles, who are attached to the synagogue and hear Moses preached, will more likely understand how they should live among their Jewish brothers and sisters. The relocation of Paul's mission from synagogue to house may well imperil the sabbath reading of Moses and thus make more likely the "gentilizing" of Christian faith. The pervasiveness of the Jewish character of this Corinthian house, however, where its first members are Jewish and its location is in close proximity to the synagogue, ensures that Moses will be read there. The implication that the transition from synagogue to household church will not necessarily jeopardize its Jewish heritage is strengthened by Stephen's speech that criticized the reification of a particular place as inherently sacred. The crucial issue in this new dispensation of salvation's history is not where the faith community worships but who is worshiped.

**18:9-11.** The visions of Acts prophesy the church's mission; the opening formula "One night the Lord [= Jesus] said to Paul in a vision" (18:9), then, is anticipatory of the story's plotline. The antagonism of certain Jews toward Paul's mission (see 18:6) will continue (see 18:12; 9:16). In this context of escalating tensions Jesus does not say to Paul "do not be afraid" because he would intervene to end Paul's mission and inaugurate more halcyon days. Rather, he promises physical protection so that Paul may continue to speak and grow the church in Corinth. Jesus' comment that "there are many in this city who are my people [λαός *laos*])" (18:10) again is prophetic of future conversions not only from among the Jews (= Sosthenes, 18:17), who are the people (*laos*) of God (see 4:10, et. al.), but also from among the Gentiles as the continuing fulfillment of Amos's prophecy that God would call out "a people" (*laos;* 15:14) from the Gentiles (see 15:17). Drawing strength from the Lord's exhortation, Paul stays on in Corinth for "a year and six months," during which he continues his prophetic ministry of "teaching the word of God among them" (18:11; see 4:31).

**18:12-17.** The conflict implied and protection promised in the Lord's vision to Paul is here fulfilled in a remarkable manner, and providing addi-

tional insight in how Luke's shaping of Acts instructs his readers about the nature of God's sovereignty (see Introduction, "Acts as Confession"). The central character of this episode is the Achaian proconsul Gallio (52 CE), the political name of Seneca's older brother and member of his influential Roman family. Achaia is the most important region of Roman Greece and therefore the importance of Gallio's pedigree is enhanced by the location of his post.

At the elevated center of the city's *agora* is the "tribunal" (βῆμα *bēma*) where public pronouncements are heard and important court cases settled. This is where Paul's Jewish opponents bring him, apparently so Gallio can dispose of their legal grievances against this rogue teacher of Israel. Their accusations are similar to those brought by Hellenist Jews against Stephen before another tribunal (6:13-14; cf. 16:20-21) and therefore probably should be glossed by that earlier indictment. In this Roman setting, however, Paul is charged with breaking Roman (not Jewish) law in Corinth (not Jerusalem). The legal presumption is that Judaism is an approved religion of the empire and that what Paul taught was outside of religious boundaries approved by "official" Israel. In this limited sense, then, Paul's proclamation that Jesus is God's Messiah and Israel's Savior is "contrary to the [Roman] law" (18:13).

Gallio intervenes before Paul can speak—a literary convention of Luke to add drama and importance to what comes next—and renders a legal verdict, which is paradigmatic for every Roman verdict from this point forward in Acts. His speech asserts crucial judgments about Paul's mission in the Diaspora. The first is that the relevant legal "matter" of the Jewish complaint against Paul does not pertain to a "crime [ἀδίκημα *adikēma*] or serious villainy" (18:14).[599] Gallio's reference to *adikēma* is more than a reference to an important Hellenistic *topos* for criminal vice; it also denotes religious impurity. The irony of his commentary on Paul's legal innocence is that it helps to render Luke's judgment about Paul's theological innocence, which is the real motive of the complaint against him. In this sense, Gallio infers that Paul is "Torah pure" and for this reason his case should be

599. The grammatical construction of Gallio's declaration is a "first-class conditional," which states something as a matter-of-fact.

tossed out of a *Jewish* courtroom even as it is dismissed from his Roman court.

This implied sense is made explicit by Gallio's second judgment: This "matter" concerns "words [= resurrection] and names [= Messiah, Jesus] and your own law [= Israel's Scripture], see to it yourselves" (18:15). Gallio nicely expresses a central point of Luke's apologia: Paul's mission and message take place *within* the purview of Israel's traditions and destiny, not outside of them. The disputes provoked are deeply religious in nature, pertaining to Paul's messianic reading of Scripture that proves Jesus is Messiah (see 18:4-5). Gallio's refusal to make a judgment confirms that such a conflict falls in a "legal" category over which Roman law and therefore a Roman court has no jurisdiction.

Gallio's brusque dismissal of the case[600] will come to symbolize Rome's prudent if sometimes heavy-handed neutrality toward Paul's mission. Some scholars have argued, against the evidence supplied by his Acts, that Luke intends to rehabilitate Rome's relationship with the church as an element of his "catholicizing" theology that seeks conciliation of relevant parties. Luke's depiction of Rome's relationship to Paul's mission in Acts, however, is rather more realistic than this and suggests that Rome's political aloofness evinces a more benign rejection of the gospel in favor of the empire's sovereignty and security.

The final scene of this episode is bizarre but perhaps illustrates Rome's disposition toward Paul's mission (see 18:17). There is no indication in the narrative of what prompts the Jewish retaliation against Sosthenes or of whether his involvement in the case is pro or con; nor are we told who the attackers are. It could be the response of embarrassed litigants taking out their legal failure on "the official of the synagogue," who may have replaced Cristus following his conversion and forced the issue against Paul as a first (and now failed) act of his administration. Or it could be, as many suppose, that Sosthenes is also a recent convert who personifies the growing anxiety of Paul's Jewish opponents in Corinth. If so, to attack him is to attack the undesirable effect of the Christian mission on members of their synagogue.

In any case, another purpose of Luke's conclusion is to portray the mocking disinterest of Gallio (= Rome) in bad light. Gallio's casual arrogance nicely captures Luke's understanding of God's hold over the unfolding of salvation to the end of the earth and harkens back to the Lord's exhortation in Paul's dream-vision. Simply put, God's will is done. But the way it gets done is often messy and the agents of God's will are sometimes unsavory people.

---

600. The NIV translation of ἀπελαύνω (*apelaunō*, "eject") captures the sense of the text better than the NRSV. Gallio's frustration in hearing an irrelevant case is reflected in literally tossing the case (and litigants!) from the courtroom.

# REFLECTIONS

**1.** "Because Paul was a tentmaker as they were, he stayed and worked with them" (18:3 NIV). While Paul did not consider manual labor essential to his missionary strategy, his bivocationalism is nonetheless exemplary of a Jewish ethic that fully integrates one's work with one's life and service before God and neighbor (cf. 1 Thess 2:9; 4:11-12; 2 Thess 3:12). Not only is it practical for Paul to work his trade to support himself while growing a church in Corinth—especially if many converts came from the working-class poor (cf. 1 Cor 1:26)—but to work his prophetic calling "free of charge" may have been illustrative of a gospel about God's grace. Yet Paul's ability to work two jobs becomes impossible as the congregation grows. Clearly his preference is to devote himself fully to his spiritual calling and thus as soon as the congregation is able to support him and Silas and Timothy arrive to help him, Paul leaves his trade and "devoted himself exclusively to preaching" (8:5 NIV). Paul's bivocationalism is a useful pattern for clergy of new congregations to follow in our contemporary situation. However, congregations should carefully consider whether bivocationalism should be a permanent arrangement or whether they should support a full-time ministry as soon as they are able.

**2.** "Then he left the synagogue and went to the house of a man name Titius Justus . . . and many of the Corinthians who heard Paul became believers and were baptized" (18:7-8 NRSV).

The Christian congregation in Corinth moves from the local synagogue to a neighbor's home. The primary motive for doing so is not a matter of convenience or one of planting a new congregation among those outside the synagogue. Instead, Paul is prompted to leave the synagogue in order to maintain theological purity. If the "sacred" is not circumscribed by where the faith community worships but by who they worship, as Luke maintains throughout Acts, the departure of believers from one congregation for another should be precipitated only by substantial theological disagreements that cannot be resolved—and then only as a last resort (see 14:27–15:5).

# ACTS 18:18-23, INTERLUDE: PAUL'S PILGRIMAGE FROM CORINTH TO ANTIOCH

## NIV

[18]Paul stayed on in Corinth for some time. Then he left the brothers and sailed for Syria, accompanied by Priscilla and Aquila. Before he sailed, he had his hair cut off at Cenchrea because of a vow he had taken. [19]They arrived at Ephesus, where Paul left Priscilla and Aquila. He himself went into the synagogue and reasoned with the Jews. [20]When they asked him to spend more time with them, he declined. [21]But as he left, he promised, "I will come back if it is God's will." Then he set sail from Ephesus. [22]When he landed at Caesarea, he went up and greeted the church and then went down to Antioch.

[23]After spending some time in Antioch, Paul set out from there and traveled from place to place throughout the region of Galatia and Phrygia, strengthening all the disciples.

## NRSV

[18]After staying there for a considerable time, Paul said farewell to the believers[a] and sailed for Syria, accompanied by Priscilla and Aquila. At Cenchreae he had his hair cut, for he was under a vow. [19]When they reached Ephesus, he left them there, but first he himself went into the synagogue and had a discussion with the Jews. [20]When they asked him to stay longer, he declined; [21]but on taking leave of them, he said, "I[b] will return to you, if God wills." Then he set sail from Ephesus.

[22]When he had landed at Caesarea, he went up to Jerusalem[c] and greeted the church, and then went down to Antioch. [23]After spending some time there he departed and went from place to place through the region of Galatia[d] and Phrygia, strengthening all the disciples.

[a] Gk brothers    [b] Other ancient authorities read I must at all costs keep the approaching festival in Jerusalem, but I    [c] Gk went up    [d] Gk the Galatian region

# COMMENTARY

Paul's follow-up ministry among those congregations founded during earlier campaigns is an important feature of his overall missionary strategy. In the present passage that recounts various bits from Paul's itinerary following the end of his Corinthian mission (18:18), he returns to the Jerusalem church (18:22a) and then Antioch (18:22b) before "strengthening all the disciples" throughout the region of his first missionary tour (18:23). Only with the prophet's "second visitation" does he consider his work there complete.[601]

The primary function of narrative interludes in Acts is to move the reader from stage to stage—or

601. Cf. R. C. Tannehill, *The Acts of the Apostles*, vol. 2 of *The Narrative Unity of Luke-Acts: A Literary Interpretation* (Minneapolis: Fortress, 1990) 2:230.

from city (Corinth) to city (Ephesus), as is the purpose of the present text. Yet there is always a sense of continuity that coordinates Paul's mission in different cities. Thus his strategy of initiating his urban mission in the synagogue continues. In this case, he stops briefly in Ephesus but long enough to enter a synagogue and discuss Scripture's messianic meaning with the Jews he finds there (18:19), a harbinger of his future mission in that great city.

**18:18.** Acts tells us nothing of the actual circumstances that prompted Paul to conclude his Corinthian mission and sail for Roman Syria—to Jerusalem and Antioch (see vv. 22-23). Nor are we told why Priscilla and Aquila would close their tentmaking business in Corinth to accompany him. The fact that they stayed there "for a considerable time" indicates that a measure of peace resulted because of the Gallio verdict, allowing establishment of the church there.

The circumstances of Paul's voyage to Jerusalem, however, are implied by his religious practices that remain in the foreground of Luke's narrative. In this case, reference is made to Paul's ritual haircut to fulfill a vow he had made. In fact, he refuses to stay on in Ephesus, even though the response to him there is hospitable, and presses forward to Jerusalem because of the obligations of his vow. The importance of Paul's vow is more fully appreciated by recalling the concerns expressed in concluding the Jerusalem Council (see 15:20-21). Paul's pilgrimage to Jerusalem is prompted neither by his high regard for the "mother church" nor by a ministry of reconciliation within his own Antiochene congregation, which is still hurting over his split from Barnabas. His haircut, rather, symbolizes a pious Jew's vow to maintain the purity of his consecrated relations with God.

Although only a passing reference in Acts, Paul's vow is probably that of a Nazirite (lit., "consecrated one") described in Num 6:1-21. If that is the case, then his ritual haircut symbolizes his dedicated service for God and within Israel (Num 6:9, 18; *m. Nazir* 1.1–9.5). Although usually done in Jerusalem, it was sometimes allowed outside of the holy city if the consecrated servant then made a pilgrimage to the Jerusalem Temple for priestly confirmation.[602] The imperfect tense of the verb

"to vow" ($\epsilon \hat{\iota} \chi \epsilon \nu$ *eichen;* lit., "was taking a vow") may indicate that his haircut initiates a particular period that would end several months later (see 21:26). In Acts, vow taking is another indication that Paul's ministry among uncircumcised Gentiles has not contaminated his loyalty to the ancestral traditions of his Jewish faith nor his vocation as a teacher of Israel (see also 21:22-26).[603]

**18:19-21.** Luke deposits "Priscilla and Aquila"[604] in Ephesus[605] to await their encounter with Apollos (see 18:24-28), while Paul "went into the synagogue and had a discussion [$\delta \iota \alpha \lambda \acute{\epsilon} \gamma o \mu \alpha \iota$ *dialegomai;* see 17:2-3] with the Jews." Once again, the reader is expected to fill in the gaps with earlier narrative details of Paul's synagogue mission. In this case, the response to his messianic interpretation of Scripture reflects interest, which implies a request for the prophet's second visitation (see 7:35-40; 13:42-43). Although Paul is ambivalent in his response to their invitation (cf. 18:21), since his current intent is vow-keeping rather than gospel preaching, the reader is soon to learn that his promise is kept when he returns to Ephesus. Evidently, an Ephesian mission is God's will (see 19:1; cf. Rom 1:10; 1 Cor 4:19; Heb 6:3; Jas 4:15).

**18:22.** The principal issue for the interpreter is whether Luke has Paul "going up" to Jerusalem before "going down" to Antioch, for the words "to Jerusalem" are not found in the Greek text.[606] In an interlude whose most important detail is Paul's haircut and vow taking in preparation for a pilgrimage to the holy city, the reader should probably assume that Paul's return to Caesarea included

---

602. B. Witherington, *The Acts of the Apostles: A Socio-Rhetorical Commentary* (Grand Rapids: Eerdmans, 1998) 557.

603. Cf. B. Levine, *Numbers 1–20,* AB 4 (New York: Doubleday, 1993) 229-35, who notes the heroic dimension of naziritism in OT narratives, especially of Israel's Judges (e.g., Deborah, Samson, Samuel). This resonance is probably intended by Luke to gloss Paul's behavior throughout his European mission.

604. Some think the reversal of the names here and in 18:26 to "Priscilla and Aquila" (see 18:2) indicates Priscilla's role as lead teacher, who is given credit for Apollos's theological rehabilitation according to 18:24-28. See J. D. G. Dunn, *The Acts of the Apostles* (Valley Forge, Pa.: Trinity, 1996) 247.

605. Ephesus is the provincial capital of Roman Asia and a city of enormous wealth and culture. The disapora community of Jews was especially strong there, since they were granted citizenship without prejudice. Many successful archaeological expeditions have made more precise the knowledge of the city behind the biblical story of Paul's mission there. For bibliography and discussion of the literature that describes these findings and their relevance as an interpretive tool for Acts 19–20, see J. A. Fitzmyer, *The Acts of the Apostles,* AB 31 (Garden City, N.Y.: Doubleday, 1998) 634-35.

606. The Western version of 18:21 adds the note that Paul must leave in order to "spend the coming feast in Jerusalem," which clarifies the verse's ambiguous reference to "this church."

a trip to Jerusalem. Johnson argues that Luke uses the verbs ἀναβαίνω/καταβαίνω (*anabainō/ katabainō,* "going up/down") elsewhere in Acts to keep contact with Jerusalem and have a similar connotation here.[607] In paying respects to the church leadership, Paul has previously responded in good faith to the council's pastoral exhortation to Antiochene believers. He has rigorously resisted any practice that might "gentilize" his Jewish heritage or the congregations his mission has founded. Paul's visit in Antioch symbolizes his mission's solidarity with Jerusalem.

**18:23.** The catchphrase "strengthening all the disciples," which concludes this interlude, is a narrative boundary marker that cues the reader that one mission is complete, with all its obligations, and that Paul will soon venture into another (see 14:22; 20:1-3).[608] The itinerancy of missionary Paul, who "went from place to place through the region of Galatia and Phrygia," is characteristic of pastoral Paul's keenly felt motive to root new converts in teaching. This follow-up circuit to previous fields of service is an important feature of his overall mission strategy. Dunn suggests that we should understand this cultivation of the Aegean church as background for the collection of an offering for the poor and hungry believers of Palestine whom the letters mention (cf. Rom 15:25; 2 Corinthians 8–9), which may have been sparked by Paul's recent visit to Jerusalem and Antioch.[609] (See Reflections at 18:24–19:7.)

607. L. T. Johnson, *The Acts of the Apostles,* SP 5 (Collegeville, Minn.: Liturgical, 1992) 330. Dunn, *The Acts of the Apostles,* 247, however, suggests Luke remains silent of any such visit because of Paul's unpopularity in Jerusalem—as Paul will find out in no uncertain terms upon a later visit in Acts 21.

608. J. P. Polhill, *The Acts of the Apostles* (Nashville: Broadman, 1992) 390-91.

609. Dunn, *The Acts of the Apostles,* 248.

# ACTS 18:24–19:7, INTERLUDE: PAUL RETURNS TO EPHESUS

NIV

[24]Meanwhile a Jew named Apollos, a native of Alexandria, came to Ephesus. He was a learned man, with a thorough knowledge of the Scriptures. [25]He had been instructed in the way of the Lord, and he spoke with great fervor[a] and taught about Jesus accurately, though he knew only the baptism of John. [26]He began to speak boldly in the synagogue. When Priscilla and Aquila heard him, they invited him to their home and explained to him the way of God more adequately.

[27]When Apollos wanted to go to Achaia, the brothers encouraged him and wrote to the disciples there to welcome him. On arriving, he was a great help to those who by grace had believed. [28]For he vigorously refuted the Jews in public debate, proving from the Scriptures that Jesus was the Christ.

19 While Apollos was at Corinth, Paul took the road through the interior and arrived at Ephesus. There he found some disciples [2]and

a 25 Or *with fervor in the Spirit*

NRSV

[24]Now there came to Ephesus a Jew named Apollos, a native of Alexandria. He was an eloquent man, well-versed in the scriptures. [25]He had been instructed in the Way of the Lord; and he spoke with burning enthusiasm and taught accurately the things concerning Jesus, though he knew only the baptism of John. [26]He began to speak boldly in the synagogue; but when Priscilla and Aquila heard him, they took him aside and explained the Way of God to him more accurately. [27]And when he wished to cross over to Achaia, the believers[a] encouraged him and wrote to the disciples to welcome him. On his arrival he greatly helped those who through grace had become believers, [28]for he powerfully refuted the Jews in public, showing by the scriptures that the Messiah[b] is Jesus.

19 While Apollos was in Corinth, Paul passed through the interior regions and came to Ephesus, where he found some disciples. [2]He said to them, "Did you receive the Holy Spirit when you

a Gk brothers    b Or the Christ

asked them, "Did you receive the Holy Spirit when[a] you believed?"

They answered, "No, we have not even heard that there is a Holy Spirit."

[3]So Paul asked, "Then what baptism did you receive?"

"John's baptism," they replied.

[4]Paul said, "John's baptism was a baptism of repentance. He told the people to believe in the one coming after him, that is, in Jesus." [5]On hearing this, they were baptized into[b] the name of the Lord Jesus. [6]When Paul placed his hands on them, the Holy Spirit came on them, and they spoke in tongues[c] and prophesied. [7]There were about twelve men in all.

[a] 2 Or after    [b] 5 Or in    [c] 6 Or other languages

became believers?" They replied, "No, we have not even heard that there is a Holy Spirit." [3]Then he said, "Into what then were you baptized?" They answered, "Into John's baptism." [4]Paul said, "John baptized with the baptism of repentance, telling the people to believe in the one who was to come after him, that is, in Jesus." [5]On hearing this, they were baptized in the name of the Lord Jesus. [6]When Paul had laid his hands on them, the Holy Spirit came upon them, and they spoke in tongues and prophesied— [7]altogether there were about twelve of them.

# COMMENTARY

The next two stories in Acts take place in Ephesus and are related by their common interest in the continuing prominence of "John's baptism" among those with deficient knowledge of the gospel and incomplete experience of the Holy Spirit. By these stories of Apollos (18:24-28) and the Ephesian "disciples" (19:1-7), the reader is apprised of yet another element in the purview of Paul's mission: It includes the theological integration of marginal believers—those who know some of the truth but not all of it or who have experienced some of God's blessings but not to the full extent promised. In both instances, these believers are catechized and initiated into the fold of Christian fellowship to whom the Scriptures and the Spirit belong.

Apollos's remediation prepares him to contribute to Paul's ongoing Corinthian mission. Moreover, Priscilla and Aquila assume responsibility for his education in the absence of Paul. Both details of Apollos's story in Acts suggest that Paul's mission strategy is collaborative; he routinely enlists gifted colleagues to help him along the way. Priscilla and Aquila enjoy extraordinary freedom in preparing Ephesus for Paul's arrival, while at the same time Timothy and Silas are given responsibility over the Macedonian congregations. Luke's interest in the origin and positive outcome of Apollos's teaching ministry is especially noteworthy, given his future importance to the Achaian church, as Paul notes in 1 Corinthians 3–4 (see also Acts 18:1-17).

This interlude also confirms the theological fluidity within earliest Christianity, which is personified by Apollos and the Ephesian twelve, who represent all those believers (including Theophilus) whose faith is formed by an inchoate presentation of the gospel. The mentoring ministry of Priscilla and Aquila becomes paradigmatic of the church's response to this critical problem within a religious movement whose growth has far outstripped its educational resources (cf. 6:1-7).

Even though the boundary marker of this passage concerns the Holy Spirit, the subsequent story of Paul's Ephesian mission testifies to the primary cultural threats to the church's theological purity, including syncretism and magic (19:11-20) and pagan religion (19:23-41). Simply put, then, the story of Paul's Ephesian mission testifies to the importance of forming Christian faith in ways that more clearly distinguish its beliefs and practices from those of other religious options.

**18:24-26.** While Paul is revisiting the circuit of earlier missions (see v. 23), significant ministry is taking place elsewhere in Ephesus, where he had earlier left Priscilla and Aquila (see v. 19). This narrative vignette concerns their recruitment of

Apollos to help Paul in Corinth, where he had planted a vigorous Christian congregation (see vv. 1-17). Apollos's credentials to teach are impressive: He is a Jew from Alexandria, a man who is good with words, and he has a "thorough knowledge of the Scriptures."

Acts tells us nothing about the church of Alexandria in Egypt—its origins, teaching, or practices. Yet Alexandria was second in influence only to Rome. It was not only a leading center of commerce and learning with a renowned library, but it also housed one of the most important communities of diaspora Jews in the Roman Empire. The great Jewish scholar Philo lived in Alexandria, and Apollos may well have been taught by him.[610] In fact, the unusual predicate adjective λόγιος (*logios*, "eloquent") expresses a characteristic of the educated person, since training in rhetoric was an essential part of education in Greco-Roman society.

In Acts, however, the prophet's rhetorical competence results from Spirit filling (see 4:8) and is explicitly disconnected from learning (see 4:13). Luke's reference to Apollos's eloquence, then, must be considered an ironic feature of his résumé since he had not yet received the Spirit of prophecy (see v. 28). This same irony extends to his thorough knowledge of the Scriptures. Although Apollos knows Scripture well, without the filling of the Holy Spirit he is unable to interpret Scripture in the elevated ways of the prophet-like-Jesus (see 2:4; 6:10).

Apollos arrives in Ephesus "with burning enthusiasm and taught accurately [ἀκριβῶς *akribōs*] the things concerning Jesus" (v. 25). Luke's clipped comment that Apollos "knew only the baptism of John" (v. 25) cues us that the source of his "burning enthusiasm" (ζέων τῷ πνεύματι *zeōn tō pneumati*) is not the Holy Spirit; rather, this is a feature of his rhetorical eloquence: He speaks with a lively (ζέων *zeōn*) spirit (πνεῦμα *pneuma*) and so has attracted a following at Ephesus. If Apollos has experienced only John's baptism (whatever that may entail) but not yet the Holy

Spirit's (and all this entails according to Acts), the content of his teaching may be suspect. Apollos does not seem to fail in his religious (= Jewish) practice; and while his knowledge of the "way of the Lord" (cf. Luke 3:4) is "accurate" (18:25), the relevant issue probably concerns an inadequate doctrine of the Spirit. The connection of Apollos's story with the twelve disciples of Ephesus (see 19:1-7) would seem to support this conjecture (see above).[611] The implication is that Apollos has been initiated into Christian discipleship by John's baptism and that he has learned only the first lessons of Jesus, perhaps only to the time of John the Baptist's martyrdom before the cross and the empty tomb.

In any case, Priscilla and Aquila "took him aside and explained the Way of God to him more accurately" (v. 26). That his information about Jesus is incomplete is indicated by Luke's use of the comparative form of ἀκριβῶς (*akribōs*). While he knows "the way of the Lord" (ἡ ὁδὸς τοῦ κυρίου *hē hodos tou kyriou*), he does not know "the Way of God [= "The Way"; ἡ ὁδὸς τοῦ θεοῦ *hē hodos tou theou*]." "The Way" is used elsewhere in Acts only in Pauline narratives (9:2; 19:9; 22:4; 24:14, 22), which suggests it is an idiom of Luke's Pauline source and is defined by the content of Paul's gospel. If so, then Apollos's problem is that he has not yet received the Pauline seal of approval, which Priscilla and Aquila now provide him.

**18:27-28.** The results of Priscilla and Aquila's mentoring are immediate: "The believers [in Ephesus] encouraged [προτρέπτομαι *protreptomai*] him and wrote to the disciples [in Achaia] to welcome him" (v. 27). Evidently, this congregation, whose faith is cultivated by Priscilla and Aquila's teaching, recognizes Apollos's vocation and gifts. Their favorable impression of him is signaled by Luke's use of *protreptomai*, which connotes the confirmation of a newly instructed teacher, and by the writing of a letter of introduction, an act of friendship and support.

Upon his arrival, Apollos "greatly helped" in the catechesis of new believers and "powerfully refuted [διακατελέγχομαι *diakatelenchomai*] the Jews in public" from the Scriptures, now more fully

---

610. From the ancient church forward, some scholars claimed that Apollos is the author of the anonymous NT letter "To the Hebrews" because it echoes the writings of Philo, employs a hellenized (= Alexandrian) exegesis of Scripture, is similar in theological conception to Paul, and reflects an intellectual rigor that corresponds to the profile of Apollos in Acts. Others, including myself, are not convinced, mostly because the echoes of Philo are faint and the letter's theological similarity to Paul is vague.

611. Cf. F. S. Spencer, *Acts*, Readings: A New Biblical Commentary (Sheffield: Sheffield Academic, 1997) 183-84, who pairs Apollos as Paul's "forerunner" much like the Baptist is to Jesus and Philip is to Peter. However, see M. Turner, *Power from on High: The Spirit in Israel's Restoration and Witness in Luke-Acts*, JPTSS 9 (Sheffield: Sheffield Academic, 1996) 388-97.

understood. The repetition of Paul's teaching in the synagogue that "Jesus is Messiah" (see 17:2-3) would suggest that Apollos's own instruction is complete and that he has been brought into agreement with Paul's christological interpretation of Israel's Scriptures. Moreover, the powerful refutation of opponents suggests Apollos's filling with the Spirit of prophecy. The location of his public ministry in Corinth (see 19:1), however, is neither the synagogue, since Paul left it for Titius's house (see 18:6), nor the courtroom, since Gallio has closed its door (see 18:12-17). Therefore, he must be contesting unrepentant Jews in the town square. There his "eloquence" coupled with his elevated understanding of Scriptures ("showing by the scriptures") has funded teaching that "powerfully refuted" the unrepentant Jews who contest the gospel's claims.

**19:1-7.** The disciples whom Paul found upon his arrival in Ephesus are similar in theological defect to Apollos: They know John's baptism but not the Spirit's.[612] It remains unlikely that their theological similarity is due to their personal acquaintance in Ephesus, however, since these "disciples" apparently did not attend a synagogue (cf. 18:26; 19:2). Nothing is known of the lessons Priscilla and Aquila may have used for instructing Apollos about "the Way of God"; presumably their curriculum was based on what was learned from Paul. This inference also suggests that his response to the twelve of Ephesus would be similar to the unwritten instruction given earlier to Apollos by Priscilla and Aquila.

**19:1-4.** Luke refers to Paul's conversation partners without qualifying them as "disciples" (μαθηταί *mathētai*), a term otherwise used only of believers in Acts. Here it suggests that they are untrained students in search of a master teacher.[613] Their ignorance of the Holy Spirit (v. 2*b*) has placed them outside of Christian fellowship: they evidently have not yet found the synagogue where Priscilla and Aquila teach, since their subsequent responses to Paul suggest they worship God outside of the synagogue where Moses and Messiah are preached.

Paul's initial and decisive question presumes their Christian faith: "Did you receive the Holy Spirit when you became believers?" (v. 2*a*). The narrative does not indicate what prompts Paul's question or why he presumes that they are believers. Paul's query recognizes that they lack the mark of the Spirit's presence and that their theological education, therefore, is incomplete; that they "have not even heard that there is a Holy Spirit" (v. 2*b*) only sharpens Paul's interrogations. Has Luke shaped their response to underscore the theological problem? Probably so, since they would have surely learned about the Holy Spirit from this prophet who predicted that the Messiah would baptize his followers with the Holy Spirit! What they seem to lack, then, is both a more robust knowledge of the Spirit formed by an *experience* of its filling and the theological claims that are adumbrated in Acts.

A second round of questions and answers detects this root problem. As with Apollos before them, these initiates "into John's baptism" had not yet received the Spirit of prophecy (v. 3; see also 18:25). Paul insinuates his own theology into John by asserting that he taught his initiates "to believe in the one who was to come after him" (v. 4). Nowhere in the Gospels does John the Baptist ever say this; Luke's Paul infers the next logical stage of John's proclamation, since the Lord's resurrection merely confirms his prophecy that he is the Messiah and the agent of forgiveness for those baptized in his name (v. 5; see also 2:21; 13:38-39).[614] Paul's commentary on John's testimony of Jesus does however recall John the Baptist's final appearance with Jesus before his imprisonment, when the Lord makes a comparison between his own importance and John's, concluding with a dramatic warning that "whoever believes in the Son has eternal life; whoever disobeys the Son will not see life, but must endure God's wrath" (John 3:36). Read in canonical context, Paul's summary of John's teaching about the Messiah's baptism implies these same consequences in exhorting John's current disciples "to believe in the one who was to come after him" (v. 4; see also 13:44-47; 19:9).

**19:5-7.** With these clipped exchanges, the catechesis of John the Baptist's former students is

612. Cf. C. K. Barrett, *A Critical and Exegetical Commentary on the Acts of the Apostles,* 2 vols, ICC (Edinburgh: T. & T. Clark, 1994, 1998) 2:892-95.

613. The root meaning of "disciple" (μαθητής *mathētēs*) is "student," a primary connotation of Luke's use of the word here. The Ephesian twelve are itinerant "theologues" searching for a mentor to replace John; they find him in Paul.

614. E. Haenchen, *The Acts of the Apostles* (Philadelphia: Westminster, 1971) 553.

complete, and so "they were baptized in the name of the Lord Jesus" (v. 5), and "the Holy Spirit came upon them" (v. 6). Again, we should not presume a formal relationship between Christian baptism and the reception of the Holy Spirit.[615] Nor should we privilege this text over others in establishing a particular baptismal liturgy ("Paul had laid his hands on them") or evidence of the Spirit's reception ("and they spoke in tongues and prophesied," v. 6). In Luke's narrative of Paul's mission, Christian baptism is sometimes mentioned without reference to the Spirit's reception (see 16:15, 33; 18:8). Elsewhere in Acts the outpouring of the Spirit of prophecy falls prior to baptism (see 9:17-18; 10:47-48), or after baptism as here (see 2:1-4; 8:12-16, 38-39), or even at the same time as baptism (see 2:38-41). And the arrival of God's Spirit does not ensure in every case the capacity to speak in tongues *and* to prophesy (cf. 2:1-11; 8:16-7, 38-39; 10:46).[616]

The close parallelism between this case and the earlier story of the Samaritans' reception of the Spirit (see 8:14-24) clarifies the story's subtext: to authorize the Pauline mission. Unlike Simon the Great, who coveted but could not acquire Peter's apostolic "authority" to lay hands on believers as the medium for the Spirit's reception (see 8:17-19), Paul has been granted this authority. This clarification of Paul's spiritual authority cues the reader of Acts to the ensuing account of the Ephesian mission, where his prophetic powers reach their zenith.

615. This is Scripture's only narrative of the "rebaptism" of believers, and the "rebaptism" of Apollos is implied by the parallelism of his story and this one.

616. Luke's reference to the twelve's capacity to prophesy must be considered remarkable by any interpretation. It will not do simply to read this capacity to speak in tongues and prophesy in the light of 1 Corinthians 12–14 as instances of "gifts of the Spirit," for in Acts these gifts fund the church's witness to Jesus rather than the formation of the Christian community, as in Paul.

# REFLECTION

**1.** "When Priscilla and Aquila heard [Apollos], they took him aside and explained the Way of God to him more accurately" (18:26 NRSV). For all his evident gifts, Apollos is an immature teacher. He knows Scripture well, but he lacks full understanding of what he is teaching. Priscilla and Aquila tutor their protégé to maturity. A congregation's theological formation depends on its teachers; misguided teaching can result in incorrect beliefs that divert believers from the Way of God. For this reason no pastoral activity is more critical to the spiritual health of a congregation than overseeing those who instruct the flock concerning the things of God. Following the pattern of Priscilla and Aquila, mentoring young teachers includes three steps: Those mature in the faith observe the new teacher firsthand in a classroom setting, assessing the content of what is being taught to make certain it agrees with the congregation's faith statement. If there is need for remediation, mentors should schedule time outside the classroom for instruction. Finally, church leaders should make certain the person resumes teaching with the full support and encouragement of the congregation (18:27-28).

**2.** This story of Priscilla's ministry introduces and frames those famous passages within the Pauline collection that instruct Christian women to submit as good wives and mothers (1 Cor 7:34-35; Eph 5:21-24), to remain silent as good students (1 Cor 14:34; 1 Tim 2:9-12), and to circumscribe their prophetic ministry with head coverings to symbolize patriarchal claims on their lives (1 Cor 11:2-10). The relevant relationships of Christian women—to Pauline tradition, to familial obligations and the workplace, and to the local congregation and its male teachers—are subtexts of Priscilla's story. Pauline teaching about women is often obscure, but the portrait of Priscilla in Acts 18 produces a fresh angle of vision for the troublesome epistolary texts that follow. Moreover, her story coheres with the gospel witness to Jesus' relationships with his female disciples—and with Paul's statement that there is neither male nor female, for all are one in Christ (Gal 3:28). Christian women can form equal partnerships with their husbands in the workplace (18:2) and the local congregation (18:26), even taking the lead in these efforts (18:18). And female teachers can instruct men in the way of the Lord (18:26). Women in ministry produce a more robust performance of God's Word in the world (18:27-28).

# ACTS 19:8-41, PAUL'S EPHESIAN MISSION

## NIV

8Paul entered the synagogue and spoke boldly there for three months, arguing persuasively about the kingdom of God. 9But some of them became obstinate; they refused to believe and publicly maligned the Way. So Paul left them. He took the disciples with him and had discussions daily in the lecture hall of Tyrannus. 10This went on for two years, so that all the Jews and Greeks who lived in the province of Asia heard the word of the Lord.

11God did extraordinary miracles through Paul, 12so that even handkerchiefs and aprons that had touched him were taken to the sick, and their illnesses were cured and the evil spirits left them.

13Some Jews who went around driving out evil spirits tried to invoke the name of the Lord Jesus over those who were demon-possessed. They would say, "In the name of Jesus, whom Paul preaches, I command you to come out." 14Seven sons of Sceva, a Jewish chief priest, were doing this. 15 One day, the evil spirit answered them, "Jesus I know, and I know about Paul, but who are you?" 16Then the man who had the evil spirit jumped on them and overpowered them all. He gave them such a beating that they ran out of the house naked and bleeding.

17When this became known to the Jews and Greeks living in Ephesus, they were all seized with fear, and the name of the Lord Jesus was held in high honor. 18Many of those who believed now came and openly confessed their evil deeds. 19A number who had practiced sorcery brought their scrolls together and burned them publicly. When they calculated the value of the scrolls, the total came to fifty thousand drachmas.[a] 20In this way the word of the Lord spread widely and grew in power.

21After all this had happened, Paul decided to go to Jerusalem, passing through Macedonia and Achaia. "After I have been there," he said, "I must visit Rome also." 22He sent two of his helpers, Timothy and Erastus, to Macedonia, while he stayed in the province of Asia a little longer.

23About that time there arose a great distur-

[a] 19 A drachma was a silver coin worth about a day's wages.

## NRSV

8He entered the synagogue and for three months spoke out boldly, and argued persuasively about the kingdom of God. 9When some stubbornly refused to believe and spoke evil of the Way before the congregation, he left them, taking the disciples with him, and argued daily in the lecture hall of Tyrannus.[a] 10This continued for two years, so that all the residents of Asia, both Jews and Greeks, heard the word of the Lord.

11God did extraordinary miracles through Paul, 12so that when the handkerchiefs or aprons that had touched his skin were brought to the sick, their diseases left them, and the evil spirits came out of them. 13Then some itinerant Jewish exorcists tried to use the name of the Lord Jesus over those who had evil spirits, saying, "I adjure you by the Jesus whom Paul proclaims." 14Seven sons of a Jewish high priest named Sceva were doing this. 15But the evil spirit said to them in reply, "Jesus I know, and Paul I know; but who are you?" 16Then the man with the evil spirit leaped on them, mastered them all, and so overpowered them that they fled out of the house naked and wounded. 17When this became known to all residents of Ephesus, both Jews and Greeks, everyone was awestruck; and the name of the Lord Jesus was praised. 18Also many of those who became believers confessed and disclosed their practices. 19A number of those who practiced magic collected their books and burned them publicly; when the value of these books[b] was calculated, it was found to come to fifty thousand silver coins. 20So the word of the Lord grew mightily and prevailed.

21Now after these things had been accomplished, Paul resolved in the Spirit to go through Macedonia and Achaia, and then to go on to Jerusalem. He said, "After I have gone there, I must also see Rome." 22So he sent two of his helpers, Timothy and Erastus, to Macedonia, while he himself stayed for some time longer in Asia.

[a] Other ancient authorities read of a certain Tyrannus, from eleven o'clock in the morning to four in the afternoon   [b] Gk them

## NIV

bance about the Way. [24]A silversmith named Demetrius, who made silver shrines of Artemis, brought in no little business for the craftsmen. [25]He called them together, along with the workmen in related trades, and said: "Men, you know we receive a good income from this business. [26]And you see and hear how this fellow Paul has convinced and led astray large numbers of people here in Ephesus and in practically the whole province of Asia. He says that man-made gods are no gods at all. [27]There is danger not only that our trade will lose its good name, but also that the temple of the great goddess Artemis will be discredited, and the goddess herself, who is worshiped throughout the province of Asia and the world, will be robbed of her divine majesty."

[28]When they heard this, they were furious and began shouting: "Great is Artemis of the Ephesians!" [29]Soon the whole city was in an uproar. The people seized Gaius and Aristarchus, Paul's traveling companions from Macedonia, and rushed as one man into the theater. [30]Paul wanted to appear before the crowd, but the disciples would not let him. [31]Even some of the officials of the province, friends of Paul, sent him a message begging him not to venture into the theater.

[32]The assembly was in confusion: Some were shouting one thing, some another. Most of the people did not even know why they were there. [33]The Jews pushed Alexander to the front, and some of the crowd shouted instructions to him. He motioned for silence in order to make a defense before the people. [34]But when they realized he was a Jew, they all shouted in unison for about two hours: "Great is Artemis of the Ephesians!"

[35]The city clerk quieted the crowd and said: "Men of Ephesus, doesn't all the world know that the city of Ephesus is the guardian of the temple of the great Artemis and of her image, which fell from heaven? [36]Therefore, since these facts are undeniable, you ought to be quiet and not do anything rash. [37]You have brought these men here, though they have neither robbed temples nor blasphemed our goddess. [38]If, then, Demetrius and his fellow craftsmen have a grievance against anybody, the courts are open and there are pro-

## NRSV

[23]About that time no little disturbance broke out concerning the Way. [24]A man named Demetrius, a silversmith who made silver shrines of Artemis, brought no little business to the artisans. [25]These he gathered together, with the workers of the same trade, and said, "Men, you know that we get our wealth from this business. [26]You also see and hear that not only in Ephesus but in almost the whole of Asia this Paul has persuaded and drawn away a considerable number of people by saying that gods made with hands are not gods. [27]And there is danger not only that this trade of ours may come into disrepute but also that the temple of the great goddess Artemis will be scorned, and she will be deprived of her majesty that brought all Asia and the world to worship her."

[28]When they heard this, they were enraged and shouted, "Great is Artemis of the Ephesians!" [29]The city was filled with the confusion; and people[a] rushed together to the theater, dragging with them Gaius and Aristarchus, Macedonians who were Paul's travel companions. [30]Paul wished to go into the crowd, but the disciples would not let him; [31]even some officials of the province of Asia,[b] who were friendly to him, sent him a message urging him not to venture into the theater. [32]Meanwhile, some were shouting one thing, some another; for the assembly was in confusion, and most of them did not know why they had come together. [33]Some of the crowd gave instructions to Alexander, whom the Jews had pushed forward. And Alexander motioned for silence and tried to make a defense before the people. [34]But when they recognized that he was a Jew, for about two hours all of them shouted in unison, "Great is Artemis of the Ephesians!" [35]But when the town clerk had quieted the crowd, he said, "Citizens of Ephesus, who is there that does not know that the city of the Ephesians is the temple keeper of the great Artemis and of the statue that fell from heaven?[c] [36]Since these things cannot be denied, you ought to be quiet and do nothing rash. [37]You have brought these men here who are neither temple robbers nor blasphemers of our[d] goddess. [38]If therefore Demetrius and the artisans

[a] Gk they    [b] Gk some of the Asiarchs    [c] Meaning of Gk uncertain    [d] Other ancient authorities read your

consuls. They can press charges. ³⁹If there is anything further you want to bring up, it must be settled in a legal assembly. ⁴⁰As it is, we are in danger of being charged with rioting because of today's events. In that case we would not be able to account for this commotion, since there is no reason for it." ⁴¹After he had said this, he dismissed the assembly.

with him have a complaint against anyone, the courts are open, and there are proconsuls; let them bring charges there against one another. ³⁹If there is anything further[a] you want to know, it must be settled in the regular assembly. ⁴⁰For we are in danger of being charged with rioting today, since there is no cause that we can give to justify this commotion." ⁴¹When he had said this, he dismissed the assembly.

[a] Other ancient authorities read *about other matters*

# COMMENTARY

The narrative of Paul's final mission as a free man is important mostly for a canonical reason. Unlike Paul's Athenian mission, whose importance in Acts is due to the city's significance, or the paradigmatic importance of his first Asian mission with Barnabas or the European mission in Philippi, this story concentrates the reader's attention on Paul's work, on his religious authority, and ultimately on his stunning success as a Christian missionary and teacher. Ephesus was a great city and strategically situated within the Roman Empire; and in due time its church would become the center of Pauline Christianity. Yet this story is not about Ephesus or the founding of its church; it is about Paul's authoritative persona and destiny (see 19:21-22). Like Peter before him, Paul's prophetic vocation and personal status within God's redemptive program cannot be imitated by the likes of Sceva's sons, nor can they be easily trivialized, as Demetrius discovers without Paul needing to say a word in his defense (see 19:30-31)!

Compressed summaries (19:8-10, 17-20), interspersed with vivid vignettes (19:11-16) lead us to Paul's climactic confrontation with local merchants (19:23-41) to draw a "picture which stood before the eyes of the sub-apostolic Church of that Paul whom the early Church recognized and honoured and who down to Augustine and Luther stood before the Paul of the letters."[617] Perhaps this more universal Paul whom we find in Ephesus is apropos to the Pauline letter of Ephesians, which has few features of the typical occasional

letter and appears to be an encyclical letter written for the post-Pauline church. This led E. Goodspeed, for example, to hypothesize that the writing of Acts occasioned the writing of Ephesians by the same author, who was motivated to provide ongoing generations of Christian readers both a biography (Acts) and a theological introduction (the Letter to the Ephesians) to the Pauline tradition.[618] This historical thesis is now dismissed for lack of evidence. However, it serves to underscore the ongoing relevance of the Paul of Acts for the summary of Pauline teaching in Ephesians; and it testifies to the universal truth of his gospel and the continuing efficacy of God's gospel to each new generation of believers. The Paul of Acts will make this clear enough in his farewell speech to the elders of the Ephesian church (see 20:17-35). Nowhere in Acts is the importance of listening and following Paul as personal exemplar and theological mentor more forcefully depicted than in this story.

**19:8-10.** In this passage, Luke summarizes the general pattern of Paul's mission since arriving in Ephesus: Following prophetic convention, he returns to the synagogue (see 18:19-21) where over a period of "three months" he speaks "boldly" (see 4:29-31) and "argues" (see 17:2-3, 17; 18:4) persuasively "for the kingdom of God" (v. 8). The added reference to the "kingdom of God" recalls the central theme of the Lord's teaching ministry and is used in Acts to express the con-

---

617. Hanechen, *The Acts of the Apostles*, 558.

618. E. Goodspeed, *The Meaning of Ephesians* (Chicago: Chicago University Press, 1933).

tinuity between what he "began to say" according to the "first book" (see 1:1) and the ministry of his apostolic successors (see 1:3). Paul is their successor within the restored Israel both in prophetic ministry and spiritual authority (see 14:22; 28:31). Simply put, the word of God that Paul is teaching in the synagogues of the diaspora is in agreement with the word of God taught by the Lord and his apostolic successors; Paul's message and mentoring are utterly trustworthy.

In Acts, the proclamation of God's kingdom is linked to Israel's restoration (1:6); therefore, the synagogue at Ephesus is the appropriate diaspora setting to announce the good news that the Lord has acted faithfully to restore God's kingdom to Israel. As expected, however, the prophet's proclamation of God's gospel divides the house of Israel between repentant (= restored) and unrepentant Jews. On the one hand, "some stubbornly [σκληρύνω sklērynō] refused to believe [ἀπειθέω apeitheō] and spoke evil of the Way before the congregation" (v. 9a; see also 7:51; 13:45; 14:2; 18:6). The use of sklērynō in this context recalls the exodus story and the hardening of Pharaoh's heart after he stubbornly failed to respond to God's Word, brought to him by Moses (Exod 13:15). As a biblical motif, the hardened heart not only symbolizes the steadfast refusal to repent but also the loss of divine blessings that results. The irony of drawing on an important OT theme for Israel's unbelief and refusal to turn back to God to characterize the Jewish opposition only intensifies the conflict provoked within the Jewish diaspora by Paul's mission. The level of hostility is indicated in passing by the "evil" (κακολογέω kakologeō) that some spoke publicly against the Way of God (see 18:26).[619]

On the other hand, the rejection of the gospel on Paul's second visit to the synagogue (see 18:19-21) signals the conclusion of the prophet's mission to the unrepentant Jews of this city; and so he leaves their synagogue, students in tow, for "the lecture hall [σχολή scholē] of Tyrannus"

(v. 9b).[620] Their departure repeats what had earlier taken place in Corinth (see 18:6-7), a move made necessary by opposition to Paul's gospel but one that in no way undercuts the Jewish heritage of the faith. In this case, the believers who accompanied Paul are called "disciples" (μαθηταί mathētai) and the new venue is not a member's home but a scholē, term that once meant "leisure" but came to mean "school" because of the leisure time required for students to gather for learning. Nothing is known of this Tyrannus, whether he is the owner of the building or one after whom the hall is named.[621] In any case, Tyrannus Hall is the place in Ephesus where Paul's "disciples" gathered to learn from their trusted theological mentor.[622]

Luke concludes this summary by indicating Paul's length of stay in Ephesus, two years, rather than the number of converts; however, when combined with other time periods noted in this narrative (vv. 8, 22), Paul's time in Ephesus totals a period of roughly three years (see Acts 20:31). By almost any criterion, this is an extraordinarily productive season in Paul's ministry (cf. 1 Cor 16:9) and helps to explain why Ephesus became the base of his continuing influence within earliest Christianity. This is even implied by Luke's hyperbolic "all the residents of Asia, both Jews and Greeks, heard the word of the Lord" (v. 10; see also 4:4, 31; 6:7; 8:4; 12:24; 13:5; 16:32; 18:11).

**19:11-12.** Paul's depiction as an Ephesian miracle worker should not be viewed as extraordinary. The city of Ephesus was itself a center of the magic arts in the ancient world. Some citizens considered their books of magic sacred scripture and paraphernalia for mediating miraculous power as commonplace. The resolution of any confusion between miracle (which God does) and magic (which magicians do) is an important biblical theme and a subtext of this passage. More important, Luke's comment that "God did extraordinary miracles through Paul" must be read ironically, since the miracles Paul performs in Ephesus parallel stories of healing and exorcism miracles found

---

619. "The Way" not only refers to the distinctive beliefs of these Jewish messianists but also to their social solidarity—a way of living together as a community of goods. See R. Cassidy, *Society and Politics in the Acts of the Apostles* (Maryknoll, N.Y.: Orbis, 1987) 95. The "evil," perhaps, might be slandering the social values of a community of goods, not just public disagreement with a Pauline interpretation of Scripture.

620. Cf. Johnson, *The Acts of the Apostles*, 339, esp. 13 for review of his "two visitation" literary theme and why it applies here.

621. I. H. Marshall, *The Acts of the Apostles*, NTG (Sheffield: JSOT, 1992) 309, suggests that Luke "drops" this name into the narrative to honor a believer who may well have rented the hall to Paul at an affordable rate to encourage his mission.

622. The Western version of Acts adds "from eleven AM until four PM," the routine workday in the life of an ancient philosopher-educator.

in the Gospels (e.g., Mark 6:53-56 and pars.) and elsewhere in Acts (see 5:12-16). The implication is that Paul is a prophet-like-Jesus in vocation and authority.

The text is careful to qualify Paul's miracle-working activity as the action of God: "*God did extraordinary miracles through* [διά *dia*] Paul" (lit., "through the hands of Paul," v. 11, italics added; cf. 2 Cor 12:12; see also 1 Cor 1:22-23). Neither the NRSV nor the NIV is sufficiently literal to convey the sense that God's healing power is mediated by the direct touch of Paul's *hands.* This more complete image of intimate touch envisages the collaboration between God and the prophet who is the authorized medium of God's power, symbolized by laying his hands directly upon the sick or possessed person (see 3:7; 5:12; 9:17, 41; 14:3; cf. 6:6; 8:17; 13:3). Moreover, Paul evidently uses the healing formula "in the name of the Lord Jesus" (see 4:5-12) since it is this that the sons of Sceva imitate (see 19:13).

The transmission of God's healing power through Paul's hands extends also to "handkerchiefs or aprons that had touched his skin" (v. 12). There is no difference whether Paul lays hands upon the sick or is touched by them: It is Paul's persona through whom God works to heal the sick. Surely these items are the very paraphernalia used in magic shows and reflect long-standing Ephesian superstitions that magic dispensed by the paranormally gifted (or demonically enabled) make sick people whole. Critically, then, this story is placed following the summary of Paul's teaching mission, where he dispenses the "word of the Lord" to all who hear before he dispenses the Lord's healing power to all who are sick. The effect of Luke's shaping of these stories is to demythologize Paul's reputation as a magic man, as though his personal powers are due his own paranormal talent rather than God's working through him. This is a fantastic image; however, it is less due to the hagiography of a legendary Paul and more due to Luke's intent to distinguish between human magic and divine miracle. The implication is that the Pauline "word of the Lord" is safeguarded by God's extraordinary power according to God's redemptive purposes.

**19:13-16.** The story of the seven sons of Sceva is strange and has caused commentators a great deal of difficulty.[623] It almost certainly alludes to the earlier story of Simon the Great, who wanted to remain competitive with the apostles in Samaria and sought to purchase their religious authority for himself (see 8:9-24). Simon was merely chastised by Peter for his foolish simony (from whose name this term derives), but the reader is made more fully aware that apostolic authority cannot be imitated by those not chosen by the Lord to rule over Israel. With characteristic wit, Luke has a demon make this same apologia in support of Paul to the sons of Sceva, who come away in far worse shape than did Simon: "Jesus I know, and Paul I know, but who are you?" (v. 15).

The reputation of Paul's healing powers had evidently spread throughout the religious community in Ephesus, and "some itinerant Jewish exorcists" attempt to invoke the name of Jesus to liberate the possessed without having a personal relationship with him. Jesus apparently allows this practice among outsiders (see Luke 9:49-50; cf. Matt 7:21-23), since its effect is not opposed to the salvation he brings or to the religious practices of his Jewish faith. Josephus mentions exorcism as a Jewish practice and even commends it as a mark of Jewish identity.[624] The issue at stake, however, is not the Jewish practice of exorcism or even that it is practiced by outsiders in the name of Jesus. The issue is that it is practiced in imitation of this prophet-like-Jesus—the formula they use is "the Jesus whom Paul proclaims." Because Paul's miracle work is closely connected to his proclamation of the word of the Lord, which presumably is not true of these Jewish exorcists, their practice threatens to subvert his mission in Ephesus and, therefore, must be stopped.

The identification of the Jewish exorcists with the "seven sons of a Jewish high priest named Sceva" is problematical, since we know nothing of a high priest by that name.[625] Luke seems intent only to give a measure of realism to the current crisis by finding pretenders to Paul's religious authority in Ephesus, since members of priestly families

---

623. Cf. Haenchen, *The Acts of the Apostles,* 565.

624. Josephus *Antiquities of the Jews* 8:42-49.

625. The Western version of Acts erases "high," changing their father's status to that of a mere "priest." Less dramatic solutions are no less satisfying. See B. Witherington, *The Acts of the Apostles: A Socio-Rhetorical Commentary* (Grand Rapids: Eerdmans, 1998) 580-81; J. A. Fitzmyer, *The Acts of the Apostles,* AB 31 (Garden City, N.Y.: Doubleday, 1998) 650-51.

would likely be familiar with the "rules" governing the practice of exorcism. In this regard, the refusal of the "evil spirit" to respond to any of Sceva's sons is not a matter of their ignorance of liturgical formulae; they do not appear to lack technical expertise. What they lack is Paul's *authority* over demons. The use of two different verbs in the demon's witty response commends this conclusion: "Jesus I know [γινώσκω *ginōskō*], and Paul I know [ἐπίσταμαι *epistamai*], but who are you?" (v. 15). The distinction the spirit makes between two ways of knowing, which "recognizes" (*ginōskō*) the Lord's ultimate authority and "experiences firsthand" (*epistamai*) Paul's authority to evoke Jesus' name for exorcism (see 16:18), subverts any religious authority the sons of Sceva may presume to have.[626] The evil spirit's combination of Jesus and Paul "permits the Christians to make a complete break with magic."[627]

But why does Paul allow the demon to have its way with the seven sons? The spirit's mastery over the sons of a priest remains a vivid image of their personal failure to be like Paul. Yet Luke's unexpected use of the prophetic catchword "house" (οἶκος *oikos*)—the place from which Sceva's sons fled "naked and wounded"—recalls Amos's prophecy of a "re-housed" Israel (see Amos 9:11-15; 15:16-21, 28-29) to add an additional layer of meaning to this story. In response to the worries of James about the gentilizing of Jewish practices (= exorcism), Luke again posits the problem among unrepentant Jews—in this case, the Jewish exorcists who come from a priestly family—rather than in the Pauline mission.

**19:17.** The public relations fallout from this episode has an immediate effect: "All residents of Ephesus . . . [were] awestruck [ἐπέπεσεν φόβος *epepesen phobos*; lit., "fear fell"]; and the name of the Lord Jesus was praised." The thematic response of fear in Acts typically indicates the public recognition of God's visitation (see 2:43), sometimes to judge (see 5:5, 11) but always to make clear the reality of God's reign (see 4:16; 9:12). Likewise, the people's recognition of the prophet's authority through his wondrous acts is expressed

not with praise of the prophet but with praise of God, who is the source and basis of his power.

**19:18-20.** The demythologization of magic in Ephesus leads to spiritual renewal: "Many of those who became believers confessed and disclosed their [magic] practices" (v. 18). The repentance of *believers* (rather than sinners) is rare within Scripture. The sense of this text is that certain believers have continued to indulge in practicing magic after their conversion to Jesus. The result of Paul's ministry, however, is the completion of their initiation into Jesus' Lordship. In this sense, then, Luke continues to gloss James's Jerusalem exhortation to put aside the "pollutions of idols," which magic practice surely is. Based on this text, James has reason to be concerned that those converted from pagan backgrounds may well continue their former religious practices; yet, at the same time he has reason to trust in Paul's authority to turn believers from these contaminates to what enriches faith.

Luke adds a vivid image of the conclusion of magic and superstition in the Ephesian church as Paul watches "fifty thousand silver coins" worth of magic books tossed into a public bonfire and incinerated. This is an enormous expense, probably equal to fifty thousand days' wages, and symbolizes the resolve to turn from magic to miracle, from pagan writings to Israel's Scriptures, from demonic charlatans to Paul. The dispossession of demonic property also symbolizes the inability of believers to appropriate God's power as another commodity; God's power is made available only through a relationship with the Lord. To this end, then, "the word of the Lord grew mightily and prevailed [ἰσχύω *ischyō*]" in Ephesus (v. 20; see also 4:4; 14:25; 16:6; 17:11). Earlier, *ischyō* is used to express Stephen's victory over his religious rivals in Jerusalem (see 6:10) and in the near context of the demoniac's mauling of Sceva's sons (see v. 16). These prophets-like-Jesus prevail against their opponents and so authorize the word they proclaim as true, the life they live as exemplary, and the mission they lead as approved by God.

**19:21-22.** This transitional text foreshadows the plotline for the rest of Acts and for this reason performs an important role within the narrative. With the elimination of various impediments (i.e., confusion about John's baptism, magic, demon possession, sickness, pretenders to Paul's

---

626. Cf. C. K. Barrett, *A Critical and Exegetical Commentary on the Acts of the Apostles,* 2 vols, ICC (Edinburgh: T. & T. Clark, 1994, 1998) 2:910.
627. E. Haenchen, *The Acts of the Apostles* (Philadelphia: Westminster, 1971) 565.

authority), a mature community in Ephesus is now formed and Paul begins to make travel plans to return to Macedonia and Achaia before going "on to Jerusalem" (v. 21a). These plans are commensurate with his missionary strategy of returning to those churches planted during earlier missions to fortify converts' spiritual resolve and theological understanding (see 14:21-23; 18:23; 20:2). Paul's priestly tasks, as much as his prophetic tasks, are an exercise of his religious authority within the church. Toward this end, then, he plans to follow the same route he paved according to Acts 16–18. The reader suspects that his plans to visit the holy city reflect his commitments to his ancestral religion, and he will travel there as a pious pilgrim (see 20:1).[628]

What is unexpected is Paul's resolve that he "must [δεῖ dei] also see Rome" (v. 21b). The shift within the overarching geographical structure of Paul's mission in Acts from Palestine (Antioch/Jerusalem) to Rome is here noted for the first time. While Paul himself tells us that he desired to see Rome (Rom 1:10; 15:24), Luke's use of the "dei of divine necessity" implies that his travel plans include Rome because God has disclosed it to him as the city of his destiny—in what manner Acts does not tell us. In fact, Paul leaves Ephesus for Macedonia in relative calm (see 20:1); he is not forced to leave as is more typically the case.[629]

An element of Paul's collaboration with God, however, is careful planning. In this case he dispatches "two of his helpers, Timothy and Erastus, to Macedonia, while he stayed for some time longer in Asia [= Ephesus]" (v. 22). Paul's colleague Erastus is dropped into the narrative at this point, never to be mentioned again. He impresses us as yet another of Paul's associates who travels ahead with Timothy to prepare the way of the prophet-like-Jesus.

628. Drawing on Paul's letters (2 Cor 8:1-2; 9:2-4), some commentators contend that Paul's motive for including Jerusalem is to deliver the collection from Macedonian and Achaian congregations to the poor of the Judean church. The Jewish cast of Paul's profile in Acts, however, suggests rather that Paul prepares to travel to Jerusalem as a pious pilgrim to celebrate Pentecost.

629. Paul however mentions facing fierce opposition in Asia/Ephesus in 1 Cor 15:32 (cf. 2 Cor 1:8-10). In shaping his story of a triumphant Paul, Luke has edited out any clear sense of suffering or conflict—even though Acts 20:3 may allude to growing animosity among the Jews of Ephesus that prevented him from traveling overland to Antioch.

**19:23-41.** The portrayal of Paul's spiritual authority in Acts would not be complete without a controversy over property. Indeed, the dispossession of property is an important barometer of the disciple's relations with God and symbolic of the possession of authority within the community (see 4:32–5:11). While Paul's ministry in Ephesus enjoys extraordinary success—so great, in fact, that the city's merchants claim that Paul's mission has had an adverse effect upon the wealthy and prominent Artemis cult—the pagan opposition to him is nevertheless pervasive and well organized. In general terms, the story of their opposition to Paul follows the plotline of his earlier controversy in Philippi. The leader of the opposition party in Ephesus is the silversmith Demetrius (vv. 23-24; cf. 16:16b), whose arguments against Paul (vv. 25-27) echo those made by the handlers of the clairvoyant girl in Philippi (16:20-21): Paul has turned people away from traditional religion, and he is bad for business. These accusations lead to mob riot and confusion (vv. 28-32; cf. 16:22), which is only intensified by the crowd's anti-Semitism (vv. 33-34; cf. 16:20). In the present passage, the city chancellor intervenes rather than God (vv. 35-41; cf. 16:25-26; 18:12-16); however, the result is the same: The charges against Paul are dismissed, and his opposition is silenced (cf. 16:35-40).

The literary function of this parallelism between Luke's narratives of Paul's Philippian and Ephesian missions is to enclose and concentrate this phase of his work on controversy with pagans (rather than with unrepentant Jews) who are more concerned to maintain their profit margins than to hear the word of God's prophet. In this contest between God and Mammon, God's word always prevails. The disturbing anti-Semitic theme found in both stories is characteristic of pagan culture and not unique to Paul's mission.

**19:23-24.** As Paul made travel plans to revisit other congregations on his way to Jerusalem and then Rome, "no little [οὐκ ὀλίγος ouk oligos] disturbance broke out concerning the Way" (v. 23). The ringleader of this controversy is "a man named Demetrius, a silversmith who made silver shrines of Artemis, brought no little [ouk oligos] business to the artisans" (v. 24). The repeated use of litotes (a literary device to express understatement) makes it clear that the disturbance is due to business rather than to religious devotion. The phrase "no little disturbance" expresses publicly the Way's threat to "no little business." This wholesaler of devotional goods has suffered a financial downturn because of Paul's Ephesian mission! The effect conversion may have on Demetrius's business is made explicit in the earlier account of burning expensive books (see v. 19): Conversion demands a complete rejection of one's pagan past, including the destruction of religious paraphernalia—magic books along with the silver shrines that Demetrius manufactured to support the Artemis cult in Ephesus.

The Artemis cult is well known from ancient literature and modern archaeological expeditions.[630] The temple of Artemis in Ephesus was considered among the seven wonders of the ancient world and was a financial center for all of Roman Asia (hence, Demetrius's worry). Its temple functionaries provided relief to the poor and shelter for the refugee. The stature of Artemis in the pagan pantheon was due in large part to the splendor of the Ephesian temple and the practices and celebrations connected with it. In Greek religion, Artemis (= Diana in Roman religion) was Apollo's sister, the virgin goddess and defender of chastity, the huntress goddess and champion of fertility. In local religion, these various associations were integrated with still others (especially with the Great Mother of Anatolian mythology), and Artemis worship took on an indigenous character in Ephesus: It was a civil religion, and the rhythm of city life revolved around the temple and its festivals. To subvert the worship of Artemis the Great was to threaten the city's culture, its way of life, both economic and social, shaped by its routines and calendar.

**19:25-27.** Demetrius organizes a protest movement among members of his silversmith guild (v. 25a), forming a cohesive group of workers in opposition to a common threat: the Way. His speech appeals to common knowledge or experience and makes clear the threat and, therefore, the reasons for the people's protest. As we would expect, his principal anxiety is "that we get our wealth [εὐπορία *euporia*] from this business" (v. 25b). Luke's vocabulary for wealth is varied. The word Demetrius uses here for "wealth" denotes a more holistic conception than mere financial gain;

it includes one's sense of well-being. In the light of what he goes on to say, the use of this word is ironical and implies that while he has other concerns in life, including religious devotion, his perspective toward all of life is at base a materialistic one.

Demetrius again appeals to what his colleagues "see and hear"—to common knowledge—to claim that "Paul has persuaded and drawn away [μεθίστημι *methistēmi*] a considerable number of people" (v. 26a). This statement simply reports what the reader knows from the earlier account of Paul's Ephesian mission: It has been a rousing success. However, the statement testifies as well to what the narrator has not said: A large number of Paul's converts come from the Artemis cult. The word *methistēmi* denotes the kind of religious seduction that makes people turn away from their cults. (Of course, this is very bad for Demetrius's business!) His summary of Paul's message that "gods made with hands are not gods" (v. 26b) echoes Paul's Areopagus speech in Athens (see 17:24-27; cf. 7:48) and recalls from that speech his polemic against idolatry on both practical (idols are not personal) and theological (God is "the God") grounds.

In his final statement, Demetrius strings together a series of infinitives that globalize his previous claims, and he ties them to the main idea that there is danger to "all Asia and the world": "not only [for] this trade of ours—but also [for] the temple of the great goddess Artemis" (v. 27). The Artemis cult was widespread; pilgrims traveled from all corners of the empire to purchase silver shrines from craftsmen and to worship in her Ephesian temple. With the loss of Artemis's global esteem would come the loss of Demetrius's importance and income. While Demetrius may be guilty of using highly charged rhetoric and exaggerated claims of Paul's threat to incite this group of local merchants, his statement measures reality accurately. The convincing logic of Paul's message against idolatry, when coupled with his powerful persona, has shifted the center of religious authority in Ephesus from the temple of Artemis toward the lecture hall of Tyrannus.

There is a sense, however, that the interpreter's principal interest in Demetrius's commentary on Paul's universal influence should be neither historical (Was history's Paul really this influential?) nor redactional (Was Luke's Paul really this influen-

---

630. For a bibliography and abstract of these expeditions, see Fitzmyer, *The Acts of the Apostles*, 657-58.

tial?) but canonical (Is Scripture's Paul really this influential?). The effect of his repeated claim that the "whole of Asia" is persuaded by Paul's teaching (v. 26) and that he has deprived "all Asia and the world" of Artemis' devotion (v. 27), especially when considered with other similar statements in this narrative (see vv. 10, 17), is to internationalize the influence of Pauline teaching. Indeed, the teaching of his letters is universally persuasive and will result in a turning from idols every place where they are read.

**19:28-31.** Demetrius's speech has its intended effect: His audience becomes "enraged," and they cry out on cue, "Great is Artemis of the Ephesians" (v. 28). Their acclamation is in the form of a confession that well expresses both their devotion to her and their astonishment that the great Artemis cult could be under attack.[631]

The Western version of Acts adds that the Ephesians' rage carried them "into the street," which makes possible the story's logic that what began as a small labor protest resulted in a city that was filled with confusion (v. 29a). Among the details of "local color" included in this episode is the reference to the theater in Ephesus, which accommodated 24,000 people and was often used for assemblies. It is not clear why in their confusion the crowd would drag with them "Gaius and Aristarchus, Macedonians who were Paul's travel companions" (v. 29b; cf. 20:4), unless to remind the reader that this present dust-up threatens Paul's travel plans to carry the Word of God with Gaius and Aristarchus to Rome via Macedonia and Jerusalem (see vv. 21-22). Perhaps it is his concern for their safety that prompts Paul's wish "to go into the crowd"; the disciples had such a reciprocal concern for his safety that they "would not let him" (v. 30)—a decision supported by friendly provincial "officials" (v. 31).[632] The keen impression these vivid images of chaos and a mob riot create indicates a threat to the gospel far worse than reasoned debate.

**19:32-34.** The repeated description of the city's "confusion" (v. 32) perhaps explains what happens next. Haenchen refers to this passage as "an old *crux interpretum*."[633] The interpretive problems are twofold: What motivates "the Jews" to push Alexander forward "to make a defense before the people"? And what prompts Luke to include this detail in his narrative? He does not provide clear answers, nor does he tell us anything about Alexander. The implication is that the crowd's confusion exists at several levels, including religious. The Jews push Alexander forward to clarify the status of "official" Judaism within Ephesus—perhaps in relationship to the Artemis cult. From other stories in Acts, the reader might be able to recover the gist of what Alexander would have said if given half a chance by the angry mob: Surely at the center of his defense would be Judaism's status as a *religio licita* ("officially recognized religion") in the empire (see 18:12-17). In addition to this general defense, most commentators suspect that Alexander's apologia would not have given support to this protest movement against Paul or attempted to distinguish Judaism from "the Way," even though Paul had long since disassociated himself from the synagogue. For both these implied reasons he is shouted down.

And he is shouted down *as a Jew:* "But when they recognized that he was a Jew, for about two hours all shouted in unison 'Great is Artemis of the Ephesians' " (v. 34). The undertone of this dramatic scene is fiercely anti-Semitic (see 16:20; 18:17). For this reason, Luke's motive is sometimes questioned: Did he add this to the story to embarrass "the Jews"? His motive, however, is very different. Within a pagan setting, the distinction the synagogue may have made between its teaching and Paul's would have been heard with the same neutrality displayed by Gallio in Corinth (see 18:12-16) or by the handlers of the slave girl in Philippi (16:20). These pagans readily understand (although with derision) what Paul's Jewish opponents fail to admit: He is a messianic Jew who shares with them the same religious practices and sacred traditions. When compared to Paul's pronounced Jewish profile within Acts, these occurrences of anti-Semitism in the narrative of Paul's mission are heavily ironic. There is a tragic con-

---

631. Cf. Haenchen, *The Acts of the Apostles,* 573. On Luke's use of the literary conventions of Hellenistic novels, see L. T. Johnson, *The Acts of the Apostles,* SP 5 (Collegeville, Minn.: Liturgical, 1992) 348-49.

632. Luke's reference to "officials of the province" ('Ασιαρχηοί *Asiarchoi*) who are friends of Paul is remarkable. On the one hand, it supports an important missionary theme of Acts that Paul's mission has friends in high places. On the other hand, these provincial rulers exercised their civic responsibility to maintain devotion to the official Roman cults, including that of Artemis.

633. Haenchen, *The Acts of the Apostles,* 574.

tour to Luke's meaning here: While all Jews share together a fundamental opposition to the symbols of Artemis worship, pagan cult members who are polluted by idols nevertheless see this theological solidarity more clearly than do Jews.

**19:35-41.** As before in Corinth when Gallio intervened on Paul's behalf and argued against his opponents, again "the town clerk" (γραμματεύς *grammateus*; lit., "scribe") quiets and addresses the angry crowd in defense of Paul (v. 35*a*). A *grammateus* was a bureaucrat, the chief city official who kept accurate records for the city and acted as a liaison with Rome. For this reason he has a good feel for the legalities of both Paul's case and a lynch mob and is the right person to "quiet" the current situation. His speech is an example of deliberative rhetoric in which he persuades his auditors to see Paul from his perspective. Significantly, his ability to move the crowd is not a function of his status in Ephesian politics but of the reasonableness of his appeal to them.

The town clerk makes three legal statements that warrant his admonition to "be quiet and do nothing rash" against Paul and his colleagues. (1) They are neither temple robbers nor blasphemers—that is, they have done nothing against the Artemis cult that would constitute hard legal evidence against them (v. 37). (2) The mob has acted inappropriately in dragging Gaius and Aristarchus, with Paul, to the theater. There is a legal protocol in place to handle all complaints: If Demetrius and his guild have a complaint, the courts are open with proconsuls available to hear cases, "let them bring charges there [i.e., rather than here]" (v. 38). This is a compressed statement that implies that papers must be filed (perhaps with the town clerk) before a court appearance in scheduled.

(3) Finally, the town clerk moves to defer whatever accusations might be brought against Paul to "the regular assembly [i.e., and not to this one, which is an irregular assembly without judicial portfolio]" (v. 39). The clerk's case, which began with a religious appeal, concludes with a legal verdict that is a more modest version of the one rendered by Gallio (see 18:12-16). If Paul is guilty of neither sacrilege (v. 37) nor criminal behavior (vv. 38, 40), and if this is simply a matter of contested religious claims between the Artemis cult (vv. 35-36) and followers of the Way, then let the case be settled in a religious context. There is no legal case, but there is a religious case; and clearly the Paul of Acts has won that one.

The clerk's argument for prudent behavior follows the logic of another scribe, Gamaliel, before a very different courtroom (see 5:35-39). His appeal to do nothing rash is grounded in religious absolutes: Since the Artemis shrine "fell from heaven,"[634] and Ephesus is "the temple keeper" (v. 35), the gods must be for us, and Paul can do nothing that subverts true believers or the Artemis shrine. The translations of the phrase "cannot be denied" (ἀναντίρρητος . . . δέον *anantirrētos . . . deon*; lit., "necessarily undeniable") disguise Luke's striking use of δεῖ (*dei*), which elsewhere in Acts speaks of the divine necessity of an event because it agrees with biblical prophecy. In this case, the clerk's appeal allows for Paul's departure and moves him a step closer to Rome, the city of his destiny (see vv. 21-22).

---

634. Greco-Roman literature mentions several objects "fallen from heaven": Pseudo-Apollodorus *Bibliotheca 3.12.3;* Appain *Hannibal* 56; Herodian 1.11.1; Pausanias 3.12.4. Euripides, in his *Iphegenia at Tauris* 15-88, 1381-85, specifically mentions such an object's being in the temple of Artemis in Taurica. Presumably these objects were meteorites that were venerated as objects sent by the gods to show divine favor. See also Fitzmyer, *The Acts of the Apostles,* 661.

# REFLECTIONS

**1.** "A number of those who practiced magic collected their books and burned them publicly" (19:19 NRSV). Various stories that distinguish between magic and miracle are featured in Acts (see 5:12-16; 8:14-24; 13:6-12; 14:8-18). The casual observer might note there are real similarities between the magician and prophet that only lead to public confusion concerning the claims of the gospel: Both brokered power, predicted futures, and influenced people by incantation of names or by human touch. Today similar comparisons are sometimes made between well-known televangelists with healing ministries or prosperity gospels and "shamans" of the occult. In part, these comparisons persist in popular culture because the distinction made in Acts is not always made clear in the church. The Jewish exorcists who attempt to use the name of Jesus magically are mocked in Luke's story in stark contrast to the reverence reserved for the name of Jesus preached by Paul. Why? Because their practice of magic is detached from a personal relationship with Jesus; it is the precise incantation of mere words to defeat the devil, motivated finally by self-interest, and it does not work.

Do we make it clear in our teaching that the promise of God's salvation-creation power is predicated on our dependence upon Jesus and not ourselves and that it enables us to serve God's purposes and not our own? The life-changing power of the gospel is concrete and demonstrative; but its transforming effect in the believer's life aims its recipient at God rather than at a material result that serves our selfish wants. The miraculous power brokered by Paul is not a commodity dispensed to manipulate the direction of human life; rather, it is the mark of his spiritual authority that serves the missionary purposes of his prophetic vocation. In this sense, the public book burning ceremony in Ephesus is not due to the ineffectiveness of these expensive books; no doubt these books are the source of powerful magic. The burning of "magic books" (or their contemporary parallels, such as diet, therapy, self-help books) is, rather, the believer's divestment of an alternate source of power and influence that detracts from the gospel message and the Spirit's power and thereby subverts our eternal relationship with the Lord.

**2.** "There is danger not only that our trade will lose its good name, but also that the temple of the great goddess Artemis will be discredited" (19:27 NIV). Demetrius views Paul as a threat because his message and its powerful effect endanger his profit margin. Hardly prompted by crass materialism, however, the protest movement he organizes against the Way is informed by a perspective that links religion and money. Demetrius is honest in his grievances but mistaken in his core beliefs.

The church will not be the church if its principal concerns are with the economic "bottom line" and with the "big business" of being a successful institution. Rather, the church's principal concerns/core beliefs are to center on the formation of a community of goods whose vocation is to cultivate together a single-minded and profound devotion of God.

# ACTS 20:1-16, PAUL'S PILGRIMAGE TO JERUSALEM

## NIV

**20**When the uproar had ended, Paul sent for the disciples and, after encouraging them, said good-by and set out for Macedonia. ²He traveled through that area, speaking many words of encouragement to the people, and finally arrived in Greece, ³where he stayed three months. Because the Jews made a plot against him just as he was about to sail for Syria, he decided to go back through Macedonia. ⁴He was accompanied by Sopater son of Pyrrhus from Berea, Aristarchus and Secundus from Thessalonica, Gaius from Derbe, Timothy also, and Tychicus and Trophimus from the province of Asia. ⁵These men went on ahead and waited for us at Troas. ⁶But

## NRSV

**20**After the uproar had ceased, Paul sent for the disciples; and after encouraging them and saying farewell, he left for Macedonia. ²When he had gone through those regions and had given the believers[a] much encouragement, he came to Greece, ³where he stayed for three months. He was about to set sail for Syria when a plot was made against him by the Jews, and so he decided to return through Macedonia. ⁴He was accompanied by Sopater son of Pyrrhus from Beroea, by Aristarchus and Secundus from Thessalonica, by Gaius from Derbe, and by Timothy, as well as by Tychicus and Trophimus from Asia. ⁵They went

[a] Gk given them

NIV

we sailed from Philippi after the Feast of Unleavened Bread, and five days later joined the others at Troas, where we stayed seven days.

⁷On the first day of the week we came together to break bread. Paul spoke to the people and, because he intended to leave the next day, kept on talking until midnight. ⁸There were many lamps in the upstairs room where we were meeting. ⁹Seated in a window was a young man named Eutychus, who was sinking into a deep sleep as Paul talked on and on. When he was sound asleep, he fell to the ground from the third story and was picked up dead. ¹⁰Paul went down, threw himself on the young man and put his arms around him. "Don't be alarmed," he said. "He's alive!" ¹¹Then he went upstairs again and broke bread and ate. After talking until daylight, he left. ¹²The people took the young man home alive and were greatly comforted.

¹³We went on ahead to the ship and sailed for Assos, where we were going to take Paul aboard. He had made this arrangement because he was going there on foot. ¹⁴When he met us at Assos, we took him aboard and went on to Mitylene. ¹⁵The next day we set sail from there and arrived off Kios. The day after that we crossed over to Samos, and on the following day arrived at Miletus. ¹⁶Paul had decided to sail past Ephesus to avoid spending time in the province of Asia, for he was in a hurry to reach Jerusalem, if possible, by

NRSV

ahead and were waiting for us in Troas; ⁶but we sailed from Philippi after the days of Unleavened Bread, and in five days we joined them in Troas, where we stayed for seven days.

7On the first day of the week, when we met to break bread, Paul was holding a discussion with them; since he intended to leave the next day, he continued speaking until midnight. ⁸There were many lamps in the room upstairs where we were meeting. ⁹A young man named Eutychus, who was sitting in the window, began to sink off into a deep sleep while Paul talked still longer. Overcome by sleep, he fell to the ground three floors below and was picked up dead. ¹⁰But Paul went down, and bending over him took him in his arms, and said, "Do not be alarmed, for his life is in him." ¹¹Then Paul went upstairs, and after he had broken bread and eaten, he continued to converse with them until dawn; then he left. ¹²Meanwhile they had taken the boy away alive and were not a little comforted.

13We went ahead to the ship and set sail for Assos, intending to take Paul on board there; for he had made this arrangement, intending to go by land himself. ¹⁴When he met us in Assos, we took him on board and went to Mitylene. ¹⁵We sailed from there, and on the following day we arrived opposite Chios. The next day we touched at Samos, andᵃ the day after that we came to Miletus. ¹⁶For Paul had decided to sail past Ephesus, so that he might not have to spend time in Asia; he was eager to be in Jerusalem, if possible, on the day of Pentecost.

ᵃ Other ancient authorities add *after remaining at Trogyllium*

# COMMENTARY

Under the shadow of Acts 19:20-21 and with new assurances of the Way's triumph in Ephesus, Paul resumes his preparations to extend the scope of his European mission to include Rome, the city of his destiny. With growing awareness of the struggles that await him during his journey to "the end of the earth," he sets out for Jerusalem as a Jewish pilgrim to worship God on the holy day of Pentecost (see 20:16). In this collocation of three stories, details of Paul's travel itinerary and

chronology are combined to help the reader follow his progress. Mention of his colleagues and others along the way form a community of witnesses who are able to mark the pilgrim's path to the holy city. Among these is the narrator, who rejoins Paul's entourage to add another voice to the journey (see 20:5).

Scholars have long noted the vague parallelism between Paul's and the Lord's final journey to Jerusalem and posit this as another proof of his solidarity with God's Messiah, whose suffering in the holy city resulted in the salvation of Israel and the nations.[635] While the literary structure and allusions found in this passage may support that reading, its theological connection is more dubious (see below). Two parallel passages that provide Paul's travel plans for Jerusalem, complete with careful chronological markers and details of his religious intent (20:1-6, 13-16), enclose another of Luke's dramatic typological stories (20:7-12), this one of a young man named Eutychus who falls from the third story of an apartment building in Troas and then is "raised from the dead" on the "first day of the week." The rhetorical effect of this triad is to convince the reader that Paul's travel plans for Jerusalem and finally Rome (see 19:21-22) are motivated by his desire to serve God's redemptive plans and purposes.

**20:1-6.** Paul's decision to leave Ephesus had already been made before the turmoil provoked by the guild of silversmiths; it was made in response to God's will rather than to escape personal attack (see 19:21-22). For this reason his departure from the city takes place during relative calm, "after the uproar had ceased" (v. 1*a*). Before bidding farewell, Paul characteristically sends for the disciples, encourages (παρακαλέσας *parakalesas*) them, and leaves for Macedonia (v. 1*b;* see also 14:22; 15:32; 16:40). Luke's repeated use of the participle *parakalesas* in Acts recalls earlier uses, inviting the inference that Paul's ongoing encouragement includes additional teaching now made evident by a prophecy of coming tribulation that would require a mature faith and theological understanding to endure (see 14:22). The reader is not told the route Paul takes from Ephesus to Macedonia, but only that "he had gone through those regions and had given the believers much encouragement [*parakalesas*]" before arriving in Greece (v. 2), where he stayed for three months (v. 3*a;* cf. 1 Cor 16:5-6).

During his stay in Greece, Paul learns of another Jewish plot against him (see 9:24; cf. 23:30). He had originally planned "to set sail for Syria," which would have put him in Jerusalem more quickly—perhaps to celebrate Passover (see v. 6). To throw his enemies off track (cf. 23:12-24), Paul changes his plans for a sea voyage and instead retraces his overland route through Macedonia (v. 3).[636]

A list of seven traveling companions is provided but without any description of their responsibilities toward Paul and his mission (v. 4)[637] other than as an advance team sent to Troas (in Asia) to make preparations for Paul's future visit. The narrator plans to join them there (v. 5). Perhaps the intended impression is that together they represent Paul's various mission fields, often in pairs, and provide witness to his past efforts.

Following the detour through Macedonia, Paul is further delayed in Philippi in order that he and the narrator can celebrate "days of Unleavened Bread" (Passover; see Luke 22:1) before joining the others in Troas (v. 6). Evidently, the plot against his life, which required him to take this detour, also made it impossible to reach Jerusalem in time to observe Passover with other pilgrims. Yet this reference to a Philippian Passover is striking for several reasons. At the surface level of the narrative, the chronological detail anchors Paul's final journey to Jerusalem in historical time: He has seven weeks to make Jerusalem by Pentecost (see v. 16). We also recognize that this passing reference contributes to Luke's portrait of a Jewish Paul who religiously integrates the practices of his ancestral faith with the belief that the living Jesus is God's Messiah. There is then in his observance of Passover tacit allusion to James's concern that Paul's mission to the nations maintain the church's Jewish identity whenever and wherever it is threatened by potential pagan pollutants (see 15:20-21).

In this regard the location of Paul's observance of Passover—in Philippi—must be recognized as

---

635. The parallelism is as follows: (1) like Jesus before him, Paul announces his intentions to travel to Jerusalem (19:21; cf. Luke 9:31); (2) he sends delegates before him in pairs (19:22; 20:4; cf. Luke 10:1); (3) unrepentant Jews plot against his life (20:3; cf. Matt 12:14; 26:4); (4) he goes forward despite this threat (20:6, 16, see 20:22-23; cf. Luke 9:51; 13:22; 17:11); (5) he enters the Holy City a final time (21:15-17; cf. Luke 19:28).

636. The Western text of Acts adds to 20:3: "The Spirit said to him to go through Macedonia."

637. Several modern commentators speculate on the basis of Pauline letters (cf. Rom 15:25-27; 1 Cor 16:1-2; 2 Cor 9:4) that those listed here are actually collection agents who have been assigned the task of delivering an offering from Macedonian and Achaian congregations to Jerusalem. Acts makes no mention of this offering during the entire travel narrative, however, and only mentions such a "gift" vaguely and in passing in 24:17 as a small bit of Paul's defense speech—and there perhaps in reference to 11:27-30. See Haenchen, *The Acts of the Apostles,* 378-79. Johnson, *The Acts of the Apostles,* 357, notes that those listed might be members of a so-called "Pauline School" who are engaged in preserving and transmitting Pauline teaching.

theologically significant. Acts demonizes Philippi as a lawless city, full of anti-Semitic bias and without an urban synagogue before Paul arrived (see 16:11-34). By the time he left town under police escort, he had established a "house" of worship *within* city limits composed of converted God-fearing Gentiles (see 16:35-40). If any congregation of the Pauline church is a prime candidate for setting aside its Jewish heritage or being contaminated by the "pollutions of idols," it surely would have been this one. And yet here is Paul the pious Jew in Philippi celebrating Passover with a congregation of God-fearing Gentile believers!

**20:7-12.** Paul arrives with Luke in Troas, where they stay a week (20:6b). On "the first day of the week" he met with a congregation there to "break bread" and to "hold a discussion with them" (v. 7). Mention of this Sunday is the first reference in the NT of observing a Christian sabbath (cf. 1 Cor 16:2; Rev 1:10), no doubt as a continuing memorial to the Lord's resurrection (cf. Luke 24:1). In fact, images of the resurrection are found throughout this story, which should be read as a typological narrative for this reason. That is, Paul's pilgrimage to Jerusalem and mission to Rome are motivated by his vocation to proclaim that Jesus is alive, and the present episode typifies this core conviction.

This congregation probably followed traditional sabbath rules and so began worship on Saturday evening after sunset into Sunday's dawn (see v. 11).[638] The practice of "breaking bread" refers to a common meal rather than to the Lord's supper and is symbolic of their social and spiritual solidarity (see 2:45-46).[639] Such meals were opportunities to gather together for community prayer and to hear inspired teaching (see 2:42). Paul's "discussion [διαλέγομαι *dialegomai*] with them" is the central activity of worship, even as it was during his synagogue ministry (see 17:2, 17:18:4; 19:8). The implication from Luke's earlier uses of *dialegomai* is that Paul is engaged in a Bible study, interpreting the Scriptures to show that the risen Jesus is God's Messiah (see 17:3). Because of time constraints on a pilgrim's journey—Paul wants

to make it to Jerusalem in time for Pentecost—he "continued speaking until midnight" (v. 7b) in an upstairs meeting room with "many lamps" (v. 8). These circumstances are added to explain what happens next in the story: A long speech in a stuffy room well past bedtime makes falling asleep plausible. These same details, however, also allude to the gospel story in which Jesus met with his disciples in the upper room to break bread in preparation for what takes place on the first day of the week (see Matt 26:20-29; Mark 14:17-25; Luke 22:14-38).

With careful staging, then, we are introduced to the other main character of this tragicomedy, "a young man named Eutychus [= Lucky]" (v. 9a). He is precariously seated on the sill of an open window, where he dozes off and falls three stories to the ground below, to be "picked up dead" (v. 9b). In dramatic fashion reminiscent of Jesus (cf. Mark 5:40), Peter (see 9:40-41), and other prophets before him (cf. 1 Kgs 17:21-22; 2 Kgs 4:34-35), Paul resuscitates Eutychus and announces to the others, "Do not be alarmed, for his life is in him" (v. 10). Several commentators have noted Paul's matter-of-fact tone and the way he hastens back upstairs to resume his conversation without fuss or fanfare (v. 11); these commentators suggest that his pronouncement makes a diagnosis rather than declares a healing miracle.[640] Paul's life-saving action, which appears as a mere hiccup during his teaching ministry, would seem to indicate that the two actions—teaching and miracle-working—form a coherent whole to express a common resurrection theme.[641]

**20:13-16.** Paul continues his pilgrimage to Jerusalem by traveling from Troas to Miletus. He travels the first leg by land to Assos, where he meets his companions, who have arrived by boat.[642] Together they continue by sea to Miletus

---

638. Fitzmyer, *The Acts of the Apostles,* 668-69.

639. Cf. H. Conzelmann, *The Acts of the Apostles,* trans. J. Limburg et al., ed. E. J. Epp and C. R. Matthews, Hermeneia (Philadelphia: Fortress, 1987) 169, who says that in its original form this was a secular story with a popular comic touch meant to provide rhetorical relief rather than "ritual exactitude."

640. Cf. E. Haenchen, *The Acts of the Apostles* (Philadelphia: Westminster, 1971) 586.

641. The hagiographic tendency of the Western version is exemplified here by adding to 20:12 the note that Paul himself brought the boy and gave them to him alive: "When they were saying goodbye, Paul took the boy away alive; and they were not a little comforted!" While the scribes want to make certain that Paul gets credit for the miracle, they subvert Luke's intentions of portraying his power as typical of his normal prophetic routines.

642. Luke does not explain Paul's travel itinerary. Fitzmyer's suggestion that he travels by land to Assos rather than by sea for reasons of safety does not square with the persona of the Paul of Acts. See J. A. Fitzmyer, *The Acts of the Apostles,* AB 31 (Garden City, N.Y.: Doubleday, 1998) 671.

---

with stops between in Mitylene, Chios, and Samos. These Aegean ports-of-call were roughly a day's sailing apart, a standard route to take into the Miletus port. Luke's travel summary, written in the first person, concludes by reconfirming Paul's religious motive for his journey to Jerusalem: "He was eager to be in Jerusalem . . . on the day of Pentecost" (v. 16; see also 2:1). His decision to bypass Ephesus is for lack of time rather than for lack of security—although one wonders why then he should wait in Miletus for the Ephesian elders to come and bid farewell to him there unless he had reason to be concerned for his safety in Ephesus (cf. 2 Cor 1:8-10).

The pairing of Paul's observance of Passover in Philippi and his eagerness to arrive in Jerusalem to celebrate Pentecost make clear the motive for his hurried travel. There is no indication whatsoever in Acts that Luke has suppressed the "real" reason for Paul's journey—delivery of the Macedonian collection. The narrator shapes a story that depicts this prophet-like-Jesus as a practicing Jew (see v. 6). For this repentant Jew, however, the celebration of Israel's Pentecost has taken on even deeper significance as a festival for remembering that God has poured out the Holy Spirit upon God's people to empower their witness to the risen Messiah to the "end of the earth." Paul's urgency to reach Jerusalem "by the day of Pentecost" is now qualified by his prophetic vocation to carry God's word to Rome (see 19:21-2). The pilgrim's pace is set by God's plan as well as Judaism's liturgical year.

# REFLECTIONS

Then Paul "went upstairs again, broke bread and ate" (20:11 NIV). The wonderful story of Paul's resuscitation of "lucky" Eutychus illustrates the good news of Jesus' resurrection. The episode is part of a journey narrative that depicts Paul on his way to Jerusalem, stopping along his pilgrim's way to "encourage" and say his fond farewells to various congregations of disciples (see 20:1-2). Central to his ministry of encouragement is Christian fellowship (= "breaking bread") and intensive instruction. The ministries of Word and table are the twin hallmarks of authentic koinōnia, without which the church cannot be the church in the world. The Benedictine Rule, which posits great value on a community's hospitality—its table fellowship—recognizes the practical truth that the Word is better received and understood in an atmosphere of congeniality and acceptance. In this special sense, Word and Table are integral parts of a formative whole.

Amid his ministry of encouragement and in continuity with other prophets before him, Paul brokers God's life-giving power in raising Eutychus from the dead. Luke does not want the reader to dwell on the miracle, however, and so Paul resumes his ministry of the Word without pause. In one sense, this is so because there is no real dichotomy between miracle and message. Paul makes so little of this miracle because the hallmark of Christian community is not the miraculous but the message of the risen Jesus. In a religious culture that is drawn toward the spectacular, the community of believers must be ever diligent to congregate around the gospel for instruction. The Word is the thing!

# ACTS 20:17-38, PAUL'S SPEECH OF SUCCESSION

## NIV

17From Miletus, Paul sent to Ephesus for the elders of the church. 18When they arrived, he said to them: "You know how I lived the whole time I was with you, from the first day I came into the province of Asia. 19I served the Lord with great humility and with tears, although I was severely tested by the plots of the Jews. 20You know that I have not hesitated to preach anything that would be helpful to you but have taught you publicly and from house to house. 21I have declared to both Jews and Greeks that they must turn to God in repentance and have faith in our Lord Jesus.

22"And now, compelled by the Spirit, I am going to Jerusalem, not knowing what will happen to me there. 23I only know that in every city the Holy Spirit warns me that prison and hardships are facing me. 24However, I consider my life worth nothing to me, if only I may finish the race and complete the task the Lord Jesus has given me—the task of testifying to the gospel of God's grace.

25"Now I know that none of you among whom I have gone about preaching the kingdom will ever see me again. 26Therefore, I declare to you today that I am innocent of the blood of all men. 27For I have not hesitated to proclaim to you the whole will of God. 28Keep watch over yourselves and all the flock of which the Holy Spirit has made you overseers.[a] Be shepherds of the church of God,[b] which he bought with his own blood. 29I know that after I leave, savage wolves will come in among you and will not spare the flock. 30Even from your own number men will arise and distort the truth in order to draw away disciples after them. 31So be on your guard! Remember that for three years I never stopped warning each of you night and day with tears.

32"Now I commit you to God and to the word of his grace, which can build you up and give you an inheritance among all those who are sanctified. 33I have not coveted anyone's silver or gold or clothing. 34You yourselves know that these hands of mine have supplied my own needs and the

<sup></sup>

[a] 28 Traditionally bishops    [b] 28 Many manuscripts of the Lord

## NRSV

17From Miletus he sent a message to Ephesus, asking the elders of the church to meet him. 18When they came to him, he said to them:

"You yourselves know how I lived among you the entire time from the first day that I set foot in Asia, 19serving the Lord with all humility and with tears, enduring the trials that came to me through the plots of the Jews. 20I did not shrink from doing anything helpful, proclaiming the message to you and teaching you publicly and from house to house, 21as I testified to both Jews and Greeks about repentance toward God and faith toward our Lord Jesus. 22And now, as a captive to the Spirit,[a] I am on my way to Jerusalem, not knowing what will happen to me there, 23except that the Holy Spirit testifies to me in every city that imprisonment and persecutions are waiting for me. 24But I do not count my life of any value to myself, if only I may finish my course and the ministry that I received from the Lord Jesus, to testify to the good news of God's grace.

25"And now I know that none of you, among whom I have gone about proclaiming the kingdom, will ever see my face again. 26Therefore I declare to you this day that I am not responsible for the blood of any of you, 27for I did not shrink from declaring to you the whole purpose of God. 28Keep watch over yourselves and over all the flock, of which the Holy Spirit has made you overseers, to shepherd the church of God[b] that he obtained with the blood of his own Son.[c] 29I know that after I have gone, savage wolves will come in among you, not sparing the flock. 30Some even from your own group will come distorting the truth in order to entice the disciples to follow them. 31Therefore be alert, remembering that for three years I did not cease night or day to warn everyone with tears. 32And now I commend you to God and to the message of his grace, a message that is able to build you up and to give you the inheritance among all who are sanctified. 33I coveted no one's silver or gold or clothing. 34You

[a] Or And now, bound in the spirit    [b] Other ancient authorities read of the Lord    [c] Or with his own blood; Gk with the blood of his Own

NIV

needs of my companions. [35]In everything I did, I showed you that by this kind of hard work we must help the weak, remembering the words the Lord Jesus himself said: 'It is more blessed to give than to receive.' "

[36]When he had said this, he knelt down with all of them and prayed. [37]They all wept as they embraced him and kissed him. [38]What grieved them most was his statement that they would never see his face again. Then they accompanied him to the ship.

NRSV

know for yourselves that I worked with my own hands to support myself and my companions. [35]In all this I have given you an example that by such work we must support the weak, remembering the words of the Lord Jesus, for he himself said, 'It is more blessed to give than to receive.' "

36When he had finished speaking, he knelt down with them all and prayed. [37]There was much weeping among them all; they embraced Paul and kissed him, [38]grieving especially because of what he had said, that they would not see him again. Then they brought him to the ship.

# COMMENTARY

Paul's speech to the Ephesian elders at Miletus brings to fitting conclusion his controversial mission to the city of Ephesus. Because it is his only speech addressed to believers, it carries paradigmatic value for the readers of Acts. We may insinuate what Paul says to the Ephesian elders into other stories in which Paul makes pastoral house calls to organize and encourage fledgling Christian congregations. His sermon topics concerning Christian leadership and character, in which he is exemplary, are particularly relevant themes of Paul's ongoing mentoring ministry.

S. Walton has noted the centrality of the Miletus discourse to the ongoing debate over whether Luke used any of Paul's letters when writing Acts.[643] In contrast to Paul's missionary speeches or legal briefs, this one addresses a pastoral setting similar to his letters, many of which convey similar concerns and interests.[644] For this reason an analysis of this speech may prove to have special importance in understanding the relationship between the Paul of Acts and the Pauline letters.[645] All the speeches of Acts are composed

by Luke, and this one in particular is a piece of his finished portrait of Paul; however, its topics and theological conception are substantially Pauline,[646] so much so that C. Hemer thinks it possible to consider it Luke's précis of Paul's actual words, of which Luke was an auditor.[647] While the majority of modern commentators remain uncertain about whether Luke witnessed this event or had direct access to any of his letters, they concur that he at the very least used Pauline sources to compose a speech that substantially agrees with the Pauline letters in its portrait of Paul and presentation of his message.[648] What must be added to this conclusion, however, is that Luke conveys an idealized representation of a canonical Paul whose Miletus

643. S. Walton, *Leadership and Lifestyle,* SNTSMS 108 (Cambridge: Cambridge University Press, 2000). In what follows in this paragraph, I am dependent on Walton's fine study and my private conversations with him.

644. This intracanonical relationship is especially true of the so-called Pastoral Epistles (1–2 Timothy and Titus) in which the canonical Paul addresses a similar problem facing the Paul of Acts in Miletus: the continuation of the Pauline legacy in a post-Pauline setting through his appointed delegates.

645. See B. Witherington, *The Acts of the Apostles: A Socio-Rhetorical Commentary* (Grand Rapids: Eerdmans, 1998) 610, for a listing of linguistic parallels between this passage and the Pauline letters.

646. Cf. S. Porter, *Paul of Acts,* WUNT 115 (Tübingen: Mohr Siebeck, 1999) 115-18.

647. C. Hemer, "The Speeches in Acts: I. The Ephesian Elders at Miletus," *TynBul* 40 (1989) 77-85. Hemer argues against Haenchen, *The Acts of the Apostles,* 596-97, who contends that the "we" passages of Acts constitute a literary device to strengthen Luke's apology for Paul, of which this speech is a crucial element, and are therefore not based upon an auditor's historical memory.

648. Cf. G. Lüdemann, *Early Christianity According to the Traditions in Acts* (Minneapolis: Fortress, 1989) 226-30, who does not think the setting/speech is historically based. More cautious in this regard is C. K. Barrett, *A Critical and Exegetical Commentary on the Acts of the Apostles,* 2 vols, ICC (Edinburgh: T. & T. Clark, 1994, 1998) 2:963-66, who notes that Luke's agreements with Pauline tradition are especially evident with those found in the Pastoral Epistles (particularly 2 Timothy) and probably depend upon similar if not the same Pauline sources. However, see Walton, *Leadership and Lifestyle,* 193, for whom "it can be unhelpful to group the Pastorals together in an undifferentiated way" and for whom the parallels even with 2 Timothy are mostly vague and not as close as Barrett, *Acts,* 195-98, thinks.

message he intends to function as formative of Christian mission well into the future.[649]

The question of the speech's literary genre is also pertinent to any discussion of its wider role within the NT canon. There is virtual unanimity among commentators that this is Paul's farewell speech, serving to publish his "last will and testament" to a gathering of close associates and friends.[650] There is one problem with this consensus: Paul does not die in Acts. For this reason, I am inclined to consider this speech more narrowly as a "speech of succession," occasioned by Paul's departure from Ephesus when it is appropriate to charge newly appointed leaders to continue his work in his absence. In this sense, it functions within Acts in a manner similar to the opening narrative, where details of the apostolic succession of Jesus are given (see 1:3-14; also 12:1-17; cf. Luke 22:14-38; 24:36-53).[651] In that earlier story, Jesus prepares his apostles for their future ministry in light of his departure (1) by reviewing and interpreting his past suffering, proofs of his resurrection (cf. 20:7-12), and his message of God's kingdom (see 1:3); (2) against the horizon of his future ascension/departure from them (1:2); (3) and in retrospect of John's promise of the Spirit (1:4-5), (4) the Lord charges his apostles to bring a Spirit-empowered witness of him to restore Israel as a light to the nations (1:6-8). (5) The succession is completed with Jesus' departure into the heavens (1:9-11). The purpose of Jesus' final speech to his apostles is not to bid them farewell but to commission them for a future mission that continues what he has begun to do and to say as Messiah (see 1:1).[652]

If the interpreter considers Paul's Miletus speech and departure as roughly analogous in form and function to the Lord's final speech to his apostles, then the following sketch of topics emerges (see below):[653] (1) Paul rehearses his past ministry, relating his suffering and testimony (20:18b-20) (2) against the horizon of his future departure from them (20:21-25) and (3) in retrospect of his ministry among them (20:26-27). (4) Paul then charges the Ephesian elders to care for the church of God (20:28-35). (5) The succession is completed with Paul's departure from them (20:36-38). Paul's purpose is pastoral preparation; his aim is to equip his successors to continue what he has begun to do and say in Ephesus, knowing that his departure from the city and its Christian congregation is now final (20:25).

These various literary and redactional conclusions point to the value of this speech in framing an approach to Paul's epistolary witness. What the Paul of Acts says to his successors in Asia forms a rhetorical ethos that cultivates the living reader's confidence in his exemplary persona and trustworthy instruction and has lasting importance for the church catholic in every generation. By extension, then, if the Paul of Acts has lasting importance as the spiritual exemplar and theological mentor of God's people, then the Pauline letters supply his theological primer and personal testimony to their living readers who are confident of his lasting importance in their Christian formation. In this regard, the themes of his speech suggest touch-points with his letters that help to fashion a coherent theological understanding of their collective witness to "the whole counsel of God"—for example, faithful and humble leadership, costly suffering of consecrated service to God, congregational welfare over personal gain, threats against the church.[654]

Paul's discourse also concerns those who are responsible for transmitting and interpreting his legacy to others in his absence. His previous mission in Ephesus laid a foundation, and his gospel defined its theological boundaries; yet, this deposit of God's grace is under constant threat, and spiritual vigilance is required of those who are custodians of it. These Pauline inheritors are charged to imitate their mentor's faithfulness no matter the cost, without which his precious legacy has no future. By extension, if the Pauline letters are the textual precipitate of Paul's legacy, then their future in the church is predicated on faithful interpreters who firmly embrace Paul's testimony to

---

649. Cf. B. Childs, *The New Testament as Canon* (Philadephia: Fortress, 1984) 225-27.

650. Cf. Walton, *Leadership and Lifestyle,* 61-65, for a summary and evaluation of the literary conventions of the "farewell speech" in both Jewish and Greco-Roman contexts.

651. For gospel parallels, see ibid., 100-117.

652. The eschatological horizon is different between Jesus and his prophet, since the expectation is that he will return to earth to complete his messianic mission (see 1:10-11; 3:21) whereas there is no expectation of Paul's return to Ephesus (however, cf. 1 Tim 1:3; 2 Tim 1:15-18).

653. For a summary and analysis of the different proposals concerning this speech's rhetorical design, see Walton, *Leadership and Lifestyle,* 66-75.

654. Ibid., 140-98.

God's grace and imitate his faithful service to God's calling. The responsibility of interpreting Paul for the next generation of believers is no longer a matter of casting lots or of holding ecclesial office, but of good character and orthodox belief in faithful imitation of Paul.

**20:17-18a.** This brief introduction to the speech sets its stage and tone: Paul "sent a message" (μετακαλέω *metakaleō*) to Ephesus asking that the "elders [πρεσβύτεροι *presbyteroi*] of the church" meet with him in Miletus. Luke assumes that a council of elders leads in the formation of Christian congregations from the very beginning of the mission to the nations (see 11:30; 14:23; 15:6; 16:4). The use of *metakaleō* suggests that this is a meeting according to God's plans, which gives it an air of importance (see 10:32).

**20:18b-27.** The first half of Paul's speech to the Ephesian elders concentrates their attention on his legacy. It is enclosed by an apologia of his past ministry at Ephesus, which he characterizes as faithful both to his prophetic calling (vv. 18*b*-21) and to his congregants (vv. 26-27). Sandwiched between is a prophecy of his future suffering in Jerusalem (vv. 22-24) and an assertion on this basis that he will not return to Ephesus (v. 25).

**20:18b-21.** In a single Greek sentence, the Paul of Acts defends his Asian mission, centered in Ephesus, in two integral movements. The first appeals to the entire body of evidence of "how I lived among you" (cf. 1 Thess 2:1-2; 5:10-11; Phil 4:15)—a life characterized by humble service to the Lord and by costly endurance of "the plots of the Jews" (v. 19; cf. 2 Cor 1:3-11). While testimony of his "humility"[655] reflects Paul's commentary on his inward affections (cf. 2 Cor 10:1; 11:7; 1 Thess 2:6), the appeal to consider his suffering, which resulted from various plots against him, is more empirical and invites his auditors to evaluate the hard evidence in his favor. The reader too can participate in this review

by recalling the narrative of his Ephesian mission in consideration of Paul's struggles there (see 19:8-10; 20:3; cf. 20:33-34).

The second broad movement concerns the disposition of his pastoral obligations to the Ephesian church. Paul's description of prophetic tasks performed is exemplary of Christian leadership for the church's future; he will later recall these same images as characteristic of ministry that continues his legacy in his absence. He asserts that in general he "did not shrink from doing anything helpful." On the one hand, Paul does not shrink from his calling to teach the congregations ("house to house"; see 15:16-17; cf. Rom 16:5; Phlm 21) his mission has founded—unlike Judas, for example, whose betrayal of Jesus was a repudiation of his divine appointment to care for the messianic community (1:16*b*-17). On the other hand, Paul does not shrink from the message he publicly proclaims "to Jews and Greeks about repentance toward God and faith toward our Lord Jesus" (v. 21; cf. Rom 10:8-13). Not only is there a practical apostasy that Paul avoids in his regular ministry among believing households; there is also a theological apostasy that Paul avoids in defending the truth claims of the gospel, which he summarizes by the Lukan catchwords "repentance" and "faith."

**20:22-24.** The shift from apologia (retrospect) to prophecy (prospect) is signaled by the appearance of the phrase καὶ νῦν ἰδοῦ (*kai nyn idou*, "And now I . . ."). Even as Paul's faithfulness is made evident by his costly devotion to the tasks of the prophet-like-Jesus, he is also faithful or "captive/compelled" (v. 22) to/by what the "Holy Spirit testifies to me in every city that imprisonment and persecutions are waiting for me" (v. 23). Details of a particular revelation from the Spirit to Paul are not mentioned. In fact, he claims that he does not know what will happen to him in Jerusalem (cf. Rom 15:30-32). Commentators have long noted the parallelism between Paul's prophecy and the Lord's prediction of his passion in Jerusalem. While this is certainly characteristic of Luke's typological shaping of his narrative and perhaps is a subtext of this part of Paul's speech, the prophecy is still much too vague to assert that Paul's final Jerusalem visit is of a type with the Lord's. Paul did not die there, nor does he know what will happen to him there.

That he should expect suffering to await him in

655. The importance of "humility" in Paul's retrospective is intensified by its rarity. It is used only here in Acts, infrequently in the NT, and not at all in the LXX. Significantly, its NT use is mostly Pauline and posited in the virtue catalogues of Ephesians (4:2) and Colossians (2:18, 23; 3:12)—writings whose Pauline traditions are closely associated with those used by Luke. Walton, *Leadership and Lifestyle*, 75-76, suggests "humility" has Christian currency as a "coin word" of the earliest church and expresses an affection prompted by the Spirit that is at odds with well-known vices, such as excessive personal ambition or a sense of rivalry.

Jerusalem is no different from what he expects in every city, since the Lord prophesied that his mission would result in Paul's suffering for his sake (see 9:15-16). This is the inevitable effect according to Acts of preaching a message that he characterizes as "the good news of God's grace" (see 15:7-11). Further, it seems more likely that the compelling motive of Paul's journey to Jerusalem is as a religious pilgrim in keeping with his observance of Jewish practices (see v. 16) and not as a Christian martyr. While he can claim that he does not count his life of any value (v. 24*a;* cf. 2 Cor 4:7–5:10; 6:4-10; Phil 1:19-26), the revelation to which he refers must be the vision in the Spirit that indicates that Rome is the city of his destiny (see 19:21). Only Paul and the readers of Acts know that it will be Rome, with a layover in Jerusalem, where Paul will "finish my course and the ministry that I received from the Lord Jesus" (v. 24*b;* cf. 1 Cor 9:24; Phil 3:8-13).

**20:25.** For these reasons, Paul's statement of departure does not predict a Jerusalem "passion." His emphatic assertion that none of them will ever see his face again must be understood in terms of his earlier vision of a new mission field in Rome, which therefore requires his departure from and a succession of his leadership in Asia. That his farewell concerns the Roman mission and not a Jerusalem passion is indicated by repetition of the central task of his prophetic vocation in Ephesus—"proclaiming the kingdom" (see 19:8)—and recalls Jesus' paradigmatic prophecy about the inspired witness of his successors that includes teaching about God's kingdom (see 1:3, 6; 14:22; 28:23, 31; cf. 1 Cor 6:9-11; 1 Thess 2:12; Col 1:13) at the "end of the earth" (see 1:8).

**20:26-27.** Paul concludes his personal reminiscence by again declaring that he did not shrink from his prophetic obligations in proclaiming the gospel in Ephesus (see v. 20). The striking declaration that he "is not responsible for the blood of any of you" (v. 26; cf. 1 Thess 2:10) recalls his earlier indictment of unrepentant Jews in Corinth (see 18:6), which presumed that they no longer could excuse their rejection of God's gospel on grounds of their ignorance of its claims and Scripture's warrants. Paul's preaching ministry has clarified God's script of salvation's history and so to refuse his message is to refuse God's invitation. In this new setting in which Paul addresses believers the issue

is not the salvation of his auditors but their assumption of Paul's mission in Ephesus. Whether or not the foundation he has laid in that city continues to be built upon is no longer in his hands; his departure signals the official beginning of their own ministry in his absence.

The addition of a final summary of Paul's gospel, "the whole purpose [βουλή *boulē*] of God" (v. 27; cf. Eph 1:11), delineates the theological boundaries of this ecclesial foundation. Elsewhere in Acts *boulē* denotes God's sovereign purpose that is worked out in the Messiah's mission (see 2:22-23) and now in the church's mission under the aegis of the Holy Spirit (see 4:28; 5:38; 13:36; cf. Gal 1:4; Eph 1:9, 11). There is no Pauline teaching that deviates from God's *boulē;* therefore, Pauline teaching is "canonical" in congregations founded by him. The implication is that *God* views any deviation from his catechesis as apostasy and subversive of God's scripted plans for salvation's progress into the future of Ephesus.

**20:28-35.** The second half of Paul's speech shifts from a description of his past and prophecy of his future to consideration of his succession in Ephesus by the elders of the church. He charges the elders (here called ἐπίσκοποι [*episkopoi,* "overseers"] without change of meaning) with their ministry in ever-vigilant expectation of coming dangers (vv. 28-31). He goes on to exhort them to follow his and the Lord's example of leadership within a community of goods that cares for the poor (vv. 32-35).

**20:28-31.** Paul's rehearsal of the dangers that will face the elders following his departure is enclosed by his charge for them to "keep watch [προσέχω *prosechō*] over yourselves and over all the flock" (v. 28; see also 5:35*b*) and to "be alert" (γρηγορέω *grēgoreo*) to his pastoral example (v. 31). The image of a shepherd watching over his flock is a familiar biblical metaphor of the leader's provident care over Israel (cf. Exod 10:28; Deut 4:9; Ezek 14:11-12; Jer 23:2; Hos 5:1; Mic 5:4; John 10:11-16; 21:17-17) of which the Paul of Acts is exemplary. He presumes their competence to do so because "the Holy Spirit has made you overseers," which not only suggests the mediation of the Spirit's power for ministry (see 1:8) but also the Spirit's authorizing "mark" in their lives that others have recognized (see 6:3-4).

While the role of elders to pastor "the church of

God" seems clear enough, it is confused by the following relative clause "he bought [περιποιέω *peripoieō*] with his own blood [διὰ τοῦ αἵματος τοῦ ἰδίου *dia tou haimatos tou idiou*]," which is obscure both in plain meaning and in its purpose in the speech.[656] That God acquires (*peripoieō*) a people by saving them from destruction is a biblical idea and probably Paul's meaning here (cf. Ps 74:2). But that God did so by means of God's own blood is very difficult to understand theologically. A few commentators think that ἴδιος (*idios*) connotes here a term of endearment for a near relative, or "one's own" (= one's own Son, so the NRSV). Others suggest that Luke combines fragments from two Pauline formulae about "the church of God" and "Christ purchases the church for God by his blood" but in a jumbled way. He may have been grammatically careless at this point because of his lack of theological interest in the efficacy of Christ's blood in saving people from their sins. Even if Acts does include a theology of the cross elsewhere, it is clearly not of the robust variety found in the Pauline letters.[657] In any case, the general sense of Paul's vague phrase is that the church has extraordinary value for God and for this reason the elders must take their calling with utmost seriousness.

The ethos shaped by the inclusio of Paul's charge to pastoral action is of a countercultural community whose beliefs and practices are set against the social norm—which is certainly in line with the preceding narrative of his controversial Ephesian mission. Paul recognizes that his departure will occasion a serious challenge to the purity of that ethos. Two potential dangers are noted: False teachers will come as "savage wolves" from the outside (v. 29) and "from your own group" inside the flock of God (v. 30). The catchphrase echoes the Lord's reference to "savage wolves" (Matt 7:15; 10:16; Luke 10:3; John 10:12), which connotes "false prophets" within Israel—teachers of Israel who reject the messianic word. The phrase has a similar meaning in Paul's speech, except that now it is his proclamation about God's

kingdom that establishes a rule of faith that measures doctrinal purity within the church: The "savage wolf" is any teacher who distorts the truth of Pauline teaching (see 13:10; cf. Phil 2:15).

Paul's warning of false teaching within the church is unusual in Acts. The repetition and variety of references to Paul's teaching in this speech underscore the importance of theological purity in maintaining and transmitting the Pauline legacy to the next generation of believers. Further, Paul calls upon the memory of the elders to remember "that for three years I did not cease night or day to warn everyone with tears" (v. 30; cf. 2 Cor 2:4). Luke's characteristic use of hyperbole again underscores the value of Paul's personal example, which also carries canonical status within the ongoing community.

**20:32-35.** A rhetorical shift from warning to encouragement is once again marked by the καὶ νῦν (*kai nyn,* "and now")—"and now" Paul's concern for an effective succession is made more apparent to his auditors. These final lines of the speech combine blessing (v. 32) and exhortation (vv. 33-35) similar to the benedictions of Pauline letters. The main thread of Paul's speech remains fixed on his "message" (λόγος *logos*) of God's grace (see v. 24; see also 14:3; 5:32). The edifying connection of Paul's gospel with the "building up" (οἰκοδομέω *oikodomeō*) of his successors (cf. Rom 14:19; 15:2; 1 Cor 3:9; 8:1; 10:23; 14:3-5, 12, 17, 26; 2 Cor 10:8; 12:19; 13:10; 1 Thess 5:11) for their future "inheritance" (cf. Rom 15:16; 1 Cor 6:9-11; Gal 3:18; 4:30; 5:21; Titus 3:7) reflects Pauline themes expressed in Lukan vocabulary.

In the context of Acts, however, the use of *oikodomeō* to encourage the spiritual formation ("build up") of elders glosses the earlier use of ἀνοικοδομέω (*anoikodomeō*) in Amos's prophecy of a "rebuilt" Israel (see 15:16) to remind the reader that God continues to fulfill the promise of a restored Israel's mission to the nations (see 15:17-18) even in Paul's absence through the ministry of spiritually restored elders. In this regard, Paul's concluding admonitions reflect the concerns expressed by James concerning whether the mixing of uncircumcised Gentiles with repentant Jews in the synagogues of the diaspora will result in the attenuation of the Jewish legacy within the church (see 15:20-21, 29). Even though Acts has carefully

---

656. The NRSV's "the church of God that he obtained with the blood of his own Son" follows a later (and less theologically difficult) textual tradition, probably borrowing Paul's own words in Rom 8:32. The NIV is preferred simply because it follows the most essential of all text-critical rules; preference is given to the most difficult rendering as more original.

657. Cf. Barrett, *Acts,* 2:976-77.

depicted Paul and, therefore, his legacy as Jewish, the reader should note the implied connection between his final exhortations and the cautionary notes sounded earlier by James regarding the social solidarity of the community. If the principal concerns of James, however, are to maintain this sense of solidarity by abstaining from the pollutants of pagan religion, Paul's concerns are more ethical and echo the social practices of the community of goods (see 2:42-47) within an acquisitive culture such as Ephesus (see 19:25b-27): The dispossession rather than "coveting" of property is the measure of one's spiritual authority (v. 33; see 4:32-35);[658] and working with one's hands to earn one's keep (v. 34; see also 18:3) is motivated by the evident need "to support the weak" (v. 35). As with the content of what is taught, these moral norms are in imitation of Paul and obedient to the Lord's command, "It is more blessed to give than to receive."[659] The purpose of appealing to Jesus is to underscore the practical truth that the community's solidarity is only as strong as its commitment

to its own "weak" (see 4:32-35; 6:1-7). Finally it is not because of his example but because of the command of Jesus that Paul can also say that "we must [δεῖ *dei*]"—a divine necessity—help the poor and the powerless. This practice remains the social mark of the community of goods in whose life the kingdom of God has been restored by God's grace.

**20:36-38.** This concluding panel casts a poignant image of a fond farewell. The sheer weight of emotive terms Luke layers into this scene—"much weeping," "embraced Paul and kissed him," "grieving especially because . . . they would not see him again"—highlights the theme of Paul's departure from Ephesus in the speech itself (vv. 25, 29) and all that is staked out because of it. It is a mistake to conclude, however, that since Luke writes from a perspective after Paul's death he must, therefore, be writing *about* Paul's death. As has been argued earlier, the Paul of Acts addresses the importance of an orderly succession of ministry in Ephesus that is occasioned by Paul's departure for a new mission elsewhere (= Rome; see 19:21) and not by his so-called passion in Jerusalem. The finality of Paul's farewell, when "they brought him to the ship," simply makes more urgent the elders' (and the reader's) compliance with his instructions.

---

658. Paul considers "coveting" (ἐπιθυμέω *epithymeō*) Adam's original sin (cf. Rom 7:7-12) and thus appropriate to use in this closing exhortation. While his own teaching regarding the dangers of wealth is not nearly as clear as Luke's, the Corinthian correspondence is replete with his protest against those who would use their wealth to marginalize "weaker" believers (cf. 1 Cor 1:27; 8:11-12; 9:11-22; 2 Cor 7:2; 11:7-11).

659. This wisdom saying is not found in the gospel tradition (cf. Sir 4:31; *Did.* 1:5; 4:5; Luke 1:45), although it reflects the Lord's teaching (see Luke 6:35-38 and par.).

# REFLECTIONS

"Keep watch over yourselves and over all the flock, of which the Holy Spirit has made you overseers" (20:28 NRSV). There are few biblical passages more instructive of the role and character of church leaders than this one. Both in what he assumes and by what he says, Paul supplies the church of every age with the essential role model and curriculum for a course in leadership training. In describing his own trials and temptations, Paul insinuates himself into his successors minds as their prophetic exemplar: They, too, will encounter similar attacks both within and outside the congregation and must deal with them as he has. Paul assumes in his absence the continuing presence of the Holy Spirit in the congregation—the Spirit who both calls and, therefore, enables its leaders to survive these attacks and to flourish as a result.

The primary marks of the Christian leader correspond to the primary problems Paul anticipates will always threaten the Christian leader: purity, possessions, power. The peculiar definition of each envisages the nature of the countercultural community that these people have been called to lead. Those who are called by God and nurtured by God's Spirit to lead a people belonging to God should neither be trained nor be measured by secular standards of leadership. Thus, for example, the quotient of one's *purity* is measured by faithful ministry of the word of God (20:20). Especially in the Pastoral Epistles, congregational leaders are instructed to teach "sound (or "healthy") doctrine" to others, ever alert to avoid theological error and to squelch its dissemination from other sources (cf. 1 Tim 1:3-7, 10-11; 4:6-10; 2 Tim 1:8-14; 2:2; 3:1-9; Titus 1:9-11). The effectiveness of the gospel to initiate people into life with God is subverted by theological compromise. Beware of the "wolves" within and without the congregation who might threaten the purity of our rule of apostolic faith (cf. 20:29-30).

The messianic career of Jesus is the subtext of Paul's speech: He is the model the Paul of Acts follows (cf. 20:24), who in turn bids the Ephesian elders to follow his example (20:31). Strategically, then, he concludes by quoting Jesus as saying, "It is more blessed to give than to receive" (20:35). Perhaps of greater practical importance to Paul than doctrinal purity is how leaders use their *possessions* (cf. 1 Tim 6:3-10, 17-19). No interpreter of Acts denies the importance of intelligent and articulate preaching (see 19:16-34); yet, Luke knows that the world will consider such preaching specious if the church says one thing and lives another. The abstract truth of a word about God's grace is tested in the real world by whether or not the handling of our goods is also gracious rather than greedy. The motive of Christian ministry must never be monetary and momentary. Those put in charge of the spiritual formation of believers must not covet their possessions (20:33); indeed, they are to make money to redistribute it among the poor (20:34-35). In the simplicity of one's lifestyle and the sharing of one's goods the truth of God's generosity toward us all is made more concrete.

The third mark of the Christian leader according to Paul is how that person handles personal *power.* Most of us can rehearse with regret the moral failure of various Christian leaders. The media sometimes gloat in telling of these failures as though it impugns the integrity of the church's witness in the world. Perhaps it does. All too often these failures are prompted by an "arrogance of power" when those placed in positions of influence have used their high standing to coerce others to do their bidding. The leader who imitates Paul's example is drawn to ministry by the Holy Spirit to serve the redemptive interests of God and the needs of God's flock. The prophetic leader of a countercultural community is one who serves others and sets aside as unseemly the ambitious acquisition of power or pretension of self-importance. The disturbing effect Jesus had on the power brokers of his world was due to the presence of God in places where life was being shaped by norms and values contrary to God's kingdom. The kingdom preaching of the incorrigible Paul had a similar effect on the rich and famous of his day (cf. 20:22-25). So it is in our day that the mark of competent leadership is the disturbing effect a faithful life will have on those whose definition of power places personal ambition over justice and grace as God has defined it in Jesus.

# ACTS 21:1-16, PAUL'S JOURNEY INTO JERUSALEM

NIV

**21** After we had torn ourselves away from them, we put out to sea and sailed straight to Cos. The next day we went to Rhodes and from there to Patara. [2]We found a ship crossing over to Phoenicia, went on board and set sail. [3]After sighting Cyprus and passing to the south of it, we sailed on to Syria. We landed at Tyre, where our ship was to unload its cargo. [4]Finding the disciples

NRSV

**21** When we had parted from them and set sail, we came by a straight course to Cos, and the next day to Rhodes, and from there to Patara.[a] [2]When we found a ship bound for Phoenicia, we went on board and set sail. [3]We came in sight of Cyprus; and leaving it on our left, we sailed to Syria and landed at Tyre, because the

[a] Other ancient authorities add *and Myra*

NIV

there, we stayed with them seven days. Through the Spirit they urged Paul not to go on to Jerusalem. [5]But when our time was up, we left and continued on our way. All the disciples and their wives and children accompanied us out of the city, and there on the beach we knelt to pray. [6]After saying good-by to each other, we went aboard the ship, and they returned home.

[7]We continued our voyage from Tyre and landed at Ptolemais, where we greeted the brothers and stayed with them for a day. [8]Leaving the next day, we reached Caesarea and stayed at the house of Philip the evangelist, one of the Seven. [9]He had four unmarried daughters who prophesied.

[10]After we had been there a number of days, a prophet named Agabus came down from Judea. [11]Coming over to us, he took Paul's belt, tied his own hands and feet with it and said, "The Holy Spirit says, 'In this way the Jews of Jerusalem will bind the owner of this belt and will hand him over to the Gentiles.' "

[12]When we heard this, we and the people there pleaded with Paul not to go up to Jerusalem. [13]Then Paul answered, "Why are you weeping and breaking my heart? I am ready not only to be bound, but also to die in Jerusalem for the name of the Lord Jesus." [14]When he would not be dissuaded, we gave up and said, "The Lord's will be done."

[15]After this, we got ready and went up to Jerusalem. [16]Some of the disciples from Caesarea accompanied us and brought us to the home of Mnason, where we were to stay. He was a man from Cyprus and one of the early disciples.

NRSV

ship was to unload its cargo there. [4]We looked up the disciples and stayed there for seven days. Through the Spirit they told Paul not to go on to Jerusalem. [5]When our days there were ended, we left and proceeded on our journey; and all of them, with wives and children, escorted us outside the city. There we knelt down on the beach and prayed [6]and said farewell to one another. Then we went on board the ship, and they returned home.

7When we had finished[a] the voyage from Tyre, we arrived at Ptolemais; and we greeted the believers[b] and stayed with them for one day. [8]The next day we left and came to Caesarea; and we went into the house of Philip the evangelist, one of the seven, and stayed with him. [9]He had four unmarried daughters[c] who had the gift of prophecy. [10]While we were staying there for several days, a prophet named Agabus came down from Judea. [11]He came to us and took Paul's belt, bound his own feet and hands with it, and said, "Thus says the Holy Spirit, 'This is the way the Jews in Jerusalem will bind the man who owns this belt and will hand him over to the Gentiles.' "
[12]When we heard this, we and the people there urged him not to go up to Jerusalem. [13]Then Paul answered, "What are you doing, weeping and breaking my heart? For I am ready not only to be bound but even to die in Jerusalem for the name of the Lord Jesus." [14]Since he would not be persuaded, we remained silent except to say, "The Lord's will be done."

15After these days we got ready and started to go up to Jerusalem. [16]Some of the disciples from Caesarea also came along and brought us to the house of Mnason of Cyprus, an early disciple, with whom we were to stay.

[a] Or continued    [b] Gk brothers    [c] Gk four daughters, virgins,

# COMMENTARY

Pilgrim Paul is determined to reach Jerusalem in time to celebrate Pentecost (see 20:16), and the present passage follows him into the holy city (21:15-16). Luke's shaping of this entire pilgrimage narrative (20:1–21:16), while reminiscent of the Lord's final journey into Jerusalem, is hardly the prelude to Paul's "passion" as many commentators contend.[660] While Paul anticipates his

660. E.g., J. D. G. Dunn, *The Acts of the Apostles* (Valley Forge, Pa.: Trinity, 1996) 277-78.

suffering (see 20:22-23)—a prospect that is subsequently confirmed by "witnesses in every city" (see 20:23; 21:4, 10-11)—he does not die there; in any case, Rome and not Jerusalem is the city of his destiny (see 19:21). Moreover, the principal parallel between the Lord's final journey to Jerusalem and Paul's is that both end up and suffer in the holy city because both are inspired prophets who obey God's will rather than their own (21:14; see 11:18; 18:21; cf. Luke 22:42). The rhetorical effect of this parallelism reminds the reader that Paul suffers not because of what he says about himself but because of what he says about Jesus.

All the elements of a travel narrative are reflected in this passage. It is framed by Paul's itinerary from Miletus to Jerusalem. There is a sense that the emotional scenes with different congregations (21:3-6, 13-14; see also 20:36-38) transform his pilgrimage into a "farewell tour," since Paul will not visit these mission fields again. He even makes pastoral calls on congregations in Tyre and Caesarea that his mission did not establish in order to demonstrate his solidarity with those whom he had earlier persecuted (see 8:1-3).[661] Along the way Luke reports various incidents in the first person, such as Agabus's prophecy (21:10-12; see also 11:27-28), and drops important names into the story, such as Philip (21:8-9; see also 8:4-40), to add vivid color to an otherwise conventional travelogue.[662] This final stage of Paul's pilgrimage is also shaped by Luke's theological interest in portraying the spiritual authority of Paul as one called to serve God's redemptive interests as a prophet-like-Jesus. In particular, his responses to repeated prophecies of his forthcoming suffering (21:4) and captivity (21:10-11) underscore his determined obedience to God.

**21:1-6.** With the resumption of his more conventional travel narrative, Luke places himself back into the story: "*We* had parted . . . set sail . . . [and] came" to the standard portages that take sea

travelers from Miletus on "a ship bound for Phoenicia" (vv. 1-2), landing in Tyre "to unload its cargo there" (v. 3), including Paul and his entourage (v. 4). That they had to "look up" (ἀνευρίσκω *aneuriskō;* lit., "discover") the disciples (v. 4*a*) living in Tyre suggests that Paul did not evangelize this region and does not know the exact locations of its congregations. He is nevertheless determined to seek them out, knowing they are somewhere nearby since he had earlier visited them briefly with Barnabas to report the happy news of Gentile conversions (see 15:3).

During his weeklong visit, the disciples warned Paul through the Spirit "not to go on to Jerusalem" (v. 4*b*). Glossed by Paul's earlier reference to such testimonies of the Holy Spirit (see 20:23), the interpreter presumes that other prophets have received advanced warning that he would suffer in Jerusalem; for this reason his friends urge him to stay away from the city. This advice was gladly received elsewhere by those who felt the currents of public opinion turning against Paul and so quickly hustled him out of town and to safety. Why not here? Because Paul has received word from the Spirit of his future suffering in Jerusalem (see 20:22-24) as a "necessary" circumstance of his final mission to Rome (see 19:21). With this confidence, then, "when our days there were ended, we left and proceeded on our journey" (v. 5*a*).

The fond farewell to Paul at Tyre is similar to the one he had experienced in Miletus, and for a similar reason: They will not see him again. The manner of his farewell also reflects the religious motive of his journey: "We knelt down on the beach and prayed" (v. 5*b*), since through prayer a community of believers receives divine direction and benefaction (see 1:14). The emphasis on Paul's corporate escort is enforced by reference to entire families who kneel together on the beach for public prayers. It must be said that Paul is traveling to Jerusalem not to suffer, although he will, and not only as a pilgrim intent to celebrate Pentecost as a messianic Jew; he makes the pilgrimage in service of God knowing that it is "necessary" for him to do so (see 19:21; 20:24).

**21:7-9.** The role of repetition in biblical narrative is to recall and engage earlier episodes in meaningful conversation. Much has happened since Philip founded the Samaritan church and

---

661. F. S. Spencer, *The Portrait of Philip in Acts,* JSNTSS 67 (Sheffield: JSOT, 1992) 258-60, suggests that these visits in Palestine are implicitly "works of repentance" since it was Paul who had previously persecuted believers there.

662. These elements of local color, coupled with the first-person narration, has led historians to conclude that Luke draws upon accurate sources in writing this travel narrative. See G. Lüdemann, *Early Christianity According to the Traditions in Acts* (Minneapolis: Fortress, 1989) 439-40. The reader should note that the narrator takes the side of those who oppose Paul's trip to Jerusalem for reasons of personal safety (see 21:12), which indicates a more direct connection with this story than with other "we" passages in Acts.

settled in Caesarea to raise a family, including "four unmarried daughters who had the gift of prophecy" (20:8-9; see also 8:40).[663] In particular, Luke's careful titling of Philip as both "evangelist" (εὐαγγελιστής *euangelistēs;* see 8:4, 12, 40) and "one of the seven" and a companion of Stephen (see 6:3-6) recalls the chain of circumstances following Stephen's death that led Paul (= Saul) to persecute Philip and commit other Hellenist believers to prison (see 8:1-3). It was Paul who ultimately drove them beyond Jerusalem and to Caesarea to plant and cultivate these very congregations he now visits. Paul's personal reversal takes an ironic twist when he stays with Philip, shortly before making his return to Jerusalem to be persecuted and imprisoned himself as a Hellenist believer! Johnson notes that "by enmeshing Paul with [Philip], Luke reminds the reader that Paul and the narrative are completing a full circle. His trip to Jerusalem is not simply a trip to a geographical place but a return to a narrative 'place' that is, for Paul, filled with the memories and possibilities of conflict."[664] In fact, Paul will soon face hostile Jews similar to those who brought Stephen to trial (see 6:9-10), and the accusations they will level against Paul are like those brought against Stephen (see 21:28; 6:11-14). Knowing this, the reader of these stories leading to Paul's arrest cannot help but note their profound irony.

**21:10-14.** The dramatic reappearance of "a prophet named Agabus" in Acts sounds a warning to the reader: His role is to predict future crises in the holy city. Earlier he came from Jerusalem to forecast a famine (see 11:27-30); in this case he both enacts and pronounces a warning to Paul: "The Jews will bind [him] and will hand him over to the Gentiles" (v. 11; cf. Luke 9:22, 44; 18:31-33; 24:7). Agabus, who "bound his own feet and hands" with Paul's belt (v. 11), presents himself in the manner of an OT prophet whose symbolic actions personify and make vivid his message from God (cf. Isa 20:2; Jer 13:1-7; Ezek 4:1-17).[665]

Paul learns two important details about his future suffering from Agabus: Jewish opposition will instigate his suffering (see 21:27-32), and his suffering will result from being "bound" (imprisoned; see vv. 33-36) and "handed over (prosecuted; cf. Luke 9:44; 18:32) to the Gentiles" (the Roman court; see 24:1-21; cf. 28:17). Agabus offers no extended clarification on the details of his prophecy; however, Luke's narrative of Paul's arrest and trials will provide these details soon enough. The Tyrian believers (with Luke!) who misread the prophecy of Paul's suffering as an implied warning for him not to continue his pilgrimage (see v. 4) are now joined by the believers here (again with Luke): "When we heard [Agabus's prophecy], we and the people there urged him not to go up to Jerusalem" (v. 12). Perhaps their response alludes to the disciples of Jesus' story who refuse to believe Jesus' prediction that their journey to Jerusalem would end in his suffering and death.

Acts delays Paul's heartfelt response to his friends to this point in the story—immediately before entering Jerusalem. The reader knows that Paul alone possesses the correct motive of Agabus's prophecy, which is not to warn him away from Jerusalem but to quicken his resolve to go on into Jerusalem, and so from there to Rome. Agabus has authority to receive and deliver God's revelation, and others to interpret it according to their own lights. Only Paul, however, possesses additional revelation that enables him to interpret its normative meaning; and the reader of Acts knows from the Lord's prophecy of Paul's mission that he would suffer for it (see 9:16).

Luke shapes his story of Paul to reflect his spiritual authority for the church, which is reflected both by his firm correction of interpreted prophecies concerning his future suffering and by his affectionate responses to his friends. Luke portrays him as a sympathetic pastor who cares deeply for

---

663. The reference to Philip's daughters is curious because they perform no immediate role in the narrative. They may be persons known to Luke's first readers, added here to commemorate Philip's historic meeting with Paul. In any case, it serves to remind readers that Joel's prophecy of inspired "daughters" who will prophesy during "the last days" (see 2:17) is fulfilled.

664. L. T. Johnson, *The Acts of the Apostles,* SP 5 (Collegeville, Minn.: Liturgical, 1992) 371.

665. Agabus's symbolic enactment of his prophecy is the only such incident in the NT. Moreover, the introductory formula he uses—"Thus says the Holy Spirit"—is unique, although it surely corresponds to the common OT prophetic formulation "Thus says the Lord." In my judgment this account reflects Luke's perspective that the Christian prophet is inspired by the Spirit to know the word and will of God, whether in interpreting Scripture (see 2:4) or through prophetic ecstasy (see 10:19).

his flock (see 20:31): "What are you doing, weeping and breaking my heart?" (v. 13). Through their sincere entreaties and Paul's emotional response, however, his resolve "to be bound [and] even to die in Jerusalem" (v. 13; cf. Rom 15:30-32) becomes all the more apparent to everyone. Again, as with Jesus before him, his motive is that "the Lord's will be done" (v. 14; see 11:18; 18:21; cf. Luke 22:42).

**21:15-16.** Paul's authority is recognized by the whole church and they gather around him in common support as he "started to go up to Jerusalem" (v. 15). He is joined in his ascent into the holy city by "disciples from Caesarea" who delivered Paul to the home of Mnason of Cyprus, "an early disciple" and perhaps one who could recall the suffering caused by Saul's persecution of the church.[666]

666. The Western version expands the text's geography in order to clarify its chronology and smooth the awkward transition from 21:16 to 21:17. In this later reading, Mnason lived in a village about two days journey outside of Jerusalem, where Jesus spent the night.

# REFLECTIONS

"The Lord's will be done" (21:14 NIV and NRSV). Nowhere in Acts is the literary theme of suffering more clearly brought into focus than here. The Lord had earlier prophesied that Paul would suffer for his name's sake (see 9:16). Certainly Paul has already suffered persecution and public humiliation. Yet here the repetition of predictions of Paul's future suffering in Jerusalem (20:22-23; 21:4, 11) underlines the high cost of his calling. The narrative's keen emphasis on Paul's suffering is not a reflection of Lukan hagiography. What honor is due Paul is not because he suffered heroically, and he is not depicted a masochist who takes unnatural delight in his suffering. He does not heed the church's exhortation to avoid the suffering predicted by the Spirit because the Spirit also directed him to go to Jerusalem (see 19:21; 20:22). The suffering that awaits him there is one consequence (or cost) of his obedience to the Lord's call.

Suffering for Jesus is not by itself a mark of superlative devotion; nor should it ever be the motive of Christian discipleship. Believers through the ages have sometimes confused their suffering with spiritual maturity. The two are not the same, nor are they necessarily related. The cost of discipleship is not always persecution or prison. In Paul's case it is; however, he is exemplary not because he suffered but because he chose to obey the Lord's will at any cost.

# ACTS 21:17-26, PAUL MEETS WITH JAMES

NIV

17When we arrived at Jerusalem, the brothers received us warmly. 18The next day Paul and the rest of us went to see James, and all the elders were present. 19Paul greeted them and reported in detail what God had done among the Gentiles through his ministry.

20When they heard this, they praised God. Then they said to Paul: "You see, brother, how many thousands of Jews have believed, and all of them are zealous for the law. 21They have been informed that you teach all the Jews who live among the Gentiles to turn away from Moses,

NRSV

17When we arrived in Jerusalem, the brothers welcomed us warmly. 18The next day Paul went with us to visit James; and all the elders were present. 19After greeting them, he related one by one the things that God had done among the Gentiles through his ministry. 20When they heard it, they praised God. Then they said to him, "You see, brother, how many thousands of believers there are among the Jews, and they are all zealous for the law. 21They have been told about you that you teach all the Jews living among the Gentiles to forsake Moses, and that you tell them not to

NIV

telling them not to circumcise their children or live according to our customs. <sup>22</sup>What shall we do? They will certainly hear that you have come, <sup>23</sup>so do what we tell you. There are four men with us who have made a vow. <sup>24</sup>Take these men, join in their purification rites and pay their expenses, so that they can have their heads shaved. Then everybody will know there is no truth in these reports about you, but that you yourself are living in obedience to the law. <sup>25</sup>As for the Gentile believers, we have written to them our decision that they should abstain from food sacrificed to idols, from blood, from the meat of strangled animals and from sexual immorality."

<sup>26</sup>The next day Paul took the men and purified himself along with them. Then he went to the temple to give notice of the date when the days of purification would end and the offering would be made for each of them.

NRSV

circumcise their children or observe the customs. <sup>22</sup>What then is to be done? They will certainly hear that you have come. <sup>23</sup>So do what we tell you. We have four men who are under a vow. <sup>24</sup>Join these men, go through the rite of purification with them, and pay for the shaving of their heads. Thus all will know that there is nothing in what they have been told about you, but that you yourself observe and guard the law. <sup>25</sup>But as for the Gentiles who have become believers, we have sent a letter with our judgment that they should abstain from what has been sacrificed to idols and from blood and from what is strangled<sup>a</sup> and from fornication." <sup>26</sup>Then Paul took the men, and the next day, having purified himself, he entered the temple with them, making public the completion of the days of purification when the sacrifice would be made for each of them.

<sup>a</sup> Other ancient authorities lack *and from what is strangled*

# COMMENTARY

With this passage Luke begins the final section of Acts. The plotline follows the adventures of Paul, who survives legal problems with hostile Jews and ambivalent Roman courts in Jerusalem (21:17–26:32), and then with nature during a stormy sea voyage and with a poisonous serpent (27:1–28:10), before safely arriving as a prisoner in the city of his destiny (28:11-31). Through it all a faithful God safeguards Paul to Rome as promised (cf. 19:21; 23:11; 27:24), "for he is an instrument whom I have chosen to bring my name before Gentiles and kings" (9:15) at the "end of the earth" (1:8).

On the day following his safe arrival in the holy city, Paul visits James along with other leaders of the Jerusalem church (21:17-19). The topic of their conversation resumes the concerns James had earlier expressed at the Jerusalem Council: whether Paul's mission to the nations would result in contaminating the church's Jewish legacy (see 15:20-21, 28-9). There now are rumors in circulation that James's worst fears have been realized. Jerusalem believers who zealously maintain Jewish practices (21:20) have heard reports from unidentified sources that Paul teaches "Jews living

among the Gentiles to forsake Moses, and that you tell them not to circumcise their children or observe the customs" (21:21). A strategy of reconciliation is devised that allows Paul to respond to these fears: He will join with other repentant Jews in Jerusalem to purify themselves in the rite of the Nazaritic vow (see 21:22-23) in order to demonstrate that he observes and guards the law (21:24); this Paul does (21:26). Since Paul arrives in Jerusalem as a pilgrim to celebrate Pentecost (see 20:16), his easy accommodation of a purification ritual is not due to church politics but to its agreement with his religious practices as a devout Jew.

Luke's shaping of the story of Paul's final visit to Jerusalem in response to this theological crisis raises serious critical problems for the interpreter. For example, Luke has edited out any reference to Paul's Jerusalem collection (cf. 24:17). The issue is not simply his silence on the topic, when Paul makes it a critical feature of his urban mission and his relationship to the Jewish church. The more knotty problem is that the epistolary Paul makes the Jerusalem collection a condition of his Roman visitation (cf. Rom 15:22-31), which otherwise squares with Luke's narrative plotline that follows

Paul's movements from Jerusalem to Rome. Why not then mention the Jerusalem collection, since it fits nicely into Luke's narrative plotline?

It is unlikely that this most recent meeting reflects poor relations between the Jerusalem church and Paul's mission; it may be nothing more than a literary convention of Luke's storytelling, which routinely plays down the role or even silences secondary figures in order to play up the role of his central characters. The theological crisis that Paul addresses in his letters is whether Gentile converts, who are not Jewish proselytes, are nonetheless initiated into their new life with God through trusting in Jesus alone. He only rarely has occasion to address the practices of repentant Jews or the internal problems facing Jewish-Gentile congregations in the diaspora (however, see Romans 14; 1 Corinthians 8–10). Even relevant autobiographical details are rhetorically designed to illustrate the larger theological lessons learned from his mission to the nations. In Acts, these concerns have already been resolved at the Jerusalem Council, and Luke's plotline has moved on to consider another worry—namely, whether Paul's mission occasions the gentilizing of repentant Jews (rather than the Judaizing of repentant Gentiles). Luke's narrative of Paul's mission since the Jerusalem Council has adequately addressed this worry.

Yet, Luke's newest concern since Paul's Miletus speech is whether a *Pauline* legacy has any future in the church (see 20:18-35). Insofar as Luke portrays Paul as an observant Jew, the reader of Acts must insist that the legacy of Paul is not only distinctively Christian but decidedly Jewish. Because this Jewish argot is almost entirely lacking in his letters, the contribution made by the Paul of Acts to Scripture's Pauline witness is to place him among Jews even as his letters place him among Gentiles. Yet some interpreters continue to wonder whether the Paul who wrote Galatians would ever have accommodated the Jewish church's suggestion that he observe a temple rite and Mosaic law (cf. Gal 2:19-21). One can easily imagine, however, that the missionary Paul who wrote 1 Corinthians could easily adapt his "principle of accommodation" to reconcile troubled relations between discordant believers in the manner narrated by this passage (cf. 1 Cor 9:19-21).

**21:17-20a.** Despite Paul's fears to the contrary

(see Rom 15:31), he is warmly greeted by James in a spirit of generous hospitality; "and all the elders were present" (vv. 17-18; see also 15:4, 6, 22-23). This should be perceived not as foreboding but as a literary cue that the same board of church leaders who received the report of Barnabas and Paul's first mission to the nations has reconvened to hear Paul's report of his second mission. Paul rehearsed with them "one by one the things that God had done among the Gentiles through his ministry [διακονία *diakonia*]" (v. 19; see also 15:12; cf. 2:22)—things that the reader of Acts has already considered from 16:6 to this point.

The use of *diakonia* repeats a catchword of Paul's Miletus speech to the leaders of his church and recalls his abiding interest that he "may finish my course and the ministry [*diakonia*] that I received from the Lord Jesus" (20:24). This linguistic link suggests two implied reasons for Paul's visit with James: He is there to say farewell, since he already knows that Rome is his appointed destination, and he is there for confirmation from the leaders of the Jewish church of the importance of what "God had done among the Gentiles through his ministry." Their response confirms that this Pauline legacy accords with God's will: "When they heard [Paul's report], they praised God" (v. 20*a;* see also 4:21; 11:18).

**21:20b-21.** The mood of this friendly meeting quickly changes from confirmation of Paul's mission among the Gentiles to concern over his mission among the Jews (see 15:20-21). His prior testimony seems unaware of this concern since he reports nothing of his successes among repentant Jews. The effect is to take Paul by surprise as though this information is "entirely new."[667] But, of course, this has been Luke's subtext all along!

Luke sharply draws the contrast between James and Paul for rhetorical effect. On the one hand, James reports that "many thousands" (lit., "many myriads") of repentant Jews "are all zealous [ζηλωτής *zēlōtēs*]) for the law [Torah]" (21:20*b*).[668] Luke's characteristic hyperbole makes the impression keener: The Jewish Christian community in Judea is vibrant and strong, and their

---

667. E. Haenchen, *The Acts of the Apostles* (Philadelphia: Westminster, 1971) 608.

668. The Western version omits "among the Jews," no doubt a reflection of its anti-Semitism. However, the resulting text makes little sense.

strength is tied to their identity as observant Jews.[669] The adjective *zēlōtēs* characterizes these Jewish converts as "traditional," people for whom a public identity as a consecrated people belonging to God is marked by their dedicated adherence to the Torah (cf. Exod 20:4-5; Deut 4:23-24; 5:8-9; 6:14-15; Nah 1:2). Ironically, before his conversion Paul depicts his devotion to these same traditions in similar terms: He performed his ancestral traditions with "zeal," so that a consecrated life is a Torah-observant one (cf. Gal 1:14; Phil 3:6; see Acts 22:3).

This religious ethos and the Jewish identity it cultivates forge a stamp of covenant loyalty similar to the Pharisaic believers who sought clarification on the practices of uncircumcised Gentiles at the Jerusalem Council (15:5). Given the cautions of James in response (see 15:20-21, 29), we are not surprised when he becomes agitated upon hearing rumors that Paul teaches "Jews living among the Gentiles to forsake [ἀποστασίαν διδάσκεις ἀπό *apostasian didaskeis apo;* lit., "teaching apostasy against"] Moses . . . not to circumcise their children or observe the customs [ἔθος *ethos*]" (v. 21; see also 15:21; cf. 20:20, 27). The problem raised is not a soteriological matter but a sociological one. The use of *ethos* refers to those religious practices or routines within which a distinctively Jewish life is formed. From Acts 16:3 forward, the reader of Acts knows full well that these unfavorable reports are a canard. Not only is Paul an exemplary Jew who finds the vast majority of his Gentile converts in the synagogues where Moses is preached every sabbath (see 15:21), but he is careful to safeguard a Jewish *ethos* against the intrusion of magic, materialism, or pagan religion—even on those occasions when believers have been forced out of their synagogues to form indigenous "household" congregations.

**21:22-24.** The proposed strategy begins with a realistic appraisal of "what then is to be done" (v. 22*a*). Paul's presence in Jerusalem cannot be kept secret from these zealous believers: "They will certainly hear that you have come" (v. 22*b*). The present crisis cannot be evaded and appropriate action is required. For this reason the church's leadership takes neither side, nor is there time for a measured deliberation over the relevant issues at stake. Paul's spirit of conciliation is not a matter of ceding to those with greater authority or to Jerusalem's supervisory prerogatives over his mission. The autonomy of Paul's mission and his spiritual authority is beyond dispute. Rather, his willingness to accommodate himself to the circumstances of the Jerusalem congregation demonstrates his agreement with James's worry about the gentilizing of the church's Jewish legacy.

Because Paul is, indeed, a Jew who observes and guards the law (v. 24*b*), the agreed course of action is viewed as an appropriate and practical response to the current rumors. The "rite of purification" called for is roughly patterned after the OT "law of the Nazirites" (cf. Num 6:1-21) and is similar in character and purpose to the vow Paul made earlier in Cenchraea (see 18:18). The Hebrew meaning of Nazirite is "consecrated one" and refers to the laity of a congregation who are set apart for service to God. Obedience to this law symbolizes one's disciplined devotion to God and the effects such a life has on the entire community. None of the three primary vows made by the Nazirite is mentioned in the text,[670] and only the ritual of shaving one's hair after completing the pledged period is indicated (cf. Num 6:13-21). For reasons of cost and ease this ritual of termination was the rule most consistently observed in completing this vow. Nor were Nazirite vows considered acts of purification per se, or together as a "rite of purification."[671] Rather, such vow-keeping symbolizes the purity of those who make such a commitment.[672]

669. See, however, J. Jervell, *Die Apostelgeschichte*, KEK 3 (Göttingen: Vandenhoeck & Ruprecht, 1998), 524-25, who rightly cautions that Luke's hyperbole must not at the same time underestimate the vigor and success of the mission to traditional Jews in Judea as though such a mission has been superseded in Acts by Paul's mission to the nations.

670. That is, abstinence from wine, not cutting one's hair, and avoiding contact with anything dead. It should also be noted that the law of the Nazirites applies equally to men and women (cf. Num 6:2), and so Luke's specification that "four *men* are under a vow" (21:23, italics added) is required.

671. See C. K. Barrett, *A Critical and Exegetical Commentary on the Acts of the Apostles*, 2 vols, ICC (Edinburgh: T. & T. Clark, 1994, 1998) 2:1010-13, for the various possible explanations of this interpretive problem. Note also this same problem obtains to 21:26 where "days of purification" are mentioned. In brief, the critical problem is that the law of the Nazirites is not a per se rite of purification. A week-long period of purification and sacrifice is required of the Nazirite only after touching something dead (cf. Num 6:10-11).

672. Cf. B. Levine, *Numbers 1–20*, AB 4 (New York: Doubleday, 1993) 229-35, who notes the heroic dimension of naziritism in OT narratives, especially of Israel's Judges (e.g., Deborah, Samson, Samuel). Luke probably intended such resonances between the judges of the OT and the Paul of Acts.

Pilgrim Paul is inclined for religious, if not also for political, reasons to join with "four men who are under a vow" (v. 23) and to shoulder their expenses while doing so—this, too, is a resurrection practice of the community of goods. Quite apart from the Nazirite's offering of shorn hair, the "rite of purification" requires a sacrifice that exacts a considerable financial cost from the supplicant. Might this be an allusion to Paul's collection hitherto unmentioned in Acts? Probably not, and the reader knows nothing of Paul's personal financial resources. The focus of the story is on his implied willingness to make a sacrifice within a faith community whose distinctive public identity is in part the sharing of goods with their needy (see 2:42-47; 4:32-35; 6:1-2). Moreover, Paul's compliance indicates his spiritual authority, since the dispossession of wealth envisages the possession of God's Spirit.

**21:25.** Some commentators find James's reiteration of his pastoral exhortation to Antioch (see 15:29; also see 15:20) superfluous here: The reader of Acts knows well that the current crisis is not about Paul's mission among uncircumcised Gentiles but rather about his mission among repentant Jews.[673] That the exhortation is repeated here may simply reflect Luke's use of a different source or the use of a new setting where James is speaking more widely to Paul's traveling companions (including Luke) who were not present at either the Jerusalem Council or the Antiochene reading of its verdict. As I have argued, however, this repetition of James's verdict provides a narrative prompt for a review of Paul's mission in Acts: At no time has Paul allowed the "pollutions of idols" to contaminate a Jewish identity in the congregations of the diaspora church.

**21:26.** Paul complies with the request: "The next day he took the men and purified himself along with them." Although the grammar of the text does not require that all five Nazirites concluded the period of their vow at the same time, they all followed biblical protocol. The sacrifice would include cutting the hair of each man to indicate that the period of consecration had been completed according to Mosaic law. Paul has passed this test of faithfulness to the practices of his ancestral religion for all to see: "He entered the temple with them, making public the completion of the days of purification." When this hard evidence of Paul's piety and teamwork is ignored and even misconstrued, the blame must shift from him to his critics.

673. The Western version of Acts makes clarifies this by adding that Gentile believers have nothing but good things to say concerning Paul's catechesis of them. The issue is thereby more narrowly considered as a "Jewish" problem with Paul's mission.

# REFLECTIONS

**1.** "They have been told about you that you teach all the Jews among the Gentiles to forsake Moses, and that you tell them not to circumcise their children or observe the customs" (21:21 NRSV). The continuing concerns voiced about Paul by other Jewish believers in Jerusalem concern his commitment to their common religious heritage. Moses and circumcision are deeply felt religious symbols; they are observed as formative of a community's loyalties, responses, and religious zeal. To subvert them is to derail the community's progress into the future of God. Thus for these believers the past of Israel defines the present of the church. Earlier their pastor James had voiced concern that the intermingling of multiple identities, Jewish and pagan, is a practical problem that might split loyalties and confuse people (see 15:20-21, 29). The Jews of Jerusalem now have reason to be concerned about their identity and whether what Paul has wrought "among the Gentiles" will jeopardize it. Of course, the readers of Acts know Jerusalem need not worry about Paul's mission. He has steadfastly protected the church's Jewish heritage as more and more Gentiles are added to its membership rolls.

The subtext of this passage, however, is Paul's identity as a prophet-like-Jesus. The prophet's task is not to replace the old with something new, but to recover and reform the old as God's unchanging word for a new day. The very idea that Paul had compromised his Jewish heritage or subverted its transmission to a new generation of children challenges his prophetic vocation.

Thus Paul's actions to prove the reports false also defend an important ingredient of his prophetic task.

When we speak of the church as a counterculture or a prophetic community and look to Acts for authoritative models, central to what we find in the reading of Acts is the high value placed on Jewish tradition. To be the church means to recover and continue to reform the sacred traditions of Israel for a new day.

**2.** "What then is to be done?" (21:22 NRSV). The practical lesson learned from this passage is the importance of a review protocol to ensure the church's forward progress. The church often makes the mistake of implementing a new policy without including specific guidelines for future review and evaluation. Years earlier as the result of two Jerusalem assemblies, the church agreed to accept uncircumcised Gentiles as full members (cf. 11:1-18; 14:27–15:29). But James expressed his reservations regarding Paul's mission to the nations. He feared that the presence of converted pagans in an assembly of Jewish believers would compromise their Jewish identity (see above). Clearly these reservations remain (21:25), but they have been rewritten in Jewish terms (21:21). A strategy is devised that would ameliorate anxiety: Paul would demonstrate his commitment to his Jewish tradition and the formation of repentant Jews by completing with others the rite of Nazirite purification (21:26).

Taken as a whole, this passage establishes a pattern of review that a congregation could institute to measure the long-term effectiveness of some policy or program. (1) An overview of positive results is presented by relevant leaders to the church's board of elders in a setting of worship and praise to God (21:17-20*a*). What are the evidences of God's activity mediated through this policy or that program? (2) The elders may then present reports of concern from members who believe the policy or program imperils the church's witness and life (21:20*b*-21). (3) Rather than taking these reports at face value, the elders devise a test of the merits of any negative report (21:22-25). (4) The test is then implemented and its results publicly observed to determine whether the result commends the continuation of the policy or program (21:26).

# ACTS 21:27-39, PAUL'S "ARREST"

NIV

[27]When the seven days were nearly over, some Jews from the province of Asia saw Paul at the temple. They stirred up the whole crowd and seized him, [28]shouting, "Men of Israel, help us! This is the man who teaches all men everywhere against our people and our law and this place. And besides, he has brought Greeks into the temple area and defiled this holy place." [29](They had previously seen Trophimus the Ephesian in the city with Paul and assumed that Paul had brought him into the temple area.)

[30]The whole city was aroused, and the people came running from all directions. Seizing Paul, they dragged him from the temple, and immediately the gates were shut. [31]While they were trying

NRSV

[27]When the seven days were almost completed, the Jews from Asia, who had seen him in the temple, stirred up the whole crowd. They seized him, [28]shouting, "Fellow Israelites, help! This is the man who is teaching everyone everywhere against our people, our law, and this place; more than that, he has actually brought Greeks into the temple and has defiled this holy place." [29]For they had previously seen Trophimus the Ephesian with him in the city, and they supposed that Paul had brought him into the temple. [30]Then all the city was aroused, and the people rushed together. They seized Paul and dragged him out of the temple, and immediately the doors were shut. [31]While they were trying to kill him,

NIV

to kill him, news reached the commander of the Roman troops that the whole city of Jerusalem was in an uproar. [32]He at once took some officers and soldiers and ran down to the crowd. When the rioters saw the commander and his soldiers, they stopped beating Paul.

[33]The commander came up and arrested him and ordered him to be bound with two chains. Then he asked who he was and what he had done. [34]Some in the crowd shouted one thing and some another, and since the commander could not get at the truth because of the uproar, he ordered that Paul be taken into the barracks. [35]When Paul reached the steps, the violence of the mob was so great he had to be carried by the soldiers. [36]The crowd that followed kept shouting, "Away with him!"

[37]As the soldiers were about to take Paul into the barracks, he asked the commander, "May I say something to you?"

"Do you speak Greek?" he replied. [38]"Aren't you the Egyptian who started a revolt and led four thousand terrorists out into the desert some time ago?"

[39]Paul answered, "I am a Jew, from Tarsus in Cilicia, a citizen of no ordinary city. Please let me speak to the people."

NRSV

word came to the tribune of the cohort that all Jerusalem was in an uproar. [32]Immediately he took soldiers and centurions and ran down to them. When they saw the tribune and the soldiers, they stopped beating Paul. [33]Then the tribune came, arrested him, and ordered him to be bound with two chains; he inquired who he was and what he had done. [34]Some in the crowd shouted one thing, some another; and as he could not learn the facts because of the uproar, he ordered him to be brought into the barracks. [35]When Paul[a] came to the steps, the violence of the mob was so great that he had to be carried by the soldiers. [36]The crowd that followed kept shouting, "Away with him!"

[37]Just as Paul was about to be brought into the barracks, he said to the tribune, "May I say something to you?" The tribune[b] replied, "Do you know Greek? [38]Then you are not the Egyptian who recently stirred up a revolt and led the four thousand assassins out into the wilderness?" [39]Paul replied, "I am a Jew, from Tarsus in Cilicia, a citizen of an important city; I beg you, let me speak to the people."

[a] Gk *he*     [b] Gk *He*

# COMMENTARY

The Paul of Acts has the remarkable capacity to incite strong emotions of both friendship and opposition. The present text is a case of the latter. It seems that for all its good intentions, the "Nazaritic strategy" misfired even before it was fully completed (21:27a). But did it? The conspiracy against Paul's mission hatched by hostile Jews in Asia (see 20:3) had extended its reach to Jerusalem where they "had seen [Paul] in the temple [and] stirred up the whole crowd [and] seized him" (21:27b). Paul's performance of a ritual of purity evidently has had no positive effect on these outsiders whose antagonism in any case does not concern the religious practices of the Jewish Paul of Acts. This is the solution to an intramural conflict between Paul and "zealous" *repentant* Jews and does not refer to unrepentant Jews. Nowhere

in Acts is Paul accused by his Jewish opponents of impugning the traditions or practices of Israel. The Jewish opposition against Paul's mission in the diaspora is due entirely to his interpretation of the Jewish Scriptures that the risen Jesus is God's Messiah.

For this reason, the reader must consider the charges brought against Paul by "the Jews from Asia" as unfounded and disingenuous (21:28-29). Nevertheless with characteristic hyperbole and local color, Luke dramatically describes the riot that ensues (21:30-36). Stirred by passion and prejudice, the crowd drags Paul from the temple and tries to kill him. Roman soldiers intervene to rescue him from the lynch mob. In his interrogation of Paul (21:37-38), the Roman tribune reflects the general ignorance about him in the holy city.

Paul's retort to the tribune (21:39) sets the stage for his first great apologia that follows.

**21:27-29.** The reader should not be surprised to find "Jews from Asia" at the Jerusalem Temple within eyesight of Paul, since they are all there as Jewish pilgrims to celebrate Pentecost (see 2:5-9; 20:16). Paul's Asian opponents are probably from Ephesus, where the synagogue's opposition toward Paul's teaching ministry is especially keen (see 19:8-10; 20:3, 19). This is reflected in their violent reaction to seeing Paul in the Temple: They "stirred up the whole crowd . . . [and] seized [lit., "laid hands on"] him" (v. 27); and then they shout for additional help in apprehending him (v. 28*a*). Passions peak during religious festivals! A mob of opponents who act in a non-rational and unprofitable manner is a thematic element of Luke's narrative (e.g., 6:1-7; 11:1-18; 14:27–15:21).

What is somewhat more surprising is the first allegation that Paul "is teaching everyone everywhere against our people, our law, and this place" (v. 28*b*). This is patently untrue; and we have heard it all before in any case, not only as gossip circulating among "zealous" believers that Paul teaches "all the Jews living among the Gentiles to forsake Moses" (see v. 21) but also as "false" testimony in the prosecution of Stephen that he (and Jesus before him) taught against "this holy place and the law" (see 6:13).[674] The second charge is more serious and new: He "has defiled this holy place" (v. 28*c*) by bringing an unclean Gentile into the Temple. Gentiles were not allowed into the inner courts of the Temple beyond the "Court of the Gentiles" upon penalty of death—a point of law still enforced by the Roman occupation. Stone slabs inscribed in both Latin and Greek with warnings to this effect were posted throughout the temple courtyard.[675] But the evidence against Paul is circumstantial: They had earlier seen him walking the streets of downtown Jerusalem with one of his Gentile companions, Trophimus the Ephesian (see 20:4). On the basis of this sighting, his accusers infer that he must have continued his tour by taking Trophimus with him into the inner courts of the Temple—an unthinkable act for the Paul of Acts!

**21:30-36.** Luke exaggerates the crowd's violent reaction to these accusations, but the rhetorical effect explains why the "tribune of the cohort" was thereby alerted. The crowd "seized Paul and dragged him out of the temple" (v. 30) with the temple police shutting the doors behind them,[676] not because Paul's alleged desecration had made the Temple unclean for everyone but because they intended "to kill him" (v. 31)—an act that would have defiled the Temple if carried out within the inner courts.[677] The "tribune of the cohort" (v. 31),[678] later named as Claudius Lysias (see 23:26), understood well the psychology of a mob riot, that things could quickly get out of control. Therefore, "he immediately took soldiers and centurions and ran down to them . . . [and] they stopped beating Paul" (21:32) for fear that they would be arrested.

What happens next supplies the details that fulfill Agabus's prophecy: The Roman tribune arrests Paul and orders him "to be bound with two chains" (v. 33; see also 21:11, 13; cf. 22:29). Paul is in Roman hands from the outset for safekeeping. The term "inquired" (πυνθάνομαι *pynthanomai;* lit., "began to interrogate") reflects the tribune's uncertainty or ambivalence about Paul's guilt. He continues to question Paul about "who he was and what he had done," but he conveys a calming and more reasonable perspective toward him that personifies Rome's posture toward Paul throughout his imprisonment.

Lysias's persona stands in stark contrast to that of the crowd, which shouts "one thing, some another" (v. 34*a*)—an atmosphere of confusion that prevents the more rational Lysias from "learn[ing] the facts [lit., "knowing with surety"]." The uproar over Paul is just too loud and intense (v. 34*b;* see 17:5; 20:1; cf. 24:18). Such scenes are commonplace in Acts and always subvert a setting

---

674. C. C. Hill, *Hellenists and Hebrews: Reappraising Division Within the Earliest Church* (Minneapolis: Fortress, 1992) 58, suggests the possibility that Paul's faithfulness and not Stephen's (or perhaps even Jesus') is the more relevant issue for Luke and therefore he reads the accusations leveled against Paul back into the Stephen story. This presumes that the parallelism between his two accounts is not coincidental but redactional.

675. So J. A. Fitzmyer, *The Acts of the Apostles,* AB 31 (Garden City, N.Y.: Doubleday, 1998) 698.

676. Probably the inner gates, restricted to purified Jews, rather than the outer gates, open to all pilgrims. So I. H. Marshall, *The Acts of the Apostles,* NTG (Sheffield: JSOT, 1992) 348.

677. E. Haenchen, *The Acts of the Apostles* (Philadelphia: Westminster, 1971) 616.

678. A Roman cohort of soldiers consisted of at least 760 infantrymen and 240 cavalrymen. Roughly ten centurions are stationed with a cohort, each one with responsibility for 100 soldiers. The "tribune" (= commandant) of this cohort is garrisoned at the northwest corner of the temple area in the Fortress Antonia with stairway access to where the riot is taking place. The response time would have been short and fits the details of Luke's narrative.

where Paul's reasoned arguments from Scripture are heard and considered, if not always in faith. Ironically, peace is found in the barracks of pagan soldiers rather than in a synagogue of pious Jews![679] There are stairsteps leading up from the temple area to the barracks that slowed the escort's progress and so again Rome safeguarded Paul from the angry mob: The soldiers carried Paul up the steps (21:35) to the shouts of "Away with him! [= Kill him!]" (v. 36; cf. Luke 23:18; John 19:15) that continues to reverberate through the narrative of Paul's trials (cf. 22:22; 28:19).

**21:37-39.** Finally away from the rabble-rousing mob, Lysias can now hear what Paul says and observe the manner by which he speaks. The results transform their legal relationship. Paul uses Greek to make a request: "May I say something to you?" (v. 37). The tribune is surprised that Paul addresses him in Greek, not because it is rare for a Jew to speak Greek; bilingualism was commonplace in Paul's Palestine. He seems surprised that Paul speaks with a particular inflection of Greek, different from those who come to Palestine from North Africa (see 2:7-8). That is, the tribune knows now by his Greek dialect that Paul is not from Egypt and therefore cannot be "the Egyptian who recently stirred up a revolt and led the four thousand assassins out into the wilderness" (v. 38).[680] His use of οὐκ ἄρα (*ouk ara,* "Then you are not . . . ") to introduce a rhetorical question implies that Lysias first thought Paul is this wanted assassin; were it so this would have marked a military coup for him! Alas, Paul is but "a Jew, from

Tarsus" (v. 39), which perhaps explains his diction as well as his ethnicity and citizenship.[681]

Paul's biographical sketch reveals important information about who he is, which will dictate how Lysias must handle his legal case. Its literary construction, for example, combines nationality, city of origin, and statement of citizenship (= passport), reflecting a rhetorical form learned from his classical education—perhaps in Tarsus, a center of Greek culture and rhetoric.[682] Paul is an educated man. Significantly, he is a Jewish man as well, not only confirming Lysias's verdict that Paul is not the Egyptian fugitive but also implying that the real conflict the soldiers rescued him from is religious rather than political in nature. Moreover, for a Jew to be "a citizen of an important city" other than Rome is no idle boast. Typically, this would have implied that Paul is a member of a prominent family or held deed to substantial real estate holdings in the region of Tarsus.

It is on this personal basis that Paul makes his polite request known to this tribune: "I beg you, let me speak to the people [= the people of God]." His request to address this audience of religious Jews, coupled with his identity as a Jew from Tarsus, discloses the religious motive of his defense. The Paul of Acts surely knows there will be no miraculous escape from the chains that now bind him, since it fulfills prophecy; his speech does not intend to set him free but to interpret his imprisonment as an act of his faithfulness to God and for Israel.[683]

---

679. The barracks in question were the soldiers' quarters at the nearby Fortress Antonia. See Josephus *Antiquities of the Jews* 15.11.4.403-9. See also L. T. Johnson, *The Acts of the Apostles,* SP 5 (Collegeville, Minn.: Liturgical, 1992) 382.

680. Josephus speaks of this same Egyptian revolutionary, who came to Jerusalem during the time of Procurator Felix as a messianic figure and predicted the destruction of the Temple. Apparently thousands were killed in the riot that ensued but the Egyptian escaped with several thousand followers—Josephus claims thirty thousand but Luke's figure is more accurate. See Josephus *Antiquities of the Jews* 20.8.6.169-72.

681. B. Witherington, *The Acts of the Apostles: A Socio-Rhetorical Commentary* (Grand Rapids: Eerdmans, 1998) 662, argues that Paul's response to Lysias's rhetorical question is more than a legal definition of his persona; it is also a rebuttal that seeks to restore his personal dignity in response to what he took to be a racial slur or deprecating perception that he was this Egyptian renegade.

682. For a description of Tarsus and its importance in the Roman world, especially as Athen's complement well known for its excellent schools, see M. Hengel and A. Schwemer, *Paul Between Damascus and Antioch* (London: SCM, 1997) 158-67.

683. For this argument worked out in detail, see R. C. Tannehill, *The Acts of the Apostles,* vol. 2 of *The Narrative Unity of Luke-Acts: A Literary Interpretation* (Minneapolis: Fortress, 1990) 2:268-84.

# REFLECTIONS

The tribune "ordered that Paul be taken into the barracks" (21:34 NIV). Many interpreters of Acts suggest that the relationship between Lysias and Paul personifies the ideal relationship between the secular state and the church. On the one hand, Lysias's perspective toward Paul is completely free of religious interest. He has no apparent interest in the gospel or in Paul as a prophet-like-Jesus. His interrogation of Paul is calculated to determine whether he is a threat to the state's interests in Palestine, and he evaluates Paul's innocence according to Roman law. Lysias's preoccupation is Rome, not God; and perhaps this is as it should be. On the other hand, Lysias protects Paul against a threat to his life. More important, he recognizes this threat as provoked by religious rather than political disagreements, and he allows Paul the freedom to explain himself on this basis. While Lysias's Rome is no liberal democracy, his decisions about Paul exemplify an understanding of the separation between state and church that tolerates, even safeguards religious freedom.

In making this point, however, the teacher of this passage should be careful not to sacralize the state. The decisions Lysias makes personify a state concerned for a secular version of peace without any concern whether its decisions agree with God's purposes. According to Luke's model, the sovereign God, the only God, can collaborate with any pagan state interested in legal justice and concerned to safeguard the church's witness to the gospel. At the same time, this same model keenly discourages revolutionary violence as legitimate means for ensuring that God's will is done on earth as it is in heaven.

In the biblical context, one finds competing models of the relationship between the state and the church. These differing models should be pressed into service to bring "checks and balances" to any discussion of this literary theme in Acts. For example, the book of Revelation characterizes the church's relationship to the state in negative terms: "Babylon" is an evil order ruled over by the unholy trinity and demands that the faithful children of God submit to their corrupting demands or be martyred (Revelation 12–13). At the very least, the congregation's teachers should guard against any interpretation of Scripture that regards civil order as "Christian" whether by nature or in purpose.

# ACTS 21:40–23:35, PAUL DEFENDS HIMSELF BEFORE JEWS IN JERUSALEM

## NIV

[40]Having received the commander's permission, Paul stood on the steps and motioned to the crowd. When they were all silent, he said to them

**22** in Aramaic[a]: [1]"Brothers and fathers, listen now to my defense."

[2]When they heard him speak to them in Aramaic, they became very quiet.

Then Paul said: [3]"I am a Jew, born in Tarsus of Cilicia, but brought up in this city. Under Gamaliel I was thoroughly trained in the law of

[a] 40 Or possibly *Hebrew;* also in 22:2

## NRSV

[40]When he had given him permission, Paul stood on the steps and motioned to the people for silence; and when there was a great hush, he addressed them in the Hebrew[a] language, saying:

**22** "Brothers and fathers, listen to the defense that I now make before you."

2When they heard him addressing them in Hebrew,[a] they became even more quiet. Then he said:

3"I am a Jew, born in Tarsus in Cilicia, but

[a] That is, *Aramaic*

## NIV

our fathers and was just as zealous for God as any of you are today. [4]I persecuted the followers of this Way to their death, arresting both men and women and throwing them into prison, [5]as also the high priest and all the Council can testify. I even obtained letters from them to their brothers in Damascus, and went there to bring these people as prisoners to Jerusalem to be punished.

[6]"About noon as I came near Damascus, suddenly a bright light from heaven flashed around me. [7]I fell to the ground and heard a voice say to me, 'Saul! Saul! Why do you persecute me?'

[8]" 'Who are you, Lord?' I asked.

" 'I am Jesus of Nazareth, whom you are persecuting,' he replied. [9]My companions saw the light, but they did not understand the voice of him who was speaking to me.

[10]" 'What shall I do, Lord?' I asked.

" 'Get up,' the Lord said, 'and go into Damascus. There you will be told all that you have been assigned to do.' [11]My companions led me by the hand into Damascus, because the brilliance of the light had blinded me.

[12]"A man named Ananias came to see me. He was a devout observer of the law and highly respected by all the Jews living there. [13]He stood beside me and said, 'Brother Saul, receive your sight!' And at that very moment I was able to see him.

[14]"Then he said: 'The God of our fathers has chosen you to know his will and to see the Righteous One and to hear words from his mouth. [15]You will be his witness to all men of what you have seen and heard. [16]And now what are you waiting for? Get up, be baptized and wash your sins away, calling on his name.'

[17]"When I returned to Jerusalem and was praying at the temple, I fell into a trance [18]and saw the Lord speaking. 'Quick!' he said to me. 'Leave Jerusalem immediately, because they will not accept your testimony about me.'

[19]" 'Lord,' I replied, 'these men know that I went from one synagogue to another to imprison and beat those who believe in you. [20]And when the blood of your martyr[a] Stephen was shed, I

[a] 20 Or witness

## NRSV

brought up in this city at the feet of Gamaliel, educated strictly according to our ancestral law, being zealous for God, just as all of you are today. [4]I persecuted this Way up to the point of death by binding both men and women and putting them in prison, [5]as the high priest and the whole council of elders can testify about me. From them I also received letters to the brothers in Damascus, and I went there in order to bind those who were there and to bring them back to Jerusalem for punishment.

[6]"While I was on my way and approaching Damascus, about noon a great light from heaven suddenly shone about me. [7]I fell to the ground and heard a voice saying to me, 'Saul, Saul, why are you persecuting me?' [8]I answered, 'Who are you, Lord?' Then he said to me, 'I am Jesus of Nazareth[a] whom you are persecuting.' [9]Now those who were with me saw the light but did not hear the voice of the one who was speaking to me. [10]I asked, 'What am I to do, Lord?' The Lord said to me, 'Get up and go to Damascus; there you will be told everything that has been assigned to you to do.' [11]Since I could not see because of the brightness of that light, those who were with me took my hand and led me to Damascus.

[12]"A certain Ananias, who was a devout man according to the law and well spoken of by all the Jews living there, [13]came to me; and standing beside me, he said, 'Brother Saul, regain your sight!' In that very hour I regained my sight and saw him. [14]Then he said, 'The God of our ancestors has chosen you to know his will, to see the Righteous One and to hear his own voice; [15]for you will be his witness to all the world of what you have seen and heard. [16]And now why do you delay? Get up, be baptized, and have your sins washed away, calling on his name.'

[17]"After I had returned to Jerusalem and while I was praying in the temple, I fell into a trance [18]and saw Jesus[b] saying to me, 'Hurry and get out of Jerusalem quickly, because they will not accept your testimony about me.' [19]And I said, 'Lord, they themselves know that in every synagogue I imprisoned and beat those who believed in you. [20]And while the blood of your witness Stephen

[a] Gk the Nazorean   [b] Gk him

NIV

stood there giving my approval and guarding the clothes of those who were killing him.'

²¹"Then the Lord said to me, 'Go; I will send you far away to the Gentiles.' "

²²The crowd listened to Paul until he said this. Then they raised their voices and shouted, "Rid the earth of him! He's not fit to live!"

²³As they were shouting and throwing off their cloaks and flinging dust into the air, ²⁴the commander ordered Paul to be taken into the barracks. He directed that he be flogged and questioned in order to find out why the people were shouting at him like this. ²⁵As they stretched him out to flog him, Paul said to the centurion standing there, "Is it legal for you to flog a Roman citizen who hasn't even been found guilty?"

²⁶When the centurion heard this, he went to the commander and reported it. "What are you going to do?" he asked. "This man is a Roman citizen."

²⁷The commander went to Paul and asked, "Tell me, are you a Roman citizen?"

"Yes, I am," he answered.

²⁸Then the commander said, "I had to pay a big price for my citizenship."

"But I was born a citizen," Paul replied.

²⁹Those who were about to question him withdrew immediately. The commander himself was alarmed when he realized that he had put Paul, a Roman citizen, in chains.

³⁰The next day, since the commander wanted to find out exactly why Paul was being accused by the Jews, he released him and ordered the chief priests and all the Sanhedrin to assemble. Then he brought Paul and had him stand before them.

23 Paul looked straight at the Sanhedrin and said, "My brothers, I have fulfilled my duty to God in all good conscience to this day." ²At this the high priest Ananias ordered those standing near Paul to strike him on the mouth. ³Then Paul said to him, "God will strike you, you whitewashed wall! You sit there to judge me according to the law, yet you yourself violate the law by commanding that I be struck!"

⁴Those who were standing near Paul said, "You dare to insult God's high priest?"

NRSV

was shed, I myself was standing by, approving and keeping the coats of those who killed him.' ²¹Then he said to me, 'Go, for I will send you far away to the Gentiles.' "

²²Up to this point they listened to him, but then they shouted, "Away with such a fellow from the earth! For he should not be allowed to live." ²³And while they were shouting, throwing off their cloaks, and tossing dust into the air, ²⁴the tribune directed that he was to be brought into the barracks, and ordered him to be examined by flogging, to find out the reason for this outcry against him. ²⁵But when they had tied him up with thongs,ᵃ Paul said to the centurion who was standing by, "Is it legal for you to flog a Roman citizen who is uncondemned?" ²⁶When the centurion heard that, he went to the tribune and said to him, "What are you about to do? This man is a Roman citizen." ²⁷The tribune came and asked Paul,ᵇ "Tell me, are you a Roman citizen?" And he said, "Yes." ²⁸The tribune answered, "It cost me a large sum of money to get my citizenship." Paul said, "But I was born a citizen." ²⁹Immediately those who were about to examine him drew back from him; and the tribune also was afraid, for he realized that Paul was a Roman citizen and that he had bound him.

³⁰Since he wanted to find out what Paulᶜ was being accused of by the Jews, the next day he released him and ordered the chief priests and the entire council to meet. He brought Paul down and had him stand before them.

23 While Paul was looking intently at the council he said, "Brothers,ᵈ up to this day I have lived my life with a clear conscience before God." ²Then the high priest Ananias ordered those standing near him to strike him on the mouth. ³At this Paul said to him, "God will strike you, you whitewashed wall! Are you sitting there to judge me according to the law, and yet in violation of the law you order me to be struck?" ⁴Those standing nearby said, "Do you dare to insult God's high priest?" ⁵And Paul said, "I did not realize, brothers, that he was high priest; for it is written, 'You shall not speak evil of a leader of your people.' "

ᵃ Or *up for the lashes*   ᵇ Gk *him*   ᶜ Gk *he*   ᵈ Gk *Men, brothers*

⁵Paul replied, "Brothers, I did not realize that he was the high priest; for it is written: 'Do not speak evil about the ruler of your people.'*"

⁶Then Paul, knowing that some of them were Sadducees and the others Pharisees, called out in the Sanhedrin, "My brothers, I am a Pharisee, the son of a Pharisee. I stand on trial because of my hope in the resurrection of the dead." ⁷When he said this, a dispute broke out between the Pharisees and the Sadducees, and the assembly was divided. ⁸(The Sadducees say that there is no resurrection, and that there are neither angels nor spirits, but the Pharisees acknowledge them all.)

⁹There was a great uproar, and some of the teachers of the law who were Pharisees stood up and argued vigorously. "We find nothing wrong with this man," they said. "What if a spirit or an angel has spoken to him?" ¹⁰The dispute became so violent that the commander was afraid Paul would be torn to pieces by them. He ordered the troops to go down and take him away from them by force and bring him into the barracks.

¹¹The following night the Lord stood near Paul and said, "Take courage! As you have testified about me in Jerusalem, so you must also testify in Rome."

¹²The next morning the Jews formed a conspiracy and bound themselves with an oath not to eat or drink until they had killed Paul. ¹³More than forty men were involved in this plot. ¹⁴They went to the chief priests and elders and said, "We have taken a solemn oath not to eat anything until we have killed Paul. ¹⁵Now then, you and the Sanhedrin petition the commander to bring him before you on the pretext of wanting more accurate information about his case. We are ready to kill him before he gets here."

¹⁶But when the son of Paul's sister heard of this plot, he went into the barracks and told Paul.

¹⁷Then Paul called one of the centurions and said, "Take this young man to the commander; he has something to tell him." ¹⁸So he took him to the commander.

The centurion said, "Paul, the prisoner, sent for me and asked me to bring this young man to you because he has something to tell you."

*5 Exodus 22:28

6When Paul noticed that some were Sadducees and others were Pharisees, he called out in the council, "Brothers, I am a Pharisee, a son of Pharisees. I am on trial concerning the hope of the resurrection* of the dead." 7When he said this, a dissension began between the Pharisees and the Sadducees, and the assembly was divided. 8(The Sadducees say that there is no resurrection, or angel, or spirit; but the Pharisees acknowledge all three.) 9Then a great clamor arose, and certain scribes of the Pharisees' group stood up and contended, "We find nothing wrong with this man. What if a spirit or an angel has spoken to him?" 10When the dissension became violent, the tribune, fearing that they would tear Paul to pieces, ordered the soldiers to go down, take him by force, and bring him into the barracks.

11That night the Lord stood near him and said, "Keep up your courage! For just as you have testified for me in Jerusalem, so you must bear witness also in Rome."

12In the morning the Jews joined in a conspiracy and bound themselves by an oath neither to eat nor drink until they had killed Paul. 13There were more than forty who joined in this conspiracy. 14They went to the chief priests and elders and said, "We have strictly bound ourselves by an oath to taste no food until we have killed Paul. 15Now then, you and the council must notify the tribune to bring him down to you, on the pretext that you want to make a more thorough examination of his case. And we are ready to do away with him before he arrives."

16Now the son of Paul's sister heard about the ambush; so he went and gained entrance to the barracks and told Paul. 17Paul called one of the centurions and said, "Take this young man to the tribune, for he has something to report to him." 18So he took him, brought him to the tribune, and said, "The prisoner Paul called me and asked me to bring this young man to you; he has something to tell you." 19The tribune took him by the hand, drew him aside privately, and asked, "What is it that you have to report to me?" 20He answered, "The Jews have agreed to ask you to bring Paul

*Gk *concerning hope and resurrection*

¹⁹The commander took the young man by the hand, drew him aside and asked, "What is it you want to tell me?"

²⁰He said: "The Jews have agreed to ask you to bring Paul before the Sanhedrin tomorrow on the pretext of wanting more accurate information about him. ²¹Don't give in to them, because more than forty of them are waiting in ambush for him. They have taken an oath not to eat or drink until they have killed him. They are ready now, waiting for your consent to their request."

²²The commander dismissed the young man and cautioned him, "Don't tell anyone that you have reported this to me."

²³Then he called two of his centurions and ordered them, "Get ready a detachment of two hundred soldiers, seventy horsemen and two hundred spearmen*ᵃ* to go to Caesarea at nine tonight. ²⁴Provide mounts for Paul so that he may be taken safely to Governor Felix."

²⁵He wrote a letter as follows:

²⁶Claudius Lysias,

To His Excellency, Governor Felix:

Greetings.

²⁷This man was seized by the Jews and they were about to kill him, but I came with my troops and rescued him, for I had learned that he is a Roman citizen. ²⁸I wanted to know why they were accusing him, so I brought him to their Sanhedrin. ²⁹I found that the accusation had to do with questions about their law, but there was no charge against him that deserved death or imprisonment. ³⁰When I was informed of a plot to be carried out against the man, I sent him to you at once. I also ordered his accusers to present to you their case against him.

³¹So the soldiers, carrying out their orders, took Paul with them during the night and brought him as far as Antipatris. ³²The next day they let the cavalry go on with him, while they returned to

ᵃ 23 The meaning of the Greek for this word is uncertain.

down to the council tomorrow, as though they were going to inquire more thoroughly into his case. ²¹But do not be persuaded by them, for more than forty of their men are lying in ambush for him. They have bound themselves by an oath neither to eat nor drink until they kill him. They are ready now and are waiting for your consent." ²²So the tribune dismissed the young man, ordering him, "Tell no one that you have informed me of this."

²³Then he summoned two of the centurions and said, "Get ready to leave by nine o'clock tonight for Caesarea with two hundred soldiers, seventy horsemen, and two hundred spearmen. ²⁴Also provide mounts for Paul to ride, and take him safely to Felix the governor." ²⁵He wrote a letter to this effect:

²⁶"Claudius Lysias to his Excellency the governor Felix, greetings. ²⁷This man was seized by the Jews and was about to be killed by them, but when I had learned that he was a Roman citizen, I came with the guard and rescued him. ²⁸Since I wanted to know the charge for which they accused him, I had him brought to their council. ²⁹I found that he was accused concerning questions of their law, but was charged with nothing deserving death or imprisonment. ³⁰When I was informed that there would be a plot against the man, I sent him to you at once, ordering his accusers also to state before you what they have against him.ᵃ"

³¹So the soldiers, according to their instructions, took Paul and brought him during the night to Antipatris. ³²The next day they let the horsemen go on with him, while they returned to the barracks. ³³When they came to Caesarea and delivered the letter to the governor, they presented Paul also before him. ³⁴On reading the letter, he asked what province he belonged to, and when he learned that he was from Cilicia, ³⁵he said, "I will give you a hearing when your accusers arrive." Then he ordered that he be kept under guard in Herod's headquarters.ᵇ

ᵃ Other ancient authorities add *Farewell*   ᵇ Gk *praetorium*

NIV

the barracks. [33]When the cavalry arrived in Caesarea, they delivered the letter to the governor and handed Paul over to him. [34]The governor read the letter and asked what province he was from. Learning that he was from Cilicia, [35]he said, "I will hear your case when your accusers get here." Then he ordered that Paul be kept under guard in Herod's palace.

# COMMENTARY

This passage narrates the first of four episodes in which Paul defends himself in Palestine against accusations brought against him by his Jewish opponents (21:40–26:30). Luke's shaping of these four episodes forms a whole that nicely coheres around certain big ideas and vivid images that the reader should keep in mind. For example, this is a section of Acts that is more speech than story; and these speeches are typically forensic (apologia) in form and function and, therefore, are different from the missionary speeches heard to this point in Acts.[684] Perhaps the most obvious characteristic of these speeches is their Jewishness. In part this reflects Paul's effort to respond to his opponents' accusation that he is guilty of teaching against Israel's ancestral traditions. Even though his Jewish opponents attempt to ratchet up their charge to expose a political consequence (= sedition), the Roman judges who hear their case against Paul follow Gallio's earlier example (see 18:12-16) and never adjudicate its legal merit. While disinterested in the theological quotient of Paul's message or even the fact that it evidently divides the house of Israel, Rome at least comprehends that nothing he has done or said is punishable under Roman law. Surely Paul pays attention to this more political accusation, but in things said and done "off the record" rather than in his speeches, in which the topics are Jewish not

Roman and the motives religious not secular. Indeed, the singular contention of his apologia is that he has acted in conformity with God's purposes for God's people.

Paul's enduring commitment to Israel is easily observed by consideration of the internal dynamic between the basic components of his first (see 22:3-21) and the final (see 26:1-23) speeches that frame Luke's narrative of Paul's legal difficulties. In both these bracketing texts Paul begins with a brief autobiographical sketch that emphasizes his Jewish background and personal identity (22:3-5; 26:4-11) before settling on different rehearsals of his Damascus road experience and calling (22:6-16; 26:12-18; see 9:1-19a). His encounter with Jesus defines his prophetic vocation as a "light to the nations" (22:17-21; 26:19-23; cf. 13:47). Yet the house of Israel, divided over whether Jesus is the Messiah, remains divided about Paul (see 22:22-23).

What role does the defense of the Paul of Acts perform within the NT canon? In particular, how does this narrative aim form the interpreter's angle of vision toward the canonical Paul and into the Pauline letters of the NT? Without doubt Luke shapes the entire narrative of Paul's trials, and in particular his apologia, to portray him as someone who is a personal exemplar of Jewish piety and a redemptive agent of Israel's God. Paul has spiritual power, and he is an inspired interpreter of God's word—the equal of Peter and John before him and of his contemporary James. At the end of the day, Luke is disinterested in Rome's verdict on Paul and so concludes Acts without legal closure. Nothing is written of Paul's meeting with the Emperor because Luke is fundamentally *disinterested* in

---

684. The basic rhetorical structure of a Greek-styled *apologia* begins with an exordium in which the speaker commends his credentials to his audience in order to win the right to be heard; next is the *narratio,* or an edited narrative of relevant events, that delimits the "case study"; with the case before the audience, the speaker provides the *probatio,* or standard proofs—eyewitnesses, textual support, revelatory events—that might be brought forward as testimony; and the speech concludes with the *refutatio,* in which the speaker brings to focus everything said in direct response to the accusations brought forward.

what Rome thinks. Luke's interest is rather posited in Paul's status as an interpreter and carrier of God's word for God's people, which has importance for the future of the church.

In this regard, Paul emerges from his legal entanglements as a principled defender of Israel's faith whose teachings are in essential continuity with the purposes of God for Israel according to Israel's Scriptures. More important, it is on this profoundly Jewish ground that Paul now can define and defend his vocation as prophetic witness to the nations. The real meaning of his Damascus road vision and his vocation is that the God of Israel has called Paul to carry God's transforming word about God's Messiah to the nations so that all people might participate in the blessings promised first to the Jews. By rooting this claim in the Scriptures the Paul of Acts is portrayed as a defender of a truly Jewish religion. In this sense, then, it is not Paul who must change how he reads Scripture, but rather it is unrepentant Israel who must revise its hermeneutic—its "official" story of God's restoration of Israel—in the light of the gospel that Paul proclaims.[685]

The plotline of the present passage, which narrates Paul's defense before the Jews of Jerusalem, includes two speeches, the first to the people (22:1-21) and the second to the Sanhedrin (23:1-6), with a variety of responses from both Jewish audiences (22:22-23; 23:7-9) and from the Roman tribune Claudius Lysias (22:24-30; 23:10) following each. The dramatic interplay of these encounters sets the stage for the plot against Paul's life (23:12-22), which is sandwiched between a christophany repeating that Rome is his destiny (23:11) and his escape from harm's way in Jerusalem to Caesarea (23:23-35), the venue of his Roman trial, which follows.

**21:40–22:21.** In his exchange with Lysias, Paul identifies himself as a Jew from Tarsus, which is also how he begins his speech to Jerusalem's Jews. He climaxes his apologia by claiming that

God commissioned him to go "far away to the Gentiles" (22:21). The interplay between his Jewish identity (22:3-5) and his Gentile commission, with its echo of Jeremiah and Isaiah's commissions (22:6-11), frame this first speech, which includes important roles performed by the devout disciple Ananias (22:12-16) and by the Temple, the erstwhile symbol of religious Israel (22:17-20). For the Paul of Acts, the public symbol of a restored Israel in the last days of salvation's history is its vocation as light to the nations.

**21:40–22:2.** Paul quieted his audience first with a hand gesture (21:40) and then by addressing them in Hebrew (22:2). The use of language again plays a strategic role in Luke's story, as Paul shifts from the Greek used to gain the attention of his Roman captor (21:37-38) to Hebrew in order to win the sympathy of a Jewish audience. His opening line to them (his exordium) identifies his speech as a "self-defense" (an apologia). In an oral culture, as Paul's surely was, auditors would be accustomed to hearing orators speak and could follow the form and related function of their speeches. An apologia spoken in the vernacular would certainly have been apropos to Paul's situation in addressing a hostile crowd. Moreover, the use of Hebrew would have appealed to the crowd's nationalistic and ethnic passions, which would have registered at fever pitch during the feast of Pentecost (see chaps. 5–11).

**22:3-5.** In presenting his Jewish credentials Paul broadly sketches a *vita* similar to the one he had submitted to Lysias (see 21:39): "I am a Jew, born in Tarsus in Cilicia."[686] He again emphasizes that he is a Jew of the diaspora—a relevant detail, since his principal antagonists are also Jews from the diaspora. In exchange for any reference to his citizenship, which may have disenfranchised him from "the people," he speaks of a childhood during

---

685. One cannot help noting Paul's ambivalence in maintaining his Jewish identity with his Christian message—Dunn's image is of a "shuttlecock batted back and forth between the two spheres—of his twofold identity and double loyalty." See J. D. G. Dunn, *The Acts of the Apostles* (Valley Forge, Pa.: Trinity, 1996) 292. Perhaps it is this that explains his name change from "Saul" to "Paul" (see 13:9); it is a Lukan metaphor for the tensions inherent within Paul, who is Jewish and Christian, from Jerusalem and Tarsus, who is citizen of Rome and Tarsus while a loyal Israelite, and speaks as prophet-like-Jesus and philosopher-like-Socrates.

686. The construction of this Greek sentence is awkward and has led commentators to debate how to punctuate it, with implications for constructing a Pauline biography. Most follow the present translations and place a comma after "Gamaliel," which distinguishes between Tarsus as Paul's ancestral home and Jerusalem as the place of his education. See A. du Toit, "The Tale of Two Cities," *NTS* 46 (2000) 375-402. It is entirely possible, however, to follow Luke's use of three participles as three discrete stages of Paul's life and so place commas after "in this city" and "law." In this case, then, Jerusalem would have been Paul's ancestral home, where he was brought up as a child and educated as a youth before moving to Tarsus—where he evidently had close family connections (see 21:39)—after completing his education and initiation into the teachers of the Pharisaic party. See C. K. Barrett, *A Critical and Exegetical Commentary on the Acts of the Apostles,* 2 vols, ICC (Edinburgh: T. & T. Clark, 1994, 1998) 2:1034-36.

which he was "brought up in this city" and educated "at the feet of Gamaliel . . . according to our ancestral law, being zealous for God" (v. 3). These details of Paul's education are classically Pharisaic. It is hardly possible to have been initiated into the Pharisaic elite (cf. Phil 3:5-6; see also Acts 23:6) without spending a considerable apprenticeship in the holy city. Gamaliel (the Elder) is probably the same teacher Luke mentions earlier in Acts as a respected member of the Sanhedrin (see 5:34); he lived in Jerusalem at the time and was one of the foremost teachers within the Pharisaic party. To sit "at the feet" of a great teacher denotes Paul's initiation from an early age (probably at age five) into the rigorous regimen of Jewish learning (lasting at least until his Bar Mitzvah at age thirteen).

He finally characterizes his devotion to his studies with two catchwords associated with the demands of the Pharisaic school: "educated strictly" (ἀκρίβεια akribeia) and "zealous" (ζηλωτής zēlōtēs) for God. The first is used by Josephus to describe the distinctive concern of the Pharisees for precision in their interpretation and observance of the "ancestral laws."[687] In this light, the auditor may well have expected Paul to speak of his "zeal for the law" (see 21:20; cf. Gal 1:14) instead of his "zeal for God" (cf. Rom 10:2). This slight shift of emphasis from torah to God may well stand as a gentle rebuke of those whose devotion to Jewish "tradition" prevents them from hearing the truth of God's gospel. At the same time, Paul's reference to "God" may intend to provide the antecedent for his next claim that he "persecuted this Way" (v. 4; see also 9:1-2; 8:1-3; cf. 19:9, 23; 22:19): Paul did so out of his devotion to God rather than to a particular interpretation of the torah.

**22:6-11.** The three accounts of Paul's conversion and calling in Acts are broadly similar in that each describes his crusade against believers, his trip to Damascus for the purpose of imprisoning believers there, his epiphany of the living Jesus when approaching Damascus, and his entry into Damascus a changed man. The repetition of the same incident in a single composition makes it unnecessary to rehearse all its details; this version glosses the earlier one in Acts 9, and together these accounts prepare the reader for Paul's second retelling (= third version) of his conversion

story, found in Acts 26. This particular retelling of his persecution of the church with clear allusions to Stephen's case (see 22:20) repeats what the reader of Acts already knows, although in this setting the irony is unmistakable. His claims may be slightly exaggerated to cultivate the impression of his devotion to God, since nowhere in Acts do we read that Paul's actions resulted in the death of any believer, rather just in the suffering and dispersion of some (see 8:1-4). In any case, to persecute "up to the point of death" with the consent of the council of elders would have been illegal in Roman Palestine. Especially important to note is that Paul recruits this council, along with the high priest and "the [Jewish] brothers in Damascus" (22:5) as witnesses to the integrity of his Jewish pedigree.

Paul's firsthand account of his encounter with Jesus differs very little from the first narrative of this event (see 9:3-6; cf. 26:12-18). He adds the time, "about noon," which makes the account more realistic,[688] and intensifies the "great" light that "shone about" him (v. 6). Moreover, in this retelling, the Lord identifies himself more fully as "Jesus of Nazareth" (v. 8; see also 2:22; 3:6; 4:10; 6:14; 26:9), which may intend not only to locate Jesus in Palestine for his Jewish audience but also to convey an ironic allusion to the circumstances of Paul's arrest when completing his Nazirite vow, for the Greek text has "Nazorean" rather than "Nazareth."

The most obvious deviation from the narrator's account in chap. 9 is that "those who were with me saw the light but did not hear the voice of the one who was speaking to me" (22:9; see 9:7; cf. 26:13). The reason for this change is not as obvious to the interpreter, but its significance in any case must be minor. The exchange between a blinded Paul and Jesus, lacking in the first version, is here added to indicate more clearly that Paul conceives of his conversion to the living Jesus in terms of his vocation—"What am I to *do*, Lord?"—which Jesus tells him will be clarified once he gets up and goes to Damascus (22:10).[689]

---

687. Josephus *Life* 191.

688. So E. Haenchen, *The Acts of the Apostles* (Philadelphia: Westminster, 1971) 625.

689. Johnson takes δόξα (*doxa*), translated "brightness/brilliance" (22:11), more literally as "glory" to reflect what he regards as Luke's intention to connect this event with the presence of God in the world. See L. T. Johnson, *The Acts of the Apostles*, SP 5 (Collegeville, Minn.: Liturgical, 1992) 389. This makes better sense of the provocative use of "Lord" (22:10) when speaking of Jesus and of Paul's calling before a hostile Jewish audience (cf. 2 Cor 4:6).

**22:12-16.** Paul's retelling of his conversion is strategically sandwiched between his Jewish *vita* (vv. 3-5) and this expanded account of Ananias's role in his commissioning. Ananias is a "devout man according to the law and well spoken of by all the Jews" (v. 12; see also 9:10), who is recruited as a relevant witness to Paul's own religious credentials before an audience of other pious Jews. Note again the use of language—Ananias calls Paul by his Aramaic name, "Saul" (v. 13), to intensify the claim made: He is a religious Jew. Ananias has no role in Paul's second version in Acts 26, where Paul addresses an audience of secular Jews and Roman leaders.

According to this version, Ananias, who first received the Lord's prophecy of Paul's mission (see 9:15-16), now reports to Paul the substance of what he is to do. The effect of telescoping the details of Paul's healing to the simple phrase "regain your sight" (v. 13; see also 9:17-18) is to posit the auditor's attention on Ananias and his witness to Jesus' prophecy of Paul's future mission. The interplay between these two texts within Acts is made more striking since Ananias restates the Lord's prophecy in a biblical idiom: "the God of our ancestors" (see 3:13; 5:30; 7:32; 13:23) has "chosen" him to know God's will (see 13:22; 21:14) and "to see the Righteous One" (see 3:14; 7:52; cf. Luke 23:47). This combination of biblical phrases, which is asserted by a pious Jew, anchors Paul's commission to "witness to all the world" (22:15) in Jewish tradition.[690] Moreover, Paul's contested interpretation of Scripture is predicated on "what you have seen and heard," thereby making the connection between his conversion to Jesus and his commission to proclaim God's word all the more clear (cf. 1 Cor 15:1-11).

Ananias's exhortation to "get up, be baptized, and have your sins washed away, calling on his name" (v. 16; see also 2:38; 3:19) rounds out the sparse earlier account where we are told that Paul is encouraged to "be filled [= baptized] with the Holy Spirit" (see 9:18-19). The interplay supplies the full logic of Christian baptism. Baptism initiates the converted Paul—the one who calls upon the Lord's name (see 2:21; 9:14)—into the covenant community on the basis of God's forgiveness of his sins (see 2:38); and it is within the context of this community's life and vocation that the Holy Spirit empowers this prophet-like-Jesus to perform the tasks that accord with God's will.[691]

**22:17-21.** The final incident in Paul's retelling of his Damascus road calling takes the reader by surprise: Paul does not mention his Jewish opposition (see 9:23-25), and he reveals that Jesus commissioned his mission during a *second* christophany while Paul was praying in the Temple (v. 21),[692] where Jesus (rather than the "disciples") also alerted him to the Jewish threat against him and urged him to leave Jerusalem immediately (v. 18; see also 9:29-30).

Paul's version of this episode is consistent with Luke's portrait of him in Acts. Although clearly ambivalent toward the Temple as a symbol of faithful Israel, Luke employs it here as a crucial element of an apologia that proves Paul's purity: A person praying in the Temple is an unlikely candidate to desecrate it. In addition, there are certain allusions to Isaiah's temple vision (cf. Isa 6:1-10), during which he is called a prophet of God and told that Israel will resist his message,[693] both of which parallel Paul's own experiences with Jesus.[694] Echoes of Jeremiah's theophany that commissioned him a "prophet to the nations" (cf. Jer 1:5; Gal 1:15) further alert the reader to the prophetic subtext of Paul's narrative of his temple

---

690. The use of "witness" (μάρτυς *martys*) is rarely used of anyone except the Twelve and often in connection to their prophetic ministry (see 1:8, 22; 2:32; 3:15; 5:32; 10:39, 41; cf. 13:31). Luke's use of it here almost certainly recalls the earlier stories of the apostles as inspired witnesses to the risen Jesus, thereby connecting their "witness" with Paul's.

691. Cf. J. D. G. Dunn, *Baptism in the Holy Spirit* (London: SCM, 1970) 73-78.

692. G. Lüdemann, *Early Christianity According to the Traditions in Acts* (Minneapolis: Fortress, 1989) 238-40, asserts that "Paul's vision in the temple is certainly unhistorical" because Paul claims he was called to be the apostle to the nations near Damascus in Gal 1:15 and because it is so evidently Lukan in language and purpose within this Acts setting.

693. The continuing literary theme of Israel's rejection in Acts is again carefully circumscribed by Luke: In Paul's apologia it is used ironically of Paul's own theological reversal—once a rejecter of Jesus, now rejected because of him. However, the prophecy of Israel's division over the Messiah is carefully placed alongside Paul's own Jewish credentials to make certain the reader understands Isaiah's prophecy is not anti-Israel, as though Christianity were destined by God to be a Gentile religion, but is a prophecy about unrepentant Israel realized during Paul's mission.

694. Paul and Isaiah are called to their prophetic vocations by a temple vision (cf. Isa 6:1//Acts 22:17); both try to excuse themselves because neither views himself as able to do the tasks involved (cf. Isa 6:5//Acts 22:19-20); and both are "sent" and both "go" at the Lord's command (cf. Isa 6:8-10//Acts 22:21). Moreover, the prophetic connection to Paul's mission to the nations is found in Jeremiah's theophanic calling as prophet to the nations (cf. Jer 1:15//Acts 22:21; Gal 1:15). See O. Betz, "Die Vision des Paulus in Temple von Jerusalem," in *Verborum Veritas* (Wuppertal: Rolf Brockhaus, 1970) 113-23.

vision: Paul is a prophet-like-Jesus who stands in the line of Israel's prophets.

Paul's reference to "the blood of your witness Stephen" (v. 20) demonstrates the extent of his "great reversal." Paul recalls the earlier story of Stephen's martyrdom, not as a prediction of his own martyrdom but as a symbol of his own conversion. The pairing of Paul's witness to the living Jesus and the dying Stephen funds his gospel as the light "to the Gentiles/nations [ἔθνη ethnē]" (v. 21; see also 13:47; cf. Isa 49:6; Luke 2:29-35; Rom 11:13; Gal 2:7).[695] Paul delays his divinely sanctioned commission until the end of the speech to underscore the universal scope of God's word and the salvation it promises: The good news for Gentiles is that they now can share in Israel's promised blessings according to the prophets. Paul's climactic assertion that he is called to carry the word of God "far away to the Gentiles [nations]" (v. 21) not only sanctions his urban mission to distant places but underscores for his Jewish audience that his mission embodies the vocation of a faithful Israel according to the prophets (= Isaiah).

**22:22-23.** There is no good reason why the crowd should react as violently as it does: A pious Paul infers from personal experience and allusions to Scripture's prophecy that the limits of Israel's promised blessings should be extended to include repentant Gentiles (see 3:21-26).[696] But the polemical cast of Luke's story precludes reasoned debate; the church's opponents in Acts are rarely if ever reasonable! Thus, an angry mob interrupts Paul before he can provide formal proof (peroratio) of his innocence.[697] Their vitriolic shouts—"he should not be allowed to live" (v. 22)—and hostile gestures—"throwing off their cloaks" (see 14:14) and "tossing dust into the air" (v. 23; see also 13:51)—seek to silence Paul, perhaps in prepara-

tion for stoning him.[698] These actions are symbols of an unthinking, unrepentant Israel's obduracy and the hard possibility that not all of Israel will repent (see 1:11; cf. Luke 4:22-30; Rom 11:25-32). The reasons why any Jew should resent the inclusion of repentant Gentiles in the blessings of Israel's salvation are less clear (see the Commentary on 23:12-22).

**22:24-29.** The actions of the tribune suggest that he is confused as well. As a pagan outsider, he fails to pick up the controversy provoked by Paul's testimony. He sees only the mob's hostile and loud reaction and knows that Paul is guilty of something bad. Thus he resorts to an "examination by flogging"—a military routine for extracting useful information from a prisoner in an unsettled case.[699] The soldiers "stretched him out to flog him" (v. 25a) in prospect of a brutal, sometimes fatal beating. Paul is prompted by their treatment to identify himself at last as a Roman citizen to the supervisory centurion: "Is it legal for you to flog a Roman citizen who is uncondemned [ἀκατάκριτος akatakritos]?" (v. 25b; see also 16:37). The weighty word here is akatakritos, which carries two legal connotations, either of which is damning. In this quasi-legal setting, Paul could mean either that the tribune is about to mete out an unjust punishment or that his anticipated flogging is premature or arbitrary, since a "proper" investigation has not yet been conducted according to Roman law. Perhaps Paul is purposefully vague in his polite but pointed question of the centurion in order to elicit precisely the response he received.

Lysias had earlier expressed surprise when Paul reported that he was a citizen of Tarsus (see 21:39). Imagine his shock when informed that "this man is a Roman citizen" (v. 26)! If a citizen's prestige and standing are determined by the city of his citizenship, few honors were more important in Paul's Mediterranean world than Roman citizenship.[700] Evidently Paul's citizenship is inher-

---

695. This formulation of Paul's commission recalls Simeon's prophecy of a universal salvation (cf. Luke 2:29-32) and a divided house of Israel (cf. Luke 2:33-35). In this sense, the hostile response to Paul's declaration is viewed within Luke's narrative as another fulfillment of Simeon's prophecy.

696. D. Boyarin, *A Radical Jew* (Berkeley: University of California Press, 1994) 228-60, argues, however, that Paul's universalism "poses a significant challenge to Jewish notions of identity," primarily because it subverts Jewish ethnic particularity envisaged not only by its monotheism but by its "cultural specificities."

697. Speeches are routinely interrupted in Acts (see 10:44; 18:14; 23:7; 26:24), and as a literary device they aid the reader in detecting the speech's climactic point, which is scored exactly when the auditors interrupt the speaker! In this case, the Jerusalem Jews interrupt Paul when he implies that Gentiles will share in Israel's salvation. In fact, however, interrupted speeches are already complete.

698. Cf. Haenchen, *The Acts of the Apostles*, 633.

699. See B. Witherington, *The Acts of the Apostles: A Socio-Rhetorical Commentary* (Grand Rapids: Eerdmans, 1998) 676-77, for illustrations of various Roman scourges, any one of which was used to flog Paul. Flogging was legalized torture and was used in Roman Palestine to extract testimony from an accused party, typically an alien, slave, or someone from the lower classes, and only when legal briefs could not resolve a case. In this sense, then, flogging is a reflection of the tribune's indecision.

700. See J. Neyrey, "Luke's Social Location of Paul," in *History, Literature, and Society in the Book of Acts*, ed. B. Witherington (Cambridge: Cambridge University Press, 1996) 276-78.

ited, whereas Lysias's is purchased at great cost (v. 28). Citizen Lysias surely understood that among the most important rights of Roman citizenship is that of a fair public trial for a citizen accused of any crime. In Paul's case, there is no evidence of a crime—indeed, accusations, once scrutinized, turn out to be religious rather than civil in nature. For this reason, Lysias is rightly afraid of the consequences of breaking Roman law at this point (v. 29; see also 16:38-39), an offense that does not respect one's status and could result in his loss of face and high position. His fear of public embarrassment may help to explain why from this moment forward he is more restrained in his handling of Paul's legal case.

**22:30.** This transitional text reflects a more cautious Lysias intent on determining the legitimacy of the accusations leveled against Paul by his Jewish antagonists. He first releases him and then convenes the Sanhedrin by his civil authority (or that of the current Roman procurator in Palestine). Paul is the latest prophet-like-Jesus to follow the Lord in appearing before this council (cf. Luke 22:66; see 4:15; 5:21; 6:12). Paul does so, however, as a pious Pharisee and a solid Roman citizen with the protective support of the empire and the theological support of the Pharisees on the council. It will make a difference: Paul does not die in Jerusalem.

**23:1-10.** The story of Paul's informal hearing before Jerusalem's Sanhedrin is as strange as it is strategic. The meeting is arranged by Lysias to understand more clearly the religious nature of the Jewish protest against Paul's mission to the nations; it is another venue for his ongoing interrogation of Paul. By this time, Lysias understands that the issues are "nationalistic" (= Jewish) and that he has no real reason to retain Paul as a prisoner. One might even suppose that Lysias has taken an interest in Paul and that this hearing is more for his personal edification than for determinng Paul's legal standing.

For this reason the intemperate proceedings are difficult for a rational outsider such as Lysias to follow. The rules of jurisprudence certainly seem different before this council than before a Roman tribunal! Why would the high priest Ananias take offense at Paul's declaration of his "clear conscience" (v. 1) and then respond with physical abuse rather than reasoned rebuttal (v. 2)? What is

the meaning of Paul's prophecy and name-calling in retaliation (v. 3)? And why should Paul cede his high moral ground so quickly, especially with a disingenuous comment (vv. 4-5)? Paul's attempt to explain the reason for his trial (v. 6) only provokes old rivalries, and the meeting degenerates into a shouting match over Paul's religious legitimacy. Roman Lysias is left on the sidelines scratching his head over the legal politics of these Palestinian Jews (vv. 7-9). In any case, this utterly fruitless hearing ends as it began with Paul held in protective custody (v. 10).

Yet, the reader of Acts will recognize what Lysias does not: Paul's claim of Pharisaic orthodoxy (v. 6), and the division within the Sanhedrin that follows (vv. 7-9) envisages Israel's theological crisis. Israel is divided over the issue of a resurrected Messiah and therefore its national "hope" is never fully realized during these "last days" of salvation's history.

**23:1.** Paul begins his self-defense in good faith. His first statement begins with the salutation, "Brothers" (see v. 6; 1:16), which intends to stage his remarks for an audience of religious peers. For this reason, he asserts the constancy of his good reputation before God. Paul's appeal to the moral norm of a "clear conscience" may well be considered provocative in this Jewish setting since it is an idea not found in the OT but one known among Hellenist moral philosophers of the day (cf. Rom 2:15; 1 Corinthians 8–10; 2 Cor 11:12; 2 Tim 1:3).[701] Its meaning, however, is plain enough: Paul asserts that the internal motivation for all his practices is zeal to perform God's will. Haenchen wonders whether this includes Paul's behaviors prior to his conversion, such as his participation in Stephen's execution or the persecution of the church (see, e.g., 7:58; 8:1-3; 9:1; 22:4).[702] But Paul's claim obtains to his "conscience before God" and not his behaviors per se.

**23:2-5.** The motive for Ananias's order for members of his entourage standing next to Paul "to strike him on the mouth" (v. 2; cf. John 18:22), presumably in response to what he has just said, is unclear and unreasonable in any

---

701. For a full discussion of "clear conscience," see R. Wall, "Conscience," in *The Anchor Bible Dictionary,* 6 vols. (Garden City, N.Y.: Doubleday, 1992) 1:1128-30.

702. Haenchen, *The Acts of the Apostles,* 637.

case.[703] More certain is the intent of Paul's prophecy that "God will strike you, you white-washed wall!" (v. 3). On the face of it, his curse responds to the illegality of Ananias's attack upon him. With biting irony, then, Paul deigns to rebuke this high priest for judging him "according to the law" and yet acting against him "in violation of the law"—probably alluding to Lev 19:15, which condemns the punishment of the powerless innocent.

Adding texture to this surface meaning, Paul's prophecy of Ananias's demise echoes Deut 28:22 and so locates it in a biblical setting where God's curses are listed "on account of the evil of your deeds, because you have forsaken me" (Deut 28:20). An angry Paul, therefore, interprets the council's peremptory strike against him as evidence that it rejects his mission and message and, therefore, Israel's God. The other intertextual echo is of Ezek 13:10 (cf. Matt 23:27), recalling the prophet's condemnation of the hypocrisy of Israel's leaders by calling them builders of a weak wall that is obscured by a veneer of white paint. That is, Ananias's rejection of Paul's prophetic ministry among the Jews incriminates not only the high priest but also all of unrepentant Israel, who blindly follow his spiritual leadership.

Trading biblical allusions, supporters of Ananias's prerogatives as president of the Sanhedrin scold Paul for insulting "God's high priest" (v. 4), which Paul accepts by citing Torah's injunction that "you shall not speak evil of a leader of your people" (v. 5*b;* cf. Exod 22:27). He is after all Torah observant, and his appeal to the alluded Scripture warrants a public apology. But how is the reader to understand Paul's remark, "I did not realize that he was high priest"? Surely he knows Ananias is the high priest and evidently understands the council well enough to exploit its internal dynamic (see v. 6)! Johnson's solution seems right that Paul's remark is ironical and intends to be read as a "prophetic criticism of the chief priest, whose behavior makes him 'unrecognizable'" since it did not accord with his spiritual status and religious function within Israel.[704] If Johnson's

point is taken, then Luke's portrait of the Sanhedrin in Acts continues to reflect its remarkable inability to pick up the irony of prophetic criticism (see 5:38-40).

**23:6.** At this point in these hearings, which already have collapsed, Paul attempts a "diversionary tactic," similar to that employed by Greek rhetors when public debates were not going their way,[705] that mixes the Sanhedrin's volatile chemistry of Pharisees and Sadducees who are political rivals for the religious affections of the Jewish people. Significantly, Paul for the first time publicly identifies himself as "a Pharisee, a son of Pharisees," although earlier he claimed that he observed the law strictly (22:3; see also 26:5; cf. Phil 3:5)—characteristic of the Pharisee—and was trained by the Pharisee scholar Gamaliel (22:3). During the course of his legal difficulties, Luke completes Paul's public profile for benefit of the reader: He is educated in Jerusalem, a citizen of Tarsus and Rome, and a member of the Pharisee party.[706]

The reason for doing so is theological, not political.[707] We should not think that Paul's rhetorical tactic is a clever maneuver to save his life, even though it does. Rather, its principal purpose is to single out the most critical element of his interpretation of Scripture in order to place it strategically within the framework of "official" Judaism: "I am on trial concerning the hope of the resurrection of the dead."[708] The theological tradition of his Pharisaism, adapted to the church's belief in the resurrected Jesus, is the essence of the Jewish heritage of the church, without which the church cannot be the church.[709] While distinctive in their

---

703. Ananias was high priest from 47–58 CE and probably at the height of his popularity when Paul stood before him in Jerusalem. He is remembered for his volatility and his wealth—and for his assassination because of pro-Roman policies in 66 CE. See Josephus *The Jewish War* 2:426-29, 441-442. See also J. A. Fitzmyer, *The Acts of the Apostles,* AB 31 (Garden City, N.Y.: Doubleday, 1998) 717.

704. Johnson, *The Acts of the Apostles,* 397.

705. G. Kennedy, *New Testament Interpretation Through Rhetorical Criticism* (Chapel Hill: University of North Carolina Press, 1984) 135.

706. The apparent contradiction between this statement and Paul's epistolary claim that he *was* a Pharisee but is no longer (Phil 3:5) has been explained both as a reflection of Luke's theological interest to portray a Jewish Paul or as Paul's rhetorical interest to portray the "dogs" of Philippi in unfavorable light; the truth is probably someplace in between.

707. By Luke's day, however, only the Pharisees had survived the tragedy of Rome's destruction of Jerusalem; they were the dominant religious elite in the diaspora that ensued. The Sadducees were no more because the various institutions they controlled were no more after 70 CE.

708. Paul's confession is a hendiadys, a literary device in which two or more terms are joined by the conjunctive "and" so that no term is subordinate to the other(s). Thus, "hope" and "resurrection of the dead" refer to the same idea: Israel's hope is its future resurrection from the dead (Dan 12:2-3; cf. 2 Macc 7; Isa 26:19).

709. J. Jervell, *Die Apostelgeschichte,* KEK 3 (Göttingen: Vandenhoeck & Ruprecht, 1998) 555-56, points out that by this logic the Pharisaism of Paul is also the Pharisaism of Christ.

attitudes and performance of the torah, it is finally the Pharisees' *theological* distinction from the Sadducees that is most important: the "hope" that a faithful God would fulfill the biblical promise of a "resurrected" (= restored) Israel and that God's eternal reign would commence within its history (see 1:6). It is into this same theological soil that the Christian gospel is planted. Paul and the other inspired missionaries of Acts therefore proclaim the gospel that God's resurrection of Messiah Jesus is an act of divine faithfulness, first for the Jews and then also for the nations.

**23:7-9.** Luke's brief summary of the "dissension between the Pharisees and the Sadducees" illustrates in microcosm the realization of Simeon's prophecy of a divided Israel over God's gospel of the resurrected Messiah (cf. Luke 2:35). Israel's division is finally over different conceptions of its future with God. On the one hand, "Sadducees say there is no resurrection" (v. 8*a*). The theological purchase of adding "angel or spirit" is not immediately clear. There is little evidence that Sadducees denied the existence of angels and spirits, nor is it realistic since they were conservative torah-literalists and torah recognizes both angels and spirits; however, this exclusion "entirely corresponds to their this-worldly religion."[710] Fitzmyer suggests that both terms are appositive to the resurrection, specifying modes of it:[711] in the resurrection, Israel will become like angels (cf. Matt 22:30), or the resurrected "physical" (= historical) Israel will be in some sense a "spiritual" Israel (cf. 1 Cor 15:44).

On the other hand, since "Pharisees acknowledge all three" (v. 8*b*), the Sanhedrin Pharisees must at least admit the plausibility of Paul's earlier testimony of a christophany (see 22:7-11)[712] and allow the possibility that there is "nothing wrong with this man" (v. 9)—nor, the reader presumes, with his message of the resurrected Messiah. Of course, these erstwhile supporters of Paul are yet nonbelievers, so what Paul clearly reports as a vision of the living Jesus the Pharisees allow might be a "spirit or an angel."

**23:10.** From Rome's perspective nothing is settled, nor is it entirely possible to turn to the Sanhedrin for help in explaining its theological disagreements with the Way. From the reader's perspective the leadership team of official Israel is in shambles, forever fighting among itself and without competence or patience to debate the merits of a case. The Sanhedrin is no better than a common mob (see 21:29-30); both "become violent" and threaten to "tear Paul to pieces" because of their theological differences, and so the tribune in both cases must intervene and safeguard Paul back to the soldiers' barracks at the Fortress Antonia (see 21:34; 22:24).

**23:11.** Paul's vision in the Jerusalem prison is the second of a Lukan triad (see also 19:21; 27:24), indicating that Rome is the city of his destiny: "You must [δεῖ *dei*] bear witness also in Rome." The repeated use of *dei* makes it clear to the reader that Paul's future includes a mission to Rome as a "divine necessity" and that no evil can subvert what God has planned. This point is highlighted by timing, since each revelation comes to Paul at a moment of personal suffering, when it is not at all certain that the historical circumstances he finds himself in will allow God's will to be done. The intent of each vision, then, is to encourage God's servant—"Keep up your courage"—and to assert that the plans of a sovereign God will be executed, as unlikely as it may seem at the moment. The interplay between Paul's personal courage and God's transcendent sovereignty stands at the center of Luke's theological conception and shapes the plotline for the rest of Acts.[713]

**23:12-22.** This scene of conspiratorial intrigue tells of Paul's transfer from protective custody in Jerusalem under the Roman tribune Claudius Lysias to Caesarea, the setting of his formal trial before the Roman governor of Palestine, Antonius Felix. Paul's situation in Jerusalem has become ever more tenuous as a group of forty Jews consecrate themselves to carry out an assassination plot against him, evidently with the blessing of certain Sadducees on the Sanhedrin (vv. 12-15).

---

710. E. Haenchen, *The Acts of the Apostles* (Philadelphia: Westminster, 1971) 638.

711. Fitzmyer, *The Acts of the Apostles,* 719.

712. The KJV, which follows the *textus receptus,* supplies the conclusion "let us not fight against God" to the implied conditional "if a spirit or angel has spoken to him." In doing so the scribes make allusion to another Sanhedrin Pharisee, Gamaliel's, earlier commentary on the Twelve's ministry in Jerusalem that "if [the apostles' ministry/teaching] is of God, you will not be able to overthrow them—in that case you may even be found fighting against God" (5:39 NRSV).

713. Cf. C. H. Talbert, *Reading Acts* (New York: Crossroad, 1997) 203-15, who contends that 23:11 leads the entire "thought-unit" that concludes with Agrippa's verdict of Paul's innocence, though his appeal to Caesar must also be honored (26:32). The subtext of Paul's various legal steps toward Rome is that "the plan of God cannot be blocked."

While certain that the assassination plot will never succeed because of the Lord's prophecy that Paul "must" see Rome (v. 11), the reader may still wonder what provokes this intense hatred of Paul among Jews. The narrator, who is concerned only to describe the tension between them, does not explain the motives of Paul's antagonists. Their hostility toward him is evidently not with a "Jewish" Paul: His practices and pedigree are traditional. While the reader is aware that Paul's mission to the Gentiles fulfills biblical prophecy (see 13:47), it nevertheless threatens a variety of working definitions of Israel and Israel's salvation that are tied explicitly to nationalistic and ethnocentric fervor felt throughout Palestine at the time. To these Jews who plot against him, Paul is a traitor (see 21:28) and must be executed as such. Even within the church there is a deeply felt concern that Paul's mission to the nations threatens Israel's identity as God's people (see 21:21). This concern is surely exacerbated by the departure of Pauline-led congregations from various urban synagogues into self-standing house churches (see 18:7; 19:9), where Jewish leaders can no longer exercise their traditional leadership over the theological formation and social identity of these new believers.

There is also the sense that Paul's message about Jesus threatens Israel in a similar manner. Not only does his interpretation from Scripture to support the Lord's resurrection provoke long-standing tensions between the Pharisees and the Sadducees (see v. 6), his claim of the Lord's messiahship also provokes antagonism between messianists and non-messianists within religious Israel. The gospel about Jesus divides Israel. Because the plotline of Luke's narrative so closely follows Paul, the reader is easily more persuaded to think that Paul's troubles are due to his own "unconventional" practices or "controversial" profile. But Luke's account of Paul's testimony is at odds with this conclusion: He is a pious Jew and a solid citizen. I suggest that whatever parallelism the reader notes between Luke's story of Paul and Jesus' final journey to and passion in Jerusalem may well intend to draw attention to Jesus and not to an element of Luke's Pauline apologia: Paul is in trouble because of what he proclaims of the resurrected Jesus and for a restored Israel.

**23:12-15.** Acts provides very little information about either the identity or motivation of the forty Jews who joined together "in a conspiracy and bound themselves by an oath . . . until they had killed Paul" (vv. 12-13). Lysias's earlier reference to the sicarii or assassins (see 21:38) alerts the reader to the general unrest in Palestine where such violent activism was a familiar marker on the political landscape. Whatever the precise motive behind this deadly plot against Paul, it is surely religious fanaticism—indicated by their solemn oath and fast from food and drink—that drives the plotters. These are devout Jews who are dedicated to their murderous mission out of zeal to serve God and Israel. Luke no doubt intends the reader to contrast the aims of their vow with those of the Nazirite vow earlier completed by Paul and members of the Jewish church (see 21:26).

Their plan requires the cooperation of certain "chief priests and elders" (v. 14), probably among the council's Sadducean membership only, given the earlier reluctance of the council's Pharisees to condemn Paul (see v. 9). They are to request that Lysias bring Paul from the barracks of Antonia Fortress to the courtroom of the Sanhedrin, where council members would question Paul to gain "more accurate information [διαγινώσκω *diaginōskō*]" about his case (v. 15 NIV). Since *diaginōskō* is a technical term for questioning a witness to settle a case, the request would be in keeping with the tribune's wishes, even though Lysias may well have hesitated, given his earlier experience with the Sanhedrin! The assassination attempt would take place during Paul's transit from the barracks to the courtroom.

**23:16-22.** Paul's nephew, a "young man" (νεανίας *neanias*, v. 17) in his twenties, overhears rumors of the ambush and gains access to Paul (perhaps as a relative) to warn him about the danger (v. 16). The severely compressed staging of Paul's escape, which tells nothing of the circumstances that allow his nephew to learn of the plans for this "secret" conspiracy, is indicative of a narrator who wants his reader to be interested only in the safety of his central character. In that regard, this passage contains elements of the literary theme of God protecting the imprisoned servant from bodily harm by liberating intervention. The liberating agent in this case is neither angelic nor natural phenomena but a family member. The loyalty of family members who come to the rescue of another, however, is a familiar convention of ancient literature and one that is glossed by Paul's earlier reference to his family's Jerusalem residence (see 22:3).[714]

The nephew's retelling of the plot for the tribune's benefit (vv. 20-21) confirms what the reader was earlier told in a Jewish setting (see v. 15). The prompt and pliant responses, first of the centurion (vv. 17-18) and then of Lysias, envisage the nature of Paul's relations with Rome in contrast to his Jewish opposition, making the reader more sympathetic to Luke's depiction of a Rome wary of Israel's intramural squabbles. That an unnamed young man should alert an important Roman tribune that "the Jews" intend to dupe the official, and then challenge him not to be persuaded by them (v. 21) enhances Rome's popular appeal while cultivating a healthy distrust of Paul's enemies, symbolized by the secrecy of Lysias's liaison with the nephew (v. 22). Sharply put, Paul has more status in secular society as a Roman citizen than in Israel as an observant Jew and prophetic carrier of God's word. This is not to claim that Rome's perspective on Paul and his mission is favorable; rather, it is simply to assert that the Rome of Acts is more obedient to its constitutional law than unrepentant Israel of Acts is to its biblical law.

**23:23-35.** The "Jerusalem" phase of Paul's trials concludes with a change of venue from Antipatris (v. 31) to Caesarea (v. 33), where Paul will be formally tried before Governor Felix (v. 35). This is accomplished by accompaniment of a large escort of four hundred and seventy troops at a late and unexpected hour (vv. 23-25). The impression made by this clandestine military operation is that Paul's safety as a Roman citizen is of paramount concern, as evidenced by the official letter sent by Tribune Lysias to Governor Felix (vv. 26-30). In his letter, which functions as an important element of Paul's whole apologia, Lysias at last gives his verdict of Paul's innocence and so provides the narrator's summary of this initial phase of Paul's legal problems. His letter also makes clear that Rome's interest in Paul is self-centered and not theological. For this reason, no real change in Paul's situation takes place, and so upon reading Lysias's letter, Felix orders that Paul be kept im-

prisoned to await the next phase of his trials (vv. 31-35).

**23:23-25.** A detachment of roughly half of those under Lysias's command in Jerusalem are assigned to safeguard Paul's transfer to Felix. Some have regarded these as inflated numbers that reflect a convention of Luke's storytelling: God's plans for Paul are being safeguarded by Rome as well. If, however, Paul is a solid citizen and an innocent man under a death threat, then the tribune would naturally want to take extra precautions in guaranteeing Paul's safe arrival into the jurisdiction of another official (= Felix). The tribune's reputation as a soldier is at stake. Luke's subsequent comment that the bulk of these troops returned to Jerusalem after taking Paul to Antipatris (vv. 31-32), about forty-five miles northwest of Jerusalem and out of harm's way, makes sound military sense and seems to confirm the story's reliability.

**23:26-30.** Claudius Felix was the co-procurator of Roman Palestine and "governor" of Judea (52–60 CE). The Roman historian Tacitus says of Felix, a freedman with considerable influence on the emperor: "With all cruelty and lust [he] wielded the power of a king, with the mentality of a slave."[715] Perhaps for this reason Lysias' letter is carefully crafted to state the legal facts as he (and the reader) have ultimately come to understand them. His letter is an example of *litterae dimissoriae* (notice to a higher court) sent by a Roman provincial official (Claudius Lysias) and addressed to his superior ("his Excellency the governor Felix") to appeal a legal case ("This man was seized by the Jews . . . but when I had learned").[716] The facts are as the reader knows them to be: Paul is a Roman citizen who was accused and interrogated by other Jews for indiscretions outside the bounds of Roman jurisprudence; he was taken into protective custody because of a death threat and is now sent to a higher authority for legal review.

Lysias's epistolary narrative generally agrees with Luke's, but it also reflects careful editing to enhance his position with Rome. For example, the reader knows the incriminating circumstances by

---

714. L. T. Johnson, *The Acts of the Apostles,* SP 5 (Collegeville, Minn.: Liturgical, 1992) 404.

715. Tacitus *Histories* 5.9. See also J. A. Fitzmyer, *The Acts of the Apostles,* AB 31 (Garden City, N.Y.: Doubleday, 1998) 727. Felix married well and often; however, he was also an anti-Semite with particular animus against Jewish zealots, whom he treated so brutally that he was dismissed as Roman procurator in 60 CE.

716. Fitzmyer, *The Acts of the Apostles,* 726.

which Lysais learned that Paul was a Roman citizen and, therefore, "rescued him"; yet, he takes full credit in his letter without indicating his blunders along the way. We also learn from this letter that Paul's legal troubles are not yet over: "I sent [Paul] to you at once, ordering his accusers to state before you what they have against him" (v. 30). This concluding statement of Lysias's intentions sets the stage for what follows in chap. 24 and for the reiteration of unrepentant Israel's case against Paul brought forward by their prosecuting attorney, Tertullus (see 24:5-6). Finally, Lysias's letter provides Felix with Rome's legal perspective by which he should interpret these accusations: "I found that [Paul] was accused concerning questions of their law, but was charged with nothing deserving death or imprisonment" (v. 29). The reader is even more convinced that God's plans for a Pauline mission in Rome will have found willing but unwitting collaborators in the various pagan officials of Roman Palestine.

**23:31-35.** Upon arrival in Caesarea (23:33) and reading of Lysias's *litterae dimissoriae* (v. 34*a*), Felix holds a preliminary hearing to clarify the issue of jurisdiction (v. 34*b*). Although he had the option of referring Paul back to Tarsus and to the regional legate, Felix chose not to for reasons that Luke does not specify. Witherington speculates that he kept Paul's case in Caesarea because of his relations with the Cilician-Syrian legate and to make traveling plans more convenient for the plaintiffs.[717]

Paul is kept under guard in Herod's *praetorium* (= "headquarters") during his trial. The *praetorium* was a multipurpose building, serving both as the official residence of the region and as a venue for the governor to render justice. Paul is still a Roman prisoner, unjustly disposed, but he is guarded by Rome in a safe and comfortable place.

717. Witherington, *The Acts of the Apostles,* 702.

# REFLECTIONS

**1.** "Listen to the defense that I now make before you" (22:1 NRSV). The series of speeches Paul makes in this portion of Acts to defend himself against charges of criminal activity may well provide a pattern for the believer's apologia, even if in less stressful circumstances. The rhetorical function of each part of this first defense speech, its narrative setting, and the ethos it cultivates within Luke's narrative world envisage important features of an effective Christian apologetic. In general terms, the motive of Paul's apologia is to defend his mission and message as the will of God. While the subtext of his speech is therefore theological, its details are biographical. Paul offers his story as sufficient evidence that his mission and message are coordinate with God's redemptive purposes for repentant Israel according to the Scriptures. In this regard, his familial background (22:3-5), his personal experience (22:6-11), and the testimony of relevant others (pious Ananias) in support of his prophetic vocation (22:12-16) coupled with his own testimony (22:17-21) contend for Paul's understanding of his conversion to Jesus and his calling to the nations. Characteristic of all his speeches in Acts, Paul employs the cultural idiom of his audience when presenting his case. Thus, he defends his conversion and mission to a Jewish audience in their official language as a Jewish insider who adheres to the core symbols of Jewish faith. The language, form, and idiom of his apologia are adapted to changing audiences and settings, always to defend the terms of his mission.

If as Christian apologists we pattern our presentations after that of Paul, we will not be primarily interested in converting others: No appeal for repentance is given, no offer of salvation is made in the text. The purpose of a believer's apologia is to defend his or her own experience of God in the idiom of the audience as a particular expression of the manner and purpose of God's presence in the world. In this sense, the material of Christian apologetics does not consist mainly of various viable evidences (historical, archaeological, scientific, linguistic, biblical, cultural, and so on) marshaled to "prove" the truth claims of the gospel; it rather consists mainly of stories that tell of personal experiences of Christian conversions and vocation. The explicit intent of these spiritual biographies, especially in hostile settings, is not to convince and convert the rational non-believer to Jesus; rather, it is to explain clearly one's own faith in the idiom of non-believers—to give them good reason for the "hope that is in [us]" (1 Pet 3:15).

**2.** "Up to this point they listened to [Paul], but then they shouted, 'Away with such a fellow from the earth! For he should not be allowed to live!' " (22:22 NRSV). What is the reader of Acts to make of the passionate and violent responses within Israel to Paul's declaration that God's Messiah has called him to go to the unclean Gentiles (see 22:21)? Why do pious people conspire together to kill God's prophet? In part, the hostile response to Paul is due to the parochialism of his opponents, who define God's salvation in nationalistic terms. Had Paul claimed the Lord sent him with a word for Israel alone, his Jewish auditors may have continued to listen to him. Had he included the purification requirements of the Sadducees in his message of the resurrected Messiah, the Sanhedrin may have united behind him instead of dividing because of him. The danger of the gospel is that it makes particular and absolute claims about who God is, what God does, and to whom God belongs; and these claims sometimes challenge our current beliefs and traditional sensibilities. Paul's Jewish opponents disagree with his sense of vocation, as they also disagree with his interpretation of Scripture, because these are particular expressions of an absolute truth that imperil their own social requirements and religious beliefs. It is hard for any of us, no matter how spiritual-minded and earnest we are, to embrace a version of "the truth" that includes those we exclude and grants access to God's liberating grace via a different route than the one we have taken.

**3.** "When Paul noticed that some were Sadducees and others were Pharisees, he called out in the council, 'Brothers, I am a Pharisee, a son of Pharisees. I am on trial concerning the hope of the resurrection of the dead' " (23:6 NRSV). The reader of Luke's story of Paul's legal troubles cannot help but admire how clever Paul is. He is not only an effective orator but he also manages and manipulates the legal proceedings to his advantage. He inserts new information about himself at opportune moments, as he did when allowing that he is a Roman citizen at the very moment when Lysias is about to torture him (see 22:25). When standing before the Sanhedrin, he again rescues himself from a difficult situation by craftily turning his interrogation into a shouting match between the council's competing political parties. In manipulating the legal proceedings to his benefit by persuasive rhetoric and crowd control, Paul exemplifies what Jesus admonished all his disciples to be in the midst of wolves: "Be wise as serpents and innocent as doves" (Matt 10:16 NRSV).

# ACTS 24:1-27, PAUL'S ROMAN TRIAL IN CAESAREA

**NIV**

**24** Five days later the high priest Ananias went down to Caesarea with some of the elders and a lawyer named Tertullus, and they brought their charges against Paul before the governor. [2]When Paul was called in, Tertullus presented his case before Felix: "We have enjoyed a long period of peace under you, and your foresight has brought about reforms in this nation. [3]Everywhere and in every way, most excellent

**NRSV**

**24** Five days later the high priest Ananias came down with some elders and an attorney, a certain Tertullus, and they reported their case against Paul to the governor. [2]When Paul[a] had been summoned, Tertullus began to accuse him, saying:

"Your Excellency,[b] because of you we have long enjoyed peace, and reforms have been made

[a] Gk *he*    [b] Gk lacks *Your Excellency*

## NIV

Felix, we acknowledge this with profound gratitude. [4]But in order not to weary you further, I would request that you be kind enough to hear us briefly.

[5]"We have found this man to be a troublemaker, stirring up riots among the Jews all over the world. He is a ringleader of the Nazarene sect [6]and even tried to desecrate the temple; so we seized him. [8]By[a] examining him yourself you will be able to learn the truth about all these charges we are bringing against him."

[9]The Jews joined in the accusation, asserting that these things were true.

[10]When the governor motioned for him to speak, Paul replied: "I know that for a number of years you have been a judge over this nation; so I gladly make my defense. [11]You can easily verify that no more than twelve days ago I went up to Jerusalem to worship. [12]My accusers did not find me arguing with anyone at the temple, or stirring up a crowd in the synagogues or anywhere else in the city. [13]And they cannot prove to you the charges they are now making against me. [14]However, I admit that I worship the God of our fathers as a follower of the Way, which they call a sect. I believe everything that agrees with the Law and that is written in the Prophets, [15]and I have the same hope in God as these men, that there will be a resurrection of both the righteous and the wicked. [16]So I strive always to keep my conscience clear before God and man.

[17]"After an absence of several years, I came to Jerusalem to bring my people gifts for the poor and to present offerings. [18]I was ceremonially clean when they found me in the temple courts doing this. There was no crowd with me, nor was I involved in any disturbance. [19]But there are some Jews from the province of Asia, who ought to be here before you and bring charges if they have anything against me. [20]Or these who are here should state what crime they found in me when I stood before the Sanhedrin— [21]unless it was this one thing I shouted as I stood in their

[a] *6-8 Some manuscripts* him and wanted to judge him according to our law. [7]But the commander, Lysias, came and with the use of much force snatched him from our hands [8]and ordered his accusers to come before you. By

## NRSV

for this people because of your foresight. [3]We welcome this in every way and everywhere with utmost gratitude. [4]But, to detain you no further, I beg you to hear us briefly with your customary graciousness. [5]We have, in fact, found this man a pestilent fellow, an agitator among all the Jews throughout the world, and a ringleader of the sect of the Nazarenes.[a] [6]He even tried to profane the temple, and so we seized him.[b] [8]By examining him yourself you will be able to learn from him concerning everything of which we accuse him."

[9]The Jews also joined in the charge by asserting that all this was true.

[10]When the governor motioned to him to speak, Paul replied:

"I cheerfully make my defense, knowing that for many years you have been a judge over this nation. [11]As you can find out, it is not more than twelve days since I went up to worship in Jerusalem. [12]They did not find me disputing with anyone in the temple or stirring up a crowd either in the synagogues or throughout the city. [13]Neither can they prove to you the charge that they now bring against me. [14]But this I admit to you, that according to the Way, which they call a sect, I worship the God of our ancestors, believing everything laid down according to the law or written in the prophets. [15]I have a hope in God—a hope that they themselves also accept—that there will be a resurrection of both[c] the righteous and the unrighteous. [16]Therefore I do my best always to have a clear conscience toward God and all people. [17]Now after some years I came to bring alms to my nation and to offer sacrifices. [18]While I was doing this, they found me in the temple, completing the rite of purification, without any crowd or disturbance. [19]But there were some Jews from Asia—they ought to be here before you to make an accusation, if they have anything against me. [20]Or let these men here tell what crime they had found when I stood before the council, [21]unless it was this one sentence that I called out while standing before them, 'It is about

[a] Gk *Nazoreans*   [b] Other ancient authorities add *and we would have judged him according to our law.* [7]*But the chief captain Lysias came and with great violence took him out of our hands,* [8]*commanding his accusers to come before you.*   [c] Other ancient authorities read *of the dead, both of*

## NIV

presence: 'It is concerning the resurrection of the dead that I am on trial before you today.' "

²²Then Felix, who was well acquainted with the Way, adjourned the proceedings. "When Lysias the commander comes," he said, "I will decide your case." ²³He ordered the centurion to keep Paul under guard but to give him some freedom and permit his friends to take care of his needs.

²⁴Several days later Felix came with his wife Drusilla, who was a Jewess. He sent for Paul and listened to him as he spoke about faith in Christ Jesus. ²⁵As Paul discoursed on righteousness, self-control and the judgment to come, Felix was afraid and said, "That's enough for now! You may leave. When I find it convenient, I will send for you." ²⁶At the same time he was hoping that Paul would offer him a bribe, so he sent for him frequently and talked with him.

²⁷When two years had passed, Felix was succeeded by Porcius Festus, but because Felix wanted to grant a favor to the Jews, he left Paul in prison.

## NRSV

the resurrection of the dead that I am on trial before you today.' "

22But Felix, who was rather well informed about the Way, adjourned the hearing with the comment, "When Lysias the tribune comes down, I will decide your case." 23Then he ordered the centurion to keep him in custody, but to let him have some liberty and not to prevent any of his friends from taking care of his needs.

24Some days later when Felix came with his wife Drusilla, who was Jewish, he sent for Paul and heard him speak concerning faith in Christ Jesus. 25And as he discussed justice, self-control, and the coming judgment, Felix became frightened and said, "Go away for the present; when I have an opportunity, I will send for you." 26At the same time he hoped that money would be given him by Paul, and for that reason he used to send for him very often and converse with him.

27After two years had passed, Felix was succeeded by Porcius Festus; and since he wanted to grant the Jews a favor, Felix left Paul in prison.

# COMMENTARY

The second phase of the legal proceedings against Paul takes place before the Roman Procurator Felix in Caesarea, the provincial capital of Roman Palestine. Moreover, for the only time in Acts Paul is actually prosecuted. Both prosecutorial and defense speeches, and the legal protocol that organizes the plotline of this passage, follow standard Roman judicial procedures and the rhetorical conventions of professional orators (= lawyers).[718] Accordingly, the prosecution schedules its trial against the accused (24:1; see 23:35); the prosecuting attorney (Tertullus) presents the charges (24:2-8); the defendant (Paul) then responds (24:10-21); after that the case is remanded to the judge, who either renders a verdict or postpones it indefinitely (24:22-27). The

result of this carefully crafted scene is a more precise understanding of the "legal" issues that separate Paul and the Way from official Judaism.

Tertullus accuses Paul of four illegalities: He is a pest, an agitator, the ringleader of a Jewish "sect," and one who tried to defile the Temple. What is lacking in these allegations is any clear mention of Paul's mission to the Gentiles, and for obvious reasons: Paul's agitation "among all Jews throughout the world" is theological, and this present conflict is Jewish and religious and not Roman and political. Thus, at the heart of Paul's rebuttal of the charges (24:11-13) and counter accusation (24:18b-21) is his "confession" of the Way's continuity with Jewish belief (24:14-15) and behavior (24:16-18a).

The reader of Acts has heard all of this before in different words and settings. If any doubt lingers in the reader's mind concerning the spiritual authority of Paul and his lasting importance for the whole church, it should end with his apologia before

---

718. For an analysis of these forensic speeches in their ancient setting, see B. Winter, "Official Proceedings and Forensic Speeches in Acts 24–26," in *The Book of Acts in First Century Setting,* ed. B. W. Winter and A. Clarke, 6 vols. (Grand Rapids: Eerdmans, 1993–98) 1:305-36, who observes that Luke's narrative "is a cameo of some of the complexities of criminal litigation in the first century" (335).

Felix. He is no criminal, no maverick, no madman, no seller of snake oil, no intellectual lightweight or religious mediocrity; the Paul of Acts is a prophet of God whose personal intentions are above reproach, whose confession of faith is thoroughly orthodox, whose religious and social practices are blameless, and whose proclamation is rightly concentrated on Israel's hope in the resurrection of the dead. These are the very prejudgments of Paul that interpreters of the Pauline letters brings with them as they glean meaning from them for the church.

**24:1-2a.** The constituency of the Jewish delegation that arrives from Jerusalem to prosecute official Judaism's case against Paul is important to determine in advance of the trial. Acts includes only "the high priest Ananias . . . with some elders" along with the "attorney" (ῥήτωρ *rhētōr*) Tertullus who may not even be Jewish.[719] Given the council's evident division along party lines on the question of Paul's purity (see 23:9) and the implied purpose of Ananias's appearance in Caesarea to broker his influence, it seems plausible that the elders he brought with him were Sadducees. The Pharisaic cast of Paul's "confession" (24:14-18*a*) and his concluding assertion (24:21), even though expressed as quintessentially Jewish, contains an implicit polemical edge. Moreover, the Jerusalem delegation includes no Jew from the diaspora who may have been able to rebut Paul's statement that "some Jews from Asia" had falsely accused him (24:19). The impression made on the reader is that this legal team came to Caesarea without a carefully crafted brief, having only "five days" to prepare for trial against the more clever and innocent Paul.

**24:2b-4.** Tertullus's opening remarks (the exordium) conform to the rhetorical conventions of a legal argument in the ancient world. On the face of it, his shameless use of flattery intends to establish good rapport with Felix so that he will be more favorably disposed to his case against Paul. More important, however, Tertullus's description

of Felix's contribution to Jewish well-being is carefully contrived to relate directly to his allegations against Paul. That is, he wishes to convey the sentiment, however true,[720] that Felix is able to render an appropriate verdict in this case as aptly demonstrated by his administrative talent and personal "foresight" (πρόνοια *pronoia*)—a virtue that denotes one's "innate benevolence" toward citizens.[721] These virtues of peacemaking and providence make him keenly alert to the problems "all the Jews" have with Paul. For example, the statement that "because of [Felix] we have long enjoyed peace" (v. 2) implies that he will consider viable the charge that Paul is a pest and agitator who disturbs the public order. It is for this reason that Tertullus can claim that his Sadducean clients "welcome this [case/judge] in every way and everywhere with utmost gratitude" (v. 3)—as well they might, given their political alliance with Roman authority in Palestine.

Since brevity is a rhetorical virtue, Tertullus wants "to detain [Felix] no further" and promises to proceed with "brief" remarks. His request that Felix listen with "customary graciousness" conveys the desire for a fair and reasoned hearing of legal matters, perhaps even to render his case with a "non-legalist interpretation."[722] This appeal may well indicate in advance that Tertullus is clever enough to realize that the case against Paul is sparse.

**24:5-8.** The four accusations Tertullus levels against Paul iterate the allegations of the "Jews from Asia" (see 21:28). The most important of these in this Roman setting is that of sedition: Paul is "an agitator [κινοῦντα στάσεις *kinounta staseis*; lit., "stirring up discord"] among all the Jews [πᾶσιν τοῖς Ἰουδαίοις *pasin tois Ioudaiois*] throughout the world [κατὰ τὴν οἰκουμένην *kata tēn oikoumenēn*]"[723] (v. 5; see also 17:6-7;

---

719. The argument that Tertullus is Jewish rests on his use of first person when listing Judaism's charges against Paul (see 24:5-6). But this may reflect only the attorney's professional obligation to identify with his clients. On the other hand, his impersonal reference to "all the Jews" might indicate that he is a Gentile, and his apparent distinction from "the Jews who joined in the charge" (24:9) might as well. The name "Tertullus" is not Jewish, and his training as a professional orator and knowledge of Roman law would necessarily have been secular.

720. Luke would have known the historian's negative verdict that Felix was a poor governor, and his use of *captatio benevolentiae*, using compliments for rhetorical effect, is ironic then of *God's* providence. The NRSV shifts "most excellent Felix" from v. 3 to the beginning of the speech in v. 2 ("Your Excellency").

721. Winter, "Official Proceedings and Forensic Speeches in Acts 24–26," 316.

722. C. K. Barrett, *A Critical and Exegetical Commentary on the Acts of the Apostles*, 2 vols, ICC (Edinburgh: T. & T. Clark, 1994, 1998) 2:1096.

723. Johnson, *The Acts of the Apostles*, 411, translates *oikoumenē* as "empire." Barrett, *Acts*, 2:1097, adds that the intent of the charge is to extend Jerusalem s grievance against Paul to be found in every part of the empire where there exists a Jewish community.

---

18:12). This phrase echoes the Jewish church's charge that Paul is teaching "all the Jews living among the Gentiles to forsake Moses" (see 21:21). From this intratext the reader more precisely understands the Jewish concern with Paul and the controversy his mission provokes: Paul's mission and message threaten to contaminate the identity of Israel as God's people in the world. One may think as well that when Tertullus speaks of "all the Jews throughout the world" he includes both repentant and unrepentant Jews in Israel's common concern with the effect of Paul's mission "among Jews."

This "was the right charge to bring against an opponent in criminal proceedings."[724] Paul is portrayed as a subversive who threatens the Pax Romana. The failure to bring Paul's opponents from diaspora Judaism in support of this critical charge must be considered a serious weakness in the prosecution's case, as Paul himself implies (see 24:19). It should be said, however, that the prosecutor's intent is only to interest Felix in the case so that he will seek out appropriate witnesses to interrogate in arriving at a fair verdict.

From the narrator's perspective the third charge, that Paul is "ringleader of the sect of the Nazarenes,"[725] is weighty for a different reason. The meaning of "sect" (αἵρεσις hairesis) is intentionally vague since Tertullus employs it here in a pejorative sense as an element of Paul's rabble-rousing, but Luke uses this same term earlier in Acts for the Sadducean (see 5:17) and Pharisaic (see 15:5) "parties." In this more positive sense, hairesis denotes a particular interpretive tradition within a wider, more inclusive religious order or philosophical school. This meaning is implied in Paul's retort to the charge when he defends "the Way" (= "sect of the Nazarenes") as a messianic movement within Judaism, similar to the Pharisaic and Sadducean parties, and not outside its theological, moral, or traditional boundaries (see 24:14-18).

From the perspective of the Sadducean delegation from Jerusalem, the final accusation is most condemning of Paul's spiritual authority: "He even tried to profane [βεβηλόω bebēloō] the temple, and so we seized him" (v. 6). The reader knows how flawed this charge is, and given its tepid expression when compared with its more forceful sounding during the Jerusalem riots (see 21:28) Tertullus would seem to agree: There is simply no evidence that would convict Paul of this sacrilege; in fact, Paul will later claim that his religious practices in the Temple purified him (see v. 18)! The relationship between this Pharisaic prophet-like-Jesus and the Temple, considered realistically, is ambivalent at best: Is he so different from Stephen in his desire to shift the epicenter of Israel's symbolic universe from the Temple to the risen Messiah? But the issue is a legal one and, based on the evidence the narrative supplies, Paul is innocent of this charge. In fact, the second half of Tertullus's accusation that the Jews "seized him" is a falsehood. The word κρατέω (krateō), weakly translated "seize," is a legal term for "arrest." Yet the reader knows that Paul's was no legal seizure by the temple police or Roman soldiers but an illegal beating by a mob.[726]

The peroratio, which calls on Felix to interrogate Paul "concerning everything of which we accuse him" (v. 8), concludes the prosecution's case. It is revealing that Felix refuses to question Paul at this juncture of the trial, as was customary during this species of legal procedure, and chooses to examine Paul in private and outside the bounds of the trial (= Roman law).

**24:9.** "The Jews" who "joined [συνεπιτίθημι synepitithēmi] the charge" represent those who support the charges Tertullus has articulated, including the high priest and his Sadducean entourage. Their support of Tertullus against Paul is expected: He is a Pharisee who asserts, "it is about the resurrection of the dead that I am on trial" (v. 21). The military term synepitithēmi denotes a unified and strategic attack against an enemy. Paul is public enemy number one of priestly Israel.

**24:10.** Luke's précis of Paul's apologia conforms to the rhetorical conventions of the ancient world, even though his exordium is more restrained than that of Tertullus. He, too,

724. Winter, "Official Proceedings and Forensic Speeches in Acts 24–26," 320.

725. The term, "sect of the Nazarenes" derives from "Jesus from Nazareth" (see 2:22; 6:14; 22:8); however, it resonates in biting irony with its Hebrew root נזר (nzr, "to dedicate" or "to consecrate") to recall that it is Paul who performs the law of the Nazirites (see 21:26). See Barrett, Acts, 2:1098.

726. Some MSS insert vv. 6b-8a here, as noted by the NRSV and the NIV.

expresses a rhetor's confidence in Felix's expertise to judge the affairs of "this [Jewish] nation." In particular, Acts confirms that Felix is able to negotiate between the theological claims of Paul's messianic "Way" and Tertullus's official Judaism to render a fair verdict in this case (see vv. 22-23), perhaps because his wife, Drusilla, possesses a keen understanding of Israel's religious culture (see v. 24).

**24:11-13.** The main body of Paul's speech consists of three proofs of his innocence in response to the four charges made by Tertullus. The first accusation is that Paul "is a pestilent fellow," guilty of sedition (see v. 5). But the Paul of Acts comes to the holy city "to worship in Jerusalem"; he is a pilgrim who intends to celebrate Pentecost with other pious Jews (see 20:16). Moreover, examination of the public record, including his notice to the temple priests that he had completed the Nazaritic vows (see 21:26), would show that he could have been in Jerusalem for no more than twelve days—hardly sufficient time to organize a rebellion against Judaism![727]

Paul rebuts Tertullus's claim that he is a "pest" by countering that "they cannot prove [παρίστημι *paristēmi*]" that he disputed with or stirred up anyone in the Temple, synagogues, or city. The legal term *paristēmi* suggests that without sufficient evidence Paul's accusers have no basis for their charge of sedition that Felix could then assess. What the prosecution itself has asked the judge to do (v. 8) is impossible.

**24:14-16.** Paul's second proof responds to the accusation that he is the ringleader of a religious sect. Rather than protest the charge, he cleverly "admits" (ὁμολογέω *homologeō*) his association with the "sect [party] of the Nazarenes" (v. 5). Johnson calls Paul's legal maneuver a "breathtaking turn" when after a series of denials he makes a public confession of his allegiance to the beliefs and practices of this sect.[728] While the legal term *homologeō* denotes admission of guilt, Paul's use of it connotes a confession of faith: Paul confesses that he worships "the God of our ancestors" (v. 14a; see also 22:3). The clause is placed in an emphatic position in this text and underscores Paul's complete loyalty to the God of the OT. He

has invented no new God (= God of Israel; cf. 17:23-31); rather, he participates in a new "Way," or path, that gains access to God's saving mercies through God's risen Messiah (see 24:21).

Paul's worship of Israel's ancestral God is proved by his belief in "everything laid down according to the law or written in the prophets"— Israel's Scriptures (v. 14b; cf. Luke 24:44-45). Moreover, his traditional (= Pharisaic) faith is demonstrated by his theology of hope: "There will be a resurrection of both the righteous and the unrighteous" (v. 15; see also 3:20-21; 23:6; cf. Dan 12:1-3; Rev 20:11-15). His assertion that his Sadducean opponents confess belief in "this same hope" when they do not (see 23:7-8) must be understood as an element of Paul's rhetoric that plays off the ambiguity of the word "sect" (*hairesis*), which is much like our contemporary use of "cult" and can mean either religious heresy or party. The Way is not a Jewish "sect" in the sense of an alleged heresy because it shares common ground with the faith traditions of its opponents; it must be another religious "party" within Judaism.

The move from "confession of faith" to refutation of the claim that he profaned the Temple (see v. 6) is an easy one: Paul pledges, "I strive [ἀσκέω *askeō*] to have a clear [ἀπρόσκοπος *aproskopos*] conscience toward God and all people" (v. 16, author's trans.). The athletic term *askeō* is used of rigorous training in preparation for a contest and is widely used for academic or moral training, as here: Paul's disciplined devotion to Israel's God and to those religious practices or disciplines— such as temple purity—that cultivate a close relationship with God. More directly, the aim of his religious discipline is a morality that is "clear," which translates *aproskopos,* a term connoting a healthy or stable conscience (for "conscience," see 23:1). Tertullus's accusation goes to Paul's *intent* to "profane" the Temple (see v. 6); however, a person with Paul's internal spiritual goods could never intentionally subvert a religious practice (temple purity) that aims at a closer relationship with Israel's God.

**24:17-20.** The third proof frames the other two by explaining more deliberately Paul's commendable reasons for coming to Jerusalem—reasons that Rome would have endorsed and even encouraged. He does not indicate what calendar he is using in commenting that it has been "sev-

---

727. See E. Haenchen, *The Acts of the Apostles* (Philadelphia: Westminster, 1971) 652.
728. L. T. Johnson, *The Acts of the Apostles,* SP 5 (Collegeville, Minn.: Liturgical, 1992) 412.

eral years" since last visiting Jerusalem (cf. 18:22). I take it that he means many years have passed since he last made the trip as a Jewish pilgrim "to bring alms to my nation and to offer sacrifices" (v. 17). In doing so, Paul was *inside* the Temple, completing "the rite of purification" (see 21:26) and thereby could not have created a public disturbance (v. 18). The reader knows from Luke's account of this rite that Paul would have logged his time in the Temple and Felix would have had access to this official record for confirmation of his claims.

Paul's parenthetical note that his original accusers (see 21:27-28) are unavailable for Felix's interrogation is a strategic maneuver of legal defense. Sherwin-White points out that Paul's comment is in reality a "sound technical objection" since "Roman law was very strong against accusers who abandoned their charges."[729] Therefore, while Paul's larger point is that he was "inside the temple" for legitimate reasons, his proof is made even more substantive by noting the absence of those who had initially brought the charge and incited the riot that triggered Paul's legal problems.

In his final proof, the Paul of Acts makes his most important although indirect claim of innocence: He is without "crime" (ἀδίκημα *adikēma*, v. 20). As a legal term, *adikēma* underwrites his claim of innocence (see 18:14); however, it carries the connotation of religious purity as well. That is, Paul has done nothing that would have rendered him religiously impure. The entire Jerusalem ordeal has been a spiritual test of Paul's own purity in belief and practice and, indeed, of the purity of the messianic movement he represents. He has ably proved the purity of both.

**24:21.** The speech's *peroratio*, or conclusion, skillfully draws attention to the *theological* subtext of Tertullus's political charges. Paul's apologia rests on the validity of a theological claim that is distinctively Jewish in cast (so v. 15)—namely, "the resurrection of the dead" (see 23:6). The reader may well gloss Paul's closing statement by his comments to the Corinthians that "if Christ has not been raised, then our preaching is in vain and your faith is in vain" (1 Cor 15:14). His mission and message, and the controversies that swirl

around each, are reduced to this single claim, which if not true render every accusation and legal consideration moot.

**24:22-23.** The reader should assume that the narrator's explanatory comment that "Felix was rather well informed about the Way" (v. 22) implies the official's essential agreement with Paul's definition of the church's beliefs and practices (see vv. 14-16) and that it must be considered a religious "party" within normative Judaism rather than a renegade movement on its margins. The historical referent to which Luke's comment points the reader is not so much that Felix possesses an accurate understanding of Christianity. Rather, Paul assumes his competence in his *captatio*, opening compliments (see v. 10)—married as he was to a Jewess (see v. 24)—and therefore will his ability to recognize the orthodoxy of Paul's confession of faith. A postponement is called for, which indicates that Felix does not intend to keep his promise to "decide the case" when the accusers arrived.

**24:24-26.** When Paul's powerful defense apparently prompted a brief postponement of the trial, the reader is left with hope that Felix's verdict will be favorable. The real reason and extended duration of the postponement reflects Luke's ambivalence toward pagan Rome's participation in God's plans for the church's (= Paul's) mission in the world. Although there is reason to think Felix is interested in what Paul "teaches concerning faith in Christ Jesus" (v. 24), "at the same time he hoped that money would be given him by Paul" (v. 26).

Luke's repeated references to time—here to "some days later"—creates the impression that a familiar legal protocol is followed in adjudicating Paul's case. Felix's continuing interrogation of Paul was now off-the-record and in the company of "his wife Drusilla, who was Jewish." She is the youngest daughter of Herod Agrippa I (see 12:1-4, 19-23) and sister of King Agrippa II (see 25:13). While her devotion to Jewish faith is unknown, Luke's reference that she is Jewish explains why she is interested in hearing Paul's "Jewish" gospel. The reader is reminded of the Jewish shape of Paul's "confession of faith" (see vv. 14-16); this is confirmed again by Drusilla's presence at this informal hearing—it is not a legal hearing but a hearing of the gospel.

---

729. A. N. Sherwin-White, *Roman Society and Roman Law in the New Testament* (Oxford: Clarendon, 1963) 52.

The subject matter of Paul's message concerning "faith in Christ Jesus" is "righteousness [δικαιοσύνη *dikaiosynē*],[730] self-control [ἐγκράτεια *enkrateia*] and the judgment [κρίμα *krima*] to come" (v. 25). In context these topics are not Paul's lectures on a virtuous Roman administration of the sort Seneca might give Felix; rather, these are the catchwords of the Pauline gospel, glossed by his NT letters, and they expand his earlier confession of faith in Israel's ancestral God.[731] In this regard, the sequence of terms is important to consider and reflects the deep logic of his gospel. The revelation of God's "right-wising" grace (*dikaiosynē*) inaugurates a new era in salvation's history that promises forgiveness and eternal life to those who have faith in Christ Jesus (cf. Rom 3:21-26; 9:30; 10:13; Gal 3:21-22; Phil 3:8-11; Titus 3:4-7). The term translated "self-control" (*enkrateia*), otherwise known as a moral virtue, is cataloged among the Spirit's "fruit" (cf. Gal 5:23) and is a public hallmark of saving trust in God's grace. While God's future *krima* is mentioned only here in Acts, it is an important theme of Romans where the fairness of God's endtime verdict is emphasized (Rom 2:1-11; 5:16; 11:33; 13:11-14).

The interpreter should resist speculating that the source of Felix's frightened dismissal of Paul is Felix's guilty conscience (for one reason or another), pricked by Paul's teachings concerning God's coming judgment. More likely the source of his guilt is his greed. The capacity of persons to respond to God is measured by their proper use of money. Felix kept Paul in custody in the hope that "money would be given him by Paul" (v. 26). While "becoming frightened" (ἔμφοβος *emphobos*) may well indicate that Felix is alert to the hard truth about God (see 10:4; 22:9; cf. Luke 24:5, 37), his greed envisages the character of someone unable to respond to God's word in faith.

Felix's interrogation of Paul continues for two years not in search of salvation but as an illegal means of acquiring money.[732]

Here again the narrative portrays Paul as a person of financial means. Earlier James asked Paul to cover the costs of expensive sacrifices offered by four brothers (21:24); Lysias's reaction to Paul's biographical sketch suggests that his Cilician and Roman citizenships envisage personal or familial wealth (21:39; 22:27-28); and Paul's testimony to his traditional piety, which required him to bring alms to Jerusalem as part of his pilgrimage, implies that he had money to devote to Israel's coffers (24:17). This unfolding portrait of Paul's ample funds is not an allusion to his Gentile collection but to personal resources that he willingly shares with others as the mark of his spiritual authority within the church (see 4:32-35).

**24:27.** Felix's role in Acts ends in ignominy. Luke's take on him is similar to that of secular historians: Felix was a malcontent, better known for greed than for competent leadership. This text reflects another feature of Roman law, which placed a two-year term limit on the detention of a Roman citizen without an official verdict being rendered.[733] Paul should have been released; however, Felix left him in prison, "since he wanted to grant the Jews a favor." What this "favor" is, Luke does not say.[734] The presumption of this passage, made clear by the next phase of Paul's trials, is that Felix turned his case over to his successor, Porcius Festus, as a delaying tactic, perhaps to give "the Jews" (see 24:1) more time to build a more persuasive case against Paul. Their time to do so will soon run out.

Little is known of Festus because his term of office was short. Josephus characterizes him as a competent leader who worked hard to reestablish good relations with the Jews and bring a lasting peace to the region. Festus's early death prevented

---

730. The NIV's translation of *dikaiosynē* as "righteousness," which is a catchword of Jewish theology denoting God's covenant renewing ("right-wising") action (cf. Rom 3:21-26; 9:30 10:13), is preferred to the NRSV's "justice," a catchword of Hellenistic moral philosophy denoting human fairness.

731. Commentators have interpreted this Pauline (= Lukan) triad in a variety of ways. Representative are (1) Haenchen, *The Acts of the Apostles*, 660-61, who takes the three as the "central themes in the post-apostolic preaching." (2) Johnson, *The Acts of the Apostles*, 419, who understands the triad as "a sort of ethical translation of 'messianic faith' for Gentile ears." And (3) Witherington, *The Acts of the Apostles*, 715, who takes the terms as a rebuke of Felix's sexual lust for Druscilla, a beautiful woman by all accounts, which resulted in her divorce of Azizus.

732. Accepting money from prisoners in exchange for their freedom was illegal under Roman law. See Haenchen, *The Acts of the Apostles*, 661.

733. J. A. Fitzmyer, *The Acts of the Apostles*, AB 31 (Garden City, N.Y.: Doubleday, 1998) 740.

734. Johnson, *The Acts of the Apostles*, 419, notes that Josephus reports a delegation of Jewish leaders from Palestine traveled to Rome to present the Emperor with various "injustices to the Jews" for which Felix is responsible. Felix is in trouble with Rome and this "favor" may be his futile attempt to win some points with his Jewish opposition so that Rome would go easier with him. See Josephus *Antiquities of the Jews* 20.182.

him from realizing his ambitious dreams.[735] His role in God's purposes for Paul are more important, for he is the procurator who hears the

prophet's appeal to Caesar (see 25:6-12) and, in agreement with Herod Agrippa II, takes responsibility for delivering Paul to the city of his destiny (see 26:30-32).

735. See. J. B. Green, "Festus, Porcius," *ABD* 2:794-95.

# REFLECTIONS

"Felix left Paul in prison" (24:27 NRSV). The tragic subtext of Acts is how frequently people make decisions against God out of greater concern for their financial situation, political status, or some other momentary accommodation. Felix is a case in point. He sat under Paul's instruction "concerning faith in Christ Jesus" (24:24 NRSV). Paul is literally his captive audience as they discuss the ultimate issues of human existence—"righteousness, self-control, and the judgment to come" (24:25). Even though Paul's message alarms him and he realizes the charges against Paul are false, Felix postpones the "not guilty" verdict to retain custody of Paul in order to extort money from his Jewish enemies. It is his greed and not his ignorance that keeps Felix from the faith.

# ACTS 25:1-12, PAUL APPEALS TO CAESAR

NIV

**25** Three days after arriving in the province, Festus went up from Caesarea to Jerusalem, [2]where the chief priests and Jewish leaders appeared before him and presented the charges against Paul. [3]They urgently requested Festus, as a favor to them, to have Paul transferred to Jerusalem, for they were preparing an ambush to kill him along the way. [4]Festus answered, "Paul is being held at Caesarea, and I myself am going there soon. [5]Let some of your leaders come with me and press charges against the man there, if he has done anything wrong."

[6]After spending eight or ten days with them, he went down to Caesarea, and the next day he convened the court and ordered that Paul be brought before him. [7]When Paul appeared, the Jews who had come down from Jerusalem stood around him, bringing many serious charges against him, which they could not prove.

[8]Then Paul made his defense: "I have done nothing wrong against the law of the Jews or against the temple or against Caesar."

[9]Festus, wishing to do the Jews a favor, said to Paul, "Are you willing to go up to Jerusalem and stand trial before me there on these charges?"

NRSV

**25** Three days after Festus had arrived in the province, he went up from Caesarea to Jerusalem [2]where the chief priests and the leaders of the Jews gave him a report against Paul. They appealed to him [3]and requested, as a favor to them against Paul,[a] to have him transferred to Jerusalem. They were, in fact, planning an ambush to kill him along the way. [4]Festus replied that Paul was being kept at Caesarea, and that he himself intended to go there shortly. [5]"So," he said, "let those of you who have the authority come down with me, and if there is anything wrong about the man, let them accuse him."

6After he had stayed among them not more than eight or ten days, he went down to Caesarea; the next day he took his seat on the tribunal and ordered Paul to be brought. [7]When he arrived, the Jews who had gone down from Jerusalem surrounded him, bringing many serious charges against him, which they could not prove. [8]Paul said in his defense, "I have in no way committed an offense against the law of the Jews, or against the temple, or against the emperor." [9]But Festus, wishing to do the Jews a favor, asked Paul, "Do you wish to go up to Jerusalem and be tried there

[a] Gk *him*

## NIV

¹⁰Paul answered: "I am now standing before Caesar's court, where I ought to be tried. I have not done any wrong to the Jews, as you yourself know very well. ¹¹If, however, I am guilty of doing anything deserving death, I do not refuse to die. But if the charges brought against me by these Jews are not true, no one has the right to hand me over to them. I appeal to Caesar!"

¹²After Festus had conferred with his council, he declared: "You have appealed to Caesar. To Caesar you will go!"

## NRSV

before me on these charges?" ¹⁰Paul said, "I am appealing to the emperor's tribunal; this is where I should be tried. I have done no wrong to the Jews, as you very well know. ¹¹Now if I am in the wrong and have committed something for which I deserve to die, I am not trying to escape death; but if there is nothing to their charges against me, no one can turn me over to them. I appeal to the emperor." ¹²Then Festus, after he had conferred with his council, replied, "You have appealed to the emperor; to the emperor you will go."

# COMMENTARY

Nero's appointment of Porcius Festus around 60 CE as procurator of Judea signals an important shift in the politics of the region. Festus is a cunning man, full of energy, whose administration is characterized by fairness toward the Jews, especially when compared to his greedy predecessor. Unfortunately, there is not a corresponding change for the good among Jerusalem's priestly elite. Two years later, the elites of official Israel continue to plot an assassination attempt against Paul, now with Festus as their intended dupe (25:1-5; see also 23:12-22). This persistence in conspiracy implies the ongoing importance of the imprisoned Paul to regional politics. The reader of Acts is right to wonder why. On the one hand, Paul is granted freedom to receive visitors in Caesarea (see 24:23), implying that he continues to be involved in the business of the Way through the mediation of close colleagues (e.g., Timothy, Silas). On the other hand, Paul's continuing influence in Palestine may well imply that he does in fact have the support of the Jerusalem church. Contemporary Acts criticism has interpreted Luke's silence on the role of the Judean or Caesarean churches as a lack of support. However, the intense concern of the religious establishment in Jerusalem regarding Paul's influence in Palestine during his two years of enforced exile, to the extent that these pious men would use subterfuge to murder him (25:2-3), can be explained only if the Jerusalem church continued to champion his mission.

No doubt Festus has heard from Felix of the failed conspiracy against Paul and knows something of the Jewish case against him as well. He is, therefore, duly cautious in his responses and actions in dealing with the Jewish leadership team in Jerusalem. After all, his prisoner is a Roman citizen in good standing, which he has also no doubt learned from Felix (see 25:12), and the legal case against him failed to convince his predecessor of Paul's guilt. Even so, Festus listens to the ad hoc case against Paul and to his rebuttal (25:6-8) before tendering Paul the choice, "Do you wish to go up to Jerusalem and be tried there before me on these charges?" (25:9).

Although biblical narrative is wont to provide the reader with information concerning the inner motivations of its characters, we simply do not know what "favor" Festus thought he was granting "the Jews" by asking Paul such a question. He is a clever politician and he makes a strategic decision as a new ruler over an intractable region. Perhaps he believes that Paul would not leave Jerusalem alive. But the reader is also unclear as to why Paul chose this particular moment to make his appeal to the Roman Caesar. Is he afraid for his personal safety in Palestine, and thus this is his ticket out to the safety of Rome (doubtful)? Or is he prompted by his sense of judicial propriety that the allegation of sedition against Rome should be evaluated by the emperor (perhaps)? Or is he motivated by his faithfulness to his prophetic vocation to "bear witness also in Rome" (23:11). Probably the latter. Luke does not tell his readers the reason for Paul's appeal and is concerned only to narrate the result: "I am appealing to the emperor's tribunal" (25:10); "To the emperor you will go" (25:12). In any case, the interpreter is simply mistaken if concluding that this legal maneuver backfired in light of Agrippa's concluding verdict (see 26:32): Paul's decision triggers a series of events that results in his mission to Rome according to God's plan, and in some significant sense it is therefore essential to the plotline of Acts.[736]

**25:1-3.** Festus hits the ground running: "Three days" after arriving in the provincial capital, he departs on an official visit of Jerusalem, his region's other principal city, where he meets with "the high priests and the leaders of the Jews" (v. 2). The promptness of his visitation may well be an indicator of the political urgency of Paul's case. Felix had left Palestine an unstable province and a breeding ground for terrorist activity. No doubt Paul is portrayed by his Jewish opponents in inflammatory terms, since they think his mission to the nations threatens to corrode Israel's theological beliefs and social practices (see 21:21, 28; 22:21-23; 24:5-6).

The change of designation from religious "elders" (πρεσβύτεροι *presbyteroi;* see 24:1) to political "leaders" (πρῶτοι *prōtoi*) connotes a wider spectrum of leadership and may indicate a broader, better-organized attack against Paul. Festus meets with the economic, political, religious elites to deal with the "Paul problem." The positive implication is that his message is pervasive and touches every institution of Jewish life. The plural "high priests" here is unusual but probably reflects the continuing role that retired high priests play in the city's religious and political culture.[737]

Luke states the business of their private meeting sharply: They "gave Festus a report against [ἐμφάνιζω κατά *emphanizō kata*]" Paul. The repetition of *emphanizō kata,* which was also used in 24:1,

indicates the resumption of the Jewish case against Paul. The impression is that the change of procurators in Caesarea prompts a renewed effort to destroy Paul and the influence of his message about the risen Jesus. With this motive in mind, they "appealed to him and requested . . . a favor": Transfer Paul to Jerusalem for a new trial (v. 3). This is the second of three times that Paul's Jewish opponents request a favor of a Roman ruler (see v. 9; see also 24:27). Such Lukan triads frame important elements in the plotline of his narrative. Since the "favor" requested is to place Paul in harm's way, this motif intends to depict his Jewish opposition in bad light and draw attention to their immoral behavior, provoked by the sharp theological differences they have with Paul. The ambush they plan is similar to the one earlier proposed by the forty hasidim (would-be Jewish assassins; see 23:12-15), except that Paul now would be traveling from Caesarea to Jerusalem.

**25:4-5.** Festus is not, however, a witting participant in the plot to ambush and kill Paul. Initially, he insists on his prerogatives as Roman procurator. The provincial seat of his administrative and judicial power is Caesarea, not Jerusalem; therefore, "come with me and press charges against the man there" (v. 5). If Festus has an inkling of the murderous motive behind the Jewish leaders' request, he has no intention of being their dupe. In a compromise, however, he does tacitly agree to reopen Paul's case, to see if "there is anything wrong [ἄτοπος *atopos;* lit., "out of place"] about the man."

**25:6-8.** And so it is in Caesarea, upon his βῆμα (*bēma,* "seat"),[738] with the leaders of the anti-Paul movement surrounding him, that Festus orders Paul to be brought for interrogation (v. 6). The narrator leaves the reader of Acts to fill in the details of this hearing, including the "many serious charges" against Paul (v. 7; see also 21:21, 28; 24:5-6) and the details of Paul's *apologia* (v. 8; see also 23:6; 24:10-21). The final element of Luke's summary of Paul's defense is new and interesting, however: "I have in no way committed an offense . . . against the emperor" (v. 8). The effect of Luke's shaping of Paul's response is twofold.

---

736. Commentators continue to draw parallels between the Lukan stories of Paul and Jesus, and in this case their Roman trials (cf. Luke 23). See, e.g., C. K. Barrett, *A Critical and Exegetical Commentary on the Acts of the Apostles,* 2 vols, ICC (Edinburgh: T. & T. Clark, 1994, 1998) 2:1122. While the same narrator is responsible for both narratives and some linguistic parallelism is sure to exist for this reason, what is clearly important to him is that neither Jesus nor Paul is guilty of the crimes alleged and that Rome does not release either prophet.

737. According to Josephus *Antiquities of the Jews* 20.179 the high priest during Festus's short regime was Ishmael ben Phiabi. Even the contentious and unpopular former high priest Ananias (see Acts 23:2) remains influential, primarily because of his landholdings and family wealth.

738. The *bēma* is variously translated and understood by commentators. It refers to a portable rostrum or raised platform placed so that the judge can sit over the crowd to render a verdict in dramatic fashion. See Josephus *The Jewish War* 2:172; see also Acts 18:12.

Clearly it prepares the reader for the climax of the story; namely, Paul's appeal to Caesar, thereby erasing his case from Festus's docket and rendering this venue irrelevant. Yet it also seems true from the previous trial before Felix—as well as from Paul's various court hearings during his mission in the diaspora (see 16:21; 17:7)—that Paul is well aware from personal experience that the most serious charge against him is that of sedition. It is left to Paul, then, to clarify the prosecution's case against him!

**25:9.** A further compromise is now proposed by Festus. In immediate context, the requested favor of a change of venue is no mere legal maneuver. While it is certainly true that a Jerusalem trial, preferably conducted by the Sanhedrin, would be the most favorable legal option for Paul's opponents, their main intent is murder and not a change of court venue or trial judge. The Jews would be more than happy to accept Festus as judge, which he evidently requires ("be tried before me"), as long as the case is transferred to Jerusalem. Their plan is for Paul to miss his court appearance there, no matter who is presiding (see v. 3)!

Haenchen assails the historical reliability of Luke's account, which he finds "incomprehensible." In his mind, a verdict would have probably been rendered immediately following Paul's defense speech.[739] But Roloff is surely right to question Festus's integrity when asking Paul to decide between Jerusalem and Caesarea; he understands the implications for himself and for Paul very well, and chooses to ignore them for reasons of political expedience.[740] Festus's duplicity is characteristic of his role in Acts; as representative of Rome, he contributes to the overall negative portrait of Rome's relationship to Paul and his mission. While Roman law safeguards Paul to Rome under the constant threat of unrepentant Jews, and so is an unwitting collaborator with God in achieving God's purpose for Paul, Roman leaders are presented as untrustworthy and self-interested.

**25:10-12.** For this reason, Paul's response to Festus's question must be considered a sharp rebuke in character with his prophetic vocation:

"This is where I should be tried . . . as you very well know" (v. 10). His charge against Festus, rooted in moral ground, is made more convincing by Paul's willingness to pay the death penalty if his crimes justify it under Roman law; his own sense of fairness commands the very same of Festus. Both translations of Paul's last statement before making his appeal—"no one can turn me over to them" (NRSV) and "no one has the right to hand me over to them" (NIV)—miss the important wordplay between the Jewish request of Festus for a "favor" (v. 3, χάρις *charis*) and Paul's challenge to him that he cannot "turn/hand over" (χαρίζομαι *charizomai*) an innocent man to his enemies. Luke shapes Paul's retort to echo the triad of requested "favors" (vv. 3, 9; see also 24:7) in order to condemn Festus's political expedience: The prophet-like-Jesus does not play Rome's games!

The most crucial right of Paul's Roman citizenship allows him to demand a fair trial before Caesar.[741] More critically, Paul recognizes that the most important legal challenge to his innocence is that of sedition against the empire and that the emperor is the appropriate judge in this case (see above). He also must realize after two years of imprisonment that he is the ball in an ongoing game of "political football" played out between the Roman procurator and the leaders of his Jewish opposition. Paul's sharp retort to Festus's lame question would seem to indicate that he does not trust Festus to call the end to this game. It is, perhaps, a frustrated citizen, then, who concludes, contrary to the procurator's suggestion to change the trial site, "I appeal to the emperor" (v. 11). The legal wrangling stops here; Paul will soon be on his way to Rome according to divine purpose (see 23:11).

The unnamed Caesar to whom Paul appeals is probably Nero (54–68 CE). Festus would have known, informally from Felix and officially from the records kept of previous interrogations and defense speeches, that Paul is a solid citizen. Although Luke mentions no sigh of relief, Festus

---

739. E. Haenchen, *The Acts of the Apostles* (Philadelphia: Westminster, 1971) 669.

740. J. Roloff, *Die Apostelgeschichte* (Göttingen: Vandenhoeck & Ruprecht, 1981) 343.

741. Cf. Sherwin-White, *Roman Society and Roman Law in the New Testament*, 144-47. See also J. Lentz, *Luke's Portrait of Paul*, SNTSMS 77 (Cambridge: Cambridge University Press, 1993) 139-70, who argues that the appeal to Caesar serves Luke's rhetorical interests in characterizing Paul's high social class and civic reputation, and as such the growing status of Christianity within Luke's Roman world. Paul's appeal to Nero raises many questions. See also Fitzmyer, *The Acts of the Apostles*, 746, for a summary and working bibliography.

must have felt the burden of a "no-win" situation lifted from his administration. For this reason, his conference with his advisors must have been rela-tively brief, perhaps only to precisely formulate his response: "You have appealed to the emperor; to the emperor you will go" (25:12).

# REFLECTIONS

"This is where I should be tried" (25:10 NRSV). The narrative climax of Paul's trials is his direct appeal to the Caesar for justice (25:11). Yet, this exercise of Roman citizenship seems a strange action for this bold prophet-like-Jesus to take. On the one hand, the interpreter is tempted to argue that Paul's appeal is a prudent act: a change of venue (Rome) and magistrate (emperor), which is Paul's civil right to demand, will allow him to overcome Festus's moral fail-ure. Upon closer reflection, however, the interpreter realizes that Paul's initiative is prompted by his awareness that the Lord plans for him to go to Rome (see 23:11). Thus his assertion that he "should" be tried in Rome is a theological claim and not a legal maneuver: Rome is the city of Paul's destiny because it is in the script of God's plan of salvation.

The precise relationship between the provident concerns of a sovereign God and the careful and clever choices that central characters like Paul make is not always clear in Acts. What does seem clear, however, is that the collaboration between the two—a faithful God and God's faith-ful servants—is a necessary feature of God's intention to fulfill the biblical promises of salvation. Thus Paul's appeal triggers a chain of events both political (so Acts 26) and natural (so Acts 27) that takes him into Rome, where once again he personifies God's faithfulness to Israel in secur-ing the salvation of the nations to the end of the earth (see 28:23-28, 30-31). Our story becomes like Paul's when our personal decisions are weighted with divine importance—when the actions we choose to take or the words we decide to speak allow us to participate effectively in accom-plishing God's plans.

# ACTS 25:13-27, INTERLUDE: FESTUS TWICE REVIEWS PAUL'S CASE

NIV

[13]A few days later King Agrippa and Bernice arrived at Caesarea to pay their respects to Festus. [14]Since they were spending many days there, Festus discussed Paul's case with the king. He said: "There is a man here whom Felix left as a prisoner. [15]When I went to Jerusalem, the chief priests and elders of the Jews brought charges against him and asked that he be condemned.

[16]"I told them that it is not the Roman custom to hand over any man before he has faced his accusers and has had an opportunity to defend himself against their charges. [17]When they came here with me, I did not delay the case, but con-vened the court the next day and ordered the

NRSV

13After several days had passed, King Agrippa and Bernice arrived at Caesarea to welcome Festus. [14]Since they were staying there several days, Festus laid Paul's case before the king, say-ing, "There is a man here who was left in prison by Felix. [15]When I was in Jerusalem, the chief priests and the elders of the Jews informed me about him and asked for a sentence against him. [16]I told them that it was not the custom of the Romans to hand over anyone before the accused had met the accusers face to face and had been given an opportunity to make a defense against the charge. [17]So when they met here, I lost no time, but on the next day took my seat on the tri-bunal and ordered the man to be brought.

## NIV

man to be brought in. [18]When his accusers got up to speak, they did not charge him with any of the crimes I had expected. [19]Instead, they had some points of dispute with him about their own religion and about a dead man named Jesus who Paul claimed was alive. [20]I was at a loss how to investigate such matters; so I asked if he would be willing to go to Jerusalem and stand trial there on these charges. [21]When Paul made his appeal to be held over for the Emperor's decision, I ordered him held until I could send him to Caesar."

[22]Then Agrippa said to Festus, "I would like to hear this man myself."

He replied, "Tomorrow you will hear him."

[23]The next day Agrippa and Bernice came with great pomp and entered the audience room with the high ranking officers and the leading men of the city. At the command of Festus, Paul was brought in. [24]Festus said: "King Agrippa, and all who are present with us, you see this man! The whole Jewish community has petitioned me about him in Jerusalem and here in Caesarea, shouting that he ought not to live any longer. [25]I found he had done nothing deserving of death, but because he made his appeal to the Emperor I decided to send him to Rome. [26]But I have nothing definite to write to His Majesty about him. Therefore I have brought him before all of you, and especially before you, King Agrippa, so that as a result of this investigation I may have something to write. [27]For I think it is unreasonable to send on a prisoner without specifying the charges against him."

## NRSV

[18]When the accusers stood up, they did not charge him with any of the crimes[a] that I was expecting. [19]Instead they had certain points of disagreement with him about their own religion and about a certain Jesus, who had died, but whom Paul asserted to be alive. [20]Since I was at a loss how to investigate these questions, I asked whether he wished to go to Jerusalem and be tried there on these charges.[b] [21]But when Paul had appealed to be kept in custody for the decision of his Imperial Majesty, I ordered him to be held until I could send him to the emperor." [22]Agrippa said to Festus, "I would like to hear the man myself." "Tomorrow," he said, "you will hear him."

[23]So on the next day Agrippa and Bernice came with great pomp, and they entered the audience hall with the military tribunes and the prominent men of the city. Then Festus gave the order and Paul was brought in. [24]And Festus said, "King Agrippa and all here present with us, you see this man about whom the whole Jewish community petitioned me, both in Jerusalem and here, shouting that he ought not to live any longer. [25]But I found that he had done nothing deserving death; and when he appealed to his Imperial Majesty, I decided to send him. [26]But I have nothing definite to write to our sovereign about him. Therefore I have brought him before all of you, and especially before you, King Agrippa, so that, after we have examined him, I may have something to write— [27]for it seems to me unreasonable to send a prisoner without indicating the charges against him."

[a] Other ancient authorities read *with anything*    [b] Gk *on them*

# COMMENTARY

The narrator has created a confidential conversation between the Roman procurator Festus and the Palestinian ruler King Agrippa and his sister Queen Bernice[742] (25:13-22), to which he adds the *précis* of a public speech (25:23-27), in order to summarize the Roman proceedings against Paul. Agrippa and Bernice, along with their sister Drusilla (see 24:24), are members of the same notorious Herodian family whose reign during the

---

742. Bernice and Agrippa were the children of Herod Agrippa I; they lived together following the death of her husband. Although she had a reputation for piety, rumors spread of an incestuous relationship between the two. They did little to end the gossip and their relationship continued until Titus conquered Palestine and took Bernice as his Jewish mistress (only later to abandon her due to anti-Semitic sentiment in Rome when he became Caesar). Whether this is a historical subtext of the present story is impossible to determine, although it might explain their ambivalent responses to Paul.

days of Jesus (cf. Matt 2; Mark 6; Luke 23) and his apostolic successors (see Acts 12) was notorious for its bloody and brutal repression of the faith community's witness to God. The reader is right to wonder whether this family's infamy will carry over to Paul's case.

This passage uses two literary conventions of Luke's narrative style: the interlude and the double speech. The double speech functions like the double vision (e.g., 9:10-17; 10:1-16) or the follow-up letter in Acts (e.g., 15:22-29; 23:26-30) to emphasize themes that carry important theological freight. In this instance, Festus recognizes Paul's innocence of any seditious activity against Rome (see 25:25); he knows that the real issue at stake turns on a theological claim about the resurrection rather than a legal charge against Paul (see 25:18-19). At the same time, these two different versions provide different perspectives on the same events. In his second speech, Festus improves both his role in the judicial proceeding to this point (see 25:14b-17) and his political standing in Palestine by asking Agrippa and Bernice to interrogate Paul and enlighten him in this matter (see 25:20-21), presumably to aid him in writing his official report to Rome (see 25:26). Rome's take on Paul is one of persistent theological ignorance and political self-interest, which in combination ironically safeguards him from the treachery of his Jewish opponents.

**25:13-14a.** The meeting of King Agrippa and Bernice with their new colleague Festus is an act of political solidarity between Roman rulers and pro-Roman interests in the Holy Land. Because of their different backgrounds—Festus is a pagan and Agrippa and Bernice are secular Jews—Festus quickly turns to them for help in settling the long-standing "Paul problem." It is hardly conceivable that Agrippa and Bernice would not have heard of Paul from the very same "chief priests and the leaders of the Jews" who reported to Festus, since Agrippa was Roman curator of the Temple and titular head of its priestly establishment. It is reasonable, therefore, that "Festus laid Paul's case before the king" (v. 14a), even though Luke does not indicate that Paul is the primary reason for this summit.

**25:14b-21.** Festus's initial rehearsal of Paul's case follows the plotline of Luke's script (see vv. 1-12), adding new details to reflect his judicial talent.

The reference to inheriting prisoner Paul from Felix is not an implicit rebuke of his predecessor but a implicit request for help to understand the case's religious nuances. Festus also fills in gaps of what took place in his Jerusalem meeting with "the leaders of the Jews" (see v. 2); nothing is mentioned, however, about their request for a change of venue (see v. 20). Evidently, the leaders, now identified as "the chief priests and the elders" (i.e., the Sanhedrin), had initially wanted Festus to bring a guilty verdict against Paul without a trial: "They asked for a sentence against him" (v. 15). Festus states the conflict between Roman and Jewish judicial protocol with high moral tone: "It was not the custom [*ethos*] of the Romans to hand over anyone before the accused . . . had been given opportunity to make a defense [apologia] against the charge" (v. 16). No mention is made of Paul's Roman citizenship, which guarantees his right to a fair trial; nor is provision of the details of Paul's apologia necessary, since these are in mind already. Emphasis is placed as it should be on Festus, who is protector of the Roman constitution and therefore acts with due dispatch: "I lost no time . . . and ordered [Paul] be brought" (v. 17). Law and order are the hallmarks of Festus's regime!

Festus's rehearsal makes Luke's point: There is no evidence to support the Jewish case against Paul, in particular the charge of sedition to which Festus could render Rome's verdict (see 25:18). He rightly concludes that "they had certain points of disagreement with him about their own religion [δεισιδαιμονία *deisidaimonia*; lit., "superstition"]" (v. 19a) devolving into an intramural squabble over contested claims "about a certain Jesus."

The Roman pagan's negative caricature of Paul's gospel of the living Jesus as "their own superstition" (see 18:14-15), coupled with his apparent lack of knowledge "about a certain Jesus," explains why he seeks Agrippa's advice and why he has not yet rendered a verdict. Luke's intent is not yet to characterize Agrippa but rather Festus as an outsider[743] whose negative reading of the gospel remains unchanged in Acts. This is hardly Haenchen's "rehabilitated Festus,"[744] whose

---

743. So Johnson, *The Acts of the Apostles*, 426, who claims that Festus uses a pejorative "superstition" (*deisidaimonia*) because he considers Agrippa a secular Jew and "as much an outsider to these disputes as himself."

744. Haenchen, *The Acts of the Apostles*, 674-75.

queries of the more knowledgeable Agrippa and Bernice are supposedly motivated by a leading citizen's desire to do right by Rome. When Festus persists in his obduracy and is finally dismissed by Paul as a parody of self-promotion (see 26:24-29), the reader cannot maintain a positive view of Festus. In fact, his hypocrisy is revealed when he tells Agrippa and Bernice that his motive for raising the prospect of a Jerusalem venue for Paul's trial is that he "was at a loss how to investigate these questions" (25:20). We know better (see 25:9). The generally negative portrayal of Felix and Festus, both of whom act like Gallio in Acts, only intensifies what must be the central irony for Luke: These pagan outsiders grasp what his Jewish opponents do not admit—that the much disputed mission of Paul to the Gentiles/nations falls within the bounds of a Jewish ethos ("*their own* religion") and has everything to do with the much disputed message of Paul that the resurrected Jesus is God's Messiah (see 25:19).

**25:22-23.** The staging of Paul's "show trial" before King Agrippa and Queen Bernice is dramatic and carefully crafted. The pomp that testifies to the importance of Paul's speech to Agrippa makes more vivid that with this speech Paul fulfills Jesus' prophecy that he will "carry my name before kings" (see 9:15). The procession of (probably five) military commanders and civic leaders into the "audience hall" of Herod's praetorium in Caesarea is but a prelude to Paul's climactic entrance (see 25:23). The interpreter should take special note of Luke's careful use of time throughout this portion of Acts; it is as though he is narrating the chronology of the trials of Paul as their "official" court recorder.

**25:24-27.** Festus's second speech publicly reviews Paul's case in broad currents for a secular venue. Once again Festus declares Paul's innocence, without even providing a summary of the prosecution's case against him: "He has done nothing deserving death" (v. 25; see also v. 18; 24:5). Festus's request for Agrippa's involvement is surely politically motivated and reflects the insecurity of a new administration. He wishes to please his Jewish constituents by finding Paul guilty but cannot do so under Roman law; he must, therefore, depend on Agrippa either to find some guilt in Paul (not likely) or to be the one to declare him innocent and take the political heat for doing so upon himself. Since Festus already has indicated to Agrippa that the alleged "crime" against Paul is heresy—which only those more knowledgeable in Jewish theology could judge (i.e., the Sanhedrin, Bernice) and which is irrelevant in this secular setting in any case—his primary political goal is for Agrippa to declare Paul innocent, which he eventually does (see 26:31-32).

Festus's use of hyperbole when describing the scope of controversy, saying that "this man about whom the whole Jewish community petitioned me, both in Jerusalem and here" (v. 24*a*), intensifies the Jewish cast of the problem. The reader will know that in private conversation Festus had made it clear to Agrippa that only "the chief priests and the elders" had petitioned him for a guilty verdict (see v. 15). Perhaps they did so on behalf of the Jewish people and Festus took their claim at face value. If this is true, then his hyperbole simply reflects his ignorance of the Jewish problem with Paul. His expressed sentiment is certainly at odds with Acts, which has more carefully circumscribed Paul's Jewish antagonists in terms both religious—they are *unrepentant* Jews—and sociological—they are only the (often Sadducean) *leaders* of the "people" who do not speak for all the people. In this sense, Jesus and his apostolic successors provoked the very same opposition previously, and for the same reasons.

Festus's concluding remarks are interesting for two reasons. Once again Luke contrasts the rational outsider (= Festus), to whom "it seems to me unreasonable [ἄλογος *alogos;* lit., "illogical"] to send a prisoner without indicating the charges against him" (v. 27), and the various Jewish mobs (including the Sanhedrin) who have been "shouting that [Paul] ought not to live any longer" (v. 24*b*) without any evident interest in the arguments made in Paul's (and his gospel's) favor. The rational thing to do in Paul's case is to examine him and then write up a report of the findings of fact (v. 26; see also 21:34; 22:30). Since Paul has already been declared innocent and his appeal to Caesar put into the record, this public examination is not another trial to determine his guilt or innocence but a public examination or "hearing" that should lead to a clarification of the truth of the matter. It is from this angle of vision—a rational investigation into the facts surrounding the case of an innocent man—that the reader should consider Paul's final and most important apologia in Acts. (See Reflections at 26:1-32.)

# ACTS 26:1-32, PAUL DEFENDS HIMSELF BEFORE KING AGRIPPA AND BERNICE

## NIV

**26** Then Agrippa said to Paul, "You have permission to speak for yourself."

So Paul motioned with his hand and began his defense: [2]"King Agrippa, I consider myself fortunate to stand before you today as I make my defense against all the accusations of the Jews, [3]and especially so because you are well acquainted with all the Jewish customs and controversies. Therefore, I beg you to listen to me patiently.

[4]"The Jews all know the way I have lived ever since I was a child, from the beginning of my life in my own country, and also in Jerusalem. [5]They have known me for a long time and can testify, if they are willing, that according to the strictest sect of our religion, I lived as a Pharisee. [6]And now it is because of my hope in what God has promised our fathers that I am on trial today. [7]This is the promise our twelve tribes are hoping to see fulfilled as they earnestly serve God day and night. O king, it is because of this hope that the Jews are accusing me. [8]Why should any of you consider it incredible that God raises the dead?

[9]"I too was convinced that I ought to do all that was possible to oppose the name of Jesus of Nazareth. [10]And that is just what I did in Jerusalem. On the authority of the chief priests I put many of the saints in prison, and when they were put to death, I cast my vote against them. [11]Many a time I went from one synagogue to another to have them punished, and I tried to force them to blaspheme. In my obsession against them, I even went to foreign cities to persecute them.

[12]"On one of these journeys I was going to Damascus with the authority and commission of the chief priests. [13]About noon, O king, as I was on the road, I saw a light from heaven, brighter than the sun, blazing around me and my companions. [14]We all fell to the ground, and I heard a voice saying to me in Aramaic,[a] 'Saul, Saul, why

[a] 14 Or Hebrew

## NRSV

**26** Agrippa said to Paul, "You have permission to speak for yourself." Then Paul stretched out his hand and began to defend himself:

[2]"I consider myself fortunate that it is before you, King Agrippa, I am to make my defense today against all the accusations of the Jews, [3]because you are especially familiar with all the customs and controversies of the Jews; therefore I beg of you to listen to me patiently.

[4]"All the Jews know my way of life from my youth, a life spent from the beginning among my own people and in Jerusalem. [5]They have known for a long time, if they are willing to testify, that I have belonged to the strictest sect of our religion and lived as a Pharisee. [6]And now I stand here on trial on account of my hope in the promise made by God to our ancestors, [7]a promise that our twelve tribes hope to attain, as they earnestly worship day and night. It is for this hope, your Excellency,[a] that I am accused by Jews! [8]Why is it thought incredible by any of you that God raises the dead?

[9]"Indeed, I myself was convinced that I ought to do many things against the name of Jesus of Nazareth.[b] [10]And that is what I did in Jerusalem; with authority received from the chief priests, I not only locked up many of the saints in prison, but I also cast my vote against them when they were being condemned to death. [11]By punishing them often in all the synagogues I tried to force them to blaspheme; and since I was so furiously enraged at them, I pursued them even to foreign cities.

[12]"With this in mind, I was traveling to Damascus with the authority and commission of the chief priests, [13]when at midday along the road, your Excellency,[a] I saw a light from heaven, brighter than the sun, shining around me and my companions. [14]When we had all fallen to the ground, I heard a voice saying to me in the Hebrew[c] language, 'Saul, Saul, why are you

[a] Gk O king    [b] Gk the Nazorean    [c] That is, Aramaic

## NIV

do you persecute me? It is hard for you to kick against the goads.'

15"Then I asked, 'Who are you, Lord?'

" 'I am Jesus, whom you are persecuting,' the Lord replied. 16'Now get up and stand on your feet. I have appeared to you to appoint you as a servant and as a witness of what you have seen of me and what I will show you. 17I will rescue you from your own people and from the Gentiles. I am sending you to them 18to open their eyes and turn them from darkness to light, and from the power of Satan to God, so that they may receive forgiveness of sins and a place among those who are sanctified by faith in me.'

19"So then, King Agrippa, I was not disobedient to the vision from heaven. 20First to those in Damascus, then to those in Jerusalem and in all Judea, and to the Gentiles also, I preached that they should repent and turn to God and prove their repentance by their deeds. 21That is why the Jews seized me in the temple courts and tried to kill me. 22But I have had God's help to this very day, and so I stand here and testify to small and great alike. I am saying nothing beyond what the prophets and Moses said would happen— 23that the Christ*a* would suffer and, as the first to rise from the dead, would proclaim light to his own people and to the Gentiles."

24At this point Festus interrupted Paul's defense. "You are out of your mind, Paul!" he shouted. "Your great learning is driving you insane."

25"I am not insane, most excellent Festus," Paul replied. "What I am saying is true and reasonable. 26The king is familiar with these things, and I can speak freely to him. I am convinced that none of this has escaped his notice, because it was not done in a corner. 27King Agrippa, do you believe the prophets? I know you do."

28Then Agrippa said to Paul, "Do you think that in such a short time you can persuade me to be a Christian?"

29Paul replied, "Short time or long—I pray God that not only you but all who are listening to me today may become what I am, except for these chains."

*b 23 Or Messiah*

## NRSV

persecuting me? It hurts you to kick against the goads.' 15I asked, 'Who are you, Lord?' The Lord answered, 'I am Jesus whom you are persecuting. 16But get up and stand on your feet; for I have appeared to you for this purpose, to appoint you to serve and testify to the things in which you have seen me*a* and to those in which I will appear to you. 17I will rescue you from your people and from the Gentiles—to whom I am sending you 18to open their eyes so that they may turn from darkness to light and from the power of Satan to God, so that they may receive forgiveness of sins and a place among those who are sanctified by faith in me.'

19"After that, King Agrippa, I was not disobedient to the heavenly vision, 20but declared first to those in Damascus, then in Jerusalem and throughout the countryside of Judea, and also to the Gentiles, that they should repent and turn to God and do deeds consistent with repentance. 21For this reason the Jews seized me in the temple and tried to kill me. 22To this day I have had help from God, and so I stand here, testifying to both small and great, saying nothing but what the prophets and Moses said would take place: 23that the Messiah*b* must suffer, and that, by being the first to rise from the dead, he would proclaim light both to our people and to the Gentiles."

24While he was making this defense, Festus exclaimed, "You are out of your mind, Paul! Too much learning is driving you insane!" 25But Paul said, "I am not out of my mind, most excellent Festus, but I am speaking the sober truth. 26Indeed the king knows about these things, and to him I speak freely; for I am certain that none of these things has escaped his notice, for this was not done in a corner. 27King Agrippa, do you believe the prophets? I know that you believe." 28Agrippa said to Paul, "Are you so quickly persuading me to become a Christian?"*c* 29Paul replied, "Whether quickly or not, I pray to God that not only you but also all who are listening to me today might become such as I am—except for these chains."

*a Other ancient authorities read the things that you have seen*
*b Or the Christ      c Or Quickly you will persuade me to play the Christian*

NIV

³⁰The king rose, and with him the governor and Bernice and those sitting with them. ³¹They left the room, and while talking with one another, they said, "This man is not doing anything that deserves death or imprisonment."

³²Agrippa said to Festus, "This man could have been set free if he had not appealed to Caesar."

NRSV

30Then the king got up, and with him the governor and Bernice and those who had been seated with them; ³¹and as they were leaving, they said to one another, "This man is doing nothing to deserve death or imprisonment." ³²Agrippa said to Festus, "This man could have been set free if he had not appealed to the emperor."

# COMMENTARY

If Paul's appeal to Caesar is the climax of the Acts narrative of his trial, this final apologia before Agrippa, Bernice, Festus, and their political and military entourage is its denouement. There is no longer need to rebut the charges of his Jewish opponents; there is need only to define the religious movement that Paul embodies. Luke's elaborate staging of this speech point the reader to this programmatic purpose. Festus asserts that this trial intends to "examine" Paul in order that legal brief can be written for the emperor (see 25:26-27). Paul need not present himself before Agrippa as a defendant who must prove his innocence in the face of charges leveled against him. Those days in court have ended with his appeal to Caesar. Therefore, while the form of Paul's speech is forensic (see 26:2, 24), its function is not to defend his political innocence per se (however, see 26:21) but to define his prophetic vocation as the personification of the very messianic movement he now represents.

The audience of Roman delegates is important to note in this regard. Powerful and privileged people, well educated and aristocratic in bearing, Paul's auditors are people of the Roman Empire. Agrippa and Bernice are Jews to be sure; but they are pro-Roman Jews, well connected with the power elites of imperial Rome. Governor, Festus personifies in his rational self-interest and religious skepticism the enlightened pagan of the Greco-Roman world. Even though this hearing takes place in Palestine, then, Paul's audience represents the interests of the Roman Empire and thus the mission field for Paul's gospel. Reference to the legal charges against Paul have been dropped from his apologia because his Jewish opponents are no longer relevant; the future of the word of the Lord belongs to the world inhabited by the likes of Festus and Agrippa.[745]

The principal ideas in this speech are familiar to the reader of Acts, and their repetition underlines the most important elements of Paul's religious authority in the book. Once again Paul sketches his Jewish credentials for a new audience (26:4-8; see also 21:39; 22:3; 23:6; 24:14-16): he is a Pharisee, a vigorous defender of the Jewish faith, ever faithful to Israel's Scriptures rightly interpreted (so 26:22-23). He again describes in detail his persecution of "the saints" (26:9-11; see 22:4-5), his dramatic conversion to Jesus (using fresh word pictures; 26:12-15; see 22:6-11), and his subsequent commission to bear witness to his resurrection to the nations (26:16-18; see 22:17-21). It is now Jesus who commissions him to his prophetic ministry, and its recital illustrates his obedience (26:19-20) according to the Scriptures (26:22). Within the framework of this testimony, then, the opposition of those unrepentant Jews that led to his arrest hardly needs to be mentioned (26:21), for the Lord has promised to rescue him from "from your people and from the Gentiles" (26:17).

In concluding his speech, Paul integrates the two different issues that have agitated controversy about him: His mission to the Gentiles (see 22:21, 22-24) and his message of the resurrected Messiah (see 23:6, 7-10; also 24:14-16, 21; 25:19). He finally claims that according to "the prophets and

745. Being members of the Herodian family, both Agrippa and Bernice would have been regarded Jewish by both Paul and Luke. However, with Josephus, *Antiquities of the Jews* 14.15.2, Herodians were *hēmiioudaios*, "half Jewish." That is, they were half Roman or "Roman Jews" in their split allegiance and bifurcated perspective toward Israel. See J. A. Fitzmyer, *The Acts of the Apostles*, AB 31 (Garden City, N.Y.: Doubleday, 1998) 756.

Moses" the rejected Messiah is resurrected by God to "proclaim light [φῶς *phōs*] both to our people [ὁ λαός *ho laos*] and to the Gentiles [ἔθνη *ethnē*]" (26:23). The reader hears an echo of Paul's earlier reference to his mission, "so that they [*ho laos/ethnē,* 26:17) may turn from darkness to light [*phōs*])" (26:18). The "light" that illumines darkness is the core proclamation of Paul's gospel, "that they [= *ho laos/ethnē*] may receive forgiveness of sins and a place among those who are sanctified by faith in [Jesus]" (26:18). Moreover, reverberations are heard of Isaiah's prophecy of the Servant's (= Israel's) vocation as "a light [*phōs*] to the nations,/that my salvation may reach to the end of the earth" (Isa 49:6)—a prophecy whose fulfillment begins with God's Messiah (cf. Luke 2:32) and continues in the mission of Paul (see 13:47). The defense of the Paul of Acts finally turns on this claim. It is not what Rome or even Israel may think of his mission or message, for the status of Paul's religious authority in the world is determined by what God thinks. God's favorable verdict on Paul's service is therefore not rendered in terms of his political innocence (26:30-32) but rather by the salvation of those who are prospective beneficiaries of divine grace "to the end of the earth," represented here by this Roman governor and Jewish king (26:24-29).

**26:1.** Luke structures the exchange between Agrippa and Paul according to ancient rhetorical form: The expert adjudicator (= Agrippa) takes over the proceedings and gives the rhetor (= Paul) permission to speak.[746] Paul makes a familiar hand gesture (see 13:16; 19:33; 21:40)—despite his shackles (see 26:29)—and "began to defend [ἀπολογέομαι *apologeomai*] himself."[747] Because Festus has already indicated that the charges against Paul do not carry any guilt from a Roman perspective and are essentially religious in kind, Paul's defense is religious in substance as well. In fact, he does not defend himself directly against his opponents' allegations but defines himself in terms of his heavenly calling and the results of his

mission among Jews and Gentiles. It is by obeying Israel's God that Paul defends himself against the accusation that he has transgressed Israel's traditions.

The positive tone established by Agrippa should be noted as well. He does not say "I give you permission" to establish a power or hostile relationship between himself and Paul. Rather more graciously, he gives Paul the freedom to state his case autobiographically—to speak *about* and not merely "for yourself"—and to him personally.[748]

**26:2-3.** The *exordium,* or introduction, of Paul's speech briefly expresses his good fortune (*captatio benevolentiae,* or compliments for rhetorical effect) that he makes his defense before Agrippa, not because of his royal rank but because he is an expert "with all the customs [ethos] and controversies of the Jews" (26:3; see 26:10*b*). Paul addresses Agrippa personally, "King Agrippa," as though in a conversation between just the two of them. According to rhetorical rules, it is necessary for Paul to first indicate the judicial competence of his judge and to tie Agrippa's expertise directly to the very essence of his defense. Thus, when Paul repeatedly addresses Agrippa personally (26:2, 7, 13, 19), the reader presumes it is because of Agrippa's familiarity "with all the customs and controversies of the Jews."

The elegance of phrasing of Paul's opening address is perhaps best illustrated by the interplay between two unusual but similar-sounding words that enclose it: "I consider myself fortunate [μακάριος *makarios*] and therefore beg of you to listen to me patiently [μακροθύμως *makrothymōs*]." The rhetor's intent is made clear by this word-play: Paul's plea for a favorable hearing is predicated on his good fortune in having Agrippa as his judge.

**26:4-18.** In conformity to the rhetor's rules, the substance of Paul's defense once again consists of a narrative (*narratio*) of his Jewish upbringing (4-8) and the circumstances (9-11) surrounding his conversion *as a Jew* to Jesus (12-15) and his calling *as a Jew* by Jesus (16-18). His autobiography is centered by two admittedly controversial claims: First, "I stand here on trial on account of

---

746. See B. Winter, "Official Proceedings and Forensic Speeches in Acts 24–26," in *The Book of Acts in First Century Setting,* ed. B. W. Winter and A. Clarke, 6 vols. (Grand Rapids: Eerdmans, 1993–98) 327-31, who concludes that both Paul and Luke understood and carefully followed the rules of conventional rhetoric, which "regulate" how Acts narrates the case in favor of Paul and his appeal to Caesar.

747. The Western version elevates Paul's piety and importance by adding "confidently, having received the consolation of the Holy Spirit."

748. Cf. B. Witherington, *The Acts of the Apostles: A Socio-Rhetorical Commentary* (Grand Rapids: Eerdmans, 1998) 738, who also notes that for this reason Luke does not refer to Agrippa as "Herod," a name synonymous with Christian oppression.

my hope in the promise made by God to our ancestors" (26:6a); and, second, this hope is that "God raises the dead" (26:8; see 23:6).

**26:4-5.** Paul signals the transition to the *narratio* by the introductory formula μὲν οὖν (*men oun;* lit., "Now then . . . "; neither the NIV nor the NRSV picks this up). The repetition of the temporal phrases "from my youth" and "from the beginning" defines the extent of his Jewish "way of life" (see 22:3). No mention is made of Tarsus; rather, the location of his Jewish life has been "in Jerusalem" and "among my own people." Thus, those Jews from Jerusalem who now oppose him could easily be asked by Agrippa to lend witness to Paul's claim that he has lived a robust Jewish life in full public view—as his Jewish opponents "have known for a long time" (v. 5a).

Perhaps more important to his self-defense is that this thoroughly Jewish upbringing was Pharisaic in kind: "I have belonged to the strictest sect [αἵρεσις *hairesis*] of our religion [θρησκεία *thrēskeia*] and lived as a Pharisee (v. 5b). The various subtexts of Paul's text alert the reader to a fuller meaning of his religious location. His reference to the Pharisees as a *hairesis* reminds the reader of the charge leveled earlier by Tertullus against Paul that he is "a ringleader of the sect [*hairesis*] of the Nazarenes" (24:5). The implicit claim here is that he is not the member of an heretical sectarian movement within Judaism but of a legitimate "party" of pious messianists. Paul's use of the rare superlative "strictest" (ἀκριβεστάτης *akribestatēs*), which denotes the precise or accurate interpretation of biblical law characteristic of the Pharisees, only intensifies the impression of his orthodoxy. The use of *thrēskeia,* which denotes formal or recognized religious observance, instead of Festus's more cynical term for "religion" (δεισιδαιμονία *deisidaimonia*), which denotes "superstition" (see 25:19), locates Paul within the bounds of Jewish orthodoxy—a subtle point meant for Agrippa due to his expert's knowledge of a Jewish ethos.

The aorist tense of the verb "I have lived" (ἔζησα *ezēsa*) is constantive and retrospective; that is, it views the action as a whole to that point, without noting the duration of time. However, Paul is vague as to *which* point. Jervell rightly insists that the logic of Paul's apologia requires Agrippa to accept that Paul's Pharisaic "way of

life"—his piety and core beliefs—carry over to his Christian way of life (see 23:6).[749] One can hardly imagine Paul's speech a "defense" against Jewish accusations, however implicit, before an expert in Jewish ethos, however personal, if this logic were somehow otherwise. Paul's argument is not to show how "Christian" his former Judaism was, but rather to show how Jewish his current Christianity is.

**26:6-8.** For this reason, the καὶ νῦν *kai nyn* ("And now") should not be taken as a formula of contrast but of the unbroken continuity (= "And") between Paul's Pharisaic Judaism and his current (= "now") messianic Christianity. For him, the essential definition of true religion concerns "my hope [ἐλπίς *elpis*] in the promise [ἐπαγγελία *epangelia*] made by God to our ancestors" (26:6) and those religious practices that cultivate this hope by "[earnest] worship day and night" (26:7). Although not explicitly stated, the reader of Acts understands from earlier texts that Paul's reference to *elpis* is to the "hope of the resurrection" (see 23:6; 24:15; 25:19), which then explains his cryptic question, "Why is it thought incredible by any of you that God raises the dead?" (26:8). Such an expression of perplexity is deeply rooted in Pharisaism's theology of hope for the resurrection of faithful Israel to eternal life, without which every other religious belief and practice is held to in vain (cf. 1 Cor 15:12-19).

Actually, the more important term of Paul's statement—at least in Acts—is *epangelia,* which recalls God's fulfilled "promise" of the Spirit's outpouring (1:4; 2:33, 39) and of the Messiah's deliverance (13:23, 32) according to Israel's Scriptures. God's realized promises of both the Messiah and the Spirit, however, are carefully related in Acts to God's umbrella promise of a restored Israel (see 1:4-8). The centrality of Paul's belief in the resurrection and of its experience in the Spirit, the content both of what God has promised repentant Israel and of what worshiping Israel hopes, is at the center of the Christian gospel from the beginning. From Pentecost forward, prophets-like-Jesus have proclaimed a gospel that integrates these two

---

749. J. Jervell, *Die Apostelgeschichte,* KEK 3 (Göttingen: Vandenhoeck & Ruprecht, 1998) 591, although some point out that Paul's adherence to purity laws governing table fellowship in mixed company is too lax to claim for his present life a "strict" adherence to Pharisaic practices. Cf. Witherington, *The Acts of the Apostles,* 740.

resurrections of a Spirit-filled Israel and Spirit-giving Messiah. Indeed, the fact of the resurrected One signifies that Israel's hope of its own end-time resurrection has already been realized (see 3:19-22; 5:28-32).

The Greek text marks a shift in implied audience from a single person, King Agrippa, to a plural "you" (ὑμεῖς *hymeis*) to make Paul's pointed question ironical, "Why is it thought incredible by any of you that God raises the dead?" (26:8). On the face of it, Paul's apologia for the resurrection appeals to human reason to evaluate the concept of deity by a supernatural power that only the gods possess: Any deity who cannot raise the dead—or transform human existence—is not a deity worth worshiping. Yet some of his Roman auditors would no doubt find this "hope in the resurrection" the core belief of a "superstitious" religion (see 17:22; 25:19). For this reason, Paul's comment may be directed to those *not* in attendance: unrepentant Jews, especially from the party of Pharisees, who share with him the ancestral hope in a resurrected Israel but who have rejected its fulfillment in the resurrected Jesus.

**26:9-11.** Luke again uses μὲν οὖν (*men oun*, "Indeed") to introduce the next period of Paul's narratio. The reader is already familiar with this "before Jesus" stage of his story from earlier texts (see 8:1-3; 9:1-2; 22:4-5). Several features of this iteration, however, deserve attention. Most critically, the opening *men oun* suggests continuity between his beliefs as a Pharisee (vv. 6-8) and his persecution of the church (vv. 9-11). More specifically, Paul's ferocity against believers exemplifies the incredulity of unrepentant Pharisees that Jesus is God's Messiah and Israel's Lord. Ironically, *he* is one who has thought it incredible "that God raises the dead [= Jesus]," and therefore "was convinced that I ought to do many things against the name of Jesus of Nazareth" (v. 9). At issue is *not* Paul's skepticism regarding resurrection. Rather, the presumed nationalism and ethnocentrism of his Jewish faith, cultivated by a Jewish education and membership in Pharisaism, had fashioned a variety of hope posited in the nation's end-time resurrection; and so the very idea of a resurrected Messiah in the past (rather than a resurrected Israel in the future) seemed to him "incredible." His is a very different sort of skepticism from that which characterizes the secular or pagan intellectual, for

whom the very idea of a "resurrection" may seem incredible. Paul did not believe in resurrected messiahs and, therefore, thought it his religious duty to squelch this new messianic movement.

The use of "the name [ὄνομα *onoma*] of Jesus of Nazareth" once again recalls the movement of the word of the Lord in Jerusalem from the very beginning. The inspired proclamation of the word witnesses to "the name of Jesus" (4:18-19), so that "by the name of Jesus Christ of Nazareth" (4:10) and "by no other name" (see 4:12) the supplicant is saved from sins (see 2:21, 38) and healed from sickness (see 3:4, 16). The "name of Jesus" stands in Acts as a metaphor for true religion because in witness to that name the hope of a restored Israel is realized. Thus, the "many things" that Paul did "against the name" refers to his efforts to subvert the movement of the word in and beyond Jerusalem.

These efforts are enumerated in a single sentence that details "what I did in Jerusalem; with authority received from the chief priests" (26:10; see 9:2, 14; 22:5). This catalog of atrocities against "the saints" (see 9:13) confirms the standing impression of Paul's antagonism against the gospel on the other side of the Damascus road, here intensified: "I was so furiously enraged at them" (26:11). According to Paul's testimony, he: (1) "locked up many of the saints" (see 8:3; 9:13); (2) "cast my vote against them"; (3) "tried to force them to blaspheme" (see 22:5); and (4) "pursued them even to foreign cities [i.e., beyond Jerusalem]" (vv. 10-11; see also 9:1-2).

Several features of this description of Paul's hostilities are new and self-incriminating and deserve further discussion. Most important in this regard is the second: "I also cast my vote [κατήνεγκα ψῆφον *katēnenka psēphon;* lit., "to cast a voting pebble") against them when they were being condemned [ἀναιρέω *anaireō*]" (v. 10*b*). Judicial bodies routinely used pebbles when deciding verdicts and so "to cast a pebble" came to refer to the vote itself; in turn, the vote cast revealed one's truest values and core beliefs. To cast a condemning vote in this instance means to vote for the death penalty against believers: Paul's opposition to the faith is thus confirmed. Acts mentions only Stephen and the apostle James as martyrs; however, this text suggests there were others. While doubtless Luke feels no compulsion to tell the story of every Christian martyr in Acts, it is most likely that Paul's comment here is a metaphor for his intense opposition to the messianic movement in Jerusalem. Further, it is unlikely that he was a voting member of the Sanhedrin and would have had a vote to cast, although some think it possible that he was a clerk or associate of Pharisees who were and therefore participated in some indirect way in any voting that actually took place.[750] Again, however, Luke is probably using the image of a "voting pebble" as a metaphor for Paul's cooperation with malevolent forces in Jerusalem (see 7:58).

Also new is the claim that Paul punished them "often in the synagogues . . . to force them to blaspheme" (v. 11a). There is no reference to believers attending synagogues in Jerusalem, even though this perhaps could be implied from the story of Stephen's arrest (see 6:8-12; cf. 2 Cor 11:24). Yet in his earlier testimony Paul did mention that he arrested and brought believers to Jerusalem for punishment (see 22:5). The new elements in Paul's rehearsal of his opposition to the Hellenists are his attempts (evidently failed)[751] to get believers to utter publicly "anathema Jesus" or some other specifically anti-Christian slogan. Paul's opposition to believers in and around Jerusalem, then, demonstrates his profound devotion to the orthodoxy of official Judaism.

**26:12-15.** Paul's public testimony is centered by his Damascus road experience, which has shaped his identity as a prophet-like-Jesus. By this point in Acts the broad details of this experience are familiar: when traveling to persecute believers in Damascus "with the authority and commission of the chief priests" (v. 12; see also 9:1-2; 22:5), he "saw a light from heaven, brighter than the sun, shining around me and my companions" (v. 13; see also 9:3; 22:6). The intensity of the brightness is here emphasized, and Paul now includes his traveling companions as witnesses to his experience: The great light surrounded them (cf. 22:9) and "we all had fallen to the ground" (v. 14a; cf. 9:7; 22:7).

Keeping with Luke's thematic interest in the use of language, Paul notes the dialect of the

divine audition: "I heard a voice saying to me in the Hebrew (lit., "Hebrew dialect"; i.e., "Aramaic") language" (v. 14b). While metaphorical of the participatory nature of God's saving activity in the world, Paul's addition of this detail in his apologia to a Roman audience stresses the essentially Jewish cast of his story and mission. The ensuing dialogue between Jesus and Paul is as before, except the addition of the famous although cryptic aphorism, "It is hard [σκληρός *skleros*] for you to kick against the goads [κέντρον *kentron*]" (v. 14c). A *kentron* is a stick with a sharpened point used as a variety of cattle prod to goad an animal in the right direction. For Paul to "kick against the goads" is to resist God's goading. The addition of *skleros*, which is an OT metaphor for "hardening" one's resolve against God's will (cf. Exod 6:9), adds an additional layer of meaning to his implied response to the Lord's probing question, "Saul, Saul, why are you persecuting me?" Paul's persecution of Jesus indicates his stubborn refusal to obey God's redemptive plan, which includes him. Because God's plan does include Paul, it is fruitless for him to persecute Jesus.

**26:16-18.** God's plan for Paul is now disclosed. There is no mention of Paul's blindness and the witness of pious Ananias to Paul's conversion is replaced by that of Paul's traveling companions. Luke shapes this final apologia to emphasize Paul's prophetic calling and in doing so brings to the fore several elements of his portrait in Acts. Jesus "appears" to Paul "to appoint [προχειρίζομαι *procheirizomai*] you to serve [ὑπηρέτης *hyperetes*] and testify [μάρτυς *martys*] (v. 16a). The purpose of this unmediated visitation is to call Paul to a task in continuity with that of the Messiah whom God "appointed" and sent to restore Israel and the entire world (see 3:19-21). Paul's tasks are also in continuity with those of the Lord's apostolic successors who are chosen (see 1:2) and given the Spirit in order to "be my witnesses" (*martyres;* see 1:8). The Paul of Acts is not appointed to an apostolic office but to be a "servant" of the word (cf. Luke 1:2). The use of *hyperetes* almost certainly alludes to Isaiah's Servant in whose role Paul is depicted (see the Commentary on 26:18).

The content of this word of the Lord involves the things in which you have seen me and . . . those in which I will appear to you" (v. 16b; see

---

750. Cf. Witherington, *The Acts of the Apostles,* 742.
751. See C. K. Barrett, *A Critical and Exegetical Commentary on the Acts of the Apostles,* 2 vols, ICC (Edinburgh: T. & T. Clark, 1994, 1998) 2:1156.

also 22:15).[752] This testimony agrees with Paul's autobiography according to which "the revelation of Jesus Christ" supplied him with the core beliefs of his gospel (cf. Gal 1:12-16). Paul implies that the Lord promised additional appearances to enhance and direct his witness. In Acts, surely this must refer to Paul's other epiphanies, most notably the Lord's disclosure that Paul "must bear witness also in Rome"[753] (see 23:11; cf. 27:23-24). That is, Paul's vocation is supplied with both a word about the living Jesus and a city of destiny in which to proclaim it.

Jesus also promises to "rescue [ἐξαιρέω exaireō] you from your people and from the Gentiles [lit., "nations")—to whom I am sending you" (26:17). The intriguing features of this segment of Paul's commissioning revelation are twofold: First, the prospect of the Lord's "rescue" (exaireō), which is an important element of the exodus typology used both in Acts (7:10, 34; 12:11; 23:27) and in OT narrative (cf. Exod 3:8; 18:4; Ps 38:40 LXX; see also Jer 1:8,19): God rescues those that God has chosen, whether Israel from Egyptian oppression or Paul from his opponents, so that God's promises are realized. Second, even more important is Paul's note of universal opposition to his message of universal salvation. The interpreter simply cannot sustain an argument that Acts casts only "the Jews" in the "bad guys" role. Paul's comment is an effective summary of the rejection theme, which recounts how unrepentant Gentiles along with unrepentant Jews seek to subvert the progress of the word of the Lord to the end of the earth and how God "rescued" Paul from their evil machinations (see 13:44-45; 14:2, 19; 16:7, 9, 19-24; 17:5-9, 13, 32; 18:6, 12-13; 19:9, 22-24; 22:7; 23:11).

The universal scope of Paul's mission is indicated even though it is possible that "to whom" (εἰς οὕς eis hous) in v. 17 refers only to the Gentiles. Earlier, Paul's claim that his mission among the Gentiles was undertaken in obedience to God's command had incensed the Jerusalem Jews (see 22:21-23). Perhaps Paul wants now to explain and expand that earlier controversy to Agrippa. In any case, I think it best to take the antecedent of eis hous as inclusive of "the people and the Gentiles."

The religious aim of Paul's witness is set forth in a sequence of pregnant phrases that summarizes his understanding of the conversion experience.[754] The structure of 26:18 is supplied by three infinitives, "to open," "to turn," and "to receive," all of which are dependent upon the concluding action of the preceding verse, "to whom I am sending you." Simply put, God sends Paul to the nations in order "to open" them to the truth of the gospel, "to turn" them from ignorance to the light of God's gospel, with the result that they are able "to receive" forgiveness and eternal life from God.

The idiom and ideas of this important text echo Isaiah's prophecy of the Servant's calling (cf. Isa 42:6-7) and constitute of the most powerful statements of conversion in Scripture. The original sounding of Isaiah's prophecy is introduced by the Creator's declaration of the Spirit's gift (cf. 42:5), so that the Servant's calling as "a light to the nations" (cf. 42:6) "to open the eyes that are blind" (cf. 42:7) presumes the Spirit's enablement. The spiritual calculus of Isaiah's definition of Israel's calling is also the logic of Paul's self-understanding. That is, his mission to the nations and the divine forgiveness that results are impossibilities without the Spirit's inspiration.

Moreover, the Paul of Acts is a prophet-like-Jesus (cf. Luke 4:14-21) who receives the mantle of Isaiah's Servant by commission of the resurrected Lord and continues to do and say what Jesus revealed to him as the personification of Isaiah's Servant Israel. Unlike Luke's Jesus, however, whose messianic mission extended only to the Jews, Paul's mission to the nations more fully realizes Isaiah's prophecy of a faithful Israel's service to God: Paul is a witness to "the people and the Gentiles" and opens all their eyes to the truth of God. He summarizes, then, the unstated justification for the plotline of Luke's Acts: Paul's Damascus road commissioning and the com-

---

752. The NIV's "as a servant and as a witness" is more literal than the NRSV, which paraphrases the nouns *hypēretēs* and *martys* by using verbs.

753. The Greek of this phrase is convoluted and for this reason its transmission is corrupted. Its plain meaning is more plainly stated in 22:15: Paul is to bear witness to "what you have seen and heard." The problem is with the direct object με (*me*, "me"), whether to retain it (as do both translations) or not. The textual and internal evidence is equally divided. In my judgment, the NIV translation offers the best compromise: retain *me* but of its fuller sense that Paul's witness is "of me"— i.e., of the living Jesus he met on the Damascus Road.

754. For this theme in Acts, see B. Gaventa, *From Darkness to Light: Aspects of Conversion in the New Testament*, OBT (Philadelphia: Fortress, 1986) 52-95.

mencement of his mission as light to the nations (Acts 9–28) take place when God's promise of Israel's restoration had been fulfilled through the church's mission to the whole house of Israel (Acts 1–8; see 3:19-26). The timing of Paul's encounter with the living Jesus in the plotline of Acts is the effect of the formation of a repentant Israel under the leadership of the Twelve.

What follows is a description of the universal experience of all who convert from darkness (= ignorance/Satan) to light (= gospel/God) through "faith in [Jesus]" (see 2:21; 11:17; 13:38-39; 15:9-11; 20:20-21). They all share in the blessings God promised to a restored Israel: God's forgiveness (see 2:38; 5:31; 10:43; 13:38) and a thorough cleansing of sins (see 3:18-19; 20:32; cf. 15:8-11; Rom 15:16; 1 Cor 6:11).

**26:19-20.** The speech's confirmatio testifies to Paul's obedience to the Lord's visionary commission, using litotes (deliberate understatement)—"I was not disobedient"—to make the character of his response more emphatic. Paul traces his obedience by the geography of his mission, narrated by Acts and easily confirmed by its readers: "first to those in Damascus [see 9:20-22] . . . then in Jerusalem [see 9:28-29], and also to the Gentiles [vv. 13-20]." The added phrase, "and throughout the countryside of Judea," is difficult not only because of its awkward grammar (stated in the accusative case rather than in the dative as the others) but more so because nowhere does Acts indicate a Pauline mission "throughout the countryside of Judea." The shift of case is exceptional but not unknown where the phrase in the accusative bounds those items enumerated in the dative; thus, Paul's preaching "throughout the countryside of Judea" merely encompasses in general those particular missions in Damascus and Jerusalem. The latter problem is amplified, however, by Paul's claim that he was "still unkown by sight to the churches of Judea" (Gal 1:22), although he also claimed to have preached the gospel in Illyricum (cf. Rom 15:19). Different solutions have been suggested; however, the grammatical solution also settles the historical conflict if the reader takes the phrase "throughout the countryside of Judea" as iterative of Paul's Damascus and Jerusalem missions in order to demonstrate that Paul's is a Jewish missionary who goes first to the Jews before reaching out to the Gentiles.[755]

Paul repeats in different words the content of his evangelical declaration to the Jews and Gentiles (see 26:18), that "they should repent and turn to God"; but he then adds the ethical imperative "and do deeds consistent with repentance" (v. 20). Although Paul implies that two discrete responses to the gospel are required for salvation, he does not clarify the exact relationship between the sinner's turn toward God for forgiveness and the believer's works that are consistent with repentance. He has already stipulated that repentance is by faith in Jesus (v. 18), and that a thorough spiritual cleansing will result; this formulation implies that works follow from repentance. The question remains whether the forgiven believer can live a manner of life that is contrary to God's will. Clearly this is impossible for the epistolary Paul, for whom good works are the natural yield of saving faith (cf. Rom 6:1-11; Eph 2:8-10). For him there is but a single response that is required, and that is the sinner's faith in the crucified Christ's sacrifice for sin (cf. Rom 3:21-26). Repentance and "deeds consistent with repentance" constitute a seamless, mutually inclusive response to God's grace, and not two related but separate responses, as Luke's Paul implies.

**26:21.** The refutatio rebuts the original charge brought against Paul that he profaned the Temple and provides Agrippa with an apt synopsis of what has been described in detail in 21:27–25:12. According to the design of his apologia, however, Paul can now claim that his arrest is the result of his responsiveness to the Lord's calling and follows Scripture's imperative (see v. 22)—the polar opposite of what his Jewish opponents allege!

**26:22-23.** Any defense speech that follows the rhetorical rules of the day includes a plea for divine help, "for which the use of the verb [τυγχάνω] *tynchanō* ("help") is standard."[756] Paul's concluding peroratio implies that God's help has kept him safe as promised and "so I stand here" (i.e., "I am alive and well"). More important, however, God has kept him safe for this moment when he bears witness "to both small and great" (see v. 29) that Scripture's promise of salvation has been fulfilled in the Christ event. With good reason, R. O'Toole contends that this

---

755. Cf. Barrett, *Acts*, 2:1163-64.

756. Winter, "Official Proceedings and Forensic Speeches in Acts 24–26," 330; cf. F. F. Bruce, *The Acts of the Apostles*, rev. ed., NICNT (Grand Rapids: Eerdmans, 1988) 504.

text is "the christological climax of Paul's defense" if not of all Luke-Acts.[757] Nowhere in Acts is there a clearer expression that the gospel's theological substructure is a narrative of fulfillment: The Messiah's suffering and resurrection are fulfilled in the life of Jesus according to the prophesied pattern of "the prophets and Moses" (see 13:15; 24:14; also 2:16; 3:18, 21-25; 7:52; 10:43; 13:27, 40; 15:15, 32; 28:23; cf. Luke 24:44-48). The ultimate importance of this point is recognized by Agrippa, who subsequently takes it up with Paul for fuller discussion (see 26:27-28).[758]

This striking summary of Paul's testimony deserves careful attention. Earlier in the speech he asserted that Israel's national hope rests on God's promise to resurrect the dead (see 26:6-8). The more controversial calculus of Paul's apologia is that Israel's hope in the resurrection must surely be related to God's resurrection of Jesus: the promise of Israel's restoration is already being realized from the empty tomb forward. It is in this specific sense that Paul can now claim that his own testimony "to both small and great" is thoroughly Jewish and follows the redemptive script of the Jewish Scriptures—"the prophets and Moses."

The strategic repetition of "Moses" in this formula (instead of the more familiar "the law") probably intends to recall other references to "Moses" in Acts so to "thicken" the meaning of Paul's appeal to Moses in his defense. The "Moses" of Acts not only denotes the biblical torah (see 15:21), he is also the type of and a prophet of Jesus. Taken together, then, all Scripture, inclusive of the books of Moses, testifies to and confirms the Christ event to which Paul himself publicly testifies. It does so because Jesus fulfills the promise that God "will raise up for you" a prophet-like-Moses (see 3:22-23; 7:37). The prophetic pattern of Moses, in which Jesus and now Paul follow, establishes the kerygmatic core of Christian proclamation: "that the Messiah must suffer [and] . . . rise from the dead." Rejection leads to vindication according to "the prophets and Moses."

What stands out more clearly as a result of Paul's mission is Israel's identity as a light to the nations (Isa 49:6-7; see 13:47; cf. Luke 2:32). Already grounded in biblical prophecy, Paul now claims that the Messiah is not only the "first to rise from the dead" to establish Israel's hope but is also the first to "proclaim light to our people and to the Gentiles" to establish Israel's vocation (cf. 2 Tim 1:10). His implied defense is that because his own identity follows from God's Messiah who fulfills Jewish Scriptures, he must therefore be considered an exemplary Jew.

**26:24-29.** Luke often uses the interrupted speech—a speech that actually has been completed—as a rhetorical device to underline the last thing said (see 10:44). The last element of Paul's speech is not the core beliefs of the Christian kerygma—the Lord's passion and his resurrection—but rather the Lord's universal mission that he now emulates. The reader already realizes the challenge that his mission represents for Jewish notions of identity (see 22:21-23); Festus's outburst recognizes that Paul's mission to the nations challenges Roman (or secular) notions of identity as well, but for very different reasons. If the universalism of Paul's mission subverts the particularity of a Jewish identity, whose religious beliefs and practices stress Israel's special relationship with the one and only Creator God, then his messianism subverts also the relativism of Rome's ethos, which tolerates the diverse and multiple identities of its different subjects. Not only does Jesus' resurrection fulfill Israel's hope according to its Scriptures, but his present and future significance is cosmic in scope (see 3:19-21).

The persona of the Festus of Acts is that of a person of rational self-interest. His judgments of Paul's "great learning" (πολλὰ γράμματα *polla grammata*) and even of his "insanity" (μανία *mania*) are measurements of the human mind. He correctly realizes that if Paul is right in his concluding words, then the Roman way of life he personifies and champions has come to an end with Jesus. Paul's retort is in kind and appeals to prceisely what Festus values: "What I am saying [ἀποφθέγγομαι *apophthengomai*] is true [ἀλήθεια *aletheia*] and reasonable [σωφροσύνη *sophrosynē*]" (v. 25).[759] His initial response goes

---

757. Cf. R. O'Toole, *The Christological Climax of Paul's Defense,* AnBib 78 (Rome: Pontifical Biblical Institute, 1978) 101-22.

758. The grammar of this text suggests that Paul proposes discussion topics rather than that he proclaims religious beliefs. The key phrases of the gospel summary are introduced by the Greek particle εἰ (*ei*), picked up in the translations as "must" (NRSV) or "would" (NIV), which by in ancient rhetoric introduces points of debate. Agrippa follows Paul's rhetorical cue and takes up these propositions for further dialogue.

759. The NRSV plausibly translates this phrase as a hendiadys: What is "true" and "reasonable" constitutes the "sober truth."

to the genre of his speech: *apophthengomai* denotes divinely inspired speech—the speech of a prophet (see 2:4, 14). Thus, his "great learning" (*polla grammata*) derives from inspired insight into the meaning of Scripture that enables him to detect the gospel's *alētheia* (cf. 2 Cor 6:7; 11:10; Gal 2:5, 14). Hardly insane, what he says is *sōphrosynē,* a word that denotes intellectual sobriety.[760]

Paul's continual personal appeal to Agrippa throughout his apologia reaches its climax with this final exchange between them. Paul had invited dialogue when summarizing his gospel message and the divine sanction of its universal application (see v. 23). While Festus fully understands the implication of what Paul says for a Roman ethos, its Jewish cast makes it an awkward fit and more suitable for Agrippa, even though the latter is a secular Jew. His familiarity with "these things" (= Jewish Scriptures) allows Paul to "speak freely" (παρρησιάζομαι *parrēsiazomai;* lit., "boldly"). The repetition of *parrēsiazomai* cues its earlier use in Acts as characteristic of the prophet-like-Jesus who is inspired by the Spirit to proclaim the gospel (see 4:29-31). It is precisely at this moment that Paul's apologia turns into a missionary speech: To "speak freely" to Agrippa is to proclaim the word of the Lord to him.

Paul contributes two elements that frame his earlier kerygmatic claims regarding the dying and rising of the Messiah and his ministry as God's light to Jews and Gentiles. These claims are a matter of the historical record: "none of these things has escaped his notice, for this was not done in a corner" (v. 26). The apologetic purpose of this litotes is emphatically to point out that the gospel's subject matter is experiential, and it can be tested whether "true and reasonable" by any "sane" person. Christian religion is neither private nor internal; as a faith consonant with Scripture's definition, its claims are worked out within history for all to see.

Paul's query about Agrippa's belief in the prophets (v. 27) evinces his theological purpose. The subtext of the question, of course, is that Paul's messianic interpretation of the prophets

recognizes that God's promises of Israel's restoration and of an international participation in its blessings are fulfilled in the ministry, suffering, and resurrection of Jesus. He is asking Agrippa whether he believes this gospel, not whether he knows the relevant prophecies. Agrippa is quick to recognize Paul's intent: "Are you so quickly persuading me to become [ποιέω *poieō*] a Christian?" (v. 28). What is more difficult for the interpreter to discern is how seriously Agrippa takes Paul's evangelistic query. The meaning here of the verb *poieō,* which literally means "to make/perform," is unclear. Is Agrippa on the verge of "making" a Christian conversion? Perhaps. However, many commentators now understand the exchange between Agrippa and Paul to be more witty than sober.[761] Especially when considered in light of Paul's punning response, perhaps all Agrippa is asking is whether he could "perform the role" of a Christian, presumably to demonstrate both his good sense and his identity with his Jewish subjects. But to "perform a role" is not to "become" a true believer.

Paul seems to sense Agrippa's lack of resolve and puns his line in reference to "these chains"—the metaphor of Paul's commitment to the gospel. That is, Paul prays that Agrippa, indeed, "perform the role" of a believer, but not that of a bit part and rather with the firm authentic dedication exemplified by his own example: "I pray God—all who are listening to me today may become what I am [i.e., perform my role]" (v. 29).

**26:30-32.** Paul has the last word in his final apologia; its exhortation is not unlike his final words to the elders of Ephesus at Miletus (see 20:35). That both unbelieving and believing leaders should follow Paul's example underwrites the universalism of his spiritual authority. It is also noteworthy that Luke narrates the ad hoc review of Paul's hearing between the king, the governor, Bernice, and "those who had been sitting with them" in a way that echoes the Jewish Sanhedrin's conference following Peter's powerful testimony earlier in Acts (see 4:15-18; cf. 5:33-40). Rome's more favorable verdict toward Paul, which confirms his innocence, contributes to the general impression that Rome is the city of his destiny.

---

760. The two genitives that delimit Paul's prophetic speech—what he "says"—set forth what is said ("true" is an objective genitive) and how it is said ("reasonable" is a subjective genitive). See Barrett, *Acts,* 2:1168.

761. E.g., L. T. Johnson, *The Acts of the Apostles,* SP 5 (Collegeville, Minn.: Liturgical, 1992) 439-40.

There is a sense in which neither Agrippa nor Festus has authority to determine that "this man could have been set free if he had not appealed to the emperor" (26:32). Rather, it is by authority of a sovereign God that Paul will appear before Caesar in Rome (see 23:11; 27:24). And so it is that Paul's legal entanglements end, not with a bang but with a whimper. All these various decisions fund the larger script that the word of the Lord will be carried by the anointed prophet as a "light to the nations, that my salvation may reach to the end of the earth" (Isa 49:6; see 13:47).

# REFLECTIONS

**1.** "Why is it thought incredible by any of you that God raises the dead?" (26:8 NRSV). When people object to the idea or fact of the resurrection, we should ask them what sort of god is it that would make hope in the resurrection unreasonable. If there is no personal and powerful God, then the conversation ends there. Paul's incredulity that anyone might regard his Easter faith as specious, however, reflects a profoundly biblical faith. From his perspective, the resurrection makes perfect sense: What other way would a life-giving God demonstrate fidelity to the promise of new life, free from the threat of death? And what other evidence makes sense of his own conversion and calling?

For others the first Easter dawned a scandalous surprise. Even the women who came to the tomb did so out of loyalty for their fallen friend. They had witnessed his execution; and they had seen his body wrapped in burial cloth and placed in a grave, sealed with a stone. Jesus of Nazareth was dead indeed. Luke captures the women's Easter surprise: "They did not find the body" (Luke 24:3). They found the tombstone rolled away, disclosing in the grave's emptiness the cornerstone of our faith. Jesus of Nazareth is risen; God has made him Lord and Christ (see 2:36). The subtext of Acts is that without God's resurrection power Christianity would have fizzled out; our faith stands or it falls with the truth of the resurrection.

Yet, none of the New Testament writers recount the resurrection itself; they are more concerned with what results from the resurrection. The importance of Easter is envisioned by the core theological convictions of the church that are clustered around the empty tomb. We cannot glibly dismiss Jesus as another "great teacher" or "moral exemplar." The resurrection stamps him as the authoritative teacher of God's truth, so that to know him is to know God in a more personal way. The resurrection illumines his life as the incarnation of God's demand perfectly obeyed, so that to follow him is to love God and neighbor in life-giving ways. Nor can we talk about the scandal of Jesus' death as a "bad Friday" on which one more innocent man was killed by powerful leaders made blind and jealous by their self-centered ambition. The innocent one crucified on that Roman cross is none other than the Son of God, and his atoning death results in "a ransom for many" (Mark 10:45).

By God's salvation-creating grace, what began as a "bad Friday" is transformed into the church's Good Friday: In the risen Jesus, God has declared the forgiveness of our sins; our hope in God's forgiveness is not groundless. Hidden in God's resurrection of the living Lord is the promise that "he will come again to judge the living and the dead." This familiar confession of our hope, so mysterious and modest, expresses the church's profound confidence: Despite the persistence of sin and the presence of suffering, God's triumph over the evil one through the risen Christ will surely have its day.

God's resurrection of Jesus also provides incisive commentary on a right understanding of ourselves, both during the present moment and into the future. A student of mine, already the graduate of a fine university just eight years before, had enrolled for classes at my university to acquire another degree and additional skills for a second career. When I congratulated him on his desire for more education, he responded with a shrug that he had become obsolete in the marketplace. The work force no longer needed his skills and he was replaced. His story is a symbol of our contemporary "hi-tech" culture, in which we are made to feel quickly dispensable and are easily forgotten. Our individual identities are reduced to numbers stored in a computer; only rarely does our work survive as a lasting contribution, and few remember our names after we leave. The pressures and secular perceptions of our everyday world shove each of us toward oblivion. But Paul writes that by faith we participate with Christ in the results of his death and resurrection, which constitute a "new life" (Rom 6:4).

God's resurrection of Jesus is bodily and historical; likewise, God's good purposes are embodied in our own particular histories, made new by God's empowering love. On the one hand, the death of Jesus' body says "no" to the spiritual sin and natural decay that destroys the various "bodies" in which we participate—personal, familial, ecclesial, and social. Yet, on the other hand, the resurrection of Jesus' body says yes to God's life-giving power: Through the redeemed community, God can bring those decaying bodies back to life. Further, God remembered Jesus when others rejected him and God brought him back to life as indispensable humanity. Likewise, God remembers us "while we still were sinners" (Rom 5:8) and restores our true humanity (Rom 8:28-30). By God's grace, our character is transformed with Christ from bad news into good (Col 3:1-11), resulting in the revitalization of our relationships with others (Col 3:12–4:6). We are risen indeed (Eph 2:5-6)! Finally, then, the resurrection envisages the "hope of Israel"—the promise of a new creation, purged of decay and death, where a community's ordinary experience is of God's shalom (cf. 1 Cor 15:35-49).

When the risen Jesus met his former disciples, they recognized him by name (John 20:16; Luke 24:35) and were reunited with him. Likewise, at Christ's triumphant return, God will not reduce our unique individuality but will restore it completely. Because we retain our individuality, those loved ones now missed will be remembered. Those lost in this life will be found in the next, for the resurrection is about reunion too: on that first Easter, Christ with God, so that on the last Easter, us with Christ and each with one another. The resurrection is a powerful symbol that God's design for creation is purposeful. The suffering, evil, and futility all around us today is challenged by the hope of tomorrow—a hope warranted by the resurrection.

**2.** "Festus exclaimed, 'You are out of your mind, Paul! Too much learning is driving you insane!'" (26:24 NRSV). Paul's perceived insanity is noteworthy by its coherence! His final speech on Palestinian soil claims two familiar moments in his life that give shape to his Christian identity—his conversion and his calling. Yet he also insists that his Christian identity is shaped by the intellectual traditions of Israel. Paul is not converted from guilt and misery or called to a journey toward self-fulfillment. He is no guru of New Age spirituality but a devout Jew whose experiences of conversion to the resurrected Messiah and calling to a prophetic ministry are consistent with the Scriptures of Israel properly understood. These holistic claims of mind and heart, of written text and living context, are the constants of a personal testimony whose coherence does not change with shifts of audience and circumstance.

Would Paul's apologia before a sophisticated audience of rich and influential leaders sound a responsive note today? Perhaps not: Most might repeat Festus's harsh verdict. Today's society is cultivated by a scientific sophistry, convinced that all claims to universal truth must be assessed by empirical investigation. The principal disposition toward anything religious, especially if revivalist in tone, is one of deep suspicion of its intellectual integrity. Central to Paul's testimony, whether to religious Jews or sophisticated pagans, is that his conversion and calling is not his doing but the living Lord's: As Willimon has noted, "Most of the traffic on the bridge between us and God is moving toward us."[762] The subtext of Paul's testimony is that a reasonable yet radical leap of faith is required to grab hold of the theocentricity of the Christian gospel. At the end of the day, Festus and then Agrippa (26:28) remain unconvinced, not because they lacked solid evidence but because they lacked faith in a faithful God who forgives and transforms human life, both now and forevermore.

762. W. Willimon, *Acts* (Atlanta: John Knox, 1988) 180.

# ACTS 27:1-12, SETTING SAIL FOR ROME

NIV

**27** When it was decided that we would sail for Italy, Paul and some other prisoners were handed over to a centurion named Julius, who belonged to the Imperial Regiment. [2]We boarded a ship from Adramyttium about to sail for ports along the coast of the province of Asia, and we put out to sea. Aristarchus, a Macedonian from Thessalonica, was with us.

[3]The next day we landed at Sidon; and Julius, in kindness to Paul, allowed him to go to his friends so they might provide for his needs. [4]From there we put out to sea again and passed to the lee of Cyprus because the winds were against us. [5]When we had sailed across the open sea off the coast of Cilicia and Pamphylia, we landed at Myra in Lycia. [6]There the centurion found an Alexandrian ship sailing for Italy and put us on board. [7]We made slow headway for many days and had difficulty arriving off Cnidus. When the wind did not allow us to hold our course, we sailed to the lee of Crete, opposite Salmone. [8]We moved along the coast with difficulty and came to a place called Fair Havens, near the town of Lasea.

[9]Much time had been lost, and sailing had already become dangerous because by now it was after the Fast.[a] So Paul warned them, [10]"Men, I can see that our voyage is going to be disastrous and bring great loss to ship and cargo, and to our own lives also." [11]But the centurion, instead of listening to what Paul said, followed the advice of the pilot and of the owner of the ship. [12]Since the harbor was unsuitable to winter in, the majority decided that we should sail on, hoping to reach Phoenix and winter there. This was a harbor in Crete, facing both southwest and northwest.

[a] 9 That is, the Day of Atonement (Yom Kippur)

NRSV

**27** When it was decided that we were to sail for Italy, they transferred Paul and some other prisoners to a centurion of the Augustan Cohort, named Julius. [2]Embarking on a ship of Adramyttium that was about to set sail to the ports along the coast of Asia, we put to sea, accompanied by Aristarchus, a Macedonian from Thessalonica. [3]The next day we put in at Sidon; and Julius treated Paul kindly, and allowed him to go to his friends to be cared for. [4]Putting out to sea from there, we sailed under the lee of Cyprus, because the winds were against us. [5]After we had sailed across the sea that is off Cilicia and Pamphylia, we came to Myra in Lycia. [6]There the centurion found an Alexandrian ship bound for Italy and put us on board. [7]We sailed slowly for a number of days and arrived with difficulty off Cnidus, and as the wind was against us, we sailed under the lee of Crete off Salmone. [8]Sailing past it with difficulty, we came to a place called Fair Havens, near the city of Lasea.

9Since much time had been lost and sailing was now dangerous, because even the Fast had already gone by, Paul advised them, [10]saying, "Sirs, I can see that the voyage will be with danger and much heavy loss, not only of the cargo and the ship, but also of our lives." [11]But the centurion paid more attention to the pilot and to the owner of the ship than to what Paul said. [12]Since the harbor was not suitable for spending the winter, the majority was in favor of putting to sea from there, on the chance that somehow they could reach Phoenix, where they could spend the winter. It was a harbor of Crete, facing southwest and northwest.

## COMMENTARY

The last two chapters of Acts narrate Paul's dramatic journey to the city of his destiny (27:1–28:16), concluding with his mission in Rome (28:17-31). The present passage narrates the first stage of Paul's voyage to Rome; it is slowly paced, reflective of the calm before a storm. The reader is introduced to Paul's traveling companions (27:1), and a travel itinerary is provided that follows their progress from Adramyttium to Fair Havens (27:2-8). Repeated references to various delays and difficult sailing (cf. 27:3-4, 6-8) alert the attentive reader to the dangerous prospect that an experienced Paul forewarns: The delays have pushed the timetable of this voyage beyond a safe point; to continue will endanger the ship and its cargo (27:9-10). Unfortunately, the Roman soldier put in charge of this expedition votes with the majority against Paul's advice and they set sail for Cretan Phoenix against poor odds (27:11-12).

Throughout it all Paul is still a prisoner of Rome, not due to his guilt but as a safeguard for his self-appointed audience before the Caesar (see 25:10-12). In truth, Rome's political institutions—its law court, military, and provincial administration—are but the public instruments of God's sovereign purpose for Paul who will arrive safely in Rome to proclaim the word of God as a "divine necessity" (see 23:11; 26:17).

**27:1.** The narrator resumes telling his story in the first person (see 16:10). Although the first person telling of a sea voyage or shipwreck is a literary convention of ancient fiction,[763] the differences between his story in Acts and those "parallels" found in Greek novels point in another direction; namely, the narrator places himself in the story to serve as a reliable witness to Paul's heroics.[764] In this sense, Paul's responses during a stormy sea complement his earlier defense speeches to provide the reader with an even more robust portrait of his spiritual authority as a prophet-like-Jesus. Indeed, his calming effort with lives at stake is far different from that of the frightened Jonah, another prophet at the mercy of a tempestuous sea. That prophet Jonah imperiled his traveling companions while prophet Paul delivered saving grace even to his military escort symbolizes their contrasting relations with God and God's purposes: Whereas Jonah is on the run from God's calling, Paul is obedient to it. Clearly, the

Paul of Acts is an experienced traveler;[765] but surely this risky feature of his ministry only evinces his single-minded interest in serving God's will (see 20:27; cf. 2 Cor 11:25-26). Moreover, in this concluding story of Paul's travels, his authority is exhibited among Gentiles who are not connected with any synagogue.

The narrator's intention is also shown by his intimate knowledge of a Mediterranean sea voyage. The reader rightly wonders why Luke takes such care in narrating this journey when he mentions more important events only in passing. I doubt his primary reason is either to follow literary convention or to liven up an otherwise slowly paced narrative. Rather, the detailed references found in this chapter to nautical terminology, complete with documentation of weather patterns and ports of call, provide the details of a realistic drama in which Paul's prophetic vocation is more fully exemplified in relation to Gentiles.

While the narrator and Aristarchus (see 19:29; 20:4; cf. Phlm 24) accompany Paul to Italy for unstated reasons, they are clearly distinguished from Paul and "some other prisoners" who are turned over to a "centurion of the Augustan Cohort, named Julius" for safekeeping (v. 1; however, see Col 4:10).[766] Perhaps Paul is allowed traveling companions because of his status as a Roman citizen or perhaps even because of his notoriety in Palestine. Not much is known about Paul's military escort. The title "Augustan Cohort" is honorific and was probably formed from auxiliary troops in Palestine who were now returning to Rome and were given this tour as extra duty. The personal name of the centurion is given— "Julius"—not because of his importance to the story but as a feature of realistic storytelling.

**27:2-8.** With the passenger list complete, the ship is ready to embark for Rome. From Luke's itinerary, it would appear this is the first of two boats. The ferry boarded in the Asian port city of Adramyttium regularly serves only the "ports along the coast of Asia" (v. 2), and is not seaworthy for the more demanding voyage on open sea to Rome. Julius must locate and book passage on

---

763. Luke's editorial decision to include, shape, and integrate certain stories like this one suggests his familiarity with the classical literary canon, including epics such as Homer's *Odyssey* and Virgil's *Aeneid*, which tell tales of sea storms and shipwrecks. See R. Pervo, *Profit with Delight* (Philadelphia: Fortress, 1987); V. Robbins "By Land and By Sea," in *Perspectives on Luke-Acts*, ed. C. Talbert (Edinburgh: T. & T. Clark, 1978) 215-42; Johnson, *The Acts of the Apostles*, 450-52; C. H. Talbert, *Reading Acts* (New York: Crossroad, 1997) 215-25; however, see also Porter's cautionary note in S. E. Porter, *The Paul of Acts*, WUNT 115 (Tübingen: Mohr Siebeck, 1999) 12-24.

764. Cf. C. Hemer, *The Book of Acts in the Setting of Hellenistic History*, WUNT 49 (Tübingen: Mohr Siebeck, 1989) 308-34.

765. Cf. E. Haenchen, *The Acts of the Apostles* (Philadelphia: Westminster, 1971) 702-3.

766. The Western version makes clear that the timing of this transfer occurred when "the governor (= Festus) decided to send him to Caesar."

another boat that will take his ship's cargo to Rome (so v. 6). However, a series of other delays and difficulties will put him well behind schedule and lead him into stormy waters ahead. For example, he "kindly" (φιλανθρώπως *philanthrōpōs*) allows Paul to visit friends in Sidon—a privilege that reflects either Paul's good relations with Rome or his social status (so 24:23) but which nevertheless causes delay in an already tight schedule.

The primary obstacle they face to a safe journey, however, is unfavorable weather: In both boats, even though sailing under the lee of Cyprus and the lee of Crete, "the winds were against us" (vv. 4, 7). The islands did nothing to protect them from severe winds, which initially forced the boat to move more slowly northward up the coastline from Cyprus to Lycian Myra instead of westward toward the open sea and Rome. In Myra their Aegean ship is exchanged for a larger Alexandrian ship headed for Rome; however, the natural forces are still against them and so their sailing proceeds "slowly for a number of days" before they arrive at their next port "off Cnidus with difficulty." Through repeated references to the severe headwinds and the sheer difficulty of their sailing, Luke makes the impression of a slowly paced voyage. Fair Havens, where they finally find safe harbor after "a number of days" at sea, is still a long distance from Rome.

**27:9-10.** In context, Paul's warning should not be understood as a prophecy but as prudent advice illustrative of his exemplary persona; that is, his prediction is fair warning that reflects the sound wisdom of a seasoned sea traveler. He understands that because "much time had been lost" and because "the Fast" (= Day of Atonement) had already been observed (in late September or early October), the Mediterranean shipping lanes to Rome are closed for the winter. The careful reader

should not overlook that Paul's method of counting time is Jewish rather than secular: The Day of Atonement, Israel's only national fast, is the traditional means of marking Jewish time and is used by observant Jews when dating journeys and events.

Paul's dire forewarning comes true only in part, which further suggests that the narrator does not intend his readers to take it as a prophecy. While it is true that by continuing there "will be with danger and much heavy loss," only the ship and its cargo will be lost; no person will die.

**27:11-12.** Paul's authority to make such a forecast presumes his good relations with Julius. But Julius, not Paul, is in charge of this voyage; therefore, it is his choice whether or not to heed this prisoner's sound advice. He seems to make a good decision based upon good reasons and majority opinion. He listens to Paul and agrees that it would be a foolish try to sail for Rome; the prospect of making Rome on schedule is no longer tenable. He disagrees with Paul, however, that they should remain in Fair Havens. In fact, Fair Havens "was not suitable for spending the winter"; his more prudent concern, then, is to find a port where his crew and cargo, and those passengers entrusted to his care, can winter safely and comfortably. Phoenix is his intended destination.[767] After consulting the ship's captain, presumably about the prospects of making Phoenix, and the ship's owner, presumably about issues of financial liability, the decision is made to set sail "on the chance that somehow they could reach Phoenix" (27:12).

---

767. The precise location of Phoenix is disputed. Hemer, *The Book of Acts in the Setting of Hellenistic History*, 139-41, places it close to Cape Mouros on the southern coast of Crete and less than fifty miles from Fair Havens. The implication is that the harbor at Fair Havens did not protect ships from the winter's winds, which swept in from the southeast, whereas the harbor at Phoenix, which faced "southwest and northwest," protected its ships from these strong southeast winds.

# REFLECTIONS

"But the centurion paid more attention to the pilot and to the owner of the ship than to what Paul said" (27:11 NRSV). From the narrative's perspective, of course, Paul's opinion should be trusted over all others! In this case, however, Paul's expertise is due to his experience in sailing the Mediterranean Sea: There are a dozen references in Acts to voyages Paul undertakes. His opinion in this ordinary matter, then, is not due to his spiritual authority, as though God inspires insight into weather patterns in the same manner God inspires an authoritative reading of Scripture! The church often makes the mistake of thinking that one's spiritual maturity transfers to all matters of life, or, conversely, that the person who builds a successful business will be able to build strong believers as a congregational leader. The special kind of expertise that enables one to lead a congregation of believers is indicated by one's spiritual maturity and graces, even as the expertise to read weather patterns is cultivated by one's relevant experience at sea.

# ACTS 27:13-26, STORMY WEATHER

## NIV

13When a gentle south wind began to blow, they thought they had obtained what they wanted; so they weighed anchor and sailed along the shore of Crete. 14Before very long, a wind of hurricane force, called the "northeaster," swept down from the island. 15The ship was caught by the storm and could not head into the wind; so we gave way to it and were driven along. 16As we passed to the lee of a small island called Cauda, we were hardly able to make the lifeboat secure. 17When the men had hoisted it aboard, they passed ropes under the ship itself to hold it together. Fearing that they would run aground on the sandbars of Syrtis, they lowered the sea anchor and let the ship be driven along. 18We took such a violent battering from the storm that the next day they began to throw the cargo overboard. 19On the third day, they threw the ship's tackle overboard with their own hands. 20When neither sun nor stars appeared for many days and the storm continued raging, we finally gave up all hope of being saved.

21After the men had gone a long time without food, Paul stood up before them and said: "Men, you should have taken my advice not to sail from Crete; then you would have spared yourselves this damage and loss. 22But now I urge you to keep up your courage, because not one of you will be lost; only the ship will be destroyed. 23Last night an angel of the God whose I am and whom I serve stood beside me 24and said, 'Do not be afraid, Paul. You must stand trial before Caesar; and God has graciously given you the lives of all who sail with you.' 25So keep up your courage, men, for I have faith in God that it will happen just as he told me. 26Nevertheless, we must run aground on some island."

## NRSV

13When a moderate south wind began to blow, they thought they could achieve their purpose; so they weighed anchor and began to sail past Crete, close to the shore. 14But soon a violent wind, called the northeaster, rushed down from Crete.[a] 15Since the ship was caught and could not be turned head-on into the wind, we gave way to it and were driven. 16By running under the lee of a small island called Cauda[b] we were scarcely able to get the ship's boat under control. 17After hoisting it up they took measures[c] to undergird the ship; then, fearing that they would run on the Syrtis, they lowered the sea anchor and so were driven. 18We were being pounded by the storm so violently that on the next day they began to throw the cargo overboard, 19and on the third day with their own hands they threw the ship's tackle overboard. 20When neither sun nor stars appeared for many days, and no small tempest raged, all hope of our being saved was at last abandoned.

21Since they had been without food for a long time, Paul then stood up among them and said, "Men, you should have listened to me and not have set sail from Crete and thereby avoided this damage and loss. 22I urge you now to keep up your courage, for there will be no loss of life among you, but only of the ship. 23For last night there stood by me an angel of the God to whom I belong and whom I worship, 24and he said, 'Do not be afraid, Paul; you must stand before the emperor; and indeed, God has granted safety to all those who are sailing with you.' 25So keep up your courage, men, for I have faith in God that it will be exactly as I have been told. 26But we will have to run aground on some island."

*a* Gk *it*    *b* Other ancient authorities read *Clauda*    *c* Gk *helps*

# COMMENTARY

The action of the second stage of Paul's sea odyssey is determined by "a violent wind, called the northeaster" that seized his ship and drove it from the coastline out into a stormy sea (27:13-15). Now adrift and at considerable risk, the ship's vigilant crew executes a sequence of emergency actions intended to ensure the ship's structural integrity and its ability to fight the wind's forceful drift toward the Libyan sandbanks, where the ship would be pounded to destruction (27:16-20). At the nadir of their physical and emotional exhaustion, when "all hope of our being saved was at last abandoned," Paul delivers a prophetic word from "the God to whom I belong and whom I worship" that assures them all of God's favor, their eventual safety, and Paul's personal destiny (27:21-26).

**27:13-15.** Some knowledge of the southern coastline of Crete is necessary to understand the peril facing the ship's crew when traveling from Fair Havens to Phoenix for the winter (see the map "The Early Eastern Roman Empire," 4). The moderate southwest winds that pick up when clearing the harbor are ideal for sailing to the west, and they allow the boat's crew to tack toward the shoreline under the leeward protection of the island's land mass. The gentle south winds are mentioned perhaps to explain why the majority of the ship's crew is seduced into leaving Fair Havens for safer harbor. However when the ship rounds Cape Matala just eight miles down the coast, it is left exposed to much stronger wind called "the northeaster" that even experienced mariners feared; if seized by these winds nothing could prevent their ship from being pushed away from the island's natural protection and out into a dangerous and tempestuous sea.

The narrator's seafaring jargon creates a picture that those who knew the vicissitudes of the Mediterranean Sea or who had read stories of sea voyages would readily have recognized as a hopeless situation. The fatalism of Luke's report is a familiar *leitmotif* of ancient literature: Once a ship is taken hold of by gale force winds its crew can do nothing but "give way to it [= furl the ship's sails] and [be] driven" out to sea where, lives and cargo are imperiled (v. 15). The desperation of the sailors is genuine when natural forces beyond their control overwhelm their skill and experience.

**27:16-20.** The emergency protocol followed by the sailors is precipitated by the situation in which they find themselves. Fortunately, they are able to drift behind a wind hedge provided by a small island, Cauda (modern-day Gaudes), which buys them a brief moment to carry out necessary "measures" (= lit., "helps") in preparation for their inevitable battle with the northeaster (v. 16). They attach the "lifeboat" to the hull; they wrap heavy ropes around the ship to undergird its structural integrity; and the anchor is lowered to produce additional drag in the hope of keeping the ship from the hazardous "sandbars of Syrtis" in the Gulf of Sidra, where it would be pounded to pieces (v. 17).

After two days of safeguarding the ship from the destructive powers of the violent storm, the crew is forced on the third day to take even more extreme measures to save their lives: They throw cargo overboard (v. 18), and then as a last resort throw "the ship's tackle [σκευή *skeuē*] overboard" (v. 19; cf. Jonah 1:5).[768] Luke's use of a genitive absolute, "neither sun nor stars," and litotes (understatement), "no small tempest raged on," coupled with an imperfect main verb, "all hope of our being saved [σώζω *sōzō*] was at last abandoned [περιηρεῖτο *periēreito*]" (v. 20) graphically describes an impossible situation that is getting worse. Paul and his companions are literally in the same boat: lost at sea, without necessary gear, without sun or stars for guidance, and without a favorable weather forecast.

**27:21-26.** Once again Paul intervenes when all seems lost. Luke's use of *sōzō* ("save") to describe the hopelessness of the situation acquires a greater depth of meaning in Acts where salvation from harm's way or from serious illness is due to God's grace, typically mediated by God's prophet.[769] In this sense, the loss of any hope of

---

768. The meaning of σκεῦος (*skeuos*, "anchor")/*skeuē*, "tackle") is uncertain but probably refers to the ship's tacking gear. More critically, the repetition of *skeuos* recalls its use in Jonah's story when similar emergency measures are taken by the ship's crew to lighten the boat in the face of a tempestuous sea. In canonical context this intertext prepares the reader for the contrasting portraits of two prophets, Jonah and Paul, and the different ways they respond to a dire situation as representational of differing responses to God's calling (see 27:21-26).

769. B. Witherington, *The Acts of the Apostles: A Socio-Rhetorical Commentary* (Grand Rapids: Eerdmans, 1998) 767; cf. R. C. Tannehill, *The Acts of the Apostles*, vol. 2 of *The Narrative Unity of Luke-Acts: A Literary Interpretation* (Minneapolis: Fortress, 1990) 2:336-40.

rescue experienced by those on Paul's boat is an appropriate stage for the prophet to pronounce hope for a reversal of fortune when God's saving grace triumphs over elements that provoke human despair. This is precisely what Paul now does.

His brief speech is a mixture of different elements. He chides, encourages, reports and prophesies—all to encourage his companions to hope in the plan of God. Initially, Paul chides those in charge for their decision to dismiss his warning and leave Fair Havens (v. 21), which has now proven a manifestly poor judgment. The point of Paul's comment is not to engage in a round of "I told you so." Rather, his initial comment echoes his earlier forecast (see vv. 10-12) to form an ironical reminder of his personal authority in the present situation and so to prepare the reader for his following exhortation. Indeed, given this reminder, Paul's listeners are readied to hear him and heed what he says next about their (and his) future.

And what Paul tells his dispirited audience is stunning news indeed. In a setting where everyone is sapped of hope and strength, Paul exhorts his co-travelers "to keep up your courage" (v. 22; see also vv. 25, 36). Their capacity to act courageously, which seems unrealistic under the present circumstances, is prompted by a vision that proffers a different future from the one presently anticipated. Angels populate Luke's narrative world and often serve important roles as the bearers of God's messages, which typically predict, as in this case, God's saving actions (see 5:19; 7:26; 10:3; 12:7; cf. Luke 1:26; 2:9-13; 22:43). Paul need not explain or justify his angelic visitation to his pagan auditors, since divine messengers are a shared feature of their religious mythologies.[770] For their benefit, however, he does identify this particular angel as the agent of "the God to whom I belong and whom I worship" (v. 23).

His theological confession echoes Jonah's explanation, given to an earlier crew of pagan sailors during a voyage to another center of political and military power, of why his disobedience to God's calling has caused a sea storm that now imperils their lives: "I worship the Lord, the God of

heaven, who made the sea and the dry land" (Jonah 1:9). Paul's affirmation presumes, with Jonah's, the Creator's sovereign control over the course of nature as much as over the course of salvation. Unlike Jonah, however, the angel's visitation and the promise of God's salvation is the consequence of Paul's obedience to his prophetic calling. Thus his assurances of their deliverance from death, even though the cargo is lost (27:22) and the ship is grounded (v. 26), are predicated on Paul's faithfulness to God.[771]

For the third time in Acts Paul is told in different words that Rome is the city of his destiny: "Paul, you must [δεῖ *dei*] stand before the emperor" (v. 24; see also 19:21; 23:11). Once again, God's future plans for a Roman mission are disclosed to Paul during a time of personal suffering and have the practical effect of bringing comfort to him. The difference in this case is that Paul also comforts his companions with the news of his divinely ordained future: They will be rescued at sea because of their association with a prophet-like-Jesus who has been called to mediate God's saving grace to others. In fact, this speech is framed by repetition of the "*dei* of divine necessity": Paul "must [*dei*] stand before Caesar" (v. 24) and the ship "will have to [*dei*] run aground on some island" (v. 26). The rest of Luke's story tells how this divine purpose is ultimately realized—an important point to remember when interpreting the behavior of both sailors (see vv. 30-32) and soldiers (see v. 42).

Finally, the reader should note that the repetition of Paul's exhortation to have courage is now joined by his pious expression of "faith in God that it will be exactly as I have been told" (v. 25). The significance of his personal affirmation becomes clear in that others onboard remain largely unaffected by Paul's speech and have a more realistic appraisal of their present peril. Surely Luke has shaped Paul's brief speech, then, to make the ironical point more emphatic that it is *Paul's* trust in God alone—"for *I* have faith in God"—that saves his companions, in spite of their lack of trust.

---

770. Cf. Haenchen, *The Acts of the Apostles,* 705.

771. For this reason, Miles and Trompf contend that this sea story continues Paul's apologia. See G. Miles and G. Trompf, "Luke and Antiphon," *HTR* 69 (1976) 259-67.

# REFLECTIONS

" 'God has granted safety to all those who are sailing with [me].' So keep up your courage, men, for I have faith in God that it will be exactly as I have been told" (27:24-25 NRSV). One of the most intriguing theological elements of this story is Paul's relationship with his pagan traveling companions. While Paul's religious authority certainly extends to other believers in Luke's narrative world, here it also extends to non-believers. Their safe passage depends upon their relationship with him and their heeding his practical instructions (see 27:33-35). Paul's concern to keep them within the bounds of his authority (see 27:31) suggests that he assumes responsibility for their physical (if not for their spiritual) salvation. As such he personifies the scope of God's provident care over all people, but especially the role the church must perform as the agent of God's salvation. The faith in God's grace that prompts the church to petition God for the salvation of others (= "So keep up your courage, men") is legitimized not only by what God has promised in the Scriptures (= "it will be exactly as I have been told") but also by our confidence that God keeps precisely what God has promised (= "for I have faith in God").

# ACTS 27:27-44, SURVIVING THE SHIPWRECK

NIV

²⁷On the fourteenth night we were still being driven across the Adriatic[a] Sea, when about midnight the sailors sensed they were approaching land. ²⁸They took soundings and found that the water was a hundred and twenty feet[b] deep. A short time later they took soundings again and found it was ninety feet[c] deep. ²⁹Fearing that we would be dashed against the rocks, they dropped four anchors from the stern and prayed for daylight. ³⁰In an attempt to escape from the ship, the sailors let the lifeboat down into the sea, pretending they were going to lower some anchors from the bow. ³¹Then Paul said to the centurion and the soldiers, "Unless these men stay with the ship, you cannot be saved." ³²So the soldiers cut the ropes that held the lifeboat and let it fall away.

³³Just before dawn Paul urged them all to eat. "For the last fourteen days," he said, "you have been in constant suspense and have gone without food—you haven't eaten anything. ³⁴Now I urge you to take some food. You need it to survive. Not one of you will lose a single hair from his head." ³⁵After he said this, he took some bread and gave thanks to God in front of them all. Then he broke

_a 27_ In ancient times the name referred to an area extending well south of Italy.     _b 28_ Greek _twenty orguias_ (about 37 meters)
_c 28_ Greek _fifteen orguias_ (about 27 meters)

NRSV

²⁷When the fourteenth night had come, as we were drifting across the sea of Adria, about midnight the sailors suspected that they were nearing land. ²⁸So they took soundings and found twenty fathoms; a little farther on they took soundings again and found fifteen fathoms. ²⁹Fearing that we might run on the rocks, they let down four anchors from the stern and prayed for day to come. ³⁰But when the sailors tried to escape from the ship and had lowered the boat into the sea, on the pretext of putting out anchors from the bow, ³¹Paul said to the centurion and the soldiers, "Unless these men stay in the ship, you cannot be saved." ³²Then the soldiers cut away the ropes of the boat and set it adrift.

33Just before daybreak, Paul urged all of them to take some food, saying, "Today is the fourteenth day that you have been in suspense and remaining without food, having eaten nothing. ³⁴Therefore I urge you to take some food, for it will help you survive; for none of you will lose a hair from your heads." ³⁵After he had said this, he took bread; and giving thanks to God in the presence of all, he broke it and began to eat. ³⁶Then all of them were encouraged and took food for themselves. ³⁷(We were in all two hundred seventy-

## NIV

it and began to eat. ³⁶They were all encouraged and ate some food themselves. ³⁷Altogether there were 276 of us on board. ³⁸When they had eaten as much as they wanted, they lightened the ship by throwing the grain into the sea.

³⁹When daylight came, they did not recognize the land, but they saw a bay with a sandy beach, where they decided to run the ship aground if they could. ⁴⁰Cutting loose the anchors, they left them in the sea and at the same time untied the ropes that held the rudders. Then they hoisted the foresail to the wind and made for the beach. ⁴¹But the ship struck a sandbar and ran aground. The bow stuck fast and would not move, and the stern was broken to pieces by the pounding of the surf.

⁴²The soldiers planned to kill the prisoners to prevent any of them from swimming away and escaping. ⁴³But the centurion wanted to spare Paul's life and kept them from carrying out their plan. He ordered those who could swim to jump overboard first and get to land. ⁴⁴The rest were to get there on planks or on pieces of the ship. In this way everyone reached land in safety.

## NRSV

-six*persons in the ship.) ³⁸After they had satisfied their hunger, they lightened the ship by throwing the wheat into the sea.

39In the morning they did not recognize the land, but they noticed a bay with a beach, on which they planned to run the ship ashore, if they could. ⁴⁰So they cast off the anchors and left them in the sea. At the same time they loosened the ropes that tied the steering-oars; then hoisting the foresail to the wind, they made for the beach. ⁴¹But striking a reef,ᵇ they ran the ship aground; the bow stuck and remained immovable, but the stern was being broken up by the force of the waves. ⁴²The soldiers' plan was to kill the prisoners, so that none might swim away and escape; ⁴³but the centurion, wishing to save Paul, kept them from carrying out their plan. He ordered those who could swim to jump overboard first and make for the land, ⁴⁴and the rest to follow, some on planks and others on pieces of the ship. And so it was that all were brought safely to land.

ᵃ Other ancient authorities read *seventy-six*; others, *about seventy-six*
ᵇ Gk *place of two seas*

# COMMENTARY

In two weeks time Paul's ship has drifted westward from Crete to Malta.[772] Suspecting that land is near, the crew takes repeated soundings of the seabed for fear that the ship might run aground in the shallows (27:27-29). When certain sailors try to escape by lifeboat, leaving the ship in the hands of inexperienced soldiers, Paul detects their subterfuge and alerts the centurion who detains the sailors and cuts the lifeboat adrift to prevent their escape (27:30-32). The motive behind Paul's action, glossed by his earlier prophecy (see 27:21-26), is not his fear that without skilled sailors the ship would otherwise be wrecked with inevitable loss of lives and cargo: According to his prophecy, the ship and cargo have been slated for destruction but lives have not. Consistent with his other actions, Paul's report to the centurion is prompted by his prophetic calling as agent of God's salvation; his concern is for the sailors whose departure from the ship (and from his presence) would almost certainly result in their death.

At daybreak on that fateful day, Paul gathers all two hundred seventy-six persons onboard his ship for breakfast, perhaps with Eucharistic overtones commensurate with Paul's prophetic vocation (see 27:35), which is necessary in any case for their emotional and physical survival (27:33-38). A strategy is quickly devised and final preparations made for a beach landing. However, their desperate plans quickly fall to ruin as the ship is caught on a sandbar and breaks apart (27:39-41). This time renegade soldiers rather than sailors threaten to subvert Paul's prophecy by killing the prisoners, but the centurion thwarts them again and so ensures that all are brought safely to land, as Paul had predicted (27:42-44).

**27:27-29.** The Sea of Adria, where they now

772. A modern calculation of Luke's chronology of Paul's voyage confirms its accuracy: This type of boat set adrift in the face of a gale force northeaster would take about two weeks to travel from Crete to Malta. See J. Smith, *The Voyage and Shipwreck of St. Paul,* 4th ed., rev. W. Smith (London: Longmans & Green, 1880) 124-27.

find themselves, is bounded most closely by Sicily to the north. In the dead of night and in the midst of chaotic circumstances, the experienced crew rightly realizes that "they were nearing land" (v. 27), perhaps because they could hear the crashing of breakers on Malta's Point Koura. The various "soundings" they take by using a weighted line confirm they are drifting toward shore—from "twenty fathoms [120 feet]" to "fifteen fathoms [90 feet]" (v. 28). While land is a symbol of hope, a refuge from a stormy sea, the sailors also realize with terror that without adequate tackle their defenseless ship will "run on the rocks [= cliffs]" and be pounded to destruction. Luke records their final approach with a note of fatalism: After dropping four drift anchors from the stern (rather than the bow) to keep the ship from turning broadside into the strong waves, they "prayed for day to come" (v. 29).

**27:30-32.** Most commentators agree that skilled sailors would know best the futility of their present situation and the best means for escaping it.[773] Under pretense of dropping additional anchors from the bow, then, some of the crew "lowered the boat [= dinghy] into the sea" to clear the inevitable wreck (v. 30). Paul alerts the centurion of their subterfuge (v. 31), and the officer orders his soldiers to cut off their only means of escape (v. 32).

Any explanation of Paul's comment to the centurion, "Unless these men stay in this ship, you cannot be saved," must emphasize his prophetic vocation, both in the terms of his earlier prophecy (see vv. 21-26) and by his role as agent of God's saving grace. In this light, Paul's worry is surely not the safety of the ship, since its destruction is a "divine necessity" (see v. 26); nor is he hopeful that the weather will improve to elevate the chance of an orderly disembarkation by lifeboat. He has also prophesied that there will be no loss of life (see v. 22), but that this outcome will be due to God's provident care and not the efforts of a skilled crew (see v. 23). Paul's prophetic concern is for the salvation of the sailors, since safety is promised only to those who remain connected to his destiny (see v. 25). Therefore, to "stay in the ship," though doomed, is to stay within the protective hedge that surrounds the prophet of God and God's plans for him in Rome. The eschatological horizon of Paul's remark to the centurion is not an improved weather forecast but the prospect of his Roman mission, which has been confirmed a third time on board this ship (see v. 24). To escape the ship is to become detached from Paul who is the medium of God's saving grace. Paul's singular worry is for those separated from him, for this means that "you cannot be saved" by God. What appears to be their "lifeboat" is, in fact, its opposite!

The Roman centurion and the soldiers under his command set the dinghy free and remove the only means of escaping a doomed ship. Theirs is not a capricious act; rather, ironically, it is the only means of securing the sailors to the destiny of Paul who alone can broker their salvation from the stormy sea.

**27:33-38.** God's promise of salvation for the ship's passengers is sealed with a meal. The time is now daybreak when Paul encourages "all of them to take some food" (v. 33). His constant interventions during this crisis display his calm spirit and judicious concern for his traveling companions. By this point in the story he has proved his character under fire and has cultivated the trust of all who now listen to him and follow his instructions: "then all of them were encouraged and took food for themselves" (v. 36).

Commentators, ancient and modern, have noted several linguistic links between Paul's instructions to eat (v. 34) and the sequence, "he took bread; and giving thanks [εὐχαρίστησεν eucharistēsen] to God in the presence of all, he broke it and began to eat" (v. 35), and the institution of the Lord's supper.[774] Indeed, Paul urges them to eat their food, "for it will help you survive [σωτηρία sōtēria]" (v. 34): This is a meal for their salvation.[775] These connections should not be taken literally since Paul would not have celebrated the Eucharist with pagans (cf. 1 Cor 11:17-

---

773. L. T. Johnson, *The Acts of the Apostles*, SP 5 (Collegeville, Minn.: Liturgical, 1992) 454, notes several parallels in ancient literature both of the untrustworthiness of sailors and of desperate attempts to flee doomed ships by lifeboat during raging sea storms.

774. Cf. P. W. Walaskay, *"And So We Came to Rome": The Political Perspective of St. Luke*, SNTMS 49 (Cambridge: Cambridge University Press, 1983) 236-38.

775. Although *sōtēria* in this setting denotes "survival" and is rightly translated as such by NIV/NRSV, Luke does not sharply distinguish between physical (= healing/survival) and spiritual (= forgiveness) forms of being saved, salvation in its various forms is always and in every case the work of God.

26) and are in any case the actions of a pious Jew. Yet, almost certainly Luke shapes this poignant moment as typological of the "last supper" in which God's sustaining grace is dispensed to communicants by the authority of God's appointed servant. In this sense, the intent of this respite is once again to illustrate Paul's spiritual authority among pagans (in addition to Luke and Aristarchus), not only because of his competent leadership in a crisis but also because he is the source of salvation for those who follow his instruction. As Johnson notes, the importance of Paul's gesture to distribute the blessed food "in the presence of all" (v. 35) is to "present an example for them, one which in fact they imitate," for those who imitate Paul are saved (cf. 20:31-35; 1 Cor 4:16; 11:1; Phil 3:17; 4:9; 1 Thess 1:6; 2 Thess 3:7-9; 2 Tim 1:13).[776]

Having eaten this meal for their salvation, the "two hundred and seventy-six persons in the ship" (v. 37) rid themselves of an extra weight by "throwing the wheat into the sea" (v. 38), thus adding to the buoyancy of the ship and allowing the waves to carry it as close to the shoreline as possible. In all likelihood, this final emergency measure is only now possible because the storm's violence has subsided enough to allow the bottom hatches to be opened and the grain shoots to be operative. These images, narrated and implied, suggest the necessary collaboration between people and God whose aim is to save them.

**27:39-41.** In this same sense, a prudent strategy is devised to beach the ship safely (v. 39) and measures are taken to make shore: "they cast off the anchors [on either side of the stern] . . . loosened the ropes that tied the steering-oars [= rudder] . . . then hoisting the foresail to the wind, they made for the beach" (v. 40). The purpose of this combination of mariner maneuvers is to exploit their location with respect to visible land

and the natural force of the wind, while at the same time regaining maximum "hand-control" of the ship's direction. Alas, they do not make shore and run aground on a patch of "reef"—literally, "a place of two seas" or a sandbar that splits the sea into two breakers. Held fast by gravity, the ship and its crew are defenseless against the pounding sea and the stern breaks apart—but without loss of life. The practical problem remaining is how to reach land without a lifeboat (see v. 32).

**27:42-44.** There also remains a military problem, however remote: The prisoners would need to be secured, since their escape could exact severe penalties on soldiers responsible for their custody (see 12:19; 16:27). The escort's plan is to kill the prisoners (v. 42); however, this plan is flawed in two important ways. First, it is based upon the implausible premise that any passenger could "swim away and escape" through rough seas and on foreign land, which is in any case a self-contained island. Second, as with the sailors' earlier plot to flee ship by its lifeboat, a plan to kill prisoners would subvert God's plan to save all on board the ship. Remarkably, it is not Paul who intervenes in this case to save the soldiers from their actions but Julius, who "wishing to save [διασώζω diasōzō] Paul" frustrates the inopportune plans of his soldiers (27:43). Whatever his motive, Julius acts as a pagan agent of divine purpose by whom all those traveling with Paul are saved (see 27:22-26).[777] This then is the final twist of a well-told story narrated with dramatic irony: Julius's action results in the survival of everyone, who are all "brought safely to land" (27:44) not because he is able to stop his men from carrying out their plan but because by protecting Paul he ensures the fulfillment of his prophecy.

---

776. Johnson, *The Acts of the Apostles,* 455.

777. On the role of non-believers in realizing God's redemptive program, see R. C. Tannehill, *The Acts of the Apostles,* vol. 2 of *The Narrative Unity of Luke-Acts: A Literary Interpretation* (Minneapolis: Fortress, 1990) 2:340.

# REFLECTIONS

"But the centurion, wishing to save Paul, kept them from carrying out their plan" (27:43 NRSV). One feature of Luke's conception of God's sovereignty that is reflected in this story is the use of different kinds of agents to broker God's promised salvation. Luke's world is populated by prophets and angels who follow God's instructions in delivering God's word, which when followed by others realize promised blessings. What is more surprising, perhaps, is that God also uses the unsuspecting as agents of God's salvation. The Roman centurion, Julius, is a case in point. First in cutting the dinghy free (27:32) and then in keeping his soldiers from executing their prisoners, Julius kept all onboard ship within the hedge of Paul's protection and allows God's promise of their safety to be fulfilled. Julius is prompted to take these actions not out of some confidence in God's promise but because of his friendship with Paul and his concern for Paul's safety (see 27:3). The practical lesson of his example is that sometimes non-believers unwittingly collaborate with God in working out God's salvation for the sake of believers for whom they care. Our friendship with non-believers cultivates personal loyalties that sometimes prompt decisions and actions that God can use as the means to a redemptive end.

# ACTS 28:1-16, "AND SO WE CAME TO ROME"

## NIV

**28** Once safely on shore, we found out that the island was called Malta. ²The islanders showed us unusual kindness. They built a fire and welcomed us all because it was raining and cold. ³Paul gathered a pile of brushwood and, as he put it on the fire, a viper, driven out by the heat, fastened itself on his hand. ⁴When the islanders saw the snake hanging from his hand, they said to each other, "This man must be a murderer; for though he escaped from the sea, Justice has not allowed him to live." ⁵But Paul shook the snake off into the fire and suffered no ill effects. ⁶The people expected him to swell up or suddenly fall dead, but after waiting a long time and seeing nothing unusual happen to him, they changed their minds and said he was a god.

⁷There was an estate nearby that belonged to Publius, the chief official of the island. He welcomed us to his home and for three days entertained us hospitably. ⁸His father was sick in bed, suffering from fever and dysentery. Paul went in to see him and, after prayer, placed his hands on him and healed him. ⁹When this had happened, the rest of the sick on the island came and were cured. ¹⁰They honored us in many ways and when we were ready to sail, they furnished us with the supplies we needed.

¹¹After three months we put out to sea in a ship that had wintered in the island. It was an Alexandrian ship with the figurehead of the twin gods Castor and Pollux. ¹²We put in at Syracuse and stayed there three days. ¹³From there we set sail and arrived at Rhegium. The next day the

## NRSV

**28** After we had reached safety, we then learned that the island was called Malta. ²The natives showed us unusual kindness. Since it had begun to rain and was cold, they kindled a fire and welcomed all of us around it. ³Paul had gathered a bundle of brushwood and was putting it on the fire, when a viper, driven out by the heat, fastened itself on his hand. ⁴When the natives saw the creature hanging from his hand, they said to one another, "This man must be a murderer; though he has escaped from the sea, justice has not allowed him to live." ⁵He, however, shook off the creature into the fire and suffered no harm. ⁶They were expecting him to swell up or drop dead, but after they had waited a long time and saw that nothing unusual had happened to him, they changed their minds and began to say that he was a god.

7Now in the neighborhood of that place were lands belonging to the leading man of the island, named Publius, who received us and entertained us hospitably for three days. ⁸It so happened that the father of Publius lay sick in bed with fever and dysentery. Paul visited him and cured him by praying and putting his hands on him. ⁹After this happened, the rest of the people on the island who had diseases also came and were cured. ¹⁰They bestowed many honors on us, and when we were about to sail, they put on board all the provisions we needed.

11Three months later we set sail on a ship that had wintered at the island, an Alexandrian ship with the Twin Brothers as its figurehead. ¹²We put

NIV

south wind came up, and on the following day we reached Puteoli. [14]There we found some brothers who invited us to spend a week with them. And so we came to Rome. [15]The brothers there had heard that we were coming, and they traveled as far as the Forum of Appius and the Three Taverns to meet us. At the sight of these men Paul thanked God and was encouraged. [16]When we got to Rome, Paul was allowed to live by himself, with a soldier to guard him.

NRSV

in at Syracuse and stayed there for three days; [13]then we weighed anchor and came to Rhegium. After one day there a south wind sprang up, and on the second day we came to Puteoli. [14]There we found believers[a] and were invited to stay with them for seven days. And so we came to Rome. [15]The believers[a] from there, when they heard of us, came as far as the Forum of Appius and Three Taverns to meet us. On seeing them, Paul thanked God and took courage.

16When we came into Rome, Paul was allowed to live by himself, with the soldier who was guarding him.

[a] Gk *brothers*

# COMMENTARY

Paul and his co-travelers have washed ashore on the island of Melita (= Malta), where they will spend the winter. They arrive cold and wet from the sea in need of immediate warmth and long-term restoration, for they are weary survivors of a traumatic experience. Surviving a stormy sea and shipwreck, Paul also shrugs off a viper's bite (28:3-5) in further demonstration that God is protecting him for Rome (28:6; see 27:24). Even the island's "natives" recognize Paul as God's man (28:1-6) and the inspired medium of divine powers dispensed for both great and small (28:7-10). Their continuing hospitality toward Paul and the others (28:2, 7, 10) indicates a people who by nature are receptive to the truth of God's Word (28:8-9; see also 17:11). Ironically, Luke's positive judgment of a superstitious and primitive people (28:6) not only underscores the universalism of God's reign but exposes as well the obduracy of the gospel's more learned and sophisticated opponents.

Paul's journey to Rome resumes "after three months" on Malta. The details of his itinerary follow the famous Appian Way; the favorable wind conditions (28:11-13) combine with the graciousness of other believers on land in bringing Paul to Rome under God s provident care (28:14-16).

**28:1-2.** When the survivors reach the shore on bits and pieces of their wrecked ship, they learn that they have landed safely on the small island of Malta, about sixty miles south of Sicily. Because

the island is a Roman colony and its harbor a strategic stop on shipping lanes leading to Rome, the Maltese were not unfamiliar with the language and customs of their unexpected visitors from Palestine and Rome.[778] Luke, however, calls their hosts "natives" (βάρβαροι *barbaroi*)—that is, they were religious barbarians who held to superstitions about God—the "Gentiles" referred to in the Pauline letters who do not know the law and have only their conscience to guide them (cf. Rom 2:12-16).[779] His effective use of litotes underlines their moral character in implicit contrast to their theological ignorance: their hospitable response is an "unusual kindness" (28:2; lit., "no usual kindness").

Hospitality without discrimination is among the most highly regarded virtues of the ancient world. Initially the kindness of the islanders takes the form of building a bonfire on the beach to dry out

---

778. Cf. Witherington, *The Acts of the Apostles*, 775-76.

779. Other commentators contend that the *barbaroi* refer to uneducated islanders who could speak only in their "native" Punic language. See, e.g., E. Haenchen, *The Acts of the Apostles* (Philadelphia: Westminster, 1971) 713; C. K. Barrett, *A Critical and Exegetical Commentary on the Acts of the Apostles*, 2 vols, ICC (Edinburgh: T. & T. Clark, 1994, 1998) 2:1220-21; J. D. G. Dunn, *The Acts of the Apostles* (Valley Forge, Pa.: Trinity, 1996) 346. This connotation, however, seems unlikely in Acts since communication between the islanders and survivors is indicated. Moreover, archaeological evidence supports the impression of a bilingual culture on first century Malta. The only barbarism indicated by Luke's story is theological: The Maltese are much too quick to leap from the mistaken conclusion that Paul is an immoral man (28:4) to another that he is an "immortal man" (28:6).

and warm up all their stranded guests: "they kindled a fire and welcomed all of us around it." In the narrative world of Acts, hospitality is vested with theological importance. Not only does a people's benefaction toward others symbolize their "receptivity to God's visitation" (see 10:24; 15:4; 16:11-15; 20:6; 21:4),[780] it also evinces the good character necessary to recognize the truth of God's word when they see it demonstrated or hear it proclaimed. Although nowhere does Luke write that Paul proclaimed the word of God during his three-month stay in Malta, the interpreter easily fills this narrative gap in light of inferences drawn from other stories of Paul in Acts—or does the reader really believe that the Paul of Acts would remain silent about the risen Messiah? The "honors" his hospitable hosts give him at his departure confirm his importance to them (28:10).

**28:3-6.** As Paul pitches in to help build the fire, a poisonous viper is chased from its home by the heat and bites his hand. The initial interpretation of the natives regarding Paul, whom they now know only as a Roman prisoner and lucky survivor, reflects the logic of the *barbaroi's* superstitious worldview: He must be guilty of the crime he has committed after all. The reference to "justice" (ἡ Δίκη *hē Dikē*) does not denote the philosophical notion of fair play but rather an avenging "Justice" of ancient mythology that personifies those cosmic fates that dispense a person's ultimate reward or punishment for deeds done. Evidently, surviving the shipwreck is an insufficient sign of Paul's innocence; Lady Justice who has withheld her final verdict until now "has not allowed him to live" (v. 4).

Given this judgment, Paul does the unexpected: "He, however, shook off the creature into the fire and suffered no harm" (v. 5). This dramatic incident recalls the Gospel text in which the risen Jesus promises miraculous "signs" that would confirm the truth of the proclaimed gospel (Mark 16:20), among them, "they will pick up snakes in their hands" without harm (Mark 16:18; cf. Luke 10:18-19). In this new setting, the truth about Paul is disclosed to them: When he is unharmed by the viper's poison, the *barbaroi* recognize it as a "sign" that "he was a god" (v. 6; also see 14:8-

13). While their primitive theology does not allow them to fully comprehend what they have seen, their verdict about Paul invites the Christian reader to draw the obvious conclusion: Paul is indeed a divinely inspired man of God's own choosing and a carrier of God's word to the whole creation (cf. Mark 16:15) whom God is safeguarding for the ministry that awaits him in Rome.

**28:7-10.** Luke includes a snapshot of Paul's three-day visit at the estate of Publius, "the leading man of the island" (v. 7). Paul's relations with city officials is an important dimension of his mission; there is a sense in which the response of civic leaders to Paul helps to determine the response of an entire city to his prophetic ministry. Here Publius's benefaction toward Paul and his companions under difficult circumstances (v. 7) commends the entire region under his care to Paul's healing power (vv. 8-9). This healing ministry, here expressed in combination with prayer and the laying on of hands (v. 8),[781] is an important feature of Paul's prophetic ministry in Acts (see 14:8-10; 19:11-12; 20:9-10) and continues what the Lord had begun in demonstration of the triumph of God's reign (cf. Luke 4:38-44). For this reason, beginning with Jesus (cf. Luke 7:20-23) and continuing in the ministry of his successors before Paul (see 3:12-16; 6:7-8; 9:36-42), the wonders of healing ministry typically complement the gospel proclamation of God's fulfilled promises (see 14:9; 19:20; 20:11).

The vigorous response of the islanders to Paul's healing of Publius's father, who had been "seized" by a fever (v. 9; cf. Mark 1:29-34 and par.), combines with their earlier recognition of him as vested with divine authority (see v. 6) and explains why they "bestowed many honors on us . . . and put on board all the provisions we needed" (v. 10). Such a response may simply be a token gesture for all that Paul had done for the Maltese. However, the giving of possessions to the prophet is symbolic of the presence of divine grace (see 4:32-35); and we may infer from this that Paul's unexpected adventure in Malta had resulted in the salvation of

---

780. L. T. Johnson, *The Acts of the Apostles,* SP 5 (Collegeville, Minn.: Liturgical, 1992) 461.

781. Laying hands on the sick is a practice unknown in the OT and rabbinic literature; it may well have originated in the Messiah's mission as symbolic of his divine authority (see Luke 4:40). The striking juxtaposition of a medical phrase, "sick in bed with fever and dysentery," with a gesture that signifies spiritual authority indicates that the "healing is accomplished not be medical means but by prayer and laying on of hands." Haenchen, *The Acts of the Apostles,* 714.

these "natives" who now live together as a community of goods under the aegis of the Holy Spirit.

**28:11-13.** With characteristic detail, Luke charts the course from Malta to Puteoli in Italy with ports of call at Sicilian Syracuse and Rhegium on the toe of Italy in between; in Puteoli they are able to pick up the Appian Way to take into Rome. The curious addition that the Alexandrian ship Julius hired to take his contingent to Italy had "the Twin Brothers as its figurehead" may serve as an ironic recollection of the full sweep of Paul's sea odyssey. The twins Castor and Pollux, "the sons of Zeus," were astral deities venerated as saviors from stormy seas. Of course, the readers of Acts understand that they are not responsible for Paul's safety; rather, it is "the God to whom I belong and whom I worship" (27:23) who has safeguarded him and his traveling entourage for their appointed ministry to "bring salvation to the end of the earth" (see 13:47; 1:8).

**28:14-16.** Paul is not the founder of the Roman church; other evangelists and believers had already cultivated this spiritual ground in preparation for his mission (cf. Rom 15:18-29).[782] Similar to the narrative of Paul's pilgrimage to Jerusalem when he visited congregations founded by other evangelists along the way (see 21:1-17), he is greeted by believers from "as far as the Forum of Appius [= 40 miles from Rome] and Three Taverns [= 30 miles from Rome]" (v. 15) who "invited [Paul] to stay with them for seven days" (v. 14) and then accompanied him into the city (v. 16). This evocative image of a church's festive welcome depicts Paul as an important person and is evocative of Jesus' entrance into the city of his destiny on Palm Sunday. The stage is set for an important ministry in this leading city of Paul's world.

---

782. Many scholars have attempted to reconstruct the origins of Christianity in Rome. For recent efforts, see K. Donfried, ed. *The Romans Debate* (Minneapolis: Augsbury, 1977; rev. ed. London: T & T Clark, 1991). Luke refers to Priscilla and Aquila, Jewish believers who are forced from Rome and settle in Corinth where they meet and work with Paul (Acts 18). This may well indicate the Jewish origins of Roman Christianity and give insight into the ambivalent responses of Jewish leaders to Paul's presence in Rome (see 28:17-28).

Luke's spotlight again shines exclusively on Paul. The reader presumes, however, that Julius and his soldiers, as well as the ship's other prisoners, accommodated Paul's desire to spend time with believers in the Roman precinct before moving into his rented flat in Rome to await his appointment with the emperor. Perhaps this explains why the Paul of Acts arrives in Rome *twice*, the first time with the terse sentence, "And so we came to Rome [εἰς τὴν Ῥώμην *eis tēn Rhōmēn*]" (v. 14b), and again when "we came into Rome [εἰς Ῥώμη *eis Rōmē*]" (v. 16a). The reference to "the soldier who was guarding him" (v. 16b) may indicate that new arrangements had been made by Julius upon first arriving in Rome (v. 14b), separating Paul from his military escort and the other prisoners while granting him considerable freedom to meet with other believers for pastoral ministry (v. 15), before he took permanent residence in Rome (v. 16a; see also v. 30). No doubt these official allowances granted Paul reflect on his political innocence and good character; and yet the lack of attention given him in Rome—only a single ordinary soldier now watches over him—may be preparing the reader for the surprising news that Paul is a relative unknown in Rome (see v. 21).

Luke's passing comment that when Paul met with the others he "thanked God and took courage [θάρσος *tharsos*]" (v. 15) explains why Luke's plotline is so fixed upon Paul: He is an exemplar of the man of God whose ministry within a community of faith is directed toward God in thankful worship and toward others, from whom he now draws courage for the important mission that awaits him. The verbal form of *tharsos* was earlier used in the Lord's visionary exhortation for Paul to "keep up your courage [θαρσέω *tharseō*] for you must witness also in Rome" (see 23:11). The courage necessary for prophetic ministry is not a virtue that one cultivates by self-discipline or by self-confidence but by submission to the Lord.

# REFLECTIONS

"After this happened, the rest of the people on the island who had diseases also came and were cured" (28:9 NRSV). The conjunction of vivid images of hospitality and healing in this passage with the characterization of the Maltese as *barbaroi* underscores an important element of Luke's critique of religious culture: Those most open to God's word are often those without a sophisticated theology. While their theological illiteracy prevents them from precisely assessing the prophet's predicament and power (28:4-6), the Maltese finally do recognize his innocence and the authority given him by God. Their hospitality toward Paul (28:2, 7, 10) indicates that even *barbaroi* can be the sort of persons who are responsive to God's healing power and saving word. The church makes a mistake by presuming that the least, last, and lost among us do not have the spiritual capacity to detect the presence of God in the world. Indeed, they often are the most willing to position themselves before God's word in order to be found by God's grace.

# ACTS 28:17-28, PAUL'S MISSION IN ROME

## NIV

[17]Three days later he called together the leaders of the Jews. When they had assembled, Paul said to them: "My brothers, although I have done nothing against our people or against the customs of our ancestors, I was arrested in Jerusalem and handed over to the Romans. [18]They examined me and wanted to release me, because I was not guilty of any crime deserving death. [19]But when the Jews objected, I was compelled to appeal to Caesar—not that I had any charge to bring against my own people. [20]For this reason I have asked to see you and talk with you. It is because of the hope of Israel that I am bound with this chain."

[21]They replied, "We have not received any letters from Judea concerning you, and none of the brothers who have come from there has reported or said anything bad about you. [22]But we want to hear what your views are, for we know that people everywhere are talking against this sect."

[23]They arranged to meet Paul on a certain day, and came in even larger numbers to the place where he was staying. From morning till evening he explained and declared to them the kingdom of God and tried to convince them about Jesus from the Law of Moses and from the Prophets. [24]Some were convinced by what he said, but others would not believe. [25]They disagreed among themselves and began to leave after Paul had

## NRSV

17Three days later he called together the local leaders of the Jews. When they had assembled, he said to them, "Brothers, though I had done nothing against our people or the customs of our ancestors, yet I was arrested in Jerusalem and handed over to the Romans. [18]When they had examined me, the Romans[a] wanted to release me, because there was no reason for the death penalty in my case. [19]But when the Jews objected, I was compelled to appeal to the emperor—even though I had no charge to bring against my nation. [20]For this reason therefore I have asked to see you and speak with you,[b] since it is for the sake of the hope of Israel that I am bound with this chain." [21]They replied, "We have received no letters from Judea about you, and none of the brothers coming here has reported or spoken anything evil about you. [22]But we would like to hear from you what you think, for with regard to this sect we know that everywhere it is spoken against."

23After they had set a day to meet with him, they came to him at his lodgings in great numbers. From morning until evening he explained the matter to them, testifying to the kingdom of God and trying to convince them about Jesus both from the law of Moses and from the prophets.

[a] Gk *they*    [b] Or *I have asked you to see me and speak with me*

NIV

made this final statement: "The Holy Spirit spoke the truth to your forefathers when he said through Isaiah the prophet:

26 " 'Go to this people and say,
   "You will be ever hearing but never
      understanding;
   you will be ever seeing but never
      perceiving."
27 For this people's heart has become calloused;
   they hardly hear with their ears,
   and they have closed their eyes.
   Otherwise they might see with their eyes,
      hear with their ears,
      understand with their hearts
and turn, and I would heal them.'[a]

28"Therefore I want you to know that God's salvation has been sent to the Gentiles, and they will listen!"[b]

[a] 27 Isaiah 6:9,10   [b] 28 Some manuscripts listen!" 29After he said this, the Jews left, arguing vigorously among themselves.

NRSV

24Some were convinced by what he had said, while others refused to believe. 25So they disagreed with each other; and as they were leaving, Paul made one further statement: "The Holy Spirit was right in saying to your ancestors through the prophet Isaiah,

26 'Go to this people and say,
   You will indeed listen, but never understand,
      and you will indeed look, but never
         perceive.
27 For this people's heart has grown dull,
   and their ears are hard of hearing,
      and they have shut their eyes;
         so that they might not look with their
            eyes,
      and listen with their ears,
   and understand with their heart and turn—
      and I would heal them.'
28Let it be known to you then that this salvation of God has been sent to the Gentiles; they will listen."[a]

[a] Other ancient authorities add verse 29, And when he had said these words, the Jews departed, arguing vigorously among themselves

# COMMENTARY

The Paul of Acts at long last has reached Rome, the city of his destiny. That his story concludes in this city and not in Jerusalem supplies an important geographical element in Luke's theological framework. Within the symbolic universe of Luke's Jewish readers, Rome represents "the end of the earth," the most distant point on the circumference of a sacred compass whose epicenter is Jerusalem (see 2:5-11; cf. *Ps. Sol.* 8.16).[783] The Lord's orienting prophecy that the church's mission would progress from the holy city to the "end of the earth" is now fulfilled through Paul's mission in Rome (see 1:8; 13:47; cf. Isa 49:6). This concluding episode, then, is a "framing device" that brings closure to a narrative whose geographical framework is provided by this prophecy.[784]

Although his legal appeal to the emperor provides the circumstance of Paul's visit (see 25:12), he is in Rome to preach the word of God. The present passage should be read from this angle of vision and as a narrative piece within the whole of Acts (see 1:8; 9:15; 13:47; 19:21; 23:11; 27:24). In fact, only passing mention of Paul's appeal to Caesar is made (28:19a); he is not here as a citizen of Rome with legal problems to settle but as a prophet-like-Jesus with a gospel to proclaim (cf. 28:20, 23). The parallelism of plotline and portraiture of Paul's final mission in Rome and his first mission at Pisidian Antioch (see 13:13-47) underscores the consistency of his urban mission, according to which Paul meets first with the Jews of Rome (28:17-20). As a prisoner, he no longer has freedom of movement and cannot go to a Roman synagogue for worship and instruction as was his custom, so he invites the "local leaders of the Jews" to his flat for introductions—in reality a rehearsal of his previous apologia with the added

783. From a non-Jewish perspective, Rome is at the *center* of the earth, not on its margins, from which all roads radiate out. See L. Alexander, "Reading Luke-Acts From Back to Front," in *The Unity of Luke-Acts,* ed. J. Verheyden (Leuven: Leuven University Press, 1999) 426-27.
784. Cf. M. Parsons, *The Departure of Jesus in Luke-Acts,* JSNTSS 21 (Sheffield: JSOT, 1987) 156-59.

assurance that he is in Rome as a friend of Israel (see 28:19). This initial meeting ends on a hopeful note with the promise of a continuing conversation (28:21-22). True to the pattern of his interaction with other Jewish audiences, Paul is invited to address this contingent of Roman Jews in increased numbers for a second time (see 13:42-44). The subject matter of this second speech shifts attention from a personal defense of his prophetic vocation to a proclamation of the word of God (28:23). The response to his missionary message is as expected in context of Acts: Some believe, others do not. As usual there is conflict within Israel over the kerygmatic claim that Jesus is God's Messiah (28:24-25; see also 2:12-13; 4:1-4; 5:12-17; 6:8-15; 9:21-25; 13:42-47; 14:1-2; 15:4-29; 17:1-15; 18:12-17; 19:8-10; 21:17–26:29; cf. Luke 2:34). But this conflict agrees with biblical prophecy, which foretells national Israel's obduracy to the gospel (28:26-27; see also 13:46). By contrast, God-fearing Gentiles "will listen" to the word of the Lord (28:28; see also 13:47).

**28:17-20.** Paul finds a flourishing Jewish community in Rome, founded long before during the first days of the Republic. A dozen or more Roman synagogues were spiritual homes to many thousands of Jews living in various neighborhoods throughout the city.[785] The reader should assume that Luke's reference to "the local leaders of the Jews," then, refers to an alliance of important leaders from these synagogues who kept in close contact with each other and with other Jewish leaders across the empire (see v. 21). Their solidarity was especially important when securing basic rights assured by the emperor in the face of widespread antisemitic activities. Their dedication to this supervisory role is indicated by the prompt response to Paul's request for a meeting.

Paul's addresses his audience as "brothers" (ἄνδρες ἀδελφοί andres adelphoi), a formula used throughout Acts to introduce speeches shaped for Jewish audiences who at least on paper share a significant common ground of beliefs and values (see 2:29; 3:17; 7:2; 13:26, 38; 22:1; 23:1, 6). What he says to them rehearses what has already been said during his trials and therefore functions as a summary of the previous narrative:

(1) "I [have] done nothing against our people [λαός laos = Israel; see 2:47] or the customs [ἔθοι ethoi] of our ancestors" (28:17a; see 21:21, 28; 22:3; 23:6; 24:12-16; 25:8; 26:4-8). Even though Mosaic ethoi cannot save (see 15:1; cf. 13:38-39), their performance helps to shape the public identity of a people belonging to God. In this sense, Paul again asserts that the ethos of the church is Jewish.

(2) "Yet I was arrested in Jerusalem and handed over to the Romans . . . [who having] examined me . . . wanted to release me" (28:17b-18a; see 21:33; 24:2-21; 25:6-12; 26:2-29). Paul explains that he does not wear "this chain" because of criminal behavior worthy of the death penalty (so 28:18b; see 22:24; 23:28; 25:18; 26:31-32), and that the legitimacy of this verdict was proved by careful examination (cf. 24:8).

(3) "When the Jews objected . . . I had no charge to bring against my nation [ἔθνος ethnos]) (v. 19; see also 22:3; 23:6; 24:14; 26:4-5). Paul roundly and routinely denies any antipathy toward Israel, always locating himself within its faith tradition and religious culture. Paul's summary implicitly contrasts Rome's legal verdict of innocence (v. 18) and the Jewish objection that rejects Paul's messianic reading of Scripture for theological reasons. In any case, he reminds his audience, probably for rhetorical effect in an anti-Semitic cultural setting, that he has come to Rome as a Jewish prisoner rather than as a prosecutor opposed to Jewish interests. His personal ethos is shaped out of deep loyalty to his Jewish ethnos.

(4) "It is for the sake of the hope of Israel that I am bound with this chain" (v. 20; see also 23:6; 24:15; 26:6-7). Paul's highly evocative phrase, "the hope of Israel," is glossed by its earlier uses in Acts as a symbol of God's promise of Israel's restoration now fulfilled by Messiah Jesus, the Pentecost of God's Spirit, and the successes of the church's Jewish mission and finally of Paul's mission to bring the gospel's light to the nations. Paul's constant apologia is that his status as a Roman prisoner is due to his obedience to a prophetic vocation that is thoroughly Jewish in character.

**28:21-22.** With characteristic irony, the narrator shapes the Jewish response to Paul's apologia to agree with his subtext: The Jewish problem is not with the prophetic messenger but with his

---

785. Cf. J. A. Fitzmyer, *The Acts of the Apostles,* AB 31 (Garden City, N.Y.: Doubleday, 1998) 792.

message about Jesus. The lack of hostility toward Paul, which sharply contrasts with the Jerusalem Jews, is quite beside Luke's point and is historically suspect in any case.[786] The claim that Roman Jewry has "no letters from Judea" about Paul, nor intends the inception of any legal proceeding against him in Rome (v. 21), is due to their ignorance of "this sect [αἵρεσις *hairesis*] we know that everywhere . . . is spoken against" (v. 22). Luke's repetition of *hairesis* recalls the earlier confusion during Paul's Roman trial in Caesarea over whether he leads a Jewish "party" or a heretical movement (see 24:5, 14; 26:5). When combined with an apparent willingness to listen to Paul's views—"we would like to hear from you what you think"—the impression is that the leaders are simply confused about this messianic movement and desire clarity in the matter. Curiously, they do not ask Paul to clarify the relations between the believers already found in and around Rome (see vv. 15-16) and the Jews represented by these leaders; this question would seem reasonable given that Paul's arrival in Rome follows Claudius's expulsion of messianic Jews—such as Aquila and Priscilla—from the city (see 18:1-2). Perhaps they are merely interested in hearing from Paul a more conciliatory version of this controversial sect. Consistent with his pattern of prophetic ministry,[787] Luke depicts this first visit as responding to the ignorance of Jews who need yet another opportunity to "hear from you what you think."

**28:23.** The purpose of the prophet's second visitation of Jews in a particular place is to repeat God's offer of salvation so that they are without excuse (see 13:42-44; 7:35). The care with which Paul engages in this prophetic task is indicated by references to time: "they set a day to meet with him," and after assembling in Paul's flat, he examines the evidence "from morning until evening." The imperfect tense of ἐξετίθετο (*exetitheto*, "explain"), found only here in the NT, is inceptive and indicates that Paul began to teach in the morning and continued teaching throughout the day.

The topics of Paul's testimony are the two constants of persuasive gospel preaching from the beginning of Jesus' ministry (Luke 4:43; Acts 1:3) to the conclusion of Paul's: the "kingdom of God"

(see 28:31; cf. Luke 9:2; 10:9-11), which God promises to restore to Israel (see 1:6); and Messiah Jesus, through whom God's promise of a restored Israel is realized in full.[788] The mention of this core promise and its fulfillment summarizes Paul's entire gospel; it also frames his biblical hermeneutic according to which "both the law and the prophets" testify to the gospel's truth (see 24:14-15; 26:22-23; cf. Luke 24:25-27, 44-46). In bringing this testimony to Rome, then, Paul realizes the Lord's commitment to him envisaged in Jerusalem (see 23:11) and fulfills Jesus' prophecy to his apostolic successors that witness to him would be made at the "end of the earth" (see 1:8).

**28:24-25a.** Luke uses a well-known formula of conflict to describe the division within Israel provoked by his interpretation of Scripture: "some were convinced [πείθω *peithō*] by what he had said, while others refused to believe" (28:24; see 13:42-47; 17:1-5; 18:4; 19:8-10; cf. 26:28). Luke uses *peithō* elsewhere in missionary settings as a synonym for repentance (see 13:43; 17:4; 18:4); there are some who are "convinced" by Paul's interpretation of "the law of Moses and the prophets" about Jesus and repent, while still others "refuse to believe" (see 19:8-9; 23:6-9).[789] What happens in Paul's lodgings is entirely consistent with what has happened in every place the gospel has been proclaimed since the beginning of Jesus' story: The gospel of God is presented first to the Jews with clarity and conviction but with mixed results. Yet we should not suppose that Paul's mission to the Jews of Rome is a complete failure, or that the Jewish rejection of the gospel explains his success among Gentiles. The plain meaning of this text is that some Jews are convinced by Paul and become believers; and their response to his ministry in Rome is hardly hostile in any case.

**28:25b-27.** Paul's parting shot—a citation from Isaiah's prophecy (Isa 6:9-10 LXX)—has been understood by many modern interpreters as a sign of resignation with which Paul washes his hands of a future mission to Israel. However, while the Paul of the letters anticipated a national turning to

786. Cf. Barrett, *Acts,* 2:1241-42.
787. See Johnson, *The Acts of the Apostles,* 12-14, 473-74.

788. Cf. Barrett, *Acts,* 2:1243.
789. Cf. J. Jervell, *Die Apostelgeschichte,* KEK 3 (Göttingen: Vandenhoeck & Ruprecht, 1998) 625-27, 630; B. Witherington, *The Acts of the Apostles: A Socio-Rhetorical Commentary* (Grand Rapids: Eerdmans, 1998) 801-02; R. Bradley, *Luke-Acts and the Jews,* SBLMS 33 (Atlanta: Scholar's Press, 1987) 74-75.

the Messiah (cf. Rom 11:26) and is clearly frustrated when this does not immediately occur (cf. Rom 9:1-5), the Lukan Paul's appeal to Isaiah is explanatory of what he has experienced first hand now and before (see 13:44-47; 18:5-7): Not every Jew who hears the gospel believes its central claim that the risen Jesus is the promised Messiah. The tragic reality, foretold at the Lord's birth, is that the word of God about him will divide Israel into a responsive remnant for salvation and an obdurate opposition for spiritual exile (cf. Luke 2:34). The plotline of the biblical Gospels and Acts follows the fulfillment of this prophecy.[790]

In its original setting, Isaiah's prophecy of Israel's spiritual dullness (Isa 6:9-10) is featured in his commissioning as a prophet of God (cf. Isa 6:6-8). While the prophet of God is called to "go and say to this people [= Israel]" (28:26), his expectation should be of Israel's obduracy rather than of a nation's renewal: "they will listen, but never understand/look, but never perceive." Significantly, the LXX version of the prophecy that Luke uses renders the verbs describing Israel's dullness as aorist indicatives rather than as the imperatives found in the Hebrew text: "For this people's mind has grown dull [rather than "Make the mind of this people dull"] . . . ears are hard of hearing [rather than "stop their ears"] . . . close their eyes [rather than "shut their eyes"]." The rhetorical effect of this change of verbal mood is to diagnose Israel's spiritual sickness as the result of its deliberate decision to reject God's word—rather than of God's preordination or the prophet's provocation of spiritual failure. Thus the prospect of God's promised restoration of the entire nation—"and I would heal them" (28:27)—is subverted by unrepentant Jews who "refuse to believe" God's saving word (see 3:19-23).

Paul's adaptation of Isaiah's prophecy to this new missionary setting follows the lead of the Gospels (cf. Matt 13:14-15//Mark 4:12//Luke 8:10//John 12:39-40) where Jesus appeals to this prophecy to explain why some in Israel fail to understand his teaching. The Gospels give this prophecy prominent position, as Acts does here, because in the hands of Christian interpreters Isaiah provides a useful apologia to a vexing

question: Why does the Christian gospel fail to convince the majority of religious Jews? The force of this question is felt even more keenly in Acts, since its narrative of the church's mission begins amidst great optimism in Jerusalem with mass conversions of devout Jews. Although James can still report to Paul that "many thousands" of Jews continue to convert to the Lord in Palestine (see 21:20), the fruit of Paul's mission to the Jews is considerably less bountiful. In response to this concern, Luke delays his use of Isaiah's prophecy to give its message greater import as his story's conclusion. The word of God convincingly presented by the prophet does not deafen, blind, or dull Israel's reception of God's promises; those Jews who "refuse to believe" have no one to blame but themselves (cf. Rom 11:7-8).[791] Indeed, the subtext of Paul's use of the prophecy is that Israel's ambivalence toward Jesus is a piece of God's scripted salvation: On this side of the Messiah's return to earth for creation's restoration (see 3:20-21; 1:10-11), Israel will remain divided over Jesus (see 3:22-23).

The same can be said of all the nations, of course; however, God's salvation belongs first of all to a faithful Israel. For this reason Jewish rejection is considered a more serious theological crisis than the obduracy of Gentiles: While all believers from every nation share God's salvation and Spirit equally (see 10:34-35; 11:18; 15:7-11), the salvation of the nations is predicated on the restoration of repentant Israel (see 3:19-26).[792] A prophetic calculus that presumes Gentiles "will listen" because repentant Jews do so first explains why Luke attaches such importance to Paul's loyalty to his Jewish heritage (see 28:17-20) and also to the Jews who were "convinced" by Paul's gospel (see 28:23-24). The more positive response of Jews to Jesus meets the necessary precondition for his mission to go forward in Rome not only to those Gentiles who "will listen" (see 28:28) but also to "all who came to him" (28:30).

---

790. Cf. D. Tiede, *Prophecy and History in Luke-Acts* (Philadelphia: Fortress, 1980).

791. Cf. Johnson, *The Acts of the Apostles,* 476.

792. For Isaiah's nationalistic interest in Israel's salvation as integral to a universal hope in the salvation of the nations, see D. van Winkle, "The Relationship of the Nations to Yahweh and to Israel in Isaiah xl-lv," *VT* 35 (1985) 446-58. Van Winkle asserts that the restoration of God's rule in Israel is the eschatological signal to all the nations of earth that blessings promised them have drawn nigh and are received from God through Israel. I suspect something like this belief is a theological subtext of Paul's citation of Isaiah in this setting.

In this regard, we should give special note to the formula Paul uses to introduce the prophetic citation: "The Holy Spirit was right in saying to your ancestors through the prophet Isaiah" (28:25*b*). Luke uses the reference to the Holy Spirit to qualify the authority of the written word: When properly interpreted by an inspired prophet (such as Peter or Paul), the sacred text becomes the authorized conduit by which the living *vox Dei* (voice of God) is heard, thereby establishing the norm for contemporary auditors in a particular setting (see 1:16; 4:25). In a similar fashion, Paul's shift from "our people or the customs of our ancestors" (28:17) to "your ancestors" is a rhetorical device that allows him to focus the inspired meaning of the cited text on those Jews who have rejected his presentation of the gospel. That is, the Holy Spirit speaks through the biblical text a word from the living God for those among Paul's departing guests who "refuse to believe."

For this reason, Paul's retort does not argue for a more permanent or inclusive "Jewish rejection of the gospel." When Paul responds twice before to the obduracy of Jewish opponents (see 13:46-47; 18:5-6), his manifest intent is not to forgo future missionary efforts among the Jews in other places. This is true to the end of his story, where he meets and presents the gospel first to Roman Jews before inviting other interested guests to his Bible study. Dunn is therefore correct in arguing that the Paul of Acts "would have understood Isaiah as indicating the course (and frustrations) of Paul's mission to his own and Isaiah's people, not as calling on him to end it in dismissive denunciation."[793] In fact, although the prophet's words are harsh, there is no evidence of personal animosity between Paul and his departing guests. At most this text provides a realistic interpretation of why an inspired teacher of Israel should expect failure when attempting to convince the entire congregation of Israel about Jesus. To say more than this or to impute other motives to Paul's use of Isaiah is to claim more than the text allows.

**28:28.** What is the connection between the mixed response of the Jews to Paul's message, Isaiah's prophecy of unrepentant Israel's obduracy, and Paul's prophecy that Gentiles "will listen" to

him? This is the third time in Acts where the topics of Jewish rejection and Gentile acceptance of the gospel are combined (see 13:46-47; 18:5-6). Such Lukan triads are narrative constructions that assure the reader of the lasting importance of these themes; but the precise logic that combines them is not at all certain. Many commentators think that Luke shapes this final scene in light of a growing realization that the church's mission to the Jews in the Diaspora had failed and the main focus of its ministry should now be directed toward non-Jews. Luke's narrative, however, does not evince such a motive. At face value, Paul's statement that salvation "has been sent to the Gentiles" and his prediction that Gentiles "will listen" assert two additional facts that are well established by the narrative from the conversion of Cornelius forward. Even as Acts makes clear that not every Jew is unresponsive to Paul, it is equally clear that not every Gentile will listen to him. He has in fact found the most responsive Gentiles in Jewish synagogues: Those who listen most keenly to the word of God are those who have left behind the idolatries of pagan religion in exchange for those sacred places where a Jewish ethos is cultivated by the teaching of Moses (see 15:20-21). The purpose of combining the themes of Jewish rejection and Gentile acceptance in Acts is to underwrite this central irony in the plan of God's salvation: *Even when devout Jews refuse to believe the word of God persuasively presented, Gentiles whose spiritual sensibility is forged in their midst are more apt to listen.*

Finally, then, the correspondence between the themes of this present passage and those that have shaped the past ministry of Paul in Acts orients the reader toward a similar future. The ending of Acts portrays an unchanged and incorrigible Paul who welcomes all to his home in Rome to hear his "bold and unhindered" proclamation of the very same gospel he has always preached (see 28:30-31). Perhaps the point that should linger on in the reader's mind is not about Paul, or Jewish rejection, or that Gentiles will listen to the gospel, but rather about the assurance of this prophet-like-Jesus: Even though the proclamation of the word of God will provoke different responses in those who hear it, the inherent trustworthiness of its claims determines the triumphant progress of God's salvation to the end of time. Others will take this gospel up and

---

793. J. D. G. Dunn, *The Acts of the Apostles* (Valley Forge, Pa.: Trinity, 1996) 355.

preach it as boldly as Paul; some will listen while others will refuse its claims. This reality was true in the past of the church and so it will be true in the church's future, until the Lord comes back to earth in the same way he departed to inaugurate the season of universal restoration.[794]

794. The Western version adds an additional verse that repeats the sentiment of 28:25: "When he had said this, the Jews went out debating vigorously among themselves" (28:29). The rhetorical effects of this addition are to enclose 28:26-28 more clearly as Paul's commentary on the conflict his gospel has provoked within Israel and to clearly demarcate 28:30-31 as the ending of Acts.

# REFLECTIONS

"This salvation of God has been sent to the Gentiles; they will listen" (28:28 NRSV). Paul's final declaration in Acts continues to haunt the church. Interpreters ancient and modern have inferred an antisemitic motive and supersessionist theology from it: Israel's rejection of the gospel in Rome is final and justifies Paul's Gentile mission and explains its success. One of the interpretive keys of this commentary is to challenge this reading of Acts.

Frankly, Luke offers his readers little to explain the mixed results of Paul's mission to the Jews or why the church has become by his day a Gentile institution. Clearly this result does not reflect either God's longing or Paul's effort. The Paul of Acts routinely presents himself as Jewish and conforms his religious practices to Israel's. He can claim with integrity at the end of the day to seek only "the hope of Israel" (28:20). His pattern also remains constant, whether free or captive: He meets with religious Jews in Rome for worship and instruction, and so they are the first to hear his testimony from their Scriptures that God's kingdom has visited them in Jesus, their promised Messiah. Why some Jews take Paul's testimony to heart while most others do not remains a mystery to those of us who believe. At the very least, the interpreter of Acts must identify with Paul's final struggle to ground his vocation in the traditions of Israel while trying to understand why all of Israel did not happily embrace his good news. This same struggle was central to Jesus' messianic career.

Nonetheless, Acts stands as an important biblical text for reflecting upon the ongoing relationship between the church and synagogue. According to Luke's reading of Scripture's prophecy, God's plan for restoring historic Israel has always divided the "people" into those who repent and those who do not (28:25-27). The mixed response to Paul's teaching in Rome is indicative of Israel's response to the preaching of God's word beginning with Moses (see 7:35) and continuing throughout Israel's history to include the Messiah (Gospel) and his successors (Acts). God has not forsaken *repentant* Israel and relentlessly offers unrepentant Israel second chances (see 7:39; 13:44-45). The word has gone first to Israel as promised (see 3:25-26), and the mission to the nations is possible only because the church's mission to the Jews has succeeded (Acts 1-8; see 13:47). Moreover, as promised God has forgiven all in Israel who repent and turn to the Lord, restoring their covenant and leading them into a season of refreshment under the aegis of the Holy Spirit (see 3:19). Likewise, Paul's claim that "Gentiles will listen" must be glossed by the rest of Acts: Clearly not all Gentiles "listen" to the gospel (see 19:23-27). Those who do and repent are typically those attached to the prophet who teaches Moses (see 28:10; 28:23) or to the synagogue where Moses is read (see 15:21). Even though enjoying a greater measure of success among Gentiles, the Paul of Acts does not register resignation but rather persistence in trying another city and synagogue where he sometimes enjoys greater success among the Jews (see 17:11; cf. 21:20).

These same concerns are also reflected in Paul's letter to the Romans. Even though he tends to spiritualize the biblical idea of Israel in Romans (cf. 2:28-29; 9:6-12), Paul concludes the principal part of his letter by claiming that historic Israel will be restored when the Gentile mission is completed and the Messiah returns to earth to complete his mission (cf. Rom 11:25-27). This remarkable vision of Israel's future restoration not only complements Luke's understanding of Paul's mission but helps the interpreter of Acts put together the story's beginning and ending. The promise of Jesus' return (see 1:9-11) glosses Paul's response to the ambivalence of Roman Jews by adding an eschatological subtext: After all the nations are finished "listening" to the gospel according to God's timetable (see 1:7; cf. Rom 11:25) and the Messiah returns to broker God's cosmic triumph over the powers of darkness, then all Israel will understand and turn for God to heal them (see 28:27).

When the conclusion to Acts is read in this wider narrative context, especially with the Romans co-text, the interpreter may well appreciate Paul's optimism in "welcoming all [Jews and Gentiles alike] who came to him" (28:30) to hear the gospel of a faithful God and God's risen Messiah (see 28:31). Nothing has changed since Paul.

# THE ENDING OF ACTS

<sup>30</sup>For two whole years Paul stayed there in his own rented house and welcomed all who came to see him. <sup>31</sup>Boldly and without hindrance he preached the kingdom of God and taught about the Lord Jesus Christ.

30He lived there two whole years at his own expense[a] and welcomed all who came to him, <sup>31</sup>proclaiming the kingdom of God and teaching about the Lord Jesus Christ with all boldness and without hindrance.

[a] Or *in his own hired dwelling*

# COMMENTARY

The final sentence of Acts is clear enough: Paul spends two years in Rome confined to his lodgings but entertaining all who visit him without legal restraint. He boldly preaches the "kingdom of God" to all his guests and teaches them about the Lord Jesus Christ. Although this portrait of Paul coheres with the rest of Acts, the passage pricks the interpreter's curiosity because it concludes Acts without saying anything of Paul's meeting with the Roman emperor—the "official" reason why he is a prisoner in Rome. Many have speculated that Luke does not include this information because he did not know the details of what happened to Paul. Yet this hardly seems possible, since Acts was probably composed after Paul's legal difficulties were resolved. Others claim that Luke knew the outcome of Paul's case but intended to produce a trilogy of earliest Christianity that he never completed. Some speculate that he considered this biographical detail either anticlimactic (e.g., the statute of limitations ran out after two years and he was released to no great fanfare) or too tragic (e.g., he was martyred) to fit the plotline of Paul's heroic story in Acts. Some modern scholars have even speculated that an early version of Acts circulated with a longer ending that included details of Paul's trial and alleged martyrdom, but then subsequent editors of Acts erased this ending because of embarrassing testimony raised in court against Paul or more

likely against the Jewish or Roman churches that had failed to support him during his time of need.[795] Still others, myself included, find no problem with Luke's ending because it portrays Paul engaged in the routines of his prophetic vocation in the divinely ordained city of his destiny. The faithful Paul of Acts has never been much concerned about the politics of Rome, nor does he think to defend his good citizenship. When he does appeal to Rome, it is in service of his mission. In this sense, Luke may well suppose that whatever the Emperor may have decided in Paul's case is irrelevant. The silence of Acts on any of these matters, however, precludes a final solution.

**28:30-31.** The pertinent interests of the interpreter of Acts as Scripture do not concern an imagined *Urtext,* or missing information, that may contribute to an impression of Luke's "unfinished business." Rather, the interpreter's principal concern is to make sense of this passage and its role in summarizing Paul's Roman mission and also in concluding the whole book of Acts. In this regard, the terms used of both the messenger (v. 30) and his message (v. 31) are highly evocative of other

795. For various hypotheses, see H. Conzelmann, *The Acts of the Apostles,* trans. J. Limburg et al., ed. E. J. Epp and C. R. Matthews, Hermeneia (Philadelphia: Fortress, 1987) 228; S. Wilson, *The Gentiles and the Gentile Mission in Luke-Acts,* SNTSMS 23 (Cambridge: Cambridge University Press, 1973) 233-36; and B. Witherington, *The Acts of the Apostles: A Socio-Rhetorical Commentary* (Grand Rapids: Eerdmans, 1998) 807-12.

episodes in Acts and effectively bring a sense of closure to its reading. Perhaps the most important impression made by this repetition of important terms in Acts is one of permanence and continuity. No matter what has transpired since the beginning of his mission, these final images depict an exemplary Paul steadfastly obedient to his prophetic calling: He "welcomed all who came to him, proclaiming [κηρύσσω *kēryssō*] the kingdom of God and teaching [διδάσκω *didaskō*] about the Lord Jesus Christ with all boldness [παρρησία *parrēsia*] and without hindrance." Mention is made of the central theme of gospel preaching since Jesus, "the kingdom of God." Paul's own summary of his ministry at Miletus already had contained this (see 20:25; cf. 19:8; 28:23), even as the Lord had earlier instructed his apostolic successors concerning the reign of God in preparing them to bear witness to him (see 1:3, 6; 10:42; cf. Luke 24:47; 9:2). From beginning to end, the preoccupation of the prophets-like-Jesus is to preach the kingdom of God. Likewise, teaching about Jesus remains a constant of the church's missionary praxis, beginning with the Twelve (4:2, 18; 5:21) and continuing with Paul's ministry (11:26) to the end (28:31; see also 20:20). These two practices of preaching about God's kingdom, restored to a faithful Israel (see 1:6), and teaching about God's Messiah enclose the whole of Acts to remind its readers of the church's ongoing vocation. God's saving purpose for all people cannot be known otherwise.

Two other important themes emphasize the *where* and the *how* of Paul's ministry in Rome and deepen the reader's sense of closure to Acts. The hospitable Paul welcomed his religious clients into his own lodging and spoke to them concerning the word of God "with all boldness." Hospitality and makeshift meeting places for worship and Bible instruction are important themes in the second half of Acts (see 16:15, 31-34; 17:5; 18:7-8; 19:9; 20:20), not only in dispelling James's anxiety over the future of a distinctively Jewish ethos in the Pauline church (see 15:20-21) but also in showing the manner by which Amos's prophecy of God's "re-housing" Israel is fulfilled through Paul's mission to the nations (see 15:16-17). The use of *parrēsia* ("boldness") recalls how the apostles prayed for the Holy Spirit's inspiration to empower a more effective proclamation of the gospel (see 4:29-31). It is this holy boldness of prophets-like-Jesus, cultivated by living in the Spirit, which enlivens a courageous communication of the gospel (see also 2:29; 9:27-28; 13:46; 14:3; 18:26; 19:8; 22:26).

According to Luke, Paul spent two years in Rome, where he lived "at his own expense and welcomed all who came to him." Paul's freedom of movement is curtailed by his house arrest. However, his freedom to entertain guests probably reflects the ambiguity of his legal status (he is not guilty of any crime or perceived as a troublemaker by Rome) or perhaps the early years of Nero's reign (early 60s) when the Roman emperor was considerably less hostile toward Jews and Christians than later in his regime.[796] Much has been made of the reference to the duration of Paul's stay—"two whole years." Why include such a specific detail in a narrative summary? Many suppose that Luke's reference to a finite period of time suggests termination of some sort, whether Paul's release or his death.[797] However, in Acts similar references are included in summaries of Paul's urban missions to convey the impression of his commitment to a particular work under difficult circumstances (see 18:11); and I suspect Luke has this apologetic intent in mind.

Among the important characteristics of Paul's persona is his handling of finances: "He lived—at his own expense." Consistent with his Pharisaism, Luke's Jewish Paul works at a trade to support himself (see 18:3). Additionally, he may have family resources to draw upon (see 21:39; 22:3) sufficient to allow him to cover the expenses of those with whom he completed vows and sacrifices of purification (see 21:24, 26). Here he takes care of his rent, and the emphatic construction of the phrase underlines the importance Luke places on Paul's doing so. That Paul's lease is for two years and is not open-ended may well indicate a lack of permanence,[798] but for what reason is left unclear (see above). In my mind, the principal point is not of Paul's impermanence but of his rented quarters,

---

796. Cf. C. K. Barrett, *A Critical and Exegetical Commentary on the Acts of the Apostles*, 2 vols, ICC (Edinburgh: T. & T. Clark, 1994, 1998) 2:1249-50.

797. Cf. C. Hemer, *The Book of Acts in the Setting of Hellenistic History*, WUNT 49 (Tübingen: Mohr Siebeck, 1989) 383-87.

798. The phrase ἐν ἰδίω μισθώματι (*en idiō misthōmati*, "at his own expense") does not actually mention a home (οἶκος/οἰκία *oikos/oikia*), which would connote a private residence. However, Luke has already mentioned Paul's ξενία (*xenia*, "lodgings," 28:23) and need not do so here. Most now take this phrase as connoting that Paul rented (rather than purchased) his Roman *xenia*. See Witherington, *The Acts of the Apostles*, 812-13.

which nicely serves as a substitute for a local synagogue where the word of God is taught to any who come for as long as the prophet remains in Rome (see 7:44-50).

More important, Paul "welcomed all [πᾶς *pas*] who came to him." The Western version of Acts rightly adds the appositional phrase, "all Jews and Gentiles," to *pas*. Prisoner Paul continues to live within his vocation to extend the gospel of God to all people (see 9:15) in the realization of Joel's prophecy that "everyone [*pas*] who calls upon the name of the Lord will be saved" (2:21).

The two features of Paul's prophetic ministry are "preaching the kingdom of God" and "teaching about the Lord Jesus Christ" (see above). These two tasks are boldly executed by inspiration of the Spirit of prophecy (see 4:13, 29-31) "and without hindrance" (ἀκωλύτως *akōlytōs*). Luke places *akōlytōs* in the emphatic position at the end of his book not merely to characterize Paul's imprisonment as allowing him considerable personal freedom but also to characterize the unhindered and unstoppable spread of God's gospel according to God's purposes (cf. 2 Tim 2:8-13).

The final sentence of Acts is a summary, not a climax: Paul is simply being Paul in Rome. Its overall importance to Luke's narrative, therefore, is not to contribute new information but to facilitate a transition with a deep impression of the story's continuity from beginning to end. Typically Luke's summaries make literary transitions to move readers along from one episode to the next. In the case of an ending, however, there is no next stage in the telling of Luke's story. What then? Perhaps he would have his last words stage a transition from the narrative world of Acts to the considerably more complicated worlds of his readers. If that is the case, then these parting images of Paul linger on in the reader's imagination to stimulate further reflection on what it means to continue what this exemplary prophet-like-Jesus "began to do and to say" in Rome (cf. 1:1). While times and places will continue to change around us, the church's prophetic calling in "proclaiming the kingdom of God and teaching about the Lord Jesus Christ with all boldness" remains constant.

# REFLECTIONS

Paul "welcomed all who came to him, proclaiming the kingdom of God . . . with all boldness" (28:30-31 NRSV). The final sentence of Acts is a summary, not a climax. Paul is simply being Paul, ever faithful to his prophetic vocation. But this is Luke's point. His conclusion does not intend to contribute new information to his biography of Paul or to frustrate his readers by leaving out important information. The ending to Acts does what good endings to excellent stories must always do: facilitate a transition that moves readers from the narrative world to their own considerably more complicated real worlds. These parting images of Paul linger on in our collective imagination to stimulate further reflection on what it means to continue what Paul began to do and to say in Rome. We are his successors. While times and places will continue to change, the church's prophetic calling is to "proclaim the kingdom of God and teach about the Lord Jesus Christ with all boldness." The church must simply be the church.

# INTRODUCTION TO EPISTOLARY LITERATURE

## ROBERT W. WALL

This article intends neither to offer a succinct summary of each NT letter's subject matter nor to survey solutions to the various critical problems each poses; these are tasks of the individual commentaries that follow. Rather, the primary purpose is to introduce readers to the "orienting concerns" that are essential for studying and reflecting upon the NT epistolary texts as Scripture. Given the literary and theological diversity of these texts, and the complex and variegated history of their interpretation, this introduction will necessarily be selective. If my intent is served, however, both the theological subject matter of the NT letters as a whole and those interpretive strategies employed to seek and find this instruction will be brought into clearer focus.

After a *general introduction* to the letters, I will lay out a rough map of sorts, employing a familiar typology to chart three essential "worlds" that will orient readers to the Bible's epistolary literature: *behind-the-text* (the world of authors and their first audiences), *within-the-text* (the world of compositions) and *in-front-of-the-text* (the world of the audience for whom the text is Scripture).[1] These worlds are not discrete locations; rather, there is considerable overlap among them. Further, the plurality of interpretive locations reflects the current intellectual climate of biblical studies, in which modernity's dominant commitment to historical models has given way to a much wider range of methodologies that together can better discern the text's full meaning. An integrated approach to the letters, combining rather than dividing historical, literary, and theological information, may better serve the primary work of Scripture's performance within the faith community: to lead readers into a deeper understanding of the gospel of God.

## GENERAL INTRODUCTION

The NT canon includes twenty-one letters gathered in two collections, Pauline (Romans through

1. See, e.g., D. Barr, *The New Testament Story: An Introduction,* 2nd ed. (Belmont, Calif.: Wadsworth, 1995) 2-18; J. B. Green and M. Turner, "NT Commentary and Systematic Theology: Strangers or Friends?" in *Between Two Horizons* (Grand Rapids, MI: Eerdmans, 2000), 1-22.

Philemon) and non-Pauline (Hebrews through Jude), that are strategically sandwiched between the books of Acts and Revelation. Both collections are often divided and grouped according to certain judgments about their points of origin, content, or current influence—judgments that remain contested. For this reason the rubrics employed during the history of their interpretation enjoy only moderate success as explanatory constructs and sometimes even dampen the distinctive contribution each letter makes to the whole canon.

In particular, while the entire Pauline collection concerns the ministry and message of the apostle Paul, its letters are often divided into those that are "genuine" (written by Paul) and those that are "disputed" (thought to have been written after Paul's death but in the manner of his "genuine" letters). This division is intended to distinguish the theology of the "real" Paul from that of his followers. Some scholars think that an imprisoned Paul (when and where are disputed) wrote or transcribed the "prison letters" (Ephesians, Philippians, Colossians, 2 Timothy, Philemon). The themes of the "Pastoral Epistles" (1–2 Timothy and Titus, which are usually studied together and are listed among the "disputed" letters) concern the characteristics of Christian leaders as well as the organization of Christian congregations (even though 2 Timothy differs in significant ways in this regard from 1 Timothy and Titus). Still another group of Paul's letters, whose greater length and influence are deemed "major" (Romans through Galatians), is occasionally separated from the shorter letters (Ephesians through Philemon). The influence of the shorter letters is sometimes perceived as less significant in forming the church's theological understanding—a view that seems to persist among some Protestant communions.

Although scholars sometimes rearrange the thirteen Pauline letters to follow a chronological scheme, the final form of the modern NT follows the Latin Vulgate so that letters written to congregations (Romans through 2 Thessalonians) precede those written to individuals (1 Timothy through Philemon). Within each group, letters are arranged by decreasing length, even though Ephesians is slightly longer than Galatians (which may well account for its priority in early canon lists; e.g., Chester Beatty papyri from c. 200 CE and the

Muratorian canon list from c. 190 CE). It should be noted, however, that the early church arranged the Pauline corpus in different sequences and often included Hebrews.[2] Sometimes these letters were arranged according to theological importance. For example, Marcion placed Galatians first among Paul's letters, since he thought its teaching best supported his own contention that the influence of the OT (and its theology) ended with Christ. Typically, Romans is placed first in the Pauline corpus not only because of its length but also because it presumes to offer its readers the best theological introduction to the writings of Paul, a status surely justified by its history and use within the church.

Unlike the Pauline letters, which are named after those being addressed, all the letters that make up the second collection (except Hebrews) are named after their supposed authors. The placement of each within the NT once again follows their decreasing length. As with the Pauline corpus, however, other sequences are found in the early and medieval churches, perhaps indicating the estimation of their relative theological importance for the purpose of Christian formation. In the canon lists of the Roman church (e.g., those of Carthage, 397 CE) and Augustine, the Petrine correspondence is placed first, which may reflect the primacy of Peter's memory and his teaching. The present form, James–Peter–John, follows Paul's list in Gal 2:9.

The writings of this second collection are even more difficult to organize into groups of common denominators than are the Pauline letters because their literary diversity is more pronounced and their theological traditions more diverse. The rubric "non-Pauline" is used in reference to those letters that do not claim residence within the Pauline domain—no matter what others may claim for them. More important, "non-Pauline" intends to orient the reader to the presence of two discrete collections of letters and then to the reflexive relationship between them as integral epistolary parts within the biblical whole. In most cases, seven of these letters (James through Jude) are listed under the ancient rubric "catholic," or more recently "general," because it is thought they were originally encyclical epistles that circulated among

2. B. Metzger, *The Canon of the New Testament* (Oxford: Clarendon, 1987) 297-99.

geographically dispersed and ethnically mixed congregations. Missing from this and other catalogs is Hebrews, which is typically left orphaned without either a Pauline or a catholic home. Perhaps its placement within the letter canon between the Pauline and the catholic letters is strategic: Being neither and yet having elements of both, Hebrews is an effective bridge, reminding readers of the interdependent character of these two collections of letters.

A. Deissmann's well-known distinction between the "epistle," compositions of public art intended for a wide audience, and the "letter," occasional correspondence intended for private and confidential reading, supports the Pauline/catholic distinction. That is, the catholic collection is composed of epistles written as artful homilies for a general readership, whereas the Pauline letters were written for and first read by particular congregations or individuals.[3] Upon closer analysis, however, this distinction does not seem appropriate for the catholic epistles, since nowhere do James, Jude, and 2 Peter (or Hebrews) claim to address a general audience; and 3 John addresses an individual. Moreover, 1 John and James (and Hebrews) only approximate literary epistles. Nor can it be said that all these epistles are known by their author, for those from "John" (and Hebrews) are anonymous.

Despite the difficulty of forming neat and convenient groups, these letters all share a common purpose: to combine theological instruction and moral exhortation toward particular practical and pastoral ends. Each addresses the spiritual struggles and theological controversies that face ordinary believers seeking a more mature witness to their faith in Jesus Christ, often within hostile social settings. Each reflects its own particular historical occasion and theological situation, where the gospel of God is adapted to the life of God's people. Each is deeply rooted in particular interpretive traditions judged acceptable by the early church as apostolic and divinely inspired. For this reason, "catholic" is sometimes also used to classify the subject matter of these letters as applicable to every Christian congregation; they were even called the *epistulae canonicae* in the West because their divine inspiration (and so canonicity) was recognized

by "all the churches."[4] However, this sense of universal significance is true of every biblical writing whose canonical status is due in part to its perceived usefulness in the spiritual formation of every generation and congregation of believers.

## THE WORLD BEHIND THE LETTERS: CONVERSATIONS IN HISTORICAL CONTEXT

No letter began its life as a biblical writing, read by the whole church for theological understanding. Every letter was at first a pastor-teacher's written response to believers whose particular sociohistorical circumstances provoked a spiritual crisis that required theological explanation and practical resolution. The letters of the NT are occasional literature, then. That is, in every case writers adapted their core theological convictions to a particular audience's historical situation in ways that enabled their writing to be, in C. Beker's apt phrase, "a word on target."[5] Therefore, current interpreters, far removed from the social world that helped to shape the letter's subject matter, are obligated to narrow the gap by gathering and using as much historical, political, and socioeconomic information regarding the original setting as possible. The epistolary text becomes a "window" through which its ancient author and first readers/auditors (authorial audience) are viewed more clearly, their worlds and traditions more fully understood, and the events implied by the text better known.

The result is a "thickened" description of the letter's subject matter that can facilitate its present performance as the church's Scripture. Within the community of faith, rarely if ever does an interest in the "world behind the letters" marginalize the theological aspect of the text itself so that we view it merely as a historical resource. Rather, we use the tools of historical criticism to understand better the biblical text as a witness to God's revelation

---

3. A. Deissmann, *Light from the Ancient East,* trans. L. R. M Strachan, 2nd ed. (London: Hodder & Stoughton, 1928).

4. So J. Fitzmyer, "Introduction to the NT Epistles," *NJBC* (Englewood Cliffs, N.J.: Prentice Hall, 1990) 771.

5. Beker has argued that Paul is not a systematic theologian but an interpreter of the Christian gospel who adapts the unchanging convictions of his faith ("coherence") to the ever-changing "contingencies" of his audiences. According to him, then, Paul's interpretive activity seeks to make the "abiding Word of the gospel a word on target." See C. Beker, "Recasting Pauline Theology" in *Pauline Theology,* ed. J. Bassler (Minneapolis: Fortress, 1991) 1:15.

within history, within circumstances in which letters are heard or read as a "word on target." The interpreter approaches these ancient texts with historical sensitivity, then, to understand more precisely their meaning at the point of origin.

Since most NT letters deal with the concrete problems of specific communities, the letters themselves are the clearest line of sight into their social world. This methodological claim does not exclude non-biblical resources, literary or otherwise, whether from the early Roman Empire or from early Judaism. Rather, it insists only that we move outward from the epistolary literature itself to all other sources when reconstructing the world behind the letters.

## THE PAULINE COLLECTION

The most important conversation partner in the Pauline correspondence is the author. To be sure, an interpreter's decisions regarding Pauline authorship depend on prior decisions about sources. Which of the letters that claim Pauline authorship were actually written by Paul? To what extent should we trust the historical veracity of Luke's portrait of Paul in Acts? And what of the apocryphal Paul of early Christian memory and legend, which many scholars think so idealizes Paul's memory and theological trajectory that both are badly distorted? Even the autobiographical portions of the authentic letters, which many suppose offer us the best window onto the historical Paul, serve primarily an apologetical (i.e., rhetorical) purpose. Other matters, such as those related to the authorial address and the date and place of origin of a particular letter, are all part of the historical matrix that help to settle the question of Pauline authorship. We leave these decisions and discussions to the commentators on the individual letters.

On balance, however, few figures from antiquity are better known than Paul. As N. Dahl has noted, "in his letters, Paul himself comes to life."[6] Current readers of his letters have sufficient raw material to sketch a basic chronology of Paul's life and mission. This historical project has a direct bearing upon the interpretation of the Pauline letters, especially when trying to date and place them in some historical sequence or social location. The

construction of a Pauline chronology helps the interpreter to assess the development of Paul's theological conception; the subject matter of Paul's message is no longer presented as a static and systematic whole. Instead, on the basis of a chronology of his ministry and letters, the development of the most important theological themes of Pauline preaching (e.g., the promise and fulfillment of God's salvation, the results of Christ's death and resurrection, the life and witness of the church) and of the central theological controversies of his Gentile mission (e.g., election, law, theodicy, Israel) can be traced through the sequence of letters. Paul's theology was a work in process.[7]

**The Book of Acts and the Chronology of the Pauline Collection.** What is known about Paul comes to us from three sources: (1) the autobiographical portions of his letters, (2) his "authorized" biography found in the book of Acts, and (3) his "unauthorized" biography found in such apocryphal writings as *The Acts of Paul* and *Thecla*. These sources are not of equal value to Paul's chronologists. Accepting the historian's rule of favoring primary (or direct) over secondary (or mediated) evidence, preference is always granted to what Paul says about himself in his letters, even though the book of Acts contributes necessary information to fill out his epistolary portrait. Most scholars hold that Paul's portrait in Acts is the literary invention of the narrator, whose principal interests are theological and not historical. The apocryphal story of Paul is still farther removed from the historical Paul, deriving in part from the canonical Acts and in part from legend, and is thus deemed either redundant or useless as a historical resource.[8]

The most crucial task facing the chronologist is the correlation of datable events mentioned in Paul's letters or his story in Acts. Sharply stated, the primary problem is that the chronology of Paul's life according to Paul's letters differs at

6. N. Dahl, *Studies in Paul* (Minneapolis: Augsburg, 1977) 6.

7. Trobisch has argued that Paul edited and published his own letter collection (consisting of Romans, 1–2 Corinthians, and Galatians) for his client-friends. See D. Trobisch, *Paul's Letter Collection: Tracing the Origins* (Minneapolis: Fortress, 1994). Paul's purpose was to supply them with a literary testament shortly before his death that would respond in a normative way to a variety of controversies generated by his Gentile mission. Trobisch's provocative thesis suggests that it was Paul (and not Marcion) who first devised a "Christian canon" by which his other writings were understood and that there is a literary and theological unity to these four letters, concentrated by a set of core themes, that fixes and stabilizes the meaning of the entire corpus.

8. See D. R. MacDonald, *The Legend and the Apostle* (Philadelphia: Westminster, 1983).

significant points from the chronology of Paul's life according to Acts. Further, the difficulty facing the chronologist is exacerbated by the lack of any clear reference to Paul's letters in the book of Acts. Acknowledging this disparity, a growing number of scholars now follow the lead of J. Knox and try to reconstruct Paul's life using only his writings, admitting into evidence information from Acts only when it is absolutely necessary for a coherent chronology and does not contradict Paul's testimony.[9]

Yet this position is not without problems. Paul surely colors his own story with rhetorical and theological intent; and there is a growing appreciation for the historical integrity of the second half of Acts, which narrates Paul's movements from the Jerusalem Council (Acts 15) to Rome (Acts 28; Paul tells us virtually nothing about the first stage of his missionary activity [Acts 9–14],[10] and none

of his letters can be dated with any probability from this period in any case). Even if the pattern of Paul's mission according to Acts 15–28 serves the narrator's literary and theological interests, his story contains reliable information.[11] Therefore, most chronologists continue to work between Paul's letters and Acts to calculate the pivotal dates of his mission and letters.[12] The following provides a tentative chronology of Paul's life, with supporting textual evidence:

9. See J. Knox, *Chapters in a Life of Paul*, rev. ed. (Altanta: Mercer University Press, 1987); R. Jewett, *Chronology of Paul's Life* (Philadelphia: Fortress, 1979); G. Luedemann, *Paul, Apostle to the Gentiles: Studies in Chronology* (Philadelphia: Fortress, 1984).

10. See M. Hengel and A. Schwemer, *Paul Between Damascus and Antioch* (London: SCM, 1997).

11. See F. F. Bruce, *Paul: Apostle of the Heart Set Free* (Grand Rapids: Eerdmans, 1977); W. W. Gasque, *A History of the Interpretation of the Acts of the Apostles* (Peabody, Mass.: Hendrickson, 1989); C. Hemer, *The Book of Acts in the Setting of Hellenistic History*, WUNT 49 (Tübingen: JCB Mohr, 1989).

12. A complicating factor in this historical project is the profound difficulty of dating the most pivotal of these events with precision. For instance, Luedemann accepts the Claudius decree, which expelled Jews from Rome and is mentioned in Acts 18:2, as a chronological marker for Paul's Corinthian mission (and so dates his letters written from Corinth accordingly). However, he dates this decree from 41 CE rather than from the commonly accepted date of 49 CE. As a result, he dates Paul's Macedonian mission, which antedates the Jerusalem Council, and the Thessalonian correspondence, which was written from Corinth, in the early 40s. Even those who accept Luedemann's reconstruction of Paul's Macedonian mission from its narrative in Acts 18 and references in 1–2 Thessalonians and yet reject Luedemann's dating of Claudius's decree will, therefore, locate the Thessalonian correspondence several years later.

| CE | |
|---|---|
| 33 | Paul's conversion/call near Damascus (Gal 1:17; Acts 9:1-22 [22:6-21; 26:12-18]) |
| 35 | First journey to Jerusalem (Gal 1:18-20; Acts 9:26-29) |
| 47–48 | Mission from Antioch to Asia (Phil 4:15; Acts 13–14) |
| 48 | Second journey to Jerusalem: the Jerusalem Council (Gal 2:1-10; Acts 15:1-12) |
| 49 | Macedonian mission from Galatia to Athens (1 Cor 16:1; 2 Cor 11:9; Gal 4:13; 1 Thess 2:2, 3:1; Phil 4:15-16; Acts 16:6–17:34) |
| 49–52 | Claudius's decree (Acts 18:2); Corinthian mission (2 Cor 1:19; 11:7-9; 1 Thess 3:6; Acts 18:1-11) |
| **50** | **Paul writes 1–2 Thessalonians** |
| 53–56 | Ephesian Mission (1 Cor 16:1-8; Acts 19) |
| **53** | **Paul writes Galatians** |
| **54** | **Paul writes 1 Corinthians** |
| **55** | **Paul writes Philippians and Philemon** |
| **55–56** | **Paul writes 2 Corinthians** |
| 56 | Paul's "painful" return to Corinth (2 Cor 13:2; cf. 10:11; 12:21; 2:13) |
| 57 | Third visit to Corinth (2 Cor 13:1; Acts 20:1-3) |
| **57** | **Paul writes Romans** |
| 57 | Third journey to Jerusalem (Rom 15:22-27; Acts 21:15–23:30) |
| 57–59 | Imprisonment and legal "trial" in Caesarea (Acts 23:31–26:21) |
| **58** | **Paul writes Colossians (and Ephesians?)** |
| 60–62 | Arrival and imprisonment in Rome (Acts 28:15-31) |
| 62–? | Paul's Mission in Spain (Rom 15:22-4); Paul Writes to Timothy and Titus? |

The NT says nothing about Paul's death. Acts concludes without mentioning the outcome of Paul's meeting with Caesar, but Paul does mention his intent to continue the mission in Illyricum (Rom 15:19) and then to Spain, following a visit to Rome (Rom 15:22-24, 28). Most scholars suppose that the narrator of Acts knew that Paul was executed in Rome (Acts 20:22-24) but realized that mentioning it would have undermined his literary purpose to portray Paul as the triumphant successor to Jesus and the Twelve. If, however, Paul was in fact released and allowed to continue his mission in Spain until his death, then we are provided a possible provenance for his final letters to his young colleagues in distant Asia, Timothy and Titus.

**Paul and Judaism.** Most reconstructions of Paul's life mention his youth in Tarsus of Cilicia, his Roman citizenship, his education in Jerusalem, and his career within Judaism. This biography is especially dependent upon Acts, where he is portrayed as a Pharisaic Jew and Roman citizen from Tarsus (22:3) who persecutes the first followers of Jesus for religious reasons (8:1-3), but who is forgiven (7:60) by them and then commissioned (9:15-16) by this same Jesus as a prophetic "teacher of Israel." Yet, Paul touches only briefly on these elements from his early life, and the references serve his writings' rhetorical design (Gal 1:11-15; Phil 3:2-11; cf. Rom 9:1-5). Nevertheless, these elements may well provide important clues in orienting us to his letters.

For example, we know that Tarsus, where Paul was apparently born and raised in diaspora Judaism, was an impressive center of Hellenistic culture and mystery religions. There, Paul could easily have picked up his understanding of moral philosophy and rhetoric as well as pagan religion, which then informs his letters and frames his message. Especially for those interpreters who explore the meaning of Paul's writings against the backdrop of Greco-Roman moral and religious culture, this feature of his early life is crucial.[13]

Paul himself points us in another direction: to his life within Judaism as "a Hebrew, born to Hebrews, and as to Torah, a Pharisee" (Phil 3:5). This identity marker reflects the formative influence of Judaism on both his religious understanding that Christianity is the fulfillment of Judaism and his missionary belief that God's elect people include Gentiles, who are also called out of the world as heirs of God's promised salvation.

Certainly Paul's background in diaspora Judaism may have contributed important symbols to his understanding of the gospel.[14] Two brief examples must suffice to illustrate this influence:

1. Paul's Bible was the Septuagint (LXX), the Greek translation of the Hebrew Scriptures used in diaspora Judaism. While true to the spirit of Jewish faith, the process of translating Scripture interprets its meaning for a new readership, infusing relevant tendencies of that readership's world into the text. The grand themes of the Jewish faith, then, were refined and even redrawn by the LXX in an effort to communicate to its Hellenistic audience. For instance, the resonances of νόμος (*nomos*), the Greek word for "law" that translates the Hebrew תורה (*tôrâ,* "instruction"), broadens the concept's meaning within diaspora Judaism. Thus, while the Jews of the diaspora looked to the teaching of the *nomos* to settle issues of religious and moral identity (= *torah*), they also understood the law in a more abstract and philosophical way as constituting a cosmic rule, instituted by the Creator, by which all of creation is patterned. Paul's use of "law" in his letters is multiform and reflects the variegated uses of this word in Hellenistic literature.

2. Paul's willingness to cross cultural lines in preaching the gospel (1 Corinthians 9), and all the tensions he notes in doing so (Romans 12), may well have been shaped within diaspora Judaism. Many have noted that the Jews of the diaspora were caught between two very different worlds. The dominant world was non-Jewish and syncretistic, inviting compromise and assimilation. The Jews were a minority called by God to remain separate and distinctive as a witness to truth. Conflict was inevitable for those Jews trying to live in a non-Jewish world that rewarded conformity and punished deviance. The fact that Paul was a Roman citizen from birth suggests that his family was skilled in moving between both worlds—a

---

13. On the influence of Paul's Jewish upbringing upon his life and thought, see J. Neyrey, *Paul, In Other Words* (Louisville: Westminster, 1990).

14. In elaboration of this point, see the interesting debate on Paul's relationship with first-century Judaism: E. P. Sanders, *Paul and Palestinian Judaism* (Philadelphia: Fortress, 1977); J. D. G. Dunn, *Jesus, Paul and the Law* (Louisville: Westminster, 1990); and N. T. Wright, *The Climax of the Covenant* (Edinburgh: T. & T. Clark, 1991).

skill, according to Acts and his letters, that Paul learned well.

In any case, the Jewishness of Paul's theological understanding is not really altered by his conversion to Christ. The deeper logic of Paul's theology is neither shaped by Greco-Roman religious culture nor created through some profound innovation on his part. He remains Israel-oriented, a committed monotheist; he utterly rejects the dualism of his pagan culture. Further, he retains a vital interest in the doctrine of divine election, even retaining its sociological importance as a primary marker for the community's public identity. Indeed, these very interests, which are the most important to his Jewish world, are at the center of the controversies provoked during his Gentile mission.

Why, then, did his message provoke so much confusion and commotion, especially within his Jewish audience? Primarily because Paul was a "christological monotheist."[15] That is, he reworked the core symbols of his Jewish world, including its "foundational story," which celebrated God's creation, God's promised salvation, and God's Israel and *torah*, in radically christological terms. Because of Christ, the confession of monotheistic faith had now been expanded to "one God, one Lord" (1 Cor 8:6); and the social marker of God's Israel was the public confession that Jesus is Lord (Rom 10:9). Those who belong to the Lord Jesus are the very same members of eschatological Israel whom God will vindicate on the future "Day of the Lord" (= resurrection from the dead).

Central to this symbolic world is Israel's Scripture, which both nurtures and justifies Paul's theological understanding. The critical issue in this regard is how Scripture functioned in the writing of Paul's letters. In his use of *midrash* and *catenae* (or connected series) of Scripture to interpret his message, Paul shared the exegetical strategies of other first-century Jewish interpreters. At an even deeper level, Paul's letters may be read as "intertexts," as texts written in intended (and reflexive) conversation with earlier Scripture. Images or words that link Christian letters with OT Scripture frame a theological setting that discloses additional layers of Paul's strategy: to confirm that Gentiles are also members of the elect community prefigured by Israel's Scriptures.[16]

Besides his penultimate commitment to God's election of Israel at the beginning of salvation's history and his ultimate concern for God's vindication of righteous Israel at the consummation of salvation's history, still other elements of Paul's teaching can be traced back to his own Pharisaic heritage. Perhaps because Pharisaism was a lay movement, engaged in all matters of the town square and marketplace, Paul's practical account of Christian faith extends God's rule and grace to every part of the community's life. Even though his rejection of the "laws of purity" seems anti-Pharisaic, his teaching about eating in 1 Corinthians 8–11 and Romans 14, especially as it relates to church order, is deeply rooted in the social world of Pharisaism. On the one hand, the pattern of Christian fellowship, as demonstrated by how and what believers eat together, is the social marker of their solidarity as a people belonging to Christ. On the other hand, the same social patterns that control the community's eating habits distinguish it from the other religious communities/options. As with Pharisaic Judaism, Pauline Christianity places a religious value on meals, eating habits, and foods—a value that when not observed can cause divisions within the community and that when observed can divide those inside the community from those outside.

**Paul and Jesus.** These two are the most prominent figures of the NT world; thus Paul's lack of contact with the historical Jesus remains an awkward feature of his résumé. Paul seemed aware of this omission (1 Cor 15:8-11; 9:1), even defensive about it (Gal 1:11-16). On this basis, Luke's defense of Paul's authority and mission in Acts tacitly admits that Paul lacked the credentials of the original apostolic successors to Jesus (see Acts 1:21-22).

The relationship between Jesus and Paul is the subject of an old debate.[17] There are still a few who appeal to the lack of contact as evidence for a fundamental discontinuity between the two, especially regarding the ongoing role of the law within the faith community. Some even speculate as to whether Jesus or Paul is the true founder of Christianity. To be sure, generic and thematic differences between the biblical Gospels and the

---

15. So N. T. Wright, "Putting Paul Together Again," in *Pauline Theology,* ed. J. Bassler (Minneapolis: Fortress, 1991) 1:206.
16. See R. Hays, *The Echoes of Scripture in the Letters of Paul* (New Haven: Yale University Press, 1989).

17. For a fine historical survey of this debate, see J. Barclay, "Jesus and Paul," in *Dictionary of Paul and His Letters,* ed. G Hawthorne et al. (Downers Grove, Ill.: InterVarsity, 1993) 492-98.

letters contribute to this impression of discontinuity. On the surface, it seems that Paul lacked a vital interest in the details of Jesus' life. For example, although he paid heed to the dominical message, only twice does he actually cite sayings of Jesus (1 Cor 7:10-11; 9:14); on other occasions Paul alludes to his sayings (Rom 12:14, 17; 13:7; 14:12-4; 16:19; 1 Cor 11:23-25; 13:2; 1 Thess 4:2, 15; 5:2, 13, 15), often in support of his own instruction or apostolic authority. To be sure, the parables and proverbs of Jesus, so rooted in the agrarian life of rural Palestine, would have little relevance for those living in the cities of Paul's mission. However, even in those letters where Paul might have appealed to the memory of Jesus for support, he failed to do so. His teaching included a more "vertical christology," concentrated on the moment of Jesus' death and resurrection as the climax of salvation's history. As for the other great events of the Messiah's earthly ministry, there is a deafening silence.[18]

Paul's lack of personal contact with Jesus of Nazareth and the lack of crucial details from the "life of Jesus" in his letters prompt the critical issue raised by Paul in Galatians: To what extent is there continuity between the message of Jesus and his immediate successors and the message of Paul? According to Pauline autobiography, continuity exists by virtue of his personal revelation of Jesus (christophany), both "to" him on the Damascus road (Gal 1:12; cf. 2 Cor 4:6; 5:16) and "in" him by some religious experience (Gal 1:16). S. Kim takes this feature of Paul's autobiography to mean that his personal experience of Jesus on the Damascus road, along with subsequent charismatic episodes, was a primary source of Paul's christological understanding as well as of his central claim that God's saving activity results in human transformation.[19]

There is little explicit evidence from his letters that Paul was familiar with the Gospels or even with pre-Gospel stories of Jesus, the Lord's Supper

(1 Cor 10:16-17 [cf. Matt 26:27]; 11:23-26 [cf. Luke 22:14-20]), and perhaps the synoptic apocalypse (1 Thess 2:16; 4:15; 2 Thess 2:2) being important exceptions. More likely, Paul was a beneficiary of early Christian traditions or memories of Jesus' ministry from "ear" and eyewitnesses, traditions that he received from believers throughout Palestine (Jerusalem, Antioch, Syria). He sometimes mentioned these sacred traditions to his readers (1 Cor 11:2, 23; 15:1, 3; cf. Rom 6:17; 1 Thess 2:13; 2 Thess 2:15; 3:6; 1 Tim 6:3). In still other passages (e.g., Rom 3:25), Jesus tradition from the Jewish church in particular was more implicit. More critically, Paul's message was informed by the thematics of messianic monotheism, grounded in the hope that God's promise to Abraham was now fulfilled and experienced for those who trusted in the redemptive results of Jesus' messianic death. Although he modified tradition about Jesus in order to recenter the significance of the Christ-event upon the cross, the grand themes of Paul's gospel are those of the Messiah. The biblical Gospels and Pauline letters are different parts of the same theological universe.

**Paul and His Mission.** Most of Paul's autobiographical statements defend his apostolic status and describe the costs of his missionary work (e.g., Rom 1:1-15; 1 Corinthians 9; 2 Cor 1:12–2:17; 7:5-16; 11–12; Phil 1:12-26; 3:1-14; 1 Thessalonians 1–3). Indeed, this self-understanding obligates the interpreter to understand Paul's letters as "missionary-minded," written for newly formed congregations of converts whose faith and witness he was committed to maintaining and nurturing. Given this understanding, in recent years much has been made of the social and cultural contexts of Paul's missionary work, located as it was in several important urban centers of the early Roman Empire. There Paul's message of God's grace found a ready audience among social groups constituted by the urban poor and powerless, who perhaps responded more out of psychological than spiritual need.[20]

In this light, scholars analyze the themes of the Pauline letters as intended for a readership formed

18. Wenham contends that Paul knew a great deal about Jesus and had access to collections of his sayings and stories. See D. Wenham, *Paul: Follower of Jesus or Founder of Christianity?* (Grand Rapids: Eerdmans, 1995). Wenham concludes that Paul adapted the tradition implicitly and creatively in his letters in order to preserve it, not to alter or "remythologize" it. The historical-critical problem in this regard is hermeneutical—that is, a determination of how Paul represented Jesus tradition in his own voice and in a new idiom for a different audience.

19. S. Kim, *The Origin of Paul's Gospel* (Grand Rapids: Eerdmans, 1982). See also A. Segal, *Paul the Convert* (New Haven: Yale University Press, 1990).

20. For this point, see W. Meeks, *The First Urban Christians: The Social World of the Apostle Paul* (New Haven: Yale University Press, 1983); A. Malherbe, *Social Aspects of Early Christianity*, 2nd ed. (Philadelphia: Fortress, 1983) 1-28.

from alienated and displaced city people. They were written to aid new converts in discriminating between the morality and life-style of a true Israel, and that belonging to "this evil age." Paul's letters to the Corinthians and the Thessalonians, in particular, can be read as primarily concerned with these sorts of issues. A sociohistorical approach makes the interpreter more sensitive to those themes that address moral or religious conflict with the surrounding pagan culture or with the social institutions of urban life. For example, D. Meeks contends that the typical member of an urban congregation founded by the Pauline mission was an artisan or trader, perhaps because Paul was an artisan.[21] R. Jewett suggests that the artisan membership of the Thessalonian congregation was primarily poor, in keeping with Paul's description of the Macedonian church in 2 Cor 8:2-4. It appears that these believers lived a hand-to-mouth existence, dependent on the sometimes fickle benefaction of their wealthy patrons. Against this social background, the modern reader of the Thessalonian correspondence can better understand Paul's admonition to "work" (1 Thess 4:9-12; 2 Thess 3:6-13) as the measure of a life pleasing to God and appreciate his concluding exhortation to depend on the steadfast benefaction of their Lord (1 Thess 5:24; 2 Thess 3:5, 16).[22]

**The Apostle Paul and His Readers.** A final element critical to Pauline autobiography defends his role and authority as a legitimate apostle (1 Cor 15:1-11; Galatians 1–2). Since this epistolary element conforms to the conventions of Greco-Roman rhetoric, we suppose Paul's intent was to posture himself and his correspondence before his reading/hearing audience: He and, therefore, what he says have religious authority for those being addressed. Yet, the subject matter of his letter and the spiritual crisis it addressed coheres as well to the definition of this relationship between the apostle and his audience.

In recent years, those interested in constructing a critical biography of Paul have turned to other questions, primarily concerning the internal life and organization of his congregations and their interaction with their surrounding social environ-

ment and with Paul, their apostle.[23] For this work, the letters provide primary information, whether to describe the characteristics of these interactions or to analyze them using the methods of social science. To be familiar with these social contingencies is to better understand the setting in which the Pauline voice was first heard as witness to the gospel of God.

## THE NON-PAULINE COLLECTION

The eight "conversations" found in the second collection of letters (Hebrews through Jude) are sufficiently different from one another to preclude any general treatment of those historical features that may group these letters into a discrete and coherent collection. Nonetheless, these conversations were shaped by the same larger circumstances that fashioned the Pauline correspondence: the political and social institutions of the Roman Empire; the moral and philosophical thematics of Hellenistic culture; and the core theological convictions of Judaism, informed and interpreted by its Torah.

These letters, however, are grouped around a single feature of their social world that may well orient the interpreter to the distinctive subject matter of the non-Pauline letters in toto. While both collections can be read as different responses to the theological problem of theodicy, the non-Pauline letters locate the roots of this crisis in a sociological rather than a missiological setting. The primary marks of this readership were its poverty (James),[24] its social dislocation (Hebrews), and its alienation (1 Peter)[25] within a hostile environment. The readers of the general epistles suffered because they had been marginalized as a direct result of their faith (Hebrews, 2 Peter, Jude) or because the norms and values of their faith conflicted with those of the persons in charge of the present world order (James, 1 Peter). Although the conflict in the Johannine epistles is internal to the faith community, the dissidents who have left the

---

21. See Meeks, *The First Urban Christians*. See also R. Hock, *The Social Context of Paul's Ministry: Tentmaking and Apostleship* (Philadelphia: Fortress, 1980).

22. R. Jewett, *The Thessalonian Correspondence*, FFNT (Philadelphia: Fortress, 1986).

23. See G. Theissen, *The Social Setting of Pauline Christianity* (Philadelphia: Fortress, 1982); B. Holmberg, *Paul and Power* (Philadelphia: Fortress, 1980), both with special interest in the congregations at Corinth.

24. So P. Maynard-Reid, *Poverty and Wealth in James* (Maryknoll, N.Y.: Orbis, 1985).

25. So J. Elliott, *A Home for the Homeless* (Philadelphia: Fortress, 1981).

congregation are sharply castigated as "antichrists" and "deceivers" (1 John 2:18-29; 4:1-4), "who have gone out into the world" (2 John 7). Rather than being received hospitably into one's home (3 John), they are to be shunned as evil (2 John 10-11). In turn, the spiritual test occasioned by suffering required the maintenance of community solidarity during seasons of suffering and social conflict. The marks of God's Israel, then, were not primarily their beliefs, as was true of the Pauline collection, but their behaviors in response to economic poverty and sociopolitical powerlessness.

The theological foundation of their response was, as with Paul, a particular understanding of divine election. However, in the case of the non-Pauline collection, election was redefined not in terms of being Gentile converts but in terms of being socially marginal: God has called out the "poor" (Jas 2:5), the "pilgrim" (Hebrews 11), the "alien and stranger" (1 Pet 1:2; 2:9), the religious sectarians (1 John) of this world, for salvation. The diverse audiences of this collection together formed a community of outcasts for whom the realization of God's promise of socioeconomic and political reversal lay still in the future, in a different world order where the last and the least will be first and fulfilled. The problem of theodicy was concentrated on the apparent contradiction of the community's dual citizenship, which forced it to ask: "Which reign is real, God's or Caesar's?" Surviving the present age in right relationship with God in order to get to the next was the religious project; the community's final, not initial, justification by God was its theological aim.

The distinctive theological accents of this collection interpret the Christian community's struggle to remain faithful to their sacred traditions on many fronts when faithlessness was the more natural response. The keenest stress, then, is on an exemplary (not crucified) Christ—a stress well suited for a collection more ethical than theological in tone. God's will is embodied in Christ's faithfulness (Heb 12:1-4; Jas 2:1; 1 Pet 2:21-25; 1 John 3:11-17; 4:7-21). Further, the terms of Christ's obedient life both legitimate and illustrate the paraenetic traditions used by these writers to give concrete direction to their audiences. The moral exhortations transform the ambiguity of the current crisis into order and tradition (2 Peter/Jude). The eschatological consequences of the communi-

ty's defection from the truth are envisaged in the warnings and exhortations to view Jesus as the prophetic exemplar of piety. Thus to follow or imitate him during the trials and tribulations of spiritual testing will result in the future blessings of God's promised salvation (Heb 12:25-29; Jas 2:1-13; 1 Pet 3:13-19; 2 Pet 2:17-22; 1 John 3:19-24; Jude 19-20).

Finally, the writings of the non-Pauline collection fashion the social world of a pilgrim people. Suffering and oppression represent those hardships that all pilgrims must bear on their way to the "shrine." Especially in Hebrews, much of this articulates a code of conduct that prepares a people for a pilgrimage: to break from existing ties in the world outside of Christ, to launch out on a journey toward the heavenly shrine, so to enter into the full blessing promised there by God.[26] A pilgrim stands at a distance from the norms and values by which the non-believing world lives. There is an intense desire to obey God steadfastly as a condition of enduring the journey through human existence and entering into eternal life, the chief blessing awaiting the pilgrim people at their heavenly shrine. Every decision and every action prepares for and promotes that pilgrimage to the heavenly end (Heb 10:32–12:29; Jas 1:2-4, 12; 1 Pet 1:1, 6-9; 2:11-12; 2 Pet 1:4-11).

## THE WORLD WITHIN THE LETTERS: COMPOSITIONS IN LITERARY CONTEXT

Any responsible interpretation of Scripture demands consideration of the diverse literary genres and rhetorical conventions that characterize its various writings. The full meaning of any letter is not determined solely by the reconstructed history behind the text but also by the literary structure of the composition itself. The discussion of this point will concentrate on two related elements: the literary genre and the rhetorical design of the NT letter. Biblical authors crafted and communicated meaning by using conventional or recognized patterns of speech.

Written correspondence and oral conversation are closely related activities, although their simi-

---

26. For the "pilgrim" motif in Hebrews, see W. Johnsson, *Hebrews*, KPG (Atlanta: John Knox, 1980).

larity can be exaggerated.[27] Not only do letters convey what the writer might say in person, but also ancient letters were written to be read aloud to an audience (see Eph 3:2-4; Rev 1:3). The oral audience of antiquity was attuned to a speech that affects the ear. As a result, letter writers crafted literary compositions for auditors by using the same techniques of public orators, who steered their audiences and shaped their common histories for their own persuasive purposes. For example, oral communication tends to be sequential, with each new idea introduced and understood by what precedes it. The integral connection of each part of the literary whole is maintained by the repetition of catchwords (or digressions), which not only underscores the composition's unity but also draws the audience to its central point. Today's audience, constituted by silent readers rather than auditors, is more familiar with other kinds of literary markers: computer fonts and typefaces, paragraph indentations, and creative punctuation, all of which organize our reading of a written text. However, an ancient audience heard a text read and organized its subject matter according to repeated words and phrases.

Literary critics usually classify NT letters according to types of oral discourse: sermons or homilies (Hebrews, 1 John), pastoral exhortation (James, 1 Peter), classroom instruction (Romans, Ephesians), and the like. Although the message is not its medium, it certainly is true that the author's message would be lost were not his or her ideas reconstituted in a language and presented in a literary form that connected with the intended readership. In this sense, then, biblical letters are sufficiently ambiguous or elastic in meaning that their current readers, who live in far different circumstances from those to whom they were written, can still appreciate them as resources for their own theological understanding. Yet, historical questions must still be addressed. The ancient world of literature treasured the act and art of letter writing. The genre and rhetorical artistry current in the literary culture of biblical writers would naturally have informed their decisions about the medium or mode of letter writing.

Two different methods were used in writing letters. One could either write a letter personally or have it written by a skilled scribe. Several of Paul's letters hint at the use of a secretary. The secretary would not be responsible for the subject matter but would do most of the writing. For instance, most epistolary addresses name more than Paul as sender; some scholars think that Sosthenes (1 Cor 1:1) and Silvanus (1 Thess 1:1; 2 Thess 1:1) served as Paul's secretaries. The benediction to 1 Peter mentions Silvanus as its scribe (1 Pet 5:12). References to a personal signature (Gal 6:11; 2 Thess 3:17; Col 4:18) or greeting (1 Cor 16:21) may well imply that the rest was dictated; Rom 16:22 actually names Tertius as "the writer of this letter" (although a few scholars still question whether Romans 16 belongs to the "authentic" Romans letter).[28] Shorter letters, such as Philemon, were probably written by Paul alone (Phlm 19); however, longer letters, such as Romans and the Corinthian correspondence, may have required secretarial assistance. Paul's employment of different scribes to help with his correspondence may well explain the literary and linguistic differences scholars have observed between his letters.

Letters were sometimes written as literary substitutes for personal (or even "official") visits.[29] They were often written as a practical matter, because authors could not visit their congregations, even though some communities needed apostolic attention. For example, Paul's stated preference was to address a spiritual crisis directly and in person (see Rom 1:9-12), but he was not always able to do so because of imprisonment or missionary obligations. To maintain his ministry and authority in the life of a particular congregation, Paul wrote and sent letters as vehicles of his theological instruction, pastoral care, and moral counsel. These same letters, which were subsequently preserved, collected, and canonized, continue to perform a similar role and to exercise a similar authority today. That is, the letters of the NT are the authorized substitutes for apostolic per-

---

27. D. E. Aune, *The New Testament in Its Literary Environment,* LEC (Philadelphia: Westminster, 1987) 159.

28. For a defense of the integrity of Romans, see H. Gamble, *The Textual History of the Letter to the Romans,* SD 42 (Grand Rapids: Eerdmans, 1977).

29. See R. Funk, "The Apostolic *Parousia:* Form and Significance," in *Christian History and Interpretation,* ed. W. Farmer, C. F. D. Moule, and R. R. Neibuhr (Cambridge: Cambridge University Press, 1967) 249-68.

sonae and powers. By reading these letters, the audience of contemporary believers continues to "hear" apostolic "voices" and benefit from their instruction. In this way, the community of faith develops under the aegis of the Spirit into the "one holy catholic and apostolic church."

This theological conviction cues a final literary point: The NT letters were written as if their authors were actually speaking to their audiences. There is nothing artificial or contrived about the epistolary literature of the NT; its expected purpose was to instruct and to persuade its readers, and its intended aim was to enable those readers to make decisions that conformed to the faith. The interpreter must approach these writings as literary art, crafted according to the conventions of the ancient world, whose aim was theological understanding.

## THE LETTER GENRE: THE PAULINE COLLECTION

A literary genre is a conventional pattern of written speech that intends to facilitate communication from its author to an audience living in a particular social setting. The epistolary literature of the NT comprises several genres of ancient literature.[30] During the last two centuries, archaeologists have unearthed a treasure trove of Greco-Roman papyri (including Jewish) and clay tablets of the ancient Near East. Included in these finds are thousands of letters that exhibit many of the same literary structures, conventions, and functions as the letters of the NT. Although the NT letters resist formal classification, they exhibit no real literary innovation.[31] Their authors were not literati but pastors who employed the standard epistolary conventions of their day; these writers sought to communicate specific messages, not to create an innovative literary genre.

The modern interpreter approaches the letter genre in terms of its overall literary structure, the rhetorical role of its every part, and the anticipated effect each convention exacts upon the audience. For example, how should the interpreter approach the Pauline letters as a literary genre? The letters unfold according to the simple structure of the integral parts, each of which has a specific

role to perform in the effective communication of his gospel:

(1) *Greeting.* In accordance with the conventions of his literary world, Paul begins his letters by introducing himself (and cosenders or secretaries) before greeting his audience with a salutation. The purpose of such prescripts was similar to that of modern business cards, a convention of today's professional world. Business cards make introductions and help to establish relationships with potential clients. Likewise, Paul greets his readers (or auditors) in order to establish a more intimate relationship with them, thereby providing a positive setting for reading (or listening to) his message and then responding accordingly.

In Paul's letters, however, variations of this opening formula carry important theological freight. Paul intends to frame a rhetorical relationship with his first audience through the phrases he uses to introduce himself, to describe his audience, and to fashion his salutation. This relationship is usually grounded in his apostolic charisma, so that his message is received as instructive if not also normative for life and faith. Sharply put, the Pauline writings of the NT are not personal letters; they are formal "apostolic" briefs, meant to be read to the entire congregation as a word to heed and to follow.

Paul's standard salutation combines χάρις (*charis,* "grace"), an innovation on the Hellenistic salutation χαῖρε (*chaire,* "greetings"), and εἰρήνη (*eirēnē,* "peace"), the greeting found in most Jewish letters. The rhetorical effect of the salutation is twofold: It addresses the audience as beneficiaries of God's universal salvation and prefaces the subject matter of the letter by the essential promise of Paul's gospel—that salvation is entered into by "grace" and "peace" with God is the result (so Rom 5:1-2).

(2) *Thanksgiving.* The second part of a Pauline letter expresses thanksgiving for the spiritual formation of the audience. In giving thanks, Paul continues the convention of Hellenistic and Jewish letter writers who offered thanks for blessings received. There are notable exceptions to this convention, however, within the Pauline corpus. In Galatians, for instance, Paul substitutes stern rebuke for expected blessing with striking effect (Gal 1:6-9); and in 2 Corinthians, a letter to another difficult congregation, Paul offers a benediction for

30. For a survey, see Aune, *The New Testament in Its Literary Environment,* 158-82.
31. For details of this conclusion, see ibid., 183-225.

divine comfort where one would expect to find thanksgiving for his audience (2 Cor 1:3-7)! Since there is no specific addressee, the encyclical letter Ephesians (as with 1 Peter) offers thanksgiving to God in the form of a Jewish *berakah*, a liturgical prayer of thanksgiving. Personal letters to well-known colleagues (1 Timothy, Titus) need not include formal thanksgiving, which is implicit in the intimate relationship between author and reader and may not serve the hortatory character of the correspondence in any case.

In most Greco-Roman letters, divine blessings were perceived as deliverance from some physical calamity or economic ruin.[32] The phraseology of the Pauline thanksgivings is quite different, echoing rather the biblical psalms. For instance, the tone of Paul's thanksgiving is worshipful, often fashioned as a prayer that perhaps could serve as a call to worship for a public reading of his letter. Paul's thanksgiving is much like a pastor's invocation at the beginning of a worship service, exalted in language and full of important theological themes that will be taken up again in the following sermon. Long sentences are often used by Paul to evoke a sense of sustained conversation with God (e.g., 1 Cor 1:4-8; Col 1:3-8, 9-11). Only in this spiritual setting can Paul's letter be heard for edification.

Important theological themes supply the substance of Pauline thanksgiving, typically articulating God's saving action in Christ. Rhetorically, these themes bring the audience immediately to the core convictions of Paul's gospel and establish the foundation for the message that follows. Paul is careful to state the practical benefits of accepting these theological convictions. Here, in the most formal and worshipful section of his letter, Paul remains a pastor seeking to nurture his flock. He does not compose his letters from a scholar's study but from that of a pastor; the concerns of his flock press upon his heart and mind. Interpreters of Pauline writings must recognize them as missionary and pastoral in motivation.

The Pauline thanksgiving often includes a prayer for the audience's spiritual formation. Paul projects an intimate, caring attitude toward his auditors. Rhetorically, this prayer fosters a positive, constructive relationship between author and audience. The prayer is also intercessory and often hints at the crisis at hand—that is, at the vital theme of the letter. The words and phrases are not "devotional musings," detached from the main body of Paul's letter. Quite deliberately, they form the basis for what Paul will say to his readers. The prayers in Pauline thanksgivings petition God to resolve the audience's spiritual crisis that has occasioned the writing of the letter.

(3) *Main Body.* Paul next addresses the difficulties that have prompted the writing of the letter, often beginning with a transitional formula or even with a statement of a thesis (e.g., Rom 1:16-18). While the most important and longest part of his letters, the main body remains resistant to formal analysis. Generally, the style of the main body depends on the audience's social location and the circumstances that occasion the letter. Typically, Paul is interested in defending or clarifying his gospel and mission, and he uses those literary devices that help to make his case.

For example, much of the main body of Romans is fashioned as a diatribe, a Greco-Roman literary genre used by philosophers in teaching their students.[33] This kind of formal literature belongs to the classroom, where the teacher imagines himself in a debate with an opponent, who raises questions or makes objections that allow the teacher to argue (and win) his case. Paul addresses his Roman readers, then, as a teacher introducing his students to the grand themes of his gospel. Yet, Paul's self-understanding as a teacher is more deeply rooted in his Pharisaic culture. Recent scholars have made much of Paul's use of Scripture in his letters, in which *midrashim,* or interpretations of biblical texts (whether cited or "echoed"), are incorporated into Paul's arguments both to justify a point and to clarify his intended meaning.[34]

Many other literary genres are also used in the Pauline collection to advance the apostle's message and mission. These include autobiography (e.g., 1 Thess 1:2–3:13; Gal 1:10–2:21; 2 Cor

---

32. The best discussion of Pauline thanksgivings is P. T. O'Brien, *Introductory Thanksgivings in the Letters of Paul,* NovTSup 49 (Leiden: Brill, 1977).

33. For this point, see S. Stowers, *Letter Writing in Greco-Roman Antiquity,* LEC (Philadelphia: Westminster, 1986); for the form and function of the "main body" in Pauline letters, see J. White, *The Form and Function of the Body of the Greek Letter,* SBLDS 2 (Missoula, Mont.: Scholars Press, 1972).

34. See, for example, Hays, *The Echoes of Scripture in the Letters of Paul.*

1:12–2:17; 7:5-16; 10:7–12:13; Col 1:23–2:3); vice and virtue lists (e.g., Rom 1:29-31; 1 Cor 6:9-10; Gal 5:19-23; Col 3:5-9, 12-13; Eph 4:2-3; 1 Tim 1:9-10); household codes (Col 3:18–4:1; Eph 5:21–6:9); and portions of early Christian or Jewish hymns and creeds (e.g., Phil 2:6-11; Col 1:15-20; 1 Tim 3:16).

Most interpreters note that the main body of a Pauline letter reflects the interplay of two integral parts of Pauline preaching: the indicatives of theological instruction (*kerygma*) and the imperatives of moral exhortation (*paraenesis*). Paul's use of common moral traditions found in both Scripture and Greco-Roman philosophy is not arbitrary; indeed, it is a remarkable innovation of his letter genre. While the subject matter of his moral instruction was well-known and widely accepted in his cultural world, he adapted it to the crisis at hand to fashion an exhortation that is "a word on target." More critically, the interplay between theology and ethics accords with the deeper logic of Paul's gospel. This deeper logic claims that the acceptance of right beliefs, or what he refers to as "the obedience of faith" (Rom 1:5; 16:26), yields right behaviors as the result of participating by faith in Christ's death and resurrection (Col 1:9-10). Believers become in life what they have already become in Christ (so Rom 6:1-12). The internal structure of the main body of the Pauline letter, then, envisages this deeper logic; moral exhortation is adapted not only to his audience's particular situation but also to his gospel.

(4) *Benediction.* Letter writers in the ancient world usually added various greetings, specific instructions, and general exhortations to their readers in the benediction. Paul is no different, although he baptizes these literary conventions by adding the distinctive phrases of his Christian ministry. The Pauline benediction includes personal news (e.g., Rom 15:14-23), general exhortation (e.g., 1 Thess 5:12-28), more specific advice or greetings to individuals (e.g., 1 Cor 16:1-24), a recap of the letter (e.g., Rom 16:17-20; Gal 6:15-16), and a signature like that of modern letters (e.g., Gal 6:11; 2 Thess 3:17), all concluding with a benediction (his "good-bye"), typically a doxology (e.g., 2 Cor 13:13) or prayer (e.g., Rom 16:25-27) that extends the benefaction of divine grace upon his audience.

Except for the occasional "recap," the benediction falls outside the letter's main body, where he addresses the audience's spiritual crisis in a more direct fashion. Paul's concern is for the general well-being of Christian congregations, regardless of the more particular problems of the moment. Benedictions also provide us with a window onto the complex and collaborative character of Paul's mission and early Christian congregational life.

## THE RHETORICAL DESIGN OF THE NT LETTER

Not only were NT letters composed according to a variety of contemporary literary genres, but some were deliberately composed according to the ancient rules of rhetoric. Aristotle defined *rhetoric* as the public art of discovering the best possible means of persuasion on any subject matter of importance.[35] As so defined, rhetoric is hardly glib or idle conversation. Rather, antiquity understood rhetoric as the disciplined act of speaking about the pertinent issues of the public square, which combined compelling arguments with studied conclusions in a way that informed the audience and prompted its civil action. When a NT letter is approached in terms of its rhetorical art, then what is said can no longer be separated from how it is said, since both contribute to the fuller meaning of the text.

There is, of course, a rhetorical aspect to literary genre. Each part and every convention of a Pauline letter, for example, performs a persuasive role in the conversation between its author and his audience that intends to effect not only increased understanding of the theological crisis that occasioned the letter but also proper response to the writer's admonitions. Thus the rhetorical analysis of a NT letter seeks to combine an interest in how each part fits together in its overall literary design according to the rules of ancient rhetorical theory with the flow and aim of the author's argument. The anticipated result for exegesis is a keener sense of how the content and even language of the text helps to produce a particular response from a community of its readers (or auditors).

According to G. Kennedy's influential studies of ancient rhetoric, the design of a literary composi-

---

35. Aristotle *Rhetoric* 1.1.

tion depends on the kind of response sought.[36] Rhetoricians term "epideictic" those compositions that intend to persuade readers to change their understanding of the world—somewhat comparable to what the gospel calls "repentance"—and "deliberative" those compositions that iterate and reinforce beliefs and values already embraced—akin to what the gospel calls "faith." These are judgments an audience makes about itself. In his letters, Paul sometimes calls for a verdict about his own ministry or apostolic charisma—that is, for a judicial decision by the audience regarding the author's credentials (e.g., 2 Corinthians 10–12; Galatians 1–2).

H. D. Betz's analysis of Galatians as a composition shaped by the rules of judicial rhetoric illustrates this approach to the literary structure of a letter.[37] According to the rules of this type of persuasive speech, Paul begins his correspondence with (1) a *superscriptio* or "prescript" (Gal 1:1-5), in which he first identifies the charges brought against him by laying out the contrast: "neither from human commission nor from human authorities, but through Jesus Christ and God the Father" (Gal 1:1; cf. Gal 1:11-12). The body of his letter begins with (2) a *stasis,* or sharp transitional statement of why the letter is necessary (1:6-10), immediately followed by the extended (3) *narratio* (Gal 1:11–2:14), an autobiography that supplies the audience with all the necessary information (the "facts" of the matter) to make an informed choice. The critical (4) *propositio* (Gal 2:15-21) suggests a common ground, but then sets forth the "proposition" to be proved (2:19-21). The (5) *probatio,* or "proof," follows (Gal 3:1–4:31), which justifies Paul's proposal. This proof consists of several different kinds of evidences: experiential (Gal 3:1-5; 4:12-20), biblical (Gal 3:6-14, 19-25; 4:21-31), legal (Gal 3:15-18), and historical (from Christian tradition, Gal 3:26–4:11).

Paul concludes the main body of his argument with (6) an *exhortatio,* in which the countervailing position of his opponents is refuted in a series of exhortations that both warn and encourage the Galatian believers (Gal 5:1–6:10). Recent literary critics, more concerned with praxis than with aesthetics, are especially drawn to this feature of Pauline (and non-Pauline) rhetoric, which draws the audience's attention to the consequences of their choices. That is, in refuting his opponents in the Galatian churches, Paul is less concerned about the internal logic of his case and more concerned about the success of his arguments in securing a particular kind of communal ethos among his readers.

A (7) *peroratio,* or "postscript," concludes the entire composition (Gal 6:11-18); here the main points of the debate are summarized and sharpened. This final statement, which contrasts his opponents (Gal 6:12-13) with Paul (6:14-15), suggests that the letter could also be read as a more deliberative discourse in which Paul is seeking to persuade his readers to make a right decision about their beliefs. In most of the Pauline letters, however, these two styles of rhetoric—judicial and deliberative—coexist: What one thinks about Paul and his mission is decisive in one's decision about the faith. Paul seems to recognize well the most important point of rhetorical discourse: The decisions made about the message and the messenger are inseparable.[38]

## THE WORLD IN FRONT OF THE LETTERS: CONFESSIONS IN CANONICAL CONTEXT

The NT letters are more than the literary art of particular authors or mere artifacts of ancient history. These same writings belong to the Christian Bible, and their primary purpose in this biblical canon is to inform the theological understanding of believers who hear and read Scripture as "the word of the Lord." This final section, then, will consider the importance of the epistolary writings

36. G. Kennedy, *New Testament Interpretation Through Rhetorical Criticism* (Chapel Hill: University of North Carolina Press, 1984). See also his important survey, *Classical Rhetoric and Its Christian and Secular Tradition from Ancient to Modern Times* (Chapel Hill: University of North Carolina Press, 1980).

37. Betz's work has been criticized by some for trying to "pour" Galatians into a preconceived cast of judicial rhetoric, esp. the nonautobiographical sections of the book (chaps. 3–6). Longenecker, for example, contends that Paul's composition evinces a more creative and synthetic literary art that combines rhetorical conventions with those of Jewish letters and personal innovation. See R. Longenecker, *Galatians,* WBC (Dallas: Word, 1990) cix-cxiii, for a summary of criticisms against Betz and his own suggestions on the rhetorical design of Galatians.

38. Significant studies emphasizing the interpretive importance of the rhetorical design of specific non-Pauline letters include H. Attridge, *Hebrews,* Hermeneia (Philadelphia: Fortress, 1989); T. Cargal, *Restoring the Diaspora: Discursive Structure and Purpose in the Epistle of James,* SBLDS 144 (Atlanta: Scholars Press, 1993); and D. Watson, *Invention, Arrangement and Style: Rhetorical Criticism of Jude and 2 Peter,* SBLDS 104 (Atlanta: Scholars Press, 1988).

of the NT from a third perspective, complementary to the other two. This perspective recognizes their canonical authority as part of the church's Scripture and their theological affirmation as part of the church's normative witness to God. Together, these writings form a "cloud of witnesses" that continues to supply their current readers (the "canonical audience") with authorized testimonies to the word of God, revealed in Jesus of Nazareth, and thereby help to define and maintain Christian life and faith "to the end of the age." From its composition by different authors and editors to its canonization as one discrete part of the Christian Bible, and throughout the history of its interpretation and application by the church catholic, the letter canon serves the theological aim of transmitting a normative and empowering interpretation of God's gospel to each generation of the canonical audience. A "text-centered" interpretation of Scripture is ultimately a theological approach by which the faithful seek to understand what it means to be God's people today.

This orienting concern for Scripture's theological (rather than historical or literary) referentiality and for its ecclesial (rather than authorial or rhetorical) intent supplies the final and most critical interpretive clues for readers of the NT letters. When reading a biblical writing as Scripture, the interpreter must determine meaning in terms of the church's intent to enrich our faith in God and to nurture our understanding of God's gospel. In this sense, the canon and creed of God's people give shape and structure to the world "in front of" Scripture. Faithful readers do not lie prostrate under Scripture in mindless devotion, nor do they stand above Scripture in intellectual arrogance; rather, they bow "in front of" Scripture in order to grasp what may be seen of God's mystery and what may be heard of God's Word. In a world centered by faith in the mercies of God, Scripture is trusted and treasured; its principal readers, members of the faith community, undertake interpretation as a sacred activity performed in obedience to the faith. These core convictions, imbued by experiences of Scripture's empowering effects upon life and faith, forge the faithful interpreter's approach to the meaning of the NT letters for life and faith.

# READING THE LETTERS AS SCRIPTURE

The dramatic rise of scholarly interest in the NT canon in recent years has two focal points: the historical and the hermeneutical. Historians of the biblical canon are primarily interested in its formation within early Christianity, whether as a theological construct or as a literary collection. Although these historians sometimes recognize and consider substantial theological issues, they give most of their attention to the chronological development of the canon and to the ideological concerns that guided the canonizing process. For example, such scholars typically discuss the relationship between a book's authorship and its canonization in terms of how attribution of authorship influenced the reception of a particular book, both within the earliest church and later into the biblical canon.

The key interpretive issue for the church rests less upon these historical projects and more upon a theological idea: Scripture is the church's *canon* or "rule of faith." Scripture's role as the church's rule of faith presumes its trustworthy witness to him whose incarnation ultimately norms the community's faith. Only in this christological sense can one say that Scripture supplies both the subject matter for the church's theological reflection and the theological boundaries or context within which Christian theology and ethics take shape.

This conviction regarding the contributions of Scripture combines two integral beliefs: Scripture is both a "canonical collection" of sacred writings and a sacred collection of "canonical writings." In the first case, when Scripture's final literary form is privileged as a "canonical collection" (*norma normata,* or "that which *becomes* the rule")—the result of the canonical process that includes and arranges certain writings—the interpretive emphasis is on a specific and limited body of sacred writings. This emphasis not only values the Bible's subject matter for theological reflection and confession, but also discerns the very ordering of Scripture's subunits as the privileged, permanent expression of an intentioned, dynamic interaction between the faithful and their written rule of faith. Such an approach into the meaning of the biblical letters is less interested in the reconstructed history behind a particular letter or in the environs that gave that text its literary and rhetorical shape. These historical and literary interests are retained, but they are located in a later period of the letters' life when the Christian Bible took its final literary shape.[39]

While various historical constructions of the canonical process have been proposed, no one is entirely clear why the various writings eventually stabilized into the Christian Bible. Certainly, one possible reason is rhetorical or even aesthetic: Over time, different communions of believers came to recognize that particular arrangements of books were more persuasive articulations of the Word of God and performed in more useful ways within that community's life and worship. Indeed, diverse arrangements of books and collections (or "canon lists") may well suggest that different theological values were held among the numerous faith communions of the early church. Eventually, use and disuse narrowed this diversity of arrangements, and a specific form of biblical literature triumphed because it facilitated or better served its intended role as Scripture for the faith community. The theological principle suggested by the canonical process is this: The final shape of the Christian Scriptures best combines and relates its subject matter to serve the church as the literary location where theological understanding is well founded and soundly framed.

In the second case, emphasis is placed on its ongoing religious function *(norma normans,* or "that which *is* the rule") in the act of interpretation that enables biblical texts to function authoritatively in shaping the theology and guiding the praxis of the church.[40] The idea of a "canonical process" is not defined by a specific historical moment or literary product as before. Rather, it draws on the entire history of the Bible's interpretation, whenever the faith community draws upon its Scriptures to "norm" its faith and life. Beginning even before biblical texts were written and continuing today, faithful interpreters contem-

porize the meaning of their Scriptures so that the faith community might better understand what it means to be God's people.

This canonical function antedates and explains the canonical form, even as the final form facilitates those functions the faith community intended for its canon. In the ongoing act of interpretation, biblical texts "become" canonical when different interpreters pick up the same text again and again to "comfort the afflicted or afflict the comfortable." In the hands of faithful interpreters, past and present, Scripture acquires multiple meanings with the theological aim of forming a people who worship and bear witness to the one true God. In this sense the history of the Bible's formation and interpretation settled more than its final literary shape as the church's written rule of faith. The history also evinced a type of hermeneutics that contemporizes the theological quotient of biblical teaching to give it an authoritative voice for today's community whose worship and witness is again undermined by similar theological crises. What gets picked up again and again and reread over and over by God's people are these same writings that interpret the believer's spiritual testing and resolve it in a way that strengthens faith and transforms life.

The reconstructed meaning of epistolary conversations between ancient writers and their first readers, occasioned by particular sociohistorical circumstances, is now relativized and universalized within Scripture. The letters of the NT are read as *biblical* confessions that bear witness to God's ongoing relationship with current readers, rather than simply as ancient conversations between authors and first audiences. They are preserved and transmitted as Scripture precisely because they promise and demonstrate the practical authority to "norm" Christian faith and guide the life of every believer who struggles to remain faithful to God in ever-changing settings. Under the aegis of God's Spirit, these epistolary compositions, formed by the literary and rhetorical conventions of the ancient world (see above), continue to communicate the gospel and persuade a people to embrace it more fully.

What follows considers the practical importance of these observations: Two properties of the canonical process, evident in the final form and placement of the letters within the NT, are

39. The most influential studies of this approach to biblical studies come from B. Childs, *Introduction to the Old Testament as Scripture* (Phliadelphia: Fortress, 1979), and *The New Testament as Canon* (Philadelphia: Fortress, 1984).

40. Sanders understands the canonical process as orchestrated by the "hermeneutics of adaptation." See the important collection of his pioneering studies in J. A. Sanders, *From Sacred Story to Sacred Text* (Philadelphia: Fortress, 1987). For a synthesis of Childs and Sanders into another model of "canonical criticism," see R. Wall and E. Lemcio, *The New Testament as Canon,* JSNTSup 76 (Sheffield: JSOT, 1992).

Scripture's own markers that orient the canonical audience to the epistolary literature of the NT as God's Word for today.

## THE FINAL FORM OF SCRIPTURE'S MULTIPLE-LETTER CANON

The two collections of letters, pluriformed in literary shape and theological substance, raise problems and possibilities similar to those facing the interpreter of the fourfold gospel of the NT. While the multiplicity of gospels has long been a topic of scholarly investigation and comment, few have considered the relationship between the NT's two corpora of letters a matter of hermeneutical value. What possible relationship does the non-Pauline collection have with the Pauline? At the very least, the sum of all their various theologies constitutes Scripture's whole epistolary witness to God. Yet, different communions privilege different witnesses, each following a "canon within the canon" in turn. For example, the Pauline collection has served Protestant believers as the primary context for theological reflection and moral guidance. This preferential option for the Pauline witness has led some to a reductionism that either reinterprets the non-Pauline letters in Pauline terms or neglects them entirely. For example, Luther at first decanonized the book of James because it seemed to communicate a gospel contrary to the one found in Galatians and Romans. Many still read James through a Pauline filter as a way to preserve its authority. Theological coherence is maintained, then, but at a cost: James is read as a "Pauline" book, distorting or denying its distinctive message.

The witness of the full canon of letters, however, is that diverse theologies are gathered together to form a community of meaning that includes the Pauline and the non-Pauline. Moreover, there is a sense in which this epistolary whole is actually better focused by disagreement than by agreement. That is, the collection's witness to the truth is better forged by the mutual criticism of its contributors, making the whole greater than the sum of its parts. Through contrasting the theologies of Paul and James, the letter canon becomes more robust than if the contributions of James were

simply added to what Paul has already brought to the table. The full effect is more like the vibrant sound produced by a complement of different and sometimes dissonant voices. The critical point is that the recognition of the complementary, reflexive relationship between these two collections is absolutely strategic in their interpretation; one cannot be read in isolation from the other lest the canonical purpose of both be diminished. More specifically, the theological substance of the second collection of letters actually extends and enhances the theological setting for reading the first. These epistolary writings, whose names and sequence recall the faith of the "pillars" of the Jewish mission (Gal 2:7-9), provide an authorized apparatus of various checks and balances that prevent the distortion and finally deepen the church's understanding of the Pauline letters—and so of the full gospel.

A common christological formula in the *intra-canonical* conversation between Pauline and non-Pauline collections illustrates this point. According to the non-Pauline book of James, the faith community is exhorted to embrace "the faith of our Lord Jesus Christ" (Jas 2:1). This formulation is similar in phraseology to Paul's claim that the coming age of God's salvation has already been inaugurated because of Christ's own faithfulness to God's redemptive will, which is most significantly expressed in Gal 3:22 ("by the faith of Jesus Christ"), Rom 3:22 ("through the faith of Jesus Christ"), and Rom 3:26 ("the one who has the faith of Jesus"; but also in Gal 2:16; Eph 3:12; Phil 1:27; 3:9; Col 2:12; and 2 Thess 2:13).

These crucial phrases are variously translated, of course, depending on how one understands the genitive Ἰησοῦ Χριστοῦ (*Iēsou Christou*). In fact, most scholars, ancient and modern, have understood this genitive construction to be "objective": The genitive noun (*Iēsou Christou*) is the recipient or object of the action implied by the verbal noun to which it stands related (πίστις *pistis*, "faith"). Virtually every modern translation of Paul's claim, therefore, is rendered, "through/by faith in Jesus Christ." Especially since the publication of R. B. Hays's influential monograph on the Pauline formula in Gal 3:22,[41] however, an increasing number of scholars understand the

---

41. R. B. Hays, *The Faith of Jesus Christ,* SBLDS 56 (Chico, Calif.: Scholars Press, 1983).

Pauline phrase as a "subjective" genitive: The genitive noun is the subject of the action implied by the verbal noun. Thus this phrase gives expression to the personal faith of Jesus in God—"the faith of Jesus Christ"—because of which the salvation-creating grace of God now resides in the community of Jesus' disciples. In the light of this reading, the Pauline confession of the faithfulness of Jesus is taken to underscore the singular significance of his messianic death: God's salvation-creating power was publicly disclosed in the death of Jesus, whose "act of obedient self-giving on the cross became the means by which the 'promise' of God was fulfilled."[42] The object of Jesus' faith is the faithful God, who promises to bring forth life from death.

Likewise, it makes better sense of James to understand the relevant phrase's genitive construction as subjective: To "hold to the faith of the Lord Jesus Christ" (2:1) is to follow his example by not discriminating against the poor (Jas 2:2-4), who are the elect of God and heirs of God's coming kingdom (Jas 2:5). In both texts, then, the "faith of Jesus Christ" expresses his personal faith, which is embodied in his faithful actions, whether on the cross (Paul) or in his ministry among the poor (James). In each case, Jesus' faithfulness to God's will lays claim to his lordship and is exemplary for his eschatological community.

Yet, James uses the formula for a different reason and with a different meaning. Most significant, the nature of Christ's faithfulness serves a moral rather than a soteriological interest. According to James, God's will is summed up in the "royal law" that calls the community to love its (poor and powerless) neighbors (Jas 2:8). Jesus is the messianic exemplar of faithfulness to God's law (Jas 2:8-10), which prohibits playing favorites with the rich and promises life to those who care for the poor neighbor (Jas 2:12-13). There is no messianic death in James; rather, the *life* of Jesus bears witness to God's coming triumph and to the ultimate vindication of true and pure religion by caring for the needs of those in distress (Jas 1:27).

These two different ways of understanding the "faith of Jesus Christ" reflect different theologies, both normative for Christian faith. Given an interest in the complementary and reflexive character of their *intracanonical* relationship, the interpreter is obligated to consider these different conceptions of the "faith of Jesus Christ" together. At the very least, one is compelled by the witness of James to consider the significance of the exemplary life of Jesus, and particularly his treatment of the poor, as having messianic value. The resulting balance between Jesus' life and his passion brings the NT letters into greater congruity with the NT Gospels, whose narratives all make this same point. This emphasis on the utterly faithful life of Jesus corrects a tendency in Pauline hermeneutics to concentrate on Christ's death and resurrection as singularly important. Further, the profoundly ethical nature of Jesus' faithfulness helps to form an ethical Christianity that not only is more aware of social injustice but also is obligated to reject it.

On the other hand, the faith community that places emphasis exclusively on the ethical competence of Jesus' life denies the necessity of divine grace as that which both purifies the faith community and empowers its obedient and worshipful response to God. Again, what is lost is the essentially collaborative character of biblical faith, which joins God's response of grace to a needy humanity with humanity's response of obedience to a gracious God. In this case, the "faith alone" of the Pauline witness is replaced by the "works alone" of James. A christology that bears witness to both Paul and James as two discrete, yet complementary, parts of a whole looks to Christ as prototypical of the faith and faithfulness that characterize Christian faith.

## THE PLACEMENT OF THE LETTERS WITHIN SCRIPTURE

Not only is it important for the interpreter to approach the two collections of letters as partners engaged in a complementary and reflexive conversation, but it is also important to consider the *intracanonical* relationships between the letters and the other parts of the canonical whole. Both the placement and the titles of NT writings are properties of the canonical process; each is suggestive of the writings' respective roles within the canon and, therefore, properly orient (or reorient) the interpreter to the NT's subject matter.[43]

42. Ibid., 175.

43. See Wall and Lemcio, *The New Testament as Canon,* 161-207.

Quite apart from authorial intentions or the rhetorical design of individual letters, then, the final literary design of the NT canon suggests that particular units of the NT canon (Gospel, Acts, letter, Apocalypse) have particular roles to perform within the whole. In particular, the sequence of these units within the NT envisages an intentional rhetorical pattern—or "canon-logic," to use A. Outler's[44] phrase—that more effectively orients the readership to the NT's pluriform witness to God and to God's Christ. By this internal logic, readers perceive that each part of the NT has a specific role to perform, which in turn explains the rich diversity of theology, literature, and language that presents Scripture's subject matter and facilitates the performance of Scripture in nurturing the faith community's theological understanding. For example, the Gospel is placed first within the NT because its narrative of the person and work of the Messiah, when taken as a fourfold whole, provides the canonical audience with a theological and moral foundation and focal point for all that follows. And the Apocalypse is placed last because it offers a visionary conclusion to Scripture's story of God.[45]

Along with the final placement of writings and collections within the biblical canon, sometimes the title provided for the various units by the canonizing community brings to clearer focus the particular contribution of that unit to a more robust understanding of God. For example, titles were provided for anonymous compositions to locate them within authoritative traditions (e.g., the four Gospels). In the case of 1 John (and Hebrews in some translations), the title included the word "epistle," even though it follows the homily rather than the letter in literary form and original function. The intent of the added superscription is not to classify its literary genre but to clarify its function within Scripture, which approximates that of a literary letter: to instruct and encourage its faithful readers who seek theological understanding.

The titles and arrangement of writings within the NT are the results of the canonizing stage of Scripture. They shed additional light on how these compositions and collections, written centuries earlier for congregations and religious crises long since settled, may continue to bear witness to God and to God's Christ for an unknown future readership. The importance of any one biblical voice for theological understanding or ethical praxis is focused or qualified by its relationship to the other voices that constitute the whole canonical chorus. Extending this metaphor, one may even suppose that these various voices, before heard only individually or in smaller groups, became more impressive, invigorating, and even "canonical" for faith only when combined with other voices to sing their counterpunctal harmonies as the full chorus.

**The Gospels and the Letters.** The interpreter's interest in the relationship between the Jesus of the Gospels and the Jesus of the letters within the world of Scripture differs from that in the relationship within either historical or literary contexts. On the one hand, the difficulties of reconstructing the relationship between the historical Paul and the pre-gospel Jesus traditions of earliest Christianity are well known (see above); equally so are the difficulties of relating narrative (Gospels) and epistolary literature. On the other hand, the canonical approach to the relationship between Gospels and the letters is guided by theological convictions envisaged by the NT's own canon-logic. In particular, the two collections of letters, written to instruct and encourage faith communities, follow the Gospels, written as narrative interpretations of Jesus' earthly life and messianic ministry. That is, even as faith communities, constituted by the current disciples of Jesus, seek to "follow after" the teaching and example of their Lord, so, too, do the letters "follow after" the Gospels in the NT canon.[46] The very order of NT collections supplies the interpreter with a visual aid that sharpens this crucial concern: The theological aim of biblical letters is to inform and thereby fashion their readers into a people whose life and faith are patterned after the Jesus of the Gospels.

This approach suggests that there is a theology for the entire letter canon that coheres around an integrated set of beliefs, a set that is not propositional but narrative in shape. That is, the narrative of the biblical Jesus provides the readers of the

44. A. Outler, "The Logic of Canon-making and the Tasks of Canon-criticism," in *Texts and Testaments* (W. March, ed. San Antonio, TX: Trinity University Press, 1980) pp. 263-76.

45. For this point, see Wall and Lemcio, *The New Testament as Canon,* 274-98.

46. So P. Achtemeier, "Epilogue: The New Testament Becomes Normative," in H. C. Kee, *Understanding the New Testament,* 4th ed. (New York: Prentice-Hall, 1983) 367-86.

letters with a narrative substructure that puts all the pieces back together again. If most interpreters agree that the letters seek to relate gospel to life, then the subject matter of that gospel, within the canonical context, is provided by the fourfold gospel tradition. In this case, this coherent center of the letters (and all NT literature) is not defined by the reconstructed life of the historical Jesus but by the kerygmatic story of God's actions through Jesus told by the Gospels. This latter story is the presupposition for all the practical advice given and theological claims made by the NT letters.

**Acts and the Letters.** By this same canon-logic, the final placement of Acts immediately prior to the letters alerts readers to the strategic importance of Acts in providing an introduction to the letters that follow.[47] The ancient church recognized the importance of this role; a version of Acts typically circulated with early collections of the Pauline and non-Pauline letters. The production and transmission of sacred texts in antiquity was limited by size and cost; thus smaller portions of the modern NT circulated independently, in service not only of the church's budget but also of its theological agenda. In the East, for example, Acts was combined with a collection of non-Pauline letters to form a smaller, more portable manuscript called the "Apostolos,"[48] apparently in memory of Jesus' apostolic successors whose stories are told in Acts and whose names are attached to the catholic epistles.[49] In the West, the Pauline corpus was added to the collection to prove Paul's apostolic character and to vindicate the right of his letters to share canonical status with the Gospels.[50] The authors of both collections of letters are introduced and authorized by Acts; and Acts' story of the church's mission to "the end of the earth" becomes a theological primer for

its readers, making them more alert to the theological subject matter of the letters that follow. Three points will help to clarify these suggestions.

First, Acts offers biographical introductions to the authors of the letters. In the canonical context, such biographies serve a theological purpose by orienting readers to the authority (religious and moral) of apostolic authors as trustworthy carriers of the word of God. This is true even though the historical accuracy of Acts' portrait of Paul and the other leaders of earliest Christianity is still keenly debated (see above). Indeed, from Scripture's perspective Acts offers its readers a theological (rather than a chronological or historical) introduction to the letters that follow. The rhetorical and moral powers of these leaders of earliest Christianity confirm and commend the importance of the letters they wrote or that stand in their apostolic traditions.

The unstoppable expansion of Christianity into the pagan world through apostolic preaching, which Acts narrates with profound optimism, underscores the anticipated result of reading and embracing what these same agents of the divine word have written. Again, the issue is not that Acts fails as a historical resource; rather, its narrative succeeds as a resource that facilitates the theological aim of the epistolary literature. In Acts' case, the *writer's* intention to defend Paul and his Gentile mission, which especially shapes the second half of his narrative, serves well the overarching *canonical* intention to introduce Paul's letter collection as theologically normative, whether or not the author had read the letters in advance of writing Acts.

Second, Acts offers readers a narrative backdrop against which they can better understand the diverse theologies that make up both collections of letters, whether those linked with Paul and his Gentile mission or those linked with the "pillars" of the Jewish mission (so Gal 2:9). Acts retains, approves, and deepens the appreciation of the theological diversity found within this epistolary witness (see Acts 15:1-21).

Modern discussions have emphasized how the "catholicizing" narrator of Acts softens the disagreements between the leaders of earliest Christianity. What is often overlooked in making this point is that the church eventually collected and canonized a Pauline corpus whose principal

---

47. See R. W. Wall, "Acts," in *The New Interpreter's Bible*, 12 vols. (Nashville: Abingdon, 1994–2002), 10:00-00.

48. K. Aland and B. Aland, *The Text of the New Testament* (Grand Rapids: Eerdmans, 1987) 49-50.

49. D. Trobisch, *Paul's Letter Collection* (Minneapolis: Fortress, 1994) 10.

50. See B. Metzger, *The Canon of the New Testament* (Oxford: Clarendon, 1987) 257-58. E. Goodspeed, now followed by others, hypothesized that an early canon of Paul's letters, mentioned in 2 Pet 3:15-16, was produced and in circulation by the end of the first century. Goodspeed speculated that the production of this proto-canon was prompted by the publication of the book of Acts, whose story of Paul rekindled interest in his literary work. There is no evidence to support Goodspeed's thesis; it rests on the perception that a literary relationship exists between the book of Acts and the letters of Paul. In my view, such a perception became possible only later during the canonical stage of the NT, when the book of Acts and the letters were bound together for the first time in the great uncials of the ancient church.

letters were often polemical and potentially divisive. The question is never raised as to why these letters were included in the canon of a catholic church if the aim was to shape theological uniformity. Might it not be the case that the canonizing process looked to Acts not to smooth Paul's polemical edges but to interpret them?

According to Acts, the church that claims continuity with the first apostles tolerates a theological pluralism even as the apostles did, although not without controversy and confusion. The Jerusalem synod described in Acts 15 achieves a kind of theological understanding rather than a theological consensus (see Acts 15:19-21). According to Acts, the divine revelation given to the apostles forms a "pluralizing monotheism,"[51] which in turn informs two discrete missions and appropriate proclamations, Jewish and Gentile (so Gal 2:7-10). Sharply put, Acts interprets the two collections of letters in a more sectarian fashion: The Pauline corpus reflects the gospel of the Gentile mission, while the non-Pauline collection reflects the gospel(s) of the Jewish mission. However, rather than causing division within the church, such a theological diversity is now perceived as normative and necessary for the work of a God who calls both Jews and Gentiles to be the people of God.

As a context for theological reflection, Acts forces us to interpret the letters in the light of two guiding principles. First, we should expect to find theological diversity as we move from Pauline to non-Pauline letters. Second, we should expect such a diversity to be useful in forming a single people for God. Against a critical hermeneutics that tends to select a "canon within the canon" from among the various possibilities, the Bible's own recommendation is for an interpretive strategy characterized by a mutually informing and self-correcting conversation between biblical theologies.

Third, the core theological commitments of Acts guide theological reflection upon the letters. The point is not that a theology of Acts determines or even anticipates the theological subject matter of the letters but that Acts shapes a particular perspective, an abiding practical interest that influences the interpretation of the letters. For example, one may contend that the primary theological

interest of Acts is the missionary advancement of the word of God to the "end of the earth" under the aegis of the Spirit. This missionary concern then functions in theological reflection as an implicit way of thinking about and organizing the subject matter of the letters that follow. That is, a reading of the letters under the light of Acts will bring to sharper focus the identity and praxis of a missionary people who respond to the Lord's demand to be God's witness to the end of the earth. Whether or not the authorial intent of the Pauline letters is missiological, their intent in canonical context becomes missiological because the Pauline letters are interpreted in the light of the missionary Paul of Acts.

The theological orientation to the letters provided by Acts holds even for the non-Pauline letters. The audiences of the non-Pauline letters are addressed in terms of their marginal social status rather than their missionary vocation. How does the missionary perspective of Acts, then, finally inform and deepen the understanding of God's people as a faith community, the outcasts from the cultural order? In part, the response is to read the non-Pauline and Pauline letters together for a fuller understanding of mission. On the one hand, the mission of the church requires accommodation in order to spread the gospel (1 Cor 9:12b-23); on the other hand, the mission of the church must take care not to be corrupted by the values and behaviors of the world outside of Christ (Jas 1:27). This more prophetic (and complete) definition of mission, which goes out into the world yet remains unconformed to it, is confirmed by Matthew's Jesus: "I am sending you out like sheep into the midst of wolves; so be wise as serpents and innocent as doves" (Matt 10:16).

**The Letters and the Apocalypse.** The strategic relationship between the letters and the book of Revelation within the NT is made evident to the interpreter by the similarity of their literary structure and theological function. While its literary conventions are mainly apocalyptic (Rev 1:1) and its message is prophetic (Rev 1:3), the Apocalypse is composed by its author as an encyclical epistle, similar in form to Ephesians or 1 Peter, and written for the theological instruction of "the seven congregations of Asia" (Rev 1:4), whose communicants are at very different places of their spiritual journey (Revelation 2–3). The

---

51. See J. A. Sanders, *Canon and Community* (Philadelphia: Fortress, 1984) 46-68.

placement of the Apocalypse at the end of the Christian Bible envisages its role as the conclusion to Scripture's story of God. God's final triumph over death has already begun through the messianic Lamb (Revelation 5; 19–21), by whom all creation will be purified and then restored to its original intent, which is to worship God and to rule with God forever (Rev 5:9-10; 21:22-27).

Of course, the congregation's response to this great confession of Christian faith depends on its spiritual maturity. If the communicants refuse to repent of their theological immaturity or moral impurity and become "overcomers" (Rev 2:7, 11, 17, 26; 3:5, 12, 21), then the message of God's coming triumph is heard with apocalyptic terror (Rev 3:14-22). However, this same message is heard by the mature and faithful, especially in a context of suffering and spiritual testing (Rev 2:8-11; 12–13), with profound hope for their eschatological vindication (Rev 14:1-5). And these same options do not change through space and time, for "the Lord God Almighty was and is and is to come" (Rev 4:8). No less than did its first auditors, contemporary congregations approach the book of Revelation as Scripture to read and reflect upon its message of God's coming triumph, either to repent or to hope because of their fidelity to the "eternal gospel" (Rev 14:6).

This orientation to the truth of the "eternal gospel," nurtured by the Apocalypse, infuses the interpretation of the NT letters with greater power and urgency, "for the time is near" (Rev 1:3; 22:10). This is the case not because the subject matter of the letters is more finely nuanced by the canonical interplay between epistle and Apocalypse but because the principal incentive and purpose of biblical interpretation are now understood more clearly than before. The church's interpretation of the NT letters aims at obedience to their inspired instruction—obedience now excited afresh by the Apocalypse's wondrous vision of the sovereign creator's sense of justice and the slain Lamb's conquering mercy.

# BIBLIOGRAPHY

Childs, Brevard S. *The New Testament as Canon.* Philadelphia: Fortress, 1984.

Donelson, Lewis R. *From Hebrews to Revelation: A Theological Introduction.* Louisville: Westminster/John Knox, 2000.

Doty, William G. *Letters in Primitive Christianity.* GBS. Philadelphia: Fortress, 1973.

Dunn, James D. G. *The Theology of Paul the Apostle.* Grand Rapids: Eerdmans, 1998.

Fitzmyer, Joseph, S.J. *Paul and His Theology.* 2nd ed. Englewood Cliffs, N.J.: Prentice Hall, 1989.

Hengel, Martin. *Judaism and Hellenism: Studies in Their Encounter in Palestine During the Early Hellenistic Period.* 2nd ed. Minneapolis: Fortress, 1991.

McDonald, Lee M. *The Formation of the Christian Biblical Canon.* Rev. ed. Peabody, Mass.: Hendrickson, 1995.

McNamara, Martin. *Palestinian Judaism and the New Testament.* GNS 4. Wilmington, Del.: Glazier, 1983.

Meade, David G. *Pseudonymity and Canon: An Investigation into the Relationship of Authorship and Authority in Jewish and Earliest Christian Tradition.* Grand Rapids: Eerdmans, 1986.

Neyrey, Jerome. *Paul, In Other Words: A Cultural Reading of his Letters.* Louisville: Westminster, 1990.

Stambaugh, John E., and David L Balch. *The New Testament in Its Social Environment.* LEC. Philadelphia: Westminster, 1986.

Stowers, Stanley. *Letter Writing in Greco-Roman Antiquity.* LEC. Philadelphia: Westminster, 1986.

Wall, Robert. W. "Reading the New Testament in Canonical Context." In *Hearing the New Testament: Strategies for Interpretation.* Edited by Joel B. Green. Grand Rapids: Eerdmans, 1995.

Wall, Robert W., and Eugene E. Lemcio, *The New Testament as Canon.* JSNTSup 76. Sheffield: JSOT, 1992.

# THE LETTER TO THE ROMANS

INTRODUCTION, COMMENTARY, AND REFLECTIONS
BY
## N. T. WRIGHT

# THE LETTER TO THE
# ROMANS

## INTRODUCTION

R omans is neither a systematic theology nor a summary of Paul's lifework, but it is
by common consent his masterpiece. It dwarfs most of his other writings, an
Alpine peak towering over hills and villages. Not all onlookers have viewed it in the
same light or from the same angle, and their snapshots and paintings of it are sometimes
remarkably unalike. Not all climbers have taken the same route up its sheer sides, and
there is frequent disagreement on the best approach. What nobody doubts is that we are
here dealing with a work of massive substance, presenting a formidable intellectual challenge while offering a breathtaking theological and spiritual vision.

Perhaps not surprisingly, it remains the case that anyone who claims to understand
Romans fully is, almost by definition, mistaken. It is common to list saints and Christian
leaders whose lives have been changed by reading this letter; the catalog could be balanced
by a similar number who have radically misunderstood it. Troublingly, the lists would overlap. Having studied this letter intensively for much of my adult life, I, of course, believe
that my current opinions on its historical and theological meaning, though humble, are
accurate. But the example of others, and the memory of my own past changes of mind,
leave me under no illusions as to the provisional nature of my conclusions.

Equally, anyone who claimed to have read all the commentaries (let alone all the
other secondary literature) on Romans would be lying. Likewise, anyone who tried to
refer to it all, let alone enter into debate with it all, would produce an unreadable book.

I am indebted to far more colleagues, ancient and modern, than can be mentioned in the footnotes or bibliography; but the purposes of this series are better served by exposition of the view to which the author has come, with occasional debates with other major interpretations, than by endless listing of and interaction with the many alternative readings that have been put forward. At the end of almost every sentence the reader should imagine an invisible footnote: "For more information, alternative views, and secondary literature, see the recent commentaries." Though in my earlier work I studied and interacted with interpreters from many generations, I have here deliberately tried to engage in debate the more recent writers, not least the two major Roman Catholic commentaries of Fitzmyer and Byrne and the two major Protestant ones of Dunn and Moo.[1]

It has become customary to approach a biblical book by asking when, where, why, and by whom it was written and then, as a second stage, what it actually says. Some of these initial questions, fortunately, are not controversial in the case of Romans; nobody doubts that Paul wrote it in the middle to late 50s of the first century, from Corinth or somewhere nearby, while planning his final voyage to Jerusalem with the intention of going on thereafter to Rome and thence to Spain. But the remaining question, "Why?" has proved remarkably difficult. Romans stands as a reminder that "why" and "what" are more organically related than we have sometimes liked to think. Theories about why Paul wanted to write this letter to this church at this moment must remain in constant dialogue with the complex discussion of what the letter itself actually says. As in other disciplines, the greatest strengths of a hypothesis or theory are to make sense of the data, to do so within an appropriately simple overall design, and to shed light on other areas of cognate research. These large aims are in view in what follows.

## THE SHAPE AND THEME OF ROMANS

It is no good picking out a few favorite lines from Romans and hoping from them to understand the whole book. One might as well try to get the feel of a Beethoven symphony by humming over half a dozen bars from different movements. Romans is, indeed, a symphonic composition: Themes are stated and developed (often in counterpoint with each other), recapitulated in different keys, anticipated in previous movements and echoed in subsequent ones. Although the demands of a commentary mean that headings will be offered for its different sections, we should not thereby be misled into supposing that each paragraph is simply "about" one particular topic. That is not how Paul wrote, at least not here. He was far more likely, in individual sentences, paragraphs, and sections, to state a point in a condensed fashion and then steadily to unpack it, in

1. Joseph A. Fitzmyer, *Romans,* AB 33 (Garden City, N.Y.: Doubleday, 1993); Brendan Byrne, *Romans,* SP 6 (Collegeville, Minn.: Liturgical, 1996); James D. G. Dunn, *Romans 1–8,* WBC 38A (Dallas: Word, 1988); James D. G. Dunn, *Romans 9–16,* 38B (Dallas: Word, 1988); Douglas J. Moo, *The Epistle to the Romans,* NICNT (Grand Rapids: Eerdmans, 1996).

the manner of someone unfolding a map stage by stage so that each new piece offers both a fresh vision and a sense of having been contained within what had gone before. At almost no point in this letter does he offer detached reflections on isolated "topics" (13:1-7 is perhaps an exception, which is one reason, though not the main one, why some have suggested that it may be an interpolation). Although Romans, written within the general Hellenistic culture of the Greco-Roman world, shares some rhetorical features with other letters of the time and place, it is impossible either to pigeonhole it within a particular genre or to use such possible parallels to infer what the letter is about independent of full-scale consideration of its argument. We must follow the sequence of thought, the inner logic, of the whole work.

The easiest thing to determine about Romans is its basic shape. Its four sections emerge clearly: chaps. 1–4, 5–8, 9–11, and 12–16. From time to time, impressed by the way in which chap. 5 draws out and in a way completes the thought of chaps. 1–4, some writers have suggested that the key break occurs between chaps. 5 and 6 rather than between 4 and 5;[2] but most are now content with the outline suggested, not least since it is clear that the opening of chap. 5 states in summary form the themes that are then developed through to the end of chap. 8. In any case, to note the divisions is not to say that Paul is doing more than rounding off one train of thought before proceeding to a closely cognate, and logically consecutive, idea. As we shall see, the most abrupt and decisive breaks—those at the ends of chaps. 8 and 11—by no means indicate that he is now going to write "about" something else altogether. Attempts to impose a formal structure on the letter are either trivial (e.g., pointing out that the opening of chap. 1 functions as the "Greeting" and 15:14–16:27 as the "Conclusion") or tendentious (e.g., suggesting that 1:18–11:36 is the "body of the letter," thereby implying that chaps. 12–16 are a mere exhortatory postscript—a view challenged in the commentary).

In fact, to see how the different parts of the letter hang together and to understand why Paul wanted to say just this at just this moment to these people, the most important thing to do is to grasp the main theme of the letter and to see why it was important to first-century Jews in general, to Paul in particular, and to him in this setting most specifically.

**"God's Righteousness."** It is not difficult to discover the main theme of the letter. "God's gospel unveils God's righteousness": That, in effect, is Paul's own summary in 1:16-17, and the letter does, indeed, unpack this dense statement. Unfortunately, though, even this apparently simple sentence is controversial, and we must clarify what is meant and justify, at least preliminarily, the decision to treat the passage, and the letter, in this way. As often in Paul's writings, to understand one key phrase we need to draw on a range of evidence and pick our way through a minefield of arguments. Before we can even address the question of why Paul wrote this particular letter, we must examine the broader question of why a Jew like him would be concerned with this overarching issue.

---

2 . See Ulrich Wilckens, *Der Brief an die Römer,* 3 vols., EKK 6 (Zurich: Benziger, 1978–82) 1:93.

**"God's Righteousness" in Paul's Judaism: Covenant, Lawcourt, Apocalyptic.** The phrase "the righteousness of God" (δικαιοσύνη θεοῦ *dikaiosynē theou*) summed up sharply and conveniently, for a first-century Jew such as Paul, the expectation that the God of Israel, often referred to in the Hebrew Scriptures by the name YHWH, would be faithful to the promises made to the patriarchs. Many Jews of Paul's day saw Israel's story, including the biblical story but bringing it up to their own day, as a story still in search of a conclusion—a conclusion to be determined by the faithfulness of their God. As long as Israel remained under the rule of pagans, the great promises made by this God to the patriarchs, and through the prophets, had still not been fulfilled.

Thus, although the Babylonian exile had obviously come to a literal end some centuries before, the promises made at the time—promises of a glorious restoration of the nation, the Temple, and the whole Jewish way of life—were widely regarded as still awaiting complete fulfillment (see the Commentary on 9:6–10:21).[3] Loyal Jews living under the various post-Babylonian powers (Persia, Greece, Egypt, Syria, and finally Rome) continued to tell the whole story of Israel in terms of promises made to the patriarchs; of an early golden age under David and Solomon; of rebellion, decline, and exile; of a long period of waiting for restoration; and of the eventual new day of liberation that would dawn in God's good time. They believed that YHWH had entered into covenant with them to do all this; paradoxically, the exile was itself, as Jeremiah, Daniel, and others had insisted, part of the covenant, since it was the result of Israel's disobedience. But their God would remain loyal to the covenant, and this loyalty would result in the great day of liberation coming to birth at last.[4] The phrase that captures this whole train of thought, occurring in various forms in the Scriptures and post-biblical writings, is "God's righteousness," in the sense of God's loyalty to the covenant with Israel (see, e.g., Ps 33:4; Isaiah 40–55; Jer 32:41; Lam 3:23; Hos 2:20). The overtones of the phrase thus bring its semantic range very near to another great biblical theme, that of God's sure and steadfast covenant love for Israel—a point of considerable importance for understanding Romans, as we shall see.

Never leaving behind this covenantal meaning, the word "righteousness" is also shaped by the Second Temple Jewish setting of the lawcourt. In the lawcourt as

3. This is still controversial, in my view needlessly. See N. T. Wright, *The New Testament and the People of God,* vol. 1 of *Christian Origins and the Question of God* (Minneapolis: Fortress, 1992) 268-71; and *Jesus and the Victory of God,* vol. 2 of *Christian Origins and the Question of God* (London: SPCK, 1996) xvii-xviii, with reference to the massive evidence in Second Temple Judaism. See also N. T. Wright, "In Grateful Dialogue: A Response," in *Jesus and the Restoration of Israel,* ed. C. C. Newman (Downers Grove, Ill.: InterVarsity, 1999) 253-61; and J. M. Scott, ed., *Exile: Old Testament, Jewish, and Christian Conceptions* (Leiden: Brill, 1997). Even if it is not accepted that most of his contemporaries would have agreed, I would still contend that this is demonstrably Paul's own point of view. Another Pauline passage that makes excellent sense on this reading is Gal 3:10-14, on which see N. T. Wright, *The Climax of the Covenant: Christ and the Law in Pauline Theology* (Minneapolis: Fortress, 1991) chap. 7; and S. J. Hafemann, "Paul and the Exile of Israel in Galatians 3–4", in Scott, *Exile,* 329-71.

4. This sequence of thought is clearly visible in passages like Ezra 9 and Daniel 9. See Wright, *The New Testament and the People of God,* chaps. 9–10.

envisaged in the OT, all cases were considered "civil" rather than "criminal"; accuser and defendant pleaded their causes before a judge. "Righteousness" was the status of the successful party when the case had been decided; "acquitted" does not quite catch this, since that term applies only to the successful defendant, whereas if the accusation was upheld the accuser would be "righteous." "Vindicated" is thus more appropriate. The word is not basically to do with morality or behavior, but rather with status in the eyes of the court—even though, once someone had been vindicated, the word "righteous" would thus as it were work backward, coming to denote not only the legal status at the end of the trial but also the behavior that had occasioned this status.[5]

The word "righteousness" applied not only to the accuser or defendant; it also denoted the appropriate activity of the judge. His duty was clear: to be impartial, to uphold the law, to punish wrongdoing, and to defend those who, like the orphan and the widow, had nobody else to defend them. Thus the "righteousness" of the judge, on the one hand, and of the parties in the case, on the other hand, are very different things. Neither has anything directly to do with the general moral behavior or virtue of the persons concerned.

Covenant and lawcourt are far more closely linked than often imagined. Behind both categories there stands a fundamental Jewish self-perception, which, if we grasp it, will enable us to understand things Paul holds together in many passages in Romans, but which interpreters have consistently separated. Through many and various expressions of covenant theology in the biblical and post-biblical periods, a theme emerges that, though by no means central in all Second Temple Judaism, has a claim to represent a deep-rooted and biblical viewpoint. It can be stated thus: The covenant between God and Israel was established in the first place in order to deal with the problem of the world as a whole. Or, as one rabbi put it, God decided to make Adam first, knowing that if he went to the bad God would send Abraham to sort things out.[6] The covenant, in other words, was established so that the creator God could rescue the creation from evil, corruption, and disintegration and in particular could rescue humans from sin and death.

In biblical thought, sin and evil are seen in terms of injustice—that is, of a fracturing of the social and human fabric. What is required, therefore, is that justice be done, not so much in the punitive sense that phrase often carries (though punishment comes into it), but in the fuller sense of setting to rights that which is out of joint, restoring things as they should be. Insofar, then, as God's covenant with Israel was designed, at the large scale, to address the problem of human sin and the failure of creation as a whole to be what its creator had intended it to be, the covenant was the means of bringing God's justice to the whole world. Since "justice" and "righteousness" (δικαιοσύνη *dikaiosynē*)

---

5. A good example of this can be seen in Genesis 38:26, when Judah acknowledges that his daughter-in-law Tamar is in the right and he is in the wrong. This states a legal position; only secondarily, and by implication, does it comment on the morality of their respective behavior.

6. *Gen. Rab.* 14:6.

and their cognates, translate the same Hebrew and Greek originals, we discover that God's righteousness, seen in terms of covenant faithfulness and through the image of the lawcourt, was to be the instrument of putting the world to rights—of what we might call cosmic restorative justice.

The images of covenant and lawcourt thus draw together, within one complex range of imagery, a familiar Second Temple perception of the Jews' own story in relation to the rest of the world. Many Jewish writings of this period tell the story of Israel and the pagan nations in terms of a great cosmic lawsuit: When the psalmists beg God to vindicate them against their adversaries, they are expressing a characteristic standpoint (e.g., Psalm 143). The pagan nations are oppressing Israel; whether they are thought of as accusers and Israel as a defendant or whether Israel is accusing the pagans of wrongdoing is unimportant. YHWH is not simply Israel's God, but the creator of the whole world and its judge; as such, YHWH is under an obligation to set things right, not least to vindicate the oppressed. True, there are some biblical passages in which YHWH is Israel's adversary at law; but, although Paul recognizes this as a theoretical and problematic possibility (see the Commentary on 3:5), his argument sticks to the more usual conception. YHWH is the judge; the nations that make war upon Israel are to be tried and condemned; Israel is to be vindicated. This scene is classically portrayed in the seventh chapter of the book of Daniel.

It takes only a little reflection, and a little acquaintance with the Jewish history and literature of Paul's period, to see that a tension or conflict could arise between the covenantal and lawcourt meanings of "righteousness." YHWH was supposed to come to Israel's rescue because of the covenant obligations between them; but YHWH was also the judge in the cosmic court, committed to judging justly between Israel and the nations and to establishing an appropriately just rule over the whole world. Is Israel also guilty? What will YHWH do then?[7] That was a puzzle for many Jews in Paul's world, and we may suppose it had been so for Paul as well; as a zealous Pharisee (his own self-description; see Gal 1:13-14; Phil 3:6), he must have longed to see God's righteousness revealed against wicked pagans and renegade Jews alike, vindicating covenant-faithful Jews like him. Although recent scholars have emphasized that there is no evidence for the pre-Christian Paul suffering from a bad or troubled conscience in the post-Augustinian sense, we must insist that there is every reason to suppose that he agonized over the fate of Israel, longing for YHWH to act decisively in history, but uncomfortably aware that if this were to happen many Jews would face condemnation along with Gentiles.

All this brings into view a final dimension of the phrase "God's righteousness." Precisely because the term evoked covenant loyalty, on the one hand, and commitment

7. This question, and the question of "God's righteousness" that it raises, is a major theme of the book known as 4 Ezra, written after the destruction of the Temple in 70 CE. See B. W. Longenecker, *Eschatology and the Covenant: A Comparison of 4 Ezra and Romans 1–11* (Sheffield: JSOT, 1991).

to putting the whole world to rights, on the other, it was perhaps inevitable that Jews who longed for all this to happen would come to describe it in what we now call "apocalyptic" language. We need to be clear, however, what we mean by this. In common with many scholars, I use the term "apocalyptic" to denote not so much a state of mind or a set of beliefs about the future, but a way of writing that uses highly charged and coded metaphors to invest space-time reality with its cosmic or theological significance. "The stars will not give their light, and the sun and the moon will be darkened" (Isa 13:10); what Isaiah had in mind was the destruction of Babylon. Four beasts will emerge from the sea; what Daniel had in mind was the rise of great empires. "One like a son of man will come to the Ancient of Days"; what Daniel had in mind was "the saints of the most high" receiving the kingdom (Daniel 7). Even so, "God's righteousness will be revealed" was a coded way of saying that God would at last act within history to vindicate Israel. The word for "is revealed" in Rom 1:17 is ἀποκαλύπτεται (*apokalyptetai*), suggesting precisely, within the first-century Jewish world, the final unveiling within history of the secret plan that Israel's God had all along been hatching.

However, just because apocalyptic language was not designed to denote literal cosmic events (the collapse of the space-time universe, for instance), that does not mean that first-century Jews did not suppose that their God would act suddenly and swiftly to bring about these long-delayed purposes. On the contrary, as the night grew darker, as pagan power increased, and as disloyalty within Israel itself became more rife, Jews like Paul must have prayed and longed for actual space-time events that would demonstrate beyond any doubt that Israel's God was the creator and judge of all the world. Through God's actions on behalf of Israel, the world would see the truth for which it had longed, the justice for which it had striven. Since this expectation of a radically new event breaking into history is in any case what some mean by "apocalyptic," we can assert that "God's righteousness" is to be understood within a framework of thought in which "covenant," "lawcourt," and "apocalyptic" language and thought forms are joined together in mutual compatibility.

**"God's Righteousness" as Paul's Christian Question.** Paul's world of thought was a variation on the Second Temple Jewish worldview. However much his encounter with the risen Jesus on the road to Damascus challenged and changed him, and however much he saw himself as "the apostle to the Gentiles," he still thought like a Jew and, most important, regarded his own Jewishness as significant (see the Commentary on 11:1-6). He quickly came to regard the events of Jesus' death and resurrection as the apocalyptic moment for which he and others had longed, and he rethought his previous way of viewing the story of Israel and the world as a result.

This can be seen precisely in Paul's vocation to be "the apostle to the Gentiles," a theme of considerable significance for Romans. Paul did not take the message of Jesus the Messiah to the Gentiles out of mere frustration that his fellow Jews had refused it, as a kind of displacement activity, but rather out of the conviction that, if God's purposes for Israel had indeed now been fulfilled, it was time for the Gentiles to come in. As becomes increasingly clear, his Gentile mission was an eschatological activity—that is, a task to be undertaken once God had acted climactically and decisively within history. It was a key feature of the new age that had now dawned, part of Paul's sense that God's future had arrived in the present, in the person and achievement of Jesus and the power of the Spirit. Although Paul clearly believed that there was a further and final event still to come, which he describes variously at different points in his writings, the great promised "end" had already begun to happen (see particularly 1 Cor 15:20-28).

This, of course, forced him to reconsider what it was that Israel's God had promised. If this was how the promises had been fulfilled, had God suffered a change of mind? Or had Israel misunderstood God's intentions? Jesus' death and resurrection, seen as the messianic events through which Israel's God had brought the covenant story to its unexpected climax, functioned for Paul not unlike the way the fall of Jerusalem functioned for the author of 4 Ezra: as the catalyst for a serious rethinking of God's promises and intentions, God's covenant faithfulness. Paul's point, to which he stuck like a leech throughout his different debates, was that Israel's God had been true to the covenant and the promises. Paul resisted all tendencies to move toward what would later be called Marcionism.[8]

This notion emerges particularly in Paul's view of the Torah, the Jewish law, which will be touched on a good deal in the commentary. Paul's fundamental insights here, which have earned him much criticism from his fellow Jews from that day to this, are (1) to uncouple the Mosaic law from the Abrahamic covenant and thus (2) to regard the Abrahamic covenant as fulfilled "apart from the law" (3:21); (3) to see the Torah as applying to Jews and Jews only, and hence not being relevant to the eschatological period when the Gentiles were coming in to God's people; (4) to see the Torah as intensifying the problem of Adam's sin for those who were "under the Torah," and thus as something from which its adherents needed to be freed; and (5) to claim, nevertheless, that the Torah had been given by God, had performed the paradoxical tasks assigned to it, and was now strangely fulfilled in the creation of the new people of God in Christ and by the Spirit. Romans makes a substantial contribution to this complex but coherent picture.

Paul thus stuck to, and argued at length for, a view of what God had done in Jesus the Messiah according to which these events were to be seen as the fulfillment of what God had promised to the patriarchs. It was, of course, a sudden and surprising fulfillment, overturning cherished expectations, breaking in unexpectedly upon the worldview that Paul himself had cherished. Recent debates have highlighted the need to stress both the continuity, in Paul's mind, between his gospel and that which had gone before in Judaism and the discontinuity, the sense of radical newness, of a divine purpose

---

8. Marcion was a 2nd cent. CE Roman heretic who taught that the God of the Jews was a different god from that revealed in Jesus.

suddenly and shockingly unveiled. To soft-pedal either of these strong points is to miss the inner tension and dynamic of Paul's thought. It is, in particular, to miss the peculiar force and glory of the letter to the Romans.

**"God's Righteousness" as the Theme of Romans.** Romans has suffered for centuries from being made to produce vital statements on questions it was not written to answer. All that has been said so far by way of historical and theological introduction will seem strange to those traditions of reading the letter that assume its central question to be that of Martin Luther: "How can I find a gracious God?" If we start there, as many commentaries will reveal, Paul's discussion of Israel and its Torah either takes second place or, worse, is relegated to a more abstract and generalized discussion of the sin and salvation of humans in general, in which the question of Israel's fate is essentially a side issue.[9] Within such a reading, it has been common to highlight the doctrine of "justification by faith," in which humans must realize their inability to make themselves "righteous" and must instead trust God's action in Christ, because of which they will be reckoned as "righteous" despite not having obeyed "the law"—that is, a general or universal moral code.

This "righteousness," the status now enjoyed by God's people in Christ, is described in Phil 3:9 as "a righteousness from God [ἡ ἐκ θεοῦ δικαιοσύνη *hē ek theou dikaiosynē*]," from which many have suggested that this status, too, is what is referred to in Rom 1:17 and elsewhere as the *dikaiosynē theou,* "the righteousness of God."[10] Although etymologically possible, this is historically very unlikely. When the latter phrase occurs in biblical and post-biblical Jewish texts, it always refers to God's own righteousness, not to the status people have from God; and Jewish discussions of "God's righteousness" in this sense show close parallels with Paul's arguments in Romans (obvious passages include Deut 33:21; Judg 5:11; 1 Sam 12:7; Neh 9:8; Pss 45:4; 72:1-4; 103:6; Isaiah 40–55 [e.g., 41:10; 45:13; 46:12-13]; Dan 9:7-9, 14, 16; Mic 6:5; Wis 5:18; *Ps Sol.* 1:10-15; 2 Bar 44:4; 78:5; 4 Ezra 7:17-25; 8:36; 10:16; 14:32; *TDan* 6:10; 1QS 10:25-6; 11:12; 1QM 4:6). I believe the detailed exegesis will bear out this interpretation.

In particular, the flow of thought through the letter as a whole makes far more sense if we understand the statement of the theme in 1:17 as being about God and God's covenant faithfulness and justice, rather than simply about "justification."[11] It brings into focus chapters 9–11, not as an appendix to a more general treatment of sin and salvation,

---

9. See C. H. Dodd, *The Epistle of Paul to the Romans,* 2nd ed. (London: Fontana, 1959) esp. 161-63. For a recent commentary in the Reformation tradition, see P. Stuhlmacher, *Paul's Letter to the Romans: A Commentary,* trans. S. J. Hafemann (Louisville: Westminster John Knox, 1994).

10. For a classic statement of this, see C. E. B. Cranfield, *A Critical and Exegetical Commentary on the Epistle to the Romans,* ICC, 2 vols. (Edinburgh: T. & T. Clark, 1975) 91-99.

11. Statistically, the word "God" (θεός *theos*) occurs with far more frequency in Romans (once every 46 words) than any other Pauline work. See L. L. Morris, "The Theme of Romans," in *Apostolic History and the Gospel: Biblical and Historical Essays presented to F. F. Bruce on his 60th Birthday,* ed. W. W. Gasque and R. P. Martin (Exeter: Paternoster, 1970) 249-63. Paul's other letters are also, of course, "about" God, but Romans makes God and God's justice, love, and reliability its major themes.

but as the intended major climax of the whole letter; and it allows for the significance of 15:1-13 as a final summing up of the subject. Within this larger theme, there is still all the room required for that which other readings have traditionally seen as the major subject—namely, the justification and salvation of individual human beings. But in this letter at least (remembering again that this is not, after all, a systematic theology but a letter addressed to a particular situation), these vital and highly important topics are held within a larger discussion. Paul's aim, it seems, is to explain to the Roman church what God has been up to and where they might belong on the map of these purposes.

Accustomed as we are to translating *dikaiosynē* as "righteousness," we should recognize from this account that the other obvious meaning of the word, "justice," is not far away. The sense of covenant faithfulness and the sense of things being put to rights, held apart within both the Reformation and the Enlightenment as "theology and ethics" or "salvation and politics," were not far removed in the mind of a Jew like Paul. Just as the Messiah was destined to be Lord of the world, so also, and for the same reasons, God's covenant with Israel had always been intended as the means of putting God's world to rights.[12] When, therefore, God's righteousness was unveiled, the effect would be precisely that the world would receive justice—that rich, restorative, much-to-be-longed-for justice of which the psalmists had spoken with such feeling (e.g., Pss 67:4; 82:8). Even a quick skim through Romans ought to reveal that this is indeed what Paul was talking about, though of course full justification of the point awaits the detail of the commentary.

But we need to remind ourselves to whom Paul's great letter was sent. Looming up behind the various discussions of why Romans was written is an issue not usually noticed. Paul was coming to Rome with the gospel message of Jesus the Jewish Messiah, the Lord of the world, claiming that, through this message, God's justice was unveiled once and for all. Rome prided itself on being, as it were, the capital of justice, the source from which justice would flow throughout the world. The Roman goddess Iustitia, like the Caesar cult itself, was a comparative novelty in Paul's world; the temple to Iustitia was established on January 8, 13 CE, and Iustitia was among the virtues celebrated by Augustus's famous *clipeus virtutis,* the golden shield set up in the Senate house and inscribed with the emperor's virtues (27 BCE). So close is the link between the new imperial regime and the virtue Iustitia that this goddess sometimes acquires the title "Augusta."[13] So, without losing any of its deep-rooted Jewish meanings of the covenant faithfulness of the creator God, Paul's declaration that the gospel of King Jesus reveals God's *dikaiosynē* must also be read as a deliberate challenge to the imperial pretension. If it is justice you want, he implies, you will find it, but not in the

---

12. I have explored this theme in various places, e.g., N. T. Wright, *The Climax of the Covenant: Christ and the Law in Pauline Theology* (Edinburgh: T. & T. Clark; Minneapolis: Fortress, 1991) 21-26; *The New Testament and the People of God,* vol. 1 of *Christian Origins and the Question of God* (Minneapolis: Fortress, 1992) chap. 9.

13. On *Iustitia,* the Roman equivalent of *dikē,* see, e.g., Ovid *Letters from the Black Sea* 3.6.25; the *Acts of Augustus* chap. 34.

εὐαγγέλιον (*euangelion*) that announces Caesar as Lord, but in the *euangelion* of Jesus.[14] The rest of Romans will show that this meaning is indeed in Paul's mind at point after point.

Nor is this meaning an indication that Paul is, as it were, shuttling to and fro between "Jewish" and "Gentile" contexts of meaning. Part of the whole point, for him, of the Jewish claim to be the covenant people of God was that the divine purpose for the whole creation would be revealed through Israel. In other words, when God at last fulfilled the covenant, the Gentile world would see, unveiled, what its own life was about. Applied to Rome, this meant that the very Jewish, very biblically based, revelation of the divine righteousness/justice was necessarily at the same time the revelation of the true Iustitia, that which really did accomplish what Caesar's Iustitia had claimed to do—namely, the putting to rights of the entire creation. We have only to think for a moment of Isaiah 40–55 to see how similar the train of thought is: Israel's God will reveal righteousness and salvation, confronting pagan empire as the sovereign creator and rescuing the covenant people in the process. All this, too, will emerge at various points throughout the letter and the commentary.

We may, therefore, offer the following highly compressed summary account of the flow of thought in the letter, which gradually unpacks the summary statement of the introduction (1:1-17).

*Chapters 1–4:* God's gospel unveils the fact that in the Messiah, Jesus of Nazareth, the God of Israel has been true to the covenant established with Abraham and has thereby brought saving order to the whole world. In the face of a world in rebellion and a chosen people unfaithful to their commission, God has, through the surrogate faithfulness of Jesus the Messiah, created a worldwide—that is, a Jewish and Gentile—family for Abraham, marked out by the covenant sign of faith.

*Chapters 5–8:* God has thereby done what the covenant was set up to do: to address and solve the problem expressed in biblical terms as the sin of Adam. In the Messiah, Jesus, God has done for this new people what was done for Israel of old in fulfillment of the promise to Abraham: Redeemed from the Egypt of enslavement to sin, they are led through the wilderness of the present life by the Spirit (not by the Torah), and they look forward to the inheritance, which will consist of the entire redeemed creation. This is how the creator will finally put the whole world to rights. All this is the result of God's astonishing, unchanging, self-giving covenant love expressed completely and finally in the death of Jesus.

14. This point, though it was developed independently, has close analogies with the argument of Neil Elliott, *Liberating Paul: The Justice of God and the Politics of the Apostle* (Maryknoll, N.Y.: Orbis, 1994) 190-92. See also Dieter Georgi, *Theocracy in Paul's Praxis and Theology* (Minneapolis: Fortress, 1991) chap. 4, excerpted in Richard A. Horsely, ed., *Paul and Empire: Religion and Power in Roman Imperial Society* (Harrisburg, Pa.: Trinity, 1997) 148-57. See further Richard A. Horsely, ed., *Paul and Politics: Ekklesia, Israel, Imperium, Interpretation: Essays in Honor of Krister Stendahl* (Harrisburg, Pa.: Trinity, 2000) chaps. 1, 10.

*Chapters 9–11:* This section highlights the peculiar tragedy of the gospel's revelation of God's righteousness—namely, the ironic failure of Israel to believe in the Messiah. This, too, however, turns out to be held within the strange purposes of God, whereby Israel's fall, acting out on a grand scale the death of Jesus, is the means by which salvation can extend to the whole world. This cannot mean that Jews themselves are thereby forever debarred from participating in the covenant blessing; Paul himself is a counter-example, and God desires that even now, by recognizing that it is indeed their promised blessings that the Gentiles are enjoying, more of Paul's fellow Jews will come to share in new covenant membership. Gentile Christians, therefore, are warned severely against anti-Jewish arrogance. The section ends with a paean of praise for the strange but glorious purposes of God.

*Chapters 12–16:* The community that is created by this gospel must live as the true, renewed humanity, in its internal and external life. In particular, it must reflect God's intention that Jew and Gentile come together as one worshiping body in Christ. Paul's own plans are bent to this end, and his greetings to different groups in the Roman church may indicate his desire to bring together disparate groups in common worship and mission.

Such a summary, which of course depends at every point on the commentary for explanation and justification, nevertheless enables us to ask, in conclusion: How then may we understand the letter's situation, and how does the shape and detailed content of the letter address it?

## THE HISTORICAL OCCASION FOR ROMANS

The letter appears to have two main "situational" aims that surface in the great climactic passages 11:11-32 and 15:7-13. Each has in view the relationship between Jews and Gentiles; the former, however, addresses Christian Gentiles who are faced with non-Christian Jews, and the latter addresses a community in which Christian Gentiles and Christian Jews find themselves in uneasy coexistence. Although the details remain unclear, it is certain that a large proportion of Rome's substantial Jewish population had to leave the city in the late 40s CE following rioting that may have resulted from early Christian preaching among the Jewish community in Rome.[15] The expulsion edict came from the Emperor Claudius, after whose death in 54 the new emperor, Nero, rescinded his decrees, making it possible for the expelled Jews to return. This historical sequence produces a situation into which Romans fits like a glove.

15. See Wright, *The New Testament and the People of God,* 354-55; W. Wiefel, "The Jewish Community in Ancient Rome and the Origins of Roman Christianity," in *The Romans Debate,* rev. ed., ed. K. P. Donfried (Peabody, Mass.: Hendrikson, 1991) 85-101. Some scholars remain doubtful about whether the Jews were really expelled. See P. Achtemeier, "Unsearchable Judgments and Inscrutable Ways: Reflections of the Discussion of Romans," in *Pauline Theology,* vol. IV, ed. E. E. Johnson and D. M. Hay, SBLSS 4 (Atlanta: Scholars Press, 1997) 3-21; S. Mason, " 'For I Am Not Ashamed of the Gospel' (Rom. 1.16): The Gospel and the First Readers of Romans," in *Gospel in Paul: Studies on Corinthians, Galatians, and Romans for Richard N. Longenecker,* ed. L. A. Jervis and P. Richardson, JSNTSup 108 (Sheffield: Sheffield Academic, 1994) 254-87.

Consider, on the one hand, the position of Gentile Christians vis-à-vis non-Christian Jews. The Roman anti-Jewish sentiment, for which there is abundant evidence in late antiquity, would create a context in which many Romans would be glad to see the Jews gone and sorry to see them return.[16] How easy, then, would it be for the Gentile Christians who remained in Rome through the early 50s to imagine that God had somehow endorsed, at the theological level, what Caesar had enacted at the political level and that God had in fact written the hated Jews out of the covenant altogether. How easy, also, when the Jews returned to take up their property and positions in society, to suppose that, though the new faith would spread to include other Gentiles, there was no point in attempting to win over any more Jews.

But Paul was coming to Rome with a gospel that was "God's power for salvation to the Jew first and also to the Greek" (1:16). If the Roman church were to accept his gospel, and indeed to support him in his missionary intention to go on from Rome to Spain, it was vital for them to realize that, even as the apostle to the Gentiles, he remained under obligation to his fellow Jews as well. Paul's travel plans in chap. 15 are thus woven into the same picture: Having been undermined by the apparent failure of his earlier home base in Antioch to support him in his practice of incorporating believing Gentiles into the same social structure as believing Jews (see Gal 2:11-21), he was determined that in the western Mediterranean he was going to make things clear from the start.

Consider, on the other hand, the position of Christian Jews and Christian Gentiles in relation to them. Paul will have known of some Jewish Christians who had returned to Rome and who, alongside Gentile cobelievers, would now be facing the difficult question of how to live together as one family with those who cherished very different cultural traditions, not least food taboos. Paul knows that this will not be solved overnight and stresses instead a doctrine of *adiaphora:* There are some practical things over which Christians can legitimately disagree, and they should not impair common worship. Underneath it all is Paul's desire that the Scriptures should be fulfilled: "Rejoice, you Gentiles, with God's people!" (15:10, quoting Deut 32:43).

Romans 9–11 and 12–16 thus are explicable in terms of the double situation of the Roman church and Paul's agendas in addressing them. Why, then, does he write chaps. 1–8? Are they just an extended introduction, before Paul reaches his real point?

By no means. If he is to address the deep-rooted problems of the interrelationship between Jews and Gentiles within God's purposes, Paul must go down to those deep roots themselves, to the foundations of Jewish and Christian thinking: to creation and fall, covenant and Torah, to Israel's covenant failure and God's covenant faithfulness. He must show how the death and resurrection of Jesus, the basic announcement of "the

16. See Menahem Stern, *Greek and Latin Authors on Jews and Judaism,* 3 vols. (Jerusalem: Israel Academy of Sciences and Humanities, 1974). On the Jewish community in Rome see H. J. Leon, *The Jews of Ancient Rome,* rev. ed. (Peabody, Mass.: Hendrikson, 1995).

gospel," are God's solution to the complex problems of Israel and the world and how these events have called into existence a people, composed of Jew and Gentile alike, led by God's Spirit and defined not by Torah but by faith, in whom all the promises of God have come true. Only so can his hearers sense the poignant tragedy of Israel's situation in Romans 9 and so move toward the main thrust of the letter. Only so can they appreciate the subtle logic of the argument that he then mounts. And only so can they be equipped for the larger questions that hover in the background—questions of the relation of Jesus' new empire with that of Caesar, of the justice of God facing the justice of Rome.

At the same time, the chapters in which he lays the foundation for his specific arguments can stand almost on their own as a statement of what God has done in the Messiah for the whole world. Here we must be careful. Romans is a tightly knit, coherent whole with an inner logic that affects every word and sentence. But the arguments of chaps. 1–4, on the one hand, and chaps. 5–8, on the other, have their own integrity. This is perhaps particularly true of chaps. 5–8, with their christological refrains tolling like a great bell at the end of almost every section. Here, if anywhere, Paul is clearly making Jesus the lens through which one may see the saving plan of God working its way out. At the same time, one must quickly add that it is precisely this section, for just this reason, that sets up the argument of chaps. 9–11. It is not simply that, having written chaps. 1–8, he finds he has to go on to 9–11; it is just as much that, because he wants to write chaps. 9–11, he finds he must write 1–8 in this way. Thus in key passages in Romans 1–8, Paul seems deliberately to set up problems and questions that he then leaves hanging in the air, only to resume them in chaps. 9–11 (the most obvious place where this occurs is 3:1-8, on which, see the commentary).

There are, of course, many other matters often covered in an introduction to a biblical book. But these are the things of most value for the intended readers of this series to understand before proceeding further. Others will be covered at the appropriate points in the commentary itself.

## BIBLIOGRAPHY

Commentaries:

Bryan, Christopher. *A Preface to Romans: Notes on the Epistle in Its Literary and Cultural Setting.* Oxford: Oxford University Press, 2000. Brief and helpful; copious reference to frequently overlooked ancient literature; interesting and original ideas and practical comments.

Byrne, Brendan. *Romans.* SP 6. Collegeville, Minn.: Liturgical, 1996. Deep scholarship; a light and wise touch; fresh insights.

Cranfield, C. E. B. *A Critical and Exegetical Commentary on the Epistle to the Romans.* ICC. 2 vols. Edinburgh: T. & T. Clark, 1975, 1979. Already a classic. A model of lucid, wide-ranging and judicious exegesis; a major contribution not just to Romans but to NT theology as a whole.

Dunn, James D. G. *Romans 1–8* and *Romans 9–16.* WBC 38A and 38B. Dallas: Word, 1988. No stone left unturned; some of the details that crawl out from underneath (innumerable secondary discussions in the unfootnoted text) may be more than the ordinary reader wants. A major representative of the so-called new perspective on Paul.

Fitzmyer, Joseph A. *Romans*. AB 33. Garden City, N.Y.: Doubleday, 1993. Thorough on bibliography and background details, not always reliable (though often very stimulating) on theological judgments. With Byrne, the most important Roman Catholic commentary of recent years.

Käsemann, Ernst. *Commentary on Romans*. Translated by Geoffrey W. Bromiley. London: SCM, 1980. Possibly the most important book on Paul since the Second World War. Rigorous in exegesis, robustly Protestant in theology, bracing in application. Not for the beginner, but exhilarating for those ready for a challenge.

Moo, Douglas J. *The Epistle to the Romans*. NICNT. Grand Rapids: Eerdmans, 1996. The most thorough and learned of recent Protestant expositions. Solidly evangelical but not afraid to find his own way through interpretative dilemmas.

Studies on Romans:

Donfried, Karl P. *The Romans Debate*. Rev. ed. Peabody, Mass.: Hendrickson, 1991. Useful collection of 23 important essays on the background, occasion, and content of Romans.

Dunn, James D. G. *The Theology of Paul the Apostle*. Grand Rapids: Eerdmans, 1998. Full, detailed, thoroughly annotated, but clear and readable. Modeled in outline on Romans: at one level, a traditional presentation of topics in Paul; at another, many important fresh interpretations (e.g., on "works of the law") for which Dunn has become famous.

Hay, David M., and E. Elizabeth Johnson, eds. *Pauline Theology*. Vol. III: *Romans*. Minneapolis: Fortress, 1991. Papers from the SBL Pauline Theology seminar, including several important discussions.

Hays, Richard B. *Echoes of Scripture in the Letters of Paul*. New Haven: Yale University Press, 1989. Seminal monograph, already something of a classic. Explores Paul's complex use of Israel's scriptures; a one-line quotation can evoke a whole biblical passage or context, thereby revealing deeper meanings in Paul.

Horsley, Richard A., ed. *Paul and Empire: Religion and Power in Roman Imperial Society*. Harrisburg, Pa.: Trinity Press International, 1997. Essays, with important introductions by the editor, highlighting the Roman imperial context (including ideology and emperor cult), whose significance for understanding Paul is only now beginning to be felt.

Sanders, E. P. *Paul, the Law, and the Jewish People*. Philadelphia: Fortress, 1983. Sequel to the same author's *Paul and Palestinian Judaism* (Philadelphia: Fortress, 1977), which marked a watershed in Pauline studies. Detailed discussions of key texts, including several from Romans.

Wagner, J. Ross. *Heralds of the Good News: Isaiah and Paul "In Concert" in the Letter to the Romans*. NovTSup 101. Leiden: Brill, 2002. Isaiah was one of Paul's most important biblical sources; this book discusses what he did with it. Full of patient and wise scholarship on the meaning of the letter.

Wright, N. T. *The Climax of the Covenant: Christ and the Law in Pauline Theology*. Edinburgh: T. & T. Clark; Minneapolis: Fortress, 1991. Detailed discussion of key texts on christology and the law, including several on Romans.

———. *The New Testament and the People of God*. Vol. 1 of *Christian Origins and the Question of God*. London: SPCK; Minneapolis: Fortress, 1992. Early Christianity within its historical and theological settings.

# OUTLINE OF ROMANS

# ROMANS 1:1–4:25

## THE FAITHFULNESS OF GOD

### OVERVIEW

The letter's main subjects are laid out in the first four chapters. The introduction (1:1-17) offers a dense statement of the theme: In the gospel announcement of the risen Jesus as Messiah and Lord, the one true God has unveiled covenant faithfulness and justice, God's own faithfulness and justice, for the benefit of all who believe. Paul then launches into a description of the world that has worshiped other gods and has reaped a harvest of dehumanization, moral deterioration, and condemnation (1:18–3:20). Though the spearhead of this attack (1:18–2:16) corresponds to regular Jewish polemic against the pagan world, Paul sharpens it up with specifically Christian notes, and he hints that Israel itself is included in the general indictment. He turns in 2:17-29 specifically to his own people, the Jews; while endorsing their claim to be the people chosen by God to bring light to the world, their own prophets indicate that they have failed in this vocation and are in danger of relinquishing their special status.

This raises acutely these questions (3:1-9): What is the point of being part of God's chosen people in the first place? How is God righteous in the whole sequence of events? Putting off these questions for the moment with very brief answers, Paul stresses both the faithlessness of Israel and the abiding faithfulness of God. But to place the issue beyond doubt he mounts a list of biblical passages (3:10-18) that all point one way: The Jews have joined the Gentiles in the dock, with nothing to say in their defense. All are equally guilty before the impartial judge.

This conclusion poses a classic question within the world of Second Temple Judaism. What happens when God's intended covenant faithfulness appears to be in conflict with the demands of impartial justice—when the double meaning of "the righteousness of God" seems to contradict itself? Paul's answer is emphatic (3:21–4:25): In Jesus the Messiah, God has been true both to the covenant with Abraham and to the demands of justice. As a result, there is now a Jew-plus-Gentile people of God, the true children of Abraham, marked out by faith rather than works of Torah.

All this has come about "through the faithfulness of Jesus the Messiah" (3:22). Jesus has accomplished—to put it another way, God has accomplished through Jesus—what Israel failed to accomplish. God's own covenant faithfulness is thus unveiled at last, an event to which the law and prophets pointed but that they could not bring about. The "faithfulness" of the Messiah, the subject matter of the gospel itself, denotes specifically his death, seen as the culmination of his whole "obedience." This faithful obedience (or obedient faithfulness) was the means of dealing with sin and hence of creating a forgiven people. The badge of membership in the renewed people of God is faith, not works of the Torah, which would have restricted apparent membership to Jews and proselytes and would in any case have condemned everyone (since all alike are sinful). However, since the gospel of Jesus thus creates a single family for the one God of Jews and Gentiles alike, the Torah itself, in which confession of this one God is central, is strangely fulfilled.

All this has come about in fulfillment of the covenant with Abraham (4:1-25). Abraham is the father, not just of Jews, but of all who believe. In a lengthy exposition of Genesis 15 (the chapter in which God made the initial covenant with Abraham), Paul demonstrates that the promises to the patriarch were not conditioned by works (Rom 4:2-8), by circumcision (Rom 4:9-12), or by Torah

(Rom 4:13-15). God has now created, through faith, the single family promised in the first place (Rom 4:16-17), consisting of believing Jews and believing Gentiles. In a closing peroration (Rom 4:18-25), Paul echoes his indictment of pagan humanity in 1:18-32 and shows by implication how the problem has been undone. Abraham's faith is the characteristic mark of genuine, God-honoring humanity. This new family, called into being by the gospel, is marked out by faith in the God who raised Jesus from the dead (Rom 4:23-25; for Paul's view that the gospel was already, in a sense, preached to Abraham himself, see Gal 3:8).

The first main statement of Paul's thesis is thus complete. The gospel of Jesus the Messiah unveils the righteousness, the covenant faithfulness, the justice of God in such a way as to bring into being the single family promised to Abraham, character-ized by faith in this Jesus. Paul has constructed this argument in such a way as to prepare carefully for the points he wishes to address in chaps. 9–11 and 12–16. To develop these lines of thought, how-ever, and to address the questions connected with them, he needs to lay still deeper foundations. Chapters 1–4, by also leading naturally into chaps. 5–8, point to where those foundations are to be found.

# ROMANS 1:1-17, OPENING STATEMENT OF THEME: GOD'S GOSPEL AND GOD'S RIGHTEOUSNESS

## Romans 1:1-7, God's Gospel and Paul's Ministry

NIV

1 Paul, a servant of Christ Jesus, called to be an apostle and set apart for the gospel of God— ²the gospel he promised beforehand through his prophets in the Holy Scriptures ³regarding his Son, who as to his human nature was a descendant of David, ⁴and who through the Spirit[a] of holiness was declared with power to be the Son of God[b] by his resurrection from the dead: Jesus Christ our Lord. ⁵Through him and for his name's sake, we received grace and apostleship to call people from among all the Gentiles to the obe-dience that comes from faith. ⁶And you also are among those who are called to belong to Jesus Christ.

⁷To all in Rome who are loved by God and called to be saints:

Grace and peace to you from God our Father and from the Lord Jesus Christ.

<sup>a</sup> 4 Or who as to his spirit    <sup>b</sup> 4 Or was appointed to be the Son of God with power

NIV

1 Paul, a servant[a] of Jesus Christ, called to be an apostle, set apart for the gospel of God, ²which he promised beforehand through his prophets in the holy scriptures, ³the gospel con-cerning his Son, who was descended from David according to the flesh ⁴and was declared to be Son of God with power according to the spirit[b] of holi-ness by resurrection from the dead, Jesus Christ our Lord, ⁵through whom we have received grace and apostleship to bring about the obedience of faith among all the Gentiles for the sake of his name, ⁶including yourselves who are called to belong to Jesus Christ,

7To all God's beloved in Rome, who are called to be saints:

Grace to you and peace from God our Father and the Lord Jesus Christ.

<sup>a</sup> Gk slave    <sup>b</sup> Or Spirit

# COMMENTARY

Paul introduces himself in terms of his vocation and defines that vocation in terms of the gospel. The opening seven verses of the letter move swiftly from Paul to the gospel, back to Paul and his ministry, and out into the world, which includes the Roman Christians. As usual, he introduces, within the formal structure of a letter opening, the themes that will occupy him in what is to come.

**1:1-2.** Paul announces himself with the word that, above all others in his world, carried overtones of social degradation. Slaves had no rights, no property, and no prospects; they were simply there to do what they were told. Modifying this to "servant," as though Paul were a free agent who happened to have a job as a cleaner or butler, misses the point. Paul will claim no social standing in his approach to the greatest imperial capital his world had ever known.

Slave though he be, however, his master is the King before whom other kings should quail, and he can thus hold up his head not on his own account but on that of "king Jesus." By transliterating Χριστός (*Christos*) rather than translating it, most English versions of Paul have encouraged the view that the word had already become a proper name for Paul. This, however, is misleading: Paul's careful and differentiated usage of "Christ," "Jesus," and for that matter "Lord" leads to the conclusion that he intended each word to carry its own set of overtones.[17] And the overtones of "Christ"—i.e., "Messiah"—are, as we shall presently see, clearly royal: The Messiah is the anointed king of Israel who in Scripture was supposed to be the ruler of all other earthly monarchs (see, e.g., Pss 72:8-11; 89:27; Isa 11:1-4). It is because Paul is the slave announcing the king that he can call his message "gospel" (see below).[18]

Paul's two further self-designations, building on the slave-of-the-king status, are both significant for this letter. First, he is "called apostle" or "apostle by God's call" (NEB). "Call" in Paul's writings usually refers, not to the specific vocation of which a Christian may gradually become aware, but to

the moment when the gospel message of Jesus first makes its saving impact on him or her. Here, in the light of Gal 1:15-16, the two ideas seem to be run together: Paul's "conversion" was also his "vocation" to be the apostle to the nations. There is a further consonance between the words; elsewhere Paul seems to define what he means by "apostle" in terms of those who had actually seen the risen Jesus (1 Cor 9:1), alluding not least to his own moment of seeing Jesus on the Damascus road. For him, conversion and calling were both contained in the one event.

In parallel with this vocation, Paul has been marked off from others, including (it seems) from other apostles, others who had seen the risen Jesus. The word translated "set apart" (ἀφορίζω *aphorizō*) indicates God's intention: If a slave is a piece of property, the owner has set this piece apart from other uses and focused it on one in particular, the service of "the gospel." "Set apart" may also reflect, with wry irony, the self-description of a Pharisee who had considered himself "separated" from the common herd of ordinary Jews. If Paul is in any sense a Christian Pharisee, it is because he has now been separated out as a slave, given a particular commission by which he is defined from now on.

"The gospel of God" is thus at the heart of Paul's self-definition and self-understanding. The word "gospel" (εὐαγγέλιον *euangelion*) referred in early Christianity to the proclamation about Jesus before it was used to denote particular books; Paul uses the term to denote the message, or announcement, that he was making around the Mediterranean world. In Paul's Jewish world, the word looked back to Isa 40:9 and 52:7, where a messenger was to bring to Jerusalem the good news of Babylon's defeat, the end of Israel's exile, and the personal return of YHWH to Zion. In the pagan world Paul addressed, the same Greek word referred to the announcement of the accession or the birthday of a ruler or emperor. Here already we find Paul at the interface of his two worlds. His message about Jesus was both the fulfillment of prophecy, as v. 2 indicates, and the announcement of one whose rule posed a challenge to all other

---

17. See N. T. Wright, *The Climax of the Covenant: Christ and the Law in Pauline Theology* (Minneapolis: Fortress, 1991) 41-49.

18. The counterimperial overtones are well brought out by M. J. Brown, "Paul's Use of Δοῦλος Χριστοῦ Ἰησοῦ in Romans 1:1," *JBL* 120 (2001) 723-37.

rulers.[19] Though the word "gospel" itself occurs infrequently in Romans, it is truly part of the main theme, since its content, Jesus Christ, forms the substructure of the entire train of thought.

The gospel is not, strictly speaking, Paul's own property (though he refers to it as "my gospel" in 2:16); it is God's. As noted in the Introduction, the word "God" occurs far more times, proportionately, in Romans than in Paul's other writings. This letter is about the way in which, through the lens of the gospel, the covenant plan and purpose of the one true God have been unveiled before the world. Paul's view of God remained deeply Jewish; he believed that the one God of Abraham, Isaac, and Jacob, the creator of the world, had now brought world history to its climax in Jesus. Paul is urging the Roman Christians to understand this purpose, and their own place within it, so that they can then live and work appropriately and, indeed, support Paul's apostolic task as well. The fact that the gospel is God's means that Paul is entrusted with an awesome responsibility. He is like one in charge of distributing royal bounty.

**1:3a.** The gospel is a message about God's Son. This is another key phrase that, although it occurs quite seldom in the letter, naturally takes center stage. Paul, in fact, lived at a moment of transition in the history of this phrase and helped it on its way to subsequent development. In the OT, "son of God" can refer to angels (Gen 6:2; Job 1:6; 2:1; 38:7; Dan 3:25; cf. Dan 3:28; Song of Three 26). But its better known referents are Israel, adopted as God's child explicitly at the time of the exodus and looking back to that moment in order to plead for subsequent deliverance (Exod 4:22; Jer 31:9; Hos 11:1; 13:13; Mal 1:6); and the king, adopted as YHWH's firstborn son—the seed of David who is also the son of God (1 Sam 7:14 [quoted with this sense in 4Q174 10-13; cf. 4Q246 2:1]; 1 Chr 17:13; Pss 2:7; 89:26-27).[20] These two senses belong together, since in some Jewish thought the Davidic king represents Israel, so that what is true of him is true of the people. To belong to Israel, in a passage that seems to have become proverbial, is

to be "in David" or "in the son of Jesse" (1 Sam 19:43–20:2; cf. 1 Kgs 12:16; 2 Chr 10:16). The natural meaning of the phrase "God's gospel concerning his son," therefore, is "God's announcement, in fulfillment of prophecy, of the royal enthronement of the Messiah, Israel's anointed king, the lord of the world."

There is a huge difference between all this and the much later Christian usage in which "son of God" comes to be a simple predication of Jesus' divinity. We should not allow this difference, however, to obscure the fact that already in Paul, at least as early as Gal 4:1-7, we find the phrase used in a way that, while still rooted in this Jewish tradition of Israel/kingship, now draws on other Jewish imagery, such as God's sending of Wisdom, to make the point that the "son" is one sent into the world not only as a messenger but also as the personal expression of God's love and purpose. As we shall see later in Romans, the arguments work only if we postulate a fundamental identity between "the son" and God's own very self— alongside, of course, the differentiation inherent in the father/son division. This raises further questions to which Paul provides no answers, only hints. But it does suggest that the earliest Christian incarnational theology known to us remained deeply rooted in Jewish tradition, however much it was saying things no one had said before.

**1:3b-4.** The "son" is then described in a complex double statement concerning Jesus' human descent, on the one hand, and the meaning of his resurrection, on the other. Like many of Paul's more formulaic passages, this passage has generated speculation that we are here dealing with that hypothetical entity the "pre-Pauline formula," which Paul has quoted, quite possibly adapting or modifying it as he did so, in order not least to establish his credentials with an audience to whom the formula would have been familiar.[21] It is, of course, quite possible that Paul might use formulae known to his readers but not otherwise to us, and the present passage might indeed be a case in point. But it must be stressed, here and elsewhere, that the reason why Paul quoted things, if he did, was that they expressed exactly what he

19. See N. T. Wright, "Gospel and Theology in Galatians," in *Gospel in Paul: Studies on Corinthians, Galatians and Romans for Richard N. Longenecker,* ed. L. Ann Jervis and Peter Richardson, JSNTSup 108 (Sheffield: Sheffield Academic, 1994) 222-39.

20. In view of this it is extraordinary that Fitzmyer can deny the existence of an OT background for the idea. See Joseph A. Fitzmyer, *Romans,* AB 33 (Garden City, N.Y.: Doubleday, 1993) 235.

21. See ibid., 229-300; Douglas J. Moo, *The Epistle to the Romans,* NICNT (Grand Rapids: Eerdmans, 1996) 44-46. Among earlier literature, see J. D. G. Dunn, "Jesus—Flesh and Spirit: An Exposition of Romans 1.3-4," *JTS* 24 (1973) 40-68.

intended to say at the time. As we shall see throughout this commentary, the christology of 1:3-4 is by no means an isolated statement attached loosely to the front of the letter but not relevant to its contents. It is the careful, weighted, programmatic statement of what will turn out to be Paul's subtext throughout the whole epistle (see also 9:5; and 15:12, the final scriptural quotation of the main body of the letter).

In particular, the "discovery" of pre-Pauline fragments such as this has sometimes been employed as a way of distancing Paul from the precise emphases of the passage. Often this is done to make him appear less "Jewish" than the statement seems to be (see the Commentary on 3:24-26). In the present case, it is pointed out that Paul nowhere else refers to Jesus' Davidic sonship; it is often assumed (less often argued) that Paul had moved away from Jewish messianic ideas altogether.[22] Themes are more important than words; once we understand how messianic ideas functioned for Paul we discover them throughout his writings. In particular, as we shall see in its proper place, his incorporative christology ("in Christ" and similar expressions) is best explained in terms of the Messiah's role of summing up his people in himself. There is also a persistent tendency in traditional Pauline scholarship to play down Jewish messianic ideas on the grounds that this makes Paul's theology more political. One could equally well argue the other way: Because Paul's theology, and for that matter his life, was so obviously political, in senses to be explored in the commentary, it is scarcely surprising that we discover Jewish messianic ideas at the center of his writings.[23]

Whether or not Paul wrote vv. 3-4 from scratch himself (and we must guard against assuming that a writer such as Paul was incapable of dictating an apparently formulaic statement off the top of his head, especially as he had had countless occasions to sum up his message orally before a wide variety of audiences), the passage as it stands offers a striking statement of that messianic view of Jesus that we shall discover at the heart of the letter. God's son, declares Paul, was born of the seed of David and marked out as "son of God" by the resurrection. As it stands, shorn of extra explanatory (but also, to us, confusing) clauses and granted what has been said about the meaning of "God's son" in Jewish tradition, this is a reasonably straightforward two-part statement of Jesus' Messiahship.[24] (1) Jesus was born of David's line;[25] (2) the resurrection declared to the world that he really was the Messiah and had been so all along.[26] This, indeed, was almost certainly where Paul's Christian thinking began: with the recognition, at or shortly after his Damascus road experience, that the Jesus he had thought to be a false Messiah was after all the true one (cf. Gal 1:16; Acts 9:20, 22, where it is clear that "son of God" and "Messiah" are virtually interchangeable).[27]

To the first phrase Paul adds "according to the flesh," intending, of course, to clarify the sense of Jesus' Davidic descent, but also thereby opening a can of worms for the interpreter. Earlier readers, still reflected in the NIV, took the double statement as expressing Jesus' "humanity," on the one hand, and his "divinity," on the other, and thus read "according to the flesh" as referring to his "human nature." But "flesh" (σάρξ *sarx*) is never simply "human nature" for Paul; nor is it simply a reference to physical humanness as opposed to

---

22. E.g., J. A. Fitzmyer, *The Letter to Philemon,* AB 34C (New York: Doubleday, 2000) 99. I have argued elsewhere, and here reemphasize, that this is a mistake. If 2 Timothy is by Paul, we can count 2:8 as another instance. If it is not, we might speculate that 2:8 was a pre-2 Timothy formula, in which case its hypothetical author could, of course, have been Paul himself. See N. T. Wright, *The Climax of the Covenant: Christ and the Law in Pauline Theology* (Edinburgh: T. & T. Clark; Minneapolis: Fortress, 1991) part one, esp. chaps. 2 and 3.

23. On the political side of Paul's work, see Neil Elliott, *Liberating Paul: The Justice of God and the Politics of the Apostle* (Maryknoll, N.Y.: Orbis, 1994); Richard A. Horsley, ed., *Paul and Empire: Religion and Power in Roman Imperial Society* (Harrisburg, Pa.: Trinity, 1997); *Paul and Politics: Ekklesia, Israel, Imperium, Interpretation: Essays in Honor of Krister Stendahl* (Harrisburg, Pa.: Trinity, 2000). From a different angle, see B. Blumenfeld, *The Political Paul: Justice, Democracy and Kingship in a Hellenistic Framework,* JSNTSup 210 (Sheffield: Sheffield Academic, 2001).

24. Although there are no biblical texts that explicitly predict the resurrection of the Messiah ("resurrection," when it developed as a belief in the post-biblical period, was thought of as happening to all God's people simultaneously), it is possible that some at least read one of the key "son of God" passages, 2 Sam 7:12 ("I will raise up your seed after you"; cf. 1 Kings 8:20), in this sense, not least because of the LXX's καὶ ἀναστήσω τὸ σπέρμα σου (*kai anastēsō to sperma sou,* "and I will resurrect your seed").

25. "Born" is a better translation for γενομένου (*genomenou*) than "descended." Paul reveals no awareness of Jesus' supposed virginal conception and hence offers no answer to the question raised by Matthew and Luke as to how such a belief is compatible with Jesus' Davidic pedigree.

26. "Declared to be" is not misleading, but the word ὁρίζω (*horizō*) really means "marked out as."

27. On the meanings Paul gave to, and deduced from, his experience of meeting the risen Jesus, see Martin Hengel and Anna Maria Schwemer, *Paul Between Damascus and Antioch: The Unknown Years* (London: SCM, 1997) 101-5; R. N. Longenecker, ed., *The Road from Damascus: The Impact of Paul's Conversion on his Life, Thought and Ministry* (Grand Rapids: Eerdmans, 1997).

nonphysical aspects, such as soul or spirit. It is always human nature *seen as* corruptible, decaying, dying, on the one hand, and/or rebelling, deceiving, and sinning, on the other. "Flesh" always carries negative overtones somewhere on this scale, whereas for Paul being human was not something negative, but good and God-given and to be reaffirmed in the resurrection. In any case, Paul has given no hint at this stage in the letter that he intends "son of God" to be taken in an explicitly "divine" sense. Since Messiahship (which in the Jewish world, of course, carried no overtones of "divinity") is the main theme of the passage, we should be careful not to overexegete it in the light of other, fuller Pauline statements— or, indeed, of later Christian tradition.

Others have seen "according to the flesh" as Paul's way of hinting that, while Jesus was indeed of the seed of David, this was not the most significant thing about him. In other words, this was Paul's way of distancing himself from Jewish messianic beliefs in order to hurry on to the more important point about Jesus' divine sonship. This, too, is misleading for the reasons already given. The whole point of Paul's gospel is that Jesus, precisely as Israel's Messiah, is now Lord of the world. That belief informs and undergirds much of this letter.

This relationship between 1:3-4 and the rest of Romans indicates what Paul means by adding "according to the flesh" and "according to the spirit." Jesus the Messiah is the one in whom God's people find their identity and salvation; he has come where they are in order to rescue them (more fully stated in 8:3-4; cf. Gal 4:4-5). His human, "fleshly" (in Paul's sense) identity is the place where he does for Adamic humanity that which Adamic humanity could not do for itself. Verse 3 thus looks ahead to 5:12-21 and all the elements of chaps. 6–8 that follow from it. It is also evoked by 9:5, which, as we shall see, restates a very similar two-part christology, making it the ground plan of the argument of chaps. 9–11: Jesus is Israel's Messiah according to the flesh and is also (now at last explicitly) "God over all, blessed for ever."

Although, therefore, "according to the flesh" carries negative connotations, Paul is not denying or playing down Jesus' physical Davidic descent and Jewish Messiahship. They are part of God's saving plan. But, as Paul knew, Jesus' public career and horrible fate had been very different from that expected of a Messiah. We know of several other messianic movements in first-century Judaism, and none of them looked like this—though many of them ended up equally horribly and were thereby shown up as false, as non-messianic.[28]

One still frequently meets the suggestion that the pre-Christian Paul rejected Jesus' Messiahship for purely theological reasons—e.g., that Jesus had been crucified and was, therefore, according to Deuteronomy, cursed by God. This proposal comes from a milieu where "history of ideas" has ousted history itself. A crucified Messiah was a failed Messiah; no first-century Jew would have needed theological exegesis of a particular text in order to make that point. The Messiah had a task: to rebuild or cleanse the Temple, to defeat the pagans, to rescue Israel and bring God's justice to the world. Anyone who died without accomplishing these things, particularly one who attacked the Temple and died at the hands of the pagans he should have been defeating, leaving Israel unredeemed and the world still unjust, was obviously not the true Messiah. This is why it took something utterly extraordinary to make anyone suppose that Jesus was in fact the Messiah. Paul is clear: It was the resurrection that marked Jesus out as "son of God" (v. 4). The resurrection reversed the verdict that all thoughtful first-century Jews would have passed on Jesus at the time of his crucifixion. If such a Messiah could not be fitted in to existing conceptions of what Israel's God was supposed to be doing, that was too bad. The existing conceptions would have to be rethought around him. That, indeed, was the intellectual dimension of Paul's lifework.

Jesus was declared to be son of God "in power." This phrase seems to refer both to the power of God that raised Jesus from the dead (see 1 Cor 6:14; 15:24, 43; 2 Cor 13:4; Eph 1:19-20; Phil 3:10) and that thereby declared his identity as Messiah, and to the powerful nature of his sonship, through which he confronts all the powers of the world, up to and including death itself, with

---

28. On other messianic and similar movements, see N. T. Wright, *The New Testament and the People of God,* vol. 1 of *Christian Origins and the Question of God* (London: SPCK; Minneapolis: Fortress, 1992) 307-20; and *Jesus and the Victory of God,* vol. 2 of *Christian Origins and the Question of God* (London: SPCK, 1996) 481-86.

the news of a different and more effective type of power altogether. Paul, of course, sees this same power at work now, by the Spirit, through the proclamation of the gospel and in the lives of those who are "in the Messiah" (see, e.g., 1:16; 11:23; 15:13; 1 Cor 1:24; 2:4-5).

Balancing "according to the flesh" in v. 3 is "according to the spirit of holiness" in v. 4. This apparent semitism ("Spirit of holiness" for "Holy Spirit") is unique, lending some further weight to the suggestion of a pre-Pauline formula—which would, nevertheless, thereby include the characteristically Pauline flesh/spirit antithesis. It is just conceivable that Paul intends to mark, by this phrase, the difference between the Spirit by whom Jesus was raised from the dead and the Spirit, now to be known as the Spirit of Jesus, who dwells in the hearts of believers. Even though these are ultimately the same Spirit, there are two different stages of operation. The point is that, for Paul, God raised Jesus from the dead by the power of the Spirit (see 8:11), in line with scriptural promises that attributed to the breath, wind, or Spirit of God the promised new life on the other side of death, and more particularly the new hope for exiled and desolate Israel (Ezek 37:5, 9-10, 14; Joel 3:1-5; the same Hebrew word [רוח *rûaḥ*] stands for "breath," "wind," and "spirit"; so too with the Greek πνεῦμα [*pneuma*]). This formulation, therefore, provides further grounding for Paul's coming description of God's rescue, in the Messiah, of the old, fleshly humanity and God's constitution, in the Messiah, of the new humanity, "who walk not according to the flesh but according to the spirit" (8:4). This contrast has nothing to do with that dualism that denies or downgrades human physicality. The spirit was, after all, responsible in Paul's view for Jesus' bodily resurrection. Rather, it has to do with the direction of a person's life, in both senses: the question of who is directing it and the question of which route it is taking.

The spirit thus marked out Jesus as son of God "by the resurrection of the dead." The word "dead" is plural in the Greek. The NIV reads "his resurrection," which obscures the point; for Paul the Jew, "the resurrection" was something that would happen at the end, when all God's people would be raised to life together. What had happened to Jesus, Paul believed, was the bringing forward into the present of this general resurrection,

in one particular case, which still belonged organically to, and anticipated, the total "resurrection of the dead" (cf. 1 Cor 15:20-22; and see the Commentary on 6:9). This is important for understanding Paul in general and Romans in particular: Paul saw the event of Easter as the start and foretaste of God's long-promised new age, "the age to come" that he and many other Jews had been expecting.[29] The resurrection told Paul not only who Jesus was (the Messiah), but also what time it was (the start of the "age to come").

Paul's initial summary of the gospel is rounded off with Jesus' full Pauline title: "Jesus, Messiah, our Lord." "Jesus" for Paul regularly refers to the human being, Jesus of Nazareth, now risen and exalted but still the same human Jesus. When Paul writes "Christ," he still means "Messiah," the one in whom Israel's destiny is summed up and brought to proper fulfillment; the word is on its way to being a name (denoting Jesus but no longer connoting Messiahship), but it has not reached that point in Paul. "Lord" expresses both the exalted humanity of Jesus, including his superior position to all other "lords" in the world, and the sometimes explicit ascription of divinity. This is seen most clearly when Paul, speaking of Jesus, quotes passages from the LXX where "Lord" (κύριος *kyrios*) stands, as he well knew, for "YHWH," the divine name (e.g., Rom 10:13). The possessive pronoun "our" is not a way of limiting the sphere of Jesus' lordship, but of giving explicit allegiance to the one who is, for Paul, lord of the whole world, supreme over all others.

This, then, is Paul's shorthand summary of "the gospel of God." Despite the unusual diction of these verses, their meaning is not only consonant with his theological views of Jesus but is closely tied to the letter's developing line of thought. Note that for Paul "the gospel" is not a system of salvation, a message first and foremost about how human beings get saved. It is an announcement about Jesus, the Messiah, the Lord.[30]

**1:5.** The shorthand summary complete, Paul returns to his introduction of himself and his vocation. Through this Jesus, Paul has received "grace

---

29. On which see Wright, *The New Testament and the People of God,* 299-300, with other references there.

30. Moo's insistence, *Romans,* 51, that "the gospel cannot be understood without reference to the person of Christ," while true, implies that "the gospel" itself is something other than the proclamation of Jesus as Lord.

and apostleship" (possibly a hendiadys—two words used to express one idea—meaning, "the grace of apostleship") with a particular purpose: to call the ἔθνη (ethnē, "nations"), the Gentiles, into covenant relationship with the one God of Israel so that the name of Jesus might be glorified throughout the world (cf. Mal 1:5, 14).

The shorthand expression he uses to describe this relationship is "the obedience of faith." It is possible that by this dense phrase he means, as in the NIV, "the obedience that comes from faith," but it is much more likely that he means "the obedience which consists in faith."[31] "Obedience" is a more prominent theme in Romans than elsewhere in the NT (elsewhere in Paul only in 2 Cor 7:15; 10:5-6; Phlm 21). It serves as a shorthand both for the total work of Jesus the Messiah, over against that of Adam (5:19), and as the sphere or realm into which, or under the rule of which, Christians come through baptism (6:12-17). Paul can again use it as a summary of that which he seeks to bring about among the nations (15:18; cf. 16:19) and in a concluding formula that closely echoes this opening one (16:26; on the textual status of this verse see the Commentary on 16:25-27).

What overtones should we hear in this dense phrase? "Obedience" in Greek is ὑπακοή (hypakoē, a compound from the verb ἀκούω akouō, "hear"). Regularly in the LXX it translates שׁמע (šamaʿ), which carries not only the meaning "hear and obey," but also the connotation, emphasized in the regular Jewish daily prayer, of personal covenant obligations: "Hear, O Israel, YHWH our God, YHWH is one; and you shall love YHWH your God" (Deut 6:4-5). To bring the nations into "obedience" would therefore mean to bring them into the family of this one God. The fact that Paul refers explicitly to the Shema prayer at the very point when he is saying just this (3:29-30) is a further indication that this train of thought is in his mind, albeit here expressed in very compact form.

Of course, the actual notion of "obedience"—doing what one is told—is itself important. Generations of theologians have worried whether this emphasis on obedience, so early in a letter supposedly about "justification by faith alone," does not suggest the priority of good moral works

rather than pure faith.[32] Such anxiety misses the point. When Paul thinks of Jesus as Lord, he thinks of himself as a slave and of the world as being called to obedience to Jesus' lordship. His apostolic commission is not to offer people a new religious option, but to summon them to allegiance to Jesus, which will mean abandoning other loyalties. The gospel issues a command, an imperial summons; the appropriate response is obedience.

The "obedience" Paul seeks to evoke when he announces the gospel is thus not a list of moral good works but faith. Faith, as Paul explains later (10:9), consists in confessing Jesus as Lord (thereby renouncing other lords) and in believing that God raised Jesus from the dead (thereby abandoning other worldviews in which such things did or could not happen, or not to Jesus; cf. too 4:23-25). This faith is actually the human faithfulness that answers to God's faithfulness. As we will discover in chap. 3, that is why this "faith" is the only appropriate badge of membership within God's true, renewed people. Despite the anxieties of some, therefore, that Paul is undermining his own doctrine of "justification by faith" before he has even stated it, v. 5 really does look ahead to Paul's exposition of justification, even though it places that theme in a rather different context from that which some expositors have assumed.

**1:6-7.** Paul has now drawn a miniature map of God's purpose, revealed in Jesus the Messiah, proclaimed in the apostolic gospel. To this he adds a pointer: "you are here."[33] The church in Rome, predominantly Gentile, though now once again including some Jews (see the Introduction), is included among those who have given allegiance, "the obedience which consists in faith," to the gospel of Jesus. They are, therefore, literally "called of Jesus Christ." As the translations (e.g., the NIV) suggest, this can be expanded as "called to belong to Jesus Christ," but we should not thereby place the emphasis on "belong" at the expense of "called." For Paul, the "call" was God's powerful word, creating new life—creating, indeed, the response it sought, as a word of love is always capable of doing. And it is to the love of

31. C. E. B. Cranfield, *A Critical and Exegetical Commentary on the Epistle to the Romans,* ICC, 2 vols. (Edinburgh: T. & T. Clark, 1975) 66, sets out various options. See also Moo, *Romans,* 51-53.

32. This anxiety has left its mark in the NIV and in Fitzmyer's translation "commitment." See Joseph A. Fitzmyer, *Romans,* AB 33 (Garden City, N.Y.: Doubleday, 1993) 237.

33. The words "in Rome" in 1:7, and also in 1:15, are missing in a few MSS, no doubt because the letter was copied and circulated to a wider audience at an early date.

God that Paul now appeals, not for the last time: "God's beloved in Rome," he labels the church, "called to be saints." Both of these phrases, while carrying their own echoes of love and holiness, look back inevitably to the status of God's people in the past, the people whom Paul sees as now renewed and expanded so as to include believing Gentiles as well as Jews.

The greeting that follows, after this densely packed introduction of Paul and his gospel, is straightforward, though this should not deceive us into treating it lightly. "Grace" and "peace" are two of Paul's greatest words for God's gift in the

Messiah. The former reaches out to those currently in rebellion; the latter gives them the central covenant blessing. And, consonant with the gospel itself, Paul couples "the Lord Jesus Messiah" with "God our Father" as the source of these gifts. The latter phrase, too, is clearly rooted in the OT, indicating that Paul is claiming for himself and his readers the status of Israel before God—indicating, too, in the light of the gospel, that the people of God are to be seen as siblings of the firstborn son (8:29). (See Reflections at 1:16-17.)

## Romans 1:8-15, Paul's Desire to Come to Rome

### NIV

[8]First, I thank my God through Jesus Christ for all of you, because your faith is being reported all over the world. [9]God, whom I serve with my whole heart in preaching the gospel of his Son, is my witness how constantly I remember you [10]in my prayers at all times; and I pray that now at last by God's will the way may be opened for me to come to you.

[11]I long to see you so that I may impart to you some spiritual gift to make you strong— [12]that is, that you and I may be mutually encouraged by each other's faith. [13]I do not want you to be unaware, brothers, that I planned many times to come to you (but have been prevented from doing so until now) in order that I might have a harvest among you, just as I have had among the other Gentiles.

[14]I am obligated both to Greeks and non-Greeks, both to the wise and the foolish. [15]That is why I am so eager to preach the gospel also to you who are at Rome.

### NRSV

[8]First, I thank my God through Jesus Christ for all of you, because your faith is proclaimed throughout the world. [9]For God, whom I serve with my spirit by announcing the gospel[a] of his Son, is my witness that without ceasing I remember you always in my prayers, [10]asking that by God's will I may somehow at last succeed in coming to you. [11]For I am longing to see you so that I may share with you some spiritual gift to strengthen you— [12]or rather so that we may be mutually encouraged by each other's faith, both yours and mine. [13]I want you to know, brothers and sisters,[b] that I have often intended to come to you (but thus far have been prevented), in order that I may reap some harvest among you as I have among the rest of the Gentiles. [14]I am a debtor both to Greeks and to barbarians, both to the wise and to the foolish [15]— hence my eagerness to proclaim the gospel to you also who are in Rome.

[a] Gk *my spirit in the gospel*    [b] Gk *brothers*

## COMMENTARY

This section actually runs on without a break into the next one (vv. 16-17). Since, however, the latter forms such a crucial summary of the whole letter, it will be better to treat it separately.

As usual, Paul follows his introduction with a report of the prayer he offers for the recipients.

The formal style does not indicate mere formality. Paul's writing is set in the context of an ongoing ministry of prayer, and if he had to choose between praying and writing, he would have regarded prayer as more important. Here he reports his regular thanksgivings for the faith of the Roman church and his unceasing prayer that he might be able to visit them. This passes naturally into a further statement of his own apostolic vocation, amplifying what has already been said in vv. 1, 5 and explaining further his desire to come to Rome. This in turn leads to his summary of the letter's thesis in vv. 16-17.

**1:8-12.** Hyperbole it may be, but it is still no mean thing to say that the faith of the Roman church was proclaimed "in all the world." Presumably this means that travelers known to Paul, not least Jewish Christians who had had to leave Rome under Claudius, were reporting the arrival in the capital of this strange new sect, neither ethnically Jewish (all the Christians in Rome for five years being Gentiles) nor pagan. There is unlikely to be a particular reason why he stresses their "faith" here, rather than, say, obedience (as in 16:19) or love (as in Col 1:8). What matters is that they are an authentic Christian congregation, for whom Paul thanks God through Jesus the Messiah (another formula that is hardly a formality). Paul often speaks of his "unceasing" prayers, referring probably to his keeping of regular times of prayer each day, though not excluding the sense of being "in prayer" at all times, standing in the presence of God with the churches on his heart and mind.

He calls God to witness to this in a somewhat strange phrase (v. 9). Although regularly translated as "whom I serve with my spirit by announcing the gospel" (it is unclear why the NIV has "whole heart" for "spirit"), the verb in question (λατρεύω *latreuō*), when it has a divine being as its object, regularly means "worship." The thought is not so much that Paul performs service for God by announcing the gospel, but that Paul *worships* God in his spirit (cf. Phil 3:3; there may be an implied contrast with the temple cult, with its geographical focus and physical activity), and that he does so "in the gospel" (the literal translation), either in the sense that his announcing of the gospel constitutes in itself an act of worship or in the sense that he worships the God he sees revealed in "the gospel of his son" (i.e., as in v. 3, the gospel concerning the son of God).

Paul's primary request, in these constant prayers, has not been so much for the growth in Christian character of the Roman church, as we might have expected, but that he will be able, in God's good time, to visit them. However, the ultimate purpose remains similar: He hopes to be able to impart "some spiritual gift" to strengthen them. Speculation about what he had in mind in this cryptic phrase should be quickly put to rest by v. 12, which may be intended to preempt any suggestion that the Roman church, founded by someone other than Paul, was lacking anything basic in its status as a Christian community. Paul's hope is simply for the mutual encouragement that comes from meeting and sharing in fellowship with others who have the same faith (Paul expands this further in 15:14-29).

**1:13-15.** "I do not want you to be unaware." Paul's slightly heavy-handed double negative indicates caution. This springs, we may guess, from his anxiety about building on someone else's foundation (cf. 15:20). He is facing the implicit question, "Why would you, a pioneer evangelist, want to come to a place where a church already exists?" To this his answer is twofold, in both cases presenting a personal appeal.[34]

First, he has been eager to come for a long time, so that he can "reap some harvest among you, as among the other nations" (v. 13). Since there were at this time probably not more than a few dozen, or at most a couple of hundred, Christians in a city of roughly a million, this would not indicate a lack of confidence in the Roman church's own evangelistic performance or prospects. Anyway, so far his eagerness has come to nothing. "I have been prevented" may indicate a sense that God has not permitted it or perhaps that Satan has hindered it, or even both. (The Corinthian correspondence indicates well enough how Paul's plans could be thwarted; see, e.g., 2 Cor 1:15-19.) Either way, he remains undeterred.

Second, Paul's commission places him under obligation, not just to God, but to all categories of non-Jewish humanity, Greeks and barbarians, wise and foolish (v. 14). He does not mean that they have done something for him for which he owes them a return, but simply that God has entrusted him with a message for them; until he has

---

34. It is noteworthy that he here, unusually in Romans, addresses them as ἀδελφοί (*adelphoi*). The Greek word would be understood to embrace both genders (brothers and sisters); "siblings" performs this function, but is sufficiently rare in common usage to be inappropriate. "Family" is perhaps our best equivalent. "Friends," though a common alternative today, is inadequate, not least in our world of casual friendships, to express the intimacy and mutual belonging that *adelphoi* would carry for Paul and his readers.

discharged this commission he is still, in that sense, in their debt, retaining in his possession something that properly belongs to them. Thus, even though there may already be a church in Rome, his sense of obligation includes that city

also (v. 15). This double reason is presented as a personal desire and obligation, appealing to the Roman Christians as fellow Christians, members of the same family (cf. Gal 4:12-20 for a similarly personal appeal). (See Reflections at 1:16-17.)

## Romans 1:16-17, The Gospel Unveils God's Righteousness

**NIV**

[16]I am not ashamed of the gospel, because it is the power of God for the salvation of everyone who believes: first for the Jew, then for the Gentile. [17]For in the gospel a righteousness from God is revealed, a righteousness that is by faith from first to last,[a] just as it is written: "The righteous will live by faith."[b]

[a] 17 Or is from faith to faith      [b] 17 Hab. 2:4

**NRSV**

16For I am not ashamed of the gospel; it is the power of God for salvation to everyone who has faith, to the Jew first and also to the Greek. [17]For in it the righteousness of God is revealed through faith for faith; as it is written, "The one who is righteous will live by faith."[a]

[a] Or The one who is righteous through faith will live

## COMMENTARY

This brings us to the great statement of the letter's theme, which is noted in the Introduction. Paul offers it as the further explanation of his desire to come to Rome and announce the gospel there. It consists of an opening statement and two successive explanations, backed up with a scriptural quotation. This style of arguing, with clauses linked by the word "for" (γάρ *gar*), is characteristic of many passages in Romans and elsewhere. Frequently the final explanatory clause expresses the deepest thing Paul wishes to say: A is so because B; B is so because C; C is so because D; and D is thus the foundation of the whole sequence. This is undoubtedly the pattern here.[35]

**1:16.** Just as King Herod looms over much of the Gospel narratives, so also Caesar, the Roman emperor, looms unmentioned over several passages in Paul's works. Caesar was the current lord of the world, whose position was by implication challenged and threatened by the Jewish Messiah, who claimed the same role. To come to Rome with the gospel of Jesus, to announce someone

else's accession to the world's throne, therefore, was to put on a red coat and walk into a field with a potentially angry bull. (This proposal might seem to be in tension with 13:1-7, but see the commentary there).

Paul is determined not to shrink from this calling; he is "not ashamed of the gospel." There may be a hint here of the tradition of Jesus' words to the disciples about people being ashamed of him (Mark 8:38 and par.). The explanation (*gar*) for Paul's not being ashamed is not simply that he is a brazen optimist, marching cheerfully toward danger while sensible people are fleeing in the opposite direction. The explanation is that the gospel, this message about Jesus that he has outlined in vv. 3-4, is itself God's power. It not merely "possesses" God's power or "is accompanied by" God's power but simply *is* God's power. Paul has discovered in practice, in city after city, that announcing the good news—that there is one God who now claims the world as his own through the crucified and risen Jesus—is in itself powerful and that the power is all God's (cf. 1 Cor 2:4-5; 1 Thess 1:5).

Paul, as so often, has expressed this point in such a way as to evoke a biblical tradition. "In thee, O Lord, do I put my trust," says the psalmist; "let me never be ashamed, deliver me in thy righ-

35. The NIV omits the first "for" at the start of v. 16; the NRSV, the second one. Paul is eager to preach in Rome, *for* he is not ashamed, *for* the gospel is God's power, *for* in it God's righteousness is unveiled, *as it is written.* Paul's little connecting words regularly indicate the way his mind is working.

teousness" (Ps 71:1-2; cf. Pss 31:1-3; 143:1; Psalm 71 continues to emphasize the same theme in vv. 15-16, 19, 24, by which time it is the psalmist's opponents who are "ashamed," while he continues to speak of God's righteousness). "Shame" in such a context is what God's people feel when their enemies are triumphing; it is what Israel (and many other peoples) felt in Paul's day, suffering at the hands of Rome. The gospel, and the power it carries, enables Paul to share the position of the psalmist, celebrating God's righteousness and so remaining unashamed in the face of enemies and gainsayers.[36]

The power unleashed within the gospel message is "for salvation." "Salvation" is another of those "Christian" technical terms, like "son of God," for which most readers today assume a particular meaning that is actually a much later development. Paul's readers had not had the dubious benefit of expositions of "salvation" that focused simply on the state of post-mortem bliss enjoyed by the redeemed in a more or less disembodied "heaven." Of course, Paul's view of God's saving purposes included, as we shall see, the belief that death itself was now a defeated enemy; his doctrine of salvation was in that sense ultimate, not merely penultimate. It had to do, not merely with rescue from evils in the present life, but with rescue from ultimate destruction. But the context of meaning remained Jewish, and in that setting "salvation" had far more to do with the rescue of Israel from pagan oppression, from Egypt or Babylon or, now, Rome, than with "life after death." Insofar as Romans 5–8 expound Paul's theology of "salvation," it is of the utmost importance to note that the climax of that passage is the redemption of creation itself. If we are right to hear all these overtones, we will also hear in this word, in the present context, a mention of that benefit that Caesar was supposed to give to his loyal followers. As in Phil 3:20-21, Jesus turns out to be the reality of which Caesar is the parody. Just as there is only one "lord of the world," so also in the last analysis there is only one "savior."[37]

The salvation in question is "for everyone who believes." Paul will explain the significance of Christian faith in chap. 3, and further explanation will be deferred to that point. Here as there, however, part of the point of faith is that it is open to all, "to the Jew first and also to the Greek." Paul has expressed this in such a way as to insist both upon the temporal primacy of the Jew within the purposes of God ("to the Jew first," corresponding to the Messiah's mission to "the circumcised" in 15:8) and the absolute equality of status now granted to the non-Jew ("Greek" here is a way of saying "Gentile").[38] If faith is a major theme in Romans, so is the equality under the gospel of what, from the Jewish point of view, are the two great divisions of humankind. These themes, as we shall see, are inseparable. Every word, every phrase in the second half of v. 16 supports the first half; that is to say, the whole clause governed by the second "for" in the verse ("for it is God's power to salvation for all believers, Jew first but equally Greek") explains why Paul is not ashamed of the gospel.

**1:17.** The third "for," undergirding the other two, goes to the heart of the matter, explaining in turn every aspect of v. 16b. In the gospel, God's righteousness is unveiled. This revelation happens, not just in the events referred to in the gospel, true though that is, but in the very announcement of the gospel. The death and resurrection of Jesus the Messiah form the initial disclosure of God's righteousness, the major apocalyptic event that burst upon an unsuspecting world and an uncomprehending Israel; now the apocalypse happens again, every time the message about Jesus is announced, as God's righteousness is unveiled before another audience.

The gospel message about Jesus, in other words, opens people's eyes to see for the first time that *this was what God had been up to all along.* It enables Jews to see how the promises they had cherished had been fulfilled, quite otherwise than they had expected. It enables Gentiles to see that there is one true God, the God of Israel, the creator; that this God has purposed to set the world to rights at last; and that this God has now in principle accomplished that purpose. And when we

36. See R. B. Hays, *Echoes of Scripture in the Letters of Paul* (New Haven: Yale University Press, 1989) 38-39, suggesting other parallels, e.g., Isa 50:7-8.

37. See N. T. Wright, "Paul's Gospel and Caesar's Empire," in Richard A. Horsely, ed., *Paul and Politics: Ekklesia, Israel, Imperium, Interpretation: Essays in Honor of Krister Stendahl* (Harrisburg, Pa.: Trinity, 2000) 160-83.

38. See esp. C. E. B. Cranfield, *A Critical and Exegetical Commentary on the Epistle to the Romans*, ICC, 2 vols. (Edinburgh: T. & T. Clark, 1975) 90-91.

say "enables to see," we should not think merely of propositions commanding intellectual assent. Paul believed that the announcement of the gospel wielded a power that overcame the unseen forces, inside people and around them, that prevented them from responding in obedient belief and allegiance (see 2 Cor 4:1-6).

It is important to note that the NIV translation ("a righteousness from God is revealed") presupposes what I argued in the Introduction to be the wrong understanding of the phrase. Instead of God's own righteousness, it suggests that Paul is referring here to the status that Christians have as a result of God's justifying action. Although this is a possible meaning of the Greek, there is no warrant for it in Paul's Jewish background; it makes the reading of 3:21-26 very problematic; and it effectively splits off other sections of Romans, notably chaps. 9–11, from the early chapters, since in 9–11 the questions Paul is addressing are precisely those summarized in Jewish literature by the notion of God's own righteousness.

God's righteousness is revealed "through faith to faith" (NRSV). By itself this is too dense and cryptic for a modern reader to be certain of its meaning. As it stands, the phrase could mean "by faith from first to last" (NIV) or one of a number of other options.[39] But in the light of 3:21-22 and other passages, its most natural meaning is "from God's faithfulness to human faithfulness."[40] When God's action in fulfillment of the covenant is unveiled, it is because God is faithful to what has been promised; when it is received, it is received by that human faith that answers to the revelation of God in Jesus Christ, that human faith that is also faith*fulness* to the call of God in Jesus the Messiah.

Paul finishes the summary statement by quoting Hab 2:4, "the righteous shall live by faith." This innocent-looking quotation has generated enormous discussions. These have to do with the apparent shifts in meaning between the original Hebrew text ("the righteous shall live by his faithfulness"), the LXX ("the righteous shall live by my faithfulness"), and Paul's own quotation ("the righteous shall live by faith[fulness]"), and also with two particular questions: Does "by faith" modify "live" or "righteous" and where, therefore, does the emphasis fall—"the righteous shall live *by faith*" or "the one who by faith is righteous *shall have life*"? And how does Paul intend the quotation to support what has gone before? All these matters, obviously, interlock.[41]

We should avoid a minimalist solution on the last question. Some have suggested that Paul merely ransacked his mental concordance for passages in which "righteousness" and "faith" occurred side by side, came up with this passage and Gen 15:6, and proceeded to quote them in Romans 1 and 4 (and in Galatians 3) without regard for their original context and meaning. His general use of Scripture and the particular sense of this passage and of Galatians 3 indicate otherwise. We need to inquire as to the wider context of the original sentence and the echoes Paul may have intended alert readers to hear.[42]

The original passage in Habakkuk belongs within a book full of woe and puzzlement. The Chaldeans are marching against Israel; all seems lost. What is Israel's God up to in allowing it? This is, once more, the question of the righteousness, or justice, of God (this alone should warn us off the idea that Paul was quoting at random a verse that merely happened to contain his two catchwords). By way of answer, the prophet is given a vision, but it is a vision for the future, to be revealed at a later date (Hab 2:3). At the moment God's true people, the righteous within a sinful nation, "will live by faith." "Faith" here, whether the human faith, as in the Hebrew text, or God's faithfulness, as in the LXX, is the key feature of the interim period.

What does this mean in practice for the prophet? It means believing that God will eventually punish the idolatrous and violent nation (2:5-20), that God will remember mercy in the midst of

---

39. See, e.g., Schelkle who, following Augustine, sees 1:17 as describing a transference from faith in the law to faith in the gospel. For Cranfield, *Romans*, 99-100, the phrase is a rhetorical way of saying "completely by faith." See also Moo, *Romans*, 76.

40. ἐκ πίστεως . . . εἰς πίστιν (*ek pisteōs . . . eis pistin*) in 1:17 corresponds quite closely to διὰ . . . πίστεως εἰς πάντας τοὺς πιστεύοντας (*dia pisteōs . . . eis pantas tous pisteuontas*) in 3:22 (see also Gal 3:22). For this interpretation, see James D. G. Dunn, *Romans 1–8*, WBC 38A (Dallas: Word, 1988).

41. On these questions see the detailed analysis of Rikki E. Watts, " 'For I Am Not Ashamed of the Gospel': Romans 1:16-17 and Habbakuk 2:4," in *Romans and the People of God: Essays in Honor of Gordon D. Fee on the Occasion of His 65th Birthday*, ed. S. K. Soderlund and N. T. Wright (Grand Rapids: Eerdmans, 1999) 3-15.

42. On such echoes, deliberate or otherwise, see above all Hays, *Echoes of Scripture in the Letters of Paul*, 39-41. Moo, *Romans*, 77-78, seems to miss the thematic connections between Habakkuk and what Paul is here talking about.

wrath and bring salvation to Israel (3:2-19). This thematic parallel with Rom 1:18–3:20 and 3:21–4:25 is striking and continues to suggest that Paul does, indeed, have the larger context from Habakkuk in mind. Faced with pagan idolatry and arrogance, the devout first-century Jew longed for God's righteousness to break forth, bringing wrath on the nations and salvation for Israel.[43] Paul, however, has seen God's purpose unveiled in the gospel and believes, like the prophet, that this vision is the key to understanding all that will now take place. This solution to the problem of first-century Israel produces a second-order problem: Much of ethnic Israel is failing to believe the gospel, while Gentiles are coming in in droves. Paul will deal with that in due course. For the moment he contents himself with the cryptic, but evocative, quotation. He is not ashamed of the gospel, because it is God's power to salvation for all believers; because, faced with a world in idolatry and ruin, God's righteousness is revealed in the gospel, a matter of divine faithfulness reaching down and calling out the response of human faithfulness. In this setting, "the righteous shall live by faithfulness"; whether divine or human or both, Paul does not need to say. The sentence remains cryptic until we reach 3:21–4:25.

43. On the use of Hab 2:4 in this context in Second Temple Judaism, see A. Strobel, *Untersuchungen zum eschatologischen Verzögerungsproblem, auf Grund der spätjüdisch-urchristlichen Geschichte von Habakuk 2,2 ff.,* NovTSup 2 (Leiden: Brill, 1961).

Part of the strength of this exegesis of v. 17 is the sense it makes of the transition to v. 18, which has long been a puzzle to students of Paul's flow of thought. But before moving to the next section of the letter, a word is needed about the road we have traveled thus far.

Romans has been thought of for centuries as the letter in which Paul expounds his doctrine of "justification by faith." This half-truth has opened up some aspects of the letter and concealed others. As will become clear, the theological content of this substantial opening section contains "justification by faith" within it by implication, but this is not the stated theme of the letter. The theme is, to repeat once more, the revelation of God's righteousness, God's covenant faithfulness, God's justice, in and through the gospel proclamation of the crucified and risen Messiah. Like the two opening themes of a classical sonata, Paul's summary of "the gospel" in 1:3-4 and his summary of "God's righteousness" in 1:16-17 will do further business with each other as the work progresses, and their contrapuntal interweaving will support other tunes, other harmonic progressions. But this letter has announced itself as a treatment, not so much of humans, their plight and their rescue (though all of that has its proper place), but of God—God's gospel, God's righteousness. We will not understand Romans unless we grasp this from the outset and remember it throughout.

# REFLECTIONS

**1.** Despite the many surface differences between Paul's world and ours, we, too, live in an age where the question of God's righteousness, God's justice, weighs heavy upon us. The wars and atrocities of the twentieth century have left major questions in the air: How can a good God allow such things? Where was God in Auschwitz? Where is God in Rwanda? In the Balkans? Where was God on September 11, 2001? It is now the world as a whole, not simply the Jewish people, that cries out for redemption, that recognizes increasingly the folly and dehumanization of idolatry, and that asks Habakkuk's questions of "Why?" and "How long?"

Our own setting, therefore, enables us to appropriate Paul's discussion of God's righteousness, here and throughout the letter, with a sense of the coming together of "covenant faithfulness" and "justice." If God is the creator of the world, and has promised to bring all things into justice, peace, and harmony, then the cosmos as a whole, and the human race within it, is called to believe in this justice and the faithfulness that will bring it about. The church's ministry to the world in our generation includes, and perhaps even focuses upon, this task: to unveil God's righteousness once more through the gospel of Jesus, the Jewish Messiah, knowing that as this happens the power of God for salvation is unleashed, so that where there is faith the blessings of God's future may be brought forward into the present.

**2.** "The gospel," in Paul's terminology, was not primarily a message about sinful human beings and how they attained justification and salvation. We can, of course, use words however we wish, but if we are to understand and appropriate Paul we will do well to use his words in his way. For him, "the gospel" was the sovereign message, from none other than God, concerning Jesus the Messiah, God's unique son. This message was not simply the offer of a new reordering of one's private spiritual interiority, a new clearing up of a morally dysfunctional life via forgiveness for the past and new moral energy for the present. It was not simply a new vocation to live for God and for others in the world. It was, rather, news about God and about Jesus; news that this Jesus had become the spearhead of God's "age to come"; news that, within this new age, the principalities and powers, including earthly rulers, the powers of darkness, and sin and death themselves had been defeated and were now summoned to allegiance. "The gospel" was a command requiring obedience, much more than an invitation seeking a response.

Always the command comes out of the blue, unexpected and in many ways unwelcome. Paul's contemporary Jews neither expected nor wanted a crucified Messiah. Paul's contemporary Gentiles neither expected nor wanted to worship and serve a Jewish figure, still less a Jewish failure (cf. 1 Cor 1:18–2:5). Our own contemporaries, long schooled to regard the climax of world history as having occurred in Western Europe in the eighteenth century (giving birth, of course, to modern North America), neither expect nor want to hear that the true climax in fact occurred in Palestine in the first century CE. They will urge counterexamples: Surely the world has not in fact improved (did Paul say it had or would?); surely Christianity has been responsible for many great evils (in part, yes, though often demonstrably when in rebellion against the gospel itself); surely we now know that Christianity is untrue (actually, no, we don't). These objections must be taken seriously; yet they may also be smoke screens to hide the fact that the grandiose claims of "modernity" are now themselves looking increasingly threadbare. The command of the gospel is a summons to give the allegiance of body and mind, heart and soul, to Jesus; and its basis is neither more nor less than the event that constituted him in Paul's eyes as Messiah and Lord—namely, his resurrection. And it is in the proclamation of this gospel, and its acceptance in faith, that people begin to glimpse a great curtain being drawn aside and the covenant faithfulness and justice of God displayed to view. Faced with that sight, it is impossible to remain a mere spectator.

**3.** Paul's self-portrait and personal introduction in these verses is both stark and subtle. Content to be defined simply by the gospel—think how much of his personal history and background he could have mentioned here, as he prepares to visit the senior city of the empire, but chooses not to—he presents himself as a slave bearing a commission from royalty. At the same time, he will not simply barge in upon the Roman church, relying on his God-given commission to give him the necessary status. He will pray for them, thank God for them, and in that context think into their possible anxieties about his coming and meet them with a personal appeal. Conscious of the biblical story, stretching ahead into his own time and catching him up within it (see the Commentary on 9:6–10:21), he is also very aware of the human stories with which his own personal story must intertwine. His prayer functions not least as a way of ensuring, so far as he can, that these stories will work together in harmony.

**4.** Already in these opening verses we find a major theme that creates huge problems in our world, and for practicing Christians. How, we ask, can the gospel message be for both Jew and non-Jew? We stand appalled at the incalculable crimes committed against Jews in our supposedly civilized world. Many feel, understandably, that for Christians to say any word to Jews about the gospel of Jesus Christ is now inappropriate. I have wrestled with these questions elsewhere and will revisit them more than once in what follows.[44] But it is impossible to suppose that Paul, for whom Jesus' Messiahship was the central content of the gospel and for whom the Jewish question of God's righteousness had in principle been addressed and solved precisely by Jesus' messianic death and resurrection, would have been content to keep this gospel only for non-Jews. Time was when the nuances of justification by faith aroused passions around the world; these days it tends to be the political overtones of the gospel that make people angry. But these issues cannot be easily either solved or wished away, and Romans remains one of the great stimuli and sourcebooks for dealing with them.

44. See N. T. Wright, *For All God's Worth* (Grand Rapids: Eerdmans, 1997) chap. 13.

# ROMANS 1:18–3:20, THE CHALLENGE FOR GOD'S RIGHTEOUSNESS: GENTILES AND JEWS ALIKE UNDER GOD'S WRATH, GUILTY OF IDOLATRY AND WICKEDNESS

## OVERVIEW

The first major section of the letter is a courtroom scene. It opens with the sentence being passed; it moves back to explain the grounds for the verdict, highlights the problems the judge has had to cope with in hearing the case, and concludes with the guilty parties in the dock, with nothing to say in their defense.

Romans 1:18–3:20, in other words, is all about God's righteousness, both in the sense that God is the judge in the cosmic lawcourt and in the sense that God is in covenant with Israel, the covenant that causes the peculiar problems when Israel, too, is found guilty in God's sight. The whole section serves as a further explanation of 1:16-17; hence the γάρ (*gar,* "for") that links 1:18 to the previous passage (omitted in the NIV). In particular, 1:18–3:20 explains why the gospel is God's saving power for *all* who believe: because God's wrath is revealed against *all* ungodliness and wickedness (1:18), and it turns out that "all sinned, and came short of God's glory" (3:23, summing up 1:18–3:20). Apart from the gospel, there is no alternative route to salvation.

The section, though, is not simply about "the human plight." It is about God's own problem and gives a preliminary statement of God's way of dealing with it. God created humans to bear the divine image within the creation and called Israel to shine the divine light into the dark world. Faced with human rebellion and Jewish faithlessness, will God abandon these projects? This section repeatedly emphasizes that God will remain faithful, though it does not yet explain how—except that God's wrath means precisely the determination not to give evil the last word, to root out from the good creation all that defaces and destroys it. Already, therefore, we find ourselves looking ahead both to the end of chap. 8, with the renewal of humans and of creation, and to the end of chap. 11, when "all Israel shall be saved." It is because the creator God remains implacably opposed to all the forces of evil that there is hope. The revelation of wrath is itself, however paradoxically, part of the good news (see the Commentary on 2:16). As in Habakkuk, quoted in v. 17, the whole world is in turmoil, but God remains sovereign. This prepares the way for the solution: As in Habakkuk once more, God's people are defined, at this moment of crisis, in terms of faithfulness. The portion of the letter that begins with 1:18 does indeed explain and unpack what is implicit in the dense statement of 1:16-17.

Two elements of Paul's strategy throughout the section are worthy of note. First, he draws extensively on traditional Jewish critiques of the pagan world. This section, particularly the first long paragraph, echoes Wisdom 12–16, which, under the guise of describing the wickedness of the Canaanites and Egyptians at the time of the exodus, launches a polemic against paganism in general, describing it in terms of idolatry and the consequent fracturing of human society. Paul agrees with this assessment of paganism, but he goes further, and by doing so effectively undercuts Wisdom's eventual point. Wisdom argued that the Israelites, rebellious in the wilderness, escaped with punishments that served as a warning and a reminder of God's law (Wis 16:5-6, 10-11). Paul will not have it. The Jews, he declares, are just as guilty as the pagans; all alike end up in the dock (Rom 3:19-20).

Second, he argues his case by a process of gradual unfolding. At first sight, 1:18-32 seems to be directed solely against the Gentiles; but, as we shall see, at two points in particular he alludes to scriptural passages that suggest that Israel, too, has behaved in a pagan manner and will receive the appropriate reward. Then in 2:1-16 he seems to be aiming at the tradition of pagan moralism; but, not least with Wisdom in mind, it is reasonable to suppose that he is also thinking of the virtuous Jew (including his own pre-Christian self, of course), looking with disdain on the ungodly and dissolute pagan world. So when he turns explicitly to the boast of Israel in 2:17, only to deconstruct it from Scripture itself, he is bringing into the open what

has already been hinted. From then on the section focuses almost entirely on Israel: Israel failing in covenant obligations (2:17-24); Israel being upstaged by a new covenant family, which includes Gentiles (2:125-29); Israel joining the pagans in the dock (3:1-20).

A good deal of the material in 1:18–3:20 looks ahead to later passages in the letter. The devastation of humanness brought about by idolatry, described in chap. 1, is reversed through the gospel, as chaps. 4, 6, 8, and 12 bear witness. The covenant purposes of God for Israel, to which Israel was unfaithful, are fulfilled in the faithful Messiah (3:21-26; 5:12-21, and throughout). The exodus, the subtext of the Wisdom passage upon which Paul draws in 1:18-32, forms the subtext, too, of Paul's exposition of the new people of God in Christ in chaps. 5–8. Above all, the problem of God's righteousness, highlighted in the dense little argument of 3:1-8, looks ahead to the whole theme of chaps. 9–11, where Paul will draw on another image from Wisdom: the potter and the clay (Wis 15:7; cf. Wis 12:12; Rom 9:19-22). The present section, then, is far from being a mere exposé of human sinfulness. Within the architecture of the whole letter, it begins the construction of several great arches, which, having reached their various peaks in reference to Jesus the Messiah, come back to earth in the specific conclusions of the different stages of the argument.

# Romans 1:18-32, Idolatry and Dehumanized Behavior Resulting in God's Wrath

NIV

18The wrath of God is being revealed from heaven against all the godlessness and wickedness of men who suppress the truth by their wickedness, 19since what may be known about God is plain to them, because God has made it plain to them. 20For since the creation of the world God's invisible qualities—his eternal power and divine nature—have been clearly seen, being understood from what has been made, so that men are without excuse.

21For although they knew God, they neither glorified him as God nor gave thanks to him, but

NRSV

18For the wrath of God is revealed from heaven against all ungodliness and wickedness of those who by their wickedness suppress the truth. 19For what can be known about God is plain to them, because God has shown it to them. 20Ever since the creation of the world his eternal power and divine nature, invisible though they are, have been understood and seen through the things he has made. So they are without excuse; 21for though they knew God, they did not honor him as God or give thanks to him, but they became futile in their thinking, and their senseless minds were

NIV

their thinking became futile and their foolish hearts were darkened. [22]Although they claimed to be wise, they became fools [23]and exchanged the glory of the immortal God for images made to look like mortal man and birds and animals and reptiles.

[24]Therefore God gave them over in the sinful desires of their hearts to sexual impurity for the degrading of their bodies with one another. [25]They exchanged the truth of God for a lie, and worshiped and served created things rather than the Creator—who is forever praised. Amen.

[26]Because of this, God gave them over to shameful lusts. Even their women exchanged natural relations for unnatural ones. [27]In the same way the men also abandoned natural relations with women and were inflamed with lust for one another. Men committed indecent acts with other men, and received in themselves the due penalty for their perversion.

[28]Furthermore, since they did not think it worthwhile to retain the knowledge of God, he gave them over to a depraved mind, to do what ought not to be done. [29]They have become filled with every kind of wickedness, evil, greed and depravity. They are full of envy, murder, strife, deceit and malice. They are gossips, [30]slanderers, God-haters, insolent, arrogant and boastful; they invent ways of doing evil; they disobey their parents; [31]they are senseless, faithless, heartless, ruthless. [32]Although they know God's righteous decree that those who do such things deserve death, they not only continue to do these very things but also approve of those who practice them.

NRSV

darkened. [22]Claiming to be wise, they became fools; [23]and they exchanged the glory of the immortal God for images resembling a mortal human being or birds or four-footed animals or reptiles.

[24]Therefore God gave them up in the lusts of their hearts to impurity, to the degrading of their bodies among themselves, [25]because they exchanged the truth about God for a lie and worshiped and served the creature rather than the Creator, who is blessed forever! Amen.

[26]For this reason God gave them up to degrading passions. Their women exchanged natural intercourse for unnatural, [27]and in the same way also the men, giving up natural intercourse with women, were consumed with passion for one another. Men committed shameless acts with men and received in their own persons the due penalty for their error.

[28]And since they did not see fit to acknowledge God, God gave them up to a debased mind and to things that should not be done. [29]They were filled with every kind of wickedness, evil, covetousness, malice. Full of envy, murder, strife, deceit, craftiness, they are gossips, [30]slanderers, God-haters,[a] insolent, haughty, boastful, inventors of evil, rebellious toward parents, [31]foolish, faithless, heartless, ruthless. [32]They know God's decree, that those who practice such things deserve to die—yet they not only do them but even applaud others who practice them.

[a] Or God-hated

# COMMENTARY

After the lofty and evocative introduction, the body of the letter begins with energy, verve, and passion. With so many cross threads of thought going to and fro, it is best to begin by seeing it as a whole.

The thought moves from an explanation and denunciation of idolatry to an explanation and denunciation of the fracturing of human life that results from it. Paul saw no reason to dissent from

the Jewish insight that regarded "sin"—living in a less-than-fully-human fashion, missing the mark as regards God's intention for his human creatures—as the result of worshiping something other than the creator.[45] And, again with Jewish tradition, he regarded idolatry itself as culpable and thus as

45. ἁμαρτία (hamartia), Paul's regular word for "sin," does not appear in chap. 1; but when Paul uses it later to summarize the human condition, he is clearly referring back to this passage among others.

worthy of appropriate punishment, since the creation was full of the signs of the creator's hand. Over the whole sorry picture, therefore, stand the bracketing statements: The wrath of God is revealed (1:18); they know God's decree that those who do such things deserve to die (1:32).

The connecting threads of the paragraph appear in the thrice-repeated "God gave them up" (vv. 24, 26, 28). In each, Paul spotlights some aspect of human corruption and degradation that results from a failure in worship. The first is a general statement; the second, a specific comment about the fracturing of gender roles. The third is general again and gives rise to the climax of the paragraph, a sprawling, squirming catalog of vices that demonstrates in equal measure Paul's disgust at dehumanized behavior and his rhetorical skill in describing it.

**1:18-23.** The opening section, which leads up to the first of these hammer blows ("God gave them up"), introduces us to a major theme within Paul's indictment of the human race. The problem is not just wrong behavior, but wrong thought patterns—the latter, indeed, being the cause of the former. Humans suppress the truth (v. 18); they refuse to acknowledge what they in fact know (v. 21*a*); their reasoning becomes futile, their heart darkened (v. 21*b*); claiming to be wise, they become fools (v. 22). This theme echoes through the rest of the chapter (vv. 25, 28, 32) and anticipates the problem highlighted in 7:7-25, where the "wretched person" knows what ought to be done but cannot do it. Equally, it points on to 12:1-2, where the "renewal of the mind," enabling one to think clearly about what God approves, is the key to presenting the body in God's service.

**1:18.** God's wrath, a prominent theme throughout Scripture, was a major problem for an older liberal theology, which struggled, rightly enough, to avoid any suggestion of God as a malevolent despot, hurling thunderbolts at those who broke arbitrary laws.[46] The tide has turned now, and the great wickednesses of the twentieth century have reminded us that unless God remains implacably opposed to the evil that distorts and defaces creation, not least humanity, God is not a good God. Paul's whole theology, not least

the expression of it in Romans, is grounded in the robust and scripturally rooted view that the creator is neither a tyrannical despot nor an indulgent, *laissez-faire* absentee landlord, nor yet, for that matter, the mere inner or spiritual dimension of all that is. God is the creator and lover of the world. This God has a passionate concern for creation, and humans in particular, that will tolerate nothing less than the best for them.

The result is "wrath"—not just a settled attitude of hostility toward idolatry and immorality, but actions that follow from such an attitude when the one to whom it belongs is the sovereign creator. The content of this wrath is not merely the process (described in the rest of the chapter) of God's "giving people up" to the result of their own folly. That, rather, is simply the anticipation of the final judgment itself, the "death" spoken of in 1:32 and the ultimate judgment described in 2:5-6, 9. The two are, of course, organically connected. Present moral degradation (and physical, too, in many cases) anticipates the ultimate degrading of humanness in death itself.

This wrath is revealed "from heaven," in the present time. As with all of Paul's "apocalyptic" theology, the "end" expected by Second Temple Jews had split into two; the end had in one sense happened, but in another sense was yet to happen fully (see esp. 1 Cor 15:12-28). Thus, although the wrath is still to be revealed in the future (2:5), the last day has in some sense been brought forward into the present. Granted the rest of Paul's thinking about how future and present fit together, this can only mean that something in the events concerning Jesus has unveiled the wrath of God in a new way. Paul's point is not that the moral corruption of the pagan world provides a fresh revelation of God's wrath. Pagans have always behaved like that, at least when seen from Paul's Jewish standpoint. He must mean that, in some way or another, the fact of Jesus has drawn back the veil on the wrath to come.

How has this happened? The answer is provided in 2:16. God, writes Paul, will judge the secrets of humans, *according to my gospel, through the Messiah, Jesus.* Drawing on the Jewish tradition that the Messiah would be the judge of the whole world, Paul sees that his gospel involves the announcement that God has fixed a day on which the world will be called to account;

---

46. The classic statement of this position may be found in C. H. Dodd, *The Epistle of Paul to the Romans* (London: Collins Fontana, 1959) 47-50.

that the agent of this divinely appointed judgment will be none other than Jesus himself; and that the proof of the matter is to be found in Jesus' resurrection (see Acts 17:31; other links between Romans 1 and Acts 17 are noted below).

This explains the train of thought that leads Paul into 1:18. The same gospel message that functions as God's saving power (1:3-4, 16) also names the judge through whom the world will be brought to account and confirms his appointment to that role. From then on nothing can be the same again. A new moment of world history has come to birth. Between the resurrection and the final judgment, the world, whether it acknowledges it or not, lives before the unveiled gaze of the judge.

But it does not, of course, acknowledge the fact. Paul's basic charge (like so many of his introductory sentences, it contains the rest of the passage in a nutshell) is that humans, in their ungodliness and injustice, suppress the truth, and do so precisely by means of that injustice. The word rendered "wickedness" in the NRSV and the NIV is ἀδικία (adikia), not just general evil but injustice, the crucial symptom of the world's out-of-jointness. This human injustice contrasts sharply with God's justice (v. 17); Paul's language is too tightly integrated to allow for loose translation here. The truth is dangerous—so rebellious humans suppress it, hide it away, try to prevent its leaking out. Not only in war is truth an early casualty.

**1:19-21.** Characteristically, Paul fills out his initial statement with three layers of explanation. God's self-revelation has displayed what can be known; this revelation takes place in the created order, rendering all without excuse; humans have refused to honor God in the appropriate way.

These verses have had to bear the weight of debates about "natural theology" (the question of whether, and to what extent, the truth of God is accessible through the created order without the aid of special revelation).[47] As with some other doctrines that have wandered to and fro seeking

biblical support, this one has fastened upon certain brief passages, in this case the present one and a few others (notably Acts 17:22-31, which has other affinities with this passage in Romans), none of which offers a full-dress exposition of the matter, but only an allusion on the way to making some other point. Nevertheless, however brief the statement, Paul clearly does believe that when humans look at creation they are aware, at some level, of the power and divinity of the creator. The problem, of course, is that this knowledge does not save those who possess it, but only renders them guilty. Paul does not say that saving knowledge of God may be had through observing the creation; nor, however, does he say that there is nothing that can be known of God that way. Indeed, granted his belief in the renewal of the human mind by grace, we must assume that in his view the Christian can indeed discern the truth of God by observing creation. But that is not his point here. In fact, like several of his Jewish contemporaries, he believes—consonant with the Jewish belief that the world was made by a good creator—that signs of the creator are visible within this world (see, e.g., Wis 13:5).[48] But these never permit humans to gain over the creator the kind of power that comes with knowledge. On the contrary, they are simply enough to ensure that when humans rebel—as they do—they are manifestly guilty.

The appropriate response to the divine self-revelation in creation would have been worship and thanksgiving. Instead, however, human thought became futile and foolish, and human hearts (not "minds" as NRSV, though the two ideas are not far apart in Paul) became darkened. This unfolding of the dense v. 18*b* prepares the way for vv. 22, 24-25 and above all vv. 28 and 32.

**1:22-23.** The result of the refusal to know God through creation is the false boast of humans and the corruption of the worshiping instinct into idolatry. Here Paul is deliberately, though covertly, retelling the story of Genesis 3, on the one hand, and of Israel in the wilderness, on the other.

47. See the discussion in Joseph A. Fitzmyer, *Romans,* AB 33 (Garden City, N.Y.: Doubleday, 1993) 273. The question of natural theology was tightly intertwined, for German theologians in the first half of the twentieth century, with the ideology of the Third Reich and with the massive protest against it of Karl Barth. That is why, for instance, Käsemann assumes that Paul's eschatology and christology would militate against anything like the natural theology found in some Hellenistic Judaism. See Ernst Käsemann, *Commentary on Romans,* trans. Geoffrey W. Bromiley (London: SCM, 1980) 41.

48. See also Letter of Aristeas 132; 2 Bar 54:17-22; Philo *On Rewards and Punishments* 43; and, in non-Jewish sources, Pseudo-Aristotle *De Mundo* [*On the Universe*] 399ab; Epictetus *Discourses* 1.6.19. The essay by G. Bornkamm, *Early Christian Experience* (London: SCM 1969) chap. 3, remains important.

Talk of God the creator has prepared the way for the first of these. When, in Genesis 3, the serpent tempts Eve, what is on offer is fruit that will, supposedly, make humans wise (Gen 3:6). The primal sin was a matter of obeying instructions, or at least suggestions, not from the creator in whose image humans were made, but from an agent within creation itself. Instead of recognizing wisdom as an attribute of the creator, to be gained by worshiping and serving that God, humans boasted in a wisdom that consisted in supposed independence. But this wisdom consisted in the greatest folly possible—namely, giving allegiance instead to images of humans and also of birds, animals, and reptiles.

This "exchange" of God's glory for an idol echoes Ps 106:20, which speaks of Israel in the wilderness swapping the living God for the golden calf. Here Paul corrects the implicit narrative of the Wisdom of Solomon, written most likely not long before his own day, by referring back to Scripture: In Wisdom, Israel in the wilderness may commit sins, but it will receive only a mild, correcting rebuke. In general, the people stand out from the pagan Egyptians. For Paul, as for the psalmist, Israel rejected the covenant God and fell away into copying the pagans (see further the Commentary on 7:9-11; 9:15-16).[49] This not only anticipates the explicit turn in the argument at 2:17, but it also looks ahead to 7:7-12, where once again the narratives of Adam and Israel are woven together.

The first part of Paul's basic charge is now complete. The human race, called to worship and reflect the image of the creator, has turned to idolatry—and has sought to dignify it by claiming it as the true wisdom. The results follow swiftly.

**1:24-27.** "God gave them up." This repeated phrase carries scriptural echoes from Ps 81:12. This psalm is itself a hymnic telling of the exodus narrative, warning of idolatry, bemoaning the fact that Israel has not heeded the warning, and appealing for the people to return to YHWH. Thus, again, Paul's surface text describes paganism, but

the subtext quietly includes Israel in the indictment. The result, for pagan and Jew alike, is that the creator allows all to reap what they have sown. The punishment not only fits the crime, but directly results from it as well: Those who worship images of their fellow creatures must not be surprised if their own bodies are dishonored as a result of the lusts (NRSV) or desires (NIV) of their hearts (ἐπιθυμία [epithymia] need not have a negative sense, but here and elsewhere in Romans it certainly does; cf. 6:12; 7:7-8; 13:9; 13:14). This condition is further evidence of Paul's general charge, focused in a new way in v. 25: Humans have swapped God's truth for a lie and have given allegiance to that which is not God. Paul, unusually, pauses to express his own allegiance to "the creator, who is blessed for ever. Amen" in this typically Jewish word of praise.

The exchange of truth for a lie results in the second "God gave them up." After the general comment about dishonoring of bodies, Paul now describes particular "lusts of shame"—that is (so NRSV), passions that degrade human beings, making them less than the full humans they were meant to be. Paul notes homosexual practice, both female and male, adding the comment that those who do these things receive in their own persons the reward of their error (the NIV's "perversion" is perhaps too exact a word, since the Greek indicates a more general wandering off course). Out of the many things Paul could have highlighted in the pagan world, he has chosen same-sex erotic practices, not simply because Jews regarded homosexual practice as a classic example of pagan vice, but more particularly because it corresponds, in his view, to what humans in general have done in swapping God's truth for a lie.[50]

The underlying logic seems to be as follows. Those who worship the true God are, as Paul says elsewhere, renewed according to the divine image (Col 3:10). When this worship is exchanged for the worship of other gods, the result will be that this humanness, this image-bearing quality, is correspondingly distorted. Paul may suppose that in Genesis 1 it is male and female together that compose the image of God; or he may simply be taking

---

49. Several Jewish traditions regarded the golden calf incident as a critical turn in Jewish history. These are cataloged in Samuel Vollenweider, *Freiheit als neue Schöpfung*, FRLANT (Göttingen: Vandenhoeck & Ruprecht, 1989) 258. See also S. J. Hafemann, *Paul, Moses and the History of Israel: The Letter/Spirit Contrast and the Argument from Scripture in 2 Corinthians 3* (Peabody, Mass.: Hendrikson 1995) 227-31.

50. On what follows see the thorough treatment in R. A. J. Gagnon, *The Bible and Homosexual Practice: Texts and Hermeneutics* (Nashville: Abingdon, 2001) 229-303; and R. B. Hays, *The Moral Vision of the New Testament* (San Francisco: Harper, 1996) 379-406.

it for granted that heterosexual intercourse is obviously the creator's intention for genital activity. Either way, his point is that homosexual behavior is a distortion of the creator's design and that such practices are evidence, not of the intention of any specific individual to indulge in such practice for its own sake, but of the tendency within an entire society for humanness to fracture when gods other than the true one are being worshiped. The point is: Exchange your God for an idol, and you will exchange your genuine humanness for a distorted version, which will do you no good. What particular physical ailments Paul believed resulted from homosexual practice is not clear, but the last line of v. 27 is in any case an aside, rather than a main plank in the argument.

**1:28-32.** The remaining five verses, all one sentence in the Greek, fill in the picture with strokes as broad and general as the previous two verses were specific and focused. The third "God gave them up" is again a close punishment-and-crime analysis: They did not see fit to have true knowledge of God, so God gave them up to an unfit mind (neither the NRSV nor the NIV retains the wordplay that encapsulates Paul's point). And the unfit mind becomes the source of inappropriate deeds; Paul's view of sin, once more, is not that it is the breaking of arbitrary divine rules but that it is subhuman or nonhuman behavior, deeds that are unfitting for humans to perform. Such people are full, Paul says twice, of all kinds of evil; like jugs filled to overflowing with noxious liquids, they are brimful of wickedness, ready to spill over at any moment. Paul's catalog of vices, arranged for maximum rhetorical effect, reads better in

Greek than in any possible English version, ending with four resounding words: ἀσυνέτους (*asynetous*), ἀσυνθέτους (*asynthetous*), ἀστόργους (*astorgous*), and ἀνελεήμονας (*aneleēmonas*). The NIV comes closest to the verbal effect: "senseless," "faithless," "heartless," "ruthless." Paul's main concern has not been to provide an exhaustive or logically ordered list of all the ways in which idolatry defaces human behavior. His intention, rather, is to paint a picture in the richest verbal colors and patterns that he can.

The final comment (v. 32) is the most devastating. They know God's just decree (for δικαίωμα *dikaiōma* see the Commentary on 8:4)—namely, that those who do such things deserve to die. Paul is again appealing to something that, in theory at least, the whole human race is aware of. He cannot mean that all humans have heard of a law that prescribes the death penalty for certain specific types of behavior. Rather, he asserts that humans in general have an innate awareness that certain types of behavior are inherently dehumanizing, to their practitioners as well as to their victims. Those who behave in these ways are destroying themselves, and at a deep level they are aware of the fact.

Nevertheless, they not only do these things but also applaud (NRSV) those who practice them. It is one thing to live a self-destructive life-style, recognizing it for what it is, grieving over it, and urging others to avoid it if they can. It is another, more sinister, thing to call evil good and good evil. Once light and darkness have been renamed, the process of dehumanization is complete and may well prove irreversible.

# REFLECTIONS

**1.** One still meets, from time to time, the belief that there is nothing really wrong with the human race. It is unhealthy, we are told, or perhaps morbid to dwell on sin or always to be drawing attention to it; it is pathological to approve of punishment, still less retribution. It is bordering on blasphemy to suppose that God would ever be wrathful.

Romans holds these notions up to the light and exposes the counterfeit theology they contain. There is such a thing as human wickedness, and if God does not oppose it relentlessly, then God stands accused of conniving at destructive and dehumanizing practices. The generation that has known both mid-century totalitarianism and late-century apartheid and "ethnic cleansing" should be in no doubt of systemic injustice, rooted in the reality of wickedness deep within the human heart. Within such settings, "embrace" (a gentle liberal toleration of different viewpoints) is not enough; there must also be "exclusion," the making and implementing of judgments that risk pronouncing a "no" as well as a "yes." Finding the appropriate coexistence of those two is an urgent task for our day.[51]

**2.** Our generation has seen the resurgence, in the Western world, of various forms of paganism. The worship of blood and soil, and the symbols that evoke them, was characteristic of the Nazi movement and remains all too familiar within the tribal and geographical disputes that still disfigure our planet. The worship of Mammon, granting absolute sovereignty to "economic forces," whatever the human cost, is endemic in much contemporary culture of both East and West. Eros, the god of sexual love, claims millions of devotees who genuinely believe they are bound to obey its every dictate, however many times its grandiose promises prove hollow. Mars, the god of war, is worshiped by many, tolerated by many more, and still wreaks havoc. And serious nature worship is on the increase, as the old "god" of eighteenth-century Deism has disappeared from view, leaving a vacuum to be filled by the "forces" within the created order, producing various kinds of pantheism.

We cannot, then, dismiss Paul's analysis of idolatry as relevant only to his own age. In some cases we can easily see how such idolatry leads to dehumanized and dehumanizing behavior—when, for instance, worship of Mammon by the few leads to widespread poverty for the many and when, faced with the call to remit large-scale and unpayable international debt, many in positions of power and financial security kick and scream rather than give up a single dollar of "owed" interest. Paul's thesis that dehumanizing behavior is rooted in the worship of idols deserves full contemporary exploration.

**3.** Paul's comment about homosexual behavior is deeply controversial today. Attempts have been made to mitigate its force by saying (for instance) that he is only referring to a deliberate swapping from heterosexual to homosexual practice, not to what in recent years has been regarded as an innate homosexual condition, or that he was only concerned with practices directly related to idolatrous cults. As in some other matters, it would be wrong to press 1:26-27 for a full analysis of same-sex desires or practices; but equally it is wrong to minimalize or marginalize what Paul teaches here. He is not saying, as in an individualistic culture he is inevitably read as saying, that individuals who are aware of same-sex erotic tendencies or who engage in the practices that result have themselves been worshiping idols. He is not proposing a case-by-case analysis. Rather, his argument is that the existence of homosexual practice in a culture is a sign that that culture as a whole has been worshiping idols and that its God-given male-and-female order is being fractured as a result.[52]

We cannot isolate these verses from Paul's larger argument, both in this paragraph and in Romans as a whole. From this it is clear that he regards homosexual practice as a dangerous distortion of God's intention. It is quite logical to say that we disagree with Paul or that in the light of our greater knowledge of human psychology we need to reassess the matter. That can be argued either way. What we cannot do is to sideline this passage as irrelevant to Christian ethical discourse, or for that matter to the argument of Romans, or to pretend that it means something other than what it says. It is, of course, important to remind ourselves also that Romans 1 is followed at once by Romans 2, with its emphatic warning against a moral superiority complex. As the argument goes on its way, Paul's most damning condemnation is reserved, not for those who engage in what he sees as dehumanizing practices, but for those who adopt a posture of innate moral virtue while themselves failing in their most basic vocation, to be the light of the world.

---

51. See Miroslav Volf, *Exclusion and Embrace: A Theological Exploration of Identity, Otherness, and Reconciliation* (Nashville: Abingdon, 1996).

52. Much fuller treatments of this topic can be found in the works of Gagnon, *The Bible and Homosexual Practice,* and Hays, *The Moral Vision of the New Testament.*

**4.** Paul's concern with truth, and with the tendency of humans to deceive themselves about it, addresses precisely the clash in contemporary culture between modernity and postmodernity. The Western Enlightenment bequeathed an intellectual climate in which it was assumed that "truth" could be known "objectively," by scientific and similar observation. Clear and hard thought, it was supposed, would probe into and lay bare the secrets of all subjects. Suspicion about this has been aroused in recent years as post-modern thinkers have pointed out, following Friedrich Nietzsche, that claims to truth are often covert claims to power. The old Roman legal question, *cui bono?* "who stood to gain by this?" formerly restricted to criminal deeds, is now asked of every human action and statement.

Paul's warnings about the ways in which humans distort the truth and come to believe and approve lies remind us of the postmodern critique. There is such a thing as a darkened heart, a mind made foolish or futile through idolatry. The practice of injustice does indeed "suppress the truth" (1:18). However, postmodernity proves too much. Not only does it, quite appropriately, self-destruct. (How do we know that the postmodern claim about knowledge is itself true? Might not it, too, be subjective posturing?) It runs the risk of ruling out what Paul emphatically claims, that despite all suspicion there is such a thing as truth, and it can be known. However, since for Paul the truth is ultimately not something objective, discovered by observation and reason alone, but something personal, given in encounter with the living God, the debates of recent centuries are transcended within a Christian epistemology. Though modernists may sneer and postmodernists gnash their teeth at the very thought, there is in Paul's book such a thing as a mind renewed by the Spirit, and he is so bold as to suggest, in Romans and elsewhere, that this is attainable in Christ (see, e.g., 1 Cor 2:14-16).

# Romans 2:1-16, God's Impartial Judgment Leaves No Room for Moral Superiority

NIV

**2** You, therefore, have no excuse, you who pass judgment on someone else, for at whatever point you judge the other, you are condemning yourself, because you who pass judgment do the same things. [2]Now we know that God's judgment against those who do such things is based on truth. [3]So when you, a mere man, pass judgment on them and yet do the same things, do you think you will escape God's judgment? [4]Or do you show contempt for the riches of his kindness, tolerance and patience, not realizing that God's kindness leads you toward repentance?

[5]But because of your stubbornness and your unrepentant heart, you are storing up wrath against yourself for the day of God's wrath, when his righteous judgment will be revealed. [6]God "will give to each person according to what he has done." [a] [7]To those who by persistence in doing good seek glory, honor and immortality, he will

[a] 6 Psalm 62:12; Prov. 24:12

NRSV

**2** Therefore you have no excuse, whoever you are, when you judge others; for in passing judgment on another you condemn yourself, because you, the judge, are doing the very same things. [2]You say,[a] "We know that God's judgment on those who do such things is in accordance with truth." [3]Do you imagine, whoever you are, that when you judge those who do such things and yet do them yourself, you will escape the judgment of God? [4]Or do you despise the riches of his kindness and forbearance and patience? Do you not realize that God's kindness is meant to lead you to repentance? [5]But by your hard and impenitent heart you are storing up wrath for yourself on the day of wrath, when God's righteous judgment will be revealed. [6]For he will repay according to each one's deeds: [7]to those who by patiently doing good seek for glory and honor and immortality, he will give eternal

[a] Gk lacks *You say*

NIV

give eternal life. [8]But for those who are self-seeking and who reject the truth and follow evil, there will be wrath and anger. [9]There will be trouble and distress for every human being who does evil: first for the Jew, then for the Gentile; [10]but glory, honor and peace for everyone who does good: first for the Jew, then for the Gentile. [11]For God does not show favoritism.

[12]All who sin apart from the law will also perish apart from the law, and all who sin under the law will be judged by the law. [13]For it is not those who hear the law who are righteous in God's sight, but it is those who obey the law who will be declared righteous. [14](Indeed, when Gentiles, who do not have the law, do by nature things required by the law, they are a law for themselves, even though they do not have the law, [15]since they show that the requirements of the law are written on their hearts, their consciences also bearing witness, and their thoughts now accusing, now even defending them.) [16]This will take place on the day when God will judge men's secrets through Jesus Christ, as my gospel declares.

NRSV

life; [8]while for those who are self-seeking and who obey not the truth but wickedness, there will be wrath and fury. [9]There will be anguish and distress for everyone who does evil, the Jew first and also the Greek, [10]but glory and honor and peace for everyone who does good, the Jew first and also the Greek. [11]For God shows no partiality.

12All who have sinned apart from the law will also perish apart from the law, and all who have sinned under the law will be judged by the law. [13]For it is not the hearers of the law who are righteous in God's sight, but the doers of the law who will be justified. [14]When Gentiles, who do not possess the law, do instinctively what the law requires, these, though not having the law, are a law to themselves. [15]They show that what the law requires is written on their hearts, to which their own conscience also bears witness; and their conflicting thoughts will accuse or perhaps excuse them [16]on the day when, according to my gospel, God, through Jesus Christ, will judge the secret thoughts of all.

# COMMENTARY

The scene is set for final judgment. The judge is impartial; the truth will out; the world will be put to rights at last. This typically Jewish depiction of the last great assize is now transposed into a Christian key: The judgment will be "through the Messiah, Jesus" (2:16). What is more, God's impartiality means that Jews and Gentiles will be judged alike.

This paragraph, completing Paul's depiction of "the revelation of God's wrath" (1:18), appears to be addressed to anyone who, faced with the vices mentioned in chap. 1, tries to adopt a superior posture. There were, after all, many pagan moralists in Paul's world, not least in Rome itself, who disdained the behavior Paul condemns just as much as he did and who regarded their philosophy as raising them above it. The question, though, of who Paul is really talking to here is complex. This is a problem we shall meet again.

Paul adopts, here and elsewhere, the prose style known as diatribe, familiar enough from classical works of the same period, such as those of the philosopher Epictetus (and not to be confused with our contemporary meaning of the word, "bitter and abusive speech; ironical or satirical criticism").[53] In this style, the writer engages in debate with imaginary opponents, putting them on the spot, asking them rhetorical questions, answering their supposed objections. Paul had had plenty of experience of real debate and knew which arguments might come up; but he does not, we must assume, expect his real opponents, non-Christian pagans or Jews, to be reading this letter. He therefore creates a double audience: the real one (the Christians in Rome) and the fictitious one (the hypothetical opponent).[54]

53. *Merriam-Webster's Collegiate Dictionary,* 10th edn., 321.
54. On the diatribe, see S. K. Stowers, *The Diatribe and Paul's Letter to the Romans,* SBLDS 57 (Chico, Calif.: Scholars Press, 1981); "Diatribe," in *Greco-Roman Literature and the New Testament,* ed. D. E. Aune (Atlanta: Scholars Press, 1988) 71-84; and *A Rereading of Romans: Justice, Jews, and Gentiles* (New Haven: Yale University Press, 1994).

This is not designed simply to enable the Roman church to listen in on his debates and so be better equipped for similar ones themselves, though that might be important too. The point is that he wants them to think the argument through with him, to see why these things must be so and not otherwise; and the fiction of a hypothetical interlocutor enables him to do this. In particular, since part of his aim is to show that the justice of God upstages all the justice that the pagan world had to offer, he is prepared, not least in this paragraph, to use technical terms known in Stoic philosophy, taking (as he says in 2 Cor 10:5) every thought captive to obey Christ (see the Commentary on 2:14).

So far so good; but, as with chapter 1, Paul here has in mind not only pagan moralists but also Jews. This does not become explicit until 2:17 (there, too, it is a literary fiction; Paul does not expect the letter to be read by non-Christian Jews). But, just as the scriptural echoes in chapter 1 indicated that Israel shared in the idolatry and immorality of the Gentile world, so the repeated emphasis on "the Jew first and also the Greek" in 2:9-10, and the emphasis on those under the law and those outside the law being treated the same in 2:12-15, make better sense if, behind the screen of "whoever you are" in v. 1, Paul envisages as his hypothetical listener not just a pagan moralist but a moralizing Jew.

To understand this section of Romans, then, we must envisage Paul intending his Christian audience in Rome to listen in on a conversation between himself and imaginary Jewish interlocutors whom he is addressing, for the moment, as if they were pagan moralists. The multiple resonances and echoes that this complex scenario sets up go some way to explaining why the text is sometimes dense and difficult. They also prepare us for later stages of the letter, in which similar many-sided writing plays a critical part.

The thrust of 2:1-16 is that God's judgment, when it arrives, will leave all without excuse. To make this point, Paul sketches one of the fullest descriptions of the final judgment in all early Christian writing. He emphasizes that the judgment is indeed unveiled through the gospel; this may come as a surprise to modern readers, for whom "the gospel" has come to mean salvation from judgment, but for Paul "the gospel" is the announcement of Jesus as Messiah, and according

to one strand of tradition the Messiah was expected to be the judge at the last day.[55] In addition, as the psalmists never tire of repeating, judgment—the putting of things to rights at last—is itself good news for those (the majority of the human race past and present) who suffer injustice and oppression. Long exegetical tradition has schooled us to read this part of Romans as simply about individuals being shown up as sinners. This is indeed one element in Paul's argument, but it falls within his larger theme: the good news that, in Jesus the Messiah, the one God of Jews and Gentiles is finally setting the whole world to rights.

This is by no means simply bad news for all humans. To the surprise, again, of those whose traditional readings of the letter lead them to expect that Paul will here simply declare that all are sinners, so that justification can be by faith alone apart from works of the law, he announces on the contrary that at the last assize justification will be on the basis of works (v. 6), and that there will not only be tribulation and wrath for all wrongdoers, but glory, honor, immortality, eternal life, and peace for all who seek for these things in the appropriate way (vv. 7, 10).

As well as a description of the last judgment itself, Paul offers a classic apocalyptic view of the period leading up to that moment (2:4-5). Again both drawing on and interacting with the book of Wisdom, he describes God as being extremely patient, holding back from summary judgment to give people a chance to repent—but thereby inevitably storing up all the more wrath for the hard-hearted, who still refuse to do so.

**2:1-3.** The "therefore" at the start is puzzling, since the person addressed is *ex hypothesi* not guilty of the charge at the end of 1:32.[56] They at least have not called evil good and good evil. Perhaps the underlying thought is that, by standing in judgment on others while being guilty of

---

55. The tradition goes back to, e.g., Psalms 2; 72; Isa 11:1-10; in Paul's day esp. *Ps. Sol.* 17-18. This is part of the wider belief that the Messiah will be God's agent in putting the world to rights. See the material surveyed in N. T. Wright, *The New Testament and the People of God,* vol. 1 of *Christian Origins and the Question of God* (London: SPCK; Minneapolis: Fortress, 1992) 307-20.

56. F. Godet, *Commentary on Paul's Epistle to the Romans,* 2 vols. (Edinburgh: T. & T. Clark, 1880–81) 190, holds that Paul's argument runs thus: If to sin while approving of the sin is criminal, is it not more inexcusable still to condemn the sin of others while joining in it?

similar offenses (in a way yet to be explored), they have been similarly deceitful, holding up their own behavior as an example when it should in fact have been condemned.

Verse 2 is sometimes taken, as in the NRSV, as a quotation from the hypothetical interlocutor, to which Paul then responds. This is not impossible. Paul almost certainly does this sort of thing in 1 Cor 6:12-13; 8:1, 4, and in the latter two verses he introduces the phrase, as here, with "we know that." The problem with all such theories, though, is the difficulty of proving that Paul intended it and that the readers would have understood. Here the strength of the proposal is that v. 3 seems to be picking up what is said in v. 2 and tossing it back, expanding v. 1 ("you who condemn") into "you who condemn those *who do such things,*" which is what, according to the theory, the interlocutor has just done. In this case, the sequence of thought runs: "You are without excuse when you condemn others, since you are doing the same things. Yes, you will no doubt say that 'God judges those who do such things'; but when *you* judge 'those who do such things', do you really suppose that you will escape that same judgment?"

This train of thought is possible, maybe even plausible. But even in this case Paul does not dissent from the thought of v. 2; and in several other passages "we know that" introduces, not a remark from an interlocutor, but something that Paul can take for granted as common ground between himself and his hearers. It may well be, then, that v. 2 is simply Paul's preliminary move, before repeating and amplifying in v. 3 the warning of v. 1: Remember, God's judgment is in accordance with truth! In other words, there is no hiding place at the last assize.

**2:4-6.** One who presumes to stand as judge over others, whether a pagan moralist or a Jewish critic of the pagan world, may be presuming the stance outlined in Wisdom and elsewhere: God is kind and forbearing, at least toward Israel, so that Israel's sins appear as mere peccadilloes, regrettable no doubt but not serious like those of the pagans (see Wis 11:9-10; 15:1-6; 16:5-12; 18:20-25). Thus, while Paul's thought echoes that of Wisdom to the extent of seeing God mercifully allowing a space for people to repent (Wis 11:23), he urges that all need to avail themselves of this chance and that not to do so means despising God's patience and storing up wrath for the final day.

On that day God will indeed render to each according to works. Paul quotes more or less exactly from Ps 62:12 (61:13 LXX) and Prov 24:12, both of which, in context, offer warnings against pride. The psalm, which ends with the phrase quoted here, sees God's just judgment according to works as an expression of God's power and mercy. This deep-rooted Jewish tradition is not denied by Paul, but rather celebrated. If one of the purposes of the letter is to show that God's justice upstages that of Caesar and Rome, we could expect nothing less. We must reserve for a later point the important question of how this final judgment according to works, described as "justification" in v. 13, relates to the "justification by faith" spoken of in chap. 3 and elsewhere.

**2:7-11.** Paul now expands what it will mean that God judges according to works. He describes the contrasts in the sequence *a, b; b, a*: the godly and the wicked, the wicked and the godly. The first contrast, in vv. 7-8, sketches out the underlying attitude of the two classes; the second, in vv. 9-10, emphasizes their final state and insists that Jew and Gentile will be judged fairly and impartially.

The attitude of the two groups is not described in moralistic terms. Paul does not, as a rabbi might have done, produce a list of things that will qualify or disqualify for "the age to come." Rather, the one group, by "patience in well doing," *seeks for* glory, honor and immortality. Paul does not say that they earn them or grasp them; merely that they are seeking them.[57] The other group, seeking their own selfish gain,[58] does "not obey the truth, but obey injustice" (again the word is ἀδικία [*adikia*], more specific than "wickedness" or "evil"). The first group is defined in terms of that for which they seek and the means by which that quest is pursued; the second, in terms of that which is obeyed and not obeyed. We are left to fill

---

57. T. Zahn, *Der Brief des Paulus an die Römer ausgelegt,* 3rd ed. (Leipzig: Deichert, 1925), understands glory, honor, and immortality to be the objects of "give": "to those who seek eternal life, He will give glory and honor and immortality." Although this is possible, given the syntax, it is unlikely.

58. The word ἐριθεία (*eritheia*) is rare, but probably means something like this. Its only attested use before Paul (cf. Gal 5:20; 2 Cor 12:20; Phil 1:17; 2:3) is Aristotle *Politics* 5.3. See also Jas 3:14, 16. See esp. Douglas J. Moo, *The Epistle to the Romans,* NICNT (Grand Rapids: Eerdmans, 1996) 138n. 14.

in the gaps and to presume that the former do obey the truth and that the latter do not patiently seek for glory. What we are not encouraged to do is to draw up a checklist of things done and not done, to weigh them against one another and thereby to arrive at the final verdict. This suggests that Paul is being careful not to endorse the merit-measuring schemes that, despite not being at the covenantal heart of Judaism, nevertheless played some role in discussions of final judgment.

Paul then sums up the two attitudes in terms of the most general moral language (vv. 9-10): The one group works evil; the other does what is good (cf. 12:9). This time the contrast is between the two final states: tribulation and distress, on the one hand, glory and honor and peace (finding that which they had sought, in other words), on the other hand. And the great emphasis here, which colors the reading of the whole chapter, is on the universality of the judgment. Condemnation and glory will alike come "to the Jew first and also, equally, to the Greek" (the "equally" is implied by Paul's careful Greek construction, just as in 1:16).

The impartiality of God as judge is known, though not a major theme, in Jewish tradition.[59] Of course, when Jews thought reflectively, rather than urgently, on God's justice, impartiality was seen to be a vital element in it. But this is where the problem outlined in the Introduction comes into view: What happens when God's impartiality as the cosmic judge appears to conflict with the covenant promises made with Israel, to which God might also be supposed to be bound? How, so to speak, does God's lawcourt justice work together with God's covenant justice? The answer will be revealed in 3:21–4:25. For the moment, like a rich but unresolved musical sequence, Paul's argument makes its striking point, that God has no favorites, and passes on.

**2:12-13.** The whole of vv. 12-16 explains further what is involved in vv. 7-11.[60] God will judge Jew and Greek alike, in complete impartiality, *for* those without the law and those within the law will be judged justly. Paul may well be responding to an implicit Jewish interjection: "We at least have Torah; that sets us apart from the Gentiles." Here we meet for the first time a crucial point, without which much of Romans remains incomprehensible: "Those apart from the law" means quite simply "Gentiles," and "those under the law" (literally "those in the law") means "Jews." "The law," here and more or less throughout Romans, means "the Jewish law," the Torah given to Moses on Mount Sinai, the law that defines and directs Israel, enabling them (supposedly) to be God's people. Gentiles were not "under the law," unless of course they became proselytes, voluntarily submitting to the Jewish code and becoming members, of a sort, within Israel.[61]

The point of v. 12, then, is once more the justice with which the condemnation will be meted out. God will not use the Jewish law to condemn Gentile sinners, but will use it to condemn Jewish sinners. The force of v. 13 is further to undergird God's impartiality; it cannot be the case that mere possession of Torah, hearing it read in synagogue, will carry validity with God. Torah was meant to be obeyed, not merely listened to. This is the beginning of a great theme that recurs frequently in Romans: Possession of Torah had become, in much Jewish thought, a badge of privilege, a talisman, a sign that Israel was inalienably God's people. No, says Paul. What counts is doing Torah. It will take him eight or ten more chapters to explain finally what he means by "doing" Torah, and we must follow the argument through to understand him at that point (see on 8:1-4; 10:5-11). For the moment, he is content to assert the point: Israel's ethnic privilege, backed up by possession of Torah, will be of no avail at the final judgment if Israel has not kept Torah. Justification, at the last, will be on the basis of performance, not possession.

**2:14-15.** These verses, or part of them, are sometimes considered an aside, letting the main thrust of the paragraph jump from v. 13 straight to the conclusion in v. 16 (so NIV; KJV includes v. 13, too, in the bracket). This once more ignores the γάρ (*gar,* "for") that introduces the passage. Paul intends to explain something he has just said, and

59. E.g., Sir 35:15[12], with a similar phrase, reflecting, as does Paul's rare word (found only here, Col 3:25, and, in the plural, Jas 2:1; cf. similar terms in Acts 10:34; Jas 2:9), the Hebrew idiom of "receiving someone's face." On the theme, see above all J. M. Bassler, *Divine Impartiality: Paul and a Theological Axiom,* SBLDS 59 (Chico, Calif.: Scholars Press, 1982); and "Divine Impartiality in Paul's Letter to the Romans," NovT 26 (1984) 43-58.

60. Both the NRSV and the NIV, unfortunately, omit the γάρ (*gar,* "for") that links v. 12 to what precedes.

61. Virtually every book on Paul, and every commentary on at least Romans and Galatians, takes a position on the meaning of "law." An important recent collection of essays is J. D. G. Dunn, ed., *Paul and the Mosaic Law,* WUNT 89 (Tübingen: Mohr-Siebeck, 1996).

there is no need to suppose that the thought of v. 15 cannot run on into v. 16 just as well, if not better, than that of v. 12 or v. 13.

But how do vv. 14-15 explain vv. 12-13? By providing an example of doers of the Torah who are not hearers of it; people, in other words, who perform what Torah requires even though, not being Jews, they have not sat in the synagogue and heard it read. Their thoughts may be confused on the last day, but they will show that "the work of the Torah" had been written on their hearts.

Who are these Gentile law-keepers? There are three basic ways in which scholars have taken these passages.[62] Some have said, in the light of the conclusion of the larger argument in 3:19-20, that this is a purely hypothetical category. Paul is indicating that, when God judges the secrets of all hearts, *if* there should be any who succeeded in doing good, they would indeed reap the appropriate reward; but he is holding up a mirage that will disappear when the argument is complete. There may, in other words, be Gentiles who fulfill part of the law, but in the end this will count for nothing. Others have taken the opposite line and seen 2:1-16 as evidence that Paul does not after all hold that all humans are sinners. He is aware, they say, that in both the Jewish and the pagan world there are some humans who really do that which God intends, who avoid vice and practice virtue, and who will be suitably rewarded in the end.[63]

Both of these positions are difficult to maintain. The first has Paul leading his readers far further up the garden path than the demands of a rhetorical strategy would suggest. The second falls foul of Paul's emphasis on the universality of human sin, in the overarching theme stated in 1:18 and concluded in 3:20. (A further option—that the passage does not really represent Paul's thought, but is either a synagogue homily thrown in here for some reason or is a train of thought that Paul should have assimilated more fully to his own mature views—is I believe a counsel of despair.)[64] The third way through is that, just as in chapter 1

Paul was hinting at Jews sharing in the judgment that would fall on pagans, a theme waiting to be explored more fully in due course, so here he is hinting at a theme he will explore later in the letter, namely that the people in question are *Christian* Gentiles (vv. 14-15)—indeed, Christian Jews and Gentiles alike (vv. 7, 10).[65] There are problems with this reading, too, but they are not so insuperable as sometimes supposed.[66]

Throughout the section so far Paul has been saying things that cry out for further explanation, which he will provide as the letter moves forward. He is at this point sketching a scene, not filling in all the details. But by the end of chap. 2 he has revealed a little more (see on 2:25-29 below); the picture will be colored in fully in 8:1-11; 10:5-11; and 13:8-10. Paul's view, to anticipate the later argument, is that those who are in Christ, who are indwelt by the Spirit, do in fact "do the law," even though, in the case of Gentiles, they have never heard it. The law, in Paul's view, pointed to that fullness of life and obedience to God which comes about in the Messiah; those who attain that fullness of life and obedience are therefore "doing the Torah" in the senses that, to Paul, really matter. He is well aware that this is paradoxical, but well aware also that to say anything else would be to imply, which he never does, either that the Torah was a bad thing, now happily left behind, or that Gentile Christians are second-class citizens in the kingdom of the Messiah. He will have it both ways; they are not under the Torah, but at the same time they are essentially doing what Torah really wanted.

The main problem with taking vv. 14-15 to refer to Gentile Christians is the word φύσει (*physei*) in v. 14, translated "by nature" in the NIV and "instinctively" in the NRSV. It is commonly thought both that this modifies the verb "do," and that Paul here echoes Stoic thought about a "natural law."[67] Neither of these is as secure as it might appear.

*Physei* comes in the middle of the clause: ὅταν γὰρ ἔθνη τὰ μὴ νόμον ἔχοντα φύσει τὰ τοῦ

62. See K. Snodgrass, "Justification by Grace to the Doers: An Analysis of the Place of Romans 2 in the Theology of Paul," *NTS* 32 (1986) 72-93.

63. See C. H. Dodd, *The Epistle of Paul to the Romans*, 2nd ed. (London: Fontana, 1959) 61-62; H. Räisänen, *Paul and the Law* (Philadelphia: Fortress, 1983) 107; E. P. Sanders, *Paul, the Law, and the Jewish People* (Philadelphia: Fortress, 1983) 123-35.

64. See Sanders, *Paul, the Law, and the Jewish People*, 123-35.

65. See N. T. Wright, "The Law in Romans 2," in Dunn, *Paul and the Mosaic Law*, 131-50. See also C. E. B. Cranfield, *A Critical and Exegetical Commentary on the Epistle to the Romans*, ICC, 2 vols. (Edinburgh: T. & T. Clark, 1975) 159-63; S. J. Gathercole, "A Law unto Themselves: The Gentiles in Romans 2.14-15 Revisited," *JSNT* 85 (2002) 27-49.

66. See esp. the critiques of Ernst Käsemann, *Commentary on Romans*, trans. Geoffrey W. Bromiley (London: SCM, 1980) 62-66; Ulrich Wilckens, *Der Brief an die Römer*, 3 vols., EKK 6 (Zurich: Benziger, 1978–82) 1:133-37, 142-46; Moo, *Romans*, 148-52.

67. For careful discussion, see Käsemann, *Romans*, 62-66.

νόμου ποιῶσιν (*hotan gar ethnē ta mē nomon echonta* <u>physei</u> *ta tou nomou poiōsin*, "for when nations not having Torah by nature do the things of Torah"). "By nature" could, grammatically, go either way, in Greek as in that English translation. It could modify "having Torah" instead of "doing the things of Torah." (One might have expected, if Paul was going to say the first of these, that *physei* would come between τά [*ta*] and μή [*mē*], τὰ φύσει μὴ νόμον ἔχοντα [*ta physei mē nomon echonta*], but that is by no means certain; hypothetical reconstructions of what Paul might have said remain insecure.) Paul's point would then be the obvious one: that Gentiles do not, by nature—that is, by origin and parentage—possess the Torah. This is exactly the sense that Paul gives to φύσις (*physis*) thirteen verses later when, making an almost identical point, he describes Gentile Christians as ἡ ἐκ φύσεως ἀκροβυστία τὸν νόμον τελοῦσα (*he ek physeōs akrobystia ton nomon telousa*, "the by-nature uncircumcision that fulfills the Torah"). "Nature" cannot here refer to something that is common, innate, to all humans. Jews, too, are born uncircumcised; that is, in that sense, their "natural" state. It must refer to Gentile humanity as opposed to Jewish (cf. Gal 2:15). I suggest that this is so for 2:14 as well.

If it is insisted that the Stoic echoes of "natural law" are so strong in this passage as virtually to force the reading "do by nature what the law requires," I still maintain, for the reasons given earlier, that the people Paul has in mind must be Gentile Christians. In that case, however, he would be providing a polemical twist of his own to the phrase "by nature." I doubt, frankly, whether Paul would suppose that any pagan could actually fulfill the Torah "by nature" in that sense. What he would be saying, with one eye on a Stoic interlocutor, would be, in effect, "You vaunt your celebrated 'natural law,' and think you can obey it. I will show you some people who have a different sort of law in their 'natures'—because, as I shall show, their 'natures' have been renewed in Christ and by the Spirit."[68]

Further evidence in favor of this overall interpretation is provided by v. 15a. To have the work of the law "written on the heart" is one of the promises of the new covenant in Jer 31:33 (see also Jer 32:40; cf. the "new heart" in Ezek 36:26). Paul clearly believed, and elaborated this at various points, that the covenant had been renewed, according to this promise, through Jesus, and that this renewal was being implemented by the Spirit in those who were "in Christ." This phrase is a further indication that he has Christian Gentiles in mind. Their conscience bears witness to this; nothing here, or in Paul's other references to "conscience," implies that he accords this faculty the status of offering direct revelation of moral truth, and indeed he envisages, in 1 Corinthians 8, persons who have "weak" consciences and need to be treated accordingly.[69] Here the thought is simply that the Gentile Christians who, living in the Spirit, are in fact fulfilling the Torah, are aware deep within their own hearts that they are right with God.

Why then do their thoughts become confused as they approach the judgment, as the end of v. 15 indicates? Perhaps because their situation, being outside the Torah and yet fulfilling it from the heart, leaves them with questions that may produce a moment of panic in even the most settled believer. Perhaps because, as Paul has said in v. 7, they have not *earned* glory, honor, and immortality, merely sought it; they know it remains a gift, however much it will turn out to be in accordance with the life they have in fact lived. Perhaps because the doctrine of assurance, which is indeed Pauline and is based securely in Romans, especially chaps. 5–8, leaves room, as it did in Paul himself, for times of "fightings without and fears within" (2 Cor 7:5), for times of utter despair (2 Cor 1:8). Perhaps because, as the hymn writer puts it, "they who fain would serve thee best are conscious most of wrong within."[70] Paul is clear, though, about the outcome.

**2:16.** On the day of judgment—Paul has reserved this climactic statement for the end of the argument, picking up the scriptural theme of "the day of YHWH"—God will judge the secrets of human hearts. Nothing will then escape scrutiny.

---

68. See esp. Stowers, *A Rereading of Romans*, 109-18. See also T. Engberg-Pedersen, *Paul and the Stoics* (Edinburgh: T. & T. Clark, 2000) 359: Paul knows perfectly well that he is using terms that are familiar from non-Jewish philosophy and is able to use them for his own purposes without either needing to be technically "correct" or to feel himself moving in a totally alien environment. Philosophical treatments of "law" and "nature," and "being a law to oneself," include, e.g., Aristotle *Rhetoric* 1.15.3-8; *Nicomachean Ethics* 4.8.8-10; Hermogenes "On Ideas" 1.221; Dio Chrysostom *Discourses* 36:23.

69. See Eckstein, *Syneidesis*, 170-79.
70. H. Twells, "At even, ere the sun was set."

God will be seen to be just. And this judgment, as we have already noted, will be "through the Messiah, Jesus." God's justice will be revealed, fulfilling scriptural promises and putting all other justice (Caesar's included) to shame. Why so? Not least precisely because this revelation will expose and assess the secrets of all human hearts. Just as Jews cannot hide from the judgment by pleading their Jewishness, so no human can hide from the judgment by relying on outward appearances and covering up the secrets of the heart.

# REFLECTIONS

**1.** It is important not to jump too quickly into a blanket condemnation of moralism. Our culture has a strong inbuilt prejudice against moralizing. We much prefer either a laissez-faire tolerance or the street-level existentialism that reduces all morals to "do what you feel like as long as you don't hurt anyone." We are thus all too eager to read Romans 2 as a denunciation of moralism and then to feel self-righteous because we are not self-righteous. This is to miss Paul's point.

He clearly believed that morals mattered to society and to persons and was not frightened to state what those morals were and how disregarding them brought disaster. Of course, he set all this in a different context from that of either Judaism or the pagan moralists (and from that of contemporary secular or postmodern moralists, for that matter), but he did not object to people holding or propagating high moral standards. What he did object to was doing so while failing to practice what one preached. It is interesting to note that his great contemporary Seneca was criticized, both in his lifetime and after his death, for preaching one standard and living another. Seneca responded, somewhat lamely, that it is the duty of moralists to hold out the highest conceivable standard even if it turns out to be impossible for themselves. For Paul this would have been nonsense. What he objected to, here at least, was the hypocrisy of denouncing faults while secretly practicing them oneself.

**2.** This is a problem familiar from psychology. We project aspects of our character—the aspects of which we are ashamed and perhaps even ignorant—on to other people and then blame them angrily for the very same things. This happens, notoriously, between parents and children. It also occurs, for instance, when journalists (the main source of moralizing in our society), whose own lives might not always bear public scrutiny, take delight in exposing, in the rich and famous, failings of which they themselves may be privately guilty. Behind Paul's specific argument here there stands an assumption, spelled out in other places, that the Christian should be so open to the searchlight of the Spirit that the dark corners of his or her life and inner motivations are increasingly spotlighted and dealt with. Only then will an authentic holding forth of standards of behavior be possible. Only then will one be able gently and firmly to articulate a standard and to denounce evil.

**3.** Belief in a final just judgment remains excellent news for millions in our world, as it was in Paul's. Of course, when this belief is downgraded into vague hopes for a better life hereafter and vague warnings about possible unpleasant consequences of wrongdoing (or for that matter when it is artificially pumped up into shrill hell-fire denunciations and casual self-satisfied salvation-assurance), the clarity of the Christian view of future judgment is lost, and with it both the moral imperative and the true hope of the oppressed. Indeed, as Marx pointed out, projecting hope for a better life forward into the future can then be used by oppressors to keep their subjects, if not happy, at least not rebellious. But that is a parody, a caricature, of Paul's teaching. There is indeed a promise that wrongs will be put to rights, offering a strong and sure hope that can sustain those who suffer oppression and injustice. But in Jesus the Messiah this hope has come forward into the present. Those who give allegiance to Jesus, so far from being agents of oppression by reinforcing a vague future hope and hence a passivity about the present, are charged with realizing God's justice in the present time in all ways possible.

**4.** It still needs saying, though it remains difficult to say, that the creator of the world has no "favored nation clause." No one, no culture, no nation, no ethnic group, can say "because we are x, y, or z, God will be gracious to us come what may." In a world of increasing ethnic and tribal tensions, often exacerbated by different religious affiliations (including, alas, different supposedly Christian affiliations; one cannot but think of Northern Ireland), this message needs to be heard afresh.

**5.** The most disturbing application of this passage is surely to the world of professing Christians. Paul seems to take it for granted that Christians will not be in the position of his imaginary interlocutor; but we are sadly familiar with those who preach or profess allegiance to Jesus as Messiah and Lord but do not practice it. Romans 2 can serve as a second-order reminder of the folly and danger of thus presuming on God's kindness and forbearance. To name the name of Jesus is, as 2:16 makes clear, to invoke the one to whom all, especially his own, will give account.

# Romans 2:17-29, The Direct Challenge to "the Jew"

## NIV

[17]Now you, if you call yourself a Jew; if you rely on the law and brag about your relationship to God; [18]if you know his will and approve of what is superior because you are instructed by the law; [19]if you are convinced that you are a guide for the blind, a light for those who are in the dark, [20]an instructor of the foolish, a teacher of infants, because you have in the law the embodiment of knowledge and truth— [21]you, then, who teach others, do you not teach yourself? You who preach against stealing, do you steal? [22]You who say that people should not commit adultery, do you commit adultery? You who abhor idols, do you rob temples? [23]You who brag about the law, do you dishonor God by breaking the law? [24]As it is written: "God's name is blasphemed among the Gentiles because of you."[a]

[25]Circumcision has value if you observe the law, but if you break the law, you have become as though you had not been circumcised. [26]If those who are not circumcised keep the law's requirements, will they not be regarded as though they were circumcised? [27]The one who is not circumcised physically and yet obeys the law will condemn you who, even though you have the[b] written code and circumcision, are a lawbreaker.

[a] 24 Isaiah 52:5; Ezek. 36:22   [b] 27 Or who, by means of a

## NRSV

17But if you call yourself a Jew and rely on the law and boast of your relation to God [18]and know his will and determine what is best because you are instructed in the law, [19]and if you are sure that you are a guide to the blind, a light to those who are in darkness, [20]a corrector of the foolish, a teacher of children, having in the law the embodiment of knowledge and truth, [21]you, then, that teach others, will you not teach yourself? While you preach against stealing, do you steal? [22]You that forbid adultery, do you commit adultery? You that abhor idols, do you rob temples? [23]You that boast in the law, do you dishonor God by breaking the law? [24]For, as it is written, "The name of God is blasphemed among the Gentiles because of you."

25Circumcision indeed is of value if you obey the law; but if you break the law, your circumcision has become uncircumcision. [26]So, if those who are uncircumcised keep the requirements of the law, will not their uncircumcision be regarded as circumcision? [27]Then those who are physically uncircumcised but keep the law will condemn you that have the written code and circumcision but break the law. [28]For a person is not a Jew who is one outwardly, nor is true circumcision something external and physical. [29]Rather, a person is a

NIV

<sup>28</sup>A man is not a Jew if he is only one outwardly, nor is circumcision merely outward and physical. <sup>29</sup>No, a man is a Jew if he is one inwardly; and circumcision is circumcision of the heart, by the Spirit, not by the written code. Such a man's praise is not from men, but from God.

NRSV

Jew who is one inwardly, and real circumcision is a matter of the heart—it is spiritual and not literal. Such a person receives praise not from others but from God.

# COMMENTARY

We now arrive at the point to which the whole section has been building up. Israel, resting on God's special vocation, has not fulfilled that vocation, and must face the challenge from those who, though not ethnically Jewish, are now inheriting Israel's role in God's purposes.

In addressing "the Jew" Paul was, of course, talking to his own former self. More; he was aware, as 9:1-5 will make clear, of deep personal grief, witnessing "his flesh" in rebellion against the gospel message of the Jewish Messiah, Jesus. All that now follows must be seen in this light.

We should beware of the natural tendency, within our individualistic culture, to assume that when Paul uses the second-person singular ("If *you*, singular, call yourself a Jew") he is referring to a typical *individual*. Just as in chap. 7 his rhetorical use of "I" arguably indicates the nation as a whole, so here his "you" focuses and makes dramatic that which is said of the whole Jewish people. Paul is not for a moment suggesting anything so absurd as that all Jews steal, commit adultery, rob temples, and so forth. His point is rather that the national boast of ethnic Israel, that of being the creator's chosen people, is falsified if theft, adultery, and so forth are found within the nation. The presence of misbehavior within ethnic Israel renders void the national, ethnic boast; it prevents Israel from fulfilling its calling to be the light of the world.

The passage, then, is not simply part of a long demonstration that all humans are sinful. That is indeed one of the major thrusts of the section 1:18–3:20, but within that overarching purpose these verses introduce a quite different idea. Faced with a general denunciation of the pagan world, many educated Jews—including, presumably, Paul himself in his pre-Christian life—would say that this is of course true of pagans, but that God has chosen Israel as the light to the nations and has given Israel the Torah so that it can fulfill this role. Israel is the solution to the world's plight (see, among countless possible examples, 2 Bar 48:20-24). The problem he is outlining at this point in the argument, and to which he will offer a solution in the section beginning at 3:21, is not simply that all are sinful and in need of salvation, but that the bearers of the solution have become part of the problem. Israel, called to be the light of the world, has become part of the darkness. How then can God's covenant plan be fulfilled? The problem of Israel is thus also a problem for God. It is, in fact, a further dimension of the problem of God's righteousness. Only if we appreciate this will the transition from chapter 2 to chapter 3 make any sense.

Paul's turn to "the Jew" in 2:17 has some analogies with the rhetorical ploy of Amos, denouncing the surrounding nations before turning to Judah (Amos 2:4) and particularly the northern kingdom, Israel (Amos 2:6). But this is not the whole truth of this passage. For a start, as we have seen, Paul has had Israel in mind all along, hinting darkly in chap. 1 that his fellow Jews were as guilty of idolatry as were the pagans, strongly suggesting in 2:1-16 that their would-be superiority was no better than that of the pagan moralists. But his point now is not so much to bring out into the open a charge that they are sinful like the rest. He will rub that in in the middle of chap. 3 (and say it again, from another angle, in 7:7-25). The point here is that Israel *should* have been—had been called to be—the divine answer to the world's problem; and that, instead, Israel is itself fatally compromised with the very same problem. Israel's sinfulness is at the heart of the charge, but the charge itself is that the doctor, instead of healing the sick, has become infected with the disease.

The ethnic boast of "the Jew" is thereby called into question. How can a nation that so manifestly fails to be the light of the world claim to be keeping Torah? In the second paragraph of this section (2:25-29), Paul advances a stronger and more detailed form of the argument he made in 2:13-15. Supposing, he says, there exists a people, not sharing Israel's ethnic privileges, in whom the purposes of God as expressed in Torah are coming to fulfillment. Will they not thereby upstage ethnic Israel? Yes, he declares, such people are members of the renewed covenant. That is what being "a Jew" is all about.

Thus, just as Paul built into his exposition of human sin (1:18-32) elements that hinted at what was to come, so now, in the same way, he is building in to his statement of the complex problem of sin—human sin and the failure of Israel to be the solution-bearer—hints of the solution. This, too, challenges normal simplistic views of the construction of Romans. We can only fully understand 2:26-29, dense and proleptic as it is, with help from elsewhere; but when we grasp its meaning we see why Paul has included it here. Not only is the existence of a parallel company of non-ethnic "Jews" and uncircumcised "circumcision" a direct, albeit oxymoronic, challenge to Israel's ethnic boast; it sharpens up the question Paul must raise at the start of chap. 3 if the solution, when he finally unveils it in 3:21 and thereafter, is to make the full sense he intends. If God has called this parallel company of "Jews" into existence, what is the point of being a Jew, the point of there being an "Israel," in the first place? What is God up to?

**2:17.** Paul's introduction is designed as a challenge: You claim the name "Jew," but are you true to it?[71] Do you know what it really involves? Certainly a Jew such as Saul of Tarsus would be ready enough with the answer, beginning with "reliance on Torah," "boasting in God," and quite possibly the vocation to be "the light of the world."

The first two of these need more nuance. The word translated "rely" principally means "rest on"; it is a matter of finding security and comfort, not a matter of using the Torah as a ladder of good

works, up which to climb to a position of moral superiority or a self-earned salvation. The attitude Paul describes would say: "God gave Israel the Torah; our possession of it is the rock on which we stand; it is what makes us Jews God's special people."

The attitude to God is much the same. The NIV's "brag about your relationship to God" sounds as though "the Jew" is telling people about a marvelous personal friendship between him or herself and the true God; but this is not Paul's meaning. (The word "relationship" is responsible for too many fudged arguments in contemporary theology.) The NRSV's "boast of your relation to God" is a little better, but the word "relation" still sounds, in our culture, as though it is referring to a "personal relationship" in the sense of two persons engaged in active friendship. Neither expression catches the depth of the Greek, which simply and literally means "boast in God"; the point is the Jewish claim, supported throughout the Hebrew Scriptures, that the creator of the world is Israel's God, and vice versa.

The word "boast" is difficult, too. In contemporary English it is almost always negative, whereas Paul is not only capable of using it in a positive sense (e.g., 5:11), but is here both reporting and commending the attitude of "the Jew" as good and God-given. "Celebrate" would bring out the point: "the Jew" celebrates the fact of election, of being God's chosen people. Neither here nor in the verses to come does Paul regard these claims with contempt, or try to undermine them. The Torah really was given to mark out Israel as God's people. God really was "their God." Paul does not for a moment reject the specialness of Israel. At this stage in the letter, he simply questions whether those making the claim have forfeited the right to do so.

**2:18-20.** This basic picture is filled out with more of "the Jew's" self-description. Verse 18 states two ways in which Torah enables the Jew to attain true moral knowledge, as a result of which (vv. 19-20) Israel should be in a position to instruct the nations, again because of Torah. This prepares the way for the charge in vv. 21-23, which consists of four moral challenges and a question about Torah, backed up with a quote from the prophets. In this paragraph Paul is concentrating on Torah, in the following one on circumcision; these are the

---

71. It may have been a typical motif of the diatribe style to have upbraided one's opponents for not living consistently with the teaching they espouse. See Moo, *Romans,* 157; Stowers, *The Diatribe and Paul's Letter to the Romans,* 112.

badges that marked out Jews from their pagan neighbors.

Possession of Torah should enable "the Jew" to know God's will and "distinguish things that differ" (v. 18), in other words, to make moral judgments, determining what is best (NRSV) or approving what is superior (NIV; the NEB, for once, comes closest to the literal meaning with "you are aware of moral distinctions"). The point is that Torah's instruction enables the Jew to see to the heart of moral issues. As a result (vv. 19-20), Israel is in theory the light of the nations, the world's moral teacher, because in Torah Israel really does possess "the embodiment of knowledge and truth." The term μόρφωσις (*morphōsis,* translated here "embodiment") means "the outward manifestation"; Paul is acknowledging, and endorsing, a remarkably high, almost incarnational, view of Torah, which should be kept in mind during subsequent discussions.

**2:21-22.** Granted your possession of this lofty privilege, Paul enquires, what have you done with it? Remembering that the "you" in question is not "every Jewish individual," but "Israel as a whole," the answer must be: Israel has squandered its inheritance. Like the biblical prophets, one of whom he will presently quote, Paul charges Israel with infidelity (see also Ps 50:16-20 and the other passages quoted in 3:10-18). The first question serves as a heading for the others: Teacher of others, will you not teach yourself? Theft and adultery exist in Israel, both literally in many cases and spiritually wherever people "rob God" (Mal 3:8) or are unfaithful to him, as a bride to her husband (e.g., Hos 2:2-13).

The charge of temple robbery is, at first blush, more surprising, both because it seems a less obvious offense than theft or adultery and because it seems even less likely that many Jews were involved in such a practice. The best explanation is, once again, that Paul is not so interested in demonstrating that "all Jews are sinners" (as we have seen, his argument scarcely proves this point), as in showing up Israel's failure to be the light of the world. One is unlikely to demonstrate to the watching pagan world that there is a better way to be human by stealing from pagan temples. This practice, though probably not widespread, was not unknown. Some Jews had evidently used the scriptural polemic against idols to argue that,

since idols have no real existence, things given to them are nobody's property, and hence may be taken with impunity.[72] Paul's point is that the practice exists and brings discredit on Israel precisely among the people to whom "the Jew" is supposed to be acting as the light of the world. This charge shows once more (a) that his concern here is with Israel as a whole, rather than every individual within it and (b) that his point about Israel as a whole is not simply Jewish sin, important though that is, as the fact that this sin results in the failure of Israel to be God's light to the Gentile world.

**2:23-24.** This opens up the substance of the charge. The real problem is Israel's failure to bring God worldwide honor. That was the purpose for which Torah had been given. What Israel has done with Torah has instead brought dishonor: The pagan nations scorn the true God on the basis of the behavior of the covenant people. Breaking Torah nullifies boasting in Torah. Israel, in fact, is in the state spoken of by Isaiah in 52:5. Exile has come because of Israel's sin (the pagan behavior among YHWH's own people that caused YHWH's displeasure), because the pagan nations, looking at Israel, now blaspheme Israel's God. The same theme appears in other prophetic passages, notably Ezek 36:20-23, a passage that (as we shall see) Paul almost certainly has in mind as well.

As usual, Paul evokes with a single quotation a whole world of scriptural resonance. His point throughout the paragraph is something that few Jews in his day would have contested: that Israel as a whole is not living up to what YHWH would desire and that Israel's continued subservience to the pagan nations, which had begun with the Babylonian captivity, was a sign that the great promised redemption had not yet arrived. In other words, Israel's "exile" was still continuing, not in a geographical, but in a theological, spiritual, and moral sense. The prophecies of Isaiah, Ezekiel, and others had not yet been fulfilled. As the book of Daniel had emphasized, the seventy years of exile had become seventy weeks of years (Introduction,

---

72. Deut 7:25-26 and Josephus *Antiquities of the Jews* 4.287 show that the temptation existed; Josephus *Against Apion* 1.310-11 reports a pagan slander against Jews that the name Jerusalem was a pun on the word for "temple robbery" because the Jews who settled it had done so much of it; Acts 19:37 shows that the charge was likely to be levied against Jews in the pagan world. For rabbinic material, see H. L. Strack and P. Billerbeck, *Kommentar Zum Neuen Testament aus Talmud und Midrash,* 6 vols. (Munich: C. H. Becksche, 1922–61) 3:113-15.

398 [and footnote 3]). And the very point to which Paul draws attention, in both Isaiah and Ezekiel, is the point at which YHWH declares that, now that the pagans are blaspheming, and the very name of God is dishonored among them, it is time to act. Isaiah goes on at once to speak of the herald who announces good news to Zion (52:7, quoted by Paul in 10:15); Ezekiel goes on at once to speak of covenant renewal, involving a change of heart and the gift of a new spirit through which God's people will at last keep the statutes of the law. Paul, with these larger contexts in mind, has called up the one element of the prophetic critique that makes his present point—that Israel has failed in bringing honor to God's name among the nations—and also hints at the renewal of the covenant and the gift of the Spirit.

**2:25-29.** He comes at this latter point by introducing, in parallel with the point about Torah, the question of circumcision. This was not seen in Judaism as a quasi-moral "good work," or as a "ritual" designed to earn God's favor, but as a key badge of Jewish identity, marking out the Jew from the pagan world around. Bringing circumcision and Torah together, Paul declares that the former only means what it is supposed to where Torah is kept; and, once again, Torah has been broken. The badge therefore tells a lie. But if the prophecies of Ezekiel and others about covenant renewal seem to be coming true elsewhere—if there are people with new hearts, new spirits, who are keeping the ordinances of Torah—then, whether they are circumcised or not, they will by their very existence show up the brokenness, the invalidity, of the covenant membership of those who still, despite their circumcision, break Torah.

Paul's description of this parallel "Jewishness," this new sort of "circumcision," is replete with overtones of "new covenant" passages both in scripture and elsewhere in his writings. The problems that this causes, for Paul and for contemporary readers, will emerge later in the letter, together with the solutions Paul proposes (see the Commentary on 3:27-31; 8:1-11; 10:1-13).

**2:25.** The initial statement, out of which the rest emerges, is sharp. Circumcision is of value (this will be raised again in 3:1) for one who keeps Torah. In other words, keeping Torah is basic, and without it circumcision becomes an empty sign, a meaningless talisman (cf. 1 Cor 7:19, which puts

the point even more strikingly: Neither circumcision nor uncircumcision matters, since what matters is keeping God's commands! Paul must have known that this was paradoxical to the point of being funny, since the command to circumcise loomed so large in Judaism and in the written Torah itself). Indeed, to break Torah means not just that circumcision is meaningless, but that it "becomes uncircumcision"; in other words, it works in reverse, marking you out as *not* a member of God's people. It becomes a badge of exclusion rather than of inclusion (cf. Gal 5:2-6, albeit with reference to ex-pagans). Paul will have more to say on this topic (which was, of course, central in the Galatian controversy) in chap. 4.

**2:26-27.** Paul now explicitly introduces a category of people that is central to his thought and that will occupy him for much of the letter. These are people who, though uncircumcised, "keep the decrees of Torah." The words he uses are, in effect, an abbreviated version of Ezek 36:27, carrying other biblical echoes as well (notably Deut 30:16 [φυλάσσεσθαι τὰ δικαιώματα *phylassesthai ta dikaiōmata,* the same root words as here]; cf. Lev 18:5; both these passages recur in Rom 10:5-11, which develops the present thought; see the Commentary on 10:1-21). Of these people Paul declares that their uncircumcision will count as circumcision; in other words, that God will recognize their physically Gentile state, paradoxically, as the badge of their membership in Israel. As though this were not scandalous enough, Paul goes on to state that these persons, law-keeping though "naturally" uncircumcised through their Gentile origins,[73] will judge those who, despite having the "letter of the law" and physical circumcision, nevertheless transgress the law.

By referring to the law as "the letter" Paul has carefully introduced the category that will enable him to contrast two types of covenant membership in the climactic verses that now follow.

**2:28-29.** By way of explanation (γάρ *gar,* "for"; as in the NRSV; unwarrantedly omitted by the NIV), Paul sets out two types of "Jew." The section began with "the Jew" that claims that name, and

---

73. The verb here for "keep" (NRSV) or "obey" (NIV) is τελειόω (*teleioō,* "fulfill," cognate with τέλος *telos,* "end" or "goal," on which see 10:4, with the commentary there). To refer to the uncircumcision as "physical" is slightly misleading. By "naturally" Paul means, as we saw in reference to 2:14, "in that they are Gentiles." All males are "naturally uncircumcised" in the sense that they are born that way.

that calls Torah and God to witness it. Paul now transfers the name, and the validation, to a different group. In the previous verses he has referred to Gentiles who, though uncircumcised, keep the law's regulations; he can only mean Gentile Christians, since this passage, explaining what has gone before, is clearly about membership in the new, or renewed, covenant. But the primary category he is describing is not restricted to Gentiles; Paul explains the narrower point (vv. 26-27) by setting out a broader one. He most certainly regarded himself, and his fellow Jewish Christians, as part of the same new covenant people of God.

The contrast he makes is between that which is open, visible, and obvious, and that which is secret. This boils down, more or less, to the "outward/inward" distinction (NRSV, NIV, and most others), but we should beware of importing into Paul a Platonic either/or that is foreign to him. His sentences are clipped and dense at this point, and paraphrase is almost inevitable; literally, what he says is, "For the one in visibility is not a Jew, nor is the one in visibility (in the flesh) circumcision; but the one in secret is a Jew, and circumcision is of the heart, in the spirit not the letter." We should note that he does not say, as the NEB and others do, the "true" Jew, the "true" circumcision. His point is more stark. The name "Jew," and the attribute "circumcision," belong to the secret/heart/spirit people, not to the visibility/flesh/letter people (cf. Phil 3:3, where a closely accurate translation might be "the 'circumcision' means us"). It is as shocking as that. As if to emphasize that he really means it, Paul will at once go on to challenge himself on the point and to think through what follows.

In referring to the secret/heart/spirit people, Paul clearly means to designate those in whom the gospel of the Messiah has done its work. The promises of God through Deuteronomy 30, Ezekiel 36, and elsewhere have come true. God has done, in Jesus and the Spirit, what he had promised; the result is the creation of the people of the new covenant. Paul's clearest statement of this point may be found in 2 Cor 3:1-6, where the letter/spirit contrast is again prominent.[74] There are several other passages in which a similar theological understanding may be discerned, not least Romans 8 and 10. Resistance to finding the notion of "covenant" in Paul has proved remarkably strong, not least among those for whom the center of Paul's thought is the radical newness of God's action in Christ; but once it is appreciated that Paul's covenant theology is precisely about the radically new and unexpected, even shocking, way in which God has fulfilled the promises of Ezekiel and elsewhere, and that "covenant" and "apocalyptic," so far from being antithetical categories, belong closely together in Second Temple Judaism and in Paul himself, the problem should fade away.[75]

The paragraph carries a typically Pauline sting in the tail. This new covenant people, the ones who fulfill Torah whether or not they are circumcised, the ones who carry the covenant marks on their hearts rather than in their flesh—this people show that they have the right to the name "Jew" because "their praise is not from humans, but from God." Paul is alluding to, rather than making, a pun that would be obvious to an educated Jew; in Hebrew the word "Judah" means "praise." They receive the name "Jew," in other words, from God, as a gift of grace. These are the ones who can now "celebrate in God" (2:17), as he will declare in 5:11.

Paul has introduced this brief description of the new covenant people into his argument without full explanation. Within 2:17-29, its primary purpose is simply to highlight the failure of Israel to be the covenant people of the creator God, the light of the dark world. As so often, however, Paul's tantalizing asides serve other purposes as well; here he has introduced one of the major themes of the letter, to be elaborated more fully in due course and has done so not least in order to raise the questions that he will glance at in chap. 3 and then return to more fully in chaps. 9–11. In fact, 2:26-29 stands to 3:1-8 much as 5–8 stands to 9–11. Paul's thought in this letter moves in a great expanding upward spiral; when we reach chap. 8, we shall be able to look down from a greater height and see this dense little statement more or less exactly beneath us.

Like many other things in chap. 2, this passage

74. See N. T. Wright, *The Climax of the Covenant: Christ and the Law in Pauline Theology* (Edinburgh: T. & T. Clark; Minneapolis: Fortress, 1991) chap. 9.

75. This comment is in dialogue with, among others, the remarkable work of J. L. Martyn, *Galatians,* AB 33A (New York: Doubleday, 1997), and *Theological Issues in the Letters of Paul* (Nashville: Abingdon, 1997) esp. chap. 7.

must wait for further elaboration in subsequent chapters. In addition to the questions Paul asks at once at the start of chap. 3, the reader, ancient or modern, wants to know: In what sense do these people "fulfill the Torah," or "keep the ordinances of the law"? Here, as so often, the exegete needs patience, which is itself, after all, one of the fruits of the Spirit.

# REFLECTIONS

**1.** The alarming conclusions of the previous paragraph are further reinforced. Who today sets themselves up as teachers of the foolish, guides to the blind? At one level, of course, politicians and journalists—who, routinely enough in many cases, show by their own behavior that they have not taken their own advice. At a different level altogether, there are some Jews, particularly some idealistic Zionists, who cling to the belief that the modern state of Israel is supposed at last to be the light to the nations. If that were so, it would not take a particularly cynical reading of contemporary Middle Eastern social and political realities to say that things are very far from where they should be. Indeed, a good many Jews, including many who themselves live in Israel, would heartily agree. One does not have to be unsympathetic with the ambiguous plight of that state to recognize the problem; indeed, the more sympathy, the more agonizing over the way things are.

But at another level altogether, a Christian reader cannot escape the acute discomfort of saying that the church, in both its local, denominational and international manifestations, stands equally under the condemnation of a passage like this. Those who read the Sermon on the Mount in the course of regular worship hear themselves now called to be the light of the world, and to embody, in secret as well as in public, the generous love of the creator God. There are many churches, of course, where the gospel is lived out in its full transforming reality. But equally there are many that must hang their heads in shame at the question, You who would teach others, can you not teach yourself?

This question arises particularly in the question of Christian unity. Part of the point of Paul's gospel is that there is one God, who, therefore, desires one people (see on 3:30). Paul fought against splitting the church along ethnic or cultural lines; Christian denominations often reflect precisely these splits, using dogmatic differences as a cloak for continuing tribal identity. Sometimes this becomes openly scandalous, as in Northern Ireland or the Balkans. But as long as those who name the name of Jesus Christ cannot at least share the Eucharist, cannot in some cases even pray together, the name of God will continue to be blasphemed among pagans.

**2.** The claim that those who belong to the new covenant, in the Messiah and by the Spirit, are now entitled to the name "Jew" was deeply controversial in Paul's day and has again become so in the twentieth century. Until we reach Romans 9–11 we cannot attempt a full treatment of the subject; but we must note again both that Paul's writing about "the Jew" was writing about himself, and that when he spoke of the failure of his own people he did so with tears.

These concessions will not, of course, mollify those for whom any claim by Christians, including Jewish Christians, to be the people of the renewed covenant is downright offensive. The offense comes at at least three levels. First, many Jews in today's world, all too aware of centuries of persecution by soi-disant Christians, are highly sensitive to the early Christian claim that the events concerning Jesus were the fulfillment of prophecy, the unveiling of the "righteousness of God"— and in particular, of course, to the claim that Jesus of Nazareth was and is Israel's promised Messiah. To make such claims, it has again been urged in our day, is itself an act of anti-Judaism, perhaps even now of anti-Semitism (the former a rejection of Judaism as a way of life, the latter a rejection of a particular race, with overtones of nineteenth- and twentieth-century racial theories).[76]

---

76. The classic statement of this position is that of Rosemary R. Ruether, *Faith and Fratricide: The Theological Roots of Anti-Semitism* (New York: Seabury, 1974).

Second, many Christians have thought long and hard about the meaning of the ghastly events in Europe in the first half of the twentieth century and have arrived at a firm conviction that the massacre of six million Jews in the Nazi "final solution" was the result of, among other things, an emphasis on claims such as those made by Paul in this passage. The moral imperative seems then inevitable: The church must back off from all such claims and should at the most express its faith in terms of a way of spirituality, based on the Jew Jesus of Nazareth, which many non-Jews have found life-giving. A corollary has sometimes been mooted: Paul is to be rejected as a paganizer of the Jewish message of Jesus.[77]

Third, a position that many consider "modern," but which is rooted, at least in its current expressions, in the eighteenth-century Enlightenment. According to this, all religions are inadequate approximations to truth, and, despite what many of them say, none has exclusive rights to it. The appropriate stance is therefore mutual tolerance. This is, of course, a covert way of saying, among other things, that (at least) Judaism, Islam, and Christianity are all actually misleading, since all of them make, at the very heart, claims that the others are bound to deny if they are not to lose their very identity. Nevertheless, this secularized agenda has seeped into both Jewish and Christian circles, often coupled with the laudable desire for humility and mutual respect, sometimes using that as a pretext for a highly arrogant liberalism that challenges all truth claims while pressing its own with remarkable intolerance.

Two points only can be made at this stage. First, Paul's own position was that of a Christian Jew. He regarded this as natural and normal, indeed the most appropriate thing possible. Though his own vocation was to declare to the pagan world the Jewish gospel message (that the one God of the whole world, the God of Abraham, Isaac and Jacob, the God who gave the Torah, had now unveiled in Jesus the final stage of the plan to bring justice and healing to the world), he knew, and insisted in this letter, that the gospel remained "for the Jew first," however much it was also "and equally to the Greek." Any suggestion that Paul would have countenanced a split, a twin-track salvation-history, in which Jews should remain Jews and Gentiles might become Christians is without the slightest foundation in his thought or writings (see the Commentary on 9:1–11:36).[78]

Second, there is a curious anomaly within the Christian position outlined above. On the one hand, we are urged to reject non-Jewish styles of Christianity, to recover the Jewish roots of our faith, and to cherish and nourish such echoes of Jewish ways, Jewish rituals, Jewish understandings, as we can. Christian versions of Seder meals have become common. This, it seems to me, is a healthy corrective to the many ways in which Christians so easily slip into non-Jewish modes of thought, taking their color and agenda instead from the pagan world around. On the other hand, the same people who urge this agenda regularly also press upon the church the need to renounce all claim to be "the Jew," "the circumcision." "Supersession" is the magic word here, or perhaps we should say the demon-word. It is wheeled out again and again, implying that in such a view the church has taken Israel's place in God's plan, leaving no room any longer for non-Christian Israel, Israel (in Paul's phrase) "according to the flesh."

This double position is grossly inconsistent. The more we examine the Jewish roots of the Christian faith, the more we are bound to discover that all the early Christians known to us defined themselves with joy as God's Israel, living in and seeking to share the blessings of the messianic age that had dawned with Jesus, the new age for the whole world that began when Jesus rose from the dead. This is hardly supersessionism, unless we were to charge Isaiah, Ezekiel, Deuteronomy even, and figures like John the Baptist, and indeed the Essenes, with that crime as well. Making the totally Jewish claim that God will renew, or has renewed, the

---

77. See particularly Hyam Maccoby, *The Mythmaker: Paul and the Invention of Christianity* (London: Weidenfeld and Nicolson, 1986); *Paul and Hellenism* (Philadelphia: Trinity, 1991).

78. Against Lloyd Gaston, *Paul and the Torah* (Vancouver: University of British Columbia Press, 1987); John G. Gager, *The Origins of Anti-Semitism* (Oxford: Oxford University Press, 1983).

covenant, throwing its membership open far and wide, was unpopular when the prophets did it, when Jesus did it, when Paul did it. There is no easy answer to the large-scale question underneath this discussion. If there were, Paul would have given it, rather than mounting the massive argument we find in chaps. 9–11. But let us at least talk sense, however humbly, in wrestling with it.

## Romans 3:1-8, Israel's Faithlessness and God's Faithfulness

3 What advantage, then, is there in being a Jew, or what value is there in circumcision? [2]Much in every way! First of all, they have been entrusted with the very words of God.

[3]What if some did not have faith? Will their lack of faith nullify God's faithfulness? [4]Not at all! Let God be true, and every man a liar. As it is written:

"So that you may be proved right when you speak
and prevail when you judge."[a]

[5]But if our unrighteousness brings out God's righteousness more clearly, what shall we say? That God is unjust in bringing his wrath on us? (I am using a human argument.) [6]Certainly not! If that were so, how could God judge the world? [7]Someone might argue, "If my falsehood enhances God's truthfulness and so increases his glory, why am I still condemned as a sinner?" [8]Why not say—as we are being slanderously reported as saying and as some claim that we say—"Let us do evil that good may result"? Their condemnation is deserved.

[a] 4 Psalm 51:4

3 Then what advantage has the Jew? Or what is the value of circumcision? [2]Much, in every way. For in the first place the Jews[a] were entrusted with the oracles of God. [3]What if some were unfaithful? Will their faithlessness nullify the faithfulness of God? [4]By no means! Although everyone is a liar, let God be proved true, as it is written,
"So that you may be justified in your words,
and prevail in your judging."[b]
[5]But if our injustice serves to confirm the justice of God, what should we say? That God is unjust to inflict wrath on us? (I speak in a human way.) [6]By no means! For then how could God judge the world? [7]But if through my falsehood God's truthfulness abounds to his glory, why am I still being condemned as a sinner? [8]And why not say (as some people slander us by saying that we say), "Let us do evil so that good may come"? Their condemnation is deserved!

[a] Gk they    [b] Gk when you are being judged

## COMMENTARY

The force of this section is only grasped when two things are appreciated: the "symphonic" structure of the letter (see Introduction), in which themes are hinted at in advance of their full statement, and the underlying subject of God's faithfulness to the covenant and Israel's vocation to an answering faithfulness through which God's purpose for the world will be accomplished. Paul is concerned here not so much with the sinfulness of all Jews, important though that is, as with Israel's failure to carry out the divine commission, to be the means of the world's salvation. The thought remains dense and sometimes elliptical, but the clear point emerges: God remains faithful to the covenant plan even though Israel has failed in the covenant task.

Israel's failure puts God into an apparently awkward position. Will not the divine righteousness at one level generate unrighteousness at another? Paul rebuts these charges briefly without actually answering them fully; he will return to them in due course.[79] For the moment his aim is to assert the continuing faithfulness of God, despite Israel's failure; this then clears the ground for the point (which many have assumed was the only one in the entire section) that Jews have joined Gentiles in the dock, guilty as charged.

**3:1-2.** What then of Israel? The question is natural in view of the end of chap. 2. If God is capable of calling "Jews" from among the uncircumcised, what was the point of being Jewish, or being circumcised, in the first place? Paul, given the chance to offer a radically Marcionite answer (e.g., "None whatever!"), has no intention of doing so. The God revealed in Jesus Christ, as he will make clear in the next two chapters, remains the God of Abraham, the covenant God. His answer gives the clue to his real concern throughout the paragraph. The Jews were *entrusted* with God's oracles. (Paul says "in the first place," but never gets round to saying "in the second place." Until, that is, chap. 9.)

"The oracles" τὰ λόγια (*ta logia*) is an unusual phrase, found only here in Paul (it is used for the "oracles" of the prophet Balaam in Num 24:4, 16 and often for words spoken by God to Israel; e.g., Deut 33:9 and frequently in Psalm 119; in the NT, see Acts 7:38; Heb 5:12; 1 Pet 4:11). In its pagan usage it often referred to oracles in the technical sense: short utterances given, supposedly under inspiration, at shrines such as Delphi. A ruler would send emissaries to an oracular shrine, who would return entrusted with the (often cryptic) words of the deity, not for themselves but for their master. In addition, the priest or priestess at the shrine would themselves be "entrusted" by the god with the message for the recipient. This explains well enough the sense of Paul's comment. The Jews were "entrusted" with messages for the world; not simply with Torah itself, but, through their living under Torah, with words of instruction, of life and light, for the Gentile world. They were to be God's messengers. The fact that this theme is so evident in the present paragraph is further proof of the reading of 2:17-29 proposed above.

**3:3.** Paul's basic answer is the central point of the paragraph. Israel's faithlessness cannot nullify God's faithfulness. He expresses this as a question, but the Greek construction demonstrates that he clearly expects the answer "No." We should note, despite the NIV's translation "What if some did not have faith?," that Paul is not so concerned with whether they "had faith" in the sense of "Christian faith," a personal trust in the God who raises the dead, but rather with their faithfulness—faithfulness (that is) to the commission to be God's messenger people. The Greek word πίστις (*pistis*), used here for the first time in the body of the letter (i.e., since 1:17), is much broader than the English "faith," particularly in some of its theological developments, and encompasses the meanings "trustworthiness" and "loyalty" as well as what we have come to think of as its more "religious" meanings (personal trust in, and knowledge of, God and belief in true statements about God). It is clearly the broader meaning that is on view here, both in its negative form, applied to Israel (unfaithfulness, untrustworthiness) and in its positive form, applied to God (faithfulness, reliability). The πίστις θεοῦ (*pistis theou*), "God's trustworthiness," is thus clearly one aspect of, one way of referring to, the δικαιοσύνη θεοῦ (*dikaiosynē theou*), "God's righteousness." God's covenant always envisaged Israel's being faithful to the commission to be the light of the world; Israel's untrustworthiness does not abolish God's trustworthiness. It merely sharpens up the question: What will God do now?

**3:4.** To back up the point, Paul quotes Ps 51:4 [50:6 LXX], the great prayer of repentance ascribed to David after his adultery with Bathsheba.[80] The verse indicates the abject sorrow of the penitent, acknowledging that when God condemns this sin there will be no question about the rightness of the verdict. God's words are true, even if all human words prove false. It is interesting to observe that when Paul alludes to or mentions David, here and in 4:6-8, it is in connection with sin and forgiveness.[81] The psalm goes on, of course, to speak of the new heart that God will create within the penitent and the gift of the Holy Spirit—"new covenant" themes, in other words,

---

79. All the questions in this section are rhetorical, made by imaginary objectors. Paul does not wish to press them on his own account. The NIV flags this up in v. 7 by adding "someone might argue."

80. On this, see Richard B. Hays, *Echoes of Scripture in the Letters of Paul* (New Haven: Yale University Press, 1989) 48-50.

81. See 4QMMT C26. On other parallels with 4QMMT see esp. the Commentary on 10:5-8.

that tie in, via Ezekiel 36, with the close of chap. 2. The verse Paul quotes stresses that sinful humanity, and sinful Israel, can have no claim on God.

**3:5-6.** This raises an apparent problem, caused perhaps by the language of the psalm as much as anything else. It might seem as though God were acting as judge and executioner in a case where the two parties at law were Israel and—God's own self! This would constitute flagrant injustice; how could the party on trial also judge the case fairly? But Paul is quick to point out that God is not actually at law with Israel; God is the cosmic judge, who must bring justice to the whole world. Some scriptural passages do speak of God having a lawsuit against Israel, but the more fundamental truth is that God is the judge.[82]

**3:7-8.** The same objection is now put from another angle, returning to the truth/falsehood antithesis of v. 4. This is not so much a legal dilemma, but an apparent absurdity at a less formal level.

Paul slips into the first-person singular ("my falsehood," "why am I condemned?"). This does not mean that he is thinking of himself as an individual, nor simply that he is personalizing the argument for the sake of rhetorical impact. He is in effect anticipating the rhetorical move of 7:7-25 (see the commentary at that point), where the "I" is a way of talking about Israel while not seeming to stand over against "his kinsmen according to the flesh." The fact that he moves back to treating Jews in general in v. 9 strongly supports this reading. The question is then, if Israel's falsehood means that God's truthfulness shines out all the more brightly, why should God object? Surely "I" should not then be condemned—in other words, surely God cannot actually endorse what was said in 2:17-29, not least 2:27? The deepest charge against Israel in 2:17-24, after all, was that God's name was being blasphemed because of Israel's disobedience to Torah. Very well, if God's glory is enhanced by this process, surely God will now be

pleased? Why should "I" then be condemned as though "I" were a ἁμαρτωλός (hamartōlos), a "sinner," a mere pagan, one of the lesser breeds outside the Torah?[83] (This question again reflects the charge Paul has been mounting throughout the previous paragraphs: The condemnation incurred by the pagans falls on Israel as well.)

Paul does not deign to answer this question, but instead amplifies it by referring to a still more blatant attack on the integrity of his theology. Some, he says, have been slandering him (lit., "blaspheming" him; but the word had a more general sense); some are reporting him as saying "let us do evil that good may come."[84] In other words, the "evil" of Israel's failure has brought the "good" of the gospel—a point one can understand people thinking on the basis of, say, Rom 11:11-15—so why not apply the principle more generally?

Paul's only comment on this is the heavily ironic one: Here at least is someone whose condemnation is manifestly just. If nothing else about God's judgment is certain, it is thoroughly deserved by people who can say such a thing—either in general, or as a caricature of Paul's teaching.

Why has Paul allowed himself even to note these problems, providing so much puzzlement for subsequent readers, without giving answers? Part of the answer, as we hinted earlier, is that he had to acknowledge them after what he had said in 2:25-29 (and indeed 2:13-15). But a further and deeper reason, which will emerge in 3:21-26, is that the gospel itself reveals God's righteousness, precisely that righteousness that is called into question in the ways outlined so briefly here.

The fuller answer, though, comes in chaps. 9–11, where the same questions recur:

3:1, "What is the point of being a Jew?" corresponds to 9:1-5 as a whole;

3:3, "Has Israel's failure impugned the faithfulness of God to the words previously issued?" corresponds to 9:6, "It is not as though God's word had failed";

---

82. There may be here an analogy with the book of Job. Job, assuming that he and God are adversaries at law, declares his innocence; Job's comforters, making the same assumption, declare Job guilty. In fact, Job's adversary is Satan; God remains the judge and in the end clears Job's name. God and Job can both be in the right simultaneously. The parallel is not exact, but the analogy holds to this extent: God appears unjust to those who assume that God is a party in the lawsuit, rather than the judge.

83. For the usage, see Gal 2:15. A hamartōlos, from the Jewish point of view, was one who, without having the benefit of Torah, sinned as it were in the dark. When a Jew sinned the result was παράβασις (parabasis, "transgression"), breaking a known commandment. See the Commentary on 5:13-14.

84. The Greek could mean that there are two different groups making similar accusations, the former in a more slanderous fashion (reflected in the NIV). But the NRSV may be right to take the sentence as a hendiadys, a single point expressed in two parallel ways.

3:5, "Is God then unjust?" corresponds to 9:14, "Is there injustice with God?";

3:7, "Why am I still condemned?" corresponds to 9:19, "Why does God still find fault?"

3:9, as we shall see below, corresponds in all sorts of ways to 9:30–10:21. In addition, the narrative logic of chap. 3, in which the failure of Israel leads to the fresh revelation of God's righteousness (3:21-26), corresponds closely to the narrative logic of the whole of 9–11, focused particularly on 10:1-4.

We should also note that in 7:7-25 we find a much fuller presentation of Israel's failure and of the strange way in which the Torah was involved in it, which develops the thought of 2:17-29 and prepares the way for chaps. 9–11. There, too, the first-order problem is not "legalism" so much as law*breaking*. The second-order problem there is the plight of Israel, called to be under Torah and yet discovering that it condemns rather than giving life—again, not too far from 2:17-29, and ending with a cry of frustration that bears some relation to the (admittedly more cynical) questions of 3:7-8. There, too, the statement of the problem in 7:7-25 prepares the ground for the statement of the solution in 8:1-11, just as the present passage prepares for 3:21–4:25, both "solutions" hinging on the death of Jesus. All in all, then, the present paragraph is thoroughly integrated into the rest of the letter.

All this indicates how Paul's mind works as he paints on this grand theological canvas, and how vital it is, if we are to grasp his full picture, to look to other places where the same theme is treated. At the same time, we must remember the role of the passage in its own context. Paul is doing much more than rehearsing the same argument two or three times, in more detail perhaps, just for the sake of it. So what role does the rapid listing of questions in 3:1-8 play within 1:18–3:20, the section within which it belongs?

The paragraph forms a vital part of three things that are going on simultaneously here. First, it is part of the specific theme of universal human sinfulness (see below on 3:19-20). If Jews are to be included in this indictment—the basic problem being not that they are legalists or moralists, but that their boast is undercut by their own law-breaking—this raises questions that must be addressed, or at least noted, before the conclusion can be drawn (3:10-20). Thus the sequence of thought runs: 2:17-29, initial accusation against Israel; 3:1-8, weighty theological objections to such an accusation (if it is true, what does that do to your wider theology?); 3:9-20, confirming the truth of the initial accusation.

Second, the paragraph belongs also with the second-order charge that Paul levels against Israel: that, commissioned to be God's messenger people, the light of the world, it was disloyal to God and failed in the commission. Since the commission was God's answer to the problem of idolatry and dissolution (1:18-32), the problem might now seem insoluble. Paul here asserts that God will remain faithful; in other words, that despite Israel's failure the problem of universal sin will be addressed and dealt with.

Third, therefore, and overarching both of these, the paragraph is part of the larger theme of God's righteousness revealed in the gospel. The character of God is a major theme here; within vv. 2-7 alone Paul deals with God's oracles, God's faithfulness, God's truth (twice), God's justice, God's wrath, God's judgment, and God's glory. He has already argued in 1:18–2:29 that the gospel reveals God's impartial judgment, enabling one to understand present moral chaos as an anticipation of the coming wrath. Objections to this are noted in 3:1-8 (it seems to impugn God's character), and they are answered in such a way as to prepare for the description of the unveiling of God's righteousness (3:21–4:25). If God is to be true to character, if the promises are to be fulfilled, what is needed is a faithful Israelite who will act on behalf of, and in the place of, faithless Israel. Paul will argue in 3:21-26 that God has provided exactly that.

First, however, the lawcourt scene must be rounded off. The Gentile world has long since been arraigned and found guilty. Paul will now insist that all Jews belong in the dock as well, with nothing to say in their own defense. (See Reflections at 3:9-20.)

# Romans 3:9-20, Torah Puts Jews in the Dock Alongside Gentiles

## NIV

[9] What shall we conclude then? Are we any better[a]? Not at all! We have already made the charge that Jews and Gentiles alike are all under sin. [10] As it is written:

"There is no one righteous, not even one;
[11]    there is no one who understands,
    no one who seeks God.
[12] All have turned away,
    they have together become worthless;
there is no one who does good,
    not even one."[b]
[13] "Their throats are open graves;
    their tongues practice deceit."[c]
"The poison of vipers is on their lips."[d]
[14]    "Their mouths are full of cursing and
        bitterness."[e]
[15] "Their feet are swift to shed blood;
[16]    ruin and misery mark their ways,
[17] and the way of peace they do not know."[f]
[18]    "There is no fear of God before their
        eyes."[g]

[19] Now we know that whatever the law says, it says to those who are under the law, so that every mouth may be silenced and the whole world held accountable to God. [20] Therefore no one will be declared righteous in his sight by observing the law; rather, through the law we become conscious of sin.

[a] 9 Or worse    [b] 12 Psalms 14:1-3; 53:1-3; Eccles. 7:20    [c] 13 Psalm 5:9    [d] 13 Psalm 140:3    [e] 14 Psalm 10:7    [f] 17 Isaiah 59:7,8    [g] 18 Psalm 36:1

## NRSV

[9] What then? Are we any better off?[a] No, not at all; for we have already charged that all, both Jews and Greeks, are under the power of sin, [10] as it is written:
"There is no one who is righteous, not even
    one;
[11]    there is no one who has understanding,
        there is no one who seeks God.
[12] All have turned aside, together they have
        become worthless;
    there is no one who shows kindness,
        there is not even one."
[13] "Their throats are opened graves;
    they use their tongues to deceive."
"The venom of vipers is under their lips."
[14]    "Their mouths are full of cursing and
        bitterness."
[15] "Their feet are swift to shed blood;
[16]    ruin and misery are in their paths,
[17] and the way of peace they have not known."
[18]    "There is no fear of God before their eyes."

[19] Now we know that whatever the law says, it speaks to those who are under the law, so that every mouth may be silenced, and the whole world may be held accountable to God. [20] For "no human being will be justified in his sight" by deeds prescribed by the law, for through the law comes the knowledge of sin.

[a] Or at any disadvantage?

# COMMENTARY

"Whatever Torah says, it speaks to those under the law" (lit., "in the law," 3:19). This is the clue to the present paragraph, with its string of scriptural quotations. Having already argued for the universality of Gentile sin and guilt, Paul now needs to emphasize that the Jews must be seen in the dock alongside the pagans. This has been where his argument has been going for some while, but 2:17-29 and 3:1-9 are not just part of the indictment; they are aimed at answering potential objections, at getting rid of excuses, before the final word is spoken.

The biblical quotations come from Israel's Scriptures and are themselves indictments, not of pagans, but of Jews. Scripture itself, in other words, bears witness against those to whom it was entrusted, leaving the whole world accountable to God (cf. 10:19-21). Paul sums up the problem in terms of the impossibility of anyone being justified by Torah, since all Torah can now do is to point to sin. This will enable him to move at once to demonstrate how the revelation of God's right-eousness in the gospel has dealt with precisely this problem.

**3:9.** The words of v. 9 could, as they stand, bear several different meanings. Once the train of thought of the chapter as a whole is grasped, how-ever, the options are reduced effectively to one.[85] Paul has been arguing that the privileges of the Jews are real, even though they have been squan-dered; he has answered his own question of v. 1 with "much in every way." This verse asks a dif-ferent question: So, then, are we Jews in a better position, in absolute terms? Are we still, in J. B. Phillips's translation, "a march ahead" of everyone else? Since the answer is filled out not only in the second half of v. 9 but also in vv. 10-20 as a whole, we can deduce that it almost certainly should be "no, not at all."[86]

Paul now begins a lawcourt metaphor, which he will develop further in vv. 19-20. He has already laid a charge, like a plaintiff in a case; a charge against both Jews and Greeks ("Greeks" here, as usual, is a metonym for "Gentiles in gen-eral"), alleging that they are both "under sin" (NIV, taking the text exactly), i.e., "under the power of sin" (NRSV). By "already charged" he is referring back, obviously, to the argument that began in 1:18. He has not, however, mentioned the word ἁμαρτία (hamartia, "sin") up to this point and has only used the cognate verb ἁμαρτάνω (hamartanō) in 2:12, first of Gentiles and then of Jews (see also ἁμαρτωλός hamartōlos in 3:7). Clearly Paul regards "laying a charge of being under (the power of) sin" as an accurate summary of all that he has said so far. This intro-duces us to another major theme in the letter, that

of "sin" as a personified force and of the slavery of humankind to this force.

In Paul's usage, "sin" refers not just to individ-ual human acts of "sin," of missing the mark (the basic meaning of the word) as regards the divine intention for full human flourishing and fulfill-ment. "Sin" takes on a malevolent life of its own, exercising power over persons and communities. It is almost as though by "sin" Paul is referring to what in some other parts of the Bible is meant by "Satan" (though Paul can use that language too; e.g., 16:20); this is particularly striking in 7:7-25. By analyzing the human plight in this way he is able to introduce the notion of enslavement to sin (e.g., 6:20) and thereby to clear the way for his own version of the story of the exodus: for Pharaoh, read "sin"; for Passover and Red Sea, read the death and resurrection of Jesus; for the arrival at Sinai and the giving of Torah, read the Spirit; for inheriting the promised land, read the renewal of all creation. This sequence of thought, as we shall see, determines a good deal of the shape of Romans 5–8. In the present chapter this is anticipated in the dense description of the death of Jesus in 3:24-26 (on which see below).

**3:10-18.** Paul arranges his string of biblical quotations quite carefully.[87] He opens with the general charge that no one is "righteous," antici-pating the conclusion in v. 20. The rest of the description is framed by charges of impiety: Nobody understands, or seeks after God (v. 11); nobody keeps the fear of God before their eyes (v. 18). Within this, he draws up a comprehensive charge of going astray (v. 12), wicked speech (vv. 13-14), and violent behavior (vv. 15-17).

As always with Paul's biblical quotations, it is worth checking the contexts to see whether he might have intended wider reference than simply the words quoted.[88] After the opening line, which corresponds both to Eccl 7:20 and Ps 14:1, Paul quotes at length from Ps 14:53, which ends with a prayer that God would deliver Israel out of cap-tivity. He then moves to Ps 5:9, the denunciation of those whose throat is an open sepulcher and who deceive with their tongue; the previous verse

---

85. The word translated "Are we any better?" (NIV) or "Are we any better off?" (NRSV, which is to be preferred, since the word refers to position and status, not moral behavior) could also mean "Are we any worse off?"; the answer, "No, not at all" (NRSV), could mean "Not com-pletely" or "Not entirely." The translation is further complicated because the question mark we assume after the opening words Τί οὖν (Ti oun, "What then?") could belong instead after the next word, προεχόμεθα (proechometha), producing a single question, "In what way, then, are we better/worse off?" But most agree that the meaning in the NRSV is correct. For different options, see C. E. B. Cranfield, A Critical and Exegetical Commentary on the Epistle to the Romans, ICC, 2 vols. (Edinburgh: T. & T. Clark, 1975) 188-91; Joseph A. Fitzmyer, Romans, AB 33 (Garden City, N.Y.: Doubleday, 1993) 330-31; Brendan Byrne, Romans, SP 6 (Collegeville, Minn.: Liturgical, 1996) 119-20.

86. Against Cranfield, Romans, 190, who argues cautiously for "not in every respect."

87. L. E. Keck, "The Function of Romans 3:10-18—Observations and Suggestions," in God's Christ and His People: Studies in Honor of Nils Alstrup Dahl, ed. J. Jervell and W. A. Meeks (Oslo: Universitetsforlaget, 1977) 141-57, suggests that this may actually be a pre-Pauline composi-tion.

88. See Hays, Echoes of Scripture in the Letters of Paul, 50-52.

prays that YHWH would lead the psalmist "in your righteousness." Continuing in vv. 13-14 the theme of the wickedness of the mouth and tongue, Ps 140:3 adds to Paul's list of charges that the unrighteous have adders' poison under their lips, and Ps 10:7 that their mouths are full of cursing and bitterness. Both psalms beseech YHWH that he would act at last, to judge the wicked and establish the kingdom for ever. All of these wider themes, clearly, fit within the overall subject matter of Romans 1–3.

We then move in v. 15 to Isa 59:7-8, the complaint that the wicked are swift to shed blood, bring ruin and destruction, and do not know the way of peace. Of all the chapters in the Hebrew Scriptures, this is the one that most strikingly depicts YHWH discovering that there is no righteousness to be had in the world, and so putting on the clothes of righteousness and salvation to rescue the covenant people and judge their adversaries (59:16-18). The chapter ends with YHWH coming to Zion as redeemer—a passage Paul will quote in 11:26—and establishing the divine covenant with Israel, putting the divine spirit within them. Psalm 36:2, the final quotation ("there is no fear of God before their eyes"), moves on to a paean of praise of God's mercy and faithfulness (36:5), God's righteousness and judgments (v. 6), and ends with a prayer for God's mercy and righteousness to abide with Israel and for the wicked to be judged at last (36:10-12).

This is too much for coincidence. What looked at first like a repetitious list of biblical quotations, apparently laboring the point that all are deeply wicked, turns out to be a subtle sequence of thought, linking in at virtually every point with the themes from Paul's surrounding argument. The surface meaning of the text is clear, that all who are "under the law" are condemned as sinners; but the subtext is saying all the time, "Yes; and in precisely this situation God will act, because of the divine righteousness, to judge the world, to rescue the helpless, to establish the covenant." Had Paul been a composer, we may suspect that he would not only have written strong, clear tunes; he would also have been a master of harmony, counterpoint, and orchestration.

**3:19.** To conclude the matter, Paul returns to lawcourt imagery. The Torah (here taken as the whole of the Jewish scriptures, not merely as the first five books) addresses those "in the law," so that every mouth may be stopped and the whole world be accountable to God. The stopping of the mouth, by placing a hand over it, was a conventional sign to indicate that one had no more to say in one's own defense; if an obviously guilty defendant continued to speak, the court might of course order that his mouth be stopped for him (cf. Acts 23:2; the NIV's and NRSV's "silenced" describes the effect, but loses the forensic significance of the physical stopping of the mouth). The term ὑπόδικος (hypodikos, "accountable") probably carries a negative sense; not just "answerable" (which might imply that a good answer could be forthcoming), but "guilty and punishable." This is confirmed by the "because" at the start of the next verse, explaining as it does why the only evidence that can be produced is evidence of sin. The case has been heard; the defendants have no more to say; they stand in the dock awaiting the verdict, which can only go one way.

**3:20.** The διότι (dioti) that opens v. 20 certainly means "for" (NRSV) or "because," not "therefore."[89] This verse offers the logical ground for 3:19, not the other way around. The Torah speaks to those under the Torah, says Paul, with the result that every mouth is stopped, because (v. 20a) nobody will be justified by works of Torah, because (v. 20b) through Torah comes knowledge of sin.[90] To remove all doubt, turn the sequence the other way around: Torah brings knowledge of sin, therefore no one will be justified by "works of Torah," therefore when Torah speaks it leaves those "under Torah" without any defense. Paul has, no doubt, left this point (about the role of Torah in the process) until last in order that he may then state the new point of 3:21 with maximum rhetorical effect.

This verse is one of those points in a Pauline argument where each phrase needs to be weighed with particular care.

---

89. Thus the NIV, showing remarkable disregard for Paul's connecting links. The penalty for this is to be forced to alter the next connective as well: γάρ (gar), introducing the last part of the verse, means "for," not "rather," as in the NIV.

90. The NIV's "through the law we become conscious of sin" adds a first-person plural where Paul leaves the matter abstract. This sentence, which sounds like a restatement of the Lutheran view of the "preaching of the law," reflects Paul's meaning only if we remember that "we" would have to mean "those under the law" (see the Commentary on 7:7-12). In addition, "becoming conscious of sin" is not quite the same as having "knowledge of sin" (see 7:7).

To begin with the subject of the sentence: "No human being" (NRSV) and "no one" (NIV) do not capture the nuance of Paul's phrase. In alluding to Ps 143:2 [142:2 LXX], it is striking that he says, literally, "all flesh [πᾶσα σάρξ *pasa sarx*] shall not be justified."[91] "Flesh," as we saw at 1:3, is a heavily loaded term for Paul. It designates, not so much ordinary physicality as opposed to non-material existence, but rather humankind seen as physically corruptible and morally rebellious, heading for death in both senses. It can also carry the sense of Jewish "flesh," sharing the problem of "fleshly" humanity, with the "fleshly" badge of circumcision only serving to emphasize this identification. That, indeed, is an important part of the argument of Galatians. Although, therefore, Paul's "all flesh" here means the whole of humanity, it is strikingly appropriate, within his wider theology, that he should use it when insisting that the Jews must join the Gentiles as guilty defendants before the judgment seat of God.

Though Paul is not quoting the psalm verbatim, he clearly intends to refer to it. Once more he seems to have the wider scriptural context in mind.[92] Psalm 143 is a prayer invoking the faithfulness and righteousness of YHWH (Ps 143:1), pleading for deliverance, not on the basis of any merit (since, as v. 2 says, no one living is righteous before God), but simply for the sake of God's name and God's righteousness (v. 11). Though the surface level of Paul's argument demands that he quote v. 2, the underlying theme of the whole section now drawing to a close, and of that about to begin, is the righteousness of God. God, being righteous, must judge the wicked; but those who are not righteous themselves may nevertheless cast themselves on God's righteousness to find deliverance.

What, then, does Paul mean, "by works of the law shall no flesh be justified before God"? How does this relate to 2:13, where "the doers of the law" shall be justified?

The question can only be answered fully in relation to the many other passages where Paul speaks of "works of the law." But a preliminary answer may be given here, to be filled out as the

commentary progresses and with additional side-long glances at Galatians.

Justification, in this passage, is clearly a law-court term. We may remind ourselves that the Greek words "justify" (δικαιόω *dikaioō*) and "justification" (δικαίωσις *dikaiōsis*) belong to the same root as "righteous" (δίκαιος *dikaios*) and "righteousness" (δικαιοσύνη *dikaiosynē*). Attempts to clarify this in English by choosing one of the two roots and forcing it through ("just, justice" rather than "righteous, righteousness"; "rightwise, rightwising" rather than "justify," "justification") bring other problems and have not commanded general assent. As noted in the Introduction, when Paul uses this language he has three interlocking spheres of reference in mind. The language most naturally belongs in the lawcourt;[93] the overarching concept in Paul's mind is God's covenant with Israel, the covenant through which (as though in a cosmic lawcourt) the world will be put to rights. And the critical turn in the argument is eschatological: Paul's affirmation that the final lawcourt scene has been brought forward into the present, that the divine "righteousness" has been disclosed already in Jesus the Messiah.

Put simply, then, Paul's point here is that the verdict of the court, i.e., of God, cannot be that those who have "works of Torah" on their record will receive the verdict "righteous." We remind ourselves again that he is not speaking of Gentiles here, but of Jews; we already know, from 1:18–2:16, that Gentiles will not be justified as they stand. "The Jew" of 2:17 will come into court, metaphorically speaking, and "rest in the Torah," producing "works of Torah"; these, it will be claimed, demonstrate that he or she is indeed a member of Israel, part of God's covenant people. No, says Paul. To cite one's possession of Torah as support will not do. Torah will simply remind you that you are a sinner like the Gentiles. That was the point of the hints in 1:18–2:16 and of the direct charge in 2:17-29—not, as is sometimes said, that the Jews are "legalists," but that they have broken the law they were given. And transgression of Torah shows that Jews, like Gentiles, are "under the power of sin" (3:9). To appeal to

91. The LXX has πᾶς ζῶν (*pas zōn*, "every living thing"). Paul quotes the same verse, with the same alteration, in Gal 2:16. "All flesh" (*pasa sarx*) takes the mind to Isa 40:5-6.

92. See Hays, *Echoes of Scripture in the Letters of Paul*, 51-53; Richard B. Hays, "Psalm 143 and the Logic of Romans 3," *JBL* 99 (1980) 107-15.

93. Paul is assuming, of course, the ancient Jewish lawcourt, not a modern one, as Seifrid accuses me of proposing. See M. A. Seifrid, *Christ Our Righteousness: Paul's Theology of Justification* (Downers Grove: InterVarsity, 2000) 59.

Torah is like calling a defense witness who endorses what the prosecution has been saying all along. (This is the point that Paul will develop, via such apparent throwaway lines as 5:20, in 7:7-25; cf. too 1 Cor 15:56.)

What then are these "works of Torah"? How does this indictment against those who have "works of Torah" on their record square with what Paul says about himself in Phil 3:6, that concerning "righteousness in Torah" he had become "blameless"? How does it fit with wider, non-Christian evidence for Jewish beliefs about Torah in Paul's day?

The only pre-Christian Jewish text we possess that uses the phrase "works of Torah" is a recently published Dead Sea Scroll, the already well-known 4QMMT.[94] "We have indeed sent you," writes the author to his readers, "this selection of works of the Torah according to our decision, for your welfare and the welfare of your people."[95] However, this cannot be used as a template for Paul's meaning of the phrase itself, since the "works" spoken of there are (a) post-biblical rulings concerning temple purity, aimed at (b) defining one group of Jews over against others. It is clear from Romans and Galatians, as we shall see, that when Paul speaks of "works of the law" he is thinking rather of (a) biblical rules that (b) defined Jews (and proselytes) over against pagans. The phrase is, after all, quite general, and we may suppose that it had a wider currency than just Paul and Qumran, even though only they out of our surviving literature use it, and that infrequently.

The main positive thing that this Qumran text contributes to the present discussion, though, is a sense of how "works of the Torah" could function within the language of justification. The third and final section of MMT tells the story of Israel, from the promises and warnings of Deuteronomy up to the writer's own day. Deuteronomy 30 promised a historical sequence: covenantal blessing, curse, then blessing again. The initial blessing and curse, says the text, came upon Israel in the time of the monarchy, with the curse being, more or less, the exile. Now, however, the second blessing promised by the same text has come upon Israel, precisely in the life of the sect, the secretly inaugurated new covenant people, yet to be finally and publicly vindicated. The members of the sect are already marked out as the eschatological Israel, ahead of the time when they will be vindicated as such. The thing that marks them out in the present is precisely the specific "works of the Torah" that the text urges upon its readers—the detailed post-biblical regulations deemed necessary by the sect. These "works of Torah," then, were the sign that the future verdict (God's vindication of the sect) was anticipated in the present; the sect could be confident now of their membership in the renewed covenant, the community of fresh blessing, the "returned-from-exile" people spoken of in Deuteronomy 30. When we widen the horizon from the sectarian "works" mentioned in the scroll to the more fundamental biblical "works" Paul has in mind, the position he is opposing can be stated thus: "works of Torah" are the sign, in the present, of that membership in Israel, God's covenant people, which will be vindicated in the future when the long-awaited "righteousness of God" is finally unveiled in action.

It is vital to keep our balance at this point. One of the great gains of the last quarter of a century in Pauline scholarship has been to recognize that Paul's contemporaries—and Paul himself prior to his conversion—were not "legalists," if by that we mean that they were attempting to earn favor with God, to earn grace as it were, by the performance of law-prescribed works.[96] Paul's fellow

---

94. MMT (an acronym for the Hebrew words meaning "a selection of works of Torah," which, coming in line C27 of the scroll, appear to sum up the text's main thrust) is reconstructed from six Qumran fragments, none of them complete (4Q394-399). It seems to be a letter, written in the mid-second century BCE, from the leader of the Qumran group to the head of a larger group, of which the Qumran sect was once a part. For the text, translations, and preliminary discussions, see Elisha Qimron and John Strugnell, *Qumran Cave 4 V: Miqṣat Maʿaśe Ha-Torah. Discoveries in the Judaean Desert X* (Oxford: Clarendon, 1994); Geza Vermes, *The Complete Dead Sea Scrolls in English* (Harmondsworth: Penguin, 1997) 220-28; Michael Wise, Martin Abegg, Jr., and Edward Cook, *The Dead Sea Scrolls: A New Translation* (San Francisco: Harper, 1996) 358-64; Florentino García Martínez, *The Dead Sea Scrolls Translated: The Qumran Texts in English* (Leiden: Brill, 1994) 77-85. On the relation between MMT and Paul, see also the Commentary on 10:5-8. Despite Vermes (493), it now appears that the other reference sometimes suggested, 4Q174, frag. 1, 1:7, reads "works of thanksgiving" (מעשי תודה *maʿaśê-tôdâ*) rather than "works of the law" (מעשי תורה *maʿaśê-tôrâh*).

95. MMT C26-27, author's trans.

96. This so-called new perspective, associated principally with E. P. Sanders, *Paul and Palestinian Judaism* (London: SCM, 1977), has now not only taken on a life and literature of its own but has generated a growth industry of opposing publications. See, e.g., R. H. Gundry, "Grace, Works, and Staying Saved in Paul," *Biblica* 66 (1985) 1-38; C. H. Talbert, "Paul, Judaism, and the Revisionists," *CBQ* 63 (2001) 1-22; D. A. Carson, P. T. O'Brien, and M. A. Seifrid, *Justification and Variegated Nomism* (Grand Rapids: Baker Academic), whose first volume, *The Complexities of Second Temple Judaism*, appeared just as this commentary went to press.

Jews were not proto-Pelagians, attempting to pull themselves up by their moral shoelaces. They were, rather, responding out of gratitude to the God who had chosen and called Israel to be the covenant people and who had given Israel the law both as the sign of that covenant membership and as the means of making it real. Paul's critique is not that the Torah was a bad thing that the Jews should not have followed, nor that their Torah-observance was done in order to stake a claim on God that God had not already granted in the covenant. His point, rather, was that all who attempted to legitimate their covenant status by appealing to possession of Torah would find that the Torah itself accused them of sin. If "the Jew" appealed to Torah to say "This shows that I am different from the Gentiles," Torah itself, according to Paul, would say "No, it doesn't; it shows that you are the same as the Gentiles."

The "works" that were regarded in Paul's day as particularly demonstrating covenant membership were, of course, those things that marked out the Jews from their pagan neighbors, not least in the diaspora: the sabbath, the food laws, and circumcision. A strong case can therefore be made for seeing "works of the law," in Romans and Galatians, as highlighting these elements in particular.[97] This case rests on the larger thrust of Paul's argument, in which "the Jew" is appealing not to perfect performance of every last commandment, but to possession of Torah as the badge of being God's special people. Special they are, but also sinning; and sin means that the specialness is of no ultimate avail.

Why, then, could Paul say of himself, in Phil 3:6, that concerning "righteousness under the law" he was "found blameless"? Presumably he meant that, as a good Jew, he regularly used the means of forgiveness and purification that were on offer in the Temple and the sacrificial cult and took part in the great fasts and feasts through which the devout Jew was assured of God's forgiveness and favor. Thus at any moment he was a Jew in good standing; not that he had always done what Torah prescribed (we must not suppose the pre-Christian Paul to have been so ignorant of his own motivation and behavior), but that he had always repented and sought God's forgiveness through the appropriate methods. Torah, he might have said, can show me that I am a sinner and can also show me the way of forgiveness. We must assume that someone who followed this path would consider themselves "blameless according to the law."

Further discussion of this point must be postponed until we arrive at 7:7-25, since that passage needs to be factored into the argument in various ways. But one major difference between what Paul says in Philippians and what he says in Romans 3 is that in the present passage his primary concern is not to analyze every single individual and to demonstrate somehow that he or she really is sinful, but rather to show that possession of Torah itself cannot sustain the claim that "the Jew" is automatically in covenant with God, automatically a cut above the Gentiles. And, in referring to those (like his own former self) who are "under the law," he looks at them in their totality, sin included. Just as Israel cannot be affirmed in the present as the inalienable covenant people of God because of the presence, within Israel, of various kinds of sin that demonstrate the failure of the national vocation (2:17-24), so no Jews, however blameless in terms of current status, can be affirmed as they stand as complete and adequate human beings, since all alike commit sin. If God is the righteous judge, God cannot allow particular members of that nation to escape the judgment they incur just as do all Gentiles.

If, however, God is truly "righteous" in the widest senses, including that of keeping the covenant promises made long ago, how then can that "righteousness" be put into operation without contradicting itself? This question was raised extremely sharply for Paul's near-contemporaries by the fall of Jerusalem in 70 CE. For Paul, it had already been raised, and answered, by the events concerning Jesus of Nazareth. Paul is now in a position to address this question, one of the most fundamental that he and his contemporaries were ever to face.

---

97. This is argued especially by Dunn in various works. See James D. G. Dunn, *Romans 1–8*, WBC 38A (Dallas: Word, 1988) 153-60, and the other refs. there.

# REFLECTIONS

**1.** Before we "translate" or "apply" these severe and often dense verses to our own day, we must consider the relevance of their own unique meaning in Paul's own time. Part of the burden of eschatology—part of the problem, that is, of believing in a God who (though always active within the world in various ways) acted uniquely and decisively at one moment in history, and part of the problem of living on the basis of that one-off action—is that one is committed to getting inside that historical situation in all its differentness to our own day, to understanding what it was that God was up to then. Preachers of the gospel cannot escape the task of being ancient historians. The alternative is shallow anachronism.

Paul insists that God will be just and faithful, despite the faithlessness of the particular humans to whom the divine oracles had been entrusted. In the post-Enlightenment world, ironically, the goodness and justice of God are often called into account precisely because of the suggestion that God might act in a particular and decisive way, in one place and time rather than at another. The rhetoric of the last two hundred years has been in favor of broad general truths, timeless and abstract religious or ethical norms or guidelines. Projecting our hard-won (and often deeply ambiguous) democracy onto the heavens, we demand that all humans should have the same vote and voice. How, we ask, can a unique act of God be fair?

This question is, at one level, a manifestation of the old discussion, associated with Barth and others, as to whether Christianity is a "religion" or rather a "revelation." In these debates, however, it was often assumed that the Jews followed a "religion," and were indeed the archetypical manifestation of *homo religiosus,* religious humanity. (This is a major theme in the great commentary of Ernst Käsemann.) We have learned, painfully enough, the danger of such caricatured generalizations. What Saul of Tarsus and his contemporaries were longing for, in any case, was a revelation, an unveiling, the fresh action of their God within history. That was how wrongs would be put right, how justice would come at last. The irony of our changing points of view, the transformation of assumptions between Paul's day and ours, is that this idea of a specific and decisive act of God, in one place and time beyond all others, is itself now felt to be wrong or unjust. We here reach basic questions of worldview, and choices have to be made. The whole New Testament witnesses to a unique act of God, such as Saul of Tarsus had expected, but at a different level, of a totally different kind. Yes, says Paul the Apostle, God has acted in history to unveil that faithfulness of which Scripture spoke. But no, the action was not what Israel, Saul of Tarsus included, had expected.

The "modern" objection to the idea of God's acting decisively and uniquely is based, it seems, on a false impression about what such actions mean. If the main purpose of divine revelation were to convey information to humans, or to give a set of rules to be kept, then it would seem unfair and arbitrary to give these to some and then to judge the others despite their disadvantage. If the main purpose was to straighten out a few design faults in creation, to perform "miracles" that helped certain people out of insoluble or life-threatening situations, this too would seem grossly unfair; why would a good God, capable of doing this sort of thing, not do it at other times, when faced (for instance) with the chance to prevent genocide?

These are, however, by no means the only possible models of divine action in the world. All analogies are imperfect; but we can conceive of other, perhaps better, ways of looking at the question. An architect has to produce a single blueprint at one time and place, so that the building may be constructed for the benefit of all. A medical researcher has to produce medications at one time and place, so that all may eventually be cured. A gardener has to plant a fruit tree in one place and at one time, so that there may be fruit for all. God, in the Jewish thought that Paul reflects, needed to act decisively at one time and in one place, so that there might be salvation for all. We should not allow the rhetoric of modernity to rob us of the glory of the gospel:

a God with muddy boots and dirty hands, busy at the center of the mess so that all may be cleaned up and sorted out.

**2.** The question of the point of being Jewish, once its own unique dimensions have been grasped, broadens out in our own day to the question of the point of being human. This has been asked in the twentieth century over and over, as philosophers, writers, and artists, as well as theologians, have reflected on the horrors of our "civilized" world, producing ever more cunning machines for making war but still unable to invent one that will make peace. Just as the Jewish vocation was to bring God's light to the Gentiles, so the human vocation was to reflect God's image into the world. Manifest human failure to do this could lead to the equivalent, for this question, of the Marcionite rejection of Judaism as a whole, i.e., a denial of the entire God-given human vocation. This, indeed, is what we find in some New Age thinking today, with humans being regarded as simply part of the world's problem, rather than potential contributors to the solution.

But Paul would be as adamant on this point as he is on his own topic: Let God be true, though everyone should prove false. God has created humans to reflect the divine image in worship and service, and God will be true to that promise. "The righteousness of God" can be called upon to fulfill the purpose of creation, not just of Israel. How this will happen, Paul will work out from 3:21 through to the end of chap. 8. To claim that it will happen is the equivalent, for these questions, of Paul's brief and clipped responses in 3:1-8. That it has already happened is the burden of his song in 3:21–4:25, summed up in 5:12-21: God has provided an obedient human being, in whom the original purpose of Genesis 1 has at last been fulfilled (see also 1 Cor 15:20-28; Phil 3:20-21; and, further afield, the whole argument of Heb 2:5-10).

**3.** The charge of universal human sinfulness is of course as controversial today as ever. Nobody, almost by definition, likes the humiliation of recognizing their sinful condition (or, if they do, we may raise questions about their balance of mind). Just as much psychology tacitly avoids the category of "evil," preferring to see varieties of human behavior in less threatening terms, so many Christians, eager for the great acceptance, the astonishing welcome, of the gospel, use this as a reason for denying human sinfulness. But, of course, if humans are not deeply sinful the gospel is no longer astonishing; indeed, it is not good news at all, since there was no problem to which it was the shocking, startling answer. Tragically, just as those who do not understand history are condemned to repeat it, so those who turn a blind eye to wickedness are always in danger of perpetrating it. If there is no disease, why worry about precautions, let alone cure? If the human race is morally sound (no doubt with a few glitches here and there), we should eat, drink, and be merry, for tomorrow we shall live. Oddly enough, at the same time as postmodernity is urging us to be suspicious of every action, every word, and every motive, the imperative it sanctions—to be true to oneself, even though "oneself" may be constantly changing—is itself deeply suspect. Tyrants, bullies, extortioners, adulterers, and murderers are all being true to themselves. And those who look at such activities and thank God that they are not like that need once more to go deeper (2:1-16), to examine the secrets of their own hearts.

**4.** There is much to learn from the way in which Paul has pulled together the awful catalog of sin in 3:10-18. Under the surface-level indictment there is hope, precisely because this wickedness is shown up by the righteousness of God, which can then be appealed to for mercy. How easy it is for preachers either to denounce wickedness in a dualistic fashion, or to abstain from such denunciations because they sound too depressing, too dismissive. Paul's denunciations, for those with ears to hear, are always hinting at the solution. His robust faith in God's forgiving faithfulness enables him to call a spade a spade.

**5.** The dismissal of "works of the law" as the means of justification has all kinds of overtones. Paul's fundamental meaning is that no Jew can use possession of the Torah, and performance of its key symbolic "works" of ethnic demarcation, as demonstration in the present time that they belong to the eschatological people of God, the people who will inherit the age to come. Torah is incapable of performing this function: When appealed to, it reminds its possessors of their own sin.

This Israel-specific and context-specific argument and meaning, vital though it is, must send off warning signals in other spheres as well. To the Roman moralist of Paul's day, it might have said that clear thought and noble intention were not enough; the clearer the thought, the nobler the intention, the more this clarity and nobility would condemn the actual behavior. To an anxious monk of the early sixteenth century, fretting about his own justification, Paul's words rang other bells. Performance of Christian duties is not enough. Despite the Reformation, the message had still not been heard by the devout John Wesley, until a fresh hearing of Luther's commentary on Galatians caused light to dawn. In the post-Enlightenment period, many, including many Christians, have assumed that "the law," here and elsewhere, refers to the Kantian idea of a categorical moral imperative suspended over all humans, and have preached this "law" to make people recognize their guilt, in order then to declare the gospel to them.

These are important overtones of Paul's statement here, but they are not its fundamental note. If we play an overtone, thinking it to be a fundamental, we shall set off new and different sets of overtones, which will not then harmonize with Paul's original sound. Sadly, this has occurred again and again, not least within the Reformation tradition, which, eager for the universal relevance and the essential *pro me* (i.e., "for me") of the gospel, and regarding Israel mainly as a classic example of the wrong way of approaching God or "religion," has created a would-be "Pauline" theology in which half of what Paul was most eager to say in Romans has been screened out. Provided, however, one is careful to tell again the unique story of Israel and Jesus, not as an example of something else but as the fundamental truth of the gospel, many of the things the Reformers wanted to insist on can be retained and, indeed, enhanced.

# ROMANS 3:21–4:25, GOD'S FAITHFULNESS TO THE COVENANT

## OVERVIEW

It should now be clear that the great theme Paul will unveil in the new section is "the righteousness of God," meaning by that the faithfulness of God to the promises long ago announced to Israel. That divine faithfulness, which seemed to be called into question by Israel's failure to be the light for the Gentiles, is now revealed through the faithful Israelite, Jesus the Messiah. The plan has not failed; rather, it is focused on, and accomplished through, one person. Through him, God has kept the promise made to Abraham.

Paul is therefore speaking, without using the word, of the covenant. This biblical term, found occasionally in Paul, is in my view a useful and appropriate shorthand for drawing attention to the fact that in this section, as in Galatians 3, Paul is evoking one chapter in particular, namely Genesis 15. In that chapter, God established the covenant with Abraham, promising both that he would have countless descendants and that his seed would attain their inheritance by passing through slavery to freedom (Gen 15:5, 13-16). Referring to Paul's "covenantal" theology at this point, as I and others have sometimes done, means simply this: Paul intends to affirm that what God has done in Jesus the Messiah is the fulfillment of the promises to Abraham. This, indeed, is the answer, or at least the initial answer, to the string of questions in 3:1-

8. Despite the unwarranted suspicions of those who assume that to refer to the covenant is to flatten out the contours of Paul's telling of the story of God, Israel, and the world, to reduce the sharp impact of the crucifixion, or to capitulate to a particular type of Reformed theology, this proposal passes the most important test of all: It makes excellent sense of the relevant texts, as we shall now see.[98]

The place of Abraham in the argument of the present section, and its partial parallel in Galatians 3, is therefore far more than as an "example" of someone who was justified by faith, as is still commonly supposed.[99] Paul is doing something much more large-scale, much more intricately crafted, than merely "stating a doctrine" in 3:21-31 and then "offering a proof from scripture" in chap. 4. He has not merely introduced Abraham because his opponents, real or imagined, would have made Abraham a strong part of their own argument. Nor is Abraham's faith the sole or central feature of chap. 4; indeed, by making it so, as we shall see, commentators have introduced puzzles into the exegesis that disappear once the larger theme is grasped.

The proposals cited here as inadequate have entered the exegesis of Romans not least because many readers have come to the text with questions other than Paul's. In particular, the broad questions of human sin and of justification by faith have dominated the discussion, so that Paul's own much more specific questions in Romans, not least those of the coming together of Jew and Gentile in Christian faith, and of the fulfillment of the Abrahamic promises, have been marginalized, to the detriment of exegesis and, in my view, of the life of the church.

Exegesis has been hampered in particular by a misunderstanding of δικαιοσύνη θεοῦ (*dikaiosynē theou*, "the righteousness of God") in 3:21-26 (on "righteousness" language, see the Introduction). Once the wider context (of 3:1-8, on the one hand, and 4:1-25, on the other) is appreciated,

and the specific argument of 3:21-26 itself fully grasped, it is quite impossible that this phrase should mean, as NIV, "a righteousness from God," that is, the righteous status that believers enjoy as a gift from God and in God's presence. Paul does indeed hold that those who believe the gospel are reckoned "righteous" (e.g., 3:26, 28), and he can speak of this as "a righteous status *from* God" (ἡ ἐκ θεοῦ δικαιοσύνη *hē ek theou dikaiosynē,* Phil 3:9). But this status, which Paul describes in that significantly different way, is not the same thing as God's own righteousness. It results from the revelation of that righteousness, of God's salvific covenant faithfulness; the present passage is, in fact, the fullest statement of this. If we wish to press for an alternative to the technical term "righteousness," with all its attendant puzzles and possibilities for misunderstanding, perhaps the best current option is that of the NJB: "God's saving justice."

Paul declares (3:21) that the Torah and the prophets bear witness to this saving justice. What was it, then, that they said, to which God has now been faithful?

The main subject Paul expounds in this section is God's creation of a single worldwide family, composed of believing Jews and believing Gentiles alike. Since the main thing standing in the way of this achievement is human sin, the central focus of the paragraph describing how God has done it is the way God has dealt with sin through the death of Jesus. "Justification," in its Pauline contexts, regularly includes both aspects: the rescue of sinners from their sin, and the creation of the worldwide family of forgiven sinners. The universal scope of this eschatological Abrahamic family is emphasized in the "all" of 3:23 and the sustained arguments of 3:27-30; 4:9-12; 4:13-15; and 4:16-17. It is not so much that Paul, wanting to emphasize "faith," shows incidentally that it happens to bring together the different ethnic groups; rather, he wants to emphasize the coming together of Jew and Gentile in Christ and, therefore, demonstrates that this aim is achieved through faith. God's aim in calling Abraham in the first place was to put the world to rights. Only through the creation of a single forgiven family, comprising Gentiles as well as Jews, can that purpose be fulfilled.

Once this is grasped, several problems can be seen in their proper light. Despite what is some-

---

98. For the debate, see, e.g., N. T. Wright, *The Climax of the Covenant: Christ and the Law in Pauline Theology* (Edinburgh: T. & T. Clark; Minneapolis: Fortress, 1991); Richard B. Hays, *Echoes of Scripture in the Letters of Paul* (New Haven: Yale University Press, 1989). On the other side, see, J. L. Martyn, *Theological Issues in the Letters of Paul* (Nashville: Abingdon, 1997).

99. See Joseph A. Fitzmyer, *Romans,* AB 33 (Garden City, N.Y.: Doubleday, 1993) 369.

times supposed, for instance, Paul does not intend to offer here (i.e., specifically in 3:24-26) a full "doctrine of atonement." He is rather summing up a much larger train of thought, which we can observe at various points in his letters, in order to use this whole train of thought within his present argument. Romans has frequently been pulled out of shape by the insistence that it should provide full information at each point on the "topic" that dogmatic theology has been expecting at this point in the argument. Only when we allow Paul to develop his own trains of thought in his own way will we avoid doing violence to the text.

Recognizing the centrality of the Jew/Gentile question in the present argument explains Paul's running sub-theme that appears in the phrase "apart from the law" (3:21). Despite the fact that Torah and prophets bear witness to God's faithfulness, Torah itself not only sustained the division between Jew and Gentile, now overcome in Christ; it also condemned those "under the law" by showing them up as sinners. Both these themes are present in 3:21–4:25 (e.g., 3:27; 4:13-17).

Paul emphasizes throughout this section that this single worldwide family is "justified" in the present time. Thinking within the same overall frame of thought as 4QMMT, he looks ahead to the future time when God will finally make all things new and will reveal once and for all who his own people are. He has already spoken of this in 2:1-16; failure to factor that passage properly into the argument has led to the ignoring of the eschatological dimension of his teaching on justification. The whole point is this: The verdict "righteous," to be issued in the future on the basis of the totality of the life led, is brought forward into the present. But, whereas MMT regarded the performance of certain specific post-biblical purity regulations as the present defining badge of those whose future justification is thereby assured, Paul regarded faith, specifically faith in the God who raised Jesus from the dead, as this badge (see 4:24-25; 10:8-10).

Justification in the present is possible, Paul argues, because the grace of God deals with the sins of the people through the death of Jesus. The people in question are, therefore, a forgiven family (4:5-8). The covenant with Abraham existed all along to deal with the problem of Adamic humanity; the echoes of the latter in 3:23, which sums up

so much of 1:18–3:20, and the anticipation here of 5:12-21, indicate clearly enough that this is what Paul has in mind.[100] God's faithfulness, when met with answering human faithfulness, creates the genuine humanity that idolatry so cruelly distorts (4:18-22, reflecting and reversing 1:18-25). And Paul also hints at the wider purpose he believes God had in view in the original creation: The promise to Abraham and his seed was that they should inherit (not the land, but) the world (4:13; cf. 8:18-25).

God has, then, been faithful in Jesus the Messiah to the promises made to Abraham, to the covenant established with the Jewish people and, through them, with humankind and the entire creation. The short, straightforward way of saying this is: "God's righteousness has been unveiled." Chapters 5–8 will show how the revealing of this righteousness works for the wider circles of humankind and creation as a whole, laying the foundations for Paul's arguments in chaps. 9–11 and 12–16. And this divine righteousness, Paul declares, has been revealed in and through the Messiah, Jesus, for the benefit of all who believe.

The dense and unusual language of 3:24-26 is best explained on the premise that Paul is here briefly summarizing an argument he could in principle have spelled out far more fully, and to which he also alludes in many other places both in Romans and elsewhere. I regard this as preferable to the proposal, which has been adopted by several scholars, that the passage contains a pre-Pauline formula that Paul is here adapting.[101] Though the language is dense and formulaic, this is not itself an indication that Paul is quoting from a source. When the theory proposes, as it does in some forms, that he is using a formulation in which "God's righteousness" meant God's faithfulness to the covenant, but that Paul himself was broadening this into a different sense of "righteousness," we may suspect that the real motivation for the "discovery" of the formula was to protect Paul from such a "Jewish-Christian" idea.

100. See Wright, *The Climax of Covenant*, 21-26; N. T. Wright, *The New Testament and the People of God*, vol. 1 of *Christian Origins and the Question of God* (London: SPCK; Minneapolis: Fortress, 1992) 251-52.

101. See Ernst Käsemann, *Commentary on Romans*, trans. Geoffrey W. Bromiley (London: SCM, 1980) 95-100; P. Stuhlmacher, *Paul's Letter to the Romans: A Commentary*, trans. S. J. Hafemann (Louisville: Westminster John Knox, 1994) 58-59; the summary in Fitzmyer, *Romans*, 342-43.

The text, though difficult, can in fact be read adequately without recourse to this hypothesis, as I hope to show.[102]

Paul's purpose in 3:21-26 is not, then, to give a full "doctrine of atonement," a complete account of how God dealt with the sins of the world through the death of Jesus. Rather, as one part of his argument that on the cross the righteousness of God was unveiled, he is content to state, not completely *how*, but simply *that* this had been accomplished. Fuller statements elsewhere indicate that for Paul the resurrection of Jesus was also significant in God's dealing with sins (e.g., 1 Cor 15:17). Had crucifixion been the end of Jesus' story, no one would ever have ascribed saving significance to the event. The resurrection casts a retrospective coloring over the crucifixion, revealing it to be the decisive, heaven-sent saving act of God. That is presumably why, when Paul spells out the nature of Christian faith in 4:24-25, he describes it as faith "in the God who raised Jesus from the dead, who was put to death for our trespasses and raised for our justification."

Jesus' achievement is thus to have done what Israel should have done but failed to do (see 3:2-3). He has been the light of the world, the one through whom God's saving purpose has been revealed. Through him God has at last dealt with the sin of the world, the purpose for which the covenant was made. Although the statement of this is already compact, Paul can summarize this, too, in shorthand form: "the faithfulness of Jesus the Messiah" (3:22). This notion has become something of a storm center in recent debate, and all we can do here is to summarize what seems to me the correct way forward.[103]

When Paul summarizes the present train of thought in 5:12-21, he uses the term "obedience," and means something very similar to what he says here. The Messiah's "obedience unto death" (cf. Phil 2:6-8) is the critical act—an act of Jesus, and also in Paul's eyes an act of God—through which sins are dealt with, justification is assured, and the worldwide covenant family is brought into being. In making this point it is important to be clear what is not being said. Paul is not speaking of Jesus' "faith" either in the sense of the things Jesus believed, or Jesus' exemplary trust in God, or Jesus' religious experience. Nor is he suggesting that Jesus' "obedience" was somehow meritorious, so that by it he earned "righteousness" on behalf of others. That is an ingenious and far-reaching way of making Paul's language fit into a theological scheme very different from his own.[104] Rather, he is highlighting Jesus' faithful obedience, or perhaps we should say Jesus' obedient faithfulness, to the saving plan marked out for Israel, the plan by which God would save the world. On the cross Jesus accomplished what God had always intended the covenant to achieve. Where Israel as a whole had been faithless, he was faithful: 3:22 answers to 3:2-3.

Jesus' faithfulness unto death is here, as in some other Pauline passages, described in sacrificial terms (for the details, see the comments below). This is one of the trickiest passages in Paul in terms of precise nuances, but the context appears to be that reappropriation of the Levitical sacrificial language, particularly from the Day of Atonement scene in Leviticus 16, which we also find in, for instance, the Maccabaean literature (4 Macc 17:22).[105] There, as here, the setting is (1) the great wrath that hangs over Israel (and, in this case, the world), because of sin; (2) the death of the martyrs as somehow dealing with that wrath on behalf of God's people; and (3) the liberation from wrath that comes as a result. And, like the Maccabaean passage, this one arguably carries overtones also of that other great reworking of

---

102. For shrewd criticism of the theory, see Douglas J. Moo, *The Epistle to the Romans,* NICNT (Grand Rapids: Eerdmans, 1996) 220-21, 240; and, in more detail, D. A. Campbell, *The Rhetoric of Righteousness in Romans 3.21-26,* JSNTSup 65 (Sheffield: Sheffield Academic, 1992) 37-57.

103. The Greek πίστις (*pistis*) can mean "faith" or "faithfulness," "trust" or "trustworthiness." On the whole subject, see esp. L. T. Johnson, "Rom 3:21-26 and the Faith of Jesus," *CBQ* 44 (1982) 77-90; R. B. Hays, *The Faith of Jesus Christ: An Investigation of the Narrative Substructure of Galatians 3:1–4:11,* 2nd ed., SBLDS 56 (Grand Rapids: Eerdmans, 2001); S. K. Williams "Again Pistis Christou," *CBQ* 49 (1987) 431-47; M. D. Hooker, "ΠΙΣΤΙΣ ΧΡΙΣΤΟΥ," *NTS* 35 (1989) 321-42; and the debate between Hays and Dunn in *SBL 1991 Seminar Papers,* ed. E. H. Lovering (Atlanta: Scholars Press) 714-44. Fitzmyer, *Romans,* 345, and Moo, *Romans,* 225, both reject the proposal of Hays and others, while Christopher Bryan, *A Preface to Romans: Notes on the Epistle in Its Literary and Cultural Setting* (Oxford: Oxford University Press, 2000) 108-10, accepts it.

104. For discussion of this viewpoint, frequent within Reformed theology, see Moo, *Romans,* 225; R. N. Longenecker, "The Obedience of Christ in the Theology of the Early Church," in *Reconciliation and Hope: New Testament Essays on Atonement and Eschatology Presented to L. L. Morris on his 60th Birthday,* ed. R. Banks (Exeter: Paternoster, 1974) 142-52.

105. See Wright, *The New Testament and the People of God,* 276-77.

Levitical themes, the fourth Servant Song of Isaiah (Isa 52:13–53:12). Jesus is, for Paul, more than a mere martyr, but not less. Paul is here drawing together several rich biblical and post-biblical strands of thought to make the point that Jesus, in his death, completely fulfilled the saving plan of God. Through his death, sin and its results have been dealt with. Wrath has been turned away from God's people.

It is Jesus' death, therefore, that reveals God's righteousness. The puzzles of 3:1-8 are hereby resolved, at least in preliminary form. God has been faithful to the promises, while remaining impartially the God of Jews and Gentiles alike; God has dealt with sin as it merited and now rescues those who cast themselves on the divine mercy. This act of grateful trust in the God who raised Jesus is the characteristic Christian "faith," which plays such a large role in Paul's thought; it is the "obedience of faith," the proper response to grace that God always sought. Though faith has an affective content (being aware of God's presence and love), a propositional content (believing that Jesus is Lord and that God raised him from the dead), and an actively trusting content (casting oneself on God's mercy), we should not ignore the meaning the word has in the same passage when applied to Jesus: faithfulness. Paul does not so easily distinguish, as we do, between believing in God and being loyal to God. Notice how closely verbal confession and belief in the heart are linked in 10:9-10.

This faith then becomes the badge that identifies, in the present time, the members of the people of God. This is the meaning of Paul's doctrine of "justification by faith." The verdict of the last day has been brought forward into the present in Jesus the Messiah; in raising him from the dead, God declared that in him had been constituted the true, forgiven worldwide family. Justification, in Paul, is not the process or event whereby someone becomes, or grows as, a Christian; it is the declaration that someone is, in the present, a member of the people of God. This is inevitably controversial, but is I believe borne out by careful study of the relevant texts.[106] We may remind ourselves of the triple layer of meaning in Paul's "righteousness" language: The covenantal declaration, seen through the metaphorical and vital lens of the law-court, is put into operation eschatologically. The verdict to be announced in the future has been brought forward into the present. Those who believe the gospel are declared to be "in the right."

Christian faith is thus the appropriate badge of membership in God's renewed people. It is accessible to all, not, like the Torah, restricted to Jews only. It perfectly expresses both that self-abandonment that refuses to claim anything as of itself, but simply casts itself on God's mercy, and, paradoxically, that genuine humanness that honors God, trusts God's power to raise the dead, and so truly worships the true God and is remade as a true human being in God's likeness. That is the point, made finally in 4:18-22, toward which the present discussion is moving.

106. On the way in which confusion then arises through subsequent Christian theology using the term in a significantly different sense to that of Paul, see A. E. McGrath, *Iustitia Dei: A History of the Christian Doctrine of Justification,* 2 vols. (Cambridge: James Clark, 1986) 1:2-3; N. T. Wright, *What St. Paul Really Said: Was Paul of Tarsus the Real Founder of Christianity?* (Grand Rapids: Eerdmans, 1997) chap. 7. See, e.g., Gal 2:15-21, where the question of justification is not "how to become a Christian" but "whether Jewish Christians and Gentile Christians can share table fellowship."

# Romans 3:21-26, God's Righteousness Revealed Through the Faithfulness of Jesus

| NIV | NRSV |
| --- | --- |
| [21]But now a righteousness from God, apart from law, has been made known, to which the Law and the Prophets testify. [22]This righteousness from God comes through faith in Jesus Christ to all who believe. There is no difference, [23]for all have sinned and fall short of the glory of God, | 21But now, apart from law, the righteousness of God has been disclosed, and is attested by the law and the prophets, [22]the righteousness of God through faith in Jesus Christ[a] for all who believe.<br><br>*a Or through the faith of Jesus Christ* |

NIV

<sup>24</sup>and are justified freely by his grace through the redemption that came by Christ Jesus. <sup>25</sup>God presented him as a sacrifice of atonement,<sup>a</sup> through faith in his blood. He did this to demonstrate his justice, because in his forbearance he had left the sins committed beforehand unpunished— <sup>26</sup>he did it to demonstrate his justice at the present time, so as to be just and the one who justifies those who have faith in Jesus.

<sup>a</sup> 25 Or *as the one who would turn aside his wrath, taking away sin*

NIV

For there is no distinction, <sup>23</sup>since all have sinned and fall short of the glory of God; <sup>24</sup>they are now justified by his grace as a gift, through the redemption that is in Christ Jesus, <sup>25</sup>whom God put forward as a sacrifice of atonement<sup>a</sup> by his blood, effective through faith. He did this to show his righteousness, because in his divine forbearance he had passed over the sins previously committed; <sup>26</sup>it was to prove at the present time that he himself is righteous and that he justifies the one who has faith in Jesus.<sup>b</sup>

<sup>a</sup> Or *a place of atonement*     <sup>b</sup> Or *who has the faith of Jesus*

# COMMENTARY

**3:21-22a.** "But now"—commentators and preachers love to roll this vintage Pauline phrase around the palate. Expressing both logical and temporal transition, it carries all the flavor of Paul's inexhaustible excitement at what God had done in Jesus the Messiah. It was, after all, news: not a new religion, nor a new ethic, but an event through which the world, Paul himself, and the situation described in 3:19-20 had been changed forever. It was the new wine that had burst the old bottles once and for all.

The paragraph thus begun—not the only time when a couple of words hint at the entire coming train of thought—continues with a summary statement of the revelation of God's righteousness. The initial mention is flanked by carefully balanced statements about the Torah, and gives rise to the fuller proposition: God's righteousness is revealed through the faithfulness of Jesus the Messiah and is for the benefit of all who believe.

The Torah has been the main theme of vv. 19-20. The first thing Paul must now do, to emphasize the newness of the good news, is to stress that this revelation has taken place "apart from Torah." This performs two functions. Most obviously, it is Torah that has pronounced the Jews guilty, standing them in the dock alongside the pagans; if there is a new word from God, this is good news for the Jews. Less immediately obvious, but vital for Paul's developing argument, it is Torah that has erected a barrier against Gentiles; if there is a new word

from God, it may be good news for Gentiles also. This double meaning, of course, corresponds negatively to Paul's emphatic and repeated statement, "to the Jew first and also the Greek" (1:16; 2:9-10).

The revelation is, however, "witnessed to by the Torah and the Prophets." Paul could no doubt have added "and the Writings," the third division of the Hebrew Bible, containing among other things the psalms, from which he will shortly quote; but the phrase "the law and the prophets" was a regular way of summarizing the whole Jewish scripture (cf. Matt 5:17; 7:12). It is vital to Paul that the fresh revelation takes place "apart from Torah," but it is equally vital that, new though it is, it is the very thing that God promised beforehand (1:2; cf. 15:7-13, the final theological summary of the whole letter). This is not just a matter of being able to "prove" the gospel from ancient authoritative scriptures. It signals the continuity and reliability of God's purpose, which is part of the meaning of God's covenant faithfulness itself.

"The righteousness of God is revealed" (not here and in v. 22 a righteousness "from" God, as in the NIV); in other words, that for which the prophets (particularly Isaiah) and the psalmists longed had come to pass. God had unveiled the covenant plan, had drawn back the curtain on the grand design; and this had been done, not in the sense merely of communicating information, but in action, as had always been promised. "Revelation" here means more than just the passing on of knowledge, important though that is as well; it means the unveiling of God through a historical event. Though it would not be strictly accurate, it would not be a very great hyperbole to say that, for Paul, "the righteousness of God" was one of the titles of Jesus the Messiah himself. God's saving justice walked around Galilee, announced the kingdom, died on a cross, and rose again. God's plan of salvation had always required a faithful Israelite to fulfill it. Now, at last, God had provided one.

This righteousness, this world-righting covenant faithfulness, has been revealed "through the faithfulness of Jesus the Messiah." Though the phrase could mean "through faith in Jesus the Messiah," the entire argument of the section strongly suggests that it is Jesus' own πίστις (*pistis*) that is spoken of and that the word here means "faithfulness," not "faith" (see the NRSV note and the secondary literature referred to in the Overview). This is not to say that Jesus himself was "justified by faith."[107] Nor does Paul envisage him, as does Hebrews, as the "pioneer" of Christian faith, the first one to believe in the way that Christians now believe (Heb 12:1-3). Nor is his "faith" a kind of meritorious work, an "active obedience" to be then accredited to those who belong to him. To be sure, Paul would have agreed that Jesus believed in the one he called Abba, Father, and that this faith sustained him in total obedience; but this is not the point he is making here. The point here is that Jesus has offered to God, at last, the faithfulness Israel had denied (3:2-3).

A further reason why πίστις Ἰησοῦ Χριστοῦ (*pistis Iēsou Christou*) here is likely to refer to Jesus' own faithfulness is that, if taken instead to refer to the faith Christians have "in" Jesus, the next phrase ("for all who believe") becomes almost entirely redundant, adding only the (admittedly important) "all." The train of thought is clearer if we read it as "through the faithfulness of Jesus the Messiah, for the benefit of all who believe." This then corresponds closely to the reading suggested above for 1:17: from God's faithfulness to answering human faith. (It is also

very close to Gal 3:22, where similar discussions have taken place.)

The paragraph's opening statement, then, declares that God's long-awaited faithfulness has been newly disclosed in the events concerning Jesus the Messiah. His faithfulness completed the role marked out for Israel and did so for the benefit of all, Jew and Gentile alike.

**3:22b-24.** The explanation, and with it the drawing out of further meaning in the opening statement, focuses on the universality of both plight and solution. "For there is no distinction" (the NIV, as often, omits "for"); Jew and Gentile, as we have seen, are in the dock together. Verse 23 sums up 1:18–3:20, but with a new emphasis: Human rebellion led to the loss of the glory of God (cf. 1:23). "For all sinned"—the tense is aorist, indicating a single moment, despite the almost universal perfect tense ("all have sinned") in the translations (the JB is a solitary exception, but the NJB has reversed this decision, going back to the perfect). Paul seems again to be thinking of Adam, hiding under the argument as in 1:18-25 and 7:7-12, emerging into daylight only in 5:12-21. This is confirmed by the next clause, "and they come short of God's glory." Here the tense is present, the continuing result of a past event. In Jewish literature of the period, losing God's glory is closely associated with the fall of Adam, just as the sense of regaining Adam's glory is one of the key features of the expected redemption.[108]

Paul does not at once announce that the glory has been restored, that humans are as it were re-humanized in the Messiah (he will come to that in chap. 5). Instead, he announces the necessary step toward it: They are "justified" (cf. 8:30: those God justified, God glorified). Only the KJV keeps the participle of the Greek ("being justified"), which perhaps indicates that vv. 22b-23 are partly parenthetical (referring back to the point already made at length in 1:18–3:20), and that in Paul's mind v. 24 continues the main theme of the paragraph, begun in vv. 21-22a and now to be developed in detail.[109] This also explains, what Paul will repeat in v. 26, who the subject of this participle is; it is

---

107. As is argued by A. T. Hanson, *Studies in Paul's Technique and Theology* (London: SPCK, 1974) 39-51.

108. On loss of glory, see *Gen. Rab.* 12:6; *Life of Adam and Eve* 21:6. On regaining it, see 1QS 4:23; CD 3:20; 4QpPs37 3:1-2.

109. See the helpful discussions in C. E. B. Cranfield, *A Critical and Exegetical Commentary on the Epistle to the Romans,* ICC, 2 vols. (Edinburgh: T. & T. Clark, 1975) 205; Douglas J. Moo, *The Epistle to the Romans,* NICNT (Grand Rapids: Eerdmans, 1996) 227.

---

scarcely the "all" of v. 23 (except insofar as "all" here emphasizes "Jew and Gentile alike"), but rather the "all who believe" of vv. 22, 26, 28-30.

This "justification" takes place in the present time, rather than in the future as in 2:1-11. This particular "justification" is the surprising anticipation of the final verdict spoken of in that passage, and carries both the lawcourt meaning that we would expect from the sustained metaphor of 3:9, 19-20, and the covenantal meaning that we would expect from 2:17–3:8—these two being, as we have already explained, dovetailed together in Paul. It is God's declaration that those who believe are in the right; their sins have been dealt with; they are God's true covenant people, God's renewed humanity. This astonishing declaration needs explaining. How can the righteous judge, spoken of at the start of the chapter, make such an announcement about those who a moment ago were standing in the dock, guilty and without defense?

Paul offers three explanations, of which the third is then developed further. This justification happens "freely"; it is neither deserved nor paid for, but is pure gift.[110] More particularly, it is "by God's grace"—the first mention of "grace" since the introduction (1:5, 7), but another theme that is now going to dominate, particularly in chapters 5 and 6. "Grace" is one of Paul's most potent shorthand terms, carrying in its beautiful simplicity the entire story of God's love, active in Christ and the Spirit to do for humans what they could never do for themselves. This, indeed, is what he at once explains in the present passage, with the last phrase of v. 24: "through the redemption that is in the Messiah, Jesus." About this there are three vital things to grasp.

The first thing to notice is that what happened in the Messiah was the gift of God's grace. Paul has no conception, as in some medieval paintings and their accompanying theology (some of which has lingered on to this day), of a stern Father-figure on a throne with the Son pleading with him, against (as it were) his better judgment, to exercise clemency. Rather, what takes place in Jesus and supremely on the cross is all from God's side. As Paul will insist in 5:6-10, the death of Jesus reveals the love of God. God does not, so to speak, have

to be persuaded that Jesus' death makes a good enough case for sinners to be justified. It was God who initiated the movement in the first place.

The second point is the meaning of "redemption." At one level, this is a metaphor from the slave-market, but it is much more besides. As with the lawcourt setting of "justification," the obvious first level of metaphor is only the front door to the many-storied home of Paul's allusive writing. "Redemption" was, to be sure, a word with overtones of slaves being bought back, finding their freedom; but Israel could scarcely hear the word without thinking of Egypt, of Passover, of the Red Sea, the wilderness wanderings, and the promised land. Paul has already hinted that the whole human race languishes in the Egypt of sin (3:9—a point he will develop more explicitly in chapter 6); what such people need is a new exodus, the cosmic equivalent of what God did for Israel long ago. As we shall see, the exodus provides a key subtext, a hidden but very powerful metanarrative, for a good deal of the rest of the letter, particularly chapters 5-8.[111]

"Redemption," in other words, is not simply one term among others, a metaphor chosen at random as another bit of street-level color for the meaning of Jesus' death. It stands at the head of the dense statement that follows, evoking a whole world of thought, offering a biblical lens through which to view what Paul is about to say. In particular, we may notice again that in Genesis 15, the passage Paul will expound in chap. 4, God promised Abraham, as the focal point of the covenant, that his seed would dwell as slaves in a foreign land and would be rescued at the proper time (Gen 15:13-16). "The redemption that is in Christ Jesus" is thus the complete fulfillment of God's covenant promise to Abraham. This is how God's covenant faithfulness is unveiled (3:21, 26; the "redemption" of the individual is linked with "the righteousness of God" in, e.g., Ps 71:19, 23-24).

Third, this redemption happens "in the Messiah, Jesus." This is where Paul makes explicit the compressed point of 3:22, that when Jesus acts in faithfulness and obedience he does so as the

---

110. δωρεάν (dōrean) is rare in the NT but is cognate with δωρεά (dōrea, "gift" or "bounty"), which Paul uses as one way of referring back to this whole train of thought in 5:15, 17.

111. See N. T. Wright, "New Exodus, New Inheritance: The Narrative Substructure of Romans 3–8," in *Romans and the People of God: Essays in Honor of Gordon D. Fee on the Occasion of His 65th Birthday*, ed. S. K. Soderlund and N. T. Wright (Grand Rapids: Eerdmans, 1999) 26-35.

Messiah, Israel's representative, the one "in whom" Israel is summed up. We shall have more to say about "in Christ" when discussing chaps. 6–8; for the moment we notice that Paul's messianic christology is explicit here, at the point where he is stating how the world has been brought from guilt to grace. What the world needed (3:2) was a faithful Israelite, to carry out God's saving purpose. God has now provided one. And, because Israel itself has joined the rest of the world in the dock, this Messiah is also God's Israel *for* Israel. All have become disobedient, that mercy might be shown to all (11:32).

**3:25-26.** Every word and phrase in these two verses has been the subject of intense scholarly debate. It is vital to keep our bearings and remind ourselves, before examining the trees, of the shape of the forest. Paul's overall point is clearly that Jesus' death demonstrates God's righteousness, being the reason why sinners are now justified. But why has he said it like this? And what extra overtones and nuances are hereby built in to the overall argument of Romans, to be developed and picked up elsewhere?

It will not do to detach all or part of these verses, declare them a pre-Pauline fragment, and so relativize their force within the current argument. It is by no means impossible that Paul was making use, in what is after all a highly charged and densely packed statement, of phrases already familiar in early Christianity. But, here of all places, he is very unlikely to have allowed himself to say something he did not mean; and, once we have grasped the meaning of "God's righteousness" in 3:21, it should be clear that the repeated emphasis of the same point in 3:25, 26 is not (as some have said) an intrusion from a "Jewish Christian" context in which God's covenant faithfulness was important, but which Paul himself has all but left behind (see the Overview). For Paul, we must not tire of repeating, God's covenant faithfulness did not mean a reaffirmation of a supposed "favored nation clause"; nor did it mean that salvation-history proceeded in a smooth developmental line. Rather, it meant that God was fulfilling the promise to Abraham that he would have a faithful family composed of Jews and Gentiles alike. We are right, then, to see these verses as expressing the heart of that which Paul began to say in 3:21.[112]

We are right, also, to interpret this dense statement of the meaning of Jesus' death in the light of the other statements in subsequent passages. We should neither press one or two words here to say more than they do, nor forbid the recognition, by reference to other passages in the letter, of a larger world of thought in the light of which the present statement makes the sense Paul intends (cf., e.g., 4:24-5; 5:6-10, 15-21; 8:3-4; we could also, of course, appeal to other letters—notably Galatians—but it is important to keep the argument here as tight as possible).

We may remind ourselves again that the covenant was put in place precisely to deal with sin. Abraham was called so that through his family God might undo the problem of Adam—the problem (in other words) Paul has set out extensively in 1:18–3:20. This is exactly the sequence of that larger logic in which 3:21–4:25 replies to the preceding section. If, then, God has been faithful to the covenant, it must be clear that sins have indeed been dealt with. This is a matter not simply of lawcourt "justice," but of covenant theology; the latter includes the former and must not be played off against it. God's creation of a new Jew-plus-Gentile family was the aim; forgiveness of sins the necessary means.

Hence the double statement about the demonstration of God's righteousness in 3:25*b*-26, which we may take first in order to give ourselves maximum purchase on the difficult 3:25*a*. God has put Jesus forward (see below) in order to display, to prove, to demonstrate that covenant faithfulness, that saving justice, which would otherwise be called into question (3:1-8).[113] In particular, God had passed over, that is, left unpunished, acts of sin committed in former times. God, it seems (Paul here takes this for granted), had been forbearing, patient, unwilling to foreclose on the human race in general or Israel in particular. Paul

---

112. The NIV reveals the weakness of its mistranslation of 3:21 ("a righteousness from God," repeated at 3:22) when at 3:25-26 it is forced to translate the same word with "justice" and to acknowledge that the justice in question is God's. This simply deconstructs the tight logic of 3:21-26. Moo, *Romans*, 219, 240, reveals the same problem as the NIV.

113. ἔνδειξις (*endeixis*, "demonstration" or "proof") makes more emphatic the general πεφανέρωται (*pephanerōtai,* "is manifested," 3:21) and ἀποκαλύπτεται (*apokalyptetai,* "is revealed," 1:16), stressing particularly the divine answer to the possible charge of ἀδικία (*adikia*, "unrighteousness," 3:3-5).

had emphasized this in 2:3-6, where the same word is used, and he now refers back to that point.[114] The first question at issue, then—the aspect of God's righteousness that might seem to have been called into question and is now demonstrated after all—is God's proper dealing with sins—i.e., punishment. Whatever Paul is saying in the first half of v. 25, it must be such as to lead to the conclusion that now, at last, God has punished sins as they deserved.

The second half of the double statement, which occupies v. 26, repeats almost verbatim the phrase about demonstrating God's righteousness (or covenant faithfulness, or saving justice), but this time takes it in a different direction. First, Paul adds "in the present time"; this is cognate with the "but now" at the start of the paragraph and emphasizes both that the past problem has reached a present conclusion and that the future verdict has been brought forward into the present time. One does not now have to wait for a future judgment to see the covenant people of God manifested (nor, as Paul will stress in vv. 27-30, can one see this through works of Torah). They are revealed in the present time by God's action in Christ.

This means that God is now seen to be "just, and the justifier." God, as both the covenant God and the "righteous judge" of the lawcourt metaphor, displays "righteousness," not simply through dealing with sins as they deserved, but also, in his summing up of the case, through finding in favor of this category of people. We must remind ourselves again that this declaration, this decision of the judge, is what constitutes these people as "righteous." The word is primarily forensic/covenantal and only secondarily (what we would call) "ethical." God's justifying activity is the declaration that this people are "in the right," in other words, announcing the verdict in their favor. Calling them "righteous," as one must on this basis, should not be misunderstood to mean that God has after all recognized that they possess ethical characteristics that have commended themselves, caused their sins to be overlooked, and persuaded the judge that they deserved a favorable verdict. To say that they are "righteous"

means that the judge has found in their favor; or, translating back into covenantal categories, that the covenant God has declared them to be the covenant people.

The point, anyway, is that the display of God's righteousness in the death of Jesus is the basis for God's justifying declaration of this category of people.[115] As we come closer to the hardest part of the passage, v. 25a, we notice at this stage that Paul clearly intends that clause to prepare the way for this statement of God's justifying declaration. Whatever precisely Paul intends to say, it must have to do with the means by which the righteous God could, without compromising that righteousness, find in favor of the ungodly (4:5).

Paul's final description (v. 26b) of the object of God's justifying declaration is very elliptical: τὸν ἐκ πίστεως Ἰησοῦ (ton ek pisteōs Iēsou, "the one"; lit., "out of the faith[fulness] of Jesus"). (We may compare the condensed descriptions in 2:29.) Here the referent is not in doubt; the person concerned is a Christian. But is "of Jesus" an objective or subjective genitive? In other words, is Paul referring to the Christian's "faith in Jesus" (as NIV), or, as in v. 22, to Jesus' own "faith(fulness)"?[116]

It could in principle be the former. Paul has already referred to Christian faith in 3:22 (and perhaps in 3:25a, on which see below). He is about to mount an argument in 3:27-31 in which the faith of Christians is central. But he normally speaks of the object of Christian faith not as Jesus, but as God—as, for example, in the striking phrase in 4:24, "those who believe in the God who raised Jesus from the dead." Granted the importance of Jesus' faithfulness in the argument of this passage,

---

114. The phrase ἐν τῇ ἀνοχῇ τοῦ θεοῦ (en tē anochē tou theou, "in the forbearance of God") opens v. 26 in the Greek editions, but the English versions rightly treat it as part of the unit of thought at the end of 3:25.

115. The meaning of καί (kai) in 3:26 is contested. (1) If rendered "and," it implies that Paul is making two statements: (a) that God is just and (b) that God justifies the Jesus-faith people. (2) If translated "even" or "namely," Paul would be saying that God's justice in this case consists in God's justifying activity (so most commentators). If translated "even though," he would be emphasizing that God's punitive justice is satisfied by Christ's death so that now sinners can be justified (see Moo, Romans, 242). Although the theological arguments against the last of these (e.g., Fitzmyer, Romans 353; Byrne, Romans, 134) are not strong, the wider meaning of δικαιοσύνη θεοῦ (dikaiosynē theou) elsewhere in the passage suggests that the first is more likely.

116. The NRSV's note "who has the faith of Jesus" takes the genitive as subjective but implies that Paul's point would thereby be that Jesus' own "faith" is somehow either the model for Christian faith or even its substance (as though Jesus' own faith were somehow infused into the believer). It seems far more likely that, if the subjective genitive is the right reading, that πίστις (pistis) here means "faithfulness." In any case, to render ton ek pisteōs as "who has the faith" seems to strain the meaning of the Greek almost intolerably.

stated proleptically in 3:22 (see above), it is more likely that what he means here, stated still in condensed form, is that God justifies the one whose status rests on the faithful death of Jesus. Even there, of course, the notion of the believer's own faith is not absent, since it is this faith that precipitates God's announcement of the verdict in the present time. But the basis for this faith is precisely the faithfulness of Jesus seen as the manifestation of the covenant faithfulness of God.

We must now return to the opening words of v. 25, whose meaning we have seen to be constrained by vv. 25b-26. Somehow, what Paul says here is designed to explain how it is that God has now dealt with sins on the one hand and declared "the one out of the faithfulness of Jesus" to be in the right on the other.

The initial surprise, granted that such language has not made its way into Romans until now, is that v. 25a is heavily sacrificial in content. God "put Jesus forth," says Paul, using a quite rare verb many of whose LXX uses are to do with the shewbread in the Temple (cf. Exod 29:23; 40:4, 23; Lev 24:8; 2 Macc 1:8). Jesus was put forth as a ἱλαστήριον (hilastērion)—a term whose precise translation focuses the problem of the clause but is undoubtedly cultic in context. And this was effective "through his blood," again a clear sacrificial reference. How does this work? What is Paul's train of thought? Why does he here refer to Jesus' death in sacrificial terms? How does sacrificial language come together with the overarching exposition of the righteousness of God? And how does the sacrifice of Jesus mean that sins have now been dealt with, creating a "righteous" people and leaving God's righteousness unimpeachable?

The language Paul uses goes back to Leviticus. In Lev 16:2 the hilastērion was the "mercy-seat," the lid on top of the ark of the covenant, the place where God appeared in the cloud to meet with Israel (cf. Exod 25:17-22; 31:7; 35:12; 37:6-9 [38:5-8 LXX]; Num 7:89; Amos 9:1). In this chapter, which prescribes the ritual for the Day of Atonement, the "mercy-seat" has a crucial role: It is the place where Aaron is to sprinkle the blood of the bullock and goat of the sin-offering (vv. 14-15), having first lit the incense to create a cloud around the mercy-seat, so that he may not die from being in the presence of God (v. 13). The sprinkling of the blood is to make atonement for the holy place,

because of the Israelites' uncleannesses, transgressions, and sins (v. 16). The LXX verb for "make atonement for" (ἐξιλάσκεται exilasketai) is from the same root as hilastērion.

Paul's other references to Jesus' death indicate that sacrificial ideas, though not his only grid of reference, were not far from his mind when he thought of the cross. In particular, elsewhere in Romans he refers to the crucifixion in terms of the sin-offering, in a context that makes it clear that he intends this precise reference to be heard (8:3, on which see below). But he does not elsewhere refer explicitly to the great Day of Atonement. He does not, for example, develop the idea of Jesus as sacrifice, or indeed as priest, in the way we find in the Letter to the Hebrews. However, on a broader canvas it is a natural Second Temple Jewish perception to see God's faithfulness to Israel (and Israel's answering loyalty to God) expressed through the temple cult and to see God's righteousness expressed in the face of Israel's sins through the sacrifices in general and the Day of Atonement in particular. To put it another way, if Israel is in trouble because of sin, the Day of Atonement will put things to rights.[117] To that extent, what Paul has done is simply to declare that God has done the same thing on a once-for-all, grand scale; he is, in that sense, alluding to Jesus as the place where the holy God and sinful Israel meet, in such a way that Israel, rather than being judged, receives atonement.

But this does not plumb the full depths of what Paul is saying here. In particular, it does not provide an explanation of the intimate connection Paul is assuming between a human death and this sacrificial language; nor between this sacrificial death and God's dealing with Israel's sins such as would justify the immediate conclusion of v. 25b; nor between this whole complex of thought and "the righteousness of God." What other contexts of meaning were available to a Second Temple Jew that might explain all this?

The most obvious answer can be found in the stories of the Maccabaean martyrs. Whatever actually happened in the torrid years of Syrian oppression in the 160s BCE, the story as it was told in Paul's day sometimes interpreted the martyrs'

---

117. See N. T. Wright, *The New Testament and the People of God*, vol. 1 of *Christian Origins and the Question of God* (London: SPCK; Minneapolis: Fortress, 1992) 272-79.

deaths in sacrificial terms. Second Maccabees clearly regards the suffering of the martyrs as bound up with God's special purposes for Israel. Other nations, says the author, go unpunished, in the patience of God, until finally they reach the full measure of their sins; but Israel's punishment is brought forward, being visited on the righteous, in order that God's mercy may remain with Israel (2 Macc 6:12-16). Though this is not exactly Paul's meaning, there is close similarity with the thought he expresses in 2:3-6 and in the mention of God's patience in the present verse. It is in this setting that the youngest of the seven famous martyred brothers declares that their suffering will soon bring an end to the wrath of the Almighty that had justly fallen upon the whole nation (2 Macc 7:38, the climax of the speech). The writer of 4 Maccabees is even more explicit: As Eleazar is being martyred, he prays that the punishment he and the others are enduring may suffice for the nation, that his blood may be their purification, and that his life may be received in exchange for theirs (4 Macc 6:28-29). Their death, says the writer, purified the land; they became as a "ransom" (ἀντίψυχον *antipsychon*) for the sin of the nation. Through their blood, and through their death seen as a *hilastērion* (NRSV, "atoning sacrifice"), divine providence has preserved Israel.[118]

It was, then, thinkable in Paul's period that the suffering of the righteous Jew might in some way atone, as a sacrifice did, for Israel. These Maccabaean passages, in fact, belong within a larger world of thought for which there is no space here.[119] But even this does not completely explain how Paul's whole sequence of logic fits together. The Second Temple trains of thought that enabled some writers to construe martyrdom in terms of sacrificial and other redemptive actions went back, in the biblical tradition, to passages in the book of Daniel, such as 11:35 and 12:1-10, where imagery from the temple cult is applied to human suffering. And behind Daniel itself, clearly alluded to there

and in much other literature familiar in Paul's day, stands Isaiah, particularly chaps. 40–55.[120] Although the attempt to read Paul, and particularly Romans, in the light of these chapters has been controversial, the argument so far shows that there is a good deal to be said for such an allusion as at least part of the explanation of the present passage.

The major point to be made here is that in Isaiah 40–55 we have a sustained exposition of the righteousness of God, focused more and more tightly on a suffering figure who represents Israel and fulfills YHWH's purpose of being a light to the nations and whose sufferings and death are finally seen in explicitly sacrificial terms.[121] We have, that is, exactly that combination of elements that we have observed, and that are otherwise puzzling in exactly that combination, in Rom 3:21-26. In other words, the sacrifical language of 3:25, used in connection with the violent death of a righteous Jew at the hands of pagans, makes sense within the context of the current martyr stories; but those martyr stories themselves send us back, by various routes, to Isaiah 40–55; and when we get there we find just those themes that we find in Romans 3.

Neither in the fourth servant song (Isa 52:13–53:12) nor at other key points in the prophet do we find the same sacrificial language that Paul uses in 3:25. However, what we do find is that the language and thought of Isa 52:13–53:12 crop up at key points in Paul's subsequent argument, leaving us in little doubt (unless we are arguably far too stringent in what we will allow as an allusion) that Paul did indeed have this passage in mind. Thus in 4:25, summing up the entire train of thought from 3:21, Paul uses the verb παρεδόθη (*paredothē*, "he was given up"), which occurs twice in Isa 53:12, with the active form ("the Lord gave him up") in 53:6; in both cases this happened "for our sins," as in 4:25.[122] And when in 5:15, 19 Paul speaks of Jesus' act of obedience availing to justify "the many," this is a clear allusion to Isa 53:11-12 (some also see a reference to Isa 53:5 in Rom 5:1).

---

118. 17:22; an alternative reading of the passage takes *hilastērion* as adjectival, qualifying θάνατος (*thanatos*), "a propitiatory death." so H. G. R. Liddell, R. Scott, H. S. Jones, *A Greek-English Lexicon,* 9th ed. (Oxford: Oxford University Press, 1996), apparently omitting the τοῦ (*tou*) that in Rahlfs' ed. of the LXX stands before θανάτου (*thanatou*). See A. Rahlfs, *Septuaginta* (Stuttgart: Deutsche Bibelgesellschaft, 1979).

119. Fuller details in N. T. Wright, *Jesus and the Victory of God,* vol. 2 of *Christian Origins and the Question of God* (London: SPCK, 1996) 576-84.

120. See ibid., 584, 588-91, with other refs. there to both primary and secondary literature.

121. For "the righteousness of God" in Isaiah 40–55, see 46:13; 51:5-6, 8. The idea of God's covenant faithfulness, through which Israel is redeemed and creation itself is renewed, is central to the whole section, both when the phrase occurs and when it is assumed.

122. Paul uses παράπτωμα (*paraptōma,* "trespass"), not ἁμαρτία (*hamartia,* "sin") as in LXX Isa 53:5, 12, but the allusion is clear nonetheless. *Paraptōma* never occurs in LXX Isaiah.

Further afield, Paul quotes Isa 52:15 in Rom 15:21 and Isa 53:1 in Rom 10:16.

The significance of Isaiah 40–55 here lies in its ability to tie together and explain what otherwise is inexplicable, namely why Paul should imagine that the death of Jesus, described in sacrificial terms, should be supposed not only to reveal the righteousness of God but also to deal properly, i.e. punitively, with sins. The idea of punishment as part of atonement is itself deeply controversial; horrified rejection of the mere suggestion has led on the part of some to an unwillingness to discern any reference to Isaiah 40–55 in Paul.[123] But it is exactly this idea that Paul states, clearly and unambiguously, in 8:3, when he says that God "condemned sin in the flesh"—i.e., the flesh of Jesus.

All this may be of help when it comes to the precise meaning of *hilastērion*. By itself, as we saw, it meant "mercy-seat," the focal point of the great ritual of the Day of Atonement; and, thence, the place and/or the means of dealing both with wrath (or punishment) and with sin.[124] Dealing with wrath or punishment is propitiation; with sin, expiation. You propitiate a person who is angry; you expiate a sin, crime, or stain on your character. Vehement rejection of the former idea in many quarters has led some to insist that only "expiation" is in view here. But the fact remains that in 1:18–3:20 Paul has declared that the wrath of God is revealed against all ungodliness and wickedness and that despite God's forbearance this will finally be meted out; that in 5:8, and in the whole promise of 8:1-30, those who are Christ's are rescued from wrath; and that the passage in which the reason for the change is stated is 3:25-26, where we find that God, though in forbearance allowing sins to go unpunished for a while, has now revealed that righteousness, that saving justice, that causes people to be declared "righteous" even though they were sinners.

123. The hasty rejection of such a train of thought as hopelessly Anselmic is seen, for instance, in Joseph A. Fitzmyer, *Romans,* AB 33 (Garden City, N.Y.: Doubleday, 1993) 353.

124. For the mass of details, see C. E. B. Cranfield, *A Critical and Exegetical Commentary on the Epistle to the Romans,* ICC, 2 vols. (Edinburgh: T. & T. Clark, 1979) 214-18; Douglas J. Moo, *The Epistle to the Romans,* NICNT (Grand Rapids: Eerdmans, 1996) 231-36. Christopher Bryan, *A Preface to Romans: Notes on the Epistle in Its Literary and Cultural Setting* (Oxford: Oxford University Press, 2000) 112, argues, against Cranfield, that the meaning "mercy-seat" can indeed make sense here. See also P. Stuhlmacher, *Paul's Letter to the Romans: A Commentary,* trans. S. J. Hafemann (Louisville: Westminster John Knox, 1994) 58-59.

The lexical history of the word *hilastērion* is sufficiently flexible to admit of particular nuances in different contexts. Paul's context here demands that the word not only retain its sacrificial overtones (the place and means of atonement), but that it carry the note of propitiation of divine wrath—with, of course, the corollary that sins are expiated. It should go without saying that this in no way implies, what the start of the verse has already ruled out, that God is an angry malevolent tyrant who demands someone's death, or someone's blood, and is indifferent as to whose it is. The point Paul is making, carried by the word *hilastērion*, is that Jesus' death was God's answer both to the plight of the world and to the problems outlined in 3:1-8—the problems, that is, for God's own justice, truth, and faithfulness. To the objection, that sacrifices in Leviticus and other biblical texts do not seem to be propitiatory, the response must be that, as we have seen, by Paul's time sacrifical language was used in exactly this way, precisely of the righteous Israelites whose deaths somehow exhausted the divine wrath that was otherwise suspended over Israel. To see Jesus as the place where atonement is made (the narrow, focused meaning of the word) and hence as the means by which atonement is made (in the broader context of the echoes set up by the word, and the entire passage) is exactly what is needed at this point in the passage.

There remain the two phrases by which *hilastērion* is qualified: "through faith" and "by means of his blood." These are most likely intended as independent modifiers of the noun, rather than the former modifying the latter ("through faith in his blood," as though the blood of Jesus were itself the object of faith). In addition, the reading we have cautiously recommended for "faith" in 3:22 and 3:26, i.e., the faithfulness of Jesus, his obedience to the divine saving plan, inclines one to the possibility—it can hardly be stronger—that this is Paul's meaning here as well. Jesus' faithfulness was the means by which the act of atonement was accomplished, by which there took place that meeting between God and the whole world of which the mercy-seat was the advance symbol. Furthermore, just as the mercy-seat fulfilled its function when sprinkled with sacrificial blood, so Paul sees the blood of Jesus as actually instrumental in bringing about that meeting of grace and helplessness, of forgiveness and sin, that occurred on the cross. Once again, the sacrificial imagery points beyond the cult to the reality of God's self-giving act in Jesus.

I suggest, therefore, that Paul has here condensed, in typical manner, three trains of thought into a single statement, to which he will then refer back, explaining himself more fully as he does so. First, the righteousness of God is revealed in God's giving of Jesus as the faithful Israelite, through whom the covenant plan to save the world from sin will be put into operation at last, despite universal failure. Second, Jesus' faithfulness was precisely faithfulness unto death, a death understood in such sacrificial terms as would evoke not only the Day of Atonement but also the self-giving of the martyrs and, behind and greater than that, the sacrificial suffering of the Servant. Third, Jesus' self-giving faithfulness to death, seen as the act of

God, not of humans operating toward God, had the effect of turning away the divine wrath that otherwise hung over not only Israel but also the whole world. Thus is God's righteousness revealed in the gospel events of Jesus' death and resurrection: God has been true to the covenant, has dealt properly with sin, has come to the rescue of the helpless and has done so with due impartiality between Jew and Gentile. Although Jesus' death is the means by which God's righteousness is revealed, and that righteousness is the main subject of the section, Paul does not supply a more extensive treatment of Calvary. But what he says here is one of the key foundations for what he will go on to argue. In order to expound his major themes, he needs a firm basis in what subsequent writers would call atonement-theology. This passage has now provided it.

# REFLECTIONS

**1.** The most important point for all subsequent Christian generations to grasp from this dense but explosive paragraph is that the righteousness—the saving justice, the covenant faithfulness—of the creator God was unveiled once and for all in the death of Jesus, the Jewish Messiah. This claim appears counter-intuitive in the contemporary world, the usual reason given being the fact that the world, and often enough the church, does not look as if Jesus' death has made a dramatic difference to them. Justice has not come to the world. Regularly, therefore, the meaning of Jesus' death has been reduced to that of an example, albeit the supreme one, of the love of God—a general truth that happened to be exemplified in one specific instance, rather than an event through which the world became a different place. Or it has been used to construct a particular kind of "atonement theology" that rescues souls out of the world while leaving this-worldly injustice unaffected. Either way, theology and exegesis have retreated from Paul's vision of God's justice unveiled on the cross.

There are, in fact, other agendas that press upon the contemporary world and insist that nothing significant can actually have happened when Jesus died. The Renaissance world saw itself as the new beginning—the revival of the best of the past, to be sure, but the new start through which everything would now be different. Whoever invented the idea of the "Middle Ages," thereby designating their own age as the start of the new period, was not only one of the most powerful figures in the history of ideas, but also the perpetrator of the belief that the real change in history had not come about in the first century of the common era, but at some much more recent time. The Enlightenment swapped the idea that history had turned its critical corner in Palestine in the first century for the belief that the moment had happened instead in Western Europe in the eighteenth century. The tacit assumption of this point of view is the deeper reason why the Pauline claim sounds simply incredible to so many. It offers a rival eschatology to that by which our culture has lived.

The claim makes the sense it does, of course, within a broadly Jewish, i.e., biblical, worldview. It was first-century Jews like Paul who were expecting their God, the creator and covenant God, to act in history in such a way that the world might recognize the divine power and faithfulness. However, precisely because this Jewish/biblical worldview posited a God who was the creator of the whole cosmos and who intended to address all humans, neither the worldview nor the Pauline claim could ever be conceived as mere private opinions. They were for all, and if they remained meaningless for all they might be thought to have failed. Hence Paul's Gentile mission, which is in view already in 3:23-24: Jew and Gentile alike sinned, but Jew and Gentile alike are now declared to be God's people as a free gift. The revelation of God's righteousness is an event of cosmic significance.

The task of teaching Christian people to think and live on the basis of a unique event that happened in the first century, but that was the turning point of cosmic history, is therefore, hard though it may seem, one of the most Pauline tasks facing a preacher and teacher today. The resurrection (vital, though unmentioned, in the logic of this paragraph) is, of course, the event that anchors this eschatological belief; if Christ is not raised, as Paul says elsewhere (1 Cor 15:17), faith is futile and we are still in our sins. In other words, if the resurrection has not happened, God's new world has not begun. We could still use Jesus as an example, his teaching as a wonderful and teasing challenge. But none of Romans would make any sense.

**2.** God's covenant faithfulness, that saving justice of which Paul speaks, demands further exploration. The loyalty of God to promises made, the unbreakable commitment to working through Israel even when Israel became faithless, is a theme not sufficiently remarked on or thought through. But only in this light can we grasp the full meaning of Jesus' Messiahship. Only thus can we comprehend his taking on of Israel's vocation to be God's faithful partner in the project for which Abraham had originally been called.

The wider dimension at which this hints is God's faithfulness to the human project itself, and indeed to the whole cosmos. To this we shall return in chapters 5 and 8, and in the wider reflections on chapters 9–11. Because Paul eventually opens up these other dimensions, we do well to remind ourselves here that the present paragraph, though its prime focus is on how God was true to the promises made to Israel and through Israel for the world, points beyond itself to the promises and commands given by God to all humankind. The challenge is then to work out how the cross of Jesus unveils, in a decisive action, those promises as well; and how to live on the basis of the belief that it does so.

**3.** Within that, of course, the paragraph states in sharp and concise form the extraordinary and still earth-shattering proposition that the creator God has acted to provide the deeply costly remedy for the plight that hangs over all humankind. Not to be deeply moved by this is to fail to listen. "Freely . . . by God's grace . . . God set him forth . . . that God might be savingly just, and the justifier." God's initiative, energy, and commitment to carrying through the project of the justification of sinners is at the heart of Paul's message and is the true source of all genuine Christian devotion. Verses 24-26 could stand as a heading over one gospel passage after another, as though to say, "This is what this story is all about."

**4.** Within that again, these verses highlight one aspect of Paul's complex portrait of Jesus: his faithfulness. Given a vocation, he was true to it, though it cost him everything. This is not said in order to be an example, to make us feel guilty once more about our own faithfulness, our half-heartedness in pursuing our own tasks, though no doubt this may be an accidental side effect. It is a matter for awe and gratitude. Paul does not here note the way in which this action of Jesus impinges on each believer personally, but those with ears to hear will detect, just below the surface of the paragraph, his words in Galatians: The son of God loved me and gave himself for me (Gal 2:20). It is this utter faithfulness, seen as an act of love, that will sustain the whole argument of Romans from this point to the end of the letter; and it can also sustain the believer and the Christian community through all the trials that beset them. It is significant that at the point where Paul says exactly this, his normal mode of speaking about "the love of God" slips, and he speaks instead of "the love of the Messiah" (8:35). It is that kind of subtle change that tells us where his heart really is.

# Romans 3:27-31, One God, One Faith, One People

NIV

27Where, then, is boasting? It is excluded. On what principle? On that of observing the law? No, but on that of faith. 28For we maintain that a man is justified by faith apart from observing the law. 29Is God the God of Jews only? Is he not the God of Gentiles too? Yes, of Gentiles too, 30since there is only one God, who will justify the circumcised by faith and the uncircumcised through that same faith. 31Do we, then, nullify the law by this faith? Not at all! Rather, we uphold the law.

NRSV

27Then what becomes of boasting? It is excluded. By what law? By that of works? No, but by the law of faith. 28For we hold that a person is justified by faith apart from works prescribed by the law. 29Or is God the God of Jews only? Is he not the God of Gentiles also? Yes, of Gentiles also, 30since God is one; and he will justify the circumcised on the ground of faith and the uncircumcised through that same faith. 31Do we then overthrow the law by this faith? By no means! On the contrary, we uphold the law.

## COMMENTARY

The connection of this paragraph to what precedes, and the internal logic within it, have both sometimes seemed difficult.[125] This is largely due to the interpretation, within the Reformation tradition and elsewhere, that treats "justification" as meaning "how someone becomes a Christian," "law" as a general moral code rather than the Jewish Torah, and "boasting" as the activity of "legalists" who, having kept whatever moral code they may be aware of, believe that they have thereby established a claim upon God, have somehow "earned" their status of "righteousness," their designation as "righteous." Within this, Paul's contrast of "works of law" and "faith" becomes more a matter of method than content: "Works" have to do with achievement, and "faith" is the abandoning of one's own efforts and trust in God instead. Paul is thus supposed to be standing alongside Augustine in his battle against Pelagius, alongside Luther in his fight against Rome. Further, though this is not always noticed, Paul is often aligned thereby with the Enlightenment in its elevation of abstract truth against this-worldly reality ("faith" as a "spiritual" matter, "works" as having to do with material things); with the Romantic movement in its elevation of feeling over outward reality, ritual, and so on; and with twentieth-century existentialism in its insistence on being true to one's inner motivations rather than being constrained from outside. Not for nothing could Rudolf Bultmann read Heidegger into the New Testament and claim to be a good Lutheran.

It is important to say that the battles of Augustine and Luther were not entirely mistaken. Paul's whole thought is characterized by the free grace of God, and any suggestion that humans, whether Jewish or Gentile, might somehow put God in their debt, might perhaps earn their good standing within God's people, would be anathema to him. This, however, is not the issue he was facing. Contemporary studies of first-century Judaism indicate that Paul's contemporaries did not think like Pelagius or Erasmus; they were not bent on earning their justification, or their salvation, from scratch by performing the "works of the law." The overarching context of the covenant embraced all Jewish law-keeping; the most detailed exploration of what living by Torah involved must be seen as falling within the category of response to grace, rather than the attempt to merit it.[126] In any case, whether or not we allow this point, we find that some of Paul's key arguments, when taken to refer to the problem that Luther thought Paul was talking about, simply do not work. The exegesis does not come away clean. The present paragraph is a case in point (see the Commentary on chap. 4;

125. See Cranfield, *Romans,* 218.

126. This is what Sanders has famously called "covenantal nomism." See particularly E. P. Sanders, *Paul and Palestinian Judaism* (London: SCM, 1977).

9:30–10:13). The proof of the theories must lie, ultimately, in the coherence of the exegesis. Much of Galatians could be called as further evidence.

The link between 3:21-26 and 3:27-31, made initially by the "therefore" at the start of v. 27 ("then," NIV, NRSV), indicates that Paul is now drawing the conclusion he has always had in mind from the brief and dense statement of the revelation of God's righteousness in Jesus' messianic faithfulness unto death. He is returning, in fact, to the question he raised in 2:17-24, that of the "boasting" of "the Jew" (see the Commentary on 2:17). The point here is that Paul is now ruling out the "boast" whereby "the Jew" maintained a status above that of the Gentiles. Paul is not addressing the more general "boast" of the moral legalist whose system of salvation is one of self-effort, but the ethnic pride of Israel according to the flesh, supported as it was by the possession of the Torah and the performance of those "works" that set Israel apart from the pagans.

This explains the crucial turn in the paragraph. If the statements of vv. 27-28 are not true, this would mean that God is the God of Jews only, not of Gentiles also. The point of the whole paragraph, not just vv. 29-30, is that, because there is one God—the central Jewish belief, of course—there must ultimately be one people of God; and, therefore, that people must be marked out by something other than the Jewish law, which would have left a high fence down the middle of the church, with Jewish Christians on one side and Gentile Christians on the other. That, again, is the main thrust of chap. 4, to which the paragraph points in several particulars, and also of Galatians 2–3, with which the present paragraph has many points of overlap.

**3:27.** Boasting is excluded. It is always risky to guess at how onomatopoeia might have worked in an ancient language, but the verb ἐξεκλείσθη (*exekleisthē*) has, to my ear at least, the ring of a door being slammed shut. The revelation of God's righteousness in Jesus' death shuts out once for all any suggestion that there might be a special status, a "favored nation clause," for ethnic Israel. God's righteousness, in other words, has not been revealed, as had been expected, in some great victory whereby Israel overcame her enemies and obtained national liberation. It came about

through the Messiah's dying at the hands of the pagans, as the great act of atonement needed not only by Israel but also by the whole world. This is why a crucified Messiah is "a scandal to Jews" (1 Cor 1:23) and why Paul can speak of his having been "crucified with the Messiah" (Gal 2:19). A crucified Messiah is either an impossibility (as Paul would have said before his conversion) or it must spell the end of Israel's ethnic "boast." This, of course, will be followed up in a good deal more detail in chaps. 9–11.

The means of boasting's exclusion is then stated compactly. Israel's status depended on the gift and performance of Torah; how is the new arrangement undergirded? What sort of Torah sustains it? The Torah characterized by "works"? No; the Torah characterized by "faith." It is, of course, controversial to take νόμος (*nomos*) here as "Torah" throughout; a long tradition, represented by NIV, has taken it as "principle"—which then causes the mistranslation of τῶν ἔργων (*tōn ergōn;* lit., "of works") as "on [the principle] of observing the law." Paul's point is more subtle and is once again so dense here that we need to call on the fuller statements later in the letter (in this case 8:1-6; 9:30–10:13) to come to our help.[127]

He is already beginning that line of thought that, in 7:7-25, will see Torah cleared of blame, though itself helpless in the cause of justification or salvation, and that, in chap. 10, will see him describe Christian faith as that which really fulfills Torah, even where the believers, if they are Gentiles, have never heard it. Paul has already hinted at this line of thought in 2:25-29: "uncircumcised people who keep the law's decrees" is an oxymoron, unless Paul is thinking of a deeper "keeping of Torah," a "fulfillment" of Torah (2:27, τὸν νόμον τελοῦσα *ton nomon telousa*) that takes place not in the letter and the outward works that define Jew from Gentile, but in the heart (see also 1 Cor 7:19).

Paul is thus distinguishing, not for the last time in the letter, between the Torah seen in two different ways. On the one hand, there is "the Torah of works"—this is Torah seen as that which defines Israel over against the nations, witnessed by the performance of the works that Torah

---

127. On the debate, see Moo, *Romans,* 247-50 (taking the usual line that "law" means "principle"); see Cranfield, *Romans,* 219-20, whom I follow with slight modifications.

prescribes—not only sabbath, food-laws and circumcision, though these are the obvious things that, sociologically speaking, give substance to the theologically based separation.[128] On the other hand, there is the new category Paul is forging here: "the Torah of faith," in a sense yet to be explained (like many things in chap. 3), gives the indication of where the true, renewed people of God are to be found. He is unwilling, it seems, to give up the belief that the God-given Torah defines the people of God. What he has done is to deny that performing "the works of Torah," the things that define Israel ethnically, is the appropriate mode of use for Torah. Rather, the Torah is to be fulfilled through faith; in other words, where someone believes the gospel, there Torah is in fact being fulfilled, even though in a surprising way (on this whole topic, see the Commentary on 9:30–10:13).

**3:28.** Paul now explains the antithesis between "the law of works" and "the law of faith" by declaring that a person is "justified by faith apart from works of the law." This, interestingly in view of the history of interpretation, is not itself a conclusion for which he has so far argued in the present letter (despite the KJV's "we conclude" and the NEB's "for our argument is"); it is a further belief that he is simply stating, as part of his present actual argument that Jewish boasting ("we possess Torah, therefore we are inalienably God's people") is excluded by the revelation of God's covenant faithfulness. The actual argument for justification by faith comes in the next chapter. The word for "we hold" (NRSV) or "we maintain" (NIV) is in fact λογιζόμεθα (*logizometha*): "we reckon," "we calculate." Paul is reporting on a calculation that has taken place, not in the present passage, but elsewhere, which he will shortly unveil.

The greatest problem facing the contemporary reader in understanding what Paul means by "a person is justified" is that centuries of usage of the English word "justify," and of its Latin root and its French and German equivalents, have assumed that "to be justified" meant much the same as "to be converted," "to be born again," "to become a

Christian."[129] The further debates that have occurred have often taken their starting-point from there, distinguishing for instance between the beginning of the the process of becoming a Christian and the continuation of that to the end. The question of an *ordo salutis*, the sequence of events that takes a person from outright unbelief through to final salvation, has been hugely influential in some circles, and I recognize that my insistence on letting Paul say what he means by his own key terms does violence to many such well-loved frameworks of thought.[130] This is not, by the way, a matter of the so-called "new perspective" on Paul, though insights from Sanders, Dunn and others, critically sifted and factored in where appropriated, must make their contribution. It is a matter of exegesis; and when we exegete Paul we find that when he talks about what later theology denotes as "conversion" and "regeneration" he speaks of God's "call" through which, by the work of the Spirit, people come to faith. "Those God called, God justified; those God justified, God also glorified": Rom 8:30 is Paul's clearest *ordo salutis*, and we will not go far wrong if we stick to it.

Of course, what Paul means by "justification" is closely linked to the question of how people who start off as sinners end up being glorified; but the word "justify" and its cognates do not refer to the event of "conversion" or the process of Christian living, for which he uses other language (see, for instance, 1 Thess 1:5; 2:13). They refer to God's declaration that certain persons are members of the covenant people, that their sins have been dealt with. Nor is it true—as anxious opponents of the "new perspective" are wont to say—that I am here simply reverting to the old either/or made famous by Wrede and Schweitzer, that Paul only talks about justification and the law in order

128. On the symbols of Jewish identity, see Wright, *The New Testament and the People of God,* 224-41.

129. On the history of the doctrine of justification, see Alister E. McGrath, *Iustitia Dei: A History of the Christian Doctrine of Justification,* 2 vols. (Cambridge: Cambridge University Press, 1986). McGrath rightly notes (1:2-3) that the usage of the term "justification" in Christian theology does not correspond exactly to the more precise Pauline meaning; he does not draw out all the ways in which this has vitiated the exegetical endeavors of those theologians who have sought to ground their views in Paul. See N. T. Wright, *What St. Paul Really Said: Was Paul of Tarsus the Real Founder of Christianity?* (Grand Rapids: Eerdmans, 1997) chap. 7.

130. I have in mind Mark A. Seifrid, *Justification by Faith: The Origin and Development of a Central Pauline Theme,* NovTSup 68 (Leiden: Brill, 1992); and *Christ Our Righteousness: Paul's Theology of Justification* (Downers Grove: InterVarsity, 2000).

to address a particular problem in the church. When we understand the place of Israel within his vision of God's purposes for the world, the relation of Jew and Gentile can never be an incidental side-issue.

Anyway, Paul's point in the present passage is quite simply that what now marks out the covenant people of God, in the light of the revelation of God's righteousness in Jesus, is not the works of Torah that demarcate ethnic Israel, but "the law of faith," the faith that, however paradoxically, is in fact the true fulfilling of Torah. There is no problem in adding the word "alone" to the word "faith"—a tradition that goes way back beyond Luther, at least to Aquinas—as long as we recognize what it means: not that a person is "converted" by faith alone without moral effort (that is true, but it is not the truth that Paul is stressing here), nor that God's grace is always prior to human response (that is equally true, and equally not Paul's emphasis here), but that the badge of membership in God's people, the badge that enables all alike to stand on the same, flat ground at the foot of the cross, is faith.

That this is his meaning is at once demonstrated in the following verse. That those who insist on other meanings are not following his train of thought is demonstrated by the trouble they have with it.[131]

**3:29-30a.** If justification were through "works of Torah," God would be shown to be the God only of Jews; whereas in fact God is the God of Gentiles also, because God is one. If justification were through Torah, God's impartiality would be impugned (2:11), and the whole fabric of the δικαιοσύνη θεοῦ (dikaiosynē theou), the justice and faithfulness of God, would start to unravel. Here we are at the characteristic point of tension in all Paul's thought: God's faithfulness to the covenant with the Jewish patriarch, Abraham, and his descendants, can only be fulfilled through the creation of a worldwide, Jew-plus-Gentile, family. The whole question of "Paul and the Law" can only be comprehended within this framework.

What Israel has always been tempted to forget, from Paul's point of view, is that the God who made the covenant with Abraham is the creator of the whole world and that the covenant was put in place precisely in order that through Israel God might address the whole world (cf. 2:17-24; 3:2).

To prove the point, Paul quotes the most fundamental Jewish confession of faith, the *Shema:* "since God is one."[132] That which defines Israel at the deepest level, the belief in and commitment to the one God of heaven and earth, itself points to the conclusion that this one God must ultimately create a single family not only of Jews but also of Gentiles.[133] The *Shema* is itself the ultimate summary of Torah (as Jesus also believed, Mark 12:29), and this summary points away from the possession of Torah and the use of it as a national badge, toward a different sort of fulfillment altogether. The very word שמע (šama') itself, meaning "hear (and obey)," a meaning picked up in the Greek compound ὑπακούω (hypakouō, "obey [as a result of hearing]"), points to Paul's concept of ὑπακοή πίστεως (hypakoē pisteōs), "the obedience of faith" (1:5; 16:26), signaling the way in which the "faith" of which Paul spoke was, for him, the true "obedience" the Torah sought, responding of course to the "faithfulness," the "obedience," of the Messiah through which God's faithfulness was revealed. God is one, and therefore recognizes as the true covenant family all those who offer this "obedience" to the gospel, whatever their ethnic origin.

**3:30b.** Paul now explicitly draws the conclusion: God will justify circumcised and uncircumcised alike, on the basis of faith. That is, God will declare that wherever this faith is found, the believer is a true member of the covenant family. Only faith can have this role, not because faith is a superior type of religious experience to anything else, nor because faith is an easier substitute for "works," putting it within the range of the morally incompetent (it is remarkable how many people

---

131. The NIV's omission of ἤ (ē "or") at the start of the verse is a symptom of the (classical Protestant) misunderstanding that runs through its translation of the whole of 3:21-31. Fitzmyer's translation "but" (*Romans,* 359) indicates the same misunderstanding, as does Barrett's suggestion that this is a different point to the previous verse. See C. K. Barrett, *A Commentary on the Epistle to the Romans* (London: A. & C. Black, 1957) 83.

132. The *Shema,* the Jewish daily prayer to this day, begins with the words of Deut 6:4: "Hear, O Israel, YHWH our God, YHWH is one." The NIV's "since there is only one God" fails to catch both the stark emphasis of the Greek and the echoes of Deuteronomy 6.

133. For the similar (and similarly dense) argument of Gal 3:15-22, see N. T. Wright, *The Climax of the Covenant: Christ and the Law in Pauline Theology* (Edinburgh: T. & T. Clark; Minneapolis: Fortress, 1991) chap. 8. Paul makes a different, though related, use of the *Shema* in 1 Cor 8:6, on which see ibid., chap. 6. See also the Commentary on Rom 5:5; 8:28.

still suppose that this is what Paul was talking about),[134] but because faith—this faith, to be defined in 4:18-25 and 10:9—is the appropriate human stance of humility and trust before the creator and covenant God, the stance that, only possible through grace, truly reveals the heart in which new covenant membership has been inscribed by the Spirit (2:29; cf. 1 Cor 12:3; Eph 2:8-10).

Paul makes the slightest of distinctions in phraseology, suggesting that the circumcised are justified "on the grounds of" faith and the uncircumcised "through" faith (the NRSV and the NIV both have "the same" faith, perhaps bringing out the fact that the second occurrence of "faith" has the definite article in the Greek). If Paul intends any difference, it is that the circumcised are already, in a sense, within the covenant and now need to be declared true covenant members on the basis of faith, while the uncircumcised, being outside the covenant, need to come in through the doorway marked "faith." The distinction only applies to their starting-point, not to their destination or to the badge that demonstrates that they have arrived there.

**3:31.** The density of Paul's argument has led some of his readers to miss the hints he has been throwing out at various points about the way in which, in this new covenant dispensation, the Torah is in fact fulfilled. What has been most striking, following 2:12-15, 17-20, 26-27; 3:19-20 (in all of which Paul is clearly affirming Torah as God's law and its verdict as true), is the way in which, beginning with 3:21 "apart from Torah," he has now declared that "the works of Torah" cannot be the badge of membership in God's people. Being an ethnic Jew, with Torah to prove it, does not establish a special inalienable status; being circumcised is neither here nor there when it comes to justification. The natural question that must follow is: Have we then abandoned the affirmation of Torah stated up to 3:20? Do we then abolish the Torah, make it null and void, through faith? (The NIV and the NRSV, by translating "this faith," again bring out the force of the definite article.)

This is just the question some readers of Paul

are waiting for. Those who follow an ultra-Protestant reading, in which "the law" refers to the legalistic, moralistic, or ritualistic practices designed, at least in the eyes of their opponents, to establish a claim on God, and those who follow an ultra-liberal (or ultra-Romantic) reading of Paul, in which "the law" refers to any moral code imposed on human beings from without—and who have therefore celebrated the victory, respectively, of low-church piety on the one hand and spontaneity on the other—will naturally want to answer "Yes!" to this question. They will perhaps feel that Paul's own answer ("On the contrary! We uphold the law") is illogical, that it represents the old Pharisee peeping out from his hiding.[135] Or they will water it down to merely "Well, I can prove the point from scripture; watch me expound the Abraham story in the next chapter." But that is to miss the inner logic and subtlety of Paul's actual argument.

Likewise, those in the Reformed tradition who are deeply concerned for the continuity of the new covenant with the old, for the abiding validity of the Old Testament, for the rejection of all that even smells of Marcion, will find that, while their sensitivities are much closer to Paul's, their emphasis, too, is not quite his, or not at this point.[136] His answer is completely genuine. We "establish" (so NASB) Torah; that is perhaps better than "uphold" (NRSV, NIV, REB). Paul is indeed concerned that what God said in the past is shown to be right and true; he will argue the point in detail in 7:7–8:11 and 9–11. But at the moment he is doing two rather different things. First, he is drawing out the significance of having the *Shema* itself as a pointer to the Jew-plus-Gentile quality of the new family (and, behind this, of the paradoxical "fulfillment of the Torah" spoken of in 2:25-9, referring to those in whose hearts the Spirit has been at work). Second, he is pointing ahead, as so often at this stage of the letter, to the dark and

---

134. E.g., the telltale aside of W. Sanday and A. C. Headlam, *A Critical and Exegetical Commentary on the Epistle to the Romans*, 5th ed., ICC (Edinburgh: T. & T. Clark, 1902) 283, suggesting that faith is "much easier." Would they still say that at the start of the twenty-first century?

135. John A. T. Robinson, *Wrestling with Romans* (Philadelphia: Westminster, 1979) 51, describes revealingly how C. H. Dodd, arriving at 3:31*b* during the course of the NEB translation project, exclaimed, "What rubbish!" Ernst Käsemann, *Commentary on Romans*, trans. Geoffrey W. Bromiley (London: SCM, 1980) 104, declares that the verse is "incomprehensible" as a conclusion to chap. 3 and that it only makes sense as a transition to chap. 4—i.e., as saying, "I can prove this from scripture."

136. See C. E. B. Cranfield, *A Critical and Exegetical Commentary on the Epistle to the Romans*, ICC, 2 vols. (Edinburgh: T. & T. Clark, 1975) 223-24.

deep arguments yet to come, in which, through the fulfillment of God's overall purpose in Christ and by the Spirit, even Torah, with all its negative side fully allowed for, will be seen to have accomplished its strange vocation.

The rhetorical force of the paragraph, and of 3:21-31 as a whole, is thus to say that God has unveiled in Jesus the Messiah, and supremely in his death, that covenant faithfulness, that saving justice, through which the outstanding problem of sin and wrath has been dealt with, so that now a new covenant family emerges, consisting of Jews and Gentiles alike, characterized by the faith that answers to the faithfulness of the Messiah.

This is offered as a summary statement; Paul now proceeds to the detailed argument (not merely "proof from scripture") to back it up. What was the covenant with Abraham all about in the first place?

# REFLECTIONS

**1.** It was one thing for Paul, looking back at his own life "under Torah," to declare that possession of Torah, and the accomplishment of its "works," was not the way by which the people of God were demarcated. It is quite another, after a checkered history, for Christians to declare the same thing as though nothing dangerous or subversive were being said. We must never forget that Paul's gospel remained "to the Jew first and also to the Greek." He never for a moment implied that Jews were not just as much the objects of God's love and grace; indeed, the crowning passage of this letter mounts a long argument to exactly this end. It is easy for Christians who live in areas where there is little or no visible Jewish presence to make "the Jews" a soft target, repeating the slogans of former theological polemics without realizing how damaging, taken out of context, such things can be, using this straw figure as a way of attacking their own opponents without imagining that there might be some real Jews listening in on the conversation, for whom this would be deeply offensive.

Of course, we must quickly say, Paul's gospel was offensive, not only to Gentiles (who often did not take kindly to being told that there was now another lord of the world, and a Jewish one at that), but also to Jews, for whom the idea of a crucified Messiah was a contradiction in terms, while the idea that God might now admit Gentiles into the covenant family on equal terms was close to unthinkable. Contemporary Western culture, in which being inoffensive has become the supreme virtue, hops from one foot to another to avoid saying anything that anyone might take exception to, forgetting that, according to the prophet, God's word is like a hammer that breaks rock in pieces. Often, of course, it is not actually Jews who are most offended by Christian claims, but rather those post-Enlightenment thinkers for whom any idea of God acting, choosing, doing specific things, appears undemocratic, not in keeping with the spirit of our age. Mainstream Judaism, and for that matter mainstream Islam, is just as offensive to this mood as mainstream Christianity.

In particular, there is no avoiding the Pauline insistence that in Christ there is "neither Jew nor Greek." One can understand why it is that, for instance in Palestine/Israel today, there are some churches where only Arab Christians worship, and others where only Jewish Christians worship; just as one can understand why there are some churches that are black only (or, indeed, white only), not by law but by choice, in multiracial communities on both sides of the Atlantic and elsewhere. But one must insist, on the basis of Romans 3, that all such situations, understandable though they may be, are regrettable and fraught with danger. Such communities are always likely to forget the truth Paul insisted on in the present passage: that the only thing uniting Christians is their faith in the God made known in Jesus Christ. To suggest by one's social or cultural behavior that the one God has any kind of "favored nation clause" is to fly in the face of the revelation of God's righteousness in the gospel. In this context, the concept of a "national church," or "state church," needs very careful thought (the writer speaks as a member of the established Church of England) if it is not to overthrow the gospel itself.

**2.** This applies not only to churches but also to communities and nations. The post-colonial world in Africa and elsewhere has seen the resurgence of tribalism; the post-immigration world in Europe has seen the resurgence of racism; the post-Cold War world of the Balkans has seen the resurgence of enthocentric nationalism. A British writer looking at Northern Ireland, where the two militant sides are still often referred to as "Catholic" and "Protestant" (now rightly being replaced by "Republican" and "Unionist"), can only hang his head in sorrow. The church's witness, so often compromised in these situations by the easy assumption that the Christian God was on the side, shall we say, of the Orthodox Serbs against the Bosnian Muslims—or the Croatian Catholics!—must shine out again, precisely with the message of Romans and Galatians, that in Christ there is neither Jew nor Greek, and if so then certainly neither Catholic nor Protestant.[137]

**3.** This latter hard lesson—Romans, after all, has been seen for many generations as the bastion of "Protestant" theology—is of course reinforced once we realize what Paul's teaching on "justification" actually is. The Protestant polemic of half a millennium has been directed against the "religion" of Catholicism, and by extension against any teaching or practice that seems to suggest a desire to "earn" justification, favor with God, or even salvation, by the correct performance of religious or sacramental duty. It must be said, sadly, that one does indeed still find, not only in some popular expressions of Roman Catholicism but also in many Protestant churches and writings, the idea that at the last the reason why God will be merciful to humans, if that will indeed be the case, is that the humans in question have performed certain deeds that will outweigh their undoubted misdeeds. The notion of free forgiveness, of

> Nothing in my hand I bring;
> Simply to thy cross I cling;

is so vast, so shocking, so radically life-changing, that many seem to prefer, when all is said and done, a simple religion of good deeds and bad. Let it be said as clearly as possible that, though this is not basically what Paul is writing about, he would have had only one thing to say about it: It stinks.

Nevertheless, the Protestant polemic has gained more targets as it has gone on, and they have less and less to do with any questions that Paul would have recognized as relevant. The Enlightenment, by rehabilitating the dualism of the spiritual and the physical, aligned quite closely with the dualism of reason and contingent historical reality, was able to introduce within Protestantism the sense that anything to do with physical objects or behavior was somehow "worldly" as opposed to "godly," thus compounding the original Reformation protest against the theology of "works-righteousness" with a subtly different protest against Christian belief having anything to do with the present world. It is that separation, of course, against which liberation theology has made a necessary, albeit sometimes perhaps a misguided, protest.

The effect on the church's worship has also been dramatic, producing a low-church mentality in which, despite all the verbal protestations about the priority of grace, the unworthiness of the worshipers, the offer of free forgiveness and the Spirit's inspiration of all that is performed in faith, any suggestion of liturgical movement, gestures, objects, robes, or even the fact of liturgy itself, can be rejected as constituting a compromise of the gospel, a collapse back into a human-centered religion, a kind of legalism, rather than a living relationship. This attitude, frankly, owes nothing to Paul, however much it claims him as its patron saint. Of course, all worship activities can come to be regarded as "things we do to earn God's favor." But that is just as true of the still and silent Quaker meeting, of the informal (and yet often secretly formal) charismatic prayer

---

137. On this whole topic see M. Volf, *Exclusion and Embrace: A Theological Exploration of Identity, Otherness, and Reconciliation* (Nashville: Abingdon, 1996).

meeting, of the unscripted, yet totally predictable, public prayers in some "free" churches, as it is of the full Orthodox or Roman Catholic liturgy. It is time to recognize these debates, important though they may be, as having little or nothing to do with what Paul is talking about in his rejection of "justification by works."

And there is more. The Romantic movement, seeking, after the sterility of eighteenth-century Rationalism, to recapture a sense of integration with the natural world, and awe and wonder when faced with it, encouraged the belief that the only "authentic" way for humans to do anything was to act as it were spontaneously, allowing things deeply felt and known to come forth as from a hidden spring. Poetic inspiration, as practiced by the Lakeland poets, became a kind of model; the suggestion that one might have to work at a poem, to cross things out and try different words here and there, seemed shoddy, second-rate, indicative of a less-than-complete inspiration.

This view would not be maintained by many writers or philosophers today; but it has left its legacy in the Christian churches in the form of the desire for spontaneity, for freedom from rules and hence also from liturgies. (I doubt whether Luther, at least, would have recognized this movement as a legitimate extension of his theology.) And this, too, is often supposed to have something to do with "justification by faith apart from works." There is of course great value in the stumbling prayer that comes from the heart as against the beautifully phrased prayer read from a book while the heart is busy elsewhere. But many, perhaps most, of the greatest spiritual guides would regard this as a quite false antithesis. Often somebody else's words will act as lightning conductors, enabling one's belief in, and sense of, God's presence to go down to the very center of one's being. The drama of the eucharistic liturgy is the reenactment of the story of Israel, focused on Jesus and supremely on his death; to break up its lines, to avoid any sense of drama in case it became a new "works-righteousness," can itself be an act of human-centered arrogance, declaring one's independence from the very gospel events themselves. Some forms of Christianity still use Paul's words, filtered through the Reformation, the Enlightenment, and the Romantic movements, to justify practices, or the lack of them, in a way that has everything to do with personal, social, and cultural preferences and prejudices and nothing whatever to do with Paul.

Indeed, at a deeper level, Paul's positive point in this paragraph cuts against many such attitudes, bound up as they are with cultural differences (e.g., Northern European or Mediterranean cultures, with their various transatlantic offshoots). A good deal of polemic that disguises itself with theological language is in fact the determination to preserve one particular cultural way of doing things; and that itself is ruled out by Paul's whole argument. When we arrive at 14:1–15:13, the final great climax of the letter, we will discover that justification by faith, as expounded in chap. 3, is designed to result in "fellowship by faith," in which different cultures, different ways of doing things, respect and celebrate one another's practices within the fellowship of the one Lord, worshiping the one God. How the church may learn to distinguish that which is of the essence of the gospel, to be preserved at all costs, from that which is part of a local culture, and hence a matter of theological indifference, is of course a well-known and exceedingly difficult problem. To put it another way, one of the main challenges facing the Western church in the twenty-first century is how to preserve the celebration of different cultures from degeneration into a mere postmodern smorgasbord of options in which everything, including morality and theology, are up for negotiation. But for Paul it was precisely part of the essence of the gospel, of the revelation of God's impartial saving justice in Jesus, that Jews and Greeks belonged together in God's family and should learn to work that out in practice. And if that division could be overcome, how much more those that still divide Christians in our own day.

# Romans 4:1-25, The Covenant Family of Abraham

## OVERVIEW

Once we recognize the main subject of the section (3:21–4:25) and its place within Paul's larger argument, we find that chapter 4 itself comes into its own. It is not simply, as it has so often been labeled, a "proof from scripture," or even an "example," of Paul's "thesis" of justification by faith in 3:21-31 (for the idea that Paul simply ransacked his mental concordance for texts about "righteousness" and "faith" and came up with Hab 2:4 and Gen 15:6, see the Commentary on 1:17). The chapter is, in fact, a full-dress exposition of the covenant God made with Abraham in Genesis 15, showing at every point how God always intended and promised that the covenant family of Abraham would include Gentiles as well as Jews.[138] Irrespective of what we might say about a systematic presentation of Paul's ideas, in his present argument this is the main topic, to which "justification by faith" makes a vital contribution, rather than the other way round.

The three main points in the argument concern works (vv. 2-8), circumcision (vv. 9-12), and the law (vv. 13-15). In the second and third cases obviously, and in the first case arguably, the discussion does not concern the question normally supposed, of how someone becomes a Christian (and whether religious ritual, "works of the law" in that sense, has anything to do with it), but rather the question, does Abraham's family consist just of Jews, or also of Gentiles? To answer this question, Paul quotes or refers to Gen 15:6 in vv. 3, 9-12, 13, 18-22, 23, arguing in detail for its meaning in its own context and for the relation of that meaning to surrounding passages in Genesis, particularly chap. 17.

This strongly supports one particular reading of v. 1, and with it the whole argument. The question Paul faces here is whether covenant membership means, after all, coming to belong to the physical family of Abraham (the question, of course, at stake in Galatians). This reading also means that the climax of the chapter can properly be located in vv. 16-17, where the remark about Abraham being the father of many nations, so far from being a parenthesis as sometimes suggested, is in fact the answer to the question of v. 1, the decisive point in the whole sequence of thought. Abraham is indeed the "father" of the covenant people of God, but he is not the father "according to the flesh." He is the father of all, Gentile and Jew alike, who believe in the God who raised Jesus.

Genesis 15:6 ("Abram believed God, and it was reckoned to him as righteousness"), which ties the chapter tightly together, is one of only two passages in the Hebrew Scriptures that speak of something being "reckoned as righteousness" to someone (the other is Ps 106:31 [105:31 LXX], referring to Phineas; see also 4QMMT C 31, on which see below). It is not a usual phrase in classical Greek, either.[139] The Hebrew of Gen 15:6 has no word corresponding to "as" in the regular translation, but simply says ויחשבה לו צדקה (wayyaḥšĕbehā lô ṣĕdāqâ, "he reckoned it to him righteousness").[140] The LXX is as Paul quotes it. Paul does not, of course, leave the phrase cryptic; his frequent repetitions and paraphrases of it throughout the chapter give us a clear idea of what he takes it to mean. It is about trusting the God who justifies the ungodly (v. 5) and can be explained by a psalm passage about the forgiveness of sins (vv. 6-8). When the original phrase says "he reckoned it to him," the "it" is clearly Abraham's faith (v. 9); and the resulting status Abraham enjoys can then be described as "the righteousness of faith" (v. 11), in a passage where "righteousness" is directly equivalent to "covenant" in the original Genesis passage.

---

138. At this stage of the Genesis story, Abraham is still called Abram. Paul's regular title for the patriarch is Ἀβραάμ (Abraam), which corresponds to the longer form. I will follow Paul in using the longer name, although strictly it is anachronistic at this point.

139. H. G. R. Liddell, R. Scott, H. S. Jones, *A Greek-English Lexicon,* 9th ed. (Oxford: Oxford University Press, 1996) cite only Xenophon *Cyropaedia* 3.1.33.

140. The LXX clarifies the sense by adding "to" before the last word. The near parallel in Ps 106:31 [105:31 LXX] has the "to" in the Hebrew as well as the Greek.

This "faith" can then be imitated, and those who share it will also have "righteousness" reckoned to them (vv. 11, 24). Verses 18-21 describe how, having received the promise of Gen 15:5, Abraham came to believe despite all the contrary factors; this offers a remarkable midrashic account, almost psychological in content. The conclusion of the chapter demonstrates that all those who share Abraham's faith will have "righteousness" reckoned to them on this basis, so that Paul can go on at once to say "Being then justified by faith" in 5:1.

Paul is arguing, then, that Abraham's faith is the sole badge of membership in God's people, and that therefore all those who share it are "justified." He offers a description of this faith, showing, on the one hand, that it is the stance of true humanity before the creator God, reversing the rebellious and idolatrous stance of 1:18-25, and, on the other, that it is the same faith that Christians demonstrate when they believe in the God who raised Jesus from the dead. This enables him to round off Romans 1–4 with a pregnant christological formula that sums up everything he has said so far. Jesus' death has dealt with the sin described in the first three chapters; his resurrection, by demonstrating that he was indeed God's faithful one, God's "son" (1:4) and that, therefore, his death was God's victory over sin, establishes justification. And, by there alluding to Isaiah 53, Paul is able to make again the point that, though often ignored by commentators, runs most of the way through Romans 1–4: Jesus has done what Israel was called to do. His faithfulness, his obedience (as Paul will refer to it in 5:12-21) reveals the covenant faithfulness, the saving justice, of God. This perfectly prepares the way both for the development of the argument in 5–8 and for its new and decisive turn in 9–11.

A comment is necessary about why Paul goes to all the trouble of this complex argument about Abraham and his family. It has long been assumed, by those who think of Paul as opposing "Judaism," that he would not have brought Abraham into his argument (here, in chap. 9, and in Galatians 3–4) had he not been forced to do so by hypothetical "opponents." Were there, some ask, "Judaizers" or Jewish sympathizers among the Roman church, to address whom Paul felt obliged to bring Abraham into the picture? Or was he deliberately snatching the best argument away from potential opponents?[141]

These suggestions may have some secondary part to play. Paul may have been aware, in writing these passages, of people (the so-called "Judaizers," perhaps) who would appeal to Genesis in favor of a theology and practice that enshrined Jewish ethnicity as a necessary, perhaps even a sufficient, condition of membership in the people of God. We have no independent evidence for this, however; and the suggestion that Paul would not otherwise have brought Abraham into the argument strikes me as the thin end of a Marcionite wedge. Paul's whole theme in Romans is the faithfulness of God to the covenant, the divine saving justice by which the world is both condemned and rescued. Here, not as an aside, a semi-apologetic or semi-polemical exegetical footnote, but as his own choice of passage and topic, he presents the story of Abraham to show that, in Jesus Christ, God has done what had been promised from the beginning and has thereby created the family whose defining mark is faith in God the life-giver.

141. E.g., Ernst Käsemann, *Commentary on Romans,* trans. Geoffrey W. Bromiley (London: SCM, 1980) 105.

# Romans 4:1-8, Believing the Promise

| NIV | NRSV |
|---|---|
| **4** What then shall we say that Abraham, our forefather, discovered in this matter? ²If, in fact, Abraham was justified by works, he had something to boast about—but not before God. ³What does the Scripture say? "Abraham believed | **4** What then are we to say was gained by*ᵃ* Abraham, our ancestor according to the flesh? ²For if Abraham was justified by works, he has something to boast about, but not before God. |
| | *ᵃ* Other ancient authorities read *say about* |

## NIV

God, and it was credited to him as righteousness."[a]

[4]Now when a man works, his wages are not credited to him as a gift, but as an obligation. [5]However, to the man who does not work but trusts God who justifies the wicked, his faith is credited as righteousness. [6]David says the same thing when he speaks of the blessedness of the man to whom God credits righteousness apart from works:

[7] "Blessed are they
     whose transgressions are forgiven,
     whose sins are covered.
[8] Blessed is the man
     whose sin the Lord will never count
          against him."[b]

[a] 3 Gen. 15:6; also in verse 22     [b] 8 Psalm 32:1,2

## NRSV

[3]For what does the scripture say? "Abraham believed God, and it was reckoned to him as righteousness." [4]Now to one who works, wages are not reckoned as a gift but as something due. [5]But to one who without works trusts him who justifies the ungodly, such faith is reckoned as righteousness. [6]So also David speaks of the blessedness of those to whom God reckons righteousness apart from works:

[7] "Blessed are those whose iniquities are forgiven,
     and whose sins are covered;
[8] blessed is the one against whom the Lord will
          not reckon sin."

# COMMENTARY

**4:1.** "What then shall we say? Have we found Abraham to be our forefather according to the flesh?" This is not, of course, what any of the commentaries or translations say, but it has a strong claim to represent Paul's mind.[142] Three reasons stand out. First, it introduces the chapter Paul is writing, as opposed to the one that many think he should have written; in other words, a chapter about the scope and nature of Abraham's family, rather than a chapter about "justification by faith" as a doctrine about how people become Christians. This, as we shall see, results in the straightforward solution of at least one major exegetical problem. Second, it recognizes that when Paul introduces an argument with τί οὖν ἐροῦμεν ti oun eroumen, "what then shall we say?" this phrase is frequently complete in itself, requiring a question mark at once. (There is, of course, no punctuation in the earliest MSS.)

Obvious examples are 6:1; 7:7; see also τί οὖν (ti oun) in 3:9. Third, it avoids at a stroke the awkwardness of sense, and hence of translation, in the usual readings (of which the NRSV and the NIV are typical) in which Abraham is the subject of εὑρηκέναι heurēkenai, "to have found," rather than the object as in the reading proposed; since it is not clear what "to have found" could possibly mean in this context, the sense of the verb has to be stretched as in the NRSV ("was gained by") and NIV ("discovered"), neither of which lead in to what Paul is actually going to say.[143] The proposal, then, is that Paul raises in v. 1 a possible conclusion that could be drawn from what has been said so far, in order to argue against it.

At this point, however, I diverge from the meaning Hays gives to his own proposed reading. He suggests that Paul wants to say "Have we *Jews* normally considered Abraham to be our forefather only according to the flesh?" I suggest, rather, that the whole of Romans 4 hinges on the question, whether 3:21-31 means that we *Christians,* Jews and Gentiles alike, now find that we are to be members of the fleshly family of Abraham (note

142. See esp. Richard B. Hays, " 'Have We Found Abraham to Be Our Forefather According to the Flesh?' A Reconsideration of Rom. 4:1," *NovT* 27 (1985) 76-98. See also Richard B. Hays, *Echoes of Scripture in the Letters of Paul* (New Haven: Yale University Press, 1989) 54-55. The suggestion goes back at least to J. A. Bain, "Romans iv. 1," *Expository Times* 5 (1893–94) 430. It is not clear that subsequent commentators (e.g. Byrne, Fitzmyer, Moo, Bryan) have recognized the force or point of Hays's proposal; the same is true of S. K. Stowers, *A Rereading of Romans: Justice, Jews, and Gentiles* (New Haven: Yale University Press, 1994) 234, 242, who unlike them claims to follow it.

143. *Abraam* is indeclinable in Greek, and hence its grammatical role in the sentence is unclear until defined from elsewhere.

how the word "find" suddenly makes perfect sense).[144] In other words (Paul is proposing this as a hypothetical question), if in Christ God has been true to the covenant with Abraham, might that not mean, as the Galatians had been led to believe, that members of the Christ-family in fact belong to Abraham's fleshly family? When we read Romans 4 as the answer to this question, it gains in coherence and force.[145]

**4:2.** Verses 2-8 are regularly appealed to by those who still argue that Paul was after all attacking a theology of self-help legalism, in which "righteousness" is earned by moral effort. By themselves these verses might indeed bear that sense. But within the present argument they are much better understood as a further metaphorical expansion, rather than the inner substance, of Paul's point.

Paul's main argument is that "works" (i.e., of Torah) were not the reason for Abraham's justification; and the idea of "working" is then expanded metaphorically in vv. 4-5 into the idea of doing a job for which one earns wages. The critical connection is established with "for" at the start of v. 2 ("in fact" in the NIV is a loose way of making the same point) and depends on the link between "works of Torah" and "Jews only" that Paul had established in the immediately preceding verses. It is ethnic Jews who possess Torah; so if Abraham were the forefather of an ethnic family only, this family would be defined by Torah, and hence defined visibly by Torah's "works." Thus (v. 2*a*) if Abraham was reckoned to be in covenant with God (i.e., was justified) on the basis of works of Torah, he and his family would be able to "boast," in the way that Paul described in 2:17-20 and then firmly excluded in 3:27-30. Verse 2*a*, in other words, explains the question of v. 1, as follows: If Abraham's covenant membership was indeed defined in terms of "works of Torah"

(v. 2*a*), then he and his family would be able to sustain an ethnic boast, and so (v. 1) any Gentiles wishing to belong to this family would then have to consider themselves ethnic Jews—would, in other words, need to become proselytes, with the males among them becoming circumcised.

Paul's response, to be filled out as usual in what follows, is brusque: "but not before (lit., "toward") God," i.e., "not as far as God is concerned." Verse 2*b* is thus Paul's initial reaction to the suggestion, rather than part of the "if . . . then" clause of the earlier part of the verse.[146] This now forces Paul into saying what *is* true "before God," to cut the ground from under any potential ethnic boast, and to establish once and for all the non-ethnic nature of Abraham's true family, on the basis of the original covenant itself.

**4:3.** By way of explanation (γάρ *gar*, omitted in NIV), Paul quotes Gen 15:6: Abraham believed God, and it was reckoned to him as "righteousness." The word "reckoned" is a bookkeeping metaphor, indicating either the placing of something in a column of figures to be added up or the result of the addition itself; so NIV's "credited" is helpful. The Greek construction of the whole phrase, however ("to credit something *to* someone *unto* something"), is rare, and the precise meaning Paul intends must be sought principally in the Genesis account itself on the one hand and in the rest of Romans 4 on the other (Ps 106:31 and MMT C 31 largely restate the problem).

Genesis 15 opens with Abraham's puzzlement. YHWH has made great promises to him, but he has no children. Who then will inherit after him? Back comes the promise: God will give Abraham a family as numerous as the stars in heaven. This promise is what Abraham "believed," at which the writer comments that God "reckoned" it (presumably, Abraham's believing of the promise) "to him (as) righteousness." The passage goes on at once to speak of God's further promise, echoing that in chapter 12, to give Abraham the land of Canaan as his inheritance. Abraham asks how he may know that he will inherit it. God commands him to prepare a covenant ceremony, which then takes place, in which God solemnly tells him that his

---

144. R. B. Hays, "Adam, Israel, Christ," in *Pauline Theology Volume III: Romans*, ed. D. M. Hay and E. E. Johnson (Minneapolis: Fortress, 1995) 81, has graciously accepted my amendment of his proposal.

145. Bain took "according to the flesh" to modify "to have found" and, therefore, assumed that Paul was asking the question, "Have we, by our fleshly efforts, found Abraham to be our forefather?" In other words, have we attained membership in Abraham's family by performing works of the law? Fitzmyer's objection to this (Joseph A. Fitzmyer, *Romans*, AB 33 [Garden City, N.Y.: Doubleday, 1993] 371) in no way damages the reading I am proposing; Fitzmyer does not seem to have noticed that the meaning proposed by Hays is quite different from that of Bain. Stowers, claiming to agree with Hays, is actually agreeing with something more like Bain's reading.

146. So C. E. B. Cranfield, *A Critical and Exegetical Commentary on the Epistle to the Romans*, ICC, 2 vols. (Edinburgh: T. & T. Clark, 1975) 228; Douglas J. Moo, *The Epistle to the Romans*, NICNT (Grand Rapids: Eerdmans, 1996) 260.

seed will languish as slaves in a foreign country, but that God will bring them out and give them the land. The whole chapter, of which the covenant ceremony forms the climax, is thus all about Abraham's promised seed and the route by which they will come to their assured inheritance. Within this context, the key statement of 15:6, cryptic and almost unparalleled as it is, appears to be proleptic, referring forward to the covenant ceremony about to take place. Its overall meaning must then be something like: "God counted Abraham's faith as constituting covenant membership"; or "Abraham's believing the promise was seen by God as the sign that Abraham was 'in the right,' was to be upheld."

There are thus three levels of meaning in the dense phrase as Paul quotes it in 4:3.

The most obvious metaphorical level is the bookkeeping one ("reckoned"). God made an entry in Abraham's ledger, writing "faith," or more specifically "faith in this promise," in the column marked "righteousness" (i.e., "covenant membership").

The second level is the lawcourt one, which is clearly in Paul's mind through the way he develops the idea. God, as the judge, declares that Abraham's faith in this promise is the sign that he is in the right in some hypothetical lawcourt. We should be careful not to assume, as normal English usage of "righteousness" might lead us to do, that (a) "righteousness" means "moral goodness," and that (b) "faith" is then either a form of, or a substitute for, such moral goodness. When Abraham's faith is "counted as righteousness," it means that this faith is the sure sign that his acquittal or vindication has already taken place. Both of these meanings, the bookkeeping one and the lawcourt one, are metaphors.

The third and deepest level of meaning is the one that dominates the chapter: the covenant and membership within it (on "righteousness" and "covenant," see the Commentary on 4:11). Abraham's faith was the sure sign that he was in partnership with God; and God sealed this with the covenant ceremony and the detailed promises about Abraham's seed and their inheritance. Both these themes play an important role in later parts of the chapter and the letter.

We must, then, resist the easy temptation to misunderstand Paul's quotation from Genesis in either of two misleading ways. First, Paul does not mean that God was looking for a particular type of moral goodness (referred to as "righteousness") that would earn people membership in the covenant, and that, failing to find this, was prepared to accept faith as a substitute.[147] Faith, for Paul, is not a "substitute" qualification because *it is not a qualification at all*; nor is "righteousness" the same thing as moral goodness. "Righteousness," when applied to humans, is, at bottom, the status of being a member of the covenant; "faith" is the badge, the sign, that reveals that status because it is its key symptom. Once that is grasped, the way is open not just for the rest of Paul's argument in the present passage to unfold smoothly, but also for the nuances carried by faith and the law later in the letter to be understood clearly.

**4:4-5.** By way of showing what he means in 4:3, Paul develops the bookkeeping metaphor in the direction of employment and wage-earning. This is the only time he uses this metaphorical field in all his discussions of justification, and we should not allow this unique and brief sidelight to become the dominant note, as it has in much post-Reformation discussion. Verse 4 indicates the metaphorical situation that might have obtained if Abraham had after all been justified by works; v. 5, by contrast, shows the true position. Through this contrast, Paul is able to build into his developing picture two further important elements: God's declaration of justification is a matter of grace (v. 4), and it has to do with God's justifying the *ungodly* (v. 5).

The danger in a contemporary reading of the contrast is to suppose that v. 5 is a straightforward reversal of v. 4: Workers get paid not by grace but by debt, but believers get paid not by debt but by grace. This then smuggles back again the possibility that faith is something for which one gets paid, a substitute or alternative work, even if payment is *ex gratia* (the fact that we use that Latin phrase for an uncontracted payment shows how easily the language slips). The two sentences are not in fact balanced, partly because Paul pulls himself out of the bookkeeping metaphor halfway through v. 5 and returns to his main points, the lawcourt and

147. E.g., J. A. Ziesler, "Paul and Arboriculture: Romans 11:17-24," *JSNT* 24 (1985) 124.

the covenant. What Paul says in v. 5 not only contrasts with v. 4 ("working" and "not working"), but also deconstructs the whole frame of thought: The alternative to "working" is to "trust the one who justifies the ungodly."

This description of God is striking for three reasons. First, nothing so far has prepared us for the description of Abraham himself as "ungodly." In the Genesis story he has already obeyed God's call (chap. 12) and, though moments of apparent disobedience are part and parcel of the story (calling Sarah his sister rather than his wife, Gen 12:10-20; 20:1-18), he appears for the most part to be worshiping and obeying God. Does Paul mean, then, that though Abraham was not ungodly, the God in whom he believed was nevertheless the one who justifies the ungodly? Probably not. The links between v. 5 and what precedes strongly imply that Abraham is still in mind. Paul is presumably thinking of Abraham's whole history, from his background in pagan Ur through to YHWH's call and the establishing of the covenant. Jewish tradition knew of Abraham's background in idolatry and tended to regard him as the first one to protest against this and to worship the one true God instead.[148] Paul does not entirely dissent from this tradition. As he will show in the rest of the chapter, Abraham is thus the forefather quite specifically of Gentiles who come to faith, not merely of Jews. This is, in fact, the beginning of a daring theme: that Abraham is actually *more like* believing Gentiles than he is like believing Jews.

Second, God's action in justifying the ungodly is, of course, exactly what, according to Scripture, a just judge should not do. Exodus 23:7 declares, in words Paul echoes, οὐ δικαιώσεις τὸν ἀσεβῆ (*ou dikaiōseis ton asebē*), "you shall not justify the ungodly"; and Proverbs 17:15, with different phraseology but the same intent, declares that those who justify the unjust, or condemn the righteous, are alike an abomination (cf. too Deut 16:19; 27:25; Prov 17:26; Ezek 22:12; Susanna 53). Paul's striking phrase simply overthrows this in the case of God; the only possible grounds for this are the revelation of God's impartial saving justice spoken of in 3:21-26. The death of Jesus has explained why it is that God was right to pass

over former sins. That which was unjust in the human lawcourt is now contained within a higher justice, reminding us again that, just as the bookkeeping metaphor is not Paul's basic point, so the lawcourt metaphor too does not reach to the heart of what he is saying. What matters is the covenant, established by God with Abraham while he was still "ungodly," and now extended by sheer grace to any and all who, despite their ungodliness, trust in this God. The covenant was always intended to be God's means of putting the world to rights; the key moment in this promised accomplishment comes when, because of the unveiling of God's righteousness in the death of Jesus, God not only can but must declare the ungodly to be set right, to be within the covenant. Paul is here preparing for the climax of the chapter, in which he defines faith as belief in "the God who raised Jesus our Lord from the dead" (4:24). Throughout the passage, in fact, Paul is wrestling not simply with the question of Abraham's faith, but with the question of God's character and identity. He insists on seeing these in the light both of Abraham and the covenant and of the events concerning Jesus.

Third, the word "ungodly" takes us right back to the start of Paul's description of human idolatry and wickedness in 1:18: The wrath of God is revealed against all ungodliness and injustice of those who suppress the truth through injustice. That Paul intends this reference back, demonstrating how, within the Abraham story, one can see God's proposed solution for the problem of 1:18–3:20, will become clear in vv. 18-22.

One who believes in this God, therefore, will discover that this "faith" will be regarded, not as a meritorious spiritual act (how could that be, for the "ungodly"?), but as the badge of covenant membership given by God in sheer grace. And already the answer to the opening question of v. 1 is starting to emerge: We (Jewish and Gentile Christians alike) have not found Abraham to be our father according to the flesh, but according to God's promise (see the same contrast in 9:8).

**4:6-8.** Paul now calls a second witness. At one level the choice of David may be determined by the key word "reckon" in Ps 32:2 [31:2 LXX]. At another, it may be that the multiple references to sin enable him, as in v. 5, to cast an eye back again to 1:18–3:20. But it is interesting to note that David is mentioned as a forgiven sinner and thereby takes a place not merely as an example but

---

148. See L. Ginzberg, *The Legends of the Jews,* 7 vols. (Baltimore: Johns Hopkins University Press, 1998) 1:186-217.

as part of covenantal history, in one Second Temple Jewish text.[149] There, however, David is described as having been "one of the pious," and it is clear that his forgiveness is seen as stemming from his observance of Torah; the implication is, if you keep Torah you, too, will be forgiven many sins. For Paul, however, it is just a matter of God not "reckoning" sins; nothing in the psalm, or in Paul's quotation from or comment on it, implies that David had been able to claim forgiveness on any grounds whatever. It was free and undeserved. David "pronounces the blessing on the person to whom God reckons righteousness apart from works" (v. 6). This gives us a further important unpacking of "reckoning righteousness"; the psalm does go on to speak of the forgiven as "the righteous" (32:11; an important indication that "the righteous" does not, there either, mean "the

morally perfect"), and Paul can assume that "reckoning righteousness apart from works" and "not reckoning sin against someone" are equivalents. The covenant, we must always remind ourselves, was there to deal with sin; when God forgives sin, or reckons someone within the covenant, these are functionally equivalent. They draw attention to different aspects of the same event.

Paul has now laid the foundation for the specific point he wants to make, namely that Gentiles are welcome in the covenant family on the basis of faith and faith alone, without having any of the badges of Jewish membership—and, indeed, that there is an appropriateness, a natural relation as it were, between them and Abraham, precisely because of the condition he was in at the time when the covenant was established. He was then uncircumcised; he did not then possess the Torah. (See Reflections at 4:23-25.)

149. 4QMMT (C 25-26).

# Romans 4:9-15, Not by Circumcision, Not by Torah

NIV

[9]Is this blessedness only for the circumcised, or also for the uncircumcised? We have been saying that Abraham's faith was credited to him as righteousness. [10]Under what circumstances was it credited? Was it after he was circumcised, or before? It was not after, but before! [11]And he received the sign of circumcision, a seal of the righteousness that he had by faith while he was still uncircumcised. So then, he is the father of all who believe but have not been circumcised, in order that righteousness might be credited to them. [12]And he is also the father of the circumcised who not only are circumcised but who also walk in the footsteps of the faith that our father Abraham had before he was circumcised.

[13]It was not through law that Abraham and his offspring received the promise that he would be heir of the world, but through the righteousness that comes by faith. [14]For if those who live by law are heirs, faith has no value and the promise is worthless, [15]because law brings wrath. And where there is no law there is no transgression.

NRSV

[9]Is this blessedness, then, pronounced only on the circumcised, or also on the uncircumcised? We say, "Faith was reckoned to Abraham as righteousness." [10]How then was it reckoned to him? Was it before or after he had been circumcised? It was not after, but before he was circumcised. [11]He received the sign of circumcision as a seal of the righteousness that he had by faith while he was still uncircumcised. The purpose was to make him the ancestor of all who believe without being circumcised and who thus have righteousness reckoned to them, [12]and likewise the ancestor of the circumcised who are not only circumcised but who also follow the example of the faith that our ancestor Abraham had before he was circumcised.

13For the promise that he would inherit the world did not come to Abraham or to his descendants through the law but through the righteousness of faith. [14]If it is the adherents of the law who are to be the heirs, faith is null and the promise is void. [15]For the law brings wrath; but where there is no law, neither is there violation.

# COMMENTARY

**4:9-12.** Paul now repeats, in sharper form, the question of 4:1, in order to address it head-on in the light of verses 2-6. Does all that has been said about Abraham and David apply only to Jews, i.e., to the circumcised? Should Gentile Christians, in other words, be required to become circumcised if they want to inherit the Abrahamic covenant blessings, not least forgiveness of sins? In addressing this question, Paul builds on 2:25-29 and 3:30, the previous mentions of circumcision. Is what he said there about the new family, composed of uncircumcised and circumcised alike, contradicted by the story of Abraham and the terms of the original covenant? Certainly not. Beginning again from Gen 15:6, Paul is able to show (v. 10, which by its question and answer ensures that the reader cannot miss the point) that, since Abraham was not circumcised until Genesis 17, his "reckoning righteous" took place before he was circumcised; in other words, that in Genesis 15 he was an uncircumcised member of the covenant.

The stress of the paragraph thus falls not so much on the method or timing of Abraham's justification, important though that is, but on what follows from it: that uncircumcised believers are every bit as "justified" as Abraham was (v. 11*b*). Indeed, vv. 11*b*-12 seem to imply almost that uncircumcised believers are the more obvious children of Abraham and that it is circumcised ones who come in on their coattails—and even then, Paul underlines, not on the basis of their circumcision, but on the basis of their following in the footsteps of Abraham's "uncircumcised faith" (v. 12*b*). In this passage, therefore, for the rhetorical purposes of stressing the free and glad welcome that grace gives to Gentiles who believe the gospel, Paul is almost reversing the sequence of 1:16, saying, "To the Gentile believer first and foremost—and also, equally, to the Jewish believer." So far from it being necessary, in other words (still answering v. 1), for Gentile believers to "discover" Abraham as their physical father—that is, for them to get circumcised—it is necessary for Jewish people to "discover" Abraham to be their uncircumcised father—that is, to share his faith. Paul does not go on to say that they should therefore remove the marks of their circumcision,

since for him that would now be irrelevant (cf. 1 Cor 7:18-20). But his argument means that their circumcision is completely beside the point as regards covenant membership.

In case of any suggestion (as in 3:1) that circumcision is therefore a bad thing, Paul gives it a place of honor in v. 11*a*. It was a "sign or seal" of the "righteousness" that was Abraham's on the basis of the faith he had while still uncircumcised. Paul does not say here, as he does in Galatians 3, that the covenant of circumcision with Abraham's ethnic family, and for that matter the territorial covenant concerning one piece of land, was designed by God as a temporary staging-post on the way to the time when, with the coming of the Messiah and the universal availability of Abrahamic faith, all nations and all lands would be claimed by God's grace.[150] But his thought here is not far off. By designating circumcision as a sign or seal of Abraham's status of faith-demarcated righteousness, Paul reclaims it rather than renouncing it: Faith is the indication of covenant membership, and circumcision was supposed to be a pointer to that status and, apparently, to that mode of indication. The implication is that to use circumcision as a pointer to a status "according to the flesh" is to abuse the sign. This too is, then, part of Paul's developing answer to the question of v. 1.

We should note, in particular, that Paul's effortless rewording of Gen 17:11 indicates clearly, what we have argued all along, that for him a primary meaning of "righteousness" was "covenant membership." God says in Genesis that circumcision is "a sign of the covenant"; Paul says it was "a sign of righteousness." He can hardly mean this as a radical alteration or correction, but rather as an explanation.[151] The whole chapter (Genesis 15) is about the covenant that God made with Abraham, and Paul is spending his whole chapter expounding it; if he had wanted to avoid covenant theology he went about it in a strange way. Rather, we should see here powerful confirmation of the

---

150. See N. T. Wright, *The Climax of the Covenant: Christ and the Law in Pauline Theology* (Edinburgh: T. & T. Clark; Minneapolis: Fortress, 1991) chap. 8.

151. Against, e.g., Ernst Käsemann, *Commentary on Romans,* trans. Geoffrey W. Bromiley (London: SCM, 1980) 114-15; Fitzmyer, *Romans,* 381.

covenantal reading of "righteousness" language in 1:17 and 3:21-31. "He received the sign of circumcision as a seal of the covenant membership marked by the faith he had while still uncircumcised."[152]

There may be a hint here, also, that Paul is thinking of baptism as the Christian version of circumcision—a pointer to the covenant status people have in Christ, by the Spirit, and whose badge is Christian faith. He seldom uses the word "sign" or "seal," but the few occurrences of the latter root are mostly found in probably baptismal contexts (2 Cor 1:22; Eph 1:13; 4:30), and in the one passage where baptism and circumcision are brought together it is clear that, for Paul, baptism in some ways at least plays the same role within the establishment of the Christian covenant people that circumcision played within the Jewish family, i.e., that of marking out the covenant people with the sign that spoke of their unique identity (Col. 2:11-12). If this is a correct understanding, it prepares the way for the developed statement of chapter 6, where we shall pursue the point further (see also on v. 13 below).

So far, then, the argument is developing step by step. First step: Does the faith family have to regard Abraham as its physical father? No. Abraham was justified freely, by grace, without works, as was the sinful David; and this faith was faith precisely in the God who justifies the "ungodly," i.e., the Gentile idolaters, the outsiders. Second step: Abraham was justified while uncircumcised, establishing the pattern for other uncircumcised people also to be justified. "That righteousness might be reckoned to them also" in v. 11b ("also" reflects the καί [kai, "also" or "even"] that in some good MSS stands before αὐτοῖς [autois, "them"]; the NRSV and the NIV assume its omission) anticipates the conclusion of the chapter's argument: "that we too will have righteousness reckoned to us, we who believe in the God who raised Jesus" (v. 24). Paul is not, then, using Abraham primarily as an example, but as the basis of his argument about who God is and who God's people are. He is still, we must remind ourselves, expounding God's covenant faithfulness.

4:13-15. These verses do not introduce a new topic; they explain what has just been said (the NIV yet again omits the *gar,* "for"). This is a further indication that Paul is not simply going through a list of three items, "works," "circumcision," and "Torah," but is rather mounting a sustained and developing argument about the extent of Abraham's promised family. He has now reached the point he has had in mind ever since the χωρὶς νόμου (*chōris nomou*) of 3:21: Torah itself cannot be the boundary marker of the covenant family (the NIV, keeping the generalized "law" throughout these verses, is in danger of obscuring Paul's focus on the Jewish law as Israel's boundary marker; the NRSV rightly keeps the definite article ["the law"] throughout). He introduces this here as the further explanation of why circumcision is neither necessary nor sufficient for membership in this family. That would absolutize Torah as the badge of membership; but Paul has already shown that Torah simply condemns those who possess it. Torah brings wrath (4:15*a,* referring back to 3:19-20, and behind that 2:12*b*); if the divine promise is to be fulfilled, it must be in a realm apart from Torah (4:15*b,* referring back to 3:21). That is the thrust of these verses.

Into this dense statement, though, Paul has built hints of other points to be developed as his argument progresses. First, he reads the geographical promises of Genesis 15 in terms of God's intention that Abraham's "seed" would inherit, not one territory merely, but the whole cosmos. Paul is here close to one strand in Second Temple Jewish thought that developed the idea of Gen 12:3; 18:18; and 22:18 (all nations being blessed in Abraham) through the prophetic promises of Isa 11:10-14; 42:1, 6; 49:6; 54:3; 65:16; Jer 4:2; Zech 9:10 (Israel as a light to the nations, the ruler of the nations, etc.), and the psalmic visions of Ps 72:8-11 (the Messiah's worldwide dominion; cf. Exod 23:31; 1 Kgs 4:21, 24) to the post-biblical thought of Sir 44:21 (which brings together Gen 12:3 and Ps 72:8) and *Jub.* 19:21 (where Jacob's family is spoken of as Abraham's had been). One destination of this line of thought is 2 Bar 14:13; 51:3, where the promised inheritance is a new world entirely, distinct from the present one; as we shall see, this is not Paul's view (see the Commentary on 8:18-27). Paul remains distinct from the other post-biblical developments too.

---

152. For later Jewish texts referring to circumcision as a "seal" see Moo, *Romans,* 268-69.

Whereas in Sirach and Jubilees the thought, as in Psalm 72, is of a geographical expansion through which Israel, still based in the promised land, and still identified ethnically, rules an increasing area until it has brought the rest of the world into subjection, in Paul's thought ethnic, national Israel will not rule the world. God will rule the world, and will do so through Jesus the Jewish Messiah, in such a way as to bring all nations equally into God's family (see 9:5; 10:13). Paul's development of the "inheritance" theme, so important in Genesis 15 and elsewhere in the Pentateuch, here takes a decisive turn that looks ahead to 8:12-30.[153]

The point of v. 13, then, that this inheritance, promised repeatedly in Genesis, was not to be made over to Abraham's seed ("descendants" [NRSV] and "offspring" [NIV] are accurate enough, but "seed" is such an evocative biblical term, and one that Paul exploits so interestingly elsewhere, that it seems worthwhile retaining it) on the basis of Torah. This is then explained (*gar*) in v. 14. In Galatians 3:17-18 Paul argues a nearly identical point, but with a different line of thought, corresponding more to that which he has just used in the present passage in relation to circumcision: The Torah, coming later than the promise, cannot be allowed to annul it. This time he uses a different strategy but to the same end: If "those from the Torah," in other words ethnic Jews, were to be the heirs, then nobody at all would inherit. This would make faith useless (that of Abraham, we must suppose, and that of anyone trying to copy him) and would nullify the promise, since God would ultimately be giving Abraham neither a seed nor an inheritance.

Why? Paul's explanation for this cryptic conclusion, given in v. 15*a*, is terse: the law works wrath.

Putting this shorthand statement together with that in 3:19-20, we arrive at the composite that explains them both. (a) Torah shows up sin within ethnic Israel; (b) sin invokes wrath. Therefore (c) if the inheritance were confined to ethnic Israel, (d) nobody at all would inherit. Those outside would be kept there; those inside would be subject to God's wrath.[154] This does not cast a slur upon Torah; Torah is simply doing its job, and Paul affirms that it is right to do so. He does not yet address the question, raised by the similar argument in Galatians, as to why God would give the Torah (Gal 3:19); he will deal with it fully in chap. 7, having allowed the problem to build up further through similar hints in chaps. 5 and 6.

The other cryptic hint given here of the wider theological scheme invoked is in 15*b:* "Where there is no law, there is no transgression." In view of his entire earlier argument, Paul can scarcely mean by this that Gentiles, being outside the Torah, are guiltless; there is, presumably, still sin, the miscellaneous missing of God's intended target for human beings, but there is no explicit disobedience to a known commandment (NRSV, "violation"; see the Commentary on 5:14). The point, however, is that (a) Abraham, not possessing the Torah, was not in this technical sense a "transgressor"; (b) Gentiles can inherit the promises made to Abraham without finding Torah standing in their way; they are not transgressors.[155]

This prepares us for the climax of the chapter. The covenant is fulfilled in the creation of a worldwide family marked out by Abraham-like faith. (See Reflections at 4:23-25.)

---

153. See N. T. Wright, "New Exodus, New Inheritance: the Narrative Substructure of Romans 3–8," in *Romans and the People of God: Essays in Honor of Gordon D. Fee on the Occasion of his 65th Birthday,* ed. S. Soderlund and N. T. Wright (Grand Rapids: Eerdmans, 1999) 26-35.

154. Again, Paul makes a similar point in Galatians with a different argument: in 3:15-22 he urges that God promised Abraham a single "seed," i.e., family, and that since the Torah would divide the world into two (Jews and Gentiles) it cannot be allowed to stand against the promise. See Wright, *The Climax of Covenant,* chap. 8.

155. This appears at variance with Gal 3:10-14, which assumes that the Torah does put some kind of a roadblock between promise and fulfillment, which it takes the death of Jesus to deal with. See ibid., chap. 7.

# Romans 4:16-17, The Whole Family, According to the Promise

NIV

[16]Therefore, the promise comes by faith, so that it may be by grace and may be guaranteed to all Abraham's offspring—not only to those who are of the law but also to those who are of the faith of Abraham. He is the father of us all. [17]As it is written: "I have made you a father of many nations."[a] He is our father in the sight of God, in whom he believed—the God who gives life to the dead and calls things that are not as though they were.

[a] 17 Gen. 17:5

NRSV

16For this reason it depends on faith, in order that the promise may rest on grace and be guaranteed to all his descendants, not only to the adherents of the law but also to those who share the faith of Abraham (for he is the father of all of us, [17]as it is written, "I have made you the father of many nations")—in the presence of the God in whom he believed, who gives life to the dead and calls into existence the things that do not exist.

## COMMENTARY

Paul now gives the full answer to the question he asked in v. 1. This is the significance of the introductory Διὰ τοῦτο (*Dia touto*): "Thus it comes about that . . . " (cf. 5:12; 2 Cor 4:1; Paul can, of course, use the phrase in many other less climactic contexts, e.g., 1:26; 13:6). The main sentence has neither verbs, subjects nor objects, not least because Paul is hurrying on to what he most wants to say in the whole chapter: literally, "Therefore by faith, so that by grace, so that the promise might be valid for *all* the seed, not only for the one from the Torah but also for the one from the faith of Abraham."[156] The universal availability of the promise is Paul's main thrust, and he backs it up at once with the explanation that answers v. 1: Abraham is the father of all of us, as it is written, "I have made you the father of many nations."

This in turn is backed up with the great statement of the other main theme of the chapter, the character of the God in whom Abraham believed. Just as Paul answered his own hypothetical suggestion in v. 2 with the brusque remark "but not before God," so now the statement of what is in fact the case is backed up with "in the presence of the God in whom he believed, the one who gives life to the dead and calls into existence things that do not exist."

156. We may fill out the clipped and cryptic opening words of 4:16 easily enough, as do the NRSV (13 words for Paul's 5) and the NIV (12): All is by faith, so that all may be according to grace.

Faith, grace and promise, then, are vital to this chapter, but they are not its main subjects. The main subjects are Abraham, his family, and his God. This is what we should expect if the overall subject of the larger section is indeed the revelation of God's covenant faithfulness and the creation of a Jew-plus-Gentile family. The present verses have often been read exactly the other way round, resulting in the bracketing, by the NRSV, of the key statement in vv. 16b-17a (the KJV and the JB simply bracket 4:17a; the RSV begins its parenthesis after "to all his descendants"). When exegesis comes out smoothly it shows that we are approaching the text from the right angle; when it comes out awkwardly, with phrases and sentences that do not fit, we should take it as a sign that the chapter is being forced in the wrong direction. Romans 4 is not a "proof from scripture" of "justification by faith," into which Paul has inserted some remarks about the fatherhood of Abraham and the character of God; it is an exposition of the covenant God and the way in which the covenant promises to Abraham were fulfilled, with justification and faith playing their part within that overall argument. Verse 17b does indeed seem a bit abrupt, immediately after the biblical quotation; but putting v. 17a in a bracket, with or without part of v. 16, does nothing to ease the suddenness of the change of topic. The abruptness, however, corresponds closely to the opening of v. 16, where

Paul is virtually writing in shorthand, and to the suddenness of 4:2*b* ("but not before God!" which is making the same point as v. 17*b* ("in the presence of the God in whom he believed"). Once we grasp this, vv. 16-17, instead of seeming awkward and broken up, appear to sum up neatly the argument of the chapter so far.

In particular, the passage makes explicit something about the character of God as revealed (albeit to Paul's Christian hindsight) in Genesis 15, something Paul will then use brilliantly to bring his discourse round to where he wants it to be at the end of the chapter. God is the God who gives life to the dead—something the pagan gods did not even claim to do—and calls into existence things that do not exist. This is, of course, a characteristically Jewish view of the one true God, the creator and lifegiver (cf. Wis 16:13; Tob 13:2; 2 Bar 48:8; belief in God's giving life to the dead is expressed in the second of the Eighteen Benedictions, part of daily Jewish prayer); and it corresponds, within the present argument, to the description of God in v. 5 as "the God who justifies the ungodly."

Within this overall statement, there is one slightly puzzling note. In v. 16 he speaks of "the whole seed"—all Abraham's multi-ethnic family, in other words[157]—as consisting of (literally) "not the one from the Torah only but also the one from the faith of Abraham." Taken by itself, this might imply that Jews who kept Torah formed one part of the family, while the other part consisted of Gentiles who, though not having Torah, shared Abraham's faith. This possibility is ruled out by everything Paul has said from 3:19 to the present point. "The one from the Torah" is simply here a shorthand for "the Jew"; and Paul has already insisted in 4:12 that Jewish ancestry, signaled by circumcision, is only of any value if the person concerned follows in the steps of Abraham's faith (cf. 2:25-29; 10:1-13; 11:23). This should alert us to the interesting overtones of the double description of God at the end of v. 17: God is the one who gives life to the dead and calls into existence the things that do not exist (so NRSV; the NIV, closer to the Greek, has "calls things that are not as though they were"). This may perhaps correspond

to the double road into justification hinted at in 3:30. When God brings a Gentile to faith, this is a creation out of nothing; the person had no previous covenant membership of any sort. "Call" is, after all, a strange word to use of creation, but it is one of Paul's regular ways of speaking about the effect of the gospel on someone's life (see, e.g., 9:24, in a similar context). When God brings a Jew to share the faith of Abraham, this is more like a life out of death, a renewal of covenant membership after the threat of being cut off (cf. 2:25-29; 11:11-16, esp. 11:15, on which see the Commentary on 11:12-32).

Verses 16-17 form a striking and original argument that belongs recognizably within Second Temple Judaism but which cuts across the line of thought we might expect. Paul's emphasis contrasts with that of Sir 44:19-21 (NRSV):

> Abraham was the great father of a multitude of
> nations,
> and no one has been found like him in glory.
> He kept the law of the Most High,
> and entered into a covenant with him;
> he certified the covenant in his flesh,
> and when he was tested he proved faithful.
> Therefore the Lord assured him with an oath
> that the nations would be blessed through his
> offspring;
> that he would make him as numerous as the
> dust of the earth,
> and exalt his offspring like the stars,
> and give them an inheritance from sea to sea
> and from the Euphrates to the ends of the earth.

Here, Torah and circumcision are the central features, along with Abraham's near-sacrifice of Isaac (Genesis 22, which is absent from Romans 4).[158] Sirach also highlights Abraham's faith(fulness) (εὑρέθη πίστος *heurethē pistos,* "he was found faithful," 44:20), but this does not have the sense of "believing the promise" that Paul has drawn out. The two belong on the same map; but Paul's new construal, his new way of telling the story, grows directly out of what he now believes about God because of the events concerning Jesus, resulting in the establishment of the Jew-plus-Gentile family with faith as its central demarcating feature.

---

157. For "seed" as "family," see Wright, *The Climax of Covenant,* 162-68, comparing the present passage with Gal 3:15-18. See also the Commentary on 9:6-8.

158. Some have cited Gen 22:17-18 as a parallel to 4:13, but the verse is equally explicable in reference to Gen 12:3; 18:18; in other words, there is nothing specific to Genesis 22. A more likely reference to that chapter is found in Rom 8:32 (see below).

Abraham's faith is what Paul now analyzes as he draws together the threads, not only of this chapter but of the letter so far. (See Reflections at 4:23-25.)

# Romans 4:18-22, The God Who Gives Life to the Dead

## NIV

[18]Against all hope, Abraham in hope believed and so became the father of many nations, just as it had been said to him, "So shall your offspring be."[a] [19]Without weakening in his faith, he faced the fact that his body was as good as dead—since he was about a hundred years old—and that Sarah's womb was also dead. [20]Yet he did not waver through unbelief regarding the promise of God, but was strengthened in his faith and gave glory to God, [21]being fully persuaded that God had power to do what he had promised. [22]This is why "it was credited to him as righteousness."

[a] 18 Gen. 15:5

## NRSV

[18]Hoping against hope, he believed that he would become "the father of many nations," according to what was said, "So numerous shall your descendants be." [19]He did not weaken in faith when he considered his own body, which was already[a] as good as dead (for he was about a hundred years old), or when he considered the barrenness of Sarah's womb. [20]No distrust made him waver concerning the promise of God, but he grew strong in his faith as he gave glory to God, [21]being fully convinced that God was able to do what he had promised. [22]Therefore his faith[b] "was reckoned to him as righteousness."

[a] Other ancient authorities lack *already*      [b] Gk *Therefore it*

# COMMENTARY

The revelation of God's character to Abraham called forth, Paul now argues, a specific form of faith. Abraham's faith was not just a general religious belief, an awareness of "the other" or of a *mysterium tremendum*. It was a trust in specific promises that the true God had made, which, if fulfilled, would show this God to be what Paul has described in v. 17 *b:* the lifegiver, the creator out of nothing.

Paul's fulsome description of Abraham's faith and what it involves, which corresponds to nothing in previous Jewish expansions of the biblical text, seems to be designed with two things in mind. In vv. 18-22 he demonstrates that when Abraham believed this promise he was exemplifying what it meant to be truly human, in contrast to the human disintegration in 1:18–3:20. In vv. 23-25, which conclude the chapter and section, he shows that this type of faith is the same as that which Christians demonstrate when believing that God raised Jesus from the dead. This, he argues, is why Christians, whether Jews or Gentiles, share the faith of Abraham and consequently share the justification spoken of in Gen 15:6.

The theme of the unity and equality of believing Jews and believing Gentiles now fades from view. Paul concentrates instead on the nature of the faith that unites them, and on the certainty of the justification that follows. Are justification and faith then after all the main themes of chap. 4? By no means. Paul has finished in vv. 16-17 the main argument that began with 4:1; he now returns to the overall argument not only of 3:21–4:25 but of 1:18–4:25. He is rounding off the larger section of which 3:21–4:25 was the second main part. He therefore widens the horizon of chapter 4, to speak more directly of the true God, the nature of faith in the true God, and the way in which this faith is the hallmark of genuine humanness as opposed to the corrupt variety.

He thus also points forward to chapters 5–8. There, in order in turn to lay a platform for the specific arguments of 9–11 and 12–16, he leaves the discussion of the Jew-plus-Gentile nature of the family out of explicit consideration for the moment, focusing instead on the way in which the story of Israel has reached its climax, and its true recapitulation, in Christ and the Spirit.

**4:18-19.** Paul returns to Genesis 15, this time to the verse that precedes his key phrase: God showed Abraham the stars, and declared, "So shall your seed be" (Gen 15:5). This was the promise that Abraham believed. Paul has linked this with the quotation from Gen 17:5 already referred to in v. 17, "I have made you the father of many nations"; he assumes that having offspring like the stars of heaven and being the father of many nations amount to the same thing. Abraham believed this promise, he says, "Hoping against hope" (so NRSV, using a well-known English idiom that more or less matches Paul's slightly more complex phrase)—in other words, persevering in hope when all reasonable expectation ("hope" in a more neutral sense) would have urged that it was impossible. He faced the fact of his own physical condition,[159] and that of Sarah, without any weak-ening in his faith. Paul draws a veil over the various episodes such as Abraham's passing Sarah off as his sister and the whole matter of Hagar and Ishmael (Sarah: Gen 12:10-20, and particularly 20:1-18, which occurs between the promise concerning Isaac [18:1-15] and his birth [21:1-7]; Hagar: Gen 16:1-16). The feature of this faith to which Paul draws attention is its persistence in hoping for new life when Abraham's and Sarah's bodies were, in terms of potential childbearing, as good as dead because of their age. This builds on 4:17 and looks directly forward to 4:24-25.

**4:20-21.** Paul now describes Abraham's faith in lavish detail. He shows that Abraham was exactly unlike the human condition described in 1:18-32. Paul is rounding off the larger argument. This, in principle, is how humanity is restored.[160] We may tabulate this as follows:

| | |
|---|---|
| 4:17 Abraham believed in God the lifegiver, the creator | 1:20, 25 God the creator, ignored by humans |
| 4:19 Abraham's body as good as dead, yet he believed in God's promise of new life | 1:24 Human bodies dishonored because of idolatry |
| 4:20 Abraham gave glory to God | 1:21 Humans did not glorify God as God |
| 4:21 Abraham recognized God's power | 1:20 Humans knew about God's power but did not worship |
| 4:19 Abraham and Sarah given power to conceive | 1:26-27 The dishonoring of bodies by females and males turning away from one another. |

To this may be added the overall point, that Abraham in this passage worshiped, trusted, and believed the true God and so was given power to be fruitful and to obtain the promised inheritance, whereas human beings in chap. 1 turned away from the true God to idols and so were given over to dishonor, unfruitfulness and corruption. The stress on Abraham's faith/faithfulness also contrasts powerfully with the faithless Israel described in 2:17–3:20, notably at 3:3. Abraham was given grace to be in faithful covenant relation with the true God and thereby to embody and exhibit, initially in his faith and subsequently in his fruitful-ness, the marks of genuine humanity. The whole thrust of 4:20-21 is the God-centeredness and God-honoringness of Abraham's faith, worshiping and relying totally on the faithful, lifegiving creator God. This stands in close relation to what Paul had said in 3:21-22, where God's covenant faithfulness is unveiled for the benefit of those who believe.

**4:22.** Therefore, declares Paul, Abraham's faith was "reckoned to him unto righteousness." The word "therefore" could, if we were not careful, send shock waves back through Paul's previous argument. Is he really saying, after all his language about grace, that this type of faith was so special, so virtuous, so remarkable, that Abraham was

159. Some puzzled early scribes, thinking further to highlight Abraham's faith, added "not" before the verb "considered," implying that Abraham simply ignored his own physical condition. Not so: Paul's point is that Abraham took it fully into account, and still believed and hoped. The NIV ("he faced the fact") splendidly catches the force of this.

160. For more detail, see E. Adams, "Abraham's Faith and Gentile Disobedience: Textual Links Between Romans 1 and 4," *JSNT* 65 (1997) 47-66.

*rewarded* for his faith by having it "reckoned as righteousness"? Is Abraham then the one conspicuous exception, prior to Jesus Christ, to the general rule laid down in 1:18–3:20, that "none is righteous, no not one"? Why, if so, did the full redemption have to wait for two thousand more years? Why did it not happen then and there, with Abraham himself?

Paul does not address these questions, which arise for us when we determine to give Abraham his full place in Pauline theology rather than being shunted into a siding as a mere polemically useful "example." But it is clear that Paul did *not* think that Abraham's faith was meritorious, something to boast about; rather, it was his response to grace (vv. 2, 4, 16, corresponding to 3:24), the grace that had called him in the first place and that now addressed him with lifegiving promises. When, therefore, Paul says that the reason Abraham's faith was "reckoned as righteousness" was because it was this sort of faith, he does not mean that Abraham earned special favor by having a special sort of faith. He means that precisely this sort of faith, evoked by sheer grace, is evidence of that redemption and renewal of humanity as a result of which there appears evidence of a human life back on track, turned from idolatry to the worship of the true God, from disbelief to faith and from corruption to fruitfulness. Faith is the sign of life; life is the gift of God. Justification is God's declaration that where this sign of life appears, the person in whom it appears is within the covenant.

# Romans 4:23-25, The Meaning of Christian Faith

[23]The words "it was credited to him" were written not for him alone, [24]but also for us, to whom God will credit righteousness—for us who believe in him who raised Jesus our Lord from the dead. [25]He was delivered over to death for our sins and was raised to life for our justification.

[23]Now the words, "it was reckoned to him," were written not for his sake alone, [24]but for ours also. It will be reckoned to us who believe in him who raised Jesus our Lord from the dead, [25]who was handed over to death for our trespasses and was raised for our justification.

# COMMENTARY

There remains but one task for Paul, and the first section of the letter is complete. He has not talked specifically about "us" (i.e. himself and his audience) since 1:5-15. Insofar as he has been addressing anyone, it has been the hypothetical debating partner within the "diatribe" style; for the rest, the argument has remained at a general level. Now at last he places his readers on the carefully drawn map; from here the next four chapters will develop, in which "we," and "our" status before God, are a major theme. This is a vital clue to the relation between chaps. 1–4 and 5–8, to the transition between them, and to the way in which both sections together lay the foundation for the second half of the letter, which contains the more particular things Paul wants to say to the Roman church.

**4:23.** As often, Paul declares that a biblical passage had, in God's intention, a wider meaning than simply its historical reference (see, e.g., 1 Cor 9:9-10; 10:11; and above all Rom 15:4, on which see the Commentary on 15:1-13). This is not arbitrary or fanciful. Precisely because of the covenantal way Paul reads scripture, he insists that what was said and done by way of foundation determines the shape of the whole building. What God said in scripture ("it was written" is a way of saying that scripture says what God intended) opens out to include all those who share Abraham's faith—which, not surprisingly, granted the full explanation of this faith in 4:17-21, is seen as faith in God the lifegiver. Abraham's faith was evoked by the word that spoke to him of his great family, even though he was as good as dead; Christian faith is called forth by the word of the gospel, which speaks of the resurrection of Jesus from the dead (1:4) and the disclosure thereby that he was and is Israel's Messiah, the Lord of the world.

**4:24.** Christian faith is thus, for Paul, irrevocably resurrection-shaped. Like Abraham's faith, it is by no means simply a general religious awareness or trust in a remote or distant supernatural being, but gains its form, as well as its content, from the revelation of God's covenant faithfulness in the events concerning Jesus (see 10:6-13, and the Commentary thereon). "Faith," for Paul, is never a thing in itself, but is always defined, as Rom 4:16-22 makes clear, in relation to the God in whom trust is placed. The purpose of a window is not to cover one wall of the house with glass, but to let light in and to let the inhabitants see out.

Paul is careful, therefore, to speak of Christian faith as "believing in the God who raised Jesus our Lord from the dead." God, not Jesus, is the primary object of Christian faith (one of many reasons why πίστις Χριστοῦ [pistis Christou], "the faith of Christ," is more likely to mean the faithfulness of Jesus himself than the faith people put in Jesus). This description of God is important for Romans, being echoed at another memorable point, 8:11; for Paul it is axiomatic that the resurrection took place by God's initiative and power (see, e.g., 10:9; 1 Cor 6:14; 15:15; 2 Cor 4:14; 13:4; Gal 1:1. 2 Cor 4:14 is very close to the present phrase and to 8:11), so that the meaning of the event is the meaning God intends (1:4), namely, that Jesus is thereby marked out as God's Son, the Messiah, Israel's representative, the one in whom God's promises of redemption have finally come true. Confessing that Jesus is Lord, therefore, and that God raised him from the dead (10:9), means sharing the faith of Abraham; and that faith, as Paul has now argued, is the one and only badge of membership in Abraham's family. Paul does not in this passage spell out the implication, but the rest of the chapter, along with 3:27-30, should still be echoing in the mind. Because there is only one badge of membership, all those who share this faith are members of God's redeemed and forgiven people, no matter what their ancestry. Paul is not making a substantially new point at this stage in the chapter. Rather, he is for the first time putting himself and his readers on the map he has drawn. It is the map of the Abrahamic family, created by the revelation of God's righteousness in Jesus the Messiah, the family in which the distinction between Jew and Gentile, maintained by Torah in particular, is set aside once for all, the family whose sole identifying badge is Christian faith.

Remarkably enough, this verse is the first mention of Jesus' resurrection since the programmatic and formulaic 1:4.[161] But, as we have seen at various points, the rest of the argument would be incomprehensible without it. For neither the first nor the last time, Paul reveals at the very conclusion of an argument something that has been foundational to it all along. Thousands of other young Jews were crucified by the Roman authorities in the first century; several would-be Messiahs were killed one way or another. What distinguishes Jesus from the rest, quite apart from his teaching and actions (which would scarcely by themselves have sustained the sort of movement that Christianity rapidly became), was obviously the resurrection. It is what gives the crucifixion the remarkable meaning it has, enabling Paul to say, by way of a closing christological summary (this, too, anticipates the careful writing of chaps. 5–8), that Jesus was "given up because of our trespasses and raised because of our justification" (for the resurrection as giving meaning to the cross, see 1 Cor 15:17-18).

The point of this verse, then, is that those who believe the gospel of Jesus, which involves believing in the God who raised Jesus from the dead, are thereby sharing Abraham's faith, and will, like him, be reckoned "righteous" in the senses already outlined. Paul has now shown how the bald assertions of 3:27-30 are grounded in the original covenant and promise, thus explaining the λογιζόμεθα (logizometha) of 3:28: When Paul said "we reckon," "we figure it out," he was referring not so much to the argument he had already sketched in 3:21-26 as to the full picture he was intending to draw in chap. 4. Having stated in 3:28 the result of the calculation, he has now shown his detailed working.

**4:25.** All this has been accomplished, of course, through Jesus himself. Paul lays bare, in conclusion, the foundation of the whole structure.

---

161. It is also only the tenth time—and this is the 116th verse of the letter!—that the name "Jesus" has occurred in Romans (1:1, 4, 6, 7, 8; 2:16; 3:22, 24, 26; and now this passage) and only the fifth in the 99 verses since the introduction. Without Jesus, there would be nothing to say; this alerts us to the way in which Paul by no means always puts the most important parts of the logical structure of his thought into the actual rhetorical flow of a particular letter.

This was where God's righteousness, God's covenant faithfulness, God's saving justice, was displayed. Jesus "was given up for our transgressions and raised for our justification."[162]

This pregnant formulation may well have been stated in this or a similar way by Paul himself and/or by other early Christians, many times before.[163] But if it was in that sense pre-Pauline, or at least pre-Romans, Paul has used it here because it sums up exactly what he has been saying, under the general heading of 1:3-4, throughout the letter so far. (It is not, in other words, a non-Pauline formula, quoted here for merely phatic purposes, i.e. to make a pleasing Christian noise unrelated to what has gone before.) Paul has spent the best part of three chapters demonstrating that all human beings were "under the power of sin" (3:9); very well, Jesus was "given up because of our trespasses" (3:24-26, in other words, answers exactly to the problem of 1:18–3:20.) Paul has spent the last thirty or so verses arguing that because of the revelation of God's righteousness in Jesus the Messiah all who believe are justified; very well, Jesus "was raised for our justification." This is another way of saying that the lifegiving God, in whom Abraham believed and was justified, gave life to Jesus, in whom we believe and are justified. This much is at once clear. But there are other questions lurking beneath the surface.

To begin with, Paul seems to be quoting, or at least deliberately alluding to, Isa 53:5, 12 (see the Commentary on 3:24-26; see also the Commentary on 5:18-19).[164] This should not come as a surprise. Isaiah 40–55 is one of the central scriptural passages in which the righteousness of the creator God is said to be revealed, both to confound the pagan nations and their gods and to rescue sinful and wayward Israel from its sin and exile, and in which this task is accomplished supremely through the death and resurrection of "the servant of the Lord." Once we recognize the large themes that tie together Romans and the central section of Isaiah, there ought to be no problem in recognizing that when Paul alludes to one central verse in this passage in Isaiah he intends a reference to the whole. Just as 4:25 expresses for the first time the theological point that turns out to have been foundational for the whole preceding passage, so it is reasonable to suggest that Isaiah 40–55 has been implicit throughout as well.[165]

This strongly implies that, though the death of Jesus has only been mentioned so far in 3:22-26 (taking references to Jesus' "faithfulness" to include a reference to his death), it has remained basic to the whole theology of justification, and of the non-ethnic covenant family, which Paul has expounded from 3:27 through to 4:24. This, again, should not surprise us. To see the cross as the basis of the coming together of Jews and Gentiles is certainly Pauline. The cross is central to the whole argument of Gal 2:11–4:11, with its exposition of Abraham's single family, justified by faith (see also Eph 2:11-22). This prepares us for the repeated emphasis on Jesus' death in chaps. 5–8. Paul is not changing course there, but drawing out what is latent in the present section.

But what, more precisely, does the present verse say about the meaning and effect of Jesus' death and resurrection? He was handed over, says Paul, "because of" our trespasses and was raised up "because of" our justification. The word in each case is διά (dia), which, when governing the accusative (as here), indicates the reason why something happens, that "on account of which" something occurs.

The first half of the verse is fairly clear. "Our trespasses" were the reason or cause for Jesus' "handing over"; as in Isaiah, he was so identified with "us" that he suffered the fate we deserved. What then of the second half of the verse? It is much harder to envisage, let alone establish, a causal connection in Paul's mind by which "our justification" could have been the cause of Jesus' resur-

---

162. This and 5:18 are the only two occurrences of the term "justification" (δικαίωσις dikaiōsis) in the NT—surprisingly, granted its use as a technical term in Christian theology and the regular appeal made to Paul, and Romans in particular, on the topic. It is rare in classical Greek; in the LXX only at Lev 24:22; in Symmachus, at Ps 34[35]:23.

163. On the possibility that this is a pre-Pauline formulation, see P. Stuhlmacher, "Jesus' Resurrection and the View of Righteousness in the Pre-Pauline Mission Congregation," in *Reconciliation, Law and Righteousness: Essays in Biblical Theology* (Philadelphia: Fortress, 1986) 55-56.

164. In particular, the strange word παρεδόθη (paredothē, "he was given up" or "he was handed over"), not of itself the most natural word to use for the death of Jesus, is the word used in Isa 53:5 and twice in 53:12. These verses in Isaiah use the word ἁμαρτία (hamartia) for "sin," rather than παράπτωμα (paraptōma; lit., "transgression") as here.

165. On Paul's use of Isaiah, see F. Wilk, *Die Bedeutung des Jesajabuches für Paulus*, FRLANT (Göttingen: Vandenhoek und Ruprecht, 1998); J. Ross Wagner, *Heralds of the Good News: Paul and Isaiah "In Concert" in the Letter to the Romans*, NovTSup 101 (Leiden: Brill, 2002).

rection, as would be required if the two halves of the verse were as closely parallel in logic as they are in literary form. The nearest Paul comes to saying something like that is 1 Cor 15:17-18: If the Messiah has not been raised, your faith is futile and you are still in your sins. Seen from that point of view, the resurrection demonstrates that Jesus' death accomplished the forgiveness and justification of God's people; one might almost say, in those terms, that the accomplishment of justification was the "cause" of the resurrection.[166] But this seems, frankly, a strange and roundabout way of saying it, and Paul has not prepared us in Romans (or Galatians) for any such statement thus far. It seems to me more likely that two other meanings come together at this point.

First, the servant of Isaiah 53 is raised to new life after his vicarious death (53:10$b$-12); his task then, as God's righteous one, is "to make many righteous" (v. 11, alluded to in Rom 5:18-19). Carrying this meaning into Romans 4, as the allusion invites us to do, would suggest that Jesus' resurrection took place "because of our justification" in the sense of "because God intended thereby to justify us."[167] This is not exactly parallel in meaning to "because of our trespasses" in the first half of the verse, unless, of course, Paul there means "he was handed over because God intended thereby to deal with our trespasses." But it is not necessary to insist on a strict parallelism of content; Paul uses the matching form to cover, by way of a shorthand summary, the two topics that have occupied him throughout the last four chapters.

This is supported, second, by the one previous mention of the resurrection in the letter (1:4). There God declares, by raising Jesus, that he really was and is God's Son, the Messiah. The resurrection unveils to the surprised world, Israel included, that this was after all the age-old saving plan of the creator God. In particular it declares, as in a lawcourt, that God has vindicated Jesus. Jesus is shown to be in the right. His life and death were the true faithfulness for which God had created Israel in the first place. Thus, if faithful Jesus is demonstrated to be Messiah by the resurrection,

the resurrection also declares in principle that all those who belong to Jesus, all those who respond in faith to God's faithfulness revealed in him, are themselves part of the true covenant family promised to Abraham. In other words, the resurrection of Jesus can at this level be seen as the declaration of justification. And this can perfectly well be expressed as "He was raised because of our justification."

Romans 4 thus leads us to a high rock looking back over the landscape we have covered. From the same vantage point, looking ahead, we can glimpse the route we are now to take.

First, the view backward. The events concerning Jesus the Messiah, and the gospel message in which these events are announced, unveil the covenant faithfulness, the saving justice, of the creator God; because in these events the promises made to Abraham have at last been accomplished. These promises were designed to redeem the world, by creating a worldwide family in whom the grim entail of human sin and its consequences (present corruption, future wrath) would be dealt with. This has now been achieved through the sacrificial death and the resurrection of the Messiah, Jesus. Through Jesus' faithfulness, God has thus fulfilled the purpose for which the people of Israel were called into being in the first place and marked out with circumcision and Torah. Torah, however, cannot be the boundary marker of covenant membership, since it inevitably points to Israel's sin. God's creation of the non-ethnic covenant family is therefore an act of supreme grace, modeled on the way in which grace came to Abraham to begin with, bringing forgiveness of sins and present justification to all, Jew and Gentile alike, who believe in "the God who raised Jesus."

Every line in this argument, every turn in the thought, will be vital for the specific points that Paul wants to make to the church in Rome in chapters 9–11 and 12–16. From our vantage point we can see, in the distance, the outline of these passages.

In 9–11, Paul wrestles with the problem of Jewish unbelief and tells again the story of Israel, from Abraham to the Messiah and on into the future. He explains how God has in fact been faithful to the promises and how, within that framework and without smuggling in favoritism by the back door, God has not written off the Jewish people. The point of the section is found in chapter 11, where Paul warns the largely Gentile

166. This is, more or less, the account given by F. Godet, *Commentary on St. Paul's Epistle to the Romans*, 2 vols. (Edinburgh: T. & T. Clark, 1880–81) 1:311-12.

167. So most commentators, e.g., James D. G. Dunn, *Romans 1–8*, WBC 38A (Dallas: Word, 1988) 225; Douglas J. Moo, *The Epistle to the Romans*, NICNT (Grand Rapids: Eerdmans, 1996) 289.

church in Rome not to despise the non-Christian Jews, who are still the objects of God's saving love and purposes.

Then, in 12–16, Paul sets out the parameters for the church to live as the renewed humanity within a pagan society. The key is again the unity, across traditional barriers, of all who believe in the God revealed in Jesus (14:1–15:13). The latter passage closes, dramatically, with the quotation of Isa 11:10, which speaks of the Messiah and his resurrection as the means by which the Gentiles will be brought under the rule of the God of Israel (Paul uses a version of Isaiah that makes this point more clearly than most translations of the prophet indicate). Paul thereby completes a huge circle with 1:3-5. The mission and unity of the church, grounded in a covenantal understanding of what the one true God accomplished in Jesus the Messiah, are the thrusts of the last two sections.

This is not the only view, however, that we gain from the end of chapter 4. As we saw when examining Paul's gospel and the way it reveals God's justice, this message offers an implicit challenge to the world Paul and his readers inhabited—the world in which Caesar ruled supreme, in which his justice had rescued the world from chaos and had established a single empire embracing all nations. Paul is not ashamed of the gospel of Jesus, because in it God's saving justice, his covenant faithfulness, is revealed. The living God thereby upstages Caesar.

What about the landscape in between our vantage point at the end of chap. 4 and the two great sections 9–11 and 12–16? How do chaps. 5–8 grow out of 1–4 and pave the way for what is to follow? This is perhaps the central question about the thought structure of Romans. It would be artificial to answer it in any other way than by introducing chaps. 5–8, which is the next exegetical task.

# REFLECTIONS

**1.** The most important reflection to arise from Romans 4 is the non-negotiable task of persuading those who believe in Jesus as Messiah and Lord to see themselves as the children of Abraham (and indeed of Sarah). Abraham is not merely an example of a biblical character who happened to be "justified by faith"; he is, declares Paul, "the father of us all." To this picture 1 Pet 3:6, and by implication Gal 4:28-31 and Heb 11:11-12, adds that Sarah is our mother. The Pauline picture of the people of God is inescapably rooted in the history of Israel from Genesis 12 onward.

This has immediate implications. First, the Christian is committed to a rigorously non-Marcionite view of the Jewish scriptures, the history to which they bear witness, and above all the God of whom they speak. The God revealed in Jesus the Messiah is the God of Abraham; the meaning of the death and resurrection of Jesus is the meaning those events acquire when seen as the fulfillment of the promises made by this God. Christian living is characterized by faith in this God, by loyalty to the project of this God for creation, by the renewing, healing, and sanctifying power of the Spirit of this God (see chap. 8). Christians read the story of Abraham and Sarah, of Isaac and Rebekah, and of Jacob, Leah, and Rachel as their own story, as an earlier act in the great drama that reached its climax in the Messiah, Jesus (cf. 9:4-5), and has now opened up to embrace the whole world.[168] Paul struggled to persuade his Gentile converts to see themselves this way, rather than to imagine that they belonged to a new group (certainly not a new "religion"!) lately sprung up from nowhere. Largely Gentile churches in our own day need to engage in the same struggle.

Second, however, the Christian is committed to believing that this family of Abraham is not defined in terms of the Jewish law. This inevitably appears a contradiction in terms to those who, for whatever reason of personal involvement or study, know from the inside the way in which devout non-Christian Jews have thought of themselves, their traditions, and above all their

---

168. On the different "acts" of the biblical story, see N. T. Wright, *The New Testament and the People of God,* vol. 1 of *Christian Origins and the Question of God* (London: SPCK; Minneapolis: Fortress, 1992) 139-43.

Torah, from that day to this. Paul, as himself a supremely devout Jew, faced exactly this problem and made every effort to convince his readers that this surprising turn of events was in fact what had been promised and intended all along. This is the main argument of the present chapter, and indeed of Galatians 3, and it bears repeating frequently, not least in Jewish-Christian discussions. It is most revealing to compare the two quite different traditions of reading Genesis 15 in, say, Paul and the rabbinic midrashim.

The questions raised by this in our own day are not addressed in this chapter. We defer, therefore, to Romans 9–11 the matter of the continuing relationship between those who see themselves as the children of Abraham defined by faith in the lifegiving God revealed in Jesus and those who see themselves as the children of Abraham defined by the possession and keeping of the Mosaic Torah.

**2.** Within the family given by God to Abraham, there is no room for sub-definitions. It is hard to live in community on the basis of nothing more nor less than belief in the God who raised Jesus. Humans naturally gravitate toward communities of similar background, personality, speech, or indeed social position or bank balance; Christians are no exception. Within Western society, particularly in urban areas, this leads to choosing one's Christian fellowship and church membership for reasons that Paul would have regarded as irrelevant, possibly damaging. This in turn leads to the suspicion that others, whose faith is in fact every bit as well founded, are somehow less Christian, or maybe not even Christian at all, because of their different social or cultural idioms. Every effort must be made to overcome this. Once Paul had shown that the barrier between Jew and Gentile had been overcome in Jesus, and that God had wonderfully achieved the worldwide community promised originally to Abraham, there was no excuse, and there remains no excuse, for thinking that one's own culture is so deeply important, even important to the gospel, that it must not be compromised by fellowship with others who do things differently.

**3.** Within this, Christians must embody in their church life the truth articulated in 4:4-8: the fact that the family promised by God to Abraham is a family of forgiven sinners, rescued by grace alone from the personal and communal disintegration that results from idolatry and sin. The God we worship is the God who justifies the ungodly, not the pious. There is, no doubt, a danger in setting up a social or even a theological inverted snobbery, of imagining that because we are socially inferior, or poor, or casual rather than devout in worship, or even that we are morally careless rather than legalistic, that this in turn somehow establishes us, rather than the devout, as the true people of God. This, indeed, is the implication, and sometimes more than the implication, of some writing on Paul and Romans, in which the problem Paul is addressing is the problem of "religion" and the apparent human attempt to use religious practices as a means of earning God's favor.[169] But if piety will not earn God's favor, nor will impiety; if religion will not do, nor will irreligion; if moralism will not qualify us, nor will immoralism.

When this bit of ivy, which easily winds itself around church life, has been uprooted—it is not, after all, what Paul is talking about—the tree is free to use its energy for proper growth. And the point at which we need to grow continually is in making real, to ourselves and one another, and particularly in the way we structure our corporate life, the fact that we believe in, and celebrate, the God who justifies the ungodly. Forgiveness remains one of the most astonishing gifts, and the church should be the place where people are regularly astonished by it.

**4.** Romans 4 urges us to examine the way in which true faith reflects, and feeds on, the character of God, and the way in which it leads to the rehabilitation of the true image-bearingness of human beings. Abraham's faith, analyzed in detail in vv. 18-21, is focused on, and gains its character from, the true God at every turn. It looks fully at the human and worldly situation,

---

169. See esp. Käsemann's repeated talk of *homo religiosus* as the real target of Paul's polemic.

filled as it is with death and decay; it acknowledges that this is the state we are in; and it also looks steadfastly at the God who raises the dead and creates out of nothing. Worshiping this God (4:20), and acknowledging that this God has the power to deliver on promises of new life in the place of death, is fundamental to Christian faith. It is also the reversal and undoing of that idolatry outlined in 1:18-25, and therefore cannot but issue in a life that undoes and reverses the consequent behavior spoken of in 1:26-31. Paul does not develop this further here, but those who want to live with the meaning of Romans 4 cannot avoid looking further, not just to chap. 6, but also to chap. 12, where he holds out a model of remade humanity in which the faith spoken of in chap. 4 has its full effect in transforming mind, character, and behavior.

**5.** The centrality of faith in God's raising of Jesus from the dead emerges with peculiar clarity from this chapter. In Western liberalism it has often been thought quite acceptable, sometimes even desirable, sometimes actually mandatory, that one should disbelieve in the resurrection of Jesus. There is much misinformation on this topic. It is often assumed that people who believe in Jesus' bodily resurrection hold a pre-scientific worldview without knowledge of the real facts of the world. To this mentality Paul's statement in v. 19 is especially relevant. It was not the case that Abraham was living in a fool's paradise, refusing to face the facts about himself. On the contrary, he looked them in the face and went on believing in the God who raises the dead. It will not do to declare that we modern persons now "know" that no such thing as bodily resurrection occurs. It does not help to cite the fact that in all cases observable to us dead people have in fact stayed dead. The testimony of the early church was precisely that, though of course all other humans remained as dead as Abraham's and Sarah's bodies (in terms of their childbearing possibilities), in this particular case the creator God had acted in a decisive, striking and as yet unique way, to give to Jesus a new bodily life—not merely a resuscitation into the same sort of bodily existence as before, but a new dimension of bodily existence. There is, no doubt, room for endless discussion about what form precisely Jesus' resurrection took and how best we might speak of it in subsequent generations. But there is no room, as far as Paul is concerned, for that impossible hybrid, a Christian who does not in any sense believe in the resurrection of Jesus.

# ROMANS 5:1–8:39

## GOD'S PEOPLE IN CHRIST AS THE TRUE HUMANITY

### OVERVIEW

Romans 5–8 is a majestic statement of some of Paul's greatest themes. The love of God embodied in Jesus' death; the hope, even during suffering, enjoyed by God's justifed people; Jesus' reversal of Adam's sin and its effects; Christian freedom from sin, the law and death itself; the life-giving leading of the Spirit. Parts of this section are sure to feature in anyone's selection of favorite biblical passages. Countless Christians, faced with life's greatest trials, have found strength and joy in Paul's closing words: "Neither height nor depth nor any other creature shall be able to separate us from the love of God in Christ Jesus our Lord" (8:39).

At the same time, these chapters contain some of Paul's densest and most difficult writing. The Adam/Christ contrast of 5:12-21 is cryptic and elliptical: trying to read its Greek after the measured sentences of 5:1-11 is like turning from Rembrandt to Picasso. Chapter 7 has produced dozens of conflicting interpretations: it has been both hailed as a profound analysis of the human condition and dismissed as a tortured and self-contradictory rambling. The description of cosmic liberation (8:19-22) is seen by some as a great climax, by others as an irrelevant aside. The section offers, in short, just what every Pauline exegete really wants: good, strong themes to enjoy, knotty problems to puzzle over.

Not everyone has agreed that 5–8 constitute a discrete section. Some have suggested that 1:18–5:11, or even 1:18–5:21, should be seen as the real first main section of the letter, with 5:12 or 6:1 starting the new symphonic movement. Paul's argument does indeed run on without a break here, unlike the deep breath between chaps. 8 and 9 or between chaps. 11 and 12. The two main paragraphs of chap. 5 (vv. 1-11, 12-21) sum up what has gone before as well as setting out material to be fur-

ther explored (e.g., 5:9 looks back to 3:24-26 and to the "wrath" of 1:18; 5:12-21 refers back to the implicit "Adam" theme in 1:18-25; 5:20 picks up 2:17-24 and 3:19-20). The chapter and paragraph divisions of Romans are of course a late invention. If Romans had concluded with personal greetings after 5:21, some might feel let down, but nobody would suggest that 5:1-21 belonged to a different world of thought from chaps. 1–4.

Nevertheless, the subject matter of 5:1-11 and 5:12-21 contains so many differences from that of chaps. 1–4 that most exegetes have concluded, rightly in my view, that they belong more naturally with what follows than with what precedes. Paul here speaks of God's love, not (principally) God's righteousness. Abraham is not mentioned, nor (apart from 5:1-2) is faith (see also 6:8; this is not part of a discussion of "faith" per se, but refers to a particular thing that Christians believe). The whole "Jew-plus-Gentile" theme, strikingly, is never mentioned; the law is again a major theme, but "works of the law" is not. Jesus, hardly mentioned in 1:18–4:25, is everywhere. Equally telling, Paul says a good deal in chaps. 5–8 about "we" and "you," whereas in the preceding section he has not spoken of "us" until the very last verses, and the earlier "you" passages are rhetorical, addressing imaginary interlocutors, whereas here he is speaking to his own actual audience.

There is a marked contrast of style. Instead of expounding passages of Scripture, Paul develops his own line of thought, alluding to Scripture frequently, and indeed retelling one of Scripture's greatest stories, but without regular quotation or exposition of specific passages. And instead of the diatribe style and its rapid-fire verbal tennis match, addressed to imaginary debating partners, we have a sustained line of thought, addressed to "my family" (ἀδελφοί *adelphoi;* lit., "brothers," 7:1, 4; 8:12; some translations, anxious about the gender-specific "brothers," replace it with "friends," but for Paul the family identity and consequent unity of God's people is paramount), building from one point to the next with an extraordinary integration of complex thought (Paul uses elements of the previous rhetorical style in, e.g., 6:1-3, 15-16; 7:7, 13—in other words, to turn particular corners in the argument, rather than to develop particular points).

This sequence of thought is opened up initially with four paragraphs of very similar length (5:1-11, 12-21; 6:1-11, 12-23), each rounded off with a christological formula that is not just added on for effect but sums up the paragraph. This then gives rise to two larger expositions. The first concerns the law: this is introduced in 7:1-6 and developed in 7:7–8:11. While completing this subject, 8:1-11 simultaneously introduces the second theme, that of the Spirit and of Christian and cosmic hope (8:1-30). Paul then returns to the topics with which the section began (8:31-39 repeats the themes of 5:1-11, with all the rhetorical stops pulled out), concluding once more with an emphatic christological summary.

Romans 5–8, then, is a carefully crafted unit. Here, more than anywhere else in Paul's surviving writing, we have a sense of a piece that might well have been composed earlier. Some have even argued that it is just that and that its placing between Romans 1–4 and 9–11 is, in effect, the combining of two quite different writings.[170] However, even if we suppose that Paul has thought it all through ahead of time and perhaps already committed some or all of it to writing (but would he really have left the grammar of 5:12-21 like that?), we are still faced with the question: why did he insert it here? When we add that chaps. 5–8 grow naturally out of 1–4 and prepare the way for both 9–11 and 12–16, we realize that the problem is not solved by the surgeon's knife. We must enquire further how the actual train of thought of these chapters develops the larger argument that Paul is actually mounting in the letter—as opposed,

unfortunately, to the argument that various traditions, both Christian and scholarly, have assumed that he is mounting. It is easy here to analyze the trees and ignore the forest. We here offer a preliminary solution, to be filled in as the exegesis progresses.

Romans 5–8 has played a vital role in mainstream Protestant readings of Romans. If chaps. 1–4 are held to be about "justification by faith," this section, starting from this point (5:1), is about something that follows from justification. Since the Reformers' exposition of justification regularly led to the question of Christian behavior, often framed in some such way as in 6:1 or 6:15, and since the word "sanctification" occurs twice in chap. 6 (vv. 19, 22), some concluded that chaps. 1–4 were "about" "justification," and chaps. 5–8 were "about" "sanctification." However, though there is indeed a sequence of thought from justification to something else in these chapters, this particular reading is unlikely to be accurate. The scarcity of the word "sanctification," and the fact that when Paul sums up the argument in 8:30 the final line reads "those he justified, them he also *glorified*," point in a rather different direction. If 1–4 is in any sense "about" justification, we might expect 5–8 to be "about" glorification.[171]

This is strikingly confirmed by the last phrase of 5:2, which completes the introductory sentence (5:1-2), and by the argument of 8:18-25, which has a good claim to be the point toward which the rest is moving. Of course, "glorification" here serves as a shorthand for the entire Christian hope, to which Paul can equally well refer by such phrases as "eternal life" (e.g., 2:7); but the point seems to be, throughout, that what God has done in Jesus the Messiah, and what God is already doing through the Spirit, guarantees that all those who believe the gospel, and are thus "justified by faith," can be assured of their final hope. They will be delivered from wrath (5:9), in other words, "saved."[172] They will be given the new bodies of resurrection life that will correspond to that of Jesus (8:11). And, since "glory" is another way of speaking of the presence of God, dwelling in the wilderness taber

---

170. See Robin Scroggs, "Paul as Rhetorician: Two Homilies in Romans 1–11," in *Jews, Greeks and Christians: Religious Cultures in Late Antiquity: Essays in Honour of William David Davies,* ed. Robert Hamerton-Kelly and Robin Scroggs, Studies in Judaism in Late Antiquity 21(Leiden: Brill, 1976) 71-98. This is discussed, together with several other similar suggestions, by Leander E. Keck, "What Makes Romans Tick?" in *Pauline Theology,* Volume III: *Romans,* ed. David M. Hay and E. Elizabeth Johnson (Minneapolis: Fortress, 1995) 3-29.

171. I place "about" in quotation marks because it is always unwise, in Romans, to imply that a given section has one topic and only one. The writing is more complex and symphonic than that.

172. It is curious that Joseph A. Fitzmyer, *Romans,* AB 33 (Garden City, N.Y.: Doubleday, 1993) 393, supposes "salvation" to be the topic of Romans 1–4, now left behind. The only mention of the idea (even then, not the key words) in 1:18–4:25 is in 2:7, 10, which look forward precisely to chaps. 5–8.

---

nacle or the Jerusalem Temple, the line of thought that runs from 5:2 ("we celebrate the hope of God's glory") to 8:30 ("those he justified, them he also glorified") involves specifically the indwelling of God, by the Spirit. The whole passage thus emphasizes that what God did decisively in Jesus the Messiah is now to be implemented through the Spirit. Paul points to ways in which the Christian's present status and future hope determine life in the the present, but the real theme is the secure future. All is guaranteed by the unshakable love of God—which is in turn demonstrated in the death of Jesus (5:6-10; 8:31-39). This is the argument that emerges most obviously from the surface of chaps. 5–8.

Beneath the surface, however, and poking out like the tips of a huge iceberg at various key points, there runs a different theme, not so often noticed. A word is necessary about the detection of apparently submerged themes. For centuries nobody minded when exegetes declared that Romans 1–4 was "about" justification and 5–8 "about" sanctification. These were regular topics in the systematic theology that sustained many churches and preachers; it seemed reasonable that Paul should develop his argument along such lines, and some sense could be made of the text on that basis (with little exceptions like 7:7-25; 8:18-25). The fact that Paul nowhere said that this was how he was dividing his material, and that so far as we know "justification" and "sanctification" did not function in his mind (or anyone else's in the first century) in the same way as they did in the church, did not seem to matter. But when people today propose alternative underlying themes, even when they are far more plausible within the mind of a Second Temple Jew, they are often howled down. "How can you be sure?" they are asked. "Why does Paul not say it more openly if that's what he meant?"

The argument for all such interpretations is cumulative. It consists of a hypothesis that one obtains not deductively (starting with the material before us and seeing what we can deduce from it), but by induction (moving from the particular to the general) or abduction (moving from data to larger theory).[173] As in much scientific procedure, the aim is to postulate a framework that, when examined, may turn out to explain the data before us

better, with more complete satisfaction, than the alternatives.[174] Like all serious readings of literary texts, such a proposal is to be verified, or as it may be falsified, not by the knock-down arguments of pseudo-scientific "proof," nor by the largely irrelevant question as to whether Paul's first audience would have seen the point at first hearing,[175] but by the overall sense that results. There are times when the answer to the objection, "But I don't see that in the text," is "Try looking through the telescope the right way round," or perhaps, "Try looking at the forest, not just the trees."

In case it seems that one protests too much, let me propose the reading of chaps. 5–8 of which I have become convinced and that, as I shall attempt to show, allows fully both for the integrity and distinction of these chapters as a section in their own right and for their careful integration with the four chapters that precede them and the eight that follow—in other words, for the advancement of the overall argument of the letter. Paul, I suggest, is telling the story of the people of the Messiah in terms of the new exodus. Jesus' people are the liberated people, on their way home to their promised land.[176]

The theme of "new exodus" is a major topic in Second Temple Judaism. It is a central way by which Jews in Paul's day expressed, symbolized, and narrated their hopes for the future—for the time when, as the prophets had foretold, their God would repeat, on their behalf, the great acts whereby their forebears were liberated from Egypt (e.g., Isa 11:11; 35:3-10; 51:9-11; 52:4-6; Jer 16:14-15; 23:7-8; Ezek 20:33-38; Hos 2:14-23). One biblical passage in particular stands out as carrying the themes of Romans 1–11 as a whole:

---

173. On "abduction," the least known of these, see C. S. Peirce, *Collected Papers* (Cambridge, Mass.: Harvard University Press, 1958) 7:89-164.

174. For further discussion of method, see N. T. Wright, *The New Testament and the People of God,* vol. 1 of *Christian Origins and the Question of God* (London: SPCK; Minneapolis: Fortress, 1992) chaps. 2–5.

175. This will be addressed in due course. Most major pieces of writing, and for that matter music and art, reveal their depths gradually. This is not a matter of bad communication but of the impossibility of instantaneously communicating truths that function at many levels simultaneously.

176. A detailed account of the proposal is found in N. T. Wright, "New Exodus, New Inheritance: The Narrative Substructure of Romans 3–8," in *Romans and the People of God: Essays in Honor of Gordon D. Fee on the Occasion of His 65th Birthday,* ed. S. Soderlund and N. T. Wright (Grand Rapids: Eerdmans, 1999) 26-35. Though I go some way beyond either, I have learned much from Frank Thielman, "The Story of Israel and the Theology of Romans 5–8," in *Romans,* vol. 3 of *Pauline Theology,* ed. David M. May and E. Elizabeth Johnson (Minneapolis: Fortress, 1995) 169-95, and Sylvia C. Keesmaat, *Paul and His Story: (Re)Interpreting the Exodus Tradition,* JNSTSup (Sheffield: Sheffield Academic, 1999). An earlier statement of one part of the proposal is found in Ignace de la Potterie, "Le chrétien conduit par l'Esprit dans son cheminement eschatologique (Rom 8,14)," in *The Law of the Spirit in Rom 7 and 8,* ed. L. de Lorenzi (Rome: St Paul's Abbey, 1976) 209-41.

The days are surely coming, says YHWH, when I will raise up for David a righteous Branch, and he shall reign as king and deal wisely, and shall execute justice and righteousness in the land. In his days Judah will be saved and Israel will live in safety. And this is the name by which he will be called: "YHWH is our righteousness."

Therefore, the days are surely coming, says YHWH, when it shall no longer be said, "As YHWH lives who brought the people of Israel up out of the land of Egypt," but "As YHWH lives who brought out and led the offspring of the house of Israel out of the land of the north and out of all the lands where I had driven them." Then they shall live in their own land. (Jer 23:5-8)

The Messiah, the righteousness of God, and the new exodus. Allowing for Paul's new perspective, whereby the promise of the land has been redefined into the promise of inheriting the whole cosmos (4:13; 8:18-25), the pattern is exact. Paul, like many other Second Temple Jews, longed for the day when God would fulfill the promises made to Abraham by bringing Israel back from exile, repeating what had been done at the exodus. Only this time, through the work of the Messiah, it would be on a different scale. This time the whole cosmos would be involved. This would be the revelation of the righteousness of God before the whole world. Paul's mind has already been moving in this way in chaps. 2 and 4; now he will develop the picture far more extensively. If he is talking about salvation, he is talking about the new exodus.[177]

The case for this reading of chaps. 5–8 can be seen to good advantage by working backward from its most obvious point, Rom 8:12-25. Paul speaks of those who are led by the Spirit of God being God's children (8:14); the phrase is very similar to that of Deut 14:1, looking back (as do all such ascriptions of divine parentage) to Exod 4:22 (see also Isa 1:2; Hos 1:10; Sir 1:10). The contrast between "the spirit of slavery" and "the spirit of adoption" (8:15) can well be construed as the contrast between Israel in Egypt and Israel journeying through the wilderness; Paul's appeal is that his

readers should not think, as Israel sometimes did, of going back to slavery rather than on to full freedom. And the crowning point of the paragraph is that God's children are also "heirs." Paul's word here (κληρονόμοι *klēronomoi*) employs the root that occurs dozens of times in the LXX, not least in Deuteronomy, usually standing for the Hebrew roots ירשׁ (*yrš*) or נחל (*nḥl*), in reference to the promised land, or part of it, as the "inheritance" God's people would acquire when the wilderness wandering was complete. For Paul, as we saw in Rom 4:13, the promise to Abraham concerning one particular piece of land has been transformed into a promise concerning "the world" (ὁ κόσμος *ho kosmos*) or, as here, "creation" (ἡ κτίσις *hē ktisis*).

This answers to the deepest level of the problem outlined in 1:18-32. God fulfills the promise to Abraham by redeeming the human race; when the human race is redeemed, the whole creation will be set free. Paul applies to creation as a whole the same exodus language he uses of God's people in chap. 6 and elsewhere: creation itself "will be set free from its slavery to corruption, into the freedom of the glory of the children of God" (8:21). The argument is based upon a retelling of the exodus story, in which not only God's people but also the whole creation are set free from "Egypt"—that is, sin, decay, and death. God's redeemed people are given the "glory" that humans lost at the fall (3:23), receiving "the world" as their inheritance.[178] God's creation currently shares the futility and corruption of the human race; when humans are set free, creation will be liberated as well.

Within the argument of Romans, the motif of slavery and freedom goes back at least to "redemption" in 3:24, but is highlighted especially in chap. 6. In 6:16, Paul personifies "sin" and "death" as the slavemasters who have kept the human race captive, and "obedience" and "righteousness" as the new owners under whom humans find freedom. He then continues the metaphor, recognizing its limitations (6:19*a*), through to the end of

---

177. Paul uses salvation terms (from the roots σωτηρία *sōtēria*; σώζω *sōzō*; and their cognates) in Rom 5:9-10; 8:24 in such a way as to make it clear that this is another way of talking about the "glorification" and the "eternal life" that has already been mentioned, on which see below.

178. See also Matt 5:5, which uses γῆ (*gē*, "land") as the object of "shall inherit." This is ambiguous. It could refer either to the land of Israel (as in Deut 4:38) or the whole world. Cf. Acts 1:8, where "to the ends of the earth" (NRSV) translates ἕως ἐσχάτου τῆς γῆς (*heōs eschatou tēs gēs*), which could technically mean "to the ends of the land [i.e., of Israel]," but in the light of Acts as a whole seems to mean "to the ends of the world."

the chapter, and builds it in to the theme of the next section (7:6, 25). This, clearly, is anticipating the "exodus" passage about slavery and freedom in chap. 8. But 6:16-23 is the development of the earlier part of the chapter, where the key event is baptism, uniting the Christian with the Messiah in his death and resurrection. Baptism, it appears, is the event through which, by means of this uniting, those enslaved to sin and death are now set free. But baptism, elsewhere in Paul, becomes a symbolic reminder of the crossing of the Red Sea (1 Cor 10:2—a passage in which Paul is urging his readers to think of themselves as in the same position as the wilderness generation, set free from Egypt and on the way home to their inheritance).[179] My proposal is that the journey that ends in chap. 8 with the glorious inheritance began in chap. 6 with the new covenant version of the crossing of the Red Sea, the event through which the slaves are set free.

This gives a new narrative coherence to the central section of 5–8—namely, 7:1–8:11. It is not just that Paul must now address, head on, the problem of the law to which he has referred several times (3:19-20; 4:15; 5:20; 6:14). Paul, unfortunately for his interpreters, is aware of no obligation to explain all the puzzling one-liners scattered throughout his writings. He is writing a letter, after all, not a doctoral dissertation. The deeper reason for writing chap. 7 is that he is following the storyline. After the Red Sea, and before the journey to the promised inheritance, comes Mt. Sinai and the giving of the Torah.

Using the exodus-story in this way carries, of course, a certain ambiguity. Paul does not think in terms of a simple typology whereby a pattern repeats itself over and over, but of a continuing narrative in which the new sequence, for all it repeats the old and gains its meaning from that repetition, also in some senses replaces the old and even undermines it. This ambiguity comes to its head in the parallel between the law and the Spirit: Torah itself has become part of the problem, part of the thing from which one needs to be set free. Paul's task in chap. 7 is then to exonerate Torah from blame, while demonstrating that only in Christ and the Spirit can its underlying

179. See R. B. Hays, "The Conversion of the Imagination: Scripture and Eschatology in 1 Corinthians," *NTS* 45 (1999) 391-412.

intention—to give life—be realized. As an abstract theological proposition, this has always seemed difficult to maintain, and this difficulty has been produced as the reason for Paul's dense and problematic argument. When seen within the context of an overarching narrative in which the events of the exodus are recapitulated in Christ and by the Spirit, in which the promises of the law and the prophets are fulfilled "apart from the law," it makes considerably more sense, and leads naturally into the passage we have already drawn attention to as the most obvious "new exodus" allusion (8:12-25).

At the head of this whole sequence of thought stands 5:12-21, where the Messiah is set in parallel, and also sharp contrast, with Adam. Adam, of course, was the one to whom, in Scripture, the whole creation was given as his inheritance. His "glory" consisted not least in his rule over the rest of God's world. The result of the fall was that the inheritance and the glory were lost; this is the picture Paul drew in 1:18-32, and summed up in 3:23. Now, in the Messiah, inheritance and glory are given back to the human race. They are to become truly human at last. Romans 5:12-21 functions as a programmatic statement, awaiting the fuller explanation of 8:12-30.

The story is more complicated than that, of course, because Israel was itself called to be the people through whom this should happen. The failure of Israel, expounded in 2:17–3:20 and presupposed here, has left a double task to be performed. The Messiah has not only reversed the fall of Adam; he has accomplished the redemptive work of Israel. His "obedience," which means almost exactly the same as his "faithfulness" (3:22), has accomplished that for which God called Israel in the first place. Torah was not, then, the means of redemption, but rather a further part of the problem, a further twist of the knife; and God has dealt with that as well. Verses 12-21, summing up where the argument of the letter has got to so far, plant the seeds that will bear fruit for the rest of 5–8.

The theme of 5:1-11 is clear, introducing the line of thought that will be summed up at the end of chap. 8: those who are justified are also glorified, because of the love of God effective through the death of Jesus. It is the move from faith to hope; from the one-off work of the Messiah to the inaugurated, but not yet consummated, work of the Spirit. This is Paul's other great theme, here and in 5–8 as a whole: those who are on this pilgrimage know the presence of the living God, not now in the pillar of cloud and fire, but in the Holy Spirit, who pours the love of God into their hearts, so that "reconciliation" (5:10-11) is not merely a fact but an experienced fact.

What contribution, then, does Romans 5–8 make toward the developing argument of the letter as a whole?

At one level, it functions as the natural sequel to 1–4. The argument for the assurance of salvation—the argument, that is, on the surface of the text—answers to one of the main strands of thought in the opening chapters. All sinned, came short of God's glory, and faced wrath. Despite what is commonly thought, 3:21–4:25 is not Paul's main answer to this problem, but rather the groundwork for the answer. The full answer comes in 5–8: there we are told that those in Christ will escape the wrath and inherit God's glory. There it is explained that those who are justified are also glorified. There Paul shows how the human race is renewed, to bear God's image afresh in Christ (8:29).

Chapters 5–8 are also where the achievement of Jesus, supremely in his vicarious messianic death, is set out most fully. The dense and cryptic statement in 3:24-26, vital though it is, points ahead to the fuller statement in 5:6-11 and 5:15-21, which are then developed in key summaries throughout the following chapters (6:3-11; 7:4; 8:3; 8:31-39). Throughout it is clear that the death of Jesus, seen here as the ground of Christian hope and Christian life, functions as such because it is first the ground of justification. Once more, 5–8 completes the train of thought in 1–4.

The theme of assurance, and of the salvation of the human race in Christ, is given power and depth by the latent exodus-narrative. When, in Genesis 15, God promised Abraham a family, the promise was explained in terms of the exodus. Now, developing the larger vision that Paul discovered in the Abrahamic promise, the human race as a whole has its exodus: its rescue from the slavery of sin and death, the indwelling presence of God by the Spirit, the present journey through the wilderness, and the hope of the final inheritance. As in 1 Corinthians, one of Paul's aims, particularly when writing to a largely Gentile church, is to implant in their worldview the scriptural narrative through which they will discover their own place on the map of God's purposes.[180] The gospel unveils the righteousness (that is, the covenant faithfulness) of God; God's people in Christ must learn to tell the story of that faithfulness and to live within it. Again, Romans 5–8 completes a strand within chaps. 1–4.

The theme of "Jew first and also Greek," so prominent in 1–4, may be absent from the text of 5–8, but it is not forgotten or left behind. What Paul says in 5–8 he says to, and of, the church as a whole. But only his Jewish and proselyte readers had been "under the law." The freedom from the law that looms so large in the middle of this section (7:1–8:11; anticipated in 5:20-21 and 6:14-15) and that gives rise to Paul's central statement of the death of Jesus, the indwelling of the Spirit, and the promise of resurrection (8:1-11), belongs to the story of how Israel's history reached its climax in the Messiah, and did so for the benefit of the whole world. In each case, however, the completion of one line of thought raises a further question. If salvation is assured because of Jesus' messianic death and the work of the Spirit, what about the people to whom the promises were first made? If God has accomplished the true exodus, what about the people of the original exodus? How can their story be truly told in the light of the full unveiling of God's righteousness in Jesus the Messiah? The opening of Romans 9 indicates that Paul is raising exactly these questions in exactly this way. The problem addressed in Romans 9–11, therefore, is introduced precisely as the dark side of the new exodus. Furthermore, Paul's account of Israel's privileges in 9:4-5 lists the very things that throughout chaps. 1–8 have been attributed, through Christ and the Spirit, to the wider family of Abraham described in chaps. 4–8. In other words, the first eight chapters of the letter raise particular questions about God's faithfulness to ethnic Israel that must be addressed for the sake of completeness.

But it would be a mistake to see chaps. 9–11, or for that matter chaps. 12–16, simply as necessary outworkings of an inner logic latent within 1–8. That would be to collapse back once more into regarding Romans 1–8 as "the things Paul really

180. See ibid.

wants to say" and 9–16 as "the things he is now forced to deal with because of what he has said." Without sliding into the opposite mistake (supposing that chaps. 9–11 and/or 12–16 are the "really important" parts, and chaps. 1–8 a mere preliminary), it is vital to see that one of the reasons Paul has set his argument out like this is precisely so that he can move forward from here to address the major issues that face the church in Rome. We postpone more detailed examination of this point to the introduction to chaps. 9–11.

It is possible, in other words, to read Romans 5–8 without reference to what has gone before or what comes after. It stands as one of the most central and majestic statements of all that Paul most passionately believes and articulately expounds. But to take it out of its context is like looking at a tree without considering its roots or its fruits. What Paul says here grows out of chaps. 1–4 and is designed to bear fruit in chaps. 9–11 and 12–16.

# ROMANS 5:1-11, FROM FAITH TO HOPE

## OVERVIEW

The first paragraph of the new section states and develops the theme that overarches the next four chapters: those whom God justified, God also glorified. In typical fashion, this is stated densely to start with (5:1-2). It is then developed with two new elements, suffering and the Spirit (5:3-5), explained and grounded (in the death of the Messiah) (5:6-9), and finally further explained and celebrated (5:10-11). As usual, Paul's successive explanations do not add new points to the opening summary, but rather explore what is contained by implication within it.

The theme is that of inaugurated eschatology. God has accomplished the justification of sinners; God will therefore complete the task, saving those already justified from the coming wrath (cf. Phil 1:6: when God begins a work, God will complete it). God's decisive disclosure of covenant faithfulness in the death of the Messiah (3:21–4:25) is now expressed in equally covenantal language, that of God's love (5:8). The argument is simple: if God loved sinners enough for the Son to die for them, God will surely complete what was begun at such cost. Those who have left Egypt will be brought to Canaan, even though suffering awaits them on the journey. Part of Christian assurance is learning to tell this story and to understand its inner logic.

The three tenses of salvation (as they are sometimes called) are thus unveiled. Paul presupposes and builds on his exposition of justification by faith in 3:21–4:25, though in 5:9-10 he will reveal its further depths: being "justified by (Christ's) blood" is functionally equivalent to "being reconciled to God through Jesus' death." This is the past tense of God's action in the Messiah. The future tense is supplied by the word "salvation" (5:9-10); this means "rescue from the coming wrath" (5:9; cf. 1 Thess 1:10) through Jesus' life. The present tense, held between these two, consists of peace, celebration, suffering, hope, love, reconciliation and (once more) celebration.

Paul is not, then, describing a mere formal or legal transaction. The whole paragraph is suffused with the personal relationship between the justified person and the God revealed in Jesus. It is a relationship of love on both sides, in which reconciliation has replaced enmity (5:5, 10). This intimacy comes about through the gift of God's Spirit, the presence of God with the newly constituted community and within the redeemed person, not least in their present wilderness sufferings. Verses 1-11 thus reveals something that had all along been at the heart of chaps. 1–4, though often hidden underneath Paul's legal imagery and the long tradition of its forensic interpretation: all that God said to Abraham, all that God accomplished in the Messiah, was done out of love, and designed to call out an answering love. The intimacy and ecstasy of 5:1-11 are a necessary further dimension of the doctrine of justification by faith.

# Romans 5:1-5, Peace, Patience, and Hope

NIV

5 Therefore, since we have been justified through faith, we[a] have peace with God through our Lord Jesus Christ, [2]through whom we have gained access by faith into this grace in which we now stand. And we[a] rejoice in the hope of the glory of God. [3]Not only so, but we[a] also rejoice in our sufferings, because we know that suffering produces perseverance; [4]perseverance, character; and character, hope. [5]And hope does not disappoint us, because God has poured out his love into our hearts by the Holy Spirit, whom he has given us.

[a] 1,2,3 Or let us

NRSV

5 Therefore, since we are justified by faith, we[a] have peace with God through our Lord Jesus Christ, [2]through whom we have obtained access[b] to this grace in which we stand; and we[c] boast in our hope of sharing the glory of God. [3]And not only that, but we[c] also boast in our sufferings, knowing that suffering produces endurance, [4]and endurance produces character, and character produces hope, [5]and hope does not disappoint us, because God's love has been poured into our hearts through the Holy Spirit that has been given to us.

[a] Other ancient authorities read let us     [b] Other ancient authorities add by faith     [c] Or let us

# COMMENTARY

**5:1-2.** Justification results in peace with God, in access to God's loving favor, and thereby, unstoppably, to the hope of glory. Thus Paul opens the paragraph and section with a characteristically dense statement of the past event, the present result, and the future promise. The whole thing is built on what has gone before: "therefore," as often, provides a key transition.

The emphasis of v. 1 falls on "we have peace." Many good manuscripts read ἐχῶμεν (echōmen, "let us have peace," imperative), rather than ἔχομεν (echomen, "we have peace," indicative), and some scholars have made a case for this reading.[181] The argument for the indicative, though, is strong: (a) the two main verbs of the second verse are in the indicative (the second could be either, but the first seems determinative); (b) the difference between a long and a short "o" was not very marked in the pronunciation of Greek when the manuscript was being copied and perhaps redictated; (c) "peace" at the start of the paragraph relates closely to "reconciliation" at its end, and reconciliation is there spoken of not as something to be striven for, but something "we have received."

God's justice has led to peace: the echoes of the world Paul was addressing are strong. Augustus Caesar had established the Roman *Pax*, founded on *Iustitia*.[182] His successors, enjoying among their titles "Lord" and "Savior," maintained the powerful imperial myth not least through the imperial cult. Paul is revealing to his Roman audience a different justice, a different peace, in virtue of a different Lord and a different God: the God of Abraham, the world's creator, who has now established peace "through our Lord Jesus Christ." This peace, the first characteristic Paul mentions of the present tense of salvation, includes the deeply personal reconciliation between each believer and the true God, but can hardly stop there; already Paul is sowing the seeds for that communal peace he longs to see come about in the whole Roman church (14:1–15:14; see esp. 14:17, 19), the work, indeed, of "the God of peace" (15:33; 16:20). It is this peace, embracing alike each person and the whole community, that reveals to the wider world the existence and nature of the alternative empire, set up through the true Lord, the

---

181. Fitzmyer, *Romans,* 395, lists Kuss, Lagrange, and Sanday and Headlam as taking this view. See the judicious discussion in Douglas J. Moo, *The Epistle to the Romans,* NICNT (Grand Rapids: Eerdmans, 1996) 295-96.

182. For this whole theme, see esp. D. Georgi, *Theocracy in Paul's Praxis and Theology* (Minneapolis: Fortress, 1991) 79-104; reprinted in R. A. Horsley, ed., *Paul and Empire: Religion and Power in Roman Imperial Society* (Harrisburg, Pa.: Trinity, 1997) 148-57.

Messiah. In one short verse Paul manages to artic-ulate both the heart of Christian personal experi-ence and the politically subversive nature of Christian loyalty.

By way of explaining this peace, Paul uses the language of the cult: we have obtained, he says, "access" to grace, the same root being used as the regular verb for approaching the altar with a sacri-fice.[183] "Grace" is here clearly a shorthand, not so much for God's action on behalf of undeserving sinners, but for the sphere of God's continuing love. The metaphor envisages grace as a room into which Jesus has ushered all who believe,[184] a room where they now "stand," a place character-ized by the presence and sustaining love of God. Just as the Temple symbolized and actualized Israel's meeting with the gracious God, so now Jesus has effected such a meeting between this God and all who approach by faith.

The result of past justification and the present status of grace is the future hope: "we celebrate the hope of the glory of God." The NRSV's "boast" keeps the same English word that the Greek had in 2:17 and 3:27; the NIV, understandably regard-ing "boast" as purely negative, replaces it here with "rejoice."[185] Part of the difficulty is that we think of "boasting" as self-advertisement, (which we, unlike the world of Paul's day, find distaste-ful), whereas Paul's Greek has a larger signifi-cance: it has to do with the grounds for confidence when facing both present and future. Hence, "cel-ebrate": this brings together the two senses of joy and confidence. What could not be attained through Torah—namely, a secure confidence in being God's people—is on offer through Jesus Christ (see the Commentary on 8:3-4).

The content of the hope is "glory." This is an advance statement of the theme developed in 8:18, 21, 30 (cf. Col 1:27). Adam's lost glory (3:23) is regained in the Messiah: not simply

dazzling beauty, but the status and task of being God's vicegerent over creation. That this is what Paul has in mind becomes clear in 8:18-27, where the revelation of God's children and their glory leads to the liberation of the whole created order. When humans are restored to be as they were intended to be, then the whole of creation will be renewed under their lordship. At the same time, the cultic context, and the mention of the Spirit at the end of the next sentence, suggests that Paul has in mind also the glory of God dwelling in the Temple: God's glorious presence, at work already in the hearts of believers, will one day flood their whole being. This, too, is borne out by the devel-opment of the subject in chap. 8. This is the hope that supplies confidence and joy.

**5:3-5.** Paul now approaches the same result from a different angle. Present Christian existence is not simply a matter of peace with God, but also, paradoxically, of suffering. This suffering, though, is to be understood as part of a larger story that again ends with hope. This time, instead of char-acterizing the hope by "glory," Paul speaks of the indwelling Spirit, who elsewhere, not least in the climax to chaps. 5–8, is the one who guarantees the future hope for the suffering people (8:12-30). In early Christian thought, as at Qumran, the Spirit is a sign of the in-breaking new age.

So, then, we celebrate our sufferings; a typically counterintuitive Pauline comment, in our day as in his own, where suffering was more likely to be regarded as a sign of the gods' displeasure. Paul tells a different story: Suffering produces patience (the NRSV's "endurance" and the NIV's "perse-verance" both bring out aspects of the same idea, which is not so much of pressing ahead in adver-sity as simply staying put without dismay). The point of this is not simply that patience is a virtue worth cultivating, but that out of patience grows "character"—a difficult word, since, although "a person of character" implies good character, we can also speak in English of "a bad character." The Greek has the overtone of "tried and tested," what we mean when we speak of someone as "firm as a rock." This, too, is valued not so much as a virtue in its own right but because from it springs hope. On the surface, there is no obvious logic in this. The Stoicism popular in Paul's day valued patience under suffering and prized a tried and tested character, but came up with little or no

---

183. James D. G. Dunn, *Romans 1–8*, WBC 38A (Dallas: Word, 1988) 248, casts doubt on this and suggests instead the idea of approaching the emperor's throne room. This is possible as well, but προσάγω (*prosagō*, "to bring near") occurs very frequently in cultic contexts in the LXX. It is true that the verb is used of bringing the sac-rifice, not the worshiper, into God's presence (so Moo, *Romans*, 300-301), but this is hardly an objection in the light of 12:1 and 15:16.

184. Some MSS, followed by the NRSV mg., omit "by faith." Whether or not it stood in the original text, it certainly says what Paul meant.

185. See Christopher Bryan, *A Preface to Romans: Notes on the Epistle in Its Literary and Cultural Setting* (Oxford: Oxford University Press, 2000) 121n. 3, on the importance of recognizing such "hooks" to what has gone before.

hope as a result. Within Paul's narrative world, however, there was plenty of point: the long journey through the wilderness leads to the promised land. In addition, Paul had personal evidence, from his own life and that of friends and colleagues, to back up the story and theology. When the patience is Christian patience, and the tried and tested character a Christian character, the result is neither shallow optimism nor settled fatalism, but hope.

This hope does not make us ashamed. "Does not disappoint us" may well express part of the true understanding: this hope will not let us down. It will be fulfilled. In that case, the evidence he offers (the love of God in our hearts by the Spirit) functions the same way as in 8:23. It is the first-fruits and guarantee of God's ultimate saving work (see 2 Cor 1:22; 5:5; see also the Commentary on 10:11-13, where "not put to shame" is functionally equivalent to "saved"). But it is possible, not least in view of the present tense Paul chooses, that by "not ashamed" he means, rather, that the Christian's present condition, living in hope, is nothing to be ashamed of (cf. 1:16). Though Christian living is often paradoxical and deeply painful, one can hold up one's head, because the present experience of the Spirit fills the heart with love. This reading fits well with 8:24-28, where the thought of the section is coming full circle, and where Paul again wants to explain that unfulfilled hope is nothing to be ashamed of.

In this connection, it is worth giving serious consideration to the minority understanding of "the love of God" in v. 5.[186] The phrase could mean either God's love for us (subjective genitive) or our love for God (objective genitive); the NRSV and the NIV in different ways foreclose on the ambiguity, settling for the former. This is in line with most interpreters, who, rightly noting that God's love for sinners is the major theme in vv. 6-10, assume that "the love of God" in v. 5 has this meaning too. Theological reasoning has also played a part, preferring to see hope as grounded on something about God (and indeed noticing that

this is the logic of vv. 6-10) rather than something about ourselves.[187]

Nevertheless, the Spirit's work, to which Paul is here ascribing the pouring out of this love in the heart, is precisely within the innermost beings of believers, and as we have seen this is frequently referred to as the sign, foretaste and guarantee of eventual salvation. (This in no way compromises justification by grace through faith; rather, as with everything in Paul's descriptions of present Christian life, it is the result and outworking of that.) And the parallel passage in 8:24-28 indicates that Paul is well capable of speaking, precisely at this point in the argument, of "those who love God," just as in 1 Cor 2:9; 8:3, the latter in an explicit invoking of the *Shema,* the Jewish daily prayer ("Hear, O Israel: YHWH our God, YHWH is one; and you shall love YHWH your God," Deut 6:4-5.) A further argument for taking "the love of God" to mean our love for God is this: Why would Paul suggest that God's love for us was poured out into, and thus thereafter located in, our *hearts?*[188]

It is then possible, and preferable, to read "the love of God" in 5:5 as a similar allusion to the *Shema,* and to take it therefore as the objective genitive: our love for God. This then links up with two previous programmatic passages in the letter: 1:5, where Paul speaks of "the obedience of faith" as the result of the gospel, and 3:30, where the monotheism of the *Shema* undergirds justification itself. If this is right, 5:5 is tied closely to the exposition of the worldwide family of Abraham in chap. 4: the *Shema* is now fulfilled by all those who love the God revealed in Jesus the Messiah. This fits well with several other passages in the letter (e.g., 2:25-29; 8:4-9; 10:6-11), and provides a striking reason for not being ashamed to be living in hope, which is after all what the present passage is about. To find in one's heart a Spirit-given love for God is itself more than consolation. To realize that this love fulfils the central command of Torah is to discover oneself to be a member of the renewed people of God.

---

186. The word for "love," here and in 5:8; 8:35, 39, is ἀγάπη (*agapē*). As is well known, this word attained a new lease of life in early Christianity, quickly becoming used to denote the self-giving love of God in Jesus Christ, and the answering love, for God and one another, of those grasped by the gospel.

187. E.g., Moo, *Romans,* 304-5; but cf. Bryan, *A Preface to Romans,* 123, who holds the subjective view but distances himself from some of the arguments used against the objective one.

188. This was first put to me by the late G. B. Caird, and was the point that convinced him to change his mind to the objective genitive.

# Romans 5:6-11, The Death of the Messiah and the Love of God

NIV

⁶You see, at just the right time, when we were still powerless, Christ died for the ungodly. ⁷Very rarely will anyone die for a righteous man, though for a good man someone might possibly dare to die. ⁸But God demonstrates his own love for us in this: While we were still sinners, Christ died for us.

⁹Since we have now been justified by his blood, how much more shall we be saved from God's wrath through him! ¹⁰For if, when we were God's enemies, we were reconciled to him through the death of his Son, how much more, having been reconciled, shall we be saved through his life! ¹¹Not only is this so, but we also rejoice in God through our Lord Jesus Christ, through whom we have now received reconciliation.

NRSV

6For while we were still weak, at the right time Christ died for the ungodly. ⁷Indeed, rarely will anyone die for a righteous person—though perhaps for a good person someone might actually dare to die. ⁸But God proves his love for us in that while we still were sinners Christ died for us. ⁹Much more surely then, now that we have been justified by his blood, will we be saved through him from the wrath of God.ª ¹⁰For if while we were enemies, we were reconciled to God through the death of his Son, much more surely, having been reconciled, will we be saved by his life. ¹¹But more than that, we even boast in God through our Lord Jesus Christ, through whom we have now received reconciliation.

ª Gk *the wrath*

# COMMENTARY

The compact introduction over, Paul settles to a more leisurely description of how the death of Jesus, by revealing God's love for sinners and by accomplishing their justification, assures those who are justified that they will be saved at the last. This is the larger explanation (γάρ *gar*, v. 6) for the whole statement of vv. 1-5, rather than for one particular part of it. It is, equally clearly, part of the overarching theme of the whole section, since Paul returns to the same point in 8:31-39.

**5:6-8.** The outline argument is straightforward, the details occasionally tricky. Verse 6 states the basic premise, v. 7 comments on it, and v. 8 draws the conclusion. The Messiah died for the ungodly; people do not normally die even for worthy people; the Messiah's death is thus the measure of God's extraordinary love. Verse 6 emphasizes the unworthiness of the recipients of God's generosity: we were still weak, still actually ungodly.[189] This links in, deliberately no doubt, with the description

of God "justifying the ungodly" in 4:5, and prepares for the third member of the sequence in v. 8: when we were still "sinners."

God's love appeared on the scene "at the right time." Paul does not refer, we may suppose, to a particular chronological scheme (though such things were reasonably common among educated Jews looking for the coming of God's kingdom.[190] Nor is he suggesting that the Messiah's death had happened at a moment of particular weakness or sinfulness on the part of Israel and the world. (Was the human race "weaker" in the first century than before?) Rather, with hindsight, he recognized, as in Gal 4:4, that "the time had fully come" (cf. Tob 14:5). He believed that God had brought to fulfillment a plan that, though opaque before, was now open to view.

The main contrast Paul is making in what follows is between worthy people, for whom one would still be unlikely to die, and unworthy people, for whom God gave the Messiah. But v. 7 also

189. The repeated "still" (ἔτι *eti*) is hard to bring out in English, and neither the NRSV nor the NIV succeeds. Some MSS omit, and some alter, the second occurrence of the word; presumably it was felt odd even in the original.

190. See Roger T. Beckwith, *Calendar and Chronology, Jewish and Christian: Biblical, Intertestamental and Patristic Studies*, AGJU 33 (Leiden: Brill, 1996).

contains a contrast between two types of worthy people: a "righteous" person, for whom, he says, one would scarcely die, and "the good person" for whom, he says, one might even brave death.[191] Commentators have sometimes tried to portray the "righteous" here as the cold, legally correct person, in order to contrast such qualities with a warmer, more appealing goodness. But the positive overtones of the word "righteous" in Paul hardly allow for the distinction necessary if the verse is to express that meaning. One possible explanation might be that "the good man" (the word has the definite article, unlike "righteous" earlier in the verse) could actually be an allusion to Jesus himself: Paul, knowing that martyrdom was always possible (e.g., Phil 1:20-21; 2:17), might intend to say here what he says in 8:36 ("for your sake we are being killed all day long"). This is hardly provable, and may seem fanciful; but it deserves considering. The conventional, and perhaps safest, approach is to suggest that "the good man" refers to someone's benefactor.[192]

Such a death would still require huge courage and dedication. The qualification added in v. 7b has not damaged the basic contrast: what God did, freely and gladly, demonstrates a love far beyond anything human love can attain. We were, after all, not merely weak or ungodly, but actually sinners: Paul includes himself, and his fellow Jews, in a word that technically described "those outside the law," the pagans who, not possessing the law, were inevitably sinful (cf. Gal 2:15, where the word is used in this technical sense). That was our condition, Paul says, when "the Messiah died for us"— a basic statement of primitive Christian belief (cf. 4:25; 1 Cor 15:3). The "for" in "for us" is not explained, though what follows fills it out somewhat, and the frequent references to Jesus' messianic death on behalf of others in the chapters that follow develop the thought in various directions.

**5:9-10.** The love of God seen in action in the death of the Messiah is then the basis for a standard type of argument, the "how much more": If God has done the difficult thing, how much more will the easy thing now be done.[193] God has already done the unthinkable; how much more will God do something relatively obvious! Paul opens up this thought in two stages, first (v. 9) offering a conclusion in terms of justification and salvation, and then (v. 10) explaining it in terms of God's reconciling love. This, too, like so much in the present paragraph, is picked up at the end of the section (8:32).

The first stage indicates that Paul is still consciously addressing the problem stated in 1:18–3:20. "The wrath" hangs over the human race (the NRSV and the NIV both specify that the wrath is God's; this is true, but Paul does not say so here). Paul thinks in terms of a coming day of wrath, not simply the individual fate of unbelievers after death (cf. 2:5, 16). Those already justified by Jesus' sacrificial death, he says, will be rescued from this coming wrath ("by his blood," picking up 3:25, clearly refers to Jesus' death as a sacrifice; see the Commentary on 5:2; the only other Pauline references to the blood of Jesus are 1 Cor 10:16; 11:25, 27; Eph 1:7; 2:13; Col 1:20). This is the negative side of the promise whose positive side is "sharing the glory of God" (5:2). (Just to be clear: "salvation" describes the future of God's people in terms of their rescue from a terrible fate; "glorification" in terms of the status they will enjoy; "resurrection" in terms of their new embodiment the other side of death; "justification," when applied to the future as in 2:13, in terms of their acquittal in the final Assize. In each case the event is the same, the connotation different.) Hope for this rescue is securely based, Paul says, expanding 5:8, because God has already effected reconciliation when we were not just weak, ungodly, or sinful, but actually God's enemies (cf. 2 Cor 5:18-19; Eph 2:16; Col 1:19-22). The fact that this deeply personal notion is offered in explanation of, rather than in addition to, the mention of justification in the first half of v. 9 indicates that the meaning and effect of justification is to bring humans into the forgiven, reconciled family of God.

Upon whose side was the enmity? At one level, clearly, on ours; we were, says Paul, "god-haters"

---

191. The phrase τοῦ ἀγαθοῦ (*tou agathou*) could be either masc. ("the good man") or neut. ("the good thing"); most understand the former, though "the good" in the sense of "the public good" is not impossible.

192. See C. E. B. Cranfield, *A Critical and Exegetical Commentary on the Epistle to the Romans,* ICC, 2 vols. (Edinburgh: T. & T. Clark, 1975) 264-65; full discussion in A. D. Clarke, "The Good and the Just in Romans 5:7," *TyndBul* 41 (1990) 128-42.

193. Commentators regularly point out the rabbinic model of argument on which this is based; but to argue *a minori ad maius* is common to many systems of logic.

(1:30), though this word would hardly apply to many pious Jews, or even to the Gentile "god-fearers" who probably made up a significant proportion of the Roman converts. Objectively, though, Paul sees all humans as being at enmity with God through sin. Reconciliation is, after all, effected from God's side, by the initiative of love. However, Paul has just mentioned the wrath, which (as in 1:18 and 2:5-11) clearly means God's wrath. This wrath stood over against us, and God's love has saved us from it. We should not, I think, cut the knot and suggest that the enmity was on our side only. God's settled and sorrowful opposition to all that is evil included enmity against sinners. The fact that God's rescuing love has found a way of deliverance and reconciliation is part of the wonder of the gospel.

Paul here elaborates the christological basis of both reconciliation and salvation. We are reconciled, he says, through the death of God's son. This is the first mention of Jesus' divine sonship since the programmatic 1:3-4, and looks on to 8:3 and 8:32 in particular. Paul uses the title sparingly—not, it seems, from any reluctance, but rather to save it for the really weighty statements. Though "son of God" is still a messianic title for Paul, the logic of this whole passage, in which Jesus' death reveals God's reconciling love, demands that he express some identity between Jesus and God, and this is Paul's chosen way of doing just that. As in 8:3 and Gal 4:4, Jesus as "son of God" is the one sent from God to accomplish that which God alone must perform.

As in 4:25, Paul here sees the cross accomplishing one task, and the resurrection, or at least the risen life of the Messiah, accomplishing another. However, whereas in 4:25 the resurrection was associated with justification, he here assigns reconciliation (in parallel with justification in v. 9) to the cross, and salvation to Jesus' "life."[194] Presumably we should not make too hard

---

194. This is the first mention of "salvation" in the letter; "salvation" and "justification" are not the same thing in Paul's mind, however much they are confused in popular parlance.

and fast a distinction between the effect of the cross and the effect of the resurrection; for Paul the cross was always the death of the one whom the resurrection proved to be the Messiah, and the resurrection was always the raising of the crucified one. There is, however, a particular point here: being saved *in* the life of the son of God looks ahead to chap. 6, where it is precisely "in Christ" that the baptized are brought to new life, indeed, to eternal life (NRSV "by" and NIV "through" both obscure this link).

**5:11.** The final point of the paragraph is perhaps less expected: we celebrate, we boast, in God! The NIV's "rejoice," though true, does not catch either the echo of 2:17 or the note of real triumph that goes with the reversal of that passage: that which was impossible under the Torah, a boasting in God that reflected pride of race and culture, is strangely possible under the gospel. The gospel has already reduced all human boasting to nothing (3:27-30; cf. 1 Cor 1:29-31); the Christian status and hope may look foolish in the world's eyes, and is clung to in the teeth of suffering (5:3-5); but when looking at "our Lord, Jesus, the Messiah," and celebrating the reconciliation with God that he has effected, the Christian can say, with the psalmist, "this God is our God, for ever and ever; he will be our guide unto death" (Ps 48:14). Or, indeed, with Paul at the climax of the present section: "if God is for us, who can be against us?" (8:31). The non-Christian Jew of Paul's day would no doubt be as offended by this as the relativist in our own (the pagan of Paul's day, and of our own, would no doubt scoff); but Paul reflects the clear and universal early Christian claim. Those who believe in Jesus the Messiah are the true people of the creator God, the God of Abraham. That is what it means to "boast in God," to celebrate the reconciliation between the creator and those who bear the creator's image. The paragraph ends, as do most in this section, with a christological summary: We boast in God through our Lord, Jesus the Messiah. Other lords, Paul implies, should take note.

# REFLECTIONS

**1.** The deeply personal reconciliation between the creator God and the human race in and through Jesus the Messiah can hardly be explored too often, or too thoroughly. It is the theme that lies at the heart of the Christian experience and claim, the point at which believing certain things *about* God is swallowed up in personal knowledge *of* God. To be sure, it is easy to be deceived at this point, not least through the arrogance that quickly and conveniently forgets that our knowledge and love of God are but the reflex of God's knowledge and love of us (1 Cor 8:2-3). It is easy to imagine that one is knowing the living God when in fact one is worshiping, and deriving spurious comfort from, an idol of one's own imagining. That is why, as in the present paragraph, it is vital to keep Jesus, and the cross and resurrection, at the center of the picture, and to invoke the Holy Spirit through whom God's love floods our hearts.

This knowledge and love of the true God is evoked and sustained most chiefly, as here, through meditation on the death of Jesus. Again, it is possible to get things out of focus at this point, to concentrate morbidly on Jesus' suffering in the same frame of mind that lures people to drool over some great natural or human disaster. But the abuse does not detract from the reality. The Gospel writers tell the story of Jesus' last days and hours in lavish detail; those who allow themselves to be caught up within that story will discover its life-changing power. Here the entire narrative is boiled down to a single sentence: God's love is demonstrated in that, while we were yet sinners, the Messiah died for us. Those whose first thought is to analyze that statement in terms of theological or literary derivations do more damage to it, even if their analysis is accurate, than one who knows no Greek but whose heart is strangely warmed in reading it. Paul is often criticized for being too logical or lawcourt-minded. That may be true of some of his interpreters. For Paul himself, the language of the lawcourt was a powerful metaphor, but the language of love spoke literal truth.

**2.** The logic of divine love is here pressed into service as part of the argument for assurance. It is ironic that, when many Western Christians are flirting with universalism, there is simultaneously an underemphasis on the eternal security of all Christian believers. It is almost as though we are trying to say that everyone else may well be saved but that we cannot be too sure about ourselves. This may, no doubt, express a proper reaction against triumphalist arrogance, but nothing is gained by ignoring Paul's central argument, here and throughout Romans 5–8: believing and baptized Christians are assured that, by the indwelling Spirit, they will be brought to resurrection life at the last. Paul was well aware, as his other letters show, of the problems of professing Christians whose behavior seemed to make a mockery of their faith (1 Corinthians wrestles with this problem on almost every page). But one of his greatest, most securely grounded, most sustained arguments is precisely this: Those whom God justified, God also glorified. To fail to grasp this, and be grasped by it, is to miss not only the heart of Paul, but, Paul would say, the heart of God.

**3.** Celebrating one's suffering sounds depressingly morbid. Western Christians easily imbibe from our culture an inclination to regard not only the pursuit but also the attainment of happiness as an inalienable right, and if suffering strikes we look either to technology to solve it or to the lawyers to apportion the blame. Paul is unspecific here about which sufferings he means (he is more explicit in 8:35), but his approach is steady and realistic: suffering produces patience, and patience produces a tried and tested character. Neither of these qualities is much in evidence—or indeed highly prized—in contemporary Western society, which wants everything at once and wants to be free to change character according to the mood of the moment. As a result, we should not be surprised that we are in many respects a society without hope. Those who believe in Jesus the Messiah are called to model communities, familes and personal lives in which the sequence of faith, peace, suffering, patience, character and hope is lived out, sustained by the Holy Spirit's work of enabling us to know God's love and to love God in return.

**4.** The political challenge implicit in this passage should be pondered and drawn out. God has established the true peace, so different from the *pax Romana,* on the foundation of true justice, so different from the Roman *Iustitia,* and has done so through the Lord Jesus, so different from the lord Caesar. This challenge, of course, had more than a little to do with the sufferings Paul endured. The church as a whole has yet to take seriously the question of how to translate its allegiance to this Lord, who established divine justice and peace through his own death, rather than through the death of those who stood in his way, into action in the world. Comparatively little attention has been given to the question, How might God's reconciling action in Christ become the ground and model for the reconciliation of human enemies? Too often those who have focused attention on the saving death of Jesus have concentrated exclusively on its relevance for final salvation and current spiritual growth, while those who have wanted to make the gospel politically relevant have ignored Paul's theology of Jesus' death. Fresh integration is called for if we are to hear and live Paul's many-sided gospel in a new century and millennium.

# ROMANS 5:12-21, FROM ADAM TO THE MESSIAH

## NIV

[12]Therefore, just as sin entered the world through one man, and death through sin, and in this way death came to all men, because all sinned— [13]for before the law was given, sin was in the world. But sin is not taken into account when there is no law. [14]Nevertheless, death reigned from the time of Adam to the time of Moses, even over those who did not sin by breaking a command, as did Adam, who was a pattern of the one to come.

[15]But the gift is not like the trespass. For if the many died by the trespass of the one man, how much more did God's grace and the gift that came by the grace of the one man, Jesus Christ, overflow to the many! [16]Again, the gift of God is not like the result of the one man's sin: The judgment followed one sin and brought condemnation, but the gift followed many trespasses and brought justification. [17]For if, by the trespass of the one man, death reigned through that one man, how much more will those who receive God's abundant provision of grace and of the gift of righteousness reign in life through the one man, Jesus Christ.

[18]Consequently, just as the result of one trespass was condemnation for all men, so also the result of one act of righteousness was justification that brings life for all men. [19]For just as through the disobedience of the one man the many were

## NRSV

[12]Therefore, just as sin came into the world through one man, and death came through sin, and so death spread to all because all have sinned— [13]sin was indeed in the world before the law, but sin is not reckoned when there is no law. [14]Yet death exercised dominion from Adam to Moses, even over those whose sins were not like the transgression of Adam, who is a type of the one who was to come.

[15]But the free gift is not like the trespass. For if the many died through the one man's trespass, much more surely have the grace of God and the free gift in the grace of the one man, Jesus Christ, abounded for the many. [16]And the free gift is not like the effect of the one man's sin. For the judgment following one trespass brought condemnation, but the free gift following many trespasses brings justification. [17]If, because of the one man's trespass, death exercised dominion through that one, much more surely will those who receive the abundance of grace and the free gift of righteousness exercise dominion in life through the one man, Jesus Christ.

[18]Therefore just as one man's trespass led to condemnation for all, so one man's act of righteousness leads to justification and life for all. [19]For just as by the one man's disobedience the many were made sinners, so by the one man's

**NIV**

made sinners, so also through the obedience of the one man the many will be made righteous.

²⁰The law was added so that the trespass might increase. But where sin increased, grace increased all the more, ²¹so that, just as sin reigned in death, so also grace might reign through righteousness to bring eternal life through Jesus Christ our Lord.

**NRSV**

obedience the many will be made righteous. ²⁰But law came in, with the result that the trespass multiplied; but where sin increased, grace abounded all the more, ²¹so that, just as sin exercised dominion in death, so grace might also exercise dominion through justification[a] leading to eternal life through Jesus Christ our Lord.

[a] Or righteousness

# COMMENTARY

The next paragraph is as terse and cryptic as the previous one was flowing and lucid. Like an artist in a hurry, Paul paints with a few large, sweeping strokes on a giant canvas, creating an overall picture without many details. It is the picture, in bold, stark outline, of his whole argument to this point; and it may help if we think of him, then, in chaps. 6–8, standing in front of this picture to talk us through the next sequence, pointing back at the extraordinary painting to show us where his different themes belong and how they fit together. As we have seen, the overall argument of 5–8 is outlined in 5:1-11, so that in summing up where he has now got to Paul is not, as it were, making the first in a sequence of logically ordered points, but rather setting up the grid on which all that follows will be plotted.

The paragraph outlines the way in which the creator and covenant God has successfully dealt with the problem of human sin and death. The hypothesis that saw Adam hiding under the argument of 1:18-25 and in isolated statements such as 3:23 is vindicated by Paul's summarizing here where he has got to, not (as has sometimes been thought) adding a fresh point or simply providing an illustration. The opening διὰ τοῦτο (dia touto) should thus be read

not simply as "therefore," but "so it comes about that": not a new point to be deduced, but a summary, a conclusion that can be drawn because of what has been said briefly, in advance, in 5:1-11. We have seen, in miniature, that the death of Jesus, the great act of obedient covenant faithfulness, has dealt with sin, that God's love revealed on the cross will certainly bring to salvation those who are justified, and that the Spirit has been given to pour the love of God into the hearts of believers, transforming them so that they become God's true humanity. This enables us to line up the problem outlined in 1:18–3:20 (sin and death) with the solution articulated in 3:21–5:11 (justification and life) and draw the conclusions. That is what Paul does here.

The shape of the argument needs clarifying. The main point Paul is making is begun in v. 12, but broken off to allow for two different sorts of explanation and modification (vv. 13-14, 15-17). He then returns to his main statement in v. 18, further explained and restated in v. 19. Verse 20 adds a further complication, showing how the law fits within the Adam-Christ picture; v. 21 restates the point of vv. 18-19 allowing for this further dimension. Thus the shape of the paragraph is like this:

> 5:12: opening statement, awaiting completion: just as sin entered and brought death
> 5:13-14: first explanatory "aside": sin and death between Adam and Moses
> 5:15-17: second explanatory "aside": the imbalances between sin and grace
> (5:15: first imbalance; 5:16-17: second imbalance, with explanation)
> 5:18: initial completion of opening statement: just as the trespass, so the act of righteousness
> 5:19: explanation and filling out of v. 18: disobedience and obedience
> 5:20: where the Law belongs on this map: intensifying the problem, but grace deals with this too
> 5:21: triumphant conclusion: the kingdom of grace triumphs over the kingdom of sin

Within this, Paul introduces a theme almost unique in his writings, but very important within early Christianity: the clash of the kingdoms. Five out of the nine occurrences in his writings of βασιλεύω (*basileuō*, "to rule as a king," "to reign") come in these verses; one of the others, picking up this passage, is at 6:12.[195] Paul does not speak here of the kingdom of Satan, but instead personifies "sin" and "death," speaking of each as "reigning" (5:14, 17*a*, 21*a*). He does not speak here, either, of the reign of God, or even of Jesus; rather, as in the admittedly ironic 1 Cor 4:8, he speaks of believers as reigning (5:17*b*), and then finally of the reign of grace itself (5:21*b*). The last, clearly, is a personification, a periphrasis for God. This theme of kingly rule, coming so soon after the grand statement of justice, peace, and lordship (5:1), cannot but be seen as a further indication of Paul's overall mission: to announce the kingdom of God in the face of all the principalities and powers of the world, not least those of Rome itself (cf. 8:38-39 and the pregnant conclusion of Acts 28:30-31).

The other themes work in groups. Sin and death obviously belong together, and are joined by trespass,[196] disobedience, and condemnation. On the other side are grace, righteousness, free gift (χάρισμα *charisma*), gift (δωρεά *dōrea* or δώρημα *dōrēma*), act of righteousness/justification/acquittal (δικαίωμα *dikaiōma*, δικαίωσις *dikaiōsis*, and δικαιοσύνη *dikaiosynē*). There are no doubt fine distinctions between these terms, but there is also broad overlap and flexibility; we may assume that part of Paul's reason for choosing different words, in some cases at least, is to avoid repetition. To grasp the main thrust of the argument, it helps to see these two groups as solid blocks, from which Paul can draw the particular nuance he wants at any given point.

The substance of the paragraph is the parallel, and contrast, between Adam and the Messiah. Paul alludes more briefly to this in 1 Cor 15:21-22, and develops the theme in one direction in 15:45-49. The context of his thinking is the fairly widespread Second Temple Jewish belief not merely about Adam as the progenitor of the human race, and indeed the fountainhead of human sin (e.g., Wis 2:23-24; 2 Bar 17:3; 23:4; 48:42; 54:15 [but cf. 54:19]; 4 Ezra 3:7; 3:21; 7:118), but about Israel, or the righteous within Israel, as the new humanity, the inheritors of "all the glory of Adam." This theme is particularly prominent in the Qumran scrolls.[197] Adam, in other words, points forward to God's ultimate intention for the human race; reflection on Adam gives a particular shape to eschatological hope. In particular, as will be important in Romans 8, Adam's sovereignty over creation will be given to the true Adam at the end. This lies at the heart of Paul's view of Jesus' lordship (e.g., 1 Cor 15:27, quoting Ps 8:7), and also of the kingly rule of Jesus' people (5:17). This paragraph, then, demonstrates that, by fulfilling the covenant promises to Abraham, the creator God has addressed and dealt with the problem of Adam; a new humanity has come into being for whom sin and death have been conquered. "The age to come" has arrived in the present with the death and resurrection of the Messiah; those who belong to the Messiah already share in its benefits. That which Israel, or groups within Israel, thought to gain has been appropriately attained by the true Israelite, the Messiah, the obedient one. He now shares this status with all his people.

The balance between Adam and Christ, which is the main point of the paragraph, is not absolute. Verses 15-17 insert two notes of imbalance, where Paul insists that the act of Christ, and its results, far outweighs what was done, and lost, by Adam. Christ did not begin where Adam began: His task, which was actually Israel's task, the vocation outlined (but not acted upon) in 2:17-24 and 3:2, was to take the weight of the human catastrophe upon himself and deal with it. Nor was the result a mere restoration of where Adam was before: in Christ the human project, begun in Adam but never completed, has been brought to its intended goal. In both cases Christ has done what Israel was called to do.

What then of Israel itself? Would Israel not say that the Torah was given in order to enable it to escape the entail of Adam's sin? Paul takes a very different line. Following his earlier statements

---

195. The other three are 1 Cor 4:8 (twice), which belong with the occurrence in Rom 5:17, and 15:25, which speaks of the messianic reign of Jesus.

196. "Sin" is simply wrongdoing, whether or not the sinner is aware of it; "trespass" or "transgression" is disobedience to a known command.

197. E.g., 1QS 4.22-21; CD 3.20; 1QH 4.15 [= 17.15 in, e.g., Vermes]; 4Q171 3.1-2. See also Wright, "New Exodus, New Inheritance," 34n. 13.

in 2:25-29; 3:19-20; and 4:15*a,* he sees the Torah entering the picture with apparently disastrous consequences (5:20). God has, however, dealt with this too. Through Jesus Christ the righteousness of God, which is revealed apart from Torah, has become the means whereby grace can usher in the age to come (5:21, with an oblique echo of 3:21). The main statements of the paragraph, holding the subsidiary and explanatory additions in place, thus come in vv. 12, 18, and 21 (see the outline on p. 523).

The "obedience" of Jesus is thus the means by which God's faithfulness to the covenant has been effected. This theme, picking up the "faithfulness" of Jesus in chap. 3, awakens echoes both linguistic and theological from Isaiah 53, which were already hinted at in 4:25. As in Phil 2:6-11, Paul has drawn together his view of Jesus as the true Adam and the true Israel. Both themes are focused on Jesus' obedient death, seen as the act of grace by which the true God is revealed.[198]

This paragraph is not only the thematic statement out of which chaps. 6–8 are quarried; it provides, too, the groundwork for chaps. 9–11 and 12–16. Paul's basic thesis about Israel according to the flesh is that they, too, are "in Adam." This, worked out in agonizing detail in 7:1-25, is then thought through in 9:6–10:21: Israel recapitulates Adam's trespass (5:20; 7:7-11; 9:32; 11:11-12). But God has dealt with the sin of Adam, and has also dealt with that of Israel; there is therefore life and hope for Israel, too, not because Paul has smuggled in a renewed nationalism after all, but because he believes in the victory of grace. Israel, even "according to the flesh," remains the people of the Messiah (9:5); thus their "casting away" means "reconciliation for the world" (11:15, echoing 5:10). Key elements of the discussion thus grow from the thematic statements in chap. 5.

The great appeal of chaps. 12–16 is for unity in the church: "We, the many, are one body in Christ." This is worked out through the argument of 14:1–15:13 in particular. Here, working backward, we find the clue to the way in which 5:12-21 draws out the theme so prominent in 1:16–4:25—namely, the coming together of Jews and Gentiles in fulfillment of the promise to

Abraham. This subject, so far from being ignored between chaps. 4 and 9, should actually be seen as highlighted in 5:12-21, through Paul's repeated emphasis on "one man . . . for many/all." "Many" and "all," in the light of the whole thrust of 1:18–4:25, must clearly be seen as meaning "Jew and Gentile alike." The problem was universal; the solution is universal. Torah's entry into the picture (5:20) did not create a race apart; rather, it exacerbated the problem. The solution is the same for all: grace, working through God's covenant faithfulness, resulting in the life of the age to come, through Jesus, Israel's Messiah, the Lord of the world, appropriated by faith; God's love, responded to with answering love inspired by the Spirit. The appeal for the unity of the church in the letter's closing chapters (see especially 15:7-13) is firmly rooted in this same crucial paragraph. With this, we are ready for the details of the text.

**5:12.** Paul begins the great comparison between Adam and Christ, but breaks it off halfway through, to insert two explanations. On the face of it, v. 12 seems fairly straightforward, granted the story of Adam and Eve in Genesis 2–3 and its interpretation in the Judaism of Paul's day. Given a commandment, to break which meant death, the unhappy pair broke it and (eventually) died. Sin and death, here personified, continue as "characters" in Paul's narrative through to chap. 8. In terms of his overall argument for assurance, they are the forces that must be defeated if the Christian is to be sure of eternal life. In terms of his underlying new-exodus story, sin and death play the role of Pharaoh: Paul imagines them as alien powers, given access to God's world through the action of Adam. Once in, they had come to stay; staying, they seized royal power. Linked together as cause and effect, they now stride through their usurped domain, wreaking misery, decay, and corruption wherever they go. No one is exempt from their commanding authority.

Straightforward in some ways this may be. But it has created huge problems of interpretation for subsequent readers, not least those eager to press Paul for solutions to problems he was not addressing. In part these are historical problems, or at least problems about whether the history really matters: Did sin really enter the world through one man? Was death really a stranger in the world until the first *Homo sapiens* "worshiped and

---

198. See N. T. Wright, *The Climax of the Covenant: Christ and the Law in Pauline Theology* (Edinburgh: T. & T. Clark; Minneapolis: Fortress, 1991) chap. 4.

served the creature rather than the creator"? And—a question that has exercised theologians for most of the years since Paul wrote these words—in what sense did "all sin" when Adam sinned? These are questions more of interpretation than of of exegesis, but unless they are addressed they threaten to derail the contemporary reader before the paragraph has even properly begun. Since this passage constitutes the driving heart of the letter, it is vital to stay on the track.

Paul clearly believed that there had been a single first pair, whose male, Adam, had been given a commandment and had broken it. Paul was, we may be sure, aware of what we would call mythical or metaphorical dimensions to the story, but he would not have regarded these as throwing doubt on the existence, and primal sin, of the first historical pair. Our knowledge of early anthropology is of course sketchy, to put it mildly. Each time another very early skull is dug up the newspapers exclaim over the discovery of the first human beings; we have consigned Adam and Eve entirely to the world of mythology, but we are still looking for their replacements. What "sin" would have meant in the early dawn of the human race it is impossible to say; but the turning away from open and obedient relationship with the loving creator, and the turning instead toward that which, though beautiful and enticing, is not God, is such a many-sided phenomenon that it is not hard to envisage it at any stage of anthropoid development. The general popular belief that the early stories of Genesis were straightforwardly disproved by Charles Darwin is of course nonsense, however many times it is reinforced in contemporary myth-making. Things are just not that simple, in biblical theology or science.

One potentially helpful way of understanding the entry of death into the world through the first human sin is to see "death" here as more than simply the natural decay and corruption of all the created order. The good creation was nevertheless transient: evening and morning, the decay and new life of autumn and spring, pointed on to a future, a purpose, which Genesis implies it was the job of the human race to bring about. All that lived in God's original world would decay and perish, but "death" in that sense carried no sting. The primal pair were, however, threatened with a different sort of thing altogether: a "death" that

would result from sin, and involve expulsion from the garden (Gen 2:17). This death is a darker force, opposed to creation itself, unmaking that which was good, always threatening to drag the world back toward chaos. Thus, when humans turned away in sin from the creator as the one whose image they were called to bear, what might have been a natural sleep acquired a sense of shame and threat. The corruption of this darker "death" corresponded all too closely to, and seemed to be occasioned by, that turning away from the source of life, and that turning instead toward lifeless objects, which later generations would call idolatry.

The final clause in the verse is deeply controversial. Most interpreters take the opening phrase (ἐφ' ᾧ *eph' hō'*) to mean "inasmuch as," or simply "because"; death spread to all, "because" all sinned. The question is, does the verb refer to actual sins committed by all people (as in the "many sins" of v. 16), or to the primal act of Adam seen as the time when "all sinned"? Since the verb is aorist, as the NIV rightly sees ("because all sinned"), not perfect, as the NRSV implies ("because all have sinned"), it might seem better to take it as a reference to Adam, even while it is clear from 1:18–3:20 that Paul believes that all humans have committed actual sin. However, the fact that that earlier argument can be summed up with an aorist at 3:23 ("all sinned, and came short of God's glory") may indicate that too much weight should not be placed on the tense. What matters is that all human sin can now be lumped together into one. "All sinned."

Faced with this dilemma, some scholars emphasize the responsibility of each individual, while others, not least those anxious to maintain Paul's parallel between Adam and Christ, emphasize the primal sin as somehow involving all subsequent humanity (it is not necessary, to hold this view, to espouse along with it any particular theory of the mode by which sin is then transmitted). Others, maintaining a delicate balance between these alternatives (the former unlikely, the latter unwelcome), suggest that this is a shorthand way of saying that when humans actually sin, as they all do, they are not merely imitating the primal sin but acting from within a human nature, and indeed within a world, radically conditioned by that prior disobedience.

Fitzmyer has recently challenged the reading of *eph' hō* as "because," and proposed instead "with the result that."[199] This does not, he suggests, remove the sense of causality between Adam's sin and those of his descendants, but it allows for a "secondary causality," and so personal responsibility, between individual sins and individual death. The problem in this, it seems to me, is that it makes the last clause of the verse relate, not to its immediate predecessor ("and so death spread to all"), with which it seems naturally to belong because of the repeated "all," but to the first verb of the sentence ("sin entered the world"). Otherwise Paul would be saying that death spread to all, with the result that all sinned—the opposite of what he actually says throughout, which is that sin causes death.[200] Fitzmyer's proposal must, I think, be regarded as at best not proven. Paul's meaning must in any case be both that an entail of sinfulness has spread throughout the human race from its first beginnings and that each individual has contributed their own share to it. Paul offers no further clue as to how the first of these actually works or how the two interrelate.

**5:13-14.** Paul said "just as" in v. 12, but there is no corresponding "so." As most translations see, we must insert a dash or bracket at the end of v. 12; v. 13 breaks in to the train of thought, and not until v. 18 is it begun again and finally completed. Paul is here addressing a perceived problem, concerning the generations between Adam and Moses—that is, those who lived before the coming of the law. How did they know what was sinful and what was not? This might seem a rather abstruse problem; the patriarchal generations, after all, seem to have known that there was such a thing as good and evil, even though they did not always abide by it. But the underlying problem may well be that if Paul were to tie sin too closely to the Torah, he would not only have a theoretical difficulty with the period between Adam and Moses, but would also run into a more pressing problem about the status of Gentiles "without the Torah" (cf. 2:14).

What Paul needs to explain here is that sin did indeed spread to all people, including those who might at first sight (from a Jewish point of view in which sin meant breaking Torah) have seemed to be without sin. His explanation is simple: sin must have been there (5:13*a*) because death was there, ruling like a king (5:14*a*). He acknowledges (5:13*b*) that sin is not reckoned up, not logged in any register, in the absence of the law. (We might note that, although it would be easy to take "law" here in a more general sense than the Mosaic Torah, the context makes it quite clear that Torah is what Paul has in mind; a good lesson to learn for the reading of the following chapters.) As a result, the subjects over whom death ruled, though sinners, were not the same type of sinners as Adam had been, that is, sinners against a specific known commandment. They did not, he says, sin "in the likeness of the trespass of Adam." "Trespass" ("transgression," NRSV) means, as we saw, sinning against a commandment (NIV, "sin by breaking a command," is a paraphrase designed to bring this point out).

This is important for what it implies as well as what it denies. It denies that the generations between Adam and Moses, being lawless, were also sinless. But it also implies that those who come after Moses, and who do have Torah, do in fact imitate Adam. This will be further stated in 5:20, echoed in 6:14-15, and will become a major theme in chap. 7.

Adam, he says, is "a type of the one who was coming." This is one of only two places where Paul uses "type" in this technical sense (the other being 1 Cor 10:6; see also 1 Cor 10:11). The thought is of a die or stamp that leaves its impression in wax: Paul's meaning seems to be that Adam prefigured the Messiah in certain respects (other candidates for "the coming one" are sometimes suggested, but it is virtually certain that Paul intended to refer to Jesus), notably in this, that he founded a family that would bear his characteristics. Thus we may hear another hint of the coming argument. Sinning "according to the likeness of the trespass of Adam" is balanced by God's plan to bring Christians "to conform to the image of his son" (8:29). The middle term in this story is supplied, evocatively in this context, by 8:3: "God sent his own son in the likeness of sinful flesh."

Paul has thus clarified a problem that might

---

199. J. A. Fitzmyer, "The Consecutive Meaning of ἐφ' ᾧ in Romans 5.12," *NTS* 39/3 (1993) 321-39, and in his commentary (*Romans*, 413-17), where details of other views are set out.

200. So rightly Brendan Byrne, *Romans*, SP 6 (Collegeville, Minn.: Liturgical, 1996) 183.

have come back to haunt him. But he is still not ready to resume the train of thought begun in v. 12. Before he can set out the parallel between Adam and Christ, he needs to head off the idea that they are *merely* or *solely* parallel.

**5:15-17.** "But not 'as the trespass, so also the grace-gift.'" That is a more literal rendering of the opening line of this difficult sub-section. It is not simply, as with the NRSV and the NIV, that Paul is denying *similarity* between the gift and the trespass; he is denying that there is a *balance* between them. The gift far outweighs the trespass; Christ has not merely restored that which Adam lost, but has gone far beyond. The remainder of v. 15 explains, somewhat complicatedly, what Paul means. The many died because of the trespass of the one (Adam); but God's grace, and the grace-gift through the one (Jesus), abounded for the many. The imbalance here seems to be between the simple progression from sin to death and the astonishing reversal whereby, faced with the result of Adam's sin, God's grace has flourished in what had seemed a hopeless situation. The two sequences are, in other words, out of all proportion to each other: in the one case, sin bred death because that is what sin does; in the other, the gift of grace is nothing short of new creation, creation not merely out of nothing but out of anti-creation, out of death itself.

A second imbalance is then presented in v. 16, with one of Paul's most tortuous shorthand sentences: literally, "and not 'as through the one man sinning, the gift.'" Again, despite the NRSV, the NIV, and others, Paul is denying not merely similarity, but balance, this time in terms of the judicial result of the process and in particular of the conditions in which it took place. The key contrast he wishes to draw is between the one sin, which brought the sentence of condemnation, and the gift that, *after many trespasses,* brought the verdict "righteous."[201] In other words, God's action in the Messiah did not start where Adam's started, and, as it were, merely get things right this time. God's action in the Messiah began at the point where Adam's ended—with many sins, and many sinners. The result in each case is hardly comparable;

condemnation and acquittal may seem equal and opposite, but only from the point of view that they are the two alternative results from a trial. In terms of what they actually mean for the people concerned they are different sorts of things: the one a denial and ending of life itself, the other an affirmation, opening up new possibilities.

Paul offers in v. 17 a further explanation of the imbalance between Adam and Christ, this time in terms of the two "reigns." But it is not, as we might have expected, "death" or "sin" on the one hand, and "God" on the other. It is the—reign of death, far outweighed by the reign of—believers! Those who were pronounced dead under the haughty and usurping kingdom of death are themselves to be the rulers in God's new world. Paul describes believers in a roundabout and telling fashion: they are "those who receive the abundance of grace and of the gift of righteousness." Paul has spoken of "the many" on both sides of the equation (v. 15) and will do so again (v. 19); he will speak of "all humans," on both sides, in v. 18. Here, however, he presents a significant modification: it is those who "receive this gift" who will reign in life in God's kingdom (cf. 1 Cor 4:8). The rest of Paul's theology, not least in Romans, makes it clear that he is thinking of those who believe the gospel of Jesus the Messiah.

They will reign, he says, "in life." This refers, we assume, both to the resurrection state in which their final rule will take place and to the "life" of the age to come, over which they will exercise dominion. Paul seems to have got from apocalyptic tradition the belief that God's final rule would be exercised through God's people. When the Ancient of Days takes the throne, the sovereignty is given to "the people of the saints of the Most High" (Dan 7:27). Here, as throughout the passage, Paul is thinking in terms of the promised blessings that Israel hoped for in the age to come being achieved by the Messiah and shared with his people. (This, of course, is what makes 9:1-5 so poignant.)

**5:18-19.** Paul is ready at last to resume his argument where he broke it off at 5:12. The opening phrase (ἄρα οὖν *ara oun*) is resumptive as well as consequential: "so, then," not simply "therefore." The key sentence, however, in which Paul at last says what he has been waiting to say for five verses, possesses neither subject, verb, nor object

---

201. The term *dikaiōma,* usually "decree" or "righteous deed" here has the sense, according to BDAG, of *dikaiōsis,* "justification," "vindication," or "acquittal." Perhaps the form Paul used brings with it the sense of this verdict as an action of the judge.

in either half. Literally it reads "as through the trespass of the one unto all people unto condemnation, so also through the righteous act of the one unto all people unto acquittal of life."[202] There may be good theology behind this odd grammar: Paul is talking about an entire story over which he sees the creator God presiding. His non-use of subjects and verbs may have an air of reverence, as well as a positively Tacitean density.

The balance he is asserting, after all the imbalances of the previous verses, lies in the universality. Adam brings condemnation for all; Christ, justification for all. Our minds instantly raise the question of numerically universal salvation, but this is not in Paul's mind. His universalism is of the sort that holds to Christ as the way for all. "Condemnation" and "judgment" have been important themes in the letter since the second chapter; Paul here, as usual, refers to the final coming judgment, the time when there will be wrath for some and life for others (2:5-11). The theme remains central in the coming chapters, reaching its dramatic climax in 8:1 ("there is therefore now no condemnation for those in Christ Jesus") and 8:33-34 ("it is God who justifies; who will condemn?"). By referring to Jesus' messianic action on the cross (this, of course, is what the second half of the comparison in each verse has been about) in terms of an "act of righteousness" or "act of acquittal" (the word is δικαίωμα *dikaiōma,* as in v. 16), Paul again draws on the thought of 3:21-26 and 5:9-10. Christ's *dikaiōma* in the middle of history leads to God's *dikaiōsis* on the last day. What was accomplished on the cross will be effective at the final judgment.

As so often, Paul at once explains himself further (γάρ *gar*), and in doing so elaborates his meaning. This time, in v. 19, it is in terms of disobedience and obedience. With audible overtones of Isa 53:11, he declares that, as Adam's disobedience gave "the many" the status of being "sinners" (see the Commentary on 5:8) so Christ's obedience has given "the many" the status of being "righteous." Jesus, whisper the Isaianic echoes, is the servant of YHWH, whose obedient death has accomplished YHWH's saving purpose.

He has "established" or "set up" his people with a new status.

To be a "sinner" is, to be sure, more than a mere status. It involves committing actual sins. But it is the status that interests Paul here. Likewise, to be "righteous," as will be apparent in the next chapter, is more than simply status, but again it is the status that matters here. Justification, rooted in the cross and anticipating the verdict of the last day, gives people a new status, ahead of the performance of appropriate deeds.

What does Paul suppose the Messiah was obedient to? A long tradition within one strand of Reformation thought has supposed that Paul was here referring to Jesus' perfect obedience to the law.[203] In this view, Christ's "active obedience" and his "passive obedience" work together. His active obedience acquires "righteousness," which is then "reckoned" to those "in Christ"; his passive obedience, culminating in the cross, deals with his people's sins. Powerful though this thought is, and influential though it has been (even in liturgy, where "the merits and death of Christ" are sometimes mentioned in this double sense), it is almost certainly not what Paul has in mind here. The Isaianic servant, to whom reference is being made, was obedient to the saving purpose of YHWH, the plan marked out for Israel from the beginning but that, through Israel's disobedience, only the servant, as an individual, can now accomplish. The "obedience" of the Messiah in 5:19 therefore corresponds closely to the "faithfulness" of the Messiah in 3:22. It refers to his obedience to God's commission (as in 3:2), to the plan to bring salvation to the world, rather than his amassing a treasury of merit through Torah obedience. Obedience to the law would be beside the point; the law has a different, and much darker, function in the argument than is often supposed. That, indeed, is the subject of the next verse.

**5:20-21.** If a devout Second Temple Jew were telling the story of Adam and the Messiah—from, we may assume, a pre-messianic point of view—the Torah would be bound to play a large and positive part in the narrative. As Paul says in 2:17-20,

---

202. The words "of the one" in each case (ἑνός *henos,* a single word in Greek) could, instead, be an adjective modifying the noun, "through the one trespass" and "through the one righteous act." But this is less likely.

203. See R. N. Longenecker, "The Obedience of Christ in the Theology of the Early Church," in *Reconciliation and Hope* (L. L. Morris *Festschrift*), ed. R. Banks (Grand Rapids: Eerdmans, 1974) 142-52.

reflecting the attitude he himself would have had before his conversion, the Torah provides the form of knowledge and truth. It is the thing that, above all, enables Israel to escape the entail of Adam's sin, to be different from the pagan world around. Not so, he says here. When Torah came in, its effect—apparently its deliberate effect—was "to increase the trespass."

Each part of this sentence is tricky. The word that describes the law's entrance is παρεισέρχομαι (*pareiserchomai*, "came in alongside").[204] The result was that the trespass increased; was this also the intention, or just the unintended result? The NRSV opts for result; the NIV for purpose. Though the latter seems harder (why would God, giving the Torah, *intend* trespass to increase?) it is almost certainly correct; this half-verse anticipates the whole argument of 7:7-25, and there it is clear that both the law itself and the effect it had were somehow, mysteriously, intended by the giver.

The clue is to link "the trespass" with its previous occurrences in the passage, where the trespass is of course Adam's. The Torah, so far from delivering its possessors from the entail of Adam's sin, actually appears to exacerbate it for them. This is more or less, after all, what Paul already said in 3:19-20. To sin outside the law is still to sin; Paul has made that clear in 5:13-14; but to sin under the law—in other words, to transgress, to break a known commandment—is to make the problem worse. Think of sin as a small color transparency; the law puts a bright light behind it and a large screen in front of it. That is what Paul means by "increase the trespass." Just as in 2:17-24, which follows on from 1:18-32, Adam's sin is writ large in Israel. Paul is stating the theme that will dominate chap. 7.

At the moment, though, he is still painting the canvas with broad brush strokes, and he sweeps on: the problem of Adam's sin was magnified by the Torah, but God has done what Torah could not. Grace has superabounded where sin abounded—that is, in Israel itself, where the full effects of Torah's magnification of Adam's sin were felt. The superabundance of grace in Israel is presumably a further reference to the messianic work, and particularly the messianic death, in which Jesus offered to Israel's God the faithful obedience that Israel had not. In Christ, God has come to where the Torah has magnified sin, and has dealt with it. This points ahead to 8:3-4.

All this leads to the full and climactic statement of the Adam-Christ balance in v. 21. When we stand back and look at the two kingdoms, they are those of sin on the one hand and grace on the other; and if "grace" is a periphrastic (or indirect) personification for "God," we may suppose that "sin" is an indirect way of saying "Satan." Paul is once again summarizing the whole train of thought of 1:18–5:11, and doing so in a way that will launch the next phase of the letter's argument: the reign of sin is matched, and outmatched, by the reign of grace, and sin's entail of death is beaten by the entail of life that follows from grace, working through "righteousness" (not "justification," as in the NRSV). Give these words their full Pauline value, and the sequence of thought becomes clear, despite the fact that the verse is packed with technical terms. Grace (the sovereign, loving purpose of God) is ruling through covenant faithfulness (God's accomplishment in Christ of that which had been promised to Abraham), and the result is the ushering in of the age to come, "eternal life," or, better, the life of the coming age.[205] And all has happened, of course, "through Jesus the Messiah, our Lord." The outstretched arms of the crucified one, embodying the love of the creator God, provide the ultimate balance of the paragraph, the place where the kingdom of sin did its worst and the kingdom of grace its triumphant best.

---

204. Paul uses it in Gal 2:4 of false brethren secretly sneaking in; though the word need not have a negative connotation, it certainly could carry one. The NIV "was added" seems to reflect Gal 3:19, which is after all similar in topic.

205. The phrase "eternal life," the natural one for translators to choose, is nevertheless potentially misleading if it conveys the idea of an endless disembodied bliss, rather than the far more this-worldly meaning of "the life of the age to come," which sits better with the eschatological vision of, e.g., Rom 8:18-27.

# REFLECTIONS

**1.** The overwhelming impression left by these verses is the superabundance of grace. However much theologians and preachers know this with their heads, and can explain it as a theory, it remains strange and surprising that it should actually be true, that it should be the central characteristic of the world in which we—even theologians and preachers!—are called to live. Surrounded as we are day by day with so many signs and symbols of sin and death, and living in a culture that has reinvented a secularized version of the doctrine of Original Sin under the guise of the hermeneutic of suspicion (see below), all our instincts tell us that life is hard, cruel and unfair. If there are signs of life and hope, they tend to be those we make for ourselves. Our culture thus oscillates between despair and self-salvation.

Into this world the news of grace, of the undeserved gift of abundant life, bursts again and again, in the message of Jesus, offering a radical alternative, an entirely different way of construing reality, a new way of conceiving our whole experience of the world and indeed of God. At every point where the seeds of wickedness have been planted, bearing deadly fruits of all kinds, there the grace of God has been planted alongside, a vibrant plant that will take over the soil and produce a life-giving harvest. Of course, it takes faith to believe this and act on it; precisely the faith that believes that God raised Jesus from the dead, and that therefore his cross was indeed "the free gift following many trespasses," "the one man's obedience." But once the world has been glimpsed in this light, everything is different, not least Christian mission and the prayer that accompanies it.

**2.** At the center of the picture, and always worth further exploration and meditation, is the achievement of Jesus himself. Though the word "cross" is not mentioned, and though Jesus' own death is not spoken of explicitly, we should not miss the fact that in this passage we have one of Paul's fullest statements of what in shorthand we call atonement theology. People often try to glean a full theology of the cross from 3:21-26, where Paul is writing about several things at once and drawing on a dense statement of the meaning of Jesus' death in order to do so. We would do better to see that passage, together with the further statements of 4:25 and 5:6-10, as leading the eye up to the present argument, which is admittedly still terse and clipped. This is the high mountain ridge from which we look back to the earlier statements, and on to subsequent ones (6:3-11; 7:4; 8:3-4, 31-39).

Central to Paul's understanding of the cross, therefore, is the belief that it is the free gift of God to a wicked and corrupt world. This point, stressed again and again in these verses, was and is offensive to those who want to make their own unaided way through life, or who suppose that nothing much is wrong with the world or the human race, or indeed themselves. Free grace is obviously correlated, here more than anywhere else, with a radical view of human wickedness and the threat posed by death. For those who want to remain independent, being ruled by grace appears almost as much of a threat as being ruled by sin and death. But this is, of course, absurd. Grace is undeserved love in powerful action; and love seeks the well-being, the flourishing, of the beloved, not their extinction or diminution. To look love in the face and see only a threat is the self-imposed nemesis of the hermeneutic of suspicion.

But this free gift is offered through the obedience, the faithfulness, of Jesus himself. Here, as in Phil 2:6-8, Paul sees the voluntary death of Jesus as the messianic act *par excellence,* the triumphant accomplishment of that covenant plan for which Israel was called in the first place, the completion of the purpose for which God called Abraham. Not for Paul the currently fashionable idea that Jesus had not intended to die but that the church—Paul himself included!—used theological hindsight to impose upon that death a meaning Jesus himself had never envisaged. Paul's allusions in this passage to the fourth servant song, highlighting his own reference to Jesus' obedience, tell the story of one who knowingly went to the place where Israel's sin and shame, and the world's sin and shame, were heaped up together, and took the full weight on himself. How this could be, theologically speaking, is hinted at in 5:20, and will be explored further in the explosive 8:3-4.

**3.** Paul's personification of sin and death, and his highlighting of these forces as the deepest problem of humans and of the world, will win him few friends among those for whom sin is merely an outdated neurosis and death an unfortunate problem that the medical profession has not yet solved. One might have thought that the twentieth century, which elevated sin to a technological level previously unimagined, and meted out violent death to more people, more efficiently, than ever before, would have been only too glad to embrace Paul's analysis of the problem, and eager to rediscover his solution. But, as so often, the patient is fearful of hearing the true diagnosis, not least because the treatment may be humiliating. Fancy having to admit, thinks the late modern Western skeptic, that one had been wrong all along, that those boring and out-of-touch Christians had had the answers! No: we will die as we have lived, in ironic agnosticism, worshiping Heisenberg's Uncertainty Principle, maintaining consistency (even in our inconsistency!) rather than embracing salvation.

Part of the problem, of course, is that traditional Christianity has frequently operated with a truncated view of sin, limiting it to personal, and particularly sexual, immorality. These things matter enormously, of course, but there are other dimensions, of which the last century has seen so many examples, which are often untouched by traditional preaching. Equally, those preachers who have focused attention on structural evil within our world, on systematic and politically enshrined injustice, have often left the home base of Pauline theology in order to do so, not realising that there were resources there from which to launch not only critique but also promise and hope. This passage invites us to explore a reintegrated view of sin and death, rebellion and consequent dehumanization, as the major problem of humankind, and thereby to offer diagnoses of our world's ills that go to the roots of the problem and prepare the way for the cure.

**4.** As a culture, the Western world of the late twentieth century has seen the growth, and the application on a wide scale, of the hermeneutic of suspicion. Every text, every artefact, every piece of popular culture, is interrogated: whose perspective does it represent? Who is it oppressing? Who is implicitly marginalized by it? This process, fueled by the great liberationist movements, not least that of women and (in the United States) of African Americans, has pinpointed many evils, and awakened consciences to many real abuses. But left to itself it functions as the secular shadow of that kind of sub-Christian teaching where the doctrine of original sin was well known but that of free grace was somehow forgotten. It produces, in other words, a gloomy, guilty mind-set, where people feel ashamed of being what they inalienably are, and apologize for innocent actions. When we meet this in an individual, we advise them to see a psychiatrist. Someone who is always apologizing, always overeager to confess their sins, needs pastoral help. But we are well on the way to creating the social or corporate equivalent; that is perhaps what neo-moralism was bound to do. It also produces, as a reflex, a "victim culture" in which those who are, or feel, "oppressed" or "marginalized" become blameless, and any criticism of them is categorized as further oppression.

This naive new morality, a crude attempt at re-erecting ethical frameworks in the wake of the perceived failure of secularism's amorality, would do well to rediscover the Pauline doctrine of which it is the parody. A true analysis of sin, structural and personal, should lead to a true discovery of grace, again both structural and personal. Applying the Pauline doctrine of grace to the larger questions faced in our culture would mean rediscovering, beyond proper and necessary suspicion, that there is such a thing as trust, and that healthy societies, as well as individuals, thrive on it.

# ROMANS 6:1-23, BAPTISM AND FREEDOM

## OVERVIEW

The question Paul now faces is, Where do Christians live on the map of 5:12-21?

This is not quite the same question as theologians and commentators have been eager to discover at this point, namely: granted justification by grace through faith, what is the place of ethics, and of moral effort, in the Christian life? This latter question is, in fact, contained within the former, but we must not, in our eagerness for relevance, ignore Paul's actual argument. The question of 6:1, and even that of 6:15, is not, despite frequent assertions, exactly the same as that which Paul cites, and scornfully dismisses, in 3:8 ("Let us do evil that good may come"). Verse 1 is primarily about *status,* not behavior, as is apparent from the argument about status that follows in 6:2-11 (behavior is included as well, and is highlighted in 6:12-14, but it is not the primary focus). And 6:15, while clearly about behavior, introduces an important argument about the two kinds of "slavery": Paul is still concerned to get his hearers thinking about where they are within the framework of chap. 5, as is evident from the way in which the conclusion (6:23) directly echoes 5:21.

Paul's question is this: Do Christians find themselves now in the Adam solidarity or in the Christ solidarity? Do they still live under the reign of sin and death, or do they live under the reign of grace and righteousness? Since God's grace reaches down to the kingdom of sin to rescue those who are there, must Christians regard themselves as still being in that dark sphere in order that grace may do its proper work? And must they then live in the manner appropriate to that old kingdom?

To this question there can be only one answer, but the manner in which Paul gives it is revealing. Christians, he says, have left the old solidarity, and belong to the new; they must behave accordingly. The transfer is effected by dying and rising with the Messiah. And the event in which this dying and rising is accomplished is baptism.

This comes as a shock to many a good Protestant reader, accustomed to regard baptism simply as an outward expression of a believer's faith, and anxious about any suggestion that the act itself, or indeed any outward act, might actually change the way things are in the spiritual realm. (This anxiety has at least as much to do with the legacy of the Enlightenment, of Romanticism, and of Existentialism, as with the theology of the sixteenth century, let alone of the first; but that is too remote a topic for now.) The words "sacramentalism," "ritualism," and even "magical," spring naturally to mind, and are not dispelled by those writers, like Albert Schweitzer, who have been eager to assert the significance, in Paul, of physical baptism as the key event in which sinners are brought into the kingdom.[206] It is in this context that the older debates, as to whether Paul was here dependent on, or at least alluding to, the mystery religions and their initiatory practices, comes into play; the massive scholarship that has been brought to bear on this issue has now returned a negative verdict.[207] At the opposite extreme, some have suggested that Paul is not here primarily referring to the actual event of water baptism, but only using the language as a metaphor for Christian beginnings, conversion and initiation, in general.[208] As most commentators have agreed, this is unlikely. First-century Christian beginnings included water-baptism; the discussion in vv. 4-5 seems to allude to the physical rite; Paul's readers would naturally understand the passage in a literal sense. We are back with the question: what did Paul mean by baptism, and why does he suddenly introduce it here?

The most obvious explanation, and one that fills the present chapter with fresh meaning both in itself and in its relation to its surrounding context, is that Paul understood baptism in terms of the new exodus. Paul had already made this link,

206. Albert Schweitzer, *The Mysticism of Paul the Apostle* (New York: Seabury, 1968).

207. See above all A. J. M. Wedderburn, *Baptism and Resurrection: Studies in Pauline Theology Against Its Graeco-Roman Background,* WUNT (Tübingen: Mohr, 1987). James D. G. Dunn, *Romans 1–8,* WBC 38A (Dallas: Word, 1988) 309-11, offers a helpful summary of the debate.

208. Dunn, *Romans 1–8,* 311-12, 327-29, referring to his own earlier work, though careful now to stress that this does not exclude a reference to the physical act.

strikingly, in 1 Cor 10:2, speaking of the wilderness generation ("our fathers"), being "baptized into Moses in the cloud and in the sea." There he brings out the parallel between their "sacramental" experience and that of Christians, the new-exodus people, and stresses the ethical obligations that lie upon Christians as a result. As we saw in introducing chaps. 5–8, the long argument that is launched by 5:12-21 includes, toward its climax, a passage (8:12-27) in which Christians are characterized as the new wilderness generation, on their way home to the promised land, accompanied by the presence of God through the Spirit. The roots of this full statement are found here in chap. 6.

From a historical point of view this meaning is not just comprehensible, but compelling. The baptism of John is best explained as a new-exodus movement, along with other similar movements that gathered people in the wilderness and looked for signs of salvation. There is every reason to suppose both that Jesus himself saw John's baptism as the starting-point for his own work, not just chronologically but thematically, and that the earliest church likewise looked back not just to Jesus but to Jesus as the leader of the movement that had begun with John's baptism.[209] Christianity was a new-exodus movement from the beginning; baptism in the earliest church, we must assume, retained this character and overtone. Moreover, the death of Jesus at Passover time, and the meal he shared with his followers on the night he was betrayed, so interwove the theme of new exodus with the fact of Jesus' death that the two became inextricable. "The redemption" had occurred, not now when Moses led the children of Israel out of Egypt, but when Jesus died as Israel's Messiah and rose again. The movement that had begun symbolically with John at the Jordan came of age at Easter. And already Jesus himself, whose mission and vocation seem to have been given focus and direction in his own baptism by John, had used baptism as a metaphor for his own coming ordeal (Mark 10:38; Luke 12:50). We may suppose that the earliest Christian assumption about baptism was that it was *both* a dramatic symbol of the new exodus *and* a sign of Jesus' death.

This is further confirmed both by the parallel between the present sequence of thought and Col 1:13-14, and by the sense this reading makes of the rest of chap. 6. God, says Paul in Colossians,[210] "has delivered us from the power of darkness and transferred us into the kingdom of his beloved son, in whom we have redemption, the forgiveness of sins." This, as has often been pointed out, is exodus language.[211] Similarly, in our present passage, 5:21 sets up the two kingdoms, and chap. 6 argues that Christians have been liberated from the first to belong to the second. A main theme of the rest of the passage is that of the rescue of the slaves: Verse 6 speaks of no longer being enslaved to sin, v. 9 of death no longer being one's master, vv. 12-14 of sin no longer reigning over one. The whole discussion of vv. 16-23 hinges on the notion of slavery recently abandoned and freedom newly found. It simply will not do to say, concerning an argument written by a first-century Jew who has expounded the promises to Abraham two chapters before and will herald the entry into the promised land two chapters later, that this is merely a slave-market illustration taken from the Hellenistic world. It cries out to be interpreted in terms of the exodus. And when we find that the key event through which slavery is abandoned and freedom is gained consists of passing through the water, re-enacting the death of Jesus, which was already interpreted in terms of Passover imagery, the case can be closed. Exodus is not a distant echo here. It is a main theme.

We may reckon, then, that when Paul says "do you not know" in v. 3, introducing his statement about baptism and Jesus' death, this is not a rhetorical trick but a genuine assumption. Baptism would not have been seen as a miscellaneous cleansing rite, or a generalized sign of initiation, but as that which brought people into the historical narrative of the new exodus. The master-narrative had been enacted when Israel's history was focused on the Messiah and his death and resurrection. The life-stories of individual people, Jews and Greeks alike, needed then to be brought within this larger narrative by the appropriate

---

209. See N. T. Wright, *Jesus and the Victory of God,* vol. 2 of *Christian Origins and the Question of God* (London: SPCK, 1996) chap. 5.

210. I assume Colossians to be by Paul; if not, it is certainly by someone close to Paul's own mind.

211. See N. T. Wright, *The Climax of the Covenant: Christ and the Law in Pauline Theology* (Edinburgh: T. & T. Clark; Minneapolis: Fortress, 1991) 109; J. D. G. Dunn, *The Epistles to the Colossians and to Philemon,* NIGTC (Grand Rapids: Eerdmans, 1996) 80-81.

symbolic means. Just as faith in the God who raised Jesus was common for all, Jew and Gentile alike, so baptism in the name of Jesus had to be undergone by all. It constituted the new people as the single new-exodus people of the one God (cf. Gal 3:26-29). Since what was at stake was the renewal of the people of God, and indeed of the whole creation (8:18-30), the event that brought together the individual life-story and the larger story of God, Israel and Jesus would itself be tangible and physical. That event, clearly, was baptism.

The community into which the baptized person came was the family, the people, of the Messiah. I have argued in detail elsewhere that Paul's incorporative language about Jesus hinges on his understanding of messiahship; the Messiah represents his people, so that what is true of him becomes true of them. The present chapter, indeed, is one of the classic passages on this theme (others include Galatians 3). Paul, it seems, could use the word Χριστός (*Christos*) not only to refer specifically to Jesus himself as Messiah, but to the whole company of the messianic people.[212] That is why, whereas he regularly says "*through* Jesus Christ," referring to that which God has done by the agency of the human being Jesus of Nazareth, who is the Messiah and Lord, he regularly says "*in* Christ Jesus." This is not a mere stylistic variant, but a key indication that he is using the words with a sense of precision. If by *Christos* he means, along with a reference to Jesus himself, "the messianic people; the people who belong to the story of the new exodus," his language in the present chapter becomes clear. People join this family through baptism; that is, they are baptized *into Christ* (v. 3). That which is true of the Messiah is therefore now true of them; that is, what happened to him happens to them *with him,* as in the famous string of words beginning with σύν (*syn,* "with," vv. 4-8). Their status and condition now, therefore, is that they are *in Christ* (v. 11), so that his having died to sin and being alive to God is true of them also. This is the logic of incorporative Messiahship, and hence of baptism.

One of the great gains of this approach to Romans 6 is that we can move away once and for all from seeing chaps. 6–8, or even 5–8, as expressing a different kind of theology, or even a

212. Ibid., chaps. 2–3, 8.

different train of thought, from chaps. 1–4. As we noted in the introduction, the promises made by God to Abraham in Genesis 15 envisaged the exodus. Paul, expounding those promises in Romans 4, sees them fulfilled in the creation of a Jew-plus-Gentile family through the death and resurrection of Jesus, and envisages them looking forward to the time when Abraham's family will inherit the world (4:13). What more appropriate way of describing the manner of that family's coming together than through the event that evokes the exodus? More particularly, the keynote of chaps. 1–4 is "God's righteousness," which is alluded to in 5:21 as the means through which grace has come to reign through Jesus Christ. Now, in chap. 6, "righteousness" becomes a periphrastic (or indirect) way of referring to God (vv. 13, 16, 18, 19, 20; the periphrasis gives way to literal statement in v. 22). God's covenant faithfulness is the overarching characteristic of the sphere into which the Christian comes through baptism.

Nor is there any conflict between "baptism" as a physical act (a "ritual," in the loaded sense that is still sometimes used) and "faith" as an interior event—or between either of these and the flooding of the heart by the Spirit of which Paul speaks in 5:5. As a first-century Jew, Paul was happily innocent of the dualistic either/or that keeps such things apart in some contemporary Christian thinking. He was well aware of the problems that arose when baptized persons, regularly attending the eucharist, gave the lie to these symbols by the way they were living; he addresses this problem in 1 Corinthians. Yet he never draws back from his strong view of either baptism or the eucharist, never lapses back into treating them as secondary. Indeed, in the present passage one might actually say that he is urging faith on the basis of baptism: since you have been baptized, he writes, work out that what is true of Christ is true of you (v. 11). The point here is not to set out a systematic *ordo salutis* in which different things happen to the Christian, outwardly and inwardly, in a particular sequence, but to expound that which is true of the baptized and believing Christian in such a way as to make it clear that one's basic status now is with Christ rather than with Adam, in the kingdom of grace rather than with the kingdom of sin and death.

Into this sequence of thought, as with 5:20 within 5:12-21, comes the law (6:14-15). It looks at first like an odd *non sequitur,* since the law has not been mentioned in the chapter until this point: sin shall not have dominion over you, Paul says (v. 14), because you are "not under law but under grace." Place the whole discussion in the context of the end of chap. 5, however, and the problem disappears. The law has come in to the Adam/Christ dialectic on the side of Adam. If baptism brings you out of the Adam-sphere, it also brings you out of the law-sphere. Paul is arguing on a knife-edge here, since his exodus theme might have suggested that the freed slaves now needed, as at Sinai, to embrace the Torah as their way of life. He will address that question in the next chapter. For the moment he is content to

explore more thoroughly the inner meaning of slavery and freedom in relation to the human condition in general (vv. 15-23). Only when this is done will he at last turn his full attention to the question: what then do we say about the law?

Chapter 6 falls naturally into two main sections, introduced by the questions of v. 1 and v. 15. Verses 12-14 form a small paragraph that applies, and rams home, the lesson of vv. 1-11, as well as preparing the way for the second half of the chapter. The NIV's breaking of the first half of the chapter—vv. 1-4, 5-7, 8-10, 11-14—is idiosyncratic and ignores the way in which Paul builds carefully up to v. 11.

# Romans 6:1-11, Dying and Rising with the Messiah

## NIV

6 What shall we say, then? Shall we go on sinning so that grace may increase? [2]By no means! We died to sin; how can we live in it any longer? [3]Or don't you know that all of us who were baptized into Christ Jesus were baptized into his death? [4]We were therefore buried with him through baptism into death in order that, just as Christ was raised from the dead through the glory of the Father, we too may live a new life.

[5]If we have been united with him like this in his death, we will certainly also be united with him in his resurrection. [6]For we know that our old self was crucified with him so that the body of sin might be done away with,[a] that we should no longer be slaves to sin— [7]because anyone who has died has been freed from sin.

[8]Now if we died with Christ, we believe that we will also live with him. [9]For we know that since Christ was raised from the dead, he cannot die again; death no longer has mastery over him. [10]The death he died, he died to sin once for all; but the life he lives, he lives to God.

[11]In the same way, count yourselves dead to sin but alive to God in Christ Jesus.

[a] 6 Or *be rendered powerless*

## NRSV

6 What then are we to say? Should we continue in sin in order that grace may abound? [2]By no means! How can we who died to sin go on living in it? [3]Do you not know that all of us who have been baptized into Christ Jesus were baptized into his death? [4]Therefore we have been buried with him by baptism into death, so that, just as Christ was raised from the dead by the glory of the Father, so we too might walk in newness of life.

[5]For if we have been united with him in a death like his, we will certainly be united with him in a resurrection like his. [6]We know that our old self was crucified with him so that the body of sin might be destroyed, and we might no longer be enslaved to sin. [7]For whoever has died is freed from sin. [8]But if we have died with Christ, we believe that we will also live with him. [9]We know that Christ, being raised from the dead, will never die again; death no longer has dominion over him. [10]The death he died, he died to sin, once for all; but the life he lives, he lives to God. [11]So you also must consider yourselves dead to sin and alive to God in Christ Jesus.

# COMMENTARY

**6:1-2.** As so often, the tight-packed introduction contains all that is to come. The regular rhetorical opening, familiar from earlier in the letter (e.g., 3:1; 4:1), enquires what conclusion might be drawn from what has just been said, and suggests a possibility that is then firmly rebutted. The apparent logic of the question comes from 5:20-21, where Paul spoke of sin "abounding" and grace "superabounding." The question is primarily about status, with behavior included but not the sole or main topic; the NIV's "shall we go on sinning" has jumped the gun somewhat, looking ahead to vv. 12-14 rather than to the primary answer found in vv. 3-11. The NRSV's "shall we continue in sin" sounds to a contemporary ear as though it means much the same thing as the NIV, but the Greek has the definite emphasis of remaining in a place, in a status. Of course, to "remain in sin," in English and for that matter in Greek, will mean to go on committing sin, but Paul is interested here in where one *is* first and foremost; it is like saying "shall we remain in France," with the assumption that if one does one will continue to speak French. At the end of chap. 5, "sin" was a dark ruling power, not primarily a style of conduct. In those terms, Paul's whole argument is that one has been moved out of one country into another; and that *therefore* (v. 12) it is no longer appropriate to go on speaking the same language. If the logic of the question were to be upheld, one should regard oneself as forever in the kingdom of sin and death, since that is where God's grace has reached to in Christ. This is not a question Paul expected the Roman church to raise—the device is here rhetorical—but that it had been raised many times in his regular preaching and teaching there is no reason to doubt.

The question is clearly wrongheaded. With the familiar μὴ γένοιτο (*mē genoito,* "let it not be so!"), Paul states his basic answer: We are those who died to sin, so how can we live in it any longer? Without the rest of the paragraph it might be difficult to see exactly what he meant by this, so we may proceed at once to his fuller explanation, noting only that his statement about "we" is slightly stronger than the translations make out. "We are the kind of people who . . . " would be

better: "we are people whose main characteristic is precisely that we have died to sin."

**6:3.** Without the wider context it is not immediately clear, when Paul says "do you not know" (cf. 7:1), whether this is actually a new piece of information, imparted with a transparent rhetorical flourish, or something he genuinely expects his audience to be aware of. It has been argued earlier that in this instance he assumes they will know this meaning of baptism, at least in its basic form: those who are baptized into the Messiah, Jesus, are baptized into his death. Jesus himself had spoken of his death as a "baptism"; and that meaning is held in place by the larger new-exodus meaning of baptism from the time of John onward, seen through the early community's awareness of Jesus' death as linked to, and interpreted by means of, the events of Passover. We have no reason to suppose that baptism was ever a merely arbitrary entry rite, with a purpose (to mark out those who belonged) but without any meaning of its own. Like many other things in early Christianity, we have little access to early thinking on this topic, and we are heavily dependent on Paul, as our earliest source, for help. Though his fertile theological mind no doubt developed and expanded the earliest understandings more than a little, we should not question that at this point he is reflecting something that was widely known and believed in the early church.

The key word is of course "into": baptism is *into* the Messiah, and hence *into* his death. Like King David in the scriptures, the Messiah could be thought of as one "in whom" those who belonged to him were summed up. "We have ten shares in the king," said the men of Israel, "and in David also we have more than you" (2 Sam 19:43). When rebellion is sounded, it is precisely this solidarity that will be broken: "We have no portion in David, no share in the son of Jesse!" (2 Sam 20:1; 1 Kgs 12:16). What matters for Paul is the opposite movement, coming "into" the king, the Messiah; and that is effected in baptism. The point is that if the Messiah is Jesus of Nazareth, the crucified and risen one, then belonging to the messianic people means being characterized by cross and resurrection, by dying and rising. This is at the heart of that dense (and deeply personal) passage Gal 2:15-21, which contains many parallels to the present argument.

**6:4-5.** What then does it mean to be "baptized into the Messiah's death"? Paul now explains this further, and draws the preliminary conclusion to back up his original statement of v. 2. Baptism involves being "co-buried" with the Messiah; Paul employs a rare word (only here and Col 2:12 in the NT), the first in a string of *syn-* compounds, to bring out the significance that what happened to the Messiah must be regarded as having happened to those who are "in him" by baptism. The prefix *syn-* means "with," and the verb here means "co-buried"—that is, "were buried with." Those who are "in" the Messiah died with him, were buried with him. It is possible, indeed likely, that the symbolism of baptism, with the candidate being plunged under the water, naturally suggested burial to Paul; unless we assume that this is his meaning, it is not clear why he should highlight Jesus' burial rather than simply his death. That seems to be the explanation, too, for "the likeness of his death" in v. 5 (see below). But, if this visible parallel was in his mind, it was as an offshoot of a connection already established between Jesus' death and baptism, rather than its original cause.

This opens the way for the main theme of the rest of the paragraph. The Messiah's resurrection means that those who are "in the Messiah" now stand, and must walk, on resurrection ground. Some have disputed whether Paul here speaks of Christians already being raised with Christ, or whether that is an idea belonging only to Colossians and Ephesians within the larger Pauline corpus; but there should be no doubt. The whole point of the argument is that Christians no longer belong in the world of death; Paul does not here suppose that one should wait until the final bodily resurrection (8:11) before beginning to "walk in newness of life," and this "walk" is based on a present status, not merely anticipating the future reality.[213] The argument of these verses is not simply that one has died to sin and hence must not live in it anymore, but that one is already "alive to God in Christ Jesus" (v. 11) and must now live accordingly. We must allow the past tense of "glorified" in 8:30 to have its full weight (see the Commentary on 8:18-30).

This is the second point at which the programmatic statement of 1:3-4 starts to come into its own (the first being 4:24-5). From here on it will become a dominant note. The resurrection of the Messiah from among the dead is the reason why his death had any salvific meaning at all.[214] Here, and throughout chaps. 6–8, it is the ground for the hope not only of Christians but of the whole created order. Neither here nor in Colossians and Ephesians does Paul offer either an unrealized or a completely realized eschatology: the baptized are in one sense already raised, and must behave accordingly, while in another sense they are still to be raised in the future. Paul emphasizes the parts of this complex truth he needs in different contexts, and we should not play his various statements off against one another. As all theologians know, it is impossible to say everything one believes in every sentence one writes, and there are always some readers who insist on imagining that what one has left out on this occasion one does not believe.

Paul adds, apparently unnecessarily in terms of his ongoing argument, that Jesus was raised "through the glory of the Father." This is to be linked with 4:24; there, too, as in 8:11, it is the Father by whose agency Jesus was raised. Why, then, does Paul speak of God's "glory" as the agent in this event? In the light of 4:20, and further off 1:21, it appears that to recognize "the glory of God" at work in the resurrection of Jesus is part of the attitude of faith in which sin and corruption are replaced with obedience and life (see the Commentary on 4:20; see also John 11:40). The point at issue here, though, is that those who have been buried with the Messiah must reckon that, as he has been raised, they too are called to "walk" with a new quality of life. "Walk" as a metaphor for human conduct is rabbinic (הלכה *halākāh*, "walking," hence "conduct"; from הלך *hālak*, "walk"); this is the conduct that will follow from

213. So Joseph A. Fitzmyer, *Romans*, AB 33 (Garden City, N.Y.: Doubleday, 1993) 435. For the debate, see the judicious remarks of Douglas J. Moo, *The Epistle to the Romans*, NICNT (Grand Rapids: Eerdmans, 1996) 371n. 97.

214. Lit., "out from among the dead ones"; it is basic, and already formulaic, in early Christianity that, against mainstream Jewish expectation, Jesus was raised alone while the rest of the dead stayed dead. This is related, of course, to 1:4, where nevertheless Jesus' resurrection was seen as the beginning of "the resurrection of the dead."

the status, but it is the status that Paul is emphasizing. A further clue may be found here as to why Paul ascribes Jesus' resurrection to the agency of God's glory: the "glorification" that is God's gift to all the justified consists not merely in their final resurrection (cf. 8:11, 17, and 29-30), but in that which anticipates the resurrection in the present, namely, the practice of holiness of which Paul speaks both here and in 8:12-17 (see also Col 3:1-4, where exactly the same connections are made).

He offers a further explanation in v. 5, which literally reads: "for if we have been united with him in the likeness of his death, we shall also be of his resurrection." For the full English sense we must supply, as the translations do, a repetition of the first verb: "we shall also be [united with him in the likeness] of his resurrection." The word for "been united" comes from a root which means "grown together," and this, together with the word "likeness" (ὁμοίωμα homoiōma), has occasioned much debate on Paul's precise nuance. The NRSV simply says "united in a death like his," which is not quite as strong as Paul's Greek; the NIV omits the idea of "likeness" altogether. It seems to me preferable to suppose that Paul is continuing to regard baptism as in some way a re-enactment of Jesus' death, a making real for the individual of the once-for-all event of Calvary (compare again Gal 2:19-20). This would explain the unusual phrase "grown together": in baptism, the existence of the Christian is, as it were, intertwined with that of the Messiah, like two young trees whose trunks grow around one another.

The main point, however, is in the second half of the verse. Granted the identity with the Messiah's death, however we fine-tune our statement of it; the result is that the baptized will share the likeness of his resurrection also. It is just possible that Paul may have in mind the early Christian practice, reflected elsewhere in the NT, of the newly baptized being clothed in white, symbolizing their commitment to holiness of life (e.g., Col 3:12-15). This, again, would make baptism a visible prefiguring of the point at issue. But we do not have to suppose this to make sense of the verse, which looks at three results simultaneously: the ultimate future, in which the Christian is assured of resurrection (cf. 8:11); the present status, where the Christian stands on resurrection ground; and the present behavior, which must

reflect present status and anticipate the future ontological reality (see Col 3:1-4). We must, therefore, take the second half of v. 5 as indicating present status and behavior, not simply the future resurrection.[215]

**6:6-7.** Paul explains further, arriving as he does so at the central statement of the paragraph. "Knowing this"—again, one may question whether Paul expected his hearers to know this already—that "our old person was co-crucified" (another *syn-* compound, paralleled in Gal 2:19). To understand Paul's meaning we must go back again to 5:12-21. The "old self" (ὁ παλαιὸς ἡμῶν ἄνθρωπος *ho palaios hēmōn anthrōpos*), which used to be translated "our old man," denotes, not some particular part of the human person, but rather the whole person, the entire self, *seen as someone "in Adam."* Call this "the old Adam," perhaps, but that phrase, too, has too many associations with an older pietism in which this "old Adam" still lingered on somewhere in the background, causing trouble from time to time; and Paul's point is precisely that in baptism the old Adamic solidarity is decisively broken. The "old self," whole and entire, is put to death once and for all. This does not mean that the Christian cannot sin; but Paul's sharp point should be felt before caveats and nuances are allowed to dull it. In baptism the whole person leaves the Adam-world for good, leaves it by death, a final one-way journey.

The purpose of this—the divine purpose, one must assume Paul means—is "so that the body of sin might be abolished" (the NIV's "rendered powerless" is a possible meaning of the Greek, but Paul's intention seems to be to insist that this "body of sin" should be destroyed, not simply left to one side without power), "so that we should no longer be under the lordship of sin." We are still within the world of 5:21, the world of the two realms, sin and grace. Paul underlines the location of Christians on that map, emphasizing which of the two countries they now live in and (more to the point) which of the two overlords now rightfully claim their allegiance. "The body of sin" could have meant the whole human being, seen as the entity that "sin" has made its own. ("Body," as often in Paul, means not "physical body," but

---

215. The verb ("we shall be") is thus a logical future, following the "if" at the start of the verse. See Fitzmyer, *Romans,* 435, against, e.g., Dunn, *Romans 1–8,* 318. See the Commentary on 6:8.

something more like our word "person," including the physical aspect but also hinting at the "personality" that goes with it.) This would make good sense, were it not for the fact that it would then approximate very closely to the meaning of "the old self," and since the abolition of "the body of sin" is the result of the crucifixion of "the old self" they cannot be identical. It is probably better to take "body" in the wider sense of "solidarity": "the old self was crucified with Christ, so that the solidarity of sin might be broken, and we should no longer be enslaved to sin." As in 5:21, the sovereign rule of sin has been decisively challenged by grace, the grace operative in Jesus' obedient death and resurrection. When that grace enfolds the baptismal candidate, entwining the Jesus-story and the Jesus-reality with theirs, the communal solidarity that sin has created, generating the sense and the fact of helplessness as humans go along with all that sin suggests, is broken, and they are free to live under a different lordship.

Paul explains yet further with a cryptic aside (v. 7): the one who has died is freed from sin. That, at least, is what he clearly means; but the verb he uses, puzzlingly to us, is δεδικαίωται (dedikaiōtai, "has been justified"). Many commentators conclude that Paul is here invoking a well-known rabbinic principle about death paying all debts. I agree with Cranfield that this is unlikely, since Paul nowhere suggests that physical death settles all accounts in God's sight. Verse 7 is not, then, a general principle invoked to explain the more specific point of v. 6, but a comment about the one who has been co-crucified with Christ; such a one has been "justified from"—that is, cleared from—their sin.[216] Once more, we may compare Gal 2:19-20: "I through the law died to the law." Why, then, "justified," rather than "freed"? The answer must be that, unlike most of his recent readers, Paul is able to keep the law-court metaphor still running in his mind even while expounding baptism and the Christian's solidarity in Christ. The Christian's freedom from sin comes through God's judicial decision. And this judicial decision is embodied in baptism.

**6:8.** Having reached the heart of his analysis in v. 6, Paul now builds toward the conclusion in

v. 11. As usual, a terse preliminary statement (v. 8) is then filled out (vv. 9-10), before the conclusion is drawn (v. 11). The preliminary statement is this: "If we co-died with the Messiah, we believe that we shall also co-live with him" (συζάω syzaō "co-live" is another συν- [syn-] compound). This "shall," like the future in v. 5, is best taken as the logical future after "if." It obviously has a future referent as well in the eventual resurrection life, but it cannot support the conclusion of v. 11 unless it refers to the present time.

**6:9-10.** "We know" (this time we can be sure that Paul's hearers did know this, at least in principle) "that the Messiah, raised from the dead, will never die again." Jesus' resurrection was not a mere resuscitation, like those of Jairus's daughter, the widow's son at Nain, or Lazarus (Mark 5:21-34 and par.; Luke 7:11-17; John 11:1-44). It is basic to all early Christian thinking on the resurrection (Paul is, of course, our chief witness, but what he says tallies well with the strange stories in the Gospels) that what happened at Easter involved the *transformation,* not merely the revival or resuscitation, of Jesus' body, so that it entered upon a new mode of physical existence, which Paul saw as the beginning and sign of the renewal of all creation (see particularly 1 Cor 15:50-57; Phil 3:20-21). The transforming of Christians' bodies at their resurrection is modeled, in Paul's thought, on the transformation of Jesus' body at his. Transformation, new creation, had already happened within God's world, and would in the end happen on a grand scale. Paul once again insists that what happened to the Messiah happened also to those "in him." He cannot emphasize strongly enough that the rule of sin and death has been decisively broken, and that Christians are no longer subject to it. "Death has no longer any sovereignty over him"; Paul is still working out the implications of 5:21, and urging his readers to do so too.

The balanced explanation of v. 10 has rhetorical force that should not be overpressed for theological precision. The Messiah did not die "to sin" in the same sense that he now lives "to God." Paul's meaning is that the Messiah came under the rule, the sovereignty, of sin and death; not that he himself sinned, but that he came, as Paul says in 8:3, "in the likeness of sinful flesh." "To die to sin" meant, for the Messiah, that he died under its

---

216. C. E. B. Cranfield, *A Critical and Exegetical Commentary on the Epistle to the Romans,* ICC, 2 vols. (Edinburgh: T. & T. Clark, 1979) 310-11.

weight, but that in doing so he came out from its domain. And this happened ἐφάπαξ (*ephapax*), once and for all. There is no room here for the idea that the Messiah, or more especially his people, still live with a foot in both camps, or with one foot in the grave and the other by the empty tomb. Jesus, the Messiah, died once and once only, and was thereafter finished with death. If Paul had wanted to say (as some cautious interpreters, aware of the danger of a shallow perfectionism, have wanted him to say) that Christians have not completely "died to sin," that the old Adam still lingers on in some way, he has chosen an extremely misleading way of saying it.[217]

"In that he lives, he lives to God"; in other words, the life Jesus now lives he lives in God's domain, the realm of grace and righteousness. Paul has told Jesus' story in terms of the two spheres of existence in 5:12-21—which is somewhat ironic, since there he himself represented the second of the spheres—in order that, through the identity of the Messiah and his people that is now established, he might demonstrate the true status of those "in Christ."

**6:11.** The key word here is "reckon," the same root as in 4:3 and elsewhere, and with the same bookkeeping metaphor in mind. Do the sum, he says; add it up and see what it comes to. The Messiah has died, once for all, and been raised; you are, by baptism, in the Messiah; therefore, you, too, have died, once for all, and been raised. The "reckoning" in question is to take place in the believing thought-processes of the Christian. The NRSV's "consider" is fine, provided it is taken in a strong sense and not allowed to become more vague ("reflect on this"); the NIV's "count yourselves" is an attempt to keep the bookkeeping metaphor alive. The point is not, as in some

schemes of piety, that the "reckoning" *achieves* the result of dying to sin and coming alive to God, any more than someone adding up a column of figures creates the result out of nothing; it opens the eyes of mind and heart to *recognize* what is in fact true. It is here that one might almost say that Paul appeals for faith on the basis of baptism. Those who have received the sign of the new exodus in the Messiah are urged to think through, and to believe, what has in fact happened to them.

The point is this: on the map of 5:21, the Christian belongs in the second half, the kingdom of grace and righteousness, not in the first half, the kingdom of sin and death. Paul is well aware that sin remains powerful and attractive for the most well-trained Christian, and that physical death awaits all except those for whom the Lord's return comes first (see 1 Cor 9:26-7; 15:51-52). He is speaking of a different level of reality. If someone challenged him and said that sin and death were just as powerful to them as they had been before their coming to faith, he would reply that they had not yet considered the seriousness of their baptism; just as if someone claimed that, now they had been baptized, evil had no attraction whatever for them, he would no doubt reply that they had not yet considered the seriousness of sin. From his whole corpus of writings, we know that Paul was a realist, about himself, about his fellow Christians, about suffering, pain, depression, fear and death itself. These were not enemies he took lightly. But his entire argument in this chapter so far, which anticipates that of 8:31-39, is that the Christian, facing these enemies, stands already on resurrection ground. This is ultimately a truth about the Christian's Lord, the Messiah, but because of baptism it becomes a truth about the Christian himself or herself. "Reckon yourselves," calculate yourselves, count yourselves, "dead to sin and alive to God in the Messiah, Jesus." This is the full answer to the question of v. 1.

---

217. To insist on this was one of the achievements of D. Martyn Lloyd-Jones in his remarkable series of published sermons on Romans. See Lloyd-Jones, *Romans: An Exposition of Chapter 6: The New Man* (London: Banner of Truth, 1972).

# Romans 6:12-14, The End of Sin's Reign

NIV

¹²Therefore do not let sin reign in your mortal body so that you obey its evil desires. ¹³Do not offer the parts of your body to sin, as instruments of wickedness, but rather offer yourselves to God, as those who have been brought from death to life; and offer the parts of your body to him as instruments of righteousness. ¹⁴For sin shall not be your master, because you are not under law, but under grace.

NRSV

12Therefore, do not let sin exercise dominion in your mortal bodies, to make you obey their passions. ¹³No longer present your members to sin as instruments[a] of wickedness, but present yourselves to God as those who have been brought from death to life, and present your members to God as instruments[a] of righteousness. ¹⁴For sin will have no dominion over you, since you are not under law but under grace.

[a] Or weapons

# COMMENTARY

The three verses that follow are a genuine bridge from one half of the chapter to the other. They follow, obviously, as imperatives that bring the indicative of vv. 2-11 into practical reality; but they also set the terms for the discussion of slavery and freedom that is to come. They, like the rest of the chapter, still belong within, and explore, the world of 5:12-21, and vv. 20-21 in particular.

**6:12.** If the reign of sin has been broken in Christ, and if the Christian truly lives in Christ, then sin has no business continuing to rule his or her life. And it is now the Christian's responsibility to make sure that this is so. If it is asked, as well it might be, what chance sin has got to rule, if the Christian has died to it, Paul's implicit answer here has to do with the sphere over which sin, though no longer enthroned, can exercise powerful attraction: the "mortal body." The Christian still possesses a body—that is, a whole person—which will die and, indeed, in terms of ethics, must be "put to death" (8:13), since it still has desires that must not be obeyed. This "mortal body" is not far from what Paul means by "the flesh," which will be discussed in due course; it is one of his ways of indicating the continuing ambiguity of the life of the Christian, an ambiguity that in no way takes back the trenchant and definite statements made in vv. 2-11. The idea of "obedience," which, of course, belongs with the idea of being ruled by a sovereign, looks back to 5:21 and on to vv. 16-17; that of the bodily desires (ἐπιθυμίαι *epithymiai*) to 7:7-8.

**6:13.** The same appeal is now put positively, in terms of "presenting" or "offering" oneself obediently to a master—a theme that will recur frequently in the next few verses. The verb translated "present" can have sacrificial overtones, as indeed in the similar context in 12:1, but here it seems more general. The choice is stark, though Paul does not express it as an exact balance. Do not, he says, present your *members* to sin, but present your *selves* to God. Still on the map of 5:21, Paul is working within the logic of 6:1-11: it is now technically impossible for the Christian to present his own or her own *self* to sin, since the self has died with Christ and been raised "in order to live to God." What is possible—all too possible, alas—is for the Christian to present his or her *members,* the varied parts of personality, mind, or body (what some have misleadingly termed the "old Adam"), to sin.

Paul's argument here is that this is illogical. To present one's members to sin is to be out of tune with the reality of what a baptized Christian is, one who has been brought from death to life (drawing on v. 11). In spelling out the two possible courses of action, he sets the terms for the discussion of slavery that begins with v. 16: instead of sin/death and grace/righteousness, as in 5:21, it is now sin/unrighteousness and God/righteousness. Paul will now, for a few verses, actually use "righteousness" as a metonym for the whole God-side of the picture, and hence even as a metaphor for

God. He will add other terms as well, without changing the basic antithesis. For the moment he allows the argument of vv. 2-11 to issue in a clear appeal, reinforced with a promise in the next verse.

**6:14.** Sin, he says, will not have dominion over you.[218] The reason is clear; you have transferred your abode, your status. You no longer live within the sin/death solidarity, but within the grace/righteousness/life solidarity. Sin, therefore, as a power, a force to be reckoned with, may still be at large in the world, but it has no authority over the Christian. This may seem counterintuitive, but it is precisely for this reason that Romans 6 is a call to that characteristically Pauline combination of faith and clear thinking. For the moment he undergirds the claim about being quit of sin's dominion by the initially unexpected explanation: "for you are not under law but under grace."

If he had said "for you are not under sin and death but under grace and righteousness," we might have been less surprised. But clearly Paul is working toward a different point, parallel in some ways with the question of 6:1, which is now to be addressed in the second half of the chapter. Like a composer suddenly modulating into a new symphonic development, Paul turns the argument in a subtly different direction, toward the role of the law. This itself belongs within the passage

(5:20-21) that has been the basis for chap. 6 so far. The terms are set in 5:20: The law came in alongside, so that the trespass might abound, but where sin abounded, grace superabounded. Paul has restated the antithesis of 6:1-13 in terms not of 5:21 but of 5:20, in order both to ward off possible misunderstandings that might arise and to prepare for his treatment of the law in chap. 7.

The idea of being "not under the law," which occurs already in Gal 3:23 and 5:18, belongs closely with Paul's previous negative statements about Torah. God's righteousness is revealed "apart from the law" (3:21); justification is by faith "apart from works of the law" (3:28); it was "not through the law" that the promise came to Abraham and his seed that he would inherit the world (4:13), because "the law works wrath" (4:15). Romans 5:20 has hardly explained this negative point, though it has sharpened it up; the law stands on the Adam-side of the equation. It is sometimes said that Galatians has a negative view of the law, and Romans a positive one. This is a very inadequate way of describing the problem, as the evidence already demonstrates. In the present context Paul's point is plain: those who belong to Christ, who have died and been raised in baptism, do not live in the Adam solidarity, *and hence do not live under the law.* This is exactly what we find in Gal 2:19: "I through the law died to the law, that I might live to God." The implication is striking. When we set the theological explanation of 6:14*b* alongside 6:14*a,* Paul is saying that, if one did live under the law, sin *would* indeed have dominion. That will take all of chap. 7 to explain.

---

218. The word "have dominion" is not, despite the NRSV, the same as in v. 12. Here it is from κυριεύω (*kyrieuō,* "exercise lordship"; in v. 12 it is from βασιλεύω *basileuō,* "exercise kingship"). The difference is slight; cf. the NIV's "reign" (v. 12) and "be master" (v. 14).

## Romans 6:15-23, Slavery and Freedom

NIV

[15]What then? Shall we sin because we are not under law but under grace? By no means! [16]Don't you know that when you offer yourselves to someone to obey him as slaves, you are slaves to the one whom you obey—whether you are slaves to sin, which leads to death, or to obedience, which leads to righteousness? [17]But thanks be to God that, though you used to be slaves to sin, you wholeheartedly obeyed the form of teaching to

NRSV

15What then? Should we sin because we are not under law but under grace? By no means! [16]Do you not know that if you present yourselves to anyone as obedient slaves, you are slaves of the one whom you obey, either of sin, which leads to death, or of obedience, which leads to righteousness? [17]But thanks be to God that you, having once been slaves of sin, have become obedient from the heart to the form of teaching to which

## NIV

which you were entrusted. [18]You have been set free from sin and have become slaves to righteousness.

[19]I put this in human terms because you are weak in your natural selves. Just as you used to offer the parts of your body in slavery to impurity and to ever-increasing wickedness, so now offer them in slavery to righteousness leading to holiness. [20]When you were slaves to sin, you were free from the control of righteousness. [21]What benefit did you reap at that time from the things you are now ashamed of? Those things result in death! [22]But now that you have been set free from sin and have become slaves to God, the benefit you reap leads to holiness, and the result is eternal life. [23]For the wages of sin is death, but the gift of God is eternal life in[a] Christ Jesus our Lord.

[a] 23 Or through

## NRSV

you were entrusted, [18]and that you, having been set free from sin, have become slaves of righteousness. [19]I am speaking in human terms because of your natural limitations.[a] For just as you once presented your members as slaves to impurity and to greater and greater iniquity, so now present your members as slaves to righteousness for sanctification.

[20]When you were slaves of sin, you were free in regard to righteousness. [21]So what advantage did you then get from the things of which you now are ashamed? The end of those things is death. [22]But now that you have been freed from sin and enslaved to God, the advantage you get is sanctification. The end is eternal life. [23]For the wages of sin is death, but the free gift of God is eternal life in Christ Jesus our Lord.

[a] Gk the weakness of your flesh

# COMMENTARY

**6:15.** Having examined the possible drastic consequences of embracing 5:21 the wrong way, Paul now turns to the possible drastic consequences of embracing 5:21 in the light of 5:20: supposing one is no longer under law, does that mean one is now a sinner? This question, like that of 6:1, is not confined to committing actual acts of sin. As the parallel in Gal 2:17 demonstrates, part of the point is that to come out from the sphere of Torah, for a Jew, meant that one was joining the "sinners," the ἁμαρτωλοί (*hamartōloi*), the lesser breeds without the law. "Shall we then be 'sinners?' "

As Paul's answer indicates, however, this time the emphasis is far more on actual behavior and far less on status, important though that remains. Once again the terms of his argument are the two spheres in which humans can belong, and the thrust is on the appropriateness of certain types of behavior for those in the God/grace/righteousness sphere.

**6:16.** As usual, he sets up the categories in an introductory sentence. "Do you not know"—this time he is invoking a general, fairly obvious, principle of human life, not a piece of Christian teaching—"that you are slaves of the one to whom you give yourselves in obedience?" The choice is between two obediences; but in Paul's eagerness to state this he allows "obedience" to do duty both for the activity itself and for the one to whom it is offered: "whether to sin [which leads to death] or to obedience [which leads to righteousness]." The "obedience" to which one offers obedience is, of course, a periphrasis (or circumlocution); behind it stands the obedience of Christ in 5:19, enabling the word and concept to function as another synecdoche for the entire grace/righteousness sphere. This explains, though it hardly excuses, the unclarity. Paul's point is that all human existence takes place in slavery, to one slavemaster or the other; his problem is that he wants to say as well that serving God in Christ is true freedom. That is why he apologizes for the language in v. 19. The two slaveries are not equal and opposite; the difference between the slavemasters produces a totally different sort of life for those who obey them.

**6:17-19a.** Paul places his readers within the diagram of the two slaveries, casting the sentence into the form of a prayer of thanksgiving (cf. 7:25; 1 Cor 15:57, and elsewhere). They were in the Adam solidarity; now they are in the Christ solidarity (again, the transition is definite, and cannot be watered down). He makes the point twice, from different angles. First, they were slaves of sin, but now have become obedient to Christian teaching; second, they were set free from sin, and have become enslaved to righteousness. It is the latter point, with all its latent absurdity in terms of "slavery" to the very thing that sets one most truly free, that draws from him the comment "I am speaking in human terms, because of the weakness of your flesh" (v. 19a); in other words, I am using a very basic illustration, to bring the point down to a level that anyone can understand.

The first of the contrasts, that in v. 17, has surprised many readers. Why does Paul not simply say "you have become obedient to grace," or indeed "to righteousness"? Why has he developed the second half of the sentence in this unexpected way: "you have become obedient from the heart to the pattern of teaching to which you were committed"?

Commentators went through a phase, two generations ago, of questioning whether this whole clause might be a later addition to Paul's text.[219] This had more to do with wanting Paul to conform to a particular theological framework than with a serious attempt to read Romans. The "pattern of teaching" to which he is referring may well be a basic Christian confession. This could even be the baptismal confession itself, since the affirmation that Jesus is Lord, and that God raised him from the dead (cf. 10:9), is so clearly germane to what he is saying at this very point. Indeed, had he said "you were slaves of sin, but now you are under the lordship of the Messiah," no one would have questioned the verse. Dunn's suggestion, that by "the pattern of teaching" Paul is referring to Jesus Christ himself, nearly amounts to the same thing, but the phraseology of the verse points more to a particular teaching, such as we find in baptismal contexts in other letters (e.g., Col 3:1-17), than to the person of Jesus himself. What is more, instead of speaking of the teaching being given to them, he says that they were "handed over" to the teaching; something about the passivity of baptism may be reflected here, as the candidate submits to the dying and rising of the Messiah and acknowledges his lordship. This would then fit with the fresh meaning proposed by Gagnon on the basis of parallels in Hellenistic Judaism: "the imprint stamped by teaching, to which (imprint) you were handed over."[220]

The point, anyway, is that having been slaves of sin Christians have now been transformed, so that they have become obedient to this new pattern "from the heart." Though this precise phrase is unique in Paul, it fits well with his emphasis on the heart in, e.g., 2:29; 5:5; 10:8-9. This is usually connected closely to the new covenant work of the Spirit, transforming the heart from the dark condition described in 1:21 to the renewal and illumination described in 2 Cor 3:2-3; 4:5 (the NIV's "wholeheartedly" is slightly misleading; Paul's emphasis is not on how much of the heart is put into obedience, but on the fact that it comes from the heart as opposed to being mere outward conformity; cf. 2:25-29). This is the point Paul will pick up in 7:6.

The result can be stated simply though paradoxically (v. 18): liberated from sin, you were enslaved to righteousness. "Righteousness" here is not so much "virtue" or moral goodness, but rather (as Paul will eventually make clear) a periphrasis for "God"; it is the divine righteousness, revealed in the death and resurrection of the Messiah (3:21-6), the righteousness through which grace has operated (5:21). It would in any case be odd, in view of the whole chapter, to think of Christians being enslaved to "virtue," a quality they are to exhibit and even possess, rather than in some sense to God. Since Paul's basic point throughout is the exodus motif of the freeing of the slaves, he is well aware that suggesting an alternative slavery is in principle odd, and is only introduced to make the point of the alternative allegiance more sharply; he uses this human illustration, he says, (literally) "because of the weakness of your flesh." Whereas elsewhere such a phrase might refer to moral disability, it here simply denotes potential slowness of understanding. How Paul knew they would possess this "weakness of the flesh," and how he imagined this remark would not be provocative, we can only guess.

219. Bultmann led the way on this. See the discussions in the commentaries, and esp. R. A. J. Gagnon, "Heart of Wax and a Teaching That Stamps: ΤΥΠΟΣ ΔΙΔΑΧΗΣ (Rom 6:17b) Once More," *JBL* 112 (1993) 667-87, at 671-73.

220. Ibid., 687. Gagnon agrees that his analysis says nothing one way or the other about a possible set pattern of early Christian teaching; I think the two ideas fit together rather well.

**6:19b.** By way of explaining vv. 17-18 (γάρ *gar*, omitted by the NIV), Paul restates the command of v. 13, with minor variations. It is not clear how much a command can actually explain something, but it requires little elaboration to see how Paul's logic works. He is explaining the balance of the two "slaveries," and hence further unpacking the paradox of being "liberated" into a different "slavery": *just as* you once presented your members as slaves to uncleanness, *so now* present your members as slaves to righteousness. "Uncleanness" was part of the problem in 1:24, and is now one of the things at which the Christian must look back, as the Israelites looked back at the fleshpots of Egypt. Paul expands the category of the former slavery: "and to lawlessness unto lawlessness," perhaps meaning "from one degree of lawlessness to another." This word, in this context, has nothing to do with the theological category of being "not under the law"; it merely refers to wild and uncontrolled behavior.

The challenge comes in the balance of "so now" with "as then." The energy and initiative that were put into uncleanness and lawlessness must now be put into the "slavery" to righteousness, which leads to "sanctification."

Here for the first time we meet the word that for so long was regarded as stating the topic of this entire section (chaps. 5–8). It is clearly important, but not that important. Its primary meaning, in any case, is focused not so much on ethical qualities as on that which is necessary for a person to approach the presence of God; this has clear and demanding behavioral consequences, but the main emphasis takes us back to v. 11: "alive to God." (The NIV's "holiness" is therefore slightly misleading—unless one takes that term, too, in its strict sense, referring not just to behavior but to access into God's presence.) "Slaves to righteousness unto sanctification" is thus God-oriented all through. Christians owe allegiance to the God whose covenant faithfulness rescued them in Christ; the result of this allegiance is that they become fit, through the obedience that wells up from the heart, for the presence of this same God. Paul is here unpacking further what was said so densely in 5:1-2.

**6:20-22.** By way of yet further explanation, he introduces a new element, which simultaneously brings the chapter back to its starting point at 5:21

(grace reigning through righteousness to eternal life) and points forward into the new topic of chap. 7 (the "fruit" borne by the two ways of life; cf. 7:4-5; this link is obscured by the NRSV's translation of the same word here as "advantage" and the NIV's "benefit"). What, he asks, was the result of the previous slavery? It carried a certain "freedom": free from God and God's righteousness. But the old slavery was a plant that bore a particular fruit, and the fruit was shame, leading to death. The new slavery, however, which Paul at last describes explicitly as slavery "to God," produces the fruit of sanctification, which leads to the life of the age to come. We are back on familiar territory.

There is a problem about the punctuation of v. 21: Does the phrase "in regard to the things of which you are now ashamed" go with "what fruit did you have" or with "their goal is death"? The NRSV and the NIV take the former route. The NEB and the REB follow the Nestle-Aland Greek text in the latter, which is probably to be preferred because of the γάρ (*gar*), significantly untranslated in the NRSV and the NIV, at the end of the last clause ("things that now make you ashamed, *for* their end is death," REB). The thought is the mirror of that in 5:5a: hope does not make us ashamed, because it truly leads to life; sin produces shame, because it leads to death. Here "shame" is not simply associated with the feelings of disgrace or humiliation that belong to the deeds of sin themselves, but with the fact that conduct of that type leads to the human disintegration of death (cf. 1:32). The contrast is with the new slavery, slavery to God, which brings Christians into "sanctification," qualifying them for access to God's presence, and so for the life of the age to come.

**6:23.** We are, then, back with 5:21, having thoroughly explored the territory it opens up. The two paths of humankind are characterized by sin and death on the one hand, and by God and life on the other. But, as in 5:15-17, they are not balanced exactly. Sin pays wages in proportion to what has been done. God gives generously, beyond all imagining, and the measure of that gift is the death and resurrection of Jesus the Messiah: "the gift of God is eternal life in the Messiah, Jesus our Lord."

In particular, chap. 6 has explored the meaning of 5:12-21 in terms of the human renewal that results from the "new exodus" of baptism. Paul's main concern has not been, at this stage, to offer a detailed agenda for ethical action, though the general commands in chap. 6 are easily strong enough to sustain such a thing. His concern has been to emphasize that when Christians look at the Adam/Christ contrast they should be in no doubt that they belong on the "Christ" side of it. This must, of course, be put into effect by the moral effort of not letting sin reign in the "mortal body"; but this ongoing struggle is not to be thought of in terms of the Christian being some kind of a hybrid, half in Adam and half in Christ. The theology of baptism, both in terms of the "new exodus" and in terms of the dying and rising of the Messiah, prohibits such a thing. That which has happened has happened once and for all.

Paul has thus prepared the way for one of his greatest and most complex arguments. Add the Torah to this Adam/Christ contrast, and what do you get? As 5:20a indicated, an increase in "the trespass" (7:7-25). What is God's response? As 5:20b-21 stated, the gift of superabundant grace, doing that which the Torah could not (8:1-11). What is the result? The renewal of the covenant, the prophetically promised replacement of the "old letter" by the "new Spirit," resulting in nothing less than resurrection and the renewal of all creation (8:12-30). At the heart of it all stands the sending, the death and the resurrection of the Messiah, God's son, to take on himself the weight of Adamic and Torah-driven trespass, and then to welcome into new life those who through suffering and prayer are led by the Spirit toward the promised inheritance. This is where we see at last what "the obedience of the Messiah," the theological driving heart of 5:12-21, really meant.

# REFLECTIONS

**1.** Romans was not written to provide "a theology of the Christian life," but Paul's larger argument demands that at certain points he write more or less exactly that, and chapter 6 is one of the two clearest examples (the other being chapter 12). Among the principal things it insists on is that being a Christian means living from within a particular story. It is the subversive story of God and the world, focused on Israel and thence on the Messiah, and reaching its climax in the Messiah's death and resurrection. No Christian can ever tell this story too frequently, or know it too well, because it is the story that has shaped him or her in baptism and that must continue to shape thought, life, and prayer thereafter. Otherwise one will be living a lie, allowing sin to continue exercising a sovereignty to which it has no more right.

The exodus story, which stands behind so much of this chapter, remains decisive. Many parts of the Christian church, fortunately, have retained it in their liturgy, particularly at Easter and the renewal of baptismal vows, reflecting an instinct sometimes superior to that of the church's exegetes. The story of coming out of slavery into freedom—with all the new puzzles and responsibilities that freedom brings!—is the story of the gospel, the narrative within which Jesus deliberately framed his own final moments with his followers, the story on which he himself drew to give meaning to his death. And, just as the Jewish people discovered in the exodus story the character of their rescuing God, so the covenant faithfulness of this same God has been fully unveiled in the paschal events of Golgotha and Easter. Learning about the Christian life and learning about the God revealed in Jesus Christ are two sides of the same coin.

**2.** It is a measure of how deeply this narrative has been woven into the consciousness of Western culture that a great many movements, national, political, social and cultural—including some that have been opposed to each other!—have told their own stories as liberation narratives. This reflects more than simply the influence of the Magna Carta on the subsequent British world and its derivatives; it is the sign of a culture stamped with the word "freedom" at a deeper level than that. The cry for freedom is one we instinctively recognize and want to respond to. At this point the exodus story offers itself as the true story of the human race, and the Christian retelling of this story in terms of the death and resurrection of Jesus Christ must do so as well. This story, if true, cannot simply be one "little story" among others, as though it could take its place happily on the cultural smorgasbord, offering a certain kind of "religious experience," alongside other stories that effectively enslaved humans and led them off to die. Even the postmodern critique that insists that all large metanarratives are instruments of slavery appeals to, and gets its power from, one story that, it assumes, is not: and that story is precisely its own version, filtered through many layers of cultural accretions, of the exodus narrative, the freeing of the slaves from Pharaoh's yoke. The Christian gospel is, at this level, telling the story that all humans know in their bones they want to hear.

**3.** It is true that in appealing to this story all kinds of things have been said and done that in some way or other distort it, or even threaten to destroy it outright. The magicians of Egypt are also adept at producing miracles to validate their position. At the level of international politics, the word "liberation" has often simply meant that a particular country has been taken over by a different form of virtual political enslavement. At both a personal and a global level, the financial loan that announces it will set you free to do all sorts of undreamed-of things will then enslave you until you have paid it back. In terms of personal morality, the freedom of one person to expand their business empire may well be at the cost of the freedom of their neighbor to remain in business; and the freedom of people to express their sexual potential regularly results both in the diminution of the freedom of others (to put it no more strongly for the moment) and also in their own enslavement to destructive and dehumanizing habits of mind and body. Telling the story of freedom is, by itself, not enough. As Paul seems to have recognized in the second half of chap. 6, freedom from the slavery of sin involves a new kind of "liberated slavery," obedience to the God who loves us and seeks our true freedom, our true humanness. Thus we have discovered, in the political sphere, that freedom from oppressive external regimes is not enough for a struggling country, in Africa or in the Balkans; with freedom come new responsibilities, to oneself and to one's neighbors, and without these one may be worse off than in the original slavery itself.

**4.** This chapter shines a bright spotlight on the dangerous half-truth, currently fashionable, that "God accepts us as we are." Indeed, the question of 6:1 could be read as raising exactly this question: Will "God's acceptance" do as a complete grounding of Christian ethics? Emphatically not. Grace reaches where humans are, and accepts them as they are, because anything less would result in nobody's being saved. Justification is by grace alone, through faith alone. But grace is always *transformative*. God accepts us where we are, but God does not intend to leave us where we are. That would be precisely to "continue in sin, that grace might abound." Unless we are simply to write Romans 6 out of the canon, the radical inclusivity of the gospel must be matched by the radical exclusivity of Christian holiness. There is such a thing as continuing to let sin reign in one's mortal body, and it will require serious moral effort to combat this tendency. The idea that Christian holiness is to be attained by every person simply doing what comes naturally would actually be funny were it not so prevalent. True freedom is not simply the random, directionless life, but the genuine humanness that reflects the image of God. This is found under the lordship of Christ. And this lordship makes demands that are as testing and difficult as they are actually liberating.

**5.** The pattern, the motive and the moral power to live in true freedom (in other words, in "slavery" to God) are found in that weaving of our life story together with the death and resurrection of the Messiah that happens in baptism. We are all too aware that thousands, perhaps millions, of the baptized seem to have abandoned the practice of Christian faith and life; but we are nevertheless called to allow the dying and rising of Christ in which we have shared to have its force and way in our own lives. If Jesus and his dying and rising are simply a great example, we remain without hope; who seriously thinks that they can live up to that ideal in their own strength? But if the fact of the messianic events has become part of our own story through the event of baptism, and the prayer and faith that accompany it, and above all the gift of the Holy Spirit of which Paul will shortly say more—then we will indeed be able to make our own the victory of grace, to present our members, and our whole selves, as instruments of God's ongoing purposes.

# ROMANS 7:1–8:11, THE LIFE THE LAW COULD NOT GIVE

## OVERVIEW

The main theme on the surface of Romans 7—and of the first paragraph of Romans 8, which belongs closely with it—is the Jewish Law, the Torah. This conclusion is unwelcome to some, not least because it appears to make the passage irrelevant for those who have never lived "under" the Torah. But Paul is here telling the story of Israel under one particular guise; this is the story that climaxes with the story of Jesus (8:3-4), and the way in which it does so is vital for understanding the basis of Christianity.

Paul is still, in fact, unpacking the last sentences of 5:12-21, and at this point 5:20 in particular: "the law came in alongside, so that the trespass might be filled out; but where sin abounded, grace superabounded." The whole passage is held within the rubric of 5:21: "sin reigned through death, but grace reigns through righteousness to eternal life through Jesus Christ our Lord." The antithesis between the two states, which has already been explored in chap. 6 from the standpoint of baptism and the release of the slaves, is repeated or alluded to several times in the present passage: 7:5-6 serves as an introductory statement; 8:5-10 offers further development, leading toward the conclusion, with echoes of 5:21 still prominent, in 8:10-11. This is where Paul shows, more fully than before, how it is that grace, i.e., God (8:3, 11, "the one who raised the Messiah from the dead") reigns through righteousness (8:10) to eternal life, i.e., resurrection life (8:10-11), through Jesus the Messiah, God's son (8:3-4, 9-11). Here, too, we see a further explication of the programmatic statement of 1:3-4: God's gospel concerns the Son of God, David's descendant "according to the flesh" (cf. 8:3), marked out as Son of God in power by the resurrection (8:10-11). What we have here, in other words, is part of the inner meaning of Paul's gospel, and one of the central passages in the whole letter. The theology of this passage is not to be played off against "justification by faith," either theologically or in terms of its background in the history of religions. It is

part of the continuous, unbroken argument of the whole letter.

In particular, this passage stands at the heart of the great section, chaps. 5–8. If the two very different paragraphs of chap. 5 form a foundation, and chap. 6 an initial platform built on that foundation, 7:1–8:11 must be seen as the main part of the building. It is not the whole; there is a further floor to go on top (8:12-30), and the view from there will be magnificent (8:31-39); but the passage now before us forms the working heart of the section—and, as we shall see, a vital part of Paul's groundwork, also, for the argument of chaps. 9–11.

Romans 7 is not, then, a mere aside, as has sometimes been thought. True, Paul here does finally address the question that has been buzzing like an angry wasp around the edge of the argument so far: what exactly is being said about the law? Ever since 2:17-29; 3:19-21, 27-31; and 4:15 this has been a pressing matter; 5:13-14 and 5:20 sharpened it up, and 6:14-15 merely increased the tension. But it would be wrong to say, as many do, that Paul is therefore simply paying off an old debt, explaining something he should really have explained before. It is just as likely that the hints and suggestions he has already dropped are to be seen as anticipations of the argument he knew he was going to have to make, fragments of a main symphonic theme stated in advance.

What Paul is here doing, as the parallel between 7:5-6 and 2 Cor 3:1-6 should make clear, is setting out *how God has renewed the covenant in Christ and by the Spirit.* "What the Torah could not do, God has done" (8:3). The whole section is, at one level, a vindication of Torah against the imputation that it was identified with sin, or that it was responsible for death. But this vindication, which is also a vindication of the God who gave Torah in the first place, serves the larger purpose, which has been in view since at least 2:17-29, of showing how the *continuity* of God's purposes, clearly seen in 3:21–4:25 and 5:12-21, includes within its purview the *discontinuity* between the dispensation of Torah and the dispensation of the Spirit. Second Corinthians 3, in fact, functions as an oblique but important commentary on this theme, as, of course, does Galatians.[221] Covenant renewal involves, of course, covenant affirmation: to renew something is to affirm it, not to abolish it. Yet renewal also implies the transcending of the old; when, as in this case, the old involves sin and death, renewal is needed to produce righteousness and life (5:21). The logic of 5:20-21 is then worked out as follows: the renewal of the covenant (7:1–8:11) results in the renewal of creation, and of God's people with it (8:12-30).

The passage is therefore an integral part of Paul's argument for assurance. His overarching theme in chaps. 5–8 is that God glorified those whom God justified. What stands in the way of this glorification? Sin and death, of course; but also Torah. "Condemnation," in other words—eschatological condemnation, the final sentence of judgment—still appears to hang over those who have come, by faith, into the Christ-family, the worldwide Abraham-family. It is all very well to demonstrate from Genesis 15 that those who believe the gospel are declared to be God's "righteous" people. But must they not face the final judgment of which 2:1-16 spoke so powerfully? Is there not still a κατάκριμα (*katakrima*), a condemnation, awaiting them on the basis of their present behavior? Romans 7:1–8:11 is designed to show, by way of reply, that "there is therefore now no condemnation for those who are in Christ Jesus" (8:1; for the way in which this verse functions as the "conclusion" of the argument, even though coming at the start of a long final paragraph, see the Commentary on 8:1-11). Paul's analysis of Torah, and now of Christ and the Spirit, shows that the condemnation that might have been supposed to be still future has been dealt with. Those who are in Christ, who are indwelt by the Spirit, can face the future with confidence.

At the same time, as chap. 11 makes clear, Paul is anxious that those who have come out from under Torah, in some sense, should not turn and despise that God-given dispensation. With an increasing number of commentators, I assume that

Paul's audience, though predominantly Gentile, had mostly been either God-fearers or maybe even proselytes before their conversion to the Messiah, Jesus. That is, they had in some sense been "under the law," even though not, for the most part, Jews by birth. To be sure, the significance of Paul's argument in this dense and dramatic passage cannot be confined to its "relevance" to one sub-group of one church at one moment of history. If this is truly how the covenant was renewed, it is of abiding importance for all Christians at all times. If Torah, rightly understood as God's law, poses a threat to God's people, rather than a promise, the threat must be shown to have been dealt with. But, precisely because of the increasingly complex situation in the young church at large, Paul must provide, simultaneously with the argument that one is "not under the law" (precisely because he is not dealing with the Galatians, who were all too eager for the law, but with the Romans, who may have been all too eager to get rid of it!), a *vindication* of Torah against the slurs that it might all too easily incur; 7:1–8:11 accomplishes all these tasks.

The other major theme of chaps. 5–8, which here also reaches its center, is that of the new exodus. 7:7-12 contains several echoes of the story of the children of Israel at Mount Sinai. But that is just one telltale symptom of what is going on. If chap. 6 speaks of the coming through the water by which the slaves are freed, and chap. 8 speaks of the wilderness wanderings, led by the strange presence of God, through which God's people journey toward their promised "inheritance," what we should expect in between is an account of the covenant formed between God and the people, the covenant that in the biblical story took place on Sinai, with the giving of Torah on the one hand and the presence of YHWH, dwelling with Israel in the tabernacle, on the other. That, it seems, is more or less exactly what Paul has written.

With, of course, heavy irony. Torah, the original covenant bond between YHWH and Israel, has now become part of the problem. As 5:20 declared, it has exacerbated the sin of Adam. It cannot, as it stands, constitute Israel as the promised eschatological people of God, the true people of Abraham (see 4:15). The story of the new exodus is thus in tension with the story of the first one, and this tension gives the whole passage its peculiar flavor and its

---

221. See N. T. Wright, *The Climax of the Covenant: Christ and the Law in Pauline Theology* (Edinburgh: T. & T. Clark; Minneapolis: Fortress, 1991) chaps. 7–9.

central problem. I can imagine someone objecting to the scheme I have just proposed on the grounds that it appears too complicated, too clever; and the obvious response is that exactly that complexity, exactly that "cleverness," is what we then find in the detail of Romans 7. The "problem of Romans 7," as articulated in its closing summary, is of someone—the celebrated "I," about which more anon—who has been freed and who has not been freed, who appears to be both liberated and still in Egypt. This person serves the law of God with the mind, but with the flesh the law of sin. In terms of chap. 6, this person appears to be on both sides of the either/or that Paul so clearly set out: enslaved to God, enslaved to sin. The exodus both has and has not happened. This is exactly Paul's analysis of the plight of Israel under Torah. In terms of the original exodus, Israel is the free people of God. In terms of the new one, the exodus from sin and death, Israel is still in slavery. The very Torah that spoke of the original freedom reminds Israel daily of that continuing servitude, and its consequences.

Paul's view of Torah here is, however, more subtle still. As I have argued elsewhere, 8:1-11 constitutes among other things the *vindication* of Torah itself.[222] When God does what Torah wanted to do but, through no fault of its own, could not, Torah is affirmed. Torah is not, as in some sub-Pauline theological schemes, a bad thing, to be jettisoned with a sigh of relief; it is a good thing, given by God, no longer the defining boundary-marker of God's people, but given a position of honor. In particular, this passage shows the positive role that Torah has played in the history of salvation, even at the very moment when it might seem most negative. We should not miss the significance, in a Jewish writer like Paul, of the little word ἵνα (*hina*), especially when repeated. "The law came in alongside, *so that* the trespass might abound" (5:20); "sin, *so that* it might appear as sin, was working death in me through the good thing [i.e., the law]" (7:13*b*); "*so that* sin might become exceedingly sinful through the commandment" (7:13*c*). This is none other than the purpose of God; this is the reason, according to this passage, why Torah was given in the first place.[223]

The end of that line of thought comes in 8:3, where Paul affirms that, having heaped up sin into one place, God condemned it all at once. Where sin abounded through Torah, grace superabounded.

At the center of Paul's argument for assurance, therefore, and his exposition of the new exodus, we find one of his clearest statements of the meaning of Jesus' death (8:3-4). To be sure, neither here nor anywhere else does he offer a complete "doctrine of atonement." But, whereas he often refers fleetingly in the course of an argument to Jesus' death, leaving us to fill in the gaps and make assumptions about his total meaning, here the sending and death of God's son (a rare phrase, as we noted earlier, but always decisive when it appears) stands structurally at the apex of the long argument, providing relief for the tension that had built up in chap. 7, and setting the tone for what is to come. "God condemned sin in the flesh"; that is the primary reason why there is now "no condemnation for those who are in the Messiah, Jesus" (8:1). And the means whereby God passed that judicial sentence in that flesh, the flesh of Jesus, was that sin had there been drawn together into one place: "where sin abounded, grace superabounded." What appeared to be the negative work of Torah thus has the deeply positive result: God has dealt with sin once and for all on the cross, and now the life of the Spirit is given to bring the new-exodus people home to their promised inheritance (5:1-5, 6-10; 8:12-30).

It will be clear from all this what answer I give to the question that is often referred to as "the problem of Romans 7." Who is the "I" that dominates 7:7-25?

The first vital move is to rule out any possibility that Paul might here be referring to the "normal Christian." Despite the powerful advocacy of commentators like Cranfield and Dunn—and the present writer knows the force of the argument, since he held it himself for several years before coming to his present view—we must give full weight to Paul's repeated assertions, throughout 6:1–8:11, that the baptized Christian is not "in sin," not "in the flesh," not "under the law."[224] The whole

---

222. Wright, *The Climax of Covenant,* chap. 10.
223. This is confirmed by the parallel in Gal 3:21-2. When Paul says "scripture concluded all under sin," "scripture" is a periphrasis, or indirect reference, for "God."

224. See C. E. B. Cranfield, *A Critical and Exegetical Commentary on the Epistle to the Romans,* ICC, 2 vols. (Edinburgh: T. & T. Clark, 1975) 342-47; James D. G. Dunn, *Romans 1–8,* WBC 38A (Dallas: Word, 1988) 387-99. Douglas J. Moo, *The Epistle to the Romans,* NICNT (Grand Rapids: Eerdmans, 1996) 442-51, provides a careful analysis, taking a similar view to mine.

point of the argument of chap. 6 was to emphasize that the Christian is not "in Adam," but that "the old man" has died with Christ, thus being now, theologically speaking, "dead to sin and alive to God in Christ." The fact that sin could still, however illogically, "reign" in one's mortal body (6:12) does not affect this question of *status,* or the question of being "not under law, but under grace" (6:14-15). The section 6:17-18 could hardly be clearer: you were once slaves of sin, but you are now slaves of righteousness; 6:22 repeats the point. Verses 4-6 of chap. 7 then repeat it again from another point of view: "you died to the law . . . so that you might belong to another"; "when we were in the flesh, the passions of sin, through the law, were at work . . . but now we are set free from the law . . . to be enslaved in the newness of the Spirit, not in the oldness of the letter." It is simply impossible, after this oft-repeated statement, to suppose that Paul will then expound a view of the Christian in which he or she is, after all, "fleshly, sold under sin" (7:14), or that he or she is "enslaved to the law of sin" (7:25). And just in case we had still missed the point, Paul makes it abundantly clear in 8:9: "you are not in the flesh, but in the Spirit."[225]

This is not to say, of course, that normal Christian experience knows nothing of moral struggle and frustration. Part of the problem in the history of exegesis of this passage is precisely that preachers and theologians have read Romans 5–8 as a "theology of the Christian life" and, finding here a portrait of moral struggle that seemed familiar to the sensitive Christian striving after holiness and ever more aware of falling short, assumed that that was what Paul was talking about. Conversely, those who from time to time have taught that it is after all possible for a Spirit-filled Christian to be sinlessly perfect in the present life have spoken eagerly, as part of their theme, about leaving Romans 7 behind and going on to Romans 8. Romans 7 then becomes a transcript of the "experience," either of the non-Christian, or of the Christian who is still struggling to live a holy life by means of "law" (not usually conceived, in such schemes, as the Torah, but rather as a more general moral law one tries to follow by one's own efforts instead of relying on the Spirit). The debates that these and similar views have occasioned

within popular piety are as endless, in their way, as the scholarly debates that have circled around the same passage but with rather different agendas (why one should assume that scholars are not interested in holiness I do not know, but it sometimes appears to be the case, just as pietists are not always interested in what the text actually says). Many of those who have taken a firm stand on the "Christian" reading of 7:14-25 have done so, it appears, out of a desire to rebut the shallow teaching on holiness that the alternative seems to inculcate.[226]

These debates are rendered beside the point when the passage is read in its full context within the ongoing argument of Romans, and with full attention to the meaning of "the law" throughout the passage. "The law" here, to repeat, is the Mosaic law, the Torah, and this is one of Paul's fullest discussions of it. And those who are "under the law" are, basically, Jews, and, by extension, those who attach themselves to Israel, i.e., God-fearers and proselytes.

The "I" of 7:7-25, which on any showing is a remarkable rhetorical feature, may then be approached within Paul's two main controlling narratives: (a) the story of Adam and the Messiah, and (b) the new exodus. Torah intrudes within the first (5:20); Sinai is a key moment in the second. Within these, Paul appears to be speaking of Israel: of Israel under Torah; of Israel at the time when Torah arrived (7:7-12); of Israel continuing to live under Torah thereafter (7:13-25). But he is not thereby speaking of how Israel under Torah would itself analyze the problem. Though in a sense this is Paul's own story, as a Jew who had lived under Torah himself, it is not a transcript of "how it felt at the time."[227] Against this idea, and all psychologizing interpretations that have derived from it in the history of research, stands Paul's own statement in Philippians 3: in his pre-Christian life he had been "blameless" in regard to "righteousness under the law." Even granted that he is there making a different point, requiring a positive statement of his pre-Christian position, it is virtually impossible

---

225. So, rightly, Moo, *Romans,* 448.

226. See J. I. Packer, "The 'Wretched Man' Revisted: Another Look at Romans 7:14-25," in *Romans and the People of God: Essays in Honor of Gordon D. Fee on the Occasion of His 65th Birthday,* ed. S. K. Soderlund and N. T. Wright (Grand Rapids: Eerdmans, 1999) 70-81.
227. Dunn, *Romans 1–8,* 394, is right to reject such a suggestion, but he fails to see the alternative: It may not have felt like this at the time, but this is how Christian hindsight analyzes it theologically.

to square that clearly autobiographical passage with a would-be autobiographical reading of Romans 7.[228] The present passage seems, then, to be a Christian theological analysis of what was in fact the case, and indeed what is still the case for those who live "under the law," not a description of how it felt or feels. It is a vivid, rhetorically sharpened way of saying something very similar to what Paul said in 2:17-29: those who embrace Torah find that Torah turns and condemns them. It is not impossible that Paul has in mind at least a sidelong reference to the rabbinic discussion of the two "inclinations," the evil inclination and the good inclination; but his picture of the "I" is not in fact exactly like the rabbinic one, and the passage can in my view be understood without making this a central motif.[229]

The point of the "I," as a rhetorical device, then becomes clear. Though we can learn a certain amount on this topic from considerations of how "autobiographical" language was used in ancient rhetoric, the main thing this teaches us is simply that such language could be used for purposes other than literal descriptions of one's own actual experience.[230] Paul must be allowed to make his own use of the rhetorical possibility. And his motive here is not far to seek. Particularly in view of where his argument will take him in chaps. 9–11, he will not describe the plight of his "kins-folk according to the flesh" as if this were some foreign or alien concern. This is his own story, and he will feel its theological tension and pain as his own (see 9:1-5; 11:14, referring to non-Christian Jews as ἡ σάρξ μου [hē sarx mou, "my flesh"]; see also the Commentary on 3:5, 7). It is a way of not saying "they," of not distancing himself from the problem, from the plight of Israel.

Crucial to most interpretations of the "I" has been the change of tense in the middle of the long "I" passage, the switch (that is) from the past tense in vv. 7-12 to the present in vv. 14-25, with v. 13

as a bridge between them. This has sometimes been explained in terms of Paul first looking at his own previous experience, or perhaps that of someone else, in vv. 7-12, and then turning to describe his own current experience in vv. 14-25. This, though attractive within the non-exegetical schemes of thought mentioned above, is unwarranted when the letter is understood in its own terms. The change of tense has to do, rather, with the change from the description of what happened when Torah first arrived in Israel, the time when Israel recapitulated the sin of Adam (5:20a; 7:9-11), to the description of the ongoing state of those who live under the law, who find themselves caught between the one exodus and the other, freed from Egypt and yet not freed from the "Egypt" of sin and death.

Among the other things the rhetorical "I" enables Paul to accomplish is the analysis of sin under Torah in such a way as to show that the death of Jesus has provided its perfect remedy. The reference to the "sin-offering" in 8:3 (see the notes) exactly suits the context, since that sacrifice was designed to deal with unwilling or unwitting sin, and Paul has so described sin-under-the-law as to make it just that. This explains, at least in part, the lengthy descriptions of moral inability ("that which I do I know not," and so forth) in vv. 15-16, 19-20.

A further explanation for the lengthy description of "life under the law" may perhaps be found—though this can never be more than a likely guess—in the pagan parallels to 7:14-20. In a long tradition from Aristotle to Ovid and beyond, pagan moralists had observed the puzzling fact that even the most morally acute among them could see, and approve, the good, while still continuing to choose and perform evil.[231] Paul's description is at certain points strikingly reminiscent of this theme, which must have been well known among serious-minded Greeks and Romans. It is probable that Paul is deliberately echoing, or alluding to, this tradition. But why?

Help is at hand in Galatians. In Galatians 5 Paul argued, with polemical intent, that if one put oneself under the law one would simply reside once more in the realm of the "flesh." In other words,

228. This was the starting point for Krister Stendahl's epochal essay "The Apostle Paul and the Introspective Conscience of the West." See Stendahl, *Paul Among Jews and Gentiles* (Philadelphia: Fortress, 1976) 78-96.

229. Details in H. L. Strack, *Kommentar zum Neuen Testament aus Talmud und Midrasch*, 6 vols. (Munich: Beck, 1922–61) 4:466-83. See W. D. Davies, *Paul and Rabbinic Judaism: Some Rabbinic Elements in Pauline Theology*, 3rd ed. (Philadelphia: Fortress, 1980) 25-27; J. Marcus, "The Evil Inclination in the Letters of Paul," *IBS* 8 (1986) 8-21. The parallel is rejected as "incomplete" by Dunn, *Romans 1–8*, 391. See also the Qumran doctrine of "two spirits," e.g., 1QS 3:15–4:26.

230. See G. Lyons, *Pauline Autobiography: Toward a New Understanding*, SBLDS 73 (Atlanta: Scholars Press, 1985).

231. For an example roughly contemporary with Paul, see Epictetus *Discourses* 2:26.

becoming Jewish (by getting circumcised and taking on the yoke of Torah) will simply bring you back to the same pagan state as you were in before—exactly the argument of Gal 4:8-11. The parallel between Gal 5:16-18 and Romans 7 is quite close: "the flesh lusts against the Spirit," writes Paul in Gal 5:17, "and the Spirit against the flesh; and these are opposed to each other, *so that you cannot do the things you want.*" And then the punch line: "But if you are led by the Spirit, you are not under the law." Precisely the point of Rom 7:1–8:11.

What happens when we transpose this back into Romans 7? If Paul's point is that Torah increases and exacerbates the plight of humankind "in Adam" (so that, for instance, 2:17-29 places "the Jew" firmly on the map of 1:18–2:16, 3:19-20 re-emphasizes the point, and 5:20 draws it together in a striking summary), what better way of elaborating this insight than by so describing the situation of Israel under Torah as to place Israel by implication fair and square on the map of the puzzled pagan moralist? This is simultaneously, of course, a way of saying that the gospel of Jesus Christ upstages the best in the pagan tradition, too. But Paul's point, I take it, is the other way around: when Israel under Torah—including himself, Paul, in his former life!—does its best, delighting in God's law in the inner person, longing to perform it to perfection, all Israel in fact attains is the same level as—Epictetus, Seneca, and Aristotle himself. "The law came in, so that [Adamic, general-human] trespass might abound." "The flesh," that which Israel shares in common with all humankind, prevents any boast in the Torah. The Torah simply shows up sin (3:19-20).

The consonance of this exposition with what Paul has said about Torah and Israel already in the letter gives supporting weight to my overall case. And this argument then dovetails nicely with the wider allusions we have observed at regular intervals to key features of Roman culture—the gospel, the justice of God, and the peace of God, all of which challenge and upstage Caesar's equivalent. Without for a moment leaving the home base of Jewish and biblical thought that provides the foundation for all his theology, Paul has directed a typically Jewish challenge to the pagan world. Within that again—also as a typically Jewish move!—he has suggested that those who do not embrace his own construal of Judaism—i.e., allegiance to Jesus as Messiah—are themselves no better than pagans.

All that has been said so far indicates that when Paul is talking about "sin" in this passage—and the word, in one form or another, occurs over twenty times in these thirty-six verses—he means exactly what he means in the letter so far. "Sin" is a power let loose in the world, a deceptive and corrosive parasite that has entwined the whole human race in its tentacles and is slowly choking it to death. And the manifestation of sin is the performance of actions that run counter both to God's purpose for humankind in general (actions that result from idolatry, as in 1:18-32) and of actions that cut across God's law, the Torah, in particular (as in the present passage and, e.g., 6:19). There is no warrant, in other words, for the theory that was popular in Germany in the mid-twentieth century, following the expositions of Kümmel and Bultmann in particular, and is still to be found in some commentaries and expositions: that when Paul here spoke of "sin" he did not mean so much the breaking of God's law *as the attempt to keep it* and so to earn a "status" for oneself independent of God and God's grace.[232] On this view Paul was charging Israel, and all humans who live "under the law" in a sense far wider than simply the Mosaic Torah, with a kind of meta-sin; not the breaking of the law, but pride in keeping it, or in attempting to do so. This theory gained its apparent force from the combination of the Lutheran critique of "human works," the attempt by human beings to make themselves righteous, and the existentialist critique of a life lived inauthentically, by human arrogance. But it has little to commend it as exegesis of Romans 7. The problem of the "I" is not that it can perform the law but ought not to try, but that it rightly delights in the law but cannot perform it. Bultmann's exegesis ends up with a negative view of Torah that has little to do with Paul's more subtle exposition.

---

232. The famous early statement of this was in W. G. Kümmel, *Römer 7 und die Bekehrung des Paulus* (Leipzig: Hinrichs, 1929; repr. Münich: Kaiser, 1974). Bultmann's essay, originally published in 1932, was translated as "Romans 7 and the Anthropology of Paul," in *Existence and Faith: The Shorter Writings of Rudolf Bultmann* (London: Hodder and Stoughton, 1960) 173-85. Perhaps the most powerful modern exposition is that of Ernst Käsemann, *Commentary on Romans,* trans. Geoffrey W. Bromiley (London: SCM, 1980) 191-212.

Little, but perhaps not absolutely nothing. One of the effects of Romans 7, in its analysis of the plight of Israel under Torah, is to ground the further critique of Israel that Paul will mount in chaps. 9–10. There he does indeed describe Israel as "seeking to establish its own righteousness." I shall argue at that point, to be sure, that this sentence, too, cannot be taken in the Bultmannian, and indeed more broadly Lutheran, sense; that it refers, not to human works attempting to establish a moral claim upon God, but to the claim of ethnic Israel to be, permanently and inalienably, the covenant people of God. But Paul does indeed charge Israel here with a kind of meta-sin, albeit not the one Bultmann and others thought. And it is true that this charge looks back, within the spiraling argument of Romans, to the present passage, not least with Paul's assertion that Israel is "ignorant" of God's righteousness (10:3): that which Israel does, Israel does not know, as in 7:15. But the meaning of chap. 10 cannot be read back into chap. 7. Paul is not simply repeating himself. He is making a new point, developed from, but not identical to, the present one.

The present passage is notable for the sudden entry of the Spirit, like a fresh character in a play. There have been isolated hints earlier on (1:4; 2:29; 5:5), but nothing at all by way of exposition. Parallels with other passages where the Spirit plays a leading role might have led us to expect more before now (see the parallel between Romans 4 and Galatians 3, where, in v. 14, the Spirit plays a key role in fulfilling the Abrahamic promises; see also 2 Corinthians 3). It is almost as though Paul has been deliberately holding back in order now to unleash this theme with full impact. 7:6 announces what is to come: we are now slaves, he says, "in the newness of the Spirit, not in the oldness of the letter." Then at last, in 8:2-11, there are no fewer than eleven references to the Spirit, followed by a further nine in vv. 12-27.[233]

The role Paul here assigns to the Spirit is that of doing what the law could not. Or rather, this is the role Paul gives to Christ and Spirit together; we must not make the mistake, as is sometimes made,

of supposing a neat antithesis of either Law/Christ or Law/Spirit. Paul has not simply extracted "the law" from a theological scheme and dropped in "Christ" or "Spirit" instead. Things are richer and more complicated than that. He is not, after all, constructing an abstract soteriology, but telling the story of God and Israel, which reaches its strange, paradoxical, yet deliberate and consistent, climax in the sending of the Messiah and the sending of the Spirit (cf. the close parallel with Gal 4:1-7). He is describing how it is that the covenant with Abraham is fulfilled, and the covenant of the Torah renewed.

The main function he gives to the Spirit in this passage, therefore, is that of *giving life:* the life the Torah promised but could not give (7:10), the life that will consist ultimately of the resurrection of the body (8:11). But this life is not merely future. As in chap. 6, the Christian already stands on resurrection ground; and the status affirmed in 6:4-5, 8-11 is here filled out with practical content, as the Spirit who will give life to the "mortal body" anticipates the resurrection by enabling those "in Christ" to have a new mind-set, to submit truly at last to God's will, even to God's law (!), and to please God in their behavior (8:5-8; cf. 1:21-2, 28; 12:2; the last is especially important). This then gives rise to the exposition of the "wilderness wanderings" of God's renewed people (8:12-27), led by the Spirit who enables them to leave slavery behind and to live as God's children.

The Spirit can thus be spoken of in exodus-language, as having been instrumental in the ultimate liberation of God's people: "the law of the Spirit of life in Christ Jesus has set you free from the law of sin and death" (8:2). That is to say, (a) the Spirit has been located on the outline map provided by 5:21—sin and death ranged against grace, righteousness and life; (b) the Spirit is part of God's way of making grace superabound where sin abounded (5:20*b*). This is the "exodus" of chap. 6 described now in terms of the analysis of the problem in 7:7-25. Only if we keep a clear eye out for the connections in Paul's ongoing argument will we discover just how tightly woven the texture of Romans actually is, how interconnected all the themes actually are, and hence how consistently Paul is making, and developing, his main point.[234]

---

233. Depending, in the latter passage, on which references are taken as "Spirit"—i.e., God's Spirit—rather than "spirit"—i.e., the human spirit. For the whole subject see G. Fee, *God's Empowering Presence: The Holy Spirit in the Letters of Paul* (Peabody, Mass.: Hendrikson, 1994).

234. On the notion of Pauline consistency—denial of which has become a knee-jerk reaction in some quarters—see Wright, *The Climax of the Covenant,* 4-7.

What then opens up to our gaze is that Paul has described the sending of the Messiah, and the gift of the Spirit, in language that, precisely within the "new exodus" theme that characterizes so much of Romans 5–8, can be seen in terms of the presence of YHWH with Israel in the wilderness, dwelling in the tabernacle, in the pillar of cloud by day and the pillar of fire by night. The "sending" of the son, as is often enough remarked, belongs within Second Temple Jewish thought in terms of the "sending," or the coming to Israel, of Wisdom, or the Shekinah, or sometimes both together. In Sirach 24 the divine Wisdom comes to dwell in the Temple in Jerusalem, and is simultaneously embodied in the Mosaic Torah (Sir 24:8-12, 23; cf. Wis 9:9-10). We now find that the "indwelling" of the Spirit (8:9, 11) belongs very closely with the same theme. This is "Temple" language, echoing the Jewish belief that the Shekinah "dwelt" within the wilderness tabernacle and then the Temple itself. Whereas, before, the indwelling force was "sin" (7:17-18, 20), now it is the Spirit. In the two other passages where Paul says the same thing he makes the point more explicitly: you, Christians, are therefore God's new Temple (1 Cor 3:16; 2 Cor 6:16). In the latter passage Paul quotes Lev 26:11, and, as in Romans 8, goes on to expound the identity of Christians as God's sons and daughters; in 2 Cor 6:18 this involves a quotation of 2 Sam 7:14, in which the promise to David, that God will build him a house, is democratized to include not only David's son but all Christians. See also 1 Cor 6:19.

The exposition of the Spirit's work in Romans 8, therefore, belongs not only with the theme of assurance but also with that of the new exodus, confirming and filling out the picture we have drawn so far. The people of God, having come out of the Egypt of sin and death, are led through the wilderness by the Son and the Spirit, the new realities to which the old language of Wisdom, Shekinah, and even Torah itself are now seen to point. (So closely are the Son and the Spirit identified in this passage, while still being distinguished in thought, that Paul can speak of the Spirit as "the Messiah's Spirit," 8:9, and of "the Messiah" being "in you," 8:10). Paul has taken some of the central Jewish language about the way in which Israel's God is known in action, saving and leading Israel to the promised inheritance, and has reused it dramatically of Christ and the Spirit. As might be said of the parallel passage in Gal 4:1-11, so we might truly say here: from this point on, if the doctrine of the Trinity had never existed, we might be forced to reinvent it. Paul cannot say anything more exalted than this about the Messiah and the Spirit; but what he has said belongs exactly on the map of Second Temple Jewish language about YHWH, the one God of Israel, and the saving presence and action of this one God.

It only remains to draw attention to the way in which the argument of the present section advances the thought of the letter as a whole. By explaining the renewal of the covenant, the vindication of Torah, and the way in which God gives resurrection life to those in Christ, this passage fills out the argument for assurance, providing the basis for the picture of new creation that follows, and hence for the great celebration at the close of chap. 8. But, precisely because it does this by highlighting the failure of Israel according to the flesh, the failure not because of their own will but because of indwelling sin (the latent "Adam" within Israel, so to speak), it intensifies the problem that must then be dealt with in chaps. 9–11. Or, to put it the other way around (since chaps. 9–11, too, are not to be seen simply as an aside, dealing with an awkward matter that has come up in the course of the letter, but rather as one of the main things Paul wants to say), in order to show what God has been doing with the ethnic family of Abraham, Paul needs first to show in graphic detail how their life under Torah has been the means of sin's being magnified—how, in other words, "the law came in so that the trespass might abound." This is the depth-dimension of the problem of Israel that Paul must address. It is not merely that a majority of Jews has not, as it happens, believed the gospel, but rather that the God-given Torah has been part of the problem, part of their stumbling over the stumbling-stone (9:32). Israel's failure as mapped in chap. 7 is the foundation for that further failure of which Paul speaks in 9:30–10:4: Israel has been ignorant of God's righteousness, and has sought to establish its own righteousness. The problem of the church's attitude toward unbelieving Israel cannot be addressed unless this dimension is fully grasped; Paul needs, in other words, to write Romans 7–8 before he can write Romans 9–11. At the same time, the sequence of thought we have observed between 5:20; 7:13; and 8:3—the sequence in which the strange God-given purpose of Torah was to heap up sin precisely in order that it might be dealt with in the "flesh" of the Messiah—stands at the heart of Paul's analysis of Israel's strange fate in 9:14-29, and of the solution he offers in chap. 11.

Romans 7:1–8:11 also stands behind chaps. 12–16, though further in the background. The central argument of that section, presented in 14:1–15:13, is that Christians from all ethnic and cultural backgrounds should accept one another as fellow members of the family. It would be wrong to see 7:1–8:11 as merely a coded way of making this point to one or other particular group within the church, as has sometimes been suggested.[235] But it should be clear that the present passage, in its exposition of the new covenant as doing that which the Torah offered but could not perform, provides the theological groundwork for what Paul will there say.

The passage 7:1–8:11 is thus part and parcel of Paul's larger argument about the righteousness of God. (With this, indeed, the question of relevance with which this overview began—of how a passage about the Jewish law might be of abiding interest to those who have never lived "under")

it—is also answered.) This, Paul is saying, is how God has been faithful to the covenant: to the promises with Abraham, and now, strangely, even to the Torah itself. What God has done "apart from Torah" nevertheless claims, so to speak, the backing of the Torah: "the Torah and the prophets bear witness to it." And what has been done is, of course, done supremely in and through Jesus the Messiah: the death of Jesus in 8:3 is the spelling out of the "righteous act" and the "obedience" of Jesus in 5:18-19, and behind that in 3:24-26. Thus "the gospel of God" (whose content is the Son, born of David's seed according to the flesh, marked out as Son by the Spirit through the resurrection) unveils the righteousness of God. And here all this advances the specific argument: those whom God justified, them God also glorified.

The argument of the passage falls into clear paragraphs. The introduction (7:1-6) leads to the question of whether the law and sin are identical (7:7-12). This produces the second-order question, whether the good law, despite being exonerated from the first charge, is nevertheless the cause of death (7:13-20). This in turn leads to Paul's paradoxical conclusion about the law (7:21-25). Paul can then expound the divine answer (8:1-11), which also, naturally, serves as the foundation of the further exposition of life in the Spirit (8:12-30).

235. See P. Minear, *The Obedience of Faith* (London: SCM, 1971).

# Romans 7:1-6, Coming Out from Under the Law

NIV

7 Do you not know, brothers—for I am speaking to men who know the law—that the law has authority over a man only as long as he lives? [2]For example, by law a married woman is bound to her husband as long as he is alive, but if her husband dies, she is released from the law of marriage. [3]So then, if she marries another man while her husband is still alive, she is called an adulteress. But if her husband dies, she is released from that law and is not an adulteress, even though she marries another man.

[4]So, my brothers, you also died to the law through the body of Christ, that you might belong to another, to him who was raised from the dead,

NRSV

7 Do you not know, brothers and sisters[a]—for I am speaking to those who know the law—that the law is binding on a person only during that person's lifetime? [2]Thus a married woman is bound by the law to her husband as long as he lives; but if her husband dies, she is discharged from the law concerning the husband. [3]Accordingly, she will be called an adulteress if she lives with another man while her husband is alive. But if her husband dies, she is free from that law, and if she marries another man, she is not an adulteress.

[4]In the same way, my friends,[a] you have died

[a] Gk brothers

## NIV

in order that we might bear fruit to God. [5]For when we were controlled by the sinful nature,[a] the sinful passions aroused by the law were at work in our bodies, so that we bore fruit for death. [6]But now, by dying to what once bound us, we have been released from the law so that we serve in the new way of the Spirit, and not in the old way of the written code.

[a] 5 Or the flesh; also in verse 25

## NRSV

to the law through the body of Christ, so that you may belong to another, to him who has been raised from the dead in order that we may bear fruit for God. [5]While we were living in the flesh, our sinful passions, aroused by the law, were at work in our members to bear fruit for death. [6]But now we are discharged from the law, dead to that which held us captive, so that we are slaves not under the old written code but in the new life of the Spirit.

# COMMENTARY

**7:1.** The NRSV and the NIV both omit the first word of the chapter, which in Greek is the single letter ἤ (ē, "or"). As usual with Paul's connections, the word matters: he is looking back to 6:14-15. "You are not under the law . . . or do you not know that the law only rules over someone during their lifetime?" In other words, you could only assume that as a Christian you *were* still under the law if you ignored one of the most basic things about how the law operates. Paul will emphasize in the first six verses of the chapter that a death has indeed occurred that results in the Christian's being "no longer under the law."

We are still working, then, within the picture set out in chap. 6: the death of the "old human" (6:6) because of which the baptized Christian is no longer "in Adam" but rather "in Christ." With this we should recognize, too, that Paul has in mind the further twist in Adamic humanity noted in 5:20. The law intensified the Adamic problem, but grace has dealt with matters at that very point (cf. 1 Cor 15:56-57). Sin will not have dominion over those who were under the law but are now in Christ. They are no longer in the position where the law exacerbated sin; rather, they are the recipients of that grace that has superabounded where sin abounded. This is Paul's subject here.

He is speaking, he says, "to those who know the law." He calls them his family,[236] and seems to want them to identify themselves with him in this

argument, just as he is himself identifying with ethnic Israel, Israel under Torah. This, indeed, may be part of the reason why, having spoken of "I" throughout 7:7-25, he suddenly switches to the second-person singular, "you," in 8:2 (on which see the Commentary on 8:1-11). He is addressing them as people who know the law. This could, of course, mean Roman law in general, in which, as in Jewish law, death pays all debts; but in view of the subject matter it is far more likely to mean the Jewish law. When this is put together with the statement in 7:4 that "you [pl.] died to the law," it becomes the more likely that most of his addressees had actually been in some sense "under the law." Since the majority among his readers was probably Gentile, this must mean that they had been either God-fearers or proselytes. (The alternative, that he is here addressing only the Jewish minority within the Roman church, seems unlikely in view of the central role of this passage within the central section of the letter.)

The point at issue, picking up what 6:7 said about sin, is that the law can only rule a person during that person's lifetime. Death brings a person out from under the rule of the law. The commentators find parallels for this in rabbinic and other codes, but the point is so wide and obvious that we do not need to explain it further. That is hardly the case, however, with what follows.

**7:2-3.** By way of explanation, Paul offers what is sometimes taken as an illustration (the NIV adds "for example," supporting its subheading, "an illustration from marriage"). But what job does

---

236. Lit., "brothers." Paul uses this term sparingly in the main argument of Romans (1:13; 8:12; 10:1; 11:25; cf. 12:1; 15:14; 15:30; 16:17), so that its use here and in 7:4 (NRSV, "friends" at 7:4 is an unfortunate flattening down of the intimacy, and rich mutual accountability, of ἀδελφοί adelphoi) seems the more emphatic.

Paul intend this picture to do? That depends on how we see it fitting in to the rest of the passage, especially v. 4. It is frequently stated that Paul's argument does not quite work. He seems (it is said) to envisage the "marriage" being between the person concerned ("you") and the law; but then it is the person, not the law, that dies.[237] To put it like this, however, is to miss the extent to which the entire chapter, including the "marriage" scene, grows directly out of 5:20-21 and the whole of chap. 6, and continues to unfold its meaning.

The point of vv. 2-3 is not difficult: the law is the thing that binds the wife to the husband, so that if the husband dies the wife is free, both from the husband and from the law that bound her to him. Thus, while the husband is alive, she will be an adulteress if she goes with someone else, but if the husband dies she is "free from the law" (Paul is already hinting at the direction of this argument, and indeed at its roots in 6:14-15). This does not mean that the law was the "first husband," but that the law bound the woman *to* the "first husband." Thus, if she takes another husband she will not be committing adultery. So far, so good.

**7:4.** The problem can then be stated succinctly: "you" died, but "you" now belong to another! Paul is not arguing from the detail of the "illustration," seen in the abstract; he is making the point he wanted to make anyway, to which the marriage picture contributes. The latter half of the verse appears to suggest that the Christian is now, in some sense, the "bride" of Jesus the Messiah ("the one who was raised from the dead"), and it adds the extra detail, that this new union will "bear fruit for God" (for the Christian as the bride of Christ, see 2 Cor 11:2; Eph 5:25-32). This picks up the image of fruitbearing from 6:21-22, but sets it now within a context where its meaning is more precisely *child*bearing.

What then about the first half of the verse? "You died to the law"; the thought is very close to Gal 2:19, "I through the law died to the law" (another use of the "autobiographical" mode of speech, which Paul will presently adopt here). It means "by death, you came out from under the law's domain," as v. 1 implies.

237. See J. A. T. Robinson, *Wrestling with Romans* (Philadelphia: Westminster, 1979) 77-79; H. Räisänen, *Paul and the Law* (Philadelphia: Fortress, 1983) 61.

But who is it, then, that has "died"? The previous chapter gives a clear, unambiguous answer, and indeed repeats it seven times: "we died to sin" (6:2); we "were baptized into Christ's death" (6:3), "we were buried with him into death" (6:4), "we were planted with him in the likeness of his death" (6:5), "our old person was co-crucified" (6:6), "we died with Christ" (6:8), "reckon yourselves dead to sin" (6:11). It might seem tedious to list all these, were it not for the fact that chap. 6 is so little invoked to explain 7:4, and that commentators who have referred to 6:6 to do so are frequently waved away by those who insist on treating chap. 7 as though it were an entirely separate discussion. Once we link the law with sin, however (the point of 5:20, which Paul will address in 7:7), "you died to the law" can only have one meaning. "You" in the first half of 7:4 is the "former husband"; "you" in the second half is the "wife." Or, if we prefer, "you" in the first half is the "old human being" of 6:6—the "old Adam," or perhaps better "the person 'in Adam.'" "You" in the second half, at least when the "re-marriage" has occurred, is the person "in Christ." Just as later in the chapter the argument hinges on the double "I," so here it hinges on a double "you."

What then does Paul mean by qualifying "you died to the law" with the phrase "through the body of Christ"? Presumably something close to what he meant in Gal 2:19 by saying "I am crucified with Christ," as the explanation of "I through the law died to the law." Here, again, the proximity to chap. 6 should help. The whole clause appears to be a shorthand way of saying three things simultaneously: (a) the bodily death of Jesus the Messiah is the representative event through which the Messiah's people die "with him" (6:4-11); (b) you are in the Messiah by baptism, and therefore shared that death; (c) your solidarity with the Messiah can be expressed in terms of your membership in his "body." The extent to which this last thought is strongly present (see, for instance, 12:5) is a matter of debate, but not of great importance. What matters is to recognize that the thought is built on the first half of chap. 6, itself an elaboration of chap. 5.

**7:5-6.** Paul now explains v. 4 with a two-sided description of the old life and the new. This, as is widely recognized, functions as the double heading over the two following sections, 7:7-25 and

8:1-11. It also awakens echoes of the "new covenant" theology of 2 Corinthians 3; this is the means by which Paul, evoking various biblical passages, can affirm the goodness of Torah without affirming its abiding validity as the boundary-marker of God's people.

"When we were in the flesh": this striking formulation tells us once and for all that "flesh" for Paul does not mean simply the physical substance of which humans are made.[238] "The flesh" denotes physicality seen on the one hand as corruptible and on the other as rebellious; it is another way of saying "in Adam," of demarcating that humanity that is characterized by sin and consequently by death. To be "in the flesh" for Paul is to be determined by "flesh" in this sense, i.e., to live under the domain of sin and death, and thus to be in the condition marked by the first half of the various antitheses both of 5:12-21 and of 6:16-23. It does not mean, in our sense, "to be physical," in some Platonic divide between the material and the non-material (see 1 Cor 15:50: "flesh and blood" cannot inherit the kingdom of God—but the resurrected or transformed body can and will; cf. Phil 3:21). It is clear from 8:9 that Christians, even while living ordinary human lives and facing ordinary human suffering and death, are, in Paul's terminology, "not in the flesh, but in the Spirit."

Those "in the flesh" discover that "the passions of sins" are at work in them to bear fruit for death. That much we could have gathered from 5:12-21, and indeed from 1:18–2:16. But Paul adds a vital extra phrase: these passions are "through the law," which both the NRSV and the NIV gloss as "aroused by the law," in the light (no doubt) of 7:9. Paul does not at this point explain what he means, though he shortly will. Here we merely note that, strange though it is to think of the law arousing sinful passions, this is consonant with 6:14-15 and, behind that, with 5:20 yet once more.

"But now we have been released from the law." "But now" awakens echoes of 3:21 and 6:22,

introducing the moment of freedom, of redemption. The verb Paul uses is the same as in v. 2 ("she is *released* from the law concerning the husband"). Though the root meaning of the word is "annul," "make ineffective," or "abolish," which might more properly have gone with the law than with the person who is (or has been up until now) "under the law," when used of the person it must mean "discharged" or "released," the force being that they and the law have nothing more now to say to one another. Paul explains this again by reference to "our" death: "having died [to that] in which we were held captive."[239] "Having died" is another reference to the death of the "old human being," as in 6:6; "the thing which held us captive" is the law once more. And the result is, again as in chap. 6, that the old slavery has been exchanged for a new one: we now serve, literally, "in the newness of the Spirit and not in the oldness of the letter" (the word for "serve" is δουλεύω [*douleuō*, "to serve as a slave"], hence making the link with 6:16-22, as explicitly in the NRSV).

The contrast of the old and the new ways of being a slave evokes 2 Cor 3:6, where it is explicitly "new covenant" language: "God has qualified us," says Paul, "to be ministers of a new covenant, not of the letter but of the Spirit; for the letter kills, but the Spirit gives life." This generates the great contrast of 2 Cor 3:7-18, whose multiple overlapping associations with Paul's thought throughout Rom 7:1–8:11 are too numerous and complex to track here.[240] What matters for our present purpose is that, rare though Paul's explicit references to the "covenant" may be, that word can appropriately reflect something absolutely foundational to his thinking: the faithfulness of God to all that had been revealed and promised in the past. This is not undercut by the fact that, because of sin and death, it was necessary for God to do something that seemed totally new in the present. Underneath the radical discontinuity caused by the gospel's breaking in upon Israel and the world, caused indeed by the earth-shattering death of the

---

238. The NIV, translating σάρξ (*sarx*) as "the sinful nature," avoids one problem: that most readers of English assume that "flesh" means "physical substance," the stuff of which humans are composed. But it falls into another one, implying either that human nature in general is sinful or that humans have more than one "nature," of which one is "sinful." Its rendering of the verb as "when *we were controlled by* the sinful nature" is further misleading; "controlled by" is not as strong, simple, or morally all-encompassing as "in."

239. The KJV's "that being dead in which we were held," implying a reference to the death either of the law or of the old Adam, is based on a hypothetical MS reading introduced by Beza into the Greek *Textus Receptus* (1565), without any existing MS support, on the basis of his guess at Chrysostom's reading. One twelfth-century MS (no. 242) has now been found that supports it.

240. On 2 Corinthians 3, see N. T. Wright, *The Climax of the Covenant: Christ and the Law in Pauline Theology* (Edinburgh: T. & T. Clark; Minneapolis: Fortress, 1991) chap. 9.

Messiah, there remains the faithfulness of the creator and covenant God to the promises made to Abraham, and indeed to the implicit though ineffective promise in the law, the promise of new life for a worldwide family, despite the sin and death brought into the world "through the one man" (5:12).

Pauline "covenant theology," then, is not opposed to "apocalyptic" theology, to a sense of the radical inbreaking of God's judgment and salvation in Christ. The covenant provides the fuller context for that. And, as the present passage and 2 Corinthians 3 make clear, the new covenant is designed precisely to take account of the problems inherent in the original covenant. The latter was written in letters on tablets of stone, but the former is to be written on the heart.

We are here very close, too, to Rom 2:29. There Paul distinguishes "the Jew who is one in secret" from one who is so merely "in what is manifest," i.e., outwardly; and he thus contrasts "the circumcision of the heart," which is a matter of the Spirit, with "the letter." This elliptical formulation, on which see the notes, brings together several things simultaneously: the contrast of two groups of people, their characterization as "the Jew" and "the Jew outwardly," circumcision of the heart and circumcision of the flesh, and the letter and the Spirit. The point of all this for Romans 7 is to confirm that here Paul is dealing with "the Jew," living under the "letter" of the Mosaic law, and

contrasting this with the Spirit-given new life in Christ; and to show that throughout 7:1–8:11 we should keep in mind the discussion in chap. 2, which, demonstrating the inadequacy of the Torah to create and sustain ethnic Israel as God's people, pointed forward to the creation of a new people in whom God's will would be done, described somewhat oxymoronically as "the uncircumcision that keeps the law" (2:26-7). At that stage it was impossible, without more explanation, to see who was being spoken of. The present passage provides that explanation.

A new mode of service, then, has been opened up, a mode to which Torah pointed but which it could not bring to pass. God has renewed the covenant in Christ, and what the Torah could not do has now been done. The new "enslavement"—enslavement to "obedience" (6:16), to the "pattern of teaching" (6:17), to "righteousness" (6:18), to God (6:22)—is one in which the heart is transformed by the Spirit (5:5), in which the whole person is promised new life (8:10-11). This life in the Spirit will dominate chap. 8.

Verses 5-6 introduce the rest of the passage, not least by saying something so outrageously provocative that it must at once raise the question that will lead in to Paul's main argument. If "the passions of sins" are aroused by the law, what are we saying about the law? Is it virtually identical with sin itself?

# Romans 7:7-12, The Arrival of the Law: Sin Seizes Its Chance

NIV

7What shall we say, then? Is the law sin? Certainly not! Indeed I would not have known what sin was except through the law. For I would not have known what coveting really was if the law had not said, "Do not covet."[a] 8But sin, seizing the opportunity afforded by the commandment, produced in me every kind of covetous desire. For apart from law, sin is dead. 9Once I was alive apart from law; but when the commandment came, sin sprang to life and I died. 10I found that the very commandment that was

[a] 7 Exodus 20:17; Deut. 5:21

NRSV

7What then should we say? That the law is sin? By no means! Yet, if it had not been for the law, I would not have known sin. I would not have known what it is to covet if the law had not said, "You shall not covet." 8But sin, seizing an opportunity in the commandment, produced in me all kinds of covetousness. Apart from the law sin lies dead. 9I was once alive apart from the law, but when the commandment came, sin revived 10and I died, and the very commandment that promised life proved to be death to me. 11For sin, seizing an opportunity in the commandment, deceived me

| NIV | NRSV |
|---|---|
| intended to bring life actually brought death. [11]For sin, seizing the opportunity afforded by the commandment, deceived me, and through the commandment put me to death. [12]So then, the law is holy, and the commandment is holy, righteous and good. | and through it killed me. [12]So the law is holy, and the commandment is holy and just and good. |

# COMMENTARY

The new paragraph extends, not to v. 13 as in several editions and translations, but to v. 12. The larger unit (vv. 7-25) is clearly subdivided, as can be seen from Paul's careful and logical connectives, into vv. 7-12, 13-20, and 21-25. The first asks, "Is the law sin?" and answers the question by telling the story of the law's arrival on Sinai and Israel's recapitulation of the sin of Adam. This was not the law's fault; the law was the unwilling tool of sin itself. The second, following the sin/death logic that dominates the entire section, asks: "Did this good law, then, cause 'my' death?" The answer again is, No. The point this time is made by telling the story of those who live under the law, emphasizing that it is still sin, not the law—and not the "I," remarkably enough!—that is responsible. The third paragraph draws the conclusion in terms of the the double-sided law, corresponding to the double-sided "I": because of sin, the law cannot give life, and the "I" cannot attain it. This states the problem of the law, and of the "I," in the terms Paul will address in the first paragraph of chap. 8.

**7:7a.** The opening question faces at last the issue that has been in the background since 2:17-29, more sharply since 5:20, and most urgently since 7:5. If the law stirs up the passions of sins, surely this means that the law and sin are virtually identical?

**7:7b-8a.** Paul's initial response is to deny the charge ("certainly not!" NIV), and to state again the point that seemed to lead to it ("yet, if it had not been for the law I would not have known sin," NRSV; the NIV, translating ἀλλά [*alla*] as "indeed," misses the force of this: Paul is actually conceding the point that had led to the charge, not yet undergirding his emphatic rebuttal of it; cf. the similar use of *alla* in 7:13, omitted altogether by the NRSV, but correctly translated as "but" in the NIV). But

what does it mean "to know sin"? The NIV takes it simply in terms of information, knowing *about* sin: "I would not have known what sin was." The same problem is repeated in the next line, which Paul intends as an explanation (γάρ *gar*): I should not have known covetousness had the law not said "you shall not covet." This time the NRSV joins the NIV: "I would not have known what it is to covet." Yet v. 8 surely indicates something stronger than simply information (cf. 3:20: through the law comes the ἐπίγνωσις ἁμαρτίας [*epignōsis hamartias,* "the knowledge of sin"]). It is not so much that the law gave the "I" information about sin in general, and coveting in particular; the law *produced* coveting, and hence sin. Sin, that is, "seized its opportunity"[241] in the commandment (Paul regularly uses ἡ ἐντολή [*hē entolē,* "the commandment"] in this chapter, more or less as a synonym for "the law," though sometimes with specific reference to the particular commandment just quoted). And, exploiting this opportunity, sin "worked in 'me' all kinds of covetousness."[242] The law, in other words, was the channel not only for knowledge *about* sin but for knowledge *of* sin in the sense that, as a result of the process, "I" knew, from the inside, what sin meant in practice. This still, of course, appears to be an indictment of the law, though Paul is building in to his picture the description of "sin" at work that will result in the law's exoneration four verses later. The law, though weak, was not the source of the problem, merely the unwilling channel.

241. The Greek word here (ἀφορμή *aphormē*) carries the metaphorical sense of "a military base of operations," but it was regularly used in the more general sense of "an opportunity," especially with the verb Paul employs here. See BDAG.

242. In a work roughly contemporary with Paul, 4 Macc 2:5-6, a Jewish writer uses the commandment "you shall not covet" to more or less exactly the opposite effect, arguing that since the law commands this it must be the case that "reason" can overcome the passions.

But what event is Paul describing? The reference to the tenth commandment in v. 7b (Exod 20:17; Deut 5:21) might indicate that he was referring to the time when the law was first given on Mount Sinai. Alternatively, many exegetes, taking the "I" literally, have supposed Paul to be referring to his own experience on first becoming aware of the commandments, perhaps at his bar mitzvah, especially if that coincided with the onset of puberty and hence of sexual desire (the tenth commandment, as 4 Maccabees 2 implies, was often taken to refer to sexual desire in particular, while obviously being of wider application). But the larger context in Romans indicates well enough what event Paul is thinking of. 5:20, once again: the law came in, so that the trespass might abound. This is not about Paul himself; it is about the moment in Israel's history, and indeed (5:13-14) in the history of humankind, when the arrival of the law meant that, as at the beginning, humans were faced with a specific command, so that the miscellaneous sin that had existed "from Adam to Moses" (5:14) would again become "trespass," breaking a known law.

That explains, as will become clear in the next three verses, the fact that Paul seems here to be referring also to the "fall" of Genesis 3 (particularly with v. 11: sin "deceived me . . . and killed me," alluding to Gen 3:13; cf. 2 Cor 11:3). We should not attempt to decide between these two (Sinai and Eden): Paul's point is precisely that what happened on Sinai recapitulated what had happened in Eden. Other Jewish exegesis linked the two moments; Paul's view falls well within recognizable Second Temple understandings of the meaning both of covetousness and of the primal sin.[243] What he has done here is so to tell the one story, that of Israel, that echoes of the other, that of Adam, are clearly heard. This is, of course, just what we should expect if he is indeed expanding the programmatic statement in 5:20: "the law came in, so that the trespass might abound."

**7:8b-10.** Paul's next statement seems to sit uncomfortably with 5:13-14. There, sin was not *counted* apart from the law, but was "in the world" even in the absence of the law, its presence being witnessed by universal death. What then

does Paul mean, "apart from the law, sin is dead"? He seems to indicate some kind of potential life for sin beyond simply producing death; when individuals sin and die, sin is not growing, not flourishing in new ways. When, however, the law appears, then sin gains, as we might say, a new lease of life. "I was once alive apart from the law" (for the last phrase, cf. 3:21); this, we must assume, refers within Paul's controlling narrative to Israel in the pre-Mosaic state, corresponding to Adam in the garden before the fateful command had been issued. "But when the commandment arrived," i.e., on Sinai, "sin sprang to life, and I died." There may be an allusion, here and indeed throughout this passage, to the fact that, in the exodus story, the giving of the commandments was the moment when Aaron and the children of Israel made the golden calf—the incident to which some subsequent rabbinic writings looked back with sorrow as the time when Israel imbibed iniquity (see the Commentary on 1:23). Sinai and Genesis 3 still go hand in hand.

The result (v. 10b) is that the commandment that promised life proved to be death for "me" (cf. 4 Ezra 9:33-37: those who received the law and sinned perished; the law, however, does not perish but remains in its glory). The allusion to the tree of life in Genesis is hidden here under the more direct reference to Lev 18:5 (which Paul quotes in Rom 10:5, in a section belonging closely with the present one) and to the covenantal passage in Deut 30:15-20, passages that promise life for those who keep Torah (see Deut 4:1; 6:24; 8:1; cf. *Ps Sol* 14:1; see also the Commentary on 10:5-11). This is, for Paul, the real irony of Torah, and it points forward to the paradoxical fulfilling of Torah's intention by the Spirit in 8:1-11. Torah intended to give life (Paul personifies Torah, though not as obviously and regularly as he does "sin"), but because of sin all it could give was death.

**7:11.** By way of explanation, Paul repeats what he had said in v. 8 about sin "taking its opportunity" through the commandment. This time, instead of merely showing that sin produced in "me" all kinds of covetousness, he draws the conclusion: sin deceived me, and so killed me. It is at this point that the disguise of the personified "sin" is close to disappearing: we are clearly talking about the serpent in the garden, though Paul has

---

243. See *bSanh* 38b; 102a; *Exod. Rab.* 21:1; 30:7; 32:1, 7, 11. See the Commentary on 1:23 and 9:15-16; the connections between these passages are important.

told the story in such a way as to allow other levels to be heard as well, which, had he been more explicit, might have been drowned out. The preliminary picture is complete: (a) sin and the law are quite distinct; (b) sin has taken over the law, the law that promised life; (c) using it as a base of operations, sin has produced the opposite of that which the law promised. This is of course why "no human being will be justified" in God's sight on the basis of Torah (3:20); it is why the Torah became "a dispensation of death" (2 Cor 3:7-11); it is why, despite the glory of the first exodus and the first covenant, a new exodus and a renewed covenant were necessary. However, this is not the whole story. As will shortly become apparent, through Paul's raising of the necessary second question, even the apparently negative side of Torah has its remarkable and positive purpose in the strange divine plan.

**7:12.** The Torah, cleared of identity with sin, can be reaffirmed as God's law, holy and just and good. This statement ranks with 3:31*b* as among those places where Paul most vehemently affirms the goodness of the Torah, rejecting outright the road that would lead, and did lead in the next century, toward Marcionism. This, indeed, in the light of 11:11-32, may be seen as one of Paul's main aims in various parts of Romans: to warn Gentile Christian readers, especially those who had had some connection with Judaism before their conversion and would now be tempted to reject everything to do with it, against such a course. They cannot cut off the branch on which they are sitting, or rather the trunk of the tree of which they are branches (11:16-24). At the present stage of the argument, it is vital that they do not react against the Torah itself (as so many of Paul's subsequent readers, since at least the second century, have been tempted to do), but that they see instead the strange but vital role it has played within the saving purposes of the one God. Romans 7 is poised between 3:1-9 on the one hand and 9:30–10:13 on the other, facing the same question (was God's covenant with Israel simply a mistake?) and giving it the same answer (no, but its purpose was stranger than had been imagined).

# Romans 7:13-20, Living Under the Law: Sin Works Death

NIV

[13]Did that which is good, then, become death to me? By no means! But in order that sin might be recognized as sin, it produced death in me through what was good, so that through the commandment sin might become utterly sinful.

[14]We know that the law is spiritual; but I am unspiritual, sold as a slave to sin. [15]I do not understand what I do. For what I want to do I do not do, but what I hate I do. [16]And if I do what I do not want to do, I agree that the law is good. [17]As it is, it is no longer I myself who do it, but it is sin living in me. [18]I know that nothing good lives in me, that is, in my sinful nature.[a] For I have the desire to do what is good, but I cannot carry it out. [19]For what I do is not the good I want to do; no, the evil I do not want to do—this I keep on doing. [20]Now if I do what I do not want

NRSV

13Did what is good, then, bring death to me? By no means! It was sin, working death in me through what is good, in order that sin might be shown to be sin, and through the commandment might become sinful beyond measure.

14For we know that the law is spiritual; but I am of the flesh, sold into slavery under sin.[a] [15]I do not understand my own actions. For I do not do what I want, but I do the very thing I hate. [16]Now if I do what I do not want, I agree that the law is good. [17]But in fact it is no longer I that do it, but sin that dwells within me. [18]For I know that nothing good dwells within me, that is, in my flesh. I can will what is right, but I cannot do it. [19]For I do not do the good I want, but the evil I do not want is what I do. [20]Now if I do what I

*a* 18 Or *my flesh*

*a* Gk *sold under sin*

| NIV | NRSV |
|---|---|
| to do, it is no longer I who do it, but it is sin living in me that does it. | do not want, it is no longer I that do it, but sin that dwells within me. |

# COMMENTARY

Though v. 13 forms in a sense a bridge between vv. 7-12 and vv. 14-20, it stands naturally at the head of the latter section. It asks, and gives the preliminary answer to, the question that determines the direction and shape of the verses to come. Too little attention has been given to the actual arguments Paul mounts here; the passage is not a string of loosely connected musings, but a carefully structured sequence of thought. Verse 13*a* raises the question, whether the law, now proved to be good, was nevertheless the cause of death; v. 13*b* gives the initial answer, that it was sin, rather than the law, that brought death; this is then further explained (γάρ *gar*) by v. 14 and what follows. Verse 14 can hardly, then, be the start of a new section, as has so often been supposed.[244]

Verses 13-20 then further subdivide. Verses 13-16 are basically about the goodness of the law, despite sin and death in the "I"; vv. 17-20 develop the thought of the paradoxical behavior of the "I" in order to show that it is not really the "I" that is at fault, but once again sin.[245] The "I" here, as I argued in the overview, is to be seen primarily as Israel under Torah, with the point being made that, even under Torah, Israel belongs in the Adam-sphere, the realm of sin and death (5:20; cf. 6:14; 7:5).

**7:13a.** The question is the natural one, granted that Paul is still thinking in terms of 5:20-21. "Sin reigned in death," and Torah seemed to have exacerbated that rule; 7:5 has repeated the point vividly. But was the good law, now firmly distinguished from "sin," thus responsible for death? Granted that sin was responsible for the initial deceit, using Torah as a base of operations, is Torah then responsible for what happens as a result, i.e., death? Once again Paul answers: of course not! His main object will now be to back up that denial, and in so doing to advance the underlying argument about the power and sinfulness of sin itself, toward the point where it is finally dealt with (8:3).

**7:13b.** All the blame attaches once more to sin itself. Sin was at work in "me" through the law ("the good thing"); and that work of sin, not of the law itself, produced death. This is the basic explanation that goes behind the dense statement of 7:5, and exonerates Torah from willing complicity in the process. But Paul has here built into this answer a double statement of purpose: it was sin, *so that it might appear as sin,* working death in me through the law, *so that sin might become exceedingly sinful* through the commandment. This is the key to understanding not only the sequence of thought that leads from here to the decisive statement of 8:3-4 but also, in a measure, Paul's whole mature thinking about the purpose of Torah, or, better, the purpose of God in giving Torah.

We must obviously assume that the repeated ἵνα (*hina*) indicates not the intention and purpose of sin itself, but the intention and purpose of God. This reflects the similar *hina* in 5:20: the Torah came in alongside, *so that the trespass might abound.* But why would God want the trespass to abound? Surely this is counterintuitive?

Not if we understand Paul's point in this passage (and, more compactly, in Gal 3:21-2). God's way of dealing with sin, it appears, is not to hold it at arm's length. It is not a matter of damage limitation, attempting to restrict the operation of sin. Torah, apparently, was not after all given in order

---

244. James D. G. Dunn, *Romans 1–8,* WBC 38A (Dallas: Word, 1988) 377, notes the disagreement among German commentators as to where the real division occurs.

245. In Wright, *The Climax of the Covenant,* 218, I suggested that v. 17 functioned both as the conclusion to vv. 13-16 and as the beginning of the new line of thought leading to v. 20. This now seems to me wrong. Verse 16 rounds off the question about the law; νυνὶ δέ (*nyni de*) at the start of v. 17 introduces a new point, which, supported by vv. 18-19, reaches its conclusion in v. 20.

that Israel might become a sin-free zone. Rather, God's way with sin takes account of the fact that sin has infected the entire human race, Israel included, and that no law could possibly be given that would deal with the problem. If life could come by the law, then the law would have been the means of covenant membership and hence of life (Gal 3:21*b;* cf. Gal 2:21). If "the command-ment which was unto life" (Rom 7:10) really could have given life, God would not have needed to do anything further (8:3-4). No: sin needed dealing with in a more radical way, at the place where it had become resident, that is, at the heart of the human race itself. And it was Torah's pecu-liar task to draw sin to its height, to let it appear in all its true colors, to be shown up as "exceedingly sinful." Sin must be seen to be sin.

But not only seen. The point of 7:13, coupled with 5:20, is that it looks on to 8:3. God gave Torah in order to draw sin into one place, *in order that it might there be dealt with fully and finally.* Where sin abounded, there grace superabounded; and that latter phrase is, of course, a periphrastic reference to the death of Jesus as the decisive event of obedience through which sin is con-demned and the human race freed from its clutches. Thus the κατάκριμα (*katakrima*), the "condemnation," of 5:18 is removed (cf. 8:1: there is therefore now no *katakrima* for those in Christ Jesus), precisely because sin itself has been condemned once and for all (8:3). The place where it has been condemned is in the "flesh" of the Messiah, representing the Israel where "sin had abounded," and thereby representing the human race whose Adamic "flesh" was where sin had taken up residence. We shall say more about this at 8:3 itself. But it is vital that we notice already where Paul's thought is moving. The dou-ble *hina* of v. 13 points to the understanding of the cross that emerges from the entire argument.

**7:14.** In order to exonerate Torah, Paul now analyzes further the "I" that is caught up in sin and hence in death. To do this, he contrasts the true nature of Torah with the nature of the human being (and the Jew precisely as a person "in Adam"). Torah is spiritual, he says, but "I" am "fleshly," sold under sin, i.e., a bond-slave to sin. He does not here explain what he means by "spir-itual"; this is part of the vindication of Torah, and belongs with 7:12. But in appealing to the basic

spirit/flesh contrast that runs through so much of the present section, and which effectively extends and clarifies the Adam/Christ contrast of chap. 5 and the slave/free contrast of chap. 6, he is now placing Torah on the God-side, the Christ-side, of the equation, and placing the "I" on the Adam-side. (We should beware, here as elsewhere in Paul, of supposing that the spirit/flesh contrast had anything very much to do with the contrast of non-physical/physical.)[246]

He does, however, explain a bit more what he means by "of the flesh." The word here (σάρκινος *sarkinos*) is rare, and takes its meaning in Paul not so much from its original lexical force but from the heavy weight of Paul's technical term σάρξ (*sarx,* "flesh," with all its connotations; cf. 1 Cor 3:1, 3; 2 Cor 3:3; 10:4). Paul appears to use both *sarkinos* ("fleshly in *type*") and *sarkikos* ("fleshly in *charac-ter*") in both senses. The point he is making is that the "I," the Jew, Israel "according to the flesh" (cf. 9:5; 11:14; 1 Cor 10:18), belongs within the Adamic solidarity, still held as a slave within the "Egypt" of sin and death; and that the law, in its promise of life, is ontologically as well as morally mismatched with Adamic humanity, Israel included. The problem is not the Torah, but the sort of person "I" am.

**7:15.** Paul's explanation of "I am fleshly" is an account of the behavior of the "I" (that v. 15 explains v. 14 is clear from the initial γάρ [*gar,* "for"], omitted in both the NRSV and the NIV; these connectives are, as usual, all-important in keeping a grip on Paul's argumentative strategy). The initial clause is the key: "what I do, I do not know." The NRSV and the NIV, perhaps not unnaturally, flatten this out into "I do not under-stand." The word γινώσκω (*ginōskō*) can indeed mean "understand," and that is part of the mean-ing here; but the way Paul develops the thought through to 8:3 suggests that he is saying some-thing stronger than that the "I" is intellectually puzzled by its own behavior; he is referring to the

---

246. It may be for this reason that the NIV translates σάρκινος (*sarki-nos*) simply as "unspiritual." This fails, though, to highlight the link Paul is making, throughout the passage, between the σάρξ (*sarx*) in which sin has taken up residence and the *sarx* of Christ where it is dealt with (8:3), and the "fleshly" nature contrasted with the "spiritual" in 8:5-9. It is perhaps better, with the NRSV, to retain the verbal link, thus clari-fying the flow of the argument, and to explain what the key terms do and do not mean.

actions in question as "sins of *ignorance*." This is further explained (a second *gar*) in the second half of the verse in terms of *unwilling* sin: what "I" do is not what "I" want, but what "I" hate. Here is the paradox of Israel under Torah; seeing what is the right thing to do, delighting in it and wanting to perform it, and yet discovering that what is performed instead is the thing the mind had rejected as hateful. But precisely within this paradox Paul has hinted at part of the solution; ignorant sins, and unwilling sins, are both taken care of within God's atoning plan (see on 8:3).

We must stress, as with 2:17-29, that Paul is not here talking about each individual Jew. He knew himself to have been "blameless in terms of righteousness under the law" (Phil 3:6). He is talking of Israel as a whole. As a nation, Israel delighted in Torah formally and officially (as it were), but was always aware that for the most part Torah was not followed. Israel was not a holy nation, obeying Torah gladly; sin, Adamic life, was evident all through. In the light of his Damascus road experience, and his whole subsequent body of belief, Paul would turn this critique upon himself and his "former life in Judaism" (Gal 1:13), believing that even in his zeal for Torah, in fact specifically in the actions to which this zeal had led him, he had been missing the way quite radically.[247] This has to do, however, with the next major turn in the argument (9:30–10:4), and is not the primary meaning of the present paragraph. His point here is rather, through the vivid rhetorical "I," to present the plight of Israel-as-a-whole under Torah, seeing Torah's picture of a truly human life, deeply honoring to God, and constantly failing as a people to attain it.

**7:16.** The conclusion from vv. 13-15 can then be drawn, reinforcing the "certainly not" of 13*a:* If, then, I do the thing I do not wish, I agree that the law is good. In other words, any charges against Torah—that it might have been evil in itself, that it might have caused "my" death—are dropped by the "I." The "I" basically agrees with Torah, and confirms its goodness, even while observing that in its own life it cannot perform the good things Torah prescribes.

**7:17-20.** The next four verses say nothing about Torah, but concentrate wholly upon the "I" and its own relation with sin. Torah has been exonerated; Paul will presently draw conclusions about it (vv. 21-25), and will then show God's remedy for the whole situation (8:1-11). But for the moment, having thus cleared Torah of complicity in sin and death, he must focus on the "I," and particularly on its "fleshly" state, developing what was said in vv. 14*b*-15 in order to do so. Contrary to much popular opinion, this small section does not portray what is usually meant by the "cloven ego" (this increases the probability that Paul is not here dependent on the rabbinic idea of two "inclinations"; see the Overview). The "I," though frustrated, is actually, like Torah, exonerated, with the blame going (of course) to sin. Paul, having moved the problem off Torah on to the "I," now moves it one stage further, on to sin itself.

**7:17.** "Now, however"; this is a new point, getting to the heart of the problem. "It is no longer I that do it, but sin that dwells in me": a remarkable statement of not just diminished but abrogated responsibility. The "indwelling" of sin is a new idea, introduced for the first and only time in Paul's writings, perhaps formed on the analogy of the indwelling of the Spirit, which Paul will contrast with this condition in 8:9, 11. Just as blaming sin for death was Paul's means of excusing Torah from complicity, so now sin is blamed for the present "fleshly" state of the "I." The underlying point seems to be not so much that humans in general are not responsible for their evil actions ("it was sin that made me do it"), as that Israel qua Israel is not responsible for the particular sin of breaking Torah. This verse functions, then, as a new proposition, which the next two verses will explain, and which v. 20 will then restate in conclusion.

**7:18-19.** The idea of being indwelt by sin is now advanced in its negative form, to explain the remarkable statement of v. 17 (*gar*, "for," which links v. 18 to v. 17, is omitted by the NIV). It is sin that dwells within the "I," that is, within its flesh, not "a good thing." Paul may perhaps be alluding to "the good thing"—i.e., the law—as in v. 13, though this remains uncertain.[248] He would then be repeating the contrast between the Torah and

---

247. See N. T. Wright, "Paul, Arabia and Elijah (Galatians 1:17)," *JBL* 115 (1996) 683-92. In 1 Tim 1:12-16 Paul's persecution of the church is described as constituting him chief among sinners (ἁμαρτωλοί *hamartōloi*); cf. 1 Cor 15:9-11.

248. A couple of ninth-century MSS (F and G) seem to have read it this way, adding "the" before "good" (lit., "for I know that there does not dwell in me, that is, in my flesh, [the] good [thing]").

the self from v. 14. The point he is pressing, in any case, is that what indwells someone is what gives them power to perform that which otherwise they would want to do but remain incapable of: literally, "for to will lies close to me, but to perform the good, not."[249] Without something "good" "dwelling in me," the "I" cannot bring the good will into reality; again, Paul is preparing the way for the contrast with the Spirit's indwelling, doing what the law could not, in the following chapter. His further explanation in v. 19 is a near-repetition of v. 15*b*, with the addition of "good" and "bad," and the replacement of "the thing I hate" with "the thing I do not want." The effect of all this is to drive a wedge between the "I" that wills, or does not will, certain things, and the "flesh," where sin dwells and where "the good thing" does not dwell.[250] The "I," Israel according to the flesh, is then on the same side, so to speak, as Torah; but, like Torah, it is powerless to prevent sin from doing what it chooses in the flesh, and eventually bringing death.

**7:20.** The conclusion is then drawn, repeating virtually word for word what was said in v. 17, which opened the subsection: "if, then, this is indeed my state, that I do that which I do not wish, it is no longer I that do it, but sin that dwells in me." It is exceedingly rare that Paul repeats anything in this way, and it gives us pause. Why does he emphasize this point so strongly? Have traditional readings missed something within the dense jungle of chap. 7?

My suggestion is that, as well as being concerned to exonerate Torah from any blame, while nevertheless showing how it has been used within

the kingdom of sin and death, Paul is simultaneously anxious to show how the "I," though fleshly and the dwelling-place of sin, is also exonerated, though still subject to sin and death. To remind ourselves what the "I" refers to—Israel according to the flesh, Israel "in Adam," Israel whose "Adamic" condition has been exacerbated by Torah—is to glimpse the solution. Paul is concerned to say that, though all the charges laid at the door of Israel, from 2:17 onward, are true, valid, and indeed grave, *there is nothing wrong with being Israel in itself.* Just as, with 7:5-6, we were back close to Paul's argument in 2:26-9, so now we are aware of the next question and answer Paul there had to address (3:1-2): What is the advantage of being a Jew? Much in every way. As with 2:17–3:9 and 11:1-32, Paul is determined simultaneously to maintain both the God-givenness of the covenant with Israel, the goodness of being Jewish, and the impossibility of finding eschatological life through that Jewishness alone. At the heart of Paul's exposition of the effect and meaning of Torah, indeed so hidden within it as usually to go unnoticed, we find a key part of Paul's root-and-branch rejection of what would later become Marcionism. Israel itself, the "I" that continues to live under Torah, and continues to discover that it points to sin within Israel and so condemns it to death, is God-given; Israel's delight in Torah (think of Psalm 119!) is a good, not a bad, thing; the problem is simply that that which is wrong with the rest of the human race—namely, indwelling sin—is wrong with Israel too, and Torah can do nothing about it. Here, in the middle of Romans 7, we find a short passage that picks up the theme of the vindication of Israel from early in chap. 3 and anticipates the full-dress statement, as the spiral of argument gradually unwinds, in chap. 11.[251]

---

249. This time it is the NRSV that omits "for." Throughout this passage Paul varies the word he uses for "do" or "perform," variously using κατεργάζομαι (*katergazomai*), πράσσω (*prassō*), and ποιέω (*poieō*); this is almost certainly to avoid repetition, not to introduce subtle shades of meaning between different kinds of "performance" or "accomplishment."

250. The negative goes with the verb: the NRSV's "nothing good dwells within me" and the NIV's "nothing good lives in me" throw the stress in the wrong direction.

251. This is in part an answer to the question rightly raised by R. B. Hays, "Adam, Israel, Christ," in *Pauline Theology Volume III: Romans,* ed. D. M. Hay and E. E. Johnson (Minneapolis: Fortress, 1995) 82.

## Romans 7:21-25, Reflecting on the Law: God's Law and Sin's Law

### NIV

21So I find this law at work: When I want to do good, evil is right there with me. 22For in my inner being I delight in God's law; 23but I see another law at work in the members of my body, waging war against the law of my mind and making me a prisoner of the law of sin at work within my members. 24What a wretched man I am! Who will rescue me from this body of death? 25Thanks be to God—through Jesus Christ our Lord!

So then, I myself in my mind am a slave to God's law, but in the sinful nature a slave to the law of sin.

### NRSV

21So I find it to be a law that when I want to do what is good, evil lies close at hand. 22For I delight in the law of God in my inmost self, 23but I see in my members another law at war with the law of my mind, making me captive to the law of sin that dwells in my members. 24Wretched man that I am! Who will rescue me from this body of death? 25Thanks be to God through Jesus Christ our Lord!

So then, with my mind I am a slave to the law of God, but with my flesh I am a slave to the law of sin.

# COMMENTARY

**7:21.** The argument, which as we have seen has been both about the Torah and about the Israel that has lived under Torah, is now brought to its double conclusion. As usual, Paul opens with a broad statement, which is then filled out by a couple of explanatory verses, before he moves to a conclusion—though this time the conclusion is more of an outburst.

"This, then, is what I discover about the law": Paul is here drawing the conclusion from his long argument. This proposal about the meaning of 7:21 can be sharpened up by pointing out that the verb here (εὑρίσκω *heuriskō*, "I find") can have the sense, not merely of "come upon by accident," but of "reaching one's findings" as a result of a careful deliberation.[252] One could translate it, "This, then, is my conclusion about the law."

But the real problem here is: What is the "law" that he now refers to? Most commentators and translators, including the NRSV and the NIV, have supposed that what Paul finds is not "the law," but "a law"—a general principle, a theory, a fact of observation, with nothing to do with "the law," the Torah, at all: "I find it to be a law," in the sense of "a regular pattern." Such readers have then gone on to suggest that in the remaining verses of the chapter, and in the first few of chap. 8, Paul is

as it were playing with the word νόμος (*nomos,* "law"), using it in a bewildering variety of senses, few if any of which refer in any direct way to Torah.

This must be addressed case by case. But our presupposition, if we are reading Romans with an eye to its overall drift and the careful integrity of its long argument, must be that when Paul says *nomos,* here of all places at the climax of an argument about Torah, he means what he has meant throughout. Paul is well capable of wordplay; he is no stranger to rhetorical flourishes. But the questions of 7:7 and 7:13 are the questions to which his entire argument has driven him, questions precisely about Torah and its identity and effects; we are in a chapter that began with a complex argument about Torah, which grew directly out of 5:20 and 6:14 where there is no question that *nomos* meant Torah; and we are now at the point where, with the argument nearly complete, the writer is summing up, drawing the threads together. Are we really to say that at precisely this point he will start twisting and turning and saying "this then is my conclusion—that I find *a* law"?

"Certainly not!" (μὴ γένοιτο *mē genoito*), as Paul himself would say. The present verse does indeed introduce the concluding section of the passage, a section in which "the law" remains one

252. See BDAG 412.

569

of the two principal subjects (the other being the plight of the "I"). And, though this is not always noticed, Paul refers here not to a *nomos* in general but to *the* law: εὑρίσκω ἄρα τὸν νόμον (*heuriskō ara ton nomon*), "this is what I find about *the* law." The definite article is highly significant. Any first-century reader or hearer, coming fresh through the discussion of 7:1-20, where the subject in almost every verse is ὁ νόμος (*ho nomos*) in the sense of "the Torah," and then reading *heuriskō ara ton nomon*, would be bound to understand it as "this, then, is what I find about 'the law' "—"the law," that is, that has been the subject all along. The present verse must be able to stand on its own feet. Paul, it is true, is quite capable of building up gradually to a dense and difficult point, but here, when he is introducing the summing-up of a long argument, we must assume that what he says would make clear sense.

The initial conclusion picks up from the description of the "I" in vv. 15-16, 17-20, in order to work back from there to what can be concluded about "the law." "This is what I find about the law: it means for me, when I want to do the good, that to me evil lies close at hand." If Paul in 7:7-12 alluded to Adam, hinting strongly (as had already been said in 5:20) that when Torah arrived in Israel, Israel recapitulated Adam's sin, the allusion here, somewhat fainter but still audible for those with ears attuned to echoes not only of Scripture but of Jewish traditions about Scripture, is to Adam's son, Cain.[253] "Sin is lurking in wait for you," said God to Cain, facing him with the choice between good and evil. Cain, choosing evil, committed murder, and found himself a wanderer and a fugitive, bearing forever the memory of his brother's blood.[254] "Wretched man that I am," says the "I" of Romans 7; "who will deliver me from this body of death?" When Torah arrived, Israel acted out Adam's trespass; living in the present under Torah, Israel continues to act out the sad paradox of Cain. Paul will show in chap. 8 how God has addressed this problem, too.

**7:22-23.** Paul now puts together into a fresh

253. The full argument, which depends on the remarkable convergence of many Jewish traditions about Cain with what Paul says in 7:13-25 as a whole, is presented in Wright, *The Climax of the Covenant*, chap. 12.

254. Gen 4:7-16; the LXX of Gen 4:7 is so confused that one should not expect to find verbal parallels; the case is made by the multiple thematic convergence, set out in Wright, ibid.

formulation what he has said about Torah on the one hand and about the "I" on the other. This statement obviously anticipates the final conclusion of 7:25*b*, and must be taken in close conjunction with it.

At this point many commentators have again balked at reading *nomos* as "Torah" throughout. "The law of God" in v. 22 is clearly the Mosaic law, they say, but surely this phrase itself shows that Paul is then talking about a different law altogether when he says ἕτερον νόμον (*heteron nomon,* "another law") in v. 23. So too with the formulation "the law of sin" at the end of v. 23, repeated at the close of v. 25. This is clearly a *prima facie* problem for anyone who wants to interpret *nomos* as "Torah" right through the passage; yet it is a nettle that must be grasped. The point to be stressed by way of reply is that these "negative" formulations *simply pick up and spell out what Paul has said about Torah in 5:20; 7:5; and particularly 7:8-11 and 7:13.* We may compare 1 Cor 15:56: "the sting of death is sin, and the strength of sin is Torah"; the fact that Paul goes on at once to say, "Thanks be to God, who gives us the victory through our Lord Jesus Christ" (1 Cor 15:57), paralleling Rom 7:25*a* so closely, indicates well enough that this embodies the same train of thought as we find at the end of Romans 7. Paul has not said anything new here, even though he has said it in a sharp and striking fashion. Precisely by demonstrating that Torah itself is "holy, just and good" (v. 12), while simultaneously explaining how sin "worked death in me" *through* "the good thing" (v. 13), he has already stated the paradox in principle, and now simply displays it in its simplest form. Insofar as the Torah is given by God, and is in itself holy, just and good, it is something rightly to be delighted in. Insofar as Torah has been made into sin's base of operations (vv. 8, 11) it has been taken over by sin, and has become "the law of sin."

Nothing is gained by lessening the force of Paul's paradox, by avoiding the thought that Torah might be its own shadowy *doppelgänger.* This has been, after all, the whole point of the section so far, and indeed the whole point of the paradox inherent not only in 5:20 but as far back as 3:19-21. The attempt to suggest that Paul might mean something else at the climax of his argument, just when he is drawing all the threads together, reminds me of the attempt by nineteenth- and early twentieth-century musical editors to make sixteenth- and seventeenth-century choral music more palatable by removing the false relations that contain not only the harmonic logic but also, frequently, the pathos and tension of the whole piece. After all, if we say that Paul means something other than Torah by some of his uses of *nomos* in this passage, we are already saying that he is writing in a deliberately paradoxical and many-sided way; if we allow this, why not allow that he is actually referring to Torah throughout, albeit highly paradoxically and many-sidedly?

The double Torah then fits the strange double identity of the "I," of Israel under Torah. The "I" itself, as Paul has been argued in vv. 17-20, is in principle exonerated; but insofar as this "I" is in Adam, is *sarkinos* (v. 14), sin and death are at work within its "members" (v. 23, repeated; cf. 6:13, 19; 7:5, another indication that Paul is making the same point as there). In the present verses Paul expresses this duality in terms of the "mind" on the one hand and the "members" on the other, further explaining the former with the phrase "the inner person" (lit., "the inner human"; the NRSV's "my inmost self" is perhaps a shade too strong). With this "inner being" (NIV) the "I" delights in God's law; Paul may well have in mind the perfectly genuine delight that Israel, even Adamic Israel, finds in the study and contemplation of Torah, as expressed classically in Psalm 19 or 119. "To will [the good] is present with me" (v. 18); this is a reality, and it is not to be denied or mocked, for instance by those who say that "the Jew" was wrong to delight in Torah. The problem here is not "legalism" or "nomism," nor yet *homo religiosus*, but sin: that sin that has taken over Torah, made it a base of operations, and is now—continuing the implicit military metaphor from vv. 8, 11—producing a full-scale war between "another Torah," the Torah as it appears in 5:20 and 7:5, and the holy, just, and good law of God. And in this war the "I" is taken captive, a prisoner of war under the rule of "the Torah of sin." Paul, still exploring the depths of 5:20, is again describing the captivity, the enslavement, the "Egypt" of sin and death, exacerbated by Torah, from which Christ and only Christ can deliver. This, seen with Christian hindsight, is the plight of the "I," of Israel, including the pre-Christian Paul himself, under Torah.

**7:24.** Paul's famous cry of despair, put into the mouth of the "I," echoes but goes beyond the great tradition not only of the biblical psalms of lament but of subsequent Jewish lamentations such as the Qumran *Hodayot*. "Wretched man that I am": the NRSV, using the well-known phrase, for once allows the gender-specific noun, though ironically the Greek here is ἄνθρωπος (*anthrōpos,* "human being"). This, indeed, is the point: that Israel too is "in Adam," is a human being like all other human beings. Like Cain, bearing about the mark of his brother's death, the "I" finds itself unable to escape from "this body of death," referring perhaps both to its own "fleshly" state but also to the solidarity of sin, of Adamic humanity, with which it is unavoidably bound up (cf. 6:6). The problem is clearly stated: it is not so much sin itself, but the death that results from it. The promise of life held out by the law (with Eden's tantalizing tree of life remembered in the background) appears a mirage. Like a moth trying to fly to the moon, the "I," Israel under Torah, remains frustratedly earthbound. "Sin reigned in death," and Torah merely tightened the noose (5:21, in the light of 5:20); the "I" finds itself enslaved under that regime. "The sting of death is sin, and the power of sin is Torah" (1 Cor 15:56). What the "wretched person" needs is deliverance, and Paul, bringing the passage's rhetoric to its height, cries out for it: "who will deliver me?"

**7:25.** The full answer is about to be given in chap. 8, and indeed in the passage that, building on chaps. 5–8 as a whole, speaks of the salvation that is still open to ethnic Israel along with the Gentiles (chap. 11). But, as in 1 Cor 15:57, Paul cannot resist anticipating these answers right away, in an expostulation whose sense is clear even if its grammar is oblique. The answer to the question is "God"; "Thanks be to God, [the one who will deliver me] through Jesus the Messiah, our Lord." This verse looks back to 5:21, where "grace" is obviously a periphrasis for "God" (cf. too 6:23), and on to 8:3, where ὁ θεός (*ho theos,* "God") is the emphatic subject of one of the most important sentences in the entire letter. The full triple statement of Jesus' identity—Jesus, the Messiah, our Lord—serves as the weighty christological summary at the end of this stage of the argument, matching those in 4:24-25; 5:11, 21;

and 6:23, and pointing toward the christology and consequent soteriology of 8:1-11, 17, 29-30 and supremely 31-39.

Verse 25b is not an anticlimax, nor (as used sometimes to be suggested) a dislocated verse, still less a gloss introduced by a later scribe into Paul's argument.[255] The double identity of the "I," and the double identity of Torah, are stated in terms of the double slavery that has ironically characterized the whole passage. The αὐτὸς ἐγώ (*autos egō*, "I of myself"), apparently ignored by the NRSV, is emphatic, but controversial. It has, inevitably, been pressed into service to support various different readings of the whole passage. By itself, though, it cannot exercise sufficient leverage to determine the meaning of the chapter one way or another. It does, however, fit very well within the line of thought I have been expounding. "I of myself" means, I suggest, "I, Paul, as part of the solidarity of Israel according to the flesh."

We may cautiously use 9:3, the other Pauline occurrence of the same phrase, in support. There Paul expresses his solidarity with his "kinsmen according to the flesh" whom he sees in rebellion against the gospel, in a passage whose deepest point (9:14-23) is as we shall see to be understood very closely together with 7:13-25. He is saying that "I of myself" *could* pray to be accursed, cut off from the Messiah, for their sake. He does not say that this is in fact his prayer; it is what, left to himself as a Jew according to the flesh, he would pray; but that is not who he now is. He is "in the Messiah," by baptism and faith, and cannot and will not change that. He will wrestle with the problem of his "kinsmen according to the flesh"

until a better solution, better than merely exchanging his own salvation for theirs, comes to light.

The contrast between the two things that are true of the "I" is made by separating out the "mind" and the "flesh." These are both clearly used in a technical sense; we should once more beware of taking them in terms simply of a non-material thinking capacity on the one hand and physicality on the other. At the same time, we should also beware of trying to understand "mind" univocally in Paul; here it clearly refers to the intention or will spoken of in vv. 15-16, 18-21, and to the "inner person" of 7:22. It goes with the phrase "the law of my mind" in 7:23. It would be a mistake, fatal to the understanding of the whole passage, to insist that it must mean exactly what it does in two of the four other references in Romans, namely 1:28 and 12:2, where the mind is first darkened and then renewed. Clearly the "mind" in the present case, though delighting in God's law, remains powerless to put it into practice, whereas that in 12:2, being renewed by God, is the source of that full transformation in which the person is able to discover in practice what God's will actually is (cf. 8:5-8). The "I" of chap. 7 remains frustrated, rightly delighting in the Torah but finding that the solidarity of Israel with Adam prevents performance and, consequently, bars the way to life. That is the contrast Paul is emphasizing.

The Torah itself, then, simply binds Israel to Adam. Without the death of the "old human," as in 6:6 and 7:2-3, that is what Torah will inevitably do. When this plight is fully understood, however, the remedy can at last be unveiled. When the sickness is properly diagnosed, it can be treated. God has done what Torah could not do—not, of course, to indicate that Torah was bad, or not God-given, but that, through sin and the "flesh," it was weak, and could not give the life it promised.

---

255. So, rightly, e.g., Joseph A. Fitzmyer, *Romans*, AB 33 (Garden City, N.Y.: Doubleday, 1993) 477, citing various opinions. Ernst Käsemann, *Commentary on Romans*, trans. Geoffrey W. Bromiley (London: SCM, 1980) 211, declares that if v. 25b is not a gloss everything he has said so far about Paul's major topics will have to be reconsidered.

# Romans 8:1-11, God Gives Life Through the Son and the Spirit

## NIV

**8** Therefore, there is now no condemnation for those who are in Christ Jesus,[a] [2]because through Christ Jesus the law of the Spirit of life set me free from the law of sin and death. [3]For what the law was powerless to do in that it was weakened by the sinful nature,[b] God did by sending his own Son in the likeness of sinful man to be a sin offering.[c] And so he condemned sin in sinful man,[d] [4]in order that the righteous requirements of the law might be fully met in us, who do not live according to the sinful nature but according to the Spirit.

[5]Those who live according to the sinful nature have their minds set on what that nature desires; but those who live in accordance with the Spirit have their minds set on what the Spirit desires. [6]The mind of sinful man[e] is death, but the mind controlled by the Spirit is life and peace; [7]the sinful mind[e] is hostile to God. It does not submit to God's law, nor can it do so. [8]Those controlled by the sinful nature cannot please God.

[9]You, however, are controlled not by the sinful nature but by the Spirit, if the Spirit of God lives in you. And if anyone does not have the Spirit of Christ, he does not belong to Christ. [10]But if Christ is in you, your body is dead because of sin, yet your spirit is alive because of righteousness. [11]And if the Spirit of him who raised Jesus from the dead is living in you, he who raised Christ from the dead will also give life to your mortal bodies through his Spirit, who lives in you.

[a] *1* Some later manuscripts *Jesus, who do not live according to the sinful nature but according to the Spirit,*    [b] *3* Or *the flesh*; also in verses 4, 5, 8, 9, 12 and 13    [c] *3* Or *man, for sin*    [d] *3* Or *in the flesh*    [e] *6, 7* Or *mind set on the flesh*

## NRSV

**8** There is therefore now no condemnation for those who are in Christ Jesus. [2]For the law of the Spirit[a] of life in Christ Jesus has set you[b] free from the law of sin and of death. [3]For God has done what the law, weakened by the flesh, could not do: by sending his own Son in the likeness of sinful flesh, and to deal with sin,[c] he condemned sin in the flesh, [4]so that the just requirement of the law might be fulfilled in us, who walk not according to the flesh but according to the Spirit.[a] [5]For those who live according to the flesh set their minds on the things of the flesh, but those who live according to the Spirit[a] set their minds on the things of the Spirit.[a] [6]To set the mind on the flesh is death, but to set the mind on the Spirit[a] is life and peace. [7]For this reason the mind that is set on the flesh is hostile to God; it does not submit to God's law—indeed it cannot, [8]and those who are in the flesh cannot please God.

9But you are not in the flesh; you are in the Spirit,[a] since the Spirit of God dwells in you. Anyone who does not have the Spirit of Christ does not belong to him. [10]But if Christ is in you, though the body is dead because of sin, the Spirit[a] is life because of righteousness. [11]If the Spirit of him who raised Jesus from the dead dwells in you, he who raised Christ[d] from the dead will give life to your mortal bodies also through[e] his Spirit that dwells in you.

[a] Or *spirit*    [b] Here the Greek word *you* is singular number; other ancient authorities read *me* or *us*    [c] Or *and as a sin offering*    [d] Other ancient authorities read *the Christ* or *Christ Jesus* or *Jesus Christ*    [e] Other ancient authorities read *on account of*

# COMMENTARY

The first eleven verses of Romans 8 lie at the very heart of Romans 5–8 as a whole. They simultaneously complete the thought of the section that began with 7:1 and begin the majestic sequence that sweeps on through to 8:30. As tightly argued as any piece of Pauline logic, they are at the same time suffused with a sense of exultation, and celebration.

Many regular readers of the Bible will find this passage almost too well known to be any longer audible. As was once said of Shakespeare's *Hamlet,* it is "full of quotations." Liturgies and private prayers have drawn freely on it. Almost every line evokes, and has indeed produced, hundreds of sermons. Johann Sebastian Bach made it the backbone of a whole cantata (*Jesu, meine Freude*). How can we avoid the two equally unhelpful reactions of having heard it all before, on the one hand, and of focusing too narrowly on particular verses, and the theological topics they evoke, on the other? How can we hear the symphony, not just the notes?

The clue is to remind ourselves, not for the first time, that we are still watching the unfolding of the Adam/Christ contrast of 5:12-21, and in particular the exposition of the great statement in the last verse of that seminal passage. "As sin reigned in death" (and we must remind ourselves of the role of the law within that reign, as in 5:20), "so grace also reigned through righteousness to eternal life through Jesus Christ our Lord." From this tight-packed statement, the key contrast for the present passage is that between death and life: "life" is the golden thread that runs through 8:1-11, the gift of God that the law wanted to give but could not, the gift that comes because God's Son has dealt with sin and death and God's life-giving Spirit has replaced sin as the indwelling power within God's people. The promise of resurrection with which the passage concludes is not added for extra effect at the end of the paragraph. It is where the whole argument is leading.

The shape of the paragraph then becomes clear. The opening statement (v. 1) is at once explained, in Paul's usual fashion, first with another dense and cryptic statement (v. 2, linked to v. 1 with *gar*), which is in turn explained (another *gar*) by the complex and powerful statement of vv. 3-4, a sentence that has as good a claim as any to represent the very center of what Paul is saying in Romans 5–8, if not in his whole theology. Verses 1-4 together serve as the platform for the step-by-step argument that explains how precisely it is that God has given the life that the law could not. Verses 5-8 rule out any way to life for those "in the flesh," but declare that the Spirit is the key source of that life. Verses 9-10 apply this to those who are "in Christ" and hence "in the Spirit," those who have the Spirit, or indeed Christ himself, dwelling in them. And verse 11 draws the conclusion: The indwelling Spirit will give new life to the mortal body of the Christian, despite the necessity of physical death.

What has happened, of course, is that the shape of 5:21, still clearly visible in vv. 2, 10, has been filled in with the more detailed content of 7:5-6. "Sin reigned in death" has been expanded, by means of 7:5 and 7:7-25, in terms of two further factors, namely, "the law" and "flesh," and is here summarized in 8:2*b*, 7-8, and the middle phrase of 8:10 ("the body is dead because of sin"). The problem that has thereby been so carefully analyzed is equally carefully dealt with: the death of Jesus and the gift of the Spirit are shown to be exactly what was necessary. "Grace reigned through righteousness to eternal life through Jesus Christ" has been expanded, by means of 7:6, to include the Spirit as the key agent of that reign.

The paragraph thus offers, as its opening statement suggests, the ultimate response to the problem set out in 2:1-16. Final "condemnation" hangs over the heads of all people. All have sinned, and in chapter 2 it was not clear how there could be any who would come into the category Paul held out in 2:7, 10. The hints of 2:13*b*-15*a* were by themselves too oblique to build on; the fuller statement in 2:26-29 can at last be seen for what it is, an advance statement of what Paul can now say clearly. Romans 8:1-11 is focused on those who, whether circumcised or not, submit to God's law in the power of the Spirit, and in whom therefore the positive verdict, the δικαίωμα (*dikaiōma*) of the law is fulfilled. This at last explains how the verdict issued in the *present* on the evidence of faith alone (3:27-30) embodies God's justice, how (in other words) God is right to declare that Abraham's true worldwide family consists of all those who believe in the gospel. As Paul says elsewhere, the one who began a good work will bring it to completion (Phil 1:6). The Spirit who was at work in the coming to faith of those who heard the gospel (1 Thess 1:4-5; 2:13) will continue that work until the final moment of resurrection itself.

This in turn is made possible because the "condemnation" of sin, the real culprit all along, has taken place on the cross. Verse 3 refers back to the theme of Christ's "obedience" in 5:12-21, and stresses that what was done there was the act of God in Christ, not (as it were) the action of Christ upon God. The central sentence of 8:3-4, around which so many vital subordinate clauses hang like bunches of grapes on a vine, is simply this: "God . . . condemned sin." No clearer statement is found in Paul, or indeed anywhere else in all early Christian literature, of the early Christian belief that what happened on the cross was the judicial punishment of sin. Taken in conjunction with 8:1 and the whole argument of the passage, not to mention the partial parallels in 2 Cor 5:21 and Gal 3:13, it is clear that Paul intends to say that in Jesus' death the condemnation that sin deserved was meted out fully and finally, so that sinners over whose heads that condemnation had hung might be liberated from this threat once and for all.[256] This densely stated but clearly thought out atonement-theology (as it would later be known) is not the main subject of the paragraph. That place belongs to the Spirit's gift of life. But, as John saw equally clearly, the outpouring of the Spirit depends on the prior achievement of the cross (cf. John 7:37-39; 20:19-23).

The paragraph is remarkable, finally, for its dense and many-sided concentration on the work of God. In Jewish thought at this time, the activity of the one God, not least the supremely self-revealing and saving divine activity on behalf of Israel, had been spoken of in many ways. God's Word would go forth to renew Israel and the world. God's Spirit, that breathed on the waters at the beginning, would blow again like a mighty wind, animating the dead bones of God's people. God's Wisdom, the divine agent in creation, would enable humans to live truly human lives, and would be sent by God to live in Israel. God's Law, again at this period sometimes conceived as a preexistent divine agent, would guide God's people along the path of life. And God's own Presence, God's Glory, would dwell in the Temple in Jerusalem, the source of life and glory for Israel (and, in some readings, for the whole world).[257]

Paul has not expounded these aspects of the character and presence of God in any systematic fashion. But they undergird and explain this whole paragraph. The way to understand the christology of v. 3, for instance, is not simply to study the phrase "Son of God" on its own. Rather, we must observe the way in which the sending of God's Son in this passage, as part of God's doing that which the law could not, belongs, together with the indwelling of the Spirit, as part of Paul's reworking of the Jewish Wisdom theology, and *Shekinah* theology, in which God's character was revealed in the act of bringing salvation to Israel. If the main topic of the paragraph is the gift to God's people of the life the law promised but could not give, the main foundation upon which that topic is built is the saving presence of the one God of Israel in the cross of the Son and the indwelling of the Spirit.

There is thus, we even dare to say, an implicit trinitarianism in this paragraph, which becomes more explicit as chap. 8 unfolds. We glimpse, in other words, how it is that the gospel outlined in 1:3-4 does indeed reveal the δικαιοσύνη θεοῦ (*dikaiosynē theou*, 1:17), thus becoming "God's power unto salvation for all who believe" (1:16). We are still left, of course, with the question as to how this works out "to the Jew first and also to the Greek." Paul's answer to this question, given spectacularly in chaps. 9–11, is constructed with considerable care on the foundations he is laying in the present passage. Here, too, what lies at the heart of it all is a vision of God.

**8:1.** The opening statement, with its connecting "therefore" (ἄρα *ara*), comes as a shock. How can the analysis of 7:7-25 lead to such a conclusion? "I of myself . . . serve the law of sin; there is therefore now no condemnation!" The answer is that Paul has leapfrogged over the middle premise of his argument. Instead of the normal pattern of a syllogism, *a* plus *b* therefore *c* ("donkeys have crosses on their backs; this animal has a cross on its back; therefore this animal is a donkey"), Paul has created a striking effect by advancing *c* and explaining it with *b:* "I serve God's law with my mind, but sin's law with my flesh; there is *therefore* no condemnation, *because* God has dealt with sin in the flesh, and provided new life for the body." The "now" picks up the "but now" of 3:21; 7:6 (see also 5:9, 11; 6:22), emphasizing the eschatological nature of God's achievement in Christ and by the Spirit. The verdict of the last day has been brought forward into the present. This is, quite simply, the solid foundation for Christian joy.

The "condemnation" spoken of here is the final judgment that God, the righteous judge, will mete out at the last. It is the necessary reaction of the

256. On 2 Cor 5:21 see N. T. Wright, "On Becoming the Righteousness of God: 2 Corinthians 5:21," in *Pauline Theology, Volume II,* ed. D. M. Hay (Minneapolis: Fortress, 1993) 200-208.

257. For details, see N. T. Wright, *Jesus and the Victory of God,* vol. 2 of *Christian Origins and the Question of God* (London: SPCK, 1996) 629-31; M. J. Borg and N. T. Wright, *The Meaning of Jesus: Two Visions* (San Francisco: Harper, 1999) chap. 10.

justice-loving God to all injustice; of the God who created image-bearing human beings to all that defaces and destroys that likeness. Like so much in this part of Romans, it looks back to chap. 5 (here, vv. 16, 18), and behind that to 2:1-16.

The reason why there is now no condemnation is not far to seek. Sin's condemnation has been effected in the cross of God's Son (v. 3), and those who are "in the Messiah, Jesus" discover that what is true of him is now true of them. His death means that, as far as they are concerned, the condemnation that must rightly fall on sin has nothing more to do with them. Thus "in Christ Jesus" at the close of v. 1 offers not just a designation of the people for whom there is no condemnation, but, in compact form, the reason why this is the case.[258]

**8:2.** Paul's fundamental explanation for v. 1 is God's act of liberation. He has already spoken of this at length in chap. 6 and developed it in 7:1-6. As we have already seen, talk of setting slaves free is exodus language: the present paragraph is describing how those who are in the Messiah, and indwelt by the Spirit, are brought out of the Egypt of sin and death and promised citizenship in the kingdom of life. There is no question but that Paul is referring in this verse to the same composite event that he has been describing in the previous chapters—namely, the messianic (and hence representative) death of Jesus and the gift of the Spirit.

The object of this liberating act is "you," singular.[259] Some MSS, followed indeed by several translations, have "me" rather than "you" (KJV, RSV, NIV, "me"; NEB, NRSV, "you"). But "you" is sufficiently well supported to be quite possible, and sufficiently unexpected, after a long paragraph where "I" and "me" are the main focus, to be likely. Why would a scribe alter the expected "me" to "you"? At the same time, Paul is not only addressing each reader as an individual with this striking and joyful message of freedom. He is ensuring that each individual reader, not only those who had in some sense been "under the

law" and hence in the precise situation of 7:7-25, would know himself or herself to be included in this joyful news. Like those old portraits whose eyes follow each onlooker around the room, this statement of freedom is aimed at every single hearer of the letter, whoever and wherever they may be.

The liberating action has taken place "in Christ Jesus." Certainty here is impossible, but it is likely that the last phrase belongs with the verb rather than modifying either "law," "Spirit," or "life." Paul is quite capable of writing lengthy strings of mutually modifying nouns and phrases, but I think it more probable that in this instance the NIV and the NEB are correct. The NIV is wrong, though, to change "in" to "through." Paul is always careful about these prepositions; the action has taken place "in the Messiah" so that those who are "in him" may benefit from it. "There is no condemnation for those in Christ, because in Christ God has set you free."

The subject of the verb, and the description of that from which one has been liberated, presents us with a new version of the problem we encountered in 3:27-31 and 7:21-25: can Paul conceivably mean "the law," the Torah, by these uses of *nomos?* This question is linked to that in 7:21-25, since the gaoler from whom "you" are now free is described in almost identical terms here to those of 7:23, 25. As I argued there, so it seems to me compelling here that the "law" in question is not a general principle, "the old vicious circle" as J. B. Phillips renders it, but the Torah itself, seen from one angle, specifically the angle described in 4:15; 5:20; and 7:1-6 (to say nothing of 7:7-25). The situation of all humankind was "under sin and death." Torah, rightly, endorsed this verdict, tightening the grip of Adamic humanness on those who were "under" its sway, and shutting out altogether the "Gentile sinners" (Gal 2:15) who were not. God's act of liberation has broken this stranglehold once and for all.

But Paul does not actually mention God as the subject of the sentence. Can it really be that "the law of the spirit of life" is a further reference to Torah, introducing now a new facet to Torah not visible in chap. 7? Most commentators draw back from this conclusion. I am persuaded, however, that that reaction is wrong. When scaling the sheer rock of Paul's thought it is important not to lose one's

---

258. Several good MSS add, at the end of v. 1, "who do not walk according to the flesh, but according to the Spirit," thus anticipating the point to be made at the end of v. 4. This was not, as has sometimes been asserted, an attempt by later scribes to undercut the sheer grace of v. 1; nevertheless, the shorter text is certainly to be preferred.

259. C. E. B. Cranfield, *A Critical and Exegetical Commentary on the Epistle to the Romans,* ICC, 2 vols. (Edinburgh: T. & T. Clark, 1975) 377, comments, truthfully if nostalgically, on the disappearance of the singular form "thee/thou" from contemporary English, making it almost impossible to convey Paul's sharply personal address.

nerve and settle for an apparently easier path, a seemingly more natural route. The explanation of v. 2, after all, is found in vv. 3-4; and there, as the heart of the chapter so far, we find that the "righteous verdict of the law," the δικαίωμα τοῦ νόμου (*dikaiōma tou nomou*), is now fulfilled "in us who walk . . . according to the Spirit." We then find, by implication, that whereas "the mind of the flesh" does not submit to God's law, the mind of the Spirit actually does (v. 7), and that by the Spirit God will do what the law wanted to do but, through no fault of its own, was unable to do (8:3, 10-11; cf. 7:10). It is not fanciful, then, but strictly in keeping with the thrust of the whole passage, to say that when Paul speaks of "the law of the Spirit of life in Christ Jesus" he is indeed referring to Torah, in a way for which we have only distantly been prepared by 3:27, 31. After all, *ho nomos* in vv. 3, 4, and 7 is clearly Torah. How obscure do we suppose Paul to have been? More will be said on the subject when we arrive at 10:4-8, which plays a similar role in the argument of chaps. 9–11 to that played by 8:1-4 within chaps. 5–8.

It would have been easy to write "for the Spirit of life in Christ Jesus has set you free," but Paul seldom settles for the easy option. He has spent a whole chapter arguing that, despite appearances (and despite many commentators!), the Torah remains God's law, holy and just and good, and that it is not guilty of causing the death that comes to those who embrace it. Now he takes a step further: When God acts in Christ and by the Spirit the Torah is somehow involved as well, somehow present and active. Speaking of Torah, after all, was a thoroughly Jewish way of speaking of God's saving action. Though Paul has spoken with eloquent passion of the way in which Torah locks the door on those who are imprisoned within Adamic humanity, he has never forgotten its promise of life. He can therefore speak, with deliberate but comprehensible paradox, of the law itself as the agent of that which God has accomplished in the Messiah and by the Spirit.

The Torah, then—why, after all, should we be surprised at being surprised by Paul?—is the hidden agent of what God has achieved, which is the life of which the Spirit is the personal giver. This, as we saw, is the main thrust of the paragraph. And it answers the otherwise puzzling question at the start of the next verse.

**8:3-4.** What was it that the law "could not do"? Some have assumed that Paul meant by this somewhat awkward phrase (lit., "the impossible thing of the law") to refer to law-abiding behavior, as though the main thrust of the paragraph were to fall on (what we would call) the "ethical" passage of vv. 4*b*-8. This then goes with an understanding of τὸ δικαίωμα τοῦ νόμου (*to dikaiōma tou nomou*) in v. 4*a* in which δικαίωμα (*dikaiōma*) would mean "righteous decree" or "requirement" (NRSV) in the sense of moral commands to be obeyed. But (to deal with that problem first) there are two outstanding objections to this reading. First, when *dikaiōma* is used in this sense it is usually plural (e.g., 2:26; elsewhere in the NT, Luke 1:6; Heb 9:1, 10; Rev 15:4; 19:8). Second, in the passage to which the present one looks back, where *dikaiōma* is contrasted with *katakrima*, as here (5:16, 18), the *dikaiōma* is unquestionably God's righteous decree or verdict, not the required behavior of God's people. A similar use appears, in a negative sense, in 1:32. It is highly likely, therefore, that *to dikaiōma tou nomou* here refers to the verdict that the law announces rather than the behavior which it requires. And, in the light of 5:16, 18 and the argument of the present passage, this is clearly (unlike 1:32) the *positive* verdict: "do this and you will live" (cf. on 10:5). That this is the correct reading of 8:4*a*, and with it 8:3*a*, is confirmed by three things: Paul's highlighting of this intention of the law at 7:10; the whole thrust of the argument of 8:1-11 (with 5:21 in the background); and the point about the life-giving Torah in 10:5-11 (see the notes on that passage). What was impossible for the law? That it should give life. It offered it, but could not deliver.

It could not do so because it was "weak because of the flesh." Despite many commentators and preachers who have been eager to see Paul say negative things about the law, he declares, summing up the argument of chap. 7, that there was nothing wrong with it in itself. The problem lay elsewhere: in the "flesh"—not the physicality of human nature, which was God-given and will be reaffirmed in the resurrection (8:11), but in the present rebellious and corruptible state of humankind, within which sin had made its dwelling (7:18, 20, 23, 25).

The main sentence with which Paul then

explains how God has done what the law could not do must then be understood as follows: God condemned sin in the flesh of Jesus, so that the life the law offered could rightly be given to those led by the Spirit. The latter was the long-term purpose of the former, the former the necessary precondition of the latter. Each half of this double statement must now be explored in detail.

God, says Paul, condemned sin. Paul does not, unlike some, say that God condemned Jesus. True, God condemned sin in the flesh of Jesus; but this is some way from saying, as many have, that God desired to punish someone and decided to punish Jesus on everyone else's behalf. Paul's statement is more subtle than that. It is not merely about a judicial exchange, the justice of which might then be questioned (and indeed has been questioned). It is about sentence of death being passed on "sin" itself, sin as a force or power capable of deceiving human beings, taking up residence within them, and so causing their death (7:7-25). To reduce Paul's thinking about the cross to terms of a law-court exchange is to diminish and distort it theologically and to truncate it exegetically. For Paul, what was at stake was not simply God's judicial honor, in some Anselmic sense, but the mysterious power called sin, at large and destructive within God's world, needing to be brought to book, to have sentence passed and executed upon it, so that, with its power broken, God could then give the life sin would otherwise prevent. That is what happened on the cross.

For this to be done it was necessary, and Paul here spells this out, that the place where the sentence was executed was indeed the true "likeness of sinful flesh" (the NIV's repeated "sinful man" fails to highlight the link between Paul's expression here and the cognate ones elsewhere in the argument). The difficult word here translated "likeness" (ὁμοίωμα *homoiōma*) is certainly meant to indicate that Jesus' humanity was indeed the genuine article; it is not a cover for a smuggled-in Docetism in which Jesus was not actually human but only seemed to be. Why, then, has Paul not simply said "sending the son in sinful flesh"? Presumably because, though Jesus' humanity was true and genuine, Jesus was himself not guilty of sin—a remarkable fact that appears at various points within early Christian tradition (cf. John 7:18; 8:46; 2 Cor 5:21; Heb 4:15; 7:26; 1

Pet 2:22). For Paul, it would have been axiomatic that sin was not necessary to genuine humanness. Sin was an intruder, not a native inhabitant, of God's good world (5:12). To debate whether Jesus' humanity was therefore "sinful humanity" or "sinless humanity," whether "fallen" or "unfallen," seems to me beside the point. What matters is that it was genuine humanity, not a sham (cf. Phil 2:7, where ἐν ὁμοιώματι ἀνθρώπων [*en homoiōmati anthrōpōn*, "in the likeness of humans"] does not mean "like a human being, but not actually one," but rather "a true human being, bearing the true likeness." Jesus could and did suffer and die, truly and really; he was in principle capable of sinning, but unlike all other humans did not. It was God's design that, in his truly human death, sentence would be meted out on sin once for all.

But how could Jesus' human flesh, and his human death, be the appropriate locus of this judgment? Why, if Jesus was himself in some sense sinless, would it make any sense that sins be condemned in him? I have already suggested that part of the answer lies in the phrase "in Christ Jesus." Because (as the resurrection revealed) Jesus was the Messiah, he represented his whole people; what was true of him was true of them. His death could therefore be counted as theirs. That is the underlying logic, rooted in the biblical picture of Israel's monarchy, that binds the unique event of Calvary to the status of all those "in Christ" from that day to this.

But the other part of the answer is found in the whole sequence of thought that, begun deep in chap. 7, reaches its climax in this verse. This is the point envisaged by the repeated "in order that" (ἵνα *hina*) of 5:20 and 7:13, the point indeed that must be grasped if the further argument of Romans 9 is to become comprehensible. Once again we are following through the train of thought over which 5:20-21 stands like a gold-lettered heading on a page. The law came in *in order that* the trespass might abound; sin worked death through the law *in order that* it might be shown up as sin, *in order that* sin might be exceedingly sinful. The law caused sin to be heaped up in one place, to flourish and abound in that single location. As many have seen, the "place" implied in 5:20-21 was Israel. As not so many have seen, God's purpose in and through all of this—in giving the Torah with this strange intention—was that sin might be drawn together, heaped up, not just in Israel in general, but *upon Israel's true representative, the Messiah,* in order that it might there be dealt with, be condemned, once and for all. God sent the Son "in the likeness of sinful flesh" to bring this sequence to its appointed climax, that in his death Torah might do the necessary, if apparently negative, work for which it was designed. We are not far, here, from what Paul says in Gal 3:22: Scripture (i.e., God, working through the written law) shut up everything under sin, in order that the promise, effective through the faithful obedience of Jesus the Messiah, might be given to all believers. And now we are not far, either, from the conclusion to the argument of Romans 9–11: God shut up all in disobedience, in order to have mercy upon all (11:32). In the strange plan of God, to deceive and defeat "the rulers of this age" (1 Cor 2:6-8), the personified forces of Sin were lured onto the one field where they were bound to lose the decisive battle. Sin, the real culprit throughout chap. 7, needed to be condemned; on the cross, it was.[260]

Paul expands his condensed reference to the cross by adding "and as a sin-offering."[261] The phrase καὶ περὶ ἁμαρτίας (*kai peri hamartias*) can, it is true, mean simply "and to deal with sin" in a more general sense. But this is the regular phrase that, in the LXX, translates the Hebrew terms for the specific sacrifice known as the sin-offering.[262] Why would Paul refer to this sacrifice here in particular? Because in the biblical codes that deal with the whole sacrificial system the sin-offering is designed to deal, not with any and every sin, but with sin that has been committed ignorantly or unwillingly. Either one did something without realizing it was sinful; or, knowing it was sinful, one did it despite intending not to. Without one or other of these saving clauses, of

course, any sin would be deliberate, knowing the act to be wrong and intending it none the less. This, known as "sinning with a high hand," is unpardonable; the person who acts thus is to be "cut off from among the people"—that is, put to death (cf. Num 15:30-31).

The sin-offering thus answers exactly, not indeed to any and every sin (that is not what this phrase was designed to do), but to the problem so carefully analyzed in chap. 7. The "I" of 7:15, as we saw, does not "know," and does not "will," the actions committed. The sin in question is precisely, in Jewish terms, sin of ignorance, unwilling sin. When we meet, in the passage where Paul is explaining how God has dealt with the problem of chap. 7, the very phrase the LXX uses regularly to refer to the sin-offering, the sacrifice that deals with this sort of sin, there can be no excuse either for rejecting the sacrificial meaning or for ignoring the tight interlinking of the argument, and its various implications.

In particular, as we shall see when dealing with 10:3, Paul is aware that in the next stage of his argument (i.e., chaps. 9–11) he will need to stress that his kinsfolk according to the flesh are "ignorant of God's righteousness." Here the point of adding "and as a sin-offering" is to emphasize that the death of Jesus has been the means, not simply of condemning sin in general, but of dealing specifically with the problem set out in the previous chapter, the problem of the "I." Paul's argument from this point on is not focused on the problem of Israel under Torah, but it is important to show, as part of his larger statement, how Israel's peculiar plight has also been taken care of.

I have left to the end of v. 3 what is arguably the most important phrase in the whole verse. If Paul thus sees the death of Jesus as the means whereby the judicial punishment on sin itself was meted out, he blocks off the possible misunderstanding of that (as in much medieval thinking and iconography, and some more recent expressions as well) as the act of a merciful second person of the Trinity placating a hostile first person. The whole action comes from God in the first place, as in 5:6-10. Paul does not use the word "love" at this point, but his dramatic summary of the whole argument in 8:31-39 shows that this is what he has in mind. The condemnation of sin in the flesh of Jesus happened as a result of divine grace, of "God sending his own Son."

---

260. It is inadequate and misrepresents the whole drift of Paul's argument to suggest, as several have done (e.g., Fitzmyer, *Romans,* 487), that this "condemnation" simply means that sin is now merely disempowered. κατέκρινεν (*katekrinen*) in v. 3 answers directly to κατάκριμα (*katakrima*) in v. 1, and that verse scarcely means "there is no disempowerment."

261. The NIV implies that this is the main purpose of God's sending of the son, with the condemnation of sin being a new idea; but that is not how the Greek works. The NIV does, however, recognize the meaning of *kai peri hamartias* as "and as a sin offering," while the NRSV, with most translations, relegates this to a footnote.

262. E.g., Lev 5:7-8; 6:25 (LXX/MT 6:18). For full details, and a more complete presentation of the following argument, see N. T. Wright, *The Climax of the Covenant: Christ and the Law in Pauline Theology* (Edinburgh: T. & T. Clark; Minneapolis: Fortress, 1991) chap. 11.

The echo of 5:10 here, and behind that of 1:3-4, is obvious, as is the important parallel with Gal 4:4 and the anticipation of 8:32. Without leaving the home base of meaning for "Son of God"—Israel in general, the Messiah in particular (on "Son of God," see the Commentary on 1:3-4; see also Gal 2:20)—and indeed while needing precisely that for his argument to work, Paul has exploited the phrase so that it becomes a way of saying what some Second Temple Judaism said about God's action in the world and Israel through Wisdom, Torah, *Shekinah,* Word, and Spirit: that God had sent, or would send, Wisdom or the others to embody the divine presence, and to be the means of the divinely originated salvation.[263] Here and elsewhere Paul has worked from within the Second Temple Jewish awareness of God's personal action in the world and in Israel. He has exploited the image of "father and son," which already carried the messianic overtones on which his argument depends, to produce genuine and appropriate innovation from within current Jewish language about God. The fact of Jesus himself, the truly human being in whom, as the resurrection revealed, God's saving plan had been put into effect, called forth from Paul the formulation that, while rooted in the pre-Christian soil of Second Temple language about God and God's action, laid the foundations for the developed Trinitarian thought of later theologians (whose main aim, of course, was to retain Jewish-style monotheism while affirming a distinction between Father and Son). The present expression forms the middle term in a crescendo: Starting with 1:3-4 and 5:10, both of which simply refer to Jesus as God's son, 8:3 speaks of God's sending "his own son" (τὸν ἑαυτοῦ υἱόν *ton heautou huion*), and 8:32 speaks of God's not sparing, but handing over "his very own son" (ὅς γε τοῦ ἰδίου υἱοῦ οὐκ ἐφείσατο *hos ge tou idiou huiou ouk epheisato*). The sending and death of the Son of God forms, in fact, one of the key threads that run through the entire letter so far.

Verse 4 then falls into place. The introductory "so that" (the *hina,* as in 5:20 and 7:13, clearly expresses the divine purpose) states God's intention: that the righteous verdict of the law might be fulfilled "in us." The life the Torah intended, indeed longed, to give to God's people is now truly given by the Spirit (for this interpretation, see above). The balance with v. 3 might have led us to expect δικαίωσις (*dikaiōsis*) at this point, but Paul may have chosen δικαίωμα (*dikaiōma*) not least because of its formal balance with the κατάκριμα (*katakrima*) of v. 1, exactly as in 5:16.[264] As argued earlier, the *dikaiōma* could conceivably have referred to the behavior the law commanded rather than the verdict it pronounced. Paul could have said that the intended result of sin's condemnation was that God's renewed people might be able at last to do what the law required (in some sense that does not require either circumcision or observance of the food laws; cf. 2:27; 13:8-10; 14:1-23; 1 Cor 7:19). Yet the singular formulation (ignored by the NIV, which translates "righteous requirements"), taken in conjunction with the larger thrust of the paragraph as a whole, strongly suggests the reference to the law's "righteous decree" of life.

This does not, of course, exclude the former point, since it is precisely by "walking according to the Spirit" that those in Christ "seek for glory, honor and immortality" (2:7). The commandment that was "unto life" brought death because of sin residing in the flesh (7:10); now the same commandment brings life because of the indwelling Spirit. On the "life/death" choice see again Lev 18:5 and Deut 30:15-20, with the discussion below on 10:5-11.

As I pointed out earlier, this in no way compromises present justification by faith. What is spoken of here is the future verdict, that of the last day, the "day" Paul described in 2:1-16. That verdict will correspond to the present one, and will follow from (though not, in that sense, be earned or merited by), the Spirit-led life of which Paul now speaks. Once again Torah is vindicated by God's action. As a detailed analysis of Paul's underlying narrative here will reveal, Torah is the main "character" at this point in the story, and here emerges triumphant.[265]

Those who will find Torah's righteous decree fulfilled in them—those, that is, who will share in the resurrection life (8:10-11)—are those who in the present do not "walk" according to the flesh

---

263. A classic statement is found in Sirach 24, where Wisdom, sent into the world, becomes *Shekinah,* dwelling in the Temple, and is summed up in the Mosaic Torah.

264. As BDAG points out.
265. See Wright, *The Climax of the Covenant,* 204-8.

but according to the Spirit (on "walk" as a Jewish metaphor for conduct [flattened out by the NIV's "live"] see the Commentary on 6:4). Here Paul highlights the Spirit/flesh contrast, already seen in 1:3-4, which will dominate the rest of the paragraph. The "flesh," not in the sense of physicality but in the sense of rebellious and corruptible human nature, is not the sphere of existence in which the Christian lives. Paul is capable of expressing things slightly differently elsewhere, as when, for instance, he speaks in Gal 2:20 of "the life I now live in the flesh," or when he distinguishes in 2 Cor 10:3 between "walking in the flesh," which there simply means "living an ordinary human life" (albeit with the overtones of mortality and decay not far off) and "waging war according to the flesh," which means "adopting the standards of rebellious and corruptible humankind." But in the present passage, as in 7:5 ("when we were in the flesh," implying that this is no longer the case), he brings together "in the flesh" (8:8-9) with "walking according to the flesh" (8:4) and "being according to the flesh" (8:5), seeing all these expressions as referring to the status and way of life of those without faith, those not baptized, those not in Christ, those not indwelt by the Spirit. "Flesh," then, carries here its fully nuanced negative meaning, not of physicality per se, but of humanity both mortal and rebellious. And part of the point of the passage, as will become clear in chaps. 9–11, is that unbelieving Israel is precisely "in the flesh."

The contrast with "flesh" is "Spirit"; not "spirit," or "on the spiritual level," as though Paul were after all contrasting the merely physical and the merely non-physical. With 1:4 in the background, and the climax of 8:9-11 coming up in the foreground (to say nothing of 8:12-27), he is clearly referring, throughout the present paragraph, to the Holy Spirit. Romans 8 contains one of Paul's greatest expositions of the work of the Spirit, emphasizing constantly the way in which the Spirit's present work anticipates the Spirit's future work of resurrection. In the present passage, it becomes clear that the Spirit "indwells" God's people in Christ, as the *Shekinah* "indwelt" the tabernacle in the wilderness or the Temple in Jerusalem; so we should not be surprised to discover in the following paragraphs that the Spirit takes the role, within the new wilderness wander-

ings of the liberated people of God, that in the exodus story was taken by the pillar of cloud and fire. Once again Paul, as a theologian in the strict sense (that is, one who thinks and writes about God), is innovating appropriately from within the Second Temple Jewish tradition. The result, as in a more compressed form in Gal 4:4-7, is that the one God of Jewish monotheism now begins to be known in three usually (though not always) distinct ways. Though Paul does not use the language of "person" to distinguish these three ways, he sets up a universe of discourse within which some such development would ultimately appear necessary.

Here the point is simply this: through the action of the Spirit in the present, those who are in Christ are walking on the road that will lead to the resurrection of the body. Indeed, the more we allow for *Shekinah* and Temple overtones in what Paul is saying, the more a further interesting possibility opens up: that Paul is hinting, as he speaks of the resurrection of the body, of the rebuilding of the Temple. In any case, the same Spirit who will raise Christ's people at the last inspires within them in the present a life that is neither corruptible—it will stand at the judgment (cf. 1 Cor 3:10-17)—nor rebellious, but which conforms to God's will for humankind. Torah is thereby vindicated; the problem of Romans 7 is thereby solved; and, as the rest of the chapter will make clear, the whole new creation is thereby brought into view.

**8:5-6.** The next pair of verses offer a two-stage explanation of why those who walk according to the Spirit inherit life. The logic works like this: (a) The two categories, walking according to the flesh and the Spirit, are each characterized by a certain manner of thinking. (b) Whereas the thinking that goes with the flesh is death, the thinking that goes with the Spirit is "life and peace" (the NEB and the REB have coalesced the two verses, producing a single complex statement instead of a two-stage one). Paul will then develop this contrast in vv. 7-8 and 9-10, using it as the bridge into the climax and conclusion of the paragraph. Both verses begin with *gar;* it seems to me more likely that both independently explain vv. 1-4, rather than that v. 6 is intended to explain something about v. 5. (The NIV omits both connectives; the NRSV, that in v. 6; the NEB, that in v. 5. If a connection between v. 5 and v. 6 is sought, it may be that Paul is meaning "and the reason I highlight the *think-*

*ing* of flesh and Spirit is because. . . . ") When the verses are taken together, leading to the point about "life and peace" at the end of v. 6, and the flow of thought of the whole paragraph is kept in mind, then the meaning of the connections becomes apparent. Like a pianist needing to keep the coming climax of the movement in mind through a tricky middle section, it is important to sustain the theological rhythm of these verses in their context rather than treating them, as some translations and commentaries have done, as isolated remarks about what it is like to live according to the flesh and the Spirit.

Instead of "walk," Paul merely says "are": "those who *are* according to the flesh." The NIV and the NRSV both say "live;" but the Greek is simply ὄντες (*ontes*), those who "are." In the second half of v. 5 Paul omits both this and the verb for "think," so that 5*b* simply reads "but those according to the Spirit the things of the Spirit." Verse 6 follows swiftly: the thinking of the flesh is death, but the thinking of the Spirit is life and peace (the death/life contrast throughout the passage, with its echoes in 10:5-11, makes it more certain that these verses are about the true fulfillment of Torah). The Greek (τὸ φρόνημα τῆς σαρκός *to phronēma tēs sarkos* and τὸ φρόνημα τοῦ πνεύματος *to phronēma tou pneumatos*) leaves it open as to whether these expressions refer to the thinking, the thought processes, that are characteristic of flesh and Spirit in themselves and are then, as it were, incarnated in human beings, or whether the "of" is objective, as in the NRSV ("to set the mind on the flesh . . . to set the mind on the Spirit"; the NIV breaks the contrast: "the mind of sinful man . . . the mind controlled by the Spirit"). I incline somewhat to the former view: the flesh, personified, "thinks" in a certain way, which then becomes embodied in particular individuals; so too with the Spirit. Certainly the partial parallel in 8:27 suggests this meaning here too.

The reason why Paul highlights the thought-processes, rather than the outward actions, that are characteristic of flesh and Spirit will emerge as the paragraph develops, but we may draw attention to the way in which, as the argument of the letter unfolds, it is the Christian *mind* that must become the initial, and transformative, locus of renewal (12:2, contrasting with 1:22, 28). As fre-

quently in his thinking about how human beings operate, Paul here envisages *thought* as the key to action; not, however, just the process of ideas through the brain, but in the stronger sense of the settled and focused activity and concentration that characterizes the one state or the other.

The important point here, and the reason why these verses help the overall argument forward, is the contrast of "death" and "life and peace" that characterize the two "thinkings." The contrast of death and life is familiar enough in this argument, and has been so since at least chap. 5; but why (apart from the echo of 5:1) add "peace"? It is not simply that the phrase "life and peace" carries distant covenantal overtones.[266] The evidence Paul is about to adduce for his assertion that walking, or "being," "according to the Spirit" is the guarantee of "life" is precisely that "flesh-thinking" is at enmity with God, whereas "Spirit-thinking" is in tune with God. At least, that is the implication of the next verses, though this time the entire thought involves an ellipsis, which must now be explained if the paragraph is to yield its complete secret.

**8:7-8.** What follows offers itself as the further explanation of what has gone before. Verse 7 begins with διότι (*dioti*), which (despite the NRSV's idiosyncratic "for this reason") normally means "because" or "for."[267] What Paul intends to say appears to be: (a) flesh-thinking is death, Spirit-thinking is life and peace; (b) *because* flesh-thinking is hostile to God, (c) whereas Spirit-thinking is at peace with God [thus explaining "peace"]; (d) *and* the Spirit is the souce of resurrection life [thus explaining "life"]; (e) and you, therefore, being indwelt by the Spirit in the present, are assured of resurrection life in the future. What he has done, however, is to foreshorten this train of thought simply to (a) (v. 6), (b) (vv. 7-8), and a combination of (d) and (e) (vv. 9-11). For neither the first nor the last time, he has omitted to make explicit the link in the thought (here [c]) that might have clarified things for those attempting to think his thoughts after him—an ironic reflection on a paragraph one of whose central subtopics is "thinking."

---

266. "Life and peace" describes the covenant between God and Levi in Mal 2:5. See also the "covenant of peace" in Num 25:12; Isa 54:10; Ezek 34:25; 37:26; Sir 45:24. The prophetic passages in particular are full of overtones that are interesting for Romans 8.
267. The only NT examples of the meaning "therefore" given by BDAG are Acts 13:35; 20:26.

Paul does at least explain stage (b) quite fully. Picking up from 5:10, and rounding off hereby the negative line of thought expounded in chap. 7, he explains that flesh-thinking is hostile to God. Interestingly, his further explanation of this (v. 7b, introduced with *gar*, omitted by both the NIV and the NRSV), is that flesh-thinking does not submit to God's law, a point that is further explained on the grounds that it cannot. As chap. 7 has made clear, the "flesh" serves "the law of sin"; however much this may, paradoxically, turn out to be the Torah in another role, at this point "the law of God" is clearly a positive thing to which humans ought to submit, not the quasi-demonic thing some Marcionite schemes of thought have imagined. The law in its full God-given glory is, after all, a spiritual thing, so that there is a mismatch between it and the person who is "fleshly, sold under sin" (7:14 and 8:7 thus belong very closely together). The implication, of course (the omitted stage [c] in the argument), is that Spirit-thinking will now fit Torah perfectly; however counterintuitive this may seem in some theological circles, it fits well with Paul's other statements about Christian fulfillment of Torah (e.g., 2:25-9; 10:4-11; 13:8-10; perhaps also 3:27).

Paul's final and most revealing comment about flesh-thinking (v. 8) is that "those who are in the flesh" are incapable of pleasing God.[268] Despite its prominence in various Pauline passages, the idea that one can actually *please* God, or the Lord, is foreign to much thinking and writing on the apostle, perhaps because it suggests to some the thin end of a wedge that will end in works-righteousness. Paul had no such scruples (see, e.g., 12:2; 14:18; 1 Cor 7:32; 2 Cor 5:9; Eph 5:10; 1 Thess 4:1). Those in the flesh cannot please God; but, by strong and clear implication, those in the Spirit can and do.

**8:9-11.** Paul clearly believes that his readers are "in the Spirit," no longer "in the flesh." The evidence for this is that the Spirit of God dwells in them; the result is that they are assured of final resurrection. Verse 11 thus gives the complete answer

to the question of 7:24, the answer anticipated in 7:25a.

That much is clear; this is the main thrust of these three verses. But the way in which Paul has said it is complex, and potentially confusing. Three levels of complexity need to be unraveled for clarity to be attained.

First, Paul switches bewilderingly between describing Christians as being "in the Spirit" and describing the Spirit as being "in them." The latter is what Paul wants to emphasize at this point, using the image of "indwelling" that evokes the idea of the *Shekinah* dwelling in the wilderness tabernacle and the Jerusalem Temple (cf. 1 Cor 3:16; 6:19, etc.). The formulation "in the Spirit" is more of a technical description, formed ad hoc to contrast with "in the flesh"; nowhere else does Paul make this contrast in exactly this way, though there are pointers in this direction in 2:29; 7:6, and he can speak of Christian thoughts, prayers, and actions as taking place "in the Spirit" (e.g., 9:1; 14:17; 15:16; the contrast of "according to the flesh" and "according to the Spirit," as in 8:5, is found again in Gal 4:29). When speaking thus, the "in" seems to denote a basic condition or situation, rather than having precise locative force. Part of the problem in all these formulations is that Paul's picture of the Christian is not simply the mirror-opposite of his picture of the non-Christian. At one level "Spirit" contrasts with "flesh"; at another, "Spirit," as the indwelling power within the person, contrasts with "sin." At another, the Spirit is doing that which the law could not. And so on. We would be wrong therefore to accuse Paul of inconsistency in his terminology. He is carving out language to say what had not been said before. As long as we allow him to explain where he is going he will not mislead.

Second, the terms he uses to denote the indwelling Spirit move in an initially confusing fashion between "the Spirit," "the Spirit of God," "the Spirit of Christ," and then simply "Christ." This, too, we must assume, is the result of Paul hammering out patterns of thought where none had existed previously. For him, the same Spirit is the Spirit of God and of the Messiah—an interesting indication, we note with a sidelong glance, of the status the Messiah already has in his thinking!—and he can move to and fro in his description according to the particular shade or nuance of the actual point being made.

268. Paul changes the phrase from "those who are *according to* the flesh" in v. 5, apparently treating the two as identical, despite the distinction he maintains in 2 Cor 10:3 and by implication Gal 2:20; in both of these Paul speaks of being "in the flesh," meaning "still living as a human being this side of the grave," while not conducting his life "according to the flesh." In the present passage the distinction is obliterated: "you are not in the flesh," he says in v. 9.

Third, Paul also shuttles to and fro in his description of Jesus the Messiah himself. As elsewhere, he refers to him as "Messiah" not least in order to stress the solidarity between him and his people. He refers to him as "Jesus" when focusing attention on Jesus himself as a specific individual human being. This, too, enables him to impart to his statements particular nuances and subtleties within the clear overall point being made.

Verse 9, then, introduces the argument that will lead to the triumphant conclusion of v. 11, making the contrast with vv. 7-8: you, he says (the "you" is plural, placing all his readers in the picture) are not in the flesh, but in the Spirit. The evidence for this is precisely that God's Spirit dwells in them. The nuance of the middle clause of v. 9 is hard to catch, since "if" (NIV) appears too doubtful and "since" (NRSV) too certain. The Greek εἴπερ (*eiper*) hovers in between these two, meaning something like "if after all" or "if, as is indeed the case"; we may compare its use in 3:30 or 8:17. If it contains a shadow of doubt it does so within a basic affirmation. The doubt, however, is raised in the last clause of the verse, which, being introduced by δέ (*de*) also implies that the middle clause was more of an affirmation than a question: "but if anyone does not possess the Messiah's Spirit, that person does not belong to him." The equivalence of "being in Christ" and "belonging to Christ" is clear in Gal 3:27-29; these are different ways of saying the same thing, denoting the people of God as redefined around the Messiah. Paul does not at this stage of his argument want to raise serious doubts as to whether some of his readers may, after all, be sham Christians; though it is important for later debates to note that, for him, the idea of a Christian who did not possess the Spirit of Christ was a contradiction in terms. Paul's strong incorporative theology of the church is balanced by an equally strong view of the necessity of each individual member of the community being indwelt by the Spirit. The final clause in v. 9 highlights the fact that the Spirit in question is the Spirit of the Messiah. This enables Paul to draw on all that he has said about the Messiah in previous chapters to make the key point of v. 10.

If the Spirit is the Spirit of the Messiah, then the Messiah himself lives in the Christian. Paul, of course, more regularly speaks of the believer being "in Christ"; this is not interchangeable with "Christ in you," which always refers to the indwelling within believers of that divine presence, variably spoken of as Christ or the Spirit, which empowers them in the present and will transform them in the future (see also Gal 2:20; 4:19; Eph 3:17; Col 1:27). Being "in Christ," as we have seen frequently, particularly in 6:1-14, means that the Messiah's death and resurrection become true of all his people. Because of the indwelling of the Messiah's Spirit, however, this is no longer seen simply as a matter of status, but of actual power.

Paul's way of saying this in the rest of v. 10 may again appear oblique, but will be clear, yet once more, when the background in 5:21 is kept in mind. "The body is dead because of sin"; in other words, even Christians are subject to the laws of decay and death, still living as they do in "the body of humiliation" (Phil 3:21). This is not in itself intended as a description of something that results from Christ being "in you"; the logic is "if Christ is in you, then (though the body is dead) the Spirit is life." Sin has reigned in death, and since sin has indwelt believers prior to their baptism and receiving of the Spirit death must surely follow. But "grace reigns through righteousness to eternal life"; because of God's covenant faithfulness, revealed in the Messiah's saving death and resurrection, the Spirit gives life the other side of death. Artificial schemes for dividing up Romans (and indeed Paul's thought as a whole), designating the first four chapters as lawcourt theology and the next four as incorporative theology, lead to commentators expressing surprise at the use of "righteousness" here, but in the light of 5:21 there should not only be no surprise but no question as to the word's referent. The Spirit, dwelling within Christians, is the lifegiving power; Paul simply says "is life," to make the contrast with "the body is dead" in the previous clause.[269] And this is so because of God's faithfulness to the covenant, God's own righteousness (other alternatives offered to explain this sudden reference to "righteousness" include "righteous behavior," following from v. 4*b*, and the righteous status Christians have as a result of God's justifying action). We look

---

269. "Spirit" here, as in the NRSV and the REB, is more likely than a reference to the human spirit, as still in most translations, including the NIV. See also N. T. Wright, *The Climax of the Covenant: Christ and the Law in Pauline Theology* (Edinburgh: T. & T. Clark; Minneapolis: Fortress, 1991) 202; G. Fee, *God's Empowering Presence: The Holy Spirit in the Letters of Paul* (Peabody, Mass.: Hendrikson, 1994) 500.

back here all the way to Abraham, who in chap. 4 believed precisely in the life-giving power of God upon which the covenant depended, the covenant to which God has now been faithful in Jesus the Messiah. Paul's pithy formulation of all this is a sign not of imprecise thought but of rhetorical power as he hastens on to v. 11. This verse is both the goal of the argument that began in 7:1 and the foundation of the still greater argument that will take him through to 8:30.

The point of v. 11 is straightforward, and its inner logic can be spelled out as follows: (a) The Spirit dwells in you; (b) the Spirit is the Spirit of the God who raised Jesus; (c) Jesus is the Messiah, and you belong to him; (d) the God who raised Jesus the Messiah will raise all the Messiah's people, you included. Once again, this sequence of thought has been compressed tightly, almost epigrammatically. As in 4:24, summing up the train of thought at that point, God is referred to as "the one who raised Jesus from the dead," repeated here at once with the significant change of "Christ" for "Jesus"; this can only be explained on the basis that "Jesus" is the individual human being and "Christ" the one who royally represents his people, so that what is true of him is true of them. The key assumption Paul makes is that the raising of Jesus is the act of God, as in 6:4; and the conclusion is of course described at much greater length in 1 Corinthians 15. Jesus the Messiah is the firstfruits (cf. too Col 1:18), the first to rise from the dead; all those who belong to him will be raised as he was raised. This final resurrection will, like that of Jesus, be the act of none other than God. In 6:4 Paul said that Jesus was raised by the *glory* of the Father; in 1 Cor 6:14 he says that God raised the Lord, and will also raise us, by the divine *power;* here he says that God will accomplish this by his *Spirit.* A case has recently been made for the strongly attested variant reading, that God will give life to your mortal bodies *because of,* rather than "through," the indwelling Spirit (cf. NRSV margin); but the argument of the chapter seems to me to fit well with the thought that the Spirit is God's agent in the final resurrection, not merely God's reason for accomplishing this great act of new creation.[270]

This, then, is the answer to 7:24b, no longer as a bare assertion of faith (as, by itself, is 7:25a), but as a tight theological argument. Who will deliver from this body of death? Who, in other words, will give life to the dead? The law, though holy, just and good, cannot do this; God will, through Christ and by the Spirit and will thereby do what the law held out (Lev 18:5; Deut 30:15-20) but could not perform.

At the end of this central passage we may reflect on the nature of Paul's achievement so far. This is the heart of his argument for assurance (those whom God justified, them God also glorified). For the Jew—for Paul himself prior to his conversion—the basis of assurance was membership in the covenant, whose outward badges were circumcision and Torah. The story of the exodus formed the backdrop to the Jewish expectation that the covenant God would once again act within history to deliver Israel. Paul has retold the story of the exodus, the freedom story, demonstrating that the Egypt of sin and death has been decisively defeated through the death of the Messiah, and that the Spirit is now leading God's redeemed people to their promised inheritance. Baptism has marked out God's renewed people; the Spirit is now "the one thing that distinguishes those who are Christ's from those who are not."[271] The sign of the Spirit's work is first and foremost faith (1 Cor 12:3) and indeed faithfulness; and the fruit of the Spirit's work is the final resurrection. Thus is the path from justification to glorification, from "passover" to the "promised land," laid out in this passage. Paul will now develop this picture, drawing on several interlocking images from the exodus story, and widening the angle of vision to include, not just humans, but the whole created order.

270. See Fee, *God's Empowering Presence,* 543. The usual reading seems to me more probable in the light of the argument of the passage as a whole. The difference between the two is not, however, enormous.
271. Ibid., 553.

# REFLECTIONS

**1.** It is important to see this long and central argument (7:1–8:11) as a whole, before drawing small-scale lessons from its different parts, which by themselves could easily be taken in senses somewhat different from those which the overall context suggests. The passage goes to the heart of the self-identity of the people of God. Israel at its best looked to Torah as the basis of its status as the chosen people of the creator God; Paul has insisted that Torah informs Israel in no uncertain terms that it is instead simply a subset of the people of Adam, in slavery to sin and facing death. Where then can assurance be found? Only in the death of the Messiah and the life-giving presence and power of the Spirit. Insofar as the church remains the people whose family story goes back to Abraham—and Paul would insist that this is a non-negotiable part of being God's people—this story must be told again and again as part of the foundation of who the church is. It is not, in other words, simply a story about how ethnic Israel faced a particular problem and how this problem was overcome—a story that might seem somewhat remote and irrelevant to Christian living in any subsequent century, let alone two millennia later. Like the story of Jesus itself, it is the story of how God's people, the church's forebears, had to pass through the anguish of Romans 7 in order that, through the Messiah and the Spirit, new hope might be born.

**2.** Within the overarching theme of assurance, the central character in the story of 7:1–8:11 is of course Torah. This is Paul's classic defense of Torah against all the charges that might be, and perhaps were being, laid against it. Torah, he insists, is holy and just and good; it is not responsible either for sin or for death. Indeed, it just goes to show the exceeding wickedness of sin itself that it can as it were make its nest in Torah, twisting Torah so that it becomes a dark and sinister replica of itself, condemning rather than giving life. When God acts in Christ and by the Spirit to give life to those indwelt by the Spirit of Christ, Torah looks on with, as we might say, a sigh of relief and approval: this was, after all, what it had intended all along. It should be clear from this, despite those whom C. E. B. Cranfield memorably called "Marcionites and semi-, crypto-, and unwitting, Marcionites,"[272] that Paul solidly and emphatically reaffirmed the goodness and God-givenness of Torah. Any suggestion that law in general, or the law in particular, were or are shabby, second-rate, primitive, destructive of true religion, and therefore to be abolished, set aside, or treated as irrelevant in the bright new day of a law-free faith, must be ruled out. Paul's theology contains many apparent paradoxes, and this point must be held in careful tension with the next one; but nothing is gained, certainly not in understanding of Paul or attempting to live and work in the light of his writings, by the shallow rejection of Torah.

**3.** Having said all that, we must also insist, against some current attempts to reinstate or rehabilitate Torah either within the church or (for instance within contemporary Israeli society) in wider social and political contexts, that the Torah is by itself weak. Not only can it not give the life to which it points; it accents, and indeed accentuates, the Adamic condition, the sinful and death-bound position, of those who embrace it. There is always a danger within the church that some Christians, anxious about Marcionism of whatever variety, and eager to insist that the whole Bible is the Word of God, will fail to heed the words of Jesus and Paul and will attempt to live by Torah in matters (for instance) such as the death penalty. There are some Christians today, despite the letter to the Hebrews and indeed the entire temple-based christology and pneumatology of the New Testament, who seem to believe that the rebuilding of the Temple in Jerusalem could still be God's will; equally, there are some who, no doubt with considerable inconsistency (I do not hear them calling for a reappropriation of patriarchal marriage customs, for example), want to see the Jewish law as in some way(s) normative for Christians today. This is to make the mistake of treating revelation in a flat, dehistoricized fashion. As Paul's own

272. Cranfield, *Romans*, 867.

writings make abundantly clear, what we find in Scripture is above all a *narrative:* the great story of God and the world, and of God's people as the people of God *for* that world. Torah stands as the headline over that story from the time of Moses to the time of the Messiah (Galatians 3 is the classic exposition of this); but the story, which started before the giving of Torah, moves on beyond the time when Torah was the determining factor, *and Torah itself celebrates this fact.* To say that its primary role was acted out in an earlier act in the drama than that in which Paul believed himself to be living is not to diminish its God-given role, but rather to celebrate it. To say that it goes on applying equally in the era of Christ and the Spirit is to ignore not only what Jesus and Paul said at several points but, if anything more important, the story Jesus enacted in his life, death, and resurrection, the story Paul took as his starting-point. This is not, of course, to deny what is said in 10:5-11 and 13:8-10 (on which see below).

**4.** On the day I sat down to write this part of the commentary I received a letter from a parish priest, asking whether the end of Romans 7 might not reflect Paul's sense of standing vis-à-vis his kinsfolk according to the flesh much as Moses had stood in Exodus 33, seeing Israel as a whole in rebellion against God and agonizing over what could be done. This, I believe, reflects a true insight, not so much as exegesis of Romans 7 but as anticipation of Romans 9. As we have had occasion to observe, the argument of Romans proceeds in a series of long spiraling loops, and Romans 7 does indeed provide part of the foundation for what Paul will say in Romans 9, whose introduction evokes exactly the picture, proposed by my correspondent, of Moses standing between God and the rebel people. However, there may be something more to say here as well. In Galatians 1 Paul describes himself as being, in his pre-Christian days, "exceedingly zealous for the traditions of my fathers." We know that this kind of "zeal" could be described as zeal for God (cf. Acts 22:3; Rom 10:2) or for the law (Acts 21:20). When Paul wrote in Romans 7 of delighting in God's law, but observing in his "members" another law bringing about death, I think it is at least worth enquiring whether he had in mind the way in which the zeal for Torah, which he and others had been exhibiting, was not only bringing death to those they opposed but also pulling down death on themselves, driving them closer toward the brink of a war with Rome that they could not possibly win. If this is in any way a valid reflection, it offers a series of concentric circles of application, relating not only to Middle Eastern politics in the twentieth as in the first century, but also to many other areas of conflict around the world, where zeal for ancestral traditions, which may or may not have been good in their way and place, leads to idolatrous behavior that is as destructive for the perpetrators as for the victims. If Romans 7 could help the church to speak more clearly on such issues we should be grateful.

**5.** Though Paul is not, in Romans 7, writing first and foremost about the plight of the whole human race, but only about that of Israel under Torah, it is nevertheless possible to work outward from what he says to a more general analysis of the puzzle of human moral inability. This, after all, is already hinted at in his (probably deliberate) sidelong allusions to the tradition, from Aristotle to Epictetus and beyond, that spoke of approving the better course but practicing the worse. If the point of Paul's analysis is that Israel is like everyone else only more so, it is perfectly legitimate to reason back from that to what must be true of "everyone else." When we do this we find, consonant with Rom 2:1-16, that even when the human race embraces and affirms some moral code, or even some moral principle, living up to it proves impossible. This does not mean that the code or the principle was wrong or misleading; just that there is a twist within the human race, as it presently finds itself, which distorts the best intentions, and exposes self-interest at the heart of apparent altruism. A glance at political and religious leadership in the Western world (to point the finger only at my own part of the human race) would offer many examples.

Someone is bound to respond to this by saying that the same is true of Christians also. I am bound to agree. Does this not call into question my whole exegesis? Is the passage not after all about Christian existence as well as anyone else's? No. The Christian is not "under law," and is not "sold under sin." There is a great irony here. In the 1960s many people within the church, as well as outside it, trumpeted loudly that the old moral codes (they often meant the sexual ones, but it applied more widely as well) were no longer relevant, since we now knew that one should live simply by love, not by law. The moral chaos that has resulted, in mainline churches in particular, over the last generation has been pitiful to behold. When people from within that same tradition now say that Christians are no better than anyone else, it seems to me somewhat unfair to hold up as the prime evidence those parts of the church that have exhibited major disloyalty to traditional Christian teaching over many years. Why not look at the many other parts of the worldwide church where Christians today can still be spoken of, as the second-century apologists spoke of their comrades, as people in whom a different way of being human, a way of holiness and joyful self-sacrificial love, was truly being modeled? Yes, it is also true (so I am told) that the greatest saints remain conscious of depths of rebellion and unholiness within them that will not be rooted out until death itself (not even, according to some traditions, until some time after that). But there is such a thing as Christian holiness, however flawed it may still be; and these flaws, and the tensions that result, are not the same as those described in Romans 7.

**6.** The villain in the drama is Sin. Paul is capable of speaking of Satan, but he does so sparingly (only ten times in the entire Pauline corpus, and only once [16:20] in Romans). But when he speaks of Sin, he means not simply human acts of rebellion or lawbreaking, but a personified force at work in the world and in humans. He speaks of it nineteen times between 7:1 and 8:11, building on the seven occurrences in 5:12-21 and the sixteen in chap. 6. (To get some idea of the scale of this treatment, there are four references in Romans prior to 5:12, two after 8:11, and only seventeen in the whole of the rest of the Paulines.) Writing after a century in which many Western Christians have regarded it as something of a social or even liturgical faux pas to speak of sin, let alone Sin, it is important to stress that our soft-pedaling of the New Testament's analysis of the depths of the human problem has done no service to either the church or the world. Of course, there are healthy and unhealthy ways of speaking about sin. The church has often allowed itself to lapse into a dualism in which certain parts of life are labeled "sinful," in order to create an artificial sphere of "holiness" that is, in fact, no more than an imposed social convention. But to say that there is such a thing as a shallow diagnosis of the human condition is not to deny that there might be a deeper one. Politicians and the media used to pretend that a little more social progress, a little more Western-style democracy in the world, would solve the ills that were still visible. We now know that this was a lie: not only is the world not a significantly better place for having more democracy, but the Western powers themselves have been shown up as riddled with corruption, selfishness masked as public service, and sexual and financial scandals. Cynicism about the political process and those who run it has become endemic. It is time once again to hold out the analysis of human behavior offered in the New Testament. There is such a thing as Sin, which is more than the sum total of human wrongdoing. It is powerful, and this power infects even those with the best intentions. If it could make even the holy Torah its base of operations, how much more the muddled intentions of well-meaning do-gooders.

**7.** Such an analysis, comes the response, is so gloomy. It will produce a human existence dogged by guilt, paranoia, and self-hatred. Nonsense. With the diagnosis goes the remedy. Not surprisingly, of course, those who dislike the Pauline analysis of sin routinely despise the Pauline remedy—namely, the cross and the Spirit. But this double answer to the problem remains foundational to genuine Christian understanding and indeed, of course, to genuine Christian living. It is, to be sure, a deep mystery that on the cross God "condemned sin" in the flesh of the Messiah. But this stands at the heart of Christianity, offering the way forward through the Red Sea, leaving behind the Egypt of sin and death, and pointing onward to the land of promise. The victory of the cross over the principalities and powers, with sin and death as their chief, provides a solidly grounded freedom from guilt in the present; there is no need for anyone to collapse into that guilty self-absorption, which passes so quickly into self-hatred, which the older liberal denials of sin and guilt were so desperate to avoid. God's love has proved itself stronger than all the powers of darkness. Nor is there any need to fear for the future; the whole point of Romans 8 is to substantiate the great opening shout: there is therefore now no condemnation for those in Christ Jesus. This truth, which always appears surprising even to those who have known it for years, needs constant reiteration in preaching, liturgy, and pastoral counseling. No techniques in these areas can substitute for the truth. But what is needed equally urgently in today's world is the application of these truths to the wider world that has neither diagnosis nor remedy for the huge and horrible problems it faces. Since Paul goes on in Romans to show how God applies the victory of the cross to the liberation of the entire cosmos, is it too much to hope that this victory might have its effect in the realm of human society, government, and law as well as in the hearts and lives of individuals?

**8.** This brings us to the subject of Christian assurance. Once again, caricatures abound, which put many off the truth itself. Christian assurance is not self-assurance. Some self-assured people happen also to be Christians, and some Christians use their Christian assurance to give off an air of self-assurance; but distortions do not invalidate the reality. In some Christian traditions it has been customary, as a sign of humility, to question whether one can ever know in the present life that one is truly saved, just as in some others it has been customary, as a sign of sound doctrine, to proclaim one's certainty on every occasion. It is perhaps significant that the greatest New Testament step-by-step argument for Christian assurance, of which this passage forms the heart, emerges from the deepest wrestling and struggling. It comes as the answer to the cry of despair that, though Paul places it in the mouth of the Torah-loving Jew, awakens echoes across every continent and in every century. *Who shall deliver me?* God will, through Jesus Christ and by the Spirit. Christian assurance is then built up, as in the argument of 8:1-11, on the basis of what has happened in Jesus the Messiah, and on the solid and unbreakable link between the Messiah and his people, of which faith is the sign, baptism the symbol, and the Spirit the personal guarantee.

**9.** This passage sees the start of one of Paul's greatest descriptions of the indwelling of the Spirit. "If anyone does not have the Spirit of Christ, that person does not belong to him." There is no such thing in New Testament theology as a Christian who does not have the Spirit dwelling in him or her. Paul will speak in the next passage of some of the signs of that indwelling—which are by no means as narrowly defined, or as obvious, as some teachings have made out. For the moment it must be noted that there can be no split-level Christianity, no division between those who have the Spirit and those who do not. This must challenge both those whose more spectacular manifestations of the Spirit's presence tempt them to despise those with the less spectacular, and those who are in fact unwitting passengers in the church, who think of themselves as Christians but in whose heart and life the Spirit has not taken up residence, and who are still therefore living "according to the flesh," whatever form that may take. Christian assurance is always balanced by warnings against complacency. And, though this is not the main point of the paragraph, we cannot ignore the way in which the presence of the Spirit produces what we would call "ethical" consequences. Reading between the lines of Paul's compressed argument in vv. 5-8, it is clear that a person in whom the Spirit dwells will begin to be at peace with God; they will submit to God's will; they will begin to live in a way that is actually pleasing to God. Paul will spell out later more of what this looks like. He has already spoken of the love for God that the Spirit inspires in the believer (5:5). For the moment it is important to draw attention to the fact that the presence of the Spirit will make a difference not just to how someone feels, but to how they live.

**10.** As with Romans as a whole, so with this central passage: it is basically about God. The God of whom Paul speaks here is mysterious, as all true speech about God must acknowledge. The purposes of this God, in which the strange work of Torah described in 7:7-25 finds apparently a central place, are darker and more unexpected than either the devout Jew or the serious pagan, or for that matter most Christians, have allowed for. There is more to learn down this line, as chaps. 9–11 will disclose. But at the same time this one true God is now made known in two complementary and interlocking ways, which call not for intellectual recognition so much as for worship and love. This God has been made known in the sending of the Son, not so that God could remain distant and detached while someone else did the difficult and painful work, but precisely so that God might be personally and intimately present at the point where sin and death had been heaped up to their full height. To imagine for a moment a world in which incarnation and cross had never happened and could never happen—this may be a hard task for a Christian, but it is a salutary one—is to imagine a world in which the rumor of incarnate love would either never be heard or be heard as a dream that was daily defied by waking reality. Without the cross of God's Son, the Scriptures of Israel would indeed speak of a God who embodied covenant love, a God who rescued slaves so that they might be a people of praise for the sake of the world. But it would remain a private story, incredible to the outside world and increasingly puzzling within an embattled and beleaguered Israel. Without the cross, the world at large would continue to believe that might and money were the things that mattered, that sexual pleasure was the highest human good, and that killing people was the way to get things done. Alas, in much of the world, even in much of the would-be Christian world, these things are still implicitly believed. It is time for a genuinely incarnational theology to be let loose again upon the world, so that the rumor may become a report, and the report a life-changing reality. And for that to happen it is vital to grasp as well that the God who sent the Son now sends the Spirit of the Son. A fully Trinitarian theology, calling forth worship, love, and service, is the only possible basis for genuine gospel work that will bring life and hope to the world.

# ROMANS 8:12-30, THE INHERITANCE GUARANTEED

## OVERVIEW

The stage is now set for the final act of the drama that Paul has been playing out since the start of chap. 5. "Being therefore justified by faith . . . we rejoice in the hope of the glory of God"; we even rejoice in our sufferings, and our hope "does not make us ashamed, because the love of God has been poured out in our hearts through the Holy Spirit who has been given to us" (5:1-5). Spirit; hope; suffering; glory; love: these are the themes, stated in advance at the head of the argument, to which Paul has now worked his way back.

Thus 8:12-30 offers a celebratory description of present Christian existence, rooted in God's past action in Jesus Christ, assured of God's future action for Christ's people and for the whole world, and sustained in the present by the Spirit. It is the conclusion of the argument for Christian assurance, for the belief that those whom God justified God also glorified (8:30). It is also, as we have noted in advance at various places, the moment when the exodus theme, latent under so much of the argument of chaps. 5–8, comes out fully into the open: what God did for Israel at the Red Sea, what God did for Jesus at Easter, God will do not only for those who are in Christ but for the whole created order. This passage is also, therefore, the completion of the basic statement about God's righteousness, God's saving justice, God's covenant faithfulness. The covenant was established in order to put the world to rights; now we see, on the large scale, how this is to happen. God has been faithful not just to the Abrahamic promises but to the whole creation.

As we should expect, God's faithfulness is revealed in the gospel of Jesus Christ. The death and resurrection of Jesus Christ, the Son of God, are the assumed subtext of this entire section, opening out to include the dying and rising, and the adoption as God's sons and daughters, of all those "in Christ." The statement in 8:29 that God's purpose was to make Jesus the firstborn among many siblings is in fact a concise summary of these nineteen verses: "adoption" or "sonship" (the nongender-specific alternatives "siblinghood" and "son-and-daughtership" are out of the question) is a major theme, running through vv. 14, 15, 16, 17, 19, and 21 before being triumphantly summed up in v. 29.

When we put together the themes of new exodus and Christian adoption, as in this passage, they generate the theme of inheritance, which belongs closely in this passage with that of glory. In Paul's scriptural background, the "inheritance" was, of course, the land, promised to Abraham and his family, and promised again to the Israelites after the exile (see, e.g., Gen 15:7; Num 34:2; Isa 57:13; 60:21; Ezek 36:12; cf. Pss 25:13; 37:9). Now, in line with 4:13, it has become the whole world, the whole creation made by the one creator God, itself renewed and redeemed. Part of the meaning of "glory" in this passage—the glory that has been promised to all God's children in Christ—is precisely that they are to receive this inheritance. And this inheritance means that those in Christ are forever indebted to the God who promises and gives this inheritance. This, indeed, is the note on which the passage opens.

But the beating heart of the whole sequence of thought is found in Paul's description of the prayer that the Spirit inspires within God's children (vv. 15-16, 26-27). The "Abba" prayer that echoes Jesus' own prayer, and provides the clearest evidence that one is indeed a child of God, is balanced by the "inarticulate groaning" in which the Spirit calls to the Father from within the hearts of Christians, expressing the longing of all creation for full redemption. In this, too, those in Christ are conformed to the image of the Son (8:29), standing between the pain of the world and the love of God, discovering that their own sufferings, including the ones they cannot begin to comprehend, are somehow themselves becoming the vessels and vehicles of God's redeeming love.

The passage, filled as it thus is with rich themes about the Christians' status, prayer, and future hope, follows a clear line of thought that could be summed up as "debtors to God's grace." We are in debt to God, because, being God's children, we are also God's heirs (8:12-17). We are fellow heirs with Christ, since, sharing his sufferings, we also share his glory (8:17-27; v. 17 is the bridge between the two movements in the long paragraph). God is utterly and unalterably purposed to bring all those in Christ to their glorious Christ-shaped inheritance (8:28-30).

# Romans 8:12-17, Led by the Spirit

## NIV

[12]Therefore, brothers, we have an obligation—but it is not to the sinful nature, to live according to it. [13]For if you live according to the sinful nature, you will die; but if by the Spirit you put to death the misdeeds of the body, you will live, [14]because those who are led by the Spirit of God are sons of God. [15]For you did not receive a spirit that makes you a slave again to fear, but you received the Spirit of sonship.[a] And by him we cry,

[a] 15 Or adoption

## NRSV

12So then, brothers and sisters,[a] we are debtors, not to the flesh, to live according to the flesh— [13]for if you live according to the flesh, you will die; but if by the Spirit you put to death the deeds of the body, you will live. [14]For all who are led by the Spirit of God are children of God. [15]For you did not receive a spirit of slavery to fall back into fear, but you have received a spirit of adoption. When we cry, "Abba![b] Father!" [16]it is that

[a] Gk brothers   [b] Aramaic for Father

**NIV**

"*Abba,*[a] Father." [16]The Spirit himself testifies with our spirit that we are God's children. [17]Now if we are children, then we are heirs—heirs of God and co-heirs with Christ, if indeed we share in his sufferings in order that we may also share in his glory.

[a] 15 Aramaic for *Father*

**NRSV**

very Spirit bearing witness[a] with our spirit that we are children of God, [17]and if children, then heirs, heirs of God and joint heirs with Christ—if, in fact, we suffer with him so that we may also be glorified with him.

[a] Or [15]*a spirit of adoption, by which we cry, "Abba! Father!"* [16]*The Spirit itself bears witness*

# COMMENTARY

Once again it is important, reading a complex passage like this, not to get bogged down in detail but to keep in mind the overall direction and underlying argument. Paul's point is to draw the conclusion (ἄρα οὖν *ara oun,* "so then," is a quite emphatic transition) that arises not only from 7:1–8:11, but also from chaps. 5 and 6: the basic truth about Christians is that they are debtors to God, the God who has made them children and heirs. Precisely because this is the argument for assurance, it is framed as an appeal to gratitude.

**8:12-13.** Following a habit that the reader of Romans is by now used to, Paul never actually finishes the sentence he begins. "We are debtors," he says—but breaks off to say what his readers are *not* indebted to, leaving them to work out from the way the argument proceeds who they are in fact indebted to. Paul works back there quite quickly, using the flesh/spirit contrast of vv. 12-13, repeated here from vv. 5-9, as the springboard to speaking of Christians as God's children and hence heirs; so the basic import of v. 12*a* is not lost. (The NEB flattens out the paragraph opening: "It follows, my friends, that our lower nature has no claim upon us"; the sense of an unresolved harmony, driving the reader forward to the gift and promise of God, is lost.)

First, though, Paul will warn against any going back to the former way of life. Just as in 8:9 he could raise the question as to whether some of his hearers did not in fact possess the Spirit, and hence did not after all belong to the Messiah, so now he warns against continuing to live "according to the flesh." This is not, as some would have it today, a lapse into dualism, a rejection of the

God-given body and all its possibilities.[273] It is a recognition that the present body, corruptible and heading for death, is not all it might be and not all it will be in the resurrection, and that to use its possibilities and potentialities as the yardstick for what one ought to be doing is to take orders from that which will turn to dust, and so to come back again under the tyranny of death. "We are indebted, not to the flesh; live that way, and you will die."

The alternative is to see the death-bound inclinations of the present body for what they are, and to anticipate the verdict of the grave by putting them to death here and now. (The NIV rightly interprets the phrase "the deeds of the body" as the *mis*deeds of the body; Paul obviously does not want Christians to do nothing at all—the body, after all, is to be the means of grateful service to God, 12:1.) As in Col 3:5-11, which explains Paul's meaning in more detail, he sees that there are styles of behavior that, like weeds left to grow unchecked, have the capacity to take over the garden and choke all the flowers. There is only one way with such things: they must be uprooted, killed off. This is, of course, impossible for those who are still "in the flesh"; but those who are led by the Spirit will find that the Spirit's inner agency enables them, if they will, to say "no" to the practices that carry the smell of death with them.

**8:14.** The γάρ (*gar*) with which v. 14 is linked to what precedes is best understood as explaining not

---

273. Paul once again moves to and fro between "flesh" and "body," though his regular usage is to treat "flesh" as entirely negative and "body" as the locus both of present possible sin and of present commanded holiness (12:1), and above all as that which will be redeemed in the resurrection (8:11). It is "the *deeds* of the body," not the body itself, that are to be abandoned. "Flesh and blood cannot inherit God's kingdom" (1 Cor 15:50), but the body can and will.

only why this Spirit-led action of killing off "the deeds of the body" leads to life, but also the suppressed statement of that to which, or rather the one to whom, Christians are indebted. "Mortification leads to life because the Spirit that enables it also assures us of our divine adoption"; and also "We are indebted [to God], for, being led by the Spirit, we are God's children [and so God's heirs]." There may also be a further logical connection, depending on the scriptural context, not least the exodus narrative; it is because the people were God's children that holiness was enjoined upon them (see Deut 14:1; cf. Isa 1:2).

It is those who are "led by the Spirit" to whom this status of divine adoption is given. The image here is taken from the wilderness wanderings of Israel, led by the pillar of cloud and fire (Exod 13:21-22; cf. Exod 14:19, 24; 40:38; Num 9:15-23; 10:34; 14:14; Deut 1:33; Neh 9:12, 19; Pss 78:14; 105:39).[274] Those symbols of God's powerful presence are here replaced, as we might have guessed from the "indwelling" theme in 8:9-11, by the Spirit, who now does for God's people that which the tabernacling presence of God did in the wilderness, assuring them of divine adoption and leading them forward to their inheritance. The idea of Christians as God's sons and daughters is rooted in the same exodus narrative, again reapplied in the prophets (Exod 4:22; cf. Isa 1:2; Hos 1:10; 11:1). As in Gal 4:1-7, the God who sends the Son now sends the Spirit of the Son in order to adopt as sons and daughters all those in whom the Spirit dwells, or (as here, still within the exodus imagery) those who are led by the Spirit.

**8:15.** The exodus context gives depth, too, to the comment that follows. We did not receive, says Paul, a spirit of slavery; that would lead us back again into fear. In other words, the pillar of cloud and fire is not leading you back to Egypt. Having come to know God, or rather to be known by God, he says in the parallel passage in Gal 4:8-11, how can you embrace what is simply a new form of slavery? No: the Spirit you have received, precisely because it is the Spirit of Jesus, the Son, is the Spirit of sonship, of adoption.

There is a problem of punctuation to be addressed here. The last six words of v. 15 (ἐν ᾧ κράζομεν αββα ὁ πατήρ *en hō krazomen abba ho patēr*) could go with what precedes, as in the KJV ("Ye have received the Spirit of adoption, whereby we cry, Abba, Father"; see also the REB). Although the NIV treats these six words as a separate sentence, they function more in relation to what precedes than to what follows ("And by him we cry, 'Abba, Father' "). Or they could go with what follows, as in the NRSV ("you have received a spirit of adoption. When we cry, 'Abba! Father!' it is that very Spirit bearing witness with our spirit that we are children of God"). The issue is finely balanced, and not very much hangs on it; Paul clearly believes that it is by the Spirit that Christians learn from the heart to call God Father, and he clearly believes also that the Spirit, in doing this, bears witness with us that we are God's children. The NEB is perhaps the most helpful, allowing the thought to flow more seamlessly forward: "a Spirit that makes us sons, enabling us to cry 'Abba! Father!' In that cry the Spirit of God joins with our spirit in testifying. . . ."

More important than the punctuation is Paul's assumption, here and in Gal 4:6, that Christians will find themselves prompted by the Spirit to call God "Father," and to use the Aramaic word that, according to Mark 14:36, Jesus himself used in his prayer in Gethsemane (and, by implication, at other times as well). Paul's addressees were basically Greek speakers, even in Rome, where a sizable portion of the population spoke Greek rather than Latin; but this Aramaic term was clearly known as a regular form of address to God. This may imply that the Lord's Prayer, too, was known in Aramaic, but what matters above all is the sense, which Paul can presume throughout the church of whatever language, that God was known in an intimate, familial relationship for which this term, used by adults as well as children but still tender and personal, was entirely appropriate. It was a way of making one's own all the exodus promises of the Scriptures, of calling upon the God of Abraham, Isaac, and Jacob for deliverance. It was a way, above all, of making Jesus' prayers one's own, and hence of sharing the sonship of Jesus.[275] It was

---

274. Ignace de la Potterie, "Le chrétien conduit par l'Esprit dans son cheminement eschatologique (Rom 8,14)," in *The Law of the Spirit in Rom 7 and 8,* ed. L. de Lorenzi (Rome: St Paul's Abbey, 1976) 225, has shown that references to the story of Israel's being "led" through the wilderness are frequently found in conjunction, as here, with the theme of Israel as God's son or of God as Israel's father. See Deut 8:2, 5; 32:6, 12; Isa 63:14-16; Jer 3:14, 19; 31:8-9; Wis 14:3.

275. On sharing the prayer of Jesus see N. T. Wright, "The Lord's Prayer as a Paradigm of Christian Prayer," in *Into God's Presence: Prayer in the New Testament,* ed. R. L. Longenecker (Grand Rapids: Eerdmans, 2001) 132-54.

a way of expressing from the heart something at the very center of the gospel: that in Jesus the Messiah, the Son of God, the covenant faithfulness of God had been revealed for the salvation of all who believe (see 1:3-4, 16-17).

**8:16.** The result of this work of the Spirit, leading through the wilderness and inspiring the cry of "Abba," is that our own human spirit is assured that we are God's children. Throughout the passage some have questioned which uses of "spirit" refer to the Holy Spirit and which to the human spirit that each person has; some, for instance, have seen the human spirit rather than God's Spirit in 8:10, though that is increasingly a rare position. But here, as in 1 Cor 2:11, there is no question. The Spirit's very own self comes alongside our human spirit to bear witness that we are God's children.

**8:17.** This is the fulcrum about which the whole discourse now pivots. Once Paul has established that all those in Christ and indwelt by the Spirit are "children of God," the end of the argument is in sight: If we are God's children, we are also God's heirs. This is the real reason why he implied that Christians were indebted to God (8:12), and it indicates the substance of the paragraph to come. Paul quickly explains in more detail what it means to be God's heirs: It means that one is a fellow heir with the Messiah. As Christians have shared his prayer, as a symptom of their sharing in his sonship, so they will share also in his inheritance. If he is to be Lord of the world, ruling over it with sovereign and saving love, they are to share that rule, bringing redemption to the world that longs for it (cf. 1 Cor 6:2-3; Paul takes this idea for granted, strange though it may be to us, and assumes that his hearers do so too). But, as Jesus himself solemnly warned, there is a cost involved (see Mark 8:34-38). The road to the inheritance, the path to glory (the two are now, at last, seen to be more or less synonymous) lies along the road of suffering.

## Romans 8:18-30, The Renewal of All Things

[18]I consider that our present sufferings are not worth comparing with the glory that will be revealed in us. [19]The creation waits in eager expectation for the sons of God to be revealed. [20]For the creation was subjected to frustration, not by its own choice, but by the will of the one who subjected it, in hope [21]that[a] the creation itself will be liberated from its bondage to decay and brought into the glorious freedom of the children of God.

[22]We know that the whole creation has been groaning as in the pains of childbirth right up to the present time. [23]Not only so, but we ourselves, who have the firstfruits of the Spirit, groan inwardly as we wait eagerly for our adoption as sons, the redemption of our bodies. [24]For in this hope we were saved. But hope that is seen is no hope at all. Who hopes for what he already has? [25]But if we hope for what we do not yet have, we wait for it patiently.

[26]In the same way, the Spirit helps us in our

18I consider that the sufferings of this present time are not worth comparing with the glory about to be revealed to us. [19]For the creation waits with eager longing for the revealing of the children of God; [20]for the creation was subjected to futility, not of its own will but by the will of the one who subjected it, in hope [21]that the creation itself will be set free from its bondage to decay and will obtain the freedom of the glory of the children of God. [22]We know that the whole creation has been groaning in labor pains until now; [23]and not only the creation, but we ourselves, who have the first fruits of the Spirit, groan inwardly while we wait for adoption, the redemption of our bodies. [24]For in[a] hope we were saved. Now hope that is seen is not hope. For who hopes[b] for what is seen? [25]But if we hope for what we do not see, we wait for it with patience.

26Likewise the Spirit helps us in our weakness; for we do not know how to pray as we ought, but that very Spirit intercedes[c] with sighs too deep for

---

[a] 20,21 Or *subjected it in hope.* [21]*For*

[a] Or *by*   [b] Other ancient authorities read *awaits*   [c] Other ancient authorities add *for us*

## NIV

weakness. We do not know what we ought to pray for, but the Spirit himself intercedes for us with groans that words cannot express. [27]And he who searches our hearts knows the mind of the Spirit, because the Spirit intercedes for the saints in accordance with God's will.

[28]And we know that in all things God works for the good of those who love him,[a] who[b] have been called according to his purpose. [29]For those God foreknew he also predestined to be conformed to the likeness of his Son, that he might be the firstborn among many brothers. [30]And those he predestined, he also called; those he called, he also justified; those he justified, he also glorified.

[a] 28 Some manuscripts And we know that all things work together for good to those who love God   [b] 28 Or works together with those who love him to bring about what is good—with those who

## NRSV

words. [27]And God,[a] who searches the heart, knows what is the mind of the Spirit, because the Spirit[b] intercedes for the saints according to the will of God.[c]

[28]We know that all things work together for good[d] for those who love God, who are called according to his purpose. [29]For those whom he foreknew he also predestined to be conformed to the image of his Son, in order that he might be the firstborn within a large family.[e] [30]And those whom he predestined he also called; and those whom he called he also justified; and those whom he justified he also glorified.

[a] Gk the one   [b] Gk he or it   [c] Gk according to God
[d] Other ancient authorities read God makes all things work together for good, or in all things God works for good   [e] Gk among many brothers

# COMMENTARY

Paul has now reached the point he mentioned in the introduction to the whole section (5:3-5): suffering is itself a cause of celebration, because it produces patience, character, and a hope that does not leave one ashamed, because the love of God has flooded the heart through the Spirit. So here the present suffering—Paul does not at this point say what this suffering consisted of, but 8:35-39 gives several suggestions—leads to patience and hope (vv. 18, 23-24) for those in whom the love of God is present (8:28). And, just as one might have gathered from the context and layout of chap. 5, and indeed from the careful christological base of the whole argument from that point to this, the aim of it all is that the Christian should be "conformed to the image of God's Son" (8:29); or, as he says in 8:17*b,* "provided that we suffer with him so that we may also be glorified with him." Glory—the splendid reign over the world for which the human race was designed from the beginning, and the splendid form of human existence that will be appropriate for that role—was lost through sin, but regained through the Messiah in his resurrection (cf. 6:4). That which is true of him is, and will be, true of his people, and Paul will now show the route by which they must travel for this to be true of them in fact.

**8:18.** By way of explanation of his cryptic opening statement in 8:17 (the connective is *gar,* omitted in the NIV and the NRSV), Paul launches the substance of this paragraph with a somewhat expanded declaration of where his calculations about the future have taken him ("I consider" in the NIV and the NRSV translates λογίζομαι [*logizomai*], the same bookkeeping metaphor as was used in 3:28; 6:11). This is not merely a feeling or a private opinion: It is something Paul has thought through. It fits together logically. The main point, echoing 2 Cor 4:17, is that the glory that is to be revealed will far outweigh the sufferings that have to be endured in the present. The idea that, because Christians are "in Christ," the true life is already present, but hidden, and waiting to be revealed when Christ is finally revealed in glory, is familiar elsewhere in Paul (e.g., Col 3:1-4). Paul's wording here, though, is slightly unexpected: he speaks of "the glory that is to be revealed *toward* us, or *into* us (εἰς ἡμᾶς *eis hēmas*), implying not merely that we are to be shown a vision of glory (as the NRSV implies), nor simply that a glory will appear within us (as the NIV implies), but that the future revelation will bestow glory upon us, from above, as a gift. The way Paul now justifies this opening statement is to describe that future glory, and the present situation of waiting for it, in order to explain both his calculation and the present in-between situation both of creation and of the Christian—and, we might even say, of God.

**8:19-21.** The first stage of this explanation focuses on something at which Paul has hardly hinted up until now, and hardly mentions anywhere else in his writings, but which he has clearly thought out carefully and intends not just to mention but to highlight at this dramatic stage of the argument. The reason why present suffering cannot compare with the coming glory is because the whole creation is on tiptoe with excitement, waiting for God's children to be revealed as who they really are. Suddenly we have turned a corner. Whereas, up until now, it might have been possible to think that Paul was simply talking about God's salvation in relation to human beings, from here on it is clear that the entire cosmos is in view. Nor is this a strange oddity, bolted on to the outside of his theology, or of the argument of Romans, as though it were simply a bit of undigested Jewish apocalyptic speculation thrown in here for good measure. No: it is part of the revelation of God's righteousness, that covenant faithfulness that always aimed at putting the whole world to rights. This is why, as we saw in 4:13, Paul declared that God's promise to Abraham had the whole world in view.

Paul could hardly express the longing of creation more dramatically. Literally, he writes, "For the eager expectation of the creation eagerly awaits the revelation of the children of God," an obvious pleonasm (use of extra or redundant words for effect) that makes its own point. The whole creation—sun, moon, sea, sky, birds, animals, plants—is longing for the time when God's people will be revealed as God's glorious human agents, set in authority over the world. But why? Why should creation be so eager for this? And how does Paul know such a thing?

He answers by explaining the present state of creation, drawing on Genesis 3 and other Jewish traditions. Creation itself is in bondage, in slavery, and needs to have its own exodus. It has been "subjected to futility," not deliberately (it did not rebel as humankind rebelled), but because God subjected it to corruption and decay, creation's equivalent of slavery in Egypt ("the slavery which

consists in corruption," v. 21). God did this precisely in order that creation might point forward to the new world that is to be, in which its beauty and power will be enhanced and its corruptibility and futility will be done away. And, if one dare put it like this, as God sent Jesus to rescue the human race, so God will send Jesus' younger siblings, in the power of the Spirit, to rescue the whole created order, to bring that justice and peace for which the whole creation yearns. (This cannot be reduced to the old liberal Protestant "social gospel"—from which the resurrection, which Paul here presupposes, was usually bracketed out.)

The basis of Paul's belief here must be a combination of two things: the biblical promise of new heavens and new earth (Isa 65:17; 66:22), and the creation story in which human beings, made in God's image, are appointed as God's steward over creation. Putting the picture together, in the light of the observable way in which the created order is out of joint, and the clear biblical and experiential belief that the human race as a whole is in rebellion against God, Paul, in company with many other Jews, saw the two as intimately related. After the fall, the earth produced thorns and thistles. Humans continued to abuse their environment, so that one of the reasons why God sent Israel into exile, according to the Scriptures, was so that the land could at last enjoy its sabbaths (Lev 26:34-43 [cf. 25:2-5]; 2 Chr 36:21). But the answer to the problem was not (as in some New Age theories) that humans should keep their hands off creation, should perhaps be removed from the planet altogether so as not to spoil it any further. The answer, if the creator is to be true to the original purpose, is for humans to be redeemed, to take their place at last as God's imagebearers, the wise steward they were always meant to be. Paul sees that this purpose has already been accomplished in principle in the resurrection of Jesus, and that it will be accomplished fully when all those in Christ are raised and together set in saving authority over the world (see 1 Cor 15:20-28). That is why, Paul says, creation is now waiting with eager longing.

That for which creation is longing is not, then, that it might be "brought into the glorious freedom of the children of God" (NIV) or might "obtain" the same glorious freedom that those in Christ will have (RSV, NRSV). The closing words of v. 21 (lit., "unto the freedom of the glory of the children of God") could be intended to be run together like that; Greek often expresses adjectival relations through genitives. But here, in the light of the previous verses, the thought seems to be not that creation and Christians will simply all be free and glorious in the same way, together, but that the freedom for which creation longs, and which it will be liberated into, is the freedom *that comes about through the glorification of the children of God*. Paul never says that creation itself will have "glory." It will have freedom *because* God's children have glory; indeed, their glory will consist quite specifically in this, that they will be God's agents in bringing the wise, healing, restorative divine justice to the whole created order.

**8:22-27.** By way of yet further explanation (*gar;* once again omitted by the NIV and the NRSV), Paul states a broader truth about the way the world is, and about Christians within it. These verses stand at the very heart of his theological description of the Christian life, set within the still-to-be-redeemed world, on the one hand, and held within the powerful love of God, on the other. He draws once more on Jewish tradition, this time the theme of the great tribulation, the great woes, that would come upon the world in order for the new world to be born.[276] This (essentially female) image of the birth pangs of the new age is applied first to the world, then to the church, and then, remarkably enough, to the Spirit. This creates the context within which, as he wants to explain to the Roman church, patience and prayer are the appropriate stance and activity for God's people while awaiting the final redemption. Within Paul's overall argument for assurance, this is vital: he needs to explain why (if all that he has said about Christ and the Spirit is true) things are still so often so painful, and also why Christians can nevertheless be confident of God's final victory and their final redemption.

**8:22.** He deals first with creation: groaning together and travailing together, which the NIV and the NRSV rightly treat as one large idea, "groaning in labor pains." This is the present state of creation. Part of the point of the image is that the coming new world will involve, not the abolition of the present one, but its transformation: birth (particularly in the culture of Paul's day, both Jewish and pagan) speaks of new life that is at the same time the mother's own life, delighting her, despite the pain of labor, with a fresh fulfillment. This continuity between the present world and the future one is the reason, one may assume, why the present passage has been marginalized in many expositions of Paul and Romans on the part of those for whom a more dualist theology was a working assumption.

**8:23.** But how will the new world come to birth? Not of its own energy and potentiality, but only through the glorification of God's children (v. 21). That is why, within the groaning creation, the church also groans, longing for its own "adoption": longing, in other words, for the "child" to be born that is its own true self. Here we strike once more the characteristic note of "now and not yet" that runs right through Paul: we have already received "the spirit of υἱοθεσία [*huiothesia,* "sonship/adoption"]" (v. 15); we are already "children of God" (vv. 16-17); and yet there is a form of this "sonship/adoption" for which we still eagerly long. The link between present and future is made, again as usual, by the Spirit, who is the "first fruits," that part of God's future redeeming power that is brought forward into the present, so that the prayer of the child in the present time (vv. 15-16) truly points on to the future resurrection glory (vv. 11, 17).[277] This idea is closely cognate with the similar statement that the Spirit is the "guarantee," using the metaphor of a down payment, of the full salvation yet to come (e.g., 2 Cor 1:22; 5:5; Eph 1:14). Here "the firstfruits of the Spirit" looks back to 8:4*b,* 9-11, and 13*b*-17. Summing up that whole train of thought, Paul can declare, here and in vv. 26-27, that the present "groaning," though at one level a sign of the present not fully redeemed state, is at the same time a sign of the Christian's sure and certain hope.

The "adoption/sonship" of which Paul here speaks—the full and final thing of which the

---

276. See N. T. Wright, *The New Testament and the People of God,* vol. 1 of *Christian Origins and the Question of God* (London: SPCK; Minneapolis: Fortress, 1992) 277-79; *Jesus and the Victory of God,* vol. 2 of *Christian Origins and the Question of God* (London: SPCK; Minneapolis: Fortress, 1996) 577-79.

277. Paul can use the same image of Christ, as the first to be raised from the dead, guaranteeing the harvest to come (1 Cor 15:20-23) or of the first converts in a particular location (e.g., Rom 16:5; 1 Cor 16:15). See also 11:16; 2 Thess 2:13. In Jas 1:18 Christians are seen as the first-fruits of God's new creation, an idea that sits very comfortably alongside Rom 8:22. For the biblical background, see the Commentary on 11:16.

Spirit's work is the beginning and guarantee—is precisely the final redemption of the body, of which Paul has already written decisively in 8:11. "Redemption," mentioned here for the first time since the highly significant 3:24, carries once more the gentle overtones of the exodus theme that underlies so much of the present passage. We ourselves have come out of "Egypt," but our body, which still needs to have its deeds put to death (v. 13), is still awaiting redemption from the slave market (Paul uses the singular "body" rather than the expected plural, as in v. 11, but there seems no particular significance to this change). The body is intended to be glorious, splendid, fashioned after the model of Jesus' own resurrection body, no longer subject to weakness, humiliation, sickness, sin, and death (cf. 1 Cor 15:54; 2 Cor 5:1-5; Phil 3:21). The Christian in the present time is but a pale shadow of his or her future self.

**8:24-25.** "For we were saved in hope." Not in "this hope," as the NIV interprets; that, though true, is not the point Paul is making here, as the further explanation makes clear. The logic of these verses, explaining what has gone before, is as follows: (a) we ourselves groan while awaiting our complete adoption; (b) this is so because we were saved in hope; (c) if we were saved in hope, this must mean that our future salvation is not yet visible; (d) the appropriate Christian stance is therefore patient expectation. Paul's concern is to stress that, while salvation is already a reality for the Christian ("we were saved": the tense is aorist, denoting a one-off event), it carries an inevitable future component. Hope is built in to Christian experience from the start, and remains one of its central characteristics (see 5:2-5; 15:13). But if this is so, Paul is stressing, one cannot expect present Christian living to be anything other than a matter of straining forward for what is yet to come, for what is yet unseen. (See Phil 3:13; 2 Cor 4:18; the present passage makes it clear that the distinction between "seen" and "unseen" things in 2 Corinthians is contrasting present and future, not [in a Platonic fashion] the world of space, time, and matter, on the one hand, and the world of ideas, on the other). One does not anxiously scan the horizon for a boat already in port.

If this is so, the Christian is called to patience. But patience is no mere dispassionate passing of the time. The word Paul uses for "wait" here is ἀπεκδεχόμεθα (*apekdechometha*), the same root that was used in v. 19, where most interpreters recognize a note of eagerness, of excited expectation. The last three words of v. 25 thus have an almost oxymoronic flavor, with the emphasis falling not, as in most English translations, on "with patience" (lit., "through patience," δι᾽ ὑπομονῆς *di' hypomonēs*), but on "eagerly await": if we hope for what we do not yet see, then, with steady patience, we maintain an eager expectation.

Paul has now described the whole creation groaning in labor-pains; he has shown that God's people in Christ share the same struggle and groaning. Where is God in all this? Not, as in so many theological schemes ancient and modern, standing to one side, or hiding a long way off. God is present in the midst of the pain. God, indeed, is groaning in labor too.

**8:26-27.** The groaning of the church, in the midst of the groaning world, is sustained and even inspired by the groaning of the Spirit. Paul clearly intends these to be seen in parallel, since he introduces the verse with ὡσαύτως (*hōsautōs*, "in the same way"). The Spirit, he says, helps us in our weakness—or, literally, "The Spirit helps our weakness." He has not spoken of "weakness" before in the present argument, and we must assume that he uses this term to sum up the state he has just described, the state of not yet being fully redeemed. Those who cannot see that for which they eagerly hope need assistance to peer into the darkness ahead and to pray God's future into the present. It is that assistance that the Spirit provides, coming alongside to help (συναντιλαμβάνεται *synantilambanetai*; this is the word Martha used in Luke 10:40 to say what Mary should have been doing for her).

Here, as in vv. 15-16, Spirit-inspired prayer is a key part of the experience of inaugurated eschatology (cf. Zech 12:10, where, in the context of the coming great eschaton, God pours out upon the house of David, and upon Jerusalem, "the spirit of grace and supplication," producing mourning in the midst of the promised glory). It is God's intention that redeemed human beings should be set in authority over the world, should indeed thereby be the agents through whom the cosmos that still groans in travail should be set free. At the moment, however, these human beings are weak, since their own bodies, that part of creation for which they have the most immediate responsibility, are still subject to decay and death. In this condition they do not even know what to pray for, how it is that God will work through them to bring about the redemption of the world. Paul here assumes both that the church is called to the task of intercession and that the church finds this very puzzling—a double truth that most great teachers of prayer from that day to this would endorse. But, just as it is the Spirit's task to inaugurate genuine humanness within the Christian in the form of holiness (vv. 12-14) and the *Abba*-prayer (vv. 15-16), so here it is the Spirit's task to enable genuine humanness, that stance of humbly trusting God and so being set in authority over the world, which is to be anticipated in the life of intercessory prayer.

Many writers, from various standpoints, have suggested that Paul here refers to the gift of *glossolalia,* "speaking in tongues." This is quite possible in terms of Paul's belief about the latter gift and its place within the church, and a strong case can be made out for it.[278] The present writer certainly has no prejudice against finding such a reference here, as some appear to have. Yet I find it strange that Paul, if he wished to refer to speaking in tongues, for which words of the λαλέω (*laleō*) root would be used ("to speak," or, of inanimate things, "to make a noise," "to give forth a sound"; see, e.g., 1 Cor 12:30; 13:1; 14:2), should here use the word ἀλαλήτος (*alalētos,* "speechless" or "voiceless") to describe the practice. It is important to say that, if he is not referring to speaking in tongues, nor is he simply referring to silent prayer such as is commonly practiced in private Christian devotion in the contemporary Western world (in Paul's day most people would have prayed aloud, just as people used to read aloud, even when alone). Rather, he is speaking of an agonizing in prayer, a mixture of lament and longing in which, like a great swell of tide at sea, "too full for sound or foam," the weight of what is taking place has nothing to do with the waves and ripples on the surface. Whether Paul expected all his readers to know this experience in prayer (as he seems to have expected them to know the *Abba*-experi-

ence) is difficult to judge. Then as now, perhaps, his words may have come as a challenge to a deeper wrestling with the pain of the world and the church, a struggle in which, like Jacob, Christians might discover that they had after all been wrestling with God as well as with their own weak humanness, and had prevailed.

The point Paul is making, in any case, is that the Spirit's own very self[279] intercedes within the Christian precisely at the point where he or she, faced with the ruin and misery of the world, finds that there are no words left to express in God's presence the sense of futility (v. 20) and the longing for redemption. It is not (as some early scribes added to the text, followed by the NIV) that the Spirit intercedes "for us"; that misses the point, and makes Paul repeat himself in the following verse. What Paul is saying is that the Spirit, active within the innermost being of the Christian, is doing the very interceding the Christian longs to do, even though the only evidence that can be produced is inarticulate groanings.

The good news about this is that God, the living, transcendent God, is in intimate touch with the Spirit, so that these inarticulate but Spirit-assisted groanings come before God as true prayer, true intercession. To say this, Paul uses another remarkable periphrasis for God (see the Commentary on 8:11; see also the Commentary on 4:24): "the heart-searcher." The Spirit's work (lit., "the mind of the Spirit," as in 8:6), deep within the human heart, is known to the heart-searching God. We may compare 2:16; 1 Cor 4:5; 1 Thess 2:4; since these references (the first two certainly, the third arguably) are to a future judgment at which the heart's secrets will be laid bare, what we have here appears to be yet another example of inaugurated eschatology; God's searching of hearts anticipates the final putting to rights of all things (see also Heb 4:12-13). The Spirit, he says, intercedes for God's people, whom he refers to as "the saints"; he often designates Christians thus, set apart as they are for God, and this is a

---

278. See Fee, *God's Empowering Presence,* 575-86, discussing particularly the argument of another notable proponent, Ernst Käsemann.

279. It seems foolish to say "itself," since, though the noun "spirit" is neuter in Greek, the reality Paul refers to is deeply personal. The sustained metaphor of groaning in birth pangs suggests "herself"; but this, though attractive in some ways granted the fact that the word for "spirit" is feminine in Hebrew, Aramaic, and Syriac, might place too much stress on a point that is at best a matter of nuance in Paul's extended metaphor.

particularly appropriate context to do so, as God's people are caught up in the inner life of God. The Spirit's intercession is "according to God's will" (lit., "according to God"). This hints at something deeper than merely praying in the way God wants or approves; God's own life, love, and energy are involved in the process. The Christian, precisely at the point of weakness and uncertainty, of inability and struggle, becomes the place at which the triune God is revealed in person.

**8:28.** Triune? Has not Paul only spoken of the first and third persons of the Trinity? No. The suffering of the church, groaning in longing and prayer for the redemption of the world, and of the present body, is the means by which Christians are "conformed to the image of God's son" (v. 29). As usual, Paul has steadily worked his way back to the point at which he began, in this case 8:17*b:* we are fellow heirs with the Messiah, so long as we suffer with him in order that we may be glorified with him. This is the theme that dominates as the paragraph, already one of Paul's most remarkable, draws to its unique and uniquely powerful climax.

Verse 28 does not represent a completely new thought (as is sometimes implied by paragraph divisions in translations, such as the NIV and the NRSV). It is not simply an extra devotional aside about the wonderful workings of providence. It is bound in tightly to the sequence of the argument. The introductory δέ (*de*) is the "but," not of opposition, but of logic; not "I hoped he would come *but* he didn't," but rather "Donkeys like carrots; *but* this is a donkey; therefore let's give him some carrots." The train of thought is, "God knows the mind of the Spirit; *but* we know that God works all things together for good for those who love God; therefore (implicit but vital) God works all things together for good for us, we in whom the Spirit is operating." (This, after all, is where the longer paragraph started, with the Christian being in God's debt [v. 12]). The intercession spoken of in v. 26 will be heard and answered in ways that, though we cannot at present see them or even conceive them, will turn out to be that for which our groaning prayers have been yearning. "All things"—not just the groanings of the previous verses, but the entire range of experiences and events that may face God's people—are taken care of by the creator God who is planning to renew the whole creation, and us along with it.

I have assumed that "God" is the implied subject of "works together." Two other views have been taken. A minority, represented by the NEB, make "the Spirit" the implied subject. The strength of this view is that the Spirit has been a main topic, perhaps the main topic, ever since 8:1, and is the subject of the immediately preceding clause. However, the subject of the previous main sentence is God, not the Spirit; and, with several commentators I regard the sudden and unexplained change of subject at the end of v. 28 (from the Spirit to God) as a fatal objection to making the Spirit the subject here.[280] A more widely held view is that "all things" are the subject: so, famously, the KJV, "All things work together for good to them that love God." There are considerable problems with this, not least the sheer oddity, for Paul, of giving "all things" such apparent theological priority (even if we understand, as devout readers usually have, a strong theology of providence behind the statement).

The NRSV, echoing the King James, implies in its footnote that to make God the subject is to endorse the variant reading of several good MSS, according to which "God" (ὁ θεός *ho theos*) was to be read after "works together." But this is not strictly the case. Even with the shorter text (which is surely correct; it would be easy to add the word "God" but very odd to omit it), the implied subject must still be that of the previous verse—namely, "the heartsearcher": God. The verse runs on, without any indication of a change of subject, to "those whom [God] foreknew" in v. 29, and indeed to the implied subject of "called according to [God's] purpose" at the end of v. 28. Had Paul not intended "God" as the subject of συνεργεῖ (*synergei*, "works together"), in fact, he really should have specified a *change* of subject to "God" toward the end of the present verse. Paul is, of course, capable of omitting connections, subjects, verbs, and anything else that he hopes will be understood by someone clinging to the tail of his fast-moving argument. But here it seems unlikely.[281]

---

280. Despite the advocacy of G. Fee, *God's Empowering Presence: The Holy Spirit in the Letters of Paul* (Peabody, Mass.: Hendrikson, 1994) 587-90.

281. It is easier to understand the train of thought in the KJV and the NRSV, because "those who love God" comes at the end of the clause in English, making a smooth transition to "those whom he foreknew" at the start of v. 29. In Greek, however, "to those who love God" comes near the start of the verse, and the accusative case of "God" does not lend itself so easily to the necessary transition to the subject for the following verbs.

Paul, then, pulls together the threads of his treatment of the triple groaning of world, church, and Spirit. The whole letter has been about God, God's covenant faithfulness, God's gospel revealed in the Son and the Spirit, and above all—not that this is a separate topic from all those—God's love. The heart of the argument for assurance is the unshakable and sovereign love of God, and the certainty that this love will win out in the end. That, indeed, is the theme that is now emerging as the major subject of the end of the chapter. We are debtors, he says, to God, from whom we have received the Spirit of sonship/adoption, and from whom we shall receive the inheritance, the glory, the sonship/adoption in its full form; and the move from present to future is undergirded, made totally secure, by the fact that God works all things together for good to those who . . . now keep the most basic command of Torah.

That most basic command is, of course, the *Shema:* "Hear, O Israel, YHWH our God, YHWH is one; and you shall love YHWH your God." Paul has already alluded to the *Shema* more than once in the letter (1:5; 3:30; 5:5). Now he comes back to it, with a hint of the positive side of the equation of which 8:7-8 was the negative. Those in the flesh do not and cannot submit to God's law; they cannot please God; but those in the Spirit now do that which the law commanded but could not of itself produce. They love God from the heart (cf. 1 Cor 2:9; 8:3). Just as Paul can vary his epithets for God, so here he pulls out a new epithet for the people of God in Christ and by the Spirit: they are the God-lovers, in other words, the true law-keepers, the true Israel.

This epithet, "the God-lovers," is again not a new idea introduced into the passage, but sums up what has been said in vv. 15, 26-27. In v. 15, those who are led by the Spirit are taught to address God in the language of familial love. In vv. 26-27, those who groan as they await their redemption discover that from the depths of their own heart there issues an inarticulate cry of faith, hope, and love to God. This, the work of the Spirit, is what qualifies them to be described in this way in the next verse (of which the clause "to those who love God" is the first substantial part). It is as though Paul had written: "because the Spirit intercedes for God's people, calling from their own hearts with love to

God; and for those who thus love God, God works all things together for good."

This same people can also be described with another Israel-epithet: they are those who are now "called according to God's purpose." That purpose—namely, that God would sum up all things in Christ (Col 1:15-20; Eph 1:10); that God would be all in all (1 Cor 15:28); that the whole creation would be liberated into the freedom that goes with the glorification of God's children—this whole purpose was always designed to be fulfilled through the agency of God's image-bearing children, the human race. This purpose has been decisively fulfilled in Jesus Christ (5:12-21), but that which was thereby inaugurated has now to be consummated. Those in Christ are the people through whom God intends to accomplish this task. They, like Israel, are assured that they have been called for a purpose—namely, to show forth the praises of the one true God in all the world (cf. Eph 1:11-12; 1 Pet 2:9). And—this is still the thrust of v. 28—those who find themselves in this category can be assured that the purpose will be fulfilled. God will accomplish it.

**8:29-30.** In order to show the branches that they are indeed to bear blossom and fruit, Paul demonstrates that the tree is securely planted and well rooted. In order (that is) to complete his argument from justification to glorification—the argument that began with 5:1-2—he goes back behind justification itself to God's purpose and call, and behind that again to God's foreknowledge. God's purpose is the overriding thought of these verses, summing up the line of thought through the whole chapter, but particularly from v. 17: God's plan from the start was to create a Christ-shaped family, a renewed human race modeled on the Son (once again the line of thought from 1:3-4, through 5:6-10, to 8:3 emerges at a crucial point in the argument). Heirs of God, said Paul in v. 17, and *fellow heirs with the Messiah:* fellow children, younger siblings of the Firstborn (see Col 1:15, 18). This would come about through a process of God's adopted children being shaped according to the likeness of the Son. Though this process will only be complete when the body itself is transformed either in resurrection or at the Lord's coming (cf. 1 Cor 15:51-55 with Phil 3:21), it is to begin here and now precisely through the holiness, suffering, and prayer of which Paul has written in the preceding verses (see also 2 Cor 3:18).[282]

This process will bring God's renewed people to the point where they reflect the Son's *image,* just as the Son is the true image of God (2 Cor 4:4; Col 1:15; 3:10). They are, that is, to become true, because renewed, human beings. This is the point, at last, to which the long argument beginning with 1:18 was looking forward. The image of God, distorted and fractured through idolatry and immorality, is restored in Jesus the Messiah, the Son of God; and the signs of that restoration are visible in those who, like Abraham, trust in God's life-giving power and so truly worship and give glory to God (4:18-22). But the purpose is never simply that God's people in Christ should resemble him, spectacular and glorious though that promise is. As we saw in vv. 18-21, it is that, as true image-bearers, they might reflect that same image into the world, bringing to creation the healing, freedom, and life for which it longs. To be conformed to the image of God, or of God's Son, is a dynamic, not a static, concept. Reflecting God into the world is a matter of costly vocation.

That, indeed, is the thrust of vv. 28-30, which otherwise can easily degenerate, as the history of interpretation shows, into an abstract theory of personal predestination and salvation. God's purpose for those in Christ is precisely Christ-shaped. They are chosen and called in order to advance God's purpose in and for the world. The five great verbs (foreknown, foreordained, called, justified, glorified), crashing chords at the end of the movement, are all to be understood as Christ-shaped. That which is true of the Messiah is true of his people.

Conformity to the Son means, of course, conformity to his death. This is familiar enough elsewhere in Paul (e.g., Phil 3:10-11, a passage very close to the present one in theme and expression). Here it is the major subject of the unit of thought that, beginning with v. 17, reaches its climax in the present verse. It is by reproducing the likeness of the Messiah, not least in suffering and "groaning," that Paul's apostolic labor went forward; that is the subject of 2 Corinthians, especially chapters 4 and 6, and it is summarized in other passages

such as Col 1:24. But it is not merely apostles to whom the privilege of sharing the sufferings of the Messiah is granted. It is, in some measure at least, all Christians. Though the last sections of Romans 8 are often (rightly) thought of as triumphant, it should never be forgotten that the triumph is announced and celebrated, with irony and paradox, from the midst of circumstances that would be simply unbearable, were it not for faith in God the life-giver, and for the hope and above all the love that accompany this faith.

Thus, in v. 29, Paul is explaining both the general point of v. 28, that God works all things together for good, and the more specific point, what is meant by being "called according to God's purpose." The concept of "foreknowledge" is by no means simply that of God being able to see the future and so to know things in advance as we know things in retrospect (though presumably more accurately). The biblical concept of "knowing" is richer than the mere transfer of information. We might invoke Gal 1:15 as at least a partial explanation. There Paul speaks of God "setting him apart" for a particular purpose, and then "calling" him by grace; the language is reminiscent of various biblical passages, including Jer 1:5, "before I formed you in the womb I knew you; I appointed you a prophet to the nations" (cf. Isa 44:2; 49:1). In Romans, we might compare 1:1, where Paul speaks of his "call" to be an apostle and of being "set apart" for God's gospel, the latter verb (ἀφορίζω *aphorizō;* also used in Gal 1:15) being a compound from the same root as προώρισεν (*proōrisen,* "foreordained") in the present verse. God's "knowing" and "call," however, are not just for prophets and apostles but for all God's people, each in their own vocation and fashion, but all according to the same pattern of Christ. Foreknowledge is a form of love or grace; to speak thus is to speak of God reaching out, in advance of anything the person may do or think, to reveal love and to solicit an answering love, to reveal a particular purpose and to call forth obedience to it.

More particularly, this foreknowledge produces God's foreordaining purpose. The word *proōrisen,* often translated "predestined" here and in v. 30 (the NEB is an exception with "foreordained"), often sends shivers down the spines of readers because of its association with the word "destiny," and the link in much popular thinking between

---

282. On which see N. T. Wright, *The Climax of the Covenant: Christ and the Law in Pauline Theology* (Edinburgh: T. & T. Clark; Minneapolis: Fortress, 1991) chap. 9.

this and "fate" (the NJB makes matters worse on this front by simply translating "destined"). Is Paul after all a determinist, believing in a blind plan that determines everything, so that human freedom, responsibility, obedience, and love itself are after all a sham?

One can easily imagine Paul's own reaction: μὴ γένοιτο (*mē genoito,* "Certainly not!"). What we have here, rather, is an expression, as in 1:1, of God's action in setting people apart for a particular purpose, a purpose in which their cooperation, their loving response to love, their obedient response to the personal call, is itself all-important. This is not to deny the mystery of grace, the free initiative of God, and the clear divine sovereignty that is after all the major theme of this entire passage, here brought to a glorious climax. But it is to deny the common misconception, based on a two-dimensional rather than a three-dimensional understanding of how God's actions and human actions relate to each other, that sees something done by God as something not done by humans, and vice versa.

One could appeal (scholars often do) to the Hebrew, or the Middle Eastern, mind-set in which paradoxes and apparent antinomies are held together without difficulty (e.g., talk of God's building the new Temple does not mean that there will not be human architects and stonemasons). But there is more to the problem than this. God's actions and human actions are not, as it were, on the same plane. Already in describing the Spirit's work Paul has shown that the groanings that seem to come from the depths of one's own heart are actually the Spirit's groaning within; and that the heartfelt cry of familial love, *Abba,* Father, is itself likewise the result of the Spirit's prompting. Woe betide theology if discussions of grace take their coloring from the mechanistic or technological age where all actions are conceived as though performed by a set of machines. God's foreknowledge and foreordination, setting people apart in advance for particular purposes, are not equal and opposite to human desires, longings, self-questionings, obedience, and above all love. You do not take away from the one by adding to the other. Even the analogy of human love breaks down, since no lover is ever in the position of playing God to the beloved. Yet love, in which love affirms the otherness of the other at precisely the same time as appearing to merge wills, souls, hearts, and bodies into one, offers some parallels, however oblique, with the workings of divine grace. Christian faith, ultimately irreducible to any analogy, and certainly not reducible to terms simply of "yet another odd paradox," involves wholeheartedly and responsibly answering the call of sovereign love, grace, and commission with a love, gratitude, and obedience that come from the depths of one's own being and are simultaneously experienced as a response to a sovereignty, a compulsion even, to which the closest parallel remains that of the highest love.

The emphasis of vv. 29-30 falls clearly on conformity to Christ; this remains so throughout the dramatic closing words, focused on the four last aorists (pre-shaped, called, justified, glorified). All has been accomplished in Christ: the fore-shaping of Christ's people to be his younger siblings; their call through the gospel that announces his lordship; their justification by faith in the God who raised him from the dead; their glorification, so that they are now already seated in the heavenly places in him (see Eph 2:6, and in the light of that, Eph 1:20-22; Col 3:1-4). There may even be a backward glance to the story of Jesus himself: his incarnation, his baptism, his resurrection, his ascension—though this remains speculative. In any case, the christological basis explains the final aorist, which is otherwise very puzzling, coming as it does after so many futures (8:9-11, 13, 17-18, 23). All these things, including "glorification," have happened already to and in Jesus, the Messiah; and what is true of the Messiah is true of his people.

Pre-shaped; called; justified; glorified—the one link in the chain not already explained in this letter is the second. Paul uses the verb "call" in a more specific sense than some other NT writings (e.g., in the Gospels it simply means the general call to which a variety of answers might be given; e.g., Matt 22:14). For Paul the "call" is what happens when, through the preaching of the gospel (or, in his own case, the revelation of the risen Jesus; but Paul does not suppose this will happen to anyone again), the Spirit works in the heart to produce faith, hope, and love. This "call" is, in the language of an older theology, "effective"; Paul knows that not all hearers of the gospel respond in faith, but when people do he describes the event as their being "called" by God (cf. 1 Thess 1:4-5 with 2 Thess 2:13-14). This will be an important category in chap. 9 (see 9:7, 11, 24-26). Paul can use the word almost synonymously with "conversion"—that is, to describe the moment of coming to faith; though it retains the sense not of a switch in religion (that might happen as well, but it is not the point of this verb) so much as the response to a sovereign command (see 1 Cor 7:15-24; Gal 1:6, 15; Eph 4:4).

Those who respond to the gospel of Jesus Christ with "the obedience of faith"—those, that is, who are "called" in this sense—are declared by God to be part of the new covenant family, the sin-forgiven worldwide people of God, on the basis of this faith alone. "Those whom God called, God also justified"; v. 30*a* thus sums up 3:21–4:25. And those who are justified by faith now rejoice in the hope of the glory of God (5:2, the introductory summary of 5–8); in other words, "those whom God justified, God also glorified" (v. 30*b*, the concluding summary). The detailed argument is done, and the four emphatic aorists of v. 30 are the last four blows of the hammer to ensure that every vital nail in the structure is in place. The steady beat of the verbs within Paul's solemn rhetoric underscores the steady beat of God's unshakable purpose set forth in the Messiah and completed by the Spirit.

It remains to note the way in which, under the general heading of "glorification," Paul's entire future hope for Christians and the world can be spoken of in so many different but overlapping and interlocking ways. To begin with, Paul can speak simply of "life" (8:11) for the mortal body: in other words, resurrection life, the new or transformed physicality that will correspond to the physically renewed body of the risen Jesus (1 Cor 15:50-57). This is what he means, of course, by "eternal life," much misused though that phrase may be in some Christian writing to permit a non-physical interpretation of the final state. But this resurrection life is never something to be enjoyed simply for itself. Those renewed at the last, those who share the glory of the Messiah, will receive an inheritance, which will be the entire world. There they

will have tasks to perform, tasks to do with the liberation of creation from the injustice, misery, bondage, corruption, and death that at present characterize it. (This picture, set out briefly in 8:18-22, is what underlies such otherwise peculiar statements as 1 Cor 6:2; cf. Wis 3:5-9; 4:16. On the future work of the redeemed in God's new world, see Rev 21:22–22:5.) This is the "glory" of which Paul speaks. And this is the hope that puts Christians permanently in God's debt.

One final reflection may be in order, to which we shall return in due course. If it is indeed true that Paul saw the gospel, with its revelation of God's saving justice and peace, as the truth of which Caesar's "gospel," and the "justice" and "peace" that flowed from it, were parodies, it may also be the case that he intends, at this end of his argument, to hint at a particular way in which this gospel makes its way in the world, and will eventually take the world over. Caesar's cult was instantiated around the empire by means of images of Caesar himself, soon to be divine, and of his son(s), heir(s), and other family members, themselves all divinities-in-waiting. These images, housed in various places but particularly in temples of the growing Caesar-cult, were there partly in order to be worshiped, and partly in order to remind the local residents whose empire they were living in. Here, at the climax of the argument that God's saving justice and peace are revealed in the gospel of Jesus, the true Lord of the world—at the climax, also, of the passage about the Spirit dwelling within Christians, like the presence of God within the Temple—Paul states that God's purpose is for Christians to be "conformed to the image of God's Son." They are to be image-bearers, forming the Temple of the living God, the people through whom in the present as well as in the future it is to be made known that the God of Abraham is the only God, that Jesus, his Son, is the world's true Lord, and that one day the world will be liberated from its present slaveries, as Israel was from Egypt, to be the true Empire in which justice, peace, and freedom will make their home.

# REFLECTIONS

**1.** The main emphasis of the whole section is on Christian living in terms of being indebted to God's grace. Much has been said and written in the last century about a human "coming of age" that renders unnecessary and undesirable all obligation, all indebtedness, all human dependence. Anything else, we have often been told, leaves us immature as human beings. The pattern of the exodus has even been used to suggest that one ought to escape all overlordship, even including that of God. Theologies that deny this, and that insist, like Paul, on permanent indebtedness to grace, are sometimes vilified as perpetrating a bullying or dominating God. The present passage not only contradicts this, but explains that the condition of permanent indebtedness to God is not a diminution, but rather an enhancement, of full human dignity.

When one considers all that has been said in Romans about "sin" and "the flesh," to protest against grace on the grounds that one ought to be independent, standing on one's own feet, is about as sensible as a drowning person protesting against being thrown a life belt. That is basic to all Paul's theology. But this passage goes further. The biblical theology of humanness that Paul here echoes, endorses, and develops is that of being made in God's image and being remade in the image of God's Son. There can be no greater human dignity that this. To seek for a status independent of this is indeed, on the one hand, to shake one's fist, Prometheus-like, at the creator, and on the other, inevitably, to worship some part of the created order (perhaps even oneself), and so to be remade in the image of that which is enslaved to decay and death. Like human stories in which people try to live without depending on anyone, only finally to be overwhelmed by love and discover a fulfillment, a self-realization, through self-giving and self-abandonment, so the story of grace is one in which humans find themselves by losing themselves, endlessly indebted to the God whose own true self-expression was found in the self-giving love of the Son. Being indebted to grace is like the permanent indebtedness that exists between those who have given themselves freely to one another in lifelong human love: a state of wonder and gratitude in which one's own humanness is enhanced rather than diminished, ennobled rather than belittled.

**2.** Within this, the wider vista that Paul opens up is the invitation to the Christian to live within the horizon of God's new creation. This great project, the global and cosmic dimension of salvation, has begun with the resurrection of Jesus, and will continue until the whole world is transformed under the just and healing rule of God's children. Though the question of what this will look and feel like, and the question of levels of continuity and discontinuity between the present creation and the new one, are exceedingly difficult to answer, that does not mean that there will not be a reality to which, in retrospect, this language will be seen to have been a true, if inadequate, pointer—much as, with Christian hindsight, the variegated prophecies of the Old Testament can be seen, and are seen in the New Testament, as true pointers to a reality that could not, however, have been fully or adequately described by them alone.

If the Christian is called to live (to use one standard jargon) at the overlap of the old and new creations, this is hardly a matter of passive acceptance of a difficult and tense moment in God's purposes, or of sitting back to await better times when the overlap is done and the new creation fully present. Rather, as the bracing ethical imperatives of 8:12-14 and the call to groaning in prayer in 8:26-27 make clear, the Christian is to embody the tension involved in bringing the new to birth already within the old. The challenge to holiness cannot be put off until some future date; nor can the challenge to bring all things in subjection to the saving rule of God's people, a task that must begin with inarticulate prayer and continue forward from there.

It is under this rubric that all Christian work in the areas of ecology, justice, and aesthetics is to be conceived. If the creation is to be renewed, not abandoned, and if that work has already begun in the resurrection of Jesus, it will not do simply to consign the present creation to acid rain and global warming and wait for Armageddon to destroy it altogether. Christians must be in the forefront of bringing, in the present time, signs and foretastes of God's eventual full healing to bear upon the created order in all its parts and at every level. If the world is to be put to rights, brought under the saving lordship of God's restorative justice, and if that work has already been unveiled prototypically in Jesus' death and resurrection, it will not do to concentrate on individual justification while allowing wider issues of justice to go unaddressed. Christians must be in the forefront of bringing, in the present time, signs and foretastes of God's healing justice to bear upon the world that is still full of corruption, injustice, oppression, division, suspicion, and war. And if the world is to attain its full beauty and dignity as God's liberated new creation, a beauty and dignity for which the present evidences of God's grandeur within creation are just a foretaste, it will not do to regard beauty, and its creation and conservation, as a pleasant but irrelevant optional extra within a world manipulated by science, exploited by technology, and bought and sold in the economic marketplace. Christians must be in the forefront of bringing, in the present time, signs and foretastes of God's fresh beauty to birth within the world, signs of hope for what the Spirit will yet do:

> And for all this, nature is never spent;
> There lives the dearest freshness deep down things;
> And, though the last lights off the black West went
> Oh, morning, at the brown brink eastward springs—
> Because the Holy Ghost over the bent
> World broods with warm breast and with ah! bright wings.[283]

**3.** The vocation of the church to live thus in the wrinkle of time that is inaugurated eschatology is focused here on the life of prayer. Paul holds together in this passage the intimate prayer that knows exactly what to call God (i.e., *Abba*) and the groaning prayer that has no idea what to ask for or even what words to use. Prayer itself is a matter of both knowing and not knowing, of security and insecurity, of "having nothing yet possessing all things" (2 Cor 6:10). The Spirit is equally and characteristically at work at both extremes, enabling the "now" of glad and assured adoption, of the child/parent relationship with God wherein Christians grow to full human maturity without ever ceasing to be the child of this parent, and enabling also the "not yet" of groaning in travail to be expressed, in the inarticulate depths, in a way that God the heartsearcher knows, hears, and understands. The latter kind of prayer is also, it appears, part of what it means "to love God." The opening of 8:28 relates, after all, quite closely to 8:26-27, for what does it mean to love God but that in the depths of one's own heart and spirit there is a call of love, trust, and hope for which the ultimate explanation is that the Spirit is there at work?

The call to this kind of inarticulate prayer is not, it seems to me, exactly the same thing as the discipline of silence practiced by some who have made long journeys into the realms of prayer and have come back to share their insights with the rest of us. It is not simply contemplation. Nor yet is it contemplation's parody, that stream-of-consciousness prayer in which random musings and daydreams pass before the mind and are vaguely brought into the presence of God. It is, rather, an agony that would come into speech if only it could, part of whose agony indeed is that to bring it to speech, to name the problem and hence to envisage its solution, would be to attain some measure of relief. The problem of evil is not so easily solved. The achievement of the cross and resurrection, and the power of the indwelling Spirit, have not produced that kind of inaugurated eschatology where everything is now laid out neatly awaiting completion, like a row of beans ripe and ready to be picked. Let no one suppose that Paul's emphasis on what has already happened in Christ leads to that kind of casual ease about the present unredeemedness of the world, or about tasks that lie ahead. However, no one should suppose, either, that the

---

283. G. M. Hopkins, "God's Grandeur."

continuing appropriate agony of expectant prayer to which the whole church is now called casts any doubt on that other experience of which the same passage speaks, the *Abba* knowledge of God that is also based on the work of the Messiah and the gift of the Spirit. The two go together in Paul and in Christian experience.

**4.** Intercession for the world that is groaning in travail is not, then, an optional extra for the Christian. Within this, intercession for the parts of one's own life that are in trouble cannot be discounted either. There is a false humility about some protests against such intercession, discounting it as trivial or self-centered. To the contrary: the groanings of each individual, caught between redemption accomplished in Christ and redemption still awaited (8:23), are all part of the groaning of creation. As long as one does not imagine that the world, and the love of God, revolve around one's own life and concerns—as long, in other words, as one is a mature and adult child of God and not still a spiritual baby—one's own concerns have their proper place, and can indeed be the starting-point for awareness of, and hence prayer about, the wider groanings of the whole cosmos. Just because we must not be self-centered, that does not mean we should ignore the self and its concerns. If we are God's beloved children, our small as well as our great concerns matter.

**5.** Suffering is a mystery, indeed. It is to be rejected as a final good—as though the Christian were after all to embrace some kind of masochism!—and yet embraced both as a sign of the time at which we live and even as a part of the means whereby redemption comes to the world. There is a terrible danger in this very Pauline theme, which feminism and other recent movements have not been slow to point out: The redemptive value of suffering has all too often been preached by the comfortable to the uncomfortable, by the elderly to the youth going off to war, by masters to slaves, by men to women. Yet the abuse does not invalidate the use, and if *corruptio optimi pessima* is a dire warning to those in danger of corrupting the best it is also a reminder to those who are all too aware of the worst.

At the heart of Paul's picture of the suffering church is the fact that, as he says in 8:10, "the Messiah is in you." If this truth undergirds the hope of future resurrection, it also means that Christian suffering in the present is somehow "messianic," which means it is somehow, in ways that will rightly and inevitably pass our comprehension, redemptive. As we saw in the notes, 2 Corinthians was written not least as an elaboration and defense of this as applied to Paul's apostleship. For millions of Christians in the contemporary world, in places such as China, Pakistan, Indonesia, the Sudan, and elsewhere, daily suffering for the faith is simply part of what being a Christian means. When, in 1998, Westminster Abbey decided to fill the ten vacant niches on the West Front with statues of twentieth-century Christian martyrs, there was no shortage of candidates.[284] For millions of others in comfortable Western churches, such suffering as comes their way often seems incidental to the practice of faith. Yet this too can be transformed, and transformative, if brought through prayer into the divine dialogue spoken of with bated breath in 8:26-27.

**6.** In a way that is characteristic of Romans 5–8 as a whole, Jesus is seldom mentioned yet everywhere present. "Fellow heirs with the Messiah" (8:17) means being "conformed to the image of God's Son" (8:29). The pattern of Jesus—his sonship, his kingdom, his suffering, his prayer, his death, and his resurrection—shapes and undergirds the whole paragraph. Paul has certainly not allowed Jesus to become a mere cipher: he remains the assured goal, the inspiration, the companion, the pattern, the older brother. It would not be fanciful to see Gethsemane

---

284. The choices were revealing and powerfully evocative both of the worldwide spread of the faith and of the challenge still posed by the gospel to the power of the world, and vice versa: Maximilian Kolbe, Poland (1941); Manche Masemola, South Africa (1928); Janani Luwum, Uganda (1977); Grand Duchess Elizabeth of Russia (1918); Martin Luther King, USA (1969); Oscar Romero, El Salvador (1980); Dietrich Bonhoeffer, Germany (1945); Esther John, Pakistan (1960); Lucian Tapiedi, Papua New Guinea (1942); Wang Zhiming, China (1972).

standing behind 8:18-27, if not in Paul's conscious mind, nevertheless in the strong tradition of the early church reading these words (see Heb 5:7-9). It would be profitable to study the portrait of Jesus as it emerges throughout Romans 5–8, and to reflect on the way in which this picture had already made its way, within less than thirty years, into the imagination and subconscious thought of Paul and the other New Testament writers.

**7.** The rootedness of the entire discussion in the narrative theology of the exodus enables one to suggest a pattern of Christian reading of the Old Testament that is neither simply historical nor simply typological. On the one hand, it is important that the original events are seen in their own right, as the formative events of the people of Israel. (The question of what precisely happened, and of how "historical" the stories accessible to Paul and to ourselves may actually be, is not our present concern.) On the other hand, as many different strands within Second Temple Judaism bear witness, the exodus story was used as a template for the great expectations that were cherished in the time of Jesus. God would, many believed, accomplish something for which the original exodus would be both the historical starting-point and the pattern. Paul, in company with many other early Christians, believed that this had happened in Jesus' life, death, and resurrection, and in the sending of the Spirit by which the church was enabled to go forward to the promised land of new creation. This suggests a reading of the Old Testament that gives due weight to original meanings and contexts, and to different understandings that were available in the first century, while yet suggesting, as the distinctively Christian meaning, the belief that the new exodus both had happened in Jesus, and was still to happen in the resurrection and the consequent transformation of the whole created order. This, I suggest, reflects part of what Paul, and presumably the rest of the early Christian movement (since he is quoting early common tradition) meant by saying that Jesus' death and resurrection had happened "according to the scriptures" (1 Cor 15:3-4).

# ROMANS 8:31-39, NOTHING WILL SEPARATE US FROM GOD'S LOVE

31What, then, shall we say in response to this? If God is for us, who can be against us? 32He who did not spare his own Son, but gave him up for us all—how will he not also, along with him, graciously give us all things? 33Who will bring any charge against those whom God has chosen? It is God who justifies. 34Who is he that condemns? Christ Jesus, who died—more than that, who was raised to life—is at the right hand of God and is also interceding for us. 35Who shall separate us from the love of Christ? Shall trouble or hardship or persecution or famine or nakedness or danger or sword? 36As it is written:

"For your sake we face death all day long;
    we are considered as sheep to be
        slaughtered."[a]

[a] *36 Psalm 44:22*

31What then are we to say about these things? If God is for us, who is against us? 32He who did not withhold his own Son, but gave him up for all of us, will he not with him also give us everything else? 33Who will bring any charge against God's elect? It is God who justifies. 34Who is to condemn? It is Christ Jesus, who died, yes, who was raised, who is at the right hand of God, who indeed intercedes for us.[a] 35Who will separate us from the love of Christ? Will hardship, or distress, or persecution, or famine, or nakedness, or peril, or sword? 36As it is written,

"For your sake we are being killed all day long;
    we are accounted as sheep to be
        slaughtered."

[a] *Or Is it Christ Jesus . . . for us?*

NIV

[37]No, in all these things we are more than conquerors through him who loved us. [38]For I am convinced that neither death nor life, neither angels nor demons,[a] neither the present nor the future, nor any powers, [39]neither height nor depth, nor anything else in all creation, will be able to separate us from the love of God that is in Christ Jesus our Lord.

[a] 38 Or nor heavenly rulers

NRSV

[37]No, in all these things we are more than conquerors through him who loved us. [38]For I am convinced that neither death, nor life, nor angels, nor rulers, nor things present, nor things to come, nor powers, [39]nor height, nor depth, nor anything else in all creation, will be able to separate us from the love of God in Christ Jesus our Lord.

# COMMENTARY

Paul's substantial argument in chaps. 5–8 is done. The style as well as the content of 8:28-30 indicates as much. What remains is to celebrate, and to do so in a way that draws together the threads of all that has been said so far—all, that is, in chaps. 1–4 as well as 5–8, which explains the strong presence of justification, as well as glorification, in this concluding passage.

As Paul does so, the theme that emerges with particular strength is that of God's love. This is only the second time in the letter Paul has spoken explicitly of God's love (counting 5:5-8 as a single reference, if 5:5 is read the way most scholars do); yet it now becomes clear that this has been the underlying theme all through. An overemphasis in some quarters on the lawcourt setting of Paul's justification terminology has led some sensitive Christians to feel that the apostle is lacking in the great theme of God's love, so obvious (for instance) in John. This, it turns out, is a false antithesis. Not only is John's Gospel replete with forensic language and imagery, a subject that cannot be pursued here.[285] Paul's whole argument is undergirded by the emphasis on the love of God: the fact that it is the main theme in what is obviously a concluding summary proves as much, and indeed warns against taking lexicographical absence to indicate conceptual absence. The thing may be present when the word is not.

The argument of this paragraph is, in fact, the same as that of 5:6-10: that since God's love has done for Christians all that has been done in

Christ, there is no power that can shake that love now, or turn it aside from completing the job. The love of God, enjoyed already in the present, will outlast and defeat all enemies, including death itself; the close links between this passage and 1 Cor 15:20-28 indicate clearly enough where the thought is going. Love is the ultimate assurance, stronger than logic, even the great logic of Romans 5–8; love is not an idea to be worked out, but a fact, an experienced fact, something that cannot be denied any more than one can stop breathing. And if the clouds of present suffering hide the sun for a while, the unshakable evidence of God's love is seen, as Paul had already said in 5:6-10, in Jesus' death. Not much is added here to 5:6-10 in terms of actual argument; this increases the sense we had in that passage (see the notes) that 5:1-11 was a full advance statement of the entire argument of 5–8. What we have now in 8:31-39 is the performative expansion of 5:11: "we celebrate in God through our Lord Jesus the Messiah, through whom we have now received the reconciliation."

The internal theological shaping of the paragraph usually goes unnoticed amid the flurry of ideas, the problems about punctuation, the lists of potential dangers and enemies, and the general tone of celebration. Paul's argument proceeds through a series of rhetorical questions, each of which is followed, not by an answer to the question itself, but by a statement that shows that the answer must be "nobody." The first of these questions and answers is broad, introducing the set; the following three fill out and explain the first. The last two verses, explaining and celebrating the answers just given, round off the whole section of the letter with the

285. See A. E. Harvey, *Jesus on Trial: A Study in the Fourth Gospel* (London: SPCK, 1976); A. T. Lincoln, *Truth on Trial: The Lawsuit Motif in the Fourth Gospel* (Peabody, Mass.: Hendrikson, 2000).

appropriate mixture of rhetoric and solemnity. Thus the paragraph works as follows:

(A) First question and answer (introductory): if God is for us, who is against us? Answer: [nobody, because] God, having not spared his Son, will now give us all things (vv. 31-32).

(B) Second question and answer (specific focus on God): Who shall bring a charge against us? Answer: [nobody, because] God is the justifier (v. 33).

(C) Third question and answer (specific focus on Christ): Who shall condemn us? Answer: [nobody, because] Christ died, was raised, and now intercedes (v. 34).

(D) Fourth question and answer (specific focus on the link of love between God and those in Christ): Who shall separate us from God's love? Answer: none of the possible candidates, because as God's faithful people we are victorious "through the one who loved us" (vv. 35-37).

(E) Final explanation, summing up: nothing can separate us from God's love in Christ (vv. 38-39).

There may be the hint of a trinitarian shape to the B-C-D sequence (vv. 33-37), picking up and celebrating the picture of God in the chapter, and indeed the letter, so far. Though the Spirit is not mentioned, the careful structuring of questions and answers may suggest, not least in the light of 8:12-16 and particularly vv. 26-28, that the Spirit is the one through whom God's love enables those in Christ to be "more than conquerors"; or, to put it another way, that over against the list of things that might separate us from God's love, it is the Spirit who joins us to God's love, making it a fact of experience, not merely a theological belief.

Within this structure, furthermore, Paul has created a remarkable web of biblical allusions and echoes, summoning up three passages in particular.[286]

The first, in v. 32, is the story of Abraham and Isaac in Genesis 22. In that passage, Abraham's willingness to sacrifice his only beloved son is the reason given for God's greatest blessings on him; here, God's actual sacrifice of the only Son is the demonstration of a love that will thereafter stop at nothing. The role of the "binding of Isaac" in the Jewish thought of Paul's day has been controversial. Though most of the evidence for this as a major theme is later, and some indeed may have developed as a response to early Christian atonement-theology, it is likely that Paul was familiar with some rabbinic traditions in which Genesis 22 had some role to play, at least in anticipating the events of Passover night and perhaps of the Day of Atonement, in providing theological justification for God's forgiving of Israel's sins and for the liberation from slavery that would follow.[287] Whether Paul is responding to such beliefs, or whether, with his own exposition of Abraham still in mind, he is simply following through his own train of thought, it is difficult to say; but his main point is clear, that God "gave up" the only Son "on our behalf." Remarkably enough, Paul managed to write a whole chapter about Abraham (Romans 4) without mentioning this incident. Now it comes in, not however (as in some of the relevant Jewish traditions) to highlight an achievement of Abraham and Isaac, because of which ethnic Israel would receive blessing or atonement, but to emphasize, almost by contrast, the powerful love of God in going even further than Abraham had done.

The second allusion is to the (so-called) third Servant Song in Isa 50:4-9. Though, of course, much Christian tradition has understood the servant songs in specific relation to Jesus himself, as Paul himself arguably does in Phil 2:6-8, in this reworking it is the church, remarkably enough, that takes on the role of the servant, here standing before hostile adversaries, trusting totally in God, and awaiting vindication (8:33-34). However, it is precisely the church "in Christ" that can take this stance. Paul's point throughout Romans 5–8 is that the identity of the church is discovered in the Messiah. The reference to the Messiah's heavenly intercession in v. 34 may, in fact, be an allusion to Isa 53:12; and the reference to being like sheep for the slaughter within the following quotation

---

286. On which see Richard B. Hays, *Echoes of Scripture in the Letters of Paul* (New Haven: Yale University Press, 1989) 57-63.

287. On the Jewish traditions see G. Vermes, *Scripture and Tradition in Judaism* (Leiden: Brill, 1973) 193-227; B. D. Chilton and P. R. Davies, "The Aqedah: A Revised Tradition History," *CBQ* 40 (1978) 514-46; B. D. Chilton, "Isaac and the Second Night: A Consideration," *Biblica* 61 (1980) 78-88. See also Joseph A. Fitzmyer, *Romans,* AB 33 (Garden City, N.Y.: Doubleday, 1993) 531-32.

(v. 36) may again deliberately echo Isa 53:7.[288] At the same time, declaring that the Messiah is now "at God's right hand" summons up Ps 110:1, one of the most frequently cited passages in early Christian exploration of Jesus' status.[289] Jesus is now sharing the very throne of God; and his place at God's right hand was from early on seen as an encouragement to the suffering church, both because he was interceding on its behalf and because his location provided assurance of eventual vindication (see Mark 12:35-37 and par.; 14:62 and par.; Acts 2:33-34; 7:55-56; Eph 1:20; Col 3:1; Heb 1:3; 8:1; 10:12; 12:2; 1 Pet 3:22; Rev 3:21).

The third biblical reference is an explicit quotation. In v. 36 Paul quotes Ps 44:22 [43:23 LXX]: "for your sake we are being killed all day long; we are reckoned as sheep for slaughter." This psalm, like its longer cousin Psalm 89, begins by celebrating the love of God for Israel seen in terms of great victories over national enemies, all looking back, of course, to the exodus story, leading to the claim that "we have boasted in God continually" (44:8). Then the psalm turns to complaint: everything has gone wrong, the enemies are prevailing and mocking, and Israel is covered with shame (vv. 9-16). However, this is not because of Israel's disloyalty; this time at least, Israel is not guilty of disobedience, of idolatry, of breaking the covenant. God knows the secrets of the heart (v. 21). Rather, it is "for your sake" that "we are being killed all day long, and accounted as sheep for the slaughter." It is precisely by being loyal to YHWH that Israel has pulled down the wrath of the pagan nations upon its own head. Therefore, the psalm concludes: It is time for God to wake up and act, to help and redeem. It is time for God's own covenant faithfulness to be unveiled in action.

There can be little doubt that Paul had the entire context in mind, and intended the alert reader to hear its overtones of faith in the midst of tribulation, of covenant loyalty and covenant hope—in fact, of the major theme of Romans.

More particularly, the idea of it being somehow God's purpose that "we are killed all the day long" fits so closely both with the servant allusion in vv. 33-34, and with the christological focus of the whole chapter, that we can go further and suggest that Paul is here reflecting again what it means to be "conformed to the image of the Son," and to share the Messiah's sufferings and glory (vv. 17, 29). There may also be the suggestion, lurking in Paul's mind as he himself faces the charge of being a disloyal Jew, that his own sufferings are the result not of infidelity but precisely of fidelity.

By skillful use of this complex web of biblical allusion and quotation, Paul is underscoring his basic contention from 3:21 onward. Those who believe in Jesus the Messiah, who respond with love to God's loving action in his death and with faith to God's raising of him from the dead, are constituted as the renewed Israel of God. They are the true children of Abraham; they are the true servant people; they are the people who claim and sing as their own the psalms of the faithful covenant people. Law, prophets, and writings are thus called in as witnesses to the fact that, in the midst of suffering and oppression, the one God of Israel has, in long-promised redeeming love, reconstituted Israel in and around Jesus the Messiah. All who belong to Jesus are the true people of this one God.

Thus is concluded the thesis of chaps. 5–8. Thus is concluded, too, one part of the argument of 1:18–8:39. And thus is formed once again the great question that takes up the other part, and will lead into some of Paul's densest argumentation: what then about Israel according to the flesh?

**8:31.** Seven rhetorical questions—four of which are structurally important, as we have seen—make up the bulk of this paragraph. They are proffered not as a challenge to Paul's readers to think up clever answers or counterexamples but as a demonstration of the certainty of his case. As so often, the opening (in this case, the first two questions) functions as an overall statement of what is to come, which is then unpacked in successive stages.

Unlike some other occurrences of an initial "What then shall we say?" (see the Commentary on 3:1; 4:1; 6:1), the opening question is not introducing a possible conclusion that Paul will then deny. Traces of this rhetorical move still remain,

---

288. See Hays, *Echoes of Scripture in the Letters of Paul,* 63: Since the people of God are thereby suffering with Christ, "upon them is the chastisement that makes others whole, and with their stripes is creation healed."

289. See N. T. Wright, *Jesus and the Victory of God,* vol. 2 of *Christian Origins and the Question of God* (London: SPCK, 1996) 508n. 116, for details of the extensive sources, both primary and secondary.

however, in the questions that follow, all of which invite hearers to suggest reasons why the security of God's people in Christ might be less than absolute, only for Paul to deny that such reasons could be found. By adding "to these things" (NIV) or "about these things" (NRSV), Paul is rhetorically inviting responses to the argument he has just completed, rather than, as in other "what shall we say?" questions, looking for logical corollaries that might follow.

The opening challenge says it all: "if God is for us, who can be against us?" The statement that "God is for us" is about as basic a way as can be conceived of summing up the revelation of God's saving justice in the gospel. Elsewhere, of course, Paul uses "for us" in one form or another as a basic way of explaining the death of Jesus (see 5:6-8; 14:15; 1 Cor 15:3; 2 Cor 5:14-15, 21; Gal 1:4; 2:20; 3:13; Eph 5:2, 25; 1 Thess 5:10; Titus 2:14). Nowhere else is he so bold as to say simply "God is for us" (it is admittedly conditional, but only as a rhetorical device). "Who is against us?" is clearly expecting the answer "nobody"; but there are plenty of candidates lined up to be considered, once Paul has amplified this basic statement. He is writing, furthermore, not from a comfortable armchair with the world at his feet, but on his way to fulfill a difficult and dangerous mission (delivering the collection to Jerusalem) that might cost him his life for one reason (opposition from Torah-observant Jews), and to begin another perhaps even more dangerous and difficult mission (to Rome, and thence to Spain) that might cost him his life for a different reason (the clash between his gospel and Caesar's kingdom). These, together with the normal hazards of his life as a missionary, and the threats from spiritual as well as human and natural forces, will be noted presently. But Paul stands firm as a Jewish-style monotheist: there is one God, and if this God is on our side, then no force on earth or elsewhere can ultimately stand against us.

**8:32.** The third question, the rhetorical response to "who is against us," carries the force: "nobody is against us, because of what God has done." God did what even Abraham had not done: Isaac was spared, but Jesus was not (the particular echo is of Gen 22:16, where Abraham is commended, and then richly blessed, because he had not spared his only son; for the significance of this, see the Overview). God's willingness to give up

the only Son is cited as the key evidence for God's utter reliability. This fills out, exactly as we would have expected from 5:6-10, what is meant by God's being "for us."

The same passage in chap. 5 explains the rhetorical question that then emerges: "How will God, then, not also give us all things with him?"—i.e., with the only Son. If God has done the hard part, there will be no problem with the easy part. If God has given the most valuable treasure possible, everything else will follow (for "give" Paul here uses the quite rare verb χαρίζομαι [charizomai], cognate with χάρις [charis, "grace"]). Instead of amplifying the negative aspect of the question of v. 31 b ("who can be against us?"), Paul moves to the positive: God will give us all things (and therefore no power can stand against us). This way of referring to the final state of blessedness, corresponding to "salvation," "glorification," or "life," picks up from vv. 17-25 the theme of inheritance, of the fact that the world as a whole belongs to the Messiah and hence to those who are his. "All things are yours," says Paul in 1 Cor 3:21-23, anticipating the flourish at the end of the present chapter. You own the world—a statement that can only be made with integrity, perhaps, by one who was facing the perils described in v. 35. The grand, sweeping statements of assurance are balanced with the clear recognition of what is still to be faced within the inaugurated eschatology that dominates the horizon. Once again, 2 Cor 6:10 comes into view: "as having nothing, yet possessing all things."

**8:33-36.** The next two verses, continuing the sequence of rhetorical questions, have caused problems to interpreters because of uncertainty over punctuation, reflected in the different translations. RSV, for example, treats the second half of v. 33 ("It is God who justifies") as the first half of a sentence, the second being the question in v. 34a, "who is to condemn?"; and then translates the rest of v. 34, not as a statement ("It is Christ Jesus who died," NRSV), but as a question: "Is it Christ Jesus [i.e., Is it Christ Jesus who is to condemn?]?" This, indeed, is only one of many possible permutations.[290] But the most likely reading,

---

290. Cf. the NEB with the alternatives noted in its margin. For details of all options, see C. E. B. Cranfield, *A Critical and Exegetical Commentary on the Epistle to the Romans,* ICC, 2 vols. (Edinburgh: T. & T. Clark, 1975) 437-38; Douglas J. Moo, *The Epistle to the Romans,* NICNT (Grand Rapids: Eerdmans, 1996) 541.

because it accords best with the rhythm and rhetoric of the whole paragraph, is to see vv. 33*a* and 34*a* as questions to which vv. 33*b* and 34*b* give oblique answers, as, in their different ways, in the NRSV and the NIV.[291] The answers are oblique because they are not offering candidates by way of reply; they are saying, rather, that because God is the justifier, and because the Messiah has died, was raised, and now intercedes, there can indeed be no one to lay a charge against God's elect, no one to condemn. The passage then flows naturally:

a. Who can be against us? No one; God, after all, did not spare the Son (vv. 31*b*-32).

b. Who will bring a charge? No one; God, after all, is the justifier (v. 33).

c. Who will condemn? No one; Christ Jesus, after all, died, was raised, and intercedes (v. 34).

And this leads to an interesting possibility for v. 35:

d. Who will separate us from Christ's love? (Expected answer: No one; the Spirit, after all, has poured out love for God into our hearts.) Paul's answer, after a list of possible agents of separation, is, however: No, we are more than conquerors through the one who loved us (i.e., presumably God, at work by the Spirit; "through" here means "through the agency of" [διά *dia* with genitive]; a few MSS altered this to "because" [*dia* with accusative]). There may have been a trinitarian sequence in Paul's mind, such as (for instance) we find in 1 Cor 12:4-6 or Gal 4:4-7, but the exuberance of the passage has prevented it from reaching full expression.

Whatever we think about that, with vv. 33-34 we are back in the lawcourt, as in the middle of chap. 3. In 2:1-16 the whole human family faced the judgment of God; in 3:19-20 the whole world was in the dock, with no defense to offer against massive charges. Now we look around for possible accusers, and find none. Any that might appear

have to face the fact that God, the judge, is the justifier; in other words, that the verdict has already been pronounced by the judge whose righteousness has been fully displayed. And that verdict—that those in the Messiah, marked out by faith, are already to be seen as "righteous," even ahead of the final vindication—is precisely what the lawcourt dimension of "justification" is all about. We should note that at this point Paul is once again speaking of the *final* day of judgment, as in 2:1-16 and 8:1. As he looks ahead to that future moment, he puts his confidence in the *past event* of justification and hence the *present standing* of God's people that results from it, knowing that "those God justified, God also glorified." The logic of justification comes full circle.

Very well, then, if there is no one to bring a charge, is there anyone who might offer a verdict of condemnation? Leaving aside the problem of envisaging a judge other than God—and here the close link between 33*b* and 34*a* comes into play, with the echoes of Isa 50:8—all thought of a negative verdict, even supposing there were any charges to come to trial, must be put out of view by the sight of the Messiah, with the whole sweep of his accomplishment. His death was the condemnation of sin (8:3); his resurrection, the announcement that sin had been dealt with, and hence the achievement of justification (4:24-25; 1 Cor 15:17); his glorification, the glorification of his people (8:17, 29-30). Paul here adds a further element, familiar from the letter to the Hebrews (7:25; 9:24) and the first letter of John (2:1), occurring only here in his writings: the present activity of the Messiah, in his life in the heavenly realm, is to intercede on behalf of those he represents. As the servant songs have already been alluded to in this passage, it is possible that, with Jesus' atoning and justifying death also mentioned, we should detect a reference to the intercessory work of the servant of the Lord in the fourth song, at Isa 53:12.

The thought switches from the lawcourt metaphor to something that is no metaphor but the deepest reality: The love of God, which, shown forth in the Messiah, forms the unbreakable bond between God and the believer. Paul here speaks of the love of the Messiah.[292] This may

---

291. Cranfield, *Romans*, 437-38, argues in favor of the RV's variation, which is to put a colon at the end of v. 33, because of the natural link between v. 33*b* and v. 34*a*, both through the antithesis of "justify" and "condemn" and because of the echo of Isa 50:8. The sense is not seriously different from the one adopted here. The reading taken in RSV—from which the REB is not far in sense—is flawed. God would not be a likely bringer of a charge (God is the judge, not a prosecutor). True, 2:16 envisages Christ as the agent of judgment, so that to propose him as a possible pronouncer of condemnation is not totally unthinkable; but the way all of Paul's questions and answers in this paragraph function tells against this implication (present in J. B. Phillips: "Who is in a position to condemn? Only Christ, and Christ died for us"). See the Overview.

292. Two very good MSS, and some lesser ones, say "of God," but the weight of evidence is against this. It would be easy for a scribe to "correct" the text in this way to the more predictable reading, not least in the light of v. 39.

simply be a telescoped way of saying "the love of God in Christ," as in v. 39; or it may actually be a deliberate reference to the love of the Messiah himself, as in Gal 2:20 ("the Messiah loved me, and gave himself for me"; see also 2 Cor 5:14; Eph 3:19). The question Paul raises is the one that will now take him through to the close of the chapter: who can separate us from this love? As suggested above, it is possible that Paul was thinking of a "Spirit"-response to this question, to follow "God" in v. 33*b* and "Christ" in v. 34*b*. Certainly, if we take the logic of the questions, and think back through all that has been said about the Spirit in chap. 8, this would make excellent sense—just as it would be typical of Paul to interrupt himself and then hurry on to his larger conclusion leaving his readers to fill in the blanks on the way.

The actual answer to the question, in any case, is again, "No one." But there is a formidable list of potential enemies who seem bent on separating believers from God's love, and Paul must list them, place the conflict with them on the map of God's purposes for the chosen people, and declare them beaten. Paul speaks of that which he knows; he had himself faced all these enemies, except perhaps the sword, and he must have known that at any moment this too might come his way, whether judically in a Roman court or casually on the road (cf. 2 Cor 11:23-29).

Facing these foes, as he was to do again in Jerusalem and on the voyage to Rome, he took comfort in the scripturally based knowledge that this was part of the vocation of God's people. Though it seemed that calamity had sent God to sleep, had caused the Almighty to shut up his mercy, yet in fact, as the psalmist affirmed, these sufferings were after all part of the plan. For the people of God, suffering was not just something *from* which God would deliver, but something *as a result of which* God would deliver; this belief, held by some (though apparently not all) Jews of the period,[293] had for Paul and the other early Christians reached its astonishing climax in the death of Jesus, but still obtained as part of the life of the new-covenant people of God. Somehow, as Paul elsewhere affirmed of his own sufferings (2 Cor 4:7-15; Col 1:24), the suffering of Christians

was to be taken up into the ongoing purposes of God, not to add to the unique achievement of Jesus the Messiah but to embody it in the world.

If Paul has been thinking implicitly of the Spirit, this would further explain the mode of his answer in v. 37, not indeed to the question of v. 35*a*, but to the problem raised by all the instruments of suffering in v. 35*b*. "In all these things we are more than conquerors"; in other words, we are not only able to win a victory over these enemies, we are able to see them off the field entirely. This is part of the meaning of v. 32*b:* God will "give us all things" with Christ. It goes closely, of course, with the promise in 1 Cor 15:24-28, that God will put all enemies under the feet of the Messiah, the last being death itself. "The one who loved us" is most likely God, though with v. 37 poised between v. 35 and v. 39 it could equally be Christ; but the way in which this love sustains the Christian is through the agency of the Spirit, as in 8:26-27. The present tense does not imply that Paul thinks he, or his readers, are able in the present time to defeat all these enemies and so to maintain a tranquil and trouble-free pursuit of happiness. This is, in other words, a shout not of triumphalism but of exuberant faith, faith in the victory that, as Easter had proved, had already been won on the cross and would finally be won at the moment of complete liberation. "We are more than conquerors," like the claim "God also glorified them," is a past truth about the Messiah, a future truth about all his people, and hence a present reality in faith for those living on the basis of that past and in the hope of that future.

**8:38-39.** The final γάρ *gar* of this section explains the shout of triumph in terms of the settled conviction (grounded on what Paul knows about the Messiah, Jesus, the Lord of the world and "our Lord") that the one true God has poured out, through this Jesus, love of the most powerful and unbreakable kind. Even justice is not the last word about this God; love is. Of this, Paul is "persuaded" (the literal meaning), in other words, "convinced" (NIV, NRSV; cf. 14:14; 15:14). This is no passing impression, feeling, or imagination. He has thought it through and reached an unshakable conclusion.

In v. 35 Paul listed physical events, threats, and circumstances that might separate one from God's love; now he lists the forces that might stand

---

293. Cf. 2 Macc 7:9, 11, where the martyred brothers speak of their deaths as being "for the sake of God's law." See further Wright, *Jesus and the Victory of God,* 579-92.

behind those physical threats. Of these, death itself is the most obvious, at least for a Jew; some parts of the Hellenistic tradition, reflected in some later Christian thinking, saw physical death in a less threatening light, because it valued physical life less highly, but for Paul death remained the last and greatest enemy (1 Cor 15:26). "Life" is presumably not simply included as the natural pair to "death"—this list manages to avoid at least one other natural pair, "principalities and powers" (see Eph 3:10; Col 2:15)—and certainly does not refer to the "life" that is the promise of God and the gift of the Spirit. Rather, it seems to envisage the present life, with all its many delights and problems, as a potential separator between God and the believer. Angels, rulers, and powers—presumably the "rulers" here are heavenly ones, corresponding to the "elements" of Gal 4:3, 9 and Col 2:8, 20, though perhaps their earthly counterparts are not ruled out—might try to break the bond of love between God and the church, but they are a defeated rabble and, though they can make a lot of noise, they can now wield no power at the level required to separate God's people from God's love (cf. Col 2:14-15). Time present and time future, space high and low—the whole world, as we say, of space and time as it stretches out before us—

can have no power to break the love God has for those in the Messiah. (Time past is irrelevant; the cross and resurrection have dealt with anything it could do.) The chapter, and the section, end with the characteristic christological summary that demonstrates, not simply Paul's rhetorical skill (cf. 5:11, 21; 6:11, 23; 7:25*a*), but the very height and depth of his entire theology.

We are back with the picture that has been there in Romans from the beginning: God and creation, with the human race poised in between, belonging within the latter but called to reflect the image of the former. Idolatry had reversed God's intended order: humans had worshiped that which was not God, had ceded power to that which, being itself corruptible, could only bring death. Now, in the Messiah, Jesus, humanity has been restored; death has been defeated, and creation itself, so far from being shunned as essentially evil, awaits its redemption. Christian assurance, despite caricatures, is the very opposite of human arrogance; it is the fruit of humble, trusting faith. Those who follow their Messiah into the valley of the shadow of death will find that they need fear no evil. Though they sometimes seem sheep for the slaughter, yet they may trust the Shepherd, whose love will follow them all the days of their life.

# REFLECTIONS

**1.** The security of which Paul has spoken throughout Romans 5–8—the security, that is, of final glorification for all those who are justified by faith—is based firmly on the trinitarian revelation of God in the gospel, reflected at least in part in the shape of the present passage. At a time when the question of God is again central in some quarters at least, it is vital to stress that Paul's theology, agenda, spirituality, faith, and hope are all focused on this very specific God. Not for him a vague Deism, a distant God known only through a thick cloud, a God to whom there could be many routes and of whom there could be many equally valid revelations. Not for him a generalized sense of "the sacred" such as could be encountered with equal validity in all, or at least most, religious traditions. After all, the religious traditions of Paul's day included many that were demonstrably dehumanizing; the most powerful new religion in Turkey during Paul's lifetime was the cult of Caesar himself. The way to the confidence and joy of which Paul here speaks is not through a general or vague sense of religion, or indeed of God, but of the specific and focused belief and trust in this God, Father, Son, and Spirit.

It is noticeable that in the post-Christian world of the modern West this belief has been misunderstood, misrepresented, and then scorned. Trinitarian belief is labeled incomprehensible, a philosopher's dense answer to a question nobody today would ask, and is set aside in favor of either a variation on Deism's distant God, or some kind of pantheism (as in some New Age think ing), or a form of panentheism.[294] What we find in Paul, if one may coin the phrase, is instead "eschatological the-enpanism": instead of everything existing "in God," true though that may be in one sense, Paul insists that at the last "God will be all in all" (1 Cor 15:28; cf. Eph 1:15-23; 4:10). What is more, this is something to be *accomplished,* not simply a steady state of affairs. The task began with the call of Israel, reached its climax in the presence of God as a human being within the world of space, time, and matter, and is now to be implemented through the Spirit of this Jesus, until the whole creation is filled with the presence and love of God in a way that at present it is not. The created order is good, but incomplete; God intends to complete it, and thereby to liberate it. To seek for God at the moment within the created order, or to try to think or pray one's way to God solely on the basis of the created order, is at best an invalid form of realized eschatology (only when God is "all in all" will this be possible), and at worst taking the broad road toward idolatry. This is not to say that the creator is not in principle knowable through creation (see 1:19-20); only that to search for a divinity within the created order is out of the question.

It is not surprising, then, that such theological schemes do not produce the kind of assurance of which Paul speaks. Indeed, they often inveigh against it, treating assurance as mere cockiness, self-satisfaction, or spiritual arrogance. It is, of course, perfectly possible for Christians to hold a form of assurance that is guilty of any or all of those things. But once again abuse does not nullify proper use. In particular, we might suggest that a form of Christian assurance that has not actually faced the challenges of vv. 35 and 38-39 may still be at best immature; not that all Christians must face all the problems that some face some of the time, but that all should be committed to the full gospel, which will mean that hostility at either an earthly or a spiritual level will come their way sooner or later. When that happens, nothing short of a trinitarian view of God will supply the assurance that is needed. But when these trials are faced, and this God is known in the midst of them to be reliable, powerful, and above all loving—that is when one may expect to hear the shout of genuine Christian joy.

**2.** This confidence, this assurance, is kept in place by the Bible. To put it another way, the reading, praying, and singing of Scripture is one of the key ways in which trust in the triune God, and the security of this God's love in Christ, is maintained. Paul, as we saw, here brings together law, prophets, and writings in a web of allusion and echo to which (it seems to me) only the most pedantic of scholars can remain deaf, in order to say in practice what he says explicitly in 15:4: these things were written for our encouragement, "so that through patience and the comfort of the scriptures we might have hope."

For too long scholars have sneered at Paul's use of Scripture, implying that for him it was a blade of grass that could be blown in any direction by any powerful wind. Preachers have taken their cue from this, often saying quite casually that Paul's use of Scripture is simply unprincipled and peculiar; sometimes, indeed, this is used as an excuse for similarly eccentric usage on the part of the expositor. We have seen, however, that his allusions and echoes are not accidental, but fall into a clear pattern. This pattern is completely explicable on the assumption of an overall covenantal reading, in which God's people from Abraham to the Messiah form the advance guard, not of course without paradox and ambiguity, of the people now created in the Messiah and the Spirit. To be sure, there has been a dramatic and decisive explosion in the middle of the sequence, with the Messiah's shameful death and all that went with it. But this, too, Paul insists, was what the covenant God had in mind all along. The people of God in the present are not simply a creation out of nothing; they are, however unexpectedly, the family promised to Abraham. The problems faced by Abraham's family before the Messiah's coming, notably the question of how Israel's God was going to fulfill the covenant and deliver Israel, were problems Paul believed

---

294. For the last, see the winsome but to my mind ultimately unconvincing essay of Marcus J. Borg, *The God We Never Knew* (San Francisco: Harper, 1997).

had been answered in Christ. The resurgence of apparently similar problems in the church was to be answered in terms of life in Christ and the victory of the Spirit. God has revealed the divine covenant faithfulness, and the proclamation of the gospel continues to unveil it. The church's task, in its own use of the Scriptures, is to hear both the earlier stages of its own story and the continual resonances, amplified in the echo chamber of the messianic events concerning Jesus, which will inform and guide its own journey through the wilderness. Learning to hear these multiple resonances with the proper blend of imaginative attention and discipline is a major part of Christian teaching and discipleship.

**3.** This passage offers, for the first time in Romans, a description of the kinds of suffering that Paul and his fellow Christians faced in the first century. Only 2 Corinthians 6 and 11, in fact, go into more detail, though the fact of suffering is everywhere apparent. Not only is there physical affliction to be faced, some from natural causes and some from violent opposition, but there is also the constant threat from supernatural or cosmic forces. Paul does not often speak explicitly about these, but throughout his writings we sense a shadow of danger, threat, and struggle that took these and other forms.

His response, clearly, is very different from that which seeks to attain a higher state of consciousness in which physical pain and suffering are irrelevant and can be ignored. The battle is real; it matters because the physical world is God's world and cannot be played down in favor of a "spiritual" reality. Suffering comes as a result of the gospel, which, by its announcement of Jesus as Lord, challenges all other lordships, many of which, at both the cosmic and the terrestrial levels, will fight in defense. (There are many forms of Christianity on offer today that pose no threat to any principalities and powers, and indeed make a virtue of not confronting anyone with anything. What kind of authenticity can they claim?) Once more, we must not confuse the necessary confrontation between the gospel and the powers of the world with the belligerence of some would-be preachers and evangelists, who are often enough propagating not the gospel itself but a particularly brittle parody of it, which can only be defended by shouting louder. For Paul, the message of the cross and resurrection of Jesus, and his enthronement as Lord of the world, never failed to arouse the wrath of the powers in one way or another. If this message were to catch on, the world would be turned upside down, and a lot of vested interests with it.

Woe betide the church, therefore, if it becomes sidelined into offering an apparently "spiritual" version of "life, liberty, and the pursuit of happiness." A recent book by a best-selling Christian author assures us that "golf, next to marriage and parenthood, can routinely be the greatest of life's learning opportunities," and that "golf can be a wonderful spiritual path of growth toward God."[295] I have no quarrel with golf. No doubt it, like many games, can teach wise players important things about themselves. Golf can also, of course, produce special kinds of suffering, both for those who play and for those who listen afterward. But I think I know what Paul would say to these propositions—and not out of any killjoy spirit, either. The Western church is in danger of becoming so concerned with Christianity as a way to further its own goals of self-advancement that it has forgotten what its siblings in many other countries know day by day, often literally in their (broken) bones; that the gospel confronts the principalities and powers with the news that their time is up, and that the true way to Christian joy lies in discovering in practice that this message is true.

**4.** The greatest theme of the paragraph is the love of God. This topic is a vast sea to put into a small bottle; far better to swim in it or to set sail upon it. Paul speaks of God's love as the ultimate security. Learning to look at the cross and to see there the strong evidence of how much one is loved is among the most basic and vital Christian disciplines, matched by opening one's heart and life to the tidal wave of that love, displacing all other rivals. The mind is to learn, and

---

295. M. Scott Peck, *Golf and the Spirit* (New York: Harmony, 1999) 61. He claims that golf teaches humility, *kenosis,* and even grace.

the heart is to know in experience, "the love of Christ which passes knowledge" (Eph 3:19). If Christian ministry does nothing but help, encourage, and enable people along these paths, it will have done well.

But God's love is also the ultimate human fulfillment. Much of Romans 5–8 has been about the genuine model of humanness, over against the spurious models offered by sin and the flesh. In a world that is currently lurching from "I think, therefore I am" to "I shop, therefore I am," the challenge to find one's human identity in being loved—*Amor, ergo sum,* I am loved, therefore I am—is central to discovering the genuine way of being human. And when, with or without specific human loves to incarnate it, human beings discover afresh that they are loved and embraced by the God who made heaven and earth, then what is found is a fulfillment that can never be self-centered, a personal enrichment that has nothing to do with self-help programs. Being loved by the true God, we are to become truly human beings in sharing that love. Not to do so is to cast doubt upon which God it was whose love was being felt in the first place.

Once again, the themes of the letter pose a standing challenge to the imperial system of which Paul, himself a Roman citizen, was a critic from within. If it is indeed true, as some have suggested, that already at this period some in Rome thought of the "secret name" of the city as AMOR, "love" ("Roma" spelled backward), it is a further indication of something we would have to stress anyway: that a community founded on, and sustained by, the sovereign love of the creator God is a political threat, not least to anything like a totalitarian system.[296] People who find themselves loved by the Lord of the world tend not to care quite so much as others what happens to them. They care passionately about justice, and many other causes great and small, but in terms of ordinary politics they are often at best seen as mavericks (the compliment that political regimentation pays to freedom of conscience) and at worst as dangerous loose cannons. In Paul's case, believing in *amor Dei,* the Love of God, and finding himself embraced by it, and discovering an answering love in his own heart, made him a highly dangerous citizen within a system that claimed to embody love, perhaps even to be a deity with that name. Citizens within all kinds of systems today need to work out the equivalent in their own terms.

The love of God, finally, offers itself as the key to the truest mode of knowing—knowing about God, knowing about other people, knowing about the world, knowing about oneself. We have learned, often painfully, that when somebody seems to be offering you something for nothing you need to be suspicious of their motives. We have learned that expressions of love are all too often a cover for manipulation and exploitation. God help us, some today even accuse God of these things. We have learned, in other words, the hermeneutic of suspicion, which is a fancy philosophers' way of saying that we have rediscovered the doctrine of original sin by the back door, shortly after the theologians had abandoned it as being historically unfounded, psychologically unwarranted, and pastorally unhelpful. What this passage would teach us, however, as one contemporary application of Paul's message about the gospel of Jesus Christ conquering the world of sin and death, the world of which the hermeneutic of suspicion warns but from which it, like the Torah, cannot free us, is that the love of God is the deepest truth in the cosmos, and that to trust this love is to open oneself neither to manipulation nor exploitation but to a richer and fuller humanness—suffering included—than one would ever know, and to a share in the loving liberation and remaking of the cosmos itself. The love of God, in other words, proposes a hermeneutic of trust: not a casual or shallow trust of any person or proposition that comes along, but a deep and hard-won trust, a knowing that is born of being loved and of loving in return. There is much that could be said about this, but it is important at least to point out that if we are thus rediscovering the doctrine of sin, we have in Romans the greatest exposition of the victory of the God of love over sin and its consequences. We would do well to apply this to the places in the world, and in our lives, where sin still reigns in death.

296. Details in D. E. Aune, *Revelation,* 3 vols., WBC 52C (Dallas: Word, 1997) 3:926-27.

We paraphrase, in conclusion, the final two verses of the section. Paul has spoken, and we must speak, of the love of the one true God. This love of God calls across the dark intervals of meaning, reaches into the depths of human despair, embraces those who live in the shadow of death or the overbright light of present life, challenges the rulers of the world and shows them up as a sham, looks at the present with clear faith and at the future with sure hope, overpowers all powers that might get in the way, fills the outer dimensions of the cosmos, and declares to the world that God is God, that Jesus the Messiah is the world's true Lord, and that in him love has won the victory. This powerful, overmastering love grasps Paul, and sustains him in his praying, his preaching, his journeying, his writing, his pastoring, and his suffering, with the strong sense of the presence of the God who had loved him from the beginning and had put that love into action in Jesus. This is the love because of which there is no condemnation. This is the love because of which those who are justified are also surely glorified. And this is the love, seen supremely in the death of the Messiah, which reaches out to the whole world with the exodus message, the freedom message, the word of joy and justice, the word of the gospel of Jesus.

# GOD'S PROMISES AND GOD'S FAITHFULNESS

## OVERVIEW

E verything about Romans 9–11 is controversial. Even its place in the letter has been challenged: C. H. Dodd, notoriously, regarded it as an old sermon that Paul happened to have by him. He slipped it in here, Dodd suggested, even though it broke the train of thought, which would otherwise have run on smoothly from chap. 8 to chap. 12.[297] At the other extreme, many have seen this section as the real climax of the letter.[298] Exegesis has attempted to negotiate positions between these two extremes, and there is now a general consensus that the section is extremely important both within the letter and for Paul's wider theology. A good many lines of thought in other letters besides Romans, and indeed in other parts of the New Testament besides Paul, raise the question of which this is the premier discussion: What has God been doing with Israel?

Like almost every part of this letter, 9–11 has suffered from being seen as the classic treatment of certain topics—topics that interpreters have brought to Paul rather than letting him dictate his own terms. Chapter 9 has long been seen as the central NT passage on "predestination," though as we shall see the theological tradition from Augustine to Calvin (and beyond) did not grasp what Paul was actually talking about here. Subsequent debates about how people get saved have used the section to balance the options: In chap. 9 (it has been said) everything flows from divine sovereignty, in chap. 10 everything hinges on human responsibility, and in chap. 11 it turns out that God will in any case have mercy upon all.[299] More broadly, those who have seen Paul's view of God and salvation as being essentially outside space and time have discovered in this passage something that to them seems very strange: a historical "dimension" to salvation. In the light of the interpretation of the first eight chapters, this has the feel of someone who, only knowing Beethoven's symphonies in piano transcription, suddenly discovers a fully orchestrated version of the third movement of his Ninth, and discusses it as a curious sideline rather than being alerted by it to what those transcriptions had been trying to say. It remains, however, the implicit view of a good many readers who have managed, despite Paul's best efforts, to screen out the "Israel" dimension from all that has gone before.[300]

The major topic that has come to the forefront of theological discussion in the second half of the twentieth century, and is obviously much closer to what Paul is really talking about, is the question of the ethnic people Israel. The horrors of Auschwitz have haunted two generations, and we shall not quickly forget what can happen when a culture demonizes an entire people, particularly when that culture professed, in some measure at least, to be Christian. Those of us whose early years were overshadowed by the memory of the Nazi horror are simply incapable of reading texts on relevant subjects—and Romans 9–11 is certainly a relevant subject—without reflecting on the ways in which they relate to what has been a major moral question of modern times.

Yet even this reflection may produce distortions. Just as modern Pauline studies have taken

---

297. C. H. Dodd, *The Epistle of Paul to the Romans* (London: Collins Fontana, 1959) 161-63.

298. K. Stendahl, *Paul Among Jews and Gentiles* (Philadelphia: Fortress, 1976) 4; N. T. Wright, *The Climax of the Covenant: Christ and the Law in Pauline Theology* (Minneapolis: Fortress, 1992) 234; J. A. Fitzmyer, *Romans,* AB 33 (New York: Doubleday, 1993) 541.

299. So, ingeniously but inaccurately, G. B. Caird, "Predestination—Romans ix.-xi.," *Expository Times* 68 (1956–57) 324-27.

300. See the classic statement of W. Sanday and A. C. Headlam, *A Critical and Exegetical Commentary on the Epistle to the Romans,* 5th ed., ICC (Edinburgh: T. & T. Clark, 1902) 225.

account of the fact that, despite Martin Luther, Paul was not after all writing about the pope, so it may be time to pause and reflect that Paul was not after all writing about Adolf Hitler. The controversial revolution in Pauline studies that produced the so-called new perspective of the 1970s shifted attention away from late-mediaeval soul-searchings and anxieties about salvation, and placed it instead on (in Sanders's phrase) the comparison of patterns of religion.[301] It was a self-consciously post-Holocaust project, aimed not least at reminding Paul's readers of his essential Jewishness. But this should not blind us to the fact that, precisely as a Jewish person, Paul begins this section with grief and sorrow—because he sees his fellow Jews rejecting the gospel of their own Messiah. Paul is not writing a post-Enlightenment treatise about how all religions are basically the same; nor is he writing an essay on the modified version of the same project—namely, how the one God has made two equally valid covenants, one with Jews and the other with Christians.[302] Nor is he writing a postmodern tract about how everybody must tell their own story and find their own way.[303] As we shall see, these chapters remain profoundly Christian—that is, centered on Jesus as Messiah and Lord. Paul does not accommodate himself to our agendas and expectations any more than he did to those of his contemporaries.

But what is he actually saying here? What is his argument, and how does he develop it? And, looking wider, how does this section advance the argument of the letter so far? Is Romans 9–11 peripheral or central to the purpose of the letter? Here we meet once more the question of a distinction between the sequence of thought in a particular letter and the hypothetical logical order of Paul's underlying theology.[304] Part of the difficulty,

here as elsewhere, is that Romans has for so long been held to be a statement precisely of Paul's underlying theology, his most fundamental beliefs, that there has always been a tendency to assimilate the actual exegesis of this specific letter to the terms, or sequence, of what the interpreter assumes as rock-bottom Pauline thought. We must beware of this trap, while not ruling out the possibility that Paul has indeed said some things here that serve as the clearest statements of some of his fundamental themes.

It will be particularly important to note the ways in which this section does indeed build on, and develop the argument of, chaps. 1–8, and the ways in which it leads naturally into 12–16. We should note as well, however, that Paul here frequently comes back to topics and questions he handles elsewhere. The letter, we remind ourselves, has not only a linear flow but also something of a spiral shape, in which (for instance) the discussion of the law in 9:30–10:13 looks back to that in 7:1–8:11, and behind that in turn to 2:17-29—and on to some elements of 14:1–15:13.

Two questions dominate these three chapters: the question of unbelieving Israel, and the question of God's faithfulness. The two are, of course, intimately connected: the latter is raised by the former. Israel's refusal (as a whole) to believe the gospel of Jesus raises in its sharpest form the question of whether God has in fact been faithful to his promises. It is somewhat paradoxical that Paul does not spell out these questions themselves; they are, it seems, too huge and obvious. He begins the section by simply addressing them, letting them come to the surface bit by bit. His heartbreaking grief in 9:1-3 speaks eloquently of the first; his opening denial ("God's word cannot have failed!") in 9:6 shows that the second is his primary concern. And when we turn to the end of the section and find the salvation of Israel guaranteed by God's gifts, call, and overall purpose (11:26-32), we can be sure we have correctly identified the double theme.

This double theme comes to focus as the question of God's covenant faithfulness, the δικαιοσύνη θεοῦ (dikaiosynē theou), which is discussed in the Introduction and in relation to such key passages as 1:17 and 3:21-31. In case there is any question of this, the buildup of questions in 9:6, 14, and 19, echoing the questions of 3:1-9,

---

301. See the title of his epoch-making book, E. P. Sanders, *Paul and Palestinian Judaism: A Comparison of Patterns of Religion* (London: SCM, 1977).

302. J. G. Gager, *The Origins of Anti-Semitism: Attitudes Toward Judaism in Pagan and Christian Antiquity* (New York: Oxford University Press, 1983); L. Gaston, *Paul and the Torah* (Vancouver: University of British Columbia, 1987) esp. 135-50. A fuller list is in D. J. Moo, *The Epistle to the Romans,* NICNT (Grand Rapids: Eerdmans, 1996) 549. For more recent critiques of this view see E. E. Johnson, *The Function of Apocalyptic and Wisdom Traditions in Romans 9–11,* SBLDS 109 (Atlanta: Scholars Press, 1989) 176-205; R. Hvalvik, "A 'Sonderweg' for Israel: A Critical Examination of a Current Interpretation of Romans 11.25-27," *JSNT* 38 (1990) 87-107.

303. As seems to be implied in K. Stendahl, *Final Account: Paul's Letter to the Romans* (Minneapolis: Fortress, 1995) chap. 4.

304. This is similar to N. R. Petersen's distinction of "poetic sequence" and "narrative sequence." See N. T. Wright, "Romans and the Theology of Paul," in *Pauline Theology,* vol. III: *Romans,* ed. D. M. Hay and E. E. Johnson (Minneapolis: Fortress, 1995) 32.

leads Paul's discussion to the central and decisive statement of 10:3: Israel has been ignorant of God's righteousness, and, in seeking to establish a righteousness of its own, has not submitted to God's righteousness. God has done what God always promised, but this does not look like what Israel had come to expect, had come to take for granted as its automatic right. God's righteousness—which means God's faithfulness to the covenant promises, and, beyond that, God's determination that through those promises the world would be put to rights—appears to be called into question by Israel's failure to believe the gospel. The reason why Paul has to write this whole section is that a huge hole has been ripped in the story of God and Israel as he and others had imagined it. We may say, somewhat like Karl Barth, that those eagerly awaiting the divine Yes had heard instead a resounding No. Paul here explores the mystery of how nevertheless this No was the necessary preliminary to an ultimate Yes—albeit a redefined one.

Is the section, then, really after all an "aside," even if a vitally necessary one? Some have suggested so.[305] The problem of Israel's unbelief, they have proposed, is the obvious and major counter-example to Paul's thesis to this point, which is that salvation is assured to all who believe because God can be trusted to keep promises. But this, though certainly true at one level, does not yet plumb the depths of what Paul has been saying in chaps. 1–8 or will now say in chaps. 9–11. The question of Israel—of God's promises to Abraham and of how they are fulfilled—has been central, not peripheral, to the letter all through. The questions of chap. 9 are the questions Paul noted at the start of chap. 3; they were raised by 2:17-29, and are now raised again, more intensively, by chaps. 5–8. This is part of the point of 9:4-5: the privileges of Israel, there enumerated, correspond quite closely, and surely not accidentally, to the things he has been saying in 5–8. This warrants us in reading 9–11 in the light of 2:28-29, where the question of who counts as a "Jew" is critical, and where the answer is given in the language of covenant renewal—which is now open to all, Jew and Gentile alike.

If these are the questions Paul must face, how does he go about answering them? It is of primary importance in reading Romans 9–11 to realize that its backbone is *a retelling of the story of Israel, from Abraham to (Paul's) present day.* From 9:6 to 10:21, Paul is retelling the great narrative that every Jew knew. His retelling belongs with (though it subverts) other Second Temple retellings of the Jewish story: It is a retelling that speaks to what God had been doing all along, and that leaves Paul in a position to mount the fresh argument of chap. 11. If this is what the story of God and Israel in fact looks like, he is saying, the present position and obligations must be understood accordingly. Only if we fail to see the essential narrative substructure of the section do the biblical references and allusions "distract" us from the point.[306]

The way the story is told is central. There were many retellings of Israel's story current in Paul's world. Obvious examples, themselves important for Romans 9–11, include such different writings as 4 Ezra, Wisdom 10–19, and 4QMMT column C.[307] A word about each will make the point. Fourth Ezra wrestles with the question of God's faithfulness to the covenant with Israel in the face of the disaster of 70 CE.[308] Wisdom reaches back to Adam, like Paul in Romans 5, in order to concentrate on the exodus story, as I have argued that Paul did in Romans 8. The exodus story was told in Wisdom not as a bare historical account, but in order to highlight the strange sovereign ways of God, the potter who molds the clay (15:7)—and particularly as an encouragement to first-century Jews to trust this God for deliverance from the pagan heirs of ancient Egypt. A short, selective version of the story is told in 4QMMT, highlighting the covenant promises of Deuteronomy 29–30, and claiming that the promises of covenant renewal are being fulfilled in those who observe the particular ceremonial practices of the

---

305. See C. Bryan, *A Preface to Romans: Notes on the Epistle in Its Literary and Cultural Setting* (Oxford: Oxford University Press, 2000) 159. Even Moo, *Romans,* 547-52, while affirming that this section is "central," does so because he supposes that Paul is facing opposition and debate on the Jew/Gentile question.

306. Fitzmyer, *Romans,* 542.

307. Obvious NT examples are the speech of Stephen in Acts 7:2-53, whose polemical selection of material and rhetorical force are well known. See B. Witherington, *The Acts of the Apostles: A Socio-Rhetorical Commentary* (Grand Rapids: Eerdmans, 1998) 259-77. See also the shorter speech of Paul in Acts 13:13-41 and the list of heroes in Hebrews 11.

308. See esp. Johnson, *The Function of Apocalyptic and Wisdom Traditions in Romans 9–11;* B. W. Longenecker, *Eschatology and the Covenant: A Comparison of 4 Ezra and Romans 1–11* (Sheffield: Sheffield Academic, 1991).

sect (see the Commentary on 10:5-9). Like 4 Ezra, Paul tells Israel's story to vindicate God's faithfulness. Like Wisdom, he recounts the narrative to make points about the way in which God always behaves. Like the author of 4QMMT, he tells the story in order to say: this is where we belong within it. We are the heirs, the new-covenant people promised long ago. His telling, in other words, is exemplary (the story offers examples of how it is with God and Israel), but it is more importantly eschatological (the story is going somewhere and including the present readers within it). Eschatology is the framework within which examples may be understood.

The main thrust of all this, within the present letter, is to arrive at the questions of 11:1 and 11:11 with both feet on firm ground. Paul's aim throughout chap. 11 is to argue from basic principles that God still intends to save ethnic Jews. Why does he need to do this? It seems there is a danger that Gentile Christians in Rome will assume, or even argue, that God has cut unbelieving Jews out of his plan for good, has left them without hope.[309] Paul does not say that Roman Gentile Christians should themselves engage in evangelism among their unbelieving Jewish neighbors. But he declares that part of the point of his own Gentile mission—the primary focus of his work, or so he says here—is to make presently unbelieving Jews jealous, jealous of seeing their privileges now shared by non-Jews, and so to bring them to salvation through faith (11:23).

Why does he need to say this to the Roman church at this stage of its history? He does not say, but three historical answers present themselves, each of which has plausibility and may have combined to give him a sense of urgency. To begin with, Rome had a long tradition of anti-Jewish sentiment.[310] The prominence of some Jews in the imperial court had only increased the sense of many in Rome that this race of foreigners was at best a mixed blessing, at worst an enemy with a dangerous set of beliefs. Gentile Christians in Rome, especially during the period when Jews had

been expelled from the capital after the riots in the late 40s, might have found it all too easy to assimilate this popular belief: although Christianity had begun among the Jews, they might suppose, God had now written them off (see the Introduction). Second, the return of considerable numbers of Jews to Rome after Claudius's death in 54 CE—supposing for the moment the truthfulness of the various accounts of expulsion, and the probability of such a return[311]—cannot but have had an impact on the small, young church in Rome. Assuming that the church numbered no more than a few dozen (the argument would still hold if it numbered a thousand, but this is unlikely), it must have seemed threatening for thousands of Jews suddenly to reappear in the capital, for the synagogues to be full again. It would be very easy for the church to demonize them, to regard them as the enemy. Third, by the late 50s there was increasing tension in Judaea and Galilee. The crisis over Gaius's plan to set up his statue in the Temple had passed, but revolutionary fervor had not waned, and successive governors seemed to go out of their way to provoke rebellion. Any Jew hearing news of this would feel involved, even hundreds of miles away across the Mediterranean. Any Gentile Christians in Rome, particularly any groups that were influenced by the two considerations just mentioned, would be eager to distance themselves from any sense of complicity with the impending revolt. Paul himself had declared that God's wrath had come upon the Judaeans at last (1 Thess 2:16); how much more might a Gentile Christian in Rome be eager to assign unbelieving Israel to the scrap-heap of history.[312] We only have to think of Marcion, less than a century later, to see how perceptive Paul was in spotting the problems that might arise.[313]

From this perspective, we may suggest that the retelling of Israel's story in 9:6–10:21 is itself designed not only to suggest a new way of reading Israel's own history but also quietly to undermine the pretensions of Rome itself. Rome, too, told

309. Moo, *Romans,* 683-84, doubts whether Roman Gentiles really questioned Jewish salvation. It seems that the whole chapter is designed to argue the point against people whom Paul assumes challenge it.

310. See the mass of material assembled by M. Stern, *Greek and Latin Authors on Jews and Judaism,* 3 vols. (Jerusalem: Israel Academy of Sciences and Humanities, 1976). For a brief survey, see J. C. Waters, *Ethnic Issues in Paul's Letter to the Romans* (Valley Forge, Pa.: Trinity, 1993), chap. 2, esp. 28-55.

311. See N. T. Wright, *The New Testament and the People of God* (Minneapolis: Fortress, 1992) 354-55; J. D. G. Dunn, *Romans 1–8,* WBC 33A (Dallas: Word, 1988) liii; Fitzmyer, *Romans,* 30-36.

312. On 1 Thess 2:16 and its relation to Romans 9–11 see W. D. Davies, *Jewish and Pauline Studies* (London: SPCK, 1984) chap. 7; C. A. Wanamaker, *The Epistles to the Thessalonians: A Commentary on the Greek Text,* NIGTC (Grand Rapids: Eerdmans, 1990) 114-19.

313. On Marcion (d. c. 160 CE) and his significance, see J. J. Clabeaux, "Marcion," in *The Anchor Bible Dictionary,* 6 vols. (Garden City, N. Y.: 1992) 4:514-16.

stories of its own history, going back to the brothers Romulus and Remus a thousand years earlier, coming through the long story of the republic and finally arriving at the emperor who was now enthroned as lord of the world.[314] Paul, having declared in 9:5 that Jesus, the Messiah, is "God over all, blessed forever" (see below), returns to the point in 10:12: Jesus is Lord of all, Jew and Gentile alike. Israel's history, climaxing in Jesus, is designed to upstage Roman history, climaxing in Augustus. This helps to create the right atmosphere for chap. 11: This is a Jewish way of construing world history, of telling its story over against the story of pagan empire, and this is the ground that the Christian continues to stand on, the ground that makes it impossible to dismiss unbelieving Jews as forever outside God's ongoing purposes.

Paul's own role and vocation become topics within the story. His mission to the Gentiles is the necessary consequence of the covenant renewal that has taken place in Christ for the benefit of Jew and Gentile alike (10:14-15). The puzzle of its results—continuing Jewish unbelief, while Gentiles flock in—is itself to be understood in terms of the fulfillment of law and prophecy (10:16-21). But that fulfillment itself offers the key to the next stage in God's plan: "jealousy," Israel's jealousy of Gentiles who are inheriting the promises (10:19; 11:11, 14). It is this jealousy, aroused precisely by the success of Paul's work among the Gentiles, that will bring Israel to faith at last (11:14). Paul is himself an example of the fact that Jews can still be saved (11:1-6); he is part of the "remnant," in the sense there explained. But he is not just an example; he is, through his mission and the "jealousy" of his fellow Jews that results, part of the means by which God will save "some of them" (11:13-14). And all this, we must remember, is held within a discussion introduced by Paul's personal grief (9:1-2), producing an astonishing potential prayer (9:3) and a firm actual one (10:1). He is himself part of the answer to his own prayer, not by becoming "anathema from Christ," as he would have been prepared to be (9:3), but by

continuing with his vocation to the Gentiles, so that in looking-glass fashion this may bring Jews back into the family after all. The self-references that emerge from the tightly knit texture of chaps. 9–11 take their place within Paul's self-introduction as we find it in 1:8-17 and 15:14-29.

There remains one underlying introductory question. What can be said about the apparent disjunction between the subject-matter of Romans 5–8 and that of 9–11? Granted that chaps. 1–4, which are, indeed, the ground and basis of chaps. 5–8, have more in common with chaps. 9–11 in terms of subject matter, we are nevertheless left with an obvious break. To look no further, Jesus Christ is mentioned explicitly about twenty-five times in 108 verses in Romans 5–8, with numerous additional references to "he," "him," to the "one man" in whom Adam's trespass is undone, and perhaps above all to "God's son." Yet in chaps. 9–11, after the three mentions in the first five verses, all we are left with is 10:4-13 and the isolated (and textually challenged) 10:17. Even more striking, perhaps, is the vivid presence (eighteen occurrences) of the Spirit in chap. 8, and its total absence, after 9:1, until 14:17 (11:8 is hardly to be construed as a reference to the Holy Spirit; 12:11 probably refers to the human spirit). These indicators have led some, notably the influential scholar Krister Stendahl, to ask whether the entire section is in fact an exposition of a different point of view, a way of salvation in which Jesus Christ plays little or no direct part.[315]

With due deference to Stendahl, whose seminal essay on Paul started many of us thinking in fresh ways a generation ago, I regard this as misleading.[316] Romans 5–8 is a formal, almost stylized step-by-step presentation of what God has accomplished in Jesus Christ. But underneath this presentation, as we saw, is the story of Israel, looking back to its beginnings in Abraham, set in the context of God's promise to undo the effects of Adam's fall, and working through exodus, Sinai, and the wilderness wanderings on the way to the

---

314. On the ideology of the Augustan Empire see esp. P. Zanker, *The Power of Images in the Age of Augustus,* trans. A. Shapiro (Ann Arbor: University of Michigan Press, 1990); R. A. Horsley, ed., *Paul and Empire: Religion and Power in Roman Imperial Society* (Harrisburg, Pa.: Trinity Press International, 1997) esp. 10-24; and P. A. Brunt *"Laus Imperii,"* in ibid., 25-35.

315. K. Stendahl, *Paul Among Jews and Gentiles* (Philadelphia: Fortress, 1976), and *Final Account: Paul's Letter to the Romans* (Minneapolis: Fortress, 1995). Johnson, *The Function of Apocalyptic and Wisdom Traditions in Romans 9–11,* 205, agrees with Stendahl that Paul's argument is "theocentric" rather than christocentric, but insists that "Christology cannot be omitted from the agenda."

316. See K. Stendahl, "The Apostle Paul and the Introspective Conscience of the West," in *Paul Among Jews and Gentiles,* 78-96.

inheritance, the new creation promised in Isaiah. The surface story is about Jesus, the deeper dimension is about Israel. In 9–11, I suggest, it is more or less the other way around—though to be sure when Jesus the Messiah appears in 10:4-13 this is not incidental, but, like the "righteousness of God" in 10:3 with which Jesus is closely correlated, as the explicit statement of what is everywhere implicit. The surface story is that of God's people, from Abraham to Paul's own day; but the deeper dimension is the story of the Messiah's people according to the flesh (9:5).

Romans 9:5 stands at the head of chaps. 9–11, in fact, much as 1:3-4 stands at the head of chaps. 1–8 and of the letter as a whole: the opening messianic statement in the light of which everything that follows is to be understood. Israel, Paul is saying, is Messiah-focused. The long story that began with Abraham reached its climax, its goal, its τέλος (telos) in him. And Israel is also Messiah-shaped. The pattern of Israel's history (rejection, failure, and exile followed by astonishing covenant renewal) is none other than the pattern of death and resurrection. That is why, when Paul sees God's righteousness unveiled in the Messiah (10:3-4), our minds inevitably go back to 3:21-26, where it was Jesus' death in particular that accomplished God's saving plan. And that is why, when we look ahead to 11:11-16, where Paul is arguing for the restoration, the "receiving back," of Israel, he alludes to key steps in the argument of chap. 5 (see the detailed exposition). He is treating Israel as precisely the Messiah's own people, according to the flesh; his argument is that in Christ, and nowhere else, can we understand what has happened, is happening, and will happen to ethnic Israel.

Hence, crucially for the interpretation of both chaps. 5–8 and 9–11 and of the relationship between the two, the complex discussion of the Torah in 7:1–8:11 turns out to have laid foundations for the equally complex passage 9:30–10:13. The details of this must be explored in their proper place. Suffice it to say here that in this new context we encounter once more Israel's stumble over the God-given Torah, and God's once again doing, through the Messiah, what the Torah always intended, in other words, the fulfillment of the *dikaiosynē theou* (10:3-4). The strange but God-given negative purpose of the Torah (remember

the repeated ἵνα [hina] of 7:13 and the sequence of thought ending with 8:3) is picked up in the strange but God-given purpose whereby, again through the Torah, Israel trips and stumbles (10:32-33). But God's purpose goes forward to embrace the Gentiles—and Israel itself can in turn be restored. This helps, as we shall see, to explain the harsh predestinarian passages in chap. 9: the double *hina* of 7:13 has become the double ὅπως (hopōs) of 9:17. As in 7:1–8:11, so here, the purpose of God through Torah and in Israel was to draw God's history with the world to the single point of the Messiah, in order to deal with sin and death and create a new world the other side. Since this vocation could only be undertaken by the Messiah as an individual, it was necessary that Israel be led along the strange path of being God's people but being called to be cast away—just as the Messiah himself was called to be crucified for the sins of the world. That, it seems, is the logic that underlies 9:6-29 and 11:11-15, and which is focused on the central passage of the whole section: 10:1-13.[317]

If this reading of chaps. 9–11 is correct, and if in particular we are right to see 10:6-13 as an essentially "new covenant" reading of Deuteronomy 30, then we are justified in claiming that the Holy Spirit, though not explicitly mentioned in these chapters, is indeed "underneath" the argument in at least one passage. In 10:9 Paul uses language very close to that of 1 Cor 12:3, where the Spirit is the main subject. In fact, 10:9-13 is close in theme to 2:27-29, where the letter/spirit contrast is crucial. And in the final verse of the section (10:13) Paul quotes from Joel 3:5 LXX, a passage that in its best-known occurrence in the NT (Acts 2:21) was cited on the day of Pentecost as part of the interpretation of the outpouring of the Spirit. Paul has no need to stress the work of the Spirit at this point in his argument; but it is impossible to claim that these three chapters present a theology from which Christ and the Spirit have been systematically excluded. This point illustrates, incidentally, a major factor in the exegesis of the section: again and again we can find clues to Paul's meaning in the larger context of the biblical passages he quotes, not least in the

---

317. See the important study of C. K. Rowe, "Romans 10:13: What Is the Name of the Lord?" *Horizons in Biblical Theology* 22 (2000) 135-73.

light of how those passages were being read in his day.

How do chaps. 9–11 relate to the final chapters of the letter, 12–16? The question is partly answered by realizing that the central passage of that closing section consists of 14:1–15:13, which emphasizes the coming together of different cultures in obedience to the same Lord. That passage is, in that sense, the long-range outworking of the theme we have seen again and again in this letter: the faithfulness of God to Jew and Gentile alike, and their coming together in the Messiah. The main thrust of Romans 11 has to do with the attitude of Christian Gentiles to non-Christian Jews, and the main thrust of Romans 14 and 15 has to do with the mutual attitudes of Christians from different ethnic backgrounds; but the underlying theology is the same. And the historical narrative of God's people in chaps. 9–10 leaves Paul precisely with the sort of community he is addressing in chaps. 12–16: the worldwide, multiethnic people who give allegiance to Abraham's God in and through Jesus the Messiah, called now to live out their lives within the wider pagan world, needing instructions that at one level are closely analogous to those needed by Jews in their diaspora, but at another level have been rethought around the death and resurrection of the Messiah and the consequent fact that the people themselves have been redefined, given new boundary markers, called to a new sort of life.

Chapters 9–11 present, then, a complex and integrated whole, which in turn is closely integrated into the warp and woof of the rest of the letter. Building on the foundations already laid, Paul is developing one of the urgent points he wants to make to the Roman church: that they, more especially the Gentile Christians, should not despise non-Christian Jews or regard them as essentially unsavable. His personal involvement in this topic is passionate; he wears his heart on his sleeve, as he does only rarely elsewhere. (We might compare, e.g., 2 Corinthians, esp. 6:11-13, and Gal 4:12-20.) This is presumably not just because he feels strongly about the subject, but because he is bringing every rhetorical ploy to bear to convince the Roman Christians, more especially the Gentiles among them, to look at the world this way—from the point of view of a thoroughly (though subversively) Jewish telling of the world's story, leading up to the Messiah and now implementing his saving rule.[318] To treat these chapters as marginal to Romans is to misunderstand the whole; the letter will simply not work without them. But this is not merely a literary judgment. To revert to the earlier image: to ignore the fact that we have here a fully orchestrated "salvation history," and to suppose that one can then read the rest of the book as referring to an ahistorical salvation or Christian life, is to remain deaf not just to the structure and flow of the letter but to the subject Paul is dealing with. To imagine that one can bypass these chapters in the interest of a simpler or smoother reading of the letter is to settle, not just for second best here, but for a severely truncated view of everything else as well.

318. On the different types of rhetoric in play in these chapters see Christopher Bryan, *A Preface to Romans: Notes on the Epistle in Its Literary and Cultural Setting* (Oxford: Oxford University Press, 2000) 160.

# ROMANS 9:1-5, PAUL'S GRIEF OVER ISRAEL'S FAILURE TO BELIEVE, DESPITE BEING PROMISE BEARER

NIV

9 I speak the truth in Christ—I am not lying, my conscience confirms it in the Holy Spirit— ²I have great sorrow and unceasing anguish in my heart. ³For I could wish that I myself were cursed and cut off from Christ for the

NRSV

9 I am speaking the truth in Christ—I am not lying; my conscience confirms it by the Holy Spirit— ²I have great sorrow and unceasing anguish in my heart. ³For I could wish that I myself were accursed and cut off from Christ for

NIV

sake of my brothers, those of my own race, [4]the people of Israel. Theirs is the adoption as sons; theirs the divine glory, the covenants, the receiving of the law, the temple worship and the promises. [5]Theirs are the patriarchs, and from them is traced the human ancestry of Christ, who is God over all, forever praised![a] Amen.

[a] 5 Or Christ, who is over all. God be forever praised! Or Christ. God who is over all be forever praised!

NRSV

the sake of my own people,[a] my kindred according to the flesh. [4]They are Israelites, and to them belong the adoption, the glory, the covenants, the giving of the law, the worship, and the promises; [5]to them belong the patriarchs, and from them, according to the flesh, comes the Messiah,[b] who is over all, God blessed forever.[c] Amen.

[a] Gk my brothers    [b] Or the Christ    [c] Or Messiah, who is God over all, blessed forever, or Messiah. May he who is God over all be blessed forever

# COMMENTARY

The odd thing about the first five verses of Romans 9 is that Paul never states what the problem actually is. He tells us of his awful grief; he tells us how he would like to pray; he tells us why the problem is so acute. But the problem itself, like a character in a Beckett play, hovers offstage, a brooding presence, all the more powerful for never being seen directly.

We can, however, accurately infer what he is talking about both from subsequent statements and from the shape of the unfolding argument. In 10:1 he prays for the salvation of his fellow Jews; in 11:1 and 11:11 he asks the critical questions about whether they are to "fall" permanently; and in 11:23 he declares that they can be grafted in again if they do not remain in unbelief. The whole argument implies, in other words, that the problem can be stated as follows: the great majority of Paul's Jewish contemporaries have not believed the gospel of Jesus Christ, and Paul believes that they are therefore, at the moment, excluded from salvation. And this in turn generates a second-order problem, which only comes into view in 11:13 and thereafter: Paul is worried that Gentile Christians in Rome may be happy that Jews should stay forever in that condition.

This packed, tense opening statement is built around the central statement of v. 3, which is a wish or prayer that Paul feels he could express but implies he should not. Verses 1-2 build up to this with a solemn declaration of inconsolable grief; vv. 4-5 explain the enormity of the situa-

tion by listing the spectacular privileges of Paul's kinsfolk.[319]

**9:1.** The shock of the abrupt transition from the exalted heights of chap. 8 to the depths of anguish of 9:2 is made the more acute by the solemn declaration in v. 1. Why Paul needed to make such a powerful affidavit, with its triple emphasis (I'm telling the truth; I'm not lying; my conscience agrees) and its invoking of both Christ and the Spirit, we can only guess; but the guess must surely be that he knew he had an uphill struggle to persuade the Gentile Christians in Rome to concern themselves now, after the last exhilarating chapter, with the plight of Israel according to the flesh. His hearers needed to know that this was not just a rhetorical ploy to gain a little sympathy for a while. It was truly heartfelt. Elements of the solemn opening words are familiar from other contexts (2 Cor 11:31; Gal 1:20; 1 Tim 2:7), but only here in his writings does he say it so fully: "I'm speaking the truth in Christ." Paul invokes two witnesses to vouch for him: his conscience, and the Holy Spirit. The way he joins the two ("my conscience bears witness in the Holy Spirit") is revealing. Paul can speak of the conscience of the unbeliever (e.g., 2 Cor 4:2), but most of his mentions of conscience are of Christian conscience (frequently, e.g., in 1 Corinthians 8 and 10). Only here, however, does he speak of conscience and the Spirit as working in this close

---

319. Calling them his "coreligionists," as Fitzmyer does (*Romans*, 544, 582), is misleading, since it implies that what they had in common was something called "religion," so easily now misunderstood in a post-Enlightenment sense. What Paul says he has in common with them is "flesh" (v. 3).

partnership. This gives the strongest possible emphasis to what he is about to say.

**9:2.** His heart (here, as often, metaphorical for the very center of the personality) is afflicted by grief. He uses two words for this. The first is λύπη (*lupē*), which refers to a state of heart related to something sad outside itself (i.e., "sorrow," "grief"); the second is ὀδύνη (*odynē*), which refers to the state of the heart in itself—"sharp pain," "anguish." The first is "great," the second "unceasing" (presumably intended as a hendiadys: the second is also great, and the first also unceasing). We should remind ourselves that the hearers of the letter would not yet know, at this point, what he was talking about; the effect of this statement would naturally be to excite sympathy and concern. Paul has led them to the point where they may, perhaps, be ready to listen to the topic he must now raise, if only because they have learned to trust him. If he now turns to a matter of such agonizing concern to himself, they should share it as well.

**9:3.** Paul delays mentioning the people over whom he is grieving until he has expressed the most extraordinary prayer: that he himself might be cut off from the Messiah. Granted the previous eight chapters, and the promises and privileges he has enumerated to date, this prayer is shocking in the extreme.[320] Paul uses the word ἀνάθεμα (*anathema*) to describe the condition he has in mind: not only separated from the Messiah, undoing all that has been poured into the phrase "in Christ" in the previous chapters, but under a solemn religious ban (see 1 Cor 16:22; Gal 1:8-9).[321] The word carries overtones of the curse put on various people in Israelite history, and that seems to be where Paul's mind is; he cannot be unaware of the moment when the greatest prophet of old, Moses himself, stood before God at Sinai and asked that he might himself be blotted out from God's book if only the people as a whole, under condemnation for idolatry when the Torah was first given, might be spared (for the curse, see Num 21:3; Deut 7:26; for Moses' prayer, see Exod 32:30-34, a passage of considerable significance for the argument of Romans 9).

Paul declares that he could pray the same prayer; that he *could* pray it, not necessarily that he *is* doing so, for that would involve him in a direct contradiction of what he has already said in the letter. And it is possible that by describing himself as "I myself" (αὐτὸς ἐγώ *autos egō*) he intends not so much to stress "this really is me, Paul, speaking" but rather to hint, as perhaps in 7:25, that this is what "I, left to myself" might think as opposed to "I, speaking as a man in Christ." But the sentiment is so sharp that, even if he expresses it in such a way as to make it clear that he is not in fact praying like this, the reader is brought up with a shock. What can make this man, this apostle, this towering theologian of the love and justice of God, speak in such a way? The answer comes with rhetorical force: it is on behalf of "my brothers and sisters" (the NRSV's "my own people" retains inclusivity at the cost of the intimacy that ἀδελφοί [*adelphoi*] carries for Paul)—a phrase Paul elsewhere reserves for his siblings in Christ: "my kinsfolk according to the flesh" (cf. 1 Cor 10:18: βλέπετε τὸν Ἰσραὴλ κατὰ σάρκα [*blepete ton Israēl kata sarka;* lit., "consider Israel according to the flesh"]). The referent is obvious: Paul means his fellow Jews. But the way he has described them is once more designed to gain maximum sympathy from the start.

"According to the flesh" is a phrase that carries a variety of overtones, all in some ways negative (on "flesh," see the Commentary on 1:3). Here it serves to distinguish Paul's fellow Jews from his siblings in Christ, both Jewish and Gentile. (It is logically possible that the phrase here could denote all Paul's fellow Jews, including Christian ones; but the subsequent argument, not least 10:1 and 11:11-14, rules this out.) And it hints at the line of thought that is to come. Paul has shown already how God deals, in Christ, with "the flesh"; the whole of 7:1–8:11 stands behind this phrase, and points to the way in which the present situation will be dealt with in 9:6–10:13. And when, two verses on, he describes the Messiah himself as coming "from them, according to the flesh," we should realize what is going on. His "kinsfolk according to the flesh" are to be understood precisely as "the Messiah's people according to the flesh." That is their privilege, their tragedy, and their hope. The chapters to come will explain each of these.

---

320. The verb can also mean "wish," as the NIV and the NRSV take it. See E. Käsemann, *Commentary on Romans* (London: SCM, 1980) 258. But the implied parallel with Moses suggests that actual prayer to God is probably in mind. See C. E. B. Cranfield, *A Critical and Exegetical Commentary on the Epistle to the Romans,* ICC, 2 vols. (Edinburgh: T. & T. Clark, 1975) 454-57; Douglas J. Moo, *The Epistle to the Romans,* NICNT (Grand Rapids: Eerdmans, 1996) 558; Bryan, *A Preface to Romans,* 159.

321. For details on the word see Moo, *Romans,* 557n. 14.

**9:4-5.** Paul lists the privileges of his kinsfolk.[322] He does so, at one level, to heighten the immediate rhetorical force, the plea for sympathy: these are the people to whom so much has been given. At another level, the list functions as a point of high irony: most of these privileges are what he has argued in the preceding chapters now belong to those (from whatever race) who are "in the Messiah." Thus, obviously, 8:12-30 has much to say about "sonship" in Christ; chaps. 5 and 8 assure believers that the "glory" lost by Adam (3:23), is guaranteed in Christ; 7:1–8:11 tell the complex story of the "giving of the law," and its strange fulfillment in the Spirit; and chap. 4 spells out the promise to Abraham, the great patriarch. The whole letter, of course, is in one way or another about the Messiah, and 1:3-4 offered an opening statement of the gospel message of which he is the subject, a statement that stands at the head of the whole letter as this statement stands at the head of this section. The force of the list is thus to say: the privileges that now belong to all those in Christ—"not least," Paul might add, "those of you in Rome" (see 1:7, 15)—are actually the privileges God promised to Israel according to the flesh. You Christians have come, as he says explicitly in 11:17 and 15:27, to share in the spiritual blessings of Israel. You must now spare a thought, and a prayer, for their present plight.

Three of the privileges he mentions do not so obviously relate to specific earlier parts of the letter, but they are linked by implication. The title "Israelites" itself, which prepares the way for the opening discussion of 9:6, looks back to the many discussions of Israel and its privileges throughout the opening chapters, and especially 2:17–3:9.[323] The "covenants" have not been mentioned specifically before, but it is at least arguable that by this phrase Paul refers, in shorthand as it were, to the relationships God established with Abraham, with Israel through Moses, and with David. These are the subject of chap. 4 (Abraham); 7:1–8:11 (Moses); and 1:3 (taken with 15:12) (David).

Finally, Israel's "worship" has not been an explicit topic, but if we were right to see "the obedience of faith" in 1:5 as, among other things, a reference to Israel's central prayer, the *Shema Israel* (see the Commentary on 3:30; 8:28), then the worship that God commanded Israel—the true worship of the true God, as opposed to the idolatry that characterized the Gentile nations (1:18-32)—is at least implicit in much that has gone before.

The point, then, is that God, having called ethnic Israel to be the light of the world, has now shone that light lavishly on the wider world, while Israel seems to have chosen to remain in darkness. Israel, called to be God's messenger to the world (3:1-2), has seen the message successfully delivered while itself failing to give heed to it. The irony and tragedy of this situation is the reason both for Paul's anguish and for this poignant way of expressing it.

The final privilege, though, is the one through which Paul intends to view this problem and bring it to a solution. "From them,[324] according to the flesh, comes the Messiah, who is over all, God blessed for ever. Amen" (NRSV). The word order in the Greek runs thus: "from whom [is] the Messiah, the one according to the flesh, who is over all God blessed for ever, Amen [ὁ Χριστὸς τὸ κατὰ σάρκα ὁ ὢν ἐπὶ πάντων θεὸς εὐλογητὸς εἰς τοὺς αἰῶνας ἀμήν *ho Christos to kata sarka ho ōn epi pantōn theos eulogētos eis tous aiōnas amēn*]."

Word order is one thing; punctuation is another. There is little or no punctuation in the earliest manuscripts, and not much in some of the later ones. This leaves the interpreter of the NT with fascinating puzzles, of which this half-verse is one of the best known. As the various alternative translations in the NRSV and the NIV indicate, there are several possible ways of punctuating, and hence of understanding Paul's intended meaning. In particular, should there be a comma or a full stop after "according to the flesh" (κατὰ σάρκα *kata sarka*)? And should there then be any punctuation after "who is over all" and before "God blessed for ever"? If so, what?

The reason for the puzzle is obvious: does Paul here refer to the Messiah as "God"? Elsewhere, as we have seen, he certainly thinks of Jesus Christ as "son of God" in a divine, not merely messianic,

---

322. Joseph A. Fitzmyer, *Romans*, AB 33 (Garden City, N.Y.: Doubleday, 1993) 543, suggests that the omission of "election" among these privileges is significant; but this is unlikely in view of 11:28.

323. Moo, *Romans*, 561, rightly stresses that in chaps. 1–8 Paul regularly speaks of "Jews," but in chaps. 9–11 of "Israel" (exceptions being 9:24; 10:12). But this does not mean that "Israel" in chaps. 9–11 is univocal—as 9:6 signals.

324. Not "theirs," as with the rest of the list. See Moo, *Romans*, 565.

sense (e.g., 1:4; 8:3). Classic passages in other letters celebrate Jesus' divinity within a continuing framework of Jewish monotheism.[325] But this cannot settle, a priori, the question of whether in this passage he refers to him as "God," so apparently baldly, without (for instance) qualifying him as "son" (see 1 Cor 15:28). Within this large question there is a secondary one: Does the phrase "who is over all" (ὁ ὢν ἐπὶ πάντων *ho ōn epi pantōn*) belong with "Christ according to the flesh," which precedes it, or with "God blessed for ever," which follows it? These are the questions that have generated the multiple possibilities evident in the translations, of which the most important are these:[326]

i. from them comes the Messiah according to the flesh, who is over all, God blessed for ever, Amen.

ii. from them comes the Messiah according to the flesh, who is over all. God be blessed for ever, Amen.

iii. from them comes the Messiah according to the flesh. God who is over all be blessed for ever, Amen.

Grammatically the arguments weigh heavily on the side of (i); in other words, on the side of saying that Paul does indeed here ascribe divinity to Christ.[327] Of the various arguments here, perhaps the strongest is that it would be highly unusual for Paul to write an asyndetic doxology—that is, an expression of praise that is not linked to a word in the immediately preceding sentence (see, e.g., 1:25).

325. On Paul's high christology elsewhere (e.g., 1 Cor 8:6; Phil 2:6-11; Col 1:15-20), see N. T. Wright, *The Climax of the Covenant: Christ and the Law in Pauline Theology* (Minneapolis: Fortress, 1991) chaps. 4–6. Titus 2:13, though normally regarded as non-Pauline, is sometimes also cited in this connection.

326. A further option involves a textual emendation that few today would advocate. See Fitzmyer, *Romans*, 548-49.

327. With the NIV and the NRSV, following the KJV and many others, and following also UBS[3] and Nestle-Aland[27]; against the RSV and the NEB. For the detailed arguments see particularly B. M. Metzger, "The Punctuation of Rom. 9:5," in *Christ and Spirit in the New Testament: Studies in Honour of Charles Francis Digby Moule*, ed. B. Lindars and S. S. Smalley (Cambridge: Cambridge University Press, 1973) 95-112. Metzger lists eight ways in which the Greek can be punctuated and argues for the one that puts a comma after "flesh" and another one before the final "Amen." Other writings are listed in Fitzmyer, *Romans*, 548-49; Moo, *Romans*, 565-68; Bryan, *A Preface to Romans*, 170-71—all agreeing with Metzger. Commentators agreeing with the RSV and the NEB include James D. G. Dunn, *Romans 9–16*, 38B (Dallas: Word, 1988) 529; P. Stuhlmacher, *Paul's Letter to the Romans: A Commentary* (Edinburgh: T. & T. Clark, 1994) 145.

More compelling than grammar alone is the consideration of how v. 5, read according to (i) above, makes sense in its wider context. We have already remarked how the complex theological statement of the gospel in 1:3-4 serves as an introduction to the whole letter, especially to chaps. 1–8. In this statement, Jesus is described as both "of the seed of David according to the flesh" and also "son of God in power according to the spirit of holiness." This leads to an emphasis on his universal rule and a call to allegiance. A double statement in which the Messiah's "fleshly" descent is balanced by his universal sovereignty would form a close parallel to this, creating a probability that at least "who is over all" goes with "Christ." This would seem to favor (i) or (ii), but it has to be said that the abrupt final sentence of (ii) is even less likely than the longer but nevertheless "unbalanced" sentence in (iii). In other words, if 9:5 is intended to be the same kind of double statement that we find in 1:3-4, (i) is the most likely reading.

But there are also indications that Paul intended 9:5 to serve in this way—not as a detached christological statement (he was not given to sudden statements of doctrines, however important, in isolation from actual arguments), but as a kind of heading for what is to come. The whole argument of 9–11, as we have suggested, moves toward, and finally affirms, the universal sovereignty of Jesus as Messiah and Lord, with 10:4-13 as the decisive statement. Though Paul does not there call Jesus θεός (*theos*, "God"), he calls him κύριος (*kyrios*, "Lord"), in one of the many passages where he is quoting from a Septuagint passage in which *kyrios* stood unambiguously for the Tetragrammaton, the sacred name YHWH. "There is no distinction between Jew and Greek; for the same Lord is Lord of all, rich in mercy to all who call upon him; for 'all who call upon the name of the Lord shall be saved' " (10:13, quoting Joel 3:5 LXX; see the Commentary on 10:13). The stress on "all" in this central passage picks up exactly the point of "who is over all" in 9:5, and increases the strong probability that Paul intended the word "God" there to be understood as a predicate of the Messiah. Chapters 9–11 close with the intention of God toward "all" (11:32), and a burst of praise to God

(11:33-36) that also echoes the brief "blessed for ever" of 9:5 (cf. 14:5-12).

If we read v. 5 in this way, what force does it add to the opening paragraph as a whole? Just this: that the Messiah who is from Israel's own race, their highest privilege and final hope, is the very embodiment of their sovereign Lord, their covenant God. And it is he whom they have rejected; this is precisely the point Paul makes in 10:21, at the close of the main "story" of chaps. 9 and 10. Just as Israel rejected their God on Mt. Sinai, precipitating Moses into his extraordinary prayer (see above), so now Israel according to the flesh has rejected its God as he came in the flesh, precipitating Paul into his own version of that prayer and his own great, unceasing grief. Israel's highest privilege, when spurned, becomes the cause of Israel's greatest tragedy.

But even that tragedy contains within itself the seeds of hope. Just because the Messiah "according to the flesh" is also "God over all, blessed for ever," and particularly because his "flesh" was the place where God "condemned sin" (8:3), so the strange and sad story of Israel's fate, to which Paul will now turn, is designed to lead on and out into new life. Read in this way, 9:5 becomes an exact, if ironic, summary of both parts of the argument that will now unfold.

# REFLECTIONS

**1.** Paul's deep, constant, and unresolved grief is a standing rebuke to the shallowness that forbids Christians to grieve on the grounds that all shall be well. Earnest preachers have sometimes read 1 Thess 4:13 as forbidding grief of all sorts, whereas what that passage forbids is grieving of a particular kind ("after the manner of pagans who have no hope"). To hold firmly to the Christian hope is not to pass beyond grief; indeed, not to grieve is not to love, since grief is the form love takes when the beloved is taken away. Paul himself speaks elsewhere (Phil 2:27) of the grief he would have had if Epaphroditus had died ("grief upon grief," he says); no suggestion there of simply "rejoicing that his friend had gone to a better place." As long as death is real, grief is real too. If it is not acknowledged, and expressed appropriately, it can be poisonous.

At the same time, it is vital to learn the lesson that this deep and inconsolable grief can coexist with the joy and celebration that fill the previous four chapters. The many-layered texture of Christian experience has room for both, and more besides. Learning how to live with these different layers, giving each its proper place, is part of Christian maturity; pointing to this task, and helping people to engage in it, is a vital part of Christian ministry. What happens between Romans 5–8 and Romans 9–11 at the level of literature must be facilitated at the level of prayer and Christian self-understanding.

**2.** The specific grief Paul feels is not, however, for those who have died, but rather for those who have rejected the gospel of Jesus. This calls into question (as do 10:1 and 11:23) any of the easygoing universalistic solutions that have been offered from time to time: Paul really does believe that those who do not believe the gospel are, to put it no stronger, given no promises of sharing in the life of the age to come. Had there been any suggestion that his nonbelieving fellow Jews were on a parallel path to salvation, exercising their rights under a covenant different from that sealed with the blood of the Messiah, his grief would have been neither deep nor unceasing; it would have consisted merely of the frustration of their not at present seeing things from his point of view. This grief is bound to be felt by those who share Paul's theological conviction and who see close family members or friends turning away in deliberate disbelief from the gospel of Jesus.

At the same time, we should note carefully that Paul does not speak of this in terms of himself being superior to them. His grief drives him to feel that it would be better for him to be cast away and for them to be saved in his place, if that could somehow happen. Though he knows it is impossible, his instinct here shows itself, paradoxically perhaps, as a deeply Christian one, formed on the basis that God gave his own son for sinners in the first place (5:8; 8:32), generating a spirituality of self-giving even to the point of wishing to be cut off from the Messiah for the sake of others. If the belief that those who belong to the Messiah are justified and glorified (8:30) is held with total conviction, it issues not in arrogance but in grief over, and in prayer for, those who at present do not share that belief.

**3.** Here, as throughout 9–11, we face the question of the Christian stance vis-à-vis unbelieving Israel, then and now. We reserve fuller comment on this for later, but we cannot miss at this stage the difference between Paul's stance and two equal and opposite distortions. On the one hand, any church that took Romans 9:1-5 seriously would find it impossible to engage in any of the anti-Jewish, still less the anti-Semitic, rhetoric that has disfigured would-be Christian discourse for many centuries. On the other hand, Paul's position is clearly incompatible with the Enlightenment position that treats all "religions" as equally valid paths to God, or to "the divine," or the local variation on this that sees Judaism and Christianity as parallel though separate "covenants." The whole point of vv. 4-5 is that what has happened in Jesus the Messiah is indeed the paradoxical fulfillment of God's Israel-shaped promises and purposes. Only if we follow Paul's own argument through the section will we understand his own unique proposal for a way forward from this impasse. But it is already clear that we should not settle for the too-easy solutions that are still propounded in many quarters. Paul demands that we think harder, not settle for comfortable answers.

# ROMANS 9:6-29, THE STORY OF ISRAEL, FROM ABRAHAM TO THE EXILE, DISPLAYS GOD'S JUSTICE IN JUDGMENT AND MERCY

## NIV

[6]It is not as though God's word had failed. For not all who are descended from Israel are Israel. [7]Nor because they are his descendants are they all Abraham's children. On the contrary, "It is through Isaac that your offspring will be reckoned."[a] [8]In other words, it is not the natural children who are God's children, but it is the children of the promise who are regarded as Abraham's offspring. [9]For this was how the promise was stated: "At the appointed time I will return, and Sarah will have a son."[b]

[10]Not only that, but Rebekah's children had one and the same father, our father Isaac. [11]Yet, before the twins were born or had done anything good or bad—in order that God's purpose in election might stand: [12]not by works but by him who calls—she was told, "The older will serve the younger."[c] [13]Just as it is written: "Jacob I loved, but Esau I hated."[d]

[a] 7 Gen. 21:12   [b] 9 Gen. 18:10,14   [c] 12 Gen. 25:23   [d] 13 Mal. 1:2,3

## NRSV

[6]It is not as though the word of God had failed. For not all Israelites truly belong to Israel, [7]and not all of Abraham's children are his true descendants; but "It is through Isaac that descendants shall be named for you." [8]This means that it is not the children of the flesh who are the children of God, but the children of the promise are counted as descendants. [9]For this is what the promise said, "About this time I will return and Sarah shall have a son." [10]Nor is that all; something similar happened to Rebecca when she had conceived children by one husband, our ancestor Isaac. [11]Even before they had been born or had done anything good or bad (so that God's purpose of election might continue, [12]not by works but by his call) she was told, "The elder shall serve the younger." [13]As it is written,

"I have loved Jacob,
    but I have hated Esau."

[14]What then are we to say? Is there injustice

## NIV

[14]What then shall we say? Is God unjust? Not at all! [15]For he says to Moses,

"I will have mercy on whom I have mercy,
and I will have compassion on whom I
have compassion."[a]

[16]It does not, therefore, depend on man's desire or effort, but on God's mercy. [17]For the Scripture says to Pharaoh: "I raised you up for this very purpose, that I might display my power in you and that my name might be proclaimed in all the earth."[b] [18]Therefore God has mercy on whom he wants to have mercy, and he hardens whom he wants to harden.

[19]One of you will say to me: "Then why does God still blame us? For who resists his will?" [20]But who are you, O man, to talk back to God? "Shall what is formed say to him who formed it, 'Why did you make me like this?'"[c] [21]Does not the potter have the right to make out of the same lump of clay some pottery for noble purposes and some for common use?

[22]What if God, choosing to show his wrath and make his power known, bore with great patience the objects of his wrath—prepared for destruction? [23]What if he did this to make the riches of his glory known to the objects of his mercy, whom he prepared in advance for glory— [24]even us, whom he also called, not only from the Jews but also from the Gentiles? [25]As he says in Hosea:

"I will call them 'my people' who are not my
people;
and I will call her 'my loved one' who is
not my loved one,"[d]

[26]and,

"It will happen that in the very place where it
was said to them,
'You are not my people,'
they will be called 'sons of the living God.'"[e]

[27]Isaiah cries out concerning Israel:

"Though the number of the Israelites be like
the sand by the sea,
only the remnant will be saved.
[28]For the Lord will carry out
his sentence on earth with speed and finality."[f]

[29]It is just as Isaiah said previously:

[a] 15 Exodus 33:19    [b] 17 Exodus 9:16    [c] 20 Isaiah 29:16; 45:9
[d] 25 Hosea 2:23    [e] 26 Hosea 1:10    [f] 28 Isaiah 10:22,23

## NRSV

on God's part? By no means! [15]For he says to Moses,

"I will have mercy on whom I have mercy,
and I will have compassion on whom I
have compassion."

[16]So it depends not on human will or exertion, but on God who shows mercy. [17]For the scripture says to Pharaoh, "I have raised you up for the very purpose of showing my power in you, so that my name may be proclaimed in all the earth." [18]So then he has mercy on whomever he chooses, and he hardens the heart of whomever he chooses.

[19]You will say to me then, "Why then does he still find fault? For who can resist his will?" [20]But who indeed are you, a human being, to argue with God? Will what is molded say to the one who molds it, "Why have you made me like this?" [21]Has the potter no right over the clay, to make out of the same lump one object for special use and another for ordinary use? [22]What if God, desiring to show his wrath and to make known his power, has endured with much patience the objects of wrath that are made for destruction; [23]and what if he has done so in order to make known the riches of his glory for the objects of mercy, which he has prepared beforehand for glory— [24]including us whom he has called, not from the Jews only but also from the Gentiles? [25]As indeed he says in Hosea,

"Those who were not my people I will call
'my people,'
and her who was not beloved I will call
'beloved.'"

[26] "And in the very place where it was said to
them, 'You are not my people,'
there they shall be called children of the
living God."

[27]And Isaiah cries out concerning Israel, "Though the number of the children of Israel were like the sand of the sea, only a remnant of them will be saved; [28]for the Lord will execute his sentence on the earth quickly and decisively."[a] [29]And as Isaiah predicted,

"If the Lord of hosts had not left survivors[b]
to us,

[a] Other ancient authorities read *for he will finish his work and cut it short in righteousness, because the Lord will make the sentence shortened on the earth*    [b] Or *descendants*; Gk *seed*

NIV

"Unless the Lord Almighty
    had left us descendants,
we would have become like Sodom,
    we would have been like Gomorrah."[a]

[a] 29 Isaiah 1:9

NRSV

we would have fared like Sodom
and been made like Gomorrah."

# COMMENTARY

To see what Paul is doing in the passage that now follows we must recognize that he is telling a single story. Not just any old story, either; this is the story of Israel, from Abraham to the exile and beyond. This passage is the first part of the continuous narrative that runs through to 10:21. It is the story of Israel told in such a way as to bring out some often-overlooked features: the story, both in promise and fulfillment, was always a story of grace, but was simultaneously one of tragic failure, of Israel being narrowed down further and further to a final "remnant." The point of this aspect of the narrative, in Paul's telling of it, is that this, too, was not outside the purpose of God, but was what had been promised all along.

This, after all, is the surface meaning from 9:6 onward. Has Israel failed to believe the gospel? Well, maybe, but it is not as though God's word has failed; for God had always specified one son and not the other, one twin and not the other, one small group while the rest fell away, one tiny remnant while the rest were lost to view, exiled apparently forever (on "exile" as a continuing theme in Second Temple Jewish thought, see the Introduction). What God promised, God has performed. This may not be the way Israel was used to telling its story (though there are affinities here with the prayers in Ezra 9 and Daniel 9), but this narrative has a strong claim, reinforced by numerous quotations and echoes, to be biblical.

Paul is not, then, producing an abstract essay on the way in which God always works with individuals, or for that matter with nations and races. This is specifically the story of Israel, the chosen people; it is the unique story of how the creator has worked with the covenant people, to bring about the purpose for which the covenant was made in the first place. It is the story, in other words, whose climax and goal is the Messiah; that, as we shall see, is the meaning of 10:3-4.

That said, we are in a position at last to understand the vexed question of the predestinarian passages such as 9:13 and especially 9:15-23. It should not need saying, but the compartmentalized ways in which Romans has been read probably require that we should say it anyway: The key to this passage is to be found in its relation to the relevant earlier parts of the letter, particularly 7:1–8:11 (to be understood, as we saw, as an expansion of the compressed statement of 5:20-21). There, the role of the Torah was to draw "sin" on to one place, magnifying it there, making it "exceedingly sinful"—and making those "under Torah" live the puzzled life of people who delighted in Torah but found that it increased the hold that sin and death had on them. This led to the conclusion, in 8:1-4: God has now done what Torah could not, condemning "sin" in the flesh of the representative Messiah, and creating by the Spirit that which the Torah wanted to create, but could not because of the "sinful flesh."

All of this is now presupposed in the unwinding spiral argument of the letter. In the present passage and the one immediately following, the story of Israel is again presented as one of puzzlement and apparent failure, to be resolved through the Messiah and (by implication) the Spirit. Romans 9:30–10:13 is the equivalent passage, at this point in the "spiral," to 7:1–8:11, with the climax of the present passage falling at 10:3-4 as that of the earlier one did at 8:3-4. The multiple resonances between the two passages (and the earlier relevant ones such as 2:17–3:9; 3:21–4:25) are as fascinating and complex as a room full of mirrors, but the main point is this: what the Torah has accomplished in Israel, even though it appears negative, is in fact part of the larger positive purpose that God had for Israel all along, part of what God had in mind in making promises to Abraham in the first place. The mystery of Israel is seen in this: that God called Israel (Abraham and his family) to undo the sin of Adam, but that work was bound to be Christ-shaped, cross-shaped, to involve being cast away that the world might be redeemed. Just as the Torah's effect in 7:7-25 was not simply negative, but served the larger positive purpose of drawing sin (the sin of the whole world!) on to one point so that it could be dealt with there—that is, in the flesh of the Messiah, so here God's purpose in election, designed to narrow Israel down to a single point (the Messiah), had in view the extension of God's saving purpose to the whole world. That something like this has been in Paul's mind all through the letter is apparent from 2:17-29 and 4:13-25. That it is indeed his point here is underlined when, later in the section, he comes to build on it. In 11:11-12 and 11:15 he puts it like this: by their trespass salvation came to the nations; their trespass means riches for the world, their diminution means riches for the Gentiles; their casting away means reconciliation for the world. (Each of those points is a shorthand way of saying what he says extensively in 9:6–10:21, not least in 9:17 and 9:22-23, some of the verses that have been felt to be the most difficult in the whole passage, indeed in the whole letter.)

The passage divides unevenly into three: vv. 6-13, vv. 14-18, and vv. 19-29, the latter of which comprises an argument (vv. 19-24) and scriptural proofs (vv. 25-29). These sections tell the story of Israel's patriarchal foundation (vv. 6-13), then of the exodus (vv. 14-18), and then of God's judgment that led to exile and, through it, to the fulfillment of God's worldwide promise to Abraham (vv. 19-24).[328] In each case Paul shows that what God himself said, through the Torah and the prophets, is what God has done—namely, that Israel was called not to be an ever-expanding empire, but to be the appropriate context for the Messiah's coming and consequent worldwide redemptive rule.

Each section is introduced by either a question or an implied question: Has God's word failed? Is

God unjust? and Why does he find fault? These are the main questions that dominate the short but vital section 3:1-9. Verse 6 corresponds to 3:3 ("Does their faithlessness nullify God's fidelity?"), 9:14 to 3:5 ("Is God unjust to exercise wrath?"), and 9:19 to 3:7 ("Why am I still being condemned as a sinner?"). Here again we are aware of the "spiral" pattern within the line of thought of the letter as a whole. These are the questions, already raised by 2:17-29, which Paul mentioned but could not at that stage address. Now, with chaps. 3–8 behind him, he can at last return to them.

Romans 9:6-13 thus tells the story of Abraham, Isaac, and Jacob, in such a way as to say: God always intended that only some of Abraham's descendants would carry forward the saving purpose. This had nothing to do with their respective merits, but only with the divine purpose. Most of Paul's Jewish contemporaries would have been happy with this understanding of the patriarchal narratives; it was his application of the same principle to the subsequent narrative that would have been controversial.

**9:6a.** This verse opens with the statement that, as we have seen, remains thematic for the whole section to the end of chap. 11: God's word has not failed, indeed it is impossible that it should do so. There is here a thematic echo of Isa 55:11, which in turn looks back to 40:8: God's word accomplishes its purpose (see also Num 23:19; 1 Sam 15:29; Ezek 24:14). Paul will refer to Isaiah 40–55 elsewhere in this section, and this makes it the more likely that he intends some such echo; the story he tells, as does the prophet, is of Israel, God's servant people, being narrowed down to a single point through which God will fulfill a worldwide purpose, revealing the divine righteousness to all the nations.

The word for "failed" in 9:6a means, literally, "fall," and though several transferred senses such as "fail" are well attested we should note that Paul uses the language of "stumbling," "tripping up," and "falling" several times later on in the argument. The answer to the implied question is: it is Israel that has stumbled, not God's word. In fact, Israel's stumble has been because of God's own Torah (9:32f.).

**9:6b.** The exposition of Israel's story begins with a firm dogmatic statement: not all who are from Israel are in fact Israel. There is an "Israel"

---

328. Moo, *Romans*, 569, suggests that vv. 14-24 are an excursus, interrupting the main argument, which consists of vv. 6-13 and 25-29. This ignores the way in which Paul is following, and retelling, the overall biblical narrative of God's dealings with Israel. Instead, Moo allows his discussion to be overshadowed by the anachronistic debates between Calvinism and Arminianism (e.g., ibid., 587-88).

and an "Israel," just as there is an "I" that delights in Torah and "another I" in 7:21-5; here, as there, the "flesh" is set against the purposes of God. Paul has put down a marker that from this point on the word "Israel" has two referents, just as with the word "Jew" in 2:28-29. Additionally, if that earlier passage is a precedent, the second "Israel" need not be simply a subset of the first, a "true Israel" taken from within the larger group of the physical family. That, to be sure, is what we find in the next verses; but by the time we get to v. 24 the picture has broadened out as it did, proleptically, in 2:29. This double meaning of "Israel" will be crucially important when we reach 11:25-26.[329]

**9:7.** This verse offers a further explanation, in relation to Abraham. Abraham was, of course, last mentioned in chap. 4, where Paul's point was that his family consists of all, whether Jewish or Gentile, who believe the gospel of Jesus. But for the moment, at the head of the long narrative he will now lay out, his point is simply that a distinction must be made (corresponding to the distinction between "Israel" and "Israel" in v. 6*b*) between Abraham's "children" and his "seed."

But which is which? Literally the verse reads "nor [is it the case] that seed of Abraham all children." Some (including the NIV) have thought that "seed of Abraham" refers to the larger category— that is, all Abraham's physical offspring, and that "children" refers to the smaller, the chosen ones. But that seems unlikely.[330] Paul's confirmation of the point with the quotation from Gen 21:12, using "seed" as the positive, more limited category, means that we must read "seed of Abraham" as denoting the "chosen" ones. Abraham, in other words, had two "children," Ishmael and Isaac; but only one, Isaac, was designated "seed." This is strongly backed up by the following verse, where being "reckoned as seed" (NRSV, "descendants"; NIV, "offspring"; both these obscure the link with 9:29, on which see below) means "being part of the elect group, as opposed to merely physical descendants" (see the similar emphasis in 9:29).

The quote from Genesis 21 invokes that whole chapter, in which—as Paul lays out in more detail in Gal 4:21-31—a distinction is made between Abraham's older son Ishmael, born to him by the slave-girl Hagar, and Isaac, born from Sarah. The point Paul is making here is, however, different from that in Galatians. There he was distinguishing between the true family and the false in order to show the spuriousness of his opponents' claims. Here, with an eye to a very different problem— potential Gentile "boasting" against unbelieving Jews—the distinction does not relate to a particular group threatening the church, but rather to the numerous unbelieving Jews over whom, as he has emphasized, he has unceasing sorrow and anguish. He is not content to sit back and casually observe the strange ways of God.

**9:8-9.** Paul explains with another, closer, echo of Gal 4:21-31. He distinguishes the two groups in terms of "flesh" and "promise": The family divides into "children of flesh" (i.e., children merely of the physical family—remembering the close associations "flesh" gives them with Paul, as in v. 3, and with the Messiah himself, as in v. 5) and "children of promise." This ties in again to the exposition of God's promise to Abraham (4:13-22), to give him an innumerable seed (i.e., family) from "many nations." Here the picture is more focused, though in the light of chaps. 9–11 as a whole we must see the same end in view: the family in question will be brought into existence through Isaac. The promise he here quotes from Gen 18:10 (repeated in 18:14) was that Sarah would have a son. This is matriarchal history, not just patriarchal. These were the promises, along with the earlier ones discussed in chap. 4, that Abraham believed; and they referred, not to all his physical descendants, but to the chosen "seed," who was Sarah's child, Isaac. The point here, in case we missed it in the flurry of detail, is that God has done what was promised. The word of God has not failed (the "word" here refers back to 9:6). God promised a son (Genesis 18); then, when time came for a choice (Genesis 21), God reaffirmed the earlier word concerning Isaac.

**9:10.** The sequence continues in the next generation, only this time the point is more acute. Someone might have responded to the Ishmael/ Isaac story by pointing out that the boys had different mothers, or that their characters were quite

---

329. Fitzmyer, *Romans,* 560, calls the second "Israel" "the Israel of faith." This may be broadly true to Paul's thinking, but is not a phrase he ever uses.

330. With Moo, *Romans,* 575; Dunn, *Romans 9–16,* 540; against Cranfield, *Romans,* 473; Fitzmyer, *Romans,* 559-60. The NIV's reading turns partly on taking ὅτι (*hoti*), the second word in the verse, to mean "because" rather than "that" as it meant in the previous, and parallel, verse. The NIV then covers its tracks by translating σπέρμα (*sperma*) as "descendants" in v. 7*a* but as "offspring" thereafter.

different. The first objection is ruled out by Paul's introducing the next phase with Rebecca rather than with Isaac; she, the mother of them both by a single father,[331] received the promise concerning Jacob's selection. Paul's thought runs ahead of him here, producing paraphrased translations in both the NIV and the NRSV; from the way he starts the sentence, it looks as though he intends to go straight from mentioning Rebecca to quoting the promise made to her, "The elder will serve the younger." Before he gets there, he inserts three qualifying clauses. The first, occupying the rest of v. 10, explains that her children were from a single father; the second, in v. 11a, explains that at the time of the promise these children were not yet born and so had no moral track record; the third, in vv. 11b-12a, gives the reason for this pre-natal promise—namely, that it emphasizes the sovereign purpose of God. This third explanation is where the weight of the short paragraph lies. This is the lesson Paul wants to take from the story, to use later on in his argument.

**9:11-12.** The second explanation occupies center stage in this brief telling of the Jacob/Esau story: it cannot be that God's selection of Jacob had anything to do with Jacob's merits, since the promise was made before he and his brother were born. God's choice has nothing to do with merit observed. Nor (to meet the objection of a later theology) could it have been foreseen, and hence explained in terms of God's knowing how the brothers were going to turn out; Jacob's behavior as a young adult, cheating and twisting this way and that, would scarcely have earned him favor with an impartial deity. The point is, though, that Paul is not here discussing what an abstract, impartial deity would or should have done; he is discussing the long purposes of God for Israel, and through Israel for the world. Central to those purposes is the principle that all must be of grace, "not of works, but of the one who calls."

In the immediate context of Romans 9–11, this phrase sets up a resonance with 11:6, where Paul insists that the remnant that now exists, the group of those Jews who have believed in Jesus, is created by grace, not works. In that context, Paul is

ruling out any suggestion that the "remnant" is a small group of Jews who have managed, through obedience to Torah, to avoid the verdict of "disobedience" that had come on everyone else (11:32). If there is a remnant of believing Jews, they can only have come into being by the same route Paul himself took: "I through the law died to the law, that I might live to God" (Gal 2:19). Of course, the phrase "not by works" occurs in many other contexts, not least in Romans, and as we have argued elsewhere its primary emphasis is on the "works of Torah" as the practices that mark out the Jew, the one who knows and (supposedly) does God's will (cf. 2:17-24), from the surrounding pagan world. In the present passage, though the emphasis is on "works" as the doing of good rather than evil, the background in Paul's mind is most likely the regular rabbinic exegesis according to which the patriarchs were already obeying the Torah, even before it was given to Moses. Paul's point, as part of his answer to the question posed by unbelieving Israel, is that God's stated purpose always involved a division within the family. The quotation from Gen 25:23 gives us, finally, the word that was spoken to Rebecca concerning her unborn twins, reversing the natural assumption concerning the rights of the firstborn.

**9:13.** This is supported in turn by the sharp quotation from Mal 1:2-3: "I loved Jacob, but hated Esau." It will not do to flatten this down by suggesting that "hate" here really means "loved somewhat less"; even that would be arbitrary, and would merit the question of v. 14 just the same.[332] The context in Malachi makes it clear what is meant: Esau, the people of Edom, have suffered devastation, and their attempts to rebuild will be thwarted. However, in context this passage of Malachi is not written to provide "Jacob" with a sense of effortless superiority, leading to arrogance. On the contrary, it is meant to undermine such a thing, and to provoke instead a sense of gratitude for the unmerited love of God.

To repeat: Paul's aim throughout this first section (9:6-13) has been to say that God's word has not failed, because he always declared that he would work through Isaac not Ishmael, and

---

331. Or possibly "by a single act of intercourse"; the Greek expression κοίτην ἔχουσα (koitēn echousa; lit., "having a marriage bed") can refer to the marriage relationship or to an act of intercourse, or indeed simply to a seminal emission. See Moo, *Romans,* 579.

332. Against Christopher Bryan, *A Preface to Romans: Notes on the Epistle in Its Literary and Cultural Setting* (Oxford: Oxford University Press, 2000) 161; Joseph A. Fitzmyer, *Romans,* AB 33 (Garden City, N.Y.: Doubleday, 1993) 563.

through Jacob not Esau, thus setting a pattern that continued through the whole story and on to Paul's own day. This, however, raises for Paul, as it does for contemporary readers, the major question: Has God been unjust? To answer this, Paul continues the story of Israel with its next major moment: the exodus from Egypt.

**9:14-18.** When faced with a dense and difficult passage like this, one wise course is to examine its roots earlier in the letter. In this case there are at least three relevant passages.

The question of 9:14, as we saw, is parallel to that of 3:5: is God unjust to inflict wrath? There Paul answered abruptly that this could not be so, since God is the world's judge, and as such is bound to punish evil. Here as there, Paul is not talking about people who are, so to speak, morally neutral; he is talking about sinful human beings. The contexts of the quotations from Exod 33:19 and 9:16, in vv. 15 and 17, make this clear. In the first case, God is speaking to Moses about those who sinned by making the golden calf. In the second, God is speaking through Moses to Pharaoh, explaining why, despite his arrogance in opposing God's plan to set Israel free, God has not struck him dead on the spot, but has allowed him to go on, hardening his heart so that the long-term effect would be the spreading of the news of God's power and reputation.

In both cases, then, the question is not: granted that human beings are a blank slate, what is God writing on that slate? Instead, it is this: Granted that Israel has followed Adam into sin (5:20 and 7:7-25 are the second relevant passages), what will God do with it? The answer Paul gives, continuing his story of Israel from Abraham to the present day, is that God has allowed Israel, like Pharaoh, to stand—that is, he has withheld instant judgment, in order that mercy may spread into the world. This is where the third earlier passage comes into play: God's kindness is meant to lead to repentance (2:4-6), though those who do not avail themselves of the chance will become hardened, to fit them the more thoroughly for the coming judgment. That this is what Paul has in mind is clear from the reprise of the present argument in 11:25-32. As with the previous paragraph, then, it is vital that we see the present statements in the larger context of the narrative Paul is constructing from 9:6 to 10:13 and beyond. What is happening to Israel in the present time serves the purpose of God's covenant intention, to spread the gospel to all the world.

**9:14.** The question, whether God is guilty of injustice, is essentially the same question as Paul grappled with in chap. 3, that of the δικαιοσύνη θεοῦ (*dikaiosynē theou*). It has to do with God's covenanted obligation to bring salvation to the Gentiles through Israel, and with his simultaneous obligation to deal with sin; both of these are brought into sharp focus by Israel's failure. In 3:21–4:25 Paul addressed the question by declaring that the Messiah, in his faithful death and resurrection, had unveiled God's righteousness in action, for the benefit of all who believe. In the present passage he is working toward a very similar conclusion, which he gives in 9:30–10:13. In 3:5-6 he was content with a brief answer to the charge of God's injustice (God remains judge of the world, and must act accordingly). Here he spells this out in terms of the exodus story.

**9:15-16.** He begins with a statement of God's sovereignty, not in the abstract but when faced with rebellious Israel. The golden calf incident (Exodus 32) became a byword for Israel's sin, all the worse because it happened at the very moment when God was entering into solemn covenant with his people in the giving of the law and the instructions for making the tabernacle (Exodus 19–20; 24; 25–30; cf. Ps 106:19; Acts 7:41; *Exod. Rab.* 21.1; 30.7; *Pesiq. Rab.* 14.10; *Tg. Neofiti*). In that context, as Moses stood before YHWH and begged forgiveness, offering to take Israel's place in being blotted out of God's book— as Paul had thought to do in v. 3—God had declared that, though severe judgment was bound to fall, some would be spared—namely, the ones God chose. God's purposes, in other words, would continue, though all of Israel be guilty (the very point Paul insisted on in 3:4). The surprise, in other words, is not that some were allowed to fall by the wayside, but that any at all were allowed to continue as God's covenant people, carrying the promises forward to their conclusion. This, in turn, shows that the status of being God's promise-bearing people has in the last analysis nothing to do with whether Israel intends to do what God wants ("human will," NRSV; "man's desire," NIV), or whether Israel expends energy on the task ("exertion," NRSV; "effort," NIV; lit., "running";

for the "running" metaphor, see 1 Cor 9:24-26; Phil 2:16; 3:12-14). What matters, what carries the saving plan forward even though all human agents let God down, is God's own mercy. "Mercy" is in fact a key theme of these chapters, and Paul clearly sees it as such by making the transition into chap. 12. (The verb ἐλεέω [eleeō] and the noun ἔλεος [eleos] occur in 9:15-16, 18, 23 and 11:30-31 [twice] and 32; see also 15:9 and Gal 6:16. The verb οἰκτίρω [oiktirō] occurs in parallel with eleeō in 9:15, and the noun οἰκτιρμός [oiktirmos], summing up the train of thought of chaps. 9–11, in 12:1.)

**9:17-18.** The same point is made graphically with another scene from the exodus narrative, that of Moses before Pharaoh. Again Paul first quotes the passage (in this case, Exod 9:16) and then draws the implication. As with Israel after the golden calf, Pharaoh is guilty; God could have punished him at once. God has, instead, "made him to stand," "raised him up" in this sense, rather than cutting him off instantly.[333] The reason is so that God's power might be displayed in him, and that God's name might be made known in all the world. The moral Paul draws in the next verse shows that he regards God's "making Pharaoh to stand" as the equivalent of "hardening"; Exod 9:16, that is, picks up 9:12 ("the LORD hardened Pharaoh's heart"), itself part of a longer sequence (Exod 4:21; 7:3, 13, 22; 8:15, 32; 9:35; 10:1; 14:8; cf. Deut 2:30; Josh 11:20; Isa 63:17). What God has done to Pharaoh is not arbitrary. Pharaoh has already enslaved God's people and resisted the call to set them free. God has in view not the protracted punishment of Pharaoh for its own sake, but the worldwide proclamation of God's power and name. This is how the language of "hardening" works in at least one strand of Second Temple Jewish thinking. (See the suggestive 2 Macc 6:12-16: God's suspension of judgment means that the pagan nations will thereby reach the full measure of their sins, v. 14; cf. Gen 15:16; Wis 19:4. Israel, meanwhile, though chastened, is eventually granted mercy.) We ought at this point to hear echoes of earlier statements regarding Israel's disobedience (1:18-23; 2:1-11, 17-24), and to detect a line of thought that runs from those passages, through the present one, on to the decisive 11:25-26.

Paul is not, then, using the example of Pharaoh to explain that God has the right to show mercy, or to harden someone's heart, out of mere caprice. Nor is it simply that God has the right to do this sort of thing when someone is standing in the way of the glorious purpose that has been promised. The sense of this passage is gained from its place within the larger story line from 9:6–10:21—that is, as part of the story of Israel itself, told to explain what is now happening to Paul's "kinsfolk according to the flesh." God's action upon Pharaoh was part of the means, not only of rescuing Israel from slavery, but of declaring God's name to the world. In much the same way, as Paul will explain in 11:11-14, God's action at the present time upon Israel "according to the flesh" is part of the means of bringing the gospel to the nations, of declaring God's name—and, now, the name of the Lord, the name of Jesus Christ!—to the nations (10:9-13). This in turn precipitates the questions of 11:1 and 11, which deal with the problem that remains at the end of it all. Reading this part of Romans is like riding a bicycle: if you stand still for more than a moment, forgetting the onward movement both of the story of 9:6–10:21 and of the letter as a whole, you are liable to lose your balance—or, perhaps, to accuse Paul of losing his.

**9:19-24.** That, of course, is very tempting at this juncture, and Paul is well aware of it. The question of 9:19 ("Why does he still find fault?") is natural and proper, however much Paul in v. 20 rebukes the creature for answering back to the creator.[334] Paul is dealing, after all, with the topic of God's righteousness; if there is complete disjunction between God's justice and everybody else's, it would be better not to use the term at all.

But here, just when it appears that Paul is going to dig himself even deeper into the hole he seems to have dug in vv. 14-18, we must again notice where he is within the story that began at 9:6. He has begun with the patriarchs; he has continued with the exodus; now he moves to the exile.

---

333. This sense of "raised up" is very different from that of Isa 41:2; 45:13; Hab 1:6; Zech 11:16, sometimes cited as parallels. See Fitzmyer, *Romans*, 567; Moo, *Romans*, 594-95. There the meaning (expressed, in any case, with different Hebrew verbs) is "caused to appear on the stage of history."

334. Bryan, *A Preface to Romans*, 91, takes "O man" (NIV) as deliberately scornful.

There were, perhaps, other options at this point. Some tellings of Israel's story (including one attributed to Paul himself in Acts) moved from the exodus to the establishment of judges and then of the monarchy (Acts 13:17-25). But Paul here waits to mention monarchs until he reaches the king himself in 10:4. Instead, he goes to those passages where Israel, in its own tellings of its own story, knew that God had acted in judgment, to prune the nation right down to a tiny remnant—and he finds, in those same passages, the clue to what God was up to. Once more God's action, evoked in the relevant biblical passages, is to be understood within the larger purposes not only for Israel but through Israel for the world. The setting, again, is not Israel as tabula rasa, but Israel as the sinful, rebellious, idolatrous people to whom God, after years of pleading, threatening, promising, and cajoling, could in the end only respond with devastating judgment. Paul here stands on the same ground as Isaiah, Jeremiah, Daniel, and the rest, the prophets who interpreted the exile as God's necessary action not only to punish Israel for its long-term infidelity but strangely, through that process, to set forward the ultimate covenant purposes. It is not a matter of echoing this or that passage which speaks, in the abstract as it were, of particular theological doctrines; it is a matter of echoing passages that speak of God's ongoing story with Israel.[335]

The central image of this passage is that of potter and clay. Paul awakens echoes here of two biblical books, and of one written around his own time. The classic passage is Jer 18:6: the prophet watches the potter remold a spoiled vessel into another one, and hears YHWH's word announcing that the same thing will happen to Israel. Israel is acting in the stubbornness of its evil will (18:12), forgetting its God and turning to idols (18:13-17). God therefore claims the right to do with Israel what the potter does with the clay (18:5-11). This is one of Jeremiah's many images of exile and restoration: Israel will be judged severely, but a new covenant will be established the other side of that judgment (Jer 31:31-4; see Rom 2:25-29).

The second passage echoed here is Isa 29:16. The context speaks of God's judgment against an Israel that has become careless, blind in their understanding and hollow in their devotion. Somehow, God will do a new thing, after the time of judgment: God will restore the fortunes of his people. Similar themes recur in Isa 45:9, where God decides to bring Gentiles from far away both to rescue his people and to join them. The image of potter and clay makes the point that Israel has no right to complain if God does such a thing. God is, after all, the creator (45:12). More particularly, the image of potter and clay affirms God's faithfulness to the promises despite full-scale rebellion on Israel's part.[336]

The other echo is of a very different book: the Wisdom of Solomon (there are many other uses of the image in Second Temple Judaism—though most of these, like Lam 4:2, are incidental imagery, not part of a larger implicit narrative; see Sir 33:13; 38:29-30; 1QS 11:22; 1QH 1:21; 3:23-24; 4:29; 10:3; 12:26, 32; 18:12; *T. Naph.* 2.2, 4). This is one of the Second Temple Jewish books where, as in Paul himself, we find retellings of the story of Israel, particularly of the exodus, drawing out points for those who inherit the story as their own. Paul's account of Pharaoh in the previous verses came close to saying what Wisdom said in its story concerning the Canaanites: God left them unpunished for a while because he was giving them an opportunity to repent, even though he knew they were thoroughly wicked and would never change (12:3-11). In 12:12 Wisdom asks: "For who will say, 'What have you done?' Or will resist your judgment?" And the passage goes on to speak of God's unchallengable righteousness, God's justice as judge of all, God's power and sovereignty as the source of it all, and God's right to judge with mildness and forbearance if he so chooses (12:13-18). Then, in the middle of his denunciation of idolatry, the writer describes the potter who forms from the same clay "both the vessels that serve clean uses and those for contrary uses, making all alike" (15:7). In context, the point is this: those who make idols fail to realize that they are themselves made of the same clay from which they manufacture their false gods (15:8). This then forms part of the denunciation of the Egyptians in particular, the idolaters from

---

335. Against Moo, *Romans,* 603.

336. So, rightly, Bryan, *A Preface to Romans,* 162. Bryan's sensitive comments about the intimate relation of potter and clay are worth close attention.

whom God rescued Israel. The theme is not identical to Paul's, but the two writings converge in this point: faced with human evil, God has the right both to remake nations and peoples in a new way and to withhold judgment for a while in order that salvation may spread to the rest of the world.

**9:19.** The question echoes 3:6: why am I still being condemned? God is sovereign; are we not all puppets?

**9:20.** Paul again refuses to take the easy way out, to assure his readers that humans are free to do what they want. Continuing to reflect on the story of Israel, hopelessly disobedient and provoking its God to wrath and judgment, and ultimately to exile, Paul responds like Isaiah or Jeremiah. Israel has no right of appeal, no right to answer God back. This in turn echoes a more fundamental problem, that of humans as creatures cross-questioning the creator, or humans as sinners arguing with the holy God.

This is the point where, not surprisingly, some have declared that Paul's argument is hopeless. I suspect that Paul would have replied, with Anselm, that post-Enlightenment thought, like many other systems, has not yet considered the seriousness of sin. If Bonhoeffer was right that putting the knowledge of good and evil before the knowledge of God was indeed, and remains, the primal act of human rebellion, then for a human to set up a standard and demand that God keep to it already smacks of such rebellion.[337] And where the humans are themselves among the sinners who have no claim on God except for judgment, their choice is in fact between accepting that judgment at once and accepting instead God's strange purpose in remolding them to carry forward his larger plans. Paul's quotation of Isa 29:16 indicates that this is what he has in mind: the judgment on Israel, following its utter infidelity, will be the prelude to a new beginning, and Israel has no right to complain if this is so.

**9:21.** Paul then develops the basic potter-and-clay image, without leaving behind its exile-and-restoration overtones, in an echo of Wis 15:7. The potter has the right to make different vessels from the same lump, one for honorable use and one for dishonorable. This verse states the principle that vv. 22-23 will then apply to the particular case of Israel.

**9:22-23.** Supposing, he says, this is what God had in mind. The force of this two-verse sentence is: "Wouldn't that put the matter in a different light?" To answer this question, though, we have to understand what exactly Paul is saying; and there are two competing ways of doing this. The question hinges on how we read the opening participle ($\theta\epsilon\lambda\omega\nu$ *thelōn*, "willing"). Is it causal ("because God willed") or concessive ("although God willed")? The NIV ("choosing") and the NRSV ("desiring") seem to take it that Paul means "because": "God wanted to show his wrath and power, and therefore bore with patience." The NJB, however, reads it as concessive: "although all the time he wanted to reveal his retribution and demonstrate his power, [God] has with great patience gone on putting up with those. . . ." And a good case can be made for this.[338] Within the theological position Paul has sketched out in 2:1-11—echoing several roughly contemporary Jewish writings—it makes good sense to see God as not inflicting wrath, even though it has been richly deserved, but rather creating a breathing space in which there is time to appeal to Israel, and for mercy to spread to more people (see 2 Chr 36:15-16, in the context of Rom 9:11-21 as a whole). Granted, in v. 17 God declares that he wants to display his power through making Pharaoh "stand." This may mean that it is wrong to insist on a straight choice between causal and concessive meanings of "willing." Paul's basic meaning may be "although," but within that there may remain a sense that since this was what God ultimately wanted to do, his long-suffering "bearing with the vessels of wrath" may in fact have been the means whereby, in the longer term, his wrath and power would be displayed all the more clearly.

Paul is saying, then, that the context for God's action is God's right and proper desire to put the world to rights, and to do so swiftly, showing that

---

338. Similarly the JB. The NEB text has causal, and the margin has concessive. Scholars in favor of the "causal" reading include C. K. Barrett, *A Commentary on the Epistle to the Romans* (London: A. & C. Black, 1957) 189-90; C. E. B. Cranfield, *A Critical and Exegetical Commentary on the Epistle to the Romans*, ICC, 2 vols. (Edinburgh: T. & T. Clark, 1975) 493-94; Douglas J. Moo, *The Epistle to the Romans*, NICNT (Grand Rapids: Eerdmans, 1996) 605-6.; Christopher Bryan, *A Preface to Romans: Notes on the Epistle in Its Literary and Cultural Setting* (Oxford: Oxford University Press, 2000) 163. For "concessive," see F. J. Leenhardt, *The Epistle to the Romans: A Commentary* (London: Lutterworth, 1961) 258; Fitzmyer, *Romans,* 569.

---

337. D. Bonhoeffer, *Ethics* (London: SCM, 1955) 3-5.

God, the creator, is also the just judge. This, after all, is what all questions of theodicy seek: the assurance that God is both powerful and just, despite appearances. Verse 22*b* then explains why those appearances are, in fact, lacking: For the sake of longer-term fulfillment of his wider purposes (we must never forget that this argument continues to 10:12-13 and beyond), God has patiently put up with the Pharaohs of this world, who now alas include much of his own people Israel, as the prophets themselves said over and over again. They are "vessels of wrath," not in the sense of being God's agents to bring wrath on others (as with the identical Greek phrase in Jer 50[27]:25; cf. Isa 13:5; 54:16), but in the sense that they are the appropriate recipients of wrath. As throughout this chapter, Paul is speaking at two levels. He is talking of the pre-exilic generation, with whom God bore patiently despite their persistent idolatry, sending prophet after prophet to them until the only reaction left was the devastating judgment of exile. And he is talking of his own generation, those upon whom, as he said in 1 Thess 2:16, wrath was now coming "to the uttermost." His own generation belong, properly, at the end of the story (10:19-21); but, as with 9:6-13 and 9:14-18, he is looking ahead, noting the pattern of the story, even while retelling its earlier segments.

God, then, has borne with much patience the "vessels of wrath." The theme of God's patience (μακροθυμία *makrothymia*) is another link back to 2:4, and forward thereby to 11:22; 2:4 links God's patience with his kindness (χρηστότης *chrēstotēs*), which is the subject of 11:22.

As in the parable of the sheep and the goats, there is an imbalance between what is said about the "vessels of wrath" and what is said about the "vessels of mercy" (Matt 25:34, 41). The former are "fitted for destruction," leaving it at least ambiguous whether they have done this to themselves by their impenitence or whether God has somehow been involved in the process. The latter, though, have been "prepared for glory" by God himself.[339] And their glory, picking up the theme that runs from 5:2 to 8:30, is God's ultimate objective. Had God simply condemned Israel at once, following its decisive rejection of Jesus as Messiah, there would have

been no space either for Jews to repent (beginning, one may suppose, with the disciples themselves!), or for Gentiles to be brought in. Instead, God's patience has served the larger good. God will in the end still display the appropriate wrath and power, but, more important, there will be also displayed "the riches of his glory," the glory, in this case, which God will give to, or share with, the "vessels of glory."

**9:24.** The grammar at the start of the verse is tricky, because Paul never completes his "what if" sentence of vv. 22-23, but instead moves sideways from the reference to "vessels of mercy." There is no question, though, who Paul has in mind as these "vessels of mercy." It is "we, whom he has called." The language of "call," as in 8:30 and indeed 9:12, is one of his regular ways of describing the process whereby the gospel's sovereign summons evokes the obedience of faith. Paul is preparing the way for the texts from Hosea he is about to quote, in which the idea of "call" is prominent. But the point of the present verse, reached with a sense of triumph after the long journey through the mysteries of Israel's narrative, is that once the exile has done its work, once Israel has gone through the remolding that the potter has the right to accomplish, then the renewed people who emerge, the "vessels of glory," will not be drawn only from Jews, but also from Gentiles. This hugely significant point, which will become a major subject of the next section (9:30–10:21), ties the present telling of the story of Israel to that in 3:21–4:25 (cf. Galatians 3–4). This is how God is keeping his word to Abraham, the word that spoke both of an ongoing selection from within his physical family and also of the worldwide people who would eventually be brought in.

**9:25-29.** There remain the biblical quotations, two (run together) from Hosea and two from Isaiah. Together they round off the first stage of the argument of 9–11: what God said he would do is what he has in fact done. The echoes of Abraham in all these quotations make it clear that Paul intends to complete here an initial circle of argument from 9:6.

**9:25-26.** The two quotations from Hosea (2:23 [2:25 LXX] and 1:10 [2:1 LXX]) speak of restoration the other side of judgment. In their original setting they refer to the Israel that has been cast

339. On the imbalance see Bryan, *A Preface to Romans,* 163-64.

away for infidelity, and has thus become "not my people" and "not beloved." Paul takes these phrases in a wider sense, understanding them to refer to people who had never been within the covenant: Gentiles. And the "call" in question, as we just noted, is not simply a matter of the giving of a name—though in the biblical world name giving was often a sovereign act of character formation. The "call" here is the call of the gospel, through which both Jews and Gentiles are summoned to believing obedience, and hence to a new identity as "sons of God" (9:26). This looks back not only to the theme of "children of God" in 9:8, the children of promise who are "reckoned as 'seed'" (see the Commentary on 9:27-29), but also to the whole theme of sonship in 8:12-30, the theme then drawn together in the reference to υἱοθεσία (*huiothesia,* "sonship") in 9:4. Together, the two Hosea passages speak of the restoration Israel can expect after exile: it will be a strange reversal of judgment, in which a new word of grace will be spoken to a new people.

**9:27-29.** To round off the argument that began with God's promise to Abraham, Paul selects two passages from Isaiah that allude in one way or another to that promise and show what God has had to do to accomplish it. In the first passage, Isa 10:22-23, God declares that even if the Abrahamic promise (of descendants as numerous as the sand of the sea) comes true, only "a remnant" will be saved. This also forms a link with the passage from Hos 1:10 (LXX 2:1) quoted immediately before, since that verse begins with the same reference back to Gen 22:17, likening Abraham's promised family to the sand of the sea (see also Gen 13:16; 28:14; 32:12).

When faced with rebellious Israel, in other words, God's first word must be judgment. At the right time, God will act swiftly and decisively (v. 28). Isaiah 10:22 adds the phrase "overflowing in righteousness"; since God's righteousness is Paul's main topic throughout this section the quotation seems designed to strengthen his overall argument. That, presumably, is why several manuscripts have added the phrase, though Paul almost certainly left it unwritten, albeit implied.

At the same time, Isa 10:22 itself is echoed by Isa 28:22, which links us to the crucial passage about the messianic "stone" that Paul will quote from Isa 28:16 in v. 33. The present passage flows directly into the next one, where the Messiah, the one who comes "from them according to the flesh" (9:5), will be seen as the goal of the entire history laid out here. The story Paul has told in vv. 6-29 is the story of what it means for Israel to be the people of the crucified Messiah. Nothing said of Israel in all this passage lies outside that rubric. This is the hidden dimension of God's strange purpose of election: Israel has been called, exactly as in 5:20 and 7:7-25, to be the place where sin gathers itself into one place in order to be dealt with at last. Israel is the people through whom the evil of the world is funneled down on to the representative Messiah. The story of Abraham's family through the exodus and exile to the Messiah himself is a story of the cross casting its shadow ahead of it. The extraordinary things Paul says about God's strange ways with Israel, especially in 9:14-24, all reflect the theology of the cross he stated in 8:3. The judgment on Israel—including its "hardening" in unbelief!—is the result of the divine purpose, that the Messiah would bear, all by himself, the weight of the world's sin and death. This in turn looks on to the conclusion in chap. 11, as we shall see.

Out of the judgment, then, will emerge a "remnant" (v. 27). This remnant will be the "seed" (v. 29)—that is, the true "children of God" promised to Abraham (vv. 7-8). If it had not been for this, Israel would have ended up like Sodom or Gomorrah, the cities of the plain destroyed by God at the very time when he was promising Abraham that Sarah would have a son (Gen 18:16–19:29). The mention of these cities is therefore yet another link to the beginning of the argument in 9:6-9. Paul is working within a dense web of textual echoes, and the cumulative force is not only to declare that God has indeed done what he said he would do but that the pattern of devastating judgment, from which a tiny remnant would escape, is built in from the beginning (cf. Gen 19:29, in which Lot and his family escape from Sodom because "God remembered Abraham"—a foretaste of the exodus [cf. Exod 2:24 with Pss 105:8-9, 42; 106:45], and now of the new exodus that happens in the gospel).

The "remnant," the "holy seed" (cf. Isa 6:13; Ezra 9:2; Mal 2:15), is critical to Paul's argument in chap. 11, and we shall take up the theme there. For the moment we may sum up what he has achieved through this many-layered construction of texts and evocation of contexts.

He has told the story of Israel, from Abraham to the promises of return from exile. At every point the story declares that God intended to affirm, as the true covenant people, not all Abraham's physical family, but only those upon whom he decided to have mercy in order to be faithful to his promises. The background for this is found in chaps. 1–8: all Israel, like all the Gentile world, is guilty of sin, and if God simply left Israel to itself not only would it have ceased to exist long ago but the promises made through Abraham to the whole world would never have come to pass. Hence, at last, Paul has returned to the sequence of thought in 3:1-8, and has spelled out its full implications. Now he can move on in the story to the point that corresponds, at this stage of his argument, to 3:21–4:35 on the one hand and to 8:1-11 on the other. Having explained how God's righteousness requires that he deal properly with sin, he will now explain how that same righteousness, God's faithfulness to the covenant, generates a world-wide family characterized by faith in Jesus as Messiah and Lord and in God's raising of him from the dead.

# REFLECTIONS

**1.** Many readers in our own day will find Paul's argument not only opaque but—at least on the surface—repellent. Our traditions of liberal democracy, not only in Western post-Englightenment civilization but also in many Protestant churches, have made us instinctively recoil against any exercise of sovereign power, even when the one exercising it happens to be the almighty, all-wise, and all-loving creator God. We cherish our freedom, even if we use it to send ourselves or our neighbors to hell (being "free" to deal in heroin, or to perpetrate racist bigotry). Without questioning the value of the liberal democratic tradition, and without pointing out its latent ambiguities and weaknesses, we must insist that the instincts it has engendered have the capacity to cast aspersions on the God of both Jewish and Christian tradition. This, of course, was part of the intention of at least some Enlightenment thinkers. The first step toward appropriating this passage will therefore be, for many, the readiness to think again about who the creator God really is and who we are in his presence.

**2.** Within that, a second humiliation for us, the heirs of the Enlightenment, is to entertain the thought that the story of Israel is the central story of the true God and the world. This is not a new idea in Romans 9, and it will become more important in chap. 11; but to be grasped by this passage we are bound to see the story Paul tells here as the root of our own story. Romans 9:24 is where for the first time in the section we see the worldwide church, with Jew and Gentile belonging together, the long fulfillment of what God promised Abraham. The humility required of Gentile Christians in admitting that Israel's story is the groundwork, the beginning, of our own story is something that many generations of Christians have refused, with devastating results.

**3.** We are, however, in a double bind at this point. Paul's necessary language about the failure of ethnic Israel, and God's consequent judgment, "swift and decisive" (9:28), has been used as a stick with which to beat unbelieving Jews from that day to this—with, again, terrible consequences. We shall explore this further when dealing with chap. 11. But for the moment we note the double danger: danger if the church ignores its Jewish roots, danger if the church supposes that, having those Jewish roots, it can look on with anything other than tears and awe at the path God called Israel to tread, the path of being (as he says in 11:15) cast away for the reconciliation of the world. To gloat over Israel as it goes through the story Paul here lays out would be to share the mood of the gloating authorities at the foot of the cross. Israel in this passage is acting out what it means to be the Messiah's people according to the flesh. Those who cherish the death of Jesus Christ, seen in all its Pauline glory as the means of God's dealing with and forgiving their own sin and death, are here summoned to watch in horror and gratitude at the cost of that unique achievement.

The cost is borne by the people who, sometimes knowingly but mostly unknowingly, found themselves called to be members of God's bomb squad, called to take the explosive charge of the world's sin to the waste ground outside the city and there let it be detonated in safety. Paul looks on in tears as most of the team, precisely because they are proud to have this vocation, become unwilling to stand back and allow the crucified Messiah to take the full force of the explosion. By denying that Jesus, the crucified and risen one, is the Messiah, they thereby themselves become caught up in the danger zone. Paul, as we shall see in chap. 11, is anxious that they should leave before it is too late. But he is not sanguine about their chances if they refuse to do so.[340]

**4.** At a more general level, and once this overall meaning is understood, there are many moments in the passage that can be, and have been, of great comfort to those who find circumstances and obligations overwhelming them. "It isn't a matter of willing, or running, but of God's mercy" (v. 16); that text alone, even without its context, can bring solace to a troubled and anxious heart. That, indeed, is part of the point of expounding God's sovereignty: not to terrify us with the sense of an unknowable and possibly capricious deity, but to assure us that the God of creation, the God we know in Jesus Christ, overflows with mercy, and that even negative judgments have mercy in view all along, if only people will have the humility and faith to find it where it has been placed. To be able to rest in the sovereign mercy of God revealed in Jesus Christ is one of the most valuable aspects of the Christian's calling.

340. I cautiously advanced the "bomb squad" illustration in "Romans and the Theology of Paul," in *Pauline Theology, Volume III: Romans,* ed. D. M. Hay and E. E. Johnson (Minneapolis: Fortress, 1995) 30-67. R. B. Hays offered criticisms of it in his "Adam, Israel, Christ," in *Pauline Theology,* vol. III: *Romans,* ed. D. M. Hay and E. E. Johnson (Minneapolis: Fortress, 1995) 82. I still think it has merit.

# ROMANS 9:30–10:21, GOD'S COVENANT FAITHFULNESS REVEALED IN THE MESSIAH

## OVERVIEW

The second half of Paul's new version of Israel's story brings us from the exile—with the promise of a remnant, and of both Jews and Gentiles called to be God's people—up to the Messiah, and to the renewal of the covenant through him. Through this covenant renewal, the gospel message of Jesus goes out to all the world, though Israel remains recalcitrant. This is the crucial part of the story Paul is telling; it is not an aside or an excursus, but central to the argument of 9–11 as a whole.[341]

This way of reading the passage, like all other possibilities, is bound to be controversial. Yet it is, I believe, solidly based. There are two main points to note, each of which will be amplified in the detailed notes as appropriate.

341. Against Douglas J. Moo, *The Epistle to the Romans,* NICNT (Grand Rapids: Eerdmans, 1996) 618.

First, the notorious 10:4 is to be given its full value: τέλος γὰρ νόμου Χριστός (*telos gar nomou Christos*). The Messiah is the . . . end? completion? fulfillment? No: he is the goal of the Torah. The story that Torah tells—the story which Paul has been rehearsing since 9:6—comes to its appointed goal in him, as we might have guessed from 9:5, where already he is the climax and crown of the list of Israel's privileges. This reading of 10:4 holds together the entire larger section, 9:6–10:21; the verse forms a pivot around which the argument moves.

Second, Paul's reading of Deuteronomy 30:12-14 in 10:6-8 belongs with two other Second Temple readings of this passage as a prediction of the true return from exile, the covenant renewal. In both Baruch and 4QMMT we find a similar understanding of the passage, though applied to the authors' own times and groups. Paul is using the same passage to make an equivalent point. Exile, the punishment of Israel's sin, reached its height in the death of the Messiah; now, with his resurrection and universal lordship (10:9), the new order promised in Deuteronomy 30 has begun, offering a new way of "keeping Torah." Whereas, however, Baruch saw this new way as an invitation to search for the true divine Wisdom, and 4QMMT saw it as a tightening up of purity regulations in the Temple, Paul sees it as faith: confessing Jesus as Lord and believing that God raised him from the dead.

The actual story of Israel, from Abraham to covenant renewal, hinging upon the coming of the Messiah, thus reaches its actual conclusion in 10:13, with Jew and Gentile coming together under the rule of the one Lord (cf. the same conclusion in 15:7-13 and the anticipations in 2:25-29; 3:27-31; 4:13-25). The final part of the chapter (10:14-21) does not add to the narrative line, but explores what has happened at that point. An urgent mission to Gentiles is under way, leading to Gentile inclusion in God's people (10:14-18), while ethnic Israel remains recalcitrant (vv. 19-21). This sets the scene for the fresh discussion of possibilities in chap. 11. Balancing vv. 14-21, at the start of the present section, 9:30-33 does not add a new stage to the story, but sums up where Paul had got to at 9:29, with Gentiles coming in and ethnic Israel tripping up over the "stone." Both parts of this are important. Despite a long tradition of seeing "the failure of Israel" as the main theme, the incoming of Gentiles, via the apostolic mission (9:30; 10:14-18), is just as important.[342]

The discussion in 9:30–10:13 is complicated by the sudden reappearance, four times in 9:30-31, six in 10:3-6, and one final time in 10:10, of the word δικαιοσύνη (*dikaiosynē*), regularly translated "righteousness" (this is assuming that the second occurence in 10:3 is part of the original text; see the Commentary on 10:3). I argued earlier for a particular and nuanced understanding of this term, and I regard the coherence that results when this is applied to the present passage as one of the strongest arguments in favor of this understanding.

342. Against Moo, ibid., 617, and many others, including the NIV's heading for the section ("Israel's Unbelief").

Of course, what strikes one person as coherent may strike another as puzzling, and all such arguments have a necessary circularity about them (reading the word this way makes sense of the passage; reading the passage this way makes sense of the word). However, the circle need not be vicious. Let me briefly rehearse the position, as applied to the present text.

First, *dikaiosynē* here primarily denotes a status that human beings may or may not possess. It is, obviously, a status that Gentiles have come to share but which ethnic Israel as a whole seems, for the moment at least, to have forfeited, though they attempted to establish it, or something like it. The status in question is, however, available through the Messiah, and the badge of it is faith. This explains most of the occurrences in this passage (the four uses in 9:30-31, the second of the three in 10:3, the single ones in 10:4-6 and 10).

At the same time, second, the word also denotes a status that is God's (10:3, the first and third occurrences). It is possible, of course, out of context, to read these as also referring to the status human beings have, marking that status out now as "coming from God" or something similar (see the full discussion, 397-405). But not only do the earlier arguments on δικαιοσύνη θεοῦ (*dikaiosynē theou*) tell heavily in the other direction; the present context does so as well. It will not do to say "since nine out of eleven occurrences refer to a status that humans have, isn't it easier to see the other two that way as well?" Adding "of God" to a word must be allowed to make a difference! The discussion from 9:6 onward, the whole theme that concludes in 11:28-36, is ultimately about God's own character and actions; and, thus far, it has all circled around the question, Has God been faithful to his promises? In doing so, has he been guilty of ἀδικία (*adikia,* "unrighteousness")? This, as we have seen, sends us back to 3:1-8, where the main subject is God's own "righteousness."

Third, the subject matter of chaps. 9–11 indicates strongly that the ongoing theme is the covenant relationship between God and Israel. The word διαθήκη (*diathēkē*) is rare in Paul in general, and in these chapters is only found in 9:4 and 11:27. But the word "covenant" is the simplest shorthand way known to me of referring to that complex of themes that are drawn together frequently in Paul but seldom in such a concentrated fashion as here. Briefly, they comprise God's promises to Abraham; the intention that through Abraham's family God would solve the problem of sin that besets the whole human race; the Torah, with all its ambiguities, as the charter of ethnic Israel, the bond of its relationship with YHWH; and the promise of renewal, of a new mode of being God's people through which exile would be undone, a new way of serving God made possible and actual, with the whole thing being opened up, as originally envisaged, for non-Jews to share. This is what I mean, in these contexts, by "covenant."

All this—it is a story, really, but it includes elements of various sorts—is bound up with the fact that God has been δίκαιος *dikaios,* "righteous." Nor is it simply that God made covenant promises and has now kept them (as one would, in that sense, be "righteous" if one had promised to cut down a tree and had then done so). The notion of God's "righteousness" itself carries "covenantal" meaning. The great majority of occurrences of *dikaiosynē* and its cognates in the LXX reflect an underlying occurrence of צדקה (*sĕdāqâ*) and its cognates; and that Hebrew root draws together, not least in books like Isaiah, which Paul drew on extensively, what appear to us as two distinct ideas but that fused together in Jewish thought: legal rectitude or equitableness on the one hand, and covenant on the other.[343]

343. BDAG 247a states somewhat cryptically that "a strict classification of [δικαιοσύνη] in the NT is complicated by freq. interplay of abstract and concrete aspects drawn from OT and Gr-Rom. cultures, in which a sense of equitableness combines with awareness of responsibility within a social context." Quite so: and "awareness of responsibility within a social context," seen in the context of Second Temple Judaism, takes concrete form in the covenant, in the mutual covenant responsibilities of God and Israel in particular, and in the covenant status Israel had, or hoped to have.

These two ideas were not sharply distinguished by Paul, because as we have seen he believed that the covenant God made with Abraham was God's appointed means of putting to rights the world in general and the human race in particular. The covenant thus included, as one vital element, God's dealing with sin and securing forgiveness for sinners. A good deal of chaps. 1–8 is taken up with this one way or another. In the present passage, however, things are different: The word ἁμαρτία (*hamartia*) and its cognates, which occur literally dozens of times in chaps. 3–8, are found precisely once in chaps. 9–11, and that in a biblical quotation, albeit an important one (11:27, quoting Isa 27:9; cf. Jer 31:34). Thus, though in 9:30–10:13 Paul is coming back over territory already familiar from 3:21–4:25 and 7:1–8:11, the spiral of his argument has got to a different point. He can now presuppose God's dealing with sin; here his purpose is to develop the theme that was already bound up within the earlier arguments—namely, the inclusion of Jews and Gentiles together in the single family promised to Abraham.

Though the questions of sin on the one hand and the unity of Jew and Gentile on the other have been held at arm's length in much exegesis and theology, for Paul they are closely intertwined. For him, the whole point of people having their sins forgiven was so that they could then join in the single family who would together and forever sing the praises of the one creator God (15:7-13). This is how, at the level of ethnic structures as well as individual forgiveness and salvation, the world is to be put to rights. And the present section of the letter is where he explains, within the larger story of Israel, and within his overall argument about the faithfulness of God, how that has come about.

# Romans 9:30-33, Faith, Works, and the Stumbling Stone

| NIV | NRSV |
| --- | --- |
| [30]What then shall we say? That the Gentiles, who did not pursue righteousness, have obtained it, a righteousness that is by faith; [31]but Israel, who pursued a law of righteousness, has not attained it. [32]Why not? Because they pursued it not by faith but as if it were by works. They | [30]What then are we to say? Gentiles, who did not strive for righteousness, have attained it, that is, righteousness through faith; [31]but Israel, who did strive for the righteousness that is based on the law, did not succeed in fulfilling that law. [32]Why not? Because they did not strive for it on the basis of faith, but as if it were based on works. |

| NIV | NRSV |
|---|---|
| stumbled over the "stumbling stone." [33]As it is written:<br><br>"See, I lay in Zion a stone that causes men to stumble<br>    and a rock that makes them fall,<br>and the one who trusts in him will never be<br>    put to shame."[a] | They have stumbled over the stumbling stone, [33]as it is written,<br><br>"See, I am laying in Zion a stone that will<br>    make people stumble, a rock that will<br>    make them fall,<br>and whoever believes in him[a] will not be<br>    put to shame." |
| [a] 33 Isaiah 8:14; 28:16 | [a] Or trusts in it |

# COMMENTARY

The first passage of the section stands back from the detailed story Paul has told so far, and asks: Where have we got to? Without doing more than summarize the previous section, we could answer: Israel has succumbed to judgment, with only a remnant to be rescued from the condemnation of exile; meanwhile, God has used the process described in 9:14-24 as a way of now calling "vessels of glory," not only Jews but also Gentiles. This is more or less exactly what Paul now says, though he adds a new and all-important element to his explanation: the dialectic of law and faith.

**9:30.** "What then shall we say?" Sometimes when Paul says this he introduces a conclusion that might be drawn, but which he will then reject or drastically modify (see the Commentary on 4:1). It is possible that we should read the rest of the verse in this way: "What then shall we say? Shall we say that Gentiles, not seeking righteousness, have received righteousness? Well, in a sense—but it is a righteousness out of faith." But this may be overly subtle.[344] Paul certainly does want to affirm that Gentiles have attained "righteousness"; and, as he will explain in 10:6-11, this is in fact the kind of "righteousness" that the Torah always envisaged as God's gift in covenant renewal. The point is that the Gentiles who were not interested in belonging to God's covenant, who were reasonably content with their pagan beliefs and practices, have now received covenant membership, the "being-put-to-rights" status

accomplished in the Messiah. But this membership is, of course, marked out not by their keeping of the Jewish Torah—they would have had to "seek" or "strive for" that, and in any case Paul has already declared that nobody will be "put-to-rights" by the Torah (3:20)—but by faith, in the way described in chaps. 3 and 4. That is basic to his argument; he is clarifying, by reference back to what he has said earlier, what he meant in v. 24.[345]

**9:31.** Israel, however, finds itself in the opposite situation: That which it was, in fact, seeking, it has not in fact found. We expect Paul to say "Israel, pursuing righteousness, did not attain it"; but Paul seldom says just what we expect, and here he adds the twist we would only have anticipated had we realized the extent to which his thought here is grounded in 3:21–4:25 and particularly 7:1–8:11. "Israel, pursuing the law, did not attain to the law." Some scholars suggest that Paul is simply unclear, since he "undoubtedly" means that Israel had been pursuing, and did not attain, "righteousness."[346]

---

344. Though see Joseph A. Fitzmyer, *Romans,* AB 33 (Garden City, N.Y.: Doubleday, 1993) 576-77; Christopher Bryan, *A Preface to Romans: Notes on the Epistle in Its Literary and Cultural Setting* (Oxford: Oxford University Press, 2000) 165, suggesting that vv. 30*b*-31 together form a second question.

345. On "seeking righteousness," see Isa 51:1 in its context; the surrounding material in Isaiah 50–51 is very relevant to Paul's argument (despite Moo, *Romans,* 621).

346. E.g., E. P. Sanders, *Paul, the Law, and the Jewish People* (Philadelphia: Fortress, 1983) 42; Fitzmyer, *Romans,* 577-78. The NIV's "a law of righteousness" picks up the fact that Paul does not write a definite article before νόμος (*nomos,* "law"), implying that this might be something other than Torah; and, at the end of the verse, by translating simply "has not attained it," leaves the possibility open that Paul means "attained righteousness," whereas the Greek is very clear in repeating *nomos.* Since this second use is also without the article, but clearly refers to the law just mentioned, it is clear that the absence of the article in the first instance is not as significant as the translation would imply. The NRSV, following the RSV, blatantly turns the first phrase around: "Israel, who did strive for the righteousness that is based on the law." It is possible that this is what Paul meant by διώκων νόμον δικαιοσύνης (*diōkōn nomon dikaiosynēs*), but he was perfectly capable of writing διώκων τὴν δικαιοσύνην τὴν ἐν νόμῳ (*diōkōn tēn dikaiosynēn tēn en nomō*) or perhaps ἐκ νόμου (*ek nomou;* cf. Phil 3:6, 9) if that was what he meant. The JB and the NJB both fall into the same trap; the NEB and the REB stick closer to what Paul actually says.

But, as so often, if we give Paul the benefit of the doubt, and are prepared to revise our expectations, he will not let us down. The thought, in fact, is here not far from 7:21-25: the more Israel clung to the law, the more it found that evil lay close at hand, and that covenant membership could not be had that way. Paul makes this more complicated by adding "of righteousness" to the first mention of "law"; as, again, in chap. 7, he will not imply that the law was not God's law, holy and just and good (the phrase "law of righteousness" occurs in Wis 2:11, but in a very different, and scarcely relevant, context). Covenant membership would indeed have been defined by Torah had that been possible, just as the Torah would have given life had it been capable of doing so, instead of having to work with material that was doomed to die (7:10; cf. Gal 3:21). In that context, as in *Alice Through the Looking Glass,* those who were the most determined to walk toward a particular goal were the ones who never reached it, while those strolling in the opposite direction found themselves arriving at once.

**9:32a.** Paul's explanation is almost equally paradoxical. The reason Israel did not attain Torah, the covenant charter, is because they were pursuing it, not by faith, but "as though by works"—the implication being "which it never was," or at least "which was an impossible route." Here is the subtlety, so often missed, in Paul's view of the Jewish law. Paul does not suppose that the Jewish law, the Torah, is bad, shabby, or even second-rate, to be pushed out of the way in favor of something else. The law is God's law, and covenant membership is marked out by attaining to it. The only question is, what counts as "attaining to it"? The full answer to this is given, brilliantly, in 10:6-9, using the "new covenant" passage in Deuteronomy 30. But those who remember what Paul said in 8:1-11, especially 8:4-8, and behind that again in 2:25-29 and 3:27-31, may already have a clue. Strange though it may seem, there is a "keeping of the law" that is open to all, Jew and Gentile alike. This, Paul has already suggested and will shortly argue, is what, so to speak, the Torah really wanted all along. To suppose that it could be fulfilled—to suppose that covenant membership could be secured for all time—simply by the "works of the law," either in the sense of the complete list of commandments, or in the (more normal) sense of the works that marked out the Jews from their pagan neighbors, falls foul of Paul's dictum: by the works of the law shall no flesh be justified (3:20; cf. Gal 2:16). In the present context, it is the second sense of "works" that dominates the horizon. What Israel has sought, and what 9:6-29 has been at pains to deny, is an inalienable identity as God's people for all those who possess Torah, for (that is) ethnic Israel as a whole. Paul, assuming his whole argument to date, declares that this can never be the appropriate fulfillment of, or attainment to, Torah. The God who gave Torah is the God who made promises to Abraham, promises about a worldwide family. Unless we are to suppose (which Paul never does) that Torah was a bad idea that God subsequently abandoned (see the Commentary on 10:4), we must conclude that God always envisaged a kind of Torah-keeping, a kind of law-fulfillment, of a different order from that pursued so vigorously by the zealous Jews of Paul's day, including himself in his earlier days (Gal 1:14; Phil 3:4-6). The subtlety of this is allowed for here not least because Paul does not include a verb in the sentence; we are bound to supply "pursued," but the precise meaning of this is left open, so there is no problem in the idea of "pursued by faith."[347] What this means will become clearer in chapter 10.

**9:32b-33.** Drawing now on the dark theme he has expounded in vv. 6-29, particularly vv. 14-24, Paul declares that what Israel did, pursuing Torah but not attaining to it, was like a sort of tripping up; and the stone that tripped them up was put there, not by some demon, but by the covenant God himself. We are back once again with the paradox of chap. 7. The law was God's good and holy law, but when it was given sin sprang to life and "I" died (7:9). When Israel continued to live under the law, sin lay close at hand (7:21), creating a "law of sin" (7:23, 25). So, here, God's good law, placed there by God's own self, has tripped up Israel as with a stone put there on purpose. We can only begin to understand this in the light of what has already been said about God's purpose for Israel, and of what will become clear in 11:11-16. God's intention was all along that Israel should be the Messiah's people according to the flesh;

347. See Fitzmyer, *Romans,* 578-79.

that is, that like the Messiah himself they should be cast away that the world might be redeemed.

The Messiah himself provides, so it seems, the final twist to this constantly surprising little paragraph. Paul's double text about the "stone," taken from Isa 28:16 and 8:14, makes use of a motif familiar in several different strands of early Christianity, very likely going back to Jesus' own fresh use of Jewish traditions including Daniel 2.[348] But who or what is the "stone"?

One's initial impression, reading the quotation in its present setting, might be that Paul intends the stumbling-stone to be understood as the law itself. The Torah, it seems, has been at least the proximate cause of Israel's stumble; Paul has just spoken of the correct way to pursue the Torah as being by faith. Hence the marginal translation in the NRSV, "whoever trusts in it," rather than "him."[349] Further reflection, however, suggests two other options. On the one hand, there is God, who according to Isa 8:12-14 is both a sanctuary for those who fear him and a stone of stumbling for those who do not. On the other hand, however, Isa 28:16 is likely to have been understood in a messianic sense; and that, indeed, was how at least some rabbis understood Isa 8:14 too.[350] And, just as in Rom 8:9-11 we detected the theme of the rebuilt Temple, the place where God came to dwell by his Spirit, so in the present passage we would be right to hear at least the overtones of the standard Second Temple idea that the "stone," probably the Messiah, would be the "foundation" of the new "Temple," which would consist of all his followers, the community that would be established around him.[351] Whatever the strength of this resonance—and since the Temple is not mentioned in Romans we cannot easily assess this—we note, as of crucial importance, that the same text that concludes v. 33 recurs in 10:11, where it is clearly Jesus as Messiah who is meant by "him." Nor is this an isolated occurrence: Throughout 10:6-10, which is then summed up in 10:11, the faith in question is faith in, or at least focused upon, the Messiah himself. The positive link between the law and the Messiah in 10:4 (however controversial it may be to put it like this; see below) completes the circle. We conclude that Paul intends the stumbling-stone to be the Messiah himself, the one who is "of them according to the flesh" (9:5). It is through faith in him, or at least through that faith in God which has Jesus' messianic achievements at its cognitional core, that the Torah is attained, as 10:4-11 will explain in detail. Those who "attain . . . by faith," then, will not be put to shame (cf. 1:16; see also the Commentary on 10:13). And since, for Paul, Israel's Messiah according to the flesh is also "God over all" (9:5; see above), we should not be surprised that there are echoes as well, through the reference to Isaiah 8, to God as both the stumbling-stone and the object of faith.

But in what way is the Messiah the stumbling-stone? How has Israel stumbled over him? At one level the answer is obvious, and leads us back to the lacuna in 9:1-5: ethnic Israel as a whole has failed to believe in the Messiah, because his crucifixion is a scandal to them (1 Cor 1:23; Gal 5:11).[352] This is without a doubt Paul's basic referent. But behind this again lay, as he knew, the rejection by the Judaean leaders of Jesus himself on his last visit to Jerusalem, and his consequent death at the hands of the pagan authorities (see Acts 13:27-9; 1 Thess 2:15). This double answer is bound up in Paul's mind with Israel's attempt to "attain to Torah" by "works"—the attempt, which he will describe further presently, to confine grace to race, to create a covenant status for Jews and Jews only. Paul sees this attempt in fundamental conflict with Jesus the crucified Messiah, and hence with the whole covenant plan of God that has reached its goal in him. This, too, we should remind ourselves, is not, according to Romans 9,

348. See 1 Pet 2:6-8, where the two Isaiah passages are separated, with Ps 118:22 quoted in between; Matt 21:42 and pars.; Acts 4:11-12; Eph 2:20. On Jesus' use (and its Second Temple Jewish context), see N. T. Wright, *Jesus and the Victory of God, Christian Origins and the Question of God* 2 (London: SPCK, 1996) 498-500.

349. See also the NJB: "he who relies on this," i.e., on the stone—leaving the interpretative option open. So too the REB: "he who has faith in it." C. K. Barrett argues cautiously for the law as the "stone," though with a christological reference as it were waiting in the wings. See Barrett, "Romans 9.30–10.21: Fall and Reponsibility of Israel," in *Die Israelfrage nach Röm 9–11*, ed. L. de Lorenzi (Rome: St Paul vor den Mauern, 1977) 112. Fitzmyer, *Romans,* 579, proposes the gospel.

350. So *b.Sanh* 38a.

351. Isa 28:16 is quoted in 1QS 8:7-8 in reference to the community. See Wright, *Jesus and the Victory of God,* 499n. 76. See also Matt 16:18, where the notion of building a community on the "rock" belongs with the same strand of thought: B. F. Meyer, *The Aims of Jesus* (London: SCM, 1979) 185-88. The Targum on Isaiah understands the reference in this way; and see 1QS 8:7-8; 1QH 6:26-7.

352. σκάνδαλον (*skandalon*), the word translated "scandal" here, is often translated "stumbling block" (e.g., KJV, RSV, NRSV, NEB, NIV on 1 Cor 1:23); but the metaphor of tripping up is absent from its basic meaning, which is to do with enticing to sin. See BDAG 926.

something outside the many-layered purpose of God. Israel stumbled over the stumbling-stone because God "laid it in Zion." The present passage is, after all, part of an argument that "God's word has not failed" (9:6). If Israel is to be "cast away" for the "reconciliation of the world" (11:14), both

Torah and Messiah are drawn into that process. The Messiah remains the key to what God has done with Israel; or, to put it another way, Israel remains the Messiah's people according to the flesh.

# Romans 10:1-21, God's Righteousness and the Worldwide Mission

NIV

**10** Brothers, my heart's desire and prayer to God for the Israelites is that they may be saved. [2]For I can testify about them that they are zealous for God, but their zeal is not based on knowledge. [3]Since they did not know the righteousness that comes from God and sought to establish their own, they did not submit to God's righteousness. [4]Christ is the end of the law so that there may be righteousness for everyone who believes.

[5]Moses describes in this way the righteousness that is by the law: "The man who does these things will live by them."[a] [6]But the righteousness that is by faith says: "Do not say in your heart, 'Who will ascend into heaven?'[b]" (that is, to bring Christ down) [7]"or 'Who will descend into the deep?'[c]" (that is, to bring Christ up from the dead). [8]But what does it say? "The word is near you; it is in your mouth and in your heart,"[d] that is, the word of faith we are proclaiming: [9]That if you confess with your mouth, "Jesus is Lord," and believe in your heart that God raised him from the dead, you will be saved. [10]For it is with your heart that you believe and are justified, and it is with your mouth that you confess and are saved. [11]As the Scripture says, "Anyone who trusts in him will never be put to shame."[e] [12]For there is no difference between Jew and Gentile—the same Lord is Lord of all and richly blesses all who call on him, [13]for, "Everyone who calls on the name of the Lord will be saved."[f]

[14]How, then, can they call on the one they have not believed in? And how can they believe in the one of whom they have not heard? And how can they hear without someone preaching to them? [15]And how can they preach unless they are sent?

[a] 5 Lev. 18:5    [b] 6 Deut. 30:12    [c] 7 Deut. 30:13    [d] 8 Deut. 30:14    [e] 11 Isaiah 28:16    [f] 13 Joel 2:32

NRSV

**10** Brothers and sisters,[a] my heart's desire and prayer to God for them is that they may be saved. [2]I can testify that they have a zeal for God, but it is not enlightened. [3]For, being ignorant of the righteousness that comes from God, and seeking to establish their own, they have not submitted to God's righteousness. [4]For Christ is the end of the law so that there may be righteousness for everyone who believes.

5Moses writes concerning the righteousness that comes from the law, that "the person who does these things will live by them." [6]But the righteousness that comes from faith says, "Do not say in your heart, 'Who will ascend into heaven?' " (that is, to bring Christ down) [7]"or 'Who will descend into the abyss?' " (that is, to bring Christ up from the dead). [8]But what does it say?

"The word is near you,
    on your lips and in your heart"
(that is, the word of faith that we proclaim); [9]because[b] if you confess with your lips that Jesus is Lord and believe in your heart that God raised him from the dead, you will be saved. [10]For one believes with the heart and so is justified, and one confesses with the mouth and so is saved. [11]The scripture says, "No one who believes in him will be put to shame." [12]For there is no distinction between Jew and Greek; the same Lord is Lord of all and is generous to all who call on him. [13]For, "Everyone who calls on the name of the Lord shall be saved."

14But how are they to call on one in whom they have not believed? And how are they to believe in one of whom they have never heard? And how are they to hear without someone to

[a] Gk Brothers    [b] Or namely, that

NIV

As it is written, "How beautiful are the feet of those who bring good news!"[a]

[16]But not all the Israelites accepted the good news. For Isaiah says, "Lord, who has believed our message?"[b] [17]Consequently, faith comes from hearing the message, and the message is heard through the word of Christ. [18]But I ask: Did they not hear? Of course they did:

"Their voice has gone out into all the earth,
their words to the ends of the world."[c]

[19]Again I ask: Did Israel not understand? First, Moses says,

"I will make you envious by those who are
not a nation;
I will make you angry by a nation that has
no understanding."[d]

[20]And Isaiah boldly says,

"I was found by those who did not seek me;
I revealed myself to those who did not ask
for me."[e]

[21]But concerning Israel he says,

"All day long I have held out my hands
to a disobedient and obstinate people."[f]

[a] 15 Isaiah 52:7    [b] 16 Isaiah 53:1    [c] 18 Psalm 19:4    [d] 19 Deut. 32:21    [e] 20 Isaiah 65:1    [f] 21 Isaiah 65:2

NRSV

proclaim him? [15]And how are they to proclaim him unless they are sent? As it is written, "How beautiful are the feet of those who bring good news!" [16]But not all have obeyed the good news;[a] for Isaiah says, "Lord, who has believed our message?" [17]So faith comes from what is heard, and what is heard comes through the word of Christ.[b]

18But I ask, have they not heard? Indeed they have; for

"Their voice has gone out to all the earth,
and their words to the ends of the world."

[19]Again I ask, did Israel not understand? First Moses says,

"I will make you jealous of those who are not
a nation;
with a foolish nation I will make you
angry."

[20]Then Isaiah is so bold as to say,

"I have been found by those who did not
seek me;
I have shown myself to those who did not
ask for me."

[21]But of Israel he says, "All day long I have held out my hands to a disobedient and contrary people."

[a] Or gospel    [b] Or about Christ; other ancient authorities read of God

# COMMENTARY

Romans 10:1-13 must be seen as a whole if its parts are to be properly understood.[353] Too often scholars and preachers have allowed vv. 3-4 to stand almost by themselves; it is revealing that neither the NRSV nor the NIV translates the γάρ (gar, "for") that connects v. 5 to what has gone before. In Paul's mind, vv. 5-9 explain and undergird vv. 1-4, so that neither can be understood without the other, nor 1-9 as a whole apart from 10-13. In fact, the whole passage is joined together in such a close chain of explanation (vv. 2, 3, 4, and 5 all link to their predecessors with gar; vv. 5-9 then form a unit, the exegetical heart of the passage; then vv. 10, 11, 12a, 12b, and 13

all open with gar).[354] This is as tightly linked a chain as any in Paul's writings.

The main theme of the passage is the covenant renewal, and covenant redefinition, that has taken place in the Messiah. God has done what he always promised; and what he had promised, in the crucial Deuteronomy 30, was that after the punishment of exile he would restore Israel, enabling it to keep the law in a new way. The Israel of Paul's day, his kinsfolk according to the flesh, did not understand this; they did not, in other words, understand the dikaiosynē theou, the righteousness of God. They did not understand either how God had been true to the covenant all

353. Against Bryan, A Preface to Romans, 159, 175, who divides after v. 10.

354. So, rightly, C. K. Rowe, "Romans 10:13: What Is the Name of the Lord?" Horizons in Biblical Theology 22 (2000) 140-41.

along, or how he was now doing exactly what he had promised in renewing that covenant and bringing Gentiles into membership, by faith, alongside believing Jews. But the covenant renewal that has taken place in and through Jesus the Messiah, the world's true Lord, is—so Paul argues—the renewal spoken of in Deuteronomy 30. At its heart is faith: faith in this Jesus, faith that is open to all, faith by which all may be saved.

The paragraph, in fact, begins and ends with salvation (vv. 1, 13). This is what covenant renewal in the Messiah has achieved. But we should watch carefully where the emphasis of the paragraph falls. It is easy, in the midst of Paul's enthusiasm for the opening of salvation to the Gentiles, to miss the fact that the paragraph opens with his prayer that Jewish people should be saved. It is, after all, part of the argument for which 9:1-5 was the curtain raiser. In other words, when he is expounding Deuteronomy 30 in vv. 6-9 he is insisting, along with the general welcome to Gentiles, that faith in the Messiah— faith that Jesus is Lord and that God raised him from the dead—is the way to salvation for all, Jew as well as Greek. This emphasis continues in the following paragraph (vv. 14-21), which Paul exactly summarizes in 11:13-14. He celebrates his own apostleship to the Gentiles in order to provoke his Jewish kinsfolk to jealousy, and so to bring them to salvation. Verse 1 thus states the theme that remains central throughout the rest of the section.[355]

**10:1.** At the start of chap. 9 Paul expressed a wish, or prayer, which he could imagine himself praying but from which, in fact, he drew back. He knows that such a thought—that he should himself be cut off from the Messiah on behalf of his kinsfolk—is not the way forward. God did not accept that prayer when Moses offered it, and would most likely not do so now. Besides, how would the casting out of an apostle benefit his fellow Jews? If God had acted in the Messiah to renew the covenant and create a way of salvation open to all, the focus of any prayer on their behalf must be that they would attain this salvation by the route God had set up.

That is why, now, he announces the prayer that he is in fact praying: that his fellow Jews may be saved. This is the desire of his heart, the desire that springs out of the grief and pain that reside there (9:2); and this desire turns into prayer.

When, therefore, we find him a few verses later speaking enthusiastically of the way by which people come to salvation, and when this is grounded in a biblical passage that speaks of how God restores the fortunes of his people after the punishment of exile, we should conclude that it is the salvation of his fellow Jews that he has primarily in mind. If you confess . . . and believe . . . you will be saved (v. 9); belief and confession lead to salvation (v. 10); all who call upon the Lord's name will be saved (v. 13). This, to be sure, is combined with his new point in 9:24 and 9:30: Gentiles are becoming equal members in God's people. But he knows that is happening anyway. His urgent prayer is that it should happen for Jews as well.

This verse has the effect of curbing any false impressions that might be received from chap. 9. Paul addresses his readers as ἀδελφοί (adelphoi, lit. "brothers"), the same word he had used for his kinsfolk in 9:3, though he modified it there by adding "according to the flesh." He wants to draw his largely Gentile audience in Rome (11:13) to share his earnest desire for the salvation of Jews, not to allow them, through a half-understanding of chap. 9, to settle back comfortably and acquiesce in their present plight. This verse already looks forward, then, to the argument of 11:11-32; that passage cannot rightly be understood unless we see it as presupposing what is said here.

**10:2.** The sense of this verse is straightforward. Paul describes his fellow Jews, and would describe his own former self, as zealous but ignorant. Paul testifies to his kinsfolk that they have "a zeal for God," as he himself had had before his conversion (Acts 22:3; Gal 1:14; Phil 3:6). He can use the word "zeal" both in the specific sense of Jewish "zeal for Torah" or "zeal for God," referring to that burning desire for God's honor, for Torah to be upheld, which had led him to use violence to preserve "the traditions of the fathers," and in the broader sense of any burning energy that made people make much of a person or cause (e.g., 2 Cor 11:2; Gal 4:17).[356] But

---

355. So Rowe, ibid., 139-40.

356. On "zeal" in Judaism see above all M. Hengel, *The Zealots: Investigations into the Jewish Freedom Movement in the Period from Herod I Until 70 A.D.,* trans. D. Smith (Edinburgh: T. & T. Clark, 1989); and N. T. Wright, *The New Testament and the People of God,* vol. 1 of *Christian Origins and the Question of God* (London: SPCK; Minneapolis: Fortress, 1992) 170-81. The Jewish background includes Num 25:11, 13; 1 Kgs 19:10, 14; Ps 69:9; 1 Macc 2:26-7, 58; Jdt 9:4. On Paul's different senses of "zeal," see N. T. Wright, *What St Paul Really Said: Was Paul of Tarsus the Real Founder of Christianity?* (Grand Rapids: Eerdmans, 1997) chap. 2. Douglas J. Moo, *The Epistle to the Romans,* NICNT (Grand Rapids: Eerdmans, 1996) 632, is wrong to say that the concept is "uniformly praised" in the NT; he does not mention Gal 1:14 or Phil 3:6, where "zeal" leads to persecuting the church.

this zeal is, literally, "not according to knowledge" (the NRSV's "not enlightened" may perhaps import a hint of gnostic superknowledge, but Paul is talking not about private illumination but about what God has revealed in the Messiah). He will explain further in the next verse what it is that they are ignorant of.

But if the sense of v. 2 is clear, what is its connection with v. 1, the connection Paul intends with *gar,* "for" (omitted by the NRSV)? His meaning might be taken to be that they were, so to speak, halfway there; they were at least zealous for God, and it was worth praying that they might complete the rest of the journey. But this is unlikely. Even supposing that he thought their type of "zeal" would have counted as such, which Phil 3:6-7 would call into question, Paul did not suppose that salvation was a final gift that came to crown a life of unaided human virtue. The more natural connection is to see v. 2 explaining, not the appropriateness of praying for them, but their need of salvation; and the part of v. 2 that explains this is "not according to knowledge." "Salvation is what I'm praying for on their behalf; they need it because, zealous as they are, they remain without vital knowledge."

**10:3.** Paul now explains (again, with *gar*) what it is they are ignorant of, and what they have been doing as a result. Unfortunately, his meaning has remained obscure because of the different ways in which the phrase *dikaiosynē theou* and its variants have been understood, and we have some tidying up to do before we can proceed.

The NRSV (following the RSV) and the NIV assume that the first occurrence of the phrase denotes the status that God's people have, a status now bestowed upon faith; and that calling this "the righteousness of God" draws attention to the fact that this status comes from God (as opposed, say, to arising from human effort).[357] The assumption is then that the second occurrence refers to the kind of status people attempt to set up for themselves, which in much traditional interpretation has been the status of a "works-righteousness" resulting from keeping the law, or a more general moral effort.

On the basis of the arguments advanced earlier (see the Introduction; Commentary on 1:17; 3:21-26),[358] I propose a different way of reading the verse, which makes more detailed sense in itself and in its relation to the wider context. The most natural way of taking the first and third occurrences of δικαιοσύνη *dikaiosynē* in the verse are to refer to God's own "righteousness"—the quality of equitable covenant faithfulness that has been the main theme of Romans in general and of 9:6-29 in particular. The second use (τὴν ἰδίαν δικαιοσύνην *tēn idian dikaiosynēn*) refers to the covenant status that Israel according to the flesh had thought to set up for itself.[359] The verse should then be understood, I suggest, as follows: "For, being ignorant of God's righteousness, and seeking to establish a righteousness of their own, they did not submit to God's righteousness."

There is no need, in fact, for each occurrence of "righteousness" to refer to the same thing. On the contrary, the sense is much clearer if they do not. It is true that the status of "righteousness" that believers enjoy is a gift from God; but this is not, here or elsewhere, what the phrase "the righteousness of God" indicates. The final use in the verse is telling: "they did not submit to God's righteousness." This is difficult to square with the idea of "a status that comes from God"; one would "receive" this, not "submit" to it.

How then does the verse, read this way, fit in to the larger sequence of thought? As in 1:17 and 3:21-6, God's righteousness is God's own equitable covenant faithfulness, God's utterly reliable loyalty to the promises to Abraham. And the whole point of 9:6-33 is that this is what it has meant for God to be utterly reliable and loyal to his promise to Abraham. This is what "God's righteousness" looks like in practice. It is not as though the word of God has failed. The problem is that Israel according to the flesh never realized this, never understood what God was doing, in fulfillment of the promise and through the strange Messiah-shaped purpose. "God's righteousness" is

357. See W. Sanday and A. C. Headlam, *A Critical and Exegetical Commentary on the Epistle to the Romans,* 5th ed., ICC (Edinburgh: T. & T. Clark, 1902) 283, and many since. The NEB/REB have "God's way of righteousness," as though the phrase referred not so much to a status as to a method or system. The JB follows the RSV, but the NJB, interestingly, has "God's saving justice."

358. See also Fitzmyer, *Romans,* 583, against C. E. B. Cranfield, *A Critical and Exegetical Commentary on the Epistle to the Romans,* ICC, 2 vols. (Edinburgh: T. & T. Clark, 1975) 515; A. Nygren, *Commentary on Romans* (Philadelphia: Fortress, 1972) 379.

359. Several good MSS (including A and B) omit δικαιοσύνην *dikaiosynēn* in the latter phrase. It is easier to explain this in terms of scribes tidying up an apparently overly repetitive sentence than it is to explain the addition of what, by the same token, would have seemed to many a redundant occurrence.

a shorthand, here, for the entire sweep of covenantally loyal actions God has undertaken from Abraham to the Messiah. Paul's kinsfolk, like his own earlier self, have remained ignorant of it all, unaware that this was what God was up to and that it was what God had said all along.

As a result, they have not submitted to this covenant history. They have resisted it, like the wicked tenants in Jesus' parable (Mark 12:1-12 and par., culminating in the rejection—and vindication—of the "stone" the builders refused), hoping to claim the inheritance for their own. They have attempted, in other words, to set up a status of covenant membership in which the principle of 9:6-29 would be quietly set aside; this would be a status for all Jews, and only for Jews. No pruning down to a remnant; no admission of Gentiles (except by becoming full Jews through proselyte initiation). This is the "righteousness" they sought to establish: a status that would be "their own." This does not refer to a status they might have achieved by moral effort, by climbing up a ladder called "works," but to a status that would be theirs and theirs only. Romans 10:3 is a central statement of what Paul principally objects to, on the basis of the gospel, within the Judaism to which he had himself belonged. He does not regard his contemporaries as proto-Pelagians, trying to pull themselves up by their own moral bootstraps in order to be good enough for God and to earn "works-righteousness" of that sort. Rather, they believed that God's covenant with Abraham was their exclusive and inalienable possession, whereas Paul had come to believe that, through the death and resurrection of the Messiah, the long covenant story as set out in the Scriptures had all along had a different shape. Paul is not turning his back on Judaism and its traditions. He is claiming to interpret them in their own terms, through their own Scriptures, and around their own Messiah (9:4-5).

This makes good sense, too, of what follows. Verses 5-9 do not contrast, as has often been thought, moralistic self-help "righteousness" with a simple trust in God. It expounds what Deuteronomy set out as the charter for the new covenant, the return from exile. It is a contrast of eschatology, not of rival and parallel systems of justification or salvation; it is the difference between what was said to Israel in the beginning and what

was said by way of invitation to covenant renewal after the exile. And the source of it all is the covenant faithfulness of God as unveiled, in action, in the Messiah. Thus, just as in 3:21-26 the *dikaiosynē theou* was revealed through the gospel of Jesus the Messiah, crucified and risen, so now God's own righteousness, his faithfulness to the covenant, has been unveiled in the Messiah as the resurrected Lord. In both cases, the badge of belonging to the covenant people is, of course, faith. This, I submit, is the clearest reading of 10:5-9. We shall expound it more fully presently. It strongly supports the understanding of v. 3 that has just been outlined.

To sum up: Paul declares that his fellow Jews are ignorant of God's righteousness, of what God has all along been doing, in faithfulness to God's own word and promise as described in 9:6-29 and now unveiled in the Messiah. Instead, they have sought to establish a covenant membership that would be for Jews and Jews only. As a result, they have not submitted to God's covenant faithfulness, God's decisive action in Jesus the Messiah in fulfillment of the promises. Just as "the mind of the flesh" cannot "submit to God's law" (8:7), so now that same mind cannot and does not submit to God's righteousness—the righteousness to which Torah and prophets bore witness, but which Torah by itself could never produce. We are here, that is, at the point of the spiral of Paul's argument directly above 8:1-11. That should help us to understand the next verse, which presents one of the most famous problems in all of Paul.

**10:4.** The problem in this short verse does not lie in the meaning of the main theological terms. Law, Christ, righteousness, faith—we have met them all many times before. The problem comes when we put them together, and add at the front the word τέλος (*telos*). Usually translated "end," this word can, like the English "end" itself, mean both "cessation, termination" and "goal, fulfillment." At this point lexicography can offer us options, but exegesis must decide which better fits the flow of thought.

The mainstream opinion, at both scholarly and popular levels, has for many years been the Lutheran or similar understanding, in which "the law" simply leads people into works-righteousness or self-righteousness, into the attempt to achieve their own justification and salvation.[360] If we come to the verse with that assumption, it appears natural to read it, like the NEB, as "Christ ends the law and brings righteousness for everyone who has faith,"[361] or, with the JB, "But now the Law has come to an end with Christ, and everyone who has faith may be justified."[362] This reading has become extremely common at a popular level, and one is used to hearing it quoted as an excuse for any and every form of antinomianism. At that level, too, it has become a focus of controversy between broadly Lutheran views (seeing the law as a negative force) and Calvinist ones (seeing it as positive). But the broadly Lutheran view has the widest currency.

There are, however, three problems with this, simply at the level of translation of the Greek text, and much larger ones at the level of Paul's thought in the context, in Romans as a whole, and in his other letters. (To oppose the Lutheran view, by the way, is not to say that a Calvinist reading is to be accepted instead. It is after all possible that neither of the great sixteenth-century European Reformers got fully inside Paul's first-century Jewish skin.) We should note before launching into the detail that most early readers of Paul took him to mean "goal," "culmination," or something similar.[363]

The first problem is that the second half of the sentence expresses, grammatically, the result, and probably also the implicit (divine) intention, of the first. It is not a second, different point from the first. Literally translated, the verse reads "For end of law Christ unto righteousness to every believing one." In such a sentence, we assume that "Christ" is the subject, "end of (the) law" is the complement, and that Paul wants us to understand "is." But "unto righteousness to every believer" cannot be a different, second thought. There must be something about Christ's being the end of the law that, in Paul's mind, itself enables or causes "righteousness for all believers." (Nor can "unto righteousness" modify "law," making the meaning that "Christ is the end of the 'law-unto-righteousness.' ")[364] One can just about imagine such a meaning: if "the end of the law" means "the abolition of Torah," this could conceivably mean "so that now, with Torah out of the way, a different system can come into operation," but it is interesting that those translations that take the verse that way find themselves pushed toward making the second half of the verse a separate thought (NEB, REB, JB). As with 9:30-31, the text itself resists the reading that many have assumed it "must" bear.[365]

The second problem is closely linked with this. Reading *telos* as "termination" tends to push translations into turning the noun "righteousness" into a verb (RSV: "so that everyone who has faith may be justified"; so too NJB). Paul could have written ἵνα δικαιωθήσονται πάντες οἱ πιστεύοντες (*hina dikaiōthēsontai pantes hoi pisteuontes*), "so that all who believe may be justified," and no doubt what he has said is not far from this. But he has chosen to speak, not of an event, but of the status believers now have. He is saying that the Messiah's being the τέλος νόμου *telos nomou* makes that status available. And with 9:31 close behind we can see why, provided we do not lose our exegetical nerve there as well. Israel pursued the νόμον δικαιοσύνης (*nomon dikaiosynēs*), but did not attain to that νόμος (*nomos*); the Messiah is the goal of the *nomos*, resulting in *dikaiosynē* for all who "pursue" it the right way. Israel's pursuit failed because it was undertaken, not by faith, but as though Torah and the status of righteousness it offers were to be attained through works; the Messiah is the goal of the Torah so that

---

360. See Sanday and Headlam, *Romans*, 283-84: "Law as a method or principle of righteousness had been done away with in Christ." See also C. H. Dodd, *The Epistle of Paul to the Romans*, 2nd ed. (London: Fontana, 1959) 176; Ernst Käsemann, *Commentary on Romans*, trans. Geoffrey W. Bromiley (London: SCM, 1980) 282-83. Luther, interestingly, in his *Lectures on Romans*, ed. W. Pauck, LCC 15 (Philadelphia: Westminster, 1961) 288, takes "Christ is the end of the law" as an introduction to what follows, showing that "every word in the Bible points to Christ."

361. The REB has changed the verb "ends" back to a noun ("Christ is the end of the law") but still retains the unwarranted addition of an extra verb ("and brings"). The second half of the Greek sentence, though, is the result of the implied verb in the first half, not a second and different thought. The NEB margin is equally unwarranted: "Christ is the end of the law as a way to righteousness for everyone who has faith"; to take εἰς δικαιοσύνην (*eis dikaiosynēn*) with νόμου (*nomou*) in that way is grammatically very harsh.

362. The NJB, however, has changed this to: "But the Law has found its fulfilment in Christ so that all who have faith will be justified." One wonders why, in either case, "but" was preferred to "for" as the connective; but at least a connection was provided, unlike the NIV, which omits γάρ (*gar*) altogether.

363. See esp. R. Badenas, *Christ the End of the Law: Romans 10.4 in Pauline Perspective*, JSNTSup 10 (Sheffield: JSOT, 1985); and the careful discussions of Cranfield, *Romans*, 515-20; and Fitzmyer, *Romans*, 584-85.

364. So, rightly, Douglas J. Moo, *The Epistle to the Romans*, NICNT (Grand Rapids: Eerdmans, 1996) 637.

365. See too the way in which Sanday and Headlam, *Romans*, 284, are forced to say that the *gar* at the start of the verse gives the reason, not for the actual statement of v. 3, but for what was implied—namely, that the Jews were wrong in not submitting to "the divine method."

---

there may be righteousness—the righteousness of the "Torah of righteousness"!—for all who have faith. Once we allow Paul to have said what he meant, instead of saying nearly, but not quite, what we expect him to have meant, the passage will come clear.

The third problem with the mainstream reading is Paul's use of the word *telos* and its cognates elsewhere, not least in Romans itself.[366] The only other occurrences of the noun in this letter come in 6:21-22: "the end of those things is death . . . the fruit you have is unto sanctification, and its end is eternal life." By itself, we might be misled into reading the first of these as meaning "termination," but the second makes it clear that what Paul means is "goal." Sanctification leads to, points toward, eternal life, and is consummated and completed thereby. The same is true of the shameful deeds that lead to death. A similar meaning accounts for two of the other Pauline references (2 Cor 11:15; Phil 3:19). Similarly, when Paul declares "then comes the end" in 1 Cor 15:24, he does not simply mean "then everything comes to a full stop," but rather "then comes the moment when everything is accomplished and God is all in all."[367] The other references are either indeterminate or too controversial to be included as evidence.[368] So, too, with Paul's use of the cognate verb τελέω (*teleō*). Though the verb can mean "bring to an end, finish," Paul's three uses of it all carry the other sense, "accomplish, perform, fulfill." In 2 Cor 12:9 God's power is "accomplished, fulfilled, made perfect" in weakness;[369] in Gal 5:16 he speaks of "accomplishing" the works of the flesh. And in Rom 2:27, at a critical early point in the argument that anticipates both 8:1-11 and the present passage, Paul speaks of "the uncircumcision which fulfills the law [ἡ . . . ἀκροβυστία τὸν νόμον τελοῦσα *hē akrobystia ton nomon*

*telousa*]." He does not mean "which brings the law to an end," but rather "which completes, fulfills the law"—even though, of course, he has in mind a "fulfillment" that, like the one in 10:6-9, is paradoxical, involving no outward marks of Jewish covenant membership, but instead the inward marks of the spirit through whom the covenant is renewed.

This already points us to the wider context, where again the meaning "conclusion, abrogation" is challenged, and the meaning "goal, completion" supported. As we have seen, the whole passage from 9:6 onward has been a retelling of the story of Israel, from the promises to Abraham, through exodus and exile, and on toward the long-awaited covenant renewal. This is the story that Torah itself, in its widest sense, tells; this is the story, as 9:31 indicates, of how Israel has pursued "the Torah of righteousness" but has not "attained Torah." It is not that Israel has attained Torah but missed righteousness; that frequent misunderstanding, with its consequent mistranslations (see above), goes with the common, but mistaken, view of 10:4. It is, rather, that Israel has not "attained Torah," because the mode of "works" is not the way whereby one can attain it. Torah, Israel's covenant charter, leads the eye forward along the story line from Abraham all the way to the Messiah, who is the goal of Torah. That is how the story works. It is the narrative logic of the entire section.[370]

Powerful support for this reading of 10:4 is found in 2:27-29; 3:27-31; 8:1-11; and 10:5-13. More details on each are found in the relevant sections of the commentary; here we simply summarize. (Notice how the "termination" reading of *telos* in 10:4 goes with the marginalization of 2:27-29, the misreading of "law" language in 3:27-31, the ignoring of the positive view of the law in 8:1-11, and the non-eschatological reading of 10:5-9; all telltale signs that Paul's theology has been forced on to a Procrustean bed.)

In 2:17-29 not a word is said about the law being a bad thing that needed to be brought to an end. Israel's problem here is that, despite boasting in Torah, it dishonors God by breaking it (v. 23). The solution is not to abrogate Torah, but for God

---

366. See Badenas, *Christ the End of the Law*, chap. 2.

367. Against Moo, *Romans*, 638, who cites this as an instance of the meaning "termination."

368. See esp. 2 Cor 3:13, on which see N. T. Wright, *The Climax of the Covenant: Christ and the Law in Pauline Theology* (Minneapolis: Fortress, 1991) 181, esp. n. 25, where I argue that τέλος (*telos*) can be read as "goal" or "final destination," even though the phrase contains the idea of the Torah's dispensation as essentially temporary.

369. BDAG 997 lists this, strangely, as an occurrence of the first meaning, on the grounds that to bring something to an end can also mean to bring it to its consummation or perfection; but, granted that the two meanings do shade into each other, if there is a point in distinguishing them it is because there is a difference between something ceasing to exist or be valid and something finding a fuller, more complete existence and power.

370. This means that Käsemann's argument, *Romans*, 283, against a connection with 9:31-32 misses the point of the larger sequence of thought.

to find a new method whereby people can keep it. There is to be a way of Torah-observance open to uncircumcision (v. 26)—a shocking oxymoron, parallel to 1 Cor 7:19, for those aware, as Paul was, that circumcision was itself commanded in Torah. Such people are described as "the uncircumcision that fulfils Torah" (v. 27). How this happens Paul merely hints. It is a matter of secret identity, the heart, and the Spirit (2:29).

In 3:27 the critical question as to how boasting is excluded is amplified: "By what sort of Torah? A Torah of works?" and the answer comes back, "No; by a Torah of faith" (3:27). This remains cryptic, but pregnant, until the point we have now reached. God's righteousness is revealed "apart from Torah" (χωρὶς νόμου *chōris nomou,* 3:21), but justification by faith is "apart from the works of Torah [χωρὶς ἔργων νόμου *chōris ergōn nomou]*" (3:28). This corresponds exactly to the theme of 9:30–10:4. We do not overthrow the law, says Paul; on the contrary, we uphold it (3:31). So, too, 10:4 does not undermine 3:27-31; on the contrary, it reinforces it.

Romans 7:1–8:11, likewise, does not undermine Torah. It does not suggest that when God acts in Jesus Christ and by the Spirit Torah is abrogated or made to look bad. On the contrary: it is "the mind of the flesh" that cannot submit to God's law (8:7). In Christ and by the Spirit God has at last done what Torah wanted to do but could not do, that is, to give life (7:10; 8:11). This points on to the theme of 10:5-9. In fact, if we wanted to summarize 2:17-29; 3:27-31; and 7:1–8:11, one good way of doing so might be to say: "Christ (and the Spirit) are the goal of Torah, so that all who have faith, all who are in Christ Jesus, may have righteousness and life." In none of these cases, despite the frantic efforts of some exegetes and theologians, would the translation "termination" do justice to what Paul actually says.

I conclude that in 10:4 Paul does not intend to declare the law's abrogation in favor of a different "system," but rather to announce that the Messiah is himself the climax of the long story of God and Israel, the story Torah tells and in which it plays a vital though puzzling part. God's purposes in Torah, purposes both negative and positive, have reached their goal in the Messiah, and the result of that is the accessibility and availability of "righteousness" for *all* who *believe.* Both of those

emphasized words are important, underlining the contrast (a) with the restriction of "righteousness" to Jews, and (b) with the badge of covenant membership seen as "works of Torah" in the sense already discussed.

This means, too, that there is an end, a termination, to the period of time that lasts from Moses to the Messiah. That is, of course, a main theme of Gal 3:16-29. But this termination is not like the termination of a journey when the car breaks down halfway and we are left stranded in open country. It is like the termination of a journey when the car has taken us to the very place we wanted to go and can now be rested with its task completed. In that sense, every "goal" implies a "termination" of sorts, but the opposite is emphatically not the case. If I stop writing because the telephone rings, that is not the same as when I stop writing because I have finished the book.[371]

**10:5-11.** Further proof for this line of interpretation is found in these verses, a difficult but vital passage.[372] At first sight, admittedly, it seems to run the other way: here is Moses telling people to keep the Torah, and here is something called "the righteousness of faith" telling them simply to believe! It has been easy in post-Enlightenment thought to line up Paul with Deuteronomy and against Leviticus; that is what a good deal of particularly Protestant thinking has wanted to do.[373] In fact, however, once we discover what Paul is doing in these verses—and they display one of his more subtle readings of Scripture—we shall see that here, too, somewhat as in 8:1-11, he envisages the fulfillment, not the abrogation, of Torah.

For a start, it would be naive to think that Paul

371. Cf. Moo, *Romans,* 641, with Bryan, *A Preface to Romans,* 172. For other "double sense" readings see P. Achtemeier, "Unsearchable Judgments and Inscrutable Ways: Reflections of the Discussion of Romans," in *Pauline Theology,* vol. IV, ed. E. E. Johnson and D. M. Hay, SBLSS 4 (Atlanta: Scholars Press, 1997) 168; James D. G. Dunn, *Romans 9–16,* 38B (Dallas: Word, 1988) 596-98 (though leaning heavily toward "termination" as the primary meaning). Fitzmyer, *Romans,* 584-85, denies that such a double meaning is possible.

372. On which see the suggestive comments of R. B. Hays, *Echoes of Scripture in the Letters of Paul* (New Haven: Yale University Press, 1989) 73-83. For a stimulating account of the passage see E. M. Humphrey, "Why Bring the Word Down? The Rhetoric of Demonstration and Disclosure in Romans 9:30–10:21," in *Romans and the People of God: Essays in Honor of Gordon D. Fee on the Occasion of His 65th Birthday,* ed. S. K. Soderlund and N. T. Wright (Grand Rapids: Eerdmans, 1999) 129-48.

373. See Sanday and Headlam, *Romans,* 285-86; C. H. Dodd, *The Epistle of Paul to the Romans,* 2nd ed. (London: Fontana, 1959) 177; Dunn, *Romans 9–16,* 600-602; Moo, *Romans,* 643-50. Among Catholic commentators this view is taken by Fitzmyer, *Romans,* 587-89; B. Byrne, *Romans,* SP 6 (Collegeville, Minn.: Liturgical, 1996) 317-18.

supposed, or imagined his hearers might be tricked into supposing, that Deuteronomy was not a book of Moses just as much as Leviticus was. It would also be out of character for Paul to set up one passage of Scripture against another.[374] But that is only a surface point. More important is the entire context of Deuteronomy 30 (the passage Paul is working with in vv. 6-8) and the way in which it appears to have functioned in Second Temple Judaism.[375] To draw on this wider world of thought is not "eisegesis," as is sometimes suggested; it is to replace the unspoken assumption that Paul was talking about what modern readers expect him to be talking about with the hard-won historical awareness that he was more likely to be talking about what readers of his day would be expecting. The task facing the interpreter is always to think one's way into a world of thought that Paul would have taken for granted. This is the move that lies at the heart of vv. 5-11 and that, once grasped, makes sense of the entire sequence of thought.[376]

Deuteronomy 30 comes immediately after the chapters in which Moses has held out to the people the covenantal blessings and curses. The curses, it must be said, far outweigh the blessings: Deut 28:1-14 lists the blessings that will follow obedience to Torah, but vv. 15-68 give a far longer list of curses, which are then reinforced in the warnings of 29:18-28. The final and most emphatic curse is exile: Israel will not simply suffer blight, mildew, barrenness, poverty, sickness, and a hundred other evils in the land, but will ultimately be driven off the land itself, scattered among the nations of the earth (28:63-68; 29:22-28; see esp. 29:28[27]: "YHWH uprooted them from their land in his anger, wrath, and indignation, and cast them into another land, as at this day"). It is assumed that all these things will come to pass; Deut 29:4 bewails the fact that Israel has remained hard-hearted, and the curses are bound to follow.

But after they have all happened, and in particular after the exile has done its worst, then there will come a great reversal. Deuteronomy 30 is a prediction of the return from exile, pointing to the spiritual and moral renewal that will make that return possible and appropriate. Israel will return to YHWH with all its heart and soul (30:2, 6). YHWH will turn Israel's captivity around, and regather his people (vv. 3-5). YHWH will circumcise Israel's heart, to love YHWH, so that Israel may live (v. 6). Blessing will once more follow, if Israel will now be obedient (vv. 8-10). And the central blessing is life itself: God has set life before them (v. 15), the life that results from keeping the commandments (v. 16) as opposed to disobeying and so incurring death (vv. 17-18). Life is what they must choose (v. 19). They must love YHWH, obey his voice, and cleave to him, "for he is your life, and the length of your days" (v. 20). The whole chapter might be entitled, "the new obedience which brings new life."[377]

In the middle of Deuteronomy we find vv. 11-14, the passage Paul quotes in 10:6-8. The commandment is not too hard; it is not far off. You do not need someone to go up to heaven and bring it down, so that you may hear it and do it; you do not need someone to cross the sea and fetch it, so that you may hear it and do it (this language about impossible quests to the deep, or to heaven, has become proverbial in 4 Ezra 4:7-8). "The word is near you; it is in your mouth, and in your heart, so that you may do it" (v. 14). The chapter, in other words, presumes that Israel has been sent into exile and is now going to turn to YHWH from the heart, and proceeds to explain what it really means to "do" the law and so to "live." This life-giving "doing" will be a matter, not of a struggle to obey an apparently impossible law, but of heart and mouth being renewed by God's living "word." It will not be a matter of someone else teaching it to them as from a great distance. Verse 14, significantly, omits even the mention of "hearing" the commandment; it will be inside them, in their mouth and heart. We cannot but think of Jer 31:33-34: In the restoration after the exile, the people will not need to be taught the commandments, because they will be written on their hearts. And this cannot but remind us of Rom

---

374. So Bryan, *A Preface to Romans,* 174.

375. The final chapters of Deuteronomy—the conclusion of the Pentateuch—were often read eschatologically at the time. Good examples are Pseudo-Philo 19; *Testament of Moses;* and 4 Ezra (see below), on which see R. J. Bauckham, "Apocalypses," in *Justification and Variegated Nomism,* vol. I: *The Complexities of Second Temple Judaism,* ed. D. A. Carson et al. (Grand Rapids: Baker Academic, 2001) 171.

376. This is a response in part to Fitzmyer, *Romans,* 588, who considers Paul's use of Deuteronomy here to be very loose.

377. This was how the chapter was being read in the Second Temple period. See 4 Ezra 7:20-21; Bar 4:1; Sir 17:11. If Paul had wanted to play Leviticus 18 ("do this and find life") off against some other text, he could hardly have chosen a worse one; this is exactly how Deuteronomy 30 was being understood. See the Commentary on 8:5-8.

2:25-29, a passage that Paul is about to echo in 10:9-10. It should be clear already that Paul has the context, and overall meaning, of Deuteronomy 30 firmly in mind. This is anything but a clever prooftext taken out of context.

This should make it clear, too, that Paul's quotation of Lev 18:5 in 10:5 is not set in opposition to Deuteronomy 30. He is not setting up a straw person ("Moses encouraged that stupid and impossible system we know as works-righteousness") in order then to knock it down with a bit of clever but slippery eisegesis of another part of the Pentateuch. Nor, as Barth and some later writers have suggested, was Paul envisaging the Messiah himself as the one who performed the law perfectly and gained life thereby.[378] Lev 18:5 brought together two things, "doing the law" and "living": "the one who does these things shall live by them." This is what the "righteousness which is from the law" declares; that is how Leviticus 18 was heard in Paul's own day.[379] Had Paul really meant that Christ is the termination of the law, we should have expected him to oppose such a view. But he does not suppose that Deuteronomy does any such thing. It offers, he insists, a fresh explanation, granted exile and return, for what "do the law and live" might actually mean.[380] In the original passage, the lines Paul quotes each end with "so that you may do it." Here, as in 2:25-29 and elsewhere, Paul's point is that those who share Christian faith are in fact "doing the law" in the sense that Deuteronomy and Jeremiah intended. Those who believe that Jesus is Lord, and that God raised him from the dead, are the new-covenant people, the returned-from-exile people. The story of Israel in 9:6-29 took us as far as exile, pointing ahead to what might happen beyond (9:24). That

story reached its dramatic climax in the Messiah, the one upon whom the curses ultimately fell (Gal 3:13). Now all who believe in the Messiah, whether they be Jew or Gentile, are thereby "fulfilling the law"; they are "doing" it in the sense Deuteronomy 30 intended; and they thereby find "life," as 8:9-11 demonstrated, the life that Torah wanted to give but could not (7:10), the life that can now be spoken of more specifically as "salvation" (10:9, 10, 13). And that, of course, was all along the point of the paragraph (10:1-13). Paul has prayed for the salvation of his kinsfolk; now, starting with Torah itself, he has shown the way by which that salvation may be found.

Important confirmation of this reading of Deuteronomy 30 is found in one of the final Dead Sea Scrolls to be released, the so-called 4QMMT.[381] Though Pauline scholars have noted that this text speaks of "justification by works of the law," the setting of this within an explicit exegesis of Deuteronomy 30, and thus its fascinating parallel to Romans 10, has not been explored.[382]

The scroll has three sections, A, B, and C; it is C that concerns us, specifically lines 12-32. This passage begins by quoting Deut 30:1-3: when the blessing and the curse have come upon you, then you will take it to heart and return to him with all your heart and with all your soul, "at the end of time" (a significant addition), so that you may live. The text then explains that Deuteronomy is to be read as predicting a three-stage history for Israel: first blessing, then curse, then restoration and renewed blessing. The blessings, it says, came upon Israel in the days of David and Solomon (C 18). The curses then came from the time of Jeroboam son of Nebat, climaxing in the Babylonian captivity (C 18-20). But then, "at the end of days," the return from exile will happen; and this is the time the writer believes Israel is now in. This is the time, then, for making it clear what precisely the Torah now requires, so that when the final end comes "it will be reckoned to

---

378. K. Barth, *A Shorter Commentary on Romans* (London: SCM, 1959) 127; followed by C. E. B. Cranfield, *A Critical and Exegetical Commentary on the Epistle to the Romans,* ICC, 2 vols. (Edinburgh: T. & T. Clark, 1975) 521-22; Christopher Bryan, *A Preface to Romans: Notes on the Epistle in Its Literary and Cultural Setting* (Oxford: Oxford University Press, 2000) 168. Criticized by James D. G. Dunn, *Romans 9–16,* 38B (Dallas: Word, 1988) 601; Joseph A. Fitzmyer, *Romans,* AB 33 (Garden City, N.Y.: Doubleday, 1993) 587; Douglas J. Moo, *The Epistle to the Romans,* NICNT (Grand Rapids: Eerdmans, 1996) 646-47. The covenantal and narratival reading I am proposing retains the positive sense hoped for by Barth and his followers but within a much more demonstrable Second Temple line of thought.

379. Cf. Sir 17:11; 45:5; Philo *Preliminary Studies* 86-87; *Ps Sol* 14:2. Bryan, *A Preface to Romans,* 175, notes that Lev 18:5 was sometimes used in connection with Gentiles being "righteous." See bBQam 38a; bSanh 59a. See also Moo, *Romans,* 648n. 15.

380. Paul was not, then, quoting it because it was a favorite text of his opponents (against Bryan, *A Preface to Romans,* 175).

381. See note 94, p. 460.

382. A start was made by P. Grelot, "Les oeuvres de la Loi (A propos de 4Q394-398)," *RQ* 16 (December 1994) 441-48; Martin Abegg, "Paul, 'Works of the Law,' and MMT," *BAR* (November/December 1994) 52-55, 82; J. D. G. Dunn, "4QMMT and Galatians," *NTS* 43/1 (1997) 147-53; M. Bachmann, "4QMMT und Galaterbrief, מעשי התורה und ΕΡΓΑ ΝΟΜΟΥ," *ZNW* 89 (1998) 91-113 (with copious bibliography, including other works by Bachmann). For a preliminary statement of the present position see N. T. Wright, "Paul and Qumran," *Bible Review* (October 1998) 18, 54.

you as righteousness" (C 30-31). The practices of Torah in question are those outlined in parts A and B, specifically, regulations for the Temple.

Deuteronomy 30, in other words, is being read as a prediction of the eschatological time when God restores the fortunes of Israel after the exile. This eschatological time, the writer believes, is now coming to pass. Those who, in the inaugurated eschatology of the present time, observe this "selection of works of the law" (the phrase that, via its Hebrew original, gives the work its modern title),[383] are assured thereby that at the end of time they will be reckoned within God's true people. The structure of this doctrine of justification is identical to Paul's (a future "end," at which some will be vindicated, who are marked out in the present time of inaugurated eschatology by the appropriate indicators), while the content is different. The "works of the law" the writer urges are not the 613 commands in Torah. Nor are they the "works of the law" that Paul warns against, the works (circumcision, food laws, sabbath) that mark out Jews over against their pagan neighbors. Nor, again, are they "works" done to earn a moralistic or proto-Pelagian "righteousness"; they are to demonstrate fidelity to the renewed covenant.[384] They are the particular "works" that will mark out this sect, with its specific practices, over against other Jews. For Paul, the thing that marks out members of the renewed covenant, the people envisaged by Deuteronomy 30, over against all others, Jews and pagans alike, is Christian faith. And the substance and object of that faith—the death and resurrection of the Messiah, and the confession of his universal lordship—is, of course, what determines the difference.

A second striking use of Deuteronomy 30 in Second Temple Judaism is found in Baruch 3, a very different text to 4QMMT and all the more significant as a parallel use of the passage Paul is working with here.[385] The fictive setting of Baruch is the Babylonian exile; the actual setting, it is nor-

mally assumed, is in the Jewish diaspora some time in the first or second century BCE.[386] In view of the "continuing exile" theme in much Second Temple thought, however, we may question whether a geographical diaspora situation is required. What matters is that the writer (or compiler) is clearly working with the idea of "exile," and is drawing on a wide range of classic biblical texts to do so. Exile is explained, as in Daniel 9—and as in Rom 9:6-33!—with a firm belief in God's righteousness (Bar 1:15; 2:1, 6, 19-23); that is, God has carried out the warnings issued by the prophets, and also in Deuteronomy 28 and 32. In this context, what Israel needs is to learn where wisdom is to be found; here, from 3:9 onward, the writer draws on Proverbs and Job, but the setting of exile-in-need-of-restoration has not been left behind. Wisdom is, in fact, the same thing as Torah (4:1; cf. Sir 24:23), and when Israel seeks God with all its heart, holding wisdom/Torah fast, then Israel will live. In that setting, we should not be surprised that the writer draws on Deuteronomy 30 to encourage his readers to seek wisdom/Torah so as to become the true returned-from-exile people (cf. 3:7 with Deut 30:1; 4:1 with Deut 30:19).

That is the wider context within which the explicit reference to Deut 30:12-13 occurs in 3:29-30: "Who has gone up into heaven, and taken her [i.e., wisdom], and brought her down from the clouds? Who has gone over the sea, and found her, and will buy her for pure gold?" The answer is clear: it is none other than God. "He found the whole way to knowledge, and gave her to his servant Jacob, and to Israel, whom he loved. Afterward she appeared on earth and lived with humankind" (see Sir 24:8-12; Wis 9:9-10). In that context, the writer turns to exhort his kinsfolk to take courage; salvation is at hand. Significantly, much of the rest of the short book, like Romans, is replete with echoes of Isaiah 40–55. God, concludes the book, "will lead Israel with joy, in the light of his glory, with the mercy and righteousness that are with him" (5:9).

The parallel between Rom 10:6-8 and Baruch 3 is frequently noted; the overall narrative context,

---

383. MMT = מקצת מעשי התורה (*miqṣāt maʿăśê hatôrâ*), C 27.

384. I thus agree with J. D. G. Dunn about the place of "works" in Judaism as principally social or covenantal boundary markers, while disagreeing with him about the "works" in MMT being the same as those in view in Galatians.

385. Similar points could be made about 4 Ezra 4:8 (which also alludes to Ps 139:8). Another very different use of Deut 30:11-14 is in the *Gospel of Thomas*, saying 3. For rabbinic uses see SB 3.279-81.

386. See D. Mendels, "Baruch, Book of," *ABD*, 1:618-20; A. Salvesen, "Baruch," in *The Oxford Bible Commentary*, ed. J. Barton and J. Muddiman (Oxford: Oxford University Press, 2001) 699-703.

of exile and return, and the repentance required for the latter, is not. That is why some have been able to suggest that the Baruch passage is not particularly relevant for interpreting Romans.[387] If all it supplies is a parallel use of Deuteronomy 30, and a general suggestion that the "Wisdom" sought or propounded by various Jewish writers at the time might be a source for Paul's christology, we might in part agree (cf. Sir 24:5). But it supplies far more than that (though not, we should note, less). Baruch, like 4QMMT, envisages a narrative within which writer and readers find themselves at home: the narrative of exile and restoration.

For all their radical differences of style and content, 4QMMT and Baruch thus reflect a similar understanding of how God is at work in Israel's history, and what is required to be a faithful, true Jew at this moment. Both take Deuteronomy 30 as pointing to what will happen when God restores the fortunes of Israel after exile. MMT sees the intensification of Torah as what is needed; Baruch urges his readers to seek the divine wisdom in which Torah is embodied. Both see this as the way to attain the salvation that God long ago promised would succeed the time of desolation and devastation. Together they create a Second Temple context of meaning within which Paul's fresh understanding, generated by his grasp of the gospel, makes full and rich sense.

With all this in mind—Deuteronomy 30 as a whole, with its emphasis on "doing" and "living," and the eschatological reading of it in two other Second Temple writers—we may offer a preliminary reading of vv. 5-9.

First, it must be noted that the passage, introduced as it is with *gar*, is advanced as the explanation of why the Messiah is the goal of the law for righteousness to all who believe (this explanatory connection is ignored in the NRSV, the NIV, and several other translations). The *gar*, in fact, governs vv. 5-9 as a whole, not simply v. 5. Paul's explanation runs as follows: "For, while Moses does indeed write concerning Torah-

righteousness that 'the one who does them shall live in them,' what 'doing' and 'living' come to mean, when God restores Israel after exile, is defined afresh by Deuteronomy 30, not in terms of an impossible demand, but in terms of God's gift of God's own word; and this 'word' is the word of faith, faith that Jesus is Lord and that God raised him from the dead." This, taken as a whole, explains v. 4, and thereby, in turn, explains how salvation is now available for all who share this faith. In other words, while opening the promise to those of any and every ethnic background, Paul is more specifically showing how his prayer in 10:1 is to be answered. This is how God will restore the fortunes of Israel. Just as MMT urged its readers to make their status in the renewed people of God secure by particular temple regulations, and just as Baruch urged his readers to seek the divine Wisdom, so Paul urges people of every race to discover the risen Lord Jesus as Messiah and find thereby the renewed covenant membership of which Deuteronomy spoke. Verse 5 is not a statement of a legalism that Paul will then sweep aside. The δέ (*de*) that links vv. 5-6 does not indicate a direct antithesis or contradiction, but a modification, a redefinition: "Yes, Moses does write Lev 18:5; *but* its key terms are then further explained in Deuteronomy 30."[388]

But what precisely is Paul making Deuteronomy 30 out to be saying?

He introduces the citation with an allusion to an earlier passage in the same book, Deut 9:4 (cf. too 8:17). This too is significant in itself.[389] "Do not say in your heart," Moses warns Israel, "it is because of my righteousness that YHWH has brought me in to occupy this land." It is a warning, in other words, against exactly that fault that Paul had highlighted in 10:3. The chapter goes on to emphasize the way in which Israel provoked YHWH to anger at Sinai by making the golden calf, and the fact that they only survived because of Moses' intercession. These, as we have already seen, are vital parts of the biblical background Paul has in mind throughout Romans 9. Even in this

---

387. E.g., Moo, *Romans*, 652-53. A major study of the parallel was that of M. J. Suggs, " 'The Word Is Near You': Romans 10:6-10 within the Purpose of the Letter," in *Christian History and Interpretation: Studies Presented to John Knox*, ed. W. R. Farmer et al. (Cambridge: Cambridge University Press, 1967) 289-312.

388. So, rightly, Bryan, *A Preface to Romans*, 168. See also Richard B. Hays, *Echoes of Scripture in the Letters of Paul* (New Haven: Yale University Press, 1989) 76-77.

389. See Hays, *Echoes of Scripture in the Letters of Paul*, 78-79.

introductory formula the echoes of what Paul is saying throughout the argument are too strong for us to suppose that he chose the phrase at random. How much more has he chosen, now, to give a fresh and creative reading of Deuteronomy 30.[390]

We have already argued that he, like two near-contemporaries, understands the passage as predicting that renewal of the covenant that he believed to be taking place in the movement to which he belonged—that is, in Paul's case, the messianic movement of the Lord Jesus. It makes sense, therefore, consistent with his view of Jesus elsewhere, that here he casts Jesus himself in the role that other Jewish thinkers gave to Torah or to Wisdom. Jesus the Messiah is himself God's life-giving, covenant-renewing, community-defining gift to God's people. His "coming down from heaven" and his "coming up from the deep" are the events through which this gift is made available to all. This passage belongs closely with Paul's other expressions of Wisdom christology, such as Col 1:15-20.[391] The emphasis falls on the Messiah as the embodiment of God's own Wisdom, the human being in whom, as in 8:3, God does what Torah could not. And the faith that accepts and celebrates this gift is then the true wisdom, the true Torah-observance, the sign of membership in the renewed covenant. Paul's line-by-line reading of Deut 30:12-14, which has some affinities with the "pesher" exegesis found at Qumran, is not simply a fanciful allegory or metaphor, nor is it "historically outrageous."[392] Like Qumran itself, Paul saw the community he was addressing as the people of the renewed covenant. Like many Second Temple Jews, he understood Deuteronomy to be telling a story, the story in which he himself and his contemporaries were now living, the story of restoration after the curse of exile.

Why then does Paul refer to Deuteronomy 30 as "the righteousness from faith [ἡ ἐκ πίστεως δικαιοσύνη *hē ek pisteōs dikaiosynē*]"? Because this, in the light of the whole argument of the letter so far, and especially 3:21–4:25, serves as a shorthand for his belief that in the Messiah God

has at last done what he promised to Abraham, and, as here, what he promised in Deuteronomy 30. He has thereby established the renewed covenant; "righteousness," as a status that people can enjoy, denotes membership in that covenant. And the badge of membership is faith. Paul's exegesis of Deuteronomy 30 thus explains what he means by the Messiah's being the goal of Torah: this covenant renewal, this promised life for those who discover that the word is not far off, but very near to them, this status of being God's people, evidenced by faith in God's Messiah—this is what Torah envisaged all along, but in and of itself could not perform. The parallels with 7:7–8:11 should be obvious.

**10:6-7.** The two moments of the Messiah's work that Paul highlights in vv. 6-7 are his "coming down" and his "raising up." There is no problem about the latter; Jesus' resurrection has been a main presupposition of this letter from its very opening (1:4), anchoring the argument at some of its most decisive moments (4:24-25; 8:11, 34; the descent into the abyss echoes Ps 107:26). But what does Paul mean by the Messiah's "coming down from heaven"?

There are two main options. The first is to see this as a reference to his coming from God, the incarnation of God's pre-existent Wisdom. The second is to understand it as his coming from heaven in the parousia.[393] Each has something to be said for it, but in my judgment the balance of probability tilts to the first. It fits with the Wisdom christology of Col 1:15-20; it belongs with Rom 8:3, which as we have seen is anyway close in meaning to the present passage; it prepares the way for the confession κύριος Ἰησοῦς (*kyrios Iēsous*), "Jesus is Lord," in v. 9;[394] it belongs with the double emphasis on Jesus as God's son and David's son in 1:3-4; it goes with the incarnational stress of 9:5, echoed as we saw in 10:11-13. I

---

390. Against Moo, *Romans*, 651.

391. On which see N. T. Wright, *The Climax of the Covenant: Christ and the Law in Pauline Theology* (Minneapolis: Fortress, 1991) chap. 5. Paul, like Baruch, echoes the wisdom literature at various points here. See, e.g., Prov 30:4; Wis 16:13.

392. Against Hays, *Echoes of Scripture in the Letters of Paul*, 82.

393. Most ancient commentators took it to refer to the incarnation. For details and support, see C. E. B. Cranfield, *A Critical and Exegetical Commentary on the Epistle to the Romans*, ICC, 2 vols. (Edinburgh: T. & T. Clark, 1975) 524-25; Joseph A. Fitzmyer, *Romans*, AB 33 (Garden City, N.Y.: Doubleday, 1993) 590; Douglas J. Moo, *The Epistle to the Romans*, NICNT (Grand Rapids: Eerdmans, 1996) 655-56. The second is urged by Ernst Käsemann, *Commentary on Romans*, trans. Geoffrey W. Bromiley (London: SCM, 1980) 288; and James D. G. Dunn, *Romans 9–16*, 38B (Dallas: Word, 1988) 605.

394. On the "divine" nature of Jesus' "lordship," see Phil 2:10-11 in the context of the poem of Phil 2:6-11 as a whole; see also Wright, *The Climax of the Covenant*, chap. 4.

suggest that Paul intends his fresh reading of Deut 30:11-14 to say: "the covenant has been renewed, following the devastation of exile, through the Messiah's coming from God and his resurrection from the dead. This has meant that God has brought his 'word' near to you, placing it on your lips as you confess Jesus as Lord, writing it on your heart as you believe that he was raised from the dead."

**10:8.** This, he says, is the "word of faith" that "we preach." For the first time, Paul's apostolic vocation becomes part of the actual argument of chaps. 9–11; this will grow through 10:14-18, and play a crucial role in 11:13-14. From that perspective, we can see what he is saying: his own announcing of Jesus as the risen Lord, summoning people to "the obedience of faith" (1:5), is itself part of the answer to the prayer of 10:1. That is why, in v. 9, he goes on to explain that when faith happens it leads to salvation, that for which he prayed at the start of the chapter.

**10:9.** Paul then explains this with a remarkable statement, one of the clearest in all his writings, of what precisely Christian faith consists of. It is not, for him, a vague religious awareness, a general sense of the presence of a benevolent deity. It is the confession of Jesus as Lord and the belief that God raised him from the dead.

This, of course, is what undergirds the earlier argument of the letter, as is apparent from 1:3-5 and 4:24-25. Verbal confession of Jesus as Lord was a primitive baptismal formula (see Acts 22:16; 1 Cor 12:3; 2 Cor 4:5; Phil 2:11);[395] it also, from early on, lay at the heart of the confrontation between the kingdom theology of the early church and the ideology of imperial Rome. Jesus' resurrection was, for Paul, the demonstration that he really was the Messiah; his belief in Jesus as the turning-point of Jewish and world history, the bearer of God's purposes, the climax of the story of God's covenant, is unthinkable without it. The resurrection is to be understood, as always in Paul, as the action of God (see 4:24; on the centrality of Jesus' resurrection for Paul, see 1 Thess 4:14; 1 Corinthians 15). And when Paul declares that belief in Jesus' resurrection is located in the heart, he links the argument with 2:28-29 and 5:5 (see

also 2:15; 6:17; 8:27); the very core of the personality is where the renewal must take place, and belief in the resurrection is the telltale symptom of that renewal (Paul's fullest statement is 1 Corinthians 15; see also 1 Cor 6:14; 2 Cor 4:14; Gal 1:1). Belief in Jesus' resurrection is thus not an arbitrary dogmatic test, a demonstration that one is prepared to believe something ridiculous on someone else's supposed divine authority. Genuine heart-level belief can only come about, Paul believed, through the action of the Spirit in the gospel. This faith is the sure sign that the gospel has done its work.

**10:10.** He then explains v. 9 in more detail, separating out "righteousness" and "salvation." He is probably not intending to say that "belief" only goes with "righteousness," or that "confession" only belongs with "salvation"; he may well be saying nearly the same thing from two different angles. However, it is noteworthy that, unlike many people who have thought to summarize his thought, he does not normally speak of "salvation by faith," but rather "righteousness by faith" (as in v. 4, we should note that Paul uses the noun "righteousness," though the NIV and the NRSV turn this into the verb "justified"—as they do in the second half of the verse, turning "salvation" into "saved"). The two are closely correlated but not identical. "Righteousness" denotes the status people have on the basis of faith: a present legal status that anticipates the future verdict of the divine lawcourt, a present covenantal status that anticipates final affirmation of membership in God's people. "Salvation" denotes the actual rescue from sin and death effected in the future by the promised resurrection, and likewise anticipated in the present (so, e.g., 8:24). "Salvation" is not a status but an event, and it is promised to those who have "righteousness" as their status.

The connection of righteousness with faith is clear; the connection of salvation with verbal confession of Jesus as Lord is not so obvious. It may well be that Paul is thinking of "Jesus is Lord" as the baptismal confession, and that, as in Romans 6, he is understanding baptism as the present anticipation of final resurrection—that is, salvation from sin and death. This would make good sense, but, unlike most of the other places where we are able to fill in the gaps in his dense, almost shorthand writing, it is a connection he nowhere makes explicit.

---

395. See also Dunn, *Romans 9–16,* 607; Käsemann, *Romans,* 291. On "Lord" see the Commentary on 1:5 and 10:12-13 below.

**10:11.** The final explanation in the present sequence consists of the quotation from Isa 28:16, which returns us to where we were in 9:33. This helps us to appreciate the flow of thought in seeing 10:1-11 as a whole, from the prayer about more Jews being saved, through the exposition of the messianic covenant renewal in which that prayer can be answered, to the affirmation of salvation for all who believe. "The one who believes in him will not be put to shame" (the NIV's "disappointed" is weak and breaks the implied link with 1:16 [see also 5:5], not to mention 9:33; "not put to shame" is clearly intended as equivalent to "saved" in v. 13). Paul has inserted, at the start of the quotation, the little word πᾶς (*pas,* "all"). Everyone who believes in him will be saved. Here there is no question that the "him" is Jesus the Lord, the risen Messiah. But once we have understood Paul's use of Deuteronomy 30, there is no problem, either, in seeing this Jesus as the law's true fulfillment and goal. He is both the stumbling-stone and the object of faith: a scandal to Jews, folly to Greeks, but God's wisdom and power for those who are called, Jew and Greek alike (1 Cor 1:23-24). This universality is the point with which Paul will now round off the paragraph.

**10:12-13.** "There is no distinction." We are back once more, in the long and unwinding spiral, at a point as it were directly above 3:22-23. There, the fact of there being no distinction between Jew and Greek highlighted the fact that all alike were in sin, and all alike were redeemed and justified by the faithful death of the Messiah and through faith in God's covenant action in him, not some other way. The present passage has no mention either of sin, or of Jesus' death to deal with it. That is now taken for granted, and the argument has moved on round the spiral to consequent topics, already outlined in 3:27-30. Jew and Gentile come together in sharing the common faith in the same Lord (Paul is already looking ahead to chap. 14). And the "Lord" in question, while identified from the earlier verses as Jesus the Messiah, is equally the κύριος (*kyrios*) of the LXX. This is where the breathtaking assertion of 9:5, that the Messiah who belonged to Israel according to the flesh is also "God over all, blessed for ever," shows up at the heart of the argument. This is where christology determines ecclesiology—including where the church stands vis-à-vis the pagan emperor!—as

well as soteriology. "The same Lord is Lord of all."[396] That was what Caesar claimed, and it was what Paul claimed for Jesus. At the same time, Paul is picking up, and transforming, a regular Jewish theme: one God, therefore one people of Israel (cf. Zech 14:9-17).[397] Where, before, "no distinction" was explained by "for all have sinned" (3:23), now it can be explained by "for there is one Lord of all." As in 3:27-30, monotheism undergirds the universality of the gospel—though, as elsewhere in Paul, it is monotheism with Jesus at the heart of it.[398]

Paul does not stop to theorize about this christology, but unless we recognize that this is what he has in mind here we will not have grasped the heart of his argument. Romans 10:12-13 is basically a statement about God, as indeed the whole section of chaps. 9–11 is an argument about God. The idea of God being "rich," already mentioned in 9:23, looks ahead to 11:33. Paul's expression here is dense; literally, it means "being rich toward all."[399] God's own riches are the underlying subject of the section, and it is on that basis that "all who call on the name of the Lord will be saved."[400]

The "all" of Joel 2:32 (LXX 3:5) has cast its shadow before it in Paul's addition to Isa 28:16 in v. 11 and in the repeated "all" of v. 12. The quotation from Joel is a further point at which we are right to hear echoes of God's renewal of the covenant.[401] Joel 2 sits comfortably alongside Deuteronomy 30 as a powerful statement of how God will restore the fortunes of Israel after devastating judgment. When we read the whole chapter there are various echoes of what Paul has already said. The children of Zion are to rejoice in YHWH their God, because of his gift of the early rain for their vindication (εἰς δικαιοσύνην *eis dikaiosynēn*)

396. Cf. Acts 10:36. Detailed discussion in C. K. Rowe, "Romans 10:13: What Is the Name of the Lord?" *Horizons in Biblical Theology* 22 (2000) 146-50. Among Second Temple references to Israel's God as "Lord of all," see 1QapGen 20:13; 4Q409 1:6; Josephus *Antiquities of the Jews* 20:90.

397. See Rowe, "Romans 10:13," 147.

398. See Wright, *The Climax of the Covenant,* chaps. 4–6.

399. The NIV ("richly blesses all") and the NRSV ("is generous to all") do not catch the emphasis, which is on the supreme riches that belong to God and are now shared with others. It is possible for a poor person to be generous; Paul's point is (a) that God is not poor but supremely rich and (b) that God shares these riches lavishly.

400. "Call upon the name of YHWH" is a frequent biblical way of designating Israel. See Dunn, *Romans 9–16,* 610-11. For similar formulae in early Christianity, see Acts 2:21; 9:14, 21 (where the phrase is almost a definition of a Christian); 22:16 (a baptismal context); and 1 Cor 1:2; 2 Tim 2:22.

401. On the use of Joel here, see Rowe, "Romans 10:13," 152-56.

(2:23). God declares (2:26) that "my people shall never again be put to shame" (οὐ μὴ καταισχυνθῇ ὁ λαός μου *ou mē kataischynthē ho laos mou*), and repeats it with emphasis a verse later (οὐ μὴ καταισχυνθῶσιν οὐκέτι πᾶς ὁ λαός μου εἰς τὸν αἰῶνα *ou mē kataischynthōsin ouketi pas ho laos mou eis ton aiōna*, "all my people shall never, ever, ever again be put to shame"). Joel 2:26-27 is thus extremely close to Isa 28:16, supplying the "all"; perhaps we should regard the scriptural quotation in 10:11 itself as a combination of Isaiah and Joel.

Looming up behind these detailed points, we should not miss the force of v. 13 in relation to the argument of chaps. 9–11 as a whole. If "those who call on the name of the Lord" is a regular biblical designation for "Israel," then v. 13 is an exact functional equivalent of 11:26 *a:* "All Israel shall be saved."[402] Verse 13 supplies Paul's initial answer to the problem of 10:1, and suggests the correct way of understanding 11:26 *a.*

The Joel passage supplies another strong hint, which we might have guessed from where we are in the "spiral" of Paul's thought, and indeed from the other use to which the same passage is put in the NT. There is here, I suggest, an allusion to the work of the Spirit in renewing the covenant, in restoring the fortunes of God's people (see 2:27-29 and 8:1-11, both of which are thematically close to the present passage; elsewhere in NT see Acts 2:16-21, the day of Pentecost). In Joel 2:28-29, God promises to pour out the divine Spirit on all the members of the community (the "all" is again emphatic). There will be portents in heaven and on earth; and at that time "everyone who calls on the name of the Lord shall be saved, for in Mount Zion and in Jerusalem there shall be those who escape" (LXX ἀνασωζόμενος *anasōzomenos*), "and among the survivors shall be those whom the Lord calls" (καὶ εὐαγγελιζόμενοι οὓς κύριος προσκέκληται *kai euangelizomenoi hous kyrios proskeklētai*, 2:32 [LXX 3:5]). The LXX readings indicate, indeed, that for Paul this text also projects him forward into the next passage, linking with "those who preach the gospel" in Isa 52:7. But the main point to note is that here, in the close hinterland of Paul's thought, we are right to see the Spirit at work, through the preaching of the

gospel of Jesus as Lord, to bring people to faith and confession and so to righteousness and salvation. People, we note once more, of all sorts: Jew and Greek, alike and together. This is the initial answer to the prayer of 10:1.

The message of 10:5-13 is so positive and upbeat—God renewing the covenant through the dramatic, even apocalyptic, events concerning Jesus, and throwing open membership to all and sundry—that if Paul had stopped there we would wonder what the problem was. Why the grief of 9:1-5? Why the earnest prayer of 10:1? Surely all that is now needed is for the message of this new covenant, this inbreaking love of God, to be announced, and people everywhere, especially the Jewish people, whose Scriptures were being fulfilled, whose Messiah had now arrived—surely they would all believe it and enjoy the new day that was dawning? Sadly, no. The renewal of the covenant is also the word of judgment, of God's confrontation with human wickedness, including Jewish wickedness (2:17-24). The problem of chaps. 9–11 is that Israel does not want to hear such a scandalous message. Verses 14-21 do indeed take the story forward into the new world that has come into being as a result of the messianic events. But the paradox that cuts right across any sense of a smooth line, of God's purposes going ahead with no problem, comes to the fore in Israel's persistent recalcitrance. The excitement of the apostolic mission and the heartbreak of Israel's refusal come together in the final part (10:14-21) of this section (9:30–10:21), and together set the scene for chap. 11.

**10:14-21.** The key to this whole part of the chapter is found in 11:13-14: Paul celebrates his apostolic vocation to preach to the Gentiles in order to make his "flesh" jealous and so save some of them. Verses 14-15 explain, in a burst of rhetorical questions, that for the renewed covenant to operate people need to be sent with the news. This puts Paul himself on the map of biblical fulfillment (10:16-18): Isaiah 52–53 spoke of God's coming actions through the Messiah, and of the people who would take the message to the whole world, even though not everyone would listen. But, tragically (10:19-21), Israel according to the flesh remained by and large aloof from it all. They knew from their own prophecies, including Deuteronomy 32, that God would bring Gentiles

402. So, rightly, ibid., 156.

in to share their blessings; but they have remained unbelieving. This is as close as Paul gets to an explicit statement of the problem that haunts Romans 9–11 as a whole. The passage is about more than simply "Israel's accountability"; it is about the inclusion of Gentiles so as to make Israel "jealous."

**10:14-15.** Four questions and a quotation explain the need for the Gentile mission that constitutes Paul's apostolic vocation, and place it on the same map of biblical prophecy that Paul has been sketching for several verses past. The questions—a unique rhetorical device in Paul—take us from the picture we have seen in 10:5-13, of people of all sorts coming to share in the covenant blessings by faith, through to the necessity, and the biblical mandate, of the apostolic mission. For people to "call on the name of the Lord," as Joel says they must, they must first have faith; but this is impossible unless they hear of the Messiah so that they can believe in him. For this, in turn, they need someone to announce him to them; and for that, the announcers need to be "sent" (ἀποσταλῶσιν *apostalōsin*, "apostled"). So far, the argument is simply: if people are to be saved under this new covenant, what has to happen is for God to "send," to commission as "apostles," people to take the message to them. Paul adds Isa 52:7: How beautiful are the feet of the messengers of good news![403] As the following passage seems to indicate, Paul understands the message concerning YHWH's servant in Isaiah 52–53 as the message about Jesus the Messiah. The people who announce the servant-message are therefore the people who now, in his own day, proclaim Jesus. The effect of vv. 14-15 is to say: this is how my own apostolic ministry fits into the large narrative of exile and restoration, of God restoring the covenant in the Messiah and calling both Jews and Gentiles into the renewed community (9:24).

Paul's apostleship was, as he says often enough, aimed at the Gentiles (1:5; 15:18; Gal 1:16; 2:2, 7; cf. Acts 9:15; 15:12; Eph 3:8; 1 Tim 2:7). It was not his primary task to take the message to Jews, though according to Acts he regularly began by speaking in synagogues (suffering the consequences, as he describes in 2 Cor 11:24; cf. Acts 13:5, 14; 14:1; 17:1-2, 10, 17; 18:4, 19; 19:8; see also 28:17, 23). He reports in Gal 2:9 a division of labor: he and his coworkers should go to the Gentiles, leaving Peter and others to go to Jews. When, therefore, he refers to his apostleship here, we may assume he is primarily thinking of speaking to Gentiles. However, as he says in 11:13-14, this is undertaken with one eye over his shoulder to see what effect it will have on his kinsfolk.

It is possible to take another view of this passage: to see vv. 14-18, as well as vv. 19-21, referring to a (largely unsuccessful) mission to Jews.[404] This is a further example of a problem we met earlier in the letter: when does the subject turn to Israel specifically (see chap. 2, where the explicit turn to the Jews in 2:17 corresponds to the explicit statement here)?[405] Here, however, the passage itself does seem to give a clear indication of what Paul has in mind. Not only does 10:19 specify "Israel" for the first time; had that been the subject all along, Paul would most likely have been content, as in vv. 16 and 18, with a simply third-person plural verb, "they. . . . " More important, when he asks whether Israel "knew" (v. 19), the thing Israel did in fact know, highlighted with the quotation from Deut 32:21, is precisely that God would bring in Gentiles to share Israel's privileges, thus making them jealous. The probability, then, is that in vv. 14-18 he is talking about the (partially successful) Gentile mission, and that only with vv. 19-21 does he turn, by contrast, to the (mostly unsuccessful) Jewish mission. The final paragraph of the section thus corresponds to the opening (9:30-33): Gentiles (to their own surprise) are coming in, while Jews are stumbling over the "stone."

**10:16-17.** In vv. 14-15 Paul has explained the need for his mission to the Gentiles, looking back to his opening statement in 1:5. Now he refers to another element in the same verse: the

---

403. Also Nah 1:15 [2:1 LXX]; but the following verse shows it is Isaiah whom Paul has in mind. The word for "messengers" is εὐαγγελιζόμενοι (*euangelizomenoi*, "gospelers"), which echoes Joel 2:32 [3:5 LXX], the verse Paul quoted in 10:13. For the translation "timely" instead of "beautiful," see BDAG 1103; Fitzmyer, *Romans,* 595, 597; Bryan, *A Preface to Romans,* 176.

404. That is presumably the view of the NIV, which heads the section 9:30–10:21 as "Israel's Unbelief" and adds "the Israelites" as the subject of v. 16. The NRSV, starting a new paragraph at v. 18 and introducing v. 19 with "Again I ask" for Paul's ἀλλὰ λέγω (*alla legō;* lit., "but I say"), may imply the same understanding; "they" in v. 18 presumes continuity of subject with the previous verses.

405. Christopher Bryan, *A Preface to Romans: Notes on the Epistle in Its Literary and Cultural Setting* (Oxford: Oxford University Press, 2000) 177, rightly sees v. 19 as the point to which Paul is leading through his exposition of the worldwide mission.

"obedience of faith." Not everyone, he says, obeyed the gospel ("accepted," NIV, is scarcely a translation of ὑπήκουσαν [hypēkousan], but reflects instead the un-Pauline assumption that "the gospel" is something offered on a take-it-or-leave-it basis, rather than an authorized summons from the world's rightful Lord). This is unlikely to be a wry, understated comment on the large-scale failure of Jews to obey the word; that, after all, is the central problem of the entire section, not something to be introduced obliquely in this way. It is far more likely to be a comment on the Gentile mission, in which, though many did believe, many more did not.[406]

Paul's aim here is not so much to face an objection ("But, Paul, if that's how the gospel is meant to work, why doesn't everyone obey it?") but to confirm the chain of events in vv. 14-15 from a second angle, summarized in v. 17. He links this chain to the previous one by quoting a closely adjacent passage of Isaiah to the one just mentioned (i.e., Isa 52:7). "Lord, who believed our report?" (Isa 53:1); this is the prophet's plaintive cry at the start of the main section of the fourth "servant song" (52:13–53:12). Paul sees himself as embodying, in his mission, the prophetic task of announcing the Messiah to the world. The word Isaiah uses for "message" is ἀκοή (akoē). Though this word can also refer to the faculty of hearing, the act of hearing or listening, and the organ with which one hears (i.e., the ear), the meaning here is the thing that is heard: the report or message (see also Gal 3:2, 5; the KJV's "faith cometh by hearing" is thus misleading, as is "act of hearing").[407]

This enables Paul to construct the sequence in v. 17: faith comes from the message, and the message happens through "the word of the Messiah," or perhaps "the word about the Messiah," or perhaps even "the word which is the Messiah."[408] The word for "word" here is ῥῆμα (rhēma), which is rare in Paul; apart from the present passage, it is found only

in 2 Cor 12:4; 13:1 (also an OT quotation); and Eph 5:26; 6:17. He much prefers to use λόγος (logos). The chances are that he uses rhēma because his mind has still not left Deut 30:14, quoted in v. 8 (ἐγγύς σου τὸ ῥῆμά ἐστιν engys sou to rhēma estin, "the word is near you." This, indeed, may be the reason for quoting Ps 18:5 in the next verse, where "their words" (τὰ ῥήματα αὐτῶν ta rhēmata autōn) go out to the end of the earth. The causal chain Paul is establishing is not simply (a) the preached message, (b) the message as heard, and (c) faith; indeed, for there to be a significant difference between the "message" and the "word of Christ," it is likely that the latter phrase denotes something more than "what preachers like me say about the Messiah." When we put v. 17 alongside v. 8, the sequence is clearer: faith comes from the message, and the message occurs through "the word which is near you," the word that has come down from heaven and up from the depths of death, the word that is the Messiah himself, God's self-revelation, God's wisdom, Torah in person. The chain is thus (a) the "word" in this full sense, (b) the preaching of this "word" (i.e., of Jesus as Messiah and Lord), and (c) faith.

**10:18.** The worldwide "hearing" of the message is now, it seems, undergirded by the grand claim of Ps 19:4 [19:5 MT, LXX]: "their sound went out into all the world, and their words to the ends of the earth." This is offered as the answer to "did they not hear": to restrict this to Jews, when the whole point of the verse is its worldwide universality, is to force a narrow interpretative scheme onto Paul's text.[409] But what precisely Paul means is, at first sight, a puzzle. The verse can scarcely refer to Paul's own apostolic mission, since (a) the psalm refers to the glory of God displayed in the created order and (b) it suggests a universality that neither Paul nor all his fellow apostles together have yet achieved. Option (a) is especially intriguing: If the message were so effectively proclaimed by creation itself, the need for apostles, carefully set out in vv. 14-17, would be undermined. It is possible that Paul means here what he means in Col 1:23, where he speaks of the gospel having been announced to every creature under heaven; this is best taken as a reference to the cosmic message that went out at the

---

406. Against Douglas J. Moo, *The Epistle to the Romans,* NICNT (Grand Rapids: Eerdmans, 1996) 664.

407. Joseph A. Fitzmyer, *Romans,* AB 33 (Garden City, N.Y.: Doubleday, 1993) 598.

408. Many good MSS have "of God," but "of the Messiah" has decisive support and, as the more unusual phrase, is virtually certain to be right. Many scribes, like many modern commentators, will have missed the allusion back to v. 8. C. K. Barrett, *A Commentary on the Epistle to the Romans* (London: A. & C. Black, 1957) 205, has suggested that v. 17 may be a gloss, but most find this implausible.

409. Against Fitzmyer, *Romans,* 599.

resurrection of Jesus, the message that death had been defeated and that the world was now a different place.[410] This message still needed Paul as its "minister." There may be something of that here, though the explicit reference to revelation through the created order itself is hardly the same thing, and puts us in mind rather of the revelation mentioned in 1:19-20, a revelation that, though true, proved not enough to save those who received it. It is also possible that, if Paul has the rest of Psalm 19 in mind, he may have taken vv. 1-6, as well as vv. 7-11, as referring to Torah, in which case he could be celebrating the fact that the "word" of Deut 30:14 was now freely available to all, as God always intended. The link between the occurrences of *rhēma* in vv. 8 and 17-18 seems to point in this direction. That seems to me the most likely understanding, though certainty here is perhaps out of reach.[411]

The Gentile world, then, has heard the gospel. Not all have believed; but, as he said in 9:30, Gentiles who were not looking for covenant membership have received it. Meanwhile, Israel, embracing the Torah, which did indeed hold out the status of "righteousness," the prospect of covenant membership, has not attained to that Torah. Instead (and this is what is driving the whole section), Israel has to look on as outsiders come to share the blessings that had been promised, blessings to which they had looked forward for so long. This is the point with which the chapter now closes.

**10:19-21.** Did Israel not know? "Know" here is preferable to "understand" (NRSV, NIV, and several others; the NEB's "failed to recognize the message" shows that the point has been missed). Not only is it the more basic meaning of the word; the answers Paul gives, quoting from Deuteronomy 32 and Isaiah 65, are not a demonstration that Israel did after all "understand" the gospel, or recognize it for what it was. They are a demonstration that Israel had long ago been warned that Gentiles would be coming in to share, and even apparently to take over, the blessings they had been promised. What Israel could not claim ignorance of, in other

words, was not "the gospel," as is sometimes suggested, but the more specific point that Paul had stated first in 9:30-31.[412] This is what the first two quotations are about.

The first is from Deut 32:21. Deuteronomy 32 is the song of Moses, a great, sprawling poem mixing powerful praise to God and scathing indictment of Israel. It is clearly a significant passage for early Christian writers; there are three direct quotations from it in Romans alone, and numerous allusions (in Romans: Deut 32:35 at Rom 12:19; 32:43 at 15:10). The rebellious ways of Israel are detailed in Deut 32:15-18; they ungratefully spurned God after all that had been done for them. In 32:19-25 the judgments that God will visit upon them are listed. According to 32:20, they are "children who do not have faith"; and 32:21 declares that as they have provoked YHWH to jealousy with their idols, beings that are not real gods, so YHWH will make them jealous with "those who are not a people" (perhaps, in Paul's mind, an echo of 9:25-26). Paul clearly takes this as a prophecy of God's call of Gentiles to enjoy Israel's privileges.[413] He will in the next chapter use this key category of "jealousy" as the fulcrum around which to turn his crucial argument.

The second quotation is from Isa 65:1, leading to the third, which is from the following verse. Isaiah, declares Paul, announces the shocking result: "boldly" (NIV) is a reference to the stark, almost horrifying content of what is said, more than to the prophet's state of mind. Again the theme (the continuing answer to the question "did Israel not know?") is the bringing of Gentiles, who were not seeking YHWH or membership in the chosen people, into good standing, just as in 9:30-31. Isaiah 65 comes straight after the long prayer for God to intervene at the time of Israel's devastation (63:15–64:12), a prayer that Paul himself might have been imitating in 10:1. This larger passage has several echoes of Romans 9–10. God is Israel's father, whether or not Abraham acknowledges it (63:16; cf. Rom 9:7-9); God has hardened their heart, making them go astray (63:17; cf. Rom 9:17-18); Israel's righteousness is like an unclean

---

410. See N. T. Wright, *The Epistles of Paul to the Colossians and to Philemon: An Introduction and Commentary* (Grand Rapids: Eerdmans, 1986) 84-85.

411. See Richard B. Hays, *Echoes of Scripture in the Letters of Paul* (New Haven: Yale University Press, 1989) 175.

412. So Fitzmyer, *Romans*, 595, 599.

413. Sirach 50:25-26 declares that the writer's soul is vexed with two nations, Samaria and Philistia, and also with a third, which is "no nation"—namely "the foolish people who dwell at Sichar." On the various rabbinic interpretations of the "non-nations," see SB 3.284-85.

garment (64:6; cf. Rom 9:30-10:3); no one calls on YHWH's name (64:7; cf. Rom 10:13); but nevertheless God is the potter and Israel the clay (64:8; cf. Rom 9:20-23). But God's response is clear (65:1-2): "I was found by those who were not looking for me; I said 'Look, here I am' to a nation that was not calling on my name. Meanwhile, I stretched out my hands all day long to a rebellious people." Paul understands the first verse to refer, as in 9:30, to the Gentiles who are coming in even though they were not expecting or wanting to, and the second to refer, as in 9:31-3, to Israel itself, remaining recalcitrant, "unbelieving and opposing."

The argument has come full circle. Paul has brought the story up to date. From Abraham to exodus, from the exile to the Messiah; and now that the Messiah has come, the new mode of covenant membership, of Torah-observance, of "righteousness," is open, and those who confess Jesus as Lord and believe that God raised him from the dead share not only this status but also the salvation promised as a result. Paul sees Gentiles entering this heritage as he announces the gospel around the world. He is praying that his fellow Jews may enter it too. At the present time, though, he sees the majority of them as Isaiah saw them: unwilling to countenance this fresh revelation from their God. The implied question of 9:1-5, and the prayer of 10:1, are thus left hanging in the air. What will happen next? Having told his version of the story about God and Israel in the past, Paul will now move cautiously to tell a story about God and Israel in the future.

# REFLECTIONS

**1.** The most important thing Paul does in this section is to explain where he, his readers, and the people he is discussing are within God's story with Israel and the world. Learning to think like this—to understand a grand narrative that is larger than ourselves, that may be challenging or even threatening to us—is a major task for those who undertake to live with Scripture. Of course, in our day grand narratives of all sorts have been called into question. They are felt to be hegemonic, attempts to snatch or guard the citadel of power; and, of course, they can be used like that. But the story Paul tells resists all such attempts to deconstruct it. It is the story of how people who had no airs and graces of their own, no thought of being sought by Israel's God, the creator, nevertheless found themselves grasped by the divine call and love as an act of sheer grace. And it is also the story—here Paul is doing some deconstruction of his own—of the shock received by the people who thought the God-and-world story could only be told, and would always be told, with them coming out on top. The climax of their own history was a Messiah who, from their point of view, was as it were an anti-Messiah. The king came, and instead of setting his people free he died their death and invited them to follow him. Only if they do so will they find the fulfillment of their own story: He is, indeed, the true King, the world's true Lord, and will give salvation to all who call on his name.

**2.** At the level of learning to read the Bible, both the ancient Scriptures of Israel and the strange writings of the early Christians, we are bound to be struck by the sheer demand of a text like this. Isaiah, Leviticus, Deuteronomy, Isaiah again, Joel, Isaiah once more, twice more, a psalm, Deuteronomy again, then Isaiah again: and each text Paul quotes opens up a world, a story, an argument, a celebration, a warning, which needs to be understood as a whole, not simply in the short passage quoted. Paul's mental world is furnished by entire biblical arguments and sequences of thought, and when he quotes or alludes to them he wants the whole passage to resonate. And many of the texts he quotes are themselves caught up, both in their biblical originals and in the ways they were read in Second Temple Judaism, in a complex web of allusion and intertextual echo, creating more meanings, sustaining old stories and inventing new ones, so that we sometimes despair of ever recovering more than a fraction of what was in the mind not only of Paul but of a hypothetical ideal first-century reader.

We should not despair. We may never understand it all, but we can make some significant strides in the right direction. And the lesson we should learn, at the level of method and Christian education, is that (to put it crudely) it is always worth looking up references. Indeed, it is always worth having a Bible with good cross-references; the current fashion for printing Bibles without such aids to inner-biblical reference may save money, but it leaves readers thin on information that could change how they approach the text, and ultimately how they understand and live it.

**3.** The story Paul tells, of the Messiah as the climax of Israel's history and the strange stumbling of Israel and ingathering of Gentiles, is unique. He does not expect this sequence of events to be played out in other settings and at other times, or in relation to other peoples. The Messiah is not an example of a general pattern in history, still less church history. The protestant tendency to expect a revolution in each generation, and to justify it from the events of the first generation, needs to be held in check by the equally important protestant principle that the death of Jesus Christ was "once for all" (6:10).Yet a shadow from this story may indeed fall across the pages of church history from time to time. There may sometimes be people with apparent privilege who need to see themselves as "ignorant of God's righteousness, and seeking to establish their own." There may be people on the margins who need to be brought in by God's surprising and unimagined grace. And, however unique Paul's apostleship, there needs to be a steady supply of people to be "sent" to announce the message, to tell the world of its rightful Lord. Isaiah's promise of the messengers whose very feet are blessed can be just as true in the twenty-first century as it was in the first.

**4.** At the heart of the passage is the message of covenant renewal, drawn out of Deuteronomy with breathtaking and yet historically grounded exegesis. The Messiah has brought the long story of Torah to its climax and goal, and all are now summoned to the faith through which Torah finds itself strangely fulfilled, even by those who did not know it (see also 2:25-29). The challenge of this in our own day is that "new covenant" theology is deeply unwelcome to two groups of readers. The first are those for whom any continuity between God's ways with Israel in the past and God's ways now, after Calvary and Easter, is under suspicion for failing to take the cross seriously enough. This charge will not stick in the present context: The cross is woven into the very fabric of Paul's argument throughout chaps. 9–11, as the Messiah's people "according to the flesh" discover what that means in practice. The second group are those who are so concerned to stress (like Paul himself) that God has not finished with Israel according to the flesh that they are anxious about even the talk of renewal. What, they say, was wrong with things as they were? And they are ready to label as oppressive, or otherwise incorrect, any possible answer Paul or anybody today might come up with.

At this point the exegete and theologian have to hold their nerve. Just because there have been substandard versions of the Christian story that have had devastatingly awful consequences for Jews (and others, for that matter), this does not mean that the Christian, not least the serious reader of Paul, must back off from making the central Christian claim, that Jesus of Nazareth was and is Israel's Messiah and the world's true Lord, and that the one God did indeed renew the ancient covenant in and through him. Indeed, as we have remarked before, not to make claims like this is, ironically, to de-Judaize Christianity, leaving the way open for Christians to demonize Jews as "the Other." Paul takes the apparently risky route—but it is the only one available—of trying to teach his readers to think in a Messiah-shaped fashion about God's dealings with the whole world, including Israel, in the belief that this will lead, not to demonization, but to Christians being grateful to the Jewish people (9:4-5) and praying to God on their behalf (10:1). This is not the last word on the subject. The chapter that follows will insist on humility replacing arrogance. But it is certainly one of the first words that needs to be said.

**5.** The sequence of short questions in 10:14-17 has often, rightly, been seen as pointing to the vocation, which remains in force, to announce the gospel of Jesus throughout the world. Many, reading these words, have had that strange sense of being confronted with a challenge that they dare not ignore. All Christians, reading them, should at least ask themselves, and more important ask God in prayer, whether they are among those who will be "sent" as heralds, enabling women, men, and children in every country and race to hear the good news, so that some at least may come to believe. Paul never promises, any more than the prophets did (think of Isa 53:1, quoted in 10:16; think, too, of Isa 6:9-13), that this will be easy, successful, or popular. Indeed, he normally implies the opposite. But the light that keeps shining through in his writings, the joy that insists on bubbling up to the surface of the toughest argument and the saddest problem, and the sense of purpose that sustains writer and reader through the long and winding discussions, remind us that the surface problems and sufferings, many though they may be, cannot be compared with the glory that will be revealed to us.

# ROMANS 11:1-36, THE SALVATION OF "ALL ISRAEL" IN FULFILLMENT OF GOD'S UNBREAKABLE PROMISES

## OVERVIEW

The conclusion of the section brings Paul to one of the most majestic sustained arguments in all his writing. Unfortunately it is also one of the most controversial. At the very point where he wants to bring his readers to the mountaintop and show them the glorious view all around, centuries of re-reading and misreading have created a fog in which interpreters wander to and fro, speculating as to what the view might look like if only we were able to see it. And yet the main thrust of the chapter, in itself and in its place within Romans 9–11 as a whole and indeed the epistle as a whole, ought not to be in doubt.

The questions Paul raised at the start of chap. 9 had to do with God and with Israel according to the flesh. The problem he faced is that Israel has, by and large, not believed the gospel of Jesus the Messiah, and that it looks therefore not only as though Paul's kinsfolk are forfeiting salvation but also as though God's own credibility, competence, wisdom, and glory are being called into question. We should not be surprised, then, that this concluding chapter draws together the threads by talking at length, head-on, about God and Israel according to the flesh.

In particular, he seizes upon the motif of "jealousy," introduced by his quotation of Deut 32:21 in 10:19, in order to develop his central point: that the fact of Gentiles coming to share their blessings is designed to make Paul's "flesh" jealous and so bring them to salvation (11:14). The way to that salvation is along the route already mapped out so carefully in 10:1-13, on the basis of Deuteronomy 30. It is faith (11:23), by which Paul continues to mean confession that Jesus is Lord and belief that God raised him from the dead. This reading of 11:11-24, as we shall see, does full justice to the text.

In 11:25-26a, however, Paul declares that, through the strange process of the hardening of Israel and the incoming of Gentiles, "all Israel shall be saved." This has caused readers down the years to believe that what Paul ultimately had in mind was not just the coming to Christian faith, during the course of ongoing history, of more Jews who, like himself, believed the gospel, but the sudden salvation of "Israel according to the flesh" in its entirety, at the very end. Many have puzzled over what exactly this means; many theories have been advanced as to how it might happen. Does he mean all Jews alive at the end, or all Jews of every age? Will this salvation be conditional on a large-scale awakening of Christian faith, or does it occur on some parallel track of divine grace? Will it be the prelude to the parousia (11:26*b* has often been taken to refer to Jesus' "Second Coming") or the result of it? Or what?

These questions have been sharpened in the last hundred years or so by two factors. First, "dispensational" theology, popular in America in particular, has highlighted the belief that, as part of the events leading toward the "millennium," ethnic Israel must return to and be established in the Holy Land, to play a crucial role in the drama that will unfold as ancient prophecies are fulfilled. Romans 11 is seen as a critical text in predicting the eventual salvation that will follow; the internationally recognized state of Israel established in 1947 is seen as the fulfillment of prophecies in the Hebrew Bible and as foreshadowing the fulfillment of Romans 11 itself.[414] Second, the horrible devastation of European Jewry at the hands of the Nazis has led conscience-stricken Christian theologians not only to search out and blame seemingly anti-Jewish texts in the New Testament, but also to highlight the present passage as offering a "two-covenant" alternative to what is seen as "super-cessionism," the belief that Christianity has "superseded" or "replaced" Judaism.[415] The popularity of the former views among many large and vigorous churches, and of the latter in influential scholarly circles, has ensured that Romans 11 is firmly fixed in many minds as a prediction that God will act on behalf of "Israel according to the flesh" in a way that bypasses what Paul saw as the normal process of coming to Christian faith. Any attempt to argue for another view is seen by some as an an exegetical equivalent of arguing that the earth is flat. (There are other pressures as well, not least the decline of a belief in "hell" and the popularity of universalism—to which Paul is then supposed to have given support in 11:32.)

Yet to decide on the meaning of a passage first and to do the exegesis afterward is always a recipe for disaster. We have seen all along that Paul's arguments in Romans, particularly in chaps. 9–11, are tightly interwoven both within the letter itself, in the context of his other writings, and in the complex and dense web of scriptural echoes and allusions. Everything he has said so far in the letter, understood both at a surface reading and in its allusive depths, inclines the reader to believe that if Romans 11 envisages ethnic Jews coming to salvation it will be by the same route as Paul himself, that is, through faith in Jesus as Messiah.[416] Consider what he has already said. He has spoken again and again of the renewal of the covenant through the Messiah, Jesus, and by the Spirit. He has made Christian faith—belief that Jesus is Lord, and that God raised him from the dead—central to his argument and pivotal for salvation, urging that this faith, and the "life" that results from it, are what the Jewish law really intended all along. He has argued in great detail that not all Abraham's physical descendants inherit the promises, but that Abraham's family is instead opened up, through faith, to people of every race. He has listed the Messiah as the crowning privilege of ethnic Israel (9:5)—and by the Messiah he obviously means Jesus himself. As we shall see, 11:1-24 is most naturally read as continuing this line of thought, developing strands already there in the argument. Since 11:25 begins with γάρ (*gar*), we should assume that it and v. 26*a* ("and so all Israel will be saved") are an explanation of what has gone before, not a new and radically different point, and if they can be read that way, with a clear line of thought going through to v. 32, the normal canons of exegesis demand that they should be. Unless, of course, Paul has contradicted himself—a possibility that several have seized upon, with variations, as the correct solution.[417] The eventual judgment depends upon the cumulative weight of several exegetical details, and will be argued for step by step.

Paul introduces the two main stages of his argument with key questions in 11:1 and 11:11: "has God forsaken his people?" and "have they [i.e., ethnic Israel] stumbled so as to fall?" Paul answers each with an emphatic "No!" To put the same point in a positive fashion, we could paraphrase the two questions: "Can any Jews then be saved?" and "Can any more Jews then be saved?"—the

---

414. J. F. Walvoord, *Israel in Prophecy* (Grand Rapids: Zondervan, 1962); J. Fischer, *The Olive Tree Connection: Sharing Messiah with Israel* (Downers Grove: InterVarsity, 1983). The work of the so-called International Christian Embassy in Jerusalem is based on this kind of thinking.

415. On the "two-covenant" proposal of Stendahl, Gager, Gaston and others, see note 302.

416. So Joseph A. Fitzmyer, *Romans*, AB 33 (Garden City, N.Y.: Doubleday, 1993) 620; Douglas J. Moo, *The Epistle to the Romans*, NICNT (Grand Rapids: Eerdmans, 1996) 725-26.

417. See E. P. Sanders, *Paul, the Law, and the Jewish People* (Philadelphia: Fortress, 1983) 199.

answer being an emphatic "Yes!" Verses 11-32 then form one sustained argument, which breaks down into three closely interrelated sections (vv. 11-16, 17-24, 25-32), and leads into the final doxology (11:33-36).

## Romans 11:1-10, God Has Not Rejected Israel

### NIV

**11** I ask then: Did God reject his people? By no means! I am an Israelite myself, a descendant of Abraham, from the tribe of Benjamin. [2]God did not reject his people, whom he foreknew. Don't you know what the Scripture says in the passage about Elijah—how he appealed to God against Israel: [3]"Lord, they have killed your prophets and torn down your altars; I am the only one left, and they are trying to kill me"[a]? [4]And what was God's answer to him? "I have reserved for myself seven thousand who have not bowed the knee to Baal."[b] [5]So too, at the present time there is a remnant chosen by grace. [6]And if by grace, then it is no longer by works; if it were, grace would no longer be grace.[c]

[7]What then? What Israel sought so earnestly it did not obtain, but the elect did. The others were hardened, [8]as it is written:

"God gave them a spirit of stupor,
　eyes so that they could not see
　and ears so that they could not hear,
to this very day."[d]

[9]And David says:

"May their table become a snare and a trap,
　a stumbling block and a retribution for
　them.
[10]May their eyes be darkened so they cannot
　see,
　and their backs be bent forever."[e]

[a] 3 1 Kings 19:10,14　[b] 4 1 Kings 19:18　[c] 6 Some manuscripts by grace. But if by works, then it is no longer grace; if it were, work would no longer be work.　[d] 8 Deut. 29:4; Isaiah 29:10　[e] 10 Psalm 69:22,23

### NRSV

**11** I ask, then, has God rejected his people? By no means! I myself am an Israelite, a descendant of Abraham, a member of the tribe of Benjamin. [2]God has not rejected his people whom he foreknew. Do you not know what the scripture says of Elijah, how he pleads with God against Israel? [3]"Lord, they have killed your prophets, they have demolished your altars; I alone am left, and they are seeking my life." [4]But what is the divine reply to him? "I have kept for myself seven thousand who have not bowed the knee to Baal." [5]So too at the present time there is a remnant, chosen by grace. [6]But if it is by grace, it is no longer on the basis of works, otherwise grace would no longer be grace.[a]

[7]What then? Israel failed to obtain what it was seeking. The elect obtained it, but the rest were hardened, [8]as it is written,

"God gave them a sluggish spirit,
　eyes that would not see
　and ears that would not hear,
down to this very day."
[9]And David says,
"Let their table become a snare and a trap,
　a stumbling block and a retribution for
　them;
[10]let their eyes be darkened so that they cannot
　see,
　and keep their backs forever bent."

[a] Other ancient authorities add But if it is by works, it is no longer on the basis of grace, otherwise work would no longer be work

# COMMENTARY

Paul introduces the two questions that shape this concluding chapter with a solemn λέγω οὖν (*legō oun*), a formula found nowhere else in his extant writings. Elsewhere when he uses λέγω (*legō*), apart from the places where it introduces an explanation of what has just been said (e.g., 1 Cor 7:8), it introduces an emphatic statement (e.g., 12:3; 15:8); here it has a solemn ring to it: "So this is the question I must raise at last. . . ."

The first question examines what might seem a possibility after the sorrowful opening of 9:1-5 and conclusion of 10:19-21. Israel according to the flesh appears to have failed completely. God has done everything possible and no response has been forthcoming. That would generate a "replacement" theology, indeed: God would have "replaced" the Jewish people with Gentiles. But that is certainly not Paul's view. He himself is both an example of a Jew who is now part of the "remnant" spoken of in 9:27, and part of the means by which God will increase the size of that remnant. But this remnant is not a small minority for whom "works-righteousness," in the senses already explored, is after all effective. It is "according to the election of grace," that is, according to the principles enunciated in 9:6-29, the negative side of which is the "hardening" spoken of in that same passage. It is misleading, therefore, to say that the "hardening" is "only partial"; the remnant that now exists, with Paul as its example, does so not by escaping the verdict of judgment but by coming through it to new life (see Gal 2:19-21).[418]

**11:1-2a.** As often, Paul introduces a new thought by proposing a conclusion that could be drawn from what has been said and then explaining why it is wrong. "Has God rejected his people?" (so NRSV; the NIV is technically correct to make this aorist: "Did God reject his people?" but the sense seems to be that of the NRSV and most translations—i.e., perfect, the present situation that results from a past event). As evidence for his rejection of this proposal, Paul cites his own case.[419] He is a

Christian, confessing Jesus as Lord and believing that God raised him from the dead; and he, of course, is a Jew, an Israelite, from the seed of Abraham (the NRSV and the NIV have "descendant," but in view of 9:7-8 it is important to note that Paul says σπέρμα [*sperma;* lit., "seed"]). What is more, he is of the tribe of Benjamin—one of the few tribes left in his day that could trace their ancestry all the way back, being from the southern tribes, who returned after the Babylonian exile (on Paul's sense of his own Jewishness and its privileges, see 2 Cor 11:22; Gal 1:13-14; Phil 3:4-6).

His own example enables him to quote emphatically from 1 Sam 12:22: "God has not rejected his people whom he foreknew" (NRSV; on God's "foreknowledge," see the Commentary on 8:29). The quotation also fits Ps 94:14 [93:14 LXX] quite closely, with only the the the verb's tense being different; the context of Ps 94:12-16 offers some suggestive wider links with Paul's argument, but the 1 Samuel reference still appears primary. This passage brings two particular overtones into Paul's context. First, the statement is Samuel's, as part of his promise that he will never stop interceding for Israel, despite their sin and folly. Samuel stands in the tradition of Moses interceding for Israel; Paul has stood in the same tradition in 9:1-5 and 10:1, and the implication here is that he is not only an example of a Jew who has been faithful to the gospel but is also part of the means, through his prayer, of Israel's continuing not-forsakenness. He highlights this praying role, as the next part-verse makes clear (11:2*b*): the link between v. 2*a* and v. 2*b* is Elijah's intercessory task. Second, the Samuel passage is all about God's provision for Israel through the choice of the first king, Saul; and Saul was from the tribe of Benjamin. Paul, whose own Hebrew name was Saul, seems content here to suggest, by implication, that just as God provided for Israel through the choice of the Benjaminite Saul a thousand years ago, so now he has done the same thing.

**11:2b-4.** Paul more naturally, though, identifies himself with the prophetic tradition than the kingly. In 10:14-17 he appeared like Isaiah, telling the good news of the servant-Messiah. In 9:1-5 and 10:1 he has prayed like Moses, and now (as

---

418. Against Fitzmyer, *Romans,* 603.
419. The NEB's translation of μὴ γένοιτο (*mē genoito*) as "I cannot believe it!" reflects Dodd's idea that Paul's logic should have made him give the answer Yes and that only residual national pride made him answer No. See C. H. Dodd, *The Epistle of Paul to the Romans,* 2nd ed. (London: Fontana, 1959) 68, 184. See also Fitzmyer, *Romans,* 603.

it appears) like Samuel. But the prophet with whom the young Saul of Tarsus seems to have identified above all, and with whom the converted Paul still felt a strong affinity, was Elijah.[420] Paul's early "zeal" was in the tradition of Elijah's zeal against the prophets of Baal; but now he saw himself in a subsequent part of the story, standing all but alone before God as the true, and persecuted prophet, praying for the people (Paul here uses the verb ἐντυγχάνω [entygchanō, "intercede"]; his only other uses of this verb have as their subjects the Spirit [8:27] and the ascended Christ [8:34]). But, like Elijah, he receives the assurance (the word for "the divine reply" or "God's answer" is χρηματισμός [chrēmatismos, "oracle"], a word found nowhere else in the NT) that he is not alone: God has created a "remnant" of those who have not bowed the knee to Baal, "leaving" them in the manner spoken of by Isa 1:9, quoted in 9:29.

**11:5-6.** Who then is this "remnant" in Paul's day, and how do they come to have escaped the fate of the rest of the nation, so graphically portrayed in 9:6–10:21? Can it be that, despite 2:17–3:20; 7:7-25; and 9:6–10:21, there are some ethnic Jews who have succeeded in obeying Torah, attaining "their own righteousness" (10:3), and establishing a status of covenant membership based on their belonging to Abraham's physical family and maintaining its distinctive outward markers? No. These two verses make it clear that this "remnant" (λεῖμμα leimma; the only use of this word in the NT) is not a small minority for whom the way of national status actually worked, a tiny group who found that Israel's privileges could after all (in terms of Phil 3:4-7) be counted as "gain" rather than "loss." No: the present "remnant" is "chosen by grace" (NRSV, NIV), literally "in accordance to the election of grace." Paul has already spoken of God's ἐκλογή (eklogē, "selection," "choice," 9:11), and will return to it in summing up the chapter and section (11:28). In the present passage he can use the word both for the act of choosing, as here, and the ones so chosen, as in 11:7. This remnant, he emphasizes, is "not according to works," otherwise the whole principle of grace would be violated. This cannot, then,

be a small number for whom "works" are after all effective.

Paul's doctrine of the remnant in this passage is thus significantly different from that of some of his contemporaries. The best example of an opposite view comes from Qumran: the sect regarded itself as the small minority who had remained true when all others had fallen away, the diminishing number who were still holding lighted candles as the night got darker and darker.[421] Paul, characteristically, sees it the other way around: those who believe in Jesus, those who are called by God's grace, are the small but increasing number who are awake, and lighting their lamps, before the coming dawn (this is how his metaphor works in 13:11-14 and 1 Thess 5:5-10). And part of the point about this image is that if there are already some who are waking up, the other side of the dark night, then there can be more. If Paul and the other Jewish Christians are a new kind of "remnant," called by God's grace in the gospel of Jesus, there is no reason why others should not join them. That is the argument of 11:11-16 and beyond.

**11:7-10.** But for the moment he pauses one more time to describe the state of Israel according to the flesh. This is not a new point, but merely amplifies and underlines what has already been said in 9:25–10:3 and 10:19-21. While "the elect" obtained what Israel as a whole sought, Israel as a whole did not, falling instead into the condemnation already spoken of by (we are not surprised to learn) Deuteronomy and Isaiah.

**11:7.** It is possible that we should read v. 7 as opening with two questions, the second being answered by Paul's statement about "the elect": "What then? What Israel sought, did it not obtain? Well, the elect obtained it—but the rest were hardened." Whereas in 9:30-31 Paul distinguished between Israel, seeking and pursuing but not obtaining, and believing Gentiles, not seeking but obtaining, here he offers simply a division within Israel itself, the division between "the remnant" and "the rest."

Of "the rest" he says that they have been "hardened." This looks back to and summarizes one

420. See N. T. Wright, "Paul, Arabia and Elijah (Galatians 1:17)," *JBL* 115 (1996) 683-92.

421. For the "remnant" in Qumran see 1QS 8:6; 1QH 6:7-8; 1QpHab 10:13; 4QFlor 1:19; 1Q37 1:3. Fitzmyer, *Romans*, 605, sees the parallel but not the all-important difference between Qumran and Paul at this point.

strand of 9:14-24. Since it is also a vital move in the decisive statement at 11:25, it is important to understand it clearly. Paul is drawing on the Jewish tradition that runs like this: when God delays outstanding judgment, those who do not use this time of delay to repent and turn back to him will be hardened, so that their final judgment, when it comes, will be seen to be just. This apocalyptic context of "hardening" is vital; ignoring it leads interpreters either into abstract discussions of predestination and reprobation or into the idea of a temporary "hardening," which is then reversed.[422] As the analogy with Pharaoh in 9:17-18 indicates, this "hardening" is not something that comes for a while, during which something else happens, and which is then removed. The "hardening," rather, is what happens during a temporary suspension of the judgment that would otherwise have fallen, to allow time for some to escape. In the case of Pharaoh, the result was the exodus from Egypt, seen as a sign of God's glorious power and the reputation of the divine name (9:17). In the present case, the result is that there is time not only for the Gentiles to come in (11:11-15), but also for more Jews, like Paul himself, to recognize that the risen Jesus is indeed Israel's Messiah and to serve him in "the obedience of faith."

For those who do not, Paul does not need to invent comments of his own; the Jewish Scriptures themselves declare God's judgment on those within Israel who remain stubborn. Deuteronomy 29, following the long list of the curses that will fall upon disobedience and idolatry, has Moses looking sorrowfully at Israel and seeing nothing but rebellion. Isaiah 29:10, closely related to one of the most-quoted words of judgment from that prophet (i.e., Isa 6:9-10, quoted frequently in the NT: e.g., Matt 13:14-15 and par.; John 12:40; Acts 28:26-27), is taken from the devastating warning in which the saying about the potter and the clay (29:16) forms part of the indictment. These are both, obviously, contexts that have been in Paul's mind for much of the section so far; the quotations from Deuteronomy 29 and Isaiah 29 simply make more explicit what has already been said. It is the

Jewish Scriptures themselves that speak of YHWH pouring out a "spirit of stupor" (Deut 29:4 [29:3 LXX]), and making eyes not to see and ears not to hear. Tragic though it is, this is part of what God had said all along, part of what Israel already should have known (10:19). The result is that unbelieving Israel is hardened permanently; that is, there are no promises to be made of a reversal of the "hardening," except in the context of a coming to faith (see 11:23). But this does not mean that any particular individuals are unable to come to faith and so, like Paul, join the increasing "remnant"; on the contrary, some have already done so and many more will follow.[423]

The psalm quotation that follows in vv. 9-10 (Ps 69:22-23 [68:23-24 LXX]) is linked to the combined quotation from Deuteronomy and Isaiah by the reference to eyes that do not see.[424] But there is a closer link still with Paul's overall theme, and this gives us a clear indication of what Paul thinks is going on here. Elsewhere in this letter, and frequently in the NT, this psalm is seen as a prediction of the sufferings of the Messiah. (See, e.g., Rom 15:3, quoting Ps 69:9; elsewhere Matt 26:37 and Heb 12:2 quoting Ps 69:20; Matt 27:34, 48 and par. quoting Ps 69:21; John 2:17 quoting Ps 69:9; John 15:25 quoting Ps 69:4; Acts 1:20 quoting Ps 69:25). The judgment that is called down upon impenitent Israel in this passage is not something separate from the central gospel events, the events concerning Jesus. If they are the fulfillment of the sufferings portrayed in the psalm, then those who have mocked and tormented the sufferer have these judgments invoked upon them. How much thought Paul gives to the specifics of the "table" becoming a snare, a trap, a stumbling-block and a delusion it is hard to say; but he did of course hold that the pure table fellowship that excluded Gentiles (cf. Gal 2:11-21) was now done away with in the Messiah, who had himself become a "stumbling-block" to his own kinsfolk (1 Cor 1:23; Gal 5:11). This judgment is simply the other side of the coin of ethnic Israel's rejection of the crucified Messiah. The judgment, moreover, will not be

---

422. See Moo, *Romans,* 689-90. See also Rom 2:3-7, the language of which Paul picks up later in the present chapter; cf. 2 Macc 6:13-16, discussed in the Commentary on 9:14-18. In the present passage, 11:7 is to be taken closely with 11:25.

423. Moo, *Romans,* 681, seems to get this exactly the wrong way around.

424. A "snare" (παγίς *pagis*) also echoes a curse in Ps 35:8. Paul thus lines up the three elements of the Jewish Scriptures (Law, Prophets, and Writings) to demonstrate that his charge against his fellow Jews is not his own invention but is the solemn and sustained witness of their own sacred texts.

reversed; as long as ethnic Israel refuses to see the crucified one as Messiah and Lord, their eyes will be darkened (v. 10) and their back bent (cf. 2 Cor 3:14-15).[425] Though a case can be made out for understanding διὰ παντός (dia pantos) as "continually," the NRSV and the NIV are probable true to Paul's meaning to translate "for ever."[426] As the next passage will make clear, Paul does not suppose that any particular ethnic Jews are subject to this condemnation; there is always room for them to come to faith. The perpetual condemnation, as

far as this passage is concerned, lies upon the rejection of the crucified Messiah, not upon this or that person who has acquiesced in that rejection. We should not be surprised at this. Granted all that Paul has argued so far, not least in 3:21–4:25, if God's covenant faithfulness has been revealed in the death of the beloved son, we should not expect the covenant to be effective for any who reject that son, and that death, as the long-awaited unveiling of God's saving plan. But, as we should continually remind ourselves, and as Romans itself insists frequently, it is only when the word of judgment has been fully heard that the word of mercy and grace can sound forth their proper harmony. Judgment must be judgment if grace is to be grace. (See Reflections at 11:33-36.)

---

425. On which see N. T. Wright, *The Climax of the Covenant: Christ and the Law in Pauline Theology* (Minneapolis: Fortress, 1991) 178-84.

426. Against C. E. B. Cranfield, *A Critical and Exegetical Commentary on the Epistle to the Romans,* ICC, 2 vols. (Edinburgh: T. & T. Clark, 1975) 552; Fitzmyer, *Romans,* 607; Christopher Bryan, *A Preface to Romans: Notes on the Epistle in Its Literary and Cultural Setting* (Oxford: Oxford University Press, 2000) 179.

## Romans 11:11-32, "All Israel" Will Be Saved

NIV

[11]Again I ask: Did they stumble so as to fall beyond recovery? Not at all! Rather, because of their transgression, salvation has come to the Gentiles to make Israel envious. [12]But if their transgression means riches for the world, and their loss means riches for the Gentiles, how much greater riches will their fullness bring!

[13]I am talking to you Gentiles. Inasmuch as I am the apostle to the Gentiles, I make much of my ministry [14]in the hope that I may somehow arouse my own people to envy and save some of them. [15]For if their rejection is the reconciliation of the world, what will their acceptance be but life from the dead? [16]If the part of the dough offered as firstfruits is holy, then the whole batch is holy; if the root is holy, so are the branches.

[17]If some of the branches have been broken off, and you, though a wild olive shoot, have been grafted in among the others and now share in the nourishing sap from the olive root, [18]do not boast over those branches. If you do, consider this: You do not support the root, but the root supports you. [19]You will say then, "Branches were broken off so that I could be grafted in." [20]Granted. But they were broken off because of unbelief, and you stand by faith. Do not be arrogant, but be afraid.

NRSV

11So I ask, have they stumbled so as to fall? By no means! But through their stumbling[c] salvation has come to the Gentiles, so as to make Israel[d] jealous. [12]Now if their stumbling[c] means riches for the world, and if their defeat means riches for Gentiles, how much more will their full inclusion mean!

13Now I am speaking to you Gentiles. Inasmuch then as I am an apostle to the Gentiles, I glorify my ministry [14]in order to make my own people[d] jealous, and thus save some of them. [15]For if their rejection is the reconciliation of the world, what will their acceptance be but life from the dead! [16]If the part of the dough offered as first fruits is holy, then the whole batch is holy; and if the root is holy, then the branches also are holy.

17But if some of the branches were broken off, and you, a wild olive shoot, were grafted in their place to share the rich root[e] of the olive tree, [18]do not boast over the branches. If you do boast, remember that it is not you that support the root, but the root that supports you. [19]You will say, "Branches were broken off so that I might be grafted in." [20]That is true. They were broken off because of their unbelief, but you stand only through faith. So do not become proud, but stand

---

[b] Gk *transgression*   [c] Gk *them*   [c] Gk *transgression*   [d] Gk *my flesh*   [e] Other ancient authorities read *the richness*

NIV

²¹For if God did not spare the natural branches, he will not spare you either.

²²Consider therefore the kindness and sternness of God: sternness to those who fell, but kindness to you, provided that you continue in his kindness. Otherwise, you also will be cut off. ²³And if they do not persist in unbelief, they will be grafted in, for God is able to graft them in again. ²⁴After all, if you were cut out of an olive tree that is wild by nature, and contrary to nature were grafted into a cultivated olive tree, how much more readily will these, the natural branches, be grafted into their own olive tree!

²⁵I do not want you to be ignorant of this mystery, brothers, so that you may not be conceited: Israel has experienced a hardening in part until the full number of the Gentiles has come in. ²⁶And so all Israel will be saved, as it is written:

"The deliverer will come from Zion;
 he will turn godlessness away from Jacob.
²⁷ And this is*ᵃ* my covenant with them
 when I take away their sins."*ᵇ*

²⁸As far as the gospel is concerned, they are enemies on your account; but as far as election is concerned, they are loved on account of the patriarchs, ²⁹for God's gifts and his call are irrevocable. ³⁰Just as you who were at one time disobedient to God have now received mercy as a result of their disobedience, ³¹so they too have now become disobedient in order that they too may now*ᶜ* receive mercy as a result of God's mercy to you. ³²For God has bound all men over to disobedience so that he may have mercy on them all.

*ᵃ27* Or *will be*   *ᵇ27* Isaiah 59:20,21; 27:9; Jer. 31:33,34
*ᶜ31* Some manuscripts do not have *now.*

NRSV

in awe. ²¹For if God did not spare the natural branches, perhaps he will not spare you.*ᵃ* ²²Note then the kindness and the severity of God: severity toward those who have fallen, but God's kindness toward you, provided you continue in his kindness; otherwise you also will be cut off. ²³And even those of Israel,*ᵇ* if they do not persist in unbelief, will be grafted in, for God has the power to graft them in again. ²⁴For if you have been cut from what is by nature a wild olive tree and grafted, contrary to nature, into a cultivated olive tree, how much more will these natural branches be grafted back into their own olive tree.

25So that you may not claim to be wiser than you are, brothers and sisters,*ᶜ* I want you to understand this mystery: a hardening has come upon part of Israel, until the full number of the Gentiles has come in. ²⁶And so all Israel will be saved; as it is written,

"Out of Zion will come the Deliverer;
 he will banish ungodliness from Jacob."
²⁷ "And this is my covenant with them,
 when I take away their sins."

²⁸As regards the gospel they are enemies of God*ᵈ* for your sake; but as regards election they are beloved, for the sake of their ancestors; ²⁹for the gifts and the calling of God are irrevocable. ³⁰Just as you were once disobedient to God but have now received mercy because of their disobedience, ³¹so they have now been disobedient in order that, by the mercy shown to you, they too may now*ᵉ* receive mercy. ³²For God has imprisoned all in disobedience so that he may be merciful to all.

*ᵃ* Other ancient authorities read *neither will he spare you*   *ᵇ* Gk lacks *of Israel*   *ᶜ* Gk *brothers*   *ᵈ* Gk lacks *of God*   *ᵉ* Other ancient authorities lack *now*

# COMMENTARY

The major section of the chapter is a long argument, with (to be sure) pauses and breaks, but essentially to be seen as a single flow of thought. It is sent on its way by the second of the two questions that structure the chapter: Granted that Israel according to the flesh has "stumbled," has this stumble meant a permanent "fall"? Certainly not, Paul replies.

He argues the contrary in three stages. Each stage depends on, and expounds further, ideas already set out both in chaps. 9–11 and in Romans as a whole.

(1) What has happened to Israel has been for the good of the Gentiles, so there is every reason to suppose that Israel itself will become "jealous," and some of Paul's kinsfolk will thereby be saved

(11:11*b*-16). This is the point where Paul picks up language about Adam and Christ from earlier in the letter, notably chap. 5, and applies it to Israel according to the flesh.

(2) Unbelieving Jews are like branches broken off God's cultivated olive tree, while Gentiles are like wild branches grafted in surprisingly; how much more can God graft the natural branches back in "if they do not remain in unbelief" (11:23)? This argument (11:17-24) is aimed specifically against Gentile arrogance, the point to which Paul has been working around: do not, he says, suppose that you can boast against the branches without yourself becoming at risk.

(3) The mystery of God's dealings with Israel and the Gentiles is thus unveiled. The "hardening" on Israel, and the "coming in" of Gentiles, is God's means of saving "all Israel." The covenant will be fulfilled in the way God always intended, that is, by being renewed through the Messiah for the forgiveness of sins. Whenever Jewish people come to faith in Jesus as Messiah, this is a further sign that God is faithful to the promises made to the patriarchs (11:25-32). The end of this specific argument is thus the end of the whole discussion that began with 9:6. All that remains, balancing the cry of anguish in 9:1-5, is the cry of praise in 11:33-36.

**11:11-12.** Paul picks up the language of "stumbling" from 9:32-33; the words are different but the idea closely related. Have they, he asks, tripped up in such a way as to fall headlong permanently?[427] Certainly not. He advances his counterargument in two stages, vv. 11*b*-12 and vv. 13-16. Each stage further subdivides; v. 11*b* is the basic statement, with v. 12 as a further conclusion; then vv. 13-14 are his major statement, explained and elaborated by v. 15 and, in turn, v. 16.

Verse 11*b* looks back to 10:19 and on to v. 14. It adds to the discussion an element that appears new but that, it turns out, was hidden in the argument of 9:6–10:21 all along: that Israel's stumble over the stumbling-stone was not just something that happened at the same time as the Gentiles' coming in to faith, to righteousness, and to salvation itself, but was actually part of the *means by which* it happened. We can understand this at one level by saying that Israel's hardening relates to Gentile salvation somewhat as Pharaoh's hardening relates to the exodus (9:17); this, it seems, is what 9:22-24 is all about, and the point is confirmed by the echo in v. 12 of the mention there of God's "riches." Somehow, God's bearing patiently with the "vessels of wrath" is part of the intention to bring these "riches" to the Gentiles. "Through their transgression, salvation has come to the Gentiles."

But if this is so then 10:19 is also in play: this will make ethnic Jews "jealous."[428] The background to this within Romans ought to be clear from 2:17-29—and from the whole sequence of thought that runs from the major statement of Christian identity in chaps. 5–8 into the sorrowful rehearsal of the same privileges in 9:1-5. But, whereas in Deut 32:21, and its quotation in 10:19, this "jealousy" appeared purely negative, it is turned to positive effect in v. 14; and Paul is already preparing the way for this. They (Paul does not use the word "Israel" between vv. 7 and 25) have "transgressed," and the world has been enriched; they have been "diminished," and God's riches have been given to the Gentiles. How much more, then, if they are brought back up to full strength (πλήρωμα *plērōma*)?

Before we explore this "full strength," let us note, so as to be quite clear, what the whole "jealousy" theme presupposes. It assumes (as argued above) that when Gentiles come to Christian faith they do indeed come to share in the blessings God promised to Israel according to the flesh (not, interestingly, the land; see the Commentary on 4:13; 8:18-27; the whole world is now seen as God's holy land, to be redeemed in the new creation). We cannot escape the force of this and retreat into the idea that Gentile Christians have a parallel track to salvation that does not intersect with the Jewish one. Nor, therefore, can we suggest that the way for Jews now to be saved is something radically different from the way Gentiles are saved—by God's grace, through faith in Jesus as Messiah, apart from works of the law.

What then might their "full strength," their complete number, mean? This is the first moment that Paul has suggested an increase in the number

---

427. The metaphorical use of πταίω (*ptaiō*) is already found in Deut 7:25. For this use of πίπτω (*piptō*) see Rom 14:4; 1 Cor 10:12.

428. See R. H. Bell, *Provoked to Jealousy: The Origin and Purpose of the Jealousy Motif in Romans 9–11*, WUNT, 2nd series, no. 63 (Tübingen: Mohr, 1994).

of Jews who come to be not merely Abraham's physical descendants but his "seed" in the full sense of 9:7-8. Up until 10:21 the number seemed to be diminishing, whittled down to a remnant. Even in 11:1-10 this "remnant" seemed to consist simply of the small number who, like Paul, had through God's electing grace abandoned the status based on "works" and embraced the messianic faith focused on Jesus. Now for the first time he begins to say that something further may yet happen. Israel according to the flesh has been "diminished"; now it will be brought to fullness.[429] "Fullness" is itself a rare term in Paul, but there is another parallel occurrence close by in 11:25. Other parts of that verse are controversial, but at this point we are on safe ground: by the "fullness of the Gentiles," we may confidently say, Paul means "the total number of those Gentiles who believe the gospel of Jesus." He is well aware that large numbers of Gentiles do not believe it, and never will. The "fullness" will consist of all those who eventually do. There is no reason to suppose that "the fullness" of Israel will mean anything more than this: the complete number of Jews, many more than at present, who likewise come to faith in the gospel.[430]

We should note at this point the way in which vv. 11-12 echo the language and argument of 5:15-21. Paul here describes Israel's "stumble" as a παράπτωμα (paraptōma, "trespass"), echoing the key term used six times there in as many verses. What is more, the "trespass" in question forms the first half of a "how much more" argument celebrating the grace of God which overcomes human stumbling. "If, by the trespass of the one, the many died, how much more has God's grace . . . abounded to the many." "If, by the trespass of the one, death reigned . . . how much more will those who receive the gift of righteousness reign in life" (5:15, 17). A moment's thought will show what is going on. This is no accidental allusion. Paul's brief statement in 5:20 ("the law

came in so that the trespass might abound"), set out at length in 7:7-25, and developed to its final stage in 9:30-33 where the "stumbling" metaphor is crucial, indicates that through Torah Israel has recapitulated the sin of Adam, has acted it out on a grand scale. But, whereas the trespass of Adam brought sin and death to the world, the "trespass" of Israel has brought salvation and "riches" to the world! How much more, then—this is the force of 11:12—should Israel now receive "fullness." Paul's two simultaneous guiding lights for understanding Israel according to the flesh are these: Israel, like everyone else, is "in Adam"; but Israel is also, according to the flesh, the Messiah's own people. Verses 11-12 develop the first of these. The following three verses will now develop the second.

**11:13-16.** Paul moves a little closer toward his rhetorical target, which will come into full view in vv. 17-24 and then, decisively, in v. 25. He is speaking to "you Gentiles." This does not mean that all Christians in Rome were Gentiles (see Introduction). Nor does it necessarily mean that only at this point is he necessarily "turning" to them specifically.[431] Rather, this section of the letter is an argument against Gentile arrogance, against Gentiles falling into the trap of assuming an ethnic superiority, the trap Paul sees the Jews having fallen into (this is hardly, then, just an aside; the REB was right to correct the NEB's "But I have something to say to you Gentiles" to "It is to you Gentiles that I am speaking"). What Paul does not want Gentile Christians to think is that God cannot and will not save any more Jews; that, though there may be a Jewish remnant, Paul himself included, there will not be any more.

After this personal address to one part, perhaps the majority part, of the Roman church, this little argument has three moves:

1. Paul's oblique missionary intent toward his kinsfolk (vv. 13b-14): his Gentile ministry is aimed at making "his flesh" jealous and so saving some of them.
2. The explanation (v. 15): like their Messiah, their "casting away" means reconciliation for the world, and their "receiving back" will be like a resurrection.

---

429. ἥττημα (hēttēma), translated "defeat" in the NRSV and "loss" in the NIV, is a rare word (only here and 1 Cor 6:7 in the NT). The cognate verb ἡττάομαι (hēttaomai) has a range of meaning, including "to be defeated," "to be inferior," "to be weaker." Since it serves here (like "trespass" earlier in the verse) to sum up the whole sequence of 9:6–10:21 and makes the direct contrast with plērōma, a sense of "diminution" seems plausible. See, however, Moo, Romans, 688n. 26.
430. Joseph A. Fitzmyer, Romans, AB 33 (Garden City, N.Y.: Doubleday, 1993) 611, discusses several possible senses of "fullness."

431. Against ibid., 608, 612.

3. The conclusion: Israel as a whole is "holy," because of the "first fruits" and the "root." This latter image will then open up into the central argument of the passage (vv. 17-24).

**11:13-14.** Paul's aim is to exploit the "jealousy" of which Deuteronomy 32 had spoken. Knowing, certainly, what a bold and even provocative move this was, he celebrated and "glorified" the ministry he had, his call to be the apostle to the Gentiles (see the Commentary on 1:5; 10:14-17). He was taking to the Gentiles the news that Israel's God, Abraham's God, was welcoming them into the one family now reconstituted around the Messiah (4:1-25). And he was seeking to hold this up before his fellow Jews so as to make them see what was happening and, becoming jealous, long to have a share in the eschatological blessings themselves. No wonder, we think wryly, Paul was beaten in synagogues. Such conduct must have seemed a deliberate and flagrant snub to some of Israel's most cherished assumptions. But he is undaunted. This is the way that some of them will be saved—and again, with this echo of the prayer of 10:1, we should hear also the solid soteriology of 10:9-13 that explains how the prayer will be answered.

To understand the roots of his argument, we should follow the Greek closely in v. 14. He does not say "my own people" (NJB, "the people who are my own blood-relations"; NEB, "the men of my own race"), but "my flesh." This picks up his phrases in 9:3, 5 ("my kinsfolk according to the flesh," and "from them, according to the flesh, is the Messiah"). Equally important, it echoes the whole argument of 7:1–8:11. There Paul, seeing his "flesh" as the place where Adam's sin was being worked out through the Torah itself, grieved over the situation but announced that God would give resurrection life to the "mortal body." Here, echoing Romans 5–8 in various ways, he sees his "flesh" in rebellion against the gospel, following through Adam's "trespass"; and he intends to make this "flesh" jealous, and so provoke it to salvation—by the route, we must assume, that he has sketched in 10:1-13, in other words by faith. He does not expect that all his fellow Jews, or even most of them, will travel this route. Verse 14 has a sober realism about it, parallel to that of 1 Cor 9:22, where the rhetoric cried out for him to say

"all" but theology and missionary experience knew he had to say "some" ("I have become all things to all people so that by all means I might save... some"; the Greek is briefer [τοῖς πᾶσιν γέγονα πάντα, ἵνα πάντως τινὰς σώσω *tois pasin gegona panta, hina pantōs tinas sōsō*]; the rhetorical pressure to write πάντας [*pantas*] instead of τινάς [*tinas*] was too strong for some MSS). But even "some" will enable him to answer "no" to the double question of 11:1 and 11:11: God will always be faithful to the promise to Abraham. This is not, then, a contrast with "fullness" in 11:12 and "all Israel" in 11:26.[432] There will always be some of Abraham's physical descendants who are included in the true "seed." That is all that the promise envisaged; that is the whole point of 9:6-29; and God will be true to the promise.

**11:15.** The explanation sends us back again to chap. 5. Israel truly is the Messiah's people according to the flesh; it was the Messiah's death, his "casting away," that achieved "reconciliation" for the world, and it is his risen life that now provides salvation (5:10; see the Commentary on 11:21 and the parallel there with 8:32). Now, in parallel fashion, the casting away of the Messiah's fleshly kinsfolk has accomplished reconciliation for the world, and their reacceptance will mean "life from the dead."

The idea that the failure, the rebellion, the "casting away" of Israel means reconciliation for the world is clearly a development of what was said in 11:11b-12a. It is a striking way of putting the same point, attributing redemptive, salvific significance to the tragedy that has befallen Israel, a significance that can only be explained on the assumption that Paul is indeed thinking of his own Christology under the argument all along. The "rejection" is indeed, in this sense, God's rejection of Israel, not (as is sometimes suggested) Israel's rejection of God.[433] Israel has acted out the representative death of its Messiah; the Gentiles are the beneficiaries. Paul returns to the same point from yet another angle in 11:30b: You Gentiles received mercy "by their disobedience." He never explains more explicitly what he means, but something like the following can perhaps be said. Paul does not

432. Against Douglas J. Moo, *The Epistle to the Romans,* NICNT (Grand Rapids: Eerdmans, 1996) 692.
433. So Bryan, *A Preface to Romans,* 187. ἀποβολή (*apobolē*) would surely be a strange word to use for the latter idea.

envisage Israel actually "dying" for the sake of the world, as the Messiah himself has done; the Messiah's work is unique, standing over against Jew and Gentile alike. But the "hardening" that has come upon Israel, as in 9:14-24, was the necessary context for the Messiah's death, and as such has become part of the saving plan. That is one of the main points of 9:6–10:21. The "hardening," then, has been the means of suspending the judgment that might otherwise have fallen, creating a breathing space in which Gentiles can be brought in (9:24, 30). In that sense, Israel's "casting away" has been instrumental in the salvation of the Gentiles.

Israel's "receiving back again" (πρόσλημψις proslēmpsis, the only occurrence of this word in the NT) must then be explained in terms of vv. 12 and 14. If, after all that has happened, Jews come back into the family, hearing and believing the gospel as in 10:6-13, then, says Paul, the significance of this will be like a kind of resurrection. "Life from the dead" here has sometimes been taken to indicate—anticipating one reading of 11:25-26—that when Israel comes back to faith this will be the signal for, or perhaps the result of, the general resurrection.[434] But v. 15 is introduced as an explanation *gar*, not a new point. Just think, Paul is saying to the Gentile Christians in Rome: once you realize that their "casting away" was like the death of the Messiah, when they are brought back again it will be like a little Easter—and you should celebrate! He is saying what 4:17 had already indicated: Abraham's family will consist of those who are brought back from the dead (i.e., Jewish converts) and those who are created out of nothing (i.e., Gentile converts). The "now" of 11:31 strongly suggests that Paul is not postponing this hoped-for salvation to some distant future.[435]

**11:16.** This phase of the argument is drawn together, and the ground prepared for the next one, by a further conclusion (for εἰ δέ [*ei de*] as drawing the conclusion, see 8:10-11). The point of this verse is that the whole is sanctifed by the part: the lump by the first fruits, the branches by the root.

The first of these images depends on the sacrificial tradition of the Feast of Weeks, represented in Num 15:20: "Of the first of your dough you shall offer up a cake as a heave offering"; the point being that once the first part of the dough has been offered to God, the entire batch is considered holy, consecrated and ready for Israel to use.[436] The second image has no particular biblical background, but is introduced by analogy with the first in order to lead to the extended metaphor of the olive tree that then follows. In both images the referent of the second term is clear: the "whole lump" and the "branches" are of course Israel according to the flesh, the Israel that has not as yet recognized its Messiah.[437] But who or what is the first fruits? Who or what is the root?

The answer to these two is not necessarily the same. The argument so far, and some of Paul's other uses of the same image, would lead us to assume that the "first fruits" refers to the "remnant" chosen by grace, including Paul himself (see particularly 16:5; 1 Cor 16:15; 2 Thess 2:13). Some Jews according to the flesh have already been converted; that is, part of the lump of dough has already been offered to God. The rest must therefore be treated as sanctified, not as common or disposable. (By "holy" here Paul clearly does not mean "automatically saved," but rather something like "sanctified by extension" or "by their relationship"; the closest parallel is in 1 Cor 7:14, referring to the non-Christian partner and the children in a mixed marriage.)[438] In other words, Gentile Christians, recognizing the fact of a "remnant" of believing Jews, must regard other Jews as holy by extension.

It is possible to take the image of "root and branches" the same way: the remnant by grace are the root, and the branches are the as yet unbelieving Jews. But it seems harsh, in view of the way Paul develops the picture, to do so. The remnant itself, within Paul's image, consists not of a root

---

434. This interpretation goes back to Origen and is favored by, among others, Ernst Käsemann, *Commentary on Romans*, trans. Geoffrey W. Bromiley (London: SCM, 1980) 307; Fitzmyer, *Romans*, 613; Moo, *Romans*, 694-96.

435. See F. J. Leenhardt, *The Epistle to the Romans: A Commentary* (London: Lutterworth, 1961) 284-85.

436. Paul also uses the image of "first fruits" in, e.g. 8:23, (see the note there); 16:5; and elsewhere. For the Jewish context see also, e.g., Philo *Special Laws* 1:131-44.

437. It is striking that the word for "lump" (φύραμα *phyrama*) is the same as in the "potter and clay" illustration in 9:21. The point here is not the same—there the lump was clay, here it is dough—but the two passages are thematically quite close. God can and will refashion the "lump" into something that at present it is not.

438. Though the interpretation of this passage too is a matter of considerable dispute. See A. C. Thiselton, *The First Epistle to the Corinthians: A Commentary on the Greek Text*, NIGTC (Grand Rapids: Eerdmans, 2000) 527-33.

that has always been there, nor yet of branches that were never broken off, but of branches that were broken off for a short while and then grafted back in again. Otherwise Paul's protestations about grace in 11:5-6 would be undermined: the remnant really would be a permanent part of God's people, a small group for whom ethnic membership and Torah-observance really had proved valid. It is much better to take the "root" as something, or someone, more permanent; suggestions include the patriarchs, the Messiah, even God.[439] Of these I am inclined to prefer the Messiah. It is possible that Paul already has in mind the text that he will use at the climactic and concluding point of the letter's theological exposition, highlighting "the root of Jesse," whose resurrection installs him as the Gentiles' true ruler (15:12, quoting Isa 11:10). But even if that is too far away in the letter to be allowed, the Messiah has been at the center of the argument, either implicitly or explicitly, for much of chaps. 9–11, and it is the messianic pattern of casting away followed by life from the dead that Paul has been thinking through in the preceding verses. The olive tree in the illustration is Israel, the true seed of Abraham, into which wild branches have been grafted but into which, far more easily, natural branches can be regrafted. And the crowning privilege of Israel, the human and historical focus of the nation's long story as God's people, is the Messiah (9:5). It is considerably easier, I think, to see the "root" that "bears" both Gentile and Jewish Christians (11:18) as the Messiah than as the patriarchs.

Does that mean that we would be right to see the Messiah as the first fruits as well, making v. 16a more of a parallel to 1 Cor 15:20, 23? Probably not. The buried reference to the Messiah in 11:15 might sway us in this direction, but it is not necessary to take the two halves of the verse as making exactly the same point in two different ways.[440] If the καί (kai) that starts v. 16b is read as "moreover," there is no problem in seeing Paul making a transition at this point to the new picture he is about to draw. Paul of all people is adept at mixing his imagery, and in a dense and allusive argument a transition like this is perfectly comprehensible.

We conclude that 11:11-16 begins the argument that God still wants and intends to save more Jews by lining up Israel according to the flesh with both Adam and the Messiah, as the argument of chaps. 5–8 might have prepared us for. Israel has acted out both the trespass of Adam and the redemptive "casting away" of the Messiah. Within this, Paul addresses a warning to the Gentile Christians in Rome: even the Gentile mission in which he exults has this as its oblique purpose, to bring more Jews to faith and so to salvation. For Jews to embrace the gospel now, after all they have gone through, would be like resurrection from the dead. They are, after all, the relatives according to the flesh not only of the existing remnant, but of the Messiah himself.

**11:17-24.** This leads Paul to one of his most famous extended images. Paul is often criticized for his apparent failure to manage such passages; in the present case some have even mocked him for being a city dweller who did not understand horticulture![441] Paul is however well aware that what he is proposing is, in terms of the metaphor he is using, "contrary to nature" (v. 24). A gardener does not normally graft wild branches on to a cultivated stock, but the other way around, directing the energy of the wild plant toward the focused fruitfulness of the cultivated one. There are exceptions to this, noted in ancient literature; we cannot tell whether Paul knew them or not.[442] Most likely he did not: he intends us to understand that what God has done with the olive tree is a miracle of grace, not the sort of thing that people do all the time.

The olive tree in the illustration clearly stands for the people of God, the people stretching back to Abraham and now including both Gentiles and Jews (the main OT reference is Jer 11:16-17: Israel as an olive tree whose branches are broken off in judgment; see also Ps 52:8; Hos 14:6). The Messiah (most probably) is the "root" through whom the tree now gets its life (v. 17), the one

---

439. For patriarchs, see Bryan, *A Preface to Romans,* 188; Moo, *Romans,* 700. Cranfield, *Romans,* 564, takes the first fruits as the Jewish Christian remnant and the root as the patriarchs.

440. Against Bryan, *A Preface to Romans,* 188.

441. C. H. Dodd, *The Epistle of Paul to the Romans,* 2nd ed. (London: Fontana, 1959) 189.

442. See Columella *On Country Matters* 5:9:16 (contemporary with Paul); Palladius *On Grafting* 53-54 (5th cent. CE). See also Moo, *Romans,* 703n. 33, and the other sources cited there, esp. A. G. Baxter and J. A. Ziesler, "Paul and Arboriculture: Romans 11:17-24," *JSNT* 24 (1985) 25-32.

who holds the whole thing in place, enabling Gentile members to gain life (v. 18). The force of the illustration is to make the Gentile Christians realize their place within God's saving purposes; they are not the new aristocracy, they are the wild country cousins brought in, to everybody's surprise, to share the inheritance. If that is so, they have no business to give themselves airs over those of the unfortunate original family members who have for the moment been ousted. God is, after all, well capable of bringing them back again. That is the thrust of this passage.

**11:17-18.** Paul's first main point is: Do not boast. His exclusion of "boasting" in 3:27-30, ruling out any kind of Jewish boast of ethnic superiority based on possession of Torah and performance of its "works," is now balanced by this stern warning to Gentile Christians—a warning that, as the history of Marcionism bears witness, was needed but not heeded.[443] The branches that are broken off are, clearly, Jews who have not believed the gospel; Paul's view of them is not that they are on a parallel track to salvation, but that at the moment they are separated from the parent tree, gaining no life from the root. They are the ones he was grieving over in 9:1-5 and praying for in 10:1. The wild olive branches (i.e., the Gentile Christians), however, have been grafted in, and are sharing the rich oily sap that is the olive's chief glory, and that comes through the root (the NRSV's "the rich root" does not quite convey the force of the phrase, lit., "the root of the richness of the olive," i.e., the root through which the richness comes). This is yet another way of saying what Paul already said in 9:24, 30, and 10:4-13: Gentiles, to their surprise, are inheriting the blessings promised to Israel. But if that is so, they must remember their origin and refrain from crowing over those who have been, for the moment, cut off. They must remember who the Messiah is, and who they themselves are as his utter dependents. They do not support the root, as though Jesus Christ were now the private possession of Gentile Christians. He, Israel's Messiah according to the flesh, supports them. Paul's sudden use of the second person singular throughout vv. 17-24 (contrasting with the plural in vv. 13, 25-32) makes his point all the more sharply.

**11:19-21.** Paul then envisages a conversation between himself and the newly ingrafted branches. The Gentile branches will declare that other branches were broken off to make room for them— the very point, they might say, that Paul himself has made in 11:11-12 and 15. The "stumble" or "trespass" of Israel has been the occasion of Gentiles coming in. Paul does not disagree; but his point is made sharply by drawing attention to the attendant circumstances both of the breaking off of some branches and the grafting in of others. What counted then, and counts still, is faith: they were broken off because of unbelief, but you stand firm by faith (the NRSV adds "only," which as in 3:28 is a fair explanation though strictly an addition to Paul's text; on the idea of "standing," i.e., remaining firm in a particular status, see 5:2; 14:4). The accusation of unbelief or unfaithfulness (or "untrustworthiness," or "disloyalty," ἀπιστία *apistia*), goes back to 3:3; this was the basic charge leveled against Israel in the beginning of Paul's argument. Abraham is specifically contrasted with this in 4:20: he did not waver in unbelief.

This leads to a more specific warning: Gentile Christians must not just avoid boasting, but must also maintain their faithfulness. They must not permit themselves an attitude of superiority (see the Commentary on 12:3, 16), but must keep humble, in the proper fear of God. Verse 21 explains why, drawing on the fuller picture Paul has in mind that becomes explicit in v. 24: God is quite capable of doing to a Gentile church what he has done to "the natural branches." If they were not spared, perhaps God will not spare Gentiles either.[444] Here, too, there is a strange echo of an earlier passage, 8:32: God did not spare the beloved son. Once again, Paul is thinking of the Jews as the Messiah's people according to the flesh; but this time their fate is held up as a warning to Gentile Christians. This is what happens if you regard yourself as automatically part of God's people, instead of continuing by faith alone. Faith remains the only valid badge of membership; anything else will lead inevitably to "boasting."

---

443. On Marcion and his movement, see R. J. Hoffman, *Marcion: On the Restitution of Christianity* (Chico, Calif.: American Academy of Religion, 1984).

444. "Perhaps" in the NRSV translates μή πως (*mē pōs*), which is missing in some good MSS but present, and hard to explain as a gloss, in several others. See B. M. Metzger, *A Textual Commentary on the Greek New Testament* (London: United Bible Societies, 1971) 526-27. Without it, the verse reads, as in the NIV, simply "he will not spare you either." Adding "perhaps" does seem appropriately reverent at this point, though of course the more appropriate it seems the easier it is to explain it as a possible addition.

What does the threat of being cut off actually mean? After the long argument of 3:21–8:39, it is highly unlikely that Paul would envisage individual Christians being justified by faith at one moment, assured of "sharing the glory of God" (5:2; 8:30), and at another moment losing both faith and salvation. On the contrary; his regular view is that when God begins a good work, through the gospel and the spirit, that good work will come to completion (Phil 1:6). What is more likely is that this is a warning to an entire church (as, for instance, in the messages to the churches of Asia in Revelation 2–3). Individual Christians may be muddled or sinful, but they will be saved, even if only, in some cases, "as through fire" (1 Cor 3:15). A church, however, that begins to boast in the way Paul is warning against may not last another generation. The only way forward is through faith; and faith, by its very nature, means dependence on God, rather than confidence in human status, birth, privilege, or merit.

**11:22-24.** Paul sums up the argument, as is fitting for part of a larger section whose main subject is God, by drawing attention to two balancing attributes of God. These create a setting in which Gentile Christians must learn where they stand, what they risk if they do not remain there, and, particularly, what God can and will do with the Messiah's presently unbelieving kinsfolk according to the flesh. Paul has already spoken of God's "kindness" (χρηστότης *chrēstotēs*) in 2:4, in describing how God's patience and forbearance were meant to lead to repentance, and in warning that a hard and impenitent heart that refused God's generosity would lead to wrath. Now, with a not dissimilar point about to emerge (11:25), he is warning that God's blend of justice and mercy, of kindness and severity,[445] has been applied to Israel according to the flesh and will be applied to Gentile churches as well. This is backed up with a reminder of God's "power" (v. 23*b*), echoing the same point earlier in the letter (1:16, 20; 4:21; 9:17, 20).[446]

God's severity is seen in the treatment of those who have "fallen," in other words, Jewish unbelievers. In v. 11 Paul declared that they had not "stumbled so as to fall," but he was there referring to Jewish unbelievers as a whole. Paul does not ignore the fact that some have indeed fallen, nor does he rule out the possibility that some individuals may remain in that condition. He is arguing, though, that God is well capable of grafting them back in to their own olive tree, "if they do not remain in unbelief" (v. 23). As in v. 20, faith and its opposite—and in the light of 10:4-13 "faith" can here only mean explicit faith in Jesus as the risen Lord—are the determining factors. Meanwhile, God's kindness is seen in the astonishing welcome to Gentiles who were neither looking for it nor deserving of it (9:30; 10:20); but they must "remain in God's kindness," in other words, maintain their position simply by trust in God rather than by reliance on their own social, cultural, or ethnic status. If they do not, they in turn can perfectly easily be "cut off." The force of the passage does not lie on the warning about what might happen to arrogant Gentile churches, but on what can perfectly well happen to presently unbelieving Jews: God can graft them back into the olive tree, if they will only follow the path laid down in chap. 10, abandon their present "unbelief," and believe the gospel. Verse 24, explaining how it is that God is capable of grafting them back again, provides a climax to the whole chapter so far, showing incidentally that Paul knew all along how unnatural his horticultural image had been. If God, against all the normal laws of nature and gardening, can cut you out of your natural wild olive and graft you in to a cultivated olive, then the branches that have presently been cut off can certainly be grafted back in again (Paul is aware of the horticultural near-impossibility of regrafting old branches; as in 4:17 and 11:15, what he is describing is a kind of resurrection). The emphasis of the whole chapter so far falls, apparently quite deliberately, on words that stress what Paul had said in 9:1-5: Israel remains God's cultivated olive tree; Jews, even unbelieving ones, belong to it by nature; it is "their own olive tree." That is the point Paul most wants the Gentile Christians in Rome to grasp. It is the point that the following, decisive subsection will then explain fully and finally.

---

445. ἀποτομία (*apotomia*); its only NT occurrence. Joseph A. Fitzmyer, *Romans,* AB 33 (Garden City, N.Y.: Doubleday, 1993) 616, points out that Paul interestingly does not use the regular words for "mercy" (ἔλεος *eleos*) and "justice" (δικαιοσύνη *dikaiosynē*).

446. Fitzmyer, ibid., helpfully links the present passage with 1:16: "Israel's salvation cannot take place apart from the power manifested in the preaching of the gospel of Christ."

We remind ourselves, arriving at this controversial passage, what Paul at least seems to have intended chaps. 9–11 to be all about. This section is all about Israel, and all about God. Israel according to the flesh has failed to believe in the gospel of the Messiah, the gospel that is God's power to salvation to all who believe (1:16), since all who confess Jesus as Lord and believe that God raised him from the dead will be saved (10:6-11). However, God made promises to Abraham and his descendants, and God's word has not failed. That sets up the problem to which, at least in Paul's mind, the present passage is the decisive answer.

Paul continues throughout this section to address Gentile Christians; when he says "you" in vv. 28, 30-31, he refers to them specifically. In those verses (11:28-32) he outlines a scheme of interchange and mutual obligation between Gentile and Jew that looks forward to 15:7-13 (which concludes the letter's theological exposition) and also to 15:27, where the Gentiles have shared in the "spiritual things" of the Jews, and are consequently under an obligation to minister to them in "fleshly things." This interchange is grounded, it seems, in the very plan of God, as Jews and Gentiles play out their unexpected roles, bringing all the human race into "disobedience" in order to have mercy upon all (11:32). ("All," as we noted earlier, cannot here mean "all individuals without distinction," but rather "the whole human race, that is, Jew and Gentile alike.")

**11:25-27.** Before this summary (vv. 28-32), Paul pulls together his long argument into a succinct statement—too succinct, it seems, for subsequent interpreters, who have continued to puzzle over what precisely he meant. This statement consists of an introduction, with its own explanation ("For I do not want you to be ignorant, brothers and sisters, of this mystery, so that you may not think too highly of yourselves," v. 25*a;* cf. Prov 3:7, a warning against trusting one's own judgment rather than God's); a statement of what has happened to Israel (v. 25*b*); the statement that "all Israel shall be saved" (v. 26*a*); and a composite scriptural quotation (26*b*-27). Each part of this has been variously understood, and the combinations of possibilities are multiple and intricate.[447]

**11:25a.** The first thing to notice is that Paul at least thinks this passage explains what has already been said. Most translations ignore the opening "for" (few translations represent the *gar* that joins the verse to what precedes it; the NEB, however, does: "For there is a deep truth here"), but Paul is quite capable of starting a new point without that or any other connecting word, and if he wrote it, he meant it. The introduction is somewhat formal ("I do not want you to be ignorant"), a tone Paul adopts when he wants special attention (cf. 1:13; 1 Cor 10:1; 12:1; 2 Cor 1:8; 1 Thess 4:13). He emphasizes once more that the point of saying all this is lest the Gentile Christians become conceited; the phrase he uses here is not easy to translate, as the versions indicate, but the overall sense is clear.[448] So far, there is nothing to indicate that Paul is making a new point, except for one thing: the fact that he speaks of "this mystery."

"This" here clearly looks forward to the "that" (ὅτι *hoti*) later in the verse: "this mystery, namely, the fact that. . . ." Paul does not often speak of "mysteries." But the other uses both in the undoubted letters and in Ephesians and Colossians suggest that he probably intends the word to refer, not to a hidden truth open only to initiates, but to an aspect of the long-range plan and purpose of God that has now been unveiled through the gospel of Jesus the Messiah (see 16:25; 1 Cor 2:1, 7; Eph 1:9; 3:3-9; 6:19; Col 1:26-27; 2:2).[449] Calling what is still to come a "mystery" does not of itself indicate that this is a new point introduced here for the first time, different to what has been said before; that could be the case, as 1 Cor 15:51 indicates, but is by no means necessary. Rather, referring to his summary statement here as a "mystery" simply indicates that it is part of God's previously hidden plan that Paul wants his readers to understand.

---

447. Perhaps the most extreme suggestion is that of C. Plag, *Israels Wege zum Heil. Eine Untersuchung zum Römer 9 bis 11* (Stuttgart: Calwer Verlag, 1969), that 11:25-27 is an extraneous insertion into a text that, without it, would have spoken simply of the continuous conversion of some Jews.

448. The NJB's "to save you from congratulating yourselves on your own good sense" is clearly an overtranslation and perhaps misses the point from the previous verses; they are in danger not of imagining themselves to be clever, but of imagining that God is now inalienably on the side of Gentiles against Jews. See also 12:3, where a similar sense has a broader application.

449. On the background to Paul's use of "mystery," see the useful notes in Fitzmyer, *Romans,* 621; Douglas J. Moo, *The Epistle to the Romans,* NICNT (Grand Rapids: Eerdmans, 1996) 714; Christopher Bryan, *A Preface to Romans: Notes on the Epistle in Its Literary and Cultural Setting* (Oxford: Oxford University Press, 2000) 188-89.

**11:25b.** What, then, has happened to Israel? An attentive reader of 9:6–11:10 could have answered without difficulty: a hardening has come upon them. Paul has already said this in 11:7, summing up the sequence of thought in 9:14-24. And such a reader could also have said what this means: such a "hardening" is what happens, through the forbearance of God, to those who do not accept the gospel. "Hardening" is what happens when otherwise immediate judgment is postponed but people do not avail themselves of the chance to repent and believe. According to the regular Jewish tradition represented here by 2:1-11, such "hardening" has only two results. Either the person comes to their senses, recognizes God's forbearance, and repents; or they are fitted the more fully for the judgment that will ensue.

To this statement, which acts as a summary of previous material rather than a new point, Paul adds two phrases, both modifying the phrase "a hardening has occurred to Israel." The first phrase is ἀπὸ μέρους (apo merous), which often means "in part" but can also mean "for a while"; an example of each is found later in the letter ("in part," 15:15; "for a while," 15:24).[450] We should note that this phrase is normally adverbial, not adjectival, making it probable that it modifies γέγονεν (gegonen, "has happened"), rather than πώρωσις (pōrosis, "hardening"). It is unlikely, then, that Paul means "a partial hardening"; even if apo merous means "in part," it will mean "has happened in part." The temporal meaning would fit, more or less, with the phrase that follows ("until the fullness of the Gentiles comes in"), in which case it would mean that the "hardening" is temporary in the sense that it postpones judgment but cannot hold it off forever. But it is more likely that, following 11:7, it implies a division between the Israel that is hardened and the Israel that has become the "remnant": "the remnant obtained it, but the rest were hardened." This reminds us that from the very beginning of the discussion Paul made it clear that there were two categories of Abraham's children (9:7-8), and indeed two categories of "Israel" itself: "not all who are of Israel are Israel" (9:6). Paul probably means, then, that a "hardening" has "partly come" upon Israel, in other words, that while one part of "Israel" now

constitutes the "remnant," the other part of "Israel according to the flesh"—the great majority—has been "hardened."

The second modifying phrase indicates how long this "hardening" will last. It is holding back the judgment while the Gentile mission happens, and will be complete when "the fullness of the Gentiles" has come in. As we noted before, Paul does not envisage that all Gentiles everywhere will believe the gospel, any more than they have done so far. He believes, rather, that there is a mode of "completion" (perhaps, when the gospel has been announced to all the nations?) in God's mind. (It is less likely that he imagines God to have a complete mathematical number of future Gentile converts in mind.) Until this has been reached, final judgment will be delayed, leaving those still impenitent in their state of "hardening." And this "hardening," as we saw, leads to judgment, unless those subject to it come to their senses, repent, and believe (2:3-6). Otherwise we are forced to read into the sequence of vv. 25-26 a temporal progression that, as we shall see, is not what Paul has in mind.

**11:26a.** So far, Paul has still not said anything that goes beyond what we might have deduced from the entire argument to date. But that changes with "and so all Israel shall be saved." This is the sentence—a mere five words in the Greek (καὶ οὕτως πᾶς Ἰσραὴλ σωθήσεται *kai houtos pas Israēl sōthēsetai*)—around which whole new theories have been built, theories not only of a new theological position but of fresh revelations suddenly received, visions of the end suddenly unveiled, an eschatology of almost Deus ex machina proportions in which God will put everything right and leave the late-modern world, never mind Paul, with no more questions. We should make no mistake: that is the magnitude of what is regularly proposed as the meaning of this half-verse. Whether it is the last-minute large-scale conversion to Christian faith of all Jews living at the time, or even of all Jews of every age; whether it is the eventual salvation of most or even all Jews, irrespective of Christian faith; whether it is the physical and geographical return of Jews to the land of Israel in the twentieth century, and/or their formation to be the leaders of the world after the church has been snatched away to heaven; the combinations and permutations of things that have

---

450. Other examples in BDAG 633.

been taught on the basis of these five words seem endless.[451]

The main positions, though, consist of various answers given to three questions: who is "all Israel," when will its "salvation" occur, and how will it be accomplished? Cranfield lists four options for the first: (a) all the elect, Jews and Gentiles alike; (b) all the elect of the nation of Israel; (c) the whole nation of Israel, including every individual; (d) national Israel as a whole, but not necessarily every individual.[452] The options on the timing are: (a) during the course of present history; (b) immediately before the second coming; (c) at the second coming. The answers to "how" are (a) through the people concerned coming to (Christian) faith; (b) through their own faith, whatever that might be; (c) through some direct divine intervention, perhaps through the agency of Christ at his second coming, which may or may not involve some kind of Christian faith.

To speak personally for a moment. When I began my study of Romans I was strongly committed to answering either (b) or (d) to the first question, either (b) or (c) to the second, and (c) to the third: that is, to understanding Paul to be saying that a very large number from national Israel would be saved at or around the time of the second coming, through the fresh revelation of the gospel that that event would supply. I changed my mind reluctantly, because of what seemed to me strong exegetical arguments; and, though this has put me in a minority even among my friends, let alone among the guild of New Testament scholars, I have seen no reason to change my mind again. I remain convinced that the right answers are (a), (a) and (a): God will save "all Israel"—that is, the whole family of Abraham, Jew and Gentile alike; this will take place during the course of present history; it will happen through their coming to Christian faith.

The principles of sound exegesis include reading short phrases in their contexts. We shall come to vv. 26b-27 presently; that is part of the puzzle, though as we shall see it strongly supports the view of v. 26a that I shall propose. But we must be clear. The weight of the whole argument of Romans is on the side of the reading I propose. If v. 26a does indeed teach a special kind of salvation for all or most Jews, with or without Christian faith, awaiting them at the end of time, then it is exegetically out of step with the passage before it (11:1-24) and, as we shall see, with the one that follows (11:28-32); it is theologically incompatible with the entire argument of 9:6–10:21; and it undermines what Paul has emphasized again and again in Romans 1–8. If Paul has indeed, while writing the letter, received as some have suggested a fresh revelation to the effect that the whole Jewish race will at the last be saved by some special means, he did the wrong thing by adding it to what he had already written. He would have done better to put the previous eleven chapters on the fire.

In addition, there are more problems with the prevailing view than normally recognized. It is not clear why saving only the final generation of Jews would get God off the hook. That is a bit too reminiscent of some secular utopias that have justified the evils of history by reference to what will happen when progress has finally achieved its goals.[453] But if a large-scale salvation of ethnic Jews is envisaged, that is what we would have to postulate: Paul clearly does not believe that most of his own contemporaries are being or will be saved (if he did, 9:1-5 is a sham and 10:1 a mere formality). Nor is it clear why switching modes of salvation at the last moment would make God look any the less arbitrary; that is exactly what Paul has argued that God has not done up to now.[454]

But there is, fortunately, no pressing reason to move in this direction. We are not forced to suppose that "all Israel" must mean "all Jews, or all living at the time of the end." The phrase "all Israel" is familiar from at least one well-known rabbinic saying, and it is at once followed by a list of exceptions.[455] Indeed, Paul may well be echoing that saying: "All Israel has a share in the age to

---

451. A good summary of views is in Fitzmyer, *Romans,* 619-20.

452. C. E. B. Cranfield, *A Critical and Exegetical Commentary on the Epistle to the Romans,* ICC, 2 vols. (Edinburgh: T. & T. Clark, 1975) 576.

453. See the suggestive essay of R. J. Bauckham, "The Year 2000 and the End of Secular Eschatology," in *Called to One Hope: Perspectives on Life to Come,* ed. J. Colwell (Carlisle: Paternoster, 2000) 249. This is a problem for the view offered by Moo, *Romans,* 722-23, and many others.

454. Against K. Stendahl, *Paul Among Jews and Gentiles* (Philadelphia: Fortress, 1976) 28.

455. *m.Sanh.* 10:1; cf. *T. Benj.* 10:11. The phrase "all Israel" is frequent in the biblical background; see 1 Kgs 12:1; Dan 9:11. Usually it means "the great majority of Jews alive at the time," but in Mal 3:22 it means the whole nation through time.

come"; it would certainly fit with his view of "salvation" to see it as the functional equivalent of the rabbinic "age to come." And, where the rabbis provided exclusion clauses to indicate that not all ethnic Jews did in fact qualify, Paul, in exactly the way we would guess from not only the whole of Romans but also Galatians and Philippians, modifies the phrase more radically. Abraham's true family are "not those of the law only, but all who share Abraham's faith" (4:16); "the Jew is the one in secret" (2:29); "you are all one in the Messiah, Jesus, and, if you belong to the Messiah, you are Abraham's seed, heirs according to promise" (Gal 3:28-9); "it is we who are 'the circumcision,' we who . . . put no confidence in the flesh" (Phil 3:3-4). These are simply the tip of the iceberg. Paul has spent half his writing life telling his readers that Abraham's family, Israel, the Jews, the circumcision, are neither reaffirmed as they stand, nor "superseded" by a superior group, nor "replaced" with someone else—that is what he is arguing against in 11:13-24—but transformed, through the death and resurrection of Israel's own Messiah and the Spirit of Israel's own God, so that Israel is now, as was always promised, both less and more than the physical family of Abraham: less, as in 9:6-13; more, as in 4:13-25.

In particular, 9:6 gives the lie to the constantly repeated assertion that one cannot make "Israel" in 11:26 mean something different from what it means in 11:25.[456] "Not all who are of Israel are in fact Israel"; Paul opened his great argument with a clear signal that he was redefining "Israel," and here the argument comes full circle. Romans 11:25 itself notes that a division has come about within ethnic Israel. Nor does this mean that "all Israel" must simply be a subcategory of ethnic Jews. As we saw in 10:1-13, Paul there announced that he was praying for the salvation of his fellow Jews, and described in detail how such salvation would come about, in accordance with Deuteronomy and Joel: all who call on the name of the Lord will be saved (10:13). That verse, as we noted, is actually a clear pre-statement of 11:26a: "All (who call on the name of the Lord; i.e., Israel) will be saved." Paul intends that

sentence both as the answer to the question of 10:1, the question of salvation for presently unbelieving Jews, and as the indication that God's mode of salvation, held out in Deuteronomy, is one that, as 9:24 had already indicated, would include Gentiles as well. The "all" of 11:26 looks back to the "all" of 10:11-13, and behind that of 4:16 ("all the seed . . . Abraham as the father of all of us"). Paul does not intend to say something radically different in 11:26 from what he has said already. The "mystery" is not a new revelation, standing over against the previous argument. It is the unveiled righteousness of God, of which Paul believed his kinsfolk to be ignorant (10:3).

In particular, of course, 10:13 looks back to 9:5: the Messiah is "God over all." The dramatic theological redefinition in 10:13, whereby "the Lord," which in the original clearly referred to YHWH, now refers to Jesus, undergirds the dramatic redefinition of God's people, whereby "Israel," as in 9:6 and Gal 6:16, now refers to the whole people of God, Gentile and Jew together. When, therefore, at the height of one of his most careful and long, drawn-out arguments, Paul declares with dramatic irony that "all Israel shall be saved," we must stand firm against the irresponsibility that would take the phrase out of its context and insist it must mean something he has carefully ruled out over and over again. However much we might want Paul to have said something else, exegesis will not sustain it.[457]

The phrase "all Israel," then, is best taken as a polemical redefinition, in line with Paul's redefinitions of "Jew" in 2:29, of "circumcision" in 2:29 and Phil 3:3, and of "seed of Abraham" in Romans 4, Galatians 3, and Rom 9:6-9. It belongs with what seems indubitably the correct reading of "the Israel of God" in Gal 6:16.[458]

When, therefore, is this salvation of "all Israel" to take place? The key is the phrase καὶ οὕτως (kai houtōs), which introduces "all Israel shall be saved." Translating this phrase "and so," as do the

---

456. E.g., Cranfield, *Romans,* 576. Good answers to this objection are supplied by J. Jeremias, "Einige vorwiegend sprachliche Beobachtungen zu Röm 11, 25-36," in *Die Israelfrage nach Röm 9–11,* ed. L. de Lorenzi (Rome: Abtei von St Paul vor dem Mauern, 1977) 199-200, 210.

457. Against both the extreme position (God will save all or most Jews irrespective of Christian faith) and the much more plausible reading (God will save a large number of Jews at the end, through Christian faith) of Fitzmyer, *Romans,* 623-24; Moo, *Romans,* 724-25.

458. See B. Witherington, *Grace in Galatia: A Commentary on St. Paul's Letter to the Galatians* (Edinburgh: T. & T. Clark, 1998) 453; J. L. Martyn, *Galatians,* AB 33A (New York: Doubleday, 1997) 574-77. There has been a considerable shift among scholarly opinion toward this reading of Gal 6:16; we may hope to see a similar shift in relation to Rom 11:26.

---

NRSV, the NIV, and many others, is technically not incorrect; but it may be misleading if it is supposed that Paul has a temporal sequence in mind, as many commentators have urged and many translations have indicated—in other words, if we imagine that "and so" really means "and then."[459] In English, "so" can mean, effectively, "then," or even "afterward." But the Greek οὕτως (houtōs) simply does not bear this sense.[460] It regularly means "thus, in this way, after this fashion, by this means." Often occurring in a pair with καθώς (kathōs, "just as . . . even so"), it describes the manner in which, rather than the time at which, something happens. To look no further than the present epistle (though a larger search through the NT would underline the same point), in every other occurrence in Romans houtōs obviously means "in this way," and never comes close to meaning "then" or "after that" (1:15; 4:18; 5:12, 15, 18-19, 21; 6:4, 11, 19; 9:20; 10:6; 11:5, 31; 12:5; 15:20; other Pauline instances of kai houtōs include 5:12; 1 Cor 7:17, 36; 11:28; Gal 6:2; 1 Thess 4:17; in each of these cases manner, not timing, seems clearly meant). In the present context it must mean "and in this way," or "and that is the way in which." It is the difference between saying "I do all the other chores first, and wait for the right moment, *and then* I go out and work in the garden" (a temporal sequence in which the last clause represents a new point) and "Every day I water the plants, mow the lawn, and sweep up the leaves; *and so* the garden will be at its best for the great day" (an explanatory addition in which the last clause draws attention to the significance of what has been going on all the time).

Does "in this way," then, refer to what Paul has just said ("hardening has come in part on Israel, the Gentiles are being saved—yes, and that is how God is saving 'all Israel' ")? Or does it refer to what he is about to say ("and this is how God will save 'all Israel': he will do it in the way that scripture indicates")? The former is considerably more likely. Paul can on occasion reverse the normal

order of καθώς . . . οὕτως (kathōs . . . houtōs, "just as . . . even so"); an obvious example is Phil 3:17 ("mark those who behave οὕτω houtō in this way, καθώς kathōs just as you have an example"); but mostly he retains the normal order, and we would have to have good extra reason to suppose that on this occasion he reversed it.[461] In addition, the phrase καθὼς γέγραπται (kathōs gegraptai) is such a standard formula that the apparent sequence houtōs . . . kathōs is likely to be a coincidence. The best interpretation of what Paul is saying is this: "A hardening has come upon part of Israel until the fullness of the Gentiles comes in; and *that process is the way in which God will save 'all Israel.'* This is in fulfillment of the scripture. . . ." (On "hardening" see Deut 29:4; Isa 6:9-10; 29:10; 2 Macc 6:12-15; see also the Commentary on 9:14-18.)

**11:26b-27.** At this point some will no doubt protest. Surely the quotations from Isaiah that now follow are intended by Paul to refer to the parousia? And does not this mean that he is thinking, throughout this passage, of a large-scale last-minute fresh act of salvation, not the steady process of "jealousy," and consequent coming to faith, that he has spoken of throughout chap. 11 so far?

This reading of 11:26b-27 has undoubtedly been popular.[462] But it is demonstrably mistaken. Even a glance at the contexts of the passages Paul actually quotes—which is usually, as we have seen, an excellent guide to his meaning—will show that he intends these biblical quotations to describe once more the same process of God's dealing with Israel's (and the world's) sins that he has already described in 9:24-6 and especially 10:6-13, with 2:25-29 and 8:1-11 in the immediate background. These texts, read from the point of view of a Second Temple Jew like Paul, speak of the same events, of exile being undone and sins forgiven, of covenant renewed and the word of faith put in the heart by the Spirit.

---

459. Cf. the NEB's "when that has happened, the whole of Israel will be saved." Among the most explicit is the JB's "and then after this the rest of Israel will be saved as well." Significantly, the NJB has modified this to "and this is how all Israel will be saved." See Joseph A. Fitzmyer, *Romans*, AB 33 (Garden City, N.Y.: Doubleday, 1993) 622-23, against, e.g., Barrett, Käsemann. Douglas J. Moo, *The Epistle to the Romans*, NICNT (Grand Rapids: Eerdmans, 1996) 720, appears to agree, but then smuggles back a temporal sequence that the text does not suggest.

460. See H. G. Liddell et al., eds., *Greek-English Lexicon with a Revised Supplement* (Oxford: Clarendon, 1996).

461. With Fitzmyer, *Romans*, 622-23; against P. Stuhlmacher, *Paul's Letter to the Romans: A Commentary*, trans. S. J. Hafemann (Louisville: Westminster John Knox, 1994). See also the similar οὕτως . . . ὡς (houtōs . . . hōs) in 1 Cor 4:1; 9:26 (twice).

462. Ernst Käsemann, *Commentary on Romans*, trans. Geoffrey W. Bromiley (London: SCM, 1980) 313-14; C. E. B. Cranfield, *A Critical and Exegetical Commentary on the Epistle to the Romans*, ICC, 2 vols. (Edinburgh: T. & T. Clark, 1975) 578; Stuhlmacher, *Paul's Letter to the Romans*, 172. For caution on this point, see Fitzmyer, *Romans*, 624-25.

The backbone of the scriptural citation comes from Isa 59:20-21. Isaiah 59 opens with a lament for Israel's continuing sinfulness; this includes vv. 7-8, which Paul has quoted as part of his indictment in 3:15-17. Then we read of YHWH himself intervening, wearing righteousness as a breastplate and salvation as a helmet (v. 17). YHWH will bring terrible judgment, so as to be feared by the nations of the earth, from east to west (vv. 18-19). In that context, "a deliverer will come to Zion [or: he will come to Zion as deliverer], and to those in Jacob who turn from transgression." At least, that is the meaning of the MT. The LXX has already altered this to mean "the deliverer will come on behalf of Zion, and will turn ungodliness away from Jacob." Paul has altered this again; the deliverer, he says, shall come out of Zion (ἥξει ἐκ Σιὼν ὁ ῥυόμενος *hēxei ek Siōn ho rhyomenos*). Perhaps he still has Deuteronomy in mind as well, because in 33:2, the beginning of the blessing of Moses, which ends with the salvation of Israel (33:28-29), we find "The Lord comes from Sinai" (Κύριος ἐκ Σινα ἥκει *Kyrios ek Sina hēkei*).[463] So far from pulling the text toward the parousia, he seems rather to be emphasizing the opposite: the redeemer, by whom he must mean Jesus the Messiah, "comes" from Zion into all the world, like YHWH "coming" from Sinai to establish the covenant and give Israel its inheritance. As the Messiah does so, he will banish ungodliness from Jacob. Once again texts that were unambiguously about YHWH in the Scriptures are taken by Paul to refer to Jesus.[464] And once again texts that looked forward to a future event are taken by Paul, not indeed to exclude the many still-future elements of his gospel (see Romans 8 and 1 Corinthians 15),[465] but to highlight the significance of what is already happening through the gospel.

"And this," continues Isaiah, "will be my covenant with them"—at which point Paul switches text, merging seamlessly into Isaiah 27. Had he continued with Isaiah 59, the description of the "covenant," which in context is obviously the covenant renewed after the exile, would tally closely with what he has said throughout the letter so far: "this is my covenant with them, says YHWH: my spirit that is upon you, and my words which I have put in your mouth, shall not depart out of your mouth, or out of the mouth of your seed . . . from now on for ever." This language of covenant renewal, replete with echoes of Joel 2, Ezekiel 36, and Jeremiah 31, also sends us back to Deuteronomy 30, as expounded in 10:6-11. God's Spirit and God's Word, placed by God in the mouths of the people, together renew the covenant. And, to move with Paul to Isa 27:9, with strong overtones of Jer 31:33-34 (38:33-34 LXX),[466] the substance of the covenant is this: God will take away Israel's sins. This is not, then, an alternative "covenant," a way to salvation for Jews and Jews only, irrespective of the entire apocalyptic salvation history Paul has laid out in 9:6–10:21. Nor has it much to do with the "pilgrimage of the nations to Zion," anticipated in some biblical and post-biblical prophecy (e.g., Isa 2:2-3; *Ps. Sol.* 17:26-46). At most, it would be an ironic reversal of that whole idea.[467] This is the same covenant renewal Paul has spoken of again and again in the letter. The hope for Israel according to the flesh lies not in clinging to its privileged status and hoping that, despite everything, God will in the end make a way of salvation other than that revealed in Jesus the Messiah and by the Spirit. Nor does it make any sense to suppose that in the last minute massive numbers of Jews alive at the time will suddenly arrive at Christian faith. What would Gentiles alive at the time say about God's impartiality, one of the major underlying themes of the whole letter? What might they say about God's constancy? No: the hope of salvation lies in the Messiah as the τέλος νόμου (*telos nomou*), the Torah's true goal, and in the renewal that remains available through him. God's salvation must be found where God has accomplished it, revealed it, and proclaimed it.

463. On the not dissimilar re-use of Deut 33:2 in 1 Enoch 1:4 see J. J. Collins, *The Apocalyptic Imagination,* 2nd ed. (Grand Rapids: Eerdmans, 1998) 48, with the comments of R. J. Bauckham, "Apocalypses," in *Justification and Variegated Nomism,* vol. I: *The Complexities of Second Temple Judaism,* ed. D. A. Carson et al. (Grand Rapids: Baker Academic, 2002) 142n. 24.

464. We do not need to postulate that such a move had already been made in pre-Pauline Judaism: the messianic reading of Isa 59:20 in *bSanh* 98a is interesting but probably irrelevant for Paul.

465. The warning of R. B. Hays, "Adam, Israel, Christ," in *Pauline Theology Volume III: Romans,* ed. D. M. Hay and E. E. Johnson (Minneapolis: Fortress, 1995) 83, against an overrealized eschatology is well taken, but what exegetes all too often embrace here is an under-realized one.

466. Joseph A. Fitzmyer, *Romans,* AB 33 (Garden City, N.Y.: Doubleday, 1993) 625, says that the present passage is "undoubtedly" a reference to the Jeremianic "new covenant."

467. See James D. G. Dunn, *Romans 9–16,* 38B (Dallas: Word, 1988) 655; Douglas J. Moo, *The Epistle to the Romans,* NICNT (Grand Rapids: Eerdmans, 1996) 684.

The combined texts in vv. 26b-27, then, undergird, rather than undermine, all that Paul has said so far in chaps. 9–11, and indeed in chaps. 1–8. Verses 25-27 as a whole fit perfectly into the flow of the chapter's argument, instead of sticking out from it like a sore thumb. This, Paul is saying, is how God is saving "all Israel," the people promised long ago to Abraham. God is doing it, not by having two tracks, a Jewish one and a Christian one (what would the "Christian one" mean for Paul if the "Jewish" bits were removed from it?); not by having a "Christian" scheme in the present and then re-inventing a "Jewish" one at the last minute; nor by suddenly relenting and allowing a partial, last-minute version of the "favored nation clause" that had been sternly ruled out up to that point; but by God doing, throughout the period that begins with the Messiah's death and resurrection, what had always been promised in Deuteronomy, Isaiah, and elsewhere. This is probably the implication of the last clause of v. 27: *"Whenever* I take away their sins" (ὅταν ἀφέλωμαι τὰς ἁμαρτίας αὐτῶν *hotan aphelōmai tas hamartias autōn*). That is, God is providing in the present time the path and the means of covenant renewal, of forgiveness, of healing and transformation, of life in and by God's Spirit: the way (in other words) of faith. Paul meant what he said in 11:23, picking up 10:1-13: They can be grafted in again, if they do not remain in unbelief. That rules out any suggestion of a mode of salvation, or a path to salvation, which does not involve the faith spoken of in chap. 10. I therefore conclude that in this passage Paul speaks of the ultimate salvation of all God's people, not only Gentiles but also an increasing number of Jews, a salvation to be brought about through the suspension of judgment (involving the "hardening" of those who do not believe) so that the gospel could spread to the Gentile world, and so by that means ethnic Jews might become "jealous" and so come to believe in their own Messiah.

**11:28-32.** The conclusion of the argument, like the conclusion of Sibelius's Fifth Symphony, comes in a succession of crashing theological chords, hammer-blows to round off the exposition, development, and climax. We have three typically Pauline statements, the first one with its own explanation, the second one explaining and clarifying the first, and the final one explaining and rounding off the entire sequence.

**11:28-29.** Paul has now spelled out the balanced view that will enable Gentile Christians to live by faith and without arrogance. He sums it up in v. 28, explaining the second part of it in terms of God's word not having failed (cf. 9:6) in v. 29. In terms of the gospel, he says, "they" (i.e., unbelieving Jews) "are enemies on your account." The NRSV adds the words "of God" after "enemies," but this is a case of protesting too much. Saying "on your account" makes it clear enough that unbelieving Israel is not the enemy of the church, but is rather hostile to the gospel itself, opposing it as a scandal and a nonsense. That, indeed, is the problem that sparks off the entire section, the problem that is heightened because of God's elective purposes and promises (9:11). The idea that unbelieving Israel is "beloved because of the ancestors"—that is, Abraham and Sarah, Isaac and Rebecca, and Jacob (and Leah and Rachel) (9:7-13), certainly does not mean that every Jew from that day to this, or every Jew in some hypothetical final generation, will eventually be saved. It means, rather, that God's own desire, like Paul's, is for them to find salvation in the full and final way it has now been achieved and unveiled. God has not written them off; that is the main point Paul is making. The contrast of "enemies . . . beloved" puts us in mind once more of 5:6-11, which explains yet again how it is that this "beloved" status can itself be the means whereby enmity can be overcome.

Why then does Paul say that they are "beloved because of the ancestors"? Once God has made promises, focused on gifts and callings, these cannot be revoked (v. 29). The word Paul uses here for "gifts" (χαρίσματα *charismata*) is used for "gifts" such as tongues and prophecy in 1 Corinthians 12 and for more general gifts of ministry in Rom 12:6; but Paul has also used it earlier in 5:15-16; 6:23 (see also 1:11) in the sense of the gifts of life, redemption, etc. We are back again to 9:6: God's word has not failed, it cannot fail, and it will not fail. God said that Abraham's family would be the bearers, as well as the recipients, of salvation, and this is what will happen. There will always be ethnic Jews among the "true Jews" of 2:29; there will always be physically circumcised people among the "true circumcision" of Phil 3:3; there will always be some from "Israel according to the flesh" (see the Commentary on 9:1-5, comparing 1 Cor 10:18) among "all Israel." Sin may have abounded through the Torah (5:20), but that was where grace more than abounded; and God will not revoke that grace.

**11:30-31.** As often, Paul's explanation of an initial compressed statement consists of an expanded version of the same point. In the present case, he retells once more the story of 9:6–10:21, to highlight particular features of it. He does so in two parts, the past (v. 30) and the present (v. 31). You Gentiles, he says (v. 30), were once disobedient to God. Now, however, you have received mercy—all because of their disobedience! He assumes again the connection, never fully spelled out, between Jewish disobedience to the gospel and the coming to faith of Gentiles (see the Commentary on 11:11-16). The point he is stressing is that, under God, the Gentiles depend for their chance at salvation on the "casting away" of Israel according to the flesh. They should no more look down on this Israel, therefore, than they would on the Messiah himself because of his salvific death. This leads naturally to the statement of the present situation (v. 31): in the same way, they have now been disobedient, but this is so that they too may now receive mercy.

What about the extra clause, "by the mercy shown to you"? In the Greek it is much more natural to take it with the verb "they have been disobedient." But the balance of the two verses, and the sense, make it likely that the NRSV and the NIV are correct to take it with "that they may receive mercy." The sense, in fact, is exactly that of 10:19 and 11:13-14: the mercy shown to Gentiles is meant to make unbelieving Jews "jealous," and so bring them to faith and salvation. If, however, the more likely meaning of the Greek is followed, Paul's sense must be that Jewish disobedience was in some way "caused" by the mercy shown to Gentiles—a new idea to the section, which is in itself unlikely at this moment when he is summing up.[468]

But when does this mercy happen? The word "now," included in the text of both the NRSV and the NIV, is missing in some good MSS. Others, however, have it, and the fact that a few lesser ones read "subsequently" suggests that there was

a word at that point that some scribes have seen fit to alter.[469] Even if this "now" were missing, however, the earlier occurrence of the same word in v. 31, together with the hint that this mercy comes about "because of the mercy shown to you," would be enough to tell us what Paul thinks is going on. The mercy that is shown to Israel according to the flesh is not something for which they will have to wait until some putative final day; it is not, therefore, something that can get the church off the hook by postponing a serious reckoning with contemporary Judaism until a conveniently delayed eschaton—as the laissez-faire thought of the Enlightenment might urge.[470] It is available "now"; and Paul's kinsfolk can, he hopes and believes, be provoked into seeking it by being "jealous" of the way in which Israel's privileges are being enjoyed by Gentiles. And this is precisely where the section began (9:1-5).

**11:32.** The final explanatory statement, as is appropriate, is about God. In an echo of Gal 3:22, Paul declares that God has locked up the whole human race in a prison called "disobedience," in order that what they then receive will be a matter of sheer mercy (for the sense of "mercy on all," see Wis 11:23).

In order to understand and appreciate the point Paul is making, we have to cast our minds back through the long argument of the letter so far. He declared, and demonstrated, that the whole human race was under the power of sin. All were "in Adam," and Israel's Torah only bound the nation the more tightly to sin and thence to death. But Israel was nevertheless the bearer of the promise, and the promise would be honored by God even if all humans failed. The Messiah, coming as the faithful Israelite, succeeded where all others had failed; his faithful, obedient death and resurrection accomplished salvation for all who believed. But how could God bring salvation not only to Gentiles—who were so far outside that it was obvious they could only come in by sheer grace and mercy—but also to Jews? How could God prevent it from seeming as though there were, after all, a "favored nation clause"? Paul's answer is that God has imprisoned Israel, too,

---

468. On the problem, see Christopher Bryan, *A Preface to Romans: Notes on the Epistle in Its Literary and Cultural Setting* (Oxford: Oxford University Press, 2000) 193; Joseph A. Fitzmyer, *Romans,* AB 33 (Garden City, N.Y.: Doubleday, 1993) 627.

469. νῦν (*nyn*): omitted by P46, A and others; included by א, B and the first hand in D. For details see Fitzmyer, *Romans,* 628; Moo, *Romans,* 711, 735.

470. See K. Barth, *Church Dogmatics* 2.2.305.

within "disobedience," so that, if and when Jews according to the flesh come to faith in Jesus as the risen Messiah and Lord, the justification they enjoy, and the salvation they await, will be for them, as much as for Gentiles, a matter of mercy from start to finish. The word of God has not failed. God has been true to the covenant; God's righteousness has been unveiled in the gospel of Jesus the Messiah, "to the Jew first, and also equally to the Greek" (1:17). Verse 32 is the conclusion, not only to chaps. 9–11, but to the whole letter so far. (See Reflections at 11:33-36.)

# Romans 11:33-36, Praise to the All-Wise God

# COMMENTARY

The concluding doxology emphasizes the sovereignty and inscrutability of God. Paul does not think that God's ways and purposes are now still invisible; they have been revealed in the Messiah. But he does believe that without the revelation granted in the gospel nobody would ever have worked them out. And yet, seen with hindsight, God's way of putting the world to rights, God's way of doing all things from creation to new creation, turns out to be spectacularly right, full of wisdom and insight, of appropriate judgment and overflowing mercy.

This is the longest of Paul's doxologies, almost as long as his two great christological poems (Phil 2:6-11 and Col 1:15-20), and not without echoes of both. It is rooted, as his thought often is, in the Jewish Wisdom tradition (see, e.g., 1 Cor 1:17–2:16; 3:18-23; 8:1-6; cf. 2 Bar 14:8-9; 20:4; 1QH 7:26-33; 10:3-7).[471] What is revealed in the gospel of

Jesus is not something other than the wisdom that ancient Jewish sages sought and celebrated, but the very same thing now made known for the salvation of the world.

**11:33.** Paul's opening words of praise stand on the edge of a cliff, looking down into the fathomless sea of God's riches. Sometimes, in prayer, one gets a glimpse like this, and the vastness, the teeming life, the power, the overall order and beauty, are beyond words. All one can do is point, and that is what this first sentence does. Look, he says, at the riches of God; look at God's wisdom and knowledge. The historical sweep of the divine purpose; the intimate understanding of human motivation; the interlocking of justice and mercy, kindness and severity, that bear patiently with terrible human wickedness and grieve over terrible human loss and tragedy, that yearn for humans to come back to the one in whose image they were made and find true life! All this is contained in these words: riches, wisdom, and knowledge. Paul

471. See E. E. Johnson, *The Function of Apocalyptic and Wisdom Traditions in Romans 9–11,* SBLDS 109 (Atlanta: Scholars Press, 1989) 168-71.

can only stand in awe. (The NRSV's "riches *and* wisdom *and* knowledge" is more likely than the NIV's "riches *of* wisdom and knowledge.")[472]

But it is not only what God has and is. It is also what God decides and does. God's "judgments," decisions about the world and about humans, cannot be searched out. We humans glimpse them from time to time, we trace small parts of them, but for the most part they are far out of our sight, where they belong. Human arrogance seizes upon this inscrutability as a reason to doubt, to mock, or to question God's wisdom or goodness; the humility proper to faith stands in awe that the God of all creation is the God of the gospel of Jesus, whose utter trustworthiness was demonstrated once for all in Jesus' resurrection.

**11:34-35.** At the heart of the hymn of praise Paul places one more double scriptural quotation, partly from his beloved Isaiah and partly from the book of Job, the greatest of biblical wrestlings with the problem of God's justice and human suffering. "Who has known the mind of the Lord?" asks Isaiah (40:13) at the start of his mighty exposition of God's creative power, the power now placed at the service of Israel-in-exile, God's unchangeable might now to be unleashed to bring about the return from exile through the work of the servant. Paul has cast himself in the role of present-day prophet, announcing the Isaianic gospel of the servant (10:14-17); now he celebrates Isaiah's God, the one through whom that gospel is initiated and confirmed. The quotation from Job 41:11 [41:3 LXX] comes from one of the most astonishing biblical statements of the sovereignty of God over all creation. God is in nobody's debt; nobody ever gives God a gift and stands back smug in the knowledge that God must now repay. All is of grace, and only of grace; to think otherwise is not to forget merely some fine-tuned or subtle bit of theology, but rather to forget the meaning of the word "God" itself in the biblical tradition. The God whom Paul has glimpsed in the gospel, whose justice and mercy he has been expounding in this his greatest letter, is vast and mysterious as the sea, near and intimate as breath, decisive and compassionate as a Galilean holy man on his way to a cruel death. The Wisdom tradition, the prophetic tradition, the Pentateuch, the psalms—all are now

poured out in justice and mercy, through the gospel of Jesus the Messiah and the power of the Spirit. Let us not imagine that because neither Jesus nor the Spirit are named in vv. 33-36 Paul has forgotten them. If Romans 11 was not built foursquare upon Romans 8 it would not be able to stand upright.[473]

**11:36.** But stand it does, because the God of whom it speaks is the one from whom, through whom, and to whom are all things.[474] Elsewhere, when Paul uses this language (1 Cor 8:6; Col 1:15-20), he is quite explicit. Jesus the Messiah, the Lord, the Son, is the one "through whom" the one God, the Father, has acted and does act in creation and redemption. The Holy Spirit, the Spirit of the Son, is the one through whom Father and Son act together to renew the covenant with a worldwide family, to bring the "word" very near, on the lips and in the heart. Paul has no need to spell out the detail in this short doxology, because he has already painted it in from so many angles and now just wishes to stand back and gaze in wonder. To this God, he concludes, be glory forever, Amen. Giving glory to God was what humankind failed to do (1:21), which was why humankind itself fell short of that glory (3:23). Abraham, in faith, gave glory to God (4:20), believing that God was indeed able to keep the life-giving promises. Now, in hope, through the gospel of the Messiah, Jesus, the glory is restored (5:2; 8:30); but the glory remains God's, God's to give, God's to be reflected back to God, God's own forever.

In Romans 9–11 Paul belongs in the tradition of the great psalmists. He starts with an urgent problem; he wrestles with it in grief and prayer; he retells the story of Israel, laying out God's acts from of old and in the present. Finally he bursts through to a paean of praise. From this point in the letter we look back and see, as glorious mountain peaks, 4:24-25 and particularly 8:28-30 and 38-39. But where we now stand is higher than them all, so high that some climbers feel dizzy and prefer to return quickly to the lower slopes. Paul is not of such a mind. He will stay and give praise. This, he implies, is what we humans, we Jews, were made for.

---

472. See Moo, *Romans*, 741.

473. We should not ignore the parallel to v. 34 in 1 Cor 2:16, where "the Lord" is, of course, Jesus; see also 1 Cor 3:21-23. We should at least hold open the posibility that the κύριος (*kyrios*) of v. 34 is the same as that in 10:13.

474. There are similar statements in some Stoic writings (see Dunn, *Romans 9–16*, 701-2), but Paul's thought remains anchored in Judaism.

# REFLECTIONS

**1.** Of the two most urgent matters that concern today's interpreter coming to terms with Romans 11, the first is undoubtedly the way in which Christian readers today can make Paul's argument their own without losing their balance. On the one hand there lies the long, ugly tradition that Paul was doing his best to head off, the tradition of denouncing the Jews and declaring that they are an accursed race. We all know where that leads. On the other hand there lies the overreaction, the eagerness to say that Paul has no critique whatever of Israel according to the flesh, the readiness to pull his text completely out of shape if only we do not (dreaded thought!) have to be so politically ignorant, naive, or simply incorrect as to say that Jesus was and is the promised Messiah and that Paul envisages salvation coming only by the route of confessing him as Lord and believing that God raised him from the dead.

Of course, a solution lies close at hand—a solution that many preachers are only too happy to use on other texts. It is perfectly possible to say that Paul says one thing but that we, today, must believe and live by something else. The discomfort one may feel at abandoning the text as authoritative will be more than made up for by the relieved smiles of the congregation, who no longer need be shocked by attitudes that modern and postmodern thought are eager to label as arrogant, imperialistic, or exclusive—not noticing, of course, that to treat texts in this way is to be guilty, oneself, of all those things. Romans 2:1 has hemeneutical as well as ethical implications. Perhaps one problem underlying at least some post-Holocaust theology is that, being eager to avoid the hard, high, and all-embracing claims of the gospel in other areas of our lives, we are a bit too keen to point out ways in which these claims, when misapplied in the social and political sphere, have done damage, and worse than damage, to peoples and communities.

Yet the challenge of Paul's analysis of the problem of Israel remains, and perhaps only now, two generations after the Nazi Holocaust, can we start to look at it again with the clarity of hindsight not only on the 1930s and 1940s but on that which has been done, with the Holocaust as pretext, in the Middle East over the last fifty years. Christianity and Judaism are, or ought to be, close cousins, yet the very closeness highlights differences as well as similarities, claims made by both that might both be false but that cannot both be true.[475] And if Christians remain loyal to Jesus of Nazareth they cannot evade the challenge of his Messiahship, upon which is based his universal lordship. He is not a private or a tame savior, available on tap, like a favorite beer, for those who want some salvation now and then. If he is not Messiah and Lord, the whole of Christianity is indeed based on a mistake and ought to be abandoned. But what if he is?

If he is, then however much breast-beating remains appropriate for Christians after centuries of arrogance and violence toward Paul's, and Jesus', kinsfolk according to the flesh, there must still be the agony (not the easy acquiescence) that sees them still in rebellion against the gospel; there must still be the prayer (not merely the patronizing acceptance of "otherness") that seeks salvation on their behalf. It is noticeable that at no point in Romans 9–11 does Paul say that he evangelizes Jews directly. He remains the missionary to the Gentiles. We assume that Peter and others still undertake their mission to the Jews (Gal 2:9); but all that Paul will say is that his work with Gentiles is designed to make his kinsfolk jealous and so save some of them. He will pray for them; he will do his own work with one eye on them; he will take a collection, no doubt at considerable personal danger both of misunderstanding and of violence on the road, in order to make his kinsfolk see that Gentiles are sharing their blessings, their common life; and he will tell the Roman church in no uncertain terms not to write them off, not to imagine that Jews can no longer be welcomed into the family of the Messiah. That, for Paul, would be the very height of anti-Judaism.

---

475. See N. T. Wright, *The New Testament and the People of God,* vol. 1 of *Christian Origins and the Question of God* (London: SPCK; Minneapolis: Fortress, 1992) 471-76.

Here, in fact, is the crowning irony of today's attempt to appropriate Romans 9–11. For Paul, anti-Judaism would mean imagining that Jews cannot come to faith in Jesus. For many today, anti-Judaism means supposing that they can and should. There is no easy way through this dilemma. Imagine what it was like for the Prodigal Son, and his older brother, the morning after the party with the fatted calf.[476]

Paul's "solution" is itself challenging and worrying. Jews, we ask, "jealous" of Gentile Christians? The very thought is laughable in much of the modern world. The church has cut such a sorry figure, has seemingly done so much to alienate the older brother, that, for all the internal problems and divisions of contemporary Judaism, there is little reason to suppose that today's Jews look at today's Christians and say to themselves "there they are, enjoying our privileges!" To ask the question, what might the church have to be like for serious-minded Jews even to think like that for one minute, is to raise all sorts of other questions that Romans 9–11 was not written to address. But it is perhaps the right place at which to start reflecting on how those who wish to take Paul seriously might go about doing and being in our own day what he believed himself called to do and be in his own in relation to his beloved kinsfolk, his people "according to the flesh."

As one aspect of this, we can scarcely ignore, as is sometimes done as though they were a category mistake, those who in our own churches are ethnically Jewish but Christian by conviction, baptism, and life. They are Paul's heirs indeed, and need and deserve our prayers for their particular and often painful witness.

**2.** The second obvious and necessary point is that Paul nowhere gives the slightest indication that ethnic Israel will one day return to their land and set up an independent state, which will in due course become the vehicle of God's blessing to the world. Of course, in his day his kinsfolk were still living in the land and worshiping in the Temple. Most Jews were already in the Diaspora, but many were living in the holy land, and had been for centuries. There was no thought of that awful second exile, of the desolations of 70 CE and 135 CE, of the banishment to which, in the eyes of many, the creation of the modern state of Israel has provided the answer. But even if there had been, there is nothing in Romans or elsewhere in Paul to give any theological support to the latter notion. The roots of the return-to-the-land theology that has become so extraordinarily popular among some churches in our own day are to be sought in the dispensationalist speculations of the nineteenth century, not in the apostolic writings of the first. As far as Paul is concerned, the promise to Abraham and his family was that they would inherit the world (Rom 4:13), the world that would share in the freedom of the glory of God's children (8:18-27). Any attempt to give a Christian gloss to the Middle Eastern political events of 1947 and thereafter is without exegetical foundation.

**3.** At the heart of Romans 9–11 there lies the humility that recognizes God as God and does not try to second-guess or criticize what God has planned and done. Cynics and skeptics of every age, not only the much-vaunted "humankind come of age" of the Enlightenment, have of course questioned everything, challenged everything, put God in the dock and declared that such a being either does not exist or, if he/she/it does, they disapprove of his/her/its actions. Fearful that every authority is necessarily oppressive, and that every order that does not proceed from within oneself is manipulative, our present-day orthodoxy has left God on the margins, an aid to spiritual well-being for those who feel they need it. But if God is the creator, and we are creatures; if God is holy, and we are sinful—and if these two things are not so, why have we kept company with Paul in the first place?—then there is a proper and grateful humility that is neither oppressed nor manipulated, a giving glory to God that enhances and does not diminish our true humanness. There is a time to ask the hard questions, and Paul encourages us to do so.

476. See N. T. Wright, *For All God's Worth* (Grand Rapids: Eerdmans, 1997) chap. 13.

There is also a time for recognizing, like Job, that our questions have missed the point, and that God's answers are, for the best of reasons, final.

**4.** Underneath Paul's repeated warning to the Gentile Christians of Rome we hear a warning that is as important in its different ways in today's church and world as his was at the time. If Paul has criticized his kinsfolk according to the flesh for their "boast," he will also point out to the Gentiles, who in Jewish terms had nothing to boast of, that there is such a thing as inverted "boasting." Most of the "isms" of our time have their reverse side, as different social, cultural, ethnic, gender-based, and agenda-based groups clamber over one another in the anguished quest for the high moral ground. Inverted prejudice, even when completely explicable as defense or natural reaction, as the long scream of the victim, is still prejudice. Where, as in the case of Rome, it may just happen to chime in with a prejudice of long standing in the local culture, it is doubly dangerous.

**5.** The detailed argument of Romans 9–11 works through the key issue that faced Paul, the issue of unbelieving Jews and of God's faithfulness to the age-old promises. But the same argument could be applied in several other spheres. Starting from the promise to redeem the whole creation (8:18-27), one could ask the equivalent question and work through to a similar answer: has God forgotten the promise to creation? No, the argument would run if we constructed it in parallel to Romans 9–11, because the promise always envisaged death and rebirth. There are already, however, signs of rebirth, of healing and new life; and God intends that there should be more of them. Just as Paul rules out Jewish privilege on the one hand and Gentile rejection of Jews on the other, so a Christian cosmology would rule out the neo-pagan or pantheistic uncritical affirmation of the created order on the one hand and the dualist rejection of it on the other. Just because we are not pantheists there is no reason to suggest that God will not redeem the whole creation. Indeed, the categories of new covenant and redemption developed by Paul in these chapters could well prove valuable in thinking through several similar or related issues.

**6.** At the heart of many of these issues, as of Romans 9–11 itself, lies the challenge of learning to tell the story. Partly this is a matter of unlearning misleading ways of telling the story of God, the world, Israel, Jesus, and the church. It takes a certain skill to unpack the stories that are implicitly being told, in both church and world, and to make the right adjustments, additions, or deletions to bring them into line with the many-stranded but essentially quite simple story Paul himself is telling. Once that is done, and the story is regularly checked for signs of wear and tear—particularly, for signs that it is becoming self-congratulatory or triumphalistic—it becomes one of the most basic tools of Christian thinking, apologetic, and instruction. Stories, not least the large-scale story from creation to new creation, from covenant to renewed covenant, from Abraham to Moses to the Messiah to final salvation, have their own dynamic. They are bottom-line reality—arguably, if Paul is anything to go by, more bottom-line even than "doctrines." When Paul wants to confront, to comfort, to build up, to worship, his regular way of doing so, admirably displayed in these chapters, is not to offer two or three abstract doctrines. It is to tell the story and invite his readers to make it their own. That remains a prime task of Christian teaching.

# GOD'S CALL TO WORSHIP, HOLINESS, AND UNITY

## OVERVIEW

P aul may be exhilarated by the vision he has laid before us, but he is by no means exhausted. His main argument is not done yet, despite impressions to the contrary.[477] There is, to be sure, a huge turn at this point in both content and (for the most part) style. But the exposition of "the gospel" that began with 1:3-4—the gospel, that is, which announces Jesus the Messiah, whose resurrection demonstrates that he is indeed God's Son and marks him out as the world's true Lord—this exposition continues right through to its closing statement in 15:7-13, one of the most telling theological passages in the letter, which completes the huge circle begun in chapter 1. So, too, the unveiling of God's "righteousness," God's saving justice, through this gospel, is not complete until Paul has shown how the "justified" community lives its life on the basis of its shared belief in Jesus as Lord; until, that is, what we might call the κοινωνία τῆς πίστεως (koinōnia tēs pisteōs), the "fellowship of faith," matches and embodies the δικαιοσύνη τῆς πίστεως (dikaiosynē tēs pisteōs), the "righteousness of faith." And as he does so we discover that one of the major theological themes of chapters 1–11—God's bringing together of Jew and Gentile in the Messiah—now becomes also one of the major practical themes of chaps. 12–16.

But that is only the beginning. Romans 12–16 is the ultimate answer to those who suggest that Paul's "ethics" are not really related to his "theology."[478] Indeed, the way those two terms have sometimes been used implies that belief and behavior are of their very nature completely

separate human activities, whereas for Paul they are inextricably interwoven. They are the breath and blood of Christian living, the twin signs of life. Here as elsewhere we should beware of reading back into Paul the disjunctions of much later philosophy, such as that between "is" and "ought," between facts and values. Paul has little time for abstractions like "values," except as they, like every other human thought, are swept up into the revitalized human life that the gospel brings about.

That is indeed the point, and even a glance at the opening of the section (12:1-2) indicates that Paul is stitching the letter together with threads of many colors. It is not just a matter of verbal links and echoes, but of major themes now to be restated, as in a symphony, in a new key perhaps but easily recognizable by all but the tone deaf. God's "mercies" generate an appeal to those who know and have received them. The renewal and harmony of body and mind looks back to the scene of human devastation in chapter 1, to the initial reversal of this in chapter 4, and especially to the promise of restoration, beginning indeed in the present time, in chapter 8. But—in case anyone should think that therefore, despite all that was said above, the argument does indeed skip from chapter 8 to chapter 12—the underlying thrust of these verses is that Christians, Jew and Gentile alike, now offer to the one true God the full and final sacrificial worship in which Israel's worship (cf. 9:4) is made complete. It is, in fact, because of 9–11 that Paul can now explain how it is that all the forward pointers in chaps. 1–8 can now be realized. Ecclesiology—if that is the best word for Paul's rich and nuanced understanding of God's people in the Messiah—provides both context and challenge for "ethics."

So, of course, does eschatology. Romans 12:1-2

---

477. J. Ziesler, *Paul's Letter to the Romans* (Philadelphia: Trinity Press International, 1989) 290.

478. Here I agree strongly with R. B. Hays, *The Moral Vision of the New Testament: A Contemporary Introduction to New Testament Ethics* (San Francisco: Harper, 1996) esp. 16-59.

draws explicitly on the essentially Second Temple Jewish view that world history divides into two ages, the "present age" and the "age to come," and insists that the two now overlap and that Christians belong in the latter. It is not, then, that the gospel, and the power of the Spirit, simply enable Christians to do somewhat better what other people have tried to do. It is, rather, that the new day has begun to dawn, and that those who belong to the Messiah must live in its light rather than in the darkness of the present world. This indicates, incidentally but helpfully, how this whole section divides up: 12:1-2 points forward to 13:11-14, giving the first two chapters an eschatological framework within which the wide-ranging general instructions of 12:3–13:10 are to be understood (see below), before 14:1–15:13 offer more specific and detailed exposition of a particular issue.[479]

Nor are ecclesiology and eschatology absent from the final division, 15:14–16:27. Paul's travel plans (to go on, via Rome, to Spain), and his request for help (15:14-24), are tightly integrated into his vision of his own vocation as the Apostle to the Gentiles and into the inner meaning and dynamic of the gospel itself (see 1:1-7 with 1:8-15). His present preoccupation—that he is about to go to Jerusalem with a gift of money collected from Gentile churches—belongs with the same understanding (15:25-33). The unusually lengthy closing greetings (16:1-16, 21-23), and the other concluding remarks (16:17-20, 25-27), are likewise not simply tossed off to complete the letter, but make their own point in practical outworking of what has been said already.

It is striking that at several points in this section Paul seems to be echoing the teaching of Jesus himself—something that, notoriously, he does very little.[480] Specific examples will be noted below; none is uncontroversial, but the cumulative effect may be worth pondering. We cannot tell from what sources Paul knew of such material; nor can we tell (since he never here says "as Jesus taught us" or anything like it) whether the sayings were well enough known that he could appeal to

Jesus' authority by implication, or whether they were little enough known at this stage that he would have remained content for the allusions to go unnoticed. I incline to the former view; Paul, I believe, saw Jesus not simply as the crucified and risen Messiah and Lord but also as the one whose teaching articulated the way of life belonging to the new age he came to inaugurate. That this does not reduce Jesus to the status of a mere moral teacher, or cast doubt on the centrality of his death and resurrection, should be obvious.

This point is underscored by another introductory reflection. The pattern of Christian living that Paul sets out here includes the call not to be overcome by evil, but to overcome evil with good (12:21). This challenge, summarizing much of the opening chapter, is then developed further in 15:7-8, where its christological underpinnings become explicit; the pattern of overcoming evil not by revenge but by patient suffering and trust in the justice of God (12:14-21) is one of the most striking themes in early Christianity. The great theological and christological themes may be muted in this section, but we do not have to look very far to see that their lack of explicit mention is a sign, not that they are forgotten, but that they are everywhere presupposed.

To what extent, then, are these chapters "general teaching," the kind of thing Paul would have said to any church in any situation, and to what extent are they specific to the church in Rome? The attempt to tie down the instructions here, particularly those of chapters 14 and 15, to specific groups and situations in the Roman church was given a new boost by the work of Paul Minear a generation ago.[481] There is no agreement on how this works out in detail (or on how much knowledge about groups and parties in Rome Paul might actually have had), but many agree that here at least Paul has a particular aim specific to the Roman church, even if we cannot always be sure who precisely the "strong" and the "weak" may have been and to what extent they represented points of view, or church groups, familiar to Paul from other settings as well (see the Overview of 14:1–15:13). The view taken here is that chapters 12 and 13 are more general, laying foundations,

---

479. See Douglas J. Moo, *The Epistle to the Romans,* NICNT (Grand Rapids: Eerdmans, 1996) 747.

480. See particularly M. Thompson, *Clothed with Christ: The Example and Teaching of Jesus in Romans 12.1–15.13,* JSNTSup (Sheffield: Sheffield Academic, 1991).

481. P. Minear, *The Obedience of Faith: the Purposes of Paul in the Epistle to the Romans* (London: SCM, 1971).

though not without an eye to the particular situation, and that chapters 14 and 15 are more specific, though not without an eye to other situations (cf. chaps. 14–15 with 1 Corinthians 8–10, for instance) and other related issues. This in turn may help us, as more of the Roman situation comes into view, to understand better why Paul wrote this letter to this church at this moment.[482]

As we have seen, it would be wrong to drive a wedge between chaps. 1–11 and chaps. 12–16, or between two things labeled "Pauline theology" and "Pauline ethics." Paul's theology is always ethical, and his ethics are always theological, even if some of the letters (not all) seem to divide quite neatly into two sections that invite that kind of labeling (the best example is Ephesians 1–6, which is ironic in view of the majority view that it was not written by Paul; obvious counterexamples include the Corinthian and Thessalonian letters). Romans 6 and 8 are hardly nonethical, just as the present section is hardly nontheological. However, it is striking that in the present section some of the key words and themes from chaps. 1–11 are completely absent. The "righteousness"/"justice" word group (δικαιοσύνη *dikaiosynē* and its cognates) simply does not occur. "Faith" is an important theme (12:3, 6; 14:1-2, 23-24), but its meaning has sometimes been thought different from what was discussed in chapters 3–4 and 10. Jesus the Messiah is not highlighted until 13:14, though he is then omnipresent in 14:1–15:13. We should not suppose that he is absent from Paul's mind at any point in 12–13; in fact, as we shall see, the apparently incidental reference to being "in Christ" in 12:5 is probably to be taken as thematic. However, there is no extended discussion of him or his work, and no reference in these first two chapters to either his death or his resurrection. Unlike chaps. 5–8 and 9–11, there is no sense that the underlying biblical references, allusions, and echoes are evoking a larger scriptural narrative; the string of references in 15:7-13, to be sure, points to the eschatological and messianic hope of Israel, but neither there nor elsewhere in the section does Paul attempt to lay out the rest of the grand story. He has already done that, and can presuppose it here. Granted that none of this

means a move away from theology toward a detached set of behavioral instructions, what does it signify?

It signifies, I think, that Paul has completed the main structure of the letter and does not need to repeat himself. We have reached the summit of the mountain range, the place from which you can see around in all directions; but the journey must now continue, down the other side, without the strenuous work of climbing, but still with a sense of continuity in our aim and goal. From time to time Paul will refer to the height he has now reached, and perhaps to the path up which he has climbed; but what follows now, with the characteristic "therefore" (οὖν *oun*) of 12:1, is about results, not process.

The last five chapters of Romans divide naturally, then, into two: 12:1–15:13 and 15:14–16:27. The former, which is also the last major section of theological exposition in the letter, subdivides into two segments of nearly identical length: 12:1–13:14 (35 verses) and 14:1–15:13 (36 verses), the first part being more general and the second more specific. In turn 12:1–13:14 divides, though this is more complicated and disputed, into six: 12:1-2 (introduction and foundation); 12:3-13 (unity in the church through each exercising their gifts); 12:14-21 (the church's life, particularly facing those outside); 13:1-7 (responsibility toward authorities); 13:8-10 (the overriding responsibility of love); and 13:11-14 (living in the light of God's dawning day). Of these divisions, the hardest decision is whether to see 12:9-13 as belonging with 12:3-8 (the view taken here), as a separate section in itself, or as introducing 12:14-21; but this is a matter more of tidiness than of content.[483] More interesting is the place of 13:1-7; as we shall see at the relevant point, the section has often been regarded as something of a cuckoo in the nest of Romans, but in fact it goes very closely with the preceding passage, which deals with avoiding vengeance. Chapters 12 and 13, taken together, thus form a circle or chiasm:

---

482. For the view that Romans 12–13 as well as 14–15 are directed more specifically to the Roman situation see J. Moiser, "Rethinking Romans 12–15," *NTS* 36 (1990) 571-82.

483. The mention of "good and evil" in 12:9, 21 might suggest that 12:9-21 is a single section; but these are such general terms that using them as a structural marker strains the point somewhat. Against Joseph A. Fitzmyer, *Romans,* AB 33 (Garden City, N.Y.: Doubleday, 1993) 658. The word for "evil" is different (πονηρόν *ponēron* in v. 9; κακόν *kakon* in v. 21).

A    12:1-2
  B        12:3-13
    C          12:14-21
    C′         13:1-7
  B′       13:8-10
A′   13:11-14

Romans 12:1-2 set out the Christian's obligation within the dawning "age to come," which joins up

with 13:11-14. The appeal for unity and love (12:3-8, 9-13) is matched in turn by 13:8-10. This leaves 12:14–13:7 at the center of the section, dealing from two different angles with the problems of living as citizens of God's kingdom (see Phil 3:20) while also continuing to live in the "present world" with its various challenges.

# ROMANS 12:1-2, THE WORSHIP OF BODY AND MIND

NIV

**12** Therefore, I urge you, brothers, in view of God's mercy, to offer your bodies as living sacrifices, holy and pleasing to God—this is your spiritual[a] act of worship. [2]Do not conform any longer to the pattern of this world, but be transformed by the renewing of your mind. Then you will be able to test and approve what God's will is—his good, pleasing and perfect will.

[a] 1 Or reasonable

NRSV

**12** I appeal to you therefore, brothers and sisters,[a] by the mercies of God, to present your bodies as a living sacrifice, holy and acceptable to God, which is your spiritual[b] worship. [2]Do not be conformed to this world,[c] but be transformed by the renewing of your minds, so that you may discern what is the will of God—what is good and acceptable and perfect.[d]

[a] Gk brothers    [b] Or reasonable    [c] Gk age    [d] Or what is the good and acceptable and perfect will of God

# COMMENTARY

The opening two verses of the section are as dense as any passage in Paul, and as so often they state concisely a theme that will then be unpacked and explored in various different ways. The key transition word is "therefore": not the only time Paul draws an ethical conclusion in this letter (see, e.g., 6:12; 8:12), but the most obvious moment of transition between the two major parts of the letter (see Overview). But the key word that tells us what sort of material is to come is the opening παρακαλῶ (parakalō), the modern Greek word for "please," as in "Please, will you do . . . ?" This is a many-sided word for Paul, ranging from "comfort" to "exhort," and the present instance is clearly closer to the latter; but this is not an empty exhortation, trying by rhetorical force to make people do things they might otherwise not, but an appeal based squarely on what has gone before. The RSV's and the NRSV's "appeal" is therefore

preferable to the NIV's and the NJB's "urge," though the latter supplies a force to this opening sentence that should not be softened. (The NEB's and REB's "implore" sounds like a desperate and emotional begging, which is quite inappropriate.)

The ground of the exhortation is "the mercies of God." Paul has spoken of God's "mercy" often enough in the preceding chapters to make it clear that the present appeal is grounded not simply on chaps. 1–8 but on chaps. 9–11 in particular. True, the word he uses here (οἰκτιρμῶν oiktirmōn; the plural reflects underlying Hebrew usage) is unusual for Paul (ἔλεος eleos is more common, as in 11:31). But its cognate verb has occurred in his quotation of Exod 33:19 at 9:15, and it stands here as a way of summing up "the depth of God's riches and wisdom and knowledge" as invoked in 11:33.

In particular, the opening verse indicates that

the foundation of all Christian obedience is that those in Christ, indwelt by the Spirit, are to offer to God the true sacrificial worship to which the cult of the Jerusalem Temple had all along pointed. Romans 12:1 does with temple worship, in other words, what 2:25-29 did with circumcision, just as 15:7-13, at the close of the section and of the letter's great argument, envisages Jew and Gentile alike joining in worship of the true God under the lordship of the Messiah. This can hardly be overemphasized. Paul has spoken of the "worship" that was one of Israel's privileges (9:4); now he makes it clear, as with the other elements in that list, that this worship is now offered by all Christians, Jew and Gentile alike (see also 10:9-13).

This sacrificial worship, though not involving animal sacrifices, is not simply "spiritual" in the sense of "not involving physical sacrifices." Many Jews of Paul's day and before, not to mention the post-70 rabbis, spoke of nonsacrificial forms of worship as the equivalent of the temple cult. This goes back, indeed, to the psalms themselves (Ps 141:2).[484] But here, though this element is certainly present, we should not be too eager to press it. Paul envisages the sacrifices in question as being physical, indeed animal; but the animals are human, and they are not to be ritually slaughtered but "presented" to God, still alive. What are to be presented are the "bodies" of Christian worshipers. As we saw earlier, the word "body" enables Paul to look in both directions; at the Christian still living within the world of space, time, and matter, as here, and as living within the multiple pressures and temptations that this places upon us, as in 8:13 where "the deeds of the body" are indeed to be "put to death."[485] Here as there, however, the point of "body" is not that it refers to one part only of the human totality, but that it refers to the complete person seen from one point of view: the point of view in which the human being lives as a physical object within space and time. This whole self is to be "presented"—the word itself carries sacrificial overtones—to God;

this implies that we should expect Christian worship to have an emphatically bodily character, however much it is also true that worship must be, in Johannine language, "in spirit and in truth" (John 4:23). It must also be stressed that, though the primary worship, the primary "presentation" that Paul envisages, is the obedience of the whole person to the commands that follow, it would be foolish to exclude from this the actual occasions of formal and informal worship when the person is physically present and performs bodily actions in the course of that worship.

These sacrifices are "holy" (the word carries here, as often, both its sense of moral uprightness and its allusion to the temple cult; hence the NJB's "dedicated"), and "well-pleasing to God." (KJV, RSV, NRSV, "acceptable" is possible, but the word is strong and should not be watered down to give the idea that God might just about be prepared to accept these sacrifices.) Paul, unusually, repeats the word "well-pleasing" in the very next verse, making it clear that for him at least what a Christian does, in Christ and by the Spirit, gives actual pleasure to God. This is counterintuitive for many Christians, schooled to insist that nothing we do can commend ourselves to God. But Paul insists in several passages that Christian worship and obedience, holiness and unity do indeed please God, and if we have articulated his other doctrines (e.g., justification) in such a way as to exclude this notion, we have clearly misrepresented him. (See 14:18; 2 Cor 5:9; Eph 5:10; Phil 4:18; Col 3:20—all the same word as here; see also the use of ἀρέσκω [areskō] in 1 Cor 7:32; 1 Thess 2:4; 4:1; and, most strikingly, Rom 8:8, where "those in the flesh" cannot please God but, it is strongly implied, "those in the Spirit" can and do.) In fact, the alternative to "pleasing God" is not simply living at a morally neutral state, neither pleasing nor displeasing; it may well be "to please oneself" (15:1), or (in a bad sense) "to please other people" (Gal 1:10). If we want to enquire further as to how it can be that a human being, a creature and a sinner, can please the living God, the holy creator, the logic of the letter as a whole, and of Paul's arguments elsewhere, suggests that it might have something to do with being restored in God's image (see 1:18-25 and the Commentary; 8:29; Col 3:10).

Paul describes this complete human worship as

---

484. For details of later writings see N. T. Wright, *The New Testament and the People of God* (Minneapolis: Fortress, 1992) 229n. 48.

485. W. Bindemann, *Die Hoffnung der Schöpfung: Römer 8, 18-27 und die Frage einer Theologie der Befreiung von Mensch und Natur,* Neukirchener Studienbücher 14 (Neukirchen-Vluyn: Neukirchen, 1983) 102-3.

"your spiritual worship." The word translated "spiritual" by the NRSV and the NIV is not, however, πνευματικός (*pneumatikos*), as one might have imagined. It is λογικός (*logikos*), which as the KJV indicates can mean "reasonable" in the sense of "in accordance with reason." The JB offers a helpful paraphrase in this sense: a worship "that is worthy of thinking beings." In Revelation 4–5, the "beasts," representing creation, worship God totally but unreflectively, and then the twenty-four elders, representing God's people, declare that God is *worthy* of this worship, reflecting on who God is and what God has done. Similarly, Paul may here be insisting, however paradoxical this may sound to ears attuned to later dualisms, that the offering of the *body* is precisely the thing that *thinking* creatures ought to recognize as appropriate. This is more likely than that he is deliberately echoing or aping Stoic ideas in which the λόγος (*logos*) formed the true inner core of every human; there are distinct echoes, but the Stoic would not have agreed that offering one's body to God was the appropriate type of worship.[486] Paul is not highlighting a kind of worship that transcends and therefore need not include the actions of the body itself. This "logical worship," likewise, is more than simply "the worship to which our argument points," though the phrase could mean that as well and it is no doubt true.

**12:2.** The second sentence does not unpack the first, but stands alongside it as the head of the whole section. In accordance with what he has said all along, Paul sees the new age, long awaited within Judaism, as having broken in to the present age in the Messiah, and understands Christians as living at their point of overlap, needing constantly to reject the pressures of the present age and to be open to the life of the new, the life offered in the Messiah. Here is the interface, for Paul, between what scholars call "eschatology" and "ethics": because you are in fact a member of the age to come, if you are in Christ, new modes and standards of behavior are not only possible but commanded.[487] This new behavior, like the "living

sacrifices," is pleasing to God, and Christians should be able to think it out and realize why. Thus, if verse 1 focuses on the body, but with the mind being involved as well (the "reasonable worship"), v. 2 focuses on the renewal of the mind, but the result is that people, being thus transformed, can work out in practice what is the right thing to *do*.[488]

"Don't let the world around you squeeze you into its own mould" was J. B. Phillips's translation of the start of verse 2. It remains memorable, catching the sense of pressure and temptation that "the present age" (Phillips missed the eschatological nuance) constantly provides. This is not a matter of simply resisting pressure from the outside, and discovering the pure unsullied world "within." That is the road to various kinds of gnosticism, the discovery of a hidden spark that, already present, just needs to be uncovered. Rather, as Paul insisted in 1:18-32, the human mind and heart are, in their natural state, dark and rebellious, full of wickedness and evil. What is required is not for people simply to learn to live authentically, without external pressure, but for them to be renewed, so that what proceeds from the transformed mind does indeed reflect the image of God.[489] The verbs are probably in the present tense, though several manuscripts have aorist instead, reflected in the NIV's implication ("Do not conform any longer") that Paul supposes his hearers to have been conforming to the present age up to now. It is more likely that at this point in the letter he is putting forward a general command rather than a specific and urgent one.[490]

The "mind" is a key category in Paul's vision of renewal (cf. 7:25 and 8:5-8). Instead of the "unfit mind" of 1:28, Paul holds out a vision of a mind renewed, able now at last to think for itself what will please God, instead of being darkened by the deceitfulness of sin (see also the suggestive "we have the mind of the Messiah" in 1 Cor 2:16). The

---

486. See Philo *Special Laws* 1:277; Epictetus *Discourses* 1.16.20-21; 2.9.2. See also A. J. Guerra, *Romans and the Apologetic Tradition: The Purpose, Genre and Audience of Paul's Letter*, SNTSMS (Cambridge: Cambridge University Press, 1995) 157-58; T. Engberg-Pedersen, *Paul and the Stoics* (Louisville: Westminster John Knox, 2000) 262-65.

487. See the classic discussion of V. P. Furnish, *Theology and Ethics in Paul* (Nashville: Abingdon, 1968).

488. Some good MSS add "your" with "mind"; whether or not this is original, it is certainly the sense, and the NRSV and the NIV are not misleading when they insert it.

489. The particular words Paul uses (συσχηματίζεσθε *syschēmatizesthe* and μεταμορφοῦσθε *metamorphousthe*, with their root nouns σχῆμα *schēma* and μορφή *morphē*, both of which mean "outward form," "shape") should probably not be pressed for further nuances; in other words, it would not have made much difference if Paul had used συμμορφίζω (*symmorphizō*) and μετασχηματίζω (*metaschēmatizō*), both of which occur in Phil 3:10, 21.

490. So Moo, *Romans*, 755.

Christian is not meant to rely simply on lists of ethical commands, but to be able to discern (NRSV), to test and approve (NIV), what God's will is— God's will, it seems, primarily for general ethical conduct but also, perhaps, for specific decisions and occasions. Paul's vision of living sacrifice, and mind renewed, generates a picture of Christian behavior in which rules matter but are not the driving force, in which thought and reflection matter but without reducing ethics to purely situational decisions. And once again Paul insists that God's will, when found and followed, is "good, pleasing, and perfect." Fear of the various movements that go under the name "perfectionism" ought not to put us off from reflecting that, with all the ambiguities and perplexities of Christian moral life, there is such a thing as knowing and doing God's will, and that we are commanded to pursue it, as Paul indicates in 1 Cor 3:18-23, humbly but confidently.

# REFLECTIONS

**1.** Paul's transition from chapters 1–11 to 12–16 is a model of integrated theological and practical thinking and writing, and hence a notable standard for those who preach expository or doctrinal sermons. As I have said, we should beware of assuming too readily that the two parts of the letter correspond exactly to what later generations have called "doctrine" and "ethics," and we should note in particular the point at which our perception of these things shades off into the decidedly unbiblical "facts and values" distinction. For Paul, the central facts are the death and resurrection of Jesus the Messiah, the world's true Lord; but if ever facts were value-laden, these are. Genuine humanness, genuine obedient faithfulness to the one God, has appeared on earth, has suffered and been vindicated. Before this fact there are no mere spectators, only subjects and rebels.

**2.** It is interesting, though, that Paul does not at this stage appeal to the lordship of Jesus as the groundwork of his moral vision. That will come later, in chapters 14 and 15. For the moment he concentrates on the images of new sacrifice and new world, brought about by the work of Jesus. The fact that later in the chapter he seems to draw on or echo the teaching of Jesus should not weaken this observation. He will not turn Jesus into either a schoolmaster to give lessons or a policeman to make sure they are obeyed. The foundation of his ethic is what Jesus *accomplished:* the whole new world, the "age to come" of Jewish expectation, into which the baptized enter and in which they must live by the Spirit. This is where we see how important it is that in chapter 6 the Christian is precisely no longer an "old human being," but instead stands on resurrection ground. Because the resurrection itself took place within continuing earthly history, and is indeed always threatened by "historical" enquiry in the sense of would-be "scientific" historiography that excludes certain things from the start, those who are "risen with the Messiah" in the sense of Col 3:1 (which I argued earlier, despite the normal assumption, is present in Romans 6 as well) are always threatened in their moral behavior by the still-unredeemed world with its assumptions and pressures, its sneers and compromises. But the Christian is not left to struggle alone. When Paul speaks of "the renewal of the mind," he is alluding to the work of God's own self in the person of the Spirit (see again 8:5-9). The Spirit is even now at work to make the new age a reality; and the space-time location where this must happen, as in chapter 8, is none other than the actual bodies of Christians. Inaugurated eschatology begins at home.

**3.** Verses 1 and 2 offer a fine balance between sacrifice and fulfillment, between an ethic of self-denial and one of self-discovery. Even the self-discovery, however, is the discovery of the *new* self that one is called to become in Christ and by the Spirit, not the uncovering of a hidden truth or inclination that had been present all along. Grace fulfills nature, but only by putting it to death (the living sacrifice) and bringing it to life again (the renewing of the mind). Exactly as in the bracing commands of Jesus himself (e.g., Mark 8:34-38), the path of self-sacrifice is the path of self-fulfillment, as through true, whole-person worship people discover to their surprise that being truly human is not what the present age supposes. Taking up the cross is the way to life, even though believing this is never easy, whether one has been following Jesus for a single day or a lifetime.

**4.** The other more obvious balance, or, perhaps better, integration, is that of body and mind within Christian obedience. Neither insincere following of an outward code, nor the easy immorality of keeping the mind (supposedly) pure while the body can do what it likes, will suffice in the new age that began with Jesus' resurrection. Behind the body/mind integration of these verses we may hear, once again, the biblical command to love God with heart, mind, soul, and strength: the *Shema,* in fact, to which Paul has alluded before (see 1:5; 3:27-30; 5:5; 8:28) and whose fulfillment is now in sight, as it will be when the present passage is unpacked in 13:8-10.

**5.** Perhaps the most striking and pastorally relevant feature of these verses is the point already stressed in the comments: that worship and obedience of this sort really does "please God." Centuries of post-Augustine and post-Reformation thought have quite rightly emphasized the free, unmerited grace of God, and the response of faith alone, as the basis of the Christian's standing in Christ, his or her membership in the family whose sins have been dealt with through Jesus' death. But this tradition, precisely in order to avoid the impression of compromise at this central point, has often failed to give due weight to the proper and regular Pauline emphasis that those who are justified in Christ and indwelt by the Spirit can, should, and regularly do "please God," that God is delighted with them not merely because they appear "in Christ" but because of what they are, and are becoming, and are beginning to do. This has nothing whatever to do with justification, and if for a single moment anyone supposed that it did the danger of self-satisfied Pelagianism would again open up before us like a dark pit. It may be difficult to keep one's balance in these matters. But to insist on the unbalanced and unbiblical view that Christians are incapable of pleasing God, in order to avoid the equally unbalanced and unbiblical view that Christians earn God's free grace, is like avoiding railway accidents by staying safely at home. We can never avoid the danger of misunderstandings. Christian living is always a risk. But with Paul as our guide we do not need to be gloomy or defensive about this. He was used to walking tightropes.

# ROMANS 12:3-13, UNITY, LOVE, AND COMMUNITY LIVING

**NIV**

[3]For by the grace given me I say to every one of you: Do not think of yourself more highly than you ought, but rather think of yourself with sober judgment, in accordance with the measure of faith God has given you. [4]Just as each of us has one body with many members, and these members do not all have the same function, [5]so in Christ we who are many form one body, and each member belongs to all the others. [6]We have different gifts, according to the grace given us. If a

**NRSV**

[3]For by the grace given to me I say to everyone among you not to think of yourself more highly than you ought to think, but to think with sober judgment, each according to the measure of faith that God has assigned. [4]For as in one body we have many members, and not all the members have the same function, [5]so we, who are many, are one body in Christ, and individually we are members one of another. [6]We have gifts that differ according to the grace given to us: prophecy, in

NIV

man's gift is prophesying, let him use it in proportion to his[a] faith. [7]If it is serving, let him serve; if it is teaching, let him teach; [8]if it is encouraging, let him encourage; if it is contributing to the needs of others, let him give generously; if it is leadership, let him govern diligently; if it is showing mercy, let him do it cheerfully.

[9]Love must be sincere. Hate what is evil; cling to what is good. [10]Be devoted to one another in brotherly love. Honor one another above yourselves. [11]Never be lacking in zeal, but keep your spiritual fervor, serving the Lord. [12]Be joyful in hope, patient in affliction, faithful in prayer. [13]Share with God's people who are in need. Practice hospitality.

[a] 6 Or in agreement with the

NRSV

proportion to faith; [7]ministry, in ministering; the teacher, in teaching; [8]the exhorter, in exhortation; the giver, in generosity; the leader, in diligence; the compassionate, in cheerfulness.

[9]Let love be genuine; hate what is evil, hold fast to what is good; [10]love one another with mutual affection; outdo one another in showing honor. [11]Do not lag in zeal, be ardent in spirit, serve the Lord.[a] [12]Rejoice in hope, be patient in suffering, persevere in prayer. [13]Contribute to the needs of the saints; extend hospitality to strangers.

[a] Other ancient authorities read serve the opportune time

# COMMENTARY

The present passage has a good deal in common with various other Pauline exhortations to the church to live as a single community, notably 1 Corinthians 12 and Philippians 2. In both cases what really counts is that the community Paul is addressing is to be shaped by the Messiah himself. In particular, in the Messiah Christians are to strive for unity, which will come through the humility in which each thinks soberly about his or her own gifts and role rather than placing too high a value on them. In the present passage, too, we would be right to see the Messiah as the shaping force underneath the argument. We would probably be right to see the reference to the church as being "one body in the Messiah" (12:5) as standing deliberately near the head of the present section (at least 12:1–15:13) much as did the reference to the Messiah being "of their race according to the flesh" in 9:5, and indeed the fuller reference with which the letter itself opens (1:3-4). Certainly the unity of believers in the Messiah continues to be a recurring theme through to 15:13.

Verses 3-13 divide, as we have said, into 3-8 and 9-13; and vv. 3-8 themselves divide naturally into the introduction (v. 3), the main statement (vv. 4-5), and the immediate application in terms of the use of different gifts (vv. 6-8). These are intended for the whole church, not simply for a "charismatic element" within it.[491]

**12:3.** The appeal that follows is intended, it seems, to explain (γάρ gar, "for") and thereby, in usual Pauline style, to unpack the dense opening of vv. 1-2. "Offer God the true worship; be transformed by having your minds renewed; because you should be thinking as one people in the Messiah."[492] The "for" thus belongs with the whole sequence of thought, not least vv. 4-5, not simply with v. 3 itself. The basic appeal—which Paul addresses emphatically to every single one of his readers—is not just from Paul speaking on his own authority. He makes it because God has equipped him for a particular task, with "the grace given to me." Paul remained conscious—as, given his extraordinary vocation, he needed to—that he attempted the tasks he did because God had appointed him to a specific role, which he refers to in this way elsewhere both in this letter and in his other writings (1:5; 15:15; 1 Cor 3:10; 15:10; Gal 2:9; Eph 3:2, 7-8; cf. Col 1:25). Sometimes this introduces a specific reference to his ministry to the Gentiles (cf. 11:13); and since the appeal in this verse echoes quite closely that of 11:20 and

491. Against Fitzmyer, Romans, 645.
492. Against Moo, Romans, 760, whose explanation would require a "therefore" or "and so" rather than a "because."

25, where the respective places and roles of Gentile and Jew are at stake, we may suppose that that thought is not far from his mind. He is, after all, laying foundations here for chaps. 14 and 15, where that mutual relationship is again in view. But for the moment he wants to make the foundation wider and deeper, and so moves to the more general point about all Christians individually learning how to think soberly about themselves.

The appeal itself is couched in quite formal tones, with a repetition of the basic word that is hard to capture in English. "Do not overthink above what you ought to think, but think in wise-thinking ways"; that is more or less it, and as with the emphasis on the mind in 12:2 (cf. 8:5-8) it stresses the role of disciplined thinking as being at the very root of basic Christian living. Here the point is that, just as in 11:25 Gentiles should not think too highly of themselves, so here all Christians should keep guard on their own self-opinion; not, of course, that they should strive for a false or inappropriate humility but that their judgment should be sober and serious.

Paul actually sets up a standard by which one may judge oneself: "the measure of faith" God has apportioned. It is possible that by this he means that every Christian has been given a different "measure of faith," some greater, some less. That would certainly make some sense in the present passage: one should, according to that interpretation, regard oneself in terms of the amount of faith one has.[493] It might be thought, as well, that this would point on to the discussion of the "strong in faith" and the "weak in faith" in chapters 14–15. But there is more to be said for the rival view: that the "measure of faith" is the same for all. Throughout the letter so far, "faith" is the same for everybody (3:27-30): belief that Jesus is Lord and that God raised him from the dead (10:9; cf. 4:24-25). Paul's point here is not that some should give themselves airs and that others should feel inferior, but that all should exercise their varied gifts on a level one with another. The last mention of "faith," in fact, was in a very similar context: branches were broken off because of unbelief, you only stand fast because of faith, and the branches

themselves can be grafted in again if they do not remain in unbelief—so do not think too highly of yourselves! (see 11:19-25). The "measure" here, then, is not a kind of measuring-jug containing different amounts of faith, apportioned to different people, but a measuring-rod, the same for all, called "faith." It is up to each Christian to see where they come against that standard, since it is the only one that matters.[494]

**12:4-5.** One of Paul's most powerful images for explaining the combined unity and diversity of the church is that of the body; and this, alongside 1 Corinthians 12, is one of the two classic passages on the subject. (In Ephesians and Colossians a subtly different point is made, Christ there being spoken of as the head of the body; see Eph 1:22; 4:15; 5:23; Col 1:18; 2:10, 19.) The present passage differs slightly from 1 Corinthians in that there, having set up the analogy in a very similar way to the present passage, Paul says simply "so also is the Messiah," indicating an identity between the meaning of "the Messiah" (ὁ Χριστός *ho Christos*) and the many "members" who together make up his "body," his complete existence in the world of present space and time (1 Cor 12:12, 27). This needs, and immediately receives in 1 Corinthians, a clear statement of the indwelling Spirit, which, while being paralleled in various ways in Romans, is not matched in chapter 12. Instead, in Romans 12, Paul keeps the picture one stage removed from apparent total identification: "We, being many, are one body in the Messiah." (It is not clear why the NIV has put "in Christ" at the start of the sentence, distancing it from "body," or why it has translated ἐσμεν [*esmen*] as "form" rather than simply "are.") In fact, the subtle distinction between 1 Cor 12:12 and Rom 12:5 is more at the level of surface expression, and should not be taken to indicate a shift in underlying meaning; Paul can say similar things elsewhere in 1 Corinthians in a way that indicates that his thought was flexible on this point within a comprehensible framework (see, e.g., 1 Cor 6:15; 10:17). And that framework is, as we have seen several times before in Romans, Paul's belief that,

---

493. See C. K. Barrett, *A Commentary on the Epistle to the Romans* (London: A. & C. Black, 1957) 235; James D. G. Dunn, *Romans 9–16*, 38B (Dallas: Word, 1988) 721-22.

494. So Douglas J. Moo, *The Epistle to the Romans,* NICNT (Grand Rapids: Eerdmans, 1996) 761; Joseph A. Fitzmyer, *Romans,* AB 33 (Garden City, N.Y.: Doubleday, 1993) 647. Christopher Bryan, *A Preface to Romans: Notes on the Epistle in Its Literary and Cultural Setting* (Oxford: Oxford University Press, 2000) 197, suggests that the reference is to God's own faithfulness.

since the resurrection demonstrated Jesus to be the Messiah, he now in that capacity represented his people, summing them up "in" himself, so that what was true of him was now true of them. This is the logic that underlies chapter 6, and the decisive 8:1, as well as the many other "in Christ" passages elsewhere in his writings (see the Commentary on 6:1-23).[495] To be "in Christ," as here, is to be a member of the Messiah's people; to speak of "one body in Christ" is to emphasize the unity of that people despite its obvious diversity.

It is possible that Paul is aware, in using this image, that pagan writers had spoken in similar terms about "the body politic."[496] There may even be a hint, though this should not be pressed on the basis of the present passage, that Paul sees the community of the Messiah's people as an entity over against the great political entity of the time, the state of Rome (see the Commentary on 13:1-7). At the same time, it is noteworthy that, whereas he speaks of the solidarity between the Messiah and ethnic Jews in terms of "flesh" (9:4), something has happened to create a different unity, a different solidarity, which is spoken of instead in terms of "body." Compare Paul's language about "my flesh" in 11:14, the background to which is found in 2 Sam 5:1//1 Chr 11:1, where the tribes of Israel say to David, "We are your bone and flesh" (see also Judg 9:2; 2 Sam 19:12-13). This substitution of terms fits so well with Paul's regular language about the corruptible, dying self ("flesh") and the self that is to be resurrected ("body") that we may well wonder whether he is not suggesting that this new entity, the "one body in Christ" as here or the "body of Christ" as in 1 Corinthians, is as it were the resurrected version of "Israel according to the flesh."

If this is the truth of the united whole, what is true of each one individually? (See the NRSV; the NIV's "each member" does not quite catch the emphasis of the Greek, which is almost "one by one," as though Paul were doing a quick head count, pointing to each person in the room in turn.) They belong to one another. We are so used to the word "member" referring to someone who belongs to a society or club that we are in danger

of ignoring the fact that here "members" (μέλη *melē*) means "parts of the body," and belongs with the extended metaphor (the JB and the NJB bring this out by translating "parts"). In 1 Corinthians 12 Paul spells this out in terms of the metaphor: one is an eye, another a foot, and so on. Here, though the point is substantially the same (the passage, indeed, has the flavor of Paul repeating, more swiftly, something he knows he has said before), he launches straight into a list of gifts.

**12:6-8.** The gifts listed here, which he refers to as "spiritual gifts" (χαρίσματα *charismata*), is identical neither with the list in 1 Corinthians 12 nor with the similar lists in, e.g., Eph 4:11, though they overlap. It is difficult to know how much weight to put on the fact that seven "gifts" are listed here (prophecy, ministry, teaching, exhortation, giving, leading, and compassion), perhaps indicating the completeness of God's provision for the work of the church (cf. eight in 1 Cor 12:28, but this omits "interpretation," which is referred to as though it is part of the same list in 1 Cor 12:10, 30; there are five in Eph 4:11, or four if "pastors and teachers" are the same people). The list itself is incomplete in the sense that several categories mentioned elsewhere are missing. Paul does not mention "apostleship," possibly because he does not suppose there to be any "apostles" in Rome (though see 16:7). Nor does he mention tongues, interpretation, healing, or special words of knowledge, as in 1 Corinthians 12. There is probably not much of significance to be drawn from this; possibly this list is deliberately general, emphasizing "ordinary" rather than "extraordinary" gifts, because Paul does not actually know what special gifts the Christians in Rome may possess.

His main point is that just as God has given him grace for his task (v. 3), so God gives the church grace for its multiple and mutually supportive tasks, and whatever they are they must be exercised to the full extent of one's powers. The NIV supplies the verb for this ("let him use it"), which brings out Paul's intention although, as in the NRSV, there is no corresponding word in the Greek (RSV, "let us use them"; NJB, "let us devote ourselves"). It is possible that Paul intends the participle at the start of v. 6 ("having gifts") simply to modify the main verb of v. 5 ("we are one body in Christ, and individually parts belonging to one another"), and so means the list to imply "and this

---

495. For details, see N. T. Wright, *The Climax of the Covenant: Christ and the Law in Pauline Theology* (Edinburgh: T. & T. Clark, 1991; Minneapolis: Fortress, 1992) chaps. 2 and 3.
496. E.g., Plato *Republic* 462c-d; Livy 2:32; Plutarch *Arat* 24:5; *Cor* 6:2-4.

will mean that the teacher should get on and teach" and the like.

With most of the gifts in the list, the thrust of the commands is obvious: servers should serve, teachers should teach, and so on, with as much energy and skill as they can. This is clear with the second, third, and fourth "gifts," ministry (or "serving," NIV), teaching, and exhortation, where the word describing how one should exercise one's gift is simply the cognate word of the gift itself. The final three (giving, leading, showing compassion) develop the idea slightly (givers should be generous, leaders should be diligent, compassion should be shown cheerfully), and this leads naturally into the more general commands of vv. 9-13.

But what about the strange phrase in v. 6 that explains how "prophecy" should be exercised? Prophecy, it seems, should be exercised "in proportion to faith" (NRSV) or "to his faith" (NIV, supplying the "his"; NEB, "a man's"; REB, "our"; the JB paraphrases: "use [the gift of prophecy] as your faith suggests"; NJB, "we should prophesy as much as our faith tells us"). The implication is that the level or content of the "faith" will vary from prophet to prophet, and that a prophet should exercise his or her gift to the full extent of that faith. It is possible, however, that as with the "measure of faith" in v. 3 we should understand this as a reference to "the faith" as the same standard for all, so that the point is that prophets should not feel themselves at liberty to say whatever comes into their heads, but rather should speak in conscious accord with the beliefs that make the church what it is. Since this is the only NT passage in which ἀναλογία (*analogia*) occurs, we cannot gauge Paul's meaning from parallels. But its basic meaning concerns proportion within a relationship,[497] and it seems to me more likely that Paul intends to refer to the proportional relationship between the Christian faith as a whole and what individual prophets say, rather than to the proportional relationship between the gift of prophecy and the amount of faith an individual prophet may have.[498]

**12:9-13.** There then follows a more general list of ways in which individual Christians and groups or churches are to behave, ways almost all of which are concerned with building up the community as a whole (i.e., not simply with the pursuit of individual virtue or holiness as though for its own sake).

**12:9.** Love stands at the head of the list, as often in Paul (see above all 1 Corinthians 13; and also Gal 5:22). We should assume that this word refers not just to the feelings that Christians have for one another (Paul returns to that in v. 10) but to the practical care for each other that marked the early church (see 1 Thess 4:9-12; it is clear there, however, that the words φιλαδελφία [*philadelphia*] and ἀγάπη [*agapē*] are very close in meaning for Paul, so that we should not drive a wedge between vv. 9-10). There follows a string of participles and adjectives; grammatically these appear to modify the main verb of the opening sentence, even though Paul has left it unexpressed (ἡ ἀγάπη ἀνυπόκριτος *hē agapē anypokritos;* lit., "Love—genuine!"). These are the ways, in other words, in which love will show itself to be the true version rather than a counterfeit, which is all the more interesting in that the list of these ways begins with the most general of moral commands, to loathe what is evil and to cling tightly to what is good (both verbs are strong: "hate" [NRSV, NIV] is not forceful enough). This is best explained in terms of 13:10: Love will always do what is good rather than what is evil, since this will be for the good of the other person. Paul presupposes that there is a large area of moral life that does not need spelling out; everyone knows that some things are good and others evil, and at this point there will be a substantial overlap between the Christian community and their neighbors both Jewish and pagan.

**12:10-13.** The rest of the list consists of lightning sketches of ways to build up the community. There must be real affection; Christians should look up to one another (lit., they should "go first and lead the way in showing honor to one another").[499] They should not (v. 11) be lazy when it comes to diligence and eagerness (this is rather like saying "you mustn't be slow when you're being swift," which seems somewhat obvious, but

497. Cf. BDAG 67, "a state of right relationship involving proportion."

498. Against C. E. B. Cranfield, *A Critical and Exegetical Commentary on the Epistle to the Romans,* ICC, 2 vols. (Edinburgh: T. & T. Clark, 1975) 621.

499. See BDAG 869.

it appears to correspond to our phrase "not be backward in coming forward"). Their spirits must be constantly aglow, like the fire that burns in an old-fashioned stove to keep the house warm and to be ready for cooking and similar tasks. And they must regard themselves as servants of the Lord, that is, of Jesus himself.[500] Their life (v. 12) should be a steady stream of rejoicing in hope, remaining patient under suffering, and giving themselves to

prayer (again, the word Paul uses is a strong one, indicating an eager and persevering devotion—the sort of attitude that takes trouble over prayer rather than being perfunctory or "when I feel like it"). And (v. 13) they should share with Christians in need, and be eager to be hospitable, to open their home to those who may need to share it. This, again, is not something other than "love," but is part of what Paul and other early Christians meant by that large and all-embracing term.[501]

---

500. A few MSS read "serving the time" (καιρῷ *kairō* instead of κυρίῳ *kyriō*), presumably intending it in a sense something like Col 4:5; but this is almost certainly a corruption. See, however, Brendan Byrne, *Romans,* SP 6 (Collegeville, Minn.: Liturgical, 1996) 379, who suggests that it means "make the most of the time remaining."

501. On hospitality, see Heb 13:2. The NRSV's addition of "to strangers" is perhaps an overexplanation: The word φιλοξενία (*philoxenia*) and its cognates can be used for hospitality simply within the Christian community, as in 1 Pet 4:9.

# ROMANS 12:14–13:7, THE CHURCH FACING THE OUTSIDE WORLD

## OVERVIEW

It has been customary to separate out 13:1-7 from its surroundings, but though it is obviously a separate paragraph it belongs closely with the end of chapter 12. Noting this link helps a certain amount in addressing the problem that, outside the central theological questions of justification, the law, and christology, has probably vexed commentators more than anything else. What did Paul mean by "submitting to the ruling authorities" (13:1), and why did he command it?[502]

Taking 12:14-21 and 13:1-7 as two halves of a statement of Christian responsibility vis-à-vis outsiders gives to the whole of 12–13, as noted above, a certain symmetry (12:1-2 and 13:11-14 locate Christian living in its wider eschatological framework, insisting on the obedience of bodily life in the present period; 12:3-13 and 13:8-10

expound the obligation of love within the Christian community; now, in the middle, the present two paragraphs deal with the life of the church over against the surrounding world). It is true that some parts of 12:14-21, especially vv. 15-16, could be seen as speaking still of life within the church, but the transition in v. 14 is quite marked, grammatically as well as in content, and it is probably better to see those parts, though no doubt relevant in church life as well, as dealing principally with Christian responsibility toward outsiders. In particular, 12:19-20 forbids vengeance in terms that link closely to the description of the rulers' obligations in 13:4, and it seems clear that Paul intends these two passages to be mutually interpretative. There is a balance to be kept between looking outside the Christian community at threatening wolves coming to attack and looking outside at God-given civic authorities whose vocation it is to keep order and peace. If 13:1-7 had been read in this light, some old problems might have been avoided.

---

502. I leave out of further consideration the desperate expedient, still adopted by some, of striking 13:1-7 down as a later gloss. See the list in Moo, *Romans,* 791; W. Munro, *Authority in Paul and Peter: The Identification of a Pastoral Stratum in the Pauline Corpus and 1 Peter,* SNTSMS (Cambridge: Cambridge University Press, 1983) 56-67.

# Romans 12:14-21, Christian Living Amid (Possibly Hostile) Outsiders

## NIV

[14]Bless those who persecute you; bless and do not curse. [15]Rejoice with those who rejoice; mourn with those who mourn. [16]Live in harmony with one another. Do not be proud, but be willing to associate with people of low position.[a] Do not be conceited.

[17]Do not repay anyone evil for evil. Be careful to do what is right in the eyes of everybody. [18]If it is possible, as far as it depends on you, live at peace with everyone. [19]Do not take revenge, my friends, but leave room for God's wrath, for it is written: "It is mine to avenge; I will repay,"[b] says the Lord. [20]On the contrary:

"If your enemy is hungry, feed him;
    if he is thirsty, give him something to drink.
In doing this, you will heap burning coals on his head."[c]

[21]Do not be overcome by evil, but overcome evil with good.

[a] 16 Or *willing to do menial work*     [b] 19 Deut. 32:35    [c] 20 Prov. 25:21,22

## NRSV

14Bless those who persecute you; bless and do not curse them. [15]Rejoice with those who rejoice, weep with those who weep. [16]Live in harmony with one another; do not be haughty, but associate with the lowly;[a] do not claim to be wiser than you are. [17]Do not repay anyone evil for evil, but take thought for what is noble in the sight of all. [18]If it is possible, so far as it depends on you, live peaceably with all. [19]Beloved, never avenge yourselves, but leave room for the wrath of God;[b] for it is written, "Vengeance is mine, I will repay, says the Lord." [20]No, "if your enemies are hungry, feed them; if they are thirsty, give them something to drink; for by doing this you will heap burning coals on their heads." [21]Do not be overcome by evil, but overcome evil with good.

[a] Or *give yourselves to humble tasks*    [b] Gk *the wrath*

# COMMENTARY

**12:14.** The NRSV and the NIV, and most other translations, are right to treat this as opening a new paragraph (against NEB, REB). Paul switches from the string of participles to a pair of straight imperatives, with a further string of participles dependent on them (imperatives, v. 14; two infinitives, equivalent of imperatives, v. 15; three participles, explaining these, v. 16a; a further imperative, v. 16b; four participles, vv. 17-19a, giving rise to further imperatives, vv. 19-21). Instead of the Christian community taking care of one another, the attention has now shifted to those who would attack and harm them. We do not know of specific persecution in the Roman church during the 50s, but Paul assumes, here as elsewhere, that persecution will come to those who remain loyal to Jesus (1 Thess 2:14; 3:3-4; cf. 2 Tim 3:12). And the appropriate response to it is blessing, not cursing. At this point

Paul stands firmly with Jesus and the entire early Christian tradition against all other traditions known to us. The noble stories of the Maccabean martyrs typify the tradition Paul would have received: the seven brothers in 2 Maccabees 7 go to their deaths calling down solemn curses on their persecutors. But in both Jesus' teaching and his own practice there was a strikingly new note: Hostility was to be met with prayer, and violence with blessing (Matt 5:38-48; Luke 6:28-35; 23:34; Acts 7:60; 1 Cor 4:12; 1 Pet 2:20-23; 3:9; Eph 5:1 should probably be considered in this light as well).[503] It is hard to imagine this teaching becoming the norm in the church, as it clearly did from the very start, unless it was firmly rooted in the words and example of Jesus himself.

503. On prohibitions of vengeance in Judaism (usually referring only to fellow Jews, not to "enemies") see K. Yinger, "Romans 12:14-21 and Nonretaliation in Second Temple Judaism: Addressing Persecution within the Community," *CBQ* 60 (1998) 74-96.

**12:15-16.** In this context it may be best to read vv. 15-16, not as commands about the internal life of the church, but as suggesting how Christians should live alongside their pagan neighbors. They should not keep themselves aloof; if someone in the next street dies, they should be prepared to sympathize and join the funeral procession, and if someone is celebrating, they should throw their hats in the air as well. It will not do, just because the society around is potentially or actually hostile, to adopt a snooty attitude; much better to know how to establish common ground and to find ways of making friends. "Live in harmony with one another" (v. 16) is literally "thinking the same things toward one another," which sounds like the kind of bracing command Paul can sometimes issue to Christian groups (e.g., Phil 2:2); but here it seems to refer, more generally, to the call to Christians to get alongside their neighbors and fellow citizens ("associating with the lowly," or possibly "taking on menial tasks") instead of hiving off to a ghetto. The final sentence of v. 16 is a strong echo of 11:25 and 12:3; clearly the attitude Paul most wants to head off in the Roman church is superiority, either against non-Christian Jews (11:25), or against fellow-Christians (12:3), or against the wider pagan world (12:16).

**12:17-18.** Paul reiterates the basic command that runs through this paragraph: one must not repay evil for evil (see 1 Thess 5:15; and, in the background, with further echoes, Prov 20:22). Instead, one must take careful thought, prior to any given situation (this "thinking beforehand," though not implied in the NRSV or the NIV, seems to be present in the prefix of the participle προνοούμενοι [pronooumenoi]), about what will show the watching world that one can hold one's head up, with nothing to be ashamed of. Of course, there will be times when the world will not understand the points at which Christian standards will not permit those who hold them to go along with the ways of the world (cf. Eph 5:11-14; 1 Pet 4:3-5). But there will be many other times, and Christians should be on the lookout for them, when they can join in gladly and show that they, too, act according to the highest moral standards of the surrounding culture. Paul is realistic: he knows that there will be many times when living at peace with every other inhabitant of the street, let alone the city, will be impossible. But he summons Christians to make every effort in that direction.

**12:19-20.** This sets the scene for the third appeal against retaliation, which this time is explained, albeit somewhat darkly. Do not curse your persecutors (v. 14); do not repay evil for evil (v. 17); now, do not perform acts of vengeance—that is, acts that try to bring justice to bear in your own disputes. (Unusually in mid-paragraph, he addresses his readers as "beloved," perhaps already to indicate a reason why this prohibition is given: God's people are loved by God and must not imagine themselves bereft of his care and hence needing to take matters into their own hands.) The verb ἐκδικέω (ekdikeō), as its root suggests, indicates the doing of justice, which Paul is not forbidding; what he prohibits is doing it freelance, in one's own favor—in other words, what we call "vengeance."

Instead, he says, "give place to wrath." Without chapter 13 it might not be clear whether this in fact meant "let your own wrath smolder away quietly," "leave room for God's wrath," or "let the process of moral cause and effect take its course"—though the first one Paul would certainly have ruled out, the second points in the right direction, and the third might not have been foreign to him either. But with 13:4 coming up six verses later, we can be reasonably confident that he means "allow God to do justice—which may well be done through the appointed magistrates." It is impossible to act in one's own case with sufficient impartiality; which is why, as Deuteronomy 32:35 had declared, God reserves the sole right to judicial punishment (again, this shows why 13:1-7 is necessary, to make the link between God's sole right and the delegated rights of rulers). From this point of view, the traditional translation "vengeance" is misleading; what is meant is judicial punishment, which becomes "vengeance" when offended parties take the law into their own hands. Though Paul is not working here with the larger story of Deuteronomy 32, it is significant that he quotes verse 35 here, as he had quoted verse 21 in 10:19, and will quote verse 43 in 15:10; this was, clearly, a passage upon which he drew consciously and regularly.

In place of private vengeance, Paul recommends a shockingly positive line of action: feed a hungry foe, give drink to a thirsty one. He quotes here from Prov 25:21-22, and the Bible contains one or two striking examples of this practice, notably 1 Kgs 6:20-23, where Elisha commanded the king of Israel not to kill enemies who were supernaturally delivered into his hands, but to give them a banquet. In that instance, the Syrian enemies did not return to invade Israel; in Proverbs, the writer says—and Paul quotes him—that taking this course of action will heap coals of fire on the enemy's head ("and YHWH will reward you," adds Proverbs). At first sight it might look as though the coals of fire were themselves punishment (however metaphorical); but this would hardly qualify as "repaying evil with good," since the vengeful intention would still be uppermost. The "coals of fire" are almost certainly intended as the burning shame of remorse for having treated someone so badly. Though the practice of having penitents carrying a literal tray of hot coals is not widely attested, it is not impossible that it was both the source of the original metaphor in Proverbs and also an allusion that Paul's hearers might pick up.[504] The point is then that treating

enemies kindly is not only appropriate behavior in its own right, refusing the vengeance that would usurp God's prerogative; it may also have the effect of turning their hearts.

**12:21.** Paul sums up the whole paragraph with another possible allusion to the Sermon on the Mount, and to the gospel events themselves, Jesus' death and resurrection. Yes, there is evil "out there" in the world. But God's people are to meet it in the way that even God met it: with love and generous goodness. The theology of the cross, in fact, can be glimpsed under this apparently detached ethical maxim: when God came to defeat evil, this was not achieved by using an even greater evil, but by using its opposite—namely, the surprising and initially counterintuitive weapons of goodness. To be consumed with vengeful thoughts, or to be led into putting such thoughts into practice, is to keep evil in circulation, whereas the way to overthrow evil, rather than perpetuating it, is to take its force and give back goodness instead. As with the commands of verses 14 and 17, we may question whether someone in Paul's tradition of Torah-based zeal could have come to this position had it not been for the example and teaching of the Messiah himself.

504. See W. Klassen, "Coals of Fire: Sign of Repentance or Revenge?" *NTS* 9 (1962–63) 337-50.

# Romans 13:1-7, God's Call to Obedience to the Authorities

| NIV | NRSV |
|---|---|
| **13** Everyone must submit himself to the governing authorities, for there is no authority except that which God has established. The authorities that exist have been established by God. ²Consequently, he who rebels against the authority is rebelling against what God has instituted, and those who do so will bring judgment on themselves. ³For rulers hold no terror for those who do right, but for those who do wrong. Do you want to be free from fear of the one in authority? Then do what is right and he will commend you. ⁴For he is God's servant to do you good. But if you do wrong, be afraid, for he does not bear the sword for nothing. He is God's servant, an agent of wrath to bring punishment on the wrongdoer. ⁵Therefore, it is necessary to submit to the | **13** Let every person be subject to the governing authorities; for there is no authority except from God, and those authorities that exist have been instituted by God. ²Therefore whoever resists authority resists what God has appointed, and those who resist will incur judgment. ³For rulers are not a terror to good conduct, but to bad. Do you wish to have no fear of the authority? Then do what is good, and you will receive its approval; ⁴for it is God's servant for your good. But if you do what is wrong, you should be afraid, for the authority[a] does not bear the sword in vain! It is the servant of God to execute wrath on the wrongdoer. ⁵Therefore one must be subject, not only because of wrath but also because of conscience. ⁶For the same reason you also pay taxes, |
| | [a] Gk *it* |

NIV

authorities, not only because of possible punishment but also because of conscience.

⁶This is also why you pay taxes, for the authorities are God's servants, who give their full time to governing. ⁷Give everyone what you owe him: If you owe taxes, pay taxes; if revenue, then revenue; if respect, then respect; if honor, then honor.

NRSV

for the authorities are God's servants, busy with this very thing. ⁷Pay to all what is due them—taxes to whom taxes are due, revenue to whom revenue is due, respect to whom respect is due, honor to whom honor is due.

# COMMENTARY

Theological fashions change, and pressure points move from one exegetical location to another. A previous generation found Romans 9 intolerable, first reading into that chapter a doctrine of absolute predestination to salvation or damnation and then angrily rejecting it. Others have taken a similar view of Rom 1:18-32, hating the very idea of "wrath" as a theologically barbarous concept. Now, after a century in which totalitarian governments have devastated continents, decimated nations, and dehumanized millions of their subjects, it is scarcely surprising that the critical searchlight has swung around and come to rest on the little paragraph now before us. As though by some scapegoating process, these seven verses have been struck out of the canon, vilified, and blamed for untold miseries. They have enabled whole generations of critics to combine their sociopolitical instincts and prejudices with their status as professional exegetes, and to leap-frog over Paul onto what looks like the high moral ground. This is always a deeply satisfying pastime.

But when the sound and fury have died away, we are left wondering what all the fuss was about. Yes, many wicked and powerful governments have appealed to Romans 13 to justify their every move. But have people not done that with words of Jesus himself? If enemies sow weeds in a field of wheat, is the wheat farmer to be blamed? There are many parts of the Bible that can be, and have been, twisted to serve violent and self-serving ends.[505] If we cut them all out, there might be little left. Exegesis, and the determination to live at

least with its results, and perhaps even by them, is always a risk, part of the risk of an incarnational religion or faith. Romans 13 is no exception.

This paragraph, I shall suggest, neither needs nor deserves opprobrium. It is not a fully blown "Theology of Church and State"; indeed, as is often pointed out, our post-Enlightenment notion of "State" would have been foreign to Paul. One can hardly blame a writer if, in the course of a letter about something else, a small aside does not contain the full sophisticated and nuanced treatment that subsequent generations might have liked. Paul's point here is essentially quite simple; it fits into the line of thought of Romans 12–13 as a whole; it need not be wished away in an effort to undercut legitimating arguments for totalitarianism, and indeed it needs to be present for the balance of the previous chapter and paragraph to be maintained.

Many theories have been advanced, predictably, as to what Paul was talking about and why. I here list only the major ones.[506] (On the unwarranted suggestion that the entire paragraph is a gloss, see the Overview for 12:14–13:7.)

(1) This passage is a general statement about ruling authorities. It applies to all legitimate authorities all the time. It is based on a general belief in the desire of the creator God for order within all societies.[507]

---

505. See R. P. Carroll, *Wolf in the Sheepfold: The Bible as a Problem for Christianity* (London: SPCK, 1991). For the parable alluded to, see Matt 13:24-43.

506. See E. Käsemann, "Principles of the Interpretation of Romans 13," in *New Testament Questions of Today* (Philadelphia: Fortress, 1969) 196-216.

507. This seems to be the position of W. Sanday and A. C. Headlam, *A Critical and Exegetical Commentary on the Epistle to the Romans*, 5th ed. (Edinburgh: T. &. T. Clark, 1902) 369-72, though they allow for the possibility of some influence from the specific occasion of the letter. They point out (371) that later NT writings (such as 1 Tim 2:1-2; Titus 3:1; 1 Pet 2:13-17) continue to take the same line despite persecutions.

(2) It is a particular statement about the Roman Empire, based on (a) Paul's belief that it was in some sense God-given, and (b) his experience of sensible magistrates protecting him from persecution, and looking (c) for the safety of the Jewish and/or Christian community in Rome at this historical moment.[508]

(3) It is a very particular statement about the specific moment in the Roman Empire when, with a new, fresh emperor in the throne (Nero's early years were as promising as his later years were terrible), Paul believed there was at least a moment when the church should trust Rome and live content within its world.[509]

(4) It is a statement of something that is now true as a result of the victory of Jesus over the powers of the world in his death and resurrection.[510]

I regard (4) as simply mistaken. Paul does not argue his point on the basis of christology or the gospel. The passage is so close in tone and content to various Jewish writings of the period and before (see below) that there is no reason to suppose that this is a new viewpoint generated by the Christian gospel.

There are further variations within (1), (2), and (3). Maybe Paul intends the paragraph as a general statement (1), but is also influenced by elements of (2) and (3), for instance by the need to distance himself from the groundswell of Jewish resistance against Rome in the Middle East.[511] Maybe he has in mind the particular situation of a tiny Christian group, including many Jews, in the city from which Jews had been expelled a few years earlier for rioting "at the instigation of Chrestus."[512] Maybe he held view (2) or perhaps (3) at the time

of writing, but found that his subsequent experience in Roman prisons led him to a very different view, which emerges in Philippians.[513] Within subsequent interpretation, variants of (2) and (3) have been taken to mean that the passage cannot be insisted upon as relevant for all time.

There may well be elements of particular historical situations visible in the passage; but what Paul actually wrote still looks very much like a general statement about ruling authorities, not a pragmatic assessment of Rome, or the present situation.[514] This is both, so to speak, good and bad news for those who are anxious about the application of the passage to subsequent situations. The more general the passage, the less it can be taken to glorify Rome, and hence to have Paul legitimating the tyranny that within a decade or so had done grievous violence to the church. The more specific the passage (Paul making a positive comment on the Roman Empire), the easier it appears to relativize it and declare it irrelevant to other times and places. However, there is an irony in this specific reading (as in [2] and [3]). By having Paul declare that Rome is a good thing (and thereby having him say nothing much about other rulers and governments), exegesis finds itself unable to see other parts of Paul, and other parts of Romans, as subverting the Roman imperial ideology: Romans 13 is regularly appealed to as an argument against a "counterimperial" reading of the rest of Paul. However, if Paul really did intend it as a general statement, based on God's appointed order in creation (as per [1] above), the less it stands in the way of this counterimperial reading. It would be ironic if, in seeking to avoid a totalitarian reading of this one text, we make it so Rome-specific that it blinds us to the far deeper anti-imperial message of Paul's gospel as a whole.

The wider context gives good reasons to support (1), even if we want to nuance the question of how Paul's readers would have heard what he was saying. As we have suggested, 13:1-7 goes closely with 12:14-21, which we would be right to assume Paul would have said to any church at

508. For (a) see B. Blumenfeld, *The Political Paul: Justice, Democracy and Kingship in a Hellenistic Framework,* JNSTSup (Sheffield: Sheffield Academic, 2001) 389-95. For (b), see R. J. Cassidy, *Paul in Chains: Roman Imprisonment and the Letters of St. Paul* (New York: Crossroad, 2001) chap. 3 (though see below). For (c), see N. Elliott, "Romans 13:1-7 in the Context of Imperial Propaganda," in *Paul and Empire: Religion and Power in Roman Imperial Society,* ed. R. A. Horsley (Harrisburg, Pa.: Trinity Press International, 1997) 184-204.

509. See Christopher Bryan, *A Preface to Romans: Notes on the Epistle in Its Literary and Cultural Setting* (Oxford: Oxford University Press, 2000) 205, referring to Tacitus *Annals* 13.51; Suetonius *Nero* 10-18.

510. See C. E. B. Cranfield, *A Critical and Exegetical Commentary on the Epistle to the Romans,* ICC, 2 vols. (Edinburgh: T. & T. Clark, 1975) 652-55, summarizing the work of Barth, Cullmann, and others.

511. So M. J. Borg, "A New Context for Romans xiii," *NTS* 19 (1972-73) 205-18.

512. See N. T. Wright, *The New Testament and the People of God* (Minneapolis: Fortress, 1992) 354.

513. Cassidy, *Paul in Chains.*

514. Against the view that Paul had a rose-colored view of Nero's early years, see Borg, "A New Context for Romans xiii," 381. For the more general point see P. H. Towner, "Romans 13:1-7 and Paul's Missiological Perspective," in *Romans and the People of God: Essays in Honor of Gordon D. Fee on the Occasion of his 65th Birthday,* ed. S. K. Soderlund and N. T. Wright (Grand Rapids: Eerdmans, 1999) 149-69.

any time. Paul is well aware that persecution may come, and even if we date all the prison letters after Romans we are surely not going to say, with 1 Thessalonians and 2 Corinthians behind him (let alone the experiences ascribed to him in Acts), that he had a pragmatically rosy view of authorities in general. Just as in 12:14-21 he seems to have drawn on traditions about the words and actions of Jesus, so there may be a sense here, as in at least one gospel tradition, that even when they are grievously deceived and almost demonic, ruling authorities still have a certain level of divine authorization (see John 19:11; cf. the interesting exchange in Acts 23:1-5).

More especially, the point he stresses throughout 12:14-21 dovetails exactly into what he says in 13:1-7. One must not call down curses on persecutors, nor repay evil with evil, nor seek private retribution; punishment is God's business. Now we see how Paul supposed, in part at least, that God went about that business. Of course, Paul believed in a final judgment (1:32; 2:1-16; 14:10) when all wrongs would be put to rights. But he now articulates, as a central point in 13:1-7, a standard Jewish and then Christian belief: that ruling authorities are what they are because God wants order in the present world. God is not going to allow chaos to reign even in the present evil age. Chaos and anarchy enable the powerful, the rich, and the bullies to come out on top, and they invariably do. God desires that even in the present time, even in the world that has not yet confessed Jesus as Lord, there should be a measure of justice and order. The point can easily be observed by thinking of situations where magistrates and judges are perceived to be failing badly in their duty to keep this order: before too long, vigilante groups and lynch mobs arise, taking "justice" into their own hands. One of the underlying theses that binds 12:14-21 and 13:1-7 together is therefore this: justice is served not by private vengeance but by individuals trusting the authorities to keep wickedness in check. Knowledge that the authorities are there to look after such matters is a strong incentive to forswear freelance attempts at "justice."

This, as I say, looks back to many clear Jewish precedents. Isaiah spoke of pagan rulers accomplishing God's purposes. Jeremiah urged Israel in exile to pray for the welfare of Babylon, because if Babylon was prospering, Israel would as well (Isa 10:5-11; 44:28–45:5; 46:11; Jer 29:4-9; 27:6-11 [God gives Jerusalem into the hand of Nebuchadnezzar]; see also Dan 1:2; 2:21, 37-49; 4:25, 32; 5:18; Ezra 6:10; Prov 8:15-16; Bar 1:11; 1 Macc 7:33). The book of Esther turns on the potentially risky but eventually satisfactory position of Jews under pagan rule. Many Jews in the Second Temple period were happy to see God's hand in the rise, as well as the fall, of great powers, and even though the early hailing of Rome as such a power must have left an extremely bitter taste in later mouths, the principle was established, and articulated in sundry writings of Paul's period: God intends that there should be good and wise rulers, and if rulers know what their business really is they will seek divine wisdom to help them accomplish it (e.g., Wis 6:1-11).[515] Romans 13:1-7 belongs fair and square on this map. It occupies a similar space, ironically enough, to that occupied by the more moderate Pharisees, the Hillelites, who were content for the moment to live and let live (though still believing in the eventual Age to Come and the worldwide rule of the Messiah), rather than the fiercer Shammaites who would have seen such a position as a compromise. From one point of view, if Paul's conversion made him look, on this point, more like a Hillelite than the Shammaite he had been before, that only serves to emphasize how very Jewish, how "natural," a position like this would seem.[516]

But did Paul not believe, and hint at several points in Romans itself, that the gospel and rule of Jesus the Messiah, the world's true Lord, subverted the gospel and rule of Caesar, whose cult was growing fast in precisely the cities (Corinth, Ephesus, and so on) where he spent most of his time?[517] Yes; and this is perhaps part of the point. If the gospel of Jesus, God's Son, the King who will rule the nations (1:3-4; 15:12) does indeed reveal God's justice and salvation, which put to shame

---

515. See also Josephus *The Jewish War* 2.197; *Against Apion* 2.75-77.

516. On Hillel and Shammai, their "schools," and the placing of Paul within this spectrum, see Wright, *The New Testament and the People of God*, 194-203; N. T. Wright, *What St. Paul Really Said: Was Paul of Tarsus the Real Founder of Christianity?* (Grand Rapids: Eerdmans, 1997) chap. 2.

517. See Richard A. Horsely, ed. *Paul and Empire: Religion and Power in Roman Imperial Society* (Harrisburg, Pa.: Trinity Press International, 1997); and Horsely, ed., *Paul and Politics: Ekklesia, Israel, Imperium, Interpretation, Essays in Honor of Krister Stendahl* (Harrisburg, Pa.: Trinity Press International, 2000).

the similar claims of Caesar (1:16-17; Phil 2:5-11; 3:19-21); if it is true that those who accept this gospel will themselves exercise a royal reign (5:17); and if Paul suspects that his audience in Rome are getting this message—then it is all the more important to make it clear that this does not mean a holy anarchy in the present, an overrealized eschatology in which the rule of Christ has already abolished all earthly governments and magistrates. Precisely because Paul is holding out for the day when all creation will be renewed (8:1-27), when every knee shall bow at the name of Jesus (Phil 2:10-11), it is vital that the excitable little groups of Christians should not take the law into their own hands in advance.[518] In particular (and with events in Palestine in mind), it is important that his readers do not take his covert polemic against the imperial ideology as a coded call to a Christian version of the so-called fourth philosophy.[519] This is where Paul's probable awareness of the riots under Claudius, and the reputation that both Jews and Christians will have gained in Rome because of them, must come into play. God does not intend that Christians should become agents of anarchy, which would replace the tyranny of the officially powerful with the tyranny of the unofficially powerful. The ultimate overthrow of pagan power comes by other means, and Paul has outlined in Romans 5 and 8 what those means are. Rome could cope with ordinary revolutions. Rome could not cope, as history bears witness, with a community owing allegiance to the crucified and risen Messiah as the world's true Lord.

In fact, reading Romans 13 against the backdrop of the extravagant claims made within the burgeoning imperial cult highlights one point in particular. According to Paul (and the Jewish tradition in which he stands) the rulers are not themselves divine; they are set up by the one God, and they owe this God allegiance. Romans 13 constitutes a severe demotion of arrogant and self-divinizing rulers. It is an undermining of totalitarianism, not a reinforcement of it. By implication, if the rulers themselves are given the task of judging wicked people within their sphere of authority, they themselves will be judged by the God who set them up. Paul does not say this explicitly; but in 13:4 he twice describes the rulers as God's "servants" (διάκονοι *diakonoi*), and if he is capable of pointing out that God's servants in the gospel will be judged on how they have performed, there is every reason to suppose that God's "servants" within the civic community will themselves also face an ultimate tribunal (cf. 1 Cor 3:10-15; 4:1-5, having described himself and Apollos as God's *diakonoi* in 3:5; 2 Cor 5:10). This, however, is not his point at the moment (just as he does not say, in Romans 5–8, what will happen to those who are not "in Christ"), and we must remind ourselves that this is not intended as a full and balanced statement of everything Paul might have wanted to say on the subject. The main thing he wants to get across to the Roman Christians is that, even though they are servants of the Messiah Jesus, the world's rightful Lord, this does not give them carte blanche to ignore the temporary subordinates whose appointed task, whether they know it or not, is to bring at least a measure of God's order and justice to the world. Government and magistrates may be more or less good or bad; but—and this is Paul's basic point—government qua government is intended by God and should in principle command submission from Christian and non-Christian alike.

Reading Rom 13:1-7 in the context of 12:14-21 raises a question, which Paul does not here even touch on: What happens when the "persecutors" (12:14) are the same people as "the governing authorities," and are using their God-given power for that purpose? Since Paul does not raise the question here, we cannot press this passage for a hint of an answer; but we might again compare Acts 23:1-5. Even if this is merely a stylized scene constructed by Luke, it expresses the same balance we might get by reading Romans the way I have suggested, adding Philippians and the Thessalonian correspondence to the mix, and then returning with the same question. "Paul" in this story declares that God will strike the "whitewashed wall," the judge who is behaving illegally. When confronted with the news that he is addressing God's high priest, he apologizes formally, recognizing that he should not speak evil of a ruler. But he does not retract his charge that the ruler in question has behaved illegally and will be

518. I owe this point to Dr David Wenham.
519. This is the point made by Borg in "A New Context for Romans xiii." The "Fourth Philosophy" is Josephus's way of demarcating the Jewish revolutionaries as a separate party alongside the Sadducess, Pharisees, and Essenes.

judged for it. A similar pattern emerges when Acts places Paul before pagan magistrates. He will submit to their authority, but he will also remind them of their duty (see Acts 16:19-40; 22:22-29; 25:6-12). We may be right to suspect that Paul could see, not far away, the battle that would come, in which Caesar insisted on an absolute allegiance that left no room for Jesus as Lord. Less than a century later, Polycarp died at the stake because of that; but even he, it seems, held on to a view of magistracy very similar to Paul's.[520]

In particular, Paul always insists on seeing the present in the light of the future. Romans 13:1-7 does not describe a new situation brought into being by the eschatological events concerning Jesus; but the obedience of Christians to earthly magistrates takes place under the sign of ultimate judgment (cf. again 2:1-16). This does not mean, as Paul's own example bears out, that one must be politically and socially quiescent until the great renewal of all things. That is the slur made on the good name of inaugurated eschatology by those who want to insist on the full renewal right away. Preaching and living the gospel must always be announcing and following Jesus, rather than Caesar, as the true Lord. But the eschatological balance must be kept. The church must live as a sign of the coming complete kingdom of Jesus Christ; but since that kingdom is characterized by "righteousness, peace, and joy in the Holy Spirit," it cannot be inaugurated in the present by chaos, violence, and hatred (cf. 14:17). The methods of the Messiah himself (12:14-21) must be used in living out his kingdom within the present world, passing away though it may be.

Romans 13:1-7 is about the running of civic communities, and the duty of Christians toward them. It does not mention or allude to the interactions between different civic communities or nations. It was because of this that later Christians developed a theory of "just war," to argue at a new level that under certain circumstances it may be right to defend the interests of a nation or community, by force if necessary; and it is against that in particular that various pacifist movements have protested. Romans 13 is sometimes called as a witness in this discussion, but its relevance may be doubted (see the Reflections).

**13:1.** "Every person" (NRSV) is literally "every soul"—a clear enough indication, if such were needed, that by "soul" Paul means more than "the immaterial element within a human being." The word ψυχή (*psychē*) regularly refers, in the New Testament, to the whole human being seen from the point of view of the person's interior life, motivation, and intention. Here it is a way of indicating that every person as an individual must obey this command. The command itself is to "be subject" (NRSV), or "submit" (NIV, NEB/REB); not necessarily "obey" (JB, NJB), though that will usually follow. The point is that one must regard the governing authorities as having a rightful claim on one's submission. The word has echoes of military formation: one must take one's place in the appropriate rank.[521]

But who are the "authorities" to whom one owes this submission? Elsewhere in Paul there are times when the "rulers and authorities," the "principalities and powers," are primarily spiritual beings, shadowy but powerful entities that stand behind the visible and earthly rulers. This seems to be the case in, for instance, Rom 8:38-39. Sometimes it seems as though he intends to refer simultaneously to both earthly and heavenly powers; this is how 1 Cor 2:6-8 is usually read, and how Col 2:14-15 must be read. But here, though it is unlikely that Paul ever made a complete distinction between earthly and heavenly dimensions of civic authority, his primary focus is on the earthly rulers themselves. They are the ones who bear the sword (v. 4). They are the ones to whom one pays taxes (vv. 6-7).[522]

The problem, of course, at the level of understanding Paul (to postpone for a minute the question of applying him today), is that in 1 Corinthians 2, and again in Col 2:15, Paul declares that the cross of Jesus Christ has defeated the powers. How can he now suggest that one should be subject to them? The answer seems to lie, whether or not Paul wrote Colossians, in the great christological poem in the first chapter of that

520. Polycarp *Mart. Pol.* 10.2; the whole passage repays study. See also Acts 4:23-31; 1 Pet 3:13-17 within the context of the persecution presupposed by the letter as a whole; and *1 Clement* 60–61.

521. On the difference between "submission," as commanded here, and blind obedience, see Douglas J. Moo, *The Epistle to the Romans*, NICNT (Grand Rapids: Eerdmans, 1996) 797, 807-10.

522. On the whole question see W. Wink, *Naming the Powers: The Language of Power in the New Testament*, vol. 1 of *The Powers* (Philadelphia: Fortress, 1984) 45-47; C. Morrison, *The Powers That Be: Earthly Rulers and Demonic Powers in Romans 13.1-7* (London: SCM, 1960).

letter, in which it is affirmed that all things, including all powers and authorities in heaven and on earth, were created in, through, and for Christ, and are also reconciled in, through, and to him.[523] The tension, in other words, is not only between Romans 13 and Colossians 2; it is between Colossians 1 and Colossians 2. And—since Paul seldom sees the need to say everything he could in principle say on a topic every time he brings it up—it is perfectly feasible to propose that Paul in this case was stressing one of the more positive aspects of the "powers." Some have argued, as noted above, that Rom 13:1-7 belongs with Col 1:20: that Paul commands submission to the powers because they have now been reconciled in Christ. But it seems much more likely that he does so in parallel with Col 1:16: he commands submission because they are part of God's good created order. The fact that they are in rebellion does not of itself mean that submission is inappropriate.

Paul, characteristically, gives an explanation for the command: all authority is from God, and (the specific form of the general statement) the actually existing ones have been put there by God. This is not a specific commendation of the Roman Empire as against the ruling systems of other times and places; it is a general point about civic authority. It belongs with mainstream Second Temple Jewish tradition, and has parallels, including one surprising one, in the NT (e.g., Wis 6:3-10; John 19:11).

**13:2-4.** Paul backs up this initial command and explanation with a short discussion of what happens when people resist the authorities, and of the fact that these results are part of God's appointed order. Resistance incurs "condemnation," or "judgment" (NRSV, NIV) (v. 2), because rulers hold no terrors for those who do good, but only for wrongdoers (v. 3a). Paul could no doubt have given counterexamples from his own recent biography, but his point here concerns God's intended order, not its corruptions. He then turns the point around (vv. 3b-4): if you want to go about your business without fear of the authorities, do what is good, and they will praise you. That is their God-given function. They are "ministers" (*diakonoi*), "stewards" of God for this purpose: their delegated task is to praise good behavior. Conversely,

then (v. 4b), if you do evil, you should be afraid, because authority has the right and responsibility to punish. Once again, the authority is God's "steward," this time to administer punitive justice—that is, "wrath"; this is the point at which the authority *must* do what the private individual *may not* do (12:14-21)—a point regularly missed in many popular-level discussions of the judicial role of civic authority.

**13:5.** This to-and-fro discussion of the appointed role of "authority" and the way in which "you" may encounter it, for good or ill, leads Paul back to reiterate his initial command, now with an extra reason: one must therefore submit, both because the alternative is "wrath" in this sense, and also because, recognizing the God-given role of authority, the educated Christian conscience ought to become disquieted if it finds itself resisting God's "stewards." Paul does not often mention the role of conscience in Christian behavior, but when he does, as here, it appears that this is not because it is marginal in his thinking but because he takes it for granted. The word occurs elsewhere in Rom 2:15; 9:1; most of the other Pauline references occur in 1 Corinthians 8 and 10; see also 2 Cor 5:11.

**13:6-7.** Conscience, too, prescribes therefore that one must pay taxes.[524] Once again Paul gives the authorities a high status: they are God's λει-τουργοί (*leitourgoi*), public servants (in a world where "public service" regularly had cultic overtones at least, sometimes explicit association with religious functions).[525] They must therefore receive what is due to them, whether the material dues of direct and indirect taxes (that is the likely distinction between the two words used here) or the non-material dues of respect and honor. This last point shows once more, not least in relation to Paul's own practice in Acts, what is and is not meant. Paul was always ready to honor the office even while criticizing the present holder. Though of course one hopes that the holder will prove worthy of the office, and one knows that sometimes holders prove so unworthy as to need removing from office, being able to respect the

523. On Col 1:15-20 see N. T. Wright, *The Climax of the Covenant: Christ and the Law in Pauline Theology* (Minneapolis: Fortress, 1991) chap. 5.

524. Some in Rome were protesting at this time about taxation. See Tacitus *Annals* 13.50-51. Nero proposed abolishing indirect taxation altogether, but his council restrained him and less sweeping measures were instigated.

525. See BDAG 591-92.

office while at least reserving judgment about the holder is part of social and civic maturity. And, for Paul, being able to say "the existing powers are ordained by God" while living under a system that, as he makes clear elsewhere, was bristling with potential or actual blasphemy and injustice, is part of Christian maturity—a part he urges his Roman readers to make their own.

# REFLECTIONS

**1.** Romans 13 has attracted so much opprobrium, particularly in the twentieth century where most thinking Westerners developed a more than justified horror of totalitarianism, that to many it seems counterintuitive to do anything but reject it outright. Either Paul did not write it, people say, or he did not mean it like it sounds, or he was just plain wrong. Whatever else you do with this passage, it is implied, you ought not to be caught agreeing with it.

Until, of course, your house is burgled. Or someone you love is murdered. Or you are cheated in business, or even in sport. Then, quite suddenly, you want someone to be in authority. Nobody enjoys the presence of a referee or umpire when they are trying to foul an opponent, or sneak offside; but everybody appeals to them when the other side do it. Actually, we none of us want to live in a world where the bullies get away with it, except when we are planning to do the bullying ourselves.

Libertarian histories of Western culture read the story of the last millennium as one of increasing social and civic freedom. The long march from Magna Carta to universal adult suffrage was not, in fact, as smooth an upward rise to freedom as it is sometimes made out to be. Oppression and systemic injustice still exist within every Western democracy. But since we tell our story as one of dethroning authorities and discovering new freedoms, we are bound to find Romans 13 a surprise, or even a shock. Unless we are actual anarchists, however, we will soon acknowledge explicitly that all societies need some regulation, some ordering, some structure of authority; and we will soon recognize that this ordering is no use unless everyone is, at least in principle, signed up to it or, failing that, able to be coerced into going along with it.

Romans 13:1-7 then issues commands that are so obvious that they only make sense if there might be some reason in the air not to obey the civic authorities. More or less everyone in the ancient world, with the possible exception of Cynic philosophers on the one hand and occasional radical groups like the extreme Shammaite or "zealous" Jews on the other, would have shrugged their shoulders and accepted that some form of civic authority was a necessary part of an ordered world. If a moral or religious teacher took the trouble to explain the rationale for such authorities, and insisted that those who embraced that moral or religious system were bound to obey them, that would be of itself a sign of what we have, in fact, seen both elsewhere in Romans and elsewhere in Paul: that the average Christian might well have supposed that there might be grounds for not doing so. You only put up "No Smoking" signs where people are likely to want to smoke. And, since Paul himself frequently hints at what the grounds for not obeying the authorities might be, we do not need to speculate for long about them. They are the sovereignty and saving justice of the one true God, unveiled in action in the world's true Lord, Jesus the Messiah.

Romans 13, in short, carries a hidden "nevertheless" at its heart. Jesus is Lord; nevertheless, his followers must obey their earthly rulers. This is not because the rulers have somehow, in theory, already submitted to his lordship, but despite the fact that they have not done so. The authorities are part of the present world order, the good and wise structure of God's original creation. Not to submit might look like a noble piece of overrealized eschatology, claiming to belong already to the new world promised when the full day dawns (see 13:11-14); but to make that complete claim ahead of time is in fact to move toward a dualism in which the goodness of the present world, even in its not-yet-redeemed state, is denied. That, in fact, is what millenarian and similar movements have classically done.

**2.** The authority of the state, however, is strictly limited here by the rubric that stands over the whole paragraph: the rulers exist by God's will and at his pleasure. The book of Daniel is a graphic description of how this works out within a pagan world and how the people of God may find their way through the resultant moral minefield. It is noticeable that even when human rulers become fatally guilty of hubris, and court their own destruction, this does not signal the end of all human rule. Even in the apocalyptic scenario in Daniel 7, the one who eventually sits on a throne dispensing judgment is "one like a son of man." Just as there is a dialectical movement between Daniel 1–6 (the stories of human kings and God's people) and Daniel 7 (the enthronement of the Ancient of Days and the vindication of "one like a son of man," representing God's people), so in Romans 13 the Christian belongs in the tension between the present existence, owing submission to earthly rulers, and the promised future "day." Just because we have become horribly aware of the dangers of brutal, self-serving, self-justifying "governments," it does not follow that there are no errors in the opposite direction.

**3.** Putting together Rom 12:14-21 and 13:1-7 has the salutary effect of reminding us of one of the most important, if pragmatic, reasons for there being governing authorities. Private vengeance, whether individual or (as in the lynch mob) corporate, is shocking in itself and can easily spiral out of control into vendettas and generations of senseless brutality. Where authorized policing fails, or is felt to be failing, the authority vacuum is quickly filled, and the results are seldom happy. Of course, commanding people to pray for their persecutors, not to repay evil with evil, to live at peace with all, and above all not to avenge themselves, is excellent advice at a purely personal level. People who allow vengeance, however apparently justified, to dominate their motivational life will become eaten up by it. It is a way of allowing the evil that someone has done to you to continue to hold you in its power. Part of the enormous breakthrough achieved by Jesus in his teaching and death is found just here: that to suffer innocently and not to retort or retaliate is to win a far greater victory than can ever be achieved by hitting back. It is to win a victory over evil itself.

**4.** I write this in the wake of September 11, 2001—a date people will recall for decades, perhaps centuries, and shudder at the memory. Terrorist atrocities against innocent and unarmed civilians, especially on so large a scale, cry out so loudly for punishment that any comment might seem superfluous. Yet in the debates that followed that terrible day Romans 13 was frequently invoked in support of military action by the United States and its allies against other countries; and one of the great problems of Christian moral discourse has been precisely that Romans 13 does not deal with such matters. That is why "Just War" theory was invented, in an attempt to develop the idea of magistracy, of a justice that kept a society in balance, beyond the borders of a particular jurisdiction and into the realms of conflict between nations. The problem with this is, to put it perhaps oversimply, that Romans 13 is dovetailed into an argument against the taking of private vengeance (12:14-21). When punitive and retaliatory action is taken against a nation, or a group within a nation, it becomes difficult to maintain that it is judicial and legitimated by Romans 13. That is not to say that such action is wrong or unjustified, only that this text will not support it. Many have concluded, rightly in my view, that the only way forward is the establishment of a worldwide justice system that will carry moral weight across different cultures and societies. Unfortunately, one of the obstacles to this is precisely the determination of some of the more powerful nations to oppose such a thing, lest they themselves be brought to account for the ways in which they have used, and perhaps abused, their own power. Romans 13 will not help in addressing these issues, then. But the rest of Romans, setting forth God's justice, freedom, and peace over against those of Caesar, could certainly do so.

# ROMANS 13:8-10, LOVE FULFILLING THE LAW

ROMANS 13:8-10

| NIV | NRSV |
|---|---|
| [8]Let no debt remain outstanding, except the continuing debt to love one another, for he who loves his fellowman has fulfilled the law. [9]The commandments, "Do not commit adultery," "Do not murder," "Do not steal," "Do not covet,"[a] and whatever other commandment there may be, are summed up in this one rule: "Love your neighbor as yourself."[b] [10]Love does no harm to its neighbor. Therefore love is the fulfillment of the law. | [8]Owe no one anything, except to love one another; for the one who loves another has fulfilled the law. [9]The commandments, "You shall not commit adultery; You shall not murder; You shall not steal; You shall not covet"; and any other commandment, are summed up in this word, "Love your neighbor as yourself." [10]Love does no wrong to a neighbor; therefore, love is the fulfilling of the law. |
| [a] 9 Exodus 20:13-15,17; Deut. 5:17-19,21   [b] 9 Lev. 19:18 | |

## COMMENTARY

This little passage on love and the law is clearly a summary of issues that Paul lays out more fully elsewhere (e.g., Galatians 5). It reverts to the theme of 12:3-13, and it may be, as we suggested above, that Paul intends this whole section (chaps. 12–13) as some kind of chiasm (see the Overview on 12:1–16:27). Within this, 13:8-10 plays a similar role within chapters 12–16 as a whole to that played by 1 Corinthians 13 within 1 Corinthians 12–14 as a whole, identifying the characteristic that must be central to all authentic Christian community life.

The thematic difference between this passage and 12:3-13, however, is that there Paul was dealing with life within the Christian community, and here he appears to be advocating a love for neighbors of any and every persuasion. The opening words of v. 8, indeed, if read without a break from what has gone before, look as if they are simply saying "always pay your bills on time"; we must assume that he is still talking about the wider community represented by those who levy taxes and demand respect (v. 7). And this view of a wider community alerts us again to a wider reference within Romans. Just as 12:1-2 looked back to 1:18-32, seeing in Christian worship the reversal of idolatry and dehumanization, so the present passage looks back to 2:17-29 in particular. With 3:27-31; 8:1-8; and 10:5-11 in the background, Paul sketches a brief but telling picture of how the Torah is fulfilled in that love of neighbor which

will bring admiration, rather than blasphemy, from the watching world (cf. 2:16-17). Here, in other words, are the "true Jews" (see 2:28-29), those who are bringing God's light and love to the world. This coheres well with the context of Gal 5:14, the other passage where Paul says almost exactly the same thing (see also 1 Corinthians 13, where, though Paul does not mention Torah, the matchless exposition of love and its abiding permanence reminds us of Jewish eulogies of Torah or wisdom; see Sirach 24).

The passage consists, typically, of an opening statement and explanation (v. 8), followed by an extended explanation of the explanation (v. 9), leading to a summary that repeats and reinforces the original explanation (v. 10).

**13:8.** Although the idea of "debt," immediately after instructions concerning money, using the cognate word ὀφειλάς (*ophelias*, 13:17; "what is due them," NRSV; "what you owe them," NIV), is most naturally taken literally, Paul has twice already in Romans used it as a metaphor, once for his own obligation to bring the gospel to the whole world (1:14) and again to indicate the Christian's obligation to live by the Spirit and not the flesh (8:12). For the sense of obligation we may compare 4:4; 15:1, 27; the root regularly carries both literal and metaphorical meanings in early Christian writings.[526] The context thus breathes life into what

526. See BDAG 743.

might be for him a nearly dead metaphor, giving a particular force to the command to love: This is a debt, owed to everyone, that can never be discharged.

The explanation, in the second half of the verse, should not be misunderstood. Paul does not, of course, mean "Love fulfils the Torah; therefore love is the way to earn righteousness with God." He does not suppose that this was ever the purpose of Torah. Rather, the purpose of Torah was that Israel might be God's light to the world; Israel was "entrusted with God's oracles," but proved unfaithful. Those who are justified by faith "apart from the works of the Torah" (3:28) are now, perfectly logically, instructed to live as the people through whom what the Torah by itself could not do is accomplished (8:3-8; 10:1-11). People who love their neighbors thus "fulfill Torah," both in the immediate sense that they will never do any of the things Torah forbids, and in the wider sense that through them God's way of life will be seen to advantage. The Greek for "the one who loves the neighbor has fulfilled the law" could also be translated "the one who loves has fulfilled the other law" (τὸν ἕτερον νόμον *ton heteron nomon;* cf. τις ἑτέρα ἐντολή *tis hetera entolē,* "any other commandment," in v. 9). This has sometimes been adopted by exegetes with the supposed meaning that love fulfills, not Torah itself, but the "other" law—that is, the one that Jesus gave to replace it. This is very awkward in view of the quotation from the Decalogue that follows immediately; and Paul rarely uses the verb "love" absolutely, without an object. The apparent echo of *heteron nomon* in 7:23 is a pure accident.

**13:9-10.** Paul explains (γάρ *gar*) what he means by saying that love fulfills Torah. First he simply states that all the commandments are in fact summed up in the command to love (v. 9); then he sums this up to the effect that love does no evil, and draws the conclusion that love is indeed Torah's fulfillment (v. 10).[527] Loving one's neighbor is itself, of course, a command in Torah (Lev 19:18, quoted here), though not part of the Ten Commandments. Paul was not the first to see it as a summary of the whole law; this is one of

several passages in Romans 12–13 where we are right to detect echoes of the teaching of Jesus himself (Matt 22:37-39 and par.; see also Jas 2:8, where this commandment is described as the "kingly law," presumably meaning "the command given by the king," i.e., Jesus; cf. 2 Macc 3:13). The specific commands he lists here consist of four of the last five of the ten (omitting the bearing of false witness, a deficiency that one good MS and a few lesser ones tried to rectify), following the LXX order of Deut 5:17-21 (adultery, murder, theft, coveting) rather than that of Exod 20:13-17 (placing theft before murder).[528] The idea of being able to sum up Torah in a single phrase has a long history in Judaism of which Paul was no doubt well aware.[529]

Though v. 10 opens, unusually, without a verbal connection to what precedes, it is clearly intended as a summary of v. 9. It should not be supposed that the full achievement of "love" consists simply in doing no evil; as Dr. Johnson said, to do no harm is the praise of a stone, not a man. Rather, love, on its way to higher and more positive goals, takes in this negative one in a single stride: If love seeks the highest good of the neighbor, it will certainly do no wrong to him or her. We should notice that Paul leaves no room for the slippery argument whereby sexual malpractice has been routinely justified in the modern world; "love," as the summary of the law, includes the command not to commit adultery, and could never be confused with the "love" that is frequently held to excuse it. One only has to ask the question, whether adultery routinely builds up or breaks down human communities and families, to see the point. Once again, then, the "fulfillment of Torah" does not mean the performance of "good works" designed to put God in one's debt; rather (and perhaps this is why Paul writes v. 8 in this fashion), it is the discharge of one's own debt, to one's neighbor but also to God. This passage takes its place alongside Paul's several earlier statements about the Torah, confirming the positive understanding of it for

---

527. Joseph A. Fitzmyer, *Romans,* AB 33 (Garden City, N.Y.: Doubleday, 1993) 677, 679, translating οὖν (*oun,* "therefore") as if it were *gar* ("for"), misses the point that Paul is here arguing for this conclusion, not presupposing it.

528. The MT, in both Exodus and Deuteronomy, has murder, adultery, theft. It is unlikely that we should read into Paul's order any sense that it is Deuteronomy that is fulfilled, rather than Exodus, or that there is particular significance in the omission of bearing false witness.

529. See *T. Iss.* 6; *b. Shabb.* 31a, which ascribes to Hillel the saying, "That which you hate, do not do to your fellows; this is the whole law, the rest is commentary; go and learn it!"

which we argued earlier, and making it clear once again that ethical obligation is not undermined but reaffirmed by a proper understanding of justification and Christian life.

# REFLECTIONS

In the light of the suggestion that this passage belongs to some extent at least with 12:3-13, we may reflect on both together.

**1.** The obvious centrality of love within early Christian ethics is so well known that we often overlook how striking, almost revolutionary, this was. Judaism, of course, cherished the command to love, but did not highlight it in the same way. Within the pagan world there was far less emphasis on anything that approximates to the early Christian meaning of "love," modeled as it was on Jesus himself. This oversight on the part of contemporary readers goes with the more practical problem that we all give lip service to the idea of love but we do not usually reflect on how to do it. Granted the prevailing context of romanticism and existentialism, it is normally assumed that love will "just happen" as long as people are sincere and do what comes naturally. The moral history of the twentieth century should have given the lie to this, but since it is a convenient thing to believe (giving one the feel of virtue without the need for hard moral work) the belief continues unabated, being propagated by most movies, many novels, and a million shallow sermons. We urgently need moral reflection, at every level of church and society, on what exactly love is, what it means and does not mean, and more especially the steps of moral learning and effort required to attain it. The very fact that this sounds so "inauthentic" ("You mean I've got to pretend?" one can hear people asking) is a measure of how far we have allowed ethical reflection to diverge from early Christianity.

**2.** Of course, Paul wants love to be "genuine" (ἀνυπόκριτος *anypokritos,* "unhypocritical"). But here is the strange thing. If you try to treat someone you thoroughly dislike as though in fact you cared very deeply for them—if you try to think of how it is to live inside their skin and walk in their shoes—then it may well happen that a genuine sympathy arises, and from that real affection, and finally an unhypocritical love. This is, after all, more or less what Paul is commending in 12:19-21. The love of which Paul speaks is tough; not simply in the sense of "tough love" as applied to the difficult task of bringing up children, though that may be true as well, but in the sense that, since it does not spring from the emotions but from the will, love will grit its teeth and act as if the emotions were in place, trusting that they will follow in good time. If we reduce ethics to emotions, we lose not only consistency of behavior but also the very possibility of moral discourse.

**3.** The unity of the church, highlighted in 12:3-8, remains a goal to be worked for despite the apparent failure of many unity schemes of the period between 1960 and 2000. Here Paul stresses the need for humility and mutual respect between different gifts within a Christian community; when everyone is doing what they are called to do to the utmost of their powers, the whole body is in good health. The ecumenical task may consist not least in the humble recognition, between the different denominations, that we may after all have different callings—overlapping, interlocking, most likely, but perhaps different as well. This is not to minimize doctrinal differences, which still matter; nor is it to connive at the scandalous fragmentation of the body of Christ, or the "one body in Christ" as here. It is to suggest that within the greater unity for which we must work we should be prepared to allow room for the particular tasks, characteristics, and genius of the different "churches" that have grown up over the years, particularly since the Reformation. The ecumenical movements of the twentieth century had a dangerously modernist feel (bringing everything together into one grand and possibly grandiose structure); maybe the ecumenical movements of the twenty-first century, though they must avoid the postmodern trap of easygoing acceptance of all differences, which results in further fragmentation, should work at ways of humbly affirming appropriate differences while learning how to celebrate and share all we hold in common.

**4.** In particular, the common life of love in the one body should also give rise, as in 13:8-10, to the command of love for the neighboring non-Christian world. This must of course work on a daily basis at the local level, in the street, the theater, the office, the factory. There will always be room for improvement—and for humility, penitence, and fresh starts—at that level. Equally, we should not ignore the bracing call to whole churches, and to communities and even countries that think of themselves as basically Christian, to act toward their neighbors in the global village with that same love, the debt that can never be discharged. One of our major world problems, bringing a myriad other evils in its wake, is precisely financial debts that can never be discharged because the compound interest increases faster than ailing economies can service it. Since the lending countries belong to the part of the world that, rightly or wrongly, is seen as "Christian" (and in some cases sees itself thus), we can scarcely avoid the problem, with all its ironies. "Love does no wrong to a neighbor"; working out what that means personally and collectively, and putting it into practice, is one of the most urgent tasks we currently face.

# ROMANS 13:11-14, LIVING BY THE RISING SUN

[11]And do this, understanding the present time. The hour has come for you to wake up from your slumber, because our salvation is nearer now than when we first believed. [12]The night is nearly over; the day is almost here. So let us put aside the deeds of darkness and put on the armor of light. [13]Let us behave decently, as in the daytime, not in orgies and drunkenness, not in sexual immorality and debauchery, not in dissension and jealousy. [14]Rather, clothe yourselves with the Lord Jesus Christ, and do not think about how to gratify the desires of the sinful nature.[a]

[a] 14 Or the flesh

11Besides this, you know what time it is, how it is now the moment for you to wake from sleep. For salvation is nearer to us now than when we became believers; [12]the night is far gone, the day is near. Let us then lay aside the works of darkness and put on the armor of light; [13]let us live honorably as in the day, not in reveling and drunkenness, not in debauchery and licentiousness, not in quarreling and jealousy. [14]Instead, put on the Lord Jesus Christ, and make no provision for the flesh, to gratify its desires.

## COMMENTARY

Paul ends the section where he began in 12:1-2, setting the Christian's moral obligations in the context of knowing what the time is: It is almost daybreak. This is a familiar image in early Christian writing, again quite possibly going back to Jesus himself; and Paul has developed it elsewhere (1 Thess 5:1-11; see also Matt 24:42-44; 26:45; Mark 13:33-37; Luke 12:35-46; 21:36; Eph 5:8-16; the idea of staying awake to be about one's Christian tasks is also evident in Eph 6:18). This idea flows consistently from the early Christian belief that with the resurrection of Jesus God's promised new age had dawned, but that full day was yet to come (see above all 1 Cor 15:20-28). Christians therefore live in the interval between the early signs of dawn and the sunrise itself, and their behavior must be appropriate for the day, not the night. There is such a thing as appropriate and good nocturnal behavior, but as with 1 Thess 5:7 Paul takes "night" as a synecdoche (one part standing for the whole) for the types of evil behavior that flourish away from the light. There is also a trace here of the metaphor Paul develops more in 1 Thess 5:8 (and that reaches fuller expression in Eph 6:10-17): What you need, between dawn and full day, are the "weapons of light" (13:12). Finally there is the command to "put on" the Lord Jesus Christ, an idea paralleled both in Galatians (3:27) and in Eph 4:24. This paragraph, in short, though perfectly at home at this point in Romans, bringing the opening exhortation of chaps. 12–13 to an appropriate and sharp conclusion, is also a window on several aspects of Pauline ethics. It should not pass unremarked that this was the passage read by Augustine after hearing children's voices chanting "pick up and read, pick up and read"; it was the final push he needed to make a clean break with his past and devote himself entirely to God.[530]

**13:11.** Paul assumes that his readers will know what "time" it is (the word for "time" here is καιρός [kairos], a special moment rather than mere chronological time); as in 12:2, he expects them to be familiar with the idea of the old age, which is passing away, and the new age, which is dawning. (The NIV's "understanding the present time" is a somewhat ponderous way of drawing attention to the significance of what he says.) He expects them to be up before day breaks fully; this theme, with its echoes of the Easter morning stories, resonates through the early Christian sense of new creation, new life bursting through the wintry crust of the old world. It is, he insists, time to wake up.

The reason he gives is that "our salvation" is nearer now than when first we believed. Paul does not say, as many of his interpreters have supposed that he said, that the final end of which he speaks in Romans 8, 1 Corinthians 15, 1 Thessalonians 4–5, and elsewhere, will certainly come within a generation; but he knows that it might well do so, and insists that it is the more urgent that Christians behave already in the manner that will then be appropriate. Though "salvation" can refer to saving events during the present course of

history (e.g., Phil 1:19), and Paul can insist in one passage that "the day of salvation" is already present (2 Cor 6:2), here the word has its normal meaning, referring to the final day when God will renew all things in Christ and give all the justified their glorious, risen bodies, and investing that event with its sense of "rescue from disaster" (see Rom 5:9-10; 8:24, 29-30; Phil 3:20-21). The idea of the eschatological moment coming "near," which Paul repeats in the next verse, carries echoes of Jesus' original proclamation, as in Mark 1:15 and parallels: God's kingdom "is near."[531] And now, he says, it is nearer than it was at the time we became believers; this is in one sense obvious, but in another needs saying as a reminder that though to us the passage of time seems to move on without much change we should not forget that the great future moment is steadily coming closer.

**13:12.** By way of explaining what he means by saying it is time to wake up, he declares that the night is nearly over and the day is breaking, and draws the conclusion in a mixed metaphor: it is time to stop nocturnal activities and put on the "weapons" proper for daylight. (The metaphor is more obviously, and gloriously, mixed in 1 Thessalonians 5, where those who are asleep will go into labor pains, because a thief is breaking into the house, while those who are awake should not get drunk, but should put on their armor.) Though "putting on" is the normal term for clothing or protective armor, the verb anticipates v. 14, where it is "the Lord Jesus Christ" who is "put on." The weapons here are "of light," contrasting with the "works of darkness"; "of light" seems to mean "appropriate for daylight," "the weapons that children of day will need." (The NRSV and the NIV translate ὅπλα [hopla] as "armor." The word properly denotes military equipment, not primarily clothing; however, the verb here and in Eph 6:11 is ordinarily used of putting on clothes.)

**13:13-14.** Paul has in mind, clearly, what in Galatians he calls "the works of the flesh," the things that characterize humanity in rebellion against its creator (Gal 5:19). As is often pointed

---

530. Augustine *Confessions* 8.29, trans. H. Chadwick (Oxford: Oxford University Press, 1991) 152-53.

531. ἤγγικεν (ēngiken), as in v. 12; the word in this verse is ἐγγύτερον (engyteron). On the meaning of Jesus' proclamation of the "nearness" of the kingdom, see N. T. Wright, *Jesus and the Victory of God, Christian Origins and the Question of God,* vol. 2 (Minneapolis: Fortress, 1996) 471-72.

out, "flesh" here means much more than "physicality"; for "quarreling and jealousy" (NRSV) you need an unquiet spirit as well as a sharp tongue and an envious eye. Nevertheless his main target here is the abuse of the body, one's own and often that of others as well: wild parties, drinking-bouts, sexual immorality and licentiousness. These are characteristic nighttime behaviors in the literal sense that they normally happen after dark, and in Paul's metaphorical sense that they belong with the old age rather than with the new day that is dawning in Christ (see 12:2). We should not forget that "quarreling and jealousy" are put on exactly the same level as immorality; there are many churches where the first four sins are unheard of but the last two run riot.

Instead, Paul commands his readers to "put on the Lord Jesus Christ, and make no provision for the flesh" (NRSV), or, as the NIV rightly interprets, "do not think about how to gratify" the desires that come from the corruptible and rebellious side of human nature. Paul has here returned to the basic commands of 6:12-13 (where, as here in v. 12, he speaks of "weapons," though there it is the parts of the body that are to become "weapons of righteousness") and of 8:12-13. And though his particular expressions shift from passage to passage, his underlying terminology is completely consistent. The "body," which will die but be raised, must already in the present be given to God in service and worship (12:2); the "flesh" will die, and its efforts to drag the Christian down with it must be resisted. There must be no loophole, no secret areas where license is permitted, where the

"desires" of the "flesh" are tolerated, let alone encouraged (see 7:4-6).

The ultimate safeguard against the seduction of the "flesh" in this full sense is Jesus himself—the Lord, the Messiah. In Gal 3:27 it is "the Messiah" who is to be "put on"; in Eph 5:24 and Col 3:10 it is "the new human being"; but the imagery of putting on a new suit of clothes, carrying as it may well do overtones of baptism, is used in several different senses and cannot easily be systematized. (In 1 Cor 15:53-4 and 2 Cor 5:3 it is used in relation to the resurrection body; in Col 3:12 it is used of the key Christian virtues; see also the passage about baptism and behavior in Romans 6.) Frequently when Paul uses more than one name or title for Jesus the one he wishes to emphasize is placed first; here, by saying, "put on the Lord Jesus Christ," he seems to be drawing attention to the sovereignty of Jesus, not simply over the believer (who is bound to obey the one whose servant he or she is), but perhaps more particularly over the forces of evil that are ranged against the gospel and those who embrace it. The Lord Jesus Christ thus becomes the personification of "the weapons of light" in v. 12: putting him on like a suit of armor is the best protection against the powers of the present darkness (see Eph 6:12). Paul is addressing those who have already "put on Christ" in baptism (Gal 3:27). The assumption must be that he is urging them, as a regular spiritual discipline, to invoke the presence and power of Jesus as Lord of all things to be their defense against all evil, not least the evil toward which they might be lured by their own "flesh."

# REFLECTIONS

**1.** There are three things this passage highlights as basic to Christian behavior. The first is to know what time one is living at. Though as we have seen there are social and cultural reasons why it seems counterintuitive to say so, the Christian is committed to the belief that the world's new day dawned with Jesus the Messiah, and that ever since his resurrection the world has been caught in the overlap between the old and the new, seen here as the moment just before full dawn when those who know their business are already up and behaving as in the daytime. The mental, moral, emotional, and spiritual effort required to sustain a belief in inaugurated eschatology may at times seem impossible. But the effort must be made. Without it, Christian moral teaching can easily degenerate into apparently baseless, or even pointless, exhortations. Why bother staying awake at midnight?[532]

---

532. This is where the metaphor's varied NT uses can become confusing. Paul's regular night/day/staying-awake language is about getting up early and being ready for morning. Sometimes in the Gospels (see references above) it is instead about staying awake late at night so as to be ready if and when the burglar, or the master of the house, arrives unexpectedly.

**2.** The second basic point is the rejection of "the works of darkness," and the making of no provision for "the desires of the flesh." The balancing point between unbridled hedonism on the one hand and nervous dualism on the other is very delicate, and Christians who react against the excesses of the one position are often in danger of lapsing into the other. It is important to read the present passage with 12:1-2 in mind, recognizing and celebrating the goodness of the body while (as in 8:12-13) rejecting some of the characteristic things that the body gets up to—which are what Paul calls "the works of the flesh." Equally, it is important, in celebrating the goodness of the created body, and delighting in the truth articulated in the next chapter, that everything made by God is good (14:14; cf. 1 Cor 10:25-27; 1 Tim 4:4), not to be led astray into thinking that therefore all rules concerning eating, drinking, and sexual practice are now irrelevant, shown up as unnecessary and probably dualistic restrictions on God-given liberty. Far from it. There are many things that must simply be ruled out, cut off without mercy; and drunkenness and sexual immorality (which often go together, of course) are among them. "As the flesh will make its own demands, there is no need to meet it halfway."[533]

**3.** Third, there is the positive command to "put on the Lord Jesus Christ." Paul never explains what exactly he thinks will constitute obedience to this attractive-sounding but to us opaque command, or to the others like it. Since it is similar to the "putting on Christ" that occurs in baptism (Gal 3:27), we may suppose that he has in mind the spiritual discipline, through daily prayer and meditation, of invoking Jesus himself as Lord (and therefore sovereign over oneself and over all powers that might attack) and savior (and therefore able to rescue one from harm). One of the best ways of doing this, practiced in many Christian traditions, is to meditate on the Gospel narratives about Jesus, placing oneself in the position of one of the onlookers or participants in the story and allowing the presence of Jesus to be felt and known, and with that presence allowing his own struggles against evil, and his call to take up the cross and follow him, to have their full effect. The reading of a gospel passage at a daily or weekly eucharist, followed by the solemn invoking of the risen Lord and feeding on the symbols of his self-giving love, is known in many Christian traditions as an excellent way of steadily obeying this most positive of ethical commands.

533. Joseph A. Fitzmyer, *Romans,* AB 33 (Garden City, N.Y.: Doubleday, 1993) 684.

# ROMANS 14:1–15:13, GOD'S CALL TO UNITY OF LIFE AND WORSHIP ACROSS BARRIERS OF CUSTOM AND ETHNIC IDENTITY

## OVERVIEW

Romans 14:1–15:13 must be treated as a single section. The final paragraph (15:7-13), it is true, also serves as the concluding paragraph for the major theological exposition not only of chaps. 12–15 but of the letter as a whole. That is part of the effect of 15:12, which echoes the theme of 1:3-5 (Jesus as the risen Messiah, the Lord of the whole world). But, as the repetition of "welcome" in 14:1 and 15:7 indicates, 15:7-13 is a summary and indeed celebration of the point that 14:1 has introduced. These two occurences of προσλαμβάνεσθε (*proslambanesthe*), together with the note that God welcomes someone in 14:3 and that Christ welcomes "you" in 15:7*b,* are the only occurrences of the word in Paul other than Philemon 17.

This exegetical decision strongly inclines me to a particular view of the subject matter of the whole section. It is remarkable that nowhere between 14:1 and 15:6 does Paul use the words "Jew" and "Gentile," or "circumcised" and "uncircumcised." He discusses the problems faced by the little church in Rome purely in terms of the different opinions that members and groups have on matters of food, drink, and observance of special days. He talks in considerable detail about the need for patience and love rather than straining one another's consciences. He speaks in terms of the "strong" and the "weak"; he sees himself as one of the "strong," but his eventual argument (15:1-6) is that the "strong" should follow the example of the Messiah in not "pleasing themselves."

Thus far, what he says is compatible with several different readings of the situation, and scholarship has duly come up with them. Divisions and subdivisions have been analyzed with great care, but no consensus has been reached.[534] However, when we add 15:7-13, as I believe we must, we suddenly find that Paul speaks of "the circumcision" (v. 8) and "the Gentiles" (v. 9), and then concludes the entire section with a string of scriptural quotations that celebrate the fact that Gentiles are coming to join the people of the one God, under the worldwide rule of Israel's Messiah. At this point we are, of course, back on the same map as in Romans 1–11.

The best reading of this problem, I think, is that the divisions Paul knows to exist within the Roman church have at least a strong element about them of the Jew/Gentile tension that has been underneath so much of the letter. This is by no means to say that "the weak" are Jewish Christians and "the strong" are Gentile Christians.[535] Paul is himself a Jewish Christian who sees himself as one of the "strong"; and, if Galatians is anything to go by, there might well be Gentile Christians whom he would categorize as

"weak." Rather, the matters about which disagreement has arisen, threatening to thwart united worship of the one God from people of all sorts, stem not principally from other types of cultural pressures, but from the continuing varied influence of the Jewish law within parts of the Christian community.[536]

This explains why he does not mention Jews and Gentiles until the final summary paragraph. To do so earlier would give the wrong impression; the divisions within the church may well not have lain exactly down the ethnic fault-line, since as we noted there might be both "strong" and "weak" Jewish Christians and both "strong" and "weak" Gentile Christians. In addition, to mention too early in the discussion the fact that there was an element of ethnicity about the whole business would have emphasized the very thing he wanted to avoid, drawing the line more firmly in the sand and polarizing those on either side, rather than doing his best to blur the line that was in danger of being drawn, and to insist that people from either side of it should learn to live together and especially to worship together.

It should not be necessary to labor the point that all the people Paul has in mind here are Christians (unlike chapter 11, where he is speaking of Jewish non-Christians).[537] They all give allegiance to Jesus as Lord, a point he makes pivotal in 14:1-12; they all believe themselves to be sharing in the life of God's kingdom (14:17) and the service of the Messiah (14:18; 15:5, 5-6). They have a duty to one another because they are all brothers and sisters for whom the Messiah died (14:15). This section is not, then, a way of outlining how Christians should live alongside non-Christian Jewish neighbors in Rome. As we might have inferred from the present section of the letter, where chaps. 12–13 have laid a foundation and chaps. 14–15 now build on it, these are instructions for the church.

---

534. For details of the relevant discussions, see M. Reasoner, *The Strong and the Weak: Romans 14.1–15.13 in Context,* SNTSMS 103 (Cambridge: Cambridge University Press, 1999). An important alternative view is that of R. J. Karris, "Romans 14:1–15:13 and the Occasion of Romans," in *The Romans Debate,* ed. K. P. Donfried, rev. ed. (Peabody, Mass.: Hendriksen, 1991) 65-84. Karris argues that Paul did not know the Roman situation, but was generalizing from experience elsewhere (e.g., Corinth).

535. Against Douglas J. Moo, *The Epistle to the Romans,* NICNT (Grand Rapids: Eerdmans, 1996) 829, though many of the points he makes remain important.

536. Horace *Satires* 1:9:71. Horace describes how a fellow poet, Fuscus Aristius, refuses to talk business on a sabbath day for fear of offending the Jews, describing himself, having scruples about such things, as "weaker" (*infirmior*), and saying there are many others like him. This reinforces the point made in relation to Galatians: Those insisting on Jewish regulations might actually be Gentiles, while Jews like Paul and his friends might be sitting loose to them.

537. For the opposite view see Mark D. Nanos, *The Mystery of Romans: The Jewish Context of Paul's Letter* (Minneapolis: Fortress, 1996) esp. chap. 3. It is impossible to do justice here to Nanos's interesting, detailed, but ultimately unsuccessful analysis.

But we do not know as much about the church as Paul did, or at least thought he did. He assumes much that we cannot even guess. The fact that he writes such a substantial and closely argued section of the letter oriented toward this topic, in the light of the spare and brief comments on several major matters in chaps. 12–13, is a strong indication that he believed he was addressing a real, not a theoretical or merely possible, problem. His basic appeal to "welcome one another" implies that the church was divided into various groups, probably each meeting in a separate small gathering, a different house, with mutual suspicions or even antipathies. It may well be that the problem had become particularly acute when the capital's Jewish population, expelled five or six years earlier by Claudius, had after Nero's accession returned en masse, including a number of Jewish Christians who had for the time being, like Paul's friends Prisca and Aquila, been forced to live elsewhere (Rom 16:3-5; cf. Acts 18:2-3).[538] We may assume that Prisca and Aquila were themselves "strong" Jewish Christians, like Paul; but the tensions between different groups, in terms of practices that some regarded as mandatory and others as irrelevant, was bound to increase under these circumstances. It is possible that some of the tensions that had emerged in the church in Corinth, due (at an earlier stage) to the personality cults reflected in 1 Corinthians 1–4 and (at a later stage) to the "super-apostles" and/or the "false apostles," whoever they were, mentioned in 2 Corinthians, had arisen in Rome as well (was there, perhaps, a "Peter" party in Rome?). Our comparative uncertainty about the precise details of the Corinthian situation makes it difficult to do more than suggest that parallels might well have existed. We would be safe in assuming that there were several different Christian groups meeting in Rome, involving a spectrum of opinion on these and other debated issues. Paul is determined to address not just some, but all of them, and to use this opportunity to promote their unity.

The tensions we see in this section are therefore similar to those we find in 1 Corinthians 8–10, but with some significant differences. The problem in Corinth seems to have been primarily, in Witherington's choice phrase, the question of venue rather than of menu.[539] Granted that it was legitimate, other things being equal, to eat meat sold in the market even though it had probably been offered to an idol as a sacrifice, it was not legitimate for Christians to go into the idol's temple itself and take part in either the cult, or the meals, or other practices associated with it. This question does not seem to be at issue in Rome; the Christians are not, it seems, being tempted to visit idol temples, or if they are Paul does not allude to the fact. But the question of whether to eat meat, and the discussion of how to avoid offending the conscience of a fellow Christian, joins the two discussions together. It is not unlike the different discussions of justification, of the promises to Abraham, and so forth, in Romans and Galatians: a different but related situation causes Paul to draw on the same stock of ideas, producing overlap but not identity.

Paul's analysis and treatment of the problem is notable for its initial highlighting of "faith" in 14:1-2, and its return to this in 14:22-23. This raises the question, which an extended discussion like this prompts in any case: what is the relationship of the present passage to the entire letter so far? The mention of "faith" obviously gives more specific focus to this, since "faith" has been a major theme, especially in 3:21–4:25 and 9:30–10:21. At first sight it might seem as though chap. 14 had little to do with these previous passages. This is not because it is about "ethics" rather than "theology"; as we saw in introducing chapters 12–16, this is a distinction we bring to Paul rather than find in him. It is rather that when he speaks of some people being "weak in faith," and of others "believing one can eat anything" (14:1-2), this seems to have nothing to do with the meaning of "faith" in the earlier sections, where it has to do with the confession that Jesus is Lord and the belief that God raised him from the dead (10:9; cf. 4:24-25). Closer investigation, however, suggests otherwise. The first major argument of the section (14:1-12) hinges at every point on the fact that Jesus is Lord and that God raised him from the dead. The word κύριος (*kyrios;* or in one case its cognate verb) occurs no fewer than ten times

---

538. N. T. Wright, *The New Testament and the People of God,* vol. 1 of *Christian Origins and the Question of God* (London: SPCK; Minneapolis: Fortress, 1992) 354-55.

539. B. W. Witherington, "Not So Idle Thoughts About *Eidolothuton,*" *TynBull* 44 (1993) 237-54.

between v. 4 and v. 11 (the occurrence in v. 11 comes within the quotation of Isa 49:18; see below). The heart of the passage, v. 9, declares that the reason the Messiah died and rose was in order to become Lord of both dead and living; and this gives rise, as in 2:1-16, to a statement of the future judgment of God at which everything will be put to rights. When we put this together— Jesus as the crucified and risen Lord of all, with weak and strong alike together facing the future judgment and working out their present status in the light of that—we should probably conclude that this is, in fact, another variation on the same theme that Paul was offering in chaps. 3–4 and 9–10 (on the link with 4:20-21 see the Commentary on 14:23). As we might have guessed from Gal 2:11-21, the first time "justification by faith" occurs as a theme in Paul's writings, part of the meaning of this theme itself is the fact that all those who believe in Jesus as the risen Lord should be able to eat together despite cultural and ethnic differences.

This means that we should probably be open to taking "faith" in the passage as meaning something close to its meaning elsewhere in the letter; and this is in fact what we find. Paul does not imply that those who are "weak in the faith" have any less a grasp on the basic content of the faith (Jesus' resurrection and lordship) than the others; only that, like those who have a weak conscience in 1 Corinthians 8, they have not thought through and worked out the full implications of that faith. Paul is constantly hinting that they should do so, but he knows from pastoral practice that people cannot necessarily be hurried on such issues and that, provided they share the basic faith itself, its relative "strength" or "weakness" should not hinder Christian fellowship. The "weak in faith," then, are not people who only accept part of the Christian gospel; they are people whose faith, though real, has not matured to the point where they understand its full implications. Now the real

point emerges: "justification by faith" includes "fellowship by faith" as one of its key elements. All those who believe the gospel of Jesus the risen Messiah and Lord belong together in the same family. Romans 14–15 does not contain, after all, something other than Paul's central theology. It is not simply "practical instructions" that leave the deep and detailed theology of justification and the rest far behind. It is, rather, what justification by faith looks like when it sits down at table in Christian fellowship.[540] And this, as we shall see when we get to 14:9-12, is what ultimately poses a challenge to the surrounding pagan culture itself.

Romans 14:1–15:13 divides up into three segments, which then further subdivide though less obviously. The topic is introduced in 14:1-12 and is given the basic analysis and answer: The weak and the strong must recognize that they have the same Lord, the one who died and rose again to be Lord of all. There will come a judgment at which all will give account, and it is not up to one Christian to pre-empt God's right in advance. Then 14:13-23 focuses on the issue of how to cope in practice, granted that both sides agree not to condemn the other; here, as in 1 Cor 8:7-13, Paul emphasizes the importance of respecting, and not making demands on, one another's consciences. This leads to 15:1-13, which moves in two waves to the great conclusion in which all alike praise the one God. Romans 15:1-6 shows the Messiah leading the way to this united praise, in his "not pleasing himself"; 15:7-13 insists again on the mutual welcome, based on the welcoming ministry of the Messiah, and celebrates with a sudden rush of scriptural citations the coming together in worship of Jews and Gentiles under the rule of this risen Messiah, through whom the one God will supply the present church with hope, through the power of the Holy Spirit.

---

540. On the relation of the various issues in 1 Corinthians 8–10 and the present passage, see N. T. Wright, "One God, One Lord, One People: Incarnational Christology for a Church in a Pagan Environment," *Ex Aud* 7 (1991) 45-58.

# Romans 14:1-12, Judging and Being Judged

## NIV

**14** Accept him whose faith is weak, without passing judgment on disputable matters. ²One man's faith allows him to eat everything, but another man, whose faith is weak, eats only vegetables. ³The man who eats everything must not look down on him who does not, and the man who does not eat everything must not condemn the man who does, for God has accepted him. ⁴Who are you to judge someone else's servant? To his own master he stands or falls. And he will stand, for the Lord is able to make him stand.

⁵One man considers one day more sacred than another; another man considers every day alike. Each one should be fully convinced in his own mind. ⁶He who regards one day as special, does so to the Lord. He who eats meat, eats to the Lord, for he gives thanks to God; and he who abstains, does so to the Lord and gives thanks to God. ⁷For none of us lives to himself alone and none of us dies to himself alone. ⁸If we live, we live to the Lord; and if we die, we die to the Lord. So, whether we live or die, we belong to the Lord.

⁹For this very reason, Christ died and returned to life so that he might be the Lord of both the dead and the living. ¹⁰You, then, why do you judge your brother? Or why do you look down on your brother? For we will all stand before God's judgment seat. ¹¹It is written:

" 'As surely as I live,' says the Lord,
'every knee will bow before me;
every tongue will confess to God.' "ᵃ

¹²So then, each of us will give an account of himself to God.

ᵃ *11* Isaiah 45:23

## NRSV

**14** Welcome those who are weak in faith,ᵃ but not for the purpose of quarreling over opinions. ²Some believe in eating anything, while the weak eat only vegetables. ³Those who eat must not despise those who abstain, and those who abstain must not pass judgment on those who eat; for God has welcomed them. ⁴Who are you to pass judgment on servants of another? It is before their own lord that they stand or fall. And they will be upheld, for the Lordᵇ is able to make them stand.

5Some judge one day to be better than another, while others judge all days to be alike. Let all be fully convinced in their own minds. ⁶Those who observe the day, observe it in honor of the Lord. Also those who eat, eat in honor of the Lord, since they give thanks to God; while those who abstain, abstain in honor of the Lord and give thanks to God.

7We do not live to ourselves, and we do not die to ourselves. ⁸If we live, we live to the Lord, and if we die, we die to the Lord; so then, whether we live or whether we die, we are the Lord's. ⁹For to this end Christ died and lived again, so that he might be Lord of both the dead and the living.

10Why do you pass judgment on your brother or sister?ᶜ Or you, why do you despise your brother or sister?ᶜ For we will all stand before the judgment seat of God.ᵈ ¹¹For it is written,
"As I live, says the Lord, every knee shall bow to me,
and every tongue shall give praise toᵉ God."
¹²So then, each of us will be accountable to God.ᶠ

ᵃ Or *conviction*      ᵇ Other ancient authorities read *for God*
ᶜ Gk *brother*      ᵈ Other ancient authorities read *of Christ*
ᵉ Or *confess*      ᶠ Other ancient authorities lack *to God*

# COMMENTARY

**14:1.** Without a by-your-leave, Paul launches out from his broad general statement of Christian obligation into a very specific topic, which we must assume had direct relevance to the Roman Christians. There may well have been disputes and dissensions that had reached Paul's ears. He opens abruptly: "As for the one who is weak as regards faith. . . ." (The singular is important, giving the opening a sharp focus [as against NRSV, which uses plural for the sake of the inclusive pronoun that follows]. NRSV margin suggests that "conviction" is a possible alternative for "faith," but though this is possible it would break the link with earlier parts of the letter.) Paul's command is immediate and to the point: you should welcome such a person. He seems to presuppose that this had not been happening.

Another presupposition emerges at once: Paul assumes that most of those reading or hearing this letter are, like him, "strong" in the sense soon to be developed. The "weak" are perhaps a minority; perhaps not even whole worshiping groups, but individuals within groups. Paul's point is that they must be made welcome, but that this ought not to become an occasion for people to ask them about their particular views and engage them in disputes over matters that are the subject of genuine questioning. (διάκρισις [diakrisis] can have a good sense, "distinguishing," though here it seems to mean "disputes" in a bad sense; likewise, διαλογισμός [dialogismos] can have a positive or neutral sense, "reasoning," or a negative one, "grumbling," "disputing"; the range of meaning of the two words is such that the phrase could mean "disputes about disputes," and perhaps that is more or less what Paul intends to convey.)

**14:2-4.** The first instance Paul gives contains almost all the elements of the whole first paragraph: (1) naming the disputed area; (2) commanding both sides to back off from passing judgment, on the grounds of God's welcome of the other; (3) warning against "condemning"; (4) invoking the lordship of Jesus, and declaring that Jesus will vindicate either or both parties.

He begins with the issue that, we may well suppose, lay close to the heart of it all. In Antioch, Peter, Barnabas, and others had originally eaten with Gentile Christians, but had separated themselves after "certain persons came from James" (Gal 2:11-14). This is not an identical issue, but it belongs in the same family of disputes, at the center of which lay the centuries-old Jewish taboos regarding food, both what to eat, how to prepare it, and with whom and in what condition to eat it.[541] Like any such deep-rooted cultural issue, it would emerge in different forms in different

situations, but with an underlying family resemblance; and it is not difficult to imagine the context of the present warning. If most Christians in Rome seemed happy to eat non-kosher food, or to eat meat bought in a market when it had almost certainly been originally offered in sacrifice to an idol, there were bound to be some for whom this was unthinkable. It went against everything they had been taught from childhood. If Christianity was an entirely new religion they might be prepared to throw away old beliefs. Part of the point, though, was that in the Messiah God had been faithful to the covenant. The Messiah was the goal of Torah. How then could Torah's forbidding of certain foods be set aside?

These questions are not simple, and Paul could not expect every Christian to come instantly and from the heart to the same conclusion that he and many others had reached: that Torah had indeed been fulfilled but that a new age had thereby been inaugurated that, though it did not deny the goodness and God-givenness of Torah, nevertheless relativized many of its injunctions as relating to the period when God's people were a single nation (see esp. Gal 3:15-29). But already the two poles of the dispute are set up, as in v. 2: one person believes it is permissible to eat everything, while another only eats vegetables. Paul does not say whether the latter position has been taken because kosher meat was unavailable, or because all meat for sale would have been offered to idols. People would know what he was talking about, namely, the kind of scruple that, because of such dangers, reckons it is best to steer clear of meat altogether.

To say that the first person "believes" that everything may be eaten is to say that, in this person's construal of the whole Christian faith, this position is a result of their more fundamental convictions about God and Jesus. The NRSV's "Some people believe in eating anything" is misleading, (a) implying that "eating anything" is the actual object of faith (as though on principle they ate the most peculiar things they could find), whereas Paul surely means that the underlying faith they hold has this as its corollary, and (b) substituting "anything" for "everything," which gives the phrase almost a contemptuous ring (like "some people think they can get away with anything"). This is not Paul's point. He is simply reporting the fact that some Christians—himself included—

---

541. On Jewish food laws see Wright, *The New Testament and the People of God*, 237-41; N. T. Wright, *Jesus and the Victory of God*, vol. 2 of *Christian Origins and the Question of God* (London: SPCK, 1996) 396-98.

have come to the settled conviction that there are no food taboos in the kingdom of God.

Verse 3 issues the basic command and explanation that governs the whole discussion and that Paul will repeat from various angles until the final statement in 15:7. Neither party must pass judgment on the other, because God has welcomed both. Actually, Paul is a little more nuanced than this: the eater must not despise the non-eater. This can hardly be a matter of condemnation, since the non-eater is not doing anything wrong, merely not exercising a right. The attitude Paul is ruling out is like the disdain shown by a motorist who drives as fast as the law allows and looks down on someone who timidly drives at only half that speed. The non-eater, however, may well "condemn" the eater, because from that point of view eating forbidden foods is actually sinful (the NIV more or less doubles the length of the verse by expanding Paul's simple words "the eater" and "the non-eater" into full paraphrases of the two positions). The "welcome" God has already extended to both is a way of summing up the message of 3:21–5:11, as for instance in 5:2: being justified by faith, we have peace with God through our Lord Jesus Christ, through whom we have received access to this grace in which we stand. That this whole strand of thought is not far below the surface will emerge later when Paul, almost casually defining "the kingdom of God" in 14:17, does so in terms that exactly summarize 5:1-5.

In v. 4 he personalizes the point: "Who do you think you are, passing judgment on someone else's household slave?" (the NRSV's concern for inclusivity again blunts the sharp force of the sing. "you" and the sing. "slave"). The point is obvious: it is up to the master to judge the slave. For one slave to look into the next room and pass judgment on another is simply inappropriate; it shows a failure to recognize who's who. Paul expresses this in terms of "standing" and "falling" both as a metaphor for "being vindicated" as opposed to "being condemned" and, perhaps, as a hint of what the Christian "vindication" will consist in: "being made to stand" is an early Christian way of speaking about "resurrection" (see Eph 5:14; for the metaphorical use, see 11:20; 1 Cor 10:12). When Paul speaks of the Lord (or, since he is using the metaphor of household slaves, the "master" as in the NIV—though this is to obscure the empha-

sis on Jesus as Lord throughout the passage) being "able" to make the slave "stand," the word for "he is able" is δυνατεῖ (*dynatei*), cognate with words for "power" that Paul often uses in relation to God's accomplishment of the resurrection (see, e.g., Rom 1:4; 1 Cor 6:14). His main point is that the Lord, the master of all the household, is able to vindicate servants who eat meat and servants who do not; but the echoes, as he says this, are of the greater vindication that is promised at the last. Since the paragraph ends with an explicit statement of the final day of judgment, we are right to allow these echoes to be heard, and to understand the present nonjudging life of the community within its eschatological frame of reference.

**14:5-6.** Paul now adds to the picture a second cause of contention: the observation of special days. The NRSV, translating literally, brings out the interwoven nature of the argument, as "some judge" one day better than another, while "others judge" all alike. The special days are presumably regarded as "more sacred" (NIV) or "holier" (NJB) than the others, but there is no word in the Greek corresponding to this; Paul simply says "one judges a day above a day, another judges every day." It is just possible that Paul has in mind the festival days of the wider pagan world, not least the Roman Empire; but it is far more likely that he is referring to the Jewish festival days, some of which, Acts implies, he himself observed (cf. Acts 20:16; it is, of course, possible to take this as a purely chronological reference). It is interesting, if that is so, that he does not refer to the sabbath explicitly. There is an apparent tension between his open attitude in this passage and his strong condemnation of the Galatians for observing "days, and months, and seasons, and years," the sure sign that by adopting Jewish practices they were, in fact, reverting to another variety of paganism (Gal 4:10). This is the same apparent tension that we find between his open attitude toward circumcision and uncircumcision in 1 Corinthians 7 and his strong condemnation, throughout Galatians, of Gentiles getting circumcised. In both cases the tension is more apparent than real. There seems no question in Romans of erstwhile pagans believing that they had to become full Jews in order to be part of the family of Abraham. The whole emphasis of the letter runs the other way, that the Roman Christians were tempted to look down on non-Christian Jews (chaps. 9–11) and now on Christians who, whether or not because of their Jewish origins, wanted to maintain some of the food taboos and other cultural markers. The "weak" might be condemning the "strong," but the main problem seems to be that the "strong" are looking down on the "weak."

Paul's principle here, which will become more important as the chapter proceeds, is that everyone should be fully convinced in their own mind. He spells out in v. 6 what this will mean: if what is done (observing the day, eating certain foods, or not eating them) is done "to the Lord"—the sign of which, in the case of meals, is the giving of thanks to God—then there should be no cause for complaint.

**14:7-9.** Paul now explains the argument so far by grounding it in the very heart of the gospel. Verse 7, introduced with γάρ (*gar,* "for"), states the principle, which is then itself explained (*gar* in each case) in turn by vv. 8-9 (this sequence of thought is obscured in the NIV by the inexplicable paragraph break after v. 8). The essential point is that everything Christians do is done, not in relation to themselves alone, but in relation to the Lord. To "live to oneself," the position Paul rules out in v. 7, is to order one's life in relation simply to one's own background, culture, desires, and wishes; these may not be wrong in themselves, but everything must be judged in relation to the Lord himself (see the parallels to this idea in 2 Cor 5:15; Gal 2:19-20). The most basic things we do—living and dying—are done in the presence of the Lord, and for his sake: Whichever of these we do, and by implication everything else we do as well, we belong to the Lord (for the idea of "belonging" to the Lord, see Gal 3:29 ["belonging to the Messiah"] and Rom 8:9; 1 Cor 3:23; 6:19-20; 15:23; 2 Cor 10:7; Gal 5:24). In Rom 14:7-9 we are still, by implication, in the metaphorical world of masters and servants. But the mention of living and dying brings Paul to the deepest explanation of the whole business: The Messiah died and lived in order to rule as Lord over dead and living alike (v. 9).[542] This "ruling as Lord," clearly, explains the "belonging to the Lord" in v. 8: it is

the death and resurrection of Jesus the Messiah that means we now belong to him, and that constitutes him indeed as the Lord of the whole world (1:3-5; 15:12). This proves more than Paul needs to prove for the immediate argument, but it points, as we shall see, to the larger issue that stands behind the entire section. The gospel announcement that Jesus, the crucified and risen Messiah, is the Lord of the whole world is thus appealed to as the reason for unity across the barriers of custom and taboo.

**14:10-12.** Though the surface argument has developed through the discussion of particular practical matters, and words of command and advice, the underlying sequence of thought has been about God and the Lord. God welcomes all believers (v. 3); the Lord will make them stand (v. 4); the Lord is the one before whom all is done (v. 6), especially when thanks are offered to God (v. 6). The Lord is the one to whom we live or die, to whom we belong, because the Messiah died and rose to become the universal Lord (vv. 8-9). This underlying sequence now reaches its climax in what begins as another rhetorical question about condemning or despising, but is actually a statement of the final judgment, as in 2:1-16 and 2 Cor 5:10, backed up by a passage from Isaiah that was obviously of vital significance to Paul. He has declared in 12:1-2 and 13:11-14 that Christian life is lived in the light of the new age, already breaking in; this is what that eschatological perspective on communal living looks like in practice.

He begins with another question to two imaginary bystanders: "You, there! and, yes, you too!" As in v. 3, one is judging and the other is despising; presumably, again, the weak judging the strong and the strong despising the weak. As they stand there squabbling in Paul's imagination, they are suddenly commanded to look up: there before them is the tribunal, the βῆμα (*bēma*), and it belongs to none other than God.[543] This does not necessarily mean that God the father will do the judging in person; in Acts 25:10 Paul is standing before Caesar's tribunal, but they are in Caesarea, not Rome, and it is the governor Festus who is

542. It is unusual for Paul to say simply "lived" (ἔζησεν *ezēsen*) rather than "lived again" or "was raised." Several MSS, reflecting this, have made adjustments accordingly. Presumably Paul has put it like this because he wants to tie in the gospel events very tightly both to our present obligation (v. 8) and to the universal lordship of Christ (v. 9*b*), both expressed in these terms.

543. Several MSS, and Polycarp *To the Philadelphians* 6.2, have "Christ," as in 2 Cor 5:10; but the best MSS read "God." Polycarp is in any case quoting freely and probably coalescing this passage and 2 Corinthians 5 in his mind. There are several scenes in Acts involving people (including Paul) appearing before a tribunal: e.g., Acts 18:12, 16-17; 25:6, 10, 17.

actually hearing the case. We should probably understand here that Jesus, as the risen Messiah, is the actual judge, even though the court comes under the overall jurisdiction of God the creator. In any case, the point for the present is that all disputes between Christians over inessentials are now irrelevant. It is to God that all must give an account (v. 12).

In between the statement of v. 10 and the conclusion of v. 12, Paul has inserted a quotation from Isa 45:23 ("to me every knee shall bow, and every tongue shall swear to God").[544] This is introduced by "As I live, says YHWH," a phrase that occurs so often in Scripture that it seems pointless to assign it a particular reference, though Isa 49:18 is often cited.[545] This picks up the "lived" of v. 9; in other words, the "living again" of Jesus is the reason why he is thus installed as judge, which in turn is the reason why it would be wrong to collapse κύριος (*kyrios*) here into a general reference to God, rather than retaining it, however paradoxically, as a reference to Jesus as the risen Messiah and, therefore, the judge. (For "resurrection, therefore Messiah," see 1:3-4; 15:12; for "resurrection, therefore judge," see 2:16; Acts 10:42; 17:31; for "Messiah, therefore judge," see Psalms 2; 72; *Pss. Sol.* 17; 2 Tim 4:1.) The main quotation, with Phil 2:10 as a close parallel, is interesting for a number of reasons. First, it brings together (as the whole passage has done), "Lord" (*kyrios*) and "God" (θεός *theos*) in a way that both echoes the LXX usage and indicates how strong and high Paul's underlying christology is at this point (see the Commentary on 10:13). Second, it emphasizes the universal sovereignty of the God of Israel, exercised in and through the risen Messiah and Lord; this, going way beyond the detail of the present argument, alerts us again to Paul's underlying agenda (see below). Third, Paul is once again linking his argument to the theme of Isaiah 40–55, suggesting that his readers should understand their present position in terms of the overall story of that passage, the unveiling of God's righteousness through the strange work of the Servant. They are the people for whom the promises—and now the responsibilities!—are coming true.

544. Paul follows the LXX of the latter passage closely, including the extra "to God" at the end. See the detailed discussion in J. R. Wagner, *Heralds of the Good News: Isaiah and Paul "In Concert" in the Letter to the Romans*, NovTSup 101 (Leiden: Brill, 2002) 336-40.
545. For more details, see Wagner, *Heralds of the Good News*, 337-38.

Each Christian, then, must give an account of himself or herself to God. There is no tension in Paul's mind between this and 8:1, where there is no condemnation for those who are in Christ. He has already indicated in 2:1-16 that there will be a coming day when all will be judged; the fact that the Christian believer is assured of a favorable verdict on that day does not make it any less serious, as 1 Cor 3:10-17 indicates well enough. Part of his point is that in the light of the coming judgment we have no business judging one another ahead of the time. There may also be a hint that to condemn or despise a fellow Christian is itself an offense for which one should be rebuked.

In another letter Paul envisages situations where a genuine dispute between believers will have to be settled in at least a quasi-judicial fashion. He instructs the community to appoint fit persons for this purpose, on the grounds that they will themselves one day judge angels (1 Cor 6:1-8). He would rather they did not have disputes with one another at all, but if need be this would be the way to settle them, rather than referring to courts of unbelievers. Once again, there is an apparent tension with the present passage; but we must remind ourselves that Romans 14–15 is not about fraud and similar matters, but about disputes over what Paul (controversially, of course) insists on regarding as inessentials. What is more, by analogy with 13:1-7 we could point out that insofar as such persons are appointed by the community, they are not acting as private individuals.

Underneath the whole argument, as a theme at first almost out of sight but emerging gradually until it becomes clear and central in the closing verses, is Paul's implication that, if Jesus is Lord, Caesar is not. The repeated reference to Jesus as Lord throughout vv. 4-8 opens this theme, not least when it is coupled with reference to household slaves; anyone in Rome would know who the ultimate Master was, with a full household of slaves. This by itself might remain a faint echo. But when we find that the Messiah has died and lived in order to rule as Lord over dead and living alike (v. 9) we begin to see where it is leading; and when we come upon a reference to God's tribunal we realize that God and Caesar are here in explicit competition. When Paul then quotes Isa 45:23, just as in Phil 2:10-11 where the Caesar reference ought certainly to be understood,[546] we are right to see the theme in full daylight. Paul has said much more than he needs for the purpose of explaining that differences of customs are irrelevant when God has welcomed all sides, and that judging one another is inappropriate in view of the coming divine judgment. If he has labored the point to this extent, he has probably done so for a special reason; and the most obvious reason is that he is emphasizing that the kingdom to which those in Christ belong is a kingdom superior to, and destined to replace, that of Caesar. The subsequent similar hints (14:17; 15:12) offer further confirmation.

But why is Paul saying this here, in this context? He is holding out two implications for the potentially divided Roman church. On the positive side, he wants to assure them that they are truly an outpost of the coming great empire of Jesus himself, the world's true Lord. Paul, in Rome as

elsewhere in Caesar's territory (including colonies like Philippi and Corinth, and centers of imperial cult like Ephesus), is intent on maintaining communities, united in their loyalty to Jesus as Lord, right under the nose of Caesar, who prided himself on maintaining in the world a unity of peoples under his own rule as Lord. The unity of Christians across traditional barriers is a sign to the principalities and powers that a greater rule than theirs has now begun (see, e.g., Gal 4:1-11; Eph 3:10). Maintaining that unity, then, is not just a matter of preventing squabbles and bad feeling in the church. It is part of essential Christian witness to the one Lord. If the church divides along lines related to ethnic or tribal loyalty, it is still living in the world of Caesar. On the negative side, squabbles over the implications of the gospel could inflame tensions between Jewish and Christian communities in Rome, which could give Caesar an excuse for persecution; memories of the expulsion of the Jews under Claudius were still recent. Differences of cultural practice within the church should not be allowed to give Caesar a chance to exercise his delegated authority in the wrong way.

546. Not least because of the link with Phil 3:20-21, where it is explicit. See N. T. Wright, "Paul's Gospel and Caesar's Empire," in *Paul and Politics: Ekklesia, Israel, Imperium, Interpretation,* ed. R. A. Horsley (Harrisburg, Pa.: Trinity, 2000) 160-83.

# Romans 14:13-23, Conscience and the Kingdom of God

## NIV

[13]Therefore let us stop passing judgment on one another. Instead, make up your mind not to put any stumbling block or obstacle in your brother's way. [14]As one who is in the Lord Jesus, I am fully convinced that no food[a] is unclean in itself. But if anyone regards something as unclean, then for him it is unclean. [15]If your brother is distressed because of what you eat, you are no longer acting in love. Do not by your eating destroy your brother for whom Christ died. [16]Do not allow what you consider good to be spoken of as evil. [17]For the kingdom of God is not a matter of eating and drinking, but of righteousness, peace and joy in the Holy Spirit, [18]because anyone who serves Christ in this way is pleasing to God and approved by men.

[19]Let us therefore make every effort to do what

[a] 14 Or that nothing

## NRSV

13Let us therefore no longer pass judgment on one another, but resolve instead never to put a stumbling block or hindrance in the way of another.[a] [14]I know and am persuaded in the Lord Jesus that nothing is unclean in itself; but it is unclean for anyone who thinks it unclean. [15]If your brother or sister[b] is being injured by what you eat, you are no longer walking in love. Do not let what you eat cause the ruin of one for whom Christ died. [16]So do not let your good be spoken of as evil. [17]For the kingdom of God is not food and drink but righteousness and peace and joy in the Holy Spirit. [18]The one who thus serves Christ is acceptable to God and has human approval. [19]Let us then pursue what makes for peace and for mutual upbuilding. [20]Do not, for the sake of food, destroy the work of God. Everything is indeed

[a] Gk of a brother    [b] Gk brother

## NIV

leads to peace and to mutual edification. <sup>20</sup>Do not destroy the work of God for the sake of food. All food is clean, but it is wrong for a man to eat anything that causes someone else to stumble. <sup>21</sup>It is better not to eat meat or drink wine or to do anything else that will cause your brother to fall.

<sup>22</sup>So whatever you believe about these things keep between yourself and God. Blessed is the man who does not condemn himself by what he approves. <sup>23</sup>But the man who has doubts is condemned if he eats, because his eating is not from faith; and everything that does not come from faith is sin.

## NRSV

clean, but it is wrong for you to make others fall by what you eat; <sup>21</sup>it is good not to eat meat or drink wine or do anything that makes your brother or sister<sup>a</sup> stumble.<sup>b</sup> <sup>22</sup>The faith that you have, have as your own conviction before God. Blessed are those who have no reason to condemn themselves because of what they approve. <sup>23</sup>But those who have doubts are condemned if they eat, because they do not act from faith;<sup>c</sup> for whatever does not proceed from faith<sup>c</sup> is sin.<sup>d</sup>

<sup>a</sup> Gk brother    <sup>b</sup> Other ancient authorities add *or be upset or be weakened*    <sup>c</sup> Or *conviction*    <sup>d</sup> Other authorities, some ancient, add here 16.25-27

# COMMENTARY

**14:13.** All right, says Paul in one of his punning moods: if you are so keen on judging things, here is something to judge—how not to trip each other up![547] Verse 13 thus forms a bridge between the two halves of chap. 14, introducing the new theme, which is the positive side of Paul's exhortation. It is not simply a matter of giving up passing judgment on, or despising, a fellow Christian; it is a matter of taking positive thought to see how to avoid making life difficult for one another—and particularly how the "strong" can avoid making life difficult for the "weak."

The paragraph divides into two segments, each one unpacking v. 13, with a conclusion (vv. 22-23). In vv. 14-18 Paul warns that even things that are not unclean in themselves become so if someone believes them to be, and that this could mean ruin for someone lured into going against conscience. In vv. 19-23 he tells them to avoid things that make a fellow Christian trip up. These two cover very similar ground from only a slightly different angle.

**14:14-18.** In v. 14*a,* and then again in v. 20*b,* Paul insists that all foods are "clean." This was a

regular early Christian belief, though it must have been hard to hammer out and maintain (see Matt 15:11, 17-20; Mark 7:18-19; Acts 10:15, 28; 11:9; Titus 1:15). Paul says here that he knows this, and has been "persuaded in the Lord Jesus." This cannot mean simply that the belief in the cleanness of all foods is part of the truth of being "in Christ." It seems to mean either that in the course of his service of, and love for, the risen Lord, Jesus had made it clear to Paul that all foods were in fact clean; or that Paul is referring to the traditions of Jesus' own sayings known to us from Matthew and Mark. On balance, and recognizing the ways in which Romans 12–13 as well alludes to (what we think of as) gospel tradition, I think it is more likely that he means the latter. (See 1 Cor 7:10, where the contrast with Rom 14:12 indicates that Paul is aware of having access to some teaching from Jesus himself ["the Lord"], while on other matters he must think things out from scratch under the influence of the Spirit [1 Cor 7:40].)[548]

The exception noted in v. 14*b,* though, is not mentioned in the gospel traditions. The thought that one can make a clean object unclean by regarding it as such is striking, and introduces a main theme of the following verses: the importance of making up one's mind and acting accordingly. Paul would not, of course, take this to the lengths of contemporary existentialism, in which

---

547. This is completely obscured in the NIV ("stop passing judgment . . . make up your mind") and the NRSV ("resolve instead"). The KJV keeps Paul's verbal flourish ("let us not judge one another . . . but judge this rather"). J. B. Phillips attempts to catch the same echo ("Let us stop turning critical eyes on one another. If we must be critical, let us be critical of our own conduct"), though this implies that the "judging" is always negative, whereas the second "judging" is positive, as in "make a good judgment about this."

548. See M. Thompson, *Clothed with Christ: The Example and Teaching of Jesus in Romans 12.1–15.13,* JSNTSup (Sheffield: Sheffield Academic, 1991) 185-99.

any behavior at all is approved as long as it is done wholeheartedly (it being conveniently ignored that people who commit genocide, acts of terrorism, and the like are often deeply sincere). What he is allowing for, throughout this section, is that genuine Christians grow to maturity at different rates and that during this process one cannot and must not hurry or harry them to accept positions their conscience at the moment cannot allow.

In particular, one must recognize (v. 15) that actual spiritual harm is caused to people when they are put in this position, and that causing such harm is a failure in the basic Christian virtue of love (13:8-10). The *gar* at the start of v. 15 (omitted in most trans.) indicates that Paul thinks he is explaining something here, but if so it must be v. 13, not v. 14. Indeed, acting in a "strong" way can even, Paul warns here and in 1 Cor 8:10-13, cause a fellow Christian's "destruction," despite the fact that the Messiah died for them. This powerful statement presumably means that one could risk betraying a "weak" person into what was, for them, some form of pagan idolatry, and that this could jeopardize their allegiance to Jesus altogether, putting the "strong" Christian at loggerheads with the Messiah himself, who had given his life for them. Paul then juxtaposes a further command (v. 16); something may be "good" for you, but the weaker Christian may call down a curse on it—and perhaps, the implication may be, on you as well.

This is then explained in vv. 17-18, with one of Paul's rare statements about God's kingdom (other Pauline mentions of the kingdom of God: 1 Cor 4:20; 6:9-10; 15:24, 50; Gal 5:21; Eph 5:5; Col 1:13; 4:11; 1 Thess 2:12; 2 Thess 1:5; 2 Tim 4:1, 18). If, however, we avoid slavish concordance-study, we shall learn to recognize themes even when their technical shorthand is absent; and in this case there is a clear earlier discussion: 5:12-21. This is all about the reign of "grace," and of those who receive it as a gift, over against the reign of sin (see 5:14, 17, 21; cf. 6:12, 14; the key word is βασιλεύω [*basileuō*, "to rule as king"], cognate with βασιλεία [*basileia*, "kingdom"]). It forms one of Paul's central (if highly condensed) statements of the entire Christian worldview and narrative, and plays as we saw a major role in the structure of chaps. 5–8 and hence of the letter as a whole. This of itself might not lead us to postulate a connection between the present passage and chap. 5, were it not that Paul's instant definition of

God's kingdom in 14:17 happens to form a tight summary of Rom 5:1-5: God's kingdom does not mean food and drink, but "righteousness, peace, and joy in the Holy Spirit." Here we have not only stumbled upon what seems to be Paul's own summary of an earlier passage in the letter, providing an important linking of the present point right back to the most central theological matters, but also a shorthand account of what he thought "the kingdom of God" was all about. The context, both here and in chap. 5, makes it clear that this definition does not mean that the kingdom is a "spiritual" as opposed to a "worldly" matter: 5:12-21 is all about the rule of sin and the rule of grace, the two powers that compete for every cubic inch of creation and every split second of time. What Paul is emphasizing is a matter of priorities: If Rom 5:1-5 is threatened, whatever is posing the threat must take second place. Since v. 17 explains vv. 15-16 (*gar*), we must take it that Paul's meaning is as follows: you must not cause your fellow Christian to suffer, possibly even to be lost altogether, by what you eat, because Rom 5:1-5 ("justified . . . peace . . . joy . . . Holy Spirit") is the most important thing there is, and food and drink, by comparison, rate nowhere on the same scale.

This is the way to behave, he says in a final explanation of the sequence of thought (*gar* again, v. 18): you are serving the Messiah, the king, and if you do so with his kingdom as your priority (see Matt 6:33) you will be, as 12:2 insisted, "well-pleasing" to God. What is more, other people will recognize and approve what you have done.

**14:19-21.** Paul then puts a second coat of paint on the same argument. He begins with a summary of the positive aim that one should have in all these things (see too 1 Corinthians 14): peace and mutual upbuilding (v. 19). This leads to a command that covers again the ground of v. 15, but whereas he there stressed the importance of honoring, and not jeopardizing, the Messiah's achievement in his death, he here emphasizes "the work of God," perhaps meaning not simply God's work in that individual but God's work in creating the church as a whole, which should be built up, as the previous verse says, and not destroyed (cf. 1 Cor 3:17).[549] Again repeating the previous segment (v. 20*b*, echoing v. 14), Paul

---

549. Dr. N. Perrin suggests to me that "the work of God" could be an echo of Exod 32:16, where the tablets of the law are "the work of God," destroyed by Moses because of the people's idolatry.

insists that all things are pure. Whereas before, though, he then declared that food became unclean for someone who believed it so, he here makes the different point: food becomes "evil" (not just "unclean") for someone who eats it in such a way as to cause someone else to stumble. The "strong" are hereby confronted: they are right to consider all foods clean, but they must realize that some food can become unclean even for them. Paul literally says "unclean for the one who eats through stumbling"; this could mean "for the weaker Christian who eats despite the objections of conscience," but the next verse suggests that the meaning normally understood is correct.[550] Verse 21 then supports this: here is something positively right and good that "the strong" can do: to abstain from meat, or wine, or anything else that makes a fellow Christian, a "brother," that is, a member of God's family, to stumble.

**14:22-23.** Paul concludes with another second-person singular address: "You there!" He returns to the mention of "faith" as in 14:1-2: You must hold the faith you have—that is, the interpretation of faith and its outworking—as a matter between you and God. (Again we note that Paul would not say this about all possible interpretations of Christian faith; had he done so, he would scarcely have needed, for instance, to write the letters to Corinth.) He adds, unusually, a blessing on the one who can make up his or her mind and then have no scruples, no self-judgment, in following it. (Paul never elsewhere coins his own "beatitude" [for the form, see Matt 5:3-11, with its rich Jewish background]; the closest he comes is in the direct quotation of Ps 32:1-2 in Rom 4:7-8.) To "condemn oneself for what one approves" may seem somewhat oxymoronic, and there may be a note of irony here: some people may say, for convenience, that they "approve" of doing something when in fact their conscience will be nagging at them that it was wrong all the time. Or perhaps Paul is rubbing in the point of v. 20: you may sincerely

approve it, but you are blessed if, when you go ahead and eat it, you do not have to judge yourself for thereby causing another Christian to stumble.

The concluding verse of the segment (v. 23) looks back to 14:1: you must welcome the "weak," but not in order to have disputes about disputes. Here Paul uses the cognate verb to the first "dispute" word: ὁ διακρινόμενος (*ho diakrinomenos,* "the one who disputes" or "the one who doubts").[551] In addition, this looks back to a key passage, 4:20-21: Abraham did not "waver" or "doubt" in unbelief (οὐ διεκρίθη τῇ ἀπιστίᾳ *ou diekrithē tē apistia*), but "grew strong in faith" (ἐνεδυναμώθη τῇ πίστει *enedynamōthē tē pistei*), being "fully convinced" (πληροφορηθείς *plērophorētheis*) that God was able to do what God had promised. This concentration of terms that echo the present discussion in a passage leading to 5:1-5, which, as we have seen, is also in Paul's mind here, can hardly be accidental. Though Abraham had good reason in human terms to be "weak," to doubt whether God could give him a child, he believed strongly and without wavering, and this faith became the prototype of Christian faith. The present discussion has not, then, been about something other than basic Christian faith (see the Overview). Paul is seeking to nurture and fortify communities in which that faith—with that content, faith of that type of full conviction—is the basis of identity and unity.

It is perhaps with Abraham and his type of faith in mind that he makes the sharp distinction that sets such a worryingly high standard for all Christian living. To doubt is not to sin; but to act on something when one has serious doubts about it is to fall under condemnation, because the action does not flow from faith. And—a new point, though we might have expected an explanatory *gar*—everything that is not of faith is sin. In other words, you are either with Abraham or with Adam. You are either living, like Abraham, in unwavering trust in God and God's promises; or you are turning away from God and living by some other means. It may sound harsh, but within the argument it makes perfect sense. The point here is not just that the weak may be convicted of sin if, though doubting, they go ahead and eat, though that

---

550. The NRSV ("to make others fall by what you eat") and the NIV ("to eat anything that causes someone else to stumble") are both paraphrases that, while giving the correct meaning, are some way away from Paul's own dense wording. The JB has a similar reading ("if by eating you make somebody else fall away"), but this has been changed in the NJB to correspond to v. 14: "any kind [of food] can be evil for someone to whom it is an offense to eat it."

551. This negative sense of the verb (as opposed to the "neutral" regular meanings of "make a distinction, evaluate, judge") is not attested before the NT, though it appears in classical literature afterward, without dependence. See BDAG 231.

is the first and probably the main level of meaning. The further level is that the strong, knowing this, must take care lest, by eating, they entice the weak into stumbling, and so themselves sin against the weak (v. 20; cf. 1 Cor 8:12). This complex little analysis of motives, responsibilities, and results is a copy-book exercise in thinking through the delicate demands both of love (13:8-10) and of humility (12:3-8) within the Christian community.

At this point in the letter some MSS add the closing blessing, which we know as 16:25-27 (see the Commentary on 15:33).

# Romans 15:1-13, Mutual Welcome, Based on the Messiah

## NIV

**15** We who are strong ought to bear with the failings of the weak and not to please ourselves. [2]Each of us should please his neighbor for his good, to build him up. [3]For even Christ did not please himself but, as it is written: "The insults of those who insult you have fallen on me."[a] [4]For everything that was written in the past was written to teach us, so that through endurance and the encouragement of the Scriptures we might have hope.

[5]May the God who gives endurance and encouragement give you a spirit of unity among yourselves as you follow Christ Jesus, [6]so that with one heart and mouth you may glorify the God and Father of our Lord Jesus Christ.

[7]Accept one another, then, just as Christ accepted you, in order to bring praise to God. [8]For I tell you that Christ has become a servant of the Jews[b] on behalf of God's truth, to confirm the promises made to the patriarchs [9]so that the Gentiles may glorify God for his mercy, as it is written:

"Therefore I will praise you among the Gentiles;
   I will sing hymns to your name."[c]

[10]Again, it says,
"Rejoice, O Gentiles, with his people."[d]

[11]And again,

"Praise the Lord, all you Gentiles,
   and sing praises to him, all you peoples."[e]

[12]And again, Isaiah says,

"The Root of Jesse will spring up,
   one who will arise to rule over the nations;
the Gentiles will hope in him."[f]

[13]May the God of hope fill you with all joy and peace as you trust in him, so that you may overflow with hope by the power of the Holy Spirit.

[a] 3 Psalm 69:9    [b] 8 Greek *circumcision*    [c] 9 2 Samuel 22:50; Psalm 18:49    [d] 10 Deut. 32:43    [e] 11 Psalm 117:1    [f] 12 Isaiah 11:10

## NRSV

**15** We who are strong ought to put up with the failings of the weak, and not to please ourselves. [2]Each of us must please our neighbor for the good purpose of building up the neighbor. [3]For Christ did not please himself; but, as it is written, "The insults of those who insult you have fallen on me." [4]For whatever was written in former days was written for our instruction, so that by steadfastness and by the encouragement of the scriptures we might have hope. [5]May the God of steadfastness and encouragement grant you to live in harmony with one another, in accordance with Christ Jesus, [6]so that together you may with one voice glorify the God and Father of our Lord Jesus Christ.

[7]Welcome one another, therefore, just as Christ has welcomed you, for the glory of God. [8]For I tell you that Christ has become a servant of the circumcised on behalf of the truth of God in order that he might confirm the promises given to the patriarchs, [9]and in order that the Gentiles might glorify God for his mercy. As it is written,
"Therefore I will confess[a] you among the
      Gentiles,
   and sing praises to your name";
[10]and again he says,
   "Rejoice, O Gentiles, with his people";
[11]and again,
"Praise the Lord, all you Gentiles,
   and let all the peoples praise him";
[12]and again Isaiah says,
"The root of Jesse shall come,
   the one who rises to rule the Gentiles;
in him the Gentiles shall hope."
[13]May the God of hope fill you with all joy and peace in believing, so that you may abound in hope by the power of the Holy Spirit.

[a] Or *thank*

# COMMENTARY

As with the previous paragraph (14:13-23), the present one gives the appearance of saying the same thing from two not very different angles in its own two segments (15:1-6, 7-13). Both parts open with a command relating to the discussion of chap. 14; both continue with a statement of what the Messiah has done; both support and develop this with Scripture; both declare that this supplies "hope"; and both conclude with the united praise of the one God.[552] Since this passage constitutes the final climax of Romans, we should hardly be surprised at this formal, almost formulaic, repetition. The immediate point may be the practical one about mutual welcome across boundaries of custom and conscience, but the underlying message Paul wants to convey is about the glorifying of God in the united worship of Jew and Gentile together in the Messiah.

This paragraph, in fact, offers a triple conclusion: to 14:1–15:13; to 12:1–15:13; and to the letter as a whole, from its very beginning. In the context of 14:1 onward, it draws together the threads in the summons to the strong to support the weak, so that together they may praise God. Within 12:1 onward, it insists on the same humility ("not thinking of yourselves more highly than you ought") that we find in 12:3-8, and returns to the note of worship and praise with which 12:1 opened: the worship of Israel, God's people, with all the world now joining in. Within the entire letter, the paragraph celebrates the fact that through the gospel of the risen Messiah, the world's true Lord, Jew and Gentile come together in God's single family, demonstrating God's covenant faithfulness.[553] Thus, if we heard strong echoes of 5:1-5, 17, and 21 in chap. 14, we would be right to hear in the present passage strong echoes of chaps. 3–4 and 9–11, to see in the united praise of God the reversal of that human failure and Jewish failure that was spelled out so graphically in

1:18–2:29,[554] and to discover Paul, throughout this passage, returning to the primary theme of the gospel itself—God's gospel, attested in the Scriptures, concerning his Son, whose Davidic Messiahship is declared in his resurrection from the dead. Indeed, as is fitting in such a dense summary, the gospel events themselves, the death and resurrection of the Messiah and his installation as Lord, are told again through Scripture. They are applied to the point in hand, but also allowed to resonate in tune with everything that has gone before (15:3, 8-9, 12).

The first subparagraph (vv. 1-6) approaches the practical point negatively: Don't please yourselves, because the Messiah didn't please himself (15:2-3). The second (vv. 7-13) says the same thing positively: welcome one another, because the Messiah welcomed you (v. 7). Paul's two closing blessings (vv. 5-6, 13) draw together themes from a now familiar source: patience, encouragement, hope, joy, peace, faith, and the power of the Holy Spirit. These blessings are another summary and echo of 5:1-5. For those with ears to hear, Paul is saying: "This is how to obtain in practice the great central blessings I outlined at the heart of the letter. Allow 'justification by faith' to produce 'fellowship by faith,' and you will know the peace, patience, joy, and hope that the Spirit brings."

A major feature of this grand conclusion is Paul's use of the Scriptures. Psalms, Deuteronomy, and finally Isaiah—no surprises about his choice of books, or the themes he draws from them. But here, unusually, he adds a note, as though reflecting on the many-sided exposition of Scripture he has offered in this letter. The Scriptures, he says, were given to us to be the means of patience, encouragement, and hope—in other words, the very things God promises, the very things the Holy Spirit puts powerfully into effect. Scripture, it seems, is a means by which God works in the church; in Pauline language, as well as in later technical theology, it is a means of grace. The present passage exemplifies the principle it thus states:

552. So L. E. Keck, "Christology, Soteriology and the Praise of God (Romans 15:7-13)," in *The Conversation Continues: Studies in Paul and John in Honor of J. Louis Martyn,* ed. R. T. Fortna and B. R. Gaventa (Nashville: Abingdon, 1990) 86.

553. Douglas J. Moo, *The Epistle to the Romans,* NICNT (Grand Rapids: Eerdmans, 1996) 874, disagrees, noting absent themes. One cannot mention everything explicitly in a few lines; I regard the "absent" topics (justification, grace, etc.) as present by strong implication.

554. See Keck, "Christology, Soteriology, and the Praise of God," 94: "the theme of the universal praise of God is, in Paul's view, much more than a rhetorical flourish. It is the actual material soteriological alternative to the root problem of humanity: not giving praise to God or honoring God."

the crescendo of scriptural quotations in vv. 3, 9-12 lead the eye up to the source and ground of Christian faith and hope, the Messiah himself, risen to rule the world. So the letter comes full circle, back to Paul's original self-introduction as the servant of God, the apostle of the Messiah and his gospel. This leads him naturally to 15:14-33, where he sketches in, as the letter moves toward its close, his plans for completing his apostolic task.

**15:1-2.** Two commands summarize the previous discussion: the strong (including Paul himself) are under obligation to "bear with" (NIV) the weaknesses of the powerless. "The failings of the weak" (NRSV, NIV) is hardly correct; the word translated "failings" is cognate with the word for "weak" (ἀσθενής *asthenēs*) throughout the previous discussion, and the word translated "weak" here is ἀδύνατος (*adynatos*), a word Paul elsewhere only uses in 8:3. Paul has not suggested that "weakness" is a "failing"; to pull the text that way is to slant his argument. Better to see, now, a subtly new point: "these 'weaknesses' I have been speaking of—the people who possess them are 'powerless.' They are who they are, and at the moment they can't help it. Thus we who are 'strong' have an obligation to support and help them."[555] This has the advantage that it gives to the main verb of v. 1 the meaning it has elsewhere in Paul: βαστάζειν (*bastazein*) does not normally mean "put up with" in the sense of "be prepared to tolerate," but, more positively, "support, help" (Gal 6:2), or "carry" (Gal 6:5).[556] The meaning then is that the strong must help those who, through their own current powerlessless, have these "weaknesses." They must support and encourage them, not browbeat them with demands for more "strength" than they can presently muster (cf. Acts 20:35 [though the word there is the rare ἀντιλαμβάνομαι *antilambanomai*]).

In doing this, the "strong" must not seek their own advantage, must not "please themselves"; as

we saw in 12:2, this is the alternative to "pleasing God," and often "pleasing God" will—despite popular opinion to the contrary—involve precisely not "pleasing oneself." Instead (v. 2), everyone must please his or her neighbor, with a view to their good and to the upbuilding of the community (the NRSV and the NIV both make "upbuilding" relate simply to the individual neighbor, but in Paul the word regularly refers to the building up of the whole community). This is, clearly, what the love spoken of in 12:3-13 and 13:8-10 looks like at street level. It is the principle Paul himself adopts in contentious matters (1 Cor 10:31–11:1, a passage quite close to the present one).

**15:3.** This principle derives from the Messiah himself. Paul has as many ways of speaking about Jesus' messianic death as he has occasions to mention it. Here he draws on Ps 69:9 (69:10 MT; 68:10 LXX), assuming that this great poem of the suffering and vindication of the righteous Israelite found its ultimate embodiment in Israel's Messiah and his crucifixion.[557] This, he says, shows that the Messiah "did not please himself"; he assumes, too, that his hearers are familiar with the basic story of Jesus, perhaps with oral traditions of such scenes as Gethsemane in which the Messiah shrank from his fate (Mark 14:32-42 and pars.; see also John 12:27; Heb 5:7-9; Rom 15:3 may also be illuminated by Phil 2:6-8, which, if not written by Paul, is certainly endorsed by him; and 2 Cor 8:9). "Not pleasing himself" is, of course, a remarkable understatement when we consider (as Paul could and did elsewhere) the shame and horror of the cross. But it makes the point Paul needs for the moment, while beginning to sketch for the last time the story of Jesus that will reach its climax in 15:12.

**15:4.** By way of somewhat oblique explanation (*gar*) of this exegesis of the psalm, Paul states that the Scriptures in general ("whatever was written in former days," NRSV) were written for our instruction, so that through patience and the encouragement of the Scriptures we might have hope. This, as we saw, echoes 5:1-5, ascribing to

---

555. The NJB's "the susceptibilities of the weaker ones" comes toward this, but still misses the underlying point. See also the NEB/REB: "the tender scruples of the weak."

556. BDAG cites only this reference and Rev 2:3, with Ignatius Polycarp 1:2, for the meaning "bear patiently, put up with." But the Ignatius passage surely means "help" or "support"; and Rev 2:3, which uses the absolute verb without object, can simply mean "enduring" without the somewhat grudging sense of "putting up with" something.

557. For this understanding of the Messiah as the "pray-er" of the psalms, see R. B. Hays, "Christ Prays the Psalms: Paul's Use of an Early Christian Exegetical Convention," in *The Future of Christology: Essays in Honor of Leander E. Keck,* ed. A. J. Malherbe and W. A. Meeks (Minneapolis: Fortress, 1993) 122-36. The other half of the same psalm verse is quoted in reference to Jesus' cleansing of the Temple in John 2:17.

Scripture what is there effected through the Spirit on the basis of God's work of justification. Granted the theme of chap. 14, and the way in which it seems to be continued in 15:1-2, we might have expected here, on the one hand, a more specific reference to the community being built up through mutual support and readiness to give up one's rights and cultural preferences, and on the other hand a more explicit comment on the Messiah's death in relation to achieving that end. Paul, however, already has his sights on the major themes of his conclusion, and it is in the light of that larger picture that the intermediate goal of united worship will become a reality. The Scriptures, and their multiple interpretation of the Messiah's suffering, give God's people hope; and in that context (vv. 5-6) they will be able to think the same way and to glorify God together. What they need for the present is not simply willingness to do what Paul has said in 14:1–15:2, but patience and encouragement; and that is what Scripture provides (cf. 1 Macc 12:9), especially once they learn to see the story of Israel as devolved onto, and fulfilled by, Jesus the Messiah.[558]

**15:5-6.** Paul turns his thoughts into prayer, the first time he has reported a prayer in relation to the Roman church since 1:9-12, where the theme of mutual comfort was likewise prominent; he is consciously coming full circle. His prayer is that "the God of patience and comfort" will give them a united mind (lit., "to think the same thing among one another according to the Messiah Jesus").[559] This is Paul's regular appeal, whether or not he thinks a church is actually divided (see Phil 2:2-4, which, in company with 2:5-11, bears close comparison with Rom 14:1–15:13 as a whole). The object of coming to a common mind (ὁμοθυμαδόν *homothymadon,* a word found frequently in the early chapters of Acts (e.g., 1:14; 2:46; 4:24; 5:12; 7:57), is thereby to come to a common worship, literally "with one mouth." The

object of this worship, as we might have guessed from the intricate christological dance of the previous chapter, is the God who is now revealed in relation to the Lord: "the God and father of our Lord Jesus the Messiah" (see, e.g., 1 Cor 8:6; 15:28; Phil 2:11; see also the Commentary on 10:13).[560]

**15:7.** The final paragraph of the letter's theological exposition, like the final paragraph of the great central section chaps. 5–8, transforms into a coda of praise and celebration but without any loss of theological poise. Paul opens with the repeated instruction from 14:1, only this time as a command to any and all parties within the church: welcome one another, therefore (the "therefore," [διό *dio*] picks up the entire previous argument). Here, as in v. 3, the Messiah's action is the crucial basis and model for what the church must now do; again, ὁ Χριστός (*ho Christos*) undoubtedly means "Messiah," and cannot be reduced to a proper name.[561] The Messiah, as he says in the next verse, is the one in and through whom God's promises to the Jewish ancestors are fulfilled; and this short paragraph is framed at its further end also by a celebration of the Messiah's work on behalf of the whole world (v. 12). The final clause of the verse, "to the glory of God," has in view the glorifying of God in praise and worship that is the subject of the rest of the paragraph. Thus, although the Messiah's welcome is undoubtedly also glorifying to God, this clause goes more directly with the command to welcome one another: "Just as the Messiah welcomed you, so you should welcome one another in order that God may be glorified." The verse forms a typically Pauline paragraph-opening, containing the various elements that will then be developed.

**15:8-9a.** What is this messianic "welcome"? Paul explains (λέγω γάρ *legō gar*) with a complex statement of what the Messiah accomplished, reminding us of the dense messianic formulations that stand at the head of the letter as a whole (1:3-4) and of chaps. 9–11 (9:5). (There are other echoes of 9:4-5: glory, promises, patriarchs, Messiah [four out of the eight privileges there

---

558. The unexpected direction of v. 4 led Keck to propose that it be seen as an interpolation. See L. E. Keck, "Romans 15:4—An Interpolation?" in *Faith and History: Essays in Honor of Paul W. Meyer,* ed. J. T. Carroll et al. (Atlanta: Scholars Press, 1991) 125-36. I agree substantially with Hays's careful rebuttal of this ("Christ Prays the Psalms," 132-34).

559. The NIV's "a spirit of unity among yourselves as you follow Christ Jesus" manages to paraphrase out Paul's sharp meaning at both ends of the clause; Paul is talking about how they are to think, not just feel (as "a spirit" suggests to today's hearers); and "according to the Messiah," granted 15:3 and the whole epistle, is more than simply "following," however high a theology of discipleship we may have.

560. See N. T. Wright, *The Climax of the Covenant: Christ and the Law in Pauline Theology* (Minneapolis: Fortress, 1991) chaps. 2, 4, and 6.

561 So, rightly, James D. G. Dunn, *Romans 9–16,* 38B (Dallas: Word, 1988) 840.

listed]). There is good reason to suppose that Paul intends here simultaneously to explain the messianic roots of the specific appeal of v. 7, and to sum up the entire letter. This is what he, at least, thinks he has been talking about all the way through.

The heart of the statement rephrases one of Paul's central presuppositions, which has proved difficult for theologians and exegetes alike to come to terms with: it is by bringing Israel's history to its climax that God, through the Messiah, has opened the way of mercy to all the nations. It is not that God has done one thing for Jews, and another thing for Gentiles; God has designed mercy for all (11:28-32), but as 9–11 made clear, the purpose for Israel always had the Gentiles in mind, and the purpose for Gentiles was always that they would come in to the fulfilled, returned-from-exile Israel. This, indeed, is what the scriptural quotations about to be produced are taken by Paul to be saying. Thus vv. 8-9*a* should be read as follows: The Messiah became a servant of the circumcision (i.e., of ethnic Israel) in order to confirm God's truthfulness.[562]

The mention of God's truthfulness sends our minds back to 3:4, 7 ("Let God be true, though every human be false . . . if God's truthfulness abounds through my falsehood to his glory, why am I still being condemned as a sinner?" [my translation]), where it is closely correlated with God's faithfulness and righteousness: Paul has the ancient promises in mind once more. But, here as there, these promises were never simply for ethnic Israel; nor were they divided, with one part belonging to Israel and the other to the nations. The promises were both *to* Israel and *through* Israel to the world.[563] This means that we should probably take the next two clauses as both parallel and consequential: the Messiah became a servant (a) to confirm the promises to the patriarchs and (b) so that the Gentiles might glorify God for mercy—but the inclusion of Gentiles is precisely one of the central patriarchal promises Paul highlights, not least in chap. 4.[564] The statement is

dense because, as well as summing up the entire exposition of God's righteousness, echoing chapters 3–4 and 9–11 in ways too many and complex to enumerate here, Paul is still conscious of making his final appeal to the community. The Messiah became a servant of the circumcision—so you Gentile Christians should love and serve your Jewish brothers and sisters in the Messiah, and not look down on them; and this was in order that the Gentiles should join with God's ancient people in united praise—so you Jewish Christians should celebrate the fact that you have people of every race joining with you in the messianic community.

The two clauses thus play out the intertwined results of the Messiah's work (while at the same time underscoring the early Christian awareness of the fact that Jesus himself had concentrated his work on ethnic Israel, not in order to exclude Gentiles permanently but because the way to save the world was to complete Israel's destiny; cf. Matt 10:5-6; 15:21-28 and par.; John 4:22-26). "Confirming the promises made to the patriarchs" sums up chaps. 4 and 9, and concisely catches the central meaning of "God's righteousness," the major theme of the letter. Nor was this simply a matter of some unfinished business on God's part, a few promises left unfulfilled that had to be dealt with if only to avoid the charge of unfaithfulness; these promises encapsulated the single, unalterable divine saving plan for the whole world, and confirming them through the Messiah's servant ministry was the heart of God's intention.

Thus the second, and consequent, result of this ministry, "that the Gentiles might glorify God for mercy," follows both in the logic of the divine plan (and of the messianic achievement) and in the logic of Paul's appeal to the community.[565] This is the doxological correlate of justification by faith: the gathering of Gentiles into the one people of God, not by works of Torah but simply by faith in God's saving action in the Messiah, results in united praise. This, in other words, is where what appear to many exegetes as two different themes in Rom 3:21-31 (God's saving action in Jesus' death resulting in justification by faith, on the one hand, and

---

562. Granted Paul's use of Isaiah 40–55, it is not entirely fanciful to see a reference to the Isaianic "servant" here, though the word Paul uses (διάκονος *diakonos*) is very rare in the LXX, where the "servant" is referred to as παῖς (*pais*). This, however, could have been problematic for Paul, since *pais*, which basically means "child," would hardly have done in the present context.

563. There is an echo here of Mic 7:20, which sets up several relevant resonances when read in the context of 7:7-20 as a whole.

564. For a different view, see J. R. Wagner, "The Christ, Servant of Jew and Gentile: A Fresh Approach to Romans 15:8-9," *JBL* 116 (1997) 473-85.

565. The change of subject is grammatically harsh (so C. E. B. Cranfield, *A Critical and Exegetical Commentary on the Epistle to the Romans*, ICC, 2 vols. [Edinburgh: T. & T. Clark, 1975] 743), but scarcely impossible for the Paul who, precisely in his dense summaries, was capable of all sorts of shortcuts in his Greek. For the use of ὑπέρ (*hyper*) to give the reason for praise or thanksgiving, see 1 Cor 10:30. See also Wagner, "The Christ, Servant of Jew and Gentile," 479.

the coming together of Jew and Gentile on the other) are finally revealed as one and the same. This was what the Messiah's servant work was about all along.

**15:9b-11.** Paul celebrates the theme of united worship with three biblical quotations, preparing the way for a final quotation (in v. 12) that sums up the entire letter.[566] As Richard Hays has persuasively argued, the opening citation from Ps 18:49 (17:50 LXX), when read in the wider context of that psalm, is intended not simply as a messianic prophecy now fulfilled, but as a statement of the embodiment, in Jesus the Messiah, of the pattern of suffering and vindication through which (as the next verse says) God's salvation and mercy are poured out, not least "upon God's Messiah, to David and his seed for ever" (Ps 17:51 LXX). The citation thus ties in both with the mention of mercy in the earlier part of v. 9 and with the explicitly Davidic statement in v. 12, while itself making the central point that the Messiah himself, understood as the one praying in this psalm, is standing there, surrounded by Gentiles, singing God's praises.[567]

For the second citation Paul returns to Deuteronomy 32 (cf. Rom 10:19; 12:19). Here the Septuagint comes to his help; the Hebrew text simply says "Praise his people, you nations," but in the LXX of v. 43 this has become "Praise, you nations, with his people," giving Paul not only further grist to his present mill but enabling him thus to tie in this passage with the deuteronomic theme that was so important in chap. 10. He then reverts to the psalter, finding in Ps 117:1 a classic invitation to the whole world to join in the praises of Israel's God. This, after all, was and is the challenge of Jewish monotheism: that the God of Israel was the creator, the God of the whole world, and that therefore the other nations, though presently stuck in idolatry, ought eventually to come to recognize and worship the same God that Israel worshiped. How this would happen remained an almost complete mystery in the ancient Scriptures. It has been Paul's theme throughout Romans that it has now been accomplished through the Messiah and by the Spirit.

**15:12-13.** It should be no surprise, then, that as his last quotation Paul chooses, with great care, a passage from Isaiah (11:10) that says exactly what he wants to say at the climax of 14:1–15:13 and at the same time completes the circle begun in 1:3-4. The Gentiles will come to hope in the Davidic Messiah, the "root of Jesse" (for "root of Jesse" as a title for the Messiah, see Rev 5:5; 22:16); he is the one who "rises to rule the nations." The echo of 1:4 should leave us in no doubt that Paul intends a reference to Jesus' resurrection. This is what constituted him as Messiah and Lord of the whole world. Once again the wider context of Paul's citation fills in the depths of meaning he has no space to spell out: Isaiah speaks here of God's purpose to renew the whole created order, and to gather the remnant of Israel, together with the Gentile world, into the one community of salvation (Isa 11:1–12:6).[568] The idea of a risen Messiah "ruling the nations" is, further, packed with explosive political implications, especially in a letter to Rome whose own emperor claimed to rule the nations. Paul, we may suppose, has had this verse of Isaiah in mind throughout the whole letter, waiting to produce it as the final move in his entire argument.

The note that comes through is "hope," as in v. 4. This is not what we might have expected; Paul, we might have supposed, would speak of "love" in concluding a passage about mutual welcome in Christ, or of "joy" in a passage about praise. But we should not suppose that he has been careless at this of all moments, especially since he reinforces the point in v. 13, referring to God as "the God of hope" and praying that his readers may "abound in hope by the power of the Holy Spirit."

Hope was, of course, a major theme of chaps. 5–8, and echoes of that section, and of its summary introduction (5:1-5), abound here. Paul's eye seems to be on the following implied thought: that throughout its struggles to live as one community despite cultural and ethnic differences, what the community needs is precisely that eschatological perspective on their present life that is supplied in 12:2 and 13:11-14: in other words, that in order to be the people they are called to be in the present, they need a constant and lively sense of

---

566. Keck, "Christology, Soteriology and the Praise of God (Romans 15:7-13)," suggests that Paul has added these verses to an already existing tradition consisting of vv. 8 and 12. This is conceivable, but I do not think it likely.

567. See R. B. Hays, *Echoes of Scripture in the Letters of Paul* (New Haven: Yale University Press, 1989) 70-73; Hays, "Christ Prays the Psalms," 134-35.

568. Partly noted in Hays, *Echoes of Scripture in the Letters of Paul,* 73.

God's promised and assured future. That, perhaps, is one of the reasons why chaps. 12–13 were shaped as they were, framed by the eschatological hope: they were designed to provide the right basis for an appeal that would itself depend on the hope that one day Jesus Christ would be seen and acknowledged as Lord of all (14:11; 15:12). Thus the line of thought that runs from God's promise-keeping in 15:8 to God's gift of hope in 15:13 ("you can trust this God," Paul is saying; "remember what he's already done in the Messiah!") is what he believes the community should remember as it lives within "the present world," Caesar's world, in the faith that Jesus is already Lord because God raised him from the dead, and that soon every knee will bow at his name.

Hope itself is sustained, then, by the "joy and peace" with which the God of hope will fill the community. Here are the notes we would have expected: "joy" is to be experienced in the glad worship of God, and "peace" is to be known within the combined, united community (cf. 14:19). And all is sustained by the power of the Spirit, the power that raised Jesus from the dead (8:10-11) and is even now at work among those who form his one body (cf. 1:4, 16; 5:5; 8:1-11, 12-27; 12:3-5; 15:19; 1 Cor 2:4-5; 6:14; 12:12-13; 2 Cor 13:4; Eph 1:19; 3:20; Phil 3:10; Col 1:11; 1 Thess 1:5; 2 Thess 1:11).

# REFLECTIONS

**1.** Paul's appeal for unity in 14:1–15:13 is thus grounded in a solidly if incipiently trinitarian theology, and this emphasizes how important it is, for all work for unity within and between churches, that the theological foundations are laid as deeply as possible. The grand schemes for church unity that characterized much of the twentieth century were often allied, unfortunately, with the kind of theology that sat loose to detail in the hope that people would be able to agree on something a bit simpler. Perhaps in the twenty-first century the churches will come to see that unity is a plant that grows best in the deepest soil, and that by patient shared study of our most central beliefs, not least the exploration of who God really is, as revealed in Jesus the Messiah and by the Spirit, and through the shared worship to which this gives rise, we may discover new ways forward in the ecumenical endeavor.

**2.** Shared worship, indeed, is central to Paul's vision. He does not say that one should wait to share in worship until all aspects of belief and practice have been hammered out. On the contrary. He sees the mutual welcome, allowing people from very different backgrounds literally to worship together with one voice, as of the essence of the quest for a deeper unity. When we read this alongside Gal 2:11-21, we discover that this is not just a bit of good advice; it grows directly from the doctrine of justification by faith itself. The point of that doctrine is that all who confess Jesus as Lord and believe that God raised him from the dead belong in the same worshiping family, and at the same table. Shared eucharistic fellowship should not be the reward awaiting us at the end of ecumenical negotiations and agreements. It should be a central means by which we travel together along that road.

**3.** Paul's main point in Romans 14 is that there are some things that appear to divide Christians very deeply in terms of their practice but are, in fact (in the language of later theology), "things indifferent" that should not be allowed to divide them. Most Christians would agree that there are such "indifferent" matters, but the difficulty is that there is no agreement on what those matters are, and on which matters are so centrally important that to disagree on them means dividing the church. Paul clearly believed that there were many things on which it was not a matter of saying "one person believes this, another believes that"; when it was reported that a Corinthian Christian had set up with his father's wife, his reaction was not that he should be welcomed as a weaker believer but that he should be kicked out on the spot (1 Cor 5:1-5; the whole chapter is important, distinguishing as it does between the importance of continuing to have dealings with the pagan world and the importance of breaking off relations with Christians who behave in grossly pagan ways). One may imagine that for some of the "weaker" Christians in Rome the idea of eating meat that had not been certified as kosher, or that had been offered to idols, would seem just as "pagan" and hence evil as sexual immorality; indeed, granted the connection between idol-worship and licentious orgies, one can understand their point of view. But what Paul is doing here is in fact to articulate not only his view that there are some "things indifferent" that should not divide the church but also his view as to what some of the key ones are.

Significantly, they are among the central boundary-markers of Judaism: food and holy days. Romans 14 is in fact an exposition, in other terms, of justification by faith apart from works of Torah. That is why Paul himself is a "strong" Christian, and clearly believes that if and when the "weak" were able to arrive at a deeper maturity in the faith they would come to that position as well. Only when we are prepared to think through divisive issues in the light of this central doctrine will the church be able to distinguish between the things that matter and the things that do not. This plays back into the whole theme of unity. Unity is not itself a "thing indifferent," though many, probably most, Christians today regard it as such ("Some Christians believe we should all get together; others believe this doesn't matter"; can you imagine what Paul would have said to that?).

**4.** At the heart of the appeal is of course love, as in 12:3-13 and 13:8-10. Love here is not a sentimental reaction, to be provoked simply by seeing a look of hurt or disappointment on someone else's face; it is rooted in the conviction that the Messiah died for the other person, too, and that, being oneself a beneficiary of his self-giving love, one cannot deliberately put a stumbling-block in the way of another beneficiary. The family identity of God's people, in which all are brothers and sisters (in a world where family membership meant a closer tie and obligation than today's Western world imagines possible), meant that taking care of one another, and thinking how to avoid making life difficult for each other, was of prime importance.

**5.** We should not play down the political significance of this entire passage (see especially the comments on 14:10-12 and 15:12). The present disunity of the worldwide church has multiplied precisely in the historical period when, under the insidious pressure of the Enlightenment, "religion" has been carefully separated off from "politics" and kept in a sealed upper chamber ("what individuals do with their solitude") where it cannot interfere with real life. The churches have often gone along with this, imagining themselves thereby to have attained some kind of freedom. But the price of this "freedom" is that it leaves Caesar enthroned, doubly defended against any attack on the arrogance of empire that might come from the Christian gospel. First, a church that acquiesces in its own marginalization (especially if it calls it "freedom") is never likely even to comment on, let alone to engage with, the ruling powers. Second, a church that all too obviously embodies the social, ethnic, cultural, and political divisions of its surrounding world is no real challenge to the Caesars of this world. It is only when representatives of many nations worship the world's true Lord in unity that Caesar might get the hint that there is after all "another king" (Acts 17:7; cf. Eph 3:10). To settle for comfortable disunity because that way we can "be ourselves" and keep things the way we have always known them is to court disloyalty to the one Lord and failure in the church's mission to challenge the gospel of Caesar with the gospel of Jesus Christ.

**6.** We should continue to learn how to tell the story of God, the world, Israel, Jesus, and ourselves so as to bring out its full flavor. It is highly significant that when Paul comes to sum up the whole letter in 15:7-13 he does so with a compressed narrative in which all the elements of the longer stories he tells from time to time are present, selected here of course for the particular needs of the argument but nevertheless reminding us of the fuller story he could have told, and does tell elsewhere. As long as we insist on reducing Christianity to slogans and isolated "doctrines" or rules, rather than seeing it primarily as the great story of what the one God has done, through the one Lord, for the one world, we will never understand what Paul is about, or be able to recapture the excitement and many-sidedness of his writing. There has been of late a fashion for "narrative" readings of Paul. It should not be thought that this is simply a fad, a new game to play with old counters. It reflects something close to the heart of Paul's own mind: that when you want to understand who God is, what the gospel is, and what our task in the world now is, the foundation for that understanding is the narrative within which the different elements make themselves at home. Revealingly, the two elements of the narrative that much post-Enlightenment thought has screened out, but that a Pauline telling of the story can never forget, are the Israel dimension and the Caesar dimension. The inalienable Jewish roots of the gospel, and the inevitable confrontation with pagan empire, are both embedded in Paul's narrative here and elsewhere, and only when today's church comes to terms with both will it become truly faithful to Paul's vision.

# ROMANS 15:14-33, PAUL'S APOSTOLIC TRAVEL PLANS

## NIV

[14]I myself am convinced, my brothers, that you yourselves are full of goodness, complete in knowledge and competent to instruct one another. [15]I have written you quite boldly on some points, as if to remind you of them again, because of the grace God gave me [16]to be a minister of Christ Jesus to the Gentiles with the priestly duty of proclaiming the gospel of God, so that the Gentiles might become an offering acceptable to God, sanctified by the Holy Spirit.

[17]Therefore I glory in Christ Jesus in my service to God. [18]I will not venture to speak of anything except what Christ has accomplished through me in leading the Gentiles to obey God by what I have said and done— [19]by the power of signs and miracles, through the power of the Spirit. So from Jerusalem all the way around to Illyricum, I have fully proclaimed the gospel of Christ. [20]It has always been my ambition to preach the gospel where Christ was not known, so that I would not be building on someone else's foundation. [21]Rather, as it is written:

"Those who were not told about him will see,
 and those who have not heard will understand."[a]

[a] 21 Isaiah 52:15

## NRSV

[14]I myself feel confident about you, my brothers and sisters,[a] that you yourselves are full of goodness, filled with all knowledge, and able to instruct one another. [15]Nevertheless on some points I have written to you rather boldly by way of reminder, because of the grace given me by God [16]to be a minister of Christ Jesus to the Gentiles in the priestly service of the gospel of God, so that the offering of the Gentiles may be acceptable, sanctified by the Holy Spirit. [17]In Christ Jesus, then, I have reason to boast of my work for God. [18]For I will not venture to speak of anything except what Christ has accomplished[b] through me to win obedience from the Gentiles, by word and deed, [19]by the power of signs and wonders, by the power of the Spirit of God,[c] so that from Jerusalem and as far around as Illyricum I have fully proclaimed the good news[d] of Christ. [20]Thus I make it my ambition to proclaim the good news,[d] not where Christ has already been named, so that I do not build on someone else's foundation, [21]but as it is written,

"Those who have never been told of him shall see,

[a] Gk brothers  [b] Gk speak of those things that Christ has not
accomplished  [c] Other ancient authorities read of the Spirit or of
the Holy Spirit  [d] Or gospel

NIV

<sup>22</sup>This is why I have often been hindered from coming to you.

<sup>23</sup>But now that there is no more place for me to work in these regions, and since I have been longing for many years to see you, <sup>24</sup>I plan to do so when I go to Spain. I hope to visit you while passing through and to have you assist me on my journey there, after I have enjoyed your company for a while. <sup>25</sup>Now, however, I am on my way to Jerusalem in the service of the saints there. <sup>26</sup>For Macedonia and Achaia were pleased to make a contribution for the poor among the saints in Jerusalem. <sup>27</sup>They were pleased to do it, and indeed they owe it to them. For if the Gentiles have shared in the Jews' spiritual blessings, they owe it to the Jews to share with them their material blessings. <sup>28</sup>So after I have completed this task and have made sure that they have received this fruit, I will go to Spain and visit you on the way. <sup>29</sup>I know that when I come to you, I will come in the full measure of the blessing of Christ.

<sup>30</sup>I urge you, brothers, by our Lord Jesus Christ and by the love of the Spirit, to join me in my struggle by praying to God for me. <sup>31</sup>Pray that I may be rescued from the unbelievers in Judea and that my service in Jerusalem may be acceptable to the saints there, <sup>32</sup>so that by God's will I may come to you with joy and together with you be refreshed. <sup>33</sup>The God of peace be with you all. Amen.

NRSV

and those who have never heard of him shall understand."

<sup>22</sup>This is the reason that I have so often been hindered from coming to you. <sup>23</sup>But now, with no further place for me in these regions, I desire, as I have for many years, to come to you <sup>24</sup>when I go to Spain. For I do hope to see you on my journey and to be sent on by you, once I have enjoyed your company for a little while. <sup>25</sup>At present, however, I am going to Jerusalem in a ministry to the saints; <sup>26</sup>for Macedonia and Achaia have been pleased to share their resources with the poor among the saints at Jerusalem. <sup>27</sup>They were pleased to do this, and indeed they owe it to them; for if the Gentiles have come to share in their spiritual blessings, they ought also to be of service to them in material things. <sup>28</sup>So, when I have completed this, and have delivered to them what has been collected,<sup>a</sup> I will set out by way of you to Spain; <sup>29</sup>and I know that when I come to you, I will come in the fullness of the blessing<sup>b</sup> of Christ.

<sup>30</sup>I appeal to you, brothers and sisters,<sup>c</sup> by our Lord Jesus Christ and by the love of the Spirit, to join me in earnest prayer to God on my behalf, <sup>31</sup>that I may be rescued from the unbelievers in Judea, and that my ministry<sup>d</sup> to Jerusalem may be acceptable to the saints, <sup>32</sup>so that by God's will I may come to you with joy and be refreshed in your company. <sup>33</sup>The God of peace be with all of you.<sup>e</sup> Amen.

<sup>a</sup> Gk *have sealed to them this fruit*   <sup>b</sup> Other ancient authorities add *of the gospel*   <sup>c</sup> Gk *brothers*   <sup>d</sup> Other ancient authorities read *my bringing of a gift*   <sup>e</sup> One ancient authority adds 16.25-27 here

# COMMENTARY

After the exalted tone and the dense, dynamic content of the writing so far, we might expect a more gentle and pastoral tone in the rest of the chapter, rounding off what Paul wants to say before the closing greetings. We get what we expect, but only up to a point. Paul remains himself, and even when discussing in more relaxed mode his recent apostolic work and his future plans he is still drawing on the same controlling story of God, the Messiah and the world, still

appealing to Scripture to explain what he has done and is doing, still teasing readers ancient and modern with compact and allusive prose.

This is in fact one of the longest discussions Paul gives anywhere of how he conceives his apostolic work, and why he has made the decisions he has (the exception to this must be 2 Corinthians as a whole). Coming to a church he had neither founded himself nor previously visited, but where several of his colleagues and coworkers now lived, he was conscious of a need to prepare the ground and explain what he was hoping to achieve. We should perhaps remind ourselves that when we speak of the Roman church in this period we are talking of perhaps a hundred people, more or less, in a city of roughly a million. It was hardly the case that there was no room for fresh work for an apostle and evangelist. However, Paul is keen to stress that his main aim is to use Rome as a base for further work in the western Mediterranean, going all the way to Spain; and this gives us a further clue to the purpose of the letter—namely, that if the Roman church is to support him in this work it is vital that they understand the inner dynamic and perspective of the gospel as he announces it.

The passage divides into two, each part dividing again: (1) Paul's intention to complete his earlier apostolic work by traveling via Rome to Spain (15:14-24); (a) Paul's explanation of his recent apostolic work as the reason for writing the letter (vv. 14-21); (b) his intention now to come to Rome and thence to Spain (vv. 22-24); (2) his forthcoming visit to Jerusalem (vv. 25-33); (a) taking the collection to Jerusalem (vv. 25-29); (b) requesting prayer in relation to that visit (vv. 30-33). Verse 14 picks up where 1:15 had left off: now at last, in the light of everything he has said in between, Paul can explain the reasons for his forthcoming visit.

**15:14.** It is sometimes suggested that Paul had been writing to Rome in the knowledge that there were serious doctrinal problems in the church—that, for instance, there was no real understanding of justification.[569] There is, though, no reason to suggest that a verse like this one, or its predecessor at 1:8, is not meant seriously. Paul knows several of the Christians in Rome, and is confident that they are not off track, but on the contrary are good-hearted people, well instructed, and able to teach one another (νουθετέω [noutheteō] can imply "warn," "admonish," but here it simply seems to carry its neutral meaning, "instruct"). Paul, in other words, did not need to write to them because they were in bad shape, but because his apostolic vocation demanded that for his new phase of work they should be brought in as partners, and hence needed to understand in detail

where he was coming from. This is not to say that there were not potential or actual problems in the Roman church, reflected not least in 11:11-32 and 14:1–15:13, only that he does not regard these as compromising the basic integrity and maturity of the church as a whole.

**15:15-16.** Paul's own view of the letter he is now completing is that it is a "reminder." He does, after all, say at various points "You do know, don't you?" and we would probably be wrong to treat all these as merely rhetorical (e.g., 6:3; 7:1). He has put things, he says, with a degree of boldness, a statement no reader of Romans is likely to dispute.[570] Once again, as at 1:5 and 12:3, he invokes his own unique vocation by God's grace, this time to explain what he has been doing in recent years (see too 1 Cor 3:10; 15:10). We who are so familiar with the story of Paul's missionary journeys, whether from Acts (with all its attendant historical problems) or from Paul's letters themselves, may forget that he cut a strange figure in the ancient world, a wandering Jew talking, arguing, suffering, praying, celebrating, making tents, traveling, cajoling, weeping, staying in one place for a day and in another for a year, always talking about God and the Messiah, about Jesus as Lord, about the resurrection of the dead. He was like a wandering philosopher, but without many of the accoutrements and with a very different message. He was like a Jewish apologist, but the communities he founded and the company he kept, not to mention the message he brought, though soaked in Jewish Scripture from start to finish, were not something any Jew had ever dreamed of before, and not something many cared to hear. What was he up to, and why should a self-respecting community in Rome take him seriously?

No doubt many of Paul's friends in Rome could and did speak for him. But his own explanation is striking: he has been a cultic minister of the Messiah with special responsibility for the Gentile world. He has been working in the priestly service of God's gospel. His task has been to ensure that

---

569. See M. Black, *Romans,* NCB (London: Oliphants, 1973) 23, 40.

570. ἀπὸ μέρους (*apo merous*) could modify "quite boldly"—i.e., "a certain degree of boldness"; the NRSV and the NIV take it with "wrote," to mean "on some points." It is possible, and perhaps preferable, to see it as modifying "as reminding you." C. K. Barrett, *A Commentary on the Epistle to the Romans* (London: A. & C. Black, 1957) 275, takes it thus, suggesting that Paul means that part of his intention has been to remind, without saying what the other part of his intention was. He is most likely acknowledging that for some hearers it has been more than a reminder.

when the sacrificial offerings are brought before God—the sacrificial offerings that consist precisely of the Gentile world itself!—they are pleasing to God because they have been made holy by the Holy Spirit. This sudden rush of sacrificial and cultic imagery can hardly be accidental; it is not, it seems, one metaphor taken at random. Paul is after all on his way to Jerusalem to bring a highly significant, and hence contentious, gift of money (see below); the thought of going up to the Temple, like a Diaspora Jew going on pilgrimage, is clearly in his mind. But he is talking about more than a single trip or a single gift. He is talking about his entire vocation, to gather up the Gentile world and present it as a surprising but appropriate offering before the world's creator and its rightful Lord.

This is not the only time that Paul uses sacrificial and priestly language to describe his apostolic vocation, but it is the fullest and most striking such occurrence (see too Phil 2:16-17). He has already spoken of Christian obedience itself in these terms (12:1-2), and since he has just alluded to 12:3 as well (the grace given him in apostolic vocation) we may take it that he sees this as a fuller statement of the way he himself must fulfill the more general instruction he there summarized.

**15:17.** This, then, is the claim he makes in the Messiah when it comes to his priestly service "concerning the things of God" (the priestly overtones of the latter phrase [τὰ πρὸς τὸν θεόν *ta pros ton theon*] are underlined by the parallel with Heb 2:17). Though Paul can speak of his only "boast" as being "in the Lord" and in his cross (1 Cor 1:31; cf. 2 Cor 10:17; Gal 6:14), he can in fact, as in the next verse, speak also of "what God [or the Messiah] has done through me," and, in consequence, of his beloved churches as his "boast," his "joy," or his "crown" (1 Thess 2:19-20; 3:9; Phil 2:16; 4:1). It is because of this "boast" that he has felt not only able but obliged to write the letter (the NIV's "glory" avoids the apparent self-claim at the cost of Paul's resonances and underlying meaning).

**15:18-19a.** He explains this (γάρ *gar*) by speaking of what the Messiah has accomplished through him. He does so through a rather oblique double negative, perhaps indicating a certain self-consciousness: literally "I will not dare to say anything about what the Messiah has not accom-

plished through me." This may be a way of saying "I wouldn't dare to tell you any stories that aren't strictly true," or it may mean simply "I have the right to speak of what the Messiah has done through me." He then mentions swiftly the various ways in which this work has been accomplished: word and deed, the power of signs and wonders, and (though this is hardly a separable phenomenon) the power of God's Spirit. We may compare 1 Cor 2:4; 2 Cor 12:12; Gal 3:5; 1 Thess 1:5; and the various scenes in Acts, e.g., 14:8-18. Paul does not often mention this, but he clearly assumes that powerful deeds, particularly healings, were part of his gospel ministry. This is his regular modus operandi; it has led him by strange paths, but his boast is that he has thereby been faithful to his commission.

**15:19b-21.** The result is an astonishing claim: to have announced the gospel message of the Messiah in a long arc from Jerusalem in the southeast to Illyricum (the Balkan coast opposite Italy on the Adriatic sea) in the northwest. This is surprising, because we have no record, in Acts or in Paul's letters, of a trip that far north. Philippi and Thessalonica are in Macedonia (northern Greece), south of Illyricum. The claim may be hyperbole, despite v. 18, or it may reflect a missionary journey of which we know nothing, which is after all quite likely considering how many holes there are in the Acts account (cf. 2 Cor 11:23-33 with Acts 13–20). What is more, to make Jerusalem his starting-point, though in a sense validated by Gal 2:1-10, conflicts at a surface level with the picture in Acts, where Antioch was the base from which he set out and to which he returned (Acts 13:1-3; 14:26). But the fundamental point is not in doubt, nor should it be seen as less than remarkable. Before Paul began, neither Asia Minor nor Greece had heard of Jesus of Nazareth; by the time he was writing this letter, there were little communities all over that part of Caesar's empire (and it was a very significant part of Caesar's empire, including many centers of the new imperial cult) in which Jesus was being celebrated as the risen Messiah, the world's true Lord. That is in itself an astonishing achievement, and Paul must have known it.

Among his aims, he says (v. 20), is to announce the gospel in places where the Messiah had not been previously named. Conscious of being a "builder," he did not wish to go to work on someone else's "foundation" (see also 1 Cor 3:10-15; 2 Cor 10:15-16). His use of this metaphor is not uniform; in 1 Cor 3:11 he declares that there is only one possible foundation—Jesus the Messiah—so one might have supposed that it would not matter who else built on it, and indeed in the same passage he sees that other people are building on his own foundation. However, his point here may be influenced by his sense that in coming to Rome he is indeed visiting a church founded by someone else. Whether or not this was Peter, and if so whether Paul was aware of this and so was anxious to avoid any suggestion of conflict between the two of them, following previous disasters (Gal 2:11-21), we cannot easily say.

The point can, once again, be stated in terms of the Isaianic Servant theme that Paul has drawn on earlier in the letter (e.g., 10:15-16).[571] Isaiah 52:13-15 spoke of the servant being announced before nations and kings, startling them with the strange message. Paul has already seen that effect wherever he has gone; but he has also seen people come into glad submission to the Servant, whom he clearly takes here to be the Messiah (the citation serves to explain vv. 19-20).

**15:22-24.** And so—to Spain! This proposal was bound to come as a surprise. All roads led to Rome, and the church there might well have supposed that once the apostle had reached the great capital he would rest content. But Paul has his eyes on a different target. The prophets in whose works he had steeped himself spoke of the faraway coastlands and islands coming to hear of the one God, of their true Lord (Isa 11:11; 41:1; 42:4, 10; 49:1; 51:5; 60:9; see also Ps 65:5-8). Paul no doubt knows that there are islands and coastlands to be found in quite different directions (going south, for instance, or east to India and beyond), and we have no idea whether he knew of Christian missions going there, or whether he ever dreamed of visiting them himself. What we do know is that, being a Roman citizen, he was able to use his citizenship as a help in traveling within the Roman Empire, and that since Rome was itself the capital of much of the world it made sense to

go there, following his apparent strategy of taking the gospel to central points and letting it do its work from there. Seemingly the logical next step was to complete the whole circuit of the north side of the Mediterranean Sea. The southern side, too, was a busy center of Roman culture, from Egypt through Libya and Cyrene, including the important province of Africa itself (the prominent tip of contemporary Tunisia, opposite Sicily, centered on Carthage). Perhaps Paul intended to make the return journey from Spain along the southern shore.

We cannot know, and these speculations peter out in frustration. That may well be, actually, what happened to Paul as well. We have no evidence that he ever got farther than Rome, and though later legend did its best to fill in the gaps and have him complete a Spanish mission and return to Rome a second time, there is no compelling reason to accept this.

For the moment he makes four points:

First, this tireless program of activity explains why he has been so long coming to them (cf. 1:13). Elsewhere he can speak of "Satan hindering him" in his desire to visit a church; there is no mention of that here, but rather of fruitful work for the gospel (1 Thess 2:18; cf. the Holy Spirit's hindering in Acts 16:6). He has longed for many years to come to them; now at last the moment has arrived. (Or at least he supposes it has.)

Second, his aims for the eastern Mediterranean have been fulfilled; he no longer has any room for new work. This sounds extraordinary, given the tiny number of Christians we must envisage compared to the population in general; but Paul thinks of himself as a church-planter, and once he has established churches in the major centers of population and culture he has to rely on them to do for themselves the work of continued evangelism in their neighborhoods. So, with Ephesus, Philippi, Thessalonica, Athens possibly, and Corinth established—not without difficulties and anxieties!—he quite genuinely concludes that it is time to move on.

Third, he intends to make them his base for further operations, all the way to Spain. Verse 24 is important for what it does not say; it does not say that Paul intends to stamp his own apostolic authority on the Roman church, or to take over its leadership in some other way. But he does hope to

571. See J. Ross Wagner, *Heralds of the Good News: Isaiah and Paul "In Concert" in the Letter to the Romans,* NovTSup 101 (Leiden: Brill, 2002) 329-36, noting how appropriate it was to pick a text that spoke of people far away, out of earshot as it were, coming to hear the good news.

be refreshed in their company for a while (ἀπὸ μέρους [apo merous] here has its temporal, not partitive, sense; Paul is not saying that he hopes they will refresh some parts of him).

**15:25-29.** This leads Paul, with a sense of foreboding that emerges at the end of the chapter, to the immediate task in hand. He was not to know, writing this letter, that his trip to Jerusalem would indeed nearly cost him his life, and that it would be a matter of years, not weeks, before he eventually arrived in Rome (see Acts 20–28). All he knows, at the moment, is that he has put his hand to a particular plow, at considerable personal risk and cost, and that he must not turn back. He has been organizing a collection of money, throughout the churches in the Greek world, to take to the poor church in Jerusalem, whom he here refers to simply as "the saints" (vv. 25-26). Galatia, Macedonia, and Achaea have contributed generously to this—we can see that process going on, with painfully tactful hints and suggestions, in 1 Cor 16:1-4, and especially in 2 Corinthians 8 and 9—and now it falls to Paul and his companions to take the money thus raised as a gift to Jerusalem. Paul does not mention the Galatian churches here, but he does in this context in 1 Cor 16:1. (This might conceivably indicate that the Galatian churches had declined to support the venture, but we should be wary of jumping to conclusions on a point like this.) It is likely that this is in long-term fulfillment of the promise recorded in Gal 2:10: the Jerusalem leaders asked Paul and Barnabas that they would "remember the poor," meaning not poor people in general but the little and poor church in Jerusalem itself. We may compare Acts 11:27-30, where the Antioch church sends Paul and Barnabas to Jerusalem with famine relief; the relation of this passage to Galatians is disputed. The Paul of Acts 24:17 refers in one of his Roman hearings to his having brought "alms and offerings to my nation."

The collection was motivated, as Paul insists here, by much more than merely the desire, important in itself, to alleviate poverty. Paul saw it as part of a reciprocal action of Jews and Gentiles, to be understood on the larger map sketched in Romans 3–4; 9–11; and 14:1–15:13. The Gentile Christians, he says, are in debt to the Jewish ones: they have come to share in their spiritual blessings, so it is only right that they should minister to them (the word is λειτουργῆσαι *leitourgēsai*, cognate with Paul's "priestly" language about himself in v. 16) in material (σαρκικός *sarkikos*) things; this is one of the few places where the "spiritual/fleshly" contrast in Paul means more or less what it means in our contemporary parlance. But there is more going on than simply redressing a balance, however important (there are echoes here of the to-and-fro movement of 11:11-32). Paul conceives the collection, it appears, as a vital sign and means the unity between the Jewish Christians in Jerusalem (where tensions with the pagan authorities were rising and fierce zealot nationalism brewing) and the Gentile Christians in the wider world. For Gentiles to give money for Jewish Christians was a sign that the Gentiles regarded them as members of the same family; for Jewish Christians to accept it would be a sign that they in turn accepted the Gentiles as part of their family. The collection was thus designed to accomplish, *mutatis mutandis,* the same thing that Paul had been urging in 14:1–15:13.

This, it seems to me, is preferable to the rival account of Paul's motivation, which suggests that he wanted to use the collection as a means of putting Rom 10:19 and 11:13-14 into operation— that is, to provoke non-Christian Jews to "jealousy" and so save some of them—perhaps even, in some grander theories, to precipitate the great event spoken of (so many think) in 11:25-27.[572] Paul's coming with the collection would thus be a new version of the long-prophesied pilgrimage of the nations to Zion.[573] In company with some others, I see no evidence for that.[574] The "great event" turns out to be a figment of the imagination (see the Commentary on 11:25-27); in the present passage Paul is thinking of the effect on Christian Jews, not on non-Christian ones. All he says about unbelieving Jews is that he prays to be delivered from them, not that they will suddenly see the light as a result of his labors.

He sees the Jerusalem visit with the collection, however important, as essentially a detour. He has

---

572. This theory, found in many variations, is associated with J. Munck, *Paul and the Salvation of Mankind* (Atlanta: John Knox, 1959). See also K. F. Nickle, *The Collection: A Study in Paul's Strategy* (Naperville, Ill.: Allenson, 1966) 129-42.

573. See S. McKnight, *A Light Among the Gentiles: Jewish Missionary Activity in the Second Temple Period* (Minneapolis: Fortress, 1991) 47-48, drawing on Isa 2:2-4; 60:6-7, 11; Mic 4:13.

574. T. L. Donaldson, *Paul and the Gentiles: Remapping the Apostle's Convictional World* (Minneapolis: Fortress, 1997) 256.

a task to complete, and as soon as it is done he will be on his way to Rome. His language for "completing the task" is strange. The NRSV ("have delivered to them what has been collected") and the NIV ("have made sure that they have received this fruit") struggle with what Paul wrote, which literally translated reads "and have sealed to them this fruit" (cf. NJB, "and have given this harvest into their possession"). The basic import is clear: Paul wants to deliver the money safe and sound. But why put it like this? Some have thought he was referring to a literal "seal"; the money was the fruit of his labor in the Gentile world, and he would deliver it to them under his own seal (so NEB; the REB, however, has backed off from this). He may be envisaging himself as a tenant handing over fruit to the owner; or maybe the "fruit" is his whole work among the Gentiles, which this gift will "seal." Others have suggested that, since sealing is the last act before handing over an article, he simply means "when the matter is complete."[575] In any case, that is the last thing he will do—so far as he knows at present—before coming on, via Rome, to Spain. And (v. 29) he has quiet confidence in God (not in himself) that, when he comes, "the blessing of the Messiah" will accompany him as it always has before.

As with the journey to Spain, we do not know exactly what happened when Paul tried to deliver the money in Jerusalem. Acts, which goes into great detail about that visit, does not mention the money except as part of Paul's speech to Festus (24:17). But the visit, clearly, was anything but a detour. Paul, according to Acts at its most detailed, was beaten up, nearly lynched, put on trial before the high priest, then before successive Roman governors, and kept in prison for two or more years before finally appealing to Caesar, and so getting to Rome courtesy of an armed escort to stand trial in the capital. This was not, perhaps, what he had in mind in 15:28; but, being Paul, it seems unlikely that he would have objected in the long run.

**15:30-33.** Aware of the dangers he faces, he concludes with a request for prayer. The request itself is made with a solemn formality: "through our Lord Jesus the Messiah, and the love of the Spirit." The prayer itself will be a struggle: "wres-

tle together with me in prayer to God on my behalf," he urges them (the NRSV's "join me in earnest prayer" does not get the force of συναγωνίσασθαί μοι [synagōnisasthai moi]; cf. NIV, "join me in my struggle"; NEB/REB, "be my allies in the fight"; see also Col 4:12). He encourages them to a twofold prayer: first, that he will himself be rescued, snatched out of the hands of unbelievers in Judaea (he is under no illusions as to his reputation as a traitor to the nation, the law, and God); second, that his ministry will be acceptable to God's people—that is, to the Christian Jews in Jerusalem. He envisages this as a difficult and dangerous time, and he speaks of coming on to Rome afterward (v. 31) almost as if he were planning a holiday in order to recover from it. He wants to come to them in joy, through God's will, and be refreshed with and by them. It is a touching moment, and we who know how the story continued after this letter was written can only look in awe at the faith and hope of the man who planned and wrote of such things.

The letter's main content is complete. Paul adds (v. 33) a brief blessing—this time invoking "the God of peace"—and moves on to personal greetings.[576]

But not all scribes left it at that. One very early manuscript[577] inserts the concluding doxology we now think of as 16:25-27 at this point, before continuing with what we call 16:1-23 and then concluding abruptly. This interesting detail (not the only oddity in that MS) is actually the tip of the iceberg: Metzger's *Textual Commentary* takes over two pages to describe the complex evidence, and a further page to evaluate it.[578] Some MSS have the doxology both here and after 14:23; two ninth-century MSS and a derivative fourteenth-century one omit it entirely (though one leaves a space at

---

575. See C. E. B. Cranfield, *A Critical and Exegetical Commentary on the Epistle to the Romans,* ICC, 2 vols. (Edinburgh: T. & T. Clark, 1975) 774-75, discussing other possibilities as well.

576. On "the God of peace," see 2 Cor 13:11; Phil 4:9; 1 Thess 5:23; Heb 13:20; cf. 2 Thess 3:16: "the Lord of peace." The range of contexts suggests that this was a frequent early Christian title for God, though the communal peace Paul seeks to inculcate in the present section makes it particularly appropriate here.

577. P[46], dated around 200 CE.

578. B. M. Metzger, *A Textual Commentary on the Greek New Testament* (London: United Bible Societies, 1971) 533-36. Other clear discussions include Cranfield, *Romans,* 5-11; H. Gamble, *The Textual History of the Letter to the Romans: A Study in Textual and Literary Criticism* (Grand Rapids: Eerdmans, 1977); L. Hurtado, "The Doxology at the End of Romans," in *New Testament Textual Criticism: Its Significance for Exegesis. Essays in Honor of Bruce M. Metzger,* ed. E. J. Epp and G. Fee (Oxford: Clarendon, 1981) 185-99; Douglas J. Moo, *The Epistle to the Romans,* NICNT (Grand Rapids: Eerdmans, 1996) 936-37; Joseph A. Fitzmyer, *Romans,* AB 33 (Garden City, N.Y.: Doubleday, 1993) 55-67. Brendan Byrne, *Romans,* SP 6 (Collegeville, Minn.: Liturgical, 1996) 461, is wrong to state that there is a "virtually unanimous judgment" that the doxology is post-Pauline.

the end of chap. 14 as though there might be something to insert); one fourteenth-century MS has it here and then stops, omitting chap. 16 itself completely. A large number of good MSS, though, have it where it stands in printed texts today.

Many scholars have regarded 16:25-27 as a post-Pauline addition, but this judgment is reached as much on its content as on its remarkably versatile manuscript location. Since, on the basis of my reading of the rest of the letter, I judge the content to be comfortably Pauline, and since I regard it as likely that Paul would have written a fitting doxology rather than allowed the letter to stop short with a brief blessing such as 15:33 or the spurious 16:24 (see below), I belong to the considerable minority who, on balance, regard the doxology as original, and as originally coming at the end of the letter (see the Commentary on 16:25-27). It is easy to explain the other placings. Scribes faced with a longer than usual list of greetings, involving persons by then unknown, might wish to create a more usable document (i.e., one that could be read out during worship) by bringing the doxology forward. Some of the manuscript displacements are almost certainly due to the influence of the second-century teacher Marcion, who hacked this letter about as he did the rest of (what became) the New Testament, in the interests of producing a text that would validate his particular views (that the God of the Old Testament had nothing in common with the God of Jesus Christ). Some may be due to an early desire, possibly as early as Paul's lifetime, possibly even under Paul's direction, to make copies of this extraordinary letter available to churches other than Rome. T. W. Manson, famously, proposed that chap. 16 was added as a "covering letter" to enable a copy of the letter to Rome, which had stopped at the end of chap. 15, to be sent to a church where he knew far more people than he did in Rome, namely Ephesus.[579] Educated guesses of this sort have been made, and remain appropriate as ways of explaining the complex MS tradition. But they should not be taken as a solid reason for placing 16:25-27 anywhere other than where it is, still less for deleting it altogether.

579. T. W. Manson, "St. Paul's Letter to the Romans—And Others," in *Studies in the Gospels and Epistles,* ed. M. Black (Manchester: Manchester University Press, 1962) 225-41; reprinted in *The Romans Debate,* rev. ed., ed. K. P. Donfried (Peabody, Mass.: Hendriksen, 1991) 3-15.

# REFLECTIONS

**1.** Paul combines a strong belief in divine providence with an equally strong recognition that one may not always, in this life, understand what it is up to. Just as in Philemon he speculates on the possible reason why God allowed Onesimus to leave his master and come to Paul, so here he makes plans with enthusiasm but also with the request for prayer that potential disaster may be averted (see Phlm 15). "Perhaps," he says—a wonderful word for combining a belief in God's overruling mercy with a humility about how much of it we can see. He has seen God do extraordinary things through his preaching of the gospel, and he believes there are more to come; but he knows well enough from previous experience that things seldom turn out exactly as planned, and on one occasion he has had to apologize to a church—or at least explain why an apology was not necessary—because it had looked as though he was changing his plans on a whim (2 Cor 1:15-22). He had Spain in his sights; but with Jerusalem to face before he could turn westward he was not altogether sanguine about the prospects.

That was just as well. According to Acts, Jerusalem was a near-disaster, the trip to Rome happened two years late and under armed guard, and the sea might easily have swallowed Paul and his companions before they ever got to see the Seven Hills. Likewise, we do not know if Paul ever made it to Spain at all, and in the absence of evidence that he did most scholars prefer to play safe and suggest that he probably did not.

If there is a lesson to be drawn from this it is that of Prov 19:21: human minds devise many plans, but it is YHWH's purpose that will be established. Paul would have heartily agreed, even when the human mind in question is that of an apostle guided and equipped by God's Spirit. But this should not lead to a shoulder-shrugging fatalism. On the contrary. One of the most important lessons in Romans 15 might be put thus: God allowed Paul to dream of Spain in order that he might write Romans. No matter that Paul probably never reached Spain. What mattered was that he wrote this letter, which has been far more powerful and influential than any missionary visit, even by Paul himself, could ever have been. Perhaps (that word again) half our great plans, the dreams we dream for our churches and our world, and even for ourselves, are dreams God allows us to dream in order that, on the way there, we may accomplish, almost without realizing it, the crucial thing God intends us to do.

**2.** Paul cheerfully breaks into "priestly" language when speaking of his evangelistic work, in a way that he does not when speaking of presiding in worship, let alone at the eucharist. The time had not yet come, but was not very far off, when devout Christians would draw on Old Testament typology to speak of such things, and for a while the powerful metaphors could make their own points, as could Paul's. The time would come later, though, when the metaphorical status of such language was forgotten, as a new "priestly" class grew up through whom alone valid worship and teaching could be offered; and the time would then come when a large part of the church overthrew all this in the name of Paul himself. Nor has the world stood still on these matters since the Reformation. Such questions still bedevil the quest for unity Paul himself would so earnestly urge upon us.

But perhaps (once more) the time may come when we shall be able to re-explore Paul's metaphors without the sense of having to revive old factions, restore old policies, or follow an antique drum. Maybe "old men ought to be explorers," and we in the church, creaking and tottering under the weight of unnecessary baggage, could do worse than to arrive where we started and know the place for the first time. Maybe when Protestants rediscover priesthood and Catholics rediscover evangelism then both will rediscover Paul, and the fire and the rose might become one. We can always hope; and, under the rubric of the previous point, working toward that hope might achieve God's ends without us even realizing it.

**3.** The collection and use of money in the church has always been, and probably will always be, a tense and delicate matter. It is worth pondering how Paul and his companions actually carried the stuff; in the days before paper money, still less international banking and credit transfers, they were taking a huge physical risk, just as in organizing the collection Paul was taking a huge risk to his reputation, as we can see reading between the lines of 2 Corinthians 8 and 9. Paul deemed it worthwhile because he knew that money could be of symbolic as well as practical help. Once someone has given to a cause, they will be far more likely to pray for it. Once somebody has received money from an unexpected source, they will feel themselves far more bonded, more part of the family. Paul had been asked by the Jerusalem apostles to "remember the poor"; they might not approve of half of what he did and said on the mission field, but he was determined never to let them say, "he never kept his promise." The apostolic faithfulness, attempting to bring together Jew and Gentile in one community of love and praise, was meant to mirror the similar faithfulness of God. So with our fund-raising, giving of money, charity work, and indeed famine relief: we have become so sophisticated, so clinical, that we can supply a credit card number from a mobile phone while not taking our eyes off the football game on television. It would not hurt to ask, whenever Romans 15 is read: what are we doing, as a church, as individuals, that will send the symbolic as well as practical message that the church of Jesus Christ is one body, one family, and that if one suffers, all suffer?

# ROMANS 16:1-16, COMMENDATION AND GREETINGS

## NIV

**16** I commend to you our sister Phoebe, a servant[a] of the church in Cenchrea. [2]I ask you to receive her in the Lord in a way worthy of the saints and to give her any help she may need from you, for she has been a great help to many people, including me.

[3]Greet Priscilla[b] and Aquila, my fellow workers in Christ Jesus. [4]They risked their lives for me. Not only I but all the churches of the Gentiles are grateful to them. [5]Greet also the church that meets at their house.

Greet my dear friend Epenetus, who was the first convert to Christ in the province of Asia. [6]Greet Mary, who worked very hard for you. [7]Greet Andronicus and Junias, my relatives who have been in prison with me. They are outstanding among the apostles, and they were in Christ before I was. [8]Greet Ampliatus, whom I love in the Lord. [9]Greet Urbanus, our fellow worker in Christ, and my dear friend Stachys. [10]Greet Apelles, tested and approved in Christ.

Greet those who belong to the household of Aristobulus. [11]Greet Herodion, my relative.

Greet those in the household of Narcissus who are in the Lord. [12]Greet Tryphena and Tryphosa, those women who work hard in the Lord.

Greet my dear friend Persis, another woman who has worked very hard in the Lord. [13]Greet Rufus, chosen in the Lord, and his mother, who has been a mother to me, too. [14]Greet Asyncritus, Phlegon, Hermes, Patrobas, Hermas and the brothers with them. [15]Greet Philologus, Julia, Nereus and his sister, and Olympas and all the saints with them. [16]Greet one another with a holy kiss.

All the churches of Christ send greetings.

[a] 1 Or *deaconess*    [b] 3 Greek *Prisca*, a variant of *Priscilla*

## NRSV

**16** I commend to you our sister Phoebe, a deacon[a] of the church at Cenchreae, [2]so that you may welcome her in the Lord as is fitting for the saints, and help her in whatever she may require from you, for she has been a benefactor of many and of myself as well.

[3]Greet Prisca and Aquila, who work with me in Christ Jesus, [4]and who risked their necks for my life, to whom not only I give thanks, but also all the churches of the Gentiles. [5]Greet also the church in their house. Greet my beloved Epaenetus, who was the first convert[b] in Asia for Christ. [6]Greet Mary, who has worked very hard among you. [7]Greet Andronicus and Junia,[c] my relatives[d] who were in prison with me; they are prominent among the apostles, and they were in Christ before I was. [8]Greet Ampliatus, my beloved in the Lord. [9]Greet Urbanus, our co-worker in Christ, and my beloved Stachys. [10]Greet Apelles, who is approved in Christ. Greet those who belong to the family of Aristobulus. [11]Greet my relative[e] Herodion. Greet those in the Lord who belong to the family of Narcissus. [12]Greet those workers in the Lord, Tryphaena and Tryphosa. Greet the beloved Persis, who has worked hard in the Lord. [13]Greet Rufus, chosen in the Lord; and greet his mother—a mother to me also. [14]Greet Asyncritus, Phlegon, Hermes, Patrobas, Hermas, and the brothers and sisters[f] who are with them. [15]Greet Philologus, Julia, Nereus and his sister, and Olympas, and all the saints who are with them. [16]Greet one another with a holy kiss. All the churches of Christ greet you.

[a] Or *minister*    [b] Gk *first fruits*    [c] Or *Junias*; other ancient authorities read *Julia*    [d] Or *compatriots*    [e] Or *compatriot*    [f] Gk *brothers*

# COMMENTARY

Despite the brilliant suggestion of T. W. Manson that Romans 16 was a covering letter to enable Romans also to be sent to Ephesus, most scholars have continued to regard it as part of Paul's original letter, to be sent to Rome along with the rest (see the Commentary on 15:14-33). The fact that Romans contains more personal greetings than the rest of Paul's letters put together alerts us that there may be something special afoot, but this does not increase the chances of chapter 16 being intended for somewhere other than Rome. Indeed, when Paul writes to churches he knows well there is a remarkable absence of named greetings (1 and 2 Corinthians, Galatians, Philippians, 1 and 2 Thessalonians); there are a few messages from Paul's present companions, but otherwise general greetings to the church, without specification (1 Cor 16:15-18 appears to be a partial exception, but this is a commendation of the three messengers from Corinth to Paul, not a greeting as such). The closest we come is precisely two names in Colossians (4:15, 17)—significantly, another church Paul had neither founded nor visited. We could almost formulate it as a rule: if Paul knows the church, he does not name individuals. Anyone who has had to make a speech or write a letter to a community they know well will understand why. The ice is thin. Mention one, and you must mention all.

This does not by itself explain the very large number of names here, or how Paul knew so many people in Rome.[580] On the latter point, we should take it for granted that there was considerable mobility among the early Christians. Roads were good, travel as easy as it had ever been, and some people, like Phoebe in 16:1, will have been financially independent and able to move about for business or personal reasons.[581] Others, like Prisca and Aquila (v. 3), had been in both Corinth (Acts 18:2) and Ephesus (1 Cor 16:19), having traveled there with Paul (Acts 18:18); but, being originally from Rome, it was understandable that they would have returned there once the coast was clear—

that is, after Claudius's death. Nothing is more probable than that they should have stayed in touch with Paul and given him information about the little church in Rome itself, or that several other Christians of his acquaintance had already found their way there.

But why mention so many of them? Here we cannot be sure, but the situation of 14:1–15:13 suggests an obvious answer. In five cases, Paul mentions, along with a name or pair of names, the Christians within a household (16:5a, 10-11, 14-15). He may or may not have wanted to mention all the individual Christians he knew in the city, but he was certainly keen to mention all the household churches he knew: we can only guess which ones might have been "weak" and which "strong," but we can be reasonably sure he was careful to greet them all with equal enthusiasm. All sorts of things can be read into accidental omissions. Paul did not want to arrive at Rome and find that he had caused fresh divisions by appearing to favor one group over another.

**16:1-2.** In his second letter to Corinth, Paul speaks with heavy irony about needing "letters of recommendation" for or from the church there (2 Cor 3:1-3; cf. Acts 18:27; Col 4:10). They knew him and he knew them. To write a letter at all would be to lie about their relationship. But "letters of recommendation" were vital in the ancient world, where, without electronic communication, anybody could turn up in a town claiming to be somebody else. If today we still need letters of reference for employment or immigration purposes, how much more necessary were they in Paul's world.

The person he commends is Phoebe, whose home is in Cenchreae, the eastern port of Corinth (in the days before the canal, Corinth had two ports, with arrangements to drag ships across the isthmus). The implication is that Phoebe is a businesswoman who is able to travel independently, and for Paul to trust her with a letter like this speaks volumes for the respect in which she was held; so it is no surprise to discover that she is a deacon in the church. Attempts to make διάκονος (*diakonos*) mean something else fail: to call her a "servant of the church," with the NIV, does indeed

---

580. A helpful contribution is that of P. Lampe, "The Roman Christians of Romans 16," in *The Romans Debate,* rev. ed., ed. K. P. Donfried (Peabody, Mass.: Hendriksen, 1991) 216-30.

581. See L. Casson, *Travel in the Ancient World* (London: Allen & Unwin, 1974).

offer a valid translation of the word, but it merely pushes the problem on a stage, since that would either mean that Phoebe was a paid employee of the church (to do what?) or that there was an order of ministry, otherwise unknown, called "servants." "Minister" (REB) is imprecise, because that word is used for several pastoral offices in today's church; "deaconess" (RSV, JB, NJB) is inaccurate, because it implies that Phoebe belonged to a specific order, of female church workers quite different from "deacons," which would not be invented for another three hundred years.[582] She was in a position of leadership, and Paul respected her as such and expected the Roman church to do so as well. He requests, as people did and still do in such letters, the kind of help that a traveler may need; and adds his commendation on the grounds that she has herself been a benefactor to many, himself included. The word "benefactor" means much more, in Paul's world, than simply "she has been a great help" (NIV): benefaction and patronage were a vital part of the culture, and this makes Phoebe someone to be reckoned with socially and financially as well as simply a sister in the Lord and a leader—of whatever sort—in her local church.[583]

**16:3-5a.** Prisca and Aquila are known from Acts 18:2, 26; 1 Cor 16:19; and 2 Tim 4:19. Acts calls Prisca "Priscilla." They seem to have been among Paul's closest friends, being, like him, tentmakers. How they had "risked their necks" for him is not known, but clearly they were well known in both Corinth and Ephesus, being capable of setting even someone like Apollos straight in his teaching. They had now returned to Rome,

having left because of Claudius's edict. Their house is the first of the "house-churches" Paul mentions.

**16:5b-16.** The details of the names that follow are mostly of interest only in that they may possibly reflect the ethnic composition of the church, though this is inevitably speculative. Prisca and Aquila were certainly Jews, as were Andronicus, Junia, and Herodion; Mary may have been as well. Paul's comments on the persons concerned, though, are sometimes worth pondering. Epaenetus (v. 5*b*) was the "first fruits of Asia into the Messiah," which presumably means he was the first to be baptized, the sign of more to come (cf. 1 Cor 16:15, where Stephanas has the same honor in Achaea). Mary (v. 6) has "worked hard for you," perhaps in prayer (cf. Col 4:12-13).

Andronicus and Junia (v. 7) are kinsfolk of Paul (this may mean simply that they are Jewish, or, as the NRSV and the NIV suggest, closer relatives) who had been in prison with him, perhaps in Ephesus; since they had been "in Christ" before Paul himself, that must mean that they had been Christians since very early on, certainly before the gospel came to Asia Minor or indeed anywhere much outside the Levant. They were therefore themselves traveling Christians, whose journeys had already intersected with Paul's, and they had now arrived in Rome, as they had earlier "arrived in Christ," ahead of him. They are man and woman, perhaps husband and wife or possibly brother and sister.[584] This is the more interesting in that they are "of note among the apostles," presumably meaning that both of them were witnesses of the resurrection (which fits, of course, with their being "in Christ" before Paul). Junia is thus one of the female "apostles," the only one so called; though presumably others, such as Mary Magdalene, were known as such as well. On Paul's meaning of "apostle" as "witness of the resurrection," see 1 Cor 9:1 (cf. Acts 1:22); perhaps the two were among the "five hundred at once" of 1 Cor 15:6.

Ampliatus, Urbanus, Stachys, and Apelles (the last of whom could conceivably be another Jewish member of the list) are greeted briefly (vv. 8-10*a*).

---

582. See 1 Tim 3:11, which seems to refer to women who hold diaconal office (see 1 Tim 3:8). Pliny *Letters* 10.96.8 speaks of two serving women "whom they call deacons," *ministrae;* Pliny would naturally use the feminine ending to avoid apparent solecism, and this word should not be pressed to indicate that there was a separate order. Too much should not be made of the masculine form of διάκονος (*diakonos*) either, though, since the fem. form was not available and the word could be used with reference to either gender (cf. 13:4). See further the helpful note in Christopher Bryan, *A Preface to Romans: Notes on the Epistle in Its Literary and Cultural Setting* (Oxford: Oxford University Press, 2000) 184-85. On "deaconess," see *The Oxford Dictionary of the Christian Church,* 3rd ed. (Oxford: Oxford University Press, 1997) 455-56, with bibliography.

583. See BDAG 885; B. W. Winter, *Seek the Welfare of the City: Christians as Benefactors and Citizens* (Grand Rapids: Eerdmans, 1994), though curiously Rom 16:2 does not appear in the index. Other discussion and refs. in Douglas J. Moo, *The Epistle to the Romans,* NICNT (Grand Rapids: Eerdmans, 1996) 916. See esp. R. Jewett, "Paul, Phoebe, and the Spanish Mission," in *The Social World of Formative Christianity and Judaism: Essays in Tribute to Howard Clark Kee,* ed. J. Neusner et al. (Philadelphia: Fortress, 1988) 142-61.

584. The KJV has "Junia," though until recently most other versions read "Junias," the masc. form. See R. S. Cervin, "A Note Regarding the Name 'Junia(s)' in Romans 16.7," *NTS* 40/3 (1994) 464-70, demonstrating that the name is certainly fem., despite the desperate attempts of many earlier lexicographers, some MSS, and some translators to this day, to suggest otherwise.

The first three are known to Paul personally, and saying that Apelles is "approved in Christ" perhaps means simply that Paul has heard good things of him though he does not know him personally. The "family" or "household" or Aristobulus (the phrase means simply "those of Aristobulus") is perhaps another house church (v. 10*b*); it is implied that Aristobulus himself is not a member, though, and perhaps it simply means that a group of believers had grown up within his household.[585] If he was the brother of Herod (see the previous note), it would be natural to mention a "Herodion" in the next breath (v. 11*a*), presumably a freedman in the service of the household. What relation he is to Paul, or whether (as in v. 7) this simply means that he too is a fellow Jew, we cannot know. The mention of Narcissus (v. 11*b*) introduces a famous name in mid-century Rome: a freedman who rose to great heights under Claudius, only to incur the jealousy of many Romans and to be forced into suicide after Claudius's death. If this is the same man, as most assume, Christians within his household after his death would have occupied a challenging and dangerous position.

Tryphena and Tryphosa (v. 12*a*) increase the number of women in the list, as does Persis (v. 12*b*); all three hard workers in the Lord. Rufus (v. 13) may perhaps be the son of Simon of Cyrene (Mark 15:21), though it was a common enough name. His mother, who remains unnamed, had been a metaphorical mother to Paul at some stage, though in what place and circumstances we do not know. (One of the tantalizing things about this chapter is that, like watching a sequence of film clips going by too fast to take in, we catch tiny glimpses into the world of early Christianity that could be very revealing if only we could freeze the frame and ask one or two leading questions. There was clearly quite a subculture growing up, but we know very nearly nothing about it.)

Verse 14 greets five more people "and the family with them," presumably another house church (where, we want to ask, would they have been on the map of 14:1–15:13? What would they be thinking by this stage of the letter?). Verse 15 greets five more people, including two male and female pairings; some have speculated that Philologus and Julia were husband and wife, with Nereus and his sister being their children. They, with Olympas, play host to another house-church ("all the saints with them"). Verse 16 commands the church to give one another the greeting that was already in common use, "the kiss of peace" or "the holy kiss" (cf. 1 Cor 16:20; 2 Cor 13:12; 1 Thess 5:26; 1 Pet 5:14; Justin Martyr *Apology* 1:65). Christian fellowship must be embodied. A general greeting from "all the Messiah's churches" concludes the list (v. 16*b*).

What do we learn about the Roman church, or even about the purpose of the letter, from this list? Not very much; but if we are right to see the extraordinary number of names as a sign of Paul's attempt to greet the different parts of the church, perhaps including some groups that were not on good terms with one another, we might speculate on the size of the church as a whole. If there are five groups mentioned here (see above), and if each house-church had between, say, six and twenty members, the total number of Christians in Rome would be somewhere between thirty and a hundred. If the Jewish names were more likely to represent communities that still adhered to some Jewish customs (though, as we saw, this would not be true for Paul himself, nor most likely for Prisca and Aquila, and possibly not for Paul's kinsfolk—which accounts for most of the Jewish names), then we might have a sense of which were the "weak" and which the "strong." I do not think we shall ever be able to tell. It seems just as likely that there were a few "weak" members on the fringe of otherwise "strong" house-churches, needing to be welcomed in, rather than entire communities that were solidly committed to one line of practice. What we do have, then, is a small, vulnerable church, needing to know and trust one another across various boundaries; a church many of whose members were not native to Rome, living most likely in immigrant communities within particular areas; a church in which men and women alike took leadership roles; a church where families and households formed the basis of worshiping communities. There is something both attractive and frightening about this picture: enormous potential, huge risks, a community both lively and vulnerable. This is the community that will now be the first to hear one of the greatest letters in the history of the world.

---

585. On the identification of this Aristobulus with the brother of Herod Agrippa, see Moo, *Romans*, 925. The name is very rare and the identification quite plausible. This Aristobulus had died in 48/49 CE, but the household might well continue to be known under his name.

# ROMANS 16:17-20, WATCH OUT FOR DIVISIONS

| NIV | NRSV |
|---|---|
| ¹⁷I urge you, brothers, to watch out for those who cause divisions and put obstacles in your way that are contrary to the teaching you have learned. Keep away from them. ¹⁸For such people are not serving our Lord Christ, but their own appetites. By smooth talk and flattery they deceive the minds of naive people. ¹⁹Everyone has heard about your obedience, so I am full of joy over you; but I want you to be wise about what is good, and innocent about what is evil.<br><br>²⁰The God of peace will soon crush Satan under your feet.<br><br>The grace of our Lord Jesus be with you. | 17I urge you, brothers and sisters,ᵃ to keep an eye on those who cause dissensions and offenses, in opposition to the teaching that you have learned; avoid them. ¹⁸For such people do not serve our Lord Christ, but their own appetites,ᵇ and by smooth talk and flattery they deceive the hearts of the simple-minded. ¹⁹For while your obedience is known to all, so that I rejoice over you, I want you to be wise in what is good and guileless in what is evil. ²⁰The God of peace will shortly crush Satan under your feet. The grace of our Lord Jesus Christ be with you.ᶜ<br><br>ᵃ Gk *brothers*   ᵇ Gk *their own belly*   ᶜ Other ancient authorities lack this sentence |

## COMMENTARY

We might now have expected greetings from Paul's companions, and a conclusion, but before that Paul throws in a further sharp word of exhortation. It sounds, actually, as though it had escaped from another letter, though there is no textual evidence to suggest that it originated anywhere but here. Perhaps, as Paul thinks and prays about these small house-churches, he has had a sudden stab of anxiety. Do they, he wonders, need to be warned that there are fierce wolves on the loose, who will not spare the flock (cf. Acts 20:29-31)?

**16:17.** The opening warning tells them to "watch out for" (NIV) or "keep an eye on" (NRSV) those who cause dissensions and "put obstacles in your way" (NIV), going against the basic Christian teaching that they have received. They are to keep away from them (though how, within a small community, is not clear). This command echoes Paul's disciplinary warnings elsewhere (e.g., 1 Cor 5:9-13). Whatever particular problems Paul may have in mind, his language here does not seem to reflect the questions at stake in 14:1–15:13.

**16:18-20.** This is then backed up (γάρ *gar,* v. 18) with an explanation of what sort of people these may be. They are not serving "our Lord the

Messiah" (one of only two occasions when these two titles occur together in the Pauline literature without the name "Jesus," the other being Col 3:24). Instead, they are serving (literally) "their own bellies," presumably meaning "appetites" in general (so NRSV and NIV). This is standard polemical language in the Jewish world of Paul's day, and normally means that the people concerned appear to be denying or abandoning some central part of the faith or teaching; the general tone makes it difficult to insist that the problem must be the same as that in Phil 3:18-19, where similar language is used.[586] The danger they pose is that they are smooth talkers, deceiving the hearts of those who are too innocent for their own good. Paul is quick to assure his hearers that he is confident of their "obedience," since it is well known to all (cf. 1:8); but it is important that they supplement this with a mature wisdom as outlined in one of Jesus' best-known sayings, being simultaneously shrewd and innocent. See Matt 10:16, "wise as serpents, innocent as doves," the first adjective there being φρόνιμοι (*phronimoi*) rather

---

586. Christopher Bryan, *A Preface to Romans: Notes on the Epistle in Its Literary and Cultural Setting* (Oxford: Oxford University Press, 2000) 231, with references.

than σοφοί (*sophoi*) as here; the second is ἀκέραιοι (*akeraioi*) in both.[587]

Once again (v. 20) Paul concludes a train of thought with a blessing. By contrast with 15:5, 13, and 33, though, we catch a darker tone. He evokes Gen 3:15: the "God of peace will see to it that "the satan" will be crushed under your feet (cf. Luke 10:17-19, and behind that Ps 91:13; see also Rev 12:10-11; on "the God of peace," see the Commentary on 15:33). Paul elsewhere sees the new, young church vulnerable to enemy attack; it was part of his theology of new creation that the church was now, like Adam and Eve, open to fresh deceit (2 Cor 11:3). But his earlier exposition of the victory of God in Jesus Christ over the sin of Adam and all its entail (5:12-21) enables him here simply to promise that the victory promised in

Genesis will be theirs, and that it will come soon. He adds a brief greeting ("the grace of our Lord Jesus be with you"), which, like the closing doxology, has wandered to and fro in the scribal traditions; some MSS have it as v. 24, which is now regularly omitted in printed editions.

This short interjection, coming between the greetings to friends in Rome and the greetings from friends with Paul, functions rhetorically like the sudden reminder that breaks into a family farewell scene: "Don't forget to water the plants!" "Make sure you take your medicine!" It is clearly heartfelt; Paul knows that troublemakers will surface in any church. There is no reason to suppose that he is thinking specifically of the "Judaizing" problem he faced in Galatians, or whatever cognate problems he was warning against in Phil 3:2-3, 17-19. His concern is to warn against any attempt to pull church members away from the central tenets of the faith, what C. S. Lewis called "mere Christianity." However plausible the persuaders, their underlying attempt to change the ground rules of Christian faith and practice usually becomes clear before too long.

587. The dominical saying may at least "stand in the background" at this point. See P. Stuhlmacher, *Paul's Letter to the Romans: A Commentary* (Louisville: Westminster John Knox, 1994) 253; so, cautiously, James D. G. Dunn, *Romans 9–16,* 38B (Dallas: Word, 1988) 905; D. Wenham, *Paul: Follower of Jesus or Founder of Christianity?* (Grand Rapids: Eerdmans, 1995) 198. Moo, *Romans,* 932 thinks the allusion "probable."

# ROMANS 16:21-24, GREETINGS FROM PAUL'S COLLEAGUES

## NIV

21Timothy, my fellow worker, sends his greetings to you, as do Lucius, Jason and Sosipater, my relatives.
22I, Tertius, who wrote down this letter, greet you in the Lord.
23Gaius, whose hospitality I and the whole church here enjoy, sends you his greetings.

Erastus, who is the city's director of public works, and our brother Quartus send you their greetings.[a]

[a] 23 Some manuscripts *their greetings.* 24*May the grace of our Lord Jesus Christ be with all of you. Amen.*

## NRSV

21Timothy, my co-worker, greets you; so do Lucius and Jason and Sosipater, my relatives.[a]
22I Tertius, the writer of this letter, greet you in the Lord.[b]
23Gaius, who is host to me and to the whole church, greets you. Erastus, the city treasurer, and our brother Quartus, greet you.[c]

[a] Or *compatriots*     [b] Or *I Tertius, writing this letter in the Lord, greet you*     [c] Other ancient authorities add verse 24, *The grace of our Lord Jesus Christ be with all of you. Amen.*

# COMMENTARY

**16:21.** Timothy is well known to readers of Paul. According to Acts 16:1-3, he is the apostle's hand-picked younger colleague, and we see him either by Paul's side or running his errands at several points in the letters (e.g., 1 Cor 4:17; 16:10; 1 Thess 3:2, 6). Lucius, Jason, and Sosipater are not so well known, but they, like some in Rome, are kinsfolk of Paul's (see the discussion of vv. 7, 11; συγγενεῖς [*syngeneis*] may mean "fellow Jews" or it may imply a closer relation). These are a reminder that, though Paul's grief at his kinsfolk in 9:1-3 was real and deep, some of them at least were alongside him (cf. Col 4:10-11). "Jason" may be the person of that name we meet in Acts 17:5-9; "Sosipater" may be the "Sopater" of Acts 20:4.

**16:22.** Paul's amanuensis, having toiled thus far anonymously to take down the apostle's spectacular flow of thought, peeps for a moment out of hiding. Tertius is still capable of giving unsuspecting readers a fright by claiming to have "written this letter" (NRSV); the NIV softens the impact by translating "who wrote down this letter," which is, of course, what it means.[588]

**16:23a.** Gaius, in whose house the local church meets, and who is playing host to Paul himself, sends greetings. It is not clear whether he is to be identified with one of the other persons of this name in the New Testament; the most likely is the one in 1 Cor 1:14, a resident of Corinth. If, however, Paul is actually staying at Cenchreae while writing, rather than at Corinth itself, Gaius might be the host of the church where Phoebe (vv. 1-2) is a deacon. This might explain why Paul can say he is host to "all the church," perhaps unlikely in a larger city like Corinth.

**16:23b.** There is an Erastus known (from an inscription) to have held public office in Corinth at this time, and though identification is never certain this may be the same person, conveying his own greetings.[589] Quartus is not heard of anywhere else; like many others before and since, he has simply been a good though obscure Christian. He stands here for the multitudes of whom we know nothing, but who were lights of the world in their several generations.

**16:24.** This verse, omitted in what are normally regarded as the best MSS, consists simply of the repetition of the closing words of v. 20, with slight variations. Some of the MSS that include it omit the words from v. 20.

588. For discussions of scribes, shorthand, etc., at this period, see R. E. Richards, *The Secretary in the Letters of Paul,* WUNT 2.42 (Tübingen: Mohr, 1991) esp. 170-72; A. Millard, *Reading and Writing in the Time of Jesus* (New York: New York University Press, 2000) esp. 168-79.

589. Details in Moo, *Romans,* 935-36; Bryan, *A Preface to Romans,* 233.

# REFLECTIONS

**1.** To a modern Western eye, the most striking feature in the list of greetings is that nearly half the people named are women. Some of them are taking leading roles in the church. When Paul declared in Gal 3:28 that there is "no 'male and female' " in Christ, just as there is neither Jew nor Greek, slave nor free, he meant it. Some have criticized him for not making as much fuss about gender as about ethnicity, but that is largely a function of the problems he had to address in his church. If this list is anything to go by, he could take for granted something that much of the rest of church history could not.

**2.** Reading between the lines, we can see Paul taking care to greet several Christian gatherings in Rome that may have taken different positions on the issues he discusses in chaps. 14–15. Being a bridge builder between different Christian groups and opinions is hard and painstaking work; it is as easy to give a wrong impression of favoring one "side" or the other as it is hard to undo that impression once made. Today's church badly needs a new generation of bridge builders who will take the trouble to treat the different groups seriously, not only to greet them by name but, as Paul does here, to honor them for who they are and what they are doing in the Lord. The aim must then be to work with them, with integrity and imagination, to bring them into fellowship and mutual respect one with another. This is not to deny that sometimes a troublemaker must be rebuked, not courted or soothed; vv. 17-20 make that clear enough. But the point to note is that the work of patiently getting to know different Christians and their contexts is demanding, and church leaders need to give attention to it.

**3.** The blend of wisdom and innocence commended by both Paul (v. 19) and Jesus (Matt 10:16) is needed as much today as ever. Shrewdness without innocence becomes serpentine; innocence without shrewdness becomes naïveté. The laudable desire to think well of everyone needs to be tempered with the recognition that some are indeed out for their own ends and are merely giving the appearance of friendliness and piety by their skill at smooth talking. Unless this is spotted early on and confronted, trouble is stored up for later, as an untreated sore is allowed to fester.

# ROMANS 16:25-27, CONCLUDING DOXOLOGY

NIV

<sup>25</sup>Now to him who is able to establish you by my gospel and the proclamation of Jesus Christ, according to the revelation of the mystery hidden for long ages past, <sup>26</sup>but now revealed and made known through the prophetic writings by the command of the eternal God, so that all nations might believe and obey him— <sup>27</sup>to the only wise God be glory forever through Jesus Christ! Amen.

NRSV

25Now to God*ᵃ* who is able to strengthen you according to my gospel and the proclamation of Jesus Christ, according to the revelation of the mystery that was kept secret for long ages <sup>26</sup>but is now disclosed, and through the prophetic writings is made known to all the Gentiles, according to the command of the eternal God, to bring about the obedience of faith— <sup>27</sup>to the only wise God, through Jesus Christ, to whom*ᵇ* be the glory forever! Amen.*ᶜ*

*ᵃ* Gk *the one*     *ᵇ* Other ancient authorities lack *to whom.* The verse then reads, *to the only wise God be the glory through Jesus Christ forever. Amen.*     *ᶜ* Other ancient authorities lack 16.25-27 or include it after 14.23 or 15.33; others put verse 24 after verse 27

# COMMENTARY

The manuscript variations in which this closing doxology has been moved to two other places in the letter, causing other dislocations as it goes, have been discussed in the Commentary on 15:33. Hardly any copies omit it altogether, however, and the burden of proof ought to be on those (and there are many) who regard it as a post-Pauline addition. The real trouble is the content. Those who have seen Romans as basically about justification by faith balk at a summary and doxology that do not mention it. Those who regard

Ephesians and Colossians as non-Pauline find material here that reminds them of those letters, and declare that therefore this passage, too, cannot be by Paul. When others point out that there are in fact several points of contact between these three verses and the rest of Romans, including some themes that are very important but not so fashionable in traditional interpretations, that then becomes a two-edged sword: precisely, say the critics, and that is because whoever wrote it was trying, cunningly, to give the appearance of summing up the letter. Once an argument gets into that state it becomes like peace negotiations between intractable opponents: Both sides are dug in, and no advance seems possible.[590]

It is true that Paul does not normally conclude his letters with a doxology like this; but it is also true that Romans, real letter though it be, is not like the other letters. Nowhere else does Paul conclude an argument with a passage like 11:33-36, but we do not for that reason strike out that magnificent paean of praise. Nowhere else does Paul lay out so formal and careful a central statement of the Christian story as he does in chaps. 5–8, replete with closing christological formulae at the end of every stage of the argument; but nobody doubts that Paul deliberately wrote that extended statement at the center of this letter. What is more, the letter is from one point of view about worship, and designed to evoke worship. It is, uniquely in his writings, a book about God (see the Introduction), and one of the running themes is the true response to the true God as opposed to the rejection of this God and the turn to idols (1:5, 18-23; 2:17-24; 4:20-22; 5:12-21; 11:33-36; 12:1-2; 15:6, 9-13). After a book like this, written by a strongly monotheistic Jew, a doxology is just what we should expect. And Paul is a Jesus-centered monotheist, in the sense explored in 10:9-13; a doxology that remains monotheistic while having Jesus at the middle of it, even at the cost of verbal clarity, is somehow exactly right. An imitator might have tried a bit harder to get the grammar to work (see the Commentary on 16:27).

What is more, Paul did in fact introduce the letter and its major themes with a reference to "God's gospel concerning God's son," attested by holy Scriptures (1:2) and with the law and the prophets bearing witness to it (3:21). This was, he said at the start, the gospel in which God's righteousness was finally "revealed" (ἀποκαλύπτεται *apokalyptetai*, 1:17) or "manifested" (πεφανέρωται *pephanerōtai*, 3:21); so for him to speak, now, of the gospel proclamation as being "according to the revelation [ἀποκάλυψις *apokalypsis*] of the mystery that is now manifested [φανερωθέντος δὲ

νῦν *phanerōthentes de nun*]" echoes his wording at central thematic points, though not in a slavish or obvious way. Above all, the result of the gospel, in a phrase often skipped over in exegesis but placed by Paul at the center of his key introduction, is "the obedience of faith among all the nations" (1:5; cf. 15:18). When we meet in this passage a phrase almost identical to that, but not quite (substituting εἰς *eis* for ἐν *en*), it looks as though the same person has expressed things slightly differently, rather than that someone else has been cutting flowers out of Paul's garden and sorting them into a pretty but now rootless arrangement.

**16:25a.** The doxology is framed by the opening five Greek words and the final seven: To the one who is able to strengthen you . . . to whom be glory forever, amen!" God's "power" has been an important theme in the letter (1:16, 20; 4:21; 9:17, 22; 11:23), and Paul declared at the start that his aim in coming to visit the Christians in Rome was so that he might impart some spiritual gift to strengthen them (1:11). He is coming to Rome confident that the God he proclaims is able to do this, through the preaching of "my" gospel; as in 2:16, this does not mean that Paul has a different gospel from everybody else, but rather that he has been personally entrusted with it. This gospel consists, at its heart, of the proclamation of Jesus the Messiah.[591]

**16:25b-26.** This gospel proclamation, the announcement of the royal news of King Jesus, is the unveiling of God's long-kept secret. This chimes in with Ephesians (1:9; 3:3, 9) and Colossians (1:26-27), but is not to be dismissed for that reason; even if those letters were neither Pauline nor from a close associate, whoever wrote them thought that they were expressing Paul's thought. Paul's own apocalyptic language and its specific meaning (1:16-17; 3:21) is well summed up here. In an undoubtedly genuine letter Paul can make the revelation of God's mysteries a main theme (1 Cor 2:1, 7; 4:1; 13:2; 14:2; and esp. 15:51-52), and he has used the same language at a crucial moment in Romans itself (11:25).[592] This mystery, the long-concealed plan of God, has now

590. See the very clear analysis of the problem in Moo, *Romans,* 936-37. A helpful recent comment is I. H. Marshall, "Romans 16:25-27—An Apt Conclusion," in *Romans and the People of God: Essays in Honor of Gordon D. Fee on the Occasion of his 65th Birthday,* ed. S. K. Soderlund and N. T. Wright (Grand Rapids: Eerdmans, 1999) 170-84.

591. The καί (*kai*) cannot here mean "and" as though the proclamation of Jesus were something other than "my gospel"; it is either explicative ("namely") or intensive ("even"). See BDAG, 495-96.

592. This theme, then, is scarcely evidence of a "Marcionite" tendency in the doxology, despite C. K. Barrett, *The Epistle to the Romans,* 2nd ed. (London: A. & C. Black, 1971) 10-11.

been unveiled, and is made known to all the nations through the prophetic writings. Readers of Romans may well think of Isaiah and the rest when they hear the phrase "prophetic writings"; those who consider this doxology a later addition may well assume that the meaning is the supposedly apostolic writings, coming from early Christian "prophets." Perhaps Paul himself could have held these ideas together. His own writings, after all, not least Romans itself, are tightly interwoven with biblical prophecy. The revelation has happened according to the command of the eternal God (see the similar language in 1:20). Its purpose, as Paul said from the start, was to bring about the obedience of faith (see the Commentary on 1:5).

All this is designed to explain the significance of the gospel proclamation of Jesus Christ: when this gospel is announced, it enables people of every nation to see that in Jesus the veil has been drawn back on the eternal plan of the eternal God, and to respond in grateful and obedient loyalty and trust. And it is by this gospel that God is able to strengthen the young church, not least through Paul's ministry as he comes to Rome (1:11).

**16:27.** There remains a twist in the tail. Paul regularly moves with bewildering ease between the one God, conceived in thoroughly Jewish terms, and Jesus the Messiah, the Lord. In Romans itself we have seen a full incarnational theology, set out in 1:3-4 as a theme, developed in 5:6-11 and 8:3-4 in particular, restated in 9:5, developed again, strikingly, in 10:5-13, and then used afresh in 14:1-12. Paul has celebrated the "wisdom" of the one true God in 11:33. Now he puts the whole picture together with more regard for underlying theology than Greek grammar, which often comes off worst, after all, in the bustle and verve of his thinking. The NRSV sticks close to the Greek, with its teasing ambiguity: "To the only wise God, through Jesus Christ, to whom be glory forever! Amen." (The NIV has smoothed this out: "to the only wise God be glory forever through Jesus Christ"; similarly, KJV, RSV, NEB, REB, NJB, and a few [obviously secondary] MSS. The awkwardness of how the Greek actually puts it raises again the question as to whether a careful imitator would have dared to write something like this.)

The question is, To whom does the "to whom" refer? God? Or Jesus Christ? I suspect that Paul's answer would be: Yes. That, of course, is the meaning of "Amen."

# REFLECTIONS

The praise of God has been central to this letter, as the formal summing-up in 15:7-13 made clear. It should not surprise us that the letter ends in most MSS with an invocation of the one true and wise God, made known in and through Jesus the Messiah; or that Paul would draw together so many threads of his argument in this way. The ideal reader of Romans, in fact, is one who is prepared to heed a summons to love this one God with mind and heart alike, and who is ready to let that love transform his or her life at every level. If the God of Abraham, Isaac, and Jacob really is the creator, the God of the whole world, and if this God raised Jesus from the dead and thereby announced that he was and is the Messiah, the world's true Lord, then worship—"the *Shema* of faith"; the "living sacrifice"—is the ultimately appropriate response. Because humans are made in the image of this God, such worship renews them in this image, and indeed transforms them to bear the image of God's son, so that he might be the firstborn among many sons and daughters (8:29).

Part of that renewal is the renewal of the mind (12:2). Anyone who has wrestled with Romans will know the challenge of that renewal, and will discover mental muscles, as well as spiritual, that need to be stretched and trained. By summing up so much of the sheer intellectual content of the letter, this doxology challenges readers to turn that mental work, too, into praise, not to rest content with one activity for the study desk and another for the prayer desk.

Ultimately, Paul's vision of the renewed community is of united worship, based on shared faith (15:6, 8-13). The praise that rises to the one God from the renewed community will thus reflect God's righteousness, that covenant faithfulness in which the Jew first, and also equally the

Greek, are drawn into the one family. That is how the community will be most truly itself. And if it is to be strengthened for shared worship and living of this quality, what it needs, not merely at the beginning of its life but undergirding it all through, is the gospel, the royal announcement of Jesus Christ. That is what this letter has been all about.

# THE FIRST LETTER TO THE CORINTHIANS

INTRODUCTION, COMMENTARY, AND REFLECTIONS
BY
J. PAUL SAMPLEY

# THE FIRST LETTER TO THE
# CORINTHIANS

# INTRODUCTION

S ome seventeen years after the death of Jesus Christ, Paul, a Jew who had become a believer about fourteen years earlier, preached the gospel to certain gentiles— and perhaps to a few Jews—in Corinth, and a church was formed.

## THE CITY OF CORINTH

Located about forty miles to the south-southwest of Athens on the shoulder of the isthmus linking the Peloponese to the rest of Greece, Corinth is, as important ancient cities needed to be, strategically defensible: It is set back from its two more vulnerable shore towns, Lechaeum on the Bay of Corinth a couple of miles to the north, and Cenchreae on the Saronic Bay about six miles to the east; it backs up against the 1,500-foot elevation of Acrocorinth; and its abundant springs assure an adequate water supply.

In Paul's time, Corinth was a hub commercially and religiously. Corinth was perhaps best known for its artisans' products, such as bronzes, but it also did a thriving business in pottery and earthenware. Religious diversity was ensured by Corinth's location. By portaging the couple of miles across the Corinthian isthmus, shippers of goods between the regions of the eastern Mediterranean basin and Rome could avoid the considerable hazards of storms in the exposed Mediterranean Sea (see Acts 27:2-44). Sailors and travelers brought with them their religions and planted them so successfully in Corinth that modern archaeologists find evidence for most of the more than two dozen temples,

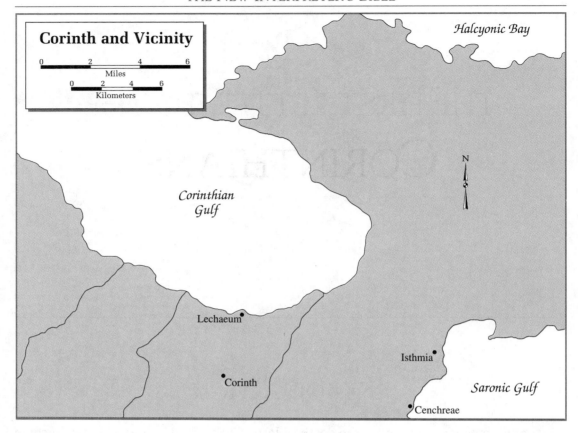

**Corinth and Vicinity**

Halcyonic Bay

Corinthian Gulf

N

Lechaeum

Isthmia

Corinth

Saronic Gulf

Cenchreae

altars, and shrines that the mid-second-century Greek chronicler Pausanias described.[1] The archaeological evidence confirms that Greek and Egyptian religious shrines coexisted there along with the Roman imperial cult. In fact, Pausanias records that alongside the forum at Corinth there was even "a temple for all the gods."[2] Also Jews, some like Prisca and Aquila, no doubt expelled by emperors Tiberius (19 CE) and Claudius (49 CE), found Corinth attractive and settled there.

Politically, Corinth enjoyed colony status, the greatest civic honor that could be accorded cities in the empire.[3] Colony status assured a special relation with the Roman Empire in which Roman laws were operative, Latin was the official governmental language (even though the populace spoke Greek and Paul's letters to Corinth are written in Greek), and as noted the imperial cult was established. Under the emperor Claudius (41–54 CE) the senate looked to Corinth even more than to Athens as the lead city of the Roman province of Achaia, and Corinth paid taxes directly to Rome well into the second century.[4] Roman proconsuls, in effect governors, went to the provinces as agents

1. Jerome Murphy-O'Connor, *St. Paul's Corinth: Texts and Archaeology* (Collegeville, Minn.: Liturgical, 1983) 78-80.

2. Pausanias 2.6–3.1.

3. See Richard E. Oster, "When Men Wore Veils to Worship: the Historical Context of 1 Corinthians 11:4," *NTS* 34 (1988) 489-93, for an excellent weighing of the significance of colony status in Corinth.

4. Victor P. Furnish, *II Corinthians* (Garden City, N.Y.: Doubleday, 1984) 9.

of imperial power; such a person was Gallio, who in 51 CE arrived in Corinth. Paul was haled before Gallio (Acts 18:12-17), and Sosthenes, who in Acts is described as the synagogue leader (ἀρχισυνάγωγος archisynagōgos, Acts 18:17), was beaten in Gallio's presence for his association with Paul and the gospel (see 1 Cor 1:1).

Whether justifiably or not, cities sometimes get a reputation, coming to be thought of as having traits, one might even say as having a sort of ethos or personality of their own. So it was with Corinth. Apart from the renowned Isthmian games that were hosted in the area every two years, Corinth was said to have a "generally superficial cultural life,"[5] which may in part ultimately be traced to Julius Caesar's reestablishment of Corinth in 44 BCE and to his populating it, along with emigrants from other parts of the empire, with eager upwardly mobile freedpersons who were unloaded from Rome's burgeoning population.[6] Understandably, the transitory nature of ancient commerce, with sailors relishing life in a city and then moving along, contributed to Corinth's becoming known as "Sin City."

Corinth's reputation for wealth without culture and for the abuse of the poor by the wealthy was so well known that Alciphron, the second- or third-century CE composer of figmentary letters reflecting bygone times, could trade on Corinth's reputation in two of his fictional letters. In one he rejoiced that he was able to escape Corinth for Athens' more friendly setting, and he characterized Corinthians as persons "without grace [or charm] and not the least convivial."[7] In the other letter, he called Corinth "the gateway to the Peloponnesus" and described it as superficially lovely enough, with its great wealth and its location "between two seas," but he found it inhabited by persons whom he once again characterized as lacking charm and grace. In the same letter he calls wealthy people's behavior disgusting, coarse, and objectionable and details the grovelling of the abject, wretched poor for the smallest morsels of food.[8] Paul's letter confirms certain details of Corinth's ethos.

Not only does Corinth have a long-standing ethos, but so does the Corinthian church. *First Clement,* a document written from the church in Rome a full generation after Paul's time, notes that the Corinthian Christians continue to "engage in partisan strife" just as in Paul's time (*1 Clem.* 47.3). Paul's letter will give evidence that the Corinthian reputation, both as a city and as a church, is well deserved.

## ESTABLISHMENT OF THE CORINTHIAN CHURCH

Paul probably arrived in Corinth for the first time in 50 CE, shortly after he had established churches in Philippi and Thessalonica, the major cities in the Roman province of Macedonia, to the north of the Aegean Sea. Our best efforts to arrive at such a date

5. Furnish, *II Corinthians,* 13.
6. Strabo 8.6.23.
7. Alciphron Letter 15.2.
8. Alciphron Letter 24.

depend on a reading of Acts 18:11 and an establishment of when the Roman provincial proconsul Gallio (whose arrival in Corinth is mentioned in Acts 18:12) was appointed. By reasonable effort we can establish that Gallio was probably appointed in the summer of 51 CE[9] and that Paul appeared before him shortly thereafter (Acts 18:12). Then, if we measure backward from that time and credit the Acts 18:11 claim that Paul had already stayed in Corinth for a year and a half prior to the time he appeared before Gallio, we deduce sometime early in 50 CE for Paul's arrival and inaugural preaching in Corinth. Furthermore, the note that 1 Corinthians is written from Ephesus (1 Cor 16:8) corroborates Acts' picture in 18:18-19 that, when he left Corinth, Paul went to Ephesus later in the summer of 51 CE after he had been haled before Gallio.

## PAUL'S EARLIEST LETTERS TO THE CORINTHIANS
## AND THE DATE OF 1 CORINTHIANS

Paul wrote the Corinthians a letter that we do not possess but that we learn about in what we call 1 Corinthians (1 Cor 5:9-12; often this lost document is referred to as the "previous letter"); so what the Bible refers to as 1 Corinthians is, in fact, Paul's second letter to them. Attempts have been made to identify 2 Cor 6:14–7:1 as a fragment of the "previous" letter, though that passage may not have been written by Paul and in any case argues that the believers should separate themselves from unbelievers, a notion contradicted in 1 Corinthians not only by the context of 1 Cor 5:9 but also by other places in which Paul clearly supposes that believers and unbelievers relate quite appropriately and openly to one another (1 Cor 7:12-16; 10:27-29; 14:24).

In the "previous" letter, Paul says that he wrote them not to associate with "immoral people," meaning by that not the immoral people of the world, because avoiding them would be an impossibility given their prevalence, but those immoral people who have become part of the believing fellowship (5:11). In part 1 Corinthians is occasioned by some ongoing Corinthian confusion regarding immorality as they had understood it in Paul's earlier—now lost—letter. The establishment of dates for the two letters must be coordinated, beginning with 1 Corinthians and then working backward to some suggestion regarding the lost "previous" letter.

Paul's travel plans mentioned at the end of 1 Corinthians (16:5-9) project a visit to Corinth (see also 1 Cor 4:21) but only after Paul stays in Ephesus until Pentecost (1 Cor 16:8), the Jewish-then-Christian festival that came fifty days after the second day of Passover. Appropriately, Paul's temporal reference has led us to assume that what we call 1 Corinthians was written in late fall or winter, leaving time for the pre-Pentecost, remaining work in Ephesus to which Paul alludes by the metaphor of the "wide door" opened to him there (1 Cor 16:9). But which fall or winter? Depending on the weight one gives Acts' portrait of Paul's work in Caesarea, Jerusalem, Antioch (Acts 18:22),

9. See Murphy-O'Connor's excellent evaluation of the evidence and choice of this date, in *St. Paul's Corinth*, 154-58.

Galatia, and Phrygia (Acts 18:23)—not to mention the time it would have taken to establish his mission in Ephesus to the point at which the "wide door" opened to him there—one may expect that 1 Corinthians was written in the fall or winter a couple of years after Paul left Corinth in late summer of 51. So the earliest reasonable estimate of the date for 1 Corinthians would be late fall or winter of 53–54 CE; at the very latest, one might stretch it to the next winter after that.

The dating of the lost letter mentioned in 1 Cor 5:9, then, would have to be enough prior to 1 Corinthians that Paul would have had occasion to discover that his effort at guidance on the issue of immorality had produced misunderstanding in the church at Corinth, though all we can say for certain is that the "previous" letter was written sometime between late summer of 51—that is, after Paul's departure from Corinth—and the fall or winter of 53 or 54.

## THE MAKEUP OF THE CORINTHIAN CHURCH

The congregation at Corinth reflects the socioeconomic and religious makeup of the city. In keeping with the "steep social pyramid"[10] that was typical of that culture, very few believers were rich, and most were poor (1 Cor 1:26). Many persons are named in 1 Corinthians or are connected to Corinth in some other New Testament writing, and we know some things about these people. Some of those who have Latin names were probably of Roman descent: Fortunatus, Quartus, and even Gaius, whose wealth is clear from Paul's description of him in Rom 16:23 as host not only of Paul but also "of the whole church" in Corinth (1 Cor 1:14). Some have Greek names: Stephanas, Achaicus, and Erastus; the latter's status and quite likely his correlate wealth are probably indicated by Paul's identification of him as Corinth's town treasurer (Rom 16:23). Some few were Jews: Aquila and Prisca, mentioned by Paul as sending greetings from Ephesus (1 Cor 16:19), were known to the Corinthians, as may be supposed from Acts 18:2 and from Paul's sweeping claim that "all the churches of the gentiles" were indebted to these two (Rom 16:3); Sosthenes, who is credited by Paul as coauthor of 1 Corinthians and whom Acts says was the leader of the Corinthian synagogue (Acts 18:17); and Apollos, whom Acts identifies as an Alexandrian Jew "well versed in the scriptures" (Acts 8:24) and was an assistant to Paul in inculcating the gospel among the Corinthians (1 Cor 3:6). In 1 Corinthians, there is absolutely no evidence of any strife or even tension in the relation of Jewish believers and gentile believers.

Not surprisingly, when one takes Alciphron's characterization of Corinth into consideration, one finds an indication that wealth and its associated status played a part in some of the struggles between Corinthian believers. Only rich persons adjudicated matters in court (chap. 6); only wealthy persons had homes and staff large enough to host the church and provide for its celebration of the Lord's supper; and only the wealthy could arrive at the dinners early enough to eat the best food and get drunk before the other, less fortunate ones could arrive (1 Cor 11:17-34).

10. Ramsay MacMullen, *Roman Social Relations 50 B.C. to A.D. 284* (New Haven: Yale University Press, 1974) 89.

Clearly, most of the Corinthian believers were gentiles. Paul, whose treatment of spiritual gifts seems determined to embrace the entire congregation (see the Commentary on 1 Cor 12:1–14:40), describes the Corinthian believers as former idolaters who *as gentiles* were misled or carried away by devotion to idols (1 Cor 12:2). The Corinthians wrote to Paul about food offered to idols (1 Cor 8:1) because in their pre-faith lives they had been free to partake in the religious festivals as a matter of course. But they are gentiles who have been taught the Scripture and traditions of Israel—surely by Paul and perhaps also by the combined efforts of Prisca, Aquila, Apollos, and Sosthenes. That Paul's churches were strongly gentile cannot be a great surprise because Paul's understanding of his call is focused on the gentiles (Rom 11:13; Gal 2:7), and when he describes his churches to the Romans he calls them "the churches of the gentiles" (Rom 16:4).

Paul successfully resocialized the gentiles who make up most of the Corinthian church into thinking of themselves as a part of the ancient people of God, as members of what he elsewhere calls the Israel of God (Gal 6:16). In fact, Paul writes to the Corinthian gentiles about "gentiles" (τὰ ἔθνη *ta ethnē*) as if the recipients can no longer be counted among those persons (12:2; 5:1; 10:20; see also Eph 2:11; 3:1; 4:17). Paul's Jewish monotheism has become theirs (1 Cor 8:4, 6). Accordingly, they view representations of other supposed deities as "idols" and meat offered in sacrifice to those deities as εἰδωλόθυτος (*eidōlothytos*, "meat offered to an idol");[11] Christ is called "our Paschal lamb" in a context in which leaven is a primary motif, without need of any explanation (5:7); the scriptures of Israel have become theirs in an authoritative fashion (see 10:26; cf. Ps 24:1); the persons in the exodus out of Egypt are unabashedly called "our ancestors" (10:1). Paul expects his readers to understand the Jewish insiders' term ἀκροβυστία (*akrobystia*) as meaning "uncircumcised" (7:18-19); they have adopted Paul's Jewish terminology for at least one day of the week, the sabbath (16:2, μία σαββάτου *mia sabbatou*); and they know the Aramaic, pre-Pauline prayer of the earliest believers, μαράνα θά (*Marana tha*, "Our Lord, come," 16:22).

## INTEGRITY AND STRUCTURE OF PAUL'S LETTER

In the past some scholars, seeing the variety of topics and failing to discern links and patterns between them, thought 1 Corinthians was made up of fragments of several letters, but now most scholars assume, as I do in this commentary, the literary integrity of 1 Corinthians.[12] Even chapter 13, whose links to the material around it are not always

---

11. Gentiles not so resocialized would have used the term ἱερόθυτος (*hierothytos*), meaning "sacrificed to a divinity." See BAGD, 372.

12. Johannes Weiss opened the debate about the integrity of 1 Corinthians, *Der erste Korintherbrief* (Göttingen: Vandenhoeck & Ruprecht, 1910), xl-xliii. Some later scholars followed him. John C. Hurd, *The Origin of 1 Corinthians* (London: SPCK, 1965; repr. Macon, Ga.: Mercer University Press, 1983) 47, is the first modern scholar to review the evidence and make a consistent case for the literary unity of 1 Corinthians. Margaret M. Mitchell, *Paul and the Rhetoric of Reconciliation* (Louisville: Westminster/John Knox, 1991) 2-5, has a good review of literature on this topic and assumes, as this commentary does, the integrity of 1 Corinthians. Hers is the strongest argument yet because she demonstrates the literary integrity of 1 Corinthians as a rhetorical whole.

explicit, functions as an encomium (see the Commentary) whose praise of love bears on what is written in the chapters on either side of it.

In one sense, the structure of 1 Corinthians is very much like other Pauline letters and, indeed, has much in common with other contemporary epistolography.[13] It opens with a salutation and thanksgiving and, after the body of the letter, closes with greetings and a blessing of the deity. On closer look, however, one sees that the letter is different from all other Pauline letters in some important particulars. Whereas Paul's letters often move toward a climactic appeal (Rom 12:1; Phil 4:2), here the *first* appeal follows directly on the thanksgiving (1:10) and is echoed in 4:16, encasing the opening chapters. Other Pauline letters seem to be dominated by one or two problems or issues that are treated by Paul's weaving them into the fabric of the letter (e.g., Philemon's concern about the runaway slave marks much of that letter; Philippians' concern with the two women's problems has recently been argued to be the main purpose in Paul's writing of that letter),[14] whereas 1 Corinthians has a string of issues or problems that Paul treats sequentially. Further, no other Pauline letter is even partially structured around answering questions that Paul's community has written to him. In 1 Corinthians, though, Paul has received a letter from the Corinthians (7:1) and needs to respond to matters they have raised in writing (see 8:1; 12:1; 16:1). Finally, the chapters that open the letter and only obliquely relate to specific Corinthian problems (chaps. 1–4) are relatively short and appear up front, setting a backdrop against which all the particular issues must be viewed. The commentary will have to inquire whether the string of issues are randomly associated or are linked to one another in some fashion.

## PAUL'S RELATION WITH THE CORINTHIANS

Paul's relationship with the Corinthians needs to be addressed in three parts. First, prior to the writing of 1 Corinthians, Paul had known the Corinthian believers for at least three years, having first evangelized there and established the church in early 50 CE, and having lived and worked with them for a year and a half that first time (Acts 18:11). The "previous" lost letter (5:9) is our primary window into what may be known about Paul and the Corinthians before 1 Corinthians. From the reference to the previous letter we may deduce some important information. First, Paul's descriptions of his efforts in that letter indicate that some, perhaps all, of the Corinthians had some confusion about Paul's teaching regarding immoral people and the need to avoid them (1 Cor 5:9-11). From 1 Corinthians it is possible to see that some of the Corinthians, in response to that earlier letter, may have tried to dissociate themselves from "immoral people" (see the question of divorcing unbelievers, 7:12-16) and even from "immorality"

13. David E. Aune, *The New Testament in Its Literary Environment* (Philadelphia: Westminster, 1987) 158-82.

14. Nils A. Dahl, "Euodia and Syntyche and Paul's Letter to the Philippians," in *The Social World of the First Christians: Essays in Honor of Wayne A. Meeks,* ed. L. M. White and O. L. Yarbrough (Minneapolis: Fortress, 1995) 3-15.

in a more general way (see married persons' thinking that they might do well to abstain from sexual intercourse, 7:2-6). Second, Paul's reference to his earlier letter suggests that he and the Corinthians were on good terms, and he readily responds to their confusion.

An additional window onto Paul's relationship with the Corinthians prior to the writing of 1 Corinthians is the letter itself; it makes no specific reference to any preceding event, to any action of Paul, or to any development among the Corinthians that, since the previous letter, has marked a change in Paul's relationship to his Corinthian followers.

First Corinthians gives abundant evidence regarding Paul's relationship to the Corinthians at the time of its composition, but the evidence has been read in a variety of ways that one could readily range along a continuum from an interpretation of 1 Corinthians as depicting Paul and the Corinthians virtually at loggerheads with one another[15] to the other extreme where the letter is read as showing that Paul and the Corinthians are on good terms with one another.[16] In either extreme and all along the interpretive continuum, no one disputes that the Corinthians are a contentious, carping bunch among themselves. But what is Paul's standing with them at the time of his writing 1 Corinthians? The evidence most often featured to claim that Paul is under heavy attack by the Corinthians is as follows:[17] Chapter 4 is taken to indicate that the Corinthians are making judgments against Paul (4:3); the "puffiness" in 4:6 is construed as "for" Apollos and "against" Paul; and Timothy is sent to reinforce Paul's own ways (4:17) in the supposed struggle. Chapters 5 and 6 are read as Paul's effort to reestablish his authority "to direct their affairs."[18] Chapter 9 is taken as a "fierce defense" of Paul in which he tries to counter their opinion that it is beneath an apostle, a wise man, to work with his own hands. The last bit of evidence on the most extreme reading of Paul as being in strife with the Corinthians is 14:37, a verse in which Paul does, indeed, brandish his authority.

Toward the other end of the continuum, where this commentary stands, one finds a stress on the call for unity among the Corinthians.[19] Rather than Paul's being on the defensive, 1:10–4:21 is Paul's censure of the Corinthians for their divisiveness; his references to himself and judgment (4:1ff.), while no doubt enhancing his own ethos, his character, serve most directly to call the divisive Corinthians to task for their fractious and thoughtless behavior toward one another.[20] The comparisons (*synkrisis*) in 4:1ff. serve the standard function of showing someone who is behaving himself properly, as in

15. Gordon D. Fee, *The First Epistle to the Corinthians* (Grand Rapids: Eerdmans, 1987), describes the letter as "combative"; e.g., "Paul is taking them on at every turn" (6); "Paul's authority is eroded" (7).

16. Mitchell, *Paul and the Rhetoric of Reconciliation*, makes a strong case that at the time of writing 1 Corinthians Paul is on good terms with the Corinthians.

17. Following Fee, *The First Epistle to the Corinthians*, 8-10.

18. Ibid., 9.

19. Mitchell, *Paul and the Rhetoric of Reconciliation*, 200, claims that the call to unity in 1:10 is the thesis statement of *"the entire letter"* (emphasis hers) and that everything subsequent serves that overriding purpose.

20. Ibid., 209-10.

the case of Paul and the other apostles, or doing it wrong, as in the case of the Corinthians;[21] and the sending of Timothy is Paul's effort to "strengthen the epistolary appeal by one who represents Paul" and is further support for his call to unity that the rest of the letter amplifies.[22] Finally, chapter 9 is not truly a "defense" but is Paul's setting up of himself as the exemplary person who forgoes the exercise of his rights in the gospel if someone might be harmed or hindered by his use of them.[23] Chapter 9 is Paul's exemplification of Christian freedom tempered by love, as the commentary will show.

Paul does relate to the Corinthians as their father in the faith (4:14) and feels responsible for them. Because he, as their father, sees problems with their conduct, he is at times harsh with them. Accordingly, he alternately warns them (4:14), shames them (6:5; 15:34), cajoles them (14:12), and encourages them (12:31; 14:20). Throughout the letter, however, his concern is to restore them to unity, to refurbish and reshape their concord, their genuine concern (his technical term for this is "love") for one another. We must be scrupulous not to tinge our reading of 1 Corinthians with the acrid atmosphere of 2 Corinthians, where matters on most fronts have deteriorated.

Between the time of 1 Corinthians and the writing of any fragment of 2 Corinthians, Paul's relationship with the Corinthians worsened. He had a "painful visit" with them when things did not go as he or they wanted (2 Cor 2:1-2). He had projected another visit and failed to show up, and some Corinthians were less than impressed (2 Cor 1:15-18). Paul's fiscal management becomes a significant problem in several ways: Some persons want to be Paul's patrons, but he refuses;[24] Paul accepts support from the Macedonians while still refusing support from the Corinthians (2 Cor 11:9); and the Corinthians' zeal for the collection destined for Jerusalem (cf. 1 Cor 16:1-4) waned considerably (2 Corinthians 8–9). But by far the most significant new development that distinguishes all of Paul's relations with the Corinthians subsequent to the time of 1 Corinthians is the arrival in Corinth of outsiders who challenge his authority (2 Cor 2:17; 3:1-3; 5:11; 10:12-18; 11:2-6, 12-15, 22-23). In 1 Corinthians the problems the Corinthians have are with one another, not with outsiders.

## PRIMARY CULTURAL PATTERNS IMPORTANT
## FOR UNDERSTANDING 1 CORINTHIANS

The Corinthians and their apostle bring certain cultural, social, and literary suppositions to their engagement with one another. Some of these suppositions need to be mentioned as a context for interpretation.

---

21. Ibid., 219-22. See also Christopher Forbes, "Comparison, Self-Praise and Irony: Paul's Boasting and the Conventions of Hellenistic Rhetoric," *NTS* 32 (1986) 2-8.

22. Mitchell, *Paul and the Rhetoric of Reconciliation*, 224-25.

23. Ibid., 244. For the best analysis of the problems with treating chap. 9 as a defense, see Mitchell's careful treatment (245) and her conclusion: "all attempts to analyze 1 Cor 9 as a true defense against actual charges have failed" (244).

24. Peter Marshall, *Enmity in Corinth: Social Conventions in Paul's Relations with the Corinthians*, WUNT 2/23 (Tübingen: Mohr/Siebeck, 1987) 218-58.

***Pater Familias.*** Paul and his readers share the knowledge that the father of the household is the one responsible for the well-being and comportment of the members of that social unit. It is the father's responsibility to inculcate values, to provide support, to enforce discipline, to train, and to protect all the members of the household. Most fundamental in carrying out these responsibilities is the father's modeling of proper behavior and comportment. The only feature of this social pattern lacking in Paul's letters is that the father trains the family members in a trade. This sweeping sense of responsibility is the proper context for Paul's epistolary efforts to have the Corinthians understand how they should properly behave (4:14-21). It also will help us to understand why it is natural for Paul—and for his readers—to set himself forward so regularly as the one who exemplifies proper life in Christ and who should, therefore, be emulated by his children in the faith.

**Honor/Shame; Praise/Blame.** The most important cultural norm in Paul's time was the attainment of honor and its equally powerful counterpart, the avoidance, or at least the minimization, of shame. Society was ordered vertically, with all persons concerned with identifying where they stood in the chain of descending power. To be sure, there were the sideward glances to see how others were doing by comparison, but decisions were made and actions were pursued with primary regard for how they would secure honor and avoid shame for oneself, how they would gain praise and limit blame. It was the understood obligation of the subordinate persons to praise and honor their benefactors, the ones on whom they found themselves dependent. The social indicators and patterns played to this structuring and to its attendant maintenance of honor. Seating assignments at social events were carefully arranged in accordance with varying degrees of status (Luke 14:7-11), and great shame was accorded anyone who breached propriety. The right to speak and, when granted, even the order in which persons were expected to speak were structured on the notions of the degree of honor.

Accordingly, when Paul writes that he does not seek to shame the Corinthians (1 Cor 4:14), when he writes something to their shame (1 Cor 6:5; 15:34), or when he mentions neither but in fact casts them in a shameworthy light (1 Cor 11:17-22), he will have hit on a hot-button item.

**Patron/Client.** In Paul's time everyone had a lord—that is, someone who could rightly be construed as being over someone else, to whom that someone else belonged or was indebted, and to whom that one was responsible. It was not just slaves who belonged to someone. Everyone right up the chain belonged to another person. Even Marcus Aurelius, the Roman emperor, mused that he was responsible to the gods. And one's comportment was understood as being keyed to pleasing one's lord, to whom one was responsible. Great effort was expended in nurturing, cultivating, and even increasing the number of one's patrons; equally prodigious care was given to one's clients to make sure that they remembered their indebtedness and to ensure that they took proper steps to show honor and praise. And so it was up and down the social ladder. One person's client was patron to many below. The power that one received from one's patron was used, by careful distribution of it to one's selected clients, and was subsequently passed on by them to clients who were then in turn indebted to them. Indebtedness and obligation were the fabric of this culture.

An abiding issue before the Corinthians in this letter is the identity of the one to whom they belong—that is Paul's way of tapping this cultural reservoir as a means of expressing the basic and defining relationship in all of life. Paul consistently reminds them that it is the Lord Jesus Christ to whom they are responsible and whom they must please. All are clients of a superior patron, and their actions are to yield honor, not shame, to their Lord. Some Corinthians seek to place themselves in the superior position with regard to other believers and thus to "lord" it over them. Status seeking will be an abiding problem with which Paul is confronted in 1 Corinthians. Paul's countercultural understanding of the gospel runs head-on into this social convention when, with its associated status seeking, it bears on how believers get along with each other.

**Stoics.** In Paul's time Stoics carried the day. One hardly needed to choose to be a Stoic or even to think of oneself as being a Stoic in certain ways; it was so much in the air that it was a part of the common coinage of life and its exchanges. Accordingly, Paul can and does use Stoic patterns and conceptions as a means of advancing his arguments and of explicating what it means to live the faith. For example, he frequently employs the Stoic conviction that certain matters are indifferent *adiaphora*, and he may even identify, as the Stoics surely did, things preferred and things not preferred from among those indifferent considerations (see 1 Corinthians 7). Another example could be Paul's conviction, expressed in different ways across the letter, that God has allocated or arranged matters as God has chosen (3:5; 7:17; 12:18, 24).

**Rhetoric and 1 Corinthians.** Rhetoric is the art of persuasion. In Paul's time, rhetoric was the basic form of education for those who could afford it. A growing body of scholarly studies of Paul show that he was indeed well tutored in rhetoric.[25] Even those not trained in rhetoric, as the majority of the Corinthians surely were not, were accustomed to it and knew its conventions by having lived in a rhetorical culture. All written and spoken words were rhetorical, so, in order to understand what was written or said, one always has to consider the rhetoric of what is there. To call something rhetorical is not to be confused with dismissing it as empty, as form prevailing over content. Everything in 1 Corinthians, therefore, is rhetorical, and we as interpreters of it must regularly inquire of its rhetorical force.

There were three types of rhetoric in those days. The first, *judicial rhetoric,* had its focus on the courtroom and generally inquired regarding what had happened in the past in order to make some judgment. The second, *deliberative rhetoric,* concerned itself with deliberations about what one should or should not do in the future, though that future

25. Duane F. Watson, "The New Testament and Greco-Roman Rhetoric: A Bibliography, *JETS* 31 (1988) 465-72, and "The New Testament and Greco-Roman Rhetoric: A Bibliographical Update," *JETS* 33 (1990) 513-24.

could be quite imminent. The third type, *epideictic rhetoric,* concerned itself with praise and blame either of an individual or of a virtue or vice and had its primary focus on the present, the way things are, or, in the case of a virtue, as things should be. In a general and overall way, documents from that time tend to fall in one of those three categories, though the rhetorical handbooks clearly caution that no rhetorician of any worth sticks to one category, but freely mixes them according to the needs of the occasion.[26] First Corinthians falls primarily into the category of deliberative rhetoric, although there are features of the letter in which Paul employs, as we shall see, some judicial rhetoric and some epideictic rhetoric.[27]

The apostle and letter writer Paul, the Corinthians and some perceived problem or problems with them, and constraints consisting, for example, of shared beliefs and experiences—all three together form the rhetorical situation that must be the context for our evaluation of 1 Corinthians.[28] The dynamic among the three can never be out of sight. In this situation our primary data consists in the letter itself. In the letter we have most directly Paul's efforts to persuade the Corinthians; we can identify Paul's strategy, what he aims for, what he values or affirms, what he considers useless, and what he denies. We have less access and certainty to whether Paul understood his recipients and whether he reflects them and what is going on there accurately. In the letter we can see Paul's assessment of the Corinthians and of what they have been doing; even there, however, in the letter itself we can sense and will actually see evidence that Paul's estimate of the maturity of the Corinthian believers is at dissonance with what they probably thought about themselves (see 3:1ff.). As tempting as it might be, we cannot assume that we can penetrate the thoughts of the persons to whom the letter was written. So, positively put, what we do have greatest access to as we approach the letter are Paul's rhetorical moves and steps, and those will be of great interest in the study that follows.

According to Demetrius of Phalerum (c. 4th cent. BCE), and regardless of which of the three types of rhetoric one used, there were really only three options available to someone, like Paul, who wanted to call upon a person or a group to alter their behavior: flattery, adverse criticism, or figured speech ("indirect speech" or the "covert hint" as it may otherwise be called).[29] In 1 Corinthians we will see that Paul at different times uses each of the three, though in the culture and in the letter the last one, "figured, indirect speech" or the "covert hint," is the most common.[30] In each case we will have to take care to interpret whatever Paul writes within the conventions appropriate to the option he employs in that section.

26. Although epideictic rhetoric focuses on praise and blame, these topics are also appropriate to and are found in judicial and deliberative rhetoric. See *Ad Herennium* 3.8.15.

27. See Mitchell, *Paul and the Rhetoric of Reconciliation,* 165, where she recognizes that 1 Corinthians 13 is an encomium.

28. See Lloyd F. Bitzer, "The Rhetorical Situation," *Philosophy and Rhetoric* 1 (1968) 1-14, esp. 6-8.

29. Demetrius of Phalerum *On Style* 9.2.66.

30. Frederick Ahl, "The Art of Safe Criticism in Greece and Rome," *AJP* 105 (1984) 204: indirect speech was "the normal mode of discourse thoughout much of Greek and Roman antiquity."

At points in the commentary it will be noted that Paul uses certain topoi or commonplaces to advance his case. For a first example, much note will be taken of exemplification. Like any good parent in that time, Paul, as the Corinthians' father in the faith, details positive and negative models of the faith and himself patterns the way his children in the faith should behave. In a second example, Paul several times employs synecdoche, a literary device in which reference is made to something by identifying one of its parts, where the part (e.g., wheels) represents and stands for the whole (e.g., car). Third, there will be several occasions to note that Paul uses a ring device called inclusio to tie together a literary unit or to finish a thought. Fourth, maxims, pithy distillations of generally accepted truths, are a feature of rhetoric in antiquity and in Paul's letters.

Paul displays a fundamental ambivalence to culture and the patterns in the world around the Corinthian believers. At times he embraces cultural conventions and patterns. At other times he distances himself and his believers from them. Perhaps such an ambivalence was unavoidable because Paul made the decision not to lead his believers to a Qumran-like isolation; perhaps it was inevitable because human transactions are always couched in culturally transmitted conventions and exchanges. Perhaps it was unavoidable because most persons have blind spots where their convictions have not fully penetrated every nook and cranny of their lives. In Paul's case, perhaps he did not carry his gospel-powered critique through consistently into every facet of his and his congregations' lives. However it happened, Paul's relation to the culture in which he and his followers lived is mixed. A few examples will illustrate the range of Paul's appropriation and critique of cultural patterns.

Beginning with an example of Paul's being critical of cultural patterns, he objects when the Corinthians use their worldly power and status to get their way in the community of believers. He severely chides the wealthy Corinthians for having taken poorer believers to court in order to have their own way (chap. 6) and for abusing their power as hosts of the Lord's supper (11:17-34). For an uncritical appropriation of cultural patterns, consider Paul's blithe assumption that men should have short hair and women should keep theirs long (11:6, 14-15). In between those extremes Paul seems to think that believers can live directly in the world, in the midst of the world's cultural patterns, without the culture's determining their stance or moral choices. We see that sort of reflection most clearly in 1 Corinthians when Paul writes about living ὡς μή (hōs mē), "as if not," which closely approximates John's expression of living "in the world" but not "of the world" (7:29-31; John 13:1; 15:19). In that passage and in its context, Paul encourages believers to live "as if not" because "the appointed time has grown short" (7:29 NRSV). Because God's purposes with the world (which include refurbishing it, Romans 8) are drawing to a close, Paul is convinced that the patterns of the world have lost their power, that believers experience a liberation from the definitional influence of social patterns and of participation in the world. Accordingly, Paul thinks that believers live their lives of faith while finding themselves within the world, whose present form is passing away (1 Cor 7:31).

## ESPECIALLY PROMINENT CONVICTIONS SEEN IN 1 CORINTHIANS

Occasionally, the commentary will elaborate on what Paul, in a particular passage, either takes for granted or alludes to with the slightest clue. In those circumstances, I will draw on the other Pauline letters as a way of illuminating what Paul and his readers took for granted without saying as much in full detail. Whatever Paul may write to any of his churches, he has a common framework in which he thinks of the gospel. The frame runs from Paul's foundational conviction on the one horizon that Christ's death and resurrection inaugurate the new creation, the redemption of creation, to the other horizon—indeed, to the end of the age at Christ's parousia when God's purposes, begun in Christ's death and resurrection, come to a conclusion.[31] This latter is a time of judgment when all will have to stand (or fall) before God and Christ and give an accounting for the life they have lived and for their actions.

For Paul, the Christian faith is lived in community. The individual is never simply and singly related to God. If "faith" is Paul's code word for right relation to God, then "love" is Paul's code word for right relation to others. Love, the proper caring for another, is the necessary expression of faith, the proper relating to God, because faith expresses itself in love (Gal 5:6). Caring for other believers, building them up, encouraging them, consoling and even warning them, are not options for believers; they are a requirement of faith. We can see this in 1 Corinthians because some of the believers there seem to have focused their attention on themselves and on God and ignored, neglected, or disregarded others; and Paul simply cannot abide it. In this sense, the whole of 1 Corinthians is a study in love.

Paul recognizes that the very constitution of community requires a sort of give-and-receive transaction between the individuals and the community. To be a believer apart from community is inconceivable for Paul. Therefore, believers must be ready to accommodate to the community. That accommodation always entails contributing to the enrichment of the fellowship by putting whatever gifts one has in service to the common good. Perhaps more problematic for modern readers, sometimes integration into the community will cause the individual to override selfishness or the rather natural desire to seek what seems so clearly in one's own self-interest. Paul's assumption is that all individuals in the association will share in the benefits of the affiliation (e.g., security, mutual care and protection, etc.). While Paul's reflections on this balance between individual and community appear at several points in 1 Corinthians, they are expressed most directly in chapter 9.

Paul is so committed to the community as the matrix of the life of faith that when he sees a conflict between the rights of the individual and the rights of the community, he will regularly recommend that the individual eschew the pursuit of individual rights and choose the community's well-being instead. First Corinthians shows this Pauline trait

31. See "The Two Horizons of Paul's Thought World," in J. Paul Sampley, *Walking Between the Times: Paul's Moral Reasoning* (Minneapolis: Fortress, 1991) 7-24.

when Paul advises that the ones who speak in tongues withhold expression of them if no one is there to interpret (14:28) and that when one is speaking and another receives a revelation, the speaker should give way (14:30). Paul exemplifies this pattern when he expresses his willingness never to eat meat if it might cause another to stumble (8:13).

We must be careful, however, because in all of his concern for the health of the community, Paul never denigrates the importance of the believer's individuality. Variety and difference are not sacrificed for community. Rather, Paul strives to integrate the distinctiveness of individuals and relishes the importance of difference to the wholesomeness of the fellowship. Accordingly, he acknowledges that different people eat all sorts of different things while others have restrictive diets (8:7-13; 10:25-31); some have homes in which to host the church, and, probably in a rhetorical overstatement, some have nothing (11:18-22); some have a few χαρίσματα (*charismata*), gifts, and others have many (12:4-11; 14:1-5); some live with the law as the defining center of their lives while others do not (9:20-21); some plant, and others water (3:6-9); and every person experiences testing as if it belonged to that person alone (10:13). But each and every one of these quite distinctively individuated persons is welcome, is important, and is even necessary to the body of Christ.

Paul assumes that believers should be responsible moral agents, that their lives are not simply driven from the heart, and that their minds should be integrated with their spirits in all of their moral reasoning. His is the integrated life, at once moral, deliberative, and spiritual—and he models it for those who would follow him. All of life, in every moment and in every situation, must be lived as ready for God's final judgment, not in quaking boots betokening lack of confidence in God's grace active in one's life, but in thankfulness to God for great and abiding mercy, ever present in good and in tough times. Contemplated conduct, therefore, must be weighed with regard to several considerations: how it expresses God's love for us, how appropriate it is to the strength of our faith, and how it affects others.

Different believers are of differing maturity. Some are "babies" in the faith; others are more mature; none are completely mature. As surely as babies learn to crawl and later walk but can carry no additional load, and as more mature persons can not only walk but also carry burdens for themselves and for others, so also Paul thinks it is with believers. Though Paul comes nearest to discussing this problem directly in Gal 6:1-5, it is an issue in 1 Corinthians, where the commentary will show that Paul thinks at least some of the Corinthians are babies in the faith and surely are not as mature as they think they are (3:1-4). Elsewhere in the letter Paul takes their fractiousness as evidence of their immaturity in the faith.

Because of that dissonance between their self-estimation and Paul's, his letter urges them to take careful stock of their standing and of their maturity. Some of the believers at Corinth have (falsely, Paul declares) thought of themselves as having arrived at the fullness of what God can bestow; they have become "arrogant" or "puffed up" as he sometimes puts it. Their arrogance is having deleterious effects on their fellow believers, who seem altogether too ready to accept their compatriots' puffy self-estimate and, with it, too low a self-estimate of themselves. Out of that low self-esteem, the less puffy Corinthians live as if they have less to offer the community of believers. A considerable part of Paul's effort in 1 Corinthians is aimed at bringing all sorts of quite different people back into full and equal participation in the community.

First Corinthians is a case study of several features of the Christian life as it has been experienced through the centuries. First, it is a classic for the problems of unity because, after all, that is one of the major problems across the issues reflected in the letter. Churches, like other social groups, are subject to fractiousness from all sorts of sources, and Corinth certainly has its share. Whether it is wealthy persons treating the poorer with disdain, or especially religiously gifted persons becoming arrogant, prideful, and disdainful of those less gifted, or persons of whatever socioeconomic bracket who think first of themselves and little about the needs of others, or persons who overestimate how strong they are in faith, or persons who have low self-esteem and cower timidly before those they consider more advanced—the list could go on—the church at Corinth has them all.

Likewise, Paul's response to those challenges of the Corinthian believers' unity is a study in distinguishing genuine unity from uniformity. Paul labors to help the Corinthians see that they truly belong to one another in Christ despite the differences of gifts and graces they exhibit. In fact, Paul goes that one better: It is precisely in the differences they bring to the community that he sees the creative, stimulating work of the Holy Spirit. The community's health and growth depend on each person's contributing what the Spirit offers through him or her to the common good of all. Without the variety and distinctiveness that each one brings, the faithful community would be a pale imitation of what it ought to be.

## 1 CORINTHIANS AS A WINDOW ON EARLY CHRISTIANITY

Paul's letters provide a vista onto the earliest known Christian communities, on churches that existed perhaps as much as a generation ahead of the time the Gospels were written. Paul, the Jew who opposed the earliest Christian movement (2 Cor 11:22; Gal 1:14; Phil 3:3-11), took the gospel to gentiles (non-Jews), who largely populated his churches. In doing so, he did not require circumcision, the traditional mark of belonging to God's people. In its place, as a ritual of admission, Paul required baptism. Even though he did not himself baptize many Corinthians (1 Cor 1:14-17), they *were* baptized. Paul gladly reasons from his convictions about baptism and its significance (1 Cor 12:13; 7:17-24). Though the congregation at Corinth was predominantly gentile (1 Cor 12:2; 8:4-6; 10:6-14), Paul clearly considers them, along with himself, to be God's children (1 Cor 1:3).

Paul's churches, like their synagogue counterparts, regularly gathered in homes.

Because the Corinthians' assemblies were so chaotic (1 Cor 14:26-33), and because the Corinthians abused the Lord's supper (1 Cor 11:17-34), we learn a great deal about their practices and about Paul's suggestions of how they ought to comport themselves.

We tend to think of the apocalyptic Paul as making sharp distinctions between his communities, their comportment, and their life-style and that of their neighbors, and from 1 Corinthians 5–6 we will see that, indeed, we should; but the separation is far from absolute. Paul thinks that believers can have dealings with unbelievers (1 Cor 10:27); indeed, some are married to unbelievers (1 Cor 7:12-16), and some unbelievers apparently freely wander into worship occasions. Paul considers none of these exchanges between believers and unbelievers as inappropriate.

## PAUL'S LETTERS

Paul's letters—all of them—are situational documents in which he writes concerning the problems he thinks need attention in that particular community of believers. First Corinthians is through and through an argument for unity that honors distinctiveness and diversity; for the believers' proper care of one another, which at the same time is grounded in an accurate self-assessment; and for the formation and upbuilding of maturity of faith that leaves no one out. First Corinthians is a textbook on moral reasoning and on the relation of the individual with the community.

Because we are not privy to what Paul and the Corinthians knew about each other and what the latter knew about Paul's teaching, we are sometimes left with having to take what appears in the letter only as a clue, an allusion, and to figure out what is the larger picture that Paul and the Corinthians may know quite well. We can sometimes reconstruct that larger picture from what we find in the other letters; indeed, we must do so if we are to understand the allusions. So from time to time the commentary will refer to what we can know from the other Pauline letters.

Thirteen New Testament letters name Paul as author, but scholars have long since wondered about the authenticity of that claim with regard to some of the letters. Concerning seven of them, 1 Corinthians included, almost no one doubts the Pauline authorship: Romans, 1 and 2 Corinthians, Galatians, Philippians, 1 Thessalonians, and Philemon.[32] After that group, though, scholarly consensus breaks down. Some scholars deem 2 Thessalonians, Colossians, and Ephesians authentic as well, but some, including me, find these letters to be what we would call Paulinist, indicating that they have come from someone in the Pauline school who writes in Paul's name and represents the Pauline tradition after the apostle has died. A smaller subset of scholars claim authenticity for the Pastoral Epistles, 1 and 2 Timothy, and Titus.[33]

32. L. E. Keck, *Paul and His Letters,* 2nd ed. (Philadelphia: Fortress, 1988) 5-6. This judgment also informed the decision of the Pauline Theology Group of the Society of Biblical Literature to focus on the seven mentioned letters. The papers from that seminar were subsequently published as *Pauline Theology,* 3 vols. (Minneapolis: Fortress, 1991–95).

33. See Luke T. Johnson, *The Writings of the New Testament* (Philadelphia: Fortress, 1986) 242-407, who argues for the authenticity of all the letters that bear Paul's name.

This commentary will pay especial attention to the six other letters about which no one has questions of Pauline authorship. Occasionally, I may refer the reader to a passage in the Paulinist tradition (2 Thessalonians, Ephesians, Colossians, 1 and 2 Timothy, and Titus) for further illumination or comparison.

## CONCLUDING NOTES

Though we know that chapter designations were added to the biblical texts only in the Middle Ages and that subdivisions into verses came about even later, nevertheless in the commentary I refer to chapters and verses as a means of handy reference. The reader of this commentary will note, however, that I cite occasions where the relatively modern divisions of the text into chapters and paragraphs and verses do not reflect the sections and turning points in Paul's argument.

The translations in the commentary and in the reflections are my own, unless otherwise indicated. In order to make clear to modern readers the semantic range of a given Greek term, I sometimes give additional possible translations of the same term by different English words separated by a slash—for example, Paul's mention of "this authority/freedom of yours" in 8:9. My hope is that such a translation will provide the readers of this commentary with additional information by which they can appreciate the different nuances that ἐξουσία (*exousia*), for example, may have in that verse.

In this commentary the recipients of 1 Corinthians are frequently referred to as "hearers" or "auditors" because the majority of the Corinthians were surely illiterate (1:26) and, therefore, dependent upon someone else to read the letter to them. So most Corinthian believers experienced this letter as a heard communication.

The term "Christian" is lacking in the commentary sections because Paul and his readers did not have this term as a self-description; it was a later development.[34]

34. My deepest gratitude goes to my wife, Sally Backus Sampley, for her love, for her careful scrutiny of this entire work, and for her numerous insightful suggestions, and to Suzanne Webber for her helpful editoral recommendations across the commentary.

## BIBLIOGRAPHY

(Author's note: Because of publication delays and other publishing commitments, I was unable to take into consideration works published since February 1997.)

Aune, David E. *The New Testament in Its Literary Environment.* Philadelphia: Westminster, 1987. A comprehensive, solid treatment of the literary context for interpreting the New Testament.

Conzelmann, Hans. *A Commentary on the First Epistle to the Corinthians.* Translated by J. W. Leitch. Hermeneia. Philadelphia: Fortress, 1975. Strong in its use of references to the Greco-Roman context for understanding Paul's points.

Fee, Gordon D. *The First Epistle to the Corinthians.* Grand Rapids: Eerdmans, 1987. A resourceful commentary, indicating standard scholarly options throughout, but reading the letter as showing Paul at loggerheads with the Corinthians.

Fitzgerald, John. *Cracks in an Earthern Vessel: An Examination of the Catalogues of Hardships in the Corinthian Correspondence.* SBLDS 99. Atlanta: Scholars Press, 1988. A thoughtful study of hardship lists in the Greco-Roman world; sheds light on Paul's usage.

Forbes, Christopher. "Comparison, Self Praise and Irony: Paul's Boasting and the Conventions of Hellenistic Rhetoric." *NTS* 32 (1986).

Krentz, Edgar M. "Military Language and Metaphors in Philippians." In *Origins and Method: Towards a New Understanding of Judaism and Christianity, Essays in Honour of John C. Hurd.* Edited by B. H. McLean. JSNTSup 88. Sheffield: Academic, 1993.

Lampe, Peter. "Theological Wisdom and the 'Word About the Cross': The Rhetorical Scheme in 1 Corinthians 1-4." *Int* 44 (1990).

Lyons, George. *Pauline Autobiography: Toward a New Understanding.* SBLDS 73. Atlanta: Scholars Press, 1985. A successfully iconoclastic rereading of Paul's autobiographical claims.

MacMullen, Ramsay. *Roman Social Relations 50 B.C. to A.D. 284.* New Haven: Yale University Press, 1974. A readable picture of the social world of that time.

Malherbe, Abraham J. "Determinism and Free Will in Paul: The Argument of 1 Corinthians 8 and 9." In *Paul in His Hellenistic Context.* Edited by T. Engberg-Pedersen. Minneapolis: Fortress, 1995.

Marshall, Peter. *Enmity in Corinth: Social Conventions in Paul's Relations with the Corinthians.* WUNT 2/23. Tübingen: Mohr/Siebeck, 1987. Friendship and enmity as a context for understanding Paul's relations with the Corinthians.

Meeks, Wayne A. *The First Urban Christians: The Social World of the Apostle Paul.* New Haven: Yale University Press, 1983. The best general treatment of Paul's relationship to his social setting.

Mitchell, Margaret M. *Paul and the Rhetoric of Reconciliation.* Louisville: Westminster/John Knox, 1991. An outstanding study of 1 Corinthians in the light of ancient rhetorical practice, social conventions, and norms.

Murphy-O'Connor, Jerome. *St. Paul's Corinth: Texts and Archaeology.* Collegeville, Minn.: Liturgical, 1983. A useful sourcebook on texts and archaeology related to Corinth.

Pogoloff, Stephen. *Logos and Sophia: The Rhetorical Situation of 1 Corinthians.* SBLDS 134. Atlanta: Scholars Press, 1992. Understands the Corinthian divisiveness as having a basis in rhetoric and associated social status, but thinks that the divisions form around Paul and Apollos.

Ramsaran, Rollin A. *Liberating Words: Paul's Use of Rhetorical Maxims in 1 Corinthians 1–10.* Valley Forge, Pa.: Trinity, 1996. Especially helpful in understanding how maxims functioned in the Greco-Roman culture and in 1 Corinthians.

Sampley, J. Paul. *Walking Between the Times: Paul's Moral Reasoning.* Minneapolis: Fortress, 1991. A study of what grounds and shapes Paul's moral reasoning.

Sigountos, J. G. "The Genre of 1 Corinthians 13." *NTS* 40 (1994).

Smit, J. "The Genre of 1 Corinthians 13 in the Light of Classical Rhetoric." *NovT* 33 (1991).

Theissen, Gerd. *The Social Setting of Pauline Christianity: Essays on Corinth.* Edited and translated by J. H. Schütz. Philadelphia: Fortress, 1982. An early and formative study on social considerations as illuminating Paul's relation to the Corinthians.

Tuckett, C. M. "The Corinthians Who Say 'There Is No Resurrection of the Dead' (1 Cor 15,12)." In *The Corinthian Correspondence.* Edited by R. Bieringer. Leuven: Leuven University Press, 1996.

Willis, W. L. *Idol Meat in Corinth: The Pauline Argument in 1 Corinthians 8 and 10.* SBLDS 68. Chico, Calif.: Scholars Press, 1985. A study of Paul's argument against the background of Hellenistic cultic meals.

Winter, B. W. "Civil Litigation in Secular Corinth and the Church. The Forensic Background to 1 Corinthians 6.1-8." *NTS* 37 (1991).

Wuellner, William. "Greek Rhetoric and Pauline Argumentation." In *Early Christian Literature and the Classical Intellectual Tradition: In honorem Robert M. Grant.* Edited by W. R. Schoedel and R. L. Wilken. Théologie Historique 54. Paris: Etudes Beauchesne, 1979.

Zaas, P. S. "Catalogues and Context: 1 Corinthians 5 and 6." *NTS* 34 (1988).

# OUTLINE OF 1 CORINTHIANS

III. 1 Corinthians 7:1-40, Paul's Response to Questions About Relations in Sociosexual Groups

    A. 7:1-7, Husbands and Wives

    B. 7:8-9, Widowers and Widows

    C. 7:10-11, Married Believers and Divorce

    D. 7:12-16, Marriage Between Believers and Unbelievers

    E. 7:17-24, Indifferent Matters: Jew, Greek, Slave, Free

    F. 7:25-28, Counsel for the Unmarried: Paul's Own Maxim

    G. 7:29-35, A Digression Regarding Life Lived Eschatologically

    H. 7:36-38, Betrothed Unmarrieds and the Idealized Responder

    I. 7:39-40, Divorce, Widowhood, and Remarriage

IV. 1 Corinthians 8:1–11:1, Paul's Response to a Corinthian Question About Eating Idol Meat

    A. 8:1-6, Their Question, Their Assumption, Paul's Rehearsal of What They Know

    B. 8:7-13, Persons Differ in Knowledge—An Imaginary and Instructive Scenario

    C. 9:1–10:13, Extended Digression Consisting of Two Examples

        9:1-27, Paul As Exemplar
          9:1-2, Identification of Paul As Free and As Apostle
          9:3-14, Paul, the One of Unexcelled Rights, Chooses Not to Use Them
          9:15-18, Paul, Free Not to Exercise His Rights, Is Bound to Preach the Gospel
          9:19-23, Paul's Evangelistic and Exemplary Adaptability
          9:24-27, Paul, the Athlete Who Takes Care Not to Be Disqualified
        10:1-13, The Exodus Retold As a Caution

    D. 10:14-22, Paul's Application: "Flee Idolatry"

    E. 10:23–11:1, A Second Summing-Up

V. 1 Corinthians 11:2–14:40, Three Worship Practices of the Community

    A. 11:2-16, Proper Comportment of Women in Worship

    B. 11:17-34, Not the Lord's Supper

G. 16:21, Autograph

H. 16:22, Enforcement Formula

I. 16:23-24, Concluding Grace

# 1 CORINTHIANS 1:1–4:21

## OPENING AND APPEAL

### OVERVIEW

Paul's undisputed letters share similar structural features. They open with a salutation, which is usually followed by a thanksgiving and the body of the letter. Somewhere in the body of the letter, most often toward the end of the body, Paul makes a direct appeal. Following the body, Paul's letters usually close with a special section of greetings. A grace always concludes Paul's letters. First Corinthians generally accords with these patterns.

## 1 CORINTHIANS 1:1-9, LETTER OPENING

### 1 Corinthians 1:1-3, Salutation

<table>
<tr><td>

NIV

1 Paul, called to be an apostle of Christ Jesus by the will of God, and our brother Sosthenes,

²To the church of God in Corinth, to those sanctified in Christ Jesus and called to be holy, together with all those everywhere who call on the name of our Lord Jesus Christ—their Lord and ours:

³Grace and peace to you from God our Father and the Lord Jesus Christ.

</td><td>

NRSV

1 Paul, called to be an apostle of Christ Jesus by the will of God, and our brother Sosthenes,

2To the church of God that is in Corinth, to those who are sanctified in Christ Jesus, called to be saints, together with all those who in every place call on the name of our Lord Jesus Christ, both their Lord[a] and ours:

3Grace to you and peace from God our Father and the Lord Jesus Christ.

[a] Gk theirs

</td></tr>
</table>

### COMMENTARY

The salutations of Paul's letters share a common structure with most letters of his time: Person A to Person B, Greetings. However, Paul elaborates each part of this structure in accordance with his particular convictions and purposes. In this letter, he identifies himself as an apostle called by God's will; Sosthenes is "the brother," meaning part of God's family (1:1; cf. Phlm 1, 7, 16, 20). When

Paul opens a letter by declaring himself an apostle, we can be certain either that there is some problem in his relationship with the readers or that he wants to reaffirm his apostolic authority as leverage for what he is about to write (see Phil 1:1; Phlm 1). The motif of calling ("election" and "choosing" are semantic alternatives) is echoed in Paul's description of his addressees (1:2) and will reappear for further reflection in 1:26-31. The Corinthians are called to be saints—that is, to live the life of sanctified ones ("saint," "sanctified," "holy" are all from the same Greek root), meaning that they are set apart for or claimed by God. Paul immediately places the Corinthian church in the larger context of all the other believers (1:2), wherever they may be, who share the trusting dependency that is implied in "calling upon the name of the Lord."

Paul radically reshapes the standard letter "greetings" into what amounts to a blessing, a benediction (1:3). All of his undisputed letters have the identical formula, perhaps because it is so foundational to the Christian life. In this opening, framing statement, grace—God's freely given, unmerited gift or favor—is featured; for Paul, God's grace not only makes possible the beginning

of faith but also sustains the believers throughout their lives; grace is the indispensable ground of the life of faith from its beginning to its end. Likewise, peace describes the believers' new relation to God (see Rom 5:1, 10). Can one possibly imagine that when Paul the Jew says "peace" he does not affirm in it the *shalom* of God's proper ordering of the world and human relations within it?

The remainder of 1:3 affirms in a definitional way believers' relation to God and to Christ. God is here depicted as father of the family with both authority and responsibility for the members; implicit is the understanding that those for whom God is father are brothers and sisters of one another. Christ is designated Lord—that is, the one to whom believers belong, who governs the lives of the believers and assures them protection.

# REFLECTIONS

**1.** We share with those Corinthians our having been called and being saints. Paul is "called"; the Corinthians are "called." In our time, we tend to think that only ministers or priests are called, but Paul views all believers as those who have been called by God ("vocation," as distinguished from "career," is a term built from the Latin equivalent of the Greek term). Paul's use of "call" is a way of affirming God's grace (see 1:3) as the ground of new life in Christ, of election (which is literally a "calling out"). All believers are called; sometimes the call has a particular task integral to it (e.g., Paul is to be apostle to the gentiles); typically, the call is to be lived directly in the life context where one is called (see 1 Cor 7:17-24); and at the judgment God will determine whether one has lived faithfully with regard to one's call. Infant baptism is the ultimate expression of God's calling people and claiming them even before they are capable of reaching out to God.

"Saints" is a specialized term in Paul's lexicon. It means "those who have been set apart for God" (Lev 11:44-45). "Called" persons are saints because God has claimed them, because God has set them apart as God's own people. Again, this is an affirmation of God's grace; to be a saint is like a trust, a stewardship, that God gives into a person's care. The same root Greek term for "saint" is found in "sanctification" (see 1:2) and "holy" (see 3:17). Modern uses of the term, so different from Paul's, assume that a person has managed to rise to an extraordinary level of moral performance. So to have someone call us a saint would be an embarrassment of inappropriateness. If we were to appropriate Paul's usage, we would know that each of us is a saint because we belong to God, apart from any question about our moral rectitude. Then we saints should live a life appropriate to our God who has called us.

**2.** Every one of Paul's letters opens with an affirmation of God's grace, and every letter closes with grace, because grace, God's freely given, unmerited gift, is the alpha and omega of the life of faith. All of life in Christ, at every point (1:4), depends on God's freely bestowed favor and is marked by God's favorable disposition toward believers. Grace is in the call that has already inaugurated our life in Christ; grace is the power of God to support and sustain us in the midst of a broken world; and grace is the assurance that, as Paul puts it, "God is for us" (see Rom 8:31-39) even in times of loss and death (1 Cor 15:57).

**3.** Though Paul's churches seem to have been house churches, localized gatherings that met in the home of one of the believers, Paul always sees believers everywhere as belonging to one another, as belonging to God's family, as those who are granted the power to call upon the name of their shared Lord. The church becomes our true family. As Jesus said: "Whoever does the will of God is my brother and sister and mother" (Mark 3:35 NRSV).

# 1 Corinthians 1:4-9, Thanksgiving

NIV

4I always thank God for you because of his grace given you in Christ Jesus. 5For in him you have been enriched in every way—in all your speaking and in all your knowledge— 6because our testimony about Christ was confirmed in you. 7Therefore you do not lack any spiritual gift as you eagerly wait for our Lord Jesus Christ to be revealed. 8He will keep you strong to the end, so that you will be blameless on the day of our Lord Jesus Christ. 9God, who has called you into fellowship with his Son Jesus Christ our Lord, is faithful.

NRSV

4I give thanks to my[a] God always for you because of the grace of God that has been given you in Christ Jesus, 5for in every way you have been enriched in him, in speech and knowledge of every kind— 6just as the testimony of[b] Christ has been strengthened among you— 7so that you are not lacking in any spiritual gift as you wait for the revealing of our Lord Jesus Christ. 8He will also strengthen you to the end, so that you may be blameless on the day of our Lord Jesus Christ. 9God is faithful; by him you were called into the fellowship of his Son, Jesus Christ our Lord.

[a] Other ancient authorities lack *my*  [b] Or *to*

# COMMENTARY

Like every moment of the life in Christ, Paul grounds his communications in thanksgiving to God ("always," 1:4). The 1 Corinthians thanksgiving lays out the scope of the Christian life, from the inception of God's grace given in Christ to the "day of our Lord," to the "end" when the Lord will be revealed, and within that framework celebrates the way the Corinthian believers have been enriched and amply supplied with χαρίσματα (*charismata*), spiritual gifts (God is the implied and understood provider). Perhaps the mention of "speech and knowledge" in 1:5 is prompted by Paul's recognition that some of the Corinthians have stressed those endowments (see 1:18–2:16) while disparaging other gifts, and he thereby makes common ground with them, even though later in the letter he will attempt to refine their understanding of "speech and knowledge." In this thanksgiving modern readers receive a fundamental clue about the letter's exigence:[35] The Corinthian believers do not

lack spiritual gifts, but they do not know how to employ them in service for the community in love. Instead, they ironically create status-oriented cliques based on what was in the first place simply a gift to them (cf. 4:7-8).

In the heart of this passage Paul's affirmation of assurance could not be stronger. The Corinthians' experience of God's enrichment of them "in every way" (1:5 NIV, NRSV) was already a "confirmation" (1:6; βεβαιόω *bebaioō*, "make firm," "establish," "confirm") of the testimony about Christ that elicited their faith in the first place. Their response was proof positive of God's calling, but that was only the beginning of their story. From that point, from their having been called and confirmed in their faith, Paul looks forward to the goal toward which God's grace is moving them—namely, "the revelation of our Lord Jesus Christ" (1:7) at the end time. That same Lord, Paul confidently assures them, will "also confirm you until the end" (1:8). What God has begun, God will assuredly bring to completion (cf. the same point in Phil 1:6). The

35. Paul Schubert, *Form and Function of the Pauline Thanksgivings* (Berlin: Töpelmann, 1939) 180.

Greek term *bebaioō*, translated here (1:6, 8) as "confirm," functions in papyri as a legal technical term meaning "properly guaranteed security"[36] and has the same stress on assurance in Paul's use of it. The guarantee is grounded in God's faithfulness (1:9)—a motif that Paul surely found grounded across his scriptures (Deut 5:10; 7:9; Pss 89:1-2; 145:13; Isa 49:7; Jer 4:2; Dan 9:4)—but must be

36. BAGD, 138.

matched by faithfulness and proper living on the part of believers. The remainder of 1 Corinthians will show that Paul has serious concerns regarding the latter. Paul's thanksgiving reminds the Corinthians of how richly they have been graced by God and of how God is faithful to carry through on what has been promised. Without saying it here, Paul sets the ground against which he can later say how much the Corinthians risk by their divisiveness and their inconsiderate treatment of each other.

# REFLECTIONS

**1.** Because believers are totally dependent on God's transforming grace for their new life in Christ, their basic response must be one of thankfulness to God (1:4); Paul expects thankfulness to God from all persons (Rom 1:21), and here he himself models it. Paul's relationship to other believers and his thankfulness to God for them is based not on whether he likes them or on whether they view issues in the world in the same way, but on the simple and profound fact that God's grace is active in them and in him. Our modern Christian community is founded on God's grace given to all, not on whether we are socially compatible and not on whether we take the same political views.

**2.** Paul defines the current life of believers by reference to the origin of faith among them ("our testimony about Christ was confirmed in you," 1:6 NIV) and to the "day of our Lord"—that is, to the end time, when Paul expects the Lord to be revealed. Thus the believers' story, our story, is always written into the larger story of what God is ultimately doing in Christ (15:1-2, 24-28); we believers are always pictured as a part of God's cosmic plan. Paul thereby protects against two dangers that are too prevalent in modern renditions of Christianity whereby faith is turned into an internal "attitudinal adjustment" or into an individualistic experience. Our lives in Christ are never just our own but always also involve how we are relating to those around us. Our life in Christ is not manifested simply by a change in attitude but must also make a difference in the choices and decisions we make, the actions we take, and the way we treat not only ourselves but also others.

# 1 CORINTHIANS 1:10–4:21, PAUL'S CONTEXTUALING OF THE LETTER

# OVERVIEW

A primary hermeneutical principle must be affirmed: Within only the broadest constraints of the literary conventions of the times—namely, that letters tended to open with salutations and thanksgivings and to close with greetings and a recognition of the gods—Paul was absolutely free to organize and arrange the contents of 1 Corinthians as he saw fit. So the arrangement of materials within the letter—what comes first, what comes next, what comes last, and so forth—is completely Paul's, and his arrangement sheds light on his purposes and goals. Accordingly, we must pay special attention to matters such as location, sequence, and association.

Roughly one-fourth of the letter, 1:10–4:21, sets the context, the background for Paul's subsequent treatment of particular problems in Corinth, identifies the Corinthian tendency toward divisiveness, and reminds the Corinthians of his exemplary and paternal caring for them. This important passage rehearses Paul's relationship to the Corinthians and theirs to the gospel.

Scholarly interpretation of these opening chapters has been dominated by two issues: (1) What is the identification of the groups that are deduced from 1:12, "Each of you says, 'I belong to Paul,' 'I belong to Apollos,' 'I belong to Cephas [Peter],' 'I belong to Christ' "? and (2) What is the nature and the source of the wisdom teaching that is reflected in 1:18–2:16 and that is assumed to have made an impact on Paul's community? Both of these scholarly traditions have some readily creditable support: (a) Wisdom and knowledge are treated at some length in the opening chapters; (b) by all the evidence the Corinthians were divisive and contentious; (c) Apollos and Paul (and Cephas?) labored with the Corinthians and, therefore, could have been persons of allegiance attachment; (d) Paul admits to having baptized some but not many of the Corinthians, leaving it clear that someone else had baptized the rest of them (1 Cor 12:13, a baptismal tradition, confirms that the Corinthian believers have indeed been baptized); and (e) in that culture, "belonging to" someone was a primary category and one that we will see Paul readily exploit in this letter (see 3:23; 6:20; 7:23).

On the issue of the identification of different "parties" or groups based on 1:12 and its "I belong" statements, scholars have rightly found most difficulty in imagining any one part of Paul's congregations anywhere who might have arrogated to themselves some especial belonging to Christ because a cardinal Pauline assertion is that all believers belong to Christ in a central, defining way (cf. 3:23). That leaves three groups, formed around Paul, Apollos, and Cephas, with perhaps some issue of allegiance to the one who did the baptizing. Since F. C. Baur[37] claimed that there really were only two groups in Corinth and that their allegiance was to Paul (and Apollos) or Cephas (and Christ), some scholars have been tempted to follow Baur's lead.[38] This reconstruction of the dynamics at Corinth supposes that the divisiveness there is between two factions that have formed competitive allegiances, some claiming Paul as their leader and others claiming Cephas (Peter) as theirs. In this construal, not adopted in this commentary, the defining struggle is between Paul and Peter, and their conflict has been reflected onto the undeniable fractiousness at Corinth. Baur's reconstruction has rightly been criticized as having a limited evidential base in Paul's letters.[39] But more tellingly for the interpretation of 1 Corinthians, we must note that Cephas's relationship to the Corinthians is unclear but not monumental in importance; surely, the Corinthians know about Cephas because Paul has taught them about him (15:5), and perhaps Cephas has been through Corinth and, maybe even with his wife, has received their hospitality (9:5). No convincing argument has ever tied particular problems or issues from the rest of the letter to any identifiable groups that could be associated with any of these leaders as distinguished from another.[40]

In fact, what is demonstrable in Corinth is that the Corinthians are given to factions, to cliques, but not that there are identifiable "groups" or "parties." There is no basis for assuming that the factional tendencies always broke on the same lines with the same people opposing others. As we will see, the church at Corinth has some problems that have clear socioeconomic power and status considerations, but particular, identifiable groups or parties within the church cannot be successfully identified. Accordingly, this commentary will treat not groups but divisions and lack of unity. In so doing we must recognize that our failure to be able to be more precise about the divisiveness may, in fact, be Paul's purposeful "fuzzing" of the

---

37. F. C. Baur, "Die Christuspartei in der korinthischen Gemeinde, der Gegensatz der petrinischen und paulinischen Christenthums in der Altesten Kirche," *Ausgewählte Werke,* ed. K. Scholder (Stuttgart: T. Frommann, 1963) 1:24-76.

38. See Michael D. Goulder, *St. Paul Versus St. Peter: A Tale of Two Missions* (Louisville: Westminster/Knox, 1994).

39. William Baird, " 'One Against the Other'; Intra-church Conflict in 1 Corinthians," in *The Conversation Continues: Studies in Paul and John in Honor of J. Louis Martyn,* ed. R. T. Fortna and B. R. Gaventa (Nashville: Abingdon, 1990) 116-36, carefully assesses and soundly, rightly rejects the line of interpretation that runs from Baur through Schmithals and that Baird identifies as Paul against "one front"— whether that be Baur's Peter or Schmithals's gnostics. The problem of 1 Corinthians is not Paul versus anyone but factions and divisions within and among the Corinthian believers.

40. L. L. Welborn, "On the Discord in Corinth: I Corinthians 1–4 and Ancient Politics," *JBL* 106 (1987) 88-89, and esp. n. 16 for some historical perspective on this failed search.

specifics as a way of avoiding reifying whatever schisms he knew to be present. In any case, on this issue we cannot penetrate with precision behind our source—namely, Paul's letter.

In these contextualizing chapters Paul does make much of wisdom, first contrasting his gospel with wisdom and then, admitting that he does deal in wisdom with mature persons, he declares that his wisdom is secret and hidden to others. Much scholarly attention has been paid to identifying the source of this wisdom and understanding whether some wisdom speculation has invaded the community.[41] As important as such questions are, if for nothing else than understanding where Paul and the Corinthians might have received or encountered such wisdom traditions, the attention of this study will be placed on the way the wisdom claims function in Paul's argumentation with the Corinthians as an act of persuasion on his part.

Our assessment of the functions of Paul's frequent references to wisdom in chaps. 1–4 must be cognizant of the fact that wisdom seems to play no explicit role in the distinct problems and issues with which chaps. 5–16 are concerned. Status, expressed in terms of boasting, puffiness, comparison, and personal practice, is a concern of the letter throughout. Paul's linking of status concerns and wisdom—which we shall see shortly—reflects the linkage in the culture of the time and allows us to see that Paul's comments about wisdom in the first four chapters set a context for him to deal with status claims throughout the letter. There is no reason to doubt that some Corinthians, quite likely responding both to Paul's repeated insistence that believers should consider what they know (more about this pattern as the letter unfolds) and to the culture's identification of sages as ones worthy of status and honor, found themselves identifying their wisdom with status and a right for respect.

While it has been stated that wisdom seems to play no explicit role in the distinct problems or issues of the letter in chaps. 5 and following, we must consider that it may be Paul more than the Corinthians who emphasizes wisdom and expounds on wisdom claims to make his points in the opening four chapters. In what follows, however, we will see that wisdom and status are very directly linked not only in that culture but also in Paul's letter, and concerns with status lace the problems Paul has with the Corinthians in the remainder of the letter. So if wisdom is not one of the Corinthian obsessions, surely status is; in any case, Paul's treatment of wisdom and its associated status lets him establish a basis in these chapters for later reflections about his readers' competitive status concerns.

One other noteworthy feature, and a key to understanding Paul's argumentation, is Paul's frequent employment of what will here be called the rival "two-way" tradition that was so prevalent not only in the wider Greco-Roman world but also among Jews at the turn of the era (Prov 28:18; Wis 5:6-7; cf. *Did.* 1-6).[42] Two rival and opposing ways or paths are depicted, and the auditors are called to take the one and avoid the other (cf. Matt 7:13-14). Much of 1:10–4:21 is constructed on such a frame.

**How to Read 1:10–4:21.** Previous studies have not taken adequate note of Paul's own clues as to how to interpret these opening four chapters. Two features of 1:10–4:21 frame the section and must provide our primary interpretive keys. First, in keeping with the rhetorical practices of the times, Paul opens and closes—encircles—the whole section with a doubled appeal (1:10; 4:16) and by doing so forms an inclusio, a frame or ring-device within which the surrounded material must be understood. His bracketing appeals thereby provide a fundamental clue as to what to look for in the intervening chapters and verses. Second, enclosed within the two appeals is Paul's explicit declaration as to his purpose in the intervening sections: He has used himself and Apollos as exemplars in order to make a point (4:6). To understand Paul's purposes in 1:10–4:21, we need to look at the doubled appeal and at the matter of Paul's exemplary treatment of himself and Apollos.

**The Doubled Appeal.** All of Paul's undisputed letters, 1 Corinthians included, arrive at a point where Paul directly implores his readers for

---

41. A sample of such efforts includes Walter Schmithals, *Gnosticism in Corinth: An Investigation of the Letters to the Corinthians*, 2nd ed., trans. J. E. Steely (Nashville: Abingdon, 1971) 141-55; R. A. Horsley, "Wisdom of Word and Words of Wisdom in Corinth," *CBQ* 39 (1977) 224-39, and "Gnosis in Corinth: 1 Corinthians 8.1-6, *NTS* 27 (1980) 32-51; and Stephen M. Pogoloff, *Logos and Sophia: The Rhetorical Situation of 1 Corinthians*, SBLDS 134 (Atlanta: Scholars Press, 1992).

42. David E. Aune, *The New Testament in Its Literary Environment*, Library of Early Christianity 8 (Philadelphia: Westminster, 1987) 197.

a response (e.g., Rom 12:1; 2 Cor 10:1; Phil 4:2). But in this respect 1 Corinthians is unusual in two ways: (1) The first appeal (1:10) occurs far earlier than in any other Pauline letter, at the beginning of what we might normally call the body of the letter, and (2) it is repeated three chapters later (4:16).

The opening appeal, based on a report from some whom Paul designates as "Chloe's people" that there is discord among the faithful at Corinth, is structured as a contrast between what the Corinthians are now—that is, torn and divided—and what Paul enjoins them to become: one in voice, mind, and opinion (1:10). Although we know nothing about the identity of Chloe and her people, we must suppose that they are in good standing with Paul and with the church at Corinth because Paul cites them as the credible source of his knowledge about the divisiveness (1:11; cf. 3:3).

The second entreaty—"Therefore I appeal to you: Become imitators of me" (4:16)—captures the intervening emphasis on exemplification, links it to Paul's appeal, and draws the opening four chapters to a close. Paul admonishes the Corinthians whose divisiveness demonstrates their lack of maturity. Though he wishes they might behave as "grown-ups" (3:1-2), he calls them his "beloved children" (4:14) and affirms his paternity: "in Christ Jesus, through the gospel, I myself begot you." He alone is their πατήρ (patēr), "father" (4:15). In the Roman world, paternity created a reciprocal responsibility between parent and children. The *pater familias* ("head of the household") was responsible for all who lived there; in particular the children's comportment and well-being were in the father's hand. The children learned by modeling after their father, learned whatever trade the household was involved with, but much more fundamentally, learned appropriate conduct. Accordingly, as their father, Paul has written in warning or admonition (4:14) and enjoins them to model after him. They would also do well to emulate Timothy, who like them is a "beloved child" but who, unlike them, understands "Paul's ways" so well that he can come to them as a teacher (4:17).

Both appeals feature contrasts: "Speak with one voice, don't have schisms" (1:10), and "Be like me, your father in the faith, not like babies" who cannot write between the lines (4:6; for this inter-pretation, see the commentary below). Both appeals acknowledge the disparity between the Corinthians' current discord and the harmony they should have in Christ. The first appeal explicitly urges unity and an end to dissension and divisiveness; the second calls simply for an emulation of Paul, who, by that time, in the intervening sections, has painted himself in his relation to Apollos as the model of cooperation and wholehearted unity in the gospel.

**Paul and Apollos As Exemplars.** Near the conclusion of 1:10–4:21, Paul baldly states his overriding purpose in the opening chapters and his means of accomplishing it. The purpose: so that the Corinthians might learn not to be puffed up in favor of one and against another. The means: Paul openly declares that, in what has preceded 4:6 ("all this"), he has used a common contemporary rhetorical device, "indirect" or "figured speech," by which he has made a point with reference to himself and Apollos as a roundabout or oblique way of critiquing the Corinthians' predilection for contentions and divisions.[43] Paul's verb in 4:6 is μετασχηματίζω (metaschēmatizō), which has a semantic range of "change the form of, transform, change," "disguise," and "say something with the aid of a figure of speech,"[44] so toward the end of the section, Paul explicitly tells the readers what he has been doing in the previous chapters.

"Frank" or "direct speech" (παρρησία parrēsia),[45] the alternative to "indirect speech," was used sparingly in Paul's time; "indirect speech" was the "normal mode of discourse" then.[46] With direct speech the writer or speaker applies the critique directly. Direct speech is argumentative and usually confrontational and leaves the speaker open to reprisal.

---

43. Benjamin Fiore, " 'Covert Allusion' in 1 Corinthians 1–4," *CBQ* 47 (1985) 85-102; David R. Hall, "A Disguise for the Wise: METASCHEMATISMOS in 1 Corinthians 4:6," *NTS* 40 (1994) 143-49; Peter Lampe, "Theological Wisdom and the 'Word About the Cross': The Rhetorical Scheme in 1 Corinthians 1–4," *Int* 44 (1990) 117-31. John Fitzgerald, *Cracks in an Earthen Vessel: An Examination of the Catalogues of Hardships in the Corinthian Correspondence*, SBLDS 99 (Atlanta: Scholars Press, 1988), traces the identification of this as a covert allusion back to J. B. Lightfoot in 1895, 119n. 10.

44. BAGD, 513.

45. See J. Paul Sampley, "Paul's Frank Speech with the Galatians and the Corinthians," in *Philodemus and the New Testament World*, NovTSup, ed. J. T. Fitzgerald, G. S. Holland, and D. Obbink (Leiden: Brill, forthcoming), and Sampley, "Frank Speech," in *Paul in the Greco-Roman World* (Harrisburg, Pa.: Trinity, forthcoming).

46. Frederick Ahl, "The Art of Safe Criticism in Greece and Rome," *AJP* 105 (1984) 204.

Indirect speech moves the discussion from the delicate, sensitive issue itself—in this instance, the discord and disharmony among the Corinthian believers—and transfers the discourse to a relatively "safe" topic where what is known or learned there can either in the act of hearing or in later reflection be transposed, ideally by Corinthian self-application, to the touchy issue of their divisiveness.[47] In this letter, the delicate issue is the Corinthians' disharmony with one another, their tendency to take sides; the safe topic is the exemplary relationship of Paul and Apollos. So when we read the references to Paul and Apollos we should recognize that they are not at all the problem. Far from it! In fact, those two leaders, in their work among the Corinthian believers, have embodied the proper harmony and unity despite their considerable dissimilarities. Rather than representing focal points for schisms, as some interpreters have suggested,[48] Paul offers himself and Apollos as models for the way dissimilar Corinthians ought to cooperate and behave in the gospel.

Having recognized Paul's acknowledged strategy of persuasion in 4:6, let us now look at Paul's references to himself and Apollos so that we can see how his "indirect speech" has served to illustrate proper Christian unity in diversity. In 1:12 Paul invites the Corinthians to think of themselves as belonging to him or to Apollos, and right away he signals that these are to be considered as just two "for instances" by adding Cephas (Paul's way of referring to Peter) to the list. Cephas's role in 1 Corinthians is minimal. Outside the opening four chapters (cf. 3:22), Cephas is mentioned only twice (9:5; 15:5), and in no way does either reference, even in the slightest hint, tie Cephas to any group or problem or issue confronting the church at Corinth. If, as I assume, there was not a group at Corinth who held allegiance to Cephas, Paul's readers would have known immediately, with the mention of Cephas, that the entire list, including Paul and Apollos, was simply illustrative and designed to make a point by analogy. Even the

modern reader of 4:6 should get that point and take it back as a guideline for reading 1:12.

But in 1:12 Paul does not stop with those belonging to Cephas. As if to ensure that no Corinthian auditors mistakenly take Paul as describing what he thinks are the social realities at Corinth, Paul parodies his own rhetorical enterprise by suggesting the unthinkable possibility that some might fancy that they belong especially to Christ as their group of allegiance. Paul's own follow-up (in 1:13) to his "I belong to Christ" parody once again shows that his purpose is illustrative with respect to himself and Apollos, as he says explicitly in 4:6. When Paul has written "I belong to Christ," he can bear it with a straight face no longer; with irony, he parodies his own parody: "Is Christ divided? Was Paul crucified for you? Or were you baptized into the name of Paul?" (1:13). Each of those questions is clearly structured, as the Greek allows, to signal that Paul expects a negative answer: Of course not!

Does Paul's writing "Each of you says . . ." (1:12) indicate that he thinks everybody in the Corinthian church has, in fact, established such an allegiance with one of the people listed—namely Paul, Apollos, or Cephas? Paul's treatment of chaos in worship in chap. 14 has a similar expression that should guide the interpreter of 1:12. In that context he advises: "Each of you has a psalm, a teaching, a revelation" (14:26). Clearly, the point is that in worship people comport themselves with discipline; the "each" functions in a distributive way to suggest that "different ones" will recite a psalm, give a teaching, share a revelation, and so forth. So also in 1:12 the "each" is to be understood in an allusive way, not as a dividing up of the congregation with no remainder.

The Paul/Apollos illustrative schema laces through these opening chapters and, following 1:12, next surfaces immediately after Paul has chided the Corinthians for still being babies in Christ when they should be more mature. His evidence that they are babies is a selective reprise of 1:10-12: "as long as there is jealousy and quarreling among you. . . . When one says, 'I belong to Paul,' and another, 'I belong to Apollos,' " that is, as long as there are divisions in the body of Christ, they are still children (3:3-4). Here, just as Paul explicitly and directly tells the reader in 4:6, Paul makes his points simply by referring to himself and Apollos alone. He does in 3:3-4 what later he

---

47. For more detail on the differences between frank and indirect speech as well as Paul's application of indirect speech to another problem, see J. Paul Sampley, "The Weak and the Strong: Paul's Careful and Crafty Rhetorical Strategy in Romans 14:1–15:13," in *The Social World of the First Christians: Essays in Honor of Wayne A. Meeks*, ed. L. M. White and O. L. Yarbrough (Minneapolis: Augsburg/Fortress, 1995) 43-46.

48. Pogoloff's very suggestive study, *Logos and Sophia*, 189-90, errs in this direction.

expressly tells the reader he has intended to do (4:6).

What does Paul expect that the Corinthians should learn from him and Apollos? His answer can be seen in 3:5-9. These two leaders are equally servants of the same Lord who called them (3:5). One planted, the other watered (3:6), they have a common purpose (3:8; lit., "are one"); and each will receive wages for his work. Because God is the one who gives the growth, the ones who plant and water are not in and of themselves anything special at all (3:7); they are simply laborers, "God's servants, working together" (3:9 NRSV); they have nothing about which they should boast or be puffed up. As surely as Paul and Apollos are "one" and should not be puffed up in favor of one or the other, so also the Corinthians should neither be divided nor boastful. Just as Paul and Apollos work together, so also should the Corinthians. Just as Paul and Apollos have individual tasks for which each will receive wages and yet have a common purpose, so also the Corinthians correspond in every detail. The Corinthian believers, as different as they are socioeconomically and as variously gifted as they may be, are all equally and collectively "God's field," "God's building" (3:9).

Later in the same chapter, it is time for perspective-keeping. The Corinthians have lost their way, become confused about basics. In their inclinations to "belong to" certain divisions and thereby achieve a boastable status (3:21), they have lost sight of their true, definitional belonging—namely, to Christ! Because they belong to Christ, who belongs to God (3:23), all partisanship, whether to Paul, to Apollos, to Cephas, or indeed (and this is the real point) to any other human leader or grouping, is inappropriate.

Between the bracketing appeals (1:10; 4:16) that encourage the Corinthians to cease their divi-

siveness and emulate their father in the gospel, Paul structures his argument around the frame provided by the references to himself and Apollos as exemplary coworkers in the gospel. So the doubled appeal and the indirect speech about himself and Apollos provide fundamental guidelines for interpreting 1:10–4:21. The doubled appeal signals Paul's profound concern, which will undergird the entire letter, that the Corinthians are schismatic—that is, they have lost sight of their true unity in Christ. Their misunderstanding and its resultant divisive behavior cue Paul concerning their immaturity, their childishness, and causes him to play the father who models maturity—and for that Paul turns to indirect speech about himself and Apollos. The Corinthians surely knew how different Paul and Apollos were from each other in so many ways; yet Paul's picture of them, especially as developed in 3:5-9, epitomizes how the Corinthian believers, themselves so different from one another, ought also to work together in the body of Christ.

In the portrait of himself and Apollos, Paul never loses sight that it is he alone who is their father; he is the one who planted. Apollos stands in second place as the one who came into the picture later and who watered what was already planted. But, as different as Paul and Apollos are and as distinct as their contributions, they are one in Christ in an exemplary fashion. The Paul/Apollos lesson is a back-to-basics illustration of Christian unity sketched broadly and consistently across 1:10–4:21 so that the Corinthians, being babies, can learn to "color within the lines," as I interpret Paul's meaning in the cryptic expression "Nothing beyond what is written" (4:6).[49]

49. Fitzgerald, *Cracks in an Earthen Vessel*, 121-28, has the best study of this problem, tracing it from Protagoras forward and indicating "a lesson that is to be learned," 124.

# 1 Corinthians 1:10-17, The Opening Appeal

**NIV**

[10]I appeal to you, brothers, in the name of our Lord Jesus Christ, that all of you agree with one another so that there may be no divisions among you and that you may be perfectly united in mind and thought. [11]My brothers, some from Chloe's household have informed me that there are

**NRSV**

10Now I appeal to you, brothers and sisters,[a] by the name of our Lord Jesus Christ, that all of you be in agreement and that there be no divisions among you, but that you be united in the

[a] Gk *brothers*

## NIV

quarrels among you. [12]What I mean is this: One of you says, "I follow Paul"; another, "I follow Apollos"; another, "I follow Cephas[a]"; still another, "I follow Christ."

[13]Is Christ divided? Was Paul crucified for you? Were you baptized into[b] the name of Paul? [14]I am thankful that I did not baptize any of you except Crispus and Gaius, [15]so no one can say that you were baptized into my name. [16](Yes, I also baptized the household of Stephanas; beyond that, I don't remember if I baptized anyone else.) [17]For Christ did not send me to baptize, but to preach the gospel—not with words of human wisdom, lest the cross of Christ be emptied of its power.

[a]12 That is, Peter    [b]13 Or in; also in verse 15

## NRSV

same mind and the same purpose. [11]For it has been reported to me by Chloe's people that there are quarrels among you, my brothers and sisters.[a] [12]What I mean is that each of you says, "I belong to Paul," or "I belong to Apollos," or "I belong to Cephas," or "I belong to Christ." [13]Has Christ been divided? Was Paul crucified for you? Or were you baptized in the name of Paul? [14]I thank God[b] that I baptized none of you except Crispus and Gaius, [15]so that no one can say that you were baptized in my name. [16](I did baptize also the household of Stephanas; beyond that, I do not know whether I baptized anyone else.) [17]For Christ did not send me to baptize but to proclaim the gospel, and not with eloquent wisdom, so that the cross of Christ might not be emptied of its power.

[a]Gk my brothers    [b]Other ancient authorities read I am thankful

# COMMENTARY

Paul, calling the Corinthians "brothers and sisters" (ἀδελφοί adelphoi, "brethren"; Paul clearly assumes that women are also included, so the suggested translation here and in the NRSV seems appropriate)[50] and thereby claiming common ground with them as children of the same Father, this time God (1:3; cf. v. 11), opens the body of the letter with an appeal that they not be schismatic but speak with one voice, one mind, and one purpose (1:10). Over against their tendency to be schismatic, Paul stacks up an overlapping variety of ways in which he thinks their unity in Christ should express itself. In 1:10 alone, where he first notes their divisiveness, Paul encases their inclination to divisiveness within three evocations of their unity. In the first, the one that is the immediate object of the appeal, he urges them all to "say the same" (NIV, "agree with one another"; NRSV, "be in agreement"), possibly evoking the reflection about precisely what believers can say together at

the very ground of their being. Clearly, from 1 Cor 12:3, Paul thinks that the central and foundational affirmation that "Jesus is Lord" is one such common claim. The second (νοῦς nous) and third (γνώμη gnōmē) common identifications have so much semantic overlap that they tend to reinforce each other because both could be translated "the same mind or outlook." Paul's point is to be seen in the overlap of the three ways, in their corroboration. His appeal to affirm the same thing and to be of the same outlook is Paul's way of declaring that what unites them ought to be far more powerful and comprehensive than what pulls them apart.

As subsequent parts of 1 Corinthians are read, the alert auditors may remember Paul's call for all the Corinthians to be of "the same mind" in 1:10 when they hear his later claim that "we ourselves have the mind of Christ" (2:16). That powerful claim identifies the shared mind that Paul yearns for the Corinthians to have and credits the Holy Spirit as making it possible (2:10-16). Though the notion of having the mind of Christ is not developed much in 1 Corinthians, we can see it elaborated in Phil 2:1-4, a passage directed at another church with dissension. There Paul follows a sim-

50. Gordon D. Fee, *The First Epistle to the Corinthians* (Grand Rapids: Eerdmans, 1987) 52n. 22, notes that "it is clear from the evidence of this letter (11:2-16) and Phil. 4:1-3 that women were participants in the worship of the community and would have been included in the 'brothers' being addressed. . . . It is therefore not pedantic, but culturally sound and biblically sensitive, for us to translate this vocative 'brothers and sisters.' "

ilar pattern—namely, he stacks up semantic over-laps, even more of them than in 1 Cor 1:10, but to the same point: "Being of the same mind, having the same love, being in full accord and of one mind" (Phil 2:2 NRSV). The unity that believers experience in Christ is supposed to be so profound and so encompassing that they share the demeanor, the outlooks, and the goals that really matter. The remainder of 1 Corinthians will make abundantly clear that Paul does not confuse unity with unifor-mity; he does not think that believers must all have the identical views on all things (cf. Rom 14:1) or that they must walk in lockstep. On the contrary, he values the distinctiveness of believers, appreciates their differences of gifts and graces (see chap. 12), and expects believers to make a range of acceptable but different moral choices (see chap. 7). The true unity of believers is established by God's grace, by Christ's love, and by the recep-tion of the Holy Spirit. These all believers share, equally and in a constitutive way.

Paul's appeal is made in "the name of our Lord Jesus Christ" (v. 10). As is clear already from 1:2, the Corinthian believers and all the faithful every-where acknowledge the shared lordship of Christ (cf. 12:3). To appeal "in the name" of that Lord should remind the readers of their baptism, the very rite by which they were brought into this new fellowship. The formula certainly reminds Paul of baptism because he uses it in his parody of their divisiveness: "Or were you baptized in the name of Paul?" Of course not! To appeal "in the name of the Lord" reminds them that Christ is their Lord and invokes his power and his election of them as the proper framework within which readers should consider Paul's petition.

The term *adelphoi* (NRSV, "brothers and sis-ters"; NIV, "brothers") occurs thirty-eight times in 1 Corinthians, more than twice as many times as in any other Pauline letter. Its frequency is a sub-tle testimony to Paul's eagerness to affirm the common, shared ground and the equal standing of all God's children, not only in their relation to Paul but especially to one another. The term depicts the reconciling resocialization of Corinthians from all sorts of social settings into the new family of God and invites them to view each other accordingly.

Divisiveness among those who are in Christ is simply unthinkable for Paul. Paul and Apollos, as

important as they have been in the life and growth of the church at Corinth—and even Cephas, whose actual relationship to the Corinthians is relatively obscure—are placed in perspective in this opening passage (1:12). The passage is bracketed by a refer-ence to Christ as Lord on one side (1:10) and the "cross of Christ" on the other (1:17). In one stroke of the pen Paul puts himself (and if himself how much more Apollos and Cephas!) and his impor-tance in perspective: "Paul wasn't crucified for you, was he? And you weren't baptized 'into the name of Paul,' were you?" (1:13 *b-c*). There is no need for an answer to these ludicrous questions, whose func-tion is to focus on the real and important issue at hand: "Christ isn't divided, is he?" Of course not. So when "there is jealousy and quarreling among you" (3:3), nothing distinguishes believers from every-body else. The way of the world has become the way of believers. (What is supposed to be outside the assembly of believers has insidiously moved inside; see the Commentary on 5:1–6:20.) The hall-mark of Christians is supposed to be unity in Christ (cf. John 13:35); Paul takes anything less than that as a sign of immaturity.

These early verses (vv. 10-17) yield some insights into the church at Corinth and into Paul. First, we learn that certain Corinthian believers were baptized by Paul, though he tries to minimize the importance of his having been the one to do it (vv. 14-16). Crispus (cf. Acts 18:8), Gaius (cf. Acts 19:29; Rom 16:23), and the household of Stephanas—that seems to cover the persons Paul can immediately recall having baptized (1:14, 16). We will learn more about Stephanas and his house-hold at the end of the letter (16:15, 17). Paul's min-imizing his role in baptism should not be construed as a depreciation of the rite. All of the Corinthians have been baptized (12:13), and their knowledge of their baptism will be an important consideration in the moral reasoning found in chaps. 7 and 12. Baptism is definitional for all believers; the identity of the baptizer is an indifferent matter. Although the Corinthians seem so concerned about status, their significance lies not in their relation to Paul—or, indeed, to any other person—but in their rela-tion to Christ and, therefore, to God.

Chloe (1:11) seems to have standing with the Corinthian church; she may have been a busi-nessperson whose agents, possibly her slaves, were on the road. Her people are a prime source for Paul's knowledge of the ways the Corinthians have become divisive (v. 11).

Second, we learn how Paul understands his calling: Christ sent him not to baptize but to evangelize (v. 17; cf. 9:19-23). Paul's identity rests not in his function as baptizer but in his preaching of the gospel. The Corinthians surely know this, too, because it was he who, by his proclamation, "planted" the church in Corinth by his preaching (3:6).

Paul's proclaiming of the gospel is not "with eloquent wisdom, so that the cross of Christ might not be emptied of its power" (v. 17). Paul's picture of the Corinthians will become clear as the letter progresses: Some of them are easily swayed by brilliant rhetoric; some have aspirations for wisdom; some are impressed by knowledge; some are awestruck by the faith and gifts of themselves and of others; some place importance in power and status. All of those persons, trading for a counterfeit, lose sight of the only true power, the power of God shown through the cross. The remainder of the letter will distinguish the real power of the cross from contenders, but in v. 17 the counterfeit is rather narrowly identified as sophisticated or cultured speech because that sets up the direction that the letter's next passage will take.

Verse 17 is the foundational statement whose significance is unpacked and refined by Paul in the following verses in which he contrasts "eloquent wisdom" with "the cross of Christ." Each of those phrases is a figure of speech (the rhetorical pattern is called synecdoche) by which the part stands for a larger whole, as, for example, "wheels" may represent or stand for a "car." The "cross of Christ," which Paul subsequently reduces even further to "cross" (v. 18), is a deliberate compression of complex affirmations into a single symbol, chosen here in part no doubt for its inescapably scandalous focus on Christ's death. Here "cross" stands for, signifies, a much larger, pivotal cluster of events so central to Paul's proclamation: the death and resurrection of Jesus Christ. For Paul, the cross, planted squarely in history, stands for the whole story of Christ's death and resurrection as a sign of God's grace and caring for human beings.

A similarly purposeful compression is found in the cryptic expression σοφία λόγου (*sophia logou;* NRSV, "eloquent wisdom"; more lit., wisdom of word or wisdom of speech), which, like

"cross of Christ" becoming "cross," is epitomized in the subsequent discussion by the single term "wisdom." The locution's precise meaning has been the subject of controversy. Many commentators, noting the heavy concentration of wisdom terminology in 1:18–2:16, have taken the recurring mention of wisdom as referring to a Greek or Jewish philosophical tradition with which, the supposition goes, some Corinthians are captivated.[51] Such an interpretation understands Paul's opening chapters as trying to free those Corinthians from their fascination with wisdom, but it encounters two difficulties: (1) What is one to make of the relative absence not only of the term "wisdom" (14 times in the first four chaps.; only once thereafter, 12:8) after chap. 4? and (2) How is one to understand the fact that wisdom does not seem to be directly responsible for a single one of the manifold problems that are treated in the rest of the letter? Such an interpretation is not necessary.

It is a feature of the culture in which Paul preached that the persons who were most directly identified with wisdom—namely, the sages—tended to be eloquent, skillful speakers. Cultured speech, eloquently delivered in a refined fashion, was the telltale of high status, of power and wealth, of education and, indeed, of wisdom.[52] In antiquity, the constellation of wealth, high status, cultured speech, and power was fixed; the sighting of any of the major stars allowed one to suppose the whole configuration. Conversely, the lack of "cleverness of speech," cultured or refined speech (possible translations of *sophia logou,* 1:17), was the certain sign of low status and, one might reasonably suppose, a corresponding lack of wisdom, wealth, and power.

Paul pointedly dissociates himself and his proclamation from clever or wise speech, from the kind of wisdom-as-status indicator in which the world, and apparently some Corinthians, put stock. In contrarian fashion, Paul takes his definition from the cross of Christ. In subsequent verses we see that Paul abbreviates these rival constellations into single and opposing terms: wisdom versus cross. To put the same point, but with a

51. See R. A. Horsley, "Gnosis in Corinth: 1 Corinthians 8.1-6," *NTS* 27 (1988) 32-51.

52. See Pogoloff's solid treatment of the strong link between social status and skill at rhetoric in antiquity: Stephen Pogoloff, *Logos and Sophia: The Rhetorical Situation of 1 Corinthians,* SBLDS 134 (Atlanta: Scholars Press, 1992) 129-53.

flexibility of terminology, there are two types of speech: one emphasizing wisdom and its associated high status, the other featuring the cross and its scandal. Paul sets up rival symbols of the way persons understand and live their lives: "Eloquent wisdom," pleasant and persuasive as it may be, comes to epitomize culturally accepted connections, associations with important persons or groups as a way of establishing one's own significance, importance, and worth; "cross," Paul's opposing symbol, demolishes all pretensions to status and standing in the world. He writes the Corinthians about his own choice not "to empty the cross of Christ" and, for the first in a long series of instances in 1 Corinthians, sets himself up as a model to be emulated. The implication is that the Corinthians, by their divisiveness, risk empty-ing the cross, nullifying its power. Cross, alternately, "Christ crucified" (1:23), Paul's opposing symbol, stands in its scandalous starkness for the ultimate in weakness and folly when considered from the standpoint represented by those who would value cultured speech and its associated social status. For the clue that wisdom is not just a matter of knowledge but also a status indicator, note that "power" opens 1:18-25 and that in v. 25 the term is set over against "weakness."

The opening appeal—to cease being divisive—therefore, is structured on the two-way pattern that is so prevalent in Paul's world and in Israel's traditions as well. In the case at hand, Paul sets the way of the cross over against the way of wisdom, the scandalous cross of Christ over against status-indicative cultured speech based on wisdom.

# REFLECTIONS

**1.** To whom do you belong? As Christians we should answer: "to Christ"; "to God." Other allegiances compete: work, possessions, status, fame, dreams, television, drugs, and so on. The sweeping biblical term for those competing affiliations is "idolatry," a topic that will surface explicitly later in the letter (5:10, 11; 6:9; 10:7), but that means having something else in the governing center of your life besides God or Christ. When you properly belong to Christ or to God, then all the other claimants either take on a proper secondary place or are removed from your life. If you have a friend whom you trust deeply, talk with that person about how you would answer this question: To whom do you belong?

**2.** With 1:10 we confront one of the problems that prompted 1 Corinthians: divisions within the church. Paul's call for the Corinthians to be "of the same mind and of the same opinion" raises certain questions for modern persons. Does unity preclude differences—differences in actions, in thoughts, in words? Does unity require uniformity of belief and behavior? This touches on an important issue about which Paul has a very sophisticated view. Paul assumes all sorts of differences among people and even credits some of the differences to the Spirit's working to enrich the body (see the argument in 12:4-26). However many differences there may be, or how distinctive the contributions to the body politic, the members of the body must never lose sight of the basis of Christian unity: the shared death with Christ in which God inaugurated their new life in Christ. Christians are united in that they share the same prior indebtedness to sin's power, the same utter need for God's grace, and the same loving redemptive power of God's mercy. Christian unity rests on that shared story, not on the opinions that believers have about issues, and not on the distinctive contributions they are enabled to make to the community of believers. It is not accidental that Paul refers to baptism in this context (1:13-16), because baptism is the ritual expression not only of believers' solidarity with Christ but also of inclusion into Christ, reception of the Spirit, and, therefore, welcome into God's family. This tension, this fundamental exploration of what is and is not Christian unity, will express itself throughout the letter.

**3.** Baptism is the ritual of admission into Christian community and has been so from the earliest days. Though individuals perform the ritual of baptism, we must be clear that it is God who does the claiming and the welcoming of the baptized persons. So it matters not who does the liturgy of baptism. In the fourth-century Donatist controversy, the issue arose as to whether a baptism done by a sinful priest was to be considered efficacious. The church in its wisdom declared that baptism is warranted by God, whose action is at its heart, not by the priest (or minister) who presides. Paul, in his depreciating of any claim that the baptizer is a status indicator, anticipates the same judgment the church rendered in the Donatist controversy (cf. Phil 1:15-18). For believers today what counts is that God claims us in baptism—each of us, equally. Some will have been immersed. Some will have been sprinkled. Some will have had water poured over them. Some will have been baptized as infants; others will have been baptized as adults. Some will have Jordan River water used. Some will have a bishop do it. But all and every one are equally claimed as God's special people and belong to one another as a result.

## 1 Corinthians 1:18-25, Christ, True Power, True Wisdom

NIV

[18]For the message of the cross is foolishness to those who are perishing, but to us who are being saved it is the power of God. [19]For it is written:

"I will destroy the wisdom of the wise;
    the intelligence of the intelligent I will
        frustrate."[a]

[20]Where is the wise man? Where is the scholar? Where is the philosopher of this age? Has not God made foolish the wisdom of the world? [21]For since in the wisdom of God the world through its wisdom did not know him, God was pleased through the foolishness of what was preached to save those who believe. [22]Jews demand miraculous signs and Greeks look for wisdom, [23]but we preach Christ crucified: a stumbling block to Jews and foolishness to Gentiles, [24]but to those whom God has called, both Jews and Greeks, Christ the power of God and the wisdom of God. [25]For the foolishness of God is wiser than man's wisdom, and the weakness of God is stronger than man's strength.

[a]19 Isaiah 29:14

NRSV

[18]For the message about the cross is foolishness to those who are perishing, but to us who are being saved it is the power of God. [19]For it is written,
"I will destroy the wisdom of the wise,
    and the discernment of the discerning I will
        thwart."

[20]Where is the one who is wise? Where is the scribe? Where is the debater of this age? Has not God made foolish the wisdom of the world? [21]For since, in the wisdom of God, the world did not know God through wisdom, God decided, through the foolishness of our proclamation, to save those who believe. [22]For Jews demand signs and Greeks desire wisdom, [23]but we proclaim Christ crucified, a stumbling block to Jews and foolishness to Gentiles, [24]but to those who are the called, both Jews and Greeks, Christ the power of God and the wisdom of God. [25]For God's foolishness is wiser than human wisdom, and God's weakness is stronger than human strength.

## COMMENTARY

Beginning in 1:18, and indeed running through 2:5, Paul takes the Corinthians "back to basics," back to the crux of the community-founding gospel he first proclaimed to them. The passage is a complex of contrasts in which Paul's purpose seems to be to create the largest possible separation or distinction. Nuance and subtlety give way to hyper-

bole. Over against the cultured speech, the "eloquent wisdom" of 1:17, and its worldly values, Paul sets the scandalous, folly ridden cross; over against the "wisdom of λόγος [*logos*]" ("speech"; cultured speech symbolizing power as the world views things), Paul offers the *logos* ("word," his preaching) of the cross. Two rival logoi, two competing claims. Here, as in 1:17 (see also Gal 5:11), "cross" simply and boldly stands for the larger complex of affirmations that Paul more frequently carries with "death and resurrection."

In the two-way tradition so widespread in antiquity (cf. Josh 24:14-27; Matt 7:13-14), Paul imagines two distinct groupings of people whom he describes as ἀπολλύμενοι (*apollymenoi,* "those who are perishing") and σωζόμενοι (*sōzomenoi,* "us who are being saved," 1:18). Paul's use of present participles in both these constructions indicates that the "perishing" and the "being saved" are simultaneous, ongoing processes. The way Paul has set it up, the Corinthians would be expected to identify with that part of humanity that is in the process of being saved (though we will see that in subsequent sections of this letter Paul wonders whether some of the Corinthians may not be in danger of slipping over to become a part of those who are perishing).

The Corinthians already know Paul's gospel and have been formed by it; a modern reader must put together the clues from a passage such as 1:18-25 and see them against a backdrop that we can reconstruct from other Pauline letters. God's decisive action in Christ's death and resurrection has inaugurated the apocalyptic end times. The new creation, the new age (= new aeon), has broken into the old world; the structure of the old world, fraught with the power of sin, is passing away (1 Cor 7:31).[53] Nonbelievers, with mind and heart darkened by the power of sin (Rom 1:21, 28), do not understand or recognize the new creation (cf. 2:8) and God's power at work in it. In fact, talk (or the word) of the cross—the ultimate symbol of shame, humiliation, and rejection—will strike nonbelievers as "folly"; but for believers it is the very power that is transforming their lives.

Paul has abandoned the former divisions of humanity into Jews and Greeks (1:22, 24) because he recognizes that God has called both Jews and Greeks (1:24). But Paul also recognizes that, by their response to the gospel, people have divided themselves into two different categories: "those who are perishing" and "us who are being saved" (cf. the same categories in 2 Cor 2:15), with the latter being understood as "those who are the called" (1:24), in this instance including everyone

in the Corinthian church (1:2) and Paul himself (1:1).

As Paul sees it, the fate of each group is not yet set, but for both a process is under way. Salvation is to be completed by God in the future. At present, believers (in 1:21 they are literally described as "the ones who are believing," once again describing the faithful as in a process; cf. 1:18), the ones called by God, are justified; they are reconciled (Rom 5:9-10). Justified, reconciled believers are in the process of moving toward salvation just as unbelievers are in the course of perishing. The "word of the cross," "Christ crucified" (1:23)—that is, the heart of Paul's proclamation—is "folly," "foolishness," even a scandal or offense (1:23) to the latter, but the "power of God" to the ones being saved (cf. Rom 1:16).

Such a transvaluation of values is what Paul attempts to describe when he calls "Christ crucified" a σκάνδαλον (*skandalon;* NIV and NRSV, "stumbling block," 1:23), from which we surely recognize our English "scandal." The term has a semantic range including "trap," "enticement to false belief," or "something that offends, repulses, elicits opposition."[54] For Paul, "Christ crucified," the very heart of the gospel proclamation, is a profound shock to the hearer. Nothing could be more unlikely than that redemption should come through the humiliating crucifixion of someone. Nothing could be more alien to the culture, its social structures and practices. To hear the scandalous gospel in such a way that one's life is transformed is to experience a *peripeteia,* an utterly shocking and fundamentally transformative turnabout. Elsewhere Paul has resorted to bold claims such as "new creation" (2 Cor 5:17) and "newness of life" (Rom 6:4) in an effort to capture some of the dynamics of the *skandalon.* Admittedly, the gospel is a *skandalon* in that it elicits opposition. Paul, like Jesus (cf. Matt 5:10-12), held that identification with the gospel would inevitably bring opposition (cf. 1 Thess 3:3-4). But the point of Paul's reference in 1:23 is not to account for opposition from outsiders—that does not seem to be a problem at this point in Corinth's life—but to ground the fundamental contrast he is stressing between the gospel and the way of the world.

53. J. Paul Sampley, *Walking Between the Times: Paul's Moral Reasoning* (Minneapolis: Fortress, 1991) 13-17.

54. BAGD, 753.

God's power is not only different from the wisdom of this world, of this age, but is also antithetical to it. Scripture confirms for Paul (note that he assumes that his readers will acknowledge the authority of Scripture) that God "will destroy the wisdom of the wise" (1:19; Isa 29:14; cf. Ps 33:10), which the subsequent rhetorical questions make clear is the wisdom of "this age" or of "the world" (1:20).

Verse 24 shows, however, that Paul does not want to write off wisdom completely, for he claims cryptically "Christ the power of God and the wisdom of God." A positive consideration of what Paul construes as true wisdom will surface for further illumination and reflection a little later in the argument (cf. 2:6). In this context, Paul identifies Christ as both the "power of God" and the "wisdom of God" (1:24). This linkage of power and wisdom should be interpreted by Paul's identification of the gospel as "the power of God for salvation" (Rom 1:16) and refers not to Christ as some incarnated wisdom but to Christ's death and resurrection as the locus of God's power effectively working in and for believers. Thus Paul's proclamation can be abbreviated to "Christ crucified" (1:23*a;* cf. 2:2) and even more concentrated as "cross" (1:18). For the present, however, Paul is content to make a hyperbolic contrast between (pretentious, human) wisdom and God's "foolishness" and to declare, "No contest!" In an enlargement of the contrast, Paul extends the metaphor to strength and weakness: "God's weakness is stronger than human strength" (1:25), showing that the wisdom talk is really also about power and status and preparing the way for the next stage of the argument.

Paul's move to attach wisdom talk to power and status is an important key to understanding not only the force of Paul's argumentation but also the internal dynamics of the Corinthian community of believers. Beneath the surface of the text, where the discussion sets one path over against another, lies the ever-present struggle for status and standing that typified Paul's time. The Corinthians are not contending about some intellectual or even theological issue as if such notions could exist in a classroom or debating hall. They are competing for status. Wisdom and its cultured speech earned status in the culture of Paul's time. Peripatetic sages, skilled in rhetoric, claimed status for themselves and exploited others for their own ends. Their teaching drew its power from capitalizing on the social conventions that accorded power and status to a teacher and to what he taught when it was persuasively expressed in eloquence. In such a human transaction, the only power at stake is the power one can evoke from hearers; the hearers generate the power by the very granting of it to a speaker. So there is a circularity in such power. The speaker elicits a willingness on the part of the hearers to credit the speaker with authority and, therefore, status. The speaker, sensing their assent, is buoyed and soars, evoking more consent from the hearers. Like a bellows-filled balloon whose inflation depends on constant pumping, so the sage and his teaching depend for their authority on constant maintenance and mutual stroking.

Paul sees that the gospel's power depends on nothing but God's own power and not at all on the social and cultural conventions of power. Some of the claims of the gospel crash head-on into such status seeking, and Paul does everything within his rhetorical power to heighten the sense of dissonance and contrast.

What are "the things that are not" (1:28)? The assertion appears in the third "God chose" statement (1:27-28). "God chose the low-born [τὰ ἀγενῆ *ta agenē;* a pointed contrast with the "well-born" of 1:26] and the despised, even the things that are not, in order to make powerless/wipe out the things that are" (1:28). This is densely packed, allusive prose, designed to fit readily within Paul's strong two-way contrast, but now the perspective has shifted from two ways to two ages. In the strongest eschatological categories Paul here describes in a few words what he will refine and expand in 7:29 when he will write of the time being shortened, and in 7:31 when he will describe the schema of this world as passing away. Believers are in transitional times; with Christ's death and resurrection, the new age, the new creation, began. In 1 Cor 1:28 God is described as choosing "the things that are not," the very phrase used of God in Rom 4:17 where God was also depicted as the one who brings life out of death. This is Paul's way of talking about the creative and redemptive power of God that is at work among the Corinthians, bringing God's own future into being at the very same time that "the things that [already] are," like the schema of this world, are passing away, being wiped out, being made powerless. Paul is describing a transitional process as radical as taking what was up and making it down and vice versa. It is a process, a transposition of cosmic proportions, that is under way by God's power; the believers are not causing it, but they surely are its beneficiaries. The prose in this verse may be densely packed, but it is Pauline basics. It should give his auditors perspective because it is clearly rehearsing something that they are supposed to know as elementary.

Paul takes the cultural pulse on another matter in this passage: How does one come to know God (1:21)? Paul's statement, merely adumbrated here but developed further elsewhere, is that in God's wisdom it is not by wisdom that one comes to know God (1:21). In other letters we can observe that Paul prefers to write of God's knowing believers (Gal 4:6). Later in 1 Corinthians Paul will look forward to that eschatological time when he will know as he has already been known (by God, understood; 13:12). Paul's convictions about grace lead him to think that the impetus for relationship with God, whether expressed in terms of faith or knowledge or whatever, moves from God to individuals, not the other way around.

# REFLECTIONS

**1.** Paul's setting of the wisdom of this world over against the wisdom of God risks misunderstanding of both. Across history people have sometimes used this passage to decry human aspirations for wisdom. In so doing, they have set faith over against wisdom, though it should be noted that Paul does not do so. Paul does not disparage wisdom per se. Rather, he casts it as wisdom versus wisdom. The wisdom of God is valued, and Paul does offer that wisdom in his preaching (2:6). At stake is the temptation for us to confuse redemption as coming from possessing the right wisdom, of mistaking salvation for thinking the proper way or having the right ideas. That is the wisdom of the world. Over against the wisdom of having the right ideas and associated status, Paul sets God's power, which has broken into sin's control of the world in the crucifixion of Christ, whom Paul calls "God's power and God's wisdom" (1:24); this power transforms and renews human beings and ultimately all of creation. The concern with wisdom is ultimately an emphasis on status. How do we weigh status in our time? Surely one way is through education, through what we know. Paul devalues the status that we might claim by our knowledge and expertise, but he does not oppose or discredit the use of our God-given minds and wisdom. What counts is not what one knows but by whom one is known.

**2.** Paul's note about not knowing God by means of wisdom (1:21) raises an important issue that has reverberated down through church history. There has always been the temptation to transform Christianity from a matter of proper relation to God (Paul's code word for that is "faith," meaning a proper trusting dependence on God to do what God has promised) to a question of holding the right ideas or opinions, to assenting to certain propositions. Some churches stress that the real test of belonging to them is on our affirmation of certain doctrinal claims (e.g., the inspiration of the Bible, the transubstantiation of the Communion elements, the virgin birth), in having the right ideas and beliefs. Paul is unfamiliar with such an interest.

**3.** At the heart of Paul's gospel is a *skandalon,* the cross. When we so frequently wear the cross as an art object, we may find it difficult to think of it as what it was: a scandalous method of capital punishment whose modern counterparts might be the electric chair or the gas chamber. At the center of worship sanctuaries stands the cross, the central symbol of the Christian faith, not a representation of money or a smiley face. We who hold on to the values of the world, whose structure is passing away, will surely stumble over the cross; we who hold on to the cross should be able to find reassurance when the world buffets and persecutes us. The cross as *skandalon* is a challenge to all rival values.

# 1 Corinthians 1:26-31, Paul's Application to the Auditors

## NIV

²⁶Brothers, think of what you were when you were called. Not many of you were wise by human standards; not many were influential; not many were of noble birth. ²⁷But God chose the foolish things of the world to shame the wise; God chose the weak things of the world to shame the strong. ²⁸He chose the lowly things of this world and the despised things—and the things that are not—to nullify the things that are, ²⁹so that no one may boast before him. ³⁰It is because of him that you are in Christ Jesus, who has become for us wisdom from God—that is, our righteousness, holiness and redemption. ³¹Therefore, as it is written: "Let him who boasts boast in the Lord."[a]

[a]31 Jer. 9:24

## NRSV

26Consider your own call, brothers and sisters:[a] not many of you were wise by human standards,[b] not many were powerful, not many were of noble birth. ²⁷But God chose what is foolish in the world to shame the wise; God chose what is weak in the world to shame the strong; ²⁸God chose what is low and despised in the world, things that are not, to reduce to nothing things that are, ²⁹so that no one[c] might boast in the presence of God. ³⁰He is the source of your life in Christ Jesus, who became for us wisdom from God, and righteousness and sanctification and redemption, ³¹in order that, as it is written, "Let the one who boasts, boast in[d] the Lord."

[a]Gk brothers   [b]Gk according to the flesh   [c]Gk no flesh
[d]Or of

# COMMENTARY

In his first effort to make a direct application to his hearers, Paul picks up a link word from the previous section: "call" (κλῆσις *klēsis*). Paul identifies the Corinthian believers as being among those called—that is, as among those people who are being saved (1:2, 24)—and further affirms his bond with them by naming them "brothers and sisters" (v. 26). Here we learn more about the congregation and about Paul's convictions regarding God's present purposes. Some few among the Corinthian believers were "wise" (σοφός *sophos*), "powerful" (δυνατός *dynatos*), and "high born" (εὐγενής *eugenēs*); most were not (1:26).[55] This demography of the Corinthian church mirrors the steep social pyramid of the culture from which the community is called.[56] There was no middle class in the Greco-Roman world. At the top of the pyramid were a few rich persons who were, therefore, automatically persons of power and status. Erastus, apparently Corinth's town treasurer (Rom 16:23), and Gaius, a host of the house church at Corinth (Rom 16:23), were no doubt among such

people. The majority of persons in that world, however, and in the church at Corinth as well, were poor and, therefore, lacked social status.

After openly recognizing the social disparity present among the Corinthian believers, Paul, in a finely crafted rhetorical structure, affirms the contrarian scheme of God's grace, introduced with a strong adversative: "nevertheless [ἀλλά *alla*] . . . God chose [ὁ θεός ἐξελέξατο *ho theos exelexato*] . . . God chose . . . God chose" (1:27-28). Similarly, the subjects of God's election are given the same emphasis by repetition of the threefold structure: God chose "the foolish things of the world . . . the weak things of the world . . . the lowborn of the world" (1:27-28) in order to "shame . . . shame . . . reduce to nothing" (vv. 27-28) their counterparts. God's purposes run counter to the structures and values of the culture; God's actions in Christ have already overturned the worldly status quo.

In a somewhat convoluted but emphatic construction, Paul declares that God's contrarian election has as its ultimate purpose the elimination of boasting: "so that all flesh [πᾶσα σάρξ *pasa sarx*] [semitism = everyone] might not boast before God" (1:29). Like every part of creation (3:21-23; 8:6; 10:26), Paul's auditors are "from God"; they are

55. Gerd Theissen, *The Social Setting of Pauline Christianity: Essays on Corinth*, ed. and trans. J. H. Schütz (Philadelphia: Fortress, 1982) 69-119.
56. Ramsay MacMullen, *Roman Social Relations 50 B.C. TO A.D. 284* (New Haven: Yale University Press, 1974) 89-94.

now "in Christ Jesus" (1:30), who became—note the shift from direct address of the Corinthians to encompass all believers, Paul included—"our wisdom, our righteousness and sanctification and redemption" (v. 30).

Boasting, a problem of considerable proportions in this letter, here emerges for the first time. But the ground for boasting's emergence has already been recognized by Paul when he associates wisdom and power (1:24) and thereby tips his hand regarding his conviction that any concern for wisdom at Corinth was sub rosa and in fact a clutching for power and its inseparable partner, status.

Verses 29 and 31 show that Paul's major concern is to undercut any basis for believers' boasting of their status with God, of their standing in Christ. How can they brag when it is God who has chosen, chosen, chosen them (1:27-28)? When most of them had no worldly prestige? When their "wisdom . . . righteousness and holiness and redemption" are all from God, and when believers have this wisdom, righteousness, holiness, and redemption only because they are in Christ Jesus, whom God has made all these things? The Corinthians hanker after wisdom; Paul does offer true wisdom, namely, Christ (1:24). By his identification of Christ with wisdom, Paul tries to convert their wisdom interests into salvation talk. The source of salvation is not what one knows or the elevated status one can hope to achieve by "having wisdom" as a sort of possession. Paul sees the whole matter almost completely the other way around. It is not what one possesses (e.g., wisdom) but who has redeemed you, who has become your Lord, that is the question. In that sense "Christ has become our wisdom," and in an effort to distinguish it from any worldly wisdom Paul refines the statement by calling forth a series of terms that are basic for Paul and that Paul more commonly used in preaching the gospel: righteousness, holiness, and redemption. Wisdom may have been a favorite of some Corinthians but Paul arrays alongside it, without apparent need for explanation, the other three: righteousness, holiness, and redemption. Righteousness (δικαιοσύνη *dikaiosynē*), whose root meaning also includes justification and justice *dikaiosynē*, is Paul's code word for the only right relation to God, namely the conferred standing that God freely bestows on those whom God has chosen (Rom 10:3; Phil 3:9). Holiness (ἁγιασμός *hagiasmos*), meaning being set apart for God,

another way of talking about being claimed by God, or being called to be a saint, is a reprise of the assertion with which the letter opened (1:2). Redemption (ἀπολύτρωσις *apolytrōsis*) is a term Paul takes from the social world of slavery where slaves were "bought with a price" (cf. ahead, 6:20; 7:23) and, therefore, were claimed by a new lord (κύριος *kyrios*) (cf. 1:31).

Christians' claims, their boasts, are always only derivative. They can boast only because God has claimed them in Christ and in Christ has given them all things, a theme that Paul will announce later (cf. 3:21-23). So, as it is written, the only boasting allowed is boasting in the Lord (v. 31; cf. Jer 9:24, which Paul has creatively altered to make explicit the connection with Christ already affirmed in v. 30; see also 1 Cor 15:31).

Two boastings appear in the text. One is unacceptable and improper; the other is appropriate and fitting. This is a typical Pauline move, seen across the corpus. For example, there is a proper and an improper walk (1 Cor 3:3; 2 Cor 10:2; Gal 5:16), a godly grief and a worldly grief (2 Cor 7:8-11), a hope grounded in faith and a hope as the world calculates things (Rom 4:18). In Jer 9:24, Paul sees confirmation that boasting in the Lord is proper (1 Cor 1:31; cf. 2 Cor 10:17 where he quotes the same Jeremiah passage again). Paul discredits self-commendation and lauds the Lord's commendation.[57] To brag about yourself is to lose track that it is God whose work has made you all that you can be. So the only boasting allowed is the one that is equivalent to expressing gratitude to God for what God has accomplished and is doing. To boast in the Lord is to credit the Lord as the source of life. Some Corinthians have lost their way on this issue and have begun to brag about themselves and their accomplishments.

As has been the case from the first appeal (1:10) forward, Paul has set the alternatives in the most hyperbolic fashion. In this passage he has done so as well. Here the alternatives are cast as "chosen" versus "wiped out" (or, as the term καταργέω [*katargeō*] may also mean, "to make powerless" or "to abolish," 1:28). Here the creator God's power to bring into being what does not exist is the same God's redemption of the lowly and the outcast

---

57. See Forbes's treatment of self-praise in antiquity: Christopher Forbes, "Comparison, Self Praise and Irony: Paul's Boasting and the Conventions of Hellenistic Rhetoric," *NTS* 32 (1986) 8-10.

and is the same God's bringing to denouement those who end up on the wrong side of this equation. The auditors would do well to make sure they know for certain which side they are on because the consequences of losing one's place are dire. Paul's rhetoric is designed to remind the Corinthians in whom God has done so much just where they stand and what is their destiny.

# REFLECTIONS

**1.** Boasting has gotten a bad reputation in Christian circles, no doubt because of persons like some of these Corinthians. The NIV corroborates that bad reputation by translating καυχάομαι (*kauchaomai*), when it is used positively, not as "boast" but as "rejoice" (Rom 5:2-3, 11) and as "glory" (Phil 3:3). Proper boasting can be a way of recognizing and celebrating what God has accomplished in one's life so far. Why should all boasting be eliminated just because some boasting can be done improperly? We Christians have trouble, sometimes, when things go well for us because we get a haughty and independent picture of how we came into such good times. We confuse our blessedness with our own effort, we diminish or eliminate God's hand in it or through it, and we lose perspective. The result can be improper boasting. By contrast, proper boasting would credit God and God's beneficence as the source of everything good and wonderful. It is like the surgeon, who after amazingly successful surgery and upon hearing the patient's expressions of gratitude, declares that it is God who deserves the glory.

**2.** The descriptions of those whom God chose (1:27-28) have their parallels in the people the four Gospels delight in showing Jesus as having fellowship with: lepers, tax collectors, prostitutes—in short, outsiders. It is ironic that while Jesus welcomed such people and Paul's church at Corinth seems to have been predominantly populated by persons of low social and economic standing, modern churches too often are not even hospitable to such. Some churches even ponder the propriety of having a food kitchen in the church because of the people it might attract. It is safe to wonder how worshipers might respond if such an outcast actually darkened the church door. Perhaps that is why 1 Peter declares that God's judgment must begin with "the household of God" (1 Pet 4:17).

# 1 Corinthians 2:1-5, Perspective-Keeping via Paul's Exemplary Pattern from the Founding Days

**NIV**

2 When I came to you, brothers, I did not come with eloquence or superior wisdom as I proclaimed to you the testimony about God.[a] [2]For I resolved to know nothing while I was with you except Jesus Christ and him crucified. [3]I came to you in weakness and fear, and with much trembling. [4]My message and my preaching were not with wise and persuasive words, but with a demonstration of the Spirit's power, [5]so that your faith might not rest on men's wisdom, but on God's power.

[a]*1 Some manuscripts as I proclaimed to you God's mystery*

**NRSV**

2 When I came to you, brothers and sisters,[a] I did not come proclaiming the mystery[b] of God to you in lofty words or wisdom. [2]For I decided to know nothing among you except Jesus Christ, and him crucified. [3]And I came to you in weakness and in fear and in much trembling. [4]My speech and my proclamation were not with plausible words of wisdom,[c] but with a demonstration of the Spirit and of power, [5]so that your faith might rest not on human wisdom but on the power of God.

[a]Gk *brothers*   [b]Other ancient authorities read *testimony*
[c]Other ancient authorities read *the persuasiveness of wisdom*

# COMMENTARY

Paul's retrospective narrative of the gospel's beginning in Corinth looks back over the three-year period since he left and selectively focuses on what he holds to be central and determinative; it also allows Paul to depict himself as having embodied the gospel to the Corinthians not only in his speech but also in his comportment. Paul's retrospective is not driven by a desire to ensure accuracy of the historical record; rather, his purpose is to be instructive, formative, and even constructive.[58] The gospel calls for proper comportment not only from the evangelist but also from the hearers. Paul's self-depiction features his exemplary and governing determination ("For I decided," 2:2) to be among them as one centered on "Christ Jesus and him crucified." Paul's inadequacies as judged by worldly standards—namely, his weakness, his fear and trembling (2:3), and his lack of flashy rhetorical style (2:4), proved a satisfactory, even fitting, medium for the transmission of the gospel of the cross and for the inauguration of the Corinthians' faith. Paul's limited eloquence and his determination to focus on the cross assured that the Corinthians' faith would be unmistakably seen for what it is: the Spirit's working as God's power in them. Neither Pauline rhetorical legerdemain nor status conferrable or available by association with Paul accounted for their faith; rather, it was God's power that seized the Corinthians and made them God's people.

For Paul the critical question is what stands at the center of the picture and by which all other parts of the picture gain their meaning and keep their perspective. Paul's answer: He made the careful decision at the beginning of his time with the Corinthians that it would be Christ and the cross, not just at the beginning but throughout. And, by implication, so it should be for the Corinthians in the present. If the crucified Christ is at the center of the picture and all else takes its definition and proportion with reference to that, then a constitutive, formative decision has been made about how the community can distinguish between what is important and what is less important or even indifferent. His statement that "we have this treasure in earthen vessels, to show that the transcendent power belongs to God and not to us" (2 Cor 4:7) can be read as a commentary on 1 Cor 2:1-5. Accordingly, boasting and concern with worldly status are out of order.

These verses contain Paul's narrative of community formation. As the apostle who brought the gospel, which he calls in an all-encompassing phrase "the mystery of God" (2:1),[59] to Corinth, Paul is free to recount the story as he sees fit and as serves his purposes in this letter, written some three years later. Note what he chooses to place at the center of the picture: "Christ Jesus and him crucified!" Neither his comportment nor his rhetoric drew attention to Paul; both, however, provided free rein to the Holy Spirit and God's power. It is no surprise, then, that Paul judges his work among the Corinthians as leaving no room for confusion; their faith is grounded on God's power, not on human wisdom or performance or status associated with sophisticated speech.

This passage exemplifies a Pauline tendency and, indeed, a standard rhetorical device known as refinement to use similar phrases to elaborate one another and to paint a rather general picture. While the similar phrases are not synonymous, neither are they technical terms and due to be distinguished by scholarly acumen. The "mystery of God" in 2:1 is identical with "my proclamation," which is the same as "my speech" in 2:4; at its heart is "Christ Jesus and him crucified" (2:2). In similar fashion, the "lofty words or wisdom" of 2:1 has a significant overlap with the "sophisticated, persuasive wisdom" of 2:4 and with the "human wisdom" of 2:5. Paul's refinement, both positively and negatively, makes sure that God's power made present through Christ's crucifixion, rather than Paul himself, stands at the center of the picture.

Paul's humility is exemplary. He who could have lorded it over the Corinthians, he who could have emphasized his role in bringing the gospel as a legitimization for his own status and authority over them, instead denigrates his own importance. He is what he is describing. In this passage he

---

58. George Lyons, *Pauline Autobiography: Toward a New Understanding*, SBLDS 73 (Atlanta: Scholars Press, 1985) 226-27.

59. Other Greek manuscripts read "the testimony of God," which would refer to Paul's own formative preaching to them, his testimony about God to them at the origin of their coming to faith. See 2:7 and 4:1.

portrays himself as having embodied the Christ-centered life in his inauguration of the gospel in Corinth. We must assume that his picture had enough verisimilitude to be recognizable to the auditors. His comportment and focus have not changed from the time he first entered Corinth to the time of his writing of 1 Corinthians. Paul presents himself as a radical contrast with those whose association with the gospel provides the ground for enhancement of personal status.

We should not be carried too far toward imagining Paul as an inadequate speaker (2:1). In 2 Cor 11:6 he acknowledges that, somewhat like Moses (Exod 4:10-11), he is unskilled in speaking, but contemporary rhetorical training urged orators to say precisely that about themselves. In that same letter fragment, however, he quotes some as saying that his letters may be powerful enough but "his bodily presence is weak and his speech disdainful" (2 Cor 10:10). While his speech may not have been eloquently delivered, the evidence across the corpus is that it was powerfully effective (cf. Gal 4:13-15; Phil 1:13-14; 1 Thess 2:13). And in the passage before us we have his understanding of why his speech, though not itself powerful, had power—God's power—nonetheless.

The passage is laced with irony. In ironic contrast, Paul reminds the auditors that the gospel focuses on Christ the crucified one, that the one who brought the gospel to them was identified not by the trappings of power and prestige but by frailty, fright, and trembling—and, at the end of these nouns, as if to emphasize his unprepossessing presence, he adds πολύς (*polys,* "much"), which in Greek can be understood to modify each of the preceding. Paul was then and is at the time of his writing the example of the one who, though he could have vaunted himself and called attention to himself, stood aside and pointed ever so clearly at Christ crucified. And the result the Corinthians know full well: The power of God, not human wisdom or cultured speech, produced faith among the Corinthians.

# REFLECTIONS

**1.** "I determined to know nothing among you except Jesus Christ and him crucified" (2:2). Paul uses hyperbole, an exaggeration, as a means of focusing on what is central. By so doing, Paul establishes that what brings Christians together and holds them together is the crucified (and risen) Lord. As we observed in 1:26, the Corinthian congregation was socioeconomically diverse, assuring that different social practices and values were represented among them. What could hold such a diverse group together other than a focus on believers' common grounding in Christ expressed in the sharing of Christ's death as represented in baptism? So today Christians of different ethnic and regional backgrounds who differ culturally, politically, and socially, can find unity if they have as their common starting point "Jesus Christ and him crucified." That is no doubt easier to say than to do. Our attention is so readily caught by our differences rather than by what holds us together in its power. If we look for unity in anything other than the cross we will become something other than the church.

**2.** We must not miss Paul's self-portrait as the stumbling, not-very-gifted speaker. Laypersons today who are asked to share their faith or to talk about the gospel in whatever way, but who are reticent to speak because they feel insecure or inadequate, could take some solace from Paul's self-portrait here. The power of one's own witness, if it is to have any, is ultimately God's power, and God has been pleased to make that power effective through all sorts of cracked, damaged vessels (cf. 2 Cor 4:7). Pastors might also receive some guidance from Paul here if they made certain that their every homiletical effort brought the heart of the gospel into engagement with their hearers.

# 1 Corinthians 2:6-16, Two Wisdoms, Two Spirits, Two Representative People

NIV

[6]We do, however, speak a message of wisdom among the mature, but not the wisdom of this age or of the rulers of this age, who are coming to nothing. [7]No, we speak of God's secret wisdom, a wisdom that has been hidden and that God destined for our glory before time began. [8]None of the rulers of this age understood it, for if they had, they would not have crucified the Lord of glory. [9]However, as it is written:

"No eye has seen,
    no ear has heard,
no mind has conceived
    what God has prepared for those who love
        him"[a]—

[10]but God has revealed it to us by his Spirit.

The Spirit searches all things, even the deep things of God. [11]For who among men knows the thoughts of a man except the man's spirit within him? In the same way no one knows the thoughts of God except the Spirit of God. [12]We have not received the spirit of the world but the Spirit who is from God, that we may understand what God has freely given us. [13]This is what we speak, not in words taught us by human wisdom but in words taught by the Spirit, expressing spiritual truths in spiritual words.[b] [14]The man without the Spirit does not accept the things that come from the Spirit of God, for they are foolishness to him, and he cannot understand them, because they are spiritually discerned. [15]The spiritual man makes judgments about all things, but he himself is not subject to any man's judgment:

[16]"For who has known the mind of the Lord
    that he may instruct him?"[c]

But we have the mind of Christ.

[a]9 Isaiah 64:4    [b]13 Or Spirit, interpreting spiritual truths to spiritual men    [c]16 Isaiah 40:13

NRSV

6Yet among the mature we do speak wisdom, though it is not a wisdom of this age or of the rulers of this age, who are doomed to perish. [7]But we speak God's wisdom, secret and hidden, which God decreed before the ages for our glory. [8]None of the rulers of this age understood this; for if they had, they would not have crucified the Lord of glory. [9]But, as it is written,

"What no eye has seen, nor ear heard,
    nor the human heart conceived,
what God has prepared for those who love
        him"—

[10]these things God has revealed to us through the Spirit; for the Spirit searches everything, even the depths of God. [11]For what human being knows what is truly human except the human spirit that is within? So also no one comprehends what is truly God's except the Spirit of God. [12]Now we have received not the spirit of the world, but the Spirit that is from God, so that we may understand the gifts bestowed on us by God. [13]And we speak of these things in words not taught by human wisdom but taught by the Spirit, interpreting spiritual things to those who are spiritual.[a]

14Those who are unspiritual[b] do not receive the gifts of God's Spirit, for they are foolishness to them, and they are unable to understand them because they are spiritually discerned. [15]Those who are spiritual discern all things, and they are themselves subject to no one else's scrutiny.

[16] "For who has known the mind of the Lord
    so as to instruct him?"

But we have the mind of Christ.

[a]Or interpreting spiritual things in spiritual language, or comparing spiritual things with spiritual    [b]Or natural

# COMMENTARY

Whereas 1:18–2:5 contrasted human weakness and human wisdom with God's power in the gospel, the present verses refine that contrast, although Paul now concedes that he does in fact speak a particular wisdom, a wisdom he describes as "not of this age [aeon]," a wisdom that is available to the "mature" and that he has already identified with Christ (1:24). Rhetorical refinement such as this dwells on the same subject but by casting the issue differently seems to be embarking on new territory and ensures the audience's continued attention. Earlier the two-way schema was (human) wisdom versus (God's) power; now it is (God's "secret and hidden") wisdom versus wisdom (of this age, of this age's rulers, and of unspiritual persons). Verses 6-16 are an elaboration, a descanting on the two-way contrast presented in vv. 1-5.

The present passage is framed on an extended opposition: There are two contending wisdoms, two opposed spirits, and, accordingly, two disparate human options, here represented by a single exemplar on each side. The passage pays especial attention to these exemplars, idealizing, on the one side, the "spiritual person" who is taught by the Holy Spirit (2:13), has access to the mysterious, otherwise hidden wisdom of God, and understands "what is truly God's" (2:11) as well as the "gifts bestowed on us by God" (2:12). We must recall that the word "Christian" had not yet been invented as an identifier in Paul's time (cf. Acts 11:26; 26:28, written some decades after Paul); "spiritual person" is probably Paul's own positive construction (cf. Gal 6:1) that properly identifies a believer with the working and inspiration of the Holy Spirit.[60] Over against this person, Paul sets the negative exemplar, the culturally valued sage, the worldly "wise person" who does not accept or receive (δέχομαι *dechomai*) "the things of the Spirit" (2:14).

We modern readers have one advantage over the Corinthians who first received this letter, who probably heard it read to them: We have the luxury of knowing what comes later in the letter and can read an earlier passage in the light of Paul's

purpose as disclosed in a subsequent passage. Verse 6 opens with an invitation for Paul's hearers to include themselves among the mature, the spiritual people, who can receive Paul's not-of-this-age wisdom, and closes by giving them the opportunity to identify themselves with the spiritual person who understands (2:14-15). It even adds the extraordinary claim, "We have the mind of Christ" (2:16). Paul's notoriously ambiguous use of "we" sometimes refers to him alone but, as here, it sometimes leaves an opening for the hearer to identify with Paul. So this passage is framed by an invitation to the Corinthians to think of themselves as mature and also to think of themselves as having the "mind of Christ," which locution in Paul usually means that persons pattern themselves after Christ (cf. Phil 2:1-5).

Imagine the shock in 3:1, however, when Paul tells the Corinthians that he cannot address them as spiritual persons; instead, he must treat them as babies in Christ. An idealized picture of where the Corinthians should be in their maturity, not where they are, is painted in 2:6-16; 3:1-4 describes where they are. In 2:6-16 Paul, like the Cynic choir master before him, sets the pitch a bit high so that more of the singers will come in on note; 3:1-4 is a reality check of some dissonance, but more on that below.

The basic two-way alternative—"those who are perishing" versus "us who are being saved"—was introduced in 1:18. Verses 6-16 elaborate that alternative and once again invite the hearers' identification, on the positive side of the alternative, with "spiritual people." On the one side is the wisdom of this present age and its rulers, who are said, literally, to be passing away (2:6). Like the "unspiritual people" mentioned in 2:14, who "do not receive the gifts of God's Spirit," those rulers, surely the temporal ones (and possibly also the cosmic powers whose ultimate destiny is expressed in 15:24), did not perceive the secret, hidden wisdom of God, so they "crucified the Lord of glory" (2:8).[61] In Paul's view there is a great, unbridgeable gulf between "those who are perishing"

---

60. See Richard Horsley, "Pneumatikos vs. Psychikos: Distinctions of Spiritual Status among the Corinthians," *HTR* 69 (1976) 269-88.

61. Those who would import gnostic concerns into their interpretation of 1 Corinthians seize on 2:7-8, but nothing here or in the opening chapters suggests that Paul has in mind any such mythological construction.

and the ones "who are being saved" (1:18), between the rulers of this age "who are blind to the Lord of glory," "who are passing away," and the Spirit-inspired persons, the "spiritual people," "who discern all things" (2:15).

The "secret and hidden" character of God's wisdom lies not just in its never having been disclosed before but also in its anticipated grandeur. Neither normal eyesight nor human imagination, as they are available to the rulers of this aeon and to unspiritual persons, can grasp "what God has prepared for those who love him" (2:9, a Pauline amalgamation of scriptural echoes; cf. Isa 52:15; 64:3 LXX). "What God has prepared" is both present already and yet not finished (cf. 1:7; 15:20-28). Without God's Spirit no one would have a clue as to the shape or grandeur of God's purpose (2:10; cf. Job 11:7). But "to those who are being saved" God has revealed the Holy Spirit as the means of fathoming "what God has prepared for those who love him" (2:9-11). Only the Spirit knows "the things of God" (2:13), and believers have received that Spirit, not the alternative, opposing spirit of the world (2:12). Believers know and can be expected to know, through the teaching of the Holy Spirit, "even the depths of God" (2:10). The Holy Spirit marks off the ones who are being saved; it enables them to recognize the Lord of glory, not to crucify him; and it helps them understand the "things bestowed . . . by God" (2:12). Only the Spirit-inspired believers, the truly mature, can understand the only true wisdom—namely, the one that Paul speaks (2:6). That is the point of the cryptic clause at the end of 2:13: Only spiritual persons understand spiritual things.

Assumed, but not argued in detail here, is Paul's deep conviction that all believers have received the Spirit (cf. Rom 8:14-17; Gal 3:1), and we have already had occasion to see Paul's reference to baptism (1:14-17), which later in this letter he associates with the reception of the Spirit (12:13). Paul's rich pneumatology is only partially in view in 2:6-16—precisely because his purposes here do not call for anything more. Later in 1 Corinthians we will see Paul's understanding that the Spirit is the provider of charismata for the good of the community (chap. 12). Nowhere in 1 Corinthians, however, would one find Paul's conviction that the Spirit joins with human spirits at the inception of faith and enables people to become God's children (Rom 8:15-16; Gal 4:6); nowhere in this letter would one learn that the Spirit helps in prayer (Rom 8:26), that the Spirit is a down payment of all that God will eschatologically give believers (2 Cor 1:22; 5:5), or that the Spirit produces fruit in the everyday lives of believers (Gal 5:22).

The phrase "those who are unspiritual" (2:14 NRSV) rightly derives its primary definition, via negativa, from Paul's predominant interest in the other group: "those who are spiritual"—that is, those with the Spirit (= all true believers). The Greek term translated "those who are unspiritual" is ψυχικός (psychikos), pertaining to the natural, not the spiritual realm. In 15:46 Paul reemploys the same contrast. Throughout 2:6-16 Paul has been concerned to set up alternatives. The spiritual person, taught by the Spirit, understands spiritual things; the natural person, out of that loop, cannot accept "things of the Spirit," indeed takes them as foolishness, and cannot understand them because they are "spiritually discerned"—that is, they can be examined and known only with the assistance of the Spirit (2:14).

Paul has shown two fundamental assumptions about people and life in these verses. First, just as there are two ways, so also all humans can be divided into two groups: those with the Spirit and those without. Second, those with the Spirit can discern (the same Greek verb appears at the end of 2:14 and is repeated twice in 2:15 and has the range of meanings "discern," "examine," and "know") everything that the unspiritual persons can plus all that is disclosed by the Spirit, who, we must recall, fathoms even the depths of God (2:10). For that reason, Paul concludes (2:15) both that the truly spiritual person "examines, knows, discerns" all things and that the truly spiritual person can claim, with Paul, that "we have the mind of Christ" (2:16).

Spiritual persons, Paul's epitome of the life of faith properly lived, are described in two complementary ways: They have received the Spirit of God (2:11), the Spirit that is from God (2:12), and they have the mind of Christ (2:16). In 1:10 Paul called upon the divisively inclined Corinthians to be united in the same mind but made no specification about which mind that might be; in 2:6-16 he now elaborates the mind both by reference to the Holy Spirit by which believers can know "even the things of God" (2:11) and by reference to

Christ, with whom believers can be of one mind (2:16; cf. Phil 2:1-11). When believers are properly guided by the Spirit and have the mind of Christ, they know what is going on, they know what matters, and they are enabled to live in accord with God's purposes.

One more claim about the spiritual person merits closer examination. According to Paul, the spiritual person is subject to the discernment or examination of "no one" (2:15). What does Paul mean here? Does "no one" refer to no one who is from among the unspiritual people? That is the most logical consideration, given his careful, insistent division of humanity into two groups with respect to their access to the Holy Spirit. But one might also ask whether this portrait of the spiritual person who is beyond examination invites any already haughty Corinthians to consider themselves as spiritual persons who are, therefore, (a) able to examine and know all things, and (b) not subject to examination by others. If so, it would seem that Paul has wandered into their camp and bids fair, by rejecting accountability, to heighten the schismatic tendencies of some Corinthians. Such an interpretation would be consistent with Paul's invitation in 2:6 for the Corinthians to think of themselves as "the mature" because Paul readily admits he does impart wisdom to such persons. To see how Paul protects himself from this trap, we will need to study 3:1-4.

Paul's mention of wisdom and rulers "of this age" (τοῦ αἰῶνος τούτου *tou aiōnos toutou*) suggests (rightly) that he thinks of multiple ages. "This age" is always pejorative for Paul (cf. 1:20; 3:18; Rom 12:2); it is an "evil age" (Gal 1:4) dominated by sin, from whose strangling grip God has delivered those who have died with Christ. Those belonging to "this age" are, like the rulers mentioned in 2:8, blinded to what is really going on in God's purpose. In Christ, the new has come, the "new creation" has begun (2 Cor 5:17; Gal 6:15). Those endowed with the Spirit of God can fathom the things of God and so can see that the newness has indeed come in Christ.

So Paul's view is that those who have died with Christ and come to newness of life (Rom 6:4) live in two ages at once. The old age, championed and defined by sin and its power, has been dealt a death blow ("the schema of this world is passing away," 1 Cor 7:31) in Christ's death and resurrec-

tion, but the old age continues, holding sway as if it thought itself to have the last word. So believers, those in Christ, live in the old age, but their citizenship is in heaven (Phil 3:20). This evil age has its idolatrous power, its own allure, and its offer of status; it bids for believers' allegiance. Believers live in this evil age—there is no alternative until Christ's parousia and the end of the age—but they walk according to the Holy Spirit (Gal 5:25). This means that believers live in this age "as if not" living in this age; for believers there is a certain eschatological detachment from the age, its values, and its goals (for more on this, see the Commentary on 7:26-31).

As we can see in this passage, Paul sometimes develops his notion of the evil age by making negative claims about "the world" (πνεῦμα τοῦ κόσμου *pneuma tou kosmou,* 2:12). We need to keep clear that Paul writes about the "world" in two very different ways, depending on his purposes. On the one hand, as here, Paul writes (negatively) of a "spirit of this world" as a means of expressing his concern that the Corinthians have brought the values of their culture, their world, into the church. The world has a putative wisdom (1 Cor 1:20), which Paul equates with the world's folly (1:27). On the other hand, for Paul, the world is God's creation, "the earth is the Lord's and its fullness" (10:26; Ps 24:1), God is the world's judge (Rom 3:6, 19), and God's faithful will inherit it (Rom 4:13; cf. Matt 5:5). In Christ's death God was reclaiming the creation, reconciling the world to God's very self (Rom 11:15; 2 Cor 5:19).

In 2:6-16 Paul makes some assumptions about how one knows whatever one knows. Paul assumes that there are two levels of perception: one that is available to everyone and on which some things can be grasped clearly enough; and another whose important insights are available only as a special gift. His understanding is grounded in his apocalyptic viewpoint, which holds that what one can perceive by unassisted human perception is surely limited and possibly distorted. Witness Paul's treatment of what he calls "the rulers of this aeon": (ἄρχοντες τοῦ αἰῶνος τούτου *archontes tou aiōnos toutou*). They did not understand what was before their eyes, deprived as they were of the mysterious and hidden wisdom of God (2:6-8), so they "crucified the Lord of glory" (2:8). Apocalyptic literature always supposes that the true story of what is going on is revealed, uncovered to chosen recipients via a dream, a vision, or, as here, by the working of God's Spirit (2:10). So for Paul it is the Holy Spirit that has disclosed what otherwise would be unknowable—namely, what God is doing in Christ. The very revelation is itself grace, a freely given, unmerited gift from God without which gift believers would be as blind as this aeon's rulers who were clueless as to God's purposes (2:8).

# REFLECTIONS

**1.** One of the great struggles across the history of the church has been how to value creation, the world, and humans' relation to it. In what sense is redemption a deliverance from the world? If one goes to an extreme one can say with docetics and gnostics that the world either was always corrupt and deficient or has become so corroded by sin and evil that salvation must be seen as an extrication of believers from the world and its morass. Paul's view is that the world has, indeed, been corrupted by human sinfulness (Rom 1:18-28) but that God's redemptive purpose in Christ is to restore all of creation to the glory it had before sin caused it to lose its former glory (Rom 8:17-25).

A further step down that same docetic (a form of christology that emphasizes Christ's divinity at the expense of his humanity) and gnostic line has been to claim that human bodies, as part of that creation, are also corrupt and irredeemable—with the inevitable claim that only the soul or spirit of a person is salvageable. But the mainstream of Christian tradition (and Paul himself!) has rejected such extreme claims about bodies (for more on Paul's understanding of body see 1 Cor 6:13; 15:35-41) and about the world as diminishing the richness of our affirmation about God as Creator and about redemption as re-creation.

If the world is not God's good creation, then our choices do not have to respect the world as our habitat. Then the world is ultimately to be escaped. Some discussion about heaven treats the world in that way. Accordingly, if the body and our fleshliness is considered alien to the inner spark or soul that is to be saved from it, then one could cite the antinomian cry, "Let us eat, drink, and be merry, for tomorrow we die." Those who hold with Paul, that the creation is God's and therefore good and that the body is good (cf. Rom 12:1), must make choices and decisions that honor their own bodies and the rest of creation.

**2.** This is the first of several places in 1 Corinthians in which Paul talks about judging, a very complex topic in this letter and no doubt inspired by a Corinthian readiness to judge one another in ways Paul found unacceptable. First, it must be said that Paul never assumes that believers "play God." It is God who judges (Rom 2:1-2; 14:12-13); it is only the Lord who can discern the secret and hidden purposes of the heart (1 Cor 4:5). A house servant either "stands or falls" (eschatological judgment terms in Paul's lexicon) before his or her own master (Rom 14:4). Others have no business meddling in what is divine prerogative, which, in Paul's view, will fully and finally take place at the return of the Lord (Rom 14:10; 2 Cor 5:10). Second, Paul marks off the borders of the community with vice lists (cf. Rom 1:29-32; 1 Cor 5:9-13; 6:9-11; 2 Cor 12:20-21; Gal 5:19-21; see the Commentary and Reflections at 1 Cor 5:9-13). Believers should steer a wide course away from the vices of these lists because such comportment is completely incompatible with membership in the body of Christ. The community has the responsibility to guard the God-given holiness of the congregation, to warn any who stray too near the borders as designated by the vice lists, and to censure anyone, like the man mentioned in 5:1-5, who has violated the sanctity of the borders. This type of judgment, which clearly from 5:5 is not final like divine judgment, but provisional and admonitory, is not only acceptable to Paul but necessary for the health of the community. An important part of community life for Paul is believers' upbuilding, encouragement, consolation, and warning of one another in the daily walk of faith (1 Cor 4:14; 14:3; 1 Thess 5:12, 14).

Modern Christians sometimes find Paul's sense of mutual responsibility troublesome. In part, also, that is because modern Christianity, in distinction from its Pauline origins, has become so intensely personalized and individualized that someone could say: "The only thing that finally matters is my own personal relation to God." In part it is because community discipline has sometimes been used as a display of power and as a cudgel to enforce a rigid conformity that Paul would not have countenanced (cf. Rom 14:2-5). The dynamics and health of Christian community would probably best be served if Christians could put into practice the delicate balance that Paul tries to achieve between personal, individual differences and distinctions on the one hand and community needs and support on the other. It is no accident that in various letters Paul expresses his concern that when one person stumbles or goes astray all suffer; when one is honored all benefit (Rom 12:15; 1 Cor 12:26; 2 Cor 11:29). Abundant sociological studies have demonstrated that communities that have no concern with standards and border keeping cannot maintain their sense of being a community.[62] So the issue is how one maintains the standards of Christian community in a way that is wholly in tune with the love and justice that all believers must honor.

**3.** Paul's letters never use the term "Christian." What moderns would call a "Christian" Paul calls a "spiritual person," that is, one who has received the Holy Spirit. So Paul's primary definition of the believer is by means of the Spirit; likewise, the reception of the Spirit is for Paul the hallmark of entry into the community. Modern Christians ought to wonder from this why so many make so little over the Spirit and its working in the life of faith and in the community. Many modern Christians are Spirit-poor; Paul and his earliest followers were Spirit-rich. It is fair to suppose that the difference lies not in the Spirit's having disappeared but in modern believers' failure to note, appreciate, and cultivate the Spirit's workings. Churches would do well to focus some of their worship life and some of their classes on understanding how the Spirit works and in discerning the Spirit in their communal and individual lives. A good place to start would be Paul's multifaceted picture of the Holy Spirit and its multifarious workings in the life of faith (see 3:16-17).

62. Peter L. Berger and Thomas Luckmann, *The Social Construction of Reality* (Garden City, N.Y.: Doubleday, 1966) 79-82.

# 1 Corinthians 3:1-4, Not Spiritual People, Babies, Merely Human

**3** Brothers, I could not address you as spiritual but as worldly—mere infants in Christ. [2]I gave you milk, not solid food, for you were not yet ready for it. Indeed, you are still not ready. [3]You are still worldly. For since there is jealousy and quarreling among you, are you not worldly? Are you not acting like mere men? [4]For when one says, "I follow Paul," and another, "I follow Apollos," are you not mere men?

**3** And so, brothers and sisters,[a] I could not speak to you as spiritual people, but rather as people of the flesh, as infants in Christ. [2]I fed you with milk, not solid food, for you were not ready for solid food. Even now you are still not ready, [3]for you are still of the flesh. For as long as there is jealousy and quarreling among you, are you not of the flesh, and behaving according to human inclinations? [4]For when one says, "I belong to Paul," and another, "I belong to Apollos," are you not merely human?

[a] Gk *brothers*

# Commentary

After 2:6-16, in which Paul painted such a lofty picture of mature, spiritual persons, 3:1-4 had to have a jarring effect upon the Corinthian hearers. Far from being mature or spiritual, Paul calls them "babies in Christ" (νήπιοι ἐν Χριστῷ *nēpioi en Christō*), and, in an effort to stress how disconnected they are from the Spirit, he three times characterizes them as "of the flesh" (3:1, 3). The Pauline alternative to being "of the Spirit" is to be "of the flesh" (σάρκινος *sarkinos*). The spiritual persons, as he just described them in 2:6-16, are the ones who are made privy to the otherwise unfathomable "depths of God" precisely by the work of the Spirit. They are the ones who should know what is going on. Their counterparts, those "of the flesh," are—given Paul's relentless two-way characterizations throughout the letter so far—the "ones who are perishing" (*apollymenoi*, 1:18), the ones who are like the *archontes tou aiōnos* "rulers of this aeon" (2:6-8). They are, as he tells them in 3:3, people without a clue.

Not content to let it go, Paul presses further regarding their immaturity: They should have been ready for solid food but could handle only milk (3:2). What is Paul's evidence of their immaturity? Their factionalism is emphasized twice over: "jealousy and quarreling" (ζῆλος καὶ ἔρις *zēlos kai eris*) (3:3, an echo of 1:10-11) and factionalism represented by Paul's oblique exemplification, "I belong to Paul," "I belong to Apollos" (3:4, a reprise of 1:12). Regrettably, nothing distinguishes the Corinthians from the persons Paul described as "unspiritual" or "natural" in 2:14: The Corinthians "behave" (περιπατέω *peripateō*) (lit., "walk") like them (3:3); the believers are divisive and contentious just like them (3:3); Corinthians forge partisan allegiances just as they do. Paul is left no other conclusion: "Are you not merely human?" (3:4), meaning, just like persons who have not been claimed by the Holy Spirit.

Later in this letter Paul will celebrate diversity and differences among the believers and credit the Holy Spirit with contributing to it and creating it. The difference is that there Paul affirms that the distinctions are inspired by the Spirit to work for and to enrich the common good (1 Cor 12:7). There diversity enriches the communion that the commu-nity shares; each person brings distinctive gifts to enrich the common, shared life in the community. In the early chapters of 1 Corinthians, Paul sees differences in a very different light. The differences are not Spirit-inspired, and they surely do not enrich the common good. Neither do they enhance the common life. In fact, the divisiveness and factionalism Paul decries destroy community, heighten individualism, and lead to boasting regarding oneself or one's associates and a denigration of others.

Implicit in Paul's chiding identification of the divisive Corinthians as babies and persons who take their cues from the flesh is the unstated counterpart—namely, that Paul has identified the truly spiritual persons as the ones he would also call mature or adult. Other letters allow us to see that Paul does, indeed, think of believers as moving from their starting point as babies in Christ toward greater and greater maturity. The life of faith is a life of growth, of maturing, of growing up. Philemon's slave Onesimus, with his conversion to the faith, has become Paul's child in the faith (Phlm 10). Paul's picture of the entry into the faith is one of a child being able to call God "Daddy" (Rom 8:15; Gal 4:6). From the babylike inception of the faith Paul expects believers to grow toward maturity. The term he uses to express that maturity is τέλειος (*teleios;* Phil 3:15), which can be translated as "perfect," "complete," "mature," "adult," or "fully developed." One who is *teleios* has reached the end or goal (*teleios*) that is appropriate. Paul even understands his own life of faith as exhibiting that same kind of growth toward full adulthood, as he tells the Philippians; though he knows he has not yet reached that goal, has not yet been perfected or become fully mature (τετελείωμαι *teteleiōmai,* Phil 3:12), he nevertheless presses on toward it.

The best that Paul can say about the Corinthians is that their understanding and comportment show that they are merely babies in the faith. Those who think of themselves as spiritual persons but who contribute to divisions in the community are immature and have an incorrect self-assessment.

Paul escalates the rhetoric: Perhaps they are not even babies in the faith (3:3). When they are schismatic, for whatever reason, the Corinthian believers are as far as possible from maturity and an understanding of what the Spirit produces. Not subtly, Paul tells the Corinthians that they have seriously overestimated themselves and their maturity of faith. Although they are still his "brothers and sisters" (3:1), they are clearly his younger, dependent siblings. The image has yet to surface explicitly in this letter, but Paul in fact considers himself their father in the faith (4:14-15). His relationship to the Corinthian believers is paradoxical. As the one who brought the gospel to the Corinthians and thereby brought them into the family of God, he is *patér*, father, the one who is ultimately responsible for all the children. On the other hand, for those who are in Christ, for those who have died with Christ, there is no distinction whatsoever (cf. Gal 3:28) because all are equally dependent upon God's grace and, accordingly, they are his brothers and sisters. Both features are true for Paul; like a father, Paul provides his children, who are also his "brothers and sisters" in Christ, some back-to-basics instruction, using himself and Apollos as models.

Throughout the opening two chapters of this letter there have been hints that Paul and at least some of the Corinthians have differing estimates of the maturity of the Corinthian believers. With 3:1-4 the discrepancy in evaluations emerges explicitly. They will not have thought of themselves as marginal babies in the faith, though that is what Paul calls them straight-out. And this will not be the last time that Paul reflects on how much his assessment of them differs from their own.

# REFLECTIONS

Paul knows that the Corinthian believers are immature because they bicker and are divisive; in fact, they are acting just like ordinary people, not believers. The Corinthians are the mother church of all subsequent squabbling churches. One of the great shames of the church is that the family of God has so many offspring who will not talk and commune with each other. Christians should find ways to honor the divinely inspired differences that we all bring to the common table without charging one another with being wrong. Different is not necessarily wrong. In the midst of our genuine differences of gifts and graces we should welcome one another in love (Rom 14:1; 15:7).

# 1 Corinthians 3:5-9, Apollos and Paul: Models

| NIV | NRSV |
|---|---|
| 5What, after all, is Apollos? And what is Paul? Only servants, through whom you came to believe—as the Lord has assigned to each his task. 6I planted the seed, Apollos watered it, but God made it grow. 7So neither he who plants nor he who waters is anything, but only God, who makes things grow. 8The man who plants and the man who waters have one purpose, and each will be rewarded according to his own labor. 9For we are God's fellow workers; you are God's field, God's building. | 5What then is Apollos? What is Paul? Servants through whom you came to believe, as the Lord assigned to each. 6I planted, Apollos watered, but God gave the growth. 7So neither the one who plants nor the one who waters is anything, but only God who gives the growth. 8The one who plants and the one who waters have a common purpose, and each will receive wages according to the labor of each. 9For we are God's servants, working together; you are God's field, God's building. |

# COMMENTARY

Apollos was merely mentioned in 1:12 and in 3:4. Now he receives more attention. All in all, we know relatively little about him. According to Acts, Apollos, an Alexandrian Jew tutored in the faith by Priscilla and Aquila, worked with the Corinthians: "He greatly helped those who through grace had become believers" (Acts 18:27). In this detail the Acts portrait concurs with Paul's claim: Apollos watered what Paul had planted (3:6). Paul differentiates his and Apollos's roles in such a way as to recognize and honor their differences, but what Paul and Apollos did is not so important as (a) that it was God working through their various efforts, and (b) that there was growth. Paul describes himself and Apollos as servants (διάκονοι *diakonoi*, 3:5), fellow workers (3:9) (συνεργοί *synergoi*), who contributed their own labors—one planted, the other watered (3:6)—"as the Lord assigned to each" (3:5). Paul's conviction that God or the Lord makes assignments to each as God or the Lord desires will be repeatedly reaffirmed later in the letter (7:17; 12:11, 18, 24*b*). The force of Paul's argumentation is lost in the NRSV and the NIV renderings of 3:8. More representative of the Greek would be the following: "The planter and the waterer are one; each will receive his own wages according to his own work." Paul and Apollos are presented as united, as one (ἕν εἰσιν *hen eisin*), though distinct exemplars for the Corinthian believers. The divinely assigned, different functions have the same source (the Lord) and the same end (growth); the individuals retain their differences but are "one," and, Paul extends the metaphor, each will receive a wage based on his own work (cf. Rom 2:6; 2 Cor 5:10). As the letter unfolds, it becomes clear that Paul thinks the Corinthians should be able to see themselves in this mirrored portrait. Implicit in the metaphor is that the Corinthians are "God's field" (3:9); they are the ones who have been the beneficiaries of Paul's planting, Apollos's watering, and God's giving of growth.

It is not surprising that Paul's chief metaphor in this passage is growth because 3:1-4 was founded on the premise that the Corinthians should have grown up more, that they should not still be babies. That passage was structured on the analogy of the family; vv. 5-6 share the presupposition of growth but move the analogy to agriculture, stressing planting and watering.

The passage closes with a refinement. The agrarian imagery gives way to architectural: "You are God's field, God's building." The building metaphor plays a prominent role in the rest of the letter, beginning in the next passage.

# REFLECTIONS

**1.** Paul uses evocative images for the church. Many of them may remind us of Jesus' parables where, for example, fields and buildings also appear. Most of Paul's metaphors feature growth, not so much of numbers as of maturing. A church is always a work-in-progress (the same point of babies who should be growing to maturity; cf. 3:1-2). They can never become satisfied with themselves, but must always be working to improve how well they reflect God's love to the world and among themselves. If we take seriously that we the church are the site where God has chosen to dwell (as Paul will develop that idea in 3:16-17; cf. Gal 2:20), then we will have to live in a way that honors God as host and guest.

Paul's images are rich with implications for the life of faith. The nurture and care of any member of God's family or any planting in God's field requires the attention and tutelage of many others. Believers' lives are always intertwined and interdependent. Accordingly, we should give more attention to the nurturing and supporting roles each person can and should play. Every believer should be both the recipient and donor of nurture and encouragement. If you do not experience both, then you should see what can be done to change the situation. One good starting point could be to make sure that you are supportive and encouraging to others. Another could be a determination to recognize and honor the points at which God's grace is working in your life.

**2.** Paul uses the Greek term *diakonos* ("servant"; the English word "deacon" comes from this term) to describe himself and Apollos. Clearly, Paul claims no special status or honor by this self-description; rather, he seems to use it as a term to describe someone whose work is a channel for God's working. When you are a conduit for God's work, when service to others is done by you, then you are a *diakonos* whether the church officially designates you as such or not. To be a deacon is not an option but an expectation of the gospel.

# 1 Corinthians 3:10-15, The Foundation and Each Person's Work

NIV

[10]By the grace God has given me, I laid a foundation as an expert builder, and someone else is building on it. But each one should be careful how he builds. [11]For no one can lay any foundation other than the one already laid, which is Jesus Christ. [12]If any man builds on this foundation using gold, silver, costly stones, wood, hay or straw, [13]his work will be shown for what it is, because the Day will bring it to light. It will be revealed with fire, and the fire will test the quality of each man's work. [14]If what he has built survives, he will receive his reward. [15]If it is burned up, he will suffer loss; he himself will be saved, but only as one escaping through the flames.

NRSV

10According to the grace of God given to me, like a skilled master builder I laid a foundation, and someone else is building on it. Each builder must choose with care how to build on it. [11]For no one can lay any foundation other than the one that has been laid; that foundation is Jesus Christ. [12]Now if anyone builds on the foundation with gold, silver, precious stones, wood, hay, straw— [13]the work of each builder will become visible, for the Day will disclose it, because it will be revealed with fire, and the fire will test what sort of work each has done. [14]If what has been built on the foundation survives, the builder will receive a reward. [15]If the work is burned up, the builder will suffer loss; the builder will be saved, but only as through fire.

# COMMENTARY

Paul planted (3:6). Shifting to the architectural metaphor, he laid the foundation (3:10) upon which others would construct. Paul the father responsible for his children (3:1-4), then Paul the planter who works the field (3:5-9), and now, with the introduction of the architectural image of building, Paul becomes the one who laid the foundation (3:10-15) upon which others must build.

Paul takes the common knowledge that the building can be no better than the foundation, that the building's future rests on the foundation's being properly laid, and declares that, like a builder who knew just how to do it properly and solidly, Paul laid the right foundation, namely, Jesus Christ. This foundation rumination is a refinement of Paul's earlier declaration that when he first came to Corinth he decided to know noth-

ing among them "except Christ and him crucified" (2:2). In the previous image Paul pictured himself as constantly and consistently focused on Christ. Now making the same point but with a building image, Paul starts with the only proper foundation—namely, Christ. But that allows him to develop the notion further: Others must build on the certified foundation; others' work must be tested; and those whose work stands the test will be rewarded.

Paul, likening himself to a "wise" (σοφός *sophos*, embracing the term for himself; NRSV, "skilled"; NIV, "expert") master builder, laid that foundation by his preaching. Earlier Paul wrote that not many of the Corinthians are wise (1:26), and he will return to that topic in 3:18-20. Will any Corinthians for whom wisdom has become a totem of status fail to notice that Paul here identifies himself as wise? Paul not only imparts wisdom (2:6), he is wise (3:10).

But wisdom is an incidental matter here. One's life, what one builds, one's work, must be appropriate to Jesus Christ, the normative foundation. That is the issue here. As with the exemplification of Paul and Apollos as God's farmworkers, so Paul's depictions of the other builders are informative descriptions of what is expected of all the Corinthians. What is built, how it is built—"Let each watch out how he or she builds" (3:9)—become metaphors for the life of faith. What in 3:1-9 was a matter of growth, whether of babies or of plants, now in 3:10-15 becomes a matter of what one constructs, of what one builds upon the foundation. Paul is convinced that all believers must build (or grow), and all will face a judgment day, "the Day" (3:13; cf. Rom 2:16; Phil 1:6; 1 Thess 5:2), in which their works (or their growth) will be tested. Verses 13-15 refer to this day, characterized in accord with the building image, as a fire, a classical eschatological image of testing (Deut 32:22; Amos 7:4; Mal 3:2). What one builds upon the foundation—"the work of each builder" (3:14), "what sort of work each has done" (3:13)—will be tested by this judgment fire. The passage plays upon the ambivalence of fire, which may destroy or may refine and purify.

Strikingly, this passage focuses on individual responsibility to build upon Jesus Christ as foundation. The possible building materials, carefully arranged in descending value from gold down to straw (3:12), are comprehensively listed because Paul's concern is not so much with which material from among this inclusive list is used but with the structure one builds. Presumably, one uses whatever materials are at hand; the list seems to suggest that any material will do. Everyone has building materials available to them. The focus is on the structure that one builds with whatever is available. "The work of each person" (3:13a, d, 14a, 15a), what one builds, not one's chosen material, is what will be tested by judgment's fire.

The reward or "wage" will be given to the one whose own work "survives" the discerning test of the judgment day's fire (3:14); if someone's work is consumed by the fire, that person suffers loss, though Paul expects that this worker may ultimately be saved "but only as through fire" (3:15). The same notion expressed here in terms of a testing with fire will be expressed later in the letter through a military image of an individual's "standing" or "falling" (10:12).

The being saved "as through fire" (ὡς διὰ πυρός *hōs dia pyros*) (3:15) is Paul's allusive reference not to fire's power to destroy—which has been the focus of most of his attention in this passage—but to fire's capacity to refine. The rich biblical imagery of fire has two nuances, and so does Paul here. Fire consumes and destroys (cf. Deut 32:22; Job 28:5; Ezek 38:22; Amos 7:4), but it also may refine and purify (cf. Ps 66:12; Isa 43:2; Zech 13:9). Paul's abiding conviction that God is known for grace, for giving new chances for redemption, leads Paul to hold out the hope that salvation may ultimately come even to the one whose work is burned up (note the similar point in 5:5; cf. Rom 5:20b). The notion of divine purification by a judgment fire is rooted in Israel's traditions (cf. Isa 1:25-28; 4:3-4). Another biblical image in Paul's scriptures may also be formative here: Israel was "like a brand snatched from the fire" (Amos 4:11; cf. Joshua, who is so described in Zech 3:2).

# REFLECTIONS

**1.** "The day," mentioned already in 1:7-8 and again in 5:5, is the time when Christ returns, when God's purposes are brought to culmination. It is a time of judgment that is mentioned across the Pauline corpus (Rom 2:5, 16; 13:12; 2 Cor 1:14; Phil 1:6, 10; 2:16; 1 Thess 5:2, 4). Paul expects that all people will be judged regarding their works at that time. The life of faith is a trust that is placed in the care of the believers, and their stewardship of this grace will face the scrutiny of divine judgment at the end time (not unlike Jesus' parables of the pounds, Luke 19:11-27, and the talents, Matt 25:14-30).

What will be weighed on judgment day is the work "of each one" (3:13). This is consistent with what Paul says in Rom 2:6 and with his later statement to these same Corinthians: "It is necessary for all of us to appear before the judgment seat of Christ so that each may receive according to what he has done in the body, whether good or bad" (2 Cor 5:10). What one does, how one builds on the foundation of Christ, how one lives up to one's calling, these are the matters on which the judgment will focus. Significantly, one's faith will not be judged; why should God judge what is, after all, a gift from God, a working of the Spirit (1 Cor 12:9)? Paul's primary subject matter in all his letters is understandably the proper comportment of the life of faith because the last judgment will focus on how one has lived the life God has given, on how one has walked in God's grace.

**2.** Each person is expected to build on the foundation that is Jesus Christ. Note that Paul does not single out any one special pre-approved building material that one has to search for like the holy grail. There is, therefore, no possible excuse for not building or not building much because of a lack of building materials. Paul's image seems to assume that one takes whatever is at hand and uses it to build. Our life of faith, therefore, is not a quest for the "right" material with which to build; instead, the life of faith involves each of us building with the material available to us. Paul's image in 3:11-13 is architectural, but later in this same letter he will make a similar point when he writes about each individual's obligation to place the Spirit-provided gifts (*charismata*), the analogue to available building materials, in service of the common good (12:7). So our building and our using the Spirit's gifts are alternative ways of talking about our responsibility to put what we have and what we are into service of God at all times.

**3.** Reward is promised here. Paul takes the normal practice of workers being paid for a job well done and projects that the same will be true at the last judgment. After Luther's proper insistence that faith alone and not works is what counts in one's standing before God, Christians have been reticent to talk of works, rewards, and payments. Surely Luther was right that gaining or earning the rewards cannot be the motivation for seeking and doing the good, for working. Gratitude, thankfulness, the glorification of God must remain the prime impulse for all that we do. But we, like Paul before us, should recognize that rewards and wages can function as an encouragment for us and others to stay on track. Paul unabashedly expects that reward, that pay-off for himself (9:23).

We must be clear, however, that Paul nowhere even hints that works can make one right with God. On the contrary, only the one who is right with God can (even must), by the assistance of God's own grace, do works that will be viewed favorably at the last day. So, it is always God's grace, that free, unmerited gift, which is at the heart of the life of faith and inspires all that one ever does, which motivates whatever building one constructs on the foundation that is Christ. The circularity of Paul's reasoning needs to be clearly understood. Grace leads to and prompts works, which in turn are recognized by God with favor. The process must spring forth from God's empowering grace—otherwise, Paul's gospel is irrecoverably distorted. Paul can exhort the Philippians to "work out your salvation with fear and trembling" only because, as the rest of the sentence makes abundantly clear, "it is God who works in you to will and to act according to his good purpose" (Phil 2:13 NIV). So rewards talk is important and proper, but is easily distorted or misunderstood.

# 1 Corinthians 3:16-17, You Are God's Temple

**NIV**

16Don't you know that you yourselves are God's temple and that God's Spirit lives in you? 17If anyone destroys God's temple, God will destroy him; for God's temple is sacred, and you are that temple.

**NRSV**

16Do you not know that you are God's temple and that God's Spirit dwells in you?[a] 17If anyone destroys God's temple, God will destroy that person. For God's temple is holy, and you are that temple.

[a] In verses 16 and 17 the Greek word for *you* is plural

## COMMENTARY

Paul refines the notion of the Corinthians' being "God's building" (θεοῦ οἰκοδομή *theou oikodomē*) (3:9). In 3:16-17 he reminds them ("Don't you know?") that they are a very special building, namely, God's temple in which God's Spirit dwells. The idea of God dwelling among the people taps Ezekiel's everlasting covenant of peace in which the Lord God pledges to put the divine sanctuary "among them forevermore" (Ezek 37:26): "My dwelling place will be with them; and I will be their God and they shall be my people" (37:27). Passage 3:10-15 stressed an individuated message: Each builder's work will be judged on the Day, and rewards will be passed out where appropriate. In his description of them as temple (3:16-17), however, Paul shifts decidedly to plurals: Together, the Corinthian believers are God's special building; they have become the dwelling place of God's Spirit. But there is a warning and a declaration. The warning: If anyone ruins, corrupts, defiles, destroys (φθείρω *phtheirō*) God's temple, then God will ruin or destroy (same verb) that person (3:17). That is the same point Paul pressed just before: The works of each individual will be judged on the last day. Paul closes the passage with his declaration, the reason that proper temple stewardship is so important: God's temple, which they are, is holy, and that temple is not to be defiled.

"Defiling the temple" deserves a further comment. As noted, the verb (*phtheirō*) has a wide semantic range, from corrupting to ruining to destroying. In 3:17*a*, at Paul's introduction of the notion that the Corinthians are God's temple, no effort is made to clarify just what action or thought Paul thinks would either corrupt or destroy God's temple. He offers no example. When the same verb is repeated in 3:17*b* about God's response to human defilement of God's temple, the mind is left to range toward speculation that Paul may anticipate that God will "destroy" such a defiler. Ancient rhetorical handbooks delighted in recommending that the same term be used, occasionally slanted one way first and another way second.[63] Paul does not have in mind the believers' destroying God's temple; he seems to be much more concerned with their defiling or spoiling the temple. But he seems equally ready to threaten that God will not simply corrupt the one who defiles, but destroy such a one. Any puzzlement that may occur to the reader at this point, however, will evaporate when Paul brings the topic back up under another ruse (yeast and Passover in 5:6-8), when he talks about a particular person, namely the man who "has his father's wife" (5:1), whom Paul views as contaminating the community, which in 3:17 is unambiguously identified as God's temple.

The notion of the Corinthians' sacredness to God, of their being set apart for God, holy to God, has surfaced occasionally in these opening chapters (cf. "saints" in 1:2; "sanctification" in 1:30), is briefly reaffirmed in 3:17, and will become a major focus in chaps. 5 and 6.

The building metaphor has allowed Paul to make several related observations: (1) The Corinthians belong to God (belonging to anyone else, Paul and Apollos included, pales in importance and can in fact be idolatrous). (2) Each believer is expected to be a builder, to produce works.

63. *Ad Herennium* 4.14.21

(3) The only foundation upon which any believer can build is that of Jesus Christ. (4) The works of individuals—that is, how they build upon Christ—will be assessed on judgment day with rewards passed out where appropriate. (5) The potential for destruction remains for each individual. (6) The Corinthians are not just any building; rather, they are a temple, a holy place where the Holy One resides, so they must be appropriately holy. And (7) God's Holy Spirit resides in them.

# REFLECTIONS

The building image, first introduced in 3:5-9, is here refined so that the readers now are invited to think of themselves as God's dwelling place, indeed, as God's temple. Gentiles and Jews at that time were familiar with the care given to protecting the holiness of temple sites as a fundamental reverence for the deity in charge; remember that ancient Corinth was peppered with temples (see the Introduction). Paul's scriptures contain the pithy claim "You shall be holy, for I the Lord your God am holy" (Lev 19:2 NRSV). In 3:16-17 Paul affirms the same connection because the one dwelling in you is holy, you, that temple, must be holy. If "you are God's temple," then proper temple honoring must require that your self (Paul's word for it would be "body") must be treated with honor. What activities of yours could be counted as dishonoring or defiling yourself, your body, as the temple of God's Holy Spirit?

The modern temptation is to read both of the "you" statements in 3:16 and the last one in 3:17 as if they were in the singular, but in fact Paul has them in the plural. Are the people of God only God's temple when they are in community, as their lives are bound up to others' in the body of Christ? A strong affirmative argument could be made. Or should Paul be understood to speak distributively so that each person can understand that he or she is God's temple? Surely, such an individualization cannot be totally ruled out. In fact, because Paul never anywhere in any of his letters imagines the life of faith as lived in isolation, it is likely that we ought to preserve both sides of the issue, but never the individual realization without that of the community.

If, indeed, "you are God's temple," then your self (Paul's word for it would be "body") must be treated with honor. Some may respond to that assertion by protesting that it is their individual right to treat their bodies as they please. Those people will need to look carefully at 6:19-20 where Paul will elaborate this point and explore further the moral consequences for one's body.

# 1 Corinthians 3:18-23, Self-Awareness and Proper Perspective

NIV

[18]Do not deceive yourselves. If any one of you thinks he is wise by the standards of this age, he should become a "fool" so that he may become wise. [19]For the wisdom of this world is foolishness in God's sight. As it is written: "He catches the wise in their craftiness"[a]; [20]and again, "The Lord knows that the thoughts of the wise are futile."[b] [21]So then, no more boasting about men! All things are yours, [22]whether Paul or Apollos or Cephas[c] or the world or life or death or the present or the future—all are yours, [23]and you are of Christ, and Christ is of God.

[a]19 Job 5:13    [b]20 Psalm 94:11    [c]22 That is, Peter

NRSV

18Do not deceive yourselves. If you think that you are wise in this age, you should become fools so that you may become wise. [19]For the wisdom of this world is foolishness with God. For it is written,

"He catches the wise in their craftiness,"
[20]and again,

"The Lord knows the thoughts of the wise,
    that they are futile."
[21]So let no one boast about human leaders. For all things are yours, [22]whether Paul or Apollos or Cephas or the world or life or death or the present or the future—all belong to you, [23]and you belong to Christ, and Christ belongs to God.

# COMMENTARY

Paul expects believers to be self-reflective. Self-deception can be avoided if one's self-estimation is properly based; as we have seen, Paul has structured these opening chapters to suggest that at least some of the Corinthians do not have an accurate self-assessment. The competing wisdoms already explicated in 2:6-7 reemerge here: The path to true wisdom may look like folly (3:18); this world's wisdom is folly with God (3:19). In Paul's view, believers are responsible moral agents; the Corinthians should have been able to keep better perspective on matters and on themselves than some of them have shown themselves able to do. Worldly wisdom and its associated status are a snare; God sees through the presumption, and so should believers; scripture warns believers that the worldly wise are readily deceived and their thoughts are futile (3:19; Job 5:12; 3:20; Ps 94:11). Believers can avoid the snare of false wisdom by maturely aiming for and attaching themselves to the secret and hidden wisdom that Paul imparts to the mature.

Further, believers can keep proper perspective only when they distinguish between what matters and what does not (3:21-23). Paul once again (cf. 1:29) warns against boasting of status gained by association with particular persons (3:21*a*). Then (3:21*b*-23), with a clever takeoff from a widespread Cynic formulation, Paul points the Corinthians toward a fuller perspective in the light of the gospel. Cynics have a form of syllogistic argument that runs thus: The wise are friends of the gods, and friends share what they have. The gods own all things; therefore, the wise have full access to all things.[64] Paul runs it the other way around: "All things are yours ... [quite a list occurs] ... all belong to you, and you belong to Christ, and Christ

belongs to God" (3:21-23). Belonging to Christ and therefore to God means that all things belong to you; therefore, boasting in human associations is out of order, showing as it does a lack of proper understanding and perspective. By extending beyond Paul and Apollos to Cephas, Paul says, in effect, "anyone." In the most sweeping fashion, Paul sketches out the implications of belonging to God in Christ and therefore possessing all things. So to belong and so to possess neutralizes, in a paradoxical way, the importance of all things including (and here Paul draws upon his pattern of listing indifferent matters) the world, life, death, things present, things to come (cf. Rom 8:38-39; 14:7-8; Gal 2:20; see also 1 Cor 4:7; 7:29-31).[65] Boasting (3:21) in anything or anyone other than God or the gospel misunderstands and misrepresents where power truly resides. Only God can establish a person's worth. Belonging to God is foundational; that is what matters. All other associations, all other belongings are at best indifferent matters and at worst idolatrous (see 4:7).

Twice in this passage Paul cites scripture as a way of seeing clearly what is important. Both of the quotations come from the wisdom traditions of Israel (Job 5:13, quoted in 1 Cor 3:19; and Ps 94:11, cited in 3:20) and are employed by Paul as a part of the (true) wisdom that believers ought to know and honor. Paul's association of the two quotations shows that he finds them much to the same point: that God knows what is going on and cuts through human pretensions and posturings. When one knows that about God one knows not to boast on human grounds (3:21). This is not the last piece on "perspective-keeping" in 1 Corinthians.

64. Diogenes Laertius 6.37, 6.72.

65. J. Paul Sampley, *Walking Between the Times: Paul's Moral Reasoning* (Minneapolis: Fortress, 1991) 77-82.

# REFLECTIONS

Paul's first explicit warning of self-deception appears in 1 Cor 3:18 (cf. 6:9; 15:33). Paul's problem with the Corinthians is their overestimation of themselves. Modern believers can experience self-deception in one of two directions, either in an overestimation or in an underestimation of themselves. To aim for too little, to love less than one would be able, would be improper stewardship of one's gifts and graces. Equally problematic, however, is an overestimation, where one thinks oneself capable of more than one's faith and love will allow. Such persons could lose themselves in their efforts to be helpful to others, to "bear one another's burdens" (Gal 6:2), because they did not properly realize their limits. They thus overreach and run the risk not only of causing somebody else harm but also of overextending themselves. Proper self-assessment or perspective-keeping will be treated by Paul at other places later in the letter (see esp. 11:17-34).

# 1 Corinthians 4:1-5, The Apostles, But Especially Paul, As Exemplary Once More

## NIV

4 So then, men ought to regard us as servants of Christ and as those entrusted with the secret things of God. ²Now it is required that those who have been given a trust must prove faithful. ³I care very little if I am judged by you or by any human court; indeed, I do not even judge myself. ⁴My conscience is clear, but that does not make me innocent. It is the Lord who judges me. ⁵Therefore judge nothing before the appointed time; wait till the Lord comes. He will bring to light what is hidden in darkness and will expose the motives of men's hearts. At that time each will receive his praise from God.

## NRSV

4 Think of us in this way, as servants of Christ and stewards of God's mysteries. ²Moreover, it is required of stewards that they be found trustworthy. ³But with me it is a very small thing that I should be judged by you or by any human court. I do not even judge myself. ⁴I am not aware of anything against myself, but I am not thereby acquitted. It is the Lord who judges me. ⁵Therefore do not pronounce judgment before the time, before the Lord comes, who will bring to light the things now hidden in darkness and will disclose the purposes of the heart. Then each one will receive commendation from God.

# COMMENTARY

Even apostles who could, with some worldly legitimacy, claim greatness are properly considered "servants/helpers of Christ" and "stewards of God's mysteries" (4:1; cf. 3:5). Chapters 1–4 are an exercise in proportionality, in keeping or regaining proper perspective, and specifically in not overestimating one's importance or standing. Paul shows the way by illustrating that apostles also must keep perspective: They are really only administrators or assistants at best. What may one reasonably ask of such stewards? That they be found trustworthily accountable [to their Lord, understood] (4:2). Once again (4:4c; cf. 3:10-15), the day of judgment puts daily life and its judgments in perspective. For Paul the only judgment that counts (again, what really matters, cf. 3:21-23) is the Lord's (4:4-5). When it comes to human judgment, whether by fellow Corinthian believers or by some secular court, Paul is like the truly spiritual persons he described in 2:15 who "discern all things, and they are themselves subject to no one else's scrutiny." The Lord will judge. The Lord can

judge because only the Lord can penetrate the secrets and know the "purposes of the heart" (4:5). That judgment is appropriately reserved for the time when the Lord comes. Besides, the only commendation or praise that matters is that which, like the wages already mentioned in 3:8, 14, God will give when one's heart (4:5) and work (3:8, 14) are tested and found true.

In 4:1-5 Paul's purposes in chaps. 1–4 emerge for all to see. He has set himself and Apollos forward as exemplars, as models who recognize that (a) they must be trustworthy, and (b) they are accountable to God or to the Lord. Instead of boasting and seeking status from their brothers and sisters in the faith, the Corinthian believers should recognize that the Lord will do the judging and then one's commendation (ἔπαινος *epainos,* "praise," "approval," "recognition"; see the same point made about wages in 3:8, 14) will come from the only source that counts—namely, God.

Once again (cf. 3:10-15), Paul's attention is turned to his individual listener, and he asks, in effect, what reward or gratification one should rightly expect from others and what one can only expect from God. Improper boasting entails the seeking of someone's approval when the only recognition that counts comes from God. Paul's eschatological frame of reference here assures his auditors that they will get recognition, if they deserve it, at the last time, when the Lord comes (3:8; cf. "the Day" in 3:13). In the meantime, believers' energy and attention should be placed on their being regularly and consistently trustworthy servants or assistants as Paul and Apollos have been.

Paul's extraordinary confidence, such that he knows of no charge that can be leveled against him (4:4), positions him as the one not only to serve as model but also, like a father (4:14), to chide the Corinthians as babies whose growth in faith and practice is retarded (3:1-2). This confidence suggests that Paul feels himself blessed as one who has carefully scrutinized his own actions and found "no reason to judge himself" (Rom 14:22 RSV).

Trustworthiness or faithfulness (πιστός *pistos*, "faithfulness," 4:2) is the bottom-line test of a steward or assistant in that time. Significantly in Paul the claim of trustworthiness is made most often about God (same term, 1 Cor 1:9; 10:13; 2 Cor 1:18; 1 Thess 5:24). God can be counted on. That is bedrock. Abraham is depicted as rightly trusting God to do what God has promised (Rom 4:20). Human faithfulness, apostolic faithfulness is derivative and reflective of God's trustworthiness. It should be no surprise that Paul's basic code word for the right relationship one has with God is πίστις (*pistis*, "faith," from the same root as *pistos*). Paul is clear that God is the ultimate judge of one's trustworthiness as a steward. Boasting about one's stewardship is not worth the breath that carries it, and God will not be misled by public relations self-promotions. As we will see when we get to 7:25, Paul does think that faithfulness, trustworthiness can be demonstrated by consistent performance over a period of time, and he thinks he has thus established his trustworthiness with the Corinthians.

# REFLECTIONS

**1.** "I am not aware of anything against myself" (4:4; cf. Job 27:6). Modern believers may read Paul's claim with utter astonishment because who among us can affirm such a clear conscience? Paul has been accurately described as having a "robust conscience."[66] For people in post-Freudian times in which we sense the convolutions of the mind and heart, not to mention a proclivity or profound capacity to self-deceive, it is difficult for us to imagine being able to utter such a claim as Paul does. One may come to terms with this disparity by elevating Paul to some special level of saintly performance, beyond the reach of most mortals—though that certainly would not be Paul's belief about himself and others. Another way may be to realize that modern persons, in part due to advancing studies of the human psyche, have a much more complex picture of the dynamics of willing and intending and interpersonal relationships than Paul had.

**2.** The central and organizing motif in the culture of Paul's time was praise and blame, another way of describing honor and shame.[67] In the Greco-Roman world, the primary goal around which life was structured and with respect to which one made decisions was the attainment of praise or honor, and its corollary, the avoidance of blame or shame. (See the Introduction for fuller discussion.) Although one may argue that similar motivations of honor and shame were basic in the early part of the twentieth century and, indeed, still function with great power in much of the world, today one can note the decline of such values in the United States and in Europe. Contemporary applications of Paul's gospel must be conscious of the way in which cultural values are shifting or have shifted from those that governed Paul's times. For modern

66. Krister Stendahl, *Paul Among Jews and Gentiles* (Philadelphia: Fortress, 1976) 80.
67. For the significance of honor in Paul's time, see Halvor Moxnes, "The Quest for Honor and the Unity of the Community in Romans 12 and in the Orations of Dio Chrysostom," in T. Engberg-Pedersen, *Paul in His Hellenistic Context* (Minneapolis: Fortress, 1995) 204-13.

Christians in much of the world, is not acquisition (and in its most exaggerated form, greed) the dominant cultural motif? The point at issue is, Where do persons such as ministers or a group such as a congregation gain leverage as they seek to engage and persuade one another and others? In Paul's time the answer would have been clear: Speak to them about how one gains honor and avoids shame or blame. That is exactly what Paul does across his letters. But if that leverage is lost or at best decreased, and another central totem, namely acquisition or greed, stands at the defining center of our culture, how does the gospel engage persons who are attuned to that totem? One answer could be to struggle to rehabilitate praise and blame. Another could be to begin the creative process of imagining how one can translate Paul's gospel from its earlier praise/blame, honor/shame context into one where acquisition is the governing motif. At its best it will surely be a subversive engagement! And perhaps Paul has already provided a starting point for such reflections in his twice-stated "All things are yours!" (3:21, 22) and in his questions in 4:7. If "All things are yours" means "All the things that matter/are important are yours" as 4:7 suggests, then one does not need to strive for that which God freely gives. Knowing that "all things are yours" should liberate one's energies to be more fully employed in serving others in love.

# 1 Corinthians 4:6-7, The Explicit Key to Paul's Strategy in Chapters 1–4

## NIV

⁶Now, brothers, I have applied these things to myself and Apollos for your benefit, so that you may learn from us the meaning of the saying, "Do not go beyond what is written." Then you will not take pride in one man over against another. ⁷For who makes you different from anyone else? What do you have that you did not receive? And if you did receive it, why do you boast as though you did not?

## NRSV

6I have applied all this to Apollos and myself for your benefit, brothers and sisters,[a] so that you may learn through us the meaning of the saying, "Nothing beyond what is written," so that none of you will be puffed up in favor of one against another. ⁷For who sees anything different in you?[b] What do you have that you did not receive? And if you received it, why do you boast as if it were not a gift?

[a] Gk brothers   [b] Or Who makes you different from another?

# COMMENTARY

Calling them "brothers and sisters" (ἀδελφοί adelphoi) and thereby stressing his common ground with his readers, Paul now explicitly discloses the rhetorical strategy that he has been pursuing in the opening section of his letter. As we noted earlier, Paul has used indirect speech, a common mode in his time, to make points to his readers—about themselves and their comportment—by making observations about himself and Apollos. Not only are Paul and Apollos exemplars of different persons being "one" in the gospel and in its life, but they have been the object lessons that Paul hopes the Corinthians will apply to themselves. These opening chapters of

the letter are a back-to-basics lesson that Paul hopes to get across so that his hearers can learn "Nothing beyond what is written" (4:6)—that is, not to paint outside the lines.[68] If they learn the most rudimentary lesson then they will not be "puffed up" (φυσιόω physioō) (watch for this term to reappear as a negative characterization of misplaced Corinthian zeal in 4:18-19; 5:2) for some and against others. Nothing is more basic to the gospel than to learn the lesson that no matter how different persons

68. John Fitzgerald, *Cracks in an Earthern Vessel: An Examination of the Catalogues of Hardships in the Corinthian Correspondence,* SBLDS 99 (Atlanta: Scholars Press, 1988) 127.

may be, they are one in Christ—and there is absolutely no place for schisms, divisiveness, boasting, or judgment. This is the babies' milk of the gospel.

Then, to drive the point home there is a reprise, with slight modification, of the earlier note that "all things are yours" (3:21-22), this time in a set of powerful questions that insist on the hearers' reflection. Paul walks the auditors through the logic of the gospel: When you are considered in the light of the gospel, what distinguishes you from anyone else? If you have nothing that you did not receive as a gift, then why do you live a lie in your boasting as if you did not receive it?

In 4:6, Paul declares that he has made his Paul-Apollos depiction across the first chapters for two reasons, namely that they may learn from Paul's portrayal of himself and Apollos and the Corinthians may stop their divisiveness. As can readily be seen in the differing translations offered by the NIV and the NRSV, Paul's meaning in the first purpose clause of 4:6 is difficult to know for certain. Some interpretations of the Greek such as the RSV ("not to go beyond what is written") left open the interpretation that Paul is here calling his auditors to live in accord with scripture either in some general sense or in the light of the particular citations he has made (e.g., avoid boasting because of Jer 9:24 as quoted in 1 Cor 1:31, and do not be superficially misled as is affirmed by the quotes of Job and Psalms in 3:19-20). But that runs into two difficulties: (1) What could it have meant "not to go beyond" those texts? and (2) The Greek construc-

tion (with the neuter article τό *to*) regularly functions to signal the beginning of a quotation such as a maxim or proverb (as the NIV and NRSV have taken it). Taken this way, the question becomes what to make of the "[Do] not [go] beyond what is written." We have seen that Paul takes the Corinthian babies back to basics in these opening chapters of 1 Corinthians. Staying within the rules, within the borders is a way Paul does moral reasoning (see the Commentaries on 5:11 and 6:9-10 for the function of the vice lists) and may, indeed, be the meaning that Paul would have established so well in his teachings earlier that this slight reference in the letter would have been expected to bring Paul's meaning (and the larger instruction) to mind for the auditors. In line with that interpretation is the suggestion that Paul has in mind the ruled slates used in the training of children in writing so that the Corinthian babies were being urged to learn the most basic things once again.[69]

The second purpose clause—"in order that you may not be puffed up in behalf of one and against another"—parallels the first in structure, although the NIV translation veils that fact, and clearly ties Paul's treatment of himself and Apollos into the Corinthian tendency toward divisiveness that was initially raised in the first appeal (1:10). So the Corinthian inclination to puffiness and boasting and to taking sides is noted in 4:6 as precisely what Paul is trying to overcome in this letter.

69. Ibid., 121-28.

# REFLECTIONS

Grace, the freely given, unmerited gift from God, itself the ground on which all the life of faith stands, is the standard by which all else is gauged. Though the term "grace" does not occur in these verses, that is what the questions in 4:7 are about. Paul's questions aim to establish the common denominator of all of life, they seek to establish or focus upon what is important by ruling some matters out of contention. To those who would vaunt themselves or whom others would lionize, Paul disarms their pretensions by frank questions: "What distinguishes you? What do you have that you have not received [as a gift, understood]? And if you receive, why do you boast as if not receiving?" (4:7). What places all believers, whether in Paul's time or in ours, on common ground is their equal dependence as ones who are the unmeriting recipients of God's grace. So who is anybody trying to fool by boasting as if this common ground of grace were not the most important fact about themselves?

# 1 Corinthians 4:8-13, The Grand Charade Seen with Evangelical Irony

## NIV

⁸Already you have all you want! Already you have become rich! You have become kings—and that without us! How I wish that you really had become kings so that we might be kings with you! ⁹For it seems to me that God has put us apostles on display at the end of the procession, like men condemned to die in the arena. We have been made a spectacle to the whole universe, to angels as well as to men. ¹⁰We are fools for Christ, but you are so wise in Christ! We are weak, but you are strong! You are honored, we are dishonored! ¹¹To this very hour we go hungry and thirsty, we are in rags, we are brutally treated, we are homeless. ¹²We work hard with our own hands. When we are cursed, we bless; when we are persecuted, we endure it; ¹³when we are slandered, we answer kindly. Up to this moment we have become the scum of the earth, the refuse of the world.

## NRSV

⁸Already you have all you want! Already you have become rich! Quite apart from us you have become kings! Indeed, I wish that you had become kings, so that we might be kings with you! ⁹For I think that God has exhibited us apostles as last of all, as though sentenced to death, because we have become a spectacle to the world, to angels and to mortals. ¹⁰We are fools for the sake of Christ, but you are wise in Christ. We are weak, but you are strong. You are held in honor, but we in disrepute. ¹¹To the present hour we are hungry and thirsty, we are poorly clothed and beaten and homeless, ¹²and we grow weary from the work of our own hands. When reviled, we bless; when persecuted, we endure; ¹³when slandered, we speak kindly. We have become like the rubbish of the world, the dregs of all things, to this very day.

# COMMENTARY

With blistering irony in his every word, Paul now exposes and ridicules those babies who, though they have a shared Lord, would lord it over others. Some in Corinth have gotten ahead of themselves. Real babies in faith, they fancy themselves ruling (which they will, but only eschatologically and equally with all other believers; cf. 6:2-3), they imagine themselves satisfied, even sated. Paul ironically joins them in their imaginings, which he treats as fantasy, and openly yearns for them to reign because, as he allows himself to suppose, he would then share the benefits of their sovereignty. As if to highlight their unreality, Paul lays out a hardship catalog as the realia of apostles. Over against the Corinthian fiction of ruling and being filled, Paul pictures apostles as condemned to death, as what seems to be a theater of the absurd played out before the world, before angels, and before people (4:9). He cannot escape the irony of the contrast: Apostles are fools, some Corinthians wise; apostles are feeble and in disre-pute, some Corinthians are strong and honored (4:10). Even in these dire circumstances apostles exemplify the gospel by not returning evil for evil; they bless, endure, and conciliate when people treat them in an opposite fashion (4:12-13). In a shift of image, it is as if apostles have become like the discardable, dirty dishwater by which the world is cleansed (4:13). Paul's hardship lists, a common feature in his letters, serve two basic functions: (1) They affirm that the real power to endure whatever comes one's way (cf. Phil 4:11-13) rests not in one's own grasp but in one's being held securely by Christ in God, and (2) they make eminently clear that the gospel never promises inoculation from distress but rather with every struggle God provides the strength to bear it or the exodus by which to escape it (see the Commentary on 1 Cor 10:1-13).

In these verses Paul opens a little window onto two of his perceptions of what is going on at Corinth. First, their divisiveness is really about power. We have seen their concerns for power in their seeking of status and in their boasting. As Paul has noted, their concerns for status and power show that they have not really gotten the picture of how different their lives in Christ should be from the social and culturally reinforced patterns of the world. They are, indeed, behaving just like children or ordinary people (3:1-4)—in either case, the point is the same. Second, at least some of these divisive Corinthians have collapsed what will truly be theirs—but only in the future—into the present and are comporting themselves as if they have "already arrived."

We have noted that the opening four chapters of 1 Corinthians are designed by Paul to establish a context for dealing with particular problems that

they are having. In the verses before us, Paul signals a note that will be played at several points throughout the letter. Its frequency suggests that it is a major and pervasive problem in the Corinthian church: Some believers are claiming for themselves that they are more advanced than other believers. These people, perhaps a minority, think that they already share God's full blessings: What God has begun in Christ is already brought to completion in them. In 4:8-13 Paul tries to shock them into the realization that God's purposes in them are really only begun; the mention of apostles suggests a contrast in that these Corinthian overestimators mistakenly think that they have achieved levels for which apostles have not even dared to reach.

# REFLECTIONS

**1.** This paragraph raises the perennial problem that believers face—namely, how much they already share in the fullness of God's gifts and how much they still await that fulfillment. Some representations of the gospel present it as "pie in the sky by and by" and assume that existence in this world is a drudge only to be endured so that some heavenly reward may be forthcoming. Some of the Corinthians have gone to the opposite extreme and seem to be claiming that in the here and now they have the fullness of all that God will ever give. Paul countenances neither extreme and invites us to consider that life in the world, even when it is beset with suffering and limitation, can be rich with God's grace so that believers can rejoice when they are suffering.

**2.** Paul depicts himself and the other apostles (4:9-13) as unwilling to respond in kind to rejection by others. They respond by blessing, enduring, and speaking kindly. Our actions should always be governed by our being centered on Christ and should reflect that grace and love. The alternative would be for us to take our cues from those around us and respond to them as they relate to us. Such a course of action has nothing to interrupt it, but, feeding on itself, it could result in a spiral of violence. Grace interrupts and derails anger and its attendant violence.

# 1 Corinthians 4:14-21, Paul Embraces and Warns His Beloved Children

NIV

[14]I am not writing this to shame you, but to warn you, as my dear children. [15]Even though you have ten thousand guardians in Christ, you do not have many fathers, for in Christ Jesus I became your father through the gospel. [16]Therefore I urge you to imitate me. [17]For this reason I am sending to you Timothy, my son whom I love, who is faithful in the Lord. He will

NRSV

[14]I am not writing this to make you ashamed, but to admonish you as my beloved children. [15]For though you might have ten thousand guardians in Christ, you do not have many fathers. Indeed, in Christ Jesus I became your father through the gospel. [16]I appeal to you, then, be imitators of me. [17]For this reason I sent[a] you

[a] Or *am sending*

## NIV

remind you of my way of life in Christ Jesus, which agrees with what I teach everywhere in every church.

<sup>18</sup>Some of you have become arrogant, as if I were not coming to you. <sup>19</sup>But I will come to you very soon, if the Lord is willing, and then I will find out not only how these arrogant people are talking, but what power they have. <sup>20</sup>For the kingdom of God is not a matter of talk but of power. <sup>21</sup>What do you prefer? Shall I come to you with a whip, or in love and with a gentle spirit?

## NRSV

Timothy, who is my beloved and faithful child in the Lord, to remind you of my ways in Christ Jesus, as I teach them everywhere in every church. <sup>18</sup>But some of you, thinking that I am not coming to you, have become arrogant. <sup>19</sup>But I will come to you soon, if the Lord wills, and I will find out not the talk of these arrogant people but their power. <sup>20</sup>For the kingdom of God depends not on talk but on power. <sup>21</sup>What would you prefer? Am I to come to you with a stick, or with love in a spirit of gentleness?

# COMMENTARY

The situation at Corinth is a complex one, for Paul and for the Corinthians. Though absent, Paul knows of the considerable socioeconomic differences among the Corinthians (1:26); he hears of the serious schisms and divisiveness among the Corinthians. But Paul is not the only person who has worked with the Corinthians; Paul laid the foundation, Paul planted, but Apollos watered (3:6); and Apollos is still in relationship with the Corinthians, though he, too, is currently absent (16:12). Others were guardians (4:15; cf. 9:5). Sylvanus and Timothy seem to have been involved in establishing the church at Corinth (2 Cor 1:19), though Timothy has been sent or is being sent, depending on how one reads 4:17. At the time of the writing of 1 Corinthians, none of the Pauline leadership is present.

In this circumstance, Paul looks back over his purposes in what he has written so far and positions himself as pre-eminent over all other guardians. He is the Corinthians' father. They are his "beloved children" (τέκνα ἀγαπητά *tekna agapēta*) (4:14) whom he begot in the gospel (4:15). His purpose has been to admonish or warn, not shame them (cf. 4:14); accordingly, he appeals to them (4:16).

In the culture of the time, parents, particularly the pater familias, exemplified proper behavior. Children were expected to learn not only trade but appropriate behavior by modeling after their fathers. Paul draws upon those cultural expectations and appeals to the Corinthians to "be imitators of me" (μιμηταί μου γίνεσθε *mimētai mou*

*ginesthe,* 4:16). This appeal echoes the first one (1:10) in which Paul urged the end of divisions. Let us review first what Paul has established across the opening chapters and second what Paul has suggested is imitable about himself in the first four chapters of this letter.

Through the family metaphor, Paul provides a moral pattern as well as a primary social grouping. All who belong to God are part of God's family and are brothers and sisters (*adelphoi,* occuring 38 times in this letter alone) to one another. On the basis of faith, gentiles are adopted, with full rights of inheritance along with their Jewish brothers and sisters, into God's family (Rom 8:14-23; Gal 4:4-7). The moral pattern is Paul, who thinks of himself as the father of all those who come to faith through his preaching (cf. Phlm 10). The Corinthian children in the faith should model after their father, as Timothy is depicted as doing (4:17). The Corinthians, still too much like babies (3:1-3), need to grow up to be like Paul their father and Timothy their brother.

We cannot ignore the string of clues across these first four chapters that status and pride of place are of great importance to some at Corinth. In the world of Paul's time, status was generally accorded to wealthy persons, and such are some of the members of the Corinthian church (1:26). Over against that cultural standard, Paul positions himself as one who knows several basic things: that true commendation comes only from God (4:5); that human boasting is out while boasting in the Lord is acceptable (1:29-31); that all will be judged solely by the work they have done (3:14); that mutual judgment is out (4:5), and that only the Lord can judge because only the Lord knows the hidden things and the "purposes of the heart" (4:5); that proper self-assessment is crucial (3:18); that, try as they may to make distinctions among themselves, they are all equally dependent on God's grace for their standing in Christ and, indeed, for all they have (3:21-33; 4:7); and that, like a loving father, Paul has broken through their folly laden pretensions and offered them milk— that is, he has taken them by the hand and led them back to the basics of the gospel (3:1). In all these Paul has shown the exemplary care that a father ought to have for his children. But in even more powerful ways he depicted himself as imitable—and to these the commentary now turns.

Paul has laced this entire letter section with references to himself and Apollos as exemplars of the faith. As different as the Corinthians know these two to be, Paul depicts himself and Apollos as persons who work together in harmony for the gospel. They are different people, their work is distinctive, they recognize that their contributions are singular, but in the gospel they are "one" (3:8); there is no boasting, no judgment, no striving for status. Instead, both Paul and Apollos comport themselves in such a way that God can provide the growth in God's own field. They, along with the rest of creation, belong to the Corinthians, and along with the Corinthians they all together belong to Christ, who belongs to God (3:22-23). Paul eschews status as the world measures it. Instead, he and Apollos are merely servants who, like everyone else, must be found trustworthy (4:2).

In a final exemplification in the opening chapters,[70] Paul stacks up all the apostles over against those people at Corinth who are inclined to make special claims about their importance, and the apostles are depicted, in blistering irony, as the opposites of praiseworthiness, as ones scorned and treated with shame. How do Paul and the other apostles respond? In an exemplary fashion: "When reviled, we bless; when persecuted, we endure; when slandered, we speak kindly" (4:12-13). And this is in the passage immediately prior to his call

for imitation of himself. We have no way to know whether the differing groups at Corinth are reviling, persecuting, or slandering one another, but as the pericope in which we find these claims is cast in a hyperbolic style, so also these may be an overstatement. Paul's hyperbolic point could be that even if others were slandering and persecuting, even if they were reviling, he as apostolic exemplar would respond with endurance and a readiness to conciliate (hints already of chap. 13). The basic point is clear: Paul sets himself up as one who does not repay just what he receives, but is enabled to represent the gospel even when he is not treated as he should be. So also, the Corinthians ought to learn from this that they need to be moved by what will later in this letter be called love as they respond to one another.

Paul closes this first section of his letter with a note of warning that puts the Corinthian response directly in the auditors' charge. Some "have become arrogant" (φυσιόω *physioō*, "puffed up"; cf. 4:6), questioning whether Paul is coming— Paul's travel plans do not always seem predictable (cf. 2 Cor 1:15-18)—but he promises not only that he will come but that they can arrange matters so that when he comes he will come as they wish him: either as the father ready to discipline them or the apostle who apparently would rather come "with love in a spirit of gentleness" (4:21). As the opening chapters have made clear, the gospel and the kingdom of God depend not on talk but power; Paul signals himself ready to come in the full power of the gospel (4:19), at which time he will check out these puffed-up, arrogant people who he suggests are long on talk and short on real power (4:19).

Paul's mentions of the kingdom of God are not frequent, but the paucity of references should not be taken as a gauge of its importance. Paul employs kingdom talk in two basic ways in his letters. The first, as reflected here in 4:20, describes what accords with God's reign and what does not. In 4:20 God's reign is positively related to power, negatively related to talk, and functions as a way of cautioning those "arrogant, puffy" people at Corinth not to put themselves in the place of having a confrontation with Paul. This reference to God's reign is formally quite like Rom 14:17, where the kingdom is indifferently related to food and drink but positively and essentially related to "righteousness and peace and joy in the Holy Spirit." Paul's refer-

---

70. Margaret Mitchell, *Paul and the Rhetoric of Reconciliation,* 39-46.

ences to "inheriting" God's kingdom (cf. Matt 25:34) function much the same way. Paul has taught the Corinthians and expects them to know that people who do the vices that Paul lists will not inherit God's kingdom or reign; the vices are absolutely disqualifying (1 Cor 6:9; 6:10; Gal 5:21; cf. Eph 5:5). One's conduct in the daily events of life must accord with God's reign or one will not be allowed to enter God's kingdom, and comportment in accord with the kingdom is required if one expects to be a part of the kingdom when God's plan is brought to its eschatological fulfillment.

Paul's other way of referring to God's reign is eschatological. Much later in 1 Corinthians, Paul depicts how he thinks God's plan, begun in the death and resurrection of Jesus Christ, will come to its full fruition. Paul writes of the end or goal (τέλος *telos*) toward which God has purposed: "Then comes the end, when he [Christ] delivers the kingdom to God, after he [Christ] has made ineffective/wiped out" all opposing powers, and the last enemy to be "made ineffective/wiped out" is death (15:24, 26). This suggests that Christ as risen Lord is in charge of the kingdom—and may we suppose, who is associated with it?—until he hands it over to God at the eschaton, at the conclusion of God's purposes.

Brandishing his authority as the father responsible for his "beloved children," Paul puts the readers on warning that they should imitate him and that they should accommodate to Timothy's representation of "Paul's ways." The reference to Paul's "ways" being those in effect in every church is designed to counter any suggestion that Paul is setting up special, singular requirements for the Corinthians (cf. a similar point in 1 Cor 15:3-11). He can warn, he can appeal—as he has done repeatedly in these opening chapters—but the outcome is totally in the Corinthians' hands. Their response will determine whether Paul has to come with a show of power or, as he seems to suggest he prefers, in a spirit of conciliation (4:21).

# REFLECTIONS

**1.** Strong modern churches foster the resocialization of their members into a recognition of themselves as a new family in Christ, especially as the secular family structure finds itself in such flux. Accordingly, congregants should be encouraged to think of themselves as a family, to care for one another appropriately, and to develop constructive ways of dealing with the inevitable points of conflict among these sisters and brothers. The pastor does not have to be father, though some parishioners will find that an instructive and comforting relationship.

**2.** Paul's call to imitate him arises out of the cultural matrix in which he and his readers live. Modeling and imitating were venerable socialization patterns that Paul found rich in potential. Paul certainly made good use of them as a way of pointing individuals and communities in the right direction. Timothy, with descriptions affirming his exemplary character, is often highlighted by Paul (16:10-11; Phil 2:19-24; 1 Thess 3:2). Other individuals are affirmed as models (16:15-18; Rom 16:1-2; 2 Cor 8:16-17). Even churches are seen as examples that inspire emulation (1 Thess 1:7-8). Churches today should self-consciously undertake to model the life of faith because their performative witness will often be more profoundly effective than words. Within the church there should also be frequent encouragement not only to live as models for other Christians but also to learn by modeling from others.

**3.** Paul's observation that the kingdom of God is power, not talk, points to his fundamental conviction that belonging to Christ is not a matter of having the "right" opinions or ideas (Rom 14:1) or of attitudinal adjustment. To be a Christian is to be claimed by the Spirit (Gal 3:1-4). The gospel is power: "It is the power of God for salvation" (Rom 1:16). When the gospel is made out to be ideas to which one assents, then faith is robbed of its power to transform. But a warning is appropriate: Some persons may come to a gradual realization that they have been taken by the Spirit; it does not have to be in a whirlwind of a moment. In fact, some may be reticent to think about the Holy Spirit's function in their lives because they never experienced the whirlwind. Oftentimes the Spirit is quiet and subtle and our hearing may not be attuned. We could try to develop greater sensitivity to the Spirit's gentle and subdued urgings within us. Like Elijah, maybe we expect God to come through with a booming utterance, when sometimes (most often?) it happens that the word comes only through a "still, small" voice (1 Kgs 19:11-12). So it is with the Spirit's workings and promptings, and perhaps we need to learn anew how to listen.

# 1 CORINTHIANS 5:1–6:20

## COMMUNITY DEFINITION AS SEEN IN TWO RELATED INSTANCES

### OVERVIEW

With the context provided by chaps. 1–4 Paul is now ready to engage some of the particular issues that concern him regarding the Corinthians. He has learned about the Corinthian believers from oral reports (1:11) and has received a letter of inquiry from them (7:1). The problems and issues are many. Where should Paul begin? Before he turns to their letter, to issues generated by them, he elects to treat two matters of his own choosing: The first centers on a man who "has his father's wife" (chap. 5), the second on the practice of some believers taking their intrachurch disputes before civil courts for adjudication (chap. 6). Before considering the texts themselves, however, some other questions and issues need to be addressed.

**Arrangement.** Why does Paul choose to start where he does? Paul has the freedom to arrange the rest of the matters in his response to the Corinthians as he sees fit. In that culture, when faced with a string of items, the first and the last are considered to be in the most emphatic positions.[71] Accordingly, what Paul puts first must be taken with seriousness by interpreters. What does his choice tell us about his estimation of the problems in Corinth and about his strategy for dealing with those problems? We will return to these questions at the end of the Commentary on 5:1–6:20.

**Literary Unity of Chapters 5 and 6.** On a cursory glance, the topics of chaps. 5 and 6 may seem unrelated, but a closer examination shows that they both deal with community definition: The first argues that what should be outside the community—namely, immorality, is wrongly inside it; the second claims that matters that

should be dealt with inside the community, disputes that ought to be resolved within the body of believers, are being treated outside it. So in both chapters, the issue is what is appropriate to life in the community and what is more properly left outside the community of faith.[72]

A series of details confirms that chaps. 5 and 6 should be read as a single literary unit. First is an inclusio that ties the opening of chap. 5—"such immorality [πορνεία *porneia*] among you" that even gentiles blush (5:1)—to the conclusion of chap. 6—"Flee from immorality" (*porneia,* 6:18). The term *porneia,* Paul's most comprehensive term for vice and wrongful living within the fellowship, and its semantic relatives lace the two chapters together (5:1, 9-11; 6:9, 13, 16, 18), and in fact provide the link to 7:2 and the next topic, but more about that later. Further, both chapters employ vice lists as a means of rehearsing the border distinctions between behavior appropriate to the community and unacceptable behavior (5:10-11; 6:9-10). Both chapters echo the believers' baptism by use of the phrase that was first mentioned in 1:2: "in the name of the Lord Jesus" (ἐν τῷ ὀνόματι τοῦ κυρίου Ἰησοῦ *en tō onomati tou Kyriou Iēsou,* 5:4; 6:11).

The two chapters conclude (6:19-20) with a reprise on the theme of the temple of the Holy Spirit (from 3:16-17) being holy and with the assertion that the Holy Spirit is residing in the believers ἐν ὑμῖν (*en hymin* "in you"), who are now implored to "Glorify God in your body" (6:20)—a clear lead-in to the subject matter of chap. 7 and, indeed, for all that follows. Though a modern English reader might not notice it, Paul has structured his opening to the two-chapter section as a striking contrast to his earlier claim that

---

71. *Ad Herennium* 3.10.17-18.

72. Wayne A. Meeks, *The First Urban Christians: The Social World of the Apostle Paul* (New Haven: Yale University Press, 1983) 129.

the Holy Spirit dwells (*en hymin,* "in you" or "among you") among the Corinthian believers as the resident power of God's grace (3:16-17). Paul opens chap. 5 with a startling declaration: Where the Holy Spirit is supposed to be dwelling (*en hymin,* "in" or "among you"), there instead, Paul says, *porneia* is *en hymin,* "among you" (5:1). So Paul begins this section with a concern about the absence of the Spirit and its supplantation by *porneia,* and he concludes the two-chapter section with a return (another inclusio) to the theme of

the Holy Spirit dwelling *en hymin,* "in you" or "among you" (6:19-20).

Present as another link between chaps. 5 and 6 is Paul's concern with judging and judgment. Believers are supposed to make certain judgments about those inside the faith community (5:12) and leave other matters of judgment to God (5:13). Another type of judging—the settling of disputes between or among believers—is appropriate within the community (6:1, 5) and is not fittingly taken to unbelievers for adjudication.

# 1 CORINTHIANS 5:1-13, THE STAIN WITHIN: A THREAT TO THE HOLINESS APPROPRIATE TO THE TEMPLE OF THE HOLY SPIRIT

### NIV

**5** It is actually reported that there is sexual immorality among you, and of a kind that does not occur even among pagans: A man has his father's wife. [2]And you are proud! Shouldn't you rather have been filled with grief and have put out of your fellowship the man who did this? [3]Even though I am not physically present, I am with you in spirit. And I have already passed judgment on the one who did this, just as if I were present. [4]When you are assembled in the name of our Lord Jesus and I am with you in spirit, and the power of our Lord Jesus is present, [5]hand this man over to Satan, so that the sinful nature[a] may be destroyed and his spirit saved on the day of the Lord.

[6]Your boasting is not good. Don't you know that a little yeast works through the whole batch of dough? [7]Get rid of the old yeast that you may be a new batch without yeast—as you really are. For Christ, our Passover lamb, has been sacrificed. [8]Therefore let us keep the Festival, not with the old yeast, the yeast of malice and wickedness, but with bread without yeast, the bread of sincerity and truth.

[9]I have written you in my letter not to associate with sexually immoral people— [10]not at all meaning the people of this world who are immoral, or

[a]*5 Or* that his body; *or* that the flesh

### NRSV

**5** It is actually reported that there is sexual immorality among you, and of a kind that is not found even among pagans; for a man is living with his father's wife. [2]And you are arrogant! Should you not rather have mourned, so that he who has done this would have been removed from among you?

[3]For though absent in body, I am present in spirit; and as if present I have already pronounced judgment [4]in the name of the Lord Jesus on the man who has done such a thing.[a] When you are assembled, and my spirit is present with the power of our Lord Jesus, [5]you are to hand this man over to Satan for the destruction of the flesh, so that his spirit may be saved in the day of the Lord.[b]

[6]Your boasting is not a good thing. Do you not know that a little yeast leavens the whole batch of dough? [7]Clean out the old yeast so that you may be a new batch, as you really are unleavened. For our paschal lamb, Christ, has been sacrificed. [8]Therefore, let us celebrate the festival, not with the old yeast, the yeast of malice and evil, but with the unleavened bread of sincerity and truth.

[9]I wrote to you in my letter not to associate with sexually immoral persons— [10]not at all

[a]*Or* on the man who has done such a thing in the name of the Lord Jesus    [b]*Other ancient authorities add* Jesus

845

the greedy and swindlers, or idolaters. In that case you would have to leave this world. [11]But now I am writing you that you must not associate with anyone who calls himself a brother but is sexually immoral or greedy, an idolater or a slanderer, a drunkard or a swindler. With such a man do not even eat.

[12]What business is it of mine to judge those outside the church? Are you not to judge those inside? [13]God will judge those outside. "Expel the wicked man from among you."[a]

[a]13 Deut. 17:7; 19:19; 21:21; 22:21,24; 24:7

meaning the immoral of this world, or the greedy and robbers, or idolaters, since you would then need to go out of the world. [11]But now I am writing to you not to associate with anyone who bears the name of brother or sister[a] who is sexually immoral or greedy, or is an idolater, reviler, drunkard, or robber. Do not even eat with such a one. [12]For what have I to do with judging those outside? Is it not those who are inside that you are to judge? [13]God will judge those outside. "Drive out the wicked person from among you."

[a]Gk brother

# COMMENTARY

The chapter opens with Paul's forceful "It is actually reported" ("Ολως ἀκούεται *Holōs akouetai*)—which has the ring of "the word has spread everywhere"—that *porneia* so extraordinarily grievous as to be off the scale is "among you" (ἐν ὑμῖν *en hymin,* 5:1), precisely where instead the Holy Spirit ought to dwell (3:16; 6:19). Nothing could be further from acceptable. Chapter 5 focuses on the situation surely known to all the believers: One of them is living with his father's wife, most likely his stepmother.

Chapter 5 closes with Paul's axiomatic recitation of a deutoronomic refrain, "Drive out the wicked one from among you" (5:13; Deut 19:19; 21:21; 22:24; 24:7). And as one reads the chapter, one can see that this scriptural sentence has shaped Paul's counsel at several points (5:2, 5, 7, 11).

Paul does not address the "man who has done this deed" (5:2), nor does he honor him with the mention of his name. Instead, he turns his attention to the other members of the congregation whom he characterizes as "puffed up" or "arrogant" (φυσιόω *physioō*). For his rebuke of them, Paul looks for some disposition as far from arrogance as possible and suggests a more fitting response would be grieving (5:2). Paul's concern is with the community and with what their response indicates about their understanding of themselves. The community's response to this man is only the first in what will be a series of problems where the standards of the world and its acceptance of such

persons have wrongly come over into the community. The other believers have an obligation to act in a defining way; they need to reaffirm the borders of proper community life and cast the "wicked one" out of their fellowship.[73] Paul's prescription is a radical step, radical in the sense of getting to the root of proper community identity and comportment.

Chapters 1–4 set up the proper contrast between the world and true believers—the rival two-way tradition—and even capitalize on Paul's general depiction of the divisive, boastful believers as behaving just like ordinary non-believers (3:3). In chap. 5 Paul inquires how the believers can tolerate conduct that even the world would find offensive: "not even among the gentiles" (5:1).

Note that Paul chides the ones who are arrogant, puffed up, boastful (5:2; cf. 4:6, 18-19). He has had the arrogant and puffy Corinthians in view from early on in this letter. They are the ones who too readily dismiss Paul's coming to Corinth (4:18), and with it challenge his authority; they are likely the same ones who are taking sides and using the gospel as part of a power game (4:6-7); they may even be the same ones whose position Paul has characterized as "already satiated, already rich, already reigning" (4:8).

Paul has undercut the ground for such arrogance by his previously made claims about God's

73. Adela Yarbro Collins, "The Function of 'Excommunication' in Paul," *HTR* 73 (1980) 259-60.

gracious election and call of the Corinthians, most of whom had no social status in the world's eye (1:26-29). God's grace toward undeserving persons—which includes everybody, according to Paul (Rom 3:22*b*-24)—is the great social leveler so that none of the Corinthians should have been "puffed up in favor of one against another" (4:6 NRSV). "What do you have that you did not receive [as a gift]? And if you received it, why do you boast as if not receiving?" (4:7; cf. 8:1). Understandably for Paul, the only boast that is acceptable is a "boast in the Lord," who has graced the believers—who of course did not deserve the grace (1:31). In unmistakable terms Paul now tells the Corinthians, "Your boast is not good!" (5:6).

Paul's earlier treatment of boasting and puffiness has been somewhat general. In chaps. 1–4 the believers' haughtiness was not identified with any particular actions or expressions of it. Now in chap. 5 Paul encounters the first specific example of how boasting has surely condoned a particular action and thereby challenged the being and identity of the community of believers. In the earlier chapters he has established that boasting is inappropriate; now he confronts a particular action that he explicitly labels πορνεία (*porneia*) and whose perpetrator he identifies with the "wicked one" of the deuteronomic refrain.

Accordingly, Paul thinks the Corinthian believers should not be elated over the man who is living in an immoral way; rather, they should have gone into mourning (5:2). Why? Because that man's action, his *porneia*, is an indictment of the entire community and of their failure to exercise proper care for one another. In 5:3-5 Paul directs them, at their next assembly, to cast him out of the fellowship: "Hand this man over to Satan" (5:5). At stake is the well-being of the community (Paul turns to this in 5:6ff.) and the future of the one who did the wrong (see the Commentary on 3:15).

The text is allusive. We may suppose that the Corinthians knew Paul's fuller thoughts from his previous discussions with them. We can only take the few clues given here and, with what we know of Paul in his other letters, try to tease out what may be Paul's suppositions embedded within the text. Paul expects to encounter *porneia* out in the world, but not in the church. God's wrath and judgment are currently being manifested in the

world against injustice and immorality (Rom 1:18-32). In the final judgment, here called "the day of the Lord" (ἡμέρα τοῦ κυρίου *hēmera tou kyriou*) (5:5; cf. 3:13), God will eradicate all evil, all sin, and those under its throes. In the meanwhile, the believers' job is to maintain proper temple holiness, which means to keep immorality (*porneia*) and injustice from tainting the fellowship of believers.

Paul's instructions to dismiss this man seem to suppose that the only hope for him in "the day of the Lord Jesus" (5:5) is for him to be cast in the meantime into the domain of Satan, where his fleshly pursuits may be unmistakably seen by him as alien to the gospel. If he were allowed to continue in fellowship, he might never, short of the judgment day, be called to account and, therefore, not be challenged to bring his comportment in line with the gospel. By excluding him from fellowship, the community will send a "wake-up call" to the man. No longer would he be able to take their acceptance and perhaps even admiration as an indicator of his being on the right path.

Regarding the man who has his father's wife, Paul develops his argument in stages, like successive transparencies superimposed on one another. Each stage supposes the previous one(s) and adds emphasis, detail, and refinement to the whole picture. In the base portrait (5:1-5), Paul identifies the situation of the man having his stepmother as incontrovertable *porneia,* chides the community not only for their arrogant response but also for their failure to remove the person and, therefore, the *porneia* from their midst; and he directs the community, at their next assembly, to give the man over to Satan—that is, to put him out of the community.

The next transparency (5:6-8) emphasizes their boasting (highlighting 5:2*a*) and draws upon the common, quotidian experience of yeast leavening dough to insinuate that the man's presence in the community insidiously functions like yeast and affects the whole lump. The note about "cleaning" out the old yeast signals that the common experience of yeast is about to be transformed to the Passover ritual of ridding the house of yeast (Exod 13:7). So the simple act of expunging yeast is transposed into ritual, proper cleansing (the notion will reappear as a link in 6:11, where washing and baptism will be associated with the readers' having been cleansed also) appropriate to Passover where

Christ is considered the Passover lamb that has been sacrificed (5:7*b*-8; cf. Exod 12:21). So just as the man of the first transparency is to be removed from the community, so also the second transparency calls the auditors to "celebrate the festival" by removing the leaven that Paul identifies with two of the most sweeping vices, κακία (*kakia,* "badness," "depravity") and πονηρία (*ponēria,* "wickedness," "baseness," 5:8). Paul's replacement virtues will be considered after a look at the third transparency, which Paul superimposes.

Paul's third transparency (5:9-13) allows him not only to reassert his main points but also to demonstrate that his recommendation in the case of this particular man is not an ad hoc opposition to this fellow. His reference to his previous (lost) letter, even though the Corinthians seem to have had some confusion as to its precise meaning, grounds Paul's recommendations to his earlier teaching. By reminding them what he had written he reinforces what he has already sketched in the two previous transparencies. The previous letter not only establishes Paul's consistency but it also serves to show the Corinthians' need for Paul's further tutelage. They should have known not to mingle with "immoral people" (πόρνοι *pornoi,* an obvious reinforcement of his rejection of *porneia* in 5:1, 9). Two verses later (5:11) Paul highlights and elaborates his earlier counsel to avoid immoral people: (a) He means immoral people who have the name "brother or sister" in Christ, not all immoral people because avoiding all of them would be an impossibility—the world is full of them; (b) he reaffirms his strong conviction that vice list conduct is inappropriate to the life of faith and once again, for added emphasis, he leads the vice list of 5:11 with πόρνος (*pornos,* "immoral person"), one more link to and reinforcement of his spurning of *porneia* in 5:1. The extended vice list (5:11) elaborates on *porneia* as symbolizing unacceptable behavior for believers and identifies any believer who does such things as due to be shunned. As if for further emphasis, Paul adds to the twice-mentioned prohibition against "mingling" (συναναμείγνυμι *synanameignymi*) (5:9, 11*a*) the injunction not even to eat with such a one (5:11; cf. 11:17-34, where the topic of eating together will be treated again and in more detail).

Paul's two main points in the entire section are consistently affirmed. First, in each of the three transparencies Paul rules out fellowship with believing brothers and sisters who are involved in *porneia* or other associated vices. Second, in each Paul assumes that it is the community's responsibility to preserve its own God-given integrity by giving to Satan, by cleansing, and by driving out the violator.

Paul's rich Jewish heritage has obviously become his readers' tradition, too, because he does not have to explain his Passover reference. He associates casting this man out of the church with the Jewish practice of cleansing the house of yeast at Passover, rejects their boasting (5:6), and urges them to realize that they are like fresh, unleavened Passover dough. This connection is confirmed by Paul's christological declaration that "our Paschal lamb, Christ, has been sacrificed" (5:7) and by his reckoning that "therefore" they should celebrate the festival by cleaning out the old yeast, which Paul identifies (5:8) with two of the most comprehensive vices that tend to show up in his and similar Stoic lists: κακία (*kakia,* "badness," "depravity") and (*ponēria,* "wickedness," "baseness"). Proper celebration of the festival takes its cue from Christ, understood as the Passover lamb, and features as a contrast two virtues as the fitting, unleavened bread (Exod 12:8, 15, 19-20): εἰλικρίνεια (*eilikrineia,* "sincerity," "purity of motive"; cf. 2 Cor 2:17) and ἀλήθεια (*alētheia,* "truthfulness," "dependability," "uprightness"). Note that in Paul's scriptures the one who eats leavened bread (= *porneia* in 1 Corinthians) is threatened with being "cut off" from Israel (Exod 12:15), from "the congregation of Israel" (Exod 12:19), a notion fully in line with Paul's use of the deuteronomic refrain explicitly quoted by him in 1 Cor 5:13.

Simply ridding the community of the *porneia* is not sufficient; something positive must be put in its place (cf. Luke 11:24-26). Paul's suggestion of replacement with sincerity and truthfulness is surely a kind of fruit of the Spirit (cf. Gal 5:22), the very Spirit whose dwelling place had been taken by *porneia* (cf. 6:19-20).

Why are these two particular virtues chosen by Paul? We cannot be certain, but Paul's further use of *eilikrineia* with the Corinthians may shed some light on its function here. In 2 Cor 1:12, where Paul writes about his own comportment, he characterizes himself as having acted "in holiness and godly sincerity," which he identifies as being powered by God's grace and which he contrasts with comportment that is based on fleshly (σαρκική *sarkikē;* NRSV, "earthly"; NIV, "worldly; not on Spirit, implied) wisdom. In the 2 Corinthians passage Paul has in mind the same two-way tradition that is already present in 1 Cor 1:21-22 and across the opening chapters: One either lives by worldly wisdom, as some of the Corinthians are inclined to do, or one lives in godly sincerity, with one's motivations pure and open for any to examine. In 2 Cor 1:12 Paul describes himself as living by that godly sincerity; in 1 Cor 5:8 he calls for the Corinthians to live in that same way.

As to why *alētheia* is chosen as the desirable virtue, we may look to the term's other appearance in 1 Corinthians and see that love "rejoices in the truth" (13:6). Paul's strong link between truthfulness and love means that to call for either is to affirm the other. So in Paul's Passover reflection, he urges the Corinthians to celebrate the festival by throwing out the evil (and the immoral person) and by featuring instead what he identifies as the unleavened bread of sincerity and truthfulness (5:8).

Paul's view of Christ's death in 5:7 fits his usual pattern of considering it a past, finished, defining event. He casts it here in Passover garb to sharpen his readers' sense that the time for cleansing the house of yeast has passed. His rhetoric, therefore, creates a sense of urgency in dealing with the man who has his father's wife. In this context, yeast becomes synonymous with contamination, which must be cast out so that the house (= temple, 3:17) and, in Paul's letter, all who reside there, may be properly holy, a motif that he will explicitly affirm in 6:19-20 as he brings this two-chapter section to a close.[74]

Maintenance of holiness and the avoidance of its counterpart, *porneia,* has been an enduring issue for the Corinthians, and the mark of this problem is visible not only across 1 Corinthians but was featured in the earlier letter (5:9-11). Paul's earlier epistolary effort to address the problem of *porneia* in the believing community did not achieve a resolution, because the matter is still up for consideration not only in 5:1-13 but also across the current letter. Let us attempt to reconstruct, from the evidence in 1 Corinthians, Paul's position

on shunning immoral persons and how it has been variously interpreted at Corinth.

Paul reminds the Corinthians that his previous letter had urged them not to "mingle/associate" (*synanameignymi*) with *pornoi,* immoral people. The repetition of the verb for "mingle" or "mix together" (5:9, 11) could suggest that it was the very term Paul had used in the previous letter. In 5:11 Paul makes clear that the troublesome mingling he had in mind was not, as some had taken it, with the immoral persons of the world. Paul's sense of logic rules out that interpretation, because then one would have had to exit the world, a ludicrous notion for Paul. He then clarifies that he meant for them to avoid nominal believers who, in fact, are immoral people; and to emphasize his point and show that the concern was not narrowly focused only on *porneia,* he elaborates a vice list of totally unacceptable behavior (5:11) that *porneia* has come in this letter to represent.

We can learn from this that for some time, perhaps from the period of their first coming into faith, the Corinthians have had immoral persons in their fellowship; the man who has his stepmother is not at all the first such, though he is acknowledged by Paul to be an extreme example. We can also learn that Paul's handling of the topic in the previous letter did not solve the matter, though we can surmise that some persons in the believing community actually tried to figure out Paul's advice and follow it. And we can learn that the earliest interpreters of one of Paul's letters, the Corinthians themselves, came up with some radically different understandings of his counsel against mingling with immoral people. Could it not be some of these very readers who concluded that they might do well to divorce their unbelieving spouses (7:12-16)? Is it an even more radical interpretation of Paul's counsel against mingling that leads some married persons to wonder if holiness and human sexuality can coexist and who, therefore, decided to abstain from sexual intercourse (7:5)? And why could not the man with his father's wife be one who took a very different reading on Paul's earlier letter, understanding that two believers could operate on a different and liberated moral code as long as both of them were believers? For such an understanding, *porneia* would be a problem only if one were involved with an unbe-

74. Ibid., 251-63.

liever. And is it not possible that the wealthy believers who adjudicate church matters by taking them to the civil courts (chap. 6) have understood Paul to say that holiness and its appropriate life are possible completely within the structures of the society? This same sort of border question, discerning the way holiness and *porneia* related, could also have contributed to the confusion over whether believers could eat meat offered to idols (cf. their letter's question in 8:1), whether believers could accept dinner invitations from unbelievers (10:27), and how to treat unbelievers when they happen into worship (14:22-25).

The matter is an important and complex one. We know that the Jewish community at Qumran, associated with the Dead Sea Scrolls, resolved the issue of minimizing the contamination of their God-given holiness by fleeing into the desert, the kind of response that Paul rejects in 5:10. But, short of escapism, how can holiness not only be lived but also honored and preserved in the world?

The proper maintenance of holiness, Paul believes, is possible while one lives directly in the world, in contact with immoral people and within the ordinary transactions of human life (cf. 7:29-31). But fellowship within the community of the faithful is to be measured by another scale: Inside the community absolutely no *porneia* is to be countenanced; immoral people who are nominal brothers and sisters in Christ must not be granted fellowship in the body of Christ. In the community *porneia* has a corrosive, corrupting, contaminating power. This same matter is treated in a different context in Romans 6, where Paul pursues the question of whether faith and sin may coexist, whether the life of faith allows the presence of sin within it. There as here the answer is the same: Faith and sin do not allow any mixture; the one precludes the other. One is either in right relation to God (faith that expresses itself in holiness living) or one is not (then one is under sin, which gains expression in immoral living). There is no middle ground, no third alternative that allows a mix. The people of God, as God's temple, must be completely and purely set apart for God. There can be no admixture of unholiness within God's family; yet God's family can and will live directly in the structures of the world, where sin and unholiness are present.

The problems of distinguishing proper from improper comportment and the holy from the immoral should have been cleared up by Paul's previous letter (5:9). Now in the present letter Paul clarifies that he had been concerned with *pornoi*, immoral persons, in the community and that believers should in fact not even have table fellowship with "someone who bears the name of 'brother' or 'sister' " if they be "immoral, or greedy, or an idolater, or an abusive person, or a drunkard, or a robber" (5:11)—repetitively strung out, as this translation tries to suggest, so as to invite the hearers to extend the list. The vice list here functions in an et cetera fashion to suggest that *porneia* serves to typify the larger problem, another instance of synecdoche; holiness is put in hazard by any comportment that crosses over the border that the vice list represents. In Paul's view, persons whose lives exemplify any of the vices are true outsiders (see the Commentary on 14:16, 23-25); they no more belong in the community than yeast belongs in the house at Passover.[75] The man living with his stepmother has, by his own comportment, become an outsider whose presence inside the community risks the holiness and well-being of all the members. By community action, the boundaries of the community must be redrawn so that this man is outside where God judges (5:13).

Believers have responsibility for comportment within the community, to monitor it and to call into question any behavior that threatens the health and wholeness, the holiness, of the community; that is what Paul probably has in mind when he asks them, "Is it not you yourselves who judge the ones inside?" (5:12). In 5:3 Paul has modeled this judgment function: He "has pronounced judgment" (reached a decision) regarding the man; he must be expelled. Parenthetically, it may be noted from 2 Cor 2:5-11 that the Corinthians subsequently put Paul's advice about monitoring community behavior into practice; in 2 Cor 2:7-8 Paul suggests that they should restore fellowship to a repentant believer.

Across his correspondence, Paul's vice lists (Rom 1:29-32; 1 Cor 6:9-11; 2 Cor 12:20-21; Gal 5:19-21) function, like a fence around the community of believers, to mark out totally unaccept-

---

75. W. A. Meeks, " 'Since Then You Would Need to Go Out of the World': Group Boundaries in Pauline Christianity," in *Critical History and Biblical Faith: New Testament Perspectives*, ed. T. J. Ryan (Villanova, Pa.: College Theological Society, 1979) 18-19.

able behavior. For Paul it is unthinkable that believers might cross over into the actions depicted in the vice lists. When a believer does, as here in chap. 5, Paul considers that the individual no longer belongs; he or she has become like an unbeliever and subject to Satan's rule and to God's direct judgment. Paul fears a contamination of the community by such a presence of *porneia*. Within the fence provided by the vice lists, Paul can embrace a broad range of conduct as long as love is put into practice, but he has no tolerance for any staining of the community's holiness. Why does he reproach the community? Because they have not understood that the wholeness of the community, the health and well-being, indeed, to use Paul's expression, the holiness of the fellowship is at risk.

By clever use of Passover analogies, such as yeast, dough, and unleavened lump, Paul elaborates the theme of believers' being God's temple that must not be corrupted. Should matters get out of hand, as in this instance, and the community find itself defiled, it must urgently move to set matters straight. In 3:17, temple honoring was set over against temple defilement. Now in 5:6-8 the intruding *porneia* is compared to yeast: Even what seems to be a "little bit" leavens the whole lump. Paul likens the believing community to their Jewish forebears who, when the paschal lamb was slain, dared not find even a hint of yeast on the premises. He reminds the believers that, in this analogy, they "really are unleavened" already (5:7), or at least are created and called to be so, and that Christ, the Passover lamb, has indeed already been slain. Accordingly, they have no option but to "clean out the old leaven" that this man represents. Then their lives will be characterized no more by the leaven of "vice and wickedness" but by the more appropriate "purity of motive and truthfulness" (5:8; cf. Rom 11:16).

In 3:17, Paul described the Corinthians as God's holy temple and warned that any threat of defilement, corruption, spoiling (φθείρω *phtheirō*, 3:17) to the temple is itself a peril to the individual who does the corruption (there it was noted that the plural was used). Here in 5:6-8 Paul makes clear that such individual corruption brings the entire community under God's judgment. The same theme will reappear, with the same key verb, in Paul's discussion of resurrection when he quotes the contemporary poetic maxim: "Bad company corrupts (*phtheirō*) good character" (15:33 NIV). Paul's final word on the subject of this man's threat to the community's well-being and holiness is the scriptural injunction to "drive out the wicked person from among you" (5:13; cf. Deut 19:19; 22:21, 24; 24:7).

# REFLECTIONS

**1.** Modern Christians often think that to raise questions regarding another person's behavior is a negative thing—and for good reason, because it can too readily be self-righteously and derogatorily delivered. But there is a legitimate question of just how fully love is carried out toward another if one never raises a question about that person's comportment no matter how far out it happens to be. Surely genuine love does not condone all actions done by loved ones. "Tough love" is an expression that suggests that love is not always "yes"; it may and must sometimes be "no" or at the very least "why?" At issue is the difference between meddling and proper responsibility. Clearly, the former is to be avoided, but the latter is an obligation of love. It may be helpful to put meddling and proper mutual responsibility on an imaginary continuum from left to right. On the right is one's clear duty; on the left is what one must avoid. In between is a range of choices, some of which will be more clearly appropriate mutual care and some of which may suggest meddling. Life's moral choices must be made in the gray area of uncertainty where the obligation of love is often clearer than our judgment about the appropriateness of our involvement in a particular gray-area situation. Not to act or to choose to be silent has its own risks—people may be harmed. For example, if one of the clergy abuses someone in the church and nothing is done about it, then the church has failed in its responsibility to care in a loving fashion for all its members. Love to the abused one should take the form of standing over against the clergy and insisting upon restorative therapy; love for the clergyperson should take the form of discipline, removal, and treatment.

**2.** The problem in all terminations of fellowship, whether in the church or between friends, is one of degree, of determining when the action falls far enough into the gray area to be harmful. Each person needs to be his or her own "gray monitor," but you might find it helpful to have occasional discussions with others about how they make their own decisions about when they think there is too much gray in a situation. Surely, excommunication in a church setting is a radical action whose very need already signals a massive failure of the fellowship to nurture and counsel its members. A church that has done its work of mutual encouragement and mutual checking properly will probably never face the need to withdraw fellowship from an individual. A church that looks the other way at its members' comportment is courting disaster. This is not "throwing the first stone." It is love's obligation for us to reflect with one another about our moral performance.

**3.** Paul's picture is one that stresses the nurturing and correcting function of the church; when the church functions as it ought, God's judgment need not enter the church. Paul does not treat the question of whether God's judgment is already being experienced by the man, but Paul is convinced that when the man is expelled, he surely comes face-to-face with God's judgment. One other angle is worth considering: Does not the church, when it knows of such vice-list-violating conduct and says nothing, encourage its member to think that the person is perhaps still within the scope of acceptable behavior?

Such a dynamic should raise for modern believers the question of how they signal affirmation and concern about the behavior of others. Surely, one response to that question will be that no one should signal to another at all, but another person might have to wonder whether there can be any real community if people do not care about how each other behaves.

**4.** Another facet of this issue may be expressed in terms of piety and holiness. For many today, religiousness, holiness is a private matter between the individual and God. But for Paul, holiness and piety, though surely grounded in individuals and in each person's behavior, are community concerns and responsibilities. They are to assemble, to turn this man over to Satan; they are to cleanse out the old leaven; and they are to celebrate the Passover festival with purity of motives and in truth. As will become evident at points across this letter, Christians stand or fall as a community, not as collected individuals. These reflections will cause problems for persons who have privatized their faith and their moral responsibility, for those who think that their moral decisions are theirs alone between themselves and God. Such an individualistic view is totally alien to Paul's picture of how the life of faith ought to be lived.

**5.** Judgment within the church is not simply a final, leave-it-to-God verdict. Note that the man is turned over to Satan with the hope or expectation that, in some way, he may be "saved on the day of the Lord" (5:5). Paul and the Corinthians may not presume to know the man's ultimate fate because his destiny is God's business, and God's grace works in mysterious ways. Decisions about maintenance of the community, its requisite holiness, and who is allowed full fellowship and participation are not decisions about damnation and salvation because these latter are not the church's dominion; they belong solely to God.

**6.** Paul's call to the Corinthians is, in effect, to "become what you are in Christ"—that is, to live up to what you have been reconstituted to be in Christ. "You really are unleavened" (5:7); live like it. Much the same point will be made in chap. 6: You really are "washed . . . sanctified . . . justified" (6:11); live like it. Paul paints the picture of what is true in Christ, reminding the believers of what God in Christ has done for them; then he calls the believers to live up to—that is, to live in accord with—their calling.

# 1 CORINTHIANS 6:1-11, WRONGFULLY CROSSING THE BORDER IN THE OTHER DIRECTION: TAKING COMMUNITY MATTERS OUT INTO THE WORLD

## NIV

**6** If any of you has a dispute with another, dare he take it before the ungodly for judgment instead of before the saints? [2]Do you not know that the saints will judge the world? And if you are to judge the world, are you not competent to judge trivial cases? [3]Do you not know that we will judge angels? How much more the things of this life! [4]Therefore, if you have disputes about such matters, appoint as judges even men of little account in the church![a] [5]I say this to shame you. Is it possible that there is nobody among you wise enough to judge a dispute between believers? [6]But instead, one brother goes to law against another—and this in front of unbelievers!

[7]The very fact that you have lawsuits among you means you have been completely defeated already. Why not rather be wronged? Why not rather be cheated? [8]Instead, you yourselves cheat and do wrong, and you do this to your brothers.

[9]Do you not know that the wicked will not inherit the kingdom of God? Do not be deceived: Neither the sexually immoral nor idolaters nor adulterers nor male prostitutes nor homosexual offenders [10]nor thieves nor the greedy nor drunkards nor slanderers nor swindlers will inherit the kingdom of God. [11]And that is what some of you were. But you were washed, you were sanctified, you were justified in the name of the Lord Jesus Christ and by the Spirit of our God.

[a]4 Or matters, do you appoint as judges men of little account in the church?

## NRSV

**6** When any of you has a grievance against another, do you dare to take it to court before the unrighteous, instead of taking it before the saints? [2]Do you not know that the saints will judge the world? And if the world is to be judged by you, are you incompetent to try trivial cases? [3]Do you not know that we are to judge angels—to say nothing of ordinary matters? [4]If you have ordinary cases, then, do you appoint as judges those who have no standing in the church? [5]I say this to your shame. Can it be that there is no one among you wise enough to decide between one believer[a] and another, [6]but a believer[a] goes to court against a believer[a]—and before unbelievers at that?

[7]In fact, to have lawsuits at all with one another is already a defeat for you. Why not rather be wronged? Why not rather be defrauded? [8]But you yourselves wrong and defraud—and believers[b] at that.

[9]Do you not know that wrongdoers will not inherit the kingdom of God? Do not be deceived! Fornicators, idolaters, adulterers, male prostitutes, sodomites, [10]thieves, the greedy, drunkards, revilers, robbers—none of these will inherit the kingdom of God. [11]And this is what some of you used to be. But you were washed, you were sanctified, you were justified in the name of the Lord Jesus Christ and in the Spirit of our God.

[a]Gk brother    [b]Gk brothers

# COMMENTARY

Apparently some Corinthian believers are taking other believers to civil courts for the settlement of disputes. It is a logical step for Paul to treat this matter at this point in the letter because, in the just-finished discussion, he has advanced the argument that judgment properly belongs inside the community.

In the Greco-Roman world, who initiated civil court cases? The answer is simple and unmistakable: only the wealthy, only the very powerful few who sat atop the steep social pyramid. We have seen (1:26) that the Corinthian church had a few such people.[76] Those wealthy people must be the ones who conduct business and settle disputes in their accustomed fashion, as they had done regularly in their life before faith came: They turn to the courts, whose verdicts followed wealth. Paul's view of this Corinthian practice is clear in the way he describes the judges in three places: Worldly judges are the persons who "wrong" others—that is, who do what is not right, not just, not righteous (ἐπὶ τῶν ἀδίκων *epi tōn adikōn,* 6:1); they are the ones who are despised or "have no standing" (NRSV) in the church (6:4); and it follows that they are "unbelievers" (6:6).[77]

Paul thinks that "the saints," his designation for all of the ones who have responded to the call of the gospel and, therefore, are the recipients of this very letter (1:2), are the ones who should be qualified to hear disputes (6:1). Paul's two-way depictions of life's basic alternatives, which he laid out so clearly and distinctively in his opening chapters (1–4), now serve to show how confused the Corinthians are and how wrong is their practice.

When faced with a problem or issue, Paul regularly refers to "what we know" and reasons from that to some advice or resolution. It is a pattern that we will see across 1 Corinthians. In the case at hand, "what we know" is mentioned in rhetorical questions that are so constructed in Greek as to expect a yes answer. "You do know, don't you, that the saints will judge the world?" (6:2). "You do know, don't you, that we will judge angels?" (6:3). Paul finds an irony in the Corinthians' going to worldly courts to settle quarrels when they, the saints, are destined to judge the very world of which those courts are so much a part. How can it be that the Corinthian saints are "incompetent for the most insignificant cases" (6:3)? When believers are destined to judge even angels, how is it possible that they cannot handle "ordinary matters" (βιωτικά *biōtika,* 6:3)? And how can they, who will ultimately judge the world and angels, lay

routine day-to-day issues before persons who have no standing in the church? It is too much for Paul: "To your shame I say this!" (6:5).

Paul's rapid-fire questions have the ring of a courtroom. Form follows function. The questions have the effect of placing the auditors, with their fascination with courts, on the witness stand; Paul adopts the stance of the one who with leading questions exposes what he takes to be the shameful conduct of the Corinthian believers.

Lying behind Paul's rebuke is his apocalyptic conviction that, in God's final judgment of sin and its grasp of the world, it is the believers who will form part of the heavenly court (cf. Dan 7:22; 12:3; Wis 3:8; Sir 4:15; 2 Esdr 9:97; *1 Enoch* 104:2; *Testament of Abraham* 1-4; 1QpHab 5:4; Matt 19:28; Rev 3:21; 20:4), who are at least present when God's final judgment takes place (cf. Isa 24:21-22). The notion that angels will face judgment may go back to the story of the sons of God, taken around the turn of the era to be angels (cf. *1 Enoch* 6–19), mentioned in Gen 6:1-6, and their improper conduct; such an interpretation lies behind 2 Pet 2:4 and Jude 6 and probably informs Paul's understanding that is reflected here in 1 Cor 6:3. Paul's questions ("Do you not know," 6:2-3) and the brevity of the discussion show that he expects the Corinthians to know and even to share his sublime picture of the end times. At no single place in the Pauline letters do we see the whole of Paul's eschatological vision; on some occasions, we see mere hints of it such as these (see 1 Cor 15:24-28). But the way Paul does not have to explain these grand claims indicates that he expects his Corinthian readers to know the assertions and the fuller story of which they are a part.

The sublimity of Paul's eschatological vision, combined with his strong and abiding conviction that judgment will surely take place at the end, mocks the trifling insignificance of the disputes that some Corinthians have dragged before public tribunals. Paul's choice of terms heightens the contrast, to the detriment of those seeking civil resolution of disputes. He uses a superlative: "If the world is to be judged by you, are you not worthy regarding the least cases?" (6:2). He associates their concerns with *biōtika,* what we might call "ordinary" or "day-to-day," "run-of-the-mill" matters that seem rather puny when compared with their anticipated end-time role of judging angels (6:3).

76. Allan Mitchell, "Rich and Poor in the Courts of Corinth: Litigiousness and Status in 1 Corinthians 6:1-11," *NTS* 39 (1993) 562-63, argues, as does this commentary, that a few wealthy believers were taking "lower status people to court, where the latter were at a disadvantage."

77. For background, see B. W. Winter, "Civil Litigation in Secular Corinth and the Church. The Forensic Background to 1 Corinthians 6.1-8," *NTS* 37 (1991) 559-72.

This section is laced with irony. First, with certain ironic rebuke aimed toward those who pride themselves on wisdom and its associated worldly status, Paul inquires, "Is there no wise person among you who could render a [fitting, just, understood] decision?" (6:5). So much for those at Corinth who saw wisdom as an avenue to power but could not see wisdom as applicable to communal strife and differences. According to Paul, lawsuits among the believers are an "utter loss" (6:7) because these very Corinthians recognize neither the nature of community in Christ nor the way believers are to deal with one another.

In parallel constructions that, as an inclusio, explicitly link back to Paul's first description of civil judges as ones who "wrong" others (6:1), Paul seeks to put the believers' strife and contention in perspective: "Why not rather be wronged? Why not rather let yourselves be robbed? Instead you yourselves wrong and rob!" (6:7-8). What characterizes the judgments rendered by unbelieving judges—namely, their wronging of others, is precisely what Paul sees has ironically become operative within the community of believers. The believers at Corinth have become precisely like those outside the faith community—yet another irony and yet one more reason why the community needs to redefine itself as distinct from the world and the latter's patterns of arrangements between and among people.

Chapter 6 and the issue of lawsuits before civil authorities raises once again the questions of community borders, of what is appropriate within the community and of how the community relates to what is going on in the world outside the church. But, in contrast to chap. 5 where *porneia* has crept into the church from the world, now the question of lawsuits raises the issue of matters that should be properly treated precisely within the community. Paul's complaint about Corinthians' going to civil courts to settle disputes is twofold, and both are ironically stated: They who value and vaunt wisdom do not have a wise person to adjudicate disputes, and they whom Paul presumes will be the experts on justice, who will sit in judgment on the world and even on angels (presumably at the end of the ages; 6:2-3), turn to persons outside the community of believers and, therefore, to judges who know nothing about justice and judging.

Paul is convinced that believers should be able to work out their differences with one another amicably and with a sense of fairness and justice; they are, after all, the ones who know the difference between ἀδικία (*adikia*, "wickedness," "injustice") and δικαιοσύνη (*dikaiosynē*, "righteousness," "justice"). But instead they turn to unjust judges for decisions of justice (6:1)! Woefully, the believers, the saints, have shirked their responsibilities to work out disputes among themselves, they have abandoned the standards that should be foundational for their communal life, and they have turned to the standards of the world.

Once again, as in chap. 5, the borders demarcating the community from the world have been breached, and here as there Paul recites a vice list as a means of marking off the distinction (6:9-10; 5:9-11).[78] The "unrighteous," those who do wrong or injustice, such as unbelieving civil judges and some within the community of faith, "will not inherit the kingdom of God" (6:9). Paul expects that the Corinthians should already know that, as the ninth rhetorical question, this one also expecting a yes answer, clearly indicates (6:9, reprised in 6:10). The listed vices function not only to reprise matters that have preceded but also to hint at those that will follow (e.g., several of the vices mentioned in 6:9-10 echo the list in 5:11; *pornoi,* "immoral ones" ties back to 5:1, 9 and ahead to 6:13-18 and 7:2; idolatry has clear links ahead to chap. 8 and to 10:19).

As in chap. 5, vice lists help Paul to distinguish acceptable behavior from unacceptable and reinforce the proper identity of believers. Paul casts the vice list in 6:9-10 to describe the former lives of some of the believers; it should no longer be descriptive of them. In the strongest contrast allowed in the Greek language (ἀλλά *alla,* "but"), Paul repeatedly dissociates his audience from the vices and the former state of their lives: "But you were washed; but you were sanctified; but you were justified" (6:11). Paul fears that the community border has been breached, that holiness has been contaminated. As a corrective, he tries to distinguish the comportment appropriate to heirs of God's kingdom.

In 6:11 the phrase "in the name of the Lord Jesus Christ" (cf. 1:10; 5:4), combined as it is with the references to the Spirit and to the readers'

---

78. P. S. Zaas, "Catalogues and Context: 1 Corinthians 5 and 6," *NTS* 34 (1988) 622-29, esp. 629.

having been "washed," makes clear that Paul is employing baptismal references as a way of positioning the Corinthians' understandings of themselves and of their new and distinctive calling in Christ. The vice lists conform to the same understanding because Paul's rhetoric is focused here on calling to mind their set-apart status as believers who should live and conduct themselves differently from the world. The same considerations should be in view as we retrospectively interpret the appearance of the identical phrase "in the name of the Lord Jesus" in 5:4. There Paul is urging the community of believers who gather in the Lord's name—that is, under Christ's power and guidance as risen Lord, to turn over to Satan the man who is sleeping with his stepmother. In both places (5:4; 6:11) the phrase serves a fundamental community-definition function; it asks the believers gathered in Christ's name to be reflective about their identity, founded in their baptism, and how they ought to live in order more fully to honor Christ's lordship. So the two appeals to "the name of the Lord" function as yet another inclusio and as another sign that the topics of chaps. 5 and 6 are interrelated in Paul's purpose.

The appearance of baptismal language—"in the name of the Lord Jesus" (*en tō onomati tou Kyriou Iēsou*)—signals several important points to the reader. First, and this ties into the earlier interpretation of chaps. 1–4, Paul is taking the auditors back to basics in chaps. 5 and 6. Second, because Paul associates baptism with entry into the faith and believers thus becoming God's children (Rom 8:14-15; Gal 4:6), Paul makes good on his claim in 3:1-2 that he must treat them as babies despite their inclination to more elevated self-estimates. Third, the inclusio of the baptismal formula in 5:4 and in 6:11 ties the content of those sections together despite the superficial sense that they deal with two distinct issues. And finally, the mention of "the Spirit of our God" in 6:11 provides the link, as yet another inclusio, that will bring chap. 6 to a close in the reprise—cast once more in a question expecting a "yes" answer because the Corinthians are supposed to know this and to live by it already—of the claim that the recipients of the letter are the temple of the Holy Spirit (6:19-20; cf. 3:16-17).

Paul has called the Corinthians "babies who are not ready [as he insinuates they should be or as they perhaps think they are] for solid food" (3:1;

4:14);[79] he has characterized them as persons whose humble social origins do not fit with their haughty self-evaluations and pretensions (1:26; 4:8); and he has gone "back to basics" with them, as one can see from the phrase "You do know, don't you . . . ?" repeated eight times—three of them in the upcoming 6:12-20—in the first six chapters (3:16; 5:6; 6:2-3, 9, 15-16, 19).

It has been noted several times since chap. 3 that Paul's estimate of the Corinthians' maturity (really immaturity) in the faith is different from the Corinthians' estimate of themselves. The two linked items in chaps. 5 and 6 are part of Paul's evidence that his estimate, not theirs, is the right one. What they ought to have known—indeed, what Paul did teach them—from their most juvenile times in the faith would have, should have kept them from the kinds of community-disruptive and destructive actions noted in the man's living with his father's wife and in their taking one another to court. The Corinthian believers have gotten ahead of themselves. They must be taken back to the basics of the life of faith and, together, build from there. As long as the church becomes like the world or the world's ways leach into the communal life of faith, the believers lack understanding and clarity on even the most basic matters.

In one other significant way Paul builds from his conviction that the Corinthians are babies. In the second delineation of vice lists in these two chapters (5:9-13; 6:9-11), Paul inquires of the believers' understandings: "You do know, don't you, that the unrighteous will not inherit God's reign?" (6:9). The talk of "inheriting the kingdom" is not frequent in Paul, but because of its appearance in another letter in a similar connection (Gal 5:21, where even there he also reminds his readers, the Galatians, that he had taught them this point earlier), it must be a traditional teaching of Paul's, and he knows he has already shared it with the Corinthians. The next verse (6:10) elaborates the same point—namely, that persons whose conduct fits the vice list will never inherit God's reign. So we find mention of inheritance alongside baptismal language ("in the name of Jesus," 6:11; 5:4) in the same way that Rom 8:15-17 depicts it, but in

79. Beverly R. Gaventa, "Mother's Milk and Ministry in 1 Corinthians 3," in *Theology and Ethics in Paul and His Interpreters: Essays in Honor of Victor Paul Furnish*, ed. E. H. Lovering, Jr., and J. L. Sumney (Nashville: Abingdon, 1996) 101-13.

Romans the baptismal connection is expressed in terms of receiving the Holy Spirit rather than with the baptismal phrase "in the name of Jesus." In Romans 8 the Spirit enables believers to become God's children, saying "Abba, Pater" ("Father" in Aramaic and in Greek, perhaps a reference to the Lord's Prayer), and then goes ahead to describe them as "heirs" of the full inheritance that God has prepared (Rom 8:17). In 1 Cor 6:9-10 Paul reminds the Corinthians that their association with *porneia* and its related vices places in jeopardy the full inheritance and place in God's reign (cf. 15:24-28) for which the thus-far working of the Spirit has qualified them, if they do not deceive themselves (6:10).

# REFLECTIONS

**1.** Disputes, differences of opinions among believers and in a church are not surprising; the way conflicts are resolved says a great deal about the maturity of the believers involved, about the health of a community of believers, about its understanding of itself and its obligations to others, and about its perception of its ultimate destiny and function in God's grand design. Believers are themselves appropriately different from one another (Paul will write about that in detail in chap. 12), so it is entirely to be expected that they will differ in their opinions about things, in their reckoning as to what is important, and in their choices of action or non-action. Fine, but love calls for them to live with one another in a respectful and caring way even when they differ. Believers should discuss with one another how they can achieve the proper respect and care when they do find themselves in a point of difference about belief or practice. Couples and good friends surely have to do this as well.

**2.** Paul discusses two types of judging in 6:1-8, and both kinds find modern expression. The one judgment is apocalyptic, cosmic, and final and occurs only at the end of the ages when believers can anticipate that they will form a subcourt under God. The other judgment is contingent and corrective. When someone today "damns" another person, we are right to object to the presumption, not only because it arrogates God's prerogative but also because it improperly absolves one from caring. Caring for others is not an option; it is an obligation. Paul assumes a connection between these two judgments: Those who will ultimately be qualified to serve in the cosmic tribunal should surely be able, already in the here and now, to handle what has been translated as "ordinary matters." Both the NIV and the NRSV translate *biōtika* as "trivial cases," which is acceptable insofar as it grasps Paul's intended contrast that has been noted here. But the translation belittles the reality that believers and churches will have differences of opinion, and sometimes quite strong ones, about "ordinary matters"—and perhaps even regarding weighty ordinary matters—that need to be resolved amicably and fairly, which Paul seems to understand.

**3.** "To have lawsuits with one another is an utter loss for you; why not rather be wronged?" (6:7). Is this Pauline position prescriptive or is it hyperbole? Supporting a Pauline overstatement designed to shock the readers are the following: the intense irony of 6:2-6 and Paul's tendency to overstatement as a means of emphasizing a point (cf. 8:13, where Paul's assertion suggests that he is prepared to become a vegetarian). If one chooses to take it as prescriptive, then one has consequent problems that call for resolution: First, is every Pauline prescription that was made for a particular congregation equally applicable to all other believers and all other congregations across all time? Second, in a litigious culture such as ours, how are believers to avoid being dupes—or, to put it in terms of Jesus' call, how are believers to be as innocent as doves and as wise as serpents (Matt 10:16)?

In either case, it may be helpful to realize that there are striking differences between Pauline churches and the social setting of most modern Christians. Paul's churches were relatively small in number; all of the believers could meet in a patron's home for worship; therefore, they all knew each other and presumably were in frequent contact with one another. In modern churches, the members often do not know one another and sometimes never share the same space with others except at worship. Further, our social structures are so much more complex that one person's involvement in business, for example, may raise liabilities about which that individual may not even be aware.

If we were to take 6:7 as prescriptive, how would we apply it in our modern settings? Clearly, Paul thought conflicts between believers ought to be resolved short of court proceedings, and that is surely still a good guideline for modern believers wherever possible. In fact, churches might do well to set up boards to assist in conflict resolution and thereby use some of the skills that members of the congregation may have, an idea certainly appropriate to Paul (6:5). Churches should aim to minimize the harm to all parties of disputes while maximizing justice. A verse such as the one before us should not be allowed to function in such a way as to ensure injustice; that would be an ultimate irony.

**4.** Moral reasoning from "what we know" is a vital pattern for Paul and could just as well be so for modern Christians. When faced with a moral choice or dilemma, Paul regularly inquires what believers know and reasons from what is known to an application concerning the issue at hand. For example, how does Paul come to the conclusion that when invited to an unbeliever's home for dinner, you are free to eat whatever is served? He knows his scriptures and remembers that we know "the earth is the Lord's and everything in it" (1 Cor 10:24, quoting Ps 24:1). To take another example, if we know that to love is not an option but an obligation, then we start the deliberation of our moral choices not by deciding whether to love a certain person; rather, we move to weigh how we might express love to this individual.

**5.** Vice lists, another example of what believers know, function to demarcate behavior that community members agree is beyond the pale. Vice lists serve to define the borders and to mark what believers assiduously must avoid in their comportment. Vice lists are a common feature in Paul's letters (Rom 1:29-32; 13:13-14; 2 Cor 12:20-21; Gal 5:19-21). A glance at the different lists shows that the terms constituting them are not consistent; the contents of the lists seem somewhat tailored toward the circumstances the given letter is addressing. In any case, the lists are not exhaustive but illustrative and are flexible as to content. In no instance is a vice labeled a sin (an important consideration in any case, but perhaps especially in our own time in dealing with matters such as Reflection 6, below, treats). Paul appears to think of sin as a power that bids to take over one's life. He refers to sins in the plural (as if they might be listed) only in materials he takes over from traditional materials that he recites.

It might be a very informative process for a modern church to start with all of Paul's virtue and vice lists and have a lengthy deliberation about what that church would establish for its own vice list; then the congregation—perhaps by highlighting some and by adding new ones—would have ownership of its own self-examination of its borders and, therefore, of its own sense of definition. A modern church could begin with 6:9-11 because there Paul has laid out both sides of the matter: (1) He has offered a vice list that serves to mark off the borders of the community by noting unacceptable behavior (6:9-10), and (2) he has identified, by a series of claims, the positive core of their identity (6:11), of who they have become in the name of Christ and in the Spirit.

**6.** In modern times two terms from the vice list in 6:9-10 have provoked especial interest. They are μαλακοί (*malakoi;* NIV and NRSV, "male prostitutes") and ἀρσενοκοῖται (*arsenokoitai;* NIV, "homosexual offenders"; NRSV, "sodomites," 6:9). The first term is used, when describing cloth, to mean "soft," but in its more general use it was pejoratively used in the contemporary culture to describe a man who was not adequately "manly" (cf. 16:13); in the cases of homosexual relations, it was used to describe the more passive one. Obviously, it would have been applied to the young boy involved with an older man. The second term was applied to men who engaged in pederasty or were sodomites; accordingly, the term was used to describe the more active male.[80]

If one knows nothing of the cultural practices and prejudices of Paul's time, one can more easily take these ancient terms from that context and make of them what one wishes. In Greek and Roman times, what we would call heterosexual married males (and one can suppose the same was true for their female counterparts) might frequently keep a boy (or in the case of wives, a girl) for their pleasure. Sometimes the kept person was a slave, who by definition would have no choice, but there were also boys who solicited sex with elders for pay. For the most part these relationships caught no special attention. Around Paul's time, however, certain prominent moralists had begun to note the more extreme, exploitative cases and to object to them.[81] All of those instances consider abuses; none of those texts concerns itself with relationships in which there is not exploitation.

Clearly, Paul thinks *porneia,* sexual immorality, and his cover-all term for immorality in general, is a characteristic of those outsiders to the faith, of gentiles who have not been converted to the faith (cf. 5:1). From his letters we can tell that Paul was a careful observer of the lives that believers and unbelievers lived. His listing of these two terms in this vice list is probably best understood as part of his general critique of the way non-believers behave. Those two terms cannot be tied to anything else in 1 Corinthians that Paul finds wrong with the Corinthians.[82]

80. BDAG 488, 109.

81. See Seneca "On Master and Slave" 7; Plutarch "Dialogue on Love" 751-52; Dio Chrysostom "Envy" 77/78.36-37, and "The Hunter" 151-52, a passage that, like Rom 1:27, decries the way some men have turned away from more socially common sexual patterns in search of increased excitement.

82. Though it is a surprisingly old publication now, Victor P. Furnish's "Homosexuality," in his *The Moral Teaching of Paul: Selected Issues* (Nashville: Abingdon, 1979) 52-82, is still one of the most balanced, thoughtful treatments of the issue.

# 1 CORINTHIANS 6:12-20, SUMMING UP AND LOOKING AHEAD

## NIV

12"Everything is permissible for me"—but not everything is beneficial. "Everything is permissible for me"—but I will not be mastered by anything. 13"Food for the stomach and the stomach for food"—but God will destroy them both. The body is not meant for sexual immorality, but for the Lord, and the Lord for the body. 14By his power God raised the Lord from the dead, and he will raise us also. 15Do you not know that your bodies are members of Christ himself? Shall I then take the members of Christ and unite them with a prostitute? Never! 16Do you not know that he who unites himself with a prostitute is one with her in body? For it is said, "The two will become one flesh."[a] 17But he who unites himself with the Lord is one with him in spirit.

18Flee from sexual immorality. All other sins a

[a]16 Gen. 2:24

## NRSV

12"All things are lawful for me," but not all things are beneficial. "All things are lawful for me," but I will not be dominated by anything. 13"Food is meant for the stomach and the stomach for food,"[a] and God will destroy both one and the other. The body is meant not for fornication but for the Lord, and the Lord for the body. 14And God raised the Lord and will also raise us by his power. 15Do you not know that your bodies are members of Christ? Should I therefore take the members of Christ and make them members of a prostitute? Never! 16Do you not know that whoever is united to a prostitute becomes one body with her? For it is said, "The two shall be one flesh." 17But anyone united to the Lord becomes one spirit with him. 18Shun fornication! Every sin that a person commits is outside the body; but the fornicator sins against the body itself. 19Or do you

[a] The quotation may extend to the word *other*

NIV

man commits are outside his body, but he who sins sexually sins against his own body. [19]Do you not know that your body is a temple of the Holy Spirit, who is in you, whom you have received from God? You are not your own; [20]you were bought at a price. Therefore honor God with your body.

NRSV

not know that your body is a temple[a] of the Holy Spirit within you, which you have from God, and that you are not your own? [20]For you were bought with a price; therefore glorify God in your body.

[a] Or sanctuary

# COMMENTARY

These verses, the first of two such passages in the letter, function as a hinge, pulling together several points and themes that have preceded and opening out to matters yet to be discussed in detail. This passage, like its parallel text in 10:23–11:1, functions as a staging point, where certain resources previously garnered are marshaled and inventoried in part though not simply to determine where author and readers are, but also to set the context for what follows. Up to this point Paul has dealt with specific actions of the Corinthians—namely, their tolerating the immorality of the man living with his stepmother, and their settling disputes in civil courts, before unbelievers.

Now, for the first time, Paul characterizes and casts up a reflection of their self-estimation: "All things are permissible for me!" (6:12). We cannot be sure what role Paul has had in formulating this maxim, but in its present form, it is probably creditable to the Corinthians. Supporting the contention that some Corinthians formulated the maxim is Paul's twice qualifying the maxim (6:12) and the individualistic cast of it ("for me"; note that when Paul next rehearses this maxim of theirs, he drops the "for me," 10:23).

Paul has a fondness for maxims and so do the Corinthians (e.g., 8:1, 4); indeed, maxims are a characteristic of Greco-Roman education and culture.[83] No doubt Paul's heavy employment of maxims in 1 Corinthians reflects the society's use of them in moral deliberation and in the education of children. In the Greco-Roman context, maxims (γνῶμαι *gnōmai;* Latin, *sententiae*) were consid-

ered epitomes of truth, of commonly shared convictions or perceptions. So they typically function as a "given" from which one argues or builds a case. Also typically, therefore, one does not refute a maxim; one may qualify it or place another maxim over against it for consideration or as a qualification of the first one.

In 6:12 Paul does not reject the Corinthians' maxim. First, he qualifies it with two additions: "but not all things are helpful" and "but I will not be mastered by anything" (6:12). Second, he lodges another maxim, whether of his own composition or not we cannot be sure, alongside theirs—"Food is for the stomach, and the stomach for food"—and, with his forceful declaration that "God will wipe out the one and the other" (6:13), he attempts a bit of perspective-keeping. In effect, he compels the readers to confront the question "Then what really matters?"

What could the Corinthian maxim—"All things are permissible for me" (6:12)—mean, and how could they, as persons standing in the Pauline tradition, have come to embrace or formulate it? Several observations are pertinent. (1) Paul never rejects the maxim (cf. 10:23 where it reappears); he does qualify it in several ways, and when he repeats it (twice) in 10:23 he modifies it by dropping the individualizing "for me," which was surely a part of their formulation of it. From this one must conclude that Paul does not take the maxim as fundamentally alien to his gospel. (2) The NRSV's translation of ἔξεστιν (*exestin*) as "lawful" is misleading; the maxim's contention has nothing to do with the law, but with what is permissible, allowable, or authorized for a believer. (3) We can see elsewhere in Paul's letters that a believer's obligation is to love (Rom 13:8), to put

83. Rollin Ramsaran, *Liberating Words: Paul's Use of Rhetorical Maxims in 1 Corinthians 1–10* (Valley Forge, Pa.: Trinity, 1996) 5-21.

one's faith, that is one's right relation to God, into expression via love (Gal 5:6). And, depending on one's measure of faith, one can make moral decisions within a wider scope if one's faith is stronger or within a narrower scope is one's faith is weaker; when doubts or waverings enter the picture, then one should not undertake the action in question (Rom 14:23).[84]

In the light of these considerations, we can imagine how some Corinthians have understood this maxim to capture their sense of freedom in Christ. First, one like the fellow who has his father's wife (5:1ff.) might in fact misjudge the strength of his faith and think that there are no moral constraints upon him, or at least that the morality of his sleeping with his stepmother is not a problem for his faith. Second, and this is even more likely, some could interpret the maxim in line with Augustine's later expression of the same sort: "Love and do what thou wilt."[85] In that statement, those who truly and properly love God will and can do as they please because they would never choose to do anything that would prove contrary to their love of God. In a similar way, Paul's Corinthian followers could think themselves thoroughly in line with Paul's teaching when they embraced the maxim in 6:12 and 10:23 as affirming a basic truth about moral reasoning in Christ: "all things [that my relationship to God allows] are permissible for me," or perhaps to take the maxim in a similar way, "all things [that truly matter] are permissible for me." "All [appropriate, fitting] things are permissible for me."

Verses 12-20 are a dense, closely ordered passage that expects some work from its auditors. Rhetorically, it is what was called "figured speech," a type of rhetoric in which rhetorical figures or tropes carry the message like pearls arranged on a string. In order to understand it, we who are not accustomed to figured speech must identify the figures and show how they work. In Paul's time figured speech was much valued and was considered powerful because it invited the hearers or readers to assess the relationship between the different figures and to make self-

application of what was heard or read. By employing this kind of address, Paul was perfectly within the normal expectations of his hearers. No signals had to be made; one simply embarked upon figured speech and expected the auditors to make not only the connections between the elements but also the application to themselves. Rhetorical handbooks are regularly insistent that the most effective rhetoric is that which minimizes the rhetor's making of application and maximizes the auditor's self-application.[86]

Let us first lay out the anatomy of 6:12-20:

1. Maxim 1 (twice stated; reflecting the attitude of some of the readers) with Pauline qualifiers (6:12; maxim 1 will be repeated twice in 10:23).
2. Maxim 2 (for perspective-keeping) with a Pauline qualifier (6:13a-b).
3. Maxim 3 (6:13c; with an embedded correctio [structure: A, not B, but A] mentioning *porneia,* linking it back to the previous discussions of immorality and ahead to 6:18 and 7:2) with a Pauline qualifier (6:14).
4. Maxim 3 opens a structure that is closed several verses later by a refinement (structure: A B, followed by a newly cast A´ B´) whose elements encapsulate, in the intervening space, what we might call "the heart of the matter":
   A: "The body is for the Lord" (6:13c)
   B: "God raised the Lord and will raise you" (6:14)
   A´: "You are not your own" (6:19b)
   B´: "You were bought with a price" (6:20a)
5. "The heart of the matter" (6:15-19a), structured around three rhetorical questions in the form of "You do know, don't you . . . ?" which signal that what is discussed in these verses is a "back-to-basics" primer regarding what the Corinthians most certainly should know and should be able to apply to their circumstances that Paul is addressing.
6. Closing injunction (6:20b, capping not only 6:12ff. but also chaps. 5–6).

Now that we have laid its structure bare, it is possible to unpack how 6:12-20 functions. By

84. J. Paul Sampley, *Walking Between the Times: Paul's Moral Reasoning* (Minneapolis: Fortress, 1991) 57-60.

85. Augustine, *Tractate on the Epistle of St. John,* trans. H. Browne, rev. and ed. J. H. Myers, in *A Select Library of the Nicene and Post-Nicene Fathers of the Christian Church* (Grand Rapids: Eerdmans, 1956) 7.8.

86. Quintilian *Institutio Oratoria* 9.2.71, LCL, recognizes that "the judge [or any hearer] will be led to . . . believe in that which he thinks he has found out for himself."

quoting maxim 1, their own saying, Paul establishes common ground with the Corinthians: "All things are permissible for me" (6:12). His attached qualifiers do not question their maxim's general claim but place alongside it another consideration—"not all things are helpful" (to be repeated in 10:23)—and allow Paul to make a personal distinction, "but I will not be mastered by anything" (6:12). What is truly "helpful" is not treated here but will be elaborated later in the letter. Immediately, however, Paul telegraphs the notion that will be developed later—namely, that while mastery by things is ruled out, mastery by the Lord is central to the life of faith (6:20).

Without introduction, maxim 2—"Food is for the stomach and the stomach is for food"—is declared (6:13); the reader is implicitly asked to make some connection of maxim 2 with maxim 1. For the person who would affirm the "no-holds-barred" sentiment of maxim 1, the second maxim would follow with an "of course" certainty: "Surely, I know what the stomach and food are made for!" Somewhat shocking, however, would be the Pauline qualifier: "And God will wipe out both the one and the other" (6:13b). God has power over all things (cf. 3:21-23); stomachs and the food they crave are not of enduring value (this is the first reference to eating, which will become the leitmotif of chaps. 8–11).

Again with no introduction, maxim 3 appears. It opens with a disclaimer and then is developed positively: "The body is not for immorality πορνεία [porneia] but for the Lord, and the Lord for the body" (6:13c).[87] By now the pattern is established. The reader should expect a Pauline qualifier, and there is one: "But God raised the Lord and will raise you through his power" (6:14). What is the reader to make of the dissonance in the claims that God will destroy food and stomach but will raise believers just as he raised the Lord? It is as if two levels of consideration vie with one another. What is important in life? Not food and the stomach. Once again, then what is important? Answer: the close connection between the "body" and its Lord, the Lord whom God has raised from

the dead and with whom believers have such an intimate bond. As Paul refines his statement of the affiliation of believers and their Lord (6:20), they are like slaves who have been purchased by a new owner and they are therefore not their own (6:19).

Maxim 3, with its bold claim that "the body is for the Lord and the Lord for the body" (6:13c), introduces a major theme of 1 Corinthians, "body" (σῶμα sōma) occurs 30 times after these verses; note its appearance already in 5:3). "Body" is not a new concept to the Corinthians: Paul clearly assumes that they know how he uses the term: "You do know, don't you, that your bodies are members of Christ?" (6:15). Modern readers can understand Paul's use of the term sōma very readily when they see it used in Rom 12:1: "I appeal to you, therefore, brothers, through the mercies of God, to present your bodies as a living sacrifice, holy and pleasing to God." Many translations rightly render it "present your selves" because for Paul sōma is a technical term that refers to one's whole self. Modern people tend to think of "having" a body; Paul thinks of people as being "bodies." Sōma, for Paul, stands for one's whole self. Accordingly, maxim 3, in light of its refinement in 6:19-20, really asserts: You, the you who in the Lord do not even own yourself (cf. Gal 2:20), are for the Lord and the Lord is for you. Because believers do not own themselves and are therefore in service of the one who owns them, they must live in a way appropriate to Christ, who became their new owner. The bond between the baptisands and their Lord could not be closer: "The body is for the Lord and the Lord for the body" (6:13c).

Believers belong to the Lord, not to porneia, the two mutually exclusive options: "You do know, don't you, that" believers are members of Christ, not members of a prostitute (πόρνη pornē, a paranomasia, or wordplay, from the term porneia, which one sees just ahead in 6:18). The stark two-way alternatives that structured the opening four chapters of this letter continue in force here. The former style of life and its previously defining relationships have been jettisoned. As Paul has been saying in chaps. 5 and 6, the old patterns and former allegiances cannot be mixed into the new life in Christ.

Paul enlists a powerful metaphor to elaborate the relationship of believers, represented as bodies, to Christ: entering into a relationship with Christ or with a prostitute. "You do know, don't

---

87. The NRSV's inconsistent translation of *porneia* prevents English readers from following Paul's use of the term (cf. 5:1; 6:13, 18; 7:2), and the NRSV's switch to "fornication" for the middle two instances, though it seems to fit the immediate context, narrows Paul's effort to illustrate a broader concern with *porneia* than simply "fornication."

you, that the one who joins himself to a prostitute is one body with her?" (6:16). Paul's fertile mind jumps from the "joining oneself" to Gen 2:24, the text from Israel's scriptures used to authenticate marriage: "A man shall leave his father and mother and join himself to his wife, and the two shall become one flesh" though he quotes only a part of the verse (6:16). The fact that he can switch from "one body" to "one flesh" suggests that the emphasis is on the oneness, the uniting. This suggestion is reinforced when Paul next develops the same thought regarding "one spirit": "The one who joins himself to the Lord is one spirit with him" (6:17). In vv. 16 and 18 Paul has laid out the two alternatives: One either joins himself to a prostitute (*pornē*; think *porneia*) or one joins himself to the Lord. Because Christians are by definition those who are joined to the Lord, Paul concludes pithily: "[Keep on] flee[ing] *porneia*" (6:18*a*; cf. 10:14). So Paul likens the relationship of believers to Christ as the proper marriage and the turning to a prostitute (*pornē*; *porneia*) as harlotry (cf. Jeremiah 2–3; Hosea 2; cf. 2 Cor 11:2). Paul's bottom-line recommendation is unequivocal, clearly stated, and succinct: "Flee *porneia*" (6:18*a*). Nothing else can proceed until the Corinthians realize that they must at all costs steer clear of any *porneia* contamination.

"The heart of the matter" (6:15-19*a*). Paul's delineation of "the heart of the matter" is structured around three questions, each of which expects a yes answer, and each of which therefore shows Paul affirming something he expects the Corinthians to understand and also to affirm. All three questions, as distinct as they are, focus on the same topic, "belonging." The first—"You do know, don't you, that your bodies are members of Christ?" (6:15)—affirms that believers as bodies, as whole persons, belong in a special way to Christ—namely, as members of Christ, a metaphor that will be elaborated in much detail in chap. 12. Paul expects the Corinthian auditors to respond to the question, in agreement with him.

The second question—"You do know, don't you, that the one who cleaves to a prostitute is one body with her?" (6:16)—employs a mundane counterpoint but still presses the issue of belonging to another, declaring that the one who clings closely to a prostitute becomes one body, one flesh, with the prostitute. Paul expects the

Corinthian auditors to accept that as given. One need not read this as indicating that the Corinthian church is having a problem with believers consorting with prostitutes. Rather, Paul takes something that he can assume every person knows as a reality in Greco-Roman cities—namely, that persons who go to a prostitute become one flesh with that person and therefore belong to the prostitute in a certain and defining sense.

The third question—"You do know, don't you, that your body is the temple of the Holy Spirit?" (6:19)—really refines the first two: The belonging that is at the heart of the issue is a very special one in which the believers are so closely bonded to Christ as to become members of Christ (of Christ's body as 12:12ff. will elaborate it). Only superficially is it like clinging to a prostitute and thus making the two one. The relationship of the believers to Christ, however, is at once more intimate and more profound: intimate because the bond is so strong, so powerful; profound because "the two are" not just "one flesh" but because the "body" has become the residence, indeed the temple, of the Holy Spirit. The Holy Spirit resides in the believers in such a way that their bodies, their very selves, have been transformed into a shrine dedicated to God, who gave them the Holy Spirit and thereby constituted them a temple (cf. 3:16-17). So this two-chapter section opens with what wrongly dwells, *porneia* (5:1), in the Corinthian believers and closes by affirming that it is the Holy Spirit who properly dwells there (6:19-20). And in the intervening verses the same point is considered by asking to whom one belongs. To whom one belongs and who or what dwells in one are the same question, simply addressed in different terms.

The next two maxims (maxim 4, 6:18*b*, and maxim 5, 6:18*c*) have proved difficult for modern interpreters.[88] The sweeping character of the claims in maxim 4, such as "every other sin" being "outside the body," raises confusion as to what is meant: Does the "every other sin," for example, include the immediately mentioned *porneia*? And how does maxim 4 fit with maxim 5, which follows and affirms that sin is indeed related to one's own body?

Maxim 4—"Every sin a person does is outside

---

88. Gordon D. Fee, *The First Epistle to the Corinthians* (Grand Rapids: Eerdmans, 1987) 261-63, summarizes previous efforts clearly.

his body" (6:18*b*)—is widely recognized as being of Corinthian origin[89] and as expressing the view of some in Corinth that, apart from *porneia,* every other sin is one that is "outside the body"—that is, no other sin is so directly related to the body as *porneia,* which always has some sense of sexual immorality. The NIV translation in fact endorses that understanding of maxim 4 by taking what would otherwise be translated as "all sin" ($\pi\hat{\alpha}\nu$ $\dot{\alpha}\mu\acute{\alpha}\rho\tau\eta\mu\alpha$ *pan hamartēma*), adding the word "other" and taking the singular noun as plural, "sins." In that way the NIV attempts to minimize the problem with which the interpreter is otherwise faced.

Maxim 5—"The immoral person sins against his own body" (6:18*c*)—is sometimes taken as Paul's critique of maxim 4, lying alongside their maxim as it does.[90] Commending such an interpretation is the strong link in maxim 5 between sin and body, which could be argued as Pauline, but it encounters the difficulty that it privatizes sin, a notion that is difficult to find in Paul's letters.

Here, however, I suggest a different interpretation of these two maxims and of their function. Both 6:18*b* and 6:18*c* are Corinthian maxims that reflect the Corinthian divisiveness even in understanding sin. Some at Corinth say in maxim 4— "All sin which a person does is outside the body"—that sin has no effect upon the body (remember: body can be understood as the self). Their argument goes as follows: If sin does not affect the body, that very body that is the Lord's, then whatever sin one does has no bearing on the body's commitment to the Lord.

Others at Corinth say in maxim 5—"The immoral man sins against his own body" (6:18*c* RSV)—implying that an individual's sin, which these among the Corinthians indeed understand to be against his own body or self, is that person's problem and is not a concern for the community. Both of these interpretations help account for the community's not being aggrieved by the behavior of the man who is sleeping with his stepmother (5:2). Advocates of maxim 4 are convinced that "sin" is of no consequence for the body or for the body's fate; such persons could believe themselves, that is their bodies, delivered beyond what they could construe as extraneous calculations regarding conduct. Champions of maxim 5 could equally well not concern themselves with the man's behavior, but for very different reasons: They could hold that his sin is against "his own body" only and does not bear upon them in any way; advocates of maxim 5 deny that an individual's sin contaminates or stains other believers. Already in chaps. 5 and 6 Paul has disagreed with both interpretations, and in 6:19, his third "You do know, don't you?" statement in 6:15-19, he tells them in back-to-basics claims just why he stands for something other than what either maxim 4 or maxim 5 reflects.

"You do know, don't you, that your body is the temple of the Holy Spirit, which you have from God, and you are not your own; you were bought with a price?" (6:19-20*a*). This passage is a foundational, definitional declaration of who believers are; it gathers together so much of what he has written to them earlier in the letter and lays the ground for all that he will write to them subsequently. The claim that believers are God's temple in which the Spirit dwells is a reprise of the assertions of 3:16-17, this time linked to "your body" and thereby undercutting the assumptions within both maxim 4 and maxim 5. Likewise, Paul's declaration that they are not their own but have been bought—Paul's analogy is the slave market in the agora or forum—by a new master (6:20, to be reprised in 7:23). In saying that the Corinthians have been "bought with a price" (6:20), Paul has no interest in answering any question as to whom the payment was made. This is not what later came to be called ransom christology in which Christ paid a price with his life so that believers could be free. Paul and his readers would have recognized that this is terminology of the slave market where slaves were regularly traded and, Paul's point, ended up with different lords or masters. Paul's concern is simply and directly to declare that the Corinthians have become subject to—that is, they belong to—a new Lord: Jesus Christ. The Corinthian believers are set apart ("holy"; 3:17) for the one who owns them and whose Spirit dwells in them. Proper "temple maintenance" is therefore a critical obligation of believers, not an option, and much less of no concern to the individual (as in maxim 4) or to the community (as in maxim 5).

89. J. Murphy-O'Connor, "Corinthian Slogans in 1 Cor. 6:12-20," *CBQ* 40 (1978) 391-93.

90. See examples of such in Fee, *The First Epistle to the Corinthians,* 261n. 57.

Three distinct metaphors coalesce to make the same point: Proper cleaving to the Lord rules out any and all rival cleavings (whether to a prostitute [*pornē*] or to *porneia*); proper obedience of the slaves to the Lord who owns them obviates all other potential allegiance to other lords; and temple maintenance proper to the Spirit who resides in the temple is obligatory.

Paul frames their maxims with his correctives. A prohibiting command—"Flee *porneia*" (6:18*a*)—introduces the Corinthian maxims, and directly following them (6:19-20) is a reaffirmation of the most important consideration the Corinthian auditors ought to know and understand, and of which Paul has already reminded them earlier—namely, that their body is the temple where the Holy Spirit has chosen to reside (3:16-17). Fleeing the *porneia* (which resides where the Holy Spirit should; 5:1), which would absolutely destroy the holiness appropriate to the Spirit's temple, therefore, is not simply an option; it is a necessity. Like an exclusive sexual commitment, holiness as a sanctum for the resident Holy Spirit requires scrupulous fidelity and stewardship of the self as body properly set aside for the Spirit.

From Paul's reference to his previous letter about *porneia* (5:9) and his clear indication that the Corinthians were confused by it, to Paul's current insistence that the body is special to the Lord and can allow of absolutely no contact with *porneia,* we can see that Paul thinks that the Corinthians themselves continue to be confused and divided regarding how they understand sin and *porneia,* Paul's catchall term for wrongful living.

Believers are one body with the Lord (6:13); they are one spirit with the Lord (6:17); and the Gen 2:24 quotation suggests that they are one flesh as well. Paul goes out of his way to affirm as fully and completely as possible the believers' belonging to Christ as an exclusive and all-embracing identity. It follows as certainly that sin and *porneia* are totally excluded (6:13); their presence cannot be countenanced in any way, by any construal. Belonging to the Lord allows no rival claim, permits no association whatsoever with sin or *porneia.* Once again, Paul capitalizes on his carefully drawn two-way tradition that he laid out so insistently in the opening chapters of this letter.

Paul's "previous letter" (5:9-10) about avoiding immoral persons (πόρνοι *pornoi*) caused confusion among believers in Corinth. Whether the Corinthians generalize to "all sin" (6:18*b*) or focus on *porneia* (6:18*c*), Paul's earlier letter had left the Corinthians divided concerning what to make of sin in general and *porneia* in particular.

What are believers to do, then? Paul's defining answer concludes this passage and, indeed, brings to a head the concerns of chaps. 5 and 6, and opens out to a consideration of the issues they have raised with Paul in their letter to him: "Therefore, glorify God in your body" (6:20*b*), clearly referring to each one's body, but perhaps also referring to the Corinthians collectively as a body, as the collective body of Christ, in which glorification of God, not backbiting and slander, should be the order of the day.

Chapters 5–6 are a study in definition. There Paul lays down the defining claim for the believers: They are those who were set apart for God, who were "bought for a price," who do not belong to themselves but to their (new) Lord, who will ultimately share with their Lord in resurrection, and whose bodies, their very selves, are members of Christ and the temple in which the Holy Spirit dwells. As persons who have nothing that was not given to them as a gift by God and therefore who are indistinguishable the one from another (4:7), believers should not form cliques as if their baseline stories are not the same but should instead "glorify God in your body" (6:20).

By noting two incidents that have come to his attention, Paul sharpens the community definition in the direction of praxis and comportment. With reference to the *porneia* of the man who "has his father's wife," Paul reflects on community borders—namely, what separates and distinguishes life in the community from that out in the world, and identifies comportment that should not be allowed inside the community. With his mention of some believers' taking others to civil courts to adjudicate disputes, he identifies what should properly stay inside the community and be resolved there. So, whether he looks to distinguish what really should be outside the community, or whether he tries to establish what should remain within and characterize the community, he is in both cases defining Christian community and identifying proper conduct appropriate to the life of faith. His message can be identified in one negative and one positive directive: "Flee *porneia*" and "Glorify God in your body." To avoid *porneia* is requisite to glorifying God in the body; glorifying God in the body necessitates fleeing *porneia*. Merely to avoid the latter does not assure the former, but simply gives proper occasion for the glorification of God to flourish when believers properly pursue it.

How is God glorified in the body? The rest of the letter is an elaboration on that notion and a demonstration of it. As will become evident, glorifying God "in your body" will at once mean (1) that individuals exercise stewardship of their own bodies, their very selves, and (2) that collectively the believers live lovingly and in an edifying fashion with each other as members of the one body that is Christ's.

# REFLECTIONS

**1.** "The body is not for *porneia* but for the Lord and the Lord for the body" (6:13). Without using the term, this is holiness talk. To be set apart for something or for someone is the root meaning of holiness. Today we tend to think of "having a body"; we might even find ourselves talking about "our bodies" as if they were another one of our possessions. For Paul, humans do not have bodies; they are bodies. *Sōma* means body in the sense of one's self—that is, who you are. It was later Christianity, after Paul and no longer dependent upon him, that fell to thinking of human beings as composed of body and some more valuable inner spark that might be termed "soul" or "spirit." Paul's Jewishness comes through handsomely in his understanding of body as who a person is; therefore, it is Paul who, when he wants to talk about God's enduring commitment to individuals, speaks of the phrase that impacted our creeds, "resurrection of the body." Paul's is a lofty and holistic view of the self, lofty because one's present self, as is, is loved and cherished by God and will be preserved by God, and holistic because Paul thinks of the human as a whole integrated being who is not only part of the "new creation" but also the object of God's redeeming love. So redemption is not the salvaging of some inner, perhaps purer essence of the individual; it is the saving of the whole being. *Sōma* is not simply flesh for Paul; one is *sōma*. Paul's profound notion of body as self, as who you are, raises issues for our understanding of how we treat our bodies, that is for how we treat ourselves. Smoking and drugs, like the lack of exercise, are abuses not only of this container that we live in but of our very selves, the selves that God has made us to be.

**2. Intimacy with the Lord.** Because life in Christ is somatic, Paul daringly writes, as did Hosea 1–3 and Ezekiel 16, of one's relation to one's Lord as like a marriage and contrasts it with a liaison with a prostitute (6:15). If our relationship to Christ is like marriage then we have two distinct angles from which to view the issue. One is to look at our marriages. If they are not in some special way a reflection of what should be an ideal relation with Christ, then it is time to work on our marriages. If our marriage is in better shape than our relation to Christ, then we should be working to improve our relation to Christ. And what can be said about marriages can be extended to other relationships by analogy. In short, how we are with the Lord should find correspondences in the other relationships of our lives.

**3.** In our individualistic society and culture, Paul's claim that "you are not your own" (6:19) will seem decidedly alien. Are we not in charge of our own lives? Can we not do as we see fit? Our own self-control is a fiction that we struggle to maintain. For Paul, and indeed for everyone in his time, nobody was without a master, a lord to whom they were in some measure responsible. Their culture was in this way a vertical one; even Marcus Aurelius, the emperor, mused about everyone being ultimately derived from and dependent upon deity.[91] Some modern people, giving lip service to equality, find a horizontal image preferable; but in reality modern cul-

---

91. Marcus Aurelius, *Meditations,* 12.26, LCL: "Nothing is a man's very own, but that his babe, his body, his very soul came forth from Him."

ture is stratified—and that not just economically—much more severely than we sometimes may want to acknowledge.

Paul's anthropology, his understanding of human nature, emerges here: All people are dependent on some being or some thing beyond themselves to give them meaning and significance (cf. Rom 14:7). So for Paul the issue is not whether one has a lord or not; one simply will have some lord. At stake is what lord one will have. Paul has taken as his model the contemporary practice of buying and selling slaves in the agora (meeting place or marketplace): "you were bought" (ἀγοράζω *agorazō*, 6:20). And, because slaves were supposed to increase their owners' honor, to make their owners look good, Paul transposes the slave's need to honor the owner into his own theological concepts and tells the Corinthians how to honor their new owner: "glorify God in your body" (6:20). In Paul's categories, the chief competing lords are sin, a power that takes over one's life and governs it (and a power that Paul thinks was the former lord of all believers; cf. Rom 3:23), or Christ, whose lordship grants perfect freedom.

One caution: "You are not your own" should not be mistaken to suggest that believers have no responsibility for their actions. In the stratified culture of Paul's time, a slave would know one's master deserved honor, and though slaves were not at their own disposal, they were certainly expected to do everything they could to bring honor to their lord. Paul thinks believers should relate in just such a fashion to Christ as their Lord, seeking his honor in all that they do. Modern Christians, though not likely to think of ourselves as slaves, might still weigh whether a contemplated action might bring honor to our Lord.

# 1 CORINTHIANS 7:1-40

## PAUL'S RESPONSE TO QUESTIONS ABOUT RELATIONS IN SOCIOSEXUAL GROUPS

## OVERVIEW

Apart from 1 Corinthians, we have no indication in the Pauline corpus that one of Paul's congregations wrote him a letter, though they may have. Some Corinthians, however, have written to Paul (7:1), apparently seeking his guidance and clarification on a range of issues (possibly including the items mentioned in 7:25; 8:1; 12:1; 16:1; cf. 16:12).

By his own arrangement of the topics and material in this letter, Paul has delayed a treatment of the Corinthians' concerns until he has two building blocks in place. The first (chaps. 1–4), by its back-to-basics push, regrounds the Corinthians in the core of the gospel, reminds them of who they are in relation to that gospel and to the world, and calls them to end their fractiousness and, following the example of their apostle, reclaim their unity around the cross. Throughout that first section Paul, their caring father in the gospel, reminds them that they are called, set aside for God in holiness and, in his protracted example of himself and Apollos, exemplifies the proper unity that should prevail among believers, a unity that fully shares the gospel and labors for it, but a unity that also honors the diversity of the participants.

The other building block is chaps. 5–6. It, too, is a lesson in fundamentals, rehearsing as it does the nature of the community, identifying how believers differ from the world and worldly practices, and attempting to clarify what is appropriately treated within the community and what should be left outside it. The unit formed by these two chapters develops a theme already laid down in the first four chapters, namely that people who live by the gospel walk in a way that is distinct from the world. The believers, as God's children, as God's farm, as God's temple, must make their moral decisions and behave in a way that honors

and glorifies the one to whom they belong. The world and its patterns, all of which are entirely familiar to Paul's readers, have leached into the community's internal transactions, and believers have looked to external patterns and practices for negotiating their differences. Paul has cleverly used two related Corinthian situations (the immoral man, chap. 5, and civil court cases, chap. 6) to sharpen their understanding not only of how differently from the world they are to behave but also of how they are to relate to one another as brothers and sisters in Christ.

The starkness of Paul's depictions of the rival two-way traditions in chaps. 1–4—people travel either one way or the other—provides the background for the reflection in chaps. 5–6 of the way the community of faith differs from the world outside. Paul uses the via negativa descriptions—which are frequently cast as depictions of how the world operates—to identify where believers should not look for establishment of their values or for their clues of what is important. To be sure, in its most radical either/or construction, which Paul has featured in the opening six chapters of this letter, to take life's cues not from God, not from the gospel but from the world is properly called "idolatry," a notion that is reflected three times in the vice lists of chaps. 5 and 6 (5:10, 11; 6:9), reappears explicitly in 10:14, and is at issue throughout. Paul's gospel has a strong countercultural critique at its heart, as may be seen in the opening chapters' regular, repeated insistence that there are (only) two ways, one belonging to the gospel and the other belonging to the world. Having carefully established his own context for treating the problems that they have raised in their letter, Paul now turns to their concerns.

From the items in the Corinthians' letter to

him, Paul chooses to deal first with marriage and what we modern people might call sexuality. Some Corinthians are confused about how to live the life of faith in the midst of the world, just the sorts of issues that Paul has already been dealing with in the letter so far. From the lengthy treatment of marriage and sexuality issues in chap. 7, we can surmise that the Corinthians are divided in their understandings of how the life of faith bears on sexual matters, and we have every reason to suppose that Paul's previous letter, which addressed how to maintain proper holiness and avoid contamination, is again a part of the Corinthians' deliberations. Some Corinthians seem to have called for sexual abstinence as the proper means of maintaining purity before God; others seem not to share that conviction, perhaps because they may be experiencing difficulty in maintaining abstinence. Their confusion is probably, in part, a direct result of Paul's earlier letter (5:9) in which he had warned them not to mingle or associate, not even to eat, with πόρνοι *pornoi,* "immoral persons," if they are named "brother or sister"—that is, if they are fellow believers (5:9, 11).

Across chapter 7 we see that some Corinthians have taken Paul's counsel to avoid πορνεία *porneia* to extremes, and they have wondered about the purity of their associations, even in marriage. This misapplication of Paul's earlier letter may have been compounded by their noting Paul's celibacy (7:7) and taking it as normative for all believers; Paul's free and frequent offering of himself as an exemplar[92] could easily have contributed to this. So in Corinth some married persons had come to wonder about the propriety of their sexuality (7:5), some marrieds and singles about whether even marriage was appropriate (7:10-11, 28), and some of those married to unbelievers about whether divorce might not be preferred as a means of maintaining holiness (7:12-15). In chap. 7 we are not confronted with an asceticism that has crept into the congregation, as some have suggested,[93] but a good-faith effort on the part of some

to respond to Paul's call for holiness. Some of Paul's followers have tried to apply what they understand of his teachings to the normal sexual practices that have been part of their lives. We see evidence of this perplexity right away when Paul opens this section of the letter by citing a Corinthian maxim: "It is good for a man not to touch a woman," a euphemistic reference to avoiding sexual intercourse (7:1). Some at Corinth have formulated this maxim as a guideline for proper living. Their maxim represents a radical effort—perhaps the most extreme among the believers at Corinth—to maintain holiness, but one that, as we shall see, Paul will find misguided.

The entire passage (7:1-40) is structured by counsels directed toward persons of different marital status: husbands and wives (7:2-7), widowers and widows (7:8-9), married who contemplate divorce (7:10-11), the "rest" (7:12-16), and virgins or unmarrieds (7:25-31). For each sociosexual group Paul maps out a preferred or better course, but for each he also countenances an alternative, concessionary but still acceptable route. Interlaced with those counsels are other components: a rumination about Jews and gentiles, slaves and free (7:17-24), and some reflections about cares (7:32-35), desire and self-control (7:36-38), and the possible remarriage of widows (7:39-40).

Paul's imminent expectation of the end of the ages is fundamental to our understanding of his advice in this chapter. From his oldest extant letter, 1 Thessalonians (see 4:13-18), to the last letter he wrote, Romans (see 13:11-14), Paul is uniformly and steadfastly convinced that God is on the brink of finishing up the creation's restoration, which was begun in Christ's death and resurrection. So also here in 1 Corinthians Paul reminds them of his teaching that "the form of this world is passing away" (7:31). "The time has grown short," he writes (7:29); "the impending crisis" (7:26 NRSV), "the present distress" (7:26 RSV; cf. 1 Thess 3:3) forces believers to act with regard to God's culminating of history. This Pauline conviction leads to the next noteworthy feature of chap. 7.

Because Paul expects the end so directly, he repeatedly counsels the Corinthians to "remain as you are" (7:20, 24, 26, 38, 40). The social structures that they encounter in the world around them are temporally bound and will not survive

---

92. Margaret M. Mitchell, *Paul and the Rhetoric of Reconciliation* (Louisville: Westminster/John Knox, 1991) 39-60.

93. Will Deming, *Paul on Marriage and Celibacy: The Hellenistic Background of 1 Corinthians 7,* SNTSMS 83 (Cambridge: Cambridge University Press, 1995) 3-4, argues convincingly that Paul's assertions in 1 Corinthians 7 do not support sexual asceticism—as much of the history of interpretation has suggested.

beyond the parousia; in fact, judging by what Paul says about slavery (7:22), those patterns and structures are already rendered indifferent and powerless. Accordingly, his counsel has an ambivalence about it. On the one side, he recognizes that the life of faith can be lived fully and faithfully in whatever circumstances one encounters (cf. his own hardship lists as examples, 4:10-13; 2 Cor 6:1-10)[94] and that being faithful does not require an overthrow of one's present social setting or status; one can remain as one is. On the other side, precisely because the structures of this age are under an eschatological sentence or verdict that will lead ultimately to their overthrow and which verdict makes them already inconsequential to one's real definition and standing before God, they can be disregarded already or lived in "as if not" living in them (see the Commentary on 7:29-31).

Two other interrelated Pauline principles emerge as the chapter unfolds: Believers should make moral choices with a view to (1) minimizing cares and anxieties, and (2) maximizing devotion to God. These themes appear most clearly in 7:32-35 where Paul's counsel about unmarried men and women opens with his declaration, "I want you to be free from care" (7:32), and closes by encouraging "your appropriate and constant devotion to the Lord, without distraction" (7:35). Paul weighs human relations in the light of these concerns and values and he counsels accordingly.

Our preliminary observations leave untouched the curious passage 7:17-24, which, though in a chapter dedicated to questions of marriage and sexuality, curiously mentions neither. Its location and function will require some accounting.

Finally, two factors must be borne in mind as we read chapter 7: (1) Paul views the life of faith as a walk, as a growth from being a baby to maturity; (2) the whole chapter must be read against the Cynic/Stoic background in which there is a fundamental effort to distinguish what really matters—that is, what really counts—from what does not matter, or from what matters less or not at all. The identification of *adiaphora*, indifferent matters, allowed Stoics to sort through all kinds of things and commitments so as to demarcate and focus upon the most important. At many points in his letters Paul employs this concept of indifferent matters as he relates to his predominantly gentile readership (cf. Rom 8:35-39; 14:8; Phil 1:10, "discern what really matters"; 4:10-13; Gal 3:28). In the passages just referenced one would find quite a list of unimportant matters including one's gender, one's social status, one's ethnic background, the way life comes to be, and even life and death themselves.

One might ask, then, what really matters to Paul. We will find many ways he expresses it: "Jesus Christ and him crucified" (1 Cor 2:2); that his readers will be "blameless at the coming of our Lord Jesus Christ" (1 Thess 5:24); and that his readers maximize their devotion to their Lord.

Among the indifferent matters, Stoics did recognize that there were "preferreds" and "not-preferreds." For example, it mattered not whether one ate sumptuously, but if one were given the opportunity to choose in such a way as not to compromise one's own integrity, then why not eat well?

To be married or not to be married was an indifferent matter to some Stoics and to Paul. Paul did not devalue marriage. But he did recognize that whether one was married or not, marriage did not have any direct or necessary bearing on one's relation to God. A married person or an unmarried person could equally well be in right relation to God or not be in right relation to God. Clearly, Paul considered that the married person has obligations to the spouse (7:1ff., 33-34). In his reflections about marriage, however, Paul freely considers preferred and not-preferred alternatives. Though he reckons marriage as an indifferent matter, Paul does have a "preferred" when he thinks about what minimizes anxiety and maximizes devotion to God (7:32-35) and when he thinks about the last-times afflictions that he is convinced his readers will experience (7:26-31, 36-38). To identify marriage as an indifferent matter is not to diminish its importance, nor is it to declare that it is outside the range of moral consideration. Matters identified as indifferent are simply placed in perspective as of relative but not ultimate importance. So, whereas marriage and nonmarriage are indifferent matters for Paul, he still has preferreds for which he aims.

We must be cautious not to expect in this chapter a full exposition of Paul's understanding of marriage and human sexuality; the chapter is not to be

---

94. John Fitzgerald, *Cracks in an Earthern Vessel: An Examination of the Catalogues of Hardships in the Corinthian Correspondence,* SBLDS 99 (Atlanta: Scholars Press, 1988) 184-201, 203-5.

confused with a manual on the family. Almost totally missing, for example, is any counsel regarding children. As is always the case in Paul's letters, he treats matters that he knows bear on his readers. He does not write general treatises and then expect his readers to apply them as they see fit. Rather, he engages the problems that he knows to be theirs, and he engages them in terms to which he has good reason to assume they resonate.

# 1 CORINTHIANS 7:1-7, HUSBANDS AND WIVES

## NIV

7 Now for the matters you wrote about: It is good for a man not to marry.[a] [2]But since there is so much immorality, each man should have his own wife, and each woman her own husband. [3]The husband should fulfill his marital duty to his wife, and likewise the wife to her husband. [4]The wife's body does not belong to her alone but also to her husband. In the same way, the husband's body does not belong to him alone but also to his wife. [5]Do not deprive each other except by mutual consent and for a time, so that you may devote yourselves to prayer. Then come together again so that Satan will not tempt you because of your lack of self-control. [6]I say this as a concession, not as a command. [7]I wish that all men were as I am. But each man has his own gift from God; one has this gift, another has that.

[a]1 Or "It is good for a man not to have sexual relations with a woman."

## NRSV

7 Now concerning the matters about which you wrote: "It is well for a man not to touch a woman." [2]But because of cases of sexual immorality, each man should have his own wife and each woman her own husband. [3]The husband should give to his wife her conjugal rights, and likewise the wife to her husband. [4]For the wife does not have authority over her own body, but the husband does; likewise the husband does not have authority over his own body, but the wife does. [5]Do not deprive one another except perhaps by agreement for a set time, to devote yourselves to prayer, and then come together again, so that Satan may not tempt you because of your lack of self-control. [6]This I say by way of concession, not of command. [7]I wish that all were as I myself am. But each has a particular gift from God, one having one kind and another a different kind.

# COMMENTARY

The chapter opens with Paul's recitation of what I have identified as a Corinthian maxim: "It is well for a man not to touch a woman." As noted earlier, maxims, by their very nature, are thought to express truth, shared convictions. The social conventions of Paul's time did not encourage the rejection of another's maxim; instead, one could amplify or qualify a maxim or one could substitute one's own maxim. In the discussion that follows, Paul's citation of the Corinthian maxim (7:1 b), he first amplifies their maxim (7:2-7) and later offers his own (7:25).

Note how Paul responds to their maxim that "it is well for a man not to touch a woman." From the previous chapters of his letter, he picks up the thread of the argument cautioning about *porneia* and writes: "Because of *porneia* each man should have his own wife" (7:2a). At first glance Paul's formulation may seem much like their maxim: Both speak to what a man might do; both recognize that a man might have a wife; and the Corinthians who formulated the maxim in 7:1 may think that they, like Paul, are trying to avoid *porneia*—they by not having connubial relations. But there any similarity between Paul's stand and the Corinthian maxim ends.

The counsel that "each man should have his own wife" (7:2a) employs the same verb Paul used in 5:1 where the man "has his father's wife"; so Paul, unlike the formulators of the maxim in 7:1b, clearly means that sexuality within marriage is a proper way of avoiding *porneia.* The Corinthian maxim commends avoiding conjugal relations altogether. Another, profound difference emerges in Paul's next statement: "and each woman should have her own husband" (7:2b), a verbatim repetition of the same pronouncement he had made regarding the husband in 7:2a, but this time applied to the wife. The Corinthians who formulated the quoted maxim are concerned with men, their rights and practices; Paul is evenhanded about what both men and women should do. Verses 3-4, surely a remarkable passage to modern ears, but perhaps not totally uncommon in Paul's time,[95] clarify Paul's distance from their maxim by depicting marriage as a relationship in which husbands and wives have equal standing and equal authority over the body of the other one.

Only when Paul has distanced himself from their maxim does he directly address (7:5) persons who, by abstaining from sexual intercourse in marriage, seem to be living according to the Corinthian maxim. He grants them what he calls a "concession" (συγγνώμη *syngnōme*)—it pointedly is not to be confused with a command—that they can agree to set aside sex and devote themselves to prayer, but only for a time lest they be overcome by temptation (7:5-6). He is convinced that they should not deprive one another, conceding that they may choose to forgo sexual intercourse for a short time in order to have (more?) time for prayer, but only if there is mutual consent. The danger: Satan will seek to exploit any lack of self-control (7:5).

The passage concludes with Paul's offering his own model of celibacy as indeed preferred, but he is fully aware not only that this is a special charisma, a gift (by God, understood) of abstinence, to him but also not practicable for most. Hence, the concession must be granted (7:6), and the advocates of the maxim would be mistaken to press it (7:1b) as if its performance were equally attainable by everyone. Some will have one gift;

others will have other gifts; and each must live in accord with and by honoring the gift or gifts that they have. He concludes: "But each has his own gift [charisma] from God, the one in one way, the other in another," a note that will be elaborated and refined in detail in chap. 12.

Paul accomplishes several things here. First, without explicitly attacking their maxim, Paul distances himself from it on several counts and in the process offers a very different picture of marriage: (1) He does not restrict his focus to what men should do; (2) he affirms that sexuality in marriage is not only appropriate but necessary for proper self-control; and (3) he treats men and women evenhandedly and claims that a fundamental reciprocity should be present in their exercise of their sexuality and in their deciding when to have intercourse and when to abstain.

Second, Paul closes this first section by stating what he considers the ideal, which happens to be his own celibate practice, which, as already noted, may well have occasioned their maxim in the first place. But Paul points out that the persons who formulated the maxim of 7:1b have erred in several ways: (1) They have taken his own celibacy as a requirement for all men. (2) In so doing, they have not recognized how charismata should function in the community (and he will have to address that again in more detail in chaps. 12–14; but see in 7:7b-c the core of the position he will develop in those later chapters: God disperses the gifts as God sees fit). (3) They have wrongly assumed that husbands are the decision makers with regard to sexuality. (4) They have too narrow a view of acceptable moral decisions and patterns that Paul thinks should properly be open to believers. Theirs may very well have been an effort to enforce uniformity of behavior as a means of achieving unity. In any case, Paul's opening treatment of husbands and wives rejects commanding or supporting one human option (such as their maxim suggests) as the only acceptable practice and offers instead what he readily characterizes as a concession (*syngnōme,* 7:6) that by comparison, with his own charisma taken as the ideal, leaves a wider range of human options possible and acceptable before God.

Third, by his opening engagement of their maxim Paul establishes the notion that believers' moral reasoning may result in a variety of accept-

---

95. See Deming, *Paul on Marriage and Celibacy,* 116-22, for strong Stoic connections for Paul's view in 7:3-4.

able responses that Paul is pleased enough to range from "better" to "good," from preferable to permissible. The pattern of "ideal" (or "better") plus a concession that is still good and acceptable characterizes Paul's counsel to every group treated in the chapter. In the rest of the chapter, the ideal, the better, the goal is typically presented first, and the concession follows. Here in 7:1-7 it goes the other way around, no doubt because the Corinthian maxim of 7:1*b* is reported in the Corinthian letter to Paul, and he chooses to engage it at the start.

Paul starts with their maxim for two reasons: Some Corinthians have formulated a maxim that is being advocated as applicable to all members of different sociosexual groupings within the church, and their maxim is probably being used to enforce a uniform behavioral pattern that Paul finds too narrowly restrictive and not adequately malleable to the diverse circumstances that different individuals within each group might experience.

The advocates of this maxim quite possibly have thought of themselves as absolutely in line with Paul, his practices, and his teachings. In fact, they may well have taken Paul's previous letter (cf. 5:9) as championing just such a sharp, stringent delineation as their maxim seems to put into practice. And it may be that they were attempting to do what Paul was affirming already in chap. 6—namely, attempting to avoid sin and *porneia* and seeking to honor proper holiness before God. So Paul has the delicate task of delineating his own, more complex moral vision from theirs without rebuking them.

In the material that follows in chap. 7, Paul turns his attention to other sociosexual groupings within the congregation, still using the pattern just identified where an ideal is pictured as the goal but where some action short of the optimum is depicted as acceptable.

# REFLECTIONS

**1.** Across the paragraphs of this literary unit, Paul's presumption is that human beings are sexual creatures for whom sexual passion, expressed in the marital context, is a legitimate and appropriate part of human experience. In our own culture, sex and sexuality are treated in two radically diverse ways. On one hand, sex and sexuality are topics about which people seldom have serious, thoughtful discussions; they are treated in a hush-hush fashion that curiously only serves to mystify them even more and helps to make possible the commercial capitalization on sex and sexuality. In the other treatment of sex and sexuality, they are used everywhere to sell everything from automobiles to toothpaste, and the entertainment media would be at a loss without them. Homes and maybe churches should be places where, in the light of the gospel, we could discuss human sexuality and its drives as a wholesome, even pleasurable part of life. Like anything else that is good, however, sex and sexuality can readily be perverted, but that possibility should neither prevent the discussion nor allow sexuality to be viewed as something intrinsically bad.

**2.** The assertions about the woman's having authority over the man's body and the man's having authority over the woman's body should give a modern Christian couple an opportunity to discuss and evaluate their practice not only of who is allowed or expected to initiate sexual intercourse but also of how authority is shared in other family decisions and practices. Paul's view of this shared authority honors both the needs and the rights of each sexual partner. And by extrapolation, wives and husbands could work at honoring one another's needs and rights in all aspects of their shared lives.

# 1 CORINTHIANS 7:8-9,
# WIDOWERS AND WIDOWS

NIV

⁸Now to the unmarried and the widows I say: It is good for them to stay unmarried, as I am. ⁹But if they cannot control themselves, they should marry, for it is better to marry than to burn with passion.

NRSV

8To the unmarried and the widows I say that it is well for them to remain unmarried as I am. ⁹But if they are not practicing self-control, they should marry. For it is better to marry than to be aflame with passion.

## COMMENTARY

Paul now considers widowers and widows (7:8-9). Although most translations of ἀγάμοις (*agamois*) settle for "unmarried" (NRSV and NIV), it should probably be translated as "widowers" for the following reasons: Biblical Greek does not have a word for "widowers"; Paul addresses single unmarrieds later in the letter (7:25-38); and the other half of the pair addressed in 7:8-9 is clearly widows (χῆραι *chērai*).

In his counsel for widowers and widows, Paul adopts the same opening that the Corinthians used for their maxim (καλόν *kalon*) and advises: "It is good/well for them to remain as I am," namely, celibate (7:8; cf. 7:7). As is his pattern throughout, however, Paul offers a concession that if self-control is a problem, they should remarry (7:9). Celibacy is the best course for widows and widowers, but remarriage is preferred over either a loss of self-control or a burning with sexual desire (7:9).

Several connections of 7:8-9 with the preceding verses emerge: Paul expects believers to discern and do the best they can. When self-control is a problem, concessions lead to an accommodating level of performance that, although clearly understood as something less than the best, is still reckoned to be acceptable behavior.

Patterns in Paul's counsel surface here and are replicated throughout his treatment of marriage and human sexuality. Across the chapter Paul establishes what he thinks is the ideal, how he thinks things ought to be, and he depicts that as the goal or paradigm toward which people ought to aim and with regard to which people should order their lives. Yet alongside each such elevated goal-setting, Paul recognizes that, for various reasons, people may not be able to achieve the ideal. And he is careful to make room for full participation in the fellowship of those who, for whatever reason, may not be able to hit the heights.

## REFLECTIONS

Paul's is not a rule-based morality. Rather, a range of responses is deemed morally appropriate. Some believers may have problems with this; they may want to assume there is one, right response in every situation. Such a view understands moral reasoning to be involved in figuring out the "right" response among the many options. Paul, however, operates with a notion of what is best and realizes that not everyone will be able to reach that. If we took Paul's view here seriously, then our wrongful judgment of one another would be less easy because we would have to grant that there is more than the one way we have figured out to respond in a given situation.

# 1 CORINTHIANS 7:10-11, MARRIED BELIEVERS AND DIVORCE

NIV

[10]To the married I give this command (not I, but the Lord): A wife must not separate from her husband. [11]But if she does, she must remain unmarried or else be reconciled to her husband. And a husband must not divorce his wife.

NRSV

10To the married I give this command—not I but the Lord—that the wife should not separate from her husband [11](but if she does separate, let her remain unmarried or else be reconciled to her husband), and that the husband should not divorce his wife.

## COMMENTARY

In this passage Paul considers whether a marriage between two believers (cf. 7:12-13) can (or should?) end in divorce. Whether this topic is simply Paul's addition or is prompted by circumstances at Corinth, Paul and his auditors know but we never shall. By means of a correctio (structure: A, not A but B), Paul pointedly bases his next counsel not on his own opinion but on a teaching of Jesus: "A wife should not separate from her husband . . . and a husband should not divorce his wife" (7:10-11). Though Paul could not have known any of the Gospels as we do—he was dead before they were written—he assuredly knew enough about the teachings of Jesus and about early Christian claims to have opposed and persecuted Christ's followers (Gal 1:23; 1 Cor 15:9). Among the teachings of Jesus that Paul clearly knew was a statement on divorce (cf. Mark 10:2-5; Matt 5:31-32; 19:9; Luke 16:18).

In Jewish practice and tradition a man could divorce his wife (Deut 24:1-4)—and for almost any reason—but a wife did not have the same right regarding her husband. Roman law and practice allowed either men or women to institute divorce.[96] Corinth, as a Roman colony city, followed Roman law in all matters so that a Corinthian wife or husband could initiate divorce. So Paul's teaching of the higher good as allowing no divorce affirms his understanding of Jesus' teaching and runs counter to the Roman law that most of his Corinthian congregation would have

known. His concession, granted in 7:11, accommodates to the rights of women under Roman colonial law.

Throughout the history of the church much has been made of Paul's choice of words: "divorce" (ἀφίημι aphiēmi, 7:11) for the husband, "separation" (χωρίζω chōrizō, 7:10) for the wife. In some times and traditions Paul's terminology has been understood to allow a man to divorce his wife, but to allow a woman only to have a legal separation from her husband. This interpretation founders on at least four grounds: (1) It anachronistically forces modern legal categories back onto ancient times; (2) it fails to appreciate that rhetorical training discouraged unnecessary repetition of the same term and encouraged alternate ways of making the same point; (3) it fails to take seriously that Paul counsels any woman who does "separate" to "remain unmarried" (ἄγαμος agamos, 7:11), so Paul himself treats chōrizō as an actual termination of the marriage; and (4) it overlooks that women are understood a few verses later to have the power to divorce (7:13).

In Paul's time the issue is at once more complex and simpler. First, the semantic ranges of the two terms overlap. In papyri, the term chōrizō not only means to leave or separate oneself from someone but also describes the separation that is divorce. Aphiēmi means not only "divorce" but also "leave," "abandon," "give up."[97] Second, in Paul's time the line between divorce and separation was often neither a legal distinction nor recorded in

---

96. Jerome Corcopino, *Daily Life in Ancient Rome: the People and the City at the Height of the Empire,* trans. E. O. Lorimer (New Haven: Yale University Press, 1940) 95-100.

97. BAGD, 125-26.

public documents. Frequently, in his era, when a marriage failed, the parties simply separated and if they were so inclined, in due time entered into another marriage, but without the modern niceties of legally dissolving the previous marriage. Anachronistic reading not only foists modern sharp distinctions between divorce and separation and modern notions of social practice and legal documentation back onto Paul's time and onto his readers but also subtly endows men with greater rights than women, a position Paul seems dedicated throughout chap. 7 to avoid.

It is much more likely that Paul has simply used two different terms for rhetorical variation, an important rhetorical convention of the times.[98] Clearly, he knows and allows that women can and do divorce—and that they can do so as believers; in 7:13 a believing woman is presumed by Paul to have the right and power to divorce (here the term is *aphiēmi,* the same one used in the end of 7:11) her husband.

If one takes "separate" and "divorce" as the use of different terms to describe the same social reality, then Paul sets the same high standard for both wife and husband. It is better if neither one

divorces a spouse, but once again Paul is prepared to make a concession. Within the formulation, however, Paul accommodates to divorce and, indeed, to divorce initiated by a wife, even though he views any divorce as less than the ideal: "If she separates, let her remain unmarried or let her be reconciled to her husband" (7:11).

Quite strikingly, Paul acknowledges that believing behavior may sometimes go counter to an explicit teaching of Jesus. Unmistakably, Paul prefers adherence to Jesus' teaching, but equally beyond question he recognizes that, a contrary teaching of Jesus notwithstanding, there may be times when women and men may need to divorce (see also 7:12-15) and that those who do divorce remain full participants in the fellowship of believers.

The post-divorce options Paul considers are "remain unmarried" and "be reconciled" (7:11). Reconciliation of humans to God and of people to people is at the heart of the gospel for Paul (2 Cor 5:14-21). So as Paul weighs the possible alternatives for divorced people, he quite naturally thinks of reconciliation. We may reasonably wonder whether his counsel to remain unmarried was driven by his conviction that the end of the ages was at hand (cf. 7:26-31; see also the Commentary on 7:25-38). (See Reflections at 7:12-16.)

98. *Ad Herennium* 4.12.18: "We shall avoid the excessive repetition of the same word."

# 1 CORINTHIANS 7:12-16, MARRIAGE BETWEEN BELIEVERS AND UNBELIEVERS

## NIV

[12]To the rest I say this (I, not the Lord): If any brother has a wife who is not a believer and she is willing to live with him, he must not divorce her. [13]And if a woman has a husband who is not a believer and he is willing to live with her, she must not divorce him. [14]For the unbelieving husband has been sanctified through his wife, and the unbelieving wife has been sanctified through her believing husband. Otherwise your children would be unclean, but as it is, they are holy.

[15]But if the unbeliever leaves, let him do so. A believing man or woman is not bound in such circumstances; God has called us to live in peace.

## NRSV

12To the rest I say—I and not the Lord—that if any believer[a] has a wife who is an unbeliever, and she consents to live with him, he should not divorce her. [13]And if any woman has a husband who is an unbeliever, and he consents to live with her, she should not divorce him. [14]For the unbelieving husband is made holy through his wife, and the unbelieving wife is made holy through her husband. Otherwise, your children would be unclean, but as it is, they are holy. [15]But if the unbelieving partner separates, let it be so; in such a case the brother or sister is not bound. It is to peace that God has called you.[b] [16]Wife, for all you

[a]Gk *brother*    [b]Other ancient authorities read *us*

NIV

¹⁶How do you know, wife, whether you will save your husband? Or, how do you know, husband, whether you will save your wife?

NRSV

know, you might save your husband. Husband, for all you know, you might save your wife.

# COMMENTARY

With divorce between believers on his mind, Paul now turns to "the rest" of the married people: those who are married to unbelieving spouses. Admitting that he lacks a pertinent teaching of the Lord (7:12), Paul must draw on other resources and convictions, three in number. First, he seems to extend Jesus' teaching to avoid divorce: Paul advises that believing spouses should not divorce unbelieving spouses if the latter are willing to remain married. Second, he gives another reason, or perhaps it is a hope: "The unbelieving husband is made holy through his wife, and the unbelieving wife is made holy through her husband" (7:14 NRSV). In chap. 5 Paul warned against contamination from the outside world, suggesting that one bit of yeast can leaven the entire lump. In 7:14 Paul affirms a different, even reverse "contagion," but this time a positive one: Sin and *porneia* have a corrosive potential; but sanctification—being claimed and set apart by and for God—also has a rub-off potential that bears on those around, not only on the unbelieving spouse but also on "your children," claiming them also as holy, meaning set apart for and belonging to God (7:14). This is a practical application of what Paul affirmed in Romans when he wrote that although sin abounds, grace abounds the more (Rom 5:20). Paul has a profound conviction that God's power to redeem is active and superabundant, breaking across barriers and through resistance. As surely as sin's power is lethal, even more so is God's power evident in those who belong to God. Not only unbelieving spouses may benefit from God's sanctifying power working through the believing spouse, but Paul assures them that "your children" are holy; they, too, are set apart for and belong to God (7:14). The life of faith is viewed as infectious. Third, he affirms that "God has called us into peace" (7:15), a theme that will emerge again in 14:33. The laconic declaration that "God has called us to peace" (7:15) is given no defense and

no elaboration by Paul, suggesting that this is a foundational claim that he expects them to know and affirm. The fact that the same expression resurfaces in 14:33 and with the same incontrovertible force confirms the reading of it here. Peacemaking, reconciliation are, after all, what Paul sees at the heart of the gospel and therefore of the life of faith (2 Cor 5:14-21; cf. Matt 5:9; Eph 4:1-6). The case of marriage between a believer and an unbeliever is an extreme test of the range of the commitment to peace. The call to peacemaking is not restricted to expression between believers alone, but also is the way believers should relate to unbelievers. This is once again the same commitment to reconciliation that was noted in 7:11. So, when counseling persons whose unbelieving spouses want divorce, Paul finds moral guidance from the conviction that believers who are able to avoid divorce are still called to peace, this time achieved precisely in the divorce itself: Grant divorce to them as a ministration of God's peace.

For two reasons we may surmise that divorce was a matter of great concern among the Corinthians: (1) Paul expends considerable papyri on it (7:10-16), and (2) he breaks into second-person, direct address at two points, when he writes about "your children" in 7:15 and when he lodges the same question to wife and husband as to whether they know that their faith may result in the salvation of their spouses (7:16).

Further, we may wonder whether the Corinthians who formulated their wisdom in the maxim "It is good for a man not to touch a woman" (7:1) may have pressed this view on married persons with the arguments that for married believers divorce would be best but, failing that, abstinence from sexual relations was required and that being married to unbelievers was simply untenable on any grounds. If so, Paul has countered their teaching in several particulars.

Finally, Paul does countenance divorce in such mixed marriages, again as less than the ideal, but only at the instance of the unbelieving spouse (7:15). Also noteworthy is that both statements about the believing husband (7:12, 14*a*) are repeated, verbatim, with regard to the believing wife (7:13, 14*b*); thus Paul continues to reflect the equal care and standing with which he has regarded males and females throughout the first sixteen verses of this chapter.

# REFLECTIONS

**1.** In treating marriages between believers and unbelievers Paul makes two remarkable claims: (1) The children are sanctified by their association with the believer, and (2) he cryptically expresses the possibility that the believing spouse might save the unbelieving spouse, male or female. Nowhere else in the entire Pauline corpus do we find such a statement of salvation being so directly ascribed to human agency. Elsewhere it is God who saves (cf. 1:18, 21); one can surely assume here also that it is God who is understood to save as well, but through the agency of love shown by the believing spouse toward the unbelieving one. What an awesome picture of the power of love between husbands and wives! The assertions that believers may sanctify their spouses and their children (7:14) complement what has been noted about good and bad models and their importance in the communal life of faith. Here we see that one's action, one's comportment is not just a private transaction between the individual and God; what one does and how one lives one's life have the potential to corrode and harm others (cf. 8:10) or to elevate and encourage others (cf. 14:3). Faith and the morality in which it expresses itself, as Paul sees them, are never totally or simply private. That is why one's faith (the right relationship to God) can never be lived without its gaining its expression in love (the right relationship to others; cf. Gal 5:6).

Think about marriage as a mutually sanctifying, mutually upbuilding relationship. Each marriage partner seeks the best for the other, encourages the other, and consoles the other when appropriate; that is love put into action. Also, when we consider our obligations to our children in light of this passage we might think of ourselves as setting them apart as special to God by refracting God's love through us to them. All of our relationships in the family are not just private transactions between us and family members; they are always done in the light of God's care and concern for each person.

**2.** Divorce is addressed at two points in this chapter: 7:10-11, 12-16. A scan of New Testament views about divorce may provide a context for some reflections about Paul's outlook. According to Mark 10:2-11, Jesus, like Paul, indicates that not-to-divorce had been the ideal but that divorce was allowed as an accommodation, in Mark's case, on account of "hardheartedness." In Matt 19:3-9 Jesus allows divorce (and remarriage) only where unchastity is involved. So when Paul takes care to note that the Lord says the wife should not divorce her husband, he no doubt is referring to the same sorts of Jesus traditions that we see in the Gospels. As indicated in the commentary, Paul's pattern throughout the chapter is to set up the ideal as the goal, but he regularly makes an accommodation to persons who for various reasons cannot attain the goal. So here the goal is conformity with Jesus' teaching that a woman not divorce her husband, but the accommodation follows immediately: "but if she does. . . ." So Paul recognizes and does not forbid divorce, though to divorce is short of the ideal. Further, Paul, in distinction from Deut 24:1-4 but in accord with Roman law, assumes that a wife may institute divorce as well as a husband.

The New Testament shows a persistent commitment to restoring relationships, to affirming peace and reconciliation. In the light of this it is not surprising that Jesus, and Paul in line with him, should counsel against a rush to divorce. Neither is it surprising that each of the noted texts reckons, for different reasons, that divorce is sometimes the chosen course. We should do everything to encourage reconciliation, not just in disputed marriages but in all of life, but we should also recognize that there are times when a marriage ought to be dissolved. Divorce should not be an early step, however, in the treatment of marriage problems.

# 1 CORINTHIANS 7:17-24, INDIFFERENT MATTERS: JEW, GREEK, SLAVE, FREE

[17]Nevertheless, each one should retain the place in life that the Lord assigned to him and to which God has called him. This is the rule I lay down in all the churches. [18]Was a man already circumcised when he was called? He should not become uncircumcised. Was a man uncircumcised when he was called? He should not be circumcised. [19]Circumcision is nothing and uncircumcision is nothing. Keeping God's commands is what counts. [20]Each one should remain in the situation which he was in when God called him. [21]Were you a slave when you were called? Don't let it trouble you—although if you can gain your freedom, do so. [22]For he who was a slave when he was called by the Lord is the Lord's freedman; similarly, he who was a free man when he was called is Christ's slave. [23]You were bought at a price; do not become slaves of men. [24]Brothers, each man, as responsible to God, should remain in the situation God called him to.

[17]However that may be, let each of you lead the life that the Lord has assigned, to which God called you. This is my rule in all the churches. [18]Was anyone at the time of his call already circumcised? Let him not seek to remove the marks of circumcision. Was anyone at the time of his call uncircumcised? Let him not seek circumcision. [19]Circumcision is nothing, and uncircumcision is nothing; but obeying the commandments of God is everything. [20]Let each of you remain in the condition in which you were called. [21]Were you a slave when called? Do not be concerned about it. Even if you can gain your freedom, make use of your present condition now more than ever.[a] [22]For whoever was called in the Lord as a slave is a freed person belonging to the Lord, just as whoever was free when called is a slave of Christ. [23]You were bought with a price; do not become slaves of human masters. [24]In whatever condition you were called, brothers and sisters,[b] there remain with God.

[a] Or *avail yourself of the opportunity*    [b] Gk *brothers*

# COMMENTARY

These eight verses are a digression. They have no explicit connection with marriage or with sexuality. Husbands and wives, divorce and sexuality—the topics on either side—are simply not mentioned in 7:17-24. After these verses Paul returns to his counsels for another class of individuals in the Corinthian congregation, virgins or unmarried (7:25ff.).

Paul clearly expects his original readers to make the connections of vv. 17-24 to what is on either side, and perhaps we modern readers can do the same once we identify what is going on inside the passage. First, we will note the structure of 7:17-24; then we will assess its function. Verses 17-24 have a two-part structure framed within three quite similar statements (7:17, 20, 24). Within that frame one finds a reflection on God's call or election, a theme that has been important in the letter from the start.

The opening sentence, structured as a chiasmus (A B B´ A´), functions like a well-balanced thesis statement for 7:17-24: "Nevertheless, to each [A] as the Lord has apportioned [B], as God has called [B´] each [A´], thus let him walk. I make this rule in all the churches" (7:17). Verse 20, echoing v. 17, says: "Each [A] in the call in which he has been called [B], in this let him remain." Verse 24 resounds and refines the same claim: "Each [A] in the circumstance where he has been called [B], brothers and sisters, in this let him remain with God." The notion of life as a walk, as a way of walking, is a commonplace in Paul's letters (cf. Rom 6:4; 13:13; 2 Cor 5:7; Gal 5:16; Phil 3:17). The theme of "remaining," first exemplified by Paul in 7:8 and reaffirmed in 7:11, emerges in 7:20 and 7:24 as a thread binding together much of his counsel about marriage and sexuality.

Verse 17 and its echoes in v. 20 and v. 24 affirm that Paul expects persons, in all of his churches, to live, specifically to walk, the gospel in the circumstances where they were called, where the grace of God engaged them. Living the gospel is the primary concern. To put it differently, how they "walk"—that is, how they comport themselves— is the key issue. Location and setting are indifferent matters; one's call is not. The gospel can flourish and be walked in any circumstance, and the living of it elevates the person and the circumstance in which the person lives. Paul does not require believers to leave their social setting. As we shall see shortly, this is partly a function of Paul's conviction that the end of the ages is near and, therefore, there is no need of altering social structures, but it also reflects his profound belief that the gospel can be fully lived wherever one is or whatever one's circumstances (cf. 2 Cor 4:7). The three kindred expressions in vv. 17, 20, and 24 frame the passage into two portions, which we now examine.

Verses 17-19 are structured around two questions with appended directions. Circumcision, even though it was a sign of being part of Israel (Gen 17:9-14), and uncircumcision (variant ways of referring to Jew and gentile; cf. Rom 2:28-29) are the first test cases to illustrate how persons should comport themselves when and where they receive their call. Was anyone circumcised—that is, was the person a Jew when called? No need to change that. Was anyone—presumably most of his Corinthian audience—called while a gentile? No need to change that. Unlike the churches in Galatia, the church at Corinth is not having even the slightest problem with circumcision or uncircumcision; the terms are mentioned in the letter only here. So Paul is reciting matters about which the Corinthians have no confusion; he is building

a case from something he knows they understand and accept. They realize that they have not been expected to become circumcised when called. Accordingly, the maxim that concludes this section will not surprise them either: "Circumcision is nothing; uncircumcision is nothing; but keeping the commandments of God [that's crucial]" (7:19). Obedience to God matters; circumcision and uncircumcision are indifferent. This clarity on an issue that is purely and simply illustrative, that builds on what they already know, prepares the way for a more complex and immediate issue for some of Paul's readers ahead in 7:20-23. Once again we see a solid Pauline principle at work: Begin with what believers know and build a ground from which to address a problem.

Verses 20-23 deal with slavery and freedom[99] and, like 7:18-19, open with a question, but unlike those previous questions of 7:18, this one is in the second-person singular and is a direct address, suggesting that this is a problem Paul knows is besetting some Corinthians: "Were you a slave when called?" "Don't let it trouble you" (NIV), or "Do not be concerned about it" (NRSV).[100] Paul's justification for why it should be of no concern is not given until a verse later (7:22), but runs as follows: True freedom is found in slavery to the Lord and does not depend on one's social status as reckoned in the world. From the perspective-keeping formulation (7:22), the world's slave is the Lord's free person and the world's free person is the Lord's slave, so, as Paul has already asked the Corinthians in this letter: "Who sees anything different in you?" (4:7 NRSV). Slavery and freedom are indifferent matters "in the Lord." But, as we have seen, the Stoic eagerness to identify "indifferent matters" (*adiaphora*) always also allowed room for distinctions within those *adiaphora* of "preferreds" and "not-preferreds." Though Paul could write to the Philippians, indicating that he knew how to get along with much and how to get along with plenty (4:12), there is nothing wrong with preferring

99. S. S. Bartchy, *MALLON CHRESAI: First-century Slavery and the Interpretation of 1 Corinthians 7:21*, SBLDS 11 (Missoula: University of Montana Press, 1973); Dale B. Martin, *Slavery as Salvation: The Metaphor of Slavery in Pauline Christianity* (New Haven: Yale University Press, 1990).

100. Neil Elliott, *Liberating Paul: The Justice of God and the Politics of the Apostle* (Maryknoll, N.Y.: Orbis, 1994) 32-40, sees in the ambiguity of Paul's cryptic Greek (μᾶλλον χρῆσαι *mallon chrēsai*) in 7:21 a call of liberation, that slaves should take the opportunity of their freedom.

plenty if one is presented with the choice. So, though Paul is clear that slavery and freedom are in a fundamental sense an *adiaphoron*, an indifferent matter, there is no reason why a believing slave who is given the chance to attain freed person status should not readily take it if he or she so desires. Freedom from slavery can surely be a "preferred."

Near the end of this passage, Paul clearly lays out what he takes to be an unavoidable truth—indeed, one that has already been affirmed in this letter: All believers have been bought by a new Lord, Jesus Christ (v. 23; 6:20). With regard to the world and its values, whether one is a slave should not be a concern; it is not an important matter, but Paul recognizes that one may have the opportunity to gain freedom and he accommodates to that (v. 21). Paul's counsel here has analogies with his advice to the groups noted earlier in chap. 7. In those cases he identified a maximum level, or what he calls "better," performance, but he always allowed for variations from that. Here in the issue of slavery he has no "better" level but instead argues from an indifferent matter (whether one is slave or free) to an allowable, "preferred" course of action.

Paul's congregations seem regularly to have had slaves in them. In the Roman world, slavery was a taken-for-granted institution. Slaves could gain their freedom in certain circumstances such as when their owners bestowed it as a reward or willed it to them at death; at times slaves could purchase their freedom. Corinth had some prominent freedmen who built proud monuments to the worldly success they achieved after they were freed, so we know that social mobility from slavery to freedom was valued by some at Corinth. Perhaps aware of that tangible social pressure, Paul accedes to their desire for freedom as reckoned in the world. This is an important concession because it shows that Paul's continued call to "remain as they are" is not an elevation of the issue of believers' status and circumstance to a level of primary importance, but a call to live, behave, walk in whatever circumstances they find themselves, in accordance with their call. The circumstances are not elevated above the life according to the gospel. Rather, the gospel, its call, and its appropriate behavior are the crucial and primary concern; the circumstances in which one finds

oneself are indifferent. Here Paul stands in line with venerable Cynic and Stoic convictions that the good life can be lived in any circumstances. So, slaves who see the opportunity to be free must walk in accord with the gospel whether they remain slaves or whether they avail themselves of the chance to be free.

The common ground that all believers, no matter their social status or ethnicity, share is that they are now "owned" by a new master, by Christ as their Lord. The last time Paul wrote in such a way in this letter he also said something else that continues to be true: "You are not your own . . . glorify God in your body" (6:19-20 NRSV). Therefore believers are not free to "become slaves of people" (7:23*b*; cf. Paul's own self-portrait in the last clause of 6:12).

What is the function of 7:17-24, and how is it accomplished? In part these verses reaffirm common ground between Paul and his readers: He and they know that circumcision and uncircumcision are indifferent matters. So, at the very least, it affirmed what they already knew—namely, that they did not have to alter their ethnicity; they did not have to become Jews, just because they came to believe in the gospel. In part, also, the readers are expected, with Paul's help, to make an analogical application of their understood indifference regarding ethnicity and a supposed indifference regarding other circumstances—these having to do with marital status—that prevailed at the time of their call.

But this explanation does not yet account for Paul's treatment of slaves and free persons. Paul's readers would have understood what Paul was doing in 7:17-24, but it may be more difficult for modern readers to see. They would have known two things that we can learn: (1) In those days it was the standard rhetorical procedure of indirect speech to put some already known, clearly understood matter or principle alongside an issue under deliberation so that the readers could make their own connections and applications. (2) Paul's readers would more readily recognize traditions that Paul had taught them than we might. As a start, let us see the structure of this passage once more as it fits into its larger context:

7:1-16    discussion of male/female
7:17-20   discussion of Jew/Greek
             (circumcised/uncircumcised)
7:21-24   discussion of slave/free
7:25-40   discussion of male/female

From 1 Cor 12:13—"For in the one Spirit we were all baptized into one body—Jews or Greeks, slaves or free—and we were all made to drink of one Spirit" (NRSV)—we can tell that the Corinthians knew the same baptismal formula— indeed, they may have heard it pronounced over them at the time of their own baptism—that we see reflected in Gal 3:28: "There is no longer Jew or Greek, there is no longer slave or free, there is no longer male or female; for all of you are one in Christ Jesus" (NRSV). The formula, no doubt a tradition composed by others and embraced by Paul, is clearly a favorite of his and is known to be affirmed by his Corinthian readers, because he explicitly argues from it in 12:13 without need for explanation or support.

Now we are in a position to see what Paul is doing by inserting 7:17-24 into the discussion of males, females, and human sexuality. In a chapter where he discusses issues relating to males and females, he has picked up the other two sets from the baptismal formula reflected in Gal 3:28 and in 1 Cor 12:13: Jew and Greek, slave and free. He has reaffirmed that whether an individual is Jew or Greek or slave or free does not matter because all persons are on equal standing and are equally important in Christ. And in so doing, he has shown the Corinthians his fulcrum for moral reasoning throughout the chapter, that is, how he has been deducing his counsels for the various groupings of males and females within the Corinthian congregation. The male/female couplet has not been left out in chap. 7 as some scholars have suggested;[101] that couplet is the subject matter throughout the chapter and so does not need repeating in vv. 17-24.

Given Paul's profound conviction that in Christ the world's distinctions between male and female no longer prevail, and faced with the Corinthian questions about sexual relations, he has set about

to imagine what the relationship between males and females would be if one took seriously that in Christ they have equal standing. As a result, Paul's interpretation throughout the chapter is characterized by an evenhanded, reciprocal, almost verbatim repetition of statements made about husbands and then applied to wives, and vice versa (7:2-4, 12-14, 16, 27, 33-34); further, though Paul does not think divorce is best, wives have just as much right to divorce as do husbands (7:10-11, 13).

Paul's purpose in chap. 7 emerges: He is doing moral reasoning concerning males and females in a way that honors their equal standing as those baptized into Christ. For Paul, those in Christ, whether male or female, are of equal status. He opens the chapter with the Corinthian maxim that radicalizes holiness and elevates men. Without explicitly rejecting the maxim, he envisions life between the sexes in the light of the baptismal formula (Gal 3:28), which is clearly a part of his conviction and, therefore, part of his regular instruction to his followers. It has already been noted that Paul's frequent course of moral reasoning is to go from problem or issue to "what we know" and to reckon from the latter toward a moral stance on the problem or issue. In this instance, Paul is presented with some questions of human sexuality and in particular with a maxim that reflects the efforts of some of his followers to deduce a moral stance appropriate to the gospel. On this occasion Paul moves from some Corinthians' solution as expressed in their maxim (7:1) and, by reference to what believers know, namely the baptismal tradition reflection in Gal 3:28 and 1 Cor 12:13 and 7:17-24, Paul constructs another, quite different picture and expresses it across chapter 7. If in Christ the world's standards and distinctions no longer pertain in any case but particularly in the relationships between male and female, what would a genuinely Christ-based ethic of human sexuality look like? Chapter 7 is a part of Paul's answer.

In 7:17-24 Paul lays down the basis on which he has reasoned in 7:1-16 and by which he will continue to reason in 7:25ff. Before he writes 7:17-24, Paul has already supposed reciprocity and equal standing for each grouping of people he has addressed; only in 7:17-24 does he signal his readers that throughout the chapter he has been operating from the baptismal formula; and with his

101. Hans Dieter Betz, *Galatians: A Commentary on Paul's Letter to the Churches in Galatia,* Hermeneia (Philadelphia: Fortress, 1979) 200, by reference to 1 Cor 12:13, accounts for the absence of the male/female pair.

deliberations about Jews/Greeks and slaves/free he invites his readers not only to perceive the key to his reasoning but also to see that the gospel, though it allows a shift of social setting for its full enactment, does not require it.

The latter is a theme that has surfaced a few times already in this letter. Some Corinthians seem to have taken Paul's call for holiness as a demand for radical breaks with or alterations of all their previous social setting and identification, as if to flee *porneia* were to flee the world and one's social setting. As he elaborates his position, Paul appears to walk a fine line in this chapter; he inclines toward urging all people to stay put, to continue to live in the same context as when they received

their call, but he recognizes that some change may be important or necessary (e.g., some may need to divorce, some may have a chance to gain freedom from slavery).

In the passages to which attention now turns, we will see why Paul finds no urgency for believers to alter their social structures or settings and how he thinks believers can live within the world without conforming to its norms. In these passages we will see that Paul continues to examine human relations in the light of the baptismal formula and its equal standing and reciprocity, and it is from this important tradition that he has deduced his maxim, which he offers in the following material.

# REFLECTIONS

**1.** Paul's vision of holiness lived within the world gives us challenges in at least two ways: to understand what holiness means and to imagine how to live it in the world, which in so many ways marches to a different drummer. Maybe it would be helpful to think of holiness as being the center of one's life. Many things vie to become the central, organizing principle of our lives: success, money, prestige, and each person can add to that list. What is at the center governs. So if it is, say, money, then decisions are made with regard to what will make the most money, what will be financially advantageous. Other concerns are ranked out in relation to the central, governing one, or are simply ignored because they do not serve the central concern. Thus it always is, no matter what is at the center of one's life. If God's love and God's purposes are at the center of your life, then all other concerns and values must take their place in rank in relation to that governing commitment. Holiness, being set apart or belonging to God, should be at the center of our lives, according to Paul. If it is and we make our choices and aversions on the basis of the primary consideration that we belong to God, then competing values are put in perspective. Then the first consideration when faced with a moral choice is not how will it affect my finances but how will it honor God's love and God's purposes. Each of us already has something that is a governing principle in the middle of our lives. Or we may have one principle in one kind of circumstance and another in a different situation. A good exercise, best done with others in open discussion, would be to share honestly what is our central, governing principle. Or we can examine a major decision and fruitfully ask what was the central value that was finally determinative in the choice that we made.

**2.** Paul's relatively quietistic counsel to "remain in the situation where called" (7:24) can be mistaken as a call to inaction, to do nothing, or even to embrace the status quo. There are circumstances that the gospel simply cannot abide and we must be unmistakably clear about that. For example, no one should remain in a physically or emotionally abusive situation. The gospel does not call for one to do that. In a similar way, Paul's counsel to "remain" should not be used as a justification for not seeking better circumstances for oneself and an improvement of one's circumstances.

**3.** We ought to appreciate and celebrate more fully that it is not just individuals who are changed for the better by their living out the gospel. Their circumstances may also be elevated by the gospel's power; their context and those persons around them may be positively affected by the reverberations of God's grace in and through them. However, there are times when the living of the gospel will set off such a reaction from those around that a believer might do well to leave those circumstances, much as Jesus is portrayed as telling his disciples to shake the dust from their feet as they left those who would ill-treat them (Matt 10:14; Luke 9:5). Even in the passage before us Paul's maxim to "remain as you are" does not become a law; it is a guideline. What an irony if it were to become the basis for a person to become entrapped in harmful or nonviable circumstances.

**4.** Paul's ready, favorable use of slavery imagery as a means of expressing proper dependence upon God (Rom 1:1; 6:11-23; 1 Cor 3:5; 4:1) should not obscure Paul's real sense of freedom, which he celebrates in Christ (cf. Gal 5:1-14) and which Augustine also affirmed when he said, "My heart is restless until it finds its rest in Thee."[102] Neither can Paul's embracing of slave imagery be transferred without caution to modern times; the use of Paul to endorse slavery in Civil War times in the United States shows those dangers. As in Paul's time, slavery is still a reality in our own time and must be consistently opposed wherever it is happening around this globe. On a more metaphorical level, slaveries are all too present; our yearning for money, for example, can place us in thrall; drug abuse is surely an invidious slavery for many persons. All such slaveries must be exposed, called into question, and the victims of them must, in every possible way, be supported and encouraged to break from them.

102. Augustine *Confessions* 1.1.

# 1 CORINTHIANS 7:25-28, COUNSEL FOR THE UNMARRIED: PAUL'S OWN MAXIM

25Now about virgins: I have no command from the Lord, but I give a judgment as one who by the Lord's mercy is trustworthy. 26Because of the present crisis, I think that it is good for you to remain as you are. 27Are you married? Do not seek a divorce. Are you unmarried? Do not look for a wife. 28But if you do marry, you have not sinned; and if a virgin marries, she has not sinned. But those who marry will face many troubles in this life, and I want to spare you this.

25Now concerning virgins, I have no command of the Lord, but I give my opinion as one who by the Lord's mercy is trustworthy. 26I think that, in view of the impending[a] crisis, it is well for you to remain as you are. 27Are you bound to a wife? Do not seek to be free. Are you free from a wife? Do not seek a wife. 28But if you marry, you do not sin, and if a virgin marries, she does not sin. Yet those who marry will experience distress in this life,[b] and I would spare you that.

[a] Or *present*   [b] Gk *in the flesh*

# COMMENTARY

After Paul's digression (7:17-24), he gives a rather protracted consideration to a last group: the virgins or unmarrieds. The term παρθένος (*parthenos*) means "unmarried" here and does not itself indicate whether the unmarried woman is betrothed, though 7:28 and 7:36-38 suggest that Paul has that reality in mind, at least there. With regard to unmarrieds Paul admits that he has no command of the Lord, but, as one who has been found trustworthy with respect to his calling, he offers his own maxim γνώμη (*gnōmē*, 7:25).[103]

103. Rollin A. Ramsaran, "More Than an Opinion: Paul's Rhetorical Maxim in First Corinthians 7:25-26," *CBQ* 57 (1995) 531-41.

Most translations depict Paul as setting forth his "opinion" (NRSV) or "judgment" (NIV, NEB), but, as we have seen, the Corinthians and Paul, like the culture of which they are a part, are very much given to maxims as a ground of moral reasoning.[104] The first section of this chapter was prompted by the Corinthians' maxim (7:1 b); Paul now offers his own, with a prefixed consideration: "I therefore reckon this to be good, because of the imminent necessity, namely, 'It is good for a person to remain as is' " (7:26). The auditors are left to ponder what Paul may have in mind with the phrase "imminent necessity," and they may think that he once again refers to the burning passion he had mentioned earlier (7:9), but it will become quite clear in vv. 28-31 that no matter how much he may have passion in view he also has in mind the impending apocalyptic conclusion of God's work already begun in Christ. In his maxim they will hear a theme that has already made its mark on the chapter: "Remain as you are" (7:8, 11, 17-24).

Immediately following his maxim, Paul addresses, directly and in the singular, unmarried persons in the congregation, giving first, as we have come to expect, his counsel concerning the ideal. Verse 27 a reminds the reader of Paul's earlier counsel to married persons and shows that his advice there was already consistent with his maxim: Those who are married should not seek divorce. Verse 27 b applies his own, newly announced maxim to the matter at hand, unmarrieds: "Are you free from a wife? Do not seek a wife." Predictably, Paul then directs his counsel to those who cannot attain the ideal, assuring that those who do marry do not sin (7:28 a-b), but "such ones [as do marry] will have worldly distress [θλῖψις *thlipsis*] which I would spare you" (7:28 c). *Thlipsis* ("distress," "affliction") refers to distress, whose origin lies in circumstances outside oneself; we can tell from other letters (Rom 8:35; 1 Thess 3:3, 7) that when Paul employs the term he usually thinks of the eschatological distress that all believers inevitably experience as God's purposes come to their conclusion—that distress Paul cannot spare the Corinthians or anyone else and in yet another digression (7:29-35) he attends to its consequences.

104. Rollin A. Ramsaran, *Liberating Words: Paul's Use of Rhetorical Maxims in 1 Corinthians 1–10* (Valley Forge, Pa.: Trinity, 1996) 6-7.

# REFLECTIONS

**1.** Paul's justification for marriage is not procreation but the need for acceptable expression of sexuality. Missing altogether in 1 Corinthians 7 is any romanticism; it is nowhere else in that culture either. Some say that notions of romantic love only began in the fourteenth century.[105] But before one dismisses Paul's view of marriage as "minimalist" or "not lofty," one should consider two matters. (1) Based on his deliberation (7:17-24) from the baptismal tradition most clearly visible in Gal 3:28, Paul argues for a fundamental reciprocity between husbands and wives (the most striking to modern ears will be that the wife has authority over the husband's body and vice versa, 7:4); and (2) form follows function in such counsel because he repeats almost verbatim his advice to women and to men (cf. 7:2-4, 10-11, 12-16, 27, 32-33).

**2.** Paul's counsel, expressed in his maxim "remain as you are" (7:26 NIV) and brought to bear on several of the exemplary cases, is powered by his abiding conviction (cf. Rom 13:11-14; 1 Thess 5:1-11) that the "schema of this world is passing away" (7:31), which process of passing creates a "present distress" (7:26) in which "the time [between now and the end] is [mercifully] shortened" (7:29). If Paul had thought differently, say that the end of the world was some distance away as many today do believe, would his counsel in particulars have been different? It is difficult to know because the only Paul we have access to is the one who thought the end was imminent and, therefore, appropriately counseled that people had no need to worry about social structures and their injustice. We do know, however, that he puts leverage on Philemon to

105. Denis de Rougemont, *Love in the Western World,* trans. M. Belgion (New York: Pantheon, 1956).

accept his former worthless slave Onesimus back, no longer as a slave but as a beloved brother in Christ (Phlm 16). We do know that he has supported slaves who desire freedom (cf. 1 Cor 7:21). It is easy to suppose that, if he had not expected an imminent parousia, he might have more strongly advocated marriage, he might have counseled widows to be more open to the idea of remarriage. Whether Paul would have or not, we must wrestle more fully with the genuine ambiguity of how to maximize our piety and holiness while dealing with the demands and distractions of daily life that we modern people experience. Further, by combining Paul's arguments here for equality and reciprocity with his claims in other places regarding the primacy of love and our obligations to encourage and build one another up, we could construct a rich, thought-provoking, and engaging model of marriage.

# 1 CORINTHIANS 7:29-35, A DIGRESSION REGARDING LIFE LIVED ESCHATOLOGICALLY

## NIV

29What I mean, brothers, is that the time is short. From now on those who have wives should live as if they had none; 30those who mourn, as if they did not; those who are happy, as if they were not; those who buy something, as if it were not theirs to keep; 31those who use the things of the world, as if not engrossed in them. For this world in its present form is passing away.

32I would like you to be free from concern. An unmarried man is concerned about the Lord's affairs—how he can please the Lord. 33But a married man is concerned about the affairs of this world—how he can please his wife—34and his interests are divided. An unmarried woman or virgin is concerned about the Lord's affairs: Her aim is to be devoted to the Lord in both body and spirit. But a married woman is concerned about the affairs of this world—how she can please her husband. 35I am saying this for your own good, not to restrict you, but that you may live in a right way in undivided devotion to the Lord.

## NRSV

29I mean, brothers and sisters,a the appointed time has grown short; from now on, let even those who have wives be as though they had none, 30and those who mourn as though they were not mourning, and those who rejoice as though they were not rejoicing, and those who buy as though they had no possessions, 31and those who deal with the world as though they had no dealings with it. For the present form of this world is passing away.

32I want you to be free from anxieties. The unmarried man is anxious about the affairs of the Lord, how to please the Lord; 33but the married man is anxious about the affairs of the world, how to please his wife, 34and his interests are divided. And the unmarried woman and the virgin are anxious about the affairs of the Lord, so that they may be holy in body and spirit; but the married woman is anxious about the affairs of the world, how to please her husband. 35I say this for your own benefit, not to put any restraint upon you, but to promote good order and unhindered devotion to the Lord.

a Gk brothers

# COMMENTARY

The first part of this new digression (7:29-31) is framed by two declarations. One depicts the believers as near the end of the age, near the time of the Lord's return, near the day of judgment: "The appointed time has grown short" (7:29; cf. 4:5). The other isolates the believers from any

inclination to live in accordance with the standards of this world: "The *schēma* [σχῆμα, "form," "outward structure"] of this world is passing away" (7:31b). Within those two framing elements Paul evokes, with only the sketchiest adumbrations, a series of snapshots of how to live in the world and yet practice detachment from the values and entanglements the world offers. The statements, all without finite verbs and without full-sentence elaborations, evince life "as if not" (*hōs mē*). The evocations invite the Corinthians to imagine the life of faith as one lived in the world but detached or disengaged from the world's values. With these snapshots or vignettes Paul answers the question of how believers can "remain as they are," namely, still living within the world, without being held captive or conformed to the values and structures of the world. The answer: Live in these structures and in these relationships "as if not," as if the world, its structures, and these relationships did not provide life with its value and meaning because one knows that the defining relationship, and therefore value, comes from one's relation to God, in Christ.

Paul has addressed this same issue, though expressed in different terms, here and there in the current letter: How is one to preserve and honor one's holiness in a world whose structure (*schēma*, 7:31) is passing away? To whom does one belong (1:12; 3:23; 6:20)? As he has done earlier, Paul continues to insist that believers do not have to withdraw from the world and from the social connections that are structured within it; instead, believers can live the life of faith within the social setting where they find themselves called by the gospel. They can "remain as they are" and avoid idolatry while walking appropriately with respect to the gospel.

The second part of the digression (7:32-35) is an amplification of Paul's claim in 7:28 that he would like to spare them worldly distress. This he develops in terms of helping them to be "free from care" (7:32*a*) and in terms of maximizing both the pleasing of the Lord and devotion to the Lord. In this amplification Paul envisions life as a sorting out of competing loyalties and rival cares or concerns. As we would expect, a Pauline ideal does emerge: It is the person, whether male (7:32-33) or female (7:34), who is free from marriage and its attendant concerns (including inevitably and rightly the desire to please one's spouse); it is the person, therefore, who is free to focus on the Lord and on pleasing the Lord. (Earlier in this letter [6:15-16], Paul has shown that he is capable of thinking of one's relation to the Lord in intimate terms of marriage.) As we would also expect, Paul

imagines and condones a concession, something less than the ideal: It is the person, whether male or female, who is "divided" (7:34), who is concerned not only about "the things of the Lord" (7:33-34) but also about "the things of the world" (7:33, 34), who is eager not only to please the Lord but also to please a spouse.

The digression concludes with a direct address to all the readers, declaring Paul's purpose in his counsel and expressing his disposition: He has sought not to put a yoke or noose (βρόχος *brochos*) upon them but to be helpful to them (cf. 6:12; 12:7). And in it all his goal has been to foster "proper, constant devotion to the Lord without distraction" (7:35). Indeed, Paul's self-description of purpose is consonant with what and how he has counseled them. He has avoided yoking them into a singular, uniform performance but has made his suggestions and given his advice with an eye to maximizing their devotion to God no matter their circumstances, all the time recognizing that different abilities and circumstances may call for some performance short of the ideal or goal.

Like the rival two-way tradition that is so prominent throughout the opening chapters of 1 Corinthians, Paul acknowledges two contending schemas (εὐσχημον *euschēmon*, 7:35, versus σχῆμα τοῦ κόσμου *schēma tou kosmou*, 7:31). The latter is the schema of this world, that, on the basis of his apocalyptic confidence, Paul declares is passing away (7:31). With that schema's passing the patterns of the world are being eclipsed. The alternate schema or pattern that Paul understands himself to be promoting in his counsels in chapter 7 is the pattern of proper, appropriate, presentable behavior (ἀλλὰ πρὸς τὸ εὐσχημον *alla pros to euschēmon*, 7:35*c*), which is then elaborated by the remainder of the sentence: "namely, uninterrupted constancy to the Lord." On the one side, the unfavored way, are the patterns of the world, its values, its modes of human relationships; on the other side, the gospel's way, is an undivided devotion to the Lord, which may be expressed in all of life's circumstances and in a range of responses, all of which are acceptable to God, but which operates on very different principles and values from the way of the world. The "proper schema" of 7:35 is the norm— so much so that Paul works from it in the next verse to describe behavior that is inappropriate—that is, not from the proper schema (7:36).

# REFLECTIONS

**1.** Although Paul believes that in some sense individuals find themselves in situations that the Lord has apportioned to them and in which they have been called by God, Paul shows across this chapter that he assumes that individuals make choices for which they are responsible, that people are capable of self-reflection and can weigh alternative actions and choose the one they deem more appropriate with regard to certain guiding principles or concerns. Persons can override their passions (an ancient concern from the Greeks forward). Self-control/self-mastery is not guaranteed, however (7:5, 8), nor does it have to be maintained in one direction if the cost is too dear (7:36).

**2.** The curious passage 7:29-32 is an exercise in perspective-keeping from which we modern believers can benefit. Given that "the time has been shortened" (7:29*a*) and that "the schema of this world is passing away" (7:31), believers relate to every indifferent matter in such a way as not to overvalue it or to confuse it with what is most important. Paul's list in 7:29-31 is illustrative of the sorts of matters that are not ultimate and should not be confused as such: marriage (7:29), mourning and rejoicing (7:30), purchasing/owning (7:30), and, a most sweeping category that functions much as an "et cetera" that includes everyone, "those who use the world" (7:31*a*). Not to confuse what matters with what does not is a constant human challenge, and one's delineation of the distinction is a road map of one's values and commitments. And all of us "use the world" (7:31*a*) in a variety of ways. When we use a disproportionate amount of the world's resources, we should have questions of conscience. All of us "use the world" in the sense of living in it, and doing so raises not only the questions of proper stewardship but also the fitting concern not to be entrapped by the world's values. The latter is Paul's concern in this passage and should be ours as well.

**3.** Paul would spare the Corinthians' "concerns" (NIV) and "anxieties" (NRSV, 7:32) and "worldly tribulations" (7:28) if he were able, but to do so is not in his control. In part the sin-burdened creation waits with eager longing for its deliverance like a woman in labor suffers the birth pangs in the delivery of the child (Rom 8:18-25). Believers are like that: They will not escape those tribulations (1 Thess 3:3). In the context of God's purposes one must honestly acknowledge the pervasive human problem of competing goods and loyalties (dedication to one's beloved and devotion to God), and one soon realizes that one can only hope to minimize, not eliminate, these particular stresses and concerns. So, in fact, Paul finally distinguishes between proper and improper anxieties and concerns. Note that life without concerns is not what the gospel promises; rather, the gospel reminds us that God's grace is always present with us in the midst of our concerns, sustaining and encouraging us (for more on this, see 1 Cor 10:1-13; cf. Rom 8:28).

**4.** For Paul the effort to please one's spouse is a taken-for-granted obligation of marriage by both husbands and wives. To be sure, it takes energy that might otherwise be placed directly in service of God, but with marriage there is also the need to please one's spouse and, notably, even one's obligations to God do not pre-empt the responsibility to please one's spouse. This is an index of how deeply Paul honors the commitments and responsibilities of marriage partners. How rich is marriage when both spouses place their obligation to please the other ahead of all competing responsibilities.

# 1 CORINTHIANS 7:36-38,
# BETHROTHED UNMARRIEDS AND
# THE IDEALIZED RESPONDER

NIV

36If anyone thinks he is acting improperly toward the virgin he is engaged to, and if she is getting along in years and he feels he ought to marry, he should do as he wants. He is not sinning. They should get married. 37But the man who has settled the matter in his own mind, who is under no compulsion but has control over his own will, and who has made up his mind not to marry the virgin—this man also does the right thing. 38So then, he who marries the virgin does right, but he who does not marry her does even better.ᵃ

ᵃ36-38 Or 36If anyone thinks he is not treating his daughter properly, and if she is getting along in years, and he feels she ought to marry, he should do as he wants. He is not sinning. He should let her get married. 37But the man who has settled the matter in his own mind, who is under no compulsion but has control over his own will, and who has made up his mind to keep the virgin unmarried—this man also does the right thing. 38So then, he who gives his virgin in marriage does right, but he who does not give her in marriage does even better.

NRSV

36If anyone thinks that he is not behaving properly toward his fiancée,ᵃ if his passions are strong, and so it has to be, let him marry as he wishes; it is no sin. Let them marry. 37But if someone stands firm in his resolve, being under no necessity but having his own desire under control, and has determined in his own mind to keep her as his fiancée,ᵃ he will do well. 38So then, he who marries his fiancéeᵃ does well; and he who refrains from marriage will do better.

ᵃ Gk virgin

# COMMENTARY

After the digression Paul's focus is clearly and fully on those unmarrieds who are betrothed, engaged. This time, however, the pattern is reversed, with the ideal being reserved for second place, for emphasis and for elaboration, and the concession leads. Building from the picture of the "proper" or "fitting" (euschēmon) relation to the Lord just mentioned in 7:35, Paul finds that if an engaged man considers that he is "behaving dishonorably" or "improperly" (ἀσχημονέω aschēmoneō) toward his betrothed, if his passions are strong (cf. the same consideration in 7:9), then "let them marry" (7:36). For such a person to marry is not to sin (7:36; cf. 7:28). Following the concession Paul presents the ideal, more fully developed here than anywhere before, which the reader must know will be some form of the guideline: "Remain as you are."

The personification of the ideal responder (7:37) is elaborate, suggesting that this is the model Paul would wish could be found in every group he has addressed in this chapter. Four important assertions identify the idealized person: (1) He or she "stands steadfast in his or her heart"; (2) he or she is not under the sway of necessity, but (3) he or she has control over the passions; and (4) he or she is "convinced in his or her own heart." Items (1) and (4) are so similar as to be an emphatic inclusio.

The detailed picture of the person who makes the ideal response accords well with Paul's own self-discipline as described in Romans and in Philemon. There Paul "knows and is persuaded" (Rom 14:14); he has no doubts or waverings (Rom 14:23); and he recognizes that moral action must not be forced, must not be by compulsion but by choice (Phlm 14). In the case at hand in 1 Cor 7:36, the stalwart-in-faith person will "keep her as his fiancée." Some basics in Paul's understanding of moral reasoning surface in 7:37. At the fore is Paul's consideration that moral decisions are grounded in one's untroubled, unshaken heart (7:37 *a*, *c*). Directly associated is Paul's concern that the individual who is faced with a moral decision not be under compulsion and not be driven by passions (7:37 *b*). Although it is not developed by Paul at this point in the letter, an individual who was so free from compulsions and passions, who was so resolved in his or her heart, would be in a position to weigh out what sort of action would be appropriate not only to one's measure of faith but also to love.

Such a person as identified here, Paul claims, "will do well" (7:37). Likewise, the one who marries his own fiancée "will do well" (7:38). So each does "well"; both responses, to marry or not to marry, are within the scope of proper moral comportment for believers. But Paul's predilection for "remaining as you are" as a means of maximizing devotion to the Lord emerges as the "better": "The one who does not marry does better" (7:38). To marry is acceptable, but it is an accommodation to limited self-control and involves a change in social status—and on both counts is devalued compared to "staying as you are."

# REFLECTIONS

Paul's idealized portrait of the ideal person merits attention. Not everybody has such an integrated moral life. Sometimes we may find ourselves more whole, sometimes more fractured. The mature believer, as Paul here assumes, is a person whose "head is screwed on straight," or as we might also put it, who is centered around a core of established values. No wind will blow this person off course hither and yon. Neither necessity nor compulsion is a primary factor in the person's moral decision. And the person's choices are not guided by the passions (anger, avarice, lust, etc.). How many of us can recognize ourselves in that portrait? Each of us can take a kind of running inventory of our moral decisions from time to time, examine our choices, and see when we come closer to that portrait and when we seem to have acted in a way alien to it. In those times when we have acted out of passion or compulsively, we can weigh whether we might do differently in another similar situation at another time.

# 1 CORINTHIANS 7:39-40, DIVORCE, WIDOWHOOD, AND REMARRIAGE

NIV

[39]A woman is bound to her husband as long as he lives. But if her husband dies, she is free to marry anyone she wishes, but he must belong to the Lord. [40]In my judgment, she is happier if she stays as she is—and I think that I too have the Spirit of God.

NRSV

39A wife is bound as long as her husband lives. But if the husband dies,[a] she is free to marry anyone she wishes, only in the Lord. [40]But in my judgment she is more blessed if she remains as she is. And I think that I too have the Spirit of God.

[a] Gk *falls asleep*

# COMMENTARY

Paul concludes his counsel regarding marriage and human sexuality with a word concerning divorce, widowhood, and remarriage. Reaffirming his earlier embrace of the Lord's teaching (7:10) as the ideal, Paul says that as long as the husband lives, the wife is bound to him. His position on that is already clear, but what happens if the husband dies?—an issue he has not addressed heretofore. Paul's concession: "She is free to marry whomever she wishes, but only in the Lord" (7:39)—the last phrase most reasonably being understood to encourage marriage to a believer.

Once again, the ideal emerges: "But she is more blessed (μακαριωτέρα *makariotera*) if she remains as she is, according to my maxim" (7:40), which he enunciated earlier in 7:26 and from which he has been deliberating right along. He concludes the whole section with what amounts to an enforcement formula: "I think that I have the Spirit of God" (7:40 RSV), an inclusio, or ring device, with 7:25, where he gave the self-estimate that he is "by the Lord's mercy trustworthy" (7:25 NRSV) and immediately introduced his maxim (7:26).

# REFLECTIONS

**1.** The NIV translates *makariotera* as "happier," the NRSV as "more blessed" (7:40). In biblical traditions, blessedness is a status conferred by God and it always requires, as a fundamental presupposition, that the person blessed be in right relationship with God. So the state of being blessed supposes a proper relation to God requisite to God's blessing being conferred. Such a person—that is, in right relation to God and accordingly conferred to a status of blessedness before God—would have good reason to be happy. But happiness, as it may be understood in modern times, is possible in isolation, as a solitary individual without reference to God, whereas blessedness is not. If happiness is at all construed as one form of pleasure, one can find (momentary?) happiness without God. Because blessedness makes clear God's presence and care for us, blessedness can happen in the midst of distress; happiness never can. Happiness does not by definition declare anything positive or negative about one's relation to God; blessedness does. (Cf. the beatitudes in Matt 5:3-12, where some translations use the unfortunately reductionist translation "Happy are those who . . . " instead of "Blessed are those who. . . .")

**2.** As we look back across this chapter, we see that Paul's advice about marriage is factored from three concerns and convictions. First, his counsel is grounded in his eschatological conviction that the time before the end is short. Second, he is concerned to maximize devotion to the Lord. Third, throughout his deliberation in chapter 7 he is guided in his counsel by the pre-Pauline baptismal formula that we see so clearly in Gal 3:28, in which distinctions between males and females in the Lord are indifferent matters. The combination of the first two provides the matrix for understanding his maxim to "remain as you are" because the time to the end is presumed to be short. The third—his creative application of the Gal 3:28 tradition—leads Paul to picture marriage as a reciprocal relationship of spouses.

Paul is a realist about human needs and human choices, and about how some of those needs and choices will impinge on one's devotion to the Lord—but his realism helps him grasp that for such a person maximizing devotion to the Lord must take place precisely in the context of those choices and needs.

Paul recognizes the power of sexual passion; he realizes that persons will need to divorce; he understands that slaves may wish freedom; and he concedes that accommodation to such drives and needs, far from being sin, is an appropriate response for believers. Throughout he is guided in his counsel by the pre-Pauline baptismal formula that we see so clearly in Gal 3:28, in which distinctions between males and females in the Lord are overcome as indifferent matters. Like the

Stoics in the world and no doubt in the Corinthian church Paul founded, Paul is able to make distinctions among indifferent matters between "preferreds" and "not-preferreds." So Paul's counsel, while affirming that in Christ there is no difference in standing of male and female, nevertheless declares his preferred: In the light of the impending end of the ages, all of them should remain as they are if possible.

**3.** A realistic view of moral reasoning undergirds this whole chapter. One may know the ideal, the best goal toward which one might aim, but, because of various factors, many of which can be beyond one's control, one may not be able to attain that goal. Paul's presumption is that we should aim as high as we possibly can, without deceiving ourselves into settling for a lesser achievement. Life does not always go as we want; we are not in control of much that happens in and around us, and matters of very different importance bid for our allegiance. Accordingly, it is crucial that we remain clearheaded regarding not only what is in our control but also what is important. Desires must not prevail over self-control (7:37). In times of moral deliberation, believers would do well to ask in scrupulous honesty: What is truly in our control? What is truly important?

# 1 CORINTHIANS 8:1–11:1

## PAUL'S RESPONSE TO A CORINTHIAN QUESTION ABOUT EATING IDOL MEAT

## OVERVIEW

With 8:1 Paul turns to a question about eating meat offered to an idol, a matter that comes from the Corinthians' letter to him. Before considering their question and Paul's response, however, a word is in order about how Paul structures his response to their question. Paul takes their rather specific question about a particular practice and uses it as an occasion for a wider elaboration of what constitutes appropriate moral reasoning and community interrelations. In the process, Paul transforms the question from one of eating, purely and simply, as they seem to have asked it, to a view in which eating becomes a metaphor for the larger issue of the proper comportment of all of life. The literary unit in which Paul accomplishes that transformation begins in 8:1 and extends through 11:1.

In this protracted section we see not only the social dynamics of the Corinthian congregation but also Paul's assessment of those dynamics. The picture in these chapters is not so different from what has emerged earlier. Some at Corinth have strong convictions and are accustomed to being heard, to taking—and being given—the lead in moral deliberation, and they seem ready to prescribe moral comportment for others. Others (we may wonder if this is not a majority) seem more accustomed to listening; they find themselves pressured to follow, and, lacking perhaps certainty of conviction and surely their own willingness to stand up and be counted, without voice or power. Perhaps some of them are even responding by trying to live and act like the more vocal and powerful persons, even though Paul considers that it may not be appropriate for them to do so (cf. 8:10-11). In what he writes, Paul must engage his followers wherever they stand in these social dynamics.

The Corinthians' way of putting the question of

8:1 shows some fundamental affinity with Paul: They have set the issue in terms of "meat offered to an idol" (εἰδωλόθυτος *eidōlothytos*), a Jewish and subsequently Christian way of referring to what others would more simply have called ἱερόθυτος (*hierothytos*), meaning something sacrificed in a temple to a deity.[106] Typically, either of these terms refers to the widespread contemporary practice of sacrificing an animal to a deity, burning some of the flesh on an altar, and eating some of it in a cultic meal, which was always a festive, social occasion. The remainder of the sacrificial animal was sold to the meat market for resale to the public. Believers like the Corinthians, even after they have come over into the faith, may still, therefore, have a range of contact with meat offered to idols: The meat is periodically available in the market for purchase (10:25); unbelieving neighbors may invite believers to dinner and serve such meat (10:27-29); and attendance at some cultic festivals is open to believers as an enviable social occasion (8:10). One might (correctly) surmise that the perennial problem of this letter emerges once again: How does one honor and protect holiness, being set apart for God, while one lives in the world, in the midst of the normal social exchanges that one encounters in Corinth?

The structure of 8:1–11:1 is as follows: 8:1-6, a clarification regarding what believers think they know and what they should know; 8:7-13, a caution that some are not clear on what they should know, and counsel about how the believers who are clear should relate to such persons; 9:1–10:13, a two-part digression in which Paul offers himself (9:1-27) and historic Israel (10:1-13) as the models

---

106. For a detailed study of Paul's argument and concerns here, see W. L. Willis, *Idol Meat in Corinth: The Pauline Argument in 1 Corinthians 8 and 10*, SBLDS 68 (Chico, Calif.: Scholars Press, 1985).

Central Corinth at the Time of Paul (about 50 CE)

0                  100 m

1. Theater
2. Market
3. Temple of Apollo or Athena
4. Fountain
5. Temple (of Hera Acraea?)
6. Stoa
7. Basilica (*possibly built after Paul's time)
8. Laecheum Road
9. Bath
10. *Peribolos* (courtyard) of Apollo
11. *Propylaea* (monumental entrance arch to Forum)
12. Statue of Athena
13. Temple of Tychē
14. Unidentified altar

15. Fountain of Poseidon
16. Temple of the Imperial Cult
17. Pantheon? (temple to all the gods)
18. Temple of Aphrodite
19. Unidentified building (temple? civic structure?)
20. Restaurant or tavern
21. Shops
22. *Bēma*
23. Sarapis shrine?
24. *Bouleutērion* (civic council chamber)
25. *Agonotheteion* (administrative office for the Isthmian Games)
26. *Tabularium* (public records office? library?)

of comportment for the community and within the community; 10:14-22, a section in which, through references to baptism and the Lord's supper, Paul returns to the question of eating meat offered to idols, this time considered in a cultic set-ting; and 10:23–11:1, a summing section, with ties back to 6:12-20, in which the Corinthians' earlier maxim about their freedom in Christ (cf. 6:12) is repeated, refined, and supplemented by Paul's call to imitation of himself and of Christ.

# 1 CORINTHIANS 8:1-6, THEIR QUESTION, THEIR ASSUMPTION, PAUL'S REHEARSAL OF WHAT THEY KNOW

### NIV

**8** Now about food sacrificed to idols: We know that we all possess knowledge.[a] Knowledge puffs up, but love builds up. [2]The man who thinks he knows something does not yet know as he ought to know. [3]But the man who loves God is known by God.

[4]So then, about eating food sacrificed to idols: We know that an idol is nothing at all in the world and that there is no God but one. [5]For even if there are so-called gods, whether in heaven or on earth (as indeed there are many "gods" and many "lords"), [6]yet for us there is but one God, the Father, from whom all things came and for whom we live; and there is but one Lord, Jesus Christ, through whom all things came and through whom we live.

[a]1 Or "We all possess knowledge," as you say

### NRSV

**8** Now concerning food sacrificed to idols: we know that "all of us possess knowledge." Knowledge puffs up, but love builds up. [2]Anyone who claims to know something does not yet have the necessary knowledge; [3]but anyone who loves God is known by him.

4Hence, as to the eating of food offered to idols, we know that "no idol in the world really exists," and that "there is no God but one." [5]Indeed, even though there may be so-called gods in heaven or on earth—as in fact there are many gods and many lords— [6]yet for us there is one God, the Father, from whom are all things and for whom we exist, and one Lord, Jesus Christ, through whom are all things and through whom we exist.

## COMMENTARY

Just as in the treatment of the first item from their letter (7:1), so also here Paul begins by repeating a maxim of some Corinthians: "We know that all of us have knowledge" (8:1*b*). Paul does not oppose or depreciate knowledge (cf. 2:6). As we have seen and will see again numerous times in 1 Corinthians, Paul readily turns to "what we know" as a resource for moral guidance and deliberation. So it is understandable that some of his followers would value and appeal to knowledge as they do here. But Paul's immediate response signals his unhappiness with their claim on two fronts: (1) "Knowledge *puffs up*," and puffiness or arrogance has already emerged as a problem at Corinth; and (2) knowledge is set over against love in such an

opposition as to remind one of the rival two-way tradition that has already been such a feature in the letter (see the Commentary on 1:10-17). Paul takes the Corinthians' claim about possessing knowledge as another indication of their eagerness to turn whatever they can toward status, prestige, and rank—which turn Paul has disparaged in 1:18-25; 2:6-13. The Corinthians who have forged this maxim—and it will not have been the whole community—have arrogated to themselves superior status and freedom based on their newfound knowledge in Christ. Of course, Paul shares some responsibility for contributing to such a misunderstanding because he believes that in Christ believers really do understand things differently (cf. his recognition of this in 2:6). But some at Corinth have used this difference to demarcate between the status of themselves and that of other believers in Christ, a stance Paul totally rejects.

Maxims, by nature, are allusive; they invite hearers to engage them and to fill out the larger picture that they evoke only in broad stroke. Let us consider the Corinthian maxim with a view to the larger picture it supposes. Their maxim—"We know that we all have knowledge" (8:1)—reflects a confidence that on its face Paul would appreciate, but Paul's response with three maxims of his own (more on that below) suggests that he finds problems with their maxim. The sweeping inclusiveness, "all of us," affirmed by their maxim simply does not correspond to reality as Paul sees it, as he says directly in 8:7. And one can surmise that their association of this maxim with the question of whether to eat idol meat suggests that they have a freedom to eat, that, as 8:9 will confirm, they have an ἐξουσία (*exousia*), a right, a freedom, and that they hold that all believers should be clear on the freedom to eat, possessing knowledge as they are all supposed to do.

The claim of some Corinthians to possess knowledge (8:1) would not have been strange in Paul's time. Stoics understood that knowledge leads to virtue, that knowledge leads to proper behavior, and that knowledge defines and enhances freedom. So the Corinthians' claim of knowledge is at the same time their assertion of their freedom, about what is permissible for them (cf. 6:12; 10:23). Paul shares with them the conviction that what one knows has a direct bearing on one's freedom to make consequent choices: For example, if one knows that there is no God but one, then concern about idols diminishes (8:4). His mention of "this authority/freedom [*exousia*] of yours" (8:9), however, separates him, as does his insistence in 8:7 that not all possess this knowledge, from those Corinthians who simply make their moral decisions from what they themselves know and who show no concern for how the resulting actions might bear on someone who did not have the same knowledge or assurance of what is permissible for them.[107] They are the ones who may have knowledge but not love (8:1).

As noted, in that culture, one usually does not directly reject someone's maxim; instead one adds a qualifier or places another maxim alongside for leverage. In this instance, Paul responds with three of his own maxims (8:1, 4, 4). Paul's first maxim—"Knowledge puffs up, but love builds up" (8:1 NRSV)—is followed by two verses of elaboration (8:2-3). With his first maxim, Paul critiques their placing of knowledge rather than love at the center of either their moral deliberation or their communal life in Christ. Paul has repeatedly been concerned that some of the Corinthians have been puffy and boastful (1:29, 31; 3:21; 4:6-7, 18, 19; 5:2, 6; and note 13:3-4), and the concern emerges here again. Over against knowledge, their definitional marker, Paul sets love. When love is at work, it can only bring about good for others, it can only accomplish or effect edification, upbuilding. Knowledge, while it is indeed important in some ways and though Paul has in fact admitted that he does indeed impart wisdom (2:6), is capable of abuse not only of others, by condescension, but of the one who claims it, by a self-estimate that is inordinate. Put differently, love keeps things in proportion, in perspective better than knowledge; knowledge without love is sure to come to nothing or even to cause harm. As Paul notes in 8:2, knowledge has a curious capacity to deceive the knower; as he will say eloquently later in this letter, "knowledge passes away" (13:8), knowledge without love reduces one to nothing (13:2) and gains nothing (13:3). Note well that knowledge is not in and of itself bad or worthy of spurn. What is wrong is knowledge that is carried away with itself, knowledge that vaunts itself as giving status, knowledge that may become a stumbling block for another, knowledge that is not put to work in love, and knowledge that eclipses love.

In the Greco-Roman world knowledge was inevitably linked to status, to a concern about where one stands in relation to others. In Paul's communities love is inextricably tied to service, to caring for one another. In 8:3 Paul tries to distinguish wrong knowing, which puts what one knows and its attendant status at the center of life, from the primal and definitional knowing that really counts: being known by God. When one knows oneself to be known by God, then love falls into place and knowing is placed in perspective. When one properly expresses love toward God,

---

107. For a careful and illuminating discussion of Stoic suppositions between Paul and the Corinthians in chaps. 8 and 9 and how those suppositions lend understanding to the connection of the two chapters in Paul's argumentation, see Abraham J. Malherbe, "Determinism and Free Will in Paul: The Argument of 1 Corinthians 8 and 9," in *Paul in His Hellenistic Context,* ed. T. Engberg-Pedersen (Minneapolis: Fortress, 1995) 231-55.

then one is known by God (8:3), then one's knowing serves God's love.

Paul touches on an abiding issue here. The problem is how believers can know that knowledge itself does not save them (that is gnosticism's claim) without going to the extreme of claiming that faith and knowledge must be set over against one another. The challenge for a believer is not to become an obscurantist, not to become a know-nothing, in short not to pit knowledge against faith. Faith, indeed, has knowledge that is appropriate to it, as Paul clearly understands (2:6). Paul regularly asks, "What do we know?" as a fundamental operation appropriate to moral reasoning. But, like any other good thing, knowledge can be used to seek status and, indeed, to lord it over others. Knowledge per se is not the problem either for Corinth or for faith; having it function properly in a loving and edifying fashion is the issue and the goal.

Verses 2-3 show that Paul thinks the Corinthians who boast that "all have knowledge" have turned things around backward. They have made themselves the measure of all things as if one's own knowing were the defining factor in one's standing or status, as if one were defined and given importance by what one knows. At stake for Paul is proper self-assessment, which for him can never begin with what one knows because that path will always lead to wrongful boasting and to an inflated self-estimate. For Paul the definitive knowing is *God's* knowing of us, which, if love for God is properly in place (cf. Deut 6:5), will result in *our being known,* in our receiving God's love in a way that not only claims us for God but also engages us in love toward others (cf. 13:9, 12).

Although the word does not appear in this context, grace is at issue here. It is not what believers know that sets them right with God and gives them to one another. The flow never runs that way for Paul. God's freely given, unmerited love claims the believers and establishes them. It is a delicate matter in Paul's understanding. One does not come to know God as many Greeks had assumed. Rather, one is known by God (Gal 4:9). All proper knowing proceeds from God and acknowledges that God's knowing precedes and grounds what believers know. God's knowing establishes, constitutes (cf. Exod 33:12, 17) believers, who then must caution themselves that their knowing is derivative and that what they know

should function as a guide to love rather than as an index of status and rank.

The Corinthians' maxim in v. 1*a* is, of course, partly right: All believers do have knowledge, and that in two senses. First, all believers who love God have been known by God and so they have the knowledge that is purely a gift of God and that we otherwise call "grace." Second, when love is properly in place, then what believers know can serve well as navigational markers for the travel along the road of faith. What believers know is supposed to help them live the life of love. But their sentential claim that "all possess knowledge" is too sweeping and not discriminating. It allows no specificity, no variation from one believer to the next. Because it is so vague and general, it provides no moral leverage for the question at hand but implies freedom to eat food offered to idols and thereby it seems to claim status. When knowledge is used as a status marker or is used to place others in jeopardy, then perspective has been lost, things have gotten turned around. And that is what Paul tells the Corinthians in 8:1-3.

With that necessary clarification about knowing and being known (vv. 2-3), Paul picks up once again their question about eating idol meat, and in his next two maxims (which he introduces with "We know" just as they have theirs) lays out the pertinent claims believers should know: "No idol in the world really exists" and "There is no God but one" (v. 4 NRSV). Paul addresses the issue on two fronts, with regard to idols and with regard to God: the first dismissively announced—idols do not truly exist—and the second the occasion for considerable elaboration—there is only the one God (cf. Deut 6:4, the *Shema,* the affirmation that stands at the center of Israel's faith). Paul's point is not just that there is a single deity. Staked out here is one's relation to that deity, the characteristics of that deity, and what we know about that deity— these are what really matter. Life must be lived in light of the deity who is in control (cf. 3:21-23). It is not an option to be unrelated to that God. Life must be lived, moral decisions must be rendered in keeping with what we know about that God. The nature of all being is imaginable only within the scope allowed by and dictated by the nature and purpose of God. A fundamental issue is engaged here: How does what one believes and knows about God bear on the relatively mundane decisions of everyday life? Paul's answer: absolutely critically and definitionally. To whom does one belong? What are the characteristics of the one to whom one belongs? These are recurring issues in 1 Corinthians because they are fundamental to living the life of faith, to understanding one's place in the world, and to moral reasoning.

Both maxims in v. 4 represent part of Paul's rich Jewish heritage that he has inculcated into the Corinthians' faith. Israel's revulsion at idols is clear (Exod 20:4-5, 23; 34:17; Lev 19:4; 26:1; Deut 4:15-20). So is its central claim, best exemplified in the *Shema* of Deut 6:4, that "God is one."

Paul identifies God as Father (echoing 1:3), which sets the context for the intense use of brother/sister concepts in 8:11-13, and, in what begins to sound like a creedal affirmation, God is described as the one who is the source of all things and the one for whom we exist (3:21-23; 8:6*b;* cf. 10:26). Paul identifies Christ as the one "through whom all things and we ourselves exist" (8:6*c*). The assertions about God and Christ reaffirm and refine what Paul already wrote in 3:21-23, that believers ideally should relate to the world and to all things as ones who know they belong to Christ, who belongs to God.

# REFLECTIONS

**1.** "Love builds up" (8:1). Love is Paul's most important concept in describing how believers rightly relate to one another, and it is so critical to his corrective of the Corinthians' interaction that he devotes a whole chapter to its elucidation (chap. 13). Love is not just a sentiment, not just a feeling, not merely a sort of disposition. Love works; it acts; it does things; and the chief thing it does is to edify, build up, cause growth in each of the persons who engages in it and who is engaged by it. Love is not a one-way street; it is more like the proverbial bad penny or like the widow's jar of meal and jug of oil (1 Kgs 17:8-16): You cannot get rid of it; it will not run out. Give it away profligately, prodigally, and it is never exhausted, nor is anyone shorted by the giving away; it does not have to be hoarded; it not only benefits the recipient, it rebounds (in a fuller form than it was sent) to the donor so that donor becomes recipient along with the other. Love works. Love transforms circumstances and people. The loved one is never again the same; the one who loves is never again the same. Love is thus a transaction but not a bartering; it is not susceptible to bargaining. Love, once under way, takes on a life of its own; like the grace on which it is built, it surprises. Love restores, love enlarges, and love makes whole. Most often that is what happens with love. But love is not a magic wand; love can be spurned and rejected; and sometimes love elicits its nearest of kin, hatred.

**2.** Idolatry is not simply the worship of an object as if it were God. So defined, idolatry would be no significant problem. Paul openly depicts idolatry here as having many gods and lords (8:5) that bid for our allegiance, that in some significant way claim us as belonging to them. The basic question, "To whom do you belong?" therefore, is ultimately a question of proper faithfulness or idolatry. When something takes over your life, begins to run it for you, then you have idolatry. Your false god or lord will be whatever apart from God governs your life. The possibilities are nearly limitless: It could be your work, your health, your desire for a boat, or perhaps a relative, such as a parent or even your children!

# 1 CORINTHIANS 8:7-13, PERSONS DIFFER IN KNOWLEDGE—AN IMAGINARY AND INSTRUCTIVE SCENARIO

## NIV

7But not everyone knows this. Some people are still so accustomed to idols that when they eat such food they think of it as having been sacrificed to an idol, and since their conscience is weak, it is defiled. 8But food does not bring us near to God; we are no worse if we do not eat, and no better if we do.

9Be careful, however, that the exercise of your freedom does not become a stumbling block to the weak. 10For if anyone with a weak conscience sees you who have this knowledge eating in an idol's temple, won't he be emboldened to eat what has been sacrificed to idols? 11So this weak brother, for whom Christ died, is destroyed by your knowledge. 12When you sin against your brothers in this way and wound their weak conscience, you sin against Christ. 13Therefore, if what I eat causes my brother to fall into sin, I will never eat meat again, so that I will not cause him to fall.

## NRSV

7It is not everyone, however, who has this knowledge. Since some have become so accustomed to idols until now, they still think of the food they eat as food offered to an idol; and their conscience, being weak, is defiled. 8"Food will not bring us close to God."[a] We are no worse off if we do not eat, and no better off if we do. 9But take care that this liberty of yours does not somehow become a stumbling block to the weak. 10For if others see you, who possess knowledge, eating in the temple of an idol, might they not, since their conscience is weak, be encouraged to the point of eating food sacrificed to idols? 11So by your knowledge those weak believers for whom Christ died are destroyed.[b] 12But when you thus sin against members of your family,[c] and wound their conscience when it is weak, you sin against Christ. 13Therefore, if food is a cause of their falling,[d] I will never eat meat, so that I may not cause one of them[e] to fall.

[a]The quotation may extend to the end of the verse    [b]Gk the weak brother . . . is destroyed    [c]Gk against the brothers    [d]Gk my brother's falling    [e]Gk cause my brother

# COMMENTARY

Paul indicates a problem, despite the confidence of the Corinthians who formulated the maxim in 8:1: "The knowledge is not shared by all" (8:7). Paul knows that there are believers at Corinth who still have it in their moral consciousness that idols do have some power and that to eat the meat is somehow to continue to show reverence for the deities they all used to recognize. For such persons, for whom the idols continue to represent power, eating causes defilement or staining (8:7; cf. Rom 14:23). In the heart of his deliberation, Paul lays down a defining premise that applies to himself and to all believers: "Food will not commend us to God!" (8:8; cf. Rom 14:10, 17).

In 8:7-13, Paul broadens the discussion from idol meat to all food for two reasons: (1) As noted, eating becomes a metaphor for living, and (2) the issue of eating idol meat is not a separate moral question that needs special, singular treatment. He makes sure that his auditors on either side of this question may understand with utter clarity his claim that *all* food, not just idol meat, is an indifferent matter in one's relation to God: "If we do not eat we are no worse off; if we do eat we are no better off" (8:8). The matter is indifferent. So, Paul thinks it is all right but not better if some, with clear moral consciousness, eat meat offered to idols; and it is all right, yes, even necessary, if others, with what he calls "weak conscience or consciousness," abstain.

Clearly, vv. 7-13 are more directly addressed to

the Corinthians who advocate the maxim "We know that all of us possess knowledge" and who accordingly think they have the "warrant" or "power" or "right" ("this liberty of yours," 8:9 NRSV; ἐξουσία [*exousia*], a term that will be the focus of attention in 9:1-18) to behave on the basis of that knowledge. This subgroup may well be the same ones who earlier in the letter were noted as championing their freedom under the maxim "All things are permissible *for me*" (6:12, italics added). The issue becomes palpable when someone with a weaker moral consciousness is tempted (Paul uses the term οἰκοδομέω [*oikodomeō*], "built up"— built up wrongly, understood; 8:10) to emulate the person of (greater) knowledge.

Paul's use of "build up" in 8:10 (NIV, "emboldened"; NRSV, "encouraged") is singular in his undisputed letters because only here he anticipates that believers may "edify," in the sense of encourage, someone to do something that person should not do, to do something that would not be helpful or appropriate to that individual. Love, properly functioning, will not encourage someone to do what is not appropriate, so improper and, therefore, false building up cannot be the work of love (8:1).

Paul refers to a person's moral consciousness (συνείδησις *syneidēsis*) being weak (8:7, 10, 12). Then in 8:11 he shortens the construction by referring to "the weak person." Although he does not directly mention "strong" people or persons with "strong moral consciousness" in vv. 7-13, he seems to be addressing them. First a word about *syneidēsis* in Paul, then some remarks about strong and weak.

Paul's laconic reference to *syneidēsis* here suggests that he has already taught the Corinthians about it and assumes they have it straight, so he feels free to use the term without elaboration. Across the corpus we can see that Paul supposes that a person's *syneidēsis* functions as a sort of moral scanner that is set off only when the contemplated action raises doubts in the mind or heart of the actor as to the act's propriety. It is the moral equivalent of a warning light. It serves the same function (and may be the same thing) as doubts or waverings (διακρίνω *diakrinō*) that one may experience in the face of a contemplated action (Rom 14:23; cf. Rom 4:20).

The reappearance of *syneidēsis* later in 1 Cor 10:23-30 confirms what we have observed and extends it. Paul supposes that each person has an individuated *syneidēsis*, which can be translated as a "moral consciousness" that is specific and pertinent only to that individual. Further, each person is to respect the moral consciousness of others so that, as in Paul's fictional dinner conversation in 10:27-29, when an individual expresses reservations about an action, the hearer must honor that person's scruples even when the contemplated action does not raise similar problems for the hearer.

This is a window onto Paul's anthropology and onto his understanding of moral reasoning. For Paul, each individual has a moral consciousness that allows a given range of actions without setting off any warning bells of impropriety or inappropriateness. Verses 7-13 show that a person's moral consciousness is directly related to one's understanding, in this instance to what one knows— that is, to what one truly understands. Paul holds (8:13) that not everyone has the understanding that idols are nothing. For *those* people, their moral consciousness is limited—that is, it is weak regarding this issue. All persons must act within the scope of their own moral consciousness. And, there is nothing wrong or inadequate about the more limited (weaker) moral consciousness. Just as food will not commend a person to God, so also knowledge does not. The scope or fullness of one's knowledge of that which one understands in such a degree as to be able to act upon it is not what commends to God, but living properly within what one understands and what one views as appropriate.

So the "weak one" is not to be considered inadequate or inferior. That person is merely at one stage or point on the growth continuum, which runs from more limited moral consciousness to a fuller moral consciousness. As the Corinthian babies in faith (3:1) are expected to grow up and mature, so believers are to care for, nurture, and build one another up in love.

Paul's way of describing the dynamics of his imaginary scenario tells us much about his understanding of community. The "weak person" is (a) "brother or sister" (4 times in vv. 11-13), (b) under the same Father (8:6), and (c) is one for "whom Christ died" (8:11). For each of these three reasons the weak person is valuable and deserving of consideration. To act without consideration toward such a brother or sister is labeled by Paul as "sinning against the brethren," and even more powerfully as "sinning against Christ!" (8:12). Christian community is founded on the one fact: Christ died for each person. That, and nothing else, is the common basis of Christian community. Therefore, to cause harm or even stumbling for someone for whom Christ died is to work calumny against Christ, who died for that person and claimed her or him as Christ's own. And because believers are brothers and sisters in Christ, any harm done to another is damaging to the family of God.

Worthy of note here is Paul's notion that sin is not an act that is purely and simply between oneself and Christ (or God). Rather, sin inevitably also affects others. So just as one's faith should always express itself in love to those around one, so sin, that broken relationship with God or Christ, always affects not only the sinner but also those in contact with the sinner (cf. 5:6-7).

Strikingly, Paul does not tell the Corinthians what they ought to do. Instead, he brings this section to a conclusion by saying what *he* would do, or not do (v. 13), and thereby offers himself as a model, as one who is at least as strong in moral consciousness as the strongest of them but who would abstain from meat altogether (probably a resort to hyperbole) rather than to scandalize or cause a brother to fall (v. 13). Paul, the radical model, shows by exemplification what is more important and what is less; and his exemplification in v. 13 paves the way for the protracted exemplification that we call chap. 9.

What began in v. 1 as a question about eating idol meat has become, by the end of the section, a question about eating meat in general—and even abstaining from eating meat when, despite one's own adequate moral consciousness, one sees that one's actions might cause harm to another member of Christ—as an example of proper consideration of others in the exercise of one's freedom in Christ. And for an elaboration of himself as moral exemplar worthy of emulation, he turns to a digression that includes chap. 9 and extends to 10:13, after which he will return to the issues raised by their question regarding meat offered to idols.

# REFLECTIONS

**1.** The Corinthians' question of what one can appropriately eat inescapably raises the question of one's relation to creation and, therefore, ultimately to God. The New Testament often portrays Jesus as giving thanks to God at the breaking of bread or at table fellowship (Mark 6:41; 8:6 and par.; 14:23 and par.; John 6:11), because whatever one eats expresses a dependence of the eater upon some of the remainder of God's creation, and therefore ultimately a dependence upon God as Creator. God of all creation is the source of all things and is the goal of human existence. Humans—and all of creation—are from God and all of human life is lived toward God. So the question of eating, precisely because it is such a perfect metaphor for describing all of life, can be weighed out ultimately and only in relation to God. Therefore, what one knows and believes about God must be factored into any decision or choice about what one eats. And if eating is a metaphor for all of life, as Paul indeed takes it to be in 10:31 at the end of this section of the letter, then whatever one decides or chooses must ultimately be decided and chosen in the light of what one knows and believes about God.

**2.** Paul describes people as having stronger and weaker moral consciousnesses because he thinks of believers as having different measures of faith (Rom 12:3), as being further along the line of development from babies in the faith (whose moral consciousness is not strongly formed or as fully instructed) to the more mature in faith. And we know from 3:1-2 that Paul thinks the Corinthians have a good many babies in the faith among them. Accordingly, he advises the Corinthians that as they make their choices they must be careful not to harm others among them who may be less mature and, therefore, *more susceptible to influence* to overreach. Wrongful building up must be a concern. Therefore, believers must factor into their moral deliberation not only how the contemplated action fits them and their relation to God but also how such an action might affect another. Believers are capable of self-control, and they are responsible for their decisions and the actions based upon them. But weaker believers must perforce look to and learn from their stronger-in-faith brothers and sisters who thus inherit a certain added responsibility to choose and to act with the weaker siblings in mind. Believers are not only responsible for themselves and their actions; they are responsible for each other and the way their deeds set examples for others.

With respect to modeling, Paul concludes the chapter by encouraging each of the auditors to model his care, his love for others. But ingredient to the chapter is also a call to the stronger-in-faith believers to take their obligations as models more seriously. Modern believers should be more self-conscious about setting a good example in each and every decision and choice and action. Even if it had no effect on others, it would surely enrich our own faithful response to God. And who knows what use God might make of it in the eyes of someone who observes us?

**3.** For Paul, sin is never simply a private act between an individual and God or Christ. Such a wrong relation with Christ or with God always inevitably spills over and harms others as well. We hear persons say that what they do with their bodies, for example, is their own business and not anybody else's. Paul would have none of that. If you harm your body, it affects others in ways you do not imagine. Sin in whatever form is corrosive not only of the individual sinner but of those proximate. Paul's notion, therefore, is totally out of joint with the modern inclination to privatize not only our relation to God but also our moral choices, both good and bad.

# 1 CORINTHIANS 9:1–10:13, EXTENDED DIGRESSION CONSISTING OF TWO EXAMPLES

## OVERVIEW

Digressions allow an author to bring a fresh perspective alongside a troublesome deliberative issue.[108] In this case, Paul's digression actually runs through 10:13 and consists of two examples, one largely positive (Paul himself, 9:1-27), one negative (most of those in the exodus, 10:1-13).[109] Paul presents himself as the example of how a believer who knows he has rights or warrants or powers behaves in love toward others so that they are properly built up (8:1) and not destroyed (8:11). Paul's digression here leaves it for the auditors to make the connection and application to their own situation.

The structure of this digression is rather straightforwardly a chiasmus (A B B´ A´). Paul is established as exemplar, as the model of one who is as free as anyone (item A) and as the Corinthians' apostle possessed of as many rights as anyone (item B) in 9:1-2. Paul's self-depiction as apostle (item B´) in 9:3-18 is of one who has rights but chooses not to exercise them. His description of his accommodating evangelistic style (9:19-23) shows his undisputed freedom (item A´) to choose for himself an ironic slavery in service of the gospel (cf. 7:21-23). The first part of the digression, that which is focused on Paul, closes with an exhortation that is cast in athletic metaphors (9:24-25) and a final offering of himself as an example (9:26-27). The structure and function of the second part of the digression (the depiction of Israel in 10:1-13) will be discussed later.

108. Wilhelm Wuellner, "Greek Rhetoric and Pauline Argumentation," *Early Christian Literature and the Classical Intellectual Tradition: In honorem Robert M. Grant,* ed. W. R. Schoedel and R. L. Wilken, Théologie Historique 54 (Paris: Etudes Beauchesne, 1979) 177-88.

109. In agreement with Wuellner, ibid., 186-87, that the digression runs from 9:1 through 10:13.

# 1 Corinthians 9:1-27, Paul As Exemplar

## 1 Corinthians 9:1-2, Identification of Paul As Free and As Apostle

NIV

NIV

9 Am I not free? Am I not an apostle? Have I not seen Jesus our Lord? Are you not the result of my work in the Lord? ²Even though I may not be an apostle to others, surely I am to you! For you are the seal of my apostleship in the Lord.

NRSV

9 Am I not free? Am I not an apostle? Have I not seen Jesus our Lord? Are you not my work in the Lord? ²If I am not an apostle to others, at least I am to you; for you are the seal of my apostleship in the Lord.

## COMMENTARY

The digression opens with two questions stated, as Greek allows, in a form that expects a yes answer. The first question—"I am free, right?"—may invite an explanation (which is at the heart of the digression's purpose) because Paul has just declared that if food causes a brother's fall Paul will simply quit eating meat (8:13). Some of his auditors may well have thought, "Some freedom!"

The second question—"I am apostle, right?"—and its attached comments about seeing Jesus (cf. 15:8) and about his having brought the gospel to them (9:1c-2) sets the stage for Paul's exemplification of apostolic comportment as a textbook study of claimable rights that go unclaimed for a purpose (9:3-18). (See Reflections at 9:24-27.)

## 1 Corinthians 9:3-14, Paul, the One of Unexcelled Rights, Chooses Not to Use Them

NIV

³This is my defense to those who sit in judgment on me. ⁴Don't we have the right to food and drink? ⁵Don't we have the right to take a believing wife along with us, as do the other apostles and the Lord's brothers and Cephas*? ⁶Or is it only I and Barnabas who must work for a living?

⁷Who serves as a soldier at his own expense? Who plants a vineyard and does not eat of its grapes? Who tends a flock and does not drink of the milk? ⁸Do I say this merely from a human point of view? Doesn't the Law say the same thing? ⁹For it is written in the Law of Moses: "Do not muzzle an ox while it is treading out the grain."* Is it about oxen that God is concerned? ¹⁰Surely he says this for us, doesn't he? Yes, this

NRSV

3This is my defense to those who would examine me. ⁴Do we not have the right to our food and drink? ⁵Do we not have the right to be accompanied by a believing wife,* as do the other apostles and the brothers of the Lord and Cephas? ⁶Or is it only Barnabas and I who have no right to refrain from working for a living? ⁷Who at any time pays the expenses for doing military service? Who plants a vineyard and does not eat any of its fruit? Or who tends a flock and does not get any of its milk?

8Do I say this on human authority? Does not the law also say the same? ⁹For it is written in the law of Moses, "You shall not muzzle an ox while it is treading out the grain." Is it for oxen that God

*5 That is, Peter    *9 Deut. 25:4

*Gk a sister as wife

NIV

was written for us, because when the plowman plows and the thresher threshes, they ought to do so in the hope of sharing in the harvest. [11]If we have sown spiritual seed among you, is it too much if we reap a material harvest from you? [12]If others have this right of support from you, shouldn't we have it all the more?

But we did not use this right. On the contrary, we put up with anything rather than hinder the gospel of Christ. [13]Don't you know that those who work in the temple get their food from the temple, and those who serve at the altar share in what is offered on the altar? [14]In the same way, the Lord has commanded that those who preach the gospel should receive their living from the gospel.

NRSV

is concerned? [10]Or does he not speak entirely for our sake? It was indeed written for our sake, for whoever plows should plow in hope and whoever threshes should thresh in hope of a share in the crop. [11]If we have sown spiritual good among you, is it too much if we reap your material benefits? [12]If others share this rightful claim on you, do not we still more?

Nevertheless, we have not made use of this right, but we endure anything rather than put an obstacle in the way of the gospel of Christ. [13]Do you not know that those who are employed in the temple service get their food from the temple, and those who serve at the altar share in what is sacrificed on the altar? [14]In the same way, the Lord commanded that those who proclaim the gospel should get their living by the gospel.

# COMMENTARY

Paul sets it forward as a mock defense (ἀπολογία *apologia*) for anyone who would "examine" (cf. 4:3-4) him, and he uses the form to make his points. This is not truly a self-defense,[110] but a rhetorical device designed to invite hearers to sort through the claims Paul is about to make. Paul uses self-description in order to set himself up as the example the Corinthians should emulate. Because form follows function, we cannot be surprised by the heavy usage of rhetorical questions; in 9:3-12 alone there are twelve. In fact, the rhetorical questions are employed in such a fashion as to put the readers on the stand, so to speak. The readers are placed in the position of being led by the inquisitor, Paul, through a series of questions that in the Greek clearly expect a yes answer. Paul's mock defense functions much as the frequent Matthean parable lead-in—"What do you think?" (Matt 18:12; 21:28)—and engages the auditors.

110. So, convincingly, Wendell Willis, "An Apostolic Apologia? The Form and Function of 1 Cor 9," *JSNT* 24 (1985) 33-48. Mitchell, while acknowledging that scholars have at times read chap. 9 as a self-defense, primarily because Paul uses the term *apologia* in 9:3, has a careful and compelling critique of that reading and instead rightly takes chapter 9 as another Pauline exemplification. See Margaret M. Mitchell, *Paul and the Rhetoric of Reconciliation* (Louisville: Westminster/John Knox, 1991) 243-49, esp. 244-55n. 330.

At issue is not whether Paul is their apostle; even if they wanted to deny that, they could not (9:1*b*-2). The Corinthians are clearly his "work in the Lord" (9:1*b*); they are the seal of his "apostleship in the Lord" (9:2*b*). Even if it were possible for other believing communities to deny Paul's apostleship (cf. paternity, 4:14), the Corinthians simply and surely could not (9:2*a*).

Paul chooses to make his case by depicting himself as the apostle of great rights and great freedom who exercises those rights and freedom (*exousia*, "warrant," "power," "right"; a term he just used in 8:9, "this *exousia* of yours," not at all or at least in a cautionary way; in 9:3-18 the term appears six times as a leitmotif of the passage, 9:4-6, 12, 18) with great care—or not at all if someone might be harmed.

Paul thinks the matter is beyond dispute—and this is the burden of his mock defense: As an apostle he has rights to receive support (9:4-6) as surely as the other apostles do; soldiers, vineyard tenders, and even shepherds have a claim of support from their labors (9:7; cf. Deut 20:6); Scripture upholds it—the law says even oxen are provisioned in return for their labor (9:8-11; Deut 25:4); temple servers eat from the sacrifices (9:13; Deut 18:1-5;

Num 18:8ff.), and the Lord declared that those preaching the gospel should get their living from it (9:14; cf. Luke 10:7; Matt 10:10). Into this stack of arguments—which must be counted as rhetorical overkill—whose purpose has been to argue decisively that he has rights that no one among the Corinthians could deny, he inserts the forceful statement: "If others enjoy this *exousia* with you, how much more do we?" (9:12). He follows it with his programmatic exemplary posturing: "We have not used this *exousia,* but we endure all things rather than give some hindrance to the gospel of Christ" (9:12).

It is a curiosity that begs for some explanation: He has spent nine verses (vv. 4-12) establishing beyond question that he has rights and in fact resumes the claim in vv. 13-14—and yet his point is that he has not exercised them. He has rights beyond the scope of anyone in the Corinthian community—"how much more do we?" (v. 12); they must, he thinks, also grant that. Yet, he pointedly reminds them that he has not used those rights. The crucial issue is, Why? The answer is already in v. 12: It is better not to exercise one's rights, even though one does not thereby give them up, than to risk hindrance to the gospel (9:12) or do harm to one of the children of the gospel (8:9), to a brother or sister for whom Christ died (8:11).

The key claim in Paul's mock defense is 9:12*b:*

"But we pass over all things in silence [στέγω *stegō*] lest we obscure [lit., "give a hindrance to"] the gospel of Christ." Each part of this dense construction merits examination. The verb in the first clause is *stegō*, which has a semantic range from "endure" or "bear" or "stand" to "pass over in silence," to "keep to oneself," or to "throw a cloak of silence" over.[111] This verb next appears in 13:7, where it describes how love works, which, as it turns out, is exactly what Paul is describing in his mock defense without once using the term: how love bears on the exercise of one's *exousia.* What Paul affirms in 9:12*b* is that he has chosen to look the other way, to disregard his rights, to overlook them across the board, because love calls for—and here he can express it in either of two ways—making sure that no obstacle is placed in the way of the gospel of Christ or in the way of one who has been the recipient of that gospel—namely, a brother or sister in Christ. He of the unexcelled rights has chosen not to employ them because of love. So his lengthy "defense" of his rights has not been made because anyone at Corinth has denied that Paul has them. Rather Paul wants the Corinthians to see that loving means not using whatever rights one has when the employment of those rights might hinder the gospel or harm one of the gospel's children. (See Reflections at 9:24-27.)

111. BAGD, 765-66.

# 1 Corinthians 9:15-18, Paul, Free Not to Exercise His Rights, Is Bound to Preach the Gospel

| NIV | NRSV |
| --- | --- |
| [15]But I have not used any of these rights. And I am not writing this in the hope that you will do such things for me. I would rather die than have anyone deprive me of this boast. [16]Yet when I preach the gospel, I cannot boast, for I am compelled to preach. Woe to me if I do not preach the gospel! [17]If I preach voluntarily, I have a reward; if not voluntarily, I am simply discharging the trust committed to me. [18]What then is my reward? Just this: that in preaching the gospel I may offer it free of charge, and so not make use of my rights in preaching it. | 15But I have made no use of any of these rights, nor am I writing this so that they may be applied in my case. Indeed, I would rather die than that—no one will deprive me of my ground for boasting! [16]If I proclaim the gospel, this gives me no ground for boasting, for an obligation is laid on me, and woe to me if I do not proclaim the gospel! [17]For if I do this of my own will, I have a reward; but if not of my own will, I am entrusted with a commission. [18]What then is my reward? Just this: that in my proclamation I may make the gospel free of charge, so as not to make full use of my rights in the gospel. |

# Commentary

Paul anticipates a possible misunderstanding of his purpose in his mock defense. Verses 15-18 counter with a flat denial that Paul's purpose in writing all this is to do now what he has never done with the Corinthians before—namely, to cash in on his apostolic rights. A remarkable self-portrait of Paul emerges in these verses: As free as he is in so many ways, he is captive to his call; he has not decided to preach the gospel; he has no choice; he is "entrusted with a commission" (v. 17 NRSV). Therefore, he is not due a "wage" ("reward," vv. 17-18 NRSV); he has no "wage," no payoff, except that in his preaching he makes the gospel of grace properly free of charge (i.e., not something that someone earns!) and that necessarily leaves him free not to take advantage of his *exousia*, his "right."

Paul is a combination of necessity and free will; he is a slave to God, a slave whose heart has been unhardened and whose mind has been renewed, and whose will has been revitalized. As to his preaching the gospel, he has no choice; he must do it or suffer the woes appropriate to his failure to do what he is called to do. Yet he freely enslaves (that is his own strong word and image) himself to all people (9:19) because of the very gospel he freely serves and offers free of charge (9:18).

In chap. 7 Paul had advised the Corinthians of the eschatological way of living "as if not" (7:29-31), and Paul now seems to be modeling before them what it would mean to live "as if not" having *exousia:* It would mean having the right and the freedom that goes with it, but it would mean also not needing to exercise the right or act out the freedom if to do so might cause any "hindrance to the gospel" or harm anyone "for whom Christ died." Paul has offered himself as "exhibit A" of the one who has abundant rights and freedom but chooses not to exercise them out of consideration—"love" is Paul's code word for this proper concern—for others.

Some scholars mistakenly say that Paul "gives up" or "renounces" his rights or freedom here[112]

and advocates the same for others, but that is to misunderstand Paul. He does not give up his freedom or his rights; instead, he decides not to exercise his freedom or his rights in certain circumstances—and that involves a very different understanding of freedom. As the letter proceeds he will describe circumstances in which believers would be free to exercise their *exousia* without fear of harming another or hindering the gospel. In fact, in the next chapter Paul will apply the principle he is here enunciating. We will read of his advising the Corinthians that they should feel free to eat whatever is sold in the meat market because, he supposes, to do so in the privacy of one's home causes neither a hindrance to the gospel nor harm to another believer's moral consciousness.

The discussion thus far in chap. 9 requires that Paul, who opened this digression with "I am free" (9:1), address directly just what this curiously abridgeble freedom in Christ means, because someone might say this sounds less like freedom and more like slavery, like being bound by someone else's limited moral consciousness. Paul treats that problem by describing his evangelistic practice (9:19-23), which once again gives the readers not only a window onto his own self-understanding but a picture of how he decides, always in service to the gospel, to accommodate to others. Freedom and slavery are now once again (cf. 7:21-23) the categories in which Paul casts his reflections; in an earlier digression Paul has already said that one's calling in the Lord relativizes not only slavery but also freedom: A slave "is a freedman of the Lord" and the free person "is a slave of Christ" (7:22). Nevertheless, Paul's claim in 9:19—"I, being free from all people, have made myself a slave to all"—must have been shocking to his contemporaries' ears: Paul, the freest of persons, is bound by the gospel, after all (9:16), and in it and for it he chooses to live the life of service to all so that he "might win the more" (9:19)—that is, so that he could carry out the call with which he is entrusted (9:17).

There is almost a playfulness in Paul's images through the heart of this digression as he uses commercial terms to talk about actions and transactions on a level quite beyond commerce. The proclaimers

---

112. C. K. Barrett, *A Commentary on the First Epistle to the Corinthians,* 2nd ed. (London: Adam & Charles Black, 1971) 200, writes of "a serious limitation" and a restriction of Paul's liberty. F. F. Bruce, *1 and 2 Corinthians,* NCBC (Grand Rapids: Eerdmans, 1971), expresses it in the following phrases: "curtail his own freedom" (83), "voluntary relinquishing of his right . . . voluntary limitation of his liberty" (86). Roman Garrison, "Paul's Use of the Athletic Metaphor in 1 Corinthians 9," *SR* 22 (1993) 214: "sacrifice of his freedom."

of the gospel "should get their living by the gospel" (9:14 NRSV; equally possible from the Greek: "should live [i.e., get their life] from the gospel"). Paul is obligated to place before (τίθημι *tithēmi,* a technical term of commerce for "depositing" or "setting aside")[113] people a gospel "free of charge" (9:18); he does not do it for the "wage" but receives a "wage" nevertheless (9:17-18*a*); and he becomes a slave to all so that he can "win" (κερδαίνω *kerdainō*) more people—that is, convert, but the term also has the semantic ring "to gain, make a profit."

113. BAGD, 816.

He does "all things" for the gospel so that he can be a "partner" (συγκοινωνός *synkoinōnos,* the term ordinarily has commercial overtones in the Greco-Roman world) in the gospel (9:23). The language is allusive; it reaches beyond itself, stretching categories, to carry unaccustomed freight, indeed to carry freight that must be expressed in concepts with which he and his hearers have some familiarity. The point never lies either on the level of commerce and transactions or in the playfulness of language, but in the truth toward which it pushes the hearers, a truth about the communal dynamics of the life of faith. (See Reflections at 9:24-27.)

# 1 Corinthians 9:19-23, Paul's Evangelistic and Exemplary Adaptability

### NIV

[19]Though I am free and belong to no man, I make myself a slave to everyone, to win as many as possible. [20]To the Jews I became like a Jew, to win the Jews. To those under the law I became like one under the law (though I myself am not under the law), so as to win those under the law. [21]To those not having the law I became like one not having the law (though I am not free from God's law but am under Christ's law), so as to win those not having the law. [22]To the weak I became weak, to win the weak. I have become all things to all men so that by all possible means I might save some. [23]I do all this for the sake of the gospel, that I may share in its blessings.

### NRSV

[19]For though I am free with respect to all, I have made myself a slave to all, so that I might win more of them. [20]To the Jews I became as a Jew, in order to win Jews. To those under the law I became as one under the law (though I myself am not under the law) so that I might win those under the law. [21]To those outside the law I became as one outside the law (though I am not free from God's law but am under Christ's law) so that I might win those outside the law. [22]To the weak I became weak, so that I might win the weak. I have become all things to all people, that I might by all means save some. [23]I do it all for the sake of the gospel, so that I may share in its blessings.

# COMMENTARY

In these verses, in which *kerdainō* appears five times, "winning" or "gaining" people for the gospel is the dominant motif; it is the governing focus of Paul's life in response to his call. Irony abounds. The one who most exemplifies freedom in Christ and who has no choice but to preach the gospel as he is called to do has freely chosen to enslave himself to all for the sake of the gospel (9:19, 23). As Paul depicts his evangelistic efforts, his voluntary slavery to all *involves a fundamental and exemplary accommodation to people as and where he*

*finds them.* To Jews, to those "under the law," Paul became as a Jew, as one under the law, though he is quick to remind his readers that he, the one who advocates living "as if not" (7:29-31), is not under the law—but all of this was for the sole purpose of winning, gaining for the gospel, the ones to whom he accommodates (9:20). The same regards gentiles, whom Paul here calls "those outside the law" and to whom he became as one outside the law—though he assures his readers that he is not outside the law of God but "in the law of Christ," probably meaning under the rule of Christ—to win them. His readers, mostly gentiles, will surely recognize what he here so pithily describes and will no doubt positively identify with him and with their experience of the gospel through him. That identification sets them up rhetorically for the next statement: "I became to the weak as a weak person, so that I might win the weak" (9:22).

As surely as Paul has made common cause with all the Corinthian believers, his explicit identification with the weak must be startling to those who imagine themselves as strong, not weak. In 9:22, Paul's voluntary identification with the weak must remind the readers of his urging them only a chapter earlier (8:10-12) to recognize that some weaker brothers and sisters may not be clear about idols and should, accordingly, not be encouraged, built up, beyond their moral consciousness.

Paul's self-portrait in this digression is complex in proportion to the dilemma he is addressing: On the one hand he pictures himself as superlative in his freedom and in his *exousia*, his "right" that pertains to his high status as an apostle, and he treats it as if he assumes that they recognize this self-portrait and readily identify with his strength and determination. On the other hand, he paints a picture of himself as a voluntary slave who, for the sake of the gospel, identifies with the weak. (This reference must surely hark back to the persons mentioned in 8:7ff. who do not possess the knowledge that idols have no real existence and that there is only one God.) Paul, the exemplary

strong, the free person, stands in an imitable way with the weak in the gospel, on account of the gospel, as a requirement of the gospel. As he does, so should every believer.

Then in the formulation—the first part of which most modern people know even if they do not know that Paul is the source of it—"I have become all things to all people in order by all means [or "at least"] to save some" (9:22*b*)—Paul tries to capture his principle of accommodation that he believes so fundamental to life lived in the gospel. His is compressed language, squeezing much into few words. Paul knows that it is not he who saves, but God. Similarly, Paul does not see in this evangelistic accommodation a loss of identity of himself or of the gospel. Intrinsic to it, however, is a fundamental principle that Paul has seized upon and that informs his entire ministry: The gospel, the power of God, always encounters and engages people where they are, where they live, in their social matrix. Inevitably, the gospel moves them and changes them, but it always comes to them, engages them, and nourishes them from that very point, as and where they are. For the concern at hand—the divisiveness of the community and the independent arrogance of some of the believers—Paul's self-portrait as one who accommodates to others, even to the weak, invites his hearers, who readily enough identify with Paul as free person, to identify with him also as voluntary servant who accommodates to the weak and to their needs for the sake of the gospel. (See Reflections at 9:24-27.)

# 1 Corinthians 9:24-27, Paul, the Athlete Who Takes Care Not to Be Disqualified

**NIV**

24Do you not know that in a race all the runners run, but only one gets the prize? Run in such a way as to get the prize. 25Everyone who competes in the games goes into strict training. They do it to get a crown that will not last; but we do it to get a crown that will last forever. 26Therefore I do not run like a man running aimlessly; I do not fight like a man beating the air. 27No, I beat my body and make it my slave so that after I have preached to others, I myself will not be disqualified for the prize.

**NRSV**

24Do you not know that in a race the runners all compete, but only one receives the prize? Run in such a way that you may win it. 25Athletes exercise self-control in all things; they do it to receive a perishable wreath, but we an imperishable one. 26So I do not run aimlessly, nor do I box as though beating the air; 27but I punish my body and enslave it, so that after proclaiming to others I myself should not be disqualified.

# COMMENTARY

As Paul draws the first part of the digression to a close, he invites his readers, so familiar with the Athenaic and Isthmian games, the latter probably having been staged no more than eight miles from Corinth and most recently less than a year prior to this writing, to think of themselves as athletes, as indeed he considers himself. In the Greco-Roman world athleticism was highly valued, athletes were honored, and every major city had an arena. The games were analogous to war; the events were often those associated with battle. This association of games and battle fits Paul's notion that God's plan is like a battle and believers must be fit and ready (cf. 2 Cor 6:7; 1 Thess 5:8). To be the very best possible athlete—the function of the "only one wins the prize" argument (9:24)—requires discipline and self-control, self-mastery[114] "in everything" as everyone in that culture surely knew; and it is this point upon which Paul seizes. Craftily using plurals in an inclusive way, Paul reminds the Corinthians that, to paraphrase, "we exercise self-control in all things . . . in order to receive an imperishable wreath or crown" as victors (9:25). Believers are like famous athletes[115] in that believers must exercise self-control "in all things" (πάντα panta, 9:25); they are unlike those athletes in that believers are running for imperishable rewards. In 9:25 Paul's emphasis lies on the single term panta, "in all things," "in everything." Typically, Paul views life as an integrated whole; all of life is to be placed in service to the gospel and others. No compartmentalization. So also here no part of life is exempt from self-control; self-indulgence must be set aside. All of his concern with self-control is Paul's modeling for his auditors the moral life lived with the full discipline and consideration of others. To be sure, some Corinthians may think of themselves as free like Paul. Now in these verses he invites them to be disciplined "in all things" as he is—not only disciplined, but also committed to voluntary slavery and identification with the weak.

114. Stanley K. Stowers, *A Rereading of Romans: Justice, Jews, and Gentiles* (New Haven: Yale University Press, 1994) 45-52, for a treatment of self-mastery in the Greco-Roman world.
115. Garrison, "Paul's Use of the Athletic Metaphor in 1 Corinthians 9," 212-14.

So it is with him, Paul says. He runs not aimlessly (unstated but assumed is that he knows the goal toward which he races). He does not simply shadowbox, but he keeps his body (= himself) under the most rigorous, deliberate discipline; indeed (to no one's surprise), he likens it to a sort of self-imposed slavery once again (9:27; cf. 9:19). And so he expects of all his readers not only rigorous, self-imposed discipline but also intentional, voluntary slavery to one another in Christ. This reference to "body" and its proper care surely echoes a similar point made earlier about proper temple maintenance of the body for the resident Holy Spirit (3:16-17). And the slavery Paul here embraces is consonant with the perfect slavery in love that is complete freedom.

Along this line it must not go unnoticed that when Paul describes the proper discipline appropriate to life in the gospel he expresses it in two verbs bearing on τὸ σῶμα (to sōma), the body, that is, his own self, understood. The verbs ὑπωπιάζω (hypōpiazō, "to treat roughly" or here "to impose discipline") and δουλαγωγέω (doulagōgeō, "to enslave or bring into subjection") surround and have as their direct object "the body, the self" (9:27). Paul has already touched on the self-mastery motif in this letter (cf. esp. in 7:38, but implicitly in 8:7-13 and 9:12b-14). In 9:26-27 Paul explicitly exemplifies the need and importance of self-mastery as a part of the daily life of the believer this side of the last judgment.

Of equal importance here is Paul's use of sōma as his self because his choice of that expression enforces significant links to what he has already written in 1 Corinthians (and will provide a ground for his comments on sōma in 1 Cor 15:35-44). As the auditor thinks back to Paul's earlier assumptions about sōma in this letter, two passages must come to mind. One is the hinge-passage (6:12-20) where Paul claims that the believing self, the sōma, belongs to the Lord in a fundamentally definitional way. The sōma is what it is in respect to the Lord, as reckoned in its relation to the Lord (6:13), and the Lord is for the sōma, which is related to the self, as in a marriage. The connection is so secure as to be expressible in the striking image: Your sōma is the temple of the Holy Spirit

(3:16-17). Paul's own exemplary self-portrait in 9:27 shows that, translating from his athletic metaphors employed there, he goes to all lengths to ensure that he practices proper temple maintenance on his own *sōma*.

The first part of the digression closes with an ironic note that may echo Paul's earlier cry of "Woe" if he does not preach the gospel. Would it not be ironic, he says, if after preaching to others he failed to practice what he preached, and, at the judgment, if he were found to be "disqualified" (*adokimos,* a technical term of athletics in which a competitor fails the test or is thrown out of the competition)? The implication is palpable: If Paul, the chosen apostle, can anticipate that he might be found disqualified in the last judgment because he did not exercise a training code and life appropriate to the gospel, then all other athletes in the gospel must reevaluate their discipline and practice and bring themselves into comportment with the gospel. With that, Paul closes the largely positive part of the digression and turns to the story of Israel's exodus out of Egypt (10:1-13) as a means of advancing his argument with a cautionary illustration precisely on this same point.

# REFLECTIONS

**1.** This entire section is a study in exemplification, an offering of models of comportment for the life of faith. Do you look for the ways in which others offer examples of living that would be worth emulating?

**2.** Paul's opening self-portrait is a study in Christian freedom. His first question, asked in Greek in such a way as to expect a positive answer, "I am free, am I not?" sets the stage for his presentation of himself as an exemplar.

What is freedom? How do we understand it? One of the most popular modern definitions is "free from all constraints and limits." In Paul's time the Stoics thought that one gained freedom by risking less, by placing less of oneself as vulnerable to the actions of Fate or to the doings of others. So one could partially characterize Stoic freedom as a retreat, a withdrawal. Is Paul's decision not to exercise his rights a retreat or withdrawal also? Paul's own discussion of freedom is focused on his right to act, to decide, or to do as he wishes.

A part of freedom is the capacity to choose the very thing that is required. There is a strangeness to the fact that love is commanded of us. How can love, which depends so much on the freedom and spontaneity of the heart, be commanded? Only because the ones commanded to love cannot imagine doing anything else! So they freely embrace what they are ordered and compelled to do. But the difference is the free embrace. Love is perfect slavery; love is perfect freedom.

**3.** Love requires discipline; it is not an accident that Paul uses boxing as a metaphor for the life of discipline (9:24-27). In order to achieve the goal (the eschatological prize of God's positive judgment), Paul models discipline where one's choices and the actions dependent upon them are not chosen with a view to what might give the most immediate personal pleasure, but are chosen with God's judgment in view—namely, that Paul might avoid being found unworthy or disqualified. So true freedom calls for sorting through the possible courses of action not first with regard to one's rights, no matter how strong or numerous they are, but with regard to what serves the well-being of others and, therefore, the common good.

Paul's final description of his exemplary self here is of the athlete, the boxer, who exercises self-discipline in all things. Paul features an irony: He who would help others by delivering the gospel to them could ironically end up disqualified (like the athlete thrown out of the competition). In this Pauline irony there is a cautionary word for all who, powered by the gospel, busy themselves so much with "helping" and "rescuing" others that they end up not taking proper care with their own self-discipline and thereby risk becoming disqualified. Giving of the self without proper care of the self can be self-destructive (cf. a similar note carried over into 10:12).

**4.** Paul's assumption throughout 9:1–10:13 is that the Corinthians do not suffer from lack of self-love and self-interest. We do not know what Paul might have said about proper self-love, but his twice-stated embrace of the command to "love your neighbor *as yourself*" (Rom 13:9; Gal 5:14; Lev 19:18) shows that he recognizes self-love as a possible base from which to reckon. In Paul's letters we have access only to his treating the balance tilted the other way, toward improper love of others. One could imagine Paul having critiqued the Corinthians as lacking proper self-love when they seem so desperate to act with no consideration/love of others. A modern Christian might do well to attempt the fashioning of such an argument because in the doing of it one would have to find a way to talk about how loving others is ultimately a form of (proper) self-love.

**5.** The "as-if-not" quality of life that Paul advocated in 7:29-31 is in chapter 9 put on display. Paul, who is the most free of all, willingly makes himself the servant of all (9:19) in behalf of the gospel. Accordingly, in some respects he lives "as if not" free; in others he lives "as if not" a slave. Put differently, service in the gospel leaves him free to be a slave of others, but in such a way that his freedom is enhanced, not lessened. Also, he relates to his indisputably considerable rights "as if not" having them. Be careful to understand: He has the rights—he and the Corinthians concede that—but he lives with them while being free from having to exercise them. Paul *insists* on his rights, enumerates them at length, and then *forgoes the exercise of his rights,* without giving them up at all. He still has the rights. He simply overrides the use of them with his concern for what serves the gospel and what serves others.

**6.** "All things to all people." This phrase, taken out of context, has come to mean all sorts of things to all sorts of people. First, the context in the letter. Paul is describing his adaptability in service of evangelism. The function of this statement is identical to that of the "I decided to know nothing among you except Christ" (2:2). Both are hyperboles designed to state unmistakably what is the governing force around which other activities are arrayed. For Paul, whatever advances the gospel is what governs his comportment. But, second, Paul relates one of the secrets of his evangelistic prowess: He goes to people, where they are, on their own terms. He does not require that they come to him or that they meet him on his own ground. He, a Jew, is apostle to gentiles, non-Jews, but they do not have to become Jews in order to be welcomed into the gospel. He knows that the gospel bridges ethnic boundaries and works its power in whatever context. Put in other terms, people do not have to possess authorized, pre-approved dippers before they can drink from the gospel. Paul custom-pours. Paul's is a noteworthy confidence that the gospel does not have to be protected by issuing it only in pre-approved containers.

What is true about the gospel is true about love, its central expression: Love always engages others, precisely where they are; it does not require them to come over or up to one's standards before it can be operative. In fact, one could argue that the only true engagement with others begins with meeting the other persons where they are; otherwise, imperialism sneaks into the picture. The careful reader of 1 Corinthians will have noticed, in the immediately preceding chapter, another illustration of Paul's willingness to adapt to others, when Paul is willing to consider becoming a vegetarian if not doing so would cause a weaker-conscienced brother or sister to stumble (8:13).

But becoming all things to all people does not involve losing or giving up one's own center, becoming gelatin-molded to whatever form appears, or losing track of what is truly important. Quite the contrary, in Paul's case it becomes absolutely critical that he know what really counts. Note Paul's description of his evangelistic strategy. When he became "as one without the law" to gentiles for whom the law was not a part of their knowledge, he knew about himself that he was "not without the law of God." Similarly, when he evangelized Jews, he became "as one under [the authority of] the law," though he knew that he himself was not under the authority of the law—meaning that the law and not God would have been the source of his life. The "as if not" character of the life of faith (see the Commentary on 7:29-35) means not only that allegiance to God is direct and all-encompassing but also that no human institution (the civil government or courts, for example) or distinction (of gender or ethnicity, for example) or practice (even of a religious sort such as keeping certain days or ritual activities) can become a primary filter that can function to separate a person from direct relationship to God. That is radical stuff. Paul is in line with a trajectory that runs from the eighth-century prophets of Israel through Jesus in which nothing, not even or especially religious requirements, stands in the way of one's relation to God. So Paul evangelizes on the principle that by preaching the gospel to all sorts of people, meeting them on their ground, he is affirming that nothing, no human institution or practice or distinction, can be permitted to hinder the communication that God cares passionately about all of God's creatures (not unlike his view in Rom 8:38-39).

# 1 Corinthians 10:1-13, The Exodus Retold As a Caution

## NIV

**10** For I do not want you to be ignorant of the fact, brothers, that our forefathers were all under the cloud and that they all passed through the sea. [2]They were all baptized into Moses in the cloud and in the sea. [3]They all ate the same spiritual food [4]and drank the same spiritual drink; for they drank from the spiritual rock that accompanied them, and that rock was Christ. [5]Nevertheless, God was not pleased with most of them; their bodies were scattered over the desert.

[6]Now these things occurred as examples[a] to keep us from setting our hearts on evil things as they did. [7]Do not be idolaters, as some of them were; as it is written: "The people sat down to eat and drink and got up to indulge in pagan revelry."[b] [8]We should not commit sexual immorality, as some of them did—and in one day twenty-three thousand of them died. [9]We should not test the Lord, as some of them did—and were killed by snakes. [10]And do not grumble, as some of them did—and were killed by the destroying angel.

[11]These things happened to them as examples and were written down as warnings for us, on whom the fulfillment of the ages has come. [12]So, if you think you are standing firm, be careful that you don't fall! [13]No temptation has seized you except what is common to man. And God is faithful; he will not let you be tempted beyond what you can bear. But when you are tempted, he will also provide a way out so that you can stand up under it.

[a]6 Or *types;* also in verse 11    [b]7 Exodus 32:6

## NRSV

**10** I do not want you to be unaware, brothers and sisters,[a] that our ancestors were all under the cloud, and all passed through the sea, [2]and all were baptized into Moses in the cloud and in the sea, [3]and all ate the same spiritual food, [4]and all drank the same spiritual drink. For they drank from the spiritual rock that followed them, and the rock was Christ. [5]Nevertheless, God was not pleased with most of them, and they were struck down in the wilderness.

6Now these things occurred as examples for us, so that we might not desire evil as they did. [7]Do not become idolaters as some of them did; as it is written, "The people sat down to eat and drink, and they rose up to play." [8]We must not indulge in sexual immorality as some of them did, and twenty-three thousand fell in a single day. [9]We must not put Christ[b] to the test, as some of them did, and were destroyed by serpents. [10]And do not complain as some of them did, and were destroyed by the destroyer. [11]These things happened to them to serve as an example, and they were written down to instruct us, on whom the ends of the ages have come. [12]So if you think you are standing, watch out that you do not fall. [13]No testing has overtaken you that is not common to everyone. God is faithful, and he will not let you be tested beyond your strength, but with the testing he will also provide the way out so that you may be able to endure it.

[a]Gk *brothers*    [b]Other ancient authorities read *the Lord*

# COMMENTARY

The digression begun in chapter 9 continues through 10:1-13 where Paul retells a cautionary version of Israel's exodus from Egypt.[116] His rendition of the exodus story sustains the note of judgment with which his own positive self-portrait ends (9:24-27). By his characterization of some of the Israelites as "idolaters" (10:7) and as ones who "practiced immorality" (10:8), Paul ties together the letter's enduring concern with πορνεία *porneia* as totally unacceptable for the life of faith (5:1; 6:13b, 18; 7:2) and the worry about idolatry that has surfaced in the Corinthians' question about eating meat offered to idols (8:1, 4). In his two earlier vice lists, Paul already anticipated his treatment of this topic and named idolatry (5:10, 11; 6:9) and *porneia* as disqualifying persons from inheriting God's reign (6:9-10). Idolatry and *porneia* are explicitly highlighted in Paul's retelling of the exodus and provide the link by which he ultimately exits the digression and makes application (10:14-22) to what was no doubt a specific problem faced by the Corinthian believers: Can they who "partake of the table of the Lord" also share what Paul pejoratively calls the "table of demons" (10:21)?

In 10:23–11:1 Paul sums up not only the argument about eating meat offered to idols (first introduced in 8:1) but links back to 6:12 where he first treated the Corinthians' slogan that "all things are permissible for me" (6:12). This passage (10:23–11:1) serves many functions: It ties together themes and concerns of the letter up to this point; it refines and extends some of the arguments made before; and it makes application to the auditors of the letter.

Typologies take past events, in this case the exodus from Egypt, or former individuals (as Abraham in Romans 4), and *by a selective retelling* of the old story become a vehicle for guidance in the present. In the retelling the author may make some explicit link to his readers, but typology invites the readers to make their own connections as well. In Paul's typological treatment of the exodus he effectively tells the old story twice, once in 10:1-4, with a warning in 10:5, and with 10:6 Paul begins an explicitly cautionary retelling of the story a second time. Clearly, Paul first tells the old story in ways designed to encourage his audi-

tors to identify with its characters. Those of the original exodus were "Our ancestors" (οἱ πατέρες ἡμῶν *hoi pateres hēmōn*) (10:1 NRSV); they, too, were baptized (10:2); they, too, partook of spiritual food and drink (10:3-4; cf. Exod 16:4, 35; 17:6; Deut 8:3; Num 20:7-11); and they, too, were related in a special way to Christ (10:4). Verse 5, with its doubly emphatic "But not," signals a transition of purpose: "But not with most of them was God pleased."

In 10:6-13 we gain an insight into one way Paul understood Scripture: Its events and characters provide examples, instructions, warnings for contemporary believers (10:6, 11). So what Paul tells about the old event and its characters should have a clear relevance for what he thinks is going on in Corinth. With 10:6, Paul's second telling of the exodus story has a very different spin. Now the persons with whom the readers were encouraged to identify in 10:1-4 turn out to be those who desired evil (v. 6), were idolaters (v. 7; Exod 32:4-6), engaged in sexual immorality (*porneia;* v. 8; Num 25:1-2), tested the Lord (v. 9; Deut 6:16; Ps 78:18; Isa 7:12), and grumbled (v. 10; cf. Num 21:5; Deut 1:26-27). God's judgment is noted in the retelling: Thousands fell in one day (v. 8; Num 25:9), snakes killed others (v. 9; Num 21:6), and others were killed by "the destroyer," that is by an avenging angel (v. 10; Exod 12:23; cf. 2 Sam 24:16; 1 Chr 21:15; Wis 18:20-25). In effect, Paul says, "Fair warning!"

What are we to make of these characterizations and the light they shed on Paul's view of the Corinthian situation? Were there grumblers or complainers in Corinth? There may well have been, though we have no other text to suggest it directly. Were there those whom Paul considered to be testing the Lord? As surely as there were any idolaters or persons engaged in *porneia,* there were persons Paul considered in danger of God's judgment (cf. 11:29-30). Not every detail of the recounted story needs to fit in a one-for-one fashion.[117] This much is clear: *Porneia* has been an

---

116. William Baird, "1 Corinthians 10:1-13," *Int* 44 (1990) 286-90.

117. On the dangers of mirror-reading—i.e., on taking every clue in the text to reveal a facet of the situation into which the letter is directed, see J. M. G. Barclay, "Mirror-Reading a Polemical Letter: Galatians as a Test Case," *JSNT* 31 (1987) 73-93, esp. 79-83; and George Lyons, *Pauline Autobiography: Toward a New Understanding,* SBLDS 73 (Atlanta: Scholars Press, 1985) 96-105.

issue in this letter (from chaps. 5 through 7) and idols, idolatry, and idol meat have been a feature as well (5:10, 11; 6:9; 8:1, 4, 7, 10; 10:7-8, 14). The gist of the account is clear: God's people—being chosen by God, being baptized, eating special food and drink—are accountable for their behavior. Neither baptism nor special edibles and potables ensure against God's judgment if the chosen ones stray or "fall" (v. 12). And there can be no mistake about it: God cannot be blamed for any falling because God never tests believers beyond what they can bear; God always graciously provides a way out, an exodus (10:13).

Paul retells the exodus from Egypt in a way that includes and admonishes his predominantly gentile audience ("our fathers," 10:1; "examples for us," 10:6; "for our instruction/warning," 10:11). The recounting of the exodus concludes with Paul's confident assertion that, along with whatever testing may come one's way, God will make "the way of escape" (RSV) or "way out" (NRSV; 10:13).

Paul's telling of the exodus invites his readers to identify with those whom Paul calls their wandering, cloud-guided forebears (10:1; Exod 13:21-22; Ps 105:39); it highlights the connections of his readers with the characters in ancient Israel by retrofitting baptism and Lord's supper motifs onto the old story: "All were baptized into Moses in the cloud and in the sea and all ate the same spiritual food and all drank the same spiritual drink" (10:2-4a). Even the rock from which they drank (Exod 17:6; Num 20:11) is identified as Christ (10:4b). The ties between Paul's readers and the old story could not be tighter.

Just at the moment when Paul's hearers should have made their most explicit identification, through the christological claim (10:4b), Paul jars his hearers with a radical shift in the trajectory of the story: "Nevertheless, with most of them God was not pleased and they were destroyed in the wilderness" (10:5). With that shocking declaration Paul pursues the downside of the exodus and, by inference, the potential jeopardy for the Corinthian believers: The people of Israel practiced idolatry and immorality; they put God to the test; and they grumbled or murmured against God (10:6-10). Given the emphasis upon idolatry and immorality in Paul's letter up to chap. 10, it is difficult to overemphasize their presence in Paul's retelling of the exodus. Paul's point to the Corinthians is ex-

plicitly stated: *Be careful that you know where and how you stand* (10:12).

Paul invites his readers to evaluate or test themselves by making a comparison with the characters in the exodus story. Like their wandering predecessors, they share in the benefits that God has provided and they are guided and nurtured by God. But they must be careful not to comport themselves, like "most" of their forebears, as persons who are tempted to idolatry and immorality and thus put God to the test. *Some* of the Corinthian believers seem to have lost their way. Paul's troubles are not with all of the Corinthians as God's problems were not with all of Israel; we may suppose that a majority of the Corinthians were living according to their faith and in consideration of others, but we do not hear from them directly, though it is safe to suppose that some of them are among those who clued Paul into the divisiveness and other problems among the community.

Paul takes the scriptural story as an example ("warning," 10:6, 11 RSV), as an instruction or warning (10:11) for him and his readers "upon whom the ends of the ages have come" (10:11; cf. 7:26, 31b). The phrase "ends of the ages" (τὰ τέλη τῶν αἰώνων *ta telē tōn aiōnōn*) is Paul's way of writing about Christ's return when God's purposes will be finished. The notion is grounded in apocalyptic speculation such as Dan 12:13 and has been mentioned by Paul already in 1 Cor 1:7-8; 7:26, 29-31 (cf. Heb 4:7 and the setting of a certain day). Accordingly, Paul calls upon each of his readers to undertake a careful self-assessment: "For this reason, let the one who thinks that he stands watch out lest he fall" (10:12). The "end of the ages" is a time of judgment when each person faces two alternatives: Either the individual will "fall" (πίπτω *piptō*), as did the twenty-three thousand in the exodus (10:8), or "stand" (ἵστημι *histēmi*; a Pauline technical term for proper grounding and remaining in God's grace; cf. Rom 5:2; 11:20; 1 Cor 15:1; 2 Cor 1:24; cf. Eph 6:13). Self-testing can give an occasion for realignment, for reorientation, in which one can make certain to steer clear of *porneia*, idolatry, and a testing of God. By altering one's course on the basis of self-examination, one can choose to stand (*histēmi*) with the exodus forebears who were faithful rather than fall (*piptō*) like those who tested God.

The passage closes (10:13) with a twist on the warning about putting the Lord to the test (10:9), turning it to a discussion of the tests that befall believers. Here Paul assures his readers that they will not be extraordinarily tested (10:13*a*) and that God, the very God of the exodus, will not let them be tested beyond their powers (10:13*b*), but with every test will provide a "way out," another exodus.

A word about Christ as the rock that followed the people in the wilderness is needed. Paul comes to the notion of the rock "following" them very readily because he notices that the location of the rock, as told in different passages in his scriptures (Ps 78:16 supposes it happened more than once; Exod 17:1-6; Num 20:2-13), is always with God's people but is mentioned first in one place and then in another and so forth. Philo, another Jew who was contemporary with Paul, identified the rock as Wisdom, who, thus personified, never abandoned God's people.[118] As the Lord's supper's food and drink are retrofitted back onto the old story so is Christ. This is easy for Paul because Paul clearly thinks of Christ as having been with God from the very beginning (cf. Phil 2:5-11).

This ends the two-part, massive digression that began in 9:1. Both sections of the digression concluded with a warning about the impending judgment and the need for the auditors to take stock and make sure they discipline themselves as Paul does (9:24-27) and avoid evil, immorality, and idolatry (10:6-13) lest they fall or be destroyed as most of their Israelite forebears were.

Why was this entire digression so long? The answer must lie in Paul's need to move the Corinthians from what they have (partially) understood into a larger and more complex picture. The digression serves two clear functions: (1) to model a proper melding of freedom with love; (2) to warn that being called and included in God's story does not inoculate believers from the responsibility to love one another and therefore to please God. Evidence across the letter shows that the Corinthians have seized onto the truth that in the gospel they are now free; Paul seems to suggest at points that their sense and practice of their new, unrestrained freedom is hazardous to themselves and to each other. Paul's lengthy digression links freedom with a concern—"love" is his code word for it—for one another. Ingredient to this attempted reconfiguration of their thinking is Paul's warning, first about himself as a potentially disqualifiable athlete and then about Israel as ones who, despite eating the special food and drinking the special drink, were struck down because God "was not pleased" with them (10:5).

The digression provides the readers a fresh angle of vision from which they can make their own applications to the questions and issues that beset them. Paul and Israel are safe targets; strong points can be made and applied to them and the readers are left with the opportunity to make self-application. The rhetorical handbooks take special note that persons who apply something to themselves are much more forceful in the application when they seem to come to the point on their own,[119] and this digression offers the auditors such an opportunity.

Taking no chances, Paul moves to make his own applications in 10:14-22 to the issue the Corinthians have raised with him about eating food offered to idols, but Paul broadens the issue to idolatry.

118. Philo *Allegorical Interpretation* 2.86.

119. Quintilian *Institutio de Oratoria* 9.2.71.

# REFLECTIONS

**1.** Exemplars can be positive or negative: We can learn how to live appropriately but also how not to. In 10:1-13 some among Israel serve as a negative model. A challenge for modern believers might be to figure out how they might learn from negative models without being non-caring, judgmental, or condescending. To be sure, the Scriptures, in their honest portrayal of humans as ones who stumble or take wrong turns, often provide, as they do for Paul in 10:1-13, a rich resource of such negative examples.

**2.** Paul's description of Israel as "our ancestors" (10:1 NRSV) to a predominantly gentile congregation is an illustration of what the creeds came to call "the communion of saints." All of God's people, whenever and wherever they were, are, or may be, are jointly and equally part of God's family. The entire biblical story is God's story, and we who have come later are having our stories woven into the ongoing saga of God's people. All of God's saints (see the Commentary on 1:2) belong to one another by God's grace.

**3.** "God will not let you be tested beyond what you can handle" (10:13). Many people know this Pauline aphorism and shake their heads in bewilderment when they find themselves in awful circumstances. Two features of the text are especially noteworthy. (1) The "yous" in the text are both in the plural, meaning that the experience of the testing and the efforts at handling it are never presumed by Paul to be borne by an individual alone. Paul's assumption is that any testing you experience is never in isolation. A death of a spouse, for example, is also a death experienced by others. And the bearing of the test, the handling of it, is never supposed by Paul to be done by an isolated individual; others will always be bearing it with the one who is tested. So the text supposes that God will not test us beyond what all of us can bear together. Paul's outlook stands in sharp contrast with the modern tendency to privatize and individualize all religious matters and experiences, even including suffering. (2) Note the context in which we find this statement about God's faithfulness not to test too hard. Paul has been writing of God's exodus deliverance of the people of Israel from slavery in Egypt (10:1-11). So the motif of deliverance should be on the reader's mind. Then Paul affirms the faithfulness of God, that God's testing will not be too severe to be borne, and concludes: "But with the testing God will make a way out [an exodus!] so that you can endure" (10:13). With every test, the faithful, dependable God will make sure it is something you collectively can handle, or God will provide an exodus just as in olden times.

**4.** In the wonders of our retelling it, the exodus has tended to become an all-glorious event, much as the shame and distress of the cross have given way to a jeweled object of beauty, but only in retrospect and only with the benefit of faith's insight. The biblical narratives show that the persons experiencing the exodus found it problematic in the extreme when they were undergoing it, and Paul reflects that in his notice of their grumbling (10:10). Would it not be fair to suggest that most exoduses are not wholeheartedly greeted when they are happening and that most exoduses seem indeed to be deliverance *only* in retrospect? So the promise of a "way out" may in fact be perceived as very troublesome at the time it is happening.

**5.** Paul's retrofitting of baptism and the Lord's supper images of eating and drinking spiritual food and drink can have a cautionary effect on believers today if they realize that those signs of God's commitment and support did not keep the ancient Israelites from stumbling and from being destroyed. Baptism and the Lord's supper are not insurance against going astray; neither are they excuses for failure to be responsible.

# 1 CORINTHIANS 10:14-22, PAUL'S APPLICATION: "FLEE IDOLATRY"

NIV

NIV

[14]Therefore, my dear friends, flee from idolatry. [15]I speak to sensible people; judge for yourselves what I say. [16]Is not the cup of thanksgiving for which we give thanks a participation in the blood of Christ? And is not the bread that we break a participation in the body of Christ? [17]Because there is one loaf, we, who are many, are one body, for we all partake of the one loaf.

[18]Consider the people of Israel: Do not those who eat the sacrifices participate in the altar? [19]Do I mean then that a sacrifice offered to an idol is anything, or that an idol is anything? [20]No, but the sacrifices of pagans are offered to demons, not to God, and I do not want you to be participants with demons. [21]You cannot drink the cup of the Lord and the cup of demons too; you cannot have a part in both the Lord's table and the table of demons. [22]Are we trying to arouse the Lord's jealousy? Are we stronger than he?

NRSV

[14]Therefore, my dear friends,[a] flee from the worship of idols. [15]I speak as to sensible people; judge for yourselves what I say. [16]The cup of blessing that we bless, is it not a sharing in the blood of Christ? The bread that we break, is it not a sharing in the body of Christ? [17]Because there is one bread, we who are many are one body, for we all partake of the one bread. [18]Consider the people of Israel;[b] are not those who eat the sacrifices partners in the altar? [19]What do I imply then? That food sacrificed to idols is anything, or that an idol is anything? [20]No, I imply that what pagans sacrifice, they sacrifice to demons and not to God. I do not want you to be partners with demons. [21]You cannot drink the cup of the Lord and the cup of demons. You cannot partake of the table of the Lord and the table of demons. [22]Or are we provoking the Lord to jealousy? Are we stronger than he?

[a] Gk my beloved    [b] Gk Israel according to the flesh

## COMMENTARY

With the digression (9:1–10:13) ended, Paul resumes the line of his argument from the end of chap. 8, where he had been reflecting about the mutual responsibility believers have for one another as they consider whether to eat meat offered to idols or not. Now in 10:14-20 he addresses the Corinthians regarding their participation in the cultic ceremonies that were a regular feature of the religions that would have been present in Corinth. Obviously, the Corinthian believers still had social contact with their unbelieving neighbors and Paul sees no problem with that (see also 10:27; 14:24). Prior to their conversion, most of the Corinthian believers would have been participants in the cultic festivals—which usually included a festal meal as a high social and religious event—so it is reasonable for them to wonder whether they can continue to take part in the festivals with their unbelieving friends. One can imagine some of the believers, especially the ones

who rightly embraced the maxims "An idol is nothing" and "There is no God but one" (8:4), positing that they could indeed take part in the cultic festivals without, as Paul would say it, "putting the Lord to the test" (10:9) or "provoking the Lord to jealousy" (10:22).

Paul's opening line on the topic, however, is not accommodating: "Flee from idolatry" (10:14 NIV). In his moral counsel, Paul, with a better-safe-than-sorry mentality, steers a wide course around perceived ethical problems or obstacles; his readers should recall an example in his own willingness never to eat meat if doing so would cause a brother or sister in Christ to stumble (8:13; see also Rom 14:23). In 10:14-22 Paul refines and particularizes his admonition to "flee from idolatry" by urging his followers to refrain from sharing table with what he dubs "demons" (10:21; cf. Deut 32:17; Ps 106:34-39; Bar 4:7).

For Paul, participation in the Lord's supper

(which itself will be a topic for further refinement in 11:17-34) is the fundamental, even defining, community action of believers. Like no other activity, this fellowship epitomizes believers' relation to Christ and to one another in pristine clarity. Cup and bread are the focal symbols (10:16-17). κοινωνία (*koinōnia*, "association," "partnership," "sharing," "fellowship," and the term from which some people speak of the Lord's supper as "communion") and related terminology ("take part in," "have a share in") lace this pericope and ground Paul's basic supposition that participation and sharing in Christ and the resulting fellowship is exclusively defining. It sets limits and boundaries that exclude any and all other rival participations.

Paul thinks his readers should know enough about Israel's practices to understand that "the ones who eat the sacrifices are partners of the altar" (10:18; cf. 9:13; i.e., they share in the food offered on the altar; cf. Lev 7:6, 15). the same with believers in Christ who drink the cup and eat the bread. And so Paul's logic follows: The same with any cultic participation! Paul thinks ahead and intercepts a possible misunderstanding: It is not that idol sacrifices are anything or that an idol is anything (10:19); he remains clear on that (8:4). The problem for Paul is that what the Corinthians' neighbors sacrifice is offered "to demons and not to God" (10:20; cf. Lev 17:7; Deut 32:17; Ps 106:37), and believers cannot risk being "partners with demons" because that is idolatry and will "provoke the Lord to jealousy" (10:22). The passage closes with an ironic intimation of divine confrontation: "We aren't stronger than the Lord, are we?" (10:22). That is why Paul thinks that fleeing idolatry or any semblance of it—that is, steering a wide course so as to avoid it—is sound advice that "sensible people" should understand (10:14-15).

Paul has reengaged the issue of eating idol meat with a strong link: "For this reason" or "Therefore [διόπερ *dioper*], my beloved, flee from idolatry" (10:14). The Lord's supper, alluded to in Paul's retelling of the exodus story (10:3) and here in 10:15ff. described for the first time in the letter, provides the base from which Paul invites his readers' reflection and assumes their assent by casting his questions in a form that expects a yes answer: Is not partaking in the Lord's supper a partnership, a sharing (*koinōnia*) in the blood and body of Christ (10:16-17)? Precisely in the Lord's supper

Paul locates the ground of all believers' being one: Because there is one loaf and because all believers share that one loaf, they, though many, are one body (10:17).

Back to basics once more: Christian unity is grounded in sharing the loaf; it depends on partaking in Christ's death. Paul expects his auditors to know this from their knowledge of Israel's practices to which he has alluded earlier (9:13): It is an inescapable principle that the ones who eat the sacrifices are "partners in the altar" (10:18), just as believers in Christ are partners in his blood and body. Paul is as certain as any of the Corinthians: An idol has no existence (10:19; cf. 8:4), but their cultic participation in Christ rules out cultic participation in pagan sacrifice, which Paul depicts negatively as an honoring of demons (10:20). Believers simply "cannot drink the cup of the Lord and the cup of demons." Just so, they "cannot share the table of the Lord and the table of demons" (10:21); to do so would be to risk provoking the Lord to jealousy (10:22, another echo of Israel's story; Deut 32:21), a turning away from the Lord to demons, a putting of the Lord to the test. Paul's recounting of the exodus from Egypt has already reminded his readers of the destruction that comes upon those who test the Lord (10:9; for more on Paul's understanding of the Lord's supper in particular, see the Commentary on 11:17-34).

Verses 14-22 comprise a remarkable text. In 8:4-13 Paul can imagine a believer's eating meat offered to idols as long as the person of weaker moral consciousness is not destroyed by this exercise of one's freedom. Similarly, just ahead in 10:25-29 he sees no necessary problem in eating idol meat in an unbelieving friend's home. Yet in 10:14-22 he absolutely forbids eating in the pagan cultic setting. Why the difference? Why the different counsel? The answer lies in Paul's special understanding of the Lord's supper's singular importance in the lives of believers. The Lord's supper is not just another meal; it is not just another get-together of believers. The Lord's supper and its worship setting are for Paul the definitive action that stands at the heart of the life of faith. In the Lord's supper believers can inescapably see that they stand only in and by God's grace; in the supper believers look with confidence toward the future when the end of the ages will come; and in the supper believers see most clearly how they relate to and with each other. The Lord's supper is like a lens through which the most important things about one's new life in Christ are absolutely brought into focus. In this sense worship at the Lord's supper allows no other participation or sharing that could in any way be confused with it. Accordingly, Paul concludes that no one who partakes of the table of the Lord can share the table of demons. Once again, Paul sees matters in rival, two-way form such that belonging to the one forbids participation in the other. And with two questions (10:22) that demand the auditors' participation, Paul echoes not only scripture (Deut 32:21) but more immediately his recent portrayal (10:9) of the ancient Israelites as the ones who tested the Lord, and

asks them if they would dare take part in the table of demons and thereby "provoke the Lord to jealousy," pretending to be "stronger than" God. The point cannot be lost on his readers: Their forebears in the exodus (10:1) tested the Lord and "twenty-three thousand fell in a single day" (10:8 NRSV), some were destroyed by serpents (10:9), and others were destroyed by the destroyer; *they* surely were not stronger than God! Now, in his pronouncement that his readers are to steer a wide course around idolatry and not participate in what he derogatorily calls the "table of demons," Paul reaps the harvest of his depiction of the consequences of the Corinthian forebears' having put the Lord to the test in the exodus. Paul's insinuation: Surely the Corinthians will not repeat the folly of their exodus forebears and risk destruction.

# REFLECTIONS

In Paul's time, sharing table, dining with someone, was the primary social symbol of acceptance, of belonging, and of mutuality. That is why so many of Jesus' teachings (cf. Luke 14:1, 7, 15) and some parables (cf. Matt 22:1-10; Luke 14:12-14) are set in a dining context. That is also why the book of Revelation depicts Jesus as knocking and asking entry, with the promise that if allowed to enter he will "go inside to him and dine with him and he with me" (Rev 3:20). Has our loss of sharing table affected our participation in the Lord's supper, not to mention our sense of sharing with our families and others for whom Christ died?

# 1 CORINTHIANS 10:23–11:1, A SECOND SUMMING-UP

NIV

[23]"Everything is permissible"—but not everything is beneficial. "Everything is permissible"—but not everything is constructive. [24]Nobody should seek his own good, but the good of others.

[25]Eat anything sold in the meat market without raising questions of conscience, [26]for, "The earth is the Lord's, and everything in it."[a]

[27]If some unbeliever invites you to a meal and you want to go, eat whatever is put before you without raising questions of conscience. [28]But if anyone says to you, "This has been offered in sacrifice," then do not eat it, both for the sake of the man who told you and for conscience' sake[b]—

[a]26 Psalm 24:1   [b]28 Some manuscripts *conscience' sake, for "the earth is the Lord's and everything in it"*

NRSV

[23]"All things are lawful," but not all things are beneficial. "All things are lawful," but not all things build up. [24]Do not seek your own advantage, but that of the other. [25]Eat whatever is sold in the meat market without raising any question on the ground of conscience, [26]for "the earth and its fullness are the Lord's." [27]If an unbeliever invites you to a meal and you are disposed to go, eat whatever is set before you without raising any question on the ground of conscience. [28]But if someone says to you, "This has been offered in sacrifice," then do not eat it, out of consideration for the one who informed you, and for the sake of conscience— [29]I mean the other's conscience, not your own. For why should my liberty be subject

## NIV

²⁹the other man's conscience, I mean, not yours. For why should my freedom be judged by another's conscience? ³⁰If I take part in the meal with thankfulness, why am I denounced because of something I thank God for?

³¹So whether you eat or drink or whatever you do, do it all for the glory of God. ³²Do not cause anyone to stumble, whether Jews, Greeks or the church of God— ³³even as I try to please everybody in every way. For I am not seeking my own good but the good of many, so that they may be saved.

11 ¹Follow my example, as I follow the example of Christ.

## NRSV

to the judgment of someone else's conscience? ³⁰If I partake with thankfulness, why should I be denounced because of that for which I give thanks?

31So, whether you eat or drink, or whatever you do, do everything for the glory of God. ³²Give no offense to Jews or to Greeks or to the church of God, ³³just as I try to please everyone in everything I do, not seeking my own advantage, but that of many, so that they may be saved.

11 ¹Be imitators of me, as I am of Christ.

# COMMENTARY

Like 6:12-20, this passage ties together themes and concerns of the letter up to this point; by recapitulation and refinement, it extends some of the arguments made before and makes application to the auditors of the letter.

*Recapitulation.* The Corinthian maxim "All things are permissible for me" (2 times in 6:12) is reprised twice to open this passage and Paul echoes his earlier concern for what builds up, for what is advantageous or helpful (6:12; 10:23). In the chapters between the two repeated sets of maxims (6:12; 10:23), Paul suggests or models proper concern for what is helpful and what builds others up by his counsels regarding marriage partners (7:2-5, 12-16), by his hyperbolic pledge to vegetarianism as an avoidance of causing someone to stumble (8:13), and by his self-portrait as the one with unexcelled rights who freely chooses not to use them if the doing so might cause harm or problems for others (chapter 9).

*Refinement.* Refining requires dwelling on a topic while seeming to move into new material; it usually involves a degree of repetition and a finding of alternate ways to make and elaborate the same point. The passage at hand is structured from their maxim—"All things are permissible"— which is itself already a near replication of 6:12. Noticeably missing—and part of the refinement— from its earlier, Corinthian form, is the individualistic "for me" that was present in 6:12. In the

intervening passages Paul has struggled to help the Corinthians see the community base and context of the Christian life; quite recently he has reminded them that they are one body because they share in the one loaf (10:17). Refinement is also present in the phrases Paul adds to their maxim: "But not everything is advantageous/helpful" and "but not everything builds up" (10:23). Their slogan, in its original form (6:12), considers moral choices *from the decision maker's standpoint;* Paul's refining additions (10:23) focus on *the well-being and edification of the community.* In the first of the section that he now brings to a close (8:1–10:22), he already identified love as that which "builds up" (8:1), so his response to their maxim claim that all things are permissible, while not denying it, calls for love to be at the center of reckoning what and how one does what may indeed be allowed. Love will always secure what is advantageous (cf. 13:4-7). In a cryptically worded injunction Paul calls for Corinthian focus on what is advantageous to the others and builds up the others: "Let no one seek his own [advantage] but that of the other one" (10:24). But their maxim—"all things are permissible"—is true also when applied to eating meat offered to idols and subsequently sold in the meat market; without questioning on account of conscience, they may eat anything sold in the meat market because scripture makes it clear that the earth and all its fullness is the Lord's (10:26; Ps 24:1; cf. 1 Cor 3:22-23). The assertion that the earth is the Lord's is an elaboration, a refinement, of Paul's earlier claims that "an idol has no existence," "there is no God but one" (8:4), and all things are from God (8:6; cf. 3:21-23).

*Recapitulation, Refinement, and Application (10:23–11:1).* With 10:25-30 Paul returns yet again to the issue about eating food offered to idols with which chapter 8 opened. Here Paul offers direct counsel that bears on their individual choices: Corinthian believers should feel conscience-free to eat whatever is sold in the meat market even though much of the meat sold there may have been offered as sacrifice in pagan religions. Paul thinks they should know themselves free to eat because scripture declares that "the earth is the Lord's and its fullness" (10:26; Ps 24:1; cf. also Pss 50:12; 89:11). Scripture accords well with the same sentiment Paul already expressed in a different way in 3:22-23: "The world . . . [and] all things are yours, yours are Christ's, and Christ is God's" (cf. 8:6).

Paul elaborates the same counsel by means of an imaginary circumstance where a believer is invited to dinner by an unbeliever (10:27-30). If the believer is inclined to accept the invitation, Paul sees no problem and, in the same wording used in 10:25 (πᾶν . . . ἐσθίετε *pan . . . esthiete,* "eat everything"—with the "everything" placed first for emphasis—without any problems for your moral consciousness) urges the believer to feel conscience-free to eat whatever is placed before him or her (10:27). The invented scenario allows Paul to explore a most important issue that he had touched upon earlier: How do one's actions impinge on others? Paul's scenario turns on someone's indicating that the entrée meat has previously been offered in sacrifice. It seems to matter little whether one interprets the identifier as a believer or not: Paul counsels respect for that person's conscience and a consequent refusal to eat the meat. This deference to others and a refusal to exercise one's own rights and freedom when it might harm others has become a leitmotif of this letter (a direct application of Paul's own patterning as reflected in 9:1-14), and the motif will continue to appear in later portions of the letter (cf. 11:33; 14:26-33 *a*).

Verses 29 *b*-30 may seem curious, but ultimately must be understood in the light of 10:31–11:1. In what has just preceded Paul has indeed been advocating a caring consideration of others by means of a self-imposed non-exercise of one's freedom when someone else's conscience might be harmed (8:9-13; 10:28-29 *a*), but he recognizes that one's freedom, though not exercised, is not to be "judged" by another's conscience (10:29 *b*). Judgment will indeed be rendered by God (Rom 14:12), but it will be on the basis of what one has done (Rom 2:6-11; 2 Cor 5:10), not on someone else's conscience but on one's own. Believers must be fully convinced (cf. 7:37; Rom 14:5) and without waverings (Rom 14:23) about whatever they, with clear conscience, choose to do. So different believers may do different things and may make distinctive moral choices and may do so quite properly. In Romans Paul makes this point with regard to keeping special days; some honor special days but others do not, and the variation in practice is fine. "Let each be fully convinced in his own mind. The one who sets one's mind on a particular day does so with respect to the Lord. And the one who eats does so with respect to the Lord, for he gives thanks to God. And the one who abstains from eating does so with respect to the Lord, and gives thanks to God" (Rom 14:5 *c*-6). But what they do must be done in love—that is, with respect for others and with a care not to do others harm but to edify them—and to honor God in thankfulness to God. If, in a spirit of thankfulness, one takes part in such a meal as Paul supposes an unbelieving friend might provide, no one should blaspheme one for that in which one partook with thankfulness (10:30).[120]

Paul's basic position emerges: No matter what one does, whether eating or drinking or whatever, "do all things to the glory of God" (10:31). This recapitulation is already an extension because the discussions from chapter 8 forward have focused on eating, but clearly, eating has become a metaphor, another use of synecdoche, for all of one's life and comportment before God.

This section also recapitulates Paul as exemplar. Throughout the letter Paul has offered himself as the model after which his children in the faith should pattern themselves. Now, at this point, he

120. D. F. Watson, "1 Corinthians 10:23-11:1 in Light of Greco-Roman Rhetoric: The Role of Rhetorical Questions," *JBL* 108 (1989) 301-18.

positions himself as example in three ways that he holds absolutely fundamental to the life of faith: (1) He tries to give no offense to anyone, here expressed in the intentionally comprehensive triad: Jews, Greeks, and God's church; (2) he tries in all things to please all people because, as he has already told his readers (cf. 9:19-23), he sees exemplary comportment as serving salvation (10:32-33); and (3) he puts into practice what he urged upon his readers in 10:24: that he does not seek his own advantage but that of the many (10:33*b*). And in all of this Paul calls upon his readers to imitate him because he is imitating Christ. To imitate Paul is to recognize that Paul is modeling after Christ.

To the modern reader it may seem that Paul is of several minds about eating meat offered to idols, allowing it in some texts (implicit consent in 8:4-6, explicit approval in 10:25 and 10:27) and prohibiting it in another (10:14-22). What is one to make of this? First, Paul's picture of the moral life is not simply a rules morality—that is, he does not generate one rule that either covers all aspects of life related to a given problem or applies equally to all believers in all circumstances. Second, the moral life is not lived alone but in community, in Christ. Third, the life in Christ is lived in the world where one interacts with unbelievers. Accordingly, Paul thinks that eating sacrificial meat in one circumstance may be fine for one person and not for another. But what may be fine for the person considered alone may not be fine if doing it might harm the other one or wrongly build up the other person. Paul seems to reason that eating meat previously offered to idols is no problem for the persons strong in faith who are clear that there are not rival gods—fine—as long as one's exercise of that freedom does not cause another to stumble (cf. the same stance in Rom 14:21). Likewise, eating sacrificial meat is no problem in an unbeliever's home—as long as no one dining there has a problem of conscience with it. In those two instances there is a consistency in Paul's reckoning.

The exception comes in Paul's ruling out the eating of meat in the cultic setting because Paul's conviction about the Lord's supper—namely, that in it one becomes united with Christ's body, does not allow him room to imagine a similar unification (he has used the daring image of becoming one flesh with a prostitute earlier to make a similar point; cf. 6:15-17) with the demons (he knows there are no other gods so he speaks instead of demons) at an idol's table. His convictions about the Lord's supper as the celebration of unity in Christ cannot logically let him condone believers' participation in the cultic worship of any other religion. "The one who cleaves to the Lord becomes one spirit with him" (6:17). "You have been bought with a price" (6:20; 7:23). At issue is "belonging to the Lord" in a totally inclusive and unmistakable way.

This passage gives access to foundational Pauline ethical considerations. The goal of all actions is to honor the Lord or God; or, in what seems to be a different way of saying the same thing, the goal of all actions is glorifying or giving thanks to God. Love, the careful weighing of how what one does may bear on another and at the same time the mode of one's consideration of others, must be factored into all decisions and into any resultant actions. Fundamental to the full expression of love is Paul's conviction that one does not seek one's own advantage as if what is good for one's self can be separated from the benefit of the others in the body of Christ, but that one must realize that one's own good is inextricably tied up with the good of all the others who are in Christ, a notion that will surface explicitly in 12:26.

We must ask what to make of Paul's two questions in 10:29*b*-30. The editors of the RSV placed a parenthesis marker between vv. 29*a* and 29*b*, no doubt sensing the shift in thought between those two parts. Prior to v. 29*b* Paul has counseled accommodation to others, but the questions of vv. 29*b*-30 indeed raise questions about the limits of such accommodation. As Paul constructs them, the two questions set forward an imaginary questioner's wrestling with the implications of what Paul has said about accommodating to the limitations of others. The questions are evocative and suggestive. They are not answered by Paul. The first question wonders why "my freedom" should be "unfavorably judged"[121]—and thereby limited!—by another's conscience (10:29*b*). The second question, though also cast as though it were from the same imaginary questioner about eating the

---

121. BAGD, 452.

entrée at Paul's fictive meal with the unbeliever, starts with a profoundly Pauline condition—"If I partake with thanks [to God, understood]"—and finishes with a strong Pauline concern, "why am I blasphemed for the very thing for which I give thanks?" We may suppose that Paul asks this question with some passion.

Before pursuing any further the interpretation of the two questions in 10:29b-30, Paul's ethical counsel needs to be considered. From chapter 8 forward he has advised forgoing the exercise of one's freedom if a brother or sister in Christ might be harmed or caused to stumble by one's contemplated action. Paul is even prepared to become a vegetarian if need be (8:13). In Paul's fictive scenario of dinner in an unbeliever's home (10:27-29a) we find the same practice, now in view of the conscience of the one who informed that the meat had been "offered in sacrifice" to some deity: Do not eat it out of consideration for the one who raised the issue (10:29a).

From these two recommendations—do not cause someone to stumble and do be considerate of others' moral consciousness—one can project an imaginary circumstance, not discussed anywhere in Paul's letters, in which each person in a congregation had a problem with some different practice and all the believers honored each of the limitations of all the others, arriving at an ethic of what might be called the "lowest common denominator." Judging from his letters, none of Paul's communities function that way, and nowhere in 1 Corinthians does Paul carry through the logic suggested here. The result would be a quite pallid community, which, rather than growing in its expression of its faith (Paul's code word for this is edification, being built up), would instead look primarily toward cutting back.

In 10:29b-30 Paul signals to his readers a caution about radicalizing—Paul knows that to be a Corinthian predilection with some of his teachings—his basic moral counsel that the one with the stronger moral consciousness forgoes the exercise of his or her freedom in the face of a weaker consciousness person. In these verses Paul recognizes that harm can happen not only to the one who has the weaker moral consciousness; some consideration also needs to be given to the person of stronger moral consciousness as well. He puts it in the form of two questions so as to prompt the reflection of his auditors. But Paul established himself in 9:1-18 as the exemplary person who never acts without consideration for others. The answer is only suggested by the question. The first question sets up the second one because the latter considers a hypothetical question of someone reviling the person who gives thanks and partakes in food with gratitude. The first question captures the issue as far as Paul has developed it to this point—namely, the limitations of one's freedom by someone with a weaker moral consciousness. The second question takes it a step beyond what Paul has considered before, to weigh the possibility that someone rebukes the person who gives thanks and partakes in food with gratitude.

Once more we need not suppose that this second question mirrors an actual happening at Corinth. More likely it represents Paul's own following through on his own logic to suppose someone who is doing just as he or she should be (giving thanks to God and partaking with gratitude) and yet being criticized. So the matter introduced in 10:29b-30 is not developed by Paul; it is merely suggested, perhaps to provoke reflection or perhaps even discussion among the Corinthians.

Paul's lengthy and detailed response to the Corinthians' question about meat offered to idols has served not only to give guidance about that particular question, but by Paul's careful shaping and developing of it, has provided him the opportunity to generalize from that issue to all of life lived in Christ together before God. In the process Paul has laid the ground for his treatment of further issues and problems that bear on the Corinthian believers' lives.

# REFLECTIONS

**1.** Note Paul's assumption in 10:15-26 about the goodness of all creation. Several points merit pondering. (1) Salvation, redemption is not achieved by extrication from the creation. (2) The creation has always given testimony to God's power and deity (Rom 1:20), but it has been subjected to sin's corruption and finds itself in bondage to decay (Rom 8:20-21). (3) The new creation has begun in Christ (2 Cor 5:16-19). (4) God's redemptive activity will not be complete until the creation is fully restored and shares in the liberty God's children already experience (Rom 8:21). One may freely eat whatever is set before him or her because "the earth belongs to the Lord" (1 Cor 10:26, quoting Ps 24:1). In the same way, one may be sexual because being sexual is a normal feature of divinely created life (1 Corinthians 7).

**2.** Here and there in Paul's letters one gets glimpses of what he considers the basic reasons for doing things. Why do you do whatever it is that you do? What is your basic motivation for doing anything in life? Of course, there are all sorts of motivations. Some persons are moved by guilt, though nowhere in Paul does one see that. Some do works in the hope that God will find them worthy of reward, but Paul rigorously opposes anything that even smacks of such a notion (e.g., Galatians). Some will do deeds to be seen and praised by others, but Paul does not countenance that. And some will do because they know that without it they will not eat. For Paul there is a basic answer to why anyone should do anything: All of one's doing should come as a grateful response to God's graceful reaching for and loving and claiming us in Jesus Christ before we were worthy, while we were unlovable. Though Paul does not state it so succinctly as John, his sense is the same: We love because God first loved us (1 John 4:19). We do deeds out of thankfulness to God, to glorify God for God's mercy and grace toward us. In that sense the Afro-American spiritual whose words proclaim "My soul is so happy that I cain't set down" captures Paul's sense that there is no way around it: The ones loved by God must reach out, they must do deeds through which love is expressed toward others. Not to do so is unthinkable.

**3.** First Corinthians 10:24 can be easily misunderstood. Some translations make misunderstanding even more likely: Consider, for example, the NIV's and the RSV's insertion of the word "good," which is totally lacking in the Greek and can be more literally translated: "Let no one seek the [thing] of one's own, but the [thing] of the other." The NRSV logically looks for the unidentified noun, signified here by [thing], in the notion of "advantage" expressed in Paul's elaboration of their maxim in 10:23*a* and echoed in the same formulation as 10:24 in 10:33.

What we actually have here is a pervasive Pauline conviction—namely, that the person who looks after his or her own self first is the person who curiously loses out even on the very goal of securing oneself. Paul learned this in Christ (11:1), who first considered what was good for humans and acted for us rather than for himself (Phil 2:5-11), and God raised him from the dead. Paul modeled that for the Philippians when he would really have preferred to leave the troubles and stresses of life in the world and go be with the Lord full-time but instead chose to stay in the world and work in their behalf (Phil 1:22-26). He urged the same response on the Philippians when he wrote to them: "Each of you should look not only to your own interests, but also to the interests of others" (2:4 NIV). Paul captures the same idea in Rom 15:2: "Let each of you please your neighbor unto the good, to edification." Without using the code word "love," Paul is writing about it. What is at stake is not a denunciation of all concern for one's self; rather it is a matter of priority, a sequencing. Love calls for people to seek the good of another; this is not an option, it is basic faithful living. The love of others should be at the center of one's purpose. Paul's conviction is that when one looks to the interests of others then one's own interests are taken care of in the process. It is almost that one who sets out to secure one's own interests can't get there from here.

But none of this must be confused with having no care for one's self. Paul adopts Jesus' embrace of the Levitical formulation: "Love your neighbor as yourself" (Lev 19:18; Rom 13:9, Gal 5:14). For that formulation to have any viability one must have a certain love for one's self. The problem, of course, is one of proportionality. How does one properly love one's self and also love one's neighbors? What is the difference between proper, proportional love of self and selfishness? The answer is to be found in one's careful self-testing, and the search to distinguish may be assisted by the active, honest, genuine love of friends.

**4.** Paul imitates Christ (11:1) by not seeking his own advantage but that of the many (10:33). Calls to imitation of Christ are across the Pauline corpus. Paul's counsels to imitation of Christ tend to focus on two areas: (1) what Christ did in giving himself for others, and, (2) the disposition of Christ toward others. Clearly, 11:1 belongs to the former, most prevalent group of references to Christ's caring for others. Other classic examples of that focus are Phil 2:1-11 and Rom 15:1-6 (cf. also texts such as 2 Cor 5:14-21). Belonging to the second type of appeal for imitation would be Paul's call for the Roman believers to welcome one another into mutual fellowship as Christ has welcomed you (Rom 15:7) and Paul's appeal that the Corinthians model Christ's meekness and his clemency, his readiness to forgive (2 Cor 10:1).

Worth noting is what is missing. Christ has already died for us, so believers are not called upon to redeem others. Also, Paul makes no attempt to psychologize Christ by imagining what Christ might have thought; nor does Paul ever write about what Christ might have done in any particular situation.

## THREE WORSHIP PRACTICES OF THE COMMUNITY

## OVERVIEW

N ext on Paul's agenda in this letter are three items, each of which, taking its cue from 10:14-22, involves the worship practices of the community (women's head covering, 11:2-16; the Lord's supper, 11:17-34; and the use of spiritual gifts, chaps. 12–14). In the structure of the middle of this letter Paul has moved from the Corinthians' question about eating idol meat (8:1) to a discussion of the central, definitive communal act of eating—namely, the Lord's supper (10:14-22). That discussion of the Lord's supper leads Paul very naturally to attach in what we call chap. 11 two other worship matters of concern to him that he links together under the heading of "traditions" (NRSV) or "teachings" (NIV; παρ-άδοσις *paradosis,* 11:2, 23). Both of these worship matters regard traditions or teachings that he acknowledges he has previously conveyed to the Corinthians (11:2, 23). He opens the section with praise for the Corinthians' "holding to the traditions" (11:2) just as he "traditioned" (11:2; using the same root term for the passing of traditions) them, but it turns out that in both matters treated in chap. 11 he objects to certain aspects of their practice.

Traditions play an important role in Paul's gospel. They provide a solid foundation upon which

the life of faith may be built and upon which moral reasoning and action may properly be grounded. When Paul confronts a problem in one of his churches he frequently rehearses what "we know" and, from that, reasons toward a solution. The traditions may come from Scripture, from others in the churches before Paul or contemporary with him (cf. 1 Cor 11:23-25; 15:3-8; Phil 2:6-11; Gal 3:28) or, as we have seen, from Paul and even from the churches he established. For Paul, such teachings provide the ground for behavior and for action; they are the navigational markers by which believers set the courses for their lives, both individually and collectively.

In the first passage (11:2-16), directed at a problem that has developed precisely because two of Paul's teachings have come into conflict with each other, much as competing goods sometimes cause problems of moral discernment, Paul tries to build a case for a particular practice that he expects in Corinth and in all of his churches. In the second (11:17-34), Paul critiques and rejects the comportment of some Corinthians at the Lord's supper and attempts to call them back to appropriate understanding and behavior.

## 1 CORINTHIANS 11:2-16, PROPER COMPORTMENT OF WOMEN IN WORSHIP

NIV

²I praise you for remembering me in everything and for holding to the teachings,ᵃ just as I passed them on to you.

ᵃ *2 Or traditions*

NRSV

2I commend you because you remember me in everything and maintain the traditions just as I handed them on to you. ³But I want you to understand that Christ is the head of every man, and

## NIV

³Now I want you to realize that the head of every man is Christ, and the head of the woman is man, and the head of Christ is God. ⁴Every man who prays or prophesies with his head covered dishonors his head. ⁵And every woman who prays or prophesies with her head uncovered dishonors her head—it is just as though her head were shaved. ⁶If a woman does not cover her head, she should have her hair cut off; and if it is a disgrace for a woman to have her hair cut or shaved off, she should cover her head. ⁷A man ought not to cover his head,ᵃ since he is the image and glory of God; but the woman is the glory of man. ⁸For man did not come from woman, but woman from man; ⁹neither was man created for woman, but woman for man. ¹⁰For this reason, and because of the angels, the woman ought to have a sign of authority on her head.

¹¹In the Lord, however, woman is not independent of man, nor is man independent of woman. ¹²For as woman came from man, so also man is born of woman. But everything comes from God. ¹³Judge for yourselves: Is it proper for a woman to pray to God with her head uncovered? ¹⁴Does not the very nature of things teach you that if a man has long hair, it is a disgrace to him, ¹⁵but that if a woman has long hair, it is her glory? For long hair is given to her as a covering. ¹⁶If anyone wants to be contentious about this, we have no other practice—nor do the churches of God.

*ᵃ 4-7 Or ⁴Every man who prays or prophesies with long hair dishonors his head. ⁵And every woman who prays or prophesies with no covering of hair on her head dishonors her head—she is just like one of the "shorn women." ⁶If a woman has no covering, let her be for now with short hair, but since it is a disgrace for a woman to have her hair shorn or shaved, she should grow it again. ⁷A man ought not to have long hair*

## NRSV

the husbandᵃ is the head of his wife,ᵇ and God is the head of Christ. ⁴Any man who prays or prophesies with something on his head disgraces his head, ⁵but any woman who prays or prophesies with her head unveiled disgraces her head—it is one and the same thing as having her head shaved. ⁶For if a woman will not veil herself, then she should cut off her hair; but if it is disgraceful for a woman to have her hair cut off or to be shaved, she should wear a veil. ⁷For a man ought not to have his head veiled, since he is the image and reflectionᶜ of God; but woman is the reflectionᶜ of man. ⁸Indeed, man was not made from woman, but woman from man. ⁹Neither was man created for the sake of woman, but woman for the sake of man. ¹⁰For this reason a woman ought to have a symbol ofᵈ authority on her head,ᵉ because of the angels. ¹¹Nevertheless, in the Lord woman is not independent of man or man independent of woman. ¹²For just as woman came from man, so man comes through woman; but all things come from God. ¹³Judge for yourselves: is it proper for a woman to pray to God with her head unveiled? ¹⁴Does not nature itself teach you that if a man wears long hair, it is degrading to him, ¹⁵but if a woman has long hair, it is her glory? For her hair is given to her for a covering. ¹⁶But if anyone is disposed to be contentious—we have no such custom, nor do the churches of God.

*ᵃ The same Greek word means man or husband   ᵇ Or head of the woman   ᶜ Or glory   ᵈ Gk lacks a symbol of   ᵉ Or have freedom of choice regarding her head*

# COMMENTARY

Women are praying and prophesying in the church at Corinth. Paul takes that practice for granted, and it is no problem (11:5, 13). A later discussion in this letter shows that prophesying is a public mode of discourse that can edify, encourage, console, or lead to conviction in the hearts of others (14:3, 24-25).¹²²

122. For two studies of prophecy in early Christianity, see David E. Aune, *Prophecy in Early Christianity and the Ancient Mediterranean World* (Grand Rapids: Eerdmans, 1983); Christopher Forbes, *Prophecy and Inspired Speech in Early Christianity and Its Hellenistic Environment* (Tübingen: J. C. B. Mohr, 1995).

Clearly, women at Corinth had heard Paul's gospel as welcoming them into full participation in the life of the church.

Even the most casual reading of 11:2-16 will discover Paul's concern: Women in Corinth, at least some of them, had stopped wearing head coverings in worship, and that bothered Paul. These verses are Paul's attempt to bring these women back in line with his teaching and with what is, in fact, the customary practice he has fostered in all of his other churches (11:16). It is reasonable to suppose that the women who had stopped wearing head coverings may have considered themselves in line with Paul's teaching about freedom in Christ, with Paul's embrace of equal standing of the sexes in the Lord (cf. 7:1-24; 12:13; Gal 3:28), with Paul's critique of persons who live according to the patterns and practices of the culture (cf. 6:1ff.), and with Paul's having welcomed women into participation in worship (e.g., praying and prophesying, 11:5).

What are we to make of these head coverings and Paul's dogged insistence that they be worn? At the outset, we must acknowledge that it is not clear just what Paul means by head coverings. The scholarly options range from "something like a shawl" or long hair that might be understood to function much like a shawl, or a more demure hairstyle in place of what might be seen as manti- cally touseled.[123] The texts simply do not allow a decisive answer. By his treatment of head coverings we can tell that Paul takes them to be customary and expects the Corinthians to have understood them as such. This is another of those instances where Paul and his readers seem to know exactly what is in dispute, but some uncertainty must remain for us.

Even though we cannot with certainty identify the head coverings, we can recognize what Paul is doing in his call for the wearing of head coverings of whatever sort. His insistence that women cover their heads in worship shows that at least on one level—namely, that in Christ there is no male or female—he has not fully carried through the social critique that he elsewhere sees implied so completely in the gospel. But even this observation must be carefully qualified because, as we shall see in what follows, Paul has what for him is an important theological basis for his position.

In these verses, although he assumes women's full participation in worship, he nevertheless wants them to wear some mark that, in fact, distinguishes them from men. His rhetoric stacks up arguments that women should comply.

This passage—in fact, all of chap. 11—is cast in the strong cultural categories of praise/honor and shame. As certainly as modern Western culture is

characterized by acquisition and competition, so surely was the Corinthians' ordered around shame and honor. The formative questions that structured the culture and that influenced behavior were: What adds to honor? What avoids or lessens shame? These were the dominant questions in Paul's time, so when Paul speaks of praising or condemning, he is relating in powerful terms of value for himself and his readers.

With this background, let us consider Paul's string of arguments—from claims about God, from culture and nature, and from Scripture—whose underlying force of logic seems to be that if all these indicators or signs point in the same direction, who would presume to go against them? Paul's first and most elaborated argument is a *theological* one (11:3-5) that builds on a claim already made in this letter and is reaffirmed later: God is over all (3:23; cf. 8:6a; 15:24, 28); next is Christ; then human beings. Paul's discussion in 11:3 assumes the same hierarchy but simply runs it in the other direction and starts, where none of his readers would have any objection, with "every man"/"husband" (ἀνδρός *andros* may mean either) having Christ as head (κεφαλή *kephalē*, "source" or "rank," 11:3a). To that claim Paul adds that the head of a "wife"/"woman" (γυνή *gynē* may mean either) is her husband (11:3b), followed directly by "and the head of Christ is God" (11:3c). Paul's readers will have been assimilated to understand that Christ is the head over all people—men and women—and that God is the head over Christ (on this last point see also 15:24, 27-28, where Paul's teaching is laid out in more detail). It is fair to wonder, however, whether the Corinthians would have already known before having heard this letter that Paul also thought that the head of a wife is her husband (11:3). Evidence suggesting that they either have not heard it before or at least have not subscribed to it in their practice is found in Paul's stacking of his arguments to bolster his position.

*Culturally,* it was considered shameful for a woman to have a shaved or bald head. Paul twice capitalizes on that cultural predisposition, first when he asserts that any woman who prays or prophesies with uncovered head dishonors her head—she might as well have her head shaved, he declares (11:5)—and, second, when he declares that a woman who will not cover her head should

123. Gordon D. Fee, *The First Epistle to the Corinthians* (Grand Rapids: Eerdmans, 1987) 496-97.

have her hair cut (off); the one is as shameful as the other (11:6).

Later in the passage he returns to the argument from the contemporary cultural practice of women, not men, having long hair, which he quite uncritically construes as a reflection of *nature's* own preferences. It is dishonorable for a man to have long hair, but long hair is a woman's mantle of glory (11:14-15). In 11:14-15 Paul caps off his reasoning with what he describes as an argument "from nature." Carefully phrased as a rhetorical question whose Greek supposes a yes answer, Paul asks: "Doesn't nature itself teach you that if a man wears long hair it is a dishonor to him, but if a woman wears long hair, it is her glory?" Rhetoricians agreed that the points of greatest importance should be placed at the beginning and at the end in a sequence such as we have here. So Paul's first argument is one of monumental proportions for him: God is over all (11:2-3). His last proof, which means that he supposes it to be powerful as well, is his argument from nature: Nature teaches that men should not have long hair but that women should. So Paul declares, and his construction of the question shows that he expects the Corinthians to agree with him. The problem, however, is that Paul's argument "from nature" is actually an argument not from nature, but from social convention—indeed, from the social convention that *he* prefers. Might there have been Corinthians who viewed what was "natural" regarding hair length in a different perspective? Quite possibly. A quotation from Musonius Rufus, a contemporary of Paul and a mentor of Epictetus among others, is instructive because it shows just how self-serving Paul's argumentation is about hair length. In a treatise entitled "On Cutting the Hair," Rufus quotes with approbation Zeno's remark that "it is quite as natural to cut the hair as it is to let it grow long."[124]

Paul calls upon *Scripture* for support, to the effect that man is the "image of God" (Gen 1:27, quoted in 11:7) and that woman was made from man (Gen 2:22, quoted in 11:12*a*). Some modern interpreters have thought that the puzzling "because of angels" comment in 11:10 might reflect Gen 6:1-4;[125] if it does not, then the

reference is another of those shared understandings between Paul and his followers that seem beyond our capacity to recover.

All of these Pauline contentions, stacked up one upon another, are designed to convince the Corinthian women that it is proper for them to wear head coverings during worship. Whatever else Paul says in 11:2-16, it remains his hope that the Corinthian women will come over to his understanding of the need for head coverings in the worship setting.

But, curiously, not all of Paul's arguments in 11:2-16 go in the direction just described. Midway through 11:2-16 Paul appears to become self-critical about the implication of his multifaceted but one-sided argument for women to wear head coverings. In his eagerness to bring the Corinthian women into conformity with the practice of women in his other churches (11:16), Paul has distinguished women/wives from and subordinated them to men/husbands—and this in a letter where he has already counterculturally reconstructed the relationship of husbands and wives in marriage (chap. 7) as one of reciprocity and parity. In the process of writing 11:2-16, Paul discovers that two of his own values are in conflict: On the one side, he wants women believers to accommodate to the culturally aligned practice of wearing head coverings; on the other side, he believes that in Christ the cultural differentiations between men and women are eschatologically challenged by the gospel.

It is important to note how Paul's argument moves. In the opening verses (11:3-10) he single-mindedly piles up one point after another, all to the end of sustaining his hierarchical distinction in praxis between men/husbands and women/wives. Then, all of a sudden, in 11:11-12 he interrupts his own argument with the particle πλήν (*plēn*, "nevertheless," "however," "but"), which is a standard Greek way to break into a previous discussion and emphasize what is very important, and it introduces what amounts to a strong counterpoint to his own argumentation advanced in 11:2-10. In 11:13*a* he calls for the Corinthians to make their own judgments in this matter, and in 11:13*b*-16 he once again returns to compiling more arguments, whose goal is to encourage the Corinthian women to decide in favor of Paul's view and cover their heads. So the bulk of the

---

124. Musonius Rufus "On Cutting the Hair" XXI.10.

125. Hans Conzelmann, *A Commentary on the First Epistle to the Corinthians*, trans. J. W. Leitch, Hermeneia (Philadelphia: Fortress, 1975) 189.

argumentation goes in the direction of head coverings, but it is significantly interrupted by Paul's reaffirmation of male/female equality that he sees in the gospel.

Thus 11:2-16 contains two competing arguments based on two distinct pictures of the order of creation. The first, and dominant one, in these verses is structured upon the repeated affirmation that God is the source of all there is, that God is over all and the head of all (3:21-23; 8:6; 15:24-28). No other gods exist; there is no rival Lord. From this basic conviction Paul posits an orderly, hierarchical universe whose structure he details in such a way as to bear on the problem he faces with the women who are not wearing the head coverings. The argument is one of source or head. Beginning with God (for all the right theological reasons), Paul traces the lineage that God is the source or head of Christ, who is the source or head of men, who are the source or head of women—and the woman who does not wear proper head covering dishonors her head, meaning not only her own head but also her husband and, one might wonder, even Christ and God. The claim that man is the source of woman probably draws on the scriptural basis of Gen 2:21-23, which says as much.

Paul knows that this picture or argument is only part of the story; it is one important way of looking at things. But logic *and his other theological convictions* lead him to recognize, counter to his main argument, that every man is, in fact, born of a woman (11:12). Not only that, but Paul has earlier preached to them and can in this letter draw upon it as established tradition that in Christ—"in the Lord" as he puts it in 11:11—there is neither male nor female (Gal 3:28; see the Commentary on 7:17-24; see also 1 Cor 12:13). So his commitment to the tradition that "in the Lord" one finds neither male nor female breaks into his earlier hierarchical argument and shapes and inspires his statement in 11:11: Nevertheless, in the Lord "woman is not independent of man or man independent of woman" (11:11 NRSV). In this portrait of the new creation, men and women are not distinguished, although he knows and reaffirms the truth of the core of the first argument—namely, "All things are from God" (11:12).

In a creative reworking of the same tradition that is found in Gal 3:28 and in 1 Cor 7:17-24 and

its context, Paul affirms that "in the Lord there is neither woman apart from man nor man apart from woman" (11:11). While he has suggested in 11:8 (cf. Gen 2:22) that woman came out of man because it served his point there to do so, it is just as surely true that "man is born of woman," as he acknowledges in 11:12*b*. And as if to keep it all in proper perspective, "all that is comes from God" (11:12*c*). Recognizing that he has now presented the Corinthians with very different lines of argument in the same passage and bearing on the same issue, he turns it over to them: "Weigh out these matters among yourselves" (11:13*a;* cf. 6:5). But without waiting for whatever they may decide, Paul stacks up more arguments favoring women wearing head coverings (11:13*b*-16) and clearly hopes the Corinthians will agree with him.

In part we may be dealing with the very nature of theological claims: Each theological assertion is partial; each theological claim is limited and gains certain important points. Not all theological claims fit neatly together without friction. Each important point gained by one theological claim usually causes some conflict with the consequences of some other theological claim. A classic example will illustrate. When one stresses that all power, glory, and honor belong to God—as the Pauline tradition does—one inevitably implies something a bit troublesome about the power of human beings. If God is all-powerful, how can we talk about human beings as having any capacity to make decisions, because choosing this or avoiding that implies not only the exercise of some power of one's own, some freedom of one's will but also inevitably some restriction on God's control? On the other side, if one posits freedom of the human will to choose, what does such an assertion inevitably imply about God's will, about God's power? One may want to hold both positions despite the associated theological ambiguities. Paul surely holds both. Another factor complicates the matter even further: Any theological assertions must take into consideration not only the problems just noted but also the complexity of life and social arrangements that add their own complicating nuances to applied theological claims. Now back to the problem of Paul and Paul's theological claims in 11:2-16.

God is surely over all in Paul's view. Such a claim, right as it is, inevitably contributes to a hierarchical vision. In dealing with idolaters' rival claims, such a conviction might be very helpful and illuminating because it could provide the framework in which one could place oneself in the line of authority and power (Paul used 1 Cor 15:3-11 in such a way; the narrative ties him into the line of divinely appointed authority). But when one is dealing, as Paul is here in 11:2-16, with intimate human exchanges and the social dynamics of his community of believers at Corinth, the conviction that God is over all can lead to stratification.

Another, related issue surfaces in this passage: What is the relation of believers to the culture of which they are a part, and how should believers relate to the norms of the culture? In 1 Corinthians, Paul has established a not altogether consistent pattern on this issue. His two-way teaching in chaps. 1–4 suggests an insurmountable breach between the way of the gospel and the way associated with the culture, but there is an incredible irony even there because in the very making of his case for separation he uses the categories of the culture to make his point. Further, he expresses astonishment that some Corinthians are resorting to the courts, a typical cultural practice, to settle intracommunal differences. In 11:17-34, Paul criticizes the wealthier Corinthians for carrying their cultural and social practices over into the Lord's supper. And yet in the passage at hand (11:2-16), Paul freely and repeatedly refers to what must be recognized as simply cultural predispositions of his time; for example, women's hair should be long, men's hair should be short, and baldness or shaved heads for women produce culturally endorsed shame.

Short of an effort at complete separation from culture, such as was attempted by the Dead Sea Scrolls community at Qumran and as apparently was pondered by some Corinthians in response to Paul's previous letter (5:9; such complete separation Paul recognizes as impractical, 5:10-11; chap. 8), Paul seems to recognize that there will always be some interaction between gospel and culture, and he even boldly co-opts cultural elements where he thinks they may be helpful to him. Overall, Paul's posture on the matter is eccentric and sporadic. Once one determines not to leave the world, as Paul clearly has decided (cf. Phil 1:23-24), then the issue is joined; then there will always be accommodations to the culture and its practices, and there will be distancing from the culture and its patterns. But in cases like Paul's one has every reason to suppose that his readers will alternately be puzzled by his eccentricity on this matter, and no doubt some will have engaged him precisely on these issues of what could be construed as inconsistency. As we have seen in this very pericope, Paul is himself a bit at loggerheads as he tries to honor two very different convictions.

These verses give us insight into not only Paul's determination but also the acuity of his mind. As to his determination, he wants a practice that the Corinthians could (and perhaps did) argue made an alien demand on them to accommodate to cultural norms of distinction between men and women. Given his lead argument (11:3-5), Paul might respond that his position was based on his theological understanding and not in cultural mores. The acuity of Paul's mind is observed, however, in his capacity to follow the logic of a position, in this instance his own, to its conclusion, to test out the ramifications of his assertions even as he is making them, and to see that his argumentation leads in some sense to a position with which he himself has some problems. We have already seen this same mental facility in Paul's awareness that the inevitable logic of his morality of concessions to weak moral consciousness leads to the problems (see the Commentary on 10:29-30).

One final note is important here. Superficially, the arguments of 1 Cor 9:1-18 and 11:2-16 appear the same because in both Paul scurries around, pulling together all sorts of culturally acknowledged practices in support of single points. In chap. 9, Paul wants to argue that, although nobody is more privileged with rights (9:12*a*) than he, he lovingly eschews the exercise of those rights because of his love of others; in 11:2-16, he wants to establish the propriety of women wearing head coverings. But the two passages are actually *distinct* in significant ways. The argument in chap. 9 begins from what Paul supposes that *everybody* already knows: that a worker is entitled to some of the fruits of his or her labors. But the argument in chap. 11 begins with what *Paul* knows—namely, that women should wear head coverings. In the former (chap. 9), Paul invites the auditors to apply to him what they already know; in the latter (chap. 11), he wants the auditors to practice what he knows. Further, the first passage uses the cultural assumptions to advocate what turns out ultimately to be countercultural: love triumphing over self-interest; the second passage uses highly selective and even ad hominem interpretations of cultural practices to support cultural conformity of women's wearing head coverings.

# REFLECTIONS

**1.** Paul's complex, convoluted rhetoric in 11:2-16 has as its primary aim getting the women to return to wearing head coverings as he expects in all his churches. In the process, two distinctive arguments, two alternative views, emerge. The primary one in these verses argues from God's primacy, structured hierarchically, and supports Paul's interest in head covering. The other stems from the view that in the Lord there is neither male nor female and is formulated out of a fundamental sense of equality between women and men.

It is tempting to ask which argument, which picture, is the "right" one, and the natural inclination would be to affirm the one that most clearly fits or supports one's own predisposition. Would it not be appropriate to admit that all of our efforts to grasp the whole picture of God's purposes are subject to human limitations of knowledge and expression and that, therefore, each vision, each picture is at best partial and incomplete? Perhaps life does not submit itself to a single story, a single accounting, a single point of moral reckoning. Perhaps that is why Paul is driven, after laying out the second argument, to call for the Corinthians to "judge for yourselves" (11:13).

A nautical metaphor might be helpful as a way of relating to these two very different pictures of "the way things ought to be" that Paul has placed alongside each other. Imagine yourself as sailing in largely unknown waters. You have a chart with certain hazards located on it and must lay out a course that avoids grounding your boat. If you can identify two visible landmarks on the chart, you can, by triangulation, calculate your exact location and navigate in such a way as to be informed by the chart. Paul offers two points on the map with his two pictures of the way things ought to be; the modern believer should be able to benefit from reference to both of them.

**2.** What could it mean today to consider God or Christ as one's head or source? Such a description must always have within it authority implications and perhaps even fundamentally definitional implications of origin and maybe even significance. With the modern drive toward independence as putatively desirable, how and in what ways can believers think of themselves as having God or Christ as their head or source? What difference would such an affirmation mean for the way one lived, for the way one related to others, for the way one made decisions of choice and aversion?

**3.** Even if most women will have no problem considering that God or Christ is their "head" or source, many wives will have difficulty thinking of their husbands as their heads or sources. What would it mean for husbands to think of their wives as their heads or sources? Would it be something like Paul's advice that a husband does not have authority over his body but that his wife does (7:4), and that a husband has no right to deny his wife conjugal rights (7:3)? Or would it be something like the Paulinist writing expressed in Ephesians when it calls for both spouses to be "mutually submissive" (Eph 5:21)? Would it be possible for married believers today to work as partners who from time to time take the leadership as head and in other times and in other occasions follow?

# 1 CORINTHIANS 11:17-34, NOT THE LORD'S SUPPER

## NIV

[17]In the following directives I have no praise for you, for your meetings do more harm than good. [18]In the first place, I hear that when you come together as a church, there are divisions among you, and to some extent I believe it. [19]No doubt there have to be differences among you to show which of you have God's approval. [20]When you come together, it is not the Lord's Supper you eat, [21]for as you eat, each of you goes ahead without waiting for anybody else. One remains hungry, another gets drunk. [22]Don't you have homes to eat and drink in? Or do you despise the church of God and humiliate those who have nothing? What shall I say to you? Shall I praise you for this? Certainly not!

[23]For I received from the Lord what I also passed on to you: The Lord Jesus, on the night he was betrayed, took bread, [24]and when he had given thanks, he broke it and said, "This is my body, which is for you; do this in remembrance of me." [25]In the same way, after supper he took the cup, saying, "This cup is the new covenant in my blood; do this, whenever you drink it, in remembrance of me." [26]For whenever you eat this bread and drink this cup, you proclaim the Lord's death until he comes.

[27]Therefore, whoever eats the bread or drinks the cup of the Lord in an unworthy manner will be guilty of sinning against the body and blood of the Lord. [28]A man ought to examine himself before he eats of the bread and drinks of the cup. [29]For anyone who eats and drinks without recognizing the body of the Lord eats and drinks judgment on himself. [30]That is why many among you are weak and sick, and a number of you have fallen asleep. [31]But if we judged ourselves, we would not come under judgment. [32]When we are judged by the Lord, we are being disciplined so that we will not be condemned with the world.

[33]So then, my brothers, when you come together to eat, wait for each other. [34]If anyone is

## NRSV

[17]Now in the following instructions I do not commend you, because when you come together it is not for the better but for the worse. [18]For, to begin with, when you come together as a church, I hear that there are divisions among you; and to some extent I believe it. [19]Indeed, there have to be factions among you, for only so will it become clear who among you are genuine. [20]When you come together, it is not really to eat the Lord's supper. [21]For when the time comes to eat, each of you goes ahead with your own supper, and one goes hungry and another becomes drunk. [22]What! Do you not have homes to eat and drink in? Or do you show contempt for the church of God and humiliate those who have nothing? What should I say to you? Should I commend you? In this matter I do not commend you!

[23]For I received from the Lord what I also handed on to you, that the Lord Jesus on the night when he was betrayed took a loaf of bread, [24]and when he had given thanks, he broke it and said, "This is my body that is for[a] you. Do this in remembrance of me." [25]In the same way he took the cup also, after supper, saying, "This cup is the new covenant in my blood. Do this, as often as you drink it, in remembrance of me." [26]For as often as you eat this bread and drink the cup, you proclaim the Lord's death until he comes.

[27]Whoever, therefore, eats the bread or drinks the cup of the Lord in an unworthy manner will be answerable for the body and blood of the Lord. [28]Examine yourselves, and only then eat of the bread and drink of the cup. [29]For all who eat and drink[b] without discerning the body,[c] eat and drink judgment against themselves. [30]For this reason many of you are weak and ill, and some have died.[d] [31]But if we judged ourselves, we would not be judged. [32]But when we are judged by the Lord, we are disciplined[e] so that we may not be condemned along with the world.

[a] Other ancient authorities read *is broken for*    [b] Other ancient authorities add *in an unworthy manner,*    [c] Other ancient authorities read *the Lord's body*    [d] Gk *fallen asleep*
[e] Or *When we are judged, we are being disciplined by the Lord*

| NIV | NRSV |
|---|---|
| hungry, he should eat at home, so that when you meet together it may not result in judgment.<br><br>And when I come I will give further directions. | 33So then, my brothers and sisters,[a] when you come together to eat, wait for one another. 34If you are hungry, eat at home, so that when you come together, it will not be for your condemnation. About the other things I will give instructions when I come.<br><br>[a] Gk brothers |

# COMMENTARY

A second worship practice, which Paul calls the "Lord's supper" and which is also based on traditions, is causing some problems at Corinth. As Paul has instituted it at Corinth, the Lord's supper is part of a full-scale meal, presumably in the home of one of the believers. As distinguished from the head-covering issue in which Paul praises the women for remembering the traditions (11:2), with the Lord's supper Paul finds nothing commendable about their practice. Their coming together for worship should be a good thing; they know the traditions of the supper, and they are observing it (how frequently we cannot know). But concerning the way they comport themselves during the meals, Paul chooses language designed to shock: Yours is not the supper of the Lord (11:20).

This passage concerns the inappropriate behavior on the part of the Corinthians and the tradition as Paul related it to them. It is worth noting that, if the Corinthians had not been making such a mockery of the supper in Paul's view, we would never have known the traditions as Paul received them or even that Paul expected his churches to observe the Lord's supper.

**11:17-22.** Can it surprise any reader of 1 Corinthians that the Corinthians' observance of the Lord's supper is a highly individualized affair? "Each one takes his own supper; and one is hungry while another is drunk" (11:21). They may have the requisite cup and bread, but they do not wait for one another before consuming them. The worshipers who arrive early eat and drink early (11:33-34). Paul thinks they "treat the church of God with contempt and put to shame the ones who do not have anything" (11:22).

Put together with what we know of the social conventions and mores of the time, we can suppose what is going on in Corinth at the Lord's supper.[126] One of the members with a large enough house—and this inevitably entails a commensurate servant staff—hosts the dinner in which the Lord's supper is observed. Some persons—this apparently breaks along economic lines also—are free to come early, and they have (the choice?) food and drink. Some get drunk (11:21). Others (Paul characterizes them as "those having nothing") perhaps get there late(r) and find, along with tipsy coworshipers, leftover food at best. (For more on the socioeconomic makeup of the congregation at Corinth, see the Commentary on 1:26-31.)[127]

The Corinthians who are abusing the Lord's supper have minimized or lost the basic Pauline sense that the life of faith is a life of community. The abusers have privatized their faith and their worship in a way that Paul finds totally unacceptable; they have lost any sense that love as the right relation to others is the proper and necessary expression of their faith as the right relation to God.

**11:23-26.** Paul credits "the Lord" as his source (cf. 1 Cor 7:10; Gal 1:12). The tradition is in the form of a narrative, a story, setting the occasion as the night of Christ's betrayal. Bread, thanksgiving (εὐχαριστέω *eucharisteō*, hence more modern reference to the supper as eucharist; 11:24), dinner, and cup (of wine) frame the narrative. (For the bread-cup sequence, see also Matt 26:26-29 and Mark 14:22-25. See also Luke

---

126. Gerd Theissen, *The Social Setting of Pauline Christianity: Essays on Corinth,* ed. and trans. J. H. Schütz (Philadelphia: Fortress, 1982) 145-74.

127. See Wayne A. Meeks, *The First Urban Christians: The Social World of the Apostle Paul* (New Haven: Yale University Press, 1983) 69-70.

22:17-20, where the order is cup-bread-cup.) The particularities within that frame show the richness of Paul's understanding of the supper.

(1) The words of institution—"Do this"—are twice linked to the phrase "in remembrance of me" (11:24-25). The idea of memory and remembering has roots that reach back into Israel and are a part of Paul's Jewish heritage. What is involved in "remembering" in Israel's traditions may be seen, for example, in Deut 26:5-11, where the narrative begins as a story told in the third person, "A wandering Aramean was my ancestor; *he* went down into Egypt and lived there as an alien, few in number," and then shifts to the second-person plural "us": "When the Egyptians treated *us* harshly and afflicted *us* . . . *we* cried to the LORD. . . . The LORD brought *us* out of Egypt" (26:5-8 NRSV). The old story becomes the tellers' story; liturgy unites the old story with the current worshipers' story. What happened back then is retold to incorporate the new tellers and hearers as a part of the narrative, as participants in the old and ongoing story. So it is with Paul's understanding of the Lord's supper. When Corinthians tell the story, it becomes *their* story; they "remember" the story in a way that ties their own lives into it in a transforming and illuminating way. As we have already seen in 10:1-13, Paul employs precisely this kind of "remembering" when he recounts the exodus to his Corinthian readers, when he describes the original exodus travelers as "*our* fathers" (10:1), and when he invites the Corinthians to picture themselves as part of the story.

(2) In eating the bread and drinking the cup, "you proclaim the Lord's death until he comes" (11:26). What is meant by "proclaim" (καταγγέλλω *katangellō*)? Although the word can mean "preach," it has a much wider sense in Paul's use of it. When people live fully the new life in Christ, their faith makes itself known, their living of their faith manifests itself to others and makes an impact on them. That is why Paul, in writing to the Thessalonians, remarks: "For the word of the Lord has sounded forth from you not only in Macedonia and Achaia, but your faith in God has gone forth everywhere so that we have no need to say anything" (1 Thess 1:8). The Thessalonians have not sent missionaries; they have lived their faith with profound zeal, and *that* has been so effective a testimony, a proclamation, that Paul has

no need to preach. Their story becomes infectious. In the same way, Paul thinks that taking part (in a proper fashion, but more on that later) in the supper is itself a "proclamation."

Paul's particular description of what is proclaimed—"Christ's death until he comes"—fits Paul's purposes at hand and also affirms his basic convictions. This particular phrase is shorthand language, capable of abbreviation among those on the inside who know and remember the whole story as Paul preaches it. The horizons of Paul's vision—indeed, the story he thinks the supper "remembers"—extend from Christ's death, on the one side, to Christ's ultimate return at the end of the ages on the other. In between—and understood—are Christ's resurrection and the association of the members of Christ's body who live in Christ until his return at the end. So Paul thinks that the supper, by what it remembers and proclaims, scans the whole story of redemption in Christ and rehearses for the believers the true scope and setting of the life they are called to live together. Every time believers take part in the supper, they rehearse God's story, who they are and where they are in God's story. If they live it as they should, their very lives will become a fitting proclamation of the gospel to the world.

(3) "This is my body which is for you" (11:24). The identification of the bread with Christ's body is present in all the traditions of the supper (Mark 14:22 and par.). Paul extends the phrase by adding "which is for you," not meaning substitution (as in "in your place") but solidarity of Christ with believers. In the eating of the bread, believers proclaim Christ as *for* believers, as "on their side," as one sees affirmed about God in Rom 8:31: "If God is *for us,* who can be against us?"

As already noted, "body" is an important term for Paul, both in the Lord's supper traditions and elsewhere in his letters, but in 1 Corinthians its significance has been set since 1 Cor 6:13*b,* where Paul declared that "the body is for the Lord and the Lord for the body" because "our bodies are members of Christ" (6:15). More immediately, Paul's first allusion to the Lord's supper (10:16-17) already made a strong point about "body": "The bread which we break, is it not a sharing κοινωνία [*koinōnia*] in the body of Christ? Because there is one bread, we the many are one body." The supper affirms in its distributing of the bread to the members that Christ's body is for believers; it is as members of Christ's body that Christians have their fundamental identity. The reference to bread is a case of synecdoche (the part stands for the whole); the bread stands for Christ's body, the church, of which all participants are members, a point that Paul develops in chap. 12.

**11:27-34.** Such an allusive frame of reference as has just been established is also necessary for the understanding of the term "body" (*sōma*) in 11:29: "For the one who eats and drinks *without discerning the body* eats and drinks judgment on himself." The immediate context for understanding "discerning the body" is Paul's concern that some Corinthians are partaking in the supper "unworthily" (11:27-34).

"Discerning the body" (διακρίνων τὸ σῶμα *diakrinōn to sōma,* 11:29) is a densely packed phrase that the Corinthians probably had been prepared to understand and that we may unpack in stages. "Discerning" is a figuring out, a reckoning that a person does or is capable of doing. The body that must be discerned cannot be separated from the just-mentioned "body of the Lord," which was identified with the bread that is eaten in the supper (11:27; on the phrase "body of Christ," see the Commentary and Reflections at 12:12-27). So inevitably discerning the body must in some fundamental sense involve a reckoning or evaluation of how well one is related to Christ, whose body is understood as "for us" in the supper traditions. But in Paul's thought the body of Christ can never be separated from the members who by God's grace are incorporated into it. So "discerning the body" is Paul's shorthand way of talking about an individual's assessment of two distinguishable but inseparable matters: how well one's life relates to Christ and how well one's love ties one to others who, though many, are one body in Christ. "The one who eats and drinks without discerning the body eats and drinks judgment on himself" (11:29).

Improper or inadequate discernment of the body leaves one vulnerable to judgment (11:29). Paul does not make it explicit here, but we can suppose, in the context of his taking the supper as remembering Christ's death until he comes, that Paul is thinking of the last judgment, God's judgment at the end time. But the reference to self-judging in the present (11:31), along with Paul's

construal of Corinthian illness as a sign of present judgment (11:30), makes it clear that Paul also has in mind a present judgment that may be brought upon oneself by improper comportment at the Lord's supper (11:29). Although all this talk about judgment, present and future, may sound threatening, there is good news in Paul's assumption: One can avoid God's present and end-time judgment. How does one elude God's judgment? By using one's self-examination (11:28*a*) in the worship context of the Lord's supper as an occasion, if need be, to redirect one's life. Such persons who by self-examination and self-correction bring themselves more fully into line with God's grace in Jesus Christ will avoid present judgment and, indeed, are already blessed. The ones who do not discern the body are, in Paul's view, already experiencing God's judgment (11:30), an eschatological foretaste of the full and final judgment. Blessing awaits "the one who finds no fault with himself regarding what he discerns" (Rom 14:22). Paul assures the Corinthians that proper self-judgment, self-assessment, assuming it becomes the occasion for self-correction, is the way to avoid divine judgment (11:31). But failing a contemporary self-correction, one may still benefit from God's presently active judgment that should serve as a wake-up call before the end time, with its final judgment of the world and of those who do not self-correct (11:32).

"Being condemned along with the world" (11:32) is not to be confused with a denigration of the cosmos or of the earth (cf. 10:26). As we saw earlier, Paul thinks that the creation is good, that it, too, has come under the power of sin, and that it, too, is being redeemed. Paul's comment about the world in 11:32 is Paul's shorthand for describing the ways of the world under the sway of sin. Again, as earlier, this is border talk whereby Paul wants to distinguish how people in the body of believers live and relate to one another differently from the way people in the outside world do.

In Paul's picture, blessing and judgment are certain to be meted out at the day of wrath (Rom 2:6-11). But judgment and blessing can also be experienced in life this side of the end. Just as surely as the wrath of God is currently being revealed against all unrighteousness (Rom 1:18), so also the righteousness of God is currently being revealed (Rom 1:17). Paul tells the Corinthians that the illness of some of them is a sign of God's judgment already at work (11:30). Regarding blessing in the present, see Rom 14:22b, where we find the Pauline beatitude "Blessed is the one who is not judging [needing to judge] himself for what he figures out and does" because one's willing and doing are so fully in harmony with God's purposes.

Verses 27-34 fit a recurring pattern in the middle chapters of 1 Corinthians in which descriptions of people's comportment (Paul's, ancient Israel's, and now the Corinthians') culminate in words of warning about judgment. Paul, though called by God as apostle, has kept an athlete's discipline so as to avoid the judgment of disqualification (9:24-27). Israel, though delivered from Egypt, was not exempted from God's judgment just because it was fed and given drink in the wilderness (10:7-13). And now the Corinthians, though privileged to sit at table for the Lord's supper, cannot hope to avoid judgment if they eat and drink "in an unworthy manner" (ἀναξίως anaxiōs), as Paul clearly thinks they are doing.

In 11:27-34 Paul calls for the Corinthians to amend their ways via self-examination in the context of the Lord's supper. "Let a person self-examine" (11:28). Others cannot do it for the individual. In fact, self-examination receives no assistance from others in the community. Paul does not lay out the reasons that the self-evaluation must be individualized and personal, but we can suppose them from his claims elsewhere regarding the hiddenness of the purposes of people's hearts (1 Cor 4:5; 14:25; Rom 2:16). Only the individual person is capable of testing and knowing why he or she did (and avoided) an action.

Paul regularly affirms the vital necessity of self-testing for believers. In 1 Corinthians all of Paul's two-way elaborations have been designed to set a context in which his auditors can see where they stand more clearly. Paul's calling the Corinthians babies (3:1-2) and treating them as such serves the same function, namely to call them to reexamine where they truly stand. In his retelling of the exodus from Egypt in 10:1-13, he already affirmed the importance of self-testing (see esp. 10:12). Elsewhere in his letters Paul urges self-examination upon his readers (cf. 2 Cor 13:5; Gal 6:4). Believers are to test themselves (11:28), their standing in the faith (2 Cor 13:5), their works (Gal

6:4); and always the purpose of such self-evaluation is so that the believers can make a midcourse correction and thereby avoid crashing headlong into God's judgment.

The Lord's supper is the preeminent context in which such self-assessment is appropriate because there the story of God's redemption through Christ is sketched from Christ's death until his return at the end of the ages, which for Paul is ineluctably the ultimate time of judgment. Proper assessment of one's self, and self-correction if need be, is pre-requisite to worthy eating and drinking in the Lord's supper (11:28).

Paul concludes this matter with what seems to be a trademark of his, a practical suggestion or two aimed at helping alleviate the immediate occasion for the problem: "Wait for one another" (11:33); "If someone is hungry, let him eat in his own house" (11:34, echoing 11:22a).

Perhaps the strangest note in 11:17-34, especially for those ancient and modern readers who have followed the frequency of Paul's efforts to minimize splits in the church as the letter has progressed, is his statement: "It is necessary that there be factions so that it may be clear who are the tried and true among you" (11:19). As noted, earlier in this letter Paul tends to invite persons among the Corinthians to identify with lofty rhetorical descriptions, only to find the rug yanked ironically from under them in a kind of shock therapy (cf. 3:1ff.). Paul concedes that there are factions at Corinth; the ideal of unity for which he has argued widely in this letter and which he will continue to advocate (chaps. 12–14) is simply not the reality. The reality is their proclivity to divisions even though not everyone is causing trouble at the Lord's supper; only some haughty (and, in the instance of the supper, likely wealthier) persons are. In 11:19 Paul turns their own thinking back on them: They who reckon themselves better than "those who have nothing" (11:22) are the ones who may ironically discover that they themselves are the ones who are not "genuine" (δόκιμος dokimos, 11:19), or "tried and true." For Paul, the term dokimos refers to a person who emerges over time as one who has passed the test, who has endured hard times and remained on course in the gospel. The "genuine" persons—or to use another, similarly freighted Pauline category, the "mature" (cf. 1 Cor 2:6; 14:20; Phil

3:15)—emerge as the ones who have continued steadfastly in their life of faith despite buffeting from the world and regardless of unjust treatment by their brothers and sisters in Christ. With this admission of differentiation, Paul does not renege on his conviction that divisions are inappropriate in the body of Christ; instead he uses the Corinthian factionalism as a means of pointing out that the ones who think themselves to be powerful and better are indeed the ones who may ultimately discover themselves as disqualified, a fate Paul has already told the readers he avoids by rigorous self-discipline (9:27; note there the same Greek term as in 11:19, but with the negating *alpha* prefixed, ἀδόκιμος [*adokimos;* NIV and NRSV, "disqualified," 9:27]). Paul's ultimate concern is to recall all of the Corinthian believers to an appropriate and worthy keeping of the Lord's supper which not only provides the proper foundation for their relation to God's whole plan in Christ but also lays down the fitting relationship between believers who are members of Christ's body that is so prominently featured in the supper ritual. Paul's counsels are driven not by a veneration of the supper properly observed but by the Corinthians' failure to have the supper function among them as it should, namely as a beacon by which to keep their lives on the proper path of faith. As for other matters, Paul assures them he will give further directions when he arrives (11:34*b*).

# REFLECTIONS

**1.** How does one *unworthily* (11:27) take part in the central ritual of the community of faith, in the eating of the bread or drinking of the cup? Paul underlines the matter's importance when he warns that unworthily partaking of the supper leaves one "liable for the body and blood of the Lord" (11:27). For Paul there are two ways one can unworthily take part, and each merits exploration: (1) One can partake without examining oneself (11:28). Or (2) one can participate while failing to "discern the body" (11:29).

Christians have an obligation to know where they stand, and the way to do that is by examining their standing before God and in Christ (7:37; 10:12; cf. 2 Cor 13:5; Gal 6:4). Without proper self-assessment, believers may lose track of where they really are in the life of faith (cf. 1 Cor 4:8-12). One's birth into the faith is associated with Christ's death; one's maturity or completion is identified with Christ's coming to mark the end of the age. The life of faith is lived from new birth to maturity or adulthood and Paul sees it ideally as a progress, as a growth in which one moves along a line between the two horizons of Christ's death on the one side and the parousia on the other.

An up-to-date assessment is crucial because we bear one another's burdens according to the measure of our own faith (Gal 6:2-4) and because each person is to put into God's service whatever degree of maturity each has at a given time. In Paul's view, the Lord's supper is the ideal place where proper self-assessment takes place. So to partake of the Lord's supper "worthily" is not to be confused with *deserving* or *meriting* God's grace (an absurdity and an impossibility on its face), but it is participating in the supper knowing that one stands only because of that grace and knowing just where one stands in one's growth toward maturity. When one properly self-assesses, then that person can take part in the service worthily.

One partakes worthily when one properly "discerns the body" (11:29).[128] No doubt Paul's mention of "body" here is generated by the words of institution (11:24), but a double-sense reference to body is clearly at work. On the one side, Paul thinks of discerning one's relation to Christ. This sense overlaps with the concern in 11:28 that a person's self-test must check out, in effect, how one relates to Christ in the present-day state of one's life. On the other side, though, is the sense already established in Paul's first mention of the Lord's supper, namely that the believers, though many, all constitute "one body" (10:17). Thus to "discern the body" is not only cryptic language for checking out one's relation to Christ, whose body is at the center of the sup-

---

128. The phrase has been understood in a variety of ways, from not realizing that the eucharistic bread is different from that of regular meals to not focusing on Christ's death as the bread is taken, but these import foreign concerns.

per, but also "discerning the body" is shorthand for checking out one's relation to all the others who along with one compose the body. So, proper discerning of the body is at once an assessing not only of one's relation to Christ but also of one's relation to all the other members of the body. Ultimately, these two facets of discerning the body are not separable because the believers are so directly and fully associated with Christ and with one another in Christ.

Therefore, the Lord's supper is communion in a double sense: It is the most intimate sharing and participation with Christ, but that communion with Christ is already also the sharing in and with other believers who by definition are also those "in Christ." The Lord's supper is for Paul both personal and communal, inextricably. The Corinthians are a study of those who have forgotten the communal nature of the Lord's supper and have pursued their own interests, perhaps with their special friends, eaten their fill, gotten drunk, and treated their poorer brothers and sisters with disregard if not scorn. So Paul assails them in two ways: First, he says it is not the Lord's supper they eat; second, he warns them that without proper discernment—that is, without recognizing how they all belong equally to one another in Christ—they eat and drink judgment upon themselves.

**2.** Paul's crediting of some Corinthians with "weakness," "sickness," and even death to God's judgment raises a very serious, fundamental theological problem. Is every illness, every evidence of human frailty a sign of God's judgment? Clearly not for Paul, because he nowhere else makes any such claim in his letters. On the contrary, his letters typically see weakness and frailty as occasions for God's grace and power. Consider some of the evidence. Paul notes Epaphroditus's brush with death and sees that God has worked positively through it (Phil 2:27). The same goes for Paul's own near death reported in 2 Cor 1:8-11. He construes the cracks in these human vessels as showing forth not God's judgment but God's transcendent power working abundantly through human frailties and weaknesses (2 Cor 4:7-12). And he happily relates that his own "thorn in the flesh" becomes to him a sign that God's grace is adequate to whatever is at hand and that God's "power is made perfect in weakness" (2 Cor 12:9). (What that thorn is, though fascinating to ponder, is not important. The important thing is Paul's seeking to be free of it.) What, then, are we to make of Paul's claim in 11:30? It appears to be purely a onetime occurrence in Paul's letters and a function of Paul's (overwrought?) rhetorical effort to drive home a point.

How would Christians be able to discern whether God's judgment was at work in a particular illness or physical problem? I dare suggest that only the individual in question might be able to sort through that issue, and that no one else is *ever* in a position to pronounce upon it. A much more important communal effort might be to see how we other believers can join together with the person who is suffering to help him or her bear the burden this side of a God-given exoduslike deliverance that Paul promised in 10:13.

Furthermore, to say that God's judgment was present in a particular illness or problem would not necessarily be the same thing as saying that God caused the illness or the problem. Hearts do give out; immune systems fail or decay; accidents do happen—and all without God having to be considered in any way the cause. But can God work through any and all of these circumstances? Paul's answer to that question is a clear "Yes." Paul shared with the Romans his conviction that, for those who are loving God (the present participle expressing continuing action), God "works unto the good" in all things (Rom 8:28). Our translation "unto the good," though a bit wooden, preserves the sense of the Greek, namely that God, while not at all said to be causing the circumstances, nevertheless actively works in the things that happen, always seeking the good for those who are in right relation with God. If God's blessing can come through the circumstances in which believers find themselves, why should it not also be possible to assert that God's judgment can work through events and situations affecting those persons who live in opposition to God? Noteworthy it is that Paul thinks the end purpose of God's judgment experienced in one's life is self-correction and a reestablishment of one's life on the right track: Chastening—instruction, training, discipline such as a father might do—may occasion a reorientation "in order that we may not be condemned with the world," in the last and final judgment (11:32).

# 1 CORINTHIANS 12:1–14:40, THE PROPER FUNCTION OF SPIRITUAL GIFTS

## OVERVIEW

These chapters are the longest sustained treatment of a problem in the letter, even slightly longer than the section 8:1–11:1. The importance of the issue addressed in chaps. 12–14 is attested not only by its length but also by its position in the letter, coming so late after so many other matters that provide a context. At the heart of the extended treatment lies what is often called "the hymn of love" (chap. 13). While echoing some themes that emerged in his earlier treatment of other problems and issues, the encomium of love provides the base for Paul's counsel in the two chapters that lie on either side. Chapter 12 opens with an item from their letter (12:1; cf. 7:1) and is the third topic in the sequence that relates to worship practices in Corinth (11:2-34).

In the remainder of chap. 12, Paul acknowledges that the Corinthians have problems with spiritual gifts, and, after affirming the basic claim that the Holy Spirit is the power that makes life under Christ's lordship possible, Paul joins with the Corinthians in their recognition of the differences they experience in their Christian life together, appreciates the differences, accounts for them as part of the divine plan, and attempts to reintegrate the differences into what he sees as God's overall purpose. Chapter 14 builds from love's foundational power to refocus the Corinthians' collective life away from competition for status, moves it toward the mutuality of the upbuilding that is the hallmark of love (8:1), and closes, in typical Pauline fashion, with some practical suggestions.

Paul widens the issue from the Corinthians' question about spiritual matters or spiritualists and treats the proper function of "spiritual gifts" (χάρισματα charismata) within the community of believers. Toward that end, Paul affirms the constitutive role of the Spirit in allocating the charismata in individual believers as the Spirit wishes and for the common good. Such distribution by the Spirit rightly causes the various gifts, each of which is equally important for the enrichment of the community, to appear randomly distributed to the members. The resulting variety has no correlation with status or importance of each recipient but achieves its significance only in respect to what the variety adds to the communal life in Christ. As members of the body of Christ, all individuals have equal standing and importance; and they should use the Spirit-apportioned gifts as a way of caring for and seeking the common good of all.

## 1 Corinthians 12:1-3, Identification of Topic and Basics About the Spirit

NIV

**12** Now about spiritual gifts, brothers, I do not want you to be ignorant. ²You know that when you were pagans, somehow or other you were influenced and led astray to mute idols. ³Therefore I tell you that no one who is speaking by the Spirit of God says, "Jesus be cursed," and no one can say, "Jesus is Lord," except by the Holy Spirit.

NRSV

**12** Now concerning spiritual gifts,[a] brothers and sisters,[b] I do not want you to be uninformed. ²You know that when you were pagans, you were enticed and led astray to idols that could not speak. ³Therefore I want you to understand that no one speaking by the Spirit of God ever says "Let Jesus be cursed!" and no one can say "Jesus is Lord" except by the Holy Spirit.

[a] Or *spiritual persons*    [b] Gk *brothers*

# COMMENTARY

The passage begins with what must be a Corinthian question (12:1). Paul responds with a positioning piece, yet another back-to-basics review (12:2-3).

Paul's discussion of *charismata* is probably generated by the Corinthians' letter to him. The section opens with περὶ δὲ τῶν πνευματικῶν (*peri de tōn pneumatikōn*), which can be translated either as "now concerning spiritual things/gifts" or "now concerning spiritual persons." The former translation, favored by the NIV and the NRSV, honors that spiritual gifts do become the chief topic of chaps. 12–14, though the term *charismata* does not occur in 12:1. We know from the thanksgiving (1:4-9) that Paul thinks that the Corinthians were not "lacking in any spiritual gifts" (*charismata*, 1:7 NRSV). The Spirit has generously endowed them with all sorts of gifts. They have abundant evidence of the Spirit's having come among them to dwell (3:16). Now in chaps. 12–14 it becomes clear that this very abundance and the Corinthians' construal of it has become such a problem in their communal life that Paul must address it.

The second translation—"now concerning spiritual persons"—builds from Paul's having set up earlier in the letter the designation "spiritualists" or "those who are spiritual" as a way of referring to mature Christians (2:13-16). This latter translation would then be open to the interpretation that some Corinthians have written inquiring about persons who are making elitist claims on the basis of what they might credit as special or unusually mature Spirit connections. In one sense, all of Paul's followers are properly called "spiritualists" because the Holy Spirit is the hallmark, the telltale sign of the Christian life (surely Paul's point in 12:3*b*). Given the Corinthians' proclivity for claiming status and for turning most things toward that end, it would not be surprising if some of them had declared themselves to be *more* spiritual than others; with the evidence of chaps. 12–14, they may even have claimed that speaking in tongues was the highest or surest sign of being truly spiritual. Such persons may have thought that to lack the ability to speak in tongues was a sign of spiritual inferiority.

Paul opens his discussion (12:1-3) by taking his auditors back to their origins in the faith, specifically and significantly to their foundational connection with the Holy Spirit. He reminds them of how they had been idolatrous pagans (12:2) and how they came to make the basic Christian confession "Jesus is Lord" (cf. Rom 10:9; Phil 2:11) solely by the working of the Holy Spirit (12:3). Paul's "back-to-basics" move discloses his abiding conviction that the Corinthians' behavior shows them to be babies in the faith (cf. 3:1-2), a note to which he will explicitly return in 14:20.

Commentators have been concerned with what to make of the expression "Cursed be Jesus" (12:3*a*). Some interpreters have supposed that there might even be a group at Corinth who held such a slogan,[129] though if we understand how the rhetoric works, there is no need for us to make such a postulation. No one at Corinth champions such a slogan. Instead, Paul here resorts to shock language that is, after all, another, though more dramatic, Pauline move to ask what we know;[130] it is designed to elicit a "we know that" or an "of course not" mode of assent and to get them focused on the basics: "God's Spirit," the Holy Spirit, is the power at the foundation of the Christian life (cf. Rom 8:15-16, 26; Gal 3:1-2).[131] That Spirit could never allow anyone to curse Jesus; that Spirit properly dwells in the believers (3:16-17), interprets things that are otherwise beyond understanding (2:14), orients the believers to Jesus Christ, and enables believers to make the most fundamental affirmation: "Jesus is Lord." A clearer understanding of how that Spirit works should help the Corinthians come to a better comprehension of the way the Spirit's gifts ought to function within the community of believers.

---

129. For a sample of efforts to establish a group or situation in which persons might say "Cursed be Jesus," see the opening review in J. D. M. Derrett, "Cursing Jesus (I Cor. XII.3): The Jews as Religious 'Persecutors' " *NTS* 21 (1975) 544-45.

130. Hans Conzelmann, *A Commentary on the First Epistle to the Corinthians,* trans. J. W. Leitch, Hermeneia (Philadelphia: Fortress, 1975) 204, rightly calls Ἀνάθεμα Ἰησοῦς (*Anathema Iēsous*) "an *ad hoc* construction on Paul's part to form an antithesis."

131. J. M. Bassler, "1 Cor 12:3—Curse and Confession in Context," *JBL* 101 (1982) 415-18.

# REFLECTIONS

Although it is the oldest Christian confession, "Jesus is Lord" may ring strange or empty to modern ears. Perhaps it is easier to understand it today in a worship context in which Christians pledge to follow Christ. But the earliest Christians understood it also to be true in their personal lives. In fact, all of life was being dedicated to honoring Christ. Every day. Every decision. Every nook and cranny of one's being and doing. Jesus' lordship is over all of life, or it is properly over none of it. Today we tend to divide up life into sacred and secular, with the sacred being rather restricted to Sundays (and maybe only a part of that) and perhaps to a few times of daily devotion. In a like manner, we may think to restrict Christ's lordship to those sacred times of our lives and figure that in the rest of our time we can operate on a different basis, perhaps the way the rest of the world does. To say that "Jesus is Lord" has meant, from the earliest days, to refuse to have life divided into secular and sacred with two value systems operative in the two areas.

In another important way, to affirm that "Jesus is Lord" has also meant, from earliest times on, that one lived with the expectation that someday—when, we need not know—Christ will return and finish up God's purposes, which include the end of death and the healing of this broken world in which we live. So to affirm Jesus' lordship is to declare that the evil and wrongdoing in the world are unacceptable and inappropriate and that God will ultimately prevail over evil and reclaim all the world, humans and all creation, for God's own self as beloved and dear.

Some may think that they are autonomous beings, that they have no lord. In reality, however, it is often only the young who think that they are in full control of their lives. Persons who "have some miles on them" generally come to realize that, in fact, they control less than they might like to dream. True freedom, as Paul recognized, comes not in abandoning all lordship—because he thought that impossible—but in proper submission in Christ to God, who created us to be in relation. All efforts to live as if we have no lord will be a mirage, a fiction, and will ultimately fall of their own weight.

For Paul, even the most basic affirmation, "Jesus is Lord," is made possible by divine assistance—another affirmation of God's grace. But merely to mouth the formula, "Jesus is Lord," is not of interest to Paul (or to other early Christian communities; cf. Matt 7:21-23) without its marking all of our behavior.

# 1 Corinthians 12:4-11, Recognition of the Issue of Diversity and Its Significance

## NIV

[4]There are different kinds of gifts, but the same Spirit. [5]There are different kinds of service, but the same Lord. [6]There are different kinds of working, but the same God works all of them in all men.

[7]Now to each one the manifestation of the Spirit is given for the common good. [8]To one there is given through the Spirit the message of wisdom, to another the message of knowledge by means of the same Spirit, [9]to another faith by the same Spirit, to another gifts of healing by that one Spirit,

## NRSV

[4]Now there are varieties of gifts, but the same Spirit; [5]and there are varieties of services, but the same Lord; [6]and there are varieties of activities, but it is the same God who activates all of them in everyone. [7]To each is given the manifestation of the Spirit for the common good. [8]To one is given through the Spirit the utterance of wisdom, and to another the utterance of knowledge according to the same Spirit, [9]to another faith by the same Spirit, to another gifts of healing by the one Spirit, [10]to another the working of miracles, to another

NIV

<sup>10</sup>to another miraculous powers, to another prophecy, to another distinguishing between spirits, to another speaking in different kinds of tongues,<sup>a</sup> and to still another the interpretation of tongues.<sup>a</sup> <sup>11</sup>All these are the work of one and the same Spirit, and he gives them to each one, just as he determines.

<sup>a</sup> *10* Or *languages;* also in verse 28

NRSV

prophecy, to another the discernment of spirits, to another various kinds of tongues, to another the interpretation of tongues. <sup>11</sup>All these are activated by one and the same Spirit, who allots to each one individually just as the Spirit chooses.

# COMMENTARY

Paul has a distinctive problem in Corinth, a problem generated by those who misconstrue the riches and abundance manifest in the Spirit's working. Across 1 Corinthians, Paul has been distressed that the congregation of believers is rent with schisms (1:10-11; 3:3; 11:17-18). Partly, this divisiveness may be understood on socioeconomic grounds (1:26-31), as may be seen not only in richer persons' carrying others to court (6:1ff.) but also in the way the Lord's supper is being abused (11:17-22). Ironically, however, their tendency toward divisiveness has also been fueled by the way the Corinthians have perceived the workings of the Holy Spirit among them, and in chaps. 12–14 Paul addresses that problem. Diversity per se is not the problem at Corinth; for Paul, the problem lies in what the Corinthians have made of their diversity on many fronts. So Paul has to distinguish proper diversity from schisms and from divisive subgroups within the community.

In Paul's view, what should persons make of such differences? Paul is not surprised by differences among believers, and he has a variegated picture of what to make of them, as we can see from 1 Corinthians. In most places, Paul sees the differences as being inspired by the Holy Spirit and as enriching the community by God's design. So different persons have different life circumstances, different callings, and thus different *charismata.* Among these differences Paul fails to see a qualitative distinction: All of the differences are appropriate, and God uses them for the common good. That believers are, in fact, different from one another does not trouble Paul. Such differentiation is to be expected. Paul becomes concerned only when those differences (e.g., glossolalia, "speaking

in tongues") are taken as status indicators or when they lead to discrimination within the community (e.g., the inconsiderate treatment of "the ones who have nothing" at the Lord's supper).

Paul recognizes that there are apportionments of gifts, of servings, and of workings (12:4-6); therefore, people in the church properly manifest differences in gifts, in service, and in works (12:8-10)—and that is as it should be. To put it more directly, the differences among the Corinthians with regard to *charismata* are not understood by Paul as an accidentally variegated picture. Rather, the Spirit has allocated, dealt out, apportioned the gifts as the Spirit has seen fit for God's purposes.

Rhetorically structured around the word διαιρέσις (*diairesis,* "allocations"), which is repeatedly placed in first position in each of three clauses for emphasis, vv. 4-6 acknowledge that there are differences in *charismata,* in serving, and in working. The translations of *diairesis* by the NRSV ("varieties") and by the NIV ("different kinds") recognize Paul's effort to acknowledge such differences, but they miss the note of *apportionment* or *distribution* that Paul shows he has in mind when he repeats the same basic term once again in v. 11: "The one and the same Spirit produces [or works] all of these [*charismata*], distributing [διαιρέω *diaireō*] them to each just as it wishes." By Paul's choice of the term *diairesis* for his description of the diversities among the Corinthians (vv. 4-6), he anticipates the point with which the passage will emphatically conclude: The Spirit is the source of all *charismata* and allocates them to each person as the Spirit chooses.

Equally noteworthy are the conclusions of each of the first three clauses in vv. 4-6. Three different terms appear: *charismata,* "spiritual gifts"; διακονία *diakonia,* "service"; ἐνέργημα *energēma,* "workings". *Diakonia* and *energēma* signal to Paul's auditors that although the central issue of discussion will be spiritual gifts, the same observations are true about all we are granted to do as believers, whether that takes place as some service or ministry or some (more general category) work. Just as Paul took the Corinthians' question about eating (8:1) as an occasion to reflect about drinking and whatever else they do (8:1; 10:31), so also here the issues about *charismata* are placed in the broader context of whatever an individual does, whether serving or any other working.

The opening list of *charismata* (vv. 8-10) is significant. First, the Spirit is credited as the source of each manifestation. Second, the list probably gives some insight into the community at Corinth: Paul's list suggests that there may have been persons there who professed wisdom (v. 8), who healed (v. 9), who performed powerful works, who prophesied, who spoke in tongues, and who interpreted those utterances (v. 10). Furthermore, faith is listed as one of the gifts (v. 9), and, in Paul's view, all believers have been given the gift of faith; accordingly, no one can view himself or herself as being bereft of Spirit-endowed *charismata.*

Speaking in tongues, or glossolalia, is a special problem in the church at Corinth. In every list of gifts (12:10, 28, 30; 14:26; cf. 13:1, 8), tongues and interpretation of tongues are mentioned last, probably a Pauline inversion of the priority affirmed by some Corinthians, and in chap. 14 tongues (mentioned 17 times) become a focus of attention. Although not at all a purely Christian phenomenon, speaking in tongues was surely a feature of Christianity from its earliest days.[132] In the New Testament we find glossolalia in Acts and in 1 Corinthians. Paul's understanding of glossolalia is that it is Spirit-inspired utterance that is "talking with God" (14:2), that upbuilds the individual (14:4), but that without interpretation (by the glossolalist or by another) is not understandable talk and does not edify others (14:5, 19). This view contrasts with the understanding of

glossolalia in Acts 2, where the Spirit uses tongues (which can sometimes be translated "languages") as a means of transcending language barriers and thereby assists or works to advance the gospel by overcoming linguistic barriers.

At Corinth some of Paul's followers have received the gift of speaking in tongues and have made the case that, perhaps because it is so obviously present and esoteric, it is the most desirable gift. Accordingly, special status was claimed for those speaking in tongues. For Paul, it is astonishing that what is a *gift* from the Spirit and, furthermore, a gift that is allocated as the Spirit chooses, could become a basis for boasting. Therefore, while recognizing the diverse allocation of gifts, Paul's opening points in vv. 4-11 are that (1) whatever gifts one has are not given to vaunt oneself but are designed to serve the common good of the community (12:7), and that (2) "one and the same Spirit" has allocated the gifts strictly as it pleased the Spirit (12:11). So the gifts are not for our own aggrandizement but are for the community; likewise, no one can boast of having any particular gift because the Spirit has doled them out as it sees fit. Paul, therefore, dissociates gift and status and ties together gift and service to the community. Readers surely recognize that we encounter here an ongoing problem in which Paul struggles to alter the Corinthians' tendencies to individualism and boasting and tries to integrate the believers more fully into community and a sense of belonging to and serving one another in Christ.

Paul's succinct claim that the *charismata* are given "for the common good" (πρὸς τὸ συμφέρον *pros to sympheron,* v. 7) is striking in two ways. First, he claims the *charismata* for the benefit of the community and thus undercuts individual efforts at enhancing status. Second, his auditors, sophisticated rhetorically as they are, will no doubt note the echoes of the root term *sympheron* from its two significantly placed earlier occurrences in the letter (6:12; 10:23). The "common good," or more generally "what is helpful" (to others, understood), has been Paul's gloss on a Corinthian maxim twice before: "All things are permissible." In both of these instances, Paul was addressing a strong Corinthian sense of freedom in Christ: Believers can, indeed, express their faith in a broad and liberating spectrum of choices and situations. But in both 6:12 and 10:23 Paul has tried

---

132. Felicitas Goodman, *Speaking in Tongues: A Cross-cultural Study of Glossolalia* (Chicago: University of Chicago Press, 1972).

to increase the scope of consideration of their moral reckoning by saying that believers must also consider whether the projected action is indeed "helpful" (*sympheron*) to others. So against that background Paul bluntly simplifies by saying in v. 7 that *the point* of *charismata* is to help or to serve the community. Chapter 14 will be a protracted reflection along the same line—namely, that tongues and giving thanks through them may be

quite significant for the one doing it but *will not edify* (another way of describing being helpful or seeking the common good) the person who does not understand the glossolalia (cf. 14:19). Paul's appeal to "let all be done for edification" is an elaboration of the notion of doing all things, even glossolalia, in such a way as to be helpful, to seek the common good.

# 1 Corinthians 12:12-13, Introduction of Body-Member Metaphor with Baptismal Tradition

NIV

12The body is a unit, though it is made up of many parts; and though all its parts are many, they form one body. So it is with Christ. 13For we were all baptized by[a] one Spirit into one body—whether Jews or Greeks, slave or free—and we were all given the one Spirit to drink.

[a] *13* Or *with*; or *in*

NRSV

12For just as the body is one and has many members, and all the members of the body, though many, are one body, so it is with Christ. 13For in the one Spirit we were all baptized into one body—Jews or Greeks, slaves or free—and we were all made to drink of one Spirit.

# COMMENTARY

To make his case about the interdependency of believers, Paul resorts to a common, contemporary metaphor about parts of the body and their relation to one another, but only after he has once again rehearsed some more "basics" that he thinks the Corinthians should understand (12:12-13). What he writes in these verses is a refinement of what he said in vv. 2-3 about the Spirit's inaugurating his followers' lives as believers and enabling them to turn away from idolatry, but this time the refinement makes the case about the interrelatedness of believers by introducing the extended metaphor of the body. In vv. 12-13 the reference is once again to the Spirit, but this time in its inaugurating connection with baptism. It was in baptism, Paul says, that, by the working of the Spirit, they were made into one body of which they are all the "many members"—that is, every believer's shared story. No matter how many members, and no matter how different they are one from another, there is just one body, just as there is only one Spirit working in all the members. A part of

the baptismal liturgy is again reflected here: "whether Jews or Greeks, slaves or free" (v. 13; cf. 7:17-24 for an earlier reflection; see also Gal 3:28). It is conceivable that Paul is here echoing the very pronouncement that was made as each Corinthian was baptized.

With this refining piece (vv. 12-13) Paul has affirmed their unity, which was grounded in their baptism, has recognized once again their differences (in the expression "whether Jews or Greeks," etc.), and has associated the body/member imagery that carries the same dynamic into the succeeding verses for further development. Paul's implication is that as surely as individual differences, such as ethnicity and social status, were rendered "indifferent" or of no importance by the working of the Spirit in their baptism where they became one, so also any distinctions in terms of being members with distinctive characteristics and functions have no significance.

To inquire whether something is helpful—that is, serves the common good or, as the same point may be alternatively stated, is edifying of others—focuses on the goal of one's actions. Love, which Paul earlier declared "edifies" or "builds up" (8:1), is the way in which the goal is achieved. So love, edification, and common good are all intimately interconnected in Paul's sense of believers' living the proper moral life.

## 1 Corinthians 12:14-26, The Members' Proper Interrelation Within the Body

### NIV

¹⁴Now the body is not made up of one part but of many. ¹⁵If the foot should say, "Because I am not a hand, I do not belong to the body," it would not for that reason cease to be part of the body. ¹⁶And if the ear should say, "Because I am not an eye, I do not belong to the body," it would not for that reason cease to be part of the body. ¹⁷If the whole body were an eye, where would the sense of hearing be? If the whole body were an ear, where would the sense of smell be? ¹⁸But in fact God has arranged the parts in the body, every one of them, just as he wanted them to be. ¹⁹If they were all one part, where would the body be? ²⁰As it is, there are many parts, but one body.

²¹The eye cannot say to the hand, "I don't need you!" And the head cannot say to the feet, "I don't need you!" ²²On the contrary, those parts of the body that seem to be weaker are indispensable, ²³and the parts that we think are less honorable we treat with special honor. And the parts that are unpresentable are treated with special modesty, ²⁴while our presentable parts need no special treatment. But God has combined the members of the body and has given greater honor to the parts that lacked it, ²⁵so that there should be no division in the body, but that its parts should have equal concern for each other. ²⁶If one part suffers, every part suffers with it; if one part is honored, every part rejoices with it.

### NRSV

14Indeed, the body does not consist of one member but of many. ¹⁵If the foot would say, "Because I am not a hand, I do not belong to the body," that would not make it any less a part of the body. ¹⁶And if the ear would say, "Because I am not an eye, I do not belong to the body," that would not make it any less a part of the body. ¹⁷If the whole body were an eye, where would the hearing be? If the whole body were hearing, where would the sense of smell be? ¹⁸But as it is, God arranged the members in the body, each one of them, as he chose. ¹⁹If all were a single member, where would the body be? ²⁰As it is, there are many members, yet one body. ²¹The eye cannot say to the hand, "I have no need of you," nor again the head to the feet, "I have no need of you." ²²On the contrary, the members of the body that seem to be weaker are indispensable, ²³and those members of the body that we think less honorable we clothe with greater honor, and our less respectable members are treated with greater respect; ²⁴whereas our more respectable members do not need this. But God has so arranged the body, giving the greater honor to the inferior member, ²⁵that there may be no dissension within the body, but the members may have the same care for one another. ²⁶If one member suffers, all suffer together with it; if one member is honored, all rejoice together with it.

## COMMENTARY

The remainder of chap. 12 is structured around what amounts to verse-by-verse variations on the twinned themes of distribution/allocation and common good/helpfulness to others. "To each *is given the manifestation of the Spirit* for the common good" (v. 7). "One and the same *Spirit* who *distributes* to each just as it wishes" (v. 11). "But now *God has arranged* the members, every one of them, in the body as he wanted" (v. 18). But *"God has so composed* [blended, mixed, as of colors] the body" (v. 28, echoing v. 18) "And *God has arranged* in the church." The arrangement of the members, the assignments of the gifts, the composition of the body—all are from God, assigned as the Spirit or God wishes, and all are to be put in the service of others for the common good.

The "one body, many members" metaphor was a commonplace in the Greco-Roman world;[133] one can even find versions of it in which, as here, the different parts of the body argue with one another. The metaphor is aptly chosen for Paul's purposes because it maintains a claim for unity—one body—while recognizing and honoring differences—many, quite different members.

Functioning as a ring device, the one body premise is stated in v. 14 and reprised in v. 20 and thus effectively frames two distinctive treatments of the metaphor. The first metaphor (vv. 15-17) uses the analogy to address persons who have a low self-estimation, who wish they were other than who they are, and seeks to assure them of their importance, even necessity, to the body. The second metaphor (vv. 21-24) addresses those who have a low estimation of others—that is, those who think they have greater importance—and reminds these people, through a more extended elaboration, because the problem is exacerbated at Corinth, that every member is equally important to the well-being of the body. In this section Paul uses the culturally determined practice of dignifying certain parts of the body with clothing to make the case that all parts of the body are necessary, needed, and honored (vv. 22-24). God orders the body in such a way as to ensure that members have proper concern for one another, sharing not only in honor but also in suffering (vv. 23-26).

Throughout the letter Paul has openly addressed

and cautioned against an overly high self-estimation; one can readily deduce that he has a considerable problem with (at least some of) the Corinthians in this regard. Regularly he has chided them for boasting, for being puffed up, for not being as wise as they think, for being babies (3:1-3), for thinking they already reign (4:8), for believing that they stand when they may in fact be falling (10:12), and so forth. Nowhere until 12:15-17 does Paul address low self-estimation. The reason why is not far to find; most of the problems Paul explicitly faces in 1 Corinthians are prompted by persons with too vaunted a self-estimation, by people thinking that they are on the high side of a sharp status gradient, by people puffing themselves up. One may suppose that the majority of the Corinthian believers were not causing the troubles but were instead too regularly on the receiving end of them. The relatively few who boasted, who thought too highly of themselves, paraded their claims before the majority, who, it must be said, at least let them get away with their pretensions or at worst ascribed truth to their posturing. Paul's pastoral problem with the Corinthians thus has a double aspect that is, indeed, explicitly addressed in balanced proportions only here (12:12-24) in the letter: He not only must caution his readers against overestimation (as he has done so regularly throughout the letter), but also here he directly seeks to encourage the others not to think too lowly of themselves and of their importance to the one body. In this connection, it should be noted that in two previous places in the letter Paul has taken the side of the majority, of those who were subjected to the abusive practices of the well-to-do minority: resolving disputes by taking other believers to court (see chap. 6) and their treatment of the "ones who have not" at the Lord's supper (11:17-34).

133. Cf. Conzelmann, *1 Corinthians*, 211.

# REFLECTIONS

Here we encounter what is probably Paul's best-known image of the church: The church is the body of Christ. Several observations need to be made. First, the image is not Paul's only one for the church. Many others (building, temple, field) have already been noted in the commentary. Second, this image is used by Paul only when there are problems of disunity (cf. Romans 12), so we should not expect this image to illustrate all that is important to know or consider about the church.

Third, Paul starts with the assumption that the church is the body of Christ. Simply because the believers die with Christ in their baptism and are one with Christ, they are already the body of Christ. Modern Christians sometimes wonder how they might more fully become the body of Christ. That is not Paul's notion. He considers that believers as believers are already the body of Christ, and he exhorts them to relate to one another in a manner appropriate to *what they already are.*

Fourth, chapter 12, with its imagery of the body, is a case study in a conception of unity that still preserves and honors diversity. The unity of the believers is grounded in that each person is an indispensable part of the body and that, though it is unstated here, it is clearly by the grace of God that each one belongs. The individuality is honored in that each believer serves the body in a distinct—neither less nor greater—way. Christian unity neither requires uniformity nor encourages it. In the same way that the gifts are given by the Spirit as the Spirit chooses and in order to serve the common good, the distinctive members are called to be part of the body, and each is to contribute its own special and distinctive work to the well-being of the whole body. For Christians to be different is not only acceptable, but it is expected and even necessary for the richness, wholeness, and vigor of the body. Believers can differ from each other in appearance and function, in what is done (cf. 12:4-11), and even in certain opinions (cf. Rom 14:1, 5-6). Believers' unity lies in their being one in Christ, in the body together; each one of them is a person for whom Christ died, and all of them have that shared death with Christ in common; thus each has been given to the other in Christ.

Fifth, with so many modern Christians having low self-esteem, we might do well to pay special attention to Paul's insistence in 12:15-17 that all the members are *equally* important to the well-being of the body of Christ. No one is less important. No one brings less to the body of Christ.

Finally, note that Christ is not here named as the head of the body. Ephesians and Colossians alter the image of the church as the body of Christ to claim Christ's headship over the church. Paul's purpose and use of the image here in 1 Corinthians affirms the closest possible identification of Christ and the believers. The believers and Christ belong to one another, and the believers are the members of Christ's body.

# 1 Corinthians 12:27-31, Application of What Has Been Said and Anticipation of the Next Part of the Argument

## NIV

[27]Now you are the body of Christ, and each one of you is a part of it. [28]And in the church God has appointed first of all apostles, second prophets, third teachers, then workers of miracles, also those having gifts of healing, those able to help others, those with gifts of administration, and those speaking in different kinds of tongues. [29]Are all apostles? Are all prophets? Are all teachers? Do all work miracles? [30]Do all have gifts of healing? Do all speak in tongues[a]? Do all interpret? [31]But eagerly desire[b] the greater gifts.

And now I will show you the most excellent way.

[a] 30 Or *other languages*   [b] 31 Or *But you are eagerly desiring*

## NRSV

[27]Now you are the body of Christ and individually members of it. [28]And God has appointed in the church first apostles, second prophets, third teachers; then deeds of power, then gifts of healing, forms of assistance, forms of leadership, various kinds of tongues. [29]Are all apostles? Are all prophets? Are all teachers? Do all work miracles? [30]Do all possess gifts of healing? Do all speak in tongues? Do all interpret? [31]But strive for the greater gifts. And I will show you a still more excellent way.

# COMMENTARY

So far in this chapter Paul has been reestablishing "basics," a continuing motif in this letter. In 12:27-31 Paul applies "what we know" about the body to the church and, with another listing of gifts, moves a step closer to the counsel that will be delivered most fully and directly in chap. 14. As surely as God has configured the members of the human body, so it is with the body of Christ (12:27), in which God has arranged that certain gifts be assigned to certain persons. Paul's claim of priority for the apostles (14:28; cf. 9:1) reaffirms his standing, his authority, as did his reference to the Corinthians earlier as babies (3:1) and as did his claim of being their father in the faith (4:14). By listing prophets as second, only behind apostles, Paul tips his hand regarding his laudation of prophecy just ahead (in chap. 14, where we will see what Paul understands by the term).[134] The

remainder of the items integral to the list should not be of great concern because on some level they no doubt function to make sure that the reader sees prophecy near the top and speaking in tongues at or near the bottom (12:28, 30). The rhetorical questions of 12:29-30, all cast to indicate that they expect a negative answer, invite the hearers to engage themselves in a perspective-giving litany: Not everybody is endowed with all the gifts, but as Paul has said four different ways in this chapter, *the gifts are apportioned as God or the Spirit sees fit* (12:11, 18, 25, 28).

With 12:31, the argument takes a curious turn, surely designed to grasp the auditors' full attention. Paul, who has made a strong case that the gifts are, first, of equal importance, and, second, assigned, apportioned, arranged by divine fiat, now urges the Corinthians to "seek the greater gifts" (χαρίσματα τὰ μείζονα *charismata ta meizona,* 12:31). The focus is on love throughout the next chapter.

134. For a detailed consideration of the topic in its broader context, see Aune, *Prophecy in Early Christianity,* 248-62.

# REFLECTIONS

**1.** Paul lists the gifts of the Spirit in 12:4-10, 27-31 and in Rom 12:3-8. How should we understand these lists? Are they intended to be exhaustive? Illustrative? The interpretive land-mines related to spiritual gifts are numerous. First, there is the natural human tendency to look at the lists and to check ourselves against them, as we check a part to its template, to see how (or even whether) the Spirit is working one or more of those gifts (*charismata*) in our own lives. Second, we could easily assume that the lists exhaust the possibilities of the Spirit's gifts (see 1 Cor 7:7 for a charisma that is not even in a list); that if one is not an apostle or has not been working miracles or healing recently, we might conclude that this person is not the medium for the Spirit's working. Third, perhaps that one gift more than all the others is *the* gift of choice.

The lists do not agree in content. Speaking in tongues is not even mentioned in the Romans list. Faith, a charisma that, by definition, *every* believer must have, is listed as a gift in 1 Cor 12:9, so no one can look at the lists and not see himself or herself reflected in them somewhere.

Although the lists are somewhat tailored to the circumstances of the letters in which they are found, they are not exhaustive of the ways the Spirit works in believers. Rather, they are *illustrative.* Further, we may conclude that, as Paul is at pains to argue in 1 Corinthians, no one gift is superior to all of the others and that no one gift is the hallmark or telltale sign of one's being a Christian. Likewise, we see that each gift is determined and allocated by the Spirit, as the Spirit wills, as a means of enriching the community life of the believers, and that there is no limit to the number of gifts an individual may exhibit. So modern Christians should view the Pauline lists of gifts as suggestive of the multitude of ways that the Spirit works in and through the lives of individuals to enrich the shared life and the common good of the believers.

One final point: The different kinds of spiritual gifts should not be isolated from the "different kinds of service" and the "different kinds of working" that parallel and overlap in 12:4-6. So as modern believers look for signs of the Spirit's working in them, they should not look simply at the spiritual gifts; that is only one part of the Spirit's working. They should look also at their service as a sign of the Spirit's expression in them; likewise, they should consider also their different ways of working along with and through others as yet another sign of the Spirit's manifesting itself in and through them. Like grace, the Spirit works in lives in surprising ways, some of which bowl us over with their immediate power and obviousness while others may seem more like Elijah's "gentle whisper" (1 Kgs 19:12 NIV), more like silence than a whirlwind. Believers should never underestimate the power or mode of the Spirit's working even if to them its working is neither obvious nor overwhelming. Accordingly, in the shared life of faith even the actions or deeds that seem the most menial and inconsequential may be the medium through which the Holy Spirit works to enrich the common good of the faithful.

**2.** Some Corinthians have made glossolalia the most important gift, the sign of having made it to the fullness, perhaps even the zenith, of Christian life—and some others in the congregation have let them do so. Evidence may be seen in the way Paul's lists of gifts always put their first-rated gift last (12:10, 30), in the contrast of tongues and love in 13:1, and in the way glossolalia is a continuing topic in chapter 14. For Paul, glossolalia is inspired by God, is edifying of the inspired individual, is not understandable speech without the accompanying gift of interpretation but with interpretation it edifies the whole church, and is just another one of the gifts all of which are equally important for the life of the church and for the common good. Paul surely does not oppose glossolalia and expects that, with interpretation, it will be part of worship (14:26-28).

Some modern Christians, like their Corinthian counterparts before them, have overlooked Paul's arguments to the contrary and have adopted the Corinthians' mistakes: that speaking in tongues is the ultimate gift, that glossolalia signals when a person has *truly* become a full-fledged Christian, and, correspondingly, that the lack of speaking in tongues is taken as a sign of a spiritual deficit. Paul opposes each of these mistakes. In the letter to the Galatians, Paul faces a quite similar problem; there circumcision instead of glossolalia has become the same sort of talisman. In Galatians, Paul argues that the key indicator of whether people are truly believers is whether they have received the Holy Spirit (Galatians 3). What would Paul say to modern Christians who single out one particular indicator (whether it be glossolalia or the "right" ideas on the inspiration of the Bible or abortion, etc.) other than the reception of the Holy Spirit as the key indicator?

# 1 Corinthians 13:1–14:1a, Encomium on Love

## OVERVIEW

For a letter that could rightly be called a continuous reflection on love—even Paul's summary injunctions at the end of the letter conclude with "Do everything in love" (16:14 NIV)—the explicit term has been rather infrequent before chap. 13. With its pithy maxim "Love builds up," 8:1 establishes such a close identification of love and edification that subsequently in the letter the appearance of either term, "love" or "edification," should call to mind the other. The way love works or functions in the community is to bring about edification or upbuilding (another translation of the same Greek term, οἰκοδομή *oikodomē*) of others. Likewise, when Paul encourages edification of others he is simply calling for love to be put into action toward them.

Chapter 13, an encomium[135] on love, though

135. J. G. Sigountos, "The Genre of 1 Corinthians 13," *NTS* 40 (1994) 246-60; J. Smit, "The Genre of 1 Corinthians 13 in the Light of Classical Rhetoric," *NovT* 33 (1991) 193-216; Carl R. Holladay, "1 Corinthians 13: Paul as Apostolic Paradigm," in *Rhetoric and the New Testament: Essays from the 1992 Heidelberg Conference,* ed. S. E. Porter and T. H. Olbricht, JSNTSup 90 (Sheffield: JSOT, 1993) 250-64.

not explicitly identifying love as a *charisma,* or gift,[136] extols love and thereby sets the stage for the next chapter's specific application of love and its inevitable expression or by-product, upbuilding (14:3-5, 12, 17, 26), to the Corinthians' problematic practices. By the first century, an encomium was a well-established rhetorical device for praising an individual or a virtue. Typically, encomia praise in two ways: by reference to actions as a clue to character (*ethos*) and by comparison and contrast with other virtues or other praiseworthy persons. Usually, encomia open with a prologue and close with an appeal for emulation. Paul's panegyric on love meets all these criteria.

Some scholars have suggested that Paul did not compose chap. 13 but knew it from elsewhere and

incorporated it into his argument.[137] Others have posited that one can read from 12:31 to chap. 14 with no interruption of Paul's argument, that Paul did not compose chap. 13, and that a later redactor of the Pauline corpus put it where it is.[138] Surely one can construe chaps. 12–14 in that fashion, but to do so overlooks some distinct functions of chap. 13. First, the chapter gives perspective and balance to the matter at hand—namely, proper use and understanding of spiritual gifts in the Corinthian church. Second, the chapter has many significant links to the rest of the letter so that it also serves to recapitulate several concerns already registered by Paul. Third, rhetorical handbooks saw such a change of pace and concentration as a powerful way of focusing the auditors' attention. Paul is surely capable of lofty composition, and chap. 13 serves too many of his concerns not to have belonged there from the start.

---

136. Note that love is considered by Paul as a "fruit" of the Spirit (Gal 5:22). That is, love is a response, a way of living that is made possible by God's grace through the working of the Holy Spirit. It is, therefore, not simply a gift but a way of being and relating.

137. See Gordon D. Fee, *The First Epistle to the Corinthians* (Grand Rapids: Eerdmans, 1987) 626n. 5.
138. See ibid.

## 1 Corinthians 13:1-3, The Prologue

NIV

**13** If I speak in the tongues*a* of men and of angels, but have not love, I am only a resounding gong or a clanging cymbal. [2]If I have the gift of prophecy and can fathom all mysteries and all knowledge, and if I have a faith that can move mountains, but have not love, I am nothing. [3]If I give all I possess to the poor and surrender my body to the flames,*b* but have not love, I gain nothing.

*a 1* Or *languages*   *b 3* Some early manuscripts *body that I may boast*

NRSV

**13** If I speak in the tongues of mortals and of angels, but do not have love, I am a noisy gong or a clanging cymbal. [2]And if I have prophetic powers, and understand all mysteries and all knowledge, and if I have all faith, so as to remove mountains, but do not have love, I am nothing. [3]If I give away all my possessions, and if I hand over my body so that I may boast,*a* but do not have love, I gain nothing.

*a* Other ancient authorities read *body to be burned*

## COMMENTARY

The encomium's prologue (13:1-3), by reference to a series of indisputably important items, establishes love as the sine qua non of the faithful life. It does so by Paul's reminding the Corinthians of his extraordinary gifts, his grandiloquent abilities, and his potential for extravagant deeds. The auditors are asked to survey Paul as being capable of all these; his history with them allows him rea-

sonably to suggest such a range—and yet lacking love. Without love, all his gifts and powers and actions come to naught in the devastatingly pithy declaration, "I am nothing" (13:2).

Imagine the impact of these verses on the original hearers of this letter. First Corinthians has so regularly centered around Paul's offering of himself as a positive example worthy of emulation. In

**13:1-3** Paul presents himself once again as a model, but this time as a negative exemplar, as one who, though so very gifted, if lacking love, would be of no worth, no value. This rhetorical device, much like the indirect speech noted in chaps. 1–4, allows Paul to lay out some stern warnings to his auditors without risk of unduly offending them and with the added advantage that his application to himself allows, even subtly commends, that others apply the same test to themselves. The auditors can hear much more forceful and blunt criticism of themselves precisely because it is Paul's critique of his imaginary, contrary-to-fact self.

Not surprisingly, the first item is the highly touted Corinthian favorite: speaking in tongues. Paul invites the hearers to imagine him, richly endowed as they know him to be with the gift of tongues (the reference to "tongues of angels" makes clear we are not dealing with linguistic acumen; cf. 14:18-19; cf. also 7:7), but lacking love (which he assumes they know him in fact not to be): He would be a useless, perhaps even an irritating musical instrument whereas, with love, he would have been helpful and even enriching. Paul's likening his imaginary loveless self to a brassy clanging instrument no doubt anticipates his subsequent development of that image in 14:7-11.

Second is a collection of items (already mentioned, e.g., in 1:18–2:16: prophetic abilities, understanding, and wisdom) with which he assumes some Corinthians have very positive identifications. And in regard to those endowments (which the letter has also been careful to remind the Corinthians Paul certainly does not lack), Paul pictures his imaginary loveless self as "nothing" (13:2). Third are two means of gaining social notoriety and presumably status: a giving away of all one's possessions and some sort of self-immolation (cf. Rom 5:7, where it is said that someone would perhaps die for another; see also Rom 9:3, where Paul imagines himself cut off so that his Jewish brothers and sisters might be included). And without love, neither gains anything. As Paul takes his epistolary walk through their gallery of values, he escalates the shock effect of his own imaginary self-portraits, moving as he does from likening himself to a useless instrument (13:1) to his claim that he is nothing (13:2). Paul's indirect critique of their self-aggrandizement around tongues, wisdom, and understanding is implicit in his imaginary loveless, negative, contrary-to-fact self-portrait.

Extraordinary gifts, grand abilities and skills, extravagant actions—all these, ironically, are emptied of any worth without love. Furthermore, with the mention of each item, the refrains describing lovelessness become more blatantly self-indulgent, more individualistic, and more self-serving. The point, subtly but powerfully made, is that no matter how magnificent the accomplishment, power, or action, when love is missing the exercise in question becomes vain, selfish, fruitless, and individualistic; it does not even serve to accomplish its self-vaunting end. "Without love, I help myself [ὀφελοῦμαι *opheloumai*] not at all" (13:3). As one Scottish translation captures it: "I am nane the better o it."[139] Love's quest can never begin with the question "What's in it for me?" Instead, love looks first to the other and asks, "What is best for you?" "What would help you?" A few verses into chap. 14, Paul, using the same Greek term ὠφελέω (*ōpheleō*) and modeling love, asks the Corinthians not how they might help *him*, but how he might help *them* (14:6). So within a few verses he does the very thing that he prescribes for them. The proper movement of love begins with attention to the needs of the other person.

Imbedded within the prologue (13:1-3) are two convictions: (1) Love's nature is to seek not one's own needs but the needs of others, and (2) in so doing, love ultimately secures not only the other person but also one's own self. Directly ahead in the encomium Paul will make this same point; he has already made it in 1 Corinthians (10:24, 33), and elsewhere in his letters he is quite regularly insistent on this same dynamic (Phil 2:1-4; cf. Rom 13:8; 15:1-2). (See Reflections at 14:1*a*.)

---

139. *The New Testament in Scots,* trans. W. L. Lorimer (Edinburgh: Southside, 1983).

# 1 Corinthians 13:4-7, Recitation of the Acts of Love

### NIV

⁴Love is patient, love is kind. It does not envy, it does not boast, it is not proud. ⁵It is not rude, it is not self-seeking, it is not easily angered, it keeps no record of wrongs. ⁶Love does not delight in evil but rejoices with the truth. ⁷It always protects, always trusts, always hopes, always perseveres.

### NRSV

4Love is patient; love is kind; love is not envious or boastful or arrogant ⁵or rude. It does not insist on its own way; it is not irritable or resentful; ⁶it does not rejoice in wrongdoing, but rejoices in the truth. ⁷It bears all things, believes all things, hopes all things, endures all things.

## COMMENTARY

An encomium of a person recounts past actions worthy of praise; an encomium of a virtue depicts its characteristics and how it functions. In 13:4-7, love's credentials are laid out both positively, with regard for what love does and how it operates, and negatively, with regard to what it avoids and does not do. "Love waits with patience" and while waiting, it is kind and merciful (13:4). Then follows a sequence of declarations of what love is not, declarations that via negativa serve to clarify what is characteristic of love: It is not jealous, not boastful, not puffed up, not behaving disgracefully, not seeking its own purposes, not becoming irritated, not keeping score of wrongs, and not taking pleasure in unrighteousness (13:4-5a).

Then with considerable rhetorical flourish Paul concludes the characterization of love by a string of most sweeping claims about love, each beginning with the direct object (πάντα *panta*, "all things"), thereby emphasizing love's all-encompassing scope. The "all things" list opens and closes with very nearly the same point about how love functions in the present, thus highlighting these two claims: "Love passes over all things in silence" (v. 7a) and "Love bears [or endures] all things" (v. 7d). On one level these assertions are positive counterparts to the disclaimer that love does not keep track of wrongs; they represent the necessary kind of "running forgiveness" that is ingredient to any sustained relationship. On another level they establish love as the context in which the difficulties and trials of life are met. How do they do so? Because love is never held alone in one's self; love always involves another;

love always links one's self to another. This reciprocal character of love has already been acknowledged by Paul in 8:3: "If someone loves God, that person is known by God." Love is a two-way street that provides a context of mutuality, understanding, and relatedness between each person and others, between God and believers, and between believers and believers. And that is the context in which love enables us, with the support of the others who are linked in love, to bear, to endure whatever comes along. This is the same point he already made in 10:13, but this time expressed in terms of love.

The other two claims of v. 7—"love believes all things; hopes all things"—tie faith and hope to love in anticipation of v. 13. It is not surprising that faith (the same Greek term for the verb "believe") and hope should appear here together; they are inextricably tied in Paul's thought (cf. Gal 5:5-6; 1 Thess 1:3; 5:8). Faith, right relationship with God, is the basis on which one has hope regarding the future, because, through faith, one knows God's redemption in the present, one can hope—that is, one can confidently look to the future in anticipation of God's completing the work that God has already begun in the present (cf. Phil 2:12b-13).

Love's believing all things describes neither a willing disregard for reality nor naïveté nor gullibility. It is probably best to take this statement as a posture of openness along the lines of 2 Cor 5:7: "We walk through faith, not through sight." Certainly, to hope all things must be grounded in this confidence in God toward the future, a confidence whose basis is neither visible nor directly knowable, a theme to which Paul returns in 13:12. On the theological level, "walking by faith" describes a way of living in trust upon the God who is "for us" (Rom 8:31; cf. 1 Cor 11:24)—that is, the God who is benevolently disposed toward humans, who brings into being the things that do not exist, and who brings life out of death (Rom 4:17). (See Reflections at 14:1a.)

# 1 Corinthians 13:8-13, Comparison and Contrast of Love with Other Virtues

# COMMENTARY

The next standard feature of an encomium compares the virtue, in Paul's case, love, to others: "Love never ends/fails." Tongues, the favorite of some Corinthians, and prophecy, Paul's alternate favorite, which he is about to advocate in chap. 14, along with knowledge, which will become the topic a few verses later, are limited, even finite; tongues and prophecy are functions that serve the particular needs of a given community within time and history, but whose scope is limited to human performance. Faith and hope are enabled by God's grace, but God does not "believe," and nowhere does Paul say that God "hopes." God does love, however, and so do believers. So love's being and existing is tied to God's very self, and in loving, believers participate with God in a special, unique, even reciprocal way. Love never ends because God's eternal love is the ground and matrix for all human loving.

Paul's eschatological convictions shape what he says here. The present, graced as it is with God's love alive in the community at Corinth, is still only a partial reflection, like that of a mirror whose glass is not clear, of what is yet to come. Paul thinks believers live with a present down payment (2 Cor 1:22; 5:10), with partial insight, or as he will develop it in chap. 15, with the perishable and mortal but in full anticipation of the imperishable and immortal. Paul's vision stretches from his recognition that all believers are somewhere on a pilgrimage from being children in the faith, as he thinks the Corinthians are (3:1), to the time when maturity or the perfect arrives (13:10), to that time when believers no longer walk by faith but by sight, when in the eschaton they see "face to face" (13:12). So Paul anticipates that faith, as important and central as it is, will someday be transcended by the most intimate presence with God. In the meantime, Paul offers himself once again as the model of the person who is no longer a child, who has set aside childish things (13:12). When the perfect arrives, when believers see face-to-face, then Paul expects to exchange his own partial knowledge for a full knowing, then his knowing will correspond to the knowing (God's, assumed but not stated) that has preceded and made possible Paul's partial and proleptic knowing (13:12).

Corinthian interest in "knowing" and "knowledge" is once again put in perspective: Paul, who exceeds them in knowledge as he also excels them in tongues, acknowledges that he knows only "in part" and that the knowledge yet to come, at the end of the ages, so far surpasses present knowledge (note that this same sort of argument will be undertaken in chap. 15 when present glory is contrasted with future glory) as to put present knowing in a modest perspective. But all of this reflection about the partial and the perfect, the present and future knowledge, the now and then, is designed to put love and the "now" in perspective: "But now remain faith, hope, and love, these three, but the greatest of these is love" (13:13). The famous Pauline triad is most clearly present here (cf. Rom 5:1-5; Gal 5:5-6; Col 1:4-5; 1 Thess 1:3; 5:8). At the heart of the Christian life are these three. Paul cannot imagine life in Christ without each part of the triad being in place and fully functioning; all three must remain whatever else may come and go or change or however different one believer is from another.

How is love greater than faith and hope? Faith, the right relation to God, makes love possible (Gal 5:6), so love presupposes faith. Does that suggest that faith is really greater? Paul has already given the cue when he introduced this whole comparative section of the encomium: "Love never fails/ends" (v. 8). Hope, a conviction and a yearning lodged in the heart of the individual, clearly ends when that for which one hopes is finally achieved. Faith, also a human commitment, though not possible without God's grace, may end; one may fall from faith (cf. Gal 3:3-5). By contrast, love, grounded as it is in God and a signal and eternal characteristic of God's commitment toward all creatures, is the one disposition that believers share most fully with God. And that love is eternal.

Love is "greatest" in three senses. First, its eternality, allowing it to be present fully now and yet guaranteed to be present also when the eschatological time brings about that toward which we have believed and hoped, establishes it as superlative. Second, it is greatest when Paul thinks of the Corinthian fascination with gifts, each of which is transient. Faith, hope, and love endure; gifts do not. Gifts are finite; they are given to persons who employ them for a period within the community. Love is the matrix of the life of faith; God's love for people becomes the force that enables them to love others. Third, the "greatest" lack of the Corinthians is love. They are well endowed with gifts, as Paul recognized already in the thanksgiving (1:7). They are quite zealous regarding spiritual matters; Paul acknowledges that, and he urges them to "seek to abound in building up the church"; if one keeps in mind the connection Paul has made in 8:1, that love builds up, one can see that he is in effect saying that they should seek to abound in loving one another (cf. 16:14). They have become too fixated on gifts and have failed to live love toward one another. In that sense, also, the greatest need for them is love. (See Reflections at 14:1a.)

# 1 Corinthians 14:1a, The Encomium's Conclusion, the Appeal for Emulation

| NIV | NRSV |
|---|---|
| **14** Follow the way of love and eagerly desire spiritual gifts, | **14** Pursue love and strive for the spiritual gifts, |

# COMMENTARY

An encomium typically ends with a call for hearers to be like the person praised or to put in practice the highlighted virtue. Paul follows the expectation: "Pursue love" (14:1*a*). Curiously, the term "love" makes no further appearance until 16:14 and 24, but the Pauline connection between love and upbuilding is so fully established (cf. 8:1) that he no longer needs to use the word "love"; he can (and does) now shift to "building up," "edification" (14:3-5, 12, 17, 26), and he is in fact talking about love without using the term. He can shift his focus to edification not only for rhetorical purposes (the rhetorical handbooks warn about overusing a term and recommend substituting another for it)[140] but also for his paraenetic purposes (he is interested not in lip service to a virtue, but in the real practice of love that by its very nature and function results in the upbuilding of others and in the edification of the church).

140. *Ad Herennium* 4.12.18.

# REFLECTIONS

**1.** Paul's encomium of love is one of the loftiest expressions in literature. Its function is to place love, in many of its aspects, in the center of the community's reflection, which location is itself symbolic of love's centrality to the life of faith. Love is the absolutely indispensable feature of the believing life (13:3); without love, no matter how many possessions one has or how prominent one is, one is lost and as good as dead. Some of Paul's assertions about love call for reflection.

(1) "Love always protects" (NIV); "Love bears all things" (NRSV); "Love passes over all things in silence" (13:7*a*). In this pithy statement Paul captures an essential characteristic of love: Not only does love not keep score of past better and worse moments and actions, but it also looks the other way, as it were. When we reflect even about friendship we know that our friendships continue precisely because we are willing to give our friends a break, to give them the benefit of the doubt, and even to overlook slights or inadvertences. If friendship depends on that, then how much more so love.

In extreme circumstances, however, love may not call for passing over something in silence; it may not allow us to look the other way and ignore it. When, for example, a person is abused physically, emotionally, or sexually, this verse cannot be invoked as a reason for the victim to bear it or for the perpetrator to be protected. In matters of fundamental justice and the protection of less powerful persons preyed on by others, love requires that its handmaiden justice be brought to bear. Then, love must protect the victim, not the victimizer. Therefore, love "bears all things" insofar as they do not harm another of God's creatures. Churches have an obligation to be counted foursquare on seeing that love is always hand in hand with justice. There is an irony about love: The very capacity to overlook, not to keep score—which is so vitally important to the functioning of love and to the wholeness of community—leaves love vulnerable to exploitation. And the community of believers, one and all, must be eternally vigilant to avoid or expose that exploitation—in a loving fashion.

(2) There is an ambiguity about love that resists common sense: In seeking the good of the other, one finds one's own good. Intuition would suggest that we take care of ourselves first and if anything or any time is left over, then we turn to others. But Paul supposes that one's good is not achievable apart from the well-being of others in the body of Christ to which all believers equally belong. So there is a circularity to love, starting from God's love of us, which love renews us and remakes us whole, and moving ineluctably until it gains expression toward others as a way of responding in thankfulness to God's love. In that sense, love cannot be held; it cannot be seized; it is realized fully only in its being shared with someone else. We who have been fully

loved by God honor and relish that love most completely only in the sharing of it with others. So, to look after the interests of others is inescapably to benefit all persons in the community and therefore to benefit oneself.

This sense of caring for others, however, can become a smoke screen for failing to attend to one's own needs, for hiding one's own desperation and deficiencies. Ideally, Paul supposes that believers ought to have accurate self-assessments, to know where they stand, where their strengths and weaknesses are, and to build upon the strengths and actively work to shore up the weaknesses. As great as it is, love founders when it is used as an excuse either to avoid proper self-care or to cloud proper self-assessment. Without the proper self-testing that Paul has consistently expected, love cannot properly engage the self one truly is with the needs of another.

There is an analogy in what Paul says about knowing and being known (13:12). God knows us perfectly; what we now know is partial and filled with enigmas, but Paul anticipates that the time is coming when he will know as Paul himself is known already by God. God's knowing, like God's loving, precedes and gives power to our knowing and our loving. Our partial knowing, like our so-far only partial loving, is capable of improvement and growth by God's grace until that end time when we will know as we are known and love as we are loved.

(3) If mountains come and go, but love endures; if love is greater even than faith and hope, then not only does our loving endure beyond us but our loving is our enduring legacy as well. Granted, our loving and its legacy can take many forms. If we took it seriously that our loving was our enduring legacy, then what reorganization would be needed in our lives, in our stewardship of our time, energy, and resources to honor and maximize that legacy?

**2.** This chapter, or part of it, is read at many wedding ceremonies—and appropriately so, because Paul has recognized some fundamentals about love no matter how it is understood. But it would be a mistake to assume that Paul here has in mind romantic love that is powered by one's yearning for and infatuation with a marriage partner. The love of which Paul writes so eloquently is a love that does not originate in one individual and reach out to another. Rather, the love celebrated in this text comes from God, claims us, and through us reaches out to others, not simply to another person whom we wish for our spouse. The love about which Paul writes, then, can never find its sole object in another single individual but reaches out through and beyond that other person. It is therefore surely appropriate to read this passage at weddings where love is affirmed between two individuals, but never without the sense that the love between those two is first not of their own origination but also that its goal can never be fully realized in its focus on one another. True love, as Paul sees it, always begins with God and always reaches beyond one's self to others. The Pauline notion of love never stops on just one other person, no matter how special, but reaches through the loved one(s) to God's broken world in which this new couple now pledge to make their life together.

**3.** A commonplace in the history of art depicts Faith, Hope, and Charity (from the Latin *caritas*, for "love") as three women. You can see them, for example, in El Greco's *Modena Triptych*, in which they stand together in the foreground of the crucifixion. In this same painting, El Greco employs a further artistic convention when he depicts Charity (Love) as being surrounded by numerous children clinging to her legs and being carried in her arms. Artists have long understood that love is known by her offspring and characterized by having children too numerous to count.

# 1 Corinthians 14:1*b*-40, Paul's Affirmation of Edification and Practical Suggestions

## OVERVIEW

This large block opens and closes with the same thought: "Seek to prophesy" (14:1*b*, 39). Across the rather extended passage, Paul argues that prophecy is superior to tongues because prophecy "builds up," "edifies" the community, and thereby serves the common good (12:7). Paul has to walk a fine line; he needs to put tongues into their proper perspective without denigrating them. So the closing note of this chapter is designed to ward off the Corinthians' tendency to extremes: "Do not prohibit the speaking in tongues" (14:39). A sort of formula emerges in Paul's reflections: Tongues plus interpretation equals or results in edification for the community; tongues without interpretation builds up only the one speaking in tongues (14:4).

The leitmotif of the section is edification, the fruit of love between and among believers (8:1). The Corinthian church's problem is not a lack of spiritual gifts (1:7), but rather the proper employment of them for the common good (12:7), for mutual upbuilding and enrichment of the communal life of faith. Some in Corinth have privatized and personalized the gifts in an attempt to enhance their own status and well-being. Paul seeks to re-

incorporate those persons and their gifts into service of the community of believers. His strategy is to stress prophecy, which he apparently thinks not only is available to everyone (14:1*b*, 39) but also builds up others.

This section, thoroughly praxis-oriented and practical in its application throughout and containing a mix of arguments including some exemplification of how things should and should not be, is governed by the question of what most edifies the community. Paul signals his answer in the opening verses: Prophecy is preferred over tongues unless the latter are accompanied by interpretation, in which case the effect is also edification. Once again Paul sets himself as the example of the one whose spirituality integrates the mind and the spirit and whose comportment in worship corresponds to his earlier-described evangelist efforts (9:19-23). He leaves no one out, neither members of the community nor those in the position of novices (see more on this in 14:13-19) nor unbelievers who might happen into the community's worship. The remainder of the chapter gives some practical suggestions, a Pauline hallmark, and closes with an enforcement statement.

# 1 Corinthians 14:1*b*-12, Edification Valued Over Glossolalia

**NIV**

especially the gift of prophecy. ²For anyone who speaks in a tongue*a* does not speak to men but to God. Indeed, no one understands him; he utters mysteries with his spirit.*b* ³But everyone who prophesies speaks to men for their strengthening, encouragement and comfort. ⁴He who speaks in a tongue edifies himself, but he who prophesies edifies the church. ⁵I would like every one of you to speak in tongues,*c* but I would rather have you

*a 2 Or another language; also in verses 4, 13, 14, 19, 26 and 27*
*b 2 Or by the Spirit    c 5 Or other languages; also in verses 6, 18, 22, 23 and 39*

**NRSV**

and especially that you may prophesy. ²For those who speak in a tongue do not speak to other people but to God; for nobody understands them, since they are speaking mysteries in the Spirit. ³On the other hand, those who prophesy speak to other people for their upbuilding and encouragement and consolation. ⁴Those who speak in a tongue build up themselves, but those who prophesy build up the church. ⁵Now I would like all of you to speak in tongues, but even more to prophesy. One who prophesies is greater than one who

## NIV

prophesy. He who prophesies is greater than one who speaks in tongues,[a] unless he interprets, so that the church may be edified.

⁶Now, brothers, if I come to you and speak in tongues, what good will I be to you, unless I bring you some revelation or knowledge or prophecy or word of instruction? ⁷Even in the case of lifeless things that make sounds, such as the flute or harp, how will anyone know what tune is being played unless there is a distinction in the notes? ⁸Again, if the trumpet does not sound a clear call, who will get ready for battle? ⁹So it is with you. Unless you speak intelligible words with your tongue, how will anyone know what you are saying? You will just be speaking into the air. ¹⁰Undoubtedly there are all sorts of languages in the world, yet none of them is without meaning. ¹¹If then I do not grasp the meaning of what someone is saying, I am a foreigner to the speaker, and he is a foreigner to me. ¹²So it is with you. Since you are eager to have spiritual gifts, try to excel in gifts that build up the church.

[a] 5 Or other languages; also in verses 6, 18, 22, 23 and 39

## NRSV

speaks in tongues, unless someone interprets, so that the church may be built up.

6Now, brothers and sisters,[a] if I come to you speaking in tongues, how will I benefit you unless I speak to you in some revelation or knowledge or prophecy or teaching? ⁷It is the same way with lifeless instruments that produce sound, such as the flute or the harp. If they do not give distinct notes, how will anyone know what is being played? ⁸And if the bugle gives an indistinct sound, who will get ready for battle? ⁹So with yourselves; if in a tongue you utter speech that is not intelligible, how will anyone know what is being said? For you will be speaking into the air. ¹⁰There are doubtless many different kinds of sounds in the world, and nothing is without sound. ¹¹If then I do not know the meaning of a sound, I will be a foreigner to the speaker and the speaker a foreigner to me. ¹²So with yourselves; since you are eager for spiritual gifts, strive to excel in them for building up the church.

[a] Gk brothers

# COMMENTARY

Throughout the chapter, Paul is careful not to disparage speaking in tongues. Tongues are a language spoken to God (v. 2), a praying of one's spirit (v. 14), a means of thanksgiving (v. 17). Tongues edify the speaker (v. 4). In one respect like all the languages in the world, speaking in tongues is also capable of transmitting meaning, but Paul is convinced the meaning is carried in the interpretation (vv. 5, 11, 13). Speaking in tongues must not be prohibited (v. 39).

But there are limitations and problems with speaking in tongues. Paul uses analogies: If harps and flutes do not play distinctive notes, who will recognize the tune (v. 7)? And more pointedly, because Paul thinks of believers as being a part of God's battle force, if the bugle does not sound a distinct call, who will prepare for battle (v. 8)? It is the same with foreign languages, all of which he credits with power; but they do not convey meaning if the hearer does not understand them (vv. 11, 16).

As laudable as Paul's portrait of tongues is, his argument attempts to transfer the Corinthian high valuation of tongues to an affirmation of the superiority of prophecy—precisely because Paul believes that prophecy edifies the community. Can we discern what Paul means by prophecy?[141] Paul presumes that his auditors know what he means, so we never receive a definition. But we can gain some insight by noting the functions Paul describes. Prophecy edifies others (v. 3), and it edifies the church (vv. 4-5); it consoles and encourages others (vv. 3, 31). It seems to be roughly equivalent, at least in Paul's exemplification and exercise of it, to instruction, to the sharing of some communication, to engagement with someone else's suffering or loss (vv. 19, 31).

141. The best studies that set the background for understanding Paul's use of the term are David E. Aune, *Prophecy in Early Christianity and the Ancient Mediterranean World* (Grand Rapids: Eerdmans, 1983); Christopher Forbes, *Prophecy and Inspired Speech in Early Christianity and Its Hellenistic Environment* (Tübingen: J. C. B. Mohr, 1995).

In Paul's picture of the way prophecy should actually function in worship, two or three prophets speak, one at a time (14:31), and others weigh out what the prophets have said (14:29). Thus prophecy does not have axiomatic, automatic authority, but may be *granted* authority after community reflection and assent. Paul holds that all persons may prophesy; it is a gift that is available to all (14:24, 31). Finally, prophecy makes sense to novices and unbelievers and may therefore set off a sequence that ultimately could result in the acclamation "Surely God is among you!" (14:25; cf. 3:16; see also the Commentary on 5:1). Prophecy functions to reprove novices and unbelievers, to call them to account, to disclose "the hidden things of their hearts" with the result that they fall on their knees before God, affirming God's presence in the community's worship. So it appears that prophecy, according to Paul, was not to be confused with telling the future; instead, it seems to be a statement intended for and applicable to the community and to those in worship, a declaration that becomes the basis for discussion and assessment—not only of what the prophet has said but also of how it applies to the lives of the auditors. Prophecy is appropriate to a range of human experiences as suggested by edification, consolation, encouragement, and learning (14:3, 31), so it seems able to bear on all aspects of the communal life of the believers.

A potential trap awaits Paul, however, as he pursues his strategy to put speaking in tongues in perspective by stressing the superior importance of prophecy in the life of the church. He faces a congregation among whom some have insisted—and others have conceded—that glossolalia is the pre-eminent gift, signifying special status and power. Paul's strategy in chap. 14 is to accommodate to the notion that if there is a superior gift, then it must be prophecy. How does Paul avoid having the same status-centered confusion transferred from tongues to prophecy? Several ways: (1) He declares that speaking in tongues, properly accompanied with interpretation, is equivalent to prophecy in that both result in edification of the community (14:5). (2) He describes prophecy as open to all persons equally (14:24, 31) and, therefore, implicitly invites the participation of all believers. (3) Most important, he argues that anyone zealous for spiritual things—and who among the glossalalists would not so describe themselves?—should seek to abound in edifying the church (14:12). Paul's most sweeping goal statement regarding edification is 14:26 (itself a refinement of 14:12): "Let all things be done for building up" (NRSV; the NIV translation chooses the less precise "strengthening" and inserts an unnecessary restriction, "the church"). With Paul's close, early identification of love and edification in 8:1, Paul's prescription in 14:26 could just as well have been formulated as follows: "Let all things be done in love," but he appropriately saves exactly that formulation for the capstone of the entire letter in 16:14.

# REFLECTIONS

In chapter 14, edification—that is, "what builds up"—is the test of every contemplated action in the life of the community. The readers who remember Paul's epigram "Love builds up" (8:2) can see the connection with chapter 13 where love is praised. When love works in the community, the community is built up, not necessarily or primarily in numbers, though it would be surprising if the numbers did not also increase, because love has an infectious quality. Love usually brings out the best in the ones loving and in the ones being loved; love usually elicits love in response. And inevitably all who love, are loved, and love in return are built up and encouraged in the most powerful way. Paul's word to those Corinthians who are eager to excel in everything is probably a good word to believers today: "Seek to excel in the edification of the church" (14:12).

# 1 Corinthians 14:13-19, How to Be Outstanding in Edifying

**NIV**

¹³For this reason anyone who speaks in a tongue should pray that he may interpret what he says. ¹⁴For if I pray in a tongue, my spirit prays, but my mind is unfruitful. ¹⁵So what shall I do? I will pray with my spirit, but I will also pray with my mind; I will sing with my spirit, but I will also sing with my mind. ¹⁶If you are praising God with your spirit, how can one who finds himself among those who do not understand*ᵃ* say "Amen" to your thanksgiving, since he does not know what you are saying? ¹⁷You may be giving thanks well enough, but the other man is not edified.

¹⁸I thank God that I speak in tongues more than all of you. ¹⁹But in the church I would rather speak five intelligible words to instruct others than ten thousand words in a tongue.

ᵃ *16 Or among the inquirers*

**NRSV**

13Therefore, one who speaks in a tongue should pray for the power to interpret. ¹⁴For if I pray in a tongue, my spirit prays but my mind is unproductive. ¹⁵What should I do then? I will pray with the spirit, but I will pray with the mind also; I will sing praise with the spirit, but I will sing praise with the mind also. ¹⁶Otherwise, if you say a blessing with the spirit, how can anyone in the position of an outsider say the "Amen" to your thanksgiving, since the outsider does not know what you are saying? ¹⁷For you may give thanks well enough, but the other person is not built up. ¹⁸I thank God that I speak in tongues more than all of you; ¹⁹nevertheless, in church I would rather speak five words with my mind, in order to instruct others also, than ten thousand words in a tongue.

# COMMENTARY

Paul has just urged those who are zealous about spiritual matters (v. 12) to focus their energies on edification. Specifically for glossolalists that would mean praying for the capacity to interpret because tongues plus interpretation leads to edification (v. 13).

Glossolalia is limited in two important respects. First, it does not engage others who might be there when the church meets; without interpretation, tongues will mean nothing to other believers and to any unbelievers who might happen to be present. Second, glossolalia does not engage the whole person; only the spirit, not the mind, is involved.

Paul has to make certain that the Corinthians understand that his critique of their use of tongues does not spring from any jealousy of their gift: He speaks in tongues "more than you all" (v. 18) but, like his emulatable self-portrait in chapter 9, through self-discipline he forgoes the practice of his gift of tongues when he is in church because, reaching for hyperbole to emphasize his point, he would rather speak a few words "with his mind" that make sense to others than a myriad of words in a tongue (v. 19). So his critique of their practice

is not grounded in jealousy, because he excels them in tongues, as he expects them to remember.

Individual ancient Greek manuscripts were written entirely in capital letters or entirely in lower case letters, so all translators must decide when capitalization is appropriate and when it is not. Of course, given modern practices, some terms are clearly to be capitalized and others just as surely are not, but sometimes, as here in v. 15, translators and interpreters of the ancient Greek are faced with an ambivalence regarding whether capitalization is appropriate. In 14:15, the issue is how to translate τῷ πνεύματι (*tō pneumati*)—that is, whether the reference is (simply) to one's own spirit or to the Holy Spirit (which Paul frequently enough calls simply "the Spirit," as this phrase could here be translated; cf. 2:4, 10-11, 13-14). Supporting capitalizing it and understanding that Paul is writing about praying and singing with the assistance of the Holy Spirit is Paul's statement in Rom 8:26 that when we do not know how to pray as necessary, the Spirit intercedes for us in sighs too deep for words. On the other side, that the term "spirit" should not be capitalized and should therefore be taken as referring to the human spirit, is the parallel construction in 14:15-16 with "the mind" (ὁ νοῦς *ho nous*) where that referent is clearly to the individual's "mind." There is also a third possibility that must be considered here—namely, that the primary referent of πνεῦμα (*pneuma,* "spirit"), read in the light of its paralleled reference to mind, here is indeed the human spirit as the commitment of one's life, but that for Paul the Holy Spirit's assistance in praying cannot be ruled out of the picture. In this third possibility, then, the reference to *pneuma* is actually double, both to the human spirit and to the Holy Spirit.

Two patterns of piety are in contention here. The one piety, which stresses what we might call the vertical axis—namely, one's relation to God, and minimizes or treats as secondary the horizontal axis—namely, one's relation to others, is represented by some of the Corinthians. This piety takes primary consideration for one's self and one's relation to God; one's gift is interpreted as a sign of one's importance, of one's recognition by God, and of God's special favor; one's spirit, not one's mind, is seen as the source of one's praying, singing, and blessing; and, most significant, this piety, when it does consider others, always secondarily and sometimes condescendingly takes little cognizance of others because it is so primarily and directly focused on the individual and God. In the portion of the letter at hand, this vertical piety is represented most directly by those who seem to be vaunting their capacity to speak in tongues. The remainder of the letter shows other instances where many among the Corinthian believers, perhaps also driven by such a piety, failed to weigh or perhaps even to be concerned with the way one's actions affect another in the community of believers.

Paul advocates an alternative piety and exemplifies it for them in his self-reflection in chap. 14. Paul's piety embraces the central tenet of the vertical piety: that one's relation to God is fundamental, but goes on to recognize that proper relation to God always already places one in relation to others in Christ. Paul's piety always lovingly integrates all of the believers actively into one's calculations and behavior; it involves the whole self, spirit *and* mind, into one's life as an ongoing act of worship; it views one's gift or gifts as graciously given to serve the common good; and it never acts without consideration for others.

As their father in the faith (cf. v. 20), Paul exemplifies this second piety. In his first portrait of himself in this large section he invites them to imagine his coming to them and speaking only in tongues (v. 6). Of what use would (even) he be to them, he inquires. No edification of others, no building up would take place. He would be useless unless he also spoke to them some revelation, knowledge, prophecy, or teaching (v. 6). His second self-portrait (v. 14) imagines himself being engaged with the community by praying in a tongue and thus engaging only his spirit but not his mind. Praying in tongues, as powerful and important a gift as it is, employs only one's spirit; Paul says one's mind is "unfruitful" when speaking in tongues (v. 14). Unable to condone anything less than full employment of himself or anyone else in service to God (cf. Rom 12:1), Paul resolves to pray, sing, and bless not only with his spirit but also with his mind (vv. 15-16). Here, as in his discussion of what could properly be eaten (chaps. 8–10—to "whatever you eat," Paul added, "whatever you drink or whatever you do" (10:31), thus extending from one exemplary action to suggest something about the pattern of the entirely integrated and faithful life), Paul moves from the specific issue under discussion, tongues, to the broader practice of one's whole life, here exemplified in "singing" and "blessing." After reminding his auditors that he speaks in tongues "more than all of you" (14:18), Paul concludes his self-portrait with a hyperbolic declaration that, *in church,* he would prefer to speak a few words with his mind rather than myriad words in a tongue (14:19). Why? Because otherwise, others are not engaged, they are not instructed (and one could presumably add the other benefits that have been noted across this chapter: They are not built up, consoled, encouraged; they learn nothing).

Parenthetically and incidentally, we probably gain some insight into Paul's own spirituality in this discussion. When he is alone he readily prays in tongues as a means of speaking with God (14:18, 28). When, however, he is with others in the worshiping community, he wants his life integrated with that of others; no one can be left out; no one can be treated as unimportant. Further, when he is with others in the worshiping community he feels obligated to engage his whole self, his mind and his spirit, in the worship and in its relationship to others. Otherwise, one takes less seriously than one should the obligation to be a channel for edification of others; otherwise, one might miss the edification that others have to offer. And prayer is not the totality of the properly worshipful life: Singing and blessing, to mention just two, are illustrative of the way the whole life ought to be integrated into worship.

# REFLECTIONS

**1.** Paul insists that he prays not only with the spirit (Spirit) but also with the mind, and he sings not only with the spirit (Spirit) but also with the mind. He represents an integration, a wholeness in his life and in his expression of his faith. Because the life of faith is rightly so much a matter of internal disposition, so much a product of the inspiration of the Holy Spirit, as Paul says, joining with our spirits (Rom 8:16), the temptation has been to maximize the spirit-characteristic of the life of faith and minimize if not eliminate the function of the mind. But as we have seen, Paul does not compartmentalize the life of faith into some segment of the person; instead, the whole person, mind and spirit and heart, is renewed and is placed in service of God, its Creator and redeemer. So Paul exemplifies what he hopes his hearers can aspire to: an integrated presentation of their whole selves and their whole lives as a thanksgiving offering, holy and acceptable to God (Rom 12:1). No part of one's being is left out of full employment in service to God; no aspect of life is relegated as outside the scope of God's concern. Paul's is a holistic, integrated view of the individual—and indeed of all of life before God. Put more directly into modern categories, Paul does not separate life into spiritual and secular, religious and the rest of life, Sundays and the remainder of the week. All of life—equally and fully—is under the dominion of God, and every aspect of one's being is placed in service to God.

Paul is radically different from modern persons who compartmentalize their lives into sacred times and secular ones, into spiritual occasions and the rest of life's experience. The connection between worship and all of life is important for Paul. Questions of moral comportment bear as equally on the way one behaves at an unbeliever's home (10:27-29) as on how one conducts one's life in worship. Worship mirrors life as it should be lived and reflects on life as the worshipers have lived it. Ideally, all of life is worship (Rom 12:1). Just as surely as God's grace is the basis of all of life, every day and every moment, so all of life is offered up to God as a thanksgiving for God's grace and bountiful gifts (1 Cor 4:7; 14:16). Understanding this helps interpreters to comprehend how Paul can call upon his followers to "pray without ceasing"—because all of life is an enacted response to and conversation with God.

**2.** Individual edification is all right, but not the ideal. Paul critiques individualism, even pious individualism, in which an individual "may give thanks well, but the other person is not edified" (14:17). Paul's is a radical affront to the modern tendency to privatize religion, piety, and one's sources of morality. For Paul, the important thing is not just how the individual is with God. Such a privatization of faith is unthinkable and unacceptable for Paul. Faith without community may not be completely bogus, but it is not the real thing, according to Paul. Without community, something so important is missing that the thing itself is called into question. Testifying of one's faith or bearing witness to others is not what Paul is thinking about. He cannot imagine faith of an individualistic piety that thrives without community, without others being positively affected and encouraged by the living of it. Put another way, no proper relation to God is possible without others in support and others who benefit.

# 1 Corinthians 14:20-40, A Series of Problems in the Corinthians' Fellowship

## OVERVIEW

Throughout the last half of chap. 14 a series of issues receive special treatment. Paul's insistence on building up one another and the church provides the immediate context in which he treats the problems.

## 1 CORINTHIANS 14:20-25, COMPORTMENT AS IT BEARS ON UNBELIEVERS AND NOVICES

### NIV

²⁰Brothers, stop thinking like children. In regard to evil be infants, but in your thinking be adults. ²¹In the Law it is written:

"Through men of strange tongues
  and through the lips of foreigners
I will speak to this people,
  but even then they will not listen to me,"ᵃ
says the Lord.

²²Tongues, then, are a sign, not for believers but for unbelievers; prophecy, however, is for believers, not for unbelievers. ²³So if the whole church comes together and everyone speaks in tongues, and some who do not understandᵇ or some unbelievers come in, will they not say that you are out of your mind? ²⁴But if an unbeliever or someone who does not understandᵇ comes in while everybody is prophesying, he will be convinced by all that he is a sinner and will be judged by all, ²⁵and the secrets of his heart will be laid bare. So he will fall down and worship God, exclaiming, "God is really among you!"

ᵃ21 Isaiah 28:11,12    ᵇ23 Or some inquirer

### NRSV

20Brothers and sisters,ᵃ do not be children in your thinking; rather, be infants in evil, but in thinking be adults. ²¹In the law it is written,
  "By people of strange tongues
    and by the lips of foreigners
  I will speak to this people;
    yet even then they will not listen to me,"
says the Lord.²²Tongues, then, are a sign not for believers but for unbelievers, while prophecy is not for unbelievers but for believers. ²³If, therefore, the whole church comes together and all speak in tongues, and outsiders or unbelievers enter, will they not say that you are out of your mind? ²⁴But if all prophesy, an unbeliever or outsider who enters is reproved by all and called to account by all. ²⁵After the secrets of the unbeliever's heart are disclosed, that person will bow down before God and worship him, declaring, "God is really among you."

ᵃ Gk brothers

## COMMENTARY

What about unbelievers and their interchange with believers? Believers and unbelievers in Corinth, in sharp distinction from Thessalonica, have easy and comfortable interaction. In Corinth, some believers are married to unbelievers (7:12-16). Further, Paul can speculate about an invitation to dinner at an unbeliever's home (10:27-29). And unbelievers apparently are sometimes present at worship occasions (14:23-24).

Paul expressed concern that an unbeliever who encounters Corinthian worship, as chaotic as it has been, will mistake the worship of God for the worship in other contemporary temples of hellenistic religions—that is, they will think Paul's followers are simply ecstatically mad (14:23). But even worse, if the unbeliever does not understand what is being said, then he or she will escape the process where such a person's being called to account may ultimately lead to the affirmation of God's presence, in other words to faith. So even in such inadvertant descriptions of worship, Paul holds that believers have an obligation not only to be considerate of unbelievers, but also to expose them to the cutting edge of the gospel.

The text not only comments about unbelievers; it also mentions those "who do not understand" (NIV), "outsiders" (NRSV)—whose identification is a bit more complex (14:16, 23-24). The NRSV translation "outsider" lends itself to be understood as another way—indeed so taken it would be a redundant one—of describing an unbeliever.

The term ἰδιώτης (idiōtēs) describes a person who is "unskilled" (cf. 2 Cor 11:6), who is an amateur, one who is untrained, one who is a non-expert as distinguished from a specialist. That range of meanings does not require that we think of persons so designated as "outsiders" to the believing community; they may simply be less adept, less skilled, less trained than some other believers. In 14:16 the representative person described as an idiōtēs, though set over against an imagined person who is speaking in tongues, is nevertheless considered able not only to say the "Amen" that Paul and his communities have adopted from Jewish synagogue practice (14:16) but also to be "built up" if only the person could understand what was being said (14:17). Paul consistently reserves the notion of edification as applicable to believers, so the person in "the position of an idiōtēs" is a believer, not an unbeliever.

Paul's introduction of this representative person gives telling clues as to how to understand it. First, the person is not simply declared to be a novice, but ὁ ἀναπληρῶν τὸν τόπον τοῦ ἰδιώτου (ho anaplērōn ton topon tou idiōtou), "one who is in the situation of a novice/beginner." So the phrase can readily be understood to describe someone who, in comparison with others who are more skilled, is in a relatively disadvantaged situation. Second, at other points in Paul's letters, indeed, even in 1 Corinthians (cf. 2:6; 3:1-2), Paul has distinguished between more mature, more advanced spiritual persons and their younger, less mature counterparts, babies in the faith. Third, because this imagined novice believer is mentioned in the context of speaking in tongues, we may suppose that this representative person is *unskilled in tongues and in their interpretation*. So Paul's

employment of the phrase "like a novice" here in 14:16 is a reference to a believer who is clearly like a beginner when compared with other believers and their employment of their charismata of speaking in and interpreting tongues. After this rather full picture of the one "in the situation of being a novice," Paul can shorten his subsequent references to *idiōtēs* (14:23-24) and expect the auditor to remember the cluster of clues identifying the person in the first place (14:16). Therefore, the one "in the position of being an *idiōtēs*" is an imagined believer who is "untrained, unskilled" in speaking (and in interpreting) tongues.

When the term *idiōtēs* reappears, it is linked chiastically (A B B′ A′) with the term "unbeliever" (14:23-24) in such a way as to tighten the identification, as if to suggest that to leave a fellow believer, even (or especially?) if that person is "like a novice," out of full participation in worship redefines the border and nature of community so that the person "unskilled" in tongues and in their interpretation is made *equivalent to an unbeliever* and is treated in such a condescending way as to deny the novice's having any standing inside the community. Treated in such a way the one "like a novice" becomes in effect like an unbeliever. In light of such inconsiderate treatment of novices by more-skilled-in-tongues believers, the unbeliever and the *idiōtēs* might as well be one when it comes to their relationship to the community: both may conclude that the tongues speakers are mad; neither will be brought to account. For Paul, such an exclusionary redefinition of the community of believers is scandalously unacceptable and grows from not properly "discerning the body" (11:29). No wonder Paul introduces this paragraph with a warning to grow up and not to be children, but adults (14:20).

The section concludes (14:25) by noting that the chaos of the Corinthians' worship may prevent the unbeliever and the novice from being called to account. Their mistreatment of novices leaches over into a mistreatment of unbelievers so that neither the unbeliever nor the novice will be able to declare what ought to be most obvious: "Surely God is ἐν ὑμῖν [en hymin, "among you," "in you"]" (v. 25). To be sure, Paul's actual words may be structured by his recollection of Isa 45:14 or Zech 8:23, but for their meaning here we must be guided by the context where they appear. We need not assume that there is a direct epiphany where God "appears" to the observer. Rather, Paul has given the readers the clues concerning what he means and how to take this expression. The most important clue is that the believers are early said to be God's building or dwelling place (3:9), God's temple (3:16-17) where the Holy Spirit dwells *en hymin,* "among you," "in you." In 14:25 the unbeliever can ideally deduce that God is in the community's midst only when the community lives and worships together in such a way as to reflect God and God's redemptive purposes in having established the community in the first place.

# REFLECTIONS

The obligations of worshipers to those who come in from outside is to comport themselves in such a way as to be transparent to God—that is, to behave as people who show God dwelling in or among them (14:25). Though the hearer does not explicitly find the building motif in chapter 14, it is present by implication. "You are God's building" (3:9). "You do know, don't you, that you are the temple of God and that the Spirit of God dwells among you? . . . The temple of God is holy and you yourselves are that temple" (3:16-17). Paul reminds the Corinthians that an outsider should see God reflected in their communal and worship life. In all that it does, the community should mirror its God. In biblical traditions as here in 14:25, when God is truly revealed observers fall to their faces in obeisance. What would it mean for a congregation to fellowship and to worship together in such a way that an outsider would be convinced that God is among them? Paul gives a clue as it relates to the Corinthians' worship: Their worship has become a time of competition, a time when chaos results because each is so eager to show the Spirit's work; God is a God not of unruliness but a God of peace (14:33). Therefore, their worship should reflect the orderliness of God's peace. So, today worshipers should do their "service" to God in such a way that God is honored, so that God's presence, God's identity, God's character shows through. If we took it seriously that all of our actions reflect the God we serve, then some of us would be embarrassed to step back and observe ourselves.

# 1 CORINTHIANS 14:26-33, DISORDERLY WORSHIP

## NIV

26What then shall we say, brothers? When you come together, everyone has a hymn, or a word of instruction, a revelation, a tongue or an interpretation. All of these must be done for the strengthening of the church. 27If anyone speaks in a tongue, two—or at the most three—should speak, one at a time, and someone must interpret. 28If there is no interpreter, the speaker should keep quiet in the church and speak to himself and God.

29Two or three prophets should speak, and the others should weigh carefully what is said. 30And if a revelation comes to someone who is sitting down, the first speaker should stop. 31For you can all prophesy in turn so that everyone may be instructed and encouraged. 32The spirits of prophets are subject to the control of prophets. 33For God is not a God of disorder but of peace.

As in all the congregations of the saints,

## NRSV

26What should be done then, my friends?[a] When you come together, each one has a hymn, a lesson, a revelation, a tongue, or an interpretation. Let all things be done for building up. 27If anyone speaks in a tongue, let there be only two or at most three, and each in turn; and let one interpret. 28But if there is no one to interpret, let them be silent in church and speak to themselves and to God. 29Let two or three prophets speak, and let the others weigh what is said. 30If a revelation is made to someone else sitting nearby, let the first person be silent. 31For you can all prophesy one by one, so that all may learn and all be encouraged. 32And the spirits of prophets are subject to the prophets, 33for God is a God not of disorder but of peace.

(As in all the churches of the saints,

[a] Gk *brothers*

# COMMENTARY

We have seen that speaking in tongues has predominated in the worship of the Corinthians, contributing to the sense of chaos and disorder. Much of chap. 14 has argued that prophecy will best serve the community and that tongues are fine as long as there is an interpreter. Now, however, Paul reverts to his habituated response of making practical suggestions. As Paul earlier recommended that instead of defiling the Lord's supper people could eat at home before coming together (11:34), so now he makes sweeping, practical suggestions about their pattern of worship.

Keeping in mind that edification should be the guideline for whatever is done ("Let all things be done for edification," 14:26), Paul first suggests that all persons present should participate in worship. None may be left out or excluded. The skilled ones must be sure that the novices have full participation. When the believers come together for worship, different ones among them offer a psalm, a teaching, a revelation, a tongue, an interpretation (14:26). Second, if there be speaking in tongues (clearly Paul imagines that glossolalia is not a necessary part of worship and just as surely is not to be excluded from worship if an interpreter is available), Paul suggests that it be limited to a couple or three times and then serially and always with interpretation (14:27) so that no unskilled person is made to feel like an outsider. Third, prophecy is treated in the same manner as tongues: Two or three prophets may speak. Fourth, "one at a time" seems to be a pervasive concern (14:27, 31) and its purpose is clear: "so that all may learn and all may be encouraged" (14:31). Paul anticipates a claim that whatever is Spirit-inspired must immediately be granted a sort of *ex cathedra* authority when he says that others present at worship must weigh or pass judgment on what is said (14:29). He also heads off an objection of Spirit-filled persons that they are "beside themselves," captive to the Spirit, and are therefore unable to control themselves: "the spirits of prophets are subject to the prophets" (14:32).

Nowhere in Paul's undisputed letters do we find information on leadership patterns in worship. Clearly, Paul supposes the worshipers to be the significant participants (11:4-5, 26-33*a*). The

Spirit, as the giver of the gifts, is understood as the source of inspiration to the participants. Most striking in his worship suggestions, however, is Paul's expectation that when two or three prophets have spoken, then "let the others weigh [pass judgment on] what is said" (14:29). These prophets are not persons who undertake to tell the future, but they are ones whose speech edifies, encourages, and consoles the community (14:3), so prophecy is a word addressed to the gathered people of God about their lives in the present. It is not enough, however, that someone claims to speak in behalf of the Spirit; automatic, unthinking assent is not to be blindly granted by the hearers. Instead, the "others"—because Paul believes that all can prophesy, the "others" probably means all the others—weigh what is said in a given prophetic utterance so as to decide whether to add their affirmative "Amen" to what is said. This is indeed a practical application of his earlier exemplary declaration that he prays and sings not only with his spirit but also with his mind (14:14-15).

Paul's suggestions regarding worship (14:26-33*a*) are not themselves to be confused with a structure or order of worship per se; his comments are very specifically aimed at the particular circumstances at Corinth where tongues have played a disproportionate role. Within his comments, however, are some abiding Pauline themes: Each one participates and contributes; all things are to be done for edification; deference to others is appropriate and fundamental in worship as in all of life; and all should learn and be encouraged.

"The spirits of the prophets are subject to the prophets" (14:32). By this Paul means that prophetic inspiration is to be kept under control by the prophet or prophets who receive it. There is no excuse for using the work of the Spirit as an occasion to override the concern for the needs and well-being of others. In what Paul here writes about prophecy, he makes a practical application of his own boxing metaphor to others (9:24-27), picturing himself as exercising self-control, self-discipline so that he not be disqualified.

Orderly Spirit-inspired worship is properly available to each and every one of the believers. Paul's warrant for his insistence upon orderly worship is stated in maxim form at the end of the paragraph: "For God is not the God of disorder [unruliness] but the God of peace—as in all the churches of the saints" (14:33), taking the last phrase as finishing the preceding paragraph and assuring the Corinthians that Paul's concern to establish orderly worship is not a position imposed only on the Corinthians. We can read the phrase "as in all the churches of the saints" as attached to the Pauline maxim about God because all ancient manuscripts of the New Testament were written one letter immediately after the other, with no spaces, no punctuation marks, no sentence and paragraph markers.

# REFLECTIONS

Paul's assumptions about worship services should be considered afresh for today. First, church leadership so often filters down to a few people carrying most of the load, in worship and in other aspects of the church's life. Why is that? In part, it is a natural tendency: Those who do well are deferred to by others. But partly it is also a failure to carry through Paul's assumption that no one should be left out of participation; it is a failure to be ingenious about finding avenues of participation great and small for each and every one. Some will be bashful and reticent and will gladly turn participation over to others; monopoly of participation will harden into habit all around. Second, Paul thinks deference and thoughtfulness of others ought to be the rule when the church comes together. Perhaps those who naturally take leadership ought to put a restraining harness on themselves and have the patience to wait for others—and they surely must be careful not to arrogate to themselves the notion that nothing would happen if they themselves did not do it. Why not put some of that energy into encouraging others to step forward, into making it easier for them to take their first steps? That would be genuinely and fully thoughtful not only of others but also constructive for the community life of faith.

## 1 CORINTHIANS 14:34-36, WOMEN SPEAKING

### NIV

[34]women should remain silent in the churches. They are not allowed to speak, but must be in submission, as the Law says. [35]If they want to inquire about something, they should ask their own husbands at home; for it is disgraceful for a woman to speak in the church.

[36]Did the word of God originate with you? Or are you the only people it has reached?

### NRSV

[34]women should be silent in the churches. For they are not permitted to speak, but should be subordinate, as the law also says. [35]If there is anything they desire to know, let them ask their husbands at home. For it is shameful for a woman to speak in church.[a] [36]Or did the word of God originate with you? Or are you the only ones it has reached?)

[a] Other ancient authorities put verses 34-35 after verse 40

# COMMENTARY

This harsh passage, urging women's silence in church and subordination to their husbands, with an unspecified reference to "the law" as support, is probably an insertion by an editor who subsequently took this Pauline letter and brought it into conformity with the practices regarding women in his own subsequent-to-Paul time.

Whereas Paul wrote his specific letters to unique churches in different settings, someone, sometime later, collected them and assumed that what Paul wrote to one community might be of value for other communities (cf. an early step along that path in Col 4:16).[142] In the process of bringing the letter collection together, someone edited the correspondence; the degree of alterations is unknowable to us.[143] The results of the editing can easiest be seen in 2 Corinthians where some scholars find fragments of as many as five letters.[144] For the clearest example, compare the polemical and defensive tone and temper of 2 Corinthians 10–13 with the relatively irenic and reconciled tone of the opening chapters of 2 Corinthians. Other changes such as excisions were also made; for example, the references to "in Rome" in Rom 1:7, 15 were dropped in later manuscripts presumably to make Romans a more universal letter that could be employed in places other than Rome.

Here in 1 Cor 14:34-36 we are probably faced with a later insertion of a text whose posture is at odds not only with Paul's relationships with women in other churches but also with what Paul has said about women earlier in 1 Corinthians. It will be helpful to review the evidence on both counts.

Verses 34-36, with their injunction of women's silence and assertion of their subordination to men, vary from what we have seen in the rest of 1 Corinthians. First, it is clear that women *are* praying and prophesying in the church at Corinth (11:5) and Paul not only makes no effort to stop it, but he seems to assume that it is quite proper; he simply wants women to wear head coverings in the worship setting. Efforts to interpret 11:5 in line with 14:34 may claim that the praying in question was silent prayer and that the women were just speaking among themselves, though there is no hint in 11:5 that such was the case. In fact, the material just treated about prophecy in chap. 14 makes clear that for Paul prophecy is available to everyone and involves speaking in church in such a manner that the "others" may weigh what is said (14:29). So the women at Corinth were in fact speaking, as were the men, during worship. Second, note how Paul used the tradition reflected most clearly in Gal 3:28— "there is neither male nor female"—to reckon the fundamental reciprocity between women and men in marriage and human sexuality (chap. 7). Third, it is Chloe's people who inform Paul of the bickering at Corinth (1:11). We do not know much about Chloe—the Corinthians and Paul knew her very well—but we may suppose that she was a woman of standing with the church (she is named) and a wealthy person whose agents (her servants, perhaps) saw Paul possibly in their pursuit of her business interests.

Further, 14:34-36 is singular when weighed against the picture and roles of women in all of the other undisputed Pauline letters (more on Colossians, Ephesians, and the Pastoral Epistles below). Phoebe, a deacon in the church at Cenchreae, just six miles from Corinth, is praised and commended as Paul's patron (Rom 16:1-2). Euodia and Syntyche, even though they are currently having some personal problems, have "struggled alongside" Paul in the gospel and it appears that their names are in the "book of life" (Phil 4:2-3). Apphia is one of the persons addressed in the letter we call Philemon (Phlm 2). Prisca, dubbed a "fellow worker" (Rom 16:3), and over a half-dozen other women are singled out for greetings and recognition in Romans 16. Clearly, from the way Paul describes the women in his letters they were significant workers in the churches and in the gospel. In the six undisputed letters apart from 1 Corinthians, *no passage suggests any limitation on the roles or functions of women in the Pauline churches.*

Ephesians and Colossians present a different picture; indeed, it is more in line with 1 Cor 14:34-36. Both Ephesians and Colossians, assumed here and by many to be products of Pauline disciples after Paul's death but written in his name, argue for the subordination of wives to their husbands (Eph 5:22-24; Col 3:18).[145] The Pastoral Epistles, 1 and 2 Timothy and Titus, thought here and by some others to be products of yet another, subsequent generation that dates after

142. Nils A. Dahl, "The Particularity of the Pauline Epistles as a Problem in the Ancient Church," in *Neotestamentica et patristica: Eine Freundesgabe, Herrn Prof. Dr. Oscar Cullmann zu seinem 60. Geburtstag ueberreicht,* ed. W. C. van Unnik (Leiden: Brill, 1962) 261-71.

143. Bart D. Ehrman, *The Orthodox Corruption of Scripture: The Effect of Early Christological Controversies on the Text of the New Testament* (New York: Oxford University Press, 1993).

144. Furnish, *II Corinthians,* 32-35.

145. See Walter Bujard, *Stilanalytische Untersuchungen zum Kolosserbrief als Beitrag zur Methodik von Sprachvergleichen,* SUNT 11 (Göttingen: Vandenhoeck & Ruprecht, 1973).

Ephesians and Colossians in the Pauline tradition, take the matter a step farther, also arguing for submission of women and for the silence of women (1 Tim 2:11-12; cf. Titus 2:5; 1 Pet 3:1) and justify this subordination, as does 1 Cor 14:34, by reference to "the law" (1 Tim 2:13-14).

One might, therefore, describe a trajectory in the early decades of Christianity where Paul, the earliest writer in the New Testament, welcomes women into full participation in the life and work of the gospel and into the worship it generates. As the Pauline tradition was carried on beyond Paul's death (mid 60s CE), and as Paul's assurance of the imminent end of the ages failed to materialize, Paul's followers felt increasing pressure to reaccommodate to the social structures and practices of their unbelieving neighbors.[146] Ephesians and Colossians represent one stage of reaccommodation; the Pastoral Epistles yet another. When one looks at 1 Cor 14:34-36 against that trajectory, one finds that it fits best with the view of women projected in the Pastoral Epistles. If Paul's letters were collected around the turn of the first and second centuries, as is a reasonable assumption, a time sometimes also argued for the writing of the Pastoral Epistles, then the redactor could readily have inserted 1 Cor 14:34-36 to bring the picture of Corinth's worship practices in line with what he thought appropriate in his own time. The result: Women should be silent in church and submissive to their husbands, despite the fact that neither of these positions is sustained by the rest of 1 Corinthians nor by the six other undisputed Pauline letters that we can be sure came from the hand of Paul.

If 14:34-36 was not inserted by a later redactor of the Pauline corpus, then two interpretations merit attention. One, the passage calling for silence from women is in a series of matters where Paul enjoins silence upon a certain subgroup within the church rather than see them intrude on other people's worship (14:28, 30). In the first injunction, he advises glossolalists to keep silent if no interpreters are present (14:29). In the second, he says that if someone gets a revelation while a prophet is speaking, the prophet should be silent. In all three cases, deference to others, a pattern argued in detail in chap. 9, is urged. These counsels to silence stand as a part of his tendency to offer practical suggestions that are designed to serve the well-being of the community.

Two, the interpretation of 14:34-36 as authentic must account for 14:36, a rather stern rebuke, and identify for what subgroup the reprimand is intended. Generally, it has been assumed to be directed at the women, who are now told to be subordinate (14:34) although it makes limited sense in that way. Alternatively, it could as readily be understood as addressed to some men in the congregation who claim in a maxim that *they* have formulated, in line with much of their culture, that "it is shameful for a woman to speak in church" (14:35*b*).[147] It could be a maxim formulated by the same persons who advocated that "it is good for a man not to touch a woman" (see the Commentary on 7:1) and could be generated by a male-dominated faction that tried in several ways, in opposition to Paul, to relegate women to a lesser role in the life of the community. Read in this way, 14:36 would be Paul's challenge of the men's hybris reflected in their maxim by asking: "Was it from you that the word of God went out? Or, has it arrived at you only?"

---

146. David L. Balch, *Let Wives Be Submissive: The Domestic Code in 1 Peter,* SBLMS 26 (Chico, Calif.: Scholars Press, 1981) 81.

147. For three very important studies that continue to argue for the authenticity of 1 Cor 14:33*b*-36, see L. A. Jervis, "1 Corinthians 14.34-35: A Reconsideration of Paul's Limitation of the Free Speech of Some Corinthian Women," *JSNT* 58 (1995) 51-74; Elisabeth Schüssler-Fiorenza, *In Memory of Her: A Feminist Theological Reconstruction of Christian Origins* (New York: Crossroad, 1985) 230-33; and Margaret M. Mitchell, *Paul and the Rhetoric of Reconciliation* (Louisville: Westminster/John Knox, 1991) 281-82n. 536.

# REFLECTIONS

The passage 14:34-36 has attracted much attention, and well it should because it is subject to very different interpretations. Whether one takes these verses as authentic or not, they do stand in the canon. Let us here reflect on the interpretations that consider 14:34-36 as having been written by Paul. All the interpretations that take the passage as authentic share one factor that we modern Christians should not fail to notice: All of them suppose that the verses are Paul's response to a very particular and peculiar situation that has emerged at Corinth. Each of them assumes that Paul is not making church policy de novo or in general, but is reacting to a special problem regarding women at Corinth. Already in this commentary we have seen that where Paul perceives a certain action to be a threat to the health of the community, he will advise a "steer-clear" course and will model such care for his followers. About himself, for example, he has depicted himself as ready to be a vegetarian if his own freedom to eat meat risks harm for any brother or sister for whom Christ died (1 Cor 8:13). So the passage is, first, a response to a particular problem that Paul has encountered only at Corinth. Second, Paul is given to practical suggestions and to counsels that "play it safe," that ask for people to forgo the exercise of their rights when their freedom might otherwise lead them to live and do in a certain way (see the discussion of freedom and one's rights in the Commentary on 9:1-27). It is an irony of the greatest gravity that Paul's counsel in these verses, when taken as authentic, has come to function for some Christians as a polity dictate that keeps modern women from being able to speak in church. As a result, countless numbers of women who are just as clearly called and moved by the Holy Spirit as their male counterparts are kept from placing that calling and movement in service to the community of believers by taking part in some form of ministry. For such people, Paul's particular and situational counsel, written long ago to treat an unusual problem in a church at Corinth, has been reified into church law that is presumed to apply to all women, preventing them from taking full part in the ministry of the church for all time.

The interpretation adopted in this commentary, that 14:34-36 is a later interpolation from a time when Paul's letters were collected and redacted and when women were once again called upon to be submissive as we see in the subsequently written Pastoral Epistles (1 Tim 2:11; 3:4; Titus 2:5; cf. 1 Pet 3:1), is called for by two features already noted in the letter: (1) His counsels about marriage and human sexuality took care to acknowledge that the same rights belong to men and to women, to husbands and to wives (1 Cor 7:2-5); and (2) Paul has already assumed that women are praying and prophesying in church and he treats that activity as quite appropriate (1 Cor 11:5).

# 1 CORINTHIANS 14:37-40, SECTION CLOSING; ENFORCEMENT STATEMENT

## NIV

[37]If anybody thinks he is a prophet or spiritually gifted, let him acknowledge that what I am writing to you is the Lord's command. [38]If he ignores this, he himself will be ignored.[a]

[39]Therefore, my brothers, be eager to prophesy, and do not forbid speaking in tongues. [40]But everything should be done in a fitting and orderly way.

[a] 38 Some manuscripts *If he is ignorant of this, let him be ignorant*

## NRSV

37Anyone who claims to be a prophet, or to have spiritual powers, must acknowledge that what I am writing to you is a command of the Lord. 38Anyone who does not recognize this is not to be recognized. 39So, my friends,[a] be eager to prophesy, and do not forbid speaking in tongues; 40but all things should be done decently and in order.

[a] Gk *my brothers*

# COMMENTARY

With a claim and a suggestion, Paul concludes the whole section that began in 12:1. The claim: Those whose self-assessment inclines them to think of themselves as a prophet or a spiritual person (see the Commentary on 12:1) should recognize the truth of what Paul has written (he accords what he has written the status of a "command of the Lord," 14:37; cf. 7:10). The suggestion: Those who do not recognize, meaning grant authority to, what he has said, should themselves not be recognized (14:38).

Tongues and prophecy surface one last time in a recapitulation: The Corinthians should be zealous to prophesy, and they should not ban tongues (14:39). Paul has a flair for generalizing from the specifics, and he does so once again as he concludes this section. As the question of food offered to idols (8:1) became the occasion for branching out into several issues regarding eating and ultimately eating became synecdoche (one part stands for a larger whole) for all of life (cf. 10:31), so also here tongues and prophecy lead Paul quite naturally to an all-encompassing assertion: "Let all things be done exemplarily and in order" (14:40). The term translated here "exemplarily" (εὐσχημόνως

*euschēmonōs;* "fitting," NIV; "decently," NRSV) is a technical term for Paul, signaling a life lived in such a way that it becomes exemplary—that is, so that it becomes a pattern that informs and inspires others. In a summary appeal in Romans, Paul calls upon the Romans to "walk as models [*euschēmonōs*] as in the daylight" because they have "put on the Lord Jesus Christ" (surely baptismal imagery; see Rom 13:13-14). Likewise, when Paul caps off his admonitions to the Thessalonians, he writes that all his admonitions are so that the Thessalonian believers may "walk as models [*euschēmonōs*] for those outside" the church (1 Thess 4:12). So also the Corinthians are to do "all things . . . as models," which, one can readily see for Paul, includes doing them in good order. Whereas the modeling of the Thessalonians is to be especially for the outsiders, in 1 Corinthians Paul is concerned with believers' modeling not only for those inside the community of faith but also for unbelievers (10:28-29; 14:23-25). So the section concludes on the continuing Pauline concern with the Corinthians to encourage them to care about and for one another, to employ love in all their relations, and, therefore, to edify one another.

# REFLECTIONS

If a picture is worth a thousand words, how much more effective is one's life lived in an exemplary way. Often people rightly learn more from us by our actions, by the way we live and by the choices we make than they do from our declarations. Whether we speak or not, we are always writing a script of our values with our deeds, by what we choose to do and by what we avoid. In a way that might challenge us, Paul thinks that believers should reflect the same exemplary walk to persons outside the faith as well as to those within it.

# 1 CORINTHIANS 15:1-58

## Discourse on Resurrection

## Overview

Now Paul comes to the last major issue addressed in this letter. Rhetoricians recognized that the first and the last of a series were the places where the most important points should be lodged.[148] So, from his placement of it, we have every reason to expect that Paul considered what we call chapter 15 to be of utmost significance. And Paul does not disappoint us: The topic is nothing less than the gospel itself (15:1). From the first words it is clear that Paul reaches back to his original encounter with the Corinthians, when he initially preached the gospel to them and they believed.

Paul's recitation of the tradition that he passed on to them as the heart of his preaching (15:3-11)—namely, a sort of truncated passion narrative[149] with a special focus on Christ's death, resurrection, and appearance to witnesses, forms an inclusio, a ring construction with his early declaration in this letter that when he came to them he knew "only Jesus Christ and him crucified" (2:1-2). So the letter opens and closes with a reaffirmation that the focus of Paul's gospel with them has been Christ's death and resurrection; that was the core of his founding gospel, and Paul brings his letter to its highest point in a discourse about resurrection and its bearing on the life of faith.

Paul's words in 15:1-2 carefully reconstruct his first contact with them, affirm their reception of his gospel "in which they [still] stand," and point toward their salvation—but this idyllic, panoramic survey crashes head-on into the conditional and cautionary words Paul directly adds: "*If* (εἰ *ei*) you hold fast, *unless* (εἰ μή *ei mē*) you have believed in vain" (15:2).

This entire letter has had a back-to-basics quality where Paul seems ever determined to circle back and pick up the little children who have strayed, become lost, or not grown as much as he had hoped. Prior to chapter 15 it has been particular matters, some more critical, some more peripheral, about which the Corinthians have lost proper focus. Now, however, at stake in Paul's view is the heart of the gospel, their standing in it, and their understanding of it.

Paul gives no clue that this discourse has been prompted by their letter to him. So, precisely what has occasioned it? One can suppose, given that its subject is identified by Paul as the very gospel in which they stand, and given its location at a point of maximum emphasis, that Paul thinks of this matter as *bearing on everything that has preceded it.* As we get into the discourse we will see that one particular misunderstanding about resurrection catches Paul's direct attention.

The major blocks of Paul's argument in chapter 15 are as follows. Paul's early rehearsal of his foundational teaching, based upon and substantiated by received Christian tradition, reminds the Corinthians of the outlines of the gospel he preached to them, the foundation he laid for them (15:3-11). In the next section we can see that some Corinthians appear to be confused about "the resurrection of the dead" (15:12-34). Then, with the help of a fictive interlocutor, Paul is able to make basic affirmations about continuity and contrast of the present life of faith and the yet-to-be-fullness of the life of faith (15:35-57). The discourse closes with a recapitulation and peroration (15:58).

---

148. *Ad Herennium* 3.10.18: "The strongest arguments should be placed at the beginning and at the end. . . . And as for the rest, since what has been said last is easily committed to memory, it is useful, when ceasing to speak, to leave some very strong argument fresh in the hearer's mind."

149. Along with "the motifs of pre-existence and incarnation," according to Richard Hays, *The Faith of Jesus: An Investigation of the Narrative Substructure of Calatians 3:1-4:11,* SBLDS 56 (Chico, Calif.: Scholars, 1983) 256-57.

Before proceeding to an examination of the particulars, however, a feature of chapter 15 must be noted. In this section Paul casts his argument, his flow of thought, in extreme language.[150] Nothing is moderated. This is language designed to shock, to call to attention, as we have just noted even in 15:2. Paul not only returns to basics, he shakes the foundations. One can deduce from this that Paul takes the matter at hand with utmost seriousness and expects his hearers to do the same. At stake, in other words, is not some optional or peripheral issue. At issue is nothing less than the heart of the gospel as it can be lived in the world.

Consider how Paul has taken matters to the extreme (as a way of gaining attention and of focusing on what really matters). In the opening nineteen verses he dares to raise the question at three points whether their faith will have amounted to nothing, will have been in vain, or is useless (15:2, 14, 17). He urges them not to be deceived (15:33); he calls them back to their senses (15:34); he conjures up a representative Corinthian spokesman and dubs him "foolish" or "ignorant" (ἄφρων *aphrōn*) (15:36); he speaks of their shame, which we have seen previously in the letter is a hot-button cultural norm (15:34). At the same time that he exposes what he takes to be their folly, he writes just as dramatically of the awesome and unassailable power of God that is working through Jesus Christ to attain the culmination of God's plan: He portrays Christ's ultimate giving over of the kingdom to God when all powers, and among them eventually even death, will be—again the strongest of verbs—set aside, abolished, wiped out (καταργέω *katargeō*, 15:24, 26; cf. 1:28; 6:13). Paul sees a radical dissonance between what God is doing and the Corinthians' life patterns and convictions, and he fears that they are risking their access to sharing in God's redemptive purposes. Nothing less than extremes in rhetoric and in warnings will adequately portray the gravity of what is at stake. Accordingly, Paul lays out his argument so that the Corinthians will not, indeed cannot miss the discrepancy between what they are believing and doing and what God is doing.

Implicit in Paul's understanding is the conviction that once one is in faith—that is, in right relationship with God, once one is justified by or reconciled to God, one can stumble, one can fall (cf. 1 Cor 10:12) from grace, can fall from faith and become once again slaves to sin. For Paul, in the unquestioned letters (see the Introduction), salvation is consistently a future finishing up of what God has already begun in Christ. For Paul believers are not currently saved, they are not already perfected or matured (cf. Phil 3:12-15). As 15:2 suggests, they are on their way toward salvation; and God's grace and power will take them there, "if they hold fast." The letter to the Galatians is good evidence of Paul's belief that reconciled, justified believers can fall from faith (cf. Gal 3:3; 4:8-11; 5:4; 6:9).

At issue between Paul and the Corinthians in chapter 15 is not only their understanding of resurrection, but the way that understanding bears on their behavior. For Paul, what one believes has a direct connection with how one behaves, or at least it ought to, and what one does ought to reflect what one believes. Paul can come at it either way: He can see wrongful conduct and suppose that there is some failure in proper belief, or he can reason from what one believes and reckon what behavior is appropriate to that belief. Chapter 15 starts from the declaration of what he and they believe and only then moves to comportment or to the difference the belief ought to make for one's viewing of human options.[151]

The Corinthians, or at least some among them, have misunderstandings about what Paul and his relayed tradition meant when they spoke of the "resurrection of the dead." Paul puts it in the form of a question, which he lodges after he has recited the foundational teaching seen in 15:3-11: "But if it is preached that 'Christ has been raised from the dead' [15:4], then how can some among you say 'There is no resurrection of the dead'?" (15:12). With these introductory observations, we can now turn to a closer examination of the passages, the flow of the argument, and an elaboration of Paul's rhetorical purposes.

---

150. D. F. Watson, "Paul's Rhetorical Strategy in 1 Corinthians 15," in S. E. Porter and T. H. Olbricht, eds., *Rhetoric and the New Testament: Essays from the 1992 Heidelberg Conference,* JSNTSup 90 (Sheffield: JSOT 1993) 231-49.

151. By contrast, chapter 7, or even chapter 8, moved from questions about proper behavior to concerns about what believers know, and then proceeded with applications to how they should behave.

# 1 CORINTHIANS 15:1-2, BROAD-BRUSH SCOPE OF THE LIFE OF FAITH

NIV

**15** Now, brothers, I want to remind you of the gospel I preached to you, which you received and on which you have taken your stand. [2]By this gospel you are saved, if you hold firmly to the word I preached to you. Otherwise, you have believed in vain.

NRSV

**15** Now I would remind you, brothers and sisters,[a] of the good news[b] that I proclaimed to you, which you in turn received, in which also you stand, [2]through which also you are being saved, if you hold firmly to the message that I proclaimed to you—unless you have come to believe in vain.

[a] Gk brothers    [b] Or gospel

## COMMENTARY

Paul's introduction to the expansive discourse on resurrection, indicating as it does that the heart of the gospel is at issue, gives clues of its importance to Paul. Paul rehearses; he reminds them in what amounts to a chain-like argument, each link of which has some special connection to "the gospel": The gospel he preached to them is the gospel they received; the gospel they received is the very one in which they, like supposedly stalwart warriors, stand (cf. Eph 6:14; Rom 14:4); that gospel in and by which they stand is the channel through which they will ultimately be saved. In such a short rhetorical sequence, Paul has sketched their entire Christian biography, from their conversion under Paul's preaching, to their being lifted up and caused to stand so as to take their part in God's great and final conquest of sin and its fruit, death, and he has even sketched their relation to the gospel out to its culmination: "Through the gospel you shall be saved" (15:2a). This fits Paul's picture of the gospel in every detail. Paul has full confidence that, as he wrote the Philippians, the God who has begun such a work in them will surely bring it to completion (Phil 1:6). God is faithful, trustworthy (1:9; 10:13; 2 Cor 1:18; 1 Thess 5:24). Because it depends entirely upon God, Paul is sure that God's plan will be brought to fulfillment. So Paul can confidently write to the Corinthians that they "shall be saved"—that is, that they shall be included in salvation, insofar as it depends on God.

What a shocking thought, then, for Paul to ponder, in his very next words, whether the Corinthians have believed in vain. What if their commitment to the gospel proved pointless and powerless? Attached to these sweeping claims about the gospel are two cautionary notes: One raises the possibility that they might not "hold fast" or "keep in one's memory" (εἰ κατέχετε *ei katechete,* 15:2c) the very gospel on which their life in Christ is founded; the other raises the even more astonishing specter that they might have believed in vain, that all their believing might prove fruitless or end in failure (15:2d). Absolutely nothing in the letter so far has suggested that any of the Corinthian believers have ever entertained the thought that all of this might end in nothing, an ephemeral dream that vanishes like the morning's dew. With 15:2 Paul has moved the question of the Corinthians' destiny to the center of the discussion and will return to it after he reviews "what we know" in 15:3-11.

A minor but significant point is that Paul opens the discourse by calling them "brothers and sisters," thus identifying himself with them and them with him as he undertakes this crucial discussion. The discourse culminates with Paul once again identifying them, this time with emphasis, as "my beloved brothers and sisters" (15:58) and exhorting them to stay the course. (See Reflections at 15:3-11.)

# 1 CORINTHIANS 15:3-11, THE FOUNDATIONAL TEACHING

NIV

[3]For what I received I passed on to you as of first importance[a]: that Christ died for our sins according to the Scriptures, [4]that he was buried, that he was raised on the third day according to the Scriptures, [5]and that he appeared to Peter,[b] and then to the Twelve. [6]After that, he appeared to more than five hundred of the brothers at the same time, most of whom are still living, though some have fallen asleep. [7]Then he appeared to James, then to all the apostles, [8]and last of all he appeared to me also, as to one abnormally born.

[9]For I am the least of the apostles and do not even deserve to be called an apostle, because I persecuted the church of God. [10]But by the grace of God I am what I am, and his grace to me was not without effect. No, I worked harder than all of them—yet not I, but the grace of God that was with me. [11]Whether, then, it was I or they, this is what we preach, and this is what you believed.

[a] 3 Or *you at the first*   [b] 5 Greek *Cephas*

NRSV

3For I handed on to you as of first importance what I in turn had received: that Christ died for our sins in accordance with the scriptures, 4and that he was buried, and that he was raised on the third day in accordance with the scriptures, 5and that he appeared to Cephas, then to the twelve. 6Then he appeared to more than five hundred brothers and sisters[a] at one time, most of whom are still alive, though some have died.[b] 7Then he appeared to James, then to all the apostles. 8Last of all, as to one untimely born, he appeared also to me. 9For I am the least of the apostles, unfit to be called an apostle, because I persecuted the church of God. 10But by the grace of God I am what I am, and his grace toward me has not been in vain. On the contrary, I worked harder than any of them—though it was not I, but the grace of God that is with me. 11Whether then it was I or they, so we proclaim and so you have come to believe.

[a] Gk *brothers*   [b] Gk *fallen asleep*

## COMMENTARY

With a recitation, in traditional form as he received it, Paul reminds them of the gospel they received from him (15:3-10). He suggests it is the same gospel that all the apostles preach (15:11); it is surely the gospel he first preached to them and that they believed (2:1-2). And from Paul's other letters we can see that it is indeed the gospel that he apparently preached in all his churches. Central among its claims is the death and resurrection of Jesus Christ (15:3-4). The actual sequence in the traditional formulation recited in 15:3-11 is: Christ died for "your sins" (though Paul, apart from traditional materials such as these that mention "sins," speaks of sin in the singular and as a power); he was buried; he was raised (the so-called divine passive, indicating that it was God who did the raising) on the third day; and the risen Lord appeared to a sequence of people among whom Paul counts himself as the very last. This is what all churches have as a foundation belief; it is what Paul believes; and it is what he knows the Corinthians believe. Thus the Corinthians are reminded not only of the gospel that they believe, but also that their connection to it is through Paul, enhancing his own ethos and status among them and thereby reinforcing the leverage that he will use with them in what follows.

Paul has written his own story into the tradition that he has received and passed on to them. Most scholars hold that 15:3-5 is the core of the tradition that Paul has received and that he adds other traditions of appearances in the ensuing verses. Those appearances are the occasion for him to weave his own story into the older story. With 15:11 he weaves his auditors' story into the whole.

Paul's self-portrait in his recounting of the traditions is telling. Each detail of it will play an important role in the remainder of the discourse. Paul's own life is paradigmatic for all believers. No previous action of his merits God's favor (Paul's persecution of "the church of God" showed his unworthiness; 15:9), but God's grace is sufficient to transform even such a person as Paul who directly and defiantly opposes God's purpose ("by God's grace I am what I am"; 15:10a). Paul confidently asserts that God's grace in him in his preaching the gospel "has not been in vain" (15:10b), a potentially striking contrast from his cautionary word to them about their faith possibly being in vain (15:2; cf. his reprise of this concern in 15:14, 58).

Paul goes out of his way to highlight his labors in a hyperbolic fashion: He claims to have labored "harder than all of" the other apostles, but he quickly puts his own works in perspective because they are not really so much his works as God's grace working though him (15:10c). Though the Corinthians had never set themselves so directly in opposition to God's plans as Paul did by his persecution of believers, they, too, lived in their sin(s) before the gospel came to them. Also, like Paul, God's grace has demonstratively proved effective in their lives; in a subsequent letter to these same people, Paul will be able to describe what happened in and with them as a "new creation" (2 Cor 5:17).

They and he both know that the transformative power of God has worked effectively in their lives; that is not at issue for even a second. So Paul's labor—read God's grace—among them has already proved effective; that is not in dispute. What *is* at issue is whether the Corinthians will stand firm in their faith and therefore whether they will ultimately be saved (15:2a). How are they in danger of falling? The rest of chapter 15 gives us insights and answers.

Paul's discussion of his work (15:10) introduces a theme that will receive attention in this discourse; in fact its importance as a topic is seen in its being a ring device, an *inclusio,* which by appearing also at the close of chapter 15 (15:58), encircles the whole discussion with the significance of what one does. The place and importance of works in relation to faith can cause some confusion. To minimize the confusion, let us put Paul's view in formulaic fashion: Work(s) can never lead to faith, that is, to right relation to God; but faith, when properly functioning, always produces work(s). In 15:10 Paul is very clear that his working is really not his in an independent way, but is "the grace of God [working] with him." The same connection is expressed in Phil 2:12-13 where Paul calls upon the Philippians to work out their own salvation "because God is the one working in you" toward that end (cf. also 1 Thess 2:13). Believers cannot separate their own work from the ongoing work of God (Paul's code word for this is "grace") in them.

# REFLECTIONS

**1.** Basic confessions such as this sketch out the narrative that is at the heart of Paul's preaching. See also Phil 2:1-13 and Galatians 3.[152] In both of these latter passages, just as in 1 Cor 15:3-11, the foundational Christian story is recounted. In Christ's death and resurrection, God has laid claim on God's own creatures, or, to put it differently, God has loved us unlovely people. In the account at hand, Paul laces his own story into the old story. We modern readers can see our own lives linked to the creed in similar ways. Like Paul, we had no special merit—indeed, we may have been living in a way that turned its back on God's grace. Like Paul, we, too, take the tradition that we have received and we transmit it to those who follow us, not only in our retelling of the old story but, from Paul's perspective more importantly, in our living it in an exemplary fashion. As chapter 15 unfolds we will also see that the old story has a direct impact on how we behave and even more fundamentally on why we act or do.

**2.** Compare the space Paul devotes to the old creedal story prior to his mention of himself with the number of verses he uses to tie his own story into the foundational story. Each of us

152. Hays, *Faith of Jesus,* 247.

should be able to tell our own saga as it ties into our collective basic story of Christ's death and resurrection. Some of us will have come to faith through the tender caring of our parents or some other relative. Others will have found our mothers and fathers in the faith outside our biological families. But each of us is indebted to those who carried the faith from the past to the present and mediated it to us. Dare we do less for those who follow us?

# 1 CORINTHIANS 15:12-34, HOW CAN SOME SAY THERE IS NO RESURRECTION OF THE DEAD?

## NIV

[12]But if it is preached that Christ has been raised from the dead, how can some of you say that there is no resurrection of the dead? [13]If there is no resurrection of the dead, then not even Christ has been raised. [14]And if Christ has not been raised, our preaching is useless and so is your faith. [15]More than that, we are then found to be false witnesses about God, for we have testified about God that he raised Christ from the dead. But he did not raise him if in fact the dead are not raised. [16]For if the dead are not raised, then Christ has not been raised either. [17]And if Christ has not been raised, your faith is futile; you are still in your sins. [18]Then those also who have fallen asleep in Christ are lost. [19]If only for this life we have hope in Christ, we are to be pitied more than all men.

[20]But Christ has indeed been raised from the dead, the firstfruits of those who have fallen asleep. [21]For since death came through a man, the resurrection of the dead comes also through a man. [22]For as in Adam all die, so in Christ all will be made alive. [23]But each in his own turn: Christ, the firstfruits; then, when he comes, those who belong to him. [24]Then the end will come, when he hands over the kingdom to God the Father after he has destroyed all dominion, authority and power. [25]For he must reign until he has put all his enemies under his feet. [26]The last enemy to be destroyed is death. [27]For he "has put everything under his feet." [a] Now when it says that "everything" has been put under him, it is clear that this does not include God himself, who put everything under Christ. [28]When he has done this, then the

[a] 27 Psalm 8:6

## NRSV

12Now if Christ is proclaimed as raised from the dead, how can some of you say there is no resurrection of the dead? [13]If there is no resurrection of the dead, then Christ has not been raised; [14]and if Christ has not been raised, then our proclamation has been in vain and your faith has been in vain. [15]We are even found to be misrepresenting God, because we testified of God that he raised Christ—whom he did not raise if it is true that the dead are not raised. [16]For if the dead are not raised, then Christ has not been raised. [17]If Christ has not been raised, your faith is futile and you are still in your sins. [18]Then those also who have died[a] in Christ have perished. [19]If for this life only we have hoped in Christ, we are of all people most to be pitied.

20But in fact Christ has been raised from the dead, the first fruits of those who have died.[a] [21]For since death came through a human being, the resurrection of the dead has also come through a human being; [22]for as all die in Adam, so all will be made alive in Christ. [23]But each in his own order: Christ the first fruits, then at his coming those who belong to Christ. [24]Then comes the end,[b] when he hands over the kingdom to God the Father, after he has destroyed every ruler and every authority and power. [25]For he must reign until he has put all his enemies under his feet. [26]The last enemy to be destroyed is death. [27]For "God[c] has put all things in subjection under his feet." But when it says, "All things are put in subjection," it is plain that this does not include the one who put all things in subjection under him. [28]When all things are subjected to him, then the

[a] Gk fallen asleep   [b] Or Then come the rest   [c] Gk he

## NIV

Son himself will be made subject to him who put everything under him, so that God may be all in all.

²⁹Now if there is no resurrection, what will those do who are baptized for the dead? If the dead are not raised at all, why are people baptized for them? ³⁰And as for us, why do we endanger ourselves every hour? ³¹I die every day—I mean that, brothers—just as surely as I glory over you in Christ Jesus our Lord. ³²If I fought wild beasts in Ephesus for merely human reasons, what have I gained? If the dead are not raised,

"Let us eat and drink,
for tomorrow we die."ᵃ

³³Do not be misled: "Bad company corrupts good character." ³⁴Come back to your senses as you ought, and stop sinning; for there are some who are ignorant of God—I say this to your shame.

ᵃ 32 Isaiah 22:13

## NRSV

Son himself will also be subjected to the one who put all things in subjection under him, so that God may be all in all.

29Otherwise, what will those people do who receive baptism on behalf of the dead? If the dead are not raised at all, why are people baptized on their behalf?

30And why are we putting ourselves in danger every hour? ³¹I die every day! That is as certain, brothers and sisters,ᵃ as my boasting of you—a boast that I make in Christ Jesus our Lord. ³²If with merely human hopes I fought with wild animals at Ephesus, what would I have gained by it? If the dead are not raised,

"Let us eat and drink,
for tomorrow we die."

³³Do not be deceived:
"Bad company ruins good morals."
³⁴Come to a sober and right mind, and sin no more; for some people have no knowledge of God. I say this to your shame.

ᵃGk brothers

# COMMENTARY

Paul addresses the general issue of the *resurrection of the dead,* which he has heard some Corinthians doubt, using as leverage his and their assumption that Christ was raised from the dead. Paul's argument in chapter 15 confirms this interpretation. The *resurrection of Christ* is not seriously disputed by anyone in Corinth; the resurrection of the dead is. The resurrection of Christ is grounded in Paul's traditionally based preaching that is at the foundation of their belief, as he reminds them (15:3-11). In what follows, Paul does not argue *that* Christ was raised from the dead—they do not dispute that; rather he argues *from* the shared affirmation that Christ was raised from the dead. The contrary-to-fact consideration, "if Christ was not raised from the dead," designed to shock his readers and to focus their attention, is met with prohibitive and unthinkable consequences for Paul and for the Corinthians: "Then our preaching is empty and your faith is empty; and I am found a false witness of God . . . your faith is useless and you are still in your sins" (15:14-17). After such dismissive rheto-

ric there is no more mention of any dispute whether Christ has been raised; instead, the discussion shifts to the true topic of dispute, namely the *resurrection of the dead,* and with it the question of when believers will share in a resurrection like Christ's.

How are we to understand the claim of some that "there is no resurrection of the dead"? Just what could they have meant by such an assertion? Resurrection was not a widespread notion in the world at that time. Greek and Roman views of resurrection ranged from assumptions that it was impossible to reckoning that it might happen in an occasional, isolated miraculous event. Some older scriptures of Israel note a few resurrections (1 Kgs 17:17; 2 Kgs 4:18; 13:20) and a few of Israel's later writings expect a future general resurrection (Isa 26:19; Dan 12:2; cf. Job 19:25-27; Ezek 37:1-14). Pharisaic Judaism, whose most notable exemplar in the New Testament is Paul, held, against the Sadducees, for a resurrection.[153] In the light of

153. Josephus *The Jewish War* 2.165; *Antiquities of the Jews* 18.16.

this information, it is likely that Paul's affirmation of the resurrection of the dead was a striking claim or bit of news for his largely gentile audience in Corinth when he first preached to them. So it is not too surprising that some of Paul's followers in Corinth continued in doubt or came to doubt about resurrection of dead people, though we should note that even those who doubted that dead people might ultimately be raised could have conceded that Christ rose as one of those occasional, isolated miraculous events. Because Paul treats the Corinthians who said "There is no resurrection of the dead" as members of the community, it is safe to suppose that they still hold that Christ was raised from the dead. This interpretation is supported by the fact that Paul, though he briefly entertains the notion, for the sake of argument, that Christ was not raised (15:13-20), simply asserts in 15:21 that *Christ was raised* and builds his case from that fundamental and apparently widespread Corinthian believers' claim.

For Paul, the linkage is indissoluble between the claim that Christ was raised and the assertion that believers likewise will be raised from the dead. The latter follows from the former because Christ was the "firstborn within a large family" (Rom 8:29 NRSV) whose resurrection guarantees the same for all his brothers and sisters; Paul makes the same point to the Corinthians in 15:23 by calling Christ the "first fruits" of the whole resurrection harvest. Indeed, his opening argument assumes and builds from that hinge: If Christ was raised, then believers will also be raised, in due time (15:12-23).

Across the undisputed letters Paul clearly anticipates that believers will be raised, will share a resurrection like Christ's, at the end time. Believers are not yet raised; they do not yet share in the resurrection (cf. the post-Pauline Eph 2:6 and Col 2:12). Because believers have died with Christ, because they have died to sin, they do already "walk in newness of life" (Rom 6:4) and they are already part of the new creation (2 Cor 5:17). Paul's view about believers not yet sharing the resurrection corresponds to his view noted above that believers are not yet saved. Believers are not yet raised, neither are they yet saved, but God's initial and ongoing work leads them toward that τέλος (*telos*), that goal—if they hold fast (15:2), if they stand firm (15:58).

Evidence from the different parts of 1 Corinthians suggests that while some may have believed that there was no resurrection of the dead, they and/or others may also have transformed the notion of resurrection from what it was for Paul, namely an eschatological, end-of-the-age event, to a spiritualized way of understanding the new life in Christ in the present. Such a transposition of Paul's fundamental preaching not only denies Paul's gospel's claim that death as the final enemy will be destroyed (15:26), but severely alters the way in which persons live and move and have their being in this world, before the parousia. So two, distinguishable problems tie to the Corinthian denial of the resurrection of the dead: First, believers who deny the resurrection of the dead view life in this world, short of the consummation of God's purposes, as the only and total chance they have to find significance and fulfillment for themselves and their lives, as in some way approximating here and now as much as possible (sharing) something of a resurrection vaguely like Christ's own; and second, the *telos* or goal toward which the believing life is directed is lost as a moral guideline to believers.

Paul's scathing sarcasm in 4:8-11 is directed precisely at such persons who have collapsed into the present what for Paul remains future, namely *already* sharing the kingdom: "Already you are satiated, already you have become rich, apart from us you have reigned!" So there are some Corinthian believers who have vaunted that they have already arrived at the fullness of the life of faith that Paul expects only at the parousia. They hold that they have advanced beyond their former peers in the faith. It is such persons who may have among them the man "who has his father's wife" (5:1), who are arrogant (5:2), who feel themselves beyond normal moral restraints, who lord it over others at the supper (11:17-34), and perhaps even those who have the highly visible gift of glossolalia (12-14). The persons whom Paul chides as "already" reigning, rich, and filled (4:8-11) could be the same ones who deny the resurrection of the dead *as a future event,* who have transformed Paul's not-until-the-end-of-the-age resurrection of believers and therefore the final defeat of the ultimate enemy, death (15:26) into a spiritualized claim to have achieved *already* some exceptional quality of life that they may very well have called "resurrection." Paul's future expectation of the resurrection of the dead has been transposed by these Corinthians into a present experience.[154]

A dissonance has come to exist between Paul's view of things and their own. Paul's own preaching about sharing Christ's death, dying with Christ, and walking in newness of life (Rom 6:4) lends itself to such a transformation because a hearer could assume that "walking in newness of life" really meant some sort of "resurrection" in the present. It is not difficult to imagine some among the Corinthians taking the newness of life to be what resurrection really means, available as it is already in the present and minimizing or even denying a future resurrection of the dead. Likewise, a few of Paul's other striking claims about the future may have led some to claim that they already enjoyed many or all of the extraordinary powers that Paul envisions in the future. As seen in 1 Corinthians, among those endtime powers that might erroneously be taken as present capacities are: Then believers will judge the world (6:2) and angels (6:3); then believers who have steered clear of the vices will inherit the kingdom (6:9; note that Paul makes clear in 15:50 that inheriting the kingdom is a future event). In fact, until the end time it is Christ, not believers, who reigns "until he has put all his enemies under his feet" (15:25; cf. 4:8).

Because of Paul's strong conviction that Christ is the firstborn of many brothers and sisters, the first fruits of the resurrection, he cannot but see a denial of resurrection of the dead as a denial of Christ's having been raised from the dead. To deny the resurrection of the dead—and therefore also Christ's resurrection—is worse than losing an important claim. It is to believe in vain and thus to remain in one's sins (15:17). That is the force of Paul's rhetoric in 15:12-19. For Paul, the two claims—that Christ has been raised and that others will be raised—are inseparable. The one leads ineluctably, *but only later,* to the other; the latter is simply the yet-to-be finishing of what God has begun in the former. So the future resurrection of the dead is a consequence of Christ's having been raised. God's faithfulness assures that. To question either—the future resurrection of the dead or

Christ's resurrection—is to raise questions about the other, and Paul can countenance questioning neither. To put it in different terms, Christ's resurrection was not some unusual event sequestered into the byways of history for Paul; it was the transformative event that marked the turn of history and linked it directly to God's culminating but not yet finished purposes in all of creation. Christ's having been raised by God has as its consequence that others will be raised from the dead, and therefore that death itself will ultimately be defeated—and all of this has credibility because every bit of it rests on God's power and purpose, neither of which can or will be qualified by human reticence, recalcitrance, or failure.

With 15:20-28 Paul elaborates upon the basic teaching that he gave them (15:3-11) and that became the foundation of their faith in which they supposedly stand. Christ, having indeed been raised from among the dead people, is twice designated "first fruits" (ἀπαρχή *aparchē*) (15:20, 23) of those who are sleeping—a euphemism for those who are dead. The mention of "first fruits" refers to the scripturally based practice of sanctifying the whole crop by offering the "first fruits" to God (Exod 23:19). In this way Paul affirms that Christ's resurrection promises or secures the future resurrection of those who belong to Christ. So without using the terms, the "first fruits" claims are language of promise, guarantee, and confidence.

Paul's first mention of Christ as "first fruits" (15:20) introduces a double typological elaboration (15:21-23) in which Paul invites the readers to reaffirm their identification with Christ, while Adam is made to symbolize all of those who are destined for death, and Christ is affirmed as the means through which believers are made alive (a theme to which he will return in 15:45-49). The Adam-Christ typology is a commonplace in Paul, appearing in 15:21-22, 45-49 and again in Rom 5:14-21. Biblical typologies work in predictable ways: They always take a person or an event and, by a selective retelling, highlight some point or points that the author wants to make to readers (see another Pauline typology in 10:1-13). When Paul lays out his Adam-Christ comparison and contrast he seeks neither to write history nor to describe some sequence in sacred history, but to call his readers to realize more fully what they have in Christ. So the comments about Adam are

---

154. See C.M. Tuckett, "No Resurrection of the Dead (1 Cor 15,12)," in *The Corinthian Correspondence,* ed. R. Bieringer (Leuven: Leuven University Press, 1996) 274.

backformed from the beliefs about Christ and are used to elaborate, via negativa, not only the significance of Christ for the readers but also the richness of the believers' new life. In 15:22, the point is that the death produced by their solidarity with Adam is ultimately overcome in Christ. (For more on the Adam-Christ typology, see the Commentary on 15:48-50 where Paul returns to it.)

With the second reference to Christ as "first fruits" of the resurrection of all believers (15:23), Paul introduces what was likely a shocking rebuke to those who had spiritualized the resurrection and thereby arrogated such status into the present: "But each in its own turn" (15:23 NIV). The proper order: Christ the first fruits, then only after that those who belong to Christ, at his parousia; in other words, when God's cosmic purposes are brought to fulfillment—and Paul once again elaborates upon his basic teaching by sketching out the final picture of the culmination of God's plan, as follows. Paul drives the "proper order" point home by detailing what will happen at the eschaton and not before. At the end, Christ will give the kingdom, the reign, to God, but only after Christ has laid waste all rule and authority and enemy, including that "last enemy" (θάνατος *thanatos*), death, which God had placed under Christ's feet (a reference to Ps 110:1). Until that time there is no resurrection of the dead and the final defeat of death.

As he sketches the grandeur of God's culminating purposes, Paul's language drifts toward doxology: In the end, even Christ will be made subject to God, who is already in 3:23 credited as being the one to whom all else, including Christ, belongs and who in 8:6 is declared to be the one from whom are all things and for whom people exist (cf. 11:3). The goal: so that "God may be all in all" (NRSV and NIV). How misguided of some of the Corinthians to write themselves into the divine script in an arrogant, previous, and presumptuous way, as if they had already arrived or already reigned (cf. 4:8-13)! To them Paul addresses his comment: "Each in the proper order" (15:23).

Paul then pushes his argument by asking rhetorical questions first about some persons whom he mentions in the third person ("they") and second about himself. Admittedly, Paul's purposes in the rhetorical questions are more certainly accessible than some of the practices to which the questions

refer. The questions suggest to the readers the folly of their practices *if the dead are not ever to be raised*. First, the persons Paul describes as "those who are being baptized in behalf of the dead" (15:29). This is another of those matters about which Paul and the Corinthians surely understood one another but which we cannot hope to fathom. The most obvious reading of the text would suggest that there are some at Corinth (note that Paul does not address them directly, but writes about them as an example) who are being baptized in behalf of dead persons, perhaps as representatives of dear ones who either never had a chance to respond to the gospel or who had died while being drawn to the faith. But the truth is that we simply do not know. Most surprising is that Paul did not oppose the practice, which seems to suppose either that grace is transferrable or that one can be a surrogate believer for another. Instead, Paul uses it to expose its folly if there is no resurrection of the dead.

Second, Paul refers to himself and his own labors and struggles (15:30-32a) in a fashion that we can see across the corpus of his letters: He is the one who works against incredible obstacles to proclaim the gospel, whose perdurance in the face of hardships marks him out as trustworthy (cf. 2 Cor 4:7-12; 6:1-10; 11:21b-29; Rom 8:31-39),[155] but in this instance his response to hardships gives him the opportunity to focus the question *why* he continues to struggle and work so hard if there is no resurrection of the dead. Paul stacks up phrases to highlight his continuous perils: He is in danger every hour; in effect he dies daily (cf. 2 Cor 6:9 NIV: "dying, and yet we live on"); at the very time of his writing of this letter he is locked in a struggle (wrestling "wild beasts"; see below) in Ephesus. And in the middle of the litany he dares to boast of his work in their behalf, in bringing the gospel to them (cf. 15:10-11), which by its placement pictures his work in their behalf as a part of the whole fabric of his life in service of the gospel and empowered by the grace of God in Christ, who is the Lord of the Corinthians and of Paul. Then, to cap it off, Paul declares, "If the dead are not raised, 'let us eat and drink because tomorrow we die' " (15:32b-c), quoting Isa 22:13, and emphasizing the futility and meaninglessness of life if death has the final word.

155. Fitzgerald, *Earthen Vessel,* 65-70, 203-5.

What does Paul mean when he says "I die daily" (15:31)? The immediate context on either side gives the first clues. "Why are we in danger every hour?" precedes (15:30) and "If, figuratively speaking, I fought wild animals in Ephesus, what good does it do?" follows (15:32). This is hardship talk, which Paul often employs as a sign of his endurance and trustworthiness, but here it is used to highlight the question: Why go to all this apostolic trouble if death has the final word? Paul's answer lies in his deep conviction that in sharing Christ's death believers become one with his suffering, and the powers of the old age vent their anger against the believers so that there is always θλῖψις (*thlipsis*), his technical term for end-times suffering and tribulation (see 1 Cor 7:28). The same point is made when he later writes about "always carrying in the body the death of Jesus" (2 Cor 4:10 NRSV). His dying daily, as indeed his carrying in the body the death of Jesus, is his shorthand way of saying that day-by-day his close identification with Christ's death and his service to his call place him in (hourly and daily) danger. Paul accomplishes one other point here as well: To those Corinthians who claim already to have "arrived," to have experienced a spiritual sort of resurrection, Paul, the exemplary leader whom no one outperforms, readily identifies himself solely with the death of Jesus and contents himself to wait for the not-yet-realized resurrection of the dead that will only come, in his view, at the end, when Christ returns.

The section concludes with three directives addressed to the Corinthian believers: (1) "Do not be foolish: 'Bad company ruins good morals'" (15:33; quoting the maxim that ultimately may be traced back to the Greek author Menander; cf. another maxim to the same point already in 5:6*b*). (2) "Come to your senses as you ought" (15:34*a*) and (3) "Do not sin" (15:34*b*), with the latter probably surprising the hearers that Paul should construe their actions as in any way representing sin. They have to be warned against sinning; some of them have no knowledge of God; Paul openly declares that he speaks to their shame—all of this is Paul pushing the hearers to the limits, his trying to shock them back to their (better) senses. Why? Because he has come to the heart of the matter: Life in this world, immersed as it is in suffering and brokenness, and work in behalf of the gospel, can all be reduced to folly if there is no resurrection of the dead, if indeed death has the victory, and if indeed death has the last word. Human striving and achieving, even if inspired by the grace of God, is emptied of all its significance if death is the final verdict. How is one's work, indeed one's very essence, one's innermost being more than a whisper if it all ends in death? Paul posits that the resurrection of the dead, which is the logical and necessary outcome of the already-accomplished resurrection of Christ, gives life in the present its meaning, allows and even demands that one enter struggles on behalf of the gospel, and assures that life's struggles and hardships have meaning, a meaning that is ensured by God and that will survive death's sting. Another index that this is indeed the heart of the matter may be seen in Paul's returning to the topic and indeed concluding the discourse on the note that believers know "that in the Lord your labor is not in vain" (15:58). But more on that later.

# REFLECTIONS

**1.** Whereas most modern understandings of faith focus on *what one believes,* Paul tends to think of faith as the *dynamic, proper relation of people to God.* For Paul, "faith" is his code word for right relation to God; faith is not static, but dynamic, that is, full of power. A deficiency of the English language contributes to the modern understanding because English lacks a verb formed on the same root word as the noun "faith." For the verb, English shifts to "believe," which suggests content or assent to propositions. Not so Greek, where verb and noun are formed on the same root. An important understanding of faith emerges in chapter 15. If Christ has not been raised from the dead, then at stake is not just some wrong belief, some erroneous idea, but faith has lost its *power*—"your faith is ματαία [*mataia,* "empty," "fruitless," "useless," "powerless"]"—and there are disastrous consequences: "You are still in your sins," those who have died in Christ have perished (15:17-18), and the struggles and labor of daily life have no meaning. Faith is the powerfully established, powerfully effective, and productive right relationship to God.

**2.** A final battle is a typical feature of end-time apocalyptic depictions (cf. Wis 5:17-20; Isa 59:16-19; Rev 19:11-21; Eph 6:10-17) such as Paul's (Rom 8:37-39; 2 Cor 10:3-4; 1 Thess 5:8-9). In the battle God defeats the enemies, variously and somewhat vaguely identified by Paul as the "rulers of this age" (2:6, 8) and "every rule, every authority and power" (15:24). But twice Paul identifies "the last enemy" as yet-to-be-destroyed death (15:26, 54-57). As Paul clearly says, sin, understood as a power, is death's sting; put differently, sin leads to death. Death is effective because it is sin's work, and sin, were it not for God's grace in Jesus Christ, would indeed have the last word. Sin's power was broken in Christ's death and resurrection, though it still stalks about seeking to make a beachhead (Rom 7:8, 11), an offensive landing point from which it can achieve control of one's life by whatever means possible. But believers, having been freed from the lordship of sin and having come under a new Lord, Jesus Christ, are free from the power of sin. And, in Paul's picture most fully elaborated in chapter 15, at the end time when every competing rule and authority and power is finally destroyed, then death also will be destroyed. Then believers will share in Christ's resurrection, death will be no more, and "we shall all be changed."

Anyone who has lost a dear one knows what Paul means when he speaks of the finality of death as an enemy. The utter irretrievability of the lost one sends shock waves of grief. Similarly, those who have faced a terrifying medical diagnosis know death as an ultimate threat. Paul's message, as simple as it is profound, is that death will not have the last word; God will. Paul is not very clear about just how that happens or what it will be like, but he is categorical that God will not allow death to eclipse what we or our loved ones are and the loving that we and they have done.

Sin as a power maneuvering to take advantage of us is one of Paul's great insights. Paul has no truck with the common notion of sin as a wrong deed, as a particular action or set of actions that one should not do. Rather sin is a crafty power that tries to take control of one's life and thereby entice one away from proper dependence upon God. Sin is a primary rival to God and to Christ regarding control over one's life. The deviousness of sin can be seen in its use of even good things, to take some Pauline examples, the law, relations between individuals, and even the practice of one's piety, to take control of our lives.

**3.** Paul sounds a decidedly future note in these verses. In most of Paul's letters, and indeed in much of 1 Corinthians, Paul is concerned with the present, with how believers live and relate to one another now. To be sure, he thinks they benefit from looking back and from looking forward, but his largest concern is with present comportment. Part of that focus may come from his concern that his followers can fall away from the grace in which they stand; part of it surely comes with his conviction that the future belongs to God and that God is working it out as pleases God, so that believers do not have the job of securing the future but of living in such a fashion as to be acceptable to God, as to be coordinated with God's plan.

In most of Paul's letters, Paul stresses continuity between the present lives of the believers and God's ultimate plan into which they are being led by the Spirit. Philippians and its "upward call" and "pressing on" (3:13-14) would be a good example. So would 1 Thessalonians with its repeated encouragement to "do so more and more" (4:1, 10). First Corinthians has also made that connection of continuity. But, as we have seen, some at Corinth have collapsed God's future, for Paul, God's yet uncompleted work, into the present. They are the butt of Paul's irony in 4:8-11 where he depicts them as "already" in the kingdom, "already" filled, and "already" rich. Such also are the ones who "deny the resurrection of the dead" (15:12). So in chapter 15 Paul tries to maintain the delicate balance between properly appreciating and celebrating what believers *already* have in Christ and yet clearly recognizing what they have *not yet* received but can with confidence anticipate.

Paul's balance between already and not yet may be difficult for modern Christians to appropriate. Paul was as clear as we that believers were different from non-believers in their comportment of their lives and in the values they affirmed in them. In that sense some believers are like all other believers. But Paul realizes that believers come in all stripes and sizes, ranging from babies in the faith to mature believers. As much joy and assurance as any believers have in their present life, though, they cannot possibly have the fullness of all that God will do for and with them. At present they and all of God's new creation are "works in progress," and that is worth celebrating. But they are not yet complete, not yet finished; God is not yet done with them and with God's purposes with the universe. If we take that to heart, a couple of things should follow: (1) We will continue to press on, to strive to live in accord with God's good and ongoing purposes; and (2) we will be cautious about getting carried away in a boastful way and we will avoid hyperventilating about how wonderful we are.

# 1 CORINTHIANS 15:35-57, A FICTIVE CHARACTER ALLOWS PAUL TO WRITE ABOUT CONTINUITY AND CHANGE

## NIV

35But someone may ask, "How are the dead raised? With what kind of body will they come?" 36How foolish! What you sow does not come to life unless it dies. 37When you sow, you do not plant the body that will be, but just a seed, perhaps of wheat or of something else. 38But God gives it a body as he has determined, and to each kind of seed he gives its own body. 39All flesh is not the same: Men have one kind of flesh, animals have another, birds another and fish another. 40There are also heavenly bodies and there are earthly bodies; but the splendor of the heavenly bodies is one kind, and the splendor of the earthly bodies is another. 41The sun has one kind of splendor, the moon another and the stars another; and star differs from star in splendor.

42So will it be with the resurrection of the dead. The body that is sown is perishable, it is raised imperishable; 43it is sown in dishonor, it is raised in glory; it is sown in weakness, it is raised in power; 44it is sown a natural body, it is raised a spiritual body.

If there is a natural body, there is also a spiritual body. 45So it is written: "The first man Adam became a living being"[a]; the last Adam, a life-giving spirit. 46The spiritual did not come first, but

[a]45 Gen. 2:7

## NRSV

35But someone will ask, "How are the dead raised? With what kind of body do they come?" 36Fool! What you sow does not come to life unless it dies. 37And as for what you sow, you do not sow the body that is to be, but a bare seed, perhaps of wheat or of some other grain. 38But God gives it a body as he has chosen, and to each kind of seed its own body. 39Not all flesh is alike, but there is one flesh for human beings, another for animals, another for birds, and another for fish. 40There are both heavenly bodies and earthly bodies, but the glory of the heavenly is one thing, and that of the earthly is another. 41There is one glory of the sun, and another glory of the moon, and another glory of the stars; indeed, star differs from star in glory.

42So it is with the resurrection of the dead. What is sown is perishable, what is raised is imperishable. 43It is sown in dishonor, it is raised in glory. It is sown in weakness, it is raised in power. 44It is sown a physical body, it is raised a spiritual body. If there is a physical body, there is also a spiritual body. 45Thus it is written, "The first man, Adam, became a living being"; the last Adam became a life-giving spirit. 46But it is not the spiritual that is first, but the physical, and then the spiritual. 47The first man was from the earth, a

## NIV

the natural, and after that the spiritual. [47]The first man was of the dust of the earth, the second man from heaven. [48]As was the earthly man, so are those who are of the earth; and as is the man from heaven, so also are those who are of heaven. [49]And just as we have borne the likeness of the earthly man, so shall we[a] bear the likeness of the man from heaven.

[50]I declare to you, brothers, that flesh and blood cannot inherit the kingdom of God, nor does the perishable inherit the imperishable. [51]Listen, I tell you a mystery: We will not all sleep, but we will all be changed— [52]in a flash, in the twinkling of an eye, at the last trumpet. For the trumpet will sound, the dead will be raised imperishable, and we will be changed. [53]For the perishable must clothe itself with the imperishable, and the mortal with immortality. [54]When the perishable has been clothed with the imperishable, and the mortal with immortality, then the saying that is written will come true: "Death has been swallowed up in victory."[b]

[55]"Where, O death, is your victory?
    Where, O death, is your sting?"[c]

[56]The sting of death is sin, and the power of sin is the law. [57]But thanks be to God! He gives us the victory through our Lord Jesus Christ.

[a]49 Some early manuscripts *so let us*    [b]54 Isaiah 25:8    [c]55 Hosea 13:14

## NRSV

man of dust; the second man is[a] from heaven. [48]As was the man of dust, so are those who are of the dust; and as is the man of heaven, so are those who are of heaven. [49]Just as we have borne the image of the man of dust, we will[b] also bear the image of the man of heaven.

[50]What I am saying, brothers and sisters,[c] is this: flesh and blood cannot inherit the kingdom of God, nor does the perishable inherit the imperishable. [51]Listen, I will tell you a mystery! We will not all die,[d] but we will all be changed, [52]in a moment, in the twinkling of an eye, at the last trumpet. For the trumpet will sound, and the dead will be raised imperishable, and we will be changed. [53]For this perishable body must put on imperishability, and this mortal body must put on immortality. [54]When this perishable body puts on imperishability, and this mortal body puts on immortality, then the saying that is written will be fulfilled:

"Death has been swallowed up in victory."
[55] "Where, O death, is your victory?
    Where, O death, is your sting?"
[56]The sting of death is sin, and the power of sin is the law. [57]But thanks be to God, who gives us the victory through our Lord Jesus Christ.

[a]Other ancient authorities add *the Lord*    [b]Other ancient authorities read *let us*    [c]Gk *brothers*    [d]Gk *fall asleep*

# COMMENTARY

In order to advance his concerns Paul turns to a time-honored rhetorical device of having "a certain person" (τί τι) raise issues that allow Paul the opportunity to include all the Corinthians. In what amounts to a refinement of the matter that capped off the previous section of his argument—namely, how does the future resurrection of the dead bear on actions in the present—Paul uses his interlocutor's queries as an occasion to reflect on two interconnected issues: (1) the continuity between the present and future life in Christ and (2) the change that will take place between the present and the future.

By personifying the inquisitor, Paul allows the Corinthians to make some identification with the questioner and with the issues, but at the same time it gives him some liberty to be abrasive with the fictive inquisitor without the Corinthians necessarily viewing it as so direct an attack upon them. So they can freely identify with the questions, but when Paul attacks the interlocutor they can distance themselves from the heat of the attack. The character, another example of indirect speech (cf. chaps. 1–4), gives Paul and his hearers some freedom in the exchange and allows for greater clarity to be achieved by bolder comments.

The fictive person's first question "How are the dead raised?" might be of interest to the Corinthians but it is never answered per se; Paul is free to let it go because he has conjured up this fictive person and, like a ventriloquist with his dummy, Paul can have him say what he will and can just as freely ignore what he says once the attention of the hearers is secured. Instead, the second question, "With what bodies do they [the dead] come?" (15:35), with its reference to "body," becomes the focus of Paul's reflections. Paul rebukes the questioner, calling him a "Foolish/ignorant person." The reader is left to wonder whether the fictive person is an ignoramus because he asked the first question or the second. That ambiguity leaves Paul clear to abandon the first question and to undertake an elaborate argument whose burden is that the bodies of things differ, a point Paul will later in the discourse elaborate with regard to resurrection. Paul then takes the interlocutor to the experience of sowing and planting, common enough among persons living in an agrarian culture, and an image he has used already in this letter (3:6-8) with reference to himself.

This fictive person's foolishness lies in not recognizing what everybody is supposed to know, and Paul is at liberty to set him straight. Paul cleverly leaves his audience in the position of going along with him in a knowing way: What one plants does not make life unless it dies, and when one sows one plants not the body that will be but a simple seed to which "God gives a body just as God has chosen" and "each of the seeds has its own body" (15:38). Paul elaborates: The same could be said for flesh, the flesh of folks, of beasts, of birds, and of fish—each is of a distinctive kind of body (15:39). Likewise, when it comes to glory and heavenly and earthly bodies, the sun, the moon, and the stars, all these different bodies have glory, but the glory differs from one to the next. And so it is with all bodies, as Paul is quick to argue (15:42).

Using the most basic analogies and observable phenomena available to every human's experience, Paul makes a very sophisticated set of points. First, what one plants is and is not what grows. Plant a radish seed and one does get a radish, but one plants only a seed and what one harvests is really quite different from the seed, though still a radish. Flesh, bodies, and glory are all variable, distinguishable, and true-to-kind on some sort of dependable pattern[156] that Paul attributes to

God just as he earlier in this letter five times affirmed that God arranges matters as God wishes them to be (cf. 3:5; 7:17; 12:18, 24, 28). Second, along with this clarity and dependability there are also mystery and change. To demonstrate this, Paul uses examples that allow him to speak of continuity along with difference. So it is body he writes about, but there are different sorts of bodies, some heavenly, some earthly. And flesh may be flesh, but some of it belongs to people, some to domesticated animals, and some to birds, though it is still all flesh. The same with glory: sun, moon, and stars—and even stars vary in glory. Such a description allows Paul to note commonality but also to honor distinctiveness.

"Thus it is with the resurrection of the dead," Paul asserts (15:42), and by a reprise of his sowing-and-reaping image (last mentioned in 15:36-37) he stresses the *distinctions* between what is sowed and what is reaped but—and this is the genius of his claim—without denying that there is at the same time some fundamental continuity. One can transpose Paul's rhetoric onto a chart:

| Sown | Raised |
|---|---|
| corruption | incorruption |
| dishonor | glory |
| weakness | power |
| unspiritual | spiritual body |
| (ψυχικόν / psychikon) | |
| body | |

The list of contrasts draws to a close when Paul reintroduces the "body" concept and says: "If there is a natural body, there is also a spiritual body," stressing that in either case it is body, but a body that is changed—and with that the focus shifts to change and "body" becomes the means by which both the change and the continuity are affirmed, but the change is highlighted.

Verses 42-50 are an elaborate and creative development from the humble example of the seed, which is transformed with its planting and sprouting. Paul claims continuity and discontinuity between what we already are and what we shall be and thereby seizes a most complex but important set of factors about the new-but-not-yet-complete life in Christ. The continuity between now and not yet is expressed in that what is planted as a body is a body when raised; those who are of the

---

156. The Stoics (cf. Seneca, Letter 124, Reason and the True Good) and Epicureans (cf. Lucretius *On the Nature of Things* 2.700-729) would have argued to the same point.

earth are the very ones who will be the ones who are of heaven; the ones bearing the image of the man of dust will surely bear the image of the man of heaven. The discontinuity is a temporal one, often elsewhere expressed in Paul's frequent categories of "now" and "not yet" but here stated by the use of "first" and "second," "first" and "last," and "sown" and "raised." Both claims—that there is significant continuity and noteworthy discontinuity between the present life of believers and their future, completed life—are important to the richness of the gospel and to Paul's purposes in this chapter.

Paul, knowing that Gen 2:7 (LXX) calls Adam a "living being" (εἰς ψυχὴν ζῶσαν *eis psychēn zōsan*), undertakes a refinement of his Adam-Christ typology, which was introduced in 15:21-22 and calls Christ a "life-giving spirit" (15:45). Once again, a chart may be helpful:

| *The First Adam* | *The Last Adam* |
| --- | --- |
| living being | life-giving spirit |
| the physical | the spiritual |
| made of earth | from heaven |
| those who are of the earth | those who are of heaven |
| the εἰκών (*eikōn,* "stamp") of the earth | the *eikōn* (stamp) of heaven |

The two Adams are clearly types, representing alternative and mutually exclusive identifications or solidarities. This is yet another case of Paul's on-going theme "to whom does one belong?" As in the Sown/Raised chart, so here Paul is eager to mark off two modes of being, two ways of belonging. Humans can live in the world with one or the other allegiance, one or the other mark of belonging. This is much the same point that he made with the Philippians, but with a very different set of metaphors, when he wrote about living in the world but having their citizenship in heaven (Phil 3:20; cf. 1:27, which would best be translated as "discharge your obligations as citizens worthy of the gospel").

Paul's strongest statement of distinction and separation comes at the end of the two-Adams typology when he affectionately addresses the Corinthians as siblings and uses traditional language to declare, echoing his earlier claim of 6:9, that "flesh and blood cannot inherit the kingdom of God, nor the corruptible inherit the incorruptible" (15:50). The two sides of both charts are not simply to be assimilated to one another; this is yet another expression of his rival two-way mode of thinking that has been manifest from the very first chapters of this letter. Why should he be so pointed in this unless it is his view that some at Corinth are in fact attempting such an inheritance? Just as Paul shocked some of the Corinthians with his earlier blunt declaration "But each in its own order" (15:23*a*), declaring that Christ alone had already experienced resurrection, so here toward the end of this section Paul once again sounds the same theme when he says, with redundancy for emphasis: "But the spiritual is not first, but the physical, then the spiritual" (15:46).

In what we have depicted as two charts, Paul has laid out rich material, not because he has now decided to share some of his theological wisdom that he has earlier admitted to having (2:6), but for the purpose of bringing the Corinthians' thinking into shape so that their behavior will follow properly from it. Paul derides those who think that they already reign (4:8) and declares that "flesh and blood," that is, human beings living in this world, cannot have access to reigning, to the kingdom, not yet, not without radical and fundamental change to which he now turns in 15:51-57.

Usually in his letters Paul labors to lead his readers into a vision that the life already begun in Christ opens out toward God's future in strong continuity and growth so that one "presses on," works for improvement, and matures (cf. Phil 1:25; 3:12-15). There are two places in the seven undisputedly authentic letters, however, where he highlights a contrast between what believers already have and what they will inherit when the parousia comes: Romans 8 (though affirming continuity as well; e.g., Rom 8:28-39) and here in 1 Corinthians 15. In chap. 15, Paul shares with the Corinthians what he terms a "mystery" (μυστήριον *mystērion*), a disclosure, which, like 15:23*b*-28, depicts what lies ahead, toward the consummation, for all believers. Paul's "we shall not all sleep" (15:51*b*) expresses the conviction that all of his undisputed letters share, namely that the end is imminent, so much so that not all will die before the parousia of Christ.

The important claim, however, is the next: "But we shall all be changed" (15:51*c*, emphatically reaffirmed in 15:52). All believers must be changed; none have arrived, not even Paul (cf. Phil 3:12), who takes backseat to none in terms of growth and strength of faith. And certainly all the Corinthians, including those who have collapsed future into present and claim already to share the resurrection in the present, must be changed.

A trumpet reference (15:52) ties Paul's comments into his larger apocalyptic scenario of a final and determinative battle (cf. 1 Thess 4:16; 5:6-10). Verse 53 opens with a particle (δεῖ *dei*) that would literally be translated "it is necessary," signaling divine action enacting God's plan, extending the picture and once again expressing some continuity between the left and right sides of the charts above: When the dead are raised incorruptible (15:52), then the corruptible will have been cloaked with the incorruptible (cf. the similar image of being further clothed, in 2 Cor 5:4). Then what is mortal will have been cloaked with immortality, and then death, the last enemy (15:26), will finally be destroyed. Paul's claim of a fundamental continuity makes clear that his view of resurrection does not consist of snatching just a soul or spirit from some to-be-discarded body.

This picture of the last times, designed as it is to give perspective to the Corinthians, moves to closure by identifying the Hosean "sting" of death with sin (Hos 13:14, quoted in 15:55). The connection of "sin leading to death," which is presupposed in 15:56, is such a commonplace as to be formulaic in Paul's letters (cf. Rom 6:16, 21, 23). And, though it seems gratuitous, that is, it appears to have nothing to do with any controversy the Corinthians seem to be having, Paul makes what for him is a ready linkage, that the law provides a fertile setting for sin: namely, that sin delights in the law (though the law itself must not be identified with sin; Rom 7:7-12) and sees in it an unrivaled opportunity to find powerful leverage by which it may bring people under its (sin's) sway (15:56).

Paul brings the main part of the discourse to a close with a "grace," a thanksgiving to God, who, by grace, "is giving us the victory [an echo from the Isa 25:8 quote in 15:54; note also the trumpet in 15:52] through our Lord Jesus Christ" (15:57). The present participle τῷ διδόντι (*tō didonti*) points to God's current and ongoing action in bringing and giving to believers the victory. Paul affirms the process that is under way with Christ's death and that will culminate in the redemption of all of creation. Believers as part of the new creation are already enjoying the benefits of God's redemptive and creative activity. Just as the schema of this world is passing away (1 Cor 7:31) due to God's indictment of sin's sway over creation, so Paul here at the end of this discourse breaks into thankfulness to God for incorporating the believers into God's victorious redemptive work.

# REFLECTIONS

**1.** A fundamental Pauline premise is that everything has a body (σῶμα *sōma*) as God has chosen (this statement is an echo of 12:18, there about spiritual gifts); nothing exists apart from *sōma*. His example of grain serves him well: The grain appears one way before planting and takes on another form after it has been planted (read "dies" 15:36) and comes up sprouted. No surprise in this; all of creation works the same way. Everything has a body as God has chosen and seeds of those bodies come true to form. In fact, the whole universe, terrestrial and celestial, is composed of distinctive bodies, each with its own particular glory.

Significant dangers attend the overemphasis that Paul here tries to correct. To declare, as some Corinthians have, that the fullness of all that God will give is available in the present, without and before a restoration of all of creation and its accompanying end of suffering and struggle, misleads persons about their present circumstances and about the grandeur of what God is ultimately under way to do: about their present because it caters to the illusory sense that salvation is an individual matter (cf. the "for me" in the Corinthians' maxims in 6:12), which a person can receive fully in the present without the larger social web, and indeed without all of God's broken world being redeemed; and about the final grandeur because it suggests that God's ultimate purposes have concluded with the individual in question, so that a smaller God is presupposed. To think that God's ultimate redemptive purposes are focused in some exclusive way on saving me (or even someone very dear to me) is filled with hubris and arrogance on my side and manifests a failure to see the vastness and the cosmic proportion of God's whole redemptive plan.

Accordingly, Paul's concluding refrain "We shall all be changed" (15:51, 52) is his confident affirmation that God, who has begun this work in believers, will bring it to completion (Phil 1:6), but it is also his sobering caution to those Corinthians who have gotten ahead of themselves by claiming already to have experienced some sort of spiritual resurrection.

**2.** The element of discontinuity, of surprise or of difference between what is now and what is in God's future, is a natural consequence of Paul's central affirmation that God's grace lies at the outset of the life of faith and undergirds every moment of it from the beginning of faith until God's culminating purposes arrive. Grace has two aspects, the one probably featured more regularly than the other. First, grace is the welcome power of God freely given because God wants to do it, and totally unmerited because we in no sense deserve it. It is what has opened up the life of faith to each of us and therefore is worthy of considerable celebration and thankfulness. The other side of grace, however, is that it turns lives upside down—if we were to speak of grace in terms of baseball, grace would at least be a curveball, and sometimes might appear as a "spitter." Grace can be very unsettling. It changes lives and people often resist and resent change, even if it might be liberating as grace's change always turns out to be. Grace's breaking into lives does not always look on the surface or at first glance even as grace, but more as discombobulation. The time when believers sing God's praises for grace most easily is after it has shaken up their world and after they have come to perceive it for what it is. Grace is frequently visible (sometimes only visible) as grace, for what it *really* is, only in retrospect.

# 1 CORINTHIANS 15:58, RECAPITULATION AND PERORATION

| NIV | NRSV |
|---|---|
| [58]Therefore, my dear brothers, stand firm. Let nothing move you. Always give yourselves fully to the work of the Lord, because you know that your labor in the Lord is not in vain. | [58]Therefore, my beloved,[a] be steadfast, immovable, always excelling in the work of the Lord, because you know that in the Lord your labor is not in vain.  <br> [a] Gk *beloved brothers* |

# COMMENTARY

Typically in Paul's time, speakers and writers who came to the end of such an eloquent address as this chapter would highlight and tie together various important themes and call for a response. So it is here. With a forceful "Therefore," Paul addressed the Corinthians very affectionately as "Brothers and sisters, my beloved." His one injunction to them is "Stand firm, immovable," but he then unfolds just how they are to stand fast. Believers stand firm and immovable by "abound-

ing in the work of the Lord always," and they can throw themselves passionately and unreservedly into that work because they should understand the resurrection and what it tells us about life and work in this world: namely, that their labor (note the singular, see below) in the Lord is not in vain, not empty.

Paul's call to them to "be steadfast" (cf. also Col 1:23) is elaborated by three participles that describe how and what they are to do in order to be steadfast. First, they are to be "immovable" (ἀμετακίνητοι *ametakinētoi*), which depicts their ability to stand against whatever winds or experiences buffet them, because of their confidence that God will bring to completion what God has begun in them through Christ (cf. Rom 4:21; Phil 1:6). That is how they can be steadfast. The first participle, "immovable," if it were there alone, might suggest that to "be steadfast" is to hold tight or to stand still. Second, Paul describes what they do to stay steadfast—and interestingly it is not by hunkering down and holding tight. They stand fast by "abounding always in the work of the Lord" (15:58). And they can abound in the work of the Lord because they know, the third participle, "that their labor is not in vain in the Lord" (15:58).

These claims are rich in content, dense in expression and significance, and profound in implication. All these affirmations undergird and explicate Paul's final exhortation: "Stand fast." When transposed to nautical imagery it would be "Stay the course." Paul makes the same argument with the Galatians, there in athletic terminology: You were running well; don't be distracted, lose your way, or turn back (Gal 5:7; 4:9).

So this discourse has moved from its opening where Paul shockingly raised the specter that their faith and his labor might be in vain (15:2), to a clarification about life-in-this-world-in-light-of-the-expected-resurrection, which affirms that actions and struggles and work "in the Lord" are significant and vital.

Special note should be taken that "the work [ἔργον *ergon*] of the Lord" and "your [ὑμῶν *hymōn*, plural] labor [κόπος *kopos*, singular] in the Lord" both employ the singular regarding the Lord's work or labor (two different Greek terms meaning the same thing here) and the believers' collective effort. We must ask why Paul uses the singular here. The answer lies in Paul's fundamental commitment to the life of faith as a life in community. There is not a list of pre-approved "works" or "labors" of the Lord that individuals must go out and do as solo agents; Paul supposes a much more community-grounded and integrated effort in which all the deeds of the community, and indeed all the actions of all the individuals within it, are coordinated into *a shared work and a common labor* in the Lord. Surely, believers do different things; just as they have different gifts, so also their

actions are distinctive. As believers' faith is one and they are therefore united in it (cf. 1 Thess 1:8), so their work, their labor is one because God's singular love is expressed in their varied work.

This reference to labor/work is a critical matter for Paul, for his own thinking, for his actions in behalf of the gospel, and for his communities because it raises the most fundamental of human questions: What do we make of our strivings? What enduring significance do our actions have? Is there meaning to the struggles of our lives? Why does one do anything that one does? These questions are made most poignant by death, which threatens to erase not only the believers themselves but also what the believers have done. Paul's letters show that he and his readers are not immune to such questions. Note how many times he raises the matter of whether he has been "running in vain," a phrase that for him raises the question of the worth of his labor—and even of his life—in behalf of the gospel (Gal 2:2; 4:11; Phil 2:16; 1 Thess 3:5; these references represent rhetorical pressure on the readers of those letters, not self-doubt on Paul's part).

We must now examine the connection Paul sees between life in the present, with its moral dilemmas and choices, with its striving and its yearning, and the finishing up of God's purposes, which still lies in the (imminent) future. The best clues of this interconnection in chapter 15 come in three verses that we now consider in sequence: "If in this life we have hoped in Christ only, we are of all people most to be pitied" (15:19); "If in the way people understand things, I wrestled wild beasts in Ephesus, what good does it do? 'Eat and drink because tomorrow we die'!" (15:32); and the just-noted climax of the discourse, "Therefore, brothers and sisters, my beloved, be firm, immovable, always abounding in the work of the Lord, knowing that your labor in the Lord is not empty" (15:58).

Has God's decisive strike against sin and its power obviated any need for the believers to do anything? Clearly the ultimate power is God's power, in Paul's view. If 2 Thessalonians is any evidence, some of Paul's followers have come to the conclusion that they need not work, that they simply stand idly by and await God's powerful completion of what God has begun. At issue in 1 Corinthians 15 is the question of whether it matters what Paul or they do, whether their labor is in vain.

For an insight, consider what Paul says about himself and his labor. He puts it in the most dramatic of forms, namely, his wrestling of wild beasts—no doubt a figurative reference to the great opposition he is encountering—in Ephesus from whence he writes this letter (16:8-9).[157] Does his laboring in behalf of the gospel in the face of adversaries amount to anything? One answer could be to throw up one's hands in despair at the meaninglessness of life and its struggles and embrace the libertine life because "tomorrow we die." If death has the final word on the meaning of life, then why would one choose wrestling wild beasts over pleasure (eating and drinking)? Paul's life shows that he has chosen the wrestling; his thought expressed in chapter 15 equally testifies that Paul has confidence that "the work of the Lord" and their "labor in the Lord" is not in vain. Why? Because death and its sting of defeat is not the last word. Death, sin's sting and the last enemy, will ultimately be overcome for all believers. Christ's resurrection as "first fruits" (15:20, 23) is the surety that the remainder of the resurrection harvest of believers will be made good. So what one does and what one is in Christ is ultimately valued, valuable, and preserved, beyond death's futile grasp. Thus, one not only can wrestle beasts wherever one is, but one must be part of the great cosmic plan, the battle with evil, in which God is engaged. Engagement, struggle, labor, doing "the work of the Lord" are not an option that believers might choose; they are an obligation. Faith does not have works as simply an option that may or may not be exercised. Faith requires that works be done. Faith is incomplete— one might even say it is not truly faith—until it expresses itself in deeds. Unwritten in this chapter but supposed is that believers have to exercise moral judgment in the choices that they make, that being in Christ has obligated them, with renewed minds (Rom 12:2), to be responsible moral agents. In the terms of this chapter, moral discernment entails their figuring out what indeed is their proper "labor in the Lord," and then abounding in it always, because they know that their "labor in the Lord is not in vain" (15:58; cf. Paul's exemplary self-portraits in this respect in 3:8ff. and in 15:10).

157. Abraham Malherbe, "The Beasts at Ephesus," *JBL* 87 (1968) 79-80.

"If in this life we have hoped in Christ only, we are of all people most to be pitied" (15:19). As Paul has constructed it, this first clause has a certain ambiguity. At issue in its interpretation is what the term "only" modifies. (a) If one takes it to mean "if in this life we have only hoped in Christ," then the question is whether this life, even in Christ, has significance in its own right, that is, whether the life of faith is realized only as a hope whose fulfillment is delayed until a later time. Though Paul does not address that issue directly in chapter 15, elsewhere Paul is clear that the present life in Christ is rich and vibrant; the life of faith is not simply an anticipated life, recognized in the present only or primarily as a hope (cf. 1 Cor 13:13; Rom 5:1). (b) If one takes it to mean "in this life only we have hoped in Christ," then the question is what connection there is between this life and the life to come. Given the way 15:35 introduces a fictive character who asks about the kind of body the dead will have, and Paul's response to the question in 15:36, we must say that Paul is concerned with the significance this bodily life has in light of the renewed and grander bodily life that awaits the believers at the parousia.

*The importance of chapter 15 in the letter.* By its position as the last major item in the letter chapter 15 caps off the body of the letter. We have seen that it attempts to correct a mistaken assumption among some Corinthians that they already share in some spiritualized resurrection that moves them to what they consider a special plateau, where they deserve honor and where they are no longer bound by certain moral restraints. And, looking back from this point we have been able to see the several places in the letter where such a mistaken notion of the resurrection may actually have been operative. We must also note that chapter 15, while it deals with resurrection as a topic, nevertheless weaves together some of the themes of the preceding chapters: (1) The opening (15:1-2) has the same comprehensive sweep across the whole of the believing life that is captured in Paul's traditions about the Lord's supper where what one proclaims there is of equal scope: "the Lord's death until he comes" (11:26). (2) The indissoluble linkage between Christ's resurrection, already accomplished, and believers' coming resurrection, which is affirmed in so many ways in chapter 15, was already declared in 6:14. (3) The cosmic portrayal of Christ and his role in God's purpose has been a theme across the letter (3:23; 8:6; 11:3), a theme that is elaborated even more in 15:21-28. (4) The 15:38 claim that God gives a body to different seeds as God chooses is a direct restatement of divine prerogative asserted three times with regard to the distribution of charismata in the congregation (12:11, 18, 24). (5) The declaration that flesh and blood will not be able to inherit the kingdom of God, which provides the basis for the additional formula, "nor the perishable inherit the imperishable" (15:50*b*), is an echo of 6:9. (6) The reference to one's labor in the Lord not being in vain should call to mind Paul's own self-portrait as a laborer along with Apollos in 3:5-9. Resurrection is the premise on which all of life and all of one's workings or deeds or accomplishments rest. All of one's work in the Lord is not only necessary but also eternally significant.

These thematic and behavioral ties of chapter 15 to the remainder of the letter emphasize the culminating and grounding role this major discussion plays not only in the structure of the letter but also in the understanding and discerning of the moral choices that believers face as they try to live a faithful life of love for one another in a broken world while they await the parousia of their Lord. As the Lord's supper provided the framework within which the believers live the scope of their lives—from Christ's death until he comes—so also the anticipated resurrection endorses, elevates, and sanctifies daily life as a mode of acceptable and thankful offering of themselves to the very God who will faithfully care for them before, in, and beyond death.

# REFLECTIONS

**1.** This grand section ends on a note about work and labor, but that is a theme that showed itself earlier in Paul's comments about being in constant danger for his association with the gospel and about his so-called wrestling with wild beasts in Ephesus. Paul writes 1 Corinthians from Ephesus (16:8) where he notes appreciatively the "wide door" open for his work there. His evidence? Much opposition (16:9). So Paul is wrestling "wild beasts" at Ephesus because of his identification with and presentation of the gospel. The dangers and opposition raise a fundamental question: Why go to all that trouble, effort, and danger? If there is no resurrection, if life is to be lived simply for the value one can tease out of the moment, there is certainly no reason to work, much less to place oneself in harm's way. But, on the other hand, if one's life is truly secure with God, what does that suggest about anxiety brought about by opposition?

As the Corinthians exemplify for us, one's convictions about the resurrection are crucial to the way one handles one's life. If one is convinced that one's salvation is already accomplished, already secure in its fullness, then one might conclude that moral restraints no longer prevail, that one is free to eat, drink, and be merry in whatever way one sees fit, and that one has no need to labor or exert one's self—especially if doing so might land one in difficult circumstances. Such persons, thinking they already had it made, would act as if they deny that Paul's anticipated judgment day has any bearing on their decisions and actions, and might even assume that their works will not be considered at the judgment (cf. Rom 2:6-8; 2 Cor 5:10).

Paul's own life, filled to the brim as it was with work on behalf of the gospel and with that work's attendant risks and opposition, is a resounding answer of another sort, based on his own understanding of the resurrection. (This ties back to the discussion of freedom in the reflections on chapter 9.) Because of Paul's unshakable confidence that God will finish—by vanquishing the last enemy, death—the good work begun in Christ, Paul knows that God will not forsake him, no matter what others may do and no matter what may befall him. This confidence frees Paul from others and frees him for others. This confidence spurs Paul to work, to risk and to brook opposition on behalf of the gospel and his call. Granted, it would not warrant any and every risk; note well that even as Paul did not go right back to Thessalonica when it was apparent that he might be harmed or killed if he did, so we are not describing a blind, unthinking, foolhardy faith.

But we would not expect foolhardy faith and unnecessary risk-taking from someone like Paul who insists that his reasonable worship of God (Rom 12:1) involves the regular and full employment of his mind as well as his spirit (14:14-15). When one knows oneself truly secure with God, one is free to serve God with a purity and openness of heart, despite the opposition such a service will surely generate.

No Christian should expect to arrive at that confidence and certainty right away; it is a matter of growth and maturity in faith today, just as it was in Paul's time. Instead of spending one's energies lamenting over not already sharing Paul's confidence, one would do far better to use those energies to build and practice one's faith so that it might grow into such a relationship. It is an effort that other believers and God will support and nourish.

A church convinced of its security in God's grace can therefore be liberated from the social pressures to conform to the culture and can take a public stand where there are matters of justice and human well-being at stake. Such a church can represent the gospel by its public declarations about social issues and by its hands-on involvement with the problems that bedevil our communities. Then the church would be doing the "work" that it is called to do.

**2.** Note that Paul links one's labors with the "work of God." It is not all labor or work that Paul praises and assures of value, but those labors that attest to God's work in and through one. So Paul's is not a paean of work or busyness for its own sake, but only insofar as one's own labors cohere with the work that God is up to. In fact, though Paul does not do so, one could suggest testing a contemplated action against what one understood about God's work that we see in Christ. One's labors in the Lord endure just as surely as does one's love (1 Cor 13:13); so properly to labor in God's work is at the same time to walk in love. Ours is a world where we seem to have construed our individual worth by reference to our busyness, as if to tell one another how busy we are is an index of our importance and goodness. Next time a friend tells you how busy they are, you might do them a favor to ask them, Why? and To what end? Of course, as surely as you do that work of friendship toward someone else, you should be ready to be asked the same questions.

**3.** The taunt "Death, where is your sting?" is an awesome one. This childlike standing unabashedly before death and shaking a defiant fist in its face is possible for believers only because they know the rest of the story, namely that death is the "final enemy," yet to be destroyed, but which will be ultimately and finally overcome in God's final triumph. To ask where death's sting is now, as a friend or loved one dies, is not to deny that the person has died, it is not to deny that we have felt and do feel death's sting, and it is not to deny that we feel grief and loss over that death. As Paul uses it, the taunt confidently looks at death and its sting in the present from beyond death, from the standpoint of God's final and completed purposes. *Then* God's power mercifully will have raised the dead; *then* God will have dealt death the sting-removing final blow; and *then* (and now already in confident hope) we may say with Paul that death is overcome by life.

4. We know the grand design of what God is doing in the overall scheme of things because the story moves from Christ's death and resurrection toward the ultimate fulfillment of all of God's promises, toward the redemption of God's creatures and cosmos. We can be part of that story by God's grace and if our lives are conduits for love. Not that we should think of ourselves as bringing God's kingdom. It is God's reign and God is bringing it. At issue for each of us is whether and how fully we will live our lives as a channel through which God's love and mercy can flow to the world and to all of God's creatures.

## ONE MORE CORINTHIAN QUESTION, PAUL'S PLANS, AND LETTER CLOSING

### OVERVIEW

The major points of the letter now having been concluded, Paul turns to a sequence of closing matters, the first of which the Corinthians seem to have raised with him in their letter (cf. 7:1), though it could have come through the Corinthian emissaries.

## 1 CORINTHIANS 16:1-4, RESPONSE TO A QUERY ABOUT THE COLLECTION

**16** Now about the collection for God's people: Do what I told the Galatian churches to do. ²On the first day of every week, each one of you should set aside a sum of money in keeping with his income, saving it up, so that when I come no collections will have to be made. ³Then, when I arrive, I will give letters of introduction to the men you approve and send them with your gift to Jerusalem. ⁴If it seems advisable for me to go also, they will accompany me.

**16** Now concerning the collection for the saints: you should follow the directions I gave to the churches of Galatia. ²On the first day of every week, each of you is to put aside and save whatever extra you earn, so that collections need not be taken when I come. ³And when I arrive, I will send any whom you approve with letters to take your gift to Jerusalem. ⁴If it seems advisable that I should go also, they will accompany me.

### COMMENTARY

The Corinthians have written Paul about the collection. The term "collection" (λογεία *logeia*), suggesting a gathering of funds for a special purpose, appears only here (16:1-4) in the Pauline corpus, but refers to the onetime offering to which he committed himself in Jerusalem (Gal 2:1-10, esp. 2:10). At the Jerusalem conference he promised that he would pull together from his largely gentile churches a goodwill offering as a demonstration, as an affirmation of Christian unity to what he otherwise calls the "saints" or the "poor among the saints in Jerusalem" (Rom 15:26). His

letters, apart from 1 Corinthians, show that Paul devotes considerable time and energy to making good on this offering (cf. Rom 15:25-28; 2 Corinthians 8–9) across about a two year span (2 Cor 8:10). We know from 2 Corinthians that the Corinthians initially responded readily to the opportunity to take part in this collection, but that their earlier zeal was lost with the passage of time (8:11). When 1 Corinthians was written, the Corinthian believers were willing participants in this generous undertaking, and Paul's response suggests that their concerns were on the logistics of how to gather it and what its disposition might be. Unlike 2 Corinthians, one finds in 1 Corinthians no hint of contention, confusion, or diminution of zeal about participation in the collection.

Paul, who is in Ephesus and has gone through the Roman province of Galatia to get there, tells the Corinthians that on the matter of the collection he recommends the steps he gave to the Galatian believers on the same topic (16:1). What follows (16:2) is a suggested pattern of regular setting aside so that when Paul arrives they will already have the (presumably substantial) collection ready. A couple of features are noteworthy: (1) The reference in the Greek is to a regular practice of each person setting apart contributions every Sabbath. From such nomenclature of days, we see how completely resocialized these gentiles were to the whole sense that they belonged to the family of God, whose roots are traceable directly to the people of Israel. It is fully understandable that they would embrace a collection aimed to show their solidarity with their believing brothers and sisters in Jerusalem. (2) There is a difficult phrase in 16:2 that the NIV ("set aside a sum . . . income") and the NRSV ("save whatever extra you earn") take distinctively but which generally suggests that each person is to "treasure up" according to how well the person gets along. We probably cannot be more precise as to Paul's meaning than that. Second Corinthians 8:13-15 may be read as an elaboration of his intended meaning here: Equity requires that whatever abundance one has should be put in service of those in need, and he sees scriptural support for this arrangement in Ex 16:18 (NRSV)—"those who gathered much had nothing over, and those who gathered little had no shortage"—which he cites there (2 Cor 8:15).

A similar notion about the collection appears in Romans 15 where Paul expresses a fundamental reciprocity among believers. There, those who have received much (the gentile believers) are indebted to those through whom they received (namely the Jewish believers who preceded them into the faith) and therefore should readily embrace the opportunity to give as they are able (Rom 15:27). On the basis of ability, each is to give to others according to the others' needs. This collection meets the general test of believers' caring for one another in proportion to what they have to offer (cf. 1 Cor 12:7).

At the time of his writing of 1 Corinthians Paul does not anticipate that he will go with the collection to Jerusalem, so he advises them that when he does come to see them next they should have the collection ready and that they can certify certain representatives whom Paul will credentialize with letters; those persons can accompany this "gift" ($\dot{\eta}$ $\chi\acute{\alpha}\rho\iota\varsigma$ *hē charis,* "grace," "gift") to Jerusalem. Earlier Paul asked, "What do you have that you have not received as a gift?" (4:7). So what the Corinthians offer to the Jerusalem saints is but the grace of God working through them, and the offering then finally is not really only to the Jerusalem saints but ultimately to God, the source of all gifts great and small. Paul closes his comments on the collection by saying that if he does decide to attend to the delivery of the collection to Jerusalem, those designated representatives will go with him. By this means he maintains his own leadership role (16:4).

# REFLECTIONS

Paul's comments across the corpus about the collection for the saints in Jerusalem give significant insights into his broader understanding of stewardship. Paul supposes that all believers will be moved to care for others who are in need (cf. the mutuality of Rom 15:27), that each should give in accord with how well one is getting along (16:2; cf. a similar concern in 2 Cor 8:11-15), and that what one contributes is literally a "grace" (16:3). The NIV and NRSV reasonably translate *charis* as "gift" because that is the linguistic center of the concept. But we might do well to think of it as "offering grace" to others because it at once reflects that any giving we do is equivalent to prayerful thankfulness, and is always in response to God's own "grace," which was freely bestowed on us while we were still sinners and which is the ongoing reckoning point by which our lives are lived and nourished day by day. So grace goes around: It comes from God, it is shared by offering such as we have with others, and all that resounds to God's glory. But caution: the grace that we share is not to be confused or identified with any degree of "success" or "prosperity" we have, so that we come to think of ourselves who have more as "more blessed" and those who have less as "less blessed." An identification with "offering grace" might also mean that the thanks over meals would be understood to have connection not only to eating but also to include giving and sharing with others.

# 1 CORINTHIANS 16:5-9, PROJECTED VISIT PLANS AND PRESENT PURPOSES

**NIV**

⁵After I go through Macedonia, I will come to you—for I will be going through Macedonia. ⁶Perhaps I will stay with you awhile, or even spend the winter, so that you can help me on my journey, wherever I go. ⁷I do not want to see you now and make only a passing visit; I hope to spend some time with you, if the Lord permits. ⁸But I will stay on at Ephesus until Pentecost, ⁹because a great door for effective work has opened to me, and there are many who oppose me.

**NRSV**

5I will visit you after passing through Macedonia—for I intend to pass through Macedonia— ⁶and perhaps I will stay with you or even spend the winter, so that you may send me on my way, wherever I go. ⁷I do not want to see you now just in passing, for I hope to spend some time with you, if the Lord permits. ⁸But I will stay in Ephesus until Pentecost, ⁹for a wide door for effective work has opened to me, and there are many adversaries.

## COMMENTARY

Most of Paul's letters contain, usually in a closing section, some indication of his plans for the present, and they often project visits to the letter recipients. And 1 Corinthians is no exception, for here he assures the Corinthians that, though he expects to stay at Ephesus through Pentecost, he then looks forward to traveling through Macedonia (a land trip, rather than an Aegean crossing, in other words) on his way for what he hopes may be an extended (across the winter) time with the Corinthians, the Lord willing (16:7). As if it is his normal practice with them, he mentions that at the end of his visit he will expect them to help him along his way wherever he is led to go next (cf. the same treatment expected for Timothy in 16:11; cf. also Rom 15:24; 2 Cor 1:16). His present purposes keep him in Ephesus, the largest city in the Roman Empire after Rome, because he sees what he calls a "great and effective door" opened to him (16:9).

## REFLECTIONS

Paul's interpretation of opposition (16:9) as a sign that he is on the right track may seem strange to the modern reader who is concerned with not causing any distress, with not making any waves. Jesus clearly warns that those who pursue righteousness for his sake will experience opposition and affliction, even though they are simultaneously promised blessedness and a share in God's reign (Matt 5:10). Believers should not be surprised by opposition, and at times even by suffering because of identification with the gospel. To be yoked to Jesus by dedication to justice is, as Jesus' words have it, an easy yoke, and his burden is light (Matt 11:30), precisely because he helps carry it. Jesus never said, "Have no enemies." Instead, he told us to relate to our enemies in love (Matt 5:44). So believers will have enemies, will experience opposition for the sake of the gospel. We will have to be careful—and here other believers can no doubt be of service—to distinguish enmity and opposition for the sake of the gospel from that generated in response to our own greed, self-centeredness or peevishness. Knowledge that walking according to the gospel will produce enmity can only be descriptive, never a license, never prescriptive.

# 1 CORINTHIANS 16:10-12, TRAVEL PLANS OF PAUL'S ASSOCIATES

### NIV

[10]If Timothy comes, see to it that he has nothing to fear while he is with you, for he is carrying on the work of the Lord, just as I am. [11]No one, then, should refuse to accept him. Send him on his way in peace so that he may return to me. I am expecting him along with the brothers.

[12]Now about our brother Apollos: I strongly urged him to go to you with the brothers. He was quite unwilling to go now, but he will go when he has the opportunity.

### NRSV

10If Timothy comes, see that he has nothing to fear among you, for he is doing the work of the Lord just as I am; [11]therefore let no one despise him. Send him on his way in peace, so that he may come to me; for I am expecting him with the brothers.

12Now concerning our brother Apollos, I strongly urged him to visit you with the other brothers, but he was not at all willing[a] to come now. He will come when he has the opportunity.

[a] Or it was not at all God's will for him

## COMMENTARY

Verses 10-11 are a commendation of Timothy, who along with Titus are Paul's doubles. Are we to suppose that Timothy and the Corinthians have had some troubles? Perhaps. If so, Paul uses his own authority to encourage a proper welcome and support of Timothy. In any case, Paul's characterization of Timothy is significant because it functions exactly as we have seen Paul's own self-descriptions, namely, to set the pattern for others in the community to follow. In fact, Paul's description ties Timothy explicitly and directly to himself: "for he works the work of the Lord just as I do" (16:10). Given that chapter 15 closed with the emphasis on doing the work of the Lord and one's labor in the Lord not being in vain (15:58),

the reprise of that model in the portrait of Timothy is not accidental but intended for emulation. Paul's note that he is expecting Timothy (and his entourage) as Timothy comes through Corinth to Ephesus expresses an interest to follow up on the matter of their treatment of Timothy much as Paul's projected visit to Philemon's house (Phlm 22).

Apollos, who throughout this letter seems to be on good terms with Paul (cf. 3:5-9), has been contacted by Paul and urged to go to Corinth. Apollos clearly has his own self-determination, and Paul reports that he has chosen not to go to Corinth at present but will come when the occasion presents itself (16:12). (See Reflections at 16:13-14.)

# 1 CORINTHIANS 16:13-14, CONCLUDING ADMONITIONS

**NIV**

¹³Be on your guard; stand firm in the faith; be men of courage; be strong. ¹⁴Do everything in love.

**NRSV**

13Keep alert, stand firm in your faith, be courageous, be strong. ¹⁴Let all that you do be done in love.

## COMMENTARY

Often at the end of letters Paul has a series of pithy admonitions and quite frequently, as is the case here, the injunctions touch on central or fundamental issues in the letter (2 Cor 13:11; Gal 6:14-16).[158] The first two admonitions—"Be on watch" and "Stand (firm)" are military imagery from Paul's apocalyptic vision that believers are part of God's army who are to be on alert, at their battle stations (cf. 1 Thess 5:6, 10); the second also has the eschatological aspect of standing before the judgment seat and being found worthy, hence the addition "in the faith" (10:12; 15:1; cf. Rom 14:10).[159] While the third—"Conduct your-selves in a courageous way"—and fourth—"Be strong"—injunctions probably reflect Ps 30:24 LXX (31:25) and may also have battle significance, they also certainly relate to Paul's chiding the Corinthians for being childish, for being babies in the faith, and for not having grown more mature in the faith.

As is typically the case in Greco-Roman rhetoric, the most important injunction is reserved for last, and, appropriately, is the most elaborate in form: "Let all the things that you do be done in love" (16:14). As noted earlier, love is what is most missing in the multifarious transactions of the Corinthians, so Paul's final injunction calls for love to be the guiding presence in *all* that the Corinthians do.

158. David E. Aune, *The New Testament in Its Literary Environment* (Philadelphia: Westminster, 1987) 191; J. A. D. Weima, *Neglected Endings: The Significance of the Pauline Letter Closings,* JSNTSup 101 (Sheffield: JSOT, 1994).

159. Edgar M. Krentz, "Military Language and Metaphors in Philippians," in *Origins and Method: Towards a New Understanding of Judaism and Christianity, Essays in Honour of John C. Hurd,* ed. B. H. McLean, JSNTSup 88 (Sheffield: Sheffield Academic Press, 1993) 109. In a yet-unpublished "Notes for a Future Study," circulated on request, Krentz writes: "The anarthrous use of five imperatives indicates heightened intensity. All fit well into the military semantic field."

## REFLECTIONS

Paul's summary call to the Corinthians is an appropriate summary call to all believers everywhere: "Let everything of yours be done in love" (16:14). One never has to apologize for loving, but one may have to distinguish attempts at loving with actually loving. How frustrating and puzzling it is to attempt to love when the intended person or persons do not perceive it as love. Paul Tillich, the theologian, wrote that revelation was not revelation until it was received by someone. So, also, love is not fully love simply in its attempt; it is genuinely love only when it is received as love. Loving is not a science. It must ever be reinvented afresh in every new situation. Oftentimes you will not know whether love has genuinely been received. Loving is a little like Noah on the high seas, sending the dove out day by day. Some days the dove will come home without any sign of its having sighted land; but, fortunately, on other days it just may come home with a branch in its beak, signifying that it has indeed found some fruitfulness. Love's duty is to send the dove, day by day. And perhaps it is best to expect nothing in return because then the love is genuinely given without strings attached. Then when the dove does bring the branch home on occasion, it can be an especial time for rejoicing. How frustrating and puzzling it is to attempt to love when the intended person or persons do not perceive it as love.

# 1 CORINTHIANS 16:15-18, COMMENDATIONS OF STEPHANAS AND OTHERS

## NIV

15You know that the household of Stephanas were the first converts in Achaia, and they have devoted themselves to the service of the saints. I urge you, brothers, 16to submit to such as these and to everyone who joins in the work, and labors at it. 17I was glad when Stephanas, Fortunatus and Achaicus arrived, because they have supplied what was lacking from you. 18For they refreshed my spirit and yours also. Such men deserve recognition.

## NRSV

15Now, brothers and sisters,[a] you know that members of the household of Stephanas were the first converts in Achaia, and they have devoted themselves to the service of the saints; 16I urge you to put yourselves at the service of such people, and of everyone who works and toils with them. 17I rejoice at the coming of Stephanas and Fortunatus and Achaicus, because they have made up for your absence; 18for they refreshed my spirit as well as yours. So give recognition to such persons.

[a] Gk brothers

# COMMENTARY

Stephanas is one of the pillars of the Corinthian church. His family was the first that Paul baptized there (1:16; 16:15), and he was part of a three-person delegation who visited Paul and no doubt filled him in on what was happening at Corinth. Perhaps they even delivered the letter from the Corinthians to Paul (7:1).

Paul's commendations have exemplary purpose, that is, they, like Paul's autobiographical portraits, highlight model-worthy ways of living: These people "devoted themselves to the service [εἰς διακονίαν *eis diakonian*] of the saints" (16:15 NIV). Paul urges recognition of (16:18) and submission to (16:16) such persons, and, in a sweep-

ing extension, "to all who come together in the work [συνεργοῦντι *synergounti*] and who labor [κοπιῶντι *kopiōnti*, in it, understood]" (16:16). Note well that this extension places Stephanas and all who work like him in line with Paul and his own self-portrait (3:6; 4:12; cf. 15:58). Such persons are exemplary because of their διακονία (*diakonia*), their service, which Paul identifies as refreshing of everyone's spirit (16:18). Parenthetically, one should also note that once again "the work" and "labor" both appear here as they did in 15:58, and both are once again in the singular because all contribute to the "work of the Lord" by their own labors.

# REFLECTIONS

Paul commends Stephanas's household because "they have devoted themselves to the service [*diakonia*] of the saints" and sets them forward as the pattern others ought to follow (16:15-16). This is the same circularity noted earlier about love. Persons who have benefited from God's grace must move in love toward others, they must, each and every one of them, engage in service, in ministry toward others. Love received is love that demands to be given, passed along to, shared with others. Service to others is not simply an option; it is the very heart of life according to the gospel.

# 1 CORINTHIANS 16:19-20, GREETINGS

| NIV | NRSV |
| --- | --- |
| ¹⁹The churches in the province of Asia send you greetings. Aquila and Priscilla*a* greet you warmly in the Lord, and so does the church that meets at their house. ²⁰All the brothers here send you greetings. Greet one another with a holy kiss. | 19The churches of Asia send greetings. Aquila and Prisca, together with the church in their house, greet you warmly in the Lord. ²⁰All the brothers and sisters*a* send greetings. Greet one another with a holy kiss. |
| *a19* Greek *Prisca*, a variant of *Priscilla* | *a* Gk *brothers* |

# COMMENTARY

Paul's location at the time of writing, Ephesus, is in the Roman province of Asia (roughly modern Turkey). Aquila and Prisca, the Jewish believers who were expelled from Rome with the other Jews under Claudius's ban in 49 CE (cf. Rom 16:3-4; Acts 18:2), have a house church in Ephesus also. Paul reports greetings from "all the Asian churches" and from Aquila, Prisca, the church in their house, and all the other believers there (16:19). The greetings section closes, as do many of Paul's letters, with his urging the auditors to greet one another with a "holy kiss," obviously another bit of Pauline pressure to have them show the signs of friendship and affection that could genuinely signal the end of their divisiveness (16:20; cf. Rom 16:16; 2 Cor 13:12; 1 Thess 5:26).

# 1 CORINTHIANS 16:21, AUTOGRAPH

| NIV | NRSV |
| --- | --- |
| ²¹I, Paul, write this greeting in my own hand. | 21I, Paul, write this greeting with my own hand. |

## COMMENTARY

In some of his letters Paul takes the pen from his scribe and adds his own personalizing touch (cf. Gal 6:11; Phlm 19). By doing so, Paul adds the full force of his authority to all of the letter and to all that has been written in it.

# 1 CORINTHIANS 16:22, ENFORCEMENT FORMULA

| NIV | NRSV |
|---|---|
| [22]If anyone does not love the Lord—a curse be on him. Come, O Lord[a]! | [22]Let anyone be accursed who has no love for the Lord. Our Lord, come![a] |
| [a]22 In Aramaic the expression *Come, O Lord* is *Marana tha*. | [a] Gk *Marana tha*. These Aramaic words can also be read *Maran atha*, meaning *Our Lord has come* |

## COMMENTARY

Occasionally Paul closes his letters with a formula of enforcement, warning regarding specific matters (cf. Gal 6:17). Here, Paul makes a foundational affirmation, one which it would be difficult to imagine any Corinthian not sharing: "if anyone does not have friendship with/love the Lord" (16:22; φιλεῖ τὸν κύριον *philei ton kyrion*), but that may, indeed, serve Paul quite well as he has sought at points in this letter to remind the Corinthians of the simple basis of their unity, namely, their relation to the Lord. The consequences of failure to love the Lord are stark: "Let that person be *anathema* (ἀνάθεμα)/accursed," cut off from the community (cf. 5:1-5; Gal 1:8). Paul concludes this section with the eschatological prayer, preserved in Aramaic, the sister language of Hebrew and probably reflecting a well-established, pre-Pauline prayer of the earliest churches: *Marana tha*, "Our Lord, come." This prayerful call for Christ's parousia echoes the Lord's supper ("you proclaim the Lord's death until he comes," 11:26 NRSV) and the resurrection discourse's introduction (15:3-11), which sketched matters out to the believers' expected but still future salvation.

## REFLECTIONS

Paul's call for the Lord to come is his imploring God to bring to conclusion God's redemptive work begun in Jesus Christ. The same sort of response lies behind the cry "Amen, come Lord Jesus" with which the book of Revelation closes (22:20; cf. the "come," which greets the opening of each of the first four seals in Rev 6:1, 3, 5, 7; cf. Rev 22:17). For Paul, God's foreshortening of the time ("the time [before the end] is shortened"; 1 Cor 7:29a) is a sign of God's mercy. Thus, Paul's call and the modern Christian's call for our Lord to come—as we see it in some contemporary liturgies—is at once a recognition that we survive and even thrive in the midst of present tribulations and distress only by the grace of God, and is at the same time an urgent plea for deliverance, for an end to suffering, for a vindication of our faithfulness, and for a complete dawning of God's reign.

# 1 CORINTHIANS 16:23-24, CONCLUDING GRACE

NIV

²³The grace of the Lord Jesus be with you. ²⁴My love to all of you in Christ Jesus. Amen.*

*24 Some manuscripts do not have *Amen*.

NRSV

²³The grace of the Lord Jesus be with you. ²⁴My love be with all of you in Christ Jesus.*

*Other ancient authorities add *Amen*

## COMMENTARY

All of Paul's letters open with a call for grace to be upon the readers, and likewise all of his letters close with a standard "grace to you" (Rom 16:20*b;* 2 Cor 13:14; Gal 6:18; Phil 4:23; 1 Thess 5:28; and Phlm 25). Grace is the be-all and end-all of the life of faith; God's grace is not just important at the outset of the life of faith, it is also the very ground of being in all of life, from beginning to end.

As this closing grace starts out in 1 Cor 16:23— "the grace of our Lord Jesus Christ be with you"— nothing is unusual, but the way Paul concludes it ties once again into the problem the letter addresses: "My love be with all of you in Christ Jesus" (16:24). Paul, who has called for love from them to one another (most recently in the summary injunctions; 16:14), now practices what he has preached and affirms his love for *all of them* in Christ Jesus. To the very end of the letter Paul models for them what they most need. And he closes without siding with any group or clique against another. His love is for *all* of them in Christ Jesus. Love for the Lord (16:22) is the sine qua non of belonging in the Christian community, and because all believers are equally in Christ, then love for the Lord calls for, even requires, love of all those who are in Christ. Paul models for them that love as he wishes God's grace upon them.

## REFLECTIONS

The letter that opened with grace (1:3) closes with an affirmation of grace (16:23), symbolizing that all the concerns of the letter—and indeed all of life—are enclosed in and supported simply and profoundly by God's grace. Without God's grace we cannot begin the day and face its challenges and opportunities; without God's grace we cannot make the most of the opportunities and find the strength to meet the challenges; and without God's grace we cannot find the peace that allows us to let go of all our unfinished work when the night comes and we must rest.

# TRANSLITERATION SCHEMA

## HEBREW AND ARAMAIC TRANSLITERATION

Consonants:

| | | | | | | | | | |
|---|---|---|---|---|---|---|---|---|---|
| א | = | ʾ | ט | = | ṭ | פ or ף | = | p |
| ב | = | b | י | = | y | צ or ץ | = | ṣ |
| ג | = | g | כ or ך | = | k | ק | = | q |
| ד | = | d | ל | = | l | ר | = | r |
| ה | = | h | מ or ם | = | m | שׂ | = | ś |
| ו | = | w | נ or ן | = | n | שׁ | = | š |
| ז | = | z | ס | = | s | ת | = | t |
| ח | = | ḥ | ע | = | ʿ | | | |

Masoretic Pointing:

| Pure-long | | | Tone-long | | | Short | | | Composite *shewa* | | |
|---|---|---|---|---|---|---|---|---|---|---|---|
| הָ | = | â | | = | ā | | = | a | | = | ǎ |
| ֵי or ֶי | = | ê | | = | ē | | = | e | or | = | ě |
| ִי or ִי | = | î | | | | | = | i | | | |
| ֹ or וֹ | = | ô | | = | ō | | = | o | | = | ŏ |
| ֻ or וּ | = | û | | | | | = | u | | | |

## GREEK TRANSLITERATION

| | | | | | | | | |
|---|---|---|---|---|---|---|---|---|
| α | = | a | ι | = | i | ρ | = | r |
| β | = | b | κ | = | k | σ or ς | = | s |
| γ | = | g | λ | = | l | τ | = | t |
| δ | = | d | μ | = | m | υ | = | y |
| ε | = | e | ν | = | n | φ | = | ph |
| ζ | = | z | ξ | = | x | χ | = | ch |
| η | = | ē | ο | = | o | ψ | = | ps |
| θ | = | th | π | = | p | ω | = | ō |

# INDEX OF MAPS, CHARTS, AND ILLUSTRATIONS

# ABBREVIATIONS

| | |
|---|---|
| BCE | Before the Common Era |
| CE | Common Era |
| c. | circa |
| cf. | compare |
| chap(s). | chapter(s) |
| d. | died |
| Dtr | Deuteronomistic historian |
| esp. | especially |
| fem. | feminine |
| HB | Hebrew Bible |
| lit. | literally |
| l(l). | line(s) |
| LXX | Septuagint |
| masc. | masculine |
| mg. | margin |
| MS(s) | manuscript(s) |
| MT | Masoretic Text |
| n.(n.) | note(s) |
| neut. | neuter |
| NT | New Testament |
| OL | Old Latin |
| OT | Old Testament |
| par. | parallel(s) |
| pl(s). | plate(s) |
| sing. | singular |
| v(v). | verse(s) |
| Vg | Vulgate |
| \\ | between Scripture references indicates parallelism |

## Names of Biblical Books (with the Apocrypha)

| | | | |
|---|---|---|---|
| Gen | Nah | 1–4 Kgdms | John |
| Exod | Hab | Add Esth | Acts |
| Lev | Zeph | Bar | Rom |
| Num | Hag | Bel | 1–2 Cor |
| Deut | Zech | 1–2 Esdr | Gal |
| Josh | Mal | 4 Ezra | Eph |
| Judg | Ps (Pss) | Jdt | Phil |
| 1–2 Sam | Job | Ep Jer | Col |
| 1–2 Kgs | Prov | 1–4 Macc | 1–2 Thess |
| Isa | Ruth | Pr Azar | 1–2 Tim |
| Jer | Cant | Pr Man | Titus |
| Ezek | Eccl | Sir | Phlm |
| Hos | Lam | Sus | Heb |
| Joel | Esth | Tob | Jas |
| Amos | Dan | Wis | 1–2 Pet |
| Obad | Ezra | Matt | 1–3 John |
| Jonah | Neh | Mark | Jude |
| Mic | 1–2 Chr | Luke | Rev |

### Names of Pseudepigraphal and Early Patristic Works

| | |
|---|---|
| *2 Apoc. Bar.* | Syriac *Apocalypse of Baruch* |
| *1-2-3 Enoch* | Ethiopic, Slavonic, Hebrew *Enoch* |
| *Apoc. Abr.* | *Apocalypse of Abraham* |
| *1-2 Clem.* | *1-2 Clement* |
| *Jub.* | *Jubilees* |
| *Pss. Sol.* | *Psalms of Solomon* |
| *Did.* | *Didache* |
| *T. Benj.* | *Testament of Benjamin* |
| *T. Dan* | *Testament of Dan* |
| *T. Iss.* | *Testament of Issachar* |
| *Bibl. Ant.* | Ps.-Philo, *Biblical Antiquities* |

### Names of Dead Sea Scrolls and Related Texts

| | |
|---|---|
| CD | Cairo text of the *Damascus Document* |
| Q | Qumran |
| 1Q, 2Q, etc. | Numbered caves of Qumran, yielding written material; sometimes followed by abbreviation of biblical or apocryphal book |
| 1QH | *Thanksgiving Hymns* (Qumran Cave 1) |
| 1QM | *War Scroll* (Qumran Cave 1) |
| 1QS | *Rule of the Community* (Qumran Cave 1) |
| 4QMMT | *Halakhic Letter* (Qumran Cave 4) |
| 4QTestim | *Testimonia* text from Qumran Cave 4 |
| 4Q394-399 | 4QMMT$^a$ (*Miqsat Ma'aśê ha-Torah$^a$*) |
| 4Q175.5-8 | 4QTest (*Testimonia*) |
| 11QT | *Temple Scroll* from Qumran Cave 11 |

### Orders and Tractates in Mishnaic and Related Literature

| | |
|---|---|
| *Tg. Neof.* | *Targum Neofiti I* |
| *Sanh.* | *Sanhedrin* |

### Other Rabbinic Works

| | |
|---|---|
| *Pesiq. R.* | *Pesiqta Rabbati* |
| *Rab.* | *Rabbah* (following abbreviation of biblical book: *Gen. Rab.* [with periods] = *Genesis Rabbah*) |

### Greek Manuscripts and Ancient Versions

| | |
|---|---|
| P$^{46}$ | Third-century Greek Papyris manuscript of the Gospels |

### Names of Nag Hammadi Tractates

### Commonly Used Periodicals, Reference Works, and Serials

| | |
|---|---|
| AB | Anchor Bible |
| ABD | D. N. Freedman (ed.), *Anchor Bible Dictionary* |
| ACNT | Augsburg Commentaries on the New Testament |
| AGJU | Arbeiten zur Geschichte des antiken Judentums und des Urchristentums |
| *AJP* | *American Journal of Philology* |
| *ABT* | *Australian Biblical Review* |
| AnBib | Analecta biblica |
| *BBR* | *Bulletin for Biblical Research* |
| BDAG | W. Bauer, W. F. Arndt, F. W. Gingrich and F. W. Danker, *Greek-English Lexicon of the New Testament and Other Early Christian Literature,* 2nd ed. Chicago, 1979; 3rd ed. Chicago, 2000 |
| *BDF* | F. Blass, A. Debrunner, and R. W. Funk, *A Greek Grammar of the New Testament* |
| BETL | Bibliotheca ephemeridum theologicarum lovaniensium |
| *Bib* | *Biblica* |
| *BibInt* | *Biblical Interpretation* |
| BNTC | Black's New Testament Commentaries |
| *BTB* | *Biblical Theology Bulletin* |
| *CBQ* | *Catholic Biblical Quarterly* |
| ConBNT | Coniectanea neotestamentica |
| EKKNT | Evangelisch-katholischer Kommentar zum Neuen Testament |
| *Ex Aud* | *Ex Auditu* |
| *ExpTim* | *Expository Times* |
| FRLANT | Forschungen zur Religion und Literatur des Alten und Neuen Testaments |
| GNS | Good News Studies |
| GTA | Göttinger theologische Arbeiten |
| HDR | Harvard Disssertations in Religion |

| | |
|---|---|
| HNT | Handbuch zum Neuen Testament |
| HTKNT | Herders theologischer Kommentar zum Neuen Testament |
| *HTR* | *Harvard Theological Review* |
| IBC | Interpretation: A Bible Commentary for Teaching and Preaching |
| *IBS* | *Irish Biblical Studies* |
| ICC | International Critical Commentary |
| Int | Interpretation |
| JB | Jerusalem Bible |
| *JBL* | *Journal of Biblical Literature* |
| *JETS* | *Journal of the Evangelical Theological Society* |
| *JSNT* | *Journal for the Study of the New Testament* |
| JSNTSup | Journal for the Study of the New Testament—Supplement Series |
| *JSOT* | *Journal for the Study of the Old Testament* |
| JSPTSS | Journal of the Study of Pentecostal Theology Supplement Series |
| *JTS* | *Journal of Theological Studies* |
| KEK | Kritisch-exegetischer Kommentar über das Neue Testament |
| KJV | King James Version |
| LCL | Loeb Classical Library |
| NCB | New Century Bible |
| NEB | New English Bible |
| *NIB* | *New Interpreter's Bible* |
| NICNT | New International Commentary on the New Testament |
| NICOT | New International Commentary on the Old Testament |
| NIGTC | The New International Greek Testament Commentary |
| NIV | New International Version |
| NJB | New Jerusalem Bible |
| *NovT* | *Novum Testamentum* |
| NovTSup | Novum Testamentum Supplements |
| NRSV | New Revised Standard Verion |
| NTC | New Testament in Context |
| NTG | New Testament Guides |
| *NTS* | *New Testament Studies* |
| *NTT* | *Norsk Teologisk Tidsskrift* |
| *OBC* | *Oxford Bible Commentary* |
| OBT | Overtures to Biblical Theology |
| REB | Revised English Bible |
| RSV | Revised Standard Version |
| SB | H. L. Strack and P. Billerbeck, *Kommentar zum Neuen Testament aus Talmud und Midrasch,* 5 vols. 1922–56 |
| SBL | Society of Biblical Literature |
| SBLDS | SBL Dissertation Series |
| SBLMS | SBL Monograph Series |
| SNTSMS | Society for New Testament Studies Monograph Series |
| SP | Sacra Pagina |
| *SR* | *Studies in Religion/Sciences religieuses* |
| SUNT | Studien zur Umwelt des Neuen Testaments |
| DNT | G. Kittel and G. Friedrich (eds.), *Theological Dictionary of the New Testament* |
| THKNT | Theologischer Handkommentar zum Neuen Testament |
| *TynBul* | *Tyndale Bulletin* |
| UBSGNT | United Bible Societies *Greek New Testament* |
| *VT* | *Vetus Testamentum* |
| WBC | Word Biblical Commentary |
| *WTJ* | *Westminster Theological Journal* |
| WUNT | Wissenschaftliche Untersuchungen zum Neuen Testament |
| *ZNW* | *Zeitschrift für die neutestamentliche Wissenschaft und die Kunde de älteren Kirche* |